The Sporting News

COMPLETE HOCKEY BOOK

1992-93 EDITION

Editor/Complete Hockey Book
CRAIG CARTER

The Sporting News

PUBLISHING CO.

Thomas G. Osenton, President and Chief Operating Officer; **Kathy Kinkeade**, Vice President/Production; **William N. Topaz**, Director/Information Development; **Gary Levy**, Editor; **Mike Nahrstedt**, Managing Editor; **Joe Hoppel**, Senior Editor; **Tom Dienhart, Dave Sloan and Larry Wigge**, Associate Editors; **Mark Shimabukuro**, Assistant Editor; **Kyle Barry, Bill Bayer, Lee Hart, Kevin Hormuth, Craig Mulcahy, Michelle Poston, George Puro, David Ressner and Terry Shea**, Editorial Assistants; **Bill Perry**, Director of Graphic Presentation; **Mike Bruner**, Art Director/Yearbooks and Books; **Gary Brinker**, Director of Information Systems.

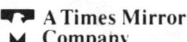

A Times Mirror Company

CONTENTS

ON THE COVER: Mario Lemieux led Pittsburgh to a sweep of Chicago in the 1992 Stanley Cup finals as the Penguins captured their second consecutive National Hockey League championship. (Photo by David Klutho)

ISBN: 0-89204-438-1

10 9 8 7 6 5 4 3 2 1

1992-93
NHL SEASON

NHL DIRECTORY

LEAGUE OFFICES

OFFICERS

President-elect
Gilbert Stein
Executive vice president
Brian F. O'Neill
Vice president of finance and treasurer
Kenneth G. Sawyer
Vice president, hockey operations
Jim Gregory
Vice president, NHL project development
Ian "Scotty" Morrison
Vice president, broadcasting
Joel Nixon
Vice president, marketing/public relations
Steve Ryan

MONTREAL OFFICE

Address
Sun Life Building
1155 Metcalfe Street
Montreal, Que., Canada H3B 2W2
Phone
514-871-9220
FAX
514-871-1663
Executive vice president
Brian F. O'Neill
Director of administration
Phil Scheuer
Assistant director of administration
Steve Hatzepetros
Director of central registry
Garry Lovegrove
Assistant director of central registry
Madeleine Supino
Director, information systems
Mario Carangi
Assistant director, information systems
Miranda Ishak
Asst. director, planning and development, information systems
Luc Coulombe
Controller
Joseph DeSousa
Assistant controller
Mary Skiadopoulos
Manager, pension administration
Lynne Blagrave
Accounting supervisor
Donna Gillman

NEW YORK OFFICE

Address
650 Fifth Avenue
33rd Floor
New York, NY 10019

Phone
212-398-1100
FAX
212-245-8221
President-elect
Gilbert Stein
Vice president, broadcasting
Joel Nixon
Director of broadcasting/G.M., publishing and video division
Stu Hackel
Vice president, finance and treasurer
Kenneth G. Sawyer

TORONTO OFFICE

Address
75 International Blvd.
Suite 300
Rexdale, Ont. M9W 6L9
Phone
416-798-0809
FAX
416-798-0819
Vice president of hockey operations
Jim Gregory
Director of officiating
Bryan Lewis
Assistant director of officiating
Wally Harris
Coordinator of development
Will Norris
Supervisor of officials
John D'Amico
Officiating coach
Dave Newell
Director of central scouting
Frank Bonello
Central scouting administration
John Andersen
Assistant director of security
Al Wiseman
Executive director of communications
Gary Meagher
Director, editorial and information systems
Susan Elliott
Statistician/information officer
Benny Ercolani
Information officer
Greg Inglis

NHL ENTERPRISES, INC.

Address
1633 Broadway
40th Floor
New York, NY 10019

Phone
212-767-4600
FAX
212-767-4646
President, NHL Enterprises, Inc.
Steve Ryan
Controller
Walter Luby
Assistant controllers
Patricia Cassell-Cooper
Mary McCarthy
Assistant director, special events
Maria Pace Buettel
Senior vice president, general counsel
Richard Zanno
General manager, publishing
Michael A. Berger
Director of administration
Janet Meyers

PROMOTIONAL LICENSING DIVISION

Executive director
Steve Flatow
Director, sponsor services
Sarah S. Galvin

RETAIL LICENSING DIVISION

General manager
Fred Scalera
Senior vice president
J. Robert Carey
Licensing and marketing director-collectibles
Ilene Kent
Licensing contract manager
James Haskins
Regional sales manager, Eastern region
Brian Jennings
Regional sales manager, Western region
Bill Tighe
Special projects coordinator
Ann Kiely
Director, non-apparel products
Judith Salsberg

EVENT MARKETING

General manager
Frank Supovitz
Director
Karen Hovsepian
Coordinators
Mindy Kopper
Maria Sutherland
Assistant
Tracy McCloskey

NHL DIRECTORY

1992-93 NHL SEASON

NHL DIRECTORY

BOSTON BRUINS
WALES CONFERENCE/ADAMS DIVISION

1992-93 SCHEDULE

OCTOBER

S	M	T	W	T	F	S
4	5	6	7	8 HAR H	9	10 NYI H
11	12 OTT H	13	14	15 SJ	16	17 LA
18	19	20	21	22 CAL	23 EDM	24
25 VAN	D 26	27	28	29 LA H	30	31 CHI H

NOVEMBER

S	M	T	W	T	F	S
1	2	3	4	5 QUE H	6	7 NYR H
8	9	10	11 BUF	12 CAL H	13	14 TOR H
15	16 MON	17	18	19 NYI H	20	21 PHI H
22	23 OTT	24	25 WAS	26	27 HAR H	D 28 HAR
29	30 QUE					

DECEMBER

S	M	T	W	T	F	S
		1	2	3 MON H	4	5 D NJ
6 PHI	7	8	9 BUF	10 OTT H	11	12 MON
13	14 BUF H	15	16	17	18 DET	19 WAS H
20	21	22 TB H	23	24	25	26 HAR
27 NYR	28	29 WIN H	30	31 MIN		

JANUARY

S	M	T	W	T	F	S
					1	2 HAR H
3	4	5 PIT	6	7 QUE H	8	9 NJ H
10	11	12 BUF H	13	14 PIT H	15	16 PHI H
17	18 D SJ H	19 NYI	20	21 PHI	22	23 NJ H
24	25 MON	26 QUE	27	28 WIN H	29	30 NYI
31						

FEBRUARY

S	M	T	W	T	F	S
	1	2 EDM H	3 QUE	4	5	6 *
7	8	9 STL	10	11 CHI	12	13
14 TB	15	16	17 MON	18	19	20 TOR
21	22	23	24	25 MIN H	26	27 D WAS H
28						

MARCH

S	M	T	W	T	F	S
	1 MON H	2	3	4 VAN H	5	6 D STL H
7	8	9 PIT	10	11 MON H	12	13 D OTT H
14	15 NYR	16	17	18 OTT	19	20 D DET H
21	22 HAR H	23	24 BUF	25 MON H	26	27 D PIT H
28	29	30 HAR	31			

APRIL

S	M	T	W	T	F	S
				1	2	3 D BUF H
4 BUF	D 5	6 QUE	7	8 QUE H	9	10 MON
11 OTT H	12	13	14 OTT	15	16	17

1992-93 SEASON

CLUB DIRECTORY

Owner and governor
Jeremy M. Jacobs
Alternative governor
Louis Jacobs
Alternate governor, president and G.M.
Harry Sinden
Vice president
Tom Johnson
Assistant general manager
Mike Milbury
Assistant to the president
Nate Greenberg
Director of administration
Dale Hamilton
Coach
Brain Sutter
Assistant coach
Tom McVie
Coord. of minor league player personnel/ scouting
Bob Tindall

Director of player evaluation
Bart Bradley
Scouting staff
Jim Morrison
Andre Lachapelle
Joe Lyons
Don Saatzer
Lars Waldner
Marcel Pelletier
Jean Ratelle
Harvey Keck
Sven-Ake Svensson
Controller
Bob Vogel
Trainer
Jim Narrigan
Athletic therapist
Don Worden
Equipment manager
Ken Fleger
Director of media relations
Heidi Holland

DRAFT CHOICES

Rnd. Player	Ht./Wt.	Overall	Pos.	1991-92 club
1—Dmitri Kvartelnov ...	5-11/180	16	F	San Diego (IHL)
3—Sergei Zholtok........	6-0/183	55	F	Riga, Latvia
5—Scott Bailey............	6-0/195	112	G	Spokane (WHL)
6—Jiri Dopita..............	6-4/202	133	F	Olomouc, Czech.
6—Grigor Panteleyv......	5-9/194	136	F	Riga, Latvia
8—Kurt Seher	6-1/180	184	D	Seattle (WHL)
9—Mattias Timander ...	6-1/191	208	D	MoDo, Sweden
10—Chris Crombie	6-2/197	232	LW	London (OHL)
11—Denis Cheruyako		256	D	CIS
11—Eugene Pavlov		257	D	SKA Leningrad, CIS

MISCELLANEOUS DATA

Home ice (capacity)
Boston Garden (14,448)
Address
150 Causeway Street
Boston, MA 02114
Business phone
617-227-3206

Rink dimensions
191 feet by 83 feet
Club colors
Gold, black and white
Minor league affiliations
Providence (AHL)
Johnstown (IHL)

SCHEDULE KEY

*All-Star Game at Montreal.
H—Home game.   D—Day game (any game starting before 4 p.m.).
NOTE: At press time, two games at neutral sites had yet to be announced.

TRAINING CAMP ROSTER

No.	FORWARDS	Ht./Wt.	Place	BORN Date	NHL exp.	1991-92 clubs
18	Brent Ashton (LW/C) ...	6-1/200	Saskatoon, Sask.	5-18-60	13	Winnipeg, Boston
34	Lyndon Byers (RW)	6-1/200	Nipawin, Sask.	2-29-64	9	Maine (AHL), Boston
51	Brian Dobbin (RW)	5-11/195	Petrolia, Ont.	8-18-66	5	Maine (AHL), New Haven (AHL), Boston
50	Clark Donatelli (LW)	5-10/180	Providence, R.I.	11-22-67	2	U.S. Nat./Olym., Boston
46	Ted Donato (C)	5-10/170	Dedham, Mass.	4-28-68	1	U.S. Nat./Olym., Boston
	Jiri Dopita (C)	6-4/202	Sumperk, Czech.	12-2-68	0	DS Olomouc (Czech.)
16	Peter Douris (RW)	6-1/195	Toronto	2-19-66	6	Maine (AHL), Boston
45	Steve Heinze (RW)	5-11/180	Lawrence, Mass.	1-30-70	1	U.S. Nat./Olym., Boston
10	Ken Hodge (C)	6-1/200	Windsor, Ont.	4-13-66	3	Maine (AHL), Boston
42	Brent Hughes (LW)	5-11/180	New Westminster, B.C.	4-5-66	3	Baltimore (AHL), Maine (AHL), Boston
49	Joe Juneau (C)	6-0/175	Pont-Rouge, Que.	1-5-68	1	Can. Nat./Olym., Boston
	Dmitri Kvartalnov (LW)..	5-11/180	Voskresensk, U.S.S.R.	3-25-66	0	San Diego (IHL)
12	Steve Leach (RW)	5-11/200	Cambridge, Mass.	1-16-66	7	Boston
44	Glen Murray (RW)	6-2/200	Halifax, N.S.	11-1-72	1	Sudbury (OHL), Boston
8	Cam Neely (RW)	6-1/210	Comox, B.C.	6-6-65	9	Boston
12	Adam Oates (C)	5-11/190	Weston, Ont.	8-27-62	7	St. Louis, Boston
19	Dave Poulin (C)	5-11/190	Mississauga, Ont.	12-17-58	10	Boston
17	Dave Reid (LW)	6-1/205	Toronto	5-15-64	9	Maine (AHL), Boston
38	Vladimir Ruzicka (C)	6-3/212	Most, Czech.	6-6-63	3	Boston
20	Bob Sweeney (C/RW)	6-3/200	Boxborough, Mass.	1-25-64	6	Maine (AHL), Boston
41	Dave Thomlinson (LW).	6-1/195	Edmonton, Alta.	10-22-66	3	Maine (AHL), Boston
	Sergei Zholtok (LW)	6-0/185	Riga, U.S.S.R.	12-2-72	0	Riga (CIS)

No.	DEFENSEMEN	Ht./Wt.	Place	Date	exp.	1991-92 clubs
43	Bob Beers.....................	6-2/200	Cheektowaga, N.Y.	5-20-67	3	Maine (AHL), Boston
77	Ray Bourque..................	5-11/210	Montreal	12-28-60	13	Boston
6	Glen Featherstone..........	6-4/215	Toronto	7-8-68	4	Boston
43	Matt Hervey..................	5-11/195	Los Angeles	5-16-66	2	Maine (AHL), Boston
28	Gord Murphy	6-1/180	Willowdale, Ont.	2-23-67	4	Philadelphia, Boston
	Gordie Roberts..............	6-1/195	Detroit	10-2-57	13	Pittsburgh
32	Don Sweeney	5-11/170	St. Stephen, N.B.	8-17-66	4	Boston
26	Glen Wesley	6-1/195	Red Deer, Alta.	10-2-68	3	Boston
36	Jim Wiemer	6-4/210	Sudbury, Ont.	1-9-61	9	Maine (AHL), Boston

No.	GOALTENDERS	Ht./Wt.	Place	Date	exp.	1991-92 clubs
	Scott Bailey	5-11/185	Calgary, Alta.	5-2-72	0	Spokane (WHL)
30	Mike Bales	6-1/180	Saskatoon, Sask.	8-6-71	0	Ohio State (CCHA)
	John Blue	5-10/185	Huntington Beach, Calif.	2-9-66	0	Maine (AHL)
33	Matt Delguidice	5-9/170	West Haven, Conn.	3-5-67	2	Maine (AHL), Boston
1	Reggie Lemelin	5-11/170	Sherbrooke, Que.	11-19-54	14	Boston
35	Andy Moog	5-8/170	Penticton, B.C.	2-18-60	12	Boston
	Mike Parson..................	6-0/170	Listowel, Ont.	3-3-70	0	Johnstown (ECHL), Maine (AHL)

1991-92 REVIEW

INDIVIDUAL STATISTICS

SCORING

	Games	G	A	Pts.	Pen.	+/-	PPG	SHG	Shots	Shooting Pct.
Ray Bourque...	80	21	60	81	56	11	7	1	334	6.3
Vladimir Ruzicka.......................................	77	39	36	75	48	-10	18	0	228	17.1
Stephen Leach..	78	31	29	60	147	-8	12	0	243	12.8
Craig Janney*..	53	12	39	51	20	1	3	0	90	13.3
Bob Carpenter..	60	25	23	48	46	-3	6	1	171	14.6
Glen Wesley..	78	9	37	46	54	-9	4	0	211	4.3
Brent Ashton*..	61	17	22	39	47	-4	6	1	124	13.7
Adam Oates*..	26	10	20	30	10	-5	3	0	73	13.7
Andy Brickley...	23	10	17	27	2	6	5	0	28	35.7
Peter Douris...	54	10	13	23	10	9	0	0	107	9.3
Bob Sweeney	63	6	14	20	103	-9	0	1	70	8.6
Joe Juneau...	14	5	14	19	4	6	2	0	38	13.2
Ken Hodge..	42	6	11	17	10	-8	3	1	62	9.7
Dave Reid...	43	7	7	14	27	5	2	1	70	10.0
Stephane Quintal*.....................................	49	4	10	14	77	-8	0	0	52	7.7
Don Sweeney..	75	3	11	14	74	-9	0	0	92	3.3
Garry Galley*..	38	2	12	14	83	-3	1	0	51	3.9
Cam Neely..	9	9	3	12	16	9	1	0	30	30.0
Chris Nilan *...	39	5	5	10	186	-5	0	0	33	15.2
Nevin Markwart*..	18	3	6	9	44	2	0	0	12	25.0
Jeff Lazaro...	27	3	6	9	31	4	0	0	46	6.5
Barry Pederson*..	32	3	6	9	8	-5	1	0	41	7.3

	Games	G	A	Pts.	Pen.	+/-	PPG	SHG	Shots	Shooting Pct.
Gordon Murphy*	42	3	6	9	51	2	0	0	82	3.7
Jim Wiemer	47	1	8	9	84	10	0	0	60	1.7
Scott Arniel	29	5	3	8	20	5	0	0	34	14.7
Dave Poulin	18	4	4	8	18	-2	0	1	31	12.9
Stephen Heinze	14	3	4	7	6	-1	0	0	29	10.3
Gord Hynes	15	0	5	5	6	8	0	0	16	0.0
Bob Beers	31	0	5	5	29	-13	0	0	25	0.0
Glen Murray	5	3	1	4	0	2	1	0	20	15.0
Chris Winnes	24	1	3	4	6	-6	0	0	20	5.0
Lou Crawford	19	2	1	3	9	-6	0	0	14	14.3
Ted Donato	10	1	2	3	8	-1	0	0	13	7.7
Wes Walz*	15	0	3	3	12	-3	0	0	17	0.0
Andy Moog (goalie)	62	0	3	3	52	0	0	0	0	0.0
Brent Hughes	8	1	1	2	38	1	0	0	10	10.0
Lyndon Byers	31	1	1	2	129	-5	0	0	12	8.3
John Byce	3	1	0	1	0	-1	1	0	2	50.0
Jozef Stumpel	4	1	0	1	0	1	0	0	3	33.3
Brian Dobbin	7	1	0	1	22	0	0	0	4	25.0
Glen Featherstone	7	1	0	1	20	-2	0	0	8	12.5
Petri Skriko*	9	1	0	1	6	-3	1	0	20	5.0
Ralph Barahona	3	0	1	1	0	1	0	0	0	0.0
Shayne Stevenson	5	0	1	1	2	1	0	0	3	0.0
Rejean Lemelin (goalie)	8	0	1	1	2	0	0	0	0	0.0
Clark Donatelli	10	0	1	1	22	-8	0	0	7	0.0
Dave Thomlinson	12	0	1	1	17	-2	0	0	12	0.0
Matt Hervey	16	0	1	1	55	-5	0	0	8	0.0
Jack Capuano	2	0	0	0	0	-1	0	0	1	0.0
Matt Glennon	3	0	0	0	2	0	0	0	2	0.0
Petr Prajsler	3	0	0	0	2	-1	0	0	3	0.0
Alan Stewart*	4	0	0	0	17	-1	0	0	1	0.0
Jim Vesey	4	0	0	0	0	0	0	0	1	0.0
Daniel Berthiaume (goalie)*	8	0	0	0	0	0	0	0	0	0.0
Matt Delguidice (goalie)	10	0	0	0	2	0	0	0	0	0.0

GOALTENDING

	Games	Min.	Goals	SO	Avg.	W	L	T	Shots	Sv. Pct.
Daniel Berthiaume*	8	399	21	0	3.16	1	4	2	156	.865
Andy Moog	62	3640	196	1	3.23	28	22	9	1727	.887
Rejean Lemelin	8	407	23	0	3.39	5	1	0	210	.890
Matt Delguidice	10	424	28	0	3.96	2	5	1	239	.883

Empty-net goals (do not count against a goaltender's average): Moog, 7.
*Played with two or more NHL teams.

RESULTS

OCTOBER

3—N.Y. Rangers	W	5-3
5—N.Y. Islanders	L	3-4
7—At N.Y. Rangers	L	*1-2
9—At Buffalo	T	*4-4
12—Montreal	L	0-6
17—At Vancouver	T	*3-3
19—At San Jose	W	4-1
24—At St. Louis	L	5-6
26—At Minnesota	L	0-4
27—At Chicago	W	6-3
31—Los Angeles	L	2-4

NOVEMBER

2—Detroit	W	4-1
4—At N.Y. Islanders	L	4-6
5—At Pittsburgh	T	*5-5
7—Calgary	T	*4-4
9—New Jersey	W	4-0
14—Quebec	W	5-2
16—At Hartford	W	*5-4
20—At Buffalo	L	1-3
22—At Washington	L	3-6
23—Buffalo	W	7-4
25—At Montreal	L	3-4
27—At N.Y. Islanders	W	3-2
29—Montreal	W	*5-4

DECEMBER

1—Hartford	W	5-4
5—Quebec	T	*2-2
7—Philadelphia	L	3-5
8—At N.Y. Rangers	L	0-4
10—At Quebec	L	2-5
12—Montreal	W	5-2
14—Toronto	W	4-3
19—Pittsburgh	L	4-6
21—Edmonton	W	6-3
22—At Montreal	L	2-3
26—Hartford	W	3-2
27—At Buffalo	L	1-8
29—At Winnipeg	W	6-3
31—At Detroit	W	5-3

JANUARY

2—Winnipeg	L	1-3
4—Buffalo	W	4-2
8—At Montreal	L	2-3
9—Quebec	W	5-4
11—Philadelphia	W	5-1
15—At Hartford	W	4-3
16—Hartford	W	*4-3
22—At Toronto	W	5-2
23—Montreal	L	1-3
25—At Hartford	T	*4-4
27—Minnesota	W	3-2
28—At Quebec	W	4-2
30—Calgary	W	3-1

FEBRUARY

1—Buffalo	T	*2-2
4—At Winnipeg	T	*3-3
6—At Philadelphia	L	1-5
8—New Jersey	L	4-6
9—Pittsburgh	W	6-3
13—At St. Louis	L	0-4
17—At Los Angeles	L	3-6
19—At Calgary	L	4-6
21—At Edmonton	W	5-3
23—At Vancouver	L	*1-2
27—Toronto	W	4-2
29—Washington	T	*5-5

MARCH

1—At Washington	W	4-1
3—At Hartford	L	0-4
5—Vancouver	T	*2-2
7—Chicago	L	1-2
8—At Chicago	L	0-4
11—At Buffalo	L	3-6
14—At Quebec	W	*5-4
15—Los Angeles	W	5-1
19—St. Louis	L	1-4
21—Edmonton	L	3-4
23—San Jose	W	7-6
26—At New Jersey	L	2-4
28—Buffalo	W	*4-3
31—At Quebec	W	*5-4

APRIL

12—Quebec	T	*1-1
13—Hartford	W	6-3
15—At Montreal	T	*4-4

*Denotes overtime game.

BUFFALO SABRES
WALES CONFERENCE/ADAMS DIVISION

1992-93 SCHEDULE

OCTOBER
S	M	T	W	T	F	S
4	5	6	7	8 QUE H	9	10 HAR
11 MON H	12	13 PIT	14	15	16 TB H	17 WAS
18	19	20	21 CHI H	22	23 SJ H	24
25	26	27	28 TOR	29	30 OTT H	31 OTT

NOVEMBER
S	M	T	W	T	F	S
1	2 NYR	3	4	5 SJ	6	7 LA
8	9	10	11 BOS H	12	13 HAR H	14 NYI
15	16	17 PIT	18	19	20	21 MIN H
22 PHI	23	24	25 QUE H	26	27 OTT H	28
29 OTT	30 MON					

DECEMBER
S	M	T	W	T	F	S
		1	2	3	4 NYI H	5
6 NJ H	7 QUE	8	9 BOS H	10	11 HAR H	12 HAR
13 BOS	14	15	16	17	18	19 MON
20 TOR H	21	22	23 WAS H	24	25	26
27 PIT H D	28	29	30	31 NYR H		

JANUARY
S	M	T	W	T	F	S
					1	2 OTT
3 STL H	4	5	6 HAR	7	8 NYI H	9
10 CAL H	11	12 BOS	13	14	15 VAN	16
17 EDM	18	19 CAL	20	21	22 QUE H	23 QUE
24	25	26 PHI	27 WAS H	28	29 NYR H	30
31 EDM H D						

FEBRUARY
S	M	T	W	T	F	S
	1	2	3 HAR H	4	5	6 *
7	8 OTT	9	10 WIN	11	12 VAN H	13
14 PIT H	15	16	17 HAR	18	19 NJ	20
21	22	23	24 DET H	25	26 MON H	27 MON
28						

MARCH
S	M	T	W	T	F	S
	1	2	3 NYR	4	5 HAR H	6
7 WIN H	8	9	10 QUE	11	12	13 HAR D
14 LA D	15	16 STL	17	18	19	20 TB D
21	22 MON	23	24 BOS H	25 CHI	26	27
28 OTT H	29	30 WAS	31 NJ H			

APRIL
S	M	T	W	T	F	S
				1	2	3 BOS D
4 BOS H D	5	6 MIN	7	8	9 DET	10 D
11 QUE H	12	13 MON H	14	15 PHI H	16	17

1992-93 SEASON

CLUB DIRECTORY

Chairman of the board and president
Seymour H. Knox III
Vice chairman of the board and counsel
Robert O. Swados
Vice chairman of the board
Robert E. Rich Jr.
Treasurer
Joseph T. J. Stewart
Assistant to the president
Seymour H. Knox IV
Senior vice president, administration
Mitchell Owen
Senior vice president, finance
Robert W. Pickel
General manager
Gerry Meehan
Director of hockey operations and coach
John Muckler
Assistant coaches
John Tortorella
John Van Boxmeer
Assistant to the general manager
Craig Ramsay
Director of player personnel
Don Luce

Director of scouting
Rudy Migay
Coordinator of minor league professional development
Joe Crozier
Scouting staff
Don Barrie
Jack Bowman
Larry Carriere
Dennis McIvor
Paul Merritt
Mike Racicot
Frank Zywiec
Director of communications
Paul Wieland
Director of public relations
John Gurtler
Director of information
Budd Bailey
Trainer
Jim Pizzutelli
Assistant trainer
Rip Simonick
Equipment supervisor
John Allaway

DRAFT CHOICES

Rnd.	Player	Ht./Wt.	Overall	Pos.	1991-92 club
1	David Cooper	6-2/204	11	D	Medicine Hat (WHL)
2	Jozef Cierny	6-2/176	35	RW	Zvolen, Czech.
3	Ondrej Steiner	6-1/176	59	C	Skoda Plzen, Czech.
4	Dean Melanson	5-11/211	80	D	St. Hyacinthe (QMJHL)
4	Matthew Barnaby	6-0/170	83	LW	Beauport (QMJHL)
5	Markus Ketterer	5-11/169	107	G	Jokerit, Finland
5	Yuri Khmylev	6-1/196	108	F	Krylja Sovetov, CIS
6	Paul Rushforth	6-0/189	131	C	North Bay (OHL)
8	Dean Tiltgen	5-11/175	179	C	Tri-City (WHL)
9	Todd Simon	5-10/188	203	C	Niagara Falls (OHL)
10	Rick Kowalsky	6-0/184	227	RW	Sault Ste. Marie (OHL)
11	Chris Clancy	6-2/198	251	LW	Cornwall (OHL)

MISCELLANEOUS DATA

Home ice (capacity)
Memorial Auditorium
(16,325, including standees)
Address
Memorial Auditorium
140 Main St.
Buffalo, NY 14202
Business phone
716-856-7300 or 800-333-7825

Rink dimensions
193 feet by 84 feet
Club colors
Blue, white and gold
Minor league affiliations
Erie (ECHL)
Rochester (AHL)

SCHEDULE KEY
*All-Star Game at Montreal.
H—Home game.   D—Day game (any game starting before 4 p.m.).
NOTE: At press time, two games at neutral sites had yet to be announced.

TRAINING CAMP ROSTER

No.	FORWARDS	Ht./Wt.	Place	Born Date	NHL exp.	1991-92 clubs
	Dave Andreychuk (LW) .	6-3/225	Hamilton, Ont.	9-29-63	10	Buffalo
28	Donald Audette (RW)	5-8/182	Laval, Que.	9-23-69	3	Buffalo
8	Doug Bodger	6-2/213	Chemainus, B.C.	6-18-66	8	Buffalo
29	Bob Corkum (C/RW)	6-2/212	Salisbury, Mass.	12-18-67	2	Rochester (AHL), Buffalo
	Jason Dawe (LW)	5-10/195	North York, Ont.	5-29-73	0	Peterborough (OHL)
34	Gord Donnelly (RW/D) .	6-1/202	Montreal	4-5-62	9	Winnipeg, Buffalo
14	Dave Hannan (C)...........	5-10/185	Sudbury, Ont.	11-26-61	11	Can. Nat./Olym., Toronto, Buffalo
10	Dale Hawerchuk (C)	5-11/190	Toronto	4-4-63	11	Buffalo
16	Pat LaFontaine (C)	5-10/177	St. Louis	2-22-65	9	Buffalo
	Steve Ludzik (C)............	5-11/195	Toronto	4-3-62	9	Rochester (AHL)
27	Brad May (LW)	6-0/209	Toronto	11-29-71	1	Buffalo
89	Alexander Mogilny	5-11/187	Khabarovsk, U.S.S.R.	2-18-69	3	Buffalo
17	Colin Patterson (C/RW) .	6-2/195	Rexdale, Ont.	5-11-60	9	Buffalo
18	Wayne Presley (RW).....	5-11/180	Dearborn, Mich.	3-23-65	8	San Jose, Buffalo
32	Rob Ray (LW)	6-0/203	Stirling, Ont.	6-8-68	3	Buffalo
	Brad Rubachuk (C)	5-11/180	Winnipeg, Man.	6-11-70	0	Rochester (AHL)
	Jiri Sejba (RW/LW)	5-10/193	Pardubice, Czech.	7-22-62	1	Rochester (AHL)
19	Tony Tanti (RW)	5-9/180	Toronto	9-7-63	11	Buffalo
15	Randy Wood (RW/LW) ..	6-0/195	Princeton, N.J.	10-12-63	6	N.Y. Islanders, Buffalo
	DEFENSEMEN					
	Greg Brown..................	6-0/185	Hartford, Conn.	3-7-70	1	U.S. Nat./Olym., Rochester (AHL)
26	Keith Carney.................	6-2/205	Pawtucket, R.I.	2-3-70	1	Rochester (AHL), Buffalo
39	Brian Curran.................	6-4/220	Toronto	11-5-63	9	Rochester (AHL), Buffalo
47	Bill Houlder	6-3/218	Thunder Bay, Ont.	3-11-67	5	Rochester (AHL), Buffalo
3	Grant Ledyard	6-2/200	Winnipeg, Man.	11-19-61	8	Buffalo
24	Randy Moller	6-2/207	Red Deer, Alta.	8-23-63	10	N.Y. Rangers, Buffalo
5	Mike Ramsey	6-3/195	Minneapolis	12-3-60	13	Buffalo
41	Ken Sutton	6-0/198	Edmonton, Alta.	5-11-69	2	Buffalo
7	Petr Svoboda	6-1/175	Most, Czech.	2-14-66	8	Montreal, Buffalo
	GOALTENDERS					
	Stephane Beauregard	5-11/185	Cowansville, Que.	1-10-68	3	Winnipeg
	John Bradley	6-0/165	Pawtucket, R.I.	2-6-68	0	Erie (ECHL), Rochester (AHL)
	Tom Draper..................	5-11/180	Outremont, Que.	11-20-66	3	Rochester (AHL), Buffalo
	David Littman	6-0/183	Cranston, R.I.	6-13-67	2	Rochester (AHL), Buffalo
30	Clint Malarchuk.............	6-0/185	Grande, Alta.	5-1-61	10	Rochester (AHL), Buffalo
31	Daren Puppa.................	6-3/205	Kirkland Lake, Ont.	3-23-65	7	Rochester (AHL), Buffalo

1991-92 REVIEW

INDIVIDUAL STATISTICS

SCORING

	Games	G	A	Pts.	Pen.	+/-	PPG	SHG	Shots	Shooting Pct.
Dale Hawerchuk	77	23	75	98	27	-22	13	0	242	9.5
Pat LaFontaine	57	46	47	93	98	10	23	0	203	22.7
Dave Andreychuk	80	41	50	91	71	-9	†28	0	337	12.2
Alexander Mogilny	67	39	45	84	73	7	15	0	236	16.5
Donald Audette	63	31	17	48	75	-1	5	0	153	20.3
Doug Bodger	73	11	35	46	108	1	4	0	180	6.1
Randy Wood*	70	20	16	36	65	-9	7	1	185	10.8
Tony Tanti	70	15	16	31	100	-4	6	1	133	11.3
Christian Ruuttu	70	4	21	25	76	-7	0	2	108	3.7
Kevin Haller*	58	6	15	21	75	-13	2	0	76	7.9
Grant Ledyard	50	5	16	21	45	-4	0	0	87	5.7
Ken Sutton	64	2	18	20	71	5	0	0	81	2.5
Dave Snuggerud*	55	3	15	18	36	-3	0	0	75	4.0
Brad May	69	11	6	17	309	-12	1	0	82	13.4
Mike Ramsey	66	3	14	17	67	8	0	0	55	5.5
Colin Patterson	52	4	8	12	30	-4	0	2	33	12.1
Jay Wells*	41	2	9	11	157	-3	0	0	26	7.7
Rob Ray	63	5	3	8	354	-9	0	0	29	17.2
Pierre Turgeon*	8	2	6	8	4	-1	0	0	14	14.3
Petr Svoboda*	13	1	6	7	52	-8	0	0	23	4.3
Dave Hannan*	12	2	4	6	48	1	0	2	8	25.0
Bob Corkum	20	2	4	6	21	-9	0	0	23	8.7
Gord Donnelly*	67	2	3	5	305	-7	0	0	25	8.0
Brad Miller	42	1	4	5	192	-5	0	0	30	3.3
Wayne Presley*	12	2	2	4	57	2	0	0	21	9.5
Rick Vaive	20	1	3	4	14	-2	0	0	25	4.0
Randy Moller*	13	1	2	3	59	1	0	0	19	5.3

	Games	G	A	Pts.	Pen.	+/-	PPG	SHG	Shots	Shooting Pct.
Keith Carney	14	1	2	3	18	-3	1	0	17	5.9
Uwe Krupp*	8	2	0	2	6	0	0	0	13	15.4
Tom Draper (goalie)	26	0	2	2	2	0	0	0	0	0.0
Bill Houlder	10	1	0	1	8	-2	0	0	18	5.6
Darrin Shannon*	1	0	1	1	0	1	0	0	2	0.0
Benoit Hogue*	3	0	1	1	0	0	0	0	6	0.0
Jody Gage	9	0	1	1	2	-1	0	0	9	0.0
Randy Hillier*	28	0	1	1	48	-14	0	0	18	0.0
Lou Franceschetti	1	0	0	0	0	0	0	0	0	0.0
Dave Littman (goalie)	1	0	0	0	0	0	0	0	0	0.0
Pete Ciavaglia	2	0	0	0	0	1	0	0	1	0.0
Darcy Loewen	2	0	0	0	2	0	0	0	1	0.0
Brian Curran	3	0	0	0	14	0	0	0	1	0.0
Dave McLlwain*	5	0	0	0	2	-3	0	0	5	0.0
Clint Malarchuk (goalie)	29	0	0	0	6	0	0	0	0	0.0
Daren Puppa (goalie)	33	0	0	0	2	0	0	0	0	0.0

GOALTENDING

	Games	Min.	Goals	SO	Avg.	W	L	T	Shots	Sv. Pct.
Tom Draper	26	1403	75	1	3.21	10	9	5	712	.895
Clint Malarchuk	29	1639	102	0	3.73	10	13	3	903	.887
Daren Puppa	33	1757	114	0	3.89	11	14	4	932	.878
Dave Littman	1	60	4	0	4.00	0	1	0	29	.862

Empty-net goals (do not count against a goaltender's average): Draper, 2; Malarchuk, 1; Puppa, 1.
*Played with two or more NHL teams.
†Led league.

RESULTS

OCTOBER

4—Pittsburgh	L	4-5
5—At Washington	L	1-3
9—Boston	T	*4-4
12—At Quebec	W	5-4
13—Vancouver	L	1-3
16—At Montreal	L	1-5
18—Montreal	W	3-1
19—At Hartford	L	1-4
25—San Jose	W	3-1
27—Hartford	W	5-1
30—At Detroit	L	1-3

NOVEMBER

1—Montreal	L	1-5
2—At Montreal	L	0-5
7—At Philadelphia	L	2-5
8—Philadelphia	W	*4-3
12—At San Jose	W	7-1
14—At Los Angeles	T	*2-2
16—At Calgary	W	5-4
20—Boston	W	3-1
22—Chicago	W	2-0
23—At Boston	L	4-7
27—Quebec	T	*4-4
29—N.Y. Rangers	L	*4-5
30—At Quebec	L	3-4

DECEMBER

4—At Winnipeg	L	4-5
7—At Hartford	T	*6-6
8—Calgary	L	2-4
11—St. Louis	L	3-6
13—Hartford	L	4-8
14—At Montreal	L	2-4
18—Washington	T	*2-2
20—Edmonton	T	*4-4
21—At Toronto	W	4-1
23—At Hartford	L	3-4
27—Boston	W	8-1
28—At New Jersey	L	0-3
31—St. Louis	W	4-3

JANUARY

3—N.Y. Islanders	W	5-2
4—At Boston	L	2-4
7—At Philadelphia	T	*5-5
8—Quebec	W	4-2
10—Edmonton	W	8-2
12—N.Y. Rangers	W	6-3
14—At N.Y. Rangers	L	2-6
15—At New Jersey	T	*8-8
21—At St. Louis	L	4-5
23—At Pittsburgh	W	*5-4
25—At Montreal	W	4-3
26—Winnipeg	W	5-2
29—At Detroit	T	*4-4
31—Montreal	W	5-3

FEBRUARY

1—At Boston	T	*2-2
4—Washington	W	7-3
7—Minnesota	L	0-2

9—Los Angeles	L	4-5
11—At Hartford	L	1-5
12—Detroit	L	4-9
14—San Jose	W	7-6
16—Hartford	W	5-4
19—At Vancouver	L	5-6
23—At Edmonton	L	2-5
25—At Calgary	W	5-3
29—At Pittsburgh	L	2-5

MARCH

1—Chicago	L	1-3
3—At Quebec	T	*4-4
6—New Jersey	W	5-4
8—N.Y. Islanders	L	2-6
11—Boston	W	6-3
14—At N.Y. Islanders	L	1-4
15—Quebec	W	6-4
17—At Minnesota	L	1-3
19—At Los Angeles	W	8-2
22—At Chicago	W	6-2
25—Toronto	W	5-2
28—At Boston	L	*3-4
29—Hartford	T	*2-2
31—At Minnesota	L	3-5

APRIL

12—Montreal	W	3-1
14—At Quebec	L	3-7
15—Quebec	L	3-4

*Denotes overtime game.

CALGARY FLAMES
CAMPBELL CONFERENCE/SMYTHE DIVISION

1992-93 SCHEDULE

OCTOBER
S	M	T	W	T	F	S
4	5	6 LA H	7	8 EDM H	9	10 TOR H
11	12	13	14	15 LA	16	17 SJ
18	19	20 LA H	21	22 BOS H	23	24
25 EDM	26	27	28 WIN	29	30 WAS H	31 MIN H

NOVEMBER
S	M	T	W	T	F	S
1	2 VAN H	3	4 VAN	5 OTT H	6	7
8 QUE	D 9 MON	10	11 HAR	12 BOS	13	14 TB
15	16	17	18	19 VAN H	20	21 NYI H
22	23	24	25 SJ H	26	27 TB H	28 CHI H
29	30					

DECEMBER
S	M	T	W	T	F	S
		1	2 WIN H	3	4 STL H	5
6	7 EDM H	8 EDM	9	10	11 TOR	12 OTT
13 DET	14 NYR	15	16	17	18	19 LA H
20	21 EDM H	22	23 WIN	24	25	26
27 EDM	28	29	30	31 MON H		

JANUARY
S	M	T	W	T	F	S
					1	2 PHI H
3	4	5 WIN H	6	7 STL	8	9 D PIT
10 BUF	11	12 NYI	13	14 PHI	15	16 MIN
17	18	19 BUFF H	20	21	22 WIN H	23 PIT H
24	25	26 DET H	27	28 LA	29	30 SJ
31						

FEBRUARY
S	M	T	W	T	F	S
	1	2 WAS	3 NJ	4	5	6 *
7	8	9	10 SJ H	11	12 QUE H	13 HAR H
14	15	16	17 TOR	18	19 DET	20
21 CHI	D 22	23 SJ	24	25	26 NYR H	27 SJ H
28						

MARCH
S	M	T	W	T	F	S
	1	2 LA	3	4 STL	5	6 TB
7	8	9	10	11 DET H	12	13 NJ H
14 VAN H	15	16 CHI H	17	18	19	20
21 WIN	D 22	23	24 STL H	25	26 VAN	27
28 TOR H	29	30 WIN H	31			

APRIL
S	M	T	W	T	F	S
				1 MIN H	2	3 D SJ
4 SJ	5	6 LA	7	8	9 VAN H	10
11 VAN	D 12	13 EDM	14	15 SJ H	16	17

1992-93 SEASON

CLUB DIRECTORY

Owners
Harley N. Hotchkiss
Norman L. Kwong
Sonia Scurfield
Byron J. Seaman
Daryl K. Seaman
President and alternate governor
W.C. "Bill" Hay
General manager
Doug Risebrough
Vice president, business and finance
Clare Rhyasen
Vice president, hockey operations
Al MacNeil
Vice president, broadcasting
Leo Ornest
Vice president, marketing
Lanny McDonald
Assistant general manager
Al Coates
Head Coach
Dave King
Assistant coaches
Guy Charron
Jamie Hislop
Goaltending consultant
Glenn Hall

Director of public relations
Rick Skaggs
Assistant public relations director
Mike Burke
Chief scout
Gerry Blair
Scouts
Al Godfrey
Ray Clearwater
Jiri Hrdina
Ian McKenzie
Lou Reycroft
Gerry McNamara
Guy Lapointe
Scouting staff
David Mayville
Lars Norrman
Tom Thompson
Pekka Rautakallio
Glen Giovanacci
Controller
Lynne Tosh
Trainer
Jim "Bearcat" Murray
Equipment manager
Bobby Stewart

DRAFT CHOICES

Rnd. Player	Ht./Wt.	Overall	Pos.	1991-92 club
1—Corey Stillman	6-0/174	6	LW	Windsor (OHL)
2—Chris O'Sullivan	6-2/180	30	D	Catholic Mem. H.S., Boston
3—Mathias Johansson	6-1/189	54	F	Farjestad, Sweden
4—Robert Svehla	6-0/185	78	D	Dukla Trencin, Czech.
5—Sami Helenius	6-5/200	102	D	Jokerit, Finland
6—Ravil Yakubov	6-1/187	126	F	Dynamo Moscow, CIS
6—Joel Bouchard	6-0/180	129	D	Verdun (QMJHL)
7—Pavel Rajnoha	6-0/185	150	D	ZPS Zlin, Czech.
8—Ryan Mulhern	6-1/180	174	C	Canterbury (Conn.) Prep
9—Brandon Carper	6-2/190	198	D	Bowling Green St. (CCHA)
10—Jonas Hoglund	6-1/187	222	RW	Farjestad, Sweden
11—Andrei Potaichuk		246	RW	Krylja Sovetov, CIS

MISCELLANEOUS DATA

Home ice (capacity)
The Olympic Saddledome (20,133)
Address
P.O. Box 1540
Station M
Calgary, Alta. T2P 3B9
Business phone
403-261-0475

Rink dimensions
200 feet by 85 feet
Club colors
Red, white and gold
Minor league affiliation
Salt Lake (IHL)

SCHEDULE KEY

*All-Star Game at Montreal.
H—Home game.   D—Day game (any game starting before 4 p.m.).
NOTE: At press time, two games at neutral sites had yet to be announced.

TRAINING CAMP ROSTER

No.	FORWARDS	Ht./Wt.	Place	BORN Date	NHL exp.	1991-92 clubs
16	Craig Berube (LW)	6-2/195	Calihoo, Alta.	12-17-65	6	Toronto, Calgary
14	Theoren Fleury (C/RW)	5-6/155	Oxbow, Sask.	6-29-68	4	Calgary
27	Tomas Forslund (RW)	6-0/185	Falun, Sweden	11-24-68	1	Salt Lake City (IHL), Calgary
17	Marc Habscheid (RW)	6-0/185	Swift Current, Sask.	3-1-63	11	Calgary
37	Todd Harkins (C)	6-3/210	Cleveland	10-8-68	1	Salt Lake City (IHL), Calgary
12	Paul Kruse (LW)	6-0/202	Merritt, B.C.	3-15-70	2	Salt Lake City (IHL), Calgary
11	Gary Leeman (RW/D)	6-0/175	Toronto	2-19-64	10	Toronto, Calgary
32	Chris Lindberg (LW)	6-1/185	Fort Francis, Ont.	4-16-67	1	Can. Nat./Olym., Calgary
42	Sergei Makarov (RW)	5-11/185	Chelyabinsk, U.S.S.R.	6-19-58	3	Calgary
25	Joe Nieuwendyk (C)	6-1/175	Oshawa, Ont.	9-10-66	6	Calgary
29	Joel Otto (C)	6-4/220	Elk River, Minn.	10-29-61	8	Calgary
28	Paul Ranheim (LW)	6-0/195	St. Louis	1-25-66	4	Calgary
26	Robert Reichel (C)	5-10/185	Litvinov, Czech.	6-25-71	2	Calgary
10	Gary Roberts (LW)	6-1/190	North York, Ont.	5-23-66	6	Calgary
22	Ronnie Stern (RW)	6-0/195	Ste. Ag. Des Mont, Que.	1-11-67	5	Calgary
	Cory Stillman (C)	6-0/174	Peterborough, Ont.	12-20-73	0	Windsor (OHL)
33	Carey Wilson (C/RW)	6-2/205	Winnipeg, Man.	5-19-62	9	Calgary
	C.J. Young (RW)	5-10/180	Waban, Mass.	1-1-68	0	U.S. Nat/Olym.
	DEFENSEMEN					
21	Alexander Godynyuk	6-0/207	Kiev, U.S.S.R.	1-27-70	2	Toronto, Salt Lake City (IHL), Calgary
5	Kevan Guy	6-3/202	Edmonton, Alta.	7-16-65	6	Salt Lake City (IHL), Calgary
4	Jim Kyte	6-5/220	Ottawa	3-21-64	10	Salt Lake City (IHL), Calgary
2	Al MacInnis	6-2/196	Inverness, N.S.	7-11-63	11	Calgary
3	Frantisek Musil	6-3/215	Pardubice, Czech.	12-17-64	6	Calgary
7	Michel Petit	6-1/185	St. Malo, Que.	2-12-64	10	Toronto, Calgary
6	Greg Smyth	6-3/195	Oakville, Ont.	4-23-66	6	Halifax (AHL), Quebec, Calgary
20	Gary Suter	6-0/190	Madison, Wis.	6-24-64	7	Calgary
18	Trent Yawney	6-3/185	Hudson Bay, Sask.	9-29-65	5	Indianapolis (IHL), Calgary
	GOALTENDERS					
37	Trevor Kidd	6-2/176	St. Boniface, Man.	3-26-72	1	Can. Nat./Olym., Calgary
	Jason Muzzatti	6-1/190	Toronto	2-3-70	0	Salt Lake City (IHL)
35	Jeff Reese	5-9/155	Brantford, Ont.	3-24-66	5	Toronto, Calgary
30	Mike Vernon	5-9/170	Calgary, Alta.	2-24-63	9	Calgary

1991-92 REVIEW

INDIVIDUAL STATISTICS

SCORING

	Games	G	A	Pts.	Pen.	+/-	PPG	SHG	Shots	Shooting Pct.
Gary Roberts	76	53	37	90	207	32	15	0	196	†27.0
Al MacInnis	72	20	57	77	83	13	11	0	304	6.6
Theoren Fleury	80	33	40	73	133	0	11	1	225	14.7
Sergei Makarov	68	22	48	70	60	14	6	0	83	26.5
Joe Nieuwendyk	69	22	34	56	55	-1	7	0	137	16.1
Gary Suter	70	12	43	55	128	1	4	0	189	6.3
Robert Reichel	77	20	34	54	32	1	8	0	181	11.0
Paul Ranheim	80	23	20	43	32	16	1	3	159	14.5
Doug Gilmour*	38	11	27	38	46	12	4	1	64	17.2
Joel Otto	78	13	21	34	161	-10	5	1	105	12.4
Carey Wilson	42	11	12	23	37	-6	4	2	74	14.9
Ronnie Stern	72	13	9	22	338	0	0	1	96	13.5
Marc Habscheid	46	7	11	18	42	-11	2	0	60	11.7
Tomas Forslund	38	5	9	14	12	-6	0	0	48	10.4
Jamie Macoun*	37	2	12	14	53	10	1	0	58	3.4
Trent Yawney	47	4	9	13	45	-5	1	0	33	12.1
Michel Petit*	36	3	10	13	79	2	3	0	68	4.4
Frank Musil	78	4	8	12	103	12	1	1	71	5.6
Gary Leeman*	29	2	7	9	27	-11	1	0	50	4.0
Mark Osiecki	50	2	7	9	24	-4	1	0	44	4.5
Chris Lindberg	17	2	5	7	17	3	0	0	19	10.5
Mike Vernon (goalie)	63	0	7	7	8	0	0	0	0	0.0
Craig Berube*	36	1	4	5	155	-3	0	0	27	3.7
Ric Nattress*	18	0	5	5	31	0	0	0	23	0.0
Paul Kruse	16	3	1	4	65	1	0	0	12	25.0
Martin Simard	21	1	3	4	119	-4	1	0	11	9.1
Tim Hunter	30	1	3	4	167	2	0	0	19	5.3
Nevin Markwart*	10	2	1	3	25	-2	0	0	4	50.0

	Games	G	A	Pts.	Pen.	+/-	PPG	SHG	Shots	Shooting Pct.
Tim Sweeney	11	1	2	3	4	0	0	0	16	6.3
Neil Sheehy	35	1	2	3	119	-7	0	0	19	5.3
Greg Smyth*	7	1	1	2	15	7	0	0	10	10.0
Stephane Matteau*	4	1	0	1	19	2	0	0	7	14.3
Richard Zemlak	5	0	1	1	42	-2	0	0	4	0.0
Alexander Godynyuk*	6	0	1	1	4	-2	0	0	12	0.0
Jeff Reese (goalie)*	12	0	1	1	12	0	0	0	0	0.0
Jim Kyte	21	0	1	1	107	2	0	0	13	0.0
Warren Sharples (goalie)	1	0	0	0	0	0	0	0	0	0.0
Darryl Olsen	1	0	0	0	0	-2	0	0	3	0.0
Trevor Kidd (goalie)	2	0	0	0	0	0	0	0	0	0.0
Kevan Guy	3	0	0	0	2	2	0	0	3	0.0
Todd Harkins	5	0	0	0	7	-2	0	0	4	0.0
Rick Wamsley (goalie)*	9	0	0	0	0	0	0	0	0	0.0
Rich Chernomaz	11	0	0	0	6	-9	0	0	21	0.0

GOALTENDING

	Games	Min.	Goals	SO	Avg.	W	L	T	Shots	Sv. Pct.
Mike Vernon	63	3640	217	0	3.58	24	30	9	1853	.883
Warren Sharples	1	65	4	0	3.69	0	0	1	40	.900
Jeff Reese*	12	587	37	0	3.78	3	2	2	290	.872
Trevor Kidd	2	120	8	0	4.00	1	1	0	56	.857
Rick Wamsley*	9	457	34	0	4.46	3	4	0	226	.850

Empty-net goals (do not count against a goaltender's average): Reese, 2; Vernon, 2; Kidd, 1.
*Played with two or more NHL teams.
†Led league.

RESULTS

OCTOBER
4—Edmonton	W	9-2
6—At Winnipeg	L	3-5
8—At San Jose	L	3-4
10—At Los Angeles	W	7-1
12—At Edmonton	L	1-3
15—Minnesota	W	6-3
17—Toronto	W	6-4
19—At Vancouver	L	2-5
22—At Minnesota	W	4-2
24—At Chicago	W	5-2
26—At St. Louis	T	*2-2
30—New Jersey	L	2-5

NOVEMBER
1—At Winnipeg	W	*7-6
4—At N.Y. Rangers	L	0-4
6—At Hartford	W	3-2
7—At Boston	T	*4-4
9—At Toronto	W	6-1
12—Detroit	L	*4-5
14—Vancouver	T	*2-2
16—Buffalo	L	4-5
21—Vancouver	W	3-2
22—At Vancouver	L	*5-6
25—Winnipeg	T	*3-3
28—Los Angeles	W	5-3
30—San Jose	L	1-2

DECEMBER
3—At Detroit	L	2-5
5—At New Jersey	L	3-6
7—At Montreal	L	1-5
8—At Buffalo	W	4-2
10—At Washington	L	1-4
14—Detroit	L	*3-4
17—Winnipeg	W	7-4
19—Quebec	T	*5-5
21—At Winnipeg	L	2-7
23—At Edmonton	L	3-5
28—Philadelphia	W	5-1
29—Los Angeles	W	6-2
31—Montreal	W	*3-2

JANUARY
4—Edmonton	L	2-3
5—At Edmonton	W	3-2
8—San Jose	W	10-3
10—Pittsburgh	W	7-5
13—At Montreal	T	*2-2
14—At Quebec	W	5-3
16—At N.Y. Rangers	L	4-6
22—N.Y. Rangers	T	*4-4
24—At San Jose	W	3-2
25—At Los Angeles	L	3-4
27—Chicago	L	*3-4
30—At Boston	L	1-3

FEBRUARY
1—At Washington	L	2-5
2—At N.Y. Islanders	L	3-6
5—Quebec	W	5-3
7—At Winnipeg	L	1-4
11—N.Y. Islanders	L	1-3
13—Washington	T	*4-4
15—At St. Louis	L	2-7
16—At Chicago	T	*5-5
19—Boston	W	6-4
21—Los Angeles	W	9-7
23—At San Jose	W	4-2
25—Buffalo	L	3-5
27—Philadelphia	L	0-3

MARCH
1—At Vancouver	L	0-11
3—Pittsburgh	L	3-6
5—Toronto	T	*5-5
7—St. Louis	W	5-1
10—At Pittsburgh	L	2-5
12—At Philadelphia	L	*4-5
14—Vancouver	L	4-6
16—Hartford	L	3-4
19—San Jose	W	3-1
21—At Los Angeles	L	2-5
24—Edmonton	T	*4-4
26—Los Angeles	W	7-2
28—Minnesota	W	4-3
31—Edmonton	W	5-2

APRIL
12—Winnipeg	L	3-4
15—At San Jose	W	4-3
16—At Vancouver	T	*4-4

*Denotes overtime game.

CHICAGO BLACKHAWKS
CAMPBELL CONFERENCE/NORRIS DIVISION

1992-93 SCHEDULE

OCTOBER

S	M	T	W	T	F	S
4	5	6	7 TB	8	9	10 STL
11 TB H	12	13	14	15 EDM H	16	17 TOR
18 VAN H	19	20	21 BUF	22 NJ H	23	24
25 DET H	26	27	28	29 PHI H	30	31 BOS

NOVEMBER

S	M	T	W	T	F	S
1 SJ H	2	3	4	5 TOR H	6	7 D QUE
8 PIT H	9	10	11	12 STL H	13	14 D MIN
15 MIN H	16	17 DET	18	19 LA	20	21 SJ
22	23 VAN	24	25	26	27 EDM	28 CAL
29	30					

DECEMBER

S	M	T	W	T	F	S
		1	2	3 TOR H	4	5 TOR
6 MON H	7	8 DET	9	10 NYI H	11	12 MIN
13	14	15	16	17 WIN H	18	19 D PHI
20 MIN H	21	22	23 OTT	24	25	26 STL H
27 DET H	28	29 DET	30	31 TB H		

JANUARY

S	M	T	W	T	F	S
					1	2 D WAS
3 WIN H	4	5	6	7 EDM H	8	9 STL
10 LA H	11	12 MIN	13	14 MIN H	15	16 TOR
17 TOR H	18	19 WIN	20	21 WAS H	22	23 D HAR
24 VAN H	25	26	27 VAN	28	29 SJ	30 LA
31						

FEBRUARY

S	M	T	W	T	F	S
	1	2	3 DET	4	5	*
7	8	9	10	11 BOS H	12	13 D PIT
14 DET H	15	16	17	18 LA H	19	20
21 D CAL H	22	23	24	25 TB	26	27 D DET
28 STL H						

MARCH

S	M	T	W	T	F	S
	1	2	3	4 QUE H	5 NJ	6
7 D OTT H	8	9	10	11 NYR H	12	13
14 D EDM	15	16 CAL	17	18	19	20 MON
21 TB H	22	23	24	25 BUF H	26 NYR	27
28 HAR H	29	30	31			

APRIL

S	M	T	W	T	F	S
				1 DET H	2	3 STL
4 STL H	5	6	7	8 NYI H	9	10 D TB
11 D TB H	12	13 MIN	14	15 TOR H	16	17

1992-93 SEASON

CLUB DIRECTORY

President
William W. Wirtz
Vice president
Arthur M. Wirtz Jr.
Vice president and asst. to the president
Thomas N. Ivan
Senior vice president
Bob Pulford
General manager
Mike Keenan
Assistant general manager
Jack Davison
Director of player personnel
Bob Murray
Head coach
Darryl Sutter
Assistant coaches
Rich Preston
Paul Baxter

Scouts
Jimmy Walker
Dave Lucas
Kerry Davison
Michel Dumas
Jim Pappin
Jan Spieczny
Duane Sutter
Steve Lyons
Brian DeBruyn
Russ Huston
Public relations
Jim DeMaria
Trainer
Mike Gapski
Lou Varga
Randy Lacey

DRAFT CHOICES

Rnd. Player	Ht./Wt.	Overall	Pos.	1991-92 club
1—Sergei Krivokrasov.	5-11/174	12	RW	Central Red Army, CIS
2—Jeff Shantz.............	6-0/184	36	C	Regina (WHL)
2—Sergei Klimovich.....	6-2/189	41	C	Dynamo Moscow, CIS
4—Andy McIntyre........	6-1/190	89	LW	Saskatoon (WHL)
5—Tim Hogan..............	6-2/180	113	D	U. of Michigan (CCHA)
6—Gerry Skrypec.........	5-11/186	137	D	Ottawa (OHL)
7—Mike Prokopec	6-1/175	161	RW	Cornwall (OHL)
8—Layne Roland	6-1/215	185	RW	Portland (WHL)
9—David Hymovitz.......	5-11/170	209	LW	Thayer (Mass.) Academy
10—Richard Raymond ...	6-1/187	233	D	Cornwall (OHL)

MISCELLANEOUS DATA

Home ice (capacity)
Chicago Stadium (17,317)
Address
1800 W. Madison Street
Chicago, IL 60612
Business phone
312-733-5300

Rink dimensions
185 feet by 85 feet
Club colors
Red, black and white
Minor league affiliation
Indianapolis (IHL)

SCHEDULE KEY

*All-Star Game at Montreal.
H—Home game.   D—Day game (any game starting before 4 p.m.).
NOTE: At press time, two games at neutral sites had yet to be announced.

TRAINING CAMP ROSTER

No.	FORWARDS	Ht./Wt.	Place	Born Date	NHL exp.	1991-92 clubs
22	Rob Brown (RW)	5-11/185	Kingston, Ont.	4-10-68	5	Hartford, Chicago
	Stefan Elvenas (RW)	6-1/183	Lund, Sweden	3-30-70	0	Rogle (Sweden)
14	Greg Gilbert (LW)	6-1/191	Mississauga, Ontario	1-22-62	11	Chicago
16	Michel Goulet (LW)	6-1/195	Peribonqua, Que.	4-21-60	13	Chicago
33	Dirk Graham (LW/RW)	5-11/190	Regina, Sask.	7-29-59	9	Chicago
23	Stu Grimson (LW)	6-5/220	Kamloops, B.C.	5-20-65	4	Indianapolis (IHL), Chicago
34	Tony Horacek (LW)	6-4/215	Vancouver, B.C.	2-3-67	3	Philadelphia, Chicago
11	Tony Hrkac (C)	5-11/170	Thunder Bay, Ont.	7-7-66	6	San Jose, Chicago
20	Mike Hudson (C/LW)	6-1/185	Guelph, Ont.	2-6-67	4	Chicago
	Sergei Krivokrasov	5-11/175	Angarsk, U.S.S.R.	4-15-74	0	CSKA Moscow (CIS)
28	Steve Larmer (RW)	5-10/189	Peterborough, Ont.	6-16-61	12	Chicago
11	Brad Lauer (RW)	6-0/195	Humbolt, Sask.	10-27-66	6	Indianapolis (IHL), N.Y. Islanders, Chicago
26	Jocelyn Lemieux (RW)	5-10/200	Mont Laurier, Que.	11-18-67	6	Chicago
32	Stephane Matteau (LW)	6-3/195	Rouyn, Que.	9-2-69	2	Calgary, Chicago
19	Dean McAmmond (C)	5-11/185	Grand Cache, Alta.	6-15-73	1	Prince Albert (WHL), Chicago
10	Brian Noonan (C/RW)	6-1/180	Boston	5-29-65	5	Chicago
27	Jeremy Roenick (C)	6-0/170	Boston	1-17-70	4	Chicago
12	Brent Sutter (C)	5-11/180	Viking, Alta.	6-10-62	12	N.Y. Islanders, Chicago
	Kerry Toporowski (RW)	6-2/212	Prince Albert, Sask.	4-9-71	0	Indianapolis (IHL)
53	Sean Williams (C)	6-1/182	Oshawa, Ont.	1-28-68	1	Indianapolis (IHL), Chicago
	DEFENSEMEN					
47	Adam Bennett	6-4/206	Georgetown, Ont.	3-30-71	1	Indianapolis (IHL), Chicago
4	Keith Brown	6-1/195	Corner Brook, Nfld.	5-6-60	13	Chicago
25	Rod Buskas	6-1/200	Wetaskiwin, Alta.	1-7-61	10	Los Angeles, Chicago
7	Chris Chelios	6-1/192	Chicago	1-25-62	9	Chicago
45	Karl Dykhuis	6-3/200	Sept-Iles, Que.	7-8-72	1	Longeueil (QMJHL), Chicago
3	Igor Kravchuk	6-1/200	Ufa, U.S.S.R.	9-13-66	1	Central Red Army (CIS), Unified Olym., Chicago
6	Frantisek Kucera	6-2/205	Prague, Czech.	2-3-68	2	Indianapolis (IHL), Chicago
2	Bryan Marchment	6-1/198	Scarborough, Ont.	5-1-69	4	Chicago
8	Cam Russell	6-4/175	Halifax, N.S.	1-12-69	3	Indianapolis (IHL), Chicago
5	Steve Smith	6-4/215	Glasgow, Scotland	4-30-63	8	Chicago
	GOALTENDERS					
30	Ed Belfour	5-11/182	Carman, Man.	4-21-65	4	Chicago
	Roch Belley	5-10/170	Hull, Que.	8-12-71	0	Indianapolis (IHL)
31	Dominik Hasek	5-11/165	Pardubice, Czech.	1-29-65	2	Indianapolis (IHL), Chicago
50	Ray LeBlanc	5-10/170	Fitchburg, Mass.	10-24-64	1	U.S. Nat./Olym., Indianapolis (IHL), Chicago
29	Jimmy Waite	6-0/163	Sherbrooke, Que.	4-15-69	4	Hershey (AHL), Indianapolis (IHL), Chicago

1991-92 REVIEW

INDIVIDUAL STATISTICS

SCORING

	Games	G	A	Pts.	Pen.	+/-	PPG	SHG	Shots	Shooting Pct.
Jeremy Roenick	80	53	50	103	98	23	22	3	234	22.6
Steve Larmer	80	29	45	74	65	10	11	2	292	9.9
Michel Goulet	75	22	41	63	69	20	9	0	176	12.5
Chris Chelios	80	9	47	56	245	24	2	2	239	3.8
Brent Sutter*	61	18	32	50	30	-5	7	1	185	9.7
Dirk Graham	80	17	30	47	89	-5	6	1	222	7.7
Brian Noonan	65	19	12	31	81	9	4	0	154	12.3
Steve Smith	76	9	21	30	304	23	3	0	153	5.9
Mike Hudson	76	14	15	29	92	-11	2	1	97	14.4
Keith Brown	57	6	10	16	69	7	2	1	105	5.7
Jocelyn Lemieux	78	6	10	16	80	-2	0	0	103	5.8
Rob Brown*	25	5	11	16	34	-1	3	0	41	12.2
Steve Konroyd*	49	2	14	16	65	4	0	0	70	2.9
Bryan Marchment	58	5	10	15	168	-4	2	0	55	9.1
Stephane Matteau*	20	5	8	13	45	3	1	0	31	16.1
Frantisek Kucera	61	3	10	13	36	3	1	0	82	3.7
Greg Gilbert	50	7	5	12	35	-4	0	0	45	15.6
Adam Creighton*	11	6	6	12	16	-1	2	0	32	18.8
Mike Peluso	63	6	3	9	†408	1	2	0	32	18.8
Igor Kravchuk	18	1	8	9	4	-3	0	0	40	2.5
Mike Stapleton	19	4	4	8	8	0	1	0	32	12.5

	Games	G	A	Pts.	Pen.	+/-	PPG	SHG	Shots	Shooting Pct.
Dan Vincelette	29	3	5	8	56	-6	0	0	28	10.7
Steve Thomas*	11	2	6	8	26	-3	0	0	35	5.7
John Tonelli*	33	1	7	8	37	2	0	0	29	3.4
Tony Horacek*	12	1	4	5	21	2	0	0	10	10.0
Stu Grimson	54	2	2	4	234	-2	0	0	23	8.7
Karl Dykhuis	6	1	3	4	4	-1	1	0	12	8.3
Rod Buskas*	42	0	4	4	80	-12	0	0	22	0.0
Tony Hrkac*	18	1	2	3	6	4	0	0	22	4.5
Dean McAmmond	5	0	2	2	0	-2	0	0	4	0.0
Ryan McGill	9	0	2	2	20	1	0	0	15	0.0
Ed Belfour (goalie)	52	0	2	2	38	0	0	0	0	0.0
Jim Waite (goalie)	17	0	1	1	0	0	0	0	0	0.0
Raymond LeBlanc (goalie)	1	0	0	0	0	0	0	0	0	0.0
Adam Bennett	5	0	0	0	12	1	0	0	6	0.0
Shawn Byram	1	0	0	0	0	0	0	0	1	0.0
Cam Russell	19	0	0	0	34	-8	0	0	9	0.0
Rob Conn	2	0	0	0	2	1	0	0	3	0.0
Brad Lauer*	6	0	0	0	4	-3	0	0	6	0.0
Sean Williams	2	0	0	0	4	0	0	0	0	0.0
Rick Lanz	1	0	0	0	2	0	0	0	0	0.0
Jeff Jackson	1	0	0	0	2	0	0	0	0	0.0
Paul Gillis*	2	0	0	0	6	-3	0	0	1	0.0
Dominik Hasek (goalie)	20	0	0	0	8	0	0	0	0	0.0

GOALTENDING

	Games	Min.	Goals	SO	Avg.	W	L	T	Shots	Sv. Pct.
Raymond LeBlanc	1	60	1	0	1.00	1	0	0	22	.955
Dominik Hasek	20	1014	44	1	2.60	10	4	1	413	.893
Ed Belfour	52	2928	132	‡5	2.70	21	18	10	1241	.894
Jim Waite	17	877	54	0	3.69	4	7	4	347	.844

Empty-net goals (do not count against a goaltender's average): Belfour, 4; Waite, 1.
*Played with two or more NHL teams.
†Led league.
‡Tied for league lead.

RESULTS

OCTOBER

3—Detroit	T	*3-3
5—At Minnesota	L	2-4
6—New Jersey	L	*2-4
10—Vancouver	W	7-6
12—At Washington	W	7-2
13—San Jose	W	7-3
17—Edmonton	W	4-2
19—At St. Louis	T	*4-4
20—St. Louis	L	1-4
22—At Pittsburgh	T	*4-4
24—Calgary	L	2-5
26—At Hartford	W	4-2
27—Boston	L	3-6
31—N.Y. Islanders	W	4-3

NOVEMBER

2—At Minnesota	L	3-4
3—Minnesota	T	*4-4
7—Quebec	W	4-2
9—At Montreal	L	2-4
10—Hartford	W	3-0
14—Toronto	W	3-0
16—At Toronto	T	*2-2
17—St. Louis	W	5-1
19—At Detroit	L	1-4
22—At Buffalo	L	0-2
27—At Edmonton	L	2-6
29—At Vancouver	L	2-5

DECEMBER

1—At Winnipeg	L	*2-3
5—Los Angeles	W	6-2
7—At N.Y. Islanders	W	5-2
8—Minnesota	W	7-2
10—At Detroit	L	3-5
14—At Philadelphia	T	*1-1
15—Philadelphia	T	*4-4
19—Montreal	W	6-4
21—At New Jersey	T	*1-1
22—St. Louis	W	5-2
26—At St. Louis	L	1-3
27—Winnipeg	T	*3-3
29—Detroit	L	4-6
31—At Minnesota	L	2-6

JANUARY

2—N.Y. Rangers	L	3-4
4—At Toronto	W	4-2
5—Minnesota	W	5-2
9—Toronto	W	2-0
10—At Winnipeg	L	2-6
12—Washington	W	4-2
14—At Philadelphia	T	*1-1
16—Toronto	W	4-0
23—Quebec	W	4-2
25—At Minnesota	W	2-0
27—At Calgary	W	*4-3
29—At Edmonton	W	4-3
30—At Vancouver	L	1-4

FEBRUARY

1—At Los Angeles	L	0-2
5—At San Jose	L	2-5
8—At St. Louis	W	3-1
13—Los Angeles	T	*2-2
16—Calgary	T	*5-5
20—New Jersey	T	*4-4
22—At Detroit	L	1-2
23—St. Louis	W	4-2
25—At N.Y. Rangers	L	1-4
27—Detroit	W	4-2
29—At Toronto	L	*5-6

MARCH

1—At Buffalo	W	3-1
5—N.Y. Islanders	T	*4-4
7—At Boston	W	2-1
8—Boston	W	4-0
10—San Jose	W	5-1
11—At N.Y. Rangers	L	1-7
15—Pittsburgh	L	3-4
19—Minnesota	W	4-1
21—At Toronto	W	3-1
22—Buffalo	L	2-6
26—At Quebec	W	*5-4
28—At Hartford	W	5-1
29—Toronto	W	5-1
31—At Detroit	T	*3-3

APRIL

| 12—Detroit | L | 1-2 |
| 14—At St. Louis | L | 3-5 |

*Denotes overtime game.

DETROIT RED WINGS
CAMPBELL CONFERENCE/NORRIS DIVISION

1992-93 SCHEDULE

OCTOBER

S	M	T	W	T	F	S
4	5	6 WIN	7	8 LA	9	10 SJ
11	12	13	14	15 QUE H	16	17 EDM H
18	19	20 WIN H	21	22 PIT	23	24 STL
25 CHI	26	27	28 SJ H	29	30 TOR H	31 TOR

NOVEMBER

S	M	T	W	T	F	S
1	2	3	4 MON H	5	6 HAR H	7 MON
8	9	10	11 TB	12	13 PIT H	14 HAR
15	16	17 CHI H	18	19 WIN H	20 WAS	21
22	23 TB H	24	25 STL H	26	27 LA H	28 STL
29 WAS H	30					

DECEMBER

S	M	T	W	T	F	S
		1	2 NYR	3 MIN H	4	5 TB
6	7	8 CHI H	9 TOR	10	11 PHI H	12
13	14 CAL H	15 OTT	16	17	18 BOS H	19 MIN
20	21	22 TOR H	23	24	25	26 TOR
27	28	29 CHI H	30	31 OTT H		

JANUARY

S	M	T	W	T	F	S
					1	2 QUE
3	4 TOR H	5	6	7	8 VAN H	9
10	11 STL H	12	13 TB H	14	15 SJ H	16
17 PHI	18	19 NYR H	20	21 STL H	22	23 STL
24	25	26 CAL	27 EDM	28	29	30 VAN
31						

FEBRUARY

S	M	T	W	T	F	S
	1	2	3 CHI H	4	5	6 *
7	8	9 NJ H	10	11 LA	12	13 STL
14 CHI	15	16	17 TB H	18	19 CAL H	20
21 D MIN	22	23	24 BUF	25	26	27 D CHI H
28 NJ						

MARCH

S	M	T	W	T	F	S
	1	2 NYI	3	4	5 TOR H	6
7 MIN	8	9	10 EDM	11 CAL	12	13
14 D SJ	15	16	17	18 MIN H	19	20 D BOS
21 D MIN	22	23 NYI H	24	25	26	27 TB
28	29 LA H	30	31			

APRIL

S	M	T	W	T	F	S
				1	2 CHI	3 D VAN H
4	5	6	7	8 TB	9	10 D BUF H
11	12	13	14	15 MIN H	16	17

1992-93 SEASON

CLUB DIRECTORY

Owner and president
Michael Ilitch
Owner and secretary/treasurer
Marian Ilitch
Executive vice president
James Lites
General counsel
Denise Ilitch Lites
Senior vice president
Jim Devellano
General manager and coach
Bryan Murray
Assistant G.M./hockey operations director
Nick Polano
Associate coach
Doug MacLean
Assistant coach
Dave Lewis
Goaltending coach
Phil Myre
Pro scouting director
Dan Belisle
Director of amateur scouting
Ken Holland
USA scouting director
Billy Dea

Western hockey league scout
Wayne Meier
Western USA scout
Chris Coury
Eastern USA scout
Mike Addesa
Northern Ontario scout
Dave Polano
Eastern Canada scout
John Stanton
European scouts
Hakan Andersson
Vladimir Havluj
Director of public relations
Bill Jamieson
Director of advertising sales
Terry Murphy
Athletic therapist
John Wharton
Athletic trainer
Mark Brennan
Assistant trainer
TBA

DRAFT CHOICES

Rnd.	Player	Ht./Wt.	Overall	Pos.	1991-92 club
1	Curtis Bowen	6-1/189	22	LW	Ottawa (OHL)
2	Darren McCarty	6-1/214	46	RW	Belleville (OHL)
3	Sylvain Cloutier	6-0/195	70	C	Guelph (OHL)
5	Mike Sullivan	6-1/190	118	C	Reading (Mass.) H.S.
6	Jason MacDonald	6-0/195	142	RW	Owen Sound (OHL)
7	Greg Scott	6-2/191	166	G	Niagara Falls (OHL)
8	Justin Krall	6-2/170	183	D	Omaha (Junior A, Tier II)
8	C.J. Denomme	5-11/180	189	G	Kitchener (OHL)
9	Jeff Walker	6-4/190	214	D	Peterborough (OHL)
10	Daniel McGillis	6-2/220	238	D	Hawkesbury (Jr. A, Tier II)
11	Ryan Bach	6-1/180	262	G	Notre Dame (Tier II)

MISCELLANEOUS DATA

Home ice (capacity)
Joe Louis Arena (19,275)
Address
600 Civic Center Drive
Detroit, MI 48226
Business phone
313-567-7333

Rink dimensions
200 feet by 85 feet
Club colors
Red and white
Minor league affiliations
Adirondack (AHL)
Toledo (ECHL)

SCHEDULE KEY

*All-Star Game at Montreal.
H—Home game.   D—Day game (any game starting before 4 p.m.).
NOTE: At press time, two games at neutral sites had yet to be announced.

No.	FORWARDS	Ht./Wt.	Place	BORN Date	NHL exp.	1991-92 clubs
11	Shawn Burr (LW)	6-1/180	Sarnia, Ont.	7-1-66	8	Detroit
12	Jimmy Carson (C)	6-1/200	Southfield, Mich.	7-20-68	6	Detroit
	Dino Ciccarelli (RW)	5-10/175	Sarnia, Ont.	2-8-60	12	Washington
25	Troy Crowder (RW)	6 3/200	Sudbury, Ont.	5-3-68	4	Detroit
47	Jim Cummins (RW)	6-2/200	Dearborn, Mich.	5-17-70	1	Adirondack (AHL), Detroit
91	Sergei Fedorov (C)	6-1/191	Minsk, U.S.S.R.	12-13-69	2	Detroit
14	Brent Fedyk (RW)	6-0/195	Yorkton, Sask.	3-8-67	5	Adirondack (AHL), Detroit
17	Gerard Gallant (LW)	5-10/185	Summerside, P.E.I.	9-2-63	8	Detroit
28	Sheldon Kennedy (RW)	5-11/170	Brandon, Man.	6-15-69	3	Adirondack (AHL), Detroit
13	Vyacheslav Kozlov (C)	5-10/172	Voskresensk, U.S.S.R.	5-3-72	1	Red Army (CIS), Detroit
22	Martin Lapointe (RW)	5-11/197	Lachine, Que.	9-12-73	1	Laval (QMJHL), Detroit
46	Marc Potvin (RW)	6-1/185	Ottawa	1-29-67	2	Adirondack (AHL), Detroit
55	Keith Primeau (LW/C)	6-4/220	Toronto	11-24-71	2	Adirondack (AHL), Detroit
24	Bob Probert (RW)	6-3/215	Windsor, Ont.	6-5-65	7	Detroit
26	Ray Sheppard (RW)	6-1/182	Pembroke, Ont.	5-27-66	5	Detroit
	Gary Shuchuk (C)	5-10/185	Edmonton, Alta.	2-17-67	1	Adirondack (AHL)
	Mike Sillinger (C)	5-10/191	Regina, Sask.	6-29-71	2	Adirondack (AHL)
	Chris Tancill (C)	5-10/185	Livonia, Mich.	2-7-68	2	Springfield (AHL), Hartford, Adirondack (AHL), Detroit
21	Paul Ysebaert (LW)	6-1/190	Sarnia, Ont.	5-15-66	4	Detroit
19	Steve Yzerman (C)	5-11/183	Cranbrook, B.C.	5-9-65	9	Detroit
	DEFENSEMEN					
	Serge Anglehart	6-2/190	Hull, Que.	4-18-70	0	Adirondack (AHL)
3	Steve Chiasson	6-0/202	Barrie, Ont.	4-14-67	6	Detroit
8	Bobby Dollas	6-2/212	Montreal	1-31-65	7	Adirondack (AHL), Detroit
	Mark Howe	5-11/185	Detroit	5-28-55	13	Philadelphia
16	Vladimir Konstantinov	5-11/176	Murmansk, U.S.S.R.	3-19-67	1	Detroit
	Gord Kruppke	6-1/200	Edmonton, Alta.	4-2-69	1	Adirondack (AHL)
5	Nicklas Lidstrom	6-2/180	Vasteras, Sweden	4-28-70	1	Detroit
	Christopher Luongo	6-0/180	Detroit	3-17-67	1	Adirondack (AHL)
2	Brad McCrimmon	5-11/197	Dodsland, Sask.	3-29-59	12	Detroit
	Dimitri Motkov	6-3/190	Moscow, U.S.S.R.	2-23-71	0	Red Army (CIS)
33	Yves Racine	6-0/185	Matane, Que.	2-7-69	3	Detroit
	Bob Wilkie	6-2/200	Calgary, Alta.	2-11-69	1	Adirondack (AHL)
	Jason York	6-2/195	Nepean, Ont.	5-20-70	0	Adirondack (AHL)
	GOALTENDERS					
32	Tim Cheveldae	5-11/180	Melville, Sask.	2-15-68	4	Detroit
	Dave Gagnon	6-0/185	Essex, Ont.	10-31-67	1	Toledo (ECHL), Fort Wayne (IHL)
31	Scott King	6-1/170	Thunder Bay, Ont.	6-25-67	2	Toledo (ECHL), Adirondack (AHL), Detroit
34	Greg Millen	5-9/160	Toronto	6-25-57	14	Maine (AHL), San Diego (IHL), Detroit
37	Vince Riendeau	5-10/185	St. Hyacinthe, Que.	4-20-66	5	St. Louis, Adirondack (AHL), Detroit

1991-92 REVIEW

INDIVIDUAL STATISTICS

SCORING

	Games	G	A	Pts.	Pen.	+/-	PPG	SHG	Shots	Shooting Pct.
Steve Yzerman	79	45	58	103	64	26	9	†8	295	15.3
Sergei Fedorov	80	32	54	86	72	26	7	2	249	12.9
Paul Ysebaert	79	35	40	75	55	†44	3	4	211	16.6
Jimmy Carson	80	34	35	69	30	17	11	0	150	22.7
Ray Sheppard	74	36	26	62	27	7	11	1	178	20.2
Nicklas Lidstrom	80	11	49	60	22	36	5	0	168	6.5
Shawn Burr	79	19	32	51	118	26	2	0	140	13.6
Kevin Miller	80	20	26	46	53	6	3	1	130	15.4
Bob Probert	63	20	24	44	276	16	8	0	96	20.8
Gerard Gallant	69	14	22	36	187	16	4	0	116	12.1
Steve Chiasson	62	10	24	34	136	22	5	0	143	7.0
Vladimir Konstantinov	79	8	26	34	172	25	1	0	108	7.4
Brad McCrimmon	79	7	22	29	118	39	2	1	94	7.4
Yves Racine	61	2	22	24	94	-6	1	0	103	1.9
Keith Primeau	35	6	10	16	83	9	0	0	27	22.2
Brent Fedyk	61	5	8	13	42	-5	0	0	60	8.3
Sheldon Kennedy	27	3	8	11	24	-2	0	0	33	9.1
Alan Kerr	58	3	8	11	133	1	0	0	41	7.3
Doug Crossman	26	0	8	8	14	8	0	0	21	0.0
Brad Marsh	55	3	4	7	53	8	0	0	29	10.3

	Games	G	A	Pts.	Pen.	+/-	PPG	SHG	Shots	Shooting Pct.
Brian MacLellan	23	1	5	6	38	4	0	0	17	5.9
Bobby Dollas	27	3	1	4	20	4	0	1	26	11.5
Tim Cheveldae (goalie)	72	0	4	4	6	0	0	0	0	0.0
Johan Garpenlov*	16	1	1	2	4	2	0	0	13	7.7
Vyacheslav Kozlov	7	0	2	2	2	-2	0	0	9	0.0
Marc Potvin	5	1	0	1	52	-2	0	0	4	25.0
Dennis Vial	27	1	0	1	72	1	0	0	6	16.7
Martin Lapointe	4	0	1	1	5	2	0	0	2	0.0
Allan Bester (goalie)	1	0	0	0	0	0	0	0	0	0.0
Jim Cummins	1	0	0	0	7	0	0	0	0	0.0
Scott King (goalie)	1	0	0	0	0	0	0	0	0	0.0
Chris Tancill*	1	0	0	0	0	0	0	0	0	0.0
Vincent Riendeau (goalie)*	2	0	0	0	0	0	0	0	0	0.0
Rick Zombo*	3	0	0	0	15	-3	0	0	1	0.0
Troy Crowder	7	0	0	0	35	0	0	0	2	0.0
Greg Millen (goalie)	10	0	0	0	0	0	0	0	0	0.0
Bob McGill*	12	0	0	0	21	-3	0	0	6	0.0

GOALTENDING

	Games	Min.	Goals	SO	Avg.	W	L	T	Shots	Sv. Pct.
Vincent Riendeau*	2	87	2	0	1.38	2	0	0	31	.935
Greg Millen	10	487	22	0	2.71	3	2	3	212	.896
Tim Cheveldae	72	†4236	226	2	3.20	‡38	23	9	†1978	.886
Scott King	1	16	1	0	3.75	0	0	0	5	.800
Allan Bester	1	31	2	0	3.87	0	0	0	9	.778

Combined shutout—Cheveldae & Riendeau.
Empty-net goals (do not count against a goaltender's average): Millen, 2; Cheveldae, 1.
*Played with two or more NHL teams.
†Led league.
‡Tied for league lead.

RESULTS

OCTOBER

3—At Chicago	T	*3-3
5—At Toronto	L	5-8
10—Montreal	L	1-4
12—At Minnesota	L	2-3
15—Edmonton	W	3-1
17—St. Louis	W	6-3
19—At Quebec	W	6-1
23—Winnipeg	L	2-3
25—Toronto	W	4-0
26—At Toronto	L	1-6
28—Los Angeles	L	3-4
30—Buffalo	W	3-1

NOVEMBER

1—Hartford	W	8-5
2—At Boston	L	1-4
5—Minnesota	L	2-3
7—St. Louis	W	10-3
8—At Washington	W	5-4
10—St. Louis	W	6-4
12—At Calgary	W	*5-4
14—At San Jose	T	*3-3
16—At Los Angeles	W	5-3
19—Chicago	W	4-1
22—Minnesota	W	4-3
23—At Minnesota	T	*2-2
25—Washington	W	5-4
30—At St. Louis	L	3-7

DECEMBER

3—Calgary	W	5-2
6—N.Y. Rangers	W	*6-5
7—At New Jersey	T	*2-2
10—Chicago	W	5-3
12—Quebec	W	4-1
14—At Calgary	W	*4-3
15—At Edmonton	W	4-1
17—At Vancouver	L	1-2
21—At Los Angeles	W	5-2
28—At Toronto	W	5-4
29—At Chicago	W	6-4
31—Boston	L	3-5

JANUARY

3—Toronto	W	6-4
4—At St. Louis	W	6-2
7—N.Y. Islanders	L	2-5
9—Minnesota	W	9-4
11—Edmonton	T	*5-5
14—At N.Y. Islanders	L	2-6
16—Pittsburgh	T	*3-3
21—Philadelphia	W	7-3
23—Vancouver	L	1-3
25—At New Jersey	W	7-0
29—Buffalo	T	*4-4
31—New Jersey	L	3-6

FEBRUARY

1—At Montreal	L	*3-4
3—At Pittsburgh	T	*4-4
5—Washington	W	4-1
7—Toronto	L	3-4

9—At N.Y. Rangers	T	*5-5
11—At Toronto	L	3-4
12—At Buffalo	W	9-4
15—San Jose	W	11-1
17—St. Louis	W	5-3
20—Toronto	W	3-2
22—Chicago	W	2-1
23—At Hartford	W	4-0
27—At Chicago	L	2-4
29—At St. Louis	W	3-2

MARCH

3—Winnipeg	L	3-4
5—Minnesota	L	2-4
7—At Quebec	T	*4-4
8—At Montreal	l	1-4
12—At St. Louis	W	5-4
14—At Minnesota	L	1-4
15—At Winnipeg	T	*1-1
17—At San Jose	W	5-4
20—N.Y. Rangers	L	2-4
22—At Philadelphia	L	3-4
24—Pittsburgh	W	4-3
28—Vancouver	W	3-1
29—At N.Y. Islanders	W	6-2
31—Chicago	T	*3-3

APRIL

12—At Chicago	W	2-1
14—At Minnesota	W	7-4

*Denotes overtime game.

EDMONTON OILERS
CAMPBELL CONFERENCE/SMYTHE DIVISION

1992-93 SCHEDULE

OCTOBER

S	M	T	W	T	F	S
4	5	6 VAN H	7	8 CAL	9	10 VAN
11 TOR H	12	13	14 WIN H	15 CHI	16	17 DET
18	19	20 TB	21	22	23 BOS H	24
25 CAL H	26	27	28 MIN H	29	30	31 WAS H

NOVEMBER

S	M	T	W	T	F	S
1	2	3 OTT H	4	5	6 WIN H	7 MIN
8	9	10 STL	11	12 SJ	13	14 LA
15	16	17	18 VAN H	19	20	21 VAN
22 NYI H	23	24	25 LA H	26	27 CHI H	28 TB H
29	30					

DECEMBER

S	M	T	W	T	F	S
		1 SJ	2	3 VAN	4	5 STL H
6	7 CAL	8 CAL H	9	10 MIN	11	12 TB
13	14	15	16 VAN H	17	18 LA H	19
20	21 CAL	22	23 SJ H	24	25	26
27 CAL H	28	29 MON H	30	31 WIN		

JANUARY

S	M	T	W	T	F	S
					1	2 TB H
3 PHI H	4	5 STL	6	7 CHI	8	9 WAS
10 PHI	11	12	13 WIN H	14	15 HAR H	16
17 BUF H	18	19 LA H	20	21	22 PIT H	23 WIN
24	25	26	27 DET H	28	29	30
31 D BUF						

FEBRUARY

S	M	T	W	T	F	S
	1	2 BOS	3 OTT	4	5	6 *
7	8	9 LA	10	11	12 SJ H	13
14 D QUE H	15	16 NYI	17	18 PIT	19	20 D HAR
21 MON	22	23 QUE	24	25	26	27 NYR H
28 SJ H						

MARCH

S	M	T	W	T	F	S
	1	2	3	4 WIN H	5	6 LA
7 SJ	8	9	10 DET H	11	12 NJ H	13
14 D CHI H	15	16	17 NYR	18 NJ	19	20 TOR
21	22	23	24	25	26 LA H	27 TOR H
28	29	30	31 MIN H			

APRIL

S	M	T	W	T	F	S
				1	2	3 WIN H
4	5	6 SJ	7 VAN	8	9	10
11 D WIN H	12	13 CAL H	14	15 WIN	16	17

1992-93 SEASON

CLUB DIRECTORY

Owner/governor
Peter Pocklington
Alternate governor
Glen Sather
General counsels
Bob Lloyd
Gary Frohlich
President/general manager
Glen Sather
Coach
Ted Green
Assistant coach
Ron Low
Kevin Primeau
Exec. V.P./assistant general manager
Bruce MacGregor
Vice president, finance
Werner Baum
Executive secretary
Betsy Dolinsky

Director of public relations
Bill Tuele
Coord. of publications & statistics
Steve Knowles
Director of player personnel/chief scout
Barry Fraser
Scouting staff
Lorne Davis
Ace Bailey
Ed Chadwick
Matti Vaisanen
Harry Howell
Athletic trainer
Barrie Stafford
Assistant trainer
Lyle Kulchisky
Athletic trainer/therapist
Ken Lowe
Team physician
Dr. Gordon Cameron

DRAFT CHOICES

Rnd. Player	Ht./Wt.	Overall	Pos.	1991-92 club
1—Joe Hulbig	6-3/212	13	LW	St. Sebastian H.S., Needham, Mass.
2—Martin Reichel	6-1/180	37	RW	Freiburg, Germany
3—Simon Roy	6-1/177	61	D	Shawinigan (QMJHL)
3—Kirk Maltby	6-0/180	65	RW	Owen Sound (OHL)
4—Ralph Intranuovo	5-8/170	96	C	Sault Ste. Marie (OHL)
5—Joachim Gage	6-0/200	109	G	Portland (WHL)
7—Steve Gibson	6-0/204	157	LW	Windsor (OHL)
8—Kyuin Shim	6-2/190	181	RW	Sherwood Park (Tier II)
8—Colin Schmidt	5-11/185	190	C	Regina Midgets
9—Marko Tuomainen	6-2/190	205	RW	Clarkson College (ECAC)
11—Bryan Rasmussen	6-1/180	253	LW	St. Louis Park (Minn.) H.S.

MISCELLANEOUS DATA

Home ice (capacity)
Northlands Coliseum (17,503)
Address
Edmonton, Alta. T5B 4M9
Business phone
403-474-8561

Rink dimensions
200 feet by 85 feet
Club colors
Blue, orange and white
Minor league affiliation
Cape Breton (AHL)

SCHEDULE KEY

*All-Star Game at Montreal.
H—Home game. D—Day game (any game starting before 4 p.m.).
NOTE: At press time, two games at neutral sites had yet to be announced.

TRAINING CAMP ROSTER

No.	FORWARDS	Ht./Wt.	Place	Born Date	NHL exp.	1991-92 clubs
42	Josef Beranek (C)	6-2/185	Litvinov, Czech.	10-25-69	1	Edmonton
16	Kelly Buchberger (LW)	6-2/210	Langenburg, Sask.	12-12-66	6	Edmonton
	Dan Currie (LW)	6-2/195	Burlington, Ont.	3-15-68	2	Cape Breton (AHL), Edmonton
21	Vincent Damphousse	6-1/190	Montreal	12-17-67	6	Edmonton
	Louie DeBrusk (LW)	6-1/205	Cambridge, Ont.	3-19-71	1	Cape Breton (AHL), Edmonton
20	Martin Gelinas (LW)	5-11/195	Shawinigan, Que.	6-5-70	4	Edmonton
85	Petr Klima (LW/RW)	6-0/190	Chaomutov, Czech.	12-23-64	7	Edmonton
14	Craig MacTavish (C)	6-1/195	London, Ont.	8-15-58	13	Edmonton
12	David Maley (C)	6-3/200	Beaver Dam, Wis.	4-24-63	7	New Jersey, Edmonton
27	Scott Mellanby (RW)	6-1/205	Montreal	6-11-66	7	Edmonton
8	Joe Murphy (RW)	6-1/190	London, Ont.	10-16-67	6	Edmonton
9	Bernie Nicholls (C)	6-0/185	Haliburton, Ont.	6-24-61	11	N.Y. Rangers, Edmonton
	Shjon Podein (C)	6-2/200	Rochester, Minn.	3-5-68	0	Cape Breton (AHL)
	Steve Rice (RW)	6-0/210	Waterloo, Ont.	5-26-71	2	Cape Breton (AHL), Edmonton
18	Craig Simpson (LW)	6-2/195	London, Ont.	2-15-67	7	Edmonton
17	Scott Thornton (C)	6-2/200	London, Ont.	1-9-71	2	Cape Breton (AHL), Edmonton
10	Esa Tikkanen (LW)	6-1/200	Helsinki, Finland	1-25-65	8	Edmonton
	Shaun Van Allen (C)	6-1/200	Shaunavon, Sask.	8-29-67	1	Cape Breton (AHL)
	Tyler Wright (C)	5-11/175	Canora, Sask.	4-6-73	0	Swift Current (WHL)
	DEFENSEMEN					
6	Brian Glynn	6-4/224	Iserlohn, West Germany	11-23-67	5	Minnesota, Edmonton
34	Greg Hawgood	5-10/190	St. Albert, Alta.	8-10-68	5	Cape Breton (AHL), Edmonton
2	Chris Joseph	6-2/210	Burnaby, B.C.	9-10-69	5	Cape Breton (AHL), Edmonton
35	Francois Leroux	6-6/221	St. Adele, Que.	4-18-70	4	Cape Breton (AHL), Edmonton
4	Kevin Lowe	6-2/195	Lachute, Que.	4-15-59	13	Edmonton
36	Norm Maciver	5-11/180	Thunder Bay, Ont.	9-8-64	6	Edmonton
24	Dave Manson	6-2/192	Prince Albert, Sask.	1-27-67	6	Edmonton
28	Craig Muni	6-3/200	Toronto	7-19-62	10	Edmonton
22	Luke Richardson	6-4/210	Ottawa	3-26-69	5	Edmonton
25	Geoff Smith	6-3/200	Edmonton, Alta.	3-7-69	3	Edmonton
	Brad Werenka	6-2/204	Two Hills, Alta.	2-12-69	0	Cape Breton (AHL)
	GOALTENDERS					
31	Norm Foster	5-9/175	Vancouver, B.C.	2-10-65	2	Cape Breton (AHL), Edmonton
	Peter Ing	6-2/170	Toronto	4-28-69	3	Cape Breton (AHL), Edmonton
30	Bill Ranford	5-10/170	Brandon, Man.	12-14-66	7	Edmonton
32	Ron Tugnutt	5-11/155	Scarborough, Ont.	10-22-67	5	Halifax (AHL), Quebec, Edmonton
	Andrew Verner	6-0/194	Weston, Ont.	11-10-72	0	Peterborough (OHL)

1991-92 REVIEW

INDIVIDUAL STATISTICS

SCORING

	Games	G	A	Pts.	Pen.	+/-	PPG	SHG	Shots	Shooting Pct.
Vincent Damphousse	80	38	51	89	53	10	12	1	247	15.4
Joe Murphy	80	35	47	82	52	17	10	2	193	18.1
Craig Simpson	79	24	37	61	80	8	6	0	128	18.8
Scott Mellanby	80	23	27	50	197	5	7	0	159	14.5
Bernie Nicholls*	49	20	29	49	60	5	7	0	115	17.4
Dave Manson	79	15	32	47	220	9	7	0	206	7.3
Kelly Buchberger	79	20	24	44	157	9	0	4	90	22.2
Anatoli Semenov	59	20	22	42	16	12	3	0	105	19.0
Norm Maciver	57	6	34	40	38	20	2	0	69	8.7
Petr Klima	57	21	13	34	52	-18	5	0	107	19.6
Craig MacTavish	80	12	18	30	98	-1	0	2	86	14.0
Martin Gelinas	68	11	18	29	62	14	1	0	94	11.7
Esa Tikkanen	40	12	16	28	44	-8	6	2	117	10.3
Josef Beranek	58	12	16	28	18	-2	0	0	79	15.2
Mark Lamb	59	6	22	28	46	4	2	0	61	9.8
Luke Richardson	75	2	19	21	118	-9	0	0	85	2.4
Geoff Smith	74	2	16	18	43	-5	0	0	61	3.3
Greg Hawgood	20	2	11	13	22	19	0	0	24	8.3
Kevin Lowe	55	2	8	10	107	-4	0	0	33	6.1
David Maley*	23	3	6	9	46	8	0	0	31	9.7
Brian Glynn*	25	2	6	8	6	11	0	1	29	6.9
Craig Muni	54	2	5	7	34	11	0	0	38	5.3
Jeff Beukeboom*	18	0	5	5	78	4	0	0	7	0.0
Troy Mallette*	15	1	3	4	36	-1	0	0	9	11.1
Louie DeBrusk	25	2	1	3	124	4	0	0	7	28.6
Peter Ing (goalie)	12	0	3	3	0	0	0	0	0	0.0

	Games	G	A	Pts.	Pen.	+/-	PPG	SHG	Shots	Shooting Pct.
Bill Ranford (goalie)	67	0	3	3	4	0	0	0	0	0.0
David Shaw*	12	1	1	2	8	-8	0	0	15	6.7
Dan Currie	7	1	0	1	0	-1	0	0	3	33.3
Scott Thornton	15	0	1	1	43	-6	0	0	11	0.0
Martin Rucinsky*	2	0	0	0	0	-3	0	0	1	0.0
Steven Rice	3	0	0	0	2	-2	0	0	2	0.0
Ron Tugnutt (goalie)*	3	0	0	0	2	0	0	0	0	0.0
Francois Leroux	4	0	0	0	7	-1	0	0	0	0.0
Chris Joseph	7	0	0	0	8	-1	0	0	5	0.0
Norm Foster (goalie)	10	0	0	0	2	0	0	0	0	0.0

GOALTENDING

	Games	Min.	Goals	SO	Avg.	W	L	T	Shots	Sv. Pct.
Norm Foster	10	439	20	0	2.73	5	3	0	183	.891
Bill Ranford	67	3822	228	1	3.58	27	26	10	1971	.884
Peter Ing	12	463	33	0	4.28	3	4	0	252	.869
Ron Tugnutt*	3	124	10	0	4.84	1	1	0	73	.863

Empty-net goals (do not count against a goaltender's average): Ranford, 5; Ing, 1.
*Played with two or more NHL teams.

| RESULTS |

OCTOBER

4—At Calgary	L		2-9
6—Los Angeles	T		*2-2
8—At Los Angeles	L		3-6
10—At St. Louis	L		*2-3
12—Calgary	W		3-1
15—At Detroit	L		1-3
17—At Chicago	L		2-4
19—At N.Y. Islanders	W		4-2
20—At N.Y. Rangers	W		4-3
23—Washington	L		5-6
26—Vancouver	W		5-4
27—At Vancouver	W		6-3
30—St. Louis	T		*2-2

NOVEMBER

1—New Jersey	L		1-3
3—At Vancouver	L		2-7
6—N.Y. Islanders	W		5-3
8—At San Jose	L		2-6
9—At Los Angeles	T		*4-4
13—At Pittsburgh	L		*4-5
14—At Philadelphia	L		1-3
16—At Quebec	W		6-2
18—At Montreal	L		0-1
23—Winnipeg	L		0-4
27—Chicago	W		6-2
29—San Jose	T		*4-4

DECEMBER

1—Vancouver	W		7-0
3—Pittsburgh	W		5-3

6—At Winnipeg	T		*4-4
8—San Jose	W		3-1
10—At Vancouver	W		7-4
12—At San Jose	L		3-6
14—Winnipeg	W		7-5
15—Detroit	L		1-4
18—At Toronto	W		7-5
20—At Buffalo	T		*4-4
21—At Boston	L		3-6
23—Calgary	W		5-3
28—Los Angeles	L		4-9
29—Montreal	L		1-3

JANUARY

2—At Los Angeles	L		3-5
4—At Calgary	W		3-2
5—Calgary	L		2-3
8—At Winnipeg	L		2-5
10—At Buffalo	L		2-8
11—At Detroit	T		*5-5
13—At Minnesota	W		7-4
15—Vancouver	L		3-5
21—San Jose	W		9-2
23—N.Y. Rangers	L		1-3
25—At San Jose	L		2-5
28—At Vancouver	W		5-3
29—Chicago	L		3-4
31—Hartford	W		4-1

FEBRUARY

2—Quebec	W		8-2
5—Montreal	W		2-1

7—N.Y. Islanders	W		4-2
11—At Minnesota	W		5-4
13—At Hartford	W		3-1
15—At Philadelphia	L		5-8
16—At Toronto	L		5-7
19—Los Angeles	W		4-3
21—Boston	L		3-5
23—Buffalo	W		5-2
26—Winnipeg	W		6-1
28—Philadelphia	W		4-2

MARCH

1—At Winnipeg	W		4-2
4—Toronto	L		2-5
6—St. Louis	W		5-3
11—New Jersey	T		*2-2
14—Hartford	W		3-1
17—At Pittsburgh	L		5-6
19—At New Jersey	W		5-3
21—At Boston	W		4-3
22—At Washington	L		2-6
24—At Calgary	T		*4-4
27—Minnesota	W		5-3
29—Los Angeles	T		*2-2
31—At Calgary	L		2-5

APRIL

12—San Jose	W		6-4
14—Winnipeg	L		2-6

*Denotes overtime game.

— 23 —

HARTFORD WHALERS
WALES CONFERENCE/ADAMS DIVISION

1992-93 SCHEDULE

OCTOBER

S	M	T	W	T	F	S
4	5	6 MON H	7	8 BOS	9	10 BUF H
11	12 NYR	13	14 OTT H	15	16	17 PIT H
18	19	20 NJ	21	22 OTT	23	24 NYI
25	26	27	28 NJ H	29	30	31 LA H

NOVEMBER

S	M	T	W	T	F	S
1	2	3 QUE H	4	5	6 DET	7 WAS H
8	9	10	11 CAL H	12	13 BUF	14
15	16	17	18 STL H	19 OTT	20	21 D QUE
22	23	24	25 MON H	26	27 D BOS	28 BOS H
29	30					

DECEMBER

S	M	T	W	T	F	S
		1 STL	2	3 SJ	4	5 LA
6	7	8	9 OTT H	10	11 BUF	12 BUF H
13	14	15	16 WAS H	17	18 WAS	19 NYR H
20	21 MON	22	23 TB	24	25	26 BOS H
27 NJ	28	29 STL †	30	31 QUE H		

JANUARY

S	M	T	W	T	F	S
					1	2 BOS
3 MIN H	4	5	6 BUF H	7	8	9 QUE H
10 MON H	11	12	13 MON	14	15 EDM	16 VAN
17	18	19 WAS ‡	20	21 SJ H	22	23 D CHI H
24 PHI	25	26	27 MON	28 OTT	29	30 WIN H
31						

FEBRUARY

S	M	T	W	T	F	S
	1	2	3 BUF	4	5	6 *
7	8	9	10	11	12 WIN	13 CAL
14	15	16	17 BUF H	18	19	20 D EDM H
21 D PIT H	22	23	24 PHI H	25	26	27 QUE
28 NYI H						

MARCH

S	M	T	W	T	F	S
	1	2	3 NJ H	4	5 BUF	6 VAN H
7	8 QUE	9	10 TOR	11	12	13 D BUF H
14 D PHI H	15	16 TB	17	18	19 WAS	20
21	22 BOS	23	24 MON H	25	26	27 MIN
28 CHI	29	30 BOS H	31			

APRIL

S	M	T	W	T	F	S
				1 PIT	2	3 OTT H
4	5 NYR	6	7 OTT	8	9	10 QUE
11 TOR H	12	13	14 NYI H	15 NYI	16	17

1992-93 SEASON

CLUB DIRECTORY

Managing general partner and governor
  Richard H. Gordon
President and alternate governor
  Emile Francis
General manager
  Brian Burke
Assistant general manager
  Ken Schinkel
Assistant to the general manager
  Tom Rowe
Special asst. to the managing gen. partner
  Gordie Howe
Vice president, marketing and sales
  Rick Francis
Treasurer
  Michael J. Amendola
Director of advertising sales
  Richard Chmura
Director of ticket operations and sales
  Jim Baldwin
Director of public relations
  John H. Forslund
Public relations assistant
  Mary Lynn Gorman

Chief statistician, assistant director of public relations and archivist
  Frank Polnaszek
Coach
  Paul Holmgren
Assistant coach
  Darcy Regier
Director of pro scouting
  Kevin Maxwell
Scouts
  Leo Boivin
  Steve Brklacich
  Claude Larose
  Bruce Haralson
  Fred Gore
  Roger Borough
  Willy Lindstrom
Trainer
  Frank "Bud" Goveira
Equipment manager
  Skip Cunningham
Strength and conditioning coach
  Doug McKenney

DRAFT CHOICES

Rnd. Player	Ht./Wt.	Overall	Pos.	1991-92 club
1—Robert Petrovicky...	5-11/172	9	C	Dukla Trencin, Czech.
2—Andrei Nikolishin	5-11/189	47	LW	Dynamo Moscow, CIS
3—Jan Vopat..............	6-0/198	57	D	Litvinov, Czech.
4—Kevin Smyth...........	6-2/217	79	LW	Moose Jaw (WHL)
4—Jason McBain	6-2/178	81	D	Portland (WHL)
6—Jarret Reid	5-10/180	143	C	Sault Ste. Marie (OHL)
7—Ken Belanger.........	6-3/189	153	LW	Ottawa (OHL)
8—Konstatin Korotkov	5-9/174	177	F	Spartak, CIS
9—Greg Zwakman.......	6-2/182	201	D	Edina (Minn.) H.S.
10—Steven Halko..........	6-1/183	225	D	Thornhill (Junior A)
11—Joacim Esbjors		249	D	Frolunda, Sweden

MISCELLANEOUS DATA

Home ice (capacity)
  Hartford Civic Center (15,635)
Address
  242 Trumbull Street
  8th Floor
  Hartford, CT 06103
Business phone
  203-728-3366

Rink dimensions
  200 feet by 85 feet
Club colors
  Silver and green
Minor league affiliation
  Springfield (AHL)

SCHEDULE KEY

*All-Star Game at Montreal.
H—Home game.   D—Day game (any game starting before 4 p.m.).
†At Louisville, Ky.   ‡At Charleston, S.C.

No.	FORWARDS	Ht./Wt.	Place	BORN Date	NHL exp.	1991-92 clubs
23	James Black (C)	5-11/185	Regina, Sask.	8-15-69	3	Springfield (AHL), Hartford
21	Andrew Cassels (C)	6-0/192	Mississauga, Ont.	7-23-69	3	Hartford
20	Yvon Corriveau (LW)	6-1/202	Welland, Ont.	2-8-67	7	Springfield (AHL), Hartford
12	Murray Craven (C/LW)	6-2/185	Medicine Hat, Alta.	7-20-64	10	Philadelphia, Hartford
11	John Cullen (C)	5-10/187	Puslinch, Ont.	8-2-64	4	Hartford
7	Randy Cunneyworth	6-0/180	Etobicoke, Ont.	5-10-61	9	Hartford
18	Paul Cyr (LW)	5-10/180	Port Alberni, B.C.	10-31-63	10	Springfield (AHL), Hartford
41	Joe Day (C)	5-11/180	Chicago	5-11-68	1	Springfield (AHL), Hartford
44	Paul Gillis (C)	5-11/198	Toronto	12-31-63	10	Indianapolis (IHL), Chicago, Hartford
14	Chris Govedaris (LW)	6-0/200	Toronto	2-2-70	2	Springfield (AHL)
17	Mark Greig (RW)	5-11/190	High River, Alta.	1-25-70	2	Springfield (AHL), Hartford
24	Bobby Holik (RW)	6-3/210	Jihlava, Czech.	1-1-71	2	Hartford
	Tim Kerr (RW)	6-3/228	Windsor, Ont.	1-5-60	12	N.Y. Rangers
	Nick Kypreos (LW)	6-0/195	Toronto	6-4-66	3	Washington
33	Jim McKenzie (LW)	6-3/210	Gull Lake, Sask.	11-3-69	3	Hartford
	Mikael Nylander (C)	5-11/176	Stockholm, Sweden	10-3-72	0	Swed. Nat., AIK Solna (Sweden), Swed. Nat. Jr.
	Robert Petrovicky (C)	5-11/172	Kosice, Czech.	10-26-73	0	Dukla Trencin (Czech.)
47	Michel Picard (LW)	5-11/190	Beauport, Que.	11-7-69	2	Springfield (AHL), Hartford
37	Patrick Poulin (LW)	6-1/208	Vanier, Que.	4-23-73	1	St. Hyacinthe (QMJHL), Hartford
8	Geoff Sanderson (C)	6-0/185	Hay River, N.W.T.	2-1-72	2	Hartford
36	Daniel Shank (RW)	5-10/190	Montreal	5-12-67	3	Adirondack (AHL), Springfield (AHL), Hartford
16	Pat Verbeek (LW)	5-9/190	Sarnia, Ont.	5-24-64	10	Hartford
38	Terry Yake (C)	5-11/175	New Westminister, B.C.	10-22-68	4	Springfield (AHL), Hartford
	DEFENSEMEN					
	Jim Agnew	6-1/190	Deloraine, Man.	3-21-66	5	Vancouver
6	Adam Burt	6-0/190	Detroit	1-15-69	4	Hartford
64	Shawn Evans	6-3/195	Kingston, Ont.	9-7-65	2	Springfield (AHL)
	Martin Hamrlik	5-11/176	Zlin, Czech.	5-6-73	0	ZPS Zlin (Czech.)
27	Doug Houda	6-2/200	Blairmore, Alta.	6-3-66	6	Hartford
4	Dan Keczmer	6-1/190	Mt. Clemens, Mich.	5-25-68	2	U.S. Nat., Springfield (AHL), Hartford
5	Steve Konroyd	6-1/195	Scarborough, Ont.	2-10-61	12	Chicago, Hartford
29	Randy Ladouceur	6-2/220	Brockville, Ont.	6-30-60	10	Hartford
	Allen Pedersen	6-3/210	Edmonton, Alta.	1-13-65	6	Minnesota
46	Todd Richards	6-0/190	Robbinsdale, Minn.	10-20-66	2	Springfield (AHL), Hartford
45	John Stevens	6-1/195	Completon, N.B.	5-4-66	4	Springfield (AHL), Hartford
3	Zarley Zalapski	6-1/210	Edmonton, Alta.	4-22-68	5	Hartford
	GOALTENDERS					
49	Mario Gosselin	5-8/160	Thetford Mines, Que.	6-15-63	8	Springfield (AHL)
50	Mike Lenarduzzi	6-0/165	Mississauga, Ont.	9-14-72	0	Sudbury (OHL), S. Ste. Marie (OHL), Ottawa (OHL)
40	Frank Pietrangelo	5-10/185	Niagara Falls, Ont.	12-17-64	5	Pittsburgh, Hartford
35	Kay Whitmore	5-11/165	Sudbury, Ont.	4-10-67	4	Hartford

1991-92 REVIEW

INDIVIDUAL STATISTICS

SCORING

	Games	G	A	Pts.	Pen.	+/-	PPG	SHG	Shots	Shooting Pct.
John Cullen	77	26	51	77	141	-28	10	0	172	15.1
Pat Verbeek	76	22	35	57	243	-16	10	0	163	13.5
Zarley Zalapski	79	20	37	57	120	-7	4	0	230	8.7
Murray Craven*	61	24	30	54	38	-4	8	4	133	18.0
Mikael Andersson	74	18	29	47	14	18	1	3	149	12.1
Bobby Holik	76	21	24	45	44	4	1	0	207	10.1
Andrew Cassels	67	11	30	41	18	3	2	2	99	11.1
Rob Brown*	42	16	15	31	39	-14	13	0	65	24.6
Geoff Sanderson	64	13	18	31	18	5	2	0	98	13.3
Brad Shaw	62	3	22	25	44	1	0	0	101	3.0
Adam Burt	66	9	15	24	93	-16	4	0	89	10.1
Marc Bergevin	75	7	17	24	64	-13	4	1	96	7.3
Mark Hunter	63	10	13	23	159	-8	5	0	92	10.9
Yvon Corriveau	38	12	8	20	36	5	3	0	69	17.4
Randy Cunneyworth	39	7	10	17	71	-5	0	0	63	11.1
Steve Konroyd*	33	2	10	12	32	-5	1	0	56	3.6
James Black	30	4	6	10	10	-4	1	0	54	7.4

HARTFORD WHALERS

1992-93 NHL SEASON

HARTFORD WHALERS

	Games	G	A	Pts.	Pen.	+/-	PPG	SHG	Shots	Shooting Pct.
Randy Ladouceur	74	1	9	10	127	-1	0	0	59	1.7
Doug Houda	56	3	6	9	125	-2	1	0	40	7.5
Michel Picard	25	3	5	8	6	-2	1	0	41	7.3
Jim McKenzie	67	5	1	6	87	-6	0	0	34	14.7
Kevin Dineen*	16	4	2	6	23	-6	1	0	28	14.3
Mark Greig	17	0	5	5	6	7	0	0	18	0.0
Barry Pederson*	5	2	2	4	0	-2	1	0	6	33.3
Ed Kastelic	25	1	3	4	61	-4	0	0	4	25.0
John Stevens	21	0	4	4	19	-4	0	0	13	0.0
Paul Cyr	17	0	3	3	19	-4	0	0	20	0.0
Joe Day	24	0	3	3	10	-2	0	0	13	0.0
Daniel Shank	13	2	0	2	18	-4	0	0	10	20.0
Terry Yake	15	1	1	2	4	-2	0	0	12	8.3
Paul Gillis*	12	0	2	2	48	0	0	0	6	0.0
Peter Sidorkiewicz (goalie)	35	0	1	1	2	0	0	0	0	0.0
Kay Whitmore (goalie)	45	0	1	1	16	0	0	0	0	0.0
Jergus Baca	1	0	0	0	0	-1	0	0	1	0.0
Dan Keczmer	1	0	0	0	0	-1	0	0	2	0.0
Patrick Poulin	1	0	0	0	2	-1	0	0	0	0.0
Frank Pietrangelo (goalie)*	5	0	0	0	0	0	0	0	0	0.0
Lee Norwood*	6	0	0	0	16	0	0	0	1	0.0
Todd Richards	6	0	0	0	2	-2	0	0	3	0.0
Mike Tomlak	6	0	0	0	0	-2	0	0	10	0.0
Chris Tancill*	10	0	0	0	2	-6	0	0	13	0.0

GOALTENDING

	Games	Min.	Goals	SO	Avg.	W	L	T	Shots	Sv. Pct.
Frank Pietrangelo*	5	306	12	0	2.35	3	1	1	156	.923
Peter Sidorkiewicz	35	1995	111	2	3.34	9	19	6	940	.882
Kay Whitmore	45	2567	155	3	3.62	14	21	6	1292	.880

Empty-net goals (do not count against a goaltender's average): Sidorkiewicz, 3; Whitmore, 2.
*Played with two or more NHL teams.

RESULTS

OCTOBER

5—At Quebec	L	2-4	
8—Montreal	T	*2-2	
12—N.Y. Rangers	W	5-2	
14—At Montreal	W	4-3	
16—At Winnipeg	W	3-2	
19—Buffalo	W	4-1	
23—San Jose	W	3-0	
26—Chicago	L	2-4	
27—At Buffalo	L	1-5	
30—Los Angeles	T	*4-4	

NOVEMBER

1—At Detroit	L	5-8
2—At Pittsburgh	W	6-5
6—Calgary	L	2-3
9—At St. Louis	W	4-3
10—At Chicago	L	0-3
12—Quebec	W	5-4
14—Montreal	T	*2-2
16—Boston	L	*4-5
17—At Toronto	W	3-1
22—At New Jersey	L	2-8
23—Washington	L	2-3
25—At Quebec	L	2-5
27—At Philadelphia	W	7-3
30—Montreal	W	3-2

DECEMBER

1—At Boston	L	4-5
4—Toronto	L	0-3
7—Buffalo	T	*6-6
13—At Buffalo	W	8-4
14—N.Y. Rangers	L	2-6
17—N.Y. Islanders	L	2-4
19—New Jersey	L	1-4
21—At Montreal	L	*2-3
23—Buffalo	W	4-3
26—At Boston	L	2-3
28—At Quebec	L	1-4
29—N.Y. Islanders	W	6-4

JANUARY

2—Quebec	W	4-1
4—Washington	T	*2-2
9—At N.Y. Islanders	L	1-2
11—At Montreal	L	2-3
15—Boston	L	3-4
16—At Boston	L	*3-4
21—Winnipeg	T	*3-3
25—Boston	T	*4-4
26—At Montreal	L	1-3
28—Minnesota	L	3-4
31—At Edmonton	L	1-4

FEBRUARY

1—At Vancouver	T	*4-4
4—At San Jose	L	5-6
6—At Los Angeles	T	*5-5
9—Minnesota	T	*4-4
11—Buffalo	W	5-1
13—Edmonton	L	1-3
15—At New Jersey	L	1-4
16—At Buffalo	L	4-5
19—Montreal	T	*2-2
22—Quebec	W	4-0
23—Detroit	L	0-4
25—St. Louis	L	2-5
27—At Pittsburgh	W	8-4
29—At Minnesota	W	*5-4

MARCH

1—At N.Y. Rangers	L	4-9
3—Boston	W	4-0
5—Quebec	L	4-10
7—Vancouver	L	1-5
9—At Quebec	L	0-2
11—Los Angeles	W	4-0
13—At Winnipeg	W	1-0
14—At Edmonton	L	1-3
16—At Calgary	W	4-3
18—At Vancouver	L	2-3
21—San Jose	L	4-5
22—Pittsburgh	T	*2-2
24—At Washington	W	8-2
26—At St. Louis	L	2-7
28—Chicago	L	1-3
29—At Buffalo	T	*2-2

APRIL

12—Philadelphia	W	4-2
13—At Boston	L	3-6
15—At Philadelphia	W	*4-3

*Denotes overtime game.

LOS ANGELES KINGS
CAMPBELL CONFERENCE/SMYTHE DIVISION

1992-93 SCHEDULE

OCTOBER

S	M	T	W	T	F	S
4	5	6 CAL	7	8 DET	9	10 WIN H
11	12	13 SJ H	14	15 CAL H	16	17 BOS H
18	19	20 CAL	21	22	23 WIN	24 MIN
25	26	27 NYI	28	29 BOS	30	31 HAR

NOVEMBER

S	M	T	W	T	F	S
1	2	3	4	5 NJ H	6	7 BUF H
8 SJ	9	10 WIN	11	12 VAN H	13	14 EDM H
15 VAN	16	17 SJ	18	19 CHI H	20	21 TOR H
22	23	24	25 EDM	26	27 DET	28 TOR
29	30					

DECEMBER

S	M	T	W	T	F	S
		1	2	3 PIT H	4	5 HAR H
6	7	8	9	10 QUE H	11	12 STL H
13	14	15 TB H	16	17	18 EDM	19 CAL
20	21	22 VAN H	23	24	25	26 SJ
27	28	29 PHI H	30	31 VAN		

JANUARY

S	M	T	W	T	F	S
					1	2 MON H
3	4	5	6 TB H	7	8 WIN	9
10 CHI	11	12 OTT	13	14 NJ	15	16 WIN H
17	18	19 EDM	20	21 VAN H	22	23 NYR H
24	25	26 SJ H	27	28 CAL H	29	30 CHI H
31						

FEBRUARY

S	M	T	W	T	F	S
	1	2 QUE	3 MON	4	5	6 *
7	8	9 EDM H	10	11 DET H	12	13 WAS H
14	15 D VAN H	16	17 MIN	18 CHI	19	20 D WAS
21	22 TB	23	24	25 STL	26	27 TOR H
28						

MARCH

S	M	T	W	T	F	S
	1	2 CAL H	3	4 OTT H	5	6 EDM H
7	8	9 NYR	10	11 PIT	12	13 D PHI
14 D BUF	15	16 WIN H	17	18 NYI H	19	20 STL H
21	22	23	24 VAN	25	26 EDM	27
28 D WIN	29 DET	30	31 TOR			

APRIL

S	M	T	W	T	F	S
				1	2	3 D MIN H
4	5	6 CAL H	7	8 SJ H	9	10 SJ
11	12	13 VAN	14	15 VAN H	16	17

1992-93 SEASON

CLUB DIRECTORY

Owner/chairman
Bruce McNall
Assistant to the chairman
Rogatien Vachon
President
Roy A. Mlakar
Vice president, public relations
Scott J. Carmichael
Vice president administration/marketing
Robert Moor
General manager
Nick Beverley
Coach
Barry Melrose
Assistant coaches
Cap Raeder
Rick Wilson
Administrative assistant to general manager
John Wolf

Director of amateur scouting
Bob Owen
Scouting staff
Alex Smart
Jim Anderson
Serge Blanchard
Jan Lindgren
Mark Miller
Al Murray
Don Perry
Ted O'Connor
Serge Aubry
Director of media relations
TBA
Media relations assistant
Adam Fell
Trainers
Pete Demers
Peter Millar
Mark O'Neill

DRAFT CHOICES

Rnd.	Player	Ht./Wt.	Overall	Pos.	1991-92 club
2—	Justin Hocking	6-4/205	39	D	Spokane (WHL)
3—	Sandy Allan	6-0/175	63	G	North Bay (OHL)
4—	Kevin Brown	6-1/212	87	RW	Belleville (OHL)
5—	Jeff Shevalier	5-11/178	111	LW	North Bay (OHL)
6—	Raymond Murray	6-1/178	135	LW	Michigan State U. (CCHA)
9—	Magnus Wernblom	6-0/178	207	RW	MoDo, Sweden
10—	Ryan Pisiak	6-2/186	231	RW	Swift Current (WHL)
11—	Jukka Tiilikainen	6-0/172	255	RW	Espoo, Finland

MISCELLANEOUS DATA

Home ice (capacity)
The Great Western Forum (16,005)
Address
3900 West Manchester Blvd.
Inglewood, CA 90305
Business phone
310-419-3160

Rink dimensions
200 feet by 85 feet
Club colors
Black, white and silver
Minor league affiliation
Phoenix (IHL)

SCHEDULE KEY

*All-Star Game at Montreal.
H—Home game.   D—Day game (any game starting before 4 p.m.).
NOTE: At press time, two games at neutral sites had yet to be announced.

TRAINING CAMP ROSTER

BORN

No.	FORWARDS	Ht./Wt.	Place	Date	NHL exp.	1991-92 clubs
8	Scott Bjugstad (RW)	6-1/185	St. Paul, Minn.	6-2-61	7	Phoenix (IHL), Los Angeles
	Frank Breault (RW)	5-11/190	Acton Valley, Que.	5-11-67	2	Phoenix (IHL),Los Angeles
	Sylvain Couturier (C)	6-2/205	Greenfield Park, Que.	4-23-68	3	Phoenix (IHL), Los Angeles
11	Mike Donnelly (LW)	5-11/185	Livonia, Mich.	10-10-63	6	Los Angeles
21	Tony Granato (LW)	5-10/185	Downers Grove, Ill.	7-25-64	4	Los Angeles
99	Wayne Gretzky (C)	6-0/170	Brantford, Ont.	1-26-61	13	Los Angeles
27	Jim Hiller (RW)	6-2/200	Pt. Alberni, B.C.	5-13-69	0	Northern Michigan (WCHA)
14	Kyosti Karjalainen	6-1/190	Gavle, Sweden	6-19-67	1	Phoenix (IHL), Los Angeles
37	Bob Kudelski (C)	6-1/200	Springfield, Mass.	3-3-64	5	Los Angeles
17	Jari Kurri (RW)	6-1/195	Helsinki, Finland	5-18-60	11	Los Angeles
	Robert Lang (C)	6-2/180	Telplice, Czech.	12-19-70	0	Czech. Nat., Litvinov (Czech.)
	Guy Leveque (C)	5-11/170	Kingston, Ont.	12-28-72	0	Cornwall (OHL)
44	John McIntyre (C/LW)	6-1/175	Ravenswood, Ont.	4-29-69	3	Los Angeles
33	Marty McSorley (RW)	6-1/225	Hamilton, Ont.	5-18-63	9	Los Angeles
23	Corey Millen (C)	5-7/168	Cloquet, Minn.	4-29-64	3	Binghamton (AHL), N.Y. Rangers, Los Angeles
29	Jay Miller (LW/D)	6-2/210	Wellesley, Mass.	7-16-60	7	Los Angeles
20	Luc Robitaille (LW)	6-0/190	Montreal	2-17-66	6	Los Angeles
7	Tomas Sandstrom (RW)	6-2/200	Jakobstad, Finland	9-4-64	8	Los Angeles
18	Dave Taylor (RW)	6-0/195	Levack, Ont.	12-4-55	15	Los Angeles
	Sean Whyte (RW)	6-0/198	Sudbury, Ont.	5-4-70	1	Phoenix (IHL), Los Angeles

DEFENSEMEN

No.		Ht./Wt.	Place	Date	NHL exp.	1991-92 clubs
26	Peter Ahola	6-3/205	Espoo, Finland	5-14-68	1	Phoenix (IHL), Los Angeles
4	Rob Blake	6-3/215	Simcoe, Ont.	12-10-69	3	Los Angeles
	Rene Chapeldaine	6-1/195	Weyburn, Sask.	9-27-66	2	Phoenix (IHL), Los Angeles
77	Paul Coffey	6-0/200	Weston, Ont.	6-1-61	12	Pittsburgh, Los Angeles
	Paul Holden	6-3/210	Kitchner, Ont.	3-15-70	0	Phoenix (IHL)
22	Charlie Huddy	6-0/210	Oshawa, Ont.	6-2-59	12	Los Angeles
	Darryl Sydor	6-0/205	Edmonton, Alta.	3-13-72	1	Kamloops (WHL), Los Angeles
56	Brent Thompson	6-2/175	Calgary, Alta.	1-9-71	1	Phoenix (IHL), Los Angeles
5	Timothy Watters	5-11/185	Kamloops, B.C.	7-25-59	11	Phoenix (IHL),Los Angeles
	Alexei Zhitnik	5-10/178	Kiev, U.S.S.R.	10-10-72	0	CSKA Moscow (CIS)

GOALTENDERS

No.		Ht./Wt.	Place	Date	NHL exp.	1991-92 clubs
31	Darryl Gilmour	6-0/171	Winnipeg, Man.	2-13-67	0	Phoenix (IHL)
	David Goverde	6-0/210	Toronto	4-9-70	1	New Haven (AHL), Phoenix (IHL), Los Angeles
32	Kelly Hrudey	5-10/189	Edmonton, Alta.	1-13-61	9	Los Angeles
	Robb Stauber	5-11/180	Duluth, Minn.	11-25-67	1	Phoenix (IHL)
1	Steve Weeks	5-11/170	Scarborough, Ont.	6-30-58	12	N.Y. Islanders, Los Angeles

1991-92 REVIEW

INDIVIDUAL STATISTICS

SCORING

	Games	G	A	Pts.	Pen.	+/-	PPG	SHG	Shots	Shooting Pct.
Wayne Gretzky	74	31	+90	121	34	-12	12	2	215	14.4
Luc Robitaille	80	44	63	107	95	-4	26	0	240	18.3
Tony Granato	80	39	29	68	187	4	7	2	223	17.5
Jari Kurri	73	23	37	60	24	-24	10	1	167	13.8
Mike Donnelly	80	29	16	45	20	5	0	1	197	14.7
Bob Kudelski	80	22	21	43	42	-15	2	1	155	14.2
Corey Millen*	46	20	21	41	44	3	8	1	89	22.5
Tomas Sandstrom	49	17	22	39	70	-2	5	0	147	11.6
Brian Benning*	53	2	30	32	99	4	0	0	102	2.0
Dave Taylor	77	10	19	29	63	10	0	0	81	12.3
Marty McSorley	71	7	22	29	268	-13	2	1	119	5.9
John McIntyre	73	5	19	24	100	0	0	0	40	12.5
Charlie Huddy	56	4	19	23	43	-10	2	1	109	3.7
Rob Blake	57	7	13	20	102	-5	5	0	131	5.3
Peter Ahola	71	7	12	19	101	12	0	0	74	9.5
Larry Robinson	56	3	10	13	37	1	0	0	46	6.5
Jay Miller	67	4	7	11	249	-8	0	0	32	12.5
Randy Gilhen*	33	3	6	9	14	-3	0	1	32	9.4
Kyosti Karjalainen	28	1	8	9	12	4	0	0	20	5.0
Tim Watters	37	0	7	7	92	-2	0	0	29	0.0
Scott Bjugstad	22	2	4	6	10	-1	0	0	25	8.0
Darryl Sydor	18	1	5	6	22	-3	0	0	18	5.6
Paul Coffey*	10	1	4	5	25	-3	0	0	25	4.0
Brent Thompson	27	0	5	5	89	-7	0	0	18	0.0

	Games	G	A	Pts.	Pen.	+/-	PPG	SHG	Shots	Shooting Pct.
Sylvain Couturier	14	3	1	4	2	-3	0	0	21	14.3
Jim Thomson	45	1	2	3	162	-1	0	0	24	4.2
Jeff Chychrun*	26	0	3	3	76	-4	0	0	22	0.0
Frank Breault	6	1	0	1	30	0	0	0	6	16.7
David Goverde (goalie)	2	0	1	1	0	0	0	0	0	0.0
Ilkka Sinisalo	3	0	1	1	2	0	0	0	3	0.0
Steve Weeks (goalie)*	7	0	1	1	0	0	0	0	0	0.0
Rene Chapdelaine	16	0	1	1	10	0	0	0	6	0.0
Kelly Hrudey (goalie)	60	0	1	1	12	0	0	0	0	0.0
Sean Whyte	3	0	0	0	0	-1	0	0	0	0.0
Shawn McCosh	4	0	0	0	4	0	0	0	2	0.0
Rod Buskas*	5	0	0	0	11	-1	0	0	1	0.0
Daniel Berthiaume (goalie)*	19	0	0	0	0	0	0	0	0	0.0

GOALTENDING

	Games	Min.	Goals	SO	Avg.	W	L	T	Shots	Sv. Pct.
Kelly Hrudey	60	3509	197	1	3.37	26	17	†13	1916	.897
Daniel Berthiaume*	19	979	66	0	4.04	7	10	1	541	.878
Steve Weeks*	7	252	17	0	4.05	1	3	0	136	.875
David Goverde	2	120	9	0	4.50	1	1	0	63	.857

Empty-net goals (do not count against a goaltender's average). Hrudey, 4; Berthiaume, 2; Weeks, 1.
*Played with two or more NHL teams.
†Led league.

RESULTS

OCTOBER

4—At Winnipeg	W	6-3
6—At Edmonton	T	*2-2
8—Edmonton	W	6-3
10—Calgary	L	1-7
12—Winnipeg	T	*3-3
16—San Jose	W	8-5
19—Minnesota	W	5-2
22—At New Jersey	L	2-5
23—At N.Y. Rangers	L	2-7
26—At N.Y. Islanders	W	4-2
28—At Detroit	W	4-3
30—At Hartford	T	*4-4
31—At Boston	W	4-2

NOVEMBER

2—At Toronto	W	5-2
7—Vancouver	L	3-4
9—Edmonton	T	*4-4
11—At Winnipeg	L	2-6
12—At Vancouver	L	2-8
14—Buffalo	T	*2-2
16—Detroit	L	3-5
19—At San Jose	W	*3-2
21—N.Y. Rangers	W	6-1
23—San Jose	W	6-4
26—Toronto	T	*4-4
28—At Calgary	L	3-5
30—New Jersey	L	1-4

DECEMBER

3—At San Jose	L	*2-3
5—At Chicago	L	2-6
7—At Quebec	L	5-7
12—Winnipeg	W	2-1
14—Vancouver	T	*4-4
17—Minnesota	L	1-2
21—Detroit	L	2-5
26—San Jose	W	5-3
28—At Edmonton	W	9-4
29—At Calgary	L	2-6
31—Vancouver	L	3-5

JANUARY

2—Edmonton	W	5-3
4—Philadelphia	W	7-3
7—At Pittsburgh	W	5-2
9—At Philadelphia	L	2-5
10—At Washington	L	4-7
12—At New Jersey	L	2-5
14—San Jose	T	*3-3
16—Washington	T	*2-2
22—At Minnesota	T	*3-3
23—At St. Louis	W	6-5
25—Calgary	W	4-3
28—St. Louis	T	*3-3
30—N.Y. Rangers	L	1-4

FEBRUARY

1—Chicago	W	2-0
4—N.Y. Islanders	L	1-2
6—Hartford	T	*5-5
8—At Pittsburgh	W	4-3

9—At Buffalo	W	5-4
11—At St. Louis	L	2-3
13—At Chicago	T	*2-2
15—Washington	W	6-3
17—Boston	W	6-3
19—At Edmonton	L	3-4
21—At Calgary	L	7-9
23—At Winnipeg	W	4-2
25—At Vancouver	W	4-3
27—Quebec	W	4-2
29—Montreal	W	5-3

MARCH

3—Philadelphia	W	4-1
4—At San Jose	W	4-3
7—Pittsburgh	W	5-3
9—Toronto	W	4-1
11—At Hartford	L	0-4
14—At Montreal	L	2-5
15—At Boston	L	1-5
17—Winnipeg	W	5-4
19—Buffalo	L	2-8
21—Calgary	W	5-2
26—At Calgary	L	2-7
27—At Winnipeg	L	4-6
29—At Edmonton	T	*2-2

APRIL

12—At Vancouver	W	6-1
14—Vancouver	L	2-3

*Denotes overtime game.

MINNESOTA NORTH STARS
CAMPBELL CONFERENCE/NORRIS DIVISION

1992-93 SCHEDULE

OCTOBER
S	M	T	W	T	F	S
4	5	6 STL	7	8 STL H	9	10 TB H
11	12	13	14	15 STL	16	17 MON
18 TOR	19	20	21	22 QUE H	23	24 LA H
25	26	27	28 EDM	29	30 VAN	31 CAL

NOVEMBER
S	M	T	W	T	F	S
1	2	3	4	5 NYI H	6	7 EDM H
8	9	10 PIT H	11	12 WIN H	13	14 D CHI H
15 CHI	16	17	18 WAS H	19 TB	20	21 BUF
22	23	24	25 VAN H	26	27 NYR H	28 SJ H
29	30 NYR					

DECEMBER
S	M	T	W	T	F	S
		1 OTT	2	3 DET	4	5 QUE
6	7	8	9	10 EDM H	11	12 CHI H
13	14	15 TOR H	16	17	18	19 DET H
20 CHI	21	22 STL H	23	24	25	26 WIN H
27 WIN	28	29	30	31 BOS H		

JANUARY
S	M	T	W	T	F	S
					1	2 NYI
3 HAR	4	5	6 NJ	7 PIT	8	9 TB H
10	11	12 CHI H	13	14 CHI	15	16 CAL H
17	18	19 TB	20	21 OTT H	22	23 D VAN H
24 TB	25	26 TOR	27	28 NJ H	29	30 TB H
31						

FEBRUARY
S	M	T	W	T	F	S
	1 VAN	2	3 SJ	4	5	6 *
7	8	9	10 WAS H	11 TB	12	13 TOR
14 TOR H	15	16	17 LA H	18	19	20 D PHI H
21 D DET H	22	23	24	25 BOS	26	27 STL
28 WIN						

MARCH
S	M	T	W	T	F	S
	1	2	3 TOR	4	5	6 MON H
7 DET H	8	9 SJ H	10	11	12	13 STL
14 STL H	15	16 PHI	17	18 DET	19	20
21 D DET H	22	23	24	25 TOR H	26	27 HAR H
28	29	30	31 EDM			

APRIL
S	M	T	W	T	F	S
				1 CAL	2	3 D LA
4	5	6 BUF H	7	8	9	10 STL H
11 STL	12	13 CHI H	14	15 DET	16	17

1992-93 SEASON

CLUB DIRECTORY

Owner, president, CEO and governor
Norman N. Green
Alternate governors
Pat Forciea
Vice president/general manager and coach
Bob Gainey
Sr. V.P. of sales and properties
John Thomas
V.P. of communications and operations
Pat Forciea
V.P. of finance and administration
Pat Hoffman
Legal counsel
John Blackshaw
Coach
Bob Gainey
Assistant coach
Doug Jarvis
Director of player personnel
Les Jackson
Director of team services
Doug Armstrong

Chief scout
Dennis Patterson
Scouts
Craig Button
Doug Overton
Director of corporate sales
Matt Colford
Director of merchandising
Peter Jocketty
Dir. of communications & media relations
Joan St. Peter
Assistant director of communications
Dan Stuchal
Director of ticket sales
Tom Vannelli
Head trainer
Dave Surprenant
Assistant trainer
Dave Smith
Equipment manager
Mark Baribeau

DRAFT CHOICES

Rnd. Player	Ht./Wt.	Overall	Pos.	1991-92 club
2—Jarkko Varvio	5-9/172	34	RW	HPK, Finland
3—Jeff Bes	6-0/186	58	C	Guelph (OHL)
4—Jere Lehtinen	6-0/183	88	F	Espoo, Finland
6—Michael Johnson	6-3/172	130	D	Ottawa (OHL)
7—Kyle Peterson	6-3/195	154	C	Thunder Bay (Jr. A, Tier II)
8—Juha Lind	5-11/161	178	C	Jokerit, Finland
9—Lars Edstrom	5-11/185	202	LW	Lulea, Sweden
10—Jeff Romfo	6-0/185	226	C	Blaine (Minn.) H.S.
11—Jeffrey Moen	6-1/170	250	G	Roseville (Minn.) H.S.

MISCELLANEOUS DATA

Home ice (capacity)
Met Center (15,274)
Address
7901 Cedar Avenue S.
Bloomington, MN 55425
Business phone
612-853-9333

Rink dimensions
200 feet by 85 feet
Club colors
Black, gold, green and white
Minor league affiliation
Kalamazoo (IHL)

SCHEDULE KEY

*All-Star Game at Montreal.
H—Home game.   D—Day game (any game starting before 4 p.m.).
NOTE: At press time, two games at neutral sites had yet to be announced.

No.	FORWARDS	Ht./Wt.	Place	BORN Date	NHL exp.	1991-92 clubs
23	Brian Bellows (LW)	5-11/195	St. Catharines, Ont.	9-1-64	10	Minnesota
7	Neal Broten (C)	5-9/170	Roseau, Minn.	11-29-59	12	Minnesota
11	Marc Bureau (C)	6-1/190	Trois-Rivieres, Que.	5-17-66	3	Kalamazoo (IHL), Minnesota
27	Shane Churla (RW)	6-1/200	Fernie, B.C.	6-24-65	6	Minnesota
20	Mike Craig (RW)	6-1/180	London, Ont.	6-6-71	2	Minnesota
22	Ulf Dahlen (RW)	6-2/195	Ostersund, Sweden	1-12-67	5	Minnesota
10	Gaetan Duchesne (LW)	5-11/200	Quebec City	7-11-62	11	Minnesota
14	Todd Elik (C)	6-1/200	Brampton, Ont.	4-15-66	3	Minnesota
15	Dave Gagner (C)	5-10/188	Chatham, Ont.	12-11-64	8	Minnesota
12	Stewart Gavin (RW)	6-0/190	Ottawa	3-15-60	12	Minnesota
31	Mark Janssens (C/LW)	6-3/216	Surrey, B.C.	5-19-68	5	Binghamton (AHL), N.Y. Rangers, Kalamazoo (IHL), Minnesota
29	Trent Klatt (RW)	6-1/205	Robbinsdale, Minn.	1-30-71	1	U. of Minnesota (WCHA), Minnesota
	Cal McGowan (C)	6-1/185	Sidney, NE.	6-19-70	0	Kalamazoo (IHL)
	Mitch Messier (RW)	6-2/200	Regina, Sask.	8-21-65	4	Kalamazoo (IHL)
25	Kip Miller (C)	5-10/185	Lansing, Mich.	6-11-69	2	Halifax (AHL), Quebec, Kalamazoo (IHL), Minnesota
9	Mike Modano (RW/C)	6-3/190	Livonia, Mich.	6-7-70	4	Minnesota
16	Brian Propp (LW)	5-10/195	Lanigan, Sask.	2-15-59	13	Minnesota
18	Bobby Smith (C)	6-4/210	North Sydney, N.S.	2-12-58	14	Minnesota
21	Derrick Smith (LW)	6-2/215	Scarborough, Ont.	1-22-65	8	Kalamazoo (IHL), Minnesota
	DEFENSEMEN					
32	Brad Berry	6-2/190	Bashaw, Alta.	4-1-65	6	Kalamazoo (IHL), Minnesota
	Enrico Ciccone	6-4/200	Montreal	4-10-70	1	Kalamazoo (IHL), Minnesota
4	Chris Dahlquist	6-1/190	Fridley, Minn.	12-14-62	7	Minnesota
28	Derian Hatcher	6-5/205	Sterling Heights, Mich.	6-4-72	1	Minnesota
	Paul Jerrard	5-10/185	Winnipeg, Man.	4-20-65	1	Kalamazoo (IHL)
6	Jim Johnson	6-1/190	New Hope, Minn.	8-9-62	7	Minnesota
3	Craig Ludwig	6-3/217	Rhinelander, Wis.	3-15-61	10	Minnesota
	Richard Matvichuk	6-2/190	Edmonton, Sask.	2-5-73	0	Saskatoon (WHL)
26	David Shaw	6-2/204	St. Thomas, Ont.	5-25-64	10	N.Y. Rangers, Edmonton, Minnesota
	Tommy Sjodin	5-11/190	Sundsvall, Sweden	8-13-65	0	Brynas (Sweden)
24	Mark Tinordi	6-4/205	Red Deer, Alta.	5-9-66	5	Minnesota
	GOALTENDERS					
30	Jon Casey	5-10/155	Grand Rapids, Minn.	8-29-62	7	Kalamazoo (IHL), Minnesota
	Larry Dyck	5-11/180	Winkler, Man.	12-15-65	0	Kalamazoo (IHL)
	Steve Guenette	5-10/175	Gloucester, Ont.	11-13-65	0	Kalamazoo (IHL)
	Jeff Levy	5-11/160	Salt Lake City	12-9-70	0	New Hampshire (H. East)
	Mike Torchia	5-11/215	Toronto	2-23-72	0	Kitchener (OHL)
35	Darcy Wakaluk	5-11/180	Pincher Creek, Alta.	3-14-66	3	Kalamazoo (IHL), Minnesota

1991-92 REVIEW

INDIVIDUAL STATISTICS

SCORING

	Games	G	A	Pts.	Pen.	+/-	PPG	SHG	Shots	Shooting Pct.
Mike Modano	76	33	44	77	46	-9	5	0	256	12.9
Brian Bellows	80	30	45	75	41	-20	12	1	255	11.8
Dave Gagner	78	31	40	71	107	-4	17	0	229	13.5
Ulf Dahlen	79	36	30	66	10	-5	16	1	216	16.7
Todd Elik	62	14	32	46	125	0	4	3	118	11.9
Bobby Smith	68	9	37	46	109	-24	3	0	129	7.0
Brian Propp	51	12	23	35	49	-3	4	0	115	10.4
Neal Broten	76	8	26	34	16	-15	4	1	119	6.7
Mike Craig	67	15	16	31	155	-12	4	0	136	11.0
Mark Tinordi	63	4	24	28	179	-13	4	0	93	4.3
Gaetan Duchesne	73	8	15	23	102	6	0	2	106	7.5
Jim Johnson	71	4	10	14	102	11	0	0	86	4.7
Brian Glynn*	37	2	12	14	24	-16	0	0	53	3.8
Chris Dahlquist	74	1	13	14	68	-10	0	0	63	1.6
Basil McRae	59	5	8	13	245	-14	0	0	64	7.8
Derian Hatcher	43	8	4	12	88	7	0	0	51	15.7
Craig Ludwig	73	2	9	11	54	0	0	0	51	3.9
Marc Bureau	46	6	4	10	50	-5	0	0	53	11.3
Stewart Gavin	35	5	4	9	27	0	0	1	49	10.2
Rob Ramage	34	4	5	9	69	-4	2	0	63	6.3
David Shaw*	37	0	7	7	49	-5	0	0	49	0.0
Derrick Smith	33	2	4	6	33	-8	0	0	29	6.9

	Games	G	A	Pts.	Pen.	+/-	PPG	SHG	Shots	Shooting Pct.
Shane Churla	57	4	1	5	278	-12	0	0	42	9.5
Steve Maltais	12	2	1	3	2	-1	0	0	6	33.3
Kip Miller*	3	1	2	3	2	-1	1	0	3	33.3
Jon Casey (goalie)	52	0	2	2	26	0	0	0	0	0.0
Allen Pedersen	29	0	1	1	10	-1	0	0	17	0.0
Trent Klatt	1	0	0	0	0	0	0	0	1	0.0
Steve Martinson	1	0	0	0	9	0	0	0	0	0.0
Scott Sandelin	1	0	0	0	0	-1	0	0	1	0.0
Mark Janssens*	3	0	0	0	0	-1	0	0	1	0.0
Brad Berry	7	0	0	0	6	-1	0	0	2	0.0
Enrico Ciccone	11	0	0	0	48	-2	0	0	2	0.0
Darcy Wakaluk (goalie)	36	0	0	0	20	0	0	0	0	0.0

GOALTENDING

	Games	Min.	Goals	SO	Avg.	W	L	T	Shots	Sv. Pct.
Darcy Wakaluk	36	1905	104	1	3.28	13	19	1	874	.881
Jon Casey	52	2911	165	2	3.40	19	23	5	1401	.882

Empty-net goals (do not count against a goaltender's average): Casey, 6; Wakaluk, 3.
*Played with two or more NHL teams.

RESULTS

OCTOBER

5—Chicago	W	4-2
10—Quebec	W	3-2
12—Detroit	W	3-2
15—At Calgary	L	3-6
17—At San Jose	W	8-2
19—At Los Angeles	L	2-5
22—Calgary	L	2-4
24—Philadelphia	L	2-5
26—Boston	W	4-0
29—At N.Y. Rangers	L	2-3
31—At Pittsburgh	L	1-8

NOVEMBER

2—Chicago	W	4-3
3—At Chicago	T	*4-4
5—At Detroit	W	3-2
6—At Toronto	L	3-4
9—Pittsburgh	L	2-3
12—Toronto	W	7-0
16—At St. Louis	L	3-5
19—N.Y. Islanders	L	4-7
22—At Detroit	L	3-4
23—Detroit	T	*2-2
29—Toronto	L	2-3
30—At Toronto	W	4-3

DECEMBER

3—St. Louis	T	*3-3
4—St. Louis	W	5-2
7—Washington	L	2-4

8—At Chicago	L	2-7
10—New Jersey	W	4-3
12—At Vancouver	L	5-7
14—At San Jose	W	3-2
17—At Los Angeles	W	2-1
21—Philadelphia	L	0-3
26—At Winnipeg	W	3-2
28—St. Louis	W	5-2
31—Chicago	W	6-2

JANUARY

2—At St. Louis	L	1-6
4—Vancouver	W	4-3
5—At Chicago	L	2-5
7—At Washington	W	5-3
9—At Detroit	L	4-9
11—San Jose	W	7-4
13—Edmonton	L	4-7
15—At Montreal	W	5-2
22—Los Angeles	T	*3-3
25—Chicago	L	0-2
27—At Boston	L	2-3
28—At Hartford	W	4-3
30—At Philadelphia	L	3-5

FEBRUARY

1—N.Y. Rangers	L	1-2
3—Toronto	W	4-2
5—At Toronto	L	*2-3
7—At Buffalo	W	2-0
9—At Hartford	T	*4-4
11—Edmonton	L	4-5

13—Winnipeg	W	6-1
15—Pittsburgh	W	5-2
17—At Montreal	L	0-8
18—At Quebec	L	0-4
21—At N.Y. Rangers	L	4-5
22—At N.Y. Islanders	L	1-2
24—At New Jersey	W	3-1
26—Montreal	L	1-4
29—Hartford	L	*4-5

MARCH

1—At Toronto	L	2-6
3—At Washington	W	3-1
5—At Detroit	W	4-2
8—Winnipeg	W	4-2
10—At St. Louis	L	2-5
11—Toronto	L	0-3
14—Detroit	W	4-1
17—Buffalo	W	3-1
19—At Chicago	L	1-4
21—At Quebec	L	2-4
24—Vancouver	L	2-4
27—At Edmonton	L	3-5
28—At Calgary	L	3-4
31—Buffalo	W	5-3

APRIL

12—St. Louis	T	*1-1
14—Detroit	L	4-7
16—At St. Louis	L	3-5

*Denotes overtime game.

MONTREAL CANADIENS
WALES CONFERENCE/ADAMS DIVISION

1992-93 SCHEDULE

OCTOBER

S	M	T	W	T	F	S
4	5	6 HAR	7	8 OTT	9	10 PIT H
11 BUF	12	13	14	15 PIT H	16	17 MIN H
18	19 STL H	20	21 SJ H	22	23 NYR	24 PHI
25	26	27	28 TB H	29	30	31 NYR H

NOVEMBER

S	M	T	W	T	F	S
1	2 WIN H	3	4 DET	5	6	7 DET H
8	9 CAL H	10	11 NJ	12	13	14 PHI H
15	16 BOS H	17 OTT	18	19 QUE	20	21 OTT H
22	23 WAS H	24	25 HAR	26	27	28 VAN H
29	30 BUF H					

DECEMBER

S	M	T	W	T	F	S
		1	2	3 BOS	4	5 WIN
6 CHI	7	8	9	10	11	12 BOS H
13 NYR	14	15	16 QUE H	17 QUE	18	19 BUF H
20	21 HAR H	22	23 NYI H	24	25	26
27 VAN	28	29 EDM	30	31 CAL		

JANUARY

S	M	T	W	T	F	S
					1	2 LA
3	4	5 SJ	6	7	8	9 TOR H
10 HAR	11	12	13 HAR H	14 QUE	15	16 NYR H
17	18	19	20 NJ H	21	22 NJ	23 TOR
24	25 BOS H	26	27 HAR H	28	29	30 D OTT H
31 D PHI H						

FEBRUARY

S	M	T	W	T	F	S
	1	2	3 LA H	4	5	6 *
7	8	9 NYI	10	11 PHI	12	13 OTT
14	15	16	17 BOS H	18	19	20 OTT H
21 EDM H	22	23 STL	24	25	26 BUF	27 BUF H
28						

MARCH

S	M	T	W	T	F	S
	1 BOS	2	3 TB	4	5	6 MIN
7	8	9	10 NYI H	11 BOS	12	13 QUE H
14	15	16	17	18 QUE	19	20 CHI H
21	22 BUF H	23	24 HAR	25 BOS	26	27 OTT H
28	29	30	31 QUE H			

APRIL

S	M	T	W	T	F	S
				1	2 WAS	3 NYI
4	5	6	7 PIT	8	9	10 BOS H
11	12 WAS H	13 BUF	14	15	16	17

1992-93 SEASON

CLUB DIRECTORY

Chairman of the board, pres. and governor
Ronald Corey
V.P. hockey and managing director
Serge Savard
Senior vice president, corporate affairs
Jean Beliveau
Vice president, Forum operations
Aldo Giampaolo
Vice president, finance and administration
Fred Steer
Assistant to managing director
Jacques Lemaire
Director of recruitment and assistant to managing director
Andre Boudrias
Coach
Jacques Demers
Assistant coaches
Jacques Laperriere
Charlie Thiffault

Goaltending instructor
Francois Allaire
Director of player development and scout
Claude Ruel
Chief scout
Doug Robinson
Director of public relations
Claude Mouton
Director of press relations
Michele Lapointe
Club physician
Dr. D.G. Kinnear
Athletic trainer
Gaetan Lefebvre
Equipment manager
Eddy Palchak
Assistants to the equipment manager
Pierre Gervais
Robert Boulanger

DRAFT CHOICES

Rnd. Player	Ht./Wt.	Overall	Pos.	1991-92 club
1—David Wilkie	6-1/202	20	C	Kamloops (WHL)
2—Valeri Bure	5-9/155	33	RW	Spokane (WHL)
2—Keli Corpse	5-11/176	44	C	Kingston (OHL)
3—Craig Rivet	6-1/172	68	D	Kingston (OHL)
4—Louis Bernard	6-1/198	82	D	Drummondville (QMJHL)
4—Marc Lamothe	6-1/186	92	G	Kingston (OHL)
5—Don Chase	5-11/190	116	C	Springfield (Junior B)
6—Martin Sychra	6-1/172	140	C	Zetor Brno, Czech.
7—Christian Proulx	5-11/188	164	D	St. Jean (QMJHL)
8—Michael Burman	6-0/186	188	D	North Bay (OHL)
9—Earl Cronan	6-1/195	212	LW	St. Mark's (Mass.) H.S.
10—Trent Cavicchi	6-3/190	236	G	Dartmouth (N.S.) Midgets
11—Hiroyuki Miura	6-3/170	260	F	Japanese National Team

MISCELLANEOUS DATA

Home ice (capacity)
Montreal Forum (16,197)
Address
2313 St. Catherine Street West
Montreal, Que. H3H 1N2
Business phone
514-932-2582

Rink dimensions
200 feet by 85 feet
Club colors
Red, white and blue
Minor league affiliation
Fredericton (AHL)

SCHEDULE KEY

*All-Star Game at Montreal.
H—Home game.　　D—Day game (any game starting before 4 p.m.).
NOTE: At press time, two games at neutral sites had yet to be announced.

TRAINING CAMP ROSTER

			BORN		NHL	
No.	FORWARDS	Ht./Wt.	Place	Date	exp.	1991-92 clubs
22	Benoit Brunet (LW)	5-11/184	Montreal	8-24-68	3	Fredericton (AHL), Montreal
	Jim Campbell (C)	6-1/175	Worchester, Mass.	4-3-73	0	Hull (QMJHL)
21	Guy Carbonneau (C)	5-11/184	Sept Iles, Que.	3-18-60	11	Montreal
	Patrik Carnback (LW)	6-0/189	Goteborg, Sweden	2-1-68	0	Vastra Frolunda (Sweden)
27	Shayne Corson (LW/C)	6-0/201	Barrie, Ont.	8-13-66	7	Montreal
6	Russ Courtnall (RW)	5-11/183	Victoria, B.C.	6-3-65	9	Montreal
15	Paul DiPietro (C)	5-9/181	S. Ste. Marie, Ont.	9-8-70	1	Fredericton (AHL), Montreal
45	Gilbert Dionne (LW)	6-0/194	Drummondville, Que.	9-19-70	2	Fredericton (AHL), Montreal
36	Todd Ewen (RW)	6-2/220	Saskatoon, Sask.	3-26-66	6	Montreal
41	Brent Gilchrist (C)	5-11/181	Moose Jaw, Sask.	4-3-67	4	Montreal
12	Mike Keane (RW)	5-10/178	Winnipeg, Man.	5-29-67	4	Montreal
	Patrik Kjellberg (LW)	6-2/196	Falun, Sweden	6-17-69	0	AIK Solna (Sweden)
	Steve Larouche	5-11/180	Rouyn, Que.	4-14-71	0	Fredericton (AHL)
	Patrick Lebeau	5-10/173	St. Jerome, Que.	3-17-70	1	Fredericton (AHL)
47	Stephan Lebeau (C)	5-10/172	Sherbrooke, Que.	2-28-68	4	Montreal
17	John LeClair (LW)	6-2/205	St. Albans, Vt.	7-5-69	2	Fredericton (AHL), Montreal
35	Michael McPhee (LW)	6-1/203	Sydney, N.S.	2-14-60	9	Montreal
11	Kirk Muller (LW)	6-0/205	Kingston, Ont.	2-8-66	8	Montreal
30	Chris Nilan (RW)	6-0/205	Boston	2-9-58	13	Boston, Montreal
18	Denis Savard (C)	5-10/175	Pointe Gatineau, Que.	2-4-61	12	Montreal
39	Brian Skrudland (C)	6-0/196	Peace River, Alta.	7-31-63	7	Montreal
	Turner Stevenson	6-3/200	Prince George, B.C.	5-18-72	0	Seattle (WHL)
	Vladimir Vujtek (LW)	5-11/175	O., Severomoravsky, Cz.	2-17-72	1	Tri-City (WHL), Montreal
	DEFENSEMEN					
	Brent Bilodeau	6-4/220	Dallas, Tex.	3-27-73	0	Seattle (WHL), Swift Current (WHL)
43	Patrice Brisebois	6-2/175	Montreal	1-27-71	2	Fredericton (AHL), Montreal
	Eric Charron	6-3/190	Verdun, Que.	1-14-70	0	Fredericton (AHL)
5	Alain Cote	6-0/200	Montmagny, Que.	4-14-67	7	Fredericton (AHL), Montreal
48	J.J. Daigneault	5-11/185	Montreal	10-12-65	7	Montreal
28	Eric Desjardins	6-1/200	Rouyn, Que.	6-14-69	4	Montreal
34	Donald Dufresne	6-1/206	Quebec City	4-10-67	4	Fredericton (AHL), Montreal
14	Kevin Haller	6-2/183	Trochu, Alta.	12-5-70	3	Rochester (AHL), Buffalo, Montreal
38	Sean Hill	6-0/195	Duluth, Minn.	2-14-70	2	U.S. Nat./Olym., Fredericton (AHL)
3	Sylvain Lefebvre	6-2/204	Richmond, Que.	10-14-67	3	Montreal
24	Lyle Odelein	5-10/206	Quill Lake, Sask.	7-21-68	3	Montreal
8	Mathieu Schneider	5-11/189	New York	6-12-69	4	Montreal
	GOALTENDERS					
	Frederic Chabot	5-10/160	Hebertville, Que.	2-12-68	1	Winston-Salem (ECHL), Fredericton (AHL)
40	Andre Racicot	5-11/165	Rouyn-Noranda, Que.	6-9-69	3	Fredericton (AHL), Montreal
33	Patrick Roy	6-0/182	Quebec City	10-5-65	8	Montreal

1991-92 REVIEW

INDIVIDUAL STATISTICS

SCORING

	Games	G	A	Pts.	Pen.	+/-	PPG	SHG	Shots	Shooting Pct.
Kirk Muller	78	36	41	77	86	15	15	1	191	18.8
Denis Savard	77	28	42	70	73	6	12	1	174	16.1
Stephan Lebeau	77	27	31	58	14	18	13	0	178	15.2
Shayne Corson	64	17	36	53	118	15	3	0	165	10.3
Brent Gilchrist	79	23	27	50	57	29	2	0	146	15.8
Mike Keane	67	11	30	41	64	16	2	0	116	9.5
Guy Carbonneau	72	18	21	39	39	2	1	1	120	15.0
Eric Desjardins	77	6	32	38	50	17	4	0	141	4.3
Gilbert Dionne	39	21	13	34	10	7	7	0	90	23.3
Matt Schneider	78	8	24	32	72	10	2	0	194	4.1
Mike McPhee	78	16	15	31	63	6	0	0	146	11.0
Russ Courtnall	27	7	14	21	6	6	0	1	63	11.1
Petr Svoboda *	58	5	16	21	94	9	1	0	88	5.7
Sylvain Turgeon	56	9	11	20	39	-4	6	0	99	9.1
John LeClair	59	8	11	19	14	5	3	0	73	11.0
J.J. Daigneault	79	4	14	18	36	16	2	0	108	3.7
Sylvain Lefebvre	69	3	14	17	91	9	0	0	85	3.5
Benoit Brunet	18	4	6	10	14	4	0	0	37	10.8
Paul DiPietro	33	4	6	10	25	5	0	0	27	14.8
Patrice Brisebois	26	2	8	10	20	9	0	0	37	5.4

	Games	G	A	Pts.	Pen.	+/-	PPG	SHG	Shots	Shooting Pct.
Lyle Odelein	71	1	7	8	212	15	0	0	43	2.3
Brian Skrudland	42	3	3	6	36	-4	0	0	51	5.9
Patrick Roy (goalie)	67	0	5	5	4	0	0	0	0	0.0
Kevin Haller*	8	2	2	4	17	4	1	0	9	22.2
Chris Nilan*	17	1	3	4	74	-1	0	0	22	4.5
Mario Roberge	20	2	1	3	62	3	0	0	7	28.6
Todd Ewen	46	1	2	3	130	3	0	0	19	5.3
Alain Cote	13	0	3	3	22	7	0	0	6	0.0
Vladimir Vujtek	2	0	0	0	0	-1	0	0	1	0.0
Donald Dufresne	3	0	0	0	2	2	0	0	2	0.0
Ed Ronan	3	0	0	0	0	0	0	0	1	0.0
Jesse Belanger	4	0	0	0	0	-1	0	0	4	0.0
Andre Racicot (goalie)	9	0	0	0	0	0	0	0	0	0.0
Roland Melanson (goalie)	9	0	0	0	0	0	0	0	0	0.0

GOALTENDING

	Games	Min.	Goals	SO	Avg.	W	L	T	Shots	Sv. Pct.
Patrick Roy	67	3935	155	‡5	†2.36	36	22	8	1806	†.914
Roland Melanson	9	492	22	2	2.68	5	3	0	195	.887
Andre Racicot	9	436	23	0	3.17	0	3	3	219	.895

Empty-net goals (do not count against a goaltender's average): Roy, 7.
*Played with two or more NHL teams.
†Led league.
‡Tied for league lead.

RESULTS

OCTOBER

3—Toronto	W	4-3	
5—N.Y. Rangers	L	*1-2	
8—At Hartford	T	*2-2	
10—At Detroit	W	4-1	
12—At Boston	W	6-0	
14—Hartford	L	3-4	
16—Buffalo	W	5-1	
18—At Buffalo	L	1-3	
19—At Philadelphia	W	1-0	
23—Quebec	W	*3-2	
24—At Quebec	W	5-0	
26—Pittsburgh	W	4-1	
30—Winnipeg	W	6-1	

NOVEMBER

1—At Buffalo	W	5-1	
2—Buffalo	W	5-0	
4—New Jersey	W	*3-2	
6—At N.Y. Rangers	W	4-1	
8—At New Jersey	L	2-3	
9—Chicago	W	4-2	
11—Washington	L	2-4	
14—At Hartford	T	*2-2	
16—Philadelphia	L	1-3	
18—Edmonton	W	1-0	
21—At Quebec	L	2-5	
23—Quebec	W	5-3	
25—Boston	W	4-3	
27—At Washington	L	1-3	
29—At Boston	L	*4-5	
30—At Hartford	L	2-3	

DECEMBER

4—Vancouver	L	0-3	
5—At N.Y. Islanders	W	5-4	
7—Calgary	W	5-1	
9—At Toronto	W	4-1	
12—At Boston	L	2-5	
14—Buffalo	W	4-2	
16—St. Louis	W	4-2	
19—At Chicago	L	4-6	
21—Hartford	W	*3-2	
22—Boston	W	3-2	
26—At Quebec	W	4-1	
29—At Edmonton	W	3-1	
31—At Calgary	L	*2-3	

JANUARY

4—At San Jose	W	*1-0	
8—Boston	W	3-2	
11—Hartford	W	3-2	
13—Calgary	T	*2-2	
15—At Minnesota	L	2-5	
16—At St. Louis	T	*6-6	
23—At Boston	W	3-1	
25—Buffalo	L	3-4	
26—Hartford	W	3-1	
29—New Jersey	L	3-4	
31—At Buffalo	L	3-5	

FEBRUARY

1—Detroit	W	*4-3	
4—At Vancouver	L	3-5	
5—At Edmonton	L	1-2	
8—At Toronto	L	4-6	
10—Vancouver	W	8-3	
12—San Jose	W	6-1	
15—Quebec	T	*4-4	
17—Minnesota	W	8-0	
19—At Hartford	T	*2-2	
22—Pittsburgh	W	2-1	
23—Quebec	T	*3-3	
26—At Minnesota	W	4-1	
28—At San Jose	T	*3-3	
29—At Los Angeles	L	3-5	

MARCH

3—At N.Y. Islanders	W	4-3	
7—N.Y. Islanders	W	8-2	
8—Detroit	W	4-1	
11—At Quebec	L	4-5	
14—Los Angeles	W	5-2	
16—At N.Y. Rangers	L	1-4	
18—Philadelphia	L	3-4	
21—St. Louis	T	*3-3	
25—At Winnipeg	T	*2-2	
27—At Washington	L	3-4	
28—At Pittsburgh	L	3-6	

APRIL

12—At Buffalo	L	1-3	
15—Boston	T	*4-4	

*Denotes overtime game.

NEW JERSEY DEVILS
WALES CONFERENCE/PATRICK DIVISION

1992-93 SCHEDULE

OCTOBER
S	M	T	W	T	F	S
4	5	6 NYI H	7	8	9 PHI	10 NYR H
11	12 WAS H	13	14 NYR	15	16	17 PHI H
18	19	20 HAR H	21	22	23 CHI	24 PIT H
25	26	27	28 HAR	29	30 NYI H	31 NYI

NOVEMBER
S	M	T	W	T	F	S
1	2	3	4	5 LA	6	7 SJ
8	9	10	11 MON H	12	13 WAS H	14 WAS
15	16	17	18	19	20 PIT H	21 PIT
22	23	24	25 OTT	26	27	28 QUE
29	30					

DECEMBER
S	M	T	W	T	F	S
		1 TOR H	2	3 OTT	4	5 D BOS H
6 BUF	7	8	9 WAS H	10	11 PIT H	12 PIT
13	14	15 WIN	16	17	18 TB	19
20	21 NYR H	22	23 NYR	24	25	26
27 HAR H	28	29 QUE	30	31		

JANUARY
S	M	T	W	T	F	S
					1 D WAS	2 WIN H
3	4 NYR	5	6 MIN H	7	8 OTT H	9 BOS
10	11	12 VAN H	13	14 LA H	15	16 D NYI H
17	18	19 MON	20	21	22 MON H	23 BOS
24	25	26 NYI	27	28 MIN	29	30 STL
31						

FEBRUARY
S	M	T	W	T	F	S
	1	2	3 CAL H	4	5	6 ★
7	8 NYR H	9 DET	10	11	12	13 D PHI H
14 D PHI	15	16	17 STL H	18	19 BUF H	20
21 QUE H	22	23 PIT	24	25 PHI	26	27 D OTT H
28 DET H						

MARCH
S	M	T	W	T	F	S
	1	2	3 HAR	4	5 CHI H	6
7 PHI H	8	9 VAN	10	11	12 EDM	13 CAL
14	15	16	17	18 EDM H	19	20 D QUE H
21 PHI	22	23 TB H	24	25 NYI	26	27 D WAS
28	29 SJ H	30	31 BUF			

APRIL
S	M	T	W	T	F	S
				1	2	3 TOR
4	5	6	7 NYR H	8	9	10 WAS
11 NYI H	12	13	14 PIT H	15 PIT	16	17

1992-93 SEASON

CLUB DIRECTORY

Chairman
John J. McMullen
President and general manager
Lou Lamoriello
Executive vice president
Max McNab
Coach
Herb Brooks
Assistant coaches
Dave Farrish
Doug Sulliman
Goaltending coach
Warren Strelow
Strength coach
Dimitri Lopuchin
Director, public and media relations
David Freed
Assistant director, media relations
Mike Levine

Public & media relations assistant
George Moreira
Director of player personnel
Marshall Johnston
Assistant director of player personnel
David Conte
Scouts
Claude Carrier
Frank Jay
Ed Thomlinson
Milt Fisher
Glen Dirk
Dan Labraaten
Les Widdifield
Marcel Pronovost
Fernie Flaman
Joe Mahoney
Bob Sauve

DRAFT CHOICES

Rnd.	Player	Ht./Wt.	Overall	Pos.	1991-92 club
1	Jason Smith	6-3/183	18	D	Regina (WHL)
2	Sergei Brylin	5-9/176	42	C	CSKA Moscow, CIS
3	Cale Hulse	6-3/205	66	D	Portland (WHL)
4	Vitali Tomilin	6-0/183	90	F	Krylja Sovetov, CIS
4	Scott McCabe	6-4/189	94	D	Detroit Midgets
5	Ryan Black	6-0/180	114	LW	Peterborough (OHL)
6	Daniel Trebil	6-3/185	138	D	Jefferson H.S., Bloomington, Min.
7	Geordie Kinnear	6-1/200	162	D	Peterborough (OHL)
8	Stephane Yelle	6-1/162	186	C	Oshawa (OHL)
9	Jeff Toms	6-3/180	210	LW	Sault Ste. Marie (OHL)
10	Heath Weenk	6-3/210	234	D	Regina (WHL)
11	Vladimir Yakovenko	5-11/174	258	G	Spartak, CIS

MISCELLANEOUS DATA

Home ice (capacity)
Byrne Meadowlands Arena (19,040)
Address
P.O. Box 504
East Rutherford, N.J. 07073
Business phone
201-935-6050

Rink dimensions
200 feet by 85 feet
Club colors
Red, black and white
Minor league affiliation
Utica (AHL)

SCHEDULE KEY

*All-Star Game at Montreal.
H—Home game.   D—Day game (any game starting before 4 p.m.).
NOTE: At press time, two games at neutral sites had yet to be announced.

TRAINING CAMP ROSTER

No.	FORWARDS	Ht./Wt.	Place	BORN Date	NHL exp.	1991-92 clubs
11	Dave Barr (RW)	6-1/195	Edmonton, Alta.	11-30-60	11	Utica (AHL), New Jersey
24	Douglas Brown (RW)	5-10/180	Southborough, Mass.	6-12-64	6	New Jersey
9	Tom Chorske (RW)	6-1/205	Minneapolis	9-18-66	3	New Jersey
33	Zdeno Ciger (LW)	6-1/190	Martin, Czech.	10-19-69	2	New Jersey
32	Pat Conacher (LW)	5-8/190	Edmonton, Alta.	5-1-59	10	New Jersey
34	Jim Dowd (C)	6-1/185	Brick, N.J.	12-25-68	1	Utica (AHL), New Jersey
	David Emma (C)	5-9/175	Cranston, R.I.	1-14-69	0	U.S. Nat./Olym., Utica (AHL)
12	Bill Guerin (C/RW)	6-2/190	Wilbraham, Mass.	11-9-70	1	Utica (AHL), New Jersey
22	Claude Lemieux (RW)	6-1/215	Buckingham, Que.	7-16-65	9	New Jersey
15	John MacLean (RW)	6-0/200	Oshawa, Ont.	11-20-64	9	New Jersey
8	Troy Mallette (C/LW)	6-2/190	Sudbury, Ont.	2-25-70	3	Edmonton, New Jersey
21	Randy McKay (RW)	6-1/185	Montreal	1-25-67	4	New Jersey
12	Jason Miller (C)	6-1/190	Edmonton, Alta.	3-1-71	2	Utica (AHL), New Jersey
	Janne Ojanen (C)	6-2/200	Tampere, Finland	4-9-68	3	New Jersey
44	Stephane Richer (RW)	6-2/200	Buckingham, Que.	6-7-66	8	New Jersey
20	Alexander Semak (C)	5-9/190	Ufa, U.S.S.R.	2-11-66	1	Dynamo Moscow (CIS), Utica (AHL), New Jersey
10	Jarrod Skalde (C)	6-0/170	Niagara Falls, Ont.	?-26-71	?	Utica (AHL), New Jersey
26	Peter Stastny (C)	6-1/200	Bratislava, Czech.	9-18-56	12	New Jersey
17	Patrik Sundstrom (C)	6-1/200	Skelleftea, Sweden	12-14-61	10	New Jersey
	Kevin Todd (C)	5-10/175	Winnipeg, Man.	5-4-68	3	New Jersey
19	Claude Vilgrain (RW)	6-1/205	Port-au-Prince, Haiti	3-1-63	3	New Jersey
25	Valeri Zelepukin (RW)	5-11/180	Voskresensk, U.S.S.R.	9-17-68	1	Utica (AHL), New Jersey
	DEFENSEMEN					
6	Tommy Albelin	6-1/190	Stockholm, Sweden	5-21-64	5	Utica (AHL), New Jersey
3	Ken Daneyko	6-0/210	Windsor, Ont.	4-17-64	9	New Jersey
23	Bruce Driver	6-0/185	Toronto	4-29-62	9	New Jersey
2	Viacheslav Fetisov	6-1/220	Moscow, U.S.S.R.	5-20-58	3	New Jersey
7	Alexei Kasatonov	6-1/215	Leningrad, U.S.S.R.	10-14-59	3	New Jersey
27	Scott Niedermayer	6-0/200	Edmonton, Alta.	8-31-73	1	Kamloops (WHL), New Jersey
28	Myles O'Connor	5-11/165	Calgary, Alta.	4-2-67	2	Utica (AHL), New Jersey
4	Scott Stevens	6-2/215	Kitchener, Ont.	4-1-64	10	New Jersey
5	Eric Weinrich	6-1/210	Roanoke, Va.	12-19-66	4	New Jersey
	GOALTENDERS					
1	Craig Billington	5-10/170	London, Ont.	9-11-66	3	New Jersey
29	Martin Brodeur	6-1/190	Montreal	5-6-72	1	St. Hyacinthe (QMJHL), New Jersey
30	Chad Erickson	5-10/175	Minneapolis	8-21-70	1	Utica (AHL), New Jersey
29	Chris Terreri	5-8/155	Warwick, R.I.	11-15-64	5	New Jersey

1991-92 REVIEW

INDIVIDUAL STATISTICS

SCORING

	Games	G	A	Pts.	Pen.	+/-	PPG	SHG	Shots	Shooting Pct.
Claude Lemieux	74	41	27	68	109	9	13	1	296	13.9
Stephane Richer	74	29	35	64	25	-1	5	1	240	12.1
Kevin Todd	80	21	42	63	69	8	2	0	131	16.0
Peter Stastny	66	24	38	62	42	6	10	1	142	16.9
Scott Stevens	68	17	42	59	124	24	7	1	156	10.9
Claude Vilgrain	71	19	27	46	74	27	1	1	88	21.6
Bruce Driver	78	7	35	42	66	5	3	1	205	3.4
Alexei Kasatonov	76	12	28	40	70	14	3	2	107	11.2
Tom Chorske	76	19	17	36	32	8	0	3	143	13.3
Randy McKay	80	17	16	33	246	6	2	0	111	15.3
Eric Weinrich	76	7	25	32	55	10	5	0	97	7.2
Valeri Zelepukin	44	13	18	31	28	11	3	0	94	13.8
Doug Brown	71	11	17	28	27	17	1	2	140	7.9
Laurie Boschman	75	8	20	28	121	9	0	0	89	9.0
Viacheslav Fetisov	70	3	23	26	108	11	0	0	70	4.3
David Maley*	37	7	11	18	58	0	1	0	42	16.7
Dave Barr	41	6	12	18	32	9	0	1	49	12.2
Zdeno Ciger	20	6	5	11	10	-2	1	0	33	18.2
Alexander Semak	25	5	6	11	0	5	0	0	45	11.1
Pat Conacher	44	7	3	10	16	0	0	1	38	18.4
Ken Daneyko	80	1	7	8	170	7	0	0	57	1.8
Troy Mallette*	17	3	4	7	43	7	0	0	19	15.8
Jarrod Skalde	15	2	4	6	4	-1	0	0	25	8.0
Patrik Sundstrom	17	1	3	4	8	-5	1	0	16	6.3

	Games	G	A	Pts.	Pen.	+/-	PPG	SHG	Shots	Shooting Pct.
Tommy Albelin	19	0	4	4	4	7	0	0	18	0.0
Jon Morris	7	1	2	3	6	-6	1	0	5	20.0
Walt Poddubny	7	1	2	3	6	-1	0	0	9	11.1
Myles O'Connor	9	0	2	2	13	-2	0	0	13	0.0
Neil Brady	7	1	0	1	4	1	0	0	3	33.3
Scott Niedermayer	4	0	1	1	2	1	0	0	4	0.0
Bill Guerin	5	0	1	1	9	1	0	0	8	0.0
Craig Billington (goalie)	26	0	1	1	2	0	0	0	0	0.0
Chris Terreri (goalie)	54	0	1	1	13	0	0	0	0	0.0
Jim Dowd	1	0	0	0	0	0	0	0	0	0.0
Alan Stewart*	1	0	0	0	5	0	0	0	0	0.0
Jeff Christian	2	0	0	0	2	0	0	0	1	0.0
Chad Erickson (goalie)	2	0	0	0	0	0	0	0	0	0.0
Jason Miller	3	0	0	0	0	0	0	0	1	0.0
Martin Brodeur (goalie)	4	0	0	0	0	0	0	0	0	0.0

GOALTENDING

	Games	Min.	Goals	SO	Avg.	W	L	T	Shots	Sv. Pct.
Craig Billington	26	1363	69	2	3.04	13	7	1	637	.892
Chris Terreri	54	3186	169	1	3.18	22	22	10	1511	.888
Martin Brodeur	4	179	10	0	3.35	2	1	0	85	.882
Chad Erickson	2	120	9	0	4.50	1	1	0	55	.836

Empty-net goals (do not count against a goaltender's average): Billington, 2.
*Played with two or more NHL teams.

RESULTS

OCTOBER
5—St. Louis	W	7-2
6—At Chicago	W	*4-2
8—Quebec	W	6-5
12—Pittsburgh	W	4-1
13—At Philadelphia	L	2-4
16—At N.Y. Rangers	L	2-4
18—At Washington	L	5-6
19—Washington	L	1-5
22—Los Angeles	W	5-2
24—At Pittsburgh	W	4-2
26—San Jose	W	9-0
29—At Vancouver	L	3-4
30—At Calgary	W	5-2

NOVEMBER
1—At Edmonton	W	3-1
4—At Montreal	L	*2-3
8—Montreal	W	3-2
9—At Boston	L	0-4
12—Philadelphia	W	5-2
14—N.Y. Islanders	L	3-4
16—Winnipeg	L	0-1
20—Washington	W	*6-5
22—Hartford	W	8-2
23—At Philadelphia	T	*5-5
27—At Pittsburgh	L	4-8
30—At Los Angeles	W	4-1

DECEMBER
5—Calgary	W	6-3
7—Detroit	T	*2-2
8—At Philadelphia	T	*2-2
10—At Minnesota	L	3-4
13—Pittsburgh	L	3-4
14—At N.Y. Islanders	T	*3-3
19—At Hartford	W	4-1
21—Chicago	T	*1-1
23—At N.Y. Rangers	L	0-3
26—At N.Y. Islanders	T	*5-5
28—Buffalo	W	3-0
29—Washington	L	3-4
31—At Pittsburgh	W	7-4

JANUARY
2—Pittsburgh	W	4-0
4—N.Y. Rangers	W	6-4
9—St. Louis	W	4-3
11—Toronto	L	3-4
12—Los Angeles	W	5-2
15—Buffalo	T	*8-8
24—At Washington	W	5-2
25—Detroit	L	0-7
29—At Montreal	W	4-3
31—At Detroit	W	6-3

FEBRUARY
1—At Toronto	L	4-6
4—Philadelphia	W	3-1
6—At St. Louis	L	1-4
8—At Boston	W	6-4
9—At Quebec	W	2-1
13—Vancouver	W	5-3
15—Hartford	W	4-1
16—N.Y. Rangers	W	4-2
18—Philadelphia	W	*4-3
20—At Chicago	T	*4-4
21—At Winnipeg	L	4-6
24—Minnesota	L	1-3
25—At Toronto	T	*5-5
28—N.Y. Islanders	L	*2-3
29—At N.Y. Islanders	W	3-1

MARCH
2—N.Y. Rangers	L	1-7
4—At N.Y. Rangers	W	5-4
6—At Buffalo	L	4-5
7—At Washington	L	*2-3
11—At Edmonton	T	*2-2
12—At Vancouver	L	1-2
14—At San Jose	L	2-3
19—Edmonton	L	3-5
21—N.Y. Islanders	T	*2-2
22—At N.Y. Rangers	L	3-6
24—San Jose	W	4-3
26—Boston	W	4-2
28—Quebec	W	5-2
29—At Philadelphia	L	4-5

APRIL
12—Washington	L	3-4
13—Pittsburgh	W	5-1
15—At N.Y. Islanders	L	0-7

*Denotes overtime game.

NEW YORK ISLANDERS
WALES CONFERENCE/PATRICK DIVISION

1992-93 SCHEDULE

OCTOBER
S	M	T	W	T	F	S
4	5	6 NJ	7	8 PIT	9	10 BOS
11	12	13	14	15 PHI	16	17 NYR H
18 NYR	19	20 PHI H	21	22	23 WAS H	24 HAR H
25	26	27 LA H	28	29	30 NJ	31 NJ H

NOVEMBER
S	M	T	W	T	F	S
1	2	3 PIT	4	5 MIN	6	7 TB H
8	9	10	11	12 PHI	13	14 BUF H
15	16	17	18	19 BOS	20	21 CAL
22 EDM	23	24 WIN	25	26	27 D PHI	28 PHI H
29	30					

DECEMBER
S	M	T	W	T	F	S
		1 PIT H	2	3	4 BUF	5 WAS H
6	7 TB	8	9	10 CHI	11	12 WIN H
13	14	15	16	17 OTT H	18	19 D PIT
20 D QUE	21	22	23 MON	24	25	26 NYR H
27	28	29 TOR H	30	31 STL		

JANUARY
S	M	T	W	T	F	S
					1	2 MIN H
3	4	5 QUE H	6	7	8 BUF	9 VAN H
10	11	12 CAL H	13	14 WAS H	15	16 D NJ
17 OTT	18	19 BOS H	20	21	22	23 PHI H
24	25	26 NJ H	27	28 PIT	29	30 BOS H
31						

FEBRUARY
S	M	T	W	T	F	S
	1 NYR H	2	3 TOR	4	5	6 *
7	8	9 MON H	10	11	12 NYR	13 NYR H
14	15	16 EDM H	17	18 STL H	19	20 D PIT H
21	22	23 WAS H	24	25 QUE	26	27 D PHI
28 HAR						

MARCH
S	M	T	W	T	F	S
	1	2 DET H	3	4	5	6
7 D WAS	8	9 PHI H	10 MON	11	12	13 PIT H
14 WAS H	15	16 SJ	17	18 LA	19	20 VAN
21	22	23 DET	24	25 NJ H	26	27 SJ H
28	29	30 PHI H	31			

APRIL
S	M	T	W	T	F	S
				1	2 NYR	3 MON H
4	5	6 WAS	7	8 CHI H	9	10 OTT H
11 NJ	12	13	14 HAR	15 HAR H	16	17

1992-93 SEASON

CLUB DIRECTORY

Owner
John O. Pickett Jr.
Chairman of the board and G.M.
William A. Torrey
President
John H. Krumpe
General counsel
William M. Skehan
Vice president/administration & CEO
Arthur J. McCarthy
Vice president
Joseph H. Dreyer
Coach
Al Arbour
Assistant coaches
Lorne Henning
Ken Morrow
Assistant G.M.
Don Maloney
Publicity director
Greg Bouris
Assistant publicity director
Catherine Schutte
Publicity assistant
Eric Mirlis

Controller
Ralph Sellitti
Director of public affairs
Jill Knee
Director of sales
Jim Johnson
Dir. of community rel. & amateur hockey
Bob Nystrom
Dir. of scouting
Gerry Ehman
Scouting staff
Harry Boyd
Richard Green
Earl Ingarfield
Hal Laycoe
Bert Marshall
Mario Saraceno
Jack Vivian
Athletic trainer
Ed Tyburski
Equipment manager
John Doolan
Assistant equipment manager
Terry Murphy

DRAFT CHOICES

Rnd. Player	Ht./Wt.	Overall	Pos.	1991-92 club
1—Darius Kasparaitis .	5-11/187	5	D	Dynamo Moscow, CIS
3—Jarrett Deuling	5-11/194	56	LW	Kamloops (WHL)
5—Tomas Klimt	6-1/183	104	C	Plzeden, Czech.
5—Ryan Duthie	5-10/180	105	C	Spokane (WHL)
6—Derek Armstrong	5-11/180	128	C	Sudbury (OHL)
7—Vladimir Grachev	6-0/178	152	RW	Dynamo Moscow, CIS
7—Steve O'Rourke	6-1/190	159	RW	Tri-City (WHL)
8—Jason Widmer	6-0/205	176	D	Lethbridge (WHL)
9—Daniel Paradis	6-2/185	200	C	Chicoutimi (QMJHL)
10—David Wainwright...	6-0/193	224	D	Thayer (Mass.) Academy
11—Andrei Vasiljev	5-8/174	248	RW	CSKA, CIS

MISCELLANEOUS DATA

Home ice (capacity)
Nassau Veterans Memorial Coliseum
(16,297)
Address
Uniondale, NY 11553
Business phone
516-794-4100

Rink dimensions
200 feet by 85 feet
Club colors
Blue, white and orange
Minor league affiliations
Capital District (AHL)
Richmond (ECHL)

SCHEDULE KEY

*All-Star Game at Montreal.
H—Home game. D—Day game (any game starting before 4 p.m.).
NOTE: At press time, two games at neutral sites had yet to be announced.

TRAINING CAMP ROSTER

No.	FORWARDS	Ht./Wt.	Place (BORN)	Date	NHL exp.	1991-92 clubs
17	Bill Berg (LW)	6-1/198	St. Catharines, Ont.	10-21-67	3	Capital District (AHL), N.Y. Islanders
9	Dave Chyzowski (LW)	6-1/190	Edmonton, Alta.	7-11-71	3	Capital District (AHL), N.Y. Islanders
11	Adam Creighton (C)	6-5/210	Burlington, Ont.	6-2-65	9	Chicago, N.Y. Islanders
15	Brad Dalgarno (RW)	6-3/215	Vancouver, B.C.	8-8-67	7	Capital District (AHL), N.Y. Islanders
20	Ray Ferraro (C)	5-10/185	Trail, B.C.	8-23-64	8	N.Y. Islanders
14	Tom Fitzgerald (RW/C)	6-1/197	Melrose, Mass.	8-28-68	4	Capital District (AHL), N.Y. Islanders
	Patrick Flatley (RW)	6-2/200	Toronto	10-3-63	9	N.Y. Islanders
33	Benoit Hogue (C)	5-10/190	Repentigny, Que.	10-28-66	5	Buffalo, N.Y. Islanders
27	Derek King (LW)	6-1/210	Hamilton, Ont.	2-11-67	6	N.Y. Islanders
10	Claude Loiselle (C)	5-11/195	Ottawa	5-29-63	11	Toronto, N.Y. Islanders
24	Daniel Marois (RW)	6-0/190	Montreal	10-3-68	5	Toronto, N.Y. Islanders
39	Hubie McDonough (C)	5-9/173	Manchester, N.H.	7-8-63	4	Capital District (AHL), N.Y. Islanders
38	Marty McInnis (C/LW)	5-10/165	Weymouth, Mass.	6-2-70	1	U.S. Nat./Olym., N.Y. Islanders
	Zigmund Palffy (LW)	5-10/169	Skalica, Czech.	5-5-72	0	Dukla Trencin (Czech.)
	Greg Parks (C)	5-9/180	Edmonton, Alta.	3-25-67	2	Capital District (AHL), N.Y. Islanders
	Chris Taylor (C)	6-1/190	Stratford, Ont.	3-6-72	0	London (OHL)
32	Steve Thomas (LW)	5-11/185	Stockport, Eng.	7-15-63	8	Chicago, N.Y. Islanders
34	Graeme Townshend	6-2/225	Kingston, Jamaica	10-2-65	3	Capital District (AHL), N.Y. Islanders
77	Pierre Turgeon (C)	6-1/203	Rouyn, Que.	8-29-69	5	Buffalo, N.Y. Islanders
25	David Volek (LW/RW)	6-0/190	Prague, Czech.	8-16-66	4	N.Y. Islanders
17	Mick Vukota (RW)	6-2/215	Saskatoon, Sask.	9-14-66	5	N.Y. Islanders

DEFENSEMEN

No.	DEFENSEMEN	Ht./Wt.	Place	Date	NHL exp.	1991-92 clubs
2	Dean Chynoweth	6-2/190	Saskatoon, Sask.	10-30-68	4	Capital District (AHL), N.Y. Islanders
3	Jeff Finley	6-2/185	Edmonton, Alta.	4-14-67	5	Capital District (AHL), N.Y. Islanders
	Darius Kasparaitis	5-11/187	Elektrenai, U.S.S.R.	10-16-72	0	Dynamo Moscow (CIS), Unified Olym.
4	Uwe Krupp	6-6/235	Cologne, West Germany	6-24-65	7	Buffalo, N.Y. Islanders
28	Tom Kurvers	6-0/197	Minneapolis	9-14-62	8	N.Y. Islanders
7	Scott Lachance	6-2/197	Charlottesville, Va.	10-22-72	1	U.S. Nat./Olym., N.Y. Islanders
	Vladimir Malakhov	6-2/207	Sverdlovsk, U.S.S.R.	8-30-68	0	Unified Olym. (CIS)
6	Wayne McBean	6-2/185	Calgary, Alta.	2-21-69	5	N.Y. Islanders
8	Jeff Norton	6-2/195	Cambridge, Mass.	11-25-65	5	N.Y. Islanders
36	Gary Nylund	6-4/192	Surrey, B.C.	10-28-63	10	Capital District (AHL), N.Y. Islanders
47	Rich Pilon	6-1/211	Saskatoon, Sask.	4-30-68	4	N.Y. Islanders
37	Dennis Vaske	6-2/210	Rockford, Ill.	10-11-67	2	Capital District (AHL), N.Y. Islanders

GOALTENDERS

No.	GOALTENDERS	Ht./Wt.	Place	Date	NHL exp.	1991-92 clubs
30	Mark Fitzpatrick	6-2/190	Toronto	11-13-68	4	Capital District (AHL), N.Y. Islanders
35	Glenn Healy	5-10/185	Pickering, Ont.	8-23-62	6	N.Y. Islanders
1	Danny Lorenz	5-10/183	Murrayville, B.C.	12-12-69	2	Capital District (AHL), N.Y. Islanders

1991-92 REVIEW

INDIVIDUAL STATISTICS

SCORING

	Games	G	A	Pts.	Pen.	+/-	PPG	SHG	Shots	Shooting Pct.
Pierre Turgeon*	69	38	49	87	16	8	13	0	193	19.7
Ray Ferraro	80	40	40	80	92	25	7	0	154	26.0
Derek King	80	40	38	78	46	-10	21	0	189	21.2
Benoit Hogue*	72	30	45	75	67	30	8	0	143	21.0
Steve Thomas*	71	28	42	70	71	11	3	0	210	13.3
Dave Volek	74	18	42	60	35	0	4	1	167	10.8
Tom Kurvers	74	9	47	56	30	-18	6	0	132	6.8
Patrick Flatley	38	8	28	36	31	14	4	1	76	10.5
Uwe Krupp*	59	6	29	35	43	13	2	0	115	5.2
Adam Creighton*	66	15	9	24	102	-4	2	0	108	13.9
Dave McLlwain*	54	8	15	23	28	-8	1	1	71	11.3
Jeff Norton	28	1	18	19	18	2	0	1	34	2.9
Tom Fitzgerald	45	6	11	17	28	-3	0	2	71	8.5
Joe Reekie	54	4	12	16	85	15	0	0	59	6.8
Bill Berg	47	5	9	14	28	-18	1	0	60	8.3
Jeff Finley	51	1	10	11	26	-6	0	0	25	4.0
Brent Sutter*	8	4	6	10	6	-5	1	0	21	19.0
Hubie McDonough	33	7	2	9	15	-4	1	1	31	22.6
Marty McInnis	15	3	5	8	0	6	0	0	24	12.5
Rob DiMaio	50	5	2	7	43	-23	0	2	43	11.6
Dan Marois*	12	2	5	7	18	2	0	0	19	10.5
Richard Pilon	65	1	6	7	183	-1	0	0	27	3.7
Wayne McBean	25	2	4	6	18	11	0	1	51	3.9
Mick Vukota	74	0	6	6	293	-6	0	0	34	0.0
Scott Lachance	17	1	4	5	9	13	0	0	20	5.0

	Games	G	A	Pts.	Pen.	+/-	PPG	SHG	Shots	Shooting Pct.
Randy Wood*	8	2	2	4	21	-3	0	0	30	6.7
Brad Dalgarno	15	2	1	3	12	-8	1	0	17	11.8
Graeme Townshend	7	1	2	3	0	6	0	0	6	16.7
Claude Loiselle*	11	1	1	2	13	-3	0	0	10	10.0
Dave Chyzowski	12	1	1	2	17	-4	0	0	18	5.6
Mark Fitzpatrick (goalie)	30	0	2	2	8	0	0	0	0	0.0
Brad Lauer*	8	1	0	1	2	-2	0	1	12	8.3
Dean Chynoweth	11	1	0	1	23	-3	0	0	6	16.7
Gary Nylund	7	0	1	1	10	-3	0	0	5	0.0
Glenn Healy (goalie)	37	0	1	1	18	0	0	0	0	0.0
Dennis Vaske	39	0	1	1	39	5	0	0	26	0.0
Ken Baumgartner*	44	0	1	1	202	-10	0	0	11	0.0
Rich Kromm	1	0	0	0	0	0	0	0	0	0.0
Greg Parks	1	0	0	0	2	0	0	0	0	0.0
Danny Lorenz (goalie)	2	0	0	0	0	0	0	0	0	0.0
Brad Turner	3	0	0	0	0	1	0	0	1	0.0
Rick Green	4	0	0	0	0	-1	0	0	2	0.0
Randy Hillier*	8	0	0	0	11	-3	0	0	5	0.0
Steve Weeks (goalie)*	23	0	0	0	2	0	0	0	0	0.0

GOALTENDING

	Games	Min.	Goals	SO	Avg.	W	L	T	Shots	Sv. Pct.
Mark Fitzpatrick	30	1743	93	0	3.20	11	13	5	949	.902
Steve Weeks*	23	1032	62	0	3.60	9	4	2	566	.890
Glenn Healy	37	1960	124	1	3.80	14	16	4	1045	.881
Danny Lorenz	2	120	10	0	5.00	0	2	0	60	.833

Empty-net goals (do not count against a goaltender's average): Fitzpatrick, 5; Healy, 4; Lorenz, 1.
*Played with two or more NHL teams.

RESULTS

OCTOBER
5—At Boston	W	4-3
9—At N.Y. Rangers	L	3-5
12—Philadelphia	W	5-4
13—At Quebec	T	*1-1
15—Pittsburgh	L	*6-7
17—At Pittsburgh	L	5-8
19—Edmonton	L	2-4
22—Winnipeg	T	*1-1
26—Los Angeles	L	2-4
29—San Jose	W	8-4
31—At Chicago	L	3-4

NOVEMBER
2—Washington	L	4-7
4—Boston	W	6-4
6—At Edmonton	L	3-5
9—At San Jose	L	3-4
10—At Vancouver	L	0-6
14—At New Jersey	W	4-3
16—N.Y. Rangers	W	4-2
19—At Minnesota	W	7-4
20—At Winnipeg	L	1-3
23—At Pittsburgh	T	*2-2
27—Boston	L	2-3
29—At Washington	W	3-2
30—Washington	W	8-1

DECEMBER
5—Montreal	L	4-5
7—Chicago	L	2-5
10—St. Louis	T	*7-7
11—At Toronto	W	5-4
14—New Jersey	T	*3-3
17—At Hartford	W	4-2
19—At Philadelphia	L	2-6
21—At St. Louis	L	2-6
23—Pittsburgh	L	3-6
26—New Jersey	T	*5-5
28—N.Y. Rangers	W	5-4
29—At Hartford	L	4-6

JANUARY
1—At Washington	L	5 8
3—At Buffalo	L	2-5
4—Quebec	W	5-2
7—At Detroit	W	5-2
9—Hartford	W	2-1
11—St. Louis	L	3-6
12—At Philadelphia	L	3-4
14—Detroit	W	6-2
16—Philadelphia	W	4-3
23—Toronto	L	3-4
25—Pittsburgh	L	3-5
30—At Pittsburgh	W	8-5

FEBRUARY
1—Philadelphia	T	*5-5
2—Calgary	W	6-3
4—At Los Angeles	W	2-1
6—At Vancouver	W	*5-4
7—At Edmonton	L	2-4
11—At Calgary	W	3-1
14—At N.Y. Rangers	L	2-9
15—Vancouver	W	3-1
17—Winnipeg	W	*5-4
20—N.Y. Rangers	W	6-2
22—Minnesota	W	2-1
23—Washington	L	1-4
25—At Philadelphia	L	1-4
28—At New Jersey	W	*3-2
29—New Jersey	L	1-3

MARCH
3—Montreal	L	3-4
5—At Chicago	T	*4-4
7—At Montreal	L	2-8
8—At Buffalo	W	6-2
10—Philadelphia	W	5-2
12—At Pittsburgh	L	4-6
14—Buffalo	W	4-1
15—At Washington	L	2-5
18—At N.Y. Rangers	T	*1-1
21—At New Jersey	T	*2-2
24—At Quebec	L	2-5
26—San Jose	W	7-4
28—N.Y. Rangers	W	4-1
29—Detroit	L	2-6

APRIL
12—At Toronto	W	6-2
13—At Washington	T	*1-1
15—New Jersey	W	7-0

*Denotes overtime game.

NEW YORK RANGERS
WALES CONFERENCE/PATRICK DIVISION

1992-93 SCHEDULE

OCTOBER
S	M	T	W	T	F	S
4	5	6	7	8	9 WAS	10 NJ
11	12 HAR H	13	14 NJ H	15	16	17 NYI
18 NYI H	19	20	21 WAS H	22	23 MON H	24 OTT
25	26 PHI H	27	28	29 QUE H	30	31 MON

NOVEMBER
S	M	T	W	T	F	S
1	2 BUF H	3	4 PHI H	5	6	7 BOS
8	9 TB H	10	11 WAS H	12	13	14 QUE
15	16	17	18	19 PHI	20	21 WIN
22	23 PIT H	24	25 PIT	26	27 MIN	28
29	30 MIN H					

DECEMBER
S	M	T	W	T	F	S
		1	2 DET H	3	4 WAS	5
6 TOR H	7	8	9	10	11 TB	12
13 MON H	14	15 CAL H	16	17 STL	18	19 HAR
20	21 NJ	22	23 NJ H	24	25	26 NYI
27 BOS H	28	29 WAS	30	31 BUF		

JANUARY
S	M	T	W	T	F	S
					1	2 PIT
3	4 NJ H	5	6 OTT H	7	8	9 D PHI
10	11 VAN H	12	13 WAS H	14	15	16 MON
17	18 DET	19	20	21	22	23 LA
24	25	26	27 WIN H	28	29 BUF	30 TOR
31						

FEBRUARY
S	M	T	W	T	F	S
	1 NYI	2	3 PHI H	4	5	6 *
7	8 NJ	9	10 PIT H	11	12 NYI H	13 NYI
14	15 D STL H	16	17	18	19	20 SJ
21	22	23	24 VAN	25	26 CAL	27 EDM
28						

MARCH
S	M	T	W	T	F	S
	1	2	3 BUF H	4	5 PIT H	6 QUE
7	8	9 LA H	10	11 CHI	12	13 WAS
14	15 BOS H	16	17 EDM H	18	19 SJ H	20
21	22 OTT	23	24 PHI H	25	26 CHI H	27
28 QUE H	29	30	31			

APRIL
S	M	T	W	T	F	S
				1	2 NYI H	3
4 WAS	5 D HAR H	6	7 NJ H	8	9 PIT H	10 PIT
11 PHI	12	13	14 WAS H	15	16	17

1992-93 SEASON

CLUB DIRECTORY

Governor
Stanley R. Jaffe
President and general manager
Neil Smith
Vice president, legal affairs
Kevin Billet
Director of communications
Barry Watkins
Director of marketing
Kevin Kennedy
Dir. of alumni/rel. & spec. projects
Maureen Brady
Alternate NHL governors
Neil Smith
Kevin Billet
Bob Gutkowski
Assistant G.M., player development
Larry Pleau
Coach
Roger Neilson
Assistant coach
Colin Campbell

Scouting staff
Tony Feltrin
Herb Hammond
Lou Jankowski
Martin Madden
David McNab
Christer Rockstrom
Scouting coordinator
Bill Short
Manager of team services
Matthew Loughran
Manager of communications
Kevin McDonald
Team physician and orthopedic surgeon
Barton Nisonson, M.D.
Medical trainer
Dave Smith
Equipment trainer
Joe Murphy
Assistant trainers
Larry Nastasi
Tim Paris

DRAFT CHOICES

Rnd. Player	Ht./Wt.	Overall	Pos.	1991-92 club
1—Peter Ferraro	5-10/175	24	C	Waterloo (USHL)
2—Mattias Norstrom	6-1/196	48	D	AIK, Sweden
3—Eric Cairns	6-5/217	72	D	Detroit (OHL)
4—Chris Ferraro	6-10/175	85	RW	Waterloo (USHL)
5—Dimitri Starostenko	6-0/185	120	W	CSKA Moscow, CIS
6—David Dal Grande	6-5/195	144	D	Ottawa (Junior A, Tier II)
7—Matt Oates	6-3/204	168	LW	Miami of Ohio Univ. (CCHA)
8—Mickey Elick	6-1/180	192	D	Calgary (Tier II)
9—Dan Brierley	6-2/185	216	D	Choate (Conn.) Prep
10—Vladimir Vorobiev	6-0/183	240	RW	CIS

MISCELLANEOUS DATA

Home ice (capacity)
Madison Square Garden (18,200)
Address
4 Pennsylvania Plaza
New York, NY 10001
Business phone
212-465-6000

Rink dimensions
200 feet by 85 feet
Club colors
Blue, red and white
Minor league affiliation
Binghamton (AHL)

SCHEDULE KEY

*All-Star Game at Montreal.
H—Home game.   D—Day game (any game starting before 4 p.m.).
NOTE: At press time, two games at neutral sites had yet to be announced.

TRAINING CAMP ROSTER

No.	FORWARDS	Ht./Wt.	Place (BORN)	Date	NHL exp.	1991-92 clubs
33	Tony Amonte (RW)	6-0/186	Weymouth, Mass.	8-2-70	2	N.Y. Rangers
	Dave Archibald (C/LW) .	6-1/190	Chilliwack, B.C.	4-14-69	3	Can. Nat./Olym.
	Ric Bennett (LW)	6-3/215	Springfield, Mass.	7-24-67	3	Binghamton (AHL), N.Y. Rangers
47	Paul Broten (RW)	5-11/183	Roseau, Minn.	10-27-65	3	N.Y. Rangers
28	Tie Domi (RW)	5-10/198	Windsor, Ont.	11-1-69	3	N.Y. Rangers
20	Jan Erixon (LW)	6-0/192	Skelleftea, Sweden	7-8-62	9	N.Y. Rangers
22	Mike Gartner (RW)	6-0/188	Ottawa	10-29-59	13	N.Y. Rangers
16	Randy Gilhen (C)	6-0/192	Zweibrucken, W. Germany	6-13-63	7	Los Angeles, N.Y. Rangers
9	Adam Graves (LW)	6-0/203	Toronto	4-12-68	5	N.Y. Rangers
19	Kris King (LW/C)	5-11/208	Bracebridge, Ont.	2-18-66	5	N.Y. Rangers
26	Joey Kocur (RW)	6-0/209	Calgary, Alta.	12-21-64	8	N.Y. Rangers
	Alexei Kovalev	6-1/189	Moscow	2-24-73	0	Dynamo Moscow (USSR)
	Brian McReynolds (C)	6-1/180	Penetanguishene, Ont.	1-5-65	2	Binghamton (AHL)
11	Mark Messier (C)	6-1/202	Edmonton, Alta.	1-18-61	13	N.Y. Rangers
13	Sergei Nemchinov (C)	6-0/199	Moscow, U.S.S.R.	1-14-64	1	N.Y. Rangers
25	John Ogrodnick (LW)	6-0/208	Ottawa	6-20-59	13	N.Y. Rangers
	Mike Stevens (C/LW)	5-11/195	Kitchener, Ont.	12-30-65	4	St. John's (AHL), Binghamton (AHl)
8	Darren Turcotte (C)	6-0/178	Boston	3-2-68	4	N.Y. Rangers
49	Doug Weight (C)	5-11/196	Warren, Mich.	1-21-71	1	Binghamton (AHL), N.Y. Rangers
	DEFENSEMEN					
	Peter Andersson	6-0/187	Orebro, Sweden	8-29-65	0	Malmo (Sweden)
23	Jeff Beukeboom	6-4/223	Ajax, Ont.	3-28-65	7	Edmonton, N.Y. Rangers
6	Joe Cirella	6-3/207	Hamilton, Ont.	5-9-63	11	N.Y. Rangers
44	Per Djoos	5-11/196	Mora, Sweden	5-11-68	2	N.Y. Rangers
14	Mark Hardy	5-11/190	Semaden, Switzerland	2-1-59	13	N.Y. Rangers
2	Brian Leetch	5-11/190	Corpus Christi, Tex.	3-3-68	5	N.Y. Rangers
3	James Patrick	6-2/192	Winnipeg, Man.	6-14-63	9	N.Y. Rangers
5	Normand Rochefort	6-1/212	Trois-Rivieres, Que.	1-28-61	12	N.Y. Rangers
	Michael Stewart	6-2/197	Calgary, Alta.	3-30-72	0	Michigan State (CCHA)
24	Jay Wells	6-1/210	Paris, Ont.	5-18-59	13	Buffalo, N.Y. Rangers
	Sergei Zubov	6-0/187	Moscow, U.S.S.R.	7-22-70	0	CSKA (USSR)
	GOALTENDERS					
	Mike Gilmore	5-10/173	Detroit	3-11-68	0	Michigan State (CCHA)
	Corey Hirsch	5-10/170	Medicine Hat, Alta.	7-1-72	0	Kamloops (WHL)
35	Mike Richter	5-11/182	Philadelphia	9-22-66	3	N.Y. Rangers
	Boris Rousson	6-2/195	Val d'Or, Que.	6-14-70	0	Binghamton (AHL)
34	John Vanbiesbrouck	5-8/172	Detroit	9-4-63	10	N.Y. Rangers

1991-92 REVIEW

INDIVIDUAL STATISTICS

SCORING

	Games	G	A	Pts.	Pen.	+/-	PPG	SHG	Shots	Shooting Pct.
Mark Messier	79	35	72	107	76	31	12	4	212	16.5
Brian Leetch	80	22	80	102	26	25	10	1	245	9.0
Mike Gartner	76	40	41	81	55	11	15	0	286	14.0
James Patrick	80	14	57	71	54	34	6	0	148	9.5
Tony Amonte	79	35	34	69	55	12	9	0	234	15.0
Adam Graves	80	26	33	59	139	19	4	4	228	11.4
Sergei Nemchinov	73	30	28	58	15	19	2	0	124	24.2
Darren Turcotte	71	30	23	53	57	11	13	1	216	13.9
John Ogrodnick	55	17	13	30	22	6	3	0	110	15.5
Doug Weight	53	8	22	30	23	-3	0	0	72	11.1
Paul Broten	74	13	15	28	102	14	0	3	96	13.5
Kris King	79	10	9	19	224	13	0	0	97	10.3
Per Djoos	50	1	18	19	40	7	1	0	39	2.6
Tim Kerr	32	7	11	18	12	-5	5	0	56	12.5
Jan Erixon	46	8	9	17	4	13	0	1	51	15.7
Joe Cirella	67	3	12	15	121	11	1	0	58	5.2
Randy Gilhen*	40	7	7	14	14	5	0	0	67	10.4
Joey Kocur	51	7	4	11	121	-4	0	0	72	9.7
Jeff Beukeboom*	56	1	10	11	122	19	0	0	41	2.4
Randy Moller*	43	2	7	9	78	-15	0	0	44	4.5
Mark Hardy	52	1	8	9	65	33	0	0	42	2.4
Tie Domi	42	2	4	6	246	-4	0	0	20	10.0
Corey Millen*	11	1	4	5	10	-1	0	0	20	5.0

— 43 —

	Games	G	A	Pts.	Pen.	+/-	PPG	SHG	Shots	Shooting Pct.
Rob Zamuner	9	1	2	3	2	0	0	0	11	9.1
John Vanbiesbrouck (goalie)	45	0	3	3	23	0	0	0	1	0.0
Normand Rochefort	26	0	2	2	31	-10	0	0	18	0.0
Eric Bennett	3	0	1	1	2	0	0	0	2	0.0
Jeff Bloemberg	3	0	1	1	0	1	0	0	5	0.0
David Shaw*	10	0	1	1	15	1	0	0	6	0.0
Peter Fiorentino	1	0	0	0	0	0	0	0	2	0.0
Bernie Nicholls*	1	0	0	0	0	-1	0	0	2	0.0
Jody Hull	3	0	0	0	2	-4	0	0	4	0.0
Mark Janssens*	4	0	0	0	5	-1	0	0	0	0.0
Jay Wells*	11	0	0	0	24	2	0	0	4	0.0
Mike Richter (goalie)	41	0	0	0	6	0	0	0	0	0.0

GOALTENDING

	Games	Min.	Goals	SO	Avg.	W	L	T	Shots	Sv. Pct.
John Vanbiesbrouck	45	2526	120	2	2.85	27	13	3	1331	.910
Mike Richter	41	2298	119	3	3.11	23	12	2	1205	.901

Empty-net goals (do not count against a goaltender's average): Vanbiesbrouck, 4; Richter, 3.
*Played with two or more NHL teams.

RESULTS

OCTOBER

3—At Boston	L	3-5
5—At Montreal	W	*2-1
7—Boston	W	*2-1
9—N.Y. Islanders	W	5-3
11—At Washington	L	1-5
12—At Hartford	L	2-5
14—Washington	L	3-5
16—New Jersey	W	4-2
19—At Pittsburgh	W	5-4
20—Edmonton	L	3-4
23—Los Angeles	W	7-2
26—At Quebec	W	5-3
29—Minnesota	W	3-2
31—Quebec	W	5-4

NOVEMBER

2—At Philadelphia	W	4-2
4—Calgary	W	4-0
6—Montreal	L	1-4
8—Toronto	T	*3-3
11—Pittsburgh	W	3-1
13—Washington	L	3-5
16—At N.Y. Islanders	L	2-4
19—At Vancouver	W	4-3
21—At Los Angeles	L	1-6
23—At St. Louis	W	3-0
27—At Winnipeg	L	2-3
29—At Buffalo	W	*5-4

DECEMBER

2—Philadelphia	W	4-2

6—At Detroit	L	*5-6
8—Boston	W	4-0
10—At Pittsburgh	L	3-5
13—At Washington	W	5-3
14—At Hartford	W	6-2
16—San Jose	W	*4-3
18—Philadelphia	W	6-3
21—At Pittsburgh	W	7-5
23—New Jersey	W	3-0
26—At Washington	W	8-6
28—At N.Y. Islanders	L	4-5
29—Pittsburgh	L	3-6
31—At Winnipeg	W	5-2

JANUARY

2—At Chicago	W	4-3
4—At New Jersey	L	4-6
6—Winnipeg	W	4-2
8—St. Louis	L	3-5
11—At Quebec	W	7-2
12—At Buffalo	L	3-6
14—Buffalo	W	6-2
16—Calgary	W	6-4
22—At Calgary	T	*4-4
23—At Edmonton	W	3-1
28—At San Jose	W	4-2
30—At Los Angeles	W	4-1

FEBRUARY

1—At Minnesota	W	2-1
5—Pittsburgh	W	4-3

7—At Washington	L	2-6
9—Detroit	T	*5-5
12—Vancouver	W	5-2
14—N.Y. Islanders	W	9-2
16—At New Jersey	L	2-4
17—Vancouver	T	*3-3
20—At N.Y. Islanders	L	2-6
21—Minnesota	W	5-4
23—Philadelphia	W	*2-1
25—Chicago	W	4-1

MARCH

1—Hartford	W	9-4
2—At New Jersey	W	7-1
4—New Jersey	L	4-5
7—At Philadelphia	L	4-5
9—Washington	L	2-5
11—Chicago	W	7-1
14—At St. Louis	W	6-0
16—Montreal	W	4-1
18—N.Y. Islanders	T	*1-1
20—At Detroit	W	4-2
22—New Jersey	W	6-3
24—At Philadelphia	W	4-3
25—Philadelphia	W	4-1
28—At N.Y. Islanders	L	1-4

APRIL

14—At Toronto	L	2-4
16—Pittsburgh	W	7-1

*Denotes overtime game.

OTTAWA SENATORS
WALES CONFERENCE/ADAMS DIVISION

1992-93 SCHEDULE

OCTOBER

S	M	T	W	T	F	S
4	5	6	7	8 MON H	9	10 QUE
11	12 BOS	13	14 HAR	15	16 WAS	17
18	19	20	21	22 HAR H	23	24 NYR H
25	26	27 PIT H	28	29	30 BUF	31 BUF H

NOVEMBER

S	M	T	W	T	F	S
1	2	3 EDM H	4	5 CAL	6 VAN	7
8	9 TOR H	10	11 QUE H	12	13 TB	14
15 PHI	16	17 MON H	18	19 HAR H	20	21 MON
22	23 BOS H	24	25 NJ H	26	27 BUF	28
29 BUF H	30					

DECEMBER

S	M	T	W	T	F	S
		1 MIN H	2	3 NJ H	4	5 PHI H
6	7 WAS H	8	9 HAR	10 BOS	11	12 CAL H
13	14	15 DET H	16	17 NYI	18	19 TOR
20	21 WAS H	22	23 CHI H	24	25	26 QUE
27 QUE H	28	29	30	31 DET		

JANUARY

S	M	T	W	T	F	S
					1	2 BUF H
3	4	5	6 NYR	7	8 H	9 NJ
10 D	11	12 LA H	13	14 STL H	15	16 PIT
17 NYI H	18	19 QUE H	20	21 MIN	22	23 WAS
24	25	26 STL	27	28 HAR H	29	30 D MON
31						

FEBRUARY

S	M	T	W	T	F	S
	1	2 WIN H	3 EDM H	4	5	6 *
7	8 BUF H	9 PHI	10	11	12	13 MON H
14	15	16	17	18 QUE	19	20 MON
21	22 WIN	23	24	25 PIT H	26	27 D NJ
28 QUE H						

MARCH

S	M	T	W	T	F	S
	1	2 SJ	3	4 LA	5	6
7 CHI	8 D	9	10	11	12	13 D BOS
14	15	16	17	18 BOS H	19	20 PIT
21	22 NYR H	23	24	25 TB H	26	27 MON
28 BUF	29	30	31			

APRIL

S	M	T	W	T	F	S
				1 QUE H	2	3 HAR
4	5	6	7 HAR H	8	9	10 NYI
11 BOS	12	13 QUE	14 BOS H	15	16	17

1992-93 SEASON

CLUB DIRECTORY

Chairman and governor
Bruce M. Firestone

Alternate governor
Rod Bryden

CEO and alternate governor
Randy J. Sexton

General Manager
Mel Bridgman

Head coach
Rick Bowness

Assistant coaches
E.J. MacGuire
Alain Vigneault

Director of player personnel
John Ferguson

Head equipment trainer
Ed Georgica

Administrative assistant
Diane Coughlan

Vice president of marketing
Jim Steel

Director of sales
Brian McKenna

Director of media relations
Laurent Benoit

Media relations assistant
TBA

DRAFT CHOICES

Rnd. Player	Ht./Wt.	Overall	Pos.	1991-92 club
1—Alexei Yashin	6-2/189	2	C	Dynamo Moscow, CIS
2—Chad Penney	6-0/196	25	LW	North Bay (OHL)
3—Patrick Traverse	6-3/173	50	D	Shawinigan (QMJHL)
4—Radek Hamr	5-11/167	73	D	Sparta Praha, Czech.
5—Daniel Guerard	6-4/211	98	RW	Victoriaville (QMJHL)
6—Al Sinclair	6-3/210	121	D	U. of Michigan (CCHA)
7—Jaroslav Miklenda	6-1/176	146	G	Olomouc, Czech.
8—Jay Kenney	6-2/190	169	D	Canterbury (Conn.) Prep
9—Claude Savoie	5-11/182	194	RW	Victoriaville (QMJHL)
10—Jake Grimes	6-1/196	217	C	Belleville (OHL)
11—Tomas Jelinek		242	LW	Czech. National Team
11—Petter Ronnquist	5-10/154	264	G	Nacka, Sweden

MISCELLANEOUS DATA

Home ice (capacity)
Ottawa Civic Centre (10,266)

Address
301 Moodie Drive
Nepean, Ont. K2H 9C4

Business phone
613-726-0540

Rink dimensions
200 feet by 85 feet

Club colors
Black, red and gold

Minor league affiliation
New Haven (AHL)

SCHEDULE KEY

*All-Star Game at Montreal.
H—Home game.　　　D—Day game (any game starting before 4 p.m.).
NOTE: At press time, two games at neutral sites had yet to be announced.

TRAINING CAMP ROSTER

No.	FORWARDS	Ht./Wt.	Place	BORN Date	NHL exp.	1991-92 clubs
	Blair Atcheynum (RW) .	6-2/190	Estevan, Sask.	4-20-69	0	Springfield (AHL)
	Laurie Boschman (C)....	6-0/185	Major, Sask.	6-4-60	13	New Jersey
	Mark Freer (C)..............	5-10/180	Peterborough, Ont.	7-14-68	4	Hershey (AHL), Philadelphia
	Jake Grimes (C)............	6-1/196	Montreal	9-13-72	0	Belleville (OHL)
	Jody Hull (RW).............	6-2/203	Petrolia, Ont.	2-2-69	4	Binghamton, N.Y. Rangers
	Tomas Jelinek (RW)	5-9/189	Prague, Czech.	4-29-62	0	HPK Hameenlinna (Czech.)
	Mark Lamb (C).............	5-9/180	Swift Current, Sask.	8-3-64	7	Edmonton
	Jeff Lazaro (LW)	5-10/180	Waltham, Mass.	3-21-68	2	Maine (AHL), Boston
	Lonnie Loach (LW)	5-10/180	New Liskeard, Ont.	4-14-68	0	Adirondack (AHL)
	Darcy Loewen (LW)	5-10/192	Calgary, Alta.	2-26-69	3	Rochester (AHL), Buffalo
	Andrew McBain (RW) ...	6-1/205	Toronto	1-18-65	9	Milwaukee (IHL), Vancouver
	Rob Murphy (C)............	6-3/210	Hull, Que.	4-7-69	5	Milwaukee (IHL), Vancouver
	Mike Peluso (LW).........	6-4/200	Hibbing, Minn.	11-8-65	3	Indianapolis (IHL), Chicago
	Chad Penney (LW)	6-0/195	Labrador City, Nfld.	9-18-73	0	Can. Nat., North Bay (OHL)
	Sylvain Turgeon (LW)	6-0/195	Noranda, Que.	1-17-65	9	Montreal
	DEFENSEMEN					
	Ken Hammond	6-1/190	London, Ont.	8-23-63	7	San Jose
	Dominic Lavoie.............	6-2/205	Montreal	11-21-67	4	Peoria (IHL), St. Louis
	Brad Miller	6-4/226	Edmonton, Alta.	7-23-69	4	Rochester (AHL), Buffalo
	Mark Osiecki..................	6-2/200	St. Paul, Minn.	7-23-68	1	Salt Lake City (IHL), Calgary
	Kent Paynter	6-0/185	Summerside, P.E.I.	4-27-65	5	Moncton (AHL), Winnipeg
	Darren Rumble	6-1/195	Barrie, Ont.	1-23-69	1	Hershey (AHL)
	Brad Shaw	6-0/190	Cambridge, Ont.	4-28-64	7	Hartford
	Patrick Traverse	6-3/178	Montreal	3-14-74	0	Shawinigan (QMJHL)
	John Van Kessel (RW) ..	6-4/193	Bridgewater, Ont.	12-19-69	0	Phoenix (IHL)
	GOALTENDERS					
	Mark Laforest................	5-11/190	Welland, Ont.	7-10-62	5	Binghamton (AHL)
	Darrin Madeley..............	5-11/165	Holland Landing, Ont.	2-25-68	0	L. Superior St. (CCHA)
	Peter Sidorkiewicz..........	5-9/180	Dabrown Bialostocka, Pol.	6-29-63	5	Hartford

LEADING SCORERS ON FIRST-YEAR EXPANSION TEAMS

Team	Season	Team points leader	G.	A.	Pts.	NHL points leader
Pittsburgh Penguins ...	1967-68	Andy Bathgate	30	29	59	Stan Mikita, Chicago—87
Los Angeles Kings	1967-68	Ed Joyal	23	34	57	Stan Mikita, Chicago—87
Minnesota North Stars ...	1967-68	Wayne Connelly	35	21	56	Stan Mikita, Chicago—87
St. Louis Blues..............	1967-68	Red Berenson*	22	29	51	Stan Mikita, Chicago—87
Philadelphia Flyers..........	1967-68	Lou Angotti	12	37	49	Stan Mikita, Chicago—87
Oakland Seals†..............	1967-68	Gerry Ehman‡	20	25	45	Stan Mikita, Chicago—87
Buffalo Sabres	1970-71	Gilbert Perreault	38	34	72	Phil Esposito, Boston—152
Vancouver Canucks	1970-71	Andre Boudrias	25	41	66	Phil Esposito, Boston—152
Atlanta Flames§............	1972-73	Bob Leiter	26	34	60	Phil Esposito, Boston—130
New York Islanders	1972-73	Billy Harris	28	22	50	Phil Esposito, Boston—130
Kansas City Scouts x	1974-75	Simon Nolet	26	32	58	Bobby Orr, Boston—135
Washington Capitals......	1974-75	Tommy Williams	22	36	58	Bobby Orr, Boston—135
Edmonton Oilers y	1979-80	Wayne Gretzky	51	z86	a137	Wayne Gretzky & Marcel Dionne, L.A.—137
Hartford Whalers y	1979-80	Mike Rogers	44	61	105	Wayne Gretzky & Marcel Dionne, L.A.—137
Quebec Nordiques y	1979-80	Real Cloutier	42	46	88	Wayne Gretzky & Marcel Dionne, L.A.—137
Winnipeg Jets y	1979-80	Morris Lukowich	35	39	74	Wayne Gretzky & Marcel Dionne, L.A.—137
San Jose Sharks............	1991-92	Pat Falloon	25	34	59	Mario Lemieux, Pittsburgh—131

*Berenson started season with N.Y. Rangers, gaining three points for a two-team total of 54.
†Became Cleveland Barons after 1975-76 season; Barons merged with Minnesota North Stars after 1977-78 season.
‡Ted Hampson collected 27 points for Detroit and 27 for Oakland for a two-team total of 54.
§Became Calgary Flames after 1979-80 season.
xBecame Colorado Rockies after 1975-76 season; became New Jersey Devils after 1981-82 season.
yEntered NHL during a merger with the World Hockey Association.
zLed league.
aTied for league lead.

PHILADELPHIA FLYERS
WALES CONFERENCE/PATRICK DIVISION

1992-93 SCHEDULE

OCTOBER

S	M	T	W	T	F	S
4	5	6 PIT	7	8	9 NJ H	10 WAS
11	12	13 QUE	14	15 NYI H	16	17 NJ
18 WIN H	19	20 NYI	21	22 VAN H	23	24 MON H
25 NYR	26	27	28	29 CHI	30	31 STL

NOVEMBER

S	M	T	W	T	F	S
1	2	3	4 NYR	5	6	7 D STL H
8	9	10	11	12 NYR H	13	14 MON
15 OTT H	16	17	18	19 NYR	20	21 BOS
22 BUF H	23	24	25	26	27 D NYI H	28 NYI
29	30					

DECEMBER

S	M	T	W	T	F	S
		1	2	3 QUE H	4	5 OTT
6 BOS H	7	8	9	10	11 DET	12 WAS H
13	14	15 PIT	16	17 PIT H	18	19 D CHI H
20 TB	21	22	23 PIT H	24	25	26 WAS
27	28	29 LA	30 SJ	31		

JANUARY

S	M	T	W	T	F	S
					1	2 CAL
3 EDM	4	5	6	7 WAS H	8	9 D NYR H
10 EDM H	11	12	13	14 CAL H	15	16 BOS
17 DET H	18	19	20	21 BOS H	22	23 NYI
24 HAR H	25	26	27 BUF H	28	29 QUE H	30 D PIT
31 D MON						

FEBRUARY

S	M	T	W	T	F	S
	1	2	3 NYR	4	5	*
7	8	9 OTT H	10	11 MON H	12	13 D NJ
14 D NJ H	15	16	17	18 VAN	19	20 D MIN
21	22	23	24 HAR	25 NJ H	26	27 D NYI H
28						

MARCH

S	M	T	W	T	F	S
	1	2 PIT H	3	4	5 WAS	6
7 NJ	8	9 NYI	10	11 WAS H	12	13 D LA H
14 D HAR	15	16 MIN H	17	18 PIT	19	20
21 NJ	22	23	24 NYR	25 SJ H	26	27 QUE
28	29	30 NYI	31			

APRIL

S	M	T	W	T	F	S
				1	2 TOR H	3 D TB H
4	5	6 WIN	7	8 WAS H	9	10 TOR
11	12	13 NYR H	14	15 BUF	16	17

1992-93 SEASON

CLUB DIRECTORY

Chairman of the executive committee
Edward M. Snider
President
Jay T. Snider
Chairman of the board emeritus
Joseph C. Scott
Senior vice president
Bob Clarke
Executive vice presidents
Keith Allen
Ron Ryan
General manager
Russ Farwell
Assistant general manager
John Blackwell
Coach
Bill Dineen
Assistant coaches
Craig Hartsburg
Ken Hitchcock
Goaltending instructor
Bernie Parent
Phys. conditioning and rehabilitation coach
Pat Croce
Director of pro scouting
Bill Barber
Pro scout and player dev. coordinator
Kevin McCarthy

Scouts
Inge Hammarstrom
Jerry Melnyk
Glen Sonmor
Red Sullivan
Vaclav Slansky
Simon Nolet
Blair Reid
Vice president, communications
John Brogan
Director of public relations
Rodger Gottlieb
Assistant director of public relations
Jill Vogel
Ticket manager
Ceil Baker
Vice president, sales
Jack Betson
Director of team services
Joe Kadlec
Athletic therapist
Gary Smith
Trainers
Jim Evers
Harry Bricker
Vice president, finance
Bob Baer
Team physician
Jeffrey Hartzell, M.D.

DRAFT CHOICES

Rnd. Player	Ht./Wt.	Overall	Pos.	1991-92 club
1—Ryan Sittler	6-2/185	7	LW	Nichols H.S., Buffalo, N.Y.
1—Jason Bowen	6-4/210	15	LW	Tri-City (WHL)
2—Denis Metlyuk	5-10/183	31	C	Lada Tagliatti, CIS
5—Vladislav Bouline	6-4/196	103	D	Dizelast Pena, Czech.
6—Roman Zolotov	6-1/183	127	D	Dynamo Moscow, CIS
7—Kirk Daubenspeck	6-0/170	151	G	Culver (Wis.) Military Acad.
8—Claude Jutras	6-0/188	175	RW	Hull (QMJHL)
9—Jonas Hakansson	6-1/207	199	RW	Malmo, Sweden
10—Chris Herperger	6-0/190	223	LW	Swift Current (WHL)
11—Patrice Paquin	6-2/192	247	LW	Beauport (QMJHL)

MISCELLANEOUS DATA

Home ice (capacity)
The Spectrum (17,382)
Address
Pattison Place
Philadelphia, PA 19148
Business phone
215-465-4500

Rink dimensions
200 feet by 85 feet
Club colors
Orange, white and black
Minor league affiliation
Hershey (AHL)

SCHEDULE KEY

*All-Star Game at Montreal.
H—Home game.   D—Day game (any game starting before 4 p.m.).
NOTE: At press time, two games at neutral sites had yet to be announced.

TRAINING CAMP ROSTER

No.	FORWARDS	Ht./Wt.	Place —BORN—	Date	NHL exp.	1991-92 clubs
25	Keith Acton (C)	5-8/170	Newmarket, Ont.	4-15-58	13	Philadelphia
40	Claude Boivin (LW)	6-2/210	St. Foy, Que.	3-1-70	1	Hershey (AHL), Philadelphia
17	Rod Brind'Amour (LW)	6-1/202	Ottawa	8-9-70	4	Philadelphia
21	Dave Brown (RW)	6-5/205	Saskatoon, Sask.	10-12-62	10	Philadelphia
	Vyatcheslav Butsayev	6-2/200	Tolyatti, U.S.S.R.	6-13-70	0	Central Red Army (CIS)
46	Al Conroy (C)	5-8/170	Calgary, Alta.	1-17-66	1	Hershey (AHL), Philadelphia
	Rod Dallman (RW)	6-0/195	Quesnel, B.C.	1-26-67	3	Hershey (AHL), Philadelphia
	Kimbi Daniels (C)	5-10/184	Brandon, Man.	1-19-72	2	Seattle (WHL), Philadelphia
20	Kevin Dineen (RW)	5-10/180	Quebec City	10-28-63	8	Hartford, Philadelphia
66	Yanick Dupre (LW)	6-0/195	Montreal	11-20-72	1	Longueuil (QMJHL), Philadelphia
9	Pelle Eklund (C)	5-10/175	Stockholm, Sweden	3-22-63	7	Philadelphia
26	Martin Hostak (C)	6-3/205	Hradec Kralove, Czech.	11-11-67	2	Hershey (AHL), Philadelphia
	Chris Jensen (RW)	5-11/180	Fort St. John, B.C.	10-28-63	6	Hershey (AHL), Philadelphia
	Gregory Johnson (C)	5-11/180	Thunder Bay, Ont.	3-16-71	0	North Dakota (WCHA)
47	Brad Jones (RW)	6-0/195	Sterling Heights, Mich.	6-26-65	6	Philadelphia
11	Steve Kasper (C)	5-8/175	Montreal	9-28-61	12	Philadelphia
15	Dale Kushner (RW)	6-1/195	Terrace, B.C.	6-13-66	3	Hershey (AHL), Philadelphia
	Eric Lindros (C)	6-5/225	London, Ont.	2-28-73	0	Can. Nat./Olym., Oshawa (OHL)
23	Andrei Lomakin (LW)	5-10/176	Voskresensk, U.S.S.R.	4-3-64	1	Philadelphia
24	Pat Murray (RW)	6-3/195	Stratford, Ont.	8-20-69	2	Hershey (AHL), Philadelphia
	Clayton Norris (RW)	6-2/200	Edmonton, Alta.	3-8-72	0	Medicine Hat (WHL)
14	Mark Pederson (LW)	6-2/196	Prelate, Sask.	1-14-68	3	Philadelphia
8	Mark Recchi (RW)	5-10/185	Kamloops, B.C.	2-1-68	4	Pittsburgh, Philadelphia
	Mikael Renberg (RW)	6-2/183	Pitea, Sweden	5-5-72	0	Lulea (Sweden)
	Chris Simon (LW)	6-3/230	Wawa, Ont.	1-30-72	0	Ottawa (OHL), S. Ste. Marie (OHL)
48	Reid Simpson (LW)	6-1/210	Flin Flon, Man.	5-21-69	1	Hershey (AHL), Philadelphia
36	Wes Walz (C)	5-10/181	Calgary, Alta.	5-15-70	3	Maine (AHL), Boston, Hershey (AHL), Philadelphia

	DEFENSEMEN					
	Steve Beadle	5-11/190	Lansing, Mich.	5-30-68	4	Hershey (AHL)
19	Brian Benning	6-0/175	Edmonton, Alta.	6-10-66	8	Los Angeles, Philadelphia
29	Terry Carkner	6-3/212	Smith Falls, Ont.	3-7-66	6	Philadelphia
	Eric Dandenault	6-0/193	Sherbrooke, Que.	3-10-70	0	Hershey (AHL)
44	Corey Foster	6-3/204	Ottawa	10-27-69	2	Hershey (AHL), Philadelphia
3	Garry Galley	5-11/190	Ottawa	4-16-63	8	Boston, Philadelphia
6	Dan Kordic	6-5/220	Edmonton, Alta.	4-18-71	1	Philadelphia
42	Moe Mantha	6-2/197	Lakewood, O.	1-21-61	12	U.S. Nat./Olym., Winnipeg, Philadelphia
	Ryan McGill	6-2/198	Prince Albert, Sask.	2-28-69	1	Indianapolis (IHL), Chicago, Hershey (AHL)
	Terran Sandwith	6-4/210	Edmonton, Alta.	4-17-72	0	Brandon (WHL), Saskatoon (WHL)
	Dimitri Yushkevich	5-11/187	Yaroslavl, U.S.S.R.	11-19-71	0	Jaroslav (C.S.S.R.)

	GOALTENDERS					
	Marc D'Amour	5-9/185	Sudbury, Ont.	4-29-61	2	Hershey (AHL)
	Yanick Degrace	5-11/175	Lameque, N.B.	4-16-71	0	Hershey (AHL)
	Scott Lagrand	6-1/170	Potsdam, N.Y.	2-11-70	0	Boston Col. (H. East)
	Ray Letourneau	5-11/190	Lewistown, N.H.	1-14-69	0	Roanoke Valley (ECHL), Hershey (AHL)
33	Dominic Roussel	6-1/180	Hull, Que.	2-22-70	1	Hershey (AHL), Philadelphia
	Tommy Soderstrom	5-9/163	Stockholm, Sweden	7-17-69	0	Djurgarden (Sweden)

1991-92 REVIEW

INDIVIDUAL STATISTICS

SCORING

	Games	G	A	Pts.	Pen.	+/-	PPG	SHG	Shots	Shooting Pct.
Rod Brind'Amour	80	33	44	77	100	-3	8	4	202	16.3
Kevin Dineen*	64	26	30	56	130	1	5	3	197	13.2
Mike Ricci	78	20	36	56	93	-10	11	2	149	13.4
Steve Duchesne	78	18	38	56	86	-7	7	2	229	7.9
Mark Pederson	58	15	25	40	22	14	4	0	94	16.0
Dan Quinn	67	11	26	37	26	-13	6	0	101	10.9
Kerry Huffman	60	14	18	32	41	1	4	0	123	11.4
Andrei Lomakin	57	14	16	30	26	-6	2	0	82	17.1
Rick Tocchet*	42	13	16	29	102	3	4	0	107	12.1
Mark Recchi*	22	10	17	27	18	-5	4	0	54	18.5
Mark Howe	42	7	18	25	18	18	6	0	63	11.1
Per-Erik Eklund	51	7	16	23	4	0	1	2	74	9.5

	Games	G	A	Pts.	Pen.	+/-	PPG	SHG	Shots	Shooting Pct.
Claude Boivin	58	5	13	18	187	-2	0	0	46	10.9
Garry Galley*	39	3	15	18	34	1	2	0	74	4.1
Brad Jones	48	7	10	17	44	-2	0	0	67	10.4
Keith Acton	50	7	10	17	98	-4	0	0	79	8.9
Terry Carkner	73	4	12	16	195	-14	0	1	70	5.7
Brian Benning*	22	2	12	14	35	-9	2	0	50	4.0
Mark Freer	50	6	7	13	18	-1	0	0	41	14.6
Kjell Samuelsson*	54	4	9	13	76	1	0	0	63	6.3
Allan Conroy	31	2	9	11	74	1	0	0	25	8.0
Gordon Murphy*	31	2	8	10	33	-4	0	0	50	4.0
Corey Foster	25	3	4	7	20	-14	1	0	67	4.5
Dave Brown	70	4	2	6	81	-11	0	0	50	8.0
Murray Craven*	12	3	3	6	8	2	1	0	19	15.8
Steve Kasper	16	3	2	5	10	-3	0	1	13	23.1
Dale Kushner	19	3	2	5	18	-5	0	0	19	15.8
Tony Horacek*	34	1	3	4	51	-9	0	0	22	4.5
Dan Kordic	46	1	3	4	126	1	0	0	27	3.7
Jiri Latal	10	1	2	3	4	1	0	0	22	4.5
Ron Hextall (goalie)	45	0	3	3	35	0	0	0	0	0.0
Kimbi Daniels	25	1	1	2	4	-4	0	0	16	6.3
Ken Wregget (goalie)*	23	0	2	2	0	0	0	0	0	0.0
Wes Walz*	2	1	0	1	0	1	0	0	2	50.0
Pat Murray	9	1	0	1	0	3	0	0	8	12.5
Martin Hostak	5	0	1	1	2	-1	0	0	8	0.0
Dominic Roussel (goalie)	17	0	1	1	2	0	0	0	0	0.0
Yanick Dupre	1	0	0	0	0	0	0	0	0	0.0
Reid Simpson	1	0	0	0	0	0	0	0	0	0.0
Rod Dallman	2	0	0	0	5	0	0	0	2	0.0
Chris Jensen	2	0	0	0	0	-1	0	0	2	0.0
Moe Mantha*	5	0	0	0	2	0	0	0	7	0.0

GOALTENDING

	Games	Min.	Goals	SO	Avg.	W	L	T	Shots	Sv. Pct.
Dominic Roussel	17	922	40	1	2.60	7	8	2	437	.908
Ron Hextall	45	2668	151	3	3.40	16	21	6	1294	.883
Ken Wregget*	23	1259	75	0	3.57	9	8	3	557	.865

Empty-net goals (do not count against a goaltender's average): Hextall, 6; Wregget, 1.
*Played with two or more NHL teams.

RESULTS

OCTOBER
4—At Washington	L	2-5
6—At Pittsburgh	T	*2-2
10—Pittsburgh	L	3-6
12—At N.Y. Islanders	L	4-5
13—New Jersey	W	4-2
17—Quebec	W	5-3
19—Montreal	L	0-1
24—At Minnesota	W	5-2
25—At Winnipeg	L	0-2
31—San Jose	W	5-2

NOVEMBER
2—N.Y. Rangers	L	2-4
5—At St. Louis	W	4-3
7—Buffalo	W	5-2
8—At Buffalo	L	*3-4
12—At New Jersey	L	2-5
14—Edmonton	W	3-1
16—At Montreal	W	3-1
17—Winnipeg	L	1-2
20—At Pittsburgh	L	2-5
23—New Jersey	T	*5-5
27—Hartford	L	3-7
29—Pittsburgh	L	3-9
30—At Pittsburgh	L	1-5

DECEMBER
2—At N.Y. Rangers	L	2-4
5—Washington	L	3-6
7—At Boston	W	5-3

8—New Jersey	T	*2-2
12—Toronto	T	*1-1
14—Chicago	T	*1-1
15—At Chicago	T	*4-4
18—At N.Y. Rangers	L	3-6
19—N.Y. Islanders	W	6-2
21—At Minnesota	W	3-0
22—Washington	W	*4-3
27—At Vancouver	T	*1-1
28—At Calgary	L	1-5

JANUARY
3—At San Jose	L	1-3
4—At Los Angeles	L	3-7
7—Buffalo	T	*5-5
9—Los Angeles	W	5-2
11—At Boston	L	1-5
12—N.Y. Islanders	W	4-3
14—Chicago	T	*1-1
16—At N.Y. Islanders	L	3-4
21—At Detroit	L	3-7
23—Winnipeg	L	0-1
25—At Toronto	L	4-6
28—Washington	W	3-2
30—Minnesota	W	5-3

FEBRUARY
1—At N.Y. Islanders	T	*5-5
2—St. Louis	W	5-1
4—At New Jersey	L	1-3
6—Boston	W	5-1
8—At Quebec	W	3-0

13—Quebec	W	3-2
15—Edmonton	W	8-5
16—Pittsburgh	T	*3-3
18—At New Jersey	L	*3-4
22—At Washington	L	5-7
23—At N.Y. Rangers	L	*1-2
25—N.Y. Islanders	W	4-1
27—At Calgary	W	3-0
28—At Edmonton	L	2-4

MARCH
1—At San Jose	W	1-0
3—At Los Angeles	L	1-4
7—N.Y. Rangers	W	5-4
8—Vancouver	L	3-7
10—At N.Y. Islanders	L	2-5
12—Calgary	W	*5-4
14—Washington	W	3-1
18—At Montreal	W	4-3
20—At Washington	W	7-6
22—Detroit	W	4-3
24—N.Y. Rangers	L	3-4
25—At N.Y. Rangers	L	1-4
29—New Jersey	W	5-4
31—At Pittsburgh	L	5-6

APRIL
12—At Hartford	L	2-4
13—Toronto	W	6-2
15—Hartford	L	*3-4

*Denotes overtime game.

— 49 —

PITTSBURGH PENGUINS
WALES CONFERENCE/PATRICK DIVISION

PITTSBURGH PENGUINS

1992-93 NHL SEASON

PITTSBURGH PENGUINS

1992-93 SCHEDULE

OCTOBER

S	M	T	W	T	F	S
4	5	6 PHI H	7	8 NYI H	9	10 MON
11	12	13 BUF H	14	15 MON H	16	17 HAR
18	19	20 VAN H	21	22 DET H	23	24 NJ
25	26	27 OTT	28	29 STL	30	31

NOVEMBER

S	M	T	W	T	F	S
1 TB	2	3 NYI H	4	5 STL H	6	7 TOR
8 CHI	9	10 MIN	11	12 QUE H	13 DET	14
15	16	17 BUF H	18	19	20 NJ	21 NJ H
22 NYR	23	24	25 NYR H	26	27 WAS	28 WAS H
29	30					

DECEMBER

S	M	T	W	T	F	S
		1 NYI	2	3 LA	4	5 D SJ
6	7	8 WIN H	9	10	11 NJ	12 NJ H
13	14	15 PHI H	16	17 PHI	18	19 D NYI H
20	21 QUE H	22	23 PHI	24	25	26
27 D BUF	28	29	30	31 TOR H		

JANUARY

S	M	T	W	T	F	S
					1	2 NYR H
3	4	5 BOS H	6	7 MIN H	8	9 D CAL H
10 WIN	11	12	13	14 BOS	15	16 OTT H
17	18	19 VAN	20	21	22 EDM	23 CAL
24	25	26 WAS H	27	28 NYI H	29	30 D PHI H
31 D WAS						

FEBRUARY

S	M	T	W	T	F	S
	1	2	3	4	5	6 ✱
7	8	9	10 NYR	11	12	13 D CHI H
14 BUF	15	16	17	18 EDM H	19	20 D NYI
21 HAR	22	23 NJ H	24	25 OTT	26	27 D TB H
28 D WAS						

MARCH

S	M	T	W	T	F	S
	1	2 PHI	3	4	5 NYR	6
7	8	9 BOS H	10	11 LA H	12	13 NYI
14	15	16	17	18 PHI H	19	20 OTT H
21	22	23 SJ H	24	25 WAS H	26	27 D BOS
28 D WAS	29	30	31			

APRIL

S	M	T	W	T	F	S
				1	2 HAR H	3 QUE
4 NJ	5	6	7 MON H	8	9 NYR	10 NYR H
11	12	13	14 NJ	15 NJ H	16	17

1992-93 SEASON

CLUB DIRECTORY

Owners
Howard Baldwin
Morris Belzberg
Thomas Ruta
President and governor
Howard Baldwin
General counsel
Paul Martha
Executive V.P. and general manager
Craig Patrick
Exec. V.P. and chief financial officer
Donn Patton
Coach
Scotty Bowman
Assistant coaches
Rick Kehoe
Pierre McGuire
Rick Paterson
Barry Smith
Scouts
Greg Malone
Les Binkley
John Gill
Charlie Hodge
Ralph Cox
Gilles Meloche

Executive vice president, marketing
Bill Barnes
V.P. public and community relations
Phil Langan
Vice president, marketing
Bill Cox
Vice president, communications & sales
Bill Strong
Controller
Kevin Hart
Director of press relations
Cindy Himes
Assistant director of press relations
Harry Sanders
Director of ticket sales
Jeff Mercer
Trainer
Skip Thayer
Strength coach
John Welday
Equipment manager
Steve Latin
Team assistant
Howard Baldwin Jr.
Team physician
Dr. Charles Burke

DRAFT CHOICES

Rnd.	Player	Ht./Wt.	Overall	Pos.	1991-92 club
1	Martin Straka	5-10/178	19	C	Skoda Pizen, Czech.
2	Marc Hussey	6-4/182	43	D	Moose Jaw (WHL)
3	Travis Thiessen	6-3/203	67	D	Moose Jaw (WHL)
4	Todd Klassen	6-0/204	91	D	Tri-City (WHL)
5	Philipp De Rouville	6-1/183	115	G	Verdun (QMJHL)
6	Artem Kopot	5-10/183	139	D	Chelyabinsk, CIS
7	Jan Alinc	6-1/176	163	RW	Litvinov, Czech.
8	Fran Bussey	6-3/182	187	C	Duluth (Minn.) H.S.
9	Brian Bonin	5-9/165	211	C	White Bear Lake (Min.) H.S.
10	Brian Callahan	6-1/180	235	C	Belmont Hill (Mass.) H.S.

MISCELLANEOUS DATA

Home ice (capacity)
Civic Arena (16,164)
Address
Gate No. 9
Pittsburgh, PA 15219
Business phone
412-642-1800

Rink dimensions
200 feet by 85 feet
Club colors
Black, gold and white
Minor league affiliation
Cleveland (IHL)

SCHEDULE KEY

*All-Star Game at Montreal.
H—Home game.　　D—Day game (any game starting before 4 p.m.).
NOTE: At press time, two games at neutral sites had yet to be announced.

TRAINING CAMP ROSTER

No.	FORWARDS	Ht./Wt.	BORN Place	Date	NHL exp.	1991-92 clubs
29	Phil Bourque (LW)	6-1/196	Chelmsford, Mass.	6-8-62	8	Pittsburgh
	Jeff Daniels (LW)	6-1/200	Oshawa, Ont.	6-24-68	2	Muskegon (IHL), Pittsburgh
12	Bob Errey (LW)	5-10/182	Montreal	9-21-64	9	Pittsburgh
10	Ron Francis (C)	6-2/200	S. Ste. Marie, Ont.	3-1-63	11	Pittsburgh
68	Jaromir Jagr (RW)	6-2/208	Kladno, Czech.	2-15-72	2	Pittsburgh
20	Jamie Leach (RW)	6-1/205	Winnipeg, Man.	8-25-69	3	Muskegon (IHL), Pittsburgh
66	Mario Lemieux (C)	6-4/210	Montreal	10-5-65	8	Pittsburgh
24	Troy Loney (LW)	6-3/209	Bow Island, Alta.	9-21-63	9	Pittsburgh
15	Shawn McEachern (C)	6-0/190	Waltham, Mass.	2-28-69	1	U.S. Nat./Olym., Pittsburgh
34	Dave Michayluk (LW)	5-10/189	Wakaw, Sask.	5-18-62	3	Muskegon (IHL)
7	Joe Mullen (RW)	5-9/180	New York	2-26-57	12	Pittsburgh
	Glenn Mulvenna (C)	5-11/187	Calgary, Alta.	2-18-67	1	Muskegon (IHL), Pittsburgh
	Markus Naslund (RW)	5-11/174	Harnosand, Sweden	7-30-73	0	MoDo (Sweden)
45	Mike Needham (RW)	5-10/185	Calgary, Alta.	4-4-70	1	Muskegon (IHL)
18	Ken Priestlay (C)	5-10/190	Vancouver, B.C.	8-24-67	6	Muskegon (IHL), Pittsburgh
25	Kevin Stevens (LW)	6-3/215	Brockton, Mass.	4-15-65	5	Pittsburgh
	Martin Straka (C)	5-9/172	Plzen, Czech.	9-3-72	0	Skoda Plzen (Czech.)
92	Rick Tocchet (RW)	6-0/205	Scarborough, Ont.	4-9-64	8	Philadelphia, Pittsburgh
19	Bryan Trottier (C)	5-11/195	Val Marie, Sask.	7-17-56	17	Pittsburgh

No.	DEFENSEMEN	Ht./Wt.	Place	Date	NHL exp.	1991-92 clubs
6	Jeff Chychrun	6-4/215	Lasalle, Que.	5-3-66	6	Phoenix (IHL), Los Angeles, Pittsburgh
	Gord Dineen	6-0/195	Toronto	9-21-62	10	Muskegon (IHL), Pittsburgh
	Bryan Fogarty	6-1/190	Montreal	6-11-69	3	Muskegon (IHL), New Haven (AHL), Halifax (AHL), Quebec
	Jamie Heward	6-2/194	Regina, Sask.	3-30-71	0	Muskegon (IHL)
3	Grant Jennings	6-3/210	Hudson Bay, Sask.	5-5-65	5	Pittsburgh
55	Larry Murphy	6-1/210	Scarborough, Ont.	3-8-61	12	Pittsburgh
	Todd Nelson	6-1/201	Prince Albert, Sask.	5-15-69	1	Muskegon (IHL), Pittsburgh
2	Jim Paek	6-1/194	Seoul, South Korea	4-7-67	2	Pittsburgh
23	Kjell Samuelsson	6-6/235	Tyngsryd, Sweden	10-18-58	7	Philadelphia, Pittsburgh
5	Ulf Samuelsson	6-1/195	Fagersta, Sweden	3-26-64	8	Pittsburgh
22	Paul Stanton	6-0/200	Boston	6-22-67	2	Pittsburgh

No.	GOALTENDERS	Ht./Wt.	Place	Date	NHL exp.	1991-92 clubs
35	Tom Barrasso	6-3/212	Boston	3-31-65	9	Pittsburgh
	Rob Dopson	6-0/200	Smith Falls, Ont.	8-21-67	0	Muskegon (IHL)
31	Ken Wregget	6-1/195	Brandon, Man.	3-25-64	9	Philadelphia, Pittsburgh

1991-92 REVIEW

INDIVIDUAL STATISTICS

SCORING

	Games	G	A	Pts.	Pen.	+/-	PPG	SHG	Shots	Shooting Pct.
Mario Lemieux	64	44	87	†131	94	27	12	4	249	17.7
Kevin Stevens	80	54	69	123	254	8	19	0	325	16.6
Joe Mullen	77	42	45	87	30	12	14	0	226	18.6
Larry Murphy	77	21	56	77	48	33	7	2	206	10.2
Mark Recchi*	58	33	37	70	78	-16	16	1	156	21.2
Jaromir Jagr	70	32	37	69	34	12	4	0	194	16.5
Paul Coffey*	54	10	54	64	62	4	5	0	207	4.8
Ron Francis	70	21	33	54	30	-7	5	1	121	17.4
Bob Errey	78	19	16	35	119	1	0	3	122	15.6
Rick Tocchet*	19	14	16	30	49	12	4	1	59	23.7
Bryan Trottier	63	11	18	29	54	-11	3	1	102	10.8
Phil Bourque	58	10	16	26	58	-6	0	1	51	19.6
Troy Loney	76	10	16	26	127	-5	0	0	94	10.6
Gordie Roberts	73	2	22	24	87	19	1	0	29	6.9
Jiri Hrdina	56	3	13	16	16	4	0	0	51	5.9
Ulf Samuelsson	62	1	14	15	206	2	1	0	75	1.3
Ken Priestlay	49	2	8	10	4	5	0	0	20	10.0
Paul Stanton	54	2	8	10	62	-8	0	0	70	2.9
Jamie Leach	38	5	4	9	8	-2	1	0	32	15.6
Grant Jennings	53	4	5	9	104	-1	0	2	35	11.4
Jim Paek	49	1	7	8	36	0	0	0	33	3.0
Peter Taglianetti	44	1	3	4	57	7	0	0	23	4.3
Shawn McEachern	15	0	4	4	0	1	0	0	14	0.0
Tom Barrasso (goalie)	57	0	4	4	30	0	0	0	0	0.0
Kjell Samuelsson*	20	1	2	3	34	0	0	0	28	3.6

	Games	G	A	Pts.	Pen.	+/-	PPG	SHG	Shots	Shooting Pct.
Jeff Chychrun*	17	0	1	1	35	-8	0	0	4	0.0
Gord Dineen	1	0	0	0	0	-2	0	0	0	0.0
Glen Mulvenna	1	0	0	0	2	-1	0	0	0	0.0
Todd Nelson	1	0	0	0	0	0	0	0	0	0.0
Jeff Daniels	2	0	0	0	0	0	0	0	0	0.0
Frank Pietrangelo (goalie)*	5	0	0	0	0	0	0	0	0	0.0
Ken Wregget (goalie)*	9	0	0	0	2	0	0	0	0	0.0
Wendell Young (goalie)	18	0	0	0	0	0	0	0	0	0.0
Jay Caufield	50	0	0	0	175	-6	0	0	16	0.0

GOALTENDING

	Games	Min.	Goals	SO	Avg.	W	L	T	Shots	Sv. Pct.
Tom Barrasso	57	3329	196	1	3.53	25	22	9	1702	.885
Wendell Young	18	838	53	0	3.79	7	6	0	476	.889
Ken Wregget*	9	448	31	0	4.15	5	3	0	202	.847
Frank Pietrangelo*	5	225	20	0	5.33	2	1	0	130	.846

Empty-net goals (do not count against a goaltender's average): Young, 4; Barrasso, 2.
*Played with two or more NHL teams.
†Led league.

RESULTS

OCTOBER
4—At Buffalo	W		5-4
6—Philadelphia	T		*2-2
10—At Philadelphia	W		6-3
12—At New Jersey	L		1-4
15—At N.Y. Islanders	W		*7-6
17—N.Y. Islanders	W		8-5
19—N.Y. Rangers	L		4-5
22—Chicago	T		*4-4
24—New Jersey	L		2-4
26—At Montreal	L		1-4
29—Washington	L		0-8
31—Minnesota	W		8-1

NOVEMBER
2—Hartford	L		5-6
5—Boston	T		*5-5
8—At Winnipeg	W		3-1
9—At Minnesota	W		3-2
11—At N.Y. Rangers	L		1-3
13—Edmonton	W		*5-4
15—At Washington	L		2-6
18—At Quebec	W		7-3
20—Philadelphia	W		5-2
23—N.Y. Islanders	T		*2-2
27—New Jersey	W		8-4
29—At Philadelphia	W		9-3
30—Philadelphia	W		5-1

DECEMBER
3—At Edmonton	L		3-5

5—At San Jose	W		8-0
7—At St. Louis	L		1-6
10—N.Y. Rangers	W		5-3
13—At New Jersey	W		4-3
14—Washington	L		2-7
17—San Jose	W		10-2
19—At Boston	W		6-4
21—N.Y. Rangers	L		5-7
23—At N.Y. Islanders	W		6-3
26—Toronto	W		12-1
28—At Washington	W		6-2
29—At N.Y. Rangers	W		6-3
31—New Jersey	L		4-7

JANUARY
2—At New Jersey	L		0-4
4—Winnipeg	W		3-2
7—Los Angeles	L		2-5
10—At Calgary	L		5-7
12—At Vancouver	W		4-3
16—At Detroit	T		*3-3
23—Buffalo	L		*4-5
25—At N.Y. Islanders	W		5-3
26—At Washington	L		4-6
28—Winnipeg	L		0-4
30—N.Y. Islanders	L		5-8

FEBRUARY
1—St. Louis	W		4-1
3—Detroit	T		*4-4
5—At N.Y. Rangers	L		3-4
8—Los Angeles	L		3-4

9—At Boston	L		3-6
15—At Minnesota	L		2-5
16—At Philadelphia	T		*3-3
18—Toronto	W		7-1
20—Quebec	T		*4-4
22—At Montreal	L		1-2
25—At Washington	L		3-5
27—Hartford	L		4-8
29—Buffalo	W		5-2

MARCH
3—At Calgary	W		6-3
6—At San Jose	W		7-3
7—At Los Angeles	L		3-5
10—Calgary	W		5-2
12—N.Y. Islanders	W		6-4
14—At Toronto	L		3-6
15—At Chicago	W		4-3
17—Edmonton	W		6-5
19—Quebec	W		6-3
22—At Hartford	T		*2-2
24—At Detroit	L		3-4
26—Vancouver	W		7-3
28—Montreal	W		6-3
31—Philadelphia	W		6-5

APRIL
13—At New Jersey	L		1-5
15—Washington	W		4-1
16—At N.Y. Rangers	L		1-7

*Denotes overtime game.

QUEBEC NORDIQUES
WALES CONFERENCE/ADAMS DIVISION

1992-93 SCHEDULE

OCTOBER

S	M	T	W	T	F	S
4	5	6	7	8 BUF	9	10 OTT H
11	12	13 PHI H	14	15 DET	16	17 STL H
18	19	20	21 STL	22 MIN	23	24 TB
25	26	27 TB H	28	29 NYR	30	31 WIN H

NOVEMBER

S	M	T	W	T	F	S
1	2	3 HAR	4	5 BOS	6	7 D CHI H
8 D CAL H	9	10	11 OTT	12 PIT	13	14 NYR H
15	16	17	18	19 MON H	20	21 D HAR H
22 D WAS H	23	24	25 BUF	26 TOR	27	28 NJ H
29	30 BOS H					

DECEMBER

S	M	T	W	T	F	S
		1	2	3 PHI	4	5 MIN H
6	7 BUF H	8	9	10 LA	11	12 SJ
13 VAN	14	15	16 MON	17 MON H	18	19
20 D NYI H	21 PIT	22	23	24	25	26 OTT H
27 OTT	28	29 NJ H	30	31 HAR		

JANUARY

S	M	T	W	T	F	S
				1	2 DET H
3	4	5 NYI	6	7 BOS	8	9 HAR
10	11	12	13	14 MON H	15	16 SJ H
17	18	19 OTT	20	21	22 BUF	23 BUF H
24	25	26 BOS H	27	28 PHI	29 WAS	30
31						

FEBRUARY

S	M	T	W	T	F	S
	1	2 LA H	3 BOS H	4	5	6 *
7	8	9 VAN H	10	11	12 CAL	13
14 D EDM	15	16	17	18 OTT H	19	20
21 NJ	22	23 EDM H	24	25 NYI H	26	27 HAR H
28 OTT						

MARCH

S	M	T	W	T	F	S
	1	2 WIN	3	4 CHI	5	6 NYR H
7	8 HAR H	9	10 BUF H	11	12	13 MON
14	15 TOR H	16	17	18 MON H	19	20 D NJ
21	22	23 WAS	24	25	26	27 PHI H
28 NYR	29	30	31 MON			

APRIL

S	M	T	W	T	F	S
				1 OTT	2	3 PIT H
4	5	6 BOS H	7	8 BOS	9	10 HAR H
11 BUF	12	13 OTT H	14	15	16	17

1992-93 SEASON

CLUB DIRECTORY

President and governor
Marcel Aubut
General manager and coach
Pierre Page
Assistant to the general manager
Gilles Leger
Assistant coaches
Don Jackson
Andre Savard
V.P./administration and finance
Jean Laflamme
V.P./marketing and communications
Jean D. Legault
Director of public relations
Richard Thibault
Director of corporate and community affairs
Guy Lafleur
Supervisor of press relations
Jean Martineau
Coordinator of public relations
Nicole Bouchard
Scouts/pro hockey and special assignment
Orval Tessier
Dave Draper

Chief scout
Pierre Gauthier
Assistant to the chief scout
Darwin Bennett
Scouts
Ross Ainsworth
Don Boyd
Herb Boxer
Yvon Gendron
Michel Georges
Mark Kelley
Bengt Lundholm
Frank Moberg
Jacques Noel
Don Paarup
Dan Summers
Team doctor
Dr. Pierre Beauchemin
Trainers
Rene Lacasse
Rene Lavigueur
Jacques Lavergne

DRAFT CHOICES

Rnd. Player	Ht./Wt.	Overall	Pos.	1991-92 club
1—Todd Warriner	6-1/172	4	LW	Windsor (OHL)
2—Paul Brousseau	6-2/212	28	RW	Hull (QMJHL)
2—Tuomas Gronman	6-2/190	29	D	Tacoma (WHL)
3—Emman'l Fernandez	6-0/168	52	G	Laval (QMJHL)
4—Ian McIntyre	6-0/184	76	LW	Beauport (QMJHL)
5—Charlie Wasley	6-2/173	100	D	St. Paul (Junior A, Tier II)
6—Paxton Schulte	6-2/210	124	LW	Spokane (WHL)
7—Martin Lepage	6-1/185	148	D	Hull (QMJHL)
8—Mike Jickling	5-11/191	172	C	Spokane (WHL)
9—Steve Passmore	5-9/165	196	G	Victoria (WHL)
10—Anson Carter	6-1/175	220	C	Wexford (Ont.) (Junior B)
11—Aaron Ellis	6-1/170	244	G	Culver (Wis.) Military Acad.

MISCELLANEOUS DATA

Home ice (capacity)
Quebec Colisee (15,399)
Address
2205 Avenue du Colisee
Quebec, Que. G1L 4W7
Business phone
418-529-8441

Rink dimensions
200 feet by 85 feet
Club colors
Blue, white and red
Minor league affiliation
Halifax (AHL)

SCHEDULE KEY

*All-Star Game at Montreal.
H—Home game.   D—Day game (any game starting before 4 p.m.).
NOTE: At press time, two games at neutral sites had yet to be announced.

TRAINING CAMP ROSTER

No.	FORWARDS	Ht./Wt.	Place	BORN Date	NHL exp.	1991-92 clubs
28	Jamie Baker (C)	6-0/190	Nepean, Que.	8-31-66	3	Halifax (AHL), Quebec
44	Gino Cavallini (LW)	6-2/215	Toronto	11-24-62	8	St. Louis, Quebec
21	Stephane Charbonneau	6-2/195	Ste-Adele, Que.	6-27-70	1	Halifax (AHL), Quebec
	Daniel Dore	6-3/202	St. Jerome, Que.	4-9-70	2	Greensboro (ECHL), Halifax (AHL)
18	Mike Hough (LW)	6-1/192	Montreal	2-6-63	6	Quebec
17	Valeri Kamensky (LW)	6-2/198	Voskresensk, U.S.S.R.	4-18-66	1	Quebec
47	Claude Lapointe (C)	5-9/173	Ville Emard, Que.	10-11-68	2	Quebec
53	Bill Lindsay (LW)	5-11/185	Big Fork, Mont.	5-17-71	1	Tri-City (WHL), Quebec
20	Mike McNeill (RW)	6-1/175	Winona, Minn.	7-22-66	2	Halifax (AHL), Quebec
25	Stephane Morin (C)	6-0/175	Montreal	3-27-69	3	Halifax (AHL), Quebec
11	Owen Nolan (RW)	6-1/194	Belfast, No. Ireland	2-12-72	2	Quebec
23	Greg Paslawski (RW)	5-11/190	Kindersley, Sask.	8-25-61	9	Quebec
22	Scott Pearson (LW)	6-1/205	Cornwall, Ont.	12-19-69	4	Halifax (AHL), Quebec
14	Herb Raglan (RW)	6-0/205	Peterborough, Ont.	8-5-67	7	Quebec
	Mike Ricci (C)	6-0/190	Scarborough, Ont.	10-27-71	2	Philadelphia
37	Martin Rucinsky (LW)	5-11/178	Most, Czech.	3-11-71	1	Cape Breton (AHL), Edmonton, Halifax (AHL), Quebec
60	Andy Rymsha	6-3/210	St. Catharines, Ont.	12-10-68	1	New Haven (AHL), Halifax (AHL), Quebec
19	Joe Sakic (C)	5-11/185	Burnaby, B.C.	7-7-69	4	Quebec
	Everett Sanipass (LW)	6-2/204	Big Cove, N.B.	2-13-68	5	Halifax (AHL)
41	Doug Smail (LW)	5-9/175	Moose Jaw, Sask.	9-2-57	12	Quebec
13	Mats Sundin (RW)	6-2/190	Sollentuna, Sweden	2-13-71	2	Quebec
21	John Tonelli (LW/C)	6-1/190	Hamilton, Ont.	3-23-57	14	Chicago, Quebec
15	Tony Twist (LW)	6-1/212	Sherwood Park, Alta.	5-9-68	3	Quebec
24	Wayne Van Dorp (LW)	6-4/225	Vancouver, B.C.	5-19-61	6	Halifax (AHL), Quebec
45	Mark Vermette (RW)	6-1/203	Cochenour, Ont.	10-3-67	4	Halifax (AHL), Quebec
	DEFENSEMEN					
	Steve Duchesne	5-11/195	Sept-Illes, Que.	6-30-65	6	Philadelphia
	Leonard Esau	6-3/195	Meadow Lake, Sask.	3-16-68	1	St. John's (AHL), Toronto
29	Steven Finn	6-0/198	Laval, Que.	8-20-66	7	Quebec
52	Adam Foote	6-1/180	Toronto	7-10-71	1	Halifax (AHL), Quebec
5	Alexei Gusarov	6-2/170	Leningrad, U.S.S.R.	7-8-64	2	Halifax (AHL), Quebec
	Kerry Huffman	6-3/205	Peterborough, Ont.	1-3-68	6	Philadelphia
42	Jon Klemm	6-3/200	Cranbrook, B.C.	1-6-70	1	Halifax (AHL), Quebec
50	Dan Lambert	5-8/177	St. Boniface, Man.	1-12-70	2	Halifax (AHL), Quebec
7	Curtis Leschyshyn	6-1/205	Thompson, Man.	9-21-69	4	Halifax (AHL), Quebec
38	David Marcinyshyn	6-3/210	Edmonton, Alta.	2-4-67	2	Halifax (AHL), Quebec
4	Mikhail Tatarinov	5-10/194	Penza, U.S.S.R.	7-16-66	2	Quebec
27	Randy Velischek	6-0/200	Montreal	2-10-62	10	Halifax (AHL), Quebec
6	Craig Wolanin	6-3/205	Grosse Point, Mich.	7-27-67	7	Quebec
	Scott Young (RW)	6-0/190	Clinton, Mass.	10-1-67	4	U.S. Nat./Olym.
	GOALTENDERS					
32	Jacques Cloutier	5-7/168	Noranda, Que.	1-3-60	10	Quebec
31	Stephane Fiset	6-0/175	Montreal	6-17-70	3	Halifax (AHL), Quebec
	Ron Hextall	6-3/192	Winnipeg, Man.	5-3-64	6	Philadelphia
34	John Tanner	6-3/182	Cambridge, Ont.	3-17-71	3	New Haven (AHL), Halifax (AHL), Quebec

1991-92 REVIEW

INDIVIDUAL STATISTICS

SCORING

	Games	G	A	Pts.	Pen.	+/-	PPG	SHG	Shots	Shooting Pct.
Joe Sakic	69	29	65	94	20	5	6	3	217	13.4
Mats Sundin	80	33	43	76	103	-19	8	2	231	14.3
Owen Nolan	75	42	31	73	183	-9	17	0	190	22.1
Greg Paslawski	80	28	17	45	18	-12	5	1	134	20.9
Mike Hough	61	16	22	38	77	-1	6	2	92	17.4
Mikhail Tatarinov	66	11	27	38	72	8	5	0	191	5.8
Claude Lapointe	78	13	20	33	86	-8	0	2	95	13.7
Doug Smail	46	10	18	28	47	-11	0	1	72	13.9
Alexei Gusarov	68	5	18	23	22	-9	3	0	66	7.6
Valeri Kamensky	23	7	14	21	14	-1	2	0	42	16.7
Herb Raglan	62	6	14	20	120	-5	0	0	79	7.6
Jamie Baker	52	7	10	17	32	-5	3	0	77	9.1
Curtis Leschyshyn	42	5	12	17	42	-28	3	0	61	8.2
Dan Lambert	28	6	9	15	22	-5	2	0	42	14.3
Kip Miller*	36	5	10	15	12	-21	1	0	46	10.9

	Games	G	A	Pts.	Pen.	+/-	PPG	SHG	Shots	Shooting Pct.
Bryan Fogarty	20	3	12	15	16	-15	0	0	30	10.0
Marc Fortier	39	5	9	14	33	-7	2	0	42	11.9
Craig Wolanin	69	2	11	13	80	-12	0	0	71	2.8
Steven Finn	65	4	7	11	194	-9	0	0	63	6.3
Stephane Morin	30	2	8	10	14	-2	0	0	41	4.9
Wayne Van Dorp	24	3	5	8	109	5	0	0	19	15.8
Gino Cavallini*	18	1	7	8	4	-1	0	0	39	2.6
Adam Foote	46	2	5	7	44	-4	0	0	55	3.6
John Tonelli*	19	2	4	6	14	-7	2	0	16	12.5
Bill Lindsay	23	2	4	6	14	-6	0	0	35	5.7
Randy Velischek	38	2	3	5	22	-3	0	0	23	8.7
Mike McNeill	26	1	4	5	8	-8	1	0	15	6.7
Scott Pearson	10	1	2	3	14	-5	0	0	14	7.1
Martin Rucinsky*	4	1	1	2	2	1	0	0	4	25.0
John Kordic	18	0	2	2	115	-3	0	0	3	0.0
Greg Smyth*	29	0	2	2	138	-10	0	0	24	0.0
Mark Vermette	10	1	0	1	8	-6	0	0	12	8.3
Jon Klemm	4	0	1	1	0	2	0	0	2	0.0
Ken McRae	10	0	1	1	31	-5	0	0	10	0.0
Tony Twist	44	0	1	1	164	-3	0	0	9	0.0
Don Barber*	2	0	0	0	0	-1	0	0	1	0.0
Stephane Charbonneau	2	0	0	0	0	-2	0	0	4	0.0
Dave Karpa	4	0	0	0	14	-2	0	0	2	0.0
Kevin Kaminski	5	0	0	0	45	-2	0	0	6	0.0
Dave Marcinyshyn	5	0	0	0	26	-1	0	0	3	0.0
Andy Rymsha	6	0	0	0	23	-3	0	0	4	0.0
John Tanner (goalie)	14	0	0	0	4	0	0	0	0	0.0
Stephane Fiset (goalie)	23	0	0	0	6	0	0	0	0	0.0
Jacques Cloutier (goalie)	26	0	0	0	6	0	0	0	0	0.0
Ron Tugnutt (goalie)*	30	0	0	0	0	0	0	0	0	0.0

GOALTENDING

	Games	Min.	Goals	SO	Avg.	W	L	T	Shots	Sv. Pct.
John Tanner	14	796	46	1	3.47	1	7	4	394	.883
Stephane Fiset	23	1133	71	1	3.76	7	10	2	646	.890
Jacques Cloutier	26	1345	88	0	3.93	6	14	3	712	.876
Ron Tugnutt*	30	1583	106	1	4.02	6	17	3	782	.864

Empty-net goals (do not count against a goaltender's average): Tugnutt, 5; Fiset, 1; Tanner, 1.
*Played with two or more NHL teams.

RESULTS

OCTOBER

5—Hartford	W	4-2
8—At New Jersey	L	5-6
10—At Minnesota	L	2-3
12—Buffalo	L	4-5
13—N.Y. Islanders	T	*1-1
17—At Philadelphia	L	3-5
19—Detroit	L	1-6
23—At Montreal	L	*2-3
24—Montreal	L	0-5
26—N.Y. Rangers	L	3-5
29—Winnipeg	W	7-2
31—At N.Y. Rangers	L	4-5

NOVEMBER

2—San Jose	W	6-3
7—At Chicago	L	2-4
10—Washington	L	3-10
12—At Hartford	L	4-5
14—At Boston	L	2-5
16—Edmonton	L	2-6
18—Pittsburgh	L	3-7
21—Montreal	W	5-2
23—At Montreal	L	3-5
25—Hartford	W	5-2
27—At Buffalo	T	*4-4
28—At St. Louis	L	2-5
30—Buffalo	W	4-3

DECEMBER

3—Vancouver	W	3-0
5—At Boston	T	*2-2
7—Los Angeles	W	7-5
10—Boston	W	5-2
12—At Detroit	L	1-4
14—St. Louis	L	2-4
17—At Washington	L	1-3
19—At Calgary	T	*5-5
21—At San Jose	L	1-4
22—At Vancouver	T	*6-6
26—Montreal	L	1-4
28—Hartford	W	4-1
30—Toronto	W	5-2

JANUARY

2—At Hartford	L	1-4
4—At N.Y. Islanders	L	2-5
8—At Buffalo	L	2-4
9—At Boston	L	4-5
11—N.Y. Rangers	L	2-7
14—Calgary	L	3-5
21—Vancouver	L	3-5
23—At Chicago	L	2-4
25—Winnipeg	W	2-1
28—Boston	L	2-4
29—At Toronto	L	2-5
31—At Winnipeg	T	*4-4

FEBRUARY

2—At Edmonton	L	2-8
5—At Calgary	L	3-5
8—Philadelphia	L	0-3
9—New Jersey	L	1-2
11—Washington	L	3-4
13—At Philadelphia	L	2-3
15—At Montreal	T	*4-4
18—Minnesota	W	4-0
20—At Pittsburgh	T	*4-4
22—At Hartford	L	0-4
23—At Montreal	T	*3-3
26—At San Jose	L	4-7
27—At Los Angeles	L	2-4

MARCH

3—Buffalo	T	*4-4
5—At Hartford	W	10-4
7—Detroit	T	*4-4
9—Hartford	W	2-0
11—Montreal	W	5-4
14—Boston	L	*4-5
15—At Buffalo	L	4-6
17—At Toronto	L	*3-4
19—At Pittsburgh	L	3-6
21—Minnesota	W	4-2
24—N.Y. Islanders	W	5-2
26—Chicago	T	*4-5
28—At New Jersey	L	2-5
31—Boston	L	*4-5

APRIL

12—At Boston	T	*1-1
14—Buffalo	W	7-3
15—At Buffalo	W	4-3

*Denotes overtime game.

— 55 —

ST. LOUIS BLUES
CAMPBELL CONFERENCE/NORRIS DIVISION

1992-93 SCHEDULE

OCTOBER
S	M	T	W	T	F	S
4	5	6 MIN H	7	8 MIN	9	10 CHI H
11	12	13 TB H	14	15 MIN H	16	17 QUE
18	19 MON	20	21 QUE H	22	23	24 DET H
25	26 SJ H	27	28	29	30	31 PHI H

NOVEMBER
S	M	T	W	T	F	S
1	2	3 TB	4	5 PIT	6	7 D PHI
8	9	10 EDM H	11	12 CHI	13	14 WIN H
15	16 TOR	17	18 HAR	19	20	21 TB H
22	23	24	25 DET	26 VAN H	27	28 DET H
29	30					

DECEMBER
S	M	T	W	T	F	S
		1 HAR H	2	3	4 CAL	5 EDM
6	7 VAN	8	9	10 SJ	11	12 LA
13	14	15	16	17 NYR H	18	19 WIN H
20	21	22 MIN	23	24	25	26 CHI
27 TOR H	28	29	30	31 NYI H		

JANUARY
S	M	T	W	T	F	S
					1	2 TOR
3 BUF	4	5 EDM H	6	7 CAL H	8	9 CHI H
10	11 DET	12	13 TOR	14 OTT	15	16 TB
17	18	19 TOR H	20	21 DET	22	23 DET H
24	25	26 OTT H	27	28 TB	29	30 NJ H
31						

FEBRUARY
S	M	T	W	T	F	S
1 TOR H	2	3 WIN	4	5	6 *	
7	8	9 BOS H	10	11 WAS H	12	13 DET H
14	15 D NYR	16	17 NJ	18 NYI	19	20
21 D WAS	22	23 MON H	24	25 LA H	26	27 MIN H
28 CHI						

MARCH
S	M	T	W	T	F	S
	1	2	3	4 CAL H	5	6 D BOS
7	8	9	10	11 SJ H	12	13 MIN H
14 MIN	15	16 BUF H	17	18	19	20 LA
21	22 VAN	23	24 CAL	25	26 WIN	27
28	29	30 VAN H	31			

APRIL
S	M	T	W	T	F	S
				1	2	3 CHI H
4 CHI	5	6 TB	7	8	9	10 MIN
11 MIN H	12	13 TOR	14	15 TB H	16	17

1992-93 SEASON

CLUB DIRECTORY

Board of directors
Michael F. Shanahan
Jud Perkins
Al Kerth
Ed Trusheim
Andy Craig
Larry Alexander
Chairman of the board
Michael F. Shanahan
President
Jack J. Quinn
Vice president/general manager
Ronald Caron
Vice president/director of sales
Bruce Affleck
V.P./dir. of player personnel and scouting/ assistant general manager
Ted Hampson
Vice president/coach
Bob Plager
V.P./dir. of broadcast sales
Matt Hyland
V.P./dir. of finance and administration
Jerry Jasiek
V.P./dir. of marketing and P.R.
Susie Mathieu

Assistant general manager
Bob Berry
Assistant director of scouting
Jack Evans
Western Canada/U.S. scout
Pat Ginnell
Scouts
Matt Keator
Paul MacLean
Assistant coaches
Wayne Thomas
Harold Snepsts
Dir. of promotions/community relations
Tracy Lovasz
Assistant directors of public relations
Jeff Trammel
Mike Caruso
Head trainer
Tom Nash
Assistant trainer
TBA
Equipment manager
Frank Burns

DRAFT CHOICES

Rnd. Player	Ht./Wt.	Overall	Pos.	1991-92 club
2—Igor Korolev	6-1/176	38	RW	Dynamo Moscow, CIS
3—Vitali Karamnov......	6-2/185	62	LW	Dynamo Moscow, CIS
3—Vitali Prokhorov......	5-9/185	64	LW	Spartak, CIS
4—Lee Leslie	6-4/191	86	LW	Prince Albert (WHL)
6—Bob Lachance	5-11/175	134	RW	Springfield (Junior B)
7—Ian Laperriere	6-0/191	158	C	Drummondville (QMJHL)
7—Lance Burns............	6-3/208	160	C	Lethbridge (WHL)
8—Igor Boldin.............	5-11/185	180	RW	Spartak, CIS
8—Nicholas Naumenko	5-11/180	182	D	Dubuque (Jr. A, Tier II)
9—Todd Harris	6-3/199	206	D	Tri-City (WHL)
10—Yuri Gunko	6-1/176	230	D	Sokol Kiev, CIS
11—Wade Salzman	6-3/192	259	G	Duluth East (Minn.) H.S.

MISCELLANEOUS DATA

Home ice (capacity)
St. Louis Arena (17,188)
Address
5700 Oakland Avenue
St. Louis, MO 63110-1397
Business phone
314-781-5300

Rink dimensions
200 feet by 85 feet
Club colors
Blue, gold, red and white
Minor league affiliation
Peoria (IHL)

SCHEDULE KEY
*All-Star Game at Montreal.
H—Home game.   D—Day game (any game starting before 4 p.m.).
NOTE: At press time, two games at neutral sites had yet to be announced.

— 56 —

TRAINING CAMP ROSTER

No.	FORWARDS	Ht./Wt.	Place	Born Date	NHL exp.	1991-92 clubs
28	Bob Bassen (C)	5-10/180	Calgary, Alta.	5-6-65	7	St. Louis
	Igor Boldin (C)	5-11/175	CIS		0	Spartak Moscow (CIS)
36	Philippe Bozon (C)	5-10/180	Chamoix, France	11-30-66	1	Chamonix (France), French Olym., St. Louis
39	Kelly Chase (RW)	5-11/195	Porcupine Plain, Sask.	10-25-67	3	St. Louis
27	Dave Christian (RW)	6-0/195	Warroad, Minn.	5-12-59	13	St. Louis
7	Nelson Emerson (C)	5-11/178	Hamilton, Ont.	8-17-67	2	St. Louis
17	Denny Felsner (RW)	6-0/195	Warren, Mich.	4-29-70	1	U. of Michigan (CCHA), St. Louis
	Derek Frenette (LW)	6-1/205	Montreal	7-13-71	0	Peoria (IHL)
16	Brett Hull (RW)	5-10/203	Belleville, Ont.	8-9-64	7	St. Louis
15	Craig Janney (C)	6-1/190	Hartford, Conn.	9-26-67	5	Boston, St. Louis
	Vitali Karamnov (LW)	6-2/185	Moscow, U.S.S.R.	7-6-68	0	Dynamo Moscow (CIS)
10	Dave Lowry (LW)	6-1/195	Sudbury, Ont.	1-14-65	7	St. Louis
26	David Mackey (LW)	6-4/210	New Westminster, B.C.	7-24-66	4	Peoria (IHL), St. Louis
	Kevin Miehm (C)	6-2/197	Kitchener, Ont.	9-10-69	0	Peoria (IHL)
	Vitali Prokhorov (LW)	5-9/185	Moscow, U.S.S.R.	12-25-66	0	Spartak Moscow (CIS), Unified Olym.
	Jason Ruff (LW)	6-3/195	Kelowna, B.C.	1-27-70	0	Peoria (IHL)
19	Brendan Shanahan (LW)	6-3/210	Mimico, Ont.	1-23-69	5	St. Louis
23	Rich Sutter (RW)	5-11/188	Viking, Alta.	12-2-63	10	St. Louis
22	Ron Sutter (C)	6-0/180	Viking, Alta.	12-2-63	10	St. Louis
18	Ron Wilson (C)	5-9/180	Toronto	5-13-56	12	St. Louis
	DEFENSEMEN					
6	Murray Baron	6-3/215	Prince George, B.C.	6-1-67	3	St. Louis
	Jeff Batters	6-2/215	Victoria, B.C.	10-23-70	0	Alaska-Anchorage (Ind.)
21	Jeff Brown	6-1/204	Ottawa	4-30-66	7	St. Louis
5	Garth Butcher	6-0/204	Regina, Sask.	1-8-63	11	St. Louis
14	Paul Cavallini	6-1/210	Toronto	10-13-65	6	St. Louis
2	Curt Giles	5-8/175	The Pas, Man.	10-30-58	13	Can. Nat./Olym., St. Louis
44	Bret Hedican	6-2/195	St. Paul, Minn.	8-10-70	1	U.S. Nat./Olym., St. Louis
	Daniel Laperriere	6-1/180	Laval, Que.	3-28-69	0	St. Lawrence (ECAC)
	Jason Marshall	6-2/190	Cranbrook, B.C.	2-22-71	1	Peoria (IHL), St. Louis
33	Stephane Quintal	6-3/220	Boucherville, Que.	10-22-68	4	Boston, St. Louis
4	Rick Zombo	6-1/195	Des Plaines, Ill.	5-8-63	8	Detroit, St. Louis
	GOALTENDERS					
40	Guy Hebert	5-11/180	Troy, N.Y.	1-7-67	1	Peoria (IHL), St. Louis
31	Curtis Joseph	5-11/182	Keswick, Ont.	4-29-67	3	St. Louis
	Geoff Sarjeant	5-9/175	Newmarket, Ont.	11-30-69	0	Michigan Tech (WCHA)

1991-92 REVIEW

INDIVIDUAL STATISTICS

SCORING

	Games	G	A	Pts.	Pen.	+/-	PPG	SHG	Shots	Shooting Pct.
Brett Hull	73	+70	39	109	48	-2	20	5	+408	17.2
Brendan Shanahan	80	33	36	69	171	-3	13	0	215	15.3
Adam Oates*	54	10	59	69	12	-4	3	0	118	8.5
Nelson Emerson	79	23	36	59	66	-5	3	0	143	16.1
Jeff Brown	80	20	39	59	38	8	10	0	214	9.3
Ron Sutter	68	19	27	46	91	9	5	4	106	17.9
Dave Christian	78	20	24	44	41	2	1	3	142	14.1
Craig Janney*	25	6	30	36	2	5	3	0	37	16.2
Paul Cavallini	66	10	25	35	95	7	3	1	164	6.1
Bob Bassen	79	7	25	32	167	12	0	0	101	6.9
Ron Wilson	64	12	17	29	46	10	5	2	100	12.0
Rich Sutter	77	9	16	25	107	7	0	1	113	8.0
Dave Lowry	75	7	13	20	77	-11	0	0	85	8.2
Garth Butcher	68	5	15	20	189	5	0	0	50	10.0
Rick Zombo*	64	3	15	18	46	4	0	0	47	6.4
Gino Cavallini*	48	9	7	16	40	-8	0	0	72	12.5
Michel Mongeau	36	3	12	15	6	-2	2	0	23	13.0
Lee Norwood*	44	3	11	14	94	14	1	0	51	5.9
Murray Baron	67	3	8	11	94	-3	0	0	55	5.5
Curtis Joseph (goalie)	60	0	9	9	12	0	0	0	0	0.0
Stephane Quintal*	26	0	6	6	32	-3	0	0	19	0.0
Philippe Bozon	9	1	3	4	4	5	0	0	19	5.3
Darin Kimble	46	1	3	4	166	-3	0	0	12	8.3
Kelly Chase	46	1	2	3	264	-6	0	0	29	3.4
Curt Giles	13	1	1	2	8	-3	0	0	4	25.0

	Games	G	A	Pts.	Pen.	+/-	PPG	SHG	Shots	Shooting Pct.
Jason Marshall	2	1	0	1	4	0	0	0	2	50.0
Bret Hedican	4	1	0	1	0	1	0	0	1	100.0
Dave Mackey	19	1	0	1	49	-4	0	0	12	8.3
Denny Felsner	3	0	1	1	1	0	0	0	2	0.0
Dominic Lavoie	6	0	1	1	10	-3	0	0	11	0.0
Guy Hebert (goalie)	13	0	1	1	0	0	0	0	0	0.0
Mario Marois*	17	0	1	1	38	-3	0	0	11	0.0
Rob Robinson	22	0	1	1	8	-4	0	0	9	0.0
Ron Hoover	1	0	0	0	0	0	0	0	1	0.0
Randy Skarda	1	0	0	0	0	0	0	0	0	0.0
Vincent Riendeau (goalie)*	3	0	0	0	0	0	0	0	0	0.0
Pat Jablonski (goalie)	10	0	0	0	4	0	0	0	0	0.0

GOALTENDING

	Games	Min.	Goals	SO	Avg.	W	L	T	Shots	Sv. Pct.
Guy Hebert	13	738	36	0	2.93	5	5	1	393	.908
Curtis Joseph	60	3494	175	2	3.01	27	20	10	1953	.910
Vincent Riendeau*	3	157	11	0	4.20	1	2	0	96	.885
Pat Jablonski	10	468	38	0	4.87	3	6	0	259	.853

Empty-net goals (do not count against a goaltender's average): Joseph, 5; Jablonski, 1.
*Played with two or more NHL teams.
†Led league.

RESULTS

OCTOBER
5—At New Jersey	L	2-7
7—At Toronto	L	0-3
10—Edmonton	W	*3-2
12—San Jose	W	6-3
15—Toronto	W	5-1
17—At Detroit	L	3-6
19—Chicago	T	*4-4
20—At Chicago	W	4-1
24—Boston	W	6-5
26—Calgary	T	*2-2
28—At Toronto	T	*1-1
30—At Edmonton	T	*2-2

NOVEMBER
1—At Vancouver	W	3-2
3—At Winnipeg	T	*3-3
5—Philadelphia	L	3-4
7—At Detroit	L	3-10
9—Hartford	L	3-4
10—At Detroit	L	4-6
14—Winnipeg	W	*2-1
16—Minnesota	W	5-3
17—At Chicago	L	1-5
20—Toronto	W	5-2
23—N.Y. Rangers	L	0-3
28—Quebec	W	5-2
30—Detroit	W	7-3

DECEMBER
3—At Minnesota	T	*3-3
4—At Minnesota	L	2-5
7—Pittsburgh	W	6-1
10—At N.Y. Islanders	T	*7-7
11—At Buffalo	W	6-3
14—At Quebec	W	4-2
16—At Montreal	L	2-4
19—San Jose	W	4-0
21—N.Y. Islanders	W	6-2
22—At Chicago	L	2-5
26—Chicago	W	3-1
28—At Minnesota	L	2-5
31—At Buffalo	L	3-4

JANUARY
2—Minnesota	W	6-1
4—Detroit	L	2-6
6—At Toronto	L	*2-3
8—At N.Y. Rangers	W	5-3
9—At New Jersey	L	3-4
11—At N.Y. Islanders	W	6-3
14—Washington	L	1-6
16—Montreal	T	*6-6
21—Buffalo	W	5-4
23—Los Angeles	L	5-6
25—Vancouver	L	*0-1
28—At Los Angeles	T	*3-3
30—At San Jose	W	4-2

FEBRUARY
1—At Pittsburgh	L	1-4
2—At Philadelphia	L	1-5
6—New Jersey	W	4-1
8—Chicago	L	1-3
11—Los Angeles	W	3-2
13—Boston	W	4-0
15—Calgary	W	7-2
17—At Detroit	L	3-5
19—At Winnipeg	W	4-3
22—Toronto	W	4-3
23—At Chicago	L	2-4
25—At Hartford	W	5-2
27—Washington	W	7-3
29—Detroit	L	2-3

MARCH
2—At Vancouver	W	5-3
6—At Edmonton	L	3-5
7—At Calgary	L	1-5
10—Minnesota	W	5-2
12—Detroit	L	4-5
14—N.Y. Rangers	L	0-6
17—At Washington	L	4-6
19—At Boston	W	4-1
21—At Montreal	T	*3-3
23—At Toronto	L	2-3
26—Hartford	W	7-2
28—Toronto	L	2-3

APRIL
12—At Minnesota	T	*1-1
14—Chicago	W	5-3
16—Minnesota	W	5-3

*Denotes overtime game.

SAN JOSE SHARKS
CAMPBELL CONFERENCE/SMYTHE DIVISION

1992-93 SCHEDULE

OCTOBER
S	M	T	W	T	F	S
4	5	6	7	8 WIN H	9	10 DET H
11	12	13 LA	14	15 BOS H	16	17 CAL H
18	19	20	21 MON	22	23 BUF	24 TOR
25	26 STL	27	28 DET	29	30 TB	31

NOVEMBER
S	M	T	W	T	F	S
1 CHI	0	0	4	5 BUF H	6	7 NJ H
8 LA H	9	10 VAN	11	12 EDM H	13	14 VAN H
15	16	17 LA H	18	19 TOR H	20	21 CHI H
22	23	24	25 CAL	26	27 WIN	28 MIN
29	30					

DECEMBER
S	M	T	W	T	F	S
		1 EDM H	2	3 HAR H	4	5 D PIT H
6	7	8	9 VAN	10 STL H	11	12 QUE H
13	14	15	16 TB H	17	18 VAN	19 VAN H
20	21 WIN	22	23 EDM	24	25	26 LA H
27	28	29 VAN	30 PHI H	31		

JANUARY
S	M	T	W	T	F	S
					1	2 VAN H
3	4	5 MON H	6	7	8 TOR	9
10 D OTT	11	12 WIN	13	14	15 DET	16 QUE
17	18 D BOS	19	20	21 HAR	22	23 TB
24	25	26 LA	27	28	29 CHI H	30 CAL H
31						

FEBRUARY
S	M	T	W	T	F	S
	1 TB H	2	3 MIN H	4	5	6 *
7	8	9	10 CAL	11	12 EDM	13
14 D WIN	15	16 WAS H	17	18 WIN H	19	20 NYR H
21	22	23 CAL H	24	25 TOR H	26	27 CAL
28 EDM						

MARCH
S	M	T	W	T	F	S
	1	2 OTT H	3	4	5	6
7 EDM H	8	9 MIN	10	11 STL	12	13
14 D DET H	15	16 NYI H	17	18	19 NYR	20
21 D WAS	22	23 PIT	24	25 PHI	26	27 NYI
28	29 NJ	30	31			

APRIL
S	M	T	W	T	F	S
				1 WIN H	2	3 D CAL H
4 CAL H	5	6 EDM H	7	8 LA	9	10 LA H
11	12	13	14	15 CAL	16	17

1992-93 SEASON

CLUB DIRECTORY

Co-owner & chairman
George Gund III
Co-owner & vice chairman
Gordon Gund
President & chief executive officer
Arthur L. Savage
Exec. vice president, finance
Grant Rollin
Exec. V.P., marketing and broadcasting
Matt Levine
Exec. vice president, building operations
Frank Jirik
Vice president/dir. of hockey operations
Dean Lombardi
Vice president/dir. of player personnel
Chuck Grillo
Vice president/coach
George Kingston
Associate coach
Bob Murdoch
Assistant coach
Drew Remenda
Strength coach
George Kinnear
Scouting coordinator
Joe Will
Executive assistant to general manager
Brenda Knight

Director of media relations
Tim Bryant
Assistant director of media relations
Ken Arnold
Media relations assistant
Jill Freeman
Scouting staff
Bob Gernander
Ray Payne
Konstantin Krylov
Larry Ross
Bob Freidlander
Ben Hays
Sakari Pietila
Pat Funk
Jack Morganstern
Deborah Wright
Head trainer
Tom Woodcock
Equipment manager
Jeff Croop
Assistant equipment manager
Arne Pappin
Team physician
Dr. Arthur Ting
Director of ticket operations
Daniel DeBoer

DRAFT CHOICES

Rnd. Player	Ht./Wt.	Overall	Pos.	1991-92 club
1—Mike Rathje	6-5/203	3	D	Medicine Hat (WHL)
1—Andrei Nazarov	6-4/209	10	LW	Dynamo Moscow, CIS
3—Alex. Cherbayev	6-0/180	51	F	Chimik, CIS
4—Jan Caloun	5-10/176	75	F	Litvinov, Czech.
5—Marcus Ragnarsson	6-1/200	99	D	Djurgarden, Sweden
6—Michal Sykora	6-4/198	123	D	Tacoma (WHL)
7—Eric Bellerose	6-1/202	147	LW	Trois-Rivieres (QMJHL)
8—Ryan Smith	6-2/200	171	D	Brandon (WHL)
9—Chris Burns	6-1/185	195	G	Thunder Bay (Junior A)
10—Alex. Kholomeyev	6-1/194	219	RW	CIS
11—Victor Ignatjev	6-3/198	243	RW	Riga, CIS

MISCELLANEOUS DATA

Home ice (capacity)
Cow Palace (11,100)
Address
10 Almaden Blvd.
Suite 600
San Jose, CA 95113
Business phone
408-287-7070

Rink dimensions
185 feet by 85 feet
Club colors
Pacific teal, gray, black and white
Minor league affiliation
Kansas City (IHL)

SCHEDULE KEY
*All-Star Game at Montreal.
H—Home game.   D—Day game (any game starting before 4 p.m.).
NOTE: At press time, two games at neutral sites had yet to be announced.

TRAINING CAMP ROSTER

No.	FORWARDS	Ht./Wt.	Place	Date	NHL exp.	1991-92 clubs
			BORN			
37	Don Barber (LW)	6-1/205	Victoria, B.C.	12-2-64	4	Winnipeg, Halifax (AHL), Quebec, San Jose
16	Perry Berezan (C)	6-2/190	Edmonton, Alta.	12-5-64	8	San Jose
15	David Bruce (LW)	5-11/190	Thunder Bay, Ont.	10-7-64	6	Kansas City (IHL), San Jose
33	Dale Craigwell (C)	5-11/180	Toronto	4-24-71	1	Kansas City (IHL), San Jose
8	Dean Evason (C)	5-10/180	Flin Flon, Man.	8-22-64	9	San Jose
17	Pat Falloon (RW)	5-11/192	Foxwarren, Man.	9-22-72	1	San Jose
10	Johan Garpenlov (LW)	5-11/185	Stockholm, Sweden	3-21-68	2	Adirondack (AHL), Detroit, San Jose
11	Kelly Kisio (C)	5-9/183	Peace River, Alta.	9-18-59	10	San Jose
40	Mikhail Kravets (LW)	5-10/182	Leningrad, U.S.S.R.	11-12-63	1	Kansas City (IHL), San Jose
9	Brian Lawton (C)	6-0/180	New Brunswick, N.J.	6-29-65	8	San Jose
19	Brian Mullen (RW)	5-10/180	New York	3-16-62	10	San Jose
36	Jeff Odgers (LW)	6-0/195	Spy Hill, Sask.	5-31-69	1	Kansas City (IHL), San Jose
28	J.F. Quintin (LW)	6-0/187	St. Jean, Que.	5-28-69	1	Kansas City (IHL), San Jose
18	Dave Snuggerud (LW)	6-0/170	Minnetonka, Minn.	6-20-66	3	Buffalo, San Jose
47	Mike Sullivan (C)	6-2/193	Marshfield, Mass.	2-28-68	1	Kansas City (IHL), San Jose
43	Ray Whitney (C)	5-9/160	Edmonton, Alta.	5-8-72	1	San Diego (IHL), San Jose
	DEFENSEMEN					
34	Michael Colman	6-3/218	Stoneham, Mass.	8-4-68	1	Kansas City (IHL), San Jose
23	Link Gaetz (LW)	6-2/223	Vancouver, B.C.	10-2-68	3	San Jose
13	Rick Lessard	6-2/206	Timmons, Ont.	1-9-68	3	Kansas City (IHL), San Jose
38	Pat MacLeod	5-11/190	Melfort, Sask.	6-15-69	2	Kansas City (IHL), San Jose
4	Jayson More	6-1/190	Souris, Man.	1-12-69	3	Kansas City (IHL), San Jose
	Sandis Ozolnich	6-1/189	Riga, U.S.S.R.	8-3-72	0	Riga (CIS), Kansas City (IHL)
	Mike Rathje	6-5/195	Manville, Alta.	5-11-74	0	Medicine Hat (WHL)
45	Claudio Scremin	6-2/200	Burnaby, B.C.	5-28-68	1	Kansas City (IHL), San Jose
	Michal Sykora	6-3/195	Pardubice, Czech.	7-5-73	0	Tacoma (WHL)
5	Neil Wilkinson	6-3/180	Selkirk, Man.	8-15-67	3	San Jose
3	David Williams	6-2/195	Plainfield, N.J.	8-25-67	1	Kansas City (IHL), San Jose
24	Doug Wilson	6-1/187	Ottawa	7-5-57	15	San Jose
2	Rob Zettler	6-3/195	Sept Iles, Que.	3-8-68	4	San Jose
	Doug Zmolek	6-1/195	Rochester, Minn.	11-3-70	0	U. of Minnesota
	GOALTENDERS					
31	Wade Flaherty	6-0/170	Terreace, B.C.	1-11-68	1	Kansas City (IHL), San Jose
30	Jeff Hackett	6-1/180	London, Ont.	6-1-68	3	San Jose
1	Brian Hayward	5-10/180	Georgetown, Ont.	6-25-60	10	Kansas City (IHL), San Jose
32	Arturs Irbe	5-7/180	Riga, U.S.S.R.	2-2-67	1	Kansas City (IHL), San Jose

1991-92 REVIEW

INDIVIDUAL STATISTICS

SCORING

	Games	G	A	Pts.	Pen.	+/-	PPG	SHG	Shots	Shooting Pct.
Pat Falloon	79	25	34	59	16	-32	5	0	181	13.8
Brian Mullen	72	18	28	46	66	-14	5	3	168	10.7
David Bruce	60	22	16	38	46	-20	10	1	137	16.1
Brian Lawton	59	15	22	37	42	-25	7	0	131	11.5
Kelly Kisio	48	11	26	37	54	-7	2	3	68	16.2
Doug Wilson	44	9	19	28	26	-38	4	0	123	7.3
David Williams	56	3	25	28	40	-13	2	0	91	3.3
Dean Evason	74	11	15	26	99	-22	1	0	88	12.5
Wayne Presley*	47	8	14	22	76	-29	3	0	114	7.0
Perry Berezan	66	12	7	19	30	-26	4	1	112	10.7
Mike Sullivan	64	8	11	19	15	-18	1	0	72	11.1
Neil Wilkinson	60	4	15	19	107	-11	1	0	95	4.2
Jay More	46	4	13	17	85	-32	1	0	60	6.7
Steve Bozek	58	8	8	16	27	-30	2	0	105	7.6
Dale Craigwell	32	5	11	16	8	-3	4	0	38	13.2
Pat MacLeod	37	5	11	16	4	-32	3	0	77	6.5
Paul Fenton	60	11	4	15	33	-39	3	2	96	11.5
Ken Hammond	46	5	10	15	82	-17	2	0	93	5.4
Link Gaetz	48	6	6	12	326	-27	3	0	73	8.2
Perry Anderson	48	4	8	12	143	-17	0	0	57	7.0
Tony Hrkac*	22	2	10	12	4	-2	0	0	31	6.5
Jeff Odgers	61	7	4	11	217	-21	0	0	64	10.9
Johan Garpenlov*	12	5	6	11	4	-2	1	0	21	23.8

	Games	G	A	Pts.	Pen.	+/-	PPG	SHG	Shots	Shooting Pct.
Rob Zettler	74	1	8	9	99	-23	0	0	72	1.4
Bob McGill*	62	3	1	4	70	-34	0	1	56	5.4
Don Barber*	12	1	3	4	2	-7	0	0	17	5.9
Jean-Francois Quintin	8	3	0	3	0	2	0	0	12	25.0
Ray Whitney	2	0	3	3	0	-1	0	0	4	0.0
Craig Coxe	10	2	0	2	19	-4	0	0	11	18.2
Rick Lessard	8	0	2	2	16	-4	0	0	4	0.0
Jeff Hackett (goalie)	42	0	2	2	8	0	0	0	0	0.0
Mike McHugh	8	1	0	1	14	-3	0	0	5	20.0
Mark Pavelich	2	0	1	1	4	-2	0	0	0	0.0
Kevin Evans	5	0	1	1	25	0	0	0	4	0.0
Dave Snuggerud*	11	0	1	1	4	-12	0	0	19	0.0
Arturs Irbe (goalie)	13	0	1	1	0	0	0	0	0	0.0
Michael Colman	15	0	1	1	32	-8	0	0	7	0.0
Jarmo Myllys (goalie)	27	0	1	1	2	0	0	0	0	0.0
Mikhail Kravets	1	0	0	0	0	0	0	0	2	0.0
Peter Lappin	1	0	0	0	0	0	0	0	2	0.0
Wade Flaherty (goalie)	3	0	0	0	0	0	0	0	0	0.0
John Carter	4	0	0	0	0	-2	0	0	5	0.0
Ed Courtenay	5	0	0	0	0	-6	0	0	7	0.0
Brian Hayward (goalie)	7	0	0	0	14	0	0	0	0	0.0
Claudio Scremin	13	0	0	0	25	-4	0	0	18	0.0

GOALTENDING

	Games	Min.	Goals	SO	Avg.	W	L	T	Shots	Sv. Pct.
Jeff Hackett	42	2314	148	0	3.84	11	27	1	1366	.892
Wade Flaherty	3	178	13	0	4.38	0	3	0	120	.892
Arturs Irbe	13	645	48	0	4.47	2	6	3	365	.868
Brian Hayward	7	305	25	0	4.92	1	4	0	177	.859
Jarmo Myllys	27	1374	115	0	5.02	3	18	1	862	.867

Empty-net goals (do not count against a goaltender's average): Myllys, 6; Flaherty, 2; Hackett, 1; Irbe, 1.
*Played with two or more NHL teams.

RESULTS

OCTOBER

4—At Vancouver	L	3-4
5—Vancouver	L	2-5
8—Calgary	W	4-3
10—Winnipeg	L	4-5
12—At St. Louis	L	3-6
13—At Chicago	L	3-7
16—At Los Angeles	L	5-8
17—Minnesota	L	2-8
19—Boston	L	1-4
23—At Hartford	L	0-3
25—At Buffalo	L	1-3
26—At New Jersey	L	0-9
29—At N.Y. Islanders	L	4-8
31—At Philadelphia	L	2-5

NOVEMBER

2—At Quebec	L	3-6
4—At Toronto	L	1-4
8—Edmonton	W	6-2
9—N.Y. Islanders	W	4-3
12—Buffalo	L	1-7
14—Detroit	T	*3-3
16—At Vancouver	L	0-1
19—Los Angeles	L	*2-3
22—Toronto	L	1-3
23—At Los Angeles	L	4-6
26—Vancouver	W	4-1
29—At Edmonton	T	*4-4
30—At Calgary	W	2-1

DECEMBER

3—Los Angeles	W	*3-2
5—Pittsburgh	L	0-8
8—At Edmonton	L	1-3
10—Winnipeg	T	*3-3
12—Edmonton	W	6-3
14—Minnesota	L	2-3
16—At N.Y. Rangers	L	*3-4
17—At Pittsburgh	L	2-10
19—At St. Louis	L	0-4
21—Quebec	W	4-1
26—At Los Angeles	L	3-5
28—Vancouver	L	2-3

JANUARY

3—Philadelphia	W	3-1
4—Montreal	L	*0-1
7—At Vancouver	L	1-4
8—At Calgary	L	3-10
11—At Minnesota	L	4-7
12—At Winnipeg	W	4-3
14—At Los Angeles	T	*3-3
21—At Edmonton	L	2-9
24—Calgary	L	2-3
25—Edmonton	W	5-2
28—N.Y. Rangers	L	2-4
30—St. Louis	L	2-4

FEBRUARY

2—At Winnipeg	L	0-6
4—Hartford	W	6-5
5—Chicago	W	5-2

9—At Washington	L	2-6
12—At Montreal	L	1-6
14—At Buffalo	L	6-7
15—At Detroit	L	1-11
18—Washington	L	2-4
21—Vancouver	L	3-5
23—Calgary	L	2-4
26—Quebec	W	7-4
28—Montreal	T	*3-3

MARCH

1—Philadelphia	L	0-1
4—Los Angeles	L	3-4
6—Pittsburgh	L	3-7
8—Toronto	W	4-1
10—At Chicago	L	1-5
11—At Winnipeg	L	0-3
14—New Jersey	W	3-2
17—Detroit	L	4-5
19—At Calgary	L	1-3
21—At Hartford	W	5-4
23—At Boston	L	6-7
24—At New Jersey	L	3-4
26—At N.Y. Islanders	L	4-7
29—At Winnipeg	L	5-6

APRIL

12—At Edmonton	L	4-6
15—Calgary	L	3-4
16—Winnipeg	L	3-5

*Denotes overtime game.

TAMPA BAY LIGHTNING
CAMPBELL CONFERENCE/NORRIS DIVISION

1992-93 SCHEDULE

OCTOBER

S	M	T	W	T	F	S
4	5	6	7 CHI H	8	9	10 MIN
11 CHI	12	13 STL	14	15 TOR	16 BUF	17
18	19	20 EDM H	21	22 TOR H	23	24 QUE H
25	26	27 QUE	28 MON	29	30 SJ H	31

NOVEMBER

S	M	T	W	T	F	S
1 PIT H	2	3 STL H	4	5	6 WAS H	7 NYI
8 NYR	9	10	11 DET H	12	13 OTT H	14 CAL H
15	16	17 WIN H	18	19 MIN H	20	21 STL
22	23 DET	24 TOR	25	26	27 CAL	28 EDM
29	30					

DECEMBER

S	M	T	W	T	F	S
		1	2	3	4	5 DET H
6	7 NYI H	8	9	10	11 NYR H	12 EDM H
13	14	15 LA	16 SJ	17	18 NJ H	19
20	21	22 PHI H	23 HAR H	24	25	26
27	28	29	30	31 CHI		

JANUARY

S	M	T	W	T	F	S
					1	2 EDM H
3 VAN	4	5	6 LA	7	8	9 MIN
10 TOR	11	12	13 DET	14	15	16 STL H
17 WAS H	18	19 MIN H	20	21 TOR H	22	23 SJ H
24 MIN H	25	26	27	28 STL H	29	30 MIN
31						

FEBRUARY

S	M	T	W	T	F	S
	1 SJ	2	3 VAN	4	5	6 *
7	8	9 TOR H	10	11 MIN H	12	13
14 BOS H	15	16	17 DET	18	19 TOR	20
21	22 LA H	23	24	25 CHI H	26	27 D PIT
28						

MARCH

S	M	T	W	T	F	S
	1	2	3 MON H	4	5	6 CAL H
7	8	9 WIN H	10	11	12 TOR	13
14 D WIN	15	16 HAR H	17	18 TOR H	19	20 D BUF H
21 CHI	22	23 NJ	24	25 OTT	26	27 DET H
28	29	30	31			

APRIL

S	M	T	W	T	F	S
				1 VAN H	2	3 D PHI
4	5	6 STL H	7	8 DET H	9	10 D CHI H
11 D CHI	12	13 WIN	14	15 STL	16	17

1992-93 SEASON

CLUB DIRECTORY

Pres., Lightning Partners, Ltd.
Yoshio Nakamura
Governor
David LeFevre
Pres., general manager and alt. gov.
Phil Esposito
Executive V.P., treasurer and alt. gov.
Mel Lowell
Vice president, secretary
Henry Paul
General partner representative
Chris Phillips
Director of hockey operations
Tony Esposito
Head coach
Terry Crisp
Assistant coach
Wayne Cashman
Chief financial officer
Mark Anderson
Accounting manager
Vincent Ascanio
Vice president, communications
Gerry Helper
Media relations manager
Barry Hanrahan
Vice president, sales and marketing
Steve Donner

Director of promotions
Carrie Esposito
Director of corporate sales
Anne Webb
Director of sales
Jon Swensson
Director of merchandising
Kevin Murphy
Director of season subscriptions
Jackie Staney
Head scout
John Chapman
Scouting staff
Angelo Bumbacco
Jacques Campeau
Jake Goertzen
Doug Macauley
Don Murdoch
Richard Rose
Jonathan Sparrow
Luke Williams
Head trainer
Skip Thayer
Assistant trainer
John Forristall
Equipment manager
Jocko Cayer

DRAFT CHOICES

Rnd.	Player	Ht./Wt.	Overall	Pos.	1991-92 club
1	Roman Hamrlik	6-2/189	1	D	ZPS Zlin, Czech.
2	Drew Bannister	6-1/193	26	D	Sault Ste. Marie (OHL)
3	Brent Gretzky	5-10/160	49	C	Belleville (OHL)
4	Aaron Gavey	6-1/169	74	C	Sault Ste. Marie (OHL)
5	Brantt Myhres	6-3/195	97	RW	Lethbridge (WHL)
6	Martin Tanguay	5-11/185	122	C	Verdun (QMJHL)
7	Derek Wilkinson	6-0/160	145	G	Detroit (OHL)
8	Dennis Maxwell	6-0/188	170	C	Niagara Falls (OHL)
9	Andrew Kemper	6-2/186	193	D	Seattle (WHL)
10	Marc Tardif	6-1/199	218	LW	Shawinigan (QMJHL)
11	Tom MacDonald	5-11/190	241	C	Sault Ste. Marie (OHL)

MISCELLANEOUS DATA

Home ice (capacity)
Expo Hall at
Florida State Fairgrounds (10,400)
Address
501 East Kennedy Blvd.
Tampa, Fla. 33602
Business phone
813-229-2658

Rink dimensions
192 feet by 85 feet
Club colors
Black, blue, silver and white
Minor league affiliations
Atlanta (IHL)

SCHEDULE KEY

*All-Star Game at Montreal.
H—Home game.   D—Day game (any game starting before 4 p.m.).
NOTE: At press time, two games at neutral sites had yet to be announced.

| | | TRAINING CAMP ROSTER | | |

No.	FORWARDS	Ht./Wt.	Place	BORN Date	NHL exp.	1991-92 clubs
	Mikael Andersson (LW) .	5-11/185	Malmo, Sweden	5-10-66	7	Hartford
	Jean Blouin..................	6-0/195	Montreal	2-26-71	0	Laval (QMJHL)
	Tim Bergland (RW)	6-3/194	Crookston, Minn.	1-11-65	3	Baltimore (AHL), Washington
	Brian Bradley (C)	5-10/177	Kitchener, Ont.	1-21-65	7	Toronto
	Jock Callander (RW).....	6-1/188	Regina, Sask.	4-23-61	4	Muskegon (IHL)
	Danton Cole (RW)	5-11/189	Pontiac, Mich.	1-10-67	3	Winnipeg
	Rob DiMaio (C)	5-10/190	Calgary, Alta.	2-19-68	4	N.Y. Islanders
	Brent Gretzky (C)	5-11/160	Brantford, Ont.	2-20-72	0	Belleville (OHL)
	Mike Hartman (LW)	6-0/192	W. Bloomfield, Mich.	2-7-67	6	Winnipeg
	Darin Kimble (RW)	6-2/205	Lucky Lake, Sask.	11-22-68	4	St. Louis
	Chris Kontos.................	6-1/195	Toronto	12-10-63	7	Can. Nat. Team
	Jason Lafreniere (C)	5-11/185	St. Catharines, Ont.	12-6-66	3	San Diego (IHL), Germany
	Steve Maltais (LW)	6-2/210	Arvida, Ont.	1-25-69	3	Halifax (AHL), Kalamazoo (IHL), Minnesota
	Basil McRae (LW)	6-2/205	Beaverton, Ont.	1-5-61	11	Minnesota
	Michel Mongeau (C)......	5-9/190	Nun's Island, Que.	2-9-65	3	Peoria (IHL), St. Louis
	Keith Osborne (RW)	6-1/180	Toronto	4-2-69	1	St. John's (AHL)
	Anatoli Semenov (LW) ...	6-2/190	Moscow, U.S.S.R.	3-5-62	3	Edmonton
	Martin Simard (RW)......	6-3/215	Montreal	6-25-66	2	Halifax (AHL), Salt Lake City (IHL), Calgary
	Shayne Stevenson..........	6-1/190	Newmarket, Ont.	10-26-70	2	Maine (AHL), Boston
	John Tucker	6-0/200	Windsor, Ont.	9-29-64	8	Asiago (Italy)
	Steve Tuttle (RW)	6-1/200	Vancouver, B.C.	1-5-66	3	Peoria (IHL)
	Dan Vincelette (LW)	6-2/202	Verdun, Que.	8-1-67	6	Indianapolis (IHL), Chicago
	Rob Zamuner (LW/C) ...	6-2/202	Oakville, Ont.	9-17-69	1	Binghamton (AHL), N.Y. Rangers
	DEFENSEMEN					
	Drew Bannister	6-1/195	Belleville, Ont.	9-4-74	0	Sault Ste. Marie (OHL)
	Marc Bergevin	6-0/185	Montreal	8-11-65	8	Hartford
	Jeff Bloemberg	6-0/205	Listowel, Ont.	1-31-68	2	Binghamton (AHL), N.Y. Rangers
	Shawn Chambers	6-2/200	Royal Oaks, Mich.	10-11-66	5	Baltimore (AHL), Washington
	Doug Crossman	6-2/190	Peterborough, Ont.	6-30-60	12	Detroit
	Roman Hamrlik............	6-2/189	Gottwaldov, Czech.	4-12-74	0	ZPS Zlin (Czech.)
	Bob McGill	6-1/193	Edmonton, Alta.	4-27-62	11	San Jose, Detroit
	Rob Ramage	6-2/205	Byron, Ont.	1-11-59	13	Minnesota
	Joe Reekie	6-3/215	Victoria, B.C.	2-22-65	7	Capital District (AHL), N.Y. Islanders
	Stephane Richer	6-2/212	Hull, Que.	4-28-66	0	Fredericton (AHL)
	Rob Robinson	6-1/214	St. Catharines, Ont.	4-19-67	1	Peoria (IHL), St. Louis
	Peter Taglianetti	6-2/195	Framingham, Mass.	8-15-63	8	Pittsburgh
	GOALTENDERS					
	Jean-Claude Bergeron...	6-2/192	Havreziue, Que.	10-14-68	1	Fredericton (AHL), Peoria (IHL)
	Mike Greenlay	6-3/200	Vitoria, Brazil	9-15-68	1	Cape Breton (AHL), Knoxville (ECHL)
	Pat Jablonski................	6-0/178	Toledo, O.	6-20-67	3	Peoria (IHL), St. Louis
	Wendell Young	5-8/181	Halifax, N.S.	8-1-63	7	Pittsburgh

FIRST-YEAR RECORDS OF NHL EXPANSION TEAMS

(Ranked by points)

Team	Season	Games	W.	L.	T.	Pts.	Division, Conference
Philadelphia Flyers.........................	1967-68	74	31	32	11	73	West Division
Hartford Whalers*	1979-80	80	27	34	19	73	Norris Division, Wales Conference
Los Angeles Kings...........................	1967-68	74	31	33	10	72	West Division
St. Louis Blues.............................	1967-68	74	27	31	16	70	West Division
Minnesota North Stars......................	1967-68	74	27	32	15	69	West Division
Edmonton Oilers*	1979-80	80	28	39	13	69	Smythe Division, Campbell Conference
Pittsburgh Penguins........................	1967-68	74	27	34	13	67	West Division
Atlanta Flames†............................	1972-73	78	25	38	15	65	West Division
Buffalo Sabres.............................	1970-71	78	24	39	15	63	East Division
Quebec Nordiques*	1979-80	80	25	44	11	61	Adams Division, Wales Conference
Vancouver Canucks.........................	1970-71	78	24	46	8	56	East Division
Winnipeg Jets*.............................	1979-80	80	20	49	11	51	Smythe Division, Campbell Conference
Oakland Seals‡.............................	1967-68	74	15	42	17	47	West Division
Kansas City Scouts§........................	1974-75	80	15	54	11	41	Smythe Division, Campbell Conference
San Jose Sharks............................	1991-92	80	17	58	5	39	Smythe Division, Campbell Conference
New York Islanders.........................	1972-73	78	12	60	6	30	East Division
Washington Capitals........................	1974-75	80	8	67	5	21	Norris Division, Wales Conference

*Entered NHL during a merger with the World Hockey Association.
†Became Calgary Flames after 1979-80 season.
‡Became Cleveland Barons after 1975-76 season; Barons merged with Minnesota North Stars after 1977-78 season.
§Became Colorado Rockies after 1975-76 season; became New Jersey Devils after 1981-82 season.

TORONTO MAPLE LEAFS
CAMPBELL CONFERENCE /NORRIS DIVISION

1992-93 SCHEDULE

OCTOBER
S	M	T	W	T	F	S
4	5	6	7 WAS H	8	9	10 CAL
11 EDM	12	13	14	15 TB H	16	17 CHI H
18 MIN H	19	20	21	22 TB	23	24 SJ H
25	26	27	28 BUF H	29	30 DET	31 DET H

NOVEMBER
S	M	T	W	T	F	S
1	2	3	4	5 CHI	6	7 PIT H
8	9 OTT	10	11	12	13	14 BOS
15	16 STL H	17	18	19 SJ	20	21 LA
22	23	24 TB H	25	26 QUE H	27	28 LA H
29	30					

DECEMBER
S	M	T	W	T	F	S
		1	2 NJ	3 CHI	4	5 CHI H
6 NYR	7	8	9 DET H	10	11 CAL H	12
13	14	15 MIN	16	17	18	19 OTT H
20 BUF	21	22 DET	23	24	25	26 DET H
27 STL	28	29 NYI	30	31 PIT		

JANUARY
S	M	T	W	T	F	S
					1	2 STL H
3	4 DET	5	6 VAN H	7	8 SJ H	9 MON
10	11 TB H	12	13 STL H	14	15	16 CHI H
17 CHI	18	19 STL	20	21 TB	22	23 MON H
24	25	26 MIN H	27	28	29	30 NYR H
31						

FEBRUARY
S	M	T	W	T	F	S
	1 STL	2	3 NYI H	4	5	6 *
7	8	9 TB	10	11 VAN H	12	13 MIN H
14 MIN	15	16	17 CAL H	18	19 TB	20 BOS H
21 VAN	22	23	24	25 SJ	26	27 LA
28						

MARCH
S	M	T	W	T	F	S
	1	2	3 MIN H	4	5 DET	6 WIN H
7	8	9 WAS	10 HAR H	11	12 TB H	13
14	15 QUE	16	17	18 TB	19	20 EDM H
21	22	23 WIN	24	25 MIN	26	27 EDM
28 CAL	29	30	31 LA H			

APRIL
S	M	T	W	T	F	S
				1 PHI	2	3 NJ H
4	5	6	7	8 WIN	9	10 PHI H
11 HAR	12	13 STL H	14	15 CHI	16	17

1992-93 SEASON

CLUB DIRECTORY

Chairman of the board and CEO
Steve A. Stavro
President, COO and general manager
Cliff Fletcher
Secretary-treasurer
J. Donald Crump
Alternate governor
Cliff Fletcher
Alternate governor and counsel
Brian P. Bellmore
Dir. of bus. operations and communications
Bob Stellick
Special consultant to the president
Darryl Sittler
Director of pro scouting
Floyd Smith
Director of player development
Tom Watt
Coach
Pat Burns
Assistant coaches
Mike Kitchen
Mike Murphy
Director of scouting
Pierre Dorion
Scouts
George Armstrong
Dick Duff
Anders Hedberg

Peter Johnson
Garth Malarchuk
Dan Marr
Jim Bzdel
Jack Gardiner
Bob Johnson
Doug Woods
Dick Bouchard
Public relations coordinator
Pat Park
Public relations assistant
Mark Hillier
Athletic therapist
Chris Broadhurst
Trainers
Dan Lemelin
Brian Papineau
Controller
Ian Clarke
Director of marketing and advertising
Bill Cluff
Box office manager
Irwin "Patty" Patoff
Team doctors
Dr. Michael Clarfield
Dr. Darrell Olgilvie-Harris
Dr. Leith Douglas
Dr. Michael Easterbrook
Dr. Simon McGrail

DRAFT CHOICES

Rnd. Player	Ht./Wt.	Overall	Pos.	1991-92 club
1—Brandon Convery....	6-0/180	8	F	Sudbury (OHL)
1—Grant Marshall........	6-1/185	23	RW	Ottawa (OHL)
4—Nikolai Borschevsky..	5-9/180	77	F	Spartak, CIS
4—Mark Raiter	6-4/220	95	D	Saskatoon (WHL)
5—Janne Gronvall........	6-3/187	101	D	Lukko, Finland
5—Chris Deruiter	6-2/190	106	RW	Kingston (OHL)
6—Mikael Hakansson..	6-1/176	125	D	NACKA, Sweden
7—Patrik Augusta		149	RW	Dukla Jihlava, Czech.
8—R. Vandenbussche...	5-11/184	173	RW	Cornwall (OHL)
9—Wayne Clarke	6-2/175	197	RW	RPI (ECAC)
10—Sergei Simonov	6-1/183	221	D	Kristall Saratov, CIS
11—Nathan Dempsey	6-0/160	245	D	Regina (WHL)

MISCELLANEOUS DATA

Home ice (capacity)
Maple Leafs Garden
(15,842, including standees)
Address
60 Carlton Street
Toronto, Ont. M5B 1L1
Business phone
416-977-1641

Rink dimensions
200 feet by 85 feet
Club colors
Blue and white
Minor league affiliation
St. John's (AHL)

SCHEDULE KEY
*All-Star Game at Montreal.
H—Home game.   D—Day game (any game starting before 4 p.m.).
NOTE: At press time, two games at neutral sites had yet to be announced.

No.	FORWARDS	Ht./Wt.	Place —BORN—	Date	NHL exp.	1991-92 clubs
10	Glenn Anderson (RW) ...	6-1/190	Vancouver, B.C.	10-2-60	12	Toronto
8	Ken Baumgartner	6-0/200	Flin Flon, Man.	3-11-66	5	N.Y. Islanders, Toronto
	Nikolai Borschevsky.......	5-9/180	Tomsk, U.S.S.R.	1-12-65	0	Spartak Moscow (CIS)
14	Rob Cimetta (LW)	6-0/190	Toronto	2-15-70	4	St. John's (AHL), Toronto
17	Wendel Clark (LW)	5-11/194	Kelvington, Sask.	10-25-66	7	Toronto
	Michael Eastwood (C)	6-2/190	Cornwall, Ont.	7-1-67	1	St. John's (AHL), Toronto
71	Mike Foligno (RW)	6-2/200	Sudbury, Ont.	1-29-59	13	Toronto
93	Doug Gilmour (C)	5-11/164	Kingston, Ont.	6-25-63	9	Calgary, Toronto
	Todd Hawkins (RW)......	6-1/195	Kingston, Ont.	8-2-66	3	St. John's (AHL), Toronto
	Greg Johnston (RW/C).	6-1/190	Barrie, Ont.	1-14-65	9	St. John's (AHL), Toronto
26	Mike Krushelnyski (C)....	6-2/200	Montreal	4-27-60	11	Toronto
11	Guy Larose (C/LW)	5-10/175	Hull, Que.	7-31-67	3	Binghamton (AHL), St. John's (AHL), Toronto
18	Kent Manderville (LW) .	6-3/195	Edmonton, Alta.	4-12-71	1	Can. Nat./Olym., Toronto
	Kevin McClelland (RW) ..	6-2/205	Oshawa, Ont.	7-4-62	11	St. John's (AHL), Toronto
7	David McLlwain (RW)	6-0/190	Seaforth, Ont.	1-9-67	5	Winnipeg, Buffalo, N.Y. Islanders, Toronto
	Ken McRae (C)	6-1/195	Finch, Ont.	4-23-68	5	Halifax (AHL), Quebec
21	Mark Osborne (LW)	6-2/200	Toronto	8-13-61	11	Winnipeg, Toronto
12	Rob Pearson (RW)	6-1/180	Oshawa, Ont.	8-3-71	1	St. John's (AHL), Toronto
24	David Sacco (C)	6-0/190	Medford, Mass.	7-31-70	0	Boston U. (Hockey East)
	Joe Sacco (LW)	6-1/180	Medford, Mass.	2-4-69	2	U.S. Nat./Olym., Toronto
	Dave Tomlinson (C)	5-11/180	North Vancouver, B.C.	5-8-68	1	St. John's (AHL), Toronto
25	Peter Zezel (C)	5-11/200	Toronto	4-22-65	8	Toronto
	DEFENSEMEN					
	Drake Berehowsky	6-1/211	Toronto	1-3-72	2	North Bay (OHL), Toronto
4	Dave Ellett	6-2/200	Cleveland	3-30-64	8	Toronto
23	Todd Gill......................	6-0/185	Brockville, Ont.	11-9-65	8	Toronto
33	Bob Halkidis	6-0/200	Toronto	3-5-66	8	Toronto
34	Jamie Macoun	6-2/200	Newmarket, Ont.	8-17-61	10	Calgary, Toronto
15	Dimitri Mironov	6-2/191	Moscow, U.S.S.R.	12-25-65	1	Soviet Wings (CIS), Unified Olym., Toronto
2	Ric Nattress..................	6-2/208	Hamilton, Ont.	5-25-62	10	Calgary, Toronto
3	Bob Rouse	6-2/210	Surrey, B.C.	6-18-64	9	Toronto
28	Darryl Shannon	6-2/195	Barrie, Ont.	6-21-68	4	Toronto
	GOALTENDERS					
31	Grant Fuhr	5-10/181	Spruce Grove, Alta.	9-28-62	11	Toronto
29	Felix Potvin	6-0/185	Anjou, Que.	6-23-71	1	St. John's (AHL), Toronto
	Damian Rhodes	6-0/170	St. Paul, Minn.	5-28-69	1	St. John's (AHL)
30	Rick Wamsley	5-11/185	Simcoe, Ont.	5-25-59	12	Calgary, Toronto

1991-92 REVIEW

INDIVIDUAL STATISTICS

SCORING

	Games	G	A	Pts.	Pen.	+/-	PPG	SHG	Shots	Shooting Pct.
Glenn Anderson	72	24	33	57	100	-13	5	0	188	12.8
Dave Ellett	79	18	33	51	95	-13	9	1	225	8.0
Peter Zezel	64	16	33	49	26	-22	4	0	125	12.8
Doug Gilmour*	40	15	34	49	32	13	6	0	104	14.4
Wendel Clark..............................	43	19	21	40	123	-14	7	0	158	12.0
Brian Bradley.............................	59	10	21	31	48	-3	4	0	78	12.8
Mike Bullard...............................	65	14	14	28	42	-19	7	0	140	10.0
Dan Marois*	63	15	11	26	76	-36	4	0	140	10.7
Rob Pearson	47	14	10	24	58	-16	6	0	79	17.7
Mike Krushelnyski.......................	72	9	15	24	72	-5	0	2	100	9.0
Bob Rouse..................................	79	3	19	22	97	-20	1	0	115	2.6
Gary Leeman*	34	7	13	20	44	-1	3	0	91	7.7
Lucien DeBlois*	54	8	11	19	39	-3	0	1	75	10.7
Todd Gill....................................	74	2	15	17	91	-22	1	0	82	2.4
Jamie Macoun*	39	3	13	16	18	0	2	0	71	4.2
Ric Nattress*	36	2	14	16	32	-1	0	0	43	4.7
Claude Loiselle*	64	6	9	15	102	-21	1	0	91	6.6
Guy Larose	34	9	5	14	27	-8	0	0	60	15.0
Mike Foligno	33	6	8	14	50	-3	2	0	41	14.6
Michel Petit*	34	1	13	14	85	-17	1	0	61	1.6
Craig Berube*	40	5	7	12	109	-2	1	0	42	11.9

	Games	G	A	Pts.	Pen.	+/-	PPG	SHG	Shots	Shooting Pct.
Joe Sacco	17	7	4	11	4	8	0	0	40	17.5
Darryl Shannon	48	2	8	10	23	-17	1	0	50	4.0
Alexander Godynyuk*	31	3	6	9	59	-12	1	0	30	10.0
Rob Cimetta	24	4	3	7	12	5	0	0	31	12.9
Bob Halkidis	46	3	3	6	145	-9	0	0	36	8.3
Mark Osborne*	11	3	1	4	8	-2	0	2	16	18.8
Dave Hannan*	35	2	2	4	16	-10	0	1	24	8.3
Tom Fergus*	11	1	3	4	4	-11	0	0	24	4.2
Kent Manderville	15	0	4	4	0	1	0	0	14	0.0
Dave McLlwain*	11	1	2	3	4	1	0	0	12	8.3
Mike Eastwood	9	0	2	2	4	-4	0	0	6	0.0
Dimitri Mironov	7	1	0	1	0	-4	0	0	7	14.3
Kevin Maguire	8	1	0	1	4	-4	0	0	8	12.5
Greg Johnston	3	0	1	1	5	-1	0	0	2	0.0
Kevin McClelland	18	0	1	1	33	-3	0	0	5	0.0
Grant Fuhr (goalie)	65	0	1	1	4	0	0	0	0	0.0
Drake Berehowsky	1	0	0	0	0	0	0	0	0	0.0
Leonard Esau	2	0	0	0	0	0	0	0	0	0.0
Todd Hawkins	2	0	0	0	0	0	0	0	0	0.0
Ken Linseman	2	0	0	0	2	-2	0	0	0	0.0
Dave Tomlinson	3	0	0	0	2	-1	0	0	6	0.0
Felix Potvin (goalie)	4	0	0	0	0	0	0	0	0	0.0
Jeff Reese (goalie)*	8	0	0	0	0	0	0	0	0	0.0
Rick Wamsley (goalie)*	8	0	0	0	0	0	0	0	0	0.0
Ken Baumgartner*	11	0	0	0	23	1	0	0	5	0.0

GOALTENDING

	Games	Min.	Goals	SO	Avg.	W	L	T	Shots	Sv. Pct.
Felix Potvin	4	210	8	0	2.29	0	2	1	120	.933
Jeff Reese*	8	413	20	1	2.91	1	5	1	210	.905
Grant Fuhr	65	3774	†230	2	3.66	25	†33	5	1933	.881
Rick Wamsley*	8	428	27	0	3.79	4	3	0	218	.876

Empty-net goals (do not count against a goaltender's average): Fuhr, 7; Potvin, 1; Reese, 1.
*Played with two or more NHL teams.
†Led league.

RESULTS

OCTOBER

3—At Montreal	L	3-4	
5—Detroit	W	8-5	
7—St. Louis	W	3-0	
9—Washington	L	4-5	
12—Vancouver	L	1-2	
15—At St. Louis	L	1-5	
17—At Calgary	L	4-6	
19—At Winnipeg	L	2-4	
21—At Vancouver	L	1-4	
25—At Detroit	L	0-4	
26—Detroit	W	6-1	
28—St. Louis	T	*1-1	

NOVEMBER

1—At Washington	L	0-4	
2—Los Angeles	L	2-5	
4—San Jose	W	4-1	
6—Minnesota	W	4-3	
8—At N.Y. Rangers	T	*3-3	
9—Calgary	L	1-6	
12—At Minnesota	L	0-7	
14—At Chicago	L	0-3	
16—Chicago	T	*2-2	
17—Hartford	L	1-3	
20—At St. Louis	L	2-5	
22—At San Jose	W	3-1	
26—At Los Angeles	T	*4-4	
29—At Minnesota	W	3-2	
30—Minnesota	L	3-4	

DECEMBER

4—At Hartford	W	3-0	
7—Vancouver	W	6-3	
9—Montreal	L	1-4	
11—N.Y. Islanders	L	4-5	
12—At Philadelphia	T	*1-1	
14—At Boston	L	5-7	
18—Edmonton	L	5-7	
20—At Washington	L	3-4	
21—Buffalo	L	1-4	
23—Winnipeg	W	3-1	
26—At Pittsburgh	L	1-12	
28—Detroit	L	4-5	
30—At Quebec	L	2-5	

JANUARY

3—At Detroit	L	4-6	
4—Chicago	L	2-4	
6—St. Louis	W	*3-2	
9—At Chicago	L	0-2	
11—At New Jersey	W	4-3	
16—At Chicago	L	0-4	
22—Boston	L	2-5	
23—At N.Y. Islanders	W	4-3	
25—Philadelphia	W	6-4	
29—Quebec	W	5-2	

FEBRUARY

1—New Jersey	W	6-4	
3—At Minnesota	L	2-4	
5—Minnesota	W	*3-2	

7—At Detroit	W	4-3	
8—Montreal	W	6-4	
11—Detroit	W	4-3	
15—Winnipeg	L	1-3	
16—Edmonton	W	7-5	
18—At Pittsburgh	L	1-7	
20—At Detroit	L	2-3	
22—At St. Louis	L	3-4	
25—New Jersey	T	*5-5	
27—At Boston	L	2-4	
29—Chicago	W	*6-5	

MARCH

1—Minnesota	W	6-2	
4—At Edmonton	W	5-2	
5—At Calgary	T	*5-5	
8—At San Jose	L	1-4	
9—At Los Angeles	L	1-4	
11—At Minnesota	W	3-0	
14—Pittsburgh	W	6-3	
17—Quebec	W	*4-3	
21—Chicago	L	1-3	
23—St. Louis	W	3-2	
25—At Buffalo	L	2-5	
28—At St. Louis	W	3-2	
29—At Chicago	L	1-5	

APRIL

12—N.Y. Islanders	L	2-6	
13—At Philadelphia	L	2-6	
14—N.Y. Rangers	W	4-2	

*Denotes overtime game.

VANCOUVER CANUCKS
CAMPBELL CONFERENCE/SMYTHE DIVISION

1992-93 SCHEDULE

OCTOBER
S	M	T	W	T	F	S
4	5	6 EDM	7	8	9	10 EDM H
11	12 WIN H	13	14	15	16 WIN	17
18 CHI	19	20 PIT	21	22 PHI	23	24
25 D	26	27	28 WAS H	29	30 MIN H	31
BOS H						

NOVEMBER
S	M	T	W	T	F	S
1	2 CAL	3	4 CAL H	5	6 OTT H	7
8 D WIN H	9	10 SJ H	11	12 LA	13	14 SJ
15	16 LA H	17	18 EDM H	19 CAL	20	21 EDM H
22	23 CHI H	24	25 MIN	26 STL	27	28 MON
29	30					

DECEMBER
S	M	T	W	T	F	S
		1	2	3 EDM H	4	5
6	7 STL H	8	9 SJ H	10	11	12
13 QUE H	14	15	16 EDM	17	18 SJ H	19 SJ
20	21	22 LA	23	24	25	26
27 MON H	28	29 SJ H	30	31 LA H		

JANUARY
S	M	T	W	T	F	S
					1	2 SJ
3 TB H	4	5	6 TOR	7	8 DET	9 NYI
10	11 NYR	12 NJ	13	14	15 BUF H	16 HAR H
17	18	19 PIT H	20	21 LA	22	23 D MIN
24 CHI	25	26	27 CHI H	28	29	30 DET H
31						

FEBRUARY
S	M	T	W	T	F	S
	1 MIN H	2	3 TB H	4	5	6 ★
7	8	9 QUE	10	11 TOR	12 BUF	13
14 LA	15 D	16	17	18 PHI H	19	20 WIN H
21	22 TOR H	23	24 NYR H	25	26 WIN	27
28						

MARCH
S	M	T	W	T	F	S
	1	2 WAS	3	4 BOS	5	6 HAR
7	8	9 NJ H	10	11 WIN	12	13
14 CAL	15	16	17	18 WIN H	19	20 NYI H
21	22 STL H	23	24 LA H	25	26 CAL H	27
28	29	30 STL	31			

APRIL
S	M	T	W	T	F	S
				1	2 TB	3 D DET
4 OTT	5	6	7 EDM H	8	9 CAL	10
11 CAL H	12 D	13 LA H	14	15 LA	16	17

1992-93 SEASON

CLUB DIRECTORY

Chairman of the board
Frank A. Griffiths
Vice chairman and governor
Arthur R. Griffiths
President, general manager, head coach
Pat Quinn
V.P./Dir. of marketing and communications
Glen Ringdal
Vice president of finance and administration
Carlos Mascarenhas
Director of media and public relations
Steve Tambellini
Director of hockey operations
George McPhee
Director of player personnel
Mike Penny
Director of hockey information
Steve Frost
Public relations assistant
Gail Nishi
Assistant coaches
Rick Ley
Stan Smyl
Ron Wilson

Strength coach
Wayne Wilson
Director of amateur scouting
Mike Penny
Director of pro scouting
Murray Oliver
Scouts
Ron Delorme
Jack McCartan
Noel Price
Ken Slater
Paul McIntosh
Ed McColgan
Scott Carter
Jack Birch
Dir. of special events and ticket operations
Lynn Harrison
Medical trainer
Larry Ashley
Equipment trainer
Pat O'Neill
Team doctors
Dr. Ross Davidson
Dr. David Lawson

DRAFT CHOICES

Rnd. Player	Ht./Wt.	Overall	Pos.	1991-92 club
1—Libor Polasek	6-3/198	21	C	TJ Vikovice, Czech.
2—Mike Peca	5-11/163	40	C	Ottawa (OHL)
2—Michael Fountain	6-0/176	45	G	Oshawa (OHL)
3—Jeff Connolly	6-0/185	69	C	St. Sebastian HS, Needham, Mass.
4—Brent Tully	6-3/184	93	D	Peterborough (OHL)
5—Brian Loney	6-1/195	110	RW	Ohio State (CCHA)
5—Adrian Aucoin	6-1/194	117	D	Boston U. (Hockey East)
6—Jason Clark	6-0/180	141	C	St. Thomas (Junior B)
7—Scott Hollis	5-11/183	165	RW	Kingston (OHL)
9—Sonny Mignacca	5-8/178	213	G	Medicine Hat (WHL)
10—Mark Wotton	5-11/187	237	D	Saskatoon (WHL)
11—Aaron Boh	6-2/177	261	D	Spokane (WHL)

MISCELLANEOUS DATA

Home ice (capacity)
Pacific Coliseum (16,123)
Address
100 North Renfrew St.
Vancouver, B.C. V5K 3N7
Business phone
604-254-5141

Rink dimensions
200 feet by 85 feet
Club colors
White, black, red and gold
Minor league affiliation
Milwaukee (IHL)

SCHEDULE KEY
*All-Star Game at Montreal.
H—Home game.   D—Day game (any game starting before 4 p.m.).
NOTE: At press time, two games at neutral sites had yet to be announced.

TRAINING CAMP ROSTER

No.	FORWARDS	Ht./Wt.	Place (BORN)	Date	NHL exp.	1991-92 clubs
8	Greg Adams (LW)	6-3/198	Nelson, B.C.	8-1-63	8	Vancouver
31	Shawn Antoski (LW)	6-4/245	Brantford, Ont.	5-25-70	2	Milwaukee (IHL), Vancouver
	Cam Brown	6-1/210	Saskatoon, Sask.	5-15-69	1	Columbus (ECHL), Milwaukee (IHL)
10	Pavel Bure (LW)	5-9/170	Moscow, U.S.S.R.	3-31-71	1	Vancouver
14	Geoff Courtnall (LW)	6-1/190	Victoria, B.C.	8-18-62	9	Vancouver
15	Tom Fergus (C)	6-0/176	Chicago	6-16-62	11	Toronto, Vancouver
58	Robert Kron (LW)	5-10/175	Brno, Czech.	2-27-67	2	Vancouver
16	Trevor Linden (C)	6-4/185	Medicine Hat, Alta.	4-11-70	4	Vancouver
27	Sergio Momesso (LW)	6-3/215	Montreal	9-4-65	8	Vancouver
19	Petr Nedved (C)	6-3/185	Liberec, Czech.	12-9-71	2	Vancouver
29	Gino Odjick (LW)	6-3/220	Maniwaki, Que.	9-7-70	2	Vancouver
	Libor Polasek (C)	6-3/198	Vitkovice, Czech.	4-22-74	0	TJ Vitkovice (Czech.)
7	Cliff Ronning (C)	5-8/175	Vancouver, B.C.	10-1-65	6	Vancouver
25	Jim Sandlak (RW)	6-3/220	Kitchener, Ont.	12-12-66	7	Vancouver
	Alex Stojanov (LW)	6-4/225	Windsor, Ont.	4-25-73	0	Guelph (OHL)
23	Garry Valk (LW/RW)	6-1/190	Edmonton, Alta.	11-27-67	2	Vancouver
9	Ryan Walter (C/LW)	6-0/200	New Westminster, B.C.	4-23-58	14	Vancouver

	DEFENSEMEN	Ht./Wt.	Place	Date	NHL exp.	1991-92 clubs
44	Dave Babych	6-2/215	Edmonton, Alta.	5-23-61	12	Vancouver
	Jassen Cullimore	6-5/225	Simcoe, Ont.	12-4-72	0	Peterborough (OHL)
4	Gerald Diduck	6-2/207	Edmonton, Alta.	4-6-65	8	Vancouver
22	Robert Dirk	6-4/218	Regina, Sask.	8-20-66	5	Vancouver
	Don Gibson	6-1/210	Deloraine, Man.	12-29-67	1	Milwaukee (IHL)
	Jason Herter	6-1/190	Hafford, Sask.	10-2-70	0	Milwaukee (IHL)
3	Doug Lidster	6-1/200	Kamloops, B.C.	10-18-60	9	Vancouver
21	Jyrki Lumme	6-1/207	Tampere, Finland	7-16-67	4	Vancouver
5	Dana Murzyn	6-2/200	Regina, Sask.	12-9-66	7	Vancouver
6	Adrien Plavsic	6-1/190	Montreal	1-13-70	3	Can. Nat./Olym., Vancouver
	Jiri Slegr	5-11/190	Litvinov, Czech.	5-30-71	0	Litvinov (Czech.), Czech. Olym.
	Phil Von Steffanelli	6-1/183	Vancouver, B.C.	4-10-69	0	Milwaukee

	GOALTENDERS	Ht./Wt.	Place	Date	NHL exp.	1991-92 clubs
	Corrie D'Alessio	5-11/155	Cornwall, Ont.	9-9-69	0	Milwaukee (IHL)
	Jason Fitzsimmons	5-11/185	Regina, Sask.	6-3-71	0	Moose Jaw (WHL)
35	Troy Gamble	5-11/195	Toronto	4-7-67	4	Milwaukee (IHL), Vancouver
1	Kirk McLean	6-0/185	Willowdale, Ont.	6-26-66	7	Vancouver

1991-92 REVIEW

INDIVIDUAL STATISTICS

SCORING

	Games	G	A	Pts.	Pen.	+/-	PPG	SHG	Shots	Shooting Pct.
Trevor Linden	80	31	44	75	101	3	6	1	201	15.4
Cliff Ronning	80	24	47	71	42	18	6	0	216	11.1
Igor Larionov	72	21	44	65	54	7	10	3	97	21.6
Pavel Bure	65	34	26	60	30	0	7	3	268	12.7
Greg Adams	76	30	27	57	26	8	13	1	184	16.3
Geoff Courtnall	70	23	34	57	116	-6	12	0	281	8.2
Jyrki Lumme	75	12	32	44	65	25	3	1	106	11.3
Sergio Momesso	58	20	23	43	198	16	2	0	153	13.1
Jim Sandlak	66	16	24	40	176	22	3	0	122	13.1
Petr Nedved	77	15	22	37	36	-3	5	0	99	15.2
Tom Fergus*	44	14	20	34	17	1	6	0	79	17.7
Doug Lidster	66	6	23	29	39	9	3	0	89	6.7
Dave Babych	75	5	24	29	63	-2	4	0	148	3.4
Gerald Diduck	77	6	21	27	229	-3	2	0	128	4.7
Garry Valk	65	8	17	25	56	3	2	1	93	8.6
Ryan Walter	67	6	11	17	49	6	1	1	73	8.2
Dana Murzyn	70	3	11	14	147	15	0	1	99	3.0
Gino Odjick	65	4	6	10	348	-1	0	0	68	5.9
Adrien Plavsic	16	1	9	10	14	4	0	0	21	4.8
Robert Dirk	72	2	7	9	126	6	0	0	44	4.5
Randy Gregg	21	1	4	5	24	-3	0	0	19	5.3
Kirk McLean (goalie)	65	0	5	5	0	0	0	0	0	0.0
Robert Kron	36	2	2	4	2	-9	0	0	49	4.1
Andrew McBain	6	1	0	1	0	-1	0	0	11	9.1
Rob Murphy	6	0	1	1	6	-2	0	0	2	0.0
Robin Bawa	2	0	0	0	0	0	0	0	1	0.0
Shawn Antoski	4	0	0	0	29	-1	0	0	6	0.0

	Games	G	A	Pts.	Pen.	+/-	PPG	SHG	Shots	Shooting Pct.
Jay Mazur	5	0	0	0	2	-2	0	0	3	0.0
Troy Gamble (goalie)	19	0	0	0	8	0	0	0	0	0.0
Jim Agnew	24	0	0	0	56	-1	0	0	9	0.0

GOALTENDING

	Games	Min.	Goals	SO	Avg.	W	L	T	Shots	Sv. Pct.
Kirk McLean	65	3852	176	‡5	2.74	‡38	17	9	1780	.901
Troy Gamble	19	1009	73	0	4.34	4	9	3	518	.859

Empty-net goals (do not count against a goaltender's average): McLean, 1.
*Played with two or more NHL teams.
‡Tied for league lead.

RESULTS

OCTOBER

4—San Jose	W	4-3
5—At San Jose	W	5-2
8—At Winnipeg	W	*3-2
10—At Chicago	L	6-7
12 At Toronto	W	2-1
13—At Buffalo	W	3-1
17—Boston	T	*3-3
19—Calgary	W	5-2
21—Toronto	W	4-1
24—Washington	W	3-1
26—At Edmonton	L	4-5
27—Edmonton	L	3-6
29—New Jersey	W	4-3

NOVEMBER

1—St. Louis	L	2-3
3—Edmonton	W	7-2
5—Winnipeg	T	*2-2
7—At Los Angeles	W	4-3
10—N.Y. Islanders	W	6-0
12—Los Angeles	W	8-2
14—At Calgary	T	*2-2
16—San Jose	W	1-0
19—N.Y. Rangers	L	3-4
21—At Calgary	L	2-3
22—Calgary	W	*6-5
26—At San Jose	L	1-4
29—Chicago	W	5-2

DECEMBER

1—At Edmonton	L	0-7
3—At Quebec	L	0-3
4—At Montreal	W	3-0
7—At Toronto	L	3-6
10—Edmonton	L	4-7
12—Minnesota	W	7-5
14—At Los Angeles	T	*4-4
17—Detroit	W	2-1
19—Winnipeg	W	3-1
22—Quebec	T	*6-6
27—Philadelphia	T	*1-1
28—At San Jose	W	3-2
31—At Los Angeles	W	5-3

JANUARY

3—At Washington	T	*3-3
4—At Minnesota	L	3-4
7—San Jose	W	4-1
12—Pittsburgh	L	3-4
14—At Winnipeg	W	4-2
15—At Edmonton	W	5-3
21—At Quebec	W	5-3
23—At Detroit	W	3-1
25—At St. Louis	W	*1-0
28—Edmonton	L	3-5
30—Chicago	W	4-1

FEBRUARY

1—Hartford	T	*4-4
4—Montreal	W	5-3
6—N.Y. Islanders	L	*4-5
10—At Montreal	L	3-8
12—At N.Y. Rangers	L	2-5
13—At New Jersey	L	3-5
15—At N.Y. Islanders	L	1-3
17—At N.Y. Rangers	T	*3-3
19—Buffalo	W	6-5
21—At San Jose	W	5-3
23—Boston	W	*2-1
25—Los Angeles	L	3-4
28—Winnipeg	W	5-3

MARCH

1—Calgary	W	11-0
2—St. Louis	L	3-5
5—At Boston	T	*2-2
7—At Hartford	W	5-1
8—At Philadelphia	W	7-3
12—New Jersey	W	2-1
14—At Calgary	W	6-4
18—Hartford	W	3-2
20—Winnipeg	T	*2-2
22—At Winnipeg	L	1-5
24—At Minnesota	W	4-2
26—At Pittsburgh	L	3-7
28—At Detroit	L	1-3
29—At Washington	L	4-7

APRIL

12—Los Angeles	L	1-6
14—At Los Angeles	W	3-2
16—Calgary	T	*4-4

*Denotes overtime game.

WASHINGTON CAPITALS
WALES CONFERENCE/PATRICK DIVISION

 WASHINGTON CAPITALS 1992-93 NHL SEASON WASHINGTON CAPITALS

1992-93 SCHEDULE

OCTOBER

S	M	T	W	T	F	S
4	5	6	7 TOR	8	9 NYR H	10 PHI H
11	12 NJ	13	14	15	16 OTT H	17 BUF H
18	19	20	21 NYR	22	23 NYI H	24
25	26 WIN	27	28 VAN	29	30 CAL	31 EDM

NOVEMBER

S	M	T	W	T	F	S
1	2	3	4	5	6 TB H	7 HAR
8	9	10	11 NYR	12	13 NJ	14 NJ H
15	16	17	18 MIN H	19	20 DET H	21
22 D QUE	23 MON	24	25 BOS H	26	27 PIT H	28 PIT
29	30 DET					

DECEMBER

S	M	T	W	T	F	S
		1	2	3	4 NYR H	5 NYI
6	7 OTT	8	9 NJ	10	11 WIN H	12 PHI
13	14	15	16 HAR	17	18 HAR H	19 BOS
20	21 OTT	22	23 BUF	24	25	26 PHI H
27	28	29 NYR H	30	31		

JANUARY

S	M	T	W	T	F	S
					1 D NJ H	2 D CHI H
3	4	5	6 PHI	7	8	9 EDM H
10	11	12	13 NYR	14 NYI	15	16
17 TB	18	19	20	21 CHI	22	23 OTT H
24	25	26 PIT	27 BUF	28	29 QUE H	30
31 D PIT H						

FEBRUARY

S	M	T	W	T	F	S
	1	2 CAL H	3	4	5	6 ★
7	8	9 MIN	10	11 STL	12	13 LA
14	15	16 SJ	17	18	19	20 D LA H
21 STL H	22	23 NYI	24	25	26	27 D BOS
28 D PIT H						

MARCH

S	M	T	W	T	F	S
	1	2 VAN H	3	4	5 PHI H	6
7 D NYI H	8	9 TOR H	10	11 PHI	12	13 NYR H
14 NYI	15	16	17	18	19 HAR H	20
21 D SJ H	22	23 QUE H	24	25 PIT	26	27 NJ H
28 D PIT H	29	30 BUF H	31			

APRIL

S	M	T	W	T	F	S
				1	2 MON H	3
4 D NYR H	5	6 NYI H	7	8 PHI	9	10 NJ H
11	12 MON	13	14 NYR	15	16	17

1992-93 SEASON

CLUB DIRECTORY

Chairman and governor
Abe Pollin
President and alternate governor
Richard M. Patrick
Vice president and general manager
David Poile
Legal counselors and alternate governors
David M. Osnos
Peter O'Malley
Vice president of finance
Edmund Stelzer
Vice president/marketing
Lew Strudler
Director of public relations
Lou Corletto
Assistant director of marketing
Debi Angus
Director of community relations
Yvon Labre
Director of promotions and advertising
Charles Copeland
Admin. assistant to public relations
Julie Hensley
Admin. assistant to the general manager
Pat Young
Coach
Terry Murray
Assistant coach
John Perpich
Strength and conditioning coach
Frank Costello

Dir. of player personnel and recruitment
Jack Button
Professional scout
Paul Gardner
Chief Eastern scout
Hugh Rogers
Chief Western scout
Craig Channell
Chief U.S. scout
Jack Barzee
Chief Quebec scout
Gilles Cote
Scouts
Keith Allain
Rudy Crha
Fred Devereaux
Michel Goulet
Mike Humitz
Eje Johansson
Kelly Pratt
Bud Quinn
Richard Rothermel
Bob Schmidt
Dan Sylvester
Darrell Young
Trainer
Stan Wong
Assistant trainer/head equipment manager
Doug Shearer

DRAFT CHOICES

Rnd. Player	Ht./Wt.	Overall	Pos.	1991-92 club
1—Sergei Gonchar	6-0/178	14	D	Dynamo Moscow, CIS
2—Jim Carey	6-2/190	32	G	Catholic Mem. H.S., Boston.
3—Stefan Ustorf	5-11/169	53	F	Kausbeuren, Germany
3—Martin Gendron	5-8/182	71	RW	St. Hyacinthe (QMJHL)
5—John Varga	5-9/172	119	LW	Tacoma (WHL)
7—Mark Matier	6-1/190	167	D	Sault Ste. Marie (OHL)
8—Mike Mathers	5-10/188	191	LW	Kamloops (WHL)
9—Brian Stagg	6-2/177	215	RW	Kingston (OHL)
10—Gregory Callahan	6-3/200	239	D	Belmont Hill (Mass.) H.S.
11—Billy Jo MacPherson	6-1/200	263	LW	Oshawa (OHL)

MISCELLANEOUS DATA

Home ice (capacity)
Capital Centre (18,130)
Address
Landover, MD 20785
Business phone
301-386-7000
Rink dimensions
200 feet by 85 feet

Club colors
Red, white and blue
Minor league affiliations
Baltimore (AHL)
Hampton-Roads (ECHL)

SCHEDULE KEY

*All-Star Game at Montreal.
H—Home game.   D—Day game (any game starting before 4 p.m.).
NOTE: At press time, two games at neutral sites had yet to be announced.

— 70 —

TRAINING CAMP ROSTER

No.	FORWARDS	Ht./Wt.	Place	BORN Date	NHL exp.	1991-92 clubs
	Mike Boback (C)	5-11/180	Mt. Clemens, Mich.	8-13-70	0	Providence College (Hockey East)
12	Peter Bondra (RW)	5-11/180	Luck, U.S.S.R.	2-7-68	2	Washington
18	Randy Burridge (LW)	5-9/180	Fort Erie, Ont.	1-7-66	7	Washington
11	Bobby Carpenter (LW)	6-0/190	Beverly, Mass.	7-13-63	11	Boston
19	John Druce (RW)	6-0/200	Peterborough, Ont.	2-23-66	4	Washington
24	Jeff Greenlaw (RW)	6-1/230	Toronto	2-28-68	4	Baltimore (AHL), Washington
32	Dale Hunter (C)	5-10/198	Petrolia, Ont.	7-31-60	12	Washington
	Mark Hunter (RW)	6-0/205	Petrolia, Ont.	11-12-62	11	Hartford
	Martin Jiranek (C)	5-11/170	Bashaw, Alta.	10-3-69	0	Bowling Green (CCHA)
	Keith Jones (RW)	6-2/190	Brantford, Ont.	11-8-68	1	Western Michigan (CCHA), Baltimore
	Dimitri Khristich (C)	6-2/190	Kiev, U.S.S.R.	7-23-69	2	Washington
	Steve Konowalchuk (C)	6-0/180	Salt Lake City	11-11-72	1	Portland (WHL), Baltimore (AHL), Washington
21	Todd Krygier (C)	5-11/180	Northville, Mich.	10-12-65	3	Washington
23	Paul MacDermid (RW)	6-1/205	Chesley, Ont.	4-14-63	11	Winnipeg, Washington
16	Alan May (RW)	6-1/200	Swan Hills, Alta.	1-14-65	5	Washington
10	Kelly Miller (LW)	5-11/195	Lansing, Mich.	3-3-63	8	Washington
	Kevin Miller (RW)	5-9/170	Lansing, Mich.	8-9-65	4	Detroit
	Jeff Nelson (C)	6-0/180	Prince Albert, Sask.	12-18-72	0	Prince Albert (WHL)
	Pat Peake (C)	6-0/195	Detroit	5-28-73	0	Detroit (OHL), Baltimore
20	Michal Pivonka (C)	6-2/198	Kladno, Czech.	1-28-66	6	Washington
17	Mike Ridley (C)	6-1/200	Winnipeg, Man.	7-8-63	7	Washington
	Reggie Savage (RW)	5-10/187	Montreal	5-1-70	0	Baltimore (AHL)
	Steve Seftel (LW)	6-3/200	Kitchener, Ont.	5-14-68	1	Baltimore (AHL)
	DEFENSEMEN					
3	Sylvain Cote	6-0/190	Quebec City	1-19-66	8	Washington
4	Kevin Hatcher	6-4/225	Detroit	9-9-66	8	Washington
34	Al Iafrate	6-3/220	Dearborn, Mich.	3-21-66	8	Washington
6	Calle Johansson	5-11/205	Goteborg, Sweden	2-14-67	5	Washington
5	Rod Langway	6-3/225	Maag, Formosa	5-3-57	14	Washington
	Jim Mathieson	6-1/209	Kindersley, Sask.	1-24-70	1	Baltimore (AHL)
2	Ken Sabourin	6-3/205	Scarborough, Ont.	4-28-66	4	Baltimore (AHL), Washington
28	Brad Schlegel	5-10/190	Kitchener, Ont.	7-22-68	1	Can. Nat./Olym., Baltimore (AHL), Washington
	John Slaney	5-11/180	St. John's, Nfld.	2-7-72	0	Cornwall (OHL), Baltimore (AHL)
	Jason Woolley	6-0/190	Toronto	7-27-69	1	Can. Nat./Olym., Baltimore (AHL), Washington
	GOALTENDERS					
33	Don Beaupre	5-9/165	Kitchener, Ont.	9-19-61	12	Baltimore (AHL), Washington
	Byron Dafoe	5-11/175	Duncan, B.C.	2-25-71	0	Hampton Roads (ECHL), New Haven (AHL), Baltimore (AHL)
	Duane Derksen	6-1/180	St. Boniface, Man.	7-7-68	0	U. of Wisconsin (WCHA)
39	Jim Hrivnak	6-2/185	Montreal	5-28-68	3	Baltimore (AHL), Washington
	Olaf Kolzig	6-3/205	Johannesburg, S. Africa	4-6-70	1	Hampton Roads (ECHL), Baltimore (AHL)

1991-92 REVIEW

INDIVIDUAL STATISTICS

SCORING

	Games	G	A	Pts.	Pen.	+/-	PPG	SHG	Shots	Shooting Pct.
Michal Pivonka	80	23	57	80	47	10	7	4	177	13.0
Dale Hunter	80	28	50	78	205	-2	13	0	110	25.5
Dino Ciccarelli	78	38	38	76	78	-10	13	0	279	13.6
Dimitri Khristich	80	36	37	73	35	24	14	1	188	19.1
Mike Ridley	80	29	40	69	38	3	5	5	123	23.6
Randy Burridge	66	23	44	67	50	-4	9	0	131	17.6
Peter Bondra	71	28	28	56	42	16	4	0	158	17.7
Calle Johansson	80	14	42	56	49	2	5	2	119	11.8
Kevin Hatcher	79	17	37	54	105	18	8	1	246	6.9
Kelly Miller	78	14	38	52	49	20	0	1	144	9.7
Al Iafrate	78	17	34	51	180	1	6	0	151	11.3
Sylvain Cote	78	11	29	40	31	7	6	0	151	7.3
John Druce	67	19	18	37	39	14	1	0	129	14.7
Todd Krygier	67	13	17	30	107	-1	1	0	127	10.2
Alan May	75	6	9	15	221	-7	0	0	43	14.0
Rod Langway	64	0	13	13	22	11	0	0	32	0.0
Mike Lalor*	64	5	7	12	64	14	0	0	54	9.3

	Games	G	A	Pts.	Pen.	+/-	PPG	SHG	Shots	Shooting Pct.
Dave Tippett	30	2	10	12	16	2	0	0	26	7.7
Nick Kypreos	65	4	6	10	206	-3	0	0	28	14.3
Paul MacDermid*	15	2	5	7	43	2	0	0	21	9.5
Tim Bergland	22	1	4	5	2	-3	0	0	18	5.6
Jeff Greenlaw	5	0	1	1	34	-1	0	0	3	0.0
Brad Schlegel	15	0	1	1	0	-4	0	0	7	0.0
Mike Liut (goalie)	21	0	1	1	2	0	0	0	0	0.0
Steve Konowalchuk	1	0	0	0	0	0	0	0	1	0.0
Jason Woolley	1	0	0	0	0	1	0	0	2	0.0
Shawn Chambers	2	0	0	0	2	-3	0	0	1	0.0
Jim Hrivnak (goalie)	12	0	0	0	0	0	0	0	0	0.0
Ken Sabourin	19	0	0	0	48	-5	0	0	12	0.0
Don Beaupre (goalie)	54	0	0	0	30	0	0	0	0	0.0

GOALTENDING

	Games	Min.	Goals	SO	Avg.	W	L	T	Shots	Sv. Pct.
Don Beaupre	54	3108	166	1	3.20	29	17	6	1435	.884
Jim Hrivnak	12	605	35	0	3.47	6	3	0	274	.872
Mike Liut	21	1123	70	1	3.74	10	7	2	558	.875

Empty-net goals (do not count against a goaltender's average): Beaupre, 2; Hrivnak, 1; Liut, 1.
*Played with two or more NHL teams.

RESULTS

OCTOBER

4—Philadelphia	W	5-2
5—Buffalo	W	3-1
9—At Toronto	W	5-4
11—N.Y. Rangers	W	5-1
12—Chicago	L	2-7
14—At N.Y. Rangers	W	5-3
18—New Jersey	W	6-5
19—At New Jersey	W	5-1
23—At Edmonton	W	6-5
24—At Vancouver	L	1-3
27—At Winnipeg	L	5-6
29—At Pittsburgh	W	8-0

NOVEMBER

1—Toronto	W	4-0
2—At N.Y. Islanders	W	7-4
8—Detroit	L	4-5
10—At Quebec	W	10-3
11—At Montreal	W	4-2
13—At N.Y. Rangers	W	5-3
15—Pittsburgh	W	6-2
20—At New Jersey	L	*5-6
22—Boston	W	6-3
23—At Hartford	W	3-2
25—At Detroit	L	4-5
27—Montreal	W	3-1
29—N.Y. Islanders	L	2-3
30—At N.Y. Islanders	L	1-8

DECEMBER

5—At Philadelphia	W	6-3
7—At Minnesota	W	4-2
8—At Winnipeg	L	3-4
10—Calgary	W	4-1
13—N.Y. Rangers	L	3-5
14—At Pittsburgh	W	7-2
17—Quebec	W	3-1
18—At Buffalo	T	*2-2
20—Toronto	W	4-3
22—At Philadelphia	L	*3-4
26—N.Y. Rangers	L	6-8
28—Pittsburgh	L	2-6
29—At New Jersey	W	4-3

JANUARY

1—N.Y. Islanders	W	8-5
3—Vancouver	T	*3-3
4—At Hartford	T	*2-2
7—Minnesota	L	3-5
10—Los Angeles	W	7-4
12—At Chicago	L	2-4
14—At St. Louis	W	6-1
16—At Los Angeles	T	*2-2
24—New Jersey	L	2-5
26—Pittsburgh	W	6-4
28—At Philadelphia	L	2-3

FEBRUARY

1—Calgary	W	5-2
4—At Buffalo	L	3-7
5—At Detroit	L	1-4
7—N.Y. Rangers	W	6-2
9—San Jose	W	6-2
11—At Quebec	W	4-3
13—At Calgary	T	*4-4
15—At Los Angeles	L	3-6
18—At San Jose	W	4-2
22—Philadelphia	W	7-5
23—At N.Y. Islanders	W	4-1
25—Pittsburgh	W	5-3
27—At St. Louis	L	3-7
29—At Boston	T	*5-5

MARCH

1—Boston	L	1-4
3—Minnesota	L	1-3
6—Winnipeg	T	*3-3
7—New Jersey	W	*3-2
9—At N.Y. Rangers	W	5-2
14—At Philadelphia	L	1-3
15—N.Y. Islanders	W	5-2
17—St. Louis	W	6-4
20—Philadelphia	L	6-7
22—Edmonton	W	6-2
24—Hartford	L	2-8
27—Montreal	W	4-3
29—Vancouver	W	7-4

APRIL

12—At New Jersey	W	4-3
13—N.Y. Islanders	T	*1-1
15—At Pittsburgh	L	1-4

*Denotes overtime game.

WINNIPEG JETS
CAMPBELL CONFERENCE/SMYTHE DIVISION

1992-93 SCHEDULE

OCTOBER

S	M	T	W	T	F	S
4	5	6 DET H	7	8 SJ	9	10 LA
11	12 VAN	13	14 EDM H	15	16 VAN H	17
18 PHI	19	20 DET	21	22	23 LA H	24
25	26 WAS H	27	28 CAL H	29	30	31 QUE

NOVEMBER

S	M	T	W	T	F	S
1	2 MON	3	4	5	6 EDM H	7
8 VAN	D 9	10 LA H	11	12 MIN	13	14 STL
15	16	17 TB	18 DET	19	20	21 NYR H
22	23	24 NYI H	25	26	27 SJ H	28
29	30					

DECEMBER

S	M	T	W	T	F	S
		1	2 CAL	3	4	5 MON H
6	7	8 PIT	9	10	11 WAS	12 NYI
13	14	15 NJ H	16	17 CHI	18	19 STL
20	21 SJ H	22	23 CAL H	24	25	26 MIN
27 MIN H	28	29 BOS H	30	31 EDM H		

JANUARY

S	M	T	W	T	F	S
					1	2 NJ
3 CHI	4	5 CAL	6	7	8 LA H	9
10 PIT H	11	12 SJ H	13 EDM	14	15	16 LA
17	18	19 CHI H	20	21	22 CAL	23 EDM H
24	25	26	27 NYR	28 BOS	29	30 HAR
31						

FEBRUARY

S	M	T	W	T	F	S
	1	2	3 STL H	4	5	6 *
	OTT					
7	8	9	10 BUF H	11	12 HAR H	13
14 D 15	16	17	18 SJ	19	20 VAN	
SJ H						
21	22 OTT H	23	24	25	26 VAN H	27
28 MIN H						

MARCH

S	M	T	W	T	F	S
	1	2 QUE H	3	4 EDM	5	6 TOR
7 BUF	8	9 TB	10	11	12 VAN H	13
14 D 15	16 LA	17	18 VAN	19	20	
TB H						
21 D 22	23 TOR H	24	25	26 STL H	27	
CAL H						
28 D 29	30 CAL	31				
LA H						

APRIL

S	M	T	W	T	F	S
				1 SJ	2	3 EDM
4	5	6 PHI H	7	8 TOR H	9	10
11 EDM	D 12	13 TB H	14	15 EDM H	16	17

1992-93 SEASON

CLUB DIRECTORY

President and governor
Barry L. Shenkarow
Alternate governors
Bill Davis
Michael A. Smith
Vice president and general manager
Michael A. Smith
Asst. G.M./director of hockey operations
Dennis McDonald
Director of finance and adminstration
Don Binda
Exec. asst to V.P. and G.M.
Pat MacDonald
Director of communications
Mike O'Hearn
Director of community relations
Lori Summers
Vice president of marketing
Madeline Hanson
Director of team services
Murray Harding

Coach
John Paddock
Assistant coaches
Terry Simpson
Glen Williamson
Director of amateur scouting
Bill Lesuk
Scouts
Mike Antonovich
Connie Broden
Sean Coady
Larry Hornung
Tom Savage
Joe Yannetti
Athletic therapists
Jim Ramsay
Phil Walker
Equipment managers
Craig Heisinger
Stan Wilson

DRAFT CHOICES

Rnd. Player	Ht./Wt.	Overall	Pos.	1991-92 club
1—Sergei Bautin	6-3/185	17	D	Dynamo Moscow, CIS
2—Boris Mironv	6-3/196	27	D	CSKA Moscow, CIS
3—Jeremy Stevenson	6-1/212	60	LW	Cornwall (OHL)
4—Mark Visheau	6-4/197	84	D	London (OHL)
6—Alexander Alexeyev	6-0/185	132	D	Novgorod, CIS
7—Artur Oktyabrev	5-11/183	155	D	Central Red Army, CIS
7—Andrei Raisky	6-2/185	156	LW	Ust-Amenogorsk, CIS
9—Nikolai Khaibulin	6-0/167	204	G	Yekaterinburg, CIS
10—Yevgeny Garanin	6-0/180	228	C	Khimik, CIS
10—Teemu Numminen	6-2/190	229	C	Stoneham (Mass.) H.S.
11—Andrei Karpovtsev	6-2/211	252	RW	Dynamo Moscow, CIS
11—Ivan Vologzaninov	5-11/165	254	LW	Sokol Kiev, CIS)

MISCELLANEOUS DATA

Home ice (capacity)
Winnipeg Arena (15,393)
Address
15-1430 Maroons Road
Winnipeg, Man. R3G 0L5
Business phone
204-982-5387

Rink dimensions
200 feet by 85 feet
Club colors
Blue, red and white
Minor league affiliations
Fort Wayne (IHL)
Moncton (AHL)

SCHEDULE KEY

*All-Star Game at Montreal.
H—Home game. D—Day game (any game starting before 4 p.m.).
NOTE: At press time, two games at neutral sites had yet to be announced.

TRAINING CAMP ROSTER

No.	FORWARDS	Ht./Wt.	BORN Place	Date	NHL exp.	1991-92 clubs
14	Stu Barnes (C)	5-10/175	Edmonton, Alta.	12-25-70	1	Moncton (AHL), Winnipeg
38	Luciano Borsato (C)	5-10/165	Richmond Hill, Ont.	1-7-66	2	Moncton (AHL), Winnipeg
40	Evgeny Davydov (LW)	6-1/185	Chelyabinsk, U.S.S.R.	5-27-67	1	Unified Olym. (CIS), Winnipeg
91	Kris Draper (C/LW)	5-11/190	Toronto	5-24-71	1	Moncton (AHL), Winnipeg
36	Mike Eagles (C)	5-10/180	Susex, N.B.	3-7-63	8	Winnipeg
15	Pat Elynuik (RW)	6-0/185	Foam Lake, Sask.	10-30-67	5	Winnipeg
28	Bob Joyce (LW)	6-1/195	St. Johns, N.B.	7-11-66	5	Moncton (AHL), Winnipeg
	Jan Kaminsky (LW)	6-2/176	Penza, U.S.S.R.	7-28-71	0	Dynamo Moscow (CIS)
37	John LeBlanc (LW/RW)	6-1/195	Campbellton, N.B.	1-21-64	4	Moncton (AHL), Winnipeg
	Scott Levins (RW)	6-3/200	Portland, Ore.	1-30-70	0	Moncton (AHL)
19	Troy Murray (C)	6-1/195	Winnipeg, Man.	7-31-62	11	Winnipeg
16	Ed Olczyk (C/RW/LW)	6-1/200	Chicago	8-16-66	8	Winnipeg
	Pekka Peltola (RW)	6-2/196	Helsinki, Finland	6-24-65	0	Finland
21	Russ Romaniuk (LW)	6-0/185	Winnipeg, Man.	6-9-70	1	Moncton (AHL), Winnipeg
	Christian Ruuttu (C)	5-11/192	Lappeenranta, Finland	2-20-64	6	Buffalo
	Teemu Selanne (RW)	6-0/180	Helsinki, Finland	3-7-70	0	Finland Olym., Jokerit (Fin.)
34	Darrin Shannon (LW)	6-2/200	Barrie, Ont.	12-8-69	4	Buffalo, Winnipeg
25	Thomas Steen (C)	5-10/195	Tocksmark, Sweden	6-8-60	11	Winnipeg
7	Keith Tkachuk (C/LW)	6-2/200	Melrose, Mass.	3-28-72	1	U.S. Nat./Olym., Winnipeg
	Alexei Zhamnov (C)	6-1/187	Moscow, U.S.S.R.	10-1-70	0	Dynamo Moscow (CIS)
	DEFENSEMEN					
	Sergei Bautin	6-3/185	Murmansk, U.S.S.R.	3-11-67	0	Dynamo Moscow (CIS)
8	Randy Carlyle	5-10/200	Sudbury, Ont.	4-19-56	16	Winnipeg
44	Shawn Cronin	6-2/210	Flushing, Mich.	8-20-63	4	Winnipeg
	Dimitri Filimonov	6-4/207	Perm, U.S.S.R.	10-14-71	0	Dynamo Moscow (CIS)
6	Phil Housley	5-10/179	St. Paul, Minn.	3-9-64	10	Winnipeg
26	Dean Kennedy	6-2/200	Redvers, Sask.	1-18-63	9	Winnipeg
22	Mike Lalor	6-0/190	Fort Erie, Ont.	3-8-63	7	Washington, Winnipeg
	Jukka Marttila	6-0/185	Tampere, Finland	4-15-68	0	Tappara (Finland)
27	Teppo Numminen	6-1/190	Tampere, Finland	7-3-68	4	Winnipeg
4	Fredrik Olausson	6-2/200	Vaxsjo, Sweden	10-5-66	6	Winnipeg
	GOALTENDERS					
35	Bob Essensa	6-0/160	Toronto	1-14-65	4	Winnipeg
	Sean Gauthier	5-11/194	Sudbury, Ont.	3-28-71	0	Fort Wayne (IHL), Moncton (AHL)
1	Mike O'Neill	5-7/155	Montreal	11-3-67	1	Fort Wayne (IHL), Moncton (AHL), Winnipeg
	Allain Roy	5-10/165	Campbelltown, N.B.	2-6-70	0	Harvard University (ECAC)
31	Rick Tabaracci	5-10/185	Toronto	1-2-69	3	Moncton (AHL), Winnipeg

1991-92 REVIEW

INDIVIDUAL STATISTICS

SCORING

	Games	G	A	Pts.	Pen.	+/-	PPG	SHG	Shots	Shooting Pct.
Phil Housley	74	23	63	86	92	-5	11	0	234	9.8
Ed Olczyk	64	32	33	65	67	11	12	0	245	13.1
Fredrik Olausson	77	20	42	62	34	-31	13	1	227	8.8
Pat Elynuik	60	25	25	50	65	-2	9	0	127	19.7
Troy Murray	74	17	30	47	69	-13	5	2	156	10.9
Darrin Shannon*	68	13	26	39	41	5	3	0	91	14.3
Teppo Numminen	80	5	34	39	32	15	4	0	143	3.5
Thomas Steen	38	13	25	38	29	5	10	0	75	17.3
Luciano Borsato	56	15	21	36	45	-6	5	0	81	18.5
Paul MacDermid*	59	10	11	21	151	-8	2	0	71	14.1
Stu Barnes	46	8	9	17	26	-2	4	0	75	10.7
Mike Eagles	65	7	10	17	118	-17	0	1	60	11.7
Mark Osborne*	43	4	12	16	65	-8	0	0	50	8.0
Doug Evans	30	7	7	14	68	2	1	0	39	17.9
Danton Cole	52	7	5	12	32	-15	1	2	65	10.8
Igor Ulanov	27	2	9	11	67	5	0	0	23	8.7
Randy Carlyle	66	1	9	10	54	4	0	0	84	1.2
Aaron Broten	25	4	5	9	14	2	0	0	29	13.8
Mike Hartman	75	4	4	8	264	-10	0	0	89	4.5
Keith Tkachuk	17	3	5	8	28	0	2	0	22	13.6
Russ Romaniuk	27	3	5	8	18	2	2	0	32	9.4
John LeBlanc	16	6	1	7	6	-6	5	0	32	18.8
Evgeny Davydov	12	4	3	7	8	7	2	0	32	12.5
Phil Sykes	52	4	2	6	72	-12	0	0	34	11.8
Bryan Erickson	10	2	4	6	0	9	0	0	16	12.5

	Games	G	A	Pts.	Pen.	+/-	PPG	SHG	Shots	Shooting Pct.
Dean Kennedy	18	2	4	6	21	2	0	0	20	10.0
Mike Lalor*	15	2	3	5	14	11	0	0	20	10.0
Petri Skriko*	15	2	3	5	4	-1	0	0	27	7.4
Mario Marois*	34	1	3	4	34	-8	0	1	32	3.1
Moe Mantha*	12	0	4	4	6	0	0	0	10	0.0
Shawn Cronin	65	0	4	4	271	-11	0	0	25	0.0
Lucien DeBlois*	11	1	2	3	2	1	0	0	15	6.7
Don Barber*	11	0	3	3	4	2	0	0	6	0.0
Kris Draper	10	2	0	2	2	0	0	0	19	10.5
Dave McLlwain*	3	1	1	2	2	1	0	0	3	33.3
Bob Essensa (goalie)	47	0	2	2	2	0	0	0	0	0.0
Brent Ashton*	7	1	0	1	4	-3	0	0	6	16.7
Rob Murray	9	0	1	1	18	-2	0	0	2	0.0
Rick Tabaracci (goalie)	18	0	1	1	4	0	0	0	0	0.0
Bob Joyce	1	0	0	0	0	0	0	0	0	0.0
Michael O'Neill (goalie)	1	0	0	0	0	0	0	0	0	0.0
Jason Cirone	3	0	0	0	2	0	0	0	1	0.0
Gord Donnelly*	4	0	0	0	11	-5	0	0	5	0.0
Rudy Poeschek	4	0	0	0	17	-5	0	0	1	0.0
Kent Paynter	5	0	0	0	4	-1	0	0	6	0.0
Stephane Beauregard (goalie)	26	0	0	0	0	0	0	0	0	0.0

GOALTENDING

	Games	Min.	Goals	SO	Avg.	W	L	T	Shots	Sv. Pct.
Bob Essensa	47	2627	126	‡5	2.88	21	17	6	1407	.910
Stephane Beauregard	26	1267	61	2	2.89	6	8	6	611	.900
Rick Tabaracci	18	966	52	0	3.23	6	7	3	470	.889
Michael O'Neill	1	13	1	0	4.62	0	0	0	7	.857

Empty-net goals (do not count against a goaltender's average): Essensa, 2; Beauregard, 1; Tabaracci, 1.
*Played with two or more NHL teams.
‡Tied for league lead.

RESULTS

OCTOBER
4—Los Angeles	L	3-6
6—Calgary	W	5-3
8—Vancouver	L	*2-3
10—At San Jose	W	5-4
12—At Los Angeles	T	*3-3
16—Hartford	L	2-3
19—Toronto	W	4-2
22—At N.Y. Islanders	T	*1-1
23—At Detroit	W	3-2
25—Philadelphia	W	2-0
27—Washington	W	6-5
29—At Quebec	L	2-7
30—At Montreal	L	1-6

NOVEMBER
1—Calgary	L	*6-7
3—St. Louis	T	*3-3
5—At Vancouver	T	*2-2
8—Pittsburgh	L	1-3
11—Los Angeles	W	6-2
14—At St. Louis	L	*1-2
16—At New Jersey	W	1-0
17—At Philadelphia	W	2-1
20—N.Y. Islanders	W	3-1
23—At Edmonton	W	4-0
25—At Calgary	T	*3-3
27—N.Y. Rangers	W	3-2

DECEMBER
1—Chicago	W	*3-2
4—Buffalo	W	5-4
6—Edmonton	T	*4-4
8—Washington	W	4-3
10—At San Jose	T	*3-3
12—At Los Angeles	L	1-2
14—At Edmonton	L	5-7
17—At Calgary	L	4-7
19—At Vancouver	L	1-3
21—Calgary	W	7-2
23—At Toronto	L	1 3
26—Minnesota	L	2-3
27—At Chicago	T	*3-3
29—Boston	L	3-6
31—N.Y. Rangers	L	2-5

JANUARY
2—At Boston	W	3-1
4—At Pittsburgh	L	2-3
6—At N.Y. Rangers	L	2-4
8—Edmonton	W	5-2
10—Chicago	W	6-2
12—San Jose	L	3-4
14—Vancouver	L	2-4
21—At Hartford	T	*3-3
23—At Philadelphia	W	1-0
25—At Quebec	L	1-2
26—At Buffalo	L	2-5
28—At Pittsburgh	W	4-0
31—Quebec	T	*4-4

FEBRUARY
2—San Jose	W	6-0

4—Boston	T	*3-3
7—Calgary	W	4-1
13—At Minnesota	L	1-6
15—At Toronto	W	3-1
17—At N.Y. Islanders	L	*4-5
19—St. Louis	L	3-4
21—New Jersey	W	6-4
23—Los Angeles	L	2-4
26—At Edmonton	L	1-6
28—At Vancouver	L	3-5

MARCH
1—Edmonton	L	2-4
3—At Detroit	W	4-3
6—At Washington	T	*3-3
8—At Minnesota	L	2-4
11—San Jose	W	3-0
13—Hartford	L	0-1
15—Detroit	T	*1-1
17—At Los Angeles	L	4-5
20—At Vancouver	T	*2-2
22—Vancouver	W	5-1
25—Montreal	T	*2-2
27—Los Angeles	W	6-4
29—San Jose	W	6-5

APRIL
12—At Calgary	W	4-3
14—At Edmonton	W	6-2
16—At San Jose	W	5-3

*Denotes overtime game.

SCHEDULE

DAY BY DAY

NOTE: At press time, two games at neutral sites for each team had yet to be added to the schedule.

*Denotes afternoon game.

TUESDAY, OCTOBER 6
Montreal at Hartford
N.Y. Islanders at New Jersey
Philadelphia at Pittsburgh
Detroit at Winnipeg
Minnesota at St. Louis
Los Angeles at Calgary
Vancouver at Edmonton

WEDNESDAY, OCTOBER 7
Washington at Toronto
Chicago at Tampa Bay

THURSDAY, OCTOBER 8
Hartford at Boston
Quebec at Buffalo
Montreal at Ottawa
N.Y. Islanders at Pittsburgh
Detroit at Los Angeles
St. Louis at Minnesota
Winnipeg at San Jose
Edmonton at Calgary

FRIDAY, OCTOBER 9
N.Y. Rangers at Washington
New Jersey at Philadelphia

SATURDAY, OCTOBER 10
N.Y. Islanders at Boston
Buffalo at Hartford
Ottawa at Quebec
Pittsburgh at Montreal
N.Y. Rangers at New Jersey
Philadelphia at Washington
Toronto at Calgary
Detroit at San Jose
Tampa Bay at Minnesota
Chicago at St. Louis
Winnipeg at Los Angeles
Edmonton at Vancouver

SUNDAY, OCTOBER 11
Montreal at Buffalo
Toronto at Edmonton
Tampa Bay at Chicago

MONDAY, OCTOBER 12
Ottawa at Boston
Hartford at N.Y. Rangers
Washington at New Jersey
Winnipeg at Vancouver

TUESDAY, OCTOBER 13
Buffalo at Pittsburgh
Philadelphia at Quebec
Tampa Bay at St. Louis
San Jose at Los Angeles

WEDNESDAY, OCTOBER 14
Ottawa at Hartford
New Jersey at N.Y. Rangers
Edmonton at Winnipeg

THURSDAY, OCTOBER 15
Boston at San Jose
Montreal at Pittsburgh
Quebec at Detroit
N.Y. Islanders at Philadelphia
Tampa Bay at Toronto

Edmonton at Chicago
Minnesota at St. Louis
Calgary at Los Angeles

FRIDAY, OCTOBER 16
Tampa Bay at Buffalo
Ottawa at Washington
Vancouver at Winnipeg

SATURDAY, OCTOBER 17
Boston at Los Angeles
Pittsburgh at Hartford
Buffalo at Washington
Minnesota at Montreal
St. Louis at Quebec
N.Y. Rangers at N.Y. Islanders
Philadelphia at New Jersey
Chicago at Toronto
Edmonton at Detroit
Calgary at San Jose

SUNDAY, OCTOBER 18
N.Y. Islanders at N.Y. Rangers
Winnipeg at Philadelphia
Minnesota at Toronto
Vancouver at Chicago

MONDAY, OCTOBER 19
St. Louis at Montreal

TUESDAY, OCTOBER 20
Hartford at New Jersey
Philadelphia at N.Y. Islanders
Vancouver at Pittsburgh
Winnipeg at Detroit
Edmonton at Tampa Bay
Los Angeles at Calgary

WEDNESDAY, OCTOBER 21
Chicago at Buffalo
San Jose at Montreal
Quebec at St. Louis
Washington at N.Y. Rangers

THURSDAY, OCTOBER 22
Boston at Calgary
Hartford at Ottawa
Quebec at Minnesota
New Jersey at Chicago
Vancouver at Philadelphia
Detroit at Pittsburgh
Toronto at Tampa Bay

FRIDAY, OCTOBER 23
Boston at Edmonton
San Jose at Buffalo
Montreal at N.Y. Rangers
N.Y. Islanders at Washington
Los Angeles at Winnipeg

SATURDAY, OCTOBER 24
Hartford at N.Y. Islanders
N.Y. Rangers at Ottawa
Montreal at Philadelphia
Quebec at Tampa Bay
Pittsburgh at New Jersey
San Jose at Toronto
Detroit at St. Louis
Los Angeles at Minnesota

SUNDAY, OCTOBER 25
Boston at Vancouver*
Detroit at Chicago
Calgary at Edmonton

MONDAY, OCTOBER 26
Philadelphia at N.Y. Rangers
Washington at Winnipeg
San Jose at St. Louis

TUESDAY, OCTOBER 27
Pittsburgh at Ottawa
Tampa Bay at Quebec
Los Angeles at N.Y. Islanders

WEDNESDAY, OCTOBER 28
New Jersey at Hartford
Buffalo at Toronto
Tampa Bay at Montreal
Washington at Vancouver
San Jose at Detroit
Minnesota at Edmonton
Calgary at Winnipeg

THURSDAY, OCTOBER 29
Los Angeles at Boston
Quebec at N.Y. Rangers
Philadelphia at Chicago
Pittsburgh at St. Louis

FRIDAY, OCTOBER 30
Ottawa at Buffalo
N.Y. Islanders at New Jersey
Washington at Calgary
Toronto at Detroit
San Jose at Tampa Bay
Minnesota at Vancouver

SATURDAY, OCTOBER 31
Chicago at Boston
Los Angeles at Hartford
Buffalo at Ottawa
N.Y. Rangers at Montreal
Winnipeg at Quebec
New Jersey at N.Y. Islanders
Philadelphia at St. Louis
Washington at Edmonton
Detroit at Toronto
Minnesota at Calgary

SUNDAY, NOVEMBER 1
Pittsburgh at Tampa Bay
San Jose at Chicago

MONDAY, NOVEMBER 2
Buffalo at N.Y. Rangers
Winnipeg at Montreal
Vancouver at Calgary

TUESDAY, NOVEMBER 3
Quebec at Hartford
Ottawa at Edmonton
N.Y. Islanders at Pittsburgh
St. Louis at Tampa Bay

WEDNESDAY, NOVEMBER 4
Montreal at Detroit
Philadelphia at N.Y. Rangers
Calgary at Vancouver

THURSDAY, NOVEMBER 5

Quebec at Boston
Buffalo at San Jose
Ottawa at Calgary
N.Y. Islanders at Minnesota
New Jersey at Los Angeles
St. Louis at Pittsburgh
Toronto at Chicago

FRIDAY, NOVEMBER 6

Hartford at Detroit
Ottawa at Vancouver
Tampa Bay at Washington
Edmonton at Winnipeg

SATURDAY, NOVEMBER 7

N.Y. Rangers at Boston
Washington at Hartford
Buffalo at Los Angeles
Detroit at Montreal
Chicago at Quebec*
Tampa Bay at N.Y. Islanders
New Jersey at San Jose
St. Louis at Philadelphia*
Pittsburgh at Toronto
Edmonton at Minnesota

SUNDAY, NOVEMBER 8

Calgary at Quebec*
Pittsburgh at Chicago
Winnipeg at Vancouver*
Los Angeles at San Jose

MONDAY, NOVEMBER 9

Toronto at Ottawa
Calgary at Montreal
Tampa Bay at N.Y. Rangers

TUESDAY, NOVEMBER 10

Pittsburgh at Minnesota
Edmonton at St. Louis
Los Angeles at Winnipeg
San Jose at Vancouver

WEDNESDAY, NOVEMBER 11

Boston at Buffalo
Calgary at Hartford
Quebec at Ottawa
Montreal at New Jersey
Washington at N.Y. Rangers
Detroit at Tampa Bay

THURSDAY, NOVEMBER 12

Calgary at Boston
Quebec at Pittsburgh
N.Y. Islanders at Philadelphia
St. Louis at Chicago
Winnipeg at Minnesota
Edmonton at San Jose
Vancouver at Los Angeles

FRIDAY, NOVEMBER 13

Hartford at Buffalo
Ottawa at Tampa Bay
Washington at New Jersey
Pittsburgh at Detroit

SATURDAY, NOVEMBER 14

Toronto at Boston
Detroit at Hartford
Buffalo at N.Y. Islanders
Philadelphia at Montreal
N.Y. Rangers at Quebec
New Jersey at Washington
Calgary at Tampa Bay
Chicago at Minnesota*
Winnipeg at St. Louis
Edmonton at Los Angeles
Vancouver at San Jose

SUNDAY, NOVEMBER 15

Ottawa at Philadelphia
Minnesota at Chicago

MONDAY, NOVEMBER 16

Boston at Montreal
St. Louis at Toronto
Los Angeles at Vancouver

TUESDAY, NOVEMBER 17

Buffalo at Pittsburgh
Montreal at Ottawa
Chicago at Detroit
Winnipeg at Tampa Bay
Los Angeles at San Jose

WEDNESDAY, NOVEMBER 18

St. Louis at Hartford
Minnesota at Washington
Vancouver at Edmonton

THURSDAY, NOVEMBER 19

N.Y. Islanders at Boston
Hartford at Ottawa
Montreal at Quebec
N.Y. Rangers at Philadelphia
Toronto at San Jose
Winnipeg at Detroit
Minnesota at Tampa Bay
Chicago at Los Angeles
Vancouver at Calgary

FRIDAY, NOVEMBER 20

Pittsburgh at New Jersey
Detroit at Washington

SATURDAY, NOVEMBER 21

Philadelphia at Boston
Hartford at Quebec*
Minnesota at Buffalo
Ottawa at Montreal
N.Y. Islanders at Calgary
N.Y. Rangers at Winnipeg
New Jersey at Pittsburgh
Toronto at Los Angeles
Tampa Bay at St. Louis
Chicago at San Jose
Edmonton at Vancouver

SUNDAY, NOVEMBER 22

Buffalo at Philadelphia
Washington at Quebec*
N.Y. Islanders at Edmonton

MONDAY, NOVEMBER 23

Boston at Ottawa
Washington at Montreal
Pittsburgh at N.Y. Rangers
Tampa Bay at Detroit
Chicago at Vancouver

TUESDAY, NOVEMBER 24

N.Y. Islanders at Winnipeg
Tampa Bay at Toronto

WEDNESDAY, NOVEMBER 25

Boston at Washington
Montreal at Hartford
Quebec at Buffalo
New Jersey at Ottawa
N.Y. Rangers at Pittsburgh
St. Louis at Detroit
Vancouver at Minnesota
San Jose at Calgary
Los Angeles at Edmonton

THURSDAY, NOVEMBER 26

Quebec at Toronto
Vancouver at St. Louis

FRIDAY, NOVEMBER 27

Hartford at Boston*
Ottawa at Buffalo
N.Y. Islanders at Philadelphia*
N.Y. Rangers at Minnesota
Pittsburgh at Washington
Los Angeles at Detroit
Tampa Bay at Calgary
Chicago at Edmonton
San Jose at Winnipeg

SATURDAY, NOVEMBER 28

Boston at Hartford
Vancouver at Montreal
New Jersey at Quebec
Philadelphia at N.Y. Islanders
Washington at Pittsburgh
Los Angeles at Toronto
Detroit at St. Louis
Tampa Bay at Edmonton
Chicago at Calgary
San Jose at Minnesota

SUNDAY, NOVEMBER 20

Buffalo at Ottawa

MONDAY, NOVEMBER 30

Boston at Quebec
Buffalo at Montreal
Minnesota at N.Y. Rangers
Washington at Detroit

TUESDAY, DECEMBER 1

Hartford at St. Louis
Minnesota at Ottawa
Pittsburgh at N.Y. Islanders
Toronto at New Jersey
Edmonton at San Jose

WEDNESDAY, DECEMBER 2

Detroit at N.Y. Rangers
Winnipeg at Calgary

THURSDAY, DECEMBER 3

Montreal at Boston
Hartford at San Jose
New Jersey at Ottawa
Quebec at Philadelphia
Pittsburgh at Los Angeles
Toronto at Chicago
Minnesota at Detroit
Edmonton at Vancouver

FRIDAY, DECEMBER 4

N.Y. Islanders at Buffalo
N.Y. Rangers at Washington
St. Louis at Calgary

SATURDAY, DECEMBER 5

Boston at New Jersey*
Hartford at Los Angeles
Philadelphia at Ottawa
Montreal at Winnipeg
Minnesota at Quebec
Washington at N.Y. Islanders
Pittsburgh at San Jose*
Chicago at Toronto
Detroit at Tampa Bay
St. Louis at Edmonton

SUNDAY, DECEMBER 6

Boston at Philadelphia
New Jersey at Buffalo
Montreal at Chicago
Toronto at N.Y. Rangers

MONDAY, DECEMBER 7

Buffalo at Quebec
Washington at Ottawa

— 77 —

N.Y. Islanders at Tampa Bay
St. Louis at Vancouver
Edmonton at Calgary

TUESDAY, DECEMBER 8

Winnipeg at Pittsburgh
Chicago at Detroit
Calgary at Edmonton

WEDNESDAY, DECEMBER 9

Boston at Buffalo
Ottawa at Hartford
Washington at New Jersey
Detroit at Toronto
San Jose at Vancouver

THURSDAY, DECEMBER 10

Ottawa at Boston
Quebec at Los Angeles
N.Y. Islanders at Chicago
St. Louis at San Jose
Edmonton at Minnesota

FRIDAY, DECEMBER 11

Hartford at Buffalo
N.Y. Rangers at Tampa Bay
Pittsburgh at New Jersey
Philadelphia at Detroit
Winnipeg at Washington
Calgary at Toronto

SATURDAY, DECEMBER 12

Boston at Montreal
Buffalo at Hartford
Calgary at Ottawa
Quebec at San Jose
Winnipeg at N.Y. Islanders
New Jersey at Pittsburgh
Washington at Philadelphia
Edmonton at Tampa Bay
Chicago at Minnesota
St. Louis at Los Angeles

SUNDAY, DECEMBER 13

Montreal at N.Y. Rangers
Quebec at Vancouver

MONDAY, DECEMBER 14

Buffalo at Boston
Calgary at Detroit

TUESDAY, DECEMBER 15

Detroit at Ottawa
Calgary at N.Y. Rangers
New Jersey at Winnipeg
Philadelphia at Pittsburgh
Toronto at Minnesota
Tampa Bay at Los Angeles

WEDNESDAY, DECEMBER 16

Washington at Hartford
Quebec at Montreal
Tampa Bay at San Jose
Vancouver at Edmonton

THURSDAY, DECEMBER 17

Ottawa at N.Y. Islanders
Montreal at Quebec
N.Y. Rangers at St. Louis
Pittsburgh at Philadelphia
Winnipeg at Chicago

FRIDAY, DECEMBER 18

Boston at Detroit
Hartford at Washington
New Jersey at Tampa Bay
Los Angeles at Edmonton
San Jose at Vancouver

SATURDAY, DECEMBER 19

Washington at Boston
N.Y. Rangers at Hartford
Buffalo at Montreal
Ottawa at Toronto
N.Y. Islanders at Pittsburgh*
Chicago at Philadelphia*
Detroit at Minnesota
Winnipeg at St. Louis
Los Angeles at Calgary
Vancouver at San Jose

SUNDAY, DECEMBER 20

Toronto at Buffalo
N.Y. Islanders at Quebec*
Philadelphia at Tampa Bay
Minnesota at Chicago

MONDAY, DECEMBER 21

Hartford at Montreal
Washington at Ottawa
Quebec at Pittsburgh
N.Y. Rangers at New Jersey
San Jose at Winnipeg
Edmonton at Calgary

TUESDAY, DECEMBER 22

Tampa Bay at Boston
Toronto at Detroit
St. Louis at Minnesota
Vancouver at Los Angeles

WEDNESDAY, DECEMBER 23

Tampa Bay at Hartford
Washington at Buffalo
Chicago at Ottawa
N.Y. Islanders at Montreal
New Jersey at N.Y. Rangers
Pittsburgh at Philadelphia
Calgary at Winnipeg
San Jose at Edmonton

SATURDAY, DECEMBER 26

Boston at Hartford
Ottawa at Quebec
N.Y. Rangers at N.Y. Islanders
Philadelphia at Washington
Detroit at Toronto
St. Louis at Chicago
Winnipeg at Minnesota
Los Angeles at San Jose

SUNDAY, DECEMBER 27

Boston at N.Y. Rangers
Hartford at New Jersey
Pittsburgh at Buffalo*
Quebec at Ottawa
Montreal at Vancouver
Toronto at St. Louis
Detroit at Chicago
Minnesota at Winnipeg
Calgary at Edmonton

TUESDAY, DECEMBER 29

Boston at Winnipeg
Montreal at Edmonton
New Jersey at Quebec
Toronto at N.Y. Islanders
N.Y. Rangers at Washington
Philadelphia at Los Angeles
Chicago at Detroit
San Jose at Vancouver

WEDNESDAY, DECEMBER 30

Philadelphia at San Jose

THURSDAY, DECEMBER 31

Boston at Minnesota
Quebec at Hartford
N.Y. Rangers at Buffalo
Ottawa at Detroit
Montreal at Calgary
N.Y. Islanders at St. Louis
Toronto at Pittsburgh
Tampa Bay at Chicago
Edmonton at Winnipeg
Los Angeles at Vancouver

FRIDAY, JANUARY 1

New Jersey at Washington*

SATURDAY, JANUARY 2

Hartford at Boston
Buffalo at Ottawa
Montreal at Los Angeles
Detroit at Quebec
Minnesota at N.Y. Islanders
N.Y. Rangers at Pittsburgh
Winnipeg at New Jersey
Philadelphia at Calgary
Chicago at Washington*
St. Louis at Toronto
Tampa Bay at Edmonton
Vancouver at San Jose

SUNDAY, JANUARY 3

Minnesota at Hartford
St. Louis at Buffalo
Philadelphia at Edmonton
Tampa Bay at Vancouver
Winnipeg at Chicago

MONDAY, JANUARY 4

New Jersey at N.Y. Rangers
Toronto at Detroit

TUESDAY, JANUARY 5

Boston at Pittsburgh
Montreal at San Jose
Quebec at N.Y. Islanders
Edmonton at St. Louis
Winnipeg at Calgary

WEDNESDAY, JANUARY 6

Buffalo at Hartford
Ottawa at N.Y. Rangers
Minnesota at New Jersey
Vancouver at Toronto
Tampa Bay at Los Angeles

THURSDAY, JANUARY 7

Quebec at Boston
Washington at Philadelphia
Minnesota at Pittsburgh
Edmonton at Chicago
Calgary at St. Louis

FRIDAY, JANUARY 8

N.Y. Islanders at Buffalo
Ottawa at New Jersey
San Jose at Toronto
Vancouver at Detroit
Los Angeles at Winnipeg

SATURDAY, JANUARY 9

New Jersey at Boston
Quebec at Hartford
Toronto at Montreal
Vancouver at N.Y. Islanders
N.Y. Rangers at Philadelphia*
Calgary at Pittsburgh*
Edmonton at Washington
Tampa Bay at Minnesota
Chicago at St. Louis

SUNDAY, JANUARY 10
Montreal at Hartford
Calgary at Buffalo
San Jose at Ottawa*
Edmonton at Philadelphia
Pittsburgh at Winnipeg
Los Angeles at Chicago

MONDAY, JANUARY 11
Vancouver at N.Y. Rangers
Tampa Bay at Toronto
St. Louis at Detroit

TUESDAY, JANUARY 12
Buffalo at Boston
Los Angeles at Ottawa
Calgary at N.Y. Islanders
Vancouver at New Jersey
Chicago at Minnesota
San Jose at Winnipeg

WEDNESDAY, JANUARY 13
Hartford at Montreal
Washington at N.Y. Rangers
St. Louis at Toronto
Tampa Bay at Detroit
Winnipeg at Edmonton

THURSDAY, JANUARY 14
Pittsburgh at Boston
St. Louis at Ottawa
Montreal at Quebec
Washington at N.Y. Islanders
Los Angeles at New Jersey
Calgary at Philadelphia
Minnesota at Chicago

FRIDAY, JANUARY 15
Hartford at Edmonton
Buffalo at Vancouver
San Jose at Detroit

SATURDAY, JANUARY 16
Philadelphia at Boston
Hartford at Vancouver
Ottawa at Pittsburgh
N.Y. Rangers at Montreal
San Jose at Quebec
N.Y. Islanders at New Jersey*
Chicago at Toronto
St. Louis at Tampa Bay
Calgary at Minnesota
Winnipeg at Los Angeles

SUNDAY, JANUARY 17
Buffalo at Edmonton
N.Y. Islanders at Ottawa
Detroit at Philadelphia
Washington at Tampa Bay
Toronto at Chicago

MONDAY, JANUARY 18
San Jose at Boston*

TUESDAY, JANUARY 19
Boston at N.Y. Islanders
Buffalo at Calgary
Quebec at Ottawa
N.Y. Rangers at Detroit
Pittsburgh at Vancouver
Toronto at St. Louis
Minnesota at Tampa Bay
Chicago at Winnipeg
Los Angeles at Edmonton

WEDNESDAY, JANUARY 20
New Jersey at Montreal

THURSDAY, JANUARY 21
Boston at Philadelphia
San Jose at Hartford
Ottawa at Minnesota
Washington at Chicago
Toronto at Tampa Bay
St. Louis at Detroit
Vancouver at Los Angeles

FRIDAY, JANUARY 22
Quebec at Buffalo
Montreal at New Jersey
Pittsburgh at Edmonton
Winnipeg at Calgary

SATURDAY, JANUARY 23
New Jersey at Boston
Chicago at Hartford*
Buffalo at Quebec
Ottawa at Washington
Montreal at Toronto
Philadelphia at N.Y. Islanders
N.Y. Rangers at Los Angeles
Pittsburgh at Calgary
Detroit at St. Louis
San Jose at Tampa Bay
Vancouver at Minnesota*
Edmonton at Winnipeg

SUNDAY, JANUARY 24
Hartford at Philadelphia
Minnesota at Tampa Bay
Vancouver at Chicago

MONDAY, JANUARY 25
Boston at Montreal

TUESDAY, JANUARY 26
Boston at Quebec
Buffalo at Philadelphia
Ottawa at St. Louis
New Jersey at N.Y. Islanders
Washington at Pittsburgh
Minnesota at Toronto
Detroit at Calgary
San Jose at Los Angeles

WEDNESDAY, JANUARY 27
Hartford at Montreal
Washington at Buffalo
Winnipeg at N.Y. Rangers
Detroit at Edmonton
Chicago at Vancouver

THURSDAY, JANUARY 28
Winnipeg at Boston
Hartford at Ottawa
Quebec at Philadelphia
N.Y. Islanders at Pittsburgh
New Jersey at Minnesota
St. Louis at Tampa Bay
Calgary at Los Angeles

FRIDAY, JANUARY 29
N.Y. Rangers at Buffalo
Quebec at Washington
Chicago at San Jose

SATURDAY, JANUARY 30
Boston at N.Y. Islanders
Winnipeg at Hartford
Ottawa at Montreal*
N.Y. Rangers at Toronto
New Jersey at St. Louis
Philadelphia at Pittsburgh*
Detroit at Vancouver
Tampa Bay at Minnesota
Chicago at Los Angeles
Calgary at San Jose

SUNDAY, JANUARY 31
Edmonton at Buffalo*
Philadelphia at Montreal*
Pittsburgh at Washington*

MONDAY, FEBRUARY 1
Winnipeg at Ottawa
N.Y. Rangers at N.Y. Islanders
Toronto at St. Louis
Tampa Bay at San Jose
Minnesota at Vancouver

TUESDAY, FEBRUARY 2
Edmonton at Boston
Los Angeles at Quebec
Calgary at Washington

WEDNESDAY, FEBRUARY 3
Boston at Quebec
Hartford at Buffalo
Edmonton at Ottawa
Los Angeles at Montreal
N.Y. Islanders at Toronto
Philadelphia at N.Y. Rangers
Calgary at New Jersey
Chicago at Detroit
Tampa Bay at Vancouver
St. Louis at Winnipeg
Minnesota at San Jose

SATURDAY, FEBRUARY 6
All-Star Game at Montreal

MONDAY, FEBRUARY 8
Buffalo at Ottawa
N.Y. Rangers at New Jersey

TUESDAY, FEBRUARY 9
Boston at St. Louis
Ottawa at Philadelphia
Montreal at N.Y. Islanders
Vancouver at Quebec
New Jersey at Detroit
Washington at Minnesota
Toronto at Tampa Bay
Edmonton at Los Angeles

WEDNESDAY, FEBRUARY 10
Buffalo at Winnipeg
Pittsburgh at N.Y. Rangers
San Jose at Calgary

THURSDAY, FEBRUARY 11
Boston at Chicago
Montreal at Philadelphia
Washington at St. Louis
Vancouver at Toronto
Detroit at Los Angeles
Minnesota at Tampa Bay

FRIDAY, FEBRUARY 12
Hartford at Winnipeg
Vancouver at Buffalo
Quebec at Calgary
N.Y. Islanders at N.Y. Rangers
San Jose at Edmonton

SATURDAY, FEBRUARY 13
Hartford at Calgary
Montreal at Ottawa
N.Y. Rangers at N.Y. Islanders
Philadelphia at New Jersey*
Chicago at Pittsburgh*
Washington at Los Angeles
Minnesota at Toronto
Detroit at St. Louis

SUNDAY, FEBRUARY 14
Boston at Tampa Bay
Pittsburgh at Buffalo

— 79 —

Quebec at Edmonton*
New Jersey at Philadelphia*
Toronto at Minnesota
Detroit at Chicago
San Jose at Winnipeg*

MONDAY, FEBRUARY 15
St. Louis at N.Y. Rangers*
Vancouver at Los Angeles*

TUESDAY, FEBRUARY 16
Edmonton at N.Y. Islanders
Washington at San Jose

WEDNESDAY, FEBRUARY 17
Boston at Montreal
Buffalo at Hartford
St. Louis at New Jersey
Calgary at Toronto
Tampa Bay at Detroit
Los Angeles at Minnesota

THURSDAY, FEBRUARY 18
Ottawa at Quebec
St. Louis at N.Y. Islanders
Philadelphia at Vancouver
Edmonton at Pittsburgh
Los Angeles at Chicago
Winnipeg at San Jose

FRIDAY, FEBRUARY 19
Buffalo at New Jersey
Tampa Bay at Toronto
Calgary at Detroit

SATURDAY, FEBRUARY 20
Boston at Toronto
Edmonton at Hartford*
Ottawa at Montreal
Pittsburgh at N.Y. Islanders*
N.Y. Rangers at San Jose
Philadelphia at Minnesota*
Los Angeles at Washington*
Winnipeg at Vancouver

SUNDAY, FEBRUARY 21
Pittsburgh at Hartford*
Edmonton at Montreal
Quebec at New Jersey
St. Louis at Washington*
Detroit at Minnesota*
Calgary at Chicago*

MONDAY, FEBRUARY 22
Ottawa at Winnipeg
Toronto at Vancouver
Los Angeles at Tampa Bay

TUESDAY, FEBRUARY 23
Montreal at St. Louis
Edmonton at Quebec
Washington at N.Y. Islanders
New Jersey at Pittsburgh
Calgary at San Jose

WEDNESDAY, FEBRUARY 24
Philadelphia at Hartford
Detroit at Buffalo
N.Y. Rangers at Vancouver

THURSDAY, FEBRUARY 25
Minnesota at Boston
Pittsburgh at Ottawa
N.Y. Islanders at Quebec
New Jersey at Philadelphia
Toronto at San Jose
Chicago at Tampa Bay
Los Angeles at St. Louis

FRIDAY, FEBRUARY 26
Montreal at Buffalo
N.Y. Rangers at Calgary
Vancouver at Winnipeg

SATURDAY, FEBRUARY 27
Washington at Boston*
Hartford at Quebec
Buffalo at Montreal
Ottawa at New Jersey*
N.Y. Islanders at Philadelphia*
N.Y. Rangers at Edmonton
Tampa Bay at Pittsburgh*
Toronto at Los Angeles
Chicago at Detroit*
Minnesota at St. Louis
San Jose at Calgary

SUNDAY, FEBRUARY 28
N.Y. Islanders at Hartford
Quebec at Ottawa
Detroit at New Jersey
Pittsburgh at Washington*
St. Louis at Chicago
Minnesota at Winnipeg
San Jose at Edmonton

MONDAY, MARCH 1
Montreal at Boston

TUESDAY, MARCH 2
Ottawa at San Jose
Quebec at Winnipeg
Detroit at N.Y. Islanders
Pittsburgh at Philadelphia
Vancouver at Washington
Calgary at Los Angeles

WEDNESDAY, MARCH 3
New Jersey at Hartford
Buffalo at N.Y. Rangers
Montreal at Tampa Bay
Minnesota at Toronto

THURSDAY, MARCH 4
Vancouver at Boston
Ottawa at Los Angeles
Quebec at Chicago
Calgary at St. Louis
Winnipeg at Edmonton

FRIDAY, MARCH 5
Hartford at Buffalo
Pittsburgh at N.Y. Rangers
Chicago at New Jersey
Philadelphia at Washington
Toronto at Detroit

SATURDAY, MARCH 6
St. Louis at Boston*
Vancouver at Hartford
Montreal at Minnesota
N.Y. Rangers at Quebec
Winnipeg at Toronto
Calgary at Tampa Bay
Edmonton at Los Angeles

SUNDAY, MARCH 7
Winnipeg at Buffalo
Ottawa at Chicago*
N.Y. Islanders at Washington*
Philadelphia at New Jersey
Detroit at Minnesota
Edmonton at San Jose

MONDAY, MARCH 8
Hartford at Quebec

TUESDAY, MARCH 9
Boston at Pittsburgh
Philadelphia at N.Y. Islanders
Los Angeles at N.Y. Rangers
New Jersey at Vancouver
Toronto at Washington
Winnipeg at Tampa Bay
San Jose at Minnesota

WEDNESDAY, MARCH 10
Hartford at Toronto
Buffalo at Quebec
N.Y. Islanders at Montreal
Detroit at Edmonton

THURSDAY, MARCH 11
Montreal at Boston
N.Y. Rangers at Chicago
Washington at Philadelphia
Los Angeles at Pittsburgh
Detroit at Calgary
San Jose at St. Louis

FRIDAY, MARCH 12
New Jersey at Edmonton
Tampa Bay at Toronto
Vancouver at Winnipeg

SATURDAY, MARCH 13
Ottawa at Boston*
Buffalo at Hartford*
Quebec at Montreal
Pittsburgh at N.Y. Islanders
N.Y. Rangers at Washington
New Jersey at Calgary
Los Angeles at Philadelphia*
Minnesota at St. Louis

SUNDAY, MARCH 14
Philadelphia at Hartford*
Los Angeles at Buffalo*
Washington at N.Y. Islanders
Detroit at San Jose*
Tampa Bay at Winnipeg*
Chicago at Edmonton*
St. Louis at Minnesota
Vancouver at Calgary

MONDAY, MARCH 15
Boston at N.Y. Rangers
Toronto at Quebec

TUESDAY, MARCH 16
Hartford at Tampa Bay
Buffalo at St. Louis
N.Y. Islanders at San Jose
Minnesota at Philadelphia
Chicago at Calgary
Winnipeg at Los Angeles

WEDNESDAY, MARCH 17
Edmonton at N.Y. Rangers

THURSDAY, MARCH 18
Boston at Ottawa
Montreal at Quebec
N.Y. Islanders at Los Angeles
Edmonton at New Jersey
Philadelphia at Pittsburgh
Toronto at Tampa Bay
Minnesota at Detroit
Winnipeg at Vancouver

FRIDAY, MARCH 19
Hartford at Washington
San Jose at N.Y. Rangers

SATURDAY, MARCH 20
Detroit at Boston*
Buffalo at Tampa Bay*

Ottawa at Pittsburgh
Chicago at Montreal
Quebec at New Jersey*
N.Y. Islanders at Vancouver
Edmonton at Toronto
St. Louis at Los Angeles

SUNDAY, MARCH 21
New Jersey at Philadelphia
San Jose at Washington*
Detroit at Minnesota*
Tampa Bay at Chicago
Calgary at Winnipeg*

MONDAY, MARCH 22
Hartford at Boston
Buffalo at Montreal
N.Y. Rangers at Ottawa
St. Louis at Vancouver

SUNDAY, MARCH 23
Quebec at Washington
N.Y. Islanders at Detroit
Tampa Bay at New Jersey
San Jose at Pittsburgh
Toronto at Winnipeg

WEDNESDAY, MARCH 24
Boston at Buffalo
Montreal at Hartford
Philadelphia at N.Y. Rangers
St. Louis at Calgary
Los Angeles at Vancouver

THURSDAY, MARCH 25
Montreal at Boston
Buffalo at Chicago
Tampa Bay at Ottawa
New Jersey at N.Y. Islanders
San Jose at Philadelphia
Washington at Pittsburgh
Toronto at Minnesota

FRIDAY, MARCH 26
Chicago at N.Y. Rangers
St. Louis at Winnipeg
Calgary at Vancouver
Los Angeles at Edmonton

SATURDAY, MARCH 27
Pittsburgh at Boston*
Hartford at Minnesota
Ottawa at Montreal
Philadelphia at Quebec
San Jose at N.Y. Islanders
New Jersey at Washington*
Toronto at Edmonton
Detroit at Tampa Bay

SUNDAY, MARCH 28
Hartford at Chicago
Ottawa at Buffalo
Quebec at N.Y. Rangers
Pittsburgh at Washington*
Toronto at Calgary
Los Angeles at Winnipeg*

MONDAY, MARCH 29
San Jose at New Jersey
Los Angeles at Detroit

TUESDAY, MARCH 30
Boston at Hartford
Buffalo at Washington
Philadelphia at N.Y. Islanders
Vancouver at St. Louis
Winnipeg at Calgary

WEDNESDAY, MARCH 31
New Jersey at Buffalo
Quebec at Montreal
Los Angeles at Toronto
Minnesota at Edmonton

THURSDAY, APRIL 1
Hartford at Pittsburgh
Quebec at Ottawa
Toronto at Philadelphia
Detroit at Chicago
Vancouver at Tampa Bay
Minnesota at Calgary
Winnipeg at San Jose

FRIDAY, APRIL 2
Montreal at Washington
N.Y. Islanders at N.Y. Rangers

SATURDAY, APRIL 3
Buffalo at Boston*
Ottawa at Hartford
Montreal at N.Y. Islanders
Pittsburgh at Quebec
New Jersey at Toronto
Tampa Bay at Philadelphia*
Vancouver at Detroit*
Chicago at St. Louis
Minnesota at Los Angeles*
Winnipeg at Edmonton
Calgary at San Jose*

SUNDAY, APRIL 4
Boston at Buffalo*
Vancouver at Ottawa
N.Y. Rangers at Washington*
Pittsburgh at New Jersey
St. Louis at Chicago
Calgary at San Jose

MONDAY, APRIL 5
Hartford at N.Y. Rangers

TUESDAY, APRIL 6
Boston at Quebec
Buffalo at Minnesota
N.Y. Islanders at Washington
Philadelphia at Winnipeg
St. Louis at Tampa Bay
Calgary at Los Angeles
Edmonton at San Jose

WEDNESDAY, APRIL 7
Hartford at Ottawa
Montreal at Pittsburgh

N.Y. Rangers at New Jersey
Edmonton at Vancouver

THURSDAY, APRIL 8
Quebec at Boston
Chicago at N.Y. Islanders
Washington at Philadelphia
Toronto at Winnipeg
Detroit at Tampa Bay
San Jose at Los Angeles

FRIDAY, APRIL 9
Pittsburgh at N.Y. Rangers
Vancouver at Calgary

SATURDAY, APRIL 10
Boston at Montreal
Hartford at Quebec
Buffalo at Detroit*
Ottawa at N.Y. Islanders
N.Y. Rangers at Pittsburgh
New Jersey at Washington
Philadelphia at Toronto
Chicago at Tampa Bay*
St. Louis at Minnesota
Los Angeles at San Jose

SUNDAY, APRIL 11
Ottawa at Boston
Toronto at Hartford
Quebec at Buffalo
N.Y. Islanders at New Jersey
Tampa Bay at Chicago*
Minnesota at St. Louis
Winnipeg at Edmonton*
Calgary at Vancouver*

MONDAY, APRIL 12
Washington at Montreal
N.Y. Rangers at Philadelphia

TUESDAY, APRIL 13
Montreal at Buffalo
Ottawa at Quebec
St. Louis at Toronto
Tampa Bay at Winnipeg
Chicago at Minnesota
Calgary at Edmonton
Los Angeles at Vancouver

WEDNESDAY, APRIL 14
Boston at Ottawa
N.Y. Islanders at Hartford
Washington at N.Y. Rangers
Pittsburgh at New Jersey

THURSDAY, APRIL 15
Hartford at N.Y. Islanders
Philadelphia at Buffalo
New Jersey at Pittsburgh
Toronto at Chicago
Minnesota at Detroit
Tampa Bay at St. Louis
Edmonton at Winnipeg
San Jose at Calgary
Vancouver at Los Angeles

1991-92 NHL REVIEW

REGULAR SEASON

FINAL STANDINGS

CLARENCE CAMPBELL CONFERENCE

JAMES NORRIS DIVISION

	G	W	L	T	Pts.	GF	GA	Home	Away	Div. Rec.
Detroit Red Wings	80	43	25	12	98	320	256	24-12- 4	19-13- 8	19-10- 3
Chicago Blackhawks	80	36	29	15	87	257	236	23- 9- 8	13-20- 7	15-12- 5
St. Louis Blues	80	36	33	11	83	279	266	25-12- 3	11-21- 8	11-17- 4
Minnesota North Stars	80	32	42	6	70	246	278	20-16- 4	12-26- 2	12-16- 4
Toronto Maple Leafs	80	30	43	7	67	234	294	21-16- 3	9-27- 4	14-16- 2

CONN SMYTHE DIVISION

	G	W	L	T	Pts.	GF	GA	Home	Away	Div. Rec.
Vancouver Canucks	80	42	26	12	96	285	250	23-10- 7	19-16- 5	20-10- 5
Los Angeles Kings	80	35	31	14	84	287	296	20-11- 9	15-20- 5	16-13- 6
Edmonton Oilers	80	36	34	10	82	295	297	22-13- 5	14-21- 5	15-14- 6
Winnipeg Jets	80	33	32	15	81	251	244	20-14- 6	13-18- 9	15-14- 6
Calgary Flames	80	31	37	12	74	296	305	19-14- 7	12-23- 5	16-15- 4
San Jose Sharks	80	17	58	5	39	219	359	14-23- 3	3-35- 2	8-24- 3

PRINCE OF WALES CONFERENCE

CHARLES F. ADAMS DIVISION

	G	W	L	T	Pts.	GF	GA	Home	Away	Div. Rec.
Montreal Canadiens	80	41	28	11	93	267	207	27- 8- 5	14-20- 6	16-10- 6
Boston Bruins	80	36	32	12	84	270	275	23-11- 6	13-21- 6	16-10- 6
Buffalo Sabres	80	31	37	12	74	289	299	22-13- 5	9-24- 7	12-14- 6
Hartford Whalers	80	26	41	13	65	247	283	13-17-10	13-24- 3	10-16- 6
Quebec Nordiques	80	20	48	12	52	255	318	18-19- 3	2-29- 9	11-15- 6

LESTER PATRICK DIVISION

	G	W	L	T	Pts.	GF	GA	Home	Away	Div. Rec.
New York Rangers	80	50	25	5	105	321	246	28- 8- 4	22-17- 1	19-15- 1
Washington Capitals	80	45	27	8	98	330	275	25-12- 3	20-15- 5	22-12- 1
Pittsburgh Penguins	80	39	32	9	87	343	308	21-13- 6	18-19- 3	16-16- 3
New Jersey Devils	80	38	31	11	87	289	259	24-12- 4	14-19- 7	14-16- 5
New York Islanders	80	34	35	11	79	291	299	20-15- 5	14-20- 6	13-15- 7
Philadelphia Flyers	80	32	37	11	75	252	273	22-11- 7	10-26- 4	10-20- 5

INDIVIDUAL LEADERS

SCORING

TOP SCORERS

	Games	G	A	Pts.	Pen.	+/-	PPG	SHG	Shots	Shooting Pct.
Mario Lemieux, Pittsburgh	64	44	87	*131	94	27	12	4	249	17.7
Kevin Stevens, Pittsburgh	80	54	69	123	254	8	19	0	325	16.6
Wayne Gretzky, Los Angeles	74	31	*90	121	34	-12	12	2	215	14.4
Brett Hull, St. Louis	73	*70	39	109	48	-2	20	5	*408	17.2
Luc Robitaille, Los Angeles	80	44	63	107	95	-4	26	0	240	18.3
Mark Messier, N.Y. Rangers	79	35	72	107	76	31	12	4	212	16.5
Jeremy Roenick, Chicago	80	53	50	103	98	23	22	3	234	22.6
Steve Yzerman, Detroit	79	45	58	103	64	26	9	*8	295	15.3
Brian Leetch, N.Y. Rangers	80	22	80	102	26	25	10	1	245	9.0
Adam Oates, St. Louis-Boston	80	20	79	99	22	-9	6	0	191	10.5
Dale Hawerchuk, Buffalo	77	23	75	98	27	-22	13	0	242	9.5
Mark Recchi, Pittsburgh-Philadelphia	80	43	54	97	96	-21	20	1	210	20.5
Pierre Turgeon, Buffalo-N.Y. Islanders	77	40	55	95	20	7	13	0	207	19.3
Joe Sakic, Quebec	69	29	65	94	20	5	6	3	217	13.4
Pat LaFontaine, Buffalo	57	46	47	93	98	10	23	0	203	22.7
Dave Andreychuk, Buffalo	80	41	50	91	71	-9	*28	0	337	12.2
Gary Roberts, Calgary	76	53	37	90	207	32	15	0	196	*27.0
Vincent Damphousse, Edmonton	80	38	51	89	53	10	12	1	247	15.4
Joe Mullen, Pittsburgh	77	42	45	87	30	12	14	0	226	18.6
Doug Gilmour, Calgary-Toronto	78	26	61	87	78	25	10	1	168	15.5
Craig Janney, Boston-St. Louis	78	18	69	87	22	6	6	0	127	14.2

The scoring leader is awarded the Art Ross Memorial Trophy.
*Indicates league-leading figure.

Games

Steve Konroyd, Chicago/Hartford	82
Steve Thomas, Chi./NYI	82
Many tied with	80

Points

Mario Lemieux, Pittsburgh	131
Kevin Stevens, Pittsburgh	123
Wayne Gretzky, Los Angeles	121
Brett Hull, St. Louis	109
Luc Robitaille, Los Angeles	107
Mark Messier, N.Y. Rangers	107
Jeremy Roenick, Chicago	103
Steve Yzerman, Detroit	103
Brian Leetch, N.Y. Rangers	102
Adam Oates, St. Louis/Boston	99

Points by a defenseman

Brian Leetch, N.Y. Rangers	102
Phil Housley, Winnipeg	86
Ray Bourque, Boston	81
Larry Murphy, Pittsburgh	77
Al MacInnis, Calgary	77

Goals

Brett Hull, St. Louis	70
Kevin Stevens, Pittsburgh	54
Gary Roberts, Calgary	53
Jeremy Roenick, Chicago	53
Pat LaFontaine, Buffalo	46
Steve Yzerman, Detroit	45
Mario Lemieux, Pittsburgh	44
Luc Robitaille, Los Angeles	44
Mark Recchi, Pit./Phi.	43
Owen Nolan, Quebec	42
Joe Mullen, Pittsburgh	42

Assists

Wayne Gretzky, Los Angeles	90
Mario Lemieux, Pittsburgh	87
Brian Leetch, N.Y. Rangers	80
Adam Oates, St. Louis/Boston	79
Dale Hawerchuk, Buffalo	75
Mark Messier, N.Y. Rangers	72
Craig Janney, Boston/St. Louis	69
Kevin Stevens, Pittsburgh	69
Joe Sakic, Quebec	65
Phil Housley, Winnipeg	63
Luc Robitaille, Los Angeles	63

Power-play goals

Dave Andreychuk, Buffalo	28
Luc Robitaille, Los Angeles	26
Pat LaFontaine, Buffalo	23
Jeremy Roenick, Chicago	22
Derek King, N.Y. Islanders	21

Shorthanded goals

Steve Yzerman, Detroit	8
Brett Hull, St. Louis	5
Mike Ridley, Washington	5
Many tied with	4

First goals

Brett Hull, St. Louis	16
Stephen Leach, Boston	11
Kevin Stevens, Pittsburgh	10
Pat LaFontaine, Buffalo	9
Owen Nolan, Quebec	9

Game-winning goals

Jeremy Roenick, Chicago	13
Brett Hull, St. Louis	9
Steve Yzerman, Detroit	9
Claude Lemieux, New Jersey	8
Mike Modano, Minnesota	8
Vincent Damphousse, Edmonton	8
Tony Granato, Los Angeles	8

Game-tying goals

Claude Lemieux, New Jersey	3
Gary Roberts, Calgary	3
Vladimir Ruzicka, Boston	3
Many tied with	2

Shots

Brett Hull, St. Louis	408
Dave Andreychuk, Buffalo	337
Ray Bourque, Boston	334
Kevin Stevens, Pittsburgh	325
Al MacInnis, Calgary	304

Shooting percentage
(80 shots minimum)

Gary Roberts, Calgary	27.0
Sergei Makarov, Calgary	26.5
Ray Ferraro, N.Y. Islanders	26.0
Dale Hunter, Washington	25.5
Sergei Nemchinov, N.Y. Rangers	24.2

Plus/minus

Paul Ysebaert, Detroit	44
Brad McCrimmon, Detroit	39
Nicklas Lidstrom, Detroit	36
James Patrick, N.Y. Rangers	34
Larry Murphy, Pittsburgh	33

Consecutive-game point streaks

Brett Hull, St. Louis	25
Pierre Turgeon, Buf./NYI	18
Dave Andreychuk, Buffalo	17

Brian Leetch, N.Y. Rangers	17
Gary Roberts, Calgary	16
Derek King, N.Y. Islanders	16

Consecutive-game goal streaks

Brett Hull, St. Louis	10
Steve Yzerman, Detroit	9
Pat LaFontaine, Buffalo	6
Mario Lemieux, Pittsburgh	6
Mike Modano, Minnesota	6
Dimitri Khristich, Washington	6
Sergei Makarov, Calgary	6
Sergei Nemchinov, N.Y. Rangers	6

Consecutive-game assist streaks

Brian Leetch, N.Y. Rangers	15
Joe Sakic, Quebec	12
Mario Lemieux, Pittsburgh	10
Craig Janney, Boston/St. Louis	10
Tom Kurvers, N.Y. Islanders	9
Mario Lemieux, Pittsburgh	9
Brian Leetch, N.Y. Rangers	9
Larry Murphy, Pittsburgh	9

Most games scoring three or more goals

Brett Hull, St. Louis	8
Pat LaFontaine, Buffalo	4
Kevin Stevens, Pittsburgh	4
Mark Messier, N.Y. Rangers	3
Joe Mullen, Pittsburgh	3
Brian Noonan, Chicago	3
Steve Yzerman, Detroit	3

Points by a rookie

Tony Amonte, N.Y. Rangers	69
Kevin Todd, New Jersey	63
Pavel Bure, Vancouver	60
Nicklas Lidstrom, Detroit	60
Nelson Emerson, St. Louis	59
Pat Falloon, San Jose	59

Goals by a rookie

Tony Amonte, N.Y. Rangers	35
Pavel Bure, Vancouver	34
Donald Audette, Buffalo	31
Pat Falloon, San Jose	25
Nelson Emerson, St. Louis	23

Assists by a rookie

Nicklas Lidstrom, Detroit	49
Kevin Todd, New Jersey	42
Nelson Emerson, St. Louis	36
Tony Amonte, N.Y. Rangers	34
Pat Falloon, San Jose	34

GOALTENDING

Games

Tim Cheveldae, Detroit	72
Bill Ranford, Edmonton	67
Patrick Roy, Montreal	67
Grant Fuhr, Toronto	65
Kirk McLean, Vancouver	65

Minutes

Tim Cheveldae, Detroit	4236
Patrick Roy, Montreal	3935
Kirk McLean, Vancouver	3852
Bill Ranford, Edmonton	3822
Grant Fuhr, Toronto	3774

Goals allowed

Grant Fuhr, Toronto	230
Bill Ranford, Edmonton	228
Tim Cheveldae, Detroit	226
Mike Vernon, Calgary	217
Kelly Hrudey, Los Angeles	197

Shutouts

Ed Belfour, Chicago	5
Bob Essensa, Winnipeg	5
Kirk McLean, Vancouver	5
Patrick Roy, Montreal	5

Ron Hextall, Philadelphia	3
Mike Richter, N.Y. Rangers	3
Kay Whitmore, Hartford	3

Lowest goals-against average
(25 games played minimum)

Patrick Roy, Montreal	2.36
Ed Belfour, Chicago	2.70
Kirk McLean, Vancouver	2.74
John Vanbiesbrouck, N.Y. Rangers	2.85
Bob Essensa, Winnipeg	2.88

Highest goals-against average
(25 games played minimum)

Ron Tugnutt, Quebec/Edmonton ... 4.36
Jacques Cloutier, Quebec 3.93
Daren Puppa, Buffalo 3.89
Jeff Hackett, San Jose...................3.84
Glenn Healy, N.Y. Islanders 3.80

Games won

Tim Cheveldae, Detroit......................38
Kirk McLean, Vancouver 38
Patrick Roy, Montreal 36
Don Beaupre, Washington 29
Andy Moog, Boston 28

Best winning percentage
(25 games played minimum)

Kirk McLean, Van. (38-17-9) 664
J. Vanbiesbrouck, NYR (27-13-3) .663
Mike Richter, NYR (23-12-2) 649
Craig Billington, N.J. (13-7-1) 643
Don Beaupre, Was. (29-17-6) 615

Worst winning percentage
(25 games played minimum)

Jarmo Myllys, San Jose (3-18-1) ..159
Jeff Hackett, San Jose (11-27-1) ..295
Ron Tugnutt, Que./Edm. (7-18-3).304
Jacques Cloutier, Que. (6-14-3) 326
Peter Sidorkiewicz, Har. (9-19-6) .353

Games lost

Grant Fuhr, Toronto 33
Mike Vernon, Calgary...................... 30
Jeff Hackett, San Jose....................27
Bill Ranford, Edmonton 26
Jon Casey, Minnesota 23
Tim Cheveldae, Detroit....................23

Saves

Curtis Joseph, St. Louis 1778
Tim Cheveldae, Detroit.................. 1752
Bill Ranford, Edmonton 1743
Kelly Hrudey, Los Angeles 1719
Grant Fuhr, Toronto 1703

Highest save percentage
(25 games played minimum)

Patrick Roy, Montreal 914
Bob Essensa, Winnipeg...................910
Curtis Joseph, St. Louis 910
John Vanbiesbrouck, N.Y. Rangers .910
Mark Fitzpatrick, N.Y. Islanders......902

Lowest save percentage
(25 games played minimum)

Ken Wregget, Phi./Pit. 860
Ron Tugnutt, Quebec/Edmonton ... .864
Jarmo Myllys, San Jose 867
Daniel Berthiaume, Los Angeles......875
Jacques Cloutier, Quebec 876

STATISTICS OF PLAYERS WITH TWO OR MORE TEAMS

SCORING

	Games	G	A	Pts.	Pen.	+/-	PPG	SHG	Shots	Shooting Pct.
Brent Ashton, Winnipeg	7	1	0	1	4	-3	0	0	6	16.7
Brent Ashton, Boston	61	17	22	39	47	-4	6	1	124	13.7
Totals	68	18	22	40	51	-7	6	1	130	13.8
Don Barber, Winnipeg	11	0	3	3	4	2	0	0	6	0.0
Don Barber, Quebec	2	0	0	0	0	-1	0	0	1	0.0
Don Barber, San Jose	12	1	3	4	2	-7	0	0	17	5.9
Totals	25	1	6	7	6	-6	0	0	24	4.2
Ken Baumgartner, N.Y. Islanders	44	0	1	1	202	-10	0	0	11	0.0
Ken Baumgartner, Toronto	11	0	0	0	23	1	0	0	5	0.0
Totals	55	0	1	1	225	-9	0	0	16	0.0
Brian Benning, Los Angeles	53	2	30	32	99	4	0	0	102	2.0
Brian Benning, Philadelphia	22	2	12	14	35	-9	2	0	50	4.0
Totals	75	4	42	46	134	-5	2	0	152	2.6
Daniel Berthiaume, Los Angeles (goalie)	19	0	0	0	0	0	0	0	0	0.0
Daniel Berthiaume, Boston (goalie)	8	0	0	0	0	0	0	0	0	0.0
Totals	27	0	0	0	0	0	0	0	0	0.0
Craig Berube, Toronto	40	5	7	12	109	-2	1	0	42	11.9
Craig Berube, Calgary	36	1	4	5	155	-3	0	0	27	3.7
Totals	76	6	11	17	264	-5	1	0	69	8.7
Jeff Beukeboom, Edmonton	18	0	5	5	78	4	0	0	7	0.0
Jeff Beukeboom, N.Y. Rangers	56	1	10	11	122	19	0	0	41	2.4
Totals	74	1	15	16	200	23	0	0	48	2.1
Rob Brown, Hartford	42	16	15	31	39	-14	13	0	65	24.6
Rob Brown, Chicago	25	5	11	16	34	-1	3	0	41	12.2
Totals	67	21	26	47	73	-15	16	0	106	19.8
Rod Buskas, Los Angeles	5	0	0	0	11	-1	0	0	1	0.0
Rod Buskas, Chicago	42	0	4	4	80	-12	0	0	22	0.0
Totals	47	0	4	4	91	-13	0	0	23	0.0
Gino Cavallini, St. Louis	48	9	7	16	40	-8	0	0	72	12.5
Gino Cavallini, Quebec	18	1	7	8	4	-1	0	0	39	2.6
Totals	66	10	14	24	44	-9	0	0	111	9.0
Jeff Chychrun, Los Angeles	26	0	3	3	76	-4	0	0	22	0.0
Jeff Chychrun, Pittsburgh	17	0	1	1	35	-8	0	0	4	0.0
Totals	43	0	4	4	111	-12	0	0	26	0.0
Paul Coffey, Pittsburgh	54	10	54	64	62	4	5	0	207	4.8
Paul Coffey, Los Angeles	10	1	4	5	25	-3	0	0	25	4.0
Totals	64	11	58	69	87	1	5	0	232	4.7
Murray Craven, Philadelphia	12	3	3	6	8	2	1	0	19	15.8
Murray Craven, Hartford	61	24	30	54	38	-4	8	4	133	18.0
Totals	73	27	33	60	46	-2	9	4	152	17.8
Adam Creighton, Chicago	11	6	6	12	16	-1	2	0	32	18.8
Adam Creighton, N.Y. Islanders	66	15	9	24	102	-4	2	0	108	13.9
Totals	77	21	15	36	118	-5	4	0	140	15.0
Lucien DeBlois, Toronto	54	8	11	19	39	-3	0	1	75	10.7
Lucien DeBlois, Winnipeg	11	1	2	3	2	1	0	0	15	6.7
Totals	65	9	13	22	41	-2	0	1	90	10.0

	Games	G	A	Pts.	Pen.	+/-	PPG	SHG	Shots	Shooting Pct.
Kevin Dineen, Hartford	16	4	2	6	23	-6	1	0	28	14.3
Kevin Dineen, Philadelphia	64	26	30	56	130	1	5	3	197	13.2
Totals	80	30	32	62	153	-5	6	3	225	13.3
Gord Donnelly, Winnipeg	4	0	0	0	11	-5	0	0	5	0.0
Gord Donnelly, Buffalo	67	2	3	5	305	-7	0	0	25	8.0
Totals	71	2	3	5	316	-12	0	0	30	6.7
Tom Fergus, Toronto	11	1	3	4	4	-11	0	0	24	4.2
Tom Fergus, Vancouver	44	14	20	34	17	1	6	0	79	17.7
Totals	55	15	23	38	21	-10	6	0	103	14.6
Garry Galley, Boston	38	2	12	14	83	-3	1	0	51	3.9
Garry Galley, Philadelphia	39	3	15	18	34	1	2	0	74	4.1
Totals	77	5	27	32	117	-2	3	0	125	4.0
Johan Garpenlov, Detroit	16	1	1	2	4	2	0	0	13	7.7
Johan Garpenlov, San Jose	12	5	6	11	4	-2	1	0	21	23.8
Totals	28	6	7	13	8	0	1	0	34	17.6
Randy Gilhen, Los Angeles	33	3	6	9	14	-3	0	1	32	9.4
Randy Gilhen, N.Y. Rangers	40	7	7	14	14	5	0	0	67	10.4
Totals	73	10	13	23	28	2	0	1	99	10.1
Paul Gillis, Chicago	2	0	0	0	6	-3	0	0	1	0.0
Paul Gillis, Hartford	12	0	2	2	48	0	0	0	6	0.0
Totals	14	0	2	2	54	-3	0	0	7	0.0
Doug Gilmour, Calgary	38	11	27	38	46	12	4	1	64	17.2
Doug Gilmour, Toronto	40	15	34	49	32	13	6	0	104	14.4
Totals	78	26	61	87	78	25	10	1	168	15.5
Brian Glynn, Minnesota	37	2	12	14	24	-16	0	0	53	3.8
Brian Glynn, Edmonton	25	2	6	8	6	11	0	1	29	6.9
Totals	62	4	18	22	30	-5	0	1	82	4.9
Alexander Godynyuk, Toronto	31	3	6	9	59	-12	1	0	30	10.0
Alexander Godynyuk, Calgary	6	0	1	1	4	-2	0	0	12	0.0
Totals	37	3	7	10	63	-14	1	0	42	7.1
Kevin Haller, Buffalo	58	6	15	21	75	-13	2	0	76	7.9
Kevin Haller, Montreal	8	2	2	4	17	4	1	0	9	22.2
Totals	66	8	17	25	92	-9	3	0	85	9.4
Dave Hannan, Toronto	35	2	2	4	16	-10	0	1	24	8.3
Dave Hannan, Buffalo	12	2	4	6	48	1	0	2	8	25.0
Totals	47	4	6	10	64	-9	0	3	32	12.5
Randy Hillier, N.Y. Islanders	8	0	0	0	11	-3	0	0	5	0.0
Randy Hillier, Buffalo	28	0	1	1	48	-14	0	0	18	0.0
Totals	36	0	1	1	59	-17	0	0	23	0.0
Benoit Hogue, Buffalo	3	0	1	1	0	0	0	0	6	0.0
Benoit Hogue, N.Y. Islanders	72	30	45	75	67	30	8	0	143	21.0
Totals	75	30	46	76	67	30	8	0	149	20.1
Tony Horacek, Philadelphia	34	1	3	4	51	-9	0	0	22	4.5
Tony Horacek, Chicago	12	1	4	5	21	2	0	0	10	10.0
Totals	46	2	7	9	72	-7	0	0	32	6.3
Tony Hrkac, San Jose	22	2	10	12	4	-2	0	0	31	6.5
Tony Hrkac, Chicago	18	1	2	3	6	4	0	0	22	4.5
Totals	40	3	12	15	10	2	0	0	53	5.7
Craig Janney, Boston	53	12	39	51	20	1	3	0	90	13.3
Craig Janney, St. Louis	25	6	30	36	2	5	3	0	37	16.2
Totals	78	18	69	87	22	6	6	0	127	14.2
Mark Janssens, N.Y. Rangers	4	0	0	0	5	-1	0	0	0	0.0
Mark Janssens, Minnesota	3	0	0	0	0	-1	0	0	1	0.0
Totals	7	0	0	0	5	-2	0	0	1	0.0
Steve Konroyd, Chicago	49	2	14	16	65	4	0	0	70	2.9
Steve Konroyd, Hartford	33	2	10	12	32	-5	1	0	56	3.6
Totals	82	4	24	28	97	-1	1	0	126	3.2
Uwe Krupp, Buffalo	8	2	0	2	6	0	0	0	13	15.4
Uwe Krupp, N.Y. Islanders	59	6	29	35	43	13	2	0	115	5.2
Totals	67	8	29	37	49	13	2	0	128	6.3
Mike Lalor, Washington	64	5	7	12	64	14	0	0	54	9.3
Mike Lalor, Winnipeg	15	2	3	5	14	11	0	0	20	10.0
Totals	79	7	10	17	78	25	0	0	74	9.5
Brad Lauer, N.Y. Islanders	8	1	0	1	2	-2	0	1	12	8.3
Brad Lauer, Chicago	6	0	0	0	4	-3	0	0	6	0.0
Totals	14	1	0	1	6	-5	0	1	18	5.6
Gary Leeman, Toronto	34	7	13	20	44	-1	3	0	91	7.7
Gary Leeman, Calgary	29	2	7	9	27	-11	1	0	50	4.0
Totals	63	9	20	29	71	-12	4	0	141	6.4
Claude Loiselle, Toronto	64	6	9	15	102	-21	1	0	91	6.6
Claude Loiselle, N.Y. Islanders	11	1	1	2	13	-3	0	0	10	10.0
Totals	75	7	10	17	115	-24	1	0	101	6.9
Paul MacDermid, Winnipeg	59	10	11	21	151	-8	2	0	71	14.1
Paul MacDermid, Washington	15	2	5	7	43	2	0	0	21	9.5
Totals	74	12	16	28	194	-6	2	0	92	13.0

	Games	G	A	Pts.	Pen.	+/-	PPG	SHG	Shots	Shooting Pct.
Jamie Macoun, Calgary	37	2	12	14	53	10	1	0	58	3.4
Jamie Macoun, Toronto	39	3	13	16	18	0	2	0	71	4.2
Totals	76	5	25	30	71	10	3	0	129	3.9
David Maley, New Jersey	37	7	11	18	58	0	1	0	42	16.7
David Maley, Edmonton	23	3	6	9	46	8	0	0	31	9.7
Totals	60	10	17	27	104	8	1	0	73	13.7
Troy Mallette, Edmonton	15	1	3	4	36	-1	0	0	9	11.1
Troy Mallette, New Jersey	17	3	4	7	43	7	0	0	19	15.8
Totals	32	4	7	11	79	6	0	0	28	14.3
Moe Mantha, Winnipeg	12	0	4	4	6	0	0	0	10	0.0
Moe Mantha, Philadelphia	5	0	0	0	2	0	0	0	7	0.0
Totals	17	0	4	4	8	0	0	0	17	0.0
Nevin Markwart, Boston	18	3	6	9	44	2	0	0	12	25.0
Nevin Markwart, Calgary	10	2	1	3	25	-2	0	0	4	50.0
Totals	28	5	7	12	69	0	0	0	16	31.3
Dan Marois, Toronto	63	15	11	26	76	-36	4	0	140	10.7
Dan Marois, N.Y. Islanders	12	2	5	7	18	2	0	0	19	10.5
Totals	75	17	16	33	94	-34	4	0	159	10.7
Mario Marois, St. Louis	17	0	1	1	38	-3	0	0	11	0.0
Mario Marois, Winnipeg	34	1	3	4	34	-8	0	1	32	3.1
Totals	51	1	4	5	72	-11	0	1	43	2.3
Stephane Matteau, Calgary	4	1	0	1	19	2	0	0	7	14.3
Stephane Matteau, Chicago	20	5	8	13	45	3	1	0	31	16.1
Totals	24	6	8	14	64	5	1	0	38	15.8
Bob McGill, San Jose	62	3	1	4	70	-34	0	1	56	5.4
Bob McGill, Detroit	12	0	0	0	21	-3	0	0	6	0.0
Totals	74	3	1	4	91	-37	0	1	62	4.8
Dave McLlwain, Winnipeg	3	1	1	2	2	1	0	0	3	33.3
Dave McLlwain, Buffalo	5	0	0	0	2	-3	0	0	5	0.0
Dave McLlwain, N.Y. Islanders	54	8	15	23	28	-8	1	1	71	11.3
Dave McLlwain, Toronto	11	1	2	3	4	1	0	0	12	8.3
Totals	73	10	18	28	36	-9	1	1	91	11.0
Corey Millen, N.Y. Rangers	11	1	4	5	10	-1	0	0	20	5.0
Corey Millen, Los Angeles	46	20	21	41	44	3	8	1	89	22.5
Totals	57	21	25	46	54	2	8	1	109	19.3
Kip Miller, Quebec	36	5	10	15	12	-21	1	0	46	10.9
Kip Miller, Minnesota	3	1	2	3	2	-1	1	0	3	33.3
Totals	39	6	12	18	14	-22	2	0	49	12.2
Randy Moller, N.Y. Rangers	43	2	7	9	78	-15	0	0	44	4.5
Randy Moller, Buffalo	13	1	2	3	59	1	0	0	19	5.3
Totals	56	3	9	12	137	-14	0	0	63	4.8
Gordon Murphy, Philadelphia	31	2	8	10	33	-4	0	0	50	4.0
Gordon Murphy, Boston	42	3	6	9	51	2	0	0	82	3.7
Totals	73	5	14	19	84	-2	0	0	132	3.8
Ric Nattress, Calgary	18	0	5	5	31	0	0	0	23	0.0
Ric Nattress, Toronto	36	2	14	16	32	-1	0	0	43	4.7
Totals	54	2	19	21	63	-1	0	0	66	3.0
Bernie Nicholls, N.Y. Rangers	1	0	0	0	0	-1	0	0	2	0.0
Bernie Nicholls, Edmonton	49	20	29	49	60	5	7	0	115	17.4
Totals	50	20	29	49	60	4	7	0	117	17.1
Chris Nilan, Boston	39	5	5	10	186	-5	0	0	33	15.2
Chris Nilan, Montreal	17	1	3	4	74	-1	0	0	22	4.5
Totals	56	6	8	14	260	-6	0	0	55	10.9
Lee Norwood, Hartford	6	0	0	0	16	0	0	0	1	0.0
Lee Norwood, St. Louis	44	3	11	14	94	14	1	0	51	5.9
Totals	50	3	11	14	110	14	1	0	52	5.8
Adam Oates, St. Louis	54	10	59	69	12	-4	3	0	118	8.5
Adam Oates, Boston	26	10	20	30	10	-5	3	0	73	13.7
Totals	80	20	79	99	22	-9	6	0	191	10.5
Mark Osborne, Winnipeg	43	4	12	16	65	-8	0	0	50	8.0
Mark Osborne, Toronto	11	3	1	4	8	-2	0	0	16	18.8
Totals	54	7	13	20	73	-10	0	2	66	10.6
Barry Pederson, Hartford	5	2	2	4	0	-2	1	0	6	33.3
Barry Pederson, Boston	32	3	6	9	8	-5	1	0	41	7.3
Totals	37	5	8	13	8	-7	2	0	47	10.6
Michel Petit, Toronto	34	1	13	14	85	-17	1	0	61	1.6
Michel Petit, Calgary	36	3	10	13	79	2	3	0	68	4.4
Totals	70	4	23	27	164	-15	4	0	129	3.1
Frank Pietrangelo, Pittsburgh (goalie)	5	0	0	0	0	0	0	0	0	0.0
Frank Pietrangelo, Hartford (goalie)	5	0	0	0	0	0	0	0	0	0.0
Totals	10	0	0	0	0	0	0	0	0	0.0
Wayne Presley, San Jose	47	8	14	22	76	-29	3	0	114	7.0
Wayne Presley, Buffalo	12	2	2	4	57	2	0	0	21	9.5
Totals	59	10	16	26	133	-27	3	0	135	7.4

	Games	G	A	Pts.	Pen.	+/-	PPG	SHG	Shots	Shooting Pct.
Stephane Quintal, Boston	49	4	10	14	77	-8	0	0	52	7.7
Stephane Quintal, St. Louis	26	0	6	6	32	-3	0	0	19	0.0
Totals	75	4	16	20	109	-11	0	0	71	5.6
Mark Recchi, Pittsburgh	58	33	37	70	78	-16	16	1	156	21.2
Mark Recchi, Philadelphia	22	10	17	27	18	-5	4	0	54	18.5
Totals	80	43	54	97	96	-21	20	1	210	20.5
Jeff Reese, Toronto (goalie)	8	0	0	0	0	0	0	0	0	0.0
Jeff Reese, Calgary (goalie)	12	0	1	1	12	0	0	0	0	0.0
Totals	20	0	1	1	12	0	0	0	0	0.0
Vincent Riendeau, St. Louis (goalie)	3	0	0	0	0	0	0	0	0	0.0
Vincent Riendeau, Detroit (goalie)	2	0	0	0	0	0	0	0	0	0.0
Totals	5	0	0	0	0	0	0	0	0	0.0
Martin Rucinsky, Edmonton	2	0	0	0	0	-3	0	0	1	0.0
Martin Rucinsky, Quebec	4	1	1	2	2	1	0	0	4	25.0
Totals	6	1	1	2	2	-2	0	0	5	20.0
Kjell Samuelsson, Philadelphia	54	4	9	13	76	1	0	0	63	6.3
Kjell Samuelsson, Pittsburgh	20	1	2	3	34	0	0	0	28	3.6
Totals	74	5	11	16	110	1	0	0	91	5.5
Darrin Shannon, Buffalo	1	0	1	1	0	1	0	0	2	0.0
Darrin Shannon, Winnipeg	68	13	26	39	41	5	3	0	91	14.3
Totals	69	13	27	40	41	6	3	0	93	14.0
David Shaw, N.Y. Rangers	10	0	1	1	15	1	0	0	6	0.0
David Shaw, Edmonton	12	1	1	2	8	-8	0	0	15	6.7
David Shaw, Minnesota	37	0	7	7	49	-5	0	0	49	0.0
Totals	59	1	9	10	72	-12	0	0	70	1.4
Petri Skriko, Boston	9	1	0	1	6	-3	1	0	20	5.0
Petri Skriko, Winnipeg	15	2	3	5	4	-1	0	0	27	7.4
Totals	24	3	3	6	10	-4	1	0	47	6.4
Greg Smyth, Quebec	29	0	2	2	138	-10	0	0	24	0.0
Greg Smyth, Calgary	7	1	1	2	15	7	0	0	10	10.0
Totals	36	1	3	4	153	-3	0	0	34	2.9
Dave Snuggerud, Buffalo	55	3	15	18	36	-3	0	0	75	4.0
Dave Snuggerud, San Jose	11	0	1	1	4	-12	0	0	19	0.0
Totals	66	3	16	19	40	-15	0	0	94	3.2
Alan Stewart, New Jersey	1	0	0	0	5	0	0	0	0	0.0
Alan Stewart, Boston	4	0	0	0	17	-1	0	0	1	0.0
Totals	5	0	0	0	22	-1	0	0	1	0.0
Brent Sutter, N.Y. Islanders	8	4	6	10	6	-5	1	0	21	19.0
Brent Sutter, Chicago	61	18	32	50	30	-5	7	1	185	9.7
Totals	69	22	38	60	36	-10	8	1	206	10.7
Petr Svoboda, Montreal	58	5	16	21	94	9	1	0	88	5.7
Petr Svoboda, Buffalo	13	1	6	7	52	-8	0	0	23	4.3
Totals	71	6	22	28	146	1	1	0	111	5.4
Chris Tancill, Hartford	10	0	0	0	2	-6	0	0	13	0.0
Chris Tancill, Detroit	1	0	0	0	0	0	0	0	0	0.0
Totals	11	0	0	0	2	-6	0	0	13	0.0
Steve Thomas, Chicago	11	2	6	8	26	-3	0	0	35	5.7
Steve Thomas, N.Y. Islanders	71	28	42	70	71	11	3	0	210	13.3
Totals	82	30	48	78	97	8	3	0	245	12.2
Rick Tocchet, Philadelphia	42	13	16	29	102	3	4	0	107	12.1
Rick Tocchet, Pittsburgh	19	14	16	30	49	12	4	1	59	23.7
Totals	61	27	32	59	151	15	8	1	166	16.3
John Tonelli, Chicago	33	1	7	8	37	2	0	0	29	3.4
John Tonelli, Quebec	19	2	4	6	14	-7	2	0	16	12.5
Totals	52	3	11	14	51	-5	2	0	45	6.7
Ron Tugnutt, Quebec (goalie)	30	0	0	0	0	0	0	0	0	0.0
Ron Tugnutt, Edmonton (goalie)	3	0	0	0	2	0	0	0	0	0.0
Totals	33	0	0	0	2	0	0	0	0	0.0
Pierre Turgeon, Buffalo	8	2	6	8	4	-1	0	0	14	14.3
Pierre Turgeon, N.Y. Islanders	69	38	49	87	16	8	13	0	193	19.7
Totals	77	40	55	95	20	7	13	0	207	19.3
Wes Walz, Boston	15	0	3	3	12	-3	0	0	17	0.0
Wes Walz, Philadelphia	2	1	0	1	0	1	0	0	2	50.0
Totals	17	1	3	4	12	-2	0	0	19	5.3
Rick Wamsley, Calgary (goalie)	9	0	0	0	0	0	0	0	0	0.0
Rick Wamsley, Toronto (goalie)	8	0	0	0	0	0	0	0	0	0.0
Totals	17	0	0	0	0	0	0	0	0	0.0
Steve Weeks, N.Y. Islanders (goalie)	23	0	0	0	2	0	0	0	0	0.0
Steve Weeks, Los Angeles (goalie)	7	0	1	1	0	0	0	0	0	0.0
Totals	30	0	1	1	2	0	0	0	0	0.0
Jay Wells, Buffalo	41	2	9	11	157	-3	0	0	26	7.7
Jay Wells, N.Y. Rangers	11	0	0	0	24	2	0	0	4	0.0
Totals	52	2	9	11	181	-1	0	0	30	6.7

	Games	G	A	Pts.	Pen.	+/-	PPG	SHG	Shots	Shooting Pct.
Randy Wood, N.Y. Islanders	8	2	2	4	21	-3	0	0	30	6.7
Randy Wood, Buffalo	70	20	16	36	65	-9	7	1	185	10.8
Totals	78	22	18	40	86	-12	7	1	215	10.2
Ken Wregget, Philadelphia (goalie)	23	0	2	2	0	0	0	0	0	0.0
Ken Wregget, Pittsburgh (goalie)	9	0	0	0	2	0	0	0	0	0.0
Totals	32	0	2	2	2	0	0	0	0	0.0
Rick Zombo, Detroit	3	0	0	0	15	-3	0	0	1	0.0
Rick Zombo, St. Louis	64	3	15	18	46	4	0	0	47	6.4
Totals	67	3	15	18	61	1	0	0	48	6.3

GOALTENDING

	Games	Min.	Goals	SO	Avg.	W	L	T	Shots	Sv. Pct.
Daniel Berthiaume, Los Angeles	19	979	66	0	4.04	7	10	1	541	.878
Daniel Berthiaume, Boston	8	399	21	0	3.16	1	4	2	156	.865
Totals	27	1378	87	0	3.79	8	14	3	697	.875
Frank Pietrangelo, Pittsburgh	5	225	20	0	5.33	2	1	0	130	.846
Frank Pietrangelo, Hartford	5	306	12	0	2.35	3	1	1	156	.923
Totals	10	531	32	0	3.62	5	2	1	286	.888
Jeff Reese, Toronto	8	413	20	1	2.91	1	5	1	210	.905
Jeff Reese, Calgary	12	587	37	0	3.78	3	2	2	290	.872
Totals	20	1000	57	1	3.42	4	7	3	500	.886
Vincent Riendeau, St. Louis	3	157	11	0	4.20	1	2	0	96	.885
Vincent Riendeau, Detroit	2	87	2	0	1.38	2	0	0	31	.935
Totals	5	244	13	0	3.20	3	2	0	127	.898
Ron Tugnutt, Quebec	30	1583	106	1	4.02	6	17	3	782	.864
Ron Tugnutt, Edmonton	3	124	10	0	4.84	1	1	0	73	.863
Totals	33	1597	116	1	4.36	7	18	3	855	.864
Rick Wamsley, Calgary	9	457	34	0	4.46	3	4	0	226	.850
Rick Wamsley, Toronto	8	428	27	0	3.79	4	3	0	218	.876
Totals	17	885	61	0	4.14	7	7	0	444	.863
Steve Weeks, N.Y. Islanders	23	1032	62	0	3.60	9	4	2	566	.890
Steve Weeks, Los Angeles	7	252	17	0	4.05	1	3	0	136	.875
Totals	30	1284	79	0	3.69	10	7	2	702	.887
Ken Wregget, Philadelphia	23	1259	75	0	3.57	9	8	3	557	.865
Ken Wregget, Pittsburgh	9	448	31	0	4.15	5	3	0	202	.847
Totals	32	1707	106	0	3.73	14	11	3	759	.860

Riendeau combined with Tim Cheveldae of Detroit for a shutout.

MISCELLANEOUS

HAT TRICKS

(Players scoring three or more goals in a game)

Date	Player, Team	Opp.	Goals	Date	Player, Team	Opp.	Goals
10- 4-91	Jari Kurri, Los Angeles	Win.	3	11-23-91	Wayne Gretzky, Los Angeles	S.J.	3
10- 5-91	Wendel Clark, Toronto	Det.	3	11-29-91	Kirk Muller, Montreal	Bos.	3
10-10-91	Steve Larmer, Chicago	Van.	3	11-29-91	Kevin Stevens, Pittsburgh	Phi.	4
10-10-91	Gary Roberts, Calgary	L.A.	3	11-30-91	Brett Hull, St. Louis	Det.	3
10-12-91	Owen Nolan, Quebec	Buf.	3	11-30-91	Pierre Turgeon, N.Y. Islanders	Was.	3
10-15-91	Derek King, N.Y. Islanders	Pit.	3	12- 3-91	Steve Yzerman, Detroit	Cal.	3
10-15-91	Mario Lemieux, Pittsburgh	NYI	3	12- 4-91	Greg Adams, Vancouver	Mon.	3
10-16-91	Bob Kudelski, Los Angeles	S.J.	3	12- 5-91	Brian Noonan, Chicago	L.A.	3
10-17-91	Bob Errey, Pittsburgh	NYI	3	12- 5-91	Kevin Stevens, Pittsburgh	S.J.	3
10-18-91	David Maley, New Jersey	Was.	3	12- 7-91	Murray Craven, Hartford	Buf.	3
10-26-91	Mike Bullard, Toronto	Det.	3	12- 7-91	Jeremy Roenick, Chicago	NYI	4
10-29-91	Owen Nolan, Quebec	Win.	3	12- 8-91	Steve Larmer, Chicago	Min.	3
11- 3-91	Igor Larionov, Vancouver	Edm.	3	12-10-91	Ray Ferraro, N.Y. Islanders	St.L.	3
11- 5-91	Vladimir Ruzicka, Boston	Pit.	3	12-10-91	Brett Hull, St. Louis	NYI	3
11- 6-91	Brian Bellows, Minnesota	Tor.	3	12-13-91	Mark Messier, N.Y. Rangers	Was.	3
11- 9-91	Brett Hull, St. Louis	Har.	3	12-14-91	Vincent Damphousse, Edmonton	Win.	4
11-11-91	Stu Barnes, Winnipeg	L.A.	3	12-19-91	Steve Duchesne, Philadelphia	NYI	3
11-12-91	Pat LaFontaine, Buffalo	S.J.	3	12-20-91	Tony Tanti, Buffalo	Edm.	3
11-12-91	Ray Sheppard, Detroit	Cal.	3	12-21-91	Brett Hull, St. Louis	NYI	3
11-13-91	Kevin Stevens, Pittsburgh	Edm.	3	12-23-91	Joe Mullen, Pittsburgh	NYI	4
11-18-91	Mark Recchi, Pittsburgh	Que.	3	12-26-91	Joe Mullen, Pittsburgh	Tor.	4
11-18-91	Kevin Stevens, Pittsburgh	Que.	3	12-26-91	Michal Pivonka, Washington	NYR	3
11-19-91	Mark Messier, N.Y. Rangers	Van.	3	12-27-91	Brian Noonan, Chicago	Win.	3
11-20-91	Stephane Richer, New Jersey	Was.	3	12-28-91	Igor Larionov, Vancouver	S.J.	3
11-22-91	Dave Babych, Vancouver	Cal.	3	12-29-91	Brian Noonan, Chicago	Det.	4
11-22-91	Paul Ranheim, Calgary	Van.	3	12-29-91	Peter Stastny, New Jersey	Was.	3
11-23-91	Dave Andreychuk, Buffalo	Bos.	3	12-31-91	Brian Bellows, Minnesota	Chi.	4

Date	Player, Team	Opp.	Goals
1- 1-92	Derek King, N.Y. Islanders	Was.	3
1- 3-92	Alexander Mogilny, Buffalo	NYI	3
1- 3-92	Paul Ysebaert, Detroit	Tor.	3
1- 7-92	Ray Ferraro, N.Y. Islanders	Det.	4
1- 8-92	Brett Hull, St. Louis	NYR	3
1-10-92	Pat LaFontaine, Buffalo	Edm.	3
1-11-92	Wendel Clark, Toronto	N.J.	3
1-13-92	Joe Murphy, Edmonton	Min.	3
1-16-92	Brett Hull, St. Louis	Mon.	3
1-16-92	Kirk Muller, Montreal	St.L.	3
1-25-92	Pat LaFontaine, Buffalo	Mon.	3
1-29-92	Steve Yzerman, Detroit	Buf.	3
2- 4-92	John Cullen, Hartford	S.J.	3
2- 6-92	Luc Robitaille, Los Angeles	Har.	4
2- 9-92	John Druce, Washington	S.J.	3
2- 9-92	Vladimir Ruzicka, Boston	Pit.	4
2-10-92	Denis Savard, Montreal	Van.	3
2-12-92	Stephan Lebeau, Montreal	S.J.	3
2-12-92	Kevin Miller, Detroit	Buf.	3
2-14-92	Adam Graves, N.Y. Rangers	NYI	3
2-14-92	Dale Hawerchuk, Buffalo	S.J.	3
2-15-92	Jimmy Carson, Detroit	S.J.	3
2-15-92	Craig Janney, St. Louis	Cal.	3
2-17-92	Brent Gilchrist, Montreal	Min.	3
2-18-92	Joe Mullen, Pittsburgh	Tor.	3
2-19-92	Ronnie Stern, Calgary	Bos.	3
2-20-92	Pierre Turgeon, N.Y. Islanders	NYR	3
2-26-92	Gilbert Dionne, Montreal	Min.	3
2-27-92	Tony Granato, Los Angeles	Que.	3
2-27-92	Brett Hull, St. Louis	Was.	3
3- 1-92	Paul Broten, N.Y. Rangers	Har.	3
3- 2-92	Brett Hull, St. Louis	Van.	3
3- 5-92	Mats Sundin, Quebec	Har.	5
3- 6-92	Pat LaFontaine, Buffalo	N.J.	3
3- 6-92	Rick Tocchet, Pittsburgh	S.J.	3
3-11-92	Mike Gartner, N.Y. Rangers	Chi.	3
3-14-92	Tony Amonte, N.Y. Rangers	St.L.	3
3-16-92	Al MacInnis, Calgary	Har.	3
3-17-92	Glenn Anderson, Toronto	Que.	3
3-19-92	Dave Andreychuk, Buffalo	L.A.	4
3-20-92	Dale Hunter, Washington	Phi.	3
3-22-92	Mark Messier, N.Y. Rangers	N.J.	4
3-26-92	Gary Roberts, Calgary	L.A.	3
4-14-92	Joe Sakic, Quebec	Buf.	4
4-14-92	Steve Yzerman, Detroit	Min.	3
4-15-92	Steve Thomas, N.Y. Islanders	N.J.	4
4-16-92	Darren Turcotte, N.Y. Rangers	Pit.	3

OVERTIME GOALS

Date	Player, Team	Opponent	Time	Final score
10- 5-91	Sergei Nemchinov, N.Y. Rangers	Montreal	1:42	N.Y. Rangers 2, Montreal 1
10- 7-91	Mike Gartner, N.Y. Rangers	Boston	0:31	N.Y. Rangers 2, Boston 1
10- 8-91	Geoff Courtnall, Vancouver	Winnipeg	3:32	Vancouver 3, Winnipeg 2
10-10-91	Brett Hull, St. Louis	Edmonton	4:31	St. Louis 3, Edmonton 2
10-15-91	Phil Bourque, Pittsburgh	N.Y. Islanders	2:30	Pittsburgh 7, N.Y. Islanders 6
10-23-91	Petr Svoboda, Montreal	Quebec	3:22	Montreal 3, Quebec 2
11- 1-91	Robert Reichel, Calgary	Winnipeg	4:37	Calgary 7, Winnipeg 6
11- 4-91	Mike Keane, Montreal	New Jersey	0:38	Montreal 3, New Jersey 2
11- 8-91	Donald Audette, Buffalo	Philadelphia	1:29	Buffalo 4, Philadelphia 3
11-12-91	Ray Sheppard, Detroit	Calgary	3:36	Detroit 5, Calgary 4
11-13-91	Kevin Stevens, Pittsburgh	Edmonton	3:25	Pittsburgh 5, Edmonton 4
11-14-91	Lee Norwood, St. Louis	Winnipeg	2:31	St. Louis 2, Winnipeg 1
11-16-91	Ray Bourque, Boston	Hartford	1:39	Boston 5, Hartford 4
11-19-91	Mike Donnelly, Los Angeles	San Jose	3:47	Los Angeles 3, San Jose 2
11-20-91	Stephane Richer, New Jersey	Washington	1:41	New Jersey 6, Washington 5
11-22-91	Dave Babych, Vancouver	Calgary	2:14	Vancouver 6, Calgary 5
11-29-91	Bob Carpenter, Boston	Montreal	4:54	Boston 5, Montreal 4
11-29-91	Mark Messier, N.Y. Rangers	Buffalo	0:43	N.Y. Rangers 5, Buffalo 4
12- 1-91	Darrin Shannon, Winnipeg	Chicago	1:09	Winnipeg 3, Chicago 2
12- 3-91	Brian Mullen, San Jose	Los Angeles	0:22	San Jose 3, Los Angeles 2
12- 5-91	Sylvain Turgeon, Montreal	N.Y. Islanders	2:52	Montreal 5, N.Y. Islanders 4
12- 6-91	Brent Fedyk, Detroit	N.Y. Rangers	4:23	Detroit 6, N.Y. Rangers 5
12-14-91	Sergei Fedorov, Detroit	Calgary	2:10	Detroit 4, Calgary 3
12-16-91	Brian Leetch, N.Y. Rangers	San Jose	0:23	N.Y. Rangers 4, San Jose 3
12-21-91	Stephan Lebeau, Montreal	Hartford	4:09	Montreal 3, Hartford 2
12-22-91	Brad Jones, Philadelphia	Washington	1:10	Philadelphia 4, Washington 3
12-31-91	Paul Ranheim, Calgary	Montreal	2:33	Calgary 3, Montreal 2
1- 4-92	Guy Carbonneau, Montreal	San Jose	1:00	Montreal 1, San Jose 0
1- 6-92	Dave Ellett, Toronto	St. Louis	4:51	Toronto 3, St. Louis 2
1-16-92	Vladimir Ruzicka, Boston	Hartford	0:26	Boston 4, Hartford 3
1-23-92	Donald Audette, Buffalo	Pittsburgh	3:15	Buffalo 5, Pittsburgh 4
1-25-92	Tom Fergus, Vancouver	St. Louis	2:12	Vancouver 1, St. Louis 0
1-27-92	Mike Hudson, Chicago	Calgary	2:13	Chicago 4, Calgary 3
2- 1-92	Kirk Muller, Montreal	Detroit	2:14	Montreal 4, Detroit 3
2- 5-92	Wendel Clark, Toronto	Minnesota	0:18	Toronto 3, Minnesota 2
2- 6-92	Ray Ferraro, N.Y. Islanders	Vancouver	2:48	N.Y. Islanders 5, Vancouver 4
2-17-92	Tom Fitzgerald, N.Y. Islanders	Winnipeg	2:55	N.Y. Islanders 5, Winnipeg 4
2-18-92	Viacheslav Fetisov, New Jersey	Philadelphia	1:42	New Jersey 4, Philadelphia 3
2-23-92	Pavel Bure, Vancouver	Boston	2:52	Vancouver 2, Boston 1
2-23-92	Tony Amonte, N.Y. Rangers	Philadelphia	4:21	N.Y. Rangers 2, Philadelphia 1
2-28-92	Steve Thomas, N.Y. Islanders	New Jersey	3:48	N.Y. Islanders 3, New Jersey 2
2-29-92	Adam Burt, Hartford	Minnesota	4:58	Hartford 5, Minnesota 4
2-29-92	Wendel Clark, Toronto	Chicago	1:02	Toronto 6, Chicago 5
3- 7-92	Dale Hunter, Washington	New Jersey	2:49	Washington 3, New Jersey 2
3-12-92	Rod Brind'Amour, Philadelphia	Calgary	1:54	Philadelphia 5, Calgary 4

Date	Player, Team	Opponent	Time	Final score
3-14-92	—Bob Carpenter, Boston	Quebec	1:27	Boston 5, Quebec 4
3-17-92	—Glenn Anderson, Toronto	Quebec	2:08	Toronto 4, Quebec 3
3-26-92	—Michel Goulet, Chicago	Quebec	4:25	Chicago 5, Quebec 4
3-28-92	—Stephen Heinze, Boston	Buffalo	3:59	Boston 4, Buffalo 3
3-31-92	—Brent Hughes, Boston	Quebec	4:24	Boston 5, Quebec 4
4-12-92	—Peter Bondra, Washington	New Jersey	2:15	Washington 4, New Jersey 3
4-15-92	—Andrew Cassels, Hartford	Philadelphia	1:38	Hartford 4, Philadelphia 3

PENALTY-SHOT INFORMATION

Date	Shooter	Goaltender	Scored	Final score
10-10-91	Kevin Miller, Detroit	Patrick Roy, Montreal	Yes	Montreal 4, Detroit 1
10-12-91	Dave McLlwain, Buffalo	Ron Tugnutt, Quebec	No	Buffalo 5, Quebec 4
10-13-91	Murray Craven, Philadelphia	Chris Terreri, New Jersey	No	Philadelphia 4, New Jersey 2
10-19-91	Gino Odjick, Vancouver	Mike Vernon, Calgary	Yes	Vancouver 5, Calgary 2
10-31-91	Bob Errey, Pittsburgh	Darcy Wakaluk, Minnesota	Yes	Pittsburgh 8, Minnesota 1
11- 2-91	Wes Walz, Boston	Tim Cheveldae, Detroit	No	Boston 4, Detroit 1
11-23-91	Doug Brown, New Jersey	Ken Wregget, Philadelphia	Yes	New Jersey 5, Philadelphia 5
11-27-91	Troy Murray, Winnipeg	Mike Richter, N.Y. Rangers	No	Winnipeg 3, N.Y. Rangers 2
12- 1-91	Greg Adams, Vancouver	Bill Ranford, Edmonton	No	Edmonton 7, Vancouver 0
12-29-91	Darren Turcotte, N.Y. Rangers	Wendell Young, Pittsburgh	No	Pittsburgh 6, N.Y. Rangers 3
1- 3-92	Steve Yzerman, Detroit	Grant Fuhr, Toronto	Yes	Detroit 6, Toronto 4
1- 7-92	Dimitri Khristich, Washington	Darcy Wakaluk, Minnesota	Yes	Minnesota 5, Washington 3
1- 9-92	Craig Janney, Boston	Stephane Fiset, Quebec	No	Boston 5, Quebec 4
1-10-92	Alexander Mogilny, Buffalo	Bill Ranford, Edmonton	No	Buffalo 8, Edmonton 2
1-16-92	John Cullen, Hartford	Andy Moog, Boston	No	Boston 4, Hartford 3
1-16-92	Paul Broten, N.Y. Rangers	Mike Vernon, Calgary	Yes	N.Y. Rangers 6, Calgary 4
1-25-92	Greg Adams, Vancouver	Curtis Joseph, St. Louis	No	Vancouver 1, St. Louis 0
1-29-92	Steve Yzerman, Detroit	Daren Puppa, Buffalo	Yes	Detroit 4, Buffalo 4
2- 6-92	Luc Robitaille, Los Angeles	Kay Whitmore, Hartford	Yes	Los Angeles 5, Hartford 5
2- 7-92	Dave Andreychuk, Buffalo	Darcy Wakaluk, Minnesota	No	Minnesota 2, Buffalo 0
2-17-92	Pavel Bure, Vancouver	John Vanbiesbrouck, N.Y. Rangers	No	Vancouver 3, N.Y. Rangers 3
2-28-92	Pavel Bure, Vancouver	Rick Tabaracci, Winnipeg	Yes	Vancouver 5, Winnipeg 3
3- 3-92	Mats Sundin, Quebec	Tom Draper, Buffalo	Yes	Quebec 4, Buffalo 4
3- 8-92	Marty McInnis, N.Y. Islanders	Tom Draper, Buffalo	No	N.Y. Islanders 6, Buffalo 2
3-17-92	Ulf Dahlen, Minnesota	Daren Puppa, Buffalo	No	Minnesota 3, Buffalo 1
3-17-92	Mario Lemieux, Pittsburgh	Bill Ranford, Edmonton	No	Pittsburgh 6, Edmonton 5
3-21-92	Chris Dahlquist, Minnesota	Stephane Fiset, Quebec	No	Quebec 4, Minnesota 2
3-24-92	Murray Craven, Hartford	Don Beaupre, Washington	Yes	Hartford 8, Washington 2
4-16-92	Todd Elik, Minnesota	Curtis Joseph, St. Louis	No	St. Louis 5, Minnesota 3

TEAM STREAKS

Most consecutive games won

Montreal, Oct. 19-Nov. 6 9
Los Angeles, Feb. 23-Mar. 9 8
N.Y. Rangers, Dec. 13-26 7
N.Y. Rangers, Oct. 23-Nov. 4 6
Edmonton, Jan. 13-Feb. 13 6
New Jersey, Feb. 8-18 6
Detroit, Feb. 12-23 6

Montreal, Oct. 19-Nov. 6 9
Vancouver, Dec. 12-Jan. 3 9
Montreal, Feb. 10-28 9

Buffalo, Dec. 18-Feb. 4 11
N.Y. Rangers, Jan. 14-Mar. 1 11
Montreal, Feb. 1-Mar. 14 10

Most consecutive home games won

Detroit, Nov. 7-Dec. 12 9
Buffalo, Dec. 27-Feb. 4 9
Pittsburgh, Feb. 29-Apr. 15 9
Los Angeles, Feb. 15-Mar. 17 8

Most consecutive road games won

Washington, Oct. 29-Nov. 13 5
Pittsburgh, Dec. 13-29 5
Vancouver, Jan. 14-25 5

Most consecutive games undefeated

Winnipeg, Nov. 16-Dec. 10 11
Detroit, Nov. 7-25 10

Most consecutive home games undefeated

Chicago, Jan.-Mar. 10 13
Chicago, Oct. 31-Dec. 27 12

Most consecutive road games undefeated

Vancouver, Feb. 17-Mar. 14 6
Many tied with 5

TEAM OVERTIME GAMES

Team	OVERALL					HOME					AWAY				
	G	W	L	T	Pct.	G	W	L	T	Pct.	G	W	L	T	Pct.
N.Y. Rangers	11	5	1	5	.682	7	3	0	4	.714	4	2	1	1	.625
Toronto	11	4	0	7	.682	7	4	0	3	.786	4	0	0	4	.500
Boston	20	6	2	12	.600	9	3	0	6	.667	11	3	2	6	.545
Vancouver	17	4	1	12	.588	10	2	1	7	.550	7	2	0	5	.643
Montreal	20	6	3	11	.575	10	4	1	5	.650	10	2	2	6	.500
Detroit	16	3	1	12	.563	5	1	0	4	.600	11	2	1	8	.545
Pittsburgh	12	2	1	9	.542	8	1	1	6	.500	4	1	0	3	.625
N.Y. Islanders	16	3	2	11	.531	8	1	2	5	.438	8	2	0	6	.625
Chicago	19	2	2	15	.500	8	0	0	8	.500	11	2	2	7	.500
Buffalo	16	2	2	12	.500	7	1	1	5	.500	9	1	1	7	.500
Los Angeles	16	1	1	14	.500	9	0	0	9	.500	7	1	1	5	.500

Team	G	W	L	T	Pct.	G	W	L	T	Pct.	G	W	L	T	Pct.
		OVERALL					HOME					AWAY			
St. Louis	15	2	2	11	.500	6	2	1	3	.583	9	0	1	8	.444
Washington	12	2	2	8	.500	4	1	0	3	.625	8	1	2	5	.438
Hartford	18	2	3	13	.472	11	0	1	10	.455	7	2	2	3	.500
Philadelphia	17	2	4	11	.441	10	2	1	7	.550	7	0	3	4	.286
New Jersey	17	2	4	11	.441	8	2	2	4	.500	9	0	2	7	.389
Winnipeg	20	1	4	15	.425	9	1	2	6	.444	11	0	2	9	.409
Calgary	19	2	5	12	.421	11	1	3	7	.409	8	1	2	5	.438
Edmonton	12	0	2	10	.417	5	0	0	5	.500	7	0	2	5	.357
San Jose	9	1	3	5	.389	6	1	2	3	.417	3	0	1	2	.333
Minnesota	8	0	2	6	.375	5	0	1	4	.400	3	0	1	2	.333
Quebec	17	0	5	12	.353	6	0	3	3	.250	11	0	2	9	.409
Totals	169	52	52	117	1.000	169	30	22	117	.524	169	22	30	117	.476

STANLEY CUP PLAYOFFS

RESULTS

DIVISION SEMIFINALS

ADAMS DIVISION
Series "A"

	W	L	Pts.	GF	GA
Montreal Canadiens	4	3	8	21	18
Hartford Whalers	3	4	6	18	21

(Montreal won Adams Division semifinal, 4-3)

Sun.	April 19—Hartford 0, at Montreal 2
Tue.	April 21—Hartford 2, at Montreal 5
Thur.	April 23—Montreal 2, at Hartford 5
Sat.	April 25—Montreal 1, at Hartford 3
Mon.	April 27—Hartford 4, at Montreal 7
Wed.	April 29—Montreal 1, at Hartford 2 (a)
Fri.	May 1—Hartford 2, at Montreal 3 (b)

(a)—Yvan Corriveau scored at 0:24 (OT) for Hartford.
(b)—Russ Courtnall scored at 5:26 (2 OT) for Montreal.

Series "B"

	W	L	Pts.	GF	GA
Boston Bruins	4	3	8	19	24
Buffalo Sabres	3	4	6	24	19

(Boston won Adams Division semifinal, 4-3)

Sun.	April 19—Buffalo 3, at Boston 2
Tue.	April 21—Buffalo 2, at Boston 3 (c)
Thur.	April 23—Boston 3, at Buffalo 2
Sat.	April 25—Boston 5, at Buffalo 4 (d)
Mon.	April 27—Buffalo 2, at Boston 0
Wed.	April 29—Boston 3, at Buffalo 9
Fri.	May 1—Buffalo 2, at Boston 3

(c)—Adam Oates scored at 11:14 (OT) for Boston.
(d)—Ted Donato scored at 2:08 (OT) for Boston.

PATRICK DIVISION
Series "C"

	W	L	Pts.	GF	GA
New York Rangers	4	3	8	28	25
New Jersey Devils	3	4	6	25	28

(New York won Patrick Division semifinal, 4-3)

Sun.	April 19—New Jersey 1, at N.Y. Rangers 2
Tue.	April 21—New Jersey 7, at N.Y. Rangers 3
Thur.	April 23—N.Y. Rangers 1, at New Jersey 3
Sat.	April 25—N.Y. Rangers 3, at New Jersey 0
Mon.	April 27—N.Y. Rangers 5, at New Jersey 3
Wed.	April 29—N.Y. Rangers 3, at New Jersey 5
Fri.	May 1—New Jersey 4, at N.Y. Rangers 8

Series "D"

	W	L	Pts.	GF	GA
Pittsburgh Penguins	4	3	8	25	27
Washington Capitals	3	4	6	27	25

(Pittsburgh won Patrick Division semifinal, 4-3)

Sun.	April 19—Pittsburgh 1, at Washington 3
Tue.	April 21—Pittsburgh 2, at Washington 6
Thur.	April 23—Washington 4, at Pittsburgh 6
Sat.	April 25—Washington 7, at Pittsburgh 2
Mon.	April 27—Pittsburgh 5, at Washington 2

Wed. April 29—Washington 4, at Pittsburgh 6
Fri. May 1—Pittsburgh 3, at Washington 1

NORRIS DIVISION
Series "E"

	W	L	Pts.	GF	GA
Detroit Red Wings	4	3	8	23	19
Minnesota North Stars	3	4	6	19	23

(Detroit won Norris Division semifinal, 4-3)

Sat.	April 18—Minnesota 4, at Detroit 3
Mon.	April 20—Minnesota 4, at Detroit 2
Wed.	April 22—Detroit 5, at Minnesota 4 (e)
Fri.	April 24—Detroit 4, at Minnesota 5
Sun.	April 26—Minnesota 0, at Detroit 3
Tue.	April 28—Detroit 1, at Minnesota 0 (f)
Thur.	April 30—Minnesota 2, at Detroit 5

(e)—Yves Racine scored at 1:15 (OT) for Detroit.
(f)—Sergei Fedorov scored at 16:13 (OT) for Detroit.

Series "F"

	W	L	Pts.	GF	GA
Chicago Blackhawks	4	2	8	23	19
St. Louis Blues	2	4	4	19	23

(Chicago won Norris Division semifinal, 4-2)

Sat.	April 18—St. Louis 1, at Chicago 3
Mon.	April 20—St. Louis 5, at Chicago 3
Wed.	April 22—Chicago 4, at St. Louis 5 (g)
Fri.	April 24—Chicago 5, at St. Louis 3
Sun.	April 26—St. Louis 4, at Chicago 6
Tue.	April 28—Chicago 2, St. Louis 1

(g)—Brett Hull scored at 3:33 (2 OT) for St. Louis.

SMYTHE DIVISION
Series "G"

	W	L	Pts.	GF	GA
Vancouver Canucks	4	3	8	29	17
Winnipeg Jets	3	4	6	17	29

(Vancouver won Smythe Division semifinal, 4-3)

Sat.	April 18—Winnipeg 3, at Vancouver 2
Mon.	April 20—Winnipeg 2, at Vancouver 3
Wed.	April 22—Vancouver 2, at Winnipeg 4
Fri.	April 24—Vancouver 1, at Winnipeg 3
Sun.	April 26—Winnipeg 2, at Vancouver 8
Tue.	April 28—Vancouver 8, at Winnipeg 3
Thur.	April 30—Winnipeg 0, at Vancouver 5

Series "H"

	W	L	Pts.	GF	GA
Edmonton Oilers	4	2	8	23	18
Los Angeles Kings	2	4	4	18	23

(Edmonton won Smythe Division semifinal, 4-2)

Sat.	April 18—Edmonton 3, at Los Angeles 1
Mon.	April 20—Edmonton 5, at Los Angeles 8
Wed.	April 22—Los Angeles 3, at Edmonton 4
Fri.	April 24—Los Angeles 4, at Edmonton 3
Sun.	April 26—Edmonton 5, at Los Angeles 2
Tue.	April 28—Los Angeles 0, at Edmonton 3

DIVISION FINALS

ADAMS DIVISION
Series "I"

	W	L	Pts.	GF	GA
Boston Bruins	4	0	8	14	8
Montreal Canadiens	0	4	0	8	14

(Boston won Adams Division final, 4-0)

Sun.	May 3—Boston 6, at Montreal 4
Tue.	May 5—Boston 3, at Montreal 2 (h)
Thur.	May 7—Montreal 2, at Boston 3
Sat.	May 9—Montreal 0, at Boston 2

(h)—Peter Douris scored at 3:12 (OT) for Boston.

PATRICK DIVISION
Series "J"

	W	L	Pts.	GF	GA
Pittsburgh Penguins	4	2	8	24	19
N.Y. Rangers	2	4	4	19	24

(Pittsburgh won Patrick Division final, 4-2)

Sun.	May 3	Pittsburgh 4, at N.Y. Rangers 2
Tue.	May 5	Pittsburgh 2, at N.Y. Rangers 4
Thur.	May 7	N.Y. Rangers 6, at Pittsburgh 5 (i)
Sat.	May 9	N.Y. Rangers 4, at Pittsburgh 5 (j)
Mon.	May 11	Pittsburgh 3, at N.Y. Rangers 2
Wed.	May 13	N.Y. Rangers 1, at Pittsburgh 5

(i)—Kris King scored at 1:29 (OT) for New York.
(j)—Ron Francis scored at 2:47 (OT) for Pittsburgh.

NORRIS DIVISION
Series "K"

	W	L	Pts.	GF	GA
Chicago Blackhawks	4	0	8	11	6
Detroit Red Wings	0	4	0	6	11

(Chicago won Norris Division final, 4-0)

Sat.	May 2	Chicago 2, at Detroit 1
Mon.	May 4	Chicago 3, at Detroit 1
Wed.	May 6	Detroit 4, at Chicago 5
Fri.	May 8	Detroit 0, at Chicago 1

SMYTHE DIVISION
Series "L"

	W	L	Pts.	GF	GA
Edmonton Oilers	4	2	8	18	15
Vancouver Canucks	2	4	4	15	18

(Edmonton won Smythe Division final, 4-2)

Sat.	May 2	Edmonton 4, at Vancouver 3 (k)
Mon.	May 4	Edmonton 0, at Vancouver 4
Wed.	May 6	Vancouver 2, at Edmonton 5
Fri.	May 8	Vancouver 2, at Edmonton 3
Sun.	May 10	Edmonton 3, at Vancouver 4
Tue.	May 12	Vancouver 0, at Edmonton 3

(k)—Joe Murphy scored at 8:36 (OT) for Edmonton.

CONFERENCE CHAMPIONSHIPS

PRINCE OF WALES CONFERENCE
Series "M"

	W	L	Pts.	GF	GA
Pittsburgh Penguins	4	0	8	19	7
Boston Bruins	0	4	0	7	19

(Pittsburgh won Wales Conference title, 4-0)

Sun.	May 17	Boston 3, at Pittsburgh 4 (l)
Tue.	May 19	Boston 2, at Pittsburgh 5
Thur.	May 21	Pittsburgh 5, at Boston 1
Sat.	May 23	Pittsburgh 5, at Boston 1

(l)—Jaromir Jagr scored at 9:44 (OT) for Pittsburgh.

CLARENCE CAMPBELL CONFERENCE
Series "N"

	W	L	Pts.	GF	GA
Chicago Blackhawks	4	0	8	21	8
Edmonton Oilers	0	4	0	8	21

(Chicago won Campbell Conference title, 4-0)

Sat.	May 16	Edmonton 2, at Chicago 8
Mon.	May 18	Edmonton 2, at Chicago 4
Wed.	May 20	Chicago 4, at Edmonton 3 (m)
Fri.	May 22	Chicago 5, at Edmonton 1

(m)—Jeremy Roenick scored at 2:35 (OT) for Chicago.

STANLEY CUP FINALS

Series "O"

	W	L	Pts.	GF	GA
Pittsburgh	4	0	8	15	10
Chicago	0	4	0	10	15

(Pittsburgh won Stanley Cup championship, 4-0)

Tue.	May 26	Chicago 4, at Pittsburgh 5
Thur.	May 28	Chicago 1, at Pittsburgh 3
Sat.	May 30	Pittsburgh 1, at Chicago 0
Mon.	June 1	Pittsburgh 6, at Chicago 5

GAME SUMMARIES, STANLEY CUP FINALS

GAME 1
AT PITTSBURGH, MAY 26
Pittsburgh 5, Chicago 4

Chicago	3	1	0	—4
Pittsburgh	1	2	2	—5

FIRST PERIOD—1. Chicago—Chelios 1 (Sutter), 6:34 (pp). 2. Chicago, Goulet 3, 13:17. 3. Chicago, Graham 4 (Chelios), 13:43. 4. Pittsburgh, Bourque 3 (Tocchet, Francis), 17:26 (pp). Penalties—Hudson, Chicago (interference), 2:07; Roberts, Pittsburgh (holding), 6:27; Peluso, Chicago (hooking), 9:34; Kravchuk, Chicago (holding), 15:44; Trottier, Pittsburgh (interference), 18:39.

SECOND PERIOD—5. Chicago, Sutter 3 (Larmer, Chelios), 11:36. 6. Pittsburgh, Tocchet 5 (Stanton, McEachern), 15:24. 7. Pittsburgh, Lemieux 12 (Stevens), 16:23. Penalties—R. Brown, Chicago (roughing), 2:27; Chicago bench, served by Lemieux (too many men), 13:21.

THIRD PERIOD—8. Pittsburgh, Jagr 10, 15:05. 9. Pittsburgh, Lemieux 13 (Murphy, Francis), 19:47 (pp). Penalties—Stanton, Pittsburgh (hooking), 1:24; Murphy, Pittsburgh (hooking), 17:39; Smith, Chicago (hooking), 19:42.

Shots on goal—Chicago 11-11-12—34. Pittsburgh 15-10-14—39. Power-play opportunities—Chicago 1 of 4; Pittsburgh 2 of 6. Goalies—Chicago, Belfour, 12-2 (39 shots-34 saves). Pittsburgh, Barrasso, 13-5 (34-30). A—16,164. Referee—Andy van Hellemond. Linesmen—Kevin Collins, Gerard Gauthier.

GAME 2
AT PITTSBURGH, MAY 28
Pittsburgh 3, Chicago 1

Chicago	0	1	0	—1
Pittsburgh	1	2	0	—3

FIRST PERIOD—1. Pittsburgh, Errey 3 (Paek), 9:52 (sh). Penalties—Peluso, Chicago (roughing), 2:07; Stanton, Pittsburgh, double minor (tripping, delay of game), 7:38; Smith, Chicago (interference), 11:05; Noonan, Chicago (cross-checking), 18:36.

SECOND PERIOD—2. Chicago, Marchment 1 (Noonan, Gilbert), 10:24. 3. Pittsburgh, M. Lemieux 14 (Tocchet), 12:55 (pp). 4. Pittsburgh, M. Lemieux 15 (Tocchet, K. Samuelsson), 15:23. Penalties—Marchment, Chicago (elbowing), 12:12; Chicago bench, served by Graham (too many men), 19:43.

THIRD PERIOD—None. Penalty—Roberts, Pit (holding), 5:09.

Shots on goal—Chicago 11-4-4—19. Pittsburgh 8-11-6—25. Power-play opportunities—Chicago 0 of 3; Pittsburgh

1 of 5. Goalies—Chicago, Belfour, 12-3 (25 shots-22 saves). Pittsburgh, Barrasso, 14-5 (19-18). A—16,164. Referee—Terry Gregson. Linesmen—Swede Knox, Ray Scapinello.

GAME 3
AT CHICAGO, MAY 30
Pittsburgh 1, Chicago 0

Pittsburgh	1	0	0—1
Chicago	0	0	0—0

FIRST PERIOD—1. Pittsburgh, Stevens 12 (Paek, McEachern), 15:26. Penalties—K. Samuelsson, Pittsburgh (high-sticking), 5:43; Roberts, Pittsburgh (tripping), 11:50; Goulet, Chicago (holding), 16:47; Jagr, Pittsburgh (holding), 19:14.

SECOND PERIOD—None. Penalties—Larmer, Chicago (cross-checking), 4:38; Stanton, Pittsburgh (holding), 7:04; Chelios, Chicago (slashing), 10:56.

THIRD PERIOD—None. Penalties—Paek, Pittsburgh (interference), 10:05; Chelios, Chicago, major-game misconduct (fighting), 19:29.

Shots on goal—Pittsburgh 6-8-6—20. Chicago 13-6-8—27. Power-play opportunities—Pittsburgh 0 of 4; Chicago 0 of 5. Goalies—Pittsburgh, Barrasso, 15-5 (27 shots-27 saves). Chicago, Belfour 12-4 (20-19). A—18,472. Referee—Don Koharski. Linesmen—Gerard Gauthier, Kevin Collins.

GAME 4
AT CHICAGO, JUNE 1
Pittsburgh 6, Chicago 5

Pittsburgh	3	1	2—6
Chicago	3	1	1—5

FIRST PERIOD—1. Pittsburgh, Jagr 11 (Loney), 1:37. 2. Chicago, Graham 5 (Matteau, Chelios), 6:21. 3. Pittsburgh, Stevens 13 (M. Lemieux, Tocchet), 6:33. 4. Chicago, Graham 6 (Chelios), 6:51. 5. Pittsburgh, M. Lemieux 16 (Murphy, Stevens), 10:13 (pp). 6. Chicago, Graham 7 (Noonan, J. Lemieux), 16:18. Penalties—U. Samuelsson, Pittsburgh (interference), 7:28; Stanton, Pittsburgh, misconduct, 7:28; Gilbert, Chicago, misconduct, 7:28; Chelios, Chicago (elbowing), 8:17; Roberts, Pittsburgh (roughing), 12:44.

SECOND PERIOD—7. Pittsburgh, Tocchet 6 (M. Lemieux, Stevens), :58. 8. Chicago, Roenick 11 (Noonan, Gilbert), 15:40. Penalties—Stanton, Pittsburgh (hooking), 2:21; Tocchet, Pittsburgh (holding), 5:41.

THIRD PERIOD—9. Pittsburgh, Murphy 6 (Tocchet), 4:51. 10. Pittsburgh, Francis 8 (McEachern, Paek), 7:59. 11. Chicago, Roenick 12 (Grimson, Buskas), 11:18. Penalties—None.

Shots on goal—Pittsburgh 12-9-8—29. Chicago 8-14-7—29. Power-play opportunities—Pittsburgh 1 of 1; Chicago 0 of 4. Goalies—Pittsburgh, Barrasso, 16-5 (29 shots-24 saves). Chicago, Belfour (4-2), Hasek, 0-2 (13:24 first, 25-21). A—18,472. Referee—Andy van Hellemond. Linesmen—Swede Knox, Ray Scapinello.

INDIVIDUAL LEADERS

Goals: Mario Lemieux, Pittsburgh (16)
Assists: Ron Francis, Pittsburgh (19)
Points: Mario Lemieux, Pittsburgh (34)
Penalty minutes: Jeff Beukeboom, N.Y. Rangers (47)
Goaltending average: Ed Belfour, Chicago (2.47)
Shutouts: Tim Cheveldae, Detroit (2)
Kirk McLean, Vancouver (2)
Bill Ranford, Edmonton (2)

TOP SCORERS

	Games	G	A	Pts.	Pen.
Mario Lemieux, Pittsburgh	15	16	18	34	2
Kevin Stevens, Pittsburgh	21	13	15	28	28
Ron Francis, Pittsburgh	21	8	19	27	6
Jaromir Jagr, Pittsburgh	21	11	13	24	6
Joe Murphy, Edmonton	16	8	16	24	12
Jeremy Roenick, Chicago	18	12	10	22	12
Chris Chelios, Chicago	18	6	15	21	37
Bernie Nicholls, Edmonton	16	8	11	19	25
Rick Tocchet, Pittsburgh	14	6	13	19	24
Adam Oates, Boston	15	5	14	19	4

INDIVIDUAL STATISTICS

BOSTON BRUINS
(Lost Wales Conference finals to Pittsburgh, 4-0)
SCORING

	Games	G	A	Pts.	Pen.
Adam Oates	15	5	14	19	4
Joe Juneau	15	4	8	12	21
Ray Bourque	12	3	6	9	12
Ted Donato	15	3	4	7	4
Dave Reid	15	2	5	7	4
Glen Murray	15	4	2	6	10
Dave Poulin	15	3	3	6	22
Glen Wesley	15	2	4	6	16
Peter Douris	7	2	3	5	0
Vladimir Ruzicka	13	2	3	5	2
Stephen Leach	15	4	0	4	10
Jim Wiemer	15	1	3	4	14
Gord Hynes	12	1	2	3	6
Stephen Heinze	7	0	3	3	17
Brent Hughes	10	2	0	2	20
Bob Sweeney	14	1	0	1	25
Gordon Murphy	15	1	0	1	12
Bob Carpenter	8	0	1	1	6
Jeff Lazaro	9	0	1	1	2
Andy Moog (goalie)	15	0	1	1	17
Bob Beers	1	0	0	0	0
Clark Donatelli	2	0	0	0	0

	Games	G	A	Pts.	Pen.
Rejean Lemelin (goalie)	2	0	0	0	0
Lyndon Byers	5	0	0	0	12
Matt Hervey	5	0	0	0	6
Don Sweeney	15	0	0	0	10

GOALTENDING

	Games	Min.	Goals	SO	Avg.
Andy Moog	15	866	46 (1)	1	3.19
Rejean Lemelin	2	54	3 (1)	0	3.33

BUFFALO SABRES
(Lost Adams Division semifinals to Boston, 3-4)
SCORING

	Games	G	A	Pts.	Pen.
Pat LaFontaine	7	8	3	11	4
Dale Hawerchuk	7	2	5	7	0
Wayne Presley	7	3	3	6	14
Petr Svoboda	7	1	4	5	6
Brad May	7	1	4	5	2
Dave Andreychuk	7	1	3	4	12
Doug Bodger	7	2	1	3	2
Randy Wood	7	2	1	3	6
Tony Tanti	7	0	3	3	4
Keith Carney	7	0	3	3	0
Dave Hannan	7	2	0	2	2

	Games	G	A	Pts.	Pen.
Alexander Mogilny	2	0	2	2	0
Mike Ramsey	7	0	2	2	8
Ken Sutton	7	0	2	2	4
Bob Corkum	4	1	0	1	0
Colin Patterson	5	1	0	1	0
Gord Donnelly	6	0	1	1	0
Christian Ruuttu	3	0	0	0	6
Tom Draper (goalie)	7	0	0	0	0
Randy Moller	7	0	0	0	8
Rob Ray	7	0	0	0	2

GOALTENDING

	Games	Min.	Goals	SO	Avg.
Tom Draper	7	433	19	1	2.63

CHICAGO BLACKHAWKS

(Lost Stanley Cup finals to Pittsburgh, 4-0)

SCORING

	Games	G	A	Pts.	Pen.
Jeremy Roenick	18	12	10	22	12
Chris Chelios	18	6	15	21	37
Steve Larmer	18	8	7	15	6
Brian Noonan	18	6	9	15	30
Dirk Graham	18	7	5	12	8
Steve Smith	18	1	11	12	16
Stephane Matteau	18	4	6	10	24
Mike Hudson	16	3	5	8	26
Brent Sutter	18	3	5	8	22
Igor Kravchuk	18	2	6	8	8
Keith Brown	14	0	8	8	18
Michel Goulet	9	3	4	7	6
Rob Brown	8	2	4	6	4
Jocelyn Lemieux	18	3	1	4	33
Greg Gilbert	10	1	3	4	16
Mike Peluso	17	1	2	3	8
Brad Lauer	7	1	1	2	2
Cam Russell	12	0	2	2	2
Tony Horacek	2	1	0	1	2
Bryan Marchment	16	1	0	1	36
Rod Buskas	6	0	1	1	0
Stu Grimson	14	0	1	1	10
Dominik Hasek (goalie)	3	0	0	0	0
Tony Hrkac	3	0	0	0	2
Dean McAmmond	3	0	0	0	2
Frantisek Kucera	6	0	0	0	0
Ed Belfour (goalie)	18	0	0	0	6

GOALTENDING

	Games	Min.	Goals	SO	Avg.
Ed Belfour	18	949	39	1	2.47
Dominik Hasek	3	158	8 (1)	0	3.04

DETROIT RED WINGS

(Lost Norris Division finals to Chicago, 4-0)

SCORING

	Games	G	A	Pts.	Pen.
Sergei Fedorov	11	5	5	10	8
Ray Sheppard	11	6	2	8	4
Steve Yzerman	11	3	5	8	12
Bob Probert	11	1	6	7	28
Shawn Burr	11	1	5	6	10
Steve Chiasson	11	1	5	6	12
Jimmy Carson	11	2	3	5	0
Mike Sillinger	8	2	2	4	2
Gerard Gallant	11	2	2	4	25
Yves Racine	11	2	1	3	10
Nicklas Lidstrom	11	1	2	3	0
Alan Kerr	9	2	0	2	17
Kevin Miller	9	0	2	2	4
Paul Ysebaert	10	1	0	1	10
Bobby Dollas	2	0	1	1	0
Martin Lapointe	3	0	1	1	4
Tim Cheveldae (goalie)	11	0	1	1	6
Brad McCrimmon	11	0	1	1	8

	Games	G	A	Pts.	Pen.
Vladimir Konstantinov	11	0	1	1	16
Troy Crowder	1	0	0	0	0
Brent Fedyk	1	0	0	0	2
Marc Potvin	1	0	0	0	0
Vincent Riendeau (goalie)	2	0	0	0	0
Brad Marsh	3	0	0	0	0
Bob McGill	8	0	0	0	14
Keith Primeau	11	0	0	0	14

GOALTENDING

	Games	Min.	Goals	SO	Avg.
Tim Cheveldae	11	597	25 (1)	2	2.51
Vincent Riendeau	2	73	4	0	3.29

EDMONTON OILERS

(Lost Campbell Conference finals to Chicago, 4-0)

SCORING

	Games	G	A	Pts.	Pen.
Joe Murphy	16	8	16	24	12
Bernie Nicholls	16	8	11	19	25
Vincent Damphousse	16	6	8	14	8
Dave Manson	16	3	9	12	44
Esa Tikkanen	16	5	3	8	8
Brian Glynn	16	4	1	5	12
Petr Klima	15	1	4	5	8
Kelly Buchberger	16	1	4	5	32
Luke Richardson	16	0	5	5	45
Chris Joseph	5	1	3	4	2
Martin Gelinas	15	1	3	4	10
Craig MacTavish	16	3	0	3	28
Josef Beranek	12	2	1	3	0
Scott Mellanby	16	2	1	3	29
Norm Maciver	13	1	2	3	10
Kevin Lowe	11	0	3	3	16
Greg Hawgood	13	0	3	3	23
Anatoli Semenov	8	1	1	2	6
David Maley	10	1	1	2	4
Mark Lamb	16	1	1	2	10
Geoff Smith	5	0	1	1	6
Craig Simpson	1	0	0	0	0
Scott Thornton	1	0	0	0	0
Ron Tugnutt (goalie)	2	0	0	0	0
Craig Muni	3	0	0	0	2
Bill Ranford (goalie)	16	0	0	0	0

GOALTENDING

	Games	Min.	Goals	SO	Avg.
Ron Tugnutt	2	60	3	0	3.00
Bill Ranford	16	909	51	2	3.37

HARTFORD WHALERS

(Lost Adams Division semifinals to Montreal, 4-3)

SCORING

	Games	G	A	Pts.	Pen.
Murray Craven	7	3	3	6	6
Andrew Cassels	7	2	4	6	6
Yvon Corriveau	7	3	2	5	18
Zarley Zalapski	7	2	3	5	6
Randy Cunneyworth	7	3	0	3	9
John Cullen	7	2	1	3	12
Patrick Poulin	7	2	1	3	0
Todd Richards	5	0	3	3	4
Doug Houda	6	0	2	2	13
Mikael Andersson	7	0	2	2	6
Pat Verbeek	7	0	2	2	12
Geoff Sanderson	7	1	0	1	2
Brad Shaw	3	0	1	1	4
Paul Gillis	7	0	1	1	6
Bobby Holik	7	0	1	1	6
Steve Konroyd	7	0	1	1	2
Randy Ladouceur	7	0	1	1	11
Kay Whitmore (goalie)	1	0	0	0	0
Adam Burt	2	0	0	0	0
Mark Hunter	4	0	0	0	6

	Games	G	A	Pts.	Pen.
Marc Bergevin	5	0	0	0	2
Daniel Shank	5	0	0	0	22
Frank Pietrangelo (goalie)	7	0	0	0	0

GOALTENDING

	Games	Min.	Goals	SO	Avg.
Frank Pietrangelo	7	425	19 (1)	0	2.68
Kay Whitmore	1	19	1	0	3.16

LOS ANGELES KINGS

(Lost Smythe Division semifinals to Edmonton, 4-2)

SCORING

	Games	G	A	Pts.	Pen.
Paul Coffey	6	4	3	7	2
Luc Robitaille	6	3	4	7	12
Wayne Gretzky	6	2	5	7	2
Tony Granato	6	1	5	6	10
John McIntyre	6	0	4	4	12
Rob Blake	6	2	1	3	12
Jari Kurri	4	1	2	3	4
Tomas Sandstrom	6	0	3	3	8
Jay Miller	5	1	1	2	12
Charlie Huddy	6	1	1	2	10
Dave Taylor	6	1	1	2	4
Mike Donnelly	6	1	0	1	4
Marty McSorley	6	1	0	1	21
Kyosti Karjalainen	3	0	1	1	2
Corey Millen	6	0	1	1	6
Larry Robinson	2	0	0	0	0
Brent Thompson	4	0	0	0	4
Kelly Hrudey (goalie)	6	0	0	0	0
Bob Kudelski	6	0	0	0	0
Tim Watters	6	0	0	0	8
Peter Ahola	6	0	0	0	2

GOALTENDING

	Games	Min.	Goals	SO	Avg.
Kelly Hrudey	6	355	22 (1)	0	3.72

MINNESOTA NORTH STARS

(Lost Norris Division semifinals to Detroit, 4-3)

SCORING

	Games	G	A	Pts.	Pen.
Brian Bellows	7	4	4	8	14
Dave Gagner	7	2	4	6	8
Neal Broten	7	1	5	6	2
Mike Modano	7	3	2	5	4
Bobby Smith	7	1	4	5	6
David Shaw	7	2	2	4	10
Jim Johnson	7	1	3	4	18
Mark Tinordi	7	1	2	3	11
Ulf Dahlen	7	0	3	3	2
Todd Elik	5	1	1	2	2
Derian Hatcher	5	0	2	2	8
Mike Craig	4	1	0	1	7
Gaetan Duchesne	7	1	0	1	6
Derrick Smith	7	1	0	1	9
Craig Ludwig	7	0	1	1	19
Brian Propp	1	0	0	0	0
Brad Berry	2	0	0	0	2
Marc Bureau	5	0	0	0	14
Trent Klatt	6	0	0	0	2
Jon Casey (goalie)	7	0	0	0	0
Chris Dahlquist	7	0	0	0	6
Stewart Gavin	7	0	0	0	6

GOALTENDING

	Games	Min.	Goals	SO	Avg.
Jon Casey	7	437	22 (1)	0	3.02

MONTREAL CANADIENS

(Lost Adams Division finals to Boston, 4-0)

SCORING

	Games	G	A	Pts.	Pen.
Denis Savard	11	3	9	12	8
Kirk Muller	11	4	3	7	31
Gilbert Dionne	11	3	4	7	10
Shayne Corson	10	2	5	7	15
Eric Desjardins	11	3	3	6	4
Patrice Brisebois	11	2	4	6	6
Brent Gilchrist	11	2	4	6	6
Matt Schneider	10	1	4	5	6
Stephan Lebeau	8	1	3	4	4
J.J. Daigneault	11	0	3	3	4
Mike Keane	8	1	1	2	16
John LeClair	8	1	1	2	4
Mike McPhee	8	1	1	2	4
Russ Courtnall	10	1	1	2	4
Guy Carbonneau	11	1	1	2	6
Brian Skrudland	11	1	1	2	20
Sean Hill	4	1	0	1	2
Sylvain Turgeon	5	1	0	1	4
Chris Nilan	7	0	1	1	15
Andre Racicot (goalie)	1	0	0	0	0
Sylvain Lefebvre	2	0	0	0	2
Todd Ewen	3	0	0	0	18
Lyle Odelein	7	0	0	0	11
Kevin Haller	9	0	0	0	6
Patrick Roy (goalie)	11	0	0	0	2

GOALTENDING

	Games	Min.	Goals	SO	Avg.
Andre Racicot	1	1	0	0	0.00
Patrick Roy	11	686	30 (2)	1	2.62

NEW JERSEY DEVILS

(Lost Patrick Division semifinals to N.Y. Rangers, 4-3)

SCORING

	Games	G	A	Pts.	Pen.
Peter Stastny	7	3	7	10	19
Claude Lemieux	7	4	3	7	26
Zdeno Ciger	7	2	4	6	0
Kevin Todd	7	3	2	5	8
Randy McKay	7	1	3	4	10
Bruce Driver	7	0	4	4	2
Bill Guerin	6	3	0	3	4
Scott Stevens	7	2	1	3	29
Stephane Richer	7	1	2	3	0
Viacheslav Fetisov	6	0	3	3	8
Tom Chorske	7	0	3	3	4
Ken Daneyko	7	0	3	3	16
Tommy Albelin	1	1	1	2	0
Valeri Zelepukin	4	1	1	2	2
Pat Conacher	7	1	1	2	4
Alexei Kasatonov	7	1	1	2	12
Claude Vilgrain	7	1	1	2	17
Janne Ojanen	3	0	2	2	0
Eric Weinrich	7	0	2	2	4
Laurie Boschman	7	1	0	1	8
Martin Brodeur (goalie)	1	0	0	0	0
Alexander Semak	1	0	0	0	0
Chris Terreri (goalie)	7	0	0	0	0

GOALTENDING

	Games	Min.	Goals	SO	Avg.
Chris Terreri	7	386	23 (2)	0	3.58
Martin Brodeur	1	32	3	0	5.63

NEW YORK RANGERS

(Lost Patrick Division finals to Pittsburgh, 4-2)

SCORING

	Games	G	A	Pts.	Pen.
Mike Gartner	13	8	8	16	4
Brian Leetch	13	4	11	15	4
Mark Messier	11	7	7	14	6
Tony Amonte	13	3	6	9	2
Adam Graves	10	5	3	8	22
James Patrick	13	0	7	7	12
Kris King	13	4	1	5	14
Jeff Beukeboom	13	2	3	5	47

	Games	G	A	Pts.	Pen.
Jan Erixon	13	2	3	5	2
Sergei Nemchinov	13	1	4	5	8
Darren Turcotte	8	4	0	4	6
Doug Weight	7	2	2	4	0
Joe Cirella	13	0	4	4	23
Paul Broten	13	1	2	3	10
Randy Gilhen	13	1	2	3	2
Mark Hardy	13	0	3	3	31
Tie Domi	6	1	1	2	32
Joey Kocur	12	1	1	2	38
Jay Wells	13	0	2	2	10
Tim Kerr	8	1	0	1	0
John Ogrodnick	3	0	0	0	0
Mike Richter (goalie)	7	0	0	0	0
John Vanbiesbrouck (goalie)	7	0	0	0	2

GOALTENDING
	Games	Min.	Goals	SO	Avg.
Mike Richter	7	412	24	1	3.50
John Vanbiesbrouck	7	368	23 (2)	0	3.75

PITTSBURGH

(Winner of 1992 Stanley Cup)

SCORING
	Games	G	A	Pts.	Pen.
Mario Lemieux	15	16	18	34	2
Kevin Stevens	21	13	15	28	28
Ron Francis	21	8	19	27	6
Jaromir Jagr	21	11	13	24	6
Rick Tocchet	14	6	13	19	24
Larry Murphy	21	6	10	16	19
Troy Loney	21	4	5	9	32
Shawn McEachern	19	2	7	9	4
Paul Stanton	21	1	7	8	42
Bryan Trottier	21	4	3	7	8
Phil Bourque	21	3	4	7	25
Joe Mullen	9	3	1	4	4
Jock Callender	12	1	3	4	2
Jim Paek	19	0	4	4	6
Bob Errey	14	3	0	3	10
Kjell Samuelsson	15	0	3	3	12
Dave Michayluk	7	1	1	2	0
Gordie Roberts	19	0	2	2	32
Jiri Hrdina	20	0	2	2	16
Tom Barrasso (goalie)	21	0	2	2	4
Ulf Samuelsson	21	0	2	2	39
Mike Needham	5	1	0	1	2
Ken Wregget (goalie)	1	0	0	0	0
Jay Caufield	5	0	0	0	2
Grant Jennings	10	0	0	0	12

GOALTENDING
	Games	Min.	Goals	SO	Avg.
Tom Barrasso	21	1233	58 (1)	1	2.82
Ken Wregget	1	40	4	0	6.00

ST. LOUIS BLUES

(Lost Norris Division semifinals to Chicago, 4-2)

SCORING
	Games	G	A	Pts.	Pen.
Brett Hull	6	4	4	8	4
Nelson Emerson	6	3	3	6	21
Craig Janney	6	0	6	6	0
Brendan Shanahan	6	2	3	5	14
Ron Sutter	6	1	3	4	8
Dave Christian	4	3	0	3	0
Jeff Brown	6	2	1	3	2
Stephane Quintal	4	1	2	3	6
Garth Butcher	5	1	2	3	16
Curt Giles	3	1	1	2	0
Bob Bassen	6	0	2	2	4
Rick Zombo	6	0	2	2	12
Philippe Bozon	6	1	0	1	27
Lee Norwood	1	0	1	1	0

	Games	G	A	Pts.	Pen.
Paul Cavallini	4	0	1	1	6
Curtis Joseph (goalie)	6	0	1	1	0
Dave Lowry	6	0	1	1	20
Ron Wilson	6	0	1	1	0
Kelly Chase	1	0	0	0	7
Dave Mackey	1	0	0	0	0
Denny Felsner	1	0	0	0	0
Murray Baron	2	0	0	0	0
Darin Kimble	5	0	0	0	7
Bret Hedican	5	0	0	0	0
Rich Sutter	6	0	0	0	8

GOALTENDING
	Games	Min.	Goals	SO	Avg.
Curtis Joseph	6	379	23	0	3.64

VANCOUVER CANUCKS

(Lost Smythe Division finals to Edmonton, 4-2)

SCORING
	Games	G	A	Pts.	Pen.
Geoff Courtnall	12	6	8	14	20
Cliff Ronning	13	8	5	13	6
Trevor Linden	13	4	8	12	6
Pavel Bure	13	6	4	10	14
Jim Sandlak	13	4	6	10	22
Igor Larionov	13	3	7	10	4
Tom Fergus	13	5	3	8	6
Dave Babych	13	2	6	8	10
Adrien Plavsic	13	1	7	8	4
Jyrki Lumme	13	2	3	5	4
Petr Nedved	10	1	4	5	16
Sergio Momesso	13	0	5	5	30
Robert Kron	11	1	2	3	2
Doug Lidster	11	1	2	3	11
Ryan Walter	13	0	3	3	8
Greg Adams	6	0	2	2	4
Randy Gregg	7	0	1	1	8
Kirk McLean (goalie)	13	0	1	1	0
Robin Bawa	1	0	0	0	0
Dana Murzyn	1	0	0	0	15
Ken Hammond	2	0	0	0	6
Jim Agnew	4	0	0	0	6
Gino Odjick	4	0	0	0	6
Garry Valk	4	0	0	0	5
Gerald Diduck	5	0	0	0	10
Robert Dirk	13	0	0	0	20

GOALTENDING
	Games	Min.	Goals	SO	Avg.
Kirk McLean	13	785	33 (2)	2	2.52

WASHINGTON CAPITALS

(Lost Patrick Division semifinals to Pittsburgh, 4-3)

SCORING
	Games	G	A	Pts.	Pen.
Mike Ridley	7	0	11	11	0
Dino Ciccarelli	7	5	4	9	14
Peter Bondra	7	6	2	8	4
Al Iafrate	7	4	2	6	14
Kevin Hatcher	7	2	4	6	19
Michal Pivonka	7	1	5	6	13
Dimitri Khristich	7	3	2	5	15
Dale Hunter	7	1	4	5	16
Calle Johansson	7	0	5	5	4
Todd Krygier	5	2	1	3	4
Sylvain Cote	7	1	2	3	4
Kelly Miller	7	1	2	3	4
John Druce	7	1	0	1	2
Randy Burridge	2	0	1	1	0
Rod Langway	7	0	1	1	8
Paul MacDermid	7	0	1	1	22
Dave Tippett	7	0	1	1	0
Brad Schlegel	7	0	1	1	2
Don Beaupre (goalie)	7	0	0	0	0
Alan May	7	0	0	0	0

GOALTENDING

	Games	Min.	Goals	SO	Avg.
Don Beaupre	7	419	22 (3)	0	3.15

WINNIPEG JETS

(Lost Smythe Division semifinals to Vancouver, 4-3)

SCORING

	Games	G	A	Pts.	Pen.
Thomas Steen	7	2	4	6	2
Fredrik Olausson	7	1	5	6	4
Phil Housley	7	1	4	5	0
Aaron Broten	7	2	2	4	12
Pat Elynuik	7	2	2	4	4
Evgeny Davydov	7	2	2	4	2
Keith Tkachuk	7	3	0	3	30
Ed Olczyk	6	2	1	3	4
Randy Carlyle	5	1	0	1	6
Lucien DeBlois	5	1	0	1	2
Darrin Shannon	7	0	1	1	10

	Games	G	A	Pts.	Pen.
Phil Sykes	7	0	1	1	9
Bob Essensa (goalie)	1	0	0	0	0
Doug Evans	1	0	0	0	2
Luciano Borsato	1	0	0	0	0
Kris Draper	2	0	0	0	0
Mike Hartman	2	0	0	0	2
Dean Kennedy	2	0	0	0	0
Shawn Cronin	4	0	0	0	6
Mike Eagles	7	0	0	0	8
Mike Lalor	7	0	0	0	19
Troy Murray	7	0	0	0	2
Teppo Numminen	7	0	0	0	0
Rick Tabaracci (goalie)	7	0	0	0	0
Igor Ulanov	7	0	0	0	39

GOALTENDING

	Games	Min.	Goals	SO	Avg.
Rick Tabaracci	7	387	26	0	4.03
Bob Essensa	1	33	3	0	5.45

MISCELLANEOUS

HAT TRICKS

(Players scoring three or more goals in a game)

Date	Player, Team	Opp.	Goals	Date	Player, Team	Opp.	Goals
4-23-92	—Mario Lemieux, Pittsburgh	Was.	3	4-30-92	—Geoff Courtnall, Vancouver	Win.	3
4-24-92	—Ray Sheppard, Detroit	Min.	3	5- 6-92	—Joe Murphy, Edmonton	Van.	3
4-25-92	—Dino Ciccarelli, Washington	Pit.	4	5- 9-92	—Ron Francis, Pittsburgh	NYR	3
4-26-92	—Esa Tikkanen, Edmonton	L.A.	3	5-21-92	—Kevin Stevens, Pittsburgh	Bos.	3
4-27-92	—Mike Gartner, N.Y. Rangers	N.J.	3	6- 1-92	—Dirk Graham, Chicago	Pit.	3
4-28-92	—Pavel Bure, Vancouver	Win.	3				

OVERTIME GOALS

Date	Player, Team	Opponent	Time	Final score
4-21-92	—Adam Oates, Boston	Buffalo	11:14	Boston 3, Buffalo 2
4-22-92	—Yves Racine, Detroit	Minnesota	1:15	Detroit 5, Minnesota 4
4-22-92	—Brett Hull, St. Louis	Chicago	*3:33	St. Louis 5, Chicago 4
4-25-92	—Ted Donato, Boston	Buffalo	2:08	Boston 5, Buffalo 4
4-28-92	—Sergei Fedorov, Detroit	Minnesota	16:13	Detroit 1, Minnesota 0
4-29-92	—Yvan Corriveau, Hartford	Montreal	0:24	Hartford 2, Montreal 1
5- 1-92	—Russ Courtnall, Montreal	Hartford	*5:26	Montreal 3, Hartford 2
5- 2-92	—Joe Murphy, Edmonton	Vancouver	8:36	Edmonton 4, Vancouver 3
5- 5-92	—Peter Douris, Boston	Montreal	3:12	Boston 3, Montreal 2
5- 7-92	—Kris King, N.Y. Rangers	Pittsburgh	1:29	N.Y. Rangers 6, Pittsburgh 5
5- 9-92	—Ron Francis, Pittsburgh	N.Y. Rangers	2:47	Pittsburgh 5, N.Y. Rangers 4
5-17-92	—Jaromir Jagr, Pittsburgh	Boston	9:44	Pittsburgh 4, Boston 3
5-20-92	—Jeremy Roenick, Chicago	Edmonton	2:35	Chicago 4, Edmonton 3

*Double-overtime goal.

PENALTY-SHOT INFORMATION

Date	Shooter	Goaltender	Scored	Final score
5-11-92	Jaromir Jagr, Pittsburgh	John Vanbiesbrouck, N.Y. Rangers	Yes	Pittsburgh 3, N.Y. Rangers 2
5-13-92	Shawn McEachern, Pittsburgh	John Vanbiesbrouck, N.Y. Rangers	No	Pittsburgh 5, N.Y. Rangers 1

AWARDS

THE SPORTING NEWS

ALL-STAR TEAMS

(Vote totals in parentheses)

Patrick Roy, Montreal (246)	Goaltender	Kirk McLean, Vancouver (69)
Brian Leetch, N.Y. Rangers (259)	Defense	Phil Housley, Winnipeg (88)
Ray Bourque, Boston (215)	Defense	Chris Chelios, Chicago (22)
Kevin Stevens, Pittsburgh (239)	Left wing	Luc Robitaille, Los Angeles (41)
Mark Messier, N.Y. Rangers (200)	Center	Wayne Gretzky, Los Angeles (51)
Brett Hull, St. Louis (246)	Right wing	Joe Mullen, Pittsburgh (12)

Note: THE SPORTING NEWS All-Star Team is selected by the NHL players.

AWARD WINNERS

(Vote totals in parentheses)

Player of the Year voting: Mark Messier, N.Y. Rangers (226); Brett Hull, St. Louis (27); Kevin Stevens, Pittsburgh (22).

Rookie of the Year voting: Tony Amonte, N.Y. Rangers (130); Pavel Bure, Vancouver (96); Niklas Lidstrom, Detroit (89); Pat Falloon, San Jose (26).

Coach of the Year voting: Pat Quinn, Vancouver (6); Pat Burns, Montreal (4); Roger Neilson, N.Y. Rangers (4); Terry Murray, Washington (2).

Executive of the Year voting: Neil Smith, N.Y. Rangers (13); Pat Quinn, Vancouver (10); Bryan Murray, Detroit (3); John Ziegler, NHL president (3).

Note: THE SPORTING NEWS player and rookie awards are selected by the NHL players, the coaches award by the NHL coaches and the executive award by NHL executives.

NHL AWARD WINNERS

Art Ross Trophy: Mario Lemieux, Pittsburgh
Hart Memorial Trophy: Mark Messier, N.Y. Rangers
James Norris Memorial Trophy: Brian Leetch, N.Y. Rangers
Vezina Trophy: Patrick Roy, Montreal
Bill Jennings Trophy: Patrick Roy, Montreal
Calder Memorial Trophy: Pavel Bure, Vancouver

Lady Byng Memorial Trophy: Wayne Gretzky, Los Angeles
Conn Smythe Trophy: Mario Lemieux, Pittsburgh
Bill Masterton Memorial Trophy: Mark Fitzpatrick, N.Y. Islanders
Frank J. Selke Trophy: Guy Carbonneau, Montreal
Jack Adams Award: Pat Quinn, Vancouver
King Clancy Trophy: Ray Bourque, Boston

ENTRY DRAFT

ROUND-BY-ROUND SELECTIONS

FIRST ROUND

No.—Selecting club	Player	Pos.	Previous team (league)
1—Tampa Bay	Roman Hamrlik	D	ZPS Zlin, Czech.
2—Ottawa	Alexei Yashin	C	Dynamo Moscow, CIS
3—San Jose	Mike Rathje	D	Medicine Hat (WHL)
4—Quebec	Todd Warriner	LW	Windsor (OHL)
5—N.Y. Islanders (from Toronto)	Darius Kasparaitis	D	Dynamo Moscow, CIS
6—Calgary	Corey Stillman	LW	Windsor (OHL)
7—Philadelphia	Ryan Sittler	LW	Nichols H.S., Buffalo, N.Y.
8—Toronto (from N.Y. Islanders)	Brandon Convery	F	Sudbury (OHL)
9—Hartford	Robert Petrovicky	C	Dukla Trencin, Czech.
10—San Jose	Andrei Nazarov	LW	Dynamo Moscow, CIS
11—Buffalo	David Cooper	D	Medicine Hat (WHL)
12—Chicago (from Winnipeg)	Sergei Krivokrasov	RW	Central Red Army, CIS
13—Edmonton	Joe Hulbig	LW	St. Sebastian HS, Needham, Mass.
14—Washington	Sergei Gonchar	D	Dynamo Moscow, CIS
15—Philadelphia	Jason Bowen	LW	Tri-City (WHL)
16—Boston	Dmitri Kvartalov	F	San Diego (IHL)
17—Winnipeg (from Chicago)	Sergei Bautin	D	Dynamo Moscow, CIS
18—New Jersey	Jason Smith	D	Regina (WHL)
19—Pittsburgh	Martin Straka	C	Skoda Pizen, Czech.
20—Montreal	David Wilkie	C	Kamloops (WHL)
21—Vancouver	Libor Polasek	C	TJ Vikovice, Czech.
22—Detroit	Curtis Bowen	LW	Ottawa (OHL)
23—Toronto (from Washington)	Grant Marshall	RW	Ottawa (OHL)
24—N.Y. Rangers	Peter Ferraro	C	Waterloo (USHL)

SECOND ROUND

No.—Selecting club	Player	Pos.	Previous team (league)
25—Ottawa	Chad Penney	LW	North Bay (OHL)
26—Tampa Bay	Drew Bannister	D	Sault Ste. Marie (OHL)
27—Winnipeg	Boris Mironv	D	CSKA Moscow, CIS
28—Quebec	Paul Brousseau	RW	Hull (QMJHL)
29—Quebec (from Toronto)	Tuomas Gronman	D	Tacoma (WHL)
30—Calgary	Chris O'Sullivan	D	Catholic Memorial H.S., Boston
31—Philadelphia	Dennis Metlyuk	C	Lada Tagliatti, CIS
32—Washington (from NYI through Toronto)	Jim Carey	G	Catholic Mem. H.S., Boston.
33—Montreal (from Hartford)	Valeri Bure	RW	Spokane (WHL)
34—Minnesota	Jarkko Varvio	RW	HPK, Finland
35—Buffalo	Jozeph Cierny	RW	Zvolen, Czech.
36—Chicago (from Winnipeg)	Jeff Shantz	C	Regina (WHL)
37—Edmonton	Martin Reichel	RW	Freiburg, Germany
38—St. Louis	Igor Korolev	RW	Dynamo Moscow, CIS
39—Los Angeles	Justin Hocking	D	Spokane (WHL)
40—Vancouver (from Boston)	Mike Peca	C	Ottawa (OHL)
41—Chicago	Sergei Klimovich	C	Dynamo Moscow, CIS
42—New Jersey	Sergei Brylin	C	CSKA Moscow, CIS
43—Pittsburgh	Marc Hussey	D	Moose Jaw (WHL)
44—Montreal	Kelli Corpse	C	Kingston (OHL)
45—Vancouver	Michael Fountain	G	Oshawa (OHL)
46—Detroit	Darren McCarty	RW	Belleville (OHL)
47—Hartford (from Washington)	Andrei Nikolishin	LW	Dynamo Moscow, CIS
48—N.Y. Rangers	Mattias Norstrom	D	AIK, Sweden

THIRD ROUND

No.—Selecting club	Player	Pos.	Previous team (league)
49—Tampa Bay	Brent Gretzky	C	Belleville (OHL)
50—Ottawa	Patrick Traverse	D	Shawinigan (QMJHL)
51—San Jose	Alexander Cherbayev	F	Chimik, CIS
52—Quebec	Emmanuel Fernandez	G	Laval (QMJHL)
53—Washington (from Toronto)	Stefan Ustorf	F	Kausbeuren, Germany
54—Calgary	Mathias Johansson	F	Farjestad, Sweden
55—Boston (from Philadelphia)	Sergei Zholtok	F	Riga, Latvia
56—N.Y. Islanders	Jarrett Deuling	LW	Kamloops (WHL)
57—Hartford	Jan Vopat	D	Litvinov, Czech.
58—Minnesota	Jeff Bes	C	Guelph (OHL)

No.—Selecting club	Player	Pos.	Previous team (league)
59—Buffalo	Ondrej Steiner	C	Skoda Plzen, Czech.
60—Winnipeg	Jeremy Stevenson	LW	Cornwall (OHL)
61—Edmonton	Simon Roy	D	Shawinigan (QMJHL)
62—St. Louis	Vitali Karamnov	LW	Dynamo Moscow, CIS
63—Los Angeles	Sandy Allan	G	North Bay (OHL)
64—St. Louis (from Boston)	Vitali Prokhorov	LW	Spartak, CIS
65—Edmonton (from Chicago)	Kirk Maltby	RW	Owen Sound (OHL)
66—New Jersey	Cale Hulse	D	Portland (WHL)
67—Pittsburgh	Travis Thiessen	D	Moose Jaw (WHL)
68—Montreal	Craig Rivet	D	Kingston (OHL)
69—Vancouver	Jeff Connolly	C	St. Sebastian HS, Needham, Mass.
70—Detroit	Sylvain Cloutier	C	Guelph (OHL)
71—Washington	Martin Gendron	RW	St. Hyacinthe (QMJHL)
72—N.Y. Rangers	Eric Cairns	D	Detroit (OHL)

FOURTH ROUND

No.—Selecting club	Player	Pos.	Previous team (league)
73—Ottawa	Radek Hamr	D	Sparta Praha, Czech.
74—Tampa Bay	Aaron Gavey	C	Sault Ste. Marie (OHL)
75—San Jose	Jan Caloun	F	Litvinov, Czech.
76—Quebec	Ian McIntyre	I W	Beauport (QMJHL)
77—Toronto	Nikolai Borschevsky		Spartak, CIS
78—Calgary	Robert Svehla	D	Dukla Trencin, Czech.
79—Hartford (from Philadelphia)	Kevin Smyth	LW	Moose Jaw (WHL)
80—Buffalo (from N.Y. Islanders)	Dean Melanson	D	St. Hyacinthe (QMJHL)
81—Hartford	Jason McBain	D	Portland (WHL)
82—Montreal (from Minnesota)	Louis Bernard	D	Drummondville (QMJHL)
83—Buffalo	Matthew Barnaby	LW	Beauport (QMJHL)
84—Winnipeg	Mark Vishneau	D	London (OHL)
85—N.Y. Rangers (from Edmonton)	Chris Ferraro	RW	Waterloo (USHL)
86—St. Louis	Lee Leslie	LW	Prince Albert (WHL)
87—Los Angeles	Kevin Brown	RW	Belleville (OHL)
88—Minnesota (from Boston)	Jeri Lihtinen	F	Espoo, Finland
89—Chicago	Andy McIntyre	LW	Saskatoon (WHL)
90—New Jersey	Vitlai Tomilin	F	Krylja Sovetov, CIS
91—Pittsburgh	Todd Klassen	D	Tri-City (WHL)
92—Montreal	Marc Lamothe	G	Kingston (OHL)
93—Vancouver	Brent Tully	D	Peterborough (OHL)
94—New Jersey (from Detroit)	Scott McCabe	D	Detroit Midgets
95—Toronto (from Washington)	Mark Raiter	D	Saskatoon (WHL)
96—Edmonton (from N.Y. Rangers)	Ralph Intranuovo	C	Sault Ste. Marie (OHL)

FIFTH ROUND

No.—Selecting club	Player	Pos.	Previous team (league)
97—Tampa Bay	Brantt Myhres	RW	Lethbridge (WHL)
98—Ottawa	Daniel Guerard	RW	Victoriaville (QMJHL)
99—San Jose	Marcus Ragnarsson	D	Djurgarden, Sweden
100—Quebec	Charley Wasley	D	St. Paul (Junior A, Tier II)
101—Toronto	Janne Gronvall	D	Lukko, Finland
102—Calgary	Sami Heleanius	D	Jokerit, Finland
103—Philadelphia	Vladislav Bouline	D	Dizelast Pena, Czech.
104—N.Y. Islanders	Thomas Klimt	C	Plzeden, Czech.
105—N.Y. Islanders (from Hartford)	Ryan Duthie	C	Spokane (WHL)
106—Toronto (from Buffalo through Minnesota)	Chris Deruiter	RW	Kingston (OHL)
107—Buffalo	Markus Ketterer	G	Jokerit, Finland
108—Buffalo (from Winnipeg)	Yuri Khmylez		Krylja Sovetov, CIS
109—Edmonton	Joachim Gage	G	Portland (WHL)
110—Vancouver (from St. Louis)	Brian Loney	RW	Ohio State (CCHA)
111—Los Angeles	Jeff Shecazalier	LW	North Bay (OHL)
112—Boston	Scott Bailey	G	Spokane (WHL)
113—Chicago	Tim Hogan	D	University of Michigan (CCHA)
114—New Jersey	Ryan Black	LW	Peterborough (OHL)
115—Pittsburgh	Philipp Derouville	G	Verdun (QMJHL)
116—Montreal	Don Chase	C	Springfield (Junior B)
117—Vancouver	Adrian Autoin	D	Boston University (Hockey East)
118—Detroit	Mike Sullivan	C	Reading (Mass.) H.S.
119—Washington	John Varga	LW	Tacoma (WHL)
120—N.Y. Rangers	Dimitri Starostenko	W	CSKA Moscow, CIS

SIXTH ROUND

No.—Selecting club	Player	Pos.	Previous team (league)
121—Ottawa	Al Sinclair	D	University of Michigan (CCHA)
122—Tampa Bay	Martin Tanguay	C	Verdun (QMJHL)

No.—Selecting club	Player	Pos.	Previous team (league)
123—San Jose	Michal Sykora	D	Tacoma (WHL)
124—Quebec	Paxton Sculte	LW	Spokane (WHL)
125—Toronto	Mikael Hakansson		NACKA, Sweden
126—Calgary	Ravil Yakubov		Dynamo Moscow, CIS
127—Philadelphia	Roman Zolotov	D	Dynamo Moscow, CIS
128—N.Y. Islanders	Derek Armstrong	C	Sudbury (OHL)
129—Calgary (from Hartford)	Joel Bouchard	D	Verdun (QMJHL)
130—Minnesota	Michael Johnson	D	Ottawa (OHL)
131—Buffalo	Paul Rushforth	C	North Bay (OHL)
132—Winnipeg	Alexander Alexeyev	D	Novgorod, CIS
133—Boston (from Edmonton)	Jiri Dopita	F	Olomouc, Czech.
134—St. Louis	Bob Lachance	RW	Springfield (Junior B)
135—Los Angeles	Raymond Murray	LW	Michigan State Univ. (CCHA)
136—Boston	Grigor Panteleyz	F	Riga, Latvia
137—Chicago	Gerry Skrypec	D	Ottawa (OHL)
138—New Jersey	Daniel Trebil	D	Jefferson H.S., Bloomington, Minn.
139—Pittsburgh	Artem Kopot	D	Chelyabinsk, CIS
140—Montreal	Martin Sychra	C	Zetor Brno, Czech.
141—Vancouver	Jason Clark	C	St. Thomas (Junior B)
142—Detroit	Jason MacDonald	RW	Owen Sound (OHL)
143—Hartford (from Washington)	Jarret Reid	C	Sault Ste. Marie (OHL)
144—N.Y. Rangers	David Dal Grande	D	Ottawa (Junior A, Tier II)

SEVENTH ROUND

No.—Selecting club	Player	Pos.	Previous team (league)
145—Tampa Bay	Derek Wilkinson	G	Detroit (OHL)
146—Ottawa	Jaroslav Miklenda	G	Olomouc, Czech.
147—San Jose	Eric Bellerose	LW	Trois-Rivieres (QMJHL)
148—Quebec	Martin Lepage	D	Hull (QMJHL)
149—Toronto	Patrick Augusta	RW	Dukla Jihlava, Czech.
150—Calgary	Pavel Rajnoha	D	ZPS Zlin, Czech.
151—Philadelphia	Kirk Daubenspeck	G	Culver (Wis.) Military Academy
152—N.Y. Islanders	Vladimir Grachev	RW	Dynamo Moscow, CIS
153—Hartford	Ken Belanger	LW	Ottawa (OHL)
154—Minnesota	Kyle Peterson	C	Thunder Bay (Junior A, Tier II)
155—Winnipeg (from Buffalo)	Artur Oktyabrev	D	Central Red Army, CIS
156—Winnipeg	Andrei Raisky	LW	Ust-Amenogorsk, CIS
157—Edmonton	Steve Gibson	LW	Windsor (OHL)
158—St. Louis	Ian Laperriere	C	Drummondville (QMJHL)
159—N.Y. Islanders (from Los Angeles)	Steve O'Rourke	RW	Tri-City (WHL)
160—St. Louis (from Boston)	Lance Burns	C	Lethbridge (WHL)
161—Chicago	Mike Prokopec	RW	Cornwall (OHL)
162—New Jersey	Geordie Kinnear	D	Peterborough (OHL)
163—Pittsburgh	Jan Alinc	RW	Litvinov, Czech.
164—Montreal	Christian Proulx	D	St. Jean (QMJHL)
165—Vancouver	Scott Hollis	RW	Kingston (OHL)
166—Detroit	Greg Scott	G	Niagara Falls (OHL)
167—Washington	Mark Matier	D	Sault Ste. Marie (OHL)
168—N.Y. Rangers	Matt Oates	LW	Miami of Ohio Univ. (CCHA)

EIGHTH ROUND

No.—Selecting club	Player	Pos.	Previous team (league)
169—Ottawa	Jay Kenney	D	Canterbury (Conn.) Prep
170—Tampa Bay	Dennis Maxwell	C	Niagara Falls (OHL)
171—San Jose	Ryan Smith	D	Brandon (WHL)
172—Quebec	Mike Jickling	C	Spokane (WHL)
173—Toronto	Ryan Vandenbussche	RW	Cornwall (OHL)
174—Calgary	Ryan Mulhern	C	Canterbury (Conn.) Prep
175—Philadelphia	Claude Jutras	RW	Hull (QMJHL)
176—N.Y. Islanders	Jason Widmer	D	Lethbridge (WHL)
177—Hartford	Konstatin Korotkov		Spartak, CIS
178—Minnesota	Juha Lind	C	Jokerit, Finland
179—Buffalo	Dean Tiltgen	C	Tri-City (WHL)
180—St. Louis (from Winnipeg)	Igor Boldin	RW	Spartak, CIS
181—Edmonton	Kyuin Shim	RW	Sherwood Park (Tier II)
182—St. Louis	Nicholas Naumenko	D	Dubuque (Junior A, Tier II)
183—Detroit (from Los Angeles)	Justin Krall	D	Omaha (Junior A, Tier II)
184—Boston	Kurt Seher	D	Seattle (WHL)
185—Chicago	Layne Roland	RW	Portland (WHL)
186—New Jersey	Stephane Yelle	C	Oshawa (OHL)
187—Pittsburgh	Fran Bussey	C	Duluth (Minn.) H.S.
188—Montreal	Michael Burman	D	North Bay (OHL)
189—Detroit (from San Jose)	C.J. Denomme	G	Kitchener (OHL)

No.—Selecting club	Player	Pos.	Previous team (league)
190—Edmonton (from N.Y. Rangers)	Colin Schmidt	C	Regina Midgets
191—Washington	Mike Mathers	LW	Kamloops (WHL)
192—N.Y. Rangers	Mickey Elick	D	Calgary (Tier II)

NINTH ROUND

No.—Selecting club	Player	Pos.	Previous team (league)
193—Tampa Bay	Andrew Kemper	D	Seattle (WHL)
194—Ottawa	Claude Savoie	RW	Victoriaville (QMJHL)
195—San Jose	Chris Burns	G	Thunder Bay (Junior A)
196—Quebec	Steve Passmore	G	Victoria (WHL)
197—Toronto	Wayne Clarke	RW	RPI (ECAC)
198—Calgary	Brandon Carper	D	Bowling Green State U. (CCHA).
199—Philadelphia	Jonas Hakansson	RW	Malmo, Sweden
200—N.Y. Islanders	Daniel Paradis	C	Chicoutimi (QMJHL)
201—Hartford	Greg Zwakman	D	Edina (Minn.) H.S.
202—Minnesota	Lars Edstrom	LW	Lulea, Sweden
203—Buffalo	Todd Simon	C	Niagara Falls (OHL)
204—Winnipeg	Nikolai Khaibulin	G	Yekaterinburg, CIS
205—Edmonton	Marko Tuomainen	RW	Clarkson College (ECAC)
206 St. Louis	Todd Harris	D	Tri-City (WHL)
207—Los Angeles	Magnus Wernblom	RW	MoDo, Sweden
208—Boston	Mattias Timander	D	MoDo, Sweden
209—Chicago	David Hymovitz	LW	Thayer (Mass.) Academy
210—New Jersey	Jeff Toms	LW	Sault Ste. Marie (OHL)
211—Pittsburgh	Brian Bonin	C	White Bear Lake (Minn.) H.S.
212—Montreal	Earl Cronin	LW	St. Mark's (Mass.) H.S.
213—Vancouver	Sonny Mignacca	G	Medicine Hat (WHL)
214—Detroit	Jeff Walker	D	Peterborough (OHL)
215—Washington	Brian Stagg	RW	Kingston (OHL)
216—N.Y. Rangers	Dan Brierley	D	Choate (Conn.) Prep

10TH ROUND

No.—Selecting club	Player	Pos.	Previous team (league)
217—Ottawa	Jake Grimes	C	Belleville (OHL)
218—Tampa Bay	Marc Tardif	LW	Shawinigan (QMJHL)
219—San Jose	Alexandr Kholomeyev	RW	CIS
220—Quebec	Anson Carter	C	Wexford (Ont.) (Junior B)
221—Toronto	Sergei Simonov	D	Kristall Saratov, CIS
222—Calgary	Jonas Hoglund	RW	Farjestad, Sweden
223—Philadelphia	Chris Herperger	LW	Swift Current (WHL)
224—N.Y. Islanders	David Wainwright	D	Thayer (Mass.) Academy
225—Hartford	Steven Halko	D	Thornhill (Junior A)
226—Minnesota	Jeff Romfo	C	Blaine (Minn.) H.S.
227—Buffalo	Rick Kowalsky	RW	Sault Ste. Marie (OHL)
228—Winnipeg	Yevgeny Garanin	C	Khimik, CIS
229—Winnipeg (from Edmonton)	Teemu Numminen	C	Stoneham (Mass.) H.S.
230—St. Louis	Yuri Gunko	D	Sokol Kiev, CIS
231—Los Angeles	Ryan Pisiak	RW	Swift Current (WHL)
232—Boston	Chris Crombie	LW	London (OHL)
233—Chicago	Richard Raymond	D	Cornwall (OHL)
234—New Jersey	Heath Weenk	D	Regina (WHL)
235—Pittsburgh	Brian Callahan	C	Belmont Hill (Mass.) H.S.
236—Montreal	Trent Cavicchi	G	Dartmouth (N.S.) Midgets
237—Vancouver	Mark Wotton	D	Saskatoon (WHL)
238—Detroit	Daniel McGillis	D	Hawkesbury (Junior A, Tier II)
239—Washington	Gregory Callahan	D	Belmont Hill (Mass.) H.S.
240—N.Y. Rangers	Vladimir Vorobiev	D	CIS

11TH ROUND

No.—Selecting club	Player	Pos.	Previous team (league)
241—Tampa Bay	Tom MacDonald	C	Sault Ste. Marie (OHL)
242—Ottawa	Tomas Jelinek	LW	Czech. National Team
243—San Jose	Victor Ignatjev	RW	Riga, CIS
244—Quebec	Aaron Ellis	G	Culver (Wis.) Military Academy
245—Toronto	Nathan Dempsey	D	Regina (WHL)
246—Calgary	Andrei Potaichuk	RW	Krylja Sovetov, CIS
247—Philadelphia	Patrice Paquin	LW	Beauport (QMJHL)
248—N.Y. Islanders	Andrei Vasiljev	RW	CSKA, CIS
249—Hartford	Joacim Esbjors	D	Frolunda, Sweden
250—Minnesota	Jeffrey Moen	G	Roseville (Minn.) H.S.
251—Buffalo	Chris Clancy	LW	Cornwall (OHL)
252—Winnipeg	Andrei Karpovtsev	RW	Dynamo Moscow, CIS

No.—Selecting club	Player	Pos.	Previous team (league)
253—Edmonton	Bryan Rasmussen	LW	St. Louis Park (Minn.) H.S.
254—Winnipeg (from St. Louis)	Ivan Vologzaninov	LW	Sokol Kiev, CIS)
255—Los Angeles	Jukka Tiilikainen	RW	Espoo, Finland
256—Boston	Denis Cheruyako	D	CIS
257—Boston (from Chicago)	Eugene Pavlov	D	SKA Leningrad, CIS
258—New Jersey	Vladimir Yakovenko	G	Spartak, CIS
259—St. Louis (from Pittsburgh)	Wade Salzman	G	Duluth East (Minn.) H.S.
260—Montreal	Hirooyuki Miura	F	Japanese National Team
261—Vancouver	Aaron Boh	D	Spokane (WHL)
262—Detroit	Ryan Bach	G	Notre Dame (Tier II)
263—Washington	Billy MacPherson	LW	Oshawa (OHL)
264—Ottawa (from N.Y. Rangers)	Petter Ronnquist	G	Nacka, Sweden

NHL HISTORY

STANLEY CUP CHAMPIONS

Season	Club	Coach
1917-18	Toronto Arenas	Dick Carroll
1919-20	Ottawa Senators	Pete Green
1920-21	Ottawa Senators	Pete Green
1921-22	Toronto St. Pats	Eddie Powers
1922-23	Ottawa Senators	Pete Green
1923-24	Montreal Canadiens	Leo Dandurand
1924-25	Victoria Cougars	Lester Patrick
1925-26	Montreal Maroons	Eddie Gerard
1926-27	Ottawa Senators	Dave Gill
1927-28	New York Rangers	Lester Patrick
1928-29	Boston Bruins	Cy Denneny
1929-30	Montreal Canadiens	Cecil Hart
1930-31	Montreal Canadiens	Cecil Hart
1931-32	Toronto Maple Leafs	Dick Irvin
1932-33	New York Rangers	Lester Patrick
1933-34	Chicago Black Hawks	Tommy Gorman
1934-35	Montreal Maroons	Tommy Gorman
1935-36	Detroit Red Wings	Jack Adams
1936-37	Detroit Red Wings	Jack Adams
1937-38	Chicago Black Hawks	Bill Stewart
1938-39	Boston Bruins	Art Ross
1939-40	New York Rangers	Frank Boucher
1940-41	Boston Bruins	Cooney Weiland
1941-42	Toronto Maple Leafs	Hap Day
1942-43	Detroit Red Wings	Jack Adams
1943-44	Montreal Canadiens	Dick Irvin
1944-45	Toronto Maple Leafs	Hap Day
1945-46	Montreal Canadiens	Dick Irvin
1946-47	Toronto Maple Leafs	Hap Day
1947-48	Toronto Maple Leafs	Hap Day
1948-49	Toronto Maple Leafs	Hap Day
1949-50	Detroit Red Wings	Tommy Ivan
1950-51	Toronto Maple Leafs	Joe Primeau
1951-52	Detroit Red Wings	Tommy Ivan
1952-53	Montreal Canadiens	Dick Irvin
1953-54	Detroit Red Wings	Tommy Ivan
1954-55	Detroit Red Wings	Jimmy Skinner
1955-56	Montreal Canadiens	Toe Blake
1956-57	Montreal Canadiens	Toe Blake
1957-58	Montreal Canadiens	Toe Blake
1958-59	Montreal Canadiens	Toe Blake
1959-60	Montreal Canadiens	Toe Blake
1960-61	Chicago Black Hawks	Rudy Pilous
1961-62	Toronto Maple Leafs	Punch Imlach
1962-63	Toronto Maple Leafs	Punch Imlach
1963-64	Toronto Maple Leafs	Punch Imlach
1964-65	Montreal Canadiens	Toe Blake
1965-66	Montreal Canadiens	Toe Blake
1966-67	Toronto Maple Leafs	Punch Imlach
1967-68	Montreal Canadiens	Toe Blake
1968-69	Montreal Canadiens	Claude Ruel
1969-70	Boston Bruins	Harry Sinden
1970-71	Montreal Canadiens	Al MacNeil
1971-72	Boston Bruins	Tom Johnson
1972-73	Montreal Canadiens	Scotty Bowman
1973-74	Philadelphia Flyers	Fred Shero
1974-75	Philadelphia Flyers	Fred Shero
1975-76	Montreal Canadiens	Scotty Bowman
1976-77	Montreal Canadiens	Scotty Bowman
1977-78	Montreal Canadiens	Scotty Bowman
1978-79	Montreal Canadiens	Scotty Bowman
1979-80	New York Islanders	Al Arbour
1980-81	New York Islanders	Al Arbour
1981-82	New York Islanders	Al Arbour
1982-83	New York Islanders	Al Arbour
1983-84	Edmonton Oilers	Glen Sather
1984-85	Edmonton Oilers	Glen Sather
1985-86	Montreal Canadiens	Jean Perron
1986-87	Edmonton Oilers	Glen Sather
1987-88	Edmonton Oilers	Glen Sather
1988-89	Calgary Flames	Terry Crisp
1989-90	Edmonton Oilers	John Muckler
1990-91	Pittsburgh Penguins	Bob Johnson
1991-92	Pittsburgh Penguins	Scotty Bowman

NOTE: 1918-19 series between Montreal and Seattle cancelled after five games because of influenza epidemic.

RECORDS

REGULAR SEASON

INDIVIDUAL—CAREER

Most seasons

NHL: 26—Gordie Howe, Detroit Red Wings and Hartford Whalers, 1946-47 through 1970-71 and 1979-80.
CHL: 9—Richie Hansen, Fort Worth Texans, Salt Lake Golden Eagles, Wichita Wind, 1975-76 through 1983-84.
AHL: 20—Fred Glover, Indianapolis Caps, St. Louis Flyers, Cleveland Barons.
Willie Marshall, Pittsburgh Hornets, Rochester Americans, Hershey Bears, Providence Reds, Baltimore Clippers.
IHL: 18—Glenn Ramsay, Cincinnati Mohawks, Fort Wayne Komets, Troy Bruins, Toledo Blades, St. Paul Saints, Omaha Knights, Des Moines Oak Leafs, Toledo Hornets, Port Huron Flags, 1956-57 through 1973-74.

Most games played

NHL: 1,767—Gordie Howe, Detroit Red Wings and Hartford Whalers (26 seasons).
AHL: 1,205—Willie Marshall, Pittsburgh Hornets, Rochester Americans, Hershey Bears, Providence Reds, Baltimore Clippers (20 seasons).
IHL: 1,053—Glenn Ramsay, Cincinnati Mohawks, Fort Wayne Komets, Troy Bruins, Toledo Blades, St. Paul Saints, Omaha Knights, Des Moines Oak Leafs, Toledo Hornets, Port Huron Flags (18 seasons).
CHL: 575—Richie Hansen, Fort Worth Texans, Salt Lake Golden Eagles, Wichita Wind (9 seasons).
WHA: 551—Andre Lacroix, Philadelphia Blazers, New York Golden Blades, Jersey Knights, San Diego Mariners, Houston Aeros and New England Whalers (7 seasons).

Most goals

NHL: 801—Gordie Howe, Detroit Red Wings, Hartford Whalers (26 seasons).
IHL: 526—Joe Kastelic, Fort Wayne Komets, Troy Burins, Louisville Rebels, Muskegon Zephyrs, Muskegon Mohawks (15 seasons).
AHL: 523—Willie Marshall, Pittsburgh Hornets, Rochester Americans, Hershey Bears, Providence Reds, Baltimore Clippers (20 seasons).
WHA: 316—Marc Tardif, Quebec Nordiques (6 seasons).
CHL: 204—Richie Hansen, Fort Worth Texans, Salt Lake Golden Eagles, Wichita Wind (9 seasons).

Most assists

NHL: 1,514—Wayne Gretzky, Edmonton Oilers, Los Angeles Kings (13 seasons).
AHL: 852—Willie Marshall, Pittsburgh Hornets, Hershey Bears, Rochester Americans, Providence Reds, Baltimore Clippers (20 seasons).
IHL: 826—Len Thornson, Huntington Hornets, Indianapolis Chiefs, Fort Wayne Komets (13 seasons).
WHA: 547—Andre Lacroix, Philadelphia Blazers, Jersey Knights, San Diego Mariners, Houston Aeros, New England Whalers (7 seasons).
CHL: 374—Richie Hansen, Fort Worth Texans, Salt Lake Golden Eagles, Wichita Wind (9 seasons).

Most points

NHL: 2,263—Wayne Gretzky, Edmonton Oilers, Los Angeles Kings (13 seasons).
AHL: 1,375—Willie Marshall, Pittsburgh Hornets, Hershey Bears, Rochester Americans, Providence Reds, Baltimore Clippers (20 seasons).
IHL: 1,252—Len Thornson, Huntington Hornets, Indianapolis Chiefs, Fort Wayne Komets (13 seasons).
WHA: 798—Andre Lacroix, Philadelphia Blazers, Jersey Knights, San Diego Mariners, Houston Aeros, New England Whalers (7 seasons).
CHL: 578—Richie Hansen, Fort Worth Texans, Salt Lake Golden Eagles, Wichita Wind (9 seasons).

Most penalty minutes

NHL: 3,966—Dave "Tiger" Williams, Toronto Maple Leafs, Vancouver Canucks, Detroit Red Wings, Los Angeles Kings, Hartford Whalers (13 seasons).
AHL: 2,402—Fred Glover, Indianapolis Caps, St. Louis Flyers, Cleveland Barons (20 seasons).
IHL: 2,175—Gord Malinoski, Dayton Gems, Saginaw Gears (9 seasons).
WHA: 962—Paul Baxter, Cleveland Crusaders, Quebec Nordiques (5 seasons).
CHL: 899—Brad Gassoff, Tulsa Oilers, Dallas Black Hawks (5 seasons).

Most shutouts

NHL: 103—Terry Sawchuk, Detroit Red Wings, Boston Bruins, Los Angeles Kings, New York Rangers, Toronto Maple Leafs (20 seasons).
AHL: 45—Johnny Bower, Cleveland Barons, Providence Reds (11 seasons).
IHL: 45—Glenn Ramsay, Cincinnati Mohawks, Fort Wayne Komets, Troy Bruins, Toledo Blades, St. Paul Saints, Omaha Knights, Des Moines Oak Leafs, Toledo Hornets, Port Huron Flags (18 seasons).
WHA: 16—Ernie Wakely, Winnipeg Jets, San Diego Mariners, Houston Aeros (6 seasons).
CHL: 12—Michel Dumas, Dallas Black Hawks (4 seasons).
Mike Veisor, Dallas Black Hawks (5 seasons).

Most goals

    NHL: 92—Wayne Gretzky, Edmonton Oilers, 1981-82 season.
    WHA: 77—Bobby Hull, Winnipeg Jets, 1974-75 season.
    CHL: 77—Alain Caron, St. Louis Braves, 1963-64 season.
    IHL: 75—Dan Lecours, Milwaukee Admirals, 1982-83 season.
    AHL: 70—Stephan Lebeau, Sherbrooke Canadiens, 1988-89 season.

Most goals by a defenseman

    NHL: 48—Paul Coffey, Edmonton Oilers, 1985-86 season.
    IHL: 34—Roly McLenahan, Cincinnati Mohawks, 1955-56 season.
    CHL: 29—Dan Poulin, Nashville South Stars, 1981-82 season.
    AHL: 28—Greg Tebbutt, Baltimore Skipjacks, 1982-83 season.
    WHA: 24—Kevin Morrison, Jersey Knights, 1973-74 season.

Most assists

    NHL: 163—Wayne Gretzky, Edmonton Oilers, 1985-86 season.
    IHL: 109—John Cullen, Flint Spirits, 1987-88 season.
    WHA: 106—Andre Lacroix, San Diego Mariners, 1974-75 season.
    AHL: 89—George "Red" Sullivan, Hershey Bears, 1953-54 season.
    CHL: 81—Richie Hansen, Salt Lake Golden Eagles, 1981-82 season.

Most assists by a defenseman

    NHL: 102—Bobby Orr, Boston Bruins, 1970-71 season.
    IHL: 86—Gerry Glaude, Muskegon Zephyrs, 1962-63 season.
    WHA: 77—J. C. Tremblay, Quebec Nordiques, 1975-76 season.
    AHL: 62—Craig Levie, Nova Scotia Voyageurs, 1980-81 season.
             Shawn Evans, Nova Scotia Oilers, 1987-88 season.
    CHL: 61—Barclay Plager, Omaha Knights, 1963-64 season.

Most points

    NHL: 215—Wayne Gretzky, Edmonton Oilers, 1985-86 season.
    IHL: 157—John Cullen, Flint Spirits, 1987-88 season.
    WHA: 154—Marc Tardif, Quebec Nordiques, 1977-78 season.
    AHL: 134—Stephan Lebeau, Sherbrooke Canadiens, 1988-89 season.
    CHL: 125—Alain Caron, St. Louis Braves, 1963-64 season.

Most points by a defenseman

    NHL: 139—Bobby Orr, Boston Bruins, 1970-71 season.
    IHL: 101—Gerry Glaude, Muskegon Zephyrs, 1962-63 season.
    WHA: 89—J. C. Tremblay, Quebec Nordiques, 1972-73 and 1975-76 seasons.
    CHL: 85—Dan Poulin, Nashville South Stars, 1981-82 season.
    AHL: 84—Greg Tebbutt, Baltimore Skipjacks, 1982-83 season.

Most penalty minutes

    IHL: 648—Kevin Evans, Kalamazoo, 1986-87 season.
    NHL: 472—Dave Schultz, Philadelphia Flyers, 1974-75 season.
    AHL: 446—Robert Ray, Rochester Americans, 1988-89 season.
    CHL: 411—Randy Holt, Dallas Black Hawks, 1974-75 season.
    WHA: 365—Curt Brackenbury, Minnesota Fighting Saints and Quebec Nordiques, 1975-76 season.

Most shutouts

    NHL: 22—George Hainsworth, Montreal Canadiens, 1928-29 season.
    NHL: 15—(modern era) Tony Esposito, Chicago Black Hawks, 1969-70 season.
    IHL: 10—Charlie Hodge, Cincinnati Mohawks, 1953-54 season.
            Joe Daley, Winnipeg Jets, 1975-76 season.
    CHL: 9—Marcel Pelletier, St. Paul Rangers, 1963-64 season.
    AHL: 9—Gordie Bell, Buffalo Bisons, 1942-43 season.
    WHA: 5—Gerry Cheevers, Cleveland Crusaders, 1972-73 season.

Lowest goals against average

    NHL: 0.98—George Hainsworth, Montreal Canadiens, 1928-29 season.
    AHL: 1.79—Frank Brimsek, Providence Reds, 1937-38 season.
    IHL: 1.88—Glenn Ramsay, Cincinnati Mohawks, 1956-57 season.
    CHL: 2.16—Russ Gillow, Oklahoma City Blazers, 1967-68 season.
    WHA: 2.57—Don McLeod, Houston Aeros, 1973-74 season.

INDIVIDUAL—GAME

Most goals
NHL: 7—Joe Malone, Quebec Bulldogs vs. Toronto St. Pats, January 31, 1920.
NHL: 6—(modern era) Syd Howe, Detroit Red Wings vs. N.Y. Rangers, Feb. 3, 1944.
        Gordon "Red" Berenson, St. Louis Blues vs. Philadelphia, Nov. 7, 1968.
        Darryl Sittler, Toronto Maple Leafs vs. Boston, Feb. 7, 1976.
CHL: 6—Jim Mayer, Dallas Black Hawks, February 23, 1979.
AHL: 6—Bob Heron, Pittsburgh Hornets, 1941-42.
        Harry Pidhirny, Springfield Indians, 1953-54.
        Camille Henry, Providence Reds, 1955-56.
        Patrick Lebeau, Fredericton Canadiens, Feb. 1, 1991.
IHL: 6—Pierre Brillant, Indianapolis Chiefs, Feb. 18, 1959.
        Bryan McLay, Muskegon Zephyrs, Mar. 8, 1961.
        Elliott Chorley, St. Paul Saints, Jan. 17, 1962.
        Joe Kastelic, Muskegon Zephyrs, Mar. 1, 1962.
        Tom St. James, Flint Generals, Mar. 15, 1985.
WHA: 5—Ron Ward, New York Raiders vs. Ottawa, January 4, 1973.
        Ron Climie, Edmonton Oilers vs. N.Y. Golden Blades, November 6, 1973.
        Andre Hinse, Houston Aeros vs. Edmonton, Jan. 16, 1975.
        Vaclav Nedomansky, Toronto Toros vs. Denver Spurs, Nov. 13, 1975.
        Wayne Connelly, Minnesota Fighting Saints vs. Cincinnati Stingers, Nov. 27, 1975.
        Ron Ward, Cleveland Crusaders vs. Toronto Toros, Nov. 30, 1975.
        Real Cloutier, Quebec Nordiques fs. Phoenix Roadrunners, Oct. 26, 1976.

Most assists
AHL: 9—Art Stratton, Buffalo Bisons vs. Pittsburgh, Mar. 17, 1963.
IHL: 9—Jean-Paul Denis, St. Paul Saints, Jan. 17, 1962.
NHL: 7—Billy Taylor, Detroit Red Wings vs. Chicago, Mar. 16, 1947.
        Wayne Gretzky, Edmonton Oilers vs. Washington, Feb. 15, 1980.
WHA: 7—Jim Harrison, Alberta Oilers vs. New York, January 30, 1973.
        Jim Harrison, Cleveland Crusaders vs. Toronto, Nov. 30, 1975.
CHL: 6—Art Stratton, St. Louis Braves, 1966-67.
        Ron Ward, Tulsa Oilers, 1967-68.
        Bill Hogaboam, Omaha Knights, January 15, 1972.
        Jim Wiley, Tulsa Oilers, 1974-75.

Most points
IHL: 11—Elliott Chorley, St. Paul Saints, Jan. 17, 1962.
        Jean-Paul Denis, St. Paul Saints, Jan. 17, 1962.
NHL: 10—Darryl Sittler, Toronto Maple Leafs vs. Boston, Feb. 7, 1976.
WHA: 10—Jim Harrison, Alberta Oilers vs. New York, January 30, 1973.
AHL: 9—Art Stratton, Buffalo Bisons vs Pittsburgh, Mar. 17, 1963.
CHL: 8—Steve Vickers, Omaha Knights vs. Kansas City, Jan. 15, 1972.

Most penalty minutes
NHL: 67—Randy Holt, Los Angeles Kings vs. Philadelphia, March 11, 1979.
IHL: 63—Willie Trognitz, Dayton Gems, Oct. 29, 1977.
AHL: 54—Wally Weir, Rochester Americans vs. New Brunswick, Jan. 16, 1981.
CHL: 49—Gary Rissling, Birmingham Bulls vs. Salt Lake, Dec. 5, 1980.
WHA: 46—Dave Hanson, Birmingham Bulls vs. Indianapolis, Feb. 5, 1978.

STANLEY CUP PLAYOFFS

INDIVIDUAL—CAREER

Most years in playoffs: 20—Gordie Howe, Detroit, Hartford.
        Larry Robinson, Montreal, Los Angeles.
Most consecutive years in playoffs: 20—Larry Robinson, Montreal, Los Angeles.
Most games: 227—Larry Robinson, Montreal, Los Angeles.
Most games by goaltender: 131—Billy Smith, N.Y. Islanders.
Most goals: 95—Wayne Gretzky, Edmonton, Los Angeles.
Most assists: 211—Wayne Gretzky, Edmonton, Los Angeles.
Most points: 306—Wayne Gretzky, Edmonton, Los Angeles.
Most penalty minutes: 546—Dale Hunter, Quebec, Washington.
Most shutouts: 14—Jacques Plante, Montreal, St. Louis.

INDIVIDUAL—SEASON

Most goals: 19—Reggie Leach, Philadelphia (1975-76).
        Jari Kurri, Edmonton (1984-85).
Most goals by a defenseman: 12—Paul Coffey, Edmonton (1984-85).
Most assists: 31—Wayne Gretzky, Edmonton (1987-88).
Most assists by a defenseman: 25—Paul Coffey, Edmonton (1984-85).
Most points: 47—Wayne Gretzky, Edmonton (1984-85).

Most points by a defenseman: 37—Paul Coffey, Edmonton (1984-85).
Most penalty minutes: 141—Chris Nilan, Montreal (1985-86).
Most shutouts: 4—Clint Benedict, Montreal Maroons (1927-28).
              Dave Kerr, N.Y. Rangers (1936-37).
              Frank McCool, Toronto (1944-45).
              Terry Sawchuk, Detroit (1951-52).
              Bernie Parent, Philadelphia (1974-75).
              Ken Dryden, Montreal (1976-77).
Most consecutive shutouts: 3—Frank McCool, Toronto (1944-45).

INDIVIDUAL—GAME

Most goals: 5—Maurice Richard, Montreal vs. Toronto, March 23, 1944.
          Darryl Sittler, Toronto vs. Philadelphia, April 22, 1976.
          Reggie Leach, Philadelphia vs. Boston, May 6, 1976.
          Mario Lemieux, Pittsburgh vs. Philadelphia, April 25, 1989.
Most assists: 6—Mikko Leinonen, N.Y. Rangers vs. Philadelphia, April 8, 1982.
           Wayne Gretzky, Edmonton vs. Los Angeles, April 9, 1987.
Most points: 8—Patrik Sundstrom, New Jersey vs. Washington, April 22, 1988.
          Mario Lemieux, Pittsburgh vs. Philadelphia, April 25, 1989.

CLUB

Most Stanley Cup championships: 23—Montreal Canadiens.
Most consecutive Stanley Cup championships: 5—Montreal Canadiens.
Most final series apperances: 31—Montreal Canadiens.
Most years in playoffs: 67—Montreal Canadiens.
Most consecutive playoff appearances: 25—Boston Bruins.
Most consecutive playoff game victories: 12—Edmonton Oilers.
Most goals, one team, one game: 13—Edmonton vs. Los Angeles, April 9, 1987.
Most goals, one team, one period: 7—Montreal Canadiens vs. Toronto, March 30, 1944, 3rd period.

ART ROSS TROPHY

(Leading scorer)

Season	Player, Team	Pts.
1917-18	Joe Malone, Montreal	44
1918-19	Newsy Lalonde, Montreal	32
1919-20	Joe Malone, Quebec Bulldogs	45
1920-21	Newsy Lalonde, Montreal	41
1921-22	Punch Broadbelt, Ottawa	46
1922-23	Babe Dye, Toronto	37
1923-24	Cy Denneny, Ottawa	23
1924-25	Babe Dye, Toronto	44
1925-26	Nels Stewart, Montreal Maroons	42
1926-27	Bill Cook, N.Y. Rangers	37
1927-28	Howie Morenz, Montreal	51
1928-29	Ace Bailey, Toronto	32
1929-30	Cooney Weiland, Boston	73
1930-01	Howie Morenz, Montreal	51
1931-32	Harvey Jackson, Toronto	53
1932-33	Bill Cook, N.Y. Rangers	50
1933-34	Charlie Conacher, Toronto	52
1934-35	Charlie Conacher, Toronto	57
1935-36	Dave Schriner, N.Y. Americans	45
1936-37	Dave Schriner, N.Y. Americans	46
1937-38	Gordie Drillion, Toronto	52
1938-39	Toe Blake, Montreal	47
1939-40	Milt Schmidt, Boston	52
1940-41	Bill Cowley, Boston	62
1941-42	Bryan Hextall, N.Y. Rangers	56
1942-43	Doug Bentley, Chicago	73
1943-44	Herbie Cain, Boston	82
1944-45	Elmer Lach, Montreal	80
1945-46	Max Bentley, Chicago	61
1946-47	Max Bentley, Chicago	72
1947-48	Elmer Lach, Montreal	61
1948-49	Roy Conacher, Chicago	68
1949-50	Ted Lindsay, Detroit	78
1950-51	Gordie Howe, Detroit	86
1951-52	Gordie Howe, Detroit	86
1952-53	Gordie Howe, Detroit	95
1953-54	Gordie Howe, Detroit	81
1954-55	Bernie Geoffrion, Montreal	75
1955-56	Jean Beliveau, Montreal	88
1956-57	Gordie Howe, Detroit	89
1957-58	Dickie Moore, Montreal	84
1958-59	Dickie Moore, Montreal	96
1959-60	Bobby Hull, Chicago	81
1960-61	Bernie Geoffrion, Montreal	95
1961-62	Bobby Hull, Chicago	84
1962-63	Gordie Howe, Detroit	86
1963-64	Stan Mikita, Chicago	89
1964-65	Stan Mikita, Chicago	87
1965-66	Bobby Hull, Chicago	97
1966-67	Stan Mikita, Chicago	97
1967-68	Stan Mikita, Chicago	87
1968-69	Phil Esposito, Boston	126
1969-70	Bobby Orr, Boston	120
1970-71	Phil Esposito, Boston	152
1971-72	Phil Esposito, Boston	133
1972-73	Phil Esposito, Boston	130
1973-74	Phil Esposito, Boston	145
1974-75	Bobby Orr, Boston	135
1975-76	Guy Lafleur, Montreal	125
1976-77	Guy Lafleur, Montreal	136
1977-78	Guy Lafleur, Montreal	132
1978-79	Bryan Trottier, N.Y. Islanders	134
1979-80	Marcel Dionne, Los Angeles	137
1980-81	Wayne Gretzky, Edmonton	164
1981-82	Wayne Gretzky, Edmonton	212
1982-83	Wayne Gretzky, Edmonton	196
1983-84	Wayne Gretzky, Edmonton	205
1984-85	Wayne Gretzky, Edmonton	208
1985-86	Wayne Gretzky, Edmonton	215

Season	Player, Team	Pts.
1986-87	Wayne Gretzky, Edmonton	183
1987-88	Mario Lemieux, Pittsburgh	168
1988-89	Mario Lemieux, Pittsburgh	199
1989-90	Wayne Gretzky, Los Angeles	142
1990-91	Wayne Gretzky, Los Angeles	163
1991-92	Mario Lemieux, Pittsburgh	131

The award was originally known as the Leading Scorer Trophy. The present trophy, first given in 1947, was presented to the NHL by Art Ross, former manager-coach of the Boston Bruins. In event of a tie, the player with the most goals receives the award.

HART MEMORIAL TROPHY

(Most Valuable Player)

Season	Player, Team
1023-24	Frank Nighbor, Ottawa
1924-25	Billy Burch, Hamilton
1925-26	Nels Stewart, Montreal Maroons
1926-27	Herb Gardiner, Montreal
1927-28	Howie Morenz, Montreal
1928-29	Roy Worters, N.Y. Americans
1929-30	Nels Stewart, Montreal Maroons
1930-31	Howie Morenz, Montreal
1931-32	Howie Morenz, Montreal
1932-33	Eddie Shore, Boston
1933-34	Aurel Joliat, Montreal
1934-35	Eddie Shore, Boston
1935-36	Eddie Shore, Boston
1936-37	Babe Siebert, Montreal
1937-38	Eddie Shore, Boston
1938-39	Toe Blake, Montreal
1939-40	Ebbie Goodfellow, Detroit
1940-41	Bill Cowley, Boston
1941-42	Tom Anderson, N.Y. Americans
1942-43	Bill Cowley, Boston
1943-44	Babe Pratt, Toronto
1944-45	Elmer Lach, Montreal
1945-46	Max Bentley, Chicago
1946-47	Maurice Richard, Montreal
1947-48	Buddy O'Connor, N.Y. Rangers
1948-49	Sid Abel, Detroit
1949-50	Chuck Rayner, N.Y. Rangers
1950-51	Milt Schmidt, Boston
1951-52	Gordie Howe, Detroit
1952-53	Gordie Howe, Detroit
1953-54	Al Rollins, Chicago
1954-55	Ted Kennedy, Toronto
1955-56	Jean Beliveau, Montreal
1956-57	Gordie Howe, Detroit
1957-58	Gordie Howe, Detroit
1958-59	Andy Bathgate, N.Y. Rangers
1959-60	Gordie Howe, Detroit
1960-61	Bernie Geoffrion, Montreal
1961-62	Jacques Plante, Montreal
1962-63	Gordie Howe, Detroit
1963-64	Jean Beliveau, Montreal
1964-65	Bobby Hull, Chicago
1965-66	Bobby Hull, Chicago
1966-67	Stan Mikita, Chicago
1967-68	Stan Mikita, Chicago
1968-69	Phil Esposito, Boston
1969-70	Bobby Orr, Boston
1970-71	Bobby Orr, Boston
1971-72	Bobby Orr, Boston
1972-73	Bobby Clarke, Philadelphia
1973-74	Phil Esposito, Boston
1974-75	Bobby Clarke, Philadelphia
1975-76	Bobby Clarke, Philadelphia
1976-77	Guy Lafleur, Montreal
1977-78	Guy Lafleur, Montreal
1978-79	Bryan Trottier, N.Y. Islanders

Season	Player, Team
1979-80	Wayne Gretzky, Edmonton
1980-81	Wayne Gretzky, Edmonton
1981-82	Wayne Gretzky, Edmonton
1982-83	Wayne Gretzky, Edmonton
1983-84	Wayne Gretzky, Edmonton
1984-85	Wayne Gretzky, Edmonton
1985-86	Wayne Gretzky, Edmonton
1986-87	Wayne Gretzky, Edmonton
1987-88	Mario Lemieux, Pittsburgh
1988-89	Wayne Gretzky, Los Angeles
1989-90	Mark Messier, Edmonton
1990-91	Brett Hull, St. Louis
1991-92	Mark Messier, N.Y. Rangers

JAMES NORRIS MEMORIAL TROPHY
(Outstanding defenseman)

Season	Player, Team
1953-54	Red Kelly, Detroit
1954-55	Doug Harvey, Montreal
1955-56	Doug Harvey, Montreal
1956-57	Doug Harvey, Montreal
1957-58	Doug Harvey, Montreal
1958-59	Tom Johnson, Montreal
1959-60	Doug Harvey, Montreal
1960-61	Doug Harvey, Montreal
1961-62	Doug Harvey, N.Y. Rangers
1962-63	Pierre Pilote, Chicago
1963-64	Pierre Pilote, Chicago
1964-65	Pierre Pilote, Chicago
1965-66	Jacques Laperriere, Montreal
1966-67	Harry Howell, N.Y. Rangers
1967-68	Bobby Orr, Boston
1968-69	Bobby Orr, Boston
1969-70	Bobby Orr, Boston
1970-71	Bobby Orr, Boston
1971-72	Bobby Orr, Boston
1972-73	Bobby Orr, Boston
1973-74	Bobby Orr, Boston
1974-75	Bobby Orr, Boston
1975-76	Denis Potvin, N.Y. Islanders
1976-77	Larry Robinson, Montreal
1977-78	Denis Potvin, N.Y. Islanders
1978-79	Denis Potvin, N.Y. Islanders
1979-80	Larry Robinson, Montreal
1980-81	Randy Carlyle, Pittsburgh
1981-82	Doug Wilson, Chicago
1982-83	Rod Langway, Washington
1983-84	Rod Langway, Washington
1984-85	Paul Coffey, Edmonton
1985-86	Paul Coffey, Edmonton
1986-87	Ray Bourque, Boston
1987-88	Ray Bourque, Boston
1988-89	Chris Chelios, Montreal
1989-90	Ray Bourque, Boston
1990-91	Ray Bourque, Boston
1991-92	Brian Leetch, N.Y. Rangers

VEZINA TROPHY
(Outstanding goaltender)

Season	Player, Team	GAA
1926-27	George Hainsworth, Montreal	1.52
1927-28	George Hainsworth, Montreal	1.09
1928-29	George Hainsworth, Montreal	0.98
1929-30	Tiny Thompson, Boston	2.23
1930-31	Roy Worters, N.Y. Americans	1.68
1931-32	Charlie Gardiner, Chicago	2.10
1932-33	Tiny Thompson, Boston	1.83
1933-34	Charlie Gardiner, Chicago	1.73
1934-35	Lorne Chabot, Chicago	1.83
1935-36	Tiny Thompson, Boston	1.71
1936-37	Normie Smith, Detroit	2.13
1937-38	Tiny Thompson, Boston	1.85
1938-39	Frank Brimsek, Boston	1.60
1939-40	Dave Kerr, N.Y. Rangers	1.60
1940-41	Turk Broda, Toronto	2.60

Season	Player, Team	GAA
1941-42	Frank Brimsek, Boston	2.38
1942-43	Johnny Mowers, Detroit	2.48
1943-44	Bill Durnan, Montreal	2.18
1944-45	Bill Durnan, Montreal	2.42
1945-46	Bill Durnan, Montreal	2.60
1946-47	Bill Durnan, Montreal	2.30
1947-48	Turk Broda, Toronto	2.38
1948-49	Bill Durnan, Montreal	2.10
1949-50	Bill Durnan, Montreal	2.20
1950-51	Al Rollins, Toronto	1.75
1951-52	Terry Sawchuk, Detroit	1.98
1952-53	Terry Sawchuk, Detroit	1.94
1953-54	Harry Lumley, Toronto	1.85
1954-55	Terry Sawchuk, Detroit	1.94
1955-56	Jacques Plante, Montreal	1.86
1956-57	Jacques Plante, Montreal	2.02
1957-58	Jacques Plante, Montreal	2.09
1958-59	Jacques Plante, Montreal	2.15
1959-60	Jacques Plante, Montreal	2.54
1960-61	Johnny Bower, Toronto	2.50
1961-62	Jacques Plante, Montreal	2.37
1962-63	Glenn Hall, Chicago	2.51
1963-64	Charlie Hodge, Montreal	2.26
1964-65	Terry Sawchuk, Toronto	2.56
	Johnny Bower, Toronto	2.38
1965-66	Lorne Worsley, Montreal	2.36
	Charlie Hodge, Montreal	2.58
1966-67	Glenn Hall, Chicago	2.38
	Denis DeJordy, Chicago	2.46
1967-68	Lorne Worsley, Montreal	1.98
	Rogatien Vachon, Montreal	2.48
1968-69	Glenn Hall, St. Louis	2.17
	Jacques Plante, St. Louis	1.96
1969-70	Tony Esposito, Chicago	2.17
1970-71	Ed Giacomin, N.Y. Rangers	2.15
	Gilles Villemure, N.Y. Rangers	2.29
1971-72	Tony Esposito, Chicago	1.76
	Gary Smith, Chicago	2.41
1972-73	Ken Dryden, Montreal	2.26
1973-74	Bernie Parent, Philadelphia	1.89
	Tony Esposito, Chicago	2.04
1974-75	Bernie Parent, Philadelphia	2.03
1975-76	Ken Dryden, Montreal	2.03
1976-77	Ken Dryden, Montreal	2.14
	Michel Larocque, Montreal	2.09
1977-78	Ken Dryden, Montreal	2.05
	Michel Larocque, Montreal	2.67
1978-79	Ken Dryden, Montreal	2.30
	Michel Larocque, Montreal	2.84
1979-80	Bob Sauve, Buffalo	2.36
	Don Edwards, Buffalo	2.57
1980-81	Richard Sevigny, Montreal	2.40
	Michel Larocque, Montreal	3.03
	Denis Herron, Montreal	3.50
1981-82	Billy Smith, N.Y. Islanders	2.97
1982-83	Pete Peeters, Boston	2.36
1983-84	Tom Barrasso, Buffalo	2.84
1984-85	Pelle Lindbergh, Philadelphia	3.02
1985-86	John Vanbiesbrouck, N.Y. Rangers	3.32
1986-87	Ron Hextall, Philadelphia	3.00
1987-88	Grant Fuhr, Edmonton	3.43
1988-89	Patrick Roy, Montreal	2.47
1989-90	Patrick Roy, Montreal	2.53
1990-91	Ed Belfour, Chicago	2.47
1991-92	Patrick Roy, Montreal	2.36

The award was formerly presented to the goaltender(s) having played a minimum of 25 games for the team with the fewest goals scored against. Beginning with the 1981-82 season, it was awarded to the outstanding goaltender.

BILL JENNINGS TROPHY
(Leading goaltender)

Season	Player, Team	GAA
1981-82	Denis Herron, Montreal	2.64
	Rick Wamsley, Montreal	2.75

Season	Player, Team	GAA
1982-83	Roland Melanson, N.Y. Islanders	2.66
	Billy Smith, N.Y. Islanders	2.87
1983-84	Pat Riggin, Washington	2.66
	Al Jensen, Washington	2.91
1984-85	Tom Barrasso, Buffalo	2.66
	Bob Sauve, Buffalo	3.22
1985-86	Bob Froese, Philadelphia	2.55
	Darren Jensen, Philadelphia	3.68
1986-87	Brian Hayward, Montreal	2.81
	Patrick Roy, Montreal	2.93
1987-88	Brian Hayward, Montreal	2.86
	Patrick Roy, Montreal	2.90
1988-89	Patrick Roy, Montreal	2.47
	Brian Hayward, Montreal	2.90
1989-90	Rejean Lemelin, Boston	2.81
	Andy Moog, Boston	2.89
1990-91	Ed Belfour, Chicago	2.47
1991-92	Patrick Roy, Montreal	2.36

The award is presented to the goaltender(s) having played a minimum of 25 games for the team with the fewest goals scored against.

CALDER MEMORIAL TROPHY

(Rookie of the year)

Season	Player, Team
1932-33	Carl Voss, Detroit
1933-34	Russ Blinco, Montreal Maroons
1934-35	Dave Schriner, N.Y. Americans
1935-36	Mike Karakas, Chicago
1936-37	Syl Apps, Toronto
1937-38	Cully Dahlstrom, Chicago
1938-39	Frank Brimsek, Boston
1939-40	Kilby Macdonald, N.Y. Rangers
1940-41	John Quilty, Montreal
1941-42	Grant Warwick, N.Y. Rangers
1942-43	Gaye Stewart, Toronto
1943-44	Gus Bodnar, Toronto
1944-45	Frank McCool, Toronto
1945-46	Edgar Laprade, N.Y. Rangers
1946-47	Howie Meeker, Toronto
1947-48	Jim McFadden, Detroit
1948-49	Pentti Lund, N.Y. Rangers
1949-50	Jack Gelineau, Boston
1950-51	Terry Sawchuk, Detroit
1951-52	Bernie Geoffrion, Montreal
1952-53	Lorne Worsley, N.Y. Rangers
1953-54	Camille Henry, N.Y. Rangers
1954-55	Ed Litzenberger, Chicago
1955-56	Glenn Hall, Detroit
1956-57	Larry Regan, Boston
1957-58	Frank Mahovlich, Toronto
1958-59	Ralph Backstrom, Montreal
1959-60	Bill Hay, Chicago
1960-61	Dave Keon, Toronto
1961-62	Bobby Rousseau, Montreal
1962-63	Kent Douglas, Toronto
1963-64	Jacques Laperriere, Montreal
1964-65	Roger Crozier, Detroit
1965-66	Brit Selby, Toronto
1966-67	Bobby Orr, Boston
1967-68	Derek Sanderson, Boston
1968-69	Danny Grant, Minnesota
1969-70	Tony Esposito, Chicago
1970-71	Gilbert Perreault, Buffalo
1971-72	Ken Dryden, Montreal
1972-73	Steve Vickers, N.Y. Rangers
1973-74	Denis Potvin, N.Y. Islanders
1974-75	Eric Vail, Atlanta
1975-76	Bryan Trottier, N.Y. Islanders
1976-77	Willi Plett, Atlanta
1977-78	Mike Bossy, N.Y. Islanders
1978-79	Bobby Smith, Minnesota
1979-80	Ray Bourque, Boston
1980-81	Peter Stastny, Quebec

Season	Player, Team
1981-82	Dale Hawerchuk, Winnipeg
1982-83	Steve Larmer, Chicago
1983-84	Tom Barrasso, Buffalo
1984-85	Mario Lemieux, Pittsburgh
1985-86	Gary Suter, Calgary
1986-87	Luc Robitaille, Los Angeles
1987-88	Joe Nieuwendyk, Calgary
1988-89	Brian Leetch, N.Y. Rangers
1989-90	Sergei Makarov, Calgary
1990-91	Ed Belfour, Chicago
1991-92	Pavel Bure, Vancouver

The award was originally known as the Leading Rookie Award. It was renamed the Calder Trophy in 1936-37 and became the Calder Memorial Trophy in 1942-43, following the death of NHL President Frank Calder.

LADY BYNG MEMORIAL TROPHY

(Most gentlemanly player)

Season	Player, Team
1924-25	Frank Nighbor, Ottawa
1925-26	Frank Nighbor, Ottawa
1926-27	Billy Burch, N.Y. Americans
1927-28	Frank Boucher, N.Y. Rangers
1928-29	Frank Boucher, N.Y. Rangers
1929-30	Frank Boucher, N.Y. Rangers
1930-31	Frank Boucher, N.Y. Rangers
1931-32	Joe Primeau, Toronto
1932-33	Frank Boucher, N.Y. Rangers
1933-34	Frank Boucher, N.Y. Rangers
1934-35	Frank Boucher, N.Y. Rangers
1935-36	Doc Romnes, Chicago
1936-37	Marty Barry, Detroit
1937-38	Gordie Drillon, Toronto
1938-39	Clint Smith, N.Y. Rangers
1939-40	Bobby Bauer, Boston
1940-41	Bobby Bauer, Boston
1941-42	Syl Apps, Toronto
1942-43	Max Bentley, Chicago
1943-44	Clint Smith, Chicago
1944-45	Bill Mosienko, Chicago
1945-46	Toe Blake, Montreal
1946-47	Bobby Bauer, Boston
1947-48	Buddy O'Connor, N.Y. Rangers
1948-49	Bill Quackenbush, Detroit
1949-50	Edgar Laprade, N.Y. Rangers
1950-51	Red Kelly, Detroit
1951-52	Sid Smith, Toronto
1952-53	Red Kelly, Detroit
1953-54	Red Kelly, Detroit
1954-55	Sid Smith, Toronto
1955-56	Earl Reibel, Detroit
1956-57	Andy Hebenton, N.Y. Rangers
1957-58	Camille Henry, N.Y. Rangers
1958-59	Alex Delvecchio, Detroit
1959-60	Don McKenney, Boston
1960-61	Red Kelly, Toronto
1961-62	Dave Keon, Toronto
1962-63	Dave Keon, Toronto
1963-64	Ken Wharram, Chicago
1964-65	Bobby Hull, Chicago
1965-66	Alex Delvecchio, Detroit
1966-67	Stan Mikita, Chicago
1967-68	Stan Mikita, Chicago
1968-69	Alex Delvecchio, Detroit
1969-70	Phil Goyette, St. Louis
1970-71	John Bucyk, Boston
1971-72	Jean Ratelle, N.Y. Rangers
1972-73	Gilbert Perreault, Buffalo
1973-74	John Bucyk, Boston
1974-75	Marcel Dionne, Detroit
1975-76	Jean Ratelle, N.Y. R.-Boston
1976-77	Marcel Dionne, Los Angeles
1977-78	Butch Goring, Los Angeles
1978-79	Bob MacMillan, Atlanta

Season	Player, Team
1979-80	Wayne Gretzky, Edmonton
1980-81	Butch Goring, N.Y. Islanders
1981-82	Rick Middleton, Boston
1982-83	Mike Bossy, N.Y. Islanders
1983-84	Mike Bossy, N.Y. Islanders
1984-85	Jari Kurri, Edmonton
1985-86	Mike Bossy, N.Y. Islanders
1986-87	Joe Mullen, Calgary
1987-88	Mats Naslund, Montreal
1988-89	Joe Mullen, Calgary
1989-90	Brett Hull, St. Louis
1990-91	Wayne Gretzky, Los Angeles
1991-92	Wayne Gretzky, Los Angeles

The award was originally known as the Lady Byng Trophy. After winning the award seven times, Frank Boucher received permanent possession and a new trophy was donated to the NHL in 1936. After Lady Byng's death in 1949, the NHL changed the name to Lady Byng Memorial Trophy.

CONN SMYTHE TROPHY

(Playoff MVP)

Season	Player, Team
1964-65	Jean Beliveau, Montreal
1965-66	Roger Crozier, Detroit
1966-67	Dave Keon, Toronto
1967-68	Glenn Hall, St. Louis
1968-69	Serge Savard, Montreal
1969-70	Bobby Orr, Boston
1970-71	Ken Dryden, Montreal
1971-72	Bobby Orr, Boston
1972-73	Yvan Cournoyer, Montreal
1973-74	Bernie Parent, Philadelphia
1974-75	Bernie Parent, Philadelphia
1975-76	Reggie Leach, Philadelphia
1976-77	Guy Lafleur, Montreal
1977-78	Larry Robinson, Montreal
1978-79	Bob Gainey, Montreal
1979-80	Bryan Trottier, N.Y. Islanders
1980-81	Butch Goring, N.Y. Islanders
1981-82	Mike Bossy, N.Y. Islanders
1982-83	Billy Smith, N.Y. Islanders
1983-84	Mark Messier, Edmonton
1984-85	Wayne Gretzky, Edmonton
1985-86	Patrick Roy, Montreal
1986-87	Ron Hextall, Philadelphia
1987-88	Wayne Gretzky, Edmonton
1988-89	Al MacInnis, Calgary
1989-90	Bill Ranford, Edmonton
1990-91	Mario Lemieux, Pittsburgh
1991-92	Mario Lemieux, Pittsburgh

BILL MASTERTON MEMORIAL TROPHY

(Sportsmanship—dedication to hockey)

Season	Player, Team
1967-68	Claude Provost, Montreal
1968-69	Ted Hampson, Oakland
1969-70	Pit Martin, Chicago
1970-71	Jean Ratelle, N.Y. Rangers
1971-72	Bobby Clarke, Philadelphia
1972-73	Lowell MacDonald, Pittsburgh
1973-74	Henri Richard, Montreal
1974-75	Don Luce, Buffalo
1975-76	Rod Gilbert, N.Y. Rangers
1976-77	Ed Westfall, N.Y. Islanders
1977-78	Butch Goring, Los Angeles
1978-79	Serge Savard, Montreal
1979-80	Al MacAdam, Minnesota

Season	Player, Team
1980-81	Blake Dunlop, St. Louis
1981-82	Glenn Resch, Colorado
1982-83	Lanny McDonald, Calgary
1983-84	Brad Park, Detroit
1984-85	Anders Hedberg, N.Y. Rangers
1985-86	Charlie Simmer, Boston
1986-87	Doug Jarvis, Hartford
1987-88	Bob Bourne, Los Angeles
1988-89	Tim Kerr, Philadelphia
1989-90	Gord Kluzak, Boston
1990-91	Dave Taylor, Los Angeles
1991-92	Mark Fitzpatrick, N.Y. Islanders

Presented by the Professional Hockey Writers' Association to the player who best exemplifies the qualities of perseverance, sportsmanship and dedication to hockey.

FRANK J. SELKE TROPHY

(Best defensive forward)

Season	Player, Team
1977-78	Bob Gainey, Montreal
1978-79	Bob Gainey, Montreal
1979-80	Bob Gainey, Montreal
1980-81	Bob Gainey, Montreal
1981-82	Steve Kasper, Boston
1982-83	Bobby Clarke, Philadelphia
1983-84	Doug Jarvis, Washington
1984-85	Craig Ramsay, Buffalo
1985-86	Troy Murray, Chicago
1986-87	Dave Poulin, Philadelphia
1987-88	Guy Carbonneau, Montreal
1988-89	Guy Carbonneau, Montreal
1989-90	Rick Meagher, St. Louis
1990-91	Dirk Graham, Chicago
1991-92	Guy Carbonneau, Montreal

JACK ADAMS AWARD

(Coach of the year)

Season	Coach, Team
1973-74	Fred Shero, Philadelphia
1974-75	Bob Pulford, Los Angeles
1975-76	Don Cherry, Boston
1976-77	Scotty Bowman, Montreal
1977-78	Bobby Kromm, Detroit
1978-79	Al Arbour, N.Y. Islanders
1979-80	Pat Quinn, Philadelphia
1980-81	Red Berenson, St. Louis
1981-82	Tom Watt, Winnipeg
1982-83	Orval Tessier, Chicago
1983-84	Bryan Murray, Washington
1984-85	Mike Keenan, Philadelphia
1985-86	Glen Sather, Edmonton
1986-87	Jacques Demers, Detroit
1987-88	Jacques Demers, Detroit
1988-89	Pat Burns, Montreal
1989-90	Bob Murdoch, Winnipeg
1990-91	Brian Sutter, St. Louis
1991-92	Pat Quinn, Vancouver

KING CLANCY TROPHY

(Humanitarian contributions)

Season	Player, Team
1987-88	Lanny McDonald, Calgary
1988-89	Bryan Trottier, N.Y. Islanders
1989-90	Kevin Lowe, Edmonton
1990-91	Dave Taylor, Los Angeles
1991-92	Ray Bourque, Boston

TEAM HISTORIES

BOSTON BRUINS

YEAR-BY-YEAR RECORDS

Season	W	L	T	Pts.	Finish	W	L	Highest round	Coach
1924-25	6	24	0	12	6th	—	—		Art Ross
1925-26	17	15	4	38	4th	—	—		Art Ross
1926-27	21	20	3	45	2nd/American	*2	2	Stanley Cup finals	Art Ross
1927-28	20	13	11	51	1st/American	*0	1	Semifinals	Art Ross
1928-29	26	13	5	57	1st/American	5	0	Stanley Cup champ	Cy Denneny
1929-30	38	5	1	77	1st/American	3	3	Stanley Cup finals	Art Ross
1930-31	28	10	6	62	1st/American	2	3	Semifinals	Art Ross
1931-32	15	21	12	42	4th/American	—	—		Art Ross
1932-33	25	15	8	58	1st/American	2	3	Semifinals	Art Ross
1933-34	18	25	5	41	4th/American	—	—		Art Ross
1934-35	26	16	6	58	1st/American	1	3	Semifinals	Frank Patrick
1935-36	22	20	6	50	2nd/American	1	1	Quarterfinals	Frank Patrick
1936-37	23	18	7	53	2nd/American	1	2	Quarterfinals	Art Ross
1937-38	30	11	7	67	1st/American	0	3	Semifinals	Art Ross
1938-39	36	10	2	74	1st	8	4	Stanley Cup champ	Art Ross
1939-40	31	12	5	67	1st	2	4	Semifinals	Ralph (Cooney) Weiland
1940-41	27	8	13	67	1st	8	3	Stanley Cup champ	Ralph (Cooney) Weiland
1941-42	25	17	6	56	3rd	2	3	Semifinals	Art Ross
1942-43	24	17	9	57	2nd	4	5	Stanley Cup finals	Art Ross
1943-44	19	26	5	43	5th	—	—		Art Ross
1944-45	16	30	4	36	4th	3	4	League semifinals	Art Ross
1945-46	24	18	8	56	2nd	5	5	Stanley Cup finals	Dit Clapper
1946-47	26	23	11	63	3rd	1	4	League semifinals	Dit Clapper
1947-48	23	24	13	59	3rd	1	4	League semifinals	Dit Clapper
1948-49	29	23	8	66	2nd	1	4	League semifinals	Dit Clapper
1949-50	22	32	16	60	5th	—	—		George Boucher
1950-51	22	30	18	62	4th	†1	4	League semifinals	Lynn Patrick
1951-52	25	29	16	66	4th	3	4	League semifinals	Lynn Patrick
1952-53	28	29	13	69	3rd	5	6	League semifinals	Lynn Patrick
1953-54	32	28	10	74	4th	0	4	League semifinals	Lynn Patrick
1954-55	23	26	21	67	4th	1	4	League semifinals	Lynn Patrick, Milt Schmidt
1955-56	23	34	13	59	5th	—	—		Milt Schmidt
1956-57	34	24	12	80	3rd	5	5	Stanley Cup finals	Milt Schmidt
1957-58	27	28	15	69	4th	6	6	Stanley Cup finals	Milt Schmidt
1958-59	32	29	9	73	2nd	3	4	League semifinals	Milt Schmidt
1959-60	28	34	8	64	5th	—	—		Milt Schmidt
1960-61	15	42	13	43	6th	—	—		Milt Schmidt
1961-62	15	47	8	38	6th	—	—		Phil Watson
1962-63	14	39	17	45	6th	—	—		Phil Watson, Milt Schmidt
1963-64	18	40	12	48	6th	—	—		Milt Schmidt
1964-65	21	43	6	48	6th	—	—		Milt Schmidt
1965-66	21	43	6	48	5th	—	—		Milt Schmidt
1966-67	17	43	10	44	6th	—	—		Harry Sinden
1967-68	37	27	10	84	3rd/East	0	4	Division semifinals	Harry Sinden
1968-69	42	18	16	100	2nd/East	6	4	Division finals	Harry Sinden
1969-70	40	17	19	99	2nd/East	12	2	Stanley Cup champ	Harry Sinden
1970-71	57	14	7	121	1st/East	3	4	Division semifinals	Tom Johnson
1971-72	54	13	11	119	1st/East	12	3	Stanley Cup champ	Tom Johnson
1972-73	51	22	5	107	2nd/East	1	4	Division semifinals	Tom Johnson, Bep Guidolin
1973-74	52	17	9	113	1st/East	10	6	Stanley Cup finals	Bep Guidolin
1974-75	40	26	14	94	2nd/Adams	1	2	Preliminaries	Don Cherry
1975-76	48	15	17	113	1st/Adams	5	7	Semifinals	Don Cherry
1976-77	49	23	8	106	1st/Adams	8	6	Stanley Cup finals	Don Cherry
1977-78	51	18	11	113	1st/Adams	10	5	Stanley Cup finals	Don Cherry
1978-79	43	23	14	100	1st/Adams	7	4	Semifinals	Don Cherry
1979-80	46	21	13	105	2nd/Adams	4	6	Quarterfinals	Fred Creighton, Harry Sinden
1980-81	37	30	13	87	2nd/Adams	0	3	Preliminaries	Gerry Cheevers
1981-82	43	27	10	96	2nd/Adams	6	5	Division finals	Gerry Cheevers
1982-83	50	20	10	110	1st/Adams	9	8	Conference finals	Gerry Cheevers
1983-84	49	25	6	104	1st/Adams	0	3	Division semifinals	Gerry Cheevers
1984-85	36	34	10	82	4th/Adams	2	3	Division semifinals	Gerry Cheevers, Harry Sinden
1985-86	37	31	12	86	3rd/Adams	0	3	Division semifinals	Butch Goring
1986-87	39	34	7	85	3rd/Adams	0	4	Division semifinals	Butch Goring, Terry O'Reilly
1987-88	44	30	6	94	2nd/Adams	12	6	Conference finals	Terry O'Reilly
1988-89	37	29	14	88	2nd/Adams	5	5	Division finals	Terry O'Reilly
1989-90	46	25	9	101	1st/Adams	13	8	Stanley Cup finals	Mike Milbury

Season	W	L	T	Pts.	Finish	W	L	Highest round	Coach
1990-91	44	24	12	100	1st/Adams	10	9	Conference finals	Mike Milbury
1991-92	36	32	12	84	2nd/Adams	8	3	Conference finals	Mike Milbury

*Won-lost record does not indicate tie(s) resulting from two-game, total-goals series that year (two-game, total-goals series were played from 1917-18 through 1935-36).
†Tied after one overtime (curfew law).

FIRST-ROUND ENTRY DRAFT CHOICES

Year	Player, Overall, Last Amateur Team (League)
1969	Don Tannahill, 3, Niagara Falls (OHL)
	Frank Spring, 4, Edmonton (WCHL)
	Ivan Boldirev, 11, Oshawa (OHL)
1970	Reggie Leach, 3, Flin Flon (WCHL)
	Rick MacLeish, 4, Peterborough (OHL)
	Ron Plumb, 9, Peterborough (OHL)
	Bob Stewart, 13, Oshawa (OHL)
1971	Ron Jones, 6, Edmonton (WCHL)
	Terry O'Reilly, 14, Oshawa (OHL)
1972	Mike Bloom, 16, St. Catharines (OHL)
1973	Andre Savard, 6, Quebec (QMJHL)
1974	Don Laraway, 18, Swift Current (WCHL)
1975	Doug Halward, 14, Peterborough (OHL)
1976	Clayton Pachal, 16, New Westminster (WCHL)
1977	Dwight Foster, 16, Kitchener (OHL)
1978	Al Secord, 16, Hamilton (OHL)
1979	Ray Bourque, 8, Verdun (QMJHL)
	Brad McCrimmon, 15, Brandon (WHL)

Year	Player, Overall, Last Amateur Team (League)
1980	Barry Pederson, 18, Victoria (WHL)
1981	Norm Leveille, 14, Chicoutimi (QMJHL)
1982	*Gord Kluzak, 1, Billings (WHL)
1983	Nevin Markwart, 21, Regina (WHL)
1984	Dave Pasin, 19, Prince Albert (WHL)
1985	No first round selection
1986	Craig Janney, 13, Boston College
1987	Glen Wesley, 3, Portland (WHL)
	Stephane Quintal, 14, Granby (QMJHL)
1988	Robert Cimetta, 18, Toronto (OHL)
1989	Shayne Stevenson, 17, Kitchener (OHL)
1990	Bryan Smolinski, 21, Michigan State University
1991	Glen Murray, 18, Sudbury (OHL)
1992	Dmitri Kvartalnov, 16, San Diego (IHL)

*Designates first player chosen in draft.

FRANCHISE LEADERS

Current players in boldface

FORWARDS/DEFENSEMEN

Games
John Bucyk	1436
Wayne Cashman	1027
Ray Bourque	**950**
Terry O'Reilly	891
Rick Middleton	881
Don Marcotte	868
Dallas Smith	861
Dit Clapper	833
Milt Schmidt	776
Woody Dumart	771

Goals
John Bucyk	545
Phil Esposito	459
Rick Middleton	402
Ken Hodge Sr.	289
Wayne Cashman	277
Ray Bourque	**272**
Bobby Orr	264
Peter McNab	263
Don Marcotte	230
Milt Schmidt	229

Assists
John Bucyk	794
Ray Bourque	**743**
Bobby Orr	624

Phil Esposito	553
Wayne Cashman	516
Rick Middleton	496
Terry O'Reilly	402
Ken Hodge Sr.	385
Bill Cowley	346
Milt Schmidt	346

Points
John Bucyk	1339
Ray Bourque	**1015**
Phil Esposito	1012
Rick Middleton	898
Bobby Orr	888
Wayne Cashman	793
Ken Hodge Sr.	674
Terry O'Reilly	606
Peter McNab	587
Milt Schmidt	575

Penalty minutes
Terry O'Reilly	2095
Mike Milbury	1552
Keith Crowder	1261
Wayne Cashman	1041
Eddie Shore	1038
Ted Green	1029

GOALTENDERS

Games
Cecil Thompson	468
Frankie Brimsek	444

Eddie Johnston	443
Gerry Cheevers	416
Gilles Gilbert	277
Jim Henry	236

Shutouts
Cecil Thompson	74
Frankie Brimsek	35
Eddie Johnston	27
Gerry Cheevers	26
Jim Henry	24
Hal Winkler	19
Gilles Gilbert	16
Don Simmons	15

Goals-against average
(2400 minutes minimum)
Hal Winkler	1.56
Cecil Thompson	1.99
Charles Stewart	2.46
John Henderson	2.52
Terry Sawchuk	2.57
Frankie Brimsek	2.58
Jim Henry	2.58

Wins
Cecil Thompson	252
Frankie Brimsek	230
Gerry Cheevers	229
Eddie Johnston	182
Gilles Gilbert	155

BUFFALO SABRES

YEAR-BY-YEAR RECORDS

Season	W	L	T	Pts.	Finish	W	L	Highest round	Coach
1970-71	24	39	15	63	5th/East	—	—		Punch Imlach
1971-72	16	43	19	51	6th/East	—	—		Punch Imlach, Joe Crozier
1972-73	37	27	14	88	4th/East	2	4	Division semifinals	Joe Crozier
1973-74	32	34	12	76	5th/East	—	—		Joe Crozier
1974-75	49	16	15	113	1st/Adams	10	7	Stanley Cup finals	Floyd Smith

Season	W	L	T	Pts.	Finish	W	L	Highest round	Coach
1975-76	46	21	13	105	2nd/Adams	4	5	Quarterfinals	Floyd Smith
1976-77	48	24	8	104	2nd/Adams	2	4	Quarterfinals	Floyd Smith
1977-78	44	19	17	105	2nd/Adams	3	5	Quarterfinals	Marcel Pronovost
1978-79	36	28	16	88	2nd/Adams	1	2	Preliminaries	Marcel Pronovost, Bill Inglis
1979-80	47	17	16	110	1st/Adams	9	5	Semifinals	Scotty Bowman
1980-81	39	20	21	99	1st/Adams	4	4	Quarterfinals	Roger Neilson
1981-82	39	26	15	93	3rd/Adams	1	3	Division semifinals	Jim Roberts, Scotty Bowman
1982-83	38	29	13	89	3rd/Adams	6	4	Division finals	Scotty Bowman
1983-84	48	25	7	103	2nd/Adams	0	3	Division semifinals	Scotty Bowman
1984-85	38	28	14	90	3rd/Adams	2	3	Divison semifinals	Scotty Bowman
1985-86	37	37	6	80	5th/Adams	—	—		Jim Schoenfeld, Scotty Bowman
1986-87	28	44	8	64	5th/Adams	—	—		Scotty Bowman, Craig Ramsay, Ted Sator
1987-88	37	32	11	85	3rd/Adams	2	4	Division semifinals	Ted Sator
1988-89	38	35	7	83	3rd/Adams	1	4	Division semifinals	Ted Sator
1989-90	45	27	8	98	2nd/Adams	2	4	Division semifinals	Rick Dudley
1990-91	31	30	19	81	3rd/Adams	2	4	Division semifinals	Rick Dudley
1991-92	31	37	12	74	3rd/Adams	3	4	Division semifinals	Rick Dudley, John Muckler

FIRST-ROUND ENTRY DRAFT CHOICES

Year   Player, Overall, Last Amateur Team (League)

1970—*Gilbert Perreault, 1, Montreal (OHL)
1971—Rick Martin, 5, Montreal (OHL)
1972—Jim Schoenfeld, 5, Niagara Falls (OHL)
1973—Morris Titanic, 12, Sudbury (OHL)
1974—Lee Fogolin, 11, Oshawa (OHL)
1975—Robert Sauve, 17, Laval (QMJHL)
1976—No first round selection
1977—Ric Seiling, 14, St. Catharines (OHL)
1978—Larry Playfair, 13, Portland (WHL)
1979—Mike Ramsey, 11, University of Minnesota
1980—Steve Patrick, 20, Brandon (WHL)
1981—Jiri Dudacek, 17, Kladno (Czechoslovakia)
1982—Phil Housley, 6, South St. Paul H.S. (Minn.)
    Paul Cyr, 9, Victoria (WHL)
    Dave Andreychuk, 16, Oshawa (OHL)

Year   Player, Overall, Last Amateur Team (League)

1983—Tom Barrasso, 5, Acton Boxboro H.S. (Mass.)
    Norm Lacombe, 10, Univ. of New Hampshire
    Adam Creighton, 11, Ottawa (OHL)
1984—Bo Andersson, 18, Vastra Frolunda (Sweden)
1985—Carl Johansson, 14, Vastra Frolunda (Sweden)
1986—Shawn Anderson, 5, Team Canada
1987—*Pierre Turgeon, 1, Granby (QMJHL)
1988—Joel Savage, 13, Victoria (WHL)
1989—Kevin Haller, 14, Regina (WHL)
1990—Brad May, 14, Niagara Falls (OHL)
1991—Philippe Boucher, 13, Granby (QMJHL)
1992—David Cooper, 11, Medicine Hat (WHL)

*Designates first player chosen in draft.

FRANCHISE LEADERS

Current players in boldface

FORWARDS/DEFENSEMEN

Games

Gilbert Perreault	1191
Craig Ramsay	1070
Mike Ramsey	878
Bill Hajt	854
Don Luce	766
Dave Andreychuk	712
Rick Martin	681
Ric Seiling	664
Mike Foligno	662
Lindy Ruff	608
Phil Housley	608

Goals

Gilbert Perreault	512
Rick Martin	382
Dave Andreychuk	319
Danny Gare	267
Craig Ramsay	252
Mike Foligno	247
Rene Robert	222
Don Luce	216
Phil Housley	178
Ric Seiling	176

Assists

Gilbert Perreault	814
Craig Ramsay	420
Dave Andreychuk	391
Phil Housley	380
Rene Robert	330
Rick Martin	313
Don Luce	310
Mike Foligno	264
Mike Ramsey	248
Danny Gare	233

Points

Gilbert Perreault	1326
Dave Andreychuk	710
Rick Martin	695
Criag Ramsay	672
Phil Housley	558
Rene Robert	552
Don Luce	526
Mike Foligno	511
Danny Gare	500
Ric Seiling	376

Penalty minutes

Mike Foligno	1447
Larry Playfair	1390
Lindy Ruff	1126
Jim Schoenfeld	1025
Mike Ramsey	904

GOALTENDERS

Games

Don Edwards	307
Tom Barrasso	266
Bob Sauve	246
Roger Crozier	202
Daren Puppa	191
Jacques Cloutier	144
Dave Dryden	120
Gerry Desjardins	116

Shutouts

Don Edwards	14
Tom Barrasso	13
Roger Crozier	10
Bob Sauve	7

Goals-against average
(2400 minutes minimum)

Gerry Desjardins	2.81
Don Edwards	2.90
Dave Dryden	3.06
Bob Sauve	3.23
Roger Crozier	3.23
Tom Barrasso	3.28
Daren Puppa	3.38
Clint Malarchuk	3.40
Jacques Cloutier	3.70

Wins

Don Edwards	156
Tom Barrasso	124
Bob Sauve	119
Daren Puppa	85
Roger Crozier	74
Gerry Desjardins	66

CHICAGO BLACKHAWKS

YEAR-BY-YEAR RECORDS

Season	\-\-\-REGULAR SEASON\-\-\-					\-\-\-PLAYOFFS\-\-\-			
	W	L	T	Pts.	Finish	W	L	Highest round	Coach
1926-27	19	22	3	41	3rd/American	*0	1	Quarterfinals	Pete Muldoon
1927-28	7	34	3	17	5th/American	—	—		Barney Stanley, Hugh Lehman
1928-29	7	29	8	22	5th/American	—	—		Herb Gardiner
1929-30	21	18	5	47	2nd/American	*0	1	Quarterfinals	Tom Schaughnessy, Bill Tobin
1930-31	24	17	3	51	2nd/American	*5	3	Stanley Cup finals	Dick Irvin
1931-32	18	19	11	47	2nd/American	1	1	Quarterfinals	Dick Irvin, Bill Tobin
1932-33	16	20	12	44	4th/American	—	—		Godfrey Matheson, Emil Iverson
1933-34	20	17	11	51	2nd/American	6	2	Stanley Cup champ	Tom Gorman
1934-35	26	17	5	57	2nd/American	*0	1	Quarterfinals	Clem Loughlin
1935-36	21	19	8	50	3rd/American	1	1	Quarterfinals	Clem Loughlin
1936-37	14	27	7	35	4th/American	—	—		Clem Loughlin
1937-38	14	25	9	37	3rd/American	7	3	Stanley Cup champ	Bill Stewart
1938-39	12	28	8	32	7th	—	—		Bill Stewart, Paul Thompson
1939-40	23	19	6	52	4th	0	2	Quarterfinals	Paul Thompson
1940-41	16	25	7	39	5th	2	3	Semifinals	Paul Thompson
1941-42	22	23	3	47	4th	1	2	Quarterfinals	Paul Thompson
1942-43	17	18	15	49	5th	—	—		Paul Thompson
1943-44	22	23	5	49	4th	4	5	Stanley Cup finals	Paul Thompson
1944-45	13	30	7	33	5th	—	—		Paul Thompson, John Gottselig
1945-46	23	20	7	53	3rd	0	4	League semifinals	John Gottselig
1946-47	19	37	4	42	6th	—	—		John Gottselig
1947-48	20	34	6	46	6th	—	—		John Gottselig, Charlie Conacher
1948-49	21	31	8	50	5th	—	—		Charlie Conacher
1949-50	22	38	10	54	6th	—	—		Charlie Conacher
1950-51	13	47	10	36	6th	—	—		Ebbie Goodfellow
1951-52	17	44	9	43	6th	—	—		Ebbie Goodfellow
1952-53	27	28	15	69	4th	3	4	League semifinals	Sid Abel
1953-54	12	51	7	31	6th	—	—		Sid Abel
1954-55	13	40	17	43	6th	—	—		Frank Eddolls
1955-56	19	39	12	50	6th	—	—		Dick Irvin
1956-57	16	39	15	47	6th	—	—		Tommy Ivan
1957-58	24	39	7	55	5th	—	—		Tommy Ivan, Rudy Pilous
1958-59	28	29	13	69	3rd	2	4	League semifinals	Rudy Pilous
1959-60	28	29	13	69	3rd	0	4	League semifinals	Rudy Pilous
1960-61	29	24	17	75	3rd	6	6	Stanley Cup finals	Rudy Pilous
1961-62	31	26	13	75	3rd	6	6	Stanley Cup finals	Rudy Pilous
1962-63	32	21	17	81	2nd	2	4	League semifinals	Rudy Pilous
1963-64	36	22	12	84	2nd	3	4	League semifinals	Billy Reay
1964-65	34	28	8	76	3rd	7	7	Stanley Cup finals	Billy Reay
1965-66	37	25	8	82	2nd	2	4	League semifinals	Billy Reay
1966-67	41	17	12	94	1st	2	4	League semifinals	Billy Reay
1967-68	32	26	16	80	4th/East	5	6	Division finals	Billy Reay
1968-69	34	33	9	77	6th/East	—	—		Billy Reay
1969-70	45	22	9	99	1st/East	4	4	Division finals	Billy Reay
1970-71	49	20	9	107	1st/West	11	7	Stanley Cup finals	Billy Reay
1971-72	46	17	15	107	1st/West	4	4	Division finals	Billy Reay
1972-73	42	27	9	93	1st/West	10	6	Stanley Cup finals	Billy Reay
1973-74	41	14	23	105	2nd/West	6	5	Division finals	Billy Reay
1974-75	37	35	8	82	3rd/Smythe	3	5	Quarterfinals	Billy Reay
1975-76	32	30	18	82	1st/Smythe	0	4	Quarterfinals	Billy Reay
1976-77	26	43	11	63	3rd/Smythe	0	2	Preliminaries	Billy Reay, Bill White
1977-78	32	29	19	83	1st/Smythe	0	4	Quarterfinals	Bob Pulford
1978-79	29	36	15	73	1st/Smythe	0	4	Quarterfinals	Bob Pulford
1979-80	34	27	19	87	1st/Smythe	3	4	Quarterfinals	Eddie Johnston
1980-81	31	33	16	78	2nd/Smythe	0	3	Preliminaries	Keith Magnuson
1981-82	30	38	12	72	4th/Norris	8	7	Conference finals	Keith Magnuson, Bob Pulford
1982-83	47	23	10	104	1st/Norris	7	6	Conference finals	Orval Tessier
1983-84	30	42	8	68	4th/Norris	2	3	Division semifinals	Orval Tessier
1984-85	38	35	7	83	2nd/Norris	9	6	Conference finals	Orval Tessier, Bob Pulford
1985-86	39	33	8	86	1st/Norris	0	3	Division semifinals	Bob Pulford
1986-87	29	37	14	72	3rd/Norris	0	4	Division semifinals	Bob Pulford
1987-88	30	41	9	69	3rd/Norris	1	4	Division semifinals	Bob Murdoch
1988-89	27	41	12	66	4th/Norris	9	7	Conference finals	Mike Keenan
1989-90	41	33	6	88	1st/Norris	10	10	Conference finals	Mike Keenan
1990-91	49	23	8	106	1st/Norris	2	4	Division semifinals	Mike Keenan
1991-92	36	29	15	87	2nd/Norris	12	6	Stanley Cup finals	Mike Keenan

*Won-lost record does not indicate tie(s) resulting from two-game, total-goals series that year (two-game, total-goals series were played from 1917-18 through 1935-36).

YEAR-BY-YEAR RECORDS

Season	W	L	T	Pts.	Finish	W	L	Highest round	Coach
1972-73	25	38	15	65	7th/West	—	—		Bernie Geoffrion
1973-74	30	34	14	74	4th/West	0	4	Division semifinals	Bernie Geoffrion
1974-75	34	31	15	83	4th/Patrick	—	—		Bernie Geoffrion, Fred Creighton
1975-76	35	33	12	82	3rd/Patrick	0	2	Preliminaries	Fred Creighton
1976-77	34	34	12	80	3rd/Patrick	1	2	Preliminaries	Fred Creighton
1977-78	34	27	19	87	3rd/Patrick	0	2	Preliminaries	Fred Creighton
1978-79	41	31	8	90	4th/Patrick	0	2	Preliminaries	Fred Creighton
1979-80	35	32	13	83	4th/Patrick	1	3	Preliminaries	Al MacNeil
1980-81	39	27	14	92	3rd/Patrick	9	7	Semifinals	Al MacNeil
1981-82	29	34	17	75	3rd/Smythe	0	3	Division semifinals	Al MacNeil
1982-83	32	34	14	78	2nd/Smythe	4	5	Division finals	Bob Johnson
1983-84	34	32	14	82	2nd/Smythe	6	5	Division finals	Bob Johnson
1984-85	41	27	12	94	3rd/Smythe	1	3	Division semifinals	Bob Johnson
1985-86	40	31	9	89	2nd/Smythe	12	10	Stanley Cup finals	Bob Johnson
1986-87	46	31	3	95	2nd/Smythe	2	4	Division semifinals	Bob Johnson
1987-88	48	23	9	105	1st/Smythe	1	5	Division finals	Terry Crisp
1988-89	54	17	9	117	1st/Smythe	16	6	Stanley Cup champ	Terry Crisp
1989-90	42	23	15	99	1st/Smythe	2	4	Division semifinals	Terry Crisp
1990-91	46	26	8	100	2nd/Smythe	3	4	Division semifinals	Doug Risebrough
1991-92	31	37	12	74	5th/Smythe	—	—		Doug Risebrough, Guy Charron

FIRST-ROUND ENTRY DRAFT CHOICES

Year Player, Overall, Last Amateur Team (League)
1972—Jacques Richard, 2, Quebec (QMJHL)
1973—Tom Lysiak, 2, Medicine Hat (WCHL)
 Vic Mercredi, 16, New Westminster (WCHL)
1974—No first round selection
1975—Richcard Mulhern, 8, Sherbrooke (QMJHL)
1976—Dave Shand, 8, Peterborough (OHL)
 Harold Phillipoff, 10, New Westminster (WCHL)
1977—No first round selection
1978—Brad Marsh, 11, London (OHL)
1979—Paul Reinhart, 12, Kitchener (OHL)
1980—Denis Cyr, 13, Montreal (OHL)
1981—Al MacInnis, 15, Kitchener (OHL)

Year Player, Overall, Last Amateur Team (League)
1982—No first round selection
1983—Dan Quinn, 13, Belleville (OHL)
1984—Gary Roberts, 12, Ottawa (OHL)
1985—Chris Biotti, 17, Belmont Hill H.S. (Mass.)
1986—George Pelawa, 16, Bemidji H.S. (Minn.)
1987—Bryan Deasley, 19, University of Michigan
1988—Jason Muzzatti, 21, Michigan State University
1989—No first round selection
1990—Trevor Kidd, 11, Brandon (WHL)
1991—Niklas Sundblad, 19, AIK (Sweden)
1992—Cory Stillman, 6, Windsor (OHL)

FRANCHISE LEADERS

Current players in boldface

FORWARDS/DEFENSEMEN
Games
Jim Peplinski 705
Al MacInnis 678
Jamie Macoun 586
Tim Hunter 545
Eric Vail 539
Joel Otto 527
Paul Reinhart 517
Guy Chouinard 514
Gary Suter 511
Lanny McDonald 492

Goals
Kent Nilsson 229
Joe Nieuwendyk 219
Lanny McDonald 215
Eric Vail 206
Guy Chouinard 193
Hakan Loob 193
Joe Mullen 190
Al MacInnis 174
Jim Peplinski 161
Tom Lysiak 155

Assists
Al MacInnis 438
Gary Suter 369
Guy Chouinard 336
Paul Reinhart 335

Kent Nilsson 333
Tom Lysiak 276
Jim Peplinski 262
Eric Vail 246
Hakan Loob 236
Joel Otto 203

Points
Al MacInnis 686
Kent Nilsson 562
Guy Chouinard 529
Gary Suter 470
Eric Vail 452
Paul Reinhart 444
Tom Lysiak 431
Hakan Loob 429
Jim Peplinski 423
Joe Nieuwendyk 416

Penalty minutes
Tim Hunter 2405
Jim Peplinski 1456
Gary Roberts 1298
Joel Otto 1270
Willi Plett 1267
Al MacInnis 804
Gary Suter 742
Jamie Macoun 666

GOALTENDERS
Games
Dan Bouchard 398
Mike Vernon 355

Reggie Lemelin 324
Phil Myre 211
Pat Riggin 119
Don Edwards 114
Rick Wamsley 111

Shutouts
Dan Bouchard 20
Phil Myre 11
Reggie Lemelin 6
Pat Riggin 4
Mike Vernon 4
Rick Wamsley 4

Goals-against average
(2400 minutes minimum)
Dan Bouchard 3.03
Phil Myre 3.21
Rick Wamsley 3.21
Mike Vernon 3.35
Reggie Lemelin 3.67
Pat Riggin 3.88
Don Edwards 4.06

Wins
Mike Vernon 193
Dan Bouchard 170
Reggie Lemelin 144
Phil Myre 76
Rick Wamsley 53
Pat Riggin 50
Don Edwards 40

TEAM HISTORIES

NHL HISTORY

TEAM HISTORIES

FIRST-ROUND ENTRY DRAFT CHOICES

Year	Player, Overall, Last Amateur Team (League)
1969	J.P. Bordeleau, 13, Montreal (OHL)
1970	Dan Maloney, 14, London (OHL)
1971	Dan Spring, 12, Edmonton (WCHL)
1972	Phil Russell, 13, Edmonton (WCHL)
1973	Darcy Rota, 13, Edmonton (WCHL)
1974	Grant Mulvey, 16, Calgary (WCHL)
1975	Greg Vaydik, 7, Medicine Hat (WCHL)
1976	Real Cloutier, 9, Quebec (WHA)
1977	Doug Wilson, 6, Ottawa (OHL)
1978	Tim Higgins, 10, Ottawa (OHL)
1979	Keith Brown, 7, Portland (WHL)
1980	Denis Savard, 3, Montreal (QMJHL)
	Jerome Dupont, 15, Toronto (OHL)

Year	Player, Overall, Last Amateur Team (League)
1981	Tony Tanti, 12, Oshawa (OHL)
1982	Ken Yaremchuk, 7, Portland (WHL)
1983	Bruce Cassidy, 18, Ottawa (OHL)
1984	Ed Olczyk, 3, U.S. Olympic Team
1985	Dave Manson, 11, Prince Albert (WHL)
1986	Everett Sanipass, 14, Verdun (QMJHL)
1987	Jimmy Waite, 8, Chicoutimi (QMJHL)
1988	Jeremy Roenick, 8, Thayer Academy (Mass.)
1989	Adam Bennett, 6, Sudbury (OHL)
1990	Karl Dykhuis, 16, Hull (QMJHL)
1991	Dean McAmmond, 22, Prince Albert (WHL)
1992	Sergei Krivokrasov, 12, Central Red Army (CIS)

FRANCHISE LEADERS

Current players in boldface

FORWARDS/DEFENSEMEN

Goals

Bobby Hull	604
Stan Mikita	541
Steve Larmer	**371**
Denis Savard	351
Dennis Hull	298
Bill Mosienko	258
Ken Wharram	252
Pit Martin	243
Doug Wilson	225
Doug Bentley	217
Jim Pappin	216
Al Secord	213
Cliff Koroll	208
Eric Nesterenko	207
Troy Murray	196
John Gottselig	176
Darryl Sutter	161
Ed Litzenberger	153
Harold March	153
Chico Maki	149

Assists

Stan Mikita	926
Denis Savard	662
Doug Wilson	554
Bobby Hull	549
Steve Larmer	**482**
Pierre Pilote	400
Pit Martin	384
Bob Murray	382
Dennis Hull	342
Doug Bentley	313
Chico Maki	292
Bill Mosienko	288
Eric Nesterenko	288
Troy Murray	287
Pat Stapleton	286
Bill Hay	283
Ken Wharram	281
Tom Lysiak	275
Keith Brown	**260**
Cliff Koroll	254

Points

Stan Mikita	1467
Bobby Hull	1153
Denis Savard	1013
Steve Larmer	**853**
Doug Wilson	779
Dennis Hull	640
Pit Martin	627
Bill Mosienko	550

Ken Wharram	533
Doug Bentley	531
Bob Murray	514
Eric Nesterenko	495
Troy Murray	483
Pierre Pilote	477
Cliff Koroll	462
Jim Pappin	444
Chico Maki	441
Tom Lysiak	412
Bill Hay	386
Harold March	383

GOALTENDERS

Shutouts

Tony Esposito	74
Glenn Hall	51
Chuck Gardiner	42
Mike Karakas	28
Al Rollins	17
Denis DeJordy	13
Ed Belfour	**9**
Murray Bannerman	8
Lorne Chabot	8
Paul Goodman	6
Hugh Lehman	6

DETROIT RED WINGS

YEAR-BY-YEAR RECORDS

	REGULAR SEASON					PLAYOFFS			
Season	W	L	T	Pts.	Finish	W	L	Highest round	Coach
1926-27	12	28	4	28	5th/American	—	—		Art Duncan, Duke Keats
1927-28	19	19	6	44	4th/American	—	—		Jack Adams
1928-29	19	16	9	47	3rd/American	0	2	Quarterfinals	Jack Adams
1929-30	14	24	6	34	4th/American	—	—		Jack Adams
1930-31	16	21	7	39	4th/American	—	—		Jack Adams
1931-32	18	20	10	46	3rd/American	*0	1	Quarterfinals	Jack Adams
1932-33	25	15	8	58	2nd/American	2	2	Semifinals	Jack Adams
1933-34	24	14	10	58	1st/American	4	5	Stanley Cup finals	Jack Adams
1934-35	19	22	7	45	4th/American	—	—		Jack Adams
1935-36	24	16	8	56	1st/American	6	1	Stanley Cup champ	Jack Adams
1936-37	25	14	9	59	1st/American	6	4	Stanley Cup champ	Jack Adams
1937-38	12	25	11	35	4th/American	—	—		Jack Adams
1938-39	18	24	6	42	5th	3	3	Semifinals	Jack Adams
1939-40	16	26	6	38	5th	2	3	Semifinals	Jack Adams
1940-41	21	16	11	53	3rd	4	5	Stanley Cup finals	Jack Adams
1941-42	19	25	4	42	5th	7	5	Stanley Cup finals	Jack Adams
1942-43	25	14	11	61	1st	8	2	Stanley Cup champ	Jack Adams
1943-44	26	18	6	58	2nd	1	4	League semifinals	Jack Adams
1944-45	31	14	5	67	2nd	7	7	Stanley Cup finals	Jack Adams
1945-46	20	20	10	50	4th	1	4	League semifinals	Jack Adams
1946-47	22	27	11	55	4th	1	4	League semifinals	Jack Adams

Season	W	L	T	Pts.	Finish	W	L	Highest round	Coach
1947-48	30	18	12	72	2nd	4	6	Stanley Cup finals	Tommy Ivan
1948-49	34	19	7	75	1st	4	7	Stanley Cup finals	Tommy Ivan
1949-50	37	19	14	88	1st	8	6	Stanley Cup champ	Tommy Ivan
1950-51	44	13	13	101	1st	2	4	League semifinals	Tommy Ivan
1951-52	44	14	12	100	1st	8	0	Stanley Cup champ	Tommy Ivan
1952-53	36	16	18	90	1st	2	4	League semifinals	Tommy Ivan
1953-54	37	19	14	88	1st	8	4	Stanley Cup champ	Tommy Ivan
1954-55	42	17	11	95	1st	8	3	Stanley Cup champ	Jimmy Skinner
1955-56	30	24	16	76	2nd	5	5	Stanley Cup finals	Jimmy Skinner
1956-57	38	20	12	88	1st	1	4	League semifinals	Jimmy Skinner
1957-58	29	29	12	70	3rd	0	4	League semifinals	Jimmy Skinner, Sid Abel
1958-59	25	37	8	58	6th	—	—		Sid Abel
1959-60	26	29	15	67	4th	2	4	League semifinals	Sid Abel
1960-61	25	29	16	66	4th	6	5	Stanley Cup finals	Sid Abel
1961-62	23	33	14	60	5th	—	—		Sid Abel
1962-63	32	25	13	77	4th	5	6	Stanley Cup finals	Sid Abel
1963-64	30	29	11	71	4th	7	7	Stanley Cup finals	Sid Abel
1964-65	40	23	7	87	1st	3	4	League semifinals	Sid Abel
1965-66	31	27	12	74	4th	6	6	Stanley Cup finals	Sid Abel
1966-67	27	39	4	58	5th				Sid Abel
1967-68	27	35	12	66	6th/East	—	—		Sid Abel
1968-69	33	31	12	78	5th/East	—	—		Bill Gadsby
1969-70	40	21	15	95	3rd/East	0	4	Division semifinals	Bill Gadsby, Sid Abel
1970-71	22	45	11	55	7th/East	—	—		Ned Harkness, Doug Barkley
1971-72	33	35	10	76	5th/East	—	—		Doug Barkley, Johnny Wilson
1972-73	37	29	12	86	5th/East	—	—		Johnny Wilson
1973-74	29	39	10	68	6th/East	—	—		Ted Garvin, Alex Delvecchio
1974-75	23	45	12	58	4th/Norris	—	—		Alex Delvecchio
1975-76	26	44	10	62	4th/Norris	—	—		Ted Garvin, Alex Delvecchio
1976-77	16	55	9	41	5th/Norris	—	—		Alex Delvecchio, Larry Wilson
1977-78	32	34	14	78	2nd/Norris	3	4	Quarterfinals	Bobby Kromm
1978-79	23	41	16	62	5th/Norris	—	—		Bobby Kromm
1979-80	26	43	11	63	5th/Norris	—	—		Bobby Kromm, Ted Lindsay
1980-81	19	43	18	56	5th/Norris	—	—		Ted Lindsay, Wayne Maxner
1981-82	21	47	12	54	6th/Norris	—	—		Wayne Maxner, Billy Dea
1982-83	21	44	15	57	5th/Norris	—	—		Nick Polano
1983-84	31	42	7	69	3rd/Norris	1	3	Division semifinals	Nick Polano
1984-85	27	41	12	66	3rd/Norris	0	3	Division semifinals	Nick Polano
1985-86	17	57	6	40	5th/Norris	—	—		Harry Neale, Brad Park, Dan Belisle
1986-87	34	36	10	78	2nd/Norris	9	7	Conference finals	Jacques Demers
1987-88	41	28	11	93	1st/Norris	9	7	Conference finals	Jacques Demers
1988-89	34	34	12	80	1st/Norris	2	4	Division semifinals	Jacques Demers
1989-90	28	38	14	70	5th/Norris	—	—		Jacques Demers
1990-91	34	38	8	76	3rd/Norris	3	4	Division semifinals	Brian Murray
1991-92	43	25	12	98	1st/Norris	4	7	Division finals	Brian Murray

*Won-lost record does not indicate tie(s) resulting from two-game, total goals series that year (two-game, total-goals series were played from 1917-18 through 1935-36).

FIRST-ROUND ENTRY DRAFT CHOICES

Year   Player, Overall, Last Amateur Team (League)

1969—Jim Rutherford, 10, Hamilton (OHL)
1970—Serge Lajeunesse, 12, Montreal (OHL)
1971—Marcel Dionne, 2, St. Catharines (OHL)
1972—No first-round selection
1973—Terry Richardson, 11, New Westminster (WCHL)
1974—Bill Lochead, 9, Oshawa (OHL)
1975—Rick Lapointe, 5, Victoria (WCHL)
1976—Fred Williams, 4, Saskatoon (WCHL)
1977—*Dale McCourt, 1, St. Catharines (OHL)
1978—Willie Huber, 9, Hamilton (OHL)
          Brent Peterson, 12, Portland (WCHL)
1979—Mike Foligno, 3, Sudbury (OHL)
1980—Mike Blaisdell, 11, Regina (WHL)

1981—No first-round selection
1982—Murray Craven, 17, Medicine Hat (WHL)
1983—Steve Yzerman, 4, Peterborough (OHL)
1984—Shawn Burr, 7, Kitchener (OHL)
1985—Brent Fedyk, 8, Regina (WHL)
1986—*Joe Murphy, 1, Michigan State University
1987—Yves Racine, 11, Longueuil (QMJHL)
1988—Kory Kocur, 17, Saskatoon (WHL)
1989—Mike Sillinger, 11, Regina (WHL)
1990—Keith Primeau, 3, Niagara Falls (OHL)
1991—Martin Lapointe, 10, Laval (QMJHL)
1992—Curtis Bowen, 22, Ottawa (OHL)

*Designates first player chosen in draft.

FRANCHISE LEADERS

Current players in boldface

FORWARDS/DEFENSEMEN

Games

Gordie Howe	1687
Alex Delvecchio	1549

Marcel Pronovost	983
Norm Ullman	875
Ted Lindsay	862
Nick Libett	861
Red Kelly	846
Syd Howe	793

Reed Larson	708
Gary Bergman	706

Goals

Gordie Howe	786
Alex Delvecchio	456
Steve Yzerman	**387**

Ted Lindsay	335
Norm Ullman	324
John Ogrodnick	259
Nick Libett	217
Syd Howe	202
Gerard Gallant	**197**
Reed Larson	188

Assists

Gordie Howe	1023
Alex Delvecchio	825
Steve Yzerman	**516**
Norm Ullman	434
Ted Lindsay	393
Reed Larson	382
Red Kelly	297
Sid Abel	279
John Ogrodnick	275
Nick Libett	250

Points

Gordie Howe	1809
Alex Delvecchio	1281
Steve Yzerman	**903**
Norm Ullman	758
Ted Lindsay	728

Reed Larson	570
John Ogrodnick	534
Nick Libett	467
Sid Abel	463
Red Kelly	451

GOALTENDERS

Games

Terry Sawchuk	734
Harry Lumley	324
Jim Rutherford	314
Roger Crozier	310
Greg Stefan	299
Roy Edwards	221
Glen Hanlon	186
Norm Smith	178
Tim Cheveldae	**167**
John Mowers	152

Shutouts

Terry Sawchuk	85
Harry Lumley	26
Roger Crozier	20
Clarence Dolson	17
Glenn Hall	17

Harry Holmes	17
Norm Smith	17

Goals-against average
(2400 minutes minimum)

Clarence Dolson	2.06
Harry Holmes	2.11
Glenn Hall	2.14
Alex Connell	2.25
John Ross Roach	2.26
Norm Smith	2.34
Terry Sawchuk	2.46
John Mowers	2.63
Cecil Thompson	2.65
Harry Lumley	2.73

Wins

Terry Sawchuk	352
Harry Lumley	163
Roger Crozier	130
Greg Stefan	115
Jim Rutherford	97
Roy Edwards	95
Tim Cheveldae	**78**
Norm Smith	76

EDMONTON OILERS

YEAR-BY-YEAR RECORDS

	REGULAR SEASON					PLAYOFFS			
Season	W	L	T	Pts.	Finish	W	L	Highest round	Coach
1972-73	38	37	3	79	5th	—	—		Ray Kinasewich
1973-74	38	37	3	79	3rd	1	4	League quarterfinals	Brian Shaw
1974-75	36	38	4	76	5th	—	—		Brian Shaw, Bill Hunter
1975-76	27	49	5	59	4th	0	4	League quarterfinals	Clare Drake, Bill Hunter
1976-77	34	43	4	72	4th	1	4	League quarterfinals	Bep Guidolin, Glen Sather
1977-78	38	39	3	79	5th	1	4	League quarterfinals	Glen Sather
1978-79	48	30	2	98	1st	6	7	Avco World Cup finals	Glen Sather
1979-80	28	39	13	69	4th/Smythe	0	3	Preliminaries	Glen Sather
1980-81	29	35	16	74	4th/Smythe	5	4	Quarterfinals	Glen Sather
1981-82	48	17	15	111	1st/Smythe	2	3	Division semifinals	Glen Sather
1982-83	47	21	12	106	1st/Smythe	11	5	Stanley Cup finals	Glen Sather
1983-84	57	18	5	119	1st/Smythe	15	4	Stanley Cup champ	Glen Sather
1984-85	49	20	11	109	1st/Smythe	15	3	Stanley Cup champ	Glen Sather
1985-86	56	17	7	119	1st/Smythe	6	4	Division finals	Glen Sather
1986-87	50	24	6	106	1st/Smythe	16	5	Stanley Cup champ	Glen Sather
1987-88	44	25	11	99	2nd/Smythe	16	2	Stanley Cup champ	Glen Sather
1988-89	38	34	8	84	3rd/Smythe	3	4	Division semifinals	Glen Sather
1989-90	38	28	14	90	2nd/Smythe	16	6	Stanley Cup champ	John Muckler
1990-91	37	37	6	80	3rd/Smythe	9	9	Conference finals	John Muckler
1991-92	36	34	10	82	3rd/Smythe	8	8	Conference finals	Ted Green

NOTE: Member of World Hockey Association from 1972-73 through 1978-79.

FIRST-ROUND ENTRY DRAFT CHOICES

Year   Player, Overall, Last Amateur Team (League)
1979—Kevin Lowe, 21, Quebec (QMJHL)
1980—Paul Coffey, 6, Kitchener (OHL)
1981—Grant Fuhr, 8, Victoria (WHL)
1982—Jim Playfair, 20, Portland (WHL)
1983—Jeff Beukeboom, 19, Sault Ste. Marie (OHL)
1984—Selmar Odelein, 21, Regina (WHL)
1985—Scott Metcalfe, 20, Kingston (OHL)
1986—Kim Issel, 21, Prince Albert (WHL)
1987—Peter Soberlak, 21, Swift Current (WHL)
1988—Francois Leroux, 19, St. Jean (QMJHL)

Year   Player, Overall, Last Amateur Team (League)
1989—Jason Soules, 15, Niagara Falls (OHL)
1990—Scott Allison, 17, Prince Albert (WHL)
1991—Tyler Wright, 12, Swift Current (WHL)
         Martin Rucinsky, 20, Litvinov (Czech.)
1992—Joe Hulbig, 13, St. Sebastian H.S. (Mass.)

 NOTE: Edmonton chose Dave Dryden, Bengt Gustafsson
and Ed Mio as priority selections before the 1979 expansion
draft.

FRANCHISE LEADERS

Current players in boldface

FORWARDS/DEFENSEMEN

Games

Kevin Lowe	**966**
Mark Messier	851
Glenn Anderson	828

Jari Kurri	754
Wayne Gretzky	696
Charlie Huddy	694
Dave Hunter	653
Lee Fogolin	586
Craig MacTavish	**553**
Paul Coffey	532

Goals

Wayne Gretzky	583
Jari Kurri	474
Glenn Anderson	413
Mark Messier	392
Paul Coffey	209
Esa Tikkanen	**164**

Craig Simpson	161
Craig MacTavish	129
Dave Hunter	119
Mike Krushelnyski	95

Assists
Wayne Gretzky	1086
Mark Messier	642
Jari Kurri	569
Glenn Anderson	483
Paul Coffey	460
Kevin Lowe	295
Charlie Huddy	287
Esa Tikkanen	239
Steve Smith	172
Dave Hunter	171

Points
Wayne Gretzky	1669
Jari Kurri	1043
Mark Messier	1034
Glenn Anderson	896
Paul Coffey	669
Esa Tikkanen	403

Charlie Huddy	368
Kevin Lowe	368
Craig Simpson	319
Dave Hunter	290

Penalty minutes
Kevin McClelland	1298
Kevin Lowe	1164
Mark Messier	1122
Steve Smith	1080
Dave Semenko	976
Lee Fogolin	886
Kelly Buchberger	800
Dave Hunter	776
Glenn Anderson	771
Jeff Beukeboom	733

GOALTENDERS

Games
Grant Fuhr	423
Andy Moog	235
Bill Ranford	218
Eddie Mio	77

Ron Low	67
Jim Corsi	26
Gary Edwards	15

Shutouts
Grant Fuhr	9
Andy Moog	4
Bill Ranford	3
Eddie Mio	1

Goals-against average
(2400 minutes minimum)
Bill Ranford	3.35
Andy Moog	3.61
Grant Fuhr	3.69
Eddie Mio	4.02
Ron Low	4.03

Wins
Grant Fuhr	226
Andy Moog	143
Bill Ranford	96
Ron Low	30
Eddie Mio	25
Jim Corsi	8

HARTFORD WHALERS

YEAR-BY-YEAR RECORDS

	REGULAR SEASON					PLAYOFFS			
Season	W	L	T	Pts.	Finish	W	L	Highest round	Coach
1972-73	46	30	2	94	1st	12	3	Avco World Cup champ	Jack Kelley
1973-74	43	31	4	90	1st	3	4	League quarterfinals	Ron Ryan
1974-75	43	30	5	91	1st	2	4	League quarterfinals	Ron Ryan, Jack Kelley
1975-76	33	40	7	73	3rd	6	4	League semifinals	Jack Kelley, Don Blackburn
									Harry Neale
1976-77	35	40	6	76	4th	1	4	League quarterfinals	Harry Neale
1977-78	44	31	5	93	2nd	8	6	Avco World Cup finals	Harry Neale
1978-79	37	34	9	83	4th	5	5	League semifinals	Bill Dineen, Don Blackburn
1979-80	27	34	19	73	4th/Norris	0	3	Preliminaries	Don Blackburn
1980-81	21	41	18	60	4th/Norris	—	—		Don Blackburn, Larry Pleau
1981-82	21	41	18	60	5th/Adams	—	—		Larry Pleau
1982-83	19	54	7	45	5th/Adams	—	—		Larry Kish, Larry Pleau, John Cunniff
1983-84	28	42	10	66	5th/Adams	—	—		Jack Evans
1984-85	30	41	9	69	5th/Adams	—	—		Jack Evans
1985-86	40	36	4	84	4th/Adams	6	4	Division finals	Jack Evans
1986-87	43	30	7	93	1st/Adams	2	4	Division semifinals	Jack Evans
1987-88	35	38	7	77	4th/Adams	2	4	Division semifinals	Jack Evans, Larry Pleau
1988-89	37	38	5	79	4th/Adams	0	4	Division semifinals	Larry Pleau
1989-90	38	33	9	85	4th/Adams	3	4	Division semifinals	Rick Ley
1990-91	31	38	11	73	4th/Adams	2	4	Division semifinals	Rick Ley
1991-92	26	41	13	65	4th/Adams	3	4	Division semifinals	Jim Roberts

NOTE: Member of World Hockey Association from 1972-73 through 1978-79.

FIRST-ROUND ENTRY DRAFT CHOICES

Year Player, Overall, Last Amateur Team (League)
1979—Ray Allison, 18, Brandon (WHL)
1980—Fred Arthur, 8, Cornwall (QMJHL)
1981—Ron Francis, 4, Sault Ste. Marie (OHL)
1982—Paul Lawless, 14, Windsor (OHL)
1983—Sylvain Turgeon, 2, Hull (QMJHL)
      David A. Jensen, 20, Lawrence Academy (Mass.)
1984—Sylvain Cote, 11, Quebec (QMJHL)
1985—Dana Murzyn, 5, Calgary (WHL)
1986—Scott Young, 11, Boston University
1987—Jody Hull, 18, Peterborough (OHL)

Year Player, Overall, Last Amateur Team (League)
1988—Chris Govedaris, 11, Toronto (OHL)
1989—Robert Holik, 10, Jihlava (Czechoslovakia)
1990—Mark Greig, 15, Lethbridge (WHL)
1991—Patrick Poulin, 9, St. Hyacinthe (QMJHL)
1992—Robert Petrovicky, Dukla Trencin (Czech.)

NOTE: Hartford chose Jordy Douglas, John Garrett and Mark Howe as priority selections before the 1979 expansion draft.

FRANCHISE LEADERS

FORWARDS/DEFENSEMEN
Games
Ron Francis	714
Kevin Dineen	489
Dave Tippett	483

Current players in boldface

Ulf Samuelsson	463
Joel Quenneville	457
Ray Ferraro	442
Dean Evason	434
Sylvain Cote	382
Paul MacDermid	373
Sylvain Turgeon	370

Goals
Ron Francis	264
Blaine Stoughton	219
Kevin Dineen	214
Sylvain Turgeon	178
Ray Ferraro	157
Pat Verbeek	109

Ray Neufeld	106
Dean Evason	87
Mark Johnson	85
Mike Rogers	85

Assists

Ron Francis	557
Kevin Dineen	262
Dave Babych	196
Ray Ferraro	194
Blaine Stoughton	158
Sylvain Turgeon	150
Dean Evason	148
Mark Howe	147
Ulf Samuelsson	144
Ray Neufeld	131

Points

Ron Francis	821
Kevin Dineen	446
Blaine Stoughton	377
Ray Ferraro	351
Sylvain Turgeon	328
Dave Babych	240
Dean Evason	235

Pat Verbeek	228
Ray Neufeld	226
Mike Rogers	210
Mark Johnson	203

Penalty minutes

Torrie Robertson	1368
Ulf Samuelsson	1108
Kevin Dineen	1029
Pat Verbeek	717
Paul MacDermid	706
Dean Evason	617
Ron Francis	540
Ed Kastelic	485
Chris Kotsopoulos	443
Ray Ferraro	417

GOALTENDERS

Games

Mike Liut	252
Greg Millen	219
Peter Sidorkiewicz	178
John Garrett	122
Steve Weeks	94

Kay Whitmore	75
Mike Veisor	69
Al Smith	30

Shutouts

Mike Liut	13
Peter Sidorkiewicz	8
Greg Millen	4
Steve Weeks	4

Goals-against average
(2400 minutes minimum)

Peter Sidorkiewicz	3.33
Mike Liut	3.36
Kay Whitmore	3.61
Steve Weeks	3.68
Greg Millen	4.25
John Garrett	4.28
Mike Veisor	4.87

Wins

Mike Liut	115
Peter Sidorkiewicz	71
Greg Millen	62
Steve Weeks	42
John Garrett	36

LOS ANGELES KINGS

YEAR-BY-YEAR RECORDS

	REGULAR SEASON					PLAYOFFS			
Season	W	L	T	Pts.	Finish	W	L	Highest round	Coach
1967-68	31	33	10	72	2nd/West	3	4	Division semifinals	Red Kelly
1968-69	24	42	10	58	4th/West	4	7	Division finals	Red Kelly
1969-70	14	52	10	38	6th/West	—	—		Hal Laycoe, Johnny Wilson
1970-71	25	40	13	63	5th/West	—	—		Larry Regan
1971-72	20	49	9	49	7th/West	—	—		Larry Regan, Fred Glover
1972-73	31	36	11	73	6th/West	—	—		Bob Pulford
1973-74	33	33	12	78	3rd/West	1	4	Division semifinals	Bob Pulford
1974-75	42	17	21	105	2nd/Norris	1	2	Preliminaries	Bob Pulford
1975-76	38	33	9	85	2nd/Norris	5	4	Quarterfinals	Bob Pulford
1976-77	34	31	15	83	2nd/Norris	4	5	Quarterfinals	Bob Pulford
1977-78	31	34	15	77	3rd/Norris	0	2	Preliminaries	Ron Stewart
1978-79	34	34	12	80	3rd/Norris	0	2	Preliminaries	Bob Berry
1979-80	30	36	14	74	2nd/Norris	1	3	Preliminaries	Bob Berry
1980-81	43	24	13	99	2nd/Norris	1	3	Preliminaries	Bob Berry
1981-82	24	41	15	63	4th/Smythe	4	6	Division finals	Parker MacDonald, Don Perry
1982-83	27	41	12	66	5th/Smythe	—	—		Don Perry
1983-84	23	44	13	59	5th/Smythe	—	—		Don Perry, Rogie Vachon, Roger Neilson
1984-85	34	32	14	82	4th/Smythe	0	3	Division semifinals	Pat Quinn
1985-86	23	49	8	54	5th/Smythe	—	—		Pat Quinn
1986-87	31	41	8	70	4th/Smythe	1	4	Division semifinals	Pat Quinn, Mike Murphy
1987-88	30	42	8	68	4th/Smythe	1	4	Division semifinals	Mike Murphy, Rogie Vachon Robbie Ftorek
1988-89	42	31	7	91	2nd/Norris	4	7	Division finals	Robbie Ftorek
1989-90	34	39	7	75	4th/Smythe	4	6	Division finals	Tom Webster
1990-91	46	24	10	102	1st/Smythe	6	6	Division finals	Tom Webster
1991-92	35	31	14	84	2nd/Smythe	2	4	Division semifinals	Tom Webster

FIRST-ROUND ENTRY DRAFT CHOICES

Year   Player, Overall, Last Amateur Team (League)
1969—No first-round selection
1970—No first-round selection
1971—No first-round selection
1972—No first-round selection
1973—No first-round selection
1974—No first-round selection
1975—Tim Young, 16, Ottawa (OHL)
1976—No first-round selection
1977—No first-round selection
1978—No first-round selection
1979—Jay Wells, 16, Kingston (OHL)
1980—Larry Murphy, 4, Peterborough (OHL)
     Jim Fox, 10, Ottawa (OHL)

Year   Player, Overall, Last Amateur Team (League)
1981—Doug Smith, 2, Ottawa (OHL)
1982—No first-round selection
1983—No first-round selection
1984—Craig Redmond, 6, Canadian Olympic Team
1985—Craig Duncanson, 9, Sudbury (OHL)
     Dan Gratton, 10, Oshawa (OHL)
1986—Jimmy Carson, 2, Verdun (QMJHL)
1987—Wayne McBean, 4, Medicine Hat (WHL)
1988—Martin Gelinas, 7, Hull (QMJHL)
1989—No first-round selection
1990—Darryl Sydor, 7, Kamloops (WHL)
1991—No first-round selection
1992—No first-round selection

FRANCHISE LEADERS

Current players in boldface

FORWARDS/DEFENSEMEN

Games

Dave Taylor	1030
Marcel Dionne	921
Butch Goring	736
Mike Murphy	673
Jay Wells	604
Bernie Nicholls	602
Mark Hardy	589
Jim Fox	578
Bob Berry	539
Juha Widing	502

Goals

Marcel Dionne	550
Dave Taylor	421
Bernie Nicholls	327
Luc Robitaille	285
Butch Goring	275
Charlie Simmer	222
Mike Murphy	194
Jim Fox	186
Wayne Gretzky	166
Bob Berry	159

Assists

Marcel Dionne	757
Dave Taylor	626
Bernie Nicholls	431
Wayne Gretzky	428

Butch Goring	384
Luc Robitaille	307
Jim Fox	292
Mike Murphy	262
Mark Hardy	244
Charlie Simmer	244

Points

Marcel Dionne	1307
Dave Taylor	1047
Bernie Nicholls	758
Butch Goring	659
Wayne Gretzky	594
Luc Robitaille	592
Jim Fox	478
Charlie Simmer	466
Mike Murphy	456
Bob Berry	350

Penalty minutes

Dave Taylor	1512
Jay Wells	1446
Marty McSorley	1161
Jay Miller	865
Mark Hardy	827

GOALTENDERS

Games

Rogie Vachon	389
Mario Lessard	240
Kelly Hrudey	175
Gary Edwards	155

Roland Melanson	119
Gerry Desjardins	103
Bob Janecyk	102
Dennis DeJordy	86

Shutouts

Rogie Vachon	32
Mario Lessard	9
Gerry Desjardins	7
Gary Edwards	7
Kelly Hrudey	7

Goals-against average
(2400 minutes minimum)

Rogie Vachon	2.86
Wayne Rutledge	3.34
Gary Edwards	3.39
Kelly Hrudey	3.40
Gerry Desjardins	3.52
Daniel Berthiaume	3.54
Dennis DeJordy	3.73
Mario Lessard	3.74
Doug Keans	4.08

Wins

Rogie Vachon	171
Mario Lessard	92
Kelly Hrudey	84
Gary Edwards	54
Bob Janecyk	41
Roland Melanson	40
Glenn Healy	37

MINNESOTA NORTH STARS

YEAR-BY-YEAR RECORDS

	REGULAR SEASON					PLAYOFFS			
Season	W	L	T	Pts.	Finish	W	L	Highest round	Coach
1967-68	27	32	15	69	4th/West	7	7	Division finals	Wren Blair
1968-69	18	43	15	51	6th/West	—	—		Wren Blair, John Muckler
1969-70	19	35	22	60	3rd/West	2	4	Division semifinals	Wren Blair, Charlie Burns
1970-71	28	34	16	72	4th/West	6	6	Division finals	Jack Gordon
1971-72	37	29	12	86	2nd/West	3	4	Division semifinals	Jack Gordon
1972-73	37	30	11	85	3rd/West	2	4	Division semifinals	Jack Gordon
1973-74	23	38	17	63	7th/West	—	—		Jack Gordon, Parker MacDonald
1974-75	23	50	7	53	4th/Smythe	—	—		Jack Gordon, Charlie Burns
1975-76	20	53	7	47	4th/Smythe	—	—		Ted Harris
1976-77	23	39	18	64	2nd/Smythe	0	2	Preliminaries	Ted Harris
1977-78	18	53	9	45	5th/Smythe	—	—		Ted Harris, Andre Beaulieu, Lou Nanne
1978-79	28	40	12	68	4th/Adams	—	—		Harry Howell, Glen Sonmor
1979-80	36	28	16	88	3rd/Adams	8	7	Semifinals	Glen Sonmor
1980-81	35	28	17	87	3rd/Adams	12	7	Stanley Cup finals	Glen Sonmor
1981-82	37	23	20	94	1st/Norris	1	3	Division semifinals	Glen Sonmor, Murray Oliver
1982-83	40	24	16	96	2nd/Norris	4	5	Division finals	Glen Sonmor, Murray Oliver
1983-84	39	31	10	88	1st/Norris	7	9	Conference finals	Bill Maloney
1984-85	25	43	12	62	4th/Norris	5	4	Division finals	Bill Maloney, Glen Sonmor
1985-86	38	33	9	85	2nd/Norris	2	3	Division semifinals	Lorne Henning
1986-87	30	40	10	70	5th/Norris	—	—		Lorne Henning, Glen Sonmor
1987-88	19	48	13	51	5th/Norris	—	—		Herb Brooks
1988-89	27	37	16	70	3rd/Norris	1	4	Division semifinals	Pierre Page
1989-90	36	40	4	76	4th/Norris	3	4	Division semifinals	Pierre Page
1990-91	27	39	14	68	4th/Norris	14	9	Stanley Cup finals	Bob Gainey
1991-92	32	42	6	70	4th/Norris	3	4	Division semifinals	Bob Gainey

FIRST-ROUND ENTRY DRAFT CHOICES

Year Player, Overall, Last Amateur Team (League)
1969—Dick Redmond, 5, St. Catharines (OHL)
      Dennis O'Brien, 14, St. Catharines (OHL)
1970—No first-round selection
1971—No first-round selection
1972—Jerry Byers, 12, Kitchener (OHL)
1973—No first-round selection
1974—Doug Hicks, 6, Flin Flon (WCHL)
1975—Brian Maxwell, 4, Medicine Hat (WCHL)

Year Player, Overall, Last Amateur Team (League)
1976—Glen Sharpley, 3, Hull (QMJHL)
1977—Brad Maxwell, 7, New Westminster (WCHL)
1978—*Bobby Smith, 1, Ottawa (OHL)
1979—Craig Hartsburg, 6, Birmingham (WHA)
      Tom McCarthy, 10, Oshawa (OHL)
1980—Brad Palmer, 16, Victoria (WHL)
1981—Ron Meighan, 13, Niagara Falls (OHL)
1982—Brian Bellows, 2, Kitchener (OHL)

1983—*Brian Lawton, 1, Mount St. Charles H.S. (R.I.)
1984—David Quinn, 13, Kent H.S. (Ct.)
1985—No first-round selection
1986—Warren Babe, 12, Lethbridge (WHL)
1987—Dave Archibald, 6, Portland (WHL)
1988—*Mike Modano, 1, Prince Albert (WHL)

1989—Doug Zmolek, 7, John Marshall H.S. (Minn.)
1990—Derian Hatcher, 8, North Bay (OHL)
1991—Richard Matvichuk, 8, Saskatoon (WHL)
1992—No first-round selection
*Designates first player chosen in draft.

FRANCHISE LEADERS

Current players in boldface

FORWARDS/DEFENSEMEN

Games

Neal Broten	794
Curt Giles	760
Brian Bellows	753
Fred Barrett	730
Bill Goldsworthy	670
Lou Nanne	635
Tom Reid	615
Steve Payne	613
Dino Ciccarelli	602
J.P. Parise	588

Goals

Brian Bellows	342
Dino Ciccarelli	332
Bill Goldsworthy	267
Neal Broten	237
Steve Payne	228
Bobby Smith	180
Tim Young	178
Danny Grant	176
J.P. Parise	154
Dave Gagner	154

Assists

Neal Broten	526
Brian Bellows	380
Bobby Smith	362
Dino Ciccarelli	319

Tim Young	316
Craig Hartsburg	315
J.P. Parise	242
Bill Goldsworthy	239
Steve Payne	238
Gordie Roberts	224

Points

Neal Broten	763
Brian Bellows	722
Dino Ciccarelli	651
Bobby Smith	542
Bill Goldsworthy	506
Tim Young	494
Steve Payne	466
Craig Hartsburg	413
J.P. Parise	396
Danny Grant	353

Penalty minutes

Basil McRae	1567
Willi Plett	1137
Brad Maxwell	1031
Shane Churla	908
Dennis O'Brien	836
Gordie Roberts	832
Craig Hartsburg	818
Bob Rouse	735

GOALTENDERS

Games

Cesare Maniago	420
Gilles Meloche	328

Don Beaupre	316
Jon Casey	265
Pete LoPresti	173
Kari Takko	131
Gump Worsley	107

Shutouts

Cesare Maniago	26
Jon Casey	9
Gilles Meloche	9
Pete LoPresti	5

Goals-against average
(2400 minutes minimum)

Gump Worsley	2.62
Cesare Maniago	3.17
Jon Casey	3.26
Gilles Gilbert	3.39
Gary Edwards	3.44
Gilles Meloche	3.51
Don Beaupre	3.74
Kari Takko	3.87
Gary Smith	3.92
Fern Rivard	3.98

Wins

Cesare Maniago	143
Gilles Meloche	141
Don Beaupre	126
Jon Casey	102
Pete LoPresti	43

MONTREAL CANADIENS

YEAR-BY-YEAR RECORDS

	REGULAR SEASON					PLAYOFFS			
Season	W	L	T	Pts.	Finish	W	L	Highest round	Coach
1917-18	13	9	0	26	1st/3rd	1	1	Semifinals	George Kennedy
1918-19	10	8	0	20	1st/2nd	†*6	3	Stanley Cup finals	George Kennedy
1919-20	13	11	0	26	2nd/3rd	—	—		George Kennedy
1920-21	13	11	0	26	3rd/2nd	—	—		George Kennedy
1921-22	12	11	1	25	3rd	—	—		Leo Dandurand
1922-23	13	9	2	28	2nd	1	1	Quarterfinals	Leo Dandurand
1923-24	13	11	0	26	2nd	6	0	Stanley Cup champ	Leo Dandurand
1924-25	17	11	2	36	3rd	3	3	Stanley Cup finals	Leo Dandurand
1925-26	11	24	1	23	7th	—	—		Cecil Hart
1926-27	28	14	2	58	2nd/Canadian	*1	1	Semifinals	Cecil Hart
1927-28	26	11	7	59	1st/Canadian	*0	1	Semifinals	Cecil Hart
1928-29	22	7	15	59	1st/Canadian	0	3	Semifinals	Cecil Hart
1929-30	21	14	9	51	2nd/Canadian	*5	0	Stanley Cup champ	Cecil Hart
1930-31	26	10	8	60	1st/Canadian	6	4	Stanley Cup champ	Cecil Hart
1931-32	25	16	7	57	1st/Canadian	1	3	Semifinals	Cecil Hart
1932-33	18	25	5	41	3rd/Canadian	*0	1	Quarterfinals	Newsy Lalonde
1933-34	22	20	6	50	2nd/Canadian	*0	1	Quarterfinals	Newsy Lalonde
1934-35	19	23	6	44	3rd/Canadian	*0	1	Quarterfinals	Newsy Lalonde, Leo Dandurand
1935-36	11	26	11	33	4th/Canadian	—	—		Sylvio Mantha
1936-37	24	18	6	54	1st/Canadian	2	3	Semifinals	Cecil Hart
1937-38	18	17	13	49	3rd/Canadian	1	2	Quarterfinals	Cecil Hart
1938-39	15	24	9	39	6th	1	2	Quarterfinals	Cecil Hart, Jules Dugal
1939-40	10	33	5	25	7th	—	—		Pit Lepine
1940-41	16	26	6	38	6th	1	2	Quarterfinals	Dick Irvin
1941-42	18	27	3	39	6th	1	2	Quarterfinals	Dick Irvin
1942-43	19	19	12	50	4th	1	4	League semifinals	Dick Irvin
1943-44	38	5	7	83	1st	8	1	Stanley Cup champ	Dick Irvin
1944-45	38	8	4	80	1st	2	4	League semifinals	Dick Irvin
1945-46	28	17	5	61	1st	8	1	Stanley Cup champ	Dick Irvin
1946-47	34	16	10	78	1st	6	5	Stanley Cup finals	Dick Irvin
1947-48	20	29	11	51	5th	—	—		Dick Irvin

Season			REGULAR SEASON					PLAYOFFS	
Season	W	L	T	Pts.	Finish	W	L	Highest round	Coach
1948-49	28	23	9	65	3rd	3	4	League semifinals	Dick Irvin
1949-50	29	22	19	77	2nd	1	4	League semifinals	Dick Irvin
1950-51	25	30	15	65	3rd	5	6	Stanley Cup finals	Dick Irvin
1951-52	34	26	10	78	2nd	4	7	Stanley Cup finals	Dick Irvin
1952-53	28	23	19	75	2nd	8	4	Stanley Cup champ	Dick Irvin
1953-54	35	24	11	81	2nd	7	4	Stanley Cup finals	Dick Irvin
1954-55	41	18	11	93	2nd	7	5	Stanley Cup finals	Dick Irvin
1955-56	45	15	10	100	1st	8	2	Stanley Cup champ	Toe Blake
1956-57	35	23	12	82	2nd	8	2	Stanley Cup champ	Toe Blake
1957-58	43	17	10	96	1st	8	2	Stanley Cup champ	Toe Blake
1958-59	39	18	13	91	1st	8	3	Stanley Cup champ	Toe Blake
1959-60	40	18	12	92	1st	8	0	Stanley Cup champ	Toe Blake
1960-61	41	19	10	92	1st	2	4	League semifinals	Toe Blake
1961-62	42	14	14	98	1st	2	4	League semifinals	Toe Blake
1962-63	28	19	23	79	3rd	1	4	League semifinals	Toe Blake
1963-64	36	21	13	85	1st	3	4	League semifinals	Toe Blake
1964-65	36	23	11	83	2nd	8	5	Stanley Cup champ	Toe Blake
1965-66	41	21	8	90	1st	8	2	Stanley Cup champ	Toe Blake
1966-67	32	25	13	77	2nd	6	4	Stanley Cup finals	Toe Blake
1967-68	42	22	10	54	1st/East	12	1	Stanley Cup champ	Toe Blake
1968-69	46	19	11	103	1st/East	12	2	Stanley Cup champ	Claude Ruel
1969-70	38	22	16	92	5th/East	—	—		Claude Ruel
1970-71	42	23	13	97	3rd/East	12	8	Stanley Cup champ	Claude Ruel, Al MacNeil
1971-72	46	16	16	108	3rd/East	2	4	Division semifinals	Scotty Bowman
1972-73	52	10	16	120	1st/East	12	5	Stanley Cup champ	Scotty Bowman
1973-74	45	24	9	99	2nd/East	2	4	Division semifinals	Scotty Bowman
1974-75	47	14	19	113	1st/Norris	6	5	Semifinals	Scotty Bowman
1975-76	58	11	11	127	1st/Norris	12	1	Stanley Cup champ	Scotty Bowman
1976-77	60	8	12	132	1st/Norris	12	2	Stanley Cup champ	Scotty Bowman
1977-78	59	10	11	129	1st/Norris	12	3	Stanley Cup champ	Scotty Bowman
1978-79	52	17	11	115	1st/Norris	12	4	Stanley Cup champ	Scotty Bowman
1979-80	47	20	13	107	1st/Norris	6	4	Quarterfinals	Bernie Geoffrion, Claude Ruel
1980-81	45	22	13	103	1st/Norris	0	3	Preliminaries	Claude Ruel
1981-82	46	17	17	109	1st/Adams	2	3	Division semifinals	Bob Berry
1982-83	42	24	14	98	2nd/Adams	0	3	Division semifinals	Bob Berry
1983-84	35	40	5	75	4th/Adams	9	6	Conference finals	Bob Berry, Jacques Lemaire
1984-85	41	27	12	94	1st/Adams	6	6	Division finals	Jacques Lemaire
1985-86	40	33	7	87	2nd/Adams	15	5	Stanley Cup champ	Jean Perron
1986-87	41	29	10	92	2nd/Adams	10	7	Conference finals	Jean Perron
1987-88	45	22	13	103	1st/Adams	5	6	Division finals	Jean Perron
1988-89	53	18	9	115	1st/Adams	14	7	Stanley Cup finals	Pat Burns
1989-90	41	28	11	93	3rd/Adams	5	6	Division finals	Pat Burns
1990-91	39	30	11	89	2nd/Adams	7	6	Division finals	Pat Burns
1991-92	41	28	11	93	1st/Adams	4	7	Division finals	Pat Burns

†1918-19 series abandoned with no Cup holder due to influenza epidemic.
*Won-lost record does not indicate tie(s) resulting from two-game, total-goals series that year (two-game, total-goals series were played from 1917-18 through 1935-36).

FIRST-ROUND ENTRY DRAFT CHOICES

Year   Player, Overall, Last Amateur Team (League)

1969—*Rejean Houle, 1, Montreal (OHL)
      Marc Tardif, 2, Montreal (OHL)
1970—Ray Martiniuk, 5, Flin Flon (WCHL)
      Chuck Lefley, 6, Canadian Nationals
1971—*Guy Lafleur, 1, Quebec (QMJHL)
      Chuck Arnason, 7, Flin Flon (WCHL)
      Murray Wilson, 11, Ottawa (OHL)
1972—Steve Shutt, 4, Toronto (OHL)
      Michel Larocque, 6, Ottawa (OHL)
      Dave Gardner, 8, Toronto (OHL)
      John Van Boxmeer, 14, Guelph (SOJHL)
1973—Bob Gainey, 8, Peterborough (OHL)
1974—Cam Connor, 5, Flin Flon (WCHL)
      Doug Risebrough, 7, Kitchener (OHL)
      Rick Chartraw, 10, Kitchener (OHL)
      Mario Tremblay, 12, Montreal (OHL)
      Gord McTavish, 15, Sudbury (OHL)
1975—Robin Sadler, 9, Edmonton (WCHL)
      Pierre Mondou, 15, Montreal (QMJHL)
1976—Peter Lee, 12, Ottawa (OHL)
      Rod Schutt, 13, Sudbury (OHL)
      Bruce Baker, 18, Ottawa (OHL)
1977—Mark Napier, 10, Birmingham (WHA)
      Normand Dupont, 18, Montreal (QMJHL)

Year   Player, Overall, Last Amateur Team (League)

1978—Danny Geoffrion, 8, Cornwall (QMJHL)
      Dave Hunter, 17, Sudbury (OHL)
1979—No first-round selection
1980—*Doug Wickenheiser, 1, Regina (WHL)
1981—Mark Hunter, 7, Brantford (OHL)
      Gilbert Delorme, 18, Chicoutimi (QMJHL)
      Jan Ingman, 19, Farjestads (Sweden)
1982—Alain Heroux, 19, Chicoutimi (QMJHL)
1983—Alfie Turcotte, 17, Portland (WHL)
1984—Petr Svoboda, 5, Czechoslovakia
      Shayne Corson, 8, Brantford (OHL)
1985—Jose Charbonneau, 12, Drummondville (QMJHL)
      Tom Chorske, 16, Minneapolis SW H.S. (Minn.)
1986—Mark Pederson, 15, Medicine Hat (WHL)
1987—Andrew Cassels, 17, Ottawa (OHL)
1988—Eric Charron, 20, Trois-Rivieres (QMJHL)
1989—Lindsay Vallis, 13, Seattle (WHL)
1990—Turner Stevenson, 12, Seattle (WHL)
1991—Brent Bilodeau, 17, Seattle (WHL)
1992—David Wilkie, 20, Kamloops (WHL)

*Designates first player chosen in draft.

FRANCHISE LEADERS

Current players in boldface

FORWARDS/DEFENSEMEN
Games
Henri Richard	1256
Larry Robinson	1202
Bob Gainey	1160
Jean Beliveau	1125
Claude Provost	1005
Maurice Richard	978
Yvan Cournoyer	968
Guy Lafleur	961
Serge Savard	917
Doug Harvey	890

Goals
Maurice Richard	544
Guy Lafleur	518
Jean Beliveau	507
Yvan Cournoyer	428
Steve Shutt	408
Bernie Geoffrion	371
Jacques Lemaire	366
Henri Richard	358
Aurele Joliat	270
Mario Tremblay	258

Assists
Guy Lafleur	728
Jean Beliveau	712
Henri Richard	688
Larry Robinson	686
Jacques Lemaire	469
Yvan Cournoyer	435
Maurice Richard	421
Elmer Lach	408
Guy Lapointe	406
Bernie Geoffrion	388

Points
Guy Lafleur	1246
Jean Beliveau	1219
Henri Richard	1046
Maurice Richard	965
Larry Robinson	883
Yvan Cournoyer	863
Jacques Lemaire	835
Steve Shutt	776
Bernie Geoffrion	759
Elmer Lach	623

Penalty minutes
Chris Nilan	**2248**
Maurice Richard	1285
John Ferguson	1214
Mario Tremblay	1043
Doug Harvey	1042
Jean Beliveau	1029
Doug Risebrough	959

Henri Richard	928
Tom Johnson	897
Shayne Corson	**891**

GOALTENDERS
Games
Jacques Plante	556
Ken Dryden	397
Bill Durnan	383
Patrick Roy	**356**
Georges Vezina	328
George Hainsworth	321
Gerry McNeil	276
Wilf Cude	249
Charlie Hodge	236
Michel Larocque	231

Shutouts
George Hainsworth	74
Jacques Plante	58
Ken Dryden	46
Bill Durnan	34
Gerry McNeil	28
Wilf Cude	22
Charlie Hodge	21
Patrick Roy	**18**
Michel Larocque	17
Gump Worsley	16

NEW JERSEY DEVILS

YEAR-BY-YEAR RECORDS

	REGULAR SEASON					PLAYOFFS			
Season	W	L	T	Pts.	Finish	W	L	Highest round	Coach
1974-75	15	54	11	41	5th/Smythe	—	—		Bep Guidolin
1975-76	12	56	12	36	5th/Smythe	—	—		Bep Guidolin, Sid Abel, Eddie Bush
1976-77	20	46	14	54	5th/Smythe	—	—		John Wilson
1977-78	19	40	21	59	2nd/Smythe	0	2	Preliminaries	Pat Kelly
1978-79	15	53	12	42	5th/Smythe	—	—		Pat Kelly, Bep Guidolin
1979-80	19	48	13	51	6th/Smythe	—	—		Don Cherry
1980-81	22	45	13	57	5th/Smythe	—	—		Billy MacMillan
1981-82	18	49	13	49	5th/Smythe	—	—		Bert Marshall, Marshall Johnston
1982-83	17	49	14	48	5th/Patrick	—	—		Billy MacMillan
1983-84	17	56	7	41	5th/Patrick	—	—		Billy MacMillan, Tom McVie
1984-85	22	48	10	54	5th/Patrick	—	—		Doug Carpenter
1985-86	28	49	3	59	5th/Patrick	—	—		Doug Carpenter
1986-87	29	45	6	64	6th/Patrick	—	—		Doug Carpenter
1987-88	38	36	6	82	4th/Patrick	11	9	Conference finals	Doug Carpenter, Jim Schoenfeld
1988-89	27	41	12	66	5th/Patrick	—	—		Jim Schoenfeld
1989-90	37	34	9	83	2nd/Patrick	2	4	Division semifinals	Jim Schoenfeld, John Cunniff
1990-91	32	33	15	79	4th/Patrick	3	4	Division semifinals	John Cunniff, Tom McVie
1991-92	38	31	11	87	4th/Patrick	3	4	Division semifinals	Tom McVie

FIRST-ROUND ENTRY DRAFT CHOICES

Year   Player, Overall, Last Amateur Team (League)
1974—Wilf Paiement, 2, St. Catharines (OHL)
1975—Barry Dean, 2, Medicine Hat (WCHL)
1976—Paul Gardner, 11, Oshawa (OHL)
1977—Barry Beck, 2, New Westminster (WCHL)
1978—Mike Gillis, 5, Kingston (OHL)
1979—*Rob Ramage, 1, Birmingham (WHA)
1980—Paul Gagne, 19, Windsor (OHL)
1981—Joe Cirella, 5, Oshawa (OHL)
1982—Rocky Trottier, 8, Billings (WHL)
        Ken Daneyko, 18, Seattle (WHL)
1983—John MacLean, 6, Oshawa (OHL)
1984—Kirk Muller, 2, Guelph (OHL)

Year   Player, Overall, Last Amateur Team (League)
1985—Craig Wolanin, 3, Kitchener (OHL)
1986—Neil Brady, 3, Medicine Hat (WHL)
1987—Brendan Shanahan, 2, London (OHL)
1988—Corey Foster, 12, Peterborough (OHL)
1989—Bill Guerin, 5, Springfield (Mass.) Jr.
        Jason Miller, 18, Medicine Hat (WHL)
1990—Martin Brodeur, 20, St. Hyacinthe (QMJHL)
1991—Scott Niedermayer, 3, Kamloops (WHL)
        Brian Rolston, 11, Detroit Compuware Jr.
1992—Jason Smith, 18, Regina (WHL)

*Designates first player chosen in draft.

FRANCHISE LEADERS

Current players in boldface

FORWARDS/DEFENSEMEN

Games
Aaron Broten	641
Kirk Muller	556
John MacLean	546
Ken Daneyko	529
Bruce Driver	512
Joe Cirella	503
Mike Kitchen	474
Pat Verbeek	463
Wilf Paiement	392
Gary Croteau	390

Goals
John MacLean	217
Kirk Muller	185
Pat Verbeek	170
Aaron Broten	162
Wilf Paiement	150
Paul Gagne	106
Brendan Shanahan	96
Gary Croteau	92
Mark Johnson	89
Doug Sulliman	86

Assists
Kirk Muller	335
Aaron Broten	307

Bruce Driver	240
John MacLean	224
Wilf Paiement	183
Patrik Sundstrom	160
Joe Cirella	159
Pat Verbeek	151
Mel Bridgman	148
Mark Johnson	140

Points
Kirk Muller	520
Aaron Broten	469
John MacLean	441
Wilf Paiement	336
Pat Verbeek	321
Bruce Driver	297
Patrik Sundstrom	246
Mark Johnson	229
Mel Bridgman	224
Brendan Shanahan	214

Penalty minutes
Ken Daneyko	1470
Pat Verbeek	943
Joe Cirella	938
John MacLean	785
David Maley	683
Kirk Muller	572
Wilf Paiement	558
Perry Anderson	553

Rob Ramage	529
Brendan Shanahan	524

GOALTENDERS

Games
Chico Resch	267
Sean Burke	162
Chris Terreri	157

Shutouts
Sean Burke	4
Craig Billington	2
Chris Terreri	2
Alain Chevrier	1
Doug Favell	1
Ron Low	1
Bill McKenzie	1
Bill Oleschuk	1
Chico Resch	1
Sam St. Laurent	1

Goals-against average
(2400 minutes minimum)
Chris Terreri	3.16
Sean Burke	3.66
Hardy Astrom	3.76
Doug Favell	3.84

Wins
Chico Resch	67
Sean Burke	62
Chris Terreri	61

NEW YORK ISLANDERS

YEAR-BY-YEAR RECORDS

	REGULAR SEASON					PLAYOFFS			
Season	W	L	T	Pts.	Finish	W	L	Highest round	Coach
1972-73	12	60	6	30	8th/East	—	—		Phil Goyette, Earl Ingarfield
1973-74	19	41	18	56	8th/East	—	—		Al Arbour
1974-75	33	25	22	88	3rd/Patrick	9	8	Semifinals	Al Arbour
1975-76	42	21	17	101	2nd/Patrick	7	6	Semifinals	Al Arbour
1976-77	47	21	12	106	2nd/Patrick	8	4	Semifinals	Al Arbour
1977-78	48	17	15	111	1st/Patrick	3	4	Quarterfinals	Al Arbour
1978-79	51	15	14	116	1st/Patrick	6	4	Semifinals	Al Arbour
1979-80	39	28	13	91	2nd/Patrick	15	6	Stanley Cup champ	Al Arbour
1980-81	48	18	14	110	1st/Patrick	15	3	Stanley Cup champ	Al Arbour
1981-82	54	16	10	118	1st/Patrick	15	4	Stanley Cup champ	Al Arbour
1982-83	42	26	12	96	2nd/Patrick	15	5	Stanley Cup champ	Al Arbour
1983-84	50	26	4	104	1st/Patrick	12	9	Stanley Cup finals	Al Arbour
1984-85	40	34	6	86	3rd/Patrick	4	6	Division finals	Al Arbour
1985-86	39	29	12	90	3rd/Patrick	0	3	Division semifinals	Al Arbour
1986-87	35	33	12	82	3rd/Patrick	7	7	Division finals	Terry Simpson
1987-88	39	31	10	88	1st/Patrick	2	4	Division semifinals	Terry Simpson
1988-89	28	47	5	61	6th/Patrick	—	—		Terry Simpson, Al Arbour
1989-90	31	38	11	73	4th/Patrick	1	4	Division semifinals	Al Arbour
1990-91	25	45	10	60	6th/Patrick	—	—		Al Arbour
1991-92	34	35	11	79	5th/Patrick	—	—		Al Arbour

FIRST-ROUND ENTRY DRAFT CHOICES

Year Player, Overall, Last Amateur Team (League)
1972—*Billy Harris, 1, Toronto (OHL)
1973—*Denis Potvin, 1, Ottawa (OHL)
1974—Clark Gillies, 4, Regina (WCHL)
1975—Pat Price, 11, Vancouver (WHA)
1976—Alex McKendry, 14, Sudbury (OHL)
1977—Mike Bossy, 15, Laval (QMJHL)
1978—Steve Tambellini, 15, Lethbridge (WCHL)
1979—Duane Sutter, 17, Lethbridge (WHL)
1980—Brent Sutter, 17, Red Deer (AJHL)
1981—Paul Boutilier, 21, Sherbrooke (QMJHL)
1982—Pat Flatley, 21, University of Wisconsin
1983—Pat LaFontaine, 3, Verdun (QMJHL)
       Gerald Diduck, 16, Lethbridge (WHL)

Year Player, Overall, Last Amateur Team (League)
1984—Duncan MacPherson, 20, Saskatoon (WHL)
1985—Brad Dalgarno, 6, Hamilton (OHL)
       Derek King, 13, Sault Ste. Marie (OHL)
1986—Tom Fitzgerald, 17, Austin Prep (Mass.)
1987—Dean Chynoweth, 13, Medicine Hat (WHL)
1988—Kevin Cheveldayoff, 16, Brandon (WHL)
1989—Dave Chyzowski, 2, Kamloops (WHL)
1990—Scott Scissons, 6, Saskatoon (WHL)
1991—Scott Lachance, 4, Boston University
1992—Darius Kasparaitis, 5, Dynamo Moscow (CIS)

*Designates first player chosen in draft.

FRANCHISE LEADERS

Current players in boldface

FORWARDS/DEFENSEMEN

Games
Bryan Trottier	1123
Denis Potvin	1080
Bob Nystrom	900
Clark Gillies	872
Bob Bourne	814
Mike Bossy	752
Brent Sutter	694
Billy Smith	675
Billy Harris	623
Stefan Persson	622

Goals
Mike Bossy	573
Bryan Trottier	500
Denis Potvin	310
Clark Gillies	304
Pat LaFontaine	287
Brent Sutter	287
Bob Bourne	238
Bob Nystrom	235
John Tonelli	206
Billy Harris	184

Assists
Bryan Trottier	853
Denis Potvin	742
Mike Bossy	553
Clark Gillies	359

John Tonelli	338
Brent Sutter	323
Stefan Persson	317
Bob Bourne	304
Pat LaFontaine	279
Bob Nystrom	278

Points
Bryan Trottier	1353
Mike Bossy	1126
Denis Potvin	1052
Clark Gillies	663
Brent Sutter	610
Pat LaFontaine	566
John Tonelli	544
Bob Bourne	542
Bob Nystrom	513
Billy Harris	443

Penalty minutes
Garry Howatt	1466
Denis Potvin	1354
Bob Nystrom	1248
Mick Vukota	**1140**
Clark Gillies	891
Duane Sutter	891
Bryan Trottier	798
Gerry Hart	783
Brent Sutter	761
Alan Kerr	691

GOALTENDERS

Games
Billy Smith	675
Chico Resch	282
Kelly Hrudey	241
Roland Melanson	136
Glenn Healy	**129**
Mark Fitzpatrick	**90**
Gerry Desjardins	80

Shutouts
Chico Resch	25
Billy Smith	22
Kelly Hrudey	6

Goals-against average
(2400 minutes minimum)
Chico Resch	2.56
Roland Melanson	3.14
Billy Smith	3.16
Mark Fitzpatrick	**3.38**
Kelly Hrudey	3.46
Glenn Healy	**3.51**

Wins
Billy Smith	304
Chico Resch	157
Kelly Hrudey	106
Roland Melanson	77
Glenn Healy	**44**
Mark Fitzpatrick	**34**
Gerry Desjardins	14

NEW YORK RANGERS

YEAR-BY-YEAR RECORDS

	REGULAR SEASON					PLAYOFFS			
Season	W	L	T	Pts.	Finish	W	L	Highest round	Coach
1926-27	25	13	6	56	1st/American	*0	1	Semifinals	Lester Patrick
1927-28	19	16	9	47	2nd/American	*5	3	Stanley Cup champ	Lester Patrick
1928-29	21	13	10	52	2nd/American	*3	2	Stanley Cup finals	Lester Patrick
1929-30	17	17	10	44	3rd/American	*1	2	Semifinals	Lester Patrick
1930-31	19	16	9	47	3rd/American	2	2	Semifinals	Lester Patrick
1931-32	23	17	8	54	1st/American	3	4	Stanley Cup finals	Lester Patrick
1932-33	23	17	8	54	3rd/American	*6	1	Stanley Cup champ	Lester Patrick
1933-34	21	19	8	50	3rd/American	*0	1	Quarterfinals	Lester Patrick
1934-35	22	20	6	50	3rd/American	*1	1	Semifinals	Lester Patrick
1935-36	19	17	12	50	4th/American	—	—		Lester Patrick
1936-37	19	20	9	47	3rd/American	6	3	Stanley Cup finals	Lester Patrick
1937-38	27	15	6	60	2nd/American	1	2	Quarterfinals	Lester Patrick
1938-39	26	16	6	58	2nd	3	4	Semifinals	Lester Patrick
1939-40	27	11	10	64	2nd	8	4	Stanley Cup champ	Frank Boucher
1940-41	21	19	8	50	4th	1	2	Quarterfinals	Frank Boucher
1941-42	29	17	2	60	1st	2	4	Semifinals	Frank Boucher
1942-43	11	31	8	30	6th	—	—		Frank Boucher
1943-44	6	39	5	17	6th	—	—		Frank Boucher
1944-45	11	29	10	32	6th	—	—		Frank Boucher
1945-46	13	28	9	35	6th	—	—		Frank Boucher
1946-47	22	32	6	50	5th	—	—		Frank Boucher
1947-48	21	26	13	55	4th	2	4	League semifinals	Frank Boucher
1948-49	18	31	11	47	6th	—	—		Frank Boucher, Lynn Patrick
1949-50	28	31	11	67	4th	7	5	Stanley Cup finals	Lynn Patrick
1950-51	20	29	21	61	5th	—	—		Neil Colville
1951-52	23	34	13	59	5th	—	—		Neil Colville, Bill Cook
1952-53	17	37	16	50	6th	—	—		Bill Cook
1953-54	29	31	10	68	5th	—	—		Frank Boucher, Muzz Patrick
1954-55	17	35	18	52	5th	—	—		Muzz Patrick
1955-56	32	28	10	74	3rd	1	4	League semifinals	Phil Watson
1956-57	26	30	14	66	4th	1	4	League semifinals	Phil Watson
1957-58	32	25	13	77	2nd	2	4	League semifinals	Phil Watson
1958-59	26	32	12	64	5th	—	—		Phil Watson
1959-60	17	38	15	49	6th	—	—		Phil Watson, Alf Pike
1960-61	22	38	10	54	5th	—	—		Alf Pike
1961-62	26	32	12	64	4th	2	4	League semifinals	Doug Harvey

Season	W	L	T	Pts.	Finish	W	L	Highest round	Coach
					REGULAR SEASON			PLAYOFFS	
1962-63	22	36	12	56	5th	—	—		Muzz Patrick, Red Sullivan
1963-64	22	38	10	54	5th	—	—		Red Sullivan
1964-65	20	38	12	52	5th	—	—		Red Sullivan
1965-66	18	41	11	47	6th	—	—		Red Sullivan, Emile Francis
1966-67	30	28	12	72	4th	0	4	League semifinals	Emile Francis
1967-68	39	23	12	90	2nd/East	2	4	Division semifinals	Emile Francis
1968-69	41	26	9	91	3rd/East	0	4	Division semifinals	Bernie Geoffrion, Emile Francis
1969-70	38	22	16	92	4th/East	2	4	Division semifinals	Emile Francis
1970-71	49	18	11	109	2nd/East	7	6	Division finals	Emile Francis
1971-72	48	17	13	109	2nd/East	10	6	Stanley Cup finals	Emile Francis
1972-73	47	23	8	102	3rd/East	5	5	Division finals	Emile Francis
1973-74	40	24	14	94	3rd/East	7	6	Division finals	Larry Popein, Emile Francis
1974-75	37	29	14	88	2nd/Patrick	1	2	Preliminaries	Emile Francis
1975-76	29	42	9	67	4th/Patrick	—	—		Ron Stewart, John Ferguson
1976-77	29	37	14	72	4th/Patrick	—	—		John Ferguson
1977-78	30	37	13	73	4th/Patrick	1	2	Preliminaries	Jean-Guy Talbot
1978-79	40	29	11	91	3rd/Patrick	11	7	Stanley Cup finals	Fred Shero
1979-80	38	32	10	86	3rd/Patrick	4	5	Quarterfinals	Fred Shero
1980-81	30	36	14	74	4th/Patrick	7	7	Semifinals	Fred Shero, Craig Patrick
1981-82	39	27	14	92	2nd/Patrick	5	5	Division finals	Herb Brooks
1982-83	35	35	10	80	4th/Patrick	5	4	Division finals	Herb Brooks
1983-84	42	29	9	93	4th/Patrick	2	3	Division semifinals	Herb Brooks
1984-85	26	44	10	62	4th/Patrick	0	3	Division semifinals	Herb Brooks, Craig Patrick
1985-86	36	38	6	78	4th/Patrick	8	8	Conference finals	Ted Sator
1986-87	34	38	8	76	4th/Patrick	2	4	Division semifinals	Ted Sator, Tom Webster, Phil Esposito
1987-88	36	34	10	82	4th/Patrick	—	—		Michel Bergeron
1988-89	37	35	8	82	3rd/Patrick	0	4	Division semifinals	Michel Bergeron, Phil Esposito
1989-90	36	31	13	85	1st/Patrick	5	5	Division finals	Roger Neilson
1990-91	36	31	13	85	2nd/Patrick	2	4	Division semifinals	Roger Neilson
1991-92	50	25	5	105	1st/Patrick	6	7	Division finals	Roger Neilson

*Won-lost record does not indicate tie(s) resulting from two-game, total goals series that year (two-game, total-goals series were played from 1917-18 through 1935-36).

FIRST-ROUND ENTRY DRAFT CHOICES

Year — Player, Overall, Last Amateur Team (League)

1969 — Andre Dupont, 8, Montreal (OHL)
Pierre Jarry, 12, Ottawa (OHL)
1970 — Normand Gratton, 11, Montreal (OHL)
1971 — Steve Vickers, 10, Toronto (OHL)
Steve Durbano, 13, Toronto (OHL)
1972 — Albert Blanchard, 10, Kitchener (OHL)
Bobby MacMillan, 15, St. Catharines (OHL)
1973 — Rick Middleton, 14, Oshawa (OHL)
1974 — Dave Maloney, 14, Kitchener (OHL)
1975 — Wayne Dillon, 12, Toronto (WHA)
1976 — Don Murdoch, 6, Medicine Hat (WCHL)
1977 — Lucien DeBlois, 8, Sorel (QMJHL)
Ron Duguay, 13, Sudbury (OHL)
1978 — No first-round selection

1979 — Doug Sulliman, 13, Kitchener (OHL)
1980 — Jim Malone, 14, Toronto (OHL)
1981 — James Patrick, 9, Prince Albert (AJHL)
1982 — Chris Kontos, 15, Toronto (OHL)
1983 — Dave Gagner, 12, Brantford (OHL)
1984 — Terry Carkner, 14, Peterborough (OHL)
1985 — Ulf Dahlen, 7, Ostersund (Sweden)
1986 — Brian Leetch, 9, Avon Old Farms Prep (Ct.)
1987 — Jayson More, 10, New Westminster (WCHL)
1988 — No first-round selection
1989 — Steven Rice, 20, Kitchener (OHL)
1990 — Michael Stewart, 13, Michigan State University
1991 — Alexei Kovalev, 15, Dynamo Moscow (USSR)
1992 — Peter Ferraro, 24, Waterloo (USHL)

FRANCHISE LEADERS

Current players in boldface

FORWARDS/DEFENSEMEN

Games

Harry Howell	1160
Rod Gilbert	1065
Ron Greschner	982
Walt Tkaczuk	945
Jean Ratelle	862
Vic Hadfield	838
Jim Neilson	810
Andy Bathgate	719
Steve Vickers	698
Dean Prentice	666

Goals

Rod Gilbert	406
Jean Ratelle	336
Andy Bathgate	272
Vic Hadfield	262
Camille Henry	256
Steve Vickers	246
Bill Cook	228
Walt Tkaczuk	227
Don Maloney	195
Bryan Hextall	187

Assists

Rod Gilbert	615
Jean Ratelle	481
Andy Bathgate	457
Walt Tkaczuk	451
Ron Greschner	431
Steve Vickers	340
James Patrick	**339**
Vic Hadfield	310
Don Maloney	307
Brad Park	283

Points

Rod Gilbert	1021
Jean Ratelle	817
Andy Bathgate	729
Walt Tkaczuk	678
Ron Greschner	610
Steve Vickers	586
Vic Hadfield	572
Don Maloney	502
Camille Henry	478
James Patrick	**438**

Penalty minutes

Ron Greschner	1226
Harry Howell	1147
Don Maloney	1113
Vic Hadfield	1036
Nick Fotiu	970

GOALTENDERS

Games

Gump Worsley	583
Ed Giacomin	539
John Vanbiesbrouck	**401**

Chuck Rayner	377	
Dave Kerr	324	
John Davidson	222	
Gilles Villemure	184	

Shutouts

Ed Giacomin	49
Dave Kerr	40
John Ross Roach	30
Chuck Rayner	24
Gump Worsley	24

Lorne Chabot	21

Goals-against average
(2400 minutes minimum)

Lorne Chabot	1.61
Dave Kerr	2.07
John Ross Roach	2.16
Andy Aitkenhead	2.42
Johnny Bower	2.62
Gilles Villemure	2.62
Ed Giacomin	2.73

Wins

Ed Giacomin	266
Gump Worsley	204
John Vanbiesbrouck	**180**
Dave Kerr	157
Chuck Rayner	123
Gilles Villemure	96
John Davidson	93

OTTAWA SENATORS

FIRST-ROUND ENTRY DRAFT CHOICES

Year   Player, Overall, Last Amateur Team (League)
1992—Alexei Yashin, 2, Dynamo Moscow (CIS)

1992 EXPANSION DRAFT CHOICES

No.	Player	Pos.	Last team	No.	Player	Pos.	Last team
1	Peter Sidorkiewicz	G	Hartford	12	Rob Murphy	C	Vancouver
2	Mark Laforest	G	N.Y. Rangers	13	Mark Lamb	C	Edmonton
3	Brad Shaw	D	New Jersey	14	Laurie Boschman	C	New Jersey
4	Darren Rumble	D	Philadelphia	15	Jim Thomson	F	Los Angeles
5	Dominic Lavoie	D	St. Louis	16	Lonnie Loach	LW	Detroit
6	Brad Miller	D	Buffalo	17	Mark Freer	C	Philadelphia
7	Ken Hammond	D	Vancouver	18	Chris Lindberg	F	Calgary
8	Kent Paynter	D	Winnipeg	19	Jeff Lazaro	LW	Boston
9	John Van Kessel	D	Los Angeles	20	Darcy Loewen	LW	Buffalo
10	Sylvain Turgeon	LW	Montreal	21	Blair Atcheynum	RW	Hartford
11	Mike Peluso	LW	Chicago				

PHILADELPHIA FLYERS

YEAR-BY-YEAR RECORDS

	REGULAR SEASON					PLAYOFFS			
Season	W	L	T	Pts.	Finish	W	L	Highest round	Coach
1967-68	31	32	11	73	1st/West	3	4	Division semifinals	Keith Allen
1968-69	20	35	21	61	3rd/West	0	4	Division semifinals	Keith Allen
1969-70	17	35	24	58	5th/West	—	—		Vic Stasiuk
1970-71	28	33	17	73	3rd/West	0	4	Division semifinals	Vic Stasiuk
1971-72	26	38	14	66	5th/West	—	—		Fred Shero
1972-73	37	30	11	85	2nd/West	5	6	Division finals	Fred Shero
1973-74	50	16	12	112	1st/West	12	5	Stanley Cup champ	Fred Shero
1974-75	51	18	11	113	1st/Patrick	12	5	Stanley Cup champ	Fred Shero
1975-76	51	13	16	118	1st/Patrick	8	8	Stanley Cup finals	Fred Shero
1976-77	48	16	16	112	1st/Patrick	4	6	Semifinals	Fred Shero
1977-78	45	20	15	105	2nd/Patrick	7	5	Semifinals	Fred Shero
1978-79	40	25	15	95	2nd/Patrick	3	5	Quarterfinals	Bob McCammon, Pat Quinn
1979-80	48	12	20	116	1st/Patrick	13	6	Stanley Cup finals	Pat Quinn
1980-81	41	24	15	97	2nd/Patrick	6	6	Quarterfinals	Pat Quinn
1981-82	38	31	11	87	3rd/Patrick	1	3	Division semifinals	Pat Quinn, Bob McCammon
1982-83	49	23	8	106	1st/Patrick	0	3	Division semifinals	Bob McCammon
1983-84	44	26	10	98	3rd/Patrick	0	3	Division semifinals	Bob McCammon
1984-85	53	20	7	113	1st/Patrick	12	7	Stanley Cup finals	Mike Keenan
1985-86	53	23	4	110	1st/Patrick	2	3	Division semifinals	Mike Keenan
1986-87	46	26	8	100	1st/Patrick	15	11	Stanley Cup finals	Mike Keenan
1987-88	38	33	9	85	2nd/Patrick	3	4	Division semifinals	Mike Keenan
1988-89	36	36	8	80	4th/Patrick	10	9	Conference finals	Paul Holmgren
1989-90	30	39	11	71	6th/Patrick	—	—		Paul Holmgren
1990-91	33	37	10	76	5th/Patrick	—	—		Paul Holmgren
1991-92	32	37	11	75	6th/Patrick	—	—		Paul Holmgren, Bill Dineen

FIRST-ROUND ENTRY DRAFT CHOICES

Year Player, Overall, Last Amateur Team (League)	Year Player, Overall, Last Amateur Team (League)
1969—Bob Currier, 6, Cornwall (QMJHL)	1972—Bill Barber, 7, Kitchener (OHL)
1970—No first-round selection	1973—No first-round selection
1971—Larry Wright, 8, Regina (WCHL)	1974—No first-round selection
Pierre Plante, 9, Drummondville (QMJHL)	1975—*Mel Bridgeman, 1, Victoria (WCHL)

Year	Player, Overall, Last Amateur Team (League)
1976	Mark Suzor, 17, Kingston (OHL)
1977	Kevin McCarthy, 17, Winnipeg (WCHL)
1978	Behn Wilson, 6, Kingston (OHL)
	Ken Linseman, 7, Birmingham (WHA)
	Dan Lucas, 14, Sault Ste. Marie (OHL)
1979	Brian Propp, 14, Brandon (WHL)
1980	Mike Stothers, 21, Kingston (OHL)
1981	Steve Smith, 16, Sault Ste. Marie (OHL)
1982	Ron Sutter, 4, Lethbridge (WHL)
1983	No first-round selection
1984	No first-round selection

Year	Player, Overall, Last Amateur Team (League)
1985	Glen Seabrooke, 21, Peterborough (OHL)
1986	Kerry Huffman, 20, Guelph (OHL)
1987	Darren Rumble, 20, Kitchener (OHL)
1988	Claude Boivin, 14, Drummondville (QMJHL)
1989	No first-round selection
1990	Mike Ricci, 4, Peterborough (OHL)
1991	Peter Forsberg, 6, Modo (Sweden)
1992	Ryan Sittler, 7, Nichols H.S. (N.Y.)
	Jason Bowen, 15, Tri-City (WHL)

*Designates first player chosen in draft.

FRANCHISE LEADERS

Current players in boldface

FORWARDS/DEFENSEMEN

Games
Bobby Clarke	1144
Bill Barber	903
Brian Propp	790
Joe Watson	746
Bob Kelly	741
Rick MacLeish	741
Gary Dornhoefer	725
Ed Van Impe	617
Jim Watson	613
Reggie Leach	606

Goals
Bill Barber	420
Brian Propp	369
Tim Kerr	363
Bobby Clarke	358
Rick MacLeish	328
Reggie Leach	306
Rick Tocchet	215
Gary Dornhoefer	202
Ilkka Sinisalo	199
Dave Poulin	161

Assists
Bobby Clarke	852
Brian Propp	480
Bill Barber	463
Rick MacLeish	369
Mark Howe	342

Gary Dornhoefer	316
Tim Kerr	287
Pelle Eklund	**280**
Murray Craven	272
Rick Tocchet	247

Points
Bobby Clarke	1210
Bill Barber	883
Brian Propp	849
Rick MacLeish	697
Tim Kerr	650
Gary Dornhoefer	518
Reggie Leach	514
Mark Howe	480
Rick Tocchet	462
Murray Craven	424

Penalty minutes
Rick Tocchet	1683
Paul Holmgren	1600
Andre Dupont	1505
Bobby Clarke	1453
Dave Schultz	1386
Bob Kelly	1285
Gary Dornhoefer	1256
Dave Brown	**1114**
Glen Cochrane	1110

GOALTENDERS

Games
Bernie Parent	486
Ron Hextall	**281**

Doug Favell	215
Pete Peeters	179
Wayne Stephenson	165
Pelle Lindbergh	157
Bob Froese	144

Shutouts
Bernie Parent	50
Doug Favell	16
Bob Froese	12
Wayne Stephenson	10

Goals-against average
(2400 minutes minimum)
Bernie Parent	2.42
Bob Froese	2.74
Wayne Stephenson	2.77
Doug Favell	2.78
Pete Peeters	3.19
Rick St. Croix	3.23
Ron Hextall	3.27
Pelle Lindbergh	3.30

Wins
Bernie Parent	232
Ron Hextall	130
Wayne Stephenson	93
Bob Froese	92
Pelle Lindbergh	87

PITTSBURGH PENGUINS

YEAR-BY-YEAR RECORDS

	REGULAR SEASON					PLAYOFFS			
Season	W	L	T	Pts.	Finish	W	L	Highest round	Coach
1967-68	27	34	13	67	5th/West	—	—		Red Sullivan
1968-69	20	45	11	51	5th/West	—	—		Red Sullivan
1969-70	26	38	12	64	2nd/West	6	4	Division finals	Red Kelly
1970-71	21	37	20	62	6th/West	—	—		Red Kelly
1971-72	26	38	14	66	4th/West	0	4	Division semifinals	Red Kelly
1972-73	32	37	9	73	5th/West	—	—		Red Kelly, Ken Schinkel
1973-74	28	41	9	65	5th/West	—	—		Ken Schinkel, Marc Boileau
1974-75	37	28	15	89	3rd/Norris	5	4	Quarterfinals	Marc Boileau
1975-76	35	33	12	82	3rd/Norris	1	2	Preliminaries	Marc Boileau, Ken Schinkel
1976-77	34	33	13	81	3rd/Norris	1	2	Preliminaries	Ken Schinkel
1977-78	25	37	18	68	4th/Norris	—	—		Johnny Wilson
1978-79	36	31	13	85	2nd/Norris	2	5	Quarterfinals	Johnny Wilson
1979-80	30	37	13	73	3rd/Norris	2	3	Preliminaries	Johnny Wilson
1980-81	30	37	13	73	3rd/Norris	2	3	Preliminaries	Eddie Johnston
1981-82	31	36	13	75	4th/Patrick	2	3	Division semifinals	Eddie Johnston
1982-83	18	53	9	45	6th/Patrick	—	—		Eddie Johnston
1983-84	16	58	6	38	6th/Patrick	—	—		Lou Angotti
1984-85	24	51	5	53	5th/Patrick	—	—		Bob Berry
1985-86	34	38	8	76	5th/Patrick	—	—		Bob Berry
1986-87	30	38	12	72	5th/Patrick	—	—		Bob Berry
1987-88	36	35	9	81	6th/Patrick	—	—		Pierre Creamer

Season	REGULAR SEASON W	L	T	Pts.	Finish	PLAYOFFS W	L	Highest round	Coach
1988-89	40	33	7	87	2nd/Patrick	7	4	Division finals	Gene Ubriaco
1989-90	32	40	8	72	5th/Patrick	—	—		Gene Ubriaco, Craig Patrick
1990-91	41	33	6	88	1st/Patrick	16	8	Stanley Cup champ	Bob Johnson
1991-92	39	32	9	87	3rd/Patrick	16	5	Stanley Cup champ	Scotty Bowman

FIRST-ROUND ENTRY DRAFT CHOICES

Year	Player, Overall, Last Amateur Team (League)
1969	No first-round selection
1970	Greg Polis, 7, Estevan (WCHL)
1971	No first-round selection
1972	No first-round selection
1973	Blaine Stoughton, 7, Flin Flon (WCHL)
1974	Pierre Larouche, 8, Sorel (QMJHL)
1975	Gord Laxton, 13, New Westminster (WCHL)
1976	Blair Chapman, 2, Saskatoon (WCHL)
1977	No first-round selection
1978	No first-round selection
1979	No first-round selection
1980	Mike Bullard, 9, Brantford (OHL)
1981	No first-round selection
1982	Rich Sutter, 10, Lethbridge (WHL)

Year	Player, Overall, Last Amateur Team (League)
1983	Bob Errey, 15, Peterborough (OHL)
1984	*Mario Lemieux, 1, Laval (QMJHL)
	Doug Bodger, 9, Kamloops (WHL)
	Roger Belanger, 16, Kingston (OHL)
1985	Craig Simpson, 2, Michigan State University
1986	Zarley Zalapski, 4, Team Canada
1987	Chris Joseph, 5, Seattle (WHL)
1988	Darrin Shannon, 4, Windsor (OHL)
1989	Jamie Heward, 16, Regina (WHL)
1990	Jaromir Jagr, 5, Poldi Kladno (Czech.)
1991	Markus Naslund, 16, Modo (Sweden)
1992	Martin Straka, 19, Skoda Plzen (Czech.)

*Designates first player chosen in draft.

FRANCHISE LEADERS

Current players in boldface

FORWARDS/DEFENSEMEN

Games

Jean Pronovost	753
Rick Kehoe	722
Ron Stackhouse	621
Ron Schock	619
Dave Burrows	573
Bob Errey	**518**
Mario Lemieux	**517**
Syl Apps	495
Greg Malone	495
Troy Loney	**450**

Goals

Mario Lemieux	**408**
Jean Pronovost	316
Rick Kehoe	312
Mike Bullard	186
Syl Apps	151
Greg Malone	143
Lowell MacDonald	140
Kevin Stevens	**140**
Bob Errey	**124**
Ron Schock	124

Assists

Mario Lemieux	**606**
Syl Apps	349
Paul Coffey	332
Rick Kehoe	324
Jean Pronovost	287

Ron Schock	280
Ron Stackhouse	277
Randy Carlyle	257
Greg Malone	221
Mike Bullard	175

Points

Mario Lemieux	**1014**
Rick Kehoe	636
Jean Pronovost	603
Syl Apps	500
Paul Coffey	440
Ron Schock	404
Greg Malone	364
Mike Bullard	361
Ron Stackhouse	343
Randy Carlyle	323

Penalty minutes

Rod Buskas	959
Troy Loney	**881**
Bryan Watson	871
Paul Baxter	851
Gary Rissling	832
Russ Anderson	684
Jim Johnson	658

GOALTENDERS

Games

Denis Herron	290
Les Binkley	196
Tom Barrasso	**173**
Michel Dion	151

Greg Millen	135
Roberto Romano	123
Jim Rutherford	115
Gilles Meloche	104
Wendell Young	101
Gary Inness	100

Shutouts

Les Binkley	11
Denis Herron	6
Dunc Wilson	5

Goals-against average
(2400 minutes minimum)

Al Smith	3.07
Les Binkley	3.12
Jim Rutherford	3.14
Gary Inness	3.34
Dunc Wilson	3.53
Michel Plasse	3.59
Gilles Meloche	3.65
Andy Brown	3.78
Tom Barrasso	**3.83**
Greg Millen	3.83

Wins

Denis Herron	88
Tom Barrasso	**77**
Les Binkley	58
Greg Millen	57
Roberto Romano	45
Jim Rutherford	44

QUEBEC NORDIQUES

YEAR-BY-YEAR RECORDS

Season	REGULAR SEASON W	L	T	Pts.	Finish	PLAYOFFS W	L	Highest round	Coach
1972-73	33	40	5	71	5th	—	—		Maurice Richard, Maurice Filion
1973-74	38	36	4	80	5th	—	—		Jacques Plante
1974-75	46	32	0	92	1st	8	7	Avco World Cup finals	Jean-Guy Jendron
1975-76	50	27	4	104	2nd	1	4	League quarterfinals	Jean-Guy Jendron
1976-77	47	31	3	97	1st	12	5	Avco World Cup champ	Marc Boileau
1977-78	40	37	3	83	4th	5	6	League semifinals	Marc Boileau
1978-79	41	34	5	87	2nd	0	4	League semifinals	Jacques Demers

Season	W	L	T	Pts.	Finish	W	L	Highest round	Coach
				REGULAR SEASON				**PLAYOFFS**	
1979-80	25	44	11	61	5th/Adams	—	—		Jacques Demers
1980-81	30	32	18	78	4th/Adams	2	3	Preliminaries	Maurice Filion, Michel Bergeron
1981-82	33	31	16	82	4th/Adams	7	9	Conference finals	Michel Bergeron
1982-83	34	34	12	80	4th/Adams	1	3	Division semifinals	Michel Bergeron
1983-84	42	28	10	94	3rd/Adams	5	4	Division finals	Michel Bergeron
1984-85	41	30	9	91	2nd/Adams	9	9	Conference finals	Michel Bergeron
1985-86	43	31	6	92	1st/Adams	0	3	Division semifinals	Michel Bergeron
1986-87	31	39	10	72	4th/Adams	7	6	Division finals	Michel Bergeron
1987-88	32	43	5	69	5th/Adams	—	—		Andre Savard, Ron Lapointe
1988-89	27	46	7	61	5th/Adams	—	—		Ron Lapointe, Jean Perron
1989-90	12	61	7	31	5th/Adams	—	—		Michel Bergeron
1990-91	16	50	14	46	5th/Adams	—	—		Dave Chambers
1991-92	20	48	12	52	5th/Adams	—	—		Dave Chambers, Pierre Page

NOTE: Member of World Hockey Association from 1972-73 through 1978-79.

FIRST-ROUND ENTRY DRAFT CHOICES

Year	Player, Overall, Last Amateur Team (League)
1979	Michel Goulet, 20, Birmingham (WHA)
1980	No first-round selection
1981	Randy Moller, 11, Lethbridge (WHL)
1982	David Shaw, 13, Kitchener (OHL)
1983	No first-round selection
1984	Trevor Steinburg, 15, Guelph (OHL)
1985	Dave Latta, 15, Kitchener (OHL)
1986	Ken McRae, 18, Sudbury (OHL)
1987	Bryan Fogarty, 9, Kingston (OHL)
	Joe Sakic, 15, Swift Current (WHL)

Year	Player, Overall, Last Amateur Team (League)
1988	Curtis Leschyshyn, 3, Saskatoon (WHL)
	Daniel Dore, 5, Drummondville (QMJHL)
1989	*Mats Sundin, 1, Nacka (Sweden)
1990	*Owen Nolan, 1, Cornwall (OHL)
1991	*Eric Lindros, 1, Oshawa (OHL)
1992	Todd Warriner, 4, Windsor (OHL)

*Designates first player chosen in draft.
NOTE: Quebec chose Paul Baxter, Richard Brodeur and Garry Lariviere as priority selections before the 1979 expansion draft.

FRANCHISE LEADERS

Current players in boldface

FORWARDS/DEFENSEMEN

Games

Michel Goulet	813
Peter Stastny	737
Alain Cote	696
Anton Stastny	650
Paul Gillis	576
Dale Hunter	523
Randy Moller	508
Normand Rochefort	480
Steven Finn	**405**
Mario Marois	403

Goals

Michel Goulet	456
Peter Stastny	380
Anton Stastny	252
Dale Hunter	140
Joe Sakic	**139**
Real Cloutier	122
Marc Tardif	116
Alain Cote	103
Wilf Paiement	102
Marian Stastny	98

Assists

Peter Stastny	668
Michel Goulet	489
Anton Stastny	384
Dale Hunter	318
Joe Sakic	**227**
Alain Cote	190
Real Cloutier	162
Mario Marois	162
Paul Gillis	146
Marian Stastny	143

Points

Peter Stastny	1048
Michel Goulet	945
Anton Stastny	636
Dale Hunter	458
Joe Sakic	**366**
Alain Cote	293
Real Cloutier	284
Marc Tardif	244
Marian Stastny	241
Paul Gillis	233

Penalty minutes

Dale Hunter	1545
Paul Gillis	1351
Steven Finn	**1126**
Randy Moller	1002
Mario Marois	778
Peter Stastny	687
Gord Donnelly	668
Wilf Paiement	619
Michel Goulet	613
Wally Weir	535

GOALTENDERS

Games

Dan Bouchard	225
Mario Gosselin	192
Ron Tugnutt	150
Clint Malarchuk	140
Michel Dion	62
Jacques Cloutier	**41**
Michel Plasse	41
Mario Brunetta	40

Shutouts

Mario Gosselin	6
Dan Bouchard	5
Clint Malarchuk	5

Goals-against average
(2400 minutes minimum)

Dan Bouchard	3.59
Clint Malarchuk	3.63
Mario Gosselin	3.67
Michel Dion	4.02
Ron Tugnutt	4.07

Wins

Dan Bouchard	107
Mario Gosselin	79
Clint Malarchuk	62
Ron Tugnutt	35
Michel Dion	15
Richard Sevigny	13

ST. LOUIS BLUES

YEAR-BY-YEAR RECORDS

Season	W	L	T	Pts.	Finish	W	L	Highest round	Coach
				REGULAR SEASON				**PLAYOFFS**	
1967-68	27	31	16	70	3rd/West	8	10	Stanley Cup finals	Lynn Patrick, Scotty Bowman
1968-69	37	25	14	88	1st/West	8	4	Stanley Cup finals	Scotty Bowman
1969-70	37	27	12	86	1st/West	8	8	Stanley Cup finals	Scotty Bowman

Season	W	L	T	Pts.	Finish	W	L	Highest round	Coach
1970-71	34	25	19	87	2nd/West	2	4	Division semifinals	Al Arbour, Scotty Bowman
1971-72	28	39	11	67	3rd/West	4	7	Division finals	Sid Abel, Bill McCreary, Al Arbour
1972-73	32	34	12	76	4th/West	1	4	Division semifinals	Al Arbour, Jean-Guy Talbot
1973-74	26	40	12	64	6th/West	—	—		Jean-Guy Talbot, Lou Angotti
1974-75	35	31	14	84	2nd/Smythe	0	2	Preliminaries	Lou Angotti, Lynn Patrick, Garry Young
1975-76	29	37	14	72	3rd/Smythe	1	2	Preliminaries	Garry Young, Lynn Patrick, Leo Boivin
1976-77	32	39	9	73	1st/Smythe	0	4	Quarterfinals	Emile Francis
1977-78	20	47	13	53	4th/Smythe	—	—		Leo Boivin, Barclay Plager
1978-79	18	50	12	48	3rd/Smythe	—	—		Barclay Plager
1979-80	34	34	12	80	2nd/Smythe	0	3	Preliminaries	Barclay Plager, Red Berenson
1980-81	45	18	17	107	1st/Smythe	5	6	Quarterfinals	Red Berenson
1981-82	32	40	8	72	3rd/Norris	5	5	Division finals	Red Berenson, Emile Francis
1982-83	25	40	15	65	4th/Norris	1	3	Division semifinals	Emile Francis, Barclay Plager
1983-84	32	41	7	71	2nd/Norris	6	5	Division finals	Jacques Demers
1984-85	37	31	12	86	1st/Norris	0	3	Division semifinals	Jacques Demers
1985-86	37	34	9	83	3rd/Norris	10	9	Conference finals	Jacques Demers
1986-87	32	33	15	79	1st/Norris	2	4	Division semifinals	Jacques Martin
1987-88	34	38	8	76	2nd/Norris	5	5	Division finals	Jacques Martin
1988-89	33	35	12	78	2nd/Norris	5	5	Division finals	Brian Sutter
1989-90	37	34	9	83	2nd/Norris	7	5	Division finals	Brian Sutter
1990-91	47	22	11	105	2nd/Norris	6	7	Division finals	Brian Sutter
1991-92	36	33	11	83	3rd/Norris	2	4	Division semifinals	Brian Sutter

FIRST-ROUND ENTRY DRAFT CHOICES

Year Player, Overall, Last Amateur Team (League)

1969—No first-round selection
1970—No first-round selection
1971—Gene Carr, 4, Flin Flon (WCHL)
1972—Wayne Merrick, 9, Ottawa (OHL)
1973—John Davidson, 5, Calgary (WCHL)
1974—No first-round selection
1975—No first-round selection
1976—Bernie Federko, 7, Saskatoon (WCHL)
1977—Scott Campbell, 9, London (OHL)
1978—Wayne Babych, 3, Portland (WCHL)
1979—Perry Turnbull, 2, Portland (WHL)
1980—Rik Wilson, 12, Kingston (OHL)

Year Player, Overall, Last Amateur Team (League)

1981—Marty Ruff, 20, Lethbridge (WHL)
1982—No first-round selection
1983—No first-round selection
1984—No first-round selection
1985—No first-round selection
1986—Jocelyn Lemieux, 10, Laval (QMJHL)
1987—Keith Osborne, 12, North Bay (OHL)
1988—Rod Brind'Amour, 9, Notre Dame Academy (Sask.)
1989—Jason Marshall, 9, Vernon (B.C.) Tier II
1990—No first-round selection
1991—No first-round selection
1992—No first-round selection

FRANCHISE LEADERS

Current players in boldface

FORWARDS/DEFENSEMEN

Games

Bernie Federko 927
Brian Sutter 779
Garry Unger 662
Bob Plager 615
Barclay Plager 614
Larry Patey 603
Red Berenson 519
Gary Sabourin 463
Jack Brownschidle 455
Gino Cavillini 454

Goals

Bernie Federko 352
Brian Sutter 303
Garry Unger 292
Brett Hull 275
Red Berenson 172
Jorgen Pettersson 161
Wayne Babych 155
Joe Mullen 151
Doug Gilmour 149
Perry Turnbull 139

Assists

Bernie Federko 721
Brian Sutter 334
Garry Unger 283
Red Berenson 240

Rob Ramage 229
Adam Oates 228
Doug Gilmour 205
Blake Dunlop 201
Wayne Babych 190
Barclay Plager 187

Points

Bernie Federko 1073
Brian Sutter 636
Garry Unger 575
Brett Hull 451
Red Berenson 412
Doug Gilmour 354
Wayne Babych 345
Joe Mullen 335
Jorgen Pettersson 332
Rob Ramage 296

Penalty minutes

Brian Sutter 1786
Barclay Plager 1115
Rob Ramage 998
Bob Gassoff 866
Perry Turnbull 829

GOALTENDERS

Games

Mike Liut 347
Greg Millen 209
Rick Wamsley 154
Glenn Hall 140

Ed Staniowski 137
Vincent Riendeau 122
Ernie Wakely 111
Eddie Johnston 108

Shutouts

Glenn Hall 16
Mike Liut 10
Jacques Plante 10
Greg Millen 8
Ernie Wakely 8

Goals-against average
(2400 minutes minimum)

Jacques Plante 2.07
Glenn Hall 2.43
Ernie Wakely 2.77
Jacques Caron 3.02
Curtis Joseph 3.09
Wayne Stephenson 3.12
Vincent Riendeau 3.34
Eddie Johnston 3.36
John Davidson 3.37
Rick Wamsley 3.41
Greg Millen 3.43

Wins

Mike Liut 151
Greg Millen 85
Rick Wamsley 75
Glenn Hall 58
Vincent Riendeau 58

SAN JOSE SHARKS

YEAR-BY-YEAR RECORDS

Season	REGULAR SEASON					PLAYOFFS			Coach
	W	L	T	Pts.	Finish	W	L	Highest round	
1991-92	17	58	5	39	6th/Smythe	—	—		George Kingston

FIRST-ROUND ENTRY DRAFT CHOICES

Year Player, Overall, Last Amateur Team (League)
1991—Pat Falloon, 2, Spokane (WHL)

Year Player, Overall, Last Amateur Team (League)
1992—Mike Rathje, 3, Medicine Hat (WHL)
Andrei Nazarov, 10, Dynamo Moscow (CIS)

FRANCHISE LEADERS

Current players in boldface

FORWARDS/DEFENSEMEN

Games

Pat Falloon	79
Dean Evason	74
Rob Zettler	74
Brian Mullen	72
Perry Berezan	66
Mike Sullivan	64
Bob McGill	62
Jeff Odgers	61
David Bruce	60
Paul Fenton	60
Neil Wilkinson	60

Goals

Pat Falloon	25
David Bruce	22
Brian Mullen	18
Brian Lawton	15
Perry Berezan	12
Dean Evason	11
Paul Fenton	11
Kelly Kisio	11
Doug Wilson	9
Wayne Presley	8
Mike Sullivan	8
Steve Bozek	8

Assists

Pat Falloon	34
Brian Mullen	28
Kelly Kisio	26
David Williams	25
Brian Lawton	22
Doug Wilson	19
David Bruce	16
Dean Evason	15
Neil Wilkinson	15
Wayne Presley	14

Points

Pat Falloon	59
Brian Mullen	46
David Bruce	38
Brian Lawton	37
Kelly Kisio	37
Doug Wilson	28
David Williams	28
Dean Evason	26
Wayne Presley	22
Perry Berezan	19
Mike Sullivan	19
Neil Wilkinson	19

Penalty minutes

Link Gaetz	326
Jeff Odgers	217
Perry Anderson	143

Neil Wilkinson	107
Dean Evason	99
Rob Zettler	99
Jay More	85
Ken Hammond	82
Wayne Presley	76
Bob McGill	70

GOALTENDERS

Games

Jeff Hackett	42
Jarmo Myllys	27
Arturs Irbe	13
Brian Hayward	7
Wade Flaherty	3

Shutouts
Never accomplished

Goals-against average
(1200 minutes minimum)

Jeff Hackett	3.84
Jarmo Myllys	5.02

Wins

Jeff Hackett	11
Jarmo Myllys	3
Arturs Irbe	2
Brian Hayward	1

TAMPA BAY LIGHTNING

FIRST-ROUND ENTRY DRAFT CHOICES

Year Player, Overall, Last Amateur Team (League)
1992—*Roman Hamrlik, 1, Zlin (Czech.)
*Designates first player chosen in draft.

1992 EXPANSION DRAFT CHOICES

No.	Player	Pos.	Last team	No.	Player	Pos.	Last team
1	Wendell Young	G	Pittsburgh	12	Mike Hartman	LW	Winnipeg
2	Frederic Chabot	G	Montreal	13	Basil McRae	LW	Minnesota
3	Joe Reekie	D	N.Y. Islanders	14	Rob DiMaio	C	N.Y. Islanders
4	Shawn Chambers	D	Washington	15	Steve Maltais	LW	Quebec
5	Peter Taglianetti	D	Pittsburgh	16	Dan Vincelette	LW	Chicago
6	Bob McGill	D	Detroit	17	Tim Bergland	RW	Washington
7	Jeff Bloemberg	D	N.Y. Rangers	18	Brian Bradley	C	Toronto
8	Doug Crossman	D	Quebec	19	Keith Osborne	RW	Toronto
9	Rob Ramage	D	Minnesota	20	Shayne Stevenson	RW	Boston
10	Michel Mongeau	C	St. Louis	21	Tim Hunter	F	Calgary
11	Anatoli Semenov	LW	Edmonton				

TORONTO MAPLE LEAFS

YEAR-BY-YEAR RECORDS

		REGULAR SEASON					PLAYOFFS		
Season	W	L	T	Pts.	Finish	W	L	Highest round	Coach
1927-28	18	18	8	44	4th/Canadian	—	—		Alex Roveril, Conn Smythe
1928-29	21	18	5	47	3rd/Canadian	2	2	Semifinals	Alex Roveril, Conn Smythe
1929-30	17	21	6	40	4th/Canadian	—	—		Alex Roveril, Conn Smythe
1930-31	22	13	9	53	2nd/Canadian	*0	1	Quarterfinals	Conn Smythe, Art Duncan
1931-32	23	18	7	53	2nd/Canadian	5	2	Stanley Cup champ	Art Duncan, Dick Irvin
1932-33	24	18	6	54	1st/Canadian	4	5	Stanley Cup finals	Dick Irvin
1933-34	26	13	9	61	1st/Canadian	2	3	Semifinals	Dick Irvin
1934-35	30	14	4	64	1st/Canadian	3	4	Stanley Cup finals	Dick Irvin
1935-36	23	19	6	52	2nd/Canadian	4	5	Stanley Cup finals	Dick Irvin
1936-37	22	21	5	49	3rd/Canadian	0	2	Quarterfinals	Dick Irvin
1937-38	24	15	9	57	1st/Canadian			Stanley Cup finals	Dick Irvin
1938-39	19	20	9	47	3rd	5	5	Stanley Cup finals	Dick Irvin
1939-40	25	17	6	56	3rd	6	4	Stanley Cup finals	Dick Irvin
1940-41	28	14	6	62	2nd	3	4	Semifinals	Hap Day
1941-42	27	18	3	57	2nd	8	5	Stanley Cup champ	Hap Day
1942-43	22	19	9	53	3rd	2	4	League semifinals	Hap Day
1943-44	23	23	4	50	3rd	1	4	League semifinals	Hap Day
1944-45	24	22	4	52	3rd	8	5	Stanley Cup champ	Hap Day
1945-46	19	24	7	45	5th	—	—		Hap Day
1946-47	31	19	10	72	2nd	8	3	Stanley Cup champ	Hap Day
1947-48	32	15	13	77	1st	8	1	Stanley Cup champ	Hap Day
1948-49	22	25	13	57	4th	8	1	Stanley Cup champ	Hap Day
1949-50	31	27	12	74	3rd	3	4	League semifinals	Hap Day
1950-51	41	16	13	95	2nd	†8	2	Stanley Cup champ	Joe Primeau
1951-52	29	25	16	74	3rd	0	4	League semifinals	Joe Primeau
1952-53	27	30	13	67	5th	—	—		Joe Primeau
1953-54	32	24	14	78	3rd	1	4	League semifinals	King Clancy
1954-55	24	24	22	70	3rd	1	4	League semifinals	King Clancy
1955-56	24	33	13	61	4th	1	4	League semifinals	King Clancy
1956-57	21	34	15	57	5th	—	—		Howie Meeker
1957-58	21	38	11	53	6th	—	—		Billy Reay
1958-59	27	32	11	65	4th	5	7	Stanley Cup finals	Billy Reay, Punch Imlach
1959-60	35	26	9	79	2nd	4	6	Stanley Cup finals	Punch Imlach
1960-61	39	19	12	90	2nd	1	4	League semifinals	Punch Imlach
1961-62	37	22	11	85	2nd	8	4	Stanley Cup champ	Punch Imlach
1962-63	35	23	12	82	1st	8	2	Stanely Cup champ	Punch Imlach
1963-64	33	25	12	78	3rd	8	6	Stanely Cup champ	Punch Imlach
1964-65	30	26	14	74	4th	2	4	League semifinals	Punch Imlach
1965-66	34	25	11	79	3rd	0	4	League semifinals	Punch Imlach
1966-67	32	27	11	75	3rd	8	2	Stanley Cup champ	Punch Imlach
1967-68	33	31	10	76	5th/East	—	—		Punch Imlach
1968-69	35	26	15	85	4th/East	0	4	Division semifinals	Punch Imlach
1969-70	29	34	13	71	6th/East	—	—		John McLellan
1970-71	37	33	8	82	4th/East	2	4	Division semifinals	John McLellan
1971-72	33	31	14	80	4th/East	1	4	Division semifinals	John McLellan
1972-73	27	41	10	64	6th/East	—	—		John McLellan
1973-74	35	27	16	86	4th/East	0	4	Division semifinals	Red Kelly
1974-75	31	33	16	78	3rd/Adams	2	5	Quarterfinals	Red Kelly
1975-76	34	31	15	83	3rd/Adams	5	5	Quarterfinals	Red Kelly
1976-77	33	32	15	81	3rd/Adams	4	5	Quarterfinals	Red Kelly
1977-78	41	29	10	92	3rd/Adams	4	2	Quarterfinals	Roger Neilson
1978-79	34	33	13	81	3rd/Adams	4	7	Quarterfinals	Roger Neilson
1979-80	35	40	5	75	4th/Adams	0	3	Preliminaries	Floyd Smith
1980-81	28	37	15	71	5th/Adams	0	3	Preliminaries	Punch Imlach, Joe Crozier
1981-82	20	44	16	56	5th/Norris	—	—		Mike Nykoluk
1982-83	28	40	12	68	3rd/Norris	1	3	Division semifinals	Mike Nykoluk
1983-84	26	45	9	61	5th/Norris	—	—		Mike Nykoluk
1984-85	20	52	8	48	5th/Norris	—	—		Dan Maloney
1985-86	25	48	7	57	4th/Norris	6	4	Division finals	Dan Maloney
1986-87	32	42	6	70	4th/Norris	7	6	Division finals	John Brophy
1987-88	21	49	10	52	4th/Norris	2	4	Division semifinals	John Brophy
1988-89	28	46	6	62	5th/Norris	—	—		John Brophy, George Armstrong
1989-90	38	38	4	80	3rd/Norris	1	4	Division semifinals	Doug Carpenter
1990-91	23	46	11	57	5th/Norris	—	—		Doug Carpenter, Tom Watt
1991-92	30	43	7	67	5th/Norris	—	—		Tom Watt

*Won-lost record does not indicate tie(s) resulting from two-game, total-goals series that year (two-game, total-goals series were played from 1917-18 through 1935-36).
†Tied after one overtime (curfew law).

FIRST-ROUND ENTRY DRAFT CHOICES

Year   Player, Overall, Last Amateur Team (League)
1969—Ernie Moser, 9, Esteven (WCHL)
1970—Darryl Sittler, 8, London (OHL)
1971—No first-round selection
1972—George Ferguson, 11, Toronto (OHL)
1973—Lanny McDonald, 4, Medicine Hat (WCHL)
       Bob Neely, 10, Peterborough (OHL)
       Ian Turnbull, 15, Ottawa (OHL)
1974—Jack Valiquette, 13, Sault Ste. Marie (OHL)
1975—Don Ashby, 6, Calgary (WCHL)
1976—No first-round selection
1977—John Anderson, 11, Toronto (OHA)
       Trevor Johansen, 12, Toronto (OHA)
1978—No first-round selection
1979—Laurie Boschman, 9, Brandon (WHL)
1980—No first-round selection
1981—Jim Benning, 6, Portland (WHL)

Year   Player, Overall, Last Amateur Team (League)
1982—Gary Nylund, 3, Portland (WHL)
1983—Russ Courtnall, 7, Victoria (WHL)
1984—Al Iafrate, 4, U.S. Olympics/Belleville (OHL)
1985—*Wendel Clark, 1, Saskatoon (WHL)
1986—Vincent Damphousse, 6, Laval (QMJHL)
1987—Luke Richardson, 7, Peterborough (OHL)
1988—Scott Pearson, 6, Kingston (OHL)
1989—Scott Thornton, 3, Belleville (OHL)
       Rob Pearson, 12, Belleville (OHL)
       Steve Bancroft, 21, Belleville (OHL)
1990—Drake Berehowsky, 10, Kingston (OHL)
1991—No first-round selection
1992—Brandon Convery, Sudbury (OHL)
       Grant Marshall, Ottawa (OHL)

*Designates first player chosen in draft.

FRANCHISE LEADERS

Current players in boldface

FORWARDS/DEFENSEMEN

Games
George Armstrong 1187
Tim Horton 1185
Borje Salming 1099
Dave Keon 1062
Ron Ellis 1034
Bob Pulford 947
Darryl Sittler 844
Ron Stewart 838
Bob Baun 739
Frank Mahovlich 720

Goals
Darryl Sittler 389
Dave Keon 365
Ron Ellis 332
Rick Vaive 299
George Armstrong 296
Frank Mahovlich 296
Bob Pulford 251
Ted Kennedy 231
Lanny McDonald 219
Syl Apps 201

Assists
Borje Salming 620
Darryl Sittler 527
Dave Keon 493

George Armstrong 417
Tim Horton 349
Ted Kennedy 329
Bob Pulford 312
Ron Ellis 308
Norm Ullman 305
Ian Turnbull 302

Points
Darryl Sittler 916
Dave Keon 858
Borje Salming 768
George Armstrong 713
Ron Ellis 640
Frank Mahovlich 597
Bob Pulford 563
Ted Kennedy 560
Rick Vaive 537
Norm Ullman 471

Penalty minutes
Dave Williams 1670
Tim Horton 1389
Borje Salming 1292
Red Horner 1264
Bob Baun 1155
Wendel Clark 1035

Goaltenders

Games
Turk Broda 629
Johnny Bower 472

Mike Palmateer 296
Harry Lumley 267
Lorne Chabot 214
Bruce Gamble 210
Ken Wregget 200

Shutouts
Turk Broda... 62
Harry Lumley 34
Lorne Chabot 33
Johnny Bower 32
George Hainsworth 19

Goals-against average
(2400 minutes minimum)
John Ross Roach 2.00
Al Rollins 2.05
Lorne Chabot 2.20
Harry Lumley 2.21
George Hainsworth 2.26
Jacques Plante 2.46
Johnny Bower 2.51
Turk Broda 2.53
Bernie Parent 2.59
Don Simmons 2.71

Wins
Turk Broda 302
Johnny Bower 220
Mike Palmateer 129
Lorne Chabot 108
Harry Lumley 104

VANCOUVER CANUCKS

YEAR-BY-YEAR RECORDS

Season	W	L	T	Pts.	Finish	W	L	Highest round	Coach
1970-71	24	46	8	56	6th/East	—	—		Hal Laycoe
1971-72	20	50	8	48	7th/East	—	—		Hal Laycoe
1972-73	22	47	9	53	7th/East	—	—		Vic Stasiuk
1973-74	24	43	11	59	7th/East	—	—		Bill McCreary, Phil Maloney
1974-75	38	32	10	86	1st/Smythe	1	4	Quarterfinals	Phil Maloney
1975-76	33	32	15	81	2nd/Smythe	0	2	Preliminaries	Phil Maloney
1976-77	25	42	13	63	4th/Smythe	—	—		Phil Maloney, Orland Kurtenbach
1977-78	20	43	17	57	3rd/Smythe	—	—		Orland Kurtenbach
1978-79	25	42	13	63	2nd/Smythe	1	2	Preliminaries	Harry Neale
1979-80	27	37	16	70	3rd/Smythe	1	3	Preliminaries	Harry Neale
1980-81	28	32	20	76	3rd/Smythe	0	3	Preliminaries	Harry Neale
1981-82	30	33	17	77	2nd/Smythe	11	6	Stanley Cup finals	Harry Neale, Roger Neilson
1982-83	30	35	15	75	3rd/Smythe	1	3	Division semifinals	Roger Neilson
1983-84	32	39	9	73	3rd/Smythe	1	3	Division semifinals	Roger Neilson, Harry Neale
1984-85	25	46	9	59	5th/Smythe	—	—		Bill Laforge, Harry Neale
1985-86	23	44	13	59	4th/Smythe	0	3	Division semifinals	Tom Watt

Season	\u2014REGULAR SEASON\u2014					\u2014PLAYOFFS\u2014			
Season	W	L	T	Pts.	Finish	W	L	Highest round	Coach
1986-87	29	43	8	66	5th/Smythe	—	—		Tom Watt
1987-88	25	46	9	59	5th/Smythe	—	—		Bob McCammon
1988-89	33	39	8	74	4th/Smythe	3	4	Division semifinals	Bob McCammon
1989-90	25	41	14	64	5th/Smythe	—	—		Bob McCammon
1990-91	28	43	9	65	4th/Smythe	2	4	Division semifinals	Bob McCammon, Pat Quinn
1991-92	42	26	12	96	1st/Smythe	6	7	Division finals	Pat Quinn

FIRST-ROUND ENTRY DRAFT CHOICES

Year — Player, Overall, Last Amateur Team (League)

1970—Dale Tallon, 2, Toronto (OHL)
1971—Jocelyn Guevremont, 3, Montreal (OHL)
1972—Don Lever, 3, Niagara Falls (OHL)
1973—Dennis Ververgaert, 3, London (OHL)
   Bob Dailey, 9, Toronto (OHL)
1974—No first-round selection
1975—Rick Blight, 10, Brandon (WCHL)
1976—No first-round selection
1977—Jere Gillis, 4, Sherbrooke (QMJHL)
1978—Bill Derlago, 4, Brandon (WCHL)
1979—Rick Vaive, 5, Birmingham (WHA)
1980—Rick Lanz, 7, Oshawa (OHL)
1981—Garth Butcher, 10, Regina (WHL)

1982—Michel Petit, 11, Sherbrooke (QMJHL)
1983—Cam Neely, 9, Portland (WHL)
1984—J.J. Daigneault, 10, Can. Ol./Longueuil (QMJHL)
1985—Jim Sandlak, 4, London (OHL)
1986—Dan Woodley, 7, Portland (WHL)
1987—No first-round selection
1988—Trevor Linden, 2, Medicine Hat (WHL)
1989—Jason Herter, 8, University of North Dakota
1990—Petr Nedved, 2, Seattle (WHL)
   Shawn Antoski, 18, North Bay (OHL)
1991—Alex Stojanov, 7, Hamilton (OHL)
1992—Libor Polasek, 21, TJ Vikovice (Czech.)

FRANCHISE LEADERS

Current players in boldface

FORWARDS/DEFENSEMEN
Games
Stan Smyl 896
Harold Snepsts 781
Dennis Kearns 677
Thomas Gradin 613
Garth Butcher 610

Goals
Stan Smyl 262
Tony Tanti 250
Thomas Gradin 197
Don Lever 186
Petri Skriko 171

Assists
Stan Smyl 411
Thomas Gradin 353
Dennis Kearns 290
Andre Boudrias 267
Doug Lidster 223

Points
Stan Smyl 673
Thomas Gradin 550
Tony Tanti 470
Don Lever 407

Andre Boudrias 388

Penalty minutes
Garth Butcher 1668
Stan Smyl 1556
Harold Snepsts 1446
Tiger Williams 1314
Jim Sandlak 661

GOALTENDERS
Games
Richard Brodeur 377
Kirk McLean 252
Gary Smith 208
Dunc Wilson 148
Glen Hanlon 137
Frank Caprice 102
Curt Ridley 96
Cesare Maniago 93
Gary Bromley 73
Steve Weeks 66

Shutouts
Gary Smith 11
Kirk McLean 10
Richard Brodeur 6
Glen Hanlon 5
Gary Bromley 3

Ken Lockett 2
Cesare Maniago 2
Dunc Wilson 2

Goals-against average
(2400 minutes minimum)
Kirk McLean 3.25
Gary Smith 3.33
Steve Weeks 3.44
Glen Hanlon 3.56
Gary Bromley 3.63
Cesare Maniago 3.68
Curt Ridley 3.80
Richard Brodeur 3.87
Dunc Wilson 3.93
John Garrett 4.11

Wins
Richard Brodeur 126
Kirk McLean 100
Gary Smith 72
Glen Hanlon 43
Frank Caprice 31
Cesare Maniago 27
Gary Bromley 25
Curt Ridley 25
Dunc Wilson 24
John Garrett 22

WASHINGTON CAPITALS

YEAR-BY-YEAR RECORDS

Season	\u2014REGULAR SEASON\u2014					\u2014PLAYOFFS\u2014			
Season	W	L	T	Pts.	Finish	W	L	Highest round	Coach
1974-75	8	67	5	21	5th/Norris	—	—		Jim Anderson, Red Sullivan
									Milt Schmidt
1975-76	11	59	10	32	5th/Norris	—	—		Milt Schmidt, Tom McVie
1976-77	24	42	14	62	4th/Norris	—	—		Tom McVie
1977-78	17	49	14	48	5th/Norris	—	—		Tom McVie
1978-79	24	41	15	63	4th/Norris	—	—		Dan Belisle
1979-80	27	40	13	67	5th/Patrick	—	—		Dan Belisle, Gary Green
1980-81	26	36	18	70	5th/Patrick	—	—		Gary Green
1981-82	26	41	13	65	5th/Patrick	—	—		Gary Green, Roger Crozier
									Bryan Murray
1982-83	39	25	16	94	3rd/Patrick	1	3	Division semifinals	Bryan Murray
1983-84	48	27	5	101	2nd/Patrick	4	4	Division finals	Bryan Murray

	REGULAR SEASON						**PLAYOFFS**			
Season	W	L	T	Pts.	Finish	W	L	Highest round	Coach
1984-85	46	25	9	101	2nd/Patrick	2	3	Division semifinals	Bryan Murray
1985-86	50	23	7	107	2nd/Patrick	5	4	Division finals	Bryan Murray
1986-87	38	32	10	86	2nd/Patrick	3	4	Division semifinals	Bryan Murray
1987-88	38	33	9	85	2nd/Patrick	7	7	Division finals	Bryan Murray
1988-89	41	29	10	92	1st/Patrick	2	4	Division semifinals	Bryan Murray
1989-90	36	38	6	78	3rd/Patrick	8	7	Conference finals	Bryan Murray, Terry Murray
1990-91	37	36	7	81	3rd/Patrick	5	6	Division finals	Terry Murray
1991-92	45	27	8	98	2nd/Patrick	3	4	Division semifinals	Terry Murray

FIRST - ROUND ENTRY DRAFT CHOICES

Year	Player, Overall, Last Amateur Team (League)
1974	*Greg Joly, 1, Regina (WCHL)
1975	Alex Forsyth, 18, Kingston (OHA)
1976	*Rick Green, 1, London (OHL)
	Greg Carroll, 15, Medicine Hat (WCHL)
1977	Robert Picard, 3, Montreal (QMJHL)
1978	Ryan Walter, 2, Seattle (WCHL)
	Tim Coulis, 18, Hamilton (OHL)
1979	Mike Gartner, 4, Cincinnati (WHA)
1980	Darren Veitch, 5, Regina (WHL)
1981	Bobby Carpenter, 3, St. John's H.S. (Mass.)
1982	Scott Stevens, 5, Kitchener (OHL)
1983	No first-round selection

Year	Player, Overall, Last Amateur Team (League)
1984	Kevin Hatcher, 17, North Bay (OHL)
1985	Yvon Corriveau, 19, Toronto (OHL)
1986	Jeff Greenlaw, 19, Team Canada
1987	No first-round selection
1988	Reggie Savage, 15, Victoriaville (QMJHL)
1989	Olaf Kolzig, 19, Tri-City (WHL)
1990	John Slaney, 9, Cornwall (OHL)
1991	Pat Peake, 14, Detroit (OHL)
	Trevor Halverson, 21, North Bay (OHL)
1992	Sergei Gonchar, 14, Dynamo Moscow (CIS)

*Designates first player chosen in draft.

FRANCHISE LEADERS

Current players in boldface

FORWARDS/DEFENSEMEN

Games

Mike Gartner	758
Rod Langway	**705**
Bengt Gustafsson	629
Scott Stevens	601
Bobby Gould	600
Kevin Hatcher	**530**
Dave Christian	504
Larry Murphy	453
Gaetan Duchesne	451
Kelly Miller	**435**

Goals

Mike Gartner	397
Bengt Gustafsson	196
Dave Christian	193
Dennis Maruk	182
Bobby Carpenter	177
Mike Ridley	**166**
Bobby Gould	134
Alan Haworth	129
Guy Charron	118
Ryan Walter	114

Assists

Mike Gartner	392
Bengt Gustafsson	359
Scott Stevens	331
Larry Murphy	259
Dennis Maruk	249
Mike Ridley	**229**
Dave Christian	224
Michal Pivonka	**213**
Kevin Hatcher	**208**
Dale Hunter	**193**

Points

Mike Gartner	789
Bengt Gustafsson	555
Dennis Maruk	431
Scott Stevens	429
Dave Christian	417
Mike Ridley	**395**
Bobby Carpenter	367
Larry Murphy	344
Michal Pivonka	**318**
Kevin Hatcher	**307**

Penalty minutes

Scott Stevens	1630
Dale Hunter	**1131**
Alan May	824
Kevin Hatcher	**779**
Mike Gartner	770
Yvon Labre	756
Greg Adams	694
Gord Lane	614

GOALTENDERS

Games

Al Jensen	173
Don Beaupre	158
Ron Low	145
Pat Riggin	143
Pete Peeters	139
Bernie Wolfe	120
Clint Malarchuk	96

Goals-against average
(2400 minutes minimum)

Pat Riggin	3.02
Don Beaupre	**3.03**
Pete Peeters	3.06
Bob Mason	3.16
Al Jensen	3.26
Clint Malarchuk	3.31
Gary Inness	3.64
Wayne Stephenson	3.65
Jim Bedard	3.94
Mike Palmateer	4.03

Wins

Al Jensen	94
Don Beaupre	**77**
Pete Peeters	70
Pat Riggin	67
Clint Malarchuk	40
Bob Mason	35
Ron Low	30
Mike Liut	27
Wayne Stephenson	22
Dave Parro	21

WINNIPEG JETS

YEAR-BY-YEAR RECORDS

	REGULAR SEASON						**PLAYOFFS**			
Season	W	L	T	Pts.	Finish	W	L	Highest round	Coach
1972-73	43	31	4	90	1st	9	5	Avco World Cup finals	Nick Mickoski, Bobby Hull
1973-74	34	39	5	73	4th	0	4	League quarterfinals	Nick Mickoski, Bobby Hull
1974-75	38	35	5	81	3rd	—	—		Rudy Pilous
1975-76	52	27	2	106	1st	12	1	Avco World Cup champ	Bobby Kromm
1976-77	46	32	2	94	2nd	11	9	Avco World Cup finals	Bobby Kromm
1977-78	50	28	2	102	1st	8	1	Avco World Cup champ	Larry Hillman
1978-79	39	35	6	84	3rd	8	2	Avco World Cup champ	Larry Hillman, Tom McVie

Season	W	L	T	Pts.	Finish	W	L	Highest round	Coach
1979-80	20	49	11	51	5th/Smythe	—	—		Tom McVie
1980-81	9	57	14	32	6th/Smythe	—	—		Tom McVie, Bill Sutherland, Mike Smith
1981-82	33	33	14	80	2nd/Norris	1	3	Division semifinals	Tom Watt
1982-83	33	39	8	74	4th/Smythe	0	3	Division semifinals	Tom Watt
1983-84	31	38	11	73	3rd/Smythe	0	3	Division semifinals	Tom Watt, Barry Long
1984-85	43	27	10	96	2nd/Smythe	3	5	Division finals	Barry Long
1985-86	26	47	7	59	3rd/Smythe	0	3	Division semifinals	Barry Long, John Ferguson
1986-87	40	32	8	88	3rd/Smythe	4	6	Division finals	Dan Maloney
1987-88	33	36	11	77	3rd/Smythe	1	4	Division semifinals	Dan Maloney
1988-89	26	42	12	64	5th/Smythe	—	—		Dan Maloney, Rick Bowness
1989-90	37	32	11	85	3rd/Smythe	3	4	Division semifinals	Bob Murdoch
1990-91	26	43	11	63	5th/Smythe	—	—		Bob Murdoch
1991-92	33	32	15	81	4th/Smythe	3	4	Division semifinals	John Paddock

NOTE: Member of World Hockey Association from 1972-73 through 1978-79.

FIRST-ROUND ENTRY DRAFT CHOICES

Year Player, Overall, Last Amateur Team (League)
1979—Jimmy Mann, 19, Sherbrooke (QMJHL)
1980—David Babych, 2, Portland (WHL)
1981—*Dale Hawerchuk, 1, Cornwall (QMJHL)
1982—Jim Kyte, 12, Cornwall (OHL)
1983—Andrew McBain, 8, North Bay (OHL)
        Bobby Dollas, 14, Laval (QMJHL)
1984—No first-round selection
1985—Ryan Stewart, 18, Kamloops (WHL)
1986—Pat Elynuik, 8, Prince Albert (WHL)
1987—Bryan Marchment, 16, Belleville (OHL)

Year Player, Overall, Last Amateur Team (League)
1988—Teemu Selanne, 10, Jokerit (Finland)
1989—Stu Barnes, 4, Tri-City (WHL)
1990—Keith Tkachuk, 19, Malden Cath. H.S. (Mass.)
1991—Aaron Ward, 5, University of Michigan
1992—Sergei Bautin, 17, Dynamo Moscow (CIS)

*Designates first player chosen in draft.
  NOTE: Winnipeg chose Scott Campbell, Morris Lukowich and Markus Mattsson as priority selections before the 1979 expansion draft.

FRANCHISE LEADERS

Current players in boldface

FORWARDS/DEFENSEMEN
Games
Thomas Steen 763
Dale Hawerchuk 713
Doug Smail 691
Randy Carlyle **542**
Ron Wilson 536

Goals
Dale Hawerchuk 379
Paul MacLean 248
Thomas Steen 218
Doug Smail 189
Morris Lukowich 168

Assists
Dale Hawerchuk 550

Thomas Steen 461
Paul MacLean 270
Dave Babych 248
Laurie Boschman 227

Points
Dale Hawerchuk 929
Thomas Steen 679
Paul MacLean 518
Doug Smail 397
Laurie Boschman 379

Penalty minutes
Laurie Boschman 1338
Jim Kyte 772
Tim Watters 760
Paul MacLean 726
Randy Carlyle **722**

Gord Donnelly 715

GOALTENDERS
Shutouts
Bob Essensa **11**
Daniel Berthiaume 4
Markus Mattsson 3
Stephane Beauregard 2
Dan Bouchard 2
Doug Soetaert 2
Ed Staniowski 2

Wins
Bob Essensa **64**
Brian Hayward 63
Daniel Berthiaume 50
Eldon Reddick 41

MINOR LEAGUES

AMERICAN HOCKEY LEAGUE

LEAGUE OFFICE

Address
425 Union Street
West Springfield, MA 01089
Phone
413-781-2030
FAX
413-733-4767
Chairman of the board
Robert W. Clarke
President and treasurer
Jack A. Butterfield
Vice president and general counsel
Macgregor Kilpatrick

Vice president, secretary
Gordon C. Anziano
Exec. dir. of marketing and communications
Robert Ohrablo
Statistician
Hellen Schoeder
Board of governors
Adirondack—TBA
Baltimore—Thomas Ebright
Binghamton—James McCoy
Cape Breton—Bruce MacGregor
Capital District—Ned Harkness

Fredericton—Andre Boudrias
Halifax—Gilles Leger
Hamilton—Patrick J. Hickey
Hershey—Jay Feaster
Moncton—TBA
New Haven—Peter Shipman
Providence—Edward Anderson
Rochester—Randy Scott
St. John's—Cliff Fletcher
Springfield—Peter R. Cooney
Utica—Lou Lamoriello
Honorary governor—George Sage

TEAMS

ADIRONDACK RED WINGS

President
Michael Ilitch
Governor
TBA
Alternate governor
Bryan Murray
General counsel
Denise Ilitch-Lites
Executive vice president
Jim Lites
Director of operations
Jack Kelley
General manager/coach
TBA
Dir. of marketing and promotions
Don Ostrom
Director of media relations
Bill Miller
Director of public relations/broadcaster
Bob Crawford
Trainer
David Casey
Home ice
Glens Falls Civic Center
Address
1 Civic Center Plaza
Glens Falls, NY 12801
Seating Capacity
4,806
NHL affiliation
Detroit Red Wings
Phone
518-798-0366
FAX
518-798-0816

BALTIMORE SKIPJACKS

President and governor
Thomas Ebright
Vice president
John M. Haas
Secretary/treasurer
Gary Fisher
Alternate govorner/G.M./coach
Barry Trotz
Assistant coach
TBA
Vice president/asstistant G.M.
Alan Rakvin
Dir. public and community relations
Margaret Robinson

Director of merchandising
Joyce Ebright
Director of marketing and sales
Sherrie Petti
Athletic trainer
Dan Redmond
Equipment manager
Rich Oberlin
Home ice
Baltimore Arena
Address
Suite 412
201 W. Baltimore Street
Baltimore, MD 21201
Seating Capacity
11,025
NHL affiliation
Washington Capitals
Phone
301-727-0703
FAX
301-547-8445

BINGHAMTON RANGERS

President
James R. McCoy
Vice president
Robert W. Carr Jr.
Governor/mang. part./sec./treasurer
Thomas Mitchell
V.P. of marketing and communications
Jason Siegel
General manager/alternate governor
Neil Smith
Coach
Ron Smith
Director of broadcasting
David Miller
Director of sales
Ron Mitchell
Director of promotions
Patrick Snyder
Home ice
Broome County Veterans Memorial
Arena
Address
One Stuart Street
Binghamton, NY 13901
Seating Capacity
4,805
NHL affiliation
New York Rangers

Phone
607-723-8937
FAX
607-724-6892

CAPE BRETON OILERS

President
Glen Sather
Governor
Bruce MacGregor
General manager
Dave Andrews
Coach
George Burnett
Secretary/public relations
Cheryl Clarke
Director of player personnel
Barry Fraser
Athletic therapist
Conrad Lackten
Trainer
TBA
Home ice
Centre 200
Address
481 George Street
Sydney, Nova Scotia B1T 6R7
Seating Capacity
4,763
NHL affiliation
Edmonton Oilers
Phone
902-562-0780
FAX
902-562-1806

CAPITAL DISTRICT ISLANDERS

Chairman/governor
Albert W. Lawrence
Vice chairman/governor
Ned Harkness
President
Garry Kearns
Board member
Steve Dworsky
General manager/alternate governor
David J. Hanson
Vice president of finance and marketing
Charles B. Staro
Coach
Butch Goring

Controller
 Phyllis Janes
Counsel
 John Hughes
Director of marketing and promotions
 Kevin P. Earl
Dir. of public relations and marketing
 Geoffrey S. Knapp
Marketing representatives
 Irma Staro Magee
 Megan Selfridge
Home ice
 RPI Houston Field House
Address
 275 River Street
 Troy, NY 12180
Seating Capacity
 5,203
NHL affiliation
 New York Islanders
Phone
 518-272-0203
FAX
 518-272-0281

FREDERICTON CANADIENS

President/alternate governor
 Peter Adams
Governor
 Andre Boudrias
Managing director
 Jacques Lemaire
Coach
 Paulin Bordeleau
Director of operations
 Wayne Gamble
Director of marketing and sales
 Russ Newton
Controller
 Allen Lynch
Equipment manager
 Patrick Langlois
Athletic therapist
 Jacques Parent
Home ice
 Aitken University Centre
Address
 P.O. Box HABS
 Fredericton, N.B. E3B 4Y2
Seating Capacity
 3,583
NHL affiliation
 Montreal Canadiens
Phone
 506-459-4227
FAX
 506-457-4250

HALIFAX CITADELS

Governor
 Gilles Leger
General manager/coach
 Clement Jodoin
Assistant coach
 Dean Hopkins
Administrative manager
 Scott Ferguson
Sales manager
 Dave Stevenson
Controller
 Tom Krzyski
Athletic therapist
 Matthew Sokolowski
Equipment manager
 Chris McQuaid

Home ice
 Halifax Metro-Centre
Address
 5284 Duke Street
 Halifax, N.S. B3J 3L2
Seating capacity
 9,629
NHL affiliation
 Quebec Nordiques
Phone
 902-421-1600
FAX
 902-425-5260

HAMILTON CANUCKS

President/chief executive officer
 Patrick J. Hickey
Vice president of operations
 Matthew W. Newsom
Dir. of communications and promotions
 Catherine Galea
Sales and marketing
 Kenneth Cook
Administrative assistant
 Carolyn Marchese-Blanche
Home ice
 Copp Coliseum
Address
 85 York Blvd.
 Hamilton, Ont. L8R 3L4
Seating capacity
 17,500 (approx.)
NHL affiliation
 Vancouver Canucks
Phone
 416-546-1122
FAX
 416-522-2138

HERSHEY BEARS

Chairman/chief executive officer
 J. Bruce McKinney
General manager
 Jay Feaster
Asst. G.M./dir. hockey operations
 Doug Yingst
Coach
 Mike Eaves
Head trainer
 Dan Stuck
Assistant trainer
 Rusty Pearl
Publicity/sales coordinator
 Scott Smith
Operations manager
 Tom Stephens
Operations supervisor
 Wilbur Hallman
Home ice
 Hersheypark Arena
Address
 P.O. Box 866
 Hershey, PA 17033
Seating capacity
 7,256
NHL affiliation
 Philadelphia Flyers
Phone
 717-534-3380
FAX
 717-534-3383

MONCTON HAWKS

Chairman
 TBA

Governor
 TBA
President
 TBA
Coach/general manager
 Dave Farrish
Home ice
 Moncton Coliseum
Address
 P.O. Box 2940, Station A
 Moncton, N.B. E1C 8T8
Seating Capacity
 6,802
NHL affiliation
 Winnipeg Jets
Phone
 506-857-4000
FAX
 506-859-8919

NEW HAVEN SENATORS

Chairman/governor
 Peter H. Shipman
President/alternate governor
 TBA
Alternate governor
 Lawrence Zicklin
Coach
 TBA
V.P./chief financial officer
 Henry W. Bradbury
V.P./assistant general manager
 TBA
Director of press relations
 Jan MacDonald
Home ice
 Veterans Memorial Coliseum
Address
 P.O. Box 1444
 New Haven, CT 06506
Seating capacity
 8,765
NHL affiliation
 Ottawa Senators
Phone
 203-787-0101
FAX
 203-787-9461

PROVIDENCE BRUINS

Chairman/CEO/governor
 Edward Anderson
President/treasurer/alternate governor
 Frank DuRoss
Coach
 Mike O'Connell
Business manager
 Jeff Fear
Marketing/sales
 Alfred Passarelli
Media/public relations/broadcasting
 Joe Beninati
Head trainer
 Jerry Foster
Equipment manager
 Peter Henderson
Home ice
 Providence Civic Center
Address
 P.O. Box 1329
 Providence, RI 02903
Seating capacity
 12,000
NHL affiliation
 Boston Bruins

AHL

MINOR LEAGUES

AHL

Phone
401-273-5000
FAX
401-273-5004

ROCHESTER AMERICANS

Chairman of the board
Lawrence Lovejoy
Governor/general manager
Randy Scott
Coach
Don Lever
Assistant coach
Terry Martin
P.R. director/broadcaster
Don Stevens
Director of media relations
Jeff Holbrook
Executive assistant
Michele Butz
Director of sales
Tony Gentile
Account executive
Chris Palin
Director of marketing
Joe Baumann
Athletic trainer
Kent Weisbeck
Home ice
Rochester War Memorial
Address
100 Exchange Street
Rochester, NY 14614
Seating capacity
6,973
NHL affiliation
Buffalo Sabres
Phone
716-454-5335
FAX
716-454-3954

ST. JOHN'S MAPLE LEAFS

President/governor
Cliff Fletcher

Alternate governor
Floyd Smith
Alternate governor
Bob Stellick
Head coach
Marc Crawford
Assistant coach
Joel Quenneville
Director of administration
Glenn Stanford
Dir. of media and team relations
Chris Reed
Home ice
St. John's Memorial Stadium
Address
18 Argyle Street
St. John's, Newfoundland A1A 1V3
Seating capacity
3,910
NHL affiliation
Toronto Maple Leafs
Phone
709-726-1010
FAX
709-726-1511

SPRINGFIELD INDIANS

President
Peter R. Cooney
Governor
James J. Coogan
Alternate governor
Brian Burke
Accountant
Dennis J. Fusco
General manager
Bruce Landon
Coach
Jay Leach
Business manager
Martha Knapp
Trainer
Webb Sommer
Equipment manager
Ralph Calvanese
Home ice
Springfield Civic Center

Address
P.O. Box 4896
Springfield, MA 01101
Seating capacity
7,452
NHL affiliation
Hartford Whalers
Phone
413-736-4546
FAX
413-788-6786

UTICA DEVILS

Chairman
John J. McMullen
President and governor
Lou Lamoriello
Alternate governor
Mike O'Neil
Head coach
Robbie Ftorek
Director of operations
Paul D'Aiuto
Director of marketing
Virginia Roher
Dir. public/media relations
William Dowsland
Marketing and adm. asst.
TBA
Athletic trainer
Robert Bill
Equipment manager
Scott Moon
Auditorium exec. dir.
Murray Sislen
Home ice
Utica Memorial Auditorium
Address
400 Oriskany St. West
Utica, NY 13502
Seating capacity
3,857
NHL affiliation
New Jersey Devils
Phone
315-724-2126
FAX
315-724-2136

1991-92 REGULAR SEASON

FINAL STANDINGS

ATLANTIC DIVISION

Team	G	W	L	T	Pts.	GF	GA
Fredericton	80	43	27	10	96	314	254
St. John's	80	39	29	12	90	325	285
Cape Breton	80	36	34	10	82	336	330
Moncton	80	32	38	10	74	285	299
Halifax	80	25	38	17	67	280	324

NORTHERN DIVISION

Team	G	W	L	T	Pts.	GF	GA
Springfield	80	43	29	8	94	308	277
Adirondack	80	40	36	4	84	335	309
New Haven	80	39	37	4	82	305	309
Capital District	80	32	37	11	75	261	289
Maine	80	23	47	10	56	296	352

SOUTHERN DIVISION

Team	G	W	L	T	Pts.	GF	GA
Binghamton	80	41	30	9	91	318	277
Rochester	80	37	31	12	86	292	248
Hershey	80	36	33	11	83	313	337
Utica	80	34	40	6	74	268	313
Baltimore	80	28	42	10	66	287	320

INDIVIDUAL LEADERS

Goals: Dan Currie, Cape Breton (50)
Assists: Shaun Van Allen, Cape Breton (84)
Points: Shaun Van Allen, Cape Breton (113)
Penalty minutes: Kirk Tomlinson, Adirondack (356)
Goaltending average: Frederic Chabot, Fredericton (2.69)
Shutouts: Stephane Fiset, Halifax (3)
David Littman, Rochester (3)

	Games	G	A	Pts.
Greg Parks, Capital District	70	36	57	93
Dan Currie, Cape Breton	66	50	42	92
Simon Wheeldon, Baltimore	78	38	53	91
Chris Tancill, Spr.-Ad.	67	48	41	89
John Purves, Baltimore	78	43	46	89
Lonnie Loach, Adirondack	67	37	49	86
Len Barrie, Hershey	75	42	43	85
Don Biggs, Binghamton	74	32	50	82
Jody Gage, Rochester	67	40	40	80
Gary Shuchuk, Adirondack	79	32	48	80
Paul Willett, New Haven	69	29	51	80
Bill McDougall, Ad.-C.B.	67	36	42	78
Shawn Evans, Springfield	80	11	67	78
Yanic Perreault, St. John's	62	38	38	76
Tyler Larter, Moncton	68	25	51	76

TOP SCORERS

	Games	G	A	Pts.
Shaun Van Allen, Cape Breton	77	29	84	113
Tim Tookey, Hershey	80	36	69	105
Stan Drulin, New Haven	77	49	53	102
Peter Ciavaglia, Rochester	77	37	61	98
John Anderson, New Haven	68	41	54	95
Andrew McKim, St. John's	79	43	50	93

INDIVIDUAL STATISTICS

ADIRONDACK RED WINGS

SCORING

	Games	G	A	Pts.	Pen.
Lonnie Loach	67	37	49	86	69
Gary Shuchuk	79	32	48	80	48
Chris Tancill	50	36	34	70	42
Mike Sillinger	64	25	41	66	26
Ken Quinney	63	31	29	60	33
Bill McDougall	45	28	24	52	112
Sheldon Kennedy	46	25	24	49	56
Keith Primeau	42	21	24	45	89
Daniel Shank	27	13	21	34	112
Stewart Malgunas	69	4	28	32	82
Marc Potvin	51	13	16	29	314
Micah Aivazoff	61	9	20	29	50
Chris Luongo	80	6	20	26	60
Jason York	49	4	20	24	32
Jim Cummins	65	7	13	20	338
Kelly Hurd	35	9	7	16	16
Derek Mayer	25	4	11	15	31
Kirk Tomlinson	54	3	12	15	356
Gord Kruppke	65	3	9	12	208
Guy Dupuis	49	3	6	9	59
Brad McCaughey	6	4	4	8	0
Max Middendorf	6	3	5	8	12
Pete Stauber	25	2	5	7	14
Bobby Dollas	19	1	6	7	33
Johan Garpenlov	9	3	3	6	6
Dennis Vial	20	2	4	6	107
Bob Wilkie	7	1	4	5	6
Dave Flanagan	11	3	1	4	2
Mike Butters	13	1	3	4	46
Alex Roberts	16	1	3	4	12
Allan Bester (goalie)	22	0	4	4	2
Darin Banister	26	0	3	3	32
Brent Fedyk	1	0	2	2	0
Phil Crowe	6	1	0	1	29
Bob Jones	1	0	1	1	0
Rob Krauss	7	0	1	1	32
Serge Anglehart	16	0	1	1	43
Mark Reimer (goalie)	25	0	1	1	4
Mike Casselman	1	0	0	0	0
Bob Boughner	1	0	0	0	7
Jason Firth	2	0	0	0	0
Vincent Riendeau (goalie)	3	0	0	0	0
Scott King (goalie)	33	0	0	0	2

GOALTENDING

	Games	Min.	Goals	SO	Avg.
Vincent Riendeau	3	179	8(4)	0	2.68
Scott King	33	1904	112	0	3.53
Allan Bester	22	1268	78(2)	0	3.69
Mark Reimer	25	1459	99(6)	0	4.07

BALTIMORE SKIPJACKS

SCORING

	Games	G	A	Pts.	Pen.
Simon Wheeldon	78	38	53	91	62
John Purves	78	43	46	89	47
Reggie Savage	77	42	28	70	51
Brent Hughes	55	25	29	54	190
Todd Hlushko	74	16	35	51	113
Craig Duncanson	46	20	26	46	98
Mark Ferner	57	7	38	45	67
Ken Lovsin	77	11	24	35	60
Bobby Reynolds	53	12	18	30	39
Tim Taylor	65	9	18	27	131
Jiri Vykoukal	56	1	21	22	47
Trevor Halverson	74	10	11	21	181
Tim Bergland	11	6	10	16	5
Chris Clarke	46	3	12	15	18
John Byce	20	9	5	14	4
Jeff Greenlaw	37	6	8	14	57
Steve Martell	42	5	7	12	120
Ken Sabourin	30	3	8	11	106
Jim Mathieson	74	2	9	11	206
Jason Woolley	15	1	10	11	6
Martin Jiranek	8	2	8	10	0
Steve Seftel	18	2	6	8	27
Wade Bartley	20	0	7	7	25
John Slaney	6	2	4	6	0
Keith Jones	6	2	4	6	0
Victor Gervais	21	1	5	6	37
Shawn Chambers	5	2	3	5	9
Dennis Smith	17	1	4	5	23
Randy Pearce	12	2	2	4	8
Harry Mews	5	1	3	4	10
Jim Hrivnak (goalie)	22	0	3	3	0
Richie Walcott	51	1	1	2	277
Steve Konowalchuk	3	1	1	2	0
Bob Babcock	26	0	2	2	55
Olaf Kolzig (goalie)	28	0	2	2	6
Pat Peake	3	1	0	1	4
Brad Schlegel	2	0	1	1	0
Byron Dafoe (goalie)	33	0	1	1	4
Dave Morissette	2	0	0	0	6
Don Beaupre (goalie)	3	0	0	0	0
Bill Kovacs	4	0	0	0	0
Rob Leask	4	0	0	0	0

GOALTENDING

	Games	Min.	Goals	SO	Avg.
Don Beaupre	3	184	10	0	3.26
Jim Hrivnak	22	1303	73(2)	0	3.36
Byron Dafoe	33	1847	119(5)	0	3.87
Olaf Kolzig	28	1503	105(6)	1	4.19

BINGHAMTON RANGERS

SCORING

	Games	G	A	Pts.	Pen.
Don Biggs	74	32	50	82	122
Ross Fitzpatrick	76	34	38	72	32
Bob Zamuner	61	19	53	72	42
Jody Hull	69	34	31	65	28
Chris Cichocki	75	28	29	57	132
Mike Hurlbut	79	16	39	55	64
Brian McReynolds	48	19	28	47	22
Jeff Bloemberg	66	6	41	47	22
Steven King	66	27	15	42	56
Ric Bennett	69	19	23	42	112
Mark Janssens	55	10	23	33	109
Daniel Lacroix	52	12	20	32	149
Mike Stevens	44	15	15	30	87
Shaun Sabol	72	5	19	24	123
Guy Larose	30	10	11	21	36
Joe Paterson	49	7	10	17	115
Doug Weight	9	3	14	17	2
Corey Millen	15	8	7	15	44
Peter Laviolette	50	4	10	14	50
Peter Fiorentino	70	2	11	13	340
Eric Germain	47	3	6	9	86
Mario Thyer	9	2	7	9	0
Murray Duval	15	1	6	7	8
Kord Cernich	5	1	3	4	6
Darren Colbourne	1	1	1	2	0
Mark Laforest (goalie)	43	0	2	2	18
Glen Goodall	6	0	2	2	0
John Mokosak	28	0	2	2	123
Tom Karalis	2	0	1	1	0
Randy Moller	3	0	1	1	0
Sam St. Laurent (goalie)	1	0	0	0	0
John Vary	1	0	0	0	0
Pat Cavanagh	4	0	0	0	0
Jason Prosofsky	4	0	0	0	5
David Quinn	19	0	0	0	6
Boris Rousson (goalie)	38	0	0	0	4

GOALTENDING

	Games	Min.	Goals	SO	Avg.
Boris Rousson	38	2261	123(5)	1	3.26
Mark Laforest	43	2559	146(1)	1	3.42
Sam St. Laurent	1	20	2	0	6.00

CAPE BRETON OILERS

SCORING

	Games	G	A	Pts.	Pen.
Shaun VanAllen	77	29	84	113	80
Dan Currie	66	50	42	92	39
Greg Hawgood	56	20	55	75	26
Shjon Podein	80	30	24	54	46
Steven Rice	45	32	20	52	38
Tomas Kapusta	67	18	33	51	55
Tomas Srsen	68	19	27	46	79
Craig Fisher	60	20	25	45	28
Chris Joseph	63	14	29	43	72
Max Middendorf	51	20	19	39	108
Tim Tisdale	69	12	26	38	30
Francois Leroux	61	7	22	29	114
Brad Werenka	66	6	21	27	95
Bill McDougall	22	8	18	26	36
Richard Borgo	52	10	14	24	90
Martin Rucinsky	35	11	12	23	34
Scott Thornton	49	9	14	23	40
Collin Bauer	55	7	15	22	36
Marc Laforge	59	0	14	14	341
Peter Soberlak	22	4	7	11	25
David Haas	16	3	7	10	32
John Blessman	27	2	8	10	16
Jason Soules	51	0	9	9	44
Dean Antos	15	1	5	4	2
Louise DeBrusk	28	2	2	4	73

	Games	G	A	Pts.	Pen.
Norm Foster (goalie)	29	0	4	4	2
John Kordic	12	2	1	3	141
Wayne Cowley (goalie)	11	0	2	2	0
Trevor Sim	2	0	1	1	0
Gary St. Pierre	1	0	0	0	5
Eugeny Belosheikin (goalie)	3	0	0	0	0
Mike Greenlay (goalie)	3	0	0	0	0
Bruce Campbell	4	0	0	0	0
Eldon Reddick (goalie)	16	0	0	0	4
Peter Ing (goalie)	24	0	0	0	2

GOALTENDING

	Games	Min.	Goals	SO	Avg.
Eldon Reddick	16	765	45(1)	0	3.53
Wayne Cowley	11	644	42(2)	0	3.91
Peter Ing	24	1411	92(2)	0	3.91
Eugeny Belosheikin	3	183	12	0	3.93
Norm Foster	29	1699	119(3)	0	4.20
Mike Greenlay	3	144	12	0	5.00

CAPITAL DISTRICT ISLANDERS

SCORING

	Games	G	A	Pts.	Pen.
Greg Parks	70	36	57	93	84
Brent Grieve	74	34	32	66	84
Phil Huber	71	26	32	58	85
Richard Kromm	76	16	39	55	36
Travis Green	71	23	27	50	10
Lee Giffin	77	19	26	45	58
Graeme Townshend	61	14	23	37	94
David Chyzowski	55	15	18	33	121
Hubie McDonough	21	11	18	29	14
Iain Fraser	45	9	11	20	24
Wayne Doucet	60	11	7	18	116
Brad Dalgarno	14	7	8	15	34
Jeff Sharples	31	3	12	15	18
Derek Laxdal	49	7	7	14	61
Dean Ewen	41	5	8	13	106
Dennis Vaske	31	1	11	12	59
Rick Hayward	27	3	8	11	139
Dean Chynoweth	43	4	6	10	164
Jeff Finley	20	1	9	10	6
Brad Turner	35	3	6	9	17
Rob Vanderydt	19	3	5	8	2
Joni Lehto	26	2	5	7	6
Stephane Robitaille	11	1	5	6	2
Vern Smith	17	1	5	6	6
John Blum	51	0	6	6	76
Joe Reekie	3	2	2	4	2
Jim Culhane	37	1	3	4	58
Kevin Cheveldayoff	44	0	4	4	110
Dean Trboyevich	22	0	3	3	65
Chris Pryor	22	0	3	3	12
Tom Fitzgerald	4	1	1	2	4
Barry Dreger	2	1	1	2	5
Jeff Jablonski	4	1	1	2	0
Bill Berg	3	0	2	2	16
Sean LeBrun	14	0	2	2	15
Danny Lorenz (goalie)	53	0	2	2	0
Alex Roberts	5	0	1	1	6
Joseph Capprini (goalie)	2	0	0	0	0
Scott McCrady	4	0	0	0	14
Gary Nylund	4	0	0	0	0
Will Averill	12	0	0	0	0
Mark Fitzpatrick (goalie)	14	0	0	0	8
Jamie McLennan (goalie)	18	0	0	0	4

GOALTENDING

	Games	Min.	Goals	SO	Avg.
Mark Fitzpatrick	14	782	39	0	2.99
Danny Lorenz	53	3050	181(1)	2	3.56
Jamie McLennan	18	952	60(3)	1	3.78
Joseph Capprini	2	77	5	0	3.90

FREDERICTON CANADIENS

SCORING

	Games	G	A	Pts.	Pen.
Patrick Lebeau	55	33	38	71	48
Jesse Belanger	65	30	41	71	26
Stephane Richer	80	17	47	64	74
Ed Ronan	78	25	34	59	82
Pierre Sevigny	74	22	37	59	145
Paul DiPietro	43	26	31	57	52
Steve Larouche	74	21	35	56	41
Gilbert Dionne	29	19	27	46	20
John Ferguson	62	18	21	39	74
Patrice Brisebois	53	12	27	39	51
Lindsay Vallis	71	10	19	29	84
Tom Sagissor	57	12	15	27	111
Sean Hill	42	7	20	27	65
Darcy Simon	58	9	11	20	308
Donald Dufresne	31	8	12	20	60
Norman Desjardins	50	9	9	18	62
Luc Gauthier	80	4	14	18	252
Marc Labellé	02	7	10	17	238
Benoit Brunet	6	7	9	16	27
John LeClair	8	7	7	14	10
Eric Charron	59	2	11	13	98
Alain Cote	20	1	10	11	24
Gerry Fleming	37	4	6	10	133
Steve Veilleux	53	3	7	10	122
Greg MacEachern	20	0	5	5	12
Mario Roberge	6	1	2	3	20
Andre Racicot (goalie)	28	0	2	2	6
Les Kuntar (goalie)	11	0	1	1	4
Frederic Chabot (goalie)	30	0	1	1	4
Brent Fleetwood	3	0	0	0	0
Jean C. Bergeron (goalie)	13	0	0	0	0

GOALTENDING

	Games	Min.	Goals	SO	Avg.
Les Kuntar	11	638	26(1)	0	2.45
Frederic Chabot	30	1761	79(3)	2	2.69
Andre Racicot	28	1666	86(2)	0	3.10
Jean C. Bergeron	13	791	57	0	4.32

HALIFAX CITADELS

SCORING

	Games	G	A	Pts.	Pen.
Ken McRae	52	30	41	71	184
Denis Chasse	73	26	35	61	254
David Marcinyshyn	74	10	42	52	138
Stephane Charbonneau	64	22	25	47	183
Kevin Kaninski	63	18	27	45	329
Mark Vernette	44	21	18	39	39
Niclas Anderson	57	8	26	34	41
Mike Dagenais	69	11	21	32	143
Dan Lambert	47	3	28	31	33
Stephane Morin	30	17	13	30	29
Kip Miller	24	9	17	26	8
Marc Fortier	16	9	16	25	44
Ivan Matulik	41	7	16	23	32
Don Barber	25	12	10	22	8
Sergei Kharin	40	10	12	22	15
Jon Klemm	70	6	13	19	40
Mike McNeil	30	10	8	18	20
Ed Ward	51	7	11	18	65
David Espe	43	4	7	11	22
Andy Rymsha	44	4	7	11	54
Wayne Van Dorp	15	5	5	10	54
Serge Roberge	66	2	8	10	319
Randy Velischek	16	3	6	9	0
Martin Simard	10	5	3	8	26
Everett Sanipass	7	3	5	8	31
Steve Maltais	10	3	3	6	0
Gerald Bzdel	35	0	6	6	42
Jamie Baker	9	5	0	5	12
Daniel Dore	29	4	1	5	45
Bruce Major	16	1	3	4	11

	Games	G	A	Pts.	Pen.
Greg Smyth	9	1	3	4	35
Scott Pearson	5	2	1	3	4
Dean Zayonce	24	0	3	3	26
Rob Reimer	10	1	1	2	0
Martin Rucinsky	7	1	1	2	6
Curtis Leschyshyn	6	0	2	2	4
Adam Foote	6	0	1	1	2
Ron Tugnutt (goalie)	8	0	1	1	2
Darren Cossar (goalie)	1	0	0	0	0
Jocelyn Provost (goalie)	1	0	0	0	0
Bryan Fogarty	2	0	0	0	2
David Karpa	2	0	0	0	4
Alexei Gusarov	3	0	0	0	0
Daryl Noren	3	0	0	0	0
Mike Butters	6	0	0	0	25
Scott Gordon (goalie)	7	0	0	0	2
Mario Doyon	9	0	0	0	22
John Tanner (goalie)	12	0	0	0	2
Eric Dubois	14	0	0	0	8
Stephane Fiset (goalie)	29	0	0	0	16
Patrick LaBrecque (goalie)	29	0	0	0	6

GOALTENDING

	Games	Min.	Goals	SO	Avg.
Darren Cossar	1	25	1	0	2.40
John Tanner	12	672	29(2)	2	2.59
Scott Gordon	7	424	27	0	3.82
Stephane Fiset	29	1675	110(4)	3	3.94
Ron Tugnutt	8	447	30(1)	0	4.03
Patrick LaBrecque	29	1570	114	0	4.36
Jocelyn Provost	1	60	6	0	6.00

HERSHEY BEARS

SCORING

	Games	G	A	Pts.	Pen.
Tim Tookey	80	36	69	105	63
Len Barrie	75	42	43	85	78
Chris Jensen	71	38	33	71	134
Darren Rumble	79	12	54	66	118
Martin Hostak	63	27	36	63	77
Pat Murray	69	19	43	62	25
Bill H. Armstrong	64	26	22	48	185
Al Conroy	47	17	28	45	90
Jamie Cooke	66	15	26	41	49
Wes Walz	41	13	28	41	37
Dave Fenyves	68	4	24	28	29
Mark Freer	31	13	11	24	38
Eric Dandenault	69	6	13	19	149
Reid Simpson	60	11	7	18	145
Rod Dallman	31	4	13	17	114
Dale Kushner	46	9	7	16	98
William Armstrong	80	2	14	16	159
Corey Foster	19	5	9	14	26
Mike Stothers	70	3	8	11	152
Claude Boivin	20	4	5	9	96
Toni Porkka	64	3	5	8	34
Ryan McGill	17	3	5	8	67
Steve Morrow	31	1	2	3	6
Steve Beadle	6	0	2	2	0
Ray Letourneau (goalie)	15	0	2	2	2
Marc D'Amour (goalie)	21	0	1	1	16
Yanick Degrace (goalie)	2	0	0	0	0
Lance Pitlick	4	0	0	0	6
Nick Vitucci (goalie)	4	0	0	0	0
Jim Waite (goalie)	11	0	0	0	2
Dominic Roussel (goalie)	35	0	0	0	4

GOALTENDING

	Games	Min.	Goals	SO	Avg.
Yanick Degrace	2	125	6	0	2.88
Dominic Roussel	35	2040	121(2)	1	3.56
Jim Waite	11	631	44(1)	0	4.18
Marc D'Amour	21	1073	79	0	4.42
Nick Vitucci	4	191	15	0	4.71
Ray Letourneau	15	791	67(2)	0	5.08

MAINE MARINERS

SCORING

	Games	G	A	Pts.	Pen.
Ralph Barahona	74	27	32	59	39
Mike Walsh	76	27	24	51	42
John Byce	55	29	21	50	41
Chris Winnes	45	12	35	47	30
Petr Prajsler	61	12	33	45	88
Jack Capuano	74	14	26	40	35
Brian Dobbin	33	21	15	36	14
Dennis Smith	59	2	32	34	63
Shayne Stevenson	54	10	23	33	150
Lou Crawford	54	17	15	32	171
Brad Tiley	62	7	22	29	36
Bob Beers	33	6	23	29	24
Mike Rossetti	52	10	15	25	72
Wes Walz	21	13	11	24	38
Dave Thomlinson	25	9	11	20	36
Andy Brickley	14	5	15	20	2
Matt Glennon	32	6	12	18	13
Barry Pederson	14	5	13	18	6
Ken Hodge	19	6	11	17	4
Jim Vesey	10	6	7	13	13
Jeff Lazaro	21	8	4	12	32
Rick Allain	66	1	11	12	249
Nevin Markwart	17	4	7	11	32
Brian Martin	11	4	7	11	2
Brent Hughes	12	6	4	10	34
Lyndon Byers	11	5	4	9	47
Scott Arniel	14	4	4	8	8
Matt Hervey	36	1	7	8	47
Peter Douris	12	4	3	7	2
David Jensen	15	2	5	7	0
Dave Reid	12	1	5	6	4
Steve Rooney	13	2	3	5	17
Oleg Znarok	6	3	1	4	11
Steve Bancroft	26	1	3	4	45
John Blue (goalie)	43	0	4	4	14
Mark Krys	28	1	2	3	18
Jeff Napierala	16	0	3	3	0
Shawn Wheeler	10	2	0	2	36
Chris Grassie	19	1	1	2	15
Sergei Shendelev	24	0	2	2	10
Bob Sweeney	1	1	0	1	0
Brian Ferreira	9	1	0	1	0
Jim Wiemer	3	0	1	1	4
Greg Millen (goalie)	11	0	1	1	34
Matt Delguidice (goalie)	25	0	1	1	10
Nick Vitucci (goalie)	1	0	0	0	0
Howard Rosenblatt	2	0	0	0	9
Pasi Schalin	5	0	0	0	0
Mike Parson (goalie)	12	0	0	0	0

GOALTENDING

	Games	Min.	Goals	SO	Avg.
Nick Vitucci	1	65	3	0	2.77
Mike Parson	12	645	37(1)	0	3.44
Greg Millen	11	599	37(2)	0	3.71
Matt Delguidice	25	1369	101(5)	0	4.43
John Blue	43	2168	165(1)	1	4.57

MONCTON HAWKS

SCORING

	Games	G	A	Pts.	Pen.
Tyler Larter	68	25	51	76	156
Jason Cirone	64	32	27	59	124
John LeBlanc	56	31	22	53	24
Bob Joyce	66	19	29	48	51
Rob Cowie	64	11	30	41	89
Scott Levins	69	15	18	33	271
Kent Paynter	62	3	30	33	71
Stu Barnes	30	13	19	32	10
Rob Murray	60	16	15	31	247
Russ Romaniuk	45	16	15	31	25

	Games	G	A	Pts.	Pen.
Warren Rychel	36	14	15	29	211
Kris Draper	61	11	18	29	113
Mark Kumpel	41	11	18	29	12
Darren Veitch	61	6	23	29	47
Ken Gernander	43	8	18	26	9
Rudy Poeschek	63	4	18	22	170
Craig Duncanson	19	12	9	21	6
Tod Hartje	38	9	9	18	35
Claude Julien	48	2	15	17	10
Dallas Eakins	67	3	13	16	136
Doug Evans	10	7	8	15	10
Lee Davidson	43	3	12	15	32
Derek Langille	62	4	9	13	77
Tony Joseph	42	6	5	11	118
Luciano Borsato	14	2	7	9	39
Rick Tabaracci (goalie)	23	0	3	3	10
Mike O'Neill (goalie)	32	0	3	3	4
Dean Morton	6	1	1	2	15
Craig Martin	11	1	1	2	70
Eric Germain	3	0	2	2	4
Aaron Broten	4	0	2	2	0
Igor Ulanov	3	0	1	1	16
Dave MacIntyre	6	0	1	1	0
Leonard Devuono	1	0	0	0	0
Allain Harvey (goalie)	1	0	0	0	0
Alan Perry (goalie)	2	0	0	0	0
Denis Roy (goalie)	2	0	0	0	0
Brett MacDonald	3	0	0	0	2
Chris Kiene	5	0	0	0	11
Tom Karalis	6	0	0	0	4
Sean Gauthier (goalie)	25	0	0	0	4

GOALTENDING

	Games	Min.	Goals	SO	Avg.
Mike O'Neill	32	1902	108(3)	1	3.41
Rick Tabaracci	23	1313	80(1)	0	3.66
Sean Gauthier	25	1415	88	1	3.73
Alan Perry	2	129	9	0	4.19
Allain Harvey	1	60	7	0	7.00
Denis Roy	1	20	3	0	9.00

NEW HAVEN NIGHTHAWKS

SCORING

	Games	G	A	Pts.	Pen.
Stan Drulia	77	49	53	102	46
John Anderson	68	41	54	95	24
Paul Willett	69	29	51	80	68
Kent Hulst	80	21	39	60	59
David Latta	76	18	27	45	100
Mario Doyon	64	11	29	40	44
Trevor Stienburg	66	17	22	39	201
Scott Schneider	59	16	23	39	29
Brian Dobbin	33	16	21	37	20
David Haas	50	13	23	36	97
Jeff Jackson	30	10	14	24	60
Andrei Kovalev	33	11	12	23	31
Mike McEwen	51	4	19	23	32
Dave Baseggio	31	3	19	22	8
Jerry Tarrant	74	0	21	21	45
Daryl Noren	34	11	9	20	22
Jerome Bechard	62	8	11	19	129
Brad Turner	32	6	11	17	58
Jim Sprott	54	4	11	15	140
Lou Franceschetti	25	6	7	13	59
Al Tuer	68	2	10	12	199
Eric Ricard	38	2	9	11	85
Scott Arniel	11	3	3	6	10
Oleg Mikoulchik	30	3	3	6	63
Andy Rymsha	16	0	5	5	20
Darryl Williams	13	0	2	2	69
Trevor Pochipinski	8	0	2	2	4
Mike Butters	2	1	0	1	5
Bryan Fogarty	4	0	1	1	6
Rick Barkovich	5	0	1	1	0
Eric Dubois	1	0	0	0	2

	Games	G	A	Pts.	Pen.
Jeff Jablonski	1	0	0	0	0
Scott Gordon (goalie)	4	0	0	0	0
Bill Pye (goalie)	4	0	0	0	0
Vern Smith	4	0	0	0	5
Dave Trombley	4	0	0	0	0
Dave Goverde (goalie)	5	0	0	0	6
Byron Dafoe (goalie)	7	0	0	0	0
Sergei Shendelev	7	0	0	0	10
John Tanner (goalie)	16	0	0	0	16
George Maneluk (goalie)	54	0	0	0	10

GOALTENDING

	Games	Min.	Goals	SO	Avg.
Scott Gordon	4	239	11(1)	0	2.76
Byron Dafoe	7	364	22	0	3.63
George Maneluk	54	2863	175(5)	1	3.67
John Tanner	16	908	57(1)	0	3.77
Dave Goverde	5	248	17(1)	0	4.11
Bill Pye	4	200	19	0	5.70

ROCHESTER AMERICANS

SCORING

	Games	G	A	Pts.	Pen.
Peter Ciavaglia	77	37	61	98	16
Jody Gage	67	40	40	80	54
Jiri Sejba	59	27	31	58	36
Jason Winch	73	23	35	58	24
Dan Frawley	78	28	23	51	208
Lou Franceschetti	49	15	25	40	64
Greg Brown	56	8	30	38	25
Don McSween	75	6	32	38	60
Brad Rubachuk	70	18	16	34	201
Lindy Ruff	62	10	24	34	110
Bill Houlder	42	8	26	34	16
Chris Snell	65	5	27	32	66
Darcy Loewen	73	11	20	31	193
Bob Corkum	52	16	12	28	47
Steve Ludzik	45	6	22	28	88
Joel Savage	59	8	14	22	39
Dave Baseggio	29	5	11	16	14
Ian Boyce	20	5	8	13	4
Sean O Donnell	77	4	9	13	193
Rick Vaive	12	4	9	13	4
Keith Carney	24	1	10	11	2
Ed Zawatsky	14	4	6	10	2
David Littman (goalie)	61	0	5	5	8
Brad Miller	27	0	4	4	113
David DiVita	25	1	2	3	59
Brian Curran	36	0	3	3	122
Steve Smith	3	1	0	1	0
Andy Pritchard	2	1	0	1	0
Peter Ambroziak	2	0	1	1	0
Tom Draper (goalie)	9	0	1	1	0
Tony Iob	1	0	0	0	0
Clint Malarchuk (goalie)	2	0	0	0	2
Daren Puppa (goalie)	2	0	0	0	2
Kevin Haller	4	0	0	0	18
Bob Fleming	5	0	0	0	29
John Bradley (goalie)	6	0	0	0	2
Bill Pye (goalie)	7	0	0	0	0

GOALTENDING

	Games	Min.	Goals	SO	Avg.
Clint Malarchuk	2	120	3	1	1.50
Bill Pye	7	272	13(2)	0	2.87
David Littman	61	3558	174(6)	3	2.93
John Bradley	6	248	13	1	3.15
Tom Draper	9	531	28	0	3.16
Daren Puppa	2	119	9	0	4.54

ST. JOHN'S MAPLE LEAFS

SCORING

	Games	G	A	Pts.	Pen.
Andrew McKim	79	43	50	93	79

	Games	G	A	Pts.	Pen.
Yanic Perreault	62	38	38	76	19
Greg Johnston	63	28	45	73	33
Todd Hawkins	66	30	27	57	139
Dave Tomlinson	75	23	34	57	75
Todd Gillingham	66	12	35	47	306
Jeff Serowik	78	11	34	45	60
Mike Eastwood	61	18	25	43	28
Brad Aitken	59	12	27	39	169
Len Esau	78	9	29	38	68
Joel Quenneville	73	7	23	30	58
Rob Pearson	27	15	14	29	107
Keith Osborne	53	11	16	27	21
Kevin Maguire	30	11	15	26	112
Mike Stevens	30	13	11	24	65
Curtis Hunt	52	5	18	23	106
Kevin McClelland	34	7	15	22	199
Bruce Bell	45	5	16	21	70
Rob Cimetta	19	4	13	17	23
Mike MacWilliam	44	7	8	15	301
Guy Larose	15	7	7	14	26
Ted Crowley	29	5	4	9	33
Mark Ferner	15	1	8	9	0
Guy Lehoux	67	1	7	8	134
Rob Mendel	39	1	4	5	26
Felix Potvin (goalie)	35	0	3	3	6
Greg Walters	10	0	2	2	20
Cory Banika	2	1	0	1	2
Jeff Perry	6	0	1	1	4
Damian Rhodes (goalie)	44	0	1	1	8
Mike Jackson	1	0	0	0	0
Mike Moes	1	0	0	0	0
David Schill (goalie)	2	0	0	0	0
Robert Horyna (goalie)	7	0	0	0	0

GOALTENDING

	Games	Min.	Goals	SO	Avg.
Felix Potvin	35	2070	101(1)	2	2.93
Damian Rhodes	43	2454	148(8)	0	3.62
Robert Horyna	7	220	17	0	4.64
David Schill	2	113	10	0	5.31

SPRINGFIELD INDIANS

SCORING

	Games	G	A	Pts.	Pen.
Shawn Evans	80	11	67	78	81
Joe Day	50	33	25	58	92
Terry Yake	53	21	34	55	63
Mike McHugh	70	23	31	54	51
Mark Greig	50	20	27	47	38
Yvon Corriveau	39	26	15	41	40
James Black	47	15	25	40	33
Chris Govedaris	43	14	25	39	55
Michel Picard	40	21	17	38	44
Denis Chalifoux	66	17	20	37	26
Mike Tomlak	39	16	21	37	24
Blair Atcheynum	62	16	21	37	64
Paul Cyr	43	11	18	29	30
Todd Richards	43	6	23	29	33
Brian Chapman	73	3	26	29	245
Daniel Shank	31	9	19	28	83
Jergus Baca	64	6	20	26	88
Kerry Russell	47	10	14	24	44
Scott Daniels	54	7	15	22	213
Chris Tancill	17	12	7	19	20
John Stevens	45	1	12	13	73
Karl Johnson	34	1	11	12	17
Dan Keczmer	18	3	4	7	10
Jukka Suonalainen	46	1	5	6	55
Scott Humeniuk	28	2	3	5	27
Jeff Harding	17	1	4	5	27
Mario Gosselin (goalie)	47	0	5	5	4
Kelly Ens	10	0	2	2	10
Chris Bright	8	1	0	1	6
Paul Cohen (goalie)	20	1	0	1	2
Scott Morrow	2	0	1	1	0

	Games	G	A	Pts.	Pen.
Scott Eichstadt	1	0	0	0	0
Lance Madsen (goalie)	4	0	0	0	0
Cam Brauer	5	0	0	0	6
Daryl Reaugh (goalie)	22	0	0	0	2
Corey Beaulieu	52	0	0	0	157

GOALTENDING

	Games	Min.	Goals	SO	Avg.
Paul Cohen	20	1126	58(2)	0	3.09
Mario Gosselin	47	2606	142(1)	0	3.27
Daryl Reaugh	22	1005	63(3)	0	3.76
Lance Madsen	4	96	8	0	5.00

UTICA DEVILS

SCORING

	Games	G	A	Pts.	Pen.
Jim Dowd	78	17	42	59	47
Jason Miller	71	23	32	55	31
Jeff Christian	76	27	24	51	198
Myles O'Connor	66	9	39	48	184
Brian Sullivan	70	23	24	47	58
Brent Severyn	80	11	33	44	211
Neil Brady	33	12	30	42	28
Mike Bodnarchuk	76	21	19	40	36
Jarrod Skalde	62	20	20	40	56
Ben Hankinson	77	17	16	33	186
Valeri Zelepukhin	22	20	9	29	8
Daryn McBride	51	10	19	29	47
Todd Copeland	80	4	23	27	96
Bill Guerin	22	13	10	23	6
Matt Ruchty	73	9	14	23	250
Bill Huard	62	9	11	20	233
Dean Malkoc	66	1	11	12	274
Jamie Huscroft	50	4	7	11	224
David Emma	15	4	7	11	12
Tommy Albelin	11	4	6	10	4
Petr Kuchyna	53	3	6	9	22
Kevin Kerr	19	3	3	6	25
Alexander Semak	7	3	2	5	0
Jon Morris	7	1	4	5	0
Kevin Dean	23	0	3	3	6
Rob Krauss	5	0	1	1	14
Doug Dadswell (goalie)	22	0	1	1	10
Corey Schwab (goalie)	24	0	1	1	8
Chad Erickson (goalie)	44	0	1	1	0
Dave Barr	1	0	0	0	7
Kris Miller	1	0	0	0	0
Jason Simon	1	0	0	0	12
Patrik Sundstrom	1	0	0	0	0
David Craievich	9	0	0	0	4

GOALTENDING

	Games	Min.	Goals	SO	Avg.
Doug Dadswell	22	1168	67(1)	0	3.44
Chad Erickson	43	2341	147(1)	2	3.77
Corey Schwab	24	1322	95(2)	0	4.31

PLAYERS WITH TWO OR MORE TEAMS

SCORING

	Games	G	A	Pts.	Pen.
Scott Arniel, New Haven	11	3	3	6	10
Scott Arniel, Maine	14	4	4	8	8
Totals	25	7	7	14	18
Dave Baseggio, Rochester	29	5	11	16	14
Dave Baseggio, New Haven	31	3	19	22	8
Totals	60	8	30	38	22
Mike Butters, Adirondack	13	1	3	4	46
Mike Butters, Halifax	6	0	0	0	25
Mike Butters, New Haven	2	1	0	1	5
Totals	21	2	3	5	76
John Byce, Maine	55	29	21	50	41
John Byce, Baltimore	20	9	5	14	4
Totals	75	38	26	64	45

	Games	G	A	Pts.	Pen.
Byron Dafoe, New Haven (g)	7	0	0	0	0
Byron Dafoe, Baltimore (g)	33	0	1	1	4
Totals	40	0	1	1	4
Brian Dobbin, New Haven	33	16	21	37	20
Brian Dobbin, Maine	33	21	15	36	14
Totals	66	37	36	73	34
Mario Doyon, Halifax	9	0	0	0	22
Mario Doyon, New Haven	64	11	29	40	44
Totals	73	11	29	40	66
Eric Dubois, New Haven	1	0	0	0	0
Eric Dubois, Halifax	14	0	0	0	8
Totals	15	0	0	0	10
Craig Duncanson, Baltimore	46	20	26	46	98
Craig Duncanson, Moncton	19	12	9	21	6
Totals	65	32	35	67	104
Mark Ferner, Baltimore	57	7	38	45	67
Mark Ferner, St. John's	15	1	8	9	6
Totals	72	8	46	54	73
Bryan Fogarty, Halifax	2	0	0	0	2
Bryan Fogarty, New Haven	4	0	1	1	6
Totals	6	0	1	1	8
Lou Franceschetti, New Haven	25	6	7	13	59
Lou Franceschetti, Rochester	49	15	25	40	64
Totals	74	21	32	53	123
Eric Germain, Moncton	3	0	2	2	4
Eric Germain, Binghamton	47	3	6	9	86
Totals	50	3	8	11	90
Scott Gordon, Halifax (g)	9	0	0	0	2
Scott Gordon, New Haven (g)	4	0	0	0	0
Totals	13	0	0	0	2
David Haas, Cape Breton	16	3	7	10	32
David Haas, New Haven	50	13	23	36	97
Totals	66	16	30	46	129
Brent Hughes, Baltimore	55	25	29	54	190
Brent Hughes, Maine	12	6	4	10	34
Totals	67	31	33	64	224
Jeff Jablonski, New Haven	1	0	0	0	0
Jeff Jablonski, Capital District	4	1	1	2	0
Totals	5	1	1	2	0
Tom Karalis, Moncton	6	0	0	0	4
Tom Karalis, Binghamton	2	0	1	1	0
Totals	8	0	1	1	4
Rob Krauss, Adirondack	7	0	1	1	32
Rob Krauss, Utica	5	0	1	1	14
Totals	12	0	2	2	46
Guy Larose, Binghamton	30	10	11	21	36
Guy Larose, St. John's	15	7	7	14	26
Totals	45	17	18	35	62
Bill McDougall, Adirondack	45	28	24	52	112
Bill McDougall, Cape Breton	22	8	18	26	36
Totals	67	36	42	78	148
Max Middendorf, Cape Breton	51	20	19	39	108
Max Middendorf, Adirondack	6	3	5	8	12
Totals	57	23	24	47	120
Daryl Noren, Halifax	3	0	0	0	0
Daryl Noren, New Haven	34	11	9	20	22
Totals	37	11	9	20	22
Bill Pye, Rochester (g)	7	0	0	0	0
Bill Pye, New Haven (g)	4	0	0	0	0
Totals	11	0	0	0	0
Alex Roberts, Adirondack	16	1	3	4	12
Alex Roberts, Capital District	5	0	1	1	6
Totals	21	1	4	5	18
Martin Rucinsky, Cape Breton	35	11	12	23	34
Martin Rucinsky, Halifax	7	1	1	2	6
Totals	42	12	13	25	40
Andy Rymsha, New Haven	16	0	5	5	20
Andy Rymsha, Halifax	44	4	7	11	54
Totals	60	4	12	16	74
Daniel Shank, Adirondack	27	13	21	34	112
Daniel Shank, Springfield	31	9	19	28	83
Totals	58	22	40	62	195
Sergei Shendelev, Maine	24	0	2	2	10
Sergei Shendelev, New Haven	7	0	0	0	10
Totals	31	0	2	2	20

	Games	G	A	Pts.	Pen.
Dennis Smith, Maine	59	2	32	34	63
Dennis Smith, Baltimore	17	1	4	5	23
Totals	76	3	36	39	86
Vern Smith, New Haven	4	0	0	0	5
Vern Smith, Capital District	17	1	5	6	6
Totals	21	1	5	6	11
Mike Stevens, St. John's	30	13	11	24	65
Mike Stevens, Binghamton	44	15	15	30	87
Totals	74	28	26	54	152
Chris Tancill, Springfield	17	12	7	19	20
Chris Tancill, Adirondack	50	36	34	70	42
Totals	67	48	41	89	62
John Tanner, New Haven (g)	16	0	0	0	16
John Tanner, Halifax (g)	12	0	0	0	2
Totals	28	0	0	0	18
Brad Turner, New Haven	32	6	11	17	58
Brad Turner, Capital District	35	3	6	9	17
Totals	67	9	17	26	75
Nick Vitucci, Maine (g)	1	0	0	0	0
Nick Vitucci, Hershey (g)	4	0	0	0	0
Totals	5	0	0	0	0
Wes Walz, Maine	21	13	11	24	38
Wes Walz, Hershey	41	13	28	41	37
Totals	62	26	39	65	75

GOALTENDING

	Games	Min.	Goals	SO	Avg.
Byron Dafoe, N.H.	7	364	22	0	3.63
Byron Dafoe, Bal.	33	1847	119(5)	0	3.87
Totals	40	2211	141(5)	0	3.83
Scott Gordon, Hal.	7	424	27	0	3.82
Scott Gordon, N.H.	4	239	11(1)	0	2.76
Totals	11	663	38(1)	0	3.44
Bill Pye, Rochester	7	272	13(2)	0	2.87
Bill Pye, New Haven	4	200	19	0	5.70
Totals	11	472	32(2)	0	4.07
John Tanner, N.H.	16	908	57(1)	0	3.77
John Tanner, Halifax	12	672	29(2)	2	2.59
Totals	28	1580	86(3)	2	3.27
Nick Vitucci, Maine	1	65	3	0	2.77
Nick Vitucci, Hershey	4	191	15	0	4.71
Totals	5	256	18	0	4.22

( )—Empty-net goals (do not count against a goaltender's average).

1992 CALDER CUP PLAYOFFS

RESULTS

FIRST ROUND

Series "A"

	W	L	Pts.	GF	GA
Moncton	4	3	8	21	21
Fredericton	3	4	6	21	21

(Moncton won series, 4-3)

Series "B"

	W	L	Pts.	GF	GA
St. John's	4	1	8	26	20
Cape Breton	1	4	2	20	26

(St. John's won series, 4-1)

Series "C"

	W	L	Pts.	GF	GA
Springfield	4	3	8	26	25
Capital District	3	4	6	25	26

(Springfield won series, 4-3)

Series "D"

	W	L	Pts.	GF	GA
Adirondack	4	1	8	23	16
New Haven	1	4	2	16	23

(Adirondack won series, 4-1)

Series "E"

	W	L	Pts.	GF	GA
Binghamton	4	0	8	21	15
Utica	0	4	0	15	21

(Binghamton won series, 4-0)

Series "F"

	W	L	Pts.	GF	GA
Rochester	4	2	8	20	16
Hershey	2	4	4	16	20

(Rochester won series, 4-2)

SECOND ROUND

Series "G"

	W	L	Pts.	GF	GA
St. John's	4	0	8	26	13
Moncton	0	4	0	13	26

(St. John's won series, 4-0)

Series "H"

	W	L	Pts.	GF	GA
Adirondack	4	0	8	13	5
Springfield	0	4	0	5	13

(Adirondack won series, 4-0)

Series "J"

	W	L	Pts.	GF	GA
Rochester	4	3	8	22	20
Binghamton	3	4	6	20	22

(Rochester won series, 4-3)

DIVISION CHAMPIONS ROUND

Series "K"

	W	L	Pts.	GF	GA
Adirondack	2	1	4	10	8
Rochester	1	2	2	8	10

(Adirondack won series, 2-1)

FINALS—FOR THE CALDER CUP

Series "L"

	W	L	Pts.	GF	GA
Adirondack	4	3	8	27	23
St. John's	3	4	6	23	27

(Adirondack won series, 4-3)

— 155 —

INDIVIDUAL LEADERS

Goals: Lonnie Loach, Adirondack (13)
Assists: Mike Sillinger, Adirondack (19)
Points: Mike Sillinger, Adirondack (28)
Penalty minutes: Todd Gillingham, St. John's (80)
Goaltending average: Allan Bester, Adirondack (2.56)
Shutouts: Allan Bester, Adirondack (1)
David Littman, Rochester (1)
Mike O'Neill, Moncton (1)

TOP SCORERS

	Games	G	A	Pts.
Mike Sillinger, Adirondack	15	9	19	28
Andrew McKim, St. John's	16	11	12	23
Mike Eastwood, St. John's	16	9	10	19
Ken Quinney, Adirondack	19	7	12	19
Lonnie Loach, Adirondack	19	13	4	17
Rob Zamuner, Binghamton	11	8	9	17
Chris Tancill, Adirondack	19	7	9	16
Mark Ferner, St. John's	14	2	14	16
Yanick Perreault, St. John's	16	7	8	15
Greg Johnston, St. John's	16	8	6	14
Jody Gage, Rochester	16	5	9	14
Sheldon Kennedy, Adirondack	16	5	9	14
Kent Manderville, St. John's	12	5	9	14

INDIVIDUAL STATISTICS

ADIRONDACK RED WINGS

(Winner of 1991 Calder Cup playoffs)

SCORING

	Games	G	A	Pts.	Pen.
Mike Sillinger	15	9	19	28	12
Ken Quinney	19	7	12	19	9
Lonnie Loach	19	13	4	17	10
Chris Tancill	19	7	9	16	31
Sheldon Kennedy	16	5	9	14	12
Gary Shuchuk	19	4	9	13	18
Bobby Dollas	18	7	4	11	22
Micah Aivazoff	19	2	8	10	25
Marc Potvin	19	5	4	9	57
Chris Luongo	19	3	5	8	10
Stewart Malgunas	18	2	6	8	28
Keith Primeau	9	1	7	8	27
Bob Wilkie	16	2	5	7	12
Kelly Hurd	8	1	4	5	2
Martin Lapointe	8	2	2	4	4
Dennis Vial	17	1	3	4	43
Bruce Boudreau	4	1	1	2	2
Kirk Tomlinson	8	1	0	1	17
Max Middendorf	5	0	1	1	16
Jason York	5	0	1	1	0
Gord Kruppke	16	0	1	1	52
Guy Dupuis	3	0	0	0	4
Jim Cummins	5	0	0	0	19
Allan Bester (goalie)	19	0	0	0	12

GOALTENDING

	Games	Min.	Goals	SO	Avg.
Allan Bester	19	1174	50(2)	1	2.56

BINGHAMTON RANGERS

(Lost quarterfinals to Rochester, 4-3)

SCORING

	Games	G	A	Pts.	Pen.
Rob Zamuner	11	8	9	17	8
Mike Stevens	11	7	6	13	45
Jeff Bloemberg	11	1	10	11	10
Don Biggs	11	3	7	10	8
Chris Cichocki	6	5	4	9	4
Mike Hurlbut	11	2	7	9	8
Peter Laviolette	11	2	7	9	9
Jody Hull	11	5	2	7	4
Daniel Lacroix	11	2	4	6	28
Doug Weight	4	1	4	5	6
Brian McReynolds	7	2	2	4	12
Ross Fitzpatrick	10	1	3	4	2
Shaun Sabol	11	1	2	3	10
Steven King	10	2	0	2	14
Darren Colbourne	2	1	0	1	0

	Games	G	A	Pts.	Pen.
Peter Fiorentino	5	0	1	1	24
John Mokosak	9	0	1	1	14
Ric Bennett	11	0	1	1	23
Mark Laforest (goalie)	11	0	1	1	4
David Quinn	2	0	0	0	0
Eric Germain	3	0	0	0	0
Mario Thyer	3	0	0	0	0
Joe Paterson	5	0	0	0	4

GOALTENDING

	Games	Min.	Goals	SO	Avg.
Mark Laforest	11	662	34(1)	0	3.08

CAPE BRETON OILERS

(Lost in first round to St. John's, 4-1)

SCORING

	Games	G	A	Pts.	Pen.
Shaun VanAllen	5	3	7	10	14
Dan Currie	5	4	5	9	4
Steven Rice	5	4	4	8	10
Shjon Podein	5	3	1	4	2
Greg Hawgood	3	2	2	4	0
Tomas Srsen	5	2	2	4	4
Tomas Kapusta	5	1	2	3	2
Brad Werenka	5	0	3	3	6
Chris Joseph	5	0	2	2	8
Scott Thornton	5	1	0	1	8
Bill McDougall	4	0	1	1	8
John Blessman	5	0	1	1	2
John Kordic	5	0	1	1	53
Wayne Cowley (goalie)	1	0	0	0	0
Craig Fisher	1	0	0	0	0
Peter Ing (goalie)	1	0	0	0	0
Tim Tisdale	2	0	0	0	2
Collin Bauer	3	0	0	0	7
Richard Borgo	3	0	0	0	6
Norm Foster (goalie)	3	0	0	0	0
Marc Laforge	4	0	0	0	24
Francois Leroux	5	0	0	0	8

GOALTENDING

	Games	Min.	Goals	SO	Avg.
Wayne Cowley	1	61	3	0	2.95
Norm Foster	3	193	14	0	4.35
Peter Ing	1	60	9	0	9.00

CAPITAL DISTRICT ISLANDERS

(Lost in first round to Springfield, 4-3)

SCORING

	Games	G	A	Pts.	Pen.
Greg Parks	7	5	8	13	4

	Games	G	A	Pts.	Pen.
Jeff Sharples	7	6	5	11	4
Lee Giffin	7	3	3	6	18
Richard Kromm	7	2	3	5	6
Brent Grieve	7	3	1	4	16
Chris Pryor	7	2	2	4	18
Rob Vanderydt	7	0	4	4	2
Travis Green	7	0	4	4	21
Derek Laxdal	4	1	1	2	10
Dean Chynoweth	6	1	1	2	39
David Chyzowski	6	1	1	2	23
Wayne Doucet	7	1	1	2	6
Phil Huber	7	0	2	2	10
Graeme Townshend	4	0	2	2	0
Stephane Robitaille	7	0	1	1	2
John Blum	1	0	0	0	2
Kevin Cheveldayoff	7	0	0	0	22
Rick Hayward	7	0	0	0	58
Danny Lorenz (goalie)	7	0	0	0	4

GOALTENDING

	Games	Min.	Goals	SO	Avg.
Danny Lorenz	7	442	25(1)	0	3.39

FREDERICTON CANADIENS

(Lost in first round to Moncton, 4-3)

SCORING

	Games	G	A	Pts.	Pen.
Patrick Lebeau	7	4	5	9	10
Paul DiPietro	7	3	4	7	8
Ed Ronan	7	5	1	6	6
Jesse Belanger	7	3	3	6	2
Stephane Richer	7	0	5	5	18
Sean Hill	7	1	3	4	6
Luc Gauthier	7	1	1	2	26
John Ferguson	5	1	1	2	4
Pierre Sevigny	7	1	1	2	26
Tom Sagissor	3	0	2	2	2
Mario Roberge	7	0	2	2	20
Eric Charron	6	1	0	1	4
Steve Larouche	7	1	0	1	0
Lindsay Vallis	4	0	1	1	7
Alain Cote	7	0	1	1	4
Gerry Fleming	1	0	0	0	7
John LeClair	2	0	0	0	4
Marc Labelle	3	0	0	0	6
Darcy Simon	4	0	0	0	13
Frederic Chabot (goalie)	7	0	0	0	2
Donald Dufresne	7	0	0	0	10

GOALTENDING

	Games	Min.	Goals	SO	Avg.
Frederic Chabot	7	457	20(1)	0	2.63

HERSHEY BEARS

(Lost in first round to Rochester, 4-2)

SCORING

	Games	G	A	Pts.	Pen.
Tim Tookey	6	4	2	6	4
Al Conroy	6	4	2	6	12
Bill H. Armstrong	6	2	2	4	6
Pat Murray	6	1	2	3	0
Wes Walz	6	1	2	3	0
Martin Hostak	6	1	2	3	2
Mark Freer	6	0	3	3	2
Darren Rumble	6	0	3	3	2
Ryan McGill	6	1	1	2	4
Dave Fenyves	6	1	1	2	10
Corey Foster	6	1	1	2	5
Len Barrie	3	0	2	2	32
Dale Kushner	6	0	2	2	23
Chris Jensen	6	0	1	1	2

	Games	G	A	Pts.	Pen.
Mike Stothers	6	0	1	1	6
William Armstrong	3	0	0	0	2
Eric Dandenault	3	0	0	0	4
Lance Pitlick	3	0	0	0	4
Jim Waite (goalie)	6	0	0	0	0

GOALTENDING

	Games	Min.	Goals	SO	Avg.
Jim Waite	6	360	19(1)	0	3.17

MONCTON HAWKS

(Lost quarterfinals to St. John's, 4-0)

SCORING

	Games	G	A	Pts.	Pen.
Stu Barnes	11	3	9	12	6
Craig Duncanson	11	6	4	10	10
Tyler Larter	10	5	5	10	33
Russ Romaniuk	10	5	4	9	19
Kent Paynter	11	2	6	8	25
Scott Levins	11	3	4	7	30
Darren Veitch	11	0	6	6	2
John LeBlanc	10	3	2	5	8
Bob Joyce	10	0	5	5	9
Dave MacIntyre	11	2	2	4	16
Dallas Eakins	11	2	1	3	16
Ken Gernander	8	1	1	2	2
Rob Cowie	5	1	1	2	0
Jason Cirone	10	1	1	2	8
Rudy Poeschek	11	0	2	2	46
Kris Draper	4	0	1	1	6
Claude Julien	4	0	1	1	4
Tony Joseph	6	0	1	1	25
Rob Murray	8	0	1	1	56
Derek Langille	1	0	0	0	0
Sean Gauthier (goalie)	2	0	0	0	0
Mark Kumpel	2	0	0	0	0
Mike O'Neill (goalie)	11	0	0	0	0

GOALTENDING

	Games	Min.	Goals	SO	Avg.
Mike O'Neill	11	670	43(2)	1	3.85
Sean Gauthier	2	26	2	0	4.62

NEW HAVEN NIGHTHAWKS

(Lost in first round to Adirondack, 4-0)

SCORING

	Games	G	A	Pts.	Pen.
Stan Drulia	5	2	4	6	4
Jeff Jackson	5	0	5	5	6
Paul Willett	5	3	1	4	2
Kent Hulst	5	2	2	4	0
Oleg Mikoulchik	4	1	3	4	6
John Anderson	4	0	4	4	0
David Haas	5	3	0	3	13
Jerome Bechard	5	0	3	3	7
Jerry Tarrant	5	1	1	2	4
David Latta	5	1	1	2	4
Scott Schneider	4	1	1	2	7
Mario Doyon	5	1	1	2	2
Rene Chapdelaine	4	0	2	2	0
Eric Ricard	2	1	0	1	2
Andrei Kovalev	1	0	1	1	0
Al Tuer	4	0	1	1	12
Shawn McCosh	5	0	1	1	0
Trevor Stienburg	1	0	0	0	2
Scott Gordon (goalie)	2	0	0	0	2
Dave Baseggio	3	0	0	0	2
George Maneluk (goalie)	3	0	0	0	0
Jim Sprott	3	0	0	0	17

GOALTENDING	Games	Min.	Goals	SO	Avg.
George Maneluk	3	216	13(1)	0	3.61
Scott Gordon	2	119	9(1)	0	4.54

GOALTENDING	Games	Min.	Goals	SO	Avg.
Damian Rhodes	6	331	16(1)	0	2.90
Felix Potvin	11	642	41(2)	0	3.83

ROCHESTER AMERICANS
(Lost semifinals to Adirondack, 2-1)

SCORING

	Games	G	A	Pts.	Pen.
Jody Gage	16	5	9	14	10
Dan Frawley	16	7	5	12	35
Don McSween	16	5	6	11	18
Bill Houlder	16	5	6	11	4
Rick Vaive	16	4	4	8	10
Lou Franceschetti	15	3	5	8	31
Jason Winch	12	2	6	8	0
Peter Ciavaglia	6	2	5	7	6
Greg Brown	16	1	5	6	4
Bob Corkum	8	0	6	6	8
Brad Rubachuk	13	4	0	4	19
Ian Boyce	16	3	1	4	0
Lindy Ruff	13	0	4	4	16
Steve Ludzik	14	2	1	3	8
Chris Snell	10	2	1	3	6
Sean O'Donnell	16	1	2	3	21
Joel Savage	9	2	0	2	8
Keith Carney	2	0	2	2	0
Darcy Loewen	4	0	1	1	8
Scott Thomas	9	0	1	1	17
John Bradley (goalie)	1	0	0	0	0
Bill Pye (goalie)	1	0	0	0	0
Jiri Sejba	2	0	0	0	0
Brad Miller	11	0	0	0	61
David Littman (goalie)	15	0	0	0	4

GOALTENDING	Games	Min.	Goals	SO	Avg.
Bill Pye	1	60	2	0	2.00
David Littman	15	879	43(1)	1	2.94
John Bradley	1	20	2	0	6.00

ST. JOHN'S MAPLE LEAFS
(Lost finals to Adirondack, 4-3)

SCORING

	Games	G	A	Pts.	Pen.
Andrew McKim	16	11	12	23	4
Mike Eastwood	16	9	10	19	16
Mark Ferner	14	2	14	16	39
Yanic Perreault	16	7	8	15	4
Greg Johnston	16	8	6	14	10
Kent Manderville	12	5	9	14	14
Jeff Serowik	16	4	9	13	22
Bruce Bell	10	4	7	11	8
Todd Gillingham	16	4	7	11	80
Kevin Maguire	11	3	7	10	43
Rob Cimetta	10	3	7	10	24
Rob Pearson	13	5	4	9	40
Dave Tomlinson	12	4	5	9	6
Curtis Hunt	12	1	5	6	36
Drake Berehowsky	6	0	5	5	21
Ted Crowley	10	3	1	4	11
Joe Sacco	1	1	1	2	0
Len Esau	13	0	2	2	14
Todd Hawkins	7	1	0	1	10
Terry Chitaroni	2	0	1	1	5
Keith Osborne	4	0	1	1	2
Kevin McClelland	5	0	1	1	9
Joel Quenneville	16	0	1	1	10
Mike MacWilliam	2	0	0	0	8
Damian Rhodes (goalie)	6	0	0	0	0
Felix Potvin (goalie)	11	0	0	0	2

SPRINGFIELD INDIANS
(Lost quarterfinals to Adirondack, 4-0)

SCORING

	Games	G	A	Pts.	Pen.
Mike McHugh	11	4	7	11	25
Daniel Shank	8	8	0	8	48
Shawn Evans	11	0	8	8	16
Terry Yake	8	3	4	7	2
Jergus Baca	11	0	6	6	20
James Black	10	3	2	5	18
Chris Govedaris	11	3	2	5	25
Brian Chapman	10	2	2	4	25
John Stevens	11	1	3	4	27
Paul Cyr	11	0	3	3	12
Todd Richards	8	0	3	3	2
Michel Picard	11	2	0	2	34
Kerry Russell	5	1	1	2	2
Blair Atcheyman	6	1	1	2	2
Mark Greig	9	1	1	2	20
Denis Chalifoux	4	1	0	1	4
Jukka Suonalainan	9	1	0	1	12
Mike Lenarduzzi (goalie)	1	0	0	0	0
Patrick Poulin	1	0	0	0	0
Daryl Reaugh (goalie)	1	0	0	0	0
Corey Beaulieu	2	0	0	0	2
Dan Keczmer	4	0	0	0	6
Scott Morrow	5	0	0	0	9
Paul Cohen (goalie)	6	0	0	0	8
Mario Gosselin (goalie)	6	0	0	0	2
Scott Daniels	10	0	0	0	32

GOALTENDING	Games	Min.	Goals	SO	Avg.
Daryl Reaugh	1	39	1	0	1.54
Mike Lenarduzzi	1	39	2	0	3.08
Mario Gosselin	6	319	18	0	3.39
Paul Cohen	6	282	16(1)	0	3.40

UTICA DEVILS
(Lost in first round to Binghamton, 4-0)

SCORING

	Games	G	A	Pts.	Pen.
Jarrod Skalde	4	3	1	4	8
Ben Hankinson	4	3	1	4	2
Todd Copeland	4	2	2	4	2
Jim Dowd	4	2	2	4	4
Bill Guerin	4	1	3	4	14
Jason Miller	4	1	3	4	0
Brian Sullivan	4	0	4	4	6
David Emma	4	1	1	2	2
Bill Huard	4	1	1	2	4
Mike Bodnarchuk	4	0	2	2	0
Dean Malkoc	4	0	2	2	6
Scott Pellerin	3	1	0	1	0
Brent Severyn	4	0	1	1	4
David Craievich	1	0	0	0	4
Doug Dadswell (goalie)	2	0	0	0	0
Chad Erickson (goalie)	2	0	0	0	2
Jeff Christian	4	0	0	0	16
Petr Kuchyna	4	0	0	0	2
Matt Ruchty	4	0	0	0	25

GOALTENDING	Games	Min.	Goals	SO	Avg.
Doug Dadswell	2	119	8(1)	0	4.03
Chad Erickson	2	127	11(1)	0	5.20

1991-92 AWARD WINNERS

ALL-STAR TEAMS

First team	Pos.	Second team
Felix Potvin, St. John's	G	Dave Littman, Rochester
Greg Hawgood, Cape Breton	D	Joel Quenneville, St. John's
Shawn Evans, Springfield	D	Stephane Richer, Fred.
Shaun Van Allen, C.B.	C	Tim Tookey, Hershey
Chris Tancill, Adirondack	RW	Stan Drulia, New Haven
John Anderson, New Haven	LW	Dan Currie, Cape Breton

TROPHY WINNERS

John B. Sollenberger Trophy: Shaun Van Allen, Cape Breton
Les Cunningham Plaque: John Anderson, New Haven
Harry (Hap) Holmes Memorial Trophy: David Littman, Rochester
Dudley (Red) Garrett Memorial Trophy: Felix Potvin, St. John's
Eddie Shore Plaque: Greg Hawgood, Cape Breton
Fred Hunt Memorial Award: John Anderson, New Haven
Louis A.R. Pieri Memorial Award: Doug Carpenter, New Haven
Baz Bastien Trophy: Felix Potvin, St. John's
Jack Butterfield Trophy: Allan Bester, Adirondack

ALL-TIME AWARD WINNERS

JOHN B. SOLLENBERGER TROPHY
(Leading scorer)

Season	Player, Team
1936-37	Jack Markle, Syracuse
1937-38	Jack Markle, Syracuse
1938-39	Don Deacon, Pittsburgh
1939-40	Norm Locking, Syracuse
1940-41	Les Cunningham, Cleveland
1941-42	Pete Kelly, Springfield
1942-43	Wally Kilrea, Hershy
1943-44	Tommy Burlington, Cleveland
1944-45	Bob Gracie, Pittsburgh
	Bob Walton, Pittsburgh
1945-46	Les Douglas, Indianapolis
1946-47	Phil Hergesheimer, Philadelphia
1947-48	Carl Liscombe, Providence
1948-49	Sid Smith, Pittsburgh
1949-50	Les Douglas, Cleveland
1950-51	Ab DeMarco, Buffalo
1951-52	Ray Powell, Providence
1952-53	Eddie Olson, Cleveland
1953-54	George Sullivan, Hershey
1954-55	Eddie Olson, Cleveland
1955-56	Zellio Toppazzini, Providence
1956-57	Fred Glover, Cleveland
1957-58	Willie Marshall, Hershey
1958-59	Bill Hicke, Rochester
1959-60	Fred Glover, Cleveland
1960-61	Bill Sweeney, Springfield
1961-62	Bill Sweeney, Springfield
1962-63	Bill Sweeney, Springfield
1963-64	Gerry Ehman, Rochester
1964-65	Art Stratton, Buffalo
1965-66	Dick Gamble, Rochester
1966-67	Gordon Labossiere, Quebec
1967-68	Simon Nolet, Quebec
1968-69	Jeannot Gilbert, Hershey
1969-70	Jude Drouin, Montreal
1970-71	Fred Speck, Baltimore
1971-72	Don Blackburn, Providence
1972-73	Yvon Lambert, Nova Scotia
1973-74	Steve West, New Haven
1974-75	Doug Gibson, Rochester
1975-76	Jean-Guy Gratton, Hershey
1976-77	Andre Peloffy, Springfield
1977-78	Gord Brooks, Philadelphia
	Rick Adduono, Rochester
1978-79	Bernie Johnston, Maine
1979-80	Norm Dube, Nova Scotia
1980-81	Mark Lofthouse, Hershey
1981-82	Mike Kasczyki, New Brunswick
1982-83	Ross Yates, Binghamton
1983-84	Claude Larose, Sherbrooke
1984-85	Paul Gardner, Binghamton
1985-86	Paul Gardner, Rochester
1986-87	Tim Tookey, Hershey
1987-88	Bruce Boudreau, Springfield

Season	Player, Team
1988-89	Stephan Lebeau, Sherbrooke
1989-90	Paul Ysebaert, Utica
1990-91	Kevin Todd, Utica
1991-92	Shaun Van Allen, Cape Breton

LES CUNNINGHAM PLAQUE
(Most Valuable Player)

Season	Player, Team
1947-48	Carl Liscombe, Providence
1948-49	Carl Liscombe, Providence
1949-50	Les Douglas, Cleveland
1950-51	Ab DeMarco, Buffalo
1951-52	Ray Powell, Providence
1952-53	Eddie Olson, Cleveland
1953-54	George "Red" Sullivan, Hershey
1954-55	Ross Lowe, Springfield
1955-56	Johnny Bower, Providence
1956-57	Johnny Bower, Providence
1957-58	Johnny Bower, Cleveland
1958-59	Bill Hicke, Rochester
	Rudy Migay, Rochester
1959-60	Fred Glover, Cleveland
1960-61	Phil Maloney, Buffalo
1961-62	Fred Glover, Cleveland
1962-63	Denis DeJordy, Buffalo
1963-64	Fred Glover, Cleveland
1964-65	Art Stratton, Buffalo
1965-66	Dick Gamble, Rochester
1966-67	Mike Nykoluk, Hershey
1967-68	Dave Creighton, Providence
1968-69	Gilles Villemure, Buffalo
1969-70	Gilles Villemure, Buffalo
1970-71	Fred Speck, Baltimore
1971-72	Garry Peters, Boston
1972-73	Billy Inglis, Cincinnati
1973-74	Art Stratton, Rochester
1974-75	Doug Gibson, Rochester
1975-76	Ron Andruff, Nova Scotia
1976-77	Doug Gibson, Rochester
1977-78	Blake Dunlop, Maine
1978-79	Rocky Saganiuk, New Brunswick
1979-80	Norm Dube, Nova Scotia
1980-81	Pelle Lindbergh, Maine
1981-82	Mike Kasczyki, New Brunswick
1982-83	Ross Yates, Binghamton
1983-84	Mal Davis, Rochester
	Garry Lariviere, St. Catharines
1984-85	Paul Gardner, Binghamton
1985-86	Paul Gardner, Rochester
1986-87	Tim Tookey, Hershey
1987-88	Jody Gage, Rochester
1988-89	Stephan Lebeau, Sherbrooke
1989-90	Paul Ysebaert, Utica
1990-91	Kevin Todd, Utica
1991-92	John Anderson, Hew Haven

HARRY (HAP) HOLMES MEMORIAL TROPHY
(Outstanding goaltender)

Season	Player, Team
1936-37	Bert Gardiner, Philadelphia
1937-38	Frank Brimsek, Providence
1938-39	Alfie Moore, Hershey
1939-40	Moe Roberts, Cleveland
1940-41	Chuck Rayner, Springfield
1941-42	Bill Beveridge, Cleveland
1942-43	Gordie Bell, Buffalo
1943-44	Nick Damore, Hershey
1944-45	Yves Nadon, Buffalo
1945-46	Connie Dion, St. Louis-Buffalo
1946-47	Baz Bastien, Pittsburgh
1947-48	Baz Bastien, Pittsburgh
1948-49	Baz Bastien, Pittsburgh
1949-50	Gil Mayer, Pittsburgh
1950-51	Gil Mayer, Pittsburgh
1951-52	Johnny Bower, Cleveland
1952-53	Gil Mayer, Pittsburgh
1953-54	Jacques Plante, Buffalo
1954-55	Gil Mayer, Pittsburgh
1955-56	Gil Mayer, Pittsburgh
1956-57	Johnny Bower, Providence
1957-58	Johnny Bower, Cleveland
1958-59	Bob Perreault, Hershey
1959-60	Ed Chadwick, Rochester
1960-61	Marcel Paille, Springfield
1961-62	Marcel Paille, Springfield
1962-63	Denis DeJordy, Buffalo
1963-64	Roger Crozier, Pittsburgh
1964-65	Gerry Cheevers, Rochester
1965-66	Les Binkley, Cleveland
1966-67	Andre Gill, Hershey
1967-68	Bob Perreault, Rochester
1968-69	Gilles Villemure, Buffalo
1969-70	Gilles Villemure, Buffalo
1970-71	Gary Kurt, Cleveland
1971-72	Dan Bouchard, Boston
	Ross Brooks, Boston
1972-73	Michel Larocque, Nova Scotia
1973-74	Jim Shaw, Nova Scotia
	Dave Elenbaas, Nova Scotia
1974-75	Ed Walsh, Nova Scotia
	Dave Elenbaas, Nova Scotia
1975-76	Dave Elenbaas, Nova Scotia
	Ed Walsh, Nova Scotia
1976-77	Ed Walsh, Nova Scotia
	Dave Elenbaas, Nova Scotia
1977-78	Bob Holland, Nova Scotia
	Maurice Barrette, Nova Scotia
1978-79	Pete Peeters, Maine
	Robbie Moore, Maine
1979-80	Rick St. Croix, Maine
	Robbie Moore, Maine
1980-81	Pelle Lindbergh, Maine
	Robbie Moore, Maine
1981-82	Bob Janecyk, New Brunswick
	Warren Skorodenski, New Brunswick
1982-83	Brian Ford, Fredericton
	Clint Malarchuk, Fredericton
1983-84	Brian Ford, Fredericton
1984-85	Jon Casey, Baltimore
1985-86	Sam St. Laurent, Maine
	Karl Friesen, Maine
1986-87	Vincent Riendeau, Sherbrooke
1987-88	Vincent Riendeau, Sherbrooke
	Jocelyn Perreault, Sherbrooke
1988-89	Randy Exelby, Sherbrooke
	Francois Gravel, Sherbrooke
1989-90	Jean Claude Bergeron, Sherbrooke
	Andre Racicot, Sherbrooke
1990-91	David Littman, Rochester
	Darcy Wakaluk, Rochester
1991-92	David Littman, Rochester

Beginning with the 1983-84 season, the award goes to the top goaltending team with each goaltender having played a minimum of 25 games for the team with the fewest goals against.

DUDLEY (RED) GARRETT MEMORIAL TROPHY
(Top rookie)

Season	Player, Team
1947-48	Bob Solinger, Cleveland
1948-49	Terry Sawchuk, Indianapolis
1949-50	Paul Meger, Buffalo
1950-51	Wally Hergesheimer, Cleveland
1951-52	Earl "Dutch" Reibel, Indianapolis
1952-53	Guyle Fielder, St. Louis
1953-54	Don Marshall, Buffalo
1954-55	Jimmy Anderson, Springfield
1955-56	Bruce Cline, Providence
1956-57	Boris "Bo" Elik, Cleveland
1957-58	Bill Sweeney, Providence
1958-59	Bill Hicke, Rochester
1959-60	Stan Baluik, Providence
1960-61	Ronald "Chico" Maki, Buffalo
1961-62	Les Binkley, Cleveland
1962-63	Doug Robinson, Buffalo
1963-64	Roger Crozier, Pittsburgh
1964-65	Ray Cullen, Buffalo
1965-66	Mike Walton, Rochester
1966-67	Bob Rivard, Quebec
1967-68	Gerry Desjardins, Cleveland
1968-69	Ron Ward, Rochester
1969-70	Jude Drouin, Montreal
1970-71	Fred Speck, Baltimore
1971-72	Terry Caffery, Cleveland
1972-73	Ron Anderson, Boston
1973-74	Rick Middleton, Providence
1974-75	Jerry Holland, Providence
1975-76	Greg Holst, Providence
	Pierre Mondou, Nova Scotia
1976-77	Rod Schutt, Nova Scotia
1977-78	Norm Dupont, Nova Scotia
1978-79	Mike Meeker, Binghamton
1979-80	Darryl Sutter, New Brunswick
1980-81	Pelle Lindbergh, Maine
1981-82	Bob Sullivan, Binghamton
1982-83	Mitch Lamoureux, Baltimore
1983-84	Claude Verret, Rochester
1984-85	Steve Thomas, St. Catharines
1985-86	Ron Hextall, Hershey
1986-87	Brett Hull, Moncton
1987-88	Mike Richard, Binghamton
1988-89	Stephan Lebeau, Sherbrooke
1989-90	Donald Audette, Rochester
1990-91	Patrick Lebeau, Fredericton
1991-92	Felix Potvin, St. John's

EDDIE SHORE PLAQUE
(Outstanding defenseman)

Season	Player, Team
1958-59	Steve Kraftcheck, Rochester
1959-60	Larry Hillman, Providence
1960-61	Bob McCord, Springfield
1961-62	Kent Douglas, Springfield
1962-63	Marc Reaume, Hershey
1963-64	Ted Harris, Cleveland
1964-65	Al Arbour, Rochester
1965-66	Jim Morrison, Quebec
1966-67	Bob McCord, Pittsburgh
1967-68	Bill Needham, Cleveland
1968-69	Bob Blackburn, Buffalo
1969-70	Noel Price, Springfield
1970-71	Marshall Johnston, Cleveland
1971-72	Noel Price, Nova Scotia
1972-73	Ray McKay, Cincinnati
1973-74	Gordon Smith, Springfield
1974-75	Joe Zanussi, Providence

Season	Player, Team
1975-76	Noel Price, Nova Scotia
1976-77	Brian Engblom, Nova Scotia
1977-78	Terry Murray, Maine
1978-79	Terry Murray, Maine
1979-80	Rick Vasko, Adirondack
1980-81	Craig Levie, Nova Scotia
1981-82	Dave Farrish, New Brunswick
1982-83	Greg Tebbutt, Baltimore
1983-84	Garry Lariviere, St. Catharines
1984-85	Richie Dunn, Binghamton
1985-86	Jim Wiemer, New Haven
1986-87	Brad Shaw, Binghamton
1987-88	Dave Fenyves, Hershey
1988-89	Dave Fenyves, Hershey
1989-90	Eric Weinrich, Utica
1990-91	Norm Maciver, Cape Breton
1991-92	Greg Hawgood, Cape Breton

FRED HUNT MEMORIAL AWARD

(Sportsmanship, determination and dedication)

Season	Player, Team
1977-78	Blake Dunlop, Maine
1978-79	Bernie Johnston, Maine
1979-80	Norm Dube, Nova Scotia
1980-81	Tony Cassolato, Hershey
1981-82	Mike Kasczyki, New Brunswick
1982-83	Ross Yates, Binghamton
1983-84	Claude Larose, Sherbrooke
1984-85	Paul Gardner, Binghamton
1985-86	Steve Tsujiura, Maine
1986-87	Glenn Merkosky, Adirondack
1987-88	Bruce Boudreau, Springfield
1988-89	Murray Eaves, Adirondack
1989-90	Murray Eaves, Adirondack
1990-91	Glenn Merkosky, Adirondack
1991-92	John Anderson, New Haven

LOUIS A.R. PIERI MEMORIAL AWARD

(Top coach)

Season	Coach, Team
1967-68	Vic Stasiuk, Quebec
1968-69	Frank Mathers, Hershey
1969-70	Fred Shero, Buffalo
1970-71	Terry Reardon, Baltimore
1971-72	Al MacNeil, Nova Scotia
1972-73	Floyd Smith, Cincinnati

Season	Coach, Team
1973-74	Don Cherry, Rochester
1974-75	John Muckler, Providence
1975-76	Chuck Hamilton, Hershey
1976-77	Al MacNeil, Nova Scotia
1977-78	Bob McCammon, Maine
1978-79	Parker MacDonald, New Haven
1979-80	Doug Gibson, Hershey
1980-81	Bob McCammon, Maine
1981-82	Orval Tessier, New Brunswick
1982-83	Jacques Demers, Fredericton
1983-84	Gene Ubriaco, Baltimore
1984-85	Bill Dineen, Adirondack
1985-86	Bill Dineen, Adirondack
1986-87	Larry Pleau, Binghamton
1987-88	John Paddock, Hershey
	Mike Milbury, Maine
1988-89	Tom McVie, Utica
1989-90	Jimmy Roberts, Springfield
1990-91	Don Lever, Rochester
1991-92	Doug Carpenter, New Haven

BAZ BASTIEN TROPHY

(Coaches pick as top goaltender)

Season	Player, Team
1983-84	Brian Ford, Fredericton
1984-85	Jon Casey, Baltimore
1985-86	Sam St. Laurent, Maine
1986-87	Mark Laforest, Adirondack
1987-88	Wendell Young, Hershey
1988-89	Randy Exelby, Sherbrooke
1989-90	Jean Claude Bergeron, Sherbrooke
1990-91	Mark Laforest, Binghamton
1991-92	Felix Potvin, St. John's

JACK BUTTERFIELD TROPHY

(Calder Cup playoff MVP)

Season	Player, Team
1983-84	Bud Stefanski, Maine
1984-85	Brian Skrudland, Sherbrooke
1985-86	Tim Tookey, Hershey
1986-87	Dave Fenyves, Rochester
1987-88	Wendell Young, Hershey
1988-89	Sam St. Laurent, Adirondack
1989-90	Jeff Hackett, Springfield
1990-91	Kay Whitmore, Springfield
1991-92	Alan Bester, Adirondack

ALL-TIME LEAGUE CHAMPIONS

	REGULAR-SEASON CHAMPION		PLAYOFF CHAMPION	
SEASON	Team	Coach	Team	Coach
1936-37	E—Philadelphia	Herb Gardiner	Syracuse	Eddie Powers
	W—Syracuse	Eddie Powers		
1937-38	E—Providence	Bun Cook	Providence	Bun Cook
	W—Cleveland	Bill Cook		
1938-39	E—Philadelphia	Herb Gardiner	Cleveland	Bill Cook
	W—Hershey	Herb Mitchell		
1939-40	E—Providence	Bun Cook	Providence	Bun Cook
	W—Indianapolis	Herb Lewis		
1940-41	E—Providence	Bun Cook	Cleveland	Bill Cook
	W—Cleveland	Bill Cook		
1941-42	E—Springfield	Johnny Mitchell	Indianapolis	Herb Lewis
	W—Indianapolis	Herb Lewis		
1942-43	—Hershey	Cooney Weiland	Buffalo	Art Chapman
1943-44	E—Hershey	Cooney Weiland	Buffalo	Art Chapman
	W—Cleveland	Bun Cook		
1944-45	E—Buffalo	Art Chapman	Cleveland	Bun Cook
	W—Cleveland	Bun Cook		
1945-46	E—Buffalo	Frank Beisler	Buffalo	Frank Beisler
	W—Indianapolis	Earl Seibert		
1946-47	E—Hershey	Don Penniston	Hershey	Don Penniston
	W—Cleveland	Bun Cook		
1947-48	E—Providence	Terry Reardon	Cleveland	Bun Cook
	W—Cleveland	Bun Cook		
1948-49	E—Providence	Terry Reardon	Providence	Terry Reardon
	W—St. Louis	Ebbie Goodfellow		

SEASON	REGULAR-SEASON CHAMPION Team	Coach	PLAYOFF CHAMPION Team	Coach
1949-50	E—Buffalo	Roy Goldsworthy	Indianapolis	Ott Heller
	W—Cleveland	Bun Cook		
1950-51	E—Buffalo	Roy Goldsworthy	Cleveland	Bun Cook
	W—Cleveland	Bun Cook		
1951-52	E—Hershey	John Crawford	Pittsburgh	King Clancy
	W—Pittsburgh	King Clancy		
1952-53	—Cleveland	Bun Cook	Cleveland	Bun Cook
1953-54	—Buffalo	Frank Eddolls	Cleveland	Bun Cook
1954-55	—Pittsburgh	Howie Meeker	Pittsburgh	Howie Meeker
1955-56	—Providence	John Crawford	Providence	John Crawford
1956-57	—Providence	John Crawford	Cleveland	Jack Gordon
1957-58	—Hershey	Frank Mathers	Hershey	Frank Mathers
1958-59	—Buffalo	Bobby Kirk	Hershey	Frank Mathers
1959-60	—Springfield	Pat Egan	Springfield	Pat Egan
1960-61	—Springfield	Pat Egan	Springfield	Pat Egan
1961-62	E—Springfield	Pat Egan	Springfield	Pat Egan
	W—Cleveland	Jack Gordon		
1962-63	E—Providence	Fern Flaman	Buffalo	Billy Reay
	W—Buffalo	Billy Reay		
1963-64	E—Quebec	Floyd Curry	Cleveland	Fred Glover
	W—Pittsburgh	Vic Stasiuk		
1964-65	E—Quebec	Bernie Geoffrion	Rochester	Joe Crozier
	W—Rochester	Joe Crozier		
1965-66	E—Quebec	Bernie Geoffrion	Rochester	Joe Crozier
	W—Rochester	Joe Crozier		
1966-67	E—Hershey	Frank Mathers	Pittsburgh	Baz Bastien
	W—Pittsburgh	Baz Bastien		
1967-68	E—Hershey	Frank Mathers	Rochester	Joe Crozier
	W—Rochester	Joe Crozier		
1968-69	E—Hershey	Frank Mathers	Hershey	Frank Mathers
	W—Buffalo	Fred Shero		
1969-70	E—Montreal	Al MacNeil	Buffalo	Fred Shero
	W—Buffalo	Fred Shero		
1970-71	E—Providence	Larry Wilson	Springfield	John Wilson
	W—Baltimore	Terry Reardon		
1971-72	E—Boston	Armond Guidolin	Nova Scotia	Al MacNeil
	W—Baltimore	Terry Reardon		
1972-73	E—Nova Scotia	Al MacNeil	Cincinnati	Floyd Smith
	W—Cincinnati	Floyd Smith		
1973-74	N—Rochester	Don Cherry	Hershey	Chuck Hamilton
	S—Baltimore	Terry Reardon		
1974-75	N—Providence	John Muckler	Springfield	Ron Stewart
	S—Virginia	Doug Barkley		
1975-76	N—Nova Scotia	Al MacNeil	Nova Scotia	Al MacNeil
	S—Hershey	Chuck Hamilton		
1976-77	—Nova Scotia	Al MacNeil	Nova Scotia	Al MacNeil
1977-78	N—Maine	Bob McCammon	Maine	Bob McCammon
	S—Rochester	Duane Rupp		
1978-79	N—Maine	Bob McCammon	Maine	Bob McCammon
	S—New Haven	Parker MacDonald		
1979-80	N—New Brunswick	Joe Crozier-Lou Angotti	Hershey	Doug Gibson
	S—New Haven	Parker MacDonald		
1980-81	N—Maine	Bob McCammon	Adirondack	Tom Webster-J.P. LeBlanc
	S—Hershey	Bryan Murray		
1981-82	N—New Brunswick	Orval Tessier	New Brunswick	Orval Tessier
	S—Binghamton	Larry Kish		
1982-83	N—Fredericton	Jacques Demers	Rochester	Mike Keenan
	S—Rochester	Mike Keenan		
1983-84	N—Fredericton	Earl Jessiman	Maine	John Paddock
	S—Baltimore	Gene Ubriaco		
1984-85	N—Maine	Tom McVie-John Paddock	Sherbrooke	Pierre Creamer
	S—Binghamton	Larry Pleau		
1985-86	N—Adirondack	Bill Dineen	Adirondack	Bill Dineen
	S—Hershey	John Paddock		
1986-87	N—Sherbrooke	Pierre Creamer	Rochester	John Van Boxmeer
	S—Rochester	John Van Boxmeer*		
1987-88	N—Maine	Mike Milbury	Hershey	John Paddock
	S—Hershey	John Paddock		
1988-89	N—Sherbrooke	Jean Hamel	Adirondack	Bill Dineen
	S—Adirondack	Bill Dineen		
1989-90	N—Sherbrooke	Jean Hamel	Springfield	Jimmy Roberts
	S—Rochester	John Van Boxmeer		
1990-91	N—Springfield	Jimmy Roberts	Springfield	Jimmy Roberts
	S—Rochester	Don Lever		
1991-92	N—Springfield	Jay Leach	Adirondack	Barry Melrose
	S—Binghamton	Ron Smith		
	A—Fredericton	Paulin Bordeleau		

*Rochester awarded division championship based on season-series record.

INTERNATIONAL HOCKEY LEAGUE

LEAGUE OFFICE

Commissioner
N. Thomas Berry Jr.
Chairman of the board of governors
Russell A. Parker
Vice chairman of the board of governors
Joseph E. Tierney Jr.
Consultants
N.R. (Bud) Poile/Jack Riley
Legal counsel
Robert P. Ufer
Director of marketing
Michael G. McCall

Director of information
Michael A. Meyers
Address
3850 Priority Way
South Drive
Suite 104
Indianapolis, IN 46240
Phone
317-573-3888
FAX
317-573-3880

Board of governors
Atlanta—David Bergman
Cincinnati—Doug Kirchhofer
Cleveland—Larry Gordon
Fort Wayne—Steven Franke
Indianapolis—Ray Compton
Kalamazoo—Ted Parfet
Kansas City—Russ Parker
Milwaukee—Joseph E. Tierney Jr.
Peoria—Bruce Saurs
Phoenix—Lyle Abraham
Salt Lake—Tim Howells
San Diego—Bill Comrie

TEAMS

ATLANTA KNIGHTS

Governor
David Bergman
General manager
Richard Adler
Coach
Gene Ubriaco
Public relations director
Dean Sever
Marketing director
Bob Bryant
Home ice
Omni Coliseum (15,207)
Address
100 Techwood Drive
Atlanta, GA 30303
NHL affiliation
Tampa Bay Lightning
Phone
404-525-5800
FAX
404-525-0044

CINCINNATI CYCLONES

Governor and general manager
Doug Kirchhofer
Coach
Dennis Desrosiers
Director of marketing
Mark Meisner
Director of public relations
Terry Ficorelli
Home ice
Cincinnati Gardens (10,326)
Address
2250 Seymour Avenue
Cincinnati, OH 45212
NHL affiliation
TBA
Phone
513-531-7825
FAX
513-531-0209

CLEVELAND LUMBERJACKS

Governor and general manager
Larry Gordon
Coach
Phil Russell

Director of public relations
Ken Mather
Director of marketing
John Gentile
Home ice
Richfield Coliseum (17,480)
Address
600 Superior Avenue
Suite 1300
Cleveland, OH 44114
NHL affiliation
Pittsburgh Penguins
Phone
216-479-6888
FAX
616-479-6889

FORT WAYNE KOMETS

Governor
Steven Franke
General manager
David Franke
Coach
Al Sims
Public relations director
Derek Ray
Marketing director
Michael Franke
Home ice
Allen County Memorial Coliseum
(8,022)
Address
4000 Parnell
Fort Wayne, IN 46805
NHL affiliation
TBA
Phone
219-483-0011
FAX
219-483-3899

INDIANAPOLIS ICE

Governor and general manager
Ray Compton
Coach
John Marks
Director of marketing
Brad Beery
Director of public relations
Tom Weisenbach

Home ice
Indiana State Fairgrounds Coliseum
(8,233)
Address
1202 East 38th Street
Indianapolis, IN 46205
NHL affiliation
Chicago Blackhawks
Phone
317-924-1234
FAX
317-924-1248

KALAMAZOO WINGS

Governor
Ted Parfet
General manager
Bill Inglis
Coach
Bob Hoffmeyer
Director of public relations/marketing
Steve Doherty
Director of broadcasting
Mike Miller
Home ice
Wings Stadium (5,113)
Address
3620 Van Rick Drive,
Kalamazoo, MI 49002
NHL affiliation
Minnesota North Stars
Phone
616-349-9772
FAX
616-345-6584

KANSAS CITY BLADES

Governor
Russ Parker
General manager
Doug Soetaert
Coach
Kevin Constantine
Director of public relations/marketing
Jim Loria
Home ice
Kemper Arena (16,000)
Address
1800 Genessee
Kansas City, MO 64102

MILWAUKEE ADMIRALS

NHL affiliation
San Jose Sharks
Phone
816-842-5233
FAX
816-842-5610

Governor
Joseph E. Tierney Jr.
General manager
Phil Wittliff
Coach
Curt Fraser
Public relations director
Doug Pettit
Director of marketing
Mike Wojciechowski
Home ice
Bradley Center (17,809)
Address
1001 North Fourth Street
Milwaukee, WI 53203
NHL affiliation
Vancouver Canucks
Phone
414-227-0550
FAX
414-227-0568

PEORIA RIVERMEN

Governor
Bruce Saurs
General manager
Denis Cyr
Coach
Rick Meagher
Director of public relations/marketing
Ted Cox

Home ice
Peoria Civic Center (9,074)
Address
201 S. W. Jefferson
Peoria, IL 61602
NHL affiliation
St. Louis Blues
Phone
309-676-1040
FAX
309-676-2488

PHOENIX ROADRUNNERS

Governor
Lyle Abraham
General manager
Adam Keller
Coach
TBA
Director of public relations
Dave Tunell
Director of marketing
Michael Whitsitt
Home ice
Veterans Memorial Coliseum (13,737)
Address
1826 West McDowell Road
Phoenix, AZ 85007
NHL affiliation
Los Angeles Kings
Phone
602-340-0001
FAX
602-340-0041

SALT LAKE GOLDEN EAGLES

Governor and general manager
Tim Howells

Coach
Bob Francis
Director of marketing
Jay Francis
Director of public relations
Mark Kelly
Home ice
Delta Center (10,387)
Address
351 W. South Temple
Salt Lake City, UT 84101
NHL affiliation
Calgary Flames
Phone
801-325-2300
FAX
801-325-2314

SAN DIEGO GULLS

Governor
Bill Comrie
General manager
Don Waddell
Coach
Rick Dudley
Public relations director
Chris Ello
Marketing director
Steve Violetta
Home ice
San Diego Sports Arena (13,200)
Address
3780 Hancock Street
Suite "G"
San Diego, CA 92110
NHL affiliation
TBA
Phone
619-688-1800
FAX
619-688-1808

1991-92 REGULAR SEASON

FINAL STANDINGS

EAST DIVISION

Team	G	W	L		Pts.	GF	GA
Fort Wayne	82	52	22	(8)	112	340	287
Muskegon	82	41	28	(13)	95	306	293
Milwaukee	82	38	36	(8)	84	306	309
Kalamazoo	82	37	35	(10)	84	292	312
Indianapolis	82	31	41	(10)	72	272	329

WEST DIVISION

Team	G	W	L		Pts.	GF	GA
Kansas City	82	56	22	(4)	116	302	248
Peoria	82	48	25	(9)	105	333	300
San Diego	82	45	28	(9)	99	340	298
Salt Lake	82	33	40	(9)	75	252	304
Phoenix	82	29	46	(7)	65	275	338

( )—Indicates overtime losses and are worth one point.

INDIVIDUAL LEADERS

Goals: Dmitri Kvartalnov, San Diego (60)
Assists: Len Hachborn, San Diego (73)
Points: Dmitri Kvartalnov, San Diego (118)
Penalty minutes: Chris McRae, Fort Wayne (413)
Goaltending average: Arturs Irbe, Kansas City (2.46)
Shutouts: Rob Dopson, Muskegon (4)
Mike O'Neill, Fort Wayne (4)

TOP SCORERS

	Games	G	A	Pts.
Dmitri Kvartalnov, San Diego	77	60	58	118
Jock Callander, Muskegon	81	42	70	112
Len Hachborn, San Diego	70	34	73	107
Scott Gruhl, Fort Wayne	78	44	61	105
Dave Michayluk, Muskegon	82	39	63	102

	Games	G	A	Pts.
Ray Whitney, San Diego	63	36	54	90
Colin Chin, Fort Wayne	73	35	55	90
Steve Tuttle, Peoria	71	43	46	89
Jean-Marc Richard, Fort Wayne	82	18	68	86
Bruce Boudreau, Fort Wayne	77	34	50	84
Eric Murano, Milwaukee	80	35	48	83
Gary Emmons, Kansas City	80	29	54	83
Mike Needham, Muskegon	80	41	37	78
Andrew McBain, Milwaukee	65	24	54	78
Shawn Heaphy, Salt Lake	76	41	36	77
Yves Heroux, Peoria	80	41	36	77
Mitch Messier, Kalamazoo	77	43	33	76
Kevin Miehm, Peoria	66	21	53	74
Jeff Rohlicek, Indianapolis	82	30	43	73
Jason Ruff, Peoria	67	27	45	72

FORT WAYNE KOMETS

SCORING

	Games	G	A	Pts.	Pen.
Scott Gruhl	78	44	61	105	196
Colin Chin	73	35	55	90	64
Jean-Marc Richard	82	18	68	86	109
Bruce Boudreau	77	34	50	84	100
Kory Kocur	69	25	40	65	68
Peter Hankinson	75	25	38	63	44
Bob Lakso	68	31	29	60	10
Chris McRae	60	20	14	34	413
Darin Smith	61	11	22	33	165
Ian Boyce	38	12	15	27	29
Carey Lucyk	79	5	18	23	81
Kelly Hurd	30	13	9	22	12
Bob Jay	76	1	19	20	119
Bob Jones	51	6	13	19	176
Mark Turner	49	8	10	18	68
Grant Richison	48	6	10	16	84
Lee Davidson	22	4	10	14	30
Ken Gernander	13	7	6	13	2
Todd Flichel	64	3	10	13	79
Steve Fletcher	60	8	3	11	320
Serge Roy	34	6	5	11	40
Scott Shaunessy	53	3	8	11	243
Guy Dupuis	10	2	7	9	0
Dennis Holland	6	2	4	6	21
Mike O'Neill (goalie)	33	0	2	2	4
Dan Wiebe	2	1	0	1	11
Chris Clifford (goalie)	2	0	1	1	2
Sean Gauthier (goalie)	18	0	1	1	8
Dusty Imoo (goalie)	15	0	1	1	0
Eldon Reddick (goalie)	14	0	1	1	2
Tom Karalis	1	0	0	0	2
Craig Levie	1	0	0	0	0
Kevin Scott	1	0	0	0	0
Boyd Sutton	1	0	0	0	2
Dave Gagnon (goalie)	2	0	0	0	0
Doug Melnyk	2	0	0	0	0
Bill Pye (goalie)	8	0	0	0	0
Craig Martin	24	0	0	0	115

GOALTENDING

	Games	Min.	Goals	SO	Avg.
Chris Clifford	2	120	4	0	2.00
Eldon Reddick	14	787	40	1	3.05
Mike O'Neill	33	1858	97	4	3.13
Dave Gagnon	2	125	7	0	3.36
Sean Gauthier	18	978	59(1)	1	3.62
Dusty Imoo	15	681	42(2)	0	3.70
Bill Pye	8	451	29	0	3.86

INDIANAPOLIS ICE

SCORING

	Games	G	A	Pts.	Pen.
Sean Williams	79	29	36	65	89
Mike Stapleton	59	18	40	58	65
Jeff Rohlicek	59	25	32	57	28
Brad Lauer	57	24	30	54	46
Trevor Dam	79	19	23	42	132
Shawn Byram	69	18	21	39	154
Craig Woodcroft	75	21	17	38	67
Rob Conn	72	19	16	35	100
Tracy Egeland	66	20	11	31	214
Steve Bancroft	36	8	23	31	49
Milan Tichy	49	6	23	29	28
Ryan McGill	40	7	19	26	170
Paul Gillis	42	10	15	25	170
Jeff Sirkka	71	3	17	20	146
Justin Lafayette	51	7	10	17	37
Adam Bennett	59	4	10	14	89
Cam Russell	41	4	9	13	78
Martin Desjardines	36	4	7	11	52

	Games	G	A	Pts.	Pen.
Jeff Jackson	18	3	7	10	41
Dan Vincelette	16	5	3	8	84
Dave Hakstol	35	1	6	7	30
Michael Speer	54	0	6	6	67
Owen Lessard	41	3	2	5	53
Trent Yawney	9	2	3	5	12
Jim Johannson	11	2	2	4	4
Frantisek Kucera	7	1	2	3	4
Kerry Toporowski	18	1	2	3	206
Stu Grimson	5	1	1	2	17
Jim Playfair	23	1	1	2	53
Brad Treliving	14	1	0	1	13
Jim Ballantine	2	0	1	1	0
Mike Peluso	4	0	1	1	15
Chris Norton	8	0	1	1	12
Roch Belley (goalie)	25	0	1	1	6
Ray LeBlanc (goalie)	25	0	1	1	16
Mark Reimer (goalie)	6	0	0	0	0
Jim Waite (goalie)	13	0	0	0	10
Dominik Hasek (goalie)	20	0	0	0	2

GOALTENDING

	Games	Min.	Goals	SO	Avg.
Mark Reimer	6	369	21	0	3.41
Ray LeBlanc	25	1468	84(1)	2	3.43
Dominik Hasek	20	1162	69(2)	1	3.56
Roch Belley	25	1270	88(3)	0	4.16
Jim Waite	13	702	53(2)	0	4.53

KALAMAZOO WINGS

SCORING

	Games	G	A	Pts.	Pen.
Mitch Messier	77	43	33	76	42
Steve Gotaas	72	34	29	63	115
Scott Robinson	78	29	27	56	58
Steve Maltais	48	25	31	56	51
Tim Lenardon	73	27	24	51	37
Mario Thyer	46	17	28	45	0
Cal McGowan	77	13	30	43	62
Warren Rychel	45	15	20	35	165
Jim Nesich	80	13	19	32	85
Roy Mitchell	69	3	26	29	102
Paul Jerrard	76	4	24	28	123
Ross Wilson	31	18	6	24	38
Brad Berry	65	5	18	23	90
Scott Sandelin	49	3	18	21	32
Enrico Ciccone	53	4	16	20	406
Doug Barrault	60	5	14	19	26
Bobby Reynolds	13	8	10	18	19
Brian Straub	29	2	12	14	45
Dave Moylan	49	2	10	12	59
Greg Spenrath	69	4	7	11	237
Steve Herniman	64	4	6	10	271
Marc Bureau	7	2	8	10	2
Craig Coxe	6	4	5	9	13
Kip Miller	6	1	8	9	4
Derrick Smith	6	1	5	6	4
Wayne Gagne	3	0	4	4	2
Tony Joseph	15	2	0	2	51
Larry Dyck (goalie)	57	0	2	2	12
Tyler Larter	3	0	2	2	4
Paul Marshall	21	0	2	2	8
Jeff Harding	6	1	0	1	63
Nick Beaulieu	1	0	1	1	0
Darrin Colborne	1	0	1	1	0
Mike Reier	2	0	1	1	0
Todd Bojcun (goalie)	1	0	0	0	0
Darcy Wakaluk (goalie)	1	0	0	0	2
Mark Janssens	2	0	0	0	2
Jackson Penney	2	0	0	0	0
Jon Casey (goalie)	4	0	0	0	2
Rod Houk (goalie)	4	0	0	0	2
Steve Guenette (goalie)	21	0	0	0	0

IHL

MINOR LEAGUES

IHL

GOALTENDING

	Games	Min.	Goals	SO	Avg.
Jon Casey	4	250	11	0	2.64
Rod Houk	4	199	10(1)	0	3.02
Larry Dyck	56	3305	195(1)	0	3.54
Steve Guenette	21	1094	70(1)	1	3.84
Darcy Wakaluk	1	60	7	0	7.00
Todd Bojcun	1	60	10	0	10.00

KANSAS CITY BLADES

SCORING

	Games	G	A	Pts.	Pen.
Gary Emmons	80	29	54	83	60
Peter Lappin	78	28	30	58	41
Larry DePalma	62	28	29	57	188
Jeff Madill	62	32	20	52	167
Kevin Evans	66	10	39	49	342
Duane Joyce	80	12	32	44	62
Mikhail Kravets	74	10	32	42	172
Craig Coxe	51	17	21	38	106
Ron Handy	38	16	19	35	30
Gordie Frantti	55	17	15	32	40
Pat MacLeod	45	9	21	30	19
Dean Kolstad	74	9	20	29	83
Claudio Scremin	70	5	23	28	44
Ed Courtenay	36	14	12	26	46
John Carter	42	11	15	26	116
Dale Craigwell	48	6	19	25	29
Rick Lessard	46	3	16	19	117
Sandis Ozolnich	34	6	9	15	20
Tom Pederson	20	6	9	15	16
David Bruce	7	5	5	10	6
Jean-Franco Quintin	21	4	6	10	29
Mike Sullivan	10	2	8	10	8
Ryan Fox	24	3	5	8	33
Murray Garbutt	25	2	6	8	19
Andy Akervik	22	1	5	6	12
David Williams	18	2	3	5	22
Jeff Odgers	12	2	2	4	56
Mike Colman	59	0	4	4	130
Troy Frederick	13	0	3	3	29
John Blessman	25	0	2	2	24
Mike Hiltner	2	0	2	2	2
Jayson More	2	0	2	2	4
Artuo Irbe (goalie)	32	0	1	1	12
Wade Flaherty (goalie)	43	0	1	1	18
Kevin Sullivan	5	0	1	1	0
Brian Hayward (goalie)	2	0	0	0	0
Stephane Brochu	3	0	0	0	2
Jarmo Myllys (goalie)	5	0	0	0	2

GOALTENDING

	Games	Min.	Goals	SO	Avg.
Brian Hayward	2	119	3(1)	1	1.51
Artur Irbe	32	1955	80(4)	0	2.46
Jarmo Myllys	5	307	15	0	2.93
Wade Flaherty	43	2603	140(3)	1	3.23

MILWAUKEE ADMIRALS

SCORING

	Games	G	A	Pts.	Pen.
Eric Murano	80	35	48	83	61
Andrew McBain	65	24	54	78	132
Rob Murphy	73	26	38	64	141
Jeff Larmer	76	27	35	62	22
Paul Guay	81	24	33	57	93
Carl Valimont	71	14	31	45	81
Ladislav Tresl	48	15	28	43	64
Robin Bawa	70	27	14	41	238
Jay Mazur	56	17	20	37	49
Neil Eisenhut	76	13	23	36	26
Phil Von Stefenelli	80	2	34	36	40
Shawn Antoski	52	17	16	33	346
Ian Kidd	80	9	24	33	75
Dennis Snedden	49	13	13	26	18

	Games	G	A	Pts.	Pen.
Jason Herter	56	7	18	25	34
Randy Boyd	42	7	9	16	80
Don Gibson	35	6	9	15	105
Cam Brown	51	6	8	14	179
Troy Neumeier	72	1	9	10	55
Igor Vyazmikin	8	3	5	8	2
Dave Capuano	9	2	6	8	8
Jeff Napierala	18	2	2	4	0
Brian Blad	58	1	3	4	162
Bob Mason (goalie)	51	0	4	4	22
Corrie D'Alessio (goalie)	27	0	1	1	2
Troy Gamble (goalie)	9	0	1	1	2
Darin Bader	4	0	0	0	5

GOALTENDING

	Games	Min.	Goals	SO	Avg.
Bob Mason	51	3024	171(6)	1	3.39
Troy Gamble	9	521	31(1)	0	3.57
Corrie D'Alessio	27	1435	96(1)	0	4.01

MUSKEGON LUMBERJACKS

SCORING

	Games	G	A	Pts.	Pen.
Jock Callander	81	42	70	112	160
Dave Michayluk	82	39	63	102	154
Mike Needham	80	41	37	78	83
Perry Ganchar	65	29	20	49	65
Gord Dineen	79	8	37	45	83
Glenn Mulvenna	70	15	27	42	24
Todd Nelson	80	6	35	41	46
Daniel Gauthier	68	19	18	37	28
Jeff Daniels	44	19	16	35	38
Sandy Smith	64	15	18	33	109
Mark Major	80	13	18	31	302
Paul Dyck	73	6	21	27	40
Jamie Heward	54	6	21	27	37
Jason Smart	45	10	14	24	49
Dale Henry	39	5	17	22	28
Paul Laus	75	0	21	21	248
Eric Brule	70	4	14	18	48
Ken Priestlay	13	4	11	15	6
Gil Delorme	60	6	6	12	89
Jean Blouin	19	4	5	9	12
Jim Latos	27	4	4	8	54
Brian Fogarty	8	2	4	6	30
Joel Gardner	5	1	2	3	2
Dave Shute	7	1	2	3	6
Christian LeLonde	3	0	3	3	0
Jamie Leach	3	1	1	2	2
Robert Melanson	7	0	2	2	2
Rob Dopson (goalie)	29	0	1	1	4
Mark Kachowski	6	0	0	0	9
Bruce Racine (goalie)	27	0	0	0	24
Alain Morissette (goalie)	31	0	0	0	0

GOALTENDING

	Games	Min.	Goals	SO	Avg.
Rob Dopson	28	1655	90(1)	4	3.26
Alain Morissette	31	1796	100(1)	1	3.34
Bruce Racine	27	1559	91	1	3.50

PEORIA RIVERMEN

SCORING

	Games	G	A	Pts.	Pen.
Steve Tuttle	71	43	46	89	22
Yves Heroux	80	41	36	77	72
Kevin Miehm	66	21	53	74	22
Jason Ruff	67	27	45	72	148
Richard Pion	82	21	50	71	173
Ron Hoover	71	27	34	61	30
Michael Mongeau	32	21	34	55	77
Brian McKee	65	15	38	53	54
Dominic Lavoie	58	20	32	52	87
Mark Bassen	82	18	23	41	228

	Games	G	A	Pts.	Pen.
Dave Mackey	35	20	17	37	90
Randy Skarda	57	8	24	32	64
Brian Pellerin	70	7	16	23	231
Jason Marshall	78	4	18	22	178
Kyle Reeves	60	12	7	19	92
Doug Evans	16	5	14	19	38
Bruce Shoebottom	79	4	12	16	234
Butch Kaebel	30	3	11	14	6
Joe Hawley	40	6	7	13	42
Derek Frenette	46	2	11	13	51
Rob Robinson	35	1	10	11	29
Rob Tustian	48	2	5	7	76
Greg Poss	18	1	4	5	41
Terry Hollinger	1	0	2	2	0
Mike Mudd (goalie)	2	0	0	0	0
Alain Raymond (goalie)	6	0	0	0	0
Dan Fowler	8	0	0	0	25
Pat Jablonski (goalie)	8	0	0	0	0
Jaan Luik	8	0	0	0	2
Francis Ouellette (goalie)	12	0	0	0	0
Jean C. Bergeron (goalie)	27	0	0	0	6
Guy Hebert (goalie)	29	0	0	0	4

GOALTENDING

	Games	Min.	Goals	SO	Avg.
Francis Ouellette	12	700	37(1)	0	3.17
Guy Hebert	29	1731	98(1)	0	3.40
Pat Jablonski	8	493	29	1	3.53
Jean C. Bergeron	27	1632	96	1	3.53
Mike Mudd	2	60	4	0	4.00
Alain Raymond	6	370	27	0	4.38

PHOENIX ROADRUNNERS

SCORING

	Games	G	A	Pts.	Pen.
Sean Whyte	72	24	30	54	113
Shawn McCosh	71	21	32	53	118
Marc Saumier	70	19	23	42	310
Ilkka Sinisalo	42	19	21	40	32
Sylvain Couturier	39	19	20	39	68
Kyosti Karjalainen	43	14	22	36	30
Iain Duncan	46	12	24	36	103
Frank Breault	51	11	10	00	40
Tim Breslin	45	8	21	29	12
Mike Vukonich	68	17	11	28	21
Scott Bjugstad	28	14	14	28	12
Darryl Williams	48	8	19	27	219
Chris Norton	62	12	14	26	44
Bill O'Dwyer	39	9	17	26	12
Rene Chapdelaine	62	4	22	26	87
Rick Lanz	38	7	14	21	21
Kevin MacDonald	76	7	14	21	304
Ross Wilson	28	9	9	18	81
Brent Thompson	42	4	13	17	139
Jeff Rohlicek	23	5	11	16	32
Derek Booth	35	2	11	13	58
Bob Berg	24	2	8	10	18
John Van Kessel	44	2	6	8	247
Peter Ahola	7	3	3	6	34
Paul Holden	47	3	3	6	63
Soren True	21	3	3	6	12
Steve Jaques	13	2	4	6	69
Brandy Semchuk	15	1	5	6	6
David Tretowicz	16	3	2	5	14
Kris Miller	16	1	2	3	17
Mike Ruark	16	1	2	3	91
Vern Smith	16	1	2	3	25
Jim Maher	9	0	3	3	21
Igor Vyazmikin	6	0	3	3	8
Tim Watters	5	0	3	3	6
David Goverde (goalie)	36	0	2	2	19
Robb Stauber (goalie)	22	0	2	2	10
Jim Thomson	2	1	0	1	0
Darryl Gilmour (goalie)	30	0	1	1	4
Joe Paterson	2	0	0	0	2

	Games	G	A	Pts.	Pen.
Jeff Chychrun	3	0	0	0	6
Barry Niecar	5	0	0	0	9

GOALTENDING

	Games	Min.	Goals	SO	Avg.
Robb Stauber	22	1242	80(1)	0	3.86
David Goverde	35	1951	129(2)	1	3.97
Darryl Gilmour	30	1774	120(2)	0	4.06

SALT LAKE GOLDEN EAGLES

SCORING

	Games	G	A	Pts.	Pen.
Shawn Heaphy	76	41	36	77	85
Todd Harkins	72	32	30	62	67
Rich Chernomaz	66	20	40	60	201
Kevin Wortman	82	12	34	46	34
Dennis Holland	72	20	25	45	102
Darryl Olsen	59	7	33	40	80
Bryan Deasley	65	12	23	35	67
Tim Harris	71	11	21	32	91
Todd Strueby	61	15	16	31	72
Paul Kruse	57	14	15	29	267
Kerry Clark	74	12	14	26	266
Kevin Grant	73	7	16	23	181
Kevan Melrose	82	5	14	19	187
Richard Zemlak	60	5	14	19	204
Kevan Guy	60	3	14	17	89
Tomas Forslund	22	10	6	16	25
Darren Banks	55	5	5	10	303
Martin Simard	11	3	7	10	51
Darren Stolk	65	2	8	10	68
Corey Lyons	26	3	3	6	4
Jason Muzzatti (goalie)	52	0	6	6	47
David Struch	12	4	1	5	8
C.J. Young	9	2	2	4	2
Alexander Godynyuk	17	2	1	3	24
Peter Kasowski	9	1	2	3	2
Kevin Dahl	13	0	2	2	12
Matt Hoffman	4	0	1	1	6
Jim Kyte	6	0	1	1	9
Dean Trboyevich	5	0	1	1	7
Todd Gillingham	1	0	0	0	2
Mark Osiecki	1	0	0	0	0
Mark Woolf	1	0	0	0	0
Neil Sheely	6	0	0	0	34
Scott Sharples (goalie)	35	0	0	0	4

GOALTENDING

	Games	Min.	Goals	SO	Avg.
Jason Muzzatti	52	3033	167(4)	2	3.30
Scott Sharples	35	1936	121(4)	0	3.75

SAN DIEGO GULLS

SCORING

	Games	G	A	Pts.	Pen.
Dmitri Kvartalnov	77	60	58	118	16
Len Hachborn	70	34	73	107	124
Ray Whitney	63	36	54	90	12
Rob Nichols	77	30	35	65	228
Larry Floyd	71	18	45	63	58
Alan Hepple	82	6	35	41	191
Sergei Starikov	70	7	31	38	42
Soren True	45	18	19	37	31
Ron Duguay	60	18	18	36	32
Darcy Norton	63	19	16	35	66
Steve Martinson	70	18	15	33	279
Denny Lambert	71	17	14	31	229
Keith Gretzky	62	12	19	31	10
Derek Mayer	30	7	16	23	47
Kord Cernich	64	5	18	23	53
Brent Sapergia	23	14	6	20	23
Brian Straub	43	3	16	19	75
Alan Leggett	55	2	16	18	21
Glen Goodall	19	1	11	12	10

	Games	G	A	Pts.	Pen.
Andrei Kvartalnov	20	6	5	11	8
Steve Shaunessy	27	1	5	6	183
Dave Korol	30	2	3	5	27
Guy Gadowsky	9	1	4	5	13
Jason Simon	13	1	4	5	45
Murray Duval	10	1	2	3	6
Jason Lafreniere	5	1	2	3	2
Kent Hawley	1	0	2	2	0
Randy Hillier	6	0	2	2	4
Marc Laniel	10	0	2	2	16
Patrick Cavanagh	6	0	1	1	37
Bruce Hoffort (goalie)	26	0	1	1	14
Rick Knickle (goalie)	46	0	1	1	10
Charlie Simmer	1	0	0	0	0
Rod Houk (goalie)	2	0	0	0	0
Rick Barkovich	3	0	0	0	0
Rob Krauss	3	0	0	0	4
Sean Burke (goalie)	7	0	0	0	0
Scott Drevitch	7	0	0	0	13
Greg Millen (goalie)	5	0	0	0	0
Mitch Wilson	12	0	0	0	55
Jason Prosofsky	31	0	0	0	111

GOALTENDING

	Games	Min.	Goals	SO	Avg.
Sean Burke	7	424	17(1)	0	2.41
Rick Knickle	46	2686	155(2)	0	3.46
Bruce Hoffort	26	1474	89(1)	0	3.62
Greg Millen	5	296	20	0	4.05
Rod Houk	2	80	6	0	4.50

PLAYERS WITH TWO OR MORE TEAMS

SCORING

	Games	G	A	Pts.	Pen.
Craig Coxe, Kansas City	51	17	21	38	106
Craig Coxe, Kalamazoo	6	4	5	9	13
Totals	57	21	26	47	119
Dennis Holland, Fort Wayne	6	2	4	6	21
Dennis Holland, Salt Lake	72	20	25	45	102
Totals	78	22	29	51	123
Rod Houk, San Diego (goalie)	2	0	0	0	0
Rod Houk, Kalamazoo (goalie)	4	0	0	0	2
Totals	6	0	0	0	2
Chris Norton, Indianapolis	8	0	1	1	12
Chris Norton, Phoenix	62	12	14	26	44
Totals	70	12	15	27	56
Jeff Rohlicek, Phoenix	23	5	11	16	32
Jeff Rohlicek, Indianapolis	59	25	32	57	28
Totals	82	30	43	73	60
Brian Straub, San Diego	43	3	16	19	75
Brian Straub, Kalamazoo	29	2	12	14	45
Totals	72	5	28	33	120
Soren True, San Diego	45	18	19	37	31
Soren True, Phoenix	21	3	3	6	12
Totals	66	21	22	43	43
Igor Vyazmikin, Milwaukee	8	3	5	8	2
Igor Vyazmikin, Phoenix	6	0	3	3	8
Totals	14	3	8	11	10
Ross Wilson, Phoenix	28	9	9	18	81
Ross Wilson, Kalamazoo	31	18	6	24	38
Totals	59	27	15	42	119

GOALTENDING

	Games	Min.	Goals	SO	Avg.
Rod Houk, San Diego	2	80	6	0	4.50
Rod Houk, Kalamazoo	4	199	10(1)	0	3.02

1992 TURNER CUP PLAYOFFS

RESULTS

QUARTERFINALS

WEST DIVISION
Series "A"

	W	L	Pts.	GF	GA
Kansas City	4	1	8	25	12
Salt Lake	1	4	2	12	25

(Kansas City won series, 4-1)

Series "B"

	W	L	Pts.	GF	GA
Peoria	4	0	8	16	6
San Diego	0	4	0	6	16

(Peoria won series, 4-0)

Series "C"

	W	L	Pts.	GF	GA
Kalamazoo	4	3	8	26	23
Fort Wayne	3	4	6	23	26

(Kalamazoo won series, 4-3)

Series "D"

	W	L	Pts.	GF	GA
Muskegon	4	1	8	27	17
Milwaukee	1	4	2	17	27

(Muskegon won series, 4-1)

SEMIFINALS

WEST DIVISION
Series "E"

	W	L	Pts.	GF	GA
Kansas City	4	2	8	28	20
Peoria	2	4	4	20	28

(Kansas City won series, 4-2)

EAST DIVISION
Series "F"

	W	L	Pts.	GF	GA
Muskegon	4	1	8	25	17
Kalamazoo	1	4	2	17	25

(Muskegon won series, 4-1)

TURNER CUP FINALS

Series "G"

	W	L	Pts.	GF	GA
Kansas City	4	0	8	22	12
Muskegon	0	4	0	12	22

(Kansas City won series, 4-0)

INDIVIDUAL LEADERS

Goals: Ron Handy, Kansas City (13)
Assists: Michel Mongeau, Peoria (14)
Points: Ron Handy, Kansas City (21)
Penalty minutes: Scott Robinson, Kalamazoo (86)
Goaltending average: Guy Hebert, Peoria (2.26)
Shutouts: None

TOP SCORERS

	Games	G	A	Pts.
Ron Handy, Kansas City	15	13	8	21
Larry DePalma, Kansas City	15	7	13	20
Gary Emmons, Kansas City	15	6	13	19
Michel Mongeau, Peoria	10	5	14	19
Perry Ganchar, Muskegon	14	9	9	18
Dave Michayluk, Muskegon	13	9	8	17
Ed Courtenay, Kansas City	15	8	9	17
Duane Joyce, Kansas City	15	6	11	17
Ken Priestlay, Muskegon	13	5	11	16
John Carter, Kansas City	15	6	9	15
Kevin Evans, Kansas City	14	2	13	15

INDIVIDUAL STATISTICS

FORT WAYNE KOMETS

(Lost quarterfinals to Kalamazoo, 4-3)

SCORING

	Games	G	A	Pts.	Pen.
Colin Chin	7	3	6	9	8
Bruce Boudreau	7	3	4	7	10
Lee Davidson	7	2	5	7	8
Phil Berger	4	3	3	6	0
Kory Kocur	7	3	3	6	49
Jean-Marc Richard	7	0	5	5	20
Scott Gruhl	6	2	2	4	48
Peter Hankinson	7	1	3	4	2
Kelly Hurd	3	3	0	3	9
Mark Turner	5	2	0	2	6
Bob Jay	7	0	2	2	4
Darin Smith	5	0	2	2	8
Grant Richison	5	0	2	2	9
Chris McRae	5	1	0	1	44
Scott Shaunessy	7	0	1	1	27
Scott White	1	0	0	0	2
Sean Gauthier (goalie)	2	0	0	0	0
Bob Jones	3	0	0	0	10
Steve Fletcher	5	0	0	0	14
Todd Flichel	7	0	0	0	2
Carey Lucyk	7	0	0	0	10
Eldon Reddick (goalie)	7	0	0	0	2

GOALTENDING

	Games	Min.	Goals	SO	Avg.
Eldon Reddick	7	369	18(1)	0	2.93
Sean Gauthier	2	48	7	0	8.75

KALAMAZOO WINGS

(Lost semifinals to Muskegon, 4-1)

SCORING

	Games	G	A	Pts.	Pen.
Steve Gotaas	12	4	10	14	20
Kip Miller	12	3	9	12	12
Ross Wilson	11	9	1	10	6
Tim Lenardon	12	5	5	10	4
Jim Nesich	12	3	7	10	12
Bobby Reynolds	12	5	4	9	4
Scott Robinson	11	2	6	8	86
Paul Jerrard	12	1	7	8	31
Mitch Messier	12	3	3	6	25
Craig Coxe	10	2	4	6	37
Dave Moylan	7	1	4	5	16
Roy Mitchell	11	1	4	5	18
Brian Straub	11	0	5	5	6
Mark Janssens	11	1	2	3	22
Warren Rychel	8	0	3	3	51
Brad Berry	5	2	0	2	6
Scott Sandelin	11	1	1	2	2
Enrico Ciccone	10	0	1	1	58

Larry Dyck (goalie)	12	0	1	1	2
Steve Herniman	1	0	0	0	0
Cal McGowan	1	0	0	0	2
Rod Houk (goalie)	3	0	0	0	0

GOALTENDING

	Games	Min.	Goals	SO	Avg.
Larry Dyck	12	690	43(1)	0	3.74
Rod Houk	3	41	3(1)	0	4.39

KANSAS CITY BLADES

(Winner of 1992 Turner Cup playoffs)

SCORING

	Games	G	A	Pts.	Pen.
Ron Handy	15	13	8	21	8
Larry DePalma	15	7	13	20	34
Gary Emmons	15	6	13	19	8
Ed Courtenay	15	8	9	17	15
Duane Joyce	15	6	11	17	8
John Carter	15	6	9	15	18
Kevin Evans	14	2	13	15	70
Mikhail Kravets	15	6	8	14	12
Jean-Franco Quintin	13	2	10	12	29
Dale Craigwell	12	4	7	11	4
Dean Kolstad	15	3	6	9	8
Sandis Ozolnich	15	2	5	7	22
Tom Pederson	13	1	6	7	14
Claudio Scremin	15	1	6	7	14
Pat MacLeod	11	1	4	5	4
Jeff Madill	6	2	2	4	30
Jeff Odgers	9	3	0	3	13
Peter Lappin	4	2	1	3	0
Artur Irbe (goalie)	15	0	3	3	4
Wade Flaherty (goalie)	1	0	0	0	0
Gordie Frantti	2	0	0	0	0
Mike Colman	3	0	0	0	4
Rick Lessard	3	0	0	0	2

GOALTENDING

	Games	Min.	Goals	SO	Avg.
Wade Flaherty	1	1	0	0	0.00
Artur Irbe	15	914	44	0	2.89

MILWAUKEE ADMIRALS

(Lost quarterfinals to Muskegon, 4-1)

SCORING

	Games	G	A	Pts.	Pen.
Eric Murano	5	3	4	7	0
Jay Mazur	5	2	3	5	0
Jeff Larmer	5	1	4	5	4
Robin Bawa	5	2	2	4	8
Paul Guay	3	2	1	3	7
Andrew McBain	5	1	2	3	10

MINOR LEAGUES

IHL

	Games	G	A	Pts.	Pen.
Phil Von Stefenelli	5	1	2	3	2
Neil Eisenhut	2	1	2	3	0
Rob Murphy	5	0	3	3	2
Shawn Antoski	5	2	0	2	20
Ladislav Tresl	5	1	1	2	6
Carl Valimont	5	0	2	2	4
Don Gibson	4	1	0	1	7
Dennis Snedden	4	0	1	1	2
Randy Boyd	2	0	1	1	2
Ian Kidd	5	0	1	1	11
Cam Brown	1	0	0	0	0
Jason Herter	1	0	0	0	2
Corrie D'Alessio (goalie)	2	0	0	0	0
Bob Mason (goalie)	3	0	0	0	0
Troy Neumeier	3	0	0	0	0
Brian Blad	5	0	0	0	0

GOALTENDING

	Games	Min.	Goals	SO	Avg.
Bob Mason	3	179	15	0	5.03
Corrie D'Alessio	2	119	12	0	6.05

MUSKEGON LUMBERJACKS
(Lost finals to Kansas City, 4-0)
SCORING

	Games	G	A	Pts.	Pen.
Perry Ganchar	14	9	9	18	18
Dave Michayluk	13	9	8	17	4
Ken Priestlay	13	5	11	16	10
Jock Callander	10	4	10	14	13
Todd Nelson	14	1	11	12	4
Glenn Mulvenna	14	5	6	11	11
Sandy Smith	14	7	2	9	4
Jeff Daniels	10	5	4	9	9
Daniel Gauthier	9	3	6	9	8
Mike Needham	8	4	4	8	6
Paul Laus	14	2	5	7	70
Gord Dineen	14	2	4	6	33
Jamie Heward	14	1	4	5	4
Dale Henry	14	1	4	5	36
Gil Delorme	7	2	2	4	12
Mark Major	12	1	3	4	29
Paul Dyck	14	1	3	4	4
Eric Brule	5	0	4	4	2
Mark Kachowski	4	2	0	2	16
Jim Latos	6	0	1	1	10
Robert Melanson	1	0	0	0	0
Bruce Racine (goalie)	1	0	0	0	0
Alain Morissette (goalie)	2	0	0	0	0
Rob Dopson (goalie)	12	0	0	0	0

GOALTENDING

	Games	Min.	Goals	SO	Avg.
Rob Dopson	12	697	40(1)	0	3.44
Alain Morissette	2	97	9	0	5.57
Bruce Racine	1	60	6	0	6.00

PEORIA RIVERMEN
(Lost semifinals to Kansas City, 4-2)
SCORING

	Games	G	A	Pts.	Pen.
Michel Mongeau	10	5	14	19	8
Jason Ruff	10	7	7	14	19
Steve Tuttle	10	4	8	12	4
Ron Hoover	10	4	4	8	4
Dominic Lavoie	10	3	4	7	12
Kevin Miehm	10	3	4	7	2
Yves Heroux	8	5	1	6	6
Richard Pion	9	3	1	4	30
Mark Bassen	10	0	4	4	15
Brian Pellerin	10	1	2	3	49
Derek Frenette	10	0	3	3	4
Brian McKee	6	1	1	2	12
Rob Robinson	10	0	2	2	12

	Games	G	A	Pts.	Pen.
Terry Hollinger	5	0	1	1	0
Jason Marshall	10	0	1	1	16
Rob Tustian	2	0	1	1	0
Butch Kaebel	3	0	0	0	0
Guy Hebert (goalie)	4	0	0	0	0
Jean C. Bergeron (goalie)	6	0	0	0	0
Randy Skarda	7	0	0	0	14
Bruce Shoebottom	10	0	0	0	33

GOALTENDING

	Games	Min.	Goals	SO	Avg.
Guy Hebert	4	239	9(1)	0	2.26
Jean C. Bergeron	6	352	24	0	4.09

SALT LAKE GOLDEN EAGLES
(Lost quarterfinals to Kansas City, 4-1)
SCORING

	Games	G	A	Pts.	Pen.
Shawn Heaphy	5	2	2	4	2
Tomas Forslund	5	2	2	4	2
Darryl Olsen	5	2	1	3	4
Rich Chernomaz	5	1	2	3	10
Paul Kruse	5	1	2	3	19
Todd Harkins	5	1	1	2	6
Dennis Holland	4	0	2	2	2
Kevin Wortman	5	1	0	1	0
Kerry Clark	5	1	0	1	34
Todd Strueby	3	1	0	1	6
Tim Harris	3	0	1	1	4
Kevan Guy	5	0	1	1	4
C.J. Young	5	0	1	1	4
Scott Sharples (goalie)	1	0	0	0	2
Bryan Deasley	2	0	0	0	4
Richard Zemlak	3	0	0	0	0
Jason Muzzatti (goalie)	4	0	0	0	2
Kevin Dahl	5	0	0	0	13
Kevan Melrose	5	0	0	0	4
Darren Stolk	5	0	0	0	2

GOALTENDING

	Games	Min.	Goals	SO	Avg.
Jason Muzzatti	4	247	18	0	4.37
Scott Sharples	1	60	7	0	7.00

SAN DIEGO GULLS
(Lost quarterfinals to Peoria, 4-0)
SCORING

	Games	G	A	Pts.	Pen.
Dmitri Kvartalnov	4	2	0	2	2
Rob Nichols	4	1	1	2	8
Steve Martinson	4	1	1	2	15
Larry Floyd	4	0	2	2	0
Len Hachborn	4	0	2	2	17
Kord Cernich	3	1	0	1	0
Kent Hawley	3	1	0	1	4
Alan Leggett	2	0	1	1	2
Jason Simon	3	0	1	1	9
Ron Duguay	4	0	1	1	0
Alan Hepple	4	0	1	1	6
Andrei Kvartalnov	1	0	0	0	0
Steve Shaunessy	1	0	0	0	2
Keith Gretzky	2	0	0	0	2
Rick Knickle (goalie)	2	0	0	0	0
Dave Korol	2	0	0	0	0
Sean Burke (goalie)	3	0	0	0	0
Denny Lambert	3	0	0	0	10
Derek Mayer	4	0	0	0	20
Darcy Norton	4	0	0	0	2
Sergei Starikov	4	0	0	0	0
Ray Whitney	4	0	0	0	0

GOALTENDING

	Games	Min.	Goals	SO	Avg.
Rick Knickle	2	78	3	0	2.31
Sean Burke	3	160	13	0	4.88

IHL

1991-92 AWARD WINNERS

ALL-STAR TEAMS

First team	Pos.	Second team
Arturs Irbe, Kansas City	G	Rick Knickle, San Diego
Jean-Marc Richard, F.W.	D	Dominic Lavoie, Peoria
Gord Dineen, Muskegon	D	Pat McLeod, Kansas City
Dmitri Kvartalnov, S.D.	LW	Dave Michayluk, Musk.
Jock Callander, Muskegon	C	Len Hachborn, San Diego
Steve Tuttle, Peoria	RW	Scott Gruhl, Fort Wayne

TROPHY WINNERS

James Gatschene Memorial Trophy: Dmitri Kvartalnov, S.D.
Leo P. Lamoureux Memorial Trophy: Dmitri Kvartalnov, S.D.
James Norris Memorial Trophy: Arturs Irbe, Kansas City
Wade Flaherty, Kansas City
Governors Trophy: Jean-Marc Richard, Fort Wayne
Garry F. Longman Memorial Trophy: Dmitri Kvartalnov, S.D.
Ken McKenzie Trophy: Kevin Wortman, Salt Lake
Commissioner's Trophy: Kevin Constantine, Kansas City
N.R. (Bud) Poile Trophy: Ron Handy, Kansas City
Fred A. Huber Trophy: Kansas City Blades
Joseph Turner Memorial Cup Winner: Kansas City Blades

ALL-TIME AWARD WINNERS

JAMES GATSCHENE MEMORIAL TROPHY
(Most Valuable Player)

Season	Player, Team
1946-47	Herb Jones, Detroit Auto Club
1947-48	Lyle Dowell, Det. Bright's Goodyears
1948-49	Bob McFadden, Det. Jerry Lynch
1949-50	Dick Kowcinak, Sarnia
1950-51	John McGrath, Toledo
1951-52	Ernie Dick, Chatham
1952-53	Donnie Marshall, Cincinnati
1953-54	No award given
1954-55	Phil Goyette, Cincinnati
1955-56	George Hayes, Grand Rapids
1956-57	Pierre Brillant, Indianapolis
1957-58	Pierre Brillant, Indianapolis
1958-59	Len Thornson, Fort Wayne
1959-60	Billy Reichart, Minneapolis
1960-61	Len Thornson, Fort Wayne
1961-62	Len Thornson, Fort Wayne
1962-63	Len Thornson, Fort Wayne
	Eddie Lang, Fort Wayne
1963-64	Len Thornson, Fort Wayne
1964-65	Chick Chalmers, Toledo
1965-66	Gary Schall, Muskegon
1966-67	Len Thornson, Fort Wayne
1967-68	Len Thornson, Fort Wayne
	Don Westbrooke, Dayton
1968-69	Don Westbrooke, Dayton
1969-70	Cliff Pennington, Des Moines
1970-71	Lyle Carter, Muskegon
1971-72	Len Fontaine, Port Huron
1972-73	Gary Ford, Muskegon
1973-74	Pete Mara, Des Moines
1974-75	Gary Ford, Muskegon
1975-76	Len Fontaine, Port Huron
1976-77	Tom Mellor, Toledo
1977-78	Dan Bonar, Fort Wayne
1978-79	Terry McDougall, Fort Wayne
1979-80	Al Dumba, Fort Wayne
1980-81	Marcel Comeau, Saginaw
1981-82	Brent Jarrett, Kalamazoo
1982-83	Claude Noel, Toledo
1983-84	Darren Jensen, Fort Wayne
1984-85	Scott Gruhl, Muskegon
1985-86	Darrell May, Peoria
1986-87	Jeff Pyle, Saginaw
	Jock Callander, Muskegon
1987-88	John Cullen, Flint
1988-89	Dave Michayluk, Muskegon
1989-90	Michel Mongeau, Peoria
1990-91	David Bruce, Peoria
1991-92	Dmitri Kvartalnov, San Diego

LEO P. LAMOUREUX MEMORIAL TROPHY
(Leading scorer)

Season	Player, Team
1946-47	Harry Marchand, Windsor
1947-48	Dick Kowcinak, Det. Auto Club
1948-49	Leo Richard, Toledo
1949-50	Dick Kowcinak, Sarnia
1950-51	Herve Parent, Grand Rapids
1951-52	George Parker, Grand Rapids
1952-53	Alex Irving, Milwaukee
1953-54	Don Hall, Johnstown
1954-55	Phil Goyette, Cincinnati
1955-56	Max Mekilok, Cincinnati
1956-57	Pierre Brillant, Indianapolis
1957-58	Warren Hynes, Cincinnati
1958-59	George Ranieri, Louisville
1959-60	Chick Chalmers, Louisville
1960-61	Ken Yackel, Minneapolis
1961-62	Len Thornson, Fort Wayne
1962-63	Moe Bartoli, Minneapolis
1963-64	Len Thornson, Fort Wayne
1964-65	Lloyd Maxfield, Port Huron
1965-66	Bob Rivard, Fort Wayne
1966-67	Len Thornson, Fort Wayne
1967-68	Gary Ford, Muskegon
1968-69	Don Westbrooke, Dayton
1969-70	Don Westbrooke, Dayton
1970-71	Darrel Knibbs, Muskegon
1971-72	Gary Ford, Muskegon
1972-73	Gary Ford, Muskegon
1973-74	Pete Mara, Des Moines
1974-75	Rick Bragnalo, Dayton
1975-76	Len Fontaine, Port Huron
1976-77	Jim Koleff, Flint
1977-78	Jim Johnston, Flint
1978-79	Terry McDougall, Fort Wayne
1979-80	Al Dumba, Fort Wayne
1980-81	Marcel Comeau, Saginaw
1981-82	Brent Jarrett, Kalamazoo
1982-83	Dale Yakiwchuk, Milwaukee
1983-84	Wally Schreiber, Fort Wayne
1984-85	Scott MacLeod, Salt Lake
1985-86	Scott MacLeod, Salt Lake
1986-87	Jock Callander, Muskegon
	Jeff Pyle, Saginaw
1987-88	John Cullen, Flint
1988-89	Dave Michayluk, Muskegon
1989-90	Michel Mongeau, Peoria
1990-91	Lonnie Loach, Fort Wayne
1991-92	Dmitri Kvartalnov, San Diego

The award was originally known as the George H. Wilkinson Trophy from 1946-47 through 1959-60.

JAMES NORRIS MEMORIAL TROPHY
(Outstanding goaltender)

Season	Player, Team
1955-56	Bill Tibbs, Troy
1956-57	Glenn Ramsey, Cincinnati
1957-58	Glenn Ramsey, Cincinnati
1958-59	Don Rigazio, Louisville
1959-60	Rene Zanier, Fort Wayne
1960-61	Ray Mikulan, Minneapolis
1961-62	Glenn Ramsey, Omaha
1962-63	Glenn Ramsey, Omaha
1963-64	Glenn Ramsey, Toledo
1964-65	Chuck Adamson, Fort Wayne
1965-66	Bob Sneddon, Port Huron
1966-67	Glenn Ramsey, Toledo
1967-68	Tim Tabor, Muskegon
	Bob Perani, Muskegon
1968-69	Pat Rupp, Dayton
	John Adams, Dayton
1969-70	Gaye Cooley, Des Moines
	Bob Perreault, Des Moines
1970-71	Lyle Carter, Muskegon
1971-72	Glenn Resch, Muskegon
1972-73	Robbie Irons, Fort Wayne
	Don Atchison, Fort Wayne
1973-74	Bill Hughes, Muskegon
1974-75	Bob Volpe, Flint
	Merlin Jenner, Flint
1975-76	Don Cutts, Muskegon
1976-77	Terry Richardson, Kalamazoo
1977-78	Lorne Molleken, Saginaw
	Pierre Chagnon, Saginaw
1978-79	Gord Laxton, Grand Rapids
1979-80	Larry Lozinski, Kalamazoo
1980-81	Claude Legris, Kalamazoo
	Georges Gagnon, Kalamazoo
1981-82	Lorne Molleken, Toledo
	Dave Tardich, Toledo
1982-83	Lorne Molleken, Toledo
1983-84	Darren Jensen, Fort Wayne
1984-85	Rick Heinz, Peoria
1985-86	Rick St. Croix, Fort Wayne
	Pokey Reddick, Fort Wayne
1986-87	Alain Raymond, Fort Wayne
	Michel Dufour, Fort Wayne
1987-88	Steve Guenette, Muskegon
1988-89	Rick Knickle, Fort Wayne
1989-90	Jimmy Waite, Indianapolis
1990-91	Guy Hebert, Peoria
	Pat Jablonski, Peoria
1991-92	Arturs Irbe, Kansas City
	Wade Flaherty, Kansas City

GOVERNORS TROPHY
(Outstanding defenseman)

Season	Player, Team
1964-65	Lionel Repka, Fort Wayne
1965-66	Bob Lemieux, Muskegon
1966-67	Larry Mavety, Port Huron
1967-68	Carl Brewer, Muskegon
1968-69	Al Breaule, Dayton
	Moe Benoit, Dayton
1969-70	John Gravel, Toledo
1970-71	Bob LaPage, Des Moines
1971-72	Rick Pagnutti, Fort Wayne
1972-73	Bob McCammon, Port Huron
1973-74	Dave Simpson, Dayton
1974-75	Murry Flegel, Muskegon
1975-76	Murry Flegel, Muskegon
1976-77	Tom Mellor, Toledo
1977-78	Michel LaChance, Milwaukee
1978-79	Guido Tenesi, Grand Rapids
1979-80	John Gibson, Saginaw
1980-81	Larry Goodenough, Saginaw
1981-82	Don Waddell, Saginaw
1982-83	Jim Burton, Fort Wayne
	Kevin Willison, Milwaukee
1983-84	Kevin Willison, Milwaukee
1984-85	Lee Norwood, Peoria
1985-86	Jim Burton, Fort Wayne
1986-87	Jim Burton, Fort Wayne
1987-88	Phil Bourque, Muskegon
1988-89	Randy Boyd, Milwaukee
1989-90	Brian Glynn, Salt Lake
1990-91	Brian McKee, Fort Wayne
1991-92	Jean-Marc Richard, Fort Wayne

GARRY F. LONGMAN MEMORIAL TROPHY
(Outstanding rookie)

Season	Player, Team
1961-62	Dave Richardson, Fort Wayne
1962-63	John Gravel, Omaha
1963-64	Don Westbrooke, Toledo
1964-65	Bob Thomas, Toledo
1965-66	Frank Golembrowsky, Port Huron
1966-67	Kerry Bond, Columbus
1967-68	Gary Ford, Muskegon
1968-69	Doug Volmar, Columbus
1969-70	Wayne Zuk, Toledo
1970-71	Corky Agar, Flint
	Herb Howdle, Dayton
1971-72	Glenn Resch, Muskegon
1972-73	Danny Gloor, Des Moines
1973-74	Frank DeMarco, Des Moines
1974-75	Rick Bragnalo, Dayton
1975-76	Sid Veysey, Fort Wayne
1976-77	Ron Zanussi, Fort Wayne
	Garth MacGuigan, Muskegon
1977-78	Dan Bonar, Fort Wayne
1978-79	Wes Jarvis, Port Huron
1979-80	Doug Robb, Milwaukee
1980-81	Scott Vanderburgh, Kalamazoo
1981-82	Scott Howson, Toledo
1982-83	Tony Fiore, Flint
1983-84	Darren Jensen, Fort Wayne
1984-85	Gilles Thibaudeau, Flint
1965-66	Guy Benoit, Muskegon
1986-87	Michel Mongeau, Saginaw
1987-88	Ed Belfour, Saginaw
	John Cullen, Flint
1988-89	Paul Ranheim, Salt Lake
1989-90	Rob Murphy, Milwaukee
1990-91	Nelson Emerson, Peoria
1991-92	Dmitri Kvartalnov, Kansas City

KEN McKENZIE TROPHY
(Outstanding American-born rookie)

Season	Player, Team
1977-78	Mike Eruzione, Toledo
1978-79	Jon Fontas, Saginaw
1979-80	Bob Janecyk, Fort Wayne
1980-81	Mike Labianca, Toledo
	Steve Janaszak, Fort Wayne
1981-82	Steve Salvucci, Saginaw
1982-83	Paul Fenton, Peoria
1983-84	Mike Krensing, Muskegon
1984-85	Bill Schafhauser, Kalamazoo
1985-86	Brian Noonan, Saginaw
1986-87	Ray LeBlanc, Flint
1987-88	Dan Woodley, Flint
1988-89	Paul Ranheim, Salt Lake
1989-90	Tim Sweeney, Salt Lake
1990-91	C.J. Young, Salt Lake
1991-92	Kevin Wortman, Salt Lake

COMMISSIONER'S TROPHY
(Coach of the year)

Season	Coach, Team
1984-85	Rick Ley, Muskegon
	Pat Kelly, Peoria
1985-86	Rob Laird, Fort Wayne
1986-87	Wayne Thomas, Salt Lake
1987-88	Rick Dudley, Flint
1988-89	B. J. MacDonald, Muskegon
	Phil Russell, Muskegon
1989-90	Darryl Sutter, Indianapolis
1990-91	Bob Plager, Peoria
1991-92	Kevin Constantine, Kansas City

N.R. (BUD) POILE TROPHY
(Playoff MVP)

Season	Player, Team
1984-85	Denis Cyr, Peoria
1985-86	Jock Callander, Muskegon
1986-87	Rick Heinz, Salt Lake
1987-88	Peter Lappin, Salt Lake
1988-89	Dave Michayluk, Muskegon
1989-90	Mike McNeill, Indianapolis
1990-91	Michel Mongeau, Peoria
1991-92	Ron Handy, Kansas City

The award was originally known as the Turner Cup Playoff MVP from 1984-85 through 1988-89.

ALL-TIME LEAGUE CHAMPIONS

	REGULAR-SEASON CHAMPION		PLAYOFF CHAMPION	
Season	Team	Coach	Team	Coach
1945-46	No trophy awarded		Detroit Auto Club	Jack Ward
1946-47	Windsor Staffords	Jack Ward	Windsor Spitfires	Ebbie Goodfellow
1947-48	Windsor Hettche Spitfires	Dent-Goodfellow	Toledo Mercurys	Andy Mulligan
1948-49	Toledo Mercurys	Andy Mulligan	Windsor Hettche Spitfires	Jimmy Skinner
1949-50	Sarnia Sailors	Dick Kowcinak	Catham Maroons	Bob Stoddart
1950-51	Grand Rapids Rockets	Lou Trudell	Toledo Mercurys	Alex Wood
1951-52	Grand Rapids Rockets	Lou Trudell	Toledo Mercurys	Alex Wood
1952-53	Cincinnati Mohawks	Buddy O'Conner	Cincinnati Mohawks	Buddy O'Conner
1953-54	Cincinnati Mohawks	Roly McLenahan	Cincinnati Mohawks	Roly McLenahan
1954-55	Cincinnati Mohawks	Roly McLenahan	Cincinnati Mohawks	Roly McLenahan
1955-56	Cincinnati Mohawks	Roly McLenahan	Cincinnati Mohawks	Roly McLenahan
1956-57	Cincinnati Mohawks	Roly McLenahan	Cincinnati Mohawks	Roly McLenahan
1957-58	Cincinnati Mohawks	Bill Gould	Indiana. Chiefs	Leo Lamoureux
1958-59	Louisville Rebels	Leo Gasparini	Louisville Rebels	Leo Gasparini
1959-60	Fort Wayne Komets	Ken Ullyot	St. Paul Saints	Fred Shero
1960-61	Minneapolis Millers	Ken Yachel	St. Paul Saints	Fred Shero
1961-62	Muskegon Zephrys	Moose Lallo	Muskegon Zephrys	Moose Lallo
1962-63	Fort Wayne Komets	Ken Ullyot	Fort Wayne Komets	Ken Ullyot
1963-64	Toledo Blades	Moe Benoit	Toledo Blades	Moe Benoit
1964-65	Port Huron Flags	Lloyd Maxfield	Fort Wayne Komets	Eddie Long
1965-66	Muskegon Mohawks	Moose Lallo	Port Huron Flags	Lloyd Maxfield
1966-67	Dayton Gems	Warren Back	Toledo Blades	Terry Slater
1967-68	Muskegon Mohawks	Moose Lallo	Muskegon Mohawks	Moose Lallo
1968-69	Dayton Gems	Larry Wilson	Dayton Gems	Larry Wilson
1969-70	Muskegon Mohawks	Moose Lallo	Dayton Gems	Larry Wilson
1970-71	Muskegon Mohawks	Moose Lallo	Port Huron Flags	Ted Garvin
1971-72	Muskegon Mohawks	Moose Lallo	Port Huron Flags	Ted Garvin
1972-73	Fort Wayne Komets	Marc Boileau	Fort Wayne Komets	Marc Boileau
1973-74	Des Moines Capitals	Dan Belisle	Des Moines Capitals	Dan Belisle
1974-75	Muskegon Mohawks	Moose Lallo	Toledo Goaldiggers	Ted Garvin
1975-76	Dayton Gems	Ivan Prediger	Dayton Gems	Ivan Prediger
1976-77	Saginaw Gears	Don Perry	Saginaw Gears	Don Perry
1977-78	Fort Wayne Komets	Gregg Pilling	Toledo Goaldiggers	Ted Garvin
1978-79	Grand Rapids Owls	Moe Bartoli	Kalamazoo Wings	Bill Purcell
1979-80	Kalamazoo Wings	Doug McKay	Kalamazoo Wings	Doug McKay
1980-81	Kalamazoo Wings	Doug McKay	Saginaw Gears	Don Perry
1981-82	Toledo Goaldiggers	Bill Inglis	Toledo Goaldiggers	Bill Inglis
1982-83	Toledo Goaldiggers	Bill Inglis	Toledo Goaldiggers	Bill Inglis
1983-84	Fort Wayne Komets	Ron Ullyot	Flint Generals	Dennis Desrosiers
1984-85	Peoria Rivermen	Pat Kelly	Peoria Rivermen	Pat Kelly
1985-86	Fort Wayne Komets	Rob Laird	Muskegon Lumberjacks	Rick Ley
1986-87	Fort Wayne Komets	Rob Laird	Salt Lake Golden Eagles	Wayne Thomas
1987-88	Muskegon Lumberjacks	Rick Ley	Salt Lake Golden Eagles	Paul Baxter
1988-89	Muskegon Lumberjacks	B.J. MacDonald	Muskegon Lumberjacks	B.J. MacDonald
1989-90	Muskegon Lumberjacks	B.J. MacDonald	Indianapolis Ice	Darryl Sutter
1990-91	Peoria Rivermen	Bob Plager	Peoria Rivermen	Bob Plager
1991-92	Kansas City Blades	Kevin Constantine	Kansas City Blades	Kevin Constantine

The IHL regular-season champion is awarded the Fred A. Huber Trophy and the playoff champion is awarded the Joseph Turner Memorial Cup.

The regular-season championship award was originally called the J.P. McGuire Trophy from 1946-47 through 1953-54.

EAST COAST HOCKEY LEAGUE

LEAGUE OFFICE

President/commissioner
Patrick Kelly

Director of information
Doug Price

Administrative secretary
June Kelly

Address
AA 520
Mart Office Building
800 Briar Creek Road
Charlotte, NC 28205

Phone
704-358-3658

FAX
704-358-3560

NOTE: League known as Atlantic Coast Hockey League from 1981-82 through 1986-87, and All American Hockey League during 1987-88.

TEAMS

BIRMINGHAM BULLS

President/general manager
Bob Polk
Coach
TBA
Director of publications
Tim Woodburn
Address
P.O. Box 13347
Birmingham, AL 35202-3347
Phone
205-458-8833
FAX
205-458-8489

COLUMBUS CHILL

President/general manager
David Paitson
Director of marketing
Alan Karpick
Coach
Terry Ruskowski
Address
1460 West Lane Avenue
Columbus, OH 43221
Phone
614-488-4455 or 614-488-4576
FAX
614-488-4576

DAYTON BOMBERS

President
Bud Ginger
General manager
Arnold W. Johnson
Coach
Claude Noel
Director of communications/broadcasting
Tom Michaels
Director of marketing
Jennifer Emmons
Address
P.O. Box 5952
Dayton, OH 45405
Phone
513-277-3765
FAX
513-278-3007

ERIE PANTHERS

Team owners
Jim Clark
Jim Wallin
Keith Lustig, M.D.
Duane Wallin

Coach and general manager
Ron Hansis
Director of marketing and media relations
Gary Thomas
Address
Erie Civic Center
809 French Street
Erie, PA 16501-1260
Mailing address
P.O. Box 6116
Erie, PA 16512-6116
Phone
814-455-3936
FAX
814-456-8287

GREENSBORO MONARCHS

Team owner
Greensboro Monarchs Hockey Inc.
Coach and general manager
Jeff Brubaker
Operations manager
Morris Jeffreys
Promotions
Mark Wylam
Director of marketing
Mark Wylam
Address
Greensboro Coliseum
1921 W. Lee Street
Greensboro, NC 27403
Phone
919-852-6170
FAX
919-852-6259

HAMPTON ROADS ADMIRALS

Team owner
Blake Cullen
Coach
John Brophy
General manager
Pat Nugent
Director of public relations
Kelly Patterson
Address
Scope Plaza
P.O. Box 299
Norfolk, VA 23501
Phone
804-640-1212
FAX
804-640-8447

JOHNSTOWN CHIEFS

Team owners
Henry Brabham IV
John Daley

General manager
John Daley
Coach
Eddie Johnstone
Director of communications/broadcasting
David Mishkin
Address
Cambria County War Memorial Arena
326 Napoleon Street
Johnstown, PA 15901
Phone
814-539-1799
FAX
814-536-1316

KNOXVILLE CHEROKEES

Team owners
Rob Stooksbury, president
Kim Simmons Thomas, V.P.
Bob Thomas, secretary/treasurer
John Staley Jr., M.D.
Harry Taylor
Coach
Barry Smith
Address
Civic Coliseum
500 E. Church St.
Knoxville, TN 37915
Phone
615-546-6707
FAX
615-546-5521

LOUISVILLE ICEHAWKS

President/general manager
Leo Huntsinger
Coach
Warren Young
Marketing/sales director
John J. Allgeier
Address
P.O. Box 37130
Louisville, KY 40233
Phone
502-367-7797
FAX
502-367-7352

NASHVILLE KNIGHTS

Owner and general manager
W. Godfrey Wood
Coach/director of hockey operations
Nick Fotiu
Vice president/marketing
Craig Jenkins
Vice president of operations
Scott Greer

Address
 Municipal Auditorium
 417 4th Ave. North
 Nashville, TN 37201
Phone
 615-255-7825
FAX
 615-255-0024

RALEIGH ICECAPS

President
 Peter Bock
Director of operations
 Jay Snead
Coach
 Kurt Kleinendorst
Address
 P.O. Box 33228
 Raleigh, NC 27636
Phone
 919-755-0022
FAX
 919-755-0899

RICHMOND RENEGADES

Owner and general manager
 Allan B. Harvie Jr.
Coach
 Roy Sommer
Director of operations
 Belinda Wiggins
Dir. of comm. and media relations
 Brian Hamilton

Address
 Richmond Coliseum
 601 East Leigh Street
 Richmond, VA 23219
Phone
 804-643-7825
FAX
 804-649-0651

ROANOKE VALLEY RAMPAGE

President
 Lawrence Revo
General manager
 TBA
Coach
 Steve Gatzos
Director of marketing
 Shirley Woolwine
Address
 P.O. Box 310
 Vinton, VA 24179
Phone
 703-345-3557
FAX
 703-344-2983

TOLEDO STORM

President/general manager
 Barry Soskin
Coach
 Chris McSorley

Director of public relations
 Jeff Gibbons
Address
 Toledo Sports Arena
 One Main Street
 Toledo, OH 43605
Phone
 419-691-0200
FAX
 419-698-8998

WHEELING THUNDERBIRDS

President
 Ed Broyhill
General manager
 Larry Kish
Office manager
 Stacey Guthrie
Director of media relations
 Mark Mead
Coach
 Doug Sauter
Address
 P.O. Box 6563
 Wheeling, WV 26003
Mailing Address
 P.O. Box 4507
 Winston-Salem, NC 27115-4507
Phone
 304-234-4626
FAX
 304-234-4846

1991-92 REGULAR SEASON

FINAL STANDINGS

EAST DIVISION

Team	G	W	L	Pts.	GF	GA
Greensboro	64	43	17 (4)	90	297	292
Hampton Roads	64	42	20 (2)	86	298	220
Winston-Salem	64	36	24 (4)	76	270	245
Richmond	64	30	27 (7)	67	263	263
Raleigh	64	25	33 (6)	56	228	284
Roanoke Valley	64	21	36 (7)	49	236	313
Knoxville	64	20	36 (8)	48	265	355

( )—Indicates overtime losses and are worth one point.

WEST DIVISION

Team	G	W	L	Pts.	GF	GA
Toledo	64	46	15 (3)	95	367	240
Cincinnati	64	36	20 (8)	80	329	284
Johnstown	64	36	23 (5)	77	294	248
Erie	64	33	27 (4)	70	284	309
Dayton	64	32	26 (6)	70	305	300
Louisville	64	31	25 (8)	70	315	306
Columbus	64	25	30 (9)	59	298	341
Nashville	64	24	36 (4)	52	246	335

INDIVIDUAL LEADERS

Goals: Darren Colbourne, Dayton (69)
Assists: Mike Reier, Dayton (75)
Points: Phil Berger, Greensboro (130)
Penalty minutes: Barry Dreger, Columbus (362)
Goaltending average: Frederic Chabot, Winston-Salem (2.94)
Shutouts: Mike James, Roanoke Valley (4)

	Games	G	A	Pts.
Mark Woolf, Roanoke Valley	63	50	51	101
Brad McCaughey, Toledo	58	56	44	100
Martin Bergeron, Louisville	64	39	61	100
Mike Casselman, Toledo	61	39	60	99
Mike Reier, Dayton	63	23	75	98
Craig Charron, Cincinnati	64	41	55	96
Doug Lawrence, Erie	60	19	74	93
Ed Zawatsky, Erie	48	42	49	91
Brett Stewart, Roanoke Valley	64	33	58	91
Martin St. Amour, Cincinnati	60	44	44	88
Daryl Noren, Greensboro	37	36	52	88
Greg Puhalski, Toledo	46	29	58	87
Jason Christie, Columbus	61	28	56	84
Scott White, Greensboro	57	21	63	84

TOP SCORERS

	Games	G	A	Pts.
Phil Berger, Greensboro	60	60	70	130
Darren Colbourne, Dayton	64	69	50	119
Mark Green, Johnstown	64	68	49	117
Mike Maurice, Toledo	62	39	72	111
Sheldon Gorski, Louisville	55	56	54	110
Trevor Jobe, Nashville/Richmond	62	54	49	103

INDIVIDUAL STATISTICS

CINCINNATI CYCLONES

SCORING

	Games	G	A	Pts.	Pen.
Craig Charron	64	41	55	96	97
Martin St. Amour	60	44	44	88	183
Kevin Scott	61	35	41	76	69
Steve Cadieux	48	38	30	68	112

	Games	G	A	Pts.	Pen.
Bob Wallwork	63	22	46	68	48
Tom Neziol	54	20	45	65	46
Chris Marshall	51	21	38	59	203
Kevin Kerr	37	27	18	45	203
Shaun Clouston	33	16	27	43	42
Howie Rosenblatt	50	26	16	42	235
David Craievich	50	11	29	40	166

	Games	G	A	Pts.	Pen.
Kevin Dean	30	3	22	25	43
Daryn McBride	19	7	15	22	62
Dan Beaudette	31	8	10	18	32
Rob Krauss	44	3	14	17	247
Scott Luik	21	2	10	12	26
Steve Shaunessy	40	0	12	12	241
Jaan Luik	20	2	9	11	40
Larry Rooney	20	0	10	10	16
Jay Rose	31	5	1	6	80
Daniel Elsener	11	0	6	6	17
Doug Melnyk	22	0	6	6	22
Pete Schure	6	2	1	3	57
Dusty Imoo (goalie)	9	0	2	2	0
David Moore	5	0	1	1	2
Jeff Hogdon	8	0	1	1	2
Corey Schwab (goalie)	8	0	1	1	4
Doug Dadswell (goalie)	24	0	1	1	8
Mark Romaine (goalie)	28	0	0	0	2
An Fu Wong	1	0	0	0	0

GOALTENDING

	Games	Min.	Goals	SO	Avg.
Dusty Imoo	9	535	33	0	3.70
Doug Dadswell	24	1361	89	0	3.92
Corey Schwab	8	450	31	0	4.13
Mark Romaine	27	1544	124	0	4.82

COLUMBUS CHILL

SCORING

	Games	G	A	Pts.	Pen.
Jason Christie	61	28	56	84	218
Kevin Alexander	64	29	52	81	38
Jim Ballantine	61	30	46	76	32
Kurt Semandel	61	26	36	62	72
Len Soccio	38	24	34	58	149
Frank LaScala	59	34	23	57	138
Trent Kaese	28	28	22	50	56
Don Cranato	40	10	32	42	28
Alain Deeks	46	15	24	39	73
Mark Cipriano	48	17	14	31	333
E.J. Sauer	34	6	23	29	73
Brad Treliving	49	4	25	29	170
Barry Dreger	57	4	24	28	362
Joey Mittelsteadt	59	7	15	22	296
Cam Brown	10	11	6	17	64
Jason Taylor	21	7	9	16	147
Jeff Napierala	13	7	6	13	10
Rob Lewis	45	2	11	13	55
Phil Crowe	32	4	7	11	145
Rob Sangster	15	3	5	8	158
Stanislav Komarov	7	2	4	6	23
Al Novakowski	9	0	1	1	61
Alain Harvey (goalie)	36	0	1	1	2
Todd Decker	4	0	1	1	0
Mark Romaine (goalie)	7	0	0	0	10
Chris Varga	2	0	0	0	2
Doug Brown (goalie)	18	0	0	0	2
Kevin Marion (goalie)	6	0	0	0	0
Steve Wachter (goalie)	3	0	0	0	0
Kevin Sawchuk (goalie)	1	0	0	0	0
Lance Madson (goalie)	1	0	0	0	0
Andre Bouliane (goalie)	2	0	0	0	0
Chris Puscian (goalie)	2	0	0	0	0
Roger Rougelot (goalie)	3	0	0	0	0

GOALTENDING

	Games	Min.	Goals	SO	Avg.
Lance Madson	1	60	2	0	2.00
Roger Rougelot	3	139	10	0	4.32
Alain Harvey	36	1941	146	1	4.51
Kevin Sawchuk	1	12	1	0	5.00
Doug Brown	18	936	80	0	5.13
Andre Bouliane	2	114	10	0	5.26
Kevin Marion	6	239	25	0	6.28
Mark Romaine	7	309	34	0	6.60
Chris Puscian	2	35	4	0	6.86
Steve Wachter	3	84	11	0	7.86

DAYTON BOMBERS

SCORING

	Games	G	A	Pts.	Pen.
Darren Colbourne	64	69	50	119	70
Mike Reier	63	23	75	98	76
Derek Crawford	61	37	37	74	231
Shawn Howard	64	30	38	68	46
Sylvain Fleury	59	27	30	57	13
Paul Marshall	36	19	29	48	32
Jeff Green	23	12	17	29	21
Joe Tonello	63	3	26	29	44
Nick Beaulieu	29	14	14	28	48
Keith Miller	24	13	13	26	14
Jaan Luik	38	3	21	24	38
Jackson Penney	16	12	10	22	38
Butch Kaebel	30	4	18	22	13
Ray Edwards	23	5	10	15	120
Mike Green	58	3	12	15	65
Glen Wisser	23	7	7	14	22
Matt Johnson	49	1	12	13	24
Scott Luik	13	5	7	12	14
Chris Newans	23	4	8	12	42
Jay Moore	10	5	6	11	6
Darryl Mitchell	12	3	8	11	18
Joe Hawley	7	3	6	9	12
John Sullivan	12	1	3	4	40
Bruce Wolanin	20	1	2	3	13
Sylvain Mayer	11	0	2	2	89
Mike Hassman	8	1	0	1	2
Stanislav Komarov	2	0	1	1	0
Alex Daviault	20	0	0	0	135
Ray DeSouza	4	0	0	0	2
Brian Fleury	4	0	0	0	0
Dusty Imoo (goalie)	4	0	0	0	7
Francis Ouelette (goalie)	8	0	0	0	0
Everett Caldwell	1	0	0	0	0
Todd Bojcun (goalie)	29	0	0	0	12
Rod Houk (goalie)	33	0	0	0	12

GOALTENDING

	Games	Min.	Goals	SO	Avg.
Francis Ouelette	8	493	35	0	4.26
Rod Houk	33	1775	130	1	4.39
Todd Bojcun	28	1392	105	0	4.53
Dusty Imoo	4	204	16	0	4.71

ERIE PANTHERS

SCORING

	Games	G	A	Pts.	Pen.
Doug Lawrence	60	19	74	93	120
Ed Zawatsky	48	42	49	91	62
Peter Buckeridge	59	31	47	78	82
Ryan Kummu	62	25	51	76	230
Bill Gall	53	15	31	46	28
Dave Pergola	43	19	18	37	44
Scot Johnston	53	24	12	36	85
Bob Fleming	54	11	21	32	161
Andrew Ross	36	13	16	29	53
Shane McFarlane	36	10	18	28	29
John Gladiator	58	7	21	28	112
Glen Goodall	14	6	20	26	12
Pat Cavanagh	35	8	14	22	220
Bob Bodak	28	9	11	20	48
Tim Roberts	31	5	12	17	25
Darrin Amundson	21	8	7	15	17
Derek Clancey	16	7	6	13	24
Murray Duval	19	5	8	13	26
Dave DiVita	21	2	10	12	46
Vern Smith	8	3	5	8	6
Steve Wienke	36	2	6	8	61
John Batten	15	4	2	6	49
Jason Prosofsky	7	2	2	4	28
Carl Sasyn	27	0	4	4	28

	Games	G	A	Pts.	Pen.
Jason Brousseau	11	2	1	3	9
Scott Burfoot	1	2	1	3	0
Steve Marcolini	6	1	2	3	19
John Bradley (goalie)	16	0	3	3	6
Dwaine Hutton	4	2	0	2	6
Mark Gowans (goalie)	46	0	2	2	2
Kurt Johnson	3	0	1	1	0
Tom Sprague	7	0	1	1	4
Dusty Imoo (goalie)	1	0	0	0	0
Steve Wachter (goalie)	1	0	0	0	0
Bill Pye (goalie)	5	0	0	0	0

GOALTENDING

	Games	Min.	Goals	SO	Avg.
Bill Pye	5	310	22	0	4.26
John Bradley	15	810	59	0	4.37
Mark Gowans	46	2674	210	0	4.71
Dusty Imoo	1	60	8	0	8.00
Steve Wachter	1	9	2	0	13.33

GREENSBORO MONARCHS

SCORING

	Games	G	A	Pts.	Pen.
Phil Berger	60	60	70	130	158
Daryl Noren	37	36	52	88	48
Scott White	57	21	63	84	204
Shawn Wheeler	52	36	36	72	301
Eric Lemarque	55	29	37	66	110
Boyd Sutton	51	17	28	45	10
Chris Laganas	63	22	21	43	294
Timo Makela	61	5	34	39	43
Peter Sentner	54	10	16	26	66
Eric Dubois	36	7	17	24	62
Roger Larche	9	12	9	21	29
Mike Butters	32	6	15	21	185
John Devereaux	32	5	16	21	77
Chris Wolanin	61	5	10	15	127
Rob Bateman	53	2	11	13	121
Gord Cruikshank	7	6	6	12	0
Ed Ward	12	4	8	12	21
Todd Gordon	45	2	9	11	171
Mike McCormick	31	6	4	10	110
Dean Zayonce	26	2	7	9	151
Brennan Maley	14	2	2	4	27
Brian Cook	10	1	2	3	8
Darren Nauss	8	0	3	3	0
Nick Vitucci (goalie)	42	0	3	3	26
Greg Menges (goalie)	31	0	2	2	25
Daniel Dore	6	1	0	1	34
Rob Reimer	4	0	1	1	2
John Blessman	2	0	0	0	14
Joel Clark (goalie)	1	0	0	0	0

GOALTENDING

	Games	Min.	Goals	SO	Avg.
Joel Clark	1	7	0	0	0.00
Nick Vitucci	42	2358	136	1	3.46
Greg Menges	31	1523	105	0	4.14

HAMPTON ROADS ADMIRALS

SCORING

	Games	G	A	Pts.	Pen.
Randy Pearce	55	32	46	78	134
Victor Gervais	44	30	43	73	79
Billy Nolan	58	26	34	60	91
Mike Chighisola	40	24	35	59	95
Brian Martin	28	30	22	52	82
Rod Taylor	40	26	24	50	29
Al MacIsaac	56	18	29	47	120
Dennis McEwen	61	15	28	43	97
Steve Martell	20	9	25	34	34
Wade Bartley	43	8	26	34	75

	Games	G	A	Pts.	Pen.
Harry Mews	15	15	17	32	31
Keith Whitmore	45	10	20	30	70
Steve Poapst	55	8	20	28	29
Murray Hood	18	4	23	27	6
Steve Mirabile	22	12	13	25	27
Shawn Snesar	57	5	17	22	272
John East	43	2	17	19	127
Dave Morissette	47	6	10	16	293
Jiri Vykoutal	9	3	9	12	12
Paul Krepelka	33	6	5	11	59
Scott Johnson	20	2	9	11	8
Kurt Kabat	18	4	6	10	50
Darcy Kaminski	24	2	5	7	110
Mark Bernard (goalie)	40	0	4	4	6
Pat Bingham	5	0	2	2	56
Chris Clarke	3	0	2	2	2
Richie Walcott	7	1	0	1	23
David Cooper (goalie)	5	0	1	1	0
Darrin Amundson	5	0	1	1	0
Phil Esposito	2	0	0	0	2
Olaf Kolzig (goalie)	14	0	0	0	31
Pete Siciliano	9	0	0	0	21
Byron Dafoe (goalie)	10	0	0	0	2

GOALTENDING

	Games	Min.	Goals	SO	Avg.
Byron Dafoe	10	562	26	1	2.78
Olaf Kolzig	14	847	41	0	2.90
Mark Bernard	40	2327	130	3	3.35
David Cooper	5	125	15	0	7.20

JOHNSTOWN CHIEFS

SCORING

	Games	G	A	Pts.	Pen.
Mark Green	64	68	49	117	44
Bruce Coles	43	32	45	77	113
Brian Ferreira	39	26	50	76	94
Bob Woods	63	18	43	61	44
Dave MacIntyre	63	21	37	58	84
Matt Glennon	30	9	46	55	77
Rob Hrytsak	47	19	27	46	68
Perry Florio	63	10	35	45	247
Doug Weiss	64	14	30	44	23
Ted Miskolczi	38	25	15	40	71
Andy Bezeau	28	11	10	21	142
Mark Krys	43	8	12	20	73
Christian Lariviere	62	3	16	19	142
Mike Rossetti	14	10	8	18	29
Mike McCormick	19	4	9	13	22
Eric Reisman	32	0	12	12	50
Scott McCrady	10	0	7	7	44
John Mooney	8	3	3	6	15
Chuck Wiegand	14	3	2	5	19
Jeff Beaudin	31	2	3	5	72
Mike Roberts	40	1	4	5	24
Pat Penner	7	2	1	3	0
Mike Sanderson	6	1	2	3	4
Steve Beadle	4	1	1	2	4
Everton Blackwin	11	1	1	2	17
Dan Poirier	3	1	1	2	9
Doug Sinclair	18	1	0	1	142
Mike Parson (goalie)	17	0	1	1	2
Stan Reddick (goalie)	42	0	1	1	8
Chris Grassie	3	0	0	0	10
Chris Harvey (goalie)	4	0	0	0	4
Mark Cascagnette	6	0	0	0	17
Phil Esposito	3	0	0	0	4
Tony Silvestri	5	0	0	0	0
Sean Callanan (goalie)	1	0	0	0	0
John Fletcher (goalie)	6	0	0	0	0
Craig Shepherd	2	0	0	0	0

GOALTENDING

	Games	Min.	Goals	SO	Avg.
John Fletcher	6	318	13	0	2.45
Mike Parson	17	994	61	1	3.68
Stan Reddick	42	2352	151	0	3.85
Chris Harvey	4	193	12	0	4.04
Sean Callanan	1	6	1	0	10.00

KNOXVILLE CHEROKEES

SCORING

	Games	G	A	Pts.	Pen.
Greg Pankewicz	59	41	39	80	214
Bruno Villeneuve	48	38	35	73	12
Troy Mick	48	23	38	61	24
Joel Gardner	36	20	34	54	30
Dave Shute	57	18	35	53	91
Shawn Lillie	39	15	28	43	6
Roman Hubalek	50	14	27	41	24
Chad Thompson	46	11	20	31	50
Mike Gober	25	16	11	27	103
Brett Lawrence	36	13	7	20	28
Dean McDonald	30	4	15	19	59
Steve Ryding	31	4	12	16	28
Jody Praznik	19	4	12	16	17
Jamie Dabanovich	36	4	9	13	23
Karl Clauss	42	4	9	13	29
Lance Marciano	29	1	12	13	54
Tommi Virkkunen	14	2	9	11	12
Robert Melanson	49	0	11	11	186
Trevor Forsythe	23	3	7	10	56
Ron Evans	10	3	6	9	18
Larry Bernard	5	3	6	9	11
Jim Latos	10	5	2	7	24
Rich Schelling	17	2	5	7	18
Jay Luknowski	5	1	6	7	0
Greg Simeone	11	1	6	7	9
Greg Long	4	3	3	6	4
John Staerker	9	2	4	6	8
Eric Rochette	22	1	5	6	38
Ken Maffia	6	2	3	5	2
Andrew Ross	9	2	3	5	2
Dominic Hardy	4	3	1	4	7
Steve Rohlik	6	1	3	4	4
Dean Anderson (goalie)	38	0	3	3	46
Bruce Wolanin	4	0	2	2	0
Brett Barnett	2	1	0	1	0
John Fletcher (goalie)	2	0	1	1	0
Daryl Harpe	2	0	1	1	4
Curtis Brown	1	0	1	1	0
Andy Stewart (goalie)	1	0	1	1	0
Brian Bellefeville	1	0	1	1	0
Carl Sasyn	3	0	1	1	0
Craig Shepherd	7	0	1	1	14
Phil Esposito	6	0	1	1	33
John Kershaw	1	0	0	0	0
Jason Glickman (goalie)	3	0	0	0	4
Geno Pare	7	0	0	0	33
Michael Gampler	3	0	0	0	0
Donald Blishen (goalie)	2	0	0	0	2
Rocky Johnson	1	0	0	0	0
Mike Lawrence	1	0	0	0	0
Greg Ware	2	0	0	0	0
Don Borgeson	4	0	0	0	49
Mike Chighisola	3	0	0	0	0
Mike Greenlay (goalie)	27	0	0	0	8
Alain Morissette (goalie)	1	0	0	0	0
Pierre Calder	13	0	0	0	27

GOALTENDING

	Games	Min.	Goals	SO	Avg.
Andy Stewart	1	33	2	0	3.64
Alain Morissette	1	65	5	0	4.62
Mike Greenlay	27	1415	113	1	4.79
Dean Anderson	37	2004	188	0	5.63
Jason Glickman	3	180	18	0	6.00
Donald Blishen	2	100	10	0	6.00
John Fletcher	2	79	10	0	7.59

LOUISVILLE ICEHAWKS

SCORING

	Games	G	A	Pts.	Pen.
Sheldon Gorski	55	56	54	110	94
Martin Bergeron	64	39	61	100	134
Trevor Buchanan	62	38	28	66	259
Brian Cook	38	18	43	61	44
Chris Bright	46	17	39	56	61
Chris Smith	58	20	33	53	15
Rob Reimer	36	26	22	48	27
Chad Biafore	62	2	45	47	155
Kelly Ens	34	20	24	44	45
Trevor Smith	40	10	22	32	64
Chris Scheid	45	10	18	28	19
Scott Humeniuk	26	7	21	28	93
Paul Gherardi	25	13	11	24	26
Scott Eichstadt	37	10	12	22	27
Mitch Wilson	25	9	11	20	144
Eric Richard	23	4	13	17	8
David Moore	38	1	15	16	40
Terry Virtue	23	1	15	16	58
Cam Brauer	44	2	10	12	182
Mark Holick	24	5	3	8	152
Patrick Cloutier	9	2	4	6	30
Corey Beaulieu	8	1	5	6	60
Brian Bellefeville	7	3	1	4	4
Jim Burke	14	1	3	4	90
Martin Lacombe	18	0	2	2	115
Brian Puhalski	4	0	1	1	16
Scott Patterson	3	0	1	1	0
Chris Clifford (goalie)	56	0	1	1	8
Sean Provost	1	0	0	0	0
Sylvain Mayer	2	0	0	0	6
Doug Bacon	2	0	0	0	5
Ron Aubrey	10	0	0	0	36
Joe Bossi	3	0	0	0	2
Kurt Johnson	3	0	0	0	0
Geno Pare	3	0	0	0	0
Roger Rougelot (goalie)	1	0	0	0	0
Lance Madson (goalie)	17	0	0	0	0

GOALTENDING

	Games	Min.	Goals	SO	Avg.
Chris Clifford	56	3151	223	1	4.25
Lance Madson	17	712	68	0	5.73
Roger Rougelot	1	21	5	0	14.29

NASHVILLE KNIGHTS

SCORING

	Games	G	A	Pts.	Pen.
Jeff Jablonski	63	36	39	75	74
Mike Seaton	63	25	38	63	48
Mike de Carle	62	28	27	55	205
Rob Dumas	63	9	37	46	215
Trevor Jobe	28	18	19	37	81
Jim Ritchie	54	20	14	34	39
Brock Kelly	52	13	19	32	223
Sean Tomalty	45	17	14	31	27
Chuck Wiegand	36	20	9	29	61
Darryl Mitchell	41	7	20	27	63
Mark Hilton	44	6	17	23	46
Kevin Sullivan	26	7	11	18	33
Steve Chelios	24	5	11	16	47
Angelo Russo	32	5	11	16	26
Tim Doyle	30	3	11	14	28
Chris Grassie	34	1	11	12	80
Chris Newans	9	6	5	11	16
Glen Engevik	14	5	6	11	20
Gord Cruikshank	17	4	7	11	8
Dan Rolfe	39	0	11	11	44
Scott Taylor	38	3	7	10	146
Sean Dooley	19	2	7	9	13
Mike Hiltner	8	2	4	6	20
Troy Volhoffer	6	1	3	4	7
Mike Sanderson	4	2	1	3	2

	Games	G	A	Pts.	Pen.
Dan Poirier	16	1	2	3	75
Don Parsons	3	0	3	3	0
Tyler Green	5	0	1	1	5
Dominic Hardy	2	0	1	1	0
Bob Bowse	7	0	1	1	2
Paul Cohen (goalie)	18	0	1	1	16
John Fletcher (goalie)	11	0	1	1	4
David Gatti	3	0	1	1	0
Ron High (goalie)	1	0	0	0	0
Roger Rougelot (goalie)	6	0	0	0	0
Nick Sereggela (goalie)	10	0	0	0	2
Chris Harvey (goalie)	20	0	0	0	16
Bryan LaFort (goalie)	12	0	0	0	4

GOALTENDING

	Games	Min.	Goals	SO	Avg.
Chris Harvey	20	956	68	0	4.27
Paul Cohen	17	894	68	0	4.56
Nick Sereggela	10	471	42	0	5.35
Bryan LaFort	11	582	52	0	5.36
John Fletcher	11	583	54	0	5.56
Roger Rougelot	8	325	35	0	6.46
Ron High	1	40	6	0	9.00

RALEIGH ICECAPS

SCORING

	Games	G	A	Pts.	Pen.
Rick Barkovich	58	31	36	67	141
Jim Powers	62	34	28	62	67
Jeff Tomlinson	44	14	34	48	26
Lyle Wildgoose	41	20	23	43	10
Kris Miller	42	12	27	39	78
Kirby Lindal	39	15	20	35	52
Barry Niecar	46	10	18	28	229
Gord Cruikshank	27	13	13	26	34
Steve Mirabile	42	12	10	22	37
Todd Person	47	11	11	22	30
Greg Walters	18	9	13	22	30
Trevor Pochipinski	38	5	15	20	15
Dave Doucette	46	3	14	17	12
Brad Gratton	16	8	5	13	2
Mike Chighisola	13	4	7	11	39
Chris Newans	13	5	4	9	26
Jerry Dineen	31	4	5	9	26
Sean Cowan	38	0	8	8	72
Bruno Villeneuve	8	5	2	7	9
Tim Doyle	35	0	6	6	16
Dana Janis	9	2	3	5	2
Bill LaCouture	11	1	4	5	7
Alex Daviault	11	1	4	5	56
Scott Feasby	20	0	5	5	47
Jeff Perry	8	2	2	4	18
Jamie Reidy	8	1	3	4	10
Peter Heine	17	0	4	4	4
Darrell Newman	16	0	4	4	13
Angelo Russo	7	2	1	3	10
Mike Hiltner	4	1	2	3	5
Brandy Semchuk	5	1	2	3	16
Rob Mendel	10	0	3	3	12
Pat Caron	3	0	2	2	31
Mike Mudd (goalie)	16	0	2	2	2
Wayne Cowley (goalie)	38	0	2	2	18
Kyle McDonough	2	1	0	1	6
Stephane Venne	3	1	0	1	0
Dean McDonald	4	0	1	1	0
Chris Harvey (goalie)	5	0	1	1	4
Roman Trebaticky	5	0	1	1	0
Mark Romaine (goalie)	1	0	0	0	0
Paul Rossi	2	0	0	0	2
Chad Thompson	2	0	0	0	0
Mark Casagnette	3	0	0	0	9
Brett Lawrence	3	0	0	0	0
Wayne Marion (goalie)	3	0	0	0	0
Roger Rougelot (goalie)	5	0	0	0	0
Sylvain Mayer	6	0	0	0	104

GOALTENDING

	Games	Min.	Goals	SO	Avg.
Wayne Cowley	38	2213	137	1	3.71
Chris Harvey	5	305	24	0	4.72
Mike Mudd	15	919	74	0	4.83
Mark Romaine	1	60	5	0	5.00
Roger Rougelot	5	219	19	0	5.21
Wayne Marion	3	159	16	0	6.04

RICHMOND RENEGADES

SCORING

	Games	G	A	Pts.	Pen.
Dave Aiken	63	31	36	67	25
Trevor Jobe	34	36	30	66	74
Paul Rutherford	64	28	30	58	34
Scott Drevitch	49	7	42	49	26
Brendan Flynn	64	12	34	46	63
Bob Berg	37	19	14	33	65
Steve Scheifele	29	11	20	31	25
Guy Gadowsky	21	16	14	30	51
Rob Vanderydt	49	12	18	30	27
Jim McGeough	24	16	12	28	34
Will Averill	33	3	23	26	18
Pat Bingham	47	10	14	24	148
Kevin Sullivan	30	14	8	22	33
Andy Akervick	30	9	12	21	32
Kirby Lindal	18	8	11	19	30
Mark Kuntz	46	6	13	19	187
Larry Rooney	41	3	10	13	57
Todd Drevitch	61	2	11	13	162
Trevor Converse	13	4	7	11	75
Joni Lehto	18	2	9	11	10
Doug Melnyk	18	2	9	11	22
Lyle Wildgoose	13	5	4	9	27
Dean Trboyevich	23	1	6	7	100
Scott Johnson	6	2	4	6	0
Greg Bignell	12	1	2	3	42
Dan Rolfe	11	1	1	2	29
Alex Roberts	2	1	1	2	2
Andy Bezeau	12	1	1	2	71
Marco Fuster	5	0	2	2	4
Pete Liptrott	10	0	2	2	59
Dan Fowler	1	0	1	1	22
Jamie McLennan (goalie)	32	0	1	1	20
Dean Williamson	2	0	1	1	2
Jon Gustafson (goalie)	35	0	1	1	6
Joseph Capprini (goalie)	4	0	0	0	0
Sean Lebrun	2	0	0	0	2
Bob Desjardins (goalie)	1	0	0	0	0

GOALTENDING

	Games	Min.	Goals	SO	Avg.
Bob Desjardins	1	65	4	0	3.69
Jamie McLennan	32	1837	114	0	3.72
Jon Gustafson	32	1771	117	1	3.96
Joseph Capprini	4	195	15	0	4.62

ROANOKE VALLEY REBELS

SCORING

	Games	G	A	Pts.	Pen.
Mark Woolf	63	50	51	101	93
Brett Stewart	64	33	58	91	115
Peter Kasowski	36	26	50	76	49
Wayne Muir	46	12	19	31	168
Ron Jones	56	17	12	29	163
Brian Bellefeville	37	16	12	28	119
Graham Garden	42	5	21	26	202
Terry Virtue	38	4	22	26	165
Mike Barlage	51	5	20	25	249
Corey Lyons	22	10	13	23	13
Bill Harrington	46	11	9	20	42
Bill Whitfield	60	6	14	20	40
Ken Moran	49	6	12	18	19
Bob Kennedy	31	7	10	17	26
Scott Eichstadt	26	6	9	15	14

	Games	G	A	Pts.	Pen.
Trevor Smith	26	4	9	13	8
Devin Derkson	51	3	6	9	144
Marco Fuster	7	1	6	7	35
Frank Bialowas	23	4	2	6	150
Steve Chelios	18	2	4	6	44
Ken Blum	30	3	2	5	64
Dana Janis	15	1	4	5	8
Joe Potskin	9	1	2	3	2
Roman Trebaticky	3	1	2	3	0
Bill LaCouture	14	1	2	3	12
Ben Wyzansky	2	0	3	3	0
Jeff Tomlinson	6	1	1	2	4
Ray Letourneau (goalie)	5	0	2	2	4
Doug Brown (goalie)	4	0	0	0	0
Greg Simeone	5	0	0	0	21
James Baker	3	0	0	0	7
Jerry Higgins	1	0	0	0	0
Jeff Hogdon	1	0	0	0	0
Don Bogeson	1	0	0	0	2
Paul Rossi	2	0	0	0	0
Greg Neish	3	0	0	0	14
Ken Maffia	5	0	0	0	2
Mike Mudd (goalie)	14	0	0	0	2
Al Novakowski	2	0	0	0	5
Darrell Newman	2	0	0	0	0
Dan Bouchard (goalie)	11	0	0	0	0
Mike James (goalie)	45	0	0	0	24

GOALTENDING

	Games	Min.	Goals	SO	Avg.
Doug Brown	4	150	9	0	3.60
Mike James	45	2446	162	4	3.97
Mike Mudd	13	661	62	0	5.63
Dan Bouchard	11	364	38	0	6.26
Ray Letourneau	5	245	33	0	8.80

TOLEDO STORM

SCORING

	Games	G	A	Pts.	Pen.
Mike Maurice	62	39	72	111	51
Brad McCaughey	58	56	44	100	29
Mike Casselman	61	39	60	99	83
Greg Puhalski	46	29	58	87	14
Don Stone	64	26	44	70	10
Dave Flanagan	46	34	29	63	64
Bruce MacDonald	42	29	26	55	32
Byron Lomow	56	18	32	50	242
Dan Wiebe	42	29	19	48	124
Alex Roberts	27	13	27	40	49
Darin Banister	27	3	29	32	68
Jody Praznik	37	3	27	30	26
Pete Stauber	25	7	21	28	46
Derek Booth	20	3	17	20	46
Tony Burns	34	8	9	17	36
Ron Aubrey	32	5	12	17	293
Bob Boughner	28	3	10	13	79
Ed Ljubicic	20	8	2	10	97
Pat Pylypuik	51	2	8	10	226
Sean Cowan	17	4	5	9	45
Ken Alexander	34	1	8	9	52
Derek Clancey	5	2	5	7	0
Mike Gober	5	3	2	5	26
Greg Bignell	22	0	5	5	167
Paul Rossi	3	1	2	3	0
Ken Blum	8	0	2	2	2
Dave Stewart	3	0	2	2	2
Mike Williams (goalie)	44	0	2	2	18
Jeff Green	4	1	0	1	2
Rick Judson	2	1	0	1	2
Scott King (goalie)	7	0	1	1	0
Paul Cohen (goalie)	6	0	0	0	6
Joe Matty (goalie)	1	0	0	0	0
Dave Gagnon (goalie)	7	0	0	0	4
Mark Romaine (goalie)	3	0	0	0	10
Dave Tench	1	0	0	0	0

	Games	G	A	Pts.	Pen.
Mark Reimer (goalie)	1	0	0	0	2
Phil Crowe	2	0	0	0	0

GOALTENDING

	Games	Min.	Goals	SO	Avg.
Joe Matty	1	0	0	0	0.00
Mark Reimer	2	119	6	0	3.03
Dave Gagnon	7	354	18	0	3.05
Paul Cohen	6	333	17	1	3.06
Scott King	7	424	25	0	3.54
Mike Williams	44	2490	158	0	3.81
Mark Romaine	4	140	11	0	4.71

WINSTON-SALEM THUNDERBIRDS

SCORING

	Games	G	A	Pts.	Pen.
Devin Edgerton	64	40	42	82	53
Craig Endean	54	25	46	71	27
Dan Woodley	57	24	42	66	102
Brent Fleetwood	56	27	32	59	73
Trevor Sim	53	25	29	54	110
Marc Laniel	57	15	36	51	90
Darren Schwartz	55	25	21	46	345
Derek DeCosty	58	30	14	44	56
Trevor Senn	41	16	25	41	196
Dean Antos	43	9	31	40	56
John Uniac	38	4	16	20	39
Doug Greschuk	64	2	16	18	138
Claude Barthe	54	3	13	16	136
Peter Heine	39	3	9	12	72
Doug Bacon	27	5	5	10	166
Tim Roberts	18	1	8	9	7
Bruce Coles	13	2	6	8	37
Derek Clancey	9	4	3	7	2
Riel Bellegarde	16	3	4	7	4
Ed McMillan	9	2	2	4	17
Gary St. Pierre	6	2	2	4	4
Jay Moore	6	1	3	4	11
John Devereaux	2	1	1	2	2
Alexandre Legault	7	1	1	2	9
Bill Campbell	3	0	2	2	0
Jerry Dineen	7	0	2	2	16
Chris Scheid	3	0	2	2	2
Lee McMillan	4	0	1	1	28
Ken Blum	8	0	1	1	14
Geno Pare	7	0	1	1	19
Jocelyn Provost (goalie)	3	0	0	0	0
Chris Puscian (goalie)	1	0	0	0	0
Joe Crowley	6	0	0	0	0
Tom Dennis (goalie)	5	0	0	0	12
Mike Millham (goalie)	38	0	0	0	8
Frederic Chabot (goalie)	25	0	0	0	12

GOALTENDING

	Games	Min.	Goals	SO	Avg.
Frederic Chabot	24	1449	71	0	2.94
Tom Dennis	5	304	20	0	3.95
Mike Millham	36	1996	137	1	4.12
Jocelyn Provost	3	120	9	0	4.50
Chris Puscian	1	20	4	0	12.00

PLAYERS WITH TWO OR MORE TEAMS

SCORING

	Games	G	A	Pts.	Pen.
Darrin Amundson, Erie	21	8	7	15	17
Darrin Amundson, H.R.	5	0	1	1	0
Totals	26	8	8	16	17
Ron Aubrey, Louisville	10	0	0	0	36
Ron Aubrey, Toledo	32	5	12	17	293
Totals	42	5	12	17	329
Doug Bacon, Louisville	2	0	0	0	5
Doug Bacon, Winston-Salem	27	5	5	10	166
Totals	29	5	5	10	171

	Games	G	A	Pts.	Pen.
Brian Bellefeville, Roanoke	37	16	12	28	119
Brian Bellefeville, Louisville	7	3	1	4	4
Brian Bellefeville, Knoxville	1	0	1	1	0
Totals	45	19	14	33	123
Andy Bezeau, Johnstown	28	11	10	21	142
Andy Bezeau, Richmond	12	1	1	2	71
Totals	40	12	11	23	213
Greg Bignell, Toledo	22	0	5	5	167
Greg Bignell, Richmond	12	1	2	3	42
Totals	34	1	7	8	209
Pat Bingham, Hampton Roads	5	0	2	2	56
Pat Bingham, Richmond	47	10	14	24	148
Totals	52	10	16	26	204
Ken Blum, Toledo	8	0	2	2	2
Ken Blum, Winston-Salem	8	0	1	1	14
Ken Blum, Roanoke	30	3	2	5	64
Totals	46	3	5	8	80
Doug Brown (g), Roanoke	4	0	0	0	0
Doug Brown (g), Columbus	18	0	0	0	2
Totals	22	0	0	0	2
Steve Cascagnette, Raleigh	3	0	0	0	9
Steve Cascagnette, Johnstown	6	0	0	0	17
Totals	9	0	0	0	26
Steve Chelios, Nashville	24	5	11	16	47
Steve Chelios, Roanoke	18	2	4	6	44
Totals	42	7	15	22	91
Mike Chighisola, H.R.	40	24	35	59	95
Mike Chighisola, Raleigh	13	4	7	11	39
Mike Chighisola, Knoxville	3	0	0	0	0
Totals	56	28	42	70	134
Derek Clancey, Toledo	5	2	5	7	0
Derek Clancey, Winston-Salem	9	4	3	7	2
Derek Clancey, Erie	16	7	6	13	24
Totals	30	13	14	27	26
Paul Cohen (g), Toledo	6	0	0	0	6
Paul Cohen (g), Nashville	18	0	1	1	16
Totals	24	0	1	1	22
Bruce Coles, Winston-Salem	13	2	6	8	37
Bruce Coles, Johnstown	43	32	45	77	113
Totals	56	34	51	85	150
Brian Cook, Greensboro	10	1	2	3	8
Brian Cook, Louisville	38	18	43	61	44
Totals	48	19	45	64	52
Sean Cowan, Toledo	17	4	5	9	45
Sean Cowan, Raleigh	38	0	8	8	72
Totals	55	4	13	17	117
Phil Crowe, Columbus	32	4	7	11	145
Phil Crowe, Toledo	2	0	0	0	0
Totals	34	4	7	11	145
Gord Cruikshank, Raleigh	27	13	13	26	34
Gord Cruikshank, Nashville	17	4	7	11	8
Gord Cruikshank, Greensboro	7	6	6	12	0
Totals	51	23	26	49	42
Alex Daviault, Raleigh	11	1	4	5	56
Alex Daviault, Dayton	20	0	0	0	135
Totals	31	1	4	5	191
John Devereaux, W.S.	2	1	1	2	2
John Devereaux, Greensboro	32	5	16	21	77
Totals	34	6	17	23	79
Jerry Dineen, Winston-Salem	7	0	2	2	16
Jerry Dineen, Raleigh	31	4	5	9	26
Totals	38	4	7	11	42
Tim Doyle, Raleigh	35	0	6	6	16
Tim Doyle, Nashville	30	3	11	14	28
Totals	65	3	17	20	44
Scott Eichstadt, Louisville	37	10	12	22	27
Scott Eichstadt, Roanoke	26	6	9	15	14
Totals	63	16	21	37	41
Phil Esposito, Hampton Roads	2	0	0	0	2
Phil Esposito, Johnstown	3	0	0	0	4
Phil Esposito, Knoxville	6	0	1	1	33
Totals	11	0	1	1	39
John Fletcher (g), Knoxville	2	0	1	1	0
John Fletcher (g), Johnstown	6	0	0	0	0
John Fletcher (g), Nashville	1	0	1	1	4
Totals	9	0	2	2	4
Marco Fuster, Roanoke	7	1	6	7	35
Marco Fuster, Richmond	5	0	2	2	4
Totals	12	1	8	9	39
Mike Gober, Toledo	5	3	2	5	26
Mike Gober, Knoxville	25	16	11	27	103
Totals	30	19	13	32	129
Chris Grassie, Johnstown	3	0	0	0	10
Chris Grassie, Nashville	34	1	11	12	80
Totals	37	1	11	12	90
Jeff Green, Toledo	4	1	0	1	2
Jeff Green, Dayton	23	12	17	29	21
Totals	27	13	17	30	23
Dominic Hardy, Knoxville	4	3	1	4	7
Dominic Hardy, Nashville	2	0	1	1	0
Totals	6	3	2	5	7
Chris Harvey (g), Johnstown	4	0	0	0	4
Chris Harvey (g), Nashville	20	0	0	0	16
Chris Harvey (g), Raleigh	5	0	1	1	4
Totals	29	0	1	1	24
Peter Heine, Raleigh	17	0	4	4	4
Peter Heine, Winston-Salem	39	3	9	12	72
Totals	56	3	13	16	76
Mike Hiltner, Nashville	8	2	4	6	20
Mike Hiltner, Raleigh	4	1	2	3	5
Totals	12	3	6	9	25
Jeff Hogdon, Roanoke	1	0	0	0	0
Jeff Hogdon, Cincinnati	8	0	1	1	2
Totals	9	0	1	1	2
Dusty Imoo (g), Dayton	4	0	0	0	7
Dusty Imoo (g), Erie	1	0	0	0	0
Dusty Imoo (g), Cincinnati	9	0	2	2	0
Totals	14	0	2	2	7
Dana Janis, Raleigh	9	2	3	5	2
Dana Janis, Roanoke	15	1	4	5	8
Totals	24	3	7	10	10
Trevor Jobe, Richmond	34	36	30	66	74
Trevor Jobe, Nashville	28	18	19	37	81
Totals	62	54	49	103	155
Kurt Johnson, Louisville	3	0	0	0	0
Kurt Johnson, Erie	3	0	1	1	0
Totals	6	0	1	1	0
Scott Johnson, Richmond	6	2	4	6	0
Scott Johnson, Hampton Roads	20	2	9	11	8
Totals	26	4	13	17	8
Stanislav Komarov, Columbus	7	2	4	6	23
Stanislav Komarov, Dayton	2	0	1	1	0
Totals	9	2	5	7	23
Bill LaCouture, Raleigh	11	1	4	5	7
Bill LaCouture, Roanoke	14	1	2	3	12
Totals	25	2	6	8	19
Brett Lawrence, Raleigh	3	0	0	0	0
Brett Lawrence, Knoxville	36	13	7	20	28
Totals	39	13	7	20	28
Kirby Lindal, Richmond	18	8	11	19	30
Kirby Lindal, Raleigh	39	15	20	35	52
Totals	57	23	31	54	82
Jaan Luik, Cincinnati	20	2	9	11	40
Jaan Luik, Dayton	38	3	21	24	38
Totals	58	5	30	35	78
Scott Luik, Cincinnati	21	2	10	12	26
Scott Luik, Dayton	13	5	7	12	14
Totals	34	7	17	24	40
Lance Madson (g), Columbus	1	0	0	0	0
Lance Madson (g), Louisville	17	0	0	0	0
Totals	18	0	0	0	0
Ken Maffia, Knoxville	6	2	3	5	2
Ken Maffia, Roanoke	5	0	0	0	2
Totals	11	2	3	5	4
Sylvain Mayer, Louisville	2	0	0	0	6
Sylvain Mayer, Raleigh	6	0	0	0	104
Sylvain Mayer, Dayton	11	0	2	2	89
Totals	19	0	2	2	199
Mike McCormick, Greensboro	31	6	4	10	110
Mike McCormick, Johnstown	19	4	9	13	22
Totals	50	10	13	23	132

	Games	G	A	Pts.	Pen.
Dean McDonald, Knoxville	30	4	15	19	59
Dean McDonald, Raleigh	4	0	1	1	0
Totals	34	4	16	20	59
Doug Melnyk, Cincinnati	22	0	6	6	22
Doug Melnyk, Richmond	18	2	9	11	22
Totals	40	2	15	17	44
Steve Mirabile, Raleigh	42	12	10	22	37
Steve Mirabile, Hampton Roads	22	12	13	25	27
Totals	64	24	23	47	64
Darryl Mitchell, Nashville	41	7	20	27	63
Darryl Mitchell, Dayton	12	3	8	11	18
Totals	53	10	28	38	81
David Moore, Cincinnati	5	0	1	1	2
David Moore, Louisville	38	1	15	16	40
Totals	43	1	16	17	42
Jay Moore, Winston-Salem	6	1	3	4	11
Jay Moore, Dayton	10	5	6	11	6
Totals	16	6	9	15	17
Mike Mudd (g), Roanoke	14	0	0	0	2
Mike Mudd (g), Raleigh	16	0	2	2	2
Totals	30	0	2	2	4
Chris Newans, Raleigh	13	5	4	9	26
Chris Newans, Dayton	23	4	8	12	42
Chris Newans, Nashville	9	6	5	11	16
Totals	45	15	17	32	84
Darrell Newman, Raleigh	16	0	4	4	13
Darrell Newman, Roanoke	2	0	0	0	0
Totals	18	0	4	4	13
Al Novakowski, Columbus	9	0	1	1	61
Al Novakowski, Roanoke	2	0	0	0	5
Totals	11	0	1	1	66
Geno Pare, Knoxville	7	0	0	0	33
Geno Pare, Winston-Salem	7	0	1	1	19
Geno Pare, Louisville	3	0	0	0	0
Totals	17	0	1	1	52
Dan Poirier, Johnstown	3	1	1	2	9
Dan Poirier, Nashville	16	1	2	3	75
Totals	19	2	3	5	84
Jody Praznik, Toledo	37	3	27	30	26
Jody Praznik, Knoxville	19	4	12	16	17
Totals	56	7	39	46	43
Chris Puscian (g), W.S.	1	0	0	0	0
Chris Puscian (g), Columbus	2	0	0	0	0
Totals	3	0	0	0	0
Rob Reimer, Greensboro	4	0	1	1	2
Rob Reimer, Louisville	36	26	22	48	27
Totals	40	26	23	49	29
Alex Roberts, Toledo	27	13	27	40	49
Alex Roberts, Richmond	2	1	1	2	2
Totals	29	14	28	42	51
Tim Roberts, Erie	31	5	12	17	25
Tim Roberts, Winston-Salem	18	1	8	9	7
Totals	49	6	20	26	32
Dan Rolfe, Richmond	11	1	1	2	29
Dan Rolfe, Nashville	39	0	11	11	44
Totals	50	1	12	13	73
Mark Romaine (g), Cincinnati	28	0	0	0	2
Mark Romaine (g), Raleigh	1	0	0	0	0
Mark Romaine (g), Toledo	3	0	0	0	10
Mark Romaine (g), Columbus	7	0	0	0	10
Totals	39	0	0	0	22
Larry Rooney, Richmond	41	3	10	13	57
Larry Rooney, Cincinnati	20	0	10	10	16
Totals	61	3	20	23	73
Andrew Ross, Erie	36	13	16	29	53
Andrew Ross, Knoxville	9	2	3	5	2
Totals	45	15	19	34	55
Paul Rossi, Toledo	3	1	2	3	0
Paul Rossi, Raleigh	2	0	0	0	2
Paul Rossi, Roanoke	2	0	0	0	0
Totals	7	1	2	3	2
Roger Rougelot (g), Nashville	6	0	0	0	0
Roger Rougelot (g), Raleigh	5	0	0	0	0
Roger Rougelot (g), Louisville	1	0	0	0	0
Roger Rougelot (g), Columbus	3	0	0	0	0
Totals	15	0	0	0	0

	Games	G	A	Pts.	Pen.
Angelo Russo, Raleigh	7	2	1	3	10
Angelo Russo, Nashville	32	5	11	16	26
Totals	39	7	12	19	36
Mike Sanderson, Nashville	4	2	1	3	2
Mike Sanderson, Johnstown	6	1	2	3	4
Totals	10	3	3	6	6
Carl Sasyn, Erie	27	0	4	4	28
Carl Sasyn, Knoxville	3	0	1	1	0
Totals	30	0	5	5	28
Chris Scheid, Winston-Salem	3	0	2	2	2
Chris Scheid, Louisville	45	10	18	28	19
Totals	48	10	20	30	21
Craig Shepherd, Knoxville	7	0	1	1	14
Craig Shepherd, Johnstown	2	0	0	0	0
Totals	9	0	1	1	14
Greg Simeone, Roanoke	5	0	0	0	21
Greg Simeone, Knoxville	11	1	6	7	9
Totals	16	1	6	7	30
Trevor Smith, Louisville	40	10	22	32	64
Trevor Smith, Roanoke	26	4	9	13	8
Totals	66	14	31	45	72
Kevin Sullivan, Nashville	26	7	11	18	33
Kevin Sullivan, Richmond	30	14	8	22	33
Totals	56	21	19	40	66
Chad Thompson, Raleigh	2	0	0	0	0
Chad Thompson, Knoxville	46	11	20	31	50
Totals	48	11	20	31	50
Roman Trebaticky, Raleigh	5	0	1	1	0
Roman Trebaticky, Roanoke	3	1	2	3	0
Totals	8	1	3	4	0
Jeff Tomlinson, Roanoke	6	1	1	2	4
Jeff Tomlinson, Raleigh	44	14	34	48	26
Totals	50	15	35	50	30
Bruno Villeneuve, Knoxville	48	38	35	73	12
Bruno Villeneuve, Raleigh	8	5	2	7	9
Totals	56	43	37	80	21
Terry Virtue, Roanoke	38	4	22	26	165
Terry Virtue, Louisville	23	1	15	16	58
Totals	61	5	37	42	223
Steve Wachter (g), Columbus	3	0	0	0	0
Steve Wachter (g), Erie	1	0	0	0	0
Totals	4	0	0	0	0
Chuck Wiegand, Nashville	36	20	9	29	61
Chuck Wiegand, Johnstown	14	3	2	5	19
Totals	50	23	11	34	80
Lyle Wildgoose, Richmond	13	5	4	9	27
Lyle Wildgoose, Raleigh	41	20	23	43	10
Totals	54	25	27	52	37
Bruce Wolanin, Knoxville	4	0	2	2	0
Bruce Wolanin, Dayton	20	1	2	3	13
Totals	24	1	4	5	13

GOALTENDING

	Games	Min.	Goals	SO	Avg.
Doug Brown, Roa.	4	150	9	0	3.60
Doug Brown, Col.	18	936	80	0	5.13
Totals	22	1086	89	0	4.92
Paul Cohen, Tol.	6	333	17	1	3.06
Paul Cohen, Nash.	17	894	68	0	4.56
Totals	23	1227	85	1	4.16
John Fletcher, Knox.	2	79	10	0	7.59
John Fletcher, John.	6	318	13	0	2.45
John Fletcher, Nash.	11	583	54	0	5.56
Totals	19	980	77	0	4.71
Chris Harvey, John.	4	193	12	0	4.04
Chris Harvey, Nash.	20	956	68	0	4.27
Chris Harvey, Ral.	5	305	24	0	4.72
Totals	29	1454	104	0	4.29
Dusty Imoo, Day.	4	204	16	0	4.71
Dusty Imoo, Erie	1	60	8	0	8.00
Dusty Imoo, Cin.	9	535	33	0	3.70
Totals	14	799	57	0	4.28
Lance Madson, Col.	1	60	2	0	2.00
Lance Madson, Lou.	17	712	68	0	5.73
Totals	18	772	70	0	5.44
Mike Mudd, Roa.	13	661	62	0	5.63
Mike Mudd, Ral.	15	919	74	0	4.83
Totals	28	1580	136	0	5.16

	Games	Min.	Goals	SO	Avg.
Chris Puscian, W.S....	1	20	4	0	12.00
Chris Puscian, Col.	2	35	4	0	6.86
Totals..................	3	55	8	0	8.73
Mark Romaine, Cin. ...	27	1544	124	0	4.82
Mark Romaine, Ral. ...	1	60	5	0	5.00
Mark Romaine, Tol. ...	4	140	11	0	4.71
Mark Romaine, Col. ...	7	309	34	0	6.60
Totals..................	39	2053	174	0	5.09

	Games	Min.	Goals	SO	Avg.
Roger Rougelot, Nash.	6	325	35	0	6.46
Roger Rougelot, Ral...	5	219	19	0	5.21
Roger Rougelot, Lou...	1	21	5	0	14.29
Roger Rougelot, Col...	3	139	10	0	4.32
Totals..................	15	704	69	0	5.88
Steve Wachter, Col. ...	3	84	11	0	7.86
Steve Wachter, Erie....	1	9	2	0	13.33
Totals..................	4	93	13	0	8.39

1992 RILEY CUP PLAYOFFS

RESULTS

EAST DIVISION
FIRST ROUND
Series "A"

	W	L	Pts.	GF	GA
Greensboro	4	3	8	28	18
Roanoke Valley	3	4	6	18	28

(Greensboro won series, 4-3)

Series "B"

	W	L	Pts.	GF	GA
Hampton Roads	3	1	6	18	16
Raleigh	1	3	2	16	18

(Hampton Roads won series, 3-1)

Series "C"

	W	L	Pts.	GF	GA
Richmond....................................	3	2	6	19	22
Winston-Salem	2	3	4	22	19

(Richmond won series, 3-2)

SEMIFINALS
Series "D"

	W	L	Pts.	GF	GA
Hampton Roads	2	0	4	12	4
Richmond....................................	0	2	0	4	12

(Hampton Roads won series, 2-0)

FINALS
Series "E"

	W	L	Pts.	GF	GA
Hampton Roads	3	1	6	13	10
Greensboro	1	3	2	10	13

(Hampton Roads won series, 3-1)

WEST DIVISION
FIRST ROUND
Series "A"

	W	L	Pts.	GF	GA
Louisville	4	1	8	23	16
Toledo	1	4	2	16	23

(Louisville won series, 4-1)

Series "B"

	W	L	Pts.	GF	GA
Cincinnati	3	0	6	21	6
Dayton	0	3	0	6	21

(Cincinnati won series, 3-0)

Series "C"

	W	L	Pts.	GF	GA
Johnstown	3	1	6	16	9
Erie..	1	3	2	9	16

(Johnstown won series, 3-1)

SEMIFINALS
Series "D"

	W	L	Pts.	GF	GA
Cincinnati	2	0	4	15	2
Johnstown	0	2	0	2	15

(Cincinnati won series, 2-0)

FINALS
Series "E"

	W	L	Pts.	GF	GA
Louisville	3	1	6	22	17
Cincinnati	1	3	2	17	22

(Louisville won series, 3-1)

RILEY CUP FINALS
Series "F"

	W	L	Pts.	GF	GA
Hampton Roads	4	0	8	21	8
Louisville	0	4	0	8	21

(Hampton Roads won series, 4-0)

INDIVIDUAL LEADERS

Goals: Rod Taylor, Hampton Roads (16)
Assists: Harry Mews, Hampton Roads (15)
Points: Rod Taylor, Hampton Roads (26)
Penalty minutes: Mike Butters, Greensboro (91)
Goaltending average: Mark Bernard, Hampton Roads (2.62)
Shutouts: Mark Bernard, Hampton Roads (1)
 Stan Reddick, Johnstown (1)

TOP SCORERS

	Games	G	A	Pts.
Rod Taylor, Hampton Roads	14	16	10	26
Harry Mews, Hampton Roads	13	10	15	25
Sheldon Gorski, Louisville..................	13	14	8	22
Phil Berger, Greensboro	11	8	13	21
Steve Cadieux, Cincinnati	9	12	7	19
Chris Bright, Louisville......................	13	9	8	17
Dennis McEwen, Hampton Roads......	14	8	6	14
Victor Gervais, Hampton Roads	14	6	8	14
Gord Cruikshank, Greensboro	11	6	8	14
Randy Pearce, Hampton Roads	11	5	9	14
Martin Bergeron, Louisville	13	3	11	14

ECHL

MINOR LEAGUES

ECHL

INDIVIDUAL STATISTICS

CINCINNATI CYCLONES

(Lost West Division finals to Louisville, 3-1)

SCORING

	Games	G	A	Pts.	Pen.
Steve Cadieux	9	12	7	19	4
Chris Marshall	9	4	9	13	30
Martin St. Amour	9	4	9	13	18
Kevin Kerr	9	4	9	13	64
Bobby Wallwork	9	5	7	12	6
Shaun Clouston	9	6	5	11	8
Howie Rosenblatt	9	3	8	11	55
Craig Charron	9	5	5	10	10
David Craievich	8	1	8	9	15
Tom Neziol	9	1	8	9	4
Larry Rooney	9	2	6	8	6
Kevin Scott	9	5	2	7	17
Kevin Dean	9	1	6	7	8
Jay Ross	9	0	2	2	21
Corey Schwab (goalie)	9	0	1	1	0
Rob Kraus	1	0	0	0	7

GOALTENDING

	Games	Min.	Goals	SO	Avg.
Corey Schwab	9	540	29	0	3.22

DAYTON BOMBERS

(Lost in first round to Cincinnati, 3-0)

SCORING

	Games	G	A	Pts.	Pen.
Paul Marshall	3	1	3	4	20
Sylvain Fleury	3	3	0	3	2
Mike Reier	3	1	1	2	2
Darren Colbourne	3	1	0	1	14
Jaan Luik	3	0	1	1	4
Matt Johnson	3	0	1	1	2
Shawn Howard	3	0	1	1	4
Nick Beaulieu	3	0	1	1	2
Joe Tonello	3	0	1	1	2
Rod Houk (goalie)	2	0	0	0	2
Derek Crawford	3	0	0	0	14
Jeff Green	3	0	0	0	0
Ray Edwards	3	0	0	0	18
Darryl Mitchell	3	0	0	0	2
Mike Green	3	0	0	0	4
Francis Ouelette (goalie)	2	0	0	0	0

GOALTENDING

	Games	Min.	Goals	SO	Avg.
Francis Ouelette	2	111	10	0	5.41
Rod Houk	2	69	10	0	8.70

ERIE PANTHERS

(Lost in first round to Johnstown, 3-1)

SCORING

	Games	G	A	Pts.	Pen.
Ed Zawatsky	4	3	0	3	0
Jason Prosofsky	4	1	2	3	18
Peter Buckeridge	4	1	2	3	2
Ryan Kummu	4	0	3	3	29
Doug Lawrence	4	1	1	2	35
Glen Goodall	4	1	1	2	2
Bob Fleming	4	0	2	2	15
Murray Duval	4	1	0	1	4
David Pergola	4	1	0	1	2
Mark Gowans (goalie)	1	0	1	1	0
Bill Gall	4	0	1	1	6
John Gladiator	4	0	1	1	11
Bill Pye (goalie)	4	0	0	0	0
Dave DiVita	4	0	0	0	7

	Games	G	A	Pts.	Pen.
Scot Johnston	4	0	0	0	4
Tom Sprague	4	0	0	0	4

GOALTENDING

	Games	Min.	Goals	SO	Avg.
Mark Gowans	1	20	0	0	0.00
Bill Pye	4	220	15	0	4.09

GREENSBORO MONARCHS

(Lost East Division finals to Hampton Roads, 3-1)

SCORING

	Games	G	A	Pts.	Pen.
Phil Berger	11	8	13	21	56
Gord Cruikshank	11	6	8	14	8
Shawn Wheeler	11	6	6	12	47
Roger Larche	11	3	9	12	45
Eric Dubois	11	4	4	8	40
John Devereaux	11	3	4	7	10
Scott White	8	1	6	7	12
Mike Butters	10	4	1	5	91
Todd Gordon	6	2	3	5	24
Timo Makela	9	1	4	5	4
Chris Laganas	10	0	4	4	28
Chris Wolanin	11	0	3	3	12
Boyd Sutton	11	0	2	2	2
Rob Bateman	7	0	1	1	8
Nick Vitucci (goalie)	11	0	1	1	4
Greg Menges (goalie)	1	0	0	0	0
Eric Lemarque	3	0	0	0	8
Peter Sentner	4	0	0	0	12

GOALTENDING

	Games	Min.	Goals	SO	Av
Greg Menges	1	3	0	0	0.0
Nick Vitucci	11	673	30	0	2.6

HAMPTON ROADS ADMIRALS

(Winner of Riley Cup playoffs)

SCORING

	Games	G	A	Pts.	Pen.
Rod Taylor	14	16	10	26	26
Harry Mews	13	10	15	25	30
Dennis McEwen	14	8	6	14	19
Victor Gervais	14	6	8	14	20
Randy Pearce	11	5	9	14	56
Steve Mirabile	13	3	10	13	4
Wade Bartley	14	4	8	12	38
Al Maclsaac	14	1	9	10	43
Steve Martell	11	4	5	9	47
Billy Nolan	14	4	4	8	14
Keith Whitmore	14	1	5	6	12
Steve Poapst	14	1	4	5	12
Dave Morissette	13	1	3	4	74
Shawn Snesar	14	0	2	2	21
Mark Bernard (goalie)	14	0	1	1	12
Paul Krepelka	4	0	0	0	0
Kurt Kabat	4	0	0	0	6

GOALTENDING

	Games	Min.	Goals	SO	Avg.
Mark Bernard	14	871	38	1	2.62

JOHNSTOWN CHIEFS

(Lost West Division semifinals to Cincinnati, 2-0)

SCORING

	Games	G	A	Pts.	Pen.
Matt Glennon	6	2	4	6	25
Brian Ferriera	6	1	5	6	53

	Games	G	A	Pts.	Pen.
Bob Woods	6	4	1	5	14
Mike Rossetti	6	3	2	5	12
Mark Green	6	2	3	5	4
Bruce Coles	6	3	1	4	12
Christian Lariviere	6	1	3	4	24
Dave McIntyre	6	1	2	3	4
Mike Roberts	6	0	2	2	8
Mike McCormick	5	1	0	1	2
Scott McCrady	3	0	1	1	4
Jeff Beaudin	6	0	1	1	18
Ted Miscolozi	4	0	1	1	2
Stan Reddick (goalie)	4	0	1	1	0
Mike Parson (goalie)	5	0	0	0	0
Doug Weiss	5	0	0	0	9
Perry Florio	6	0	0	0	21

GOALTENDING

	Games	Min.	Goals	SO	Avg.
Stan Reddick	4	136	9	1	3.97
Mike Parson	5	224	15	0	4.02

LOUISVILLE ICEHAWKS

(Lost Riley Cup finals to Hampton Roads, 4-0)

SCORING

	Games	G	A	Pts.	Pen.
Sheldon Gorski	13	14	8	22	15
Chris Bright	13	9	8	17	18
Martin Bergeron	13	3	11	14	36
Brian Cook	12	6	6	12	28
Scott Humeniuk	13	1	11	12	33
Chris Smith	13	2	9	11	4
Kelly Ens	13	6	4	10	50
Terry Virtue	13	0	8	8	49
Trevor Buchanan	13	3	4	7	77
Chad Biafore	13	1	6	7	69
Rob Reimer	12	4	2	6	2
Paul Gherardi	13	2	4	6	15
Chris Scheid	2	1	2	3	0
David Moore	13	1	1	2	11
Cam Brauer	13	0	1	1	28
Chris Clifford (goalie)	13	0	1	1	2
Lance Madson (goalie)	1	0	0	0	0

GOALTENDING

	Games	Min.	Goals	SO	Avg.
Lance Madson	1	21	1	0	2.86
Chris Clifford	13	780	53	0	4.08

RALEIGH ICECAPS

(Lost in first round to Hampton Roads, 3-1)

SCORING

	Games	G	A	Pts.	Pen.
Rick Barkovich	4	4	3	7	18
Kris Miller	4	2	3	5	8
Jim Powers	4	2	3	5	2
Lyle Wildgoose	4	1	4	5	2
Trevor Pochipinski	4	0	5	5	18
Barry Niecar	4	4	0	4	22
Greg Walters	4	1	2	3	8
Jeff Tomlinson	4	1	2	3	6
Bruno Villeneuve	4	0	2	2	2
Kirby Lindal	4	1	0	1	8
Brandy Semchuk	2	1	0	1	4
Dave Doucette	2	0	1	1	2
Jeff Perry	4	0	1	1	11
Rob Mendel	4	0	0	0	2
Sean Cowan	4	0	0	0	8
Chris Harvey (goalie)	4	0	0	0	0

GOALTENDING

	Games	Min.	Goals	SO	Avg.
Chris Harvey	4	249	17	0	4.10

RICHMOND RENEGADES

(Lost East Division semifinals to Hampton Roads, 2-0)

SCORING

	Games	G	A	Pts.	Pen.
Brendan Flynn	7	3	5	8	0
Dave Aiken	7	5	2	7	0
Kevin Sullivan	7	3	4	7	4
Guy Gadowsky	5	4	2	6	4
Scott Drevitch	7	0	5	5	4
Alex Roberts	6	2	2	4	29
Pat Bingham	6	2	2	4	71
Andy Akervick	7	0	4	4	33
Bob Berg	6	2	1	3	0
Mark Kuntz	7	1	2	3	52
Paul Rutherford	5	1	1	2	2
Jim McGeough	7	0	2	2	8
Doug Melnyk	7	0	1	1	13
Todd Drevitch	7	0	1	1	30
Greg Bignell	6	0	1	1	40
Jon Gustafson (goalie)	6	0	1	1	2
Bob Desjardins (goalie)	1	0	0	0	0

GOALTENDING

	Games	Min.	Goals	SO	Avg.
Jon Gustafson	6	357	26	0	4.37
Bob Desjardins	1	60	8	0	8.00

ROANOKE VALLEY REBELS

(Lost in first round to Greensboro, 4-3)

SCORING

	Games	G	A	Pts.	Pen.
Peter Kasowski	7	2	8	10	10
Brett Stewart	7	2	7	9	13
Mark Woolf	7	6	2	8	4
Cory Lyons	7	4	3	7	4
Ben Wyzansky	7	1	4	5	7
Bill Harrington	6	1	1	2	6
Scott Eichstadt	7	1	1	2	18
Wayne Muir	7	1	1	2	36
Trevor Smith	4	0	1	1	5
Ken Blum	7	0	1	1	19
Devin Derkson	6	0	0	0	34
Bill Whitfield	7	0	0	0	6
Frank Bialowas	3	0	0	0	34
Mike Barlage	7	0	0	0	34
Ron Jones	5	0	0	0	34
Graham Garden	1	0	0	0	2
Mike James (goalie)	7	0	0	0	0

GOALTENDING

	Games	Min.	Goals	SO	Avg.
Mike James	7	427	28	0	3.93

TOLEDO STORM

(Lost in first round to Louisville, 4-1)

SCORING

	Games	G	A	Pts.	Pen.
Don Stone	5	2	4	6	6
Pete Stauber	5	2	3	5	46
Dave Flanagan	5	4	0	4	4
Greg Puhalski	5	2	2	4	11
Brad McCaughey	3	1	3	4	0
Darin Banister	5	1	3	4	14
Bruce MacDonald	5	0	4	4	22
Mike Maurice	5	1	2	3	6
Bob Boughner	5	2	0	2	15
Ken Alexander	5	0	2	2	13
Ron Aubrey	3	0	1	1	57
Mike Casselman	5	0	1	1	6
Mike Williams (goalie)	1	0	0	0	0
Pat Pylypuik	5	0	0	1	38
Phil Crowe	5	0	0	0	58
Mark Reimer (goalie)	4	0	0	0	0

GOALTENDING				
	Games	Min.	Goals	SO	Avg.
Mark Reimer	4	249	17	0	4.10
Mike Williams	1	59	6	0	6.10

WINSTON-SALEM THUNDERBIRDS

(Lost in first round to Richmond, 3-2)

SCORING

	Games	G	A	Pts.	Pen.
Trevor Sim	5	7	2	9	4
Marc Laniel	5	2	5	7	4
Devin Edgerton	5	2	5	7	2
Dean Antos	5	1	6	7	0
Craig Endean	4	1	6	7	2
Derek DeCosty	5	4	2	6	8

	Games	G	A	Pts.	Pen.
Dan Woodley	5	3	3	6	2
Darren Schwartz	5	1	4	5	61
Tim Roberts	5	1	1	2	2
John Uniac	5	0	2	2	2
Mike Millham (goalie)	2	0	0	0	0
Brent Fleetwood	4	0	0	0	7
Doug Greschuk	5	0	0	0	4
Pete Heine	3	0	0	0	19
Doug Bacon	4	0	0	0	44
Trevor Senn	4	0	0	0	60
Tom Dennis (goalie)	4	0	0	0	0

GOALTENDING				
	Games	Min.	Goals	SO	Avg.
Mike Millham	2	75	4	0	3.20
Tom Dennis	4	222	14	0	3.78

1991-92 AWARD WINNERS

ALL-STAR TEAMS

First team	Pos.	Second team
Nick Vitucci, Greensboro	G	Stan Reddick, Johnstown
Scott White, Greensboro	D	Marc Laniel, Win.-Salem
Ryan Kummu, Erie	D	Kris Miller, Raleigh
Mark Green, Johnstown	LW	Mike Casselman, Toledo
Mike Maurice, Toledo	C	Martin Bergeron, Louisville
Darren Colbourne, Dayton	RW	Phil Berger, Greensboro

Coach of the Year: Doug Sauter, Winston-Salem

TROPHY WINNERS

Most Valuable Player: Phil Berger, Greensboro
Scoring leader: Phil Berger, Greensboro
Outstanding defenseman: Scott White, Greensboro
Rookie of the Year: Darren Colbourne, Dayton
Playoff MVP: Mark Bernard, Hampton Roads
Coach of the Year: Doug Sauter, Winston-Salem

ALL-TIME AWARD WINNERS

MOST VALUABLE PLAYER

Season	Player, Team
1981-82	Dave MacQueen, Salem
1982-83	Rory Cava, Carolina
1983-84	Paul O'Neill, Virginia
1984-85	Barry Tabobondung, Erie
1985-86	Joe Curran, Carolina
1986-87	Peter DeArmas, Virginia
1987-88	John Torchetti, Carolina
1988-89	Daryl Harpe, Erie
1989-90	Bill McDougall, Erie
1990-91	Stan Drulia, Knoxville
1991-92	Phil Berger, Greensboro

TOP GOALTENDER

Season	Player, Team
1981-82	Gilles Moffet, Salem
1982-83	Yves Dechene, Carolina
1983-84	Darrell May, Erie
1984-85	Dan Olson, Carolina
1985-86	Ray LeBlanc, Carolina
1986-87	Dana Demole, Virginia
1987-88	Tim Flanigan, Virginia
1988-89	Scott Gordon, Johnstown
1989-90	Alain Raymond, Hampton-Roads
1990-91	Dean Anderson, Knoxville
1991-92	Frederic Chabot, Winston-Salem

TOP SCORER

Season	Player, Team
1981-82	Dave MacQueen, Salem
1982-83	Dave Watson, Carolina
1983-84	Rob Clavette, Pinebridge-Erie
1984-85	Paul Mancini, Erie
1985-86	Dave Herbst, Erie
1986-87	Doug McCarthy, Carolina
1987-88	John Torchetti, Carolina
1988-89	Daryl Harpe, Erie
1989-90	Bill McDougall, Erie
1990-91	Stan Drulia, Knoxville
1991-92	Phil Berger, Greensboro

PLAYOFF MVP

Season	Player, Team
1984-85	Brian Carroll, Carolina
1985-86	Bob Dore, Carolina
1986-87	Peter DeArmas, Virginia
	Dana Demole, Virginia
1987-88	Tim Flanigan, Virginia
1988-89	Nick Vitucci, Carolina
1989-90	Wade Flaherty, Greensboro
1990-91	Dave Gagnon, Hampton Roads
	Dave Flanagan, Hampton Roads
1991-92	Mark Bernard, Hampton Roads

ROOKIE OF THE YEAR

Season	Player, Team
1984-85	Kurt Rugenius, Mohawk Valley
	Todd Bjorkstrand, Pinebridge
1985-86	Bobby Williams, New York
1986-87	Scott Knutson, Carolina
	Scott Curwin, Virginia
1987-88	Mike Sparago, Virginia
	Dean Dixon, Carolina
1988-89	Tom Sasso, Johnstown
1989-90	Bill McDougall, Erie
1990-91	Dan Gauthier, Knoxville
1991-92	Darren Colbourne, Dayton

COACH OF THE YEAR

Season	Coach, Team
1981-82	Bill Horton, Mohawk Valley
1982-83	Jim Mikol, Erie
1983-84	Paul O'Neill, Virginia
1984-85	Frank Perkins, Pinebridge
1985-86	Rick Dudley, Carolina
1986-87	John Tortorella, Virginia
1987-88	John Tortorella, Virginia
1988-89	Ron Hansis, Erie
1989-90	Dave Allison, Virginia
1990-91	Don Jackson, Knoxville
1991-92	Doug Sauter, Winston-Salem

MINOR LEAGUES

ECHL

TOP DEFENSEMAN

Season	Player, Team
1988-89	Kelly Szautner, Erie
1989-90	Bill Whitfield, Virginia
1990-91	Brett McDonald, Nashville
1991-92	Scott White, Greensboro

ALL-TIME LEAGUE CHAMPIONS

REGULAR-SEASON CHAMPION / PLAYOFF CHAMPION

Season	Team	Coach	Team	Coach
1981-82	Salem Raiders	Pat Kelly	Mohawk Valley Stars	Bill Horton
1982-83	Carolina Thunderbirds	Rick Dudley	Carolina Thunderbirds	Rick Dudley
1983-84	Carolina Thunderbirds	Rick Dudley	Erie Golden Blades	Bill Horton
1984-85	Carolina Thunderbirds	Rick Dudley	Carolina Thunderbirds	Rick Dudley
1985-86	Carolina Thunderbirds	Rick Dudley	Carolina Thunderbirds	Rick Dudley
1986-87	Virginia Lancers	John Tortorella	Virginia Lancers	John Tortorella
1987-88	Virginia Lancers	John Tortorella	Virginia Lancers	John Tortorella
1988-89	Erie Panthers	Ron Hansis	Carolina Thunderbirds	Brendon Watson
1989-90	Winston-Salem Thunderbirds	C. McSorley, J. Fraser	Greensboro Monarchs	Jeff Brubaker
1990-91	Knoxville Cherokees	Don Jackson	Hampton Roads Admirals	John Brophy
1991-92	Toledo Storm	Chris McSorley	Hampton Roads Admirals	John Brophy

The ECHL playoff champion is awarded the Bob Payne Trophy.

MAJOR JUNIOR LEAGUES

CANADIAN HOCKEY LEAGUE

GENERAL INFORMATION

The Canadian Hockey League is an alliance of the three Major Junior leagues—Ontario Hockey League, Quebec Major Junior Hockey League and Western Hockey League. After the regular season, the three leagues compete in a round-robin tournament to decide the Memorial Cup championship. Originally awarded to the national Junior champion, the Memorial Cup later signified Junior A supremacy (after Junior hockey in Canada was divided into "A" and "B" classes). Beginning in 1971, when Junior A hockey was split into Major Junior and Tier II Junior A, the Memorial Cup was awarded to the Major Junior champion.

LEAGUE OFFICE

Address
305 Milner Ave.
Scarborough, Ont. M1B 3V4
Phone
416-298-3523
FAX
416-298-3187
President
Ed Chynoweth

Vice presidents
David E. Branch
Gilles Courteau
Director of information
Jim Price
Directors
Dr. R.L. Vaughan
Marcel Robert
Rick Brodsky

Director of officiating
Richard Doerksen
Member leagues
Ontario Hockey League
Quebec Major Junior Hockey League
Western Hockey League

1992 MEMORIAL CUP

FINAL STANDINGS

Team (League)	W	L	Pts.	GF	GA
Kamloops (WHL)	4	1	8	23	14
Sault Ste. Marie (OHL)	3	1	6	18	13
Seattle (WHL)	1	3	2	12	18
College Francais (QMJHL)	0	3	0	5	13

RESULTS

SATURDAY, MAY 9
Seattle 5, College Francais 3
Sault Ste. Marie 6, Kamloops 3

SUNDAY, MAY 10
Kamloops 4, College Francais 0

TUESDAY, MAY 12
Sault Ste. Marie 4, College Francais 2

WEDNESDAY, MAY 13
Sault Ste. Marie 4, Seattle 3

THURSDAY, MAY 14
Kamloops 3, Seattle 1

SATURDAY, MAY 16
Kamloops 8, Seattle 3

FINAL
SUNDAY, MAY 17
Kamloops 5, Sault Ste. Marie 4

TOP TOURNAMENT SCORERS

	Games	G	A	Pts.
Mike Mathers, Kamloops	5	4	*6	*10
Zac Boyer, Kamloops	5	*5	4	9
Colin Miller, Sault Ste. Marie	4	3	4	7
Scott Niedermayer, Kamloops	5	2	5	7
Chris Simon, Sault Ste. Marie	4	3	3	6
Jarret Reid, Sault Ste. Marie	4	3	3	6
Craig Lyons, Kamloops	5	3	3	6
Todd Johnson, Kamloops	5	4	0	4
George Zajankala, Seattle	4	3	1	4
Tony Iob, Sault Ste. Marie	4	2	2	4
Ralph Intranuovo, S. Ste. Marie	4	1	3	4
Steve Yule, Kamloops	5	1	3	4

*Indicates tournament leader.

1991-92 AWARD WINNERS

ALL-STAR TEAMS

First team	Pos.	Second team
Corey Hirsch, Kamloops	G	Mike Fountain, Oshawa
Scott Niedermayer, Kam.	D	Richard Matvichuk, Sask.
Drake Berehowsky, N. Bay	D	Darryl Sydor, Kamloops
Patrick Poulin, St. Hy.	LW	Todd Warriner, Windsor
Todd Simon, Niagara Falls	C	Steve Konowalchuk, Port.
Darren McCarty, Belleville	RW	Turner Stevenson, Seattle

Coach of the Year: Bryan Maxwell, Spokane

TROPHY WINNERS

Player of the year: Charles Poulin, St. Hyacinthe
Plus/minus award: Dean McAmmond, Prince Albert
Rookie of the year: Alexandre Daigle, Victoriaville
Defenseman of the year: Drake Berehowsky, North Bay
Goaltender of the year: Corey Hirsch, Kamloops
Scholastic player of the year: Nathan LaFayette, Cornwall
Coach of the year: Bryan Maxwell, Spokane
Executive of the year: Bert Templeton, North Bay
Most sportsmanlike player of the year: Martin Gendron, St. Hy.
Top draft prospect award: Todd Warriner, Windsor

HISTORY

ALL-TIME MEMORIAL CUP WINNERS

Season	Team	Season	Team	Season	Team
1918-19	Univ. of Toronto Schools	1922-23	Univ. of Manitoba-Winnipeg	1926-27	Owen Sound Greys
1919-20	Toronto Canoe Club	1923-24	Owen Sound Greys	1927-28	Regina Monarchs
1920-21	Winnipeg Falcons	1924-25	Regina Pats	1928-29	Toronto Marlboros
1921-22	Fort William War Veterans	1925-26	Calgary Canadians	1929-30	Regina Pats

Season	Team	Season	Team	Season	Team
1930-31	Winnipeg Elmwoods	1951-52	Guelph Biltmores	1972-73	Toronto Marlboros
1931-32	Sudbury Wolves	1952-53	Barrie Flyers	1973-74	Regina Pats
1932-33	Newmarket	1953-54	St. Catharines Tee Pees	1974-75	Toronto Marlboros
1933-34	Toronto St. Michael's	1954-55	Toronto Marlboros	1975-76	Hamilton Fincups
1934-35	Winnipeg Monarchs	1955-56	Toronto Marlboros	1976-77	New Westminster Bruins
1935-36	West Toronto Redmen	1956-57	Flin Flon Bombers	1977-78	New Westminster Bruins
1936-37	Winnipeg Monarchs	1957-58	Ottawa-Hull Jr. Canadiens	1978-79	Peterborough Petes
1937-38	St. Boniface Seals	1958-59	Winnipeg Braves	1979-80	Cornwall Royals
1938-39	Oshawa Generals	1959-60	St. Catharines Tee Pees	1980-81	Cornwall Royals
1939-40	Oshawa Generals	1960-61	Tor. St. Michael's Majors	1981-82	Kitchener Rangers
1940-41	Winnipeg Rangers	1961-62	Hamilton Red Wings	1982-83	Portland Winter Hawks
1941-42	Portage la Prairie	1962-63	Edmonton Oil Kings	1983-84	Ottawa 67's
1942-43	Winnipeg Rangers	1963-64	Toronto Marlboros	1984-85	Prince Albert Raiders
1943-44	Oshawa Generals	1964-65	Niagara Falls Flyers	1985-86	Guelph Platers
1944-45	Toronto St. Michael's	1965-66	Edmonton Oil Kings	1986-87	Medicine Hat Tigers
1945-46	Winnipeg Monarchs	1966-67	Toronto Marlboros	1987-88	Medicine Hat Tigers
1946-47	Toronto St. Michael's	1967-68	Niagara Falls Flyers	1988-89	Swift Current Broncos
1947-48	Port Arthur W. End Bruins	1968-69	Montreal Jr. Canadiens	1989-90	Oshawa Generals
1948-49	Montreal Royals	1969-70	Montreal Jr. Canadiens	1990-91	Spokane Chiefs
1949-50	Montreal Jr. Canadiens	1970-71	Quebec Remparts	1991-92	Kamloops Blazers
1950-51	Barrie Flyers	1971-72	Cornwall Royals		

ALL-TIME AWARD WINNERS

PLAYER OF THE YEAR AWARD

Season	Player, Team
1974-75	Ed Staniowski, Regina
1975-76	Peter Lee, Ottawa
1976-77	Dale McCourt, Ste. Catharines
1977-78	Bobby Smith, Ottawa
1978-79	Pierre LaCroix, Trois-Rivieres
1979-80	Doug Wickenheiser, Regina
1980-81	Dale Hawerchuk, Cornwall
1981-82	Dave Simpson, London
1982-83	Pat LaFontaine, Verdun
1983-84	Mario Lemieux, Laval
1984-85	Dan Hodgson, Prince Albert
1985-86	Luc Robitaille, Hull
1986-87	Rob Brown, Kamloops
1987-88	Joe Sakic, Swift Current
1988-89	Bryan Fogarty, Niagara Falls
1989-90	Mike Ricci, Peterborough
1990-91	Eric Lindros, Oshawa
1991-92	Charles Poulin, St. Hyacinthe

PLUS/MINUS AWARD

Season	Player, Team
1986-87	Rob Brown, Kamloops
1987-88	Marc Saumier, Hull
1988-89	Bryan Fogarty, Niagara Falls
1989-90	Len Barrie, Kamloops
1990-91	Eric Lindros, Oshawa
1991-92	Dean McAmmond, Prince Albert

ROOKIE OF THE YEAR AWARD

Season	Player, Team
1987-88	Martin Gelinas, Hull
1988-89	Yanic Perreault, Trois-Rivieres
1989-90	Petr Nedved, Seattle
1990-91	Philippe Boucher, Granby
1991-92	Alexandre Daigle, Victoriaville

DEFENSEMAN OF THE YEAR AWARD

Season	Player, Team
1987-88	Greg Hawgood, Kamloops
1988-89	Bryan Fogarty, Niagara Falls
1989-90	John Slaney, Cornwall
1990-91	Patrice Brisebois, Drummondville
1991-92	Drake Berehowsky, North Bay

GOALTENDER OF THE YEAR AWARD

Season	Player, Team
1987-88	Stephane Beauregard, St. Jean
1988-89	Stephane Fiset, Victoriaville
1989-90	Trevor Kidd, Brandon
1990-91	Felix Potvin, Chicoutimi
1991-92	Corey Hirsch, Kamloops

SCHOLASTIC PLAYER OF THE YEAR AWARD

Season	Player, Team
1987-88	Darrin Shannon, Windsor
1988-89	Jeff Nelson, Prince Albert
1989-90	Jeff Nelson, Prince Albert
1990-91	Scott Niedermayer, Kamloops
1991-92	Nathan LaFayette, Cornwall

COACH OF THE YEAR AWARD

Season	Coach, Team
1987-88	Alain Vigneault, Hull
1988-89	Joe McDonnell, Kitchener
1989-90	Ken Hitchcock, Kamloops
1990-91	Joe Canale, Chicoutimi
1991-92	Bryan Maxwell, Spokane

EXECUTIVE OF THE YEAR AWARD

Season	Executive, Team or League
1988-89	John Horman, QMJHL
1989-90	Russ Farwell, Seattle
1990-91	Sherwood Bassin, Sault Ste. Marie
1991-92	Bert Templeton, North Bay

MOST SPORTSMANLIKE PLAYER OF THE YEAR AWARD

Season	Player, Team
1989-90	Andrew McKim, Hull
1990-91	Pat Falloon, Spokane
1991-92	Martin Gendron, St. Hyacinthe

TOP DRAFT PROSPECT AWARD

Season	Player, Team
1990-91	Eric Lindros, Oshawa
1991-92	Todd Warriner, Windsor

ONTARIO HOCKEY LEAGUE

LEAGUE OFFICE

Commissioner
David E. Branch
Chairman of the board
Dr. Robert Vaughan
Director of administration
Herb Morell

Director of hockey operations
Ted Baker
Director of officiating
Ken Bodendistel
Director of central scouting
Jack Ferguson

Address
305 Milner Avenue
Suite 208
Scarborough, Ontario M1B 3V4
Phone
416-299-8700

1991-92 REGULAR SEASON

FINAL STANDINGS

MATT LEYDEN DIVISION

Team	G	W	L	T	Pts.	GF	GA
Peterborough	66	41	18	7	89	319	256
North Bay	66	40	21	5	85	323	259
Cornwall	66	38	22	6	82	328	289
Sudbury	66	33	27	6	72	331	320
Oshawa	66	31	26	9	71	274	273
Ottawa	66	32	30	4	68	280	251
Belleville	66	27	27	12	66	314	293
Kingston	66	16	44	6	38	241	316

HAP EMMS DIVISION

Team	G	W	L	T	Pts.	GF	GA
Sault Ste. Marie	66	41	19	6	88	335	229
Niagara Falls	66	39	23	4	82	307	254
London	66	37	25	4	78	310	260
Kitchener	66	29	30	7	65	283	282
Windsor	66	25	33	8	58	272	316
Owen Sound	66	23	41	2	48	260	315
Detroit	66	23	42	1	47	279	353
Guelph	66	4	51	11	19	235	425

INDIVIDUAL LEADERS

Goals: Darren McCarty, Belleville (55)
Assists: Brett Seguin, Ottawa (100)
Points: Todd Simon, Niagara Falls (146)
Penalty minutes: David Benn, Detroit (305)
Goaltending average: Fred Brathwaite, London (3.31)
Shutouts: Fred Brathwaite, London (4)

	Games	G	A	Pts.
Ralph Intranuovo, Sault	65	50	63	113
Jake Grimes, Belleville	66	44	69	113
Colin Miller, Sault	66	37	73	110
Jason Dawe, Peterborough	66	53	55	108
Mike Harding, Peterborough	64	44	61	105
Jeff Bes, Guelph	62	40	62	102
Scott Hollis, Oshawa	66	47	54	101
Chris Crombie, London	66	45	55	100
Jeff Reid, Cornwall	65	43	57	100
Ryan Kuwabara, Ottawa	66	43	57	100
Kevin Brown, Niagara Falls	64	42	58	100
Andrew Brunette, Owen Sound	66	51	47	98
Jason Firth, North Bay	53	25	72	97
Kevin MacKay, Windsor	64	32	63	95
Jamie Matthews, Sudbury	64	26	69	95

TOP SCORERS

	Games	G	A	Pts.
Todd Simon, Niagara Falls	66	53	93	146
Brett Seguin, Ottawa	64	34	100	134
John Spoltore, North Bay	66	47	84	131
Darren McCarty, Belleville	65	55	72	127
Chris Taylor, London	66	48	74	122
Brent Gretzky, Belleville	62	43	78	121

INDIVIDUAL STATISTICS

BELLEVILLE BULLS

SCORING

	Games	G	A	Pts.	Pen.
Darren McCarty	65	55	72	127	177
Brent Gretzky	62	43	78	121	37
Jake Grimes	66	44	69	113	18
Scott Boston	65	13	71	84	89
Tony Cimellaro	48	39	44	83	51
Kevin Brown	66	24	24	48	52
Darren Hurley	66	15	26	41	138
Shayne Antoski	41	16	17	33	16
Aaron Morrison	39	14	17	31	111
Dan Preston	53	4	16	20	26
Craig Fraser	22	8	10	18	74
Blair Scott	41	3	15	18	83
Doug Doull	62	6	11	17	123
Rick Marshall	62	3	14	17	124
Paul McCallion	23	4	10	14	30
Dale Chokan	36	2	9	11	40
Mark Donahue	23	6	3	9	32
Dominic Belanger	52	5	4	9	18
Daniel Godbout	60	1	8	9	44
Gairin Smith	11	1	7	8	22

	Games	G	A	Pts.	Pen.
Keith Redmond	16	1	7	8	52
Greg Bailey	50	1	7	8	36
Ryan Merritt	6	3	1	4	2
Brian Mielko	25	1	3	4	4
Marcello Fabrizi	13	2	1	3	5
Rob Kingham	22	0	3	3	20
Chris Varga	7	0	2	2	2
Ian Keiller	47	0	2	2	69
Gord Dulmage	2	0	1	1	0
Rob Stopar (goalie)	4	0	1	1	0
Scott Osborne	10	0	1	1	2
Greg Dreveny (goalie)	61	0	1	1	8
Rod MacCormick	1	0	0	0	0
James Sheehan	3	0	0	0	4
Richard Gallace (goalie)	9	0	0	0	0

GOALTENDING

	Games	Min.	Goals	SO	Avg.
Richard Gallace	9	372	26	0	4.19
Greg Dreveny	61	3528	249(4)	1	4.23
Rob Stopar	4	135	14	0	6.22

( )—Empty-net goals (do not count against a goal-tender's average).

CORNWALL ROYALS

SCORING

	Games	G	A	Pts.	Pen.
Jeff Reid	65	43	57	100	69
Tom Nemeth	66	25	49	74	33
Nathan LaFayette	66	28	45	73	26
Chris Clancy	66	28	38	66	117
Shayne Gaffar	59	25	35	60	17
John Slaney	34	19	41	60	43
Guy Leveque	37	23	36	59	40
Mark DeSantis	66	10	45	55	105
Dave Lemay	66	10	31	41	87
Jeremy Stevenson	63	15	23	38	176
Gord Pell	28	11	27	38	12
Rival Fullum	30	18	15	33	38
Sam Oliveira	57	12	20	32	12
Ryan VandenBussche	61	13	15	28	230
Mike Prokopec	59	12	15	27	75
Todd Walker	65	7	19	26	21
Richard Raymond	60	6	15	21	55
J.A. Schneider	25	9	11	20	91
Larry Courville	60	8	12	20	80
David Babcock	30	2	7	9	18
Matt McGuffin	18	0	6	6	29
Paul Andrea	29	2	3	5	17
Alan Letang	47	1	4	5	16
Jason Meloche	24	0	3	3	45
Rob Dykeman (goalie)	39	0	2	2	12
Matt Hogan	3	1	0	1	0
Ilpo Kauhanen (goalie)	31	0	1	1	20
Joe Benninger (goalie)	1	0	0	0	0
Rainer Giberson	1	0	0	0	2
Dave Roberts	1	0	0	0	0

GOALTENDING

	Games	Min.	Goals	SO	Avg.
Rob Dykeman	39	2232	150(1)	1	4.03
Ilpo Kaukanen	31	1711	130(1)	0	4.56
Joe Benninger	1	60	7	0	7.00

DETROIT COMPUWARE AMBASSADORS

SCORING

	Games	G	A	Pts.	Pen.
Pat Peake	53	41	52	93	44
Jeff Gardiner	58	30	42	72	11
Todd Harvey	58	21	43	64	141
John Wynne	65	18	43	61	46
Chris Skoryna	62	23	32	55	13
Bob Wren	62	13	36	49	58
Mark Lawrence	28	19	26	45	54
J.D. Eaton	65	17	18	35	136
Chris Varga	54	14	15	29	15
John Pinches	65	9	20	29	36
Tony McCabe	34	8	20	28	22
Jeff Kostuch	64	10	15	25	16
Craig Fraser	29	12	12	24	10
Mark Donahue	23	8	10	18	16
Pat Barton	31	8	10	18	36
Keith Redmond	25	6	12	18	61
Aaron Morrison	25	9	8	17	30
Blair Scott	28	1	16	17	68
David Benn	61	4	12	16	305
Eric Cairns	64	1	11	12	237
Chris Phelps	54	1	10	11	52
Derek Etches	16	3	6	9	0
Ryan Merritt	7	1	5	6	17
Rob Kinghan	35	1	5	6	47
Glen Craig	62	1	4	5	76
Paul Doherty	21	0	4	4	18
Jamie Shea (goalie)	24	0	3	3	4
Derek Wilkinson (goalie)	38	0	2	2	4
Jeff Smith	4	0	1	1	0
John Finnie (goalie)	1	0	0	0	0
Chris Pickersgill	3	0	0	0	0
Brent Thombs (goalie)	3	0	0	0	0

	Games	G	A	Pts.	Pen.
James Sheehan	4	0	0	0	11
Taylor Clarke	7	0	0	0	16
Jeff Nolan	7	0	0	0	0
Brad Teichmann (goalie)	15	0	0	0	2

GOALTENDING

	Games	Min.	Goals	SO	Avg.
Derek Wilkinson	38	1943	138(3)	1	4.26
Brent Thombs	3	151	14	0	5.56
Jamie Shea	24	1105	110(3)	0	5.97
Brad Teichmann	15	730	76(2)	0	6.25
John Finnie	1	42	7	0	10.00

GUELPH STORM

SCORING

	Games	G	A	Pts.	Pen.
Jeff Bes	62	40	62	102	123
Bill Kovacs	55	35	38	73	61
Sylvain Cloutier	62	35	31	66	74
Brent Pope	65	10	38	48	108
Wade Whiten	48	16	21	37	61
Alek Stojanov	33	12	15	27	91
Jeff Pawluk	61	12	15	27	100
Brent Watson	50	7	18	25	140
Dave Anderson	33	4	21	25	34
Kayle Short	39	4	19	23	81
Todd Bertuzzi	47	7	14	21	145
Grant Pritchett	56	1	16	17	50
Kevin Reid	39	8	8	16	76
Mike Hartwick	27	4	7	11	77
Ken Ruddick	36	4	7	11	58
Chris McMurtry	55	2	9	11	56
Mike Cote	32	6	4	10	56
Gairin Smith	12	5	5	10	15
Bill LaForge	23	2	7	9	17
Duane Harmer	55	2	7	9	72
Toby Burkitt	26	4	4	8	21
Todd Gleason	17	1	6	7	18
Craig Lutes	18	3	2	5	11
Ken Blum	6	2	3	5	0
Kelvin Solari	46	1	4	5	75
Sean Brown	17	2	2	4	24
Shane Johnson	29	2	2	4	10
Trevor Renkers	10	1	3	4	12
Matt Turek	23	1	3	4	20
Brian Murphy	20	2	1	3	38
Steve Pottie	34	0	3	3	0
Rob Leask	7	0	1	1	15
Ben Hendrick (goalie)	1	0	0	0	0
Dan DeGurse	2	0	0	0	0
George Dourian (goalie)	6	0	0	0	4
Angelo Amore (goalie)	7	0	0	0	0
Scott Jenkins	7	0	0	0	17
Dan Tanevski (goalie)	49	0	0	0	36

GOALTENDING

	Games	Min.	Goals	SO	Avg.
George Dourian	6	334	27	0	4.85
Angelo Amore	7	225	23	0	6.13
Dan Tanevski	49	1873	199(4)	0	6.37
Steve Pottie	34	1559	167(1)	0	6.43
Ben Hendrick	1	30	4	0	8.00

KINGSTON FRONTENACS

SCORING

	Games	G	A	Pts.	Pen.
Keli Corpse	65	31	52	83	20
Chris Gratton	62	27	39	66	35
Dave Stewart	65	15	45	60	143
John Vary	54	11	38	49	102
Alastair Still	62	20	22	42	81
Justin Morrison	23	18	21	39	63
Steve Parson	39	18	20	38	24
Gord Harris	37	15	21	36	33

	Games	G	A	Pts.	Pen.
Greg Clancy	39	14	22	36	13
Brian Stagg	65	17	14	31	21
Cory Johnson	66	10	20	30	12
Craig Rivet	66	5	21	26	97
Bill Robinson	40	13	11	24	16
Mike Dawson	63	4	19	23	101
Shawn Caplice	63	6	9	15	108
Joel Yates	58	2	12	14	186
Kevin King	42	4	9	13	11
Tony Bella	47	1	8	9	23
Marc Lamothe (goalie)	42	0	5	5	4
Chris Scharf	59	4	0	4	37
Jason Wadel	52	3	1	4	34
Rod Pasma	23	2	1	3	68
Peter McGlynn (goalie)	19	1	1	2	28
Blake Martin	4	0	1	1	2
Mike Yacynuk	8	0	1	1	2
Jason Beaton	10	0	1	1	32
Brad Teichmann	13	0	1	1	2
Trevor Doyle	26	0	1	1	19
Brandon Coleman	1	0	0	0	0
Trent Cull	18	0	0	0	31

GOALTENDING

	Games	Min.	Goals	SO	Avg.
Peter McGlynn	19	1000	74(2)	1	4.44
Brad Teichmann	13	630	49	0	4.67
Marc Lamothe	42	2378	189(2)	1	4.77

KITCHENER RANGERS

SCORING

	Games	G	A	Pts.	Pen.
Yvan Corbin	61	41	37	78	17
Jamie Caruso	55	27	48	75	81
Chris LiPuma	61	13	59	72	115
Trevor Gallant	55	22	36	58	28
Mike Polano	52	24	30	54	96
Norm Dezainde	64	19	24	43	53
Shayne McCosh	62	7	36	43	46
Gib Tucker	34	12	26	38	16
Derek Gauthier	59	20	17	37	82
Brad Barton	64	9	26	35	160
Tyler Ertel	24	16	18	34	48
Eric Manlow	59	12	20	32	17
Gary Miller	55	4	23	27	73
Gairin Smith	38	13	13	26	65
Tim Spitzig	62	8	13	21	87
Tony McCabe	31	8	12	20	34
Jason Gladney	65	2	18	20	54
Marc Robillard	65	10	6	16	16
Paul McCallion	35	3	11	14	27
Jack Williams	11	3	7	10	9
Mike Torchia (goalie)	55	0	8	8	26
Darren Bell	5	5	1	6	4
Chris Kraemer	21	2	4	6	47
Robert Frayn	21	1	5	6	51
Dale Chokan	15	0	4	4	14
Justin Cullen	33	0	4	4	52
Dennis Bonvie	7	1	1	2	23
Chris Shushack	36	1	0	1	4
Shamus Gregga (goalie)	2	0	0	0	0
Rod Saarinen	2	0	0	0	0
Jason Zohil	3	0	0	0	18
Jason Stevenson	8	0	0	0	0
C. Jay Denomme (goalie)	21	0	0	0	2

GOALTENDING

	Games	Min.	Goals	SO	Avg.
Mike Torchia	55	3042	203(2)	1	4.00
C. Jay Denomme	21	881	63(2)	0	4.29
Shamus Gregga	2	80	12	0	9.00

LONDON KNIGHTS

SCORING

	Games	G	A	Pts.	Pen.
Chris Taylor	66	48	74	122	57
Chris Crombie	66	45	55	100	100
Dennis Purdie	54	38	37	75	153
Scott McKay	64	30	45	75	97
Brett Marietti	57	25	27	52	59
Barry Potomski	61	19	32	51	224
Paul Wolanski	44	11	35	46	57
Sean O'Reilly	64	9	36	45	152
Dave Gilmore	65	13	26	39	65
Mark Visheau	66	5	31	36	104
Brad Smyth	58	17	18	35	93
Greg Ryan	34	5	26	31	46
Jason Allison	65	11	18	29	15
Aaron Nagy	38	9	19	28	17
Nick Stajduhar	66	6	15	21	62
Kelly Reed	41	3	18	21	25
Steve Smillie	60	4	12	16	13
Troy Sweet	26	1	8	9	21
Gord Ross	55	2	6	8	49
Cory Evans	55	2	5	7	101
Rick Corriveau	4	0	7	7	6
Derrick Crane	15	5	1	6	39
Brent Brownlee (goalie)	36	0	4	4	2
Drew Herendeen	17	1	1	2	10
Jason Glover	2	1	0	1	2
Jason Skellett	1	0	1	1	2
Dave Anderson	3	0	1	1	2
Brian Stacey	16	0	1	1	6
Chris Dubecki (goalie)	1	0	0	0	0
Dave Kindree	1	0	0	0	0
Mark Williams (goalie)	2	0	0	0	0
Jamie Watts	4	0	0	0	0
Gerry Arcella (goalie)	16	0	0	0	0
Fred Brathwaite (goalie)	23	0	0	0	4

GOALTENDING

	Games	Min.	Goals	SO	Avg.
Fred Brathwaite	23	1325	61	4	2.76
Mark Williams	2	80	4	0	3.00
Gerry Arcella	16	542	40	0	4.43
Brent Brownlee	36	2000	151	0	4.53
Chris Dubecki	1	40	4	0	6.00

NIAGARA FALLS THUNDER

SCORING

	Games	G	A	Pts.	Pen.
Todd Simon	66	53	93	146	70
Kevin Brown	64	42	58	100	12
Rick Corriveau	54	21	57	78	72
Ethan Moreau	62	20	35	55	39
Steve Staios	65	11	42	53	122
Geoff Rawson	64	17	33	50	50
Scott Campbell	55	13	37	50	100
Dan Krisko	60	16	33	49	23
Dennis Maxwell	66	20	26	46	139
Dale Junkin	62	20	19	39	22
Mike DeCoff	49	20	14	34	49
Todd Wetzel	66	13	17	30	51
Mark Cardiff	62	10	16	26	36
Tom Moores	59	10	13	23	46
Jason Clarke	63	5	15	20	215
Neil Fewster	65	4	12	16	72
Ryan Tocher	58	4	8	12	53
Ken Blum	10	3	3	6	16
John Johnson	3	4	1	5	2
Jason Coles	58	0	5	5	68
Matt McGuffin	30	1	2	3	18
David Babcock	24	0	1	1	26
Manny Legace (goalie)	43	0	1	1	10
Gord Duffy	1	0	0	0	0
Brian Holk	1	0	0	0	0
Mike Teutenberg (goalie)	1	0	0	0	0

	Games	G	A	Pts.	Pen.
Tom Yurcich	1	0	0	0	2
Rick Girhiny	2	0	0	0	0
Steve Mercer	2	0	0	0	0
Paul Wolanski	3	0	0	0	0
Brad Love	4	0	0	0	0
Greg Scott (goalie)	31	0	0	0	15

GOALTENDING

	Games	Min.	Goals	SO	Avg.
Manny Legace	43	2384	143(5)	0	3.60
Greg Scott	31	1585	103	0	3.90
Mike Teutenberg	1	18	3	0	10.00

NORTH BAY CENTENNIALS

SCORING

	Games	G	A	Pts.	Pen.
John Spoltore	66	47	84	131	31
Jason Firth	53	25	72	97	22
Drake Berehowsky	62	19	63	82	147
Jack Williams	53	40	35	75	31
Bill Lang	62	24	37	61	101
Billy Wright	63	26	32	58	72
Jeff Shevalier	64	28	29	57	26
Chad Penney	57	25	27	52	93
Ryan Merritt	45	25	20	45	103
Mark Lawrence	24	13	14	27	21
Michael Burman	63	3	22	25	64
Rob Thorpe	57	6	16	22	56
Jamie Caruso	13	9	10	19	10
Paul Rushforth	65	8	11	19	24
Allan Cox	61	1	17	18	124
Jason MacDonald	17	5	8	13	50
Wade Gibson	44	2	10	12	63
Dennis Bonvie	49	0	12	12	261
Shayne Antoski	11	6	5	11	4
Brad Brown	49	2	9	11	170
Pat Barton	27	4	6	10	22
James Sheehan	44	2	3	5	14
Bryan Drury	13	0	4	4	34
Dave Szabo	47	2	1	3	23
Paul Doherty	24	0	3	3	25
Ian Blanchfield	6	1	1	2	0
Gary Miller	13	0	2	2	16
Ron Bertrand (goalie)	43	0	2	2	21
Brad Shepard	15	0	1	1	19
Sandy Allan (goalie)	34	0	1	1	10
Brent Rowley	1	0	0	0	0
Peter Papadogiannis (goalie)	2	0	0	0	0
Dominic Belanger	13	0	0	0	2

GOALTENDING

	Games	Min.	Goals	SO	Avg.
Ron Bertrand	43	2200	138(1)	2	3.76
Sandy Allan	34	1747	112(1)	0	3.85
Peter Papadogiannis	2	38	7	0	11.05

OSHAWA GENERALS

SCORING

	Games	G	A	Pts.	Pen.
Scott Hollis	66	47	54	101	183
Jason Weaver	61	29	42	71	159
Matt Hoffman	50	25	41	66	93
Trevor Burgess	65	16	43	59	80
B.J. MacPherson	60	20	32	52	108
Mark Deazeley	66	19	21	40	215
Rob Leask	49	13	27	40	90
Jan Benda	61	12	23	35	68
Darryl LaFrance	48	12	20	32	24
Eric Lindros	13	9	22	31	54
Markus Brunner	35	10	17	27	25
Stephane Yelle	55	12	14	26	20
Troy Sweet	40	7	19	26	56
Jason Arnott	57	9	15	24	12

	Games	G	A	Pts.	Pen.
Brian Grieve	66	4	20	24	80
Wade Simpson	64	5	11	16	104
Jean-Paul Davis	21	3	11	14	18
Todd Bradley	48	3	11	14	60
Jason Campeau	51	6	7	13	19
Sean Brown	38	2	8	10	65
Craig Lutes	17	5	3	8	17
Kevin Spero	56	4	2	6	20
Joe Cook	59	1	4	5	84
Mike Cote	14	1	3	4	8
Neil Iserhoff	12	0	4	4	0
Dave Anderson	7	0	3	3	5
Ken Shepard (goalie)	7	0	2	2	6
John Carr	2	0	0	0	0
Mike Mortimer	2	0	0	0	0
Darren McClellan	3	0	0	0	4
Brent Brownlee (goalie)	6	0	0	0	0
Fred Brathwaite (goalie)	24	0	0	0	4
Mike Fountain (goalie)	40	0	0	0	12

GOALTENDING

	Games	Min.	Goals	SO	Avg.
Ken Shepard	7	265	16	1	3.62
Fred Brathwaite	24	1248	81	0	3.89
Mike Fountain	40	2260	149(1)	1	3.96
Brent Brownlee	6	235	26	0	6.64

OTTAWA 67's

SCORING

	Games	G	A	Pts.	Pen.
Brett Seguin	64	34	100	134	70
Ryan Kuwabara	66	43	57	100	84
Grant Marshall	61	32	51	83	132
Peter Ambroziak	49	32	49	81	50
Curt Bowen	65	31	45	76	94
Jeff Ricciardi	61	15	41	56	220
Grayden Reid	54	10	26	36	18
Gerry Skrypec	65	6	21	27	105
Mike Peca	27	8	17	25	32
Zbynek Kukacka	66	13	10	23	24
Steve Washburn	59	5	17	22	10
Shean Donovan	58	11	8	19	14
Matt Stone	49	13	5	18	112
Chris Coveny	65	5	10	15	74
Greg Clancy	12	5	7	12	11
Chris Gignac	35	3	6	9	7
Bill Hall	48	3	6	9	30
Greg Ryan	33	1	8	9	27
Mike Johnson	63	1	8	9	49
Ken Belanger	51	4	4	8	174
Doug Minor	14	3	1	4	28
Pat Curcio	20	1	3	4	0
Wade Gibson	11	0	4	4	31
Chris Simon	2	1	1	2	24
Mark O'Donnell	14	0	1	1	2
Dan Ryder (goalie)	24	0	1	1	4
Tyson Johnson (goalie)	2	0	0	0	0
Steve Pottie (goalie)	2	0	0	0	0
Mark Rigby	3	0	0	0	0
Rick Pollard (goalie)	5	0	0	0	2
Chris Shushack	6	0	0	0	2
Brad Spry	12	0	0	0	21
Mike Lenarduzzi (goalie)	18	0	0	0	0
Sean Spencer (goalie)	27	0	0	0	2
Sean Gawley	31	0	0	0	6

GOALTENDING

	Games	Min.	Goals	SO	Avg.
Dan Ryder	24	1380	55(2)	3	2.39
Mike Lenarduzzi	18	986	60	1	3.65
Sean Spencer	27	1165	91(1)	0	4.69
Rick Pollard	5	238	19(1)	0	4.79
Steve Pottie	2	120	11	0	5.50
Tyson Johnson	2	100	11	0	6.60

OWEN SOUND PLATERS

SCORING

	Games	G	A	Pts.	Pen.
Andrew Brunette	66	51	47	98	42
Kirk Maltby	64	50	41	91	99
Jim Brown	65	37	51	88	64
Justin Morrison	36	9	43	52	106
Brock Woods	61	10	37	47	201
Scott Walker	53	7	31	38	128
Jason MacDonald	42	17	19	36	129
Geordie Maynard	49	13	15	28	125
Rick Morton	63	1	27	28	192
Steve Parson	27	10	17	27	19
Willie Skilliter	66	7	15	22	8
Jeff Smith	56	7	14	21	62
Luigi Calce	61	10	8	18	75
Wyatt Buckland	58	6	9	15	77
Troy Hutchinson	65	3	10	13	39
Gord Dickie	54	5	7	12	11
Grayden Reid	8	2	10	12	4
Aaron Nagy	29	5	5	10	30
Jason Buetow	26	4	5	9	8
Shawn Krueger	55	0	9	9	78
Steve Walker	9	2	3	5	2
Jeff Perry	7	0	5	5	8
Jason Hughes	55	0	5	5	53
Rob MacKenzie	25	3	1	4	4
Mark Vilneff	22	1	3	4	6
Jason Skellett	6	0	3	3	2
Wade Gibson	4	0	2	2	0
Sean Basilio (goalie)	37	0	1	1	0
Greg Clancy	2	0	0	0	0
Brodie Coffin	2	0	0	0	0
Jamie Grimoldby	2	0	0	0	0
Joe Tuori	3	0	0	0	2
Mike Majewski	5	0	0	0	18
Geoff Schnare (goalie)	8	0	0	0	0
Jamie Storr (goalie)	34	0	0	0	10

GOALTENDING

	Games	Min.	Goals	SO	Avg.
Jamie Storr	34	1733	128(4)	0	4.43
Sean Basilio	37	1968	160	1	4.88
Geoff Schnare	8	270	23	1	5.11

PETERBOROUGH PETES

SCORING

	Games	G	A	Pts.	Pen.
Jason Dawe	66	53	55	108	55
Mike Harding	64	44	61	105	111
John Johnson	52	45	39	84	24
Mike Tomlinson	61	19	50	69	83
Chris Pronger	63	17	45	62	90
Dale McTavish	60	25	31	56	59
Bryan Gendron	61	19	32	51	213
Ryan Black	66	18	33	51	57
Jassen Cullimore	54	9	37	46	65
Don O'Neill	57	14	27	41	102
Brent Tully	65	9	23	32	65
Dave Roche	62	10	17	27	134
Doug Searle	64	3	24	27	144
Geordie Kinnear	63	5	16	21	195
Chris Longo	25	5	14	19	16
Colin Wilson	62	7	10	17	36
Kelly Vipond	42	5	8	13	19
Chad Grills	32	4	4	8	8
Matt St. Germain	44	4	4	8	32
Jeff Walker	40	2	1	3	18
Andrew Verner (goalie)	53	0	3	3	16
Shawn Heins	49	1	1	2	73
Scott Turner	29	1	0	1	14
Shawn Healey	2	0	1	1	2
Greg Bailey	1	0	0	0	0
Jude Rutland	4	0	0	0	2
Chad Lang (goalie)	16	0	0	0	0

GOALTENDING

	Games	Min.	Goals	SO	Avg.
Andrew Verner	53	3123	190(3)	1	3.65
Chad Lang	16	886	63	0	4.27

SAULT STE. MARIE GREYHOUNDS

SCORING

	Games	G	A	Pts.	Pen.
Ralph Intranuovo	65	50	63	113	44
Colin Miller	66	37	73	110	52
Jarret Reid	61	53	40	93	67
Rick Kowalsky	66	25	44	69	119
Tony Iob	42	28	34	62	157
Shaun Imber	66	5	54	59	23
Jason Denomme	60	24	32	56	116
David Matsos	61	23	22	45	34
Chris Simon	31	19	25	44	143
Mark Matier	66	4	27	31	68
Tom MacDonald	52	11	15	26	139
Drew Bannister	64	4	21	25	122
Perry Pappas	53	12	10	22	68
Wade Whitten	20	5	16	21	20
Aaron Gavey	48	7	11	18	27
Mike DeCoff	13	4	11	15	26
Jeff Toms	35	9	5	14	0
Brian Goudie	65	2	12	14	216
Todd Gleason	44	0	12	12	38
Gary Roach	41	2	9	11	6
Brad Baber	35	3	7	10	31
Kiley Hill	32	4	3	7	28
Jonas Rudberg	8	2	4	6	0
Kevin Reid	21	2	4	6	50
Briane Thompson	42	0	4	4	17
Chris Grenville	10	0	2	2	9
Kevin Hodson (goalie)	50	0	2	2	12
Rob Stopar	6	0	1	1	0
Bob Harrison (goalie)	6	0	0	0	0
Tim Bacik (goalie)	7	0	0	0	0
Mike Lenarduzzi (goalie)	9	0	0	0	4
Chris Shushack	9	0	0	0	0
Jason Julian	11	0	0	0	11

GOALTENDING

	Games	Min.	Goals	SO	Avg.
Bob Harrison	6	285	12(1)	1	2.53
Rob Stopar	6	260	11	0	2.54
Kevin Hodson	50	2722	151(3)	0	3.33
Tim Bacik	7	246	15(3)	0	3.66
Mike Lenarduzzi, SSM	9	486	33	0	4.07

SUDBURY WOLVES

SCORING

	Games	G	A	Pts.	Pen.
Jamie Matthews	64	26	69	95	30
Derek Armstrong	66	31	54	85	22
Glen Murray	54	37	47	84	93
Jason Young	55	26	56	82	49
Shawn Rivers	64	26	54	80	34
Terry Chitaroni	51	31	47	78	119
Brandon Convery	44	40	27	67	44
Rod Hinks	66	35	21	56	62
Barrie Moore	62	15	38	53	57
Mike Peca	39	16	34	50	61
Bernie John	60	4	33	37	21
Barry Young	60	6	19	25	110
Kyle Blacklock	66	4	21	25	26
Jamie Rivers	55	3	13	16	20
Mike Yeo	43	5	8	13	60
Tim Favot	60	2	11	13	10
Jason Zohil	53	6	6	12	144
Darren Dougan	16	3	8	11	0
Leonard MacDonald	28	2	7	9	78
Sean Gagnon	4	3	4	7	60
Darren Bell	5	3	4	7	6
Bill Kovacs	5	3	4	7	8

	Games	G	A	Pts.	Pen.
Bob MacIsaac	52	2	5	7	27
Kayle Short	25	0	3	3	38
George Dourian (goalie)	30	0	3	3	4
Derek Etches	7	2	0	2	2
Joel Sandie	8	0	2	2	22
Mike Lenarduzzi (goalie)	22	0	2	2	6
Todd Jones	2	0	1	1	7
Steve Potvin	6	0	1	1	16
Dan Ryder (goalie)	23	0	1	1	8
Carmelo Giurleo (goalie)	1	0	0	0	0
Jason Warner	1	0	0	0	0
Todd McKee	2	0	0	0	2
Aaron Beals (goalie)	3	0	0	0	0
Chris Fraser	5	0	0	0	4
Kelvin Solari	5	0	0	0	0

GOALTENDING

	Games	Min.	Goals	SO	Avg.
Aaron Beals	3	64	4	0	3.75
Mike Lenarduzzi	22	1201	84(1)	2	4.20
Dan Ryder	23	1157	91	0	4.72
George Dourian	30	1552	133(4)	0	5.14
Carmelo Giurleo	1	20	3	0	9.00

WINDSOR SPITFIRES

SCORING

	Games	G	A	Pts.	Pen.
Kevin MacKay	64	32	63	95	77
Cory Stillman	53	29	61	90	59
Steve Gibson	63	49	40	89	41
Bill Bowler	66	25	63	88	28
Todd Warriner	50	41	42	83	66
Jason Stos	63	22	48	70	114
Steve Smith	46	7	19	26	63
Craig Lutes	31	7	17	24	29
Tom Sullivan	63	5	14	19	223
John Copley	62	3	15	18	72
Gord Harris	28	9	7	16	27
Robert Frayn	37	6	8	14	46
David Myles	38	7	6	13	48
Leonard MacDonald	29	4	9	13	67
Ryan O'Neill	52	4	8	12	52
Jamie Allison	59	4	8	12	70
Brady Blain	59	2	9	11	8
Eric Stamp	46	5	5	10	156
Mike Hartwick	30	3	6	9	59
Rod Pasma	27	3	4	7	59
Peter Allison	50	1	5	6	39
Trent Cull	32	0	6	6	66
Todd Hunter (goalie)	36	0	6	6	8
Craig Binns	54	1	4	5	61
Reuben Castella	39	0	4	4	58
Marcus Middleton	13	2	0	2	26
Matt Mullin (goalie)	45	0	2	2	6
Earl St. Hilare	7	1	0	1	0
Jeff Bramham	7	0	1	1	2
Lain Schubert	1	0	0	0	5
Brad Teichmann	2	0	0	0	2

GOALTENDING

	Games	Min.	Goals	SO	Avg.
Brad Teichmann	2	80	5	0	3.75
Matt Mullin	45	2263	172(1)	0	4.56
Todd Hunter	36	1661	137(1)	2	4.95

PLAYERS WITH TWO OR MORE TEAMS

SCORING

	Games	G	A	Pts.	Pen.
Dave Anderson, London	3	0	1	1	2
Dave Anderson, Oshawa	7	0	3	3	5
Dave Anderson, Guelph	33	4	21	25	34
Totals	43	4	25	29	41

	Games	G	A	Pts.	Pen.
Shayne Antoski, North Bay	11	6	5	11	4
Shayne Antoski, Belleville	41	16	17	33	16
Totals	52	22	22	44	20
David Babcock, Niagara Falls	24	0	1	1	26
David Babcock, Cornwall	30	2	7	9	18
Totals	54	2	8	10	44
Greg Bailey, Peterborough	1	0	0	0	0
Greg Bailey, Belleville	50	1	7	8	36
Totals	51	1	7	8	36
Pat Barton, North Bay	27	4	6	10	22
Pat Barton, Detroit	31	8	10	18	36
Totals	58	12	16	28	58
Dominic Belanger, North Bay	13	0	0	0	2
Dominic Belanger, Belleville	52	5	4	9	18
Totals	65	5	4	9	20
Darren Bell, Sudbury	5	3	4	7	6
Darren Bell, Kitchener	5	5	1	6	4
Totals	10	8	5	13	10
Ken Blum, Guelph	6	2	3	5	0
Ken Blum, Niagara Falls	10	3	3	6	16
Totals	16	5	6	11	10
Dennis Bonvie, Kitchener	7	1	1	2	23
Dennis Bonvie, North Bay	49	0	12	12	261
Totals	56	1	13	14	284
Fred Brathwaite, Oshawa (g)	24	0	0	0	4
Fred Brathwaite, London (g)	23	0	0	0	4
Totals	47	0	0	0	8
Sean Brown, Guelph	17	2	2	4	24
Sean Brown, Oshawa	38	2	8	10	65
Totals	55	4	10	14	89
Brent Brownlee, London (g)	36	0	4	4	2
Brent Brownlee, Oshawa (g)	6	0	0	0	0
Totals	42	0	4	4	2
Jamie Caruso, North Bay	13	9	10	19	10
Jamie Caruso, Kitchener	55	27	48	75	81
Totals	68	36	58	94	91
Dale Chokan, Belleville	36	2	9	11	40
Dale Chokan, Kitchener	15	0	4	4	14
Totals	51	2	13	15	54
Greg Clancy, Ottawa	12	5	7	12	11
Greg Clancy, Owen Sound	2	0	0	0	0
Greg Clancy, Kingston	39	14	22	36	13
Totals	53	19	29	48	24
Rick Corriveau, London	4	0	7	7	6
Rick Corriveau, Niagara Falls	54	21	57	78	72
Totals	58	21	64	85	78
Mike Cote, Oshawa	14	1	3	4	8
Mike Cote, Guelph	32	6	4	10	21
Totals	46	7	7	14	29
Trent Cull, Windsor	32	0	6	6	66
Trent Cull, Kingston	18	0	0	0	31
Totals	50	0	6	6	97
Mike DeCoff, Sault Ste. Marie	13	4	11	15	26
Mike DeCoff, Niagara Falls	49	20	14	34	49
Totals	62	24	25	49	75
Paul Doherty, Detroit	21	0	4	4	18
Paul Doherty, North Bay	24	0	3	3	25
Totals	45	0	7	7	43
Mark Donahue, Detroit	23	8	10	18	16
Mark Donahue, Belleville	23	6	3	9	32
Totals	46	14	13	27	48
George Dourian, Guelph (g)	6	0	0	0	4
George Dourian, Sudbury (g)	30	0	3	3	4
Totals	36	0	3	3	8
Derek Etches, Sudbury	7	2	0	2	2
Derek Etches, Detroit	16	3	6	9	0
Totals	23	5	6	11	2
Craig Fraser, Belleville	22	8	10	18	74
Craig Fraser, Detroit	29	12	12	24	10
Totals	51	20	22	42	144
Robert Frayn, Kitchener	21	1	5	6	51
Robert Frayn, Windsor	37	6	8	14	46
Totals	58	7	13	20	97
Wade Gibson, Ottawa	11	0	4	4	31
Wade Gibson, Owen Sound	4	0	2	2	0

MAJOR JUNIOR LEAGUES

	Games	G	A	Pts.	Pen.
Wade Gibson, North Bay	44	2	10	12	63
Totals	59	2	16	18	94
Todd Gleason, Guelph	17	1	6	7	18
Todd Gleason, Sault Ste. Marie	44	0	12	12	38
Totals	61	1	18	19	56
Gord Harris, Kingston	37	15	21	36	33
Gord Harris, Windsor	28	9	7	16	27
Totals	65	24	28	52	60
Mike Hartwick, Guelph	27	4	7	11	77
Mike Hartwick, Windsor	30	3	6	9	59
Totals	57	7	13	20	136
John Johnson, Niagara Falls	3	4	1	5	2
John Johnson, Peterborough	52	45	39	84	24
Totals	55	49	40	89	26
Rob Kingham, Detroit	35	1	5	6	47
Rob Kingham, Belleville	22	0	3	3	20
Totals	57	1	8	9	67
Bill Kovacs, Sudbury	5	3	4	7	8
Bill Kovacs, Guelph	55	35	38	73	61
Totals	60	38	42	80	69
Mark Lawrence, Detroit	28	19	26	45	54
Mark Lawrence, North Bay	24	13	14	27	21
Totals	52	32	40	72	75
Rob Leask, Guelph	7	0	1	1	15
Rob Leask, Oshawa	49	13	27	40	90
Totals	56	13	28	41	105
Mike Lenarduzzi, SSM (goalie)	9	0	0	0	4
Mike Lenarduzzi, Ottawa (g)	18	0	0	0	0
Mike Lenarduzzi, Sudbury (g)	22	0	2	2	6
Totals	49	0	2	2	10
Craig Lutes, Oshawa	17	5	3	8	17
Craig Lutes, Guelph	18	3	2	5	11
Craig Lutes, Windsor	31	7	17	24	29
Totals	66	15	22	37	57
Jason MacDonald, North Bay	17	5	8	13	50
Jason MacDonald, Owen Sound	42	17	19	36	129
Totals	59	22	27	49	179
Leonard MacDonald, Windsor	29	4	9	13	67
Leonard MacDonald, Sudbury	28	2	7	9	78
Totals	57	6	16	22	145
Tony McCabe, Kitchener	31	8	12	20	34
Tony McCabe, Detroit	34	8	20	28	22
Totals	65	16	32	48	56
Paul McCallion, Kitchener	35	3	11	14	27
Paul McCallion, Belleville	23	4	10	14	30
Totals	58	7	21	28	57
Matt McGuffin, Cornwall	18	0	6	6	29
Matt McGuffin, Niagara Falls	30	1	1	2	18
Totals	48	1	7	8	47
Ryan Merritt, Detroit	7	1	5	6	17
Ryan Merritt, Belleville	6	3	1	4	2
Ryan Merritt, North Bay	45	25	20	45	103
Totals	58	29	26	55	122
Gary Miller, North Bay	13	0	2	2	16
Gary Miller, Kitchener	55	4	23	27	73
Totals	68	4	25	29	89
Aaron Morrison, Belleville	39	14	17	31	111
Aaron Morrison, Detroit	25	9	8	17	30
Totals	64	23	25	46	141
Justin Morrison, Kingston	23	18	21	39	63
Justin Morrison, Owen Sound	36	9	43	52	106
Totals	59	27	64	91	169
Aaron Nagy, London	38	9	19	28	17
Aaron Nagy, Owen Sound	29	5	5	10	30
Totals	67	14	24	38	47
Steve Parson, Owen Sound	27	10	17	27	19
Steve Parson, Kingston	39	18	20	38	24
Totals	66	28	37	65	43
Rod Pasma, Kingston	23	2	1	3	68
Rod Pasma, Windsor	27	3	4	7	59
Totals	50	5	5	10	127
Mike Peca, Sudbury	39	16	34	50	61
Mike Peca, Ottawa	27	8	17	25	32
Totals	66	24	51	75	93
Steve Pottie, Ottawa (goalie)	2	0	0	0	0

	Games	G	A	Pts.	Pen.
Steve Pottie, Guelph (goalie)	34	0	3	3	0
Totals	36	0	3	3	0
Keith Redmond, Belleville	16	1	7	8	52
Keith Redmond, Detroit	25	6	12	18	61
Totals	41	7	19	26	113
Grayden Reid, Owen Sound	8	2	10	12	4
Grayden Reid, Ottawa	54	10	26	36	18
Totals	62	12	36	48	22
Kevin Reid, Sault Ste. Marie	21	2	4	6	50
Kevin Reid, Guelph	39	8	8	16	76
Totals	60	10	12	22	126
Greg Ryan, London	34	5	26	31	46
Greg Ryan, Ottawa	33	1	8	9	27
Totals	67	6	34	40	73
Dan Ryder, Sudbury (goalie)	23	0	1	1	8
Dan Ryder, Ottawa (goalie)	24	0	1	1	4
Totals	47	0	2	2	12
Blair Scott, Belleville	41	3	15	18	83
Blair Scott, Detroit	28	1	16	17	68
Totals	69	4	31	35	151
James Sheehan, Detroit	4	0	0	0	11
James Sheehan, Belleville	3	0	0	0	4
James Sheehan, North Bay	44	2	3	5	14
Totals	51	2	3	5	29
Kayle Short, Guelph	39	4	19	23	81
Kayle Short, Sudbury	25	0	3	3	38
Totals	64	4	22	26	119
Chris Shushack, S. Ste. Marie	9	0	0	0	0
Chris Shushack, Ottawa	6	0	0	0	2
Chris Shushack, Kitchener	36	1	0	1	4
Totals	51	1	0	1	6
Chris Simon, Ottawa	2	1	1	2	24
Chris Simon, Sault Ste. Marie	31	19	25	44	143
Totals	33	20	26	46	167
Jason Skellett, Owen Sound	6	0	3	3	2
Jason Skellett, London	1	0	1	1	2
Totals	7	0	4	4	4
Gairin Smith, Guelph	12	5	5	10	15
Gairin Smith, Belleville	11	1	7	8	22
Gairin Smith, Kitchener	38	13	13	26	65
Totals	61	19	25	44	102
Kelvin Solari, Sudbury	5	0	0	0	0
Kelvin Solari, Guelph	46	1	4	5	75
Totals	51	1	4	5	75
Rob Stopar, Belleville (goalie)	4	0	1	1	0
Rob Stopar, S. Ste. Marie (g)	6	0	1	1	0
Totals	10	0	2	2	0
Troy Sweet, Oshawa	40	7	19	26	56
Troy Sweet, London	26	1	8	9	21
Totals	66	8	27	35	77
Brad Teichmann, Detroit (g)	15	0	0	0	2
Brad Teichmann, Windsor (g)	2	0	0	0	2
Brad Teichmann, Kingston (g)	13	0	1	1	2
Totals	30	0	1	1	6
Chris Varga, Belleville	7	0	2	2	2
Chris Varga, Detroit	54	14	15	29	15
Totals	61	14	17	31	17
Wade Whitten, Sault Ste. Marie	20	5	16	21	20
Wade Whiten, Guelph	48	16	21	37	61
Totals	68	21	37	58	81
Jack Williams, Kitchener	11	3	7	10	9
Jack Williams, North Bay	53	40	35	75	31
Totals	64	43	42	85	40
Paul Wolanski, Niagara Falls	3	0	0	0	0
Paul Wolanski, London	44	11	35	46	57
Totals	47	11	35	46	57
Jason Zohil, Kitchener	3	0	0	0	18
Jason Zohil, Sudbury	53	6	6	12	144
Totals	56	6	6	12	162

GOALTENDING

	Games	Min.	Goals	SO	Avg.
Fred Brathwaite, Osh.	24	1248	81	0	3.89
Fred Brathwaite, Lon.	23	1325	61	4	2.76
Totals	47	2573	142	4	3.31

	Games	Min.	Goals	SO	Avg.
Brent Brownlee, Osh...	6	235	26	0	6.64
Brent Brownlee, Lon...	36	2000	151	0	4.53
Totals..................	42	2235	177	0	4.75
George Dourian, Gue..	6	334	27	0	4.85
George Dourian, Sud. .	30	1552	133(4)	0	5.14
Totals..................	36	1886	160(4)	0	5.09
Mike Lenarduzzi, SSM	9	486	33	0	4.07
Mike Lenarduzzi, Ott. .	18	986	60	1	3.65
Mike Lenarduzzi, Sud.	22	1201	84(1)	2	4.20
Totals..................	49	2673	177(1)	3	3.97
Steve Pottie, Ottawa...	2	120	11	0	5.50
Steve Pottie, Guelph ..	34	1559	167(1)	0	6.43
	36	1679	178(1)	0	6.36

	Games	Min.	Goals	SO	Avg.
Dan Ryder, Sudbury ..	23	1157	91	0	4.72
Dan Ryder, Ottawa	24	1380	55(2)	3	2.39
Totals..................	47	2537	146(2)	3	3.45
Rob Stopar, Belleville .	4	135	14	0	6.22
Rob Stopar, SSM........	6	260	11	0	2.54
Totals..................	10	395	25	0	3.80
Brad Teichmann, Det.	15	730	76(2)	0	6.25
Brad Teichmann, W....	2	80	5	0	3.75
Brad Teichmann, King.	13	630	49	0	4.67
Totals..................	30	1440	130(2)	0	5.42

( )—Empty-net goals (do not count against a goal-tender's average).

1992 J. ROSS ROBERTSON CUP PLAYOFFS

RESULTS

LEYDEN DIVISION

QUARTERFINALS

Series "A"

	W	L	Pts.	GF	GA
Belleville...	1	4	2	17	32
North Bay.......................................	4	1	8	32	17

(North Bay won series, 4-1)

Series "B"

	W	L	Pts.	GF	GA
Ottawa	4	2	8	31	22
Cornwall..	2	4	4	22	31

(Ottawa won series, 4-2)

Series "C"

	W	L	Pts.	GF	GA
Oshawa	3	4	6	20	26
Sudbury	4	3	8	26	20

(Sudbury won series, 4-3)

SEMIFINALS

Series "D"

	W	L	Pts.	GF	GA
Ottawa	1	4	2	11	17
Peterborough.................................	4	1	8	17	11

(Peterborough won series, 4-1)

Series "E"

	W	L	Pts.	GF	GA
Sudbury	0	4	0	5	19
North Bay.......................................	4	0	8	19	5

(North Bay won series, 4-0)

FINALS

Series "F"

	W	L	Pts.	GF	GA
North Bay.......................................	4	1	8	29	14
Peterborough.................................	1	4	2	14	29

(North Bay won series, 4-1)

EMMS DIVISION

QUARTERFINALS

Series "A"

	W	L	Pts.	GF	GA
Detroit...	3	4	6	28	38
Niagara Falls..................................	4	3	8	38	28

(Niagara Falls won series, 4-3)

Series "B"

	W	L	Pts.	GF	GA
Owen Sound..................................	1	4	2	17	28
London..	4	1	8	28	17

(London won series, 4-1)

Series "C"

	W	L	Pts.	GF	GA
Windsor	3	4	6	19	22
Kitchener	4	3	8	22	19

(Kitchener won series, 4-3)

SEMIFINALS

Series "D"

	W	L	Pts.	GF	GA
Kitchener	3	4	6	18	30
Sault Ste. Marie.............................	4	3	8	30	18

(Sault Ste. Marie won series, 4-3)

Series "E"

	W	L	Pts.	GF	GA
London..	1	4	2	15	20
Niagara Falls..................................	4	1	8	20	15

(Niagara Falls won series, 4-1)

FINALS

Series "F"

	W	L	Pts.	GF	GA
Niagara Falls..................................	1	4	2	19	32
Sault Ste. Marie.............................	4	1	8	32	19

(Sault Ste. Marie won series, 4-1)

J. ROSS ROBERTSON CUP FINALS

Series "G"

	W	L	Pts.	GF	GA
North Bay.......................................	3	4	6	22	27
Sault Ste. Marie.............................	4	3	8	27	22

(Sault Ste. Marie won series, 4-3)

MAJOR JUNIOR LEAGUES

INDIVIDUAL LEADERS

Goals: Mark Lawrence, North Bay (23)
Assists: John Spoltore, North Bay (28)
Points: Todd Simon, Niagara Falls (41)
John Spoltore, North Bay (41)
Penalty minutes: Dennis Bonvie, North Bay (91)
Goaltending average: Ron Bertrand, North Bay (2.84)
Shutouts: Ron Bertrand, North Bay (1)
Kevin Hodson, Sault Ste. Marie (1)
Matt Mullin, Windsor (1)

TOP SCORERS

	Games	G	A	Pts.
Todd Simon, Niagara Falls	17	17	24	41
John Spoltore, North Bay	21	13	28	41
Mark Lawrence, North Bay	21	23	12	35
Tony Iob, Sault Ste. Marie	19	17	17	34
Colin Miller, Sault Ste. Marie	19	10	23	33
Drake Berehowsky, North Bay	21	7	24	31
Chad Penney, North Bay	21	13	17	30
Jason Firth, North Bay	21	10	15	25
Ralph Intranuovo, Sault Ste. Marie	18	10	14	24
Chris Taylor, London	10	8	16	24

INDIVIDUAL STATISTICS

BELLEVILLE BULLS

(Lost Leyden Division quarterfinals to North Bay, 4-1)

SCORING

	Games	G	A	Pts.	Pen.
Tony Cimellaro	5	6	4	10	10
Scott Boston	5	0	6	6	10
Kevin Brown	5	1	4	5	8
Darren McCarty	5	1	4	5	13
Jake Grimes	5	4	0	4	0
Mark Donahue	5	3	0	3	2
Shayne Antoski	5	1	2	3	2
Darren Hurley	5	1	2	3	7
Paul McCallion	5	0	2	2	4
Dan Preston	5	0	2	2	5
Doug Doull	5	0	1	1	9
Daniel Godbout	5	0	1	1	5
Richard Gallace (goalie)	2	0	0	0	0
Greg Bailey	5	0	0	0	2
Dominic Belanger	5	0	0	0	2
Greg Dreveny (goalie)	5	0	0	0	0
Craig Fraser	5	0	0	0	2
Ian Keiller	5	0	0	0	0
Rob Kinghan	5	0	0	0	12
Rick Marshall	5	0	0	0	5

GOALTENDING

	Games	Min.	Goals	SO	Avg.
Richard Gallace	2	71	4	0	3.38
Greg Dreveny	5	229	26(2)	0	6.81

CORNWALL ROYALS

(Lost Leyden Division quarterfinals to Ottawa, 4-2)

SCORING

	Games	G	A	Pts.	Pen.
John Slaney	6	3	8	11	0
Guy Leveque	6	3	5	8	2
Nathan LaFayette	6	2	5	7	16
Rival Fullum	6	4	1	5	2
Tom Nemeth	6	3	2	5	4
Jeff Reid	6	1	4	5	6
Jeremy Stevenson	6	3	1	4	4
Chris Clancy	6	1	2	3	4
Mark DeSantis	6	1	2	3	7
Shayne Gaffar	6	1	1	2	2
Ryan VandenBussche	6	0	2	2	9
David Babcock	6	0	1	1	10
Dave Lemay	6	0	1	1	21
Sam Oliveira	6	0	1	1	0
Ilpo Kauhanen (goalie)	2	0	0	0	0
Rob Dykeman (goalie)	5	0	0	0	2
Larry Courville	6	0	0	0	8
Alan Letang	6	0	0	0	2
Mike Prokopec	6	0	0	0	2
Todd Walker	6	0	0	0	0

GOALTENDING

	Games	Min.	Goals	SO	Avg.
Rob Dykeman	5	274	22	0	4.82
Ilpo Kauhanen	2	101	9	0	5.35

DETROIT COMPUWARE AMBASSADORS

(Lost Emms Division quarterfinals to Niagara Falls, 4-3)

SCORING

	Games	G	A	Pts.	Pen.
Pat Peake	7	8	9	17	10
Todd Harvey	7	3	5	8	30
Bob Wren	7	3	4	7	19
John Wynne	7	2	5	7	4
Chris Skoryna	7	2	3	5	11
Aaron Morrison	6	1	3	4	10
Keith Redmond	7	1	3	4	49
Tony McCabe	6	3	0	3	2
Jeff Gardiner	6	1	2	3	0
Chris Varga	5	0	3	3	0
Chris Phelps	7	0	3	3	10
Blair Scott	7	0	3	3	23
Pat Barton	6	1	1	2	4
Glen Craig	7	0	2	2	9
John Pinches	4	1	0	1	5
J.D. Eaton	7	1	0	1	13
Jeff Kostuch	7	1	0	1	7
Brent Thombs (goalie)	1	0	0	0	0
Jamie Shea (goalie)	3	0	0	0	0
David Benn	7	0	0	0	50
Eric Cairns	7	0	0	0	31
Derek Wilkinson (goalie)	7	0	0	0	0

GOALTENDING

	Games	Min.	Goals	SO	Avg.
Jamie Shea	3	74	5	0	4.05
Derek Wilkinson	7	313	28	0	5.37
Brent Thombs	1	33	4(1)	0	7.27

KITCHENER RANGERS

(Lost Emms Division semifinals to Sault Ste. Marie, 4-3)

SCORING

	Games	G	A	Pts.	Pen.
Tyler Ertel	14	10	9	19	46
Chris LiPuma	14	4	9	13	34
Trevor Gallant	14	5	6	11	4
Derek Gauthier	14	4	6	10	8
Norm Dezainde	10	3	5	8	15
Yvan Corbin	14	3	4	7	6
Eric Manlow	14	2	5	7	10
Jamie Caruso	11	3	2	5	6
Gairin Smith	5	1	2	3	6
Brad Barton	14	1	2	3	14
Chris Kraemer	14	1	2	3	2
Shayne McCosh	14	1	2	3	28
Jason Gladney	14	1	1	2	14

	Games	G	A	Pts.	Pen.
Gary Miller	14	1	1	2	24
C.J. Denomme (goalie)	1	0	0	0	0
Mike Polano	3	0	0	0	2
Tim Spitzig	4	0	0	0	2
Marc Robillard	14	0	0	0	0
Chris Shushack	14	0	0	0	0
Jason Stevenson	14	0	0	0	0
Mike Torchia (goalie)	14	0	0	0	6

GOALTENDING

	Games	Min.	Goals	SO	Avg.
Mike Torchia	14	900	47	0	3.13
C.J. Denomme	1	20	2	0	6.00

LONDON KNIGHTS

(Lost Emms Division semifinals to Niagara Falls, 4-1)

SCORING

	Games	G	A	Pts.	Pen.
Chris Taylor	10	8	16	24	0
Dennis Purdie	10	5	10	15	26
Sean O'Reilly	10	2	12	14	12
Chris Crombie	8	5	8	13	0
Scott McKay	10	3	8	11	8
Paul Wolanski	10	4	6	10	10
Brett Marietti	10	5	4	9	11
Barry Potomski	10	5	1	6	22
Nick Stajudhar	10	1	4	5	10
Mark Visheau	10	0	4	4	27
Brad Smyth	10	2	0	2	8
Troy Sweet	10	1	1	2	2
Dave Gilmore	10	0	2	2	6
Cory Evans	4	1	0	1	0
Jason Glover	10	1	0	1	4
Steve Smillie	4	0	1	1	4
Fred Brathwaite (goalie)	10	0	1	1	2
Jason Allison	7	0	0	0	0
Jason Skellett	8	0	0	0	4
Derrick Crane	9	0	0	0	2
Kelly Reed	10	0	0	0	8

GOALTENDING

	Games	Min.	Goals	SO	Avg.
Fred Brathwaite	10	615	36(1)	0	3.51

NIAGARA FALLS THUNDER

(Lost Emms Division finals to Sault Ste. Marie, 4-1)

SCORING

	Games	G	A	Pts.	Pen.
Todd Simon	17	17	24	41	36
Kevin Brown	17	11	11	22	12
Rick Corriveau	17	5	16	21	36
Geoff Rawson	17	6	10	16	30
Steve Staios	17	7	8	15	27
Mike DeCoff	16	5	10	15	23
Dennis Maxwell	17	4	9	13	32
Dan Krisko	17	3	10	13	4
Ethan Moreau	17	4	6	10	4
Dale Junkin	17	4	4	8	12
Jason Clarke	17	3	3	6	84
Mark Cardiff	17	2	4	6	14
Todd Wetzel	17	3	2	5	24
Scott Campbell	15	1	3	4	33
Tom Moores	17	1	2	3	14
Manny Legace (goalie)	14	0	2	2	4
Jason Coles	17	1	0	1	9
Brad Love	1	0	0	0	0
Brian Holk	3	0	0	0	0
Greg Scott (goalie)	5	0	0	0	0
Neil Fewster	7	0	0	0	2
Matt McGuffin	10	0	0	0	0
Ryan Tocher	16	0	0	0	2

GOALTENDING

	Games	Min.	Goals	SO	Avg.
Manny Legace	14	791	56	0	4.25
Greg Scott	5	240	19	0	4.75

NORTH BAY CENTENNIALS

(Lost J. Ross Robertson Cup finals to Sault Ste. Marie, 4-3)

SCORING

	Games	G	A	Pts.	Pen.
John Spoltore	21	13	28	41	25
Mark Lawrence	21	23	12	35	36
Drake Berehowsky	21	7	24	31	22
Chad Penney	21	13	17	30	9
Jason Firth	21	10	15	25	29
Jack Williams	21	10	10	20	20
Jeff Shevalier	21	5	11	16	25
Michael Burman	21	3	12	15	21
Bill Lang	21	5	8	13	38
Rob Thorpe	21	8	4	12	23
Billy Wright	19	4	4	8	27
Brad Brown	18	0	6	6	43
Allan Cox	21	0	6	6	51
Wade Gibson	21	1	3	4	20
Paul Rushforth	19	0	2	2	6
Ron Bertrand (goalie)	21	0	2	2	14
Dennis Bonvie	21	0	1	1	91
Ian Blanchard	1	0	0	0	0
Ian Blanchfield	1	0	0	0	0
Stephan Rivard	2	0	0	0	0
Sandy Allan (goalie)	3	0	0	0	0
Paul Doherty	3	0	0	0	2
Perry Ohm	6	0	0	0	2
Dave Szabo	15	0	0	0	0
James Sheehan	21	0	0	0	4

GOALTENDING

	Games	Min.	Goals	SO	Avg.
Ron Bertrand	2	1247	59(2)	1	2.84
Sandy Allan	3	18	2	0	6.67

OSHAWA GENERALS

(Lost Leyden Division quarterfinals to Sudbury, 4-3)

SCORING

	Games	G	A	Pts.	Pen.
Matt Hoffman	7	6	9	15	10
Scott Hollis	7	7	3	10	8
B.J. MacPherson	7	2	5	7	27
Rob Leask	7	1	4	5	4
Trevor Burgess	7	0	3	3	8
Stephane Yelle	7	2	0	2	2
Jan Benda	7	1	1	2	12
Joe Cook	6	0	2	2	0
Sean Brown	7	1	0	1	4
Jean-Paul Davis	7	0	1	1	8
Brian Grieve	7	0	1	1	6
Darryl LaFrance	7	0	1	1	2
John Carr	1	0	0	0	0
Ken Shepard (goalie)	1	0	0	0	0
Jason Weaver	3	0	0	0	6
Todd Bradley	5	0	0	0	8
Jason Campeau	6	0	0	0	0
Markus Brunner	7	0	0	0	2
Mark Deazeley	7	0	0	0	16
Mike Fountain (goalie)	7	0	0	0	4
Wade Simpson	7	0	0	0	2
Kevin Spero	7	0	0	0	4

GOALTENDING

	Games	Min.	Goals	SO	Avg.
Ken Shepard	1	2	0	0	0.00
Mike Fountain	7	428	26	0	3.64

OTTAWA 67's

(Lost Leyden Division semifinals to Peterborough, 4-1)

SCORING

	Games	G	A	Pts.	Pen.
Brett Seguin	11	8	10	18	16
Grant Marshall	11	6	11	17	11
Mike Peca	11	6	10	16	6
Ryan Kuwabara	10	6	5	11	9
Jeff Ricciardi	11	3	8	11	45
Peter Ambroziak	11	3	7	10	33
Curtis Bowen	11	3	7	10	11
Chris Coveny	11	2	3	5	12
Steve Washburn	11	2	3	5	4
Greg Ryan	11	0	3	3	18
Grayden Reid	11	0	2	2	2
Matt Stone	10	1	0	1	21
Shean Donovan	11	1	0	1	5
Mike Johnson	11	1	0	1	14
Gerry Skrypec	5	0	1	1	8
Pat Curcio	8	0	1	1	4
Bill Hall	11	0	1	1	11
Zbynek Kukacka	11	0	1	1	0
Sean Spencer (goalie)	1	0	0	0	0
Ken Belanger	11	0	0	0	24
Dan Ryder (goalie)	11	0	0	0	6

GOALTENDING

	Games	Min.	Goals	SO	Avg.
Sean Spencer	1	48	1	0	1.25
Dan Ryder	11	626	38	0	3.64

OWEN SOUND PLATERS

(Lost Emms Division quarterfinals to London, 4-1)

SCORING

	Games	G	A	Pts.	Pen.
Scott Walker	5	0	7	7	8
Kirk Maltby	5	3	3	6	18
Andrew Brunette	5	5	0	5	8
Justin Morrison	5	3	2	5	11
Jim Brown	5	1	4	5	4
Luigi Calce	5	2	1	3	2
Brock Woods	5	0	3	3	16
Willie Skilliter	5	1	1	2	0
Jason MacDonald	5	0	2	2	8
Jeff Smith	5	0	2	2	2
Wyatt Buckland	4	1	0	1	0
Troy Hutchinson	5	1	0	1	0
Aaron Nagy	5	0	1	1	0
Sean Basilio (goalie)	1	0	0	0	0
Mark Vilneff	2	0	0	0	0
Geordie Maynard	4	0	0	0	16
Gord Dickie	5	0	0	0	0
Jason Hughes	5	0	0	0	8
Shawn Krueger	5	0	0	0	2
Rick Morton	5	0	0	0	8
Jamie Storr (goalie)	5	0	0	0	0

GOALTENDING

	Games	Min.	Goals	SO	Avg.
Sean Basilio	1	5	0	0	0.00
Jamie Storr	5	299	28	0	5.62

PETERBOROUGH PETES

(Lost Leyden Division finals to North Bay, 4-1)

SCORING

	Games	G	A	Pts.	Pen.
Chris Longo	10	5	6	11	16
Mike Harding	10	6	4	10	29
Jassen Cullimore	10	3	6	9	8
John Johnson	10	2	7	9	15
Chris Pronger	10	1	8	9	28
Dale McTavish	10	2	5	7	11
Doug Searle	10	1	5	6	16

	Games	G	A	Pts.	Pen.
Jason Dawe	4	5	0	5	0
Bryan Gendron	10	2	2	4	36
Mike Tomlinson	10	2	2	4	22
Ryan Black	7	1	1	2	11
Don O'Neill	10	1	1	2	17
Geordie Kinnear	10	0	2	2	36
Jeff Walker	6	0	1	1	0
Matt St. Germain	9	0	1	1	9
Colin Wilson	10	0	1	1	4
Chad Lang (goalie)	2	0	0	0	0
Shawn Heins	7	0	0	0	5
Kelly Vipond	7	0	0	0	0
Dave Roche	10	0	0	0	34
Brent Tully	10	0	0	0	2
Andrew Verner (goalie)	10	0	0	0	2

GOALTENDING

	Games	Min.	Goals	SO	Avg.
Andrew Verner	10	539	30 (1)	0	3.34
Chad Lang	2	65	9	0	8.31

SAULT STE. MARIE GREYHOUNDS

(Winner of 1992 J. Ross Robertson Cup playoffs)

SCORING

	Games	G	A	Pts.	Pen.
Tony Iob	19	17	17	34	45
Colin Miller	19	10	23	33	18
Ralph Intranuovo	18	10	14	24	12
Jarret Reid	19	5	13	18	17
Jason Denomme	18	7	9	16	14
Rick Kowalsky	19	6	10	16	39
Shaun Imber	19	4	12	16	6
Chris Simon	11	5	8	13	49
Drew Bannister	16	3	10	13	36
Tom MacDonald	19	3	7	10	31
David Matsos	19	4	5	9	6
Perry Pappas	19	4	4	8	12
Mark Matier	19	3	5	8	14
Brian Goudie	17	2	5	7	45
Aaron Gavey	19	5	1	6	10
Todd Gleason	19	0	2	2	12
Kiley Hill	5	1	0	1	0
Jeff Toms	16	0	1	1	2
Rob Stopar (goalie)	1	0	0	0	0
Briane Thompson	6	0	0	0	4
Brad Baber	8	0	0	0	0
Peter Johansson	9	0	0	0	4
Gary Roach	9	0	0	0	4
Kevin Hodson (goalie)	18	0	0	0	4

GOALTENDING

	Games	Min.	Goals	SO	Avg.
Kevin Hodson	18	1116	54 (1)	1	2.90
Rob Stopar	1	60	4	0	4.00

SUDBURY WOLVES

(Lost Leyden Division semifinals to North Bay, 4-0)

SCORING

	Games	G	A	Pts.	Pen.
Jamie Matthews	11	2	11	13	4
Terry Chitaroni	11	7	5	12	39
Glen Murray	11	7	4	11	18
Barrie Moore	11	0	7	7	12
Brandon Convery	5	3	2	5	4
Jason Young	11	3	2	5	14
Rod Hinks	11	2	3	5	6
Bernie John	11	0	5	5	2
Derek Armstrong	9	2	2	4	2
Shawn Rivers	11	0	4	4	10
Mike Yeo	11	2	1	3	2
Leonard MacDonald	8	0	3	3	19
Barry Young	11	2	0	2	27
Kyle Blacklock	11	1	1	2	4

	Games	G	A	Pts.	Pen.
Kayle Short	8	0	2	2	23
Mike Lenarduzzi (goalie)	11	0	2	2	0
Sean Gagnon	5	0	1	1	0
George Dourian (goalie)	1	0	0	0	0
Bob MacIssac	5	0	0	0	5
Darren Dougan	8	0	0	0	4
Jamie Rivers	8	0	0	0	0
Tim Favot	10	0	0	0	2
Jason Zohil	11	0	0	0	14

GOALTENDING

	Games	Min.	Goals	SO	Avg.
George Dourian	1	20	1	0	3.00
Mike Lenarduzzi	11	651	38	0	3.50

WINDSOR SPITFIRES

(Lost Emms Division quarterfinals to Kitchener, 4-3)

SCORING

	Games	G	A	Pts.	Pen.
Todd Warrinor	7	5	4	9	0
Kevin MacKay	7	3	4	7	6
Cory Stillman	7	2	4	6	8

	Games	G	A	Pts.	Pen.
Jason Stos	7	0	6	6	14
Steve Gibson	7	4	1	5	6
Bill Bowler	7	2	3	5	13
Jamie Allison	4	1	1	2	2
Tom Sullivan	7	1	1	2	16
Brady Blain	7	1	0	1	2
Matt Mullin (goalie)	6	0	1	1	4
John Copley	7	0	1	1	12
Rod Pasma	7	0	1	1	18
Todd Hunter (goalie)	2	0	0	0	0
Eric Stamp	3	0	0	0	0
Peter Allison	7	0	0	0	0
Craig Binns	7	0	0	0	6
Robert Frayn	7	0	0	0	10
Gord Harris	7	0	0	0	2
Mike Hartwick	7	0	0	0	8
Craig Lutes	7	0	0	0	6
Ryan O'Neill	7	0	0	0	2

GOALTENDING

	Games	Min.	Goals	SO	Avg.
Todd Hunter	2	138	5	0	2.17
Matt Mullin	6	326	17	1	3.13

1991-92 AWARD WINNERS

ALL-STAR TEAMS

First team	Pos.	Second team
Mike Fountain, Oshawa	G	Andrew Verner, Pet.
Drake Berehowsky, N. Bay	D	Jassen Cullimore, Pet.
Scott Boston, Belleville	D	Jeff Ricciardi, Ottawa
Todd Warriner, Windsor	LW	Chris Crombie, London
Todd Simon, Niagara Falls	C	John Spoltore, North Bay
Darren McCarty, Belleville	RW	Scott Hollis, Oshawa

Coach of the Year: George Burnett, Niagara Falls

TROPHY WINNERS

Red Tilson Trophy: Todd Simon, Niagara Falls
Eddie Powers Memorial Trophy: Todd Simon, Niagara Falls
Dave Pinkney Trophy: Kevin Hodson, Sault Ste. Marie
Max Kaminsky Trophy: Drake Berehowsky, North Bay
William Hanley Trophy: John Spoltore, North Bay
Emms Family Award: Chris Gratton, Kingston
Matt Leyden Trophy: George Burnett, Niagara Falls
Jim Mahon Memorial Trophy: Darren McCarty, Belleville
F.W. Dinty Moore Trophy: Sandy Allan, North Bay
Leo Lalonde Memorial Trophy: John Spoltore, North Bay
Hamilton Spectator Trophy: Peterborough Petes
J. Ross Robertson Cup: Sault Ste. Marie Greyhounds

ALL-TIME AWARD WINNERS

RED TILSON TROPHY

(Outstanding player)

Season	Player, Team
1944-45	Doug McMurdy, St. Catharines
1945-46	Tod Sloan, St. Michael's
1946-47	Ed Sanford, St. Michael's
1947-48	George Armstrong, Stratford
1948-49	Gil Mayer, Barrie
1949-50	George Armstrong, Marlboros
1950-51	Glenn Hall, Windsor
1951-52	Bill Harrington, Kitchener
1952-53	Bob Attersley, Oshawa
1953-54	Brian Cullen, St. Catharines
1954-55	Hank Ciesla, St. Catharines
1955-56	Ron Howell, Guelph
1956-57	Frank Mahovlich, St. Michael's
1957-58	Murray Oliver, Hamilton
1958-59	Stan Mikita, St. Catharines
1959-60	Wayne Connelly, Peterborough
1960-61	Rod Gilbert, Guelph
1961-62	Pit Martin, Hamilton
1962-63	Wayne Maxner, Niagara Falls
1963-64	Yvan Cournoyer, Montreal
1964-65	Andre Lacroix, Peterborough
1965-66	Andre Lacroix, Peterborough
1966-67	Mickey Redmond, Peterborough
1967-68	Walt Tkaczuk, Kitchener
1968-69	Rejean Houle, Montreal
1969-70	Gilbert Perreault, Montreal
1970-71	Dave Gardner, Marlboros

Season	Player, Team
1971-72	Don Lever, Niagara Falls
1972-73	Rick Middleton, Oshawa
1973-74	Jack Valiquette, Sault Ste. Marie
1974-75	Dennis Maruk, London
1975-76	Peter Lee, Ottawa
1976-77	Dale McCourt, St. Catharines
1977-78	Bobby Smith, Ottawa
1978-79	Mike Foligno, Sudbury
1979-80	Jim Fox, Ottawa
1980-81	Ernie Godden, Windsor
1981-82	Dave Simpson, London
1982-83	Doug Gilmour, Cornwall
1983-84	John Tucker, Kitchener
1984-85	Wayne Groulx, Sault Ste. Marie
1985-86	Ray Sheppard, Cornwall
1986-87	Scott McCrory, Oshawa
1987-88	Andrew Cassels, Ottawa
1988-89	Bryan Fogarty, Niagara Falls
1989-90	Mike Ricci, Peterborough
1990-91	Eric Lindros, Oshawa
1991-92	Todd Simon, Niagara Falls

EDDIE POWERS MEMORIAL TROPHY

(Scoring champion)

Season	Player, Team
1933-34	J. Groboski, Oshawa
1934-35	J. Good, Toronto Lions
1935-36	John O'Flaherty, West Toronto
1936-37	Billy Taylor, Oshawa

Season	Player, Team
1937-38	Hank Goldup, Tor. Marlboros
1938-39	Billy Taylor, Oshawa
1939-40	Jud McAtee, Oshawa
1940-41	Gaye Stewart, Tor. Marlboros
1941-42	Bob Wiest, Brantford
1942-43	Norman "Red" Tilson, Oshawa
1943-44	Ken Smith, Oshawa
1944-45	Leo Gravelle, St. Michael's
1945-46	Tod Sloan, St. Michael's
1946-47	Fleming Mackell, St. Michael's
1947-48	George Armstrong, Stratford
1948-49	Bert Giesebrecht, Windsor
1949-50	Earl Reibel, Windsor
1950-51	Lou Jankowski, Oshawa
1951-52	Ken Laufman, Guelph
1952-53	Jim McBurney, Galt
1953-54	Brian Cullen, St. Catharines
1954-55	Hank Ciesla, St. Catharines
1955-56	Stan Baliuk, Kitchener
1956-57	Bill Sweeney, Guelph
1957-58	John McKenzie, St. Catharines
1958-59	Stan Mikita, St. Catharines
1959-60	Chico Maki, St. Catharines
1960-61	Rod Gilbert, Guelph
1961-62	Andre Boudrias, Montreal
1962-63	Wayne Maxner, Niagara Falls
1963-64	Andre Boudrias, Montreal
1964-65	Ken Hodge, St. Catharines
1965-66	Andre Lacroix, Peterborough
1966-67	Derek Sanderson, Niagara Falls
1967-68	Tom Webster, Niagara Falls
1968-69	Rejean Houle, Montreal
1969-70	Marcel Dionne, St. Catharines
1970-71	Marcel Dionne, St. Catharines
1971-72	Bill Harris, Toronto
1972-73	Blake Dunlop, Ottawa
1973-74	Jack Valiquette, Sault Ste. Marie
	Rick Adduono, St. Catharines
1974-75	Bruce Boudreau, Toronto
1975-76	Mike Kaszycki, Sault Ste. Marie
1976-77	Dwight Foster, Kitchener
1977-78	Bobby Smith, Ottawa
1978-79	Mike Foligno, Sudbury
1979-80	Jim Fox, Ottawa
1980-81	John Goodwin, Sault Ste. Marie
1981-82	Dave Simpson, London
1982-83	Doug Gilmour, Cornwall
1983-84	Tim Salmon, Kingston
1984-85	Dave MacLean, Belleville
1985-86	Ray Sheppard, Cornwall
1986-87	Scott McCrory, Oshawa
1987-88	Andrew Cassels, Ottawa
1988-89	Bryan Fogarty, Niagara Falls
1989-90	Keith Primeau, Niagara Falls
1990-91	Eric Lindros, Oshawa
1991-92	Todd Simon, Niagara Falls

DAVE PINKNEY TROPHY

(Top team goaltending)

Season	Player, Team
1948-49	Gil Mayer, Barrie
1949-50	Don Lockhart, Marlboros
1950-51	Don Lockhart, Marlboros
	Lorne Howes, Barrie
1951-52	Don Head, Marlboros
1952-53	John Henderson, Marlboros
1953-54	Dennis Riggin, Hamilton
1954-55	John Albani, Marlboros
1955-56	Jim Crockett, Marlboros
1956-57	Len Broderick, Marlboros
1957-58	Len Broderick, Marlboros
1958-59	Jacques Caron, Peterborough
1959-60	Gerry Cheevers, St. Michael's
1960-61	Bud Blom, Hamilton
1961-62	George Holmes, Montreal

Season	Player, Team
1962-63	Chuck Goddard, Peterborough
1963-64	Bernie Parent, Niagara Falls
1964-65	Bernie Parent, Niagara Falls
1965-66	Ted Quimet, Montreal
1966-67	Peter MacDuffe, St. Catharines
1967-68	Bruce Mullet, Montreal
1968-69	Wayne Wood, Montreal
1969-70	John Garrett, Peterborough
1970-71	John Garrett, Peterborough
1971-72	Michel Larocque, Ottawa
1972-73	Mike Palmateer, Toronto
1973-74	Don Edwards, Kitchener
1974-75	Greg Millen, Peterborough
1975-76	Jim Bedard, Sudbury
1976-77	Pat Riggin, London
1977-78	Al Jensen, Hamilton
1978-79	Nick Ricci, Niagara Falls
1979-80	Rick LaFerriere, Peterborough
1980-81	Jim Ralph, Ottawa
1981-82	Marc D'Amour, Sault Ste. Marie
1982-83	Peter Sidorkiewicz, Oshawa
	Jeff Hogg, Oshawa
1983-84	Darren Pang, Ottawa
	Greg Coram, Ottawa
1984-85	Scott Mosey, Sault Ste. Marie
	Marty Abrams, Sault Ste. Marie
1985-86	Kay Whitmore, Peterborough
	Ron Tugnutt, Peterborough
1986-87	Sean Evoy, Oshawa
	Jeff Hackett, Oshawa
1987-88	Todd Bojcun, Peterborough
	John Tanner, Peterborough
1988-89	Todd Bojcun, Peterborough
	John Tanner, Peterborough
1989-90	Jeff Wilson, Peterborough
	Sean Gauthier, Kingston
1990-91	Kevin Hodson, Sault Ste. Marie
	Mike Lenarduzzi, Sault Ste. Marie
1991-92	Kevin Hodson, Sault Ste. Marie

MAX KAMINSKY TROPHY

(Outstanding defenseman)

Season	Player, Team
1969-70	Ron Plumb, Peterborough
1970-71	Jocelyn Guevremont, Montreal
1971-72	Denis Potvin, Ottawa
1972-73	Denis Potvin, Ottawa
1973-74	Jim Turkiewicz, Peterborough
1974-75	Mike O'Connell, Kingston
1975-76	Rick Green, London
1976-77	Craig Hartsburg, S. Ste. Marie
1977-78	Brad Marsh, London
	Rob Ramage, London
1978-79	Greg Theberge, Peterborough
1979-80	Larry Murphy, Peterborough
1980-81	Steve Smith, Sault Ste. Marie
1981-82	Ron Meighan, Niagara Falls
1982-83	Allan MacInnis, Kitchener
1983-84	Brad Shaw, Ottawa
1984-85	Bob Halkidis, London
1985-86	Terry Carkner, Peterborough
	Jeff Brown, Sudbury
1986-87	Kerry Huffman, Guelph
1987-88	Darryl Shannon, Windsor
1988-89	Bryan Fogarty, Niagara Falls
1989-90	John Slaney, Cornwall
1990-91	Chris Snell, Ottawa
1991-92	Drake Berehowsky, North Bay

WILLIAM HANLEY TROPHY

(Most gentlemanly)

Season	Player, Team
1960-61	Bruce Draper, St. Michael's
1961-62	Lowell MacDonald, Hamilton

Season	Player, Team
1962-63	Paul Henderson, Hamilton
1963-64	Fred Stanfield, St. Catharines
1964-65	Jimmy Peters, Hamilton
1965-66	Andre Lacroix, Peterborough
1966-67	Mickey Redmond, Peterborough
1967-68	Tom Webster, Niagara Falls
1968-69	Rejean Houle, Montreal
1969-74	No award presented
1974-75	Doug Jarvis, Peterborough
1975-76	Dale McCourt, Hamilton
1976-77	Dale McCourt, St. Catharines
1977-78	Waynbe Gretzky, S.S. Marie
1978-79	Sean Simpson, Ottawa
1979-80	Sean Simpson, Ottawa
1980-81	John Goodwin, Sault Ste. Marie
1981-82	Dave Simpson, London
1982-83	Kirk Muller, Guelph
1983-84	Kevin Conway, Kingston
1984-85	Scott Tottle, Peterborough
1985-86	Jason Lafreniere, Belleville
1986-87	Scott McCrory, Oshawa
	Keith Gretzky, Hamilton
1987-88	Andrew Cassels, Ottawa
1988-89	Kevin Miehm, Oshawa
1989-90	Mike Ricci, Peterborough
1990-91	Dale Craigwell, Oshawa
1991-92	John Spoltore, North Bay

EMMS FAMILY AWARD

(Rookie of the year)

Season	Player, Team
1972-73	Dennis Maruk, London
1973-74	Jack Valiquette, Sault Ste. Marie
1974-75	Danny Shearer, Hamilton
1975-76	John Travella, Sault Ste. Marie
1976-77	Yvan Joly, Ottawa
1977-78	Wayne Gretzky, S.S. Marie
1978-79	John Goodwin, Sault Ste. Marie
1979-80	Bruce Dowie, Toronto
1980-81	Tony Tanti, Oshawa
1981-82	Pat Verbeek, Sudbury
1982-83	Bruce Cassidy, Ottawa
1983-84	Shawn Burr, Kitchener
1984-85	Derek King, Sault Ste. Marie
1985-86	Lonnie Loach, Guelph
1986-87	Andrew Cassels, Ottawa
1987-88	Rick Corriveau, London
1988-89	Owen Nolan, Cornwall
1989-90	Chris Longo, Peterborough
1990-91	Cory Stillman, Windsor
1991-92	Chris Gratton, Kingston

MATT LEYDEN TROPHY

(Coach of the year)

Season	Coach, Team
1971-72	Gus Bodnar, Oshawa
1972-73	George Armstrong, Toronto
1973-74	Jack Bownass, Kingston
1974-75	Bert Templeton, Hamilton
1975-76	Jerry Toppazzini, Sudbury
1976-77	Bill Long, London
1977-78	Bill White, Oshawa
1978-79	Gary Green, Peterborough
1979-80	Dave Chambers, Toronto
1980-81	Brian Kilrea, Ottawa
1981-82	Brian Kilrea, Ottawa
1982-83	Terry Crisp, Sault Ste. Marie
1983-84	Tom Barrett, Kitchener

Season	Coach, Team
1984-85	Terry Crisp, Sault Ste. Marie
1985-86	Jacques Martin, Guelph
1986-87	Paul Theriault, Oshawa
1987-88	Dick Todd, Peterborough
1988-89	Joe McDonnell, Kitchener
1989-90	Larry Mavety, Kingston
1990-91	George Burnett, Niagara Falls
1991-92	George Burnett, Niagara Falls

JIM MAHON MEMORIAL TROPHY

(Top scoring right wing)

Season	Player, Team
1971-72	Bill Harris, Toronto
1972-73	Dennis Ververgaert, London
1973-74	Dave Gorman, St. Catharines
1974-75	Mark Napier, Toronto
1975-76	Peter Lee, Ottawa
1976-77	John Anderson, Toronto
1977-78	Dino Ciccarelli, London
1978 70	Mike Foligno, Sudbury
1979-80	Jim Fox, Ottawa
1980-81	Tony Tanti, Oshawa
1981-82	Tony Tanti, Oshawa
1982-83	Ian MacInnis, Cornwall
1983-84	Wayne Presley, Kitchener
1984-85	Dave MacLean, Belleville
1985-86	Ray Sheppard, Cornwall
1986-87	Ron Goodall, Kitchener
1987-88	Sean Williams, Oshawa
1988-89	Stan Drulia, Niagara Falls
1989-90	Owen Nolan, Cornwall
1990-91	Rob Pearson, Oshawa
1991-92	Darren McCarty, Belleville

F.W. DINTY MOORE TROPHY

(Lowest average by a rookie goalie)

Season	Player, Team
1975-76	Mark Locken, Hamilton
1976-77	Barry Heard, London
1977-78	Ken Ellacott, Peterborough
1978-79	Nick Ricci, Niagara Falls
1979-80	Mike Vezina, Ottawa
1980-81	John Vanbiesbrouck, Sault Ste. Marie
1981-82	Shawn Kilroy, Peterborough
1982-83	Dan Burrows, Belleville
1983-84	Jerry Iuliano, Sault Ste. Marie
1984-85	Ron Tugnutt, Peterborough
1985-86	Paul Henriques, Belleville
1986-87	Jeff Hackett, Oshawa
1987-88	Todd Bojcun, Peterborough
1988-89	Jeff Wilson, Kingston
1989-90	Sean Basilio, London
1990-91	Kevin Hodson, Sault Ste. Marie
1991-92	Sandy Allan, North Bay

LEO LALONDE MEMORIAL TROPHY

(Overage player of the year)

Season	Player, Team
1983-84	Don McLaren, Ottawa
1984-85	Dunc MacIntyre, Belleville
1985-86	Steve Guenette, Guelph
1986-87	Mike Richard, Toronto
1987-88	Len Soccio, North Bay
1988-89	Stan Drulia, Niagara Falls
1989-90	Iain Fraser, Oshawa
1990-91	Joey St. Aubin, Kitchener
1991-92	John Spoltore, North Bay

ALL-TIME LEAGUE CHAMPIONS

	REGULAR-SEASON CHAMPION	PLAYOFF CHAMPION
Season	Team	Team
1933-34	No trophy awarded	St. Michael's College
1934-35	No trophy awarded	Kitchener
1935-36	No trophy awarded	West Toronto Redmen
1936-37	No trophy awarded	St. Michael's College
1937-38	No trophy awarded	Oshawa Generals
1938-39	No trophy awarded	Oshawa Generals
1939-40	No trophy awarded	Oshawa Generals
1940-41	No trophy awarded	Oshawa Generals
1941-42	No trophy awarded	Oshawa Generals
1942-43	No trophy awarded	Oshawa Generals
1943-44	No trophy awarded	Oshawa Generals
1944-45	No trophy awarded	St. Michael's College
1945-46	No trophy awarded	St. Michael's College
1946-47	No trophy awarded	St. Michael's College
1947-48	No trophy awarded	Barrie Flyers
1948-49	No trophy awarded	Barrie Flyers
1949-50	No trophy awarded	Guelph Biltmores
1950-51	No trophy awarded	Barrie Flyers
1951-52	No trophy awarded	Guelph Biltmores
1952-53	No trophy awarded	Barrie Flyers
1953-54	No trophy awarded	St. Catharines Tee Pees
1954-55	No trophy awarded	Toronto Marlboros
1955-56	No trophy awarded	Toronto Marlboros
1956-57	No trophy awarded	Guelph Biltmores
1957-58	St. Catharines Tee Pees	Toronto Marlboros
1958-59	St. Catharines Tee Pees	Peterborough TPTs
1959-60	Toronto Marlboros	St. Catharines Tee Pees
1960-61	Guelph Royals	St. Michael's College
1961-62	Montreal Jr. Canadiens	Hamilton Red Wings
1962-63	Niagara Falls Flyers	Niagara Falls Flyers
1963-64	Toronto Marlboros	Toronto Marlboros
1964-65	Niagara Falls Flyers	Niagara Falls Flyers
1965-66	Peterborough Petes	Oshawa Generals
1966-67	Kitchener Rangers	Toronto Marlboros
1967-68	Kitchener Rangers	Niagara Falls Flyers
1968-69	Montreal Jr. Canadiens	Montreal Jr. Canadiens
1969-70	Montreal Jr. Canadiens	Montreal Jr. Canadiens
1970-71	Peterborough Petes	St. Catharines Black Hawks
1971-72	Toronto Marlboros	Peterborough Petes
1972-73	Toronto Marlboros	Toronto Marlboros
1973-74	Kitchener Rangers	St. Catharines Black Hawks
1974-75	Toronto Marlboros	Toronto Marlboros
1975-76	Sudbury Wolves	Hamilton Steelhawks
1976-77	St. Catharines Fincups	Ottawa 67's
1977-78	Ottawa 67's	Peterborough Petes
1978-79	Peterborough Petes	Peterborough Petes
1979-80	Peterborough Petes	Peterborough Petes
1980-81	Sault St. Marie Greyhounds	Kitchener Rangers
1981-82	Ottawa 67's	Kitchener Rangers
1982-83	Sault Ste. Marie Greyhounds	Oshawa Generals
1983-84	Kitchener Rangers	Ottawa 67's
1984-85	Sault Ste. Marie Greyhounds	Sault Ste. Marie Greyhounds
1985-86	Peterborough Petes	Guelph Platers
1986-87	Oshawa Generals	Oshawa Generals
1987-88	Windsor Compuware Spitfires	Windsor Compuware Spitfires
1988-89	Kitchener Rangers	Peterborough Petes
1989-90	Oshawa Generals	Oshawa Generals
1990-91	Oshawa Generals	Sault Ste. Marie Greyhounds
1991-92	Peterborough Petes	Sault Ste. Marie Greyhounds

The OHL regular-season champion is awarded the Hamilton Spectator Trophy and the playoff champion is awarded the J. Ross Robertson Cup.

QUEBEC MAJOR JUNIOR HOCKEY LEAGUE

LEAGUE OFFICE

President and executive director
Gilles Courteau
Statistician
Richard Blouin

Communications assistant
Manon Gagnon
Administrative assistant
Marie Claude Dubois

Address
110 Rue de la Barre
Bureau 210
Longueuil, Quebec J4K 1A3
Phone
514-442-3590

1991-92 REGULAR SEASON

FINAL STANDINGS

ROBERT LE BEL DIVISION

Team	G	W	L	T	Pts.	GF	GA
Longueuil	70	40	17	5	101	350	233
Hull	70	41	24	5	87	331	259
Laval	70	38	27	5	81	306	276
St. Hyacinthe	70	35	28	7	77	332	274
Granby	70	25	42	3	53	291	355
St. Jean	70	24	43	3	51	250	336

FRANK DILIO DIVISION

Team	G	W	L	T	Pts	GF	GA
Trois-Rivieres	70	45	21	4	94	333	221
Shawinigan	70	37	27	6	80	279	273
Chicoutimi	70	31	33	6	68	279	304
Drummondville	70	28	39	3	59	285	319
Beauport	70	25	40	5	55	257	298
Victoriaville	70	16	52	2	34	243	388

INDIVIDUAL LEADERS

Goals: Martin Gendron, St. Hyacinthe (71)
Assists: Charles Poulin, St. Hyacinthe (97)
Points: Pat Poulin, St. Hyacinthe (138)
Penalty minutes: Matthew Barnaby, Beauport (476)
Goaltending average: Jean-Francois Labbe, T-R (3.10)
Shutouts: Johnny Lorenzo, Shawinigan (3)

	Games	G	A	Pts.
Robert Guillet, Longueuil	67	56	62	118
Carl Boudreau, Trois-Rivieres	69	47	68	115
Alexandre Daigle, Victoriaville	66	35	75	110
Eric Bellerose, Trois-Rivieres	70	44	65	109
Todd Sparks, Hull	61	28	76	104
Jim Bermingham, Laval	65	37	66	103
Michel St. Jacques, Chicoutimi	69	44	53	97
Dave Chouinard, Longueuil	69	34	63	97
Rene Corbet, Drummondville	56	46	50	96
Yves Sarault, Trois-Rivieres	68	44	52	96
Paul Brousseau, Hull	57	35	61	96
David St. Pierre, Longueuil	59	40	55	95
Sebastien Parent, Chicoutimi	70	25	70	95
Dominic Maltais, Beauport	67	53	41	94

TOP SCORERS

	Games	G	A	Pts.
Patrick Poulin, St. Hyacinthe	56	52	86	138
Martin Gendron, St. Hyacinthe	69	71	66	137
Charles Poulin, St. Hyacinthe	68	38	97	135
Hugues Mongeon, Laval	62	53	77	130
Hugo Proulx, Drummondville	66	45	79	124
Marc Rodgers, Longueuil	65	44	76	120

INDIVIDUAL STATISTICS

BEAUPORT HARFANGS

SCORING

	Games	G	A	Pts.	Pen.
Dominic Maltais	67	53	41	94	179
Simon Toupin	70	46	45	91	64
Patrick Genest	60	37	33	70	32
Matthew Barnaby	63	29	37	66	476
Ian McIntyre	63	29	32	61	250
Eric Cool	45	13	48	61	44
Carl Leblanc	63	7	54	61	191
Martin Roy	69	9	27	36	160
Herve Lapointe	63	8	23	31	234
Charlie Boucher	66	8	21	29	20
Patrice Paquin	60	10	15	25	169
Reginald Brezeault	60	2	18	20	324
Daniel Laflamme	67	5	13	18	94
Martin Lacombe	34	4	13	17	312
Jamie Bird	62	0	17	17	25
Gregg Pineo	64	10	4	14	90
Eric Moreau	56	3	6	9	2
Jean-Guy Trudel	56	1	4	5	20
Radoslav Balaz	24	2	1	3	14
Jean-Francois Picard	27	2	1	3	23
Brandon Piccarreto	52	0	2	2	31
Stephane Gachet	21	0	0	0	4

	Games	G	A	Pts.	Pen.
Steeve Dubuc (goalie)	1	—	—	—	0
Alain Gauthier (goalie)	26	—	—	—	6
Marcel Cousineau (goalie)	67	—	—	—	16

GOALTENDING

	Games	Min.	Goals	SO	Avg.
Marcel Cousineau	67	3673	241	0	3.94
Alain Gauthier	26	1198	111	0	5.56
Steeve Dubuc	1	37	4	0	6.54

CHICOUTIMI SAGUENEENS

SCORING

	Games	G	A	Pts.	Pen.
Michel St. Jacques	69	44	53	97	22
Sebastien Parent	70	25	70	95	101
Daniel Paradis	70	42	47	89	97
Danny Beauregard	59	33	53	86	28
Patrice Martineau	65	41	31	72	128
Steve Gosselin	64	11	42	53	99
Eric Meloche	59	16	32	48	121
Carl Wiseman	60	17	25	42	4
Dave Tremblay	68	14	15	29	4
Martin Beaupre	49	5	22	27	114
Dany Larochelle	64	3	18	21	53

	Games	G	A	Pts.	Pen.
Patrick Clement	66	4	15	19	164
Dave Belliveau	65	14	4	18	53
Carl Blondin	53	10	8	18	4
Christian Caron	47	3	14	17	13
Martin Lamarche	62	2	6	8	62
Alen Kerr	38	1	7	8	145
Patrick Lacombe	67	1	6	7	367
Dany Girard	68	0	6	6	28
Rodney Petawabano	55	1	4	5	48
Patrick Lampron	32	0	2	2	57
Michel Guinois	1	0	1	1	0
Sylvain Careau (goalie)	16	—	—	—	0
Hugo Hamelin (goalie)	16	—	—	—	4
Sylvain Rodrigue (goalie)	59	—	—	—	0

GOALTENDING

	Games	Min.	Goals	SO	Avg.
Sylvain Rodrigue	59	3046	202	1	3.98
Sylvain Careau	16	674	52	1	4.63
Hugo Hamelin	16	559	45	0	4.83

DRUMMONDVILLE VOLTIGEURS

SCORING

	Games	G	A	Pts.	Pen.
Hugo Proulx	66	45	79	124	82
Rene Colbert	56	46	50	96	90
Ian Laperriere	70	28	49	77	160
Eric Plante	66	27	33	60	88
Dave Whittom	58	15	35	50	392
Stephane Paradis	66	18	25	43	62
Eric Marcoux	58	8	32	40	195
Vincent Tremblay	43	15	24	39	72
Louis Bernard	70	8	24	32	59
Sylvain Ducharme	67	10	20	30	100
Alexandre Duchesne	67	6	11	17	51
Eric Duchesne	50	8	8	16	214
David Lessard	64	2	14	16	49
Eric Rochette	33	2	10	12	66
Paul-Emile Exantus	38	6	5	11	53
Alain Nasreddine	61	1	9	10	78
Alexandre Gaumond	42	1	6	7	17
Jonathan Dubois	26	2	4	6	31
Patrick Larose	24	1	3	4	79
Bruce McHugh	43	1	2	3	56
Patrick Miller (goalie)	3	—	—	—	0
Yves Loubier (goalie)	17	—	—	—	6
Pierre Gagnon (goalie)	59	—	—	—	16

GOALTENDING

	Games	Min.	Goals	SO	Avg.
Pierre Gagnon	59	3401	237	1	4.18
Yves Loubier	17	740	64	1	5.18
Patrick Miller	3	109	10	0	5.49

GRANBY BISONS

SCORING

	Games	G	A	Pts.	Pen.
Martin Balleux	70	36	45	81	34
Robin Bouchard	65	29	26	55	150
Patrick Grise	69	25	27	52	55
Sebastien Fortier	62	14	31	45	65
Martin Larochelle	69	12	28	40	47
Jacques Parent	66	22	17	39	76
Pierre Fillion	63	12	24	36	92
Yannick Frechette	54	10	24	34	96
Martin Rozon	63	6	20	26	43
Patrick Lamoureux	64	5	18	23	72
Jacques Blouin	67	1	19	20	118
Eric Beauvais	66	6	10	16	46
Benoit Therrien	52	1	12	13	71
Eric Joyal	56	1	11	12	93
Sylvain Brisson	63	4	7	11	47
Pierre Calder	51	2	9	11	161
Louis-Andre Morin	50	2	7	9	85

	Games	G	A	Pts.	Pen.
Dominic Grand'maison	48	1	6	7	117
Pascal Gagnon	47	0	4	4	47
Sebastien Dupuis (goalie)	10	—	—	—	0
Martin Brochu (goalie)	52	—	—	—	6

GOALTENDING

	Games	Min.	Goals	SO	Avg.
Martin Brochu	52	2772	218	0	4.72
Sebastien Dupuis	10	470	44	0	5.62

HULL OLYMPIQUES

SCORING

	Games	G	A	Pts.	Pen.
Todd Sparks	61	28	76	104	140
Paul Brousseau	57	35	61	96	54
Jim Campbell	64	41	44	85	51
Claude Jutras	66	25	41	66	321
Joel Blain	60	24	35	59	146
Sebastie Bordeleau	62	26	32	58	91
Pierre-Franc Lalonde	47	23	22	45	34
Joseph Napolitano	64	21	21	42	208
Michal Longauer	68	13	25	38	65
Joey Deliva	44	18	17	35	11
Shane Doiron	66	14	21	35	147
Steven Dion	70	12	23	35	212
Eric Lecompte	60	16	17	33	138
Francois Paquette	51	6	23	29	14
Frederic Boivin	64	14	13	27	392
Harold Hersh	52	9	14	23	47
Eric Lavigne	46	4	17	21	101
Martin Lepage	69	2	10	12	71
Jacques Auger	48	2	9	11	130
Sylvain Lapointe	67	0	11	11	65
Paul MacDonald	42	0	4	4	16
Thierry Mayer	14	1	1	2	36
Yanik Francoeur (goalie)	4	—	—	—	4
Yanick Degrace (goalie)	35	—	—	—	2
Marc Legault (goalie)	37	—	—	—	2

GOALTENDING

	Games	Min.	Goals	SO	Avg.
Marc Legault	37	2032	114	1	3.37
Yanick Degrace	35	1970	112	0	3.41
Yanik Francoeur	4	156	16	0	6.16

LAVAL TITANS

SCORING

	Games	G	A	Pts.	Pen.
Hugues Mongeon	62	53	77	130	35
Jim Bermingham	65	37	66	103	88
Sandy McCarthy	62	39	51	90	326
Philippe Boucher	65	29	48	77	83
Eric Veilleux	60	31	40	71	87
Benoit Larose	70	11	53	64	171
Marc Beaucage	67	24	38	62	117
Martin Lapointe	31	25	30	55	84
Jean Blouin	25	27	21	48	44
Michael Gaul	50	6	38	44	44
Jean Roberge	54	20	20	40	66
Yanick Dube	65	14	19	33	8
Brant Blackned	67	17	15	32	48
Giuseppe Argento	46	6	8	14	218
Yan St. Pierre	46	2	9	11	34
Petr Valenta	62	1	10	11	125
Philip Gathercole	42	4	6	10	26
John Kovacs	51	3	7	10	181
Dany Michaud	64	1	7	8	45
Daniel Arsenault	24	0	5	5	98
Greg MacEachern	11	0	4	4	22
Martin Chaput	49	0	2	2	92
Sylvain Blouin	28	0	0	0	23
Francois Leblanc (goalie)	10	—	—	—	2
Emmanuel Fernandez (goalie)	31	—	—	—	2

GOALTENDING

	Games	Min.	Goals	SO	Avg.
Emmanuel Fernandez.	31	1593	99	1	3.73
Francois Leblanc	10	521	40	0	4.61

LONGUEUIL COLLEGE-FRANCAIS

SCORING

	Games	G	A	Pts.	Pen.
Marc Rodgers	65	44	76	120	109
Robert Guillet	67	56	62	118	104
Dave Chouinard	69	34	63	97	40
David St. Pierre	59	40	55	95	98
Martin Tanguay	67	41	50	91	117
Mario Nobili	52	27	48	75	184
Dominic Rheaume	70	32	41	73	47
Yanick Dupre	40	26	31	57	69
Yan Arsenault	56	13	38	51	49
Joel Bouchard	70	9	37	46	55
Donald Brashear	65	18	24	42	283
Pascal Vincent	70	8	27	35	42
Carl Lamothe	67	6	29	35	22
Stacy Dallaire	64	9	21	30	133
Jean-Martin Morin	65	11	16	27	44
Karl Dykhuis	29	5	19	24	55
Etienne Lavoie	63	0	17	17	309
Francois Rivard	66	4	7	11	27
Pierre Gendron	40	1	6	7	15
Jean-Seba Lefebvre	46	0	1	1	47
Andrej Dobrota	19	0	0	0	2
Simon Arial	22	0	0	0	15
Philippe De Rouville (goalie)	34	—	—	—	6
Eric Raymond (goalie)	50	—	—	—	12

GOALTENDING

	Games	Min.	Goals	SO	Avg.
Philippe De Rouville	34	1854	99	2	3.20
Eric Raymond	50	2938	167	2	3.41

ST. HYACINTHE LASERS

SCORING

	Games	G	A	Pts.	Pen.
Patrick Poulin	56	52	86	138	58
Martin Gendron	69	71	66	137	45
Charles Poulin	68	38	97	135	113
Hugues Laliberte	60	33	39	72	56
Normand Paquet	69	19	46	65	29
Jean-Franco Gregoire	67	23	37	60	55
Yves Meunier	64	27	20	47	115
Dean Melanson	42	8	19	27	158
Carl Menard	52	12	13	25	17
Patrick Belisle	53	8	16	24	11
Yannik Lemay	37	1	21	22	16
Alain Cote	61	4	15	19	86
Martin Lajeunesse	68	2	16	18	52
Martin Beauchamp	26	11	5	16	20
Stephane Huard	45	7	9	16	29
Stan Melanson	62	3	13	16	207
Martin Trudel	65	2	14	16	53
Etienne Thibault	54	2	9	11	57
Sebastien Berube	56	0	5	5	57
Dany Fortin	22	1	2	3	12
Jean-Guy Daigneault	26	0	3	3	23
David Desnoyers	43	0	3	3	72
Jean-Francois Rivard (goalie)	15	—	—	—	2
Stephane Menard (goalie)	22	—	—	—	0
Martin Brodeur (goalie)	48	—	—	—	39

GOALTENDING

	Games	Min.	Goals	SO	Avg.
Martin Brodeur	48	2846	161	2	3.39
Jean-Francois Rivard	15	738	55	1	4.47
Stephane Menard	22	1121	85	0	4.55

ST. JEAN LYNX

SCORING

	Games	G	A	Pts.	Pen.
Samuel Groleau	70	32	53	85	70
Patrick Carignan	67	27	43	70	51
Marquis Mathieu	70	20	36	56	166
Lino Salvo	67	21	33	54	42
Mil Sukovic	60	20	23	43	135
Stephane St. Amour	62	19	24	43	80
Richard Aimonetto	60	14	16	30	67
Patrick Deraspe	62	16	12	28	155
Steve Ares	60	16	10	26	235
Denis Beauchamp	56	8	12	20	138
Stephane Desjardins	63	4	16	20	174
Nathan Morin	62	7	12	19	274
Christian Proulx	68	1	17	18	180
Raymond Delarosbil	70	3	13	16	147
Jean-Alain Schneider	40	3	12	15	112
Sebastien Moreau	57	2	7	9	50
Eric Alarie	25	3	5	8	27
Stephane Madore	39	1	4	5	69
Eric O'Connor	44	2	2	4	91
Luc Corriveau	7	0	1	1	0
Jean-Chri Honorez	3	0	0	0	0
Patrick Laferiere (goalie)	2	—	—	—	4
Jean-Pascal Lemelin (goalie)	31	—	—	—	0
Jean-Francois Gagnon (goalie)	32	—	—	—	12

GOALTENDING

	Games	Min.	Goals	SO	Avg.
Patrick Laferiere	2	120	8	0	4.00
Jean-Pascal Lemelin	31	1649	121	1	4.40
Jean-Francois Gagnon	32	1433	127	1	5.32

SHAWINIGAN CATARACTES

SCORING

	Games	G	A	Pts.	Pen.
Richard Hamelin	69	32	50	82	45
Jean Imbeau	69	33	47	80	71
Francois Groleau	65	8	70	78	74
Steve Dontigny	50	33	43	76	80
Alain Savage	69	23	39	62	60
Jean-Francois Jomphe	44	28	33	61	69
Marc Tardif	55	25	34	59	214
Pierre Allard	70	19	37	56	99
Stefan Simoes	60	19	24	43	63
Mario Therrien	69	11	27	38	129
Marc Savard	71	8	23	31	78
Pascal Lebrasseur	69	9	18	27	81
Simon Roy	63	3	24	27	24
Francois Bourdeau	70	6	19	25	85
Alain Cote	65	12	8	20	70
Serge Labelle	49	2	15	17	296
Jeremy Caissie	64	8	8	16	44
Patrick Traverse	59	3	11	14	12
Jean-Franc Laroche	34	4	6	10	19
Steve Laplante	58	1	1	2	80
Andre Alie	3	0	0	0	0
Jocelyn Charbonneau	45	0	0	0	13
Sebastien Plouffe (goalie)	23	—	—	—	4
Johnny Lorenzo (goalie)	52	—	—	—	48

GOALTENDING

	Games	Min.	Goals	SO	Avg.
Johnny Lorenzo	52	2813	166	3	3.54
Sebastien Plouffe	23	1192	84	1	4.23

TROIS-RIVIERES DRAVEURS

SCORING

	Games	G	A	Pts.	Pen.
Carl Boudreau	69	47	68	115	71
Eric Bellerose	70	44	65	109	133
Yves Sarault	68	44	52	96	106
Patrick Nadeau	68	28	62	90	134

	Games	G	A	Pts.	Pen.
Dave Paquet	66	36	39	75	112
Carl Fleury	65	17	39	56	76
Stephane Julien	64	13	41	54	103
Travor Duhaime	66	24	28	52	184
Claude Poirier	69	8	39	47	110
Pascal Rheaume	65	17	20	37	84
Steve Searles	63	17	18	35	238
Paolo Racicot	48	5	30	35	204
Jason Downey	68	7	27	34	277
Joe Crowley	41	11	13	24	124
Nicolas Turmel	53	10	12	22	53
Pascal Trepanier	53	4	18	22	125
Dave Boudreault	54	8	13	21	52
Stephan Viens	66	4	9	13	243
Eric Messier	58	2	10	12	28
Charles Paquette	60	1	7	8	101
Pascal Veilleux	34	2	1	3	12
Jocelyn Thibault (goalie)	30	—	—	—	2
Jean-Francois Labbe (goalie)	48	—	—	—	35

GOALTENDING

	Games	Min.	Goals	SO	Avg.
Jocelyn Thibault	30	1497	77	0	3.09
Jean-Francois Labbe	48	2749	142	1	3.10

VICTORIAVILLE TIGRES

SCORING

	Games	G	A	Pts.	Pen.
Alexandre Daigle	66	35	75	110	63
Claude Savoie	69	39	40	79	140

	Games	G	A	Pts.	Pen.
Jocelyn Langlois	70	29	32	61	51
Patrick Bisaillon	52	31	27	58	70
Nicolas Lefebvre	68	18	36	54	126
Hughes Bouchard	71	8	27	35	167
Christian Tardif	67	12	19	31	34
Pascal Bernier	67	8	22	30	84
Daniel Guerard	31	5	16	21	66
Stephane Larocque	50	8	10	18	77
Pascal Chiasson	64	1	17	18	93
Daniel Germain	62	3	14	17	72
Mario Dumoulin	67	3	13	16	117
Sebastien Tremblay	48	2	14	16	175
Carl Poirier	56	8	7	15	43
Martin Woods	60	3	12	15	193
Ian Laterreur	52	5	8	13	35
Marc Thibeault	48	2	4	6	133
Alexandre Laporte	44	1	4	5	43
Martin Laitre	35	1	0	1	160
Michel Cormier	3	0	1	1	0
Danick Lepine (goalie)	15	—	—	—	12
Patrick Charbonneau (goalie)	37	—	—	—	29

GOALTENDING

	Games	Min.	Goals	SO	Avg.
Patrick Charbonneau	37	1943	163	0	5.03
Danick Lepine	15	714	69	0	5.80

1992 PRESIDENT CUP PLAYOFFS

RESULTS

QUARTERFINALS

Series "A"

	W	L	Pts.	GF	GA
Longueuil	4	2	8	23	22
St. Hyacinthe	2	4	4	22	23

(Longueuil won series, 4-2)

Series "B"

	W	L	Pts.	GF	GA
Laval	4	2	8	28	24
Hull	2	4	4	24	28

(Laval won series, 4-2)

Series "C"

	W	L	Pts.	GF	GA
Trois-Rivieres	4	0	8	21	8
Drummondville	0	4	0	8	21

(Trois-Rivieres won series, 4-0)

Series "D"

	W	L	Pts.	GF	GA
Shawinigan	4	0	8	22	15
Chicoutimi	0	4	0	15	22

(Shawinigan won series, 4-0)

SEMIFINALS

Series "E"

	W	L	Pts.	GF	GA
Longueuil	4	2	8	25	19
Shawinigan	2	4	4	19	25

(Longueuil won series, 4-2)

Series "F"

	W	L	Pts.	GF	GA
Trois-Rivieres	4	0	8	26	5
Laval	0	4	0	5	26

(Trois-Rivieres won series, 4-0)

FINALS

Series "G"

	W	L	Pts.	GF	GA
Longueuil	4	3	8	26	26
Trois-Rivieres	3	4	6	26	26

(Longueuil won series, 4-3)

Goals: Robert Guillet, Longueuil (14)
Dominic Rheaume, Longueuil (14)
Assists: Eric Bellerose, Trois-Rivieres (16)
Points: Robert Guillet, Longueuil (25)
Penalty minutes: Donald Brashear, Longueuil (98)
Goaltending average: Jean-Francois Labbe, T-R (2.50)
Shutouts: Philippe DeRouville, Longueuil (1)
Jean-Francois Labbe, Trois-Rivieres (1)

TOP SCORERS

	Games	G	A	Pts.
Robert Guillet, Longueuil..............	19	14	11	25
Carl Boudreau, Trois-Rivieres...........	15	10	13	23
Eric Bellerose, Trois-Rivieres........	15	7	16	23
Dave Paquet, Trois-Rivieres	15	10	11	21
Martin Tanguay, Longueuil..............	19	8	13	21
Yves Sarault, Trois-Rivieres...........	15	10	10	20
Francois Groleau, Shawinigan	10	5	15	20
Yanick Dupre, Longueuil.................	19	9	9	18
Dominic Rheaume, Longueuil	19	14	3	17
Patrick Nadeau, Trois-Rivieres........	15	7	10	17

CHICOUTIMI SAGUENEENS

(Lost quarterfinals to Shawinigan, 4-0)

SCORING

	Games	G	A	Pts.	Pen.
Sebastine Parent	3	3	5	8	19
Daniel Paradis	4	4	3	7	8
Patrice Martineau	3	1	5	6	18
Michel St. Jacques	4	2	2	4	4
Danny Beauregard	4	1	3	4	2
Dave Tremblay	4	0	4	4	0
Eric Meloche	3	1	2	3	2
Steve Gosselin	4	1	2	3	8
Carl Wiseman	3	2	0	2	0
Dany Larochelle	4	0	2	2	4
Patrick Clement	4	0	1	1	4
Christian Caron	1	0	0	0	0
Michel Guinois	2	0	0	0	0
Dave Belliveau	4	0	0	0	16
Carl Blondi	4	0	0	0	4
Dany Girard	4	0	0	0	9
Alen Kerr	4	0	0	0	0
Patrick Lacombe	4	0	0	0	21
Martin Lamarche..........................	4	0	0	0	0
Patrick Lampron	4	0	0	0	0
Sylvain Rodrigue (goalie)	4	—	—	—	2

GOALTENDING

	Games	Min.	Goals	SO	Avg.
Sylvain Rodrigue	4	254	20	0	4.72

DRUMMONDVILLE VOLTIGEURS

(Lost quarterfinals to Trois-Rivieres, 4-0)

SCORING

	Games	G	A	Pts.	Pen.
Ian Laperriere	4	2	2	4	9
Hugo Prouix	4	3	0	3	11
Rene Corbet	4	1	2	3	17
Eric Plante	4	1	2	3	4
Sylvain Ducharme	4	0	2	2	4
Eric Rochette	4	0	2	2	20
Eric Duchesne	4	1	0	1	2
Stephane Paradis	2	0	1	1	0
Louis Bernard	4	0	1	1	4
Patrick Larose	1	0	0	0	0
Alexandre Duchesne	3	0	0	0	0
Alexandre Gaumond......................	3	0	0	0	12
Eric Marcoux	3	0	0	0	4
Jonathan Dubois	4	0	0	0	15
Paul-Emile Exantus	4	0	0	0	0
David Lessard............................	4	0	0	0	0
Bruce McHugh	4	0	0	0	0
Alain Nasreddine	4	0	0	0	17
Vincent Tremblay	4	0	0	0	2

	Games	G	A	Pts.	Pen.
Dave Whittom..............................	4	0	0	0	53
Yves Loubier (goalie)	2	—	—	—	2
Pierre Gagnon (goalie)	3	—	—	—	15

GOALTENDING

	Games	Min.	Goals	SO	Avg.
Pierre Gagnon	3	132	9	0	4.08
Yves Loubier..............	2	107	11	0	6.19

HULL OLYMPIQUES

(Lost quarterfinals to Laval, 4-2)

SCORING

	Games	G	A	Pts.	Pen.
Todd Sparks	6	2	9	11	12
Jim Campbell	6	7	3	10	8
Paul Brousseau	6	3	5	8	10
Shane Doiron	6	3	4	7	14
Francois Paquette	5	1	6	7	4
Joel Blain	6	4	2	6	27
Sebastien Bordeleau	5	0	3	3	23
Pierre-Francois Lalonde...............	6	1	1	2	2
Sylvain Lapointe	6	1	1	2	10
Claude Jutras............................	6	0	2	2	34
Joey Deliva	4	0	2	2	2
Michal Longauer	6	1	0	1	9
Eric Lecompte............................	6	1	0	1	4
Steven Dion	5	0	1	1	21
Jacques Auger............................	6	0	1	1	10
Paul MacDonald	1	0	0	0	0
Joseph Napolitano	4	0	0	0	18
Frederic Boivin	6	0	0	0	27
Eric Lavigne	6	0	0	0	32
Martin Lepage	6	0	0	0	4
Yanick Degrace (goalie)	2	—	—	—	0
Marc Legault (goalie)	6	—	—	—	6

GOALTENDING

	Games	Min.	Goals	SO	Avg.
Marc Legault	6	330	24	0	4.36
Yanick Degrace	2	31	4	0	7.64

LAVAL TITANS

(Lost semifinals to Trois-Rivieres, 4-0)

SCORING

	Games	G	A	Pts.	Pen.
Martin Lapointe	10	4	10	14	32
Jean Blouin	10	5	8	13	41
Benoit Larose............................	10	5	6	11	20
Philippe Boucher	10	5	6	11	8
Sandy McCarthy..........................	8	4	5	9	81
Jim Bermingham	10	3	6	9	28
Eric Veilleux............................	10	3	5	8	27

	Games	G	A	Pts.	Pen.
Hugues Mongeon	10	2	4	6	8
Jean Roberge	10	0	4	4	18
Petr Valenta	10	1	1	2	4
Yanick Dube	10	0	2	2	2
Michael Gaul	10	0	2	2	20
Brant Blackned	10	1	0	1	6
Greg MacEachern	10	0	1	1	29
Philip Gathercole	1	0	0	0	0
Dany Michaud	5	0	0	0	0
John Kovacs	7	0	0	0	32
Sylvain Blouin	9	0	0	0	35
Daniel Arsenault	10	0	0	0	61
Yan St. Pierre	10	0	0	0	12
Francois Leblanc (goalie)	4	—	—	—	0
Emmanuel Fernandez (goalie)	9	—	—	—	0

GOALTENDING

	Games	Min.	Goals	SO	Avg.
Francois Leblanc	4	134	11	0	4.91
Emmanuel Fernandez	9	468	39	0	5.00

LONGUEUIL COLLEGE-FRANCAIS

Winner of 1992 President Cup playoffs)

SCORING

	Games	G	A	Pts.	Pen.
Robert Guillet	19	14	11	25	26
Martin Tanguey	19	8	13	21	32
Yanick Dupre	19	9	9	18	20
Dominic Rheaume	19	14	3	17	16
Marc Rodgers	18	3	13	16	26
Mario Nobill	18	6	9	15	10
Dave Chouinard	19	3	10	13	10
Karl Dykhuis	17	0	12	12	14
David St. Pierre	15	3	6	9	15
Yan Arsenault	11	1	7	8	6
Joel Bouchard	19	1	7	8	20
Stacy Dallaire	19	4	3	7	45
Pascal Vincent	18	1	6	7	14
Donald Brashear	18	4	2	6	98
Jean-Martin Morin	18	3	3	6	8
Etienne Lavoie	15	0	5	5	21
Carl Lamothe	16	0	2	2	7
Simon Arial	2	0	0	0	2
Andrej Dobrota	8	0	0	0	0
Francois Rivard	17	0	0	0	0
Pierre Gendron	19	0	0	0	11
Philippe De Rouville (goalie)	11	—	—	—	0
Eric Raymond (goalie)	11	—	—	—	0

GOALTENDING

	Games	Min.	Goals	SO	Avg.
Philippe De Rouville	11	593	28	1	2.83
Eric Raymond	11	571	39	0	4.09

ST. HYACINTHE LASERS

(Lost quarterfinals to Longueuil, 4-2)

SCORING

	Games	G	A	Pts.	Pen.
Martin Gendron	6	7	4	11	14
Jean-Franco Gregoire	6	3	8	11	2
Hugues Laliberte	6	1	7	8	9
Normand Paquet	6	1	4	5	4
Yannik Lemay	6	2	2	4	0
Charles Poulin	6	2	2	4	20
Patrick Poulin	5	2	2	4	4
Martin Beauchamp	6	3	0	3	0
Dean Melanson	6	1	2	3	25
David Desnoyers	6	0	1	1	2
Martin Lajeunesse	6	0	1	1	0
Carl Menard	6	0	1	1	2
Yves Meunier	6	0	1	1	12
Stan Melanson	6	0	1	1	22
Etienne Thibault	1	0	0	0	0
Patrick Belisle	2	0	0	0	0

	Games	G	A	Pts.	Pen.
Sebastien Berube	4	0	0	0	2
Alain Cote	6	0	0	0	10
Stephane Huard	6	0	0	0	10
Martin Trudel	6	0	0	0	13
Stephane Menard (goalie)	1	—	—	—	0
Martin Brodeur (goalie)	5	—	—	—	4

GOALTENDING

	Games	Min.	Goals	SO	Avg.
Martin Brodeur	5	317	14	0	2.65
Stephane Menard	1	60	9	0	9.00

SHAWINIGAN CATARACTES

(Lost semifinals to Longueuil, 4-2)

SCORING

	Games	G	A	Pts.	Pen.
Francois Groleau	10	5	15	20	8
Jean-Francois Jomphe	10	6	10	16	10
Alain Savage	10	6	6	12	18
Richard Hamelin	10	3	7	10	2
Stefan Simoes	10	6	3	9	14
Jean Imbeau	10	4	5	9	14
Marc Tardif	10	0	8	8	57
Pierre Allard	10	3	4	7	8
Alain Cote	10	5	1	6	7
Simon Roy	10	1	4	5	9
Mario Therrien	10	1	4	5	22
Marc Savard	10	1	3	4	20
Francois Bourdeau	10	0	2	2	12
Pascal Lebrasseur	10	0	2	2	23
Jean-Franc Laroche	10	0	1	1	14
Jocelyn Charbonneau	2	0	0	0	0
Serge Labelle	9	0	0	0	26
Jeremy Caissie	9	0	0	0	0
Patrick Traverse	10	0	0	0	4
Sebastien Plouffe (goalie)	1	—	—	—	0
Johnny Lorenzo (goalie)	10	—	—	—	4

GOALTENDING

	Games	Min.	Goals	SO	Avg.
Sebastien Plouffe	1	20	1	0	3.00
Johnny Lorenzo	10	600	39	0	3.90

TROIS-RIVIERES DRAVEURS

(Lost finals to Longueuil, 4-3)

SCORING

	Games	G	A	Pts.	Pen.
Carl Boudreau	15	10	13	23	6
Eric Bellerose	15	7	16	23	26
Dave Paquet	15	10	11	21	25
Yves Sarault	15	10	10	20	18
Patrick Nadeau	15	7	10	17	14
Jason Downey	15	5	11	16	72
Claude Poirier	15	1	11	12	16
Stephane Julien	15	4	7	11	11
Travor Duhaime	14	0	11	11	36
Carl Fleury	15	4	6	10	33
Pascal Rheaume	14	5	4	9	23
Pascal Trepanier	15	3	5	8	21
Dave Boudreault	15	2	6	8	12
Eric Messier	15	2	2	4	13
Paolo Racicot	13	1	2	3	24
Stephan Viens	13	1	0	1	12
Nicolas Turmel	15	1	0	1	16
Steve Searles	14	0	1	1	21
Pascal Veilleux	1	0	0	0	0
Charles Paquette	6	0	0	0	2
Jocelyn Thibault (goalie)	3	—	—	—	0
Jean-Francois Labbe (goalie)	15	—	—	—	0

GOALTENDING

	Games	Min.	Goals	SO	Avg.
Jocelyn Thibault	3	110	4	0	2.19
Jean-Francois Labbe	15	791	33	1	2.50

1991-92 AWARD WINNERS

ALL-STAR TEAMS

First team	Pos.	Second team
J.-Francois Labbe, T-R	G	Martin Brodeur, St. Hy.
Francois Groleau, Shaw.	LD	Benoit Larose, Laval
Yan Arsenault, Longueuil	RD	Philippe Boucher, Laval
Patrick Poulin, St. Hy.	LW	Yves Sarault, T-R
Charles Poulin, St. Hy.	C	Alexandre Daigle, Vic.
Martin Gendron, St. Hy.	RW	Robert Guillet, Longueuil

Coach of the Year: Alain Sanscartier, Shawinigan

TROPHY WINNERS

Frank Selke Trophy: Martin Gendron, St. Hyacinthe
Michel Bergeron Trophy: Alexandre Daigle, Victoriaville
Raymond Lagace Trophy: Philippe DeRouville, Longueuil
Jean Beliveau Trophy: Patrick Poulin, St. Hyacinthe
Michel Briere Trophy: Charles Poulin, St. Hyacinthe
Marcel Robert Trophy: Simon Toupin, Beauport
Mike Bossy Trophy: Paul Brousseau, Hull
Emile "Butch" Bouchard Trophy: Francois Groleau, Shawinigan
Jacques Plante Trophy: Jean-Francois Labbe, Trois-Rivieres
Guy Lafleur Trophy: Robert Guillet, Longueuil
Robert LeBel Trophy: Trois-Rivieres Draveurs
John Rougeau Trophy: Longueuil College Francais
President Cup: Longueuil College Francais

ALL-TIME AWARD WINNERS

FRANK SELKE TROPHY

(Most gentlemanly player)

Season	Player, Team
1970-71	Norm Dube, Sherbrooke
1971-72	Gerry Teeple, Cornwall
1972-73	Claude Larose, Drummondville
1973-74	Gary MacGregor, Cornwall
1974-75	Jean-Luc Phaneuf, Montreal
1975-76	Norm Dupont, Montreal
1976-77	Mike Bossy, Laval
1977-78	Kevin Reeves, Montreal
1978-79	Ray Bourque, Verdun
	Jean-Francois Sauve, Trois-Rivieres
1979-80	Jean-Francois Sauve, Trois-Rivieres
1980-81	Claude Verret, Trois-Rivieres
1981-82	Claude Verret, Trois-Rivieres
1982-83	Pat LaFontaine, Verdun
1983-84	Jerome Carrier, Verdun
1984-85	Patrick Emond, Chicoutimi
1985-86	Jimmy Carson, Verdun
1986-87	Luc Beausoleil, Laval
1987-88	Stephan Lebeau, Shawinigan
1988-89	Steve Cadieux, Shawinigan
1989-90	Andrew McKim, Hull
1990-91	Yanic Perreault, Trois-Rivieres
1991-92	Martin Gendron, St. Hyacinthe

MICHEL BERGERON TROPHY

(Top rookie forward)

Season	Player, Team
1969-70	Serge Martel, Verdun
1970-71	Bob Murphy, Cornwall
1971-72	Bob Murray, Cornwall
1972-73	Pierre Larouche, Sorel
1973-74	Mike Bossy, Laval
1974-75	Dennis Pomerleau, Hull
1975-76	Jean-Marc Bonamie, Shawinigan
1976-77	Rick Vaive, Sherbrooke
1977-78	Norm Rochefort, Trois-Rivieres
	Denis Savard, Montreal
1978-79	Alan Grenier, Laval
1979-80	Dale Hawerchuk, Cornwall
1980-81	Claude Verret, Trois-Rivieres
1981-82	Sylvain Turgeon, Hull
1982-83	Pat LaFontaine, Verdun
1983-84	Stephane Richer, Granby
1984-85	Jimmy Carson, Verdun
1985-86	Pierre Turgeon, Granby
1986-87	Rob Murphy, Laval
1987-88	Martin Gelinas, Hull
1988-89	Yanic Perreault, Trois-Rivieres

Season	Player, Team
1989-90	Martin Lapointe, Laval
1990-91	Rene Corbet, Drummondville
1991-92	Alexandre Daigle, Victoriaville

Prior to 1980-81 season, award was given to QMJHL rookie of the year.

RAYMOND LAGACE TROPHY

(Top rookie defenseman or goaltender)

Season	Player, Team
1980-81	Billy Campbell, Montreal
1981-82	Michel Petit, Sherbrooke
1982-83	Bobby Dollas, Laval
1983-84	James Gasseau, Drummondville
1984-85	Robert Desjardins, Shawinigan
1985-86	Stephane Guerard, Shawinigan
1986-87	Jimmy Waite, Chicoutimi
1987-88	Stephane Beauregard, St. Jean
1988-89	Karl Dykhuis, Hull
1989-90	Francois Groleau, Shawinigan
1990-91	Philippe Boucher, Granby
1991-92	Philippe DeRouville, Longueuil

JEAN BELIVEAU TROPHY

(Scoring leader)

Season	Player, Team
1969-70	Luc Simard, Trois-Rivieres
1970-71	Guy Lafleur, Quebec
1971-72	Jacques Richard, Quebec
1972-73	Andre Savard, Quebec
1973-74	Pierre Larouche, Sorel
1974-75	Norm Dupont, Montreal
1975-76	Richard Dalpe, Trois-Rivieres
	Sylvain Locas, Chicoutimi
1976-77	Jean Savard, Quebec
1977-78	Ron Carter, Sherbooke
1978-79	Jean-Francois Sauve, Trois-Rivieres
1979-80	Jean-Francois Sauve, Trois-Rivieres
1980-81	Dale Hawerchuk, Cornwall
1981-82	Claude Verret, Trois-Rivieres
1982-83	Pat LaFontaine, Verdun
1983-84	Mario Lemieux, Laval
1984-85	Guy Rouleau, Longueuil
1985-86	Guy Rouleau, Hull
1986-87	Marc Fortier, Chicoutimi
1987-88	Patrice Lefebvre, Shawinigan
1988-89	Stephane Morin, Chicoutimi
1989-90	Patrick Lebeau, Victoriaville
1990-91	Yanic Perreault, Trois-Rivieres
1991-92	Patrick Poulin, St. Hyacinthe

MICHEL BRIERE TROPHY

(Most Valuable Player)

Season	Player, Team
1972-73	Andre Savard, Quebec
1973-74	Gary MacGregor, Cornwall
1974-75	Mario Viens, Cornwall
1975-76	Peter Marsh, Sherbrooke
1976-77	Lucien DeBlois, Sorel
1977-78	Kevin Reeves, Montreal
1978-79	Pierre Lacroix, Trois-Rivieres
1979-80	Denis Savard, Montreal
1980-81	Dale Hawerchuk, Cornwall
1981-82	John Chabot, Sherbrooke
1982-83	Pat LaFontaine, Verdun
1983-84	Mario Lemieux, Laval
1984-85	Daniel Berthiaune, Chicoutimi
1985-86	Guy Rouleau, Hull
1986-87	Robert Desjardins, Longueuil
1987-88	Marc Saumier, Hull
1988-89	Stephane Morin, Chicoutimi
1989-90	Andrew McKim, Hull
1990-91	Yanic Perreault, Trois-Rivieres
1991-92	Charles Poulin, St. Hyacinthe

MARCEL ROBERT TROPHY

(Top scholastic/athletic performer)

Season	Player, Team
1981-82	Jacques Sylvestre, Granby
1982-83	Claude Gosselin, Quebec
1983-84	Gilbert Paiement, Chicoutimi
1984-85	Claude Gosselin, Longueuil
1985-86	Bernard Morin, Laval
1986-87	Patrice Tremblay, Chicoutimi
1987-88	Stephane Beauregard, St. Jean
1988-89	Daniel Lacroix, Granby
1989-90	Yanic Perreault, Trois-Rivieres
1990-91	Benoit Larose, Laval
1991-92	Simon Toupin, Beauport

MIKE BOSSY TROPHY

(Top pro prospect)

Season	Player, Team
1980-81	Dale Hawerchuk, Cornwall
1981-82	Michel Petit, Sherbrooke
1982-83	Pat LaFontaine, Verdun
	Sylvain Turgeon, Hull
1983-84	Mario Lemieux, Laval
1984-85	Jose Charbonneau, Drummondville
1985-86	Jimmy Carson, Verdun
1986-87	Pierre Turgeon, Granby
1987-88	Daniel Dore, Drummondville
1988-89	Patrice Brisebois, Laval
1989-90	Karl Dykhuis, Hull
1990-91	Philippe Boucher, Granby
1991-92	Paul Brousseau, Hull

Originally known as Association of Journalism of Hockey Trophy from 1980-81 through 1982-83.

EMILE "BUTCH" BOUCHARD TROPHY

(Top defenseman)

Season	Player, Team
1975-76	Jean Gagnon, Quebec
1976-77	Robert Picard, Montreal
1977-78	Mark Hardy, Montreal
1978-79	Ray Bourque, Verdun
1979-80	Gaston Therrien, Quebec
1980-81	Fred Boimistruck, Cornwall
1981-82	Paul Andre Boutilier, Sherbrooke
1982-83	J.J. Daigneault, Longueuil
1983-84	Billy Campbell, Verdun
1984-85	Yves Beaudoin, Shawinigan
1985-86	Sylvain Cote, Hull

Season	Player, Team
1986-87	Jean Marc Richard, Chicoutimi
1987-88	Eric Desjardins, Granby
1988-89	Yves Racine, Victoriaville
1989-90	Claude Barthe, Victoriaville
1990-91	Patrice Brisebois, Drummondville
1991-92	Francois Groleau, Shawinigan

JACQUES PLANTE TROPHY

(Top goaltender)

Season	Player, Team
1969-70	Michael Deguise, Sorel
1970-71	Reynald Fortier, Quebec
1971-72	Richard Brodeur, Cornwall
1972-73	Pierre Perusee, Quebec
1973-74	Claude Legris, Sorel
1974-75	Nick Sanza, Sherbrooke
1975-76	Tim Bernhardt, Cornwall
1976-77	Tim Bernhardt, Cornwall
1977-78	Tim Bernhardt, Cornwall
1978-79	Jacques Cloutier, Trois-Rivieres
1979-80	Corrado Micalef, Sherbrooke
1980-81	Michel Dufour, Sorel
1981-82	Jeff Barratt, Montreal
1982-83	Tony Haladuick, Laval
1983-84	Tony Haladuick, Laval
1984-85	Daniel Berthiaume, Chicoutimi
1985-86	Robert Desjardins, Hull
1986-87	Robert Desjardins, Longueuil
1987-88	Stephane Beauregard, St. Jean
1988-89	Stephane Fiset, Victoriaville
1989-90	Pierre Gagnon, Victoriaville
1990-91	Felix Potvin, Chicoutimi
1991-92	Jean-Francois Labbe, Trois-Rivieres

GUY LAFLEUR TROPHY

(Playoff MVP)

Season	Player, Team
1977-78	Richard David, Trois-Rivieres
1978-79	Jean-Francois Sauve, Trois-Rivieres
1979-80	Dale Hawerchuk, Cornwall
1980-81	Alain Lemieux, Trois-Rivieres
1981-82	Michel Morissette, Sherbrooke
1982-83	Pat LaFontaine, Verdun
1983-84	Mario Lemieux, Laval
1984-85	Claude Lemieux, Verdun
1985-86	Sylvain Cote, Hull
	Luc Robitaille, Hull
1986-87	Marc Saumier, Longueuil
1987-88	Marc Saumier, Hull
1988-89	Donald Audette, Laval
1989-90	Denis Chalifoux, Laval
1990-91	Felix Potvin, Chicoutimi
1991-92	Robert Guillet, Longueuil

ROBERT LeBEL TROPHY

(Best team defensive average)

Season	Team
1977-78	Trois-Rivieres Draveurs
1978-79	Trois-Rivieres Draveurs
1979-80	Sherbrooke Beavers
1980-81	Sorel Black Hawks
1981-82	Montreal Juniors
1982-83	Shawinigan Cataracts
1983-84	Shawinigan Cataracts
1984-85	Shawinigan Cataracts
1985-86	Hull Olympiques
1986-78	Longueuil Chevaliers
1987-88	St. Jean Castors
1988-89	Hull Olympiques
1989-90	Victoriaville Tigres
1990-91	Chicoutimi Sagueneens
1991-92	Trois-Rivieres Draveurs

REGULAR-SEASON CHAMPION	PLAYOFF CHAMPION
Season Team	**Team**
1969-70—Quebec Remparts	Quebec Remparts
1970-71—Quebec Remparts	Quebec Remparts
1971-72—Cornwall Royals	Cornwall Royals
1972-73—Quebec Remparts	Quebec Remparts
1973-74—Sorel Black Hawks	Quebec Remparts
1974-75—Sherbrooke Beavers	Sherbrooke Beavers
1975-76—Sherbrooke Beavers	Quebec Remparts
1976-77—Quebec Remparts	Sherbrooke Beavers
1977-78—Trois-Rivieres Draveurs	Trois-Rivieres Draveurs
1978-79—Trois-Rivieres Draveurs	Trois-Rivieres Draveurs
1979-80—Sherbrooke Beavers	Cornwall Royals
1980-81—Cornwall Royals	Cornwall Royals
1981-82—Sherbrooke Beavers	Sherbrooke Beavers
1982-83—Laval Voisins	Verdun Juniors
1983-84—Laval Voisins	Laval Voisins
1984-85—Shawinigan Cataracts	Verdun Junior Canadiens
1985-86—Hull Olympiques	Hull Olympiques
1986-87—Granby Bisons	Longueuil Chevaliers
1987-88—Hull Olympiques	Hull Olympiques
1988-89—Trois-Rivieres Draveurs	Laval Titans
1989-90—Victoriaville Tigres	Laval Titans
1990-91—Chicoutimi Sagueneens	Chicoutini Saguenees
1991-92—Longueuil College Francais	Longueuil College Francais

The QMJHL regular-season champion is awarded the John Rougeau Trophy and the playoff champion is awarded the Presidents Cup

The John Rougeau Trophy was originally called the Governors Trophy from 1969-70 through 1982-83.

WESTERN HOCKEY LEAGUE

LEAGUE OFFICE

Note: League was known as Canadian Major Junior Hockey League in 1966-67 and Western Canadian Hockey League from 1967-68 through 1976-77.

Address
602-5920 Macleod Trail S.
Calgary, Alberta T2H 0K2
Phone
403-253-8113

President
Ed Chynoweth
Vice president
Richard Doerksen

Executive assistant
Norman Dueck
Statistician
Stu Judge

1991-92 REGULAR SEASON

FINAL STANDINGS

EAST DIVISION

Team	G	W	L	T	Pts.	GF	GA
Prince Albert	72	50	20	2	102	356	261
Medicine Hat	72	48	24	0	96	336	264
Saskatoon	72	38	29	5	81	315	260
Lethbridge	72	39	31	2	80	350	284
Swift Current	72	35	33	4	74	296	313
Moose Jaw	72	33	36	3	69	279	316
Regina	72	31	36	5	67	300	298
Brandon	72	11	55	6	28	246	356

WEST DIVISION

Team	G	W	L	T	Pts.	GF	GA
Kamloops	72	51	17	4	106	351	226
Spokane	72	37	29	6	80	267	270
Tri-City	72	35	35	2	72	363	376
Seattle	72	33	34	5	71	292	285
Portland	72	31	37	4	66	314	342
Tacoma	72	24	43	5	53	273	346
Victoria	72	15	52	5	35	231	372

INDIVIDUAL LEADERS

Goals: Kevin Riehl, Medicine Hat (65)
    Kevin St. Jacques, Lethbridge (65)
Assists: Brian Sakic, Tri-City (83)
Points: Kevin St. Jacques, Lethbridge (140)
Penalty minutes: John Badduke, Portland (515)
Goaltending average: Corey Hirsch, Kamloops (2.72)
Shutouts: Corey Hirsch, Kamloops (5)

	Games	G	A	Pts.
Jeff Nelson, Prince Albert	64	48	65	113
Zac Boyer, Kamloops	70	40	69	109
Steve Konowalchuk, Portland	64	51	53	104
Andrew Schneider, Swift Current	63	44	60	104
Donevan Hextall, Prince Albert	71	33	71	104
Jason Krywulak, Swift Current	72	43	59	102
Vladimir Vujtek, Tri-City	53	41	61	102
Todd Holt, Swift Current	66	47	54	101
Lee Leslie, Prince Albert	72	52	48	100
Radek Sip, Lethbridge	71	38	62	100
Shayne Green, Kamloops	71	43	55	98
Dan Kesa, Prince Albert	62	46	51	97
Brad Zavisha, Lethbridge	70	51	44	95
Craig Lyons, Kamloops	65	44	51	95
Jiri Beranek, Portland	72	31	63	94

TOP SCORERS

	Games	G	A	Pts.
Kevin St. Jacques, Lethbridge	71	65	75	140
Terry Degner, Tri-City	72	58	81	139
Brian Sakic, Tri-City	72	45	83	128
Kevin Riehl, Medicine Hat	69	65	50	115
Chris Schmidt, Moose Jaw	72	60	54	114

INDIVIDUAL STATISTICS

BRANDON WHEAT KINGS

SCORING

	Games	G	A	Pts.	Pen.
Bobby House	71	35	42	77	133
Marty Murray	68	20	36	56	22
Brian Purdy	47	24	29	53	24
Mike Maneluk	68	23	30	53	102
Chris Johnston	66	21	24	45	113
Jeff Hoad	72	14	20	34	176
Todd Dutiaume	71	14	17	31	10
Ryan Smith	71	7	24	31	88
Chris Constant	34	5	21	26	78
Merv Priest	51	10	12	22	50
Darrin Ritchie	45	11	10	21	20
Terran Sanwith	41	6	14	20	145
Stu Scantlebury	63	6	14	20	136
Craig Geekie	69	5	14	19	52
Rob Puchniak	71	1	18	19	303
Mike Chrun	25	4	12	16	30
Jesse Wilson	27	7	7	14	21
Mark Kolesar	56	6	7	13	36

	Games	G	A	Pts.	Pen.
Greg Gatto	17	5	5	10	75
Dan Kopec	48	5	4	9	127
Jeff Jubenville	31	4	4	8	96
Dwayne Gylywoychuk	70	2	4	6	163
Sean McFatridge	22	2	3	5	104
Kevin Schmalz	36	2	3	5	102
Mike Vandenberghe	16	0	5	5	42
Cam Danyluk	5	3	0	3	16
Colin Cloutier	3	1	1	2	0
Hardy Sauter	6	1	1	2	7
Glen Webster	7	2	0	2	60
Carlos Bye	3	0	1	1	4
Chris Osgood (goalie)	16	0	1	1	6
Kevin Robertson	1	0	0	0	0
Tim Slukynsky	1	0	0	0	0
Jason Smith	1	0	0	0	0
Pete Leboutillier	2	0	0	0	5
Jeff Bloski (goalie)	3	0	0	0	0
Jeff Staples	3	0	0	0	0
Aaron Boh	4	0	0	0	4
Dean Intwert (goalie)	13	0	0	0	2

	Games	G	A	Pts.	Pen.
Shawn Dietrich (goalie)	14	0	0	0	4
Rick Geisel (goalie)	18	0	0	0	6
Andrew Reimer (goalie)	20	0	0	0	6

GOALTENDING

	Games	Min.	Goals	SO	Avg.
Chris Osgood	16	890	60	1	4.04
Dean Intwert	13	638	45(2)	0	4.23
Andrew Reimer	20	1136	92	1	4.86
Shawn Dietrich	14	681	59(2)	0	5.20
Rick Geisel	18	979	85(2)	0	5.21
Jeff Bloski	3	73	9	0	7.40

KAMLOOPS BLAZERS

SCORING

	Games	G	A	Pts.	Pen.
Zac Boyer	70	40	69	109	90
Shayne Green	71	43	55	98	167
Craig Lyons	65	44	51	95	80
Mike Mather	70	30	40	70	103
Jarrett Deuling	68	28	26	54	79
Joff Watchorn	71	19	29	48	140
Darryl Sydor	29	9	39	48	43
Todd Johnson	55	14	31	45	12
Ed Patterson	38	19	25	44	120
Craig Bonner	67	15	28	43	172
Lance Johnson	63	16	25	41	109
David Wilkie	71	12	28	40	153
Scott Niedermayer	35	7	32	39	61
Scott Loucks	49	8	14	22	121
Rod Stevens	57	8	13	21	30
Jarrett Bousquet	58	6	15	21	156
Steve Yule	61	7	10	17	257
Rob Lelacheur	27	6	8	14	90
Scott Ferguson	62	4	10	14	148
Darcy Tucker	26	3	10	13	42
Ryan Huska	44	4	5	9	33
Fred Hettle	16	1	8	9	54
Tyson Nash	33	1	6	7	62
Ryan Harrison	9	2	4	6	11
Jarret Zukiwsky	10	0	5	5	74
Michal Sup	14	0	4	4	27
Corey Hirsch (goalie)	48	0	4	4	16
Len Forshner	8	2	1	3	37
Chris Murray	33	1	1	2	218
Dale Masson (goalie)	29	0	2	2	6
Roland Ramoser	2	1	0	1	2
Dan Blasko	7	1	0	1	4
Mark Bell	1	0	0	0	0
Antti Boman	1	0	0	0	0

GOALTENDING

	Games	Min.	Goals	SO	Avg.
Corey Hirsch	48	2732	124(1)	5	2.72
Dale Masson	29	1645	101	1	3.68

LETHBRIDGE HURRICANES

SCORING

	Games	G	A	Pts.	Pen.
Kevin St. Jacques	71	65	75	140	159
Radek Sip	71	38	62	100	95
Rob Hartnell	57	41	49	90	174
Terry Hollinger	65	23	62	85	155
Brad Zavisha	59	44	40	84	160
Shane Peacock	67	35	45	80	217
Darcy Werenka	69	17	58	75	56
Brad Zimmer	69	27	28	55	73
Al Kinisky	56	9	24	33	121
Lance Burns	71	15	11	26	147
Domenic Pittis	65	6	17	23	48
Jason Widmer	40	2	19	21	181
Todd MacIsaac	61	6	14	20	145
Jamie Pushor	49	2	15	17	232
Jason Sorochan	30	8	7	15	95
Brantt Myhres	53	4	11	15	359

	Games	G	A	Pts.	Pen.
Cadrin Smart	62	0	12	12	64
Lee Sorochan	67	2	9	11	155
Darcy Austin (goalie)	59	0	5	5	23
Slade Stephenson	54	1	3	4	312
Jason Knight	29	2	1	3	79
Maurice Meagher	59	2	1	3	112
Travis Munday	18	1	0	1	19
Derek Jones	6	0	1	1	0
Jason McBain	13	0	1	1	12
David Trofimenkoff (goalie)	21	0	1	1	0
Blaine Fomradas	2	0	0	0	4
Duane Maruschak	7	0	0	0	4
Trevor Pennock	16	0	0	0	57

GOALTENDING

	Games	Min.	Goals	SO	Avg.
David Trofimenkoff	21	1080	67	0	3.72
Darcy Austin	59	3267	212(5)	0	3.89

MEDICINE HAT TIGERS

SCORING

	Games	G	A	Pts.	Pen.
Kevin Reihl	69	65	50	115	125
Rob Niedermayer	71	32	46	78	97
Clayton Norris	69	26	39	65	300
Stacy Roest	72	22	43	65	20
David Cooper	72	17	47	64	176
Olaf Kjenstad	70	24	32	56	102
Cam Danyluk	52	27	26	53	158
Evan Marble	70	8	45	53	100
Scott Townsend	72	16	30	46	43
Scott Lindsay	71	21	18	39	84
Dana Rieder	72	15	23	38	48
Lanny Watkins	65	14	20	34	53
Mike Rathje	67	11	23	34	109
Bryan McCabe	68	6	24	30	177
Jon Duval	69	4	26	30	171
Lorne Toews	65	14	11	25	199
Mike Vandenberghe	49	2	16	18	101
Ryan Petz	67	7	10	17	43
Darby Walker	28	3	1	4	64
Curtis Cardinal	18	2	2	4	17
Jeramie Heistad	19	0	3	3	52
Patrik Ondrlsik	3	0	1	1	2
Sonny Mignacca (goalie)	56	0	1	1	30
Glen McGillivray	2	0	0	0	10
Dean Intwert (goalie)	4	0	0	0	12
Mark Pethke (goalie)	5	0	0	0	0
Chris Osgood (goalie)	15	0	0	0	16

GOALTENDING

	Games	Min.	Goals	SO	Avg.
Chris Osgood	15	819	44	0	3.22
Sonny Mignacca	56	3207	189(4)	2	3.54
Dean Intwert	4	178	13(1)	0	4.38
Mark Pethke	5	158	13	0	4.94

MOOSE JAW WARRIORS

SCORING

	Games	G	A	Pts.	Pen.
Chris Schmidt	72	60	54	114	16
Kevin Smyth	71	30	55	85	114
Scott Allison	72	37	45	82	238
Dean Dorchak	45	26	37	63	38
Travis Thiessen	72	9	50	59	112
Kevin Master	72	11	40	51	94
Derek Kletzel	51	22	27	49	81
Marc Hussey	72	7	34	34	203
Russ West	71	15	16	31	180
Chris Brandt	61	12	17	29	42
Jeff Petruic	67	17	7	24	109
Jeff Budai	69	6	17	23	150

WHL

MAJOR JUNIOR LEAGUES

WHL

	Games	G	A	Pts.	Pen.
Fred Hettle	53	4	13	17	94
Jarret Zukiwsky	42	9	7	16	227
Todd Johnson	13	2	12	14	7
Kent Staniforth	64	2	8	10	338
Chris Armstrong	43	2	7	9	19
Jason Fitzsimmons (goalie)	60	0	8	8	99
David Jesiolowski	63	2	5	7	130
Travis Stevenson	61	1	3	4	72
Peter Cox	11	2	1	3	38
Kim Deck	18	2	1	3	28
Lonnie Bohonos	8	1	1	2	0
Bill Hooson	58	0	2	2	184
Shayne Sieker	1	0	1	1	2
Garfield Henderson	22	0	1	1	4
Scott Ducharmie	1	0	0	0	0
Matthew Desmarais	2	0	0	0	0
Rod Gorrill	2	0	0	0	0
Jody Lehman (goalie)	2	0	0	0	0
Sean Selmser	2	0	0	0	0
Ryan Smyth	2	0	0	0	0
Lee Jacques	2	0	0	0	0
Christian Twomey	4	0	0	0	5
Tyler Lovering	7	0	0	0	0
Ian Layton	17	0	0	0	23
Jason Carey (goalie)	22	0	0	0	31

GOALTENDING

	Games	Min.	Goals	SO	Avg.
Jason Fitzsimmons	60	3286	222(6)	0	4.05
Jason Carey	22	1021	82	0	4.82
Jody Lehman	2	66	6	0	5.45

PORTLAND WINTER HAWKS

SCORING

	Games	G	A	Pts.	Pen.
Steve Konowalchuk	64	51	53	104	95
Jiri Beranek	72	31	63	94	46
Chris Rowland	70	34	31	65	246
Adam Deadmarsh	68	30	30	60	111
Layne Roland	67	28	31	59	80
Colin Foley	71	20	39	59	96
Dennis Saharchuk	72	19	28	47	85
Brandon Smith	70	12	32	44	63
Chad Seibel	72	4	39	43	290
Brandon Coates	69	20	17	37	133
Jason McBain	54	9	23	32	95
Gordon Pell	27	15	15	30	66
Nick Vachon	25	9	19	28	46
Cale Hulse	70	4	18	22	250
John Badduke	67	6	13	19	515
Brad Zavisha	11	7	4	11	18
Nolan Pratt	22	2	9	11	13
Mike Williamson	69	2	9	11	171
Rick Mearns	42	4	5	9	56
Peter Cox	12	2	5	7	46
Shawn Stone	43	2	4	6	19
Dave Cammock	57	1	4	5	163
Joaquin Gage (goalie)	63	0	5	5	39
Kelly Harris	30	1	2	3	165
Ryan Van Steinburg	37	0	3	3	157
Shayne Sieker	7	1	1	2	22
Brantt Myhres	4	0	2	2	22
Jason Weimer	2	0	1	1	0
Scott Langkow (goalie)	1	0	0	0	0
Dean Whitney (goalie)	4	0	0	0	0
Adam Murray	12	0	0	0	38
Corey Jones (goalie)	14	0	0	0	4

GOALTENDING

	Games	Min.	Goals	SO	Avg.
Scott Langkow	1	33	2	0	3.64
Joaquin Gage	63	3635	269(6)	2	4.44
Corey Jones	14	594	52(1)	0	5.25
Dean Whitney	4	110	11(1)	0	6.00

PRINCE ALBERT RAIDERS

SCORING

	Games	G	A	Pts.	Pen.
Jeff Nelson	64	48	65	113	84
Donevan Hextall	71	33	71	104	105
Lee J. Leslie	72	52	48	100	70
Dan Kesa	62	46	51	97	201
Dean McAmmond	63	37	54	91	189
Curt Regnier	58	30	42	72	98
Jeff Gorman	71	23	31	54	79
Dave Neilson	66	25	23	48	304
Darren Van Impe	69	9	37	46	129
Troy Hjertaas	66	8	26	34	305
Jason Kwiatkowski	69	7	19	26	87
Barkley Swenson	61	11	14	25	110
Shane Zulyniak	67	1	19	20	173
Jason Renard	56	6	8	14	237
Ryan Pisiak	56	5	7	12	60
Darren Perkins	65	4	7	11	221
Jeff Lank	56	2	8	10	26
Nic Polychronopoulos	62	2	4	6	121
Merv Haney	47	1	4	5	21
Jamie Linden	4	2	1	3	8
Jason Klassen	55	1	2	3	2
Shane Toporowski	6	2	0	2	2
Travis Laycock (goalie)	58	0	2	2	4
Brian Kostur	2	1	0	1	2
Kendall Sidoruk (goalie)	1	0	0	0	0
Jay Fitzpatrick	2	0	0	0	0
Mike McGhan	2	0	0	0	2
Darren Wright	2	0	0	0	2
Denis Pederson	10	0	0	0	6
Stan Matwijiw (goalie)	19	0	0	0	0

GOALTENDING

	Games	Min.	Goals	SO	Avg.
Travis Laycock	58	3383	192(1)	0	3.41
Stan Matwijiw	19	955	63(1)	0	3.96
Kendall Sidoruk	1	21	4	0	11.43

REGINA PATS

SCORING

	Games	G	A	Pts.	Pen.
Frank Kovacs	69	46	45	91	274
Jeff Shantz	72	39	50	89	75
Lloyd Pelletier	67	46	42	88	71
Louis Dumont	66	32	47	79	62
Derek Eberle	72	14	45	59	114
Jason Smith	62	9	29	38	168
Garry Pearce	46	14	20	34	27
Brad Scott	69	12	21	33	155
Kerry Biette	52	15	13	28	88
Niklas Barklund	64	16	11	27	53
Chris Constant	19	11	16	27	45
Trevor Hannas	58	8	18	26	96
Nathan Dempsey	70	4	22	26	72
Heath Weenk	68	3	22	25	125
Gib Tucker	28	4	16	20	18
Jamie Hayden	72	4	16	20	119
A.J. Kelham	49	4	10	14	35
Terry Bendera	18	4	7	11	52
Ken Richardson	58	4	7	11	185
Rob McCaig	43	2	5	7	82
Kelly Harris	18	1	4	5	79
Niko Ovaska	20	0	5	5	32
Jeff Friesen	4	3	1	4	2
Josh Erdman	9	1	3	4	27
Jason Young	6	1	1	2	14
Mike Crespeigne	20	1	1	2	108
Greg Story	2	0	2	2	0
Tony Frenette	3	1	0	1	0
Brad Bagu	16	1	0	1	19
Jason Gibson	5	0	1	1	5
Barry Becker (goalie)	20	0	1	1	0
Mike Risdale (goalie)	61	0	1	1	4

	Games	G	A	Pts.	Pen.
Jason Clague (goalie)	1	0	0	0	0
Jason Morris	1	0	0	0	0
Vernon Beardy	1	0	0	0	0
Devin Grimeau	4	0	0	0	2
Russ Gronick	4	0	0	0	24
Craig Kinney	5	0	0	0	0
Darcy Jerome	6	0	0	0	21
Danny Pilling	8	0	0	0	2
Hal Christiansen	21	0	0	0	29

GOALTENDING

	Games	Min.	Goals	SO	Avg.
Jason Clague	1	60	2	0	2.00
Mike Risdale	61	3521	232(4)	1	3.95
Barry Becker	20	817	60	0	4.41

SASKATOON BLADES

SCORING

	Games	G	A	Pts.	Pen.
Ryan Fujita	72	38	44	82	103
Derek Tibbatts	72	34	40	74	31
Shane Calder	71	25	48	73	176
Glen Gulutzan	71	19	54	73	49
Mark Franks	63	34	24	58	39
David Struce	47	29	26	55	34
Jeff Buchanan	72	17	37	54	143
Richard Matvichuk	58	14	40	54	126
Shawn Yakimishyn	56	21	32	53	292
James Startup	71	13	35	48	70
Mark Wotton	64	11	25	36	92
Andy MacIntyre	55	22	13	35	66
Paul Buczkowski	45	9	16	25	37
Sean McFatridge	44	6	10	16	213
Mark Raiter	72	2	12	14	354
Chad Michalchuk	58	3	10	13	111
Chad Rusnak	29	3	6	9	16
Jason Becker	55	6	2	8	23
Bryce Goebel	71	1	7	8	42
Rhett Trombley	50	3	4	7	221
Terran Sanwith	18	2	5	7	53
Jason Knight	25	1	3	4	34
Trevor Robins (goalie)	50	0	4	4	61
Mike Carr	9	1	2	3	6
Rob Lelacheur	10	1	2	3	78
Jason Knox	4	0	3	3	4
David Hunchak	9	0	2	2	0
Norman Maracle (goalie)	29	0	2	2	4
Jason Northard	1	0	0	0	0
Chad Allan	1	0	0	0	2
Richard Gibbs	1	0	0	0	0
Andrew Reimer (goalie)	1	0	0	0	0
Trent Coghill	2	0	0	0	0
Rhett Warrener	2	0	0	0	0
Joey Chivers	3	0	0	0	2
Mark Goodkey	3	0	0	0	0

GOALTENDING

	Games	Min.	Goals	SO	Avg.
Andrew Reimer	1	60	3	0	3.00
Norman Maracle	29	1529	87(1)	1	3.41
Trevor Robins	50	2794	163(6)	0	3.50

SEATTLE THUNDERBIRDS

SCORING

	Games	G	A	Pts.	Pen.
Mike Kennedy	71	42	47	89	134
Darren McAusland	71	27	46	73	85
Blake Knox	63	26	35	61	280
Craig Chapman	70	24	33	57	184
Turner Stevenson	58	20	32	52	304
Jeff Sebastian	72	15	33	48	144
Duane Maruschak	62	20	23	43	41
Kurt Seher	55	15	23	38	103
Joel Dyck	59	9	25	34	185

	Games	G	A	Pts.	Pen.
Dody Wood	37	13	19	32	232
Jesse Wilson	38	11	19	30	32
George Zajankala	49	13	14	27	197
Chris Wells	64	13	8	21	80
Troy Hyatt	46	8	13	21	45
Eric Bouchard	69	8	13	21	75
Kimby Daniels	19	7	14	21	133
Jeff Jubenville	34	4	9	13	169
Brendan Witt	67	3	9	12	212
Andrew Kemper	68	2	9	11	90
Andy MacIntyre	12	6	2	8	18
Tyler Quiring	12	2	5	7	6
Al Kinisky	7	2	1	3	27
Brent Bilodeau	7	1	2	3	43
Erin Thornton	7	0	3	3	34
Ryan Brown	60	1	1	2	230
Shawn Dietrich (goalie)	15	0	2	2	12
Chad Rusnak	5	0	1	1	9
Glen Webster	6	0	1	1	76
Chris Osgood (goalie)	21	0	1	1	18
Paul Nicolls	28	0	1	1	25
Mike Power (goalie)	1	0	0	0	0
Jason Heuppleheuser	1	0	0	0	0
Milt Mastad	2	0	0	0	0
Kees Roodbol	2	0	0	0	0
Jeff Peddigrew	2	0	0	0	0
Rick Geisel (goalie)	4	0	0	0	0
Mike McKinlay	4	0	0	0	2
Rob Tallas (goalie)	14	0	0	0	2
Andrew Reimer (goalie)	27	0	0	0	18

GOALTENDING

	Games	Min.	Goals	SO	Avg.
Chris Osgood	21	1217	65(2)	1	3.20
Shawn Dietrich	15	788	49	0	3.73
Andrew Reimer	27	1428	89	0	3.74
Rob Tallas	14	708	52	0	4.41
Mike Power	1	70	7	0	6.00
Rick Geisel	4	189	20(1)	0	6.35

SPOKANE CHIEFS

SCORING

	Games	G	A	Pts.	Pen.
Paxton Schulte	70	42	42	84	222
Mike Jickling	69	30	44	74	92
Frank Evans	63	11	52	63	215
Hardy Sauter	66	13	48	61	81
Steve Junker	58	28	32	60	110
Ryan Duthie	67	23	37	60	119
Valerie Bure	53	27	22	49	78
Mark Szoke	62	20	22	42	335
Craig Reichert	68	13	20	33	86
Jared Bednar	62	7	17	24	200
Aaron Boh	55	3	19	22	209
Brian Purdy	24	5	14	19	14
Tyler Romanchuk	57	9	8	17	260
Jamie Linden	60	7	10	17	302
Randy Toye	60	5	12	17	70
Shane Maitland	26	4	8	12	139
Geoff Grandberg	69	2	10	12	70
Justin Hocking	71	4	6	10	309
Greg Gatto	35	3	7	10	138
Mike Gray	67	4	3	7	330
Danny Faassen	50	3	2	5	127
Brad Toporowski	47	1	4	5	69
Cam Danyluk	6	0	4	4	37
Bram Vanderkracht	13	3	0	3	25
Scott Bailey (goalie)	65	0	3	3	83
Craig Fletcher	2	0	0	0	0
Regan Simpson	2	0	0	0	2
Jeremy Stasiuk	2	0	0	0	0
Jason Padollan	2	0	0	0	2
Kurtis Boutet	4	0	0	0	0
Jeremy Warring (goalie)	14	0	0	0	4

GOALTENDING

	Games	Min.	Goals	SO	Avg.
Scott Bailey	65	3748	206(6)	1	3.30
Jeremy Warring	14	645	58	0	5.40

SWIFT CURRENT BRONCOS

SCORING

	Games	G	A	Pts.	Pen.
Andy Schneider	63	44	60	104	120
Jason Krywulak	72	43	59	102	70
Todd Holt	66	47	54	101	155
Tyler Wright	63	36	46	82	295
Brent Bilodeau	56	10	47	57	118
Ashley Buckberger	67	23	22	45	38
Trent McCleary	72	23	22	45	240
Dan Sherstenka	71	7	30	37	131
Chris Herperger	72	14	19	33	44
Rick Girard	45	14	17	31	6
Mark Stowe	48	12	17	29	32
Regan Mueller	22	7	13	20	0
Len MacAusland	70	3	12	15	155
John McMulkin	64	5	5	10	12
Jason Borvath	63	3	7	10	148
Keith McCambridge	72	1	4	5	94
Kevin Koopman (goalie)	60	0	5	5	30
Joel Dyck	5	1	3	4	4
Shane Hnidy	56	1	3	4	11
Mark McCoy	41	0	3	3	37
Robert Struch	18	2	0	2	9
Dody Wood	3	0	2	2	14
Matt Young	55	0	2	2	23
Chris Low	5	0	1	1	0
Darren Watson	2	0	0	0	7
Jason Watson	2	0	0	0	0
Blake Knox	4	0	0	0	34
Ryan MacNevin	4	0	0	0	2
Kurt Seher	5	0	0	0	25
Ryan McConnell	11	0	0	0	0
Bram Vanderkracht	16	0	0	0	64
Ken Zilka	23	0	0	0	19
Jarrod Daniel (goalie)	24	0	0	0	0
Jeremy Riehl	47	0	0	0	4

GOALTENDING

	Games	Min.	Goals	SO	Avg.
Kevin Koopman	60	3367	234(1)	1	4.17
Jarrod Daniel	24	1013	76(2)	1	4.50

TACOMA ROCKETS

SCORING

	Games	G	A	Pts.	Pen.
Jeff Whittle	66	42	45	87	98
Allen Egeland	72	35	39	74	135
Jamie Black	71	33	37	70	79
John Varga	72	25	34	59	93
Van Burgess	60	25	27	52	151
Kevin Malgunas	64	18	25	43	273
Laurie Billeck	65	14	29	43	168
Michal Sykora	61	13	23	36	66
Trevor Fraser	67	9	26	35	353
Scott Thomas	68	7	22	29	50
Tuomas Gronman	61	5	18	23	102
Mike Piersol	52	4	14	18	77
Ryan Strain	52	4	11	15	153
Toby Weishaar	53	8	6	14	89
Dave McMillen	72	4	9	13	399
Drew Schoneck	68	1	9	10	171
Peter Cox	40	6	2	8	119
Lasse Pirjeta	16	5	2	7	4
Cory Stock	44	3	4	7	38
Gary Audette	13	4	2	6	18
Jason Knox	19	1	4	5	38
Shane Maitland	18	3	0	3	114
Travis Kelln	10	1	2	3	21
Joey Young	46	2	0	2	66

	Games	G	A	Pts.	Pen.
Dennis Pinfold	33	1	1	2	50
Darryl Onofrychuk (goalie)	13	0	1	1	4
Kelly Thiessen (goalie)	25	0	1	1	0
Jeff Calvert (goalie)	46	0	1	1	2
Chad Vestergaard	1	0	0	0	0
Jason Young	3	0	0	0	0
Kris Webster	3	0	0	0	0
Kevin Borzell	3	0	0	0	2
Curtis Friesen	4	0	0	0	2
Tyler Romanchuk	4	0	0	0	2
Rhett Trombley	7	0	0	0	42

GOALTENDING

	Games	Min.	Goals	SO	Avg.
Kelly Thiessen	25	1444	97(3)	0	4.03
Jeff Calvert	46	2508	200(4)	1	4.78
Darryl Onofrychuk	13	438	42	0	5.75

TRI-CITY AMERICANS

SCORING

	Games	G	A	Pts.	Pen.
Terry Degner	72	58	81	139	83
Brian Sakic	72	45	83	128	55
Vladimir Uvjtex	53	41	61	102	114
Bill Lindsay	42	34	59	93	111
Cory Dosdall	69	37	43	80	343
Todd Klassen	69	23	42	65	60
Dean Tiltgen	69	29	34	63	43
Jason Smith	62	17	39	56	55
Todd Harris	58	7	27	34	113
Jamie Barnes	62	16	15	31	48
Darren Hastman	66	11	13	24	116
Adam Rettschlag	47	7	8	15	82
Mirsad Mujcin	65	5	10	15	300
Trevor Sherban	55	2	12	14	110
Chad Cabana	57	5	8	13	175
Dan O'Rourke	46	4	8	12	197
Steve O'Rourke	42	3	9	12	45
Mark Toljanich	65	2	9	11	62
Jason Bowen	19	5	3	8	135
Kory Mullin	49	2	5	7	82
Fran DeFrenza	11	3	1	4	8
Jodi Murphy	58	3	1	4	259
David Hebky	9	2	2	4	4
Jeff Fancy	14	1	2	3	58
Jeff Cej	20	1	2	3	2
Mark Goodkey	13	0	3	3	6
Todd Esselmont	7	0	2	2	4
Byron Penstock (goalie)	33	0	2	2	12
Mark Dawkins (goalie)	50	0	2	2	6
Jason Peters	3	0	1	1	2
Scott Adair	13	0	1	1	92
Damon Langkow	1	0	0	0	0
Lance Leslie (goalie)	3	0	0	0	0
Dennis Pinfold	4	0	0	0	2

GOALTENDING

	Games	Min.	Goals	SO	Avg.
Lance Leslie	3	151	10	0	3.97
Mark Dawkins	50	2573	211(3)	0	4.92
Byron Penstock	33	1644	151(1)	0	5.51

VICTORIA COUGARS

SCORING

	Games	G	A	Pts.	Pen.
Gerry St. Cyr	70	38	55	93	407
Scott Fukami	69	49	43	92	12
Ross Harris	70	25	29	54	53
David Hebky	50	14	26	40	28
Matt Smith	69	10	24	34	387
Travis Kelln	60	6	25	31	10
Mike Barrie	54	15	15	30	165
Shea Esselmont	72	12	18	30	100
Brent Thurston	42	8	20	28	240
Ryan Pellaers	71	13	10	23	50

	Games	G	A	Pts.	Pen.
Kane Chaloner	67	7	13	20	44
Steve Lingren	70	4	14	18	103
Fran DeFrenza	59	8	9	17	127
Randy Chadney	66	5	9	14	62
Darcy Mattersdorfer	66	4	6	10	24
Dwayne Newman	72	2	8	10	178
Todd Harris	12	1	8	9	55
Chris Catellier	66	0	6	6	153
Chris Hawes	40	4	1	5	349
Brad Bagu	10	0	5	5	37
Jeff Fancy	42	1	3	4	197
Craig Fletcher	25	2	2	4	24
Matt Recchi	15	1	3	4	28
Cam Bristow	13	1	1	2	40
Michel Michon	13	0	2	2	13
Steve Passmore (goalie)	71	0	2	2	92
Andrew Laming	5	1	0	1	6
Kevin Robertson	16	0	1	1	7
Byron Briske	1	0	0	0	0
Derek Jones	2	0	0	0	0
Mike Leclerc	2	0	0	0	0
Gary Fialkosky (goalie)	2	0	0	0	0
Bud Bowell	6	0	0	0	0
Dave Hamilton (goalie)	8	0	0	0	11

GOALTENDING

	Games	Min.	Goals	SO	Avg.
Gary Fialkosky	2	54	4	0	4.44
Steve Passmore	71	4228	347(7)	0	4.92
Dave Hamilton	8	108	14	0	7.78

PLAYERS WITH TWO OR MORE TEAMS

SCORING

	Games	G	A	Pts.	Pen.
Brad Bagu, Victoria	10	0	5	5	37
Brad Bagu, Regina	16	1	0	1	19
Totals	26	1	5	6	56
Brent Bilodeau, Seattle	7	1	2	3	43
Brent Bilodeau, Swift Current	56	10	47	57	118
Totals	63	11	49	60	161
Aaron Boh, Brandon	4	0	0	0	4
Aaron Boh, Spokane	55	3	19	22	209
Totals	59	3	19	22	213
Chris Constant, Brandon	34	5	21	26	78
Chris Constant, Regina	19	11	16	27	45
Totals	53	16	37	53	123
Peter Cox, Moose Jaw	11	2	1	3	38
Peter Cox, Portland	12	2	5	7	46
Peter Cox, Tacoma	40	6	2	8	119
Totals	63	10	8	18	203
Cam Danyluk, Spokane	6	0	4	4	37
Cam Danyluk, Brandon	5	3	0	3	16
Cam Danyluk, Medicine Hat	52	27	26	53	158
Totals	63	30	30	60	211
Fran DeFrenza, Tri-City	11	3	1	4	8
Fran DeFrenza, Victoria	59	8	9	17	127
Totals	70	11	10	21	135
Shawn Dietrich, Brandon (g)	14	0	0	0	4
Shawn Dietrich, Seattle (g)	15	0	2	2	12
Totals	29	0	2	2	16
Joel Dyck, Swift Current	5	1	3	4	4
Joel Dyck, Seattle	59	9	25	34	185
Totals	64	10	28	38	189
Jeff Fancy, Tri-City	14	1	2	3	58
Jeff Fancy, Victoria	42	1	3	4	197
Totals	56	2	5	7	255
Craig Fletcher, Spokane	2	0	0	0	0
Craig Fletcher, Victoria	25	2	2	4	24
Totals	27	2	2	4	24
Greg Gatto, Spokane	35	3	7	10	138
Greg Gatto, Brandon	17	5	5	10	75
Totals	52	8	12	20	213
Rick Geisel, Seattle (goalie)	4	0	0	0	2
Rick Geisel, Brandon (goalie)	18	0	0	0	6
Totals	22	0	0	0	8

	Games	G	A	Pts.	Pen.
Mark Goodkey, Tri-City	13	0	3	3	6
Mark Goodkey, Saskatoon	3	0	0	0	0
Totals	16	0	3	3	6
Kelly Harris, Portland	30	1	2	3	165
Kelly Harris, Regina	18	1	4	5	79
Totals	48	2	6	8	244
Todd Harris, Victoria	12	1	8	9	55
Todd Harris, Tri-City	58	7	27	34	113
Totals	70	8	35	43	168
David Hebky, Tri-City	9	2	2	4	4
David Hebky, Victoria	50	14	26	40	28
Totals	59	16	28	44	32
Fred Hettle, Kamloops	16	1	8	9	54
Fred Hettle, Moose Jaw	53	4	13	17	94
Totals	69	5	21	26	148
Dean Intwert, Brandon (goalie)	13	0	0	0	2
Dean Intwert, Medicine Hat (g)	4	0	0	0	12
Totals	17	0	0	0	14
Todd Johnson, Moose Jaw	13	2	12	14	7
Todd Johnson, Kamloops	55	14	31	45	12
Totals	68	16	43	59	19
Derek Jones, Lethbridge	6	0	1	1	0
Derek Jones, Victoria	2	0	0	0	0
Totals	8	0	1	1	0
Jeff Jubenville, Seattle	34	4	9	13	169
Jeff Jubenville, Brandon	31	4	4	8	96
Totals	65	8	13	21	265
Al Kinisky, Seattle	7	2	1	3	27
Al Kinisky, Lethbridge	56	9	24	33	121
Totals	63	11	25	36	148
Travis Kelln, Tacoma	10	1	2	3	21
Travis Kelln, Victoria	60	6	25	31	10
Totals	70	7	27	34	31
Jason Knight, Lethbridge	29	2	1	3	79
Jason Knight, Saskatoon	25	1	3	4	34
Totals	54	3	4	7	113
Blake Knox, Swift Current	4	0	0	0	34
Blake Knox, Seattle	63	26	35	61	280
Totals	67	26	35	61	314
Jason Knox, Saskatoon	4	0	3	3	4
Jason Knox, Tacoma	19	1	4	5	38
Totals	23	1	7	8	42
Rob Lelacheur, Saskatoon	10	1	2	3	78
Rob Lelacheur, Kamloops	27	6	8	14	90
Totals	37	7	10	17	168
Jamie Linden, Prince Albert	4	2	1	3	8
Jamie Linden, Spokane	60	7	10	17	302
Totals	64	9	11	20	310
Andy MacIntyre, Seattle	12	6	2	8	18
Andy MacIntyre, Saskatoon	55	22	13	35	66
Totals	67	28	15	43	84
Shane Maitland, Spokane	26	4	8	12	139
Shane Maitland, Tacoma	18	3	0	3	114
Totals	44	7	8	15	253
Duane Maruschak, Lethbridge	7	0	0	0	4
Duane Maruschak, Seattle	62	20	23	43	41
Totals	69	20	23	43	45
Jason McBain, Lethbridge	13	0	1	1	12
Jason McBain, Portland	54	9	23	32	95
Totals	67	9	24	33	107
Sean McFatridge, Saskatoon	44	6	10	16	213
Sean McFatridge, Brandon	22	2	3	5	104
Totals	66	8	13	21	317
Brantt Myhres, Portland	4	0	2	2	22
Brantt Myhres, Lethbridge	53	4	11	15	359
Totals	57	4	13	17	381
Chris Osgood, Medicine Hat (g)	15	0	0	0	16
Chris Osgood, Brandon (goalie)	16	0	1	1	6
Chris Osgood, Seattle (goalie)	21	0	1	1	18
Totals	52	0	2	2	40
Dennis Pinfold, Tri-City	4	0	0	0	2
Dennis Pinfold, Tacoma	33	1	1	2	50
Totals	37	1	1	2	52
Brian Purdy, Brandon	47	24	29	53	24
Brian Purdy, Spokane	24	5	14	19	14
Totals	71	29	43	72	38

	Games	G	A	Pts.	Pen.
Andrew Reimer, Saskatoon (g) .	1	0	0	0	0
Andrew Reimer, Seattle (g)	27	0	0	0	18
Andrew Reimer, Brandon (g)	20	0	0	0	6
Totals	48	0	0	0	24
Kevin Robertson, Brandon	1	0	0	0	0
Kevin Robertson, Victoria	16	0	1	1	7
Totals	17	0	1	1	7
Tyler Romanchuk, Tacoma	4	0	0	0	2
Tyler, Romanchuk, Spokane	57	9	8	17	260
Totals	61	9	8	17	262
Chad Rusnak, Saskatoon	29	3	6	9	16
Chad Rusnak, Seattle	5	0	1	1	9
Totals	34	3	7	10	25
Terran Sanwith, Brandon	41	6	14	20	145
Terran Sanwith, Saskatoon	18	2	5	7	53
Totals	59	8	19	27	198
Hardy Sauter, Brandon	6	1	1	2	7
Hardy Sauter, Spokane	66	13	48	61	81
Totals	72	14	49	63	88
Kurt Seher, Swift Current	5	0	0	0	25
Kurt Seher, Seattle	55	15	23	38	103
Totals	60	15	23	38	128
Shayne Sieker, Portland	7	1	1	2	22
Shayne Sieker, Moose Jaw	1	0	1	1	2
Totals	8	1	2	3	24
Jason Smith, Brandon	1	0	0	0	0
Jason Smith, Tri-City	62	17	39	56	55
Totals	63	17	39	56	55
Rhett Trombley, Tacoma	7	0	0	0	42
Rhett Trombley, Saskatoon	50	3	4	7	221
Totals	57	3	4	7	263
Mike Vandenberghe, Brandon	16	0	5	5	42
Mike Vandenberghe, M.H.	49	2	16	18	101
Totals	65	2	21	23	143
Bram Vanderkracht, Spokane	13	3	0	3	25
Bram Vanderkracht, S.C.	16	0	0	0	64
Totals	29	3	0	3	89

	Games	G	A	Pts.	Pen.
Glen Webster, Brandon	7	2	0	2	60
Glen Webster, Seattle	6	0	1	1	76
Totals	13	2	1	3	136
Jesse Wilson, Seattle	38	11	19	30	32
Jesse Wilson, Brandon	27	7	7	14	21
Totals	65	18	26	44	53
Dody Wood, Seattle	37	13	19	32	232
Dody Wood, Swift Current	3	0	2	2	14
Totals	40	13	21	34	246
Brad Zavisha, Portland	11	7	4	11	18
Brad Zavisha, Lethbridge	59	44	40	84	160
Totals	70	51	44	95	178
Jarret Zukiwsky, Kamloops	10	0	5	5	74
Jarret Zukiwsky, Moose Jaw	42	9	7	16	227
Totals	52	9	12	21	301

GOALTENDING

	Games	Min.	Goals	SO	Avg.
Shawn Dietrich, Bran.	14	681	59(2)	0	5.20
Shawn Dietrich, Sea...	15	788	49	0	3.73
Totals	29	1469	108	0	4.41
Rick Geisel, Seattle....	4	189	20(1)	0	6.35
Rick Geisel, Brandon ..	18	979	85(2)	0	5.21
Totals	22	1168	105	0	5.39
Dean Intwert, Bran....	13	638	45(2)	0	4.23
Dean Intwert, M.H.	4	178	13(1)	0	4.38
Totals	17	816	58	0	4.26
Chris Osgood, M.H. ...	15	819	44	0	3.22
Chris Osgood, Bran. ...	16	890	60	1	4.04
Chris Osgood, Seattle.	21	1217	65(2)	1	3.20
Totals	52	2926	169	2	3.47
Andrew Reimer, Sask.	1	60	3	0	3.00
Andrew Reimer, Sea...	27	1428	89	0	3.74
Andrew Reimer, Bran.	20	1136	92	1	4.86
Totals	48	2624	184	1	4.21

( )—Empty-net goals (do not count against a goaltender's average).

1992 PLAYOFFS

RESULTS

EAST DIVISION PRELIMINARY

Series "A"

	W	L	Pts.	GF	GA
Prince Albert	4	0	8	33	14
Moose Jaw	0	4	0	14	33

(Prince Albert won series, 4-0)

Series "B"

	W	L	Pts.	GF	GA
Swift Current	4	0	8	18	12
Medicine Hat	0	4	0	12	18

(Swift Current won series, 4-0)

Series "C"

	W	L	Pts.	GF	GA
Saskatoon	4	1	8	28	17
Lethbridge	1	4	2	17	28

(Saskatoon won series, 4-1)

WEST DIVISION PRELIMINARY

Series "D"

	W	L	Pts.	GF	GA
Kamloops	4	0	8	31	7
Tacoma	0	4	0	7	31

(Kamloops won series, 4-0)

Series "E"

	W	L	Pts.	GF	GA
Spokane	4	2	8	29	27
Portland	2	4	4	27	29

(Spokane won series, 4-2)

Series "F"

	W	L	Pts.	GF	GA
Seattle	4	1	8	21	15
Tri-City	1	4	2	15	21

(Seattle won series, 4-1)

EAST DIVISION SEMIFINALS

Series "G"

	W	L	Pts.	GF	GA
Saskatoon	3	1	6	12	9
Swift Current	1	3	2	9	12

(Saskatoon won series, 3-1)

WEST DIVISION SEMIFINALS

Series "H"

	W	L	Pts.	GF	GA
Seattle	3	1	6	16	15
Spokane	1	3	2	15	16

(Seattle won series, 3-1)

EAST DIVISION FINALS

Series "I"

	W	L	Pts.	GF	GA
Saskatoon	4	2	8	30	17
Prince Albert	2	4	4	17	30

(Saskatoon won series, 4-2)

WEST DIVISION FINALS

Series "J"

	W	L	Pts.	GF	GA
Kamloops	4	2	8	25	14
Seattle	2	4	4	14	25

(Kamloops won series, 4-2)

FINALS

Series "K"

	W	L	Pts.	GF	GA
Kamloops	4	3	8	28	19
Saskatoon	3	4	6	19	28

(Kamloops won series, 4-3)

INDIVIDUAL LEADERS

Goals: Ryan Fujita, Saskatoon (13)
Assists: Kevin Boyer, Kamloops (20)
Points: Kevin Boyer, Kamloops (29)
Penalty minutes: Brendan Witt, Seattle (84)
Goaltending average: Corey Hirsch, Kamloops (2.20)
Shutouts: Corey Hirsch, Kamloops (2)

TOP SCORERS

	Games	G	A	Pts.
Zac Boyer, Kamloops	17	9	20	29
Jeff Buchanan, Saskatoon	22	10	14	24
Dean McAmmond, Prince Albert	10	12	11	23
Scott Niedermayer, Kamloops	17	9	14	23
David Struch, Saskatoon	22	8	15	23
Ryan Fujita, Saskatoon	22	*13	9	22
Shayne Green, Kamloops	17	10	11	21
Jeff Nelson, Prince Albert	9	7	14	21
Craig Lyons, Kamloops	17	7	14	21
Mark Franks, Saskatoon	22	10	10	20

INDIVIDUAL STATISTICS

KAMLOOPS BLAZERS

(Winner of 1992 WHL playoffs)

SCORING

	Games	G	A	Pts.	Pen.
Zac Boyer	17	9	20	29	16
Scott Niedermayer	17	9	14	23	28
Shayne Green	17	10	11	21	32
Craig Lyons	17	7	14	21	10
Darryl Sydor	17	3	15	18	18
Mike Mathers	16	10	7	17	17
Jarrett Deuling	17	10	6	16	18
Todd Johnson	13	5	8	13	12
David Wilkie	16	6	5	11	19
Jeff Watchorn	17	4	5	9	19
Lance Johnson	15	5	3	8	10
Rod Stevens	15	2	2	4	0
Jarret Bousquet	16	0	4	4	25
Steve Yule	17	2	1	3	37
Lenn Forshener	10	1	2	3	30
Scott Loucks	15	1	2	3	21
Rob Lelacheur	13	0	3	3	29
Scott Ferguson	12	0	2	2	21
Ryan Huska	6	0	1	1	0
Darcy Tucker	9	0	1	1	16
Corey Hirsch (goalie)	16	0	1	1	2
Ed Patterson	1	0	0	0	0
Dale Masson (goalie)	2	0	0	0	0
Craig Bonner	3	0	0	0	8
Tyson Nash	4	0	0	0	0
Chris Murray	5	0	0	0	10

GOALTENDING

	Games	Min.	Goals	SO	Avg.
Corey Hirsch	16	954	35(1)	2	2.20
Dale Masson	2	70	4	0	3.43

LETHBRIDGE HURRICANES

(Lost East Division preliminaries to Saskatoon, 4-1)

SCORING

	Games	G	A	Pts.	Pen.
Shane Peacock	5	2	5	7	2
Radek Sip	5	2	3	5	4
Rob Hartnell	5	1	4	5	12
Brad Zavisha	5	3	1	4	18
Kevin St. Jacques	3	2	2	4	2
Jason Widmer	5	0	4	4	9
Darcy Werenka	5	2	1	3	0

	Games	G	A	Pts.	Pen.
Terry Hollinger	5	1	2	3	13
Brad Zimmer	5	2	0	2	10
Domenic Pittis	5	0	2	2	4
Lee Sorochan	5	0	2	2	6
Jason Sorochan	3	1	0	1	9
Lance Burns	4	1	0	1	5
Todd MacIsaac	5	0	1	1	18
Slade Stephenson	3	0	0	0	14
Maurice Meagher	3	0	0	0	4
Al Kinisky	4	0	0	0	0
Jamie Pushor	5	0	0	0	33
Cadrin Smart	5	0	0	0	0
Brantt Myhres	5	0	0	0	36
Darcy Austin (goalie)	5	0	0	0	0

GOALTENDING

	Games	Min.	Goals	SO	Avg.
Darcy Austin	5	303	28	0	5.54

MEDICINE HAT TIGERS

(Lost East Division preliminaries to Swift Current, 4-0)

SCORING

	Games	G	A	Pts.	Pen.
Rob Niedermayer	4	2	3	5	2
David Cooper	4	1	4	5	8
Kevin Riehl	4	2	2	4	4
Lanny Watkins	4	3	0	3	0
Stacy Roest	4	2	1	3	0
Evan Marble	4	0	3	3	12
Dana Rieder	4	2	0	2	7
Olaf Kjenstad	4	0	2	2	2
Mike Rathje	4	0	1	1	2
Mike Vandenberghe	4	0	1	1	13
Jon Duval	4	0	1	1	11
Scott Townsend	4	0	1	1	2
Scott Lindsay	4	0	1	1	6
Clayton Norris	2	0	0	0	9
Ryan Petz	3	0	0	0	0
Darby Walker	3	0	0	0	0
Sonny Mignacca (goalie)	4	0	0	0	0
Bryan McCabe	4	0	0	0	6
Cam Danyluk	4	0	0	0	6
Lorne Toews	4	0	0	0	10

GOALTENDING

	Games	Min.	Goals	SO	Avg.
Sonny Mignacca	4	240	17(1)	0	4.25

MOOSE JAW WARRIORS

(Lost East Division preliminaries to Prince Albert, 4-0)

SCORING

	Games	G	A	Pts.	Pen.
Dean Dorchak	4	3	3	6	2
Jeff Budai	4	2	2	4	2
Chris Schmidt	3	1	3	4	0
Kevin Smyth	4	1	3	4	6
Kevin Masters	4	2	1	3	2
Russ West	4	0	3	3	15
Scott Allison	3	1	1	2	25
Marc Hussey	4	1	1	2	0
Fred Hettle	4	1	1	2	0
Jarrett Zukiwsky	4	1	1	2	13
Derek Kletzel	2	0	2	2	0
Travist Thiessen	4	0	2	2	8
Jeff Petruic	4	1	0	1	0
Chris Brandt	4	0	1	1	2
Bill Hoosen	1	0	0	0	0
Curtis Brown	1	0	0	0	0
Sean Selmser	2	0	0	0	0
Jason Carey (goalie)	2	0	0	0	0
Jason Fitzsimmons (goalie)	4	0	0	0	0
Travis Stevenson	4	0	0	0	0
David Jesiolowski	4	0	0	0	7
Kent Staniforth	4	0	0	0	4
Chris Armstrong	4	0	0	0	0

GOALTENDING

	Games	Min.	Goals	SO	Avg.
Jason Carey	2	53	5	0	5.66
Jason Fitzsimmons	4	186	27(1)	0	8.71

PORTLAND WINTER HAWKS

(Lost West Division preliminaries to Spokane, 4-2)

SCORING

	Games	G	A	Pts.	Pen.
Steve Konowalchuk	6	3	6	9	12
Brandon Smith	6	3	5	8	4
Jiri Beranek	6	5	2	7	8
Adam Deadmarsh	6	3	3	6	13
Chris Rowland	6	2	4	6	28
Layne Roland	6	3	2	5	10
Gordon Pell	6	2	3	5	8
Colin Foley	6	1	4	5	8
Nolan Pratt	6	1	3	4	12
Nick Vachon	6	0	3	3	14
John Badduke	6	1	1	2	42
Chad Seibel	6	1	1	2	32
Mike Williamson	6	0	2	2	21
Dennis Saharchuk	6	0	2	2	11
Cale Hulse	6	0	2	2	27
Rick Mearns	6	1	0	1	0
Jason McBain	6	1	0	1	13
Brandon Coates	6	0	1	1	6
Joaquin Gage (goalie)	6	0	0	0	0

GOALTENDING

	Games	Min.	Goals	SO	Avg.
Joaquin Gage	6	366	28(1)	0	4.59

PRINCE ALBERT RAIDERS

(Lost East Division finals to Saskatoon, 4-2)

SCORING

	Games	G	A	Pts.	Pen.
Dean McAmmond	10	12	11	23	26
Jeff Nelson	9	7	14	21	18
Dan Kesa	10	9	10	19	27
Lee J. Leslie	10	6	6	12	12
Curt Regnier	10	1	9	10	2
Donevan Hextall	10	3	6	9	10
David Neilson	10	4	3	7	21
Darren Van Impe	8	1	5	6	10
Barkley Swenson	8	3	1	4	12

	Games	G	A	Pts.	Pen.
Jason Kwiatkowski	10	1	3	4	16
Shane Toporowski	7	2	1	3	6
Jeff Gorman	10	0	3	3	12
Merv Haney	9	1	1	2	2
Nick Polychronopoulos	9	0	2	2	16
Denis Pederson	7	0	1	1	13
Darren Perkins	10	0	1	1	25
Ryan Pisiak	1	0	0	0	0
Stan Matwijiw (goalie)	1	0	0	0	0
Jason Klassen	3	0	0	0	0
Jeff Lank	9	0	0	0	2
Travis Laycock (goalie)	10	0	0	0	0
Shane Zulyniak	10	0	0	0	8
Troy Hjertaas	10	0	0	0	28

GOALTENDING

	Games	Min.	Goals	SO	Avg.
Stan Matwijiw	1	20	1	0	3.00
Travis Laycock	10	580	43	0	4.45

SASKATOON BLADES

(Lost WHL finals to Kamloops, 4-3)

SCORING

	Games	G	A	Pts.	Pen.
Jeff Buchanan	22	10	14	24	39
David Struch	22	8	15	23	26
Ryan Fujita	22	13	9	22	21
Mark Franks	22	10	10	20	12
Derek Tibbatts	22	7	11	18	6
Shane Calder	22	5	13	18	50
Glen Gulutzan	18	3	14	17	16
Shawn Yakimishyn	22	6	8	14	60
James Startup	22	5	8	13	31
Andy MacIntyre	22	10	2	12	17
Richard Matvichuk	22	1	9	10	61
Mark Wotton	21	2	6	8	22
Mark Raiter	22	0	7	7	45
Chad Michalchuk	22	2	4	6	23
Trevor Robins (goalie)	9	0	3	3	10
Terran Sandwith	18	2	1	3	28
Jason Becker	22	2	1	3	0
Paul Buczkowski	4	2	0	2	0
Rhett Trombley	18	1	1	2	53
David Hunchak	1	0	0	0	0
Clarke Wilm	1	0	0	0	0
Jason Knight	10	0	0	0	17
Norm Maracle (goalie)	15	0	0	0	0
Bryce Goebel	18	0	0	0	5

GOALTENDING

	Games	Min.	Goals	SO	Avg.
Norm Maracle	15	860	37(1)	0	2.58
Trevor Robins	9	473	32(1)	0	4.06

SEATTLE THUNDERBIRDS

(Lost West Division finals to Kamloops, 4-2)

SCORING

	Games	G	A	Pts.	Pen.
Mike Kennedy	15	11	6	17	20
Kimbi Daniels	15	5	10	15	27
Kurt Seher	15	3	12	15	32
Turner Stevenson	15	9	3	12	55
Duane Maruschak	15	4	8	12	4
Darren McAusland	15	5	6	11	21
Blake Knox	15	4	7	11	57
Jeff Sebastian	15	3	7	10	40
Joel Dyck	15	4	5	9	28
George Zajankala	15	1	3	4	37
Criag Chapman	15	1	3	4	22
Tyler Quiring	12	0	3	3	16
Brendan Witt	15	1	1	2	84
Ryan Brown	14	0	2	2	38
Eric Bouchard	15	0	1	1	9
Chris Osgood (goalie)	15	0	1	1	26

	Games	G	A	Pts.	Pen.
Andrew Kemper	1	0	0	0	0
Mike McKinlay	3	0	0	0	0
Shawn Dietrich (goalie)	3	0	0	0	0
Brent Duncan	6	0	0	0	33
Chris Wells	11	0	0	0	15
Paul Nicolls	12	0	0	0	11
Troy Hyatt	15	0	0	0	11

GOALTENDING

	Games	Min.	Goals	SO	Avg.
Chris Osgood	15	904	51(1)	0	3.38
Shawn Dietrich	3	23	3	0	7.83

SPOKANE CHIEFS

(Lost West Division semifinals to Seattle, 3-1)

SCORING

	Games	G	A	Pts.	Pen.
Valeri Bure	10	11	6	17	10
Ryan Duthie	10	5	10	15	18
Mike Jickling	10	7	6	13	20
Steve Junker	10	6	7	13	18
Mark Szoko	10	4	7	11	19
Paxton Schulte	10	2	8	10	48
Hardy Sauter	10	1	8	9	17
Frank Evans	10	2	3	5	43
Jason Podollan	10	3	1	4	16
Jared Bednar	7	2	1	3	9
Justin Hocking	10	0	3	3	28
Aaron Boh	8	0	2	2	17
Brian Purdy	8	0	2	2	8
Geoff Grandberg	10	0	2	2	4
Scott Bailey (goalie)	10	0	2	2	4
Craig Reichert	4	1	0	1	4
Randy Toye	5	0	0	0	5
Danny Faasen	5	0	0	0	0
Mike Gray	6	0	0	0	11
Brad Toporowski	7	0	0	0	13
Tyler Romanchuk	10	0	0	0	41
Jamie Linden	10	0	0	0	69

GOALTENDING

	Games	Min.	Goals	SO	Avg.
Scott Bailey	10	605	43	0	4.26

SWIFT CURRENT BRONCOS

(Lost East Division semifinals to Saskatoon, 3-1)

SCORING

	Games	G	A	Pts.	Pen.
Andy Schneieder	8	4	9	13	8
Jason Krywulak	8	4	8	12	6
Todd Holt	8	4	5	9	10
Tyler Wright	8	2	5	7	16
Dan Sherstenka	8	2	5	7	6
Brent Bilodeau	8	2	3	5	11
Dody Wood	7	2	1	3	37
Ashley Buckberger	8	2	1	3	2
Trent McCleary	8	1	2	3	16
Rick Girard	8	2	0	2	2
Mark Stowe	8	1	1	2	8
Jason Horvath	8	0	2	2	13
Regan Mueller	8	1	0	1	0
Kevin Koopman (goalie)	8	0	1	1	2
Chris Herperger	8	0	1	1	9
Jarrod Daniel (goalie)	1	0	0	0	0
Shane Hnidy	4	0	0	0	0
John McMulkin	5	0	0	0	0
Len MacAusland	8	0	0	0	10
Keith McCambridge	8	0	0	0	2
Matt Young	8	0	0	0	0

GOALTENDING

	Games	Min.	Goals	SO	Avg.
Jarrod Daniel	1	0	0	0	0.00
Kevin Koopman	8	486	24	0	2.96

TACOMA ROCKETS

(Lost West Division preliminaries to Kamloops, 4-0)

SCORING

	Games	G	A	Pts.	Pen.
Kevin Malgunas	4	4	1	5	36
Van Burgess	4	1	3	4	4
Johnn Varga	4	1	2	3	0
Michal Sykora	4	0	2	2	2
Jamie Black	4	1	0	1	0
Tuomas Gronman	4	0	1	1	2
Laurie Billeck	4	0	1	1	18
Trevor Fraser	4	0	1	1	2
Allan Egeland	4	0	1	1	18
Dave McMillen	4	0	1	1	13
Joey Young	1	0	0	0	0
Dennis Pinfold	2	0	0	0	0
Kelly Thiessen (goalie)	2	0	0	0	0
Potor Cox	2	0	0	0	4
Shane Maitland	2	0	0	0	11
Jeff Calvert (goalie)	3	0	0	0	0
Cory Stock	3	0	0	0	4
Toby Weishaar	3	0	0	0	7
Ryan Strain	3	0	0	0	5
Scott Thomas	4	0	0	0	4
Mike Piersol	4	0	0	0	4
Drew Schoneck	4	0	0	0	11
Jeff Whittle	4	0	0	0	2

GOALTENDING

	Games	Min.	Goals	SO	Avg.
Jeff Calvert	3	152	19	0	7.50
Kelly Thiessen	2	88	12	0	8.18

TRI-CITY AMERICANS

(Lost West Division preliminaries to Seattle, 4-1)

SCORING

	Games	G	A	Pts.	Pen.
Brian Sakic	5	4	4	8	14
Terry Degner	5	3	3	6	6
Bill Lindsay	3	2	3	5	16
Jason Smith	5	0	4	4	4
Todd Harris	5	1	2	3	8
Dean Tiltgen	5	2	0	2	6
Trevor Sherban	5	1	1	2	32
Dan O'Rourke	5	0	2	2	26
Jamie Barnes	5	0	2	2	19
Kory Mullin	5	1	0	1	6
Mirsad Mujcin	5	1	0	1	11
Steve O'Rourke	2	0	1	1	2
Chad Cabana	4	0	1	1	21
Jason Bowen	5	0	1	1	42
Lance Leslie (goalie)	2	0	0	0	0
Darren Hastman	3	0	0	0	2
Mark Dawking (goalie)	4	0	0	0	0
Mark Toljanich	4	0	0	0	2
Adam Rettschlag	4	0	0	0	4
Todd Klassen	5	0	0	0	2
Cory Dosdall	5	0	0	0	28
Jodi Murphy	5	0	0	0	14

GOALTENDING

	Games	Min.	Goals	SO	Avg.
Mark Dawkins	4	245	12(1)	0	2.94
Lance Leslie	2	80	8	0	6.00

1991-92 AWARD WINNERS

ALL-STAR TEAMS

EAST DIVISION

First team	Pos.	Second team
Trevor Robins, Saskatoon	G	Sonny Mignacca, M. Hat
Richard Matvichuk, Sask.	D	Brent Bilodeau, Swift Cur.
David Cooper, M. Hat	D	Mike Rathje, Medicine Hat
Brad Zavisha, Lethbridge	LW	Donevan Hextall, P.A.
Kevin St. Jacques, Leth.	C	Jeff Nelson, Prince Albert
Chris Schmidt, Moose Jaw	RW	Frank Kovacs, Regina
		Clayton Norris, Med. Hat

WEST DIVISION

First team	Pos.	Second team
Corey Hirsch, Kamloops	G	Scott Bailey, Spokane
Darryl Sydor, Kamloops	D	Frank Evans, Spokane
Scott Niedermayer, Kam.	D	Todd Klassen, Tri-City
Vladimir Vujtek, Tri-City	LW	Billy Lindsay, Tri-City
Steve Konowalchuk, Port.	C	Terry Degner, Tri-City
Turner Stevenson, Seattle	LW	Mike Kennedy, Seattle

TROPHY WINNERS

Four Broncos Memorial Trophy: Steve Konowalchuk, Portland
Bob Clarke Trophy: Kevin St. Jacques, Lethbridge
Jim Piggott Memorial Trophy: Ashley Buckberger, Swift Current
Brad Hornung Trophy: Steve Junker, Spokane
Bill Hunter Trophy: Richard Matvichuk, Saskatoon
Del Wilson Trophy: Corey Hirsch, Kamloops
Player of the Year: Corey Hirsch, Kamloops
Dunc McCallum Memorial Trophy: Bryan Maxwell, Spokane
Scott Munro Memorial Trophy: Kamloops Blazers
Msgr. Athol Murray Memorial Trophy: Kamloops Blazers

ALL-TIME AWARD WINNERS

FOUR BRONCOS MEMORIAL TROPHY

(Most valuable player—selected by coaches)

Season	Player, Team
1966-67	Gerry Pinder, Saskatoon
1967-68	Jim Harrison, Estevan
1968-69	Bobby Clarke, Flin Flon
1969-70	Reggie Leach, Flin Flon
1970-71	Ed Dyck, Calgary
1971-72	John Davidson, Calgary
1972-73	Dennis Sobchuk, Regina
1973-74	Ron Chipperfield, Brandon
1974-75	Bryan Trottier, Lethbridge
1975-76	Bernie Federko, Saskatoon
1976-77	Barry Beck, New Westminster
1977-78	Ryan Walter, Seattle
1978-79	Perry Turnbull, Portland
1979-80	Doug Wickenheiser, Regina
1980-81	Steve Tsujiura, Medicine Hat
1981-82	Mike Vernon, Calgary
1982-83	Mike Vernon, Calgary
1983-84	Ray Ferraro, Brandon
1984-85	Cliff Ronning, New Westminster
1985-86	Emanuel Viveiros, Prince Albert (East Div.)
	Rob Brown, Kamloops (West Division)
1986-87	Joe Sakic, Swift Current (East Division)
	Rob Brown, Kamloops (West Division)
1987-88	Joe Sakic, Swift Current
1988-89	Stu Barnes, Tri-City
1989-90	Glen Goodall, Seattle
1990-91	Ray Whitney, Spokane
1991-92	Steve Konowalchuk, Portland

BOB CLARKE TROPHY

(Top scorer)

Season	Player, Team
1966-67	Gerry Pinder, Saskatoon
1967-68	Bobby Clarke, Flin Flon
1968-69	Bobby Clarke, Flin Flon
1969-70	Reggie Leach, Flin Flon
1970-71	Chuck Arnason, Flin Flon
1971-72	Tom Lysiak, Medicine Hat
1972-73	Tom Lysiak, Medicine Hat
1973-74	Ron Chipperfield, Brandon
1974-75	Mel Bridgman, Victoria
1975-76	Bernie Federko, Saskatoon
1976-77	Bill Derlago, Brandon
1977-78	Brian Propp, Brandon

Season	Player, Team
1978-79	Brian Propp, Brandon
1979-80	Doug Wickenheiser, Regina
1980-81	Brian Varga, Regina
1981-82	Jack Callander, Regina
1982-83	Dale Derkatch, Regina
1983-84	Ray Ferraro, Brandon
1984-85	Cliff Ronning, New Westminster
1985-86	Rob Brown, Kamloops
1986-87	Rob Brown, Kamloops
1987-88	Joe Sakic, Swift Current
	Theo Fleury, Moose Jaw
1988-89	Dennis Holland, Portland
1989-90	Len Barrie, Kamloops
1990-91	Ray Whitney, Spokane
1991-92	Kevin St. Jacques, Lethbridge

The award was originally known as the Bob Brownridge Memorial Trophy

JIM PIGGOTT MEMORIAL TROPHY

(Rookie of the year)

Season	Player, Team
1966-67	Ron Garwasiuk, Regina
1967-68	Ron Fairbrother, Saskatoon
1968-69	Ron Williams, Edmonton
1969-70	Gene Carr, Flin Flon
1970-71	Stan Weir, Medicine Hat
1971-72	Dennis Sobchuk, Regina
1972-73	Rick Blight, Brandon
1973-74	Cam Connor, Flin Flon
1974-75	Don Murdoch, Medicine Hat
1975-76	Steve Tambellini, Lethbridge
1976-77	Brian Propp, Brandon
1977-78	John Orgrodnick, New Westminster
	Keith Brown, Portland
1978-79	Kelly Kisio, Calgary
1979-80	Grant Fuhr, Victoria
1980-81	Dave Michayluk, Regina
1981-82	Dale Derkatch, Regina
1982-83	Dan Hodgson, Prince Albert
1983-84	Cliff Ronning, New Westminster
1984-85	Mark Mackay, Moose Jaw
1985-86	Neil Brady, Medicine Hat (East Division)
	Ron Shudra, Kamloops, (West Division)
	Dave Waldie, Portland (West Division)
1986-87	Joe Sakic, Swift Current (East Division)
	Dennis Holland, Portland (West Division)
1987-88	Stu Barnes, New Westminster

Season	Player, Team
1988-89	Wes Walz, Lethbridge
1989-90	Petr Nedved, Seattle
1990-91	Donevan Hextall, Prince Albert
1991-92	Ashley Buckberger, Swift Current

The award was originally known as the Stewart "Butch" Paul Memorial Trophy.

BRAD HORNUNG TROPHY

(Most sportsmanlike player)

Season	Player, Team
1966-67	Morris Stefaniw, Estevan
1967-68	Bernie Blanchette, Saskatoon
1968-69	Bob Liddington, Calgary
1969-70	Randy Rota, Calgary
1970-71	Lorne Henning, Estevan
1971-72	Ron Chipperfield, Brandon
1972-73	Ron Chipperfield, Brandon
1973-74	Mike Rogers, Calgary
1974-75	Danny Arndt, Saskatoon
1975-76	Blair Chapman, Saskatoon
1976-77	Steve Tambellini, Lethbridge
1977-78	Steve Tambellini, Lethbridge
1978-79	Errol Rausse, Seattle
1979-80	Steve Tsujiura, Medicine Hat
1980-81	Steve Tsujiura, Medicine Hat
1981-82	Mike Moller, Lethbridge
1982-83	Darren Boyko, Winnipeg
1983-84	Mark Lamb, Medicine Hat
1984-85	Cliff Ronning, New Westminster
1985-86	Randy Smith, Saskatoon (East Division)
	Ken Morrison, Kamloops (West Division)
1986-87	Len Nielsen, Regina (East Division)
	Dave Archibald, Portland (West Division)
1987-88	Craig Endean, Regina
1988-89	Blair Atcheynum, Moose Jaw
1989-90	Bryan Bosch, Lethbridge
1990-91	Pat Falloon, Spokane
1991-92	Steve Junker, Spokane

The award was originally known as the Frank Boucher Memorial Trophy for most gentlemanly player.

BILL HUNTER TROPHY

(Top defenseman)

Season	Player, Team
1966-67	Barry Gibbs, Estevan
1967-68	Gerry Hart, Flin Flon
1968-69	Dale Hoganson, Estevan
1969-70	Jim Hargreaves, Winnipeg
1970-71	Ron Jones, Edmonton
1971-72	Jim Watson, Calgary
1972-73	George Pesut, Saskatoon
1973-74	Pat Price, Saskatoon
1974-75	Rick LaPointe, Victoria
1975-76	Kevin McCarthy, Winnipeg
1976-77	Barry Beck, New Westminster
1977-78	Brad McCrimmon, Brandon
1978-79	Keith Brown, Portland
1979-80	David Babych, Portland
1980-81	Jim Benning, Portland
1981-82	Gary Nylund, Portland
1982-83	Gary Leeman, Regina
1983-84	Bob Rouse, Lethbridge
1984-85	Wendel Clark, Saskatoon
1985-86	Emanuel Viveiros, Prince Albert (East Division)
	Glen Wesley, Portland (West Division)
1986-87	Wayne McBean, Medicine Hat (East Division)
	Glen Wesley, Portland (West Division)
1987-88	Greg Hawgood, Kamloops
1988-89	Dan Lambert, Swift Current
1989-90	Kevin Haller, Regina
1990-91	Darryl Sydor, Kamloops
1991-92	Richard Matvichuk, Saskatoon

DEL WILSON TROPHY

(Top goaltender)

Season	Player, Team
1966-67	Ken Brown, Moose Jaw
1967-68	Chris Worthy, Flin Flon
1968-69	Ray Martyniuk, Flin Flon
1969-70	Ray Martyniuk, Flin Flon
1970-71	Ed Dyck, Calgary
1971-72	John Davidson, Calgary
1972-73	Ed Humphreys, Saskatoon
1973-74	Garth Malarchuk, Calgary
1974-75	Bill Oleschuk, Saskatoon
1975-76	Carey Walker, New Westminster
1976-77	Glen Hanlon, Brandon
1977-78	Bart Hunter, Portland
1978-79	Rick Knickle, Brandon
1979-80	Kevin Eastman, Victoria
1980-81	Grant Fuhr, Victoria
1981-82	Mike Vernon, Calgary
1982-83	Mike Vernon, Calgary
1983-84	Ken Wregget, Lethbridge
1984-85	Troy Gamble, Medicine Hat
1985-86	Mark Fitzpatrick, Medicine Hat
1986-87	Kenton Rein, Prince Albert (East Division)
	Dean Cook, Kamloops (West Division)
1987-88	Troy Gamble, Spokane
1988-89	Danny Lorenz, Seattle
1989-90	Trevor Kidd, Brandon
1990-91	Jamie McLennan, Lethbridge
1991-92	Corey Hirsch, Kamloops

PLAYER OF THE YEAR

(Selected by fans and media)

Season	Player, Team
1974-75	Ed Staniowski, Regina
1975-76	Bernie Federko, Saskatoon
1976-77	Kevin McCarthy, Winnipeg
1977-78	Ryan Walter, Seattle
1978-79	Brian Propp, Brandon
1979-80	Doug Wickenheiser, Regina
1980-81	Barry Pederson, Victoria
1981-82	Mike Vernon, Calgary
1982-83	Dean Evason, Kamloops
1983-84	Ray Ferraro, Brandon
1984-85	Dan Hodgson, Prince Albert
1985-86	Emanuel Viveiros, Prince Albert
1986-87	Rob Brown, Kamloops
1987-88	Joe Sakic, Swift Current
1988-89	Dennis Holland, Portland
1989-90	Wes Walz, Lethbridge
1990-91	Ray Whitney, Spokane
1991-92	Corey Hirsch, Kamloops

DUNC McCALLUM MEMORIAL TROPHY

(Coach of the year)

Season	Coach, Team
1968-69	Scotty Munro, Calgary
1969-70	Pat Ginnell, Flin Flon
1970-71	Pat Ginnell, Flin Flon
1971-72	Earl Ingarfield, Regina
1972-73	Pat Ginnell, Flin Flon
1973-74	Stan Dunn, Swift Current
1974-75	Pat Ginnell, Victoria
1975-76	Ernie McLean, New Westminster
1976-77	Dunc McCallum, Brandon
1977-78	Jack Shupe, Victoria
	Dave King, Billings
1978-79	Dunc McCallum, Brandon
1979-80	Doug Sauter, Calgary
1980-81	Ken Hodge, Portland
1981-82	Jack Sangster, Seattle
1982-83	Darryl Lubiniecki, Saskatoon
1983-84	Terry Simpson, Prince Albert
1984-85	Doug Sauter, Medicine Hat

Season	Coach, Team
1985-86	Terry Simpson, Prince Albert
1986-87	Ken Hitchcock, Kam. (W. Division)
	Graham James, S. Curr. (E. Div.)
1987-88	Marcel Comeau, Saskatoon

Season	Coach, Team
1988-89	Ron Kennedy, Medicine Hat
1989-90	Ken Hitchcock, Kamloops
1990-91	Tom Renney, Kamloops
1991-92	Bryan Maxwell, Spokane

ALL-TIME LEAGUE CHAMPIONS

REGULAR-SEASON CHAMPION

PLAYOFF CHAMPION

Season	Team	Team (Playoff)
1966-67	Edmonton Oil Kings	Moose Jaw Canucks
1967-68	Flin Flon Bombers	Estevan Bruins
1968-69	Flin Flon Bombers	Flin Flon Bombers
1969-70	Flin Flon Bombers	Flin Flon Bombers
1970-71	Edmonton Oil Kings	Edmonton Oil Kings
1971-72	Calgary Centennials	Edmonton Oil Kings
1972-73	Saskatoon Blades	Medicine Hat Tigers
1973-74	Regina Pats	Regina Pats
1974-75	Victoria Cougars	New Westminster Bruins
1975-76	New Westminster Bruins	New Westminster Bruins
1976-77	New Westminster Bruins	New Westminster Bruins
1977-78	Brandon Wheat Kings	New Westminster Bruins
1978-79	Brandon Wheat Kings	Brandon Wheat Kings
1979-80	Portland Winter Hawks	Regina Pats
1980-81	Victoria Cougars	Victoria Cougars
1981-82	Lethbridge Broncos	Portland Winter Hawks
1982-83	Saskatoon Blades	Lethbridge Broncos
1983-84	Kamloops Junior Oilers	Kamloops Junior Oilers
1984-85	Prince Albert Raiders	Prince Albert Raiders
1985-86	Medicine Hat Tigers	Kamloops Blazers
1986-87	Kamloops Blazers	Medicine Hat Tigers
1987-88	Saskatoon Blades	Medicine Hat Tigers
1988-89	Swift Current Broncos	Swift Current Broncos
1989-90	Kamloops Blazers	Kamloops Blazers
1990-91	Kamloops Blazers	Spokane Chiefs
1991-92	Kamloops Blazers	Kamloops Blazers

The WHL regular-season champion is awarded the Scott Munro Memorial Trophy and the playoff champion is awarded the Msgr. Athol Murray Memorial Trophy.

COLLEGE HOCKEY

1991-92 SEASON

NCAA TOURNAMENT

EAST REGIONAL
(Providence, R.I.)
Michigan State 4, Boston University 2
Wisconsin 4, New Hampshire 2
Michigan State 3, Maine 2
Wisconsin 5, St. Lawrence 2

WEST REGIONAL
(Detroit)
Lake Superior State 7, Alaska-Anchorage 3
Northern Michigan 8, Clarkson 4
Lake Superior State 8, Minnesota 3
Michigan 7, Northern Michigan 6

SEMIFINAL SERIES
(Albany, N.Y.)
Lake Superior State 4, Michigan State 2
Wisconsin 4, Michigan 2

CHAMPIONSHIP GAME
(Albany, N.Y.)
Lake Superior State 5, Wisconsin 3

ALL-TOURNAMENT TEAM

Player	Pos.	College
Darrin Madeley	G	Lake Superior State
Mark Astley	D	Lake Superior State
Barry Richter	D	Wisconsin
Paul Constantin	F	Lake Superior State
Brian Rolston	F	Lake Superior State
Jason Zent	F	Wisconsin

NCAA Most Valuable Player: Paul Constantin, Lake Superior St.

ALL-AMERICA TEAMS

	EAST		
First team	Pos.	Second team	
Parris Duffus, Cornell	G	Scott LaGrand, Boston Col.	
		Christian Soucy, Vermont	
Mike Brewer, Brown	D	Tom Dion, Boston U.	
Dan LaPerriere, St. Lawr.	D	Rob Gaudreau, Providence	
Scott Pellerin, Maine	F	Dominic Amodeo, N.H.	
Jean-Yves Roy, Maine	F	Dale Band, Colgate	
David Sacco, Boston U.	F	Mike Lappin, St. Lawrence	

	WEST		
First team	Pos.	Second team	
Darrin Madeley, L. Sup. St.	G	Duane Derksen, Wisconsin	
Mark Astley, L. Sup. St.	D	Chris Hynnes, Colorado Col.	
Joby Messier, Michigan St.	D	Doug Zmolek, Minnesota	
Dallas Drake, N. Michigan	F	Jim Hiller, N. Michigan	
Denny Felsner, Michigan	F	Greg Johnson, N. Dakota	
Dwayne Norris, Michigan St.	F	Larry Olimb, Minnesota	

HISTORY

TOURNAMENT CHAMPIONS

Year	Champion	Coach	Score	Runner-up	Most outstanding player
1948	Michigan	Vic Heyliger	8-4	Dartmouth	Joe Riley, F, Dartmouth
1949	Boston College	John Kelley	4-3	Dartmouth	Dick Desmond, G, Dartmouth
1950	Colorado College	Cheddy Thompson	13-4	Boston University	Ralph Bevins, G, Boston University
1951	Michigan	Vic Heyliger	7-1	Brown	Ed Whiston, G, Brown
1952	Michigan	Vic Heyliger	4-1	Colorado College	Kenneth Kinsley, G, Colorado College
1953	Michigan	Vic Heyliger	7-3	Minnesota	John Matchefts, F, Michigan
1954	Rensselaer	Ned Harkness	5-4*	Minnesota	Abbie Moore, F, Rensselaer
1955	Michigan	Vic Heyliger	5-3	Colorado College	Philip Hilton, D, Colorado College
1956	Michigan	Vic Heyliger	7-5	Michigan Tech	Lorne Howes, G, Michigan
1957	Colorado College	Thomas Bedecki	13-6	Michigan	Bob McCusker, F, Colorado College
1958	Denver	Murray Armstrong	6-2	North Dakota	Murray Massier, F, Denver
1959	North Dakota	Bob May	4-3*	Michigan State	Reg Morelli, F, North Dakota
1960	Denver	Murray Armstrong	5-3	Michigan Tech	Bob Marquis, F, Boston University
					Barry Urbanski, G, Boston University
					Louis Angotti, F, Michigan Tech
1961	Denver	Murray Armstrong	12-2	St. Lawrence	Bill Masterton, F, Denver
1962	Michigan Tech	John MacInnes	7-1	Clarkson	Louis Angotti, F, Michigan Tech
1963	North Dakota	Barney Thorndycraft	6-5	Denver	Al McLean, F, North Dakota
1964	Michigan	Allen Renfrew	6-3	Denver	Bob Gray, G, Michigan
1965	Michigan Tech	John MacInnes	8-2	Boston College	Gary Milroy, F, Michigan Tech
1966	Michigan State	Amo Bessone	6-1	Clarkson	Gaye Cooley, G, Michigan State
1967	Cornell	Ned Harkness	4-1	Boston University	Walt Stanowski, D, Cornell
1968	Denver	Murray Armstrong	4-0	North Dakota	Gerry Powers, G, Denver
1969	Denver	Murray Armstrong	4-3	Cornell	Keith Magnuson, D, Denver
1970	Cornell	Ned Harkness	6-4	Clarkson	Daniel Lodboa, D, Cornell
1971	Boston University	Jack Kelley	4-2	Minnesota	Dan Brady, G, Boston University
1972	Boston University	Jack Kelley	4-0	Cornell	Tim Regan, G, Boston University
1973	Wisconsin	Bob Johnson	4-2	Vacated	Dean Talafous, F, Wisconsin

Year	Champion	Coach	Score	Runner-up	Most outstanding player
1974	Minnesota	Herb Brooks	4-2	Michigan Tech	Brad Shelstad, G, Minnesota
1975	Michigan Tech	John MacInnes	6-1	Minnesota	Jim Warden, G, Michigan Tech
1976	Minnesota	Herb Brooks	6-4	Michigan Tech	Tom Vanelli, F, Minnesota
1977	Wisconsin	Bob Johnson	6-5*	Michigan	Julian Baretta, G, Wisconsin
1978	Boston University	Jack Parker	5-3	Boston College	Jack O'Callahan, D, Boston University
1979	Minnesota	Herb Brooks	4-3	North Dakota	Steve Janaszak, G, Minnesota
1980	North Dakota	John Gasparini	5-2	Northern Michigan	Doug Smail, F, North Dakota
1981	Wisconsin	Bob Johnson	6-3	Minnesota	Marc Behrend, G, Wisconsin
1982	North Dakota	John Gasparini	5-2	Wisconsin	Phil Sykes, F, North Dakota
1983	Wisconsin	Jeff Sauer	6-2	Harvard	Marc Behrend, G, Wisconsin
1984	Bowling Green State	Jerry York	5-4*	Minnesota-Duluth	Gary Kruzich, G, Bowling Green State
1985	Rensselaer	Mike Addesa	2-1	Providence	Chris Terreri, G, Providence
1986	Michigan State	Ron Mason	6-5	Harvard	Mike Donnelly, F, Michigan State
1987	North Dakota	John Gasparini	5-3	Michigan State	Tony Hrkac, F, North Dakota
1988	Lake Superior State	Frank Anzalone	4-3*	St. Lawrence	Bruce Hoffort, G, Lake Superior State
1989	Harvard	Bill Cleary	4-3*	Minnesota	Ted Donato, F, Harvard
1990	Wisconsin	Jeff Sauer	7-3	Colgate	Chris Tancill, F, Wisconsin
1991	Northern Michigan	Rick Comley	8-7*	Boston University	Scott Beattie, F, Northern Michigan
1992	Lake Superior State	Jeff Jackson	5-3	Wisconsin	Paul Constantin, F, Lake Superior State

*Overtime.

ALL-TIME TOURNAMENT RECORDS

	Visits	W	L	GF	GA	Pct.	Finished 1st	Finished 2nd
Colgate	1	3	1	10	11	.750	0	1
Michigan	15	24	10	203	125	.706	7	2
‡Wisconsin	13	26	11	158	112	.703	5	2
North Dakota	13	22	11	132	102	.667	5	3
Denver	11	17	9	121	73	.654	5	2
#Lake Superior State	6	12	8	93	68	.600	2	0
*Northeastern	2	3	2	25	24	.600	0	0
Michigan Tech	10	13	9	118	85	.591	3	4
†Michigan State	13	22	16	162	140	.579	2	2
#Rensselaer Polytechnic Institute	6	8	6	52	50	.567	2	0
Northern Michigan	5	7	6	61	59	.538	1	1
Minnesota	17	22	19	224	198	.537	3	6
Boston University	18	23	23	196	199	.500	3	3
Maine	5	9	9	74	77	.500	0	0
Merrimack	1	2	2	14	16	.500	0	0
Yale	1	1	1	7	5	.500	0	0
Cornell	9	9	10	66	71	.474	2	2
Providence	6	9	11	71	73	.450	0	1
Clarkson	11	11	14	83	109	.444	0	3
Dartmouth	5	4	5	38	37	.444	0	0
Minnesota-Duluth	3	4	5	33	34	.444	0	1
*Bowling Green State	9	8	12	66	88	.400	1	0
Colorado College	9	6	10	76	84	.375	2	2
†Harvard	14	13	22	132	159	.371	1	2
Brown	3	2	4	28	38	.333	0	1
Boston College	18	13	27	141	105	.325	1	2
Alaska-Anchorage	3	2	5	22	39	.286	0	0
St. Lawrence	12	5	21	76	123	.192	0	2
New Hampshire	5	2	9	37	60	.182	0	0
‡Lowell	1	0	1	5	11	.000	0	0
St. Cloud State	1	0	2	5	10	.000	0	0
Vermont	1	0	2	2	10	.000	0	0
Western Michigan	1	0	2	4	11	.000	0	0

(Denver also participated in 1973 tournament but its record was voided by the NCAA in 1977 upon discovery of violations by the University. The team had finished second in '73.)
*Bowling Green State and Northeastern played to a 2-2 tie in 1981-82.
†Harvard and Michigan State played to a 3-3 tie in 1982-83.
#Lake Superior State and RPI played to a 3-3 tie in 1984-85.
‡Wisconsin and Lowell played to a 4-4 tie in 1987-88.
Hobey Baker Memorial Trophy (Top college hockey player in U.S.): Scott Pellerin, Maine.

HOBEY BAKER AWARD WINNERS

(Top college hockey player in United States)

Year	Player, College
1981	Neal Broten, Minnesota
1982	George McPhee, Bowling Green St.
1983	Mark Fusco, Harvard
1984	Tom Kurvers, Minnesota-Duluth
1985	Bill Watson, Minnesota-Duluth
1986	Scott Fusco, Harvard
1987	Tony Hrkac, North Dakota
1988	Robb Stauber, Minnesota
1989	Lane MacDonald, Harvard
1990	Kip Miller, Michigan State
1991	David Emma, Boston College
1992	Scott Pellerin, Maine

CENTRAL COLLEGIATE HOCKEY ASSOCIATION

1991-92 SEASON

FINAL STANDINGS

	W	L	T	GF	GA	Pct.
Michigan (32-9-3)..........	22	7	3	150	104	.734
Lake Superior St. (30-9-4)	20	8	4	141	78	.688
Michigan State (25-11-8)	18	7	7	149	105	.672
Western Mich. (16-14-6) .	14	12	6	119	114	.531
Miami of Ohio (17-17-6)..	12	14	6	124	145	.469
Ferris State (13-18-7)....	11	15	6	102	127	.438
Ill.-Chicago (10-20-6)	8	18	6	101	132	.344
Ohio State (12-21-5)	8	19	5	134	182	.328
Bowling Green (8-21-5) ..	7	20	5	123	156	.297

Overall record in parentheses.

PLAYOFF RESULTS

QUARTERFINALS

Michigan 4, Ohio State 2
Michigan 9, Ohio State 4
(Michigan won series, 2-0)

Michigan State 5, Ferris State 2
Michigan State 4, Ferris State 1
(Michigan State won series, 2-0)

Lake Superior State 3, Illinois-Chicago 1
Lake Superior State 9, Illinois-Chicago 2
(Lake Superior State won series, 2-0)

Miami of Ohio 3, Western Michigan 1
Miami of Ohio 4, Western Michigan 3 (OT)
(Miami of Ohio won series, 2-0)

SEMIFINALS

Lake Superior State 5, Michigan State 3
Michigan 6, Miami of Ohio 2

CONSOLATION GAME

Michigan State 8, Miami 5

CHAMPIONSHIP GAME

Lake Superior State 3, Michigan 1

ALL-STAR TEAMS

First team	Pos.	Second team
Darrin Madeley, L.S.S.	G	Jon Hillebrandt, Ill.-Chi.
Mark Astley, L.S.S.	D	Joe Cook, Miami of Ohio
Joby Messier, Michigan St.	D	Steve Barnes, L.S.S.
Denny Felsner, Michigan	F	Sandy Moger, L.S.S.
Dwayne Norris, Mich. St.	F	Peter Holmes, Bowling Green
Keith Jones, W. Michigan	F	Martin Jiranek, B'ling Green

AWARD WINNERS

Player of the year: Dwayne Norris, Michigan State
Rookie of the year: Brian Loney, Ohio State
Coach of the year: George Gwozdecky, Miami of Ohio
Leading scorer: Denny Felsner, Michigan
Playoff MVP: Darrin Madeley, Lake Superior State

INDIVIDUAL STATISTICS

BOWLING GREEN STATE

SCORING

	Pos.	Class	Games	G	A	Pts.	Pen.
Peter Holmes..........	F	Sr.	34	26	34	60	38
Martin Jiranek	F	Sr.	34	25	28	53	46
Brett Harkins	F	Jr.	34	8	39	47	32
Dan Bylsma	F	Sr.	34	11	14	25	24
Brian Holzinger	F	Fr.	30	14	8	22	36
Jim Solly	F	Sr.	34	10	11	21	45
Jeff Wells	D	So.	31	5	13	18	20
Brandon Carper	D	Fr.	34	2	16	18	44
Sean Pronger	F	Fr.	34	9	7	16	28
Todd Reirden	D	So.	33	8	7	15	34
Llew Ncwana	F	Sr.	34	5	10	15	36
Aris Brimanis	F/D	So.	32	2	9	11	38
Rick Mullins	F	Jr.	25	3	3	6	10
Otis Plageman	D	Sr.	26	1	5	6	22
Ty Eigner	F	Jr.	33	2	2	4	8
Glen Mears............	D	So.	32	1	2	3	38
Greg de Vries	D	Fr.	24	0	3	3	20
Paul Basic.............	F	Jr.	26	1	1	2	6
Tom Glantz............	F	Fr.	14	0	2	2	0
Angelo Libertucci ..	G	Jr.	18	0	2	2	6
Ken Klee	D	Jr.	10	0	1	1	14
Will Clarke	G	Fr.	14	0	1	1	0
Nathan Cressman..	G	Fr.	5	0	0	0	0
Rick Lacroix..........	F	So.	5	0	0	0	2
Keith Redmond	F	So.	8	0	0	0	14

GOALTENDING

	Games	W	L	T	Min.	GA	Avg.
Will Clarke	14	4	9	1	797	50	3.76
Angelo Libertucci	18	3	8	4	1002	81	4.85
Nathan Cressman	5	1	4	0	269	32	7.14

FERRIS STATE

SCORING

	Pos.	Class	Games	G	A	Pts.	Pen.
Tim Christian	F	Fr.	37	14	15	29	34
Norm Krumpschmid ..	F	Sr.	37	11	18	29	26
John Gruden	D	So.	37	9	14	23	24
Kelly Sorensen.......	F	Sr.	38	7	14	21	59
Daniel Chaput	D	Jr.	34	5	16	21	56
Jeff Jestadt...........	F	Jr.	34	12	7	19	21
Tom O'Rourke	F	Sr.	37	10	9	19	70
Aaron Asp	F	Jr.	33	9	10	19	14
Dave Karpa	D	So.	34	7	12	19	124
Gary Kitching.........	F	Fr.	36	7	9	16	52
Doug Smith	F	So.	20	4	7	11	22
Daryl Filipek	D	Jr.	31	4	6	10	28
John Duff	F	Fr.	37	3	7	10	32
Kevin Moore	F	Jr.	29	2	8	10	16
Robb McIntyre	F	Fr.	32	4	3	7	48
Mike Jorgensen	F	Sr.	14	3	4	7	6
Brad Burnham	F	Fr.	26	1	6	7	12
Colin Dodunski.......	D	Fr.	36	2	3	5	52
Mike May	F	Jr.	20	1	4	5	20
Kevin Doherty	D	Fr.	10	2	2	4	12
Mike Kolenda	D	Fr.	35	1	2	3	46
Luke Harvey	F	Fr.	16	1	1	2	8
Pat Mazzoli	G	So.	18	0	1	1	0
Rod Grandfield	F	Sr.	15	0	0	0	2
Craig Lisko............	G	So.	26	0	0	0	0

GOALTENDING

	Games	W	L	T	Min.	GA	Avg.
Craig Lisko.............	26	8	11	4	1374	73	3.19
Pat Mazzoli	18	5	7	3	939	71	4.54

ILLINOIS-CHICAGO

SCORING

	Pos.	Class	Games	G	A	Pts.	Pen.
Chris MacDonald	F	Fr.	36	11	27	38	58
Mark Zdan	F	Fr.	36	19	17	36	48
Rick Judson	F	Sr.	36	17	19	36	26
Derek Knorr	F	Fr.	35	12	16	28	86
Chris Watson	F	So.	32	6	14	20	32
Shannon Finn	D	Fr.	36	6	14	20	80
Brad Smiley	F	Sr.	27	9	8	17	14
Link Bessert	F	Jr.	33	9	5	14	52
Jim Maher	D	Sr.	34	5	9	14	52
Eric Schneider	D	Sr.	36	5	7	12	40
Jeff Blum	D	Fr.	35	3	9	12	65
Mike Dennis	D	So.	35	3	9	12	52
Randy Zulinick	F	Sr.	29	5	5	10	16
Mike Real	F	Jr.	33	3	6	9	24
Mark Ottenbreit	F	Jr.	19	2	5	7	24
Jim Richardson	F	Fr.	29	2	5	7	4
Erik Magsamen	F	Sr.	26	1	5	6	10
Bob Gohde	D	Fr.	29	1	4	5	18
Cory Hextall	F	Jr.	28	2	2	4	18
Justin O'Connor	F	Fr.	12	1	2	3	14
Jon Hillebrandt	G	Fr.	31	0	3	3	0
Troy Florell	F	Jr.	8	1	1	2	24
Rob Mottau	D	Fr.	23	0	1	1	22
Gary Mangino	G	Sr.	1	0	0	0	0
Jeff Featherstone	G	So.	4	0	0	0	0
Damian Holland	G	Sr.	7	0	0	0	2

GOALTENDING

	Games	W	L	T	Min.	GA	Avg.
Jeff Featherstone	4	1	0	1	125	5	2.39
Jon Hillebrandt	31	7	19	4	1754	121	4.14
Damian Holland	7	2	1	1	285	22	4.63
Gary Mangino	1	0	0	0	24	2	4.90

LAKE SUPERIOR STATE

SCORING

	Pos.	Class	Games	G	A	Pts.	Pen.
Paul Constantin	F	Sr.	43	21	31	52	48
Sandy Moger	F	Sr.	42	26	25	51	111
Mark Astley	D	Sr.	43	12	37	49	65
Vincent Faucher	F	Sr.	42	23	25	48	88
Brian Rolston	F	Fr.	41	18	28	46	16
Clayton Beddoes	F	So.	42	16	28	44	26
Steve Barnes	D	So.	43	3	28	31	37
Wayne Strachan	F	Fr.	42	12	18	30	35
John Hendry	F	Jr.	43	13	13	26	59
Dean Hulett	F	Jr.	37	10	15	25	66
Michael Smith	D	Jr.	43	8	17	25	34
Jay Ness	F	So.	42	9	10	19	20
Mike Morin	F	Fr.	37	10	5	15	26
Kurt Miller	F	So.	15	6	7	13	32
Rob Valicevic	F	Fr.	36	8	4	12	12
Tim Hanley	D	Fr.	38	3	8	11	14
Mike Bachusz	F	Jr.	37	2	5	7	12
Jim Peters	D	So.	34	2	4	6	55
Darren Wetherill	D	So.	31	1	5	6	52
Darrin Madeley	G	Jr.	38	0	4	4	4
Dan Angelelli	F	Fr.	23	0	3	3	34
Jason Welch	F	Fr.	2	0	1	1	4
Blaine Lacher	G	Fr.	10	0	1	1	0
Brian Lukowski	G	Jr.	1	0	0	0	0
Brad Willner	D	Fr.	16	0	0	0	8

GOALTENDING

	Games	W	L	T	Min.	GA	Avg.
Darrin Madeley	38	25	6	4	2144	74	2.07
Blaine Lacher	10	5	3	0	413	23	3.34
Brian Lukowski	1	0	0	0	30	2	4.00

MIAMI OF OHIO

SCORING

	Pos.	Class	Games	G	A	Pts.	Pen.
Ken House	F	Sr.	40	27	23	50	22
Joe Cook	D	Jr.	38	15	26	41	58
Brian Savage	F	So.	40	24	16	40	43
Enrico Blasi	F	So.	40	15	22	37	18
Chris Bergeron	F	Jr.	40	13	23	36	22
Andrew Miller	F	Fr.	40	9	16	25	32
Bobby Marshall	D	So.	40	5	20	25	48
Marc Boxer	F	Fr.	32	4	18	22	40
Matt Oates	F	Fr.	40	8	13	21	42
Jason Mallon	F	Fr.	40	6	13	19	74
Brendan Curley	F	Jr.	33	9	9	18	48
Trent Eigner	D	So.	39	7	11	18	43
Dan Carter	F	Fr.	36	5	12	17	56
Terry Ouimet	F	Jr.	29	9	6	15	4
Dan Daikawa	D	Fr.	40	1	6	7	36
Joey Saban	F	Jr.	18	4	2	6	6
Rob Fischer	D	Sr.	39	0	6	6	54
Stephen Rohr	F	So.	21	1	3	4	26
Steve Wilson	D	Sr.	39	1	3	4	61
Derek Block	F	Fr.	10	2	1	3	0
Jason Crane	F	Fr.	5	0	2	2	8
Shawn Penn	F	Fr.	7	0	0	0	4
Rene Vonlanthen	F	So.	13	0	0	0	20
R. Shulmistra	G	So.	19	0	0	0	2
Mark Michaud	G	Sr.	31	0	0	0	4

GOALTENDING

	Games	W	L	T	Min.	GA	Avg.
Mark Michaud	31	14	12	4	1577	112	4.26
Richard Shulmistra	19	3	5	2	850	67	4.73

MICHIGAN

SCORING

	Pos.	Class	Games	G	A	Pts.	Pen.
Denny Felsner	F	Sr.	44	42	52	94	48
Brian Wiseman	F	So.	44	27	44	71	76
David Oliver	F	So.	44	31	27	58	32
David Roberts	F	Jr.	44	16	42	58	48
Ted Kramer	F	Sr.	44	17	14	31	52
Patrick Neaton	D	Jr.	43	10	20	30	62
Mark Ouimet	F	Jr.	40	10	19	29	30
Cam Stewart	F	So.	44	13	15	28	106
Mike Helber	F	Sr.	43	8	13	21	26
Aaron Ward	D	So.	42	7	12	19	64
Chris Tamer	D	Jr.	43	4	15	19	125
Mike Stone	F	So.	43	8	10	18	16
Dan Stiver	F	Jr.	41	8	8	16	8
Mike Knuble	F	Fr.	43	7	8	15	48
Tim Hogan	D	Fr.	34	2	8	10	34
David Harlock	D	Jr.	44	1	6	7	80
Doug Evans	D	Sr.	38	2	3	5	32
Rick Willis	F	Fr.	32	1	4	5	42
Al Sinclair	D	Fr.	22	0	4	4	30
Ron Sacka	F	Fr.	15	1	1	2	16
Steve Shields	G	So.	37	0	2	2	18
Chris Gordon	G	So.	14	0	1	1	0
Anton Fiodorov	F	Fr.	1	0	0	0	0
Al Loges	G	Fr.	1	0	0	0	0
V. Nedomansky	F	Sr.	1	0	0	0	0
David Wright	F	So.	1	0	0	0	0

GOALTENDING

	Games	W	L	T	Min.	GA	Avg.
Steve Shields	37	27	7	2	2091	98	2.81
Chris Gordon	14	5	2	1	546	42	4.62
Al Loges	1	0	0	0	20	2	6.00

MICHIGAN STATE

SCORING

	Pos.	Class	Games	G	A	Pts.	Pen.
Dwayne Norris	F	Sr.	44	44	39	83	62
Peter White	F	Sr.	44	26	51	77	32
Bryan Smolinski	F	Jr.	44	30	35	65	59
Steve Suk	F	Fr.	44	11	41	52	24
Rem Murray	F	Fr.	44	13	38	51	18
Rob Woodward	F	Jr.	43	14	16	30	64

— 233 —

	Pos.	Class	Games	G	A	Pts.	Pen.
Joby Messier..........	D	Sr.	44	13	16	29	85
Nicolas Perreault...	D	So.	44	12	11	23	77
Bart Turner............	F	So.	44	9	7	16	36
Steve Guolla..........	F	Fr.	36	4	9	13	8
Michael Burkett.....	F	So.	33	7	5	12	42
Wes McCauley.......	D	Jr.	42	2	10	12	42
Kelly Harper..........	F	So.	36	4	5	9	2
Bill Shalawylo........	F	Jr.	23	3	5	8	12
Scott Worden.........	F	So.	44	1	7	8	36
Doug Garbarz........	D	Sr.	40	1	5	6	56
Steve Norton..........	D	So.	44	0	6	6	38
Matt Albers...........	F	Fr.	27	2	2	4	14
Michael Stewart	D	Jr.	8	1	3	4	6
Michael Thompson	F	Jr.	17	1	2	3	12
Scott Dean	F	Fr.	21	1	2	3	26
Mike Gilmore.........	G	Sr.	36	0	1	1	4
Mike Buzak	G	Fr.	7	0	1	1	2
Eric Kruse	G	Fr.	8	0	0	0	2
Charlie Elliott........	D	Jr.	16	0	0	0	2

GOALTENDING

	Games	W	L	T	Min.	GA	Avg.
Eric Kruse	8	5	1	1	363	17	2.81
Mike Gilmore............	36	16	10	7	2011	103	3.07
Mike Buzak	7	4	0	0	311	22	4.25

OHIO STATE
SCORING

	Pos.	Class	Games	G	A	Pts.	Pen.
David Smith	F	Sr.	36	22	41	63	81
Brian Loney	F	Fr.	37	21	34	55	109
Ron White	F	So.	38	31	13	44	18
Scott Walsh	F	Sr.	38	10	28	38	54
Rob Schriner	F	Sr.	38	23	8	31	62
Steve Richards	D	Fr.	38	11	17	28	66
Sacha Guilbault.....	F	Fr.	38	9	7	16	26
Phil Cadman	F	Jr.	38	6	9	15	19
Glenn Painter	D	Jr.	18	4	11	15	8
Eddie Choi	F	So.	30	3	8	11	14
Rob Peters.............	D	So.	28	3	7	10	53
Greg Beaucage	F/D	Sr.	35	2	7	9	110
Tim Green..............	D	So.	34	0	8	8	60
Brian Baldrica	D	Sr.	30	1	6	7	18
Bryan Riedel	F	So.	37	3	3	6	40
John Graham	D	Jr.	34	2	2	4	54
Kevin Powell	F	Fr.	11	1	2	3	10
Mike Bales	G	Jr.	36	0	3	3	10
Mike Merriman	F	So.	18	1	1	2	30

	Pos.	Class	Games	G	A	Pts.	Pen.
Matt Brandt	D	So.	18	0	2	2	12
Marty Diamond......	F	So.	4	0	1	1	8
Sandy Fraser	D	Fr.	14	0	1	1	8
Adam Smith	F	Fr.	22	0	1	1	16
Brent Convery.......	G	Fr.	1	0	0	0	0
Pat Rodgers	F	So.	2	0	0	0	0
Jim Slazyk............	G	Jr.	6	0	0	0	0
Steve Ott	F	So.	8	0	0	0	8

GOALTENDING

	Games	W	L	T	Min.	GA	Avg.
Brent Convery.........	1	0	0	0	35	3	5.18
Mike Bales	36	11	20	5	2061	180	5.24
Jim Slazyk...............	6	1	1	0	205	24	7.01

WESTERN MICHIGAN
SCORING

	Pos.	Class	Games	G	A	Pts.	Pen.
Keith Jones	F	Sr.	35	25	31	56	77
Pat Ferschweiler ...	F	Jr.	36	8	32	40	56
Colin Ward	F	So.	36	25	14	39	60
Scott Garrow..........	F	Sr.	36	15	23	38	40
Chris Belanger.......	D	Fr.	36	7	24	31	28
Ryan D'Arcy..........	F	Fr.	36	6	17	23	42
Byron Witkowski ...	F	Jr.	34	9	9	18	36
Jason Jennings	F	Jr.	35	8	9	17	52
Francois Leroux	F	Fr.	36	9	7	16	58
Mike Whitton	F	Fr.	30	6	6	12	61
Derek Schooley......	D	So.	36	3	9	12	48
Andy Suhy	D	Sr.	36	3	9	12	89
Brian Gallentine	F	Fr.	33	7	4	11	26
Brian Tulik	D	Sr.	35	1	10	11	62
Brent Brekke	D	So.	36	1	10	11	68
Joe Bonnett...........	F	Jr.	36	5	3	8	24
Lynn Zimmerman ..	F	So.	28	2	3	5	22
Craig Brown	G	So.	28	0	1	1	8
Brad Swain	D	Fr.	2	0	0	0	0
Brian Renfrew........	G	Fr.	5	0	0	0	0
Peter Wilkinson	F	Fr.	5	0	0	0	4
Rob Laurie.............	G	Sr.	6	0	0	0	0
J.P. LaRoche.........	F	Jr.	16	0	0	0	6
Brad Dawson	D	Sr.	34	0	0	0	14

GOALTENDING

	Games	W	L	T	Min.	GA	Avg.
Craig Brown	28	13	10	5	1668	89	3.20
Rob Laurie..............	6	2	1	1	294	20	4.08
Brian Renfrew.........	5	1	2	0	237	21	5.33

EASTERN COLLEGE ATHLETIC CONFERENCE

1991-92 SEASON

FINAL STANDINGS

Team	G	W	L	T	Pts.	GF	GA
Harvard (14-7-6)	22	13	3	6	32	90	59
St. Law. (20-9-2).....	22	15	6	1	31	104	66
Clarkson (22-8-1)	22	15	6	1	31	101	63
Yale (13-7-7)..........	22	11	4	7	29	103	90
Cornell (13- 10-4)	22	10	8	4	24	70	59
Brown (10- 16-4)	22	10	8	4	24	93	86
Vermont (16- 12-3)..	22	10	9	3	23	78	74
Colgate (14- 16-1) ..	22	11	11	0	22	105	108
Princeton (12- 14-1) .	22	9	12	1	19	85	92
R.P.I. (14- 14-4)	22	6	12	4	16	70	89
Dartmouth (3-21-2) .	22	3	17	2	8	60	116
Union (3-21-1)	22	2	19	1	5	61	118

Overall record in parentheses.

PLAYOFF RESULTS

PRELIMINARIES

Rensselaer 5, Vermont 1
Princeton 5, Colgate 4 (2 OT)

QUARTERFINALS

Rensselaer 4, Harvard 3 (OT)
St. Lawrence 6, Princeton 3
Clarkson 8, Brown 3
Cornell 4, Yale 1

SEMIFINALS

Cornell 4, Clarkson 3 (2 OT)
St. Lawrence 6, Rensselaer 5 (2 OT)

CHAMPIONSHIP GAME

St. Lawrence 4, Cornell 2

ALL-STAR TEAMS

First team	Pos.	Second team
Christian Soucy, Vermont	G	Parris Duffus, Cornell
Mike Brewer, Brown	D	Stephane Robitaille, R.P.I.
Dan LaPerriere, St. Law.	D	Jack Duffy, Yale
Dale Band, Colgate	F	Derek Chauvette, Brown
Mark Kaufmann, Yale	F	Andre Faust, Princeton
Mike Lappin, St. Lawrence	F	Hugo Belanger, Clarkson

AWARD WINNERS

Player of the year: Dan LaPerriere, St. Lawrence
Rookie of the year: Christian Soucy, Vermont
Coach of the year: Tim Taylor, Yale
Leading scorer: Dale Band, Colgate
Playoff MVP: Dan LaPerriere, St. Lawrence

INDIVIDUAL STATISTICS

BROWN

SCORING

	Pos.	Class	Games	G	A	Pts.	Pen.
Mike Brewer...........	D	Sr.	28	13	34	47	62
Derek Chauvette....	F	Jr.	30	12	30	42	21
Scott Hanley	F	Jr.	28	15	20	35	67
Mike Ross...............	F	Jr.	29	14	19	33	79
Tim Chase..............	D	Jr.	29	19	10	29	25
Eric Trach..............	F	Fr.	25	4	14	18	9
Sascha Pogor.........	F	Jr.	27	6	10	16	42
Chris Kaban...........	F	So.	20	7	7	14	22
James O'Brien........	D	Jr.	28	3	11	14	47
Joey Beck...............	F	Jr.	28	11	1	12	37
Kelly Jones.............	F	So.	22	4	7	11	18
Mike Traggio..........	D	Fr.	27	1	10	11	73
Mark Fabbro...........	F	So.	20	3	4	7	18
M. Shaughnessy	F	So.	25	1	5	6	10
Todd Simpson........	D	Fr.	14	1	3	4	20
Darrin MacKay	F	Sr.	18	1	3	4	16
Joe Verderber	F	Sr.	22	1	3	4	10
Rick Olczyk	D	Sr.	23	0	4	4	46
Brendan Whittet	D	So.	7	0	3	3	8
Tony Martino	F	Fr.	15	2	0	2	0
Paul Stravato	F	Sr.	8	0	2	2	0
Kris Omicioli...........	F	Fr.	6	0	1	1	0
Pat Thompson	D	Fr.	15	1	0	1	6
Kim Hannah	F	Fr.	17	1	0	1	0
Chris Schremp	F	Sr.	1	0	0	0	0
Jeff Reschny	D	Fr.	9	0	0	0	12
Geoff Finch............	G	So.	15	0	0	0	0
Paul Ohman	D	Sr.	16	0	0	0	14
Brett Haywood.......	G	So.	18	0	0	0	4

GOALTENDING

	Games	W	L	T	Min.	GA	Avg.
Brett Haywood..........	18	6	9	2	1005	77	4.60
Geoff Finch..............	15	4	7	2	815	65	4.79

CLARKSON

SCORING

	Pos.	Class	Games	G	A	Pts.	Pen.
Steve Dubinsky......	F	Jr.	33	21	34	55	40
Hugo Belanger	F	Jr.	33	18	33	51	28
Scott Thomas	F	Jr.	30	25	21	46	62
Craig Conroy	F	So.	32	20	16	36	38
Pat Robitaille	F	Fr.	33	7	27	34	14
Todd Marchant......	F	Fr.	33	20	12	32	32
Marko Tuomainen .	F	Fr.	29	11	13	24	34
Jeff Torrey	F	Sr.	33	6	16	22	26
Ed Sabo	F	Sr.	32	8	12	20	31
S. Fotheringham ...	F	So.	33	6	14	20	36
Guy Sanderson	D	Jr.	31	4	14	18	111
Brian Mueller	D	Fr.	29	4	13	17	32
Ed Henrich	D	So.	30	2	11	13	22
Nikko Tavi	D	Jr.	33	1	12	13	23
Pat Theriault..........	F	So.	33	3	9	12	10
M. D'Orsonnens	D	Jr.	32	2	10	12	34
Dave Green	F	Jr.	33	6	3	9	6
Kent Anderson.......	D	Sr.	33	0	6	6	20
Chris Rogles	G	Jr.	19	0	2	2	8
Jerry Rosenheck.....	F	Fr.	6	1	0	1	4
Bracken Gardner ...	D	Jr.	1	0	0	0	0
Scott Hopkins	F	Jr.	6	0	0	0	0
Jason Currie	G	So.	19	0	0	0	6

GOALTENDING

	Games	W	L	T	Min.	GA	Avg.
Jason Currie	19	11	7	1	1001	48	2.88
Chris Rogles.............	19	11	3	0	996	51	3.07

COLGATE

SCORING

	Pos.	Class	Games	G	A	Pts.	Pen.
Dale Band...............	F	Sr.	28	13	40	53	20
Andrew Dickson	F	Jr.	31	15	31	46	33

	Pos.	Class	Games	G	A	Pts.	Pen.
Marcel Richard	F	So.	31	18	27	45	48
Ron Fogarty	F	Fr.	31	16	24	40	16
Clayton Fahey	F	So.	31	12	15	27	36
Jason Greyerbiehl	F	Sr.	27	11	16	27	21
Dan Gardner	F	So.	31	11	11	22	22
Chris MacKenzie	F	So.	30	9	13	22	16
Brad Dexter	D	Fr.	30	1	18	19	38
Sam Raffoul	F	So.	27	12	5	17	70
Craig deBlois	F	Jr.	30	13	3	16	73
Brent Wilde	F	So.	27	6	10	16	40
Bruce Gardiner	F	So.	23	7	8	15	77
Matt Garzone	D	Fr.	28	1	11	12	12
Alan Brown	D	Jr.	29	1	10	11	28
Troy Mohns	D	Jr.	20	1	6	7	16
Chris Ladner	D	So.	9	0	7	7	0
Bob Haddock	D	Jr.	12	2	4	6	12
Jason Craig	D	Fr.	24	0	5	5	20
Nigel Creightney	D	Fr.	29	2	1	3	28
Dan Gibson	D	So.	21	0	3	3	32
Rob Metz	F	So.	9	1	1	2	6
Ken Baker	G	Sr.	16	0	1	1	6
Jason Gates	G	Fr.	1	0	0	0	0
Shawn Murray	G	So.	15	0	0	0	0

GOALTENDING

	Games	W	L	T	Min.	GA	Avg.
Ken Baker	16	7	8	1	924	70	4.55
Shawn Murray	15	7	7	0	904	71	4.71
Jason Gates	1	0	1	0	60	9	9.00

CORNELL
SCORING

	Pos.	Class	Games	G	A	Pts.	Pen.
Joe Dragon	F	Sr.	29	10	16	26	37
Jason Vogel	F	Jr.	29	11	10	21	30
Ryan Hughes	F	Sr.	27	8	13	21	36
Karl Williams	F	Sr.	29	5	14	19	34
Phil Nobel	F	Sr.	20	11	7	18	26
Todd Chambers	D	So.	29	4	13	17	26
Stephane Gauvin	F	Sr.	29	6	10	16	28
Shaun Hannah	F	So.	28	4	11	15	30
Alex Nikolic	F	Sr.	26	5	9	14	60
Dave Burke	D	Sr.	29	5	9	14	30
Tyler McManus	F	Fr.	26	6	3	9	20
Geoff Bumstead	F	So.	21	4	5	9	16
Jim McPhee	F	Sr.	27	2	7	9	8
Russ Hammond	F	Jr.	29	5	3	8	2
Marc Deschamps	D	Sr.	25	0	7	7	60
Jake Karam	F	Fr.	27	2	4	6	4
Paul Dukovac	D	Sr.	8	2	2	4	6
Blair Ettles	D	Fr.	10	0	3	3	4
Parris Duffus	G	So.	28	0	3	3	2
Rick Davis	C	So.	11	1	1	2	2
Etienne Belzile	D	Jr.	29	1	1	2	20
Andy Bandurski	G	Fr.	3	0	0	0	0
Christian Felli	D	Fr.	24	0	0	0	10

GOALTENDING

	Games	W	L	T	Min.	GA	Avg.
Andy Bandurski	3	0	0	1	89	2	1.35
Parris Duffus	28	14	11	3	1675	74	2.65

DARTMOUTH
SCORING

	Pos.	Class	Games	G	A	Pts.	Pen.
Scott Fraser	F	So.	24	11	7	18	60
Pat Turcotte	F	Fr.	26	9	9	18	32
Dion Delmonte	F	Fr.	26	4	13	17	38
Mike Stacchi	F	Fr.	26	9	7	16	48
Tony Delcarmine	F	So.	25	5	11	16	66
Derek Geary	F	So.	26	7	6	13	30
Trevor Dodman	D	Fr.	25	3	9	12	20
Tom Wieman	F	Sr.	25	5	3	8	38
Mike Fenn	F	Sr.	16	2	6	8	10
Matt Collins	D	So.	24	2	6	8	83

	Pos.	Class	Games	G	A	Pts.	Pen.
Peter Clark	F	Jr.	26	3	4	7	18
Yannick Roussin	D	Fr.	26	3	4	7	18
Kevin Kiley	F	Sr.	20	2	3	5	18
Nate Dudley	D	Sr.	25	0	5	5	46
Greg Chapman	D	Jr.	22	2	2	4	4
Rob Kerr	F	Fr.	12	1	3	4	2
Matt Ocken	F	Sr.	22	1	3	4	28
Shawn Burt	F	Jr.	8	1	1	2	4
Eric D'Orio	D	So.	9	0	2	2	21
Mike Loga	D	So.	11	0	1	1	44
Stephen Harb	D	Fr.	12	0	1	1	6
Vern Guetens	G	Jr.	15	0	1	1	0
Mike Richardson	F	So.	1	0	0	0	0
Chad Boucher	F	Fr.	2	0	0	0	2
Jon Hess	F	Fr.	5	0	0	0	0
Matt Wilson	F	Fr.	5	0	0	0	0
Rett Waldman	F	Fr.	6	0	0	0	0
Dan Williams	D	So.	12	0	0	0	2
Mike Bracco	G	So.	15	0	0	0	0

GOALTENDING

	Games	W	L	T	Min.	GA	Avg.
Mike Bracco	15	1	11	0	735	63	5.14
Vern Guetens	15	2	10	2	833	74	5.33

HARVARD
SCORING

	Pos.	Class	Games	G	A	Pts.	Pen.
Tim Burke	F	Sr.	27	8	24	32	24
S. Flomenhoft	F	Jr.	27	14	17	31	30
Steve Martins	F	Fr.	20	13	14	27	26
Matt Mallgrave	F	Jr.	27	12	15	27	20
Brad Kowik	F	Fr.	27	10	10	20	20
Ben Coughlin	F	Fr.	26	10	9	19	20
Derek Maguire	D	So.	24	1	16	17	16
Sean McCann	D	So.	27	4	11	15	51
Cory Gustafson	F	Fr.	27	3	10	13	22
Jim Coady	F	Sr.	26	7	4	11	34
Perry Cohagen	F	Fr.	27	5	6	11	36
Lou Body	D	So.	22	1	9	10	23
Rich Defreitas	D	So.	27	1	8	9	10
Brian Farrell	F	So.	9	5	3	8	8
Gus Gardner	F	So.	26	3	3	6	12
Bryan Lowsinger	D	Fr.	18	1	5	6	4
Chris Baird	F	So.	22	3	2	5	10
Kevin Sneddon	D	Sr.	17	2	3	5	10
Brian McCormack	D	So.	26	0	5	5	24
M. Breistroff	F	So.	21	0	4	4	24
Dave Kilpatrick	F	So.	6	0	1	1	2
Brian Connolly	F	Sr.	1	0	0	0	0
Greg Hess	F	Sr.	2	0	0	0	2
Sean Wenham	D	So.	4	0	0	0	0
Chuck Hughes	G	So.	12	0	0	0	2
Allain Roy	G	Sr.	15	0	0	0	8

GOALTENDING

	Games	W	L	T	Min.	GA	Avg.
Allain Roy	15	9	4	2	919	39	2.55
Chuck Hughes	12	5	3	4	739	38	3.09

PRINCETON
SCORING

	Pos.	Class	Games	G	A	Pts.	Pen.
Andre Faust	F	Sr.	27	14	21	35	38
Terry Morris	F	Jr.	24	16	16	32	24
Matt Zilinskas	F	Jr.	26	13	16	29	26
Mike McKee	D	Sr.	27	12	17	29	34
Brian Bigelow	F	Jr.	25	9	12	21	18
Ian Sharp	F	Fr.	26	8	10	18	32
Troy Ewanchyna	F	So.	25	4	14	18	16
Jeff Kampersal	D	Fr.	27	7	10	17	36
Scott Sinson	F	Jr.	23	4	11	15	12
Sean O'Brien	D	So.	27	3	10	13	38
Sverre Sears	D	Jr.	25	3	9	12	62
Dan Slatalla	F	Sr.	21	5	4	9	23

	Pos.	Class	Games	G	A	Pts.	Pen.
Chris Stewart	F	Sr.	16	1	8	9	8
Mervin Kopeck	F	Fr.	23	2	4	6	6
Jack Craig	D	Sr.	27	2	3	5	50
Keith Merkler	F	Jr.	13	2	2	4	14
Miro Pasic	F	So.	12	1	1	2	10
Gavin Colquhoun	D	Fr.	20	0	2	2	24
David Scowby	F	Fr.	25	1	0	1	20
Scott Almon	D	Fr.	1	0	0	0	0
John Fust	F	Jr.	7	0	0	0	0
Chris Mitchell	F	Jr.	9	0	0	0	13
H. Schoebel	F	Fr.	9	0	0	0	4
Rod Yorke	G	Fr.	12	0	0	0	2
Craig Fiander	G	Jr.	16	0	0	0	6
Ethan Early	F	Fr.	20	0	0	0	11

GOALTENDING

	Games	W	L	T	Min.	GA	Avg.
Craig Fiander	16	7	9	0	962	63	3.93
Rod Yorke	12	5	5	1	667	50	4.50

RENSSELAER POLYTECHNIC INSTITUTE

SCORING

	Pos.	Class	Games	G	A	Pts.	Pen.
Craig Hamelin	F	Jr.	33	21	19	40	20
Ron Pasco	F	So.	33	12	23	35	34
Xavier Majic	F	So.	32	13	19	32	58
Wayne Clarke	F	Fr.	33	12	17	29	30
S. Robitaille	D	Sr.	33	5	18	23	18
Jeff Gabriel	F	So.	31	10	12	22	34
Allen Kummu	D	Jr.	31	6	14	20	54
Adam Bartell	D	Fr.	32	5	13	18	22
Eric Perardi	F	Fr.	30	8	9	17	38
Kelly Askew	F	Fr.	33	7	10	17	56
Todd Hilditch	Sr.	Sr.	33	4	13	17	90
Jeff Brick	F	Fr.	33	8	7	15	12
Zach Dargaty	D	Sr.	26	3	6	9	12
Dan Vaillant	D	Sr.	32	2	7	9	73
Brad Layzell	D	So.	31	1	8	9	44
Rick Borina	F	Sr.	32	3	2	5	18
Ivan Moore	D/F	Sr.	32	2	3	5	65
Jeff Matthews	F	Fr.	21	1	2	3	8
Cam Cuthbert	D	So.	21	1	0	1	24
Ken Kwasniewski	F	Fr.	1	0	1	1	0
Cam Matches	F	Jr.	7	0	1	1	2
Chris Maye	F	Fr.	1	0	0	0	0
Tim Carvel	G	So.	2	0	0	0	0
Sean Kennedy	G	Sr.	10	0	0	0	0
Neil Little	G	So.	28	0	0	0	6

GOALTENDING

	Games	W	L	T	Min.	GA	Avg.
Tim Carvel	2	0	0	0	19	0	0.00
Sean Kennedy	10	2	3	1	479	29	3.63
Neil Little	28	12	12	3	1330	96	3.76

ST. LAWRENCE

SCORING

	Pos.	Class	Games	G	A	Pts.	Pen.
Mike Lappin	F	Sr.	33	25	37	62	24
Dan Laperriere	D	Sr.	32	8	45	53	36
Chris Wells	F	Sr.	33	15	21	36	40
Martin Lacroix	F	Sr.	22	17	18	35	24
Greg Carvel	F	Jr.	34	12	22	34	23
Lee Albert	F	So.	33	15	17	32	16
Eric Lacroix	F	So.	34	11	21	32	40
Chris Lappin	D	Sr.	34	9	17	26	40
Spencer Meany	F	So.	30	12	8	20	123
Ted Dent	F	Sr.	32	6	9	15	28
Gerard Verbeek	F	Jr.	30	6	8	14	12
John Massoud	F	Jr.	24	7	6	13	8
Mike Allain	F	So.	33	4	9	13	38
Mike McCourt	D	So.	32	2	9	11	22
Ted Beattie	D	Jr.	34	1	7	8	64
Mark McGeough	F	So.	23	3	3	6	22
Brian Kapeller	F	Fr.	29	3	3	6	66

	Pos.	Class	Games	G	A	Pts.	Pen.
M. Terwilliger	D	Jr.	30	0	5	5	4
Dan Skene	F	Fr.	9	2	1	3	8
Cade Blackburn	F	Fr.	10	1	1	2	0
John Roderick	D	Jr.	28	1	1	2	42
Scott Celentano	D	So.	12	0	2	2	14
Brady Giroux	G	So.	11	0	1	1	0
Dave MacTavish	G	Jr.	2	0	0	0	0
P. Spagnoletti	G	So.	25	0	0	0	6

GOALTENDING

	Games	W	L	T	Min.	GA	Avg.
P. Spagnoletti	25	16	6	2	1472	73	2.98
Brady Giroux	11	6	4	0	590	36	3.66
Dave MacTavish	2	0	0	0	13	1	4.62

UNION

SCORING

	Pos.	Class	Games	G	A	Pts.	Pen.
Craig Ferrero	F	Sr.	25	15	17	32	58
Bill Railton	F	Sr.	24	11	15	26	106
Dalton Menhall	F	Sr.	25	13	8	21	90
Jayson Flowers	F	So.	23	9	9	18	16
Rick Clifford	F	Sr.	25	6	12	18	16
Scott Whitney	D	Sr.	25	2	16	18	56
Chris Albert	F	Fr.	25	5	9	14	24
Tim Cregan	F	Sr.	18	5	5	10	22
Rick Burchill	D	Sr.	23	4	6	10	72
Bill McKenna	D	So.	22	1	6	7	38
Dean Goulet	D	Fr.	25	1	6	7	20
Cory Holbrough	F	Fr.	16	2	3	5	22
Jeff Jiampetti	F	So.	20	1	4	5	11
Matt Kelley	D	Fr.	20	1	4	5	22
Greg Steele	D	Jr.	18	0	4	4	12
Kevin Sullivan	F	So.	13	2	1	3	10
Wally Bzdell	F	So.	9	1	2	3	12
Alex McClellan	D	Fr.	12	1	2	3	14
Greg Eccleston	D	Jr.	19	1	1	2	10
Gary Edmands	D	Fr.	14	0	2	2	20
Jon Quint	F	So.	13	1	0	1	10
Dalton Gustafson	F	Sr.	1	0	0	0	0
Jim Helkie	G	Jr.	1	0	0	0	0
Shayne White	G	Sr.	1	0	0	0	0
Keith Darby	F	Fr.	2	0	0	0	0
Dave Tessitore	F	Fr.	6	0	0	0	0
Byron Smith	D	So.	11	0	0	0	14
Mike Gallant	G	Fr.	12	0	0	0	0
Steve Battiston	F	So.	15	0	0	0	0
Luigi Villa	G	Fr.	16	0	0	0	4

GOALTENDING

	Games	W	L	T	Min.	GA	Avg.
Shayne White	1	0	1	0	61	5	4.92
Mike Gallant	12	0	9	0	627	53	5.07
Luigi Villa	16	3	10	1	758	70	5.54
Jim Helkie	1	0	1	0	60	8	8.00

VERMONT

SCORING

	Pos.	Class	Games	G	A	Pts.	Pen.
Nick Perreault	F	So.	31	16	17	33	30
Dom Ducharme	F	Fr.	31	13	19	32	20
Jim Larkin	F	Sr.	29	15	16	31	32
Aaron Miller	D	Jr.	31	3	16	19	36
Tim Fingerhut	F	So.	30	9	9	18	14
Mike McLaughlin	F	Sr.	30	9	9	18	34
Rob Pattison	F	So.	25	6	12	18	8
Toby Kearkey	F	Jr.	31	6	11	17	36
T. Lehouiller	F	Jr.	31	10	4	14	24
Brendan Creagh	D	Jr.	21	6	7	13	10
Bill Lincoln	F	Fr.	28	5	6	11	34
Corey Machanic	D	So.	29	3	8	11	24
Jeremy Benoit	D	Sr.	26	2	9	11	20
Joe McCarthy	D	Jr.	26	2	7	9	21
Jason Williams	D	Fr.	29	1	7	8	34
Leif Selstad	F	Sr.	9	3	3	6	4

— 237 —

COLLEGE HOCKEY

	Pos.	Class	Games	G	A	Pts.	Pen.
Brian Leddy	F	Fr.	27	3	3	6	22
Scott MacDonald	D	Fr.	28	0	6	6	18
Kevin Monty	F	Jr.	10	1	4	5	4
Mike Larkin	D	Fr.	14	2	2	4	14
Ted Madden	D	Sr.	23	0	2	2	4
Christian Soucy	G	Fr.	30	0	2	2	2
Bo Beckman	F	Jr.	14	1	0	1	6
Daniel Eppler	D	So.	4	0	1	1	2
Tom Quinn	D	Fr.	1	0	0	0	0
John Barto	G	Jr.	2	0	0	0	0
Jim Beraldi	G	So.	2	0	0	0	0

GOALTENDING

	Games	W	L	T	Min.	GA	Avg.
Christian Soucy	30	15	11	3	1773	84	2.84
John Barto	2	1	1	0	95	5	3.16
Jim Beraldi	2	0	0	0	21	4	11.43

YALE

SCORING

	Pos.	Class	Games	G	A	Pts.	Pen.
Mark Kaufmann	F	Jr.	27	25	20	45	18
John Sather	F	Sr.	27	14	19	33	6
James Lavish	F	Jr.	26	16	13	29	44
Jack Duffy	D	Jr.	27	3	24	27	74
Martin Leroux	F	So.	27	9	17	26	20
Craig Ferguson	F	Sr.	27	9	14	23	26
Jeff Blaeser	F	Sr.	24	8	15	23	4
Peter Allen	D	Jr.	26	6	12	18	26

	Pos.	Class	Games	G	A	Pts.	Pen.
Andy Weidenbach	F	Fr.	26	6	11	17	35
S. Matusovich	D	Sr.	27	3	13	16	52
Y. Chiasson	F	Jr.	27	10	4	14	40
Stephen Maltby	F	Jr.	25	4	5	9	31
Jason Cipolla	F	Fr.	27	3	6	9	42
Jim Mackey	D	So.	27	1	7	8	44
Steve Lombardi	F	Fr.	14	2	3	5	2
Mike O'Brien	F	Sr.	27	1	4	5	12
Pelle Bildtsen	D	So.	8	1	2	3	4
Dave Cochran	D	So.	14	0	2	2	18
Dean Malish	D	Jr.	25	0	2	2	14
Jeff Williams	F	Jr.	2	0	1	1	0
Dan Nyberg	D	Fr.	7	0	1	1	4
John Hockin	G	Jr.	16	0	1	1	0
Garrison Smith	D	Fr.	1	0	0	0	2
Glen Johnson	F	So.	2	0	0	0	0
Todd Caricato	F	So.	3	0	0	0	0
Mike Cullinane	D	So.	3	0	0	0	2
Chris Barbanti	F	Fr.	4	0	0	0	4
Nadew Befekadu	G	Sr.	4	0	0	0	2
Richard Giroux	D	Fr.	4	0	0	0	2
Todd Sullivan	G	Fr.	10	0	0	0	2

GOALTENDING

	Games	W	L	T	Min.	GA	Avg.
John Hockin	16	5	4	5	894	58	3.89
Todd Sullivan	10	6	3	1	567	37	3.92
Nadew Befekadu	4	2	0	1	190	14	4.42

HOCKEY EAST

1991-92 SEASON

FINAL STANDINGS

Team	G	W	L	T	Pts.	GF	GA
Maine (31-4-2)	21	17	2	2	36	115	54
New Hamp. (22-13-2)	21	13	6	2	28	94	75
Providence (21-13-2)	21	11	8	2	24	99	79
Boston U. (22-9-4) ...	21	10	7	4	24	92	88
Boston Col. (14-18-3)	21	9	10	2	20	68	76
Lowell (11-19-4)	21	6	11	4	16	75	91
N'eastern (15-20-0) ..	21	6	15	0	12	70	103
Merrimack (13-21-0)	21	4	17	0	8	60	102

Overall record in parentheses.

PLAYOFF RESULTS

QUARTERFINALS

Providence 7, Lowell 0
Boston College 5, Boston University 2
New Hampshire 4, Northeastern 2
Maine 7, Merrimack 0

SEMIFINALS

Maine 7, Boston College 3
New Hampshire 5, Providence 2

CHAMPIONSHIP GAME

Maine 4, New Hampshire 1

ALL-STAR TEAMS

First team	Pos.	Second team
Mark Richards, Lowell	G	Garth Snow, Maine
Tom Dion, Boston U.	D	Chris Imes, Maine
Rob Gaudreau, Providence	D	Kevin O'Sullivan, Boston U.
Mike Boback, Providence	F	Jim Montgomery, Maine
Scott Pellerin, Maine	F	Scott Morrow, New Hamp.
David Sacco, Boston U.	F	Jean-Yves Roy, Maine

AWARD WINNERS

Player of the year: Scott Pellerin, Maine
Rookie of the year: Ian Moran, Boston College
Chad Quenneville, Providence
Coach of the year: Jack Parker, Boston University
Leading scorer: Mike Boback, Providence
Playoff MVP: Scott Pellerin, Maine

INDIVIDUAL STATISTICS

BOSTON COLLEGE
SCORING

	Pos.	Class	Games	G	A	Pts.	Pen.
David Franzosa	C	Sr.	35	18	35	53	38
Marc Beran	F	Jr.	35	22	20	42	45
Jack Callahan.......	F	So.	35	15	11	26	52
Joe Cleary	D	Sr.	29	5	20	25	66
Michael Spalla	D	So.	35	7	16	23	22
John Joyce.............	F	So.	35	9	13	22	32
Ian Morgan	D	Fr.	30	2	16	18	44
Ryan Haggerty	C	Fr.	34	12	5	17	16
Todd Hall..............	D	Fr.	33	2	10	12	14
Rob Canavan	F	Fr.	30	7	4	11	28
Jason Rathbone.....	F	Sr.	35	3	7	10	30
Sal Manganaro	F	Fr.	35	4	4	8	18
Ron Pascucci	D	Jr.	35	2	6	8	30
Jim Krayer	F	Fr.	31	2	3	5	2
Mike McCarthy	C	Fr.	34	2	2	4	10
Scott Zygulski	D	Jr.	32	0	4	4	24
Brett Stickney	C	Fr.	29	1	2	3	10
Mike Delay	D	Sr.	34	1	2	3	28
Jerry Buckley	F	Fr.	30	2	0	2	46
Scott LaGrand	G	Jr.	30	0	1	1	2
Mike Sparrow........	G	Fr.	4	0	0	0	2
Josh Singewald	G	Fr.	8	0	0	0	2

GOALTENDING

	Games	W	L	T	Min.	GA	Avg.
Josh Singewald	8	3	2	1	308	19	3.69
Scott LaGrand	30	11	16	2	1750	108	3.70
Mike Sparrow...........	4	0	0	0	54	7	7.71

BOSTON UNIVERSITY
SCORING

	Pos.	Class	Games	G	A	Pts.	Pen.
David Sacco...........	F	Jr.	35	14	33	47	30
Mike Pomichter.....	F	Fr.	35	11	27	38	14
Petteri Koskimaki ..	F	Jr.	33	19	18	37	12
Mike Prendergast ..	F	Fr.	32	19	15	34	49
Steve Thornton......	F	Fr.	29	11	16	27	10

	Pos.	Class	Games	G	A	Pts.	Pen.
Mark Bavis.............	F	Jr.	35	9	18	27	30
Mike Bavis	F	Jr.	35	11	14	25	32
Kaj Linna...............	D	Fr.	33	7	14	21	46
Kevin O'Sullivan	D	Jr.	33	3	18	21	62
Doug Friedman	F	So.	35	11	8	19	42
John Lilley	F	Fr.	24	9	9	18	43
Tom Dion	D	Sr.	35	5	12	17	34
Rich Brennan	D	Fr.	31	4	13	17	54
Nick Vachon	F	So.	16	6	7	13	10
Jon Pratt	F	So	29	8	4	12	42
Adrian Aucoin........	D	Fr.	33	2	10	12	62
David Dahlberg......	F	Jr.	29	2	9	11	10
Jon Jenkins	F	Fr.	32	4	4	8	14
M. Brownschidle....	D	Sr.	26	2	6	8	6
Dan Donato	D	So.	6	1	3	4	2
Stephen Foster	D	So.	12	0	4	4	12
Ken Rausch	F	Fr.	11	0	2	2	0
Jon Jacques	F	Fr.	7	1	0	1	2
Scott Cashman	G	Jr.	21	0	1	1	18
John McKersie	G	Fr.	8	0	0	0	0
Derek Herlofsky	G	Fr.	9	0	0	0	2

GOALTENDING

	Games	W	L	T	Min.	GA	Avg.
Derek Herlofsky	9	7	1	1	537	22	2.46
John McKersie..........	8	3	2	1	396	23	3.48
Scott Cashman	21	12	6	2	1209	77	3.82

LOWELL
SCORING

	Pos.	Class	Games	G	A	Pts.	Pen.
Mike Murray	F	So.	31	22	15	37	40
Dan O'Connell	F	Jr.	34	16	17	33	64
Shane Henry	F	So.	30	11	18	29	4
Dave Gatti	F	Sr.	27	12	16	28	22
Dave Stevens	F	Jr.	31	12	15	27	26
Ian Hebert	F	So.	34	7	16	23	24
Greg Carter	F	Sr.	34	11	11	22	14
Don Parsons	F	Sr.	32	7	15	22	34

— 239 —

	Pos.	Class	Games	G	A	Pts.	Pen.
Dave Pensa	F	Jr.	33	8	9	17	32
Gerry Daley	F	Jr.	31	5	9	14	38
Tim Smallwood	D	Jr.	30	1	10	11	34
Kerry Angus	D	Fr.	32	0	11	11	14
Normand Bazin	F	So.	30	4	6	10	22
Travis Tucker	D	So.	32	1	7	8	77
Keith Carney	D	Jr.	22	1	6	7	24
Aaron Kriss	D	Fr.	29	1	4	5	22
Mark Carlson	F	Jr.	23	3	1	4	20
Eric Brown	F	Fr.	21	2	1	3	2
Tomi Maarni	D	Sr.	5	1	2	3	4
Jeremy Tabb	F	Fr.	6	1	2	3	2
Andy Borggaard	F	Fr.	14	1	1	2	8
Scott Meehan	D	Jr.	34	0	2	2	28
Adam Hooper	D	Fr.	17	0	1	1	8
Dwayne Roloson	G	So.	12	0	0	0	6
Mark Richards	G	Sr.	23	0	0	0	6

GOALTENDING

	Games	W	L	T	Min.	GA	Avg.
Mark Richards	23	8	11	4	1393	97	4.18
Dwayne Roloson	12	3	8	0	660	52	4.73

MAINE
SCORING

	Pos.	Class	Games	G	A	Pts.	Pen.
Jim Montgomery	F	Jr.	37	21	44	65	46
Scott Pellerin	F	Sr.	37	32	25	57	54
Jean-Yves Roy	F	Jr.	35	32	24	56	62
Brian Downey	F	Sr.	37	19	32	51	29
Cal Ingraham	F	Jr.	37	15	30	45	22
Patrice Tardif	F	So.	31	18	20	38	14
Martin Robitaille	F	Sr.	31	5	22	27	8
Chris Imes	D	Jr.	31	4	19	23	22
Kent Salfi	F	Jr.	33	12	10	22	4
Matt Martin	D	So.	30	4	14	18	46
Jason Weinrich	D	So.	36	1	15	16	18
Eric Fenton	F/D	Jr.	22	7	8	15	18
Randy Olson	F	Sr.	19	10	4	14	4
Andy Silverman	D	Fr.	30	2	9	11	18
Wayne Conlan	F	Fr.	22	8	1	9	10
Dave LaCouture	F	Jr.	28	5	4	9	30
Tony Link	D	Sr.	34	3	6	9	44
Lee Saunders	D	So.	13	1	8	9	8
Dan Murphy	D	Jr.	36	0	6	6	44
Mike Barkley	F	Sr.	15	1	4	5	14
Jim Burcar	D	Fr.	12	1	3	4	6
Steve Widmeyer	F	Jr.	23	1	2	3	20
Steve Tepper	F	Sr.	16	0	3	3	20
Garth Snow	G	Jr.	31	0	3	3	10
Devin Mintz	F	Jr.	3	1	1	2	0
Martin Mercier	F	Jr.	15	0	1	1	10
Rob Howland	G	Jr.	6	0	0	0	2
Mike Dunham	G	So.	7	0	0	0	0

GOALTENDING

	Games	W	L	T	Min.	GA	Avg.
Mike Dunham	7	6	0	0	382	14	2.20
Garth Snow	31	25	4	2	1792	73	2.44
Rob Howland	6	0	0	0	57	3	3.18

MERRIMACK
SCORING

	Pos.	Class	Games	G	A	Pts.	Pen.
Dan Gravelle	F	Jr.	34	23	28	51	40
Teal Fowler	F	Jr.	34	20	15	35	32
Agostino Casale	F	Sr.	17	17	13	30	22
Rob Atkinson	F	So.	29	2	18	20	16
Alex Weinrich	D	Jr.	34	2	18	20	40
Bryan Miller	D	Jr.	34	5	13	18	32
Rob Kelley	D	Sr.	27	10	7	17	30
Jeff Massey	F	Sr.	32	7	8	15	30
Claude Maillet	D	Sr.	25	6	9	15	35
Brendan Locke	F	Sr.	34	4	11	15	10
Cooper Naylor	F	So.	31	2	13	15	6

	Pos.	Class	Games	G	A	Pts.	Pen.
John Barron	F	Jr.	31	6	7	13	19
Matt Crowley	F	Jr.	24	7	3	10	4
Jim Gibson	F	So.	19	5	5	10	10
Mark Cornforth	D	Fr.	23	1	9	10	40
Wayde McMillan	F	So.	19	3	6	9	6
Guy Ragault	F	Jr.	14	2	4	6	8
Don MacLeod	D	Jr.	28	1	5	6	40
Matt Adams	F	Fr.	29	2	3	5	10
Jason Pagni	D	So.	10	1	3	4	4
Matt Hayes	F	Jr.	22	0	4	4	18
Mike Flaherty	D	Fr.	22	0	3	3	23
Chris Davis	F	Fr.	2	1	1	2	0
Quentin Fendelet	F	So.	5	1	1	2	0
Mike Kelleher	F	Fr.	12	0	1	1	4
Chris Ross	F	Fr.	13	0	1	1	12
Steve D'Amore	G	Sr.	32	0	1	1	0
Brent Raftery	F	Fr.	1	0	0	0	0
Yannick Gosselin	G	Sr.	3	0	0	0	0
Matt Hentges	D	Sr.	6	0	0	0	6
Mike Doneghey	G	Jr.	8	0	0	0	0

GOALTENDING

	Games	W	L	T	Min.	GA	Avg.
Yannick Gosselin	3	1	1	0	81	5	3.70
Steve D'Amore	32	11	18	0	1714	121	4.24
Mike Doneghey	8	1	2	0	233	18	4.64

NEW HAMPSHIRE
SCORING

	Pos.	Class	Games	G	A	Pts.	Pen.
Domenic Amodeo	F	Sr.	37	26	42	68	28
Joe Flanagan	F	Sr.	37	26	34	60	12
Savo Mitrovic	F	Sr.	37	15	42	57	51
Scott Morrow	F	Sr.	35	30	23	53	65
Glenn Stewart	F	So.	37	15	11	26	39
Kevin Thomson	F	Jr.	32	13	11	24	52
Greg Klym	F	Jr.	34	6	16	22	8
Rob Donovan	F	So.	36	7	9	16	36
Jim McGrath	D	Jr.	34	2	13	15	40
Frank Messina	D	Sr.	35	2	13	15	34
Jason Dexter	F	So.	35	5	9	14	12
Bob Chebator	F	So.	36	5	6	11	24
Eric Flinton	F	Fr.	35	6	4	10	10
Jesse Cooper	D	Jr.	35	3	4	7	41
Nick Poole	F	Fr.	23	2	5	7	2
Kent Schmidtke	F	Fr.	25	1	4	5	6
Ted Russell	D	Fr.	35	0	5	5	34
Greg Blow	F	So.	15	1	3	4	31
Scott Malone	D	Fr.	27	0	4	4	52
Eric Royal	F	Fr.	14	0	3	3	2
Mike Guilbert	D	Fr.	3	2	0	2	0
Chris Jensen	D	Sr.	25	1	1	2	10
Mark McGinn	F	Sr.	4	0	0	0	2
Brett Abel	G	Jr.	6	0	0	0	0
Jeff Levy	G	So.	35	0	0	0	0

GOALTENDING

	Games	W	L	T	Min.	GA	Avg.
Jeff Levy	35	20	13	2	2030	111	3.28
Brett Abel	6	2	0	0	191	14	4.40

NORTHEASTERN
SCORING

	Pos.	Class	Games	G	A	Pts.	Pen.
Jay Schiavo	F	Jr.	35	17	28	45	8
S. Laplante	F	Jr.	35	15	28	43	22
Rob Kenny	F	Sr.	34	19	14	33	44
Dino Grossi	F	So.	31	15	11	26	50
Matt Saunders	F	Sr.	35	8	17	25	38
Jean-Franc. Aube	F	Fr.	30	8	11	19	10
Chris Foy	D	Jr.	33	8	11	19	45
Mike Taylor	F	So.	28	7	10	17	13
Darryl MacNair	D	Fr.	32	6	9	15	32
Tom O'Connor	F	So.	28	5	10	15	12
Adam Hayes	F	Jr.	31	5	8	13	22

	Pos.	Class	Games	G	A	Pts.	Pen.
Francois Bouchard	D	Fr.	34	4	9	13	28
Jason Melong	F	Fr.	22	3	10	13	12
Paul Sacco	D	Sr.	35	3	9	12	24
Geoff Lucas	F	Fr.	32	3	8	11	24
Paul Flanagan	D	Sr.	30	4	5	9	48
Keith Cyr	F	Sr.	6	2	4	6	6
Jason Kelly	D	Fr.	15	2	4	6	16
Bob Kellogg	D	So.	27	2	3	5	34
Sean Curtin	F	Sr.	16	1	4	5	6
Joel Bishop	F	So.	18	2	2	4	6
Derek Edgerly	F	So.	15	2	1	3	14
Craig Carmody	F	Fr.	13	0	2	2	2
Joe Eagan	D	So.	6	1	0	1	6
Tom Parlon	F	Fr.	7	0	1	1	2
Chris Utano	G	Jr.	4	0	0	0	0
Todd Reynolds	G	Fr.	17	0	0	0	4
Tom Cole	G	Sr.	22	0	0	0	2

GOALTENDING

	Games	W	L	T	Min.	GA	Avg.
Todd Reynolds	17	5	11	0	929	69	4.46
Tom Cole	22	10	9	0	1139	92	4.85
Chris Utano	4	0	0	0	23	3	7.90

PROVIDENCE

SCORING

	Pos.	Class	Games	G	A	Pts.	Pen.
Mike Boback	F	Sr.	36	24	48	72	34
Rob Gaudreau	F	Sr.	36	21	34	55	22

	Pos.	Class	Games	G	A	Pts.	Pen.
Craig Darby	F	Fr.	35	17	24	41	47
Chris Therien	D	So.	36	16	25	41	38
Chad Quenneville	F	Fr.	36	13	22	35	18
Bob Cowan	F	Jr.	36	13	18	31	36
Gary Socha	F	Jr.	26	11	14	25	34
Shaun Kane	D	Sr.	36	11	11	22	59
Brian Ridolfi	F	So.	21	6	16	22	36
Brady Kramer	F	Fr.	36	11	10	21	47
Erik Peterson	F	So.	32	9	5	14	26
George Breen	F	Fr.	36	8	4	12	24
Brian Jefferies	F	Jr.	21	4	3	7	15
Mark Devine	F	Jr.	26	4	2	6	8
Jon Rowe	D	Fr.	27	2	4	6	30
Mark Doshan	F	Sr.	25	3	2	5	10
Todd Huyber	D	Jr.	29	0	5	5	58
Ian Paskowski	D	So.	35	0	5	5	22
Bob Creamer	F	Sr.	13	1	3	4	8
Rob Concannon	F	So.	17	1	2	3	8
Jeff Robison	D	Sr.	33	0	3	3	20
Mike Heinke	G	So.	16	0	2	2	4
Jon Lavarro	G	Fr.	10	0	2	2	14
Brad Mullahy	G	Jr.	22	0	2	2	14
Dean Capuano	D	So.	3	0	0	0	0
David Berard	G	Sr.	4	0	0	0	0

GOALTENDING

	Games	W	L	T	Min.	GA	Avg.
David Berard	4	0	0	0	60	1	1.00
Mike Heinke	16	10	4	0	816	48	3.53
Brad Mullahy	22	11	9	2	1291	80	3.72

WESTERN COLLEGIATE HOCKEY ASSOCIATION

1991-92 SEASON

FINAL STANDINGS

Team	G	W	L	T	Pts.	GF	GA
Minnesota (33-11-0)	32	26	6	0	52	163	89
Wisconsin (27-14-2)	32	19	11	2	40	129	106
N. Mich. (25-14-3)	32	17	12	3	37	184	133
Colorado C. (18-18-5)	32	14	14	4	32	138	141
M.-Duluth (15-20-2)	32	14	16	2	30	124	137
Mich. Tech (15-22-1)	32	14	17	1	29	114	137
St. Cloud St. (14-21-2)	32	12	19	1	25	120	138
N. Dakota (17-21-1)	32	12	19	1	25	137	172
Denver (9-25-2)	32	8	22	2	18	110	166

Overall record in parentheses.

PLAYOFF RESULTS

SEMIFINALS

Northern Michigan 6, Wisconsin 3
Minnesota 5, Colorado College 1

CONSOLATION GAME

Wisconsin 5, Colorado College 3

CHAMPIONSHIP GAME

Northen Michigan 4, Minnesota 2

ALL-STAR TEAMS

First team	Pos.	Second team
Duane Derksen, Wisconsin	G	Jeff Stolp, Minnesota
Chris Hynnes, Colorado C.	D	Doug Zmolek, Minnesota
Greg Andrusak, Min.-Dul.	D	Travis Richards, Min.
Dallas Drake, N. Michigan	F	Jim Hiller, N. Michigan
Larry Olimb, Minnesota	F	Derek Plante, Min.-Duluth
Greg Johnson, N. Dakota	F	Dixon Ward, N. Dakota

AWARD WINNERS

Most Valuable Player: Duane Derksen, Wisconsin
Rookie of the year: Darby Hendrickson, Minnesota
Coach of the year: Brad Buetow, Colorado College
Leading scorer: Jim Hiller, Northern Michigan
Playoff MVP: Corwin Saurdiff, Northern Michigan

INDIVIDUAL STATISTICS

COLORADO COLLEGE
SCORING

	Pos.	Class	Games	G	A	Pts.	Pen.
Steve Strunk	F	Sr.	41	25	25	50	36
Chris Hynnes	D	Jr.	40	12	31	43	59
Jody Jaraczewski	F	So.	41	21	20	41	78
Kent Fearns	D	Fr.	41	10	27	37	48
Grant Block	F	Sr.	40	16	20	36	59
Shawn Reid	D	So.	41	12	22	34	64
R.J. Enga	F	Fr.	40	11	16	27	18
Chris Venkus	F	Sr.	27	11	13	24	49
Ryan Reynard	F	Fr.	41	12	9	21	138
Al Schuler	F/D	Sr.	41	6	13	19	30
Rik Duryea	F	Sr.	41	4	11	15	52
Chris McCafferty	F	So.	27	5	9	14	12
Brian Bethard	D	Jr.	39	4	9	13	56
Brian Bruininks	F	Sr.	40	3	8	11	29
Jim Paradise	F	So.	36	2	9	11	18
Steve Nelson	F	So.	35	8	1	9	18
Mark Peterson	D	Jr.	38	3	6	9	32
David Paxton	D	Fr.	37	2	5	7	81
Rob Shypitka	F	Fr.	22	3	3	6	12
Paul Frank	G	Fr.	20	0	3	3	0
Shawn Reddington	F	Jr.	9	0	1	1	6
Marcus Taeck	F	So.	10	0	1	1	10
Paul Badalich	G	Jr.	13	0	1	1	0
Marty Harrison	F	Fr.	1	0	0	0	4
John Steiner	D	Fr.	8	0	0	0	10
Denis Casey	G	Jr.	12	0	0	0	2

GOALTENDING

	Games	W	L	T	Min.	GA	Avg.
Paul Badalich	13	4	4	2	700	46	3.94
Denis Casey	12	6	4	1	664	44	3.97
Paul Frank	20	8	10	2	1167	81	4.16

DENVER
SCORING

	Pos.	Class	Games	G	A	Pts.	Pen.
Lance Momotani	F	Sr.	36	12	25	37	14
Jason Elders	F	Fr.	36	12	18	30	35
Brent Cary	F	Fr.	36	17	8	25	12
B. Konowalchuk	C	So.	33	8	17	25	53

	Pos.	Class	Games	G	A	Pts.	Pen.
Angelo Ricci	C	Fr.	26	10	11	21	20
Mike Naylor	C	Fr.	36	9	11	20	24
Corey Carlson	F	Jr.	25	5	15	20	34
Darren Biggs	F	Sr.	36	10	8	18	46
Paul Koch	D	Fr.	36	4	13	17	48
Chris Kenady	F	Fr.	36	8	5	13	56
Craig McMillan	D	Fr.	32	5	6	11	20
Ian DeCorby	D	So.	31	1	10	11	44
Ryan O'Leary	F	Jr.	17	5	4	9	22
John McLean	D	Fr.	36	4	5	9	36
Kevin Sobb	C	So.	35	4	4	8	2
Brett Petersen	D	Sr.	36	3	5	8	30
Mark Luger	D	So.	24	1	7	8	52
Sean Ortiz	F	Fr.	34	2	2	4	14
Ken MacArthur	C	Sr.	3	2	1	3	20
Heath Sampson	C	Fr.	19	1	1	2	6
J. Lindsay	F	So.	21	1	1	2	8
Mike Markovich	D	Sr.	3	0	1	1	10
Bryan Schoen	G	Jr.	36	0	1	1	10
Jason Van Herik	G	Fr.	7	0	0	0	0
Kevin Oztekin	F	Fr.	10	0	0	0	4

GOALTENDING

	Games	W	L	T	Min.	GA	Avg.
Bryan Schoen	36	9	25	2	2040	167	4.91
Jason Van Herik	7	0	0	0	134	18	8.07

MICHIGAN TECH
SCORING

	Pos.	Class	Games	G	A	Pts.	Pen.
John Young	C	Jr.	39	19	41	60	63
Jim Storm	F	So.	39	25	33	58	12
Jamie Steer	F	Sr.	39	26	24	50	30
Brent Peterson	F	Fr.	39	11	9	20	18
Kevin Manninen	C	So.	32	7	12	19	20
Darcy Martini	D	Sr.	17	5	13	18	58
Greg Parnell	F	Sr.	38	4	14	18	46
Layne LeBel	D	So.	37	6	11	17	26
Don Osborne	D	Jr.	33	5	8	13	40
Travis Seale	C	Fr.	38	4	9	13	10
Ken Plaquin	D	Jr.	32	3	7	10	10
Liam Garvey	D	Fr.	33	3	7	10	47

	Pos.	Class	Games	G	A	Pts.	Pen.
Tim Hartnett	F	Sr.	29	5	3	8	16
Reid McDonald	F	Sr.	38	3	5	8	14
Davis Payne	F	Sr.	24	6	1	7	71
Hugh McEwen	F	So.	16	3	3	6	30
Kirby Perrault	D	So.	39	2	2	4	60
Randy Stevens	F	Fr.	28	1	3	4	16
Randy Lewis	F	Jr.	25	2	1	3	53
Jeff Hill	D	So.	38	0	3	3	81
Justin Peca	F	Fr.	19	1	2	3	12
Darren Brkic	D	So.	10	0	2	2	8
Geoff Sarjeant	G	Sr.	23	0	2	2	2
Mike Hauswirth	F	Jr.	7	0	1	1	4
Rod Ewacha	F	Jr.	2	0	0	0	0
Jim Bonner	D	Jr.	10	0	0	0	14
Jamie Ram	G	So.	23	0	0	0	8

GOALTENDING

	Games	W	L	T	Min.	GA	Avg.
Jamie Ram	23	9	9	1	1144	83	4.35
Geoff Sarjeant	23	7	13	0	1201	90	4.50

	Pos.	Class	Games	G	A	Pts.	Pen.
Kraig Karakas	C	So.	25	2	5	7	18
Jason Bortolussi	F	Jr.	15	4	2	6	12
Brian Caruso	F	So.	29	2	3	5	34
Corey Osmak	F	So.	26	1	4	5	58
Joe Tamminen	F	Fr.	23	1	3	4	12
Brett Larson	D	Fr.	26	2	1	3	20
Rodney Miller	D	So.	11	0	2	2	22
Marc Christian	F	Fr.	14	1	0	1	10
Jerome Butler	G	Fr.	22	0	1	1	0
Scott Engen	F	Jr.	1	0	0	0	0
Garett Plotnik	F	Fr.	1	0	0	0	0
Brett Nelson	G	Sr.	6	0	0	0	0
Wayne Sager	F	Sr.	9	0	0	0	0
Tony Flint	G	Jr.	12	0	0	0	0

GOALTENDING

	Games	W	L	T	Min.	GA	Avg.
Tony Flint	12	4	7	0	706	48	4.08
Jerome Butler	22	9	11	2	1325	91	4.12
Brett Nelson	6	2	2	0	258	21	4.87

MINNESOTA
SCORING

	Pos.	Class	Games	G	A	Pts.	Pen.
Larry Olimb	C	Sr.	44	24	56	80	72
Trent Klatt	F	Jr.	44	30	36	66	78
Craig Johnson	C	So.	44	19	39	58	70
D. Hendrickson	C	Fr.	44	25	30	55	63
Travis Richards	D	Jr.	44	10	23	33	65
Steve Magnusson	C/F	Fr.	41	9	24	33	56
Cory Laylin	F	Sr.	44	19	12	31	44
Jeff Nielsen	F	So.	44	15	15	30	74
Doug Zmolek	D	Jr.	44	6	21	27	88
Justin McHugh	F/C	Fr.	41	14	9	23	34
Scott Bell	F/D	So.	44	15	7	22	80
Joe Dziedzic	F	So.	37	9	10	19	68
John Brill	F	Jr.	38	8	9	17	62
Mike Muller	D	So.	44	4	12	16	60
Chris McAlpine	D	So.	42	3	9	12	136
Eric Means	D	So.	43	1	11	12	46
Tony Bianchi	F/D	So.	24	1	4	5	2
Sean Fabian	D	Sr.	35	1	4	5	45
Todd Westlund	F	So.	22	1	3	4	14
Brandon Steege	F	Fr.	13	1	1	2	22
Jeff Stolp	G	Sr.	36	0	1	1	6
Nick Gerebi	C	Sr.	4	0	0	0	0
John O'Connell	D	Fr.	4	0	0	0	0
Jeff Callinan	G	Fr.	6	0	0	0	0
Jed Fiebelkorn	F	Fr.	7	0	0	0	10
Tom Newman	G	Jr.	12	0	0	0	0

GOALTENDING

	Games	W	L	T	Min.	GA	Avg.
Tom Newman	12	5	1	0	418	17	2.44
Jeff Stolp	36	26	9	0	2017	98	2.91
Jeff Callinan	6	2	1	0	209	15	4.32

MINNESOTA-DULUTH
SCORING

	Pos.	Class	Games	G	A	Pts.	Pen.
Derek Plante	C	Jr.	37	27	36	63	28
Doug Torrell	F	Sr.	37	22	22	44	84
Kevin Kaiser	F	Sr.	37	18	19	37	66
Greg Andrusak	D	Sr.	36	7	27	34	125
Brett Hauer	D	Jr.	33	8	14	22	40
Rusty Fitzgerald	F	Fr.	37	9	11	20	40
Chris Marinucci	C/F	So.	37	6	13	19	41
Jon Rohloff	D	Jr.	27	9	9	18	48
Joe Biondi	C/F	Jr.	34	8	6	14	10
Chris Sittlow	C	Fr.	29	4	6	10	20
Brad Penner	F/C	Jr.	31	4	6	10	12
Marty Olson	F	So.	21	5	4	9	14
Kevin Starren	D	Sr.	36	2	7	9	32
Rod Aldoff	D	Fr.	23	1	8	9	25
Jeff Parrott	D	Jr.	33	1	8	9	78

NORTH DAKOTA
SCORING

	Pos.	Class	Games	G	A	Pts.	Pen.
Greg Johnson	F	Jr.	39	20	54	74	8
Jeff McLean	F	Sr.	39	27	43	70	40
Dixon Ward	F	Sr.	38	33	31	64	90
Justin Duberman	F	Sr.	39	17	27	44	90
Dane Jackson	F	Sr.	39	23	19	42	81
Marty Schriner	F	So.	32	10	12	22	112
Brad Bombardir	D	So.	35	3	14	17	54
Donny Riendeau	F	Jr.	37	8	8	16	64
Chris Gotziaman	F	So.	38	9	6	15	47
Dave Hakstol	D	Sr.	21	3	11	14	52
Scott Kirton	F	Fr.	37	5	6	11	68
Kevin McKinnon	F	So.	39	3	7	10	18
Darren Bear	D	Fr.	36	3	5	8	52
Corey Howe	F	Fr.	36	1	6	7	50
Brad Pascall	D	Sr.	28	0	7	7	85
Lars Oxholm	D	Fr.	32	0	7	7	60
Chad Johnson	D	Jr.	32	0	6	6	41
Brett Hryniuk	F	Fr.	39	4	0	4	8
Jon Larson	D	Jr.	33	1	3	4	16
Joby Bond	F	So.	14	0	2	2	18
Jamie Burt	D	So.	19	0	2	2	18
Jarrod Olson	F/D	Fr.	1	0	0	0	0
Cory Cadden	G	So.	6	0	0	0	0
Jeff Lembke	G	Fr.	10	0	0	0	2
Todd Jones	G	Fr.	30	0	0	0	0

GOALTENDING

	Games	W	L	T	Min.	GA	Avg.
Cory Cadden	6	2	4	0	303	23	4.56
Todd Jones	30	12	14	1	1631	129	4.75
Jeff Lembke	10	3	3	0	412	41	5.97

NORTHERN MICHIGAN
SCORING

	Pos.	Class	Games	G	A	Pts.	Pen.
Jim Hiller	F	Jr.	41	31	55	86	119
Dallas Drake	C	Sr.	40	39	44	83	58
Mark Beaufait	C	Jr.	41	31	50	81	47
Scott Beattie	C	Jr.	40	28	46	74	80
Tony Szabo	F	Jr.	41	21	20	41	64
Joe Frederick	F	Jr.	38	26	8	34	122
Phil Soukoroff	D	Sr.	40	9	20	29	32
Jason Hehr	D	Fr.	42	8	17	25	38
Brent Riplinger	F	Fr.	41	12	12	24	12
Mike Harding	F	Fr.	30	7	9	16	52
Troy Johnson	F/C	Fr.	21	6	10	16	15
Greg Hadden	F	Jr.	33	6	8	14	80
Bryan Ganz	F	So.	28	2	11	13	38
Lou Melone	D	Sr.	30	2	11	13	24
Steve Carpenter	D	So.	34	2	11	13	78
Bill MacGillivray	F	Fr.	33	2	6	8	22

	Pos.	Class	Games	G	A	Pts.	Pen.
Phil Neururer	D	Sr.	26	1	6	7	16
Garett MacDonald	D	So.	36	0	6	6	86
Scott Smith	C	So.	18	2	3	5	10
Dan Ruoho	F	Jr.	18	2	2	4	26
Geoff Simpson	D	Jr.	25	1	3	4	20
Dave Huettl	D/F	Jr.	14	0	4	4	22
Corwin Saurdiff	G	Fr.	36	0	4	4	0
Chad Dameworth	D	Fr.	13	0	2	2	8
Steve Hamilton	D	Fr.	14	0	2	2	6
Steve Woog	F	So.	15	0	1	1	10
Jamie Welsh	G	So.	6	0	0	0	0
Rob Kruhlak	G	Jr.	7	0	0	0	0

GOALTENDING

	Games	W	L	T	Min.	GA	Avg.
Corwin Saurdiff	36	23	10	1	2045	121	3.55
Rob Kruhlak	7	2	2	2	367	30	4.90
Jamie Welsh	6	0	2	0	117	11	5.64

ST. CLOUD STATE

SCORING

	Pos.	Class	Games	G	A	Pts.	Pen.
Jeff Saterdalen	C	Sr.	37	16	29	45	50
Tim Hanus	F	Sr.	37	17	27	44	36
Tony Gruba	F	So.	37	14	22	36	76
Fred Knipscheer	F	Jr.	33	15	17	32	48
Sandy Gasseau	F	Fr.	36	15	16	31	67
Steve Ross	D	Jr.	37	11	16	27	32
Dan O'Shea	F	Jr.	35	10	14	24	65
Greg Hagen	F	Jr.	34	10	8	18	28
Jeff Schmidt	F	Fr.	31	5	12	17	10
Doc DelCastillo	F	Sr.	31	4	11	15	0
Jay Moser	D	Fr.	35	3	9	12	40
Brett Lievers	C	So.	16	2	10	12	12
Jordy Wingate	D	Sr.	34	2	10	12	44
Rikard Gronborg	D	Sr.	32	4	7	11	76
Noel Rahn	F	Jr.	23	8	1	9	23
Chic Pojar	F	Sr.	31	4	5	9	24
Chris Ramberg	C	Fr.	18	4	4	8	8
Todd Kennedy	D	Sr.	34	3	4	7	37
Kelly Hultgren	D	Fr.	34	0	7	7	38
Dave Holum	F	Fr.	25	1	2	3	28
Eric Johnson	F	Fr.	20	0	2	2	8
Gino Santerre	D	Fr.	5	1	0	1	22

	Pos.	Class	Games	G	A	Pts.	Pen.
Tony Burns	D	So.	5	0	1	1	6
Mike O'Hara	G	Sr.	12	0	1	1	0
Grant Sjerven	G	So.	24	0	1	1	0
Cory Fairchild	F	Fr.	4	0	0	0	0
Dave Stone	G	So.	10	0	0	0	2

GOALTENDING

	Games	W	L	T	Min.	GA	Avg.
Dave Stone	10	1	3	2	350	22	3.77
Grant Sjerven	24	9	11	0	1326	90	4.07
Mike O'Hara	12	4	7	0	557	46	4.96

WISCONSIN

SCORING

	Pos.	Class	Games	G	A	Pts.	Pen.
Jason Zent	F	So.	43	27	17	44	134
Doug Macdonald	F	Sr.	33	16	28	44	76
Barry Richter	F	Jr.	43	10	29	39	62
Blaine Moore	F	So.	43	16	20	36	52
Andrew Shier	F	So.	43	10	25	35	64
Dan Plante	F	So.	40	15	16	31	113
Brett Kurtz	F	Sr.	43	13	16	29	80
Chris Tucker	F	So.	38	13	10	23	23
Kelly Fairchild	F	Fr.	41	11	10	21	45
Brian Rafalski	D	Fr.	38	3	16	19	40
Maco Balkovec	D	Fr.	39	7	11	18	101
Jason Francisco	F	Jr.	35	10	7	17	14
Chris Nelson	D	Sr.	43	4	12	16	96
Jon Helgeson	F	Sr.	41	5	8	13	64
Jamie Spencer	F	Fr.	29	4	5	9	12
Joe Harwell	D	Sr.	41	2	7	9	83
Mike Doers	F	So.	41	3	5	8	18
Duane Derksen	G	Sr.	35	0	5	5	14
Mike Strobel	F	Fr.	32	3	0	3	16
Mark Strobel	D	Fr.	37	1	2	3	48
Matt Buss	F	So.	5	1	1	2	0
Chris Tok	D	Fr.	19	0	2	2	8
Jeff Sanderson	D	So.	3	1	0	1	2
Todd Hedlund	F	Fr.	5	0	1	1	2
Jon Michelizzi	G	Jr.	10	0	0	0	0

GOALTENDING

	Games	W	L	T	Min.	GA	Avg.
Duane Derksen	35	21	12	2	2064	110	3.20
Jon Michelizzi	10	6	2	0	530	30	3.40

1991-92 SEASON

FINAL STANDINGS

	W	L	T	GF	GA	Pct.
Alaska-Anchorage	25	8	1	193	124	.750
Alabama-Huntsville	16	12	1	150	118	.569
Kent	15	14	2	143	137	.516
Alaska-Fairbanks	17	17	1	162	146	.500
Army	11	19	1	138	163	.371
Notre Dame	11	19	1	114	153	.371
Air Force	12	22	0	138	149	.353

INDIVIDUAL STATISTICS

AIR FORCE

SCORING

	Pos.	Class	Games	G	A	Pts.	Pen.
Bob Ingraham	C	Jr.	34	14	24	38	28
Eric Rice	F	Jr.	32	21	15	36	47
John Decker	F	Fr.	34	15	21	36	42
Jason Mantaro	C	Sr.	32	14	16	30	38
Beau Bilek	D	Fr.	32	10	13	23	24
Terry Courtney	C	Jr.	28	10	10	20	113
Dan McAlister	F	Fr.	32	10	8	18	15
Brett Gallagher	F	Sr.	34	6	12	18	26
Andy Veneri	C	Fr.	34	6	12	18	40
Erik Brown	F	Fr.	27	2	11	13	33
Matt Tramonte	C	So.	30	7	5	12	16
John Sullivan	F	Fr.	34	5	7	12	25
Tony Roe	D	Sr.	30	5	6	11	62
Deron Christy	F	Jr.	29	1	9	10	16
Jeff Barlow	C	So.	24	5	4	9	6
Steve Masiello	D	Jr.	26	0	7	7	20
Tony Retka	D	So.	33	2	4	6	50
Scot Spann	D	So.	22	2	2	4	10
Doug Smalley	D	So.	22	1	2	3	27
Joe Javorski	F	Fr.	15	0	2	2	10
Mike Thode	F	Fr.	2	1	0	1	0
George Kitz	F	Fr.	4	1	0	1	2
Kevin Magalleta	F	Fr.	3	0	1	1	0
Mark Liebich	G	Sr.	30	0	1	1	0
Jeff Quinn	G	Fr.	1	0	0	0	0
Mike Benson	G	Fr.	2	0	0	0	0
Bryan Nobs	D	So.	5	0	0	0	6
Bill Benson	F	So.	7	0	0	0	2
Derec Liebel	G	Jr.	7	0	0	0	0

GOALTENDING

	Games	W	L	T	Min.	GA	Avg.
Jeff Quinn	1	0	0	0	9	0	0.00
Mark Liebich	30	8	22	0	1711	121	4.24
Mike Benson	2	2	0	0	120	9	4.50
Derec Liebel	7	2	0	0	194	15	4.64

ALABAMA-HUNTSVILLE

SCORING

	Pos.	Class	Games	G	A	Pts.	Pen.
Curt Krolak	F	Sr.	24	19	27	46	37
Graham Fair	F	So.	25	13	25	38	22
Don Burke	D	Jr.	23	12	25	37	105
Brian Beigel	F	Jr.	24	14	17	31	14
Troy Awender	F	Sr.	22	14	16	30	20
Shane Bowler	F	Fr.	24	7	18	25	6
Stuart Vitue	F	Jr.	16	10	14	24	14
Dave Slifka	D	So.	25	6	18	24	32
Doug McDonald	F	Sr.	21	5	19	24	12
Logan Lampert	F	Jr.	21	9	14	23	24
Garry Symons	F	Fr.	22	7	13	20	90
Lance West	F	Fr.	25	8	11	19	20
Mike Mooney	D	Jr.	25	7	9	16	22
Jason Acevedo	D	So.	25	4	10	14	22
Howie McEachern	D	Sr.	22	1	11	12	48
Jean-Marc Plante	F	Sr.	14	5	6	11	18
Don Erbach	D	Sr.	22	3	6	9	42

(continued)

	Pos.		Games	G	A	Pts.	Pen.
Darryl Bossence	F	So.	21	3	5	8	20
Kevin Caputo	D	Jr.	12	2	3	5	2
Mark Hernandez	F	Fr.	16	1	3	4	23
Bobby Thompson	G	Sr.	12	0	2	2	6
Brian Toffey	G	Jr.	1	0	0	0	0
Manny Butera	G	Fr.	11	0	0	0	2

GOALTENDING

	Games	W	L	T	Min.	GA	Avg.
Bobby Thompson	12	8	7	1	725	47	3.91
Manny Butera	11	6	4	0	582	58	5.97
Brian Toffey	1	0	1	0	92	13	8.37

ALASKA-ANCHORAGE

SCORING

	Pos.	Class	Games	G	A	Pts.	Pen.
Derek Donald	F	Sr.	35	23	36	59	50
Keith Morris	F	Jr.	36	24	26	50	18
Dean Larson	F	Sr.	32	21	29	50	32
Steve Bogoyevac	F	Sr.	36	20	22	42	20
Trent Pankewicz	F	Jr.	33	10	23	33	54
Brad Stewart	D	So.	35	4	27	31	16
Mark Stitt	F	Fr.	35	11	19	30	30
Kevin Brown	F	Jr.	33	9	14	23	42
Brian Kraft	F	Sr.	19	7	16	23	20
Jeff Batters	D	Sr.	34	6	17	23	86
Mitch Kean	F	Fr.	28	14	7	21	24
Garnet Deschamps	F	So.	34	10	10	20	12
Lorne Knauft	D	Jr.	35	6	13	19	72
Martin Bakula	D	So.	29	5	14	19	24
Troy Norcross	F	Fr.	34	7	7	14	58
Paul Williams	F	Fr.	27	6	8	14	14
Jim Tobin	F	Jr.	32	4	9	13	47
Jim Mayes	F	Sr.	35	5	7	12	43
Todd Green	F	Fr.	11	0	2	2	6
Trent Leggett	F	Fr.	5	1	0	1	2
Erik Hodne	F	Fr.	7	0	1	1	6
Paul Krake	G	Sr.	28	0	1	1	2
Bryan Herring	F	Jr.	1	0	0	0	0
Cotton Gore	F	Fr.	3	0	0	0	0
Randy Sperry	F	So.	3	0	0	0	4
Shaun Gravistin	G	Jr.	9	0	0	0	0
Scott Millar	D	Jr.	35	0	0	0	57

GOALTENDING

	Games	W	L	T	Min.	GA	Avg.
Paul Krake	28	19	8	0	1646	94	3.43
Shaun Gravistin	9	8	0	1	523	30	3.44

ALASKA-FAIRBANKS

SCORING

	Pos.	Class	Games	G	A	Pts.	Pen.
Shawn Ulrich	F	Jr.	35	16	32	48	89
Dean Fedorchuk	F	So.	35	29	14	43	45
Wayne Sawchuk	F	Jr.	31	21	19	40	84
Tavis MacMillan	F	So.	27	7	28	35	52
Don Lester	D	So.	35	5	27	32	24
Todd Skoglund	F	So.	31	12	14	26	112
Wade Klippenstein	F	Jr.	33	12	13	25	108

INDEPENDENTS

	Pos.	Class	Games	G	A	Pts.	Pen.
Doug Raycroft	F	Jr.	32	13	6	19	30
Lorne Kannigan	F	So.	30	9	9	18	18
Brian Sutton	D	Jr.	33	4	13	17	26
Derby Bognar.........	D	Jr.	34	3	14	17	58
Scott Keyes...........	F	So.	33	10	6	16	12
Warren Carter	F	Fr.	34	3	12	15	20
Jason Eckel	F	Fr.	17	5	9	14	4
Corey Spring	F	Fr.	35	3	8	11	30
Derek Linnell..........	D	Sr.	29	3	7	10	24
Kirk Patton	D	So.	34	3	4	7	26
Marcel Aubin	D	Fr.	16	1	6	7	22
Chris O'Rourke.......	F	So.	13	1	5	6	71
Glenn Odishaw.......	D	So.	22	1	1	2	31
Chris Carney	F	Fr.	3	1	0	1	0
Travis Powell	D	So.	17	0	1	1	10
Todd Henderson ...	G	Jr.	20	0	1	1	0
Brian Fish	G	Fr.	4	0	0	0	2
Nathan Rose	F	Jr.	4	0	0	0	0
Kevin Dillard	F	So.	13	0	0	0	0
Jamie Loewen	G	Sr.	14	0	0	0	0

GOALTENDING

	Games	W	L	T	Min.	GA	Avg.
Jamie Loewen	14	8	4	1	816	52	3.83
Todd Henderson ...	20	8	12	0	1111	80	4.32
Brian Fish	4	1	1	0	182	14	4.61

ARMY
SCORING

	Pos.	Class	Games	G	A	Pts.	Pen.
Rick Berube..........	F	Jr.	29	16	21	37	28
Rick Randazzo	F	Jr.	31	13	23	36	44
Chad Sundem........	F	Jr.	31	15	18	33	16
Mark Stachelski	F	Fr.	30	11	22	33	53
Scott Tardif...........	F	Sr.	25	18	13	31	30
Bob Mansell	F	Jr.	29	10	18	28	8
R. MacLaughlin	F	Fr.	24	9	14	23	10
Milt Smith.............	F	So.	31	7	12	19	30
Ross Erzar	F	Sr.	21	12	5	17	20
Michael Landers....	D	So.	30	4	12	16	16
Chris Mead...........	D	Sr.	28	4	11	15	45
Kevin Backus.........	D	Jr.	29	1	11	12	18
Chris Soucie..........	D	Sr.	26	3	7	10	16
Sean Hennessy	D	Fr.	28	1	8	9	36
Justin Lambert	F	Jr.	20	3	4	7	6
Larry Seward	F	So.	15	2	4	6	0
John Compton........	D	So.	27	1	5	6	36
David Pilarski	F	So.	10	1	4	5	14
Chad Palodichuk ...	F	Fr.	13	3	1	4	2
Eric Kindgren	F	Jr.	12	2	2	4	6
Derek Huffer	F	So.	8	1	2	3	2
Scott Gardiner	F	Jr.	6	0	3	3	2
Craig Fellman	F	Fr.	7	1	1	2	0
Dan Carey	F	Jr.	11	0	2	2	2
Scott Boyle	G	Jr.	12	0	2	2	2
Brian Bolio	G	Fr.	5	0	1	1	0
Ronald Adimey	G	Fr.	7	0	1	1	0
Brett Funck............	D	So.	9	0	1	1	2
Dean Wegner	F	Jr.	13	0	1	1	14
Steve Burke	F	Jr.	1	0	0	0	0
Tim Hocking...........	F	Fr.	1	0	0	0	0
Matthew Posner	F	So.	1	0	0	0	0
Ted Doyle	F	Fr.	2	0	0	0	0
Sam Pearson.........	G	So.	2	0	0	0	0
Troy Eigner	F	Fr.	5	0	0	0	2
Jay McDonald........	D	Fr.	5	0	0	0	2
Brandon Hayes	G	Sr.	15	0	0	0	0

GOALTENDING

	Games	W	L	T	Min.	GA	Avg.
Brian Bolio	5	3	1	1	275	17	3.71
Ronald Adimey	7	2	3	0	342	28	4.92
Brandon Hayes........	15	2	11	0	737	63	5.13
Scott Boyle	12	4	4	0	472	44	5.59
Sam Pearson...........	2	0	0	0	46	9	11.79

KENT
SCORING

	Pos.	Class	Games	G	A	Pts.	Pen.
Claude Morin	F	Fr.	31	21	18	39	12
Steve McLean	F	So.	29	13	16	29	22
Dean Sylvester	F	Fr.	31	7	21	28	10
Ross Antonini	F	Jr.	31	14	12	26	54
Neal Purdon	F	So.	28	17	5	22	20
Barry Cummins	D	Fr.	29	7	15	22	26
Jay Neal	D	Jr.	27	8	13	21	28
Tim Evans..............	F	Jr.	29	11	9	20	36
Bob Krosky	F	So.	29	6	13	19	54
Kevin McPherson ..	F	So.	29	9	9	18	12
Brian Mulcahy	F	So.	30	9	7	16	50
Roger Mischke	D	So.	24	4	11	15	36
Lane Gunderson	D	Fr.	22	5	4	9	10
Rick Carter............	F	Sr.	31	3	6	9	14
Gregg Fesette	D	Jr.	28	1	7	8	56
Ken Eddy	D	Jr.	20	1	6	7	16
Kip Guenther	F	Sr.	26	4	2	6	21
Steve Chalupnik	D	So.	16	0	6	6	10
Matt Brait..............	D	Jr.	30	0	5	5	68
Brent Mahoney	F	Jr.	27	2	2	4	34
Dan Duffy..............	D	Jr.	9	0	3	3	12
Brad Baxter	F	Jr.	3	1	0	1	2
Mario Lacasse	G	Fr.	11	0	1	1	2
Paul Dixon	G	So.	9	0	0	0	0
Scott Shaw............	G	Jr.	18	0	0	0	14

GOALTENDING

	Games	W	L	T	Min.	GA	Avg.
Mario Lacasse	11	4	1	1	456	30	3.95
Paul Dixon	8	4	4	0	418	28	4.02
Scott Shaw............	18	7	9	1	1002	79	4.73

NOTRE DAME
SCORING

	Pos.	Class	Games	G	A	Pts.	Pen.
Curtis Janicke	F	Jr.	31	12	38	50	68
Lou Zadra	F	Sr.	31	24	23	47	44
Sterling Black	F	Jr.	30	12	22	34	18
Michael Curry	F	Sr.	30	11	11	22	42
Matt Osiecki...........	D	So.	30	4	18	22	46
Dan Sawyer	D	Jr.	31	7	13	20	44
Troy Cusey............	F	Fr.	30	8	6	14	16
Brent Lamppa	F	Fr.	31	6	6	12	18
John Rushin...........	F	Fr.	17	8	2	10	30
Scott Vickman	D	Sr.	26	1	9	10	52
Pat Arendt.............	F	Sr.	30	3	5	8	20
Kevin Patrick	D	Jr.	31	3	5	8	20
Tim Litchard	F	So.	25	4	3	7	8
Tom Miniscalco	F	Jr.	21	2	2	4	20
Robert Copeland	D	Sr.	26	2	2	4	20
Jeff Hasselman	F	Fr.	30	2	2	4	8
Chris Tschupp	F	So.	13	1	3	4	8
Eric Gregoire	D	Jr.	17	0	4	4	12
Jason Konesco	D	So.	14	2	1	3	14
David Bankoske.....	F	Sr.	2	1	1	2	4
Dan Marvin	F	Jr.	29	1	1	2	14
Tom Arkell	D	So.	5	0	1	1	4
Brent Lothrop	G	So.	8	0	1	1	0
Justin Arcangel	D	So.	12	0	1	1	4
Steve Soderling	F	Fr.	12	0	1	1	4
Cullen Hegarty	F	So.	1	0	0	0	0
Mark Wainwright ..	F	Fr.	2	0	0	0	0
Mike Wilary	F	Fr.	4	0	0	0	0
Carey Nemeth	F	Fr.	6	0	0	0	0
Greg Louder	G	So.	18	0	0	0	0
Carl Picconato	G	Jr.	8	0	0	0	0

GOALTENDING

	Games	W	L	T	Min.	GA	Avg.
Brent Lothrop	8	4	3	0	390	27	4.15
Greg Louder	18	5	13	0	1055	88	5.00
Carl Picconato	8	2	3	1	419	35	5.01

CANADIAN COLLEGES

ATLANTIC UNIVERSITIES ATHLETIC ASSOCIATION, 1991-92 SEASON

FINAL STANDINGS

KELLY DIVISION

Team	G	W	L	T	Pts.	GF	GA
Acadia University......	24	18	4	2	38	124	73
Dalhousie University ..	25	13	8	4	30	118	99
St. Mary's University .	26	9	13	4	22	117	126
St. Francis Xavier U. ..	26	9	14	3	21	86	118
U. Col. of Cape Breton.	26	7	15	4	18	120	142

MACADAM DIVISION

Team	G	W	L	T	Pts.	GF	GA
U. of New Brunswick ..	26	18	7	1	37	141	94
U. of P. Edward Island	24	13	9	2	28	126	101
St. Thomas University	26	11	14	1	23	119	135
Univ. de Moncton.......	25	9	14	2	20	110	121
Mount Allison Univ.	24	7	16	1	15	97	149

PLAYOFF RESULTS

KELLY DIVISION SEMIFINALS

St. Mary's 6, Dalhousie 5 (2 OT)
Dalhousie 5, St. Mary's 1
Dalhousie 9, St. Mary's 1

Acadia 7, St. Francis Xavier 0
Acadia 6, St. Francis Xavier 2

MACADAM DIVISION SEMIFINALS

Prince Edward Island 5, St. Thomas 3
Prince Edward Island 3, St. Thomas 2

New Brunswick 4, Moncton 2
New Brunswick 3, Moncton 2

KELLY DIVISION FINALS

Dalhousie 5, Acadia 3
Acadia 5, Dalhousie 4
Acadia 6, Dalhousie 3

MACADAM DIVISION FINALS

Prince Edward Island 6, New Brunswick 5 (3 OT)
Prince Edward Island 4, New Brunswick 2

LEAGUE FINALS

Acadia 12, Prince Edward Island 1
Acadia 4, Prince Edward Island 3 (2 OT)

ALL-STAR TEAMS

Kelly Division	Pos.	Macadam Division
Pat McGarry, Dalhousie	G	Chris Somers, N.B.
Kevin Knopp, Acadia	D	Wayne MacPhee, P.E.I.
Tim Gilligan, St. Mary's	D	Garth Joy, St. Thomas
George Dupont, Acadia	F	Shane MacEachern, P.E.I.
Joe Suk, Dalhousie	F	Mathiew Beliveau, Moncton
Craig Teeple, St. Mary's	F	Brent Grant, St. Thomas

AWARD WINNERS

Most Valuable Player: Craig Teeple, St. Mary's
Rookie of the year: Jerrett DeFazio, St. Mary's
Coach of the year: Tom Coolen, Acadia
Leading scorer: Craig Teeple, St. Mary's

CANADA WEST UNIVERSITY ATHLETIC ASSOCIATION, 1991-92 SEASON

FINAL STANDINGS

Team	G	W	L	T	Pts.	GF	GA
Regina (22-12-3).....	28	19	6	3	41	159	111
Alberta (26-9-5).....	28	17	6	5	39	137	100
Calgary* (22-16-4)..	28	15	11	2	32	121	119
Manitoba (19-16-2) .	28	14	13	1	29	121	111
Lethbridge (18-19-3).	28	12	13	3	27	123	129
Sask.* (16-18-1).....	28	13	14	1	27	109	110
Brit. Col.* (16-17-3) .	28	11	14	3	25	110	137
Brandon† (6-32-3)...	28	1	25	2	4	88	150

Overall record in parentheses.
*Won one game due to forfeit.
†Lost three games due to forfeit.

PLAYOFF RESULTS

SEMIFINALS

Regina 7, Manitoba 6
Regina 6, Manitoba 1

Calgary 4, Alberta 3 (OT)
Alberta 6, Calgary 5
Alberta 6, Calgary 4

FINALS

Alberta 5, Regina 3
Alberta 4, Regina 3

ALL-STAR TEAMS

First team	Pos.	Second team
Roydon Gunn, Sask.	G	Craig Lumbard, Regina
Ian Herbers, Alberta	D	Denis Carignan, Regina
Garth Premak, Alberta	D	Bart Cote, Regina
Adam Morrison, Alberta	F	LenNielsen, Regina
Troy Edwards, Regina	F	Wayde Bucsis, Sask.
Craig Streu, Manitoba	F	Grant Delcourt, B.C.

AWARD WINNERS

Most Valuable Player: Roydon Gunn, Saskatchewan
Rookie of the year: Craig Lumbard, Regina
Most gentlemanly player: Darrin McKechnie, Regina
Coach of the year: Bill Liskowich, Regina
Leading scorer: Adam Morrison, Alberta

ONTARIO UNIVERSITIES ATHLETIC ASSOCIATION, 1991-92 SEASON

FINAL STANDINGS

EAST DIVISION

Team	G	W	L	T	Pts.	GF	GA
Que. at Trois-Rivieres .	22	17	4	1	35	140	66
McGill University	22	15	5	2	32	103	68
University of Toronto .	22	14	6	2	30	113	70
York University..........	22	11	8	3	25	98	80
University of Ottawa ..	22	10	10	2	22	119	94
Concordia University .	22	8	12	2	18	91	94
Queen's University	22	4	17	1	9	81	135
Ryerson Poly. Inst.	22	0	22	0	0	55	217

WEST DIVISION

Team	G	W	L	T	Pts.	GF	GA
U. of Western Ontario.	22	16	5	1	33	119	65
University of Waterloo.	22	16	6	0	32	120	68
University of Guelph..	22	15	7	0	30	142	94
Wilfrid Laurier Univ...	22	13	7	2	28	102	74
University of Windsor	22	12	10	0	24	109	95
Laurentian University	22	7	14	1	15	105	119
Brock University........	22	7	14	1	15	104	137
Royal Military College	22	2	20	0	4	56	181

PLAYOFF RESULTS

EAST DIVISION QUARTERFINALS

Toronto 5, Concordia 3
York 5, Ottawa 3

WEST DIVISION QUARTERFINALS

Guelph 7, Laurentian 1
Laurier 7, Windsor 1

EAST DIVISION SEMIFINALS

McGill 4, Toronto 2
Toronto 4, McGill 1
Toronto 2, McGill 1

Quebec at Trois-Rivieres 5, York 2
Quebec at Trois-Rivieres 6, York 3

WEST DIVISION SEMIFINALS

Guelph 2, Waterloo 1
Waterloo 4, Guelph 2
Guelph 6, Waterloo 3

Laurier 4, Western 3 (OT)
Laurier 4, Western 3 (OT)

EAST DIVISION FINALS

Toronto 5, Quebec at Trois-Rivieres 4 (2 OT)
Quebec at Trois-Rivieres 8, Toronto 3
Quebec at Trois-Rivieres 6, Toronto 1

WEST DIVISION FINALS

Guelph 3, Laurier 2 (2 OT)
Laurier 4, Guelph 2
Laurier 7, Guelph 4

LEAGUE FINALS

Quebec at Trois-Rivieres 8, Laurier 2

ALL-STAR TEAMS

EAST DIVISION

First team	Pos.	Second team
Denis Desbiens, UQTR	G	Robert Desjardins, Con.
Mark Haarmann, Toronto	D	Francois Loranger, UQTR
Marc Picard, UQTR	D	Guy Girouard, York
Stephane Groleau, UQTR	F	Steve Simoni, Ottawa
Martin Raymond, McGill	F	Doug Cherepacha, Toronto
Mike Fiset, Ottawa	F	Benoit Gosselin, UQTR

WEST DIVISION

First team	Pos.	Second team
Mark Seguin, Windsor	G	Steve Udvari, Waterloo
Steve Perkovic, Guelph	D	Larry Rucchin, Laurier
Corey Keenan, Waterloo	D	Doug Jones, Ontario
Rob Arabski, Guelph	F	Mark McCreary, Laurier
Steve Rucchin, Ontario	F	Darren Snyder, Waterloo
Dave Lorentz, Waterloo	F	Rod Anthony, Windsor

AWARD WINNERS

East Division Most Valuable Player: Denis Desbiens, UQTR
West Division Most Valuable Player: Rob Arabski, Guelph
East Division rookie of the year: Patrick Jeanson, McGill
West Division rookie of the year: Jeff Wilson, Guelph
East Division most gentlemanly player: Doug Cherepacha, Toronto
West Division most gentlemanly player: Dave Lorentz, Waterloo
East Division coach of the year: Paul Titanic, Toronto
West Division coach of the year: Rick Cranker, Windsor
Leading scorer: Rod Anthony, Windsor
Playoff MVP: Francois Loranger, Quebec at Trois-Rivieres

INDEX OF TEAMS

NHL, MINOR LEAGUES, MAJOR JUNIOR LEAGUES

COLLEGE TEAMS

EXPLANATION OF FOOTNOTES AND ABBREVIATIONS

*Led league.
†Tied for league lead.

POSITIONS: C: center. **D:** defenseman. **G:** goaltender. **LW:** left winger. **RW:** right winger.

STATISTICS: A: assists. **Avg.:** goals-against average. **G:** goals. **GA:** goals against. **Gms.:** games. **L:** losses. **Min.:** minutes. **Pen.:** penalty minutes. **Pts:** points. **SO:** shutouts. **T:** ties. **W:** wins.

LEAGUES: AAHL: All American Hockey League. **ACHL:** Atlantic Coast Hockey League. **AHL:** American Hockey League. **AJHL:** Alberta Junior Hockey League. **AUAA:** Atlantic Universities Athletic Association. **BCJHL:** British Columbia Junior Hockey League. **CAHL:** Central Alberta Hockey League. **CAJHL:** Central Alberta Junior Hockey League. **Can. College:** Canadian College. **Can.HL:** Canadian Hockey League. **CCHA:** Central Collegiate Hockey Association. **CHL:** Central Hockey League. **CIS:** Commonwealth of Independent States. **COJHL:** Central Ontario Junior Hockey League. **CPHL:** Central Professional Hockey League. **CWUAA:** Canada West University Athletic Association. **Conn. H.S.:** Connecticut High School. **Czech.:** Czechoslovakia. **ECAC:** Eastern College Athletic Conference. **ECAC-II:** Eastern College Athletic Conference, Division II. **ECHL:** East Coast Hockey League. **EHL:** Eastern Hockey League. **GWHC:** Great Western Hockey Conference. **Hoc. East:** Hockey East. **IHL:** International Hockey League. **Ill. H.S.:** Illinois High School. **Indiana H.S.:** Indiana High School. **Int'l:** International. **KIJHL:** Kootenay International Junior Hockey League. **Mass. H.S.:** Massachusetts High School. **Md. H.S.:** Maryland High School. **Mich. H.S.:** Michigan High School. **Minn. H.S.:** Minnesota High School. **MJHL:** Manitoba Junior Hockey League. **MTHL:** Metro Toronto Hockey League. **NAHL:** North American Hockey League. **NAJHL:** North American Junior Hockey League. **NCAA-II:** National Collegiate Athletic Association, Division II. **N.D. H.S.:** North Dakota High School. **NEJHL:** New England Junior Hockey League. **NHL:** National Hockey League. **N.H. H.S.:** New Hampshire High School. **N.J. H.S.:** New Jersey High School. **NSJHL:** Nova Scotia Junior Hockey League. **N.S.Jr.A:** Nova Scotia Junior A. **N.Y. H.S.:** New York High School. **NYMJHL:** New York Major Junior Hockey League. **NYOHL:** North York Ontario Hockey League. **ODHA:** Ottawa & District Hockey Association. **OHA:** Ontario Hockey Association. **OHA Jr. A:** Ontario Hockey Association Junior A. **OHA Mjr. Jr. A:** Ontario Hockey Association Major Junior A. **OHA Senior:** Ontario Hockey Association Senior. **OHL:** Ontario Hockey League. **O. H.S.:** Ohio High School. **OJHA:** Ontario Junior Hockey Association. **OJHL:** Ontario Junior Hockey League. **OMJHL:** Ontario Major Junior Hockey League. **OPJHL:** Ontario Provincial Junior Hockey League. **OUAA:** Ontario Universities Athletic Association. **PCJHL:** Peace Caribou Junior Hockey League. **PEIHA:** Prince Edward Island Hockey Association. **PEIJHL:** Prince Edward Island Junior Hockey League. **QMJHL:** Quebec Major Junior Hockey League. **R.I. H.S.:** Rhode Island High School. **SAJHL:** Southern Alberta Junior Hockey League. **SJHL:** Saskatchewan Junior Hockey League. **Sask. H.S.:** Saskatchewan High School. **SOJHL:** Southern Ontario Junior Hockey League. **Swed. Jr.:** Sweden Junior. **Switz.:** Switzerland. **TBAHA:** Thunder Bay Amateur Hockey Association. **TBJHL:** Thunder Bay Junior Hockey League. **USHL:** United States Hockey League. **USSR:** Union of Soviet Socialist Republics. **Vt. H.S.:** Vermont High School. **W. Germany, W. Ger.:** West Germany. **WCHA:** Western Collegiate Hockey Association. **WCHL:** Western Canada Hockey League. **WHA:** World Hockey Association. **WHL:** Western Hockey League. **Wisc. H.S.:** Wisconsin High School. **Yukon Sr.:** Yukon Senior.

EXPLANATION OF AWARDS

NHL AWARDS: Alka-Seltzer Plus Award: plus/minus leader. **Art Ross Trophy:** leading scorer. **Bill Masterton Memorial Trophy:** perseverance, sportsmanship and dedication to hockey. **Bud Light/NHL Man of the Year:** service to community; called Budweiser/NHL Man of the Year prior to 1990-91. **Budweiser/NHL Man of the Year:** service to community; renamed Bud Light/NHL Man of the Year in 1990-91. **Calder Memorial Trophy:** rookie of the year. **Conn Smythe Trophy:** most valuable player in playoffs. **Dodge Performance of the Year Award:** most outstanding performance. **Dodge Performer of the Year Award:** most outstanding performer in regular season. **Dodge Ram Tough Award:** highest combined total of power play, shorthanded, game-winning and game-tying goals. **Emery Edge Award:** plus/minus leader; awarded from 1982-83 through 1987-88. **Frank J. Selke Trophy:** best defensive forward. **Hart Memorial Trophy:** most valuable player. **Jack Adams Award:** coach of the year. **James Norris Memorial Trophy:** outstanding defenseman. **King Clancy Memorial Trophy:** humanitarian contributions. **Lady Byng Memorial Trophy:** most gentlemanly player. **Lester B. Pearson Award:** outstanding player as selected by NHL Players' Association. **Lester Patrick Trophy:** outstanding service to hockey in U.S. **Trico Goaltender Award:** best save percentage. **Vezina Trophy:** best goaltender; awarded to goalkeeper(s) having played minimum of 25 games for team with fewest goals scored against prior to 1981-82. **Viking Award:** outstanding Swedish-born player as voted on by Swedish-born NHL players. **William M. Jennings Trophy:** goalkeeper(s) having played minimum of 25 games for team with fewest goals scored against.

MINOR LEAGUE AWARDS: Baz Bastien Trophy: top goaltender (AHL). **Bobby Orr Trophy:** best defenseman (CHL). **Bob Gassoff Award:** most improved defenseman (CHL). **Commissioner's Trophy:** coach of the year (IHL). **Don Ashby Memorial Trophy:** ironman award (CHL). **Dudley (Red) Garrett Memorial Trophy:** rookie of the year (AHL). **Eddie Shore Plaque:** outstanding defenseman (AHL). **Fred Hunt Memorial Award:** sportsmanship, determination and dedication (AHL). **Garry F. Longman Memorial Trophy:** outstanding rookie (IHL). **Governors Trophy:** outstanding defenseman (IHL). **Harry (Hap) Holmes Memorial Trophy:** goaltender(s) having played minimum of 25 games for team with fewest goals scored against (AHL); awarded to outstanding goaltender prior to 1983-84. **Jack Butterfield Trophy:** Calder Cup Playoffs MVP (AHL). **Jake Milford Trophy:** coach of the year (CHL). **James Gatschene Memorial Trophy:** most valuable player (IHL). **James Norris Memorial Trophy:** outstanding goaltender (IHL). **John B. Sollenberger Trophy:** leading scorer (AHL); originally called Wally Kilrea Trophy, later changed to Carl Liscombe Trophy until summer of 1955. **Ken McKenzie Trophy:** outstanding U.S.-born rookie (IHL). **Ken McKenzie Trophy:** top rookie (CHL). **Leo P. Lamoureux Memorial Trophy:** leading scorer (IHL); originally called George H. Wilkinson Trophy from 1946-47 through 1959-60. **Les Cunningham Plaque:** most valuable player (AHL). **Louis A.R. Pieri Memorial Award:** top coach (AHL). **Max McNab Trophy:** playoff MVP (CHL). **N.R. (Bud) Poile Trophy:** playoff MVP (IHL); originally called Turner Cup Playoff MVP from 1984-85 through 1988-89. **Phil Esposito Trophy:** leading scorer (CHL). **Terry Sawchuk Trophy:** top goaltenders (CHL). **Tommy Ivan Trophy:** most valuable player (CHL). **Turner Cup Playoff MVP:** playoff MVP (IHL); renamed N.R. (Bud) Poile Trophy in 1989-90.

MAJOR JUNIOR LEAGUE AWARDS: Association of Journalists for Major Junior League Hockey Trophy: top pro prospect (QMJHL); renamed Michael Bossy Trophy in 1983-84. **Bill Hunter Trophy:** top defenseman (WHL); called Top Defenseman Trophy prior to 1987-88 season. **Bob Brownridge Memorial Trophy:** top scorer (WHL); later renamed Bob Clarke Trophy. **Bobby Smith Trophy:** scholastic player of the year (OHL). **Bob Clarke Trophy:** top scorer (WHL); originally called Bob Brownridge Memorial Trophy. **Brad Hornung Trophy:** most sportsmanlike player (WHL); called Frank Boucher Memorial Trophy for most gentlemanly player prior to 1987-88 season. **Dave Pinkney Trophy:** top team goaltending (OHL). **Del Wilson Trophy:** top goaltender (WHL); called Top Goaltender Trophy prior to 1987-88 season. **Des Instructeurs Trophy:** rookie of the year (QMJHL); awarded to top rookie forward since 1981-82 season; renamed Michel Bergeron Trophy in 1985-86. **Dunc McCallum Memorial Trophy:** coach of the year (WHL). **Eddie Powers Memorial Trophy:** scoring champion (OHL). **Emile (Butch) Bouchard Trophy:** best defenseman (QMJHL). **Emms Family Award:** rookie of the year (OHL). **Four Broncos Memorial Trophy:** most valuable player as selected by coaches (WHL); called Most Valuable Player Trophy prior to 1987-88 season. **Frank Boucher Memorial Trophy:** most gentlemanly player (WHL); renamed Brad Hornung Trophy during 1987-88 season. **Frank J. Selke Trophy:** most gentlemanly player (QMJHL). **F.W. (Dinty) Moore Trophy:** rookie goalie with best goals-against average (OHL). **George Parsons Trophy:** sportsmanship in Memorial Cup (Can.HL). **Guy Lafleur Trophy:** most valuable player during playoffs (QMJHL). **Hap Emms Memorial Trophy:** outstanding goaltender in Memorial Cup (Can.HL). **Jacques Plante Trophy:** best goaltender (QMJHL). **Jean Beliveau Trophy:** leading point scorer (QMJHL). **Jim Mahon Memorial Trophy:** top scoring right winger (OHL). **Jim Piggott Memorial Trophy:** rookie of the year (WHL); originally called Stewart (Butch) Paul Memorial Trophy. **Leo Lalonde Memorial Trophy:** overage player of the year (OHL). **Marcel Robert Trophy:** top scholastic/athletic performer (QMJHL). **Matt Leyden Trophy:** coach of the year (OHL). **Max Kaminsky Trophy:** outstanding defenseman (OHL); awarded to most gentlemanly player prior to 1969-70. **Michael Bossy Trophy:** top pro prospect (QMJHL); originally called Association of Journalism of Hockey Trophy from 1980-81 through 1982-83. **Michel Bergeron Trophy:** top rookie forward (QMJHL); awarded to rookie of the year prior to 1980-81 season. **Michel Briere Trophy:** most valuable player (QMJHL). **Most Valuable Player Trophy:** most valuable player (WHL); renamed Four Broncos Memorial Trophy during 1987-88 season. **Raymond Lagace Trophy:** top rookie defenseman or goaltender (QMJHL). **Red Tilson Trophy:** outstanding player (OHL). **Shell Cup:** awarded to offensive player of the year and defensive player of the year (QMJHL). **Stafford Smythe Memorial Trophy:** most valuable player of Memorial Cup (Can.HL). **Stewart (Butch) Paul Memorial Trophy:** rookie of the year (WHL); renamed Jim Piggott Memorial Trophy during 1987-88 season. **Top Defenseman Trophy:** top defenseman (WHL); renamed Bill Hunter Trophy during 1987-88 season. **Top Goaltender Trophy:** top goaltender (WHL); renamed Del Wilson Trophy during 1987-88 season. **William Hanley Trophy:** most gentlemanly player (OHL).

COLLEGE AWARDS: Adam Kryczka Trophy: top goaltender (CWUAA). **Hobey Baker Memorial Trophy:** top college hockey player in U.S. **Senator Joseph A. Sullivan Trophy:** outstanding player in Canadian Interuniversity Athletic Union.

OTHER AWARDS: Gold Stick Award: Europe's top player. **Izvestia Trophy:** leading scorer (USSR).

A

ACTON, KEITH
C, FLYERS

PERSONAL: Born April 15, 1958, at Newmarket, Ont. . . . 5-8/170. . . . Shoots left. . . . Full name: Keith Edward Acton.

TRANSACTIONS/CAREER NOTES: Selected by Montreal Canadiens in sixth round (eighth Canadiens pick, 103rd overall) of NHL entry draft (June 15, 1978). . . . Traded by Canadiens with RW Mark Napier and third-round pick in 1984 draft previously acquired from Toronto Maple Leafs (C Ken Hodge) to Minnesota North Stars for C Bobby Smith (October 1983). . . . Injured left wrist (April 20, 1984). . . . Traded by North Stars to Edmonton Oilers for D Moe Mantha (January 22, 1988). . . . Broke nose (December 14, 1988). . . . Traded by Oilers with sixth-round pick in 1991 draft (D Dimitri Yushkevich) to Philadelphia Flyers for RW Dave Brown (February 7, 1989). . . . Traded by Flyers with G Pete Peeters to Winnipeg Jets for future considerations (September 28, 1989). . . . Traded by Jets with G Pete Peeters to Philadelphia Flyers for fifth-round pick in 1991 draft previously acquired from Maple Leafs (C Juha Ylonen) (October 3, 1989); Jets did not have to surrender future considerations in a previous deal for Shawn Cronin (the NHL fined both Flyers and Jets $10,000 for violating a league by-law against loaning players to another team). . . . Underwent elbow surgery (September 1990). . . . Sprained knee (October 1990); missed three games. . . . Fractured wrist (November 27, 1991); missed 26 games.
HONORS: Named to AHL All-Star second team (1979-80).

Season Team	League	REGULAR SEASON					PLAYOFFS				
		Gms.	G	A	Pts.	Pen.	Gms.	G	A	Pts.	Pen.
74-75—Wexford Jr. B	MTHL	43	23	29	52	46	—	—	—	—	—
75-76—Peterborough	OHA Mj. Jr. A	35	9	17	26	30	—	—	—	—	—
76-77—Peterborough	OMJHL	65	52	69	121	93	4	1	4	5	6
77-78—Peterborough	OMJHL	68	42	86	128	52	21	10	8	18	16
78-79—Nova Scotia	AHL	79	15	26	41	22	10	4	2	6	4
79-80—Nova Scotia	AHL	75	45	53	98	38	6	1	2	3	8
—Montreal	NHL	2	0	1	1	0	—	—	—	—	—
80-81—Montreal	NHL	61	15	24	39	74	2	0	0	0	6
81-82—Montreal	NHL	78	36	52	88	88	5	0	4	4	16
82-83—Montreal	NHL	78	24	26	50	63	3	0	0	0	0
83-84—Montreal	NHL	9	3	7	10	4	—	—	—	—	—
—Minnesota	NHL	62	17	38	55	60	15	4	7	11	12
84-85—Minnesota	NHL	78	20	38	58	90	9	4	4	8	6
85-86—Minnesota	NHL	79	26	32	58	100	5	0	3	3	6
86-87—Minnesota	NHL	78	16	29	45	56	—	—	—	—	—
87-88—Minnesota	NHL	46	8	11	19	74	—	—	—	—	—
—Edmonton	NHL	26	3	6	9	21	7	2	0	2	16
88-89—Edmonton	NHL	46	11	15	26	47	—	—	—	—	—
—Philadelphia	NHL	25	3	10	13	64	16	2	3	5	18
89-90—Philadelphia	NHL	69	13	14	27	80	—	—	—	—	—
90-91—Philadelphia	NHL	76	14	23	37	131	—	—	—	—	—
91-92—Philadelphia	NHL	50	7	10	17	98	—	—	—	—	—
NHL totals		863	216	336	552	1050	62	12	21	33	80

ADAMS, GREG
LW, CANUCKS

PERSONAL: Born August 1, 1963, at Nelson, B.C. . . . 6-3/198. . . . Shoots left. . . . Full name: Greg G. Adams.
COLLEGE: Northern Arizona.
TRANSACTIONS/CAREER NOTES: Signed as free agent by New Jersey Devils (June 25, 1984). . . . Tore tendon in right wrist (April 1986). . . . Traded by Devils with G Kirk McLean to Vancouver Canucks for C Patrik Sundstrom, a fourth-round pick in 1988 draft (LW Matt Ruchty) and the option to flip second-round picks in 1988 draft; Devils exercised option and selected LW Jeff Christian and Canucks selected D Leif Rohlin (September 1987). . . . Fractured ankle (February 1989). . . . Fractured cheekbone (January 4, 1990); missed 12 games. . . . Sprained left knee (October 17, 1990); missed 12 games. . . . Sprained forearm, wrist and abdomen (February 27, 1991). . . . Suffered concussion (October 8, 1991); missed one game.

Season Team	League	REGULAR SEASON					PLAYOFFS				
		Gms.	G	A	Pts.	Pen.	Gms.	G	A	Pts.	Pen.
80-81—Kelowna	BCJHL	47	40	50	90	16	—	—	—	—	—
81-82—Kelowna	BCJHL	45	31	42	73	24	—	—	—	—	—
82-83—Northern Arizona Univ.	Indep.	29	14	21	35	46	—	—	—	—	—
83-84—Northern Arizona Univ.	Indep.	47	40	50	90	16	—	—	—	—	—
84-85—Maine	AHL	41	15	20	35	12	11	3	4	7	0
—New Jersey	NHL	36	12	9	21	14	—	—	—	—	—
85-86—New Jersey	NHL	78	35	42	77	30	—	—	—	—	—
86-87—New Jersey	NHL	72	20	27	47	19	—	—	—	—	—
87-88—Vancouver	NHL	80	36	40	76	30	—	—	—	—	—
88-89—Vancouver	NHL	61	19	14	33	24	7	2	3	5	2
89-90—Vancouver	NHL	65	30	20	50	18	—	—	—	—	—
90-91—Vancouver	NHL	55	21	24	45	10	5	0	0	0	2
91-92—Vancouver	NHL	76	30	27	57	26	6	0	2	2	4
NHL totals		523	203	203	406	171	18	2	5	7	8

AGNEW, JIM
D, WHALERS

PERSONAL: Born March 21, 1966, at Deloraine, Man. . . . 6-1/190. . . . Shoots left.
TRANSACTIONS/CAREER NOTES: Selected by Vancouver Canucks as underage junior in eighth round (10th Canucks pick, 157th overall) of NHL entry draft (June 9, 1984). . . . Tore knee ligaments (March 18, 1990). . . . Sprained left knee ligaments (November 19, 1990); missed 19 games. . . .

Resprained left knee ligaments (January 6, 1991). . . . Signed as free agent by Hartford Whalers (June 29, 1992).
HONORS: Named to WHL All-Star first team (1985-86). . . . Named to IHL All-Star second team (1989-90).

Season Team	League	REGULAR SEASON					PLAYOFFS				
		Gms.	G	A	Pts.	Pen.	Gms.	G	A	Pts.	Pen.
82-83—Brandon	WHL	14	1	1	2	9	—	—	—	—	—
83-84—Brandon	WHL	71	6	17	23	107	12	0	1	1	39
84-85—Brandon	WHL	19	3	15	18	82	—	—	—	—	—
—Portland	WHL	44	5	24	29	223	6	0	2	2	44
85-86—Portland	WHL	70	6	30	36	386	9	0	1	1	48
86-87—Vancouver	NHL	4	0	0	0	0	—	—	—	—	—
—Fredericton	AHL	67	0	5	5	261	—	—	—	—	—
87-88—Vancouver	NHL	10	0	1	1	16	—	—	—	—	—
—Fredericton	AHL	63	2	8	10	188	14	0	2	2	43
88-89—Milwaukee	IHL	47	2	10	12	181	11	0	2	2	34
89-90—Milwaukee	IHL	51	4	10	14	238	—	—	—	—	—
—Vancouver	NHL	7	0	0	0	36	—	—	—	—	—
90-91—Vancouver	NHL	20	0	0	0	81	—	—	—	—	—
—Milwaukee	IHL	3	0	0	0	33	—	—	—	—	—
91-92—Vancouver	NHL	24	0	0	0	56	4	0	0	0	6
NHL totals		65	0	1	1	189	4	0	0	0	6

AHOLA, PETER
D, KINGS

PERSONAL: Born May 14, 1968, at Espoo, Finland. . . . 6-3/205. . . . Shoots left. . . . Full name: Peter Kristian Ahola.
COLLEGE: Boston University.
TRANSACTIONS/CAREER NOTES: Signed as free agent by Los Angeles Kings (April 5, 1991).
HONORS: Named to NCAA All-America East second team (1990-91).

Season Team	League	REGULAR SEASON					PLAYOFFS				
		Gms.	G	A	Pts.	Pen.	Gms.	G	A	Pts.	Pen.
89-90—Boston University	Hockey East	43	3	20	23	65	—	—	—	—	—
90-91—Boston University	Hockey East	39	12	24	36	88	—	—	—	—	—
91-92—Los Angeles	NHL	71	7	12	19	101	6	0	0	0	2
—Phoenix	IHL	7	3	3	6	34	—	—	—	—	—
NHL totals		71	7	12	19	101	6	0	0	0	2

AITKEN, BRADLEY
LW, MAPLE LEAFS

PERSONAL: Born October 30, 1967, at Scarborough, Ont. . . . 6-3/200. . . . Shoots left.
TRANSACTIONS/CAREER NOTES: Traded by Peterborough Petes with future considerations to Sault Ste. Marie Greyhounds for RW Graeme Bonar (February 1986). . . . Selected by Pittsburgh Penguins as underage junior in third round (third Penguins pick, 46th overall) of NHL entry draft (June 21, 1986). . . . Separated shoulder (October 1986); missed three weeks. . . . Traded by Penguins to Edmonton Oilers for RW Kim Issel (March 5, 1991). . . . Signed as free agent by Toronto Maple Leafs (July 30, 1991).

Season Team	League	REGULAR SEASON					PLAYOFFS				
		Gms.	G	A	Pts.	Pen.	Gms.	G	A	Pts.	Pen.
84-85—Peterborough	OHL	63	18	26	44	36	—	—	—	—	—
85-86—Peterborough	OHL	48	9	28	37	77	—	—	—	—	—
—Sault Ste. Marie	OHL	20	8	19	27	11	—	—	—	—	—
87-88—Pittsburgh	NHL	5	1	1	2	0	—	—	—	—	—
—Muskegon	IHL	74	32	31	63	128	1	0	0	0	0
88-89—Muskegon	IHL	74	35	30	65	139	13	5	5	10	75
89-90—Muskegon	IHL	46	10	23	33	172	—	—	—	—	—
—Fort Wayne	IHL	13	5	2	7	57	5	2	1	3	12
—Phoenix	IHL	8	2	1	3	18	—	—	—	—	—
90-91—Muskegon	IHL	44	14	17	31	143	—	—	—	—	—
—Kansas City	IHL	6	4	6	10	2	—	—	—	—	—
—Pittsburgh	NHL	6	0	1	1	25	—	—	—	—	—
—Edmonton	NHL	3	0	1	1	0	—	—	—	—	—
—Cape Breton	AHL	6	2	3	5	17	3	0	2	2	6
91-92—St. John's	AHL	59	12	27	39	169	—	—	—	—	—
NHL totals		14	1	3	4	25					

AIVAZOFF, MICAH
C/LW, RED WINGS

PERSONAL: Born May 4, 1969, at Powell River, B.C. . . . 6-0/185. . . . Shoots left.
TRANSACTIONS/CAREER NOTES: Selected by Los Angeles Kings in sixth round (sixth Kings pick, 109th overall) of NHL entry draft (June 11, 1988).

Season Team	League	REGULAR SEASON					PLAYOFFS				
		Gms.	G	A	Pts.	Pen.	Gms.	G	A	Pts.	Pen.
85-86—Victoria	WHL	27	3	4	7	25	—	—	—	—	—
86-87—Victoria	WHL	72	18	39	57	112	5	1	0	1	2
87-88—Victoria	WHL	69	26	57	83	79	8	3	4	7	14
88-89—Victoria	WHL	70	35	65	100	136	8	5	7	12	2
89-90—New Haven	AHL	77	20	39	59	71	—	—	—	—	—
90-91—New Haven	AHL	79	11	29	40	84	—	—	—	—	—
91-92—Adirondack	AHL	61	9	20	29	50	†19	2	8	10	25

ALBELIN, TOMMY
D, DEVILS

PERSONAL: Born May 21, 1964, at Stockholm, Sweden.... 6-1/190.... Shoots left.
TRANSACTIONS/CAREER NOTES: Selected by Quebec Nordiques in eighth round (seventh Nordiques pick, 152nd overall) of NHL entry draft (June 8, 1983).... Traded by Nordiques to New Jersey Devils for a fourth-round pick in 1989 draft (LW Niclas Andersson) (December 12, 1988).... Injured right knee (March 2, 1990); missed four games.

Season	Team	League	REGULAR SEASON Gms.	G	A	Pts.	Pen.	PLAYOFFS Gms.	G	A	Pts.	Pen.
82-83	Djurgarden	Sweden	17	2	5	7	4	6	1	0	1	2
83-84	Djurgarden	Sweden	37	9	8	17	36	4	0	1	1	2
84-85	Djurgarden	Sweden	32	9	8	17	22	8	2	1	3	4
85-86	Djurgarden	Sweden	35	4	8	12	26	—	—	—	—	—
86-87	Djurgarden	Sweden	33	7	5	12	49	2	0	0	0	0
87-88	Quebec	NHL	60	3	23	26	47	—	—	—	—	—
88-89	Halifax	AHL	8	2	5	7	4	—	—	—	—	—
	Quebec	NHL	14	2	4	6	27	—	—	—	—	—
	New Jersey	NHL	46	7	24	31	40	—	—	—	—	—
89-90	New Jersey	NHL	68	6	23	29	63	—	—	—	—	—
90-91	Utica	AHL	14	4	2	6	10	—	—	—	—	—
	New Jersey	NHL	47	2	12	14	44	3	0	1	1	2
91-92	New Jersey	NHL	19	0	4	4	4	1	1	1	2	0
	Utica	AHL	11	4	6	10	4	—	—	—	—	—
NHL totals			**254**	**20**	**90**	**110**	**225**	**4**	**1**	**2**	**3**	**2**

ALEXEYEV, ALEXANDER
D, JETS

PERSONAL: Born March 23, 1974, at Kiev, U.S.S.R.... 5-11/198.... Shoots left.
TRANSACTIONS/CAREER NOTES: Selected by Winnipeg Jets in sixth round (fifth Jets pick, 132nd overall) of NHL entry draft (June 20, 1992).

Season	Team	League	REGULAR SEASON Gms.	G	A	Pts.	Pen.	PLAYOFFS Gms.	G	A	Pts.	Pen.
90-91	Sokol Kiev	USSR	5	0	0	0	2	—	—	—	—	—
91-92	Sokol Kiev	CIS	25	1	5	6	22	—	—	—	—	—

ALLAN, SANDY
G, KINGS

PERSONAL: Born January 22, 1974, at Nassau, Bahamas.... 6-0/175.... Shoots left.
HIGH SCHOOL: Chippewa Secondary School (North Bay, Ont.).
TRANSACTIONS/CAREER NOTES: Selected by Los Angeles Kings in third round (second Kings pick, 63rd overall) of NHL entry draft (June 20, 1992).
HONORS: Won F.W. (Dinty) Moore Trophy (1991-92).

Season	Team	League	REGULAR SEASON Gms.	Min.	W	L	T	GA	SO	Avg.	PLAYOFFS Gms.	Min.	W	L	GA	SO	Avg.
91-92	North Bay	OHL	34	1747	18	5	4	112	0	3.85	3	18	0	0	2	0	6.67

ALLISON, SCOTT
LW, OILERS

PERSONAL: Born April 22, 1972, at St. Boniface, Man.... 6-4/194.... Shoots left.
TRANSACTIONS/CAREER NOTES: Selected by Edmonton Oilers in first round (first Oilers pick, 17th overall) of NHL entry draft (June 16, 1990).

Season	Team	League	REGULAR SEASON Gms.	G	A	Pts.	Pen.	PLAYOFFS Gms.	G	A	Pts.	Pen.
88-89	Prince Albert	WHL	51	6	9	15	37	3	0	0	0	0
89-90	Prince Albert	WHL	66	22	16	38	73	11	1	4	5	8
90-91	Prince Albert	WHL	37	0	6	6	44	—	—	—	—	—
	Portland	WHL	44	5	17	22	105	—	—	—	—	—
91-92	Moose Jaw	WHL	72	37	45	82	238	3	1	1	2	25

AMBROZIAK, PETER
LW, SABRES

PERSONAL: Born September 15, 1971, at Ottawa.... 6-0/191.... Shoots left.
TRANSACTIONS/CAREER NOTES: Selected by Buffalo Sabres in fourth round (fourth Sabres pick, 72nd overall) of NHL entry draft (June 22, 1991).

Season	Team	League	REGULAR SEASON Gms.	G	A	Pts.	Pen.	PLAYOFFS Gms.	G	A	Pts.	Pen.
88-89	Ottawa	OHL	50	8	15	23	11	12	1	2	3	2
89-90	Ottawa	OHL	60	13	19	32	37	4	0	0	0	2
90-91	Ottawa	OHL	62	30	32	62	56	17	15	9	24	24
91-92	Rochester	AHL	2	0	1	1	0	—	—	—	—	—
	Ottawa	OHL	49	32	49	81	50	11	3	7	10	33

AMONTE, TONY
RW, RANGERS

PERSONAL: Born August 2, 1970, at Weymouth, Mass.... 6-0/186.... Shoots left.... Full name: Anthony Lewis Amonte.
HIGH SCHOOL: Thayer Academy (Braintree, Mass.).
COLLEGE: Boston University.

TRANSACTIONS/CAREER NOTES: Selected by New York Rangers in fourth round (third Rangers pick, 68th overall) of NHL entry draft (June 11, 1988)....Separated shoulder (December 29, 1990).
HONORS: Named to Hockey East All-Rookie team (1989-90)....Named to Hockey East All-Star second team (1990-91)....Named to NHL All-Rookie team (1991-92).

		REGULAR SEASON					PLAYOFFS				
Season Team	League	Gms.	G	A	Pts.	Pen.	Gms.	G	A	Pts.	Pen.
86-87—Thayer Academy	Mass. H.S.		25	32	57		—	—	—	—	—
87-88—Thayer Academy	Mass. H.S.		30	38	68		—	—	—	—	—
88-89—Team USA Juniors	Int'l	7	1	3	4		—	—	—	—	—
89-90—Boston University	Hockey East	41	25	33	58	52	—	—	—	—	—
90-91—Boston University	Hockey East	38	31	37	68	82	2	0	2	2	2
—New York Rangers	NHL	—	—	—	—	—	13	3	6	9	2
91-92—New York Rangers	NHL	79	35	34	69	55	15	3	8	11	4
NHL totals		79	35	34	69	55	15	3	8	11	4

ANDERSON, GLENN
RW, MAPLE LEAFS

PERSONAL: Born October 2, 1960, at Vancouver, B.C....6-1/190....Shoots left.... Full name: Glenn Chris Anderson.
COLLEGE: Denver.
TRANSACTIONS/CAREER NOTES: Selected by Edmonton Oilers in fourth round (third Oilers pick, 69th overall) of NHL entry draft (August 9, 1979)....Underwent knee surgery to remove bone chips (November 1900)....Underwent nose surgery to correct breathing problem (Spring 1982)....Suspended eight games by NHL for fighting (December 13, 1985)....Pulled side muscle (November 1988)....Fined $500 for deliberately breaking the cheekbone of RW Tomas Sandstrom (February 28, 1990)....Missed first four games of 1990-91 season due to contract dispute (October 1990)....Injured thigh (March 5, 1991); missed two games....Traded by Oilers with G Grant Fuhr and LW Craig Berube to Toronto Maple Leafs for LW Vincent Damphousse, D Luke Richardson, G Peter Ing, C Scott Thornton and future considerations (September 19, 1991).
RECORDS: Shares NHL single-game playoff record for most points in one period—4 (April 6, 1988).

		REGULAR SEASON					PLAYOFFS				
Season Team	League	Gms.	G	A	Pts.	Pen.	Gms.	G	A	Pts.	Pen.
77-78—Bellingham Jr. A	BCJHL	58	61	64	125	96	—	—	—	—	—
—New Westminster	WCHL	1	0	1	1	2	—	—	—	—	—
78-79—Seattle	WHL	2	0	1	1	0	—	—	—	—	—
—University of Denver	WCHA	40	26	29	55	58	—	—	—	—	—
79-80—Canadian Olympic Team	Int'l	49	21	21	42	46	—	—	—	—	—
—Seattle	WHL	7	5	5	10	4	—	—	—	—	—
80-81—Edmonton	NHL	58	30	23	53	24	9	5	7	12	12
81-82—Edmonton	NHL	80	38	67	105	71	5	2	5	7	8
82-83—Edmonton	NHL	72	48	56	104	70	16	10	10	20	32
83-84—Edmonton	NHL	80	54	45	99	65	19	6	11	17	33
84-85—Edmonton	NHL	80	42	39	81	69	18	10	16	26	38
85-86—Edmonton	NHL	72	54	48	102	90	10	8	3	11	14
86-87—Edmonton	NHL	80	35	38	73	65	21	14	13	27	59
87-88—Edmonton	NHL	80	38	50	88	58	19	9	16	25	49
88-89—Edmonton	NHL	79	16	48	64	93	7	1	2	3	8
89-90—Edmonton	NHL	73	34	38	72	107	22	10	12	22	20
90-91—Edmonton	NHL	74	24	31	55	59	18	6	7	13	41
91-92—Toronto	NHL	72	24	33	57	100	—	—	—	—	—
NHL totals		900	437	516	953	871	164	81	102	183	314

ANDERSON, PERRY
LW

PERSONAL: Born October 14, 1961, at Barrie, Ont....6-1/225....Shoots left....Full name: Perry Lynn Anderson.
HIGH SCHOOL: North Park (Brantford, Ont.).
TRANSACTIONS/CAREER NOTES: Selected by St. Louis Blues as an underage junior in sixth round (fifth Blues pick, 117th overall) of NHL entry draft (June 11, 1980)....Broke bone in foot (March 1984)....Traded by Blues to New Jersey Devils for C Rick Meagher and a 12th-round pick in 1986 draft (LW Bill Butler) (August 1985). ...Strained abdominal muscle (January 13, 1986); missed eight games....Suffered concussion (January 1988)....Strained rotator cuff (October 1988)....Sprained right knee (January 1989)....Separated left shoulder (March 1989)....Underwent surgery to left knee (August 1990)....Signed as free agent by San Jose Sharks (July 8, 1991)....Injured jaw (November 30, 1991); missed 18 games.
HONORS: Named to OHL All-Star second team (1981-82).

		REGULAR SEASON					PLAYOFFS				
Season Team	League	Gms.	G	A	Pts.	Pen.	Gms.	G	A	Pts.	Pen.
78-79—Kingston	OMJHL	60	6	13	19	85	5	2	1	3	6
79-80—Kingston	OMJHL	63	17	16	33	52	3	0	0	0	6
80-81—Kingston	OMJHL	38	9	13	22	118	—	—	—	—	—
—Brantford	OMJHL	31	8	27	35	43	6	4	2	6	15
81-82—Salt Lake City	IHL	71	32	32	64	117	2	1	0	1	2
—St. Louis	NHL	5	1	2	3	0	10	2	0	2	4
82-83—Salt Lake City	IHL	57	23	19	42	140	—	—	—	—	—
—St. Louis	NHL	18	5	2	7	14	—	—	—	—	—
83-84—Montana	CHL	8	7	3	10	34	—	—	—	—	—
—St. Louis	NHL	50	7	5	12	195	9	0	0	0	27

Season Team	League	REGULAR SEASON					PLAYOFFS				
		Gms.	G	A	Pts.	Pen.	Gms.	G	A	Pts.	Pen.
84-85—St. Louis	NHL	71	9	9	18	146	3	0	0	0	7
85-86—New Jersey	NHL	51	7	12	19	91	—	—	—	—	—
86-87—New Jersey	NHL	57	10	9	19	105	—	—	—	—	—
87-88—New Jersey	NHL	60	4	6	10	222	10	0	0	0	113
88-89—New Jersey	NHL	39	3	6	9	128	—	—	—	—	—
89-90—Utica	AHL	71	13	17	30	128	5	0	0	0	24
90-91—New Jersey	NHL	1	0	0	0	5	4	0	1	1	10
—Utica	AHL	68	19	14	33	245	—	—	—	—	—
91-92—San Jose	NHL	48	4	8	12	143	—	—	—	—	—
NHL totals		400	50	59	109	1049	36	2	1	3	161

ANDERSSON, MIKAEL
LW, LIGHTNING

PERSONAL: Born May 10, 1966, at Malmo, Sweden.... 5-11/185.... Shoots left.... Full name: Bo Mikael Andersson.

TRANSACTIONS/CAREER NOTES: Selected by Buffalo Sabres in first round (first Sabres pick, 18th overall) of NHL entry draft (June 9, 1984).... Sprained ankle, missed three weeks (March 3, 1987).... Twisted ankle (March 1988).... Sprained neck and shoulder (December 1988).... Selected by Hartford Whalers in 1989 NHL waiver draft (October 2, 1989).... Bruised left knee (December 13, 1989).... Reinjured knee (February 9, 1990).... Pulled right hamstring (March 8, 1990).... Reinjured hamstring (March 17, 1990).... Reinjured hamstring (April 1990).... Underwent surgery to left knee (May 14, 1990).... Suffered from the flu (October 4, 1990); missed two games.... Pulled groin (January 1991).... Injured toe (October 26, 1991); missed one game.... Injured groin (December 17, 1991); missed three games.... Suffered chip fracture to foot (April 12, 1992).... Signed as free agent by Tampa Bay Lightning (July 8, 1992).

Season Team	League	REGULAR SEASON					PLAYOFFS				
		Gms.	G	A	Pts.	Pen.	Gms.	G	A	Pts.	Pen.
83-84—Vastra Frolunda	Sweden	12	0	2	2	6	—	—	—	—	—
84-85—Vastra Frolunda	Sweden	32	16	11	27	18	6	3	2	5	2
85-86—Rochester	AHL	20	10	4	14	6	—	—	—	—	—
—Buffalo	NHL	33	1	9	10	4	—	—	—	—	—
86-87—Rochester	AHL	42	6	20	26	14	9	1	2	3	2
—Buffalo	NHL	16	0	3	3	0	—	—	—	—	—
87-88—Rochester	AHL	35	12	24	36	16	—	—	—	—	—
—Buffalo	NHL	37	3	20	23	10	1	1	0	1	0
88-89—Buffalo	NHL	14	0	1	1	4	—	—	—	—	—
—Rochester	AHL	56	18	33	51	12	—	—	—	—	—
89-90—Hartford	NHL	50	13	24	37	6	5	0	3	3	2
90-91—Hartford	NHL	41	4	7	11	8	—	—	—	—	—
—Springfield	AHL	26	7	22	29	10	18	†10	8	18	12
91-92—Hartford	NHL	74	18	29	47	14	7	0	2	2	6
NHL totals		265	39	93	132	46	13	1	5	6	8

ANDERSSON, PETER
D, RANGERS

PERSONAL: Born August 29, 1965, at Orebro, Sweden.... 6-0/187.... Shoots left.
TRANSACTIONS/CAREER NOTES: Selected by New York Rangers in fourth round (fifth Rangers pick, 73rd overall) of NHL entry draft (June 8, 1983).

Season Team	League	REGULAR SEASON					PLAYOFFS				
		Gms.	G	A	Pts.	Pen.	Gms.	G	A	Pts.	Pen.
83-84—Farjestad	Sweden	36	4	7	11	22	—	—	—	—	—
84-85—Farjestad	Sweden	35	5	12	17	24	—	—	—	—	—
85-86—Farjestad	Sweden	34	6	10	16	18	—	—	—	—	—
86-87—Farjestad	Sweden	32	9	8	17	32	—	—	—	—	—
87-88—Farjestad	Sweden	38	14	20	34	44	—	—	—	—	—
88-89—Farjestad	Sweden	33	6	17	23	44	—	—	—	—	—
89-90—Malmo	Sweden-II	—	—	—	—	—	—	—	—	—	—
90-91—Malmo	Sweden	34	9	17	26	26	—	—	—	—	—
91-92—Malmo	Sweden	40	12	20	32	18	—	—	—	—	—

ANDREYCHUK, DAVE
LW, SABRES

PERSONAL: Born September 29, 1963, at Hamilton, Ont.... 6-3/225.... Shoots right.... Full name: David Andreychuk.
TRANSACTIONS/CAREER NOTES: Selected by Buffalo Sabres as underage junior in first round (third Sabres pick, 16th overall) of NHL entry draft (June 9, 1982). ... Sprained knee (March 1983).... Fractured collarbone (March 1985).... Twisted knee (September 1985).... Injured right knee (September 1986).... Strained medial collateral ligaments in left knee (November 27, 1988).... Broke left thumb (February 18, 1990).
MISCELLANEOUS: Played with Team Canada in World Junior Championships (1982-83).

Season Team	League	REGULAR SEASON					PLAYOFFS				
		Gms.	G	A	Pts.	Pen.	Gms.	G	A	Pts.	Pen.
80-81—Oshawa	OMJHL	67	22	22	44	80	10	3	2	5	20
81-82—Oshawa	OHL	67	58	43	101	71	3	1	4	5	16
82-83—Oshawa	OHL	14	8	24	32	6	—	—	—	—	—
—Buffalo	NHL	43	14	23	37	16	4	1	0	1	4

Season Team	League	REGULAR SEASON Gms.	G	A	Pts.	Pen.	PLAYOFFS Gms.	G	A	Pts.	Pen.
83-84—Buffalo	NHL	78	38	42	80	42	2	0	1	1	2
84-85—Buffalo	NHL	64	31	30	.61	54	5	4	2	6	4
85-86—Buffalo	NHL	80	36	51	87	61	—	—	—	—	—
86-87—Buffalo	NHL	77	25	48	73	46	—	—	—	—	—
87-88—Buffalo	NHL	80	30	48	78	112	6	2	4	6	0
88-89—Buffalo	NHL	56	28	24	52	40	5	0	3	3	0
89-90—Buffalo	NHL	73	40	42	82	42	6	2	5	7	2
90-91—Buffalo	NHL	80	36	33	69	32	6	2	2	4	8
91-92—Buffalo	NHL	80	41	50	91	71	7	1	3	4	12
NHL totals		711	319	391	710	516	41	12	20	32	32

ANDRUSAK, GREG
D, PENGUINS

PERSONAL: Born November 14, 1969, at Cranbrook, B.C.... 6-1/180.... Shoots right. ... Full name: Greg Frederick Andrusak.
COLLEGE: Minnesota-Duluth.
TRANSACTIONS/CAREER NOTES: Selected by Pittsburgh Penguins in fifth round (fifth Penguins pick, 88th overall) of NHL entry draft (June 11, 1988).
HONORS: Named to WCHA All-Star first team (1991-92).

Season Team	League	REGULAR SEASON Gms.	G	A	Pts.	Pen.	PLAYOFFS Gms.	G	A	Pts.	Pen.
86-87—Kelowna	BCJHL	45	10	24	34	95	—	—	—	—	—
87-88—Minnesota-Duluth	WCHA	37	4	5	9	42	—	—	—	—	—
88-89—Minnesota-Duluth	WCHA	35	4	8	12	74	—	—	—	—	—
—Canadian National Team..	Int'l	2	0	0	0	0	—	—	—	—	—
89-90—Minnesota-Duluth	WCHA	35	5	29	34	74	—	—	—	—	—
90-91—Canadian National Team..	Int'l	53	4	11	15	34	—	—	—	—	—
91-92—Minnesota-Duluth	WCHA	36	7	27	34	125	—	—	—	—	—

ANGLEHART, SERGE
D, RED WINGS

PERSONAL: Born April 18, 1970, at Hull, Que.... 6-2/190.... Shoots right.
TRANSACTIONS/CAREER NOTES: Selected by Detroit Red Wings as underage junior in second round (second Red Wings pick, 38th overall) of NHL entry draft (June 11, 1988).... Suspended one game by QMJHL for being aggressor in fight (March 26, 1989).... Traded by Drummondville Voltigeurs with LW Claude Boivin and a fifth-round draft pick to Laval Titans for D Luc Doucet, D Brad MacIsaac and second- and third-round draft picks (February 15, 1990).

Season Team	League	REGULAR SEASON Gms.	G	A	Pts.	Pen.	PLAYOFFS Gms.	G	A	Pts.	Pen.
87-88—Drummondville	QMJHL	44	1	8	9	122	17	0	3	3	19
88-89—Drummondville	QMJHL	39	6	15	21	89	3	0	0	0	37
—Adirondack	AHL	—	—	—	—	—	2	0	0	0	0
89-90—Laval	QMJHL	48	2	19	21	131	10	1	6	7	69
90-91—Adirondack	AHL	52	3	8	11	113	—	—	—	—	—
91-92—Adirondack	AHL	16	0	1	1	43	—	—	—	—	—

ANTOSKI, SHAWN
LW/RW, CANUCKS

PERSONAL: Born May 25, 1970, at Brantford, Ont.... 6-4/245.... Shoots left.
TRANSACTIONS/CAREER NOTES: Injured knee ligament (December 1988).... Separated shoulder (March 1989).... Selected by Vancouver Canucks in first round (second Canucks pick, 18th overall) of NHL entry draft (June 17, 1989).... Suffered sore back (December 1991).

Season Team	League	REGULAR SEASON Gms.	G	A	Pts.	Pen.	PLAYOFFS Gms.	G	A	Pts.	Pen.
87-88—North Bay	OHL	52	3	4	7	163	—	—	—	—	—
88-89—North Bay	OHL	57	6	21	27	201	9	5	3	8	24
89-90—North Bay	OHL	59	25	31	56	201	5	1	2	3	17
90-91—Milwaukee	IHL	62	17	7	24	330	5	1	2	3	10
—Vancouver	NHL	2	0	0	0	0	—	—	—	—	—
91-92—Milwaukee	IHL	52	17	16	33	346	5	2	0	2	20
—Vancouver	NHL	4	0	0	0	29	—	—	—	—	—
NHL totals		6	0	0	0	29					

ARCHIBALD, DAVE
C/LW, RANGERS

PERSONAL: Born April 14, 1969, at Chilliwack, B.C.... 6-1/190.... Shoots left.... Full name: David Archibald.
TRANSACTIONS/CAREER NOTES: Underwent shoulder surgery (January 1984).... Lacerated hand (October 1986).... Selected as underage junior by Minnesota North Stars in first round (first North Stars pick, sixth overall) of NHL entry draft (June 13, 1987).... Injured shoulder (September 1987).... Suffered sore back (February 1989).... Traded by North Stars to New York Rangers for D Jayson More (November 1, 1989).

Season Team	League	REGULAR SEASON Gms.	G	A	Pts.	Pen.	PLAYOFFS Gms.	G	A	Pts.	Pen.
84-85—Portland	WHL	47	7	11	18	10	3	0	2	2	0
85-86—Portland	WHL	70	29	35	64	56	15	6	7	13	11

Season Team	League	REGULAR SEASON					PLAYOFFS				
		Gms.	G	A	Pts.	Pen.	Gms.	G	A	Pts.	Pen.
86-87—Portland	WHL	65	50	57	107	40	20	10	18	28	11
87-88—Minnesota	NHL	78	13	20	33	26	—	—	—	—	—
88-89—Minnesota	NHL	72	14	19	33	14	—	—	—	—	—
89-90—Minnesota	NHL	12	1	5	6	6	5	0	1	1	0
—New York Rangers	NHL	19	2	3	5	6	—	—	—	—	—
—Flint	IHL	41	14	38	52	16	4	3	2	5	0
90-91—Canadian National Team	Int'l	29	19	12	31	20	—	—	—	—	—
91-92—Canadian National Team	Int'l	58	20	43	63	62	—	—	—	—	—
—Canadian Olympic Team	Int'l	8	7	1	8	18	—	—	—	—	—
NHL totals		181	30	47	77	52	5	0	1	1	0

ARMSTRONG, BILL
LW, FLYERS

PERSONAL: Born June 25, 1966, at London, Ont. . . . 6-2/195. . . . Shoots left. . . . Full name: William Harold Armstrong.
COLLEGE: Western Michigan.
TRANSACTIONS/CAREER NOTES: Signed as free agent by Philadelphia Flyers (May 16, 1989).

Season Team	League	REGULAR SEASON					PLAYOFFS				
		Gms.	G	A	Pts.	Pen.	Gms.	G	A	Pts.	Pen.
86-87—Western Michigan Univ.	CCHA	43	13	20	33	86	—	—	—	—	—
87-88—Western Michigan Univ.	CCHA	41	22	17	39	88	—	—	—	—	—
88-89—Western Michigan Univ.	CCHA	40	23	19	42	97	—	—	—	—	—
89-90—Hershey	AHL	58	10	6	16	99	—	—	—	—	—
90-91—Philadelphia	NHL	1	0	1	1	0	—	—	—	—	—
—Hershey	AHL	70	36	27	63	150	6	2	8	10	19
91-92—Hershey	AHL	64	26	22	48	185	6	2	2	4	6
NHL totals		1	0	1	1	0					

ARMSTRONG, BILL
D, FLYERS

PERSONAL: Born May 18, 1970, at Richmond Hill, Ont. . . . 6-5/220. . . . Shoots left. . . . Full name: William C. Armstrong.
TRANSACTIONS/CAREER NOTES: Selected by Philadelphia Flyers in third round (fifth Flyers pick, 46th overall) of NHL entry draft (June 16, 1990).

Season Team	League	REGULAR SEASON					PLAYOFFS				
		Gms.	G	A	Pts.	Pen.	Gms.	G	A	Pts.	Pen.
86-87—Barrie Jr. B	OHA	45	1	11	12	45	—	—	—	—	—
87-88—Toronto	OHL	64	1	10	11	99	—	—	—	—	—
88-89—Toronto	OHL	64	1	16	17	82	—	—	—	—	—
89-90—Dukes of Hamilton	OHL	18	0	2	2	38	—	—	—	—	—
—Niagara Falls	OHL	4	0	1	1	17	—	—	—	—	—
—Oshawa	OHL	41	2	8	10	115	17	0	7	7	39
90-91—Hershey	AHL	56	1	9	10	117	1	0	0	0	0
91-92—Hershey	AHL	†80	2	14	16	159	3	0	0	0	2

ARMSTRONG, DEREK
C, ISLANDERS

PERSONAL: Born April 23, 1973, at Ottawa. . . . 6-0/180. . . . Shoots right.
HIGH SCHOOL: Lo-Ellen Park Secondary School (Sudbury, Ont.).
TRANSACTIONS/CAREER NOTES: Selected by New York Islanders in sixth round (fifth Islanders pick, 128th overall) of NHL entry draft (June 20, 1992).

Season Team	League	REGULAR SEASON					PLAYOFFS				
		Gms.	G	A	Pts.	Pen.	Gms.	G	A	Pts.	Pen.
89-90—Hawkesbury	COJHL	48	8	10	18	30	—	—	—	—	—
90-91—Sudbury	OHL	2	0	2	2	0	—	—	—	—	—
—Hawkesbury	COJHL	54	27	45	72	49	—	—	—	—	—
91-92—Sudbury	OHL	66	31	54	85	22	9	2	2	4	2

ARNIEL, SCOTT
LW/C, BRUINS

PERSONAL: Born September 17, 1962, at Kingston, Ont. . . . 6-1/170. . . . Shoots left.
TRANSACTIONS/CAREER NOTES: Selected by Winnipeg Jets as underage junior in second round (second Jets pick, 22nd overall) of NHL entry draft (June 10, 1981). . . . Traded by Jets to Buffalo Sabres for LW Gilles Hamel (June 21, 1986). . . . Bruised abdominal muscle (March 1988). . . . Suffered concussion (April 9, 1990). . . . Traded by Sabres with D Phil Housley, RW Jeff Parker and a first-round pick in 1990 draft (C Keith Tkachuk) to Jets for C Dale Hawerchuk, a first-round pick in 1990 draft (LW Brad May) and future considerations (June 16, 1990); RW Greg Paslawski sent to Sabres to complete deal (February 5, 1991). . . . Traded by Jets to Boston Bruins for future considerations (November 22, 1991). . . . Strained shoulder (December 1, 1991); missed four games. . . . Fractured right thumb (January 1992).

Season Team	League	REGULAR SEASON					PLAYOFFS				
		Gms.	G	A	Pts.	Pen.	Gms.	G	A	Pts.	Pen.
79-80—Cornwall	QMJHL	61	22	28	50	51	—	—	—	—	—
80-81—Cornwall	QMJHL	68	52	71	123	102	19	14	19	33	24
81-82—Cornwall	OHL	24	18	26	44	43	—	—	—	—	—
—Winnipeg	NHL	17	1	8	9	14	3	0	0	0	0

Season Team	League	REGULAR SEASON					PLAYOFFS				
		Gms.	G	A	Pts.	Pen.	Gms.	G	A	Pts.	Pen.
82-83—Winnipeg	NHL	75	13	5	18	46	2	0	0	0	0
83-84—Winnipeg	NHL	80	21	35	56	68	2	0	0	0	5
84-85—Winnipeg	NHL	79	22	22	44	81	8	1	2	3	9
85-86—Winnipeg	NHL	80	18	25	43	40	3	0	0	0	12
86-87—Buffalo	NHL	63	11	14	25	59	—	—	—	—	—
87-88—Buffalo	NHL	73	17	23	40	61	6	0	1	1	5
88-89—Buffalo	NHL	80	18	23	41	46	5	1	0	1	4
89-90—Buffalo	NHL	79	18	14	32	77	5	1	0	1	4
90-91—Winnipeg	NHL	75	5	17	22	87	—	—	—	—	—
91-92—New Haven	AHL	11	3	3	6	10	—	—	—	—	—
—Boston	NHL	29	5	3	8	20	—	—	—	—	—
—Maine	AHL	14	4	4	8	8	—	—	—	—	—
NHL totals		730	149	189	338	599	34	3	3	6	39

ASHTON, BRENT
LW/C, BRUINS

PERSONAL: Born May 18, 1960, at Saskatoon, Sask. . . . 6-1/200. . . . Shoots left. . . . Full name: Brent Kenneth Ashton.

TRANSACTIONS/CAREER NOTES: Selected by Vancouver Canucks as underage junior in second round (second Canucks pick, 26th overall) of NHL entry draft (August 9, 1979). . . . Injured knee ligament; missed parts of 1979-80 season. . . . Traded by Canucks with a fourth-round pick in 1982 draft (LW Tom Martin) to Winnipeg Jets as compensation for Canucks signing of C Ivan Hlinka, a Czechoslovakian player drafted by Jets in a special draft on May 28, 1981 (July 15, 1981). . . . Traded by Jets with a third-round pick in 1982 draft (C Dave Kasper) to Colorado Rockies for RW Lucien DeBlois (July 15, 1981). . . . Traded by New Jersey Devils to Minnesota North Stars for D Dave Lewis (October 3, 1983). . . . Traded by North Stars with D Brad Maxwell to Quebec Nordiques for LW Tony McKegney and RW Bo Berglund (December 14, 1984). . . . Injured hip (October 1985); missed two weeks. . . . Tore left knee ligaments (September 1986). . . . Traded by Nordiques with D Gilbert Delorme and RW Mark Kumpel to Detroit Red Wings for LW John Ogrodnick, C Doug Shedden and LW Basil McRae (January 17, 1987). . . . Traded by Red Wings to Jets for RW Paul MacLean (June 13, 1988). . . . Strained ligaments in right knee (March 15, 1989); missed three games. . . . Pulled groin (November 1, 1990); missed six games. . . . Broke nose and jaw (March 8, 1991). . . . Traded by Jets to Boston Bruins for RW Petri Skriko (October 29, 1991). . . . Underwent knee surgery (April 9, 1992).

Season Team	League	REGULAR SEASON					PLAYOFFS				
		Gms.	G	A	Pts.	Pen.	Gms.	G	A	Pts.	Pen.
75-76—Saskatoon	WCHL	11	3	4	7	11	—	—	—	—	—
76-77—Saskatoon	WCHL	54	26	25	51	84	—	—	—	—	—
77-78—Saskatoon	WCHL	46	38	28	66	47	—	—	—	—	—
78-79—Saskatoon	WHL	62	64	55	119	80	11	14	4	18	5
79-80—Vancouver	NHL	47	5	14	19	11	4	1	0	1	6
80-81—Vancouver	NHL	77	18	11	29	57	3	0	0	0	0
81-82—Colorado	NHL	80	24	36	60	26	—	—	—	—	—
82-83—New Jersey	NHL	76	14	19	33	47	—	—	—	—	—
83-84—Minnesota	NHL	68	7	10	17	54	12	1	2	3	22
84-85—Minnesota	NHL	29	4	7	11	15	—	—	—	—	—
—Quebec	NHL	49	27	24	51	38	18	6	4	10	13
85-86—Quebec	NHL	77	26	32	58	64	3	2	1	3	9
86-87—Quebec	NHL	46	25	19	44	17	—	—	—	—	—
—Detroit	NHL	35	15	16	31	22	16	4	9	13	6
87-88—Detroit	NHL	73	26	27	53	50	16	7	5	12	10
88-89—Winnipeg	NHL	75	31	37	68	36	—	—	—	—	—
89-90—Winnipeg	NHL	79	22	34	56	37	7	3	1	4	2
90-91—Winnipeg	NHL	61	12	24	36	58	—	—	—	—	—
91-92—Winnipeg	NHL	7	1	0	1	4	—	—	—	—	—
—Boston	NHL	61	17	22	39	47	—	—	—	—	—
NHL totals		940	274	332	606	583	79	24	22	46	68

ASTLEY, MARK
D, SABRES

PERSONAL: Born March 30, 1969, at Calgary, Alta. . . . 5-11/185. . . . Shoots left.
COLLEGE: Lake Superior State (Mich.).
TRANSACTIONS/CAREER NOTES: Selected by Buffalo Sabres in 10th round (ninth Sabres pick, 194th overall) of NHL entry draft (June 17, 1989). . . . Hospitalized with strep pneumonia (March 14, 1990).
HONORS: Named to CCHA All-Star second team (1990-91). . . . Named to CCHA All-Star first team (1991-92).

Season Team	League	REGULAR SEASON					PLAYOFFS				
		Gms.	G	A	Pts.	Pen.	Gms.	G	A	Pts.	Pen.
87-88—Calgary Canucks	AJHL	52	25	37	62	106	—	—	—	—	—
88-89—Lake Superior State	CCHA	42	3	12	15	26	—	—	—	—	—
89-90—Lake Superior State	CCHA	43	7	25	32	74	—	—	—	—	—
90-91—Lake Superior State	CCHA	45	19	27	46	50	—	—	—	—	—
91-92—Lake Superior State	CCHA	43	12	37	49	65	—	—	—	—	—

ATCHEYNUM, BLAIR
RW, SENATORS

PERSONAL: Born April 20, 1969, at Estevan, Sask. . . . 6-2/190. . . . Shoots right.
TRANSACTIONS/CAREER NOTES: Selected by Swift Current Broncos in special compensation draft to replace players injured and killed in a December 30, 1986 bus crash (February 1987). . . . Traded by Broncos to Moose Jaw Warriors for D Tim

Logan (February 1987). . . . Selected by Hartford Whalers in third round (second Whalers pick, 52nd overall) of NHL entry draft (June 17, 1989). . . . Suffered concussion (January 12, 1991). . . . Selected by Ottawa Senators in NHL expansion draft (June 18, 1992).

HONORS: Won Brad Hornung Trophy (1988-89). . . . Named to WHL All-Star first team (1988-89).

Season Team	League	REGULAR SEASON					PLAYOFFS				
		Gms.	G	A	Pts.	Pen.	Gms.	G	A	Pts.	Pen.
85-86—North Battleford	SJHL	35	25	20	45	50	—	—	—	—	—
86-87—Saskatoon	WHL	21	0	4	4	4	—	—	—	—	—
—Swift Current	WHL	5	2	1	3	0	—	—	—	—	—
—Moose Jaw	WHL	12	3	0	3	2	—	—	—	—	—
87-88—Moose Jaw	WHL	60	32	16	48	52	—	—	—	—	—
88-89—Moose Jaw	WHL	71	70	68	138	70	7	2	5	7	13
89-90—Binghamton	AHL	78	20	21	41	45	—	—	—	—	—
90-91—Springfield	AHL	72	25	27	52	42	13	0	6	6	6
91-92—Springfield	AHL	62	16	21	37	64	6	1	1	2	2

AUCOIN, ADRIAN
D, CANUCKS

PERSONAL: Born July 3, 1973, at London, Ont. . . . 6-1/194. . . . Shoots right.
COLLEGE: Boston University.
TRANSACTIONS/CAREER NOTES: Selected by Vancouver Canucks in fifth round (seventh Canucks pick, 117th overall) of NHL entry draft (June 20, 1992).

Season Team	League	REGULAR SEASON					PLAYOFFS				
		Gms.	G	A	Pts.	Pen.	Gms.	G	A	Pts.	Pen.
91-92—Boston University	Hockey East	33	2	10	12	62	—	—	—	—	—

AUDETTE, DONALD
RW, SABRES

PERSONAL: Born September 23, 1969, at Laval, Que. . . . 5-8/182. . . . Shoots right.
TRANSACTIONS/CAREER NOTES: Selected by Buffalo Sabres in ninth round (eighth Sabres pick, 183rd overall) of NHL entry draft (June 17, 1989). . . . Broke left hand (February 11, 1990); missed seven games. . . . Bruised thigh (September 1990). . . . Bruised thigh (October 1990); missed five games. . . . Tore left knee ligaments (November 16, 1990). . . . Underwent surgery to left knee (December 10, 1990). . . . Sprained ankle (December 14, 1991); missed eight games. . . . Injured knee (March 31, 1992).

HONORS: Won Guy Lafleur Trophy (1988-89). . . . Named to QMJHL All-Star first team (1988-89). . . . Won Dudley (Red) Garrett Memorial Trophy (1989-90). . . . Named to AHL All-Star first team (1989-90).

Season Team	League	REGULAR SEASON					PLAYOFFS				
		Gms.	G	A	Pts.	Pen.	Gms.	G	A	Pts.	Pen.
86-87—Laval	QMJHL	66	17	22	39	36	14	2	6	8	10
87-88—Laval	QMJHL	63	48	61	109	56	14	7	12	19	20
88-89—Laval	QMJHL	70	76	85	161	123	17	*17	12	29	43
89-90—Rochester	AHL	70	42	46	88	78	15	9	8	17	29
—Buffalo	NHL	—	—	—	—	—	2	0	0	0	0
90-91—Rochester	AHL	5	4	0	4	2	—	—	—	—	—
—Buffalo	NHL	8	4	3	7	4	—	—	—	—	—
91-92—Buffalo	NHL	63	31	17	48	75	—	—	—	—	—
NHL totals		71	35	20	55	79	2	0	0	0	0

BABCOCK, BOB
D, CAPITALS

PERSONAL: Born August 3, 1968, at Agincourt, Ont. . . . 6-1/220. . . . Shoots left. . . . Full name: Bob Frank Babcock.
TRANSACTIONS/CAREER NOTES: Selected by Washington Capitals as underage junior in 10th round (11th Capitals pick, 208th overall) of NHL entry draft (June 21, 1986). . . . Suspended 10 games by AHL for fighting (December 10, 1989).

Season Team	League	REGULAR SEASON					PLAYOFFS				
		Gms.	G	A	Pts.	Pen.	Gms.	G	A	Pts.	Pen.
85-86—Sault Ste. Marie	OHL	50	1	7	8	185	—	—	—	—	—
86-87—Sault Ste. Marie	OHL	62	7	8	15	243	4	0	0	0	11
87-88—Sault Ste. Marie	OHL	8	0	2	2	30	—	—	—	—	—
—Cornwall	OHL	42	0	16	16	120	—	—	—	—	—
88-89—Cornwall	OHL	42	0	9	9	163	18	1	3	4	29
89-90—Baltimore	AHL	67	0	4	4	249	6	0	0	0	23
90-91—Washington	NHL	1	0	0	0	0	—	—	—	—	—
—Baltimore	AHL	38	0	3	3	112	—	—	—	—	—
91-92—Baltimore	AHL	26	0	2	2	55	—	—	—	—	—
NHL totals		1	0	0	0	0					

BABYCH, DAVE
D, CANUCKS

PERSONAL: Born May 23, 1961, at Edmonton, Alta. . . . 6-2/215. . . . Shoots left. . . . Full name: David Michael Babych. . . . Brother of Wayne Babych, right winger for four NHL teams (1978-79 to 1986-87).
TRANSACTIONS/CAREER NOTES: Selected by Winnipeg Jets as underage junior in first round (first Jets pick, second overall) of NHL entry draft (June 11, 1980). . . . Separated shoulder (March 1984). . . . Suffered back

spasms (December 1984). . . . Traded by Jets to Hartford Whalers for RW Ray Neufeld (November 21, 1985). . . . Injured hip (January 1987); missed 12 games. . . . Lacerated right hand (March 16, 1989), missed six games. . . . Bruised neck (March 1990). . . . Underwent surgery to right wrist (October 29, 1990); missed 44 games. . . . Broke right thumb (February 8, 1991); missed remainder of the season. . . . Selected by Minnesota North Stars in 1991 NHL expansion draft (May 30, 1991). . . . Traded by North Stars to Vancouver Canucks for Craig Ludwig. It was part of a three-club deal that saw D Tom Kurvers go from Canucks to the Islanders for Ludwig (June 22, 1991). . . . Suffered sore back (November 3, 1991); missed one game.

HONORS: Won AJHL Top Defenseman Trophy (1977-78). . . . Won AJHL Rookie of the Year Trophy (1977-78). . . . Named to AJHL All-Star first team (1977-78). . . . Won Top Defenseman Trophy (1979-80). . . . Named to WHL All-Star first team (1979-80).

			REGULAR SEASON					PLAYOFFS				
Season Team	League	Gms.	G	A	Pts.	Pen.	Gms.	G	A	Pts.	Pen.
77-78—Portland	WCHL	6	1	3	4	4	—	—	—	—	—
—Fort Saskatchewan	AJHL	56	31	69	100	37	—	—	—	—	—
78-79—Portland	WHL	67	20	59	79	63	25	7	22	29	22
79-80—Portland	WHL	50	22	60	82	71	8	1	10	11	2
80-81—Winnipeg	NHL	69	6	38	44	90	—	—	—	—	—
81-82—Winnipeg	NHL	79	19	49	68	92	4	1	2	3	29
82-83—Winnipeg	NHL	79	13	61	74	56	3	0	0	0	0
83-84—Winnipeg	NHL	66	18	39	57	62	3	1	1	2	0
84-85—Winnipeg	NHL	78	13	49	62	78	8	2	7	9	6
85-86—Winnipeg	NHL	19	4	12	16	14	—	—	—	—	—
—Hartford	NHL	62	10	43	53	36	8	1	3	4	14
86-87—Hartford	NHL	66	8	33	41	44	6	1	2	1	14
87-88—Hartford	NHL	71	14	36	50	54	6	3	2	5	2
88-89—Hartford	NHL	70	6	41	47	54	4	1	5	6	2
89-90—Hartford	NHL	72	6	37	43	62	7	1	2	3	0
90-91—Hartford	NHL	8	0	6	6	4	—	—	—	—	—
91-92—Vancouver	NHL	75	5	24	29	63	13	2	6	8	10
NHL totals		814	122	468	590	709	62	13	29	42	77

BACA, JERGUS
D, WHALERS

PERSONAL: Born April 1, 1965, at Kosice, Czechoslovakia. . . . 6-2/211. . . . Shoots left.
TRANSACTIONS/CAREER NOTES: Selected by Hartford Whalers in seventh round (sixth Whalers pick, 141st overall) of NHL entry draft (June 16, 1990). . . . Bruised shoulder (October 1990).

			REGULAR SEASON					PLAYOFFS				
Season Team	League	Gms.	G	A	Pts.	Pen.	Gms.	G	A	Pts.	Pen.
89-90—Kosice	Czech.	47	9	16	25		—	—	—	—	—
90-91—Hartford	NHL	9	0	2	2	14	—	—	—	—	—
—Springfield	AHL	57	6	23	29	89	18	3	13	16	18
91-92—Springfield	AHL	64	6	20	26	88	11	0	6	6	20
—Hartford	NHL	1	0	0	0	0	—	—	—	—	—
NHL totals		10	0	2	2	14					

BADER, DARIN
LW, CANUCKS

PERSONAL: Born April 2, 1971, at Edmonton, Alta. . . . 6-0/202. . . . Shoots left.
TRANSACTIONS/CAREER NOTES: Injured knee and underwent surgery (August 1989). . . . Selected by Vancouver Canucks in fourth round (fourth Canucks pick, 65th overall) of NHL entry draft (June 16, 1990).

			REGULAR SEASON					PLAYOFFS				
Season Team	League	Gms.	G	A	Pts.	Pen.	Gms.	G	A	Pts.	Pen.
87-88—Saskatoon	WHL	53	5	9	14	73	10	2	0	2	11
88-89—Saskatoon	WHL	66	19	14	33	214	8	7	3	10	25
89-90—Saskatoon	WHL	54	26	31	57	107	10	6	4	10	30
90-91—Saskatoon	WHL	40	35	32	67	105	—	—	—	—	—
91-92—Milwaukee	IHL	4	0	0	0	5	—	—	—	—	—

BAILEY, SCOTT
G, BRUINS

PERSONAL: Born May 2, 1972, at Calgary, Alta. . . . 5-11/185. . . . Shoots left.
TRANSACTIONS/CAREER NOTES: Selected by Boston Bruins in fifth round (Bruins third pick, 112th overall) of NHL entry draft (June 20, 1992).
HONORS: Won WHL (West) Rookie of the Year Award (1990-91). . . . Named to WHL (West) All-Star second team (1990-91 and 1991-92).

			REGULAR SEASON							PLAYOFFS					
Season Team	League	Gms.	Min.	W	L	T	GA	SO	Avg.	Gms.	Min.	W	L	GA	SO	Avg.
88-89—Moose Jaw	WHL	2	34				7	0	12.35	—	—	—	—	—	—	—
90-91—Spokane Chiefs	WHL	46	2537	33	11	0	157	4	3.71	—	—	—	—	—	—	—
91-92—Spokane Chiefs	WHL	65	3748	34	23	5	206	1	3.30	10	605	5	5	43	0	4.26

BAKER, JAMIE
C, NORDIQUES

PERSONAL: Born August 31, 1966, at Nepean, Que. . . . 6-0/190. . . . Shoots left. . . . Full name: James Paul Baker.
COLLEGE: St. Lawrence (N.Y.).
TRANSACTIONS/CAREER NOTES: Selected by Quebec Nordiques in NHL supplemental draft (June 10, 1988). . . . Broke left ankle (December 30, 1988). . . . Sprained ankle (January 9, 1992); missed two games.

Season Team	League	Gms.	G	A	Pts.	Pen.	Gms.	G	A	Pts.	Pen.
		REGULAR SEASON					**PLAYOFFS**				
85-86—St. Lawrence University ...	ECAC	31	9	16	25	52	—	—	—	—	—
86-87—St. Lawrence University ...	ECAC	32	8	24	32	59	—	—	—	—	—
87-88—St. Lawrence University ...	ECAC	38	26	28	54	44	—	—	—	—	—
88-89—St. Lawrence University ...	ECAC	13	11	16	27	16	—	—	—	—	—
89-90—Quebec	NHL	1	0	0	0	0	—	—	—	—	—
—Halifax..............................	AHL	74	17	43	60	47	6	0	0	0	7
90-91—Quebec	NHL	18	2	0	2	8	—	—	—	—	—
—Halifax..............................	AHL	50	14	22	36	85	—	—	—	—	—
91-92—Halifax..............................	AHL	9	5	0	5	12	—	—	—	—	—
—Quebec	NHL	52	7	10	17	32	—	—	—	—	—
NHL totals.................................		71	9	10	19	40					

BALES, MIKE
G, BRUINS

PERSONAL: Born August 6, 1971, at Saskatoon, Sask. . . . 6-1/180. . . . Shoots left. . . . Full name: Michael Raymond Bales.
COLLEGE: Ohio State.
TRANSACTIONS/CAREER NOTES: Selected by Boston Bruins in fifth round (fourth Bruins pick, 105th overall) of NHL entry draft (June 16, 1990).

Season Team	League	Gms.	Min.	W	L	T	GA	SO	Avg.	Gms.	Min.	W	L	GA	SO	Avg.
		REGULAR SEASON								**PLAYOFFS**						
88-89—Estevan	SJHL	44	2412				197	1	4.90	—	—	—	—	—	—	—
89-90—Ohio State....................	CCHA	21	1117	6	13	2	95	0	5.10	—	—	—	—	—	—	—
90-91—Ohio State....................	CCHA	*39	*2180	11	24	3	*184	0	5.06	—	—	—	—	—	—	—
91-92—Ohio State....................	CCHA	36	2061	11	20	5	*180		5.24	—	—	—	—	—	—	—

BANCROFT, STEVE
D, BLACKHAWKS

PERSONAL: Born October 6, 1970, at Toronto. . . . 6-1/215. . . . Shoots left.
TRANSACTIONS/CAREER NOTES: Underwent surgery to left shoulder (April 1989). . . . Selected by Toronto Maple Leafs in first round (third Maple Leafs pick, 21st overall) of NHL entry draft (June 17, 1989). . . . Traded by Maple Leafs to Boston Bruins for LW Rob Cimetta (November 9, 1990). . . . Traded by Bruins with 11th-round pick in 1993 draft to Chicago Blackhawks for 11th-round pick in 1992 draft and 12th-round pick in 1993 draft (January 8, 1992).

Season Team	League	Gms.	G	A	Pts.	Pen.	Gms.	G	A	Pts.	Pen.
		REGULAR SEASON					**PLAYOFFS**				
86-87—St. Catharines Jr. B..........	OHA	11	5	8	13	20	—	—	—	—	—
87-88—Belleville Bulls................	OHL	56	1	8	9	42	—	—	—	—	—
88-89—Belleville Bulls................	OHL	66	7	30	37	99	5	0	2	2	10
89-90—Belleville Bulls................	OHL	53	10	33	43	135	11	3	9	12	38
90-91—Newmarket......................	AHL	9	0	3	3	22	—	—	—	—	—
—Maine................................	AHL	53	2	12	14	46	2	0	0	0	2
91-92—Maine................................	AHL	26	1	3	4	45	—	—	—	—	—
—Indianapolis	IHL	36	8	23	31	49	—	—	—	—	—

BANNISTER, DREW
D, LIGHTNING

PERSONAL: Born September 4, 1974, at Belleville, Ont. . . . 6-1/195. . . . Shoots right.
HIGH SCHOOL: Bawating Collegiate School (Sault Ste. Marie, Ont.).
TRANSACTIONS/CAREER NOTES: Selected by Tampa Bay Lightning in second round (second Lightning pick, 26th overall) of NHL entry draft (June 20, 1992).
HONORS: Named to Memorial Cup All-Star team (1991-92).

Season Team	League	Gms.	G	A	Pts.	Pen.	Gms.	G	A	Pts.	Pen.
		REGULAR SEASON					**PLAYOFFS**				
90-91—Sault Ste. Marie	OHL	41	2	8	10	51	4	0	0	0	0
91-92—Sault Ste. Marie	OHL	64	4	21	25	122	16	3	10	13	36

BARAHONA, RALPH
C, BRUINS

PERSONAL: Born November 16, 1965, at Lakewood, Calif. . . . 5-10/180. . . . Shoots right. . . . Full name: Ralph J. Barahona.
COLLEGE: Wisconsin-Stevens Point.
TRANSACTIONS/CAREER NOTES: Signed as free agent by Boston Bruins (September 1990).

Season Team	League	Gms.	G	A	Pts.	Pen.	Gms.	G	A	Pts.	Pen.
		REGULAR SEASON					**PLAYOFFS**				
88-89—Wisconsin-Stevens Point	NCAA-II	41	33	47	80		—	—	—	—	—
89-90—Wisconsin-Stevens Point	NCAA-II	35	22	30	52	18	—	—	—	—	—
90-91—Maine..............................	AHL	72	24	33	57	14	2	1	1	2	0
—Boston	NHL	3	2	1	3	0	—	—	—	—	—
91-92—Maine..............................	AHL	74	27	32	59	39	—	—	—	—	—
—Boston	NHL	3	0	1	1	0	—	—	—	—	—
NHL totals.................................		6	2	2	4	0					

BARBER, DON
LW, SHARKS

PERSONAL: Born December 2, 1964, at Victoria, B.C. . . . . 6-1/205. . . . Shoots left. . . . Full name: Donald Frederick Barber.
COLLEGE: Bowling Green State.
TRANSACTIONS/CAREER NOTES: Selected by Edmonton Oilers as underage junior in sixth round (fifth Oilers pick, 120th overall) of NHL entry draft (June 8, 1983). . . . Traded by Oilers with C Marc Habscheid and D Emanuel Viveiros to Minnesota North Stars for RW Gord Sherven and C Don Biggs (December 20, 1985). . . . Injured knee (October 1987). . . . Traded by North Stars with future considerations to Winnipeg Jets for LW Doug Smail (November 7, 1990). . . . Claimed on waivers by Quebec Nordiques (November 12, 1991). . . . Traded by Nordiques to San Jose Sharks for C Murray Garbutt (March 7, 1992).

			REGULAR SEASON					PLAYOFFS			
Season Team	League	Gms.	G	A	Pts.	Pen.	Gms.	G	A	Pts.	Pen.
82-83—Kelowna	BCJHL	35	26	31	57	54	—	—	—	—	—
83-84—St. Albert	AJHL	53	42	38	80	74	—	—	—	—	—
84-85—Bowling Green State	CCHA	39	15	12	27	44	—	—	—	—	—
85-86—Bowling Green State	CCHA	35	21	22	43	64	—	—	—	—	—
86-87—Bowling Green State	CCHA	43	29	34	63	109	—	—	—	—	—
87-88—Bowling Green State	CCHA	38	18	47	65	60	—	—	—	—	—
88-89—Minnesota	NHL	23	8	5	13	8	4	1	1	2	2
—Kalamazoo	IHL	39	14	17	31	23	—	—	—	—	—
89-90—Kalamazoo	IHL	10	4	4	8	38	—	—	—	—	—
—Minnesota	NHI	44	15	19	34	32	7	3	3	6	8
90-91—Minnesota	NHL	7	0	0	0	4	—	—	—	—	—
—Winnipeg	NHL	16	1	2	3	14	—	—	—	—	—
—Moncton	AHL	38	17	21	38	32	9	4	6	10	8
91-92—Winnipeg	NHL	11	0	3	3	4	—	—	—	—	—
—Quebec	NHL	2	0	0	0	0	—	—	—	—	—
—Halifax	AHL	25	12	10	22	8	—	—	—	—	—
—San Jose	NHL	12	1	3	4	2	—	—	—	—	—
NHL totals		115	25	32	57	64	11	4	4	8	10

BARNABY, MATTHEW
LW/RW, SABRES

PERSONAL: Born May 4, 1973, at Ottawa. . . . 6-0/170. . . . Shoots right.
TRANSACTIONS/CAREER NOTES: Selected by Buffalo Sabres in fourth round (fifth Sabres pick, 83rd overall) of NHL entry draft (June 20, 1992).

			REGULAR SEASON					PLAYOFFS			
Season Team	League	Gms.	G	A	Pts.	Pen.	Gms.	G	A	Pts.	Pen.
90-91—Beauport	QMJHL	52	9	5	14	262	—	—	—	—	—
91-92—Beauport	QMJHL	63	29	37	66	*476	—	—	—	—	—

BARNES, STU
C, JETS

PERSONAL: Born December 25, 1970, at Edmonton, Alta. . . . 5-10/175. . . . Shoots right. . . . Full name: Stu D. Barnes.
TRANSACTIONS/CAREER NOTES: Selected by Winnipeg Jets in first round (first Jets pick, fourth overall) of NHL entry draft (June 17, 1989).
HONORS: Won Jim Piggott Memorial Trophy (1987-88). . . . Named to WHL All-Star second team (1987-88). . . . Won Four Broncos Memorial Trophy (1988-89). . . . Named to WHL All-Star first team (1988-89).

			REGULAR SEASON					PLAYOFFS			
Season Team	League	Gms.	G	A	Pts.	Pen.	Gms.	G	A	Pts.	Pen.
86-87—St. Albert	AJHL	57	43	32	75	80	—	—	—	—	—
87-88—New Westminster	WHL	71	37	64	101	88	5	2	3	5	6
88-89—Tri-City Americans	WHL	70	59	82	141	117	7	6	5	11	10
89-90—Tri-City Americans	WHL	63	52	92	144	165	7	1	5	6	26
90-91—Canadian National Team	Int'l	53	22	27	49	68	—	—	—	—	—
91-92—Winnipeg	NHL	46	8	9	17	26	—	—	—	—	—
—Moncton	AHL	30	13	19	32	10	11	3	9	12	6
NHL totals		46	8	9	17	26					

BARON, MURRAY
D, BLUES

PERSONAL: Born June 1, 1967, at Prince George, B.C. . . . 6-3/215. . . . Shoots left. . . . Full name: Murray D. Baron.
COLLEGE: North Dakota.
TRANSACTIONS/CAREER NOTES: Selected by Philadelphia Flyers as underage player in eighth round (seventh Flyers pick, 167th overall) of NHL entry draft (June 21, 1986). . . . Separated left shoulder (October 5, 1989). . . . Underwent surgery to have bone spur removed from foot (April 1990). . . . Traded by Flyers with C Ron Sutter to St. Louis Blues for C Rod Brind'Amour and C Dan Quinn (September 22, 1991). . . . Injured shoulder (December 3, 1991); missed seven games.

			REGULAR SEASON					PLAYOFFS			
Season Team	League	Gms.	G	A	Pts.	Pen.	Gms.	G	A	Pts.	Pen.
84-85—Vernon	BCJHL	37	5	9	14	93	—	—	—	—	—
85-86—Vernon	BCJHL	49	15	32	47	176	7	1	2	3	13
86-87—Univ. of North Dakota	WCHA	41	4	10	14	62	—	—	—	—	—
87-88—Univ. of North Dakota	WCHA	41	1	10	11	95	—	—	—	—	—
88-89—Univ. of North Dakota	WCHA	40	2	6	8	92	—	—	—	—	—
—Hershey	AHL	9	0	3	3	8	—	—	—	—	—

Season Team	League	REGULAR SEASON					PLAYOFFS				
		Gms.	G	A	Pts.	Pen.	Gms.	G	A	Pts.	Pen.
89-90—Hershey	AHL	50	0	10	10	101	—	—	—	—	—
—Philadelphia	NHL	16	2	2	4	12	—	—	—	—	—
90-91—Hershey	AHL	6	2	3	5	0	—	—	—	—	—
—Philadelphia	NHL	67	8	8	16	74	—	—	—	—	—
91-92—St. Louis	NHL	67	3	8	11	94	2	0	0	0	2
NHL totals		150	13	18	31	180	2	0	0	0	2

BARR, DAVE
RW, DEVILS

PERSONAL: Born November 30, 1960, at Edmonton, Alta. . . . 6-1/195. . . . Shoots right. . . . Full name: David Angus Barr.

TRANSACTIONS/CAREER NOTES: Signed as free agent by Boston Bruins (September 28, 1981). . . . Traded by Bruins to New York Rangers for C/RW Dave Silk (October 5, 1983). . . . Traded by Rangers with third-round pick in 1984 draft (G Alan Perry) and cash to St. Louis Blues for C Larry Patey and NHL rights to RW Bob Brooke (March 5, 1984). . . . Sprained knee (March 19, 1986). . . . Traded by Blues to Hartford Whalers for D Tim Bothwell (October 21, 1986). . . . Traded by Whalers to Detroit Red Wings for D Randy Ladouceur (January 12, 1987). . . . Separated right shoulder (November 1987). . . . Broke right foot (December 1987). . . . Broke right ankle (March 14, 1991). . . . Sent to New Jersey Devils with RW Randy McKay as compensation for Red Wings signing free agent RW Troy Crowder (September 1991). . . . Separated left shoulder (September 21, 1991); missed first nine games of season. . . . Lacerated tendon and artery in wrist (February 21, 1992); missed final 21 games of season.

Season Team	League	REGULAR SEASON					PLAYOFFS				
		Gms.	G	A	Pts.	Pen.	Gms.	G	A	Pts.	Pen.
77-78—Pincher Creek	AJHL	60	16	32	48	53	—	—	—	—	—
78-79—Edmonton	WHL	72	16	19	35	61	—	—	—	—	—
79-80—Lethbridge	WHL	60	16	38	54	47	—	—	—	—	—
80-81—Lethbridge	WHL	72	26	62	88	106	10	4	10	14	4
81-82—Erie	AHL	76	18	48	66	29	—	—	—	—	—
—Boston	NHL	2	0	0	0	0	5	1	0	1	0
82-83—Baltimore	AHL	72	27	51	78	67	—	—	—	—	—
—Boston	NHL	10	1	1	2	7	10	0	0	0	2
83-84—New York Rangers	NHL	6	0	0	0	2	—	—	—	—	—
—Tulsa	CHL	50	28	37	65	24	—	—	—	—	—
—St. Louis	NHL	1	0	0	0	0	5	0	1	1	15
84-85—St. Louis	NHL	75	16	18	34	32	2	0	0	0	2
85-86—St. Louis	NHL	75	13	38	51	70	11	1	1	2	14
86-87—St. Louis	NHL	2	0	0	0	0	—	—	—	—	—
—Hartford	NHL	30	2	4	6	19	—	—	—	—	—
—Detroit	NHL	37	13	13	26	49	13	1	0	1	14
87-88—Detroit	NHL	51	14	26	40	58	16	5	7	12	22
88-89—Detroit	NHL	73	27	32	59	69	6	3	1	4	6
89-90—Detroit	NHL	62	10	25	35	45	—	—	—	—	—
—Adirondack	AHL	9	1	14	15	17	—	—	—	—	—
90-91—Detroit	NHL	70	18	22	40	55	—	—	—	—	—
91-92—New Jersey	NHL	41	6	12	18	32	—	—	—	—	—
—Utica	AHL	1	0	0	0	7	—	—	—	—	—
NHL totals		535	120	191	311	438	68	11	10	21	75

BARRASSO, TOM
G, PENGUINS

PERSONAL: Born March 31, 1965, at Boston. . . . 6-3/212. . . . Shoots right. . . . Full name: Thomas Barrasso.

HIGH SCHOOL: Acton-Boxborough (Mass.).

TRANSACTIONS/CAREER NOTES: Selected by Buffalo Sabres in first round (first Sabres pick, fifth overall) of NHL entry draft (June 8, 1983). . . . Suffered chip fracture of ankle (November 1987). . . . Pulled groin (April 9, 1988). . . . Traded by Sabres with a third-round pick in 1990 draft to Pittsburgh Penguins for D Doug Bodger and LW Darrin Shannon (November 12, 1988). . . . Pulled groin muscle (Janurary 17, 1989). . . . Injured shoulder (March 1989). . . . Underwent surgery to right wrist (October 30, 1989); missed 21 games. . . . Pulled groin (February 1990). . . . Granted leave of absence to be with daughter as she underwent cancer treatment in Los Angeles (February 9, 1990). . . . Rejoined the Penguins (March 19, 1990). . . . Bruised right hand (October 29, 1991); missed two games. . . . Bruised right ankle (December 26, 1991); missed three games. . . . Suffered back spasms (March 1992); missed three games.

HONORS: Won Vezina Trophy (1983-84). . . . Won Calder Memorial Trophy (1983-84). . . . Named to THE SPORTING NEWS All-Star second team (1983-84, 1984-85 and 1987-88). . . . Named to NHL All-Star first team (1983-84). . . . Named to NHL All-Rookie team (1983-84). . . . Shared William M. Jennings Trophy with Bob Sauve (1984-85). . . . Named to NHL All-Star second team (1984-85).

RECORDS: Shares NHL single-season playoff record for most wins by a goaltender—16 (1991-92).

MISCELLANEOUS: Member of U.S. National Junior Team (1983).

Season Team	League	REGULAR SEASON							PLAYOFFS					
		Gms.	Min.	W	L	T	GA	SO	Avg.	Gms.	Min.	W	L	GA	SO	Avg.
81-82—Acton-Boxborough HS	Mass. HS	23	1035				32	7	1.86	—	—	—	—	—	—	—
82-83—Acton-Boxborough HS	Mass. HS	23	1035				17	10	0.99	—	—	—	—	—	—	—
83-84—Buffalo	NHL	42	2475	26	12	3	117	2	2.84	3	139	0	2	8	0	3.45
84-85—Rochester	AHL	5	267	3	1	1	6	1	1.35	—	—	—	—	—	—	—
—Buffalo	NHL	54	3248	25	18	10	144	*5	*2.66	5	300	2	3	22	0	4.40
85-86—Buffalo	NHL	60	*3561	29	24	5	214	2	3.61	—	—	—	—	—	—	—
86-87—Buffalo	NHL	46	2501	17	23	2	152	2	3.65	—	—	—	—	—	—	—

Season Team	League	Gms.	Min.	W	L	T	GA	SO	Avg.	Gms.	Min.	W	L	GA	SO	Avg.
87-88—Buffalo	NHL	54	3133	25	18	8	173	2	3.31	4	224	1	3	16	0	4.29
88-89—Buffalo	NHL	10	545	2	7	0	45	0	4.95	—	—	—	—	—	—	—
—Pittsburgh	NHL	44	2406	18	15	7	162	0	4.04	11	631	7	4	40	0	3.80
89-90—Pittsburgh	NHL	24	1294	7	12	3	101	0	4.68	—	—	—	—	—	—	—
90-91—Pittsburgh	NHL	48	2754	27	16	3	165	1	3.59	20	1175	12	7	51	+1	*2.60
91-92—Pittsburgh	NHL	57	3329	25	22	9	196	1	3.53	*21	*1233	*16	5	*58	1	2.82
NHL totals		439	25246	201	167	50	1469	15	3.49	64	3702	38	24	195	2	3.16

BARRIE, LEN
C, FLYERS

PERSONAL: Born June 4, 1969, at Kimberly, B.C.... 6-0/190.... Shoots right.
TRANSACTIONS/CAREER NOTES: Selected by Edmonton Oilers in sixth round (seventh Oilers pick, 124th overall) of NHL entry draft (June 11, 1988).... Broke finger (March 1989).... Traded by Victoria Cougars to Kamloops Blazers for RW Mark Cipriano (August 1989).... Signed as free agent by Philadelphia Flyers (February 8, 1990).
HONORS: Won CHL Plus/Minus Award (1989-90).... Won Bob Clarke Trophy (1989-90).... Named to WHL All-Star first team (1989-90).

Season Team	League	Gms.	G	A	Pts.	Pen.	Gms.	G	A	Pts.	Pen.
85-86—Calgary Spurs	AJHL	23	7	14	21	86	—	—	—	—	—
—Calgary	WHL	32	3	0	3	18	—	—	—	—	—
86-87—Calgary	WHL	34	13	13	26	81	—	—	—	—	—
—Victoria	WHL	34	7	6	13	92	5	0	1	1	15
87-88—Victoria	WHL	70	37	49	86	192	8	2	0	2	29
88-89—Victoria	WHL	67	39	48	87	157	7	5	2	7	23
89-90—Philadelphia	NHL	1	0	0	0	0	—	—	—	—	—
—Kamloops	WHL	70	*85	*100	*185	108	17	†14	23	†37	24
90-91—Hershey	AHL	63	26	32	58	60	7	4	0	4	12
91-92—Hershey	AHL	75	42	43	85	78	3	0	2	2	32
NHL totals		1	0	0	0	0					

BARTLEY, WADE
D, CAPITALS

PERSONAL: Born May 16, 1970, at Killarney, Man.... 6-0/190.... Shoots right.... Full name: Wade A. Bartley.
COLLEGE: North Dakota.
TRANSACTIONS/CAREER NOTES: Tore knee cartilage (November 1986).... Selected by Washington Capitals in second round (third Capitals pick, 41st overall) of NHL entry draft (June 11, 1988).

Season Team	League	Gms.	G	A	Pts.	Pen.	Gms.	G	A	Pts.	Pen.
86-87—Dauphin	MJHL	36	4	24	28	55	—	—	—	—	—
87-88—Dauphin	MJHL	47	10	64	74	104	—	—	—	—	—
88-89—Univ. of North Dakota	WCHA	32	1	1	2	8	—	—	—	—	—
89-90—Sudbury	OHL	60	23	36	59	53	7	1	4	5	10
90-91—Baltimore	AHL	2	0	0	0	0	—	—	—	—	—
—Sudbury	OHL	47	11	37	48	57	5	1	3	4	4
91-92—Hampton Roads	ECHL	43	8	26	34	75	14	4	8	12	38
—Baltimore	AHL	20	0	7	7	25	—	—	—	—	—

BASSEN, BOB
C, BLUES

PERSONAL: Born May 6, 1965, at Calgary, Alta.... 5-10/180.... Shoots left.... Son of Hank Bassen, goalie, Chicago Blackhawks, Detroit Red Wings and Pittsburgh Penguins (1954-55 through 1967-68).
TRANSACTIONS/CAREER NOTES: Signed as free agent by New York Islanders (October 19, 1984).... Injured knee (October 12, 1985).... Traded by Islanders with D Steve Konroyd to Chicago Blackhawks for D Gary Nylund and D Marc Bergevin (November 25, 1988).... Selected by St. Louis Blues in 1990 NHL waiver draft for $25,000 (October 2, 1990).
HONORS: Named to WHL All-Star first team (1984-85).... Named to IHL All-Star first team (1989-90).

Season Team	League	Gms.	G	A	Pts.	Pen.	Gms.	G	A	Pts.	Pen.
82-83—Medicine Hat	WHL	4	3	2	5	0	3	0	0	0	4
83-84—Medicine Hat	WHL	72	29	29	58	93	14	5	11	16	12
84-85—Medicine Hat	WHL	65	32	50	82	143	10	2	8	10	39
85-86—New York Islanders	NHL	11	2	1	3	6	3	0	1	1	0
—Springfield	AHL	54	13	21	34	111	—	—	—	—	—
86-87—New York Islanders	NHL	77	7	10	17	89	14	1	2	3	21
87-88—New York Islanders	NHL	77	6	16	22	99	6	0	1	1	23
88-89—New York Islanders	NHL	19	1	4	5	21	—	—	—	—	—
—Chicago	NHL	49	4	12	16	62	10	1	1	2	34
89-90—Indianapolis	IHL	73	22	32	54	179	12	3	8	11	33
—Chicago	NHL	6	1	1	2	8	—	—	—	—	—
90-91—St. Louis	NHL	79	16	18	34	183	13	1	3	4	24
91-92—St. Louis	NHL	79	7	25	32	167	6	0	2	2	4
NHL totals		397	44	87	131	635	52	3	10	13	106

B

BASSEN, MARK
C

PERSONAL: Born May 9, 1969, at Calgary, Alta. . . . 5-10/170. . . . Shoots right. . . . Son of Hank Bassen, goalie, Chicago Blackhawks, Detroit Red Wings and Pittsburgh Penguins (1954-55 through 1967-68); and brother of Bob Bassen, center, St. Louis Blues.
TRANSACTIONS/CAREER NOTES: Signed as free agent by Philadelphia Flyers (October 12, 1989). . . . Signed as free agent by St. Louis Blues (August 1991).

Season Team	League	REGULAR SEASON					PLAYOFFS				
		Gms.	G	A	Pts.	Pen.	Gms.	G	A	Pts.	Pen.
86-87—Calgary	WHL	4	1	1	2	2	—	—	—	—	—
87-88—Lethbridge	WHL	70	19	28	47	48	—	—	—	—	—
88-89—Lethbridge	WHL	7	1	4	5	12	—	—	—	—	—
—Brandon	WHL	65	31	65	96	74	—	—	—	—	—
89-90—Hershey	AHL	57	5	9	14	128	—	—	—	—	—
90-91—Hershey	AHL	42	3	1	4	86	—	—	—	—	—
91-92—Peoria	IHL	82	18	23	41	228	10	0	4	4	15

BATTERS, JEFF
D, BLUES

PERSONAL: Born October 23, 1970, at Victoria, B.C. . . . 6-2/215. . . . Shoots right. . . . Full name: Jeffrey William Batters.
COLLEGE: Alaska-Anchorage.
TRANSACTIONS/CAREER NOTES: Selected by St. Louis Blues in seventh round (seventh Blues pick, 135th overall) of NHL entry draft (June 17, 1989).

Season Team	League	REGULAR SEASON					PLAYOFFS				
		Gms.	G	A	Pts.	Pen.	Gms.	G	A	Pts.	Pen.
88-89—Alaska-Anchorage	Indep.	33	8	14	22	123	—	—	—	—	—
89-90—Alaska-Anchorage	Indep.	34	6	9	15	102	—	—	—	—	—
90-91—Alaska-Anchorage	Indep.	39	16	14	30	90	—	—	—	—	—
91-92—Alaska-Anchorage	Indep.	34	6	17	23	86	—	—	—	—	—

BAUER, COLLIN
D, OILERS

PERSONAL: Born September 6, 1970, at Edmonton, Alta. . . . 6-1/180. . . . Shoots left.
TRANSACTIONS/CAREER NOTES: Selected by Edmonton Oilers in third round (fourth Oilers pick, 61st overall) of NHL entry draft (June 11, 1988). . . . Fractured three vertebrae and a rib (November 11, 1990).
HONORS: Named to WHL (East) All-Star team (1988-89).

Season Team	League	REGULAR SEASON					PLAYOFFS				
		Gms.	G	A	Pts.	Pen.	Gms.	G	A	Pts.	Pen.
86-87—Saskatoon	WHL	61	1	25	26	37	11	0	6	6	10
87-88—Saskatoon	WHL	70	9	53	62	66	10	2	5	7	16
88-89—Saskatoon	WHL	61	17	62	79	71	8	1	8	9	8
89-90—Saskatoon	WHL	29	4	25	29	49	10	1	8	9	14
90-91—Cape Breton	AHL	40	4	14	18	18	4	1	1	2	4
91-92—Cape Breton	AHL	55	7	15	22	36	3	0	0	0	7

BAUMGARTNER, KEN
D/LW, MAPLE LEAFS

PERSONAL: Born March 11, 1966, at Flin Flon, Man. . . . 6-0/200. . . . Shoots left. . . . Full name: Ken James Baumgartner.
TRANSACTIONS/CAREER NOTES: Selected by Buffalo Sabres as underage junior in 12th round (12th Sabres pick, 245th overall) of NHL entry draft (June 15, 1985). . . . Traded by Sabres with D Larry Playfair and RW Sean McKenna to Los Angeles Kings for D Brian Engblom and C Doug Smith (January 29, 1986). . . . Traded by Kings with C Hubie McDonough to New York Islanders for RW Mikko Makela (November 29, 1989). . . . Fractured right orbital bone (December 19, 1991); missed 14 games. . . . Traded by Islanders with C Dave McLlwain to Toronto Maple Leafs for C Claude Loiselle and RW Daniel Marois (March 10, 1992).

Season Team	League	REGULAR SEASON					PLAYOFFS				
		Gms.	G	A	Pts.	Pen.	Gms.	G	A	Pts.	Pen.
83-84—Prince Albert	WHL	57	1	6	7	203	—	—	—	—	—
84-85—Prince Albert	WHL	60	3	9	12	252	13	1	3	4	*89
85-86—Prince Albert	WHL	70	4	23	27	277	20	3	9	12	112
86-87—Chur	Switzerland			Statistics unavailable.							
—New Haven	AHL	13	0	3	3	99	6	0	0	0	60
87-88—Los Angeles	NHL	30	2	3	5	189	5	0	1	1	28
—New Haven	AHL	48	1	5	6	181	—	—	—	—	—
88-89—Los Angeles	NHL	49	1	3	4	286	5	0	0	0	8
—New Haven	AHL	10	1	3	4	26	—	—	—	—	—
89-90—Los Angeles	NHL	12	1	0	1	28	—	—	—	—	—
—New York Islanders	NHL	53	0	5	5	194	4	0	0	0	27
90-91—New York Islanders	NHL	78	1	6	7	282	—	—	—	—	—
91-92—New York Islanders	NHL	44	0	1	1	202	—	—	—	—	—
—Toronto	NHL	11	0	0	0	23	—	—	—	—	—
NHL totals		277	5	18	23	1204	14	0	1	1	63

BAUTIN, SERGEI
D, JETS

PERSONAL: Born March 11, 1967, at Murmansk, U.S.S.R. . . . 6-3/185. . . . Shoots left.
TRANSACTIONS/CAREER NOTES: Selected by Winnipeg Jets in first round (first Jets pick, 17th overall) of NHL entry draft (June 20, 1992).

Season Team	League	REGULAR SEASON Gms.	G	A	Pts.	Pen.	PLAYOFFS Gms.	G	A	Pts.	Pen.
90-91—Dynamo Moscow	USSR	33	2	0	2	28	—	—	—	—	—
91-92—Dynamo Moscow	CIS	37	1	3	4	88	—	—	—	—	—

BAVIS, MARK
C, RANGERS

PERSONAL: Born March 13, 1970, at Roslindale, Mass.... 6-0/175.... Shoots left.... Full name: Mark Lawrence Bavis.
HIGH SCHOOL: Catholic Memorial (Boston), then Cushing Academy (Ashburnham, Mass.).
COLLEGE: Boston University.
TRANSACTIONS/CAREER NOTES: Selected by New York Rangers in ninth round (10th Rangers pick, 181st overall) of NHL entry draft (June 17, 1989).

Season Team	League	REGULAR SEASON Gms.	G	A	Pts.	Pen.	PLAYOFFS Gms.	G	A	Pts.	Pen.
87-88—Catholic Memorial H.S.	Mass. H.S.	19	16	26	42		—	—	—	—	—
88-89—Cushing Academy	Mass. H.S.	29	27	31	58	18	—	—	—	—	—
89-90—Boston University	Hockey East	44	6	5	11	50	—	—	—	—	—
90-91—Boston University	Hockey East	40	5	18	23	47	—	—	—	—	—
91-92—Boston University	Hockey East	35	9	18	27	30	—	—	—	—	—

BAWA, ROBIN
RW, CANUCKS

PERSONAL: Born March 26, 1966, at Chemainus, B.C.... 6-2/214.... Shoots right.
TRANSACTIONS/CAREER NOTES: Signed as free agent by Washington Capitals (May 22, 1987).... Traded by Capitals to Vancouver Canucks for future considerations (August 1, 1991).
HONORS: Named to WHL All-Star first team (1986-87).

Season Team	League	REGULAR SEASON Gms.	G	A	Pts.	Pen.	PLAYOFFS Gms.	G	A	Pts.	Pen.
82-83—Kamloops	WHL	66	10	24	34	17	7	1	2	3	0
83-84—Kamloops	WHL	64	16	28	44	40	13	4	2	6	4
84-85—New Westminster	WHL	26	4	6	10	20	—	—	—	—	—
—Kamloops	WHL	26	2	13	15	25	15	4	9	13	14
85-86—Kamloops	WHL	63	29	43	72	78	16	5	13	18	4
86-87—Kamloops	WHL	62	57	56	113	91	13	6	7	13	22
87-88—Fort Wayne	IHL	55	12	27	39	239	6	1	3	4	24
88-89—Baltimore	AHL	75	23	24	47	205	—	—	—	—	—
89-90—Baltimore	AHL	61	7	18	25	189	11	1	2	3	49
—Washington	NHL	5	1	0	1	6	—	—	—	—	—
90-91—Fort Wayne	IHL	72	21	26	47	381	18	4	4	8	87
91-92—Milwaukee	IHL	70	27	14	41	238	5	2	2	4	8
—Vancouver	NHL	2	0	0	0	0	1	0	0	0	0
NHL totals		7	1	0	1	6	1	0	0	0	0

BEAUPRE, DON
G, CAPITALS

PERSONAL: Born September 19, 1961, at Kitchener, Ont.... 5-9/165.... Shoots left.... Full name: Donald William Beaupre.
TRANSACTIONS/CAREER NOTES: Selected by Minnesota North Stars as underage junior in second round (second North Stars pick, 37th overall) of NHL entry draft (June 11, 1980).... Bruised ribs (October 1981).... Sprained knee (February 1985).... Pulled groin muscle (December 1987).... Traded by North Stars to Washington Capitals for rights to D Claudio Scremin (November 1, 1988).... Injured ligaments in right thumb (January 31, 1990); missed nine games.... Pulled left groin (October 30, 1990); missed 12 games.
HONORS: Named to OMJHL All-Star first team (1979-80).

Season Team	League	REGULAR SEASON Gms.	Min.	W	L	T	GA	SO	Avg.	PLAYOFFS Gms.	Min.	W	L	GA	SO	Avg.
78-79—Sudbury	OMJHL	54	3248				*259	2	4.78	10	600			44		4.40
79-80—Sudbury	OMJHL	59	3447	28	29	2	248	0	4.32	9	552	5	4	38	0	4.13
80-81—Minnesota	NHL	44	2585	18	14	11	138	0	3.20	6	360	4	2	26	0	4.33
81-82—Nashville	CHL	5	299	2	3	0	25	0	5.02	—						
—Minnesota	NHL	29	1634	11	8	9	101	0	3.71	2	60	0	1	4	0	4.00
82-83—Birmingham	CHL	10	599	8	2	0	31	0	3.11	—						
—Minnesota	NHL	36	2011	19	10	5	120	0	3.58	4	245	2	2	20	0	4.90
83-84—Salt Lake City	CHL	7	419	2	5	0	30	0	4.30	—						
—Minnesota	NHL	33	1791	16	13	2	123	0	4.12	13	781	6	7	40	1	3.07
84-85—Minnesota	NHL	21	1770	10	17	3	109	1	3.69	4	184	1	1	12	0	3.91
85-86—Minnesota	NHL	52	3073	25	20	6	182	1	3.55	5	300	2	3	17	0	3.40
86-87—Minnesota	NHL	47	2622	17	20	6	174	1	3.98	—						
87-88—Minnesota	NHL	43	2288	10	22	3	161	0	4.22	—						
88-89—Minnesota	NHL	1	59	0	1	0	3	0	3.05	—						
—Kalamazoo	IHL	3	179	1	2	0	9	0	3.02	—						
—Baltimore	AHL	30	1715	14	12	2	102	0	3.57	—						
—Washington	NHL	11	578	5	4	0	28	1	2.91	—						
89-90—Washington	NHL	48	2793	23	18	5	150	2	3.22	8	401	4	3	18	0	2.69
90-91—Baltimore	AHL	2	120	2	0	0	3	0	1.50	—						
—Washington	NHL	45	2572	20	18	3	113	*5	2.64	11	624	5	5	29	†1	2.79
91-92—Baltimore	AHL	3	184	1	1	1	10	0	3.26	—						
—Washington	NHL	54	3108	29	17	6	166	1	3.20	7	419	3	4	22	0	3.15
NHL totals		464	26884	203	182	59	1568	12	3.50	60	3374	27	28	188	2	3.34

BEAUREGARD, STEPHANE
G, SABRES

PERSONAL: Born January 10, 1968, at Cowansville, Que. . . . 5-11/185. . . . Shoots right.

TRANSACTIONS/CAREER NOTES: Selected by Winnipeg Jets in third round (third Jets pick, 52nd overall) of NHL entry draft (June 11, 1988). . . . Suffered hip flexor (October 29, 1991); missed four games. . . . Traded by Jets to Buffalo Sabres for C Christian Ruuttu and future considerations (June 15, 1992).

HONORS: Won Jacques Plante Trophy (1987-88). . . . Won Raymond Lagace Trophy (1987-88). . . . Won Marcel Robert Trophy (1987-88). . . . Named to QMJHL All-Star first team (1987-88).

			REGULAR SEASON							PLAYOFFS						
Season Team	League	Gms.	Min.	W	L	T	GA	SO	Avg.	Gms.	Min.	W	L	GA	SO	Avg.
86-87—St. Jean	QMJHL	13	785	6	7	0	58	0	4.43	5	260	1	3	26	0	6.00
87-88—St. Jean	QMJHL	*66	*3766	38	20	3	229	2	*3.65	7	423	3	4	34	0	4.82
88-89—Moncton	AHL	15	824	4	8	2	62	0	4.51	—						
—Fort Wayne	IHL	16	830	9	5	0	43	0	3.11	9	484	4	4	21	*1	*2.60
89-90—Fort Wayne	IHL	33	1949	20	8	3	115	1	3.54	—						
—Winnipeg	NHL	19	1079	7	8	3	59	0	3.28	4	238	1	3	12	0	3.03
90-91—Winnipeg	NHL	16	836	3	10	1	55	0	3.95	—						
—Moncton	AHL	9	504	3	4	1	20	1	2.38	1	60	1	0	1	0	1.00
—Fort Wayne	IHL	32	1761	14	13	2	109	0	3.71	*19	*1158	10	9	57	2	2.95
91-92—Winnipeg	NHL	26	1267	6	8	6	61	2	2.89	—						
NHL totals		61	3182	16	26	10	175	2	3.30	4	238	1	3	12	0	3.03

BEERS, BOB
D, BRUINS

PERSONAL: Born May 20, 1967, at Cheektowaga, N.Y. . . . 6-2/200. . . . Shoots right. . . . Full name: Robert C. Beers.

COLLEGE: Northern Arizona, then Maine.

TRANSACTIONS/CAREER NOTES: Selected by Boston Bruins in 11th round (10th Bruins pick, 220th overall) of NHL entry draft (June 15, 1985). . . . Broke right leg (May 9, 1990). . . . Underwent surgery to remove pin from right hip (December 10, 1990); missed four games. . . . Suffered tendinitis in right hip (January 6, 1991).

HONORS: Named to NCAA All-America East second team (1988-89). . . . Named to Hockey East All-Star second team (1988-89).

		REGULAR SEASON					PLAYOFFS				
Season Team	League	Gms.	G	A	Pts.	Pen.	Gms.	G	A	Pts.	Pen.
85-86—Northern Arizona Univ.	Indep.	28	11	39	50	96	—				
86-87—University of Maine	Hockey East	38	0	13	13	46	—				
87-88—University of Maine	Hockey East	41	3	11	14	72	—				
88-89—University of Maine	Hockey East	44	10	27	37	53	—				
89-90—Maine	AHL	74	7	36	43	63	—				
—Boston	NHL	3	0	1	1	6	14	1	1	2	18
90-91—Maine	AHL	36	2	16	18	21	—				
—Boston	NHL	16	0	1	1	10	6	0	0	0	4
91-92—Boston	NHL	31	0	5	5	29	1	0	0	0	0
—Maine	AHL	33	6	23	29	24	—				
NHL totals		50	0	7	7	45	21	1	1	2	22

BELANGER, JESSE
C, CANADIENS

PERSONAL: Born June 15, 1969, at St. Georges Beauce, Que. . . . 6-0/170. . . . Shoots right.

TRANSACTIONS/CAREER NOTES: Signed as free agent by Montreal Canadiens (October 3, 1990).

		REGULAR SEASON					PLAYOFFS				
Season Team	League	Gms.	G	A	Pts.	Pen.	Gms.	G	A	Pts.	Pen.
87-88—Granby	QMJHL	69	33	43	76	10	5	3	3	6	0
88-89—Granby	QMJHL	67	40	63	103	26	4	0	5	5	0
89-90—Granby	QMJHL	67	53	54	107	53	—				
90-91—Fredericton	AHL	75	40	58	98	30	6	2	4	6	0
91-92—Fredericton	AHL	65	30	41	71	26	7	3	3	6	2
—Montreal	NHL	4	0	0	0	0	—				
NHL totals		4	0	0	0	0					

BELFOUR, ED
G, BLACKHAWKS

PERSONAL: Born April 21, 1965, at Carman, Man. . . . 5-11/182. . . . Shoots left. . . . Full name: Edward Belfour.

COLLEGE: North Dakota.

TRANSACTIONS/CAREER NOTES: Signed as free agent by Chicago Blackhawks (June 1987).

HONORS: Named top goaltender in Manitoba Junior Hockey League (1985-86). . . . Named to WCHA All-Star first team (1986-87). . . . Named to NCAA All-America West second team (1986-87). . . . Shared Garry F. Longman Memorial Trophy with John Cullen (1987-88). . . . Named to IHL All-Star first team (1987-88). . . . Named Rookie of the Year by THE SPORTING NEWS (1990-91). . . . Won the Vezina Trophy (1990-91). . . . Won the Calder Memorial Trophy (1990-91). . . . Won the William M. Jennings Trophy (1990-91). . . . Won Trico Goaltender Award (1990-91). . . . Named to THE SPORTING NEWS All-Star first team (1990-91). . . . Named to NHL All-Star first team (1990-91). . . . Named to the NHL All-Rookie Team (1990-91).

			REGULAR SEASON							PLAYOFFS						
Season Team	League	Gms.	Min.	W	L	T	GA	SO	Avg.	Gms.	Min.	W	L	GA	SO	Avg.
85-86—Winkler	MJHL	48	2880				124	1	2.58	—						
86-87—Univ. of North Dakota	WCHA	34	2049	29	4	0	81	3	2.37	—						
87-88—Saginaw	IHL	61	*3446	32	25	0	183	3	3.19	9	561	4	5	33	0	3.53

Season Team	League	REGULAR SEASON								PLAYOFFS						
		Gms.	Min.	W	L	T	GA	SO	Avg.	Gms.	Min.	W	L	GA	SO	Avg.
88-89—Chicago	NHL	23	1148	4	12	3	74	0	3.87	—	—	—	—	—	—	—
—Saginaw	IHL	29	1760	12	10	0	92	0	3.14	5	298	2	3	14	0	2.82
89-90—Can. National Team	Int'l	33	1808				93		3.09	—	—	—	—	—	—	—
—Chicago	NHL	—	—	—	—	—	—	—	—	9	409	4	2	17	0	2.49
90-91—Chicago	NHL	*74	*4127	*43	19	7	170	4	*2.47	6	295	2	4	20	0	4.07
91-92—Chicago	NHL	52	2928	21	18	10	132	†5	2.70	18	949	12	4	39	1	*2.47
NHL totals		149	8203	68	49	20	376	9	2.75	33	1653	18	10	76	1	2.76

BELLEY, ROCH
G, BLACKHAWKS

PERSONAL: Born August 12, 1971, at Hull, Que.... 5-10/170.... Shoots left.
TRANSACTIONS/CAREER NOTES: Selected by Chicago Blackhawks in fourth round (11th Blackhawks pick, 176th overall of NHL entry draft (June 22, 1991).

Season Team	League	REGULAR SEASON								PLAYOFFS						
		Gms.	Min.	W	L	T	GA	SO	Avg.	Gms.	Min.	W	L	GA	SO	Avg.
87-88—Gloucester	COJHL	34	1805				151	0	5.02	—	—	—	—	—	—	—
88-89—Gloucester	COJHL	36	1932				175	2	5.43	—	—	—	—	—	—	—
89-90—Niagara Falls	OHL	23	1029				114	0	6.65	—	—	—	—	—	—	—
90-91—Niagara Falls	OHL	45	2525	26	8	7	155	1	3.68	—	—	—	—	—	—	—
91-92—Indianapolis	IHL	25	1270	4	12	3	88	0	4.16	—	—	—	—	—	—	—

BELLOWS, BRIAN
LW, NORTH STARS

PERSONAL: Born September 1, 1964, at St. Catharines, Ont.... 5-11/195.... Shoots right.
TRANSACTIONS/CAREER NOTES: Separated shoulder (November 1981); coached Kitchener Rangers for two games while recovering (became the youngest coach in OHL history at 17 years old).... Selected by Minnesota North Stars as underage junior in first round (first North Stars pick, second overall) of NHL entry draft (June 9, 1982).... Suffered tendinitis in elbow (October 1984).... Injured wrist (October 1986), missed 13 games.... Strained abdominal muscles (February 1989); missed 20 games.... Bruised left knee (September 1990). ...Strained hip and groin (December 18, 1990).
HONORS: Named to Memorial Cup All-Star team (1980-81).... Won George Parsons Trophy (1981-82).... Named to OHL All-Star first team (1981-82).... Named to THE SPORTING NEWS All-Star second team (1989-90).... Named to NHL All-Star second team (1989-90).

Season Team	League	REGULAR SEASON					PLAYOFFS				
		Gms.	G	A	Pts.	Pen.	Gms.	G	A	Pts.	Pen.
80-81—Kitchener	OMJHL	66	49	67	116	23	16	14	13	27	13
81-82—Kitchener	OHL	47	45	52	97	23	15	16	13	29	11
82-83—Minnesota	NHL	78	35	30	65	27	9	5	4	9	18
83-84—Minnesota	NHL	78	41	42	83	66	16	2	12	14	6
84-85—Minnesota	NHL	78	26	36	62	72	9	2	4	6	9
85-86—Minnesota	NHL	77	31	48	79	46	5	5	0	5	16
86-87—Minnesota	NHL	65	26	27	53	54	—	—	—	—	—
87-88—Minnesota	NHL	77	40	41	81	81	—	—	—	—	—
88-89—Minnesota	NHL	60	23	27	50	55	5	2	3	5	8
89-90—Minnesota	NHL	80	55	44	99	72	7	4	3	7	10
90-91—Minnesota	NHL	80	35	40	75	43	23	10	19	29	30
91-92—Minnesota	NHL	80	30	45	75	41	7	4	4	8	14
NHL totals		753	342	380	722	557	81	34	49	83	111

BELZILE, ETIENNE
D, FLAMES

PERSONAL: Born May 2, 1972, at Quebec City.... 6-1/180.... Shoots left.
COLLEGE: Cornell.
TRANSACTIONS/CAREER NOTES: Selected by Calgary Flames in second round (fourth Flames pick, 41st overall) of NHL entry draft (June 16, 1989).

Season Team	League	REGULAR SEASON					PLAYOFFS				
		Gms.	G	A	Pts.	Pen.	Gms.	G	A	Pts.	Pen.
89-90—Cornell University	ECAC	28	1	4	5	18	—	—	—	—	—
90-91—Cornell University	ECAC	32	2	3	5	38	—	—	—	—	—
91-92—Cornell University	ECAC	29	1	1	2	20	—	—	—	—	—

BENNETT, ADAM
D, BLACKHAWKS

PERSONAL: Born March 30, 1971, at Georgetown, Ont.... 6-4/206.... Shoots right.
TRANSACTIONS/CAREER NOTES: Separated both shoulders (1987-88).... Selected by Chicago Blackhawks in first round (first Blackhawks pick, sixth overall) of NHL entry draft (June 17, 1989).
HONORS: Named to OHL All-Star second team (1990-91).

Season Team	League	REGULAR SEASON					PLAYOFFS				
		Gms.	G	A	Pts.	Pen.	Gms.	G	A	Pts.	Pen.
86-87—Georgetown Jr. B	OHA	1	0	0	0	0	—	—	—	—	—
87-88—Georgetown Jr. B	OHA	32	9	31	40	63	—	—	—	—	—
88-89—Sudbury	OHL	66	7	22	29	133	—	—	—	—	—
89-90—Sudbury	OHL	65	18	43	61	116	7	1	2	3	23
90-91—Sudbury	OHL	54	21	29	50	123	5	1	2	3	11
—Indianapolis	IHL	3	0	1	1	12	2	0	0	0	0
91-92—Indianapolis	IHL	59	4	10	14	89	—	—	—	—	—
—Chicago	NHL	5	0	0	0	12	—	—	—	—	—
NHL totals		5	0	0	0	12					

BENNETT, RIC
LW, RANGERS

PERSONAL: Born July 24, 1967, at Springfield, Mass. . . . 6-3/215. . . . Shoots left. . . . Full name: Eric John Bennett.
HIGH SCHOOL: Wilbraham and Monson Academy (Mass.).
COLLEGE: Providence.
TRANSACTIONS/CAREER NOTES: Selected by Minnesota North Stars in third round (fourth North Stars pick, 54th overall) of NHL entry draft (June 21, 1986). . . . Rights traded by North Stars with C Brian Lawton and LW Igor Liba to New York Rangers for D Mark Tinordi, D Paul Jerrard, C Mike Sullivan, RW Brett Barnett and the Los Angeles Kings third-round pick in 1989 draft (C Murray Garbutt) (October 11, 1988). . . . Underwent surgery to left knee (January 24, 1990).
HONORS: Named to NCAA All-America East second team (1988-89). . . . Named to Hockey East All-Star second team (1989-90).

Season Team	League	REGULAR SEASON Gms.	G	A	Pts.	Pen.	PLAYOFFS Gms.	G	A	Pts.	Pen.
85-86—Wilbraham Monson Acad.	Mass. H.S.	20	30	39	69	25	—	—	—	—	—
86-87—Providence College	Hockey East	32	15	12	27	34	—	—	—	—	—
87-88—Providence College	Hockey East	33	9	16	25	70	—	—	—	—	—
88-89—Providence College	Hockey East	32	14	32	46	74	—	—	—	—	—
89-90—Providence College	Hockey East	31	12	24	36	74	—	—	—	—	—
—New York Rangers	NHL	6	1	0	1	5	—	—	—	—	—
90-91—Binghamton	AHL	71	27	32	59	206	10	2	1	3	27
—New York Rangers	NHL	6	0	0	0	6	—	—	—	—	—
91-92—Binghamton	AHL	69	19	23	42	112	11	0	1	1	23
—New York Rangers	NHL	3	0	1	1	2	—	—	—	—	—
NHL totals		**15**	**1**	**1**	**2**	**13**	—	—	—	—	—

BENNING, BRIAN
D, FLYERS

PERSONAL: Born June 10, 1966, at Edmonton, Alta. . . . 6-0/175. . . . Shoots left. . . . Brother of Jim Benning, defenseman, Toronto Maple Leafs and Vancouver Canucks (1981-82 through 1989-90).
TRANSACTIONS/CAREER NOTES: Cracked bone in right wrist (December 1983); missed 38 games. . . . Selected by St.Louis Blues as underage junior in second round (first Blues pick, 26th overall) of NHL entry draft (June 9, 1984). . . . Broke right leg (December 28, 1984). . . . Traded by Blues to Los Angeles Kings for a third-round pick in 1991 draft (November 10, 1989). . . . Underwent appendectomy (March 6, 1990); missed three weeks. . . . Suspended three games by NHL for cross-checking (September 28, 1990). . . . Suffered back spasms (December 1990). . . . Injured groin (October 22, 1991); missed three games. . . . Traded by Kings with D Jeff Chychrun and a first-round pick in 1992 draft to Pittsburgh Penguins for D Paul Coffey (February 19, 1992). . . . Traded by Penguins with RW Mark Recchi and a first-round pick in 1992 draft previously acquired from Kings to Philadelphia Flyers for RW Rick Tocchet, D Kjell Samuelsson, G Ken Wregget and a third-round pick in 1992 draft (February 19, 1992).
HONORS: Named to NHL All-Rookie team (1986-87).

Season Team	League	REGULAR SEASON Gms.	G	A	Pts.	Pen.	PLAYOFFS Gms.	G	A	Pts.	Pen.
83-84—Portland	WHL	38	6	41	47	108	—	—	—	—	—
84-85—Kamloops	WHL	17	3	18	21	26	—	—	—	—	—
—St. Louis	NHL	4	0	2	2	0	—	—	—	—	—
85-86—Team Canada	Int'l	60	6	13	19	43	—	—	—	—	—
—St. Louis	NHL	—	—	—	—	—	6	1	2	3	13
86-87—St. Louis	NHL	78	13	36	49	110	6	0	4	4	9
87-88—St. Louis	NHL	77	8	29	37	107	10	1	6	7	25
88-89—St. Louis	NHL	66	8	26	34	102	7	1	1	2	11
89-90—St. Louis	NHL	7	1	1	2	2	—	—	—	—	—
—Los Angeles	NHL	48	5	18	23	104	7	0	2	2	10
90-91—Los Angeles	NHL	61	7	24	31	127	12	0	5	5	6
91-92—Los Angeles	NHL	53	2	30	32	99	—	—	—	—	—
—Philadelphia	NHL	22	2	12	14	35	—	—	—	—	—
NHL totals		**416**	**46**	**178**	**224**	**686**	**48**	**3**	**20**	**23**	**74**

BERANEK, JOSEF
C, OILERS

PERSONAL: Born October 25, 1969, at Litvinov, Czechoslovakia. . . . 6-2/185. . . . Shoots left.
TRANSACTIONS/CAREER NOTES: Selected by Edmonton Oilers in fourth round (third Oilers pick, 78th overall) of NHL entry draft (June 17, 1989).

Season Team	League	REGULAR SEASON Gms.	G	A	Pts.	Pen.	PLAYOFFS Gms.	G	A	Pts.	Pen.
87-88—CHZ Litvinov	Czech.	14	7	4	11	12	—	—	—	—	—
88-89—CHZ Litvinov	Czech.	32	18	10	28	47	—	—	—	—	—
—Czechoslovakia Nat. Jr.	Czech.	5	2	7	9	2	—	—	—	—	—
89-90—Dukla Trencin	Czech.	49	16	21	37		—	—	—	—	—
90-91—CHZ Litvinov	Czech.	50	27	27	54	98	—	—	—	—	—
91-92—Edmonton	NHL	58	12	16	28	18	12	2	1	3	0
NHL totals		**58**	**12**	**16**	**28**	**18**	**12**	**2**	**1**	**3**	**0**

BEREHOWSKY, DRAKE
D, MAPLE LEAFS

PERSONAL: Born January 3, 1972, at Toronto. . . . 6-1/211. . . . Shoots right.
TRANSACTIONS/CAREER NOTES: Injured knees and underwent reconstructive surgery (October 13, 1989); missed remainder of season. . . . Selected by Toronto Maple Leafs in first round (first Maple Leafs pick, 10th overall) of NHL entry draft (June 16, 1990).

HONORS: Won Can.HL Defenseman of the Year Award (1991-92).... Won Max Kaminsky Trophy (1991-92).... Named to Can.HL All-Star first team (1991-92).... Named to OHL All-Star first team (1991-92).

			REGULAR SEASON					PLAYOFFS			
Season Team	League	Gms.	G	A	Pts.	Pen.	Gms.	G	A	Pts.	Pen.
87-88—Barrie Jr. B	OHA	40	10	36	46	81	—	—	—	—	—
88-89—Kingston	OHL	63	7	39	46	85	—	—	—	—	—
89-90—Kingston	OHL	9	3	11	14	28	—	—	—	—	—
90-91—Toronto	NHL	8	0	1	1	25	—	—	—	—	—
—Kingston	OHL	13	5	13	18	28	—	—	—	—	—
—North Bay	OHL	26	7	23	30	51	10	2	7	9	21
91-92—North Bay	OHL	62	19	63	82	147	21	7	24	31	22
—Toronto	NHL	1	0	0	0	0	—	—	—	—	—
—St. John's	AHL	—	—	—	—	—	6	0	5	5	21
NHL totals		9	0	1	1	25					

BEREZAN, PERRY
C, SHARKS

PERSONAL: Born December 5, 1964, at Edmonton, Alta.... 6-2/190.... Shoots right.... Full name: Perry Edmund Berezan.
COLLEGE: North Dakota.
TRANSACTIONS/CAREER NOTES: Selected by Calgary Flames as underage junior in third round (third Flames pick, 55th overall) of NHL entry draft (June 8, 1983).... Suffered sinus problems (February 1986); missed eight games.... Broke ankle (March 19, 1986).... Injured groin (November 1986).... Underwent surgery for groin injury (March 1987).... Injured groin (November 1987).... Lacerated hand (February 1988).... Traded by Flames with RW Shane Churla to Minnesota North Stars for LW Brian MacLellan and a fourth-round pick in 1989 draft (C Robert Reichel) (March 4, 1989).... Suffered concussion (October 1989).... Sprained ankle (December 18, 1989); missed eight games.... Broke nose (March 1990).... Signed as free agent by San Jose Sharks (October 10, 1991).... Sprained knee (October 23, 1991); missed five games.
HONORS: Named to WCHA All-Star second team (1984-85).

			REGULAR SEASON					PLAYOFFS			
Season Team	League	Gms.	G	A	Pts.	Pen.	Gms.	G	A	Pts.	Pen.
81-82—St. Albert	AJHL	47	16	36	52	47	—	—	—	—	—
82-83—St. Albert	AJHL	57	37	40	77	110	—	—	—	—	—
83-84—Univ. of North Dakota	WCHA	44	28	24	52	29	—	—	—	—	—
84-85—Univ. of North Dakota	WCHA	42	23	35	58	32	—	—	—	—	—
—Calgary	NHL	9	3	2	5	4	2	1	0	1	4
85-86—Calgary	NHL	55	12	21	33	39	8	1	1	2	6
86-87—Calgary	NHL	24	5	3	8	24	2	0	2	2	7
87-88—Calgary	NHL	29	7	12	19	66	8	0	2	2	13
88-89—Calgary	NHL	35	4	4	8	21	—	—	—	—	—
—Minnesota	NHL	16	1	4	5	4	5	1	2	3	4
89-90—Minnesota	NHL	64	3	12	15	31	5	1	0	1	0
90-91—Kalamazoo	IHL	2	0	0	0	2	—	—	—	—	—
—Minnesota	NHL	52	11	6	17	30	1	0	0	0	0
91-92—San Jose	NHL	66	12	7	19	30	—	—	—	—	—
NHL totals		350	58	71	129	249	31	4	7	11	34

BERG, BILL
LW, ISLANDERS

PERSONAL: Born October 21, 1967, at St. Catharines, Ont.... 6-1/198.... Shoots left.... Full name: William Berg.... Brother of Bob Berg, left winger in Los Angeles Kings system.
TRANSACTIONS/CAREER NOTES: Broke ankle (March 1985).... Selected by New York Islanders as underage junior in third round (third Islanders pick, 59th overall) of NHL entry draft (June 21, 1986). ... Injured knee (October 1986).... Separated shoulder (May 1990).... Fractured left foot (November 9, 1991); missed 12 games.
MISCELLANEOUS: Moved from defense to left wing (1990).

			REGULAR SEASON					PLAYOFFS			
Season Team	League	Gms.	G	A	Pts.	Pen.	Gms.	G	A	Pts.	Pen.
84-85—Grimsby Jr. B	OHA	42	10	22	32	153	—	—	—	—	—
85-86—Toronto	OHL	64	3	35	38	143	4	0	0	0	19
86-87—Toronto	OHL	57	3	15	18	138	—	—	—	—	—
—Springfield	AHL	4	1	1	2	4	—	—	—	—	—
87-88—Springfield	AHL	76	6	26	32	148	7	0	3	3	31
—Peoria	IHL	5	0	1	1	8					
88-89—New York Islanders	NHL	7	1	2	3	10	—	—	—	—	—
—Springfield	AHL	69	17	32	49	122	—	—	—	—	—
89-90—Springfield	AHL	74	12	42	54	74	15	5	12	17	35
90-91—New York Islanders	NHL	78	9	14	23	67	—	—	—	—	—
91-92—New York Islanders	NHL	47	5	9	14	28	—	—	—	—	—
—Capital District	AHL	3	0	2	2	16	—	—	—	—	—
NHL totals		132	15	25	40	105					

BERG, BOB
LW, KINGS

PERSONAL: Born July 2, 1970, at Beamsville, Ont.... 6-1/190.... Shoots left.... Brother of Bill Berg, left winger, New York Islanders.
TRANSACTIONS/CAREER NOTES: Selected by Los Angeles Kings in third round (third Kings pick, 49th overall) of NHL entry draft (June 16, 1990).... Traded by Niagara Falls Thunder to Sudbury Wolves

B

for a sixth-round draft pick (January 10, 1991).
HONORS: Named to OHL All-Star first team (1989-90).

			REGULAR SEASON					PLAYOFFS				
Season	Team	League	Gms.	G	A	Pts.	Pen.	Gms.	G	A	Pts.	Pen.
85-86	Grimsby Jr. B	OHA	40	22	12	34	73	—	—	—	—	—
86-87	Grimsby Jr. B	OHA	36	13	16	29	115	—	—	—	—	—
87-88	Belleville	OHL	61	15	27	42	59	—	—	—	—	—
88-89	Belleville	OHL	66	33	51	84	88	5	1	3	4	8
89-90	Belleville	OHL	66	48	49	97	124	8	2	2	4	14
90-91	Niagara Falls	OHL	12	8	4	12	11	—	—	—	—	—
	Sudbury	OHL	23	12	15	27	34	5	2	1	3	6
	New Haven	AHL	19	0	1	1	8	—	—	—	—	—
91-92	Phoenix	IHL	24	2	8	10	18	—	—	—	—	—
	Richmond	ECHL	37	19	14	33	65	6	2	1	3	0

BERGERON, JEAN-CLAUDE
G, LIGHTNING

PERSONAL: Born October 14, 1968, at Havreziue, Que. . . . 6-2/192. . . . Shoots left.

TRANSACTIONS/CAREER NOTES: Selected by Montreal Canadiens in fifth round (sixth Canadiens pick, 104th overall of NHL entry draft (June 11, 1988). . . . Traded by Canadiens to Tampa Bay Lightning for G Frederic Chabot (June 18, 1992).
HONORS: Named to AHL All-Star first team (1989-90). . . . Won Baz Bastien Trophy (1989-90). . . . Shared Harry (Hap) Holmes Memorial Trophy with Andre Racicot (1989-90).

			REGULAR SEASON							PLAYOFFS					
Season	Team	League	Gms.	Min.	W	L	T	GA	SO	Avg.	Gms.	Min.	W	L	GA	SO	Avg.
85-86	Shawinigan	QMJHL	33	1796				156	0	5.21	—	—			—	—	—
86-87	Verdun	QMJHL	52	2991				*306	0	6.14	—	—			—	—	—
87-88	Verdun	QMJHL	49	2715	13	31	3	*265	0	5.86	—	—			—	—	—
88-89	Verdun	QMJHL	44	2417	8	34	1	199	0	4.94	—	—			—	—	—
	Sherbrooke	AHL	5	302	4	1	0	18	0	3.58	—	—			—	—	—
89-90	Sherbrooke	AHL	40	2254	21	8	7	103	2	*2.74	9	497	6	2	28	0	3.38
90-91	Montreal	NHL	19	941	7	6	2	59	0	3.76	—	—			—	—	—
	Fredericton	AHL	18	1083	12	6	0	59	1	3.27	10	546	5	5	32	0	3.52
91-92	Fredericton	AHL	13	791	5	7	1	57	0	4.32	—	—			—	—	—
	Peoria	IHL	27	1632	14	9	3	96	1	3.53	6	352	3	3	24	0	4.09
NHL totals			19	941	7	6	2	59	0	3.76							

BERGERON, MARTIN
C

PERSONAL: Born January 20, 1968, at Verdun, Que. . . . 6-0/185. . . . Shoots left.
TRANSACTIONS/CAREER NOTES: Selected by New York Rangers in fifth round (fourth Rangers pick, 99th overall) of NHL entry draft (June 11, 1988).
HONORS: Named to ECHL All-Star second team (1991-92).

			REGULAR SEASON					PLAYOFFS				
Season	Team	League	Gms.	G	A	Pts.	Pen.	Gms.	G	A	Pts.	Pen.
85-86	Drummondville	QMJHL	74	14	34	48	65	23	0	1	1	25
86-87	Drummondville	QMJHL	66	36	58	94	83	8	5	8	13	0
87-88	Drummondville	QMJHL	69	45	64	109	99	17	12	14	26	24
88-89	Drummondville	QMJHL	68	55	81	136	95	4	3	1	4	4
	Denver	IHL	1	0	1	1	0	—	—	—	—	—
89-90	Erie	ECHL	59	30	58	88	109	7	3	4	7	20
90-91	Binghamton	AHL	41	11	22	33	31	—	—	—	—	—
	San Diego	IHL	9	4	4	8	16	—	—	—	—	—
91-92	Louisville	ECHL	64	39	61	100	134	13	3	11	14	36

BERGEVIN, MARC
D, LIGHTNING

PERSONAL: Born August 11, 1965, at Montreal. . . . 6-0/185. . . . Shoots left.
TRANSACTIONS/CAREER NOTES: Selected by Chicago Blackhawks as underage junior in third round (third Blackhawks pick, 59th overall) of NHL entry draft (June 8, 1983). . . . Sprained neck (March 18, 1987). . . . Traded by Blackhawks with D Gary Nylund to New York Islanders for D Steve Konroyd and C Bob Bassen (November 25, 1988). . . . Bruised ribs (November 25, 1989). . . . Broke hand (May 1990). . . . Traded by Islanders to Hartford Whalers for future considerations (October 31, 1990). . . . Signed as free agent by Tampa Bay Lightning (July 9, 1992).

			REGULAR SEASON					PLAYOFFS				
Season	Team	League	Gms.	G	A	Pts.	Pen.	Gms.	G	A	Pts.	Pen.
82-83	Chicoutimi	QMJHL	64	3	27	30	113	—	—	—	—	—
83-84	Chicoutimi	QMJHL	70	10	35	45	125	—	—	—	—	—
	Springfield	AHL	7	0	1	1	2	—	—	—	—	—
84-85	Springfield	AHL	—	—	—	—	—	4	0	0	0	0
	Chicago	NHL	60	0	6	6	54	6	0	3	3	2
85-86	Chicago	NHL	71	7	7	14	60	3	0	0	0	0
86-87	Chicago	NHL	66	4	10	14	66	3	1	0	1	2
87-88	Chicago	NHL	58	1	6	7	85	—	—	—	—	—
	Saginaw	IHL	10	2	7	9	20	—	—	—	—	—
88-89	Chicago	NHL	11	0	0	0	18	—	—	—	—	—
	New York Islanders	NHL	58	2	13	15	62	—	—	—	—	—
89-90	New York Islanders	NHL	18	0	4	4	30	—	—	—	—	—
	Springfield	AHL	47	7	16	23	66	17	2	11	13	16

Season	Team	League	Gms.	G	A	Pts.	Pen.	Gms.	G	A	Pts.	Pen.
				REGULAR SEASON					PLAYOFFS			
90-91	—Hartford	NHL	4	0	0	0	4	—	—	—	—	—
	—Capital District	AHL	7	0	5	5	6	—	—	—	—	—
	—Springfield	AHL	58	4	23	27	85	18	0	7	7	26
91-92	—Hartford	NHL	75	7	17	24	64	5	0	0	0	2
	NHL totals		421	21	63	84	443	17	1	3	4	6

BERGLAND, TIM
RW, LIGHTNING

PERSONAL: Born January 11, 1965, at Crookston, Minn. . . . 6-3/194. . . . Shoots right. . . . Full name: Timothy Daniel Bergland.
HIGH SCHOOL: Lincoln (Thief River Falls, Minn.).
COLLEGE: Minnesota.
TRANSACTIONS/CAREER NOTES: Selected by Washington Capitals as underage junior in fourth round (first Capitals pick, 75th overall) of NHL entry draft (June 8, 1983). . . . Selected by Tampa Bay Lightning in NHL expansion draft (June 18, 1992).

Season	Team	League	Gms.	G	A	Pts.	Pen.	Gms.	G	A	Pts.	Pen.
				REGULAR SEASON					PLAYOFFS			
82-83	—Lincoln High School	Minn. H.S.	20	26	22	48		—	—	—	—	—
83-84	—University of Minnesota	WCHA	24	4	11	15	4	—	—	—	—	—
84-85	—University of Minnesota	WCHA	46	7	12	19	16	—	—	—	—	—
85-86	—University of Minnesota	WCHA	48	11	16	27	26	—	—	—	—	—
86-87	—University of Minnesota	WCHA	49	18	17	35	48	—	—	—	—	—
87-88	—Fort Wayne	IHL	13	2	1	3	9	—	—	—	—	—
	—Binghamton	AHL	63	21	26	47	31	4	0	0	0	0
88-89	—Baltimore	AHL	78	24	29	53	39	—	—	—	—	—
89-90	—Baltimore	AHL	47	12	19	31	55	—	—	—	—	—
	—Washington	NHL	32	2	5	7	31	15	1	1	2	8
90-91	—Washington	NHL	47	5	9	14	21	11	1	1	2	12
	—Baltimore	AHL	15	8	9	17	16	—	—	—	—	—
91-92	—Washington	NHL	22	1	4	5	2	—	—	—	—	—
	—Baltimore	AHL	11	6	10	16	5	—	—	—	—	—
	NHL totals		101	8	18	26	54	26	2	2	4	20

BERNARD, LOUIS
D, CANADIENS

PERSONAL: Born July 10, 1974, at Victoriaville, Que. . . . 6-1/203. . . . Shoots right.
TRANSACTIONS/CAREER NOTES: Selected by Montreal Canadiens in fourth round (fifth Canadiens pick, 82nd overall) of NHL entry draft (June 20, 1992).

Season	Team	League	Gms.	G	A	Pts.	Pen.	Gms.	G	A	Pts.	Pen.
				REGULAR SEASON					PLAYOFFS			
91-92	—Drummondville	QMJHL	70	8	24	32	59	4	0	1	1	4

BERRY, BRAD
D, NORTH STARS

PERSONAL: Born April 1, 1965, at Bashaw, Alta. . . . 6-2/190. . . . Shoots left. . . . Full name: Bradley L. Berry.
COLLEGE: North Dakota.
TRANSACTIONS/CAREER NOTES: Selected by Winnipeg Jets in second round (third Jets pick, 29th overall) of NHL entry draft (June 8, 1983). . . . Signed as free agent by Minnesota North Stars (October 14, 1991).

Season	Team	League	Gms.	G	A	Pts.	Pen.	Gms.	G	A	Pts.	Pen.
				REGULAR SEASON					PLAYOFFS			
83-84	—North Dakota	WCHA	32	2	7	9	8	—	—	—	—	—
84-85	—North Dakota	WCHA	40	4	26	30	26	—	—	—	—	—
85-86	—North Dakota	WCHA	40	6	29	35	26	—	—	—	—	—
	—Winnipeg	NHL	13	1	0	1	10	3	0	0	0	0
86-87	—Winnipeg	NHL	52	2	8	10	60	7	0	1	1	14
87-88	—Winnipeg	NHL	48	0	6	6	75	—	—	—	—	—
	—Moncton	AHL	10	1	3	4	14	—	—	—	—	—
88-89	—Winnipeg	NHL	38	0	9	9	45	—	—	—	—	—
	—Moncton	AHL	38	3	16	19	39	—	—	—	—	—
89-90	—Winnipeg	NHL	12	1	2	3	6	1	0	0	0	0
	—Moncton	AHL	38	1	9	10	58	—	—	—	—	—
90-91	—Brynas	Sweden	38	3	1	4	38	—	—	—	—	—
91-92	—Kalamazoo	IHL	65	5	18	23	90	5	2	0	2	6
	—Minnesota	NHL	7	0	0	0	6	2	0	0	0	2
	NHL totals		170	4	25	29	202	13	0	1	1	16

BERTHIAUME, DANIEL
G

PERSONAL: Born January 26, 1966, at Longueuil, Que. . . . 5-9/151. . . . Shoots left.
TRANSACTIONS/CAREER NOTES: Traded by Drummondville Voltigeurs to Chicoutimi Sagueneens for RW Simon Massie (October 1984). . . . Selected by Winnipeg Jets as underage junior in third round (third Jets pick, 60th overall) of NHL entry draft (June 15, 1985). . . . Pulled chest muscle (March 1, 1988). . . . Suspended by Jets for failing to report to Moncton (October 4, 1988); suspension lifted (October 11, 1988). . . . Suspended by Moncton (November 4, 1988); suspension lifted (November 29, 1988). . . . Injured shoulder and suspended eight games by AHL for altercation (December 17, 1988). . . . Traded by Jets to Minnesota North Stars for future considerations (January 22, 1990). . . . Injured knee (February 13, 1990); missed 13 games. . . . Traded by North Stars to Los Angeles Kings for LW Craig Duncanson (September 6, 1990). . . . Suffered concussion (December 5, 1991); missed two

games.... Traded by Kings to Boston Bruins for future considerations (January 20, 1992).... Traded by Bruins to Jets for LW Doug Evans (June 10, 1992).... Released by Jets (July 28, 1992).
HONORS: Won Michel Briere Trophy (1984-85).... Won Jacques Plante Trophy (1984-85).

Season	Team	League	REGULAR SEASON							PLAYOFFS						
			Gms.	Min.	W	L	T	GA	SO	Avg.	Gms.	Min.	W	L	GA	SO	Avg.
83-84—Drummondville	QMJHL	28	1562				131	0	5.03	—	—	—	—	—	—	—
84-85—Drummondville/Chicoutimi	QMJHL	*59	*3347	40	11	2	215	†2	3.85	†14	770	8	6	*51	0	3.97
85-86—Chicoutimi	QMJHL	*66	*3718	34	29	3	*286	1	4.62	9	580	4	5	36	0	3.72
—Winnipeg	NHL	—	—	—	—	—	—	—	—	1	68	0	1	4	0	3.53
86-87—Sherbrooke	AHL	7	420	4	3	0	23	0	3.29	—	—	—	—	—	—	—
—Winnipeg	NHL	31	1758	18	7	3	93	1	3.17	8	439	4	4	21	0	2.87
87-88—Winnipeg	NHL	56	3010	22	19	7	176	2	3.51	5	300	1	4	25	0	5.00
88-89—Winnipeg	NHL	9	443	0	8	0	44	0	5.96	—	—	—	—	—	—	—
—Moncton	AHL	21	1083	6	9	2	76	0	4.21	3	180	1	2	11	0	3.67
89-90—Winnipeg	NHL	24	1387	10	11	3	86	1	3.72	—	—	—	—	—	—	—
—Minnesota	NHL	5	240	1	3	0	14	0	3.50	—	—	—	—	—	—	—
90-91—Los Angeles	NHL	37	2119	20	11	4	117	1	3.31	—	—	—	—	—	—	—
91-92—Los Angeles	NHL	19	979	7	10	1	66	0	4.04	—	—	—	—	—	—	—
—Boston	NHL	8	399	1	4	2	21	0	3.16	—	—	—	—	—	—	—
NHL totals		189	10335	79	73	20	617	5	3.58	14	807	5	9	50	0	3.72

BERUBE, CRAIG
LW, FLAMES

PERSONAL: Born December 17, 1965, at Calihoo, Alta.... 6-2/195.... Shoots left.
TRANSACTIONS/CAREER NOTES: Signed as free agent by Philadelphia Flyers (March 19, 1986).... Sprained left knee (March 1988).... Traded by Flyers with RW Scott Mellanby and C Craig Fisher to Edmonton Oilers for RW Dave Brown, D Corey Foster and the NHL rights to RW Jari Kurri (May 30, 1991).... Traded by Oilers with G Grant Fuhr and RW/LW Glenn Anderson to Toronto Maple Leafs for LW Vincent Damphousse, D Luke Richardson, G Peter Ing, C Scott Thornton and future considerations (September 19, 1991). ... Traded by Maple Leafs with D Alexander Godynyuk, RW Gary Leeman, D Michel Petit and G Jeff Reese to Calgary Flames for C Doug Gilmour, D Jamie Macoun, LW Kent Manderville, D Ric Nattress and G Rick Wamsley (January 2, 1992).

Season	Team	League	REGULAR SEASON					PLAYOFFS				
			Gms.	G	A	Pts.	Pen.	Gms.	G	A	Pts.	Pen.
82-83—Williams Lake	PCJHL	33	9	24	33	99	—	—	—	—	—
—Kamloops	WHL	4	0	0	0	0	—	—	—	—	—
83-84—New Westminster	WHL	70	11	20	31	104	8	1	2	3	5
84-85—New Westminster	WHL	70	25	44	69	191	10	3	2	5	4
85-86—Kamloops	WHL	32	17	14	31	119	—	—	—	—	—
—Medicine Hat	WHL	34	14	16	30	95	25	7	8	15	102
86-87—Hershey	AHL	63	7	17	24	325	—	—	—	—	—
—Philadelphia	NHL	7	0	0	0	57	5	0	0	0	17
87-88—Hershey	AHL	31	5	9	14	119	—	—	—	—	—
—Philadelphia	NHL	27	3	2	5	108	—	—	—	—	—
88-89—Hershey	AHL	7	0	2	2	19	—	—	—	—	—
—Philadelphia	NHL	53	1	1	2	199	16	0	0	0	56
89-90—Philadelphia	NHL	74	4	14	18	291	—	—	—	—	—
90-91—Philadelphia	NHL	74	8	9	17	293	—	—	—	—	—
91-92—Toronto	NHL	40	5	7	12	109	—	—	—	—	—
—Calgary	NHL	36	1	4	5	155	—	—	—	—	—
NHL totals		311	22	37	59	1212	21	0	0	0	73

BES, JEFF
C, N. STARS

PERSONAL: Born July 31, 1973, at Tillsonburg, Ont.... 6-0/186.... Shoots left.
HIGH SCHOOL: Bishop MacDonnell (Guelph, Ont.).
TRANSACTIONS/CAREER NOTES: Selected by Minnesota North Stars in third round (second North Stars pick, 58th overall) of NHL entry draft (June 20, 1992).

Season	Team	League	REGULAR SEASON					PLAYOFFS				
			Gms.	G	A	Pts.	Pen.	Gms.	G	A	Pts.	Pen.
87-88—Woodstock Jr. C	OHA	33	19	10	29	16	—	—	—	—	—
88-89—St. Mary's Jr. B	OHA	37	8	22	30	37	—	—	—	—	—
89-90—St. Mary's Jr. B	OHA	39	25	37	62	127	—	—	—	—	—
90-91—Dukes of Hamilton	OHL	66	23	47	70	53	4	1	4	5	4
91-92—Guelph	OHL	62	40	62	102	123	—	—	—	—	—

BESTER, ALLAN
G, RED WINGS

PERSONAL: Born March 26, 1964, at Hamilton, Ont.... 5-7/155.... Shoots left.... Full name: Allan J. Bester.
TRANSACTIONS/CAREER NOTES: Selected by Toronto Maple Leafs as underage junior in third round (third Maple Leafs pick, 48th overall) of NHL entry draft (June 8, 1983).... Sprained left knee ligaments (February, 1988); missed 14 games.... Suffered phlebitis in right leg (January, 1989).... Stretched knee ligaments (April, 1989).... Suffered from bone spurs in right heel (October, 1989).... Underwent surgery for calcium deposits on his heels (October, 1990).... Traded by Toronto Maple Leafs to Detroit Red Wings for a sixth-round pick in 1991 draft (C Alexander Kuzminsky) (March 5, 1991).
HONORS: Named to OHL All-Star first team (1982-83).... Won Jack Butterfield Trophy (1991-92).

Season	Team	League	REGULAR SEASON							PLAYOFFS						
			Gms.	Min.	W	L	T	GA	SO	Avg.	Gms.	Min.	W	L	GA	SO	Avg.
81-82—Brantford	OHL	19	970	4	11	0	68	0	4.21	—	—	—	—	—	—	—
82-83—Brantford	OHL	56	3210	29	21	3	188	0	3.51	8	480	3	3	20	†1	*2.50

Season	Team	League	REGULAR SEASON Gms.	Min.	W	L	T	GA	SO	Avg.	PLAYOFFS Gms.	Min.	W	L	GA	SO	Avg.
83-84	Brantford	OHL	23	1271	12	9	1	71	1	3.35	1	60	0	1	5	0	5.00
	Toronto	NHL	32	1848	11	16	4	134	0	4.35	—	—	—	—	—	—	—
84-85	St. Catharines	AHL	30	1669	9	18	1	133	0	4.78	—	—	—	—	—	—	—
	Toronto	NHL	15	767	3	9	1	54	1	4.22	—	—	—	—	—	—	—
85-86	St. Catharines	AHL	50	2855	23	23	3	173	1	3.64	11	637	7	3	27	0	2.54
	Toronto	NHL	1	20	0	0	0	2	0	6.00	—	—	—	—	—	—	—
86-87	Newmarket	AHL	3	190	1	0	0	6	0	1.89	—	—	—	—	—	—	—
	Toronto	NHL	36	1808	10	14	3	110	2	3.65	1	39	0	1	1	0	1.54
87-88	Toronto	NHL	30	1607	8	12	5	102	2	3.81	5	253	2	3	21	0	4.98
88-89	Toronto	NHL	43	2460	17	20	3	156	2	3.80	—	—	—	—	—	—	—
89-90	Newmarket	AHL	5	264	2	1	1	18	0	4.09	—	—	—	—	—	—	—
	Toronto	NHL	42	2206	20	16	0	165	0	4.49	—	—	—	—	—	—	—
90-91	Toronto	NHL	6	247	0	4	0	18	0	4.37	—	—	—	—	—	—	—
	Detroit	NHL	3	178	0	3	0	13	0	4.38	1	20	0	0	1	0	3.00
	Newmarket	AHL	19	1157	7	8	4	58	1	3.01	—	—	—	—	—	—	—
91-92	Detroit	NHL	1	31	0	0	0	2	0	3.87	—	—	—	—	—	—	—
	Adirondack	AHL	22	1268	13	8	0	78	0	3.69	†19	1174	*14	5	50	1	2.56
NHL totals			209	11172	69	94	16	756	7	4.06	7	312	2	3	23	0	4.42

BEUKEBOOM, JEFF

D, RANGERS

PERSONAL: Born March 28, 1965, at Ajax, Ont.... 6-4/223.... Shoots right.... Nephew of Ed Kea, defenseman, Atlanta Flames and St. Louis Blues (1973-74 through 1982-83); and cousin of Joe Nieuwendyk, center, Calgary Flames.

TRANSACTIONS/CAREER NOTES: Selected by Edmonton Oilers as underage junior in first round (first Oilers pick, 19th overall) of NHL entry draft (June 8,1983).... Injured knee (December 1984).... Lacerated knuckle (October 24, 1987).... Suspended 10 games by NHL for leaving the bench (October 2, 1988).... Sprained right knee (January 1989).... Suffered hairline fracture of ankle (February 22, 1991); missed two games.... Traded by Oilers to New York Rangers for D David Shaw (November 12, 1991), completing deal in which Oilers traded C Mark Messier with future considerations to Rangers for C Bernie Nicholls, LW Louie DeBrusk, RW Steven Rice and future considerations (October 4, 1991). ... Strained back (Match 16, 1992); missed one game.

HONORS: Named to OHL All-Star first team (1984-85).

Season	Team	League	REGULAR SEASON Gms.	G	A	Pts.	Pen.	PLAYOFFS Gms.	G	A	Pts.	Pen.
81-82	Newmarket	OPJHL	49	5	30	35	218	—	—	—	—	—
82-83	Sault Ste. Marie	OHL	70	0	25	25	143	16	1	14	15	46
83-84	Sault Ste. Marie	OHL	61	6	30	36	178	16	1	7	8	43
84-85	Sault Ste. Marie	OHL	37	4	20	24	85	16	4	6	10	47
85-86	Nova Scotia	AHL	77	9	20	29	175	—	—	—	—	—
	Edmonton	NHL	—	—	—	—	—	1	0	0	0	4
86-87	Nova Scotia	AHL	14	1	7	8	35	—	—	—	—	—
	Edmonton	NHL	44	3	8	11	124	—	—	—	—	—
87-88	Edmonton	NHL	73	5	20	25	201	7	0	0	0	16
88-89	Cape Breton	AHL	8	0	4	4	36	—	—	—	—	—
	Edmonton	NHL	36	0	5	5	94	1	0	0	0	2
89-90	Edmonton	NHL	46	1	12	13	86	2	0	0	0	0
90-91	Edmonton	NHL	67	3	7	10	150	18	1	3	4	28
91-92	Edmonton	NHL	18	0	5	5	78	—	—	—	—	—
	New York Rangers	NHL	56	1	10	11	122	13	2	3	5	*47
NHL totals			340	13	67	80	855	42	3	6	9	97

BIGGS, DON

C, RANGERS

PERSONAL: Born April 7, 1965, at Mississauga, Ont.... 5-8/180.... Shoots right.

TRANSACTIONS/CAREER NOTES: Injured knee ligaments (April 1982).... Selected by Minnesota North Stars as underage junior in eighth round (ninth North Stars pick, 156th overall) of NHL entry draft (June 8, 1983).... Traded by North Stars with RW Gord Sherven to Edmonton Oilers for C Marc Habscheid, D Emanuel Viveiros and LW Don Barber (December 20, 1985).... Signed as free agent by Philadelphia Flyers (July 17, 1987).... Suspended five games by AHL for biting (December 16, 1989).... Signed to play with Olten (Switzerland) (May 1990).... Claimed by Rochester Americans on waivers after signing contract with Hershey Bears upon returning from Switzerland (November 1, 1990).... Suspended three games by AHL for physically abusing linesman (February 1, 1991).... Traded by Flyers to New York Rangers for future considerations (August 8, 1991).

Season	Team	League	REGULAR SEASON Gms.	G	A	Pts.	Pen.	PLAYOFFS Gms.	G	A	Pts.	Pen.
82-83	Oshawa	OHL	70	22	53	75	145	16	3	6	9	17
83-84	Oshawa	OHL	58	31	60	91	149	7	4	4	8	18
84-85	Oshawa	OHL	60	48	69	117	105	5	3	4	7	6
	Springfield	AHL	6	0	3	3	0	2	1	0	1	0
	Minnesota	NHL	1	0	0	0	0	—	—	—	—	—
85-86	Springfield	AHL	28	15	16	31	46	—	—	—	—	—
	Nova Scotia	AHL	47	6	23	29	36	—	—	—	—	—
86-87	Nova Scotia	AHL	80	22	25	47	165	5	1	2	3	4
87-88	Hershey	AHL	77	38	41	79	151	12	5	†11	†16	22
88-89	Hershey	AHL	76	36	67	103	158	11	5	9	14	30
89-90	Philadelphia	NHL	11	2	0	2	8	—	—	—	—	—
	Hershey	AHL	66	39	53	92	125	—	—	—	—	—

Season	Team	League	Gms.	G	A	Pts.	Pen.	Gms.	G	A	Pts.	Pen.
				REGULAR SEASON					PLAYOFFS			
90-91—Olten		Switzerland				Statistics unavailable.						
—Rochester		AHL	65	31	57	88	115	15	9	*14	*23	14
91-92—Binghamton		AHL	74	32	50	82	122	11	3	7	10	8
NHL totals			12	2	0	2	8					

BILLECK, LAURIE
D, NORTH STARS

PERSONAL: Born July 2, 1971, at Dolphin, Man.... 6-3/210.... Shoots right.
TRANSACTIONS/CAREER NOTES: Injured shoulder (September 1989).... Selected by Minnesota North Stars in third round (second North Stars pick, 50th overall) of NHL entry draft (June 16, 1990).... Injured left shoulder (December 11, 1990).... Underwent surgery to left shoulder (January 24, 1991); missed remainder of season.

Season	Team	League	Gms.	G	A	Pts.	Pen.	Gms.	G	A	Pts.	Pen.
				REGULAR SEASON					PLAYOFFS			
88-89—Prince Albert		WHL	60	2	4	6	65	4	1	0	1	14
89-90—Prince Albert		WHL	67	7	28	35	135	14	2	3	5	24
90-91—Prince Albert		WHL	35	1	10	11	60	3	0	0	0	5
91-92—Tacoma		WHL	65	14	29	43	168	4	0	1	1	18

BILLINGTON, CRAIG
G, DEVILS

PERSONAL: Born September 11, 1966, at London, Ont.... 5-10/170.... Shoots left.
TRANSACTIONS/CAREER NOTES: Selected by New Jersey Devils as underage junior in second round (second Devils pick, 23rd overall) of NHL entry draft (June 9, 1984).... Suffered from mononucleosis (July, 1984).... Injured hamstring (February 15, 1992); missed two games.... Strained knee (March 11, 1992); missed six games.... Underwent arthroscopic knee surgery (April 13, 1992).
HONORS: Won Bobby Smith Trophy (1984-85).... Named to OHL All-Star first team (1984-85).

Season	Team	League	Gms.	Min.	W	L	T	GA	SO	Avg.	Gms.	Min.	W	L	GA	SO	Avg.
					REGULAR SEASON									PLAYOFFS			
82-83—London Diamonds		OPJHL	23	1338				76	0	3.41	—	—	—	—	—	—	—
83-84—Belleville		OHL	44	2335	20	19	0	162	1	4.16	1	30	0	0	3	0	6.00
84-85—Belleville		OHL	47	2544	26	19	0	180	1	4.25	14	761	7	5	47	†1	3.71
85-86—Belleville		OHL	3	180	2	1	0	11	0	3.67	†20	1133	9	6	*68	0	3.60
—New Jersey		NHL	18	902	4	9	1	77	0	5.12	—	—	—	—	—	—	—
86-87—Maine		AHL	20	1151	9	8	2	70	0	3.65	—	—	—	—	—	—	—
—New Jersey		NHL	22	1114	4	13	2	89	0	4.79	—	—	—	—	—	—	—
87-88—Utica		AHL	*59	*3404	22	27	8	*208	1	3.67	—	—	—	—	—	—	—
88-89—Utica		AHL	41	2432	17	18	6	150	2	3.70	4	219	1	3	18	0	4.93
89-90—Utica		AHL	38	2087	20	13	1	138	0	3.97	—	—	—	—	—	—	—
90-91—Can. National Team		Int'l	34	1879	17	14	2	110	2	3.51	—	—	—	—	—	—	—
91-92—New Jersey		NHL	26	1363	13	7	1	69	2	3.04	—	—	—	—	—	—	—
NHL totals			66	3379	21	29	4	235	2	4.17							

BILODEAU, BRENT
D, CANADIENS

PERSONAL: Born March 27, 1973, at Dallas.... 6-4/220.... Shoots left.
TRANSACTIONS/CAREER NOTES: Selected by Montreal Canadiens in first round (first Canadiens pick, 17th overall) of NHL entry draft (June 22, 1991).
HONORS: Named to WHL (East) All-Star second team (1991-92).

Season	Team	League	Gms.	G	A	Pts.	Pen.	Gms.	G	A	Pts.	Pen.
				REGULAR SEASON					PLAYOFFS			
88-89—St. Albert		AJHL	55	8	17	25	167	—	—	—	—	—
89-90—Seattle		WHL	68	14	29	43	170	13	3	5	8	31
90-91—Seattle		WHL	55	7	18	25	145	6	1	0	1	12
91-92—Seattle		WHL	7	1	2	3	43	—	—	—	—	—
—Swift Current		WHL	56	10	47	57	118	8	2	3	5	11

BJUGSTAD, SCOTT
LW/C, KINGS

PERSONAL: Born June 2, 1961, at St. Paul, Minn.... 6-1/185.... Shoots left.
HIGH SCHOOL: Irondale (St.Paul, Minn.).
COLLEGE: Minnesota.
TRANSACTIONS/CAREER NOTES: Selected by Minnesota North Stars in ninth round (13th North Stars pick, 181st overall) of NHL entry draft (June 10, 1981).... Pulled abdominal muscle (March 15, 1987).... Separated shoulder (October 31, 1987).... Strained knee ligaments (December 1987).... Underwent knee surgery (February 1988).... Strained left knee ligaments (September 1988).... Traded by North Stars with D Gord Dineen to Pittsburgh Penguins for D Ville Siren and C Steve Gotaas (December 17, 1988).... Suspended by Penguins for refusing to report to Muskegon Lumberjacks (March 10, 1989).... Signed as free agent by Los Angeles Kings (August 1989).... Injured groin (October 1989).... Sprained knee (April 1990).... Sprained left knee (December 20, 1990); missed five games.... Fractured nose (January 22, 1991); missed four games.... Suffered recurring abdominal strain (March 1992); missed remainder of season.

Season	Team	League	Gms.	G	A	Pts.	Pen.	Gms.	G	A	Pts.	Pen.
				REGULAR SEASON					PLAYOFFS			
79-80—University of Minnesota		WCHA	18	2	2	4	2	—	—	—	—	—
80-81—University of Minnesota		WCHA	35	12	13	25	34	—	—	—	—	—
81-82—University of Minnesota		WCHA	36	29	14	43	24	—	—	—	—	—
82-83—University of Minnesota		WCHA	44	43	48	91	30	—	—	—	—	—

Season	Team	League	Gms.	G	A	Pts.	Pen.	Gms.	G	A	Pts.	Pen.
			REGULAR SEASON					**PLAYOFFS**				
83-84	—U.S. National Team	Int'l	54	31	20	51	28	—	—	—	—	—
	—U.S. Olympic Team	Int'l	6	3	2	5	6	—	—	—	—	—
	—Minnesota	NHL	5	0	0	0	2	—	—	—	—	—
	—Salt Lake City	IHL	15	10	8	18	6	5	3	4	7	0
84-85	—Minnesota	NHL	72	11	4	15	32	—	—	—	—	—
	—Springfield	AHL	5	2	3	5	2	—	—	—	—	—
85-86	—Minnesota	NHL	80	43	33	76	24	5	0	1	1	0
86-87	—Minnesota	NHL	39	4	9	13	43	—	—	—	—	—
	—Springfield	AHL	11	6	4	10	7	—	—	—	—	—
87-88	—Minnesota	NHL	33	10	12	22	15	—	—	—	—	—
88-89	—Geneva	Switzerland				Statistics unavailable.						
	—Pittsburgh	NHL	24	3	0	3	4	—	—	—	—	—
	—Kalamazoo	IHL	4	5	0	5	4	—	—	—	—	—
89-90	—New Haven	AHL	47	45	21	66	40	—	—	—	—	—
	—Los Angeles	NHL	11	1	2	3	2	2	0	0	0	2
90-91	—Phoenix	IHL	3	7	2	9	2	—	—	—	—	—
	—Los Angeles	NHL	31	2	4	6	12	2	0	0	0	0
91-92	—Los Angeles	NHL	22	2	4	6	10	—	—	—	—	—
	—Phoenix	IHL	28	14	14	28	12	—	—	—	—	—
	NHL totals		317	76	68	144	144	9	0	1	1	2

BLACK, JAMES
C, WHALERS

PERSONAL: Born August 15, 1969, at Regina, Sask.... 5-11/185.... Shoots left.
TRANSACTIONS/CAREER NOTES: Selected by Hartford Whalers in fifth round (fourth Whalers pick, 94th overall) of NHL entry draft (June 17, 1989).

Season	Team	League	Gms.	G	A	Pts.	Pen.	Gms.	G	A	Pts.	Pen.
			REGULAR SEASON					**PLAYOFFS**				
87-88	—Portland	WHL	72	30	50	80	50	—	—	—	—	—
88-89	—Portland	WHL	71	45	51	96	57	19	13	6	19	28
89-90	—Hartford	NHL	1	0	0	0	0	—	—	—	—	—
	—Binghamton	AHL	80	37	35	72	34	—	—	—	—	—
90-91	—Hartford	NHL	1	0	0	0	0	—	—	—	—	—
	—Springfield	AHL	79	35	61	96	34	18	9	9	18	6
91-92	—Springfield	AHL	47	15	25	40	33	10	3	2	5	18
	—Hartford	NHL	30	4	6	10	10	—	—	—	—	—
	NHL totals		32	4	6	10	10					

BLACK, RYAN
LW, DEVILS

PERSONAL: Born October 25, 1973, at Guelph, Ont.... 6-1/180.... Shoots left.
HIGH SCHOOL: Thomas A. Stewart (Peterborough, Ont.).
TRANSACTIONS/CAREER NOTES: Selected by New Jersey Devils in fifth round (sixth Devils pick, 114th overall) of NHL entry draft (June 20, 1992).

Season	Team	League	Gms.	G	A	Pts.	Pen.	Gms.	G	A	Pts.	Pen.
			REGULAR SEASON					**PLAYOFFS**				
88-89	—New Hamburg Jr. C	OHA	23	3	3	6	24	—	—	—	—	—
89-90	—Elmira Jr. B	OHA	33	19	21	40	94	—	—	—	—	—
	—Waterloo Jr. B	OHA	15	5	4	9	37	—	—	—	—	—
90-91	—Peterborough	OHL	59	7	16	23	41	4	0	1	1	0
91-92	—Peterborough	OHL	66	18	33	51	57	7	1	1	2	11

BLAESER, JEFF
LW, PENGUINS

PERSONAL: Born November 5, 1970, at Parma, O.... 6-3/195.... Shoots left.... Full name: Jeffrey Michael Blaeser.
HIGH SCHOOL: St. Johns Prep (Danvers, Mass.).
COLLEGE: Princeton, then Yale.
TRANSACTIONS/CAREER NOTES: Selected by Pittsburgh Penguins in seventh round (seventh Penguins pick, 130th overall) of NHL entry draft (June 11, 1988).

Season	Team	League	Gms.	G	A	Pts.	Pen.	Gms.	G	A	Pts.	Pen.
			REGULAR SEASON					**PLAYOFFS**				
86-87	—St. John's Prep School	Mass. H.S.		15	22	37		—	—	—	—	—
87-88	—St. John's Prep School	Mass. H.S.		14	20	34		—	—	—	—	—
88-89	—Yale University	ECAC	31	8	19	27	12	—	—	—	—	—
89-90	—Yale University	ECAC	29	17	14	31	16	—	—	—	—	—
90-91	—Yale University	ECAC	29	12	15	27	8	—	—	—	—	—
91-92	—Yale University	ECAC	24	8	15	23	4	—	—	—	—	—

BLAIN, JOEL
LW, OILERS

PERSONAL: Born October 12, 1971, at Malartic, Que.... 6-0/195.... Shoots left.
TRANSACTIONS/CAREER NOTES: Selected by Edmonton Oilers in fourth round (fourth Oilers pick, 67th overall) of NHL entry draft (June 16, 1990).

Season	Team	League	Gms.	G	A	Pts.	Pen.	Gms.	G	A	Pts.	Pen.
			REGULAR SEASON					**PLAYOFFS**				
87-88	—Hull	QMJHL	51	2	7	9	25	—	—	—	—	—
88-89	—Hull	QMJHL	64	14	16	30	105	—	—	—	—	—

Season Team	League	REGULAR SEASON					PLAYOFFS				
		Gms.	G	A	Pts.	Pen.	Gms.	G	A	Pts.	Pen.
89-90—Hull	QMJHL	65	31	47	78	137	11	6	6	12	16
90-91—Hull	QMJHL	61	19	31	50	95	6	4	3	7	17
91-92—Hull	QMJHL	60	24	35	59	146	6	4	2	6	27

BLAKE, ROB
D, KINGS

PERSONAL: Born December 10, 1969, at Simcoe, Ont. . . . 6-3/215. . . . Shoots right. . . . Full name: Robert Bowlby Blake.
COLLEGE: Bowling Green State.
TRANSACTIONS/CAREER NOTES: Dislocated shoulder (April 1987). . . . Selected by Los Angeles Kings in fourth round (fourth Kings pick, 70th overall) of NHL entry draft (June 11, 1988). . . . Sprained knee (April 1990). . . . Injured knee (February 12, 1991); missed two games. . . . Injured shoulder (October 8, 1991); missed 11 games. . . . Sprained knee ligaments (November 28, 1991); missed six games. . . . Suffered from the flu (January 23, 1992); missed one game. . . . Suffered from the flu (February 13, 1992); missed one game. . . . Strained shoulder (March 14, 1992); missed four games.
HONORS: Named to CCHA All-Star second team (1988-89). . . . Named to NCAA All-America West first team (1989-90). . . . Named to CCHA All-Star first team (1989-90). . . . Named to NHL All-Rookie team (1990-91).

Season Team	League	REGULAR SEASON					PLAYOFFS				
		Gms.	G	A	Pts.	Pen.	Gms.	G	A	Pts.	Pen.
86-87—Stratford Jr. B	OHA	31	11	20	31	115	—	—	—	—	—
87-88—Bowling Green State	CCHA	36	5	8	13	72	—	—	—	—	—
88-89—Bowling Green State	CCHA	46	11	21	32	140	—	—	—	—	—
89-90—Bowling Green State	CCHA	42	23	36	59	140	—	—	—	—	—
—Los Angeles	NHL	4	0	0	0	4	8	1	3	4	4
90-91—Los Angeles	NHL	75	12	34	46	125	12	1	4	5	26
91-92—Los Angeles	NHL	57	7	13	20	102	6	2	1	3	12
NHL totals		136	19	47	66	231	26	4	8	12	42

BLOEMBERG, JEFF
D, LIGHTNING

PERSONAL: Born January 31, 1968, at Listowel, Ont. . . . 6-0/205. . . . Shoots right.
TRANSACTIONS/CAREER NOTES: Selected by New York Rangers as underage junior in fifth round (fifth Rangers pick, 93rd overall) of NHL entry draft (June 21, 1986). . . . Selected by Tampa Bay Lightning in NHL expansion draft (June 18, 1992).
HONORS: Named to AHL All-Star second team (1990-91).

Season Team	League	REGULAR SEASON					PLAYOFFS				
		Gms.	G	A	Pts.	Pen.	Gms.	G	A	Pts.	Pen.
84-85—Listowel Jr. B	OHA	31	7	14	21	73	—	—	—	—	—
85-86—North Bay	OHL	60	2	11	13	76	8	1	2	3	9
86-87—North Bay	OHL	60	5	13	18	91	21	1	6	7	13
87-88—North Bay	OHL	46	9	26	35	60	—	—	—	—	—
—Colorado	IHL	5	0	0	0	0	11	1	0	1	8
88-89—New York Rangers	NHL	9	0	0	0	0	—	—	—	—	—
—Denver	IHL	64	7	22	29	55	1	0	0	0	0
89-90—Flint	IHL	44	7	21	28	24	—	—	—	—	—
90-91—Binghamton	AHL	77	16	46	62	28	10	0	6	6	10
91-92—Binghamton	AHL	66	6	41	47	22	11	1	10	11	10
—New York Rangers	NHL	3	0	1	1	0	—	—	—	—	—
NHL totals		12	0	1	1	0					

BLUE, JOHN
G, BRUINS

PERSONAL: Born February 9, 1966, at Huntington Beach, Calif. . . . 5-10/185. . . . Shoots left.
COLLEGE: Minnesota.
TRANSACTIONS/CAREER NOTES: Selected by Winnipeg Jets in 10th round (ninth Jets pick, 197th overall) of NHL entry draft (June 21, 1986). . . . Traded by Jets to Minnesota North Stars for a seventh-round pick in 1988 draft (C Markus Akerbloom) (March 7, 1988). . . . Signed as free agent by Boston Bruins (August 1, 1991).
HONORS: Named to WCHA All-Star second team (1984-85). . . . Named to WCHA All-Star first team (1985-86).

Season Team	League	REGULAR SEASON								PLAYOFFS						
		Gms.	Min.	W	L	T	GA	SO	Avg.	Gms.	Min.	W	L	GA	SO	Avg.
83-84—Des Moines	USHL	15	753				63		5.02	—	—	—	—	—	—	—
84-85—Univ. of Minnesota	WCHA	34	1964	23	10	0	111	2	3.39	—	—	—	—	—	—	—
85-86—Univ. of Minnesota	WCHA	29	1588	20	6	0	80	3	3.02	—	—	—	—	—	—	—
86-87—Univ. of Minnesota	WCHA	33	1889	21	9	1	99	3	3.14	—	—	—	—	—	—	—
87-88—U.S. National Team	Int'l	13	588	3	4	1	33	0	3.37	—	—	—	—	—	—	—
—Kalamazoo	IHL	15	847	3	8	4	65	0	4.60	1	40	0	1	6	0	9.00
88-89—Kalamazoo	IHL	17	970	8	6	0	69	0	4.27	—	—	—	—	—	—	—
—Virginia	ECHL	10	570				38	0	4.00	—	—	—	—	—	—	—
89-90—Kalamazoo	IHL	4	232	2	1	1	18	0	4.66	—	—	—	—	—	—	—
—Phoenix	IHL	19	986	5	10	3	93	0	5.66	—	—	—	—	—	—	—
—Knoxville	ECHL	19	1000	6	10	1	85	0	5.10	—	—	—	—	—	—	—
90-91—Maine	AHL	10	545	3	4	2	22	0	2.42	1	40	0	1	7	0	10.50
—Kalamazoo	IHL	1	64	1	0	0	2	0	1.88	—	—	—	—	—	—	—
—Albany	IHL	19	1077	11	6	0	71	0	3.96	—	—	—	—	—	—	—
—Peoria	IHL	4	240	4	0	0	12	0	3.00	—	—	—	—	—	—	—
—Knoxville	ECHL	3	149	1	1	0	13	0	5.23	—	—	—	—	—	—	—
91-92—Maine	AHL	43	2168	11	*23	6	165	1	4.57	—	—	—	—	—	—	—

BOBACK, MIKE
C, CAPITALS

PERSONAL: Born August 13, 1970, at Mt. Clemens, Mich. . . . 5-11/180. . . . Shoots right. . . . Full name: Michael Boback.
COLLEGE: Providence.
TRANSACTIONS/CAREER NOTES: Selected by Washington Capitals in 10th round (12th Capitals pick, 198th overall) of NHL entry draft (June 16, 1990).
HONORS: Named to Hockey East All-Star first team (1989-90 and 1991-92).

		REGULAR SEASON					PLAYOFFS				
Season Team	League	Gms.	G	A	Pts.	Pen.	Gms.	G	A	Pts.	Pen.
88-89—Providence College	Hockey East	29	19	19	38	24	—	—	—	—	—
89-90—Providence College	Hockey East	31	13	29	42	28	—	—	—	—	—
90-91—Providence College	Hockey East	26	15	24	39	6	—	—	—	—	—
91-92—Providence College	Hockey East	36	24	*48	*72	34	—	—	—	—	—

BODGER, DOUG
D, SABRES

PERSONAL: Born June 18, 1966, at Chemainus, B.C. . . . 6-2/213. . . . Shoots left.
TRANSACTIONS/CAREER NOTES: Selected by Pittsburgh Penguins as underage junior in first round (second Penguins pick, ninth overall) of NHL entry draft (June 9, 1984). . . . Underwent surgery to remove bone chip on left foot (April 1985). . . . Sprained knee (December 1987). . . . Strained left knee (October 1988). . . . Traded by Penguins with LW Darrin Shannon to Buffalo Sabres for G Tom Barrasso and a third-round pick in 1990 draft (November 12, 1988). . . . Sprained left knee (October 1989); missed eight games. . . . Injured shoulder (December 28, 1990); missed four games. . . . Separated left shoulder (February 17, 1991); missed 18 games. . . . Reinjured left shoulder (March 30, 1991). . . . Injured eye (February 11, 1992); missed seven games.
HONORS: Named to WHL All-Star second team (1982-83). . . . Named to WHL All-Star first team (1983-84).

		REGULAR SEASON					PLAYOFFS				
Season Team	League	Gms.	G	A	Pts.	Pen.	Gms.	G	A	Pts.	Pen.
82-83—Kamloops	WHL	72	26	66	92	98	7	0	5	5	2
83-84—Kamloops	WHL	70	21	77	98	90	17	2	15	17	12
84-85—Pittsburgh	NHL	65	5	26	31	67	—	—	—	—	—
85-86—Pittsburgh	NHL	79	4	33	37	63	—	—	—	—	—
86-87—Pittsburgh	NHL	76	11	38	49	52	—	—	—	—	—
87-88—Pittsburgh	NHL	69	14	31	45	103	—	—	—	—	—
88-89—Pittsburgh	NHL	10	1	4	5	7	—	—	—	—	—
—Buffalo	NHL	61	7	40	47	52	5	1	1	2	11
89-90—Buffalo	NHL	71	12	36	48	64	6	1	5	6	6
90-91—Buffalo	NHL	58	5	23	28	54	4	0	1	1	0
91-92—Buffalo	NHL	73	11	35	46	108	7	2	1	3	2
NHL totals		562	70	266	336	570	22	4	8	12	19

BODNARCHUK, MIKE
RW, DEVILS

PERSONAL: Born March 26, 1970, at Bramalea, Ont. . . . 6-1/175. . . . Shoots right. . . . Full name: Michael Bodnarchuk.
TRANSACTIONS/CAREER NOTES: Selected by New Jersey Devils in fourth round (sixth Devils pick, 64th overall) of NHL entry draft (June 16, 1990).
HONORS: Named to OHL All-Star second team (1989-90).

		REGULAR SEASON					PLAYOFFS				
Season Team	League	Gms.	G	A	Pts.	Pen.	Gms.	G	A	Pts.	Pen.
86-87—Bramalea	MTHL	34	12	8	20	33	—	—	—	—	—
87-88—Kingston	OHL	63	12	20	32	12	—	—	—	—	—
88-89—Kingston	OHL	63	22	38	60	30	—	—	—	—	—
89-90—Kingston	OHL	66	40	59	99	31	7	2	4	6	4
90-91—Utica	AHL	69	23	32	55	28	—	—	—	—	—
91-92—Utica	AHL	76	21	19	40	36	4	0	2	2	0

BOIVIN, CLAUDE
LW, FLYERS

PERSONAL: Born March 1, 1970, at St. Foy, Que. . . . 6-2/210. . . . Shoots left.
TRANSACTIONS/CAREER NOTES: Selected by Philadelphia Flyers in first round (first Flyers pick, 14th overall) of NHL entry draft (June 11, 1988). . . . Traded by Drummondville Voltigeurs with D Serge Anglehart and a fifth-round draft pick to Laval Titans for D Luc Doucet, D Brad MacIsaac and second- and third-round draft picks (February 15, 1990).

		REGULAR SEASON					PLAYOFFS				
Season Team	League	Gms.	G	A	Pts.	Pen.	Gms.	G	A	Pts.	Pen.
87-88—Drummondville	QMJHL	63	23	26	49	233	17	5	3	8	74
88-89—Drummondville	QMJHL	63	20	36	56	218	4	0	2	2	27
89-90—Laval	QMJHL	59	24	51	75	309	13	7	13	20	59
90-91—Hershey	AHL	65	13	32	45	159	7	1	5	6	28
91-92—Hershey	AHL	20	4	5	9	96	—	—	—	—	—
—Philadelphia	NHL	58	5	13	18	187	—	—	—	—	—
NHL totals		58	5	13	18	187					

BOLDIN, IGOR
C, BLUES

PERSONAL: Born February 2, 1964, at Moscow, U.S.S.R. . . . 5-11/175. . . . Shoots left.
TRANSACTIONS/CAREER NOTES: Selected by St. Louis Blues in eighth round (eighth Blues pick, 180th overall) of NHL entry draft (June 20, 1992).

		REGULAR SEASON					PLAYOFFS				
Season Team	League	Gms.	G	A	Pts.	Pen.	Gms.	G	A	Pts.	Pen.
81-82—Spartak Moscow	USSR	3	1	0	1	0	—	—	—	—	—
82-83—Spartak Moscow	USSR	41	14	8	22	4	—	—	—	—	—

Season	Team	League	REGULAR SEASON					PLAYOFFS				
			Gms.	G	A	Pts.	Pen.	Gms.	G	A	Pts.	Pen.
83-84—Spartak Moscow		USSR	40	12	19	31	2	—	—	—	—	—
84-85—Spartak Moscow		USSR	48	10	10	20	12	—	—	—	—	—
85-86—Spartak Moscow		USSR	36	8	6	14	2	—	—	—	—	—
86-87—Spartak Moscow		USSR	40	5	8	13	8	—	—	—	—	—
87-88—Spartak Moscow		USSR	41	20	9	29	4	—	—	—	—	—
88-89—Spartak Moscow		USSR	43	9	7	16	7	—	—	—	—	—
89-90—Spartak Moscow		USSR	45	13	18	31	8	—	—	—	—	—
90-91—Spartak Moscow		USSR	43	8	15	23	8	—	—	—	—	—
91-92—Spartak Moscow		CIS	41	8	25	33	4	—	—	—	—	—

BOMBARDIR, BRAD
D, DEVILS

PERSONAL: Born May 5, 1972, at Powell River, B.C. . . . . 6-2/187. . . . Shoots left. . . . Full name: Luke Bradley Bombardir. **COLLEGE:** North Dakota. **TRANSACTIONS/CAREER NOTES:** Selected by New Jersey Devils in third round (fifth Devils pick, 56th overall) of NHL entry draft (June 16, 1990).

Season	Team	League	REGULAR SEASON					PLAYOFFS				
			Gms.	G	A	Pts.	Pen.	Gms.	G	A	Pts.	Pen.
88-89—Powell River		BCJHL	30	6	5	11	24	6	0	0	0	0
89-90—Powell River		BCJHL	60	10	35	45	93	8	2	3	5	4
90-91—Univ. of North Dakota		WCHA	33	3	6	9	18	—	—	—	—	—
91-92—Univ. of North Dakota		WCHA	35	3	14	17	54	—	—	—	—	—

BONDRA, PETER
RW, CAPITALS

PERSONAL: Born February 7, 1968, at Luck, U.S.S.R. . . . 5-11/180. . . . Shoots left. **TRANSACTIONS/CAREER NOTES:** Selected by Washington Capitals in eighth round (ninth Capitals pick, 156th overall) of NHL entry draft (June 16, 1990). . . . Dislocated left shoulder (January 17, 1991). . . . Suffered recurring shoulder problems (February 13, 1991); missed 13 games.

Season	Team	League	REGULAR SEASON					PLAYOFFS				
			Gms.	G	A	Pts.	Pen.	Gms.	G	A	Pts.	Pen.
88-89—Kosice		Czech.	40	30	10	40	20	—	—	—	—	—
89-90—Kosice		Czech.	42	29	17	46		—	—	—	—	—
90-91—Washington		NHL	54	12	16	28	47	4	0	1	1	2
91-92—Washington		NHL	71	28	28	56	42	7	6	2	8	4
NHL totals			125	40	44	84	89	11	6	3	9	6

BORGO, RICHARD
RW, OILERS

PERSONAL: Born September 25, 1970, at Thunder Bay, Ont. . . . 5-11/190. . . . Shoots right. **TRANSACTIONS/CAREER NOTES:** Selected by Edmonton Oilers in second round (second Oilers pick, 36th overall) of NHL entry draft (June 17, 1989).

Season	Team	League	REGULAR SEASON					PLAYOFFS				
			Gms.	G	A	Pts.	Pen.	Gms.	G	A	Pts.	Pen.
85-86—Thunder Bay		USHL	41	11	19	30	37	—	—	—	—	—
86-87—Kitchener		OHL	62	5	10	15	29	—	—	—	—	—
87-88—Kitchener		OHL	64	24	22	46	81	4	0	4	4	0
88-89—Kitchener		OHL	66	23	23	46	75	5	0	1	1	4
89-90—Kitchener		OHL	32	13	22	35	43	17	5	5	10	10
90-91—Kitchener		OHL	60	43	56	99	50	6	1	0	1	12
91-92—Cape Breton		AHL	52	10	14	24	90	3	0	0	0	6

BORSATO, LUCIANO
C, JETS

PERSONAL: Born January 7, 1966, at Richmond Hill, Ont. . . . 5-10/165. . . . Shoots right. . . . Full name: Luciano R. Borsato. **COLLEGE:** Clarkson (N.Y.). **TRANSACTIONS/CAREER NOTES:** Selected by Winnipeg Jets as underage junior in seventh round (seventh Jets pick, 135th overall) of NHL entry draft (June 9, 1984). **HONORS:** Named to NCAA All-America East second team (1987-88).

Season	Team	League	REGULAR SEASON					PLAYOFFS				
			Gms.	G	A	Pts.	Pen.	Gms.	G	A	Pts.	Pen.
83-84—Bramalea		MTHL	37	20	36	56	59	—	—	—	—	—
84-85—Clarkson		ECAC	33	15	17	32	37	—	—	—	—	—
85-86—Clarkson		ECAC	32	17	20	37	50	—	—	—	—	—
86-87—Clarkson		ECAC	31	16	*41	57	55	—	—	—	—	—
87-88—Clarkson		ECAC	33	15	29	44	38	—	—	—	—	—
—Moncton		AHL	3	1	1	2	0	—	—	—	—	—
88-89—Tappara		Finland	44	31	36	67	69	7	0	3	3	4
—Moncton		AHL	6	2	5	7	4	—	—	—	—	—
89-90—Moncton		AHL	1	1	0	1	0	—	—	—	—	—
90-91—Moncton		AHL	41	14	24	38	40	9	3	7	10	22
—Winnipeg		NHL	1	0	1	1	2	—	—	—	—	—
91-92—Moncton		AHL	14	2	7	9	39	—	—	—	—	—
—Winnipeg		NHL	56	15	21	36	45	1	0	0	0	0
NHL totals			57	15	22	37	47	1	0	0	0	0

BORSCHEVSKY, NIKOLAI
RW, MAPLE LEAFS

PERSONAL: Born January 12, 1965, at Tomsk, U.S.S.R. . . . 5-9/180. . . . Shoots left.
TRANSACTIONS/CAREER NOTES: Selected by Toronto Maple Leafs in fourth round (third Maple Leafs pick, 77th overall) of NHL entry draft (June 20, 1992).

Season Team	League	REGULAR SEASON					PLAYOFFS				
		Gms.	G	A	Pts.	Pen.	Gms.	G	A	Pts.	Pen.
83-84—Dynamo Moscow	USSR	34	4	5	9	4	—	—	—	—	—
84-85—Dynamo Moscow	USSR	34	5	9	14	6	—	—	—	—	—
85-86—Dynamo Moscow	USSR	31	6	4	10	4	—	—	—	—	—
86-87—Dynamo Moscow	USSR	28	1	4	5	8	—	—	—	—	—
87-88—Dynamo Moscow	USSR	37	11	7	18	6	—	—	—	—	—
88-89—Dynamo Moscow	USSR	43	7	8	15	18	—	—	—	—	—
89-90—Spartak Moscow	USSR	48	17	25	42	8	—	—	—	—	—
90-91—Spartak Moscow	USSR	45	19	16	35	16	—	—	—	—	—
91-92—Spartak Moscow	CIS	40	25	14	39	16	—	—	—	—	—

BOSCHMAN, LAURIE
C, SENATORS

PERSONAL: Born June 4, 1960, at Major, Sask. . . . 6-0/185. . . . Shoots left. . . . Full name: Laurie Joseph Boschman.
TRANSACTIONS/CAREER NOTES: Selected by Toronto Maple Leafs in first round (first Maple Leafs pick, ninth overall) of NHL entry draft (August 9, 1979). . . . Injured finger tendon (December 7, 1980). . . . Suffered from mononucleosis (January 1981). . . . Traded by Maple Leafs to Edmonton Oilers for C Walt Poddubny and Phil Drouillard (March 1982). . . . Traded by Oilers to Winnipeg Jets for RW Willy Lindstrom (March 1983). . . . Dislocated shoulder (December 7, 1983). . . . Underwent surgery to reconstruct right shoulder (April 1988). . . . Lacerated ankle (October 16, 1988). . . . Suspended eight games by NHL for high-sticking (February 8, 1990). . . . Traded by Jets to New Jersey Devils for RW Bob Brooke (September 6, 1990); Brooke refused to report to Jets, announcing he would rather retire; Jets then received a fifth-round pick in 1991 draft (LW Jan Kaminsky) as compensation. . . . Bruised shoulder (November 1990). . . . Selected by Ottawa Senators in NHL expansion draft (June 18, 1992).
HONORS: Named to WHL All-Star first team (1978-79). . . . Named to Memorial Cup All-Star team (1978-79).

Season Team	League	REGULAR SEASON					PLAYOFFS				
		Gms.	G	A	Pts.	Pen.	Gms.	G	A	Pts.	Pen.
76-77—Brandon	MJHL	47	17	40	57	139	—	—	—	—	—
—Brandon	WCHL	3	0	1	1	0	12	1	1	2	17
77-78—Brandon	WCHL	72	42	57	99	227	8	2	5	7	45
78-79—Brandon	WHL	65	66	83	149	215	22	11	23	34	56
79-80—Toronto	NHL	80	16	32	48	78	3	1	1	2	18
80-81—New Brunswick	AHL	4	4	1	5	47	—	—	—	—	—
—Toronto	NHL	53	14	19	33	178	3	0	0	0	7
81-82—Toronto	NHL	54	9	19	28	150	—	—	—	—	—
—Edmonton	NHL	11	2	3	5	37	3	0	1	1	4
82-83—Edmonton	NHL	62	8	12	20	183	—	—	—	—	—
—Winnipeg	NHL	12	3	5	8	34	3	0	1	1	12
83-84—Winnipeg	NHL	61	28	46	74	234	3	0	1	1	5
84-85—Winnipeg	NHL	80	32	44	76	180	8	2	1	3	21
85-86—Winnipeg	NHL	77	27	42	69	241	3	0	1	1	6
86-87—Winnipeg	NHL	80	17	24	41	152	10	2	3	5	32
87-88—Winnipeg	NHL	80	25	23	48	227	5	1	3	4	9
88-89—Winnipeg	NHL	70	10	26	36	163	—	—	—	—	—
89-90—Winnipeg	NHL	66	10	17	27	103	2	0	0	0	2
90-91—New Jersey	NHL	78	11	9	20	79	7	1	1	2	16
91-92—New Jersey	NHL	75	8	20	28	121	7	1	0	1	8
NHL totals		939	220	341	561	2159	57	8	13	21	140

BOUCHARD, JOEL
D, FLAMES

PERSONAL: Born January 23, 1974, at Montreal. . . . 6-0/180. . . . Shoots left.
TRANSACTIONS/CAREER NOTES: Selected by Calgary Flames in sixth round (sixth Flames pick, 129th overall) of NHL entry draft (June 20, 1992).

Season Team	League	REGULAR SEASON					PLAYOFFS				
		Gms.	G	A	Pts.	Pen.	Gms.	G	A	Pts.	Pen.
90-91—Longueuil	QMJHL	53	3	19	22	34	8	0	1	1	11
91-92—Verdun	QMJHL	70	9	37	46	55	19	1	7	8	20

BOUCHER, PHILIPPE
D, SABRES

PERSONAL: Born March 24, 1973, at St. Apollnaire, Que. . . . 6-2/189. . . . Shoots right.
TRANSACTIONS/CAREER NOTES: Selected by Buffalo Sabres in first round (first Sabres pick, 13th overall) of NHL entry draft (June 22, 1991).
HONORS: Won Can.HL Rookie of the Year Award (1990-91). . . . Won Raymond Lagace Trophy (1990-91). . . . Won Michael Bossy Trophy (1990-91). . . . Named to QMJHL All-Star second team (1990-91 and 1991-92).

Season Team	League	REGULAR SEASON					PLAYOFFS				
		Gms.	G	A	Pts.	Pen.	Gms.	G	A	Pts.	Pen.
90-91—Granby	QMJHL	69	21	46	67	92	—	—	—	—	—
91-92—Laval	QMJHL	65	29	48	77	83	10	5	6	11	8

BOUGHNER, BOB
D, RED WINGS

PERSONAL: Born March 8, 1971, at Windsor, Ont.... 5-11/201.... Shoots right.
TRANSACTIONS/CAREER NOTES: Selected by Detroit Red Wings in second round (second Red Wings pick, 32nd overall) of NHL entry draft (June 17, 1989).

Season Team	League	REGULAR SEASON					PLAYOFFS				
		Gms.	G	A	Pts.	Pen.	Gms.	G	A	Pts.	Pen.
87-88—St. Mary's Jr. B	OHA	36	4	18	22	177	—	—	—	—	—
88-89—Sault Ste. Marie	OHL	64	6	15	21	182	—	—	—	—	—
89-90—Sault Ste. Marie	OHL	49	7	23	30	122	—	—	—	—	—
90-91—Sault Ste. Marie	OHL	64	13	33	46	156	14	2	9	11	35
91-92—Adirondack	AHL	1	0	0	0	7	—	—	—	—	—
—Toledo	ECHL	28	3	10	13	79	5	2	0	2	15

BOURQUE, PHIL
LW, PENGUINS

PERSONAL: Born June 8, 1962, at Chelmsford, Mass.... 6-1/196.... Shoots left.... Full name: Phillipe Richard Bourque.
TRANSACTIONS/CAREER NOTES: Signed as free agent by Pittsburgh Penguins (July 1982).... Suffered back spasms (November 1989).... Sprained wrist (December 1990).... Suffered inflammation of left elbow (November 15, 1991); missed two games.... Strained back (December 18, 1991); missed three games.... Fractured left foot (January 10, 1992); missed nine games.... Reinjured foot (February 9, 1992); missed four games.
HONORS: Won Governors Trophy (1987-88).... Named to IHL All-Star first team (1987-88).

Season Team	League	REGULAR SEASON					PLAYOFFS				
		Gms.	G	A	Pts.	Pen.	Gms.	G	A	Pts.	Pen.
80-81—Kingston	OMJHL	47	4	4	8	46	6	0	0	0	10
81-82—Kingston	OHL	67	11	40	51	111	4	0	0	0	0
82-83—Baltimore	AHL	65	1	15	16	93	—	—	—	—	—
83-84—Baltimore	AHL	58	5	17	22	96	—	—	—	—	—
—Pittsburgh	NHL	5	0	1	1	12	—	—	—	—	—
84-85—Baltimore	AHL	79	6	15	21	164	13	2	5	7	23
85-86—Pittsburgh	NHL	4	0	0	0	2	—	—	—	—	—
—Baltimore	AHL	74	8	18	26	226	—	—	—	—	—
86-87—Pittsburgh	NHL	22	2	3	5	32	—	—	—	—	—
—Baltimore	AHL	49	15	16	31	183	—	—	—	—	—
87-88—Muskegon	IHL	52	16	36	52	66	6	1	2	3	16
—Pittsburgh	NHL	21	4	12	16	20	—	—	—	—	—
88-89—Pittsburgh	NHL	80	17	26	43	97	11	4	1	5	66
89-90—Pittsburgh	NHL	76	22	17	39	108	—	—	—	—	—
90-91—Pittsburgh	NHL	78	20	14	34	106	24	6	7	13	16
91-92—Pittsburgh	NHL	58	10	16	26	58	†21	3	4	7	25
NHL totals		344	75	89	164	435	56	13	12	25	107

BOURQUE, RAY
D, BRUINS

PERSONAL: Born December 28, 1960, at Montreal.... 5-11/210.... Shoots left.... Full name: Raymond Jean Bourque.
TRANSACTIONS/CAREER NOTES: Selected by Boston Bruins in first round (first Bruins pick, eighth overall) of NHL entry draft (August 9, 1979).... Suffered broken jaw (November 11, 1980).... Injured left shoulder (October 1981).... Fractured left wrist (April 21, 1982).... Refractured left wrist and fractured left forearm (Summer 1982).... Broke bone over left eye (October 1982).... Sprained left knee ligaments (December 10, 1988).... Bruised hip (April 7, 1990).... Bruised right shoulder (October 17, 1990); missed four games.... Fractured finger (May 5, 1992); missed remainder of playoffs.
HONORS: Named to QMJHL All-Star first team (1977-78 and 1978-79).... Won Frank J. Selke Trophy (1978-79).... Won Emile (Butch) Bouchard Trophy (1978-79).... Named NHL Rookie of the Year by THE SPORTING NEWS (1979-80).... Won Calder Memorial Trophy (1979-80).... Named to NHL All-Star first team (1979-80, 1981-82, 1983-84, 1984-85, 1986-87, 1987-88, 1989-90 through 1991-92).... Named to THE SPORTING NEWS All-Star second team (1980-81, 1982-83, 1985-86 and 1988-89).... Named to NHL All-Star second team (1980-81, 1982-83, 1985-86 and 1988-89).... Named to THE SPORTING NEWS All-Star first team (1981-82, 1983-84, 1984-85, 1986-87, 1987-88 and 1989-90 through 1991-92).... Won James Norris Memorial Trophy (1986-87, 1987-88, 1989-90, and 1990-91).... Won King Clancy Memorial Trophy (1991-92).

Season Team	League	REGULAR SEASON					PLAYOFFS				
		Gms.	G	A	Pts.	Pen.	Gms.	G	A	Pts.	Pen.
76-77—Sorel	QMJHL	69	12	36	48	61	—	—	—	—	—
77-78—Verdun	QMJHL	72	22	57	79	90	4	2	1	3	0
78-79—Verdun	QMJHL	63	22	71	93	44	11	3	16	19	18
79-80—Boston	NHL	80	17	48	65	73	10	2	9	11	27
80-81—Boston	NHL	67	27	29	56	96	3	0	1	1	2
81-82—Boston	NHL	65	17	49	66	51	9	1	5	6	16
82-83—Boston	NHL	65	22	51	73	20	17	8	15	23	10
83-84—Boston	NHL	78	31	65	96	57	3	0	2	2	0
84-85—Boston	NHL	73	20	66	86	53	5	0	3	3	4
85-86—Boston	NHL	74	19	57	76	68	3	0	0	0	4
86-87—Boston	NHL	78	23	72	95	36	4	1	2	3	0
87-88—Boston	NHL	78	17	64	81	72	23	3	18	21	26
88-89—Boston	NHL	60	18	43	61	52	10	0	4	4	6
89-90—Boston	NHL	76	19	65	84	50	17	5	12	17	16
90-91—Boston	NHL	76	21	73	94	75	19	7	18	25	12
91-92—Boston	NHL	80	21	60	81	56	12	3	6	9	12
NHL totals		950	272	742	1014	759	135	30	95	125	131

BOWEN, CURT
LW, RED WINGS

PERSONAL: Born March 24, 1974, at Kenora, Ont. . . . 6-1/189. . . . Shoots left. . . . Full name: Curtis Bowen.
HIGH SCHOOL: Ridgemont (Ottawa).
TRANSACTIONS/CAREER NOTES: Selected by Detroit Red Wings in first round (first Red Wings pick, 22nd overall) of NHL entry draft (June 20, 1992).

			REGULAR SEASON					PLAYOFFS			
Season	Team	League	Gms.	G	A	Pts.	Pen.	Gms.	G	A	Pts.	Pen.
90-91—Ottawa		OHL	42	12	14	26	31	—	—	—	—	—
91-92—Ottawa		OHL	65	31	45	76	94	11	3	7	10	11

BOWEN, JASON
LW, FLYERS

PERSONAL: Born November 11, 1973, at Courtenay, B.C. . . . 6-4/210. . . . Shoots left.
TRANSACTIONS/CAREER NOTES: Selected by Philadelphia Flyers in first round (second Flyers pick, 15th overall) of NHL entry draft (June 20, 1992).

			REGULAR SEASON					PLAYOFFS			
Season	Team	League	Gms.	G	A	Pts.	Pen.	Gms.	G	A	Pts.	Pen.
89-90—Tri-City Americans		WHL	61	8	5	13	129	7	0	3	3	4
90-91—Tri-City Americans		WHL	60	7	13	20	252	6	2	2	4	18
91-92—Tri-City Americans		WHL	19	5	3	8	135	5	0	1	1	42

BOYER, ZAC
RW, BLACKHAWKS

PERSONAL: Born October 25, 1971, at Inuvik, N.W.T. . . . 6-1/185. . . . Shoots right. . . . Full name: Zachery Boyer.
TRANSACTIONS/CAREER NOTES: Selected by Chicago Blackhawks in fourth round (sixth Blackhawks pick, 88th overall) of NHL entry draft (June 22, 1991).

			REGULAR SEASON					PLAYOFFS			
Season	Team	League	Gms.	G	A	Pts.	Pen.	Gms.	G	A	Pts.	Pen.
87-88—St. Albert		AJHL	55	16	31	47	258	—	—	—	—	—
88-89—Kamloops		WHL	42	10	17	27	22	16	9	8	17	10
89-90—Kamloops		WHL	71	24	47	71	63	17	4	4	8	8
90-91—Kamloops		WHL	64	45	60	105	58	12	6	10	16	8
91-92—Kamloops		WHL	70	40	69	109	90	17	9	*20	*29	16

BOZEK, STEVE
C/LW

PERSONAL: Born November 26, 1960, at Kelowna, B.C. . . . 5-11/180. . . . Shoots left. . . . Full name: Steven Michael Bozek.
COLLEGE: Northern Michigan.
TRANSACTIONS/CAREER NOTES: Selected by Los Angeles Kings in third round (fifth Kings pick, 52nd overall) of NHL entry draft (June 11, 1980). . . . Sprained left knee (January 20, 1983). . . . Traded by Kings to Calgary Flames for LW Kevin LaVallee and LW Carl Mokosak (June 1983). . . . Tore ligament in finger on left hand (October 1984). . . . Injured knee (March 12, 1986). . . . Strained knee ligaments (October 1987). . . . Hyperextended knee and strained back (March 1988). . . . Traded by Flames with RW Brett Hull to St. Louis Blues for D Rob Ramage and G Rick Wamsley (March 1988). . . . Traded by Blues with C Doug Gilmour, RW Mark Hunter and D/RW Michael Dark to Flames for C Mike Bullard, C Craig Coxe and D Tim Corkery (September 5, 1988). . . . Traded by Flames with D Paul Reinhart to Vancouver Canucks for a third-round pick in 1989 draft (D Veli-Pekka Kautonen) (September 6, 1988). . . . Hyperextended knee (December 1988). . . . Separated shoulder (January 23, 1991); missed 10 games. . . . Signed as free agent by San Jose Sharks (August 9, 1991).
HONORS: Named to CCHA All-Star first team (1979-80 and 1980-81). . . . Named to NCAA All-America West team (1980-81).

			REGULAR SEASON					PLAYOFFS			
Season	Team	League	Gms.	G	A	Pts.	Pen.	Gms.	G	A	Pts.	Pen.
78-79—Northern Michigan Univ.		CCHA	33	12	12	24	21	—	—	—	—	—
79-80—Northern Michigan Univ.		CCHA	41	42	47	89	32	—	—	—	—	—
80-81—Northern Michigan Univ.		CCHA	44	†35	*55	*90	46	—	—	—	—	—
81-82—Los Angeles		NHL	71	33	23	56	68	10	4	1	5	6
82-83—Los Angeles		NHL	53	13	13	26	14	—	—	—	—	—
83-84—Calgary		NHL	46	10	10	20	16	10	3	1	4	15
84-85—Calgary		NHL	54	13	22	35	6	3	1	0	1	4
85-86—Calgary		NHL	64	21	22	43	24	14	2	6	8	32
86-87—Calgary		NHL	71	17	18	35	22	4	1	0	1	2
87-88—Calgary		NHL	26	3	7	10	12	—	—	—	—	—
—St. Louis		NHL	7	0	0	0	0	7	1	1	2	6
88-89—Vancouver		NHL	71	17	18	35	64	7	0	2	2	4
89-90—Vancouver		NHL	58	14	9	23	32	—	—	—	—	—
90-91—Vancouver		NHL	62	15	17	32	32	3	0	0	0	0
91-92—San Jose		NHL	58	8	8	16	27	—	—	—	—	—
NHL totals			641	164	167	331	309	58	12	11	23	69

BOZON, PHILIPPE
C, BLUES

PERSONAL: Born November 30, 1966, at Chamoix, France. . . . 5-10/180. . . . Shoots left.
TRANSACTIONS/CAREER NOTES: Signed as free agent by St. Louis Blues (September 29, 1985). . . . On Blues inactive list while in France preparing for 1992 Olympics (1987-88 through 1990-91). . . . Returned to Blues (February 27, 1992).
HONORS: Named to QMJHL All-Star second team (1985-86).

			REGULAR SEASON					PLAYOFFS			
Season	Team	League	Gms.	G	A	Pts.	Pen.	Gms.	G	A	Pts.	Pen.
84-85—St. Jean		QMJHL	67	32	50	82	82	3	1	0	1	0
85-86—St. Jean		QMJHL	65	59	52	111	72	10	10	6	16	16
—Peoria		IHL	—	—	—	—	—	5	1	0	1	0

Season Team	League	REGULAR SEASON Gms.	G	A	Pts.	Pen.	PLAYOFFS Gms.	G	A	Pts.	Pen.
86-87—Peoria	IHL	28	4	11	15	17	—	—	—	—	—
—St. Jean	QMJHL	25	20	21	41	75	8	5	5	10	30
87-88—Mont-Blanc	France	18	11	15	26	34	10	15	6	21	6
89-90—French National Team	Int'l	—	—	—	—	—	—	—	—	—	—
—Grenoble	France	36	45	38	83	34	—	—	—	—	—
90-91—Grenoble	France	Statistics unavailable.									
91-92—Chamonix	France	10	12	8	20	20	—	—	—	—	—
—French Olympic Team	Int'l	7	3	2	5	4	—	—	—	—	—
—St. Louis	NHL	9	1	3	4	4	6	1	0	1	27
NHL totals		9	1	3	4	4	6	1	0	1	27

BRADLEY, BRIAN
C, LIGHTNING

PERSONAL: Born January 21, 1965, at Kitchener, Ont. . . . 5-10/177. . . . Shoots right. . . . Full name: Brian Walter Richard Bradley.

TRANSACTIONS/CAREER NOTES: Selected by Calgary Flames as underage junior in third round (second Flames pick, 51st overall) of NHL entry draft (June 8, 1983). . . . Traded by Flames with RW Peter Bakovic and future considerations (D Kevan Guy) to Vancouver Canucks for C Craig Coxe (March 1988). . . . Bruised knee (January 1989). . . . Broke thumb knuckle (February 1, 1990); missed seven games. . . . Traded by Canucks to Toronto Maple Leafs for D Tom Kurvers (January 12, 1991). . . . Sprained ankle (November 10, 1991); missed six games. . . . Suffered back spasms (December 10, 1991); missed two games. . . . Selected by Tampa Bay Lightning in NHL expansion draft (June 18, 1992).

Season Team	League	REGULAR SEASON Gms.	G	A	Pts.	Pen.	PLAYOFFS Gms.	G	A	Pts.	Pen.
81-82—London	OHL	62	34	44	78	34	—	—	—	—	—
82-83—London	OHL	67	37	82	119	37	3	1	0	1	0
83-84—London	OHL	49	40	60	100	24	4	2	4	6	0
84-85—London	OHL	32	27	49	76	22	8	5	10	15	4
85-86—Calgary	NHL	5	0	1	1	0	1	0	0	0	0
—Moncton	AHL	59	23	42	65	40	10	6	9	15	4
86-87—Moncton	AHL	20	12	16	28	8	—	—	—	—	—
—Calgary	NHL	40	10	18	28	16	—	—	—	—	—
87-88—Canadian Olympic Team	Int'l	51	18	23	41	42	—	—	—	—	—
—Vancouver	NHL	11	3	5	8	6	—	—	—	—	—
88-89—Vancouver	NHL	71	18	27	45	42	7	3	4	7	10
89-90—Vancouver	NHL	67	19	29	48	65	—	—	—	—	—
90-91—Vancouver	NHL	44	11	20	31	42	—	—	—	—	—
—Toronto	NHL	26	0	11	11	20	—	—	—	—	—
91-92—Toronto	NHL	59	10	21	31	48	—	—	—	—	—
NHL totals		323	71	132	203	239	8	3	4	7	10

BRADLEY, JOHN
G, SABRES

PERSONAL: Born February 6, 1968, at Pawtucket, R.I. . . . 6-0/165. . . . Shoots left. . . . Full name: John W. Bradley.

COLLEGE: Boston University.

TRANSACTIONS/CAREER NOTES: Selected by Buffalo Sabres in fourth round (fourth Sabres pick, 84th overall) of NHL entry draft (June 13, 1987).

Season Team	League	REGULAR SEASON Gms.	Min.	W	L	T	GA	SO	Avg.	PLAYOFFS Gms.	Min.	W	L	GA	SO	Avg.
86-87—New Hampton H.S.	R.I.H.S.	34	2040				96	4	2.82	—	—	—	—	—	—	—
87-88—Boston University	Hoc. East	9	523	4	4	0	40	0	4.59	—	—	—	—	—	—	—
88-89—Boston University	Hoc. East	11	583	5	4	1	53	0	5.45	—	—	—	—	—	—	—
89-90—Boston University	Hoc. East	7	377	2	3	1	20	1	3.18	—	—	—	—	—	—	—
90-91—Boston University	Hoc. East	20	1177	14	4	1	62	*3	3.16	—	—	—	—	—	—	—
91-92—Rochester	AHL	6	248	2	2	1	13	1	3.15	1	20	0	0	2	0	6.00
—Erie	ECHL	15	810	6	4	2	59	0	4.37	—	—	—	—	—	—	—

BRADY, NEIL
C, DEVILS

PERSONAL: Born April 12, 1968, at Montreal. . . . 6-2/200. . . . Shoots left. . . . Full name: Neil Patrick Brady.

TRANSACTIONS/CAREER NOTES: Selected by New Jersey Devils as underage junior in first round (first Devils pick, third overall) of NHL entry draft (June 21, 1986).

HONORS: Won Stewart (Butch) Paul Memorial Trophy (East) (1985-86).

Season Team	League	REGULAR SEASON Gms.	G	A	Pts.	Pen.	PLAYOFFS Gms.	G	A	Pts.	Pen.
84-85—Medicine Hat	WHL	—	—	—	—	—	3	0	0	0	2
85-86—Medicine Hat	WHL	72	21	60	81	104	21	9	11	20	23
86-87—Medicine Hat	WHL	57	19	64	83	126	18	1	4	5	25
87-88—Medicine Hat	WHL	61	16	35	51	110	15	0	3	3	19
88-89—Utica	AHL	75	16	21	37	56	4	0	3	3	0
89-90—New Jersey	NHL	19	1	4	5	13	—	—	—	—	—
—Utica	AHL	38	10	13	23	21	5	0	1	1	10
90-91—New Jersey	NHL	3	0	0	0	0	—	—	—	—	—
—Utica	AHL	77	33	63	96	91	—	—	—	—	—
91-92—Utica	AHL	33	12	30	42	28	—	—	—	—	—
—New Jersey	NHL	7	1	0	1	4	—	—	—	—	—
NHL totals		29	2	4	6	17					

BREAULT, FRANK
RW, KINGS

PERSONAL: Born May 11, 1967, at Acton Valley, Que. . . . 5-11/190. . . . Shoots left. . . . Full name: Francois Breault.
TRANSACTIONS/CAREER NOTES: Traded by Trois Rivieres Draveurs to Granby Bisons for a fifth-round draft pick (February 1987). . . . Signed as free agent by Los Angeles Kings (July 1988). . . . Injured cruciate ligament of right knee (December 13, 1990). . . . Bruised knee (October 28, 1991).

			REGULAR SEASON					PLAYOFFS				
Season	Team	League	Gms.	G	A	Pts.	Pen.	Gms.	G	A	Pts.	Pen.
85-86—Trois-Rivieres	QMJHL	60	15	13	28	73	—	—	—	—	—
86-87—Granby	QMJHL	60	24	33	57	134	—	—	—	—	—
87-88—Trois-Rivieres	QMJHL	28	16	19	35	108	—	—	—	—	—
—Maine	AHL	11	0	1	1	37	—	—	—	—	—
88-89—New Haven	AHL	68	21	24	45	51	—	—	—	—	—
89-90—New Haven	AHL	37	17	21	38	33	—	—	—	—	—
90-91—Los Angeles	NHL	17	1	4	5	6	—	—	—	—	—
91-92—Los Angeles	NHL	6	1	0	1	30	—	—	—	—	—
—Phoenix	IHL	54	14	19	33	40	—	—	—	—	—
NHL totals		23	2	4	6	36					

BREEN, GEORGE
RW, OILERS

PERSONAL: Born August 3, 1973, at Webster, Mass. . . . 6-2/200. . . . Shoots right. . . . Full name: George Bernard Breen.
HIGH SCHOOL: Shrewsbury (Mass.), then Cushing Academy (Ashburnham, Mass.).
COLLEGE: Providence.
TRANSACTIONS/CAREER NOTES: Selected by Edmonton Oilers in third round (third Oilers pick, 56th overall) of NHL entry draft (June 22, 1991).

			REGULAR SEASON					PLAYOFFS				
Season	Team	League	Gms.	G	A	Pts.	Pen.	Gms.	G	A	Pts.	Pen.
87-88—Shrewsbury H.S.	Mass. H.S.	20	11	9	20		—	—	—	—	—
88-89—Shrewsbury H.S.	Mass. H.S.	20	32	9	41		—	—	—	—	—
89-90—Cushing Academy	Mass. H.S.	20	9	8	17		—	—	—	—	—
90-91—Cushing Academy	Mass. H.S.	23	21	39	60		—	—	—	—	—
91-92—Providence College	Hockey East	36	8	4	12	24	—	—	—	—	—

BRENNAN, RICH
D, NORDIQUES

PERSONAL: Born November 26, 1972, at Schenectady, N.Y. . . . 6-2/200. . . . Shoots right. . . . Full name: Richard Brennan.
HIGH SCHOOL: Albany Academy (N.Y.), then Tabor Academy (Marion, Mass.).
COLLEGE: Boston University.
TRANSACTIONS/CAREER NOTES: Selected by Quebec Nordiques in third round (third Nordiques pick, 46th overall) of NHL entry draft (June 22, 1991).

			REGULAR SEASON					PLAYOFFS				
Season	Team	League	Gms.	G	A	Pts.	Pen.	Gms.	G	A	Pts.	Pen.
88-89—Albany Academy	N.Y. H.S.	25	17	30	47	57	—	—	—	—	—
89-90—Tabor Academy	N.Y. H.S.	33	12	14	26	68	—	—	—	—	—
90-91—Tabor Academy	N.Y. H.S.	34	13	37	50	91	—	—	—	—	—
91-92—Boston University	Hockey East	31	4	13	17	54	—	—	—	—	—

BRICKLEY, ANDY
LW, BRUINS

PERSONAL: Born August 9, 1961, at Melrose, Mass. . . . 5-11/200. . . . Shoots left. . . . Full name: Andrew Brickley.
COLLEGE: New Hampshire.
TRANSACTIONS/CAREER NOTES: Selected by Philadelphia Flyers in 10th round (10th Flyers pick, 210th overall) of NHL entry draft (June 11, 1980). . . . Traded by Flyers with C Ron Flockhart, C/LW Mark Taylor and first-round pick in 1984 draft (RW/C Roger Belanger) to Pittsburgh Penguins for RW Rich Sutter and second-round pick (D Greg Smyth) and third-round pick (LW David McLay) in 1984 draft (October 23, 1983). . . . Strained ankle (December 1983). . . . Released by Penguins (August 1985). . . . Signed as free agent by Maine Mariners (September 1985). . . . Suffered tendinitis in shoulder (December 1985). . . . Signed as free agent by New Jersey Devils (July 8, 1986). . . . Injured foot (September 1987). . . . Selected by Boston Bruins in 1988 waiver draft for $12,500 (October 3, 1988). . . . Strained groin (December 1988). . . . Sprained right ankle (September 24, 1989); missed nine games. . . . Tore right groin muscle (January 27, 1990); missed eight games. . . . Underwent surgery to right thigh (July 17, 1990). . . . Separated shoulder (March 1991). . . . Injured shoulder (November 16, 1991); missed 38 games.
HONORS: Named to NCAA All-America East team (1981-82). . . . Named to AHL All-Star second team (1982-83).

			REGULAR SEASON					PLAYOFFS				
Season	Team	League	Gms.	G	A	Pts.	Pen.	Gms.	G	A	Pts.	Pen.
79-80—Univ. of New Hampshire	ECAC	27	15	17	32	8	—	—	—	—	—
80-81—Univ. of New Hampshire	ECAC	31	27	25	52	16	—	—	—	—	—
81-82—Univ. of New Hampshire	ECAC	35	26	27	53	6	—	—	—	—	—
82-83—Philadelphia	NHL	3	1	1	2	0	—	—	—	—	—
—Maine	AHL	76	29	54	83	10	17	9	5	14	0
83-84—Springfield	AHL	7	1	5	6	2	—	—	—	—	—
—Pittsburgh	NHL	50	18	20	38	9	—	—	—	—	—
—Baltimore	AHL	4	0	5	5	2	—	—	—	—	—
84-85—Baltimore	AHL	31	13	14	27	8	15	†10	8	18	0
—Pittsburgh	NHL	45	7	15	22	10	—	—	—	—	—
85-86—Maine	AHL	60	26	34	60	20	5	0	4	4	0
86-87—New Jersey	NHL	51	11	12	23	8	—	—	—	—	—

Season Team	League	REGULAR SEASON Gms.	G	A	Pts.	Pen.	PLAYOFFS Gms.	G	A	Pts.	Pen.
87-88—Utica	AHL	9	5	8	13	4	—	—	—	—	—
—New Jersey	NHL	45	8	14	22	14	4	0	1	1	4
88-89—Boston	NHL	71	13	22	35	20	10	0	2	2	0
89-90—Boston	NHL	43	12	28	40	8	2	0	0	0	0
90-91—Maine	AHL	17	8	17	25	2	1	0	0	0	0
—Boston	NHL	40	2	9	11	8	—	—	—	—	—
91-92—Maine	AHL	14	5	15	20	2	—	—	—	—	—
—Boston	NHL	23	10	17	27	2	—	—	—	—	—
NHL totals		371	82	138	220	79	16	0	3	3	4

BRIGHT, CHRIS
C, WHALERS

PERSONAL: Born October 14, 1970, at Guelph, Ont. . . . 6-0/187. . . . Shoots left.
TRANSACTIONS/CAREER NOTES: Selected by Hartford Whalers in fourth round (fourth Whalers pick, 78th overall) of NHL entry draft (June 16, 1990).

Season Team	League	REGULAR SEASON Gms.	G	A	Pts.	Pen.	PLAYOFFS Gms.	G	A	Pts.	Pen.
87-88—Moose Jaw	WHL	20	2	2	4	10	—	—	—	—	—
88-89—Moose Jaw	WHL	71	18	27	45	61	7	2	0	2	6
89-90—Moose Jaw	WHL	72	36	38	74	107	—	—	—	—	—
90-91—Springfield	AHL	37	3	4	7	32	—	—	—	—	—
91-92—Springfield	AHL	8	1	0	1	6	—	—	—	—	—
—Louisville	ECHL	46	17	39	56	61	13	9	8	17	18

BRILL, JOHN
RW, PENGUINS

PERSONAL: Born December 3, 1970, at St. Paul, Minn. . . . 6-3/180. . . . Shoots left. . . . Full name: John Paul Brill.
HIGH SCHOOL: Grand Rapids (Minn.).
COLLEGE: Minnesota.
TRANSACTIONS/CAREER NOTES: Selected by Pittsburgh Penguins in third round (third Penguins pick, 58th overall) of NHL entry draft (June 17, 1989).

Season Team	League	REGULAR SEASON Gms.	G	A	Pts.	Pen.	PLAYOFFS Gms.	G	A	Pts.	Pen.
87-88—Grand Rapids H.S.	Minn. H.S.	28	15	13	28		—	—	—	—	—
88-89—Grand Rapids H.S.	Minn. H.S.	25	23	29	52	28	—	—	—	—	—
89-90—University of Minnesota	WCHA	34	2	8	10	22	—	—	—	—	—
90-91—University of Minnesota	WCHA	44	6	13	19	36	—	—	—	—	—
91-92—University of Minnesota	WCHA	38	8	9	17	62	—	—	—	—	—

BRIMANIS, ARIS
D, FLYERS

PERSONAL: Born March 14, 1972, at Cleveland. . . . 6-3/195. . . . Shoots right. . . . Full name: Aris Aldis Brimanis.
HIGH SCHOOL: Culver Military Academy (O.).
COLLEGE: Bowling Green State.
TRANSACTIONS/CAREER NOTES: Selected by Philadelphia Flyers in fourth round (third Flyers pick, 86th overall) of NHL entry draft (June 22, 1991).

Season Team	League	REGULAR SEASON Gms.	G	A	Pts.	Pen.	PLAYOFFS Gms.	G	A	Pts.	Pen.
88-89—Culver Military Academy	Indiana H.S.	38	10	13	23		—	—	—	—	—
89-90—Culver Military Academy	Indiana H.S.	37	15	10	25		—	—	—	—	—
90-91—Bowling Green State	CCHA	38	3	6	9	42	—	—	—	—	—
91-92—Bowling Green State	CCHA	32	2	9	11	38	—	—	—	—	—

BRIND'AMOUR, ROD
LW/C, FLYERS

PERSONAL: Born August 9, 1970, at Ottawa. . . . 6-1/202. . . . Shoots left. . . . Full name: Rod Jean Brind'Amour.
COLLEGE: Michigan State.
TRANSACTIONS/CAREER NOTES: Broke wrist (November 1985). . . . Selected by St. Louis Blues in first round (first Blues pick, ninth overall) of NHL entry draft (June 11, 1988). . . . Traded by Blues with C Dan Quinn to Philadelphia Flyers for C Ron Sutter and D Murray Baron (September 22, 1991).
HONORS: Named to CCHA All-Rookie Team (1988-89). . . . Named CCHA Rookie of the Year (1988-89). . . . Named to NHL All-Rookie team (1989-90).

Season Team	League	REGULAR SEASON Gms.	G	A	Pts.	Pen.	PLAYOFFS Gms.	G	A	Pts.	Pen.
87-88—Notre Dame	SJHL	56	46	61	107	136	—	—	—	—	—
88-89—Michigan State	CCHA	42	27	32	59	63	—	—	—	—	—
—St. Louis	NHL	—	—	—	—	—	5	2	0	2	4
89-90—St. Louis	NHL	79	26	35	61	46	12	5	8	13	6
90-91—St. Louis	NHL	78	17	32	49	93	13	2	5	7	10
91-92—Philadelphia	NHL	80	33	44	77	100	—	—	—	—	—
NHL totals		237	76	111	187	239	30	9	13	22	20

BRISEBOIS, PATRICE
D, CANADIENS

PERSONAL: Born January 27, 1971, at Montreal. . . . 6-2/175. . . . Shoots right.
TRANSACTIONS/CAREER NOTES: Underwent surgery on fractured right thumb (February 1988). . . . Tore ligaments in left knee (March 1988). . . . Broke left thumb (August 1988). . . . Selected by Montreal Canadiens in second round

(second Canadiens pick, 30th overall) of NHL entry draft (June 17, 1989).... Traded by Laval Titans with LW Allen Kerr to Drummondville Voltigeurs for second- and third-round picks in 1990 draft (May 26, 1990).
HONORS: Won Michael Bossy Trophy (1988-89).... Won Can.HL Defenseman of the Year Award (1990-91).... Won Emile (Butch) Bouchard Trophy (1990-91).... Named to QMJHL All-Star first team (1990-91).... Named to Memorial Cup All-Star team (1990-91).

			REGULAR SEASON					PLAYOFFS			
Season	Team	League	Gms.	G	A	Pts.	Pen.	Gms.	G	A	Pts.	Pen.
87-88—Laval		QMJHL	48	10	34	44	95	6	0	2	2	2
88-89—Laval		QMJHL	50	20	45	65	95	17	8	14	22	45
89-90—Laval		QMJHL	56	18	70	88	108	13	7	9	16	26
90-91—Montreal		NHL	10	0	2	2	4	—	—	—	—	—
—Drummondville		QMJHL	54	17	44	61	72	14	6	18	24	49
91-92—Fredericton		AHL	53	12	27	39	51	—	—	—	—	—
—Montreal		NHL	26	2	8	10	20	11	2	4	6	6
NHL totals			36	2	10	12	24	11	2	4	6	6

B

BRODEUR, MARTIN
G, DEVILS

PERSONAL: Born May 6, 1972, at Montreal.... 6-1/190.... Shoots left.
TRANSACTIONS/CAREER NOTES: Suffered pinched nerve in elbow and slight concussion (March 9, 1990).... Selected by New Jersey Devils in first round (first Devils pick, 20th overall) of NHL entry draft (June 16, 1990).
HONORS: Named to QMJHL All-Star second team (1991-92).

			REGULAR SEASON							PLAYOFFS						
Season	Team	League	Gms.	Min.	W	L	T	GA	SO	Avg.	Gms.	Min.	W	L	GA	SO	Avg.
89-90—St. Hyacinthe		QMJHL	42	2333	23	13	2	156	0	4.01	12	678	5	7	46	0	4.07
90-91—St. Hyacinthe		QMJHL	52	2946	22	24	4	162	2	3.30	4	232	0	4	16	0	4.14
91-92—St. Hyacinthe		QMJHL	48	2846	27	16	4	161	2	3.39	5	317	2	3	14	0	2.65
—New Jersey		NHL	4	179	2	1	0	10	0	3.35	1	32	0	1	3	0	5.63
NHL totals			4	179	2	1	0	10	0	3.35	1	32	0	1	3	0	5.63

BROTEN, AARON
C/LW, JETS

PERSONAL: Born November 14, 1960, at Roseau, Minn. ... 5-10/168.... Shoots left. ... Brother of Neal Broten, center, Minnesota North Stars; and brother of Paul Broten, right winger, New York Rangers.
HIGH SCHOOL: Roseau (Minn.).
COLLEGE: Minnesota.
TRANSACTIONS/CAREER NOTES: Selected by Colorado Rockies in sixth round (fifth Rockies pick, 106th overall) of NHL entry draft (June 11, 1980).... Sprained ankle (February 15, 1986).... Reinjured ankle (March 6, 1986).... Reinjured ankle (March 19, 1986).... Traded by New Jersey Devils to Minnesota North Stars for C Bob Brooke (January 5, 1990).... Suffered slight concussion (March 17, 1990).... Acquired by Quebec Nordiques in 1990 NHL waiver draft for $10,000 (October 1, 1990).... Traded by Nordiques with D Michel Petit and RW Lucien DeBlois to Toronto Maple Leafs for LW Scott Pearson and 1992 draft picks (November 17, 1990).... Separated left shoulder (January 26, 1991).... Signed as free agent by Winnipeg Jets (January 10, 1992).
HONORS: Won WCHA Rookie of the Year Award (1979-80).... Named to WCHA All-Star first team (1980-81).

			REGULAR SEASON					PLAYOFFS			
Season	Team	League	Gms.	G	A	Pts.	Pen.	Gms.	G	A	Pts.	Pen.
79-80—University of Minnesota ...		WCHA	41	25	47	72	8	—	—	—	—	—
80-81—University of Minnesota ...		WCHA	45	*47	*59	*106	24	—	—	—	—	—
—Colorado		NHL	2	0	0	0	0	—	—	—	—	—
81-82—Fort Worth		CHL	19	15	21	36	11	—	—	—	—	—
—Colorado		NHL	58	15	24	39	6	—	—	—	—	—
82-83—Wichita		CHL	4	0	4	4	0	—	—	—	—	—
—New Jersey		NHL	73	16	39	55	28	—	—	—	—	—
83-84—New Jersey		NHL	80	13	23	36	36	—	—	—	—	—
84-85—New Jersey		NHL	80	22	35	57	38	—	—	—	—	—
85-86—New Jersey		NHL	66	19	25	44	26	—	—	—	—	—
86-87—New Jersey		NHL	80	26	53	79	36	—	—	—	—	—
87-88—New Jersey		NHL	80	26	57	83	80	20	5	11	16	20
88-89—New Jersey		NHL	80	16	43	59	81	—	—	—	—	—
89-90—New Jersey		NHL	42	10	8	18	36	—	—	—	—	—
—Minnesota		NHL	35	9	9	18	22	7	0	5	5	8
90-91—Quebec		NHL	20	5	4	9	6	—	—	—	—	—
—Toronto		NHL	27	6	4	10	32	—	—	—	—	—
91-92—Moncton		AHL	4	0	2	2	0	—	—	—	—	—
—Winnipeg		NHL	25	4	5	9	14	7	2	2	4	12
NHL totals			748	187	329	516	441	34	7	18	25	40

BROTEN, NEAL
C, NORTH STARS

PERSONAL: Born November 29, 1959, at Roseau, Minn. ... 5-9/170.... Shoots left. ... Full name: Neal LaMoy Broten.... Brother of Aaron Broten, center/left winger, Winnipeg Jets; and brother of Paul Broten, right winger, New York Rangers.
HIGH SCHOOL: Roseau (Minn.).
COLLEGE: Minnesota.
TRANSACTIONS/CAREER NOTES: Selected by Minnesota North Stars in second round (third North Stars pick, 42nd overall) of NHL entry draft (August 9, 1979).... Fractured ankle (December 26, 1981).... Dislocated shoulder (October 30, 1986).... Tore shoulder ligaments (March 1987).... Separated shoulder (November 1987).... Underwent reconstructive shoulder surgery

(February 1988).... Suffered sterno-clavicular sprain (February 14, 1989).... Strained groin (December 18, 1990).
HONORS: Won WCHA Rookie of the Year Award (1978-79).... Won Hobey Baker Memorial Trophy (1980-81).... Named to NCAA All-America West team (1980-81).... Named to WCHA All-Star first team (1980-81).... Named to NCAA All-Tournament team (1980-81).
MISCELLANEOUS: Member of 1980 gold medal-winning U.S. Olympic team.

			REGULAR SEASON					PLAYOFFS				
Season	Team	League	Gms.	G	A	Pts.	Pen.	Gms.	G	A	Pts.	Pen.
78-79	University of Minnesota ...	WCHA	40	21	50	71	18	—	—	—	—	—
79-80	U.S. Olympic Team	Int'l	62	27	31	58	22	—	—	—	—	—
80-81	University of Minnesota ...	WCHA	36	17	54	71	56	—	—	—	—	—
	Minnesota	NHL	3	2	0	2	12	19	1	7	8	9
81-82	Minnesota	NHL	73	38	60	98	42	4	0	2	2	0
82-83	Minnesota	NHL	79	32	45	77	43	9	1	6	7	10
83-84	Minnesota	NHL	76	28	61	89	43	16	5	5	10	4
84-85	Minnesota	NHL	80	19	37	56	39	9	2	5	7	10
85-86	Minnesota	NHL	80	29	76	105	47	5	3	2	5	2
86-87	Minnesota	NHL	46	18	35	53	35	—	—	—	—	—
87-88	Minnesota	NHL	54	9	30	39	32	—	—	—	—	—
88-89	Minnesota	NHL	68	18	38	56	57	5	2	2	4	4
89-90	Minnesota	NHL	80	23	62	85	45	7	2	2	4	18
90-91	Minnesota	NHL	79	13	56	69	26	23	9	13	22	6
91-92	Minnesota	NHL	76	8	26	34	16	7	1	5	6	2
	NHL totals....................		794	237	526	763	437	104	26	49	75	65

BROTEN, PAUL
RW, RANGERS

PERSONAL: Born October 27, 1965, at Roseau, Minn.... 5-11/183.... Shoots right.... Brother of Aaron Broten, center/left winger, Winnipeg Jets; and brother of Neal Broten, center, Minnesota North Stars.
HIGH SCHOOL: Roseau (Minn.).
COLLEGE: Minnesota.
TRANSACTIONS/CAREER NOTES: Selected by New York Rangers in fourth round (third Rangers pick, 77th overall) of NHL entry draft (June 9, 1984).... Pulled thigh muscle (September 1990).

			REGULAR SEASON					PLAYOFFS				
Season	Team	League	Gms.	G	A	Pts.	Pen.	Gms.	G	A	Pts.	Pen.
83-84	Roseau H.S.	Minn. H.S.	26	26	29	55	4	—	—	—	—	—
84-85	University of Minnesota ...	WCHA	44	8	8	16	26	—	—	—	—	—
85-86	University of Minnesota ...	WCHA	38	6	16	22	24	—	—	—	—	—
86-87	University of Minnesota ...	WCHA	48	17	22	39	52	—	—	—	—	—
87-88	University of Minnesota ...	WCHA	62	19	26	45	54	—	—	—	—	—
88-89	Denver	IHL	77	28	31	59	133	4	0	2	2	6
89-90	Flint	IHL	28	17	9	26	55	—	—	—	—	—
	New York Rangers	NHL	32	5	3	8	26	6	1	1	2	2
90-91	New York Rangers	NHL	28	4	6	10	18	5	0	0	0	2
	Binghamton	AHL	8	2	2	4	4	—	—	—	—	—
91-92	New York Rangers	NHL	74	13	15	28	102	13	1	2	3	10
	NHL totals....................		134	22	24	46	146	24	2	3	5	14

BROUSSEAU, PAUL
RW, NORDIQUES

PERSONAL: Born September 18, 1973, at Montreal.... 6-2/212.... Shoots right.
COLLEGE: Heritage College (Orlando, Fla.).
TRANSACTIONS/CAREER NOTES: Selected by Quebec Nordiques in second round (second Nordiques pick, 28th overall) of NHL entry draft (June 20, 1992).
HONORS: Won Mike Bossy Trophy (1991-92).... Won QMJHL Top Draft Prospect Award (1991-92).

			REGULAR SEASON					PLAYOFFS				
Season	Team	League	Gms.	G	A	Pts.	Pen.	Gms.	G	A	Pts.	Pen.
89-90	Chicoutimi	QMJHL	57	17	24	41	32	7	0	3	3	0
90-91	Trois-Rivieres.................	QMJHL	67	30	66	96	48	6	3	2	5	2
91-92	Hull	QMJHL	57	35	61	96	54	6	3	5	8	10

BROWN, CAM
LW, CANUCKS

PERSONAL: Born May 15, 1969, at Saskatoon, Sask.... 6-1/210.... Shoots left.
TRANSACTIONS/CAREER NOTES: Signed as free agent by Vancouver Canucks (April 6, 1990).

			REGULAR SEASON					PLAYOFFS				
Season	Team	League	Gms.	G	A	Pts.	Pen.	Gms.	G	A	Pts.	Pen.
87-88	Brandon...........................	WHL	69	2	13	15	185	4	1	1	2	15
88-89	Brandon...........................	WHL	72	17	42	59	225	—	—	—	—	—
89-90	Brandon...........................	WHL	68	34	41	75	182	—	—	—	—	—
90-91	Vancouver.......................	NHL	1	0	0	0	7	—	—	—	—	—
	Milwaukee......................	IHL	74	11	13	24	218	3	0	0	0	0
91-92	Milwaukee......................	IHL	51	6	8	14	179	1	0	0	0	0
	Columbus.......................	ECHL	10	11	6	17	64	—	—	—	—	—
	NHL totals....................		1	0	0	0	7					

BROWN, DAVE
RW, FLYERS

PERSONAL: Born October 12, 1962, at Saskatoon, Sask.... 6-5/205.... Shoots right.... Full name: David Brown.
TRANSACTIONS/CAREER NOTES: Selected by Philadelphia Flyers in seventh round (seventh Flyers pick, 140th overall) of NHL entry draft (June 9, 1982).... Bruised shoulder (March 1985).

. . . Suspended five games by NHL for stick-swinging incident (March 1987). . . . Suspended 15 games by NHL for crosschecking (October 16, 1987). . . . Bruised left hand and wrist (January 1988). . . . Traded by Flyers to Edmonton Oilers for C Keith Acton and future considerations (February 7, 1989). . . . Lacerated face (March 3, 1989). . . . Sprained hand (March 1989). . . . Traded by Oilers with D Corey Foster and the NHL rights to RW Jari Kurri to Flyers for RW Scott Mellanby, LW Craig Berube and C Craig Fisher (May 30, 1991). . . . Injured shoulder (January 28, 1992); missed 10 games.

Season	Team	League	REGULAR SEASON					PLAYOFFS				
			Gms.	G	A	Pts.	Pen.	Gms.	G	A	Pts.	Pen.
80-81	Spokane Flyers	WHL	9	2	2	4	21	—	—	—	—	—
81-82	Saskatoon	WHL	62	11	33	44	344	5	1	0	1	4
82-83	Maine	AHL	71	8	6	14	*418	16	0	0	0	*107
	Philadelphia	NHL	2	0	0	0	5	—	—	—	—	—
83-84	Philadelphia	NHL	19	1	5	6	98	2	0	0	0	12
	Springfield	AHL	59	17	14	31	150	—	—	—	—	—
84-85	Philadelphia	NHL	57	3	6	9	165	11	0	0	0	59
85-86	Philadelphia	NHL	76	10	7	17	277	5	0	0	0	16
86-87	Philadelphia	NHL	62	7	3	10	274	26	1	2	3	59
87-88	Philadelphia	NHL	47	12	5	17	114	7	1	0	1	27
88-89	Philadelphia	NHL	50	0	3	3	100	—	—	—	—	—
	Edmonton	NHL	22	0	2	2	56	7	0	0	0	6
89-90	Edmonton	NHL	60	0	6	6	145	3	0	0	0	0
90-91	Edmonton	NHL	58	3	4	7	160	16	0	1	1	30
91-92	Philadelphia	NHL	70	4	2	6	81	—	—	—	—	—
	NHL totals		523	40	43	83	1475	77	2	3	5	209

BROWN, DOUG

RW, DEVILS

PERSONAL: Born June 12, 1964, at Southborough, Mass. . . . 5-10/180. . . . Shoots right. . . . Full name: Douglas Allen Brown. . . . Brother of Greg Brown, defenseman, Buffalo Sabres.
COLLEGE: Boston College.
TRANSACTIONS/CAREER NOTES: Signed as free agent by New Jersey Devils (August 1986). . . . Broke nose (October 1988). . . . Injured back (November 25, 1989). . . . Bruised right foot (February 13, 1991).

Season	Team	League	REGULAR SEASON					PLAYOFFS				
			Gms.	G	A	Pts.	Pen.	Gms.	G	A	Pts.	Pen.
82-83	Boston College	ECAC	22	9	8	17	0	—	—	—	—	—
83-84	Boston College	ECAC	38	11	10	21	6	—	—	—	—	—
84-85	Boston College	Hockey East	45	37	31	68	10	—	—	—	—	—
85-86	Boston College	Hockey East	38	16	40	56	16	—	—	—	—	—
86-87	Maine	AHL	73	24	34	58	15	—	—	—	—	—
	New Jersey	NHL	4	0	1	1	0	—	—	—	—	—
87-88	New Jersey	NHL	70	14	11	25	20	19	5	1	6	6
	Utica	AHL	2	0	2	2	2	—	—	—	—	—
88-89	New Jersey	NHL	63	15	10	25	15	—	—	—	—	—
	Utica	AHL	4	1	4	5	0	—	—	—	—	—
89-90	New Jersey	NHL	89	14	20	34	16	6	0	1	1	2
90-91	New Jersey	NHL	58	14	16	30	4	7	2	2	4	2
91-92	New Jersey	NHL	71	11	17	28	27	—	—	—	—	—
	NHL totals		355	68	75	143	82	32	7	4	11	10

BROWN, GREG

D, SABRES

PERSONAL: Born March 7, 1963, at Hartford, Conn. . . . 6-0/185. . . . Shoots right. . . . Full name: Gregory Curtis Brown. . . . Brother of Doug Brown, right winger, New Jersey Devils.
HIGH SCHOOL: St. Mark's (Southborough, Mass.).
COLLEGE: Boston College.
TRANSACTIONS/CAREER NOTES: Selected by Buffalo Sabres in second round (second Sabres pick, 26th overall) of NHL entry draft (June 21, 1986).
HONORS: Named to Hockey East All-Star first team (1988-89 and 1989-90). . . . Named Hockey East Player of the Year (1989-90). . . . Named to NCAA All-America East first team (1989-90).

Season	Team	League	REGULAR SEASON					PLAYOFFS				
			Gms.	G	A	Pts.	Pen.	Gms.	G	A	Pts.	Pen.
84-85	St. Marks H.S.	Mass. H.S.	24	16	24	40	12	—	—	—	—	—
85-86	St. Marks H.S.	Mass. H.S.	19	22	28	50	30	—	—	—	—	—
86-87	Boston College	Hockey East	37	10	27	37	22	—	—	—	—	—
87-88	U.S. Olympic Team	Int'l	6	0	4	4	2	—	—	—	—	—
88-89	Boston College	Hockey East	40	9	34	43	24	—	—	—	—	—
89-90	Boston College	Hockey East	42	5	35	40	42	—	—	—	—	—
90-91	Buffalo	NHL	39	1	2	3	35	—	—	—	—	—
	Rochester	AHL	31	6	17	23	16	14	1	4	5	8
91-92	Rochester	AHL	56	8	30	38	25	16	1	5	6	4
	U.S. National Team	Int'l	8	0	0	0	5	—	—	—	—	—
	U.S. Olympic Team	Int'l	7	0	0	0	2	—	—	—	—	—
	NHL totals		39	1	2	3	35					

BROWN, JEFF

D, BLUES

PERSONAL: Born April 30, 1966, at Ottawa. . . . 6-1/204. . . . Shoots right.
TRANSACTIONS/CAREER NOTES: Selected by Quebec Nordiques as underage junior in second round (second Nordiques pick, 36th overall) of NHL entry draft (June 9, 1984). . . . Traded by Nordiques to St. Louis Blues for G Greg Millen and C Tony Hrkac (December 13, 1989). . . . Broke left

B

ankle; (February 14, 1991); missed 13 games.
HONORS: Shared Max Kaminsky Trophy with Terry Carkner (1985-86).... Named to OHL All-Star first team (1985-86).

Season Team	League	REGULAR SEASON					PLAYOFFS				
		Gms.	G	A	Pts.	Pen.	Gms.	G	A	Pts.	Pen.
81-82—Hawkesbury	COJHL	49	12	47	59	72	—	—	—	—	—
82-83—Sudbury	OHL	65	9	37	46	39	—	—	—	—	—
83-84—Sudbury	OHL	68	17	60	77	39	—	—	—	—	—
84-85—Sudbury	OHL	56	16	48	64	26	—	—	—	—	—
85-86—Sudbury	OHL	45	22	28	50	24	4	0	2	2	11
—Quebec	NHL	8	3	2	5	6	1	0	0	0	0
—Fredericton	AHL	—	—	—	—	—	1	0	1	1	0
86-87—Fredericton	AHL	26	2	14	16	16	—	—	—	—	—
—Quebec	NHL	44	7	22	29	16	13	3	3	6	2
87-88—Quebec	NHL	78	16	37	53	64	—	—	—	—	—
88-89—Quebec	NHL	78	21	47	68	62	—	—	—	—	—
89-90—Quebec	NHL	29	6	10	16	18	—	—	—	—	—
—St. Louis	NHL	48	10	28	38	37	12	2	10	12	4
90-91—St. Louis	NHL	67	12	47	59	39	13	3	9	12	6
91-92—St. Louis	NHL	80	20	39	59	38	6	2	1	3	2
NHL totals		432	95	232	327	280	45	10	23	33	14

BROWN, KEITH
D, BLACKHAWKS

PERSONAL: Born May 6, 1960, at Corner Brook, Nfld.... 6-1/195.... Shoots right.... Full name: Keith Jeffrey Brown.

TRANSACTIONS/CAREER NOTES: Selected by Chicago Blackhawks as underage junior in first round (first Blackhawks pick, seventh overall) of NHL entry draft (August 9, 1979).... Tore ligaments in right knee (December 23, 1981).... Separated right shoulder (January 26, 1983).... Strained leg (January 1985).... Broke finger (October 1985); missed 10 games.... Tore ligaments and damaged cartilage in left knee (October 1987).... Bruised shoulder (January 1990).... Bruised ribs (February 25, 1990); missed 10 games.... Bruised elbow (April 1990).... Strained shoulder (September 1990).... Bruised ribs (November 1990).... Separated left shoulder (December 16, 1990); missed 30 games.... Strained chest muscle (March 1991).... Injured eye (October 10, 1991); missed one game.... Pulled groin (November 7, 1991); missed two games.... Reinjured groin (November 19, 1991); missed two games.... Reinjured groin (December 1991); missed three games.... Sprained right ankle (January 27, 1992); missed 14 games.
HONORS: Shared WCHL Rookie of the Year Award with John Ogrodnick (1977-78).... Named to WCHL All-Star second team (1977-78).... Won Top Defenseman Trophy (1978-79).... Named to WHL All-Star first team (1978-79).

Season Team	League	REGULAR SEASON					PLAYOFFS				
		Gms.	G	A	Pts.	Pen.	Gms.	G	A	Pts.	Pen.
76-77—Fort Saskatchewan	AJHL	59	14	61	75	14	—	—	—	—	—
—Portland	WCHL	2	0	0	0	0	—	—	—	—	—
77-78—Portland	WCHL	72	11	53	64	51	8	0	3	3	2
78-79—Portland	WHL	70	11	85	96	75	25	3	*30	33	21
79-80—Chicago	NHL	76	2	18	20	27	6	0	0	0	4
80-81—Chicago	NHL	80	9	34	43	80	3	0	2	2	2
81-82—Chicago	NHL	33	4	20	24	26	4	0	2	2	5
82-83—Chicago	NHL	50	4	27	31	20	7	0	0	0	11
83-84—Chicago	NHL	74	10	25	35	94	5	0	1	1	10
84-85—Chicago	NHL	56	1	22	23	55	11	2	7	9	31
85-86—Chicago	NHL	70	11	29	40	87	3	0	1	1	9
86-87—Chicago	NHL	73	4	23	27	86	4	0	1	1	6
87-88—Chicago	NHL	24	3	6	9	45	5	0	2	2	10
88-89—Chicago	NHL	74	2	16	18	84	13	1	3	4	25
89-90—Chicago	NHL	67	5	20	25	87	18	0	4	4	43
90-91—Chicago	NHL	45	1	10	11	55	6	1	0	1	8
91-92—Chicago	NHL	57	6	10	16	69	14	0	8	8	18
NHL totals		779	62	260	322	815	99	4	31	35	182

BROWN, KEVIN
RW, KINGS

PERSONAL: Born May 11, 1974, at Birmingham, England.... 6-2/211.... Shoots right.... Full name: Kevin J. Brown.
HIGH SCHOOL: Quinte Secondary School (Belleville, Ont.).
TRANSACTIONS/CAREER NOTES: Selected by Los Angeles Kings in fourth round (third Kings pick, 87th overall) of NHL entry draft (June 20, 1992).

Season Team	League	REGULAR SEASON					PLAYOFFS				
		Gms.	G	A	Pts.	Pen.	Gms.	G	A	Pts.	Pen.
89-90—Georgetown Jr. B	OHA	31	3	8	11	59	—	—	—	—	—
90-91—Waterloo Jr. B	OHA	46	25	33	58	116	—	—	—	—	—
91-92—Belleville Bulls	OHL	66	24	24	48	52	5	1	4	5	8

BROWN, ROB
RW, BLACKHAWKS

PERSONAL: Born April 10, 1968, at Kingston, Ont.... 5-11/185.... Shoots left.... Full name: Robert Brown.
TRANSACTIONS/CAREER NOTES: Selected by Pittsburgh Penguins as underage junior in fourth round (fourth Penguins pick, 67th overall) of NHL entry draft (June 21, 1986).... Separated right shoulder (February 12, 1989), missed 12 games.... Traded by Penguins to Hartford Whalers for RW Scott Young (December 21, 1990).... Injured Adam's apple (April 5, 1991); missed one playoff game.... Traded by Whalers to Chicago Blackhawks for D Steve Konroyd (January 24, 1992).

Named to WHL All-Star first team (1985-86 and 1986-87).... Won Can.HL Player of the Year Award (1986-87)....
Won Can.HL Plus/Minus Award (1986-87).... Won WHL West Most Valuable Player Trophy (1985-86 and 1986-87)....
Won WHL Player of the Year Award (1986-87).

			REGULAR SEASON					PLAYOFFS			
Season Team	League	Gms.	G	A	Pts.	Pen.	Gms.	G	A	Pts.	Pen.
83-84—Kamloops	WHL	50	16	42	58	80	15	1	2	3	17
84-85—Kamloops	WHL	60	29	50	79	95	15	8	8	16	28
85-86—Kamloops	WHL	69	58	*115	*173	171	16	*18	*28	*46	14
86-87—Kamloops	WHL	63	*76	*136	*212	101	5	6	5	11	6
87-88—Pittsburgh	NHL	51	24	20	44	56	—	—	—	—	—
88-89—Pittsburgh	NHL	68	49	66	115	118	11	5	3	8	22
89-90—Pittsburgh	NHL	80	33	47	80	102	—	—	—	—	—
90-91—Pittsburgh	NHL	25	6	10	16	31	—	—	—	—	—
91-92—Hartford	NHL	42	16	15	31	39	—	—	—	—	—
—Chicago	NHL	25	5	11	16	34	8	2	4	6	4
NHL totals		291	133	169	302	380	19	7	7	14	26

BROWNSCHIDLE, MARK
D, JETS

PERSONAL: Born October 26, 1970, at East Amherst, N.Y.... 6-2/185....
Shoots right.... Full name: Mark D. Brownschidle.... Brother of Jack
Brownschidle, defenseman, St. Louis Blues and Hartford Whalers (1977-
78 through 1985-86); and Jeff Brownschidle, defenceman, Hartford Whal
ers (1981-82 through 1982-83).
COLLEGE: Boston University.
TRANSACTIONS/CAREER NOTES: Selected by Winnipeg Jets in fourth round (fifth Jets pick, 64th overall) of NHL entry draft (June
17, 1989).

			REGULAR SEASON					PLAYOFFS			
Season Team	League	Gms.	G	A	Pts.	Pen.	Gms.	G	A	Pts.	Pen.
87-88—Amherst Jr.	Buffalo		2	12	14		—	—	—	—	—
88-89—Boston University	Hockey East	35	0	7	7	12	—	—	—	—	—
89-90—Boston University	Hockey East	38	1	4	5	12	—	—	—	—	—
90-91—Boston University	Hockey East	13	0	1	1	10	—	—	—	—	—
91-92—Boston University	Hockey East	26	2	6	8	6	—	—	—	—	—

BRUCE, DAVID
LW, SHARKS

PERSONAL: Born October 7, 1964, at Thunder Bay, Ont.... 5-11/190.... Shoots right.
TRANSACTIONS/CAREER NOTES: Selected by Vancouver Canucks as underage junior in second
round (second Canucks pick, 30th overall) of NHL entry draft (June 8, 1983).... Suffered
from mononucleosis (November 1987).... Bruised foot (March 1988).... Tore cartilage near
thumb on left hand and underwent surgery (March 1989).... Signed as free agent by St. Louis Blues (July 1990).... Selected
by San Jose Sharks in NHL expansion draft (May 1991).... Tore abdominal muscle (March 19, 1992).
HONORS: Won James Gatschene Memorial Trophy (1990-91).... Named to IHL All-Star first team (1990-91).

			REGULAR SEASON					PLAYOFFS			
Season Team	League	Gms.	G	A	Pts.	Pen.	Gms.	G	A	Pts.	Pen.
81-82—Thunder Bay	TBJHL	35	27	31	58	74					
82-83—Kitchener	OHL	67	36	35	71	199	12	7	9	16	27
83-84—Kitchener	OHL	62	52	40	92	203	10	5	8	13	20
84-85—Fredericton	AHL	56	14	11	25	104	5	0	0	0	37
85-86—Fredericton	AHL	66	25	16	41	151	2	0	1	1	12
—Vancouver	NHL	12	0	1	1	14	1	0	0	0	0
86-87—Fredericton	AHL	17	7	6	13	73	—	—	—	—	—
—Vancouver	NHL	50	9	7	16	109	—	—	—	—	—
87-88—Fredericton	AHL	30	27	18	45	115	—	—	—	—	—
—Vancouver	NHL	28	7	3	10	57	—	—	—	—	—
88-89—Vancouver	NHL	53	7	7	14	65	—	—	—	—	—
89-90—Milwaukee	IHL	68	40	35	75	148	6	5	3	8	0
90-91—St. Louis	NHL	12	1	2	3	14	2	0	0	0	2
—Peoria	IHL	60	*64	52	116	78	18	*18	11	*29	40
91-92—Kansas City	IHL	7	5	5	10	6	—	—	—	—	—
—San Jose	NHL	60	22	16	38	46	—	—	—	—	—
NHL totals		215	46	36	82	305	3	0	0	0	2

BRUNET, BENOIT
LW, CANADIENS

PERSONAL: Born August 24, 1968, at Montreal.... 5-11/184.... Shoots left.
TRANSACTIONS/CAREER NOTES: Selected by Montreal Canadiens as underage junior in sec-
ond round (second Canadiens pick, 27th overall) of NHL entry draft (June 21, 1986)....
Injured ankle (September 1987). ... Tore left knee ligaments (September 24, 1990);
missed 24 games.... Fractured ankle (December 4, 1991).
HONORS: Named to QMJHL All-Star second team (1986-87).... Named to AHL All-Star first team (1988-89).

			REGULAR SEASON					PLAYOFFS			
Season Team	League	Gms.	G	A	Pts.	Pen.	Gms.	G	A	Pts.	Pen.
85-86—Hull	QMJHL	71	33	37	70	81	—	—	—	—	—
86-87—Hull	QMJHL	60	43	67	110	105	6	7	5	12	8
87-88—Hull	QMJHL	62	54	89	143	131	10	3	10	13	11
88-89—Montreal	NHL	2	0	1	1	0	—	—	—	—	—
—Sherbrooke	AHL	73	41	*76	117	95	6	2	0	2	4

Season Team	League	REGULAR SEASON					PLAYOFFS				
		Gms.	G	A	Pts.	Pen.	Gms.	G	A	Pts.	Pen.
89-90—Sherbrooke..................	AHL	72	32	35	67	82	12	8	7	15	20
90-91—Fredericton	AHL	24	13	18	31	16	6	5	6	11	2
—Montreal......................	NHL	17	1	3	4	0	—	—	—	—	—
91-92—Fredericton	AHL	6	7	9	16	27	—	—	—	—	—
—Montreal......................	NHL	18	4	6	10	14	—	—	—	—	—
NHL totals..........................		37	5	10	15	14					

BRYLIN, SERGEI
C, DEVILS

PERSONAL: Born January 13, 1974, at Moscow, U.S.S.R. . . . 5-9/176. . . . Shoots left.
TRANSACTIONS/CAREER NOTES: Selected by New Jersey Devils in second round (second Devils pick, 42nd overall) of NHL entry draft (June 20, 1992).

Season Team	League	REGULAR SEASON					PLAYOFFS				
		Gms.	G	A	Pts.	Pen.	Gms.	G	A	Pts.	Pen.
91-92—CSKA Moscow.................	CIS	44	1	6	7	4	—	—	—	—	—

BUCHBERGER, KELLY
LW/RW, OILERS

PERSONAL: Born December 12, 1966, at Langenburg, Sask. . . . 6-2/210. . . . Shoots left. . . . Full name: Kelly Michael Buchberger.
TRANSACTIONS/CAREER NOTES: Selected by Edmonton Oilers as underage junior in ninth round (eighth Oilers pick, 188th overall) of NHL entry draft (June 15, 1985). . . . Suspended six games by AHL for leaving bench to fight (March 30, 1988). . . . Fractured right ankle (March 1989). . . . Dislocated left shoulder (March 13, 1990). . . . Reinjured shoulder (May 4, 1990).

Season Team	League	REGULAR SEASON					PLAYOFFS				
		Gms.	G	A	Pts.	Pen.	Gms.	G	A	Pts.	Pen.
83-84—Melville	SAJHL	60	14	11	25	139	—	—	—	—	—
84-85—Moose Jaw	WHL	51	12	17	29	114	—	—	—	—	—
85-86—Moose Jaw	WHL	72	14	22	36	206	13	11	4	15	37
86-87—Nova Scotia	AHL	70	12	20	32	257	5	0	1	1	23
—Edmonton	NHL	—	—	—	—	—	3	0	1	1	5
87-88—Edmonton	NHL	19	1	0	1	81	—	—	—	—	—
—Nova Scotia	AHL	49	21	23	44	206	2	0	0	0	11
88-89—Edmonton	NHL	66	5	9	14	234	—	—	—	—	—
89-90—Edmonton	NHL	55	2	6	8	168	19	0	5	5	13
90-91—Edmonton	NHL	64	3	1	4	160	12	2	1	3	25
91-92—Edmonton	NHL	79	20	24	44	157	16	1	4	5	32
NHL totals..........................		283	31	40	71	800	50	3	11	14	75

BULJIN, VLADISLAV
D, FLYERS

PERSONAL: Born May 18, 1972, at Penza, U.S.S.R. . . . 6-4/196. . . . Shoots right.
TRANSACTIONS/CAREER NOTES: Selected by Philadelphia Flyers in fifth round (fourth Flyers pick, 103rd overall) of NHL entry draft (June 20, 1992).

Season Team	League	REGULAR SEASON					PLAYOFFS				
		Gms.	G	A	Pts.	Pen.	Gms.	G	A	Pts.	Pen.
90-91—Dizelist Penza..................	CIS	68					—	—	—	—	—
91-92—Dizelist Penza..................	CIS				Statistics unavailable.						

BULLARD, MIKE
C

PERSONAL: Born March 10, 1961, at Ottawa. . . . 5-11/198. . . . Shoots left. . . . Full name: Michael Brian Bullard.
TRANSACTIONS/CAREER NOTES: Selected by Pittsburgh Penguins as underage junior in first round (first Penguins pick, ninth overall) of NHL entry draft (June 11, 1980). . . . Suffered from mononucleosis (October 1982); missed 20 games. . . . Suffered chip fracture of left shoulder (December 1984), missed 11 games. . . . Traded by Penguins to Calgary Flames for C Dan Quinn (November 1986). . . . Traded by Flames with C Craig Coxe and D Tim Corkery to St. Louis Blues for C Doug Gilmour, RW Mark Hunter, LW Steve Bozek and D/RW Michael Dark (September 5, 1988). . . . Traded by Blues to Philadelphia Flyers for C Peter Zezel (November 29, 1988). . . . Injured hip flexor (March 1990). . . . Signed to play with Ambri Piotta in Switzerland (June 1990). . . . Traded by Flyers to Toronto Maple Leafs for option of using Maple Leafs' fourth-round pick in 1992 draft or third-round pick in 1993 draft (July 29, 1991). . . . Placed on waivers by Maple Leafs (July 28, 1992).
HONORS: Named to OMJHL All-Star second team (1979-80).

Season Team	League	REGULAR SEASON					PLAYOFFS				
		Gms.	G	A	Pts.	Pen.	Gms.	G	A	Pts.	Pen.
78-79—Brantford...................	OMJHL	66	43	56	99	66	—	—	—	—	—
79-80—Brantford...................	OMJHL	66	†66	84	150	86	11	10	6	16	29
80-81—Brantford...................	OMJHL	42	47	60	107	55	6	4	5	9	10
—Pittsburgh	NHL	15	1	2	3	19	4	3	3	6	0
81-82—Pittsburgh	NHL	75	36	27	63	91	5	1	1	2	4
82-83—Pittsburgh	NHL	57	22	22	44	60	—	—	—	—	—
83-84—Pittsburgh	NHL	76	51	41	92	57	—	—	—	—	—
84-85—Pittsburgh	NHL	57	9	11	20	125	—	—	—	—	—
85-86—Pittsburgh	NHL	77	41	42	83	69	—	—	—	—	—
86-87—Pittsburgh	NHL	14	2	10	12	17	—	—	—	—	—
—Calgary......................	NHL	57	28	26	54	34	6	4	3	7	2
87-88—Calgary......................	NHL	79	48	55	103	68	6	0	2	2	6
88-89—St. Louis	NHL	20	4	12	16	46	—	—	—	—	—
—Philadelphia	NHL	54	23	26	49	60	19	3	9	12	32

Season Team	League	REGULAR SEASON					PLAYOFFS				
		Gms.	G	A	Pts.	Pen.	Gms.	G	A	Pts.	Pen.
89-90—Philadelphia	NHL	70	27	37	64	67	—	—	—	—	—
90-91—Ambri Piotta	Switzerland	36	37	27	64		5	8	9	17	
91-92—Toronto	NHL	65	14	14	28	42	—	—	—	—	—
NHL totals		716	306	325	631	755	40	11	18	29	44

BURE, PAVEL
RW/LW, CANUCKS

PERSONAL: Born March 31, 1971, at Moscow, U.S.S.R. . . . 5-9/170. . . . Shoots left. . . . Brother of Valeri Bure, left winger in Montreal Canadiens system.
TRANSACTIONS/CAREER NOTES: Selected by Vancouver Canucks in sixth round (Canucks fourth pick, 113th overall) of NHL entry draft (June 17, 1989).
HONORS: Named Soviet League Rookie of the Year (1988-89). . . . Won Calder Memorial Trophy (1991-92).

Season Team	League	REGULAR SEASON					PLAYOFFS				
		Gms.	G	A	Pts.	Pen.	Gms.	G	A	Pts.	Pen.
87-88—CSKA	USSR	5	1	1	2	0	—	—	—	—	—
88-89—CSKA	USSR	32	17	9	26	8	—	—	—	—	—
89-90—Red Army	USSR	46	14	11	25	22	—	—	—	—	—
90-91—Red Army	USSR	46	35	12	47	24	—	—	—	—	—
91-92—Vancouver	NHL	65	34	26	60	30	13	6	4	10	14
NHL totals		65	34	26	60	30	13	6	4	10	14

BURE, VALERI
LW, CANADIENS

PERSONAL: Born June 13, 1974, at Moscow, U.S.S.R. . . . 5-10/160. . . . Shoots right. . . . Brother of Pavel Bure, right winger/left winger, Vancouver Canucks.
TRANSACTIONS/CAREER NOTES: Selected by Montreal Canadiens in second round (second Canadiens pick, 33rd overall) of NHL entry draft (June 20, 1992).

Season Team	League	REGULAR SEASON					PLAYOFFS				
		Gms.	G	A	Pts.	Pen.	Gms.	G	A	Pts.	Pen.
90-91—CSKA Moscow	USSR	3	0	0	0	0	—	—	—	—	—
91-92—Spokane Chiefs	WHL	53	27	22	49	78	10	11	6	17	10

BUREAU, MARC
C, NORTH STARS

PERSONAL: Born May 17, 1966, at Trois-Rivieres, Que. . . . 6-1/190. . . . Shoots right.
TRANSACTIONS/CAREER NOTES: Traded by Chicoutimi Sagueneens with C Stephane Roy, Lee Duhemee, Sylvain Demers and D Rene L'Ecuyer to Granby Bisons for LW Greg Choules and C Stephane Richer (January 1985). . . . Signed as free agent by Calgary Flames (May 16, 1987). . . . Suffered eye contusion (March 25, 1990); missed final two weeks of season. . . . Traded by Flames to Minnesota North Stars for a third-round pick in 1991 draft (RW Sandy McCarthy) (March 5, 1991). . . . Injured shoulder (January 13, 1992); missed four games. . . . Separated shoulder (February 15, 1992); missed five games. . . . Separated shoulder (March 1, 1992); missed eight games.
HONORS: Named to IHL All-Star second team (1990-91).

Season Team	League	REGULAR SEASON					PLAYOFFS				
		Gms.	G	A	Pts.	Pen.	Gms.	G	A	Pts.	Pen.
83-84—Chicoutimi	QMJHL	56	6	16	22	14	—	—	—	—	—
84-85—Granby	QMJHL	68	50	70	120	29	—	—	—	—	—
85-86—Chicoutimi	QMJHL	63	36	62	98	69	9	3	7	10	10
86-87—Longueuil	QMJHL	66	54	58	112	68	20	17	20	37	12
87-88—Salt Lake City	IHL	69	7	20	27	86	7	0	3	3	8
88-89—Salt Lake City	IHL	76	28	36	64	119	14	7	5	12	31
89-90—Salt Lake City	IHL	67	43	48	91	173	11	4	8	12	0
—Calgary	NHL	5	0	0	0	4	—	—	—	—	—
90-91—Calgary	NHL	5	0	0	0	2	—	—	—	—	—
—Salt Lake City	IHL	54	40	48	88	101	—	—	—	—	—
—Minnesota	NHL	9	0	6	6	4	23	3	2	5	20
91-92—Minnesota	NHL	46	6	4	10	50	5	0	0	0	14
—Kalamazoo	IHL	7	2	8	10	2	—	—	—	—	—
NHL totals		65	6	10	16	60	28	3	2	5	34

BURKE, DAVID
D, MAPLE LEAFS

PERSONAL: Born October 15, 1970, at Detroit. . . . 6-1/185. . . . Shoots left. . . . Full name: David Andrew Burke.
COLLEGE: Cornell.
TRANSACTIONS/CAREER NOTES: Selected by Toronto Maple Leafs in sixth round (sixth Maple Leafs pick, 108th overall) of NHL entry draft (June 17, 1989).

Season Team	League	REGULAR SEASON					PLAYOFFS				
		Gms.	G	A	Pts.	Pen.	Gms.	G	A	Pts.	Pen.
86-87—Detroit Compuware	NAJHL	56	7	13	20	105	—	—	—	—	—
87-88—Detroit Compuware	NAJHL	61	4	34	38	94	—	—	—	—	—
88-89—Cornell University	ECAC	30	0	3	3	24	—	—	—	—	—
89-90—Cornell University	ECAC	29	0	12	12	28	—	—	—	—	—
90-91—Cornell University	ECAC	32	2	8	10	43	—	—	—	—	—
91-92—Cornell University	ECAC	29	5	9	14	30	—	—	—	—	—

BURKE, SEAN
G, DEVILS

PERSONAL: Born January 29, 1967, at Windsor, Ont. . . . 6-3/205. . . . Shoots left.
TRANSACTIONS/CAREER NOTES: Selected by New Jersey Devils as underage junior in second round (second Devils pick, 24th overall) of NHL entry draft (June 15, 1985). . . . Injured groin (December, 1988). . . . Underwent arthroscopic surgery to right knee (September 5, 1989).
MISCELLANEOUS: Member of 1992 silver medal-winning Canadian Olympic team.

Season Team	League	REGULAR SEASON								PLAYOFFS						
		Gms.	Min.	W	L	T	GA	SO	Avg.	Gms.	Min.	W	L	GA	SO	Avg.
83-84—St. Michael's H.S.	MTHL	25	1482				120	0	4.86	—	—	—	—	—	—	—
84-85—Toronto	OHL	49	2987	25	21	3	211	0	4.24	5	266	1	3	25	0	5.64
85-86—Toronto	OHL	47	2840	16	27	3	†233	0	4.92	4	238	0	4	24	0	6.05
—Team Canada	Int'l	5	284				22	0	4.65	—	—	—	—	—	—	—
86-87—Team Canada	Int'l	46	2670				138	0	3.10	—	—	—	—	—	—	—
87-88—Can. Olympic Team	Int'l	41	2200				104	1	2.84	—	—	—	—	—	—	—
—New Jersey	NHL	13	689	10	1	0	35	1	3.05	17	1001	9	8	*57	†1	3.42
88-89—New Jersey	NHL	62	3590	22	31	9	†230	3	3.84	—	—	—	—	—	—	—
89-90—New Jersey	NHL	52	2914	22	22	6	175	0	3.60	2	125	0	2	8	0	3.84
90-91—New Jersey	NHL	35	1870	8	12	8	112	0	3.59	—	—	—	—	—	—	—
91-92—Can. National Team	Int'l	31	1721	18	6	4	75	1	2.61	—	—	—	—	—	—	—
—Can. Olympic Team	Int'l	7	429	5	2	0	17	0	2.38	—	—	—	—	—	—	—
—San Diego	IHL	7	424	4	2	1	17	0	2.41	3	160	0	3	13	0	4.88
NHL totals		162	9063	62	66	23	552	4	3.65	19	1126	9	10	65	1	3.46

BURNS, TONY

D, RED WINGS

PERSONAL: Born September 18, 1971, at Duluth, Minn. . . . 6-0/195. . . . Shoots left. . . . Full name: Anthony Michael Burns.
HIGH SCHOOL: Denfeld (Duluth, Minn.).
COLLEGE: St. Cloud State (Minn.).
TRANSACTIONS/CAREER NOTES: Injured right knee (September 2, 1988). . . . Selected by Detroit Red Wings in fifth round (fourth Red Wings pick, 87th overall) of NHL entry draft (June 16, 1990).

Season Team	League	REGULAR SEASON					PLAYOFFS				
		Gms.	G	A	Pts.	Pen.	Gms.	G	A	Pts.	Pen.
88-89—Duluth Denfeld H.S.	Minn. H.S.	29	17	25	42		—	—	—	—	—
89-90—Duluth Denfeld H.S.	Minn. H.S.	25	21	23	44		—	—	—	—	—
90-91—St. Cloud State	WCHA	32	2	6	8	31	—	—	—	—	—
91-92—St. Cloud State	WCHA	5	0	1	1	6	—	—	—	—	—
—Toledo	ECHL	34	8	9	17	36	—	—	—	—	—

BURR, SHAWN

C/LW, RED WINGS

PERSONAL: Born July 1, 1966, at Sarnia, Ont. . . . 6-1/180. . . . Shoots left.
TRANSACTIONS/CAREER NOTES: Selected by Detroit Red Wings as underage junior in first round (first Red Wings Pick, seventh overall) of NHL entry draft (June 9, 1984). . . . Separated left shoulder (May 1988).
HONORS: Won Emms Family Award (1983-84). . . . Named to OHL All-Star second team (1985-86).

Season Team	League	REGULAR SEASON					PLAYOFFS				
		Gms.	G	A	Pts.	Pen.	Gms.	G	A	Pts.	Pen.
83-84—Kitchener	OHL	68	41	44	85	50	16	5	12	17	22
84-85—Kitchener	OHL	48	24	42	66	50	4	3	3	6	2
—Detroit	NHL	9	0	0	0	2	—	—	—	—	—
—Adirondack	AHL	4	0	0	0	2	—	—	—	—	—
85-86—Kitchener	OHL	59	60	67	127	83	5	2	3	5	8
—Adirondack	AHL	3	2	2	4	2	17	5	7	12	32
—Detroit	NHL	5	1	0	1	4	—	—	—	—	—
86-87—Detroit	NHL	80	22	25	47	107	16	7	2	9	20
87-88—Detroit	NHL	78	17	23	40	97	9	3	1	4	14
88-89—Detroit	NHL	79	19	27	46	78	6	1	2	3	6
89-90—Adirondack	AHL	3	4	2	6	2	—	—	—	—	—
—Detroit	NHL	76	24	32	56	82	—	—	—	—	—
90-91—Detroit	NHL	80	20	30	50	112	7	0	4	4	15
91-92—Detroit	NHL	79	19	32	51	118	11	1	5	6	10
NHL totals		486	122	169	291	600	49	12	14	26	65

BURRIDGE, RANDY

LW, CAPITALS

PERSONAL: Born January 7, 1966, at Fort Erie, Ont. . . . 5-9/180. . . . Shoots left. . . . Full name: Randy H. Burridge.
TRANSACTIONS/CAREER NOTES: Selected by Boston Bruins in eighth round (seventh Bruins pick, 157th overall) of NHL entry draft (June 15, 1985). . . . Strained groin (March 1, 1986). . . . Suspended by AHL during playoffs (April 1987). . . . Sprained medial collateral ligament in left knee (February 6, 1990); missed 18 games. . . . Tore right knee ligaments (February 7, 1991). . . . Underwent surgery to right knee (February 13, 1991). . . . Traded by Bruins to Washington Capitals for RW Stephen Leach (June 21, 1991). . . . Partially tore left knee ligament (March 1, 1992); missed 14 games.

Season Team	League	REGULAR SEASON					PLAYOFFS				
		Gms.	G	A	Pts.	Pen.	Gms.	G	A	Pts.	Pen.
82-83—Fort Erie Jr. B	OHA	42	32	56	88	32	—	—	—	—	—
83-84—Peterborough	OHL	55	6	7	13	44	8	3	2	5	7
84-85—Peterborough	OHL	66	49	57	106	88	17	9	16	25	18
85-86—Peterborough	OHL	17	15	11	26	23	3	1	3	4	2
—Boston	NHL	52	17	25	42	28	3	0	4	4	12
—Moncton	AHL	—	—	—	—	—	3	0	2	2	2
86-87—Moncton	AHL	47	26	41	67	139	3	1	2	3	30
—Boston	NHL	23	1	4	5	16	2	1	0	1	2
87-88—Boston	NHL	79	27	28	55	105	23	2	10	12	16

Season Team	League	REGULAR SEASON Gms.	G	A	Pts.	Pen.	PLAYOFFS Gms.	G	A	Pts.	Pen.
88-89—Boston	NHL	80	31	30	61	39	10	5	2	7	8
89-90—Boston	NHL	63	17	15	32	47	21	4	11	15	14
90-91—Boston	NHL	62	15	13	28	40	19	0	3	3	39
91-92—Washington	NHL	66	23	44	67	50	2	0	1	1	0
NHL totals		425	131	159	290	325	80	12	31	43	91

BURT, ADAM
D, WHALERS

PERSONAL: Born January 15, 1969, at Detroit. . . . 6-0/190. . . . Shoots left.
TRANSACTIONS/CAREER NOTES: Suffered broken jaw (December 1985). . . . Selected by Hartford Whalers as underage junior in second round (second Whalers pick, 39th overall) of NHL entry draft (June 13, 1987). . . . Separated left shoulder (September 13, 1988). . . . Bruised hip (December 1989). . . . Dislocated left shoulder (January 19, 1989). . . . Tore medial collateral ligaments in right knee (February 16, 1991); missed remainder of season. . . . Sprained left wrist (January 11, 1992); missed six games.
HONORS: Named to OHL All-Star second team (1987-88).

Season Team	League	REGULAR SEASON Gms.	G	A	Pts.	Pen.	PLAYOFFS Gms.	G	A	Pts.	Pen.
85-86—North Bay	OHL	49	0	11	11	81	10	0	0	0	24
86-87—North Bay	OHL	57	4	27	31	138	24	1	6	7	68
87-88—North Bay	OHL	66	17	54	71	176	2	0	0	0	0
—Binghamton	AHL	—	—	—	—	—	2	1	1	2	0
88-89—North Bay	OHL	23	4	11	15	45	12	2	12	14	12
—Team USA Juniors	Int'l	7	1	6	7	—	—	—	—	—	—
—Binghamton	AHL	5	0	2	2	13	—	—	—	—	—
—Hartford	NHL	5	0	0	0	6	—	—	—	—	—
89-90—Hartford	NHL	63	4	8	12	105	2	0	0	0	0
90-91—Springfield	AHL	9	1	3	4	22	—	—	—	—	—
—Hartford	NHL	42	2	7	9	63	—	—	—	—	—
91-92—Hartford	NHL	66	9	15	24	93	2	0	0	0	0
NHL totals		176	15	30	45	267	4	0	0	0	0

BUSKAS, ROD
D, BLACKHAWKS

PERSONAL: Born January 7, 1961, at Wetaskiwin, Alta. . . . 6-1/200. . . . Shoots right. . . . Full name: Rod Dale Buskas.
TRANSACTIONS/CAREER NOTES: Selected by Pittsburgh Penguins in sixth round (fifth Penguins pick, 112th overall) of NHL entry draft (June 10, 1981). . . . Injured shoulder (February 1985). . . . Injured shoulder (November 1986). . . . Traded by Penguins to Vancouver Canucks for a sixth-round pick in 1990 draft (D Ian Moran) (October 24, 1989). . . . Broke ankle (December 13, 1989); missed 29 games. . . . Traded by Canucks with RW Tony Tanti and C Barry Pederson to Penguins for C Dan Quinn, RW Andrew McBain and C Dave Capuano (January 8, 1990). . . . Selected by Los Angeles Kings in 1990 NHL waiver draft for $10,000 (October 1, 1990). . . . Strained chest muscle (December 20, 1990). . . . Injured foot (January 22, 1991). . . . Traded by Kings to Chicago Blackhawks for D Chris Norton (October 28, 1991). . . . Bruised left foot (February 22, 1992); missed 14 games.

Season Team	League	REGULAR SEASON Gms.	G	A	Pts.	Pen.	PLAYOFFS Gms.	G	A	Pts.	Pen.
78-79—Red Deer	AJHL	37	13	22	35	63	—	—	—	—	—
—Billings	WHL	1	0	0	0	0	—	—	—	—	—
—Medicine Hat	WHL	35	1	12	13	60	—	—	—	—	—
79-80—Medicine Hat	WHL	72	7	40	47	284	—	—	—	—	—
80-81—Medicine Hat	WHL	72	14	46	60	164	5	1	1	2	8
81-82—Erie	AHL	69	1	18	19	78	—	—	—	—	—
82-83—Muskegon	IHL	1	0	0	0	9	—	—	—	—	—
—Baltimore	AHL	31	2	8	10	45	—	—	—	—	—
—Pittsburgh	NHL	41	2	2	4	102	—	—	—	—	—
83-84—Baltimore	AHL	33	2	12	14	100	10	1	3	4	22
—Pittsburgh	NHL	47	2	4	6	60	—	—	—	—	—
84-85—Pittsburgh	NHL	69	2	7	9	191	—	—	—	—	—
85-86—Pittsburgh	NHL	72	2	7	9	159	—	—	—	—	—
86-87—Pittsburgh	NHL	68	3	15	18	123	—	—	—	—	—
87-88—Pittsburgh	NHL	76	4	8	12	206	—	—	—	—	—
88-89—Pittsburgh	NHL	52	1	5	6	105	10	0	0	0	23
89-90—Vancouver	NHL	17	0	3	3	36	—	—	—	—	—
—Pittsburgh	NHL	6	0	0	0	13	—	—	—	—	—
90-91—Los Angeles	NHL	57	3	8	11	182	2	0	2	2	22
91-92—Los Angeles	NHL	5	0	0	0	11	—	—	—	—	—
—Chicago	NHL	42	0	4	4	80	6	0	1	1	0
NHL totals		552	19	63	82	1268	18	0	3	3	45

BUTCHER, GARTH
D, BLUES

PERSONAL: Born January 8, 1963, at Regina, Sask. . . . 6-0/204. . . . Shoots right.
TRANSACTIONS/CAREER NOTES: Selected by Vancouver Canucks as underage junior in first round (first Canucks pick, 10th overall) of NHL entry draft (June 10, 1981). . . . Separated shoulder (October 1984). . . . Traded by Canucks with C Dan Quinn to St. Louis Blues for LW Geoff Courtnall, D Robert Dirk, C Cliff Ronning, LW Sergio Momesso and a future draft pick (March 5, 1991). . . . Fractured bone in left foot (March 7, 1992); missed final 12 games of season.
HONORS: Named to WHL All-Star first team (1980-81 and 1981-82).

B

Season Team	League	REGULAR SEASON					PLAYOFFS				
		Gms.	G	A	Pts.	Pen.	Gms.	G	A	Pts.	Pen.
79-80—Regina Tier II	SJHL	51	15	31	46	236	—	—	—	—	—
—Regina	WHL	13	0	4	4	20	9	0	0	0	45
80-81—Regina	WHL	69	9	77	86	230	11	5	17	22	60
81-82—Regina	WHL	65	24	68	92	318	19	3	17	20	95
—Vancouver	NHL	5	0	0	0	9	1	0	0	0	0
82-83—Kamloops	WHL	5	4	2	6	4	6	4	8	12	16
—Vancouver	NHL	55	1	13	14	104	3	1	0	1	2
83-84—Fredericton	AHL	25	4	13	17	43	6	0	2	2	19
—Vancouver	NHL	28	2	0	2	34	—	—	—	—	—
84-85—Vancouver	NHL	75	3	9	12	152	—	—	—	—	—
—Fredericton	AHL	3	1		1	11	—	—	—	—	—
85-86—Vancouver	NHL	70	4	7	11	188	3	0	0	0	0
86-87—Vancouver	NHL	70	5	15	20	207	—	—	—	—	—
87-88—Vancouver	NHL	80	6	17	23	285	—	—	—	—	—
88-89—Vancouver	NHL	78	0	20	20	227	7	1	1	2	22
89-90—Vancouver	NHL	80	6	14	20	205	—	—	—	—	—
90-91—Vancouver	NHL	69	6	12	18	257	—	—	—	—	—
—St. Louis	NHL	13	0	4	4	32	13	2	1	3	54
91-92—St. Louis	NHL	68	5	15	20	189	5	1	2	3	16
NHL totals		691	38	126	164	1889	32	5	4	9	94

BUTSAYEV, VYATCHESLAV
C, FLYERS

(June 16, 1990).

PERSONAL: Born June 13, 1970, at Tolyatti, U.S.S.R. . . . . 6-2/200. . . . Shoots left.
TRANSACTIONS/CAREER NOTES: Selected by Philadelphia Flyers in sixth round (10th Flyers pick, 109th overall) of NHL entry draft

Season Team	League	REGULAR SEASON					PLAYOFFS				
		Gms.	G	A	Pts.	Pen.	Gms.	G	A	Pts.	Pen.
89-90—Central Red Army	USSR	48	13	4	17	30	—	—	—	—	—
90-91—Central Red Army	USSR	46	14	9	23	32	—	—	—	—	—
91-92—Central Red Army	USSR	36	12	13	25	26	—	—	—	—	—

BYCE, JOHN
C, CAPITALS

PERSONAL: Born September 8, 1967, at Madison, Wis. . . . . 6-0/175. . . . Shoots right. . . . Full name: John Arthur Byce.
HIGH SCHOOL: Madison Memorial (Wis.).
COLLEGE: Wisconsin.
TRANSACTIONS/CAREER NOTES: Selected by Boston Bruins in 11th round (11th Bruins pick, 220th overall) of NHL entry draft (June 15, 1985). . . . Injured knee (November 18, 1988). . . . Dislocated left shoulder (September 22, 1990); missed first six games of season. . . . Broke bone in left foot (March 15, 1991). . . . Traded by Bruins with D Dennis Smith to Washington Capitals for LW Brent Hughes and a 12th-round pick in 1992 draft (February 24, 1992).
HONORS: Named to WCHA All-Star second team (1988-89 and 1989-90). . . . Named to NCAA All-Tournament team (1989-90).

Season Team	League	REGULAR SEASON					PLAYOFFS				
		Gms.	G	A	Pts.	Pen.	Gms.	G	A	Pts.	Pen.
84-85—Madison Memorial	Wisc. H.S.	24	39	47	86	32	—	—	—	—	—
85-86—					Did not play.						
86-87—University of Wisconsin	WCHA	40	1	4	5	12	—	—	—	—	—
87-88—University of Wisconsin	WCHA	41	22	12	34	18	—	—	—	—	—
88-89—University of Wisconsin	WCHA	42	27	28	55	16	—	—	—	—	—
89-90—University of Wisconsin	WCHA	46	27	44	71	20	—	—	—	—	—
—Boston	NHL	—	—	—	—	—	8	2	0	2	2
90-91—Maine	AHL	53	19	29	48	20	—	—	—	—	—
—Boston	NHL	18	1	3	4	6	—	—	—	—	—
91-92—Maine	AHL	55	29	21	50	41	—	—	—	—	—
—Boston	NHL	3	1	0	1	0	—	—	—	—	—
—Baltimore	AHL	20	9	5	14	4	—	—	—	—	—
NHL totals		21	2	3	5	6	8	2	0	2	2

BYERS, LYNDON
RW, BRUINS

PERSONAL: Born February 29, 1964, at Nipawin, Sask. . . . . 6-1/200. . . . Shoots right. . . . Full name: Lyndon Svi Byers.
TRANSACTIONS/CAREER NOTES: Traded by Saskatoon Blades to Regina Pats for LW Todd Strueby (September 10, 1981). . . . Broke right wrist (April 1981). . . . Selected by Boston Bruins as underage junior in second round (third Bruins pick, 39th overall) of NHL entry draft (June 9, 1982). . . . Tore ligaments in right knee (September 1987). . . . Separated left shoulder (November 1987). . . . Bruised right hand (March 1988). . . . Bruised left thigh (April 1988). . . . Dislocated jaw (September 1988). . . . Separated right shoulder (December 1988). . . . Suffered inflammation of left elbow (February 1989). . . . Separated right shoulder (March 22, 1989). . . . Injured left knee (September 29, 1989); missed first seven games of season. . . . Tore tendon in left thumb (December 9, 1989); missed 14 games. . . . Broke left foot (February 1990); missed 14 games. . . . Strained quadricep (October 16, 1990); missed five games. . . . Bruised lower back (November 17, 1990); missed three games. . . . Suspended 10 games by NHL for leaving bench to fight (December 13, 1990). . . . Fractured left foot (December 16, 1990). . . . Underwent surgery to repair fractured navicular bone in left foot (February 8, 1991). . . . Refractured left foot (March 25, 1991). . . . Injured groin (October 27, 1991); missed seven games.
HONORS: Named to SCMHL All-Star second team (1980-81).

Season Team	League	REGULAR SEASON					PLAYOFFS				
		Gms.	G	A	Pts.	Pen.	Gms.	G	A	Pts.	Pen.
80-81—Notre Dame	SCMHL	37	35	42	77	106	—	—	—	—	—
81-82—Regina	WHL	57	18	25	43	169	20	5	6	11	48
82-83—Regina	WHL	70	32	38	70	153	5	1	1	2	16
83-84—Regina	WHL	58	32	57	89	154	23	17	18	35	78
—Boston	NHL	10	2	4	6	32	—	—	—	—	—
84-85—Hershey	AHL	27	4	6	10	55	—	—	—	—	—
—Boston	NHL	33	3	8	11	41	—	—	—	—	—
85-86—Boston	NHL	5	0	2	2	9	—	—	—	—	—
—Moncton	AHL	14	2	4	6	26	—	—	—	—	—
—Milwaukee	IHL	8	0	2	2	22	—	—	—	—	—
86-87—Moncton	AHL	27	5	5	10	63	—	—	—	—	—
—Boston	NHL	18	2	3	5	53	1	0	0	0	0
87-88—Maine	AHL	2	0	1	1	18	—	—	—	—	—
—Boston	NHL	53	10	14	24	236	11	1	2	3	62
88-89—Maine	AHL	4	1	3	4	2	—	—	—	—	—
—Boston	NHL	49	0	4	4	218	2	0	0	0	0
89-90—Boston	NHL	43	4	4	8	159	17	1	0	1	12
90-91—Boston	NHL	19	2	2	4	82	1	0	0	0	10
91-92—Boston	NHL	31	1	1	2	129	5	0	0	0	12
—Maine	AHL	11	5	4	9	47	—	—	—	—	—
NHL totals		261	24	42	66	959	37	2	2	4	96

BC

BYLSMA, DANIEL
LW, JETS

PERSONAL: Born September 19, 1970, at Grand Rapids, Mich. . . . 6-2/205. . . . Shoots left. . . . Full name: Daniel Brian Bylsma.
COLLEGE: Bowling Green State.
TRANSACTIONS/CAREER NOTES: Selected by Winnipeg Jets in fourth round (sixth Jets pick, 69th overall) of NHL entry draft (June 17, 1989).

Season Team	League	REGULAR SEASON					PLAYOFFS				
		Gms.	G	A	Pts.	Pen.	Gms.	G	A	Pts.	Pen.
87-88—St. Mary's Jr. B	OHA	40	30	39	69	33	—	—	—	—	—
88-89—Bowling Green State	CCHA	39	4	7	11	16	—	—	—	—	—
89-90—Bowling Green State	CCHA	44	13	17	30	32	—	—	—	—	—
90-91—Bowling Green State	CCHA	40	9	12	21	48	—	—	—	—	—
91-92—Bowling Green State	CCHA	34	11	14	25	24	—	—	—	—	—

BYRAM, SHAWN
LW, BLACKHAWKS

PERSONAL: Born September 12, 1968, at Neepawa, Man. . . . 6-2/204. . . . Shoots left.
TRANSACTIONS/CAREER NOTES: Selected by New York Islanders as underage junior in fourth round (fourth Islanders pick, 80th overall) of NHL entry draft (June 21, 1986). . . . Signed as free agent by Chicago Blackhawks (August 2, 1991).

Season Team	League	REGULAR SEASON					PLAYOFFS				
		Gms.	G	A	Pts.	Pen.	Gms.	G	A	Pts.	Pen.
85-86—Regina	WHL	46	7	6	13	45	9	0	1	1	11
86-87—Prince Albert	WHL	67	19	21	40	147	7	1	1	2	10
87-88—Prince Albert	WHL	61	23	28	51	178	10	5	2	7	27
88-89—Springfield	AHL	45	5	11	16	195	—	—	—	—	—
—Indianapolis	IHL	1	0	0	0	2	—	—	—	—	—
89-90—Springfield	AHL	31	4	4	8	30	—	—	—	—	—
—Johnstown	ECHL	8	5	5	10	35	—	—	—	—	—
90-91—Capital District	AHL	62	28	35	63	162	—	—	—	—	—
—New York Islanders	NHL	4	0	0	0	14	—	—	—	—	—
91-92—Indianapolis	IHL	69	18	21	39	154	—	—	—	—	—
—Chicago	NHL	1	0	0	0	0	—	—	—	—	—
NHL totals		5	0	0	0	14					

CAIRNS, ERIC
D, RANGERS

PERSONAL: Born June 27, 1974, at Oakville, Ont. . . . 6-6/217. . . . Shoots left.
TRANSACTIONS/CAREER NOTES: Selected by New York Rangers in third round (third Rangers pick, 72nd overall) of NHL entry draft (June 20, 1992).

Season Team	League	REGULAR SEASON					PLAYOFFS				
		Gms.	G	A	Pts.	Pen.	Gms.	G	A	Pts.	Pen.
90-91—Burlington Jr. B	OHA	37	5	16	21	120	—	—	—	—	—
91-92—Detroit	OHL	64	1	11	12	237	7	0	0	0	31

CALLANDER, JOCK
RW, LIGHTNING

PERSONAL: Born April 23, 1961, at Regina, Sask. . . . 6-1/188. . . . Shoots right. . . . Full name: John Callander. . . . Brother of Drew Callander, center, Philadelphia Flyers and Vancouver Canucks (1976-77 through 1979-80).
TRANSACTIONS/CAREER NOTES: Signed as free agent by St. Louis Blues (September 28, 1981). . . . Signed as free agent by Pittsburgh Penguins (July 31, 1987). . . . Knee surgery (October 1990). . . . Tore knee ligaments (January 19, 1991). . . . Signed as free agent by Tampa Bay Lightning (July 29, 1992).
HONORS: Won Bob Brownridge Memorial Trophy (1981-82). . . . Named Turner Cup Playoff Most Valuable Player (1985-86). . . . Shared James Gatschene Memorial Trophy with Jeff Pyle (1986-87). . . . Shared Leo P. Lamoureux Memorial Trophy with Jeff Pyle (1986-87). . . . Named to IHL All-Star first team (1986-87 and 1991-92).

Season	Team	League	Gms.	G	A	Pts.	Pen.	Gms.	G	A	Pts.	Pen.
			REGULAR SEASON					**PLAYOFFS**				
78-79	—Regina	WHL	19	3	2	5	0	—	—	—	—	—
	—Regina Blues	SJHL	42	44	42	86	24	—	—	—	—	—
79-80	—Regina	WHL	39	9	11	20	25	18	8	5	13	0
80-81	—Regina	WHL	72	67	86	153	37	11	6	7	13	14
81-82	—Regina	WHL	71	79	111	*190	59	20	13	*26	39	37
82-83	—Salt Lake City	IHL	68	20	27	47	26	6	0	1	1	9
83-84	—Montana	CHL	72	27	32	59	69	—	—	—	—	—
	—Toledo	IHL	2	0	0	0	0	—	—	—	—	—
84-85	—Muskegon	IHL	82	39	68	107	86	17	8	13	21	33
85-86	—Muskegon	IHL	82	39	72	111	121	14	*12	11	*23	12
86-87	—Muskegon	IHL	82	54	82	†136	110	15	13	7	20	23
87-88	—Muskegon	IHL	31	20	36	56	49	6	2	3	5	25
	—Pittsburgh	NHL	41	11	16	27	45	—	—	—	—	—
88-89	—Muskegon	IHL	48	25	39	64	40	7	5	5	10	30
	—Pittsburgh	NHL	30	6	5	11	20	10	2	5	7	10
89-90	—Muskegon	IHL	46	29	49	78	118	15	6	†14	20	54
	—Pittsburgh	NHL	30	4	7	11	49	—	—	—	—	—
90-91	—Muskegon	IHL	30	14	20	34	102	—	—	—	—	—
91-92	—Muskegon	IHL	81	42	70	112	160	10	4	10	14	13
	—Pittsburgh	NHL	—	—	—	—	—	12	1	3	4	2
	NHL totals		101	21	28	49	114	22	3	8	11	12

CALOUN, JAN
RW, SHARKS

PERSONAL: Born December 20, 1972, at Usti-nad-Labem, Czechoslovakia. . . . 5-10/176. . . . Shoots right.

TRANSACTIONS/CAREER NOTES: Selected by San Jose Sharks in fourth round (fourth Sharks pick, 75th overall) of NHL entry draft (June 20, 1992).

Season	Team	League	Gms.	G	A	Pts.	Pen.	Gms.	G	A	Pts.	Pen.
			REGULAR SEASON					**PLAYOFFS**				
90-91	—CHZ Litvinov	Czech.	50	28	19	47	12	—	—	—	—	—
91-92	—Chemopetrol Litvinov	Czech.	46	39	13	52		—	—	—	—	—

CAMPBELL, JAMES
C, CANADIENS

PERSONAL: Born February 3, 1973, at Worcester, Mass. . . . 6-1/175. . . . Shoots right.

HIGH SCHOOL: Lawrence Academy (Groton, Mass.), then Northwood School (Lake Placid, N.Y.).

TRANSACTIONS/CAREER NOTES: Selected by Montreal Canadiens in second round (second Canadiens pick, 28th overall) of NHL entry draft (June 22, 1991).

Season	Team	League	Gms.	G	A	Pts.	Pen.	Gms.	G	A	Pts.	Pen.
			REGULAR SEASON					**PLAYOFFS**				
88-89	—Lawrence Academy	Mass. H.S.	12	12	8	20	6	—	—	—	—	—
89-90	—Lawrence Academy	Mass. H.S.	8	14	7	21	8	—	—	—	—	—
90-91	—Northwood School	N.Y. H.S.	26	36	47	83	36	—	—	—	—	—
91-92	—Hull	QMJHL	64	41	44	85	51	6	7	3	10	8

CAPUANO, JACK
D, BRUINS

PERSONAL: Born July 7, 1966, at Cranston, R.I. . . . 6-2/210. . . . Shoots left. . . . Full name: Jack Capuano Jr. . . . Brother of Dave Capuano, center/right winger, Vancouver Canucks.

HIGH SCHOOL: Kent (Conn.).

COLLEGE: Maine.

TRANSACTIONS/CAREER NOTES: Selected by Toronto Maple Leafs in fifth round (fourth Maple Leafs pick, 88th overall) of NHL entry draft (June 9, 1984). . . . Traded by Maple Leafs with LW Paul Gagne and RW Derek Laxdal to New York Islanders for C Gilles Thibaudeau and C Mike Stevens (December 20, 1989). . . . Traded by Islanders to Vancouver Canucks for LW Jeff Rohlicek (March 6, 1990).

HONORS: Named to Hockey East All-Star second team (1986-87). . . . Named to NCAA All-America East first team (1987-88). . . . Named to Hockey East All-Star first team (1987-88). . . . Named to IHL All-Star second team (1990-91).

Season	Team	League	Gms.	G	A	Pts.	Pen.	Gms.	G	A	Pts.	Pen.
			REGULAR SEASON					**PLAYOFFS**				
83-84	—Kent	Conn. H.S.		10	8	18		—	—	—	—	—
84-85	—University of Maine	Hockey East				Statistics unavailable.						
85-86	—University of Maine	Hockey East	39	9	13	22	59	—	—	—	—	—
86-87	—University of Maine	Hockey East	42	10	34	44	20	—	—	—	—	—
87-88	—University of Maine	Hockey East	43	13	37	50	87	—	—	—	—	—
88-89	—Newmarket	AHL	74	5	16	21	52	1	0	0	0	0
89-90	—Toronto	NHL	1	0	0	0	0	—	—	—	—	—
	—Newmarket	AHL	8	0	2	2	7	—	—	—	—	—
	—Springfield	AHL	14	0	4	4	8	—	—	—	—	—
	—Milwaukee	IHL	17	3	10	13	60	6	0	1	1	12
90-91	—Milwaukee	IHL	80	20	30	50	76	6	0	1	1	2
	—Vancouver	NHL	3	0	0	0	0	—	—	—	—	—
91-92	—Maine	AHL	74	14	26	40	35	—	—	—	—	—
	—Boston	NHL	2	0	0	0	0	—	—	—	—	—
	NHL totals		6	0	0	0	0					

CARBONNEAU, GUY
C, CANADIENS

PERSONAL: Born March 18, 1960, at Sept Iles, Que... 5-11/184.... Shoots right.
TRANSACTIONS/CAREER NOTES: Selected by Montreal Canadiens as underage junior in third round (fourth Canadiens pick, 44th overall) of NHL entry draft (August 9, 1979).... Strained right knee ligaments (October 7, 1989); missed nine games.... Broke nose (October 28, 1989).... Suffered concussion (October 8, 1990).... Fractured rib (January 13, 1992); missed six games.... Injured elbow (March 2, 1992); missed one game.
HONORS: Named to QMJHL All-Star second team (1979-80).... Won Frank J. Selke Trophy (1987-88, 1988-89 and 1991-92).

Season Team	League	REGULAR SEASON Gms.	G	A	Pts.	Pen.	PLAYOFFS Gms.	G	A	Pts.	Pen.
76-77—Chicoutimi	QMJHL	59	9	20	29	8	4	1	0	1	0
77-78—Chicoutimi	QMJHL	70	28	55	83	60	—	—	—	—	—
78-79—Chicoutimi	QMJHL	72	62	79	141	47	4	2	1	3	4
79-80—Chicoutimi	QMJHL	72	72	110	182	66	12	9	15	24	28
—Nova Scotia	AHL	—	—	—	—	—	2	1	1	2	2
80-81—Montreal	NHL	2	0	1	1	0	—	—	—	—	—
—Nova Scotia	AHL	78	35	53	88	87	6	1	3	4	9
81-82—Nova Scotia	AHL	77	27	67	94	124	9	2	7	9	8
82-83—Montreal	NHL	77	18	29	47	68	3	0	0	0	2
83-84—Montreal	NHL	78	24	30	54	75	15	4	3	7	12
84-85—Montreal	NHL	79	23	34	57	43	12	4	3	7	8
85-86—Montreal	NHL	80	20	36	56	57	20	7	5	12	35
86-87—Montreal	NHL	79	18	27	45	68	17	3	8	11	20
87-88—Montreal	NHL	80	17	21	38	61	11	0	4	4	2
88-89—Montreal	NHL	79	26	30	56	44	21	4	5	9	10
89-90—Montreal	NHL	68	19	36	55	37	11	2	3	5	6
90-91—Montreal	NHL	78	20	24	44	63	13	1	5	6	10
91-92—Montreal	NHL	72	18	21	39	39	11	1	1	2	6
NHL totals		772	203	289	492	555	134	26	37	63	111

CAREY, JIM
G, CAPITALS

PERSONAL: Born May 31, 1974, at Dorchester, Mass.... 6-2/190.... Shoots left.
HIGH SCHOOL: Catholic Memorial (Boston).
TRANSACTIONS/CAREER NOTES: Selected by Washington Capitals in second round (second Capitals pick, 32nd overall) of NHL entry draft (June 20, 1992).

Season Team	League	REGULAR SEASON Gms.	Min.	W	L	T	GA	SO	Avg.	PLAYOFFS Gms.	Min.	W	L	GA	SO	Avg.
89-90—Catholic Memorial H.S..	Mass. HS	12		12	0	0				—	—	—	—	—	—	—
90-91—Catholic Memorial H.S..	Mass. HS	14		13	0	0		6		—	—	—	—	—	—	—
91-92—Catholic Memorial H.S..	Mass. HS	21	1108	19	2	0	29	6	1.57	—	—	—	—	—	—	—

CARKNER, TERRY
D, FLYERS

PERSONAL: Born March 7, 1966, at Smith Falls, Ont.... 6-3/212.... Shoots left.
TRANSACTIONS/CAREER NOTES: Selected by New York Rangers as underage junior in first round (first Rangers pick, 14th overall) of NHL entry draft (June 9, 1984).... Traded by Rangers with LW Jeff Jackson to Quebec Nordiques for LW John Ogrodnick and D David Shaw (September 1987).... Suspended 10 games by NHL for leaving the bench during fight (January 24, 1988).... Traded by Nordiques to Philadelphia Flyers for D Greg Smyth and third-round pick in 1989 draft (G John Tanner) (July 1988).... Underwent surgery to left knee (September 23, 1989); missed 15 games.... Bruised ankle (March 1990).... Bruised foot (November 23, 1991); missed two games.
HONORS: Named to OHL All-Star second team (1984-85).... Shared Max Kaminsky Trophy with Jeff Brown (1985-86).... Named to OHL All-Star first team (1985-86).

Season Team	League	REGULAR SEASON Gms.	G	A	Pts.	Pen.	PLAYOFFS Gms.	G	A	Pts.	Pen.
82-83—Brockville	COJHL	47	8	32	40	94	—	—	—	—	—
83-84—Peterborough	OHL	66	4	21	25	91	8	0	6	6	13
84-85—Peterborough	OHL	64	14	47	61	125	17	2	10	12	11
85-86—Peterborough	OHL	54	12	32	44	106	16	1	7	8	17
86-87—New Haven	AHL	12	2	6	8	56	3	1	0	1	0
—New York Rangers	NHL	52	2	13	15	120	1	0	0	0	0
87-88—Quebec	NHL	63	3	24	27	159	—	—	—	—	—
88-89—Philadelphia	NHL	78	11	32	43	149	19	1	5	6	28
89-90—Philadelphia	NHL	63	4	18	22	167	—	—	—	—	—
90-91—Philadelphia	NHL	79	7	25	32	204	—	—	—	—	—
91-92—Philadelphia	NHL	73	4	12	16	195	—	—	—	—	—
NHL totals		408	31	124	155	994	20	1	5	6	28

CARLYLE, RANDY
D, JETS

PERSONAL: Born April 19, 1956, at Sudbury, Ont.... 5-10/200.... Shoots left.... Full name: Randolph Robert Carlyle.
TRANSACTIONS/CAREER NOTES: Selected by Toronto Maple Leafs from Sudbury Wolves in second round (first Maple Leafs pick, 30th overall) of NHL entry draft (June 1, 1976).
... Broke ankle; missed parts of 1978-79 season.... Traded by Maple Leafs with C George Ferguson to Pittsburgh Penguins for D Dave Burrows (June 1978).... Injured back (October 1982).... Injured knee (January 1983).... Injured knee (March 1984).... Traded by Penguins to Winnipeg Jets for first-round pick in 1984 draft (D Doug Bodger) and player to be named after the 1983-84 season (D Moe Mantha) (March 1984).... Injured thigh (November 12, 1985); missed eight games.... Suffered whiplash (November 1986); missed nine games.... Strained neck muscles (January 18, 1989).... Bruised left knee

C

(November 5, 1989); missed nine games. . . . Missed 10 games due to death of parents (December 1989). . . . Tore ligaments in right knee (March 15, 1990). . . . Strained groin and bruised thigh (November 11, 1990); missed five games. . . . Strained triceps (February 20, 1991); missed seven games. . . . Bruised ribs (October 29, 1991); missed three games. . . . Strained abdomen (December 14, 1991); missed six games. . . . Suffered ankle contusion (January 4, 1992); missed two games.
HONORS: Named to OHA Major Junior A All-Star second team (1975-76). . . . Won James Norris Memorial Trophy (1980-81). . . . Named to NHL All-Star first team (1980-81).
MISCELLANEOUS: Does not wear a helmet.

Season Team	League	Gms.	G	A	Pts.	Pen.	Gms.	G	A	Pts.	Pen.
				REGULAR SEASON					PLAYOFFS		
73-74—Sudbury	OHA Mj. Jr. A	12	0	8	8	21	—	—	—	—	—
74-75—Sudbury	OHA Mj. Jr. A	67	17	47	64	118	15	3	6	9	21
75-76—Sudbury	OHA Mj. Jr. A	60	15	64	79	126	17	6	13	19	50
76-77—Dallas	CHL	26	2	7	9	63	—	—	—	—	—
—Toronto	NHL	45	0	5	5	51	9	0	1	1	20
77-78—Dallas	CHL	21	3	14	17	31	—	—	—	—	—
—Toronto	NHL	49	2	11	13	31	7	0	1	1	8
78-79—Pittsburgh	NHL	70	13	34	47	78	7	0	0	0	12
79-80—Pittsburgh	NHL	67	8	28	36	45	5	1	0	1	4
80-81—Pittsburgh	NHL	76	16	67	83	136	5	4	5	9	9
81-82—Pittsburgh	NHL	73	11	64	75	131	5	1	3	4	16
82-83—Pittsburgh	NHL	61	15	41	56	110	—	—	—	—	—
83-84—Pittsburgh	NHL	50	3	23	26	82	—	—	—	—	—
—Winnipeg	NHL	5	0	3	3	2	3	0	2	2	4
84-85—Winnipeg	NHL	71	13	38	51	98	8	1	5	6	13
85-86—Winnipeg	NHL	68	16	33	49	93	—	—	—	—	—
86-87—Winnipeg	NHL	71	16	26	42	93	10	1	5	6	18
87-88—Winnipeg	NHL	78	15	44	59	210	5	0	2	2	10
88-89—Winnipeg	NHL	78	6	38	44	78	—	—	—	—	—
89-90—Winnipeg	NHL	53	3	15	18	50	—	—	—	—	—
90-91—Winnipeg	NHL	52	9	19	28	44	—	—	—	—	—
91-92—Winnipeg	NHL	66	1	9	10	54	5	1	0	1	6
NHL totals		1033	147	498	645	1386	69	9	24	33	120

CARNBACK, PATRIK
LW, CANADIENS

PERSONAL: Born February 1, 1968, at Goteborg, Sweden. . . . 6-0/ 189. . . . Shoots left.
TRANSACTIONS/CAREER NOTES: Selected by Montreal Canadiens in sixth round (seventh Canadiens pick, 125th overall) of NHL entry draft (June 11, 1988).

Season Team	League	Gms.	G	A	Pts.	Pen.	Gms.	G	A	Pts.	Pen.
				REGULAR SEASON					PLAYOFFS		
86-87—Vastra Frolunda	Sweden	28	3	1	4	4	—	—	—	—	—
87-88—Vastra Frolunda	Sweden	33	16	19	35	10	—	—	—	—	—
88-89—Vastra Frolunda	Sweden	53	39	36	75	52	—	—	—	—	—
89-90—Vastra Frolunda	Sweden	40	26	27	53	34	—	—	—	—	—
90-91—Vastra Frolunda	Sweden	22	10	9	19	46	—	—	—	—	—
91-92—Vastra Frolunda	Sweden	33	17	24	41	32	—	—	—	—	—

CARNEY, KEITH
D, SABRES

PERSONAL: Born February 3, 1970, at Pawtucket, R.I. . . . 6-2/205. . . . Shoots left. . . . Full name: Keith Edward Carney.
COLLEGE: Maine.
TRANSACTIONS/CAREER NOTES: Selected by Buffalo Sabres in fourth round (third Sabres pick, 76th overall) of NHL entry draft (June 11, 1988).
HONORS: Named to Hockey East All-Rookie team (1988-89). . . . Named to NCAA All-America East second team (1989-90). . . . Named to Hockey East All-Star second team (1989-90). . . . Named to NCAA All-America East first team (1990-91). . . . Named to Hockey East All-Star first team (1990-91).

Season Team	League	Gms.	G	A	Pts.	Pen.	Gms.	G	A	Pts.	Pen.
				REGULAR SEASON					PLAYOFFS		
88-89—University of Maine	Hockey East	40	4	22	26	24	—	—	—	—	—
89-90—University of Maine	Hockey East	41	3	41	44	43	—	—	—	—	—
90-91—University of Maine	Hockey East	40	7	49	56	38	—	—	—	—	—
91-92—Rochester	AHL	24	1	10	11	2	2	0	2	2	0
—Buffalo	NHL	14	1	2	3	18	7	0	3	3	0
NHL totals		14	1	2	3	18	7	0	3	3	0

CARPENTER, BOBBY
LW, CAPITALS

PERSONAL: Born July 13, 1963, at Beverly, Mass. . . . 6-0/ 190. . . . Shoots left. . . . Full name: Robert Carpenter.
HIGH SCHOOL: St. John's Prep (Danvers, Mass.).
TRANSACTIONS/CAREER NOTES: Selected by Washington Capitals as underage junior in first round (first Capitals pick, third overall) of NHL entry draft (June 10, 1981). . . . Traded by Capitals with second-round pick in 1989 draft (RW Jason Prosofsky) to New York Rangers for C Mike Ridley, C Kelly Miller and RW Bobby Crawford (January 1, 1987). . . . Traded by Rangers with D Tom Laidlaw to Los Angeles Kings for C Marcel Dionne, C Jeff Crossman and a third-round pick in 1989 draft (March 10, 1987). . . . Tore rotator cuff (January 1988). . . . Broke right thumb and wrist (December 31, 1988). . . . Traded by Kings to Boston Bruins for C Steve Kasper and LW Jay Miller (January 23, 1989). . . . Tore ligaments of right wrist (April 1989). . . . Injured left knee (October 1990). . . . Suffered multiple fracture of left kneecap (De-

cember 8, 1990); missed remainder of season.... Injured left wrist and suffered stiffness in knee (April 5, 1991).... Strained calf (March 19, 1992).... Signed as free agent by Capitals (June 30, 1992).

Season Team	League	REGULAR SEASON					PLAYOFFS				
		Gms.	G	A	Pts.	Pen.	Gms.	G	A	Pts.	Pen.
79-80—St. John's Prep School	Mass. H.S.		28	37	65		—	—	—	—	—
80-81—St. John's Prep School	Mass. H.S.		14	24	38		—	—	—	—	—
81-82—Washington	NHL	80	32	35	67	69	—	—	—	—	—
82-83—Washington	NHL	80	32	37	69	64	4	1	0	1	2
83-84—Washington	NHL	80	28	40	68	51	8	2	1	3	25
84-85—Washington	NHL	80	53	42	95	87	5	1	4	5	8
85-86—Washington	NHL	80	27	29	56	105	9	5	4	9	12
86-87—Washington	NHL	22	5	7	12	21	—	—	—	—	—
—New York Rangers	NHL	28	2	8	10	20	—	—	—	—	—
—Los Angeles	NHL	10	2	3	5	6	5	1	2	3	2
87-88—Los Angeles	NHL	71	19	33	52	84	5	1	1	2	0
88-89—Los Angeles	NHL	39	11	15	26	16	—	—	—	—	—
—Boston	NHL	18	5	9	14	10	8	1	1	2	4
89-90—Boston	NHL	80	25	31	56	97	21	4	6	10	39
90-91—Boston	NHL	29	8	8	16	22	1	0	1	1	2
91-92—Boston	NHL	60	25	23	48	46	8	0	1	1	6
NHL totals		767	274	320	594	698	74	16	21	37	100

CARSON, JIMMY
C, RED WINGS

PERSONAL: Born July 20, 1968, at Southfield, Mich.... 6-1/200.... Shoots right.... Full name: James Carson.
TRANSACTIONS/CAREER NOTES: Selected by Los Angeles Kings as underage junior in first round (first Kings pick, second overall) of NHL entry draft (June 21, 1986).... Traded by Kings with LW Martin Gelinas and first-round picks in 1989 (traded to New Jersey), 1991 (LW Martin Rucinsky) and 1993 drafts, and cash to Edmonton Oilers for C Wayne Gretzky, RW/D Marty McSorley and LW/C Mike Krushelnyski (August 9, 1988).... Bruised right knee (September 27, 1989).... Traded by Oilers with C Kevin McClelland and a fifth-round pick in 1991 draft to Detroit Red Wings for C/RW Joe Murphy, C/LW Adam Graves, LW Petr Klima and D Jeff Sharples (November 2, 1989).... Injured right knee ligaments (February 3, 1990); missed 14 games.... Suffered from tonsillitis and mononucleosis (March 1990).... Suffered sore left shoulder (November 1990).... Strained right knee (January 11, 1991); missed 15 games. ... Underwent surgery to left shoulder ligaments (April 25, 1991).
HONORS: Won Frank J. Selke Trophy (1985-86).... Won Michael Bossy Trophy (1985-86).... Named to QMJHL All-Star second team (1985-86).... Named to NHL All-Rookie team (1986-87).

Season Team	League	REGULAR SEASON					PLAYOFFS				
		Gms.	G	A	Pts.	Pen.	Gms.	G	A	Pts.	Pen.
84-85—Verdun	QMJHL	68	44	72	116	16	—	—	—	—	—
85-86—Verdun	QMJHL	69	70	83	153	46	5	2	6	8	0
86-87—Los Angeles	NHL	80	37	42	79	22	5	1	2	3	6
87-88—Los Angeles	NHL	80	55	52	107	45	5	5	3	8	4
88-89—Edmonton	NHL	80	49	51	100	36	7	2	1	3	6
89-90—Edmonton	NHL	4	1	2	3	0	—	—	—	—	—
—Detroit	NHL	44	20	16	36	8	—	—	—	—	—
90-91—Detroit	NHL	64	21	25	46	28	7	2	1	3	4
91-92—Detroit	NHL	80	34	35	69	30	11	2	3	5	0
NHL totals		432	217	223	440	169	35	12	10	22	20

CARTER, JOHN
LW, SHARKS

PERSONAL: Born May 3, 1963, at Winchester, Mass.... 5-10/181.... Shoots left.
COLLEGE: Rensselaer Polytechnic Institute (N.Y.).
TRANSACTIONS/CAREER NOTES: Sprained knee (February 1986).... Signed as free agent by Boston Bruins (March 1986).... Bruised knee (March 1987).... Bruised knee (February 1988).... Suffered from the flu (October 31, 1990); missed two weeks.... Suffered concussion (December 1, 1990).... Signed as free agent by San Jose Sharks (August 22, 1991).
HONORS: Named to ECAC All-Star second team (1983-84).... Named to NCAA All-America East second team (1984-85).... Named to ECAC All-Star first team (1984-85).

Season Team	League	REGULAR SEASON					PLAYOFFS				
		Gms.	G	A	Pts.	Pen.	Gms.	G	A	Pts.	Pen.
82-83—R.P.I.	ECAC	29	16	22	38	33	—	—	—	—	—
83-84—R.P.I.	ECAC	38	35	39	74	52	—	—	—	—	—
84-85—R.P.I.	ECAC	37	43	29	72	52	—	—	—	—	—
85-86—R.P.I.	ECAC	27	23	18	41	68	—	—	—	—	—
—Boston	NHL	3	0	0	0	0	—	—	—	—	—
86-87—Moncton	AHL	58	25	30	55	60	6	2	3	5	5
—Boston	NHL	8	0	1	1	0	—	—	—	—	—
87-88—Boston	NHL	4	0	1	1	2	—	—	—	—	—
—Maine	AHL	76	38	38	76	145	10	4	4	8	44
88-89—Maine	AHL	24	13	6	19	12	—	—	—	—	—
—Boston	NHL	44	12	10	22	24	10	1	2	3	6
89-90—Maine	AHL	2	2	2	4	2	—	—	—	—	—
—Boston	NHL	76	17	22	39	26	21	6	3	9	45
90-91—Boston	NHL	50	4	7	11	68	—	—	—	—	—
—Maine	AHL	16	5	9	14	16	1	0	0	0	10
91-92—Kansas City	IHL	42	11	15	26	116	15	6	9	15	18
—San Jose	NHL	4	0	0	0	0	—	—	—	—	—
NHL totals		189	33	41	74	120	31	7	5	12	51

CARUSO, BRIAN
LW, FLAMES

PERSONAL: Born September 10, 1972, at Thunder Bay, Ont. . . . 6-2/225. . . . Shoots left. . . . Full name: Brian Anthony Caruso.
COLLEGE: Minnesota-Duluth.
TRANSACTIONS/CAREER NOTES: Selected by Calgary Flames in third round (fourth Flames pick, 63rd overall) of NHL entry draft (June 22, 1991).

		REGULAR SEASON					PLAYOFFS				
Season Team	League	Gms.	G	A	Pts.	Pen.	Gms.	G	A	Pts.	Pen.
88-89—Thunder Bay Flyers	USHL	68	12	26	38	58	—	—	—	—	—
89-90—Thunder Bay Flyers	USHL	56	30	46	76	78	—	—	—	—	—
90-91—Minnesota-Duluth	WCHA	31	5	6	11	24	—	—	—	—	—
91-92—Minnesota-Duluth	WCHA	29	2	3	5	34	—	—	—	—	—

CASEY, JON
G, NORTH STARS

PERSONAL: Born August 29, 1962, at Grand Rapids, Minn. . . . 5-10/155. . . . Shoots left. . . . Full name: Jonathon J. Casey.
HIGH SCHOOL: Grand Rapids (Minn.).
COLLEGE: North Dakota.
TRANSACTIONS/CAREER NOTES: Signed as free agent by Minnesota North Stars (March 1984).
HONORS: Won Harry (Hap) Holmes Memorial Trophy (1984-85). . . . Won Baz Bastien Trophy (1984-85). . . . Named to AHL All-Star first team (1984-85).

		REGULAR SEASON							PLAYOFFS						
Season Team	League	Gms.	Min.	W	L	T	GA	SO	Avg.	Gms.	Min.	W	L	GA SO	Avg.
80-81—Univ. of North Dakota	WCHA	6	300	3	1	0	19	0	3.80	—	—	—	—	— —	—
81-82—Univ. of North Dakota	WCHA	18	1038	15	3	0	48	1	2.77	—	—	—	—	— —	—
82-83—Univ. of North Dakota	WCHA	17	1020	9	6	2	42	0	2.47	—	—	—	—	— —	—
83-84—Univ. of North Dakota	WCHA	37	2180	25	10	2	115	2	3.17	—	—	—	—	— —	—
—Minnesota	NHL	2	84	1	0	0	6	0	4.29	—	—	—	—	— —	—
84-85—Baltimore	AHL	46	2646	30	11	4	116	†4	*2.63	13	689	8	3	38 0	3.31
85-86—Springfield	AHL	9	464	4	3	1	30	0	3.88	—	—	—	—	— —	—
—Minnesota	NHL	26	1402	11	11	1	91	0	3.89	—	—	—	—	— —	—
86-87—Indianapolis	CHL	31	1794	14	15	0	133	0	4.45	—	—	—	—	— —	—
—Springfield	AHL	13	770	1	8	0	56	0	4.36	—	—	—	—	— —	—
87-88—Kalamazoo	IHL	42	2541	24	13	5	154	2	3.64	7	382	3	3	26 0	4.08
—Minnesota	NHL	14	663	1	7	4	41	0	3.71	—	—	—	—	— —	—
88-89—Minnesota	NHL	55	2961	18	17	12	151	1	3.06	—	—	—	—	— —	—
89-90—Minnesota	NHL	61	3407	*31	22	4	183	3	3.22	7	415	3	4	21 1	3.04
90-91—Minnesota	NHL	55	3185	21	20	11	158	2	2.98	*23	*1205	*14	7	*61 †1	3.04
91-92—Minnesota	NHL	52	2911	19	23	5	165	2	3.40	7	437	3	4	22 0	3.02
—Kalamazoo	IHL	4	250	2	1	1	11	0	2.64	—	—	—	—	— —	—
NHL totals		265	14613	102	100	37	795	9	3.26	37	2057	20	15	104 2	3.03

CASSELS, ANDREW
C, WHALERS

PERSONAL: Born July 23, 1969, at Mississauga, Ont. . . . 6-0/192. . . . Shoots left.
TRANSACTIONS/CAREER NOTES: Broke wrist (January 1986). . . . Selected by Montreal Canadiens as underage junior in first round (first Canadiens pick, 17th overall) of NHL entry draft (June 13, 1987). . . . Sprained left knee ligaments (September 1988). . . . Separated right shoulder (November 29, 1989); missed 10 games. . . . Traded by Canadiens to Hartford Whalers for second-round pick in 1992 draft (September 17, 1991).
HONORS: Won Emms Family Award (1986-87). . . . Won Red Tilson Trophy (1987-88). . . . Won Eddie Powers Memorial Trophy (1987-88). . . . Won William Hanley Trophy (1987-88). . . . Named to OHL All-Star first team (1987-88 and 1988-89).

		REGULAR SEASON					PLAYOFFS				
Season Team	League	Gms.	G	A	Pts.	Pen.	Gms.	G	A	Pts.	Pen.
85-86—Bramalea Jr. B	OHA	33	18	25	43	26	—	—	—	—	—
86-87—Ottawa	OHL	66	26	66	92	28	11	5	9	14	7
87-88—Ottawa	OHL	61	48	*103	*151	39	16	8	*24	†32	13
88-89—Ottawa	OHL	56	37	97	134	66	12	5	10	15	10
89-90—Sherbrooke	AHL	55	22	45	67	25	12	2	11	13	6
—Montreal	NHL	6	2	0	2	2	—	—	—	—	—
90-91—Montreal	NHL	54	6	19	25	20	8	0	2	2	2
91-92—Hartford	NHL	67	11	30	41	18	7	2	4	6	6
NHL totals		127	19	49	68	40	15	2	6	8	8

CAUFIELD, JAY
RW, PENGUINS

PERSONAL: Born July 17, 1965, at Philadelphia, Pa. . . . 6-4/235. . . . Shoots right.
COLLEGE: North Dakota.
TRANSACTIONS/CAREER NOTES: Signed as free agent by New York Rangers (October 1985). . . . Injured knee (October 1986). . . . Traded by Rangers with C Dave Gagner to Minnesota North Stars for D Jari Gronstrand and D Paul Boutilier (October 1987). . . . Selected by Pittsburgh Penguins in 1988 NHL waiver draft for $40,000 (October 3, 1988). . . . Injured ankle and suffered blood poisoning (October 1988). . . . Pinched nerve in neck (December 1988). . . . Dislocated finger on right hand and underwent surgery (February 2, 1990); missed 18 games. . . . Suffered back spasms during preseason (September 1991); missed first eight games of season.

		REGULAR SEASON					PLAYOFFS				
Season Team	League	Gms.	G	A	Pts.	Pen.	Gms.	G	A	Pts.	Pen.
84-85—Univ. of North Dakota	WCHA	1	0	0	0	0	—	—	—	—	—
85-86—New Haven	AHL	42	2	3	5	40	1	0	0	0	0
—Toledo	IHL	30	5	3	8	54	—	—	—	—	—

Season Team	League	REGULAR SEASON					PLAYOFFS				
		Gms.	G	A	Pts.	Pen.	Gms.	G	A	Pts.	Pen.
86-87—New Haven	AHL	13	0	0	0	43	—	—	—	—	—
—Flint	IHL	14	4	3	7	59	—	—	—	—	—
—New York Rangers	NHL	13	2	1	3	45	3	0	0	0	12
87-88—Kalamazoo	IHL	65	5	10	15	273	6	0	1	1	47
—Minnesota	NHL	1	0	0	0	0	9	0	0	0	28
88-89—Pittsburgh	NHL	58	1	4	5	285	—	—	—	—	—
89-90—Pittsburgh	NHL	37	1	2	3	123	—	—	—	—	—
90-91—Muskegon	IHL	3	1	0	1	18	—	—	—	—	—
—Pittsburgh	NHL	23	1	1	2	71	—	—	—	—	—
91-92—Pittsburgh	NHL	50	0	0	0	175	5	0	0	0	2
NHL totals		182	5	8	13	699	17	0	0	0	42

CAVALLINI, GINO
LW, NORDIQUES

PERSONAL: Born November 24, 1962, at Toronto. . . . 6-2/215. . . . Shoots left. . . . Full name: Gino John Cavallini. . . . Brother of Paul Cavallini, defenseman, St. Louis Blues.
COLLEGE: Bowling Green State.
TRANSACTIONS/CAREER NOTES: Signed as free agent by Calgary Flames (July 1984). . . . Traded by Flames with LW Eddy Beers and D Charles Bourgeois to St. Louis Blues for D Terry Johnson, RW Joe Mullen and D Rik Wilson (February 1986). . . . Broke right hand (January 1988); missed 16 games. . . . Strained left knee (February 1989). . . . Claimed on waivers by Quebec Nordiques (February 27, 1992).

Season Team	League	REGULAR SEASON					PLAYOFFS				
		Gms.	G	A	Pts.	Pen.	Gms.	G	A	Pts.	Pen.
81-82—Toronto St. Mikes	OJHL	37	27	56	83		—	—	—	—	—
82-83—Bowling Green State	CCHA	40	8	16	24	52	—	—	—	—	—
83-84—Bowling Green State	CCHA	43	25	23	48	16	—	—	—	—	—
84-85—Moncton	AHL	51	29	19	48	28	—	—	—	—	—
—Calgary	NHL	27	6	10	16	14	3	0	0	0	4
85-86—Moncton	AHL	4	3	2	5	7	—	—	—	—	—
—Calgary	NHL	27	7	7	14	26	—	—	—	—	—
—St. Louis	NHL	30	6	5	11	36	17	4	5	9	10
86-87—St. Louis	NHL	80	18	26	44	54	6	3	1	4	2
87-88—St. Louis	NHL	64	15	17	32	62	10	5	5	10	19
88-89—St. Louis	NHL	74	20	23	43	79	9	0	2	2	17
89-90—St. Louis	NHL	80	15	15	30	77	12	1	3	4	2
90-91—St. Louis	NHL	78	8	27	35	81	13	1	3	4	2
91-92—St. Louis	NHL	48	9	7	16	40	—	—	—	—	—
—Quebec	NHL	18	1	7	8	4	—	—	—	—	—
NHL totals		526	105	144	249	473	70	14	19	33	56

CAVALLINI, PAUL
D, BLUES

PERSONAL: Born October 13, 1965, at Toronto. . . . 6-1/210. . . . Shoots left. . . . Full name: Paul Edward Cavallini. . . . Brother of Gino Cavallini, left winger, Quebec Nordiques.
HIGH SCHOOL: Henry Carr (Rexdale, Ont.).
COLLEGE: Providence.
TRANSACTIONS/CAREER NOTES: Selected by Washington Capitals as underage junior in 10th round (ninth Capitals pick, 205th overall) of NHL entry draft (June 9, 1984). . . . Traded by Capitals to St. Louis Blues for a second-round pick in 1988 draft (D Wade Bartley) (December 1987). . . . Broke hand (December 11, 1987). . . . Injured neck (December 11, 1988). . . . Dislocated left shoulder (February 25, 1989). . . . Lost tip of left index finger (December 22, 1990); missed 13 games. . . . Strained knee ligament (October 20, 1991); missed 13 games.
HONORS: Won Alka-Seltzer Plus Award (1989-90).

Season Team	League	REGULAR SEASON					PLAYOFFS				
		Gms.	G	A	Pts.	Pen.	Gms.	G	A	Pts.	Pen.
83-84—Henry Carr H.S.	MTHL	54	20	41	61	190	—	—	—	—	—
84-85—Providence College	Hockey East	45	5	14	19	64	—	—	—	—	—
85-86—Team Canada	Int'l	52	1	11	12	95	—	—	—	—	—
—Binghamton	AHL	15	3	4	7	20	6	0	2	2	56
86-87—Binghamton	AHL	66	12	24	36	188	13	2	7	9	35
—Washington	NHL	6	0	2	2	8	—	—	—	—	—
87-88—Washington	NHL	24	2	3	5	66	—	—	—	—	—
—St. Louis	NHL	48	4	7	11	86	10	1	6	7	26
88-89—St. Louis	NHL	65	4	20	24	128	10	2	2	4	14
89-90—St. Louis	NHL	80	8	39	47	106	12	2	3	5	20
90-91—St. Louis	NHL	67	10	25	35	89	13	2	3	5	20
91-92—St. Louis	NHL	66	10	25	35	95	4	0	1	1	6
NHL totals		356	38	121	159	578	49	7	15	22	86

CHABOT, FREDERIC
G, CANADIENS

PERSONAL: Born February 12, 1968, at Hebertville, Que. . . . 5-10/160. . . . Shoots right.
TRANSACTIONS/CAREER NOTES: Selected by New Jersey Devils in 10th round (10th Devils pick, 192nd overall) of NHL entry draft (June 21, 1986). . . . Signed as free agent by Montreal Canadiens (January 16, 1990). . . . Selected by Tampa Bay Lightning in NHL expansion draft (June 18, 1992). . . . Traded by Lightning to Canadiens for G Jean-Claude Bergeron (June 18, 1992).
HONORS: Named to Memorial Cup All-Star team (1981-82). . . . Named to WHL All-Star first team (1988-89).

C

Season Team	League	REGULAR SEASON Gms.	Min.	W	L	T	GA	SO	Avg.	PLAYOFFS Gms.	Min.	W	L	GA	SO	Avg.
86-87—Drummondville............	QMJHL	*62	*3508	31	29	0	293	1	5.01	8	481	2	6	40	0	4.99
87-88—Drummondville............	QMJHL	58	3276	27	24	4	237	1	4.34	*16	1019	10	6	56	†1	*3.30
88-89—Moose Jaw	WHL	26	1385				114	1	4.94	—	—	—	—	—	—	—
—Prince-Albert	WHL	28	1572				88	1	3.36	4	199	1	1	16	0	4.82
89-90—Fort Wayne	IHL	23	1208	6	13	3	87	1	4.32	—	—	—	—	—	—	—
—Sherbrooke...................	AHL	2	119	1	1	0	8	0	4.03	—	—	—	—	—	—	—
90-91—Montreal	NHL	3	108	0	0	1	6	0	3.33	—	—	—	—	—	—	—
—Fredericton	AHL	35	1800	9	15	5	122	0	4.07	—	—	—	—	—	—	—
91-92—Winston-Salem............	ECHL	25	1449	15	7	2	71	0	*2.94	—	—	—	—	—	—	—
—Fredericton	AHL	30	1761	17	9	4	79	2	*2.69	7	457	3	4	20	0	2.63
NHL totals..........................		3	108	0	0	1	6	0	3.33							

CHAMBERS, SHAWN

D, LIGHTNING

PERSONAL: Born October 11, 1966, at Royal Oaks, Mich. . . . 6-2/200. . . . Shoots left. . . . Full name: Shawn Randall Chambers.
COLLEGE: Alaska-Fairbanks.
TRANSACTIONS/CAREER NOTES: Selected by Minnesota North Stars in NHL supplemental draft (June 1987). . . . Dislocated shoulder (February 1988). . . . Separated right shoulder (September 1988). . . . Injured left knee (September 11, 1990); missed first 11 games of season. . . . Fractured left kneecap (December 5, 1990); missed three months. . . . Underwent surgery to left knee to remove piece of loose cartilage (May 1991). . . . Traded by North Stars to Washington Capitals for C Trent Klatt and LW Steve Maltais (June 21, 1991). . . . Suffered sore knee (October 1991); missed first 47 games of season. . . . Reinjured knee (January 26, 1992); missed final 31 games of season. . . . Underwent arthroscopic knee surgery (February 4, 1992). . . . Selected by Tampa Bay Lightning in NHL expansion draft (June 18, 1992).

Season Team	League	REGULAR SEASON Gms.	G	A	Pts.	Pen.	PLAYOFFS Gms.	G	A	Pts.	Pen.
85-86—Alaska-Fairbanks	Indep.	25	15	21	36	34	—	—	—	—	—
86-87—Fort Wayne	IHL	12	2	6	8	0	10	1	4	5	5
—Seattle	WHL	28	8	25	33	58	—	—	—	—	—
—Minnesota	NHL	19	1	7	8	21	—	—	—	—	—
87-88—Kalamazoo	IHL	19	1	6	7	22	—	—	—	—	—
—Minnesota	NHL	72	5	19	24	80	3	0	2	2	0
88-89—Minnesota	NHL	78	8	18	26	81	7	2	1	3	0
89-90—Minnesota	NHL	29	1	3	4	24	23	0	7	7	16
90-91—Kalamazoo	IHL	3	1	1	2	0	—	—	—	—	—
—Baltimore.........................	AHL	5	2	3	5	9	—	—	—	—	—
91-92—Washington	NHL	2	0	0	0	2	—	—	—	—	—
NHL totals................................		200	15	47	62	208	33	2	10	12	16

CHAPDELAINE, RENE

D, KINGS

PERSONAL: Born September 27, 1966, at Weyburn, Sask. . . . 6-1/195. . . . Shoots right. . . . Full name: Rene R. Chapdelaine.
COLLEGE: Lake Superior State (Mich.).
TRANSACTIONS/CAREER NOTES: Selected by Los Angeles Kings in eighth round (seventh Kings pick, 149th overall) of NHL entry draft (June 21, 1986).

Season Team	League	REGULAR SEASON Gms.	G	A	Pts.	Pen.	PLAYOFFS Gms.	G	A	Pts.	Pen.
84-85—Weyburn Red Wings	SJHL	61	3	17	20		—	—	—	—	—
85-86—Lake Superior State	CCHA	40	2	7	9	24	—	—	—	—	—
86-87—Lake Superior State	CCHA	28	1	5	6	51	—	—	—	—	—
87-88—Lake Superior State	CCHA	35	1	9	10	44	—	—	—	—	—
88-89—Lake Superior State	CCHA	46	4	9	13	52	—	—	—	—	—
89-90—New Haven	AHL	41	0	1	1	35	—	—	—	—	—
90-91—Phoenix	IHL	17	0	2	2	10	11	0	0	0	8
—New Haven.....................	AHL	65	3	11	14	49	—	—	—	—	—
—Los Angeles...................	NHL	3	0	1	1	10	—	—	—	—	—
91-92—Phoenix	IHL	62	4	22	26	87	—	—	—	—	—
—Los Angeles...................	NHL	16	0	1	1	10	—	—	—	—	—
NHL totals................................		19	0	2	2	20					

CHAPMAN, BRIAN

D, WHALERS

PERSONAL: Born February 10, 1968, at Brockville, Ont. . . . 6-0/195. . . . Shoots left.
TRANSACTIONS/CAREER NOTES: Selected by Hartford Whalers as underage junior in fourth round (third Whalers pick, 74th overall) of NHL entry draft (June 21, 1986). . . . Suspended 10 games by OHL (October 5, 1986). . . . Suspended six games by AHL for fighting (March 11, 1989). . . . Fractured left thumb (November 10, 1990).

Season Team	League	REGULAR SEASON Gms.	G	A	Pts.	Pen.	PLAYOFFS Gms.	G	A	Pts.	Pen.
84-85—Brockville	COJHL	50	11	32	43	145	—	—	—	—	—
85-86—Belleville Bulls.................	OHL	66	6	31	37	168	24	2	6	8	54
86-87—Belleville Bulls.................	OHL	54	4	32	36	142	6	1	1	2	10
—Binghamton	AHL	—	—	—	—	—	1	0	0	0	0
87-88—Belleville Bulls.................	OHL	63	11	57	68	180	6	1	4	5	13
88-89—Binghamton	AHL	71	5	25	30	216	—	—	—	—	—
89-90—Binghamton	AHL	68	2	15	17	180	—	—	—	—	—

Season Team	League	REGULAR SEASON					PLAYOFFS				
		Gms.	G	A	Pts.	Pen.	Gms.	G	A	Pts.	Pen.
90-91—Hartford	NHL	3	0	0	0	29	—	—	—	—	—
—Springfield	AHL	60	4	23	27	200	18	1	4	5	62
91-92—Springfield	AHL	73	3	26	29	245	10	2	2	4	25
NHL totals		3	0	0	0	29					

CHARBONNEAU, STEPHANE
RW, NORDIQUES

PERSONAL: Born June 27, 1970, at Ste.-Adele, Que. . . . 6-2/195. . . . Shoots right.
TRANSACTIONS/CAREER NOTES: Signed as a free agent by Quebec Nordiques (April 25, 1991).

Season Team	League	REGULAR SEASON					PLAYOFFS				
		Gms.	G	A	Pts.	Pen.	Gms.	G	A	Pts.	Pen.
87-88—Hull	QMJHL	51	10	20	30	70	11	5	8	13	12
88-89—Hull	QMJHL	64	23	29	52	142	9	2	2	4	22
89-90—Shawinigan	QMJHL	62	37	58	95	154	6	4	2	6	11
90-91—Shawinigan	QMJHL	6	4	3	7	2	—	—	—	—	—
—Chicoutimi	QMJHL	55	37	30	67	109	17	†13	9	22	43
91-92—Halifax	AHL	64	22	25	47	183	—	—	—	—	—
—Quebec	NHL	2	0	0	0	0	—	—	—	—	—
NHL totals		2	0	0	0	0					

CHARRON, ERIC
D, CANADIENS

PERSONAL: Born January 14, 1970, at Verdun, Que. . . . 6-3/192. . . . Shoots left.
TRANSACTIONS/CAREER NOTES: Selected by Montreal Canadiens in first round (first Canadiens pick, 20th overall) of NHL entry draft (June 11, 1988).

Season Team	League	REGULAR SEASON					PLAYOFFS				
		Gms.	G	A	Pts.	Pen.	Gms.	G	A	Pts.	Pen.
87-88—Trois-Rivieres	QMJHL	67	3	13	16	135	—	—	—	—	—
88-89—Sherbrooke	AHL	1	0	0	0	0	—	—	—	—	—
—Verdun	QMJHL	67	4	31	35	177	—	—	—	—	—
89-90—St. Hyacinthe	QMJHL	68	13	38	51	152	11	3	4	7	67
—Sherbrooke	AHL	—	—	—	—	—	2	0	0	0	0
90-91—Fredericton	AHL	71	1	11	12	108	2	1	0	1	29
91-92—Fredericton	AHL	59	2	11	13	98	6	1	0	1	4

CHASE, DON
C, CANADIENS

PERSONAL: Born March 17, 1974, at Springfield, Mass. . . . 5-11/190. . . . Shoots right.
TRANSACTIONS/CAREER NOTES: Selected by Montreal Canadiens in fifth round (seventh Canadiens pick, 116th overall) of NHL entry draft (June 20, 1992).

Season Team	League	REGULAR SEASON					PLAYOFFS				
		Gms.	G	A	Pts.	Pen.	Gms.	G	A	Pts.	Pen.
91-92—Springfield Jr. B	NEJHL	49	69	75	144	80	—	—	—	—	—

CHASE, KELLY
RW, BLUES

PERSONAL: Born October 25, 1967, at Porcupine Plain, Sask. . . . 5-11/195. . . . Shoots right. . . . Full name: Kelly Wayne Chase.
TRANSACTIONS/CAREER NOTES: Signed as free agent by St. Louis Blues (May 24, 1988). . . . Bruised right foot (January 1990). . . . Suffered back spasms (March 1990). . . . Suspended 10 games by NHL for fighting (March 18, 1991). . . . Injured knee (December 11, 1991); missed two games. . . . Sprained left wrist (January 14, 1992); missed three games. . . . Bruised thigh (February 2, 1992); missed five games. . . . Injured hand (February 23, 1992); missed four games.

Season Team	League	REGULAR SEASON					PLAYOFFS				
		Gms.	G	A	Pts.	Pen.	Gms.	G	A	Pts.	Pen.
85-86—Saskatoon	WHL	57	7	18	25	172	10	3	4	7	37
86-87—Saskatoon	WHL	68	17	29	46	285	11	2	8	10	37
87-88—Saskatoon	WHL	70	21	34	55	*343	9	3	5	8	32
88-89—Peoria	IHL	38	14	7	21	278	—	—	—	—	—
89-90—Peoria	IHL	10	1	2	3	76	—	—	—	—	—
—St. Louis	NHL	43	1	3	4	244	9	1	0	1	46
90-91—Peoria	IHL	61	20	34	54	406	10	4	3	7	61
—St. Louis	NHL	2	1	0	1	15	6	0	0	0	18
91-92—St. Louis	NHL	46	1	2	3	264	1	0	0	0	7
NHL totals		91	3	5	8	523	16	1	0	1	71

CHELIOS, CHRIS
D, BLACKHAWKS

PERSONAL: Born January 25, 1962, at Chicago. . . . 6-1/192. . . . Shoots right. . . . Full name: Christos K. Chelios.
COLLEGE: Wisconsin.
TRANSACTIONS/CAREER NOTES: Selected by Montreal Canadiens as underage junior in second round (fifth Canadiens pick, 40th overall) of NHL entry draft (June 10, 1981). . . . Sprained right ankle (January 1985). . . . Injured left knee (April 1985). . . . Sprained knee (December 19, 1985). . . . Reinjured knee (January 20, 1986). . . . Suffered back spasms (October 1986). . . . Broke finger of left hand (December 1987). . . . Bruised tailbone (February 7, 1988). . . . Strained left knee ligaments (February 1990). . . . Underwent surgery to repair torn abdominal muscle (April 30, 1990). . . . Traded by Canadiens with a second-round pick in 1991 draft (C Michael Pomichter) to Chicago Blackhawks for C Denis Savard

(June 29, 1990).... Lacerated left temple (February 9, 1991).
HONORS: Named to WCHA All-Star second team (1982-83).... Named to NCAA All-Tournament team (1982-83).... Named to NHL All-Rookie team (1984-85).... Won James Norris Memorial Trophy (1988-89).... Named to THE SPORTING NEWS All-Star first team (1988-89).... Named to NHL All-Star first team (1988-89).... Named to THE SPORTING NEWS All-Star second team (1990-91 and 1991-92).... Named to NHL All-Star second team (1990-91).

Season Team	League	REGULAR SEASON					PLAYOFFS				
		Gms.	G	A	Pts.	Pen.	Gms.	G	A	Pts.	Pen.
79-80—Moose Jaw	SJHL	53	12	31	43	118	—	—	—	—	—
80-81—Moose Jaw	SJHL	54	23	64	87	175	—	—	—	—	—
81-82—University of Wisconsin ...	WCHA	43	6	43	49	50	—	—	—	—	—
82-83—University of Wisconsin ...	WCHA	45	16	32	48	62	—	—	—	—	—
83-84—U.S. National Team	Int'l	60	14	35	49	58	—	—	—	—	—
—U.S. Olympic Team	Int'l	6	0	4	4	8	—	—	—	—	—
—Montreal	NHL	12	0	2	2	12	15	1	9	10	17
84-85—Montreal	NHL	74	9	55	64	87	9	2	8	10	17
85-86—Montreal	NHL	41	8	26	34	67	20	2	9	11	49
86-87—Montreal	NHL	71	11	33	44	124	17	4	9	13	38
87-88—Montreal	NHL	71	20	41	61	172	11	3	1	4	29
88-89—Montreal	NHL	80	15	58	73	185	21	4	15	19	28
89-90—Montreal	NHL	53	9	22	31	136	5	0	1	1	8
90-91—Chicago	NHL	77	12	52	64	192	6	1	7	8	46
91-92—Chicago	NHL	80	9	47	56	245	18	6	15	21	37
NHL totals		559	93	336	429	1220	122	23	74	97	269

CHERBAYEV, ALEXANDER
LW, SHARKS

PERSONAL: Born August 13, 1973, at Voskresensk, U.S.S.R. ... 6-1/ 187.... Shoots left.
TRANSACTIONS/CAREER NOTES: Selected by San Jose Sharks in third round (third Sharks pick, 51st overall) of NHL entry draft (June 20, 1992).

Season Team	League	REGULAR SEASON					PLAYOFFS				
		Gms.	G	A	Pts.	Pen.	Gms.	G	A	Pts.	Pen.
90-91—Khimik Voskresensk	USSR	16	2	2	4	0	—	—	—	—	—
91-92—Khimik Voskresensk	CIS	38	3	3	6	14	—	—	—	—	—

CHERNOMAZ, RICHARD
RW, FLAMES

PERSONAL: Born September 1, 1963, at Selkirk, Man. ... 5-8/185. ... Shoots right.
TRANSACTIONS/CAREER NOTES: Selected by Colorado Rockies as underage junior in second round (third Rockies pick, 26th overall) of NHL entry draft (June 10, 1981).... Suffered recurring pain caused by separated shoulder; missed parts of 1981-82 season.... Injured knee ligaments (January 1983).... Sprained left knee and underwent arthroscopic surgery (November 27, 1984).... Signed as free agent by Calgary Flames (August 1987).... Underwent surgery to remove ligament from right knee (November 1989); missed 13 games.
HONORS: Named to WHL All-Star first team (1982-83).... Named to IHL All-Star second team (1988-89 and 1990-91).

Season Team	League	REGULAR SEASON					PLAYOFFS				
		Gms.	G	A	Pts.	Pen.	Gms.	G	A	Pts.	Pen.
79-80—Saskatoon	SJHL	51	33	37	70	75	—	—	—	—	—
—Saskatoon	WHL	25	9	10	19	33	—	—	—	—	—
80-81—Victoria	WHL	72	49	64	113	92	15	11	15	26	38
81-82—Victoria	WHL	49	36	62	98	69	4	1	2	3	13
—Colorado	NHL	2	0	0	0	0	—	—	—	—	—
82-83—Victoria	WHL	64	71	53	124	113	12	10	5	15	18
83-84—Maine	AHL	69	17	29	46	39	2	0	1	1	0
—New Jersey	NHL	7	2	1	3	2	—	—	—	—	—
84-85—Maine	AHL	64	17	34	51	64	10	2	2	4	4
—New Jersey	NHL	3	0	2	2	2	—	—	—	—	—
85-86—Maine	AHL	78	21	28	49	82	5	0	0	0	2
86-87—Maine	AHL	58	35	27	62	65	—	—	—	—	—
—New Jersey	NHL	25	6	4	10	8	—	—	—	—	—
87-88—Calgary	NHL	2	1	0	1	0	—	—	—	—	—
—Salt Lake City	IHL	73	48	47	95	122	18	4	14	18	30
88-89—Calgary	NHL	1	0	0	0	0	—	—	—	—	—
—Salt Lake City	IHL	81	33	68	101	122	14	7	5	12	47
89-90—Salt Lake City	IHL	65	39	35	74	170	11	6	6	12	32
90-91—Salt Lake City	IHL	81	39	58	97	213	4	3	1	4	8
91-92—Salt Lake City	IHL	66	20	40	60	201	5	1	2	3	10
—Calgary	NHL	11	0	0	0	6	—	—	—	—	—
NHL totals		51	9	7	16	18					

CHEVELDAE, TIM
G, RED WINGS

PERSONAL: Born February 15, 1968, at Melville, Sask. ... 5-11/180. ... Shoots left.
TRANSACTIONS/CAREER NOTES: Selected by Detroit Red Wings as underage junior in fourth round (fourth Red Wings pick, 64th overall) of NHL entry draft (June 21, 1986).
HONORS: Named to WHL All-Star first team (1987-88).

Season Team	League	REGULAR SEASON								PLAYOFFS						
		Gms.	Min.	W	L	T	GA	SO	Avg.	Gms.	Min.	W	L	GA	SO	Avg.
84-85—Melville	SAJHL	23	1167				98	0	5.04	—	—	—	—	—	—	—
85-86—Saskatoon	WHL	36	2030	21	10	3	165	0	4.88	8	480	6	2	29	0	3.63
86-87—Saskatoon	WHL	33	1909	20	11	0	133	2	4.18	5	308	4	1	20	0	3.90
87-88—Saskatoon	WHL	66	3798	44	19	3	235	1	3.71	6	364	4	2	27	0	4.45
88-89—Detroit	NHL	2	122	0	2	0	9	0	4.43	—	—	—	—	—	—	—
—Adirondack	AHL	30	1694	20	8	0	98	1	3.47	2	99	1	0	9	0	5.45
89-90—Adirondack	AHL	31	1848	17	8	6	116	0	3.77	—	—	—	—	—	—	—
—Detroit	NHL	28	1600	10	9	8	101	0	3.79	—	—	—	—	—	—	—
90-91—Detroit	NHL	65	3615	30	26	5	*214	2	3.55	7	398	3	4	22	0	3.32
91-92—Detroit	NHL	*72	*4236	†38	23	9	226	2	3.20	11	597	3	7	25	†2	2.51
NHL totals		167	9573	78	60	22	550	4	3.45	18	995	6	11	47	2	2.83

CHEVELDAYOFF, KEVIN
D, ISLANDERS

PERSONAL: Born February 4, 1970, at Saskatoon, Sask. . . . 6-0/202. . . . Shoots right.
TRANSACTIONS/CAREER NOTES: Selected by New York Islanders in first round (first Islanders pick, 16th overall) of NHL entry draft (June 11, 1988). . . . Underwent reconstructive surgery to left knee (January 6, 1989); missed remainder of 1988-89 season and part of 1989-90 season.

Season Team	League	REGULAR SEASON					PLAYOFFS				
		Gms.	G	A	Pts.	Pen.	Gms.	G	A	Pts.	Pen.
86-87—Brandon	WHL	70	0	16	16	259	—	—	—	—	—
87-88—Brandon	WHL	71	3	29	32	265	4	0	2	2	20
88-89—Brandon	WHL	40	4	12	16	135	—	—	—	—	—
89-90—Brandon	WHL	33	5	12	17	56	—	—	—	—	—
—Springfield	AHL	4	0	0	0	0	—	—	—	—	—
90-91—Capital District	AHL	76	0	14	14	203	—	—	—	—	—
91-92—Capital District	AHL	44	0	4	4	110	7	0	0	0	22

CHIASSON, STEVE
D, RED WINGS

PERSONAL: Born April 14, 1967, at Barrie, Ont. . . . 6-0/202. . . . Shoots left.
TRANSACTIONS/CAREER NOTES: Selected by Detroit Red Wings as underage junior in third round (third Red Wings pick, 50th overall) of NHL entry draft (June 15, 1985). . . . Injured hand (October 1985). . . . Separated right shoulder (February 1988). . . . Injured foot (May 1988). . . . Injured groin (October 1988). . . . Bruised ribs (January 1989). . . . Injured ankle (February 1989). . . . Injured knee (November 29, 1990); missed three games. . . . Broke right ankle (January 2, 1991). . . . Reinjured right ankle (February 19, 1991); missed 26 games. . . . Reinjured right ankle (March 9, 1991). . . . Injured ankle (October 22, 1991); missed 14 games.
HONORS: Won Stafford Smythe Memorial Trophy (1985-86). . . . Named to Memorial Cup All-Star team (1985-86).

Season Team	League	REGULAR SEASON					PLAYOFFS				
		Gms.	G	A	Pts.	Pen.	Gms.	G	A	Pts.	Pen.
83-84—Guelph	OHL	55	1	9	10	112	—	—	—	—	—
84-85—Guelph	OHL	61	8	22	30	139	—	—	—	—	—
85-86—Guelph	OHL	54	12	29	41	126	18	10	10	20	37
86-87—Detroit	NHL	45	1	4	5	73	2	0	0	0	19
87-88—Adirondack	AHL	23	6	11	17	58	—	—	—	—	—
—Detroit	NHL	29	2	9	11	57	9	2	2	4	31
88-89—Detroit	NHL	65	12	35	47	149	5	2	1	3	6
89-90—Detroit	NHL	67	14	28	42	114	—	—	—	—	—
90-91—Detroit	NHL	42	3	17	20	80	5	3	1	4	19
91-92—Detroit	NHL	62	10	24	34	136	11	1	5	6	12
NHL totals		310	42	117	159	609	32	8	9	17	87

CHITARONI, TERRY
C, MAPLE LEAFS

PERSONAL: Born December 9, 1972, at Haileybury, Ont. . . . 5-11/200. . . . Shoots right.
TRANSACTIONS/CAREER NOTES: Selected by Toronto Maple Leafs in fourth round (second Maple Leafs pick, 69th overall) of NHL entry draft (June 22, 1991).

Season Team	League	REGULAR SEASON					PLAYOFFS				
		Gms.	G	A	Pts.	Pen.	Gms.	G	A	Pts.	Pen.
88-89—Sudbury	OHL	58	17	23	40	103	—	—	—	—	—
89-90—Sudbury	OHL	65	21	47	68	173	7	4	1	5	15
90-91—Sudbury	OHL	61	28	43	71	162	5	1	1	2	18
91-92—Sudbury	OHL	51	31	47	78	119	11	7	5	12	39
—St. John's	AHL	—	—	—	—	—	2	0	1	1	5

CHORSKE, TOM
RW, DEVILS

PERSONAL: Born September 18, 1966, at Minneapolis. . . . 6-1/205. . . . Shoots right. . . . Full name: Thomas Chorske.
HIGH SCHOOL: Southwest (Minneapolis).
COLLEGE: Minnesota.
TRANSACTIONS/CAREER NOTES: Selected by Montreal Canadiens in first round (second Canadiens pick, 16th overall) of NHL entry draft (June 15, 1985). . . . Separated shoulder (November 18, 1988); missed 11 games. . . . Suffered hip pointer (October 26, 1989). . . . Sprained right shoulder (March 14, 1991). . . . Traded by Canadiens with RW Stephane Richer to New Jersey Devils for LW Kirk Muller and G Roland Melanson (September 1991).
HONORS: Named to WCHA All-Star first team (1988-89).

C

Season Team	League	REGULAR SEASON					PLAYOFFS				
		Gms.	G	A	Pts.	Pen.	Gms.	G	A	Pts.	Pen.
84-85—Minn. Southwest H.S.	Minn. H.S.	23	44	26	70		—	—	—	—	—
85-86—University of Minnesota ...	WCHA	39	6	4	10	6	—	—	—	—	—
86-87—University of Minnesota ...	WCHA	47	20	22	42	20	—	—	—	—	—
87-88—U.S. Olympic Team	Int'l		9	16	25		—	—	—	—	—
88-89—University of Minnesota ...	WCHA	37	25	24	49	28	—	—	—	—	—
89-90—Montreal	NHL	14	3	1	4	2	—	—	—	—	—
—Sherbrooke	AHL	59	22	24	46	54	12	4	4	8	8
90-91—Montreal	NHL	57	9	11	20	32	—	—	—	—	—
91-92—New Jersey	NHL	76	19	17	36	32	7	0	3	3	4
NHL totals.................		147	31	29	60	66	7	0	3	3	4

CHRISTIAN, DAVE
RW, BLUES

PERSONAL: Born May 12, 1959, at Warroad, Minn. . . . 6-0/ 195. . . . Shoots right. . . . Full name: David W. Christian. . . . Son of Bill Christian and nephew of Roger Christian, both members of 1960 gold medal-winning U.S. Olympic team and 1964 U.S. Olympic team; and nephew of Gordon Christian, member of 1956 U.S. Olympic team.

COLLEGE: North Dakota.

TRANSACTIONS/CAREER NOTES: Selected by Winnipeg Jets in second round (second Jets pick, 40th overall) of NHL entry draft (August 9, 1979). . . . Tore shoulder muscles (December 1982); missed 25 games. . . . Traded by Jets to Washington Capitals for first-round pick in 1983 draft (D Bobby Dollas) (June 1983). . . . Traded by Capitals to Boston Bruins for LW Bob Joyce (December 13, 1989). . . . Signed as free agent by St. Louis Blues; Bruins tried to block the signing, claiming Christian was not a free agent. Blues and Bruins later arranged a trade in which Boston received D Glen Featherstone and LW Dave Thomlinson, whom they had previously signed as free agents, for Christian, a third-round pick in 1992 draft and either a seventh-round pick in 1992 draft or a sixth-round pick in 1993 draft (July 30, 1991). . . . Bruised ribs (January 16, 1992); missed one game.

MISCELLANEOUS: Member of 1980 gold medal-winning U.S. Olympic team.

Season Team	League	REGULAR SEASON					PLAYOFFS				
		Gms.	G	A	Pts.	Pen.	Gms.	G	A	Pts.	Pen.
77-78—Univ. of North Dakota	WCHA	38	8	16	24	14	—	—	—	—	—
78-79—Univ. of North Dakota	WCHA	40	22	24	46	22	—	—	—	—	—
79-80—U.S. National Team	Int'l	59	10	20	30	26	—	—	—	—	—
—U.S. Olympic Team	Int'l	7	0	8	8	6	—	—	—	—	—
—Winnipeg	NHL	15	8	10	18	2	—	—	—	—	—
80-81—Winnipeg	NHL	80	28	43	71	22	—	—	—	—	—
81-82—Winnipeg	NHL	80	25	51	76	28	4	0	1	1	2
82-83—Winnipeg	NHL	55	18	26	44	23	3	0	0	0	0
83-84—Washington	NHL	80	29	52	81	28	8	5	4	9	5
84-85—Washington	NHL	80	26	43	69	14	5	1	1	2	0
85-86—Washington	NHL	80	41	42	83	15	9	4	4	8	0
86-87—Washington	NHL	76	23	27	50	8	7	1	3	4	6
87-88—Washington	NHL	80	37	21	58	26	14	5	6	11	6
88-89—Washington	NHL	80	34	31	65	12	6	1	1	2	0
89-90—Washington	NHL	28	3	8	11	4	—	—	—	—	—
—Boston	NHL	50	12	17	29	8	21	4	1	5	4
90-91—Boston	NHL	78	32	21	53	41	19	8	4	12	4
91-92—St. Louis	NHL	78	20	24	44	41	4	3	0	3	0
NHL totals....................................		940	336	416	752	272	100	32	25	57	27

CHRISTIAN, JEFF
LW, DEVILS

PERSONAL: Born July 30, 1970, at Burlington, Ont. . . . 6-1/ 195. . . . Shoots left. . . . Full name: Jeffrey Christian.

TRANSACTIONS/CAREER NOTES: Selected by New Jersey Devils in second round (second Devils pick, 23rd overall) of NHL entry draft (June 11, 1988). . . . Traded by London Knights to Owen Sound Platers for C Todd Hlushko and D David Noseworthy (November 27, 1989). . . . Suspended three games by OHL for high-sticking (March 28, 1990).

Season Team	League	REGULAR SEASON					PLAYOFFS				
		Gms.	G	A	Pts.	Pen.	Gms.	G	A	Pts.	Pen.
86-87—Dundas Jr. C....................	OHA	29	20	34	54	42	—	—	—	—	—
87-88—London	OHL	64	15	29	44	154	9	1	5	6	27
88-89—London	OHL	60	27	30	57	221	20	3	4	7	56
89-90—London	OHL	18	14	7	21	64	—	—	—	—	—
—Owen Sound	OHL	37	19	26	45	145	10	6	7	13	43
90-91—Utica	AHL	80	24	42	66	165	—	—	—	—	—
91-92—Utica	AHL	76	27	24	51	198	4	0	0	0	16
—New Jersey.......................	NHL	2	0	0	0	2	—	—	—	—	—
NHL totals....................................		2	0	0	0	2					

CHURLA, SHANE
RW, NORTH STARS

PERSONAL: Born June 24, 1965, at Fernie, B.C. . . . 6-1/ 200. . . . Shoots right.

TRANSACTIONS/CAREER NOTES: Selected by Hartford Whalers in sixth round (fourth Whalers pick, 110th overall) of NHL entry draft (June 15, 1985). . . . Pulled stomach muscles (October 1985). . . . Suspended three games by AHL (October 5, 1986). . . . Traded by Whalers with D Dana Murzyn to Calgary Flames for D Neil Sheehy, C Carey Wilson and the rights to LW Lane MacDonald (January 1988). . . . Traded by Flames with C Perry Berezan to Minnesota North Stars for LW Brian MacLellan and a fourth-round pick in 1989 draft (C Robert Reichel) (March 4, 1989). . . . Broke wrist (April 2, 1989). . . . Bruised right hand (November 1989). . . . Suspended 10 games by NHL for fighting (December 28, 1989). . . . Underwent surgery to wrist (April 1990). . . .

Tore rib cartilage (November 17, 1990); missed five games. . . . Separated shoulder (December 11, 1990); missed seven games. . . . Separated right shoulder (January 17, 1991); missed 23 games. . . . Selected by San Jose Sharks in dispersal draft of North Stars roster (May 30, 1991). . . . Traded by Sharks to North Stars for C Kelly Kisio (June 3, 1991). . . . Suffered back spasms (January 30, 1992); missed five games. . . . Injured shoulder (March 19, 1992); missed five games.

Season Team	League	REGULAR SEASON					PLAYOFFS				
		Gms.	G	A	Pts.	Pen.	Gms.	G	A	Pts.	Pen.
83-84—Medicine Hat	WHL	48	3	7	10	115	14	1	5	6	41
84-85—Medicine Hat	WHL	70	14	20	34	*370	9	1	0	1	55
85-86—Binghamton	AHL	52	4	10	14	306	3	0	0	0	22
86-87—Binghamton	AHL	24	1	5	6	249	—	—	—	—	—
—Hartford	NHL	20	0	1	1	78	2	0	0	0	42
87-88—Binghamton	AHL	25	5	8	13	168	—	—	—	—	—
—Hartford	NHL	2	0	0	0	14	—	—	—	—	—
—Calgary	NHL	29	1	5	6	132	7	0	1	1	17
88-89—Calgary	NHL	5	0	0	0	25	—	—	—	—	—
—Salt Lake City	IHL	32	3	13	16	278	—	—	—	—	—
—Minnesota	NHL	13	1	0	1	54	—	—	—	—	—
89-90—Minnesota	NHL	53	2	3	5	292	7	0	0	0	44
90-91—Minnesota	NHL	40	2	2	4	286	22	2	1	3	90
91-92—Minnesota	NHL	57	4	1	5	278	—	—	—	—	—
NHL totals		219	10	12	22	1159	38	2	2	4	193

CHYCHRUN, JEFF
D, PENGUINS

PERSONAL: Born May 3, 1966, at Lasalle, Que. . . . 6-4/215. . . . Shoots right.
TRANSACTIONS/CAREER NOTES: Selected by Philadelphia Flyers as underage junior in second round (second Flyers pick, 37th overall) of NHL entry draft (June 9, 1984). . . . Suffered viral infection (November 1989). . . . Suffered concussion (October 11, 1990); missed three games. . . . Suffered concussion (October 23, 1990); missed three games. . . . Fractured navicular bone in left wrist and underwent surgery (November 23, 1990); missed 41 games. . . . Traded by Flyers with rights to RW Jari Kurri to Los Angeles Kings for D Steve Duchesne, C Steve Kasper and a fourth-round pick in 1991 draft (D Aris Brimanis) (May 30, 1991). . . . Underwent wrist surgery (Summer 1991); missed 25 games. . . . Traded by Kings with D Brian Benning and a first-round pick in 1992 draft to Pittsburgh Penguins for D Paul Coffey (February 19, 1992).

Season Team	League	REGULAR SEASON					PLAYOFFS				
		Gms.	G	A	Pts.	Pen.	Gms.	G	A	Pts.	Pen.
83-84—Kingston	OHL	83	1	13	14	137	—	—	—	—	—
84-85—Kingston	OHL	58	4	10	14	206	—	—	—	—	—
85-86—Kingston	OHL	61	4	21	25	127	10	2	1	3	17
—Kalamazoo	IHL	—	—	—	—	—	3	1	0	1	0
—Hershey	AHL	—	—	—	—	—	4	0	1	1	9
86-87—Hershey	AHL	74	1	17	18	239	4	0	0	0	10
—Philadelphia	NHL	1	0	0	0	4	—	—	—	—	—
87-88—Philadelphia	NHL	3	0	0	0	4	—	—	—	—	—
—Hershey	AHL	55	0	5	5	210	12	0	2	2	44
88-89—Philadelphia	NHL	80	1	4	5	245	19	0	2	2	65
89-90—Philadelphia	NHL	79	2	7	9	250	—	—	—	—	—
90-91—Philadelphia	NHL	36	0	6	6	105	—	—	—	—	—
91-92—Phoenix	IHL	3	0	0	0	6	—	—	—	—	—
—Los Angeles	NHL	26	0	3	3	76	—	—	—	—	—
—Pittsburgh	NHL	17	0	1	1	35	—	—	—	—	—
NHL totals		242	3	21	24	719	19	0	2	2	65

CHYNOWETH, DEAN
D, ISLANDERS

PERSONAL: Born October 30, 1968, at Saskatoon, Sask. . . . 6-2/190. . . . Shoots right. . . . Son of Ed Chynoweth, President of the Western Hockey League.
TRANSACTIONS/CAREER NOTES: Broke hand (September 1985). . . . Broke hand (April 1986). . . . Broke hand (October 1986). . . . Fractured rib and punctured lung (April 1987). . . . Selected by New York Islanders as underage junior in first round (first Islanders pick, 13th overall) of NHL entry draft (June 13, 1987). . . . Injured left eye (October 27, 1988); missed two months. . . . Developed Osgood-Schlatter disease, an abnormal relationship between the muscles and the growing bones (December 1988); missed remainder of season. . . . Injured ankle (October 31, 1989). . . . Sprained ligaments in right thumb (November 1989).
HONORS: Named to Memorial Cup All-Star team (1987-88).

Season Team	League	REGULAR SEASON					PLAYOFFS				
		Gms.	G	A	Pts.	Pen.	Gms.	G	A	Pts.	Pen.
85-86—Medicine Hat	WHL	69	3	12	15	208	17	3	2	5	52
86-87—Medicine Hat	WHL	67	3	18	21	285	13	4	2	6	28
87-88—Medicine Hat	WHL	64	1	21	22	274	16	0	6	6	*87
88-89—New York Islanders	NHL	6	0	0	0	48	—	—	—	—	—
89-90—New York Islanders	NHL	20	0	2	2	39	—	—	—	—	—
—Springfield	AHL	40	0	7	7	98	17	0	4	4	36
90-91—New York Islanders	NHL	25	1	1	2	59	—	—	—	—	—
—Capital District	AHL	44	1	5	6	176	—	—	—	—	—
91-92—Capital District	AHL	43	4	6	10	164	6	1	1	2	39
—New York Islanders	NHL	11	1	0	1	23	—	—	—	—	—
NHL totals		62	2	3	5	169					

C

CHYZOWSKI, DAVE
LW, ISLANDERS

PERSONAL: Born July 11, 1971, at Edmonton, Alta. . . . 6-1/190. . . . Shoots left. . . . Full name: David Chyzowski.
TRANSACTIONS/CAREER NOTES: Selected by New York Islanders in first round (first Islanders pick, second overall) of NHL entry draft (June 17, 1989).
HONORS: Named to WHL (West) All-Star first team (1988-89).

Season	Team	League	REGULAR SEASON					PLAYOFFS				
			Gms.	G	A	Pts.	Pen.	Gms.	G	A	Pts.	Pen.
87-88	Kamloops	WHL	66	16	17	33	117	18	2	4	6	26
88-89	Kamloops	WHL	68	56	48	104	139	16	15	13	28	32
89-90	Kamloops	WHL	4	5	2	7	17	17	11	6	17	46
	Springfield	AHL	4	0	0	0	7	—	—	—	—	—
	New York Islanders	NHL	34	8	6	14	45	—	—	—	—	—
90-91	Capital District	AHL	7	3	6	9	22	—	—	—	—	—
	New York Islanders	NHL	56	5	9	14	61	—	—	—	—	—
91-92	New York Islanders	NHL	12	1	1	2	17	—	—	—	—	—
	Capital District	AHL	55	15	18	33	121	6	1	1	2	23
NHL totals			102	14	16	30	123					

CIAVAGLIA, PETER
C, SABRES

PERSONAL: Born July 15, 1969, at Albany, N.Y. . . . 5-10/173. . . . Shoots left. . . . Full name: Peter Anthony Ciavaglia.
COLLEGE: Harvard.
TRANSACTIONS/CAREER NOTES: Selected by Calgary Flames in seventh round (eighth Flames pick, 145th overall) of NHL entry draft (June 13, 1987). . . . Signed as free agent by Buffalo Sabres (August 1990).
HONORS: Named to ECAC All-Star second team (1988-89). . . . Named ECAC Player of the Year (1990-91). . . . Named to NCAA All-America East second team (1990-91). . . . Named to ECAC All-Star first team (1990-91).

Season	Team	League	REGULAR SEASON					PLAYOFFS				
			Gms.	G	A	Pts.	Pen.	Gms.	G	A	Pts.	Pen.
86-87	Nichols/Wheatfield	NY Jr. B		53	84	137		—	—	—	—	—
87-88	Harvard University	ECAC	30	10	23	33	16	—	—	—	—	—
88-89	Harvard University	ECAC	34	15	48	63	36	—	—	—	—	—
89-90	Harvard University	ECAC	28	17	18	35	22	—	—	—	—	—
90-91	Harvard University	ECAC	28	24	39	63	4	—	—	—	—	—
91-92	Rochester	AHL	77	37	61	98	16	6	2	5	7	6
	Buffalo	NHL	2	0	0	0	0	—	—	—	—	—
NHL totals			2	0	0	0	0					

CICCARELLI, DINO
RW, RED WINGS

PERSONAL: Born February 8, 1960, at Sarnia, Ont. . . . 5-10/175. . . . Shoots right.
TRANSACTIONS/CAREER NOTES: Fractured midshaft of right femur (Spring 1978). . . . Signed as free agent by Minnesota North Stars (September 1979). . . . Injured shoulder (November 1984). . . . Broke right wrist (December 1984). . . . Suspended three games by NHL for making contact with linesman (October 5, 1987). . . . Suspended 10 games by NHL for stick-swinging incident (January 6, 1988). . . . Suspended by North Stars for failure to report to training camp (September 10, 1988). . . . Traded by North Stars with D Bob Rouse to Washington Capitals for RW Mike Gartner and D Larry Murphy (March 7, 1989). . . . Suffered concussion (March 8, 1989). . . . Sprained left knee (April 23, 1990). . . . Fractured right hand (October 20, 1990); missed 21 games. . . . Injured groin (March 24, 1991); missed five games. . . . Injured eye (December 4, 1991); missed one game. . . . Traded by Capitals to Detroit Red Wings for RW Kevin Miller (June 20, 1992).
HONORS: Won Jim Mahon Memorial Trophy (1977-78). . . . Named to OMJHL All-Star second team (1977-78).
RECORDS: Holds NHL single-season playoff record for most goals as a rookie—14; and points as a rookie—21 (1981).

Season	Team	League	REGULAR SEASON					PLAYOFFS				
			Gms.	G	A	Pts.	Pen.	Gms.	G	A	Pts.	Pen.
76-77	London	OMJHL	66	39	43	82	45	—	—	—	—	—
77-78	London	OMJHL	68	*72	70	142	49	9	6	10	16	6
78-79	London	OMJHL	30	8	11	19	25	7	3	5	8	0
79-80	London	OMJHL	62	50	53	103	72	5	2	6	8	15
	Oklahoma City	CHL	6	3	2	5	0	—	—	—	—	—
80-81	Oklahoma City	CHL	48	32	25	57	45	—	—	—	—	—
	Minnesota	NHL	32	18	12	30	29	19	14	7	21	25
81-82	Minnesota	NHL	76	55	51	106	138	4	3	1	4	2
82-83	Minnesota	NHL	77	37	38	75	94	9	4	6	10	11
83-84	Minnesota	NHL	79	38	33	71	58	16	4	5	9	27
84-85	Minnesota	NHL	51	15	17	32	41	9	3	3	6	8
85-86	Minnesota	NHL	75	44	45	89	53	5	0	1	1	6
86-87	Minnesota	NHL	80	52	51	103	92	—	—	—	—	—
87-88	Minnesota	NHL	67	41	45	86	79	—	—	—	—	—
88-89	Minnesota	NHL	65	32	27	59	64	—	—	—	—	—
	Washington	NHL	11	12	3	15	12	6	3	3	6	12
89-90	Washington	NHL	80	41	38	79	122	8	8	3	11	6
90-91	Washington	NHL	54	21	18	39	66	11	5	4	9	22
91-92	Washington	NHL	78	38	38	76	78	7	5	4	9	14
NHL totals			825	444	416	860	926	94	49	37	86	133

CICCONE, ENRICO
D, NORTH STARS

PERSONAL: Born April 10, 1970, at Montreal. . . . 6-4/200. . . . Shoots left.
TRANSACTIONS/CAREER NOTES: Selected by Minnesota North Stars in fifth round (fifth North Stars pick, 92nd overall) of NHL entry draft (June 16, 1990).

Season Team	League	REGULAR SEASON					PLAYOFFS				
		Gms.	G	A	Pts.	Pen.	Gms.	G	A	Pts.	Pen.
87-88—Shawinigan	QMJHL	61	2	12	14	324	—	—	—	—	—
88-89—Shawinigan/T-Rivieres	QMJHL	58	7	19	26	289	—	—	—	—	—
89-90—Trois-Rivieres	QMJHL	40	4	24	28	227	3	0	0	0	15
90-91—Kalamazoo	IHL	57	4	9	13	384	4	0	1	1	32
91-92—Kalamazoo	IHL	53	4	16	20	406	10	0	1	1	58
—Minnesota	NHL	11	0	0	0	48	—	—	—	—	—
NHL totals		11	0	0	0	48					

CICHOCKI, CHRIS
RW, RANGERS

PERSONAL: Born September 17, 1963, at Detroit. . . . 5-11/185. . . . Shoots right. **COLLEGE:** Michigan Tech.
TRANSACTIONS/CAREER NOTES: Signed as free agent by Detroit Red Wings (June 1985). . . . Traded by Red wings with third-round pick in 1987 draft to New Jersey Devils for C Mel Bridgman (March 1987). . . . Separated shoulder (January 1989); missed 17 games. . . . Traded by Devils to Hartford Whalers for RW Jim Thomson (October 31, 1989). . . . Signed as free agent by New York Rangers (September 6, 1990).
MISCELLANEOUS: Member of 1983 U.S. Junior National Team.

Season Team	League	REGULAR SEASON					PLAYOFFS				
		Gms.	G	A	Pts.	Pen.	Gms.	G	A	Pts.	Pen.
82-83—Michigan Tech	WCHA	36	12	10	22	10	—	—	—	—	—
83-84—Michigan Tech	WCHA	40	25	20	45	36	—	—	—	—	—
84-85—Michigan Tech	WCHA	40	30	24	54	14	—	—	—	—	—
85-86—Adirondack	AHL	9	4	4	8	6	—	—	—	—	—
—Detroit	NHL	59	10	11	21	21	—	—	—	—	—
86-87—Adirondack	AHL	55	31	34	65	27	—	—	—	—	—
—Detroit	NHL	2	0	0	0	2	—	—	—	—	—
—Maine	AHL	7	2	2	4	0	—	—	—	—	—
87-88—New Jersey	NHL	5	1	0	1	2	—	—	—	—	—
—Utica	AHL	69	36	30	66	66	—	—	—	—	—
88-89—New Jersey	NHL	2	0	1	1	2	—	—	—	—	—
—Utica	AHL	59	32	31	63	50	5	0	1	1	2
89-90—Utica	AHL	11	3	1	4	10	—	—	—	—	—
—Binghamton	AHL	60	21	26	47	12	—	—	—	—	—
90-91—Binghamton	AHL	80	35	30	65	70	9	0	4	4	2
91-92—Binghamton	AHL	75	28	29	57	132	6	5	4	9	4
NHL totals		68	11	12	23	27					

CIERNY, JOZEF
LW, SABRES

PERSONAL: Born May 13, 1974, at Zvolen, Czechoslovakia. . . . 6-2/176. . . . Shoots left.
TRANSACTIONS/CAREER NOTES: Selected by Buffalo Sabres in second round (second Sabres pick, 35th overall) of NHL entry draft (June 20, 1992).

Season Team	League	REGULAR SEASON					PLAYOFFS				
		Gms.	G	A	Pts.	Pen.	Gms.	G	A	Pts.	Pen.
91-92—Zvolen	Czech.	26	10	3	13	8	—	—	—	—	—

CIGER, ZDENO
LW, DEVILS

PERSONAL: Born October 19, 1969, at Martin, Czechoslovakia. . . . 6-1/190. . . . Shoots left. . . . Full name: Zdenek Ciger.
TRANSACTIONS/CAREER NOTES: Selected by New Jersey Devils in third round (third Devils pick, 54th overall) of NHL entry draft (June 11, 1988). . . . Bruised left shoulder (October 6, 1990). . . . Injured elbow (January 24, 1991). . . . Fractured right wrist (September 24, 1991); missed first 59 games of season.

Season Team	League	REGULAR SEASON					PLAYOFFS				
		Gms.	G	A	Pts.	Pen.	Gms.	G	A	Pts.	Pen.
88-89—Dukla Trencin	Czech.	32	15	21	36	18	—	—	—	—	—
89-90—Dukla Trencin	Czech.	53	18	28	46		—	—	—	—	—
90-91—New Jersey	NHL	45	8	17	25	8	6	0	2	2	4
—Utica	AHL	8	5	4	9	2	—	—	—	—	—
91-92—New Jersey	NHL	20	6	5	11	10	7	2	4	6	0
NHL totals		65	14	22	36	18	13	2	6	8	4

CIMETTA, ROB
LW, MAPLE LEAFS

PERSONAL: Born February 15, 1970, at Toronto. . . . 6-0/190. . . . Shoots left. . . . Full name: Robert Cimetta.
TRANSACTIONS/CAREER NOTES: Fractured wrist (October 1986). . . . Selected by Boston Bruins in first round (first Bruins pick, 18th overall) of NHL entry draft (June 11, 1988). . . . Traded by Bruins to Toronto Maple Leafs for D Steve Bancroft (November 9, 1990). . . . Bruised bicep (March 16, 1991). . . . Pulled groin (December 11, 1991); missed eight games.
HONORS: Named to OHL All-Star first team (1988-89).

Season Team	League	REGULAR SEASON					PLAYOFFS				
		Gms.	G	A	Pts.	Pen.	Gms.	G	A	Pts.	Pen.
86-87—Toronto	OHL	66	21	35	56	65	—	—	—	—	—
87-88—Toronto	OHL	64	34	42	76	90	4	2	2	4	7
88-89—Toronto	OHL	50	*55	47	102	89	6	3	3	6	0
—Boston	NHL	7	2	0	2	0	1	0	0	0	15

C

Season Team	League	REGULAR SEASON					PLAYOFFS				
		Gms.	G	A	Pts.	Pen.	Gms.	G	A	Pts.	Pen.
89-90—Boston	NHL	47	8	9	17	33	—	—	—	—	—
—Maine	AHL	9	3	2	5	13	—	—	—	—	—
90-91—Toronto	NHL	25	2	4	6	21	—	—	—	—	—
—Newmarket	AHL	29	16	18	34	24	—	—	—	—	—
91-92—Toronto	NHL	24	4	3	7	12	—	—	—	—	—
—St. John's	AHL	19	4	13	17	23	10	3	7	10	24
NHL totals		103	16	16	32	66	1	0	0	0	15

CIRELLA, JOE
D, RANGERS

PERSONAL: Born May 9, 1963, at Hamilton, Ont. . . . 6-3/207. . . . Shoots right.
TRANSACTIONS/CAREER NOTES: Selected by Colorado Rockies as underage junior in first round (first Rockies pick, fifth overall) of NHL entry draft (June 10, 1981). . . . Injured left knee (November 26, 1985). . . . Traded by New Jersey Devils to Quebec Nordiques for C Walt Poddubny (June 17, 1989). . . . Broke right foot (January 18, 1990). . . . Strained lower back (February 28, 1990). . . . Injured knee (October 21, 1990). . . . Traded by Nordiques to New York Rangers for C Aaron Broten and a fifth-round pick in 1991 draft (LW Bill Lindsay) (January 17, 1991). . . . Strained lower back (October 4, 1991); missed 10 games.
HONORS: Named to OHL All-Star first team (1982-83). . . . Named to Memorial Cup All-Star team (1982-83).

Season Team	League	REGULAR SEASON					PLAYOFFS				
		Gms.	G	A	Pts.	Pen.	Gms.	G	A	Pts.	Pen.
80-81—Oshawa	OMJHL	56	5	31	36	220	11	0	2	2	41
81-82—Oshawa	OHL	3	0	1	1	10	11	7	10	17	32
—Colorado	NHL	65	7	12	19	52	—	—	—	—	—
82-83—Oshawa	OHL	56	13	55	68	110	17	4	16	20	37
—New Jersey	NHL	2	0	1	1	4	—	—	—	—	—
83-84—New Jersey	NHL	79	11	33	44	137	—	—	—	—	—
84-85—New Jersey	NHL	66	6	18	24	143	—	—	—	—	—
85-86—New Jersey	NHL	66	6	23	29	147	—	—	—	—	—
86-87—New Jersey	NHL	65	9	22	31	111	—	—	—	—	—
87-88—New Jersey	NHL	80	8	31	39	191	19	0	7	7	49
88-89—New Jersey	NHL	80	3	19	22	155	—	—	—	—	—
89-90—Quebec	NHL	56	4	14	18	67	—	—	—	—	—
90-91—Quebec	NHL	39	2	10	12	59	—	—	—	—	—
—New York Rangers	NHL	19	1	0	1	52	6	0	2	2	26
91-92—New York Rangers	NHL	67	3	12	15	121	13	0	4	4	23
NHL totals		684	60	195	255	1239	38	0	13	13	98

CIRONE, JASON
C, JETS

PERSONAL: Born February 21, 1971, at Toronto. . . . 5-9/185. . . . Shoots left.
TRANSACTIONS/CAREER NOTES: Selected by Winnipeg Jets in third round (third Jets pick, 46th overall) of NHL entry draft (June 17, 1989). . . . Traded by Cornwall Royals to Windsor Spitfires for LW Rival Fullum and a second-round draft pick (January 10, 1991).

Season Team	League	REGULAR SEASON					PLAYOFFS				
		Gms.	G	A	Pts.	Pen.	Gms.	G	A	Pts.	Pen.
87-88—Cornwall	OHL	53	12	11	23	41	11	1	2	3	4
88-89—Cornwall	OHL	64	39	44	83	67	17	19	8	27	14
89-90—Cornwall	OHL	32	21	43	64	56	6	4	2	6	14
90-91—Cornwall	OHL	40	31	29	60	66	—	—	—	—	—
—Windsor	OHL	23	27	23	50	31	11	9	8	17	14
91-92—Moncton	AHL	64	32	27	59	124	10	1	1	2	8
—Winnipeg	NHL	3	0	0	0	2	—	—	—	—	—
NHL totals		3	0	0	0	2					

CLARK, JASON
C/LW, CANUCKS

PERSONAL: Born May 6, 1972, at London, Ont. . . . 6-1/180. . . . Shoots left.
TRANSACTIONS/CAREER NOTES: Selected by Vancouver Canucks in sixth round (eighth Canucks pick, 141st overall) of NHL entry draft (June 20, 1992).

Season Team	League	REGULAR SEASON					PLAYOFFS				
		Gms.	G	A	Pts.	Pen.	Gms.	G	A	Pts.	Pen.
91-92—St. Thomas Jr. B	OHA	47	25	52	77	66	—	—	—	—	—

CLARK, KERRY
RW, FLAMES

PERSONAL: Born August 21, 1968, at Kelvington, Sask. . . . 6-1/195. . . . Shoots left. . . . Brother of Wendel Clark, left winger, Toronto Maple Leafs.
TRANSACTIONS/CAREER NOTES: Selected by New York Islanders as underage junior in 10th round (12th Islanders pick, 206th overall) of NHL entry draft (June 21, 1986). . . . Broke ankle (1986-87). . . . Suspended six games by AHL for fighting (October 15, 1988). . . . Signed as free agent by Calgary Flames (July 23, 1990).

Season Team	League	REGULAR SEASON					PLAYOFFS				
		Gms.	G	A	Pts.	Pen.	Gms.	G	A	Pts.	Pen.
84-85—Regina	WHL	36	1	1	2	66	—	—	—	—	—
85-86—Regina	WHL	23	4	4	8	58	—	—	—	—	—
—Saskatoon	WHL	39	5	8	13	104	13	2	2	4	33
86-87—Saskatoon	WHL	54	12	10	22	229	8	0	1	1	23

Season	Team	League	REGULAR SEASON Gms.	G	A	Pts.	Pen.	PLAYOFFS Gms.	G	A	Pts.	Pen.
87-88—Saskatoon		WHL	67	15	11	26	241	10	2	2	4	16
88-89—Springfield		AHL	63	7	7	14	264	—	—	—	—	—
—Indianapolis		IHL	3	0	1	1	12	—	—	—	—	—
89-90—Phoenix		IHL	38	4	8	12	262	—	—	—	—	—
—Springfield		AHL	21	0	1	1	73	—	—	—	—	—
90-91—Salt Lake City		IHL	62	14	14	28	372	4	1	1	2	12
91-92—Salt Lake City		IHL	74	12	14	26	266	5	1	0	1	34

CLARK, WENDEL
LW, MAPLE LEAFS

PERSONAL: Born October 25, 1966, at Kelvington, Sask. . . . 5-11/194. . . . Shoots left. . . . Brother of Kerry Clark, right winger in Calgary Flames system.
TRANSACTIONS/CAREER NOTES: Selected by Toronto Maple Leafs as underage junior in first round (first Maple Leafs pick, first overall) of NHL entry draft (June 15, 1985). . . . Suffered from virus (November 1985). . . . Broke right foot (November 26, 1985); missed 14 games. . . . Suffered back spasms (November 1987); missed 23 games. . . . Suffered tendinitis in right shoulder (October 1987). . . . Reinjured back (February 1988); missed 90 regular season games before returning to lineup (March 1, 1989). . . . Suffered recurrance of back problems (October 1989). . . . Bruised muscle above left knee (November 4, 1989); missed seven games. . . . Tore ligament of right knee (January 26, 1990); missed 29 games. . . . Separated left shoulder (December 18, 1990). . . . Pulled rib cage muscle (February 6, 1991); missed 12 games. . . . Partially tore knee ligaments (October 7, 1991); missed 12 games. . . . Strained knee ligaments (November 6, 1991); missed 24 games.
HONORS: Won Top Defenseman Trophy (1984-85). . . . Named to WHL East All-Star first team (1984-85). . . . Named NHL Rookie of the Year by THE SPORTING NEWS (1985-86). . . . Named to NHL All-Rookie team (1985-86).

Season	Team	League	REGULAR SEASON Gms.	G	A	Pts.	Pen.	PLAYOFFS Gms.	G	A	Pts.	Pen.
83-84—Saskatoon		WHL	72	23	45	68	225	—	—	—	—	—
84-85—Saskatoon		WHL	64	32	55	87	253	3	3	3	6	7
85-86—Toronto		NHL	66	34	11	45	227	10	5	1	6	47
86-87—Toronto		NHL	80	37	23	60	271	13	6	5	11	38
87-88—Toronto		NHL	28	12	11	23	80	—	—	—	—	—
88-89—Toronto		NHL	15	7	4	11	66	—	—	—	—	—
89-90—Toronto		NHL	38	18	8	26	116	5	1	1	2	19
90-91—Toronto		NHL	63	18	16	34	152	—	—	—	—	—
91-92—Toronto		NHL	43	19	21	40	123	—	—	—	—	—
NHL totals			333	145	94	239	1035	28	12	7	19	104

CLARKE, CHRIS
D, CAPITALS

PERSONAL: Born August 6, 1967, at Arnprior, Ont. . . . 6-0/185. . . . Shoots left. . . . Full name: Christopher James Clarke.
COLLEGE: Western Michigan.
TRANSACTIONS/CAREER NOTES: Selected by Washington Capitals in 10th round (eighth Capitals pick, 204th overall) of NHL entry draft (June 13, 1987). . . . Injured jaw (January 1989).

Season	Team	League	REGULAR SEASON Gms.	G	A	Pts.	Pen.	PLAYOFFS Gms.	G	A	Pts.	Pen.
86-87—Pembrooke		BCJHL	—	—	—	—	—	—	—	—	—	—
87-88—Western Michigan Univ.		CCHA	42	7	32	39	64	—	—	—	—	—
88-89—Western Michigan Univ.		CCHA	38	3	21	24	51	—	—	—	—	—
89-90—Western Michigan Univ.		CCHA	39	2	21	23	55	—	—	—	—	—
90-91—Western Michigan Univ.		CCHA	41	4	23	27	68	—	—	—	—	—
91-92—Baltimore		AHL	46	3	12	15	18	—	—	—	—	—
—Hampton Roads		ECHL	3	0	2	2	2	—	—	—	—	—

CLEARY, JOSEPH
D, BLACKHAWKS

PERSONAL: Born January 17, 1970, at Buffalo, N.Y. . . . 6-0/190. . . . Shoots right. . . . Full name: Joseph Patrick Cleary.
HIGH SCHOOL: Cushing Academy (Ashburnham, Mass.).
COLLEGE: Boston College.
TRANSACTIONS/CAREER NOTES: Selected by Chicago Blackhawks in fifth round (fourth Blackhawks pick, 92nd overall) of NHL entry draft (June 11, 1988). . . . Suspended two games for fighting (December 8, 1990).

Season	Team	League	REGULAR SEASON Gms.	G	A	Pts.	Pen.	PLAYOFFS Gms.	G	A	Pts.	Pen.
86-87—Cushing Academy		Mass. H.S.		15	30	45		—	—	—	—	—
87-88—Stratford Jr. B		OHA	41	20	37	57	160	—	—	—	—	—
89-90—Boston College		Hockey East	42	5	21	26	56	—	—	—	—	—
90-91—Boston College		Hockey East	36	4	19	23	34	—	—	—	—	—
91-92—Boston College		Hockey East	29	5	20	25	66	—	—	—	—	—

CLOUTIER, JACQUES
G, NORDIQUES

PERSONAL: Born January 3, 1960, at Noranda, Que. . . . 5-7/168. . . . Shoots left.
TRANSACTIONS/CAREER NOTES: Selected by Buffalo Sabres as underage junior in third round (fourth Sabres pick, 55th overall) of NHL entry draft (August 9, 1979). . . . Suffered broken collarbone (January 1982). . . . Tore ligaments in knee (December 1984); missed remainder of season; spent the year as an assistant coach with Rochester. . . . Traded by Sabres to Chicago Blackhawks for future considerations (September, 1989); Steve Ludzik and a draft pick later sent to Sabres to complete deal. . . . Pulled groin (December 11, 1989); missed six games. . . . Strained left knee (March 25, 1990). . . . Traded by

Blackhawks to Quebec Nordiques for LW Tony McKegney (January 29, 1991).
HONORS: Won Jacques Plante Trophy (1978-79).... Named to QMJHL All-Star first team (1978-79).

Season Team	League	REGULAR SEASON								PLAYOFFS						
		Gms.	Min.	W	L	T	GA	SO	Avg.	Gms.	Min.	W	L	GA	SO	Avg.
76-77—Trois-Rivieres	QMJHL	24	1109				93	0	5.03	—	—	—	—	—	—	—
77-78—Trois-Rivieres	QMJHL	*71	*4134				240	*4	3.48	13	779			40	1	3.08
78-79—Trois-Rivieres	QMJHL	*72	*4168				218	†3	*3.14	13	780			36	0	2.77
79-80—Trois-Rivieres	QMJHL	55	3222	27	20	7	231	†2	4.30	7	420	3	4	33	0	4.71
80-81—Rochester	AHL	*61	*3478	27	27	6	*209	1	3.61	—	—	—	—	—	—	—
81-82—Rochester	AHL	23	1366	14	7	2	64	0	2.81	—	—	—	—	—	—	—
—Buffalo	NHL	7	311	5	1	0	13	0	2.51	—	—	—	—	—	—	—
82-83—Buffalo	NHL	25	1390	10	7	6	81	0	3.50	—	—	—	—	—	—	—
—Rochester	AHL	13	634	7	3	1	42	0	3.97	16	992	12	4	47	0	2.84
83-84—Rochester	AHL	*51	*2841	26	22	1	172	1	3.63	*18	*1145	9	9	*68	0	3.56
84-85—Rochester	AHL	14	803	10	2	1	36	0	2.69	—	—	—	—	—	—	—
—Buffalo	NHL	1	65	0	0	1	4	0	3.69	—	—	—	—	—	—	—
85-86—Rochester	AHL	14	835	10	2	2	38	1	2.73	—	—	—	—	—	—	—
—Buffalo	NHL	15	872	5	9	1	49	1	3.37	—	—	—	—	—	—	—
86-87—Buffalo	NHL	40	2167	11	19	5	137	0	3.79	—	—	—	—	—	—	—
87-88—Buffalo	NHL	20	851	4	8	2	67	0	4.72	—	—	—	—	—	—	—
88-89—Buffalo	NHL	36	1786	15	14	0	108	0	3.63	4	238	1	3	10	1	2.52
—Rochester	AHL	11	527	2	7	0	41	0	4.67	—	—	—	—	—	—	—
89-90—Chicago	NHL	43	2178	18	15	2	112	2	3.09	4	175	0	2	8	0	2.74
90-91—Chicago	NHL	10	403	2	3	0	24	0	3.57	—	—	—	—	—	—	—
—Quebec	NHL	15	829	3	8	2	61	0	4.41	—	—	—	—	—	—	—
91-92—Quebec	NHL	26	1345	6	14	3	88	0	3.93	—	—	—	—	—	—	—
NHL totals		238	12197	79	98	22	744	3	3.66	8	413	1	5	18	1	2.62

CLOUTIER, SYLVAIN
C, RED WINGS

PERSONAL: Born February 13, 1974, at Mt. Laurier, Que.... 6-0/192.... Shoots left.
HIGH SCHOOL: Bishop MacDonnell (Guelph, Ont.).
TRANSACTIONS/CAREER NOTES: Selected by Detroit Red Wings in third round (third Red Wings pick, 70th overall) of NHL entry draft (June 20, 1992).

Season Team	League	REGULAR SEASON					PLAYOFFS				
		Gms.	G	A	Pts.	Pen.	Gms.	G	A	Pts.	Pen.
91-92—Guelph	OHL	62	35	31	66	74	—	—	—	—	—

COFFEY, PAUL
D, KINGS

PERSONAL: Born June 1, 1961, at Weston, Ont.... 6-0/200.... Shoots left.... Full name: Paul Douglas Coffey.
TRANSACTIONS/CAREER NOTES: Selected by Edmonton Oilers in first round (first Oilers pick, sixth overall) of NHL entry draft (June 11, 1980).... Suffered recurring back spasms (December 1986); missed 10 games.... Traded by Oilers with LW Dave Hunter and RW Wayne Van Dorp to Pittsburgh Penguins for C Craig Simpson, C Dave Hannan, D Moe Mantha and D Chris Joseph (November 24, 1987).... Tore knee cartilage (December 1987).... Bruised right shoulder (November 16, 1988).... Broke finger (May 1990).... Injured back (February 27, 1991). ... Injured hip muscle (March 9, 1991).... Scratched left eye cornea (April 9, 1991).... Broke jaw (April 1991).... Pulled hip muscle (February 3, 1992); missed three games.... Traded by Penguins to Los Angeles Kings for D Brian Benning, D Jeff Chychrun and first-round pick in 1992 draft (February 19, 1992).... Suffered back spasms (March 3, 1992); missed three games.... Fractured wrist (March 17, 1992); missed five games.
HONORS: Named to OMJHL All-Star second team (1979-80).... Named to NHL All-Star second team (1980-81 through 1983-84 and 1989-90).... Named to THE SPORTING NEWS All-Star second team (1981-82 through 1983-84, 1986-87 and 1989-90).... Won James Norris Memorial Trophy (1984-85 and 1985-86).... Named to THE SPORTING NEWS All-Star first team (1984-85, 1985-86 and 1988-89).... Named to NHL All-Star first team (1984-85, 1985-86 and 1988-89).
RECORDS: Holds NHL career records for most goals by a defenseman—318; most assists by a defenseman—796; and most points by a defenseman—1,114.... Holds NHL single-season record for most goals by a defenseman—48 (1985-86).... Shares NHL single-game record for most points by a defenseman—8; and most assists by a defenseman—6 (March 14, 1986). ... Holds NHL record for most consecutive games scoring points by a defenseman—28 (1985-86).... Holds NHL single-season playoff records for most goals by a defenseman—12; assists by a defenseman—25; and points by a defenseman—37 (1985).... Holds NHL single-game playoff record for most points by a defenseman—6 (May 14, 1985).

Season Team	League	REGULAR SEASON					PLAYOFFS				
		Gms.	G	A	Pts.	Pen.	Gms.	G	A	Pts.	Pen.
77-78—Kingston	OMJHL	8	2	2	4	11	—	—	—	—	—
—North York	MTHL	50	14	33	47	64	—	—	—	—	—
78-79—Sault Ste. Marie	OMJHL	68	17	72	89	99	—	—	—	—	—
79-80—Sault Ste. Marie	OMJHL	23	10	21	31	63	—	—	—	—	—
—Kitchener	OMJHL	52	19	52	71	130	—	—	—	—	—
80-81—Edmonton	NHL	74	9	23	32	130	9	4	3	7	22
81-82—Edmonton	NHL	80	29	60	89	106	5	1	1	2	6
82-83—Edmonton	NHL	80	29	67	96	87	16	7	7	14	14
83-84—Edmonton	NHL	80	40	86	126	104	19	8	14	22	21
84-85—Edmonton	NHL	80	37	84	121	97	18	12	25	37	44
85-86—Edmonton	NHL	79	48	90	138	120	10	1	9	10	30
86-87—Edmonton	NHL	59	17	50	67	49	17	3	8	11	30
87-88—Pittsburgh	NHL	46	15	52	67	93	—	—	—	—	—
88-89—Pittsburgh	NHL	75	30	83	113	193	11	2	13	15	31

Season Team	League	REGULAR SEASON					PLAYOFFS				
		Gms.	G	A	Pts.	Pen.	Gms.	G	A	Pts.	Pen.
89-90—Pittsburgh	NHL	80	29	74	103	95	—	—	—	—	—
90-91—Pittsburgh	NHL	76	24	69	93	128	12	2	9	11	6
91-92—Pittsburgh	NHL	54	10	54	64	62	—	—	—	—	—
—Los Angeles	NHL	10	1	4	5	25	6	4	3	7	2
NHL totals		873	318	796	1114	1289	123	44	92	136	206

COLE, DANTON
RW, LIGHTNING

PERSONAL: Born January 10, 1967, at Pontiac, Mich.... 5-11/189.... Shoots right.... Full name: Danton Edward Cole.
COLLEGE: Michigan State.
TRANSACTIONS/CAREER NOTES: Selected by Winnipeg Jets in sixth round (sixth Jets pick, 123rd overall) of NHL entry draft (June 15, 1985).... Strained knee (January 26, 1992); missed 11 games.... Traded by Jets to Tampa Bay Lightning for future considerations (June 19, 1992).

Season Team	League	REGULAR SEASON					PLAYOFFS				
		Gms.	G	A	Pts.	Pen.	Gms.	G	A	Pts.	Pen.
84-85—Aurora	OHA	41	51	44	95	91	—	—	—	—	—
85-86—Michigan State	CCHA	43	11	10	21	22	—	—	—	—	—
86-87—Michigan State	CCHA	44	9	15	24	16	—	—	—	—	—
87-88—Michigan State	CCHA	46	20	36	56	00	—	—	—	—	—
88-89—Michigan State	CCHA	47	29	33	62	46	—	—	—	—	—
89-90—Winnipeg	NHL	2	1	1	2	0	—	—	—	—	—
—Moncton	AHL	80	31	42	73	18	—	—	—	—	—
90-91—Winnipeg	NHL	66	13	11	24	24	—	—	—	—	—
—Moncton	AHL	3	1	1	2	0	—	—	—	—	—
91-92—Winnipeg	NHL	52	7	5	12	32	—	—	—	—	—
NHL totals		120	21	17	38	56					

COLMAN, MICHAEL
D, SHARKS

PERSONAL: Born August 4, 1968, at Stoneham, Mass.... 6-3/218.... Shoots right.
COLLEGE: Ferris State (Mich.).
TRANSACTIONS/CAREER NOTES: Signed as free agent by San Jose Sharks (September 3, 1991).

Season Team	League	REGULAR SEASON					PLAYOFFS				
		Gms.	G	A	Pts.	Pen.	Gms.	G	A	Pts.	Pen.
87-88—Humboldt	SJHL	55	3	7	10	188	—	—	—	—	—
88-89—Humboldt	SJHL	64	3	17	20	161	—	—	—	—	—
89-90—Ferris State	CCHA	23	0	4	4	62	—	—	—	—	—
90-91—Kansas City	IHL	66	1	6	7	115	—	—	—	—	—
91-92—Kansas City	IHL	59	0	4	4	130	3	0	0	0	4
—San Jose	NHL	15	0	1	1	32	—	—	—	—	—
NHL totals		15	0	1	1	32					

CONACHER, PAT
LW, DEVILS

PERSONAL: Born May 1, 1959, at Edmonton, Alta.... 5-8/190.... Shoots left.... Full name: Patrick John Conacher.
TRANSACTIONS/CAREER NOTES: Selected by New York Rangers in fourth round (third Rangers pick, 76th overall) of NHL entry draft (August 9, 1979).... Fractured left ankle (September 21, 1980).... Injured shoulder (November 1982).... Signed as free agent by Edmonton Oilers (October 4, 1983).... Injured groin (December 1984).... Signed as free agent by New Jersey Devils (August 1985).... Sprained back (February 1988).... Bruised left shoulder (December 1988).... Underwent major reconstructive surgery to left shoulder (April 7, 1989). ... Lacerated face and lost two teeth (October 13, 1989).... Sprained left knee (April 9, 1990).... Strained left knee (September 22, 1990).... Suffered ulcer problems (February 1991).... Injured groin (October 24, 1991); missed two games.... Injured groin (December 1991).... Underwent hernia surgery (January 9, 1992); missed 34 games.

Season Team	League	REGULAR SEASON					PLAYOFFS				
		Gms.	G	A	Pts.	Pen.	Gms.	G	A	Pts.	Pen.
77-78—Billings	WCHL	72	31	44	75	105	20	15	14	29	22
78-79—Billings	WHL	39	25	37	62	50	—	—	—	—	—
—Saskatoon	WHL	33	15	32	47	37	—	—	—	—	—
79-80—New York Rangers	NHL	17	0	5	5	4	3	0	1	1	2
—New Haven	AHL	53	11	14	25	43	7	1	1	2	4
80-81—New York Rangers	NHL	—	—	—	—	—	—	—	—	—	—
81-82—Springfield	AHL	77	23	22	45	38	—	—	—	—	—
82-83—Tulsa	CHL	63	29	28	57	44	—	—	—	—	—
—New York Rangers	NHL	5	0	1	1	4	—	—	—	—	—
83-84—Moncton	AHL	28	7	16	23	30	—	—	—	—	—
—Edmonton	NHL	45	2	8	10	31	3	1	0	1	2
84-85—Nova Scotia	AHL	68	20	45	65	44	6	3	2	5	0
85-86—New Jersey	NHL	2	0	2	2	2	—	—	—	—	—
—Maine	AHL	69	15	30	45	83	5	1	1	2	11
86-87—Maine	AHL	56	12	14	26	47	—	—	—	—	—
87-88—Utica	AHL	47	14	33	47	32	—	—	—	—	—
—New Jersey	NHL	24	2	5	7	12	17	2	2	4	14
88-89—New Jersey	NHL	55	7	5	12	14	—	—	—	—	—

Season Team	League	REGULAR SEASON					PLAYOFFS				
		Gms.	G	A	Pts.	Pen.	Gms.	G	A	Pts.	Pen.
89-90—Utica	AHL	57	13	36	49	53	—	—	—	—	—
—New Jersey	NHL	19	3	3	6	4	5	1	0	1	10
90-91—Utica	AHL	4	0	1	1	6	—	—	—	—	—
—New Jersey	NHL	49	5	11	16	27	7	0	2	2	2
91-92—New Jersey	NHL	44	7	3	10	16	7	1	1	2	4
NHL totals		260	26	43	69	114	42	5	6	11	34

CONN, ROB
LW/RW, 'HAWKS

PERSONAL: Born September 3, 1968, at Calgary, Alta. . . . 6-2/200. . . . Shoots right. . . . Full name: Robert Phillip Conn.
COLLEGE: Alaska-Anchorage.
TRANSACTIONS/CAREER NOTES: Signed as free agent by Chicago Blackhawks (July 31, 1991).

Season Team	League	REGULAR SEASON					PLAYOFFS				
		Gms.	G	A	Pts.	Pen.	Gms.	G	A	Pts.	Pen.
88-89—Alaska-Anchorage	Indep.	33	21	17	38	46	—	—	—	—	—
89-90—Alaska-Anchorage	Indep.	34	27	21	48	46	—	—	—	—	—
90-91—Alaska-Anchorage	Indep.	43	28	32	60	53	—	—	—	—	—
91-92—Indianapolis	IHL	72	19	16	35	100	—	—	—	—	—
—Chicago	NHL	2	0	0	0	2	—	—	—	—	—
NHL totals		2	0	0	0	2					

CONNOLLY, JEFF
C, CANUCKS

PERSONAL: Born February 1, 1974, at Worcester, Mass. . . . 6-0/185. . . . Shoots right.
HIGH SCHOOL: Milton Academy (Mass.), then St. Sebastian's Country Day School (Needham, Mass.).
TRANSACTIONS/CAREER NOTES: Selected by Vancouver Canucks in third round (fourth Canucks pick, 69th overall) of NHL entry draft (June 20, 1992).

Season Team	League	REGULAR SEASON					PLAYOFFS				
		Gms.	G	A	Pts.	Pen.	Gms.	G	A	Pts.	Pen.
89-90—Milton Academy	Mass. H.S.	21	14	18	32		—	—	—	—	—
90-91—Milton Academy	Mass. H.S.	23	28	19	47		—	—	—	—	—
91-92—St. Sebastian's	Mass. H.S.	28	31	35	66		—	—	—	—	—

CONROY, AL
C, FLYERS

PERSONAL: Born January 17, 1966, at Calgary, Alta. . . . 5-8/170. . . . Shoots right. . . . Full name: Allan Conroy.
TRANSACTIONS/CAREER NOTES: Signed as free agent by Detroit Red Wings (August 1989). . . . Signed as free agent by Philadelphia Flyers (August 21, 1991).

Season Team	League	REGULAR SEASON					PLAYOFFS				
		Gms.	G	A	Pts.	Pen.	Gms.	G	A	Pts.	Pen.
86-87—Rapperswill	Switzerland		30	32	62		—	—	—	—	—
—Rochester	AHL	13	4	4	8	40	13	1	3	4	50
87-88—Varese	Italy	36	25	39	64		—	—	—	—	—
—Adirondack	AHL	13	5	8	13	20	11	1	3	4	41
88-89—Dortmund	Germany	46	53	78	131		—	—	—	—	—
89-90—Adirondack	AHL	77	23	33	56	147	5	0	0	0	20
90-91—Adirondack	AHL	80	26	39	65	172	2	1	1	2	0
91-92—Hershey	AHL	47	17	28	45	90	6	4	2	6	12
—Philadelphia	NHL	31	2	9	11	74	—	—	—	—	—
NHL totals		31	2	9	11	74					

CONVERY, BRANDON
C, MAPLE LEAFS

PERSONAL: Born February 4, 1974, at Kingston, Ont. . . . 6-1/180. . . . Shoots right.
HIGH SCHOOL: Lasalle Secondary School (Sudbury, Ont.).
TRANSACTIONS/CAREER NOTES: Selected by Toronto Maple Leafs in first round (first Maple Leafs pick, eighth overall) of NHL entry draft (June 20, 1992).
HONORS: Won OHL Top Prospect Award (1991-92).

Season Team	League	REGULAR SEASON					PLAYOFFS				
		Gms.	G	A	Pts.	Pen.	Gms.	G	A	Pts.	Pen.
89-90—Kingston Jr. B	OHA	42	13	25	38	4	—	—	—	—	—
90-91—Sudbury	OHL	56	26	22	48	18	5	1	1	2	2
91-92—Sudbury	OHL	44	40	27	67	44	5	3	2	5	4

COOKE, JAMIE
RW, FLYERS

PERSONAL: Born November 5, 1968, at Bramalea, Ont. . . . 6-2/206. . . . Shoots right. . . . Full name: Jamie William Cooke.
COLLEGE: Colgate.
TRANSACTIONS/CAREER NOTES: Selected by Philadelphia Flyers in seventh round (eighth Flyers pick, 140th overall) of NHL entry draft (June 11, 1988).

Season Team	League	REGULAR SEASON					PLAYOFFS				
		Gms.	G	A	Pts.	Pen.	Gms.	G	A	Pts.	Pen.
86-87—Bramalea Jr. B	OHA	37	21	28	49	46	—	—	—	—	—
87-88—Bramalea Jr. B	OHA	37	26	44	70	56	—	—	—	—	—

Season	Team	League	REGULAR SEASON Gms.	G	A	Pts.	Pen.	PLAYOFFS Gms.	G	A	Pts.	Pen.
88-89—Colgate University		ECAC	28	13	11	24	26	—	—	—	—	—
89-90—Colgate University		ECAC	38	16	20	36	24	—	—	—	—	—
90-91—Colgate University		ECAC	32	28	26	54	22	—	—	—	—	—
91-92—Hershey		AHL	66	15	26	41	49	—	—	—	—	—

COOPER, DAVID
D, SABRES

PERSONAL: Born November 2, 1973, at Ottawa.... 6-1/190.... Shoots left.
HIGH SCHOOL: Medicine Hat (Alta.).
TRANSACTIONS/CAREER NOTES: Selcted by Buffalo Sabres in first round (first Sabres pick, 11th overall) of NHL entry draft (June 20, 1992).
HONORS: Won WHL Top Prospect Award (1991-92).... Named to WHL (East) All-Star first team (1991-92).

Season	Team	League	REGULAR SEASON Gms.	G	A	Pts.	Pen.	PLAYOFFS Gms.	G	A	Pts.	Pen.
89-90—Medicine Hat		WHL	61	4	11	15	65	3	0	2	2	2
90-91—Medicine Hat		WHL	64	12	31	43	66	11	1	3	4	23
91-92—Medicine Hat		WHL	72	17	47	64	176	4	1	4	5	8

COPELAND, TODD
D, DEVILS

PERSONAL: Born May 18, 1968, at Ridgewood, N.J.... 6-2/210.... Shoots left.... Full name: John Todd Copeland.
HIGH SCHOOL: Belmont Hill (Belmont, Mass.).
COLLEGE: Miohigan.
TRANSACTIONS/CAREER NOTES: Injured knee (February 1986).... Selected by New Jersey Devils in second round (second Devils pick, 24th overall) of NHL entry draft (June 21, 1986).

Season	Team	League	REGULAR SEASON Gms.	G	A	Pts.	Pen.	PLAYOFFS Gms.	G	A	Pts.	Pen.
84-85—Belmont Hill H.S.		Mass. H.S.	23	8	25	33	18	—	—	—	—	—
85-86—Belmont Hill H.S.		Mass. H.S.	19	4	19	23	19	—	—	—	—	—
86-87—University of Michigan		CCHA	34	2	10	12	57	—	—	—	—	—
87-88—University of Michigan		CCHA	41	3	10	13	58	—	—	—	—	—
88-89—University of Michigan		CCHA	39	5	14	19	102	—	—	—	—	—
89-90—University of Michigan		CCHA	34	6	16	22	62	—	—	—	—	—
90-91—Utica		AHL	79	6	24	30	53	—	—	—	—	—
91-92—Utica		AHL	80	4	23	27	96	4	2	2	4	2

CORBET, RENE
LW, NORDIQUES

PERSONAL: Born June 25, 1973, at Victoriaville, Que.... 6-0/176.... Shoots left.
TRANSACTIONS/CAREER NOTES: Selected by Quebec Nordiques in second round (second Nordiques pick, 24th overall) of NHL entry draft (June 22, 1991).
HONORS: Won the Michel Bergeron Trophy (1990-91).... Named to QMJHL All-Rookie Team (1990-91).

Season	Team	League	REGULAR SEASON Gms.	G	A	Pts.	Pen.	PLAYOFFS Gms.	G	A	Pts.	Pen.
90-91—Drummondville		QMJHL	45	25	40	65	34	14	11	6	17	15
91-92—Drummondville		QMJHL	56	46	50	96	90	4	1	2	3	17

CORKUM, BOB
C/RW, SABRES

PERSONAL: Born December 18, 1967, at Salisbury, Mass.... 6-2/212.... Shoots right.... Full name: Robert Freeman Corkum.
HIGH SCHOOL: Triton Regional (Byfield, Mass.).
COLLEGE: Maine.
TRANSACTIONS/CAREER NOTES: Selected by Buffalo Sabres in third round (third Sabres pick, 47th overall) of NHL entry draft (June 21, 1986).... Injured hip (March 19, 1992).

Season	Team	League	REGULAR SEASON Gms.	G	A	Pts.	Pen.	PLAYOFFS Gms.	G	A	Pts.	Pen.
84-85—Triton Regional H.S.		Mass. H.S.	18	35	36	71		—	—	—	—	—
85-86—University of Maine		Hockey East	39	7	16	23	53	—	—	—	—	—
86-87—University of Maine		Hockey East	35	18	11	29	24	—	—	—	—	—
87-88—University of Maine		Hockey East	40	14	18	32	64	—	—	—	—	—
88-89—University of Maine		Hockey East	45	17	31	48	64	—	—	—	—	—
89-90—Rochester		AHL	43	8	11	19	45	12	2	5	7	16
—Buffalo		NHL	8	2	0	2	4	5	1	0	1	4
90-91—Rochester		AHL	69	13	21	34	77	15	4	4	8	4
91-92—Rochester		AHL	52	16	12	28	47	8	0	6	6	8
—Buffalo		NHL	20	2	4	6	21	4	1	0	1	0
NHL totals			28	4	4	8	25	9	2	0	2	4

CORPSE, KELI
C, CANADIENS

PERSONAL: Born May 14, 1974, at London, Ont.... 5-11/174.... Shoots left.
HIGH SCHOOL: Loyalist Collegiate (Kingston, Ont.).
TRANSACTIONS/CAREER NOTES: Selected by Montreal Canadiens in second round (third Canadiens pick, 44th overall) of NHL entry draft (June 20, 1992).

Season	Team	League	REGULAR SEASON Gms.	G	A	Pts.	Pen.	PLAYOFFS Gms.	G	A	Pts.	Pen.
89-90—London Jr. B		OHA	39	26	31	57	10	—	—	—	—	—
90-91—Kingston		OHL	58	18	33	51	34	—	—	—	—	—
91-92—Kingston		OHL	65	31	52	83	20	—	—	—	—	—

C

CORRIVEAU, RICK

D, CAPITALS

PERSONAL: Born January 6, 1971, at Welland, Ont. . . . 6-0/208. . . . Shoots left. . . . Full name: Rick Claude Corriveau. . . . Brother of Yvon Corriveau, left winger, Hartford Whalers.

TRANSACTIONS/CAREER NOTES: Injured right knee ligaments (November 6, 1988). . . . Selected by St. Louis Blues in second round (second Blues pick, 31st overall) of NHL entry draft (June 17, 1989). . . . Returned to the draft pool by Blues and selected by Washington Capitals in eighth round, 168th pick overall (June 22, 1991).

HONORS: Won Emms Family Award (1987-88).

			REGULAR SEASON					PLAYOFFS			
Season	Team	League	Gms.	G	A	Pts.	Pen.	Gms.	G	A	Pts.	Pen.
86-87—Welland Jr. B		OHA	29	9	17	26	90	—	—	—	—	—
87-88—London		OHL	63	19	47	66	51	12	4	10	14	18
88-89—London		OHL	12	4	10	14	23	1	0	0	0	0
89-90—London		OHL	63	22	55	77	63	6	4	3	7	12
90-91—London		OHL	64	27	60	87	83	7	3	7	10	16
91-92—London		OHL	4	0	7	7	6	—	—	—	—	—
—Niagara Falls		OHL	54	21	57	78	72	17	5	16	21	36

CORRIVEAU, YVON

LW, WHALERS

PERSONAL: Born February 8, 1967, at Welland, Ont. . . . 6-1/202. . . . Shoots left. . . . Brother of Rick Corriveau, defenseman in Washington Capitals system.

TRANSACTIONS/CAREER NOTES: Shoulder injury (March 1985). . . . Selected by Washington Capitals as underage junior in first round (first Capitals pick, 19th overall) of NHL entry draft (June 15, 1985). . . . Bruised thigh (November 1988). . . . Traded by Capitals to Hartford Whalers for G Mike Liut (March 5, 1990). . . . Bruised foot (October 1990).

			REGULAR SEASON					PLAYOFFS			
Season	Team	League	Gms.	G	A	Pts.	Pen.	Gms.	G	A	Pts.	Pen.
83-84—Welland Jr. B		OHA	36	16	21	37	51	—	—	—	—	—
84-85—Toronto		OHL	59	23	28	51	65	3	0	0	0	5
85-86—Toronto		OHL	59	54	36	90	75	4	1	1	2	0
—Washington		NHL	2	0	0	0	0	4	0	3	3	2
86-87—Toronto		OHL	23	14	19	33	23	—	—	—	—	—
—Binghamton		AHL	7	0	0	0	2	8	0	1	1	0
—Washington		NHL	17	1	1	2	24	—	—	—	—	—
87-88—Binghamton		AHL	35	15	14	29	64	—	—	—	—	—
—Washington		NHL	44	10	9	19	84	13	1	2	3	30
88-89—Baltimore		AHL	33	16	23	39	65	—	—	—	—	—
—Washington		NHL	33	3	2	5	62	1	0	0	0	0
89-90—Washington		NHL	50	9	6	15	50	—	—	—	—	—
—Hartford		NHL	13	4	1	5	22	4	1	0	1	0
90-91—Hartford		NHL	23	1	1	2	18	—	—	—	—	—
—Springfield		AHL	44	17	25	42	10	18	†10	6	16	31
91-92—Hartford		NHL	38	12	8	20	36	7	3	2	5	18
—Springfield		AHL	39	26	15	41	40	—	—	—	—	—
NHL totals			220	40	28	68	296	29	5	7	12	50

CORSON, SHAYNE

LW/C, CANADIENS

PERSONAL: Born August 13, 1966, at Barrie, Ont. . . . 6-0/201. . . . Shoots left.

TRANSACTIONS/CAREER NOTES: Selected by Montreal Canadiens in first round (second Canadiens pick, eighth overall) of NHL entry draft (June 9, 1984). . . . Broke jaw (January 24, 1987). . . . Strained ligament in right knee (September 1987). . . . Injured groin (March 1988). . . . Injured knee (April 1988). . . . Injured knee (April 1989). . . . Bruised left shoulder (October 29, 1989). . . . Broke toe on right foot (December 1989). . . . Suffered hip pointer (November 10, 1990); missed seven games. . . . Pulled groin (February 11, 1991).

HONORS: Named to World Junior Hockey Championship All-Star team (1986).

			REGULAR SEASON					PLAYOFFS			
Season	Team	League	Gms.	G	A	Pts.	Pen.	Gms.	G	A	Pts.	Pen.
82-83—Barrie		COJHL	23	13	29	42	87	—	—	—	—	—
83-84—Brantford		OHL	66	25	46	71	165	6	4	1	5	26
84-85—Hamilton		OHL	54	27	63	90	154	11	3	7	10	19
85-86—Hamilton		OHL	47	41	57	98	153	—	—	—	—	—
—Montreal		NHL	3	0	0	0	2	—	—	—	—	—
86-87—Montreal		NHL	55	12	11	23	144	17	6	5	11	30
87-88—Montreal		NHL	71	12	27	39	152	3	1	0	1	12
88-89—Montreal		NHL	80	26	24	50	193	21	4	5	9	65
89-90—Montreal		NHL	76	31	44	75	144	11	2	8	10	20
90-91—Montreal		NHL	71	23	24	47	138	13	9	6	15	36
91-92—Montreal		NHL	64	17	36	53	118	10	2	5	7	15
NHL totals			420	121	166	287	891	75	24	29	53	178

COTE, ALAIN

D, CANADIENS

PERSONAL: Born April 14, 1967, at Montmagny, Que. . . . 6-0/200. . . . Shoots right. . . . Full name: Alain Gabriel Cote. . . . Brother of Sylvain Cote, defenseman, Washington Capitals.

TRANSACTIONS/CAREER NOTES: Selected by Boston Bruins as underage junior in second round (first Bruins pick, 31st overall) of NHL entry draft (June 15, 1985). . . . Traded by Bruins to Washington Capitals for RW Bobby Gould (September 27, 1989). . . . Traded by Capitals to Montreal Canadiens for D Marc Deschamps (June 23, 1990). . . . Injured eye (March 30, 1991).

Season	Team	League	REGULAR SEASON					PLAYOFFS				
			Gms.	G	A	Pts.	Pen.	Gms.	G	A	Pts.	Pen.
83-84	—Quebec	QMJHL	60	3	17	20	40	—	—	—	—	—
84-85	—Quebec	QMJHL	68	9	25	34	173	—	—	—	—	—
85-86	—Granby	QMJHL	22	4	12	16	48	—	—	—	—	—
	—Moncton	AHL	3	0	0	0	0	—	—	—	—	—
	—Boston	NHL	32	0	6	6	14	—	—	—	—	—
86-87	—Granby	QMJHL	43	7	24	31	185	4	0	3	3	2
	—Boston	NHL	3	0	0	0	0	—	—	—	—	—
87-88	—Boston	NHL	2	0	0	0	0	—	—	—	—	—
	—Maine	AHL	69	9	34	43	108	9	2	4	6	19
88-89	—Maine	AHL	37	5	16	21	111	—	—	—	—	—
	—Boston	NHL	31	2	3	5	51	—	—	—	—	—
89-90	—Washington	NHL	2	0	0	0	7	—	—	—	—	—
	—Baltimore	AHL	57	5	19	24	161	3	0	0	0	9
90-91	—Montreal	NHL	28	0	6	6	26	11	0	2	2	26
	—Fredericton	AHL	49	8	19	27	110	—	—	—	—	—
91-92	—Montreal	NHL	13	0	3	3	22	—	—	—	—	—
	—Fredericton	AHL	20	1	10	11	24	7	0	1	1	4
NHL totals			111	2	18	20	120	11	0	2	2	26

COTE, SYLVAIN
D, CAPITALS

PERSONAL: Born January 19, 1966, at Quebec City.... 6-0/190.... Shoots right.... Brother of Alain Cote, defenseman, Montreal Canadiens.

TRANSACTIONS/CAREER NOTES: Selected by Hartford Whalers as underage junior in first round (first Whalers pick, 11th overall) of NHL entry draft (June 9, 1984).... Broke toe on left foot (October 28, 1989).... Sprained left knee (December 1989).... Fractured right foot (January 22, 1990).... Traded by Whalers to Washington Capitals for a second-round pick in 1992 draft (September 8, 1991).

HONORS: Won Emile (Butch) Bouchard Trophy (1985-86).... Shared Guy Lafleur Trophy with Luc Robitaille (1985-86).... Named to QMJHL All-Star first team (1985-86).... Named to World Junior Championship All-Star Team (1986).

Season	Team	League	REGULAR SEASON					PLAYOFFS				
			Gms.	G	A	Pts.	Pen.	Gms.	G	A	Pts.	Pen.
82-83	—Quebec	QMJHL	66	10	24	34	50	—	—	—	—	—
83-84	—Quebec	QMJHL	66	15	50	65	89	5	1	1	2	0
84-85	—Hartford	NHL	67	3	9	12	17	—	—	—	—	—
85-86	—Hartford	NHL	2	0	0	0	0	—	—	—	—	—
	—Hull	QMJHL	26	10	33	43	14	13	6	*28	34	22
86-87	—Binghamton	AHL	12	2	4	6	0	—	—	—	—	—
	—Hartford	NHL	67	2	8	10	20	2	0	2	2	4
87-88	—Hartford	NHL	67	7	21	28	30	6	1	1	2	4
88-89	—Hartford	NHL	78	8	9	17	49	3	0	1	1	4
89-90	—Hartford	NHL	28	4	2	6	14	5	0	0	0	0
90-91	—Hartford	NHL	73	7	12	19	17	6	0	2	2	2
91-92	—Washington	NHL	78	11	29	40	31	7	1	2	3	4
NHL totals			460	42	90	132	178	29	2	8	10	14

COURTENAY, ED
RW, SHARKS

PERSONAL: Born February 2, 1968, at Verdun, Que.... 6-4/216.... Shoots right.... Full name: Edward Courtenay.

TRANSACTIONS/CAREER NOTES: Signed as free agent by Minnesota North Stars (October 1, 1989).... Selected by San Jose Sharks in NHL dispersal draft (May 30, 1991).... Injured wrist (October 18, 1991); missed four games.

Season	Team	League	REGULAR SEASON					PLAYOFFS				
			Gms.	G	A	Pts.	Pen.	Gms.	G	A	Pts.	Pen.
87-88	—Granby	QMJHL	54	37	34	71	19	5	1	1	2	2
88-89	—Granby	QMJHL	68	59	55	114	68	4	1	1	2	22
	—Kalamazoo	IHL	1	0	0	0	0	1	0	0	0	2
89-90	—Kalamazoo	IHL	57	25	28	53	16	3	0	0	0	0
90-91	—Kalamazoo	IHL	76	35	36	71	37	8	2	3	5	12
91-92	—Kansas City	IHL	36	14	12	26	46	15	8	9	17	15
	—San Jose	NHL	5	0	0	0	0	—	—	—	—	—
NHL totals			5	0	0	0	0					

COURTNALL, GEOFF
LW, CANUCKS

PERSONAL: Born August 18, 1962, at Victoria, B.C.... 6-1/190.... Shoots left.... Brother of Russ Courtnall, right winger, Montreal Canadiens.

TRANSACTIONS/CAREER NOTES: Signed as free agent by Boston Bruins (September 1983).... Traded by Bruins with G Bill Ranford to Edmonton Oilers for G Andy Moog (March 1988).... Traded by Oilers to Washington Capitals for C Greg Adams (July 1988).... Traded by Capitals to St. Louis Blues for C Peter Zezel and D Mike Lalor (July 13, 1990).... Traded by Blues with D Robert Dirk, C Cliff Ronning, LW Sergio Momesso and a future draft pick to Vancouver Canucks for C Dan Quinn and D Garth Butcher (March 5, 1991).... Lacerated foot (February 28, 1992) and suffered from chronic fatigue (March 1992); missed nine games.

Season	Team	League	REGULAR SEASON					PLAYOFFS				
			Gms.	G	A	Pts.	Pen.	Gms.	G	A	Pts.	Pen.
80-81	—Victoria	WHL	11	3	5	8	6	15	2	1	3	7
81-82	—Victoria	WHL	72	35	57	92	100	4	1	0	1	2

C

Season Team	League	REGULAR SEASON					PLAYOFFS				
		Gms.	G	A	Pts.	Pen.	Gms.	G	A	Pts.	Pen.
83-84—Victoria	WHL	71	41	73	114	186	12	6	7	13	42
—Hershey	AHL	74	14	12	26	51	—	—	—	—	—
—Boston	NHL	5	0	0	0	0	—	—	—	—	—
84-85—Hershey	AHL	9	8	4	12	4	—	—	—	—	—
—Boston	NHL	64	12	16	28	82	5	0	2	2	7
85-86—Moncton	AHL	12	8	8	16	6	—	—	—	—	—
—Boston	NHL	64	21	17	38	61	3	0	0	0	2
86-87—Boston	NHL	65	13	23	36	117	1	0	0	0	0
87-88—Boston	NHL	62	32	26	58	108	—	—	—	—	—
—Edmonton	NHL	12	4	4	8	15	19	0	3	3	23
88-89—Washington	NHL	79	42	38	80	112	6	2	5	7	12
89-90—Washington	NHL	80	35	39	74	104	15	4	9	13	32
90-91—St. Louis	NHL	66	27	30	57	56	—	—	—	—	—
—Vancouver	NHL	11	6	2	8	8	6	3	5	8	4
91-92—Vancouver	NHL	70	23	34	57	116	12	6	8	14	20
NHL totals		578	215	229	444	779	67	15	32	47	100

COURTNALL, RUSS
RW, CANADIENS

PERSONAL: Born June 3, 1965, at Victoria, B.C. ... 5-11/183. ... Shoots right. ... Brother of Geoff Courtnall, left winger, Vancouver Canucks. **TRANSACTIONS/CAREER NOTES:** Selected by Toronto Maple Leafs as underage junior in first round (first Maple Leafs pick, seventh overall) of NHL entry draft (June 8, 1983). ... Bruised knee (November 1987). ... Suffered from virus (February 1988). ... Suffered back spasms (March 1988). ... Traded by Maple Leafs to Montreal Canadiens for RW John Kordic and a sixth-round pick in 1989 draft (RW Michael Doers) (November 7, 1988). ... Pulled muscle in right shoulder (October 8, 1991); missed 41 games. ... Injured hand (January 15, 1992); missed 12 games.

Season Team	League	REGULAR SEASON					PLAYOFFS				
		Gms.	G	A	Pts.	Pen.	Gms.	G	A	Pts.	Pen.
82-83—Victoria	WHL	60	36	61	97	33	12	11	7	18	6
83-84—Victoria	WHL	32	29	37	66	63	—	—	—	—	—
—Canadian Olympic Team	Int'l	16	4	7	11	10	—	—	—	—	—
—Toronto	NHL	14	3	9	12	6	—	—	—	—	—
84-85—Toronto	NHL	69	12	10	22	44	—	—	—	—	—
85-86—Toronto	NHL	73	22	38	60	52	10	3	6	9	8
86-87—Toronto	NHL	79	29	44	73	90	13	3	4	7	11
87-88—Toronto	NHL	65	23	26	49	47	6	2	1	3	0
88-89—Toronto	NHL	9	1	1	2	4	—	—	—	—	—
—Montreal	NHL	64	22	17	39	15	21	8	5	13	18
89-90—Montreal	NHL	80	27	32	59	27	11	5	1	6	10
90-91—Montreal	NHL	79	26	50	76	29	13	8	3	11	7
91-92—Montreal	NHL	27	7	14	21	6	10	1	1	2	4
NHL totals		559	172	241	413	320	84	30	21	51	58

COUSINEAU, MARCEL
G, BRUINS

PERSONAL: Born April 30, 1973, at Delson, Que. ... 5-10/175. ... Shoots left. **TRANSACTIONS/CAREER NOTES:** Selected by Boston Bruins in third round (third Bruins pick, 62nd overall) of NHL entry draft (June 22, 1991). **HONORS:** Named to QMJHL All-Rookie Team (1990-91).

Season Team	League	REGULAR SEASON								PLAYOFFS						
		Gms.	Min.	W	L	T	GA	SO	Avg.	Gms.	Min.	W	L	GA	SO	Avg.
90-91—Beauport	QMJHL	49	2739	13	29	3	196	1	4.29	—	—	—	—	—	—	—
91-92—Beauport	QMJHL	*67	*3673	26	*32	5	*241	0	3.94	—	—	—	—	—	—	—

COUTURIER, SYLVAIN
C/LW, KINGS

PERSONAL: Born April 23, 1968, at Greenfield Park, Que. ... 6-2/205. ... Shoots left. **TRANSACTIONS/CAREER NOTES:** Selected by Los Angeles Kings as underage junior in fourth round (third Kings pick, 65th overall) of NHL entry draft (June 21, 1986). ... Broke jaw (October 1989).

Season Team	League	REGULAR SEASON					PLAYOFFS				
		Gms.	G	A	Pts.	Pen.	Gms.	G	A	Pts.	Pen.
85-86—Laval	QMJHL	68	21	37	58	64	14	1	7	8	28
86-87—Laval	QMJHL	67	39	51	90	77	13	12	14	26	19
87-88—Laval	QMJHL	67	70	67	137	115	—	—	—	—	—
88-89—Los Angeles	NHL	16	1	3	4	2	—	—	—	—	—
—New Haven	AHL	44	18	20	38	33	10	2	2	4	11
89-90—New Haven	AHL	50	9	8	17	47	—	—	—	—	—
90-91—Los Angeles	NHL	3	0	1	1	0	—	—	—	—	—
—Phoenix	IHL	66	50	37	87	49	10	8	2	10	10
91-92—Los Angeles	NHL	14	3	1	4	2	—	—	—	—	—
—Phoenix	IHL	39	19	20	39	68	—	—	—	—	—
NHL totals		33	4	5	9	4					

COXE, CRAIG
RW, SHARKS

PERSONAL: Born January 21, 1964, at Chula Vista, Calif.... 6-4/210.... Shoots left.
TRANSACTIONS/CAREER NOTES: Selected by Detroit Red Wings as underage junior in fourth round (fourth Red Wings pick, 66th overall) of NHL entry draft (June 9, 1982).... WHL rights traded by Portland Winter Hawks to Saskatoon Blades for future considerations (October 1984).... Broke hand (October 1985); missed 13 games.... Suspended first three regular-season games by NHL for leaving penalty box in preseason game (September 1987).... Traded by Vancouver Canucks to Calgary Flames for C Brian Bradley, RW Peter Bakovic and future considerations (D Kevan Guy) (March 1988).... Traded by Flames with C Mike Bullard and D Tim Corkey to St. Louis Blues for C Doug Gilmour, RW Mark Hunter, LW Steve Bozek and D/RW Michael Dark (September 5, 1988).... Sold by Blues to Chicago Blackhawks to complete future consideration of D Rik Wilson trade made on September 27 (September 28, 1989).... Claimed by Canucks in 1989 NHL waiver draft for $15,000 (October 2, 1989).... Selected by San Jose Sharks in 1991 NHL expansion draft (May 30, 1991).

			REGULAR SEASON					PLAYOFFS			
Season Team	League	Gms.	G	A	Pts.	Pen.	Gms.	G	A	Pts.	Pen.
81-82—St. Albert	AJHL	51	17	48	65	212	—	—	—	—	—
82-83—Belleville	OHL	64	14	27	41	102	4	1	2	3	2
83-84—Belleville	OHL	45	17	28	45	90	3	2	0	2	4
84-85—Vancouver	NHL	9	0	0	0	49	—	—	—	—	—
—Fredericton	AHL	62	8	7	15	242	4	2	1	3	16
85-86—Vancouver	NHL	57	3	5	8	176	3	0	0	0	2
86-87—Fredericton	AHL	46	1	12	13	168	—	—	—	—	—
—Vancouver	NHL	15	1	0	1	31	—	—	—	—	—
87-88—Vancouver	NHL	64	5	12	17	186	—	—	—	—	—
—Calgary	NHL	7	2	3	5	32	2	1	0	1	16
88-89—St. Louis	NHL	41	0	7	7	127	—	—	—	—	—
—Peoria	IHL	8	2	7	9	38	—	—	—	—	—
89-90—Vancouver	NHL	25	1	4	5	66	—	—	—	—	—
—Milwaukee	IHL	5	0	5	5	4	—	—	—	—	—
90-91—Milwaukee	IHL	36	9	21	30	116	6	3	2	5	22
—Vancouver	NHL	7	0	0	0	27	—	—	—	—	—
91-92—San Jose	NHL	10	2	0	2	19	—	—	—	—	—
—Kansas City	IHL	51	17	21	38	106	—	—	—	—	—
—Kalamazoo	IHL	6	4	5	9	13	10	2	4	6	37
NHL totals		235	14	31	45	713	5	1	0	1	18

CRAIG, MIKE
RW, NORTH STARS

PERSONAL: Born June 6, 1971, at London, Ont.... 6-1/180.... Shoots right.
TRANSACTIONS/CAREER NOTES: Selected by Minnesota North Stars in second round (second North Stars pick, 28th overall) of NHL entry draft (June 17, 1989).... Broke fibula (January 28, 1990). ... Broke right wrist (February 4, 1991); missed 17 games.

			REGULAR SEASON					PLAYOFFS			
Season Team	League	Gms.	G	A	Pts.	Pen.	Gms.	G	A	Pts.	Pen.
86-87—Woodstock Jr. C.	OHA	32	29	19	48	64	—	—	—	—	—
87-88—Oshawa	OHL	61	6	10	16	39	7	7	0	7	11
88-89—Oshawa	OHL	63	36	36	72	34	6	3	1	4	6
89-90—Oshawa	OHL	43	36	40	76	85	17	10	16	26	46
90-91—Minnesota	NHL	39	8	4	12	32	10	1	1	2	20
91-92—Minnesota	NHL	67	15	16	31	155	4	1	0	1	7
NHL totals		106	23	20	43	187	14	2	1	3	27

CRAIGWELL, DALE
C, SHARKS

PERSONAL: Born April 24, 1971, at Toronto.... 5-11/180.... Shoots left.
COLLEGE: Toronto.
TRANSACTIONS/CAREER NOTES: Selected by San Jose Sharks in 10th round (11th Sharks pick, 199th overall) of NHL entry draft (June 22, 1991).
HONORS: Won William Hanley Trophy (1990-91).

			REGULAR SEASON					PLAYOFFS			
Season Team	League	Gms.	G	A	Pts.	Pen.	Gms.	G	A	Pts.	Pen.
88-89—Oshawa	OHL	55	9	14	23	15	6	0	0	0	0
89-90—Oshawa	OHL	64	22	41	63	39	17	7	7	14	11
90-91—Oshawa	OHL	56	27	68	95	34	16	7	16	23	9
91-92—Kansas City	IHL	48	6	19	25	29	12	4	7	11	4
—San Jose	NHL	32	5	11	16	8	—	—	—	—	—
NHL totals		32	5	11	16	8					

CRAVEN, MURRAY
C/LW, WHALERS

PERSONAL: Born July 20, 1964, at Medicine Hat, Alta.... 6-2/185.... Shoots left.
TRANSACTIONS/CAREER NOTES: Selected by Detroit Red Wings as underage junior in first round (first Red Wings pick, 17th overall) of NHL entry draft (June 9, 1982).... Injured left knee cartilage (January 15, 1983).... Traded by Red Wings with LW/C Joe Paterson to Philadelphia Flyers for C Darryl Sittler (October 1984).... Broke foot (April 16, 1987).... Hyperextended right knee and lacerated eye (November 1988).... Bruised right foot (January 1989).... Fractured left wrist (February 24, 1989). ... Fractured right wrist (April 5, 1989).... Suffered back spasms (February 1990).... Injured rotator cuff (March 24, 1990).... Traded by Flyers to Hartford Whalers for RW Kevin Dineen (November 13, 1991).... Injured groin (January 21, 1992).

Season Team	League	REGULAR SEASON Gms.	G	A	Pts.	Pen.	PLAYOFFS Gms.	G	A	Pts.	Pen.
80-81—Medicine Hat	WHL	69	5	10	15	18	5	0	0	0	2
81-82—Medicine Hat	WHL	72	35	46	81	49	—	—	—	—	—
82-83—Medicine Hat	WHL	28	17	29	46	35	—	—	—	—	—
—Detroit	NHL	31	4	7	11	6	—	—	—	—	—
83-84—Medicine Hat	WHL	48	38	56	94	53	4	5	3	8	4
—Detroit	NHL	15	0	4	4	6	—	—	—	—	—
84-85—Philadelphia	NHL	80	26	35	61	30	19	4	6	10	11
85-86—Philadelphia	NHL	78	21	33	54	34	5	0	3	3	4
86-87—Philadelphia	NHL	77	19	30	49	38	12	3	1	4	9
87-88—Philadelphia	NHL	72	30	46	76	58	7	2	5	7	4
88-89—Philadelphia	NHL	51	9	28	37	52	1	0	0	0	0
89-90—Philadelphia	NHL	76	25	50	75	42	—	—	—	—	—
90-91—Philadelphia	NHL	77	19	47	66	53	—	—	—	—	—
91-92—Philadelphia	NHL	12	3	3	6	8	—	—	—	—	—
—Hartford	NHL	61	24	30	54	38	7	3	3	6	6
NHL totals		630	180	313	493	365	51	12	18	30	34

CRAWFORD, LOU
LW, BRUINS

PERSONAL: Born November 5, 1962, at Belleville, Ont. . . . 6-0/185. . . . Shoots left. . . . Full name: Louis Crawford.
TRANSACTIONS/CAREER NOTES: Signed as free agent by Buffalo Sabres (August 1984). . . . Signed as free agent by Nova Scotia Oilers (October 1985). . . . Signed as free agent by Boston Bruins (July 6, 1989).

Season Team	League	REGULAR SEASON Gms.	G	A	Pts.	Pen.	PLAYOFFS Gms.	G	A	Pts.	Pen.
79-80—Belleville Jr. B	OHA	10	7	11	18	60	—	—	—	—	—
80-81—Kitchener	OMJHL	53	2	7	9	134	—	—	—	—	—
81-82—Kitchener	OHL	64	11	17	28	243	15	3	4	7	71
82-83—Rochester	AHL	64	5	11	16	142	13	1	1	2	7
83-84—Rochester	AHL	76	7	6	13	234	17	2	4	6	87
84-85—Rochester	AHL	70	8	7	15	213	1	0	0	0	10
85-86—Nova Scotia	AHL	78	8	11	19	214	—	—	—	—	—
86-87—Nova Scotia	AHL	35	3	4	7	48	—	—	—	—	—
87-88—Nova Scotia	AHL	65	15	15	30	170	4	1	2	3	9
88-89—Adirondack	AHL	74	23	23	46	179	9	0	6	6	32
89-90—Boston	NHL	7	0	0	0	20	1	0	0	0	0
—Maine	AHL	62	11	15	26	241	—	—	—	—	—
90-91—Maine	AHL	80	18	17	35	215	2	0	0	0	5
91-92—Maine	AHL	54	17	15	32	171	—	—	—	—	—
—Boston	NHL	19	2	1	3	9	—	—	—	—	—
NHL totals		26	2	1	3	29	1	0	0	0	0

CREIGHTON, ADAM
C, ISLANDERS

PERSONAL: Born June 2, 1965, at Burlington, Ont. . . . 6-5/210. . . . Shoots left. . . . Son of Dave Creighton, center, four NHL teams (1948-49 through 1959-60).
TRANSACTIONS/CAREER NOTES: Selected by Buffalo Sabres in first round (third Sabres pick, 11th overall) of NHL entry draft (June 8, 1983). . . . Underwent knee surgery (January 1988). . . . Sprained knee (September 1988). . . . Traded by Sabres to Chicago Blackhawks for RW Rick Vaive (December 2, 1988). . . . Suspended five games by NHL for stick-swinging incident in preseason game (September 30, 1990). . . . Sprained right hand (February 10, 1991). . . . Traded by Blackhawks with LW Steve Thomas to New York Islanders for C Brent Sutter and RW Brad Lauer (October 25, 1991).
HONORS: Won Stafford Smythe Memorial Cup (May 1984). . . . Named to Memorial Cup All-Star team (1983-84).

Season Team	League	REGULAR SEASON Gms.	G	A	Pts.	Pen.	PLAYOFFS Gms.	G	A	Pts.	Pen.
81-82—Ottawa	OHL	60	14	27	41	73	17	7	1	8	40
82-83—Ottawa	OHL	68	44	46	90	88	9	0	2	2	12
83-84—Ottawa	OHL	56	42	49	91	79	13	16	11	27	28
—Buffalo	NHL	7	2	2	4	4	—	—	—	—	—
84-85—Ottawa	OHL	10	4	14	18	23	5	6	2	8	11
—Rochester	AHL	6	5	3	8	2	5	2	1	3	20
—Buffalo	NHL	30	2	8	10	33	—	—	—	—	—
85-86—Rochester	AHL	32	17	21	38	27	—	—	—	—	—
—Buffalo	NHL	20	1	1	2	2	—	—	—	—	—
86-87—Buffalo	NHL	56	18	22	40	26	—	—	—	—	—
87-88—Buffalo	NHL	36	10	17	27	87	—	—	—	—	—
88-89—Buffalo	NHL	24	7	10	17	44	—	—	—	—	—
—Chicago	NHL	43	15	14	29	92	15	5	6	11	44
89-90—Chicago	NHL	80	34	36	70	224	20	3	6	9	59
90-91—Chicago	NHL	72	22	29	51	135	6	0	1	1	10
91-92—Chicago	NHL	11	6	6	12	16	—	—	—	—	—
—New York Islanders	NHL	66	15	9	24	102	—	—	—	—	—
NHL totals		445	132	154	286	765	41	8	13	21	113

CRONIN, SHAWN
D, JETS

PERSONAL: Born August 20, 1963, at Flushing, Mich. . . . 6-2/210. . . . Shoots left. . . . Full name: Shawn Patrick Cronin.
COLLEGE: Illinois-Chicago.
TRANSACTIONS/CAREER NOTES: Signed as free agent by Hartford Whalers (March 1986). . . . Signed as free agent by Washington Capitals (June 6, 1988). . . . Signed as free agent by Philadelphia Flyers (June 13, 1989). . . . Traded by Flyers to Winnipeg Jets for future considerations (July 21, 1989); future considerations later cancelled. . . . Bruised hand (February 1990). . . . Bruised foot (October 27, 1991); missed three games. . . . Injured ribs (December 23, 1991).

			REGULAR SEASON					PLAYOFFS				
Season	Team	League	Gms.	G	A	Pts.	Pen.	Gms.	G	A	Pts.	Pen.
82-83—Illinois-Chicago		CCHA	36	1	5	6	52	—	—	—	—	—
83-84—Illinois-Chicago		CCHA	32	0	4	4	41	—	—	—	—	—
84-85—Illinois-Chicago		CCHA	31	2	6	8	52	—	—	—	—	—
85-86—Illinois-Chicago		CCHA	38	3	8	11	70	—	—	—	—	—
86-87—Binghamton		AHL	12	0	1	1	60	10	0	0	0	41
—Salt Lake City		IHL	53	8	16	24	118	—	—	—	—	—
87-88—Binghamton		AHL	66	3	8	11	212	4	0	0	0	15
88-89—Washington		NHL	1	0	0	0	0	—	—	—	—	—
—Baltimore		AHL	75	3	9	12	267	—	—	—	—	—
89-90—Winnipeg		NHL	61	0	4	4	243	5	0	0	0	7
90-91—Winnipeg		NHL	67	1	5	0	189	—	—	—	—	—
91-92—Winnipeg		NHL	65	0	4	4	271	4	0	0	0	6
NHL totals			194	1	13	14	703	9	0	0	0	13

CROSS, CORY
D, LIGHTNING

PERSONAL: Born January 3, 1971, at Lloydminster, Alta. . . . 6-5/212. . . . Shoots left. . . . Full name: Cory James Cross.
HIGH SCHOOL: Lloydminster Comprehensive (Alta.).
COLLEGE: Alberta.
TRANSACTIONS/CAREER NOTES: Selected by Tampa Bay Lightning in NHL supplemental draft (June 19, 1992).

			REGULAR SEASON					PLAYOFFS				
Season	Team	League	Gms.	G	A	Pts.	Pen.	Gms.	G	A	Pts.	Pen.
90-91—University of Alberta		CWUAA	20	2	5	7	16	—	—	—	—	—
91-92—University of Alberta		CWUAA	39	3	10	13	76	—	—	—	—	—

CROSSMAN, DOUG
D, LIGHTNING

PERSONAL: Born June 30, 1960, at Peterborough, Ont. . . . 6-2/190. . . . Shoots left. . . . Full name: Douglas Crossman.
TRANSACTIONS/CAREER NOTES: Selected by Chicago Blackhawks as underage junior in sixth round (sixth Blackhawks pick, 112th overall) of NHL entry draft (August 9, 1979). . . . Injured thumb (February 1983). . . . Traded by Blackhawks with second-round pick in 1984 draft (RW Scott Mellanby) to Philadelphia Flyers for D Behn Wilson (June 1983). . . . Traded by Flyers to Los Angeles Kings for D Jay Wells (September 29, 1988). . . . Traded by Kings to New York Islanders to complete February 22, 1989 trade of G Kelly Hrudey from Islanders to Kings for G Mark Fitzpatrick, D Wayne McBean and future considerations (May 23, 1989). . . . Injured foot (November 6, 1990). . . . Traded by Islanders to Hartford Whalers for C Ray Ferraro (November 13, 1990). . . . Injured leg (February 12, 1991). . . . Traded by Whalers to Detroit Red Wings for D Doug Houda (February 20, 1991). . . . Selected by Tampa Bay Lightning in NHL expansion draft (June 18, 1992).
HONORS: Named to OMJHL All-Star first team (1979-80).

			REGULAR SEASON					PLAYOFFS				
Season	Team	League	Gms.	G	A	Pts.	Pen.	Gms.	G	A	Pts.	Pen.
76-77—London		OMJHL	1	0	0	0	0	—	—	—	—	—
77-78—Ottawa		OMJHL	65	4	17	21	17	—	—	—	—	—
78-79—Ottawa		OMJHL	67	12	51	63	63	4	1	3	4	0
79-80—Ottawa		OMJHL	66	20	96	116	48	11	7	6	13	19
80-81—Chicago		NHL	9	0	2	2	2	—	—	—	—	—
—New Brunswick		AHL	70	13	43	56	90	13	5	6	11	36
81-82—Chicago		NHL	70	12	28	40	24	11	0	3	3	4
82-83—Chicago		NHL	80	13	40	53	46	13	3	7	10	6
83-84—Philadelphia		NHL	78	7	28	35	63	3	0	0	0	0
84-85—Philadelphia		NHL	80	4	33	37	65	19	4	6	10	38
85-86—Philadelphia		NHL	80	6	37	43	55	5	0	1	1	4
86-87—Philadelphia		NHL	78	9	31	40	29	26	4	14	18	31
87-88—Philadelphia		NHL	76	9	29	38	43	7	1	1	2	8
88-89—New Haven		AHL	3	0	0	0	0	—	—	—	—	—
—Los Angeles		NHL	74	10	15	25	53	2	0	1	1	2
89-90—New York Islanders		NHL	80	15	44	59	54	5	0	1	1	6
90-91—New York Islanders		NHL	16	1	6	7	12	—	—	—	—	—
—Hartford		NHL	41	4	19	23	19	—	—	—	—	—
—Detroit		NHL	17	3	4	7	17	6	0	5	5	6
91-92—Detroit		NHL	26	0	8	8	14	—	—	—	—	—
NHL totals			805	93	324	417	496	97	12	39	51	105

CROWDER, TROY
RW, RED WINGS

PERSONAL: Born May 3, 1968, at Sudbury, Ont. . . . 6-4/220. . . . Shoots right.
TRANSACTIONS/CAREER NOTES: Selected by New Jersey Devils as underage junior in sixth round (sixth Devils pick, 108th overall) of NHL entry draft (June 21, 1986). . . . Left training camp (September 1989); returned (March 1990). . . . Injured left elbow (October 4,

1990). . . . Hyperextended elbow (November 1, 1990). . . . Lacerated right hand and damaged ligaments (December 29, 1990). . . . Signed as free agent by Detroit Red Wings (September 1991); Devils received C/RW Dave Barr and RW Randy McKay as compensation. . . . Strained back (October 10, 1991); missed 73 games.

Season Team	League	REGULAR SEASON					PLAYOFFS				
		Gms.	G	A	Pts.	Pen.	Gms.	G	A	Pts.	Pen.
85-86—Hamilton	OHL	55	4	4	8	178	—	—	—	—	—
86-87—North Bay	OHL	35	6	11	17	90	23	3	9	12	99
—Belleville Bulls	OHL	21	5	5	10	52	—	—	—	—	—
87-88—North Bay	OHL	9	1	2	3	44	—	—	—	—	—
—New Jersey	NHL	—	—	—	—	—	1	0	0	0	12
—Belleville Bulls	OHL	46	12	27	39	103	6	2	3	5	24
—Utica	AHL	3	0	0	0	36	—	—	—	—	—
88-89—Utica	AHL	62	6	4	10	152	2	0	0	0	25
89-90—Nashville	ECHL	3	0	0	0	15	—	—	—	—	—
—New Jersey	NHL	10	0	0	0	23	2	0	0	0	10
90-91—New Jersey	NHL	59	6	3	9	182	—	—	—	—	—
91-92—Detroit	NHL	7	0	0	0	35	1	0	0	0	0
NHL totals		76	6	3	9	240	4	0	0	0	22

CROWLEY, JOSEPH
LW, OILERS

PERSONAL: Born February 29, 1972, at Concord, Mass. . . . 6-2/195. . . . Shoots left. . . . Full name: Joseph James Crowley.
HIGH SCHOOL: Lawrence Academy (Groton, Mass.).
COLLEGE: Boston College.
TRANSACTIONS/CAREER NOTES: Suffered from mononucleosis (January 1990). . . . Selected by Edmonton Oilers in third round (third Oilers pick, 59th overall) of NHL entry draft (June 16, 1990).

Season Team	League	REGULAR SEASON					PLAYOFFS				
		Gms.	G	A	Pts.	Pen.	Gms.	G	A	Pts.	Pen.
87-88—Lawrence Academy	Mass. H.S.	24	21	23	44	34	—	—	—	—	—
88-89—Lawrence Academy	Mass. H.S.	20	13	22	35	42	—	—	—	—	—
89-90—Lawrence Academy	Mass. H.S.	10	8	5	13	14	—	—	—	—	—
90-91—Boston College	Hockey East	17	3	0	3	14	—	—	—	—	—
91-92—Trois-Rivieres	QMJHL	41	11	13	24	124	—	—	—	—	—
—Winston-Salem	ECHL	6	0	0	0	0	—	—	—	—	—

CULLEN, JOHN
C, WHALERS

PERSONAL: Born August 2, 1964, at Puslinch, Ont. . . . 5-10/187. . . . Shoots right. . . . Full name: Barry John Cullen. . . . Son of Barry Cullen, right winger, Toronto Maple Leafs and Detroit Red Wings (1955-56 through 1959-64).
COLLEGE: Boston University.
TRANSACTIONS/CAREER NOTES: Selected by Buffalo Sabres in NHL supplemental draft (1986). . . . Signed as free agent by Pittsburgh Penguins (July 1988). . . . Suffered from hepatitis (October 1989); missed seven games. . . . Pulled stomach muscle (November 17, 1990). . . . Traded by Penguins with D Zarley Zalapski and RW Jeff Parker to Whalers for C Ron Francis, D Ulf Samuelsson and D Grant Jennings (March 4, 1991). . . . Missed first three games of 1991-92 season due to contract dispute.
HONORS: Named ECAC Rookie of the Year (1983-84). . . . Named to Hockey East All-Star first team (1984-85 and 1985-86). . . . Named to NCAA All-America East second team (1985-86). . . . Named to Hockey East All-Star second team (1986-87). . . . Won James Gatschene Memorial Trophy (1987-88). . . . Won Leo P. Lamoureux Memorial Trophy (1987-88). . . . Shared Garry F. Longman Memorial Trophy with Ed Belfour (1987-88). . . . Named to IHL All-Star first team (1987-88).

Season Team	League	REGULAR SEASON					PLAYOFFS				
		Gms.	G	A	Pts.	Pen.	Gms.	G	A	Pts.	Pen.
83-84—Boston University	ECAC	40	23	33	56	28	—	—	—	—	—
84-85—Boston University	Hockey East	41	27	32	59	46	—	—	—	—	—
85-86—Boston University	Hockey East	43	25	49	74	54	—	—	—	—	—
86-87—Boston University	Hockey East	36	23	29	52	35	—	—	—	—	—
87-88—Flint	IHL	81	48	*109	*157	113	16	11	†15	26	16
88-89—Pittsburgh	NHL	79	12	37	49	112	11	3	6	9	28
89-90—Pittsburgh	NHL	72	32	60	92	138	—	—	—	—	—
90-91—Pittsburgh	NHL	65	31	63	94	83	—	—	—	—	—
—Hartford	NHL	13	8	8	16	18	6	2	7	9	10
91-92—Hartford	NHL	77	26	51	77	141	7	2	1	3	12
NHL totals		306	109	219	328	492	24	7	14	21	50

CULLIMORE, JASSEN
D, CANUCKS

PERSONAL: Born December 4, 1972, at Simcoe, Ont. . . . 6-5/225. . . . Shoots left.
TRANSACTIONS/CAREER NOTES: Selected by Vancouver Canucks in second round (second Canucks pick, 29th overall) of NHL entry draft (June 22, 1991).
HONORS: Named to OHL All-Star second team (1991-92).

Season Team	League	REGULAR SEASON					PLAYOFFS				
		Gms.	G	A	Pts.	Pen.	Gms.	G	A	Pts.	Pen.
88-89—Peterborough	OHL	20	2	1	3	6	—	—	—	—	—
89-90—Peterborough	OHL	59	2	6	8	61	11	0	2	2	8
90-91—Peterborough	OHL	62	8	16	24	74	4	1	0	1	7
91-92—Peterborough	OHL	54	9	37	46	65	10	3	6	9	8

CUMMINS, JIM
RW, RED WINGS

PERSONAL: Born May 17, 1970, at Dearborn, Mich. . . . 6-2/200. . . . Shoots right. . . . Full name: James Stephen Cummins.
COLLEGE: Michigan State.
TRANSACTIONS/CAREER NOTES: Selected by New York Rangers in fourth round (fifth Rangers

pick, 67th overall) of NHL entry draft (June 17, 1989). . . . Traded by Rangers with C Kevin Miller and D Dennis Vial to Detroit Red Wings for RW Joe Kocur and D Per Djoos (March 5, 1991).

Season Team	League	REGULAR SEASON					PLAYOFFS				
		Gms.	G	A	Pts.	Pen.	Gms.	G	A	Pts.	Pen.
87-88—Detroit Compuware..........	NAJHL	31	11	15	26	146	—	—	—	—	—
88-89—Michigan State................	CCHA	36	3	9	12	100	—	—	—	—	—
89-90—Michigan State................	CCHA	41	8	7	15	94	—	—	—	—	—
90-91—Michigan State................	CCHA	34	9	6	15	110	—	—	—	—	—
91-92—Adirondack	AHL	65	7	13	20	338	5	0	0	0	19
—Detroit	NHL	1	0	0	0	7	—	—	—	—	—
NHL totals...............		1	0	0	0	7					

CUNNEYWORTH, RANDY
LW, WHALERS

PERSONAL: Born May 10, 1961, at Etobicoke, Ont. . . . 6-0/180. . . . Shoots left. . . . Full name: Randolph William Cunneyworth.

TRANSACTIONS/CAREER NOTES: Selected by Buffalo Sabres as underage junior in eighth round (ninth Sabres pick, 167th overall) of NHL entry draft (June 11, 1980). . . . Attended Pittsburgh Penguins training camp as unsigned free agent (Summer 1985); Sabres then traded his equalization rights with RW Mike Moller to Penguins for future considerations (October 4, 1985); Penguins sent RW Pat Hughes to Sabres to complete deal (October 1985). . . . Suspended three games by NHL (January 1988). . . . Suspended five games by NHL (January 1988). . . . Fractured right foot (January 24, 1989). . . . Traded by Penguins with G Richard Tabaracci and RW Dave MoLlwain to Winnipeg Jets for RW Andrew McBain, D Jim Kyte and LW Randy Gilhen (June 17, 1989). . . . Broke bone in right foot (October 1989). . . . Traded by Jets to Hartford Whalers for C Paul MacDermid (December 13, 1989). . . . Broke tibia bone in left leg (November 28, 1990); missed 38 games. . . . Strained lower back (December 1991); missed one game. . . . Strained ankle (December 21, 1991); missed two games. . . . Strained left ankle (January 16, 1992); missed three games. . . . Reinjured ankle (February 1, 1992); missed six games.

Season Team	League	REGULAR SEASON					PLAYOFFS				
		Gms.	G	A	Pts.	Pen.	Gms.	G	A	Pts.	Pen.
79-80—Ottawa............................	OMJHL	63	16	25	41	145	11	0	1	1	13
80-81—Ottawa............................	OMJHL	67	54	74	128	240	15	5	8	13	35
—Rochester......................	AHL	1	0	1	1	2	—	—	—	—	—
—Buffalo..........................	NHL	1	0	0	0	2	—	—	—	—	—
81-82—Rochester......................	AHL	57	12	15	27	86	9	4	0	4	30
—Buffalo..........................	NHL	20	2	4	6	47	—	—	—	—	—
82-83—Rochester......................	AHL	78	23	33	56	111	16	4	4	8	35
83-84—Rochester......................	AHL	54	18	17	35	85	17	5	5	10	55
84-85—Rochester......................	AHL	72	30	38	68	148	5	2	1	3	16
85-86—Pittsburgh......................	NHL	75	15	30	45	74	—	—	—	—	—
86-87—Pittsburgh......................	NHL	79	26	27	53	142	—	—	—	—	—
87-88—Pittsburgh......................	NHL	71	35	39	74	141	—	—	—	—	—
88-89—Pittsburgh......................	NHL	70	25	19	44	156	11	3	5	8	26
89-90—Winnipeg......................	NHL	28	5	6	11	34	—	—	—	—	—
—Hartford........................	NHL	43	9	9	18	41	4	0	0	0	2
90-91—Springfield....................	AHL	2	0	0	0	5	—	—	—	—	—
—Hartford........................	NHL	32	9	5	14	49	1	0	0	0	0
91-92—Hartford........................	NHL	39	7	10	17	71	7	3	0	3	9
NHL totals...............		458	133	149	282	757	23	6	5	11	37

CURRAN, BRIAN
D, SABRES

PERSONAL: Born November 5, 1963, at Toronto. . . . 6-4/220. . . . Shoots left. **TRANSACTIONS/CAREER NOTES:** Underwent appendectomy (November 1981). . . . Selected by Boston Bruins as underage junior in second round (second Bruins pick, 22nd overall) of NHL entry draft (June 9, 1982). . . . Broke ankle (September 1982). . . . Bruised thigh (November 1984). . . . Broke leg (February 1, 1986). . . . Signed as free agent by New York Islanders (August 1986); Bruins awarded D Paul Boutilier as compensation. . . . Fractured jaw (January 12, 1988). . . . Traded by Islanders to Toronto Maple Leafs for a sixth-round pick in 1988 draft (RW Pavel Gross) (March 1988). . . . Pulled pelvic muscle (November 1988). . . . Bruised spine (December 1, 1988). . . . Dislocated right wrist (February 25, 1989). . . . Bruised left wrist (November 1990). . . . Traded by Maple Leafs with LW Lou Franceschetti to Buffalo Sabres for RW Mike Foligno and an eighth-round pick in 1991 draft (C Thomas Kucharcik) (December 17, 1990). . . . Injured shoulder (December 28, 1990); missed four games.

Season Team	League	REGULAR SEASON					PLAYOFFS				
		Gms.	G	A	Pts.	Pen.	Gms.	G	A	Pts.	Pen.
80-81—Portland	WHL	51	2	16	18	132	14	1	7	8	63
81-82—Portland	WHL	59	2	28	30	275	7	0	1	1	13
82-83—Portland	WHL	56	1	30	31	187	14	1	3	4	57
83-84—Hershey	AHL	23	0	2	2	94	—	—	—	—	—
—Boston	NHL	16	1	1	2	57	3	0	0	0	7
84-85—Hershey	AHL	4	0	0	0	19	—	—	—	—	—
—Boston	NHL	56	0	1	1	158	—	—	—	—	—
85-86—Boston	NHL	43	2	5	7	192	2	0	0	0	4
86-87—New York Islanders..........	NHL	68	0	10	10	356	8	0	0	0	51
87-88—Springfield	AHL	8	1	0	1	43	—	—	—	—	—
—New York Islanders..........	NHL	22	0	1	1	68	—	—	—	—	—
—Toronto............................	NHL	7	0	1	1	19	6	0	0	0	41
88-89—Toronto............................	NHL	47	1	4	5	185	—	—	—	—	—
89-90—Toronto............................	NHL	72	2	9	11	301	5	0	1	1	19

C

Season Team	League	REGULAR SEASON					PLAYOFFS				
		Gms.	G	A	Pts.	Pen.	Gms.	G	A	Pts.	Pen.
90-91—Toronto	NHL	4	0	0	0	7	—	—	—	—	—
—Buffalo	NHL	17	0	1	1	43	—	—	—	—	—
—Newmarket	AHL	6	0	1	1	32	—	—	—	—	—
—Rochester	AHL	10	0	0	0	36	—	—	—	—	—
91-92—Buffalo	NHL	3	0	0	0	14	—	—	—	—	—
—Rochester	AHL	36	0	3	3	122	—	—	—	—	—
NHL totals		355	6	33	39	1400	24	0	1	1	122

CURRIE, DAN

LW, OILERS

PERSONAL: Born March 15, 1968, at Burlington, Ont. . . . 6-2/195. . . . Shoots left. . . . Full name: Daniel Robert Currie.

TRANSACTIONS/CAREER NOTES: Selected by Edmonton Oilers as underage junior in fourth round (fourth Oilers pick, 84th overall) of NHL entry draft (June 21, 1986).

HONORS: Named to OHL All-Star first team (1987-88). . . . Named to AHL All-Star second team (1991-92).

Season Team	League	REGULAR SEASON					PLAYOFFS				
		Gms.	G	A	Pts.	Pen.	Gms.	G	A	Pts.	Pen.
85-86—Sault Ste. Marie	OHL	66	21	22	43	37	—	—	—	—	—
86-87—Sault Ste. Marie	OHL	66	31	52	83	53	4	2	1	3	2
87-88—Sault Ste. Marie	OHL	57	50	59	109	53	6	3	9	12	4
—Nova Scotia	AHL	3	4	2	6	0	5	4	3	7	0
88-89—Cape Breton	AHL	77	29	36	65	29	—	—	—	—	—
89-90—Cape Breton	AHL	77	36	40	76	28	—	—	—	—	—
90-91—Cape Breton	AHL	71	47	45	92	51	4	3	1	4	8
—Edmonton	NHL	5	0	0	0	0	—	—	—	—	—
91-92—Cape Breton	AHL	66	*50	42	92	39	5	4	5	9	4
—Edmonton	NHL	7	1	0	1	0	—	—	—	—	—
NHL totals		12	1	0	1	0					

CYR, PAUL

LW, WHALERS

PERSONAL: Born October 31, 1963, at Port Alberni, B.C. . . . 5-10/180. . . . Shoots left.

TRANSACTIONS/CAREER NOTES: Selected by Buffalo Sabres as underage junior in first round (second Sabres pick, ninth overall) of NHL entry draft (June 9, 1982). . . . Injured thumb (December 16, 1982). . . . Broke knuckle (March 6, 1984). . . . Pulled groin (December 13, 1985). . . . Broke ankle (August 1986). . . . Sprained knee (October 16, 1987). . . . Traded by Sabres with 10th-round pick in 1988 draft (C Eric Fenton) to New York Rangers for LW Mike Donnelly and a fifth-round pick in 1988 draft (RW Alexander Mogilny) (December 1987). . . . Sprained right knee and underwent surgery (October 1988); missed remainder of 1988-89 season and entire 1989-90 season. . . . Signed as free agent by Hartford Whalers (September 30, 1990). . . . Bruised shoulder (December 30, 1990). . . . Suffered from the flu (January 8, 1991); missed two games.

HONORS: Named to WHL All-Star second team (1981-82).

Season Team	League	REGULAR SEASON					PLAYOFFS				
		Gms.	G	A	Pts.	Pen.	Gms.	G	A	Pts.	Pen.
79-80—Nanaimo	BCJHL	60	28	52	80	202	—	—	—	—	—
80-81—Victoria	WHL	64	36	22	58	85	14	6	5	11	46
81-82—Victoria	WHL	58	52	56	108	167	4	3	2	5	12
82-83—Victoria	WHL	20	21	22	43	61	—	—	—	—	—
—Buffalo	NHL	36	15	12	27	59	10	1	3	4	6
83-84—Buffalo	NHL	71	16	27	43	52	3	0	1	1	0
84-85—Buffalo	NHL	71	22	24	46	63	5	2	2	4	15
85-86—Buffalo	NHL	71	20	31	51	120	—	—	—	—	—
86-87—Buffalo	NHL	73	11	16	27	122	—	—	—	—	—
87-88—Buffalo	NHL	20	1	1	2	38	—	—	—	—	—
—New York Rangers	NHL	40	4	13	17	41	—	—	—	—	—
88-89—New York Rangers	NHL	1	0	0	0	2	—	—	—	—	—
89-90—New York Rangers	NHL	Did not play—injured.									
90-91—Hartford	NHL	70	12	13	25	107	6	1	0	1	10
91-92—Hartford	NHL	17	0	3	3	19	—	—	—	—	—
—Springfield	AHL	43	11	18	29	30	11	0	3	3	12
NHL totals		470	101	140	241	623	24	4	6	10	31

DAFOE, BYRON

G, CAPITALS

PERSONAL: Born February 25, 1971, at Duncan, B.C. . . . 5-11/175. . . . Shoots left. . . . Full name: Byron Jaromir Dafoe.

TRANSACTIONS/CAREER NOTES: Selected by Washington Capitals in second round (second Capitals pick, 35th overall) of NHL entry draft (June 17, 1989). . . . Underwent emergency appendectomy (December 1989).

Season Team	League	REGULAR SEASON							PLAYOFFS						
		Gms.	Min.	W	L	T	GA	SO	Avg.	Gms.	Min.	W	L	GA	SO	Avg.
87-88—Juan de Fuca	BCJHL	32	1716				129	0	4.51	—	—	—	—	—	—	—
88-89—Portland	WHL	59	3279	29	24	3	*291	1	5.32	*18	*1091	10	8	*81	*1	4.45
89-90—Portland	WHL	40	2265	14	21	3	193	0	5.11	—	—	—	—	—	—	—
90-91—Portland	WHL	8	414	1	5	1	41	0	5.94	—	—	—	—	—	—	—
—Prince Albert	WHL	32	1839	13	12	4	124	0	4.05	—	—	—	—	—	—	—
91-92—New Haven	AHL	7	364	3	2	1	22	0	3.63	—	—	—	—	—	—	—
—Baltimore	AHL	33	1847	12	16	4	119	0	3.87	—	—	—	—	—	—	—
—Hampton Roads	ECHL	10	562	6	4	0	26	1	2.78	—	—	—	—	—	—	—

CD

DAGENAIS, MIKE
D, NORDIQUES

PERSONAL: Born July 22, 1969, at Ottawa.... 6-3/200.... Shoots left.... Full name: Michael Dagenais.
TRANSACTIONS/CAREER NOTES: Selected by Chicago Blackhawks in third round (fourth Blackhawks pick, 60th overall) of NHL entry draft (June 13, 1987).... Traded by Blackhawks to Quebec Nordiques for D Ryan McGill (September 26, 1991).

			REGULAR SEASON					PLAYOFFS				
Season	Team	League	Gms.	G	A	Pts.	Pen.	Gms.	G	A	Pts.	Pen.
85-86—Peterborough		OHL	45	1	3	4	40	—	—	—	—	—
86-87—Peterborough		OHL	56	1	17	18	66	12	4	1	5	20
87-88—Peterborough		OHL	66	11	23	34	125	12	1	1	2	31
88-89—Peterborough		OHL	62	14	23	37	122	13	3	3	6	12
89-90—Peterborough		OHL	44	14	26	40	74	12	4	1	5	18
90-91—Indianapolis		IHL	76	13	14	27	115	4	0	0	0	4
91-92—Halifax		AHL	69	11	21	32	143	—	—	—	—	—

DAHLEN, ULF
RW, NORTH STARS

PERSONAL: Born January 12, 1967, at Ostersund, Sweden.... 6-2/195.... Shoots right.
TRANSACTIONS/CAREER NOTES: Selected by New York Rangers in first round (first Rangers pick, seventh overall) of NHL entry draft (June 15, 1985).... Bruised shin (November 1987).... Bruised left shoulder (November 1988).... Separated right shoulder (January 1989).... Traded by Rangers with a fourth-round pick in 1990 draft and future considerations to Minnesota North Stars for RW Mike Gartner (March 6, 1990).

			REGULAR SEASON					PLAYOFFS				
Season	Team	League	Gms.	G	A	Pts.	Pen.	Gms.	G	A	Pts.	Pen.
83-84—Ostersund		Sweden	36	15	11	26	10	—	—	—	—	—
84-85—Ostersund		Sweden	36	33	26	59	20	—	—	—	—	—
85-86—Bjorkloven		Sweden	22	4	3	7	8	—	—	—	—	—
86-87—Bjorkloven		Sweden	31	9	12	21	20	6	6	2	8	4
87-88—New York Rangers		NHL	70	29	23	52	26	—	—	—	—	—
—Colorado		IHL	2	2	2	4	0	4	0	0	0	0
88-89—New York Rangers		NHL	56	24	19	43	50	—	—	—	—	—
89-90—New York Rangers		NHL	63	18	18	36	30	7	1	4	5	2
—Minnesota		NHL	13	2	4	6	0	15	2	6	8	4
90-91—Minnesota		NHL	66	21	18	39	6	7	0	3	3	2
91-92—Minnesota		NHL	79	36	30	66	10					
NHL totals			347	130	112	242	122	33	3	13	16	8

DAHLQUIST, CHRIS
D, NORTH STARS

PERSONAL: Born December 14, 1962, at Fridley, Minn.... 6-1/190.... Shoots left. ... Full name: Christopher C. Dahlquist.
COLLEGE: Lake Superior State (Mich.).
TRANSACTIONS/CAREER NOTES: Signed as free agent by Pittsburgh Penguins (May 1985).... Traded by Penguins with Jim Johnson to Minnesota North Stars for D Peter Taglianetti and D Larry Murphy (December 11, 1990).... Broke left wrist (January 1991).

			REGULAR SEASON					PLAYOFFS				
Season	Team	League	Gms.	G	A	Pts.	Pen.	Gms.	G	A	Pts.	Pen.
81-82—Lake Superior State		CCHA	39	4	10	14	18	—	—	—	—	—
82-83—Lake Superior State		CCHA	35	0	12	12	63	—	—	—	—	—
83-84—Lake Superior State		CCHA	40	4	19	23	76	—	—	—	—	—
84-85—Lake Superior State		CCHA	44	4	15	19	112	—	—	—	—	—
85-86—Baltimore		AHL	65	4	21	25	64	—	—	—	—	—
—Pittsburgh		NHL	5	1	2	3	2	—	—	—	—	—
86-87—Baltimore		AHL	51	1	16	17	50	—	—	—	—	—
—Pittsburgh		NHL	19	0	1	1	20	—	—	—	—	—
87-88—Pittsburgh		NHL	44	3	6	9	69	—	—	—	—	—
88-89—Pittsburgh		NHL	43	1	5	6	42	2	0	0	0	0
—Muskegon		IHL	10	3	6	9	14	—	—	—	—	—
89-90—Muskegon		IHL	6	1	1	2	8	—	—	—	—	—
—Pittsburgh		NHL	62	4	10	14	56	—	—	—	—	—
90-91—Pittsburgh		NHL	22	1	2	3	30	—	—	—	—	—
—Minnesota		NHL	42	2	6	8	33	23	1	6	7	20
91-92—Minnesota		NHL	74	1	13	14	68	7	0	0	0	6
NHL totals			311	13	45	58	320	32	1	6	7	26

DAIGNEAULT, J.J.
D, CANADIENS

PERSONAL: Born October 12, 1965, at Montreal.... 5-11/185.... Shoots left.... Full name: Jean-Jacques Daigneault.
TRANSACTIONS/CAREER NOTES: Underwent knee surgery (March 1984).... Selected by Vancouver Canucks as underage junior in first round (first Canucks pick, 10th overall) of NHL entry draft (June 1984).... Broke finger (March 19, 1986).... Traded by Canucks with second-round pick in 1986 draft (C Kent Hawley) and a fifth-round pick in 1987 draft to Philadelphia Flyers for RW Rich Sutter, D Dave Richter and third-round pick in 1986 draft (D Don Gibson) (June 1986).... Sprained ankle (April 12, 1987).... Traded by Flyers to Montreal Canadiens for D Scott Sandelin (November 1988).... Bruised shoulder (December 1990).... Suffered left hip pointer (March 16, 1991).... Injured knee (April 7, 1991).
HONORS: Won Emile (Butch) Bouchard Trophy (1982-83).... Named to QMJHL All-Star first team (1982-83).

Season Team	League	REGULAR SEASON					PLAYOFFS				
		Gms.	G	A	Pts.	Pen.	Gms.	G	A	Pts.	Pen.
81-82—Laval	QMJHL	64	4	25	29	41	18	1	3	4	2
82-83—Longueuil	QMJHL	70	26	58	84	58	15	4	11	15	35
83-84—Canadian Olympic Team	Int'l	62	6	15	21	40	—	—	—	—	—
—Longueuil	QMJHL	10	2	11	13	6	14	3	13	16	30
84-85—Vancouver	NHL	67	4	23	27	69	—	—	—	—	—
85-86—Vancouver	NHL	64	5	23	28	45	3	0	2	2	0
86-87—Philadelphia	NHL	77	6	16	22	56	9	1	0	1	0
87-88—Philadelphia	NHL	28	2	2	4	12	—	—	—	—	—
—Hershey	AHL	10	1	5	6	8	—	—	—	—	—
88-89—Hershey	AHL	12	0	10	10	13	—	—	—	—	—
—Sherbrooke	AHL	63	10	33	43	48	6	1	3	4	2
89-90—Sherbrooke	AHL	28	8	19	27	18	—	—	—	—	—
—Montreal	NHL	36	2	10	12	14	9	0	0	0	2
90-91—Montreal	NHL	51	3	16	19	31	5	0	1	1	0
91-92—Montreal	NHL	79	4	14	18	36	11	0	3	3	4
NHL totals		402	26	104	130	263	37	1	6	7	6

D'ALESSIO, CORRIE
G, CANUCKS

PERSONAL: Born September 9, 1969, at Cornwall, Ont. . . . 5-11/155. . . . Shoots left. . . . Full name: Corrie Vince D'Alessio.
COLLEGE: Cornell.
TRANSACTIONS/CAREER NOTES: Selected by Vancouver Canucks in sixth round (fourth Canucks pick, 107th overall) of NHL entry draft (June 11, 1988).
HONORS: Named to ECAC All-Rookie team (1987-88).

Season Team	League	REGULAR SEASON							PLAYOFFS					
		Gms.	Min.	W	L	T	GA	SO	Avg.	Gms.	Min.	W	L	GA SO	Avg.
86-87—Pembrooke	BCJHL	25	1327				95	0	4.30	—	—	—	—	—	—
87-88—Cornell University	ECAC	25	1457	17	8	0	67	0	2.76	—	—	—	—	—	—
88-89—Cornell University	ECAC	29	1684	15	13	1	96	1	3.42	—	—	—	—	—	—
89-90—Cornell University	ECAC	16	887	6	7	2	50	0	3.38	—	—	—	—	—	—
90-91—Cornell University	ECAC	24	1160	10	7	3	67	0	3.47	—	—	—	—	—	—
91-92—Milwaukee	IHL	27	1435	9	14	2	96	0	4.01	2	119	0	2	12 0	6.05

DALGARNO, BRAD
RW, ISLANDERS

PERSONAL: Born August 8, 1967, at Vancouver, B.C. . . . 6-3/215. . . . Shoots right.
TRANSACTIONS/CAREER NOTES: Selected by New York Islanders as underage junior in first round (first Islanders pick, sixth overall) of NHL entry draft (June 15, 1985). . . . Suffered concussion (November 1988). . . . Fractured orbital bone of left eye (February 21, 1989). . . . Sat out season in retirement (1989-90). . . . Bruised kidney (December 9, 1990); missed four games. . . . Lacerated jaw (January 13, 1991); missed three games. . . . Sprained left shoulder (November 27, 1991); missed four games. . . . Reinjured left shoulder (December 11, 1991); missed seven games. . . . Fractured left wrist (January 12, 1992); missed final 37 games of season. . . . Underwent shoulder surgery (April 1, 1992).

Season Team	League	REGULAR SEASON					PLAYOFFS				
		Gms.	G	A	Pts.	Pen.	Gms.	G	A	Pts.	Pen.
83-84—Markham	MTHL	40	17	11	28	59	—	—	—	—	—
84-85—Hamilton	OHL	66	23	30	53	86	—	—	—	—	—
85-86—Hamilton	OHL	54	22	43	65	79	—	—	—	—	—
—New York Islanders	NHL	2	1	0	1	0	—	—	—	—	—
86-87—Hamilton	OHL	60	27	32	59	100	—	—	—	—	—
—New York Islanders	NHL	—	—	—	—	—	1	0	1	1	0
87-88—New York Islanders	NHL	38	2	8	10	58	4	0	0	0	19
—Springfield	AHL	39	13	11	24	76	—	—	—	—	—
88-89—New York Islanders	NHL	55	11	10	21	86	—	—	—	—	—
89-90—		Did not play—retired.									
90-91—New York Islanders	NHL	41	3	12	15	24	—	—	—	—	—
—Capital District	AHL	27	6	14	20	26	—	—	—	—	—
91-92—Capital District	AHL	14	7	8	15	34	—	—	—	—	—
—New York Islanders	NHL	15	2	1	3	12	—	—	—	—	—
NHL totals		151	19	31	50	180	5	0	1	1	19

DAL GRANDE, DAVID
D, RANGERS

PERSONAL: Born July 8, 1974, at Ottawa. . . . 6-5/195. . . . Shoots left.
TRANSACTIONS/CAREER NOTES: Selected by New York Rangers in sixth round (sixth Rangers pick, 144th overall) of NHL entry draft (June 20, 1992).

Season Team	League	REGULAR SEASON					PLAYOFFS				
		Gms.	G	A	Pts.	Pen.	Gms.	G	A	Pts.	Pen.
91-92—Ottawa	COJHL	53	7	28	35	54	—	—	—	—	—

DALLMAN, ROD
RW, FLYERS

PERSONAL: Born January 26, 1967, at Quesnel, B.C. . . . 6-0/195. . . . Shoots left.
TRANSACTIONS/CAREER NOTES: Broke left ankle (October 1984). . . . Selected by New York Islanders as underage junior in eighth round (eighth Islanders pick, 118th overall) of NHL entry draft (June 15, 1985). . . . Injured shoulder (October 1986). . . . Suspended five games by AHL for knocking down linesman (November 22, 1989). . . . Strained knee ligaments (May 1990). . . . Signed as free agent by Philadelphia Flyers (August 1990).

Season Team	League	Gms.	G	A	Pts.	Pen.	Gms.	G	A	Pts.	Pen.
		REGULAR SEASON					**PLAYOFFS**				
84-85—Prince Albert	WHL	40	8	11	19	133	12	3	4	7	51
85-86—Prince Albert	WHL	59	20	21	41	198	—	—	—	—	—
86-87—Prince Albert	WHL	47	13	21	34	240	5	0	1	1	32
87-88—New York Islanders	NHL	3	1	0	1	6	—	—	—	—	—
—Springfield	AHL	59	9	17	26	355	—	—	—	—	—
88-89—New York Islanders	NHL	1	0	0	0	15	1	0	1	1	0
—Springfield	AHL	67	12	12	24	360	—	—	—	—	—
89-90—Springfield	AHL	43	10	20	30	129	15	5	5	10	59
90-91—Hershey	AHL	2	0	0	0	0	—	—	—	—	—
—San Diego	IHL	15	3	5	8	85	—	—	—	—	—
91-92—Hershey	AHL	31	4	13	17	114	—	—	—	—	—
—Philadelphia	NHL	2	0	0	0	5	—	—	—	—	—
NHL totals		6	1	0	1	26	1	0	1	1	0

DAM, TREVOR
RW, BLACKHAWKS

PERSONAL: Born April 20, 1970, at Scarborough, Ont. . . . 5-10/208. . . . Shoots right.
TRANSACTIONS/CAREER NOTES: Selected by Chicago Blackhawks in third round (second Blackhawks pick, 50th overall) of NHL entry draft (June 11, 1988).

Season Team	League	Gms.	G	A	Pts.	Pen.	Gms.	G	A	Pts.	Pen.
		REGULAR SEASON					**PLAYOFFS**				
86-87—London	OHL	64	6	17	23	88	—	—	—	—	—
87-88—London	OHL	66	25	38	63	169	12	0	3	3	19
88-89—London	OHL	66	33	59	92	111	21	9	11	20	39
89-90—London	OHL	56	20	54	74	91	6	2	5	7	15
90-91—Indianapolis	IHL	50	9	10	19	28	1	0	0	0	2
91-92—Indianapolis	IHL	79	19	23	42	132	—	—	—	—	—

D'AMOUR, MARC
G, FLYERS

PERSONAL: Born April 29, 1961, at Sudbury, Ont. . . . 5-9/185. . . . Shoots left.
TRANSACTIONS/CAREER NOTES: Signed as free agent by Calgary Flames (April 1982). . . . Pulled groin (January 28, 1986). . . . Signed as free agent by Philadelphia Flyers (September 30, 1989).
HONORS: Shared Dave Pinkney Trophy with John Vanbiesbrouck (1981-82). . . . Named to OHL All-Star first team (1981-82).

Season Team	League	Gms.	Min.	W	L	T	GA	SO	Avg.	Gms.	Min.	W	L	GA	SO	Avg.
		REGULAR SEASON								**PLAYOFFS**						
78-79—Sault Ste. Marie	OMJHL	30	1501				149	0	5.96	—						
79-80—Sault Ste. Marie	OMJHL	33	1429	16	15	0	117	0	4.91	—						
80-81—Sault Ste. Marie	OMJHL	16	653	7	1	1	38	0	3.49	14	683	5	4	41	0	3.60
81-82—Sault Ste. Marie	OHL	46	2384	28	12	1	130	1	*3.27	10	504	3	2	30	0	3.57
82-83—Colorado	CHL	42	2373	16	21	2	153	1	3.87	1	59			4	0	4.07
83-84—Colorado	CHL	36	1917	18	12	1	131	0	4.10	1	20	0	0	0	0	0.00
84-85—Salt Lake City	IHL	12	694	7	2	2	33	0	2.85	—						
—Moncton	AHL	37	2051	18	14	2	115	0	3.36	—						
85-86—Moncton	AHL	21	1129	6	9	3	72	0	3.83	5	296	1	4	20	0	4.05
—Calgary	NHL	15	560	2	4	2	32	0	3.43	—						
86-87—Binghamton	AHL	8	461	5	3	0	30	0	3.90	—						
—Salt Lake City	IHL	10	523	3	6	0	37	0	4.24	—						
87-88—Salt Lake City	IHL	*62	3245	26	19	5	177	0	3.27	*19	*1123	*12	7	*67	0	3.58
88-89—Philadelphia	NHL	1	19	0	0	0	0	0	0.00	—						
—Hershey	AHL	39	2174	19	3	3	127	0	3.51	—						
—Indianapolis	IHL	6	324				20	0	3.70	—						
89-90—Hershey	AHL	43	2505	15	20	6	148	2	3.54	—						
90-91—Hershey	AHL	28	1331	10	8	4	80	0	3.61	2	80	0	1	5	0	3.75
—Fort Wayne	IHL	3	136				9	0	3.97	—						
91-92—Hershey	AHL	21	1073	9	8	2	79	0	4.42	—						
NHL totals		16	579	2	4	2	32	0	3.32							

DAMPHOUSSE, VINCENT
LW/C, OILERS

PERSONAL: Born December 17, 1967, at Montreal. . . . 6-1/190. . . . Shoots left.
TRANSACTIONS/CAREER NOTES: Selected by Toronto Maple Leafs as underage junior in first round (first Maple Leafs pick, sixth overall) of NHL entry draft (June 21, 1986). . . . Traded by Maple Leafs with D Luke Richardson, G Peter Ing, C Scott Thornton and future considerations to Edmonton Oilers for G Grant Fuhr, LW/RW Glenn Anderson and LW Craig Berube (September 19, 1991).
HONORS: Named to QMJHL All-Star second team (1985-86).
RECORDS: Shares NHL All-Star single-game record for most goals—4 (1991).

Season Team	League	Gms.	G	A	Pts.	Pen.	Gms.	G	A	Pts.	Pen.
		REGULAR SEASON					**PLAYOFFS**				
83-84—Laval	QMJHL	66	29	36	65	25	—	—	—	—	—
84-85—Laval	QMJHL	68	35	68	103	62	—	—	—	—	—
85-86—Laval	QMJHL	69	45	110	155	70	14	9	27	36	12

Season Team	League	REGULAR SEASON					PLAYOFFS				
		Gms.	G	A	Pts.	Pen.	Gms.	G	A	Pts.	Pen.
86-87—Toronto	NHL	80	21	25	46	26	12	1	5	6	8
87-88—Toronto	NHL	75	12	36	48	40	6	0	1	1	10
88-89—Toronto	NHL	80	26	42	68	75	—	—	—	—	—
89-90—Toronto	NHL	80	33	61	94	56	5	0	2	2	2
90-91—Toronto	NHL	79	26	47	73	65	—	—	—	—	—
91-92—Edmonton	NHL	80	38	51	89	53	16	6	8	14	8
NHL totals		474	156	262	418	315	39	7	16	23	28

DANDENAULT, ERIC
D, FLYERS

PERSONAL: Born March 10, 1970, at Sherbrooke, Que. . . . 6-0/193. . . . Shoots right. **TRANSACTIONS/CAREER NOTES:** Signed as free agent by Philadelphia Flyers (October 4, 1991).

Season Team	League	REGULAR SEASON					PLAYOFFS				
		Gms.	G	A	Pts.	Pen.	Gms.	G	A	Pts.	Pen.
90-91—Drummondville	QMJHL	67	14	33	47	215	—	—	—	—	—
91-92—Hershey	AHL	69	6	13	19	149	3	0	0	0	4

DANEYKO, KEN
D, DEVILS

PERSONAL: Born April 17, 1964, at Windsor, Ont. . . . 6-0/210. . . . Shoots left. . . . Full name: Kenneth Daneyko. **TRANSACTIONS/CAREER NOTES:** Selected by Seattle Breakers from Spokane Flyers in WHL dispersal draft (December 1981). . . . Selected by New Jersey Devils as underage junior in first round (second Devils pick, 18th overall) of NHL entry draft (June 1982). . . . Fractured right fibula (November 2, 1983). . . . Suspended one game and fined $500 by NHL for playing in West Germany without permission (October 1985). . . . Injured wrist (February 25, 1987). . . . Broke nose (February 24, 1988).

Season Team	League	REGULAR SEASON					PLAYOFFS				
		Gms.	G	A	Pts.	Pen.	Gms.	G	A	Pts.	Pen.
80-81—Spokane Flyers	WHL	62	6	13	19	140	4	0	0	0	6
81-82—Spokane Flyers	WHL	26	1	11	12	147	—	—	—	—	—
—Seattle	WHL	38	1	22	23	151	14	1	9	10	49
82-83—Seattle	WHL	69	17	43	60	150	4	1	3	4	14
83-84—Kamloops	WHL	19	6	28	34	52	17	4	9	13	28
—New Jersey	NHL	11	1	4	5	17	—	—	—	—	—
84-85—New Jersey	NHL	1	0	0	0	10	—	—	—	—	—
—Maine	AHL	80	4	9	13	206	11	1	3	4	36
85-86—Maine	AHL	21	3	2	5	75	—	—	—	—	—
—New Jersey	NHL	44	0	10	10	100	—	—	—	—	—
86-87—New Jersey	NHL	79	2	12	14	183	—	—	—	—	—
87-88—New Jersey	NHL	80	5	7	12	239	20	1	6	7	83
88-89—New Jersey	NHL	80	5	5	10	283	—	—	—	—	—
89-90—New Jersey	NHL	74	6	15	21	216	6	2	0	2	21
90-91—New Jersey	NHL	80	4	16	20	249	7	0	1	1	10
91-92—New Jersey	NHL	80	1	7	8	170	7	0	3	3	16
NHL totals		529	24	76	100	1467	40	3	10	13	130

DANIELS, JEFF
LW, PENGUINS

PERSONAL: Born June 24, 1968, at Oshawa, Ont. . . . 6-1/200. . . . Shoots left. **TRANSACTIONS/CAREER NOTES:** Selected by Pittsburgh Penguins as underage junior in sixth round (sixth Penguins pick, 109th overall) of NHL entry draft (June 21, 1986).

Season Team	League	REGULAR SEASON					PLAYOFFS				
		Gms.	G	A	Pts.	Pen.	Gms.	G	A	Pts.	Pen.
84-85—Oshawa	OHL	59	7	11	18	16	—	—	—	—	—
85-86—Oshawa	OHL	62	13	19	32	23	6	0	1	1	0
86-87—Oshawa	OHL	54	14	9	23	22	15	3	2	5	5
87-88—Oshawa	OHL	64	29	39	68	59	4	2	3	5	0
88-89—Muskegon	IHL	58	21	21	42	58	11	3	5	8	11
89-90—Muskegon	IHL	80	30	47	77	39	6	1	1	2	7
90-91—Pittsburgh	NHL	11	0	2	2	2	—	—	—	—	—
—Muskegon	IHL	62	23	29	52	18	5	1	3	4	2
91-92—Pittsburgh	NHL	2	0	0	0	0	—	—	—	—	—
—Muskegon	IHL	44	19	16	35	38	10	5	4	9	9
NHL totals		13	0	2	2	2					

DANIELS, KIMBI
C, FLYERS

PERSONAL: Born January 19, 1972, at Brandon, Man. . . . 5-10/184. . . . Shoots right. **TRANSACTIONS/CAREER NOTES:** Selected by Philadelphia Flyers in third round (fifth Flyers pick, 44th overall) of NHL entry draft (June 16, 1990).

Season Team	League	REGULAR SEASON					PLAYOFFS				
		Gms.	G	A	Pts.	Pen.	Gms.	G	A	Pts.	Pen.
88-89—Swift Current	WHL	68	30	31	61	48	12	6	6	12	12
89-90—Swift Current	WHL	69	43	51	94	84	4	1	3	4	10
90-91—Philadelphia	NHL	2	0	1	1	0	—	—	—	—	—
—Swift Current	WHL	69	54	64	118	68	3	4	2	6	6
91-92—Philadelphia	NHL	25	1	1	2	4	—	—	—	—	—
—Seattle	WHL	19	7	14	21	133	15	5	10	15	27
NHL totals		27	1	2	3	4					

DARBY, CRAIG
C, CANADIENS

PERSONAL: Born September 26, 1972, at Oneida, N.Y.... 6-3/180.... Shoots right.
HIGH SCHOOL: Albany Academy (N.Y.).
TRANSACTIONS/CAREER NOTES: Selected by Montreal Canadiens in second round (third Canadiens pick, 43rd overall) of NHL entry draft (June 22, 1991).

			REGULAR SEASON					PLAYOFFS			
Season Team	League	Gms.	G	A	Pts.	Pen.	Gms.	G	A	Pts.	Pen.
89-90—Albany Academy	N.Y. H.S.	29	32	53	85		—	—	—	—	—
90-91—Albany Academy	N.Y. H.S.		33	61	94		—	—	—	—	—
91-92—Providence College	Hockey East	35	17	24	41	47	—	—	—	—	—

DAVIDSON, LEE
C, JETS

PERSONAL: Born June 30, 1968, at Winnipeg, Man.... 5-10/165.... Shoots left.... Full name: Lee A. Davidson.
COLLEGE: North Dakota.
TRANSACTIONS/CAREER NOTES: Selected by Washington Capitals in eighth round (ninth Capitals pick, 166th overall) of NHL entry draft (June 21, 1986).... Signed as free agent by Winnipeg Jets (September 4, 1990).
HONORS: Named to WCHA All-Star second team (1990).... Named to NCAA West All-American second team (1990).

			REGULAR SEASON					PLAYOFFS			
Season Team	League	Gms.	G	A	Pts.	Pen.	Gms.	G	A	Pts.	Pen.
85-86—Penticton..........................	BCJHL	48	34	74	108	90	8	2	7	9	10
86-87—Univ. of North Dakota	WCHA	41	16	12	28	65	—	—	—	—	—
87-88—Univ. of North Dakota	WCHA	40	22	24	46	74	—	—	—	—	—
88-89—Univ. of North Dakota	WCHA	41	16	37	53	60	—	—	—	—	—
89-90—Univ. of North Dakota	WCHA	45	26	49	75	66	—	—	—	—	—
90-91—Moncton	AHL	69	15	17	32	24	—	—	—	—	—
91-92—Moncton	AHL	43	3	12	15	32	—	—	—	—	—
—Fort Wayne	IHL	22	4	10	14	30	7	2	5	7	8

DAVYDOV, EVGENY
LW/RW, JETS

PERSONAL: Born May 27, 1967, at Chelyabinsk, U.S.S.R.... 6-1/185.... Shoots right.
TRANSACTIONS/CAREER NOTES: Selected by Winnipeg Jets in 12th round (14th Jets pick, 235th overall) of NHL entry draft (June 17, 1989).
MISCELLANEOUS: Member of 1992 gold medal-winning Unified Olympic team.

			REGULAR SEASON					PLAYOFFS			
Season Team	League	Gms.	G	A	Pts.	Pen.	Gms.	G	A	Pts.	Pen.
84-85—Chelyabinsk	USSR	5	1	0	1	2	—	—	—	—	—
85-86—Chelyabinsk	USSR	39	11	5	16	22	—	—	—	—	—
86-87—CSKA	USSR	32	11	2	13	8	—	—	—	—	—
87-88—CSKA	USSR	44	16	7	23	18	—	—	—	—	—
88-89—CSKA	USSR	35	9	7	16	4	—	—	—	—	—
89-90—CSKA	USSR	44	17	6	23	16	—	—	—	—	—
90-91—CSKA	USSR	44	10	10	20	26	—	—	—	—	—
91-92—Unified Olympic Team.......	Int'l	8	3	3	6		—	—	—	—	—
—Winnipeg	NHL	12	4	3	7	8	7	2	2	4	2
NHL totals................................		12	4	3	7	8	7	2	2	4	2

DAWE, JASON
LW, SABRES

PERSONAL: Born May 29, 1973, at North York, Ont.... 5-10/195.... Shoots left.
TRANSACTIONS/CAREER NOTES: Tore ankle ligaments (September 1989).... Selected by Buffalo Sabres in second round (second Sabres pick, 35th overall) of NHL entry draft (June 22, 1991).

			REGULAR SEASON					PLAYOFFS			
Season Team	League	Gms.	G	A	Pts.	Pen.	Gms.	G	A	Pts.	Pen.
89-90—Peterborough	OHL	50	15	18	33	19	12	4	7	11	4
90-91—Peterborough	OHL	66	43	27	70	43	4	3	1	4	0
91-92—Peterborough	OHL	66	53	55	108	55	4	5	0	5	0

DAY, JOE
C, WHALERS

PERSONAL: Born May 11, 1968, at Chicago.... 5-11/180.... Shoots left.... Full name: Joseph Christopher Day.
COLLEGE: St. Lawrence (N.Y.).
TRANSACTIONS/CAREER NOTES: Selected by Hartford Whalers in ninth round (eighth Whalers pick, 186th overall) of NHL entry draft (June 13, 1987).... Fractured right foot (April 4, 1992); missed playoffs.
HONORS: Named to ECAC All-Star second team (1989-90).

			REGULAR SEASON					PLAYOFFS			
Season Team	League	Gms.	G	A	Pts.	Pen.	Gms.	G	A	Pts.	Pen.
85-86—Chicago Minor Hawks	Ill.	30	23	18	41	69	—	—	—	—	—
86-87—St. Lawrence University ...	ECAC	33	9	11	20	25	—	—	—	—	—
87-88—St. Lawrence University ...	ECAC	33	23	17	40	40	—	—	—	—	—
88-89—St. Lawrence University ...	ECAC	36	21	27	48	44	—	—	—	—	—
89-90—St. Lawrence University ...	ECAC	30	18	26	44	24	—	—	—	—	—
90-91—Springfield..........................	AHL	75	24	29	53	82	18	5	5	10	27
91-92—Springfield..........................	AHL	50	33	25	58	92	—	—	—	—	—
—Hartford..............................	NHL	24	0	3	3	10	—	—	—	—	—
NHL totals.................................		24	0	3	3	10	—	—	—	—	—

DEASLEY, BRYAN
LW, FLAMES

PERSONAL: Born November 26, 1968, at Toronto. . . . 6-3/205. . . . Shoots left. . . . Full name: Bryan Thomas Deasley.
COLLEGE: Michigan.
TRANSACTIONS/CAREER NOTES: Broke ribs (February 1986). . . . Fractured wrist (January 1987). . . . Selected by Calgary Flames in first round (first Flames pick, 19th overall) of NHL entry draft (June 13, 1987). . . . Underwent ankle surgery (July 1987). . . . Traded by Flames to Quebec Nordiques for C Claude Loiselle (March 2, 1991); trade cancelled by NHL when Loiselle was claimed by Toronto Maple Leafs on waivers prior to the trade; Deasley returned to Flames.

Season Team	League	REGULAR SEASON					PLAYOFFS				
		Gms.	G	A	Pts.	Pen.	Gms.	G	A	Pts.	Pen.
85-86—St. Michael's Jr. B	ODHA	30	17	20	37	88	—	—	—	—	—
86-87—University of Michigan	CCHA	38	13	10	23	74	—	—	—	—	—
87-88—University of Michigan	CCHA	27	18	4	22	38	—	—	—	—	—
88-89—Canadian National Team	Int'l	54	19	19	38	32	—	—	—	—	—
—Salt Lake City	IHL	—	—	—	—	—	7	3	3	6	25
89-90—Salt Lake City	IHL	71	16	11	27	46	11	4	0	4	8
90-91—Salt Lake City	IHL	75	24	21	45	63	1	0	0	0	0
91-92—Salt Lake City	IHL	65	12	23	35	67	2	0	0	0	4

DEBLOIS, LUCIEN
RW, JETS

PERSONAL: Born June 21, 1957, at Joliette, Que. . . . 5-11/200. . . . Shoots right.
TRANSACTIONS/CAREER NOTES: Selected by New York Rangers from Sorel Blackhawks in first round (first Rangers pick, eighth overall) of NHL entry draft (June 14, 1977). . . . Traded by Rangers with D Mike McEwen, LW Pat Hickey, D Dean Turner and future considerations (RW Bobby Sheehan and RW Bobby Crawford) to Colorado Rockies for D Barry Beck (November 1979). . . . Pulled groin (November 1980). . . . Traded by Rockies to Winnipeg Jets for C Brent Ashton and a third-round pick in 1982 draft (C Dave Kasper) (July 1981). . . . Traded by Jets to Montreal Canadiens for LW Perry Turnbull (June 1984). . . . Pulled groin (November 6, 1984). . . . Pulled stomach muscles (January 2, 1985). . . . Sprained right knee (October 16, 1985); missed 16 games. . . . Signed as free agent by Rangers (September 1986). . . . Hyperextended right knee (January 1988). . . . Suffered bursitis in right knee (March 1988). . . . Tore bicep tendon in right shoulder (November 1988). . . . Signed as free agent by Quebec Nordiques (June 27, 1989). . . . Traded by Nordiques with C/LW Aaron Broten and D Michel Petit to Toronto Maple Leafs for LW Scott Pearson and second-round picks in 1991 and 1992 drafts. Quebec traded the second-round pick in 1991 draft to Washington on June 22, 1991 (November 17, 1990). . . . Strained neck (February 10, 1991). . . . Injured leg and developed infection (February 23, 1991). . . . Traded by Maple Leafs to Jets for RW Mark Osborne (March 10, 1992). . . . Suffered contusion to quadricep (March 1992).
HONORS: Named to QMJHL All-Star first team (1975-76 and 1976-77). . . . Won Michel Briere Trophy (1976-77).

Season Team	League	REGULAR SEASON					PLAYOFFS				
		Gms.	G	A	Pts.	Pen.	Gms.	G	A	Pts.	Pen.
73-74—Sorel	QMJHL	56	30	35	65	53	—	—	—	—	—
74-75—Sorel	QMJHL	72	46	53	99	62	—	—	—	—	—
75-76—Sorel	QMJHL	70	56	55	111	112	5	1	1	2	32
76-77—Sorel	QMJHL	72	56	78	134	131	—	—	—	—	—
77-78—New York Rangers	NHL	71	22	8	30	27	3	0	0	0	2
78-79—New York Rangers	NHL	62	11	17	28	26	9	2	0	2	4
—New Haven	AHL	7	4	6	10	6	—	—	—	—	—
79-80—New York Rangers	NHL	6	3	1	4	7	—	—	—	—	—
—Colorado	NHL	70	24	19	43	36	—	—	—	—	—
80-81—Colorado	NHL	74	26	16	42	78	—	—	—	—	—
81-82—Winnipeg	NHL	65	25	27	52	87	4	2	1	3	4
82-83—Winnipeg	NHL	79	27	27	54	69	3	0	0	0	5
83-84—Winnipeg	NHL	80	34	45	79	50	3	0	1	1	4
84-85—Montreal	NHL	51	12	11	23	20	8	2	4	6	4
85-86—Montreal	NHL	61	14	17	31	48	11	0	0	0	7
86-87—New York Rangers	NHL	40	3	8	11	27	2	0	0	0	2
87-88—New York Rangers	NHL	74	9	21	30	103	—	—	—	—	—
88-89—New York Rangers	NHL	73	9	24	33	107	4	0	0	0	4
89-90—Quebec	NHL	70	9	8	17	45	—	—	—	—	—
90-91—Quebec	NHL	14	2	2	4	13	—	—	—	—	—
—Toronto	NHL	38	10	12	22	30	—	—	—	—	—
91-92—Toronto	NHL	54	8	11	19	39	—	—	—	—	—
—Winnipeg	NHL	11	1	2	3	2	5	1	0	1	2
NHL totals		993	249	276	525	814	52	7	6	13	38

DeBRUSK, LOUIE
LW, OILERS

PERSONAL: Born March 19, 1971, at Cambridge, Ont. . . . 6-1/205. . . . Shoots left.
TRANSACTIONS/CAREER NOTES: Selected by New York Rangers in third round (fourth Rangers pick, 49th overall) of NHL entry draft (June 17, 1989). . . . Traded by Rangers with C Bernie Nicholls, RW Steven Rice and future considerations to Edmonton Oilers for C Mark Messier and future considerations (October 4, 1991); Rangers later traded D David Shaw to Oilers for D Jeff Beukeboom to complete the deal (November 12, 1991). . . . Separated shoulder (January 28, 1992); missed four games.

Season Team	League	REGULAR SEASON					PLAYOFFS				
		Gms.	G	A	Pts.	Pen.	Gms.	G	A	Pts.	Pen.
87-88—Stratford Jr. B	OHA	43	13	14	27	205	—	—	—	—	—
88-89—London	OHL	59	11	11	22	149	19	1	1	2	43
89-90—London	OHL	61	21	19	40	198	6	2	2	4	24

Season	Team	League	REGULAR SEASON Gms.	G	A	Pts.	Pen.	PLAYOFFS Gms.	G	A	Pts.	Pen.
90-91	—London	OHL	61	31	33	64	*223	7	2	2	4	14
	—Binghamton	AHL	2	0	0	0	7	2	0	0	0	9
91-92	—Edmonton	NHL	25	2	1	3	124	—	—	—	—	—
	—Cape Breton	AHL	28	2	2	4	73	—	—	—	—	—
	NHL totals		25	2	1	3	124					

DEGRACE, YANICK
G, FLYERS

PERSONAL: Born April 16, 1971, at Lameque, N.B. . . . . 5-11/175. . . . Shoots left.
TRANSACTIONS/CAREER NOTES: Selected by Philadelphia Flyers in fifth round (fourth Flyers pick, 94th overall) of NHL entry draft (June 22, 1991).

Season	Team	League	REGULAR SEASON Gms.	Min.	W	L	T	GA	SO	Avg.	PLAYOFFS Gms.	Min.	W	L	GA	SO	Avg.
90-91	—Trois-Rivieres	QMJHL	33	1726	13	11	2	97	1	3.37	—	—	—	—	—	—	—
91-92	—Hershey	AHL	2	125	0	1	1	6	0	2.88	—	—	—	—	—	—	—

DelGUIDICE, MATT
G, BRUINS

PERSONAL: Born March 5, 1967, at West Haven, Conn. . . . 5-9/170. . . . Shoots right. . . . Full name: Matthew DelGuidice.
COLLEGE: Maine.
TRANSACTIONS/CAREER NOTES: Selected by Boston Bruins in fourth round (fourth Bruins pick, 77th overall) of NHL entry draft (June 13, 1987).

Season	Team	League	REGULAR SEASON Gms.	Min.	W	L	T	GA	SO	Avg.	PLAYOFFS Gms.	Min.	W	L	GA	SO	Avg.
86-87	—St. Anselm College	ECAC-II	24	1437	11	13	0	76		3.17	—	—	—	—	—	—	—
87-88	—University of Maine	Hoc. East						Did not play — transfer student.									
88-89	—University of Maine	Hoc. East	20	1090	16	4	0	57	1	*3.14	—	—	—	—	—	—	—
89-90	—University of Maine	Hoc. East	23	1257	16	4	0	68	0	3.25	—	—	—	—	—	—	—
90-91	—Boston	NHL	1	10	0	0	0	0	0	0.00	—	—	—	—	—	—	—
	—Maine	AHL	52	2893	23	18	9	160	2	3.32	2	82	1	1	5	0	3.66
91-92	—Maine	AHL	25	1369	5	15	0	101	0	4.43	—	—	—	—	—	—	—
	—Boston	NHL	10	424	2	5	1	28	0	3.96	—	—	—	—	—	—	—
	NHL totals		11	434	2	5	1	28	0	3.87							

DePALMA, LARRY
LW, SHARKS

PERSONAL: Born October 27, 1965, at Trenton, Mich. . . . 6-0/180. . . . Shoots left.
TRANSACTIONS/CAREER NOTES: Signed as free agent by Minnesota North Stars (March 1986). . . . Injured wrist (October 1987). . . . Sprained ankle ligaments (February 1989). . . . Signed as free agent by San Jose Sharks (August 30, 1991).
HONORS: Named to WHL All-Star second team (1985-86).

Season	Team	League	REGULAR SEASON Gms.	G	A	Pts.	Pen.	PLAYOFFS Gms.	G	A	Pts.	Pen.
84-85	—New Westminster	WHL	65	14	16	30	87	10	1	1	2	25
85-86	—Saskatoon	WHL	65	61	51	112	232	13	7	9	16	58
	—Minnesota	NHL	1	0	0	0	0	—	—	—	—	—
86-87	—Springfield	AHL	9	2	2	4	82	—	—	—	—	—
	—Minnesota	NHL	56	9	6	15	219	—	—	—	—	—
87-88	—Baltimore	AHL	16	8	10	18	121	—	—	—	—	—
	—Kalamazoo	IHL	22	6	11	17	215	—	—	—	—	—
	—Minnesota	NHL	7	1	1	2	15	—	—	—	—	—
88-89	—Minnesota	NHL	43	5	7	12	102	2	0	0	0	6
89-90	—Kalamazoo	IHL	36	7	14	21	218	4	1	1	2	32
90-91	—Kalamazoo	IHL	55	27	32	59	160	11	5	4	9	25
	—Minnesota	NHL	14	3	0	3	26	—	—	—	—	—
91-92	—Kansas City	IHL	62	28	29	57	188	15	7	13	20	34
	NHL totals		121	18	14	32	362	2	0	0	0	6

DERKSEN, DUANE
G, CAPITALS

PERSONAL: Born July 7, 1968, at St. Boniface, Man. . . . 6-1/180. . . . Shoots left. . . . Full name: Duane Edward Derksen.
COLLEGE: Wisconsin.
TRANSACTIONS/CAREER NOTES: Selected by Washington Capitals in third round (fourth Capitals choice, 57th overall) of NHL entry draft (June 11, 1988).
HONORS: Named to WCHA All-Star second team (1990-91). . . . Won WCHA Most Valuable Player Award (1991-92). . . . Named to WCHA All-Star first team (1991-92).

Season	Team	League	REGULAR SEASON Gms.	Min.	W	L	T	GA	SO	Avg.	PLAYOFFS Gms.	Min.	W	L	GA	SO	Avg.
86-87	—Winkler	SOJHL	48	2140				171	1	4.79	—	—	—	—	—	—	—
87-88	—Winkler	SOJHL	38	2294				198	0	5.18	—	—	—	—	—	—	—
88-89	—Univ. of Wisconsin	WCHA	11	560				37	0	3.96	—	—	—	—	—	—	—
89-90	—Univ. of Wisconsin	WCHA	41	2345				133	2	3.40	—	—	—	—	—	—	—
90-91	—Univ. of Wisconsin	WCHA	*42	*2474				133	3	3.23	—	—	—	—	—	—	—
91-92	—Univ. of Wisconsin	WCHA	35	*2064	21	12	†2	110	0	3.20	—	—	—	—	—	—	—

D

DEROUVILLE, PHILLIPPE
G, PENGUINS

PERSONAL: Born August 7, 1974, at Arthabaska, Que. . . . 6-2/180. . . . Shoots left.
TRANSACTIONS/CAREER NOTES: Selected by Pittsburgh Penguins in fifth round (fifth Penguins pick, 115th overall) of NHL entry draft (June 20, 1992).
HONORS: Won Raymond Lagace Trophy (1991-92).

Season Team	League	Gms.	Min.	REGULAR SEASON W	L	T	GA	SO	Avg.	Gms.	Min.	PLAYOFFS W	L	GA	SO	Avg.
90-91—Longueuil	QMJHL	20	1030	13	6	0	50	0	2.91	—	—	—	—	—	—	—
91-92—Longueuil	QMJHL	34	1854	20	6	3	99	2	3.20	11	593	†7	2	28	†1	2.83

DESJARDINS, ERIC
D, CANADIENS

PERSONAL: Born June 14, 1969, at Rouyn, Que. . . . 6-1/200. . . . Shoots right.
TRANSACTIONS/CAREER NOTES: Selected by Montreal Canadiens as underage junior in second round (third Canadiens pick, 38th overall) of NHL entry draft (June 13, 1987). . . . Suffered from the flu (January 1989). . . . Pulled groin (November 2, 1989); missed seven games. . . . Sprained left ankle (January 26, 1991); missed 16 games. . . . Fractured right thumb (December 8, 1991); missed two games.
HONORS: Named to QMJHL All-Star second team (1986-87). . . . Won Emile (Butch) Bouchard Trophy (1987-88).

Season Team	League	REGULAR SEASON Gms.	G	A	Pts.	Pen.	PLAYOFFS Gms.	G	A	Pts.	Pen.
86-87—Granby	QMJHL	66	14	24	38	75	8	3	2	5	10
87-88—Granby	QMJHL	62	18	49	67	138	5	0	3	3	10
—Sherbrooke	AHL	3	0	0	0	6	4	0	2	2	2
88-89—Montreal	NHL	36	2	12	14	26	14	1	1	2	6
89-90—Montreal	NHL	55	3	13	16	51	6	0	0	0	10
90-91—Montreal	NHL	62	7	18	25	27	13	1	4	5	8
91-92—Montreal	NHL	77	6	32	38	50	11	3	3	6	4
NHL totals		230	18	75	93	154	44	5	8	13	28

DESJARDINS, MARTIN
C, BLACKHAWKS

PERSONAL: Born January 28, 1967, at Ste. Rose, Que. . . . 6-0/180. . . . Shoots left.
TRANSACTIONS/CAREER NOTES: Selected by Montreal Canadiens in fourth round (fifth Canadiens pick, 75th overall) of NHL entry draft (June 15, 1985). . . . Traded by Canadiens to Chicago Blackhawks for a future draft pick (October 11, 1990).

Season Team	League	REGULAR SEASON Gms.	G	A	Pts.	Pen.	PLAYOFFS Gms.	G	A	Pts.	Pen.
84-85—Trois-Rivieres	QMJHL	66	29	34	63	76	7	4	6	10	6
85-86—Trois-Rivieres	QMJHL	71	49	69	118	103	4	2	4	6	4
86-87—Trois-Rivieres	QMJHL	52	32	52	84	77	—	—	—	—	—
—Longueuil	QMJHL	68	39	61	100	89	19	8	10	18	18
87-88—Sherbrooke	AHL	75	34	36	70	117	5	1	1	2	8
88-89—Sherbrooke	AHL	70	17	27	44	104	6	2	7	9	21
89-90—Sherbrooke	AHL	65	21	26	47	72	12	4	†13	17	28
—Montreal	NHL	8	0	2	2	2	—	—	—	—	—
90-91—Fredericton	AHL	2	0	1	1	6	—	—	—	—	—
—Indianapolis	IHL	71	15	42	57	110	7	2	1	3	8
91-92—Indianapolis	IHL	36	4	7	11	52	—	—	—	—	—
NHL totals		8	0	2	2	2					

DESJARDINS, NORMAN
RW, CANADIENS

PERSONAL: Born March 25, 1968, at Montreal. . . . 5-10/184. . . . Shoots right.
TRANSACTIONS/CAREER NOTES: Signed as free agent by Montreal Canadiens (October 2, 1989).

Season Team	League	REGULAR SEASON Gms.	G	A	Pts.	Pen.	PLAYOFFS Gms.	G	A	Pts.	Pen.
86-87—Granby	QMJHL	52	19	22	41	61	—	—	—	—	—
—Verdun	QMJHL	14	3	5	8	45	—	—	—	—	—
87-88—Verdun	QMJHL	69	31	44	75	95	—	—	—	—	—
88-89—Longueuil	QMJHL	63	26	61	87	72	—	—	—	—	—
89-90—Sherbrooke	AHL	58	13	19	32	91	12	4	3	7	15
90-91—Fredericton	AHL	74	11	13	24	110	9	2	2	4	6
91-92—Fredericton	AHL	50	9	9	18	62	—	—	—	—	—

DEULING, JARRETT
LW, ISLANDERS

PERSONAL: Born March 4, 1974, at Vernon, B.C. . . . 6-0/198. . . . Shoots left.
HIGH SCHOOL: Norkam Secondary School (Kamloops, B.C.).
TRANSACTIONS/CAREER NOTES: Selected by New York Islanders in third round (second Islanders pick, 56th overall) of NHL entry draft (June 20, 1992).
HONORS: Won WHL playoff Most Valuable Player Award (1991-92).

Season Team	League	REGULAR SEASON Gms.	G	A	Pts.	Pen.	PLAYOFFS Gms.	G	A	Pts.	Pen.
90-91—Kamloops	WHL	48	4	12	16	43	12	5	2	7	7
91-92—Kamloops	WHL	68	28	24	52	79	17	10	6	16	18

DIDUCK, GERALD
D, CANUCKS

PERSONAL: Born April 6, 1965, at Edmonton, Alta.... 6-2/207.... Shoots right.
TRANSACTIONS/CAREER NOTES: Selected by New York Islanders as underage junior in first round (second Islanders pick, 16th overall) of NHL entry draft (June 8, 1983).... Fractured left foot (November 1987).... Fractured right hand (November 1988).... Injured knee (January 1989).... Traded by Islanders to Montreal Canadiens for D Craig Ludwig (September 4, 1990).... Traded by Canadiens to Vancouver Canucks for a fourth-round pick in 1991 draft (LW Vladimir Vujtek) (January 12, 1991).... Bruised knee (March 16, 1991).

Season Team	League	REGULAR SEASON					PLAYOFFS				
		Gms.	G	A	Pts.	Pen.	Gms.	G	A	Pts.	Pen.
81-82—Lethbridge	WHL	71	1	15	16	81	12	0	3	3	27
82-83—Lethbridge	WHL	67	8	16	24	151	20	3	12	15	49
83-84—Indianapolis	IHL	—	—	—	—	—	10	1	6	7	19
—Lethbridge	WHL	65	10	24	34	133	5	1	4	5	27
84-85—New York Islanders	NHL	65	2	8	10	80	—	—	—	—	—
85-86—New York Islanders	NHL	10	1	2	3	2	—	—	—	—	—
—Springfield	AHL	61	6	14	20	175	—	—	—	—	—
86-87—Springfield	AHL	45	6	8	14	120	—	—	—	—	—
—New York Islanders	NHL	30	2	3	5	67	14	0	1	1	35
87-88—New York Islanders	NHL	68	7	12	19	113	6	1	0	1	42
88-89—New York Islanders	NHL	65	11	21	32	155	—	—	—	—	—
89-90—New York Islanders	NHL	76	3	17	20	163	5	0	0	0	12
90-91—Montreal	NHL	32	1	2	3	39	—	—	—	—	—
—Vancouver	NHL	31	3	7	10	66	6	1	0	1	11
91-92—Vancouver	NHL	77	6	21	27	229	5	0	0	0	10
NHL totals		454	36	93	129	914	36	2	1	3	110

DiMAIO, ROB
C, LIGHTNING

PERSONAL: Born February 19, 1968, at Calgary, Alta.... 5-10/190.... Shoots right.... Full name: Robert DiMaio.
TRANSACTIONS/CAREER NOTES: Traded by Kamloops Blazers with LW Dave Mackey and C Kalvin Knibbs to Medicine Hat Tigers for LW Doug Pickel and LW Sean Pass (December 1985).... Selected by New York Islanders in sixth round (sixth Islanders pick, 118th overall) of NHL entry draft (June 13, 1987).... Suspended two games by WHL for leaving bench to fight (January 28, 1988).... Bruised left hand (February 1989).... Sprained clavicle (November 1989).... Sprained wrist (February 20, 1992); missed four games.... Reinjured wrist (February 29, 1992); missed final 17 games of season.... Underwent surgery to repair torn ligaments in wrist (March 11, 1992).... Selected by Tampa Bay Lightning in NHL expansion draft (June 18, 1992).
HONORS: Won Stafford Smythe Memorial Trophy (1987-88).... Named to Memorial Cup All-Star team (1987-88).

Season Team	League	REGULAR SEASON					PLAYOFFS				
		Gms.	G	A	Pts.	Pen.	Gms.	G	A	Pts.	Pen.
84-85—Kamloops	WHL	55	9	18	27	29	—	—	—	—	—
85-86—Kamloops	WHL	6	1	0	1	0	—	—	—	—	—
—Medicine Hat	WHL	55	20	30	50	82	—	—	—	—	—
86-87—Medicine Hat	WHL	70	27	43	70	130	20	7	11	18	46
87 88—Medicine Hat	WHL	54	47	43	90	120	14	12	19	+31	59
88-89—New York Islanders	NHL	16	1	0	1	30	—	—	—	—	—
—Springfield	AHL	40	13	18	31	67	—	—	—	—	—
89-90—New York Islanders	NHL	7	0	0	0	2	1	1	0	1	4
—Springfield	AHL	54	25	27	52	69	16	4	7	11	45
90-91—New York Islanders	NHL	1	0	0	0	0	—	—	—	—	—
—Capital District	AHL	12	3	4	7	22	—	—	—	—	—
91-92—New York Islanders	NHL	50	5	2	7	43	1	1	0	1	4
NHL totals		74	6	2	8	75	1	1	0	1	4

DINEEN, GORD
D, PENGUINS

PERSONAL: Born September 21, 1962, at Toronto.... 6-0/195.... Shoots right.... Full name: Gordon Dineen.... Brother of Kevin Dineen, right winger, Philadelphia Flyers; brother of Peter Dineen, defenseman, Los Angeles Kings and Detroit Red Wings (1986-87 and 1989-90); and son of Bill Dineen, right winger, Detroit Red Wings and Chicago Blackhawks (1953-54 through 1957-58) and current head coach, Philadelphia Flyers.
TRANSACTIONS/CAREER NOTES: Selected by New York Islanders as underage junior in second round (second Islanders pick, 42nd overall) of NHL entry draft (June 10, 1981).... Bruised ribs (January 15, 1985).... Sprained left ankle (February 1988).... Traded by Islanders with future considerations to Minnesota North Stars for D Chris Pryor (March 1988).... Traded by North Stars with LW Scott Bjugstad to Pittsburgh Penguins for D Ville Siren and C Steve Gotaas (December 17, 1988).
HONORS: Won Bobby Orr Trophy (1982-83).... Won Bob Gassoff Award (1982-83).... Named to CHL All-Star first team (1982-83).... Named to IHL All-Star first team (1991-92).

Season Team	League	REGULAR SEASON					PLAYOFFS				
		Gms.	G	A	Pts.	Pen.	Gms.	G	A	Pts.	Pen.
79-80—St. Michael's Jr. B	ODHA	42	15	35	50	103	—	—	—	—	—
80-81—Sault Ste. Marie	OMJHL	68	4	26	30	158	19	1	7	8	58
81-82—Sault Ste. Marie	OHL	68	9	45	54	185	13	1	2	3	52
82-83—Indianapolis	CHL	73	10	47	57	78	13	2	10	12	29
—New York Islanders	NHL	2	0	0	0	4	—	—	—	—	—
83-84—Indianapolis	CHL	26	4	13	17	63	9	1	1	2	28
—New York Islanders	NHL	43	1	11	12	32	—	—	—	—	—
84-85—Springfield	AHL	25	1	8	9	46	10	0	0	0	26
—New York Islanders	NHL	48	1	12	13	89	—	—	—	—	—

Season Team	League	REGULAR SEASON Gms.	G	A	Pts.	Pen.	PLAYOFFS Gms.	G	A	Pts.	Pen.
85-86—New York Islanders	NHL	57	1	8	9	81	3	0	0	0	2
—Springfield	AHL	11	2	3	5	20	—	—	—	—	—
86-87—New York Islanders	NHL	71	4	10	14	110	7	0	4	4	4
87-88—New York Islanders	NHL	57	4	12	16	62	—	—	—	—	—
—Minnesota	NHL	13	1	1	2	21	—	—	—	—	—
88-89—Kalamazoo	IHL	25	2	6	8	49	—	—	—	—	—
—Minnesota	NHL	2	0	1	1	2	—	—	—	—	—
—Pittsburgh	NHL	38	1	2	3	42	11	0	2	2	8
89-90—Pittsburgh	NHL	69	1	8	9	125	—	—	—	—	—
90-91—Muskegon	IHL	40	1	14	15	57	5	0	2	2	0
—Pittsburgh	NHL	9	0	0	0	6	—	—	—	—	—
91-92—Muskegon	IHL	79	8	37	45	83	14	2	4	6	33
—Pittsburgh	NHL	1	0	0	0	0	—	—	—	—	—
NHL totals		410	14	65	79	574	40	1	7	8	68

DINEEN, KEVIN
RW, FLYERS

PERSONAL: Born October 28, 1963, at Quebec City. . . . 5-10/180. . . . Shoots right. . . . Full name: Kevin W. Dineen. . . . Brother of Gord Dineen, defenseman, Pittsburgh Penguins; brother of Peter Dineen, defenseman, Los Angeles Kings and Detroit Red Wings (1986-87 and 1989-90); and son of Bill Dineen, right winger, Detroit Red Wings and Chicago Blackhawks (1953-54 through 1957-58) and current head coach, Philadelphia Flyers.
COLLEGE: Denver.
TRANSACTIONS/CAREER NOTES: Selected by Hartford Whalers as underage junior in third round (third Whalers pick, 56th overall) of NHL entry draft (June 9, 1982). . . . Sprained left shoulder (October 24, 1985); missed nine games. . . . Broke knuckle (January 12, 1986); missed seven games. . . . Sprained knee (February 14, 1986). . . . Suffered shoulder tendinitis (September 1988). . . . Underwent surgery to right knee cartilage (August 1, 1990). . . . Suffered hip pointer (November 28, 1990). . . . Hospitalized due to complications caused by Crohn's disease (January 1, 1991); missed eight games. . . . Injured groin (March 1991). . . . Traded by Whalers to Philadelphia Flyers for C/LW Murray Craven (November 13, 1991). . . . Sprained wrist (February 4, 1992); missed one game.
HONORS: Named to THE SPORTING NEWS All-Star second team (1986-87). . . . Named Bud Light/NHL Man of the Year (1990-91).

Season Team	League	REGULAR SEASON Gms.	G	A	Pts.	Pen.	PLAYOFFS Gms.	G	A	Pts.	Pen.
80-81—St. Michael's Jr. B	ODHA	40	15	28	43	167	—	—	—	—	—
81-82—University of Denver	WCHA	38	12	22	34	105	—	—	—	—	—
82-83—University of Denver	WCHA	36	16	13	29	108	—	—	—	—	—
83-84—Canadian Olympic Team	Int'l	—	—	—	—	—	—	—	—	—	—
84-85—Binghamton	AHL	25	15	8	23	41	—	—	—	—	—
—Hartford	NHL	57	25	16	41	120	—	—	—	—	—
85-86—Hartford	NHL	57	33	35	68	124	10	6	7	13	18
86-87—Hartford	NHL	78	40	69	109	110	6	2	1	3	31
87-88—Hartford	NHL	74	25	25	50	219	6	4	4	8	8
88-89—Hartford	NHL	79	45	44	89	167	4	1	0	1	10
89-90—Hartford	NHL	67	25	41	66	164	6	3	2	5	18
90-91—Hartford	NHL	61	17	30	47	104	6	1	0	1	16
91-92—Hartford	NHL	16	4	2	6	23	—	—	—	—	—
—Philadelphia	NHL	64	26	30	56	130	—	—	—	—	—
NHL totals		553	240	292	532	1161	38	17	14	31	101

DIONNE, GILBERT
LW, CANADIENS

PERSONAL: Born September 19, 1970, at Drummondville, Que. . . . 6-0/194. . . . Shoots left. . . . Brother of Marcel Dionne, Hall of Fame center, Detroit Red Wings, Los Angeles Kings and New York Rangers (1971-72 through 1988-89).
TRANSACTIONS/CAREER NOTES: Selected by Montreal Canadiens in fourth round (fifth Canadiens pick, 81st overall) of NHL entry draft (June 16, 1990).
HONORS: Named to NHL All-Rookie team (1991-92).

Season Team	League	REGULAR SEASON Gms.	G	A	Pts.	Pen.	PLAYOFFS Gms.	G	A	Pts.	Pen.
87-88—Niagara Falls Jr. B	OHA	38	36	48	84	60	—	—	—	—	—
88-89—Kitchener	OHL	66	11	33	44	13	5	1	1	2	4
89-90—Kitchener	OHL	64	48	57	105	85	17	13	10	23	22
90-91—Fredericton	AHL	77	40	47	87	62	9	6	5	11	8
—Montreal	NHL	2	0	0	0	0	—	—	—	—	—
91-92—Fredericton	AHL	29	19	27	46	20	—	—	—	—	—
—Montreal	NHL	39	21	13	34	10	11	3	4	7	10
NHL totals		41	21	13	34	10	11	3	4	7	10

DIPIETRO, PAUL
C, CANADIENS

PERSONAL: Born September 8, 1970, at Sault Ste. Marie, Ont. . . . 5-9/181. . . . Shoots right.
TRANSACTIONS/CAREER NOTES: Selected by Montreal Canadiens in fifth round (sixth Canadiens pick, 102nd overall) of NHL entry draft (June 16, 1990). . . . Strained hip flexor (February 12, 1992).

Season Team	League	REGULAR SEASON Gms.	G	A	Pts.	Pen.	PLAYOFFS Gms.	G	A	Pts.	Pen.
86-87—Sudbury	OHL	49	5	11	16	13	—	—	—	—	—
87-88—Sudbury	OHL	63	25	42	67	27	—	—	—	—	—

Season Team	League	REGULAR SEASON					PLAYOFFS				
		Gms.	G	A	Pts.	Pen.	Gms.	G	A	Pts.	Pen.
88-89—Sudbury	OHL	57	31	48	79	27	—	—	—	—	—
89-90—Sudbury	OHL	66	56	63	119	57	7	3	6	9	7
90-91—Fredericton	AHL	78	39	31	70	38	9	5	6	11	2
91-92—Fredericton	AHL	43	26	31	57	52	7	3	4	7	8
—Montreal	NHL	33	4	6	10	25	—	—	—	—	—
NHL totals		33	4	6	10	25	—	—	—	—	—

DIRK, ROBERT
D, CANUCKS

PERSONAL: Born August 20, 1966, at Regina, Sask. . . . 6-4/218. . . . Shoots left.
TRANSACTIONS/CAREER NOTES: Selected by St. Louis Blues as underage junior in third round (fourth Blues pick, 53rd overall) of NHL entry draft (June 9, 1984). . . . Traded by Blues with LW Geoff Courtnall, C Cliff Ronning, LW Sergio Momesso and a future draft pick to Vancouver Canucks for C Dan Quinn and D Garth Butcher. . . . Sprained ankle (November 26, 1991); missed three games. . . . Sprained knee (February 1, 1992); missed four games.
HONORS: Named to WHL All-Star second team (1985-86).

Season Team	League	REGULAR SEASON					PLAYOFFS				
		Gms.	G	A	Pts.	Pen.	Gms.	G	A	Pts.	Pen.
82-83—Regina	WHL	1	0	0	0	0	—	—	—	—	—
—Kelowna	BCJHL	40	8	23	31	87	—	—	—	—	—
83-84—Regina	WHL	62	2	10	12	64	20	1	12	13	24
84-85—Regina	WHL	69	10	34	44	97	8	0	0	0	4
85-86—Regina	WHL	72	19	60	79	140	10	3	5	8	8
86-87—Peoria	IHL	76	5	17	22	155	—	—	—	—	—
87-88—St. Louis	NHL	7	0	1	1	16	6	0	1	1	2
—Peoria	IHL	54	4	21	25	126	—	—	—	—	—
88-89—St. Louis	NHL	9	0	1	1	11	—	—	—	—	—
—Peoria	IHL	22	0	2	2	54	—	—	—	—	—
89-90—Peoria	IHL	24	1	2	3	79	3	0	0	0	0
—St. Louis	NHL	37	1	1	2	128	9	0	1	1	2
90-91—Peoria	IHL	3	0	0	0	2	—	—	—	—	—
—St. Louis	NHL	41	1	3	4	100	—	—	—	—	—
—Vancouver	NHL	11	1	0	1	20	6	0	0	0	13
91-92—Vancouver	NHL	72	2	7	9	126	13	0	0	0	20
NHL totals		177	5	13	18	401	34	0	2	2	37

DJOOS, PER
D, RANGERS

PERSONAL: Born May 11, 1968, at Mora, Sweden. . . . 5-11/196. . . . Shoots left.
TRANSACTIONS/CAREER NOTES: Selected by Detroit Red Wings in seventh round (seventh Red Wings pick, 127th overall) of NHL entry draft (June 21, 1986). . . . Underwent surgery to repair right knee cartilage (October 19, 1990). . . . Traded by Red Wings with RW Joe Kocur to New York Rangers for C Kevin Miller, D Denis Vial and RW Jim Cummins (March 5, 1991).

Season Team	League	REGULAR SEASON					PLAYOFFS				
		Gms.	G	A	Pts.	Pen.	Gms.	G	A	Pts.	Pen.
84-85—Mora	Sweden-II	20	2	3	5	2	—	—	—	—	—
85-86—Mora	Sweden-II	30	9	5	14	14	—	—	—	—	—
86-87—Brynas	Sweden	23	1	2	3	16	—	—	—	—	—
87-88—Brynas	Sweden	34	4	11	15	18	—	—	—	—	—
88-89—Brynas	Sweden	40	1	17	18	44	—	—	—	—	—
89-90—Brynas	Sweden	37	5	13	18	34	5	1	3	4	6
90-91—Adirondack	AHL	20	2	9	11	6	—	—	—	—	—
—Detroit	NHL	26	0	12	12	16	—	—	—	—	—
—Binghamton	AHL	14	1	8	9	10	9	2	2	4	4
91-92—New York Rangers	NHL	50	1	18	19	40	—	—	—	—	—
NHL totals		76	1	30	31	56					

DOBBIN, BRIAN
RW, BRUINS

PERSONAL: Born August 18, 1966, at Petrolia, Ont. . . . 5-11/195. . . . Shoots right.
TRANSACTIONS/CAREER NOTES: Selected by Philadelphia Flyers as underage junior in fifth round (sixth Flyers pick, 100th overall) of NHL entry draft (June 9, 1984). . . . Damaged ligament in right knee (September 1986). . . . Traded by Flyers with D Gord Murphy and a third-round pick in 1992 draft to Boston Bruins for D Garry Galley, C Wes Walz and future considerations (January 2, 1992). . . . Strained lower back (February 1, 1992).
HONORS: Named to AHL All-Star first team (1988-89). . . . Named to AHL All-Star second team (1989-90).

Season Team	League	REGULAR SEASON					PLAYOFFS				
		Gms.	G	A	Pts.	Pen.	Gms.	G	A	Pts.	Pen.
81-82—Mooretown Jr. C	OHA	38	31	24	55	50	—	—	—	—	—
82-83—Kingston	OHL	69	16	39	55	35	—	—	—	—	—
83-84—London	OHL	70	30	40	70	70	—	—	—	—	—
84-85—London	OHL	53	42	57	99	63	8	7	4	11	2
85-86—London	OHL	59	38	55	93	113	5	2	1	3	9
—Hershey	AHL	2	1	0	1	0	18	5	5	10	21
86-87—Hershey	AHL	52	26	35	61	66	5	4	2	6	15
—Philadelphia	NHL	12	2	1	3	14	—	—	—	—	—
87-88—Hershey	AHL	54	36	47	83	58	12	7	8	15	15
—Philadelphia	NHL	21	3	5	8	6	—	—	—	—	—

Season Team	League	REGULAR SEASON					PLAYOFFS				
		Gms.	G	A	Pts.	Pen.	Gms.	G	A	Pts.	Pen.
88-89—Philadelphia	NHL	14	0	1	1	8	2	0	0	0	17
—Hershey	AHL	59	43	48	91	61	11	7	6	13	12
89-90—Hershey	AHL	68	38	47	85	58	—	—	—	—	—
—Philadelphia	NHL	9	1	1	2	11	—	—	—	—	—
90-91—Hershey	AHL	80	33	43	76	82	7	1	2	3	7
91-92—New Haven	AHL	33	16	21	37	20	—	—	—	—	—
—Maine	AHL	33	21	15	36	14	—	—	—	—	—
—Boston	NHL	7	1	0	1	22	—	—	—	—	—
NHL totals		63	7	8	15	61	2	0	0	0	17

DOLLAS, BOBBY
D, RED WINGS

PERSONAL: Born January 31, 1965, at Montreal. . . . 6-2/212. . . . Shoots left.
TRANSACTIONS/CAREER NOTES: Selected by Winnipeg Jets as underage junior in first round (second Jets pick, 14th overall) of NHL entry draft (June 8, 1983). . . . Traded by Jets to Quebec Nordiques for RW Stu Kulak (December 1987). . . . Signed as free agent by Detroit Red Wings (October 1990). . . . Suffered from the flu (December 15, 1990); missed two games. . . . Injured leg (January 9, 1991). . . . Strained abdomen (November 7, 1991); missed 15 games.
HONORS: Won Raymond Lagace Trophy (1982-83). . . . Named to QMJHL All-Star second team (1982-83).

Season Team	League	REGULAR SEASON					PLAYOFFS				
		Gms.	G	A	Pts.	Pen.	Gms.	G	A	Pts.	Pen.
82-83—Laval	QMJHL	63	16	45	61	144	11	5	5	10	23
83-84—Laval	QMJHL	54	12	33	45	80	14	1	8	9	23
—Winnipeg	NHL	1	0	0	0	0	—	—	—	—	—
84-85—Winnipeg	NHL	9	0	0	0	0	—	—	—	—	—
—Sherbrooke	AHL	8	1	3	4	4	17	3	6	9	17
85-86—Sherbrooke	AHL	25	4	7	11	29	—	—	—	—	—
—Winnipeg	NHL	46	0	5	5	66	3	0	0	0	2
86-87—Sherbrooke	AHL	75	6	18	24	87	16	2	4	6	13
87-88—Quebec	NHL	9	0	0	0	2	—	—	—	—	—
—Moncton	AHL	26	4	10	14	20	—	—	—	—	—
—Fredericton	AHL	33	4	8	12	27	15	2	2	4	24
88-89—Halifax	AHL	57	5	19	24	65	4	1	0	1	14
—Quebec	NHL	16	0	3	3	16	—	—	—	—	—
89-90—Canadian National Team	Int'l	68	8	29	37	60	—	—	—	—	—
90-91—Detroit	NHL	56	3	5	8	20	7	1	0	1	13
91-92—Detroit	NHL	27	3	1	4	20	2	0	1	1	0
—Adirondack	AHL	19	1	6	7	33	18	7	4	11	22
NHL totals		164	6	14	20	124	12	1	1	2	15

DOMI, TIE
RW, RANGERS

PERSONAL: Born November 1, 1969, at Windsor, Ont. . . . 5-10/198. . . . Full name: Tahir Domi.
TRANSACTIONS/CAREER NOTES: Suspended indefinitely by OHL for leaving the bench during a fight (November 2, 1986). . . . Selected by Toronto Maple Leafs in second round (second Maple Leafs pick, 27th overall) of NHL entry draft (June 11, 1988). . . . Traded by Maple Leafs with G Mark Laforest to New York Rangers for RW Greg Johnston (June 28, 1990). . . . Suspended six games by AHL for pre-game fighting (November 25, 1990). . . . Sprained right knee (March 11, 1992); missed eight games.

Season Team	League	REGULAR SEASON					PLAYOFFS				
		Gms.	G	A	Pts.	Pen.	Gms.	G	A	Pts.	Pen.
85-86—Windsor Jr. B	OHA	32	8	17	25	346	—	—	—	—	—
86-87—Peterborough	OHL	18	1	1	2	79	—	—	—	—	—
87-88—Peterborough	OHL	60	22	21	43	*292	12	3	9	12	24
88-89—Peterborough	OHL	43	14	16	30	175	17	10	9	19	*70
89-90—Newmarket	AHL	57	14	11	25	285	—	—	—	—	—
—Toronto	NHL	2	0	0	0	42	—	—	—	—	—
90-91—New York Rangers	NHL	28	1	0	1	185	—	—	—	—	—
—Binghamton	AHL	25	11	6	17	219	7	3	2	5	16
91-92—New York Rangers	NHL	42	2	4	6	246	6	1	1	2	32
NHL totals		72	3	4	7	473	6	1	1	2	32

DONATELLI, CLARK
LW, BRUINS

PERSONAL: Born November 22, 1967, at Providence, R.I. . . . 5-10/180. . . . Shoots left. . . . Full name: John Clark Donatelli.
COLLEGE: Boston University.
TRANSACTIONS/CAREER NOTES: Selected by New York Rangers in fifth round (fourth Rangers pick, 98th overall) of NHL entry draft (June 9, 1984). . . . Traded by Rangers with LW Ville Kentala, D Reijo Ruotsalainen and D Jim Wiemer to Edmonton Oilers for C Mike Golden, D Don Jackson and D Miloslav Horava (October 2, 1986). . . . Signed as free agent by Minnesota North Stars (June 20, 1989). . . . Signed as free agent by Boston Bruins (March 10, 1992).
HONORS: Named to NCAA All-America East second team (1985-86). . . . Named to Hockey East All-Star second team (1985-86).

Season Team	League	REGULAR SEASON					PLAYOFFS				
		Gms.	G	A	Pts.	Pen.	Gms.	G	A	Pts.	Pen.
84-85—Boston University	Hockey East	40	17	18	35	46	—	—	—	—	—
85-86—Boston University	Hockey East	43	28	34	62	30	—	—	—	—	—
86-87—Boston University	Hockey East	37	15	23	38	46	—	—	—	—	—

Season	Team	League	REGULAR SEASON					PLAYOFFS				
			Gms.	G	A	Pts.	Pen.	Gms.	G	A	Pts.	Pen.
87-88—U.S. National Team	Int'l	50	11	27	38	26	—	—	—	—	—
—U.S. Olympic Team	Int'l	6	2	1	3	5	—	—	—	—	—
88-89—					Did not play.							
89-90—Minnesota	NHL	25	3	3	6	17	—	—	—	—	—
—Kalamazoo	IHL	27	8	9	17	47	4	0	2	2	12
90-91—San Diego	IHL	46	17	10	27	45	—	—	—	—	—
91-92—U.S. National Team	Int'l	42	13	25	38	50	—	—	—	—	—
—U.S. Olympic Team	Int'l	8	2	1	3	6	—	—	—	—	—
—Boston	NHL	10	0	1	1	22	2	0	0	0	0
NHL totals		35	3	4	7	39	2	0	0	0	0

DONATO, TED
C, BRUINS

PERSONAL: Born April 28, 1968, at Dedham, Mass. . . . 5-10/170. . . . Shoots left. . . . Full name: Edward Paul Donato.
HIGH SCHOOL: Catholic Memorial (Boston).
COLLEGE: Harvard.
TRANSACTIONS/CAREER NOTES: Selected by Boston Bruins in fifth round (fifth Bruins pick, 98th overall) of NHL entry draft (June 13, 1987). . . . Broke collarbone (November 18, 1989).
HONORS: Named to ECAC All-Star first team (1990-91).

Season	Team	League	REGULAR SEASON					PLAYOFFS				
			Gms.	G	A	Pts.	Pen.	Gms.	G	A	Pts.	Pen.
86-87—Catholic Memorial H.S.	Mass. H.S.	22	29	34	63	30	—	—	—	—	—
87-88—Harvard University	ECAC	28	12	14	26	24	—	—	—	—	—
88-89—Harvard University	ECAC	34	14	37	51	30	—	—	—	—	—
89-90—Harvard University	ECAC	16	5	6	11	34	—	—	—	—	—
90-91—Harvard University	ECAC	28	19	37	56	26	—	—	—	—	—
91-92—U.S. National Team	Int'l	52	11	22	33	24	—	—	—	—	—
—U.S. Olympic Team	Int'l	8	4	3	7	8	—	—	—	—	—
—Boston	NHL	10	1	2	3	8	15	3	4	7	4
NHL totals		10	1	2	3	8	15	3	4	7	4

D

DONNELLY, GORD
RW/D, SABRES

PERSONAL: Born April 5, 1962, at Montreal. . . . 6-1/202. . . . Shoots right. . . . Full name: Gordon Donnelly.
TRANSACTIONS/CAREER NOTES: Selected by St. Louis Blues in third round (third Blues pick, 62nd overall) of NHL entry draft (June 10, 1981). . . . Sent by Blues along with D Claude Julien to Quebec Nordiques as compensation for St. Louis signing coach Jacques Demers (August 1983). . . . Suspended five games by NHL for kneeing (October 29, 1987). . . . Suspended five games and fined $100 by NHL for pre-game fighting (February 26, 1988). . . . Suspended 10 games by NHL for hitting with stick (March 27, 1988); missed final four games of 1987-88 season and first six games of 1988-89 season. . . . Traded by Nordiques to Winnipeg Jets for D Mario Marois (December 6, 1988). . . . Fined $500 by NHL for kicking (April 12, 1990). . . . Traded by Jets with RW Dave McLlwain, a sixth-round pick in 1992 draft and future considerations to Buffalo Sabres for LW Darrin Shannon, LW Mike Hartman and D Dean Kennedy (October 11, 1991).

Season	Team	League	REGULAR SEASON					PLAYOFFS				
			Gms.	G	A	Pts.	Pen.	Gms.	G	A	Pts.	Pen.
78-79—Laval	QMJHL	71	1	14	15	79	—	—	—	—	—
79-80—Laval	QMJHL	44	5	10	15	47	—	—	—	—	—
—Chicoutimi	QMJHL	24	1	5	6	64	—	—	—	—	—
80-81—Sherbrooke	QMJHL	67	15	23	38	252	14	1	2	3	35
81-82—Sherbrooke	QMJHL	60	8	41	49	250	22	2	7	9	*106
82-83—Salt Lake City	IHL	67	3	12	15	222	6	1	1	2	8
83-84—Fredericton	AHL	30	2	3	5	146	7	1	1	2	43
—Quebec	NHL	38	0	5	5	60	—	—	—	—	—
84-85—Fredericton	AHL	42	1	5	6	134	6	0	1	1	25
—Quebec	NHL	22	0	0	0	33	—	—	—	—	—
85-86—Fredericton	AHL	37	3	5	8	103	5	0	0	0	33
—Quebec	NHL	36	2	2	4	85	1	0	0	0	0
86-87—Quebec	NHL	38	0	2	2	143	13	0	0	0	53
87-88—Quebec	NHL	63	4	3	7	301	—	—	—	—	—
88-89—Quebec	NHL	16	4	0	4	46	—	—	—	—	—
—Winnipeg	NHL	57	6	10	16	228	6	0	1	1	8
89-90—Winnipeg	NHL	55	3	3	6	222	—	—	—	—	—
90-91—Winnipeg	NHL	57	3	4	7	265	—	—	—	—	—
91-92—Winnipeg	NHL	4	0	0	0	11	—	—	—	—	—
—Buffalo	NHL	67	2	3	5	305	6	0	1	1	0
NHL totals		453	24	32	56	1699	26	0	2	2	61

DONNELLY, MIKE
LW, KINGS

PERSONAL: Born October 10, 1963, at Livonia, Mich. . . . 5-11/185. . . . Shoots left. . . . Full name: Michael Chene Donnelly.
HIGH SCHOOL: Franklin (Livonia, Mich.).
COLLEGE: Michigan State.
TRANSACTIONS/CAREER NOTES: Signed as free agent by New York Rangers (August 1986). . . . Dislocated and fractured right index finger (November 1987). . . . Traded by Rangers with a fifth-round pick in 1988 draft (RW Alexander Mogilny) to Buffalo

Sabres for LW Paul Cyr and a 10th-round pick in 1988 draft (C Eric Fenton) (December 1987).... Traded by Sabres to Los Angeles Kings for LW Mikko Makela (October 1, 1990).
HONORS: Named to NCAA All-America West first team (1985-86).

Season Team	League	REGULAR SEASON					PLAYOFFS				
		Gms.	G	A	Pts.	Pen.	Gms.	G	A	Pts.	Pen.
82-83—Michigan State	CCHA	24	7	13	20	8	—	—	—	—	—
83-84—Michigan State	CCHA	44	18	14	32	40	—	—	—	—	—
84-85—Michigan State	CCHA	44	26	21	47	48	—	—	—	—	—
85-86—Michigan State	CCHA	44	*59	38	97	65	—	—	—	—	—
86-87—New York Rangers	NHL	5	1	1	2	0	—	—	—	—	—
—New Haven	AHL	58	27	34	61	52	7	2	0	2	9
87-88—Colorado	IHL	8	7	11	18	15	—	—	—	—	—
—New York Rangers	NHL	17	2	2	4	8	—	—	—	—	—
—Buffalo	NHL	40	6	8	14	44	—	—	—	—	—
88-89—Buffalo	NHL	22	4	6	10	10	—	—	—	—	—
—Rochester	AHL	53	32	37	69	53	—	—	—	—	—
89-90—Rochester	AHL	68	43	55	98	71	16	*12	7	19	9
—Buffalo	NHL	12	1	2	3	8	—	—	—	—	—
90-91—Los Angeles	NHL	53	7	5	12	41	12	5	4	9	6
—New Haven	AHL	18	10	6	16	2	—	—	—	—	—
91-92—Los Angeles	NHL	80	29	16	45	20	6	1	0	1	4
NHL totals		229	50	40	90	131	18	6	4	10	10

DOPITA, JIRI
C, BRUINS

PERSONAL: Born December 2, 1968, at Sumperk, Czechoslovakia.... 6-4/202.... Shoots left.
TRANSACTIONS/CAREER NOTES: Selected by Boston Bruins in sixth round (fourth Bruins pick, 133rd overall) of NHL entry draft (June 20, 1992).

Season Team	League	REGULAR SEASON					PLAYOFFS				
		Gms.	G	A	Pts.	Pen.	Gms.	G	A	Pts.	Pen.
89-90—Dukla Jihlava	Czech.	5	1	2	3		—	—	—	—	—
90-91—DS Olomouc	Czech.	42	11	13	24		—	—	—	—	—
91-92—DS Olomouc	Czech.	38	23	20	43		—	—	—	—	—

DOPSON, ROB
G, PENGUINS

PERSONAL: Born August 21, 1967, at Smith Falls, Ont.... 6-0/200.
COLLEGE: Wilfrid Laurier (Ont.)
TRANSACTIONS/CAREER NOTES: Signed as free agent by Pittsburgh Penguins (July 15, 1991).

Season Team	League	REGULAR SEASON							PLAYOFFS						
		Gms.	Min.	W	L	T	GA	SO	Avg.	Gms.	Min.	W	L	GA	SO	Avg.
89-90—Wilfrid Laurier Univ.	OUAA	22	1319				57	0	2.59	—	—	—	—	—	—	—
90-91—Muskegon	IHL	24	1243				90	0	4.34	—	—	—	—	—	—	—
91-92—Muskegon	IHL	29	1655	13	12	2	90	4	3.26	12	697	8	4	40	0	3.44

DORE, DANIEL
RW, NORDIQUES

PERSONAL: Born April 9, 1970, at St. Jerome, Que.... 6-3/202.... Shoots right.
TRANSACTIONS/CAREER NOTES: Selected by Quebec Nordiques in first round (second Nordiques pick, fifth overall) of NHL entry draft (June 11, 1988).... Underwent surgery to finger (April 1989).... Underwent surgery to nose (May 1989).... Traded by Drummondville Voltigeurs with RW Denis Chasse and D Pierre-Paul Landry to Chicoutimi Sagueneens for LW Yanic Dupre, D Guy Lehoux and RW Eric Meloche (December 19, 1989).... Suffered from recurring back pain (October 11, 1990).
HONORS: Won Michael Bossy Trophy (1987-88).

Season Team	League	REGULAR SEASON					PLAYOFFS				
		Gms.	G	A	Pts.	Pen.	Gms.	G	A	Pts.	Pen.
86-87—Drummondville	QMJHL	68	23	41	64	229	8	0	1	1	18
87-88—Drummondville	QMJHL	64	24	39	63	218	17	7	11	18	42
88-89—Drummondville	QMJHL	62	33	58	91	236	4	2	3	5	14
89-90—Quebec	NHL	16	2	3	5	6	—	—	—	—	—
—Chicoutimi	QMJHL	24	6	23	29	112	6	0	3	3	27
90-91—Halifax	AHL	50	7	10	17	139	—	—	—	—	—
—Quebec	NHL	1	0	0	0	0	—	—	—	—	—
91-92—Halifax	AHL	29	4	1	5	45	—	—	—	—	—
—Greensboro	ECHL	6	1	0	1	34	—	—	—	—	—
NHL totals		17	2	3	5	6					

DOUCET, WAYNE
LW, ISLANDERS

PERSONAL: Born June 19, 1970, at Etobicoke, Ont.... 6-2/203.... Shoots left.
TRANSACTIONS/CAREER NOTES: Separated shoulder (October 1986).... Selected by New York Islanders in second round (second Islanders pick, 29th overall) of NHL entry draft (June 11, 1988).

Season Team	League	REGULAR SEASON					PLAYOFFS				
		Gms.	G	A	Pts.	Pen.	Gms.	G	A	Pts.	Pen.
86-87—Sudbury	OHL	64	20	28	48	85	—	—	—	—	—
87-88—Sudbury	OHL	23	9	4	13	53	—	—	—	—	—
—Hamilton	OHL	37	11	14	25	74	1	0	0	0	8
88-89—Kingston	OHL	59	26	43	69	89	—	—	—	—	—
—Springfield	AHL	6	2	2	4	4	—	—	—	—	—

Season	Team	League	REGULAR SEASON Gms.	G	A	Pts.	Pen.	PLAYOFFS Gms.	G	A	Pts.	Pen.
89-90—Kingston	OHL	66	32	47	79	127	7	2	5	7	18
90-91—Capital District	AHL	21	11	6	17	93	—	—	—	—	—
91-92—Capital District	AHL	60	11	7	18	116	7	1	1	2	6

DOURIS, PETER
RW, BRUINS

PERSONAL: Born February 19, 1966, at Toronto. . . . 6-1/195. . . . Shoots right.
COLLEGE: New Hampshire.
TRANSACTIONS/CAREER NOTES: Selected by Winnipeg Jets in second round (first Jets pick, 30th overall) of NHL entry draft (June 9, 1984). . . . Traded by Jets to St. Louis Blues for LW/D Kent Carlson and a 12th-round pick in 1989 draft (RW Sergei Kharin) (September 29, 1988). . . . Signed as free agent by Boston Bruins (September 1989). . . . Injured ankle (December 1990). . . . Strained hip flexor (November 1991); missed three games.

Season	Team	League	REGULAR SEASON Gms.	G	A	Pts.	Pen.	PLAYOFFS Gms.	G	A	Pts.	Pen.
83-84—Univ. of New Hampshire	ECAC	38	19	15	34	14	—	—	—	—	—
84-85—Univ. of New Hampshire	Hockey East	42	27	24	51	34	—	—	—	—	—
85-86—Team Canada	Int'l	33	16	7	23	18	—	—	—	—	—
—Winnipeg	NHL	11	0	0	0	0	—	—	—	—	—
86-87—Sherbrooke	AHL	62	14	28	42	24	17	7	*15	*22	16
—Winnipeg	NHL	6	0	0	0	0	—	—	—	—	—
87-88—Moncton	AHL	73	42	37	79	53	—	—	—	—	—
—Winnipeg	NHL	4	0	2	2	0	1	0	0	0	0
88-89—Peoria	IHL	81	28	41	69	32	4	1	2	3	0
89-90—Maine	AHL	38	17	20	37	14	—	—	—	—	—
—Boston	NHL	36	5	6	11	15	8	0	1	1	8
90-91—Maine	AHL	35	16	15	31	9	7	0	1	1	6
—Boston	NHL	39	5	2	7	9	2	3	0	3	2
91-92—Boston	NHL	54	10	13	23	10	7	2	3	5	2
—Maine	AHL	12	4	3	7	2	—	—	—	—	—
NHL totals		150	20	23	43	34	18	5	4	9	10

DOWD, JIM
C, DEVILS

PERSONAL: Born December 25, 1968, at Brick, N.J. . . . 6-1/185. . . . Shoots right. . . . Full name: James Dowd.
HIGH SCHOOL: Brick Township (N.J.).
COLLEGE: Lake Superior State (Mich.).
TRANSACTIONS/CAREER NOTES: Selected by New Jersey Devils in eighth round (seventh Devils pick, 149th overall) of NHL entry draft (June 13, 1987).
HONORS: Named to CCHA All-Star second team (1989-90). . . . Named CCHA Player of the Year (1990-91). . . . Named to NCAA All-America West first team (1990-91). . . . Named to CCHA All-Star first team (1990-91).

Season	Team	League	REGULAR SEASON Gms.	G	A	Pts.	Pen.	PLAYOFFS Gms.	G	A	Pts.	Pen.
85-86—Brick H.S.	N.J. H.S.		47	51	98		—	—	—	—	—
86-87—Brick H.S.	N.J. H.S.	24	22	33	55		—	—	—	—	—
87-88—Lake Superior State	CCHA	45	18	27	45	16	—	—	—	—	—
88-89—Lake Superior State	CCHA	46	24	35	59	40	—	—	—	—	—
89-90—Lake Superior State	CCHA	46	25	67	92	30	—	—	—	—	—
90-91—Lake Superior State	CCHA	44	24	54	78	53	—	—	—	—	—
91-92—Utica	AHL	78	17	42	59	47	4	2	2	4	4
—New Jersey	NHL	1	0	0	0	0	—	—	—	—	—
NHL totals		1	0	0	0	0					

DOYON, MARIO
D, NORDIQUES

PERSONAL: Born August 27, 1968, at Quebec City. . . . 6-0/174. . . . Shoots right.
TRANSACTIONS/CAREER NOTES: Selected by Chicago Blackhawks in sixth round (fifth Blackhawks pick, 119th overall) of NHL entry draft (June 21, 1986). . . . Traded by Blackhawks with LW Everett Sanipass and LW Dan Vincelette to Quebec Nordiques for LW Michel Goulet, G Greg Millen and a sixth-round pick in 1991 draft (March 5, 1990).

Season	Team	League	REGULAR SEASON Gms.	G	A	Pts.	Pen.	PLAYOFFS Gms.	G	A	Pts.	Pen.
85-86—Drummondville	QMJHL	71	5	14	19	129	23	5	4	9	32
86-87—Drummondville	QMJHL	65	18	47	65	150	8	1	3	4	30
87-88—Drummondville	QMJHL	68	23	54	77	233	17	3	14	17	46
88-89—Saginaw	IHL	71	16	32	48	69	6	0	0	0	8
—Chicago	NHL	7	1	1	2	6	—	—	—	—	—
89-90—Indianapolis	IHL	66	9	25	34	50	—	—	—	—	—
—Halifax	AHL	5	1	2	3	0	6	1	3	4	2
—Quebec	NHL	9	2	3	5	6	—	—	—	—	—
90-91—Halifax	AHL	59	14	23	37	58	—	—	—	—	—
—Quebec	NHL	12	0	0	0	4	—	—	—	—	—
91-92—Halifax	AHL	9	0	0	0	22	—	—	—	—	—
—New Haven	AHL	64	11	29	40	44	5	1	1	2	2
NHL totals		28	3	4	7	16					

DRAKE, DALLAS
C, RED WINGS

PERSONAL: Born February 4, 1969, at Trail, B.C. . . . 6-0/170. . . . Shoots left. . . . Full name: Dallas James Drake.
COLLEGE: Northern Michigan.
TRANSACTIONS/CAREER NOTES: Selected by Detroit Red Wings in sixth round (sixth Red Wings pick, 116th overall) of NHL entry draft (June 17, 1989).
HONORS: Named to WCHA All-Star first team (1991-92).

Season Team	League		REGULAR SEASON					PLAYOFFS				
		Gms.	G	A	Pts.	Pen.	Gms.	G	A	Pts.	Pen.
84-85—Rossland	KIJHL	30	13	37	50		—	—	—	—	—
85-86—Rossland	KIJHL	41	53	73	126		—	—	—	—	—
86-87—Rossland	KIJHL	40	55	80	135		—	—	—	—	—
87-88—Vernon	BCJHL	47	39	85	124	50	11	9	17	26	30
88-89—Northern Michigan Univ.	WCHA	45	18	24	42	26	—	—	—	—	—
89-90—Northern Michigan Univ.	WCHA	36	13	24	37	42	—	—	—	—	—
90-91—Northern Michigan Univ.	WCHA	44	22	36	58	89	—	—	—	—	—
91-92—Northern Michigan Univ.	WCHA	40	*39	44	83	58	—	—	—	—	—

DRAPER, KRIS
C/LW, JETS

PERSONAL: Born May 24, 1971, at Toronto. . . . 5-11/190. . . . Shoots left. . . . Full name: Kris Bruce Draper.
TRANSACTIONS/CAREER NOTES: Selected by Winnipeg Jets in third round (fourth Jets pick, 62nd overall) of NHL entry draft (June 17, 1989).

Season Team	League		REGULAR SEASON					PLAYOFFS				
		Gms.	G	A	Pts.	Pen.	Gms.	G	A	Pts.	Pen.
88-89—Canadian National Team	Int'l	60	11	15	26	16	—	—	—	—	—
89-90—Canadian National Team	Int'l	61	12	22	34	44	—	—	—	—	—
90-91—Winnipeg	NHL	3	1	0	1	5	—	—	—	—	—
—Moncton	AHL	7	2	1	3	2	—	—	—	—	—
—Ottawa	OHL	39	19	42	61	35	17	8	11	19	20
91-92—Moncton	AHL	61	11	18	29	113	4	0	1	1	6
—Winnipeg	NHL	10	2	0	2	2	2	0	0	0	0
NHL totals		13	3	0	3	7	2	0	0	0	0

DRAPER, TOM
G, SABRES

PERSONAL: Born November 20, 1966, at Outremont, Que. . . . 5-11/180. . . . Shoots left. . . . Full name: Thomas Edward Draper.
COLLEGE: Vermont.
TRANSACTIONS/CAREER NOTES: Selected by Winnipeg Jets in eight round (eighth Jets pick, 165th overall) of NHL entry draft (June 15, 1985). . . . Traded by Jets to St. Louis Blues for future considerations (February 28, 1991); G Jim Vesey sent to Jets by Blues to complete deal (May 24, 1991). . . . Traded by Blues to Jets for future considerations (May 24, 1991). . . . Traded by Jets to Buffalo Sabres for future considerations (June 22, 1991).
HONORS: Named to ECAC All-Star first team (1986-87). . . . Named to AHL All-Star second team (1988-89).

Season Team	League		REGULAR SEASON							PLAYOFFS						
		Gms.	Min.	W	L	T	GA	SO	Avg.	Gms.	Min.	W	L	GA	SO	Avg.
83-84—University of Vermont	ECAC	20	1205	8	12	0	82	0	4.08	—	—	—	—	—	—	—
84-85—University of Vermont	ECAC	24	1316	5	17	0	90	0	4.10	—	—	—	—	—	—	—
85-86—University of Vermont	ECAC	29	1697	15	12	1	87	1	3.08	—	—	—	—	—	—	—
86-87—University of Vermont	ECAC	29	1662	16	13	0	96	2	3.47	—	—	—	—	—	—	—
87-88—Tappara	Finland	28	1619	16	3	9	87	0	3.22	—	—	—	—	—	—	—
88-89—Moncton	AHL	54	2962	27	17	5	171	2	3.46	7	419	5	2	24	0	3.44
—Winnipeg	NHL	2	120	1	1	0	12	0	6.00	—	—	—	—	—	—	—
89-90—Moncton	AHL	51	2844	20	24	3	167	1	3.52	—	—	—	—	—	—	—
—Winnipeg	NHL	6	359	2	4	0	26	0	4.35	—	—	—	—	—	—	—
90-91—Fort Wayne	IHL	10	564	5	3	1	32	0	3.40	—	—	—	—	—	—	—
—Moncton	AHL	30	1779	15	13	2	95	1	3.20	—	—	—	—	—	—	—
—Peoria	IHL	10	584	6	3	1	36	0	3.70	4	214	2	1	10	0	2.80
91-92—Rochester	AHL	9	531	4	3	2	28	0	3.16	—	—	—	—	—	—	—
—Buffalo	NHL	26	1403	10	9	5	75	1	3.21	7	433	3	4	19	1	2.63
NHL totals		34	1882	13	14	5	113	1	3.60	7	433	3	4	19	1	2.63

DREVITCH, SCOTT
D

PERSONAL: Born September 9, 1965, at Brookline, Mass. . . . 5-10/175. . . . Shoots right. . . . Full name: Scott D. Drevitch.
COLLEGE: Lowell (Mass.).
TRANSACTIONS/CAREER NOTES: Signed as free agent by Maine Mariners (October 1988).
HONORS: Named to ECHL All-Star second team (1989-90).

Season Team	League		REGULAR SEASON					PLAYOFFS				
		Gms.	G	A	Pts.	Pen.	Gms.	G	A	Pts.	Pen.
85-86—University of Lowell	Hockey East	32	1	8	9	10	—	—	—	—	—
86-87—University of Lowell	Hockey East	35	3	25	28	24	—	—	—	—	—
87-88—University of Lowell	Hockey East	37	5	21	26	28	—	—	—	—	—
88-89—Maine	AHL	75	10	21	31	51	—	—	—	—	—
89-90—Virginia	ECHL	40	14	31	45	46	4	3	3	6	10
—Maine	AHL	13	0	1	1	10	—	—	—	—	—

Season	Team	League	REGULAR SEASON					PLAYOFFS				
			Gms.	G	A	Pts.	Pen.	Gms.	G	A	Pts.	Pen.
90-91—Albany		IHL	20	2	9	11	13	—	—	—	—	—
—Phoenix		IHL	3	0	1	1	4	—	—	—	—	—
—New Haven		AHL	14	1	6	7	4	—	—	—	—	—
91-92—San Diego		IHL	7	0	0	0	13	—	—	—	—	—
—Richmond		ECHL	49	7	42	49	26	7	0	5	5	4

DRIVER, BRUCE
D, DEVILS

PERSONAL: Born April 29, 1962, at Toronto.... 6-0/185.... Shoots left.... Full name: Bruce Douglas Driver.
COLLEGE: Wisconsin.
TRANSACTIONS/CAREER NOTES: Selected by Colorado Rockies as underage junior in sixth round (sixth Rockies pick, 108th overall) of NHL entry draft (June 10, 1981).... Underwent surgery to left knee (February 1985).... Reinjured knee (April 2, 1985).... Bruised shoulder (March 9, 1986).... Sprained ankle (February 1988).... Broke right leg in three places (December 7, 1988).... Broke rib (January 8, 1991); missed three games.... Reinjured rib (January 22, 1991); missed four games.
HONORS: Named to NCAA All-America West team (1981-82).... Named to WCHA All-Star first team (1981-82).... Named to NCAA All-Tournament Team (1982).... Named to WCHA All-Star second team (1982-83).

Season	Team	League	REGULAR SEASON					PLAYOFFS				
			Gms.	G	A	Pts.	Pen.	Gms.	G	A	Pts.	Pen.
79-80—Royal York Royals		OPJHL	43	13	57	70	102	—	—	—	—	—
80-81—University of Wisconsin		WCHA	42	5	15	20	42	—	—	—	—	—
81-82—University of Wisconsin		WCHA	46	7	37	44	84	—	—	—	—	—
82-83—University of Wisconsin		WCHA	39	16	34	50	50	—	—	—	—	—
83-84—Canadian Olympic Team		Int'l	61	11	17	28	44	—	—	—	—	—
—Maine		AHL	12	2	6	8	15	16	0	10	10	8
—New Jersey		NHL	4	0	2	2	0	—	—	—	—	—
84-85—New Jersey		NHL	67	9	23	32	36	—	—	—	—	—
85-86—Maine		AHL	15	4	7	11	16	—	—	—	—	—
—New Jersey		NHL	40	3	15	18	32	—	—	—	—	—
86-87—New Jersey		NHL	74	6	28	34	36	—	—	—	—	—
87-88—New Jersey		NHL	74	15	40	55	68	20	3	7	10	14
88-89—New Jersey		NHL	27	1	15	16	24	—	—	—	—	—
89-90—New Jersey		NHL	75	7	46	53	63	6	1	5	6	6
90-91—New Jersey		NHL	73	9	36	45	62	7	1	2	3	12
91-92—New Jersey		NHL	78	7	35	42	66	7	0	4	4	2
NHL totals			512	57	240	297	387	40	5	18	23	34

DRUCE, JOHN
RW, CAPITALS

PERSONAL: Born February 23, 1966, at Peterborough, Ont.... 6-1/200.... Shoots right.... Full name: John W. Druce.
TRANSACTIONS/CAREER NOTES: Broke collarbone (October 1983).... Tore ligaments in ankle (December 1984).... Selected by Washington Capitals in second round (second Capitals pick, 40th overall) of NHL entry draft (June 15, 1985).... Tore thumb ligaments (October 1985).

Season	Team	League	REGULAR SEASON					PLAYOFFS				
			Gms.	G	A	Pts.	Pen.	Gms.	G	A	Pts.	Pen.
83-84—Peterborough Jr. B		OHA	40	15	18	33	69	—	—	—	—	—
84-85—Peterborough		OHL	54	12	14	26	90	17	6	2	8	21
85-86—Peterborough		OHL	49	22	24	46	84	16	0	5	5	34
86-87—Binghamton		AHL	7	13	9	22	131	12	0	3	3	28
87-88—Binghamton		AHL	68	32	29	61	82	1	0	0	0	0
88-89—Washington		NHL	48	8	7	15	62	1	0	0	0	0
—Baltimore		AHL	16	2	11	13	10	—	—	—	—	—
89-90—Washington		NHL	45	8	3	11	52	15	14	3	17	23
—Baltimore		AHL	26	15	16	31	38	—	—	—	—	—
90-91—Washington		NHL	80	22	36	58	46	11	1	1	2	7
91-92—Washington		NHL	67	19	18	37	39	7	1	0	1	2
NHL totals			240	57	64	121	199	34	16	4	20	32

DRULIA, STAN
RW

PERSONAL: Born January 5, 1968, at Elmira, N.Y.... 5-10/180.... Shoots right.
TRANSACTIONS/CAREER NOTES: Selected by Pittsburgh Penguins as underage junior in 11th round (11th Penguins pick, 214th overall) of NHL entry draft (June 21, 1986).... Signed as free agent by Edmonton Oilers (May 1989).
HONORS: Won Jim Mahon Memorial Trophy (1988-89).... Won Leo Lalonde Memorial Trophy (1988-89).... Named to OHL All-Star first team (1988-89).... Won ECHL Most Valuable Player Award (1990-91).... Named to ECHL All-Star first team (1990-91).... Named to AHL All-Star second team (1991-92).

Season	Team	League	REGULAR SEASON					PLAYOFFS				
			Gms.	G	A	Pts.	Pen.	Gms.	G	A	Pts.	Pen.
84-85—Belleville Bulls		OHL	63	24	31	55	33	—	—	—	—	—
85-86—Belleville Bulls		OHL	66	43	37	80	73	—	—	—	—	—
86-87—Hamilton		OHL	55	27	51	78	26	—	—	—	—	—
87-88—Hamilton		OHL	65	52	69	121	44	14	8	16	24	12
88-89—Niagara Falls		OHL	47	52	93	145	59	17	11	*26	37	18
—Maine		AHL	3	1	1	2	0	—	—	—	—	—

D

Season Team	League	REGULAR SEASON					PLAYOFFS				
		Gms.	G	A	Pts.	Pen.	Gms.	G	A	Pts.	Pen.
89-90—Cape Breton	AHL	31	5	7	12	2	—	—	—	—	—
—Phoenix	IHL	16	6	3	9	2	—	—	—	—	—
90-91—Knoxville	ECHL	64	*63	77	*140	39	3	3	2	5	4
91-92—New Haven	AHL	77	49	53	102	46	5	2	4	6	4

DRURY, TED
C, FLAMES

PERSONAL: Born September 13, 1971, at Boston. . . . 6-0/185. . . . Shoots left. . . . Full name: Theodore Evans Drury.
HIGH SCHOOL: Fairfield College Prep School (Conn.).
COLLEGE: Harvard.
TRANSACTIONS/CAREER NOTES: Broke ankle (January 1988). . . . Selected by Calgary Flames in second round (second Flames pick, 42nd overall) of NHL entry draft (June 17, 1989).

Season Team	League	REGULAR SEASON					PLAYOFFS				
		Gms.	G	A	Pts.	Pen.	Gms.	G	A	Pts.	Pen.
87-88—Fairfield College Prep	Conn. H.S.		21	28	49		—	—	—	—	—
88-89—Fairfield College Prep	Conn. H.S.		35	31	66		—	—	—	—	—
89-90—Harvard University	ECAC	17	9	13	22	10	—	—	—	—	—
90-91—Harvard University	ECAC	26	18	18	36	22	—	—	—	—	—
91-92—U.S. National Team	Int'l	53	11	23	34	30	—	—	—	—	—
—U.S. Olympic Team	Int'l	7	1	1	2	0	—	—	—	—	—

DuBOIS, ERIC
D, NORDIQUES

PERSONAL: Born May 7, 1970, at Montreal. . . . 6-0/195. . . . Shoots right.
TRANSACTIONS/CAREER NOTES: Selected by Quebec Nordiques in fourth round (sixth Nordiques pick, 76th overall) of NHL entry draft (June 17, 1989).

Season Team	League	REGULAR SEASON					PLAYOFFS				
		Gms.	G	A	Pts.	Pen.	Gms.	G	A	Pts.	Pen.
86-87—Laval	QMJHL	61	1	17	18	29	—	—	—	—	—
87-88—Laval	QMJHL	69	8	32	40	132	14	1	7	8	12
88-89—Laval	QMJHL	68	15	44	59	126	17	1	11	12	55
89-90—Laval	QMJHL	66	9	36	45	153	13	3	8	11	29
90-91—Laval	QMJHL	57	15	45	60	122	13	3	5	8	29
91-92—New Haven	AHL	1	0	0	0	2	—	—	—	—	—
—Halifax	AHL	14	0	0	0	8	—	—	—	—	—
—Greensboro	ECHL	36	7	17	24	62	11	4	4	8	40

DUCHESNE, GAETAN
LW, NORTH STARS

PERSONAL: Born July 11, 1962, at Quebec City. . . . 5-11/200. . . . Shoots left.
TRANSACTIONS/CAREER NOTES: Selected by Washington Capitals in eighth round (eighth Capitals pick, 152nd overall) of NHL entry draft (June 10, 1981). . . . Bruised right ankle (December 30, 1981). . . . Broke finger (October 11, 1984). . . . Traded by Capitals with C Alan Haworth and a first-round pick in 1987 draft (C Joe Sakic) to Quebec Nordiques for C Dale Hunter and G Clint Malarchuk (June 1987). . . . Sprained left knee (January 26, 1988). . . . Sprained left shoulder (November 1988). . . . Traded by Nordiques to Minnesota North Stars for C Kevin Kaminski (June 18, 1989). . . . Sprained right knee (November 11, 1989); missed eight games.

Season Team	League	REGULAR SEASON					PLAYOFFS				
		Gms.	G	A	Pts.	Pen.	Gms.	G	A	Pts.	Pen.
79-80—Quebec	QMJHL	46	9	28	37	22	5	0	2	2	9
80-81—Quebec	QMJHL	72	27	45	72	63	7	1	4	5	6
81-82—Washington	NHL	74	9	14	23	46	—	—	—	—	—
82-83—Hershey	AHL	1	1	0	1	0	—	—	—	—	—
—Washington	NHL	77	18	19	37	52	4	1	1	2	4
83-84—Washington	NHL	79	17	19	36	29	8	2	1	3	2
84-85—Washington	NHL	67	15	23	38	32	5	0	1	1	7
85-86—Washington	NHL	80	11	28	39	39	9	4	3	7	12
86-87—Washington	NHL	74	17	35	52	53	7	3	0	3	14
87-88—Quebec	NHL	80	24	23	47	83	—	—	—	—	—
88-89—Quebec	NHL	70	8	21	29	56	—	—	—	—	—
89-90—Minnesota	NHL	72	12	8	20	33	7	0	0	0	6
90-91—Minnesota	NHL	68	9	9	18	18	23	2	3	5	34
91-92—Minnesota	NHL	73	8	15	23	102	7	1	0	1	6
NHL totals		814	148	214	362	543	70	13	9	22	85

DUCHESNE, STEVE
D, NORDIQUES

PERSONAL: Born June 30, 1965, at Sept-Illes, Que. . . . 5-11/195. . . . Shoots left.
TRANSACTIONS/CAREER NOTES: Signed as free agent by Los Angeles Kings (October 1984). . . . Strained left knee (January 26, 1988). . . . Separated left shoulder (November 1988). . . . Traded by Kings with C Steve Kasper and fourth-round pick in 1991 draft (D Aris Brimanis) to Philadelphia Flyers for D Jeff Chychrun and rights to RW Jari Kurri (May 30, 1991). . . . Traded by Flyers with G Ron Hextall, C Mike Ricci, C Peter Forsberg, D Kerry Huffman, first-round pick in 1993 draft, cash and future considerations to Quebec Nordiques for C Eric Lindros (June 20, 1992); Flyers sent LW Chris Simon and first-round pick in 1994 draft to Nordiques to complete deal (July 21, 1992).
HONORS: Named to NHL All-Rookie team (1986-87).

Season Team	League	REGULAR SEASON					PLAYOFFS				
		Gms.	G	A	Pts.	Pen.	Gms.	G	A	Pts.	Pen.
83-84—Drummondville	QMJHL	67	1	34	35	79	—	—	—	—	—
84-85—Drummondville	QMJHL	65	22	54	76	94	5	4	7	11	8

— 346 —

Season	Team	League	REGULAR SEASON					PLAYOFFS				
			Gms.	G	A	Pts.	Pen.	Gms.	G	A	Pts.	Pen.
85-86	New Haven	AHL	75	14	35	49	76	5	0	2	2	9
86-87	Los Angeles	NHL	75	13	25	38	74	5	2	2	4	4
87-88	Los Angeles	NHL	71	16	39	55	109	5	1	3	4	14
88-89	Los Angeles	NHL	79	25	50	75	92	11	4	4	8	12
89-90	Los Angeles	NHL	79	20	42	62	36	10	2	9	11	6
90-91	Los Angeles	NHL	78	21	41	62	66	12	4	8	12	8
91-92	Philadelphia	NHL	78	18	38	56	86	—	—	—	—	—
NHL totals			**460**	**113**	**235**	**348**	**463**	**43**	**13**	**26**	**39**	**44**

DUFRESNE, DONALD
D, CANADIENS

PERSONAL: Born April 10, 1967, at Quebec City. . . . 6-1/206. . . . Shoots left.
TRANSACTIONS/CAREER NOTES: Suffered from pneumonia (November 1984). . . . Selected by Montreal Canadiens in sixth round (eighth Canadiens pick, 117th overall) of NHL entry draft (June 15, 1985). . . . Dislocated shoulder (January 8, 1988). . . . Sprained ankle (February 1989). . . . Separated shoulder (October 5, 1989); missed 15 games. . . . Reinjured shoulder (December 9, 1989). . . . Tore ligaments in right knee (December 9, 1991); missed 15 games.
HONORS: Named to QMJHL All-Star second team (1985-86 and 1986-87).

Season	Team	League	REGULAR SEASON					PLAYOFFS				
			Gms.	G	A	Pts.	Pen.	Gms.	G	A	Pts.	Pen.
83-84	Trois-Rivieres	QMJHL	67	7	12	19	97	—	—	—	—	—
84-85	Trois-Rivieres	QMJHL	65	5	30	35	112	7	1	3	4	12
85-86	Trois-Rivieres	QMJHL	63	8	32	40	160	1	0	0	0	0
86-87	Longueuil	QMJHL	67	5	29	34	97	20	1	8	9	38
87-88	Sherbrooke	AHL	47	1	8	9	107	6	1	1	2	34
88-89	Montreal	NHL	13	0	1	1	43	6	1	1	2	4
	Sherbrooke	AHL	47	0	12	12	170	—	—	—	—	—
89-90	Montreal	NHL	18	0	4	4	23	10	0	1	1	18
	Sherbrooke	AHL	38	2	11	13	104	0	0	0	0	0
90-91	Fredericton	AHL	10	1	4	5	35	1	0	0	0	0
	Montreal	NHL	53	2	13	15	55	10	0	1	1	21
91-92	Montreal	NHL	3	0	0	0	2	—	—	—	—	—
	Fredericton	AHL	31	8	12	20	60	7	0	0	0	10
NHL totals			**87**	**2**	**18**	**20**	**123**	**26**	**1**	**3**	**4**	**43**

DUNCANSON, CRAIG
LW, CAPITALS

PERSONAL: Born March 17, 1967, at Sudbury, Ont. . . . 6-0/190. . . . Shoots left. . . . Full name: Craig Murray Duncanson.
TRANSACTIONS/CAREER NOTES: Tore knee ligaments (September 1984). . . . Selected by Los Angeles Kings as underage junior in first round (first Kings pick, ninth overall) of NHL entry draft (June 15, 1985). . . . Suffered deep leg bruise (November 23, 1986). . . . Traded by Kings to Minnesota North Stars for G Daniel Berthiaume (September 6, 1990). . . . Traded by North Stars to Winnipeg Jets for C Brian Hunt (September 6, 1990). . . . Traded by Jets with LW Brent Hughes and C Simon Wheeldon to Washington Capitals for LW Bob Joyce, D Kent Paynter and C Tyler Larter (May 21, 1991). . . . Loaned to Jets organization (February 26, 1992).

Season	Team	League	REGULAR SEASON					PLAYOFFS				
			Gms.	G	A	Pts.	Pen.	Gms.	G	A	Pts.	Pen.
82-83	St. Michael's Jr. B	ODHA	32	14	19	33	68	—	—	—	—	—
83-84	Sudbury	OHL	62	38	38	76	178	—	—	—	—	—
84-85	Sudbury	OHL	53	35	28	63	129	—	—	—	—	—
85-86	Sudbury	OHL	21	12	17	29	55	—	—	—	—	—
	Cornwall	OHL	40	31	50	81	135	6	4	7	11	2
	Los Angeles	NHL	2	0	1	1	0	—	—	—	—	—
	New Haven	AHL	—	—	—	—	—	2	0	0	0	5
86-87	Cornwall	OHL	52	22	45	67	88	5	4	3	7	20
	Los Angeles	NHL	2	0	0	0	24	—	—	—	—	—
87-88	New Haven	AHL	57	15	25	40	170	—	—	—	—	—
	Los Angeles	NHL	9	0	0	0	12	—	—	—	—	—
88-89	New Haven	AHL	69	25	39	64	200	17	4	8	12	60
	Los Angeles	NHL	5	0	0	0	0	—	—	—	—	—
89-90	Los Angeles	NHL	10	3	2	5	9	—	—	—	—	—
	New Haven	AHL	51	17	30	47	152	—	—	—	—	—
90-91	Moncton	AHL	58	16	34	50	107	9	3	11	14	31
	Winnipeg	NHL	7	2	0	2	16	—	—	—	—	—
91-92	Baltimore	AHL	46	20	26	46	98	—	—	—	—	—
	Moncton	AHL	19	12	9	21	6	11	6	4	10	10
NHL totals			**35**	**5**	**3**	**8**	**61**					

DUNHAM, MIKE
G, DEVILS

PERSONAL: Born June 1, 1972, at Johnson City, N.Y. . . . 6-2/170. . . . Shoots left. . . . Full name: Michael Francis Dunham.
HIGH SCHOOL: Canterbury (New Milford, Conn.).
COLLEGE: Maine.
TRANSACTIONS/CAREER NOTES: Selected by New Jersey Devils in third round (fourth Devils pick, 53rd overall) of NHL entry draft (June 16, 1990).

Season Team	League	Gms.	Min.	W	L	T	GA	SO	Avg.	Gms.	Min.	W	L	GA	SO	Avg.
88-89—Canterbury School.......	Conn. HS	25					63	2		—	—	—	—	—	—	—
89-90—Canterbury School.......	Conn. HS	32	1558				55		2.12	—	—	—	—	—	—	—
90-91—University of Maine	Hoc. East	23	1275	14	5	2	63	2	*2.96	—	—	—	—	—	—	—
91-92—University of Maine	Hoc. East	7	382	6	0	0	14	1	2.20	—	—	—	—	—	—	—
—U.S. National Team......	Int'l	3	157	0	1	1	10	0	3.82	—	—	—	—	—	—	—

DUPRE, YANICK
LW, FLYERS

PERSONAL: Born November 20, 1972, at Montreal. . . . 6-0/195. . . . Shoots left.
TRANSACTIONS/CAREER NOTES: Pulled ankle ligament (September 1989). . . . Traded by Chicoutimi Sagueneens with D Guy Lehoux and RW Eric Meloche to Drummondville Voltigeurs for RW Daniel Dore, RW Denis Chasse and D Pierre-Paul Landry (December 19, 1989). . . . Injured knee ligament (October 1990). . . . Selected by Philadelphia Flyers in third round (second Flyers pick, 50th overall) of NHL entry draft (June 1991).
HONORS: Named to QMJHL All-Star second team (1989).

Season Team	League	Gms.	G	A	Pts.	Pen.	Gms.	G	A	Pts.	Pen.
89-90—Drummondville................	QMJHL	53	15	19	34	69	—	—	—	—	—
90-91—Drummondville................	QMJHL	58	29	38	67	87	11	8	5	13	33
91-92—Philadelphia	NHL	1	0	0	0	0	—	—	—	—	—
—Longueuil	QMJHL	40	26	31	57	69	19	9	9	18	20
NHL totals..		1	0	0	0	0					

DUPUIS, GUY
D, RED WINGS

PERSONAL: Born May 10, 1970, at Moncton, N.B.. . . 6-2/199. . . . Shoots right.
TRANSACTIONS/CAREER NOTES: Selected by Detroit Red Wings in third round (third Red Wings pick, 47th overall) of NHL entry draft (June 11, 1988).

Season Team	League	Gms.	G	A	Pts.	Pen.	Gms.	G	A	Pts.	Pen.
86-87—Hull	QMJHL	69	5	10	15	35	8	1	2	3	2
87-88—Hull	QMJHL	69	14	34	48	72	19	3	8	11	29
88-89—Hull	QMJHL	70	15	56	71	89	9	3	3	6	8
89-90—Hull	QMJHL	70	8	41	49	96	11	1	3	4	8
90-91—Adirondack	AHL	57	4	10	14	73	—	—	—	—	—
91-92—Adirondack	AHL	49	3	6	9	59	3	0	0	0	4
—Fort Wayne	IHL	10	2	7	9	0	—	—	—	—	—

DUTHIE, RYAN
C, ISLANDERS

PERSONAL: Born September 2, 1974, at Strathmore, Alta.. . . 5-10/180. . . . Shoots right.
HIGH SCHOOL: Joel E. Ferris (Spokane, Wash.).
TRANSACTIONS/CAREER NOTES: Selected by New York Islanders in fifth round (fourth Islanders pick, 105th overall) of NHL entry draft (June 20, 1992).

Season Team	League	Gms.	G	A	Pts.	Pen.	Gms.	G	A	Pts.	Pen.
91-92—Spokane Chiefs	WHL	67	23	37	60	119	10	5	10	15	18

DUVAL, MURRAY
D, RANGERS

PERSONAL: Born January 22, 1970, at Thompson, Man.. . . 6-0/195. . . . Shoots left.
TRANSACTIONS/CAREER NOTES: Stretched left knee ligaments (January 1987). . . . Selected by New York Rangers in second round (second Rangers pick, 26th overall) of NHL entry draft (June 11, 1988). . . . Traded by Tri-City Americans with D Jason Smith to Swift Current Broncos for C Brian Sakic and RW Wade Smith (October 18, 1989).
HONORS: Named to WHL All-Star second team (1990-91).

Season Team	League	Gms.	G	A	Pts.	Pen.	Gms.	G	A	Pts.	Pen.
86-87—Spokane Chiefs	WHL	27	2	6	8	21	—	—	—	—	—
87-88—Spokane Chiefs	WHL	70	26	37	63	104	15	5	2	7	22
88-89—Spokane Chiefs	WHL	4	0	3	3	22	—	—	—	—	—
—Tri-City Americans	WHL	67	14	25	39	122	—	—	—	—	—
89-90—Tri-City Americans	WHL	7	4	4	8	10	—	—	—	—	—
—Swift Current..................	WHL	7	3	5	8	31	—	—	—	—	—
—Kamloops	WHL	56	14	36	50	94	17	8	7	15	29
90-91—Kamloops	WHL	67	47	66	113	187	12	8	5	13	30
91-92—Binghamton	AHL	15	1	6	7	8	—	—	—	—	—
—San Diego	IHL	10	1	2	3	6	—	—	—	—	—
—Erie	ECHL	19	5	8	13	26	4	1	0	1	4

DYCK, LARRY
G, NORTH STARS

PERSONAL: Born December 15, 1965, at Winkler, Man.. . . 5-11/180. . . . Shoots left.
COLLEGE: Manitoba.
TRANSACTIONS/CAREER NOTES: Signed as free agent by Minnesota North Stars (August, 1988).
HONORS: CWUAA Freshman of the Year (1986-87). . . . Named to CWUAA All-Star first team (1986-87). . . . Named to CWUAA All-Star second team (1987-88).

Season Team	League	Gms.	Min.	W	L	T	GA	SO	Avg.	Gms.	Min.	W	L	GA	SO	Avg.
86-87—University of Manitoba.	CWUAA	18	1019				61	*3	3.59	—	—	—	—	—	—	—
87-88—University of Manitoba.	CWUAA	*19	*1118				87	0	4.67	—	—	—	—	—	—	—

— 348 —

Season Team	League	REGULAR SEASON Gms.	Min.	W	L	T	GA	SO	Avg.	PLAYOFFS Gms.	Min.	W	L	GA	SO	Avg.
88-89—Kalamazoo	IHL	42	2308	17	20	2	168	0	4.37	—	—	—	—	—	—	—
89-90—Kalamazoo	IHL	36	1959	20	12	2	116	0	3.55	7	353	2	3	22	0	3.74
—Knoxville	ECHL	3	184	1	1	1	12	0	3.91	—	—	—	—	—	—	—
90-91—Kalamazoo	IHL	38	2182	21	15	0	133	1	3.66	1	60	0	1	6	0	6.00
91-92—Kalamazoo	IHL	57	**3305	25	23	6	195	0	3.54	12	690	5	7	43	0	3.74

DYKHUIS, KARL
D, BLACKHAWKS

PERSONAL: Born July 8, 1972, at Sept-Iles, Que.... 6-3/200.... Shoots left.
TRANSACTIONS/CAREER NOTES: Selected by Chicago Blackhawks in first round (first Blackhawks pick, 16th overall) of NHL entry draft (June 16, 1990).... QMJHL rights traded by Hull Olympiques to College Francais for first- and sixth-round draft picks (January 10, 1991).
HONORS: Won Raymond Lagace Trophy (1988-89).... Won Michael Bossy Trophy (1989-90).... Named to QMJHL All-Star first team (1989-90).

Season Team	League	REGULAR SEASON Gms.	G	A	Pts.	Pen.	PLAYOFFS Gms.	G	A	Pts.	Pen.
88-89—Hull	QMJHL	63	2	29	31	59	9	1	9	10	6
89-90—Hull	QMJHL	69	10	45	55	119	11	2	5	7	2
90-91—Longueuil	QMJHL	3	1	4	5	6	—	—	—	—	—
—Canadian National Team..	Int'l	—	—	—	—	—	—	—	—	—	—
91-92—Longueuil	QMJHL	29	5	19	24	55	17	0	12	12	14
—Chicago	NHL	6	1	3	4	4	—	—	—	—	—
NHL totals		6	1	3	4	4					

DZIEDZIC, JOE
LW, PENGUINS

PERSONAL: Born December 18, 1971, at Minneapolis.... 6-3/200.... Shoots left.... Full name: Joseph Walter Dziedzic.
HIGH SCHOOL: Edison (Minneapolis).
COLLEGE: Minnesota.
TRANSACTIONS/CAREER NOTES: Selected by Pittsburgh Penguins in third round (second Penguins pick, 61st overall) of NHL entry draft (June 16, 1990).

Season Team	League	REGULAR SEASON Gms.	G	A	Pts.	Pen.	PLAYOFFS Gms.	G	A	Pts.	Pen.
88-89—Minneapolis Edison H.S....	Minn. H.S.	25	47	27	74		—	—	—	—	—
89-90—Minneapolis Edison H.S....	Minn. H.S.	17	29	19	48		—	—	—	—	—
90-91—University of Minnesota ...	WCHA	20	6	4	10	26	—	—	—	—	—
91-92—University of Minnesota ...	WCHA	37	9	10	19	68	—	—	—	—	—

EAGLES, MIKE
C, JETS

PERSONAL: Born March 7, 1963, at Susex, N.B.... 5-10/180.... Shoots left.... Full name: Michael Bryant Eagles.
TRANSACTIONS/CAREER NOTES: Selected by Quebec Nordiques as underage junior in sixth round (fifth Nordiques pick, 116th overall) of NHL entry draft (June 10, 1981).... Broke hand (October 1984).... Injured ribs (February 21, 1986).... Traded by Nordiques to Chicago Blackhawks for G Bob Mason (July 1988).... Broke left hand (February 1989).... Bruised kidney (January 15, 1990); missed eight games.... Traded by Blackhawks to Winnipeg Jets for a fourth-round pick in 1991 draft (D Igor Kravchuk) (December 14, 1990).... Fractured thumb (February 17, 1992); missed 14 games.

Season Team	League	REGULAR SEASON Gms.	G	A	Pts.	Pen.	PLAYOFFS Gms.	G	A	Pts.	Pen.
79-80—Melville	SJHL	55	46	30	76	77	—	—	—	—	—
80-81—Kitchener	OMJHL	56	11	27	38	64	18	4	2	6	36
81-82—Kitchener	OHL	62	26	40	66	148	15	3	11	14	27
82-83—Kitchener	OHL	58	26	36	62	133	12	5	7	12	27
—Quebec	NHL	2	0	0	0	2	—	—	—	—	—
83-84—Fredericton	AHL	68	13	29	42	85	4	0	0	0	5
84-85—Fredericton	AHL	36	4	20	24	80	3	0	0	0	2
85-86—Quebec	NHL	73	11	12	23	49	3	0	0	0	2
86-87—Quebec	NHL	73	13	19	32	55	4	1	0	1	10
87-88—Quebec	NHL	76	10	10	20	74	—	—	—	—	—
88-89—Chicago	NHL	47	5	11	16	44	—	—	—	—	—
89-90—Indianapolis	IHL	24	11	13	24	47	13	*10	10	20	34
—Chicago	NHL	23	1	2	3	34	—	—	—	—	—
90-91—Indianapolis	IHL	25	15	14	29	47	—	—	—	—	—
—Winnipeg	NHL	44	0	9	9	79	—	—	—	—	—
91-92—Winnipeg	NHL	65	7	10	17	118	7	0	0	0	8
NHL totals		403	47	73	120	455	14	1	0	1	20

EAKINS, DALLAS
D, JETS

PERSONAL: Born January 20, 1967, at Dade City, Fla.... 6-2/195.... Shoots left.
TRANSACTIONS/CAREER NOTES: Selected by Washington Capitals as underage junior in 10th round (11th Capitals pick, 208th overall) of NHL entry draft (June 15, 1985).... Injured back (October 1988).... Signed as free agent by Winnipeg Jets (September 1989).

DE

Season	Team	League	REGULAR SEASON					PLAYOFFS				
			Gms.	G	A	Pts.	Pen.	Gms.	G	A	Pts.	Pen.
84-85—Peterborough		OHL	48	0	8	8	96	7	0	0	0	18
85-86—Peterborough		OHL	60	6	16	22	134	16	0	1	1	30
86-87—Peterborough		OHL	54	3	11	14	145	12	1	4	5	37
87-88—Peterborough		OHL	64	11	27	38	129	12	3	12	15	16
88-89—Baltimore		AHL	62	0	10	10	139	—	—	—	—	—
89-90—Moncton		AHL	75	2	11	13	189	—	—	—	—	—
90-91—Moncton		AHL	75	1	12	13	132	9	0	1	1	44
91-92—Moncton		AHL	67	3	13	16	136	11	2	1	3	16

EASTWOOD, MICHAEL
C/RW, MAPLE LEAFS

PERSONAL: Born July 1, 1967, at Cornwall, Ont. . . . 6-2/190. . . . Shoots right. . . . Full name: Michael B. Eastwood.
COLLEGE: Western Michigan.
TRANSACTIONS/CAREER NOTES: Selected by Toronto Maple Leafs in fifth round (fifth Maple Leafs pick, 91st overall) of NHL entry draft (June 13, 1987).
HONORS: Named to CCHA All-Star second team (1990-91).

Season	Team	League	REGULAR SEASON					PLAYOFFS				
			Gms.	G	A	Pts.	Pen.	Gms.	G	A	Pts.	Pen.
86-87—Pembroke		COJHL					Statistics unavailable.					
87-88—Western Michigan Univ.		CCHA	42	5	8	13	14	—	—	—	—	—
88-89—Western Michigan Univ.		CCHA	40	10	13	23	87	—	—	—	—	—
89-90—Western Michigan Univ.		CCHA	40	25	27	52	36	—	—	—	—	—
90-91—Western Michigan Univ.		CCHA	42	29	32	61	84	—	—	—	—	—
91-92—St. John's		AHL	61	18	25	43	28	16	9	10	19	16
—Toronto		NHL	9	0	2	2	4	—	—	—	—	—
NHL totals			9	0	2	2	4					

EDGERLY, DEREK
C, BLACKHAWKS

PERSONAL: Born April 3, 1971, at Malden, Mass. . . . 6-1/190. . . . Shoots left. . . . Full name: Derek Robert Edgerly.
HIGH SCHOOL: Stoneham (Mass.).
COLLEGE: Northeastern.
TRANSACTIONS/CAREER NOTES: Selected by Chicago Blackhawks in sixth round (fifth Blackhawks pick, 124th overall) of NHL entry draft (June 16, 1990).

Season	Team	League	REGULAR SEASON					PLAYOFFS				
			Gms.	G	A	Pts.	Pen.	Gms.	G	A	Pts.	Pen.
88-89—Stoneham H.S.		Mass. H.S.	18	30	12	42	10	—	—	—	—	—
89-90—Stoneham H.S.		Mass. H.S.	18	28	23	51	12	—	—	—	—	—
90-91—Northeastern University		Hockey East	34	3	11	14	12	—	—	—	—	—
91-92—Northeastern University		Hockey East	15	2	1	3	14	—	—	—	—	—

E

EGELAND, TRACY
LW, BLACKHAWKS

PERSONAL: Born August 20, 1970, at Lethbridge, Alta. . . . 6-1/180. . . . Shoots right.
TRANSACTIONS/CAREER NOTES: Injured elbow (November 1986); missed two weeks. . . . Traded by Swift Current Broncos to Medicine Hat Tigers for C Travis Kellin (August 1988). . . . Selected by Chicago Blackhawks in seventh round (fifth Blackhawks pick, 132nd overall) of NHL entry draft (June 17, 1989).

Season	Team	League	REGULAR SEASON					PLAYOFFS				
			Gms.	G	A	Pts.	Pen.	Gms.	G	A	Pts.	Pen.
86-87—Swift Current		WHL	48	3	2	5	20	—	—	—	—	—
87-88—Swift Current		WHL	63	10	22	32	34	—	—	—	—	—
88-89—Medicine Hat		WHL	42	11	12	23	64	—	—	—	—	—
—Prince Albert		WHL	24	17	10	27	24	4	0	1	1	13
89-90—Prince Albert		WHL	61	39	26	65	160	13	7	10	17	26
90-91—Indianapolis		IHL	79	17	22	39	205	7	2	1	3	21
91-92—Indianapolis		IHL	66	20	11	31	214	—	—	—	—	—

EKLUND, PELLE
C, FLYERS

PERSONAL: Born March 22, 1963, at Stockholm, Sweden. . . . 5-10/175. . . . Shoots left. . . . Full name: Per-Erik Eklund.
TRANSACTIONS/CAREER NOTES: Selected by Philadelphia Flyers in eighth round (seventh Flyers pick, 161st overall) of NHL entry draft (June 8, 1983). . . . Bruised hip (March 1988). . . . Strained left knee (October 1989). . . . Bruised right knee (November 24, 1989). . . . Strained hip flexor and stomach muscles (January 31, 1991); missed five games. . . . Bruised shoulder (November 20, 1991); missed one game. . . . Sprained knee (January 12, 1992); missed eight games. . . . Reinjured knee (February 6, 1992); missed five games. . . . Reinjured knee (February 27, 1992); missed three games. . . . Sprained knee (March 1992); missed final six games of season. . . . Underwent arthroscopic surgery to knee (April 14, 1992).
RECORDS: Holds NHL playoff record for fastest goal from the start of a period—6 seconds (April 25, 1989).
MISCELLANEOUS: Member of 1984 bronze medal-winning Swedish Olympic team. . . . Named Sweden's Athlete of the Year for 1984.

Season	Team	League	REGULAR SEASON					PLAYOFFS				
			Gms.	G	A	Pts.	Pen.	Gms.	G	A	Pts.	Pen.
81-82—Stockholm AIK		Sweden	23	2	3	5	2	—	—	—	—	—
82-83—Stockholm AIK		Sweden	34	13	17	30	14	3	1	4	5	2

Season Team	League	REGULAR SEASON Gms.	G	A	Pts.	Pen.	PLAYOFFS Gms.	G	A	Pts.	Pen.
83-84—Stockholm AIK	Sweden	35	9	18	27	24	6	6	7	13	2
84-85—Stockholm AIK	Sweden	35	16	33	49	10	—	—	—	—	—
85-86—Philadelphia	NHL	70	15	51	66	12	5	0	2	2	0
86-87—Philadelphia	NHL	72	14	41	55	2	26	7	20	27	2
87-88—Philadelphia	NHL	71	10	32	42	12	7	0	3	3	0
88-89—Philadelphia	NHL	79	18	51	69	23	19	3	8	11	2
89-90—Philadelphia	NHL	70	23	39	62	16	—	—	—	—	—
90-91—Philadelphia	NHL	73	19	50	69	14	—	—	—	—	—
91-92—Philadelphia	NHL	51	7	16	23	4	—	—	—	—	—
NHL totals		486	106	280	386	83	57	10	33	43	4

ELIK, TODD
C, NORTH STARS

PERSONAL: Born April 15, 1966, at Brampton, Ont. . . . 6-1/200. . . . Shoots left.
COLLEGE: Regina (Sask.).
TRANSACTIONS/CAREER NOTES: Signed as free agent by New York Rangers (February 26, 1988). . . . Traded by Rangers with LW Igor Liba, D Michael Boyce and future considerations to Los Angeles Kings for D Dean Kennedy and D Denis Larocque (December 12, 1988). . . . Injured near right eye (January 1991). . . . Injured thigh (February 26, 1991); missed one game. . . . Traded by Kings to Minnesota North Stars for D Charlie Huddy, LW Randy Gilhen, RW Jim Thomson and a fourth-round pick in 1991 draft (D Alexei Zhitnik) (June 22, 1991).

Season Team	League	REGULAR SEASON Gms.	G	A	Pts.	Pen.	PLAYOFFS Gms.	G	A	Pts.	Pen.
83-84—Kingston	OHL	64	5	16	21	17	—	—	—	—	—
84-85—Kingston	OHL	34	14	11	25	6	—	—	—	—	—
—North Bay	OHL	23	4	6	10	2	4	2	0	2	0
85-86—North Bay	OHL	40	12	34	46	20	10	7	6	13	0
86-87—University of Regina	CWUAA	27	26	34	60	137	—	—	—	—	—
87-88—Denver	IHL	81	44	56	100	83	12	8	12	20	9
88-89—Denver	IHL	28	20	15	35	22	—	—	—	—	—
—New Haven	AHL	43	11	25	36	31	17	10	12	22	44
89-90—Los Angeles	NHL	48	10	23	33	41	10	3	9	12	10
—New Haven	AHL	32	20	23	43	42	—	—	—	—	—
90-91—Los Angeles	NHL	74	21	37	58	58	12	2	7	9	6
91-92—Minnesota	NHL	62	14	32	46	125	5	1	1	2	2
NHL totals		184	45	92	137	224	27	6	17	23	18

ELLETT, DAVE
D, MAPLE LEAFS

PERSONAL: Born March 30, 1964, at Cleveland. . . . 6-2/200. . . . Shoots left.
COLLEGE: Bowling Green State.
TRANSACTIONS/CAREER NOTES: Selected by Winnipeg Jets as underage junior in fourth round (third Jets pick, 75th overall) of NHL entry draft (June 9, 1982). . . . Bruised thigh (March 6, 1988); missed 10 games. . . . Sprained ankle (November 16, 1988). . . . Traded by Jets with C Paul Fenton to Toronto Maple Leafs for C Ed Olczyk and LW Mark Osborne (November 10, 1990).

Season Team	League	REGULAR SEASON Gms.	G	A	Pts.	Pen.	PLAYOFFS Gms.	G	A	Pts.	Pen.
81-82—Ottawa	COJHL	50	9	35	44		—	—	—	—	—
82-83—Bowling Green State	CCHA	40	4	13	17	34	—	—	—	—	—
83-84—Bowling Green State	CCHA	43	15	39	54	9	—	—	—	—	—
84-85—Winnipeg	NHL	80	11	27	38	85	8	1	5	6	4
85-86—Winnipeg	NHL	80	15	31	46	96	3	0	1	1	0
86-87—Winnipeg	NHL	78	13	31	44	53	10	0	8	8	2
87-88—Winnipeg	NHL	68	13	45	58	106	5	1	2	3	10
88-89—Winnipeg	NHL	75	22	34	56	62	—	—	—	—	—
89-90—Winnipeg	NHL	77	17	29	46	96	7	2	0	2	6
90-91—Winnipeg	NHL	17	4	7	11	6	—	—	—	—	—
—Toronto	NHL	60	8	30	38	69	—	—	—	—	—
91-92—Toronto	NHL	79	18	33	51	95	—	—	—	—	—
NHL totals		614	121	267	388	668	33	4	16	20	22

ELVENAS, STEFAN
RW, BLACKHAWKS

PERSONAL: Born March 30, 1970, at Lund, Sweden. . . . 6-1/183. . . . Shoots left.
TRANSACTIONS/CAREER NOTES: Selected by Chicago Blackhawks in fourth round (third Blackhawks pick, 71st overall) of NHL entry draft (June 17, 1989).

Season Team	League	REGULAR SEASON Gms.	G	A	Pts.	Pen.	PLAYOFFS Gms.	G	A	Pts.	Pen.
87-88—Rogle	Sweden	36	21	17	38		—	—	—	—	—
88-89—Rogle	Sweden	35	37	29	66	16	—	—	—	—	—
89-90—Rogle	Sweden	35	18	25	43	56	—	—	—	—	—
90-91—Rogle	Sweden	32	31	11	42	20	—	—	—	—	—
91-92—Rogle	Sweden	14	19	11	30	6	—	—	—	—	—

ELYNUIK, PAT
RW, JETS

PERSONAL: Born October 30, 1967, at Foam Lake, Sask. . . . 6-0/185. . . . Shoots right. . . . Full name: Pat Gerald Elynuik.
TRANSACTIONS/CAREER NOTES: Selected by Winnipeg Jets as underage junior in first round (first Jets pick, eighth overall) of NHL entry draft (June 21, 1986). . . . Separated left shoulder

E

(March 7, 1989).... Strained groin (December 14, 1991); missed six games.... Sprained knee (February 2, 1992); missed three games.... Injured eye (March 17, 1992); missed five games.
HONORS: Named to WHL All-Star first team (1985-86 and 1986-87).

Season Team	League	REGULAR SEASON					PLAYOFFS				
		Gms.	G	A	Pts.	Pen.	Gms.	G	A	Pts.	Pen.
84-85—Prince Albert	WHL	70	23	20	43	54	13	9	3	12	7
85-86—Prince Albert	WHL	68	53	53	106	62	20	7	9	16	17
86-87—Prince Albert	WHL	64	51	62	113	40	8	5	5	10	12
87-88—Winnipeg	NHL	13	1	3	4	12	—	—	—	—	—
—Moncton	AHL	30	11	18	29	35	—	—	—	—	—
88-89—Winnipeg	NHL	56	26	25	51	29	—	—	—	—	—
—Moncton	AHL	7	8	2	10	2	—	—	—	—	—
89-90—Winnipeg	NHL	80	32	42	74	83	7	2	4	6	2
90-91—Winnipeg	NHL	80	31	34	65	73	—	—	—	—	—
91-92—Winnipeg	NHL	60	25	25	50	65	7	2	2	4	4
NHL totals		**289**	**115**	**129**	**244**	**262**	**14**	**4**	**6**	**10**	**6**

EMERSON, NELSON
C, BLUES

PERSONAL: Born August 17, 1967, at Hamilton, Ont.... 5-11/178.... Shoots right. ... Full name: Nelson Donald Emerson.
COLLEGE: Bowling Green State.
TRANSACTIONS/CAREER NOTES: Selected by St. Louis Blues in third round (second Blues pick, 44th overall) of NHL entry draft (June 15, 1985).... Fractured bone under his eye (December 28, 1991).
HONORS: Named CCHA Rookie of the Year (1986-87).... Named to NCAA All-America West second team (1987-88).... Named to CCHA All-Star first team (1987-88 and 1989-90).... Named to CCHA All-Star second team (1988-89).... Named to NCAA All-America West first team (1989-90).... Won Garry F. Longman Memorial Trophy (1990-91).... Named to IHL All-Star first team (1990-91).

Season Team	League	REGULAR SEASON					PLAYOFFS				
		Gms.	G	A	Pts.	Pen.	Gms.	G	A	Pts.	Pen.
84-85—Stratford Jr. B	OHA	40	23	38	61	70	—	—	—	—	—
85-86—Stratford Jr. B	OHA	39	54	58	112	91	—	—	—	—	—
86-87—Bowling Green State	CCHA	45	26	35	61	28	—	—	—	—	—
87-88—Bowling Green State	CCHA	45	34	49	83	54	—	—	—	—	—
88-89—Bowling Green State	CCHA	44	22	46	68	46	—	—	—	—	—
89-90—Bowling Green State	CCHA	44	30	52	82	42	—	—	—	—	—
—Peoria	IHL	3	1	1	2	0	—	—	—	—	—
90-91—St. Louis	NHL	4	0	3	3	2	—	—	—	—	—
—Peoria	IHL	73	36	79	115	91	17	9	12	21	16
91-92—St. Louis	NHL	79	23	36	59	66	6	3	3	6	21
NHL totals		**83**	**23**	**39**	**62**	**68**	**6**	**3**	**3**	**6**	**21**

EMMA, DAVID
C, DEVILS

PERSONAL: Born January 14, 1969, at Cranston, R.I.... 5-11/180.... Shoots left.... Full name: David Anaclethe Emma.
HIGH SCHOOL: Bishop Hendricken (Warwick, R.I.).
COLLEGE: Boston College.
TRANSACTIONS/CAREER NOTES: Selected by New Jersey Devils in sixth round (sixth Devils pick, 110th overall) of NHL entry draft (June 17, 1989).
HONORS: Named to Hockey East All-Star second team (1988-89).... Named to Hockey East All-Star first team (1989-90 and 1990-91).... Won Hobey Baker Memorial Trophy (1990-91).... Named Hockey East Player of the Year (1990-91).... Named to NCAA All-America East first team (1989-90 and 1990-91).

Season Team	League	REGULAR SEASON					PLAYOFFS				
		Gms.	G	A	Pts.	Pen.	Gms.	G	A	Pts.	Pen.
87-88—Boston College	Hockey East	30	19	16	35	30	—	—	—	—	—
88-89—Boston College	Hockey East	36	20	31	51	36	—	—	—	—	—
89-90—Boston College	Hockey East	42	38	34	*72	46	—	—	—	—	—
90-91—Boston College	Hockey East	39	35	46	81	44	—	—	—	—	—
91-92—U.S. National Team	Int'l	55	15	16	31	32	—	—	—	—	—
—U.S. Olympic Team	Int'l	6	0	1	1	6	—	—	—	—	—
—Utica	AHL	15	4	7	11	12	4	1	1	2	2

ERICKSON, BRYAN
RW, JETS

PERSONAL: Born March 7, 1960, at Roseau, Minn.... 5-9/170.... Shoots right.
COLLEGE: Minnesota.
TRANSACTIONS/CAREER NOTES: Fractured wrist (January 1983).... Signed as free agent by Washington Capitals (April 5, 1983).... Broke thumb (October 1984).... Traded by Capitals to Los Angeles Kings for D Bruce Shoebottom (October 31, 1985).... Injured left knee cartilage (October 23, 1986).... Traded by Kings to Pittsburgh Penguins for C Chris Kontos and a sixth-round pick in 1989 draft (C Micah Aivazoff) (February 5, 1988).... Separated shoulder (March 1988).... Signed as free agent by Winnipeg Jets (March 2, 1990).... Strained abdomen (October 12, 1991); missed 11 games.... Restrained abdomen (December 1991); missed remainder of season.
HONORS: Named to WCHA All-Star second team (1981-82).... Named to WCHA All-Star first team (1982-83).

Season Team	League	REGULAR SEASON					PLAYOFFS				
		Gms.	G	A	Pts.	Pen.	Gms.	G	A	Pts.	Pen.
79-80—University of Minnesota	WCHA	23	10	15	25	14	—	—	—	—	—
80-81—University of Minnesota	WCHA	44	39	47	86	30	—	—	—	—	—

			REGULAR SEASON					PLAYOFFS				
Season Team	League	Gms.	G	A	Pts.	Pen.	Gms.	G	A	Pts.	Pen.
81-82—University of Minnesota ...	WCHA	35	25	20	45	20	—	—	—	—	—
82-83—University of Minnesota ...	WCHA	42	35	47	82	30	—	—	—	—	—
—Hershey	AHL	1	0	1	1	0	3	3	0	3	0
83-84—Hershey	AHL	31	16	12	28	11	—	—	—	—	—
—Washington	NHL	45	12	17	29	16	8	2	3	5	7
84-85—Binghamton	AHL	13	6	11	17	8	—	—	—	—	—
—Washington	NHL	57	15	13	28	23	—	—	—	—	—
85-86—Binghamton	AHL	7	5	3	8	2	—	—	—	—	—
—New Haven	AHL	14	8	3	11	11	—	—	—	—	—
—Los Angeles.....................	NHL	55	20	23	43	36	—	—	—	—	—
86-87—Los Angeles.....................	NHL	68	20	30	50	26	3	1	1	2	0
87-88—Los Angeles.....................	NHL	42	6	15	21	20	—	—	—	—	—
—Pittsburgh	NHL	11	1	4	5	0	—	—	—	—	—
—New Haven	AHL	3	0	0	0	0	—	—	—	—	—
88-89—						Did not play.					
89-90—Moncton	AHL	13	4	7	11	4	—	—	—	—	—
90-91—Winnipeg	NHL	6	0	7	7	0	—	—	—	—	—
—Moncton	AHL	36	18	14	32	16	—	—	—	—	—
91-92—Winnipeg	NHL	10	2	4	6	0	—	—	—	—	—
NHL totals.............		294	76	113	189	121	11	3	4	7	7

ERICKSON, CHAD
G, DEVILS

PERSONAL: Born August 21, 1970, at Minneapolis.... 5-10/175.... Shoots right.... Full name: Chad Carlyle Erickson.
HIGH SCHOOL: Warroad (Minn.).
COLLEGE: Minnesota-Duluth.
TRANSACTIONS/CAREER NOTES: Selected by New Jersey Devils in seventh round (eighth Devils pick, 138th overall) of NHL entry draft (June 11, 1988).
HONORS: Named to NCAA All-America West first team (1989-90).... Named to WCHA All-Star first team (1989-90).

			REGULAR SEASON							PLAYOFFS					
Season Team	League	Gms.	Min.	W	L	T	GA	SO	Avg.	Gms.	Min.	W	L	GA	SO	Avg.
86-87—Warroad H.S.	Minn. HS	21	945				36	1	2.29	—	—	—	—	—	—	—
87-88—Warroad H.S.	Minn. HS	24	1080				33	7	1.83	—	—	—	—	—	—	—
88-89—Minnesota-Duluth.......	WCHA	15	821	5	7	1	49	0	3.58	—	—	—	—	—	—	—
89-90—Minnesota-Duluth.......	WCHA	39	2301	19	19	1	141	0	3.68	—	—	—	—	—	—	—
90-91—Minnesota-Duluth.......	WCHA	40	2393	14	19	7	*159	0	3.99	—	—	—	—	—	—	—
91-92—Utica.............................	AHL	44	2341	18	19	3	147	2	3.77	2	127	0	2	11	0	5.20
—New Jersey..................	NHL	2	120	1	1	0	9	0	4.50	—	—	—	—	—	—	—
NHL totals.............		2	120	1	1	0	9	0	4.50							

ERIXON, JAN
LW, RANGERS

PERSONAL: Born July 8, 1962, at Skelleftea, Sweden.... 6-0/192.... Shoots left.
TRANSACTIONS/CAREER NOTES: Selected by New York Rangers in second round (second Rangers pick, 30th overall) of NHL entry draft (June 10, 1981).... Bruised foot (February 1985).... Bruised leg (December 8, 1985).... Fractured tibia (January 12, 1986).... Suffered hip injury (December 1986).... Sprained right knee (October 1988).... Sprained back (February 1989).... Suffered back spasms (December 2, 1989).... Underwent surgery to lower back to repair herniated disc (May 2, 1990).... Sprained right knee (November 26, 1990); missed 24 games.... Reinjured knee (January 25, 1991); missed two games.... Injured back during preseason (September 1991); missed first nine games of season.... Injured ribs (January 6, 1992); missed five games.... Injured shoulder (February 12, 1992); missed eight games.

			REGULAR SEASON					PLAYOFFS				
Season Team	League	Gms.	G	A	Pts.	Pen.	Gms.	G	A	Pts.	Pen.
79-80—Skelleftea AIK	Sweden	32	9	3	12	22	—	—	—	—	—
80-81—Skelleftea AIK	Sweden	32	6	6	12	4	3	1	0	1	0
81-82—Skelleftea AIK	Sweden	30	7	7	14	26	—	—	—	—	—
82-83—Skelleftea AIK	Sweden	36	10	18	28		—	—	—	—	—
83-84—New York Rangers	NHL	75	5	25	30	16	5	2	0	2	4
84-85—New York Rangers	NHL	66	7	22	29	33	2	0	0	0	2
85-86—New York Rangers	NHL	31	2	17	19	4	12	0	1	1	4
86-87—New York Rangers	NHL	68	8	18	26	24	6	1	0	1	0
87-88—New York Rangers	NHL	70	7	19	26	33	—	—	—	—	—
88-89—New York Rangers	NHL	44	4	11	15	27	4	0	1	1	2
89-90—New York Rangers	NHL	58	4	9	13	8	10	1	0	1	2
90-91—New York Rangers	NHL	53	7	18	25	8	6	1	2	3	0
91-92—New York Rangers	NHL	46	8	9	17	4	13	2	3	5	2
NHL totals.............		511	52	148	200	157	58	7	7	14	16

ERREY, BOB
LW, PENGUINS

PERSONAL: Born September 21, 1964, at Montreal.... 5-10/182.... Shoots left.
TRANSACTIONS/CAREER NOTES: Selected by Pittsburgh Penguins as underage junior in first round (first Penguins pick, 15th overall) of NHL entry draft (June 8, 1983).... Sprained right knee (March 18, 1987).... Broke right wrist (October 1987).... Injured shoulder (May 9, 1992).
HONORS: Named to OHL All-Star first team (1982-83).

E

Season Team	League	Gms.	G	A	Pts.	Pen.	Gms.	G	A	Pts.	Pen.
		REGULAR SEASON					**PLAYOFFS**				
81-82—Peterborough	OHL	68	29	31	60	39	9	3	1	4	9
82-83—Peterborough	OHL	67	53	47	100	74	4	1	3	4	7
83-84—Pittsburgh	NHL	65	9	13	22	29	—	—	—	—	—
84-85—Baltimore	AHL	59	17	24	41	14	8	3	4	7	11
—Pittsburgh	NHL	16	0	2	2	7	—	—	—	—	—
85-86—Baltimore	AHL	18	8	7	15	28	—	—	—	—	—
—Pittsburgh	NHL	37	11	6	17	8	—	—	—	—	—
86-87—Pittsburgh	NHL	72	16	18	34	46	—	—	—	—	—
87-88—Pittsburgh	NHL	17	3	6	9	18	—	—	—	—	—
88-89—Pittsburgh	NHL	76	26	32	58	124	11	1	2	3	12
89-90—Pittsburgh	NHL	78	20	19	39	109	—	—	—	—	—
90-91—Pittsburgh	NHL	79	20	22	42	115	24	5	2	7	29
91-92—Pittsburgh	NHL	78	19	16	35	119	14	3	0	3	10
NHL totals		518	124	134	258	575	49	9	4	13	51

ESAU, LEONARD
D, NORDIQUES

PERSONAL: Born March 16, 1968, at Meadow Lake, Sask. . . . 6-3/195. . . . Shoots right. . . . Full name: Leonard Roy Esau.
COLLEGE: St. Cloud State (Minn.).
TRANSACTIONS/CAREER NOTES: Selected by Toronto Maple Leafs in fifth round (fifth Maple Leafs pick, 86th overall) of NHL entry draft (June 11, 1988). . . . Traded by Maple Leafs to Quebec Nordiques for C Ken McRae (July 21, 1992).

Season Team	League	Gms.	G	A	Pts.	Pen.	Gms.	G	A	Pts.	Pen.
		REGULAR SEASON					**PLAYOFFS**				
86-87—Humboldt	SJHL	57	4	26	30	278	—	—	—	—	—
87-88—Humboldt	SJHL	57	16	37	53	229	—	—	—	—	—
88-89—St. Cloud State	WCHA	35	12	27	39	69	—	—	—	—	—
89-90—St. Cloud State	WCHA	29	8	11	19	83	—	—	—	—	—
90-91—Newmarket	AHL	75	4	14	18	28	—	—	—	—	—
91-92—St. John's	AHL	78	9	29	38	68	13	0	2	2	14
—Toronto	NHL	2	0	0	0	0	—	—	—	—	—
NHL totals		2	0	0	0	0					

ESPE, DAVID
D, NORDIQUES

PERSONAL: Born November 3, 1966, at St. Paul, Minn. . . . 6-0/185. . . . Shoots left.
HIGH SCHOOL: White Bear Lake (Minn.).
COLLEGE: Minnesota.
TRANSACTIONS/CAREER NOTES: Selected by Quebec Nordiques in fourth round (fifth Nordiques pick, 78th overall) of NHL entry draft (June 15, 1985).

Season Team	League	Gms.	G	A	Pts.	Pen.	Gms.	G	A	Pts.	Pen.
		REGULAR SEASON					**PLAYOFFS**				
84-85—White Bear Lake H.S.	Minn. H.S.	21	11	16	27	30	—	—	—	—	—
85-86—University of Minnesota	WCHA	27	0	6	6	18	—	—	—	—	—
86-87—University of Minnesota	WCHA	45	4	8	12	28	—	—	—	—	—
87-88—University of Minnesota	WCHA	43	4	10	14	68	—	—	—	—	—
88-89—University of Minnesota	WCHA	47	0	11	11	61	—	—	—	—	—
89-90—Halifax	AHL	48	2	16	18	26	1	0	0	0	4
90-91—Halifax	AHL	49	5	16	21	51	—	—	—	—	—
91-92—Halifax	AHL	43	4	7	11	22	—	—	—	—	—

ESSENSA, BOB
G, JETS

PERSONAL: Born January 14, 1965, at Toronto. . . . 6-0/160. . . . Shoots left. . . . Full name: Robert Earle Essensa.
HIGH SCHOOL: Henry Carr (Rexdale, Ont.).
COLLEGE: Michigan State.
TRANSACTIONS/CAREER NOTES: Selected by Winnipeg Jets in fourth round (fifth Jets pick, 69th overall) of NHL entry draft (June 8, 1983). . . . Suffered severe lacerations to both hands and wrist (February 1985). . . . Injured groin (September 1990); missed three weeks. . . . Sprained knee (October 12, 1991); missed four games. . . . Injured left hamstring (December 8, 1991); missed four games. . . . Sprained knee (March 6, 1992); missed seven games.
HONORS: Named to CCHA All-Star first team (1984-85). . . . Named to CCHA All-Star second team (1985-86). . . . Named to NHL All-Rookie team (1989-90).

Season Team	League	Gms.	Min.	W	L	T	GA	SO	Avg.	Gms.	Min.	W	L	GA	SO	Avg.
		REGULAR SEASON								**PLAYOFFS**						
81-82—Henry Carr H.S.	MTHL	17	948				79		5.00	—	—	—	—	—	—	—
82-83—Henry Carr H.S.	MTHL	31	1840				98	2	3.20	—	—	—	—	—	—	—
83-84—Michigan State	CCHA	17	947	11	4	0	44	2	2.79	—	—	—	—	—	—	—
84-85—Michigan State	CCHA	18	1059	15	2	0	29	2	1.64	—	—	—	—	—	—	—
85-86—Michigan State	CCHA	23	1333	17	4	1	74	1	3.33	—	—	—	—	—	—	—
86-87—Michigan State	CCHA	25	1383	19	3	1	64	*2	*2.78	—	—	—	—	—	—	—
87-88—Moncton	AHL	27	1287	7	11	1	100	1	4.66	—	—	—	—	—	—	—
88-89—Winnipeg	NHL	20	1102	6	8	3	68	1	3.70	—	—	—	—	—	—	—
—Fort Wayne	IHL	22	1287	14	7	0	70	0	3.26	—	—	—	—	—	—	—
89-90—Moncton	AHL	6	358	3	3	0	15	0	2.51	—	—	—	—	—	—	—
—Winnipeg	NHL	36	2035	18	9	5	107	1	3.15	4	206	2	1	12	0	3.50
90-91—Moncton	AHL	2	125	1	0	1	6	0	2.88	—	—	—	—	—	—	—
—Winnipeg	NHL	55	2916	19	24	6	153	4	3.15	—	—	—	—	—	—	—
91-92—Winnipeg	NHL	47	2627	21	17	6	126	+5	2.88	1	33	0	0	3	0	5.45
NHL totals		158	8680	64	58	20	454	11	3.14	5	239	2	1	15	0	3.77

EVANS, DOUG
LW, BRUINS

PERSONAL: Born June 2, 1963, at Peterborough, Ont.... 5-9/178.... Shoots left.... Full name: Doug Thomas Evans.
TRANSACTIONS/CAREER NOTES: Signed as free agent by St. Louis Blues (June 10, 1985).... Separated left shoulder (September 1987).... Traded by Blues to Winnipeg Jets for C Ron Wilson (January 22, 1990).... Loaned to Peoria Rivermen (November 9, 1991); returned (December 15, 1991).... Traded by Jets to Boston Bruins for G Daniel Berthiaume (June 10, 1992).
HONORS: Named to IHL All-Star first team (1985-86).

			REGULAR SEASON					PLAYOFFS				
Season	Team	League	Gms.	G	A	Pts.	Pen.	Gms.	G	A	Pts.	Pen.
80-81	Peterborough	OMJHL	51	9	24	33	139	—	—	—	—	—
81-82	Peterborough	OHL	56	17	49	66	176	9	0	2	2	41
82-83	Peterborough	OHL	65	31	55	86	165	4	0	3	3	23
83-84	Peterborough	OHL	61	45	79	124	98	8	4	12	16	26
84-85	Peoria	IHL	81	36	61	97	189	20	18	14	32	†88
85-86	St. Louis	NHL	13	1	0	1	2	—	—	—	—	—
	Peoria	IHL	69	46	51	97	179	10	4	6	10	32
86-87	Peoria	IHL	18	10	15	25	39	—	—	—	—	—
	St. Louis	NHL	53	3	13	16	91	5	0	0	0	10
87-88	Peoria	IHL	11	4	16	20	64	—	—	—	—	—
	St. Louis	NHL	41	5	7	12	49	2	0	0	0	0
88-89	St. Louis	NHL	53	7	12	19	81	7	1	2	3	10
89-90	Peoria	IHL	42	19	28	47	128	—	—	—	—	—
	St. Louis	NHL	3	0	0	0	0	—	—	—	—	—
	Winnipeg	NHL	27	10	8	18	33	7	2	2	4	10
90-91	Winnipeg	NHL	70	7	27	34	108	—	—	—	—	—
91-92	Winnipeg	NHL	30	7	7	14	68	1	0	0	0	2
	Peoria	IHL	16	5	14	19	38	—	—	—	—	—
	Moncton	AHL	10	7	8	15	10	—	—	—	—	—
NHL totals			290	40	74	114	432	22	3	4	7	38

EVANS, KEVIN
LW, NORTH STARS

PERSONAL: Born July 10, 1965, at Peterborough, Ont.... 5-9/179.... Shoots left.... Full name: Kevin Robert Evans.
TRANSACTIONS/CAREER NOTES: Signed as free agent by Minnesota North Stars (August 8, 1988).... Suspended three games and fined $100 by IHL for fighting (December 28, 1988).... Severed five tendons and an artery (February 24, 1989).... Suspended one game and fined $300 by IHL for fighting (November 25, 1989).... Underwent reconstructive knee surgery (December 1990).... Selected by San Jose Sharks in NHL dispersal draft (May 30, 1991).... Signed as free agent by North Stars (July 17, 1992).

			REGULAR SEASON					PLAYOFFS				
Season	Team	League	Gms.	G	A	Pts.	Pen.	Gms.	G	A	Pts.	Pen.
83-84	Peterborough Jr. B	OHA	39	17	34	51	210	—	—	—	—	—
84-85	London	OHL	52	3	7	10	148	—	—	—	—	—
85-86	Victoria	WHL	66	16	39	55	*441	—	—	—	—	—
	Kalamazoo	IHL	11	3	5	8	97	6	3	0	3	56
86-87	Kalamazoo	IHL	73	19	31	50	*648	5	1	1	2	46
87-88	Kalamazoo	IHL	54	9	28	37	404	—	—	—	—	—
88-89	Kalamazoo	IHL	54	22	32	54	328	—	—	—	—	—
89-90	Kalamazoo	IHL	76	30	54	84	346	—	—	—	—	—
90-91	Minnesota	NHL	4	0	0	0	19	—	—	—	—	—
	Kalamazoo	IHL	16	10	12	22	70	—	—	—	—	—
91-92	San Jose	NHL	5	0	1	1	25	—	—	—	—	—
	Kansas City	IHL	66	10	39	49	342	14	2	13	15	70
NHL totals			9	0	1	1	44					

EVANS, SHAWN
D, WHALERS

PERSONAL: Born September 7, 1965, at Kingston, Ont.... 6-3/195.... Shoots left.... Cousin of Dennis Kearns, defenseman, Vancouver Canucks (1971-72 through 1980-81).
TRANSACTIONS/CAREER NOTES: Selected by New Jersey Devils as underage junior in second round (second Devils pick, 24th overall) of NHL entry draft (June 8, 1983).... Traded by Devils with fifth-round (C Mike Wolak) pick in 1986 draft to St. Louis Blues for LW/C Mark Johnson (September 19, 1985). ... Traded by Blues to Edmonton Oilers for RW Todd Ewen (October 15, 1986).... Signed as free agent by New York Islanders (June 20, 1988).... Signed to play with Olten, Switzerland (May 1990).... Signed as free agent with Hartford Whalers (August 14, 1991).
HONORS: Named to OHL All-Star second team (1983-84).... Named to AHL All-Star first team (1991-92).

			REGULAR SEASON					PLAYOFFS				
Season	Team	League	Gms.	G	A	Pts.	Pen.	Gms.	G	A	Pts.	Pen.
81-82	Kitchener Jr. B	OHA	21	9	13	22	55	—	—	—	—	—
82-83	Peterborough	OHL	58	7	41	48	116	4	2	0	2	12
83-84	Peterborough	OHL	67	21	88	109	116	8	1	16	17	8
84-85	Peterborough	OHL	66	16	83	99	78	16	6	18	24	6
85-86	Peoria	IHL	55	8	26	34	36	—	—	—	—	—
	St. Louis	NHL	7	0	0	0	2	—	—	—	—	—
86-87	Nova Scotia	AHL	55	7	28	35	29	5	0	4	4	6
87-88	Nova Scotia	AHL	79	8	62	70	109	5	1	1	2	40
88-89	Springfield	AHL	68	9	50	59	125					

E

Season Team	League	REGULAR SEASON Gms.	G	A	Pts.	Pen.	PLAYOFFS Gms.	G	A	Pts.	Pen.
89-90—New York Islanders	NHL	2	1	0	1	0	—	—	—	—	—
—Springfield	AHL	63	6	35	41	102	18	6	11	17	35
90-91—Olten	Switzerland				Statistics unavailable.						
—Maine	AHL	51	9	37	46	44	2	0	1	1	0
91-92—Springfield	AHL	80	11	67	78	81	11	0	8	8	16
NHL totals		9	1	0	1	2					

EVASON, DEAN
C, SHARKS

PERSONAL: Born August 22, 1964, at Flin Flon, Man. . . . 5- 10/ 180. . . . Shoots left.
TRANSACTIONS/CAREER NOTES: Selected by Kamloops Junior Oilers in WHL disperal draft of players of Spokane Flyers (December 1981). . . . Selected by Washington Capitals as underage junior in fifth round (third Capitals pick, 89th overall) of NHL entry draft (June 9, 1982). . . . Traded by Capitals with G Peter Sidorkiewicz to Hartford Whalers for LW David A. Jensen (March 1985). . . . Strained left ankle ligaments (December 14, 1988). . . . Traded by Whalers to San Jose Sharks for D Dan Keczmer (October 2, 1991). . . . Pulled abdominal muscles (January 27, 1992); missed two games.
HONORS: Won WHL Player of the Year Award (1982-83). . . . Named to WHL All-Star first team (1983-84).

Season Team	League	REGULAR SEASON Gms.	G	A	Pts.	Pen.	PLAYOFFS Gms.	G	A	Pts.	Pen.
80-81—Spokane Flyers	WHL	3	1	1	2	0	—	—	—	—	—
81-82—Kamloops	WHL	70	29	69	98	112	4	2	1	3	0
82-83—Kamloops	WHL	70	71	93	164	102	7	5	7	12	18
83-84—Kamloops	WHL	57	49	88	137	89	17	†21	20	41	33
—Washington	NHL	2	0	0	0	2	—	—	—	—	—
84-85—Binghamton	AHL	65	27	49	76	38	8	3	5	8	9
—Washington	NHL	15	3	4	7	2	—	—	—	—	—
—Hartford	NHL	2	0	0	0	0	—	—	—	—	—
85-86—Binghamton	AHL	26	9	17	26	29	—	—	—	—	—
—Hartford	NHL	55	20	28	48	65	10	1	4	5	10
86-87—Hartford	NHL	80	22	37	59	67	5	3	2	5	35
87-88—Hartford	NHL	77	10	18	28	117	6	1	1	2	2
88-89—Hartford	NHL	67	11	17	28	60	4	1	2	3	10
89-90—Hartford	NHL	78	18	25	43	138	7	2	2	4	22
90-91—Hartford	NHL	75	6	23	29	170	6	0	4	4	29
91-92—San Jose	NHL	74	11	15	26	99	—	—	—	—	—
NHL totals		525	101	167	268	720	38	8	15	23	108

EWEN, TODD
RW, CANADIENS

PERSONAL: Born March 26, 1966, at Saskatoon, Sask. . . . 6-2/220. . . . Shoots right.
TRANSACTIONS/CAREER NOTES: Selected by Edmonton Oilers as underage junior in eighth round (eighth Oilers pick, 168th overall) of NHL entry draft (June 9, 1984). . . . Traded by Oilers to St. Louis Blues for D Shawn Evans (October 15, 1986). . . . Sprained ankle (October 1987). . . . Suspended one game by NHL for third game misconduct of season (January 1988). . . . Pulled groin (October 1988). . . . Tore right eye muscle (December 1988). . . . Pulled left hamstring and bruised shoulder (February 1989). . . . Suspended 10 games by NHL for coming off bench to instigate fight during playoff game (April 18, 1989); missed three playoff games and first seven games of 1989-90 season. . . . Broke right hand (October 28, 1989). . . . Traded by Blues to Montreal Canadiens for the return of a draft pick dealt to Montreal for D Mike Lalor (December 12, 1989). . . . Strained knee ligaments and underwent surgery (November 19, 1990); missed 24 games. . . . Fractured right hand at home (February 14, 1991); missed remainder of season. . . . Separated shoulder (February 12, 1992); missed two games.

Season Team	League	REGULAR SEASON Gms.	G	A	Pts.	Pen.	PLAYOFFS Gms.	G	A	Pts.	Pen.
82-83—Vernon	BCJHL	42	20	23	43	195	—	—	—	—	—
—Kamloops	WHL	3	0	0	0	2	2	0	0	0	0
83-84—New Westminster	WHL	68	11	13	24	176	7	2	1	3	15
84-85—New Westminster	WHL	56	11	20	31	304	10	1	8	9	60
85-86—New Westminster	WHL	60	28	24	52	289	—	—	—	—	—
—Maine	AHL	—	—	—	—	—	3	0	0	0	7
86-87—Peoria	IHL	16	3	3	6	110	—	—	—	—	—
—St. Louis	NHL	23	2	0	2	84	4	0	0	0	23
87-88—St. Louis	NHL	64	4	2	6	227	6	0	0	0	21
88-89—St. Louis	NHL	34	4	5	9	171	2	0	0	0	21
89-90—Peoria	IHL	2	0	0	0	12	—	—	—	—	—
—St. Louis	NHL	3	0	0	0	11	—	—	—	—	—
—Montreal	NHL	41	4	6	10	158	10	0	0	0	4
90-91—Montreal	NHL	28	3	2	5	128	—	—	—	—	—
91-92—Montreal	NHL	46	1	2	3	130	3	0	0	0	18
NHL totals		239	18	17	35	909	25	0	0	0	87

FALLOON, PAT
RW, SHARKS

PERSONAL: Born September 22, 1972, at Foxwarren, Man. . . . 5- 11/ 192. . . . Shoots right. . . . Full name: Patrick Falloon.
TRANSACTIONS/CAREER NOTES: WHL rights traded with future considerations by Regina Pats to Spokane Chiefs for RW Jamie Heward (October 1987). . . . Tore right knee cartilage and underwent surgery (July 24, 1990). . . . Selected by San Jose Sharks in first round (first Sharks pick, second overall) of NHL entry draft (June 22, 1991).

HONORS: Named WHL West Division Rookie of the Year (1988-89).... Named to WHL All-Star second team (1988-89).... Won WHL West Division Most Sportsmanlike Player Award (1989-90).... Named to WHL All-Star first team (1989-90 and 1990-91).... Won CHL Most Sportsmanlike Player of the Year Award (1990-91).... Won Brad Hornung Trophy (1990-91). ...Won Stafford Smythe Memorial Trophy (1990-91).... Named to Memorial Cup All-Star Team (1990-91).

			REGULAR SEASON					PLAYOFFS			
Season Team	League	Gms.	G	A	Pts.	Pen.	Gms.	G	A	Pts.	Pen.
88-89—Spokane Chiefs	WHL	72	22	56	78	41	5	5	8	13	4
89-90—Spokane Chiefs	WHL	71	60	64	124	48	6	5	8	13	4
90-91—Spokane Chiefs	WHL	61	64	74	138	33	15	10	14	24	10
91-92—San Jose	NHL	79	25	34	59	16	—	—	—	—	—
NHL totals		79	25	34	59	16					

FARRELL, BRIAN
C, PENGUINS

PERSONAL: Born April 16, 1972, at Hartford, Conn.... 5-11/182.... Shoots left.... Full name: Brian Patrick Farrell. **HIGH SCHOOL:** Avon Old Farms School For Boys (Conn.). **COLLEGE:** Harvard.

TRANSACTIONS/CAREER NOTES: Selected by Pittsburgh Penguins in fifth round (fourth Penguins pick, 89th overall) of NHL entry draft (June 16, 1990).

			REGULAR SEASON					PLAYOFFS			
Season Team	League	Gms.	G	A	Pts.	Pen.	Gms.	G	A	Pts.	Pen.
88-89—Avon Old Farms H.S.	Conn. H.S.	27	13	24	37		—	—	—	—	—
89-90—Avon Old Farms H.S.	Conn. H.S.	24	22	23	45		—	—	—	—	—
90-91—Harvard University	ECAC	29	3	8	11	16	—	—	—	—	—
91-92—Harvard University	ECAC	9	5	3	8	8	—	—	—	—	—

FEATHERSTONE, GLEN
D, BRUINS

PERSONAL: Born July 8, 1968, at Toronto.... 6-4/215.... Shoots left. **TRANSACTIONS/CAREER NOTES:** Selected by St. Louis Blues as underage junior in fourth round (fourth Blues pick, 73rd overall) of NHL entry draft (June 21, 1986).... Suffered sore back (March 7, 1991); missed two games.... Signed as free agent by Boston Bruins (July 25, 1991); Bruins and Blues later arranged a trade in which Boston received Featherstone and LW Dave Thomlinson, whom they had also previously signed as a free agent, for RW Dave Christian, whom the Blues had previously signed as a free agent, a third-round pick in 1992 draft and either a seventh-round pick in 1992 draft or a sixth-round pick in 1993 draft.... Suffered hip pointer (October 5, 1991); missed three games.... Strained back (November 1991); missed remainder of season.... Underwent back surgery (November 15, 1991).

			REGULAR SEASON					PLAYOFFS			
Season Team	League	Gms.	G	A	Pts.	Pen.	Gms.	G	A	Pts.	Pen.
85-86—Windsor	OHL	49	0	6	6	135	14	1	1	2	23
86-87—Windsor	OHL	47	6	11	17	154	14	2	6	8	19
87-88—Windsor	OHL	53	7	27	34	201	12	6	9	15	47
88-89—Peoria	IHL	37	5	19	24	97	—	—	—	—	—
—St. Louis	NHL	18	0	2	2	22	6	0	0	0	25
89-90—Peoria	IHL	15	1	4	5	43	—	—	—	—	—
—St. Louis	NHL	58	0	12	12	145	12	0	2	2	47
90-91—St. Louis	NHL	68	5	15	20	204	9	0	0	0	31
91-92—Boston	NHL	7	1	0	1	20	—	—	—	—	—
NHL totals		151	6	29	35	391	27	0	2	2	103

FEDOROV, SERGEI
C, RED WINGS

PERSONAL: Born December 13, 1969, at Minsk, U.S.S.R.... 6-1/191.... Shoots left. **TRANSACTIONS/CAREER NOTES:** Selected by Detroit Red Wings in fourth round (fourth Red Wings pick, 74th overall) of NHL entry draft (June 17, 1989).... Bruised left shoulder (October 1990).... Reinjured left shoulder (January 16, 1991).

HONORS: Named to NHL All-Rookie team (1990-91).

			REGULAR SEASON					PLAYOFFS			
Season Team	League	Gms.	G	A	Pts.	Pen.	Gms.	G	A	Pts.	Pen.
85-86—Dynamo Minsk	USSR	15	6	1	7	10	—	—	—	—	—
86-87—Central Red Army	USSR	29	6	6	12	12	—	—	—	—	—
87-88—Central Red Army	USSR	48	7	9	16	20	—	—	—	—	—
88-89—Central Red Army	USSR	44	9	8	17	35	—	—	—	—	—
89-90—Central Red Army	USSR	48	19	10	29	20	—	—	—	—	—
90-91—Detroit	NHL	77	31	48	79	66	7	1	5	6	4
91-92—Detroit	NHL	80	32	54	86	72	11	5	5	10	8
NHL totals		157	63	102	165	138	18	6	10	16	12

FEDYK, BRENT
RW, RED WINGS

PERSONAL: Born March 8, 1967, at Yorkton, Sask.... 6-0/195.... Shoots right. **TRANSACTIONS/CAREER NOTES:** Selected by Detroit Red Wings as underage junior in first round (first Red Wings pick, eighth overall) of NHL entry draft (June 15, 1985).... Strained hip in Red Wings training camp (September 1985); missed three weeks.... Traded by Regina Pats with RW Ken McIntyre, LW Grant Kazuik, D Gerald Bzdel and the WHL rights to LW Kevin Kowalchuk to Seattle Thunderbirds for RW Craig Endean, C Ray Savard, Grant Chorney, C Erin Ginnell and WHL rights to LW Frank Kovacs (November 1986).... Traded by Thunderbirds to Portland Winter Hawks for future considerations (February 1987).... Injured knee (December 22, 1990); missed one game.... Suffered deep shin bruise (January 26, 1991); missed five games.... Suffered concussion (March 1991).
HONORS: Named to WHL All-Star second team (1985-86).

Season Team	League	REGULAR SEASON					PLAYOFFS				
		Gms.	G	A	Pts.	Pen.	Gms.	G	A	Pts.	Pen.
82-83—Regina	WHL	1	0	0	0	0	—	—	—	—	—
83-84—Regina	WHL	63	15	28	43	30	23	8	7	15	6
84-85—Regina	WHL	66	35	35	70	48	8	5	4	9	0
85-86—Regina	WHL	50	43	34	77	47	5	0	1	1	0
86-87—Regina	WHL	12	9	6	15	9	—	—	—	—	—
—Seattle	WHL	13	5	11	16	9	—	—	—	—	—
—Portland	WHL	11	5	4	9	6	14	5	6	11	0
87-88—Detroit	NHL	2	0	1	1	2	—	—	—	—	—
—Adirondack	AHL	34	9	11	20	22	5	0	2	2	6
88-89—Detroit	NHL	5	2	0	2	0	—	—	—	—	—
—Adirondack	AHL	66	40	28	68	33	15	7	8	15	23
89-90—Detroit	NHL	27	1	4	5	6	—	—	—	—	—
—Adirondack	AHL	33	14	15	29	24	6	2	1	3	4
90-91—Detroit	NHL	67	16	19	35	38	6	1	0	1	2
91-92—Adirondack	AHL	1	0	2	2	0	—	—	—	—	—
—Detroit	NHL	61	5	8	13	42	1	0	0	0	2
NHL totals		162	24	32	56	88	7	1	0	1	4

FELSNER, DENNY
RW, BLUES

PERSONAL: Born April 29, 1970, at Warren, Mich. . . . 6-0/195. . . . Shoots left. . . . Full name: Denny Walter Felsner.
COLLEGE: Michigan.
TRANSACTIONS/CAREER NOTES: Selected by St. Louis Blues in third round (third Blues pick, 55th overall) of NHL entry draft (June 17, 1989). . . . Injured knee (December 29, 1989).
HONORS: Named to CCHA All-Rookie team (1988-89). . . . Named to NCAA All-America West second team (1990-91). . . . Named to CCHA All-Star first team (1990-91 and 1991-92).

Season Team	League	REGULAR SEASON					PLAYOFFS				
		Gms.	G	A	Pts.	Pen.	Gms.	G	A	Pts.	Pen.
86-87—Detroit Falcons	NAJHL	37	22	33	55	18	—	—	—	—	—
87-88—Detroit Junior Red Wings	NAJHL	39	35	43	78	46	—	—	—	—	—
88-89—University of Michigan	CCHA	39	30	19	49	22	—	—	—	—	—
89-90—University of Michigan	CCHA	33	27	16	43	24	—	—	—	—	—
90-91—University of Michigan	CCHA	46	40	35	75	58	—	—	—	—	—
91-92—University of Michigan	CCHA	44	42	*52	*94	48	—	—	—	—	—
—St. Louis	NHL	3	0	1	1	0	1	0	0	0	0
NHL totals		3	0	1	1	0	1	0	0	0	0

FENTON, PAUL
LW

PERSONAL: Born December 22, 1959, at Springfield, Mass. . . . 5-11/180. . . . Shoots left. . . . Full name: Paul John Fenton.
HIGH SCHOOL: Cathedral (Springfield, Mass.).
COLLEGE: Boston University.
TRANSACTIONS/CAREER NOTES: Signed as free agent by Hartford Whalers (October 6, 1983). . . . Released by Whalers (July 1986). . . . Signed as free agent by New York Rangers (September 1986). . . . Acquired by Los Angeles Kings on waivers from Rangers (October 1987). . . . Traded by Kings to Winnipeg Jets for LW Gilles Hamel (November 25, 1988). . . . Traded by Jets with D Dave Ellett to Toronto Maple Leafs for C Ed Olczyk and LW Mark Osborne (November 10, 1990). . . . Traded by Maple Leafs with RW John Kordic to Washington Capitals for fifth-round pick in 1991 draft (C Alexei Kudashov) (January 24, 1991). . . . Traded by Capitals to Calgary Flames for D Ken Sabourin (January 24, 1991). . . . Traded by Flames to Whalers for future considerations (August 26, 1991). . . . Suffered from throat ailment (October 1991). . . . Traded by Whalers to San Jose Sharks for C Mike McHugh (October 18, 1991). . . . Injured head (February 23, 1992); missed four games.
HONORS: Won Ken McKenzie Trophy (1982-83). . . . Named to IHL All-Star second team (1982-83). . . . Named to AHL All-Star first team (1985-86). . . . Named to AHL All-Star second team (1986-87).

Season Team	League	REGULAR SEASON					PLAYOFFS				
		Gms.	G	A	Pts.	Pen.	Gms.	G	A	Pts.	Pen.
79-80—Boston University	ECAC	28	12	21	33	18	—	—	—	—	—
80-81—Boston University	ECAC	7	4	4	8	0	—	—	—	—	—
81-82—Boston University	ECAC	28	20	13	33	28	—	—	—	—	—
82-83—Peoria	IHL	82	60	51	111	53	—	—	—	—	—
—Colorado	CHL	1	0	1	1	0	3	2	0	2	2
83-84—Binghamton	AHL	78	41	24	65	67	—	—	—	—	—
84-85—Binghamton	AHL	45	26	21	47	18	—	—	—	—	—
—Hartford	NHL	33	7	5	12	10	—	—	—	—	—
85-86—Hartford	NHL	1	0	0	0	0	—	—	—	—	—
—Binghamton	AHL	75	53	35	88	87	6	2	0	2	2
86-87—New York Rangers	NHL	8	0	0	0	2	—	—	—	—	—
—New Haven	AHL	70	37	38	75	45	7	6	4	10	6
87-88—New Haven	AHL	5	11	5	16	9	—	—	—	—	—
—Los Angeles	NHL	71	20	23	43	46	5	2	1	3	2
88-89—Los Angeles	NHL	21	2	3	5	6	—	—	—	—	—
—Winnipeg	NHL	59	14	9	23	33	—	—	—	—	—
89-90—Winnipeg	NHL	80	32	18	50	40	7	2	0	2	23
90-91—Winnipeg	NHL	17	4	4	8	18	—	—	—	—	—
—Toronto	NHL	30	5	10	15	0	—	—	—	—	—
—Calgary	NHL	31	5	7	12	10	5	0	0	0	2
91-92—San Jose	NHL	60	11	4	15	33	—	—	—	—	—
NHL totals		411	100	83	183	198	17	4	1	5	27

F

FENYVES, DAVE
D, FLYERS

PERSONAL: Born April 29, 1960, at Dunnville, Ont.... 6-0/190.... Shoots left.... Full name: David Alan Fenyves.
TRANSACTIONS/CAREER NOTES: Separated shoulder (October 1977).... Signed as free agent by Buffalo Sabres (October 31, 1979).... Selected by Philadelphia Flyers during NHL waiver draft as compensation for Sabres drafting of D/RW Ed Hospodar (October 5, 1987).
HONORS: Named to OMJHL All-Star second team (1979-80).... Won Jack Butterfield Trophy (1986-87).... Named to AHL All-Star second team (1986-87).... Won Eddie Shore Plaque (1987-88 and 1988-89).... Named to AHL All-Star first team (1988-89).

Season Team	League	REGULAR SEASON					PLAYOFFS				
		Gms.	G	A	Pts.	Pen.	Gms.	G	A	Pts.	Pen.
77-78—Peterborough	OMJHL	59	3	12	15	36	—	—	—	—	—
78-79—Peterborough	OMJHL	66	2	23	25	122	19	0	5	5	18
79-80—Peterborough	OMJHL	66	9	36	45	92	14	0	3	3	14
80-81—Rochester	AHL	77	6	16	22	146	—	—	—	—	—
81-82—Rochester	AHL	73	3	14	17	68	5	0	1	1	4
82-83—Rochester	AHL	51	2	19	21	45	—	—	—	—	—
—Buffalo	NHL	24	0	8	8	14	4	0	0	0	0
83-84—Buffalo	NHL	10	0	4	4	9	2	0	0	0	7
—Rochester	AHL	70	3	16	19	55	16	1	4	5	22
84-85—Rochester	AHL	9	0	3	3	8	—	—	—	—	—
—Buffalo	NHL	60	1	0	9	27	5	0	0	0	2
85-86—Buffalo	NHL	47	0	7	7	37	—	—	—	—	—
86-87—Rochester	AHL	71	6	16	22	57	18	3	12	15	10
—Buffalo	NHL	7	1	0	1	0	—	—	—	—	—
87-88—Philadelphia	NHL	5	0	0	0	0	—	—	—	—	—
—Hershey	AHL	75	11	40	51	47	12	1	8	9	10
88-89—Philadelphia	NHL	1	0	1	1	0	—	—	—	—	—
—Hershey	AHL	79	15	51	66	41	12	2	6	8	6
89-90—Philadelphia	NHL	12	0	0	0	4	—	—	—	—	—
—Hershey	AHL	66	6	37	43	57	—	—	—	—	—
90-91—Philadelphia	NHL	40	1	4	5	28	—	—	—	—	—
—Hershey	AHL	29	4	11	15	13	7	0	3	3	6
91-92—Hershey	AHL	68	4	24	28	29	6	1	1	2	10
NHL totals		206	3	32	35	119	11	0	0	0	9

FERGUS, TOM
C, CANUCKS

PERSONAL: Born June 16, 1962, at Chicago.... 6-0/176.... Shoots left.... Full name: Thomas Joseph Fergus.
TRANSACTIONS/CAREER NOTES: Selected by Boston Bruins as underage junior in third round (second Bruins pick, 60th overall) of NHL entry draft (June 11, 1980).... Tore ligaments in left knee (January 20, 1982).... Damaged knee ligaments (February 1984).... Traded by Bruins to Toronto Maple Leafs for C Bill Derlago (September 1985).... Suffered viral infection (March 1987); missed 23 games.... Pulled groin (November 1987).... Bruised ribs (March 1988).... Pulled groin and stomach muscle (February 6, 1990).... Underwent surgery to repair torn abdominal muscle (November 1990).... Injured back and chest (March 20, 1991).... Claimed on waivers by Vancouver Canucks for $5,000 (December 18, 1991).

Season Team	League	REGULAR SEASON					PLAYOFFS				
		Gms.	G	A	Pts.	Pen.	Gms.	G	A	Pts.	Pen.
79-80—Peterborough	OMJHL	63	8	6	14	14	14	1	5	6	6
80-81—Peterborough	OMJHL	63	43	45	88	33	5	1	4	5	2
81-82—Boston	NHL	61	15	24	39	12	6	3	0	3	0
82-83—Boston	NHL	80	28	35	63	39	15	2	2	4	15
83-84—Boston	NHL	69	25	36	61	12	3	2	0	2	9
84-85—Boston	NHL	79	30	43	73	75	5	0	0	0	4
85-86—Toronto	NHL	78	31	42	73	64	10	5	7	12	6
86-87—Newmarket	AHL	1	0	1	1	0	—	—	—	—	—
—Toronto	NHL	57	21	28	49	57	2	0	1	1	2
87-88—Toronto	NHL	63	19	31	50	81	6	2	3	5	2
88-89—Toronto	NHL	80	22	45	67	48	—	—	—	—	—
89-90—Toronto	NHL	54	19	26	45	62	5	2	1	3	4
90-91—Toronto	NHL	14	5	4	9	8	—	—	—	—	—
91-92—Toronto	NHL	11	1	3	4	4	—	—	—	—	—
—Vancouver	NHL	44	14	20	34	17	13	5	3	8	6
NHL totals		690	230	337	567	479	65	21	17	38	48

FERGUSON, JOHN
LW, CANADIENS

PERSONAL: Born July 7, 1967, at Winnipeg, Man.... 6-0/192.... Shoots left.... Full name: John Stewart Ferguson Jr.... Son of John Ferguson, left winger, Montreal Canadiens (1963-64 through 1970-71), and former general manager of New York Rangers (1976 through 1978) and Winnipeg Jets of WHA (1978 through 1979).
COLLEGE: Providence.
TRANSACTIONS/CAREER NOTES: Selected by Montreal Canadiens in 12th round (fifteenth Canadiens pick, 247th overall) of NHL entry draft (June 15, 1985).

Season Team	League	REGULAR SEASON					PLAYOFFS				
		Gms.	G	A	Pts.	Pen.	Gms.	G	A	Pts.	Pen.
84-85—Winnipeg	MJHL	—	—	—	—	—	—	—	—	—	—
85-86—Providence College	Hockey East	18	1	2	3	2	—	—	—	—	—

Season Team	League	REGULAR SEASON					PLAYOFFS				
		Gms.	G	A	Pts.	Pen.	Gms.	G	A	Pts.	Pen.
86-87—Providence College	Hockey East	23	0	0	0	6	—	—	—	—	—
87-88—Providence College	Hockey East	34	0	5	5	31	—	—	—	—	—
88-89—Providence College	Hockey East	40	14	15	29	66	—	—	—	—	—
89-90—Sherbrooke	AHL	17	4	3	7	8	1	0	0	0	0
—Peoria	IHL	18	1	8	9	14	3	0	0	0	2
90-91—Fredericton	AHL	73	14	8	22	96	9	3	3	6	21
91-92—Fredericton	AHL	62	18	21	39	74	5	1	1	2	4

FERNANDEZ, EMMANUEL
G, NORDIQUES

PERSONAL: Born August 27, 1974, at Etobicoke, Ont. . . . 6-0/173. . . . Shoots left. . . . Nephew of Jacques Lemaire, center, Montreal Canadiens (1967-68 through 1978-79).
TRANSACTIONS/CAREER NOTES: Selected by Quebec Nordiques in third round (fourth Nordiques pick, 52nd overall) of NHL entry draft (June 20, 1992).

Season Team	League	REGULAR SEASON							PLAYOFFS					
		Gms.	Min.	W	L	T	GA	SO	Avg.	Gms.	Min.	W	L	GA	SO	Avg.
91-92—Laval	QMJHL	31	1593	14	13	2	99	1	3.73	9	468	3	5	†39	0	5.00

FERNER, MARK
D, MAPLE LEAFS

PERSONAL: Born September 5, 1965, at Regina, Sask. . . . 6-0/170. . . . Shoots left.
TRANSACTIONS/CAREER NOTES: Selected by Buffalo Sabres in 10th round (12th Sabres pick, 194th overall) of NHL entry draft (June 8, 1983). . . . Broke foot (March 1986). . . . Traded by Sabres to Washington Capitals for C Scott McCrory (June 1, 1989). . . . Traded by Capitals to Toronto Maple Leafs for a 12th-round pick in 1992 draft (February 27, 1992).
HONORS: Named to WHL All-Star first team (1984-85). . . . Named to AHL All-Star second team (1990-91).

Season Team	League	REGULAR SEASON					PLAYOFFS				
		Gms.	G	A	Pts.	Pen.	Gms.	G	A	Pts.	Pen.
82-83—Kamloops	WHL	69	6	15	21	81	7	0	0	0	7
83-84—Kamloops	WHL	72	9	30	39	162	14	1	8	9	20
84-85—Kamloops	WHL	69	15	39	54	91	15	4	9	13	21
85-86—Rochester	AHL	63	3	14	17	87	—	—	—	—	—
86-87—Buffalo	NHL	13	0	3	3	9	—	—	—	—	—
—Rochester	AHL	54	0	12	12	157	—	—	—	—	—
87-88—Rochester	AHL	69	1	25	26	165	7	1	4	5	31
88-89—Buffalo	NHL	2	0	0	0	2	—	—	—	—	—
—Rochester	AHL	55	0	18	18	97	—	—	—	—	—
89-90—Washington	NHL	2	0	0	0	0	—	—	—	—	—
—Baltimore	AHL	74	7	28	35	76	11	1	2	3	21
90-91—Baltimore	AHL	61	14	40	54	38	6	1	4	5	24
—Washington	NHL	7	0	1	1	4	—	—	—	—	—
91-92—Baltimore	AHL	57	7	38	45	67	—	—	—	—	—
—St. John's	AHL	15	1	8	9	6	14	2	14	16	39
NHL totals		24	0	4	4	15					

FERRARO, CHRIS
RW, RANGERS

PERSONAL: Born January 24, 1973, at Port Jefferson, N.Y. . . . 5-10/175. . . . Shoots right. . . . Twin brother of Peter Ferraro, center in New York Rangers system.
TRANSACTIONS/CAREER NOTES: Selected by New York Rangers in fourth round (fourth Rangers pick, 85th overall) of NHL entry draft (June 20, 1992).

Season Team	League	REGULAR SEASON					PLAYOFFS				
		Gms.	G	A	Pts.	Pen.	Gms.	G	A	Pts.	Pen.
90-91—Dubuque	USHL	45	53	44	97		—	—	—	—	—
91-92—Waterloo	USHL	38	49	50	99	106	—	—	—	—	—

FERRARO, PETER
C, RANGERS

PERSONAL: Born January 24, 1973, at Port Jefferson, N.Y. . . . 5-10/175. . . . Shoots right. . . . Twin brother of Chris Ferraro, right winger in New York Rangers system.
TRANSACTIONS/CAREER NOTES: Selected by New York Rangers in first round (first Rangers pick, 24th overall) of NHL entry draft (June 20, 1992).

Season Team	League	REGULAR SEASON					PLAYOFFS				
		Gms.	G	A	Pts.	Pen.	Gms.	G	A	Pts.	Pen.
90-91—Dubuque	USHL	29	21	31	52	83	—	—	—	—	—
91-92—Waterloo	USHL	42	48	53	101	168	—	—	—	—	—

FERRARO, RAY
C, ISLANDERS

PERSONAL: Born August 23, 1964, at Trail, B.C. . . . 5-10/185. . . . Shoots left.
TRANSACTIONS/CAREER NOTES: Selected by Hartford Whalers as underage junior in fifth round (fifth Whalers pick, 88th overall) of NHL entry draft (June 9, 1982). . . . Traded by Whalers to New York Islanders for D Doug Crossman (November 13, 1990).
HONORS: Won Most Valuable Player Trophy (1983-84). . . . Won Bob Brownridge Memorial Trophy (1983-84). . . . Won WHL Player of the Year Award (1983-84). . . . Named to WHL All-Star first team (1983-84).

Season Team	League	REGULAR SEASON					PLAYOFFS				
		Gms.	G	A	Pts.	Pen.	Gms.	G	A	Pts.	Pen.
81-82—Penticton	BCJHL	48	65	70	135	50	—	—	—	—	—
82-83—Portland	WHL	50	41	49	90	39	14	14	10	24	13

F

Season Team	League	REGULAR SEASON					PLAYOFFS				
		Gms.	G	A	Pts.	Pen.	Gms.	G	A	Pts.	Pen.
83-84—Brandon	WHL	72	*108	84	*192	84	11	13	15	28	20
84-85—Binghamton	AHL	37	20	13	33	29	—	—	—	—	—
—Hartford	NHL	44	11	17	28	40	—	—	—	—	—
85-86—Hartford	NHL	76	30	47	77	57	10	3	6	9	4
86-87—Hartford	NHL	80	27	32	59	42	6	1	1	2	8
87-88—Hartford	NHL	68	21	29	50	81	6	1	1	2	6
88-89—Hartford	NHL	80	41	35	76	86	4	2	0	2	4
89-90—Hartford	NHL	79	25	29	54	109	7	0	3	3	2
90-91—Hartford	NHL	15	2	5	7	18	—	—	—	—	—
—New York Islanders	NHL	61	19	16	35	52	—	—	—	—	—
91-92—New York Islanders	NHL	80	40	40	80	92	—	—	—	—	—
NHL totals		583	216	250	466	577	33	7	11	18	24

FERREIRA, BRIAN
RW

PERSONAL: Born February 1, 1968, at Falmouth, Mass. . . . 6-0/175. . . . Shoots right. . . . Full name: Brian Peter Ferreira.
HIGH SCHOOL: Falmouth (Mass.).
COLLEGE: Rensselaer Polytechnic Institute (N.Y.).
TRANSACTIONS/CAREER NOTES: Selected by Boston Bruins in eighth round (seventh Bruins pick, 160th overall) of NHL entry draft (June 21, 1986). . . . Underwent knee surgery (January 1989).

Season Team	League	REGULAR SEASON					PLAYOFFS				
		Gms.	G	A	Pts.	Pen.	Gms.	G	A	Pts.	Pen.
84-85—Falmouth H.S.	Mass. H.S.	24	31	32	63		—	—	—	—	—
85-86—Falmouth H.S.	Mass. H.S.	22	37	43	80	12	—	—	—	—	—
86-87—R.P.I.	ECAC	30	19	17	36	24	—	—	—	—	—
87-88—R.P.I.	ECAC	32	18	19	37	48	—	—	—	—	—
88-89—R.P.I.	ECAC	15	3	13	16	28	—	—	—	—	—
89-90—R.P.I.	ECAC	34	10	35	45	36	—	—	—	—	—
90-91—Maine	AHL	5	0	1	1	2	—	—	—	—	—
—Johnstown	ECHL	38	25	22	47	47	8	9	2	11	14
91-92—Maine	AHL	9	1	0	1	0	—	—	—	—	—
—Johnstown	ECHL	39	26	50	76	94	6	1	5	6	53

FETISOV, VIACHESLAV
D, DEVILS

PERSONAL: Born May 20, 1958, at Moscow, U.S.S.R. . . . 6-1/220. . . . Shoots left.
TRANSACTIONS/CAREER NOTES: Selected by Montreal Canadiens in 12th round (14th Canadiens pick, 201st overall) of NHL entry draft (June 15, 1978). . . . Selected by New Jersey Devils in eighth round (sixth Devils pick, 150th overall) of NHL entry draft (June 8, 1983). . . . Tore cartilage in left knee (November 22, 1989); missed six games. . . . Suffered bronchial pneumonia and hospitalized twice (November 28, 1990); missed 10 games.
HONORS: Won Soviet Player of the Year Award (1981-82 and 1985-86). . . . Won Gold Stick Award as Europe's top player (1983-84 and 1985-88).
MISCELLANEOUS: Member of 1980 silver medal-winning and 1984 and 1988 gold medal-winning U.S.S.R. Olympic teams.

Season Team	League	REGULAR SEASON					PLAYOFFS				
		Gms.	G	A	Pts.	Pen.	Gms.	G	A	Pts.	Pen.
76-77—Central Red Army	USSR	28	3	4	7	14	—	—	—	—	—
77-78—Central Red Army	USSR	35	9	18	27	46	—	—	—	—	—
78-79—Central Red Army	USSR	29	10	19	29	40	—	—	—	—	—
79-80—Central Red Army	USSR	37	10	14	24	46	—	—	—	—	—
80-81—Central Red Army	USSR	48	13	16	29	44	—	—	—	—	—
81-82—Central Red Army	USSR	46	15	26	41	20	—	—	—	—	—
82-83—Central Red Army	USSR	43	6	17	23	46	—	—	—	—	—
83-84—Central Red Army	USSR	44	19	30	49	38	—	—	—	—	—
84-85—Central Red Army	USSR	20	13	12	25	6	—	—	—	—	—
85-86—Central Red Army	USSR	40	15	19	34	12	—	—	—	—	—
86-87—Central Red Army	USSR	39	13	20	33	18	—	—	—	—	—
87-88—Central Red Army	USSR	46	18	17	35	26	—	—	—	—	—
88-89—Central Red Army	USSR	23	9	8	17	18	—	—	—	—	—
89-90—New Jersey	NHL	72	8	34	42	52	6	0	2	2	10
90-91—New Jersey	NHL	67	3	16	19	62	7	0	0	0	17
—Utica	AHL	1	1	1	2	0	—	—	—	—	—
91-92—New Jersey	NHL	70	3	23	26	108	6	0	3	3	8
NHL totals		209	14	73	87	222	19	0	5	5	35

FILIMONOV, DIMITRI
D, JETS

PERSONAL: Born October 14, 1971, at Perm, U.S.S.R. . . . 6-4/207. . . . Shoots right.
TRANSACTIONS/CAREER NOTES: Selected by Winnipeg Jets in third round (second Jets pick, 49th overall) of NHL entry draft (June 22, 1991).

Season Team	League	REGULAR SEASON					PLAYOFFS				
		Gms.	G	A	Pts.	Pen.	Gms.	G	A	Pts.	Pen.
90-91—Dynamo Moscow	USSR	45	4	6	10	12	—	—	—	—	—
91-92—Dynamo Moscow	CIS	38	3	2	5	12	—	—	—	—	—

FINLEY, JEFF
D, ISLANDERS

PERSONAL: Born April 14, 1967, at Edmonton, Alta.... 6-2/185.... Shoots left.
TRANSACTIONS/CAREER NOTES: Selected by New York Islanders as underage junior in third round (fourth Islanders pick, 55th overall) of NHL entry draft (June 15, 1985).... Suffered swollen left knee (September 1988).

Season Team	League	REGULAR SEASON					PLAYOFFS				
		Gms.	G	A	Pts.	Pen.	Gms.	G	A	Pts.	Pen.
83-84—Portland	WHL	5	0	0	0	0	5	0	1	1	4
—Summerland	BCJHL	49	0	21	21	14	—	—	—	—	—
84-85—Portland	WHL	69	6	44	50	57	6	1	2	3	2
85-86—Portland	WHL	70	11	59	70	83	15	1	7	8	16
86-87—Portland	WHL	72	13	53	66	113	20	1	†21	22	27
87-88—Springfield	AHL	52	5	18	23	50	—	—	—	—	—
—New York Islanders	NHL	10	0	5	5	15	1	0	0	0	2
88-89—New York Islanders	NHL	4	0	0	0	6	—	—	—	—	—
—Springfield	AHL	65	3	16	19	55	—	—	—	—	—
89-90—New York Islanders	NHL	11	0	1	1	0	5	0	2	2	2
—Springfield	AHL	57	1	15	16	41	13	1	4	5	23
90-91—Capital District	AHL	67	10	34	44	34	—	—	—	—	—
—New York Islanders	NHL	11	0	0	0	4	—	—	—	—	—
91-92—Capital District	AHL	20	1	9	10	6	—	—	—	—	—
—New York Islanders	NHL	51	1	10	11	26	—	—	—	—	—
NHL totals		87	1	16	17	51	6	0	2	2	4

FINN, STEVEN
D, NORDIQUES

PERSONAL: Born August 20, 1966, at Laval, Que.... 6-0/198.... Shoots left.
TRANSACTIONS/CAREER NOTES: Selected by Quebec Nordiques as underage junior in third round (third Nordiques pick, 57th overall) of NHL entry draft (June 9, 1984).... Separated left shoulder (January 31, 1990).... Lacerated right index finger (October 25, 1990); missed five games.... Sprained wrist (November 25, 1991); missed six games.... Sprained right wrist (February 15, 1992); missed seven games.
HONORS: Named to QMJHL All-Star second team (1984-85).

Season Team	League	REGULAR SEASON					PLAYOFFS				
		Gms.	G	A	Pts.	Pen.	Gms.	G	A	Pts.	Pen.
82-83—Laval	QMJHL	69	7	30	37	108	6	0	2	2	6
83-84—Laval	QMJHL	68	7	39	46	159	14	1	6	7	27
84-85—Laval	QMJHL	61	20	33	53	169	—	—	—	—	—
—Fredericton	AHL	4	0	0	0	14	6	1	1	2	4
85-86—Laval	QMJHL	29	4	15	19	111	14	6	16	22	57
—Quebec	NHL	17	0	1	1	28	—	—	—	—	—
86-87—Fredericton	AHL	38	7	19	26	73	—	—	—	—	—
—Quebec	NHL	36	2	5	7	40	13	0	2	2	29
87-88—Quebec	NHL	75	3	7	10	198	—	—	—	—	—
88-89—Quebec	NHL	77	2	6	8	235	—	—	—	—	—
89-90—Quebec	NHL	64	3	9	12	208	—	—	—	—	—
90-91—Quebec	NHL	71	6	13	19	228	—	—	—	—	—
91-92—Quebec	NHL	65	4	7	11	194	—	—	—	—	—
NHL totals		405	20	48	68	1131	13	0	2	2	29

FIORENTINO, PETER
D, RANGERS

PERSONAL: Born December 22, 1968, at Niagara Falls, Ont.... 6-1/205.... Shoots right.
TRANSACTIONS/CAREER NOTES: Selected by New York Rangers in 11th round (eleventh Rangers pick, 215th overall) of NHL entry draft (June 11, 1988).... Suspended three games (October 19, 1990).... Tore tendon in left ring finger (March 1991).

Season Team	League	REGULAR SEASON					PLAYOFFS				
		Gms.	G	A	Pts.	Pen.	Gms.	G	A	Pts.	Pen.
84-85—Niagara Falls Jr. B	OHA	38	7	10	17	149	—	—	—	—	—
85-86—Sault Ste. Marie	OHL	58	1	6	7	87	—	—	—	—	—
86-87—Sault Ste. Marie	OHL	64	1	12	13	187	4	2	1	3	5
87-88—Sault Ste. Marie	OHL	65	5	27	32	252	6	2	2	4	21
88-89—Sault Ste. Marie	OHL	55	5	24	29	220	—	—	—	—	—
—Denver	IHL	10	0	0	0	39	4	0	0	0	24
89-90—Flint	IHL	64	2	7	9	302	—	—	—	—	—
90-91—Binghamton	AHL	55	2	11	13	361	1	0	0	0	0
91-92—Binghamton	AHL	70	2	11	13	340	5	0	1	1	24
—New York Rangers	NHL	1	0	0	0	0	—	—	—	—	—
NHL totals		1	0	0	0	0					

FISET, STEPHANE
G, NORDIQUES

PERSONAL: Born June 17, 1970, at Montreal.... 6-0/175.... Shoots left.
TRANSACTIONS/CAREER NOTES: Selected by Quebec Nordiques in second round (third Nordiques pick, 24th overall) of NHL entry draft (June 13, 1987).... Underwent shoulder surgery (May, 1989).... Twisted knee (December 9, 1990).... Sprained left knee (January 14, 1992); missed 12 games.
HONORS: Won Can.HL Goaltender of the Year Award (1988-89).... Won Jacques Plante Trophy (1988-89).... Named to QMJHL All-Star first team (1988-89).

Season	Team	League	Gms.	Min.	W	L	T	GA	SO	Avg.	Gms.	Min.	W	L	GA	SO	Avg.
										REGULAR SEASON					PLAYOFFS		
87-88—Victoriaville	QMJHL	40	2221	14	17	4	146	1	3.94	2	163	0	2	10	0	3.68
88-89—Victoriaville	QMJHL	43	2401	25	14	0	138	1	*3.45	12	711	9	2	33	0	*2.78
89-90—Victoriaville	QMJHL	24	1383	14	6	3	63	1	2.73	*14	*790	7	6	*49	0	3.72
—Quebec	NHL	6	342	0	5	1	34	0	5.96	—	—	—	—	—	—	—
90-91—Quebec	NHL	3	186	0	2	1	12	0	3.87	—	—	—	—	—	—	—
—Halifax	AHL	36	1902	10	15	8	131	0	4.13	—	—	—	—	—	—	—
91-92—Halifax	AHL	29	1675	8	14	6	110	†3	3.94	—	—	—	—	—	—	—
—Quebec	NHL	23	1133	7	10	2	71	1	3.76	—	—	—	—	—	—	—
NHL totals		32	1661	7	17	4	117	1	4.23							

FISHER, CRAIG
C, OILERS

PERSONAL: Born June 30, 1970, at Oshawa, Ont. . . . 6-3/180. . . . Shoots left. . . . Full name: Craig Francis Fisher.
COLLEGE: Miami of Ohio.
TRANSACTIONS/CAREER NOTES: Suffered concussion (October 1987). . . . Selected by Philadelphia Flyers in third round (third Flyers pick, 56th overall) of NHL entry draft (June 11, 1988). . . . Traded by Flyers with RW Scott Mellanby and LW Craig Berube to Edmonton Oilers for RW Dave Brown, D Corey Foster and the NHL rights to RW Jari Kurri (May 30, 1991).
HONORS: Named to CCHA All-Rookie team (1988-89). . . . Named to CCHA All-Star first team (1989-90).

Season	Team	League	Gms.	G	A	Pts.	Pen.	Gms.	G	A	Pts.	Pen.
				REGULAR SEASON					PLAYOFFS			
86-87—Oshawa Jr. B	OHA	34	22	26	48	18	—	—	—	—	—
87-88—Oshawa Jr. B	OHA	36	42	34	76	48	—	—	—	—	—
88-89—Miami of Ohio	CCHA	37	22	20	42	37	—	—	—	—	—
89-90—Miami of Ohio	CCHA	39	37	29	66	38	—	—	—	—	—
—Philadelphia	NHL	2	0	0	0	0	—	—	—	—	—
90-91—Hershey	AHL	77	43	36	79	46	7	5	3	8	2
—Philadelphia	NHL	2	0	0	0	0	—	—	—	—	—
91-92—Cape Breton	AHL	60	20	25	45	28	1	0	0	0	0
NHL totals		4	0	0	0	0					

FITZGERALD, RUSTY
C, PENGUINS

PERSONAL: Born October 4, 1972, at Minneapolis. . . . 6-1/185. . . . Shoots left.
HIGH SCHOOL: William M. Kelley (Silver Bay, Minn.), then East (Duluth, Minn.).
TRANSACTIONS/CAREER NOTES: Selected by Pittsburgh Penguins in second round (second Penguins pick, 38th overall) of NHL entry draft (June 22, 1991).

Season	Team	League	Gms.	G	A	Pts.	Pen.	Gms.	G	A	Pts.	Pen.
				REGULAR SEASON					PLAYOFFS			
87-88—Silver Bay H.S.	Minn. H.S.	20	19	26	45	18	—	—	—	—	—
88-89—Silver Bay H.S.	Minn. H.S.	22	24	25	49	26	—	—	—	—	—
89-90—Silver Bay H.S.	Minn. H.S.	21	25	26	51	24	—	—	—	—	—
—Northland Jr. B	Minn.	20	11	5	16	12	—	—	—	—	—
90-91—Duluth East High School	Minn. H.S.	15	14	11	25		—	—	—	—	—
91-92—Minnesota-Duluth	WCHA	37	9	11	20	40	—	—	—	—	—

FITZGERALD, TOM
RW/C, ISLANDERS

PERSONAL: Born August 28, 1968, at Melrose, Mass. . . . 6-1/197. . . . Shoots right. . . . Full name: Thomas James Fitzgerald.
HIGH SCHOOL: Austin Prep (Reading, Mass.).
COLLEGE: Providence.
TRANSACTIONS/CAREER NOTES: Selected by New York Islanders in first round (first Islanders pick, 17th overall) of NHL entry draft (June 21, 1986). . . . Bruised left knee (November 7, 1990). . . . Strained abdominal muscle (October 22, 1991); missed 16 games.

Season	Team	League	Gms.	G	A	Pts.	Pen.	Gms.	G	A	Pts.	Pen.
				REGULAR SEASON					PLAYOFFS			
84-85—Austin Prep.	Mass. H.S.	18	20	21	41		—	—	—	—	—
85-86—Austin Prep.	Mass. H.S.	24	35	38	73		—	—	—	—	—
86-87—Providence College	Hockey East	15	2	0	2	2	—	—	—	—	—
87-88—Providence College	Hockey East	36	19	15	34	50	—	—	—	—	—
88-89—Springfield	AHL	61	24	18	42	43	—	—	—	—	—
—New York Islanders	NHL	23	3	5	8	10	—	—	—	—	—
89-90—Springfield	AHL	53	30	23	53	32	14	2	9	11	13
—New York Islanders	NHL	19	2	5	7	4	4	1	0	1	4
90-91—New York Islanders	NHL	41	5	5	10	24	—	—	—	—	—
—Capital District	AHL	27	7	7	14	50	—	—	—	—	—
91-92—New York Islanders	NHL	45	6	11	17	28	—	—	—	—	—
—Capital District	AHL	4	1	1	2	4	—	—	—	—	—
NHL totals		128	16	26	42	66	4	1	0	1	4

FITZPATRICK, MARK
G, ISLANDERS

PERSONAL: Born November 13, 1968, at Toronto. . . . 6-2/190. . . . Shoots left.
TRANSACTIONS/CAREER NOTES: Injured knee (February 1987). . . . Selected by Los Angeles Kings as underage junior in second round (second Kings pick, 27th overall) of NHL entry draft (June 13, 1987). . . . Traded by Kings with D Wayne McBean and future considerations to New York Islanders for G Kelly Hrudey (February 22, 1989); D Doug Crossman sent to the

F

Islanders on May 23 to complete the trade. . . . Developed Eosinophilic Myalgia Syndrome (EMS) after a reaction to L-Trytophan, an ingredient in a vitamin supplement (September 1990); returned to play (March 1991). . . . Suffered recurrance of EMS and underwent biopsy on right thigh (October 22, 1991); missed 10 games.

HONORS: Won Top Goaltender Trophy (1985-86). . . . Named to WHL All-Star second team (1985-86 and 1987-88). . . . Won Bill Masterton Memorial Trophy (1991-92).

				REGULAR SEASON							PLAYOFFS					
Season	Team	League	Gms.	Min.	W	L	T	GA	SO	Avg.	Gms.	Min.	W	L	GA SO	Avg.
83-84—Revelstoke	BCJHL	21	1019				90	0	5.30	—	—	—	—	— —	—
84-85—Medicine Hat	WHL	3	180				9	0	3.00	—	—	—	—	— —	—
85-86—Medicine Hat	WHL	41	2074	26	6	1	99	1	*2.86	*19	986	12	5	*58 0	3.53
86-87—Medicine Hat	WHL	50	2844	31	11	4	159	*4	3.35	*20	*1224	12	8	71 †1	3.48
87-88—Medicine Hat	WHL	63	3600	36	15	6	194	†2	*3.23	16	959	12	4	52 †1	*3.25
88-89—New Haven	AHL	18	980	10	5	1	54	1	3.31	—	—	—	—	— —	—
—Los Angeles	NHL	17	957	6	7	3	64	0	4.01	—	—	—	—	— —	—
—New York Islanders	NHL	11	627	3	5	2	41	0	3.92	—	—	—	—	— —	—
89-90—New York Islanders	NHL	47	2653	19	19	5	150	3	3.39	4	152	0	2	13 0	5.13
90-91—Capital District	AHL	12	734	3	7	2	47	0	3.84	—	—	—	—	— —	—
—New York Islanders	NHL	2	120	1	1	0	6	0	3.00	—	—	—	—	— —	—
91-92—Capital District	AHL	14	782	6	5	1	39	0	2.99	—	—	—	—	— —	—
—New York Islanders	NHL	30	1743	11	13	5	93	0	3.20	—	—	—	—	— —	—
NHL totals		107	6100	40	45	15	354	3	3.48	4	152	0	2	13 0	5.13

FITZPATRICK, ROSS
LW, RANGERS

PERSONAL: Born October 7, 1960, at Penticton, B.C. . . . 6-0/195. . . . Shoots left. . . . Full name: Ross Edward Fitzpatrick.
COLLEGE: Western Michigan.
TRANSACTIONS/CAREER NOTES: Selected by Philadelphia Flyers in seventh round (seventh Flyers pick, 147th overall) of NHL entry draft (June 11, 1980). . . . Broke hand (December 1982). . . . Underwent surgery for separated shoulder (January 10, 1985). . . . Underwent knee surgery (January 1987). . . . Suffered chip fracture of ankle bone (February 25, 1990); missed six games. . . . Signed as free agent by New York Rangers (August 1990).
HONORS: Named to CCHA All-Star first team (1980-81). . . . Named to AHL All-Star second team (1985-86 and 1989-90).

			REGULAR SEASON					PLAYOFFS			
Season	Team	League	Gms.	G	A	Pts.	Pen.	Gms.	G	A	Pts.	Pen.
77-78—Penticton	BCJHL	65	63	63	126	80	—	—	—	—	—
78-79—Western Michigan Univ.	CCHA	35	16	21	37	31	—	—	—	—	—
79-80—Western Michigan Univ.	CCHA	34	26	33	59	22	—	—	—	—	—
80-81—Western Michigan Univ.	CCHA	36	28	43	71	22	—	—	—	—	—
81-82—Western Michigan Univ.	CCHA	33	30	28	58	34	—	—	—	—	—
82-83—Maine	AHL	66	29	28	57	32	12	5	1	6	12
—Philadelphia	NHL	1	0	0	0	0	—	—	—	—	—
83-84—Springfield	AHL	45	33	30	63	28	4	3	2	5	2
—Philadelphia	NHL	12	4	2	6	0	—	—	—	—	—
84-85—Hershey	AHL	35	26	15	41	8	—	—	—	—	—
—Philadelphia	NHL	5	1	0	1	0	—	—	—	—	—
85-86—Philadelphia	NHL	2	0	0	0	0	—	—	—	—	—
—Hershey	AHL	77	50	47	97	28	17	9	7	16	10
86-87—Hershey	AHL	66	45	40	85	34	5	1	4	5	10
87-88—Hershey	AHL	35	14	17	31	12	12	†11	4	15	8
88-89—Vienna	Austria				Statistics unavailable.						
—Hershey	AHL	11	6	9	15	4	9	2	2	4	4
89-90—Hershey	AHL	74	45	*58	103	26	—	—	—	—	—
90-91—Binghamton	AHL	69	26	29	55	26	10	3	1	4	4
91-92—Binghamton	AHL	76	34	38	72	32	10	1	3	4	2
NHL totals		20	5	2	7	0					

FITZSIMMONS, JASON
G, CANUCKS

PERSONAL: Born June 3, 1971, at Regina, Sask. . . . 5-11/185. . . . Shoots left.
TRANSACTIONS/CAREER NOTES: Selected by Vancouver Canucks in 11th round (10th Canucks pick, 227th overall) of NHL entry draft (June 22, 1991).

			REGULAR SEASON							PLAYOFFS					
Season	Team	League	Gms.	Min.	W	L	T	GA	SO	Avg.	Gms.	Min.	W	L	GA SO	Avg.
89-90—Moose Jaw	WHL	28	1392	10	10	1	90	0	3.88	—	—	—	— —	—
90-91—Moose Jaw	WHL	44	2170	15	23	2	179	0	4.95	8	481	4	4	27 0	3.37
91-92—Moose Jaw	WHL	60	3286	29	28	1	222	0	4.05	4	186	0	4	27 0	8.71

FLAHERTY, WADE
G, SHARKS

PERSONAL: Born January 11, 1968, at Terreace, B.C. . . . 6-0/170. . . . Shoots right.
TRANSACTIONS/CAREER NOTES: Selected by Buffalo Sabres in ninth round (tenth Sabres pick, 181st overall) of NHL entry draft (June 11, 1988). . . . Signed as free agent by San Jose Sharks (September 3, 1991).
HONORS: Named to WHL All-Star second team (1987-88). . . . Won ECHL Playoff Most Valuable Player Award (1989-90). . . . Shared James Norris Memorial Trophy with Arturs Irbe (1991-92).

			REGULAR SEASON							PLAYOFFS					
Season	Team	League	Gms.	Min.	W	L	T	GA	SO	Avg.	Gms.	Min.	W	L	GA SO	Avg.
84-85—Kelowna Wings	WHL	1	55	0	0	0	5	0	5.45	—	—	—	— — —	—
85-86—Seattle	WHL	9	271	1	3	0	36	0	7.97	—	—	—	— — —	—
—Spokane Chiefs	WHL	5	161	0	3	0	21	0	7.83	—	—	—	— — —	—

Season Team	League	REGULAR SEASON								PLAYOFFS						
		Gms.	Min.	W	L	T	GA	SO	Avg.	Gms.	Min.	W	L	GA	SO	Avg.
86-87—Nanaimo	BCJHL	15	830				53	0	3.83	—	—	—	—	—	—	—
—Victoria	WHL	3	127	0	2	0	16	0	7.56	—	—	—	—	—	—	—
87-88—Victoria	WHL	36	2052	20	15	0	135	0	3.95	5	300	2	3	18	0	3.60
88-89—Victoria	WHL	42	2408	21	19	0	180	0	4.49	8	480	3	5	35	0	4.38
89-90—Kalamazoo	IHL	1	13	0	0	0	0	0	0.00	—	—	—	—	—	—	—
—Greensboro	ECHL	27	1308	12	10	0	96		4.40	†9	567	8	1	21	0	*2.22
90-91—Kansas City	IHL	†56	2990	16	31	4	*224	0	4.49	—	—	—	—	—	—	—
91-92—Kansas City	IHL	43	2603	26	14	3	140	1	3.23	1	1	0	0	0	0	0.00
—San Jose	NHL	3	178	0	3	0	13	0	4.38	—	—	—	—	—	—	—
NHL totals		3	178	0	3	0	13	0	4.38							

FLATLEY, PATRICK
RW, ISLANDERS

PERSONAL: Born October 3, 1963, at Toronto. . . . 6-2/200. . . . Shoots right. . . . Full name: Patrick William Flatley.
HIGH SCHOOL: Henry Carr (Rexdale, Ont.).
COLLEGE: Wisconsin.
TRANSACTIONS/CAREER NOTES: Selected by New York Islanders as underage junior in first round (first Islanders pick, 21st overall) of NHL entry draft (June 9, 1982). . . . Broke bone in left hand (April 1985). . . . Strained left knee ligaments (February 4, 1987). . . . Separated right shoulder (November 1987). . . . Injured right knee (January 1988). . . . Underwent reconstructive knee surgery (February 1988). . . . Injured right knee (December 1988). . . . Suffered sore right ankle (February 1989). . . . Re-injured right knee (March 1989). . . . Bruised right ankle (October 1989). . . . Pulled groin muscle (February 13, 1990). . . . Re-injured groin; (March 2, 1990); missed six games. . . . Sprained right knee (October 13, 1990). . . . Bruised left knee (November 30, 1990). . . . Fractured finger on left hand (February 16, 1991). . . . Fractured right thumb (December 19, 1991); missed 42 games.
HONORS: Named to NCAA All-America West team (1982-83). . . . Named to NCAA All-Tournament team (1982-83). . . . Named to WCHA All-Star first team (1982-83).

Season Team	League	REGULAR SEASON					PLAYOFFS				
		Gms.	G	A	Pts.	Pen.	Gms.	G	A	Pts.	Pen.
80-81—Henry Carr H.S.	MTHL	42	30	61	91	122	—	—	—	—	—
81-82—University of Wisconsin	WCHA	33	17	20	37	65	—	—	—	—	—
82-83—University of Wisconsin	WCHA	43	25	44	69	76	—	—	—	—	—
83-84—Canadian Olympic Team	Int'l	57	33	17	50	136	—	—	—	—	—
—New York Islanders	NHL	16	2	7	9	6	21	9	6	15	14
84-85—New York Islanders	NHL	78	20	31	51	106	4	1	0	1	6
85-86—New York Islanders	NHL	73	18	34	52	66	3	0	0	0	21
86-87—New York Islanders	NHL	63	16	35	51	81	11	3	2	5	6
87-88—New York Islanders	NHL	40	9	15	24	28	—	—	—	—	—
88-89—New York Islanders	NHL	41	10	15	25	31	—	—	—	—	—
—Springfield	AHL	2	1	1	2	2	—	—	—	—	—
89-90—New York Islanders	NHL	62	17	32	49	101	5	3	0	3	2
90-91—New York Islanders	NHL	56	20	25	45	74	—	—	—	—	—
91-92—New York Islanders	NHL	38	8	28	36	31	—	—	—	—	—
NHL totals		467	120	222	342	524	44	16	8	24	49

FLETCHER, STEVEN
D, JETS

PERSONAL: Born March 31, 1962, at Montreal. . . . 6-2/180. . . . Shoots left.
TRANSACTIONS/CAREER NOTES: Selected by Calgary Flames as underage junior in 10th round (11th Flames pick, 202nd overall) of NHL entry draft (June 11, 1980). . . . Signed as free agent by Montreal Canadiens (August 21, 1984). . . . Signed as free agent by Winnipeg Jets (July 15, 1988). . . . Traded by Jets to Philadelphia Flyers for future considerations (December 12, 1988).

Season Team	League	REGULAR SEASON					PLAYOFFS				
		Gms.	G	A	Pts.	Pen.	Gms.	G	A	Pts.	Pen.
79-80—Hull	QMJHL	61	2	14	16	183	—	—	—	—	—
80-81—Hull	QMJHL	66	4	13	17	231	—	—	—	—	—
81-82—Hull	QMJHL	60	4	20	24	230	—	—	—	—	—
82-83—Fort Wayne	IHL	34	1	9	10	115	—	—	—	—	—
—Sherbrooke	AHL	36	0	1	1	119	—	—	—	—	—
83-84—Sherbrooke	AHL	77	3	7	10	208	—	—	—	—	—
84-85—Sherbrooke	AHL	50	2	4	6	192	13	0	0	0	48
85-86—Sherbrooke	AHL	64	2	12	14	293	—	—	—	—	—
86-87—Sherbrooke	AHL	70	15	11	26	261	17	5	5	10	82
87-88—Montreal	NHL	—	—	—	—	—	1	0	0	0	5
—Sherbrooke	AHL	76	8	21	29	338	6	2	1	3	28
88-89—Hershey	AHL	29	5	8	13	91	—	—	—	—	—
—Moncton	AHL	23	1	1	2	89	—	—	—	—	—
—Winnipeg	NHL	3	0	0	0	5	—	—	—	—	—
89-90—Hershey	AHL	28	1	1	2	132	—	—	—	—	—
90-91—Fort Wayne	IHL	66	7	9	16	289	15	2	0	2	70
91-92—Fort Wayne	IHL	60	8	3	11	320	5	0	0	0	14
NHL totals		3	0	0	0	5	1	0	0	0	5

FLEURY, THEOREN
C/RW, FLAMES

PERSONAL: Born June 29, 1968, at Oxbow, Sask. . . . 5-6/155. . . . Shoots right.
TRANSACTIONS/CAREER NOTES: Selected by Calgary Flames in eighth round (ninth Flames pick, 166th overall) of NHL entry draft (June 13, 1987).
HONORS: Named to WHL All-Star first team (1986-87). . . . Shared Bob Clarke Trophy

F

with Joe Sakic (1987-88).... Named to WHL All-Star second team (1987-88).... Shared Alka-Seltzer Plus Award with Marty McSorley (1990-91).

Season Team	League	REGULAR SEASON					PLAYOFFS				
		Gms.	G	A	Pts.	Pen.	Gms.	G	A	Pts.	Pen.
84-85—Moose Jaw	WHL	71	29	46	75	82	—	—	—	—	—
85-86—Moose Jaw	WHL	72	43	65	108	124	—	—	—	—	—
86-87—Moose Jaw	WHL	66	61	68	129	110	9	7	9	16	34
87-88—Moose Jaw	WHL	65	68	92	†160	235	—	—	—	—	—
—Salt Lake City	IHL	2	3	4	7	7	8	11	5	16	16
88-89—Salt Lake City	IHL	40	37	37	74	81	—	—	—	—	—
—Calgary	NHL	36	14	20	34	46	22	5	6	11	24
89-90—Calgary	NHL	80	31	35	66	157	6	2	3	5	10
90-91—Calgary	NHL	79	51	53	104	136	7	2	5	7	14
91-92—Calgary	NHL	80	33	40	73	133	—	—	—	—	—
NHL totals		275	129	148	277	472	35	9	14	23	48

FLICHEL, TODD
D, JETS

PERSONAL: Born September 14, 1964, at Osgoode, Ont.... 6-3/195.... Shoots right.
COLLEGE: Bowling Green State.
TRANSACTIONS/CAREER NOTES: Selected by Winnipeg Jets in ninth round (10th Jets pick, 169th overall) of NHL entry draft (June 8, 1983).

Season Team	League	REGULAR SEASON					PLAYOFFS				
		Gms.	G	A	Pts.	Pen.	Gms.	G	A	Pts.	Pen.
83-84—Bowling Green State	CCHA	44	1	3	4	12	—	—	—	—	—
84-85—Bowling Green State	CCHA	42	5	7	12	62	—	—	—	—	—
85-86—Bowling Green State	CCHA	42	3	10	13	84	—	—	—	—	—
86-87—Bowling Green State	CCHA	42	4	15	19	75	—	—	—	—	—
87-88—Winnipeg	NHL	2	0	0	0	14	—	—	—	—	—
—Moncton	AHL	65	5	12	17	102	—	—	—	—	—
88-89—Moncton	AHL	74	2	29	31	81	10	1	4	5	25
—Winnipeg	NHL	1	0	0	0	0	—	—	—	—	—
89-90—Winnipeg	NHL	3	0	1	1	2	—	—	—	—	—
—Moncton	AHL	65	7	14	21	74	—	—	—	—	—
90-91—Moncton	AHL	75	8	21	29	44	9	0	0	0	8
91-92—Fort Wayne	IHL	64	3	10	13	79	7	0	0	0	2
NHL totals		6	0	1	1	16					

FLOMENHOFT, STEVEN
C, SENATORS

PERSONAL: Born May 4, 1971, at Riverwoods, Ill.... 6-0/215.... Shoots right.... Full name: Steven T. Flomenhoft.
HIGH SCHOOL: Avon Old Farms School for Boys (Conn.).
COLLEGE: Harvard.
TRANSACTIONS/CAREER NOTES: Selected by Ottawa Senators in NHL supplemental draft (June 19, 1992).

Season Team	League	REGULAR SEASON					PLAYOFFS				
		Gms.	G	A	Pts.	Pen.	Gms.	G	A	Pts.	Pen.
89-90—Harvard University	ECAC	28	5	5	10	22	—	—	—	—	—
90-91—Harvard University	ECAC	29	12	14	26	48	—	—	—	—	—
91-92—Harvard University	ECAC	27	14	17	31	30	—	—	—	—	—

FOGARTY, BRYAN
D, PENGUINS

PERSONAL: Born June 11, 1969, at Montreal.... 6-1/190.... Shoots left.
TRANSACTIONS/CAREER NOTES: Selected by Quebec Nordiques as underage junior in first round (first Nordiques pick, ninth overall) of NHL entry draft (June 13, 1987).... Traded by Kingston Raiders to Niagara Falls Thunder for D Garth Joy, LW Jason Simon, Kevin Lune and a fourth-round pick in 1989 draft (August 1988).... Underwent appendectomy (September 1989).... Underwent substance-abuse treatment (February 1991); missed one month.... Left Nordiques to report to halfway house (March 28, 1991).... Suffered from the flu (November 30, 1991); missed five games.... Traded by Nordiques to Pittsburgh Penguins for rights to RW Scott Young (March 10, 1992).
HONORS: Named to OHL All-Star first team (1986-87 and 1988-89).... Won Can.HL Player of the Year Award (1988-89).... Won Can.HL Defenseman of the Year Award (1988-89).... Won Can.HL Plus/Minus Award (1988-89).... Won Red Tilson Trophy (1988-89).... Won Eddie Powers Memorial Trophy (1988-89).... Won Max Kaminsky Trophy (1988-89).

Season Team	League	REGULAR SEASON					PLAYOFFS				
		Gms.	G	A	Pts.	Pen.	Gms.	G	A	Pts.	Pen.
84-85—Aurora	OHA	66	18	39	57	180	—	—	—	—	—
85-86—Kingston	OHL	47	2	19	21	14	10	1	3	4	4
86-87—Kingston	OHL	56	20	50	70	46	12	2	3	5	5
87-88—Kingston	OHL	48	11	36	47	50	—	—	—	—	—
88-89—Niagara Falls	OHL	60	47	*108	*155	88	17	10	22	32	36
89-90—Quebec	NHL	45	4	10	14	31	—	—	—	—	—
—Halifax	AHL	22	5	14	19	6	6	4	2	6	0
90-91—Halifax	AHL	5	0	2	2	0	—	—	—	—	—
—Quebec	NHL	45	9	22	31	24	—	—	—	—	—
91-92—Quebec	NHL	20	3	12	15	16	—	—	—	—	—
—Halifax	AHL	2	0	0	0	2	—	—	—	—	—
—New Haven	AHL	4	0	1	1	6	—	—	—	—	—
—Muskegon	IHL	8	2	4	6	30	—	—	—	—	—
NHL totals		110	16	44	60	71					

FOLIGNO, MIKE

RW, MAPLE LEAFS

PERSONAL: Born January 29, 1959, at Sudbury, Ont. . . . 6-2/200. . . . Shoots right. . . . Full name: Mike Anthony Foligno.

TRANSACTIONS/CAREER NOTES: Selected by Detroit Red Wings in first round (first Red Wings pick, third overall) of NHL entry draft (August 9, 1979). . . . Traded by Red Wings with C Dale McCourt, C Brent Peterson and future considerations to Buffalo Sabres for G Bob Sauve, D Jim Schoenfeld and LW/C Derek Smith (December 2, 1981). . . . Injured tailbone (October 31, 1982). . . . Injured shoulder (February 12, 1983). . . . Bruised kidney (December 7, 1986). . . . Suffered back spasms (February 1988). . . . Pulled rib cartilage (January 14, 1989). . . . Fractured left thumb (February 18, 1990). . . . Traded by Sabres with an eighth-round pick in 1991 draft (C Thomas Kucharcik) to Toronto Maple Leafs for D Brian Curran and LW Lou Franceschetti (December 17, 1990). . . . Tore medial collateral ligament in the left knee (December 18, 1990); missed seven games. . . . Fractured tibia (December 21, 1991); missed remainder of season.

HONORS: Won Red Tilson Trophy (1978-79). . . . Won Eddie Powers Memorial Trophy (1978-79). . . . Won Jim Mahon Memorial Trophy (1978-79). . . . Named to OMJHL All-Star first team (1978-79).

			REGULAR SEASON					PLAYOFFS				
Season Team	League	Gms.	G	A	Pts.	Pen.	Gms.	G	A	Pts.	Pen.
75-76—Sudbury	OHA Mj. Jr. A	57	22	14	36	45	—	—	—	—	—
76-77—Sudbury	OMJHL	66	31	44	75	62	—	—	—	—	—
77-78—Sudbury	OMJHL	67	47	39	86	112	—	—	—	—	—
78-79—Sudbury	OMJHL	68	65	85	*150	98	10	5	5	10	14
79-80—Detroit	NHL	80	36	35	71	109	—	—	—	—	—
80-81—Detroit	NHL	80	28	35	63	210	—	—	—	—	—
81-82—Detroit	NHL	26	13	13	26	28	—	—	—	—	—
—Buffalo	NHL	66	20	31	51	149	4	2	0	2	9
82-83—Buffalo	NHL	66	22	25	47	135	10	2	3	5	39
83-84—Buffalo	NHL	70	32	31	63	151	3	2	1	3	19
84-85—Buffalo	NHL	77	27	29	56	154	5	1	3	4	12
85-86—Buffalo	NHL	79	41	39	80	168	—	—	—	—	—
86-87—Buffalo	NHL	75	30	29	59	176	—	—	—	—	—
87-88—Buffalo	NHL	74	29	28	57	220	6	3	2	5	31
88-89—Buffalo	NHL	75	27	22	49	156	5	3	1	4	21
89-90—Buffalo	NHL	61	15	25	40	99	6	0	1	1	12
90-91—Buffalo	NHL	31	4	5	9	42	—	—	—	—	—
—Toronto	NHL	37	8	7	15	65	—	—	—	—	—
91-92—Toronto	NHL	33	6	8	14	50	—	—	—	—	—
NHL totals		920	338	362	700	1912	39	13	11	24	143

FOOTE, ADAM

D, NORDIQUES

PERSONAL: Born July 10, 1971, at Toronto. . . . 6-1/180. . . . Shoots right. . . . Full name: Adam David Vernon Foote.

TRANSACTIONS/CAREER NOTES: Selected by Quebec Nordiques in second round (second Nordiques pick, 22nd overall) of NHL entry draft (June 17, 1989). . . . Fractured right thumb (February 1992); missed remainder of season.

HONORS: Named to OHL All-Star first team (1990-91).

			REGULAR SEASON					PLAYOFFS				
Season Team	League	Gms.	G	A	Pts.	Pen.	Gms.	G	A	Pts.	Pen.
88-89—Sault Ste. Marie	OHL	66	7	32	39	120	—	—	—	—	—
89-90—Sault Ste. Marie	OHL	61	12	43	55	199	—	—	—	—	—
90-91—Sault Ste. Marie	OHL	59	18	51	69	93	14	5	12	17	28
91-92—Quebec	NHL	46	2	5	7	44	—	—	—	—	—
—Halifax	AHL	6	0	1	1	2	—	—	—	—	—
NHL totals		46	2	5	7	44					

FORSBERG, PETER

C, NORDIQUES

PERSONAL: Born July 20, 1973, at Ornskoldsvik, Sweden. . . . 6-0/181. . . . Shoots left.

TRANSACTIONS/CAREER NOTES: Selected by Philadelphia Flyers in first round (first Flyers pick, sixth overall) of NHL entry draft (June 22, 1991). . . . Traded by Flyers with G Ron Hextall, C Mike Ricci, D Steve Duchesne, D Kerry Huffman, first-round pick in 1993 draft, cash and future considerations to Quebec Nordiques for C Eric Lindros (June 20, 1992); Flyers sent LW Chris Simon and first-round pick in 1994 draft to Nordiques to complete deal (July 21, 1992).

			REGULAR SEASON					PLAYOFFS				
Season Team	League	Gms.	G	A	Pts.	Pen.	Gms.	G	A	Pts.	Pen.
89-90—MoDo	Sweden Jr.	30	15	12	27	42	—	—	—	—	—
90-91—MoDo	Sweden	23	7	10	17	22	—	—	—	—	—
91-92—MoDo	Sweden	39	9	19	28	78	—	—	—	—	—

FORSLUND, TOMAS

RW, FLAMES

PERSONAL: Born November 24, 1968, at Falun, Sweden. . . . 6-0/185. . . . Shoots left.

TRANSACTIONS/CAREER NOTES: Selected by Calgary Flames in fourth round (fourth Flames pick, 85th overall) of NHL entry draft (June 11, 1988). . . . Strained right knee (November 16, 1991); missed 11 games. . . . Strained right knee (December 17, 1991).

			REGULAR SEASON					PLAYOFFS				
Season Team	League	Gms.	G	A	Pts.	Pen.	Gms.	G	A	Pts.	Pen.
86-87—Leksand	Sweden	23	3	5	8		—	—	—	—	—
87-88—Leksand	Sweden	37	9	10	19		—	—	—	—	—
88-89—Leksand	Sweden	39	14	16	30	56	—	—	—	—	—
89-90—Leksand	Sweden	38	14	21	35	48	3	0	1	1	2
90-91—Swedish National Team	Int'l	21	6	9	15	26	—	—	—	—	—
—Leksand	Sweden	39	15	19	34	54	4	2	3	5	0

F

Season Team	League	REGULAR SEASON					PLAYOFFS				
		Gms.	G	A	Pts.	Pen.	Gms.	G	A	Pts.	Pen.
91-92—Calgary	NHL	38	5	9	14	12	—	—	—	—	—
—Salt Lake City	IHL	22	10	6	16	25	5	2	2	4	2
NHL totals		38	5	9	14	12					

FORTIER, MARC
C, NORDIQUES

PERSONAL: Born February 26, 1966, at Sherbrooke, Que. . . . 6-0/192. . . . Shoots right.
TRANSACTIONS/CAREER NOTES: Signed as free agent by Quebec Nordiques (February 3, 1987). . . . Injured groin (February 18, 1992).
HONORS: Won Jean Beliveau Trophy (1986-87). . . . Named to QMJHL All-Star first team (1986-87).

Season Team	League	REGULAR SEASON					PLAYOFFS				
		Gms.	G	A	Pts.	Pen.	Gms.	G	A	Pts.	Pen.
84-85—Chicoutimi	QMJHL	68	35	63	98	114	14	8	4	12	16
85-86—Chicoutimi	QMJHL	71	47	86	133	49	9	2	14	16	12
86-87—Chicoutimi	QMJHL	65	66	*135	*201	39	19	11	*40	*51	20
87-88—Quebec	NHL	27	4	10	14	12	—	—	—	—	—
—Fredericton	AHL	50	26	36	62	48	—	—	—	—	—
88-89—Quebec	NHL	57	20	19	39	45	—	—	—	—	—
—Halifax	AHL	16	11	11	22	14	—	—	—	—	—
89-90—Halifax	AHL	15	5	6	11	6	—	—	—	—	—
—Quebec	NHL	59	13	17	30	28	—	—	—	—	—
90-91—Halifax	AHL	58	24	32	56	85	—	—	—	—	—
—Quebec	NHL	14	0	4	4	6	—	—	—	—	—
91-92—Halifax	AHL	16	9	16	25	44	—	—	—	—	—
—Quebec	NHL	39	5	9	14	33	—	—	—	—	—
NHL totals		196	42	59	101	124					

FOSTER, COREY
D, FLYERS

PERSONAL: Born October 27, 1969, at Ottawa. . . . 6-3/204. . . . Shoots left.
TRANSACTIONS/CAREER NOTES: Selected by New Jersey Devils in first round (first Devils pick, 12th overall) of NHL entry draft (June 11, 1988). . . . Traded by Devils to Edmonton Oilers for a first-round pick in 1989 draft (C Jason Miller) (June 17, 1989). . . . Traded by Oilers with RW Dave Brown and rights to RW Jari Kurri to Philadelphia Flyers for RW Scott Mellanby, LW Craig Berube and C Craig Fisher (May 30, 1991). . . . Fractured collar bone during preseason (September 1991); missed 14 games.

Season Team	League	REGULAR SEASON					PLAYOFFS				
		Gms.	G	A	Pts.	Pen.	Gms.	G	A	Pts.	Pen.
86-87—Peterborough	OHL	30	3	4	7	4	1	0	0	0	0
87-88—Peterborough	OHL	66	13	31	44	58	11	5	9	14	13
88-89—Peterborough	OHL	55	14	42	56	42	17	1	17	18	12
—New Jersey	NHL	2	0	0	0	0	—	—	—	—	—
89-90—Cape Breton	AHL	54	7	17	24	32	1	0	0	0	0
90-91—Cape Breton	AHL	67	14	11	25	51	4	2	4	6	4
91-92—Philadelphia	NHL	25	3	4	7	20	—	—	—	—	—
—Hershey	AHL	19	5	9	14	26	6	1	1	2	5
NHL totals		27	3	4	7	20					

FOSTER, NORM
G, OILERS

PERSONAL: Born February 10, 1965, at Vancouver, B.C. . . . 5-9/175. . . . Shoots left. . . . Full name: Norman Richard Foster.
COLLEGE: Michigan State.
TRANSACTIONS/CAREER NOTES: Selected by Boston Bruins in 11th round (11th Bruins pick, 222nd overall) of NHL entry draft (June 8, 1983). . . . Traded by Bruins to Edmonton Oilers for future considerations (September 10, 1991).
HONORS: Named to NCAA All-Tournament team (1985-86).

Season Team	League	REGULAR SEASON								PLAYOFFS						
		Gms.	Min.	W	L	T	GA	SO	Avg.	Gms.	Min.	W	L	GA	SO	Avg.
81-82—Penticton	BCJHL	21	1187				58		2.93	—	—	—	—	—	—	—
82-83—Penticton	BCJHL	33	1999				156	0	4.68	—	—	—	—	—	—	—
83-84—Michigan State	CCHA	32	1814				83		2.75	—	—	—	—	—	—	—
84-85—Michigan State	CCHA	26	1531	22	4	0	67	1	2.63	—	—	—	—	—	—	—
85-86—Michigan State	CCHA	24	1414	17	5	1	87	1	3.69	—	—	—	—	—	—	—
86-87—Michigan State	CCHA	24	1383	14	7	1	90	1	3.90	—	—	—	—	—	—	—
87-88—Milwaukee	IHL	38	2001	10	22	1	170	0	5.10	—	—	—	—	—	—	—
88-89—Maine	AHL	47	2411	16	17	6	156	1	3.88	—	—	—	—	—	—	—
89-90—Maine	AHL	*64	*3664	23	28	10	*217	3	3.55	—	—	—	—	—	—	—
90-91—Maine	AHL	2	122	1	1	0	7	0	3.44	—	—	—	—	—	—	—
—Cape Breton	AHL	40	2207	15	14	7	135	1	3.67	2	128	0	2	8	0	3.75
—Boston	NHL	3	184	2	1	0	14	0	4.57	—	—	—	—	—	—	—
91-92—Cape Breton	AHL	29	1699	15	13	1	119	0	4.20	3	193	1	2	14	0	4.35
—Edmonton	NHL	10	439	5	3	0	20	0	2.73	—	—	—	—	—	—	—
NHL totals		13	623	7	4	0	34	0	3.27							

FOUNTAIN, MIKE
G, CANUCKS

PERSONAL: Born January 26, 1972, at Gravenhurst, Ont. . . . 6-0/176. . . . Shoots left. . . . Full name: Michael Fountain.
COLLEGE: Trent (Ont.).
TRANSACTIONS/CAREER NOTES: Selected by Vancouver Canucks in second round (third

F

HONORS: Named to Can.HL All-Star second team (1991-92).... Named to OHL All-Star first team (1991-92).

				REGULAR SEASON							PLAYOFFS					
Season	Team	League	Gms.	Min.	W	L	T	GA	SO	Avg.	Gms.	Min.	W	L	GA	SO	Avg.
88-89—Huntsville Jr. C	OHA	22	1306				82	0	3.77	—	—	—	—	—	—	—
89-90—Chatham Jr. B	OHA	21	1249				76	0	3.65	—	—	—	—	—	—	—
90-91—Sault Ste. Marie	OHL	7	380	5	2	0	19	0	3.00	—	—	—	—	—	—	—
—Oshawa	OHL	30	1483	17	5	1	84	0	3.40	8	292			26	0	5.34
91-92—Oshawa	OHL	40	2260	18	13	6	149	1	3.96	7	428	3	4	26	0	3.64

FOY, CHRISTOPHER
D, ISLANDERS

PERSONAL: Born September 16, 1970, at Toronto.... 6-0/190.... Shoots left.... Full name: Christopher William Foy.
HIGH SCHOOL: Thornhill Secondary School (Ont.).
COLLEGE: Northeastern.
TRANSACTIONS/CAREER NOTES: Selected by New York Islanders in NHL supplemental draft (June 19, 1992).

			REGULAR SEASON					PLAYOFFS			
Season	Team	League	Gms.	G	A	Pts.	Pen.	Gms.	G	A	Pts.	Pen.
89-90—Northeastern University	Hockey East	37	0	5	5	48	—	—	—	—	—
90-91—Northeastern University	Hockey East	33	0	3	3	20	—	—	—	—	—
91-92—Northeastern University	Hockey East	33	8	11	19	45	—	—	—	—	—

FRANCESCHETTI, LOU
RW, SABRES

PERSONAL: Born March 28, 1958, at Toronto.... 6-0/190.... Shoots left.
TRANSACTIONS/CAREER NOTES: Selected by Washington Capitals in fifth round (seventh Capitals pick, 71st overall) of NHL entry draft (June 15, 1978)....
Bruised right leg (March 1988).... Traded by Capitals to Toronto Maple Leafs
for a fifth-round pick in 1992 entry draft (C Mark Ouimet) (July 1989).... Broke bone in right foot (October 13, 1990); missed 13 games.... Traded by Maple Leafs with D Brian Curran to Buffalo Sabres for RW Mike Foligno and an eighth-round pick in 1991 draft (C Thomas Kucharcik) (December 17, 1990).... Strained knee (February 15, 1991); missed eight games.... Loaned to New Haven Nighthawks (October 11, 1991); returned (December 18, 1991).

			REGULAR SEASON					PLAYOFFS			
Season	Team	League	Gms.	G	A	Pts.	Pen.	Gms.	G	A	Pts.	Pen.
75-76—St. Catharines	OHA Mj. Jr. A	1	0	0	0	0	—	—	—	—	—
76-77—Niagara Falls	OMJHL	61	23	30	53	80	—	—	—	—	—
77-78—Niagara Falls	OMJHL	62	40	50	90	46	—	—	—	—	—
78-79—Saginaw	IHL	2	1	1	2	0	—	—	—	—	—
—Port Huron	IHL	76	45	58	103	131	—	—	—	—	—
79-80—Port Huron	IHL	15	3	8	11	31	—	—	—	—	—
—Hershey	AHL	65	27	29	56	58	14	6	9	15	32
80-81—Hershey	AHL	79	32	36	68	173	10	3	7	10	30
81-82—Washington	NHL	30	2	10	12	23	—	—	—	—	—
—Hershey	AHL	50	22	33	55	89	—	—	—	—	—
82-83—Hershey	AHL	80	31	44	75	176	5	1	2	3	16
83-84—Washington	NHL	2	0	0	0	0	3	0	0	0	8
—Hershey	AHL	73	26	34	60	130	—	—	—	—	—
84-85—Binghamton	AHL	52	29	43	72	75	—	—	—	—	—
—Washington	NHL	22	4	7	11	45	5	1	1	2	15
85-86—Washington	NHL	76	7	14	21	131	8	0	0	0	15
86-87—Washington	NHL	75	12	9	21	127	7	0	0	0	23
87-88—Washington	NHL	59	4	8	12	113	4	0	0	0	14
—Binghamton	AHL	6	2	4	6	4	—	—	—	—	—
88-89—Washington	NHL	63	7	10	17	123	6	1	0	1	8
—Baltimore	AHL	10	8	7	15	30	—	—	—	—	—
89-90—Toronto	NHL	80	21	15	36	127	5	0	1	1	26
90-91—Toronto	NHL	16	1	1	2	30	—	—	—	—	—
—Buffalo	NHL	35	1	7	8	28	6	1	0	1	2
91-92—Buffalo	NHL	1	0	0	0	0	—	—	—	—	—
—New Haven	AHL	25	6	7	13	59	—	—	—	—	—
—Rochester	AHL	49	15	25	40	64	15	3	5	8	31
NHL totals		459	59	81	140	747	44	3	2	5	111

FRANCIS, RON
C, PENGUINS

PERSONAL: Born March 1, 1963, at Sault Ste. Marie, Ont.... 6-2/200.... Shoots left.... Full name: Ronald Francis.... Cousin of Mike Liut, goaltender, Washington Capitals.
TRANSACTIONS/CAREER NOTES: Selected by Hartford Whalers as underage junior in first round (first Whalers pick, fourth overall) of NHL entry draft (June 10, 1981).... Injured eye (January 27, 1982); missed three weeks.... Strained ligaments in right knee (November 30, 1983).... Broke ankle (January 18, 1986); missed 27 games.... Broke left index finger (January 28, 1989); missed 11 games.... Broke nose (November 24, 1990).... Traded by Whalers with D Ulf Samuelsson and D Grant Jennings to Pittsburgh Penguins for C John Cullen, D Zarley Zalapski and RW Jeff Parker (March 4, 1991).

			REGULAR SEASON					PLAYOFFS			
Season	Team	League	Gms.	G	A	Pts.	Pen.	Gms.	G	A	Pts.	Pen.
80-81—Sault Ste. Marie	OMJHL	64	26	43	69	33	19	7	8	15	34
81-82—Sault Ste. Marie	OHL	25	18	30	48	46	—	—	—	—	—
—Hartford	NHL	59	25	43	68	51	—	—	—	—	—

Season Team	League	Gms.	G	A	Pts.	Pen.	Gms.	G	A	Pts.	Pen.
		REGULAR SEASON					PLAYOFFS				
82-83—Hartford	NHL	79	31	59	90	60	—	—	—	—	—
83-84—Hartford	NHL	72	23	60	83	45	—	—	—	—	—
84-85—Hartford	NHL	80	24	57	81	66	—	—	—	—	—
85-86—Hartford	NHL	53	24	53	77	24	10	1	2	3	4
86-87—Hartford	NHL	75	30	63	93	45	6	2	2	4	6
87-88—Hartford	NHL	80	25	50	75	89	6	2	5	7	2
88-89—Hartford	NHL	69	29	48	77	36	4	0	2	2	0
89-90—Hartford	NHL	80	32	69	101	73	7	3	3	6	8
90-91—Hartford	NHL	67	21	55	76	51	—	—	—	—	—
—Pittsburgh	NHL	14	2	9	11	21	24	7	10	17	24
91-92—Pittsburgh	NHL	70	21	33	54	30	21	8	*19	27	6
NHL totals		798	287	599	886	591	78	23	43	66	50

FRANZOSA, DAVID
LW, BRUINS

PERSONAL: Born November 20, 1970, at Reading, Mass. . . . 5-11/175. . . . Shoots left. . . . Full name: David Joseph Franzosa.
COLLEGE: Boston College.
TRANSACTIONS/CAREER NOTES: Selected by Boston Bruins in 11th round (11th Bruins pick, 227th overall) of NHL entry draft (June 17, 1989).

Season Team	League	Gms.	G	A	Pts.	Pen.	Gms.	G	A	Pts.	Pen.
		REGULAR SEASON					PLAYOFFS				
88-89—Boston College	Hockey East	23	2	5	7	4	—	—	—	—	—
89-90—Boston College	Hockey East	42	8	20	28	20	—	—	—	—	—
90-91—Boston College	Hockey East	39	14	19	33	14	—	—	—	—	—
91-92—Boston College	Hockey East	35	18	35	53	38	—	—	—	—	—

FRAWLEY, DANNY
RW, SABRES

PERSONAL: Born June 2, 1962, at Sturgeon Falls, Ont. . . . 6-0/193. . . . Shoots right. . . . Full name: William Daniel Frawley.
TRANSACTIONS/CAREER NOTES: Selected by Chicago Blackhawks as underage junior in 10th round (15th Blackhawks pick, 204th overall) of NHL entry draft (June 11, 1980). . . . Acquired by Pittsburgh Penguins in 1985 NHL waiver draft (October 7, 1985). . . . Underwent knee surgery (December 1987). . . . Signed as free agent by Buffalo Sabres (September 1990).

Season Team	League	Gms.	G	A	Pts.	Pen.	Gms.	G	A	Pts.	Pen.
		REGULAR SEASON					PLAYOFFS				
79-80—Sudbury	OMJHL	63	21	26	47	67	8	0	1	1	2
80-81—Cornwall	QMJHL	28	10	14	24	76	18	5	12	17	37
81-82—Cornwall	OHL	64	27	50	77	239	5	3	8	11	19
82-83—Springfield	AHL	80	30	27	57	107	—	—	—	—	—
83-84—Chicago	NHL	3	0	0	0	0	—	—	—	—	—
—Springfield	AHL	69	22	34	56	137	4	0	1	1	12
84-85—Milwaukee	IHL	26	11	12	23	125	—	—	—	—	—
—Chicago	NHL	30	4	3	7	64	1	0	0	0	0
85-86—Pittsburgh	NHL	69	10	11	21	174	—	—	—	—	—
86-87—Pittsburgh	NHL	78	14	14	28	218	—	—	—	—	—
87-88—Pittsburgh	NHL	47	6	8	14	152	—	—	—	—	—
88-89—Muskegon	IHL	24	12	16	28	35	14	6	4	10	31
—Pittsburgh	NHL	46	3	4	7	66	—	—	—	—	—
89-90—Muskegon	IHL	82	31	47	78	165	15	9	12	21	51
90-91—Rochester	AHL	74	15	31	46	152	14	4	7	11	34
91-92—Rochester	AHL	78	28	23	51	208	16	7	5	12	35
NHL totals		273	37	40	77	674	1	0	0	0	0

FREER, MARK
C, SENATORS

PERSONAL: Born July 14, 1968, at Peterborough, Ont. . . . 5-10/180. . . . Shoots left.
TRANSACTIONS/CAREER NOTES: Signed as free agent by Philadelphia Flyers (September 1986). . . . Selected by Ottawa Senators in NHL expansion draft (June 18, 1992).

Season Team	League	Gms.	G	A	Pts.	Pen.	Gms.	G	A	Pts.	Pen.
		REGULAR SEASON					PLAYOFFS				
85-86—Peterborough	OHL	65	16	28	44	24	14	3	4	7	13
86-87—Peterborough	OHL	65	39	43	82	44	12	2	6	8	5
—Philadelphia	NHL	1	0	1	1	0	—	—	—	—	—
87-88—Philadelphia	NHL	1	0	0	0	0	—	—	—	—	—
—Peterborough	OHL	63	38	71	109	63	12	5	12	17	4
88-89—Philadelphia	NHL	5	0	1	1	0	—	—	—	—	—
—Hershey	AHL	75	30	49	79	77	12	4	6	10	2
89-90—Hershey	AHL	65	28	36	64	31	—	—	—	—	—
90-91—Hershey	AHL	77	18	44	62	45	7	1	3	4	17
91-92—Hershey	AHL	31	13	11	24	38	6	0	3	3	2
—Philadelphia	NHL	50	6	7	13	18	—	—	—	—	—
NHL totals		57	6	9	15	18					

FRENETTE, DEREK
LW, BLUES

PERSONAL: Born July 13, 1971, at Montreal. . . . 6-1/205. . . . Shoots left.
COLLEGE: Ferris State (Mich.).
TRANSACTIONS/CAREER NOTES: Selected by St. Louis Blues in sixth round (sixth Blues pick, 124th overall) of NHL entry draft (June 17, 1989).

Season	Team	League	REGULAR SEASON					PLAYOFFS				
			Gms.	G	A	Pts.	Pen.	Gms.	G	A	Pts.	Pen.
88-89	Ferris State	CCHA	27	3	4	7	17	—	—	—	—	—
89-90	Ferris State	CCHA	29	1	4	5	48	—	—	—	—	—
90-91	Hull	QMJHL	66	27	42	69	72	6	4	3	7	12
—Peoria		IHL	—	—	—	—	—	6	0	0	0	0
91-92	Peoria	IHL	46	2	11	13	51	10	0	3	3	4

FUHR, GRANT
G, MAPLE LEAFS

PERSONAL: Born September 28, 1962, at Spruce Grove, Alta.... 5-10/186.... Shoots right.
TRANSACTIONS/CAREER NOTES: Selected by Edmonton Oilers in first round (first Oilers pick, eighth overall) of NHL entry draft (June 10, 1981).... Suffered partial separation of right shoulder (December 1981).... Strained left knee ligaments and underwent surgery (December 13, 1983).... Separated shoulder (February 1985).... Bruised left shoulder (November 3, 1985); missed 10 games.... Bruised left shoulder (November 1987).... Injured right knee (November 1987).... Suffered cervical neck strain (January 18, 1989).... Underwent appendectomy (September 14, 1989); missed first six games of season.... Underwent reconstructive surgery to left shoulder (December 27, 1989).... Tore adhesions in left shoulder (March 13, 1990).... Suspended six months by the NHL for admitting to using drugs earlier in career (September 27, 1990).... Traded by Oilers with RW/LW Glenn Anderson and LW Craig Berube to Toronto Maple Leafs for LW Vincent Damphousse, D Luke Richardson, G Peter Ing, C Scott Thornton and future considerations (September 19, 1991).... Sprained thumb (October 17, 1991); missed two games. ... Pulled groin (November 12, 1991); missed three games.... Sprained knee (February 11, 1992); missed four games.
HONORS: Won Stewart (Butch) Paul Memorial Trophy (1979-00).... Named to WHL All-Star first team (1979-80 and 1980-81).... Won Top Goaltender Trophy (1980-81).... Named to THE SPORTING NEWS All-Star second team (1981-82 and 1985-86).... Named to NHL All-Star second team (1981-82).... Won Vezina Trophy (1987-88).... Named to THE SPORTING NEWS All-Star first team (1987-88).... Named to NHL All-Star first team (1987-88).
RECORDS: Holds NHL single-season record for most points by a goaltender—14 (1983-84); and most games by a goaltender—75 (1987-88).... Shares NHL single-season playoff record for most wins by a goaltender—16 (1987-88).

Season	Team	League	REGULAR SEASON							PLAYOFFS						
			Gms.	Min.	W	L	T	GA	SO	Avg.	Gms.	Min.	W	L	GA	SO	Avg.
79-80	Victoria	WHL	43	2488				130	2	3.14	8	465	5	3	22	0	2.84
80-81	Victoria	WHL	59	*3448				160	†4	*2.78	15	899	12	3	45	1	3.00
81-82	Edmonton	NHL	48	2847	28	5	14	157	0	3.31	5	309	2	3	26	0	5.05
82-83	Moncton	AHL	10	604				40	0	3.97	—						
—Edmonton		NHL	32	1803	13	12	5	129	0	4.29	1	11	0	0	0	0	0.00
83-84	Edmonton	NHL	45	2625	30	10	4	171	1	3.91	16	883	11	4	44	1	2.99
84-85	Edmonton	NHL	46	2559	26	8	7	165	1	3.87	†18	*1064	*15	3	55	0	3.10
85-86	Edmonton	NHL	40	2184	29	8	0	143	0	3.93	9	541	5	4	28	0	3.11
86-87	Edmonton	NHL	44	2388	22	13	3	137	0	3.44	19	1148	14	5	47	0	2.46
87-88	Edmonton	NHL	*75	*4304	40	24	9	*246	†4	3.43	*19	*1136	*16	2	55	0	2.90
88-89	Edmonton	NHL	59	3341	23	26	6	213	1	3.83	7	417	3	4	24	1	3.45
89-90	Cape Breton	AHL	2	120				6	0	3.00	—						
—Edmonton		NHL	21	1081	9	7	3	70	1	3.89	—						
90-91	Cape Breton	AHL	4	240				17	0	4.25	—						
—Edmonton		NHL	13	778	6	4	3	39	1	3.01	17	1019	8	7	51	0	3.00
91-92	Toronto	NHL	65	3774	25	*33	5	*230	2	3.66	—						
NHL totals			488	27684	251	150	59	1700	11	3.68	111	6528	74	32	330	2	3.03

GAETZ, LINK
LW, SHARKS

PERSONAL: Born October 2, 1968, at Vancouver, B.C.... 6-2/223.... Shoots left.
TRANSACTIONS/CAREER NOTES: Suspended indefinitely by Spokane Chiefs (April 12, 1988).... Selected by Minnesota North Stars in second round (second North Stars pick, 40th overall) of NHL entry draft (June 11, 1988).... Suspended four games by IHL for high-sticking (January 23, 1989).... Suspended by North Stars for not reporting to Kansas City Blades (November 9, 1990).... Suspended by Blades for off-ice incident (February 5, 1991).... Entered in-patient alcohol abuse program (February 19, 1991).... Selected by San Jose Sharks in NHL dispersal draft (May 30, 1991).... Injured hand (October 5, 1991); missed four games.... Sprained knee (November 2, 1991); missed four games.

Season	Team	League	REGULAR SEASON					PLAYOFFS				
			Gms.	G	A	Pts.	Pen.	Gms.	G	A	Pts.	Pen.
85-86	Quesnel	PCJHL	15	0	7	7	4	—	—	—	—	—
86-87	New Westminster	WHL	44	2	7	9	52	—	—	—	—	—
—Merritt		BCJHL	7	4	2	6	27	—	—	—	—	—
—Delta		BCJHL	23	9	12	21	53	—	—	—	—	—
87-88	Spokane Chiefs	WHL	59	9	20	29	313	10	2	2	4	70
88-89	Minnesota	NHL	12	0	2	2	53	—	—	—	—	—
—Kalamazoo		IHL	37	3	4	7	192	5	0	0	0	56
89-90	Kalamazoo	IHL	61	5	16	21	318	9	2	2	4	59
—Minnesota		NHL	5	0	0	0	33	—	—	—	—	—
90-91	Kalamazoo	IHL	9	0	1	1	44	—	—	—	—	—
—Kansas City		IHL	18	1	10	11	178	—	—	—	—	—
91-92	San Jose	NHL	48	6	6	12	326	—	—	—	—	—
NHL totals			65	6	8	14	412					

GAGE, JOAQUIN
G, OILERS

PERSONAL: Born October 19, 1973, at Vancouver, B.C.... 6-1/200.... Shoots left.
COLLEGE: Portland Community College (Ore.).
TRANSACTIONS/CAREER NOTES: Selected by Edmonton Oilers in fifth round (sixth Oilers pick, 109th overall) of NHL entry draft (June 20, 1992).

FG

Season	Team	League	Gms.	Min.	W	L	T	GA	SO	Avg.	Gms.	Min.	W	L	GA	SO	Avg.
					REGULAR SEASON								PLAYOFFS				
90-91	—Bellingham Jr. A	BCJHL	16	751				64	0	5.11	—	—	—	—	—	—	—
	—Portland	WHL	3	180	0	3	0	17	0	5.67	—	—	—	—	—	—	—
91-92	—Portland	WHL	63	3635	27	30	4	269	2	4.44	6	366	2	4	28	0	4.59

GAGE, JODY
RW, SABRES

PERSONAL: Born November 29, 1959, at Toronto. . . . 6-0/190. . . . Shoots right. . . . Full name: Joseph William Gage.

TRANSACTIONS/CAREER NOTES: Selected by Detroit Red Wings in third round (second Detroit pick, 46th overall) of NHL entry draft (August 9, 1979). . . . Signed as free agent by Buffalo Sabres (August 1985). . . . Strained ankle and knee ligaments in preseason game (September 27, 1988); missed two months.

HONORS: Named to AHL All-Star first team (1985-86 and 1990-91). . . . Won Les Cunningham Plaque (1987-88).

Season	Team	League	Gms.	G	A	Pts.	Pen.	Gms.	G	A	Pts.	Pen.
				REGULAR SEASON					PLAYOFFS			
76-77	—St. Catharines	OMJHL	47	13	20	33	2	—	—	—	—	—
77-78	—Hamilton Fincups	OMJHL	32	15	18	33	19	—	—	—	—	—
	—Kitchener	OMJHL	36	17	27	44	21	9	4	3	7	4
78-79	—Kitchener	OMJHL	59	46	43	89	40	10	1	2	3	6
79-80	—Adirondack	AHL	63	25	21	46	15	5	2	1	3	0
	—Kalamazoo	IHL	14	17	12	29	0	—	—	—	—	—
80-81	—Detroit	NHL	16	2	2	4	22	—	—	—	—	—
	—Adirondack	AHL	59	17	31	48	44	17	9	6	15	12
81-82	—Adirondack	AHL	47	21	20	41	21	—	—	—	—	—
	—Detroit	NHL	31	9	10	19	2	—	—	—	—	—
82-83	—Adirondack	AHL	65	23	30	53	33	6	1	5	6	8
83-84	—Detroit	NHL	3	0	0	0	0	—	—	—	—	—
	—Adirondack	AHL	73	40	32	72	32	6	3	4	7	2
84-85	—Adirondack	AHL	78	27	33	60	55	—	—	—	—	—
85-86	—Buffalo	NHL	7	3	2	5	0	—	—	—	—	—
	—Rochester	AHL	73	42	57	99	56	—	—	—	—	—
86-87	—Rochester	AHL	70	26	39	65	60	17	*14	5	19	24
87-88	—Rochester	AHL	76	*60	44	104	46	5	2	5	7	10
	—Buffalo	NHL	2	0	0	0	0	—	—	—	—	—
88-89	—Rochester	AHL	65	31	38	69	50	—	—	—	—	—
89-90	—Rochester	AHL	75	45	38	83	42	17	4	6	10	12
90-91	—Rochester	AHL	73	42	43	85	34	15	6	10	16	14
91-92	—Rochester	AHL	67	40	40	80	54	16	5	9	14	10
	—Buffalo	NHL	9	0	1	1	2	—	—	—	—	—
	NHL totals		68	14	15	29	26					

GAGNER, DAVE
C, NORTH STARS

PERSONAL: Born December 11, 1964, at Chatham, Ont. . . . 5-10/188. . . . Shoots left.

TRANSACTIONS/CAREER NOTES: Selected by New York Rangers as underage junior in first round (first Rangers pick, 12th overall) of NHL entry draft (June 8, 1983). . . . Fractured ankle (February 5, 1986). . . . Underwent emergency appendectomy (December 1986). . . . Traded by Rangers with RW Jay Caufield to Minnesota North Stars for D Jari Gronstrad and D Paul Boutilier (October 8, 1987). . . . Broke kneecap (March 31, 1989). . . . Underwent surgery to left knee cartilage (November 11, 1990). . . . Underwent arthroscopic knee surgery (December 18, 1991); missed one game. . . . Hyperextended knee (March 17, 1992); missed one game.

HONORS: Won Bobby Smith Trophy (1982-83). . . . Named to OHL All-Star second team (1982-83).

RECORDS: Shares NHL single-game playoff record for most points in one period—4 (April 8, 1991, first period).

Season	Team	League	Gms.	G	A	Pts.	Pen.	Gms.	G	A	Pts.	Pen.
				REGULAR SEASON					PLAYOFFS			
81-82	—Brantford	OHL	68	30	46	76	31	11	3	6	9	6
82-83	—Brantford	OHL	70	55	66	121	57	8	5	5	10	4
83-84	—Canadian Olympic Team	Int'l	50	19	18	37	26	—	—	—	—	—
	—Brantford	OHL	12	7	13	20	4	6	0	4	4	6
84-85	—New Haven	AHL	38	13	20	33	23	—	—	—	—	—
	—New York Rangers	NHL	38	6	6	12	16	—	—	—	—	—
85-86	—New York Rangers	NHL	32	4	6	10	19	—	—	—	—	—
	—New Haven	AHL	16	10	11	21	11	4	1	2	3	2
86-87	—New York Rangers	NHL	10	1	4	5	12	—	—	—	—	—
	—New Haven	AHL	56	22	41	63	50	7	1	5	6	18
87-88	—Kalamazoo	IHL	14	16	10	26	26	—	—	—	—	—
	—Minnesota	NHL	51	8	11	19	55	—	—	—	—	—
88-89	—Minnesota	NHL	75	35	43	78	104	—	—	—	—	—
	—Kalamazoo	IHL	1	0	1	1	4	—	—	—	—	—
89-90	—Minnesota	NHL	79	40	38	78	54	7	2	3	5	16
90-91	—Minnesota	NHL	73	40	42	82	114	23	12	15	27	28
91-92	—Minnesota	NHL	78	31	40	71	107	7	2	4	6	8
	NHL totals		436	165	190	355	481	37	16	22	38	52

GAGNON, DAVE
G, RED WINGS

PERSONAL: Born October 31, 1967, at Essex, Ont. . . . 6-0/185. . . . Shoots left. . . . Full name: David Anthony Gagnon.

COLLEGE: Colgate.

TRANSACTIONS/CAREER NOTES: Signed as free agent by Detroit Red Wings (June 11, 1990).

... Injured hamstring (December 1, 1991).
HONORS: Named ECAC Player of the Year (1989-90).... Named to NCAA All-America East first team (1989-90).... Named to ECAC All-Star first team (1989-90).... Named to ECAC All-Tournament team (1989-90).

			REGULAR SEASON								PLAYOFFS						
Season	Team	League	Gms.	Min.	W	L	T	GA	SO	Avg.	Gms.	Min.	W	L	GA	SO	Avg.
87-88	Colgate University	ECAC	13	743	6	4	2	43	1	3.47	—	—	—	—	—	—	—
88-89	Colgate University	ECAC	28	1622	17	9	2	102	0	3.77	—	—	—	—	—	—	—
89-90	Colgate University	ECAC	33	1986	28	3	1	93	0	2.81	—	—	—	—	—	—	—
90-91	Detroit	NHL	2	35	0	1	0	6	0	10.29	—	—	—	—	—	—	—
	Adirondack	AHL	24	1356	7	8	5	94	0	4.16	—	—	—	—	—	—	—
	Hampton Roads	ECHL	10	606	7	1	2	26	2	2.57	11	696	*10	1	27	0	*2.33
91-92	Toledo	ECHL	7	354	4	2	0	18	0	3.05	—	—	—	—	—	—	—
	Fort Wayne	IHL	2	125	2	0	0	7	0	3.36	—	—	—	—	—	—	—
NHL totals			2	35	0	1	0	6	0	10.29							

GALLANT, GERARD

LW, RED WINGS

PERSONAL: Born September 2, 1963, at Summerside, P.E.I.... 5-10/190.... Shoots left.

TRANSACTIONS/CAREER NOTES: Selected by Detroit Red Wings in sixth round (fourth Red Wings pick, 107th overall) of NHL entry draft (June 10, 1981).... Broke jaw (December 11, 1985); missed 25 games.... Fined $500 by NHL for stick-swinging incident (April 8, 1909).... Suspended five games by NHL for slashing (October 7, 1989).... Suspended three games by NHL for hitting linesman (January 13, 1990).... Suffered sore back (November 1990); missed eight games.... Suffered back spasms (December 1990); missed 18 games.... Underwent surgery to remove bone spur in back (March 14, 1991); missed remainder of season.... Injured hand (February 1992); missed five games.... Strained back (March 20, 1992); missed five games.
HONORS: Named to NHL All-Star second team (1988-89).

			REGULAR SEASON					PLAYOFFS				
Season	Team	League	Gms.	G	A	Pts.	Pen.	Gms.	G	A	Pts.	Pen.
79-80	Summerside	PEIHA	45	60	55	115	90	—	—	—	—	—
80-81	Sherbrooke	QMJHL	68	41	60	101	220	14	6	13	19	46
81-82	Sherbrooke	QMJHL	58	34	58	92	260	22	14	24	38	84
82-83	St. Jean	QMJHL	33	28	25	53	139	—	—	—	—	—
	Verdun	QMJHL	29	26	49	75	105	15	†14	19	33	*84
83-84	Adirondack	AHL	77	31	33	64	195	7	1	3	4	34
84-85	Adirondack	AHL	46	18	29	47	131	—	—	—	—	—
	Detroit	NHL	32	6	12	18	66	3	0	0	0	11
85-86	Detroit	NHL	52	20	19	39	106	—	—	—	—	—
86-87	Detroit	NHL	80	38	34	72	216	16	8	6	14	43
87-88	Detroit	NHL	73	34	39	73	242	16	6	9	15	55
88-89	Detroit	NHL	76	39	54	93	230	6	1	2	3	40
89-90	Detroit	NHL	69	36	44	80	254	—	—	—	—	—
90-91	Detroit	NHL	45	10	16	26	111	—	—	—	—	—
91-92	Detroit	NHL	69	14	22	36	187	11	2	2	4	25
NHL totals			496	197	240	437	1412	52	17	19	36	174

GALLEY, GARRY

D, FLYERS

PERSONAL: Born April 16, 1963, at Ottawa.... 5-11/190.... Shoots left.
COLLEGE: Bowling Green State.
TRANSACTIONS/CAREER NOTES: Selected by Los Angeles Kings in fifth round (fourth Kings pick, 100th overall) of NHL entry draft (June 8, 1983).... Injured knee (December 8, 1985).... Traded by Kings to Washington Capitals for G Al Jensen (February 14, 1987).... Signed as free agent by Boston Bruins with Capitals getting third-round draft pick in 1989 as compensation (July 8, 1988).... Sprained left shoulder (September 30, 1989); missed first nine games of season.... Suffered lacerations to cheek, both lips and part of his neck (October 6, 1990).... Dislocated right shoulder (December 22, 1990).... Bruised left kneecap (March 23, 1991); missed two games. ... Pulled hamstring (April 17, 1991); missed three playoff games.... Traded by Bruins with C Wes Walz and future considerations to Philadelphia Flyers for D Gord Murphy, RW Brian Dobbin and third-round pick in 1992 draft (January 2, 1992).... Bruised ribs (January 9, 1992); missed one game.... Fractured foot (March 3, 1992); missed two games.
HONORS: Named to CCHA All-Star first team (1982-83).... Named to NCAA All-Tournament team (1983-84).

			REGULAR SEASON					PLAYOFFS				
Season	Team	League	Gms.	G	A	Pts.	Pen.	Gms.	G	A	Pts.	Pen.
81-82	Bowling Green State	CCHA	42	3	36	39	48	—	—	—	—	—
82-83	Bowling Green State	CCHA	40	17	29	46	40	—	—	—	—	—
83-84	Bowling Green State	CCHA	44	15	52	67	61	—	—	—	—	—
84-85	Los Angeles	NHL	78	8	30	38	82	3	1	0	1	2
85-86	Los Angeles	NHL	49	9	13	22	46	—	—	—	—	—
	New Haven	AHL	4	2	6	8	6	—	—	—	—	—
86-87	Los Angeles	NHL	30	5	11	16	57	—	—	—	—	—
	Washington	NHL	18	1	10	11	10	2	0	0	0	0
87-88	Washington	NHL	58	7	23	30	44	13	2	4	6	13
88-89	Boston	NHL	78	8	21	29	80	9	0	1	1	33
89-90	Boston	NHL	71	8	27	35	75	21	3	3	6	34
90-91	Boston	NHL	70	6	21	27	84	16	1	5	6	17
91-92	Boston	NHL	38	2	12	14	83	—	—	—	—	—
	Philadelphia	NHL	39	3	15	18	34	—	—	—	—	—
NHL totals			529	57	183	240	595	64	7	13	20	99

G

GAMBLE, TROY
G, CANUCKS

PERSONAL: Born April 7, 1967, at Toronto.... 5-11/195.... Shoots left.
TRANSACTIONS/CAREER NOTES: Selected by Vancouver Canucks as underage junior in second round (second Canucks pick, 25th overall) of NHL entry draft (June 15, 1985).... Traded by Medicine Hat Tigers with D Kevin Ekdahl to Spokane Chiefs for D Keith Van Rooyen, RW Kirby Lindal and RW Rocky Dundas (December, 1986).
HONORS: Won Top Goaltender Trophy (1984-85).... Named to WHL All-Star first team (1984-85 and 1987-88).... Won Del Wilson Trophy (1987-88).

Season	Team	League	Gms.	Min.	W	L	T	GA	SO	Avg.	Gms.	Min.	W	L	GA	SO	Avg.
83-84	Hobbema	AJHL	22	1102				90	0	4.90	—	—	—	—	—	—	—
84-85	Medicine Hat	WHL	37	2095	27	6	2	100	*3	*2.86	2	120	1	1	9	0	4.50
85-86	Medicine Hat	WHL	45	2264	28	11	0	142	0	3.76	11	530	5	4	31	0	3.51
86-87	Medicine Hat	WHL	11	646	7	3	0	46	0	4.27	—	—	—	—	—	—	—
	Spokane Chiefs	WHL	38	2157	17	17	1	163	0	4.53	5	298	0	5	35	0	7.05
	Vancouver	NHL	1	60	0	1	0	4	0	4.00	—	—	—	—	—	—	—
87-88	Spokane Chiefs	WHL	*67	*3824	35	26	1	235	0	3.69	15	875	7	8	56	†1	3.84
88-89	Vancouver	NHL	5	302	2	3	0	12	0	2.38	—	—	—	—	—	—	—
	Milwaukee	IHL	42	2198	23	9	0	138	0	3.77	11	640	5	5	35	0	3.28
89-90	Milwaukee	IHL	*56	3033	22	21	4	*213	2	4.21	—	—	—	—	—	—	—
90-91	Vancouver	NHL	47	2433	16	16	6	140	1	3.45	4	249	1	3	16	0	3.86
91-92	Vancouver	NHL	19	1009	4	9	3	73	0	4.34	—	—	—	—	—	—	—
	Milwaukee	IHL	9	521	2	4	2	31	0	3.57	—	—	—	—	—	—	—
NHL totals			72	3804	22	29	9	229	1	3.61	4	249	1	3	16	0	3.86

GANCHAR, PERRY
RW, PENGUINS

PERSONAL: Born October 28, 1963, at Saskatoon, Sask.... 5-9/180.... Shoots right.
TRANSACTIONS/CAREER NOTES: Selected by St. Louis Blues as underage junior in sixth round (third Blues pick, 113th overall) of NHL entry draft (June 9, 1982).... Traded by Blues to Montreal Canadiens for C/LW Ron Flockhart (August 26, 1985).... Traded by Canadiens to Pittsburgh Penguins for future considerations (December 17, 1987).... Injured knee (January 1988).
HONORS: Named to IHL All-Star second team (1984-85).

Season	Team	League	Gms.	G	A	Pts.	Pen.	Gms.	G	A	Pts.	Pen.
77-78	Saskatoon	WCHL	4	2	0	2	2	—	—	—	—	—
78-79	Saskatoon	SJHL	50	21	33	54	72	—	—	—	—	—
	Saskatoon	WHL	14	5	3	8	15	—	—	—	—	—
79-80	Saskatoon	WHL	70	41	24	65	116	—	—	—	—	—
80-81	Saskatoon	WHL	68	36	20	56	195	—	—	—	—	—
81-82	Saskatoon	WHL	53	38	52	90	82	5	3	3	6	17
82-83	Saskatoon	WHL	68	68	48	116	105	6	1	4	5	24
	Salt Lake City	IHL	—	—	—	—	—	1	0	1	1	0
83-84	Montana	CHL	59	23	22	45	77	—	—	—	—	—
	St. Louis	NHL	1	0	0	0	0	7	3	1	4	0
84-85	Peoria	IHL	63	41	29	70	114	20	4	11	15	49
	St. Louis	NHL	7	0	2	2	0	—	—	—	—	—
85-86	Sherbrooke	AHL	75	25	29	54	42	—	—	—	—	—
86-87	Sherbrooke	AHL	68	22	29	51	64	17	9	8	17	37
87-88	Sherbrooke	AHL	28	12	18	30	61	—	—	—	—	—
	Montreal	NHL	1	1	0	1	0	—	—	—	—	—
	Pittsburgh	NHL	30	2	5	7	36	—	—	—	—	—
88-89	Pittsburgh	NHL	3	0	0	0	0	—	—	—	—	—
	Muskegon	IHL	70	39	34	73	114	14	7	8	15	6
89-90	Muskegon	IHL	70	40	45	85	111	14	3	5	8	27
90-91	Muskegon	IHL	80	37	38	75	87	5	2	1	3	0
91-92	Muskegon	IHL	65	29	20	49	65	14	9	9	18	18
NHL totals			42	3	7	10	36	7	3	1	4	0

GARBUTT, MURRAY
C/LW, NORDIQUES

PERSONAL: Born July 29, 1971, at Hanna, Alta.... 6-1/205.... Shoots left.
TRANSACTIONS/CAREER NOTES: Selected by Minnesota North Stars in third round (third North Stars pick, 60th overall) of NHL entry draft (June 17, 1989).... Became property of San Jose Sharks as part of ownership change with North Stars (September 1990).... Traded by Sharks to Quebec Nordiques for LW Don Barber (March 7, 1992).

Season	Team	League	Gms.	G	A	Pts.	Pen.	Gms.	G	A	Pts.	Pen.
87-88	Medicine Hat	WHL	9	2	1	3	15	16	0	1	1	15
88-89	Medicine Hat	WHL	64	14	24	38	145	3	1	0	1	6
89-90	Medicine Hat	WHL	72	38	27	65	221	3	1	0	1	21
90-91	Medicine Hat	WHL	30	15	26	41	97	—	—	—	—	—
	Spokane Chiefs	WHL	31	17	19	36	90	15	4	8	12	44
91-92	Kansas City	IHL	25	2	6	8	19	—	—	—	—	—

GARPENLOV, JOHAN
LW, SHARKS

PERSONAL: Born March 21, 1968, at Stockholm, Sweden.... 5-11/185.... Shoots left.
TRANSACTIONS/CAREER NOTES: Selected by Detroit Red Wings in fifth round (fifth Red Wings pick, 85th overall) of NHL entry draft (June 9, 1984).... Traded by

Red Wings to San Jose Sharks for D Bob McGill and an eighth-round pick in 1992 draft previously acquired from Vancouver Canucks (March 10, 1992).

			REGULAR SEASON					PLAYOFFS			
Season Team	League	Gms.	G	A	Pts.	Pen.	Gms.	G	A	Pts.	Pen.
86-87—Djurgarden	Sweden	29	5	8	13	20	—	—	—	—	—
87-88—Djurgarden	Sweden	30	7	10	17	12	—	—	—	—	—
88-89—Djurgarden	Sweden	36	12	19	31	20	—	—	—	—	—
89-90—Djurgarden	Sweden	39	20	13	33	36	8	2	4	6	4
90-91—Detroit	NHL	71	18	22	40	18	6	0	1	1	4
91-92—Detroit	NHL	16	1	1	2	4	—	—	—	—	—
—Adirondack	AHL	9	3	3	6	6	—	—	—	—	—
—San Jose	NHL	12	5	6	11	4	—	—	—	—	—
NHL totals		99	24	29	53	26	6	0	1	1	4

GARTNER, MIKE
RW, RANGERS

PERSONAL: Born October 29, 1959, at Ottawa. . . . 6-0/188. . . . Shoots right. . . . Full name: Michael Alfred Gartner.

TRANSACTIONS/CAREER NOTES: Signed as underage junior by Cincinnati Stingers (August 1978). . . . Selected by Washington Capitals in first round (first Capitals pick, fourth overall) of NHL entry draft (August 9, 1979). . . . Injured eye (February 1983). . . . Underwent arthroscopic surgery to repair torn cartilage in left knee (March 1986). . . . Sprained right knee (November 1988). . . . Traded by Capitals with D Larry Murphy to Minnesota North Stars for RW Dino Ciccarelli and D Bob Rouse (March 7, 1989). . . . Underwent surgery to repair cartilage in left knee (April 14, 1989). . . . Traded by North Stars to New York Rangers for C Ulf Dahlen, fourth-round pick in 1990 draft, and future considerations (March 6, 1990).

HONORS: Won Emms Family Award (1976-77). . . . Named to OMJHL All-Star first team (1977-78).

			REGULAR SEASON					PLAYOFFS			
Season Team	League	Gms.	G	A	Pts.	Pen.	Gms.	G	A	Pts.	Pen.
75-76—St. Catharines	OHA Mj. Jr. A	3	1	3	4	0	—	—	—	—	—
76-77—Niagara Falls	OMJHL	62	33	42	75	125	—	—	—	—	—
77-78—Niagara Falls	OMJHL	64	41	49	90	56	—	—	—	—	—
78-79—Cincinnati	WHA	78	27	25	52	123	3	0	2	2	2
79-80—Washington	NHL	77	36	32	68	66	—	—	—	—	—
80-81—Washington	NHL	80	48	46	94	100	—	—	—	—	—
81-82—Washington	NHL	80	35	45	80	121	—	—	—	—	—
82-83—Washington	NHL	73	38	38	76	54	4	0	0	0	4
83-84—Washington	NHL	80	40	45	85	90	8	3	7	10	16
84-85—Washington	NHL	80	50	52	102	71	5	4	3	7	9
85-86—Washington	NHL	74	35	40	75	63	9	2	10	12	4
86-87—Washington	NHL	78	41	32	73	61	7	4	3	7	14
87-88—Washington	NHL	80	48	33	81	73	14	3	4	7	14
88-89—Washington	NHL	56	26	29	55	71	—	—	—	—	—
—Minnesota	NHL	13	7	7	14	2	5	0	0	0	0
89-90—Minnesota	NHL	67	34	36	70	32	—	—	—	—	—
—New York Rangers	NHL	12	11	5	16	6	10	5	3	8	12
90-91—New York Rangers	NHL	79	49	20	69	53	6	1	1	2	0
91-92—New York Rangers	NHL	76	40	41	81	55	13	8	8	16	4
WHA totals		78	27	25	52	123	3	0	2	2	2
NHL totals		1005	538	501	1039	918	81	30	39	69	77

GAUDREAU, ROB
RW, SHARKS

PERSONAL: Born January 20, 1970, at Providence, R.I. . . . 5-11/185. . . . Shoots right. . . . Full name: Robert Rene Gaudreau.

HIGH SCHOOL: Bishop Hendricken (R.I.).

COLLEGE: Providence.

TRANSACTIONS/CAREER NOTES: Separated shoulder (February 1987). . . . Selected by Pittsburgh Penguins in ninth round (eighth Penguins pick, 127th overall) of NHL entry draft (June 11, 1988). . . . Traded by Penguins to Minnesota North Stars for C Richard Zemlak (November 1, 1988). . . . Selected by San Jose Sharks in NHL dispersal draft (May 30, 1991).

HONORS: Named Hockey East co-Rookie of the Year with Scott Pellerin (1988-89). . . . Named to Hockey East All-Rookie team (1988-89). . . . Named to Hockey East All-Star second team (1990-91). . . . Named to Hockey East All-Star first team (1991-92).

			REGULAR SEASON					PLAYOFFS			
Season Team	League	Gms.	G	A	Pts.	Pen.	Gms.	G	A	Pts.	Pen.
86-87—Bishop Hendricken	R.I.H.S.	33	41	39	80		—	—	—	—	—
87-88—Bishop Hendricken	R.I.H.S.		52	60	112		—	—	—	—	—
88-89—Providence College	Hockey East	42	28	29	57	32	—	—	—	—	—
89-90—Providence College	Hockey East	32	20	18	38	12	—	—	—	—	—
90-91—Providence College	Hockey East	36	34	27	61	20	—	—	—	—	—
91-92—Providence College	Hockey East	36	21	34	55	22	—	—	—	—	—

GAUTHIER, DANIEL
LW, PENGUINS

PERSONAL: Born May 17, 1970, at Charlemagne, Que. . . . 6-2/190. . . . Shoots left.

TRANSACTIONS/CAREER NOTES: Selected by Pittsburgh Penguins in third round (third Penguins pick, 62nd overall) of NHL entry draft (June 11, 1988). . . . Left Victoriaville (January 2, 1990); returned (January 16, 1990).

HONORS: Won ECHL Rookie of the Year Award (1990-91). . . . Named to ECHL All-Star first team (1990-91).

G

Season	Team	League	Gms.	G	A	Pts.	Pen.	Gms.	G	A	Pts.	Pen.
			REGULAR SEASON					PLAYOFFS				
86-87	Longueuil	QMJHL	64	23	22	45	23	18	4	5	9	15
87-88	Victoriaville	QMJHL	66	43	47	90	53	5	2	1	3	0
88-89	Victoriaville	QMJHL	64	41	75	116	84	16	12	17	29	30
89-90	Victoriaville	QMJHL	62	45	69	114	32	16	8	*19	27	16
90-91	Albany	IHL	1	1	0	1	0	—	—	—	—	—
	Knoxville	ECHL	61	41	*93	134	40	2	0	4	4	4
91-92	Muskegon	IHL	68	19	18	37	28	9	3	6	9	8

GAUTHIER, LUC
D, CANADIENS

PERSONAL: Born April 19, 1964, at Longueuil, Que.... 5-9/195.... Shoots left.
TRANSACTIONS/CAREER NOTES: Signed as free agent by Montreal Canadiens (October 7, 1986).... Broke ankle (October 1987).

Season	Team	League	Gms.	G	A	Pts.	Pen.	Gms.	G	A	Pts.	Pen.
			REGULAR SEASON					PLAYOFFS				
82-83	Longueuil	QMJHL	67	3	18	21	132	—	—	—	—	—
83-84	Longueuil	QMJHL	70	8	54	62	207	—	—	—	—	—
84-85	Longueuil	QMJHL	60	13	47	60	111	—	—	—	—	—
	Flint	IHL	21	1	0	1	20	—	—	—	—	—
85-86	Saginaw	IHL	66	9	29	38	165	—	—	—	—	—
86-87	Sherbrooke	AHL	78	5	17	22	81	17	2	4	6	31
87-88	Sherbrooke	AHL	61	4	10	14	105	6	0	0	0	18
88-89	Sherbrooke	AHL	77	8	20	28	178	6	0	0	0	10
89-90	Sherbrooke	AHL	79	3	23	26	139	12	0	4	4	35
90-91	Fredericton	AHL	69	7	20	27	238	9	1	1	2	10
	Montreal	NHL	3	0	0	0	2	—	—	—	—	—
91-92	Fredericton	AHL	80	4	14	18	252	7	1	1	2	26
NHL totals			3	0	0	0	2					

GAUTHIER, SEAN
G, JETS

PERSONAL: Born March 28, 1971, at Sudbury, Ont.... 5-11/194.
TRANSACTIONS/CAREER NOTES: Selected by Winnipeg Jets in ninth round (seventh Jets pick, 181st overall) of NHL entry draft (June 22, 1991).

Season	Team	League	Gms.	Min.	W	L	T	GA	SO	Avg.	Gms.	Min.	W	L	GA	SO	Avg.
			REGULAR SEASON								PLAYOFFS						
91-92	Fort Wayne	IHL	18	978	10	4	2	59	1	3.62	2	48			7	0	8.75
	Moncton	AHL	25	1415	8	10	5	88	1	3.73	2	26			2	0	4.62

GAVEY, AARON
C, LIGHTNING

PERSONAL: Born February 22, 1974, at Sudbury, Ont.... 6-0/170.... Shoots left.
TRANSACTIONS/CAREER NOTES: Selected by Tampa Bay Lightning in fourth round (fourth Lightning pick, 74th overall) of NHL entry draft (June 20, 1992).

Season	Team	League	Gms.	G	A	Pts.	Pen.	Gms.	G	A	Pts.	Pen.
			REGULAR SEASON					PLAYOFFS				
90-91	Peterborough Jr. B	OHA	42	26	30	56	68	—	—	—	—	—
91-92	Sault Ste. Marie	OHL	48	7	11	18	27	19	5	1	6	10

GAVIN, STEWART
RW, NORTH STARS

PERSONAL: Born March 15, 1960, at Ottawa.... 6-0/190.... Shoots left.... Full name: Robert Stewart Gavin.
TRANSACTIONS/CAREER NOTES: Selected by Toronto Maple Leafs in fourth round (fourth Maple Leafs pick, 74th overall) of NHL entry draft (June 11, 1980).... Separated shoulder (October 1981).... Reinjured shoulder (December 1981).... Sprained ankle (October 1982).... Traded by Maple Leafs to Hartford Whalers for D Chris Kotsopoulos (October 7, 1985).... Strained ligaments in right ankle (December 8, 1987); missed 22 games.... Selected by Minnesota North Stars in 1988 NHL waiver draft for $7,500 (October 3, 1988).... Broke cheekbone (December 13, 1988).... Tore medial collateral ligament in left knee (November 4, 1990); missed 19 games.... Strained lower back (December 1990).... Resprained left knee ligament (January 13, 1991); missed 13 games.... Reaggravated left knee ligament injury (February 14, 1991); missed six games.... Injured groin (November 23, 1991); missed 44 games.

Season	Team	League	Gms.	G	A	Pts.	Pen.	Gms.	G	A	Pts.	Pen.
			REGULAR SEASON					PLAYOFFS				
76-77	Ottawa	OMJHL	1	0	0	0	0	—	—	—	—	—
77-78	Toronto	OMJHL	67	16	24	40	19	—	—	—	—	—
78-79	Toronto	OMJHL	61	24	25	49	83	3	1	0	1	0
79-80	Toronto	OMJHL	66	27	30	57	52	4	1	1	2	2
80-81	Toronto	NHL	14	1	2	3	13	—	—	—	—	—
	New Brunswick	AHL	46	7	12	19	42	13	1	0	1	2
81-82	Toronto	NHL	38	5	6	11	29	—	—	—	—	—
82-83	St. Catharines	AHL	6	2	4	6	17	—	—	—	—	—
	Toronto	NHL	63	6	5	11	44	4	0	0	0	0
83-84	Toronto	NHL	80	10	22	32	90	—	—	—	—	—
84-85	Toronto	NHL	73	12	13	25	38	—	—	—	—	—
85-86	Hartford	NHL	76	26	29	55	51	10	4	1	5	13
86-87	Hartford	NHL	79	20	22	42	28	6	2	4	6	10
87-88	Hartford	NHL	56	11	10	21	59	6	2	2	4	4
88-89	Minnesota	NHL	73	8	18	26	34	5	3	1	4	10

G

Season Team	League	REGULAR SEASON					PLAYOFFS				
		Gms.	G	A	Pts.	Pen.	Gms.	G	A	Pts.	Pen.
89-90—Minnesota	NHL	80	12	13	25	76	7	0	2	2	12
90-91—Minnesota	NHL	38	4	4	8	36	21	3	10	13	20
91-92—Minnesota	NHL	35	5	4	9	27	7	0	0	0	6
NHL totals		705	120	148	268	525	66	14	20	34	75

GELINAS, MARTIN
LW, OILERS

PERSONAL: Born June 5, 1970, at Shawinigan, Que.... 5-11/195.... Shoots left.
TRANSACTIONS/CAREER NOTES: Broke left clavicle (November 1983).... Suffered hairline fracture of clavicle (July 1986).... Selected by Los Angeles Kings in first round (first Kings pick, seventh overall) of NHL entry draft (June 11, 1988).... Traded by Kings with C Jimmy Carson, first-round picks in 1989 (traded to New Jersey), 1991 and 1993 drafts and cash to Edmonton Oilers for C Wayne Gretzky, RW/D Marty McSorley and LW/C Mike Krushelnyski (August 9, 1988).... Suspended five games (March 9, 1990).... Underwent shoulder surgery (June 1990).
HONORS: Won Can.HL Rookie of the Year Award (1987-88).... Won Michel Bergeron Trophy (1987-88).

Season Team	League	REGULAR SEASON					PLAYOFFS				
		Gms.	G	A	Pts.	Pen.	Gms.	G	A	Pts.	Pen.
87-88—Hull	QMJHL	65	63	68	131	74	17	15	18	33	32
88-89—Edmonton	NHL	6	1	2	3	0	—	—	—	—	—
Hull	QMJHL	41	38	39	77	31	9	5	4	9	14
89-90—Edmonton	NHL	46	17	8	25	30	20	2	3	5	6
90-91—Edmonton	NHL	73	20	20	40	34	18	3	6	9	25
91-92—Edmonton	NHL	68	11	18	29	62	15	1	3	4	10
NHL totals		193	49	48	97	126	53	6	12	18	41

GENDRON, MARTIN
RW, CAPITALS

PERSONAL: Born February 15, 1974, at Valleyfield, Que.... 5-8/180.... Shoots right.
TRANSACTIONS/CAREER NOTES: Selected by Washington Capitals in third round (fourth Capitals pick, 71st overall) of NHL entry draft (June 20, 1992).
HONORS: Named to QMJHL All-Rookie team (1990-91).... Won Can.HL Most Sportsmanlike Player of the Year Award (1991-92).... Won Shell Cup (1991-92).... Won Frank J. Selke Trophy (1991-92).... Named to QMJHL All-Star first team (1991-92).

Season Team	League	REGULAR SEASON					PLAYOFFS				
		Gms.	G	A	Pts.	Pen.	Gms.	G	A	Pts.	Pen.
90-91—St. Hyacinthe	QMJHL	55	34	23	57	33	4	1	2	3	0
91-92—St. Hyacinthe	QMJHL	69	*71	66	137	45	6	7	4	11	14

GERMAIN, ERIC
D, RANGERS

PERSONAL: Born June 26, 1966, at Quebec City.... 6-1/190.... Shoots left.
TRANSACTIONS/CAREER NOTES: Signed as free agent by Los Angeles Kings (June 1986).... Suspended 10 games by AHL for bumping into referee (March 13, 1990).... Signed as free agent by New York Rangers (July 19, 1990).

Season Team	League	REGULAR SEASON					PLAYOFFS				
		Gms.	G	A	Pts.	Pen.	Gms.	G	A	Pts.	Pen.
83-84—St. Jean	QMJHL	57	2	15	17	60	4	1	0	1	6
84-85—St. Jean	QMJHL	66	10	31	41	243	5	4	0	4	14
85-86—St. Jean	QMJHL	66	5	38	43	183	10	0	6	6	56
86-87—Flint	IHL	21	0	2	2	23	—	—	—	—	—
—Fredericton	AHL	44	2	8	10	28	—	—	—	—	—
87-88—Los Angeles	NHL	4	0	1	1	13	1	0	0	0	4
—New Haven	AHL	69	0	10	10	82	—	—	—	—	—
88-89—New Haven	AHL	55	0	9	9	93	17	0	3	3	23
89-90—New Haven	AHL	59	3	12	15	112	—	—	—	—	—
90-91—Binghamton	AHL	60	4	10	14	144	10	0	1	1	14
91-92—Binghamton	AHL	47	3	6	9	86	3	0	0	0	0
—Moncton	AHL	3	0	2	2	4	—	—	—	—	—
NHL totals		4	0	1	1	13	1	0	0	0	4

GERNANDER, KEN
LW, JETS

PERSONAL: Born June 30, 1969, at Grand Rapids, Minn.... 5-10/175.... Shoots left.... Full name: Kenneth Robert Gernander.
HIGH SCHOOL: Greenway (Coleraine, Minn.).
COLLEGE: Minnesota.
TRANSACTIONS/CAREER NOTES: Selected by Winnipeg Jets in fifth round (fourth Jets pick, 96th overall) of NHL entry draft (June 13, 1987).

Season Team	League	REGULAR SEASON					PLAYOFFS				
		Gms.	G	A	Pts.	Pen.	Gms.	G	A	Pts.	Pen.
85-86—Greenway H.S.	Minn. H.S.	23	14	23	37		—	—	—	—	—
86-87—Greenway H.S.	Minn. H.S.	26	35	34	69		—	—	—	—	—
87-88—University of Minnesota	WCHA	44	14	14	28	14	—	—	—	—	—
88-89—University of Minnesota	WCHA	44	9	11	20	2	—	—	—	—	—
89-90—University of Minnesota	WCHA	44	32	17	49	24	—	—	—	—	—
90-91—University of Minnesota	WCHA	44	23	20	43	24	—	—	—	—	—
91-92—Moncton	AHL	43	8	18	26	9	8	1	1	2	2
—Fort Wayne	IHL	13	7	6	13	2	—	—	—	—	—

G

GIBSON, DON

D, CANUCKS

PERSONAL: Born December 29, 1967, at Deloraine, Man. . . . 6-1/210. . . . Shoots right. . . . Full name: Donald Scott Gibson.
COLLEGE: Michigan State.
TRANSACTIONS/CAREER NOTES: Selected by Vancouver Canucks in third round (second Canucks pick, 49th overall) of NHL entry draft (June 21, 1986). . . . Suspended three games by CCHA for spearing and fighting (February 1988). . . . Injured knee (December 1988). . . . Injured knee (December 1989).
HONORS: Named to CCHA All-Star second team (1989-90).

Season Team	League	REGULAR SEASON					PLAYOFFS				
		Gms.	G	A	Pts.	Pen.	Gms.	G	A	Pts.	Pen.
85-86—Winkler	MJHL	34	24	29	53	210	—	—	—	—	—
86-87—Michigan State	CCHA	43	3	3	6	74	—	—	—	—	—
87-88—Michigan State	CCHA	43	7	12	19	118	—	—	—	—	—
88-89—Michigan State	CCHA	39	7	10	17	107	—	—	—	—	—
89-90—Michigan State	CCHA	44	5	22	27	167	—	—	—	—	—
—Milwaukee	IHL	1	0	0	0	4	5	0	1	1	41
90-91—Milwaukee	IHL	21	4	3	7	76	—	—	—	—	—
—Vancouver	NHL	14	0	3	3	20	—	—	—	—	—
91-92—Milwaukee	IHL	35	6	9	15	105	4	1	0	1	7
NHL totals		14	0	3	3	20					

GILBERT, GREG

LW, BLACKHAWKS

PERSONAL: Born January 22, 1962, at Mississauga, Ontario. . . . 6-1/191. . . . Shoots left. . . . Full name: Gregory Scott Gilbert.
TRANSACTIONS/CAREER NOTES: Sprained ankle (December 1979). . . . Selected by New York Islanders as underage junior in fourth round (fifth Islanders pick, 80th overall) of NHL entry draft (June 11, 1980). . . . Stretched ligaments in left ankle (September 1984). . . . Injured ligaments in knee and underwent arthroscopic surgery then major reconstructive surgery (February 27, 1985). . . . Broke jaw (October 11, 1986); missed 10 games. . . . Bruised thigh (December 7, 1986). . . . Bruised hip (February 1987). . . . Separated right shoulder (March 1987). . . . Bruised right knee (February 20, 1987). . . . Injured left foot (April 1988). . . . Suffered back spasms and injured left shoulder (February 1989). . . . Traded by Islanders to Chicago Blackhawks for fifth-round pick in 1989 draft (RW Steve Young) (March 7, 1989). . . . Broke foot (March 1989). . . . Strained abdominal muscle during practice (March 8, 1990). . . . Bruised left shoulder (September 28 ,1990); missed first eight games of season. . . . Hyperextended left knee (April 1991). . . . Pulled lateral muscle (November 13, 1991); missed two games. . . . Fracture ankle (February 16, 1992). . . . Suffered slight strain of left knee (April 4, 1992).

Season Team	League	REGULAR SEASON					PLAYOFFS				
		Gms.	G	A	Pts.	Pen.	Gms.	G	A	Pts.	Pen.
79-80—Toronto	OMJHL	68	10	11	21	35	—	—	—	—	—
80-81—Toronto	OMJHL	64	30	37	67	73	5	2	6	8	16
81-82—Toronto	OHL	65	41	67	108	119	10	4	12	16	23
—New York Islanders	NHL	1	1	0	1	0	4	1	1	2	2
82-83—Indianapolis	CHL	24	11	16	27	23	—	—	—	—	—
—New York Islanders	NHL	45	8	11	19	30	10	1	0	1	14
83-84—New York Islanders	NHL	79	31	35	66	59	21	5	7	12	39
84-85—New York Islanders	NHL	58	13	25	38	36	—	—	—	—	—
85-86—Springfield	AHL	2	0	0	0	2	—	—	—	—	—
—New York Islanders	NHL	60	9	19	28	82	2	0	0	0	9
86-87—New York Islanders	NHL	51	6	7	13	26	10	2	2	4	6
87-88—New York Islanders	NHL	76	17	28	45	46	4	0	0	0	6
88-89—New York Islanders	NHL	55	8	13	21	45	—	—	—	—	—
—Chicago	NHL	4	0	0	0	0	15	1	5	6	20
89-90—Chicago	NHL	70	12	25	37	54	19	5	8	13	34
90-91—Chicago	NHL	72	10	15	25	58	5	0	1	1	2
91-92—Chicago	NHL	50	7	5	12	35	10	1	3	4	16
NHL totals		621	122	183	305	471	100	16	27	43	148

GILCHRIST, BRENT

C, CANADIENS

PERSONAL: Born April 3, 1967, at Moose Jaw, Sask. . . . 5-11/181. . . . Shoots left.
TRANSACTIONS/CAREER NOTES: Strained medial collateral ligament (January 1985). . . . Selected by Montreal Canadiens as underage junior in sixth round (sixth Canadiens pick, 79th overall) of NHL entry draft (June 15, 1985). . . . Injured knee (January 1987). . . . Broke right index finger (November 17, 1990); missed 19 games. . . . Separated left shoulder (February 6, 1991); missed two games. . . . Reinjured left shoulder (February 13, 1991); missed five games.

Season Team	League	REGULAR SEASON					PLAYOFFS				
		Gms.	G	A	Pts.	Pen.	Gms.	G	A	Pts.	Pen.
83-84—Kelowna Wings	WHL	69	16	11	27	16	—	—	—	—	—
84-85—Kelowna Wings	WHL	51	35	38	73	58	6	5	2	7	8
85-86—Spokane Chiefs	WHL	52	45	45	90	57	9	6	7	13	19
86-87—Spokane Chiefs	WHL	46	45	55	100	71	5	2	7	9	6
—Sherbrooke	AHL	—	—	—	—	—	10	2	7	9	2
87-88—Sherbrooke	AHL	77	26	48	74	83	6	1	3	4	6
88-89—Montreal	NHL	49	8	16	24	16	9	1	1	2	10
—Sherbrooke	AHL	7	6	5	11	7	—	—	—	—	—
89-90—Montreal	NHL	57	9	15	24	28	8	2	0	2	2
90-91—Montreal	NHL	51	6	9	15	10	13	5	3	8	6
91-92—Montreal	NHL	79	23	27	50	57	11	2	4	6	6
NHL totals		236	46	67	113	111	41	10	8	18	24

G

GILES, CURT

D, BLUES

PERSONAL: Born October 30, 1958, at The Pas, Man. . . . 5-8/175. . . . Shoots left. . . . Full name: Curtis Jon Giles.
COLLEGE: Minnesota-Duluth.
TRANSACTIONS/CAREER NOTES: Selected by Minnesota North Stars in fourth round (fourth North Stars pick, 54th overall) of NHL entry draft (June 15, 1978). . . . Suffered right knee strain (February 1981). . . . Injured knee (January 1984). . . . Underwent surgery to amputate left ring finger due to a tumor that had grown into the bone (March 24, 1986). . . . Traded by North Stars with LW Tony McKegney and second-round pick in 1988 draft (C Troy Mallette) to New York Rangers for RW/C/D Bob Brooke and fourth-round pick in 1988 draft (November 13, 1986). . . . Fractured elbow (April 14, 1987). . . . Traded by Rangers to North Stars for C Byron Lomow and future considerations (November 20, 1987). . . . Injured groin (November 6, 1989). . . . Strained lower back (March 1990). . . . Sprained left knee ligament (January 25, 1991). . . . Announced retirement (October 4, 1991). . . . Signed as free agent by St. Louis Blues (February 29, 1992).
HONORS: Named to NCAA All-America team (1977-78 and 1978-79). . . . Named to WCHA All-Star first team (1977-78 and 1978-79).
MISCELLANEOUS: Member of 1992 silver-medal-winning Canadian Olympic team.

			REGULAR SEASON					PLAYOFFS				
Season	Team	League	Gms.	G	A	Pts.	Pen.	Gms.	G	A	Pts.	Pen.
75-76	Minnesota-Duluth	WCHA	34	5	17	22	76	—	—	—	—	—
76-77	Minnesota-Duluth	WCHA	37	12	37	49	64	—	—	—	—	—
77-78	Minnesota-Duluth	WCHA	34	11	36	47	62	—	—	—	—	—
78-79	Minnesota-Duluth	WCHA	30	3	38	41	38	—	—	—	—	—
79-80	Oklahoma City	CHL	42	4	24	28	05	—	—	—	—	—
	Minnesota	NHL	37	2	7	9	31	12	2	4	6	10
80-81	Minnesota	NHL	67	5	22	27	56	19	1	4	5	14
81-82	Minnesota	NHL	74	3	12	15	87	4	0	0	0	2
82-83	Minnesota	NHL	76	2	21	23	70	5	0	2	2	6
83-84	Minnesota	NHL	70	6	22	28	59	16	1	3	4	25
84-85	Minnesota	NHL	77	5	25	30	49	9	0	0	0	17
85-86	Minnesota	NHL	69	6	21	27	30	5	0	1	1	10
86-87	Minnesota	NHL	11	0	3	3	4	—	—	—	—	—
	New York Rangers	NHL	61	2	17	19	50	5	0	0	0	6
87-88	New York Rangers	NHL	13	0	0	0	10	—	—	—	—	—
	Minnesota	NHL	59	1	12	13	66	—	—	—	—	—
88-89	Minnesota	NHL	76	5	10	15	77	5	0	0	0	4
89-90	Minnesota	NHL	74	1	12	13	48	7	0	1	1	6
90-91	Minnesota	NHL	70	4	10	14	48	10	1	0	1	16
91-92	Canadian National Team	Int'l	31	3	6	9	37	—	—	—	—	—
	Canadian Olympic Team	Int'l	8	1	0	1	6	—	—	—	—	—
	St. Louis	NHL	13	1	1	2	8	3	1	1	2	0
NHL totals			847	43	195	238	693	100	6	16	22	116

GILHEN, RANDY

C, RANGERS

PERSONAL: Born June 13, 1963, at Zweibrucken, West Germany. . . . 6-0/192. . . . Shoots left.
TRANSACTIONS/CAREER NOTES: Selected by Hartford Whalers as underage junior in sixth round (sixth Whalers pick, 109th overall) of NHL entry draft (June 9, 1982). . . . Signed as free agent by Winnipeg Jets (August 1985). . . . Separated shoulder (November 16, 1988). . . . Traded by Jets with RW Andrew McBain and D Jim Kyte to Pittsburgh Penguins for C/LW Randy Cunneyworth, G Richard Tabaracci and RW Dave McIlwain (June 17, 1989). . . . Sprained knee (November 2, 1989). . . . Selected by Minnesota North Stars in NHL expansion draft (May 30, 1991). . . . Traded by North Stars with D Charlie Huddy, RW Jim Thomson and fourth-round pick in 1991 draft (D Alexei Zhitnik) to Los Angeles Kings for C Todd Elik (June 22, 1991). . . . Traded by Kings to New York Rangers for C Corey Millen (December 23, 1991).

			REGULAR SEASON					PLAYOFFS				
Season	Team	League	Gms.	G	A	Pts.	Pen.	Gms.	G	A	Pts.	Pen.
79-80	Saskatoon	SJHL	55	18	34	52	112	—	—	—	—	—
	Saskatoon	WHL	9	2	2	4	20	—	—	—	—	—
80-81	Saskatoon	WHL	68	10	5	15	154	—	—	—	—	—
81-82	Winnipeg	WHL	61	41	37	78	87	—	—	—	—	—
82-83	Winnipeg	WHL	71	57	44	101	84	3	2	2	4	0
	Hartford	NHL	2	0	1	1	0	—	—	—	—	—
	Binghamton	AHL	—	—	—	—	—	5	2	0	2	2
83-84	Binghamton	AHL	73	8	12	20	72	—	—	—	—	—
84-85	Salt Lake City	IHL	57	20	20	40	28	—	—	—	—	—
	Binghamton	AHL	18	3	3	6	9	8	4	1	5	16
85-86	Fort Wayne	IHL	82	44	40	84	48	15	10	8	18	6
86-87	Winnipeg	NHL	2	0	0	0	0	—	—	—	—	—
	Sherbrooke	AHL	75	36	29	65	44	17	7	13	20	10
87-88	Winnipeg	NHL	13	3	2	5	15	4	1	0	1	10
	Moncton	AHL	68	40	47	87	51	—	—	—	—	—
88-89	Winnipeg	NHL	64	5	3	8	38	—	—	—	—	—
89-90	Pittsburgh	NHL	61	5	11	16	54	—	—	—	—	—
90-91	Pittsburgh	NHL	72	15	10	25	51	16	1	0	1	14
91-92	Los Angeles	NHL	33	3	6	9	14	—	—	—	—	—
	New York Rangers	NHL	40	7	7	14	14	13	1	2	3	2
NHL totals			287	38	40	78	186	33	3	2	5	26

G

GILL, TODD
D, MAPLE LEAFS

PERSONAL: Born November 9, 1965, at Brockville, Ont.... 6-0/185.... Shoots left.
TRANSACTIONS/CAREER NOTES: Selected by Toronto Maple Leafs as underage junior in second round (second Maple Leafs pick, 25th overall) of NHL entry draft (June 9, 1984).... Broke bone in right foot (October 1987).... Bruised shoulder (March 1989).... Fractured finger (October 15, 1991); missed three games.... Strained back (February 8, 1992); missed three games.

Season Team	League	REGULAR SEASON Gms.	G	A	Pts.	Pen.	PLAYOFFS Gms.	G	A	Pts.	Pen.
82-83—Windsor	OHL	70	12	24	36	108	3	0	0	0	11
83-84—Windsor	OHL	68	9	48	57	184	3	1	1	2	10
84-85—Toronto	NHL	10	1	0	1	13	—	—	—	—	—
—Windsor	OHL	53	17	40	57	148	4	0	1	1	14
85-86—St. Catharines	AHL	58	8	25	33	90	10	1	6	7	17
—Toronto	NHL	15	1	2	3	28	1	0	0	0	0
86-87—Newmarket	AHL	11	1	8	9	33	—	—	—	—	—
—Toronto	NHL	61	4	27	31	92	13	2	2	4	42
87-88—Newmarket	AHL	2	0	1	1	2	—	—	—	—	—
—Toronto	NHL	65	8	17	25	131	6	1	3	4	20
88-89—Toronto	NHL	59	11	14	25	72	—	—	—	—	—
89-90—Toronto	NHL	48	1	14	15	92	5	0	3	3	16
90-91—Toronto	NHL	72	2	22	24	113	—	—	—	—	—
91-92—Toronto	NHL	74	2	15	17	91	—	—	—	—	—
NHL totals		**404**	**30**	**111**	**141**	**632**	**25**	**3**	**8**	**11**	**78**

GILLIS, PAUL
C, WHALERS

PERSONAL: Born December 31, 1963, at Toronto.... 5-11/198.... Shoots left.... Full name: Paul C. Gillis.
TRANSACTIONS/CAREER NOTES: Selected by Quebec Nordiques as underage junior in second round (second Nordiques pick, 34th overall) of NHL entry draft (June 9, 1982).... Suspended three games by NHL for scratching during a fight (November 2, 1986).... Developed Guillain-Barre Syndrome, a neurological disorder brought on by a virus (Summer 1989); missed first eight games of season.... Sprained knee (November 1989).... Separated right shoulder (September 1990); missed first 13 games of season.... Traded by Nordiques with LW Dan Vincelette to Chicago Blackhawks for C Mike McNeil and D Ryan McGill (March 5, 1991).... Traded by Blackhawks to Hartford Whalers for future considerations (January 27, 1992).... Fractured left foot (February 4, 1992); missed 22 games.

Season Team	League	REGULAR SEASON Gms.	G	A	Pts.	Pen.	PLAYOFFS Gms.	G	A	Pts.	Pen.
80-81—Niagara Falls	OMJHL	59	14	19	33	165	—	—	—	—	—
81-82—Niagara Falls	OHL	66	27	62	89	247	5	1	5	6	26
82-83—North Bay	OHL	61	34	52	86	151	6	1	3	4	26
—Quebec	NHL	7	0	2	2	2	—	—	—	—	—
83-84—Fredericton	AHL	18	7	8	15	47	—	—	—	—	—
—Quebec	NHL	57	8	9	17	59	1	0	0	0	2
84-85—Quebec	NHL	77	14	28	42	168	18	1	7	8	73
85-86—Quebec	NHL	80	19	24	43	203	3	0	2	2	16
86-87—Quebec	NHL	76	13	26	39	267	13	2	4	6	65
87-88—Quebec	NHL	80	7	10	17	164	—	—	—	—	—
88-89—Quebec	NHL	79	15	25	40	163	—	—	—	—	—
89-90—Quebec	NHL	71	8	14	22	234	—	—	—	—	—
90-91—Quebec	NHL	49	3	8	11	91	—	—	—	—	—
—Chicago	NHL	13	0	5	5	53	2	0	0	0	2
91-92—Chicago	NHL	2	0	0	0	6	—	—	—	—	—
—Indianapolis	IHL	42	10	15	25	170	—	—	—	—	—
—Hartford	NHL	12	0	2	2	48	5	0	1	1	0
NHL totals		**603**	**87**	**153**	**240**	**1458**	**42**	**3**	**14**	**17**	**158**

GILMORE, MIKE
G, RANGERS

PERSONAL: Born March 11, 1968, at Detroit.... 5-10/173.... Shoots left.
COLLEGE: Michigan State.
TRANSACTIONS/CAREER NOTES: Selected by New York Rangers in NHL supplemental draft (June 15, 1990).
HONORS: Named to CCHA All-Star second team (1990-91).

Season Team	League	REGULAR SEASON Gms.	Min.	W	L	T	GA	SO	Avg.	PLAYOFFS Gms.	Min.	W	L	GA	SO	Avg.
88-89—Michigan State	CCHA	3	74	1	0	0	5	0	4.05	—	—	—	—	—	—	—
89-90—Michigan State	CCHA	12	638	9	1	0	29	0	2.73	—	—	—	—	—	—	—
90-91—Michigan State	CCHA	22	1218	9	8	3	54	*2	2.66	—	—	—	—	—	—	—
91-92—Michigan State	CCHA	36	2011	16	10	7	103	2	3.07	—	—	—	—	—	—	—

GILMOUR, DARRYL
G, KINGS

PERSONAL: Born February 13, 1967, at Winnipeg, Man.... 6-0/171.... Shoots left.
TRANSACTIONS/CAREER NOTES: Selected by Philadelphia Flyers as underage junior in third round (third Flyers pick, 48th overall) of NHL entry draft (June 15, 1985).... Signed as free agent by Los Angeles Kings (December 15, 1989).
HONORS: Named to WHL All-Star first team (1985-86).

Season Team	League	REGULAR SEASON Gms.	Min.	W	L	T	GA	SO	Avg.	PLAYOFFS Gms.	Min.	W	L	GA	SO	Avg.
83-84—St. James	MJHL	15	900				45		3.00	—	—	—	—	—	—	—
84-85—Moose Jaw	WHL	*58	3004	15	35	0	*297	0	5.93	—	—	—	—	—	—	—

G

Season Team	League	Gms.	Min.	W	L	T	GA	SO	Avg.	Gms.	Min.	W	L	GA	SO	Avg.
				REGULAR SEASON								PLAYOFFS				
85-86—Moose Jaw	WHL	*62	*3482	19	34	3	*276	1	4.76	9	490	4	4	48	0	5.88
86-87—Moose Jaw	WHL	31	1776	14	13	2	123	2	4.16	—	—	—	—	—	—	—
—Portland	WHL	24	1460	15	7	1	111	0	4.56	19	1167	12	7	83	1	4.27
87-88—Hershey	AHL	25	1273	14	7	0	78	1	3.68	—	—	—	—	—	—	—
88-89—Hershey	AHL	38	2093	16	14	5	144	0	4.13	—	—	—	—	—	—	—
89-90—Nashville	ECHL	10	529	6	3	0	43	0	4.88	—	—	—	—	—	—	—
—New Haven	AHL	23	1356	10	11	2	85	0	3.76	—	—	—	—	—	—	—
90-91—New Haven	AHL	26	1375	5	14	3	90	1	3.93	—	—	—	—	—	—	—
—Phoenix	IHL	4	180	2	0	0	13	0	4.33	—	—	—	—	—	—	—
91-92—Phoenix	IHL	30	1774	10	15	3	120	0	4.06	—	—	—	—	—	—	—

GILMOUR, DOUG

C, MAPLE LEAFS

PERSONAL: Born June 25, 1963, at Kingston, Ont. . . . 5-11/164. . . . Shoots left. . . . Full name: Douglas Gilmour.

TRANSACTIONS/CAREER NOTES: Selected by St. Louis Blues as underage junior in seventh round (fourth Blues pick, 134th overall) of NHL entry draft (June 9, 1982). . . . Sprained ankle (October 7, 1985); missed four games. . . . Suffered concussion (January 1988). . . . Bruised shoulder (March 1988). . . . Traded by Blues with RW Mark Hunter, LW Steve Bozek and D/RW Michael Dark to Calgary Flames for C Mike Bullard, C Craig Coxe and D Tim Corkery (September 5, 1988). . . . Suffered abscessed jaw (March 1989); missed six games. . . . Broke bone in right foot (August 12, 1989). . . . Traded by Flames with D Ric Nattress, D Jamie Macoun, LW Kent Manderville and G Rick Wamsley to Toronto Maple Leafs for LW Craig Berube, D Alexander Godynyuk, LW Gary Leeman, D Michel Petit and G Jeff Reese (January 2, 1992).

HONORS: Won Red Tilson Trophy (1982-83). . . . Won Eddie Powers Memorial Trophy (1982-83). . . . Named to OHL All-Star first team (1982-83).

Season Team	League	Gms.	G	A	Pts.	Pen.	Gms.	G	A	Pts.	Pen.
			REGULAR SEASON						PLAYOFFS		
80-81—Cornwall	QMJHL	51	12	23	35	35	—	—	—	—	—
81-82—Cornwall	OHL	67	46	73	119	42	5	6	9	15	2
82-83—Cornwall	OHL	68	*70	*107	*177	62	8	8	10	18	16
83-84—St. Louis	NHL	80	25	28	53	57	11	2	9	11	10
84-85—St. Louis	NHL	78	21	36	57	49	3	1	1	2	2
85-86—St. Louis	NHL	74	25	28	53	41	19	9	12	†21	25
86-87—St. Louis	NHL	80	42	63	105	58	6	2	2	4	16
87-88—St. Louis	NHL	72	36	50	86	59	10	3	14	17	18
88-89—Calgary	NHL	72	26	59	85	44	22	11	11	22	20
89-90—Calgary	NHL	78	24	67	91	54	6	3	1	4	8
90-91—Calgary	NHL	78	20	61	81	144	7	1	1	2	0
91-92—Calgary	NHL	38	11	27	38	46	—	—	—	—	—
—Toronto	NHL	40	15	34	49	32	—	—	—	—	—
NHL totals		690	245	453	698	584	84	32	51	83	99

GLENNON, MATT

LW, BRUINS

PERSONAL: Born September 20, 1968, at Hull, Mass. . . . 6-0/185. . . . Shoots left. . . . Full name: Matthew Joseph Glennon.

COLLEGE: Boston College.

TRANSACTIONS/CAREER NOTES: Selected by Boston Bruins in sixth round (seventh Bruins pick, 119th overall) of NHL entry draft (June 13, 1987).

Season Team	League	Gms.	G	A	Pts.	Pen.	Gms.	G	A	Pts.	Pen.
			REGULAR SEASON						PLAYOFFS		
87-88—Boston College	Hockey East	16	3	3	6	16	—	—	—	—	—
88-89—Boston College	Hockey East	16	1	6	7	4	—	—	—	—	—
89-90—Boston College	Hockey East	31	7	11	18	16	—	—	—	—	—
90-91—Boston College	Hockey East	33	6	9	15	36	—	—	—	—	—
91-92—Maine	AHL	32	6	12	18	13	—	—	—	—	—
—Johnstown	ECHL	30	9	46	55	77	6	2	4	6	25
—Boston	NHL	3	0	0	0	2	—	—	—	—	—
NHL totals		3	0	0	0	2					

GLYNN, BRIAN

D, OILERS

PERSONAL: Born November 23, 1967, at Iserlohn, West Germany. . . . 6-4/224. . . . Shoots left. . . . Full name: Brian Thomas Glynn.

TRANSACTIONS/CAREER NOTES: Selected by Calgary Flames in second round (second Flames pick, 37th overall) of NHL entry draft (June 21, 1986). . . . Traded by Flames to Minnesota North Stars for D Frantisek Musil (October 26, 1990). . . . Traded by North Stars to Edmonton Oilers for D David Shaw (January 21, 1992). . . . Injured knee (March 15, 1992); missed seven games.

HONORS: Won Governors Trophy (1989-90). . . . Named to IHL All-Star first team (1989-90).

Season Team	League	Gms.	G	A	Pts.	Pen.	Gms.	G	A	Pts.	Pen.
			REGULAR SEASON						PLAYOFFS		
84-85—Saskatoon	SJHL	12	1	0	1	2	3	0	0	0	0
85-86—Saskatoon	WHL	66	7	25	32	131	13	0	3	3	30
86-87—Saskatoon	WHL	44	2	26	28	163	11	1	3	4	19
87-88—Calgary	NHL	67	5	14	19	87	1	0	0	0	0
88-89—Salt Lake City	IHL	31	3	10	13	105	14	3	7	10	31
—Calgary	NHL	9	0	1	1	19	—	—	—	—	—

G

Season	Team	League	REGULAR SEASON					PLAYOFFS				
			Gms.	G	A	Pts.	Pen.	Gms.	G	A	Pts.	Pen.
89-90	—Calgary	NHL	1	0	0	0	0	—	—	—	—	—
	—Salt Lake City	IHL	80	17	44	61	164	—	—	—	—	—
90-91	—Salt Lake City	IHL	8	1	3	4	18	—	—	—	—	—
	—Minnesota	NHL	66	8	11	19	83	23	2	6	8	18
91-92	—Minnesota	NHL	37	2	12	14	24	—	—	—	—	—
	—Edmonton	NHL	25	2	6	8	6	16	4	1	5	12
NHL totals			205	17	44	61	219	40	6	7	13	30

GODYNYUK, ALEXANDER

D, FLAMES

PERSONAL: Born January 27, 1970, at Kiev, U.S.S.R. . . . 6-0/207. . . . Shoots left.
TRANSACTIONS/CAREER NOTES: Selected by Toronto Maple Leafs in sixth round (fifth Maple Leafs pick, 115th overall) of NHL entry draft (June 16, 1990). . . . Traded by Maple Leafs with LW Craig Berube, RW Gary Leeman, D Michel Petit and G Jeff Reese to Calgary Flames for C Doug Gilmour, D Jamie Macoun, LW Kent Manderville, D Ric Nattress and G Rick Wamsley (January 2, 1992).

Season	Team	League	REGULAR SEASON					PLAYOFFS				
			Gms.	G	A	Pts.	Pen.	Gms.	G	A	Pts.	Pen.
89-90	—Sokol Kiev	USSR	38	3	2	5	31	—	—	—	—	—
90-91	—Sokol Kiev	USSR	19	3	1	4	20	—	—	—	—	—
	—Toronto	NHL	18	0	3	3	16	—	—	—	—	—
	—Newmarket	AHL	11	0	1	1	29	—	—	—	—	—
91-92	—Toronto	NHL	31	3	6	9	59	—	—	—	—	—
	—Calgary	NHL	6	0	1	1	4	—	—	—	—	—
	—Salt Lake City	IHL	17	2	1	3	24	—	—	—	—	—
NHL totals			55	3	10	13	79					

GONCHAR, SERGEI

D, CAPITALS

PERSONAL: Born April 13, 1974, at Chelyabinsk, U.S.S.R. . . . 6-0/178. . . . Shoots left.
TRANSACTIONS/CAREER NOTES: Selected by Washington Capitals in first round (first Capitals pick, 14th overall) of NHL entry draft (June 20, 1992).

Season	Team	League	REGULAR SEASON					PLAYOFFS				
			Gms.	G	A	Pts.	Pen.	Gms.	G	A	Pts.	Pen.
90-91	—Mechel Chelyabinsk	USSR	2	0	0	0	0	—	—	—	—	—
91-92	—Traktor Chelyabinsk	CIS	31	1	0	1	6	—	—	—	—	—

GORDON, SCOTT

G, NORDIQUES

PERSONAL: Born February 6, 1963, at South Easton, Mass. . . . 5-10/175. . . . Shoots left. . . . Full name: Scott Michael Gordon.
COLLEGE: Boston College.
TRANSACTIONS/CAREER NOTES: Signed as free agent by Quebec Nordiques (October 1986).
HONORS: Named to Hockey East All-Star first team (1985-86).

Season	Team	League	REGULAR SEASON							PLAYOFFS					
			Gms.	Min.	W	L	T	GA	SO	Avg.	Gms.	Min.	W	L	GA SO	Avg.
82-83	—Boston College	ECAC	9	371	3	3	0	15	0	2.43	—	—	—	—	—	—
83-84	—Boston College	ECAC	35	2034	21	13	0	127	1	3.75	—	—	—	—	—	—
84-85	—Boston College	Hoc. East	36	2179	23	11	2	131	1	3.61	—	—	—	—	—	—
85-86	—Boston College	Hoc. East	32	1851	17	8	1	112	2	3.63	—	—	—	—	—	—
86-87	—Fredericton	AHL	31	1616	9	12	2	119	0	4.42	—	—	—	—	—	—
87-88	—Baltimore	AHL	34	1638	7	17	3	145	0	5.31	—	—	—	—	—	—
88-89	—Halifax	AHL	2	116	0	2	0	10	0	5.17	—	—	—	—	—	—
	—Johnstown	ECHL	31	1839				117	†2	*3.82	*11	*647			*36 0	*3.34
89-90	—Quebec	NHL	10	597	2	8	0	53	0	5.33	—	—	—	—	—	—
	—Halifax	AHL	48	2851	28	16	3	158	0	3.33	6	340	2	4	28 0	4.94
90-91	—Quebec	NHL	13	485	0	8	0	48	0	5.94	—	—	—	—	—	—
	—Halifax	AHL	24	1410	12	10	2	87	2	3.70	—	—	—	—	—	—
91-92	—Halifax	AHL	7	424	3	3	1	27	0	3.82	—	—	—	—	—	—
	—U.S. National Team	Int'l	29	1666	13	12	3	112	0	4.03	—	—	—	—	—	—
	—U.S. Olympic Team	Int'l	1	17	0	0	0	2	0	7.06	—	—	—	—	—	—
	—New Haven	AHL	4	239	3	1	0	11	0	2.76	2	119	0	2	9 0	4.54
NHL totals			23	1082	2	16	0	101	0	5.60						

GOSSELIN, MARIO

G, WHALERS

PERSONAL: Born June 15, 1963, at Thetford Mines, Que. . . . 5-8/160. . . . Shoots left.
TRANSACTIONS/CAREER NOTES: Selected by Quebec Nordiques as underage junior in third round (third Nordiques pick, 55th overall) of NHL entry draft (June 9, 1982). . . . Injured knee (March 8, 1984); missed remainder of season. . . . Suffered from the flu (January 16, 1986); missed one game. . . . Signed as free agent by Los Angeles Kings (June 1989). . . . Suffered from the flu (October 1989). . . . Signed as free agent by Hartford Whalers (September 4, 1991).
HONORS: Named to QMJHL All-Star second team (1981-82). . . . Named to QMJHL All-Star first team (1982-83).

Season	Team	League	REGULAR SEASON							PLAYOFFS					
			Gms.	Min.	W	L	T	GA	SO	Avg.	Gms.	Min.	W	L	GA SO	Avg.
80-81	—Shawinigan	QMJHL	21	907	4	9	0	75	0	4.96	1	20	0	0	2 0	6.00
81-82	—Shawinigan	QMJHL	*60	*3404				230	0	4.05	14	788			58 0	4.42
82-83	—Shawinigan	QMJHL	46	2556	32	9	1	133	*3	*3.12	8	457	5	3	29 0	3.81

Season	Team	League	Gms.	Min.	W	L	T	GA	SO	Avg.	Gms.	Min.	W	L	GA	SO	Avg.
83-84—Can. Olympic Team......	Int'l		36	2007				126	0	3.77	—	—	—	—	—	—	—
—Quebec	NHL		3	148	2	0	0	3	1	1.22	—	—	—	—	—	—	—
84-85—Quebec	NHL		35	1960	19	10	3	109	1	3.34	17	1059	9	8	54	0	3.06
85-86—Fredericton	AHL		5	304	2	2	1	15	0	2.96	—	—	—	—	—	—	—
—Quebec	NHL		31	1726	14	14	1	111	2	3.86	1	40	0	1	5	0	7.50
86-87—Quebec	NHL		30	1625	13	11	1	86	0	3.18	11	654	7	4	37	0	3.39
87-88—Quebec	NHL		54	3002	20	28	4	189	2	3.78	—	—	—	—	—	—	—
88-89—Quebec	NHL		39	2064	11	19	3	146	0	4.24	—	—	—	—	—	—	—
—Halifax	AHL		3	183	3	0	0	9	0	2.95	—	—	—	—	—	—	—
89-90—Los Angeles	NHL		26	1226	7	11	1	79	0	3.87	3	63	0	2	3	0	2.86
90-91—Phoenix	IHL		46	2673	24	15	4	172	1	3.86	11	670	7	4	*43	0	3.85
91-92—Springfield	AHL		47	2606	28	11	5	142	0	3.27	6	319	1	4	18	0	3.39
NHL totals			218	11751	86	93	13	723	6	3.69	32	1816	16	15	99	0	3.27

GOTAAS, STEVE
C, NORTH STARS

PERSONAL: Born May 10, 1967, at Cumrose, Sask.... 5-10/180.... Shoots right. **TRANSACTIONS/CAREER NOTES:** Underwent shoulder surgery (May 1984).... Selected by Pittsburgh Penguins as underage junior in fifth round (fourth Penguins pick, 86th overall) of NIIL entry draft (June 15, 1985).... Suffered bursitis in hip (September 1987).... Injured shoulder (September 1988).... Traded by Penguins with D Ville Siren to Minnesota North Stars for LW Scott Bjugstad and D Gord Dineen (December 17, 1988).... Injured knee cap (March 1989); underwent surgery during off-season.... Underwent major reconstructive knee surgery (October 12, 1989); out until final week of season.

Season	Team	League	Gms.	G	A	Pts.	Pen.	Gms.	G	A	Pts.	Pen.
83-84—Prince Albert	WHL		65	10	22	32	47	5	0	1	1	0
84-85—Prince Albert	WHL		72	32	41	73	66	13	3	6	9	17
85-86—Prince Albert	WHL		61	40	61	101	31	—	—	—	—	—
86-87—Prince Albert	WHL		68	53	55	108	94	8	5	6	11	16
87-88—Pittsburgh	NHL		36	5	6	11	45	—	—	—	—	—
—Muskegon	IHL		34	16	22	38	4	—	—	—	—	—
88-89—Muskegon	IHL		19	9	16	25	34	—	—	—	—	—
—Kalamazoo	IHL		30	24	22	46	12	5	2	3	5	2
—Minnesota	NHL		12	1	3	4	6	3	0	1	1	12
89-90—Kalamazoo	IHL		1	1	0	1	0	2	0	0	0	2
90-91—Minnesota	NHL		1	0	0	0	2	—	—	—	—	—
—Kalamazoo	IHL		78	30	49	79	88	7	3	5	8	4
91-92—Kalamazoo	IHL		72	34	29	63	115	12	4	10	14	20
NHL totals			49	6	9	15	53	3	0	1	1	12

GOTZIAMAN, CHRIS
RW, DEVILS

PERSONAL: Born November 29, 1971, at Roseau, Minn.... 6-2/190.... Shoots right.... Full name: Christopher S. Gotziaman. **HIGH SCHOOL:** Roseau (Minn.). **COLLEGE:** North Dakota.
TRANSACTIONS/CAREER NOTES: Underwent surgery to knee cartilage (February 1988).... Selected by New Jersey Devils in second round (third Devils pick, 29th overall) of NHL entry draft (June 16, 1990).... Broke right wrist (December 1990).

Season	Team	League	Gms.	G	A	Pts.	Pen.	Gms.	G	A	Pts.	Pen.
88-89—Roseau H.S.	Minn. H.S.		25	13	18	31		—	—	—	—	—
89-90—Roseau H.S.	Minn. H.S.		28	34	31	65		—	—	—	—	—
90-91—Univ. of North Dakota	WCHA		40	11	8	19	26	—	—	—	—	—
91-92—Univ. of North Dakota	WCHA		38	9	6	15	47	—	—	—	—	—

GOULET, MICHEL
LW, BLACKHAWKS

PERSONAL: Born April 21, 1960, at Peribonqua, Que.... 6-1/195.... Shoots left. **TRANSACTIONS/CAREER NOTES:** Signed as underage junior by Birmingham Bulls (July 1978).... Selected by Quebec Nordiques in first round (first Nordiques pick, 20th overall) of NHL entry draft (August 9, 1979).... Fractured thumb (January 2, 1985).... Suspended by Quebec after leaving training camp to renegotiate contract (September 1985).... Broke finger on right hand (October 13, 1986).... Strained ligaments in left knee (October 6, 1988).... Underwent surgery to finger (May 1989).... Sprained right ankle (October 28, 1989); missed nine games.... Traded by Nordiques with G Greg Millen and sixth-round pick in 1991 draft to Chicago Blackhawks for LW Everett Sanipass, LW Dan Vincelette and D Mario Doyon (March 5, 1990).... Bruised ribs and stretched rib cartilage (March 11, 1990).... Bruised right ankle (November 1990).... Sprained right knee (March 30, 1991); missed playoffs.... Pulled groin (March 31, 1992).
HONORS: Named to QMJHL All-Star second team (1977-78).... Named to THE SPORTING NEWS All-Star second team (1982-83 and 1987-88).... Named to NHL All-Star second team (1982-83 and 1987-88).... Named to THE SPORTING NEWS All-Star first team (1983-84 through 1986-87).... Named to NHL All-Star first team (1983-84, 1985-86, and 1986-87).

Season	Team	League	Gms.	G	A	Pts.	Pen.	Gms.	G	A	Pts.	Pen.
76-77—Quebec	QMJHL		37	17	18	35	9	14	3	8	11	19
77-78—Quebec	QMJHL		72	73	62	135	109	1	0	1	1	0
78-79—Birmingham	WHA		78	28	30	58	64	—	—	—	—	—
79-80—Quebec	NHL		77	22	32	54	48	—	—	—	—	—
80-81—Quebec	NHL		76	32	39	71	45	4	3	4	7	7

G

Season Team	League	REGULAR SEASON					PLAYOFFS				
		Gms.	G	A	Pts.	Pen.	Gms.	G	A	Pts.	Pen.
81-82—Quebec	NHL	80	42	42	84	48	16	8	5	13	6
82-83—Quebec	NHL	80	57	48	105	51	4	0	0	0	6
83-84—Quebec	NHL	75	56	65	121	76	9	2	4	6	17
84-85—Quebec	NHL	69	55	40	95	55	17	11	10	21	17
85-86—Quebec	NHL	75	53	50	103	64	3	1	2	3	10
86-87—Quebec	NHL	75	49	47	96	61	13	9	5	14	35
87-88—Quebec	NHL	80	48	58	106	56	—	—	—	—	—
88-89—Quebec	NHL	69	26	38	64	67	—	—	—	—	—
89-90—Quebec	NHL	57	16	29	45	42	—	—	—	—	—
—Chicago	NHL	8	4	1	5	9	14	4	2	6	6
90-91—Chicago	NHL	74	27	38	65	65	—	—	—	—	—
91-92—Chicago	NHL	75	22	41	63	69	9	3	4	7	6
WHA totals		78	28	30	58	64					
NHL totals		970	509	568	1077	756	89	41	36	77	110

GOVEDARIS, CHRIS
LW, WHALERS

PERSONAL: Born February 2, 1970, at Toronto. . . . 6-0/200. . . . Shoots left.
TRAN SACTIONS/CAREER NOTES: Suspended two games by OHL (October 1986). . . . Selected by Hartford Whalers in first round (first Whalers pick, 11th overall) of NHL entry draft (June 11, 1988). . . . Suspended 15 games by OHL for shattering stick across another player's hip (January 22, 1989). . . . Bruised right leg (January 23, 1991); missed five games. . . . Suspended by Whalers for failure to report to AHL game (October 31, 1991); reinstated (January 3, 1992).

Season Team	League	REGULAR SEASON					PLAYOFFS				
		Gms.	G	A	Pts.	Pen.	Gms.	G	A	Pts.	Pen.
85-86—Toronto Young Nationals	MTHL	38	35	50	85		—	—	—	—	—
86-87—Toronto	OHL	64	36	28	64	148	—	—	—	—	—
87-88—Toronto	OHL	62	42	38	80	118	4	2	1	3	10
88-89—Toronto	OHL	49	41	38	79	117	6	2	3	5	0
89-90—Hartford	NHL	12	0	1	1	6	2	0	0	0	2
—Binghamton	AHL	14	3	3	6	4	—	—	—	—	—
—Dukes of Hamilton	OHL	23	11	21	32	53	—	—	—	—	—
90-91—Hartford	NHL	14	1	3	4	4	—	—	—	—	—
—Springfield	AHL	56	26	36	62	133	9	2	5	7	36
91-92—Springfield	AHL	43	14	25	39	55	11	3	2	5	25
NHL totals		26	1	4	5	10	2	0	0	0	2

GOVERDE, DAVID
G, KINGS

PERSONAL: Born April 9, 1970, at Toronto. . . . 6-0/210. . . . Shoots left.
TRANSACTIONS/CAREER NOTES: Selected by Los Angeles Kings in fifth round (fifth Kings pick, 91st overall) of NHL entry draft (June 16, 1990).

Season Team	League	REGULAR SEASON							PLAYOFFS						
		Gms.	Min.	W	L	T	GA	SO	Avg.	Gms.	Min.	W	L	GA	SO	Avg.
87-88—Windsor	OHL	10	471				28	0	3.57	—	—	—	—	—	—	—
88-89—Windsor	OHL	5	221				24	0	6.52	—	—	—	—	—	—	—
—Sudbury	OHL	39	2189				156	0	4.28	—	—	—	—	—	—	—
89-90—Sudbury	OHL	52	2941	28	12	7	182	0	3.71	7	394	3	3	25	0	3.81
90-91—Phoenix	IHL	40	2007	11	19	5	137	1	4.10	—	—	—	—	—	—	—
91-92—Phoenix	IHL	35	1951	11	19	3	129	1	3.97	—	—	—	—	—	—	—
—Los Angeles	NHL	2	120	1	1	0	9	0	4.50	—	—	—	—	—	—	—
—New Haven	AHL	5	248	1	3	0	17	0	4.11	—	—	—	—	—	—	—
NHL totals		2	120	1	1	0	9	0	4.50							

GRAHAM, DIRK
LW/RW, BLACKHAWKS

PERSONAL: Born July 29, 1959, at Regina, Sask. . . . 5-11/190. . . . Shoots right. . . . Full name: Dirk Milton Graham.
TRANSACTIONS/CAREER NOTES: Selected by Vancouver Canucks in fifth round (fifth Canucks pick, 89th overall) of NHL entry draft (August 9, 1979). . . . Signed as free agent by Minnesota North Stars (August 17, 1983). . . . Sprained wrist (November 1987); missed seven games. . . . Traded by North Stars to Chicago Blackhawks for LW Curt Fraser (January 4, 1988). . . . Fined $500 by NHL for fighting (December 28, 1989). . . . Fractured left kneecap (March 17, 1990); missed six weeks. . . . Underwent surgery to left knee (May 1990).
HONORS: Named to WHL All-Star second team (1978-79). . . . Named to IHL All-Star second team (1980-81). . . . Named to IHL All-Star first team (1982-83). . . . Named to Can.HL All-Star first team (1983-84). . . . Won Frank J. Selke Trophy (1990-91).

Season Team	League	REGULAR SEASON					PLAYOFFS				
		Gms.	G	A	Pts.	Pen.	Gms.	G	A	Pts.	Pen.
75-76—Regina Blues	SJHL	54	36	32	68	82	—	—	—	—	—
—Regina	WCHL	2	0	0	0	0	6	1	1	2	5
76-77—Regina	WCHL	65	37	28	65	66	—	—	—	—	—
77-78—Regina	WCHL	72	49	61	110	87	13	15	19	34	37
78-79—Regina	WHL	71	48	60	108	252	—	—	—	—	—
79-80—Dallas	CHL	62	17	15	32	96	—	—	—	—	—
80-81—Fort Wayne	IHL	6	1	2	3	12	—	—	—	—	—
—Toledo	IHL	61	40	45	85	88	—	—	—	—	—
81-82—Toledo	IHL	72	49	56	105	68	13	10	11	21	8
82-83—Toledo	IHL	78	70	55	125	86	11	13	7	†20	30

G

Season	Team	League	REGULAR SEASON Gms.	G	A	Pts.	Pen.	PLAYOFFS Gms.	G	A	Pts.	Pen.
83-84—Minnesota		NHL	6	1	1	2	0	1	0	0	0	2
—Salt Lake City		IHL	57	37	57	94	72	5	3	8	11	2
84-85—Springfield		AHL	37	20	28	48	41	—	—	—	—	—
—Minnesota		NHL	36	12	11	23	23	9	0	4	4	7
85-86—Minnesota		NHL	80	22	33	55	87	5	3	1	4	2
86-87—Minnesota		NHL	76	25	29	54	142	—	—	—	—	—
87-88—Minnesota		NHL	28	7	5	12	39	—	—	—	—	—
—Chicago		NHL	42	17	19	36	32	4	1	2	3	4
88-89—Chicago		NHL	80	33	45	78	89	16	2	4	6	38
89-90—Chicago		NHL	73	22	32	54	102	5	1	5	6	2
90-91—Chicago		NHL	80	24	21	45	88	6	1	2	3	17
91-92—Chicago		NHL	80	17	30	47	89	18	7	5	12	8
NHL totals			581	180	226	406	691	64	15	23	38	80

GRANATO, TONY
LW, KINGS

PERSONAL: Born July 25, 1964, at Downers Grove, Ill. . . . 5-10/185. . . . Shoots right. . . . Full name: Anthony Lewis Granato.
HIGH SCHOOL: Northwood School (Lake Placid, N.Y.).
COLLEGE: Wisconsin.
TRANSACTIONS/CAREER NOTES: Selected by New York Rangers in sixth round (fifth Rangers pick, 120th overall) of NHL entry draft (June 9, 1982). . . . Bruised foot (February 1989). . . . Traded by Rangers with RW Tomas Sandstrom to Los Angeles Kings for C Bernie Nicholls (January 20, 1990). . . . Pulled groin (January 25, 1990); missed 12 games. . . . Injured knee (March 20, 1990). . . . Tore rib cartilage (December 18, 1990); missed 10 games.
HONORS: Named to NCAA All-America West second team (1986-87). . . . Named to WCHA All-Star second team (1986-87). . . . Named to NHL All-Rookie team (1988-89).

Season	Team	League	REGULAR SEASON Gms.	G	A	Pts.	Pen.	PLAYOFFS Gms.	G	A	Pts.	Pen.
81-82—Northwood School		N.Y. H.S.	—	—	—	—	—	—	—	—	—	—
82-83—Northwood School		N.Y. H.S.	—	—	—	—	—	—	—	—	—	—
83-84—University of Wisconsin		WCHA	35	14	17	31	48	—	—	—	—	—
84-85—University of Wisconsin		WCHA	42	33	34	67	94	—	—	—	—	—
85-86—University of Wisconsin		WCHA	32	25	24	49	36	—	—	—	—	—
86-87—University of Wisconsin		WCHA	42	28	45	73	64	—	—	—	—	—
87-88—U.S. National Team		Int'l	49	40	31	71	55	—	—	—	—	—
—U.S. Olympic Team		Int'l	6	1	7	8	4	—	—	—	—	—
—Denver		IHL	22	13	14	27	36	8	9	4	13	16
88-89—New York Rangers		NHL	78	36	27	63	140	4	1	1	2	21
89-90—New York Rangers		NHL	37	7	18	25	77	—	—	—	—	—
—Los Angeles		NHL	19	5	6	11	45	10	5	4	9	12
90-91—Los Angeles		NHL	68	30	34	64	154	12	1	4	5	28
91-92—Los Angeles		NHL	80	39	29	68	187	6	1	5	6	10
NHL totals			282	117	114	231	603	32	8	14	22	71

GRANT, KEVIN
D, FLAMES

PERSONAL: Born January 9, 1969, at Toronto. . . . 6-3/210. . . . Shoots right.
TRANSACTIONS/CAREER NOTES: Injured knee ligaments (February 1, 1987). . . . Selected by Calgary Flames as underage junior in second round (third Flames pick, 40th overall) of NHL entry draft (June 13, 1987). . . . Traded by Kitchener Rangers with C Sean Stansfield and fourth-round pick in 1989 draft (Traded to Sault Ste. Marie Greyhounds) and fourth-round pick in 1990 draft to Sudbury Wolves for RW Pierre Gagnon, D John Uniac and a seventh-round pick in 1989 draft (Jamie Israel) (November 1988).

Season	Team	League	REGULAR SEASON Gms.	G	A	Pts.	Pen.	PLAYOFFS Gms.	G	A	Pts.	Pen.
85-86—Kitchener		OHL	63	2	15	17	204	5	0	1	1	11
86-87—Kitchener		OHL	52	5	18	23	125	4	0	1	1	16
87-88—Kitchener		OHL	48	3	20	23	138	4	0	1	1	4
88-89—Sudbury		OHL	60	9	41	50	186	—	—	—	—	—
—Salt Lake City		IHL	3	0	1	1	5	3	0	0	0	12
89-90—Salt Lake City		IHL	78	7	17	24	117	11	0	2	2	22
90-91—Salt Lake City		IHL	63	6	19	25	200	3	0	0	0	8
91-92—Salt Lake City		IHL	73	7	16	23	181	—	—	—	—	—

GRAVES, ADAM
LW, RANGERS

PERSONAL: Born April 12, 1968, at Toronto. . . . 6-0/203. . . . Shoots left.
TRANSACTIONS/CAREER NOTES: Bruised shoulder (February 1986). . . . Selected by Detroit Red Wings as underage junior in second round (second Red Wings pick, 22nd overall) of NHL entry draft (June 21, 1986). . . . Traded by Red Wings with C/RW Joe Murphy, LW Petr Klima and D Jeff Sharples to Edmonton Oilers for C Jimmy Carson, C Kevin McClelland and a fifth-round pick in 1991 draft (later traded to Montreal Canadiens) (November 2, 1989). . . . Signed as free agent by New York Rangers (September 2, 1991); Oilers received C/LW Troy Mallette as compensation (September 9, 1991).

Season	Team	League	REGULAR SEASON Gms.	G	A	Pts.	Pen.	PLAYOFFS Gms.	G	A	Pts.	Pen.
84-85—King City Jr. B.		OHA	25	23	33	56	29	—	—	—	—	—
85-86—Windsor		OHL	62	27	37	64	35	16	5	11	16	10
86-87—Windsor		OHL	66	45	55	100	70	14	9	8	17	32
—Adirondack		AHL	—	—	—	—	—	5	0	1	1	0

G

Season Team	League	REGULAR SEASON					PLAYOFFS				
		Gms.	G	A	Pts.	Pen.	Gms.	G	A	Pts.	Pen.
87-88—Detroit	NHL	9	0	1	1	8	—	—	—	—	—
—Windsor	OHL	37	28	†32	60	107	12	14	18	32	16
88-89—Detroit	NHL	56	7	5	12	60	5	0	0	0	4
—Adirondack	AHL	14	10	11	21	28	14	11	7	18	17
89-90—Detroit	NHL	13	0	1	1	13	—	—	—	—	—
—Edmonton	NHL	63	9	12	21	123	22	5	6	11	17
90-91—Edmonton	NHL	76	7	18	25	127	18	2	4	6	22
91-92—New York Rangers	NHL	80	26	33	59	139	10	5	3	8	22
NHL totals		297	49	70	119	470	55	12	13	25	65

GREEN, RICK

D, ISLANDERS

PERSONAL: Born February 20, 1956, at Belleville, Ont. . . . 6-3/200. . . . Shoots left. . . . Full name: Richard Douglas Green.

TRANSACTIONS/CAREER NOTES: Selected by Washington Capitals in first round (first Capitals pick, first overall) of NHL entry draft (June 1, 1976). . . . Broke right wrist; missed part of 1976-77 season. . . . Broke hand (November 1980). . . . Separated shoulder (December 14, 1981). . . . Traded by Capitals with LW Ryan Walter to Montreal Canadiens for D Rod Langway, D Brian Engblom, C Doug Jarvis and RW Craig Laughlin (September 9, 1982). . . . Injured hip (March 1983). . . . Broke right wrist (October 1983). . . . Broke rib (February 21, 1984). . . . Injured ankle (September 1985); missed first eight games of season. . . . Broke thumb (December 31, 1985). . . . Reinjured thumb (February 24, 1986). . . . Lacerated eyelid (October 1986). . . . Bruised right foot (October 1987). . . . Injured back (March 1988). . . . Suffered concussion (November 24, 1988). . . . Suffered back spasms (March 1989). . . . NHL rights traded by Canadiens to Detroit Red Wings for a fifth-round pick in 1991 draft (D Brad Layzell) (June 15, 1990). . . . Suffered swollen right knee (November 19, 1990). . . . Suffered back spasms (January 12, 1991). . . . Traded by Red Wings with future considerations to New York Islanders for RW Alan Kerr (May 28, 1991). . . . Fractured foot (January 23, 1992); missed 17 games.

HONORS: Won Max Kaminsky Trophy (1975-76). . . . Named to OHA Major Junior A All-Star first team (1975-76).

Season Team	League	REGULAR SEASON					PLAYOFFS				
		Gms.	G	A	Pts.	Pen.	Gms.	G	A	Pts.	Pen.
72-73—London	OHA Mj. Jr. A	7	0	1	1	2	—	—	—	—	—
73-74—London	OHA Mj. Jr. A	65	6	30	36	45	—	—	—	—	—
74-75—London	OHA Mj. Jr. A	65	8	45	53	68	—	—	—	—	—
75-76—London	OHA Mj. Jr. A	61	13	47	60	69	5	1	0	1	4
76-77—Washington	NHL	45	3	12	15	16	—	—	—	—	—
77-78—Washington	NHL	60	5	14	19	67	—	—	—	—	—
78-79—Washington	NHL	71	8	33	41	62	—	—	—	—	—
79-80—Washington	NHL	71	4	20	24	52	—	—	—	—	—
80-81—Washington	NHL	65	8	23	31	91	—	—	—	—	—
81-82—Washington	NHL	65	3	25	28	93	—	—	—	—	—
82-83—Montreal	NHL	66	2	24	26	58	3	0	0	0	2
83-84—Montreal	NHL	7	0	1	1	7	15	1	2	3	33
84-85—Montreal	NHL	77	1	18	19	30	12	0	3	3	14
85-86—Montreal	NHL	46	3	2	5	20	18	1	4	5	8
86-87—Montreal	NHL	72	1	9	10	10	17	0	4	4	8
87-88—Montreal	NHL	59	2	11	13	33	11	0	2	2	2
88-89—Montreal	NHL	72	1	14	15	25	21	1	1	2	6
89-90—Marano	Italy	19	5	12	17	6	10	3	6	9	4
90-91—Detroit	NHL	65	2	14	16	24	3	0	0	0	0
91-92—New York Islanders	NHL	4	0	0	0	0	—	—	—	—	—
NHL totals		845	43	220	263	588	100	3	16	19	73

GREEN, TRAVIS

C, ISLANDERS

PERSONAL: Born December 20, 1970, at Creston, B.C. . . . 6-0/196. . . . Shoots right.

TRANSACTIONS/CAREER NOTES: Selected by New York Islanders in second round (second Islanders pick, 23rd overall) of NHL entry draft (June 17, 1989). . . . Traded by Spokane Chiefs to Medicine Hat Tigers for RW Mark Woolf, D/LW Chris Lafreniere and C Frank Esposito (January 26, 1990).

Season Team	League	REGULAR SEASON					PLAYOFFS				
		Gms.	G	A	Pts.	Pen.	Gms.	G	A	Pts.	Pen.
85-86—Castlegar	KIJHL	35	30	40	70	41	—	—	—	—	—
86-87—Spokane Chiefs	WHL	64	8	17	25	27	3	0	0	0	0
87-88—Spokane Chiefs	WHL	72	33	53	86	42	15	10	10	20	13
88-89—Spokane Chiefs	WHL	72	51	51	102	79	—	—	—	—	—
89-90—Spokane Chiefs	WHL	50	45	44	89	80	—	—	—	—	—
—Medicine Hat	WHL	25	15	24	39	19	3	0	0	0	2
90-91—Capital District	AHL	73	21	34	55	26	—	—	—	—	—
91-92—Capital District	AHL	71	23	27	50	10	7	0	4	4	21

GREENLAW, JEFF

RW, CAPITALS

PERSONAL: Born February 28, 1968, at Toronto. . . . 6-1/230. . . . Shoots left. . . . Full name: Jeff Carl Greenlaw.

TRANSACTIONS/CAREER NOTES: Selected by Washington Capitals in first round (first Capitals pick, 19th overall) of NHL entry draft (June 21, 1986). . . . Suffered stress fracture of vertebrae (April 1987). . . . Suffered deep bruise in right leg (September 1989); missed 65 games.

Season Team	League	REGULAR SEASON					PLAYOFFS				
		Gms.	G	A	Pts.	Pen.	Gms.	G	A	Pts.	Pen.
84-85—St. Catharines Jr. B	OHA	33	21	29	50	141	—	—	—	—	—
85-86—Team Canada	Int'l	57	3	16	19	81	—	—	—	—	—

G

Season Team	League	REGULAR SEASON					PLAYOFFS				
		Gms.	G	A	Pts.	Pen.	Gms.	G	A	Pts.	Pen.
86-87—Washington	NHL	22	0	3	3	44	—	—	—	—	—
—Binghamton	AHL	4	0	2	2	0	—	—	—	—	—
87-88—Binghamton	AHL	56	8	7	15	142	1	0	0	0	2
—Washington	NHL	—	—	—	—	—	1	0	0	0	19
88-89—Baltimore	AHL	55	12	15	27	115	—	—	—	—	—
89-90—Baltimore	AHL	10	3	2	5	26	7	1	0	1	13
90-91—Baltimore	AHL	50	17	17	34	93	3	1	1	2	2
—Washington	NHL	10	2	0	2	10	1	0	0	0	2
91-92—Baltimore	AHL	37	6	8	14	57	—	—	—	—	—
—Washington	NHL	5	0	1	1	34	—	—	—	—	—
NHL totals		37	2	4	6	88	2	0	0	0	21

GREGG, RANDY

D

PERSONAL: Born February 19, 1956, at Edmonton, Alta. . . . 6-4/215. . . . Shoots left. . . . Full name: Randall John Gregg.

COLLEGE: Alberta (degree in medicine).

TRANSACTIONS/CAREER NOTES: Signed as free agent by Edmonton Oilers (March 1981). . . . Bruised left shoulder (December 1984). . . . Sprained left knee (January 1985). . . . Separated ribs (October 28, 1985); missed 16 games. . . . Announced retirement (September 1986). . . . Returned to Oilers (November 1986). . . . Dislocated left shoulder (March 17, 1987). . . . Pulled leg muscle (December 1988). . . . Pulled leg muscle (September 1989); missed first 21 games of season. . . . Bruised thigh (May 10, 1990). . . . Claimed by Vancouver Canucks in NHL waiver draft (October 2, 1990). . . . Injured groin (October 27, 1991); missed three games.

HONORS: Won Senator Joseph A. Sullivan Award (1978-79).

MISCELLANEOUS: Is a medical doctor.

Season Team	League	REGULAR SEASON					PLAYOFFS				
		Gms.	G	A	Pts.	Pen.	Gms.	G	A	Pts.	Pen.
75-76—University of Alberta	CWUAA	20	3	14	17	27	—	—	—	—	—
76-77—University of Alberta	CWUAA	24	9	17	26	34	—	—	—	—	—
77-78—University of Alberta	CWUAA	24	7	23	30	37	—	—	—	—	—
78-79—University of Alberta	CWUAA	24	5	16	21	47	—	—	—	—	—
79-80—Canadian National Team	Int'l	56	7	17	24	36	—	—	—	—	—
—Canadian Olympic Team	Int'l	6	1	1	2	2	—	—	—	—	—
80-81—Kokudo	Japan	35	12	18	30	30	—	—	—	—	—
81-82—Kokudo	Japan	36	12	20	32	25	—	—	—	—	—
—Edmonton	NHL	—	—	—	—	—	4	0	0	0	0
82-83—Edmonton	NHL	80	6	22	28	54	16	2	4	6	13
83-84—Edmonton	NHL	80	13	27	40	56	19	3	7	10	21
84-85—Edmonton	NHL	57	3	20	23	32	17	0	6	6	12
85-86—Edmonton	NHL	64	2	26	28	47	10	1	0	1	12
86-87—Edmonton	NHL	52	8	16	24	42	18	3	6	9	17
87-88—Canadian Olympic Team	Int'l	45	3	8	11	45	—	—	—	—	—
—Edmonton	NHL	15	1	2	3	8	19	1	8	9	24
88-89—Edmonton	NHL	57	3	15	18	28	7	1	0	1	4
89-90—Edmonton	NHL	48	4	20	24	42	20	2	6	8	16
90-91—Vancouver	NHL					Did not play.					
91-92—Vancouver	NHL	21	1	4	5	24	7	0	1	1	8
NHL totals		474	41	152	193	333	137	13	38	51	127

GREIG, MARK

RW, WHALERS

PERSONAL: Born January 25, 1970, at High River, Alta. . . . 5-11/190. . . . Shoots right.

TRANSACTIONS/CAREER NOTES: Selected by Hartford Whalers in first round (first Whalers pick, 15th overall) of NHL entry draft (June 16, 1990).

HONORS: Named to WHL (East) All-Star first team (1989-90).

Season Team	League	REGULAR SEASON					PLAYOFFS				
		Gms.	G	A	Pts.	Pen.	Gms.	G	A	Pts.	Pen.
86-87—Calgary	WHL	5	0	0	0	0	—	—	—	—	—
87-88—Lethbridge	WHL	65	9	18	27	38	—	—	—	—	—
88-89—Lethbridge	WHL	71	36	72	108	113	8	5	5	10	16
89-90—Lethbridge	WHL	65	55	80	135	149	18	11	21	32	35
90-91—Hartford	NHL	4	0	0	0	0	—	—	—	—	—
—Springfield	AHL	73	32	55	87	73	17	2	6	8	22
91-92—Hartford	NHL	17	0	5	5	6	—	—	—	—	—
—Springfield	AHL	50	20	27	47	38	9	1	1	2	20
NHL totals		21	0	5	5	6					

G

GRETZKY, BRENT

C, LIGHTNING

PERSONAL: Born February 20, 1972, at Brantford, Ont. . . . 5-11/160. . . . Shoots left. . . . Brother of Wayne Gretzky, center, Los Angeles Kings.

HIGH SCHOOL: Quinte Secondary School (Belleville, Ont.).

TRANSACTIONS/CAREER NOTES: Selected by Tampa Bay Lightning in third round (third Lightning pick, 49th overall) of NHL entry draft (June 20, 1992).

Season Team	League	REGULAR SEASON					PLAYOFFS				
		Gms.	G	A	Pts.	Pen.	Gms.	G	A	Pts.	Pen.
87-88—Brantford Jr. B	OHA	14	4	11	15	2	—	—	—	—	—
88-89—Brantford Jr. B	OHA	40	29	47	76	57	—	—	—	—	—

Season Team	League	REGULAR SEASON					PLAYOFFS				
		Gms.	G	A	Pts.	Pen.	Gms.	G	A	Pts.	Pen.
89-90—Belleville	OHL	40	29	47	76	57	11	0	0	0	2
90-91—Belleville	OHL	66	26	56	82	25	6	3	3	6	2
91-92—Belleville	OHL	62	43	78	121	37	—	—	—	—	—

GRETZKY, WAYNE

C, KINGS

PERSONAL: Born January 26, 1961, at Brantford, Ont. . . . 6-0/170. . . . Shoots left. . . . Full name: Wayne Douglas Gretzky. . . . Brother of Brent Gretzky, center in Tampa Bay Lightning system.

TRANSACTIONS/CAREER NOTES: Signed as an underage junior by Indianapolis Racers to multi-year contract (May 1978). . . . Traded by Racers with LW Peter Driscoll and G Ed Mio to Edmonton Oilers for cash and future considerations (November 1978). . . . Bruised right shoulder (January 28, 1984). . . . Underwent surgery on left ankle to remove benign growth (June 1984). . . . Twisted right knee (December 30, 1987). . . . Suffered corneal abrasion to left eye (February 19, 1988); missed three games. . . . Traded by Oilers with RW/D Marty McSorley and LW/C Mike Krushelnyski to Los Angeles Kings for C Jimmy Carson, LW Martin Gelinas, first-round picks in 1989 (traded to New Jersey), 1991 and 1993 drafts and cash (August 9, 1988). . . . Injured groin (March 17, 1990). . . . Strained lower back (March 22, 1990); missed five regular-season games and two playoff games. . . . Missed five games due to personal reasons (October 1991). . . . Sprained knee (February 25, 1992); missed one game.

HONORS: Won William Hanley Trophy (1977-78). . . . Won Emms Family Award (1977-78). . . . Named to OMJHL All-Star second team (1977-78). . . . Named WHA Rookie of the Year by THE SPORTING NEWS (1978-79). . . . Won WHA Rookie of the Year Award (1978-79). . . . Named to WHA All-Star second team (1978-79). . . . Won Hart Memorial Trophy (1979-80 through 1986-87 and 1988-89). . . . Won Lady Byng Memorial Trophy (1979-80, 1990-91 and 1991-92). . . . Named to THE SPORTING NEWS All-Star second team (1979-80, 1987-88, 1988-89 and 1991-92). . . . Named to NHL All-Star second team (1979-80 and 1987-88 through 1989-90). . . . Named NHL Player of Year by THE SPORTING NEWS (1980-81 through 1986-87). . . . Won Art Ross Memorial Trophy (1980-81 through 1986-87, 1989-90 and 1990-91). . . . Named to THE SPORTING NEWS All-Star first team (1980-81 through 1986-87 and 1990-91). . . . Named to NHL All-Star first team (1980-81 through 1986-87 and 1990-91). . . . Named Man of the Year by THE SPORTING NEWS (1981). . . . Won Lester B. Pearson Award (1981-82 through 1984-85 and 1986-87). . . . Won Emery Edge Award (1983-84, 1984-85 and 1986-87). . . . Named Canadian Athlete of the Year (1985). . . . Won Conn Smythe Trophy (1984-85 and 1987-88). . . . Won Dodge Performer of the Year Award (1984-85 through 1986-87). . . . Won Dodge Performance of the Year Award (1988-89).

RECORDS: Holds NHL career records for points—2,263; assists—1,514; overtime assists—10; most games with three or more goals—48; most 40-or-more goal seasons—12; most consecutive 40-or-more goal seasons—12 (1979-80 through 1990-91); most consecutive 60-or-more goal seasons—4 (1981-82 through 1984-85); most 100-or-more point seasons—13; most consecutive 100-or-more point seasons—13 (1979-80 through 1991-92); highest assist-per-game average—1.516; and highest points-per-game average—2.265. . . . Shares NHL career records for most consecutive 30-or more goal seasons—13 (1979-80 through 1991-92); most 50-or-more goal seasons—9; and most 60-or-more goal seasons—5. . . . Holds NHL single-season records for most goals—92 (1981-82); assists—163 (1985-86); points—215 (1985-86); games with three or more goals—10 (1981-82 and 1983-84); highest goals-per-game average—1.18 (1983-84); highest assists-per-game average—2.04 (1985-86); and highest points-per-game average—2.77 (1983-84). . . . Shares NHL single-game records for most assists—7 (February 15, 1980; December 11, 1985; and February 14, 1986); and most goals in one period—4 (February 18, 1981). . . . Holds NHL records for most consecutive games scoring points—51 (October 5, 1983 through January 28, 1984); and most consecutive games with an assist—23 (1990-91). . . . Holds NHL career playoff records for most goals—95; most assists—211; most points—306; and most games with three-or-more goals—7. . . . Shares NHL career playoff record for most game-winning goals—18. . . . Holds NHL single-season playoff records for most assists—31 (1988); and most points—47 (1985). . . . Shares NHL single-season playoff record for most shorthanded goals—3 (1983). . . . Holds NHL final-series playoff records for most assists—10 (1988); and most points—13 (1988). . . . Shares NHL single-series playoff record for most assists—14 (1985). . . . Shares NHL single-game playoff records for most assists—6 (April 9, 1987); most shorthanded goals—2 (April 6, 1983); most assists in one period—3 (done five times); and most points in one period—4 (April 12, 1987). . . . Holds NHL career All-Star game record for most goals—11. . . . Holds NHL All-Star records for most goals in one period—4 (1983); and most points in one period—4 (1983). . . . Shares NHL All-Star single-game record for most goals—4 (February 8, 1983).

Season Team	League	REGULAR SEASON					PLAYOFFS				
		Gms.	G	A	Pts.	Pen.	Gms.	G	A	Pts.	Pen.
76-77—Peterborough	OMJHL	3	0	3	3	0	—	—	—	—	—
77-78—Sault Ste. Marie	OMJHL	64	70	112	182	14	13	6	20	26	0
78-79—Indianapolis	WHA	8	3	3	6	0	—	—	—	—	—
—Edmonton	WHA	72	43	61	104	19	13	†10	10	*20	2
79-80—Edmonton	NHL	79	51	*86	†137	21	3	2	1	3	0
80-81—Edmonton	NHL	80	55	*109	*164	28	9	7	14	21	4
81-82—Edmonton	NHL	80	*92	*120	*212	26	5	5	7	12	8
82-83—Edmonton	NHL	80	*71	*125	*196	59	16	12	*26	*38	4
83-84—Edmonton	NHL	74	*87	*118	*205	39	19	13	*22	*35	12
84-85—Edmonton	NHL	80	*73	*135	*208	52	18	17	*30	*47	4
85-86—Edmonton	NHL	80	52	*163	*215	46	10	8	11	19	2
86-87—Edmonton	NHL	79	*62	*121	*183	28	21	5	*29	*34	6
87-88—Edmonton	NHL	64	40	*109	149	24	19	12	*31	*43	16
88-89—Los Angeles	NHL	78	54	†114	168	26	11	5	17	22	0
89-90—Los Angeles	NHL	73	40	*102	*142	42	7	3	7	10	0
90-91—Los Angeles	NHL	78	41	*122	*163	16	12	4	11	15	2
91-92—Los Angeles	NHL	74	31	*90	121	34	6	2	5	7	2
WHA totals		80	46	64	110	19	13	10	10	20	2
NHL totals		999	749	1514	2263	441	156	95	211	306	60

GREYERBIEHL, JASON

LW, BLACKHAWKS

PERSONAL: Born March 24, 1970, at Bramalea, Ont. . . . 6-0/175. . . . Shoots left. . . . Full name: Jason Lawrence Greyerbiehl.

COLLEGE: Colgate.

TRANSACTIONS/CAREER NOTES: Selected by Chicago Blackhawks in ninth round (seventh Blackhawks pick, 174th overall) of NHL entry draft (June 17, 1989).

G

Season Team	League	REGULAR SEASON					PLAYOFFS				
		Gms.	G	A	Pts.	Pen.	Gms.	G	A	Pts.	Pen.
87-88—Bramalea Jr. B	OHA	37	33	27	60	10	—	—	—	—	—
88-89—Colgate University	ECAC	31	6	9	15	14	—	—	—	—	—
89-90—Colgate University	ECAC	38	12	20	32	20	—	—	—	—	—
90-91—Colgate University	ECAC	30	7	14	21	12	—	—	—	—	—
91-92—Colgate University	ECAC	27	11	16	27	21	—	—	—	—	—

GRIEVE, BRENT
LW, ISLANDERS

PERSONAL: Born May 9, 1969, at Oshawa, Ont. . . . 6-1/205. . . . Shoots left.
TRANSACTIONS/CAREER NOTES: Selected by New York Islanders in fourth round (fourth Islanders pick, 65th overall) of NHL entry draft (June 17, 1989).

Season Team	League	REGULAR SEASON					PLAYOFFS				
		Gms.	G	A	Pts.	Pen.	Gms.	G	A	Pts.	Pen.
86-87—Oshawa	OHL	60	9	19	28	102	24	3	8	11	22
87-88—Oshawa	OHL	56	19	20	39	122	7	0	1	1	8
88-89—Oshawa	OHL	49	34	33	67	105	6	4	3	7	4
89-90—Oshawa	OHL	62	46	47	93	125	17	10	10	20	26
90-91—Kansas City	IHL	5	2	2	4	2	—	—	—	—	—
—Capital District	AHL	61	14	13	27	80	—	—	—	—	—
91-92—Capital District	AHL	74	34	32	66	84	7	3	1	4	16

GRIMES, JAKE
C, SENATORS

PERSONAL: Born September 13, 1972, at Montreal. . . . 6-1/196. . . . Shoots left.
TRANSACTIONS/CAREER NOTES: Selected by Ottawa Senators in 10th round (10th Senators pick, 217th overall) of NHL entry draft (June 20, 1992).

Season Team	League	REGULAR SEASON					PLAYOFFS				
		Gms.	G	A	Pts.	Pen.	Gms.	G	A	Pts.	Pen.
89-90—Belleville	OHA	66	9	12	21	11	—	—	—	—	—
90-91—Belleville	OHA	66	31	41	72	16	—	—	—	—	—
91-92—Belleville	OHA	66	44	69	113	18	—	—	—	—	—

GRIMSON, STU
LW, BLACKHAWKS

PERSONAL: Born May 20, 1965, at Kamloops, B.C. . . . 6-5/220. . . . Shoots left. . . . Full name: Stuart Grimson.
COLLEGE: Manitoba.
TRANSACTIONS/CAREER NOTES: Fractured forearm (February 1983). . . . Selected by Detroit Red Wings in 10th round (11th Red Wings pick, 186th overall) of NHL entry draft (June 8, 1983). . . . Did not sign with Detroit and returned to entry draft pool (May 1985). . . . Selected by Calgary Flames in seventh round (eighth Flames pick, 143rd overall) of entry draft (June 15, 1985). . . . Broke cheekbone (January 9, 1990). . . . Claimed on waivers by Chicago Blackhawks (October 1, 1990).

Season Team	League	REGULAR SEASON					PLAYOFFS				
		Gms.	G	A	Pts.	Pen.	Gms.	G	A	Pts.	Pen.
82-83—Regina	WHL	48	0	1	1	144	5	0	0	0	14
83-84—Regina	WHL	63	8	8	16	131	21	0	1	1	29
84-85—Regina	WHL	71	24	32	56	248	8	1	2	3	14
85-86—University of Manitoba	CWUAA	12	7	4	11	113	3	1	1	2	20
86-87—University of Manitoba	CWUAA	29	8	8	16	67	14	4	2	6	28
87-88—Salt Lake City	IHL	38	9	5	14	268	—	—	—	—	—
88-89—Calgary	NHL	1	0	0	0	5	—	—	—	—	—
—Salt Lake City	IHL	72	9	18	27	*397	15	2	3	5	*86
89-90—Salt Lake City	IHL	62	8	8	16	319	4	0	0	0	8
—Calgary	NHL	3	0	0	0	17	—	—	—	—	—
90-91—Chicago	NHL	35	0	1	1	183	5	0	0	0	46
91-92—Indianapolis	IHL	5	1	1	2	17	—	—	—	—	—
—Chicago	NHL	54	2	2	4	234	14	0	1	1	10
NHL totals		93	2	3	5	439	19	0	1	1	56

GROLEAU, FRANCOIS
D, FLAMES

PERSONAL: Born January 23, 1973, at Longueuil, Que. . . . 6-0/193. . . . Shoots left.
TRANSACTIONS/CAREER NOTES: Selected by Calgary Flames in second round (second Flames pick, 41st overall) of NHL entry draft (June 22, 1991).
HONORS: Won Raymond Lagace Trophy (1989-90). . . . Named to QMJHL All-Star second team (1989-90). . . . Won Emile (Butch) Bouchard Trophy (1991-92). . . . Named to QMJHL All-Star first team (1991-92).

Season Team	League	REGULAR SEASON					PLAYOFFS				
		Gms.	G	A	Pts.	Pen.	Gms.	G	A	Pts.	Pen.
89-90—Shawinigan	QMJHL	60	11	54	65	80	6	0	1	1	12
90-91—Shawinigan	QMJHL	70	9	60	69	70	6	0	3	3	2
91-92—Shawinigan	QMJHL	65	8	70	78	74	10	5	15	20	8

GRONMAN, TUOMAS
D, NORDIQUES

PERSONAL: Born March 22, 1974, at Vitasaari, Finland. . . . 6-2/193. . . . Shoots left.
TRANSACTIONS/CAREER NOTES: Selected by Quebec Nordiques in second round (third Nordiques pick, 29th overall) of NHL entry draft (June 20, 1992).

G

Season Team	League	REGULAR SEASON					PLAYOFFS				
		Gms.	G	A	Pts.	Pen.	Gms.	G	A	Pts.	Pen.
90-91—Rauman Lukko................	Finland	40	15	20	35	60	—	—	—	—	—
91-92—Tacoma	WHL	61	5	18	23	102	4	0	1	1	2
—Finland National Jr. Team	Int'l	7	1	0	1	10	—	—	—	—	—

GRONVALL, JANNE
D, MAPLE LEAFS

PERSONAL: Born July 17, 1973, at Rauma, Finland. . . . 6-3/187. . . . Shoots left.
TRANSACTIONS/CAREER NOTES: Selected by Toronto Maple Leafs in fifth round (fifth Maple Leafs pick, 101st overall) of NHL entry draft (June 20, 1992).

Season Team	League	REGULAR SEASON					PLAYOFFS				
		Gms.	G	A	Pts.	Pen.	Gms.	G	A	Pts.	Pen.
89-90—Lukko	Finland	5	0	0	0	0	—	—	—	—	—
90-91—Lukko	Finland	40	2	8	10	30	—	—	—	—	—
91-92—Lukko	Finland	42	2	6	8	40	2	0	0	0	0

GUAY, PAUL
RW, CANUCKS

PERSONAL: Born September 2, 1963, at Providence, R.I. . . . 6-0/185. . . . Shoots right.
HIGH SCHOOL: Mt. St. Charles (Woonsocket, R.I.).
COLLEGE: Providence.
TRANSACTIONS/CAREER NOTES: Selected by Minnesota North Stars as underage junior in sixth round (10th North Stars pick, 118th overall) of NHL entry draft (June 10, 1981). . . . Traded by North Stars with third-round pick in 1985 draft to Philadelphia Flyers for RW Paul Holmgren (February 23, 1984). . . . Traded by Flyers to Los Angeles Kings for RW Steve Seguin (October 11, 1985). . . . Traded by Kings to Boston Bruins for RW Dave Pasin (November 3, 1988). . . . Signed as free agent by New Jersey Devils (August 14, 1989). . . . Signed as free agent by New York Islanders (August 13, 1990). . . . Signed as free agent by Vancouver Canucks (August 22, 1991).
HONORS: Named to ECAC All-Star second team (1982-83).

Season Team	League	REGULAR SEASON					PLAYOFFS				
		Gms.	G	A	Pts.	Pen.	Gms.	G	A	Pts.	Pen.
79-80—Mount St. Charles H.S.	R.I.H.S.	23	18	19	37		—	—	—	—	—
80-81—Mount St. Charles H.S.	R.I.H.S.	23	28	38	66		—	—	—	—	—
81-82—Providence College	ECAC	33	23	17	40	38	—	—	—	—	—
82-83—Providence College	ECAC	42	34	31	65	83	—	—	—	—	—
83-84—U.S. National Team..........	Int'l	62	20	18	38	44	—	—	—	—	—
—U.S. Olympic Team	Int'l	6	1	0	1	8	—	—	—	—	—
—Philadelphia....................	NHL	14	2	6	8	14	3	0	0	0	4
84-85—Hershey..........................	AHL	74	23	30	53	123	—	—	—	—	—
—Philadelphia....................	NHL	2	0	1	1	0	—	—	—	—	—
85-86—Los Angeles....................	NHL	23	3	3	6	18	—	—	—	—	—
—New Haven.....................	AHL	57	15	36	51	101	5	3	0	3	11
86-87—Los Angeles....................	NHL	35	2	5	7	16	2	0	0	0	0
—New Haven.....................	AHL	6	1	3	4	11	—	—	—	—	—
87-88—New Haven.....................	AHL	42	21	26	47	53	—	—	—	—	—
—Los Angeles....................	NHL	33	4	4	8	40	4	0	1	1	8
88-89—New Haven.....................	AHL	4	4	6	10	20	—	—	—	—	—
—Los Angeles....................	NHL	2	0	0	0	2	—	—	—	—	—
—Boston............................	NHL	5	0	2	2	0	—	—	—	—	—
—Maine.............................	AHL	61	15	29	44	77	—	—	—	—	—
89-90—Utica.............................	AHL	75	25	30	55	103	5	2	2	4	13
90-91—New York Islanders..........	NHL	3	0	2	2	2	—	—	—	—	—
—Capital District................	AHL	74	26	35	61	81	—	—	—	—	—
91-92—Milwaukee......................	IHL	81	24	33	57	93	3	2	1	3	7
NHL totals.................................		**117**	**11**	**23**	**34**	**92**	**9**	**0**	**1**	**1**	**12**

GUENETTE, STEVE
G, NORTH STARS

PERSONAL: Born November 13, 1965, at Montreal. . . . 5-10/175. . . . Shoots left.
TRANSACTIONS/CAREER NOTES: Signed as free agent by Pittsburgh Penguins (June 1985). . . . Traded by Penguins to Calgary Flames for sixth-round pick in 1989 draft (RW Mike Needham) (January 9, 1989). . . . Traded by Flames to Minnesota North Stars for a seventh-round pick in 1991 draft (LW Matt Hoffman) (May 30, 1991).
HONORS: Won Leo Lalonde Memorial Trophy (1985-86). . . . Named to OHL All-Star second team (1985-86). . . . Won James Norris Memorial Trophy (1987-88). . . . Named to IHL All-Star second team (1987-88). . . . Named to IHL All-Star first team (1988-89).

Season Team	League	REGULAR SEASON							PLAYOFFS					
		Gms.	Min.	W	L	T	GA	SO	Avg.	Gms.	Min.	W	L	GA SO	Avg.
83-84—Guelph	OHL	38	1808	9	18	2	155	0	5.14	—	—	—	—	— —	—
84-85—Guelph	OHL	47	2593	16	22	4	200	1	4.63	—	—	—	—	— —	—
85-86—Guelph	OHL	50	2910	26	20	1	165	†3	3.40	†20	*1167	15	3	54 *2	*2.78
86-87—Baltimore.......................	AHL	54	3035	21	23	0	157	*5	3.10	—	—	—	—	— —	—
—Pittsburgh.....................	NHL	2	113	0	2	0	8	0	4.25	—	—	—	—	— —	—
87-88—Pittsburgh.....................	NHL	19	1092	12	7	0	61	1	3.35	—	—	—	—	— —	—
—Muskegon......................	IHL	33	1943	23	4	5	91	*4	*2.81	—	—	—	—	— —	—
88-89—Pittsburgh.....................	NHL	11	574	5	6	0	41	0	4.29	—	—	—	—	— —	—
—Salt Lake City................	IHL	30	1810	24	5	0	82	2	2.72	*13	*782	5	8	*44 0	3.38
—Muskegon......................	IHL	10	597	6	4	0	39	0	3.92	—	—	—	—	— —	—
89-90—Calgary..........................	NHL	2	119	1	1	0	8	0	4.03	—	—	—	—	— —	—
—Salt Lake City................	IHL	47	2779	22	21	4	160	0	3.45	†10	545			*35 †1	3.85

Season Team	League	REGULAR SEASON								PLAYOFFS						
		Gms.	Min.	W	L	T	GA	SO	Avg.	Gms.	Min.	W	L	GA	SO	Avg.
90-91—Calgary	NHL	1	60	1	0	0	4	0	4.00	—	—	—	—	—	—	—
—Salt Lake City	IHL	43	2521	26	13	4	137	2	3.26	2	59	0	1	9	0	9.15
91-92—Kalamazoo	IHL	21	1094	7	9	3	70	1	3.84	—	—	—	—	—	—	—
NHL totals		35	1958	19	16	0	122	1	3.74							

GUERARD, DANIEL
C/RW, SENATORS

PERSONAL: Born April 9, 1974, at Lasalle, Que. . . . 6-4/211. . . . Shoots right.
TRANSACTIONS/CAREER NOTES: Selected by Ottawa Senators in fifth round (fifth Senators pick, 98th overall) of NHL entry draft (June 20, 1992).

Season Team	League	REGULAR SEASON					PLAYOFFS				
		Gms.	G	A	Pts.	Pen.	Gms.	G	A	Pts.	Pen.
91-92—Victoriaville	QMJHL	31	5	16	21	66	—	—	—	—	—

GUERIN, BILL
C/RW, DEVILS

PERSONAL: Born November 9, 1970, at Wilbraham, Mass. . . . 6-2/190. . . . Shoots right. . . . Full name: William Robert Guerin.
COLLEGE: Boston College.
TRANSACTIONS/CAREER NOTES: Selected by New Jersey Devils in first round (first Devils pick, fifth overall) of NHL entry draft (June 17, 1989). . . . Suffered from the flu (February 1992); missed three games

Season Team	League	REGULAR SEASON					PLAYOFFS				
		Gms.	G	A	Pts.	Pen.	Gms.	G	A	Pts.	Pen.
85-86—Springfield Jr. B	NEJHL	48	26	19	45	71	—	—	—	—	—
86-87—Springfield Jr. B	NEJHL	32	34	20	54	40	—	—	—	—	—
87-88—Springfield Jr. B	NEJHL	38	31	44	75	146	—	—	—	—	—
88-89—Springfield Jr. B	NEJHL	31	32	37	69	90	—	—	—	—	—
89-90—Boston College	Hockey East	39	14	11	25	64	—	—	—	—	—
90-91—Boston College	Hockey East	38	26	19	45	102	—	—	—	—	—
91-92—U.S. National Team	Int'l	46	12	15	27	67	—	—	—	—	—
—Utica	AHL	22	13	10	23	6	4	1	3	4	14
—New Jersey	NHL	5	0	1	1	9	6	3	0	3	4
NHL totals		5	0	1	1	9	6	3	0	3	4

GUILLET, ROBERT
RW, CANADIENS

PERSONAL: Born February 22, 1972, at Montreal. . . . 5-11/189. . . . Shoots right.
TRANSACTIONS/CAREER NOTES: Selected by Montreal Canadiens in third round (fourth Canadiens pick, 60th overall) of NHL entry draft (June 16, 1990).
HONORS: Named to QMJHL All-Star first team (1990-91). . . . Won Guy Lafleur Trophy (1991-92). . . . Named to QMJHL All-Star second team (1991-92).

Season Team	League	REGULAR SEASON					PLAYOFFS				
		Gms.	G	A	Pts.	Pen.	Gms.	G	A	Pts.	Pen.
89-90—Longueuil	QMJHL	69	32	40	72	132	7	2	1	3	16
90-91—Longueuil	QMJHL	69	55	32	87	96	8	4	7	11	27
91-92—Longueuil	QMJHL	67	56	62	118	104	19	†14	11	*25	26

GUSAROV, ALEXEI
D, NORDIQUES

PERSONAL: Born July 8, 1964, at Leningrad, U.S.S.R. . . . 6-2/170. . . . Shoots left.
TRANSACTIONS/CAREER NOTES: Selected by Quebec Nordiques in 11th round (11th Nordiques pick, 213th overall) in the NHL entry draft (June 11, 1988). . . . Suffered hairline fracture of left ankle (December 15, 1990); missed seven games. . . . Hyperextended right knee (February 28, 1991). . . . Fractured finger (October 13, 1991); missed four games.
MISCELLANEOUS: Member of 1988 gold medal-winning U.S.S.R. Olympic team.

Season Team	League	REGULAR SEASON					PLAYOFFS				
		Gms.	G	A	Pts.	Pen.	Gms.	G	A	Pts.	Pen.
81-82—Leningrad SKA	USSR	20	1	2	3	16	—	—	—	—	—
82-83—Leningrad SKA	USSR	42	2	1	3	32	—	—	—	—	—
83-84—Leningrad SKA	USSR	43	2	3	5	32	—	—	—	—	—
84-85—Red Army	USSR	36	3	2	5	26	—	—	—	—	—
85-86—Red Army	USSR	40	3	5	8	30	—	—	—	—	—
86-87—Red Army	USSR	38	4	7	11	24	—	—	—	—	—
87-88—Red Army	USSR	39	3	2	5	28	—	—	—	—	—
88-89—Red Army	USSR	42	5	4	9	37	—	—	—	—	—
89-90—Red Army	USSR	42	4	7	11	42	—	—	—	—	—
90-91—Red Army	USSR	15	0	0	0	12	—	—	—	—	—
—Quebec	NHL	36	3	9	12	12	—	—	—	—	—
—Halifax	AHL	2	0	3	3	2	—	—	—	—	—
91-92—Quebec	NHL	68	5	18	23	22	—	—	—	—	—
—Halifax	AHL	3	0	0	0	0	—	—	—	—	—
NHL totals		104	8	27	35	34					

GUY, KEVAN
D, FLAMES

PERSONAL: Born July 16, 1965, at Edmonton, Alta. . . . 6-3/202. . . . Shoots right.
TRANSACTIONS/CAREER NOTES: Selected by Calgary Flames as underage junior in fourth round (fifth Flames pick, 71st overall) of NHL entry draft (June 8, 1983). . . . Traded by Flames to Vancouver Canucks to complete March 1988 deal in which Flames sent C Brian Bradley and RW Peter Bakovic

G

to Canucks for C Craig Coxe (June 1988).... Fractured bone in right foot (February 18, 1990); missed 10 games.... Traded by Canucks with RW Ronnie Stern and a fourth-round pick in 1992 draft to Flames for D Dana Murzyn and a fourth-round pick in 1992 draft (March 5, 1991).... Pulled hamstring (December 2, 1991).

			REGULAR SEASON					PLAYOFFS			
Season Team	League	Gms.	G	A	Pts.	Pen.	Gms.	G	A	Pts.	Pen.
82-83—Medicine Hat	WHL	69	7	20	27	89	5	0	3	3	16
83-84—Medicine Hat	WHL	72	15	42	57	117	14	3	4	7	14
84-85—Medicine Hat	WHL	31	7	17	24	46	10	1	2	3	2
85-86—Moncton	AHL	73	4	20	24	56	10	0	2	2	6
86-87—Moncton	AHL	46	2	10	12	38	—	—	—	—	—
—Calgary	NHL	24	0	4	4	19	4	0	1	1	23
87-88—Calgary	NHL	11	0	3	3	8	—	—	—	—	—
—Salt Lake City	IHL	61	6	30	36	49	19	1	6	7	26
88-89—Vancouver	NHL	45	2	2	4	34	1	0	0	0	0
89-90—Milwaukee	IHL	29	2	11	13	33	—	—	—	—	—
—Vancouver	NHL	30	2	5	7	32	—	—	—	—	—
90-91—Vancouver	NHL	39	1	6	7	39	—	—	—	—	—
—Calgary	NHL	4	0	0	0	4	—	—	—	—	—
91-92—Salt Lake City	IHL	60	3	14	17	89	5	0	1	1	4
—Calgary	NHL	3	0	0	0	2	—	—	—	—	—
NHL totals		156	5	20	25	138	5	0	1	1	23

HAAS, DAVID
LW, OILERS

PERSONAL: Born July 23, 1968, at Toronto.... 6-2/196.... Shoots left.... Full name: David John Haas.
TRANSACTIONS/CAREER NOTES: Selected by Edmonton Oilers as underage junior in fifth round (fifth Oilers pick, 105th overall) of NHL entry draft (June 21, 1986).... Traded by London Knights with C Kelly Cain and D Ed Kister to Kitchener Rangers for RW Peter Lisy, D Ian Pound, D Steve Marcolini and C Greg Hankkio (October 1986).... Loaned to New Haven Nighthawks (December 4, 1991).
HONORS: Named to OHL All-Star second team (1987-88).

			REGULAR SEASON					PLAYOFFS			
Season Team	League	Gms.	G	A	Pts.	Pen.	Gms.	G	A	Pts.	Pen.
85-86—London	OHL	62	4	13	17	91	5	0	1	1	0
86-87—London	OHL	5	1	0	1	5	—	—	—	—	—
—Kitchener	OHL	4	0	1	1	4	—	—	—	—	—
—Belleville	OHL	55	10	13	23	86	6	3	0	3	13
87-88—Belleville	OHL	5	1	1	2	9	—	—	—	—	—
—Windsor	OHL	58	59	46	105	237	11	9	11	20	50
88-89—Cape Breton	AHL	61	9	9	18	325	—	—	—	—	—
89-90—Cape Breton	AHL	53	6	12	18	230	4	2	2	4	15
90-91—Cape Breton	AHL	60	24	23	47	137	3	0	2	2	12
—Edmonton	NHL	5	1	0	1	0	—	—	—	—	—
91-92—Cape Breton	AHL	16	3	7	10	32	—	—	—	—	—
—New Haven	AHL	50	13	23	36	97	5	3	0	3	13
NHL totals		5	1	0	1	0					

HABSCHEID, MARC
RW, FLAMES

PERSONAL: Born March 1, 1963, at Swift Current, Sask.... 6-0/185.... Shoots right. ... Full name: Marc Joseph Habscheid.
TRANSACTIONS/CAREER NOTES: Selected by Edmonton Oilers as underage junior in sixth round (sixth Oilers pick, 113th overall) of NHL entry draft (June 10, 1981).... Suffered head injury (November 1982).... Suspended by Oilers for refusing to report to Nova Scotia Oilers (October 1985).... Traded by Oilers with LW Don Barber and D Emanuel Viveiros to Minnesota North Stars for RW Gord Sherven and C Don Biggs (December 20, 1985).... Assigned to Springfield Indians, refused to report; granted permission to join the Canadian National team in Calgary (November 1986).... Signed as free agent by Detroit Red Wings (June 9, 1989).... Injured groin (November 1990); missed eight games.... Separated shoulder (December 16, 1990); missed 10 games.... Suffered sore shoulder (February 17, 1991); missed five games.... Traded by Red Wings to Calgary Flames for LW Brian MacLellan (June 11, 1991).
HONORS: Named to WHL All-Star second team (1981-82).

			REGULAR SEASON					PLAYOFFS			
Season Team	League	Gms.	G	A	Pts.	Pen.	Gms.	G	A	Pts.	Pen.
80-81—Saskatoon	WHL	72	34	63	97	50	—	—	—	—	—
81-82—Saskatoon	WHL	55	64	87	151	74	5	3	4	7	4
—Edmonton	NHL	7	1	3	4	2	—	—	—	—	—
—Wichita	CHL	—	—	—	—	—	3	0	0	0	0
82-83—Kamloops	WHL	6	7	16	23	8	—	—	—	—	—
—Edmonton	NHL	32	3	10	13	14	—	—	—	—	—
83-84—Edmonton	NHL	9	1	0	1	6	—	—	—	—	—
—Moncton	AHL	71	19	37	56	32	—	—	—	—	—
84-85—Edmonton	NHL	26	5	3	8	4	—	—	—	—	—
—Nova Scotia	AHL	48	29	29	58	65	6	4	3	7	9
85-86—Minnesota	NHL	6	2	3	5	0	2	0	0	0	0
—Springfield	AHL	41	18	32	50	21	—	—	—	—	—
86-87—Minnesota	NHL	15	2	0	2	2	—	—	—	—	—
87-88—Canadian Olympic Team	Int'l	69	24	37	61	48	—	—	—	—	—
—Minnesota	NHL	16	4	11	15	6	—	—	—	—	—
88-89—Minnesota	NHL	76	23	31	54	40	5	1	3	4	13

Season Team	League	REGULAR SEASON					PLAYOFFS				
		Gms.	G	A	Pts.	Pen.	Gms.	G	A	Pts.	Pen.
89-90—Detroit	NHL	66	15	11	26	33	—	—	—	—	—
90-91—Detroit	NHL	46	9	8	17	22	5	0	0	0	0
91-92—Calgary	NHL	46	7	11	18	42	—	—	—	—	—
NHL totals		345	72	91	163	171	12	1	3	4	13

HACKETT, JEFF
G, SHARKS

PERSONAL: Born June 1, 1968, at London, Ont. . . . 6-1/180. . . . Shoots left.
TRANSACTIONS/CAREER NOTES: Selected by New York Islanders as underage junior in second round (second Islanders pick, 34th overall) of NHL entry draft (June 13, 1987). . . . Strained groin (May 13, 1990). . . . Selected by San Jose Sharks in NHL expansion draft (May 30, 1991). . . . Injured groin and hamstring (December 3, 1991); missed nine games. . . . Injured knee (March 23, 1992).
HONORS: Won F.W. (Dinty) Moore Trophy (1986-87). . . . Shared Dave Pinkney Trophy with Sean Evoy (1986-87). . . . Won Jack Butterfield Trophy (1989-90).

Season Team	League	REGULAR SEASON							PLAYOFFS						
		Gms.	Min.	W	L	T	GA	SO	Avg.	Gms.	Min.	W	L	GA	SO	Avg.
85-86—London Jr. B	OHA	19	1150	—	—	—	66	0	3.44	—	—	—	—	—	—	—
86-87—Oshawa	OHL	31	1672	18	9	2	85	0	3.05	15	895	8	7	40	0	2.68
87-88—Oshawa	OHL	53	3165	30	21	2	205	0	3.89	7	438	3	4	31	0	4.25
88-89—New York Islanders	NHL	13	662	4	7	0	39	0	3.53	—	—	—	—	—	—	—
—Springfield	AHL	29	1677	12	14	2	116	0	4.15	—	—	—	—	—	—	—
89-90—Springfield	AHL	54	3045	24	25	3	187	1	3.68	†17	934	10	5	*60	0	3.85
90-91—New York Islanders	NHL	30	1508	5	18	1	91	0	3.62	—	—	—	—	—	—	—
91-92—San Jose	NHL	42	2314	11	27	1	148	0	3.84	—	—	—	—	—	—	—
NHL totals		85	4484	20	52	2	278	0	3.72							

HAKANSSON, MIKAEL
C, MAPLE LEAFS

PERSONAL: Born March 31, 1974, at Stockholm, Sweden. . . . 6-1/176. . . . Shoots left.
TRANSACTIONS/CAREER NOTES: Selected by Toronto Maple Leafs in sixth round (seventh Maple Leafs pick, 125th overall) of NHL entry draft (June 20, 1992).

Season Team	League	REGULAR SEASON					PLAYOFFS				
		Gms.	G	A	Pts.	Pen.	Gms.	G	A	Pts.	Pen.
90-91—Nacka	Sweden	27	2	5	7	6	—	—	—	—	—
91-92—Nacka	Sweden	29	3	15	18	24	—	—	—	—	—

HALKIDIS, BOB
D, MAPLE LEAFS

PERSONAL: Born March 5, 1966, at Toronto. . . . 6-0/200. . . . Shoots left.
TRANSACTIONS/CAREER NOTES: Broke ankle (September 1982). . . . Reinjured ankle (November 1982); missed two weeks. . . . Selected by Buffalo Sabres as underage junior in fourth round (fourth Sabres pick, 81st overall) of NHL entry draft (June 9, 1984). . . . Dislocated right shoulder (December 4, 1985); missed 15 games. . . . Suspended six games by AHL for fighting (October 23, 1987). . . . Injured ankle (December 1987). . . . Injured shoulder (December 1988). . . . Traded by Sabres to Los Angeles Kings for D Dale DeGray (November 24, 1989). . . . Underwent surgery to left shoulder (May 1990). . . . Underwent surgery to left shoulder (October 16, 1990). . . . Signed as free agent by Toronto Maple Leafs (July 24, 1991). . . . Pulled groin (November 21, 1991); missed three games.
HONORS: Won Max Kaminsky Trophy (1984-85). . . . Named to OHL All-Star first team (1984-85).

Season Team	League	REGULAR SEASON					PLAYOFFS				
		Gms.	G	A	Pts.	Pen.	Gms.	G	A	Pts.	Pen.
82-83—London	OHL	37	3	12	15	52	—	—	—	—	—
83-84—London	OHL	51	9	22	31	123	8	0	2	2	27
84-85—London	OHL	62	14	50	64	154	8	3	6	9	22
—Buffalo	NHL	—	—	—	—	—	4	0	0	0	19
85-86—Buffalo	NHL	37	1	9	10	115	—	—	—	—	—
86-87—Buffalo	NHL	6	1	1	2	19	—	—	—	—	—
—Rochester	AHL	59	1	8	9	144	8	0	0	0	43
87-88—Rochester	AHL	15	2	5	7	50	—	—	—	—	—
—Buffalo	NHL	30	0	3	3	115	4	0	0	0	22
88-89—Buffalo	NHL	16	0	1	1	66	—	—	—	—	—
—Rochester	AHL	16	0	6	6	64	—	—	—	—	—
89-90—Rochester	AHL	18	1	13	14	70	—	—	—	—	—
—Los Angeles	NHL	20	0	4	4	56	—	—	—	—	—
—New Haven	AHL	30	3	17	20	67	—	—	—	—	—
90-91—Phoenix	IHL	4	1	5	6	6	—	—	—	—	—
—New Haven	AHL	7	1	3	4	10	—	—	—	—	—
—Los Angeles	NHL	34	1	3	4	133	3	0	0	0	0
91-92—Toronto	NHL	46	3	3	6	145	—	—	—	—	—
NHL totals		189	6	24	30	649	11	0	0	0	41

H

HALL, TODD
D, WHALERS

PERSONAL: Born January 22, 1973, at Columbia, S.C. . . . 6-1/212. . . . Shoots left.
HIGH SCHOOL: Hamden (Conn.).
TRANSACTIONS/CAREER NOTES: Selected by Hartford Whalers in third round (third Whalers pick, 53rd overall) of NHL entry draft (June 12, 1991).

Season Team	League		REGULAR SEASON					PLAYOFFS			
		Gms.	G	A	Pts.	Pen.	Gms.	G	A	Pts.	Pen.
88-89—Hamden H.S.	Conn. H.S.	24	12	21	33	6	—	—	—	—	—
89-90—Hamden H.S.	Conn. H.S.	17	10	22	32	6	—	—	—	—	—
90-91—Hamden H.S.	Conn. H.S.	23	10	15	25	12	—	—	—	—	—
91-92—Boston College	Hockey East	33	2	10	12	14	—	—	—	—	—

HALLER, KEVIN
D, CANADIENS

PERSONAL: Born December 5, 1970, at Trochu, Alta. . . . 6-2/183. . . . Shoots left.
TRANSACTIONS/CAREER NOTES: Broke leg (October 1986). . . . Broke leg (May 1987). . . . Selected by Buffalo Sabres in first round (first Sabres pick, 14th overall) of NHL entry draft (June 17, 1989). . . . Separated shoulder (May 7, 1991); missed seven games. . . . Traded by Sabres to Montreal Canadiens for D Petr Svoboda (March 10, 1992).
HONORS: Won Bill Hunter Trophy (1989-90). . . . Named to WHL (East) All-Star first team (1989-90).

Season Team	League		REGULAR SEASON					PLAYOFFS			
		Gms.	G	A	Pts.	Pen.	Gms.	G	A	Pts.	Pen.
87-88—Olds	AJHL	54	13	31	44	58	—	—	—	—	—
88-89—Regina	WHL	72	10	31	41	99	—	—	—	—	—
89-90—Regina	WHL	58	16	37	53	93	11	2	9	11	16
—Buffalo	NHL	2	0	0	0	0	—	—	—	—	—
90-91—Rochester	AHL	52	2	8	10	53	10	2	1	3	6
—Buffalo	NHL	21	1	8	9	20	6	1	4	5	10
91-92—Buffalo	NHL	58	6	15	21	75					
—Rochester	AHL	4	0	0	0	18					
—Montreal	NHL	8	2	2	4	17	9	0	0	0	6
NHL totals		89	9	25	34	112	15	1	4	5	16

HALVERSON, TREVOR
LW, CAPITALS

PERSONAL: Born April 6, 1971, at White River, Ont. . . . 6-1/193. . . . Shoots left. . . . Full name: Trevor Lloyd Halverson.
TRANSACTIONS/CAREER NOTES: Selected by Washington Capitals in first round (second Capitals pick, 21st overall) of NHL entry draft (June 22, 1991).
HONORS: Named to OHL All-Star first team (1990-91).

Season Team	League		REGULAR SEASON					PLAYOFFS			
		Gms.	G	A	Pts.	Pen.	Gms.	G	A	Pts.	Pen.
88-89—North Bay	OHL	52	8	10	18	77	—	—	—	—	—
89-90—North Bay	OHL	54	22	20	42	162	2	2	1	3	2
90-91—North Bay	OHL	64	59	36	95	128	10	3	6	9	4
91-92—Baltimore	AHL	74	10	11	21	181	—	—	—	—	—

HAMMOND, KEN
D, SENATORS

PERSONAL: Born August 23, 1963, at London, Ont. . . . 6-1/190. . . . Shoots left. . . . Full name: Kenneth Paul Hammond.
COLLEGE: Rensselaer Polytechnic Institute (N.Y.).
TRANSACTIONS/CAREER NOTES: Selected by Los Angeles Kings in eighth round (eighth Kings pick, 147th overall) of NHL entry draft (June 8, 1983). . . . Sprained knee (March 13, 1988). . . . Selected by Edmonton Oilers in 1988 NHL waiver draft for $30,000 (October 3, 1988). . . . Claimed on waivers by New York Rangers when the Oilers attempted to assign him to Cape Breton (November 1, 1988). . . . Traded by Rangers to Toronto Maple Leafs for LW Chris McRae (February 19, 1989). . . . Suffered back spasms (March 1989). . . . Sold by Maple Leafs to Boston Bruins (August 20, 1990). . . . Signed as free agent by San Jose Sharks (August 9, 1991). . . . Pulled groin (January 23, 1992); missed five games. . . . Fractured hand (February 21, 1992); missed seven games. . . . Traded by Sharks to Vancouver Canucks for an eighth-round pick in 1992 draft (March 9, 1992). . . . Underwent surgery to hand (March 1992). . . . Selected by Ottawa Senators in NHL expansion draft (June 18, 1992).
HONORS: Named to NCAA All-America East first team (1984-85). . . . Named to ECAC All-Star first team (1984-85).

Season Team	League		REGULAR SEASON					PLAYOFFS			
		Gms.	G	A	Pts.	Pen.	Gms.	G	A	Pts.	Pen.
81-82—R.P.I.	ECAC	29	2	3	5	54	—	—	—	—	—
82-83—R.P.I.	ECAC	28	4	13	17	54	—	—	—	—	—
83-84—R.P.I.	ECAC	34	5	11	16	72	—	—	—	—	—
84-85—R.P.I.	ECAC	38	11	28	39	90	—	—	—	—	—
—Los Angeles	NHL	3	1	0	1	0	3	0	0	0	4
85-86—New Haven	AHL	67	4	12	16	96	4	0	0	0	7
—Los Angeles	NHL	3	0	1	1	2	—	—	—	—	—
86-87—New Haven	AHL	66	1	15	16	76	6	0	1	1	21
—Los Angeles	NHL	10	0	2	2	11	—	—	—	—	—
87-88—New Haven	AHL	26	3	8	11	27	—	—	—	—	—
—Los Angeles	NHL	46	7	9	16	69	2	0	0	0	4
88-89—Edmonton	NHL	5	0	1	1	8	—	—	—	—	—
—New York Rangers	NHL	3	0	0	0	0	—	—	—	—	—
—Toronto	NHL	14	0	2	2	12	—	—	—	—	—
—Denver	IHL	38	5	18	23	24	—	—	—	—	—
89-90—Newmarket	AHL	75	9	45	54	106	—	—	—	—	—
90-91—Boston	NHL	1	1	0	1	2	8	0	0	0	10
—Maine	AHL	80	10	41	51	159	2	0	1	1	16
91-92—San Jose	NHL	46	5	10	15	82	—	—	—	—	—
NHL totals		131	14	25	39	186	13	0	0	0	18

HAMR, RADEK
D, SENATORS

PERSONAL: Born June 15, 1974, at Prague, Czechoslovakia.... 5-11/167.... Shoots left.
TRANSACTIONS/CAREER NOTES: Selected by Ottawa Senators in fourth round (fourth Senators pick, 73rd overall) of NHL entry draft (June 20, 1992).

			REGULAR SEASON					PLAYOFFS			
Season Team	League	Gms.	G	A	Pts.	Pen.	Gms.	G	A	Pts.	Pen.
91-92—Sparta Prague	Czech.	3	0	0	0	0	—	—	—	—	—

HAMRLIK, MARTIN
D, WHALERS

PERSONAL: Born May 6, 1973, at Zlin, Czechoslovakia.... 5-11/176.... Shoots right. ... Brother of Roman Hamrlik, defenseman in Tampa Bay Lightning system.
TRANSACTIONS/CAREER NOTES: Selected by Hartford Whalers in second round (second Whalers pick, 31st overall) of NHL entry draft (June 22, 1991).... Suffered from Lyme disease (October 1991); missed remainder of season.

			REGULAR SEASON					PLAYOFFS			
Season Team	League	Gms.	G	A	Pts.	Pen.	Gms.	G	A	Pts.	Pen.
89-90—TJ Zlin	Czech.	12	2	0	2		—	—	—	—	—
90-91—TJ Zlin	Czech.	50	8	14	22	44	—	—	—	—	—
91-92—ZPS Zlin	Czech.	4	0	2	2		—	—	—	—	—

HAMRLIK, ROMAN
D, LIGHTNING

PERSONAL: Born April 12, 1974, at Gottwaldov, Czechoslovakia. ... 6-2/190. ... Shoots left.... Brother of Martin Hamrlik, defenseman in Hartford Whalers system.
TRANSACTIONS/CAREER NOTES: Selected by Tampa Bay Lightning in first round (first Lightning pick, first overall) of NHL entry draft (June 20, 1992).

			REGULAR SEASON					PLAYOFFS			
Season Team	League	Gms.	G	A	Pts.	Pen.	Gms.	G	A	Pts.	Pen.
90-91—TJ Zlin	Czech.	14	2	2	4	18	—	—	—	—	—
91-92—ZPS Zlin	Czech.	34	5	5	10	34	—	—	—	—	—

HANKINSON, BEN
RW, DEVILS

PERSONAL: Born January 5, 1969, at Edina, Minn.... 6-2/180.... Shoots right.... Full name: Benjamin John Hankinson.... Brother of Peter Hankinson, right winger in Winnipeg Jets system.
HIGH SCHOOL: Edina (Minn.).
COLLEGE: Minnesota.
TRANSACTIONS/CAREER NOTES: Selected by New Jersey Devils in sixth round (fifth Devils pick, 107th overall) of NHL entry draft (June 13, 1987).
HONORS: Named to WCHA All-Star first team (1989-90).

			REGULAR SEASON					PLAYOFFS			
Season Team	League	Gms.	G	A	Pts.	Pen.	Gms.	G	A	Pts.	Pen.
85-86—Edina High School	Minn. H.S.		9	21	30		—	—	—	—	—
86-87—Edina High School	Minn. H.S.	26	14	20	34		—	—	—	—	—
87-88—University of Minnesota	WCHA	24	4	7	11	36	—	—	—	—	—
88-89—University of Minnesota	WCHA	43	7	11	18	115	—	—	—	—	—
89-90—University of Minnesota	WCHA	46	25	41	66	34	—	—	—	—	—
90-91—University of Minnesota	WCHA	43	19	21	40	133	—	—	—	—	—
91-92—Utica	AHL	77	17	16	33	186	4	3	1	4	2

HANKINSON, PETER
RW, JETS

PERSONAL: Born November 24, 1967, at Edina, Minn.... 5-9/170.... Shoots right. ... Brother of Ben Hankinson, right winger in New Jersey Devils system.
HIGH SCHOOL: Edina (Minn.).
COLLEGE: Minnesota.
TRANSACTIONS/CAREER NOTES: Selected by Winnipeg Jets in NHL supplemental draft (June 16, 1989).

			REGULAR SEASON					PLAYOFFS			
Season Team	League	Gms.	G	A	Pts.	Pen.	Gms.	G	A	Pts.	Pen.
86-87—University of Minnesota	WCHA	43	16	12	28	10	—	—	—	—	—
87-88—University of Minnesota	WCHA	39	25	20	45	32	—	—	—	—	—
88-89—University of Minnesota	WCHA	48	16	27	43	42	—	—	—	—	—
89-90—University of Minnesota	WCHA	45	19	12	31	116	—	—	—	—	—
90-91—Moncton	AHL	47	2	14	16	10	4	0	0	0	0
—Fort Wayne	IHL	10	1	2	3	4	—	—	—	—	—
91-92—Fort Wayne	IHL	75	25	38	63	44	7	1	3	4	2

HANNAN, DAVE
C, SABRES

PERSONAL: Born November 26, 1961, at Sudbury, Ont.... 5-10/185.... Shoots left.... Full name: David Hannan.
TRANSACTIONS/CAREER NOTES: Bruised shoulder; missed part of 1980-81 season.... Selected by Pittsburgh Penguins in 10th round (ninth Penguins pick, 196th overall) of NHL entry draft (June 10, 1981).... Traded by Penguins with C Craig Simpson, D Chris Joseph and D Moe Mantha to Edmonton Oilers for D Paul Coffey, LW Dave Hunter and RW Wayne Van Dorp (November 24, 1987).... Selected by Penguins in 1988 NHL waiver draft (October 3, 1988); LW Dave Hunter was taken by Oilers as compensation.... Suffered hip pointer (October 1988).... Sprained knee (March 1989).... Selected by Toronto Maple Leafs in 1989 NHL waiver draft for $7,500 (October 2, 1989).... Injured left knee ligaments (November 22, 1989).... Underwent surgery to left knee (December 18, 1989); missed 23 games.... Traded by Maple Leafs to Buffalo Sabres for a sixth-round pick in 1992 draft (March 10, 1992).... Injured shoulder (April 12, 1992).
MISCELLANEOUS: Member of 1992 silver medal-winning Canadian Olympic team.

Season Team	League	REGULAR SEASON					PLAYOFFS				
		Gms.	G	A	Pts.	Pen.	Gms.	G	A	Pts.	Pen.
77-78—Windsor	OMJHL	68	14	16	30	43	—	—	—	—	—
78-79—Sault Ste. Marie	OMJHL	26	7	8	15	13	—	—	—	—	—
79-80—Sault Ste. Marie	OMJHL	28	11	10	21	31	—	—	—	—	—
—Brantford	OMJHL	25	5	10	15	26	—	—	—	—	—
80-81—Brantford	OMJHL	56	46	35	81	155	6	2	4	6	20
81-82—Erie	AHL	76	33	37	70	129	—	—	—	—	—
—Pittsburgh	NHL	1	0	0	0	0	—	—	—	—	—
82-83—Baltimore	AHL	5	2	2	4	13	—	—	—	—	—
—Pittsburgh	NHL	74	11	22	33	127	—	—	—	—	—
83-84—Baltimore	AHL	47	18	24	42	98	10	2	6	8	27
—Pittsburgh	NHL	24	2	3	5	33	—	—	—	—	—
84-85—Baltimore	AHL	49	20	25	45	91	—	—	—	—	—
—Pittsburgh	NHL	30	6	7	13	43	—	—	—	—	—
85-86—Pittsburgh	NHL	75	17	18	35	91	—	—	—	—	—
86-87—Pittsburgh	NHL	58	10	15	25	56	—	—	—	—	—
87-88—Pittsburgh	NHL	21	4	3	7	23	—	—	—	—	—
—Edmonton	NHL	51	9	11	20	43	12	1	1	2	8
88-89—Pittsburgh	NHL	72	10	20	30	157	8	0	1	1	4
89-90—Toronto	NHL	39	6	9	15	55	3	1	0	1	4
90-91—Toronto	NHL	74	11	23	34	82	—	—	—	—	—
91-92—Toronto	NHL	35	2	2	4	16	—	—	—	—	—
—Canadian National Team	Int'l	3	0	0	0	2	—	—	—	—	—
—Canadian Olympic Team	Int'l	8	3	5	8	8	—	—	—	—	—
—Buffalo	NHL	12	2	4	6	48	7	2	0	2	2
NHL totals		566	90	137	227	774	30	4	2	6	18

HARDY, MARK

D, RANGERS

PERSONAL: Born February 1, 1959, at Semaden, Switzerland.... 5-11/195.... Shoots left.... Full name: Mark Lea Hardy.

TRANSACTIONS/CAREER NOTES: Selected by Los Angeles Kings in second round (third Kings pick, 30th overall) of NHL entry draft (August 9, 1979).... Underwent surgery to sublexation tendon in left wrist (October 1985); missed 25 games.... Suffered viral infection (January 1988).... Traded by Kings to New York Rangers for RW Ron Duguay (February 23, 1988).... Traded by Rangers to Minnesota North Stars for future draft considerations (LW Louie DeBrusk) (June 13, 1988).... Injured wrist (October 19, 1988).... Traded by North Stars to Rangers for LW Larry Bernard and a fifth-round pick in 1989 draft (D Rhys Hollyman) (December 10, 1988).... Sprained wrist (March 1989).... Sprained right ankle (March 3, 1990); missed 13 regular-season games and two playoff games.... Reinjured ankle (April 9, 1990); missed remainder of playoffs.... Suspended five games by NHL for stick swinging (November 16, 1990).... Strained back (November 4, 1991); missed four games.... Separated shoulder (December 31, 1991); missed 24 games.

HONORS: Won Emile (Butch) Bouchard Trophy (1977-78).... Named to QMJHL All-Star first team (1977-78).

Season Team	League	REGULAR SEASON					PLAYOFFS				
		Gms.	G	A	Pts.	Pen.	Gms.	G	A	Pts.	Pen.
75-76—Montreal	QMJHL	64	6	17	23	44	—	—	—	—	—
76-77—Montreal	QMJHL	72	20	40	60	137	12	4	8	12	14
77-78—Montreal	QMJHL	72	25	57	82	150	13	3	10	13	22
78-79—Montreal	QMJHL	67	18	52	70	117	11	5	8	13	40
79-80—Binghamton	AHL	56	3	13	16	32	—	—	—	—	—
—Los Angeles	NHL	15	0	1	1	10	4	1	1	2	9
80-81—Los Angeles	NHL	77	5	20	25	77	4	1	2	3	4
81-82—Los Angeles	NHL	77	6	39	45	130	10	1	2	3	9
82-83—Los Angeles	NHL	74	5	34	39	101	—	—	—	—	—
83-84—Los Angeles	NHL	79	8	41	49	122	—	—	—	—	—
84-85—Los Angeles	NHL	78	14	39	53	97	3	0	1	1	2
85-86—Los Angeles	NHL	55	6	21	27	71	—	—	—	—	—
86-87—Los Angeles	NHL	73	3	27	30	120	5	1	2	3	10
87-88—Los Angeles	NHL	61	6	22	28	99	—	—	—	—	—
—New York Rangers	NHL	19	2	2	4	31	—	—	—	—	—
88-89—Minnesota	NHL	15	2	4	6	26	—	—	—	—	—
—New York Rangers	NHL	45	2	12	14	45	4	0	1	1	31
89-90—New York Rangers	NHL	54	0	15	15	94	3	0	1	1	2
90-91—New York Rangers	NHL	70	1	5	6	89	6	0	1	1	30
91-92—New York Rangers	NHL	52	1	8	9	65	13	0	3	3	31
NHL totals		844	61	290	351	1177	52	4	14	18	128

HARKINS, BRETT

LW/C, ISLANDERS

PERSONAL: Born July 2, 1970, at North Ridgefield, O.... 6-1/170.... Shoots left.... Full name: Brett Alan Harkins.... Brother of Todd Harkins, center, Calgary Flames.

COLLEGE: Bowling Green State.

TRANSACTIONS/CAREER NOTES: Selected by New York Islanders in seventh round (ninth Islanders pick, 133rd overall) of NHL entry draft (June 17, 1989).

HONORS: Named to CCHA All-Rookie team (1989-90).

Season Team	League	REGULAR SEASON					PLAYOFFS				
		Gms.	G	A	Pts.	Pen.	Gms.	G	A	Pts.	Pen.
87-88—Brockville	COJHL	55	21	55	76	36	—	—	—	—	—
88-89—Detroit Compuware	NAJHL	38	23	46	69	94	—	—	—	—	—

Season Team	League	REGULAR SEASON					PLAYOFFS				
		Gms.	G	A	Pts.	Pen.	Gms.	G	A	Pts.	Pen.
89-90—Bowling Green State	CCHA	41	11	43	54	45	—	—	—	—	—
90-91—Bowling Green State	CCHA	40	22	38	60	30	—	—	—	—	—
91-92—Bowling Green State	CCHA	34	8	39	47	32	—	—	—	—	—

HARKINS, TODD
C, FLAMES

PERSONAL: Born October 8, 1968, at Cleveland.... 6-3/210.... Shoots right.... Full name: Todd Michael Harkins.... Brother of Brett Harkins, left winger/center in New York Islanders system.
COLLEGE: Miami of Ohio.
TRANSACTIONS/CAREER NOTES: Selected by Calgary Flames in second round (second Flames pick, 42nd overall) of NHL entry draft (June 11, 1988).

Season Team	League	REGULAR SEASON					PLAYOFFS				
		Gms.	G	A	Pts.	Pen.	Gms.	G	A	Pts.	Pen.
86-87—Aurora Jr. B......................	OHA	40	19	29	48	102	—	—	—	—	—
87-88—Miami of Ohio	CCHA	34	9	7	16	133	—	—	—	—	—
88-89—Miami of Ohio	CCHA	36	8	7	15	77	—	—	—	—	—
89-90—Miami of Ohio	CCHA	40	27	17	44	78	—	—	—	—	—
90-91—Salt Lake City...................	IHL	79	15	27	42	113	3	0	0	0	2
91-92—Salt Lake City...................	IHL	72	32	30	62	67	5	1	1	2	6
—Calgary............................	NHL	5	0	0	0	7	—	—	—	—	—
NHL totals....................................		5	0	0	0	7					

HARLOCK, DAVID
D, DEVILS

PERSONAL: Born March 16, 1971, at Toronto.... 6-2/195.... Shoots left.... Full name: David Alan Harlock.
COLLEGE: Michigan.
TRANSACTIONS/CAREER NOTES: Injured knee (October 1988).... Selected by New Jersey Devils in second round (second Devils pick, 24th overall) of NHL entry draft (June 16, 1990).

Season Team	League	REGULAR SEASON					PLAYOFFS				
		Gms.	G	A	Pts.	Pen.	Gms.	G	A	Pts.	Pen.
86-87—Toronto Red Wings	MTHL	86	17	55	72	60	—	—	—	—	—
87-88—Toronto Red Wings	MTHL	70	16	56	72	100	—	—	—	—	—
88-89—St. Michael's Jr. B............	ODHA	25	4	15	19	34	—	—	—	—	—
89-90—University of Michigan	CCHA	42	2	13	15	44	—	—	—	—	—
90-91—University of Michigan	CCHA	39	2	8	10	70	—	—	—	—	—
91-92—University of Michigan	CCHA	44	1	6	7	80	—	—	—	—	—

HARRIS, TIM
RW, FLAMES

PERSONAL: Born October 16, 1967, at Toronto.... 6-2/190.... Shoots right.
COLLEGE: Lake Superior State (Mich.).
TRANSACTIONS/CAREER NOTES: Selected by Calgary Flames in fourth round (fifth Flames pick, 70th overall) of NHL entry draft (June 13, 1987).

Season Team	League	REGULAR SEASON					PLAYOFFS				
		Gms.	G	A	Pts.	Pen.	Gms.	G	A	Pts.	Pen.
85-86—Pickering Jr. B	OHA	34	13	25	38	91	—	—	—	—	—
86-87—Pickering Jr. B	OHA	36	20	36	56	142	—	—	—	—	—
87-88—Lake Superior State	CCHA	43	8	10	18	79	—	—	—	—	—
88-89—Lake Superior State	CCHA	29	1	5	6	78	—	—	—	—	—
89-90—Lake Superior State	CCHA	39	6	17	23	71	—	—	—	—	—
90-91—Lake Superior State	CCHA	45	17	22	39	122	—	—	—	—	—
91-92—Salt Lake City..................	IHL	71	11	21	32	91	3	0	1	1	4

HARTMAN, MIKE
LW/RW, LIGHTNING

PERSONAL: Born February 7, 1967, at West Bloomfield, Mich.... 6-0/192.... Shoots left. ... Full name: Michael Jay Hartman.
TRANSACTIONS/CAREER NOTES: Selected by Buffalo Sabres in seventh round (eighth Sabres pick, 131st overall) of NHL entry draft (June 21, 1986).... Suffered sore back (January 1989).... Sprained right ankle (December 1, 1989); missed five games.... Reinjured right ankle (December 29, 1989); missed five games.... Injured right ankle (March 10, 1990).... Injured elbow (Novembr 3, 1990); missed seven games.... Traded by Sabres with LW Darrin Shannon and D Dean Kennedy to Winnipeg Jets for RW Dave McLlwain, D Gordon Donnelly, a sixth-round pick in 1992 draft and future considerations (October 11, 1991).... Suffered from the flu (December 1991); missed one game.... Selected by Tampa Bay Lightning in NHL expansion draft (June 18, 1992).

Season Team	League	REGULAR SEASON					PLAYOFFS				
		Gms.	G	A	Pts.	Pen.	Gms.	G	A	Pts.	Pen.
84-85—Belleville Bulls..................	OHL	49	13	12	25	119	—	—	—	—	—
85-86—Belleville Bulls..................	OHL	4	2	1	3	5	—	—	—	—	—
—North Bay........................	OHL	53	19	16	35	205	10	2	4	6	34
86-87—North Bay........................	OHL	32	15	24	39	144	19	7	8	15	88
—Buffalo.............................	NHL	17	3	3	6	69	—	—	—	—	—
87-88—Rochester........................	AHL	57	13	14	27	283	4	1	0	1	22
—Buffalo.............................	NHL	18	3	1	4	90	6	0	0	0	35
88-89—Buffalo.............................	NHL	70	8	9	17	316	5	0	0	0	34
89-90—Buffalo.............................	NHL	60	11	10	21	211	6	0	0	0	18
90-91—Buffalo.............................	NHL	60	9	3	12	204	2	0	0	0	17
91-92—Winnipeg.........................	NHL	75	4	4	8	264	2	0	0	0	2
NHL totals....................................		300	38	30	68	1154	21	0	0	0	106

H

HASEK, DOMINIK
G, BLACKHAWKS
(1991-92).

PERSONAL: Born January 29, 1965, at Pardubice, Czechoslovakia....5-11/165.
TRANSACTIONS/CAREER NOTES: Selected by Chicago Blackhawks in 10th round (11th Blackhawks pick, 199th overall) of NHL entry draft (June 8, 1983).
HONORS: Named to IHL All-Star first team (1990-91)....Named to NHL All-Rookie team

Season Team	League	Gms.	Min.	W	L	T	GA	SO	Avg.	Gms.	Min.	W	L	GA	SO	Avg.
						REGULAR SEASON							PLAYOFFS			
81-82—Pardubice	Czech.	12	661				34	0	3.09	—	—	—	—	—	—	—
82-83—Pardubice	Czech.	42	2358				105	0	2.67	—	—	—	—	—	—	—
83-84—Pardubice	Czech.	40	2304				108	0	2.81	—	—	—	—	—	—	—
84-85—Pardubice	Czech.	42	2419				131	0	3.25	—	—	—	—	—	—	—
85-86—Pardubice	Czech.	45	2689				138	0	3.08	—	—	—	—	—	—	—
86-87—Pardubice	Czech.	23	2515				103	0	2.46	—	—	—	—	—	—	—
87-88—Pardubice	Czech.	31	2265				98	0	2.60	—	—	—	—	—	—	—
88-89—Pardubice	Czech.	42	2507				114	0	2.73	—	—	—	—	—	—	—
89-90—Dukla Jihlava	Czech.	40	2251				80	0	2.13	—	—	—	—	—	—	—
90-91—Chicago	NHL	5	195	3	0	1	8	0	2.46	3	69	0	0	3	0	2.61
—Indianapolis	IHL	33	1903	20	11	4	80	*5	*2.52	1	60	1	0	3	0	3.00
91-92—Indianapolis	IHL	20	1162	7	10	3	69	1	3.56	—	—	—	—	—	—	—
—Chicago	NHL	20	1014	10	4	1	44	1	2.60	3	158	0	2	8	0	3.04
NHL totals		25	1209	13	4	2	52	1	2.58	6	227	0	2	11	0	2.91

HATCHER, DERIAN
D, NORTH STARS

PERSONAL: Born June 4, 1972, at Sterling Heights, Mich....6-5/205....Shoots left. ...Brother of Kevin Hatcher, defenseman, Washington Capitals.
TRANSACTIONS/CAREER NOTES: Underwent knee surgery (January 1989)....Selected by Minnesota North Stars in first round (first North Stars pick, eighth overall) of NHL entry draft (June 16, 1990)....Suspended 10 games by NHL (December 1991)....Fractured ankle in off-ice incident (January 19, 1992); missed 21 games.

Season Team	League	Gms.	G	A	Pts.	Pen.	Gms.	G	A	Pts.	Pen.
			REGULAR SEASON					PLAYOFFS			
88-89—Detroit G.P.D.	MNHL	51	19	35	54	100	—	—	—	—	—
89-90—North Bay	OHL	64	14	38	52	81	5	2	3	5	8
90-91—North Bay	OHL	64	13	50	63	163	10	2	10	12	28
91-92—Minnesota	NHL	43	8	4	12	88	5	0	2	2	8
NHL totals		43	8	4	12	88	5	0	2	2	8

HATCHER, KEVIN
D, CAPITALS

PERSONAL: Born September 9, 1966, at Detroit....6-4/225....Shoots right....Full name: Kevin John Hatcher....Brother of Derian Hatcher, defenseman, Minnesota North Stars.
TRANSACTIONS/CAREER NOTES: Selected by Washington Capitals as underage junior in first round (first Capitals pick, 17th overall) of NHL entry draft (June 9, 1984)....Tore cartilage in left knee (October 1987). ...Pulled groin (January 1989)....Fractured two metatarsal bones in left foot (February 5, 1989); missed 15 games.... Sprained left knee (April 27, 1990)....Did not attend Capitals training camp due to contract dispute (September 1990).... Injured right knee (November 10, 1990).
HONORS: Named to OHL All-Star second team (1984-85).

Season Team	League	Gms.	G	A	Pts.	Pen.	Gms.	G	A	Pts.	Pen.
			REGULAR SEASON					PLAYOFFS			
83-84—North Bay	OHL	67	10	39	49	61	4	2	2	4	11
84-85—North Bay	OHL	58	26	37	63	75	8	5	8	13	9
—Washington	NHL	2	1	0	1	0	1	0	0	0	0
85-86—Washington	NHL	79	9	10	19	119	9	1	1	2	19
86-87—Washington	NHL	78	8	16	24	144	7	1	0	1	20
87-88—Washington	NHL	71	14	27	41	137	14	5	7	12	55
88-89—Washington	NHL	62	13	27	40	101	6	1	4	5	20
89-90—Washington	NHL	80	13	41	54	102	11	0	8	8	32
90-91—Washington	NHL	79	24	50	74	69	11	3	3	6	8
91-92—Washington	NHL	79	17	37	54	105	7	2	4	6	19
NHL totals		530	99	208	307	777	66	13	27	40	173

HAUER, BRETT
D, CANUCKS

PERSONAL: Born July 11, 1971, at Edina, Minn....6-2/180....Shoots right....Full name: Brett Timothy Hauer....Cousin of Don Jackson, defenseman, Minnesota North Stars, Edmonton Oilers and New York Rangers (1977-78 through 1986-87).
HIGH SCHOOL: Richfield (Minn.).
COLLEGE: Minnesota-Duluth.
TRANSACTIONS/CAREER NOTES: Selected by Vancouver Canucks in fourth round (third Canucks pick, 71st overall) of NHL entry draft (June 17, 1989)....Separated shoulder (December 1990).

Season Team	League	Gms.	G	A	Pts.	Pen.	Gms.	G	A	Pts.	Pen.
			REGULAR SEASON					PLAYOFFS			
87-88—Richfield H.S.	Minn. H.S.	24	3	3	6		—	—	—	—	—
88-89—Richfield H.S.	Minn. H.S.	24	8	15	23	70	—	—	—	—	—
89-90—Minnesota-Duluth	WCHA	37	2	6	8	44	—	—	—	—	—
90-91—Minnesota-Duluth	WCHA	30	1	7	8	54	—	—	—	—	—
91-92—Minnesota-Duluth	WCHA	33	8	14	22	40	—	—	—	—	—

H

HAWERCHUK, DALE
C, SABRES

PERSONAL: Born April 4, 1963, at Toronto.... 5-11/190.... Shoots left.
TRANSACTIONS/CAREER NOTES: Selected by Winnipeg Jets as underage junior in first round (first Jets pick, first overall) of NHL entry draft (June 10, 1981).... Broke rib (April 13, 1985).... Fractured cheekbone (February 1, 1989).... Traded by Jets with first-round pick in 1990 draft (LW Brad May) to Buffalo Sabres for D Phil Housley, LW Scott Arniel, RW Jeff Parker and a first-round pick in 1990 draft (C Keith Tkachuk) (June 16, 1990).... Injured hip (March 8, 1992); missed one game.
HONORS: Won Instructeurs Trophy (1979-80).... Won Guy Lafleur Trophy (1979-80).... Named to Memorial Cup All-Star team (1979-80 and 1980-81).... Won Can.HL Player of the Year Award (1980-81).... Won Michel Briere Trophy (1980-81). ... Won Jean Beliveau Trophy (1980-81).... Won Association of Journalists for Major Junior League Hockey Trophy (1980-81).... Won CCM Trophy (1980-81).... Named to QMJHL All-Star first team (1980-81).... Named NHL Rookie of the Year by THE SPORTING NEWS (1981-82).... Won Calder Memorial Trophy (1981-82).... Named to THE SPORTING NEWS All-Star second team (1984-85).... Named to NHL All-Star second team (1984-85).
RECORDS: Holds NHL record for most assists in one period—5 (March 6, 1984).

			REGULAR SEASON					PLAYOFFS			
Season	Team	League	Gms.	G	A	Pts.	Pen.	Gms.	G	A	Pts.	Pen.
79-80—Cornwall		QMJHL	72	37	66	103	21	18	20	25	45	0
80-81—Cornwall		QMJHL	72	*81	*102	*183	69	19	15	20	35	8
81-82—Winnipeg		NHL	80	45	58	103	47	4	1	7	8	5
82-83—Winnipeg		NHL	79	40	51	91	31	3	1	4	5	8
83-84—Winnipeg		NHL	80	37	65	102	73	3	1	1	2	0
84-85—Winnipeg		NHL	80	53	77	130	74	3	2	1	3	4
85-86—Winnipeg		NHL	80	46	59	105	44	3	0	3	3	0
86-87—Winnipeg		NHL	80	47	53	100	54	10	5	8	13	4
87-88—Winnipeg		NHL	80	44	77	121	59	5	3	4	7	16
88-89—Winnipeg		NHL	75	41	55	96	28	—	—	—	—	—
89-90—Winnipeg		NHL	79	26	55	81	60	7	3	5	8	2
90-91—Buffalo		NHL	80	31	58	89	32	6	2	4	6	10
91-92—Buffalo		NHL	77	23	75	98	27	7	2	5	7	0
NHL totals			870	433	683	1116	529	51	20	42	62	49

HAWGOOD, GREG
D, OILERS

PERSONAL: Born August 10, 1968, at St. Albert, Alta.... 5-10/190.... Shoots left. ... Full name: Gregory William Hawgood.
TRANSACTIONS/CAREER NOTES: Selected by Boston Bruins as underage junior in 10th round (ninth Bruins pick, 202nd overall) of NHL entry draft (June 21, 1986).... Announced that he would play in Italy for 1990-91 season (July 1990).... Traded by Bruins to Edmonton Oilers for C Vladimir Ruzicka (October 22, 1990).
HONORS: Named to WHL (West) All-Star first team (1985-86 through 1987-88).... Won Can.HL Defenseman of the Year Award (1987-88).... Won Bill Hunter Trophy (1987-88).... Won Eddie Shore Plaque (1991-92).... Named to AHL All-Star first team (1991-92).

			REGULAR SEASON					PLAYOFFS			
Season	Team	League	Gms.	G	A	Pts.	Pen.	Gms.	G	A	Pts.	Pen.
83-84—Kamloops		WHL	49	10	23	33	39	—	—	—	—	—
84-85—Kamloops		WHL	66	25	40	65	72	—	—	—	—	—
85-86—Kamloops		WHL	71	34	85	119	86	16	9	22	31	16
86-87—Kamloops		WHL	61	30	93	123	139	—	—	—	—	—
87-88—Boston		NHL	1	0	0	0	0	3	1	0	1	0
—Kamloops		WHL	63	48	85	133	142	16	10	16	26	33
88-89—Boston		NHL	56	16	24	40	84	10	0	2	2	2
—Maine		AHL	21	2	9	11	41	—	—	—	—	—
89-90—Boston		NHL	77	11	27	38	76	15	1	3	4	12
90-91—Asiago		Italy	2			0		—	—	—	—	—
—Maine		AHL	5	0	1	1	13	—	—	—	—	—
—Cape Breton		AHL	55	10	32	42	73	4	0	3	3	23
—Edmonton		NHL	6	0	1	1	6	—	—	—	—	—
91-92—Cape Breton		AHL	56	20	55	75	26	3	2	2	4	0
—Edmonton		NHL	20	2	11	13	22	13	0	3	3	23
NHL totals			160	29	63	92	188	41	2	8	10	37

HAWKINS, TODD
RW, MAPLE LEAFS

PERSONAL: Born August 2, 1966, at Kingston, Ont.... 6-1/195.... Shoots right.
TRANSACTIONS/CAREER NOTES: Selected by Vancouver Canucks in 11th round (10th Canucks pick, 217th overall) of NHL entry draft (June 21, 1986).... Suspended two games by OHL (October 1, 1986).... Bruised hand (September 1988).... Traded by Canucks to Toronto Maple Leafs for D Brian Blad (January 22, 1991).
HONORS: Named to OHL All-Star second team (1986-87).

			REGULAR SEASON					PLAYOFFS			
Season	Team	League	Gms.	G	A	Pts.	Pen.	Gms.	G	A	Pts.	Pen.
84-85—Belleville Bulls		OHL	58	7	16	23	117	12	1	0	1	10
85-86—Belleville Bulls		OHL	60	14	13	27	172	24	9	7	16	60
86-87—Belleville Bulls		OHL	60	47	40	87	187	6	3	5	8	16
87-88—Flint		IHL	50	13	13	26	337	16	3	5	8	*174
—Fredericton		AHL	2	0	0	0	11	—	—	—	—	—
88-89—Vancouver		NHL	4	0	0	0	9	—	—	—	—	—
—Milwaukee		IHL	63	12	14	26	307	9	1	0	1	33

— 399 —

H

Season Team	League	REGULAR SEASON Gms.	G	A	Pts.	Pen.	PLAYOFFS Gms.	G	A	Pts.	Pen.
89-90—Vancouver	NHL	4	0	0	0	6	—	—	—	—	—
—Milwaukee	IHL	61	23	17	40	273	5	4	1	5	19
90-91—Milwaukee	IHL	39	9	11	20	134	—	—	—	—	—
—Newmarket	AHL	22	2	5	7	66	—	—	—	—	—
91-92—St. John's	AHL	66	30	27	57	139	7	1	0	1	10
—Toronto	NHL	2	0	0	0	0	—	—	—	—	—
NHL totals		10	0	0	0	15					

HAWLEY, JOE
C/RW, BLUES

PERSONAL: Born March 13, 1971, at Peterborough, Ont. . . . 5-10/186. . . . Shoots right.
TRANSACTIONS/CAREER NOTES: Selected by St. Louis Blues in 11th round (eighth Blues pick, 222nd overall) of NHL entry draft (June 16, 1990).

Season Team	League	REGULAR SEASON Gms.	G	A	Pts.	Pen.	PLAYOFFS Gms.	G	A	Pts.	Pen.
87-88—Peterborough	OHL	63	16	23	39	39	—	—	—	—	—
88-89—Peterborough	OHL	49	13	30	43	61	—	—	—	—	—
89-90—Peterborough	OHL	66	8	40	48	59	12	2	3	5	26
90-91—Peterborough	OHL	63	17	47	64	70	4	2	3	5	11
—Peoria	IHL	5	0	0	0	0	—	—	—	—	—
91-92—Dayton	ECHL	7	3	6	9	12	—	—	—	—	—
—Peoria	IHL	40	6	7	13	42	—	—	—	—	—

HAYWARD, BRIAN
G, SHARKS

PERSONAL: Born June 25, 1960, at Georgetown, Ont. . . . 5-10/180. . . . Shoots left. . . . Full name: Brian George Hayward.
COLLEGE: Cornell.
TRANSACTIONS/CAREER NOTES: Signed as free agent by Winnipeg Jets (September 1982). . . . Traded by Jets to Montreal Canadiens for G Steve Penney and LW Jan Ingman (August 1986). . . . Suffered back spasms (November 1987). . . . Pulled thigh muscle (December 26, 1987). . . . Injured back (February 23, 1988). . . . Suffered back spasms (November 1988). . . . Sprained left wrist (February 1990). . . . Suspended by Canadiens after missing team practice (October 8, 1990); missed a month. . . . Traded by Canadiens to Minnesota North Stars for D Jayson More (November 7, 1990). . . . Selected by San Jose Sharks in 1991 NHL dispersal draft (May 30, 1991). . . . Injured back (October 21, 1991); missed 19 games. . . . Injured back (Janaury 27, 1992).
HONORS: Named to NCAA All-America team (1981-82). . . . Named to ECAC All-Star first team (1981-82). . . . Shared William M. Jennings Trophy with Patrick Roy (1988-89).

Season Team	League	REGULAR SEASON Gms.	Min.	W	L	T	GA	SO	Avg.	PLAYOFFS Gms.	Min.	W	L	GA	SO	Avg.
78-79—Cornell University	ECAC	25	1469	18	6	0	95	0	3.88	3	179	2	1	14	0	4.69
79-80—Cornell University	ECAC	12	508	2	7	0	52	0	6.14	—						
80-81—Cornell University	ECAC	19	967	11	4	1	58	1	3.60	4	181	2	1	18	0	5.97
81-82—Cornell University	ECAC		1320	11	10	1	68	0	3.09	—						
82-83—Sherbrooke	AHL	22	1208	6	11	3	89	1	4.42	—						
—Winnipeg	NHL	24	1440	10	12	2	89	1	3.71	3	160	0	3	14	0	5.25
83-84—Sherbrooke	AHL	15	781	4	8	0	69	0	5.30	—						
—Winnipeg	NHL	28	1530	7	18	2	124	0	4.86	—						
84-85—Winnipeg	NHL	61	3436	33	17	7	220	0	3.84	6	309	2	4	23	0	4.47
85-86—Sherbrooke	AHL	3	185	2	0	1	5	0	1.62	—						
—Winnipeg	NHL	52	2721	13	28	5	217	0	4.79	2	68	0	1	6	0	5.29
86-87—Montreal	NHL	37	2178	19	13	4	102	1	2.81	13	708	6	5	32	0	2.71
87-88—Montreal	NHL	39	2247	22	10	4	107	2	2.86	4	230	2	2	9	0	2.35
88-89—Montreal	NHL	36	2091	20	13	3	101	1	2.90	2	124	1	1	7	0	3.39
89-90—Montreal	NHL	29	1674	10	12	6	94	1	3.37	1	33	0	0	2	0	3.64
90-91—Minnesota	NHL	26	1473	6	15	3	77	2	3.14	6	171	0	2	11	0	3.86
—Kalamazoo	IHL	2	120				5	0	2.50	—						
91-92—San Jose	NHL	7	305	1	4	0	25	0	4.92	—						
—Kansas City	IHL	2	119	1	1	0	3	1	1.51	—						
NHL totals		339	19095	141	142	36	1156	8	3.63	37	1803	11	18	104	0	3.46

HEALY, GLENN
G, ISLANDERS

PERSONAL: Born August 23, 1962, at Pickering, Ont. . . . 5-10/185. . . . Shoots left. . . . Full name: Glenn M. Healy.
COLLEGE: Western Michigan.
TRANSACTIONS/CAREER NOTES: Signed as free agent by Los Angeles Kings (June 1985). . . . Signed as free agent by New York Islanders (August 1989); Kings received a fourth-round pick in 1990 draft (later traded to Minnesota) as compensation. . . . Strained left ankle ligaments (October 13, 1990); missed eight games. . . . Fractured right index finger (November 10, 1991); missed five games. . . . Fractured right thumb (January 3, 1992); missed 10 games. . . . Severed tip of finger in practice and underwent reconstructive surgery (March 2, 1992); missed 13 games.
HONORS: Named to NCAA All-America West second team (1984-85). . . . Named to CCHA All-Star second team (1984-85).

Season Team	League	REGULAR SEASON Gms.	Min.	W	L	T	GA	SO	Avg.	PLAYOFFS Gms.	Min.	W	L	GA	SO	Avg.
81-82—Western Michigan U.	CCHA	27	1569	7	19	1	116	0	4.44	—						
82-83—Western Michigan U.	CCHA	30	1733	8	19	2	116	0	4.02	—						
83-84—Western Michigan U.	CCHA	38	2242	19	16	3	146	0	3.91	—						
84-85—Western Michigan U.	CCHA	37	2172	21	14	2	118		3.26	—						

Season	Team	League	REGULAR SEASON								PLAYOFFS						
			Gms.	Min.	W	L	T	GA	SO	Avg.	Gms.	Min.	W	L	GA	SO	Avg.
85-86	—Toledo	IHL	7	402				28	0	4.18	—	—	—	—	—	—	—
	—New Haven	AHL	43	2410	21	15	4	160	0	3.98	2	119	0	2	11	0	5.55
	—Los Angeles	NHL	1	51	0	0	0	6	0	7.06	—	—	—	—	—	—	—
86-87	—New Haven	AHL	47	2828	21	15	0	173	1	3.67	7	427	3	4	19	0	2.67
87-88	—Los Angeles	NHL	34	1869	12	18	1	135	1	4.33	4	240	1	3	20	0	5.00
88-89	—Los Angeles	NHL	48	2699	25	19	2	192	0	4.27	3	97	0	1	6	0	3.71
89-90	—New York Islanders	NHL	39	2197	12	19	6	128	2	3.50	4	166	1	2	9	0	3.25
90-91	—New York Islanders	NHL	53	2999	18	24	9	166	0	3.32	—	—	—	—	—	—	—
91-92	—New York Islanders	NHL	37	1960	14	16	4	124	1	3.80	—	—	—	—	—	—	—
NHL totals			212	11775	81	96	22	751	4	3.83	11	503	2	6	35	0	4.17

HEBERT, GUY

G, BLUES

PERSONAL: Born January 7, 1967, at Troy, N.Y. . . . 5-11/180. . . . Shoots left. . . . Full name: Guy Andrew Hebert.

COLLEGE: Hamilton (N.Y.).

TRANSACTIONS/CAREER NOTES: Selected by St. Louis Blues in eighth round (eighth Blues pick, 159th overall) of NHL entry draft (June 13, 1987).

HONORS: Shared James Norris Memorial Trophy with Pat Jablonski (1990-91). . . . Named to IHL All-Star second team (1990-91).

Season	Team	League	REGULAR SEASON								PLAYOFFS						
			Gms.	Min.	W	L	T	GA	SO	Avg.	Gms.	Min.	W	L	GA	SO	Avg.
86-87	—Hamilton College	NCAA-II	18	1070				40		2.24	—	—	—	—	—	—	—
87-88	—Hamilton College	NCAA-II	8	450				19		2.53	—	—	—	—	—	—	—
88-89	—Hamilton College	NCAA-II	25	1453				62		2.56	—	—	—	—	—	—	—
89-90	—Peoria	IHL	30	1706	7	13	7	124	1	4.36	2	76	0	1	5	0	3.95
90-91	—Peoria	IHL	36	2093	24	10	1	100	2	*2.87	8	458	3	4	32	0	4.19
91-92	—Peoria	IHL	29	1731	20	9	0	98	0	3.40	4	239	3	1	9	0	*2.26
	—St. Louis	NHL	13	738	5	5	1	36	0	2.93	—	—	—	—	—	—	—
NHL totals			13	738	5	5	1	36	0	2.93							

HEDICAN, BRET

D, BLUES

PERSONAL: Born August 10, 1970, at St. Paul, Minn. . . . 6-2/195. . . . Shoots left. . . . Full name: Bret Michael Hedican.

COLLEGE: St. Cloud State (Minn.).

TRANSACTIONS/CAREER NOTES: Selected by St. Louis Blues in 10th round (10th Blues pick, 198th overall) of NHL entry draft (June 11, 1988).

HONORS: Named to WCHA All-Star first team (1990-91).

Season	Team	League	REGULAR SEASON					PLAYOFFS				
			Gms.	G	A	Pts.	Pen.	Gms.	G	A	Pts.	Pen.
88-89	—St. Cloud State	WCHA	28	5	3	8	28	—	—	—	—	—
89-90	—St. Cloud State	WCHA	36	4	17	21	37	—	—	—	—	—
90-91	—St. Cloud State	WCHA	41	18	30	48	52	—	—	—	—	—
91-92	—U.S. National Team	Int'l	54	1	8	9	59	—	—	—	—	—
	—U.S. Olympic Team	Int'l	8	0	0	0	4	—	—	—	—	—
	—St. Louis	NHL	4	1	0	1	0	5	0	0	0	0
NHL totals			4	1	0	1	0	5	0	0	0	0

HEINZE, STEVE

RW, BRUINS

PERSONAL: Born January 30, 1970, at Lawrence, Mass. . . . 5-11/180. . . . Shoots right. . . . Full name: Stephen Herbert Heinze.

HIGH SCHOOL: Lawrence Academy (Groton, Mass.).

COLLEGE: Boston College.

TRANSACTIONS/CAREER NOTES: Selected by Boston Bruins in second round (second Bruins pick, 60th overall) of NHL entry draft (June 11, 1988). . . . Injured shoulder (May 1, 1992).

HONORS: Named to Hockey East All-Rookie Team (1988-89). . . . Named to NCAA All-America East first team (1989-90). . . . Named to Hockey East All-Star first team (1989-90).

Season	Team	League	REGULAR SEASON					PLAYOFFS				
			Gms.	G	A	Pts.	Pen.	Gms.	G	A	Pts.	Pen.
86-87	—Lawrence Academy	Mass. H.S.	23	26	24	50		—	—	—	—	—
87-88	—Lawrence Academy	Mass. H.S.	23	30	25	55		—	—	—	—	—
88-89	—Boston College	Hockey East	36	26	23	49	26	—	—	—	—	—
89-90	—Boston College	Hockey East	40	27	36	63	41	—	—	—	—	—
90-91	—Boston College	Hockey East	35	21	26	47	35	—	—	—	—	—
91-92	—U.S. National Team	Int'l	49	18	15	33	38	—	—	—	—	—
	—U.S. Olympic Team	Int'l	8	1	3	4	8	—	—	—	—	—
	—Boston	NHL	14	3	4	7	6	7	0	3	3	17
NHL totals			14	3	4	7	6	7	0	3	3	17

HELENIUS, SAMI

D, FLAMES

PERSONAL: Born January 22, 1974, at Helsinki, Finland. . . . 6-5/200. . . . Shoots left.

TRANSACTIONS/CAREER NOTES: Selected by Calgary Flames in fifth round (fifth Flames pick, 102nd overall) of NHL entry draft (June 20, 1992).

Season	Team	League	REGULAR SEASON					PLAYOFFS				
			Gms.	G	A	Pts.	Pen.	Gms.	G	A	Pts.	Pen.
91-92	—Jokerit Helsinki Jrs.	Finland				Statistics unavailable.						

H

HENDRICKSON, DARBY
C, MAPLE LEAFS

PERSONAL: Born August 28, 1972, at Richfield, Minn. . . . 6-0/175. . . . Shoots left.
HIGH SCHOOL: Richfield (Minn.).
TRANSACTIONS/CAREER NOTES: Selected by Toronto Maple Leafs in fourth round (third Maple Leafs pick, 73rd overall) of NHL entry draft (June 16, 1990).
HONORS: Won WCHA Rookie of the Year Award (1991-92).

Season Team	League	Gms.	G	A	Pts.	Pen.	Gms.	G	A	Pts.	Pen.
		—REGULAR SEASON—					**—PLAYOFFS—**				
87-88—Richfield H.S.	Minn. H.S.	22	12	9	21	10	—	—	—	—	—
88-89—Richfield H.S.	Minn. H.S.	22	22	20	42	12	—	—	—	—	—
89-90—Richfield H.S.	Minn. H.S.	24	23	27	50	49	—	—	—	—	—
90-91—Richfield H.S.	Minn. H.S.	27	32	29	61		—	—	—	—	—
91-92—University of Minnesota	WCHA	44	25	30	55	63	—	—	—	—	—

HEROUX, YVES
RW, BLUES

PERSONAL: Born April 27, 1965, at Terrebonne, Que. . . . 5-11/185. . . . Shoots right.
TRANSACTIONS/CAREER NOTES: Suffered foot infection (December 1981). . . . Selected by Quebec Nordiques in second round (first Nordiques pick, 32nd overall) of NHL entry draft (June 8, 1983). . . . Signed as free agent by St. Louis Blues (March 13, 1990).

Season Team	League	Gms.	G	A	Pts.	Pen.	Gms.	G	A	Pts.	Pen.
		—REGULAR SEASON—					**—PLAYOFFS—**				
82-83—Chicoutimi	QMJHL	70	41	40	81	44	5	0	4	4	8
83-84—Chicoutimi	QMJHL	56	28	25	53	67	—	—	—	—	—
—Fredericton	AHL	4	0	0	0	0	—	—	—	—	—
84-85—Chicoutimi	QMJHL	66	42	54	96	123	14	5	8	13	16
85-86—Fredericton	AHL	31	12	10	22	42	2	0	1	1	7
—Muskegon	IHL	42	14	8	22	41	—	—	—	—	—
86-87—Fredericton	AHL	37	8	6	14	13	—	—	—	—	—
—Quebec	NHL	1	0	0	0	0	—	—	—	—	—
—Muskegon	IHL	25	6	8	14	31	2	0	0	0	0
87-88—Baltimore	AHL	5	0	2	2	2	—	—	—	—	—
88-89—Flint	IHL	82	43	42	85	98	—	—	—	—	—
89-90—Peoria	IHL	14	3	2	5	4	5	2	2	4	0
90-91—Albany	IHL	45	22	18	40	46	—	—	—	—	—
—Peoria	IHL	33	16	8	24	26	17	4	4	8	16
91-92—Peoria	IHL	80	41	36	77	72	8	5	1	6	6
NHL totals		1	0	0	0	0					

HERTER, JASON
D, CANUCKS

PERSONAL: Born October 2, 1970, at Hafford, Sask. . . . 6-1/190. . . . Shoots right. . . . Full name: Jason D. Herter.
COLLEGE: North Dakota.
TRANSACTIONS/CAREER NOTES: Strained shoulder (September 1988). . . . Selected by Vancouver Canucks in first round (first Canucks pick, eighth overall) of NHL entry draft (June 17, 1989).
HONORS: Named to WCHA All-Star second team (1989-90 and 1990-91).

Season Team	League	Gms.	G	A	Pts.	Pen.	Gms.	G	A	Pts.	Pen.
		—REGULAR SEASON—					**—PLAYOFFS—**				
87-88—Notre Dame	SJHL	54	5	33	38	152	—	—	—	—	—
88-89—Univ. of North Dakota	WCHA	41	8	24	32	62	—	—	—	—	—
89-90—Univ. of North Dakota	WCHA	38	11	39	50	40	—	—	—	—	—
90-91—Univ. of North Dakota	WCHA	39	11	26	37	52	—	—	—	—	—
91-92—Milwaukee	IHL	56	7	18	25	34	1	0	0	0	2

HERVEY, MATT
D, BRUINS

PERSONAL: Born May 16, 1966, at Los Angeles. . . . 5-11/195. . . . Shoots right.
TRANSACTIONS/CAREER NOTES: Suspended six games by WHL for stick-swinging incident (November 1986). . . . Signed as free agent by Winnipeg Jets (October 1987). . . . Suffered sore back (March 23, 1992).

Season Team	League	Gms.	G	A	Pts.	Pen.	Gms.	G	A	Pts.	Pen.
		—REGULAR SEASON—					**—PLAYOFFS—**				
83-84—Victoria	WHL	67	4	19	23	89	—	—	—	—	—
84-85—Victoria	WHL	14	1	3	4	17	—	—	—	—	—
—Lethbridge	WHL	54	3	9	12	88	—	—	—	—	—
85-86—Lethbridge	WHL	60	9	17	26	110	—	—	—	—	—
86-87—Seattle	WHL	9	4	5	9	59	—	—	—	—	—
—Richmond	BCJHL	17	4	21	25	99	11	3	10	13	22
87-88—Moncton	AHL	69	9	20	29	265	—	—	—	—	—
88-89—Moncton	AHL	73	8	28	36	295	10	1	2	3	42
—Winnipeg	NHL	2	0	0	0	4	—	—	—	—	—
89-90—Moncton	AHL	47	3	13	16	168	—	—	—	—	—
90-91—Moncton	AHL	71	4	28	32	132	7	0	1	1	23
91-92—Boston	NHL	16	0	1	1	55	5	0	0	0	6
—Maine	AHL	36	1	7	8	47	—	—	—	—	—
NHL totals		18	0	1	1	59	5	0	0	0	6

HEWARD, JAMIE
D, PENGUINS

PERSONAL: Born March 30, 1971, at Regina, Sask. . . . 6-2/194. . . . Shoots right.
TRANSACTIONS/CAREER NOTES: Traded by Spokane Chiefs to Regina Pats for RW Pat Falloon and future considerations (October 1987). . . . Broke jaw (November 1988). . . . Selected by Pittsburgh Penguins in first round (first Penguins pick, 16th overall) of NHL entry draft (June 17, 1989). . . . Suffered from mononucleosis (September 1989).
HONORS: Named to WHL All-Star first team (1990-91).

			REGULAR SEASON					PLAYOFFS				
Season	Team	League	Gms.	G	A	Pts.	Pen.	Gms.	G	A	Pts.	Pen.
87-88	Regina	WHL	68	10	17	27	17	4	1	1	2	2
88-89	Regina	WHL	52	31	28	59	29	—	—	—	—	—
89-90	Regina	WHL	72	14	44	58	42	11	2	2	4	10
90-91	Regina	WHL	71	23	61	84	41	8	2	9	11	6
91-92	Muskegon	IHL	54	6	21	27	37	14	1	4	5	4

HEXTALL, DONEVAN
LW, DEVILS

PERSONAL: Born February 24, 1972, at Wolseley, Sask. . . . 6-3/190. . . . Shoots left.
TRANSACTIONS/CAREER NOTES: Selected by New Jersey Devils in second round (third Devils pick, 33rd overall) of NHL entry draft (June 22, 1991).
HONORS: Won Jim Piggott Memorial Trophy (1990-91). . . . Named to WHL (East) All-Star second team (1991-92).

			REGULAR SEASON					PLAYOFFS				
Season	Team	League	Gms.	G	A	Pts.	Pen.	Gms.	G	A	Pts.	Pen.
89-90	Prince Albert	WHL	7	1	2	3	4	—	—	—	—	—
	Weyburn Red Wings	SJHL	63	23	45	68	127	—	—	—	—	—
90-91	Prince Albert	WHL	70	30	59	89	55	3	1	3	4	0
91-92	Prince Albert	WHL	71	33	71	104	105	10	3	6	9	10

HEXTALL, RON
G, NORDIQUES

PERSONAL: Born May 3, 1964, at Winnipeg, Man. . . . 6-3/192. . . . Shoots left.
TRANSACTIONS/CAREER NOTES: Selected by Philadelphia Flyers as underage junior in sixth round (sixth Flyers pick, 119th overall) of NHL entry draft (June 9, 1982). . . . Suspended eight games by NHL for slashing (May 1987). . . . Pulled hamstring (March 7, 1989). . . . Suspended for first 12 games of 1989-90 season by NHL for attacking opposing player in final playoff game (May 11, 1989). . . . Did not attend training camp due to a contract dispute (September 1989). . . . Pulled groin (November 4, 1989). . . . Pulled hamstring (November 15, 1989). . . . Tore right groin muscle (December 13, 1989); missed 29 games. . . . Injured left groin (March 8, 1990). . . . Pulled groin (October 11, 1990); missed five games. . . . Sprained left knee medial collateral ligament (October 27, 1990); missed five weeks. . . . Tore groin muscle (March 12, 1991); missed nine games. . . . Suffered from the flu (November 14, 1991); missed one game. . . . Developed shoulder tendinitis (November 27, 1991); missed nine games. . . . Traded by Flyers with C Mike Ricci, C Peter Forsberg, D Steve Duchesne, D Kerry Huffman, first-round pick in 1993 draft, cash and future considerations to Quebec Nordiques for C Eric Lindros (June 20, 1992); Flyers sent LW Chris Simon and first-round pick in 1994 draft to Nordiques to complete deal (July 21, 1992).
HONORS: Won Dudley (Red) Garrett Memorial Trophy (1985-86). . . . Named to AHL All-Star first team (1985-86). . . . Named NHL Rookie of the Year by THE SPORTING NEWS (1986-87). . . . Won Vezina Trophy (1986-87). . . . Won Conn Smythe Trophy (1986-87). . . . Named to THE SPORTING NEWS All-Star second team (1986-87). . . . Named to NHL All-Star first team (1986-87). . . . Named to NHL All-Rookie team (1986-87).
RECORDS: Holds NHL single-season playoff record for most minutes played by a goaltender—1,540 (1987).
STATISTICAL NOTES: Scored a goal into a Washington empty net, becoming the first goalie to score a goal in Stanley Cup play (April 11, 1989).

			REGULAR SEASON							PLAYOFFS						
Season	Team	League	Gms.	Min.	W	L	T	GA	SO	Avg.	Gms.	Min.	W	L	GA	SO	Avg.
80-81	Melville	SJHL	42	2127				254	0	7.17	—	—	—	—	—	—	—
81-82	Brandon	WHL	30	1398	12	11	0	133	0	5.71	3	103	0	2	16	0	9.32
82-83	Brandon	WHL	44	2589	13	30	0	249	0	5.77	—	—	—	—	—	—	—
83-84	Brandon	WHL	46	2670	29	13	2	190	0	4.27	10	592	5	5	37	0	3.75
84-85	Kalamazoo	IHL	19	1103	6	11	1	80	0	4.35	—	—	—	—	—	—	—
	Hershey	AHL	11	555	4	6	0	34	0	3.68	—	—	—	—	—	—	—
85-86	Hershey	AHL	*53	*3061	30	19	2	174	*5	3.41	13	780	5	7	42	*1	3.23
86-87	Philadelphia	NHL	*66	*3799	37	21	6	190	1	3.00	*26	*1540	15	11	*71	†2	2.77
87-88	Philadelphia	NHL	62	3561	30	22	7	208	0	3.50	7	379	2	4	30	0	4.75
88-89	Philadelphia	NHL	64	3756	30	28	6	202	0	3.23	15	886	8	7	49	0	3.32
89-90	Philadelphia	NHL	8	419	4	2	1	29	0	4.15	—	—	—	—	—	—	—
	Hershey	AHL	1	49	1	0	0	3	0	3.67	—	—	—	—	—	—	—
90-91	Philadelphia	NHL	36	2035	13	16	5	106	0	3.13	—	—	—	—	—	—	—
91-92	Philadelphia	NHL	45	2668	16	21	6	151	3	3.40	—	—	—	—	—	—	—
	NHL totals		281	16238	130	110	31	886	4	3.27	48	2805	25	22	150	2	3.21

HILL, SEAN
D, CANADIENS

PERSONAL: Born February 14, 1970, at Duluth, Minn. . . . 6-0/195. . . . Shoots right. . . . Full name: Sean Ronald Hill.
COLLEGE: Wisconsin.
TRANSACTIONS/CAREER NOTES: Selected by Montreal Canadiens in eighth round (ninth Canadiens pick, 167th overall) of NHL entry draft (June 11, 1988). . . . Injured knee (December 29, 1990). . . . Suspended two games by WCHA for elbowing (January 18, 1991).
HONORS: Named to WCHA All-Star second team (1989-90 and 1990-91). . . . Named to NCAA All-America West second team (1990-91).

			REGULAR SEASON					PLAYOFFS				
Season	Team	League	Gms.	G	A	Pts.	Pen.	Gms.	G	A	Pts.	Pen.
88-89	University of Wisconsin	WCHA	45	2	23	25	69	—	—	—	—	—
89-90	University of Wisconsin	WCHA	42	14	39	53	78	—	—	—	—	—

Season	Team	League	REGULAR SEASON					PLAYOFFS				
			Gms.	G	A	Pts.	Pen.	Gms.	G	A	Pts.	Pen.
90-91	—University of Wisconsin ...	WCHA	37	19	32	51	122	—	—	—	—	—
	—Fredericton	AHL	—	—	—	—	—	3	0	2	2	2
	—Montreal	NHL	—	—	—	—	—	1	0	0	0	0
91-92	—Fredericton	AHL	42	7	20	27	65	7	1	3	4	6
	—U.S. National Team	Int'l	12	4	3	7	16	—	—	—	—	—
	—U.S. Olympic Team	Int'l	8	2	0	2	6	—	—	—	—	—
	—Montreal	NHL	—	—	—	—	—	4	1	0	1	2
NHL totals								5	1	0	1	2

HILLIER, RANDY
D, SABRES

PERSONAL: Born March 30, 1960, at Toronto.... 6-1/192.... Shoots left.... Full name: Randy George Hillier.

TRANSACTIONS/CAREER NOTES: Selected by Boston Bruins in fifth round (fourth Bruins pick, 102nd overall) of NHL entry draft (June 11, 1980).... Injured knee (April 19, 1982).... Injured left knee (December 1982).... Strained ligaments in right knee (April 2, 1983).... Traded by Bruins to Pittsburgh Penguins for fourth-round pick in 1985 draft (October 1984).... Underwent surgery to remove bone chips from left shoulder (December 1984); missed 20 games.... Broke finger (March 1985).... Tore knee ligaments (November 30, 1985).... Injured shoulder (November 1986).... Bruised left hand (March 12, 1987).... Tore hip muscles (October 1987).... Bruised heel (November 1987).... Bruised ribs (February 1989).... Bruised knee (March 1989).... Broke toe (April 1989).... Broke thumb (January 10, 1990); missed 10 games.... Signed as free agent by New York Islanders (June 30, 1991).... Injured shoulder (October 27, 1990).... Broke left foot (November 13, 1990); missed 34 games.... Lacerated leg (March 17, 1991). ...Signed as free agent by New York Islanders (July 1, 1991).... Traded by Islanders with C Pat LaFontaine, LW Randy Wood and future considerations to Buffalo Sabres for C Pierre Turgeon, RW Benoit Hogue, D Uwe Krupp and C Dave McLlwain (October 25, 1991).

Season	Team	League	REGULAR SEASON					PLAYOFFS				
			Gms.	G	A	Pts.	Pen.	Gms.	G	A	Pts.	Pen.
77-78	—Sudbury	OMJHL	60	1	14	15	67	—	—	—	—	—
78-79	—Sudbury	OMJHL	61	9	25	34	173	10	2	5	7	21
79-80	—Sudbury	OMJHL	60	16	49	65	143	9	3	6	9	14
80-81	—Springfield	AHL	64	3	17	20	105	6	0	2	2	36
81-82	—Erie	AHL	35	6	13	19	52	—	—	—	—	—
	—Boston	NHL	25	0	8	8	29	8	0	1	1	16
82-83	—Boston	NHL	70	0	10	10	99	3	0	0	0	4
83-84	—Boston	NHL	69	3	12	15	125	—	—	—	—	—
84-85	—Pittsburgh	NHL	45	2	19	21	56	—	—	—	—	—
85-86	—Baltimore	AHL	8	0	5	5	14	—	—	—	—	—
	—Pittsburgh	NHL	28	0	3	3	53	—	—	—	—	—
86-87	—Pittsburgh	NHL	55	4	8	12	97	—	—	—	—	—
87-88	—Pittsburgh	NHL	55	1	12	13	144	—	—	—	—	—
88-89	—Pittsburgh	NHL	68	1	23	24	141	9	0	1	1	49
89-90	—Pittsburgh	NHL	61	3	12	15	71	—	—	—	—	—
90-91	—Pittsburgh	NHL	31	2	2	4	32	8	0	0	0	24
91-92	—New York Islanders	NHL	8	0	0	0	11	—	—	—	—	—
	—Buffalo	NHL	28	0	1	1	48	—	—	—	—	—
	—San Diego	IHL	6	0	2	2	4	—	—	—	—	—
NHL totals			543	16	110	126	906	28	0	2	2	93

HIRSCH, COREY
G, RANGERS

PERSONAL: Born July 1, 1972, at Medicine Hat, Alta.... 5-10/170.... Shoots left.
TRANSACTIONS/CAREER NOTES: Selected by New York Rangers in eighth round (seventh Rangers pick, 169th overall) in NHL entry draft (June 22, 1991).
HONORS: Named to WHL West All-Star second team (1989-90).... Won Can.HL Goaltender of the Year Award (1991-92).... Won Hap Emms Memorial Trophy (1991-92)... Won Del Wilson Trophy (1991-92).... Won WHL Player of the Year Award (1991-92).... Named to Can.HL All-Star first team (1991-92).... Named to Memorial Cup All-Star team (1991-92).... Named to WHL West All-Star first team (1991-92).

Season	Team	League	REGULAR SEASON							PLAYOFFS						
			Gms.	Min.	W	L	T	GA	SO	Avg.	Gms.	Min.	W	L	GA	SO	Avg.
88-89	—Kamloops	WHL	32	1516	11	12	2	106	2	4.20	5	245			19	0	4.65
89-90	—Kamloops	WHL	63	3608	43	13	0	230	3	3.82	17	1043	14	3	60	0	3.45
90-91	—Kamloops	WHL	38	1970	26	7	1	100	3	3.05	11	623	5	6	42	0	4.04
91-92	—Kamloops	WHL	48	2732	35	10	2	124	*5	*2.72	*16	*954	*11	5	35	*2	*2.20

HOCKING, JUSTIN
D, KINGS

PERSONAL: Born January 9, 1974, at Stettler, Alta.... 6-4/210.... Shoots right.
COLLEGE: Spokane Falls Community College (Wash.).
TRANSACTIONS/CAREER NOTES: Selected by Los Angeles Kings in second round (first Kings pick, 39th overall) of NHL entry draft (June 20, 1992).

Season	Team	League	REGULAR SEASON					PLAYOFFS				
			Gms.	G	A	Pts.	Pen.	Gms.	G	A	Pts.	Pen.
90-91	—Fort Saskatchewan	AJHL	38	4	6	10	84	—	—	—	—	—
91-92	—Spokane Chiefs	WHL	71	4	6	10	309	10	0	3	3	28

HODGE, KEN
C, BRUINS

PERSONAL: Born April 13, 1966, at Windsor, Ont.... 6-1/200.... Shoots left.... Full name: Kenneth David Hodge Jr.... Son of Ken Hodge, right winger, Chicago Blackhawks, Boston Bruins and New York Rangers (1965-66 through 1977-78).
HIGH SCHOOL: St. John's Prep School (Danvers, Mass.).

COLLEGE: Boston College.
TRANSACTIONS/CAREER NOTES: Selected by Minnesota North Stars in third round (second North Stars pick, 46th overall) of NHL entry draft (June 9, 1984). . . . Injured shoulders (November 1987). . . . Reinjured shoulders (November 1987). . . . Traded by North Stars to Boston Bruins for future considerations (August 21, 1990). . . . Sprained knee (October 27, 1991); missed nine games.
HONORS: Named Hockey East Freshman of the Year (1984-85). . . . Named to NHL All-Rookie team (1990-91).

			REGULAR SEASON					PLAYOFFS			
Season Team	League	Gms.	G	A	Pts.	Pen.	Gms.	G	A	Pts.	Pen.
83-84—St. John's Prep School......	Mass. H.S.	22	25	38	63		—	—	—	—	—
84-85—Boston College	Hockey East	41	20	44	64	28	—	—	—	—	—
85-86—Boston College	Hockey East	21	11	17	28	16	—	—	—	—	—
86-87—Boston College	Hockey East	37	29	33	62	30	—	—	—	—	—
87-88—Kalamazoo	IHL	70	15	35	50	24	—	—	—	—	—
88-89—Minnesota	NHL	5	1	1	2	0	—	—	—	—	—
—Kalamazoo	IHL	72	26	45	71	34	6	1	5	6	16
89-90—Kalamazoo	IHL	68	33	53	86	19	10	5	13	18	2
90-91—Maine.............................	AHL	8	7	10	17	2	—	—	—	—	—
—Boston	NHL	70	30	29	59	20	15	4	6	10	6
91-92—Boston	NHL	42	6	11	17	10	—	—	—	—	—
—Maine.............................	AHL	19	6	11	17	4	—	—	—	—	—
NHL totals..............................		117	37	41	78	30	15	4	6	10	6

HOFFORT, BRUCE
G

PERSONAL: Born July 30, 1966, at North Battleford, Sask. . . . 5-10/185. . . . Shoots left.
COLLEGE: Lake Superior State (Mich.).
TRANSACTIONS/CAREER NOTES: Signed as free agent by Philadelphia Flyers (August, 1989).
HONORS: Named to CCHA All-Star first team (1987-88 and 1988-89). . . . Named CCHA Player of the Year (1988-89). . . . Named to NCAA All-America West first team (1988-89).

			REGULAR SEASON							PLAYOFFS					
Season Team	League	Gms.	Min.	W	L	T	GA	SO	Avg.	Gms.	Min.	W	L	GA	SO	Avg.
87-88—Lake Superior State	CCHA	*31	*1787	23	4	3	*79	*3	*2.65	—	—	—	—	—	—	—
88-89—Lake Superior State	CCHA	*44	*2595	27	10	5	*117	*3	*2.71	—	—	—	—	—	—	—
89-90—Philadelphia	NHL	7	329	3	0	2	20	0	3.65	—	—	—	—	—	—	—
—Hershey	AHL	40	2284	16	18	4	139	1	3.65	—	—	—	—	—	—	—
90-91—Philadelphia	NHL	2	39	1	0	1	3	0	4.62	—	—	—	—	—	—	—
—Hershey	AHL	18	913	3	12	1	74	0	4.86	—	—	—	—	—	—	—
—Kansas City................	IHL	18	883				68	0	4.62	—	—	—	—	—	—	—
91-92—San Diego	IHL	26	1474	11	9	4	89	0	3.62	—	—	—	—	—	—	—
NHL totals.............................		9	368	4	0	3	23	0	3.75	—	—	—	—	—	—	—

HOGAN, TIM
D, BLACKHAWKS

PERSONAL: Born January 7, 1974, at Oshawa, Ont. . . . 6-2/185. . . . Shoots right.
COLLEGE: Michigan.
TRANSACTIONS/CAREER NOTES: Selected by Chicago Blackhawks in fifth round (fifth Blackhawks pick, 113th overall) of NHL entry draft (June 20, 1992).

			REGULAR SEASON					PLAYOFFS			
Season Team	League	Gms.	G	A	Pts.	Pen.	Gms.	G	A	Pts.	Pen.
90-91—Wexford Jr. B	MTHL	33	5	19	24	46	—	—	—	—	—
91-92—University of Michigan	CCHA	34	2	8	10	34	—	—	—	—	—

HOGUE, BENOIT
C, ISLANDERS

PERSONAL: Born October 28, 1966, at Repentigny, Que. . . . 5-10/190. . . . Shoots left.
TRANSACTIONS/CAREER NOTES: Selected by Buffalo Sabres as underage junior in second round (second Sabres pick, 35th overall) of NHL entry draft (June 15, 1985). . . . Suspended six games by AHL for fighting (October 1987). . . . Suffered sore back (March 1988). . . . Broke left cheekbone (October 11, 1989); missed 20 games. . . . Sprained left ankle (March 14, 1990). . . . Traded by Sabres with C Pierre Turgeon, D Uwe Krupp and C Dave McLlwain to New York Islanders for C Pat LaFontaine, LW Randy Wood, D Randy Hillier and future considerations (October 25, 1991).

			REGULAR SEASON					PLAYOFFS			
Season Team	League	Gms.	G	A	Pts.	Pen.	Gms.	G	A	Pts.	Pen.
83-84—St. Jean	QMJHL	59	14	11	25	42	—	—	—	—	—
84-85—St. Jean	QMJHL	63	46	44	90	92	—	—	—	—	—
85-86—St. Jean	QMJHL	65	54	54	108	115	9	6	4	10	26
86-87—Rochester	AHL	52	14	20	34	52	12	5	4	9	8
87-88—Buffalo	NHL	3	1	1	2	0	—	—	—	—	—
—Rochester	AHL	62	24	31	55	141	7	6	1	7	46
88-89—Buffalo	NHL	69	14	30	44	120	5	0	0	0	17
89-90—Buffalo	NHL	45	11	7	18	79	3	0	0	0	10
90-91—Buffalo	NHL	76	19	28	47	76	5	3	1	4	10
91-92—Buffalo	NHL	3	0	1	1	0	—	—	—	—	—
—New York Islanders..........	NHL	72	30	45	75	67	—	—	—	—	—
NHL totals.............................		268	75	112	187	342	13	3	1	4	37

HOLDEN, PAUL
D, KINGS

PERSONAL: Born March 15, 1970, at Kitchner, Ont. . . . 6-3/210. . . . Shoots left.
TRANSACTIONS/CAREER NOTES: Selected by Los Angeles Kings in second round (second Kings pick, 28th overall) of NHL entry draft (June 11, 1988).
HONORS: Named to OHL All-Star second team (1989-90).

H

Season Team	League	REGULAR SEASON					PLAYOFFS				
		Gms.	G	A	Pts.	Pen.	Gms.	G	A	Pts.	Pen.
86-87—St. Thomas Jr. B	OHA	23	5	11	16	112	—	—	—	—	—
87-88—London	OHL	65	8	12	20	87	12	1	1	2	10
88-89—London	OHL	54	11	21	32	90	20	1	3	4	17
89-90—London	OHL	61	11	31	42	78	6	1	1	2	7
—New Haven	AHL	2	1	1	2	2	—	—	—	—	—
90-91—New Haven	AHL	59	2	8	10	23	—	—	—	—	—
91-92—Phoenix	IHL	47	3	3	6	63	—	—	—	—	—

HOLIK, BOBBY
RW, WHALERS

PERSONAL: Born January 1, 1971, at Jihlava, Czechoslovakia.... 6-3/210.... Shoots right.... Full name: Robert Holik.

TRANSACTIONS/CAREER NOTES: Selected by Hartford Whalers in first round (first Whalers pick, 10th overall) of NHL entry draft (June 17, 1989).... Broke right thumb (February 1990).

Season Team	League	REGULAR SEASON					PLAYOFFS				
		Gms.	G	A	Pts.	Pen.	Gms.	G	A	Pts.	Pen.
87-88—Dukla Jihlava	Czech.	31	5	9	14		—	—	—	—	—
88-89—Dukla Jihlava	Czech.	24	7	10	17		—	—	—	—	—
89-90—Dukla Jihlava	Czech.	31	12	18	30		—	—	—	—	—
90-91—Hartford	NHL	78	21	22	43	113	6	0	0	0	7
91-92—Hartford	NHL	76	21	24	45	44	7	0	1	1	6
NHL totals		154	42	46	88	157	13	0	1	1	13

HOLLAND, DENNIS
C, FLAMES

PERSONAL: Born January 30, 1969, at Vernon, B.C.... 5-10/165.... Shoots left.

TRANSACTIONS/CAREER NOTES: Selected by Detroit Red Wings as underage junior in third round (fourth Red Wings pick, 52nd overall) of NHL entry draft (June 13, 1987).... Traded by Red Wings to Calgary Flames for future considerations (October 1991).

HONORS: Won Stewart (Butch) Paul Memorial Trophy (West) (1986-87).... Named to WHL (West) All-Star first team (1987-88 and 1988-89).... Won Bob Clarke Trophy (1988-89).... Won WHL Player of the Year Award (1988-89).

Season Team	League	REGULAR SEASON					PLAYOFFS				
		Gms.	G	A	Pts.	Pen.	Gms.	G	A	Pts.	Pen.
85-86—Vernon	BCJHL	51	43	62	105	40	7	4	6	10	14
—Portland	WHL	1	3	2	5	0	—	—	—	—	—
86-87—Portland	WHL	72	36	77	113	96	20	7	14	21	20
87-88—Portland	WHL	67	58	86	144	115	—	—	—	—	—
88-89—Portland	WHL	69	*82	85	*167	120	19	15	*22	*37	18
89-90—Adirondack	AHL	78	19	34	53	53	6	1	1	2	10
90-91—Adirondack	AHL	28	8	7	15	31	2	0	0	0	4
—San Diego	IHL	45	25	30	55	129	—	—	—	—	—
91-92—Fort Wayne	IHL	6	2	4	6	21	—	—	—	—	—
—Salt Lake City	IHL	72	20	25	45	102	4	0	2	2	2

HOOVER, RON
C, BLUES

PERSONAL: Born January 9, 1965, at North Bay, Ont.... 6-0/190.... Shoots left.... Full name: Ronald Kenneth Hoover.

COLLEGE: Western Michigan.

TRANSACTIONS/CAREER NOTES: Selected by Hartford Whalers in eighth round (seventh Whalers pick, 158th overall) of NHL entry draft (June 21, 1986).... Signed as free agent by Boston Bruins (September 1, 1989).... Injured right eye (February 2, 1991); missed two weeks.... Signed as free agent by St. Louis Blues (July 23, 1991).

HONORS: Named to CCHA All-Star second team (1987-88).

Season Team	League	REGULAR SEASON					PLAYOFFS				
		Gms.	G	A	Pts.	Pen.	Gms.	G	A	Pts.	Pen.
85-86—Western Michigan Univ.	CCHA	43	10	23	33	36	—	—	—	—	—
86-87—Western Michigan Univ.	CCHA	34	7	10	17	22	—	—	—	—	—
87-88—Western Michigan Univ.	CCHA	42	39	23	62	40	—	—	—	—	—
88-89—Western Michigan Univ.	CCHA	42	32	27	59	66	—	—	—	—	—
89-90—Boston	NHL	2	0	0	0	0	—	—	—	—	—
—Maine	AHL	75	28	26	54	57	—	—	—	—	—
90-91—Maine	AHL	62	28	16	44	40	—	—	—	—	—
—Boston	NHL	15	4	0	4	31	8	0	0	0	18
91-92—Peoria	IHL	71	27	34	61	30	10	4	4	8	4
—St. Louis	NHL	1	0	0	0	0	—	—	—	—	—
NHL totals		18	4	0	4	31	8	0	0	0	18

HORACEK, TONY
LW, BLACKHAWKS

PERSONAL: Born February 3, 1967, at Vancouver, B.C.... 6-4/215.... Shoots left.

TRANSACTIONS/CAREER NOTES: Selected by Philadelphia Flyers as underage junior in seventh round (eighth eighth pick, 147th overall) of NHL entry draft (June 15, 1985).... Suspended one game by WHL for swinging stick at fans (November 1, 1987).... Suspended eight games by WHL for fighting (November 27, 1987).... Suffered broken knuckle (December 1989).... Injured left eye (March 19, 1991); missed six games.... Traded by Flyers to Chicago Blackhawks for D Ryan McGill (February 7, 1992). ...Suffered hip pointer (February 25, 1992); missed nine games.

Season Team	League	REGULAR SEASON Gms.	G	A	Pts.	Pen.	PLAYOFFS Gms.	G	A	Pts.	Pen.
84-85—Kelowna Wings	WHL	67	9	18	27	114	6	0	1	1	11
85-86—Spokane Chiefs	WHL	64	19	28	47	129	9	4	5	9	29
86-87—Spokane Chiefs	WHL	64	23	37	60	177	5	1	3	4	18
—Hershey	AHL	1	0	0	0	0	1	0	0	0	0
87-88—Hershey	AHL	1	0	0	0	0	—	—	—	—	—
—Spokane Chiefs	WHL	24	17	23	40	63	—	—	—	—	—
—Kamloops	WHL	26	14	17	31	51	18	6	4	10	73
88-89—Hershey	AHL	10	0	0	0	38	—	—	—	—	—
—Indianapolis	IHL	43	11	13	24	138	—	—	—	—	—
89-90—Philadelphia	NHL	48	5	5	10	117	—	—	—	—	—
—Hershey	AHL	12	0	5	5	25	—	—	—	—	—
90-91—Hershey	AHL	19	5	3	8	35	4	2	0	2	14
—Philadelphia	NHL	34	3	6	9	49	—	—	—	—	—
91-92—Philadelphia	NHL	34	1	3	4	51	—	—	—	—	—
—Chicago	NHL	12	1	4	5	21	2	1	0	1	2
NHL totals		128	10	18	28	238	2	1	0	1	2

HORYNA, ROBERT
G, MAPLE LEAFS

PERSONAL: Born September 10, 1970, at Hradec, Czechoslovakia. ... 5-11/185. ... Shoots left.
TRANSACTIONS/CAREER NOTES: Selected by Toronto Maple Leafs in ninth round (eighth Maple Leafs pick, 178th overall) of NHL entry draft (June 16, 1990).

Season Team	League	REGULAR SEASON Gms.	Min.	W	L	T	GA	SO	Avg.	PLAYOFFS Gms.	Min.	W	L	GA	SO	Avg.
89-90—Dukla Jihlava	Czech.	13	710				41		3.46	—	—	—	—	—	—	—
90-91—Newmarket	AHL	22	1162	8	10	2	81	0	4.18	—	—	—	—	—	—	—
91-92—St. John's	AHL	7	220	1	2	0	17	0	4.64	—	—	—	—	—	—	—

HOSTAK, MARTIN
C, FLYERS

PERSONAL: Born November 11, 1967, at Hradec Kralove, Czechoslovakia. ... 6-3/205. ... Shoots left.
TRANSACTIONS/CAREER NOTES: Selected by Philadelphia Flyers in third round (third Flyers pick, 62nd overall) of NHL entry draft (June 13, 1987).

Season Team	League	REGULAR SEASON Gms.	G	A	Pts.	Pen.	PLAYOFFS Gms.	G	A	Pts.	Pen.
86-87—Sparta Prague	Czech.	34	6	2	8		—	—	—	—	—
87-88—Sparta Prague	Czech.	26	8	9	17		—	—	—	—	—
88-89—Sparta Prague	Czech.	35	11	15	26		—	—	—	—	—
89-90—Sparta Prague	Czech.	55	31	34	65		11	4	7	11	
90-91—Hershey	AHL	11	6	2	8	2	3	1	0	1	0
—Philadelphia	NHL	50	3	10	13	22	—	—	—	—	—
91-92—Hershey	AHL	63	27	36	63	77	6	1	2	3	2
—Philadelphia	NHL	5	0	1	1	2	—	—	—	—	—
NHL totals		55	3	11	14	24					

HOUDA, DOUG
D, WHALERS

PERSONAL: Born June 3, 1966, at Blairmore, Alta. ... 6-2/200. ... Shoots right.
TRANSACTIONS/CAREER NOTES: Selected by Detroit Red Wings as underage junior in second round (second Red Wings pick, 28th overall) of NHL entry draft (June 9, 1984). ... Fractured left cheekbone (September 23, 1988). ... Injured knee and underwent surgery (November 21, 1989). ... Traded by Red Wings to Hartford Whalers for D Doug Crossman (February 20, 1991).
HONORS: Named to WHL All-Star second team (1984-85). ... Named to AHL All-Star first team (1987-88).

Season Team	League	REGULAR SEASON Gms.	G	A	Pts.	Pen.	PLAYOFFS Gms.	G	A	Pts.	Pen.
81-82—Calgary	WHL	3	0	0	0	0	—	—	—	—	—
82-83—Calgary	WHL	71	5	23	28	99	16	1	3	4	44
83-84—Calgary	WHL	69	6	30	36	195	4	0	0	0	7
84-85—Calgary	WHL	65	20	54	74	182	8	3	4	7	29
—Kalamazoo	IHL	—	—	—	—	—	7	0	2	2	10
85-86—Calgary	WHL	16	4	10	14	60	—	—	—	—	—
—Medicine Hat	WHL	35	9	23	32	80	25	4	19	23	64
—Detroit	NHL	6	0	0	0	4	—	—	—	—	—
86-87—Adirondack	AHL	77	6	23	29	142	11	1	8	9	50
87-88—Detroit	NHL	11	1	1	2	10	—	—	—	—	—
—Adirondack	AHL	71	10	32	42	169	11	0	3	3	44
88-89—Adirondack	AHL	7	0	3	3	8	—	—	—	—	—
—Detroit	NHL	57	2	11	13	67	6	0	1	1	0
89-90—Detroit	NHL	73	2	9	11	127	—	—	—	—	—
90-91—Adirondack	AHL	38	9	17	26	67	—	—	—	—	—
—Detroit	NHL	22	0	4	4	43	—	—	—	—	—
—Hartford	NHL	19	1	2	3	41	6	0	0	0	8
91-92—Hartford	NHL	56	3	6	9	125	6	0	2	2	13
NHL totals		244	9	33	42	417	18	0	3	3	21

H

HOUGH, MIKE

LW, NORDIQUES

PERSONAL: Born February 6, 1963, at Montreal. . . . 6-1/192. . . . Shoots left. . . . Full name: Mike L. Hough.

TRANSACTIONS/CAREER NOTES: Selected by Quebec Nordiques as underage junior in ninth round (seventh Nordiques pick, 181st overall) of NHL entry draft (June 9, 1982). . . . Sprained left shoulder and developed tendinitis (November 5, 1989); missed 14 games. . . . Broke right thumb (January 23, 1990); missed 12 games. . . . Injured back (November 8, 1990); missed nine games. . . . Separated left shoulder (January 15, 1991); missed three games. . . . Suffered concussion (February 10, 1991). . . . Injured knee (December 28, 1991); missed three games. . . . Fractured left thumb (February 15, 1992); missed 14 games.

Season Team	League	REGULAR SEASON					PLAYOFFS				
		Gms.	G	A	Pts.	Pen.	Gms.	G	A	Pts.	Pen.
80-81—Dixie	OPJHL	24	15	20	35	84	—	—	—	—	—
81-82—Kitchener	OHL	58	14	34	48	172	14	1	5	6	16
82-83—Kitchener	OHL	61	17	27	44	156	12	5	4	9	30
83-84—Fredericton	AHL	69	11	16	27	142	1	0	0	0	7
84-85—Fredericton	AHL	76	21	27	48	49	6	1	1	2	2
85-86—Fredericton	AHL	74	21	33	54	68	6	0	3	3	8
86-87—Quebec	NHL	56	6	8	14	79	9	0	3	3	26
—Fredericton	AHL	10	1	3	4	20	—	—	—	—	—
87-88—Fredericton	AHL	46	16	25	41	133	15	4	8	12	55
—Quebec	NHL	17	3	2	5	2	—	—	—	—	—
88-89—Halifax	AHL	22	11	10	21	87	—	—	—	—	—
—Quebec	NHL	46	9	10	19	39	—	—	—	—	—
89-90—Quebec	NHL	43	13	13	26	84	—	—	—	—	—
90-91—Quebec	NHL	63	13	20	33	111	—	—	—	—	—
91-92—Quebec	NHL	61	16	22	38	77	—	—	—	—	—
NHL totals		286	60	75	135	392	9	0	3	3	26

HOULDER, BILL

D, SABRES

PERSONAL: Born March 11, 1967, at Thunder Bay, Ont. . . . 6-3/218. . . . Shoots left. . . . Full name: William Houlder.

TRANSACTIONS/CAREER NOTES: Selected by Washington Capitals as underage junior in fourth round (fourth Capitals pick, 82nd overall) of NHL entry draft (June 15, 1985). . . . Pulled groin (January 1989). . . . Traded by Capitals to Buffalo Sabres for D Shawn Anderson (September 30, 1990).

HONORS: Named to AHL All-Star first team (1990-91).

Season Team	League	REGULAR SEASON					PLAYOFFS				
		Gms.	G	A	Pts.	Pen.	Gms.	G	A	Pts.	Pen.
83-84—Thunder Bay Beavers	TBAHA	23	4	18	22	37	—	—	—	—	—
84-85—North Bay	OHL	66	4	20	24	37	8	0	0	0	2
85-86—North Bay	OHL	59	5	30	35	97	10	1	6	7	12
86-87—North Bay	OHL	62	17	51	68	68	22	4	19	23	20
87-88—Washington	NHL	30	1	2	3	10	—	—	—	—	—
—Fort Wayne	IHL	43	10	14	24	32	—	—	—	—	—
88-89—Baltimore	AHL	65	10	36	46	50	—	—	—	—	—
—Washington	NHL	8	0	3	3	4	—	—	—	—	—
89-90—Baltimore	AHL	26	3	7	10	12	7	0	2	2	2
—Washington	NHL	41	1	11	12	28	—	—	—	—	—
90-91—Rochester	AHL	69	13	53	66	28	15	5	13	18	4
—Buffalo	NHL	7	0	2	2	4	—	—	—	—	—
91-92—Rochester	AHL	42	8	26	34	16	16	5	6	11	4
—Buffalo	NHL	10	1	0	1	8	—	—	—	—	—
NHL totals		96	3	18	21	54					

HOUSE, BOBBY

RW, BLACKHAWKS

PERSONAL: Born January 7, 1973, at Whitehorse, Yukon. . . . 6-1/200. . . . Shoots right.

TRANSACTIONS/CAREER NOTES: Traded by Spokane Chiefs with Marty Murray and G Don Blishen to Brandon Wheat Kings for G Trevor Kidd and Bart Cote (January 21, 1991). . . . Selected by Chicago Blackhawks in third round (fourth Blackhawks pick, 66th overall) of NHL entry draft (June 22, 1991).

Season Team	League	REGULAR SEASON					PLAYOFFS				
		Gms.	G	A	Pts.	Pen.	Gms.	G	A	Pts.	Pen.
88-89—Houjens	Yukon Sr.	28	36	27	63	28	—	—	—	—	—
89-90—Spokane Chiefs	WHL	64	18	16	34	74	5	0	0	0	6
90-91—Spokane Chiefs	WHL	38	11	19	30	63	—	—	—	—	—
—Brandon	WHL	23	18	7	25	14	—	—	—	—	—
91-92—Brandon	WHL	71	35	42	77	133	—	—	—	—	—

HOUSLEY, PHIL

D, JETS

PERSONAL: Born March 9, 1964, at St. Paul, Minn. . . . 5-10/179. . . . Shoots left. . . . Full name: Phil F. Housley.

HIGH SCHOOL: South St. Paul (Minn.).

TRANSACTIONS/CAREER NOTES: Selected by Buffalo Sabres as underage player in first round (first Sabres pick, sixth overall) of NHL entry draft (June 9, 1982). . . . Bruised shoulder (January 1984). . . . Suspended three games by NHL (October 1984). . . . Injured back (November 1987). . . . Bruised back (January 12, 1989). . . . Suffered hip pointer and bruised back (March 18, 1989). . . . Pulled shoulder ligaments while playing at World Cup Tournament (April 1989). . . . Traded by Sabres with LW Scott Arniel, RW Jeff Parker and a first-round pick in 1990 draft (C Keith Tkachuk) to Winnipeg Jets for C Dale Hawerchuk and a first-round pick in 1990 draft (LW Brad May) (June 16, 1990). . . . Strained abdo-

H

men (February 26, 1992); missed five games.
HONORS: Named to NHL All-Rookie team (1982-83).... Named to THE SPORTING NEWS All-Star second team (1991-92)....
Named to NHL All-Star second team (1991-92).
MISCELLANEOUS: Member of Team U.S.A. at World Junior Championships (1982).... Member of Team U.S.A. at World Cup Tournament (1982).

| Season Team | League | REGULAR SEASON | | | | | PLAYOFFS | | | | |
		Gms.	G	A	Pts.	Pen.	Gms.	G	A	Pts.	Pen.
80-81—St. Paul	USHL	6	7	7	14	6	—	—	—	—	—
81-82—South St. Paul H.S.	Minn. H.S.	22	31	34	65	18	—	—	—	—	—
82-83—Buffalo	NHL	77	19	47	66	39	10	3	4	7	2
83-84—Buffalo	NHL	75	31	46	77	33	3	0	0	0	6
84-85—Buffalo	NHL	73	16	53	69	28	5	3	2	5	2
85-86—Buffalo	NHL	79	15	47	62	54	—	—	—	—	—
86-87—Buffalo	NHL	78	21	46	67	57	—	—	—	—	—
87-88—Buffalo	NHL	74	29	37	66	96	6	2	4	6	6
88-89—Buffalo	NHL	72	26	44	70	47	5	1	3	4	2
89-90—Buffalo	NHL	80	21	60	81	32	6	1	4	5	4
90-91—Winnipeg	NHL	78	23	53	76	24	—	—	—	—	—
91-92—Winnipeg	NHL	74	23	63	86	92	7	1	4	5	0
NHL totals		760	224	496	720	502	42	11	21	32	22

HOWE, MARK
D, RED WINGS

PERSONAL: Born May 28, 1955, at Detroit.... 5-11/185.... Shoots left.... Full name: Mark Steven Howe.... Son of Gordie Howe, Hall of Fame right winger, Detroit Red Wings and Hartford Whalers (1946-47 through 1970-71 and 1979-80) and Houston Aeros and New England Whalers of WHA (1973-74 through 1978-79); and brother of Marty Howe, defenseman, Hartford Whalers and Boston Bruins (1979-80 through 1984-85) and Houston Aeros and New England Whalers of WHA (1973-74 through 1978-79).
TRANSACTIONS/CAREER NOTES: Signed by Houston Aeros (June 1972).... Traded by London Knights to Toronto Marlboros for D Larry Goodenough and C Dennis Maruk (August 1972).... Underwent corrective knee surgery; missed most of 1971-72 season.... Selected by Boston Bruins from Marlboros in second round (second Bruins pick, 25th overall) of amateur draft (May 28, 1974).... Suffered shoulder separation; missed part of 1976-77 season.... Signed as free agent by New England Whalers (June 1977).... Injured ribs; missed part of 1977-78 season.... Selected by Boston Bruins in NHL reclaim draft, but remained Hartford Whalers property as a priority selection for the expansion draft (June 9, 1979).... Suffered five-inch puncture wound to upper thigh (December 27, 1980).... Traded by Whalers to Philadelphia Flyers for C Ken Linseman, C Greg Adams and first-round pick (LW David A. Jensen) and exchange of third-round picks in 1983 draft (August 19, 1982).... Injured shoulder (February 1984).... Bruised collarbone (January 1985).... Suffered back spasms (January 1987).... Broke rib and vertebrae (September 1987).... Strained back (March 1988).... Bruised right foot (October 1988).... Pulled groin muscle (December 1988).... Sprained left knee cruciate ligament (February 1989); missed eight games.... Reinjured left knee (February 27, 1989).... Injured groin (December 22, 1989).... Injured back (January 27, 1990).... Injured back (November 3, 1990); missed four games.... Reinjured back (November 25, 1990).... Underwent surgery for herniated disk (January 18, 1991); missed 54 games.... Aggravated back injury (October 4, 1991); missed seven games.... Fractured thumb (November 23, 1991); missed 24 games.... Signed as free agent by Detroit Red Wings (July 8, 1992).
HONORS: Won Most Valuable Player and Outstanding Forward Awards (1970-71).... Named to SOJHL All-Star first team (1970-71).... Won WHA Rookie of the Year Award (1973-74).... Named to WHA All-Star second team (1973-74 and 1976-77).... Named to WHA All-Star first team (1978-79).... Named to THE SPORTING NEWS All-Star second team (1979-80). ... Named to THE SPORTING NEWS All-Star first team (1982-83, 1985-86 and 1986-87).... Named to NHL All-Star first team (1982-83, 1985-86 and 1986-87).... Won Emery Edge Award (1985-86).

| Season Team | League | REGULAR SEASON | | | | | PLAYOFFS | | | | |
		Gms.	G	A	Pts.	Pen.	Gms.	G	A	Pts.	Pen.
70-71—Detroit Junior Red Wings	SOJHL	44	37	*70	*107		—	—	—	—	—
71-72—Detroit Junior Red Wings	SOJHL	9	5	9	14		—	—	—	—	—
—U.S. Olympic Team	Int'l	—	—	—	—	—	—	—	—	—	—
72-73—Toronto	OHA Mj. Jr. A	60	38	66	104	27	—	—	—	—	—
73-74—Houston	WHA	76	38	41	79	20	14	9	10	19	4
74-75—Houston	WHA	74	36	40	76	30	13	†10	12	*22	0
75-76—Houston	WHA	72	39	37	76	38	†17	6	10	16	18
76-77—Houston	WHA	57	23	52	75	46	10	4	10	14	2
77-78—New England	WHA	70	30	61	91	32	14	8	7	15	18
78-79—New England	WHA	77	42	65	107	32	6	4	2	6	6
79-80—Hartford	NHL	74	24	56	80	20	3	1	2	3	2
80-81—Hartford	NHL	63	19	46	65	54	—	—	—	—	—
81-82—Hartford	NHL	76	8	45	53	18	—	—	—	—	—
82-83—Philadelphia	NHL	76	20	47	67	18	3	0	2	2	4
83-84—Philadelphia	NHL	71	19	34	53	44	3	0	0	0	2
84-85—Philadelphia	NHL	73	18	39	57	31	19	3	8	11	6
85-86—Philadelphia	NHL	77	24	58	82	36	5	0	4	4	0
86-87—Philadelphia	NHL	69	15	43	58	37	26	2	10	12	4
87-88—Philadelphia	NHL	75	19	43	62	62	7	3	6	9	4
88-89—Philadelphia	NHL	52	9	29	38	45	19	0	15	15	10
89-90—Philadelphia	NHL	40	7	21	28	24	—	—	—	—	—
90-91—Philadelphia	NHL	19	0	10	10	8	—	—	—	—	—
91-92—Philadelphia	NHL	42	7	18	25	18	—	—	—	—	—
WHA totals		426	208	296	504	198	74	41	51	92	48
NHL totals		807	189	489	678	415	85	9	47	56	32

H

HRDINA, JIRI
C, PENGUINS

PERSONAL: Born January 5, 1958, at Prague, Czechoslovakia.... 6-0/190.... Shoots right.
TRANSACTIONS/CAREER NOTES: Selected by Calgary Flames in eighth round (eighth Flames pick, 159th overall) of NHL entry draft (June 9, 1984).... Strained ligaments in right knee (December 16, 1989).... Traded by Flames to Pittsburgh Penguins for D Jim Kyte (December 13, 1990).... Lacerated right ankle (March 9, 1991); missed six games.... Injured ligaments in left knee (November 13, 1991); missed 13 games.... Separated left shoulder (March 19, 1992); missed three games.
MISCELLANEOUS: Member of 1984 silver medal-winning Czechoslovakian Olympic team.

			REGULAR SEASON					PLAYOFFS				
Season Team	League	Gms.	G	A	Pts.	Pen.	Gms.	G	A	Pts.	Pen.
85-86—Sparta Prague	Czech.	44	18	19	37	30	—	—	—	—	—
86-87—Sparta Prague	Czech.	31	18	18	36	24	—	—	—	—	—
87-88—Sparta Prague	Czech.	22	7	15	22	0	—	—	—	—	—
—Czech. Olympic Team	Int'l	8	2	5	7	4	—	—	—	—	—
—Calgary	NHL	9	2	5	7	2	1	0	0	0	0
88-89—Calgary	NHL	70	22	32	54	26	4	0	0	0	0
89-90—Calgary	NHL	64	12	18	30	31	6	0	1	1	2
90-91—Calgary	NHL	14	0	3	3	4	—	—	—	—	—
—Pittsburgh	NHL	37	6	14	20	13	14	2	2	4	6
91-92—Pittsburgh	NHL	56	3	13	16	16	20	0	2	2	16
NHL totals		250	45	85	130	92	45	2	5	7	24

HRIVNAK, JIM
G, CAPITALS

PERSONAL: Born May 28, 1968, at Montreal.... 6-2/185.... Shoots left.... Full name: James Richard Hrivnak.
COLLEGE: Merrimack (Mass.).
TRANSACTIONS/CAREER NOTES: Selected by Washington Capitals in third round (fourth Capitals pick, 61st overall) of NHL entry draft (June 21, 1986).
HONORS: Named to AHL All-Star second team (1989-90).

			REGULAR SEASON							PLAYOFFS					
Season Team	League	Gms.	Min.	W	L	T	GA	SO	Avg.	Gms.	Min.	W	L	GA SO	Avg.
85-86—Merrimack College	ECAC-II	21	1230	12	6	2	75	0	3.66	—	—	—	—	— —	—
86-87—Merrimack College	ECAC-II	34	1618	27	7	0	58	3	2.15	—	—	—	—	— —	—
87-88—Merrimack College	ECAC-II	37	2119	31	6	0	84	4	2.38	—	—	—	—	— —	—
88-89—Merrimack College	ECAC-II	22	1295				52	4	2.41	—	—	—	—	— —	—
—Baltimore	AHL	10	502	1	8	0	55	0	6.57	—	—	—	—	— —	—
89-90—Washington	NHL	11	609	5	5	0	36	0	3.55	—	—	—	—	— —	—
—Baltimore	AHL	47	2722	24	19	2	139	*4	3.06	6	360	4	2	19 *1	3.17
90-91—Washington	NHL	9	432	4	2	1	26	0	3.61	—	—	—	—	— —	—
—Baltimore	AHL	42	2481	20	16	6	134	1	3.24	6	324	2	3	21 0	3.89
91-92—Washington	NHL	12	605	6	3	0	35	0	3.47	—	—	—	—	— —	—
—Baltimore	AHL	22	1303	10	8	3	73	0	3.36	—	—	—	—	— —	—
NHL totals		32	1646	15	10	1	97	0	3.54						

HRKAC, TONY
C, BLACKHAWKS

PERSONAL: Born July 7, 1966, at Thunder Bay, Ont.... 5-11/170.... Shoots left.... Full name: Anthony J. Hrkac.
COLLEGE: North Dakota.
TRANSACTIONS/CAREER NOTES: Selected by St. Louis Blues as underage junior in second round (second Blues pick, 32nd overall) of NHL entry draft (June 9, 1984).... Suspended six games by coach for disciplinary reasons (January 1985).... Bruised left leg (January 1987).... Sprained shoulder (January 12, 1988).... Lacerated ankle (March 1988).... Bruised left shoulder (November 28, 1989).... Traded by Blues with G Greg Millen to Quebec Nordiques for D Jeff Brown (December 13, 1989).... Traded by Nordiques to San Jose Sharks for RW Greg Paslawski (May 30, 1991).... Injured wrist during preseason (September 1991); missed first 27 games of season.... Traded by Sharks to Chicago Blackhawks for a conditional pick in 1993 draft (February 7, 1992).
HONORS: Won Hobey Baker Memorial Trophy (1986-87).... Won WCHA Player of the Year Award (1986-87).... Named NCAA Tournament Most Valuable Player (1986-87).... Named to NCAA All-America West first team (1986-87).... Named to WCHA All-Star first team (1986-87).... Named to NCAA All-Tournament Team (1986-87).

			REGULAR SEASON					PLAYOFFS				
Season Team	League	Gms.	G	A	Pts.	Pen.	Gms.	G	A	Pts.	Pen.
83-84—Orillia	OHA	42	*52	54	*106	20	—	—	—	—	—
84-85—Univ. of North Dakota	WCHA	36	18	36	54	16	—	—	—	—	—
85-86—Team Canada	Int'l	62	19	30	49	36	—	—	—	—	—
86-87—Univ. of North Dakota	WCHA	48	46	*70	*116	48	—	—	—	—	—
—St. Louis	NHL	—	—	—	—	—	3	0	0	0	0
87-88—St. Louis	NHL	67	11	37	48	22	10	6	1	7	4
88-89—St. Louis	NHL	70	17	28	45	8	4	1	1	2	0
89-90—St. Louis	NHL	28	5	12	17	8	—	—	—	—	—
—Quebec	NHL	22	4	8	12	2	—	—	—	—	—
—Halifax	AHL	20	12	21	33	4	6	5	9	14	4
90-91—Halifax	AHL	3	4	1	5	2	—	—	—	—	—
—Quebec	NHL	70	16	32	48	16	—	—	—	—	—
91-92—San Jose	NHL	22	2	10	12	4	—	—	—	—	—
—Chicago	NHL	18	1	2	3	6	3	0	0	0	2
NHL totals		297	56	129	185	66	20	7	2	9	6

H

HRUDEY, KELLY

G, KINGS

PERSONAL: Born January 13, 1961, at Edmonton, Alta. . . . 5-10/189. . . . Shoots left. . . . Full name: Kelly Stephen Hrudey.

TRANSACTIONS/CAREER NOTES: Selected by New York Islanders as underage junior in second round (second Islanders pick, 38th overall) of NHL entry draft (June 11, 1980). . . . Traded by Islanders to Los Angeles Kings for D Wayne McBean, G Mark Fitzpatrick and future considerations (February 27, 1989); D Doug Crossman was sent to the Islanders on May 23 to complete the deal. . . . Suffered from the flu (April 1989). . . . Suffered from mononucleosis (February 1990); missed 14 games. . . . Bruised ribs (April 20, 1990).

HONORS: Named to WHL All-Star second team (1980-81). . . . Shared Terry Sawchuk Trophy with Robert Holland (1981-82 and 1982-83). . . . Won Max McNab Trophy (1981-82). . . . Named to CHL All-Star first team (1981-82 and 1982-83). . . . Won Tommy Ivan Trophy (1982-83).

						REGULAR SEASON						PLAYOFFS					
Season	Team	League	Gms.	Min.	W	L	T	GA	SO	Avg.	Gms.	Min.	W	L	GA	SO	Avg.
78-79—Medicine Hat		WHL	57	3093	12	34	7	*318	0	6.17	—	—	—	—	—	—	—
79-80—Medicine Hat		WHL	57	3049	25	23	4	212	1	4.17	13	638	6	6	48	0	4.51
80-81—Medicine Hat		WHL	55	3023	32	19	1	200	†4	3.97	4	244			17	0	4.18
—Indianapolis		CHL	—	—	—	—	—	—	—	—	2	135			8	0	3.56
81-82—Indianapolis		CHL	51	3033	27	19	4	149	1	*2.95	13	842	11	2	34	*1	*2.42
82-83—Indianapolis		CHL	47	2744	26	17	1	139	2	3.04	10	†637	*7	3	28	0	*2.64
83-84—Indianapolis		CHL	6	370	3	2	1	21	0	3.41	—	—	—	—	—	—	—
—New York Islanders		NHL	12	535	7	2	0	28	0	3.14	—	—	—	—	—	—	—
84-85—New York Islanders		NHL	41	2335	19	17	3	141	2	3.62	5	281	1	3	8	0	1.71
85-86—New York Islanders		NHL	45	2563	19	15	8	137	1	3.21	2	120	0	2	6	0	3.00
86-87—New York Islanders		NHL	46	2634	21	15	7	145	0	3.30	14	842	7	7	38	0	2.71
87-88—New York Islanders		NHL	47	2751	22	17	5	153	3	3.34	6	381	2	4	23	0	3.62
88-89—New York Islanders		NHL	50	2800	18	24	3	183	0	3.92	—	—	—	—	—	—	—
—Los Angeles		NHL	16	974	10	4	2	47	1	2.90	10	566	4	6	35	0	3.71
89-90—Los Angeles		NHL	52	2860	22	21	6	194	2	4.07	9	539	4	4	39	0	4.34
90-91—Los Angeles		NHL	47	2730	26	13	6	132	3	2.90	12	798	6	6	37	0	2.78
91-92—Los Angeles		NHL	60	3509	26	17	*13	197	1	3.37	6	355	2	4	22	0	3.72
NHL totals			416	23691	190	145	53	1357	13	3.44	64	3882	26	36	208	0	3.21

HUBER, PHIL

C, ISLANDERS

PERSONAL: Born January 10, 1969, at Calgary, Alta. . . . 5-11/187. . . . Shoots left.

TRANSACTIONS/CAREER NOTES: Selected by New York Islanders in eighth round (10th Islanders pick, 149th overall) of NHL entry draft (June 17, 1989).

HONORS: Named to WHL (West) All-Star first team (1989-90).

				REGULAR SEASON				PLAYOFFS			
Season	Team	League	Gms.	G	A	Pts.	Pen.	Gms.	G	A	Pts.	Pen.
87-88—Kamloops		WHL	63	19	30	49	54	18	3	9	12	23
88-89—Kamloops		WHL	72	54	68	122	103	16	*18	13	31	48
89-90—Kamloops		WHL	72	63	89	152	176	17	12	11	23	44
90-91—Capital District		AHL	5	1	1	2	0	—	—	—	—	—
—Richmond		ECHL	56	32	40	72	87	4	1	3	4	4
91-92—Capital District		AHL	71	26	32	58	85	7	0	2	2	10

HUDDY, CHARLIE

D, KINGS

PERSONAL: Born June 2, 1959, at Oshawa, Ont. . . . 6-0/210. . . . Shoots left. . . . Full name: Charles William Huddy.

TRANSACTIONS/CAREER NOTES: Signed as free agent by Edmonton Oilers (September 14, 1979). . . . Injured shoulder (November 10, 1980). . . . Suffered back spasms (February 1986); missed three games. . . . Broke finger (April 1986). . . . Suffered hematoma of left thigh and underwent surgery (May 7, 1988); missed six playoff games. . . . Strained hamstring (January 2, 1989). . . . Sprained right ankle (December 22, 1990); missed 17 games. . . . Broke left toe (February 16, 1991); missed nine games. . . . Twisted back (March 1991). . . . Selected by Minnesota North Stars in 1991 NHL expansion draft (May 30, 1991). . . . Traded by North Stars with LW Randy Gilhen, RW Jim Thomson and a fourth-round pick in 1991 draft (D Alexei Zhitnik) to Los Angeles Kings for C Todd Elik (June 22, 1991). . . . Injured groin (October 10, 1991); missed seven games. . . . Strained groin (November 7, 1991); missed five games. . . . Suffered chest contusion (February 1, 1992); missed seven games. . . . Suffered chest contusion (March 3, 1992); missed five games.

HONORS: Won Emery Edge Award (1982-83).

				REGULAR SEASON				PLAYOFFS			
Season	Team	League	Gms.	G	A	Pts.	Pen.	Gms.	G	A	Pts.	Pen.
77-78—Oshawa		OMJHL	59	17	18	35	81	6	2	1	3	10
78-79—Oshawa		OMJHL	64	20	38	58	108	5	3	4	7	12
79-80—Houston		CHL	79	14	34	48	46	6	1	0	1	2
80-81—Edmonton		NHL	12	2	5	7	6	—	—	—	—	—
—Wichita		CHL	47	8	36	44	71	17	3	11	14	10
81-82—Wichita		CHL	32	7	19	26	51	—	—	—	—	—
—Edmonton		NHL	41	4	11	15	46	5	1	2	3	14
82-83—Edmonton		NHL	76	20	37	57	58	15	1	6	7	10
83-84—Edmonton		NHL	75	8	34	42	43	12	1	9	10	8
84-85—Edmonton		NHL	80	7	44	51	46	18	3	17	20	17
85-86—Edmonton		NHL	76	6	35	41	55	7	0	2	2	0
86-87—Edmonton		NHL	58	4	15	19	35	21	1	7	8	21
87-88—Edmonton		NHL	77	13	28	41	71	13	4	5	9	10
88-89—Edmonton		NHL	76	11	33	44	52	7	2	0	2	4
89-90—Edmonton		NHL	70	1	23	24	56	22	0	6	6	11
90-91—Edmonton		NHL	53	5	22	27	32	18	3	7	10	10
91-92—Los Angeles		NHL	56	4	19	23	43	6	1	1	2	10
NHL totals			750	85	306	391	543	144	17	62	79	115

H

HUDSON, MIKE
C/LW, BLACKHAWKS

PERSONAL: Born February 6, 1967, at Guelph, Ont.... 6-1/185.... Shoots left.... Full name: Michael Hudson.

TRANSACTIONS/CAREER NOTES: Traded by Hamilton Steelhawks with D Keith Vanrooyen to Sudbury Wolves for C Brad Belland (October 1985).... Selected by Chicago Blackhawks as underage junior in seventh round (sixth Blackhawks pick, 140th overall) of NHL entry draft (June 21, 1986).... Lacerated right hand (December 21, 1989); missed 12 games.... Suffered elbow tendinitis (September 1990).... Underwent elbow surgery (May 1991).

Season Team	League	REGULAR SEASON Gms.	G	A	Pts.	Pen.	PLAYOFFS Gms.	G	A	Pts.	Pen.
84-85—Hamilton	OHL	50	10	12	22	13	—	—	—	—	—
85-86—Hamilton	OHL	7	3	2	5	4	—	—	—	—	—
—Sudbury	OHL	59	35	42	77	20	4	2	5	7	7
86-87—Sudbury	OHL	63	40	57	97	18	—	—	—	—	—
87-88—Saginaw	IHL	75	18	30	48	44	10	2	3	5	20
88-89—Chicago	NHL	41	7	16	23	20	10	1	2	3	18
—Saginaw	IHL	30	15	17	32	10	—	—	—	—	—
89-90—Chicago	NHL	49	9	12	21	56	4	0	0	0	2
90-91—Chicago	NHL	55	7	9	16	62	6	0	2	2	8
—Indianapolis	IHL	3	1	2	3	0	—	—	—	—	—
91-92—Chicago	NHL	76	14	15	29	92	16	3	5	8	26
NHL totals		221	37	52	89	230	36	4	9	13	54

HUFFMAN, KERRY
D, NORDIQUES

PERSONAL: Born January 3, 1968, at Peterborough, Ont.... 6-3/205.... Shoots left.... Brother-in-law of Mike Posavad, defenseman, St. Louis Blues (1985-86 through 1986-87).

TRANSACTIONS/CAREER NOTES: Selected by Philadelphia Flyers as underage junior in first round (first Flyers pick, 20th overall) of NHL entry draft (June 21, 1986).... Sprained ankle (November 1987).... Suffered calcium deposits in thigh (January 1988); missed 22 games.... Bruised right knee (March 15, 1990).... Suspended by Flyers after leaving team in dispute over ice time (November 16, 1990).... Returned to Flyers (December 10, 1990).... Suffered from tonsillitis (October 1991); missed one game.... Traded by Flyers with G Ron Hextall, C Mike Ricci, C Peter Forsberg, D Steve Duchesne, first-round pick in 1993 draft, cash and future considerations to Quebec Nordiques for C Eric Lindros (June 20, 1992); Flyers sent LW Chris Simon and first-round pick in 1994 draft to Nordiques to complete deal (July 21, 1992).

HONORS: Won Max Kaminsky Trophy (1986-87).... Named to OHL All-Star first team (1986-87).

Season Team	League	REGULAR SEASON Gms.	G	A	Pts.	Pen.	PLAYOFFS Gms.	G	A	Pts.	Pen.
84-85—Peterborough Jr. B	OHA	24	2	5	7	53	—	—	—	—	—
85-86—Guelph	OHL	56	3	24	27	35	20	1	10	11	10
86-87—Guelph	OHL	44	4	31	35	20	5	0	2	2	8
—Hershey	AHL	3	0	1	1	0	4	0	0	0	0
—Philadelphia	NHL	9	0	0	0	2	—	—	—	—	—
87-88—Philadelphia	NHL	52	6	17	23	34	2	0	0	0	0
88-89—Hershey	AHL	29	2	13	15	16	—	—	—	—	—
—Philadelphia	NHL	29	0	11	11	31	—	—	—	—	—
89-90—Philadelphia	NHL	43	1	12	13	34	—	—	—	—	—
90-91—Hershey	AHL	45	5	29	34	20	7	1	2	3	0
—Philadelphia	NHL	10	1	2	3	10	—	—	—	—	—
91-92—Philadelphia	NHL	60	14	18	32	41	—	—	—	—	—
NHL totals		203	22	60	82	152	2	0	0	0	0

HUGHES, BRENT
LW, BRUINS

PERSONAL: Born April 5, 1966, at New Westminster, B.C.... 5-11/180.... Shoots left.... Full name: Brent Allen Hughes.

TRANSACTIONS/CAREER NOTES: Traded by New Westminster Bruins to Victoria Cougars for future considerations (October 1986).... Signed as free agent by Winnipeg Jets (July 1987).... Traded by Jets with LW Craig Duncanson and C Simon Wheeldon to Washington Capitals for LW Bob Joyce, D Kent Paynter and C Tyler Larter (May 21, 1991).... Traded by Capitals with 12th-round pick in 1992 draft to Boston Bruins for RW John Byce and D Dennis Smith (February 24, 1992).

HONORS: Named to WHL All-Star first team (1986-87).

Season Team	League	REGULAR SEASON Gms.	G	A	Pts.	Pen.	PLAYOFFS Gms.	G	A	Pts.	Pen.
83-84—New Westminster	WHL	67	21	18	39	133	9	2	2	4	27
84-85—New Westminster	WHL	64	25	32	57	135	11	2	1	3	37
85-86—New Westminster	WHL	71	28	52	80	180	—	—	—	—	—
86-87—New Westminster	WHL	8	5	4	9	22	—	—	—	—	—
—Victoria	WHL	61	38	61	99	146	5	4	1	5	8
87-88—Moncton	AHL	77	13	19	32	206	—	—	—	—	—
88-89—Winnipeg	NHL	28	3	2	5	82	—	—	—	—	—
—Moncton	AHL	54	34	34	68	286	10	9	4	13	40
89-90—Moncton	AHL	65	31	29	60	277	—	—	—	—	—
—Winnipeg	NHL	11	1	2	3	33	—	—	—	—	—
90-91—Moncton	AHL	63	21	22	43	144	3	0	0	0	7
91-92—Baltimore	AHL	55	25	29	54	190	—	—	—	—	—
—Maine	AHL	12	6	4	10	34	—	—	—	—	—
—Boston	NHL	8	1	1	2	38	10	2	0	2	20
NHL totals		47	5	5	10	153	10	2	0	2	20

H

HUGHES, RYAN
C, NORDIQUES

PERSONAL: Born January 17, 1972, at Montreal. . . . 6-1/180. . . . Shoots left. . . . Full name: Ryan Laine Hughes.
COLLEGE: Cornell.
TRANSACTIONS/CAREER NOTES: Selected by Quebec Nordiques in second round (second Nordiques pick, 22nd overall) of NHL entry draft (June 16, 1990).

Season Team	League	REGULAR SEASON					PLAYOFFS				
		Gms.	G	A	Pts.	Pen.	Gms.	G	A	Pts.	Pen.
89-90—Cornell University	ECAC	28	7	16	23	35	—	—	—	—	—
90-91—Cornell University	ECAC	32	18	34	52	28	—	—	—	—	—
—Victoria	WHL	1	0	1	1	2	—	—	—	—	—
91-92—Cornell University	ECAC	27	8	13	21	36	—	—	—	—	—

HULBIG, JOE
LW, OILERS

PERSONAL: Born September 29, 1973, at Wrentham, Mass. . . . 6-3/215. . . . Shoots left.
HIGH SCHOOL: St. Sebastian's Country Day School (Needham, Mass.).
TRANSACTIONS/CAREER NOTES: Selected by Edmonton Oilers in first round (first Oilers pick, 13th overall) of NHL entry draft (June 20, 1992).

Season Team	League	REGULAR SEASON					PLAYOFFS				
		Gms.	G	A	Pts.	Pen.	Gms.	G	A	Pts.	Pen.
90-91—St. Sebastian's	Mass. H.S.		23	19	42		—	—	—	—	—
91-92—St. Sebastian's	Mass. H.S.	17	19	24	43	30	—	—	—	—	—

HULL, BRETT
RW, BLUES

PERSONAL: Born August 9, 1964, at Belleville, Ont. . . . 5-10/203. . . . Shoots right. . . . Full name: Brett A. Hull. . . . Son of Bobby Hull, Hall of Fame left winger, Chicago Blackhawks, Winnipeg Jets and Hartford Whalers (1957-58 through 1971-72 and 1979-80) and Winnipeg Jets of WHA (1972-73 through 1978-79); and nephew of Dennis Hull, left winger, Chicago Blackhawks and Detroit Red Wings (1964-65 through 1977-78).
COLLEGE: Minnesota-Duluth.
TRANSACTIONS/CAREER NOTES: Selected by Calgary Flames in sixth round (sixth Flames pick, 117th overall) of NHL entry draft (June 9, 1984). . . . Traded by Flames with LW Steve Bozek to St. Louis Blues for D Rob Ramage and G Rick Wamsley (March 7, 1988). . . . Sprained left ankle (January 15, 1991); missed two regular-season games and All-Star game. . . . Suffered back spasms (March 12, 1992); missed seven games.
HONORS: Won WCHA Freshman of the Year Award (1984-85). . . . Named to WCHA All-Star first team (1985-86). . . . Won Dudley (Red) Garrett Memorial Trophy (1986-87). . . . Named to AHL All-Star first team (1986-87). . . . Won Lady Byng Memorial Trophy (1989-90). . . . Won Dodge Ram Tough Award (1989-90 and 1990-91). . . . Named to THE SPORTING NEWS All-Star first team (1989-90 through 1991-92). . . . Named to NHL All-Star first team (1989-90 through 1991-92). . . . Named NHL Player of the Year by THE SPORTING NEWS (1990-91). . . . Won Hart Memorial Trophy (1990-91). . . . Won Lester B. Pearson Award (1990-91).
RECORDS: Holds NHL career record for highest goals-per-game average—.807. . . . Holds NHL single-season record for most goals by a right winger—86 (1990-91).
MISCELLANEOUS: Shares distinction with Bobby Hull of being the first father-son duo to win the same NHL trophy (both the Lady Byng Memorial and Hart Memorial trophies).
STATISTICAL NOTES: Became the first son of an NHL 50-goal scorer to score 50 goals in one season (1989-90).

Season Team	League	REGULAR SEASON					PLAYOFFS				
		Gms.	G	A	Pts.	Pen.	Gms.	G	A	Pts.	Pen.
82-83—Penticton	BCJHL	50	48	56	104	27	—	—	—	—	—
83-84—Penticton	BCJHL	56	*105	83	*188	20	—	—	—	—	—
84-85—Minnesota-Duluth	WCHA	48	32	28	60	24	—	—	—	—	—
85-86—Minnesota-Duluth	WCHA	42	*52	32	84	46	—	—	—	—	—
—Calgary	NHL	—	—	—	—	—	2	0	0	0	0
86-87—Moncton	AHL	67	50	42	92	16	3	2	2	4	2
—Calgary	NHL	5	1	0	1	0	4	2	1	3	0
87-88—Calgary	NHL	52	26	24	50	12	—	—	—	—	—
—St. Louis	NHL	13	6	8	14	4	10	7	2	9	4
88-89—St. Louis	NHL	78	41	43	84	33	10	5	5	10	6
89-90—St. Louis	NHL	80	*72	41	113	24	12	13	8	21	17
90-91—St. Louis	NHL	78	*86	45	131	22	13	11	8	19	4
91-92—St. Louis	NHL	73	*70	39	109	48	6	4	4	8	4
NHL totals		379	302	200	502	143	57	42	28	70	35

HULL, JODY
RW, SENATORS

PERSONAL: Born February 2, 1969, at Petrolia, Ont. . . . 6-2/203. . . . Shoots right.
TRANSACTIONS/CAREER NOTES: Strained ankle ligaments (September 1986). . . . Pulled groin (February 1987). . . . Selected by Hartford Whalers as underage junior in first round (first Whalers pick, 18th overall) of NHL entry draft (June 13, 1987). . . . Pulled hamstring (March 1989). . . . Traded by Whalers to New York Rangers for C Carey Wilson and third-round pick in 1991 draft (C Mikael Nylander) (July 9, 1990). . . . Sprained muscle of right hand (October 6, 1990). . . . Bruised left big toe (November 19, 1990); missed six games. . . . Injured knee (March 13, 1991). . . . Traded by Rangers to Ottawa Senators for future considerations (July 27, 1992).
HONORS: Named to OHL All-Star second team (1987-88).

Season Team	League	REGULAR SEASON					PLAYOFFS				
		Gms.	G	A	Pts.	Pen.	Gms.	G	A	Pts.	Pen.
84-85—Cambridge Jr. B	OHA	38	13	17	30	39	—	—	—	—	—
85-86—Peterborough	OHL	61	20	22	42	29	16	1	5	6	4
86-87—Peterborough	OHL	49	18	34	52	22	12	4	9	13	14
87-88—Peterborough	OHL	60	50	44	94	33	12	10	8	18	8

H

Season	Team	League	REGULAR SEASON Gms.	G	A	Pts.	Pen.	PLAYOFFS Gms.	G	A	Pts.	Pen.
88-89—Hartford		NHL	60	16	18	34	10	1	0	0	0	2
89-90—Binghamton		AHL	21	7	10	17	6	—	—	—	—	—
—Hartford		NHL	38	7	10	17	21	5	0	1	1	2
90-91—New York Rangers		NHL	47	5	8	13	10	—	—	—	—	—
91-92—New York Rangers		NHL	3	0	0	0	2	—	—	—	—	—
—Binghamton		AHL	69	34	31	65	28	11	5	2	7	4
NHL totals			148	28	36	64	43	6	0	1	1	4

HULSE, CALE
D, DEVILS

PERSONAL: Born November 10, 1973, at Edmonton, Alta. . . . 6-3/210. . . . Shoots right.
COLLEGE: Portland.
TRANSACTIONS/CAREER NOTES: Selected by New Jersey Devils in third round (third Devils pick, 66th overall) of NHL entry draft (June 20, 1992).

Season	Team	League	REGULAR SEASON Gms.	G	A	Pts.	Pen.	PLAYOFFS Gms.	G	A	Pts.	Pen.
90-91—Calgary Royals		AJHL	49	3	23	26	220	—	—	—	—	—
91-92—Portland		WHL	70	4	18	22	250	6	0	2	2	27

HULST, KENT
C, NORDIQUES

PERSONAL: Born April 8, 1968, at St. Thomas, Ont. . . . 6-1/180. . . . Shoots left.
TRANSACTIONS/CAREER NOTES: Traded by Belleville Bulls with future considerations to Windsor Compuware Spitfires for C Keith Gretzky (February 1986). . . . Selected by Toronto Maple Leafs as underage junior in fourth round (fourth Maple Leafs pick, 69th overall) of NHL entry draft (June 21, 1986). . . . Separated shoulder (September 1988). . . . Signed as free agent by Quebec Nordiques (September 20, 1991).

Season	Team	League	REGULAR SEASON Gms.	G	A	Pts.	Pen.	PLAYOFFS Gms.	G	A	Pts.	Pen.
84-85—St. Thomas Jr. B		OHA	47	21	25	46	29	—	—	—	—	—
85-86—Belleville		OHL	43	6	17	23	20	—	—	—	—	—
—Windsor		OHL	17	6	10	16	9	—	—	—	—	—
86-87—Windsor		OHL	37	18	20	38	49	—	—	—	—	—
—Belleville		OHL	27	13	10	23	17	6	1	1	2	0
87-88—Belleville		OHL	66	42	43	85	48	6	3	1	4	7
88-89—Belleville		OHL	45	21	41	62	43	—	—	—	—	—
—Flint		IHL	7	0	1	1	4	—	—	—	—	—
—Newmarket		AHL	—	—	—	—	—	2	1	1	2	2
89-90—Newmarket		AHL	80	26	34	60	29	—	—	—	—	—
90-91—Newmarket		AHL	79	28	37	65	57	—	—	—	—	—
91-92—New Haven		AHL	†80	21	39	60	59	5	2	2	4	0

HUNTER, DALE
C, CAPITALS

PERSONAL: Born July 31, 1960, at Petrolia, Ont. . . . 5-10/198. . . . Shoots left. . . . Full name: Dale Robert Hunter. . . . Brother of Mark Hunter, right winger, Washington Capitals; and brother of Dave Hunter, left winger, Edmonton Oilers of WHA (1978-79) and Edmonton Oilers, Pittsburgh Penguins and Winnipeg Jets (1979-80 through 1988-89).
TRANSACTIONS/CAREER NOTES: Selected by Quebec Nordiques as underage junior in second round (second Nordiques pick, 41st overall) of NHL entry draft (August 9, 1979). . . . Suspended three games by NHL (March 1984). . . . Suffered hand infection (April 21, 1985). . . . Broke lower fibula of left leg (November 25, 1986). . . . Traded by Nordiques with G Clint Malarchuk to Washington Capitals for C Alan Haworth, LW Gaeten Duchesne and first-round pick in 1987 draft (C Joe Sakic) (June 13, 1987). . . . Broke thumb (September 1988). . . . Suspended four games by NHL for elbowing D Gord Murphy (February 10, 1991).

Season	Team	League	REGULAR SEASON Gms.	G	A	Pts.	Pen.	PLAYOFFS Gms.	G	A	Pts.	Pen.
77-78—Kitchener		OMJHL	68	22	42	64	115	—	—	—	—	—
78-79—Sudbury		OMJHL	59	42	68	110	188	10	4	12	16	47
79-80—Sudbury		OMJHL	61	34	51	85	189	9	6	9	15	45
80-81—Quebec		NHL	80	19	44	63	226	5	4	2	6	34
81-82—Quebec		NHL	80	22	50	72	272	16	3	7	10	52
82-83—Quebec		NHL	80	17	46	63	206	4	2	1	3	24
83-84—Quebec		NHL	77	24	55	79	232	9	2	3	5	41
84-85—Quebec		NHL	80	20	52	72	209	17	4	6	10	*97
85-86—Quebec		NHL	80	28	42	70	265	3	0	0	0	15
86-87—Quebec		NHL	46	10	29	39	135	13	1	7	8	56
87-88—Washington		NHL	79	22	37	59	238	14	7	5	12	88
88-89—Washington		NHL	80	20	37	57	219	6	0	4	4	29
89-90—Washington		NHL	80	23	39	62	233	15	4	8	12	61
90-91—Washington		NHL	76	16	30	46	234	11	1	9	10	41
91-92—Washington		NHL	80	28	50	78	205	7	1	4	5	16
NHL totals			918	249	511	760	2674	120	29	56	85	554

HUNTER, MARK
RW, CAPITALS

PERSONAL: Born November 12, 1962, at Petrolia, Ont. . . . 6-0/205. . . . Shoots right. . . . Brother of Dale Hunter, center, Washington Capitals. Brother of Dave Hunter, left winger, Edmonton Oilers of WHA (1978-79); and Edmonton Oilers, Pittsburgh Penguins and Winnipeg Jets (1979-80 through 1988-89).

H

TRANSACTIONS/CAREER NOTES: Selected by Montreal Canadiens as underage junior in first round (first Canadians pick, seventh overall) of NHL entry draft (June 10, 1981).... Pulled tendon in right knee (November 13, 1982).... Suffered laceration under right arm (November 29, 1982).... Tore medial ligaments in right knee and underwent surgery (December 26, 1982); missed 42 games.... Injured right knee and underwent surgery (October 1983).... Injured knee (February 21, 1984).... Reinjured knee (February 1985).... Traded by Canadiens with rights to D Michael Dark and second-round (RW Herb Raglan), third-round (C Nelson Emerson), fifth-round (C Dan Brooks) and sixth-round (G Rich Burchill) picks in 1985 draft to St. Louis Blues for first-round (RW Jose Charbonneau), second-round (D Todd Richards), fourth-round (C Martin Desjardins), fifth-round (RW Tom Sagissor) and sixth-round (D Donald Dufresne) picks in 1985 draft (June 15, 1985).... Strained shoulder (March 1987).... Bruised thigh (November 3, 1987).... Strained left knee (March 22, 1988).... Traded by Blues with C Doug Gilmour, LW Steve Bozek and D/RW Michael Dark to Calgary Flames for C Mike Bullard, C Craig Coxe and D Tim Corkery (September 5, 1988).... Dislocated right shoulder (November 1988).... Suffered concussion (December 26, 1988).... Suspended three games by NHL for striking another player with stick (March 13, 1989).... Broke hand (April 13, 1989).... Strained anterior cruciate ligament of right knee (October 11, 1989); missed 11 games.... Reinjured knee (November 18, 1989).... Reinjured knee (December 1989).... Underwent surgery to right knee (December 15, 1989).... Bruised shoulder (October 30, 1990); missed seven games.... Traded by Flames to Hartford Whalers for C Carey Wilson (March 5, 1991).... Suffered thigh contusion (December 4, 1991); missed one game.... Injured shoulder (February 4, 1992); missed one game.... Traded by Whalers to Washington Capitals for LW Nick Kypreos (June 15, 1992).

			REGULAR SEASON					PLAYOFFS			
Season	Team	League	Gms.	G	A	Pts.	Pen.	Gms.	G	A	Pts.	Pen.
79-80—Brantford	OMJHL	66	34	55	89	171	11	2	8	10	27
80-81—Brantford	OMJHL	53	39	40	79	157	6	3	3	6	27
81-82—Montreal	NHL	71	18	11	29	143	5	0	0	0	20
82-83—Montreal	NHL	31	8	8	16	73	—	—	—	—	—
83-84—Montreal	NHL	22	6	4	10	42	14	2	1	3	69
84-85—Montreal	NHL	72	21	12	33	123	11	0	3	3	13
85-86—St. Louis	NHL	78	44	30	74	171	19	7	7	14	48
86-87—St. Louis	NHL	74	36	33	69	169	5	0	3	3	10
87-88—St. Louis	NHL	66	32	31	63	136	5	2	3	5	24
88-89—Calgary	NHL	66	22	8	30	194	10	2	2	4	23
89-90—Calgary	NHL	10	2	3	5	39	—	—	—	—	—
90-91—Calgary	NHL	57	10	15	25	125	—	—	—	—	—
—Hartford	NHL	11	4	3	7	40	6	5	1	6	17
91-92—Hartford	NHL	63	10	13	23	159	4	0	0	0	6
NHL totals		621	213	171	384	1414	79	18	20	38	230

HUNTER, TIM
RW, NORDIQUES

PERSONAL: Born September 10, 1960, at Calgary, Alta.... 6-2/202.... Shoots right.... Full name: Timothy Robert Hunter.

TRANSACTIONS/CAREER NOTES: Selected by Atlanta Flames in third round (fourth Flames pick, 54th overall) of NHL entry draft (August 9, 1979).... Flames franchised moved to Calgary (May 21, 1980).... Bruised hand (October 1987).... Injured right eye (October 17, 1988).... Suspended 10 games and fined $500 by NHL for leaving bench to fight (November 1, 1989).... Tore shoulder muscles (October 6, 1990); missed four games.... Reinjured shoulder (October 18, 1990).... Reinjured shoulder (December 2, 1990); missed 20 games.... Suffered back spasms (October 1991); missed one game.... Fractured left ankle (December 8, 1991); missed 39 games.... Selected by Tampa Bay Lightning in NHL expansion draft (June 18, 1992).... Traded by Lightning to Quebec Nordiques for RW Martin Simard (June 22, 1992).

			REGULAR SEASON					PLAYOFFS			
Season	Team	League	Gms.	G	A	Pts.	Pen.	Gms.	G	A	Pts.	Pen.
77-78—Kamloops	BCJHL	51	9	28	37	266	—	—	—	—	—
—Seattle	WCHL	3	1	2	3	4	—	—	—	—	—
78-79—Seattle	WHL	70	8	41	49	300	—	—	—	—	—
79-80—Seattle	WHL	72	14	53	67	311	12	1	2	3	41
80-81—Birmingham	CHL	58	3	5	8	*236	—	—	—	—	—
—Nova Scotia	AHL	17	0	0	0	62	6	0	1	1	45
81-82—Oklahoma City	CHL	55	4	12	16	222	—	—	—	—	—
—Calgary	NHL	2	0	0	0	9	—	—	—	—	—
82-83—Calgary	NHL	16	1	0	1	54	9	1	0	1	*70
—Colorado	CHL	46	5	12	17	225	—	—	—	—	—
83-84—Calgary	NHL	43	4	4	8	130	7	0	0	0	21
84-85—Calgary	NHL	71	11	11	22	259	4	0	0	0	24
85-86—Calgary	NHL	66	8	7	15	291	19	0	3	3	108
86-87—Calgary	NHL	73	6	15	21	361	6	0	0	0	51
87-88—Calgary	NHL	68	8	5	13	337	9	4	0	4	32
88-89—Calgary	NHL	75	3	9	12	*375	19	0	4	4	32
89-90—Calgary	NHL	67	2	3	5	279	6	0	0	0	4
90-91—Calgary	NHL	34	5	2	7	143	7	0	0	0	10
91-92—Calgary	NHL	30	1	3	4	167	—	—	—	—	—
NHL totals		545	49	59	108	2405	86	5	7	12	352

HURD, KELLY
RW, RED WINGS

PERSONAL: Born May 13, 1968, at Castlegar, B.C.... 5-10/170.... Shoots right.

TRANSACTIONS/CAREER NOTES: Selected by Detroit Red Wings in seventh round (sixth Red Wings pick, 143rd overall) of NHL entry draft (June 11, 1988).

HONORS: Named to WCHA All-Star second team (1990-91).

			REGULAR SEASON					PLAYOFFS			
Season	Team	League	Gms.	G	A	Pts.	Pen.	Gms.	G	A	Pts.	Pen.
86-87—Kelowna	BCJHL	50	40	53	93	121	—	—	—	—	—
87-88—Michigan Tech	WCHA	41	18	22	40	34	—	—	—	—	—

H

Season Team	League	REGULAR SEASON					PLAYOFFS				
		Gms.	G	A	Pts.	Pen.	Gms.	G	A	Pts.	Pen.
88-89—Michigan Tech	WCHA	42	18	14	32	36	—	—	—	—	—
89-90—Michigan Tech	WCHA	37	12	13	25	50	—	—	—	—	—
90-91—Michigan Tech	WCHA	35	29	22	51	44	—	—	—	—	—
91-92—Adirondack	AHL	35	9	7	16	16	8	1	4	5	2
—Fort Wayne	IHL	30	13	9	22	12	3	3	0	3	9

HUSCROFT, JAMIE

D, DEVILS

PERSONAL: Born January 9, 1967, at Creston, B.C.... 6-2/200.... Shoots right.... Full name: James Huscroft.

TRANSACTIONS/CAREER NOTES: Selected by New Jersey Devils as underage junior in ninth round (ninth Devils pick, 171st overall) of NHL entry draft (June 15, 1985).... Fractured arm (October 1986); missed eight weeks.... Traded by Seattle Thunderbirds to Medicine Hat Tigers for C Mike Schwengler (February 1987).... Fractured right wrist (October 1988).... Injured groin (December 1988).... Broke foot (January 1989); missed 19 games.

Season Team	League	REGULAR SEASON					PLAYOFFS				
		Gms.	G	A	Pts.	Pen.	Gms.	G	A	Pts.	Pen.
83-84—Portland	WHL	63	0	12	12	77	5	0	0	0	15
84-85—Seattle	WHL	69	3	13	16	273	—	—	—	—	—
85-86—Seattle	WHL	66	6	20	26	394	5	0	1	1	18
86-87—Seattle	WHL	21	1	18	19	99	20	0	3	3	0
—Medicine Hat	WHL	35	4	21	25	170	20	0	3	3	*125
87-88—Flint	IHL	3	1	0	1	2	16	0	1	1	110
—Utica	AHL	71	5	7	12	316	—	—	—	—	—
88-89—Utica	AHL	41	2	10	12	215	5	0	0	0	40
—New Jersey	NHL	15	0	2	2	51	—	—	—	—	—
89-90—New Jersey	NHL	42	2	3	5	149	5	0	0	0	16
—Utica	AHL	23	3	6	9	122	—	—	—	—	—
90-91—New Jersey	NHL	8	0	1	1	27	3	0	0	0	6
—Utica	AHL	59	3	15	18	339	—	—	—	—	—
91-92—Utica	AHL	50	4	7	11	224	—	—	—	—	—
NHL totals		65	2	6	8	227	8	0	0	0	22

HUSSEY, MARC

D, PENGUINS

PERSONAL: Born January 22, 1974, at Chatham, N.B.... 6-4/185.... Shoots right.

HIGH SCHOOL: Vanier Collegiate (Moose Jaw, Sask.).

TRANSACTIONS/CAREER NOTES: Selected by Pittsburgh Penguins in second round (second Penguins pick, 43rd overall) of NHL entry draft (June 20, 1992).

Season Team	League	REGULAR SEASON					PLAYOFFS				
		Gms.	G	A	Pts.	Pen.	Gms.	G	A	Pts.	Pen.
90-91—Moose Jaw	WHL	68	5	8	13	67	8	2	2	4	7
91-92—Moose Jaw	WHL	72	7	27	34	203	4	1	1	2	0

HYNES, GORD

D, BRUINS

PERSONAL: Born July 22, 1966, at Montreal.... 6-1/170.... Shoots left.

TRANSACTIONS/CAREER NOTES: Selected by Boston Bruins in sixth round (fifth Bruins pick, 115th overall) of NHL entry draft (June 15, 1985).

MISCELLANEOUS: Member of 1992 silver medal-winning Canadian Olympic team.

Season Team	League	REGULAR SEASON					PLAYOFFS				
		Gms.	G	A	Pts.	Pen.	Gms.	G	A	Pts.	Pen.
83-84—Medicine Hat	WHL	72	5	14	19	39	14	0	0	0	0
84-85—Medicine Hat	WHL	70	18	45	63	61	10	6	9	15	17
85-86—Medicine Hat	WHL	58	22	39	61	45	25	8	15	23	32
86-87—Moncton	AHL	69	2	19	21	21	4	0	0	0	2
87-88—Maine	AHL	69	5	30	35	65	7	1	3	4	4
88-89—Canadian National Team	Int'l	61	8	38	46	44	—	—	—	—	—
89-90—Canadian National Team	Int'l	12	3	1	4	4	—	—	—	—	—
—Varese	Italy	29	13	36	49	16	3	3	3	6	0
90-91—Canadian National Team	Int'l	57	12	30	42	62	—	—	—	—	—
91-92—Canadian National Team	Int'l	48	12	22	34	50	—	—	—	—	—
—Canadian Olympic Team	Int'l	8	3	3	6	6	—	—	—	—	—
—Boston	NHL	15	0	5	5	6	12	1	2	3	6
NHL totals		15	0	5	5	6	12	1	2	3	6

IAFRATE, AL

D, CAPITALS

PERSONAL: Born March 21, 1966, at Dearborn, Mich.... 6-3/220.... Shoots left.... Full name: Al Anthony Iafrate.

TRANSACTIONS/CAREER NOTES: Selected by Toronto Maple Leafs as underage junior in first round (first Maple Leafs pick, fourth overall) of NHL entry draft (June 9, 1984).... Bruised knee (February 1985).... Broke nose (October 2, 1985); missed five games.... Strained neck (January 29, 1986); missed six games.... Suffered stiff back (January 1988).... Broke back (October 22, 1988).... Lacerated hand (December 9, 1988).... Tore right knee ligament (March 24, 1990).... Underwent knee surgery (April 9, 1990).... Traded by Maple Leafs to Washington Capitals for D Bob Rouse and C Peter Zezel (January 16, 1991).... Took a leave of absence due to mental exhaustion (March 30, 1991).... Injured eye (February 19, 1992); missed one game.

Season Team	League	REGULAR SEASON					PLAYOFFS				
		Gms.	G	A	Pts.	Pen.	Gms.	G	A	Pts.	Pen.
83-84—U.S. National Team	Int'l	55	4	17	21	26	—	—	—	—	—
—U.S. Olympic Team	Int'l	6	0	0	0	2	—	—	—	—	—
—Belleville Bulls	OHL	10	2	4	6	2	3	0	1	1	2

Season Team	League	REGULAR SEASON					PLAYOFFS				
		Gms.	G	A	Pts.	Pen.	Gms.	G	A	Pts.	Pen.
84-85—Toronto	NHL	68	5	16	21	51	—	—	—	—	—
85-86—Toronto	NHL	65	8	25	33	40	10	0	3	3	4
86-87—Toronto	NHL	80	9	21	30	55	13	1	3	4	11
87-88—Toronto	NHL	77	22	30	52	80	6	3	4	7	6
88-89—Toronto	NHL	65	13	20	33	72	—	—	—	—	—
89-90—Toronto	NHL	75	21	42	63	135	—	—	—	—	—
90-91—Toronto	NHL	42	3	15	18	113	—	—	—	—	—
—Washington	NHL	30	6	8	14	124	10	1	3	4	22
91-92—Washington	NHL	78	17	34	51	180	7	4	2	6	14
NHL totals		580	104	211	315	850	46	9	15	24	57

IJ

ING, PETER
G, OILERS

PERSONAL: Born April 28, 1969, at Toronto. . . . 6-2/170. . . . Shoots left. . . . Full name: Peter A. Ing.
TRANSACTIONS/CAREER NOTES: Selected by Toronto Maple Leafs in third round (third Maple Leafs pick, 48th overall) of NHL entry draft (June 11, 1988). . . . Traded by Maple Leafs with LW Vincent Damphousse, D Luke Richardson, C Scott Thornton and future considerations to Edmonton Oilers for G Grant Fuhr, RW/LW Glenn Anderson and LW Craig Berube (September 19, 1991).

Season Team	League	REGULAR SEASON								PLAYOFFS						
		Gms.	Min.	W	L	T	GA	SO	Avg.	Gms.	Min.	W	L	GA	SO	Avg
86-87—Windsor	OHL	28	1615	10	11	3	105	0	3.90	5	161	4	0	9	0	3.35
87-88—Windsor	OHL	43	2422	30	7	1	125	2	3.10	3	225	2	0	7	0	1.87
88-89—Windsor	OHL	19	1043	7	7	3	76	1	4.37	—	—	—	—	—	—	—
—London	OHL	32	1848	18	11	2	104	+2	3.38	*21	*1093	11	9	*82	0	4.50
89-90—Toronto	NHL	3	182	0	2	1	18	0	5.93	—	—	—	—	—	—	—
—Newmarket	AHL	48	2829	16	19	2	184	1	3.90	—	—	—	—	—	—	—
90-91—Toronto	NHL	56	3126	16	+29	8	200	1	3.84	—	—	—	—	—	—	—
91-92—Edmonton	NHL	12	463	3	4	0	33	0	4.28	—	—	—	—	—	—	—
—Cape Breton	AHL	24	1411	9	10	4	92	0	3.91	1	60	0	1	9	0	9.00
NHL totals		71	3771	19	35	9	251	1	3.99							

INTRANUOVO, RALPH
C, OILERS

PERSONAL: Born December 11, 1973, at Scarborough, Ont. . . . 5-8/170. . . . Shoots left.
TRANSACTIONS/CAREER NOTES: Selected by Edmonton Oilers in fourth round (fifth Oilers pick, 96th overall) of NHL entry draft (June 20, 1992).

Season Team	League	REGULAR SEASON					PLAYOFFS				
		Gms.	G	A	Pts.	Pen.	Gms.	G	A	Pts.	Pen.
90-91—Sault Ste. Marie	OHL	63	25	42	67	22	14	7	13	20	17
91-92—Sault Ste. Marie	OHL	65	50	63	113	44	18	10	14	24	12

IRBE, ARTURS
G, SHARKS

PERSONAL: Born February 2, 1967, at Riga, U.S.S.R. . . . 5-7/180. . . . Shoots left.
TRANSACTIONS/CAREER NOTES: Selected by Minnesota North Stars in 10th round (11th North Stars pick, 196th overall) of NHL entry draft (June 17, 1989). . . . Selected by San Jose Sharks in NHL dispersal draft (May 30, 1991).
HONORS: Named Soviet League Rookie of the Year (1987-88). . . . Shared James Norris Memorial Trophy with Wade Flaherty (1991-92). . . . Named to IHL All-Star first team (1991-92).

Season Team	League	REGULAR SEASON								PLAYOFFS						
		Gms.	Min.	W	L	T	GA	SO	Avg.	Gms.	Min.	W	L	GA	SO	Avg.
86-87—Dynamo Riga	USSR	2	27				1	0	2.22	—	—	—	—	—	—	—
87-88—Dynamo Riga	USSR	34	1870				84	0	2.70	—	—	—	—	—	—	—
88-89—Dynamo Riga	USSR	41	2460				117	0	2.85	—	—	—	—	—	—	—
89-90—Dynamo Riga	USSR	48	2880				116	0	2.42	—	—	—	—	—	—	—
90-91—Dynamo Riga	USSR	46	2713				133	0	2.94	—	—	—	—	—	—	—
91-92—Kansas City	IHL	32	1955	24	7	1	80	0	*2.46	15	914	12	3	44	0	2.89
—San Jose	NHL	13	645	2	6	3	48	0	4.47	—	—	—	—	—	—	—
NHL totals		13	645	2	6	3	48	0	4.47							

JABLONSKI, PAT
G, LIGHTNING

PERSONAL: Born June 20, 1967, at Toledo, O. . . . 6-0/178. . . . Shoots right. . . . Brother of Jeff Jablonski, left winger in New York Islanders system.
TRANSACTIONS/CAREER NOTES: Selected by St. Louis Blues in seventh round (sixth Blues pick, 138th overall) of NHL entry draft (June 15, 1985). . . . Pulled groin (December 7, 1991); missed 26 games. . . . Traded by Blues with D Rob Robinson, RW Darin Kimble and RW Steve Tuttle to Tampa Bay Lightning for future considerations (June 19, 1992).
HONORS: Shared James Norris Memorial Trophy with Guy Hebert (1990-91).

Season Team	League	REGULAR SEASON								PLAYOFFS						
		Gms.	Min.	W	L	T	GA	SO	Avg.	Gms.	Min.	W	L	GA	SO	Avg.
84-85—Detroit Compuware	NAJHL	29	1483				95	0	3.84	—	—	—	—	—	—	—
85-86—Windsor	OHL	29	1600	6	16	4	119	1	4.46	6	263	0	3	20	0	4.56
86-87—Windsor	OHL	41	2328	22	14	2	128	+3	3.30	12	710	8	4	38	0	3.21
87-88—Windsor	OHL	18	994	14	3	0	48	2	*2.90	9	537	8	0	28	0	3.13
—Peoria	IHL	5	285	2	2	1	17	0	3.58	—	—	—	—	—	—	—
88-89—Peoria	IHL	35	2051	11	20	3	163	1	4.77	3	130	0	2	13	0	6.00

Season Team	League	Gms.	Min.	W	L	T	GA	SO	Avg.	Gms.	Min.	W	L	GA	SO	Avg.
89-90—St. Louis	NHL	4	208	0	3	0	17	0	4.90	—						
—Peoria	IHL	36	2043	14	17	4	165	0	4.85	4	223	1	3	19	0	5.11
90-91—St. Louis	NHL	8	492	2	3	3	25	0	3.05	3	90	0	0	5	0	3.33
—Peoria	IHL	29	1738	23	3	2	87	0	3.00	10	532	7	2	23	0	*2.59
91-92—St. Louis	NHL	10	468	3	6	0	38	0	4.87	—						
—Peoria	IHL	8	493	6	1	1	29	1	3.53	—						
NHL totals		22	1168	5	12	3	80	0	4.11	3	90	0	0	5	0	3.33

JACKSON, DANE
RW, CANUCKS

PERSONAL: Born May 17, 1970, at Winnipeg, Man. . . . 6-1/190. . . . Shoots right. . . . Full name: Dane K. Jackson. **COLLEGE:** North Dakota. **TRANSACTIONS/CAREER NOTES:** Selected by Vancouver Canucks in third round (third Canucks pick, 44th overall) of NHL entry draft (June 11, 1988).

Season Team	League	Gms.	G	A	Pts.	Pen.	Gms.	G	A	Pts.	Pen.
87-88—Vernon	BCJHL	50	28	32	60	99	13	7	10	17	49
88-89—Univ. of North Dakota	WCHA	30	4	5	9	33	—	—	—	—	—
89-90—Univ. of North Dakota	WCHA	44	15	11	26	56	—	—	—	—	—
90-91—Univ. of North Dakota	WCHA	37	17	9	26	79	—	—	—	—	—
91-92—Univ. of North Dakota	WCHA	39	23	19	42	81	—	—	—	—	—

JACKSON, JEFF
LW/C, BLACKHAWKS

PERSONAL: Born April 24, 1965, at Chatham, Ont. . . . 6-1/193. . . . Shoots left. **TRANSACTIONS/CAREER NOTES:** Stretched knee ligaments (January 1982). . . . Selected by Toronto Maple Leafs as underage junior in second round (second Maple Leafs pick, 28th overall) of NHL entry draft (June 8, 1983). . . . Suffered from a deteriorating hip condition (March 1987). . . . Traded by Maple Leafs with third-round pick (C Rob Zamaner) in 1989 draft to New York Rangers for LW Mark Osborne (March 5, 1987). . . . Traded by Rangers with D Terry Carkner to Quebec Nordiques for D David Shaw and LW John Ogrodnick (September 30, 1987). . . . Sprained left knee (January 1988). . . . Sprained both knees (March 1988). . . . Sprained right knee (January 26, 1989). . . . Sprained ligaments in left knee (February 1989). . . . Fractured left forearm radius bone (January 24, 1991); missed remainder of season.

Season Team	League	Gms.	G	A	Pts.	Pen.	Gms.	G	A	Pts.	Pen.
81-82—Newmarket	OHA	45	30	39	69	105	—	—	—	—	—
82-83—Brantford	OHL	64	18	25	43	63	8	1	1	2	27
83-84—Brantford	OHL	58	27	42	69	78	2	0	1	1	0
84-85—Hamilton	OHL	20	13	14	27	51	17	8	12	20	26
—Toronto	NHL	17	0	1	1	24	—	—	—	—	—
85-86—St. Catharines	AHL	74	17	28	45	122	13	5	2	7	30
—Toronto	NHL	5	1	2	3	2	—	—	—	—	—
86-87—Newmarket	AHL	7	3	6	9	13	—	—	—	—	—
—Toronto	NHL	55	8	7	15	64	—	—	—	—	—
—New York Rangers	NHL	9	5	1	6	15	6	1	1	2	16
87-88—Quebec	NHL	68	9	18	27	103	—	—	—	—	—
88-89—Quebec	NHL	33	4	6	10	28	—	—	—	—	—
89-90—Quebec	NHL	65	8	12	20	71	—	—	—	—	—
90-91—Quebec	NHL	10	3	1	4	4	—	—	—	—	—
—Halifax	AHL	25	8	17	25	45	—	—	—	—	—
91-92—Indianapolis	IHL	18	3	7	10	41	—	—	—	—	—
—Chicago	NHL	1	0	0	0	2	—	—	—	—	—
—New Haven	AHL	30	10	14	24	60	5	0	5	5	6
NHL totals		263	38	48	86	313	6	1	1	2	16

JAGR, JAROMIR
RW, PENGUINS

PERSONAL: Born February 15, 1972, at Kladno, Czechoslovakia. . . . 6-2/208. . . . Shoots left. **TRANSACTIONS/CAREER NOTES:** Selected by Pittsburgh Penguins in first round (first Penguins pick, fifth overall) of NHL entry draft (June 16, 1990). **HONORS:** Named to NHL All-Rookie team (1990-91). . . . Named to NHL/Upper Deck All-Rookie team (1990-91).

Season Team	League	Gms.	G	A	Pts.	Pen.	Gms.	G	A	Pts.	Pen.
88-89—Poldi Kladno	Czech.	39	8	10	18		—	—	—	—	—
89-90—Poldi Kladno	Czech.	51	30	30	60		—	—	—	—	—
90-91—Pittsburgh	NHL	80	27	30	57	42	24	3	10	13	6
91-92—Pittsburgh	NHL	70	32	37	69	34	†21	11	13	24	6
NHL totals		150	59	67	126	76	45	14	23	37	12

JAKS, PAULI
G, KINGS

PERSONAL: Born January 25, 1972, at Schaffhausen, Switzerland. . . . 6-0/191. . . . Shoots left. **TRANSACTIONS/CAREER NOTES:** Selected by Los Angeles Kings in fifth round (fourth Kings pick, 108th overall) of NHL entry draft (June 22, 1991).

Season Team	League	Gms.	Min.	W	L	T	GA	SO	Avg.	Gms.	Min.	W	L	GA	SO	Avg.
90-91—Ambri Piotta	Switz.	22	1247				100	0	4.81	—	—	—	—	—	—	—

JANNEY, CRAIG
C, BLUES

PERSONAL: Born September 26, 1967, at Hartford, Conn.... 6-1/190.... Shoots left.... Full name: Craig Harlan Janney.
HIGH SCHOOL: Deerfield Academy (Mass.).
COLLEGE: Boston College.
TRANSACTIONS/CAREER NOTES: Broke collarbone (December 1985).... Selected by Boston Bruins in first round (first Bruins pick, 13th overall) of NHL entry draft (June 21, 1986).... Suffered from mononucleosis (December 1986).... Pulled right groin (December 1988); missed seven games.... Tore right groin muscle (October 26, 1989); missed 21 games.... Strained left shoulder (April 5, 1990).... Sprained left shoulder (December 13, 1990).... Sprained right ankle (March 30, 1991).... Traded by Bruins with D Stephane Quintal to St. Louis Blues for C Adam Oates (February 7, 1992).
HONORS: Named to NCAA All-America East first team (1986-87).... Named to Hockey East All-Star first team (1986-87).

			REGULAR SEASON					PLAYOFFS				
Season	Team	League	Gms.	G	A	Pts.	Pen.	Gms.	G	A	Pts.	Pen.
84-85—Deerfield Academy		Mass. H.S.	17	33	35	68	6	—	—	—	—	—
85-86—Boston College		Hockey East	34	13	14	27	8	—	—	—	—	—
86-87—Boston College		Hockey East	37	28	*55	*83	6	—	—	—	—	—
87-88—U.S. National Team		Int'l	52	26	44	70	6	—	—	—	—	—
—U.S. Olympic Team		Int'l	5	3	1	4	2	—	—	—	—	—
—Boston		NHL	15	7	9	16	0	23	6	10	16	11
88-89—Boston		NHL	62	16	46	62	12	10	4	9	13	21
89-90—Boston		NHL	55	24	38	62	4	18	3	19	22	2
90-91—Boston		NHL	77	26	66	92	8	10	4	18	22	11
91-92—Boston		NHL	53	12	39	51	20	—	—	—	—	—
—St. Louis		NHL	25	6	30	36	2	6	0	6	6	0
NHL totals			287	91	228	319	46	75	17	62	79	45

JANSSENS, MARK
C/LW, NORTH STARS

PERSONAL: Born May 19, 1968, at Surrey, B.C.... 6-3/216.... Shoots left.
TRANSACTIONS/CAREER NOTES: Selected by New York Rangers as underage junior in fourth round (fourth Rangers pick, 72nd overall) of NHL entry draft (June 21, 1986). ... Fractured skull and suffered cerebral concussion (December 10, 1988).... Traded by Rangers to Minnesota North Stars for C Mario Thyer and a third-round pick in 1993 draft (March 10, 1992).

			REGULAR SEASON					PLAYOFFS				
Season	Team	League	Gms.	G	A	Pts.	Pen.	Gms.	G	A	Pts.	Pen.
84-85—Regina		WHL	70	8	22	30	51	5	1	1	2	0
85-86—Regina		WHL	71	25	38	63	146	9	0	2	2	17
86-87—Regina		WHL	68	24	38	62	209	3	0	1	1	14
87-88—Regina		WHL	71	39	51	90	202	4	3	4	7	6
—New York Rangers		NHL	1	0	0	0	0	—	—	—	—	—
—Colorado		IHL	6	2	2	4	24	12	3	2	5	20
88-89—New York Rangers		NHL	5	0	0	0	0	—	—	—	—	—
—Denver		IHL	38	19	19	38	104	4	3	0	3	18
89-90—New York Rangers		NHL	80	5	8	13	161	9	2	1	3	10
90-91—New York Rangers		NHL	67	9	7	16	172	6	3	0	3	6
91-92—New York Rangers		NHL	4	0	0	0	5	—	—	—	—	—
—Binghamton		AHL	55	10	23	33	109	—	—	—	—	—
—Minnesota		NHL	3	0	0	0	0	—	—	—	—	—
—Kalamazoo		IHL	2	0	0	0	2	11	1	2	3	22
NHL totals			160	14	15	29	338	15	5	1	6	16

JELINEK, TOMAS
RW, SENATORS

PERSONAL: Born April 29, 1962, at Prague, Czechoslovakia.... 5-9/189.... Shoots left.
TRANSACTIONS/CAREER NOTES: Selected by Ottawa Senators in 11th round (11th Senators pick, 242nd overall) of NHL entry draft (June 20, 1992).

			REGULAR SEASON					PLAYOFFS				
Season	Team	League	Gms.	G	A	Pts.	Pen.	Gms.	G	A	Pts.	Pen.
79-80—Sparta Prague		Czech.	7	0	1	1		—	—	—	—	—
80-81—Dukla Trencin		Czech.	34	5	6	11		—	—	—	—	—
81-82—Dukla Trencin		Czech.	36	9	3	12		—	—	—	—	—
82-83—Sparta Prague		Czech.	40	20	25	45		—	—	—	—	—
83-84—Sparta Prague		Czech.	43	13	5	18		—	—	—	—	—
84-85—Sparta Prague		Czech.	44	15	4	19		—	—	—	—	—
85-86—Sparta Prague		Czech.	40	7	2	9		—	—	—	—	—
86-87—Sparta Prague		Czech.	36	7	5	12		—	—	—	—	—
87-88—Sparta Prague		Czech.	45	14	11	25		—	—	—	—	—
88-89—Sparta Prague		Czech.	45	15	17	32		—	—	—	—	—
89-90—Motor Ceske-Budejovice		Czech.	48	23	20	43		—	—	—	—	—
90-91—Motor Ceske-Budejovice		Czech.	51	24	23	47		—	—	—	—	—
91-92—HPK Hameenlinna		Finland	41	24	23	47	98	—	—	—	—	—

JENNINGS, GRANT
D, PENGUINS

PERSONAL: Born May 5, 1965, at Hudson Bay, Sask.... 6-3/210.... Shoots left.
TRANSACTIONS/CAREER NOTES: Injured shoulder (1984-85) ... Signed as free agent by Washington Capitals (June 25, 1985).... Injured knee (October 1986).... Traded by Capitals with RW Ed Kastelic to Hartford Whalers for D Neil Sheehy and RW Mike Millar (July 6, 1988).... Broke left hand (October 6, 1988).... Bruised right foot (October 1988).... Sprained left shoulder (December 1988).... Underwent surgery to left shoulder (April 14, 1989).... Sprained left knee (February 7, 1990).

... Twisted knee (March 14, 1990).... Strained left ankle (September 1990).... Bruised shoulder (December 1, 1990); missed six games.... Injured shoulder (February 13, 1991).... Traded by Whalers with C Ron Francis and D Ulf Samuelsson to Pittsburgh Penguins for C John Cullen, D Zarley Zalapski and RW Jeff Parker (March 4, 1991).... Separated left shoulder (March 1991).... Bruised hand (February 15, 1992); missed seven games.... Bruised right hand (March 15, 1992); missed one game.

			REGULAR SEASON					PLAYOFFS				
Season	Team	League	Gms.	G	A	Pts.	Pen.	Gms.	G	A	Pts.	Pen.
83-84—Saskatoon		WHL	64	5	13	18	102	—	—	—	—	—
84-85—Saskatoon		WHL	47	10	24	34	134	2	1	0	1	2
85-86—Binghamton		AHL	51	0	4	4	109	—	—	—	—	—
86-87—Fort Wayne		IHL	3	0	0	0	0	—	—	—	—	—
—Binghamton		AHL	47	1	5	6	125	13	0	2	2	17
87-88—Binghamton		AHL	56	2	12	14	195	3	1	0	1	15
—Washington		NHL	—	—	—	—	—	1	0	0	0	0
88-89—Hartford		NHL	55	3	10	13	159	4	1	0	1	17
—Binghamton		AHL	2	0	0	0	2	—	—	—	—	—
89-90—Hartford		NHL	64	3	6	9	171	7	0	0	0	13
90-91—Hartford		NHL	44	1	4	5	82	—	—	—	—	—
—Pittsburgh		NHL	13	1	3	4	26	13	1	1	2	16
91-92—Pittsburgh		NHL	53	4	5	9	104	10	0	0	0	12
NHL totals			229	12	28	40	542	35	2	1	3	58

JENSEN, CHRIS
RW, FLYERS

PERSONAL: Born October 28, 1963, at Fort St. John, B.C.... 5-11/180.... Shoots right.... Full name: Chris B. Jensen.
COLLEGE: North Dakota.
TRANSACTIONS/CAREER NOTES: Selected by New York Rangers as underage player in fourth round (fourth Rangers pick, 78th overall) of NHL entry draft (June 9, 1982).... Injured knee (October 1985).... Strained shoulder (October 1986).... Shoulder surgery (April 1987).... Traded by Rangers to Philadelphia Flyers for D Michael Boyce (September 28, 1988).... Underwent surgery to knee (February 1989); missed five weeks.... Injured hand (October 1989).

			REGULAR SEASON					PLAYOFFS				
Season	Team	League	Gms.	G	A	Pts.	Pen.	Gms.	G	A	Pts.	Pen.
80-81—Kelowna		BCJHL	53	51	45	96	120	—	—	—	—	—
81-82—Kelowna		BCJHL	48	46	46	92	212	—	—	—	—	—
82-83—Univ. of North Dakota		WCHA	13	3	3	6	28	—	—	—	—	—
83-84—Univ. of North Dakota		WCHA	44	24	25	49	100	—	—	—	—	—
84-85—Univ. of North Dakota		WCHA	40	25	27	52	80	—	—	—	—	—
85-86—Univ. of North Dakota		WCHA	34	25	40	65	53	—	—	—	—	—
—New York Rangers		NHL	9	1	3	4	0	—	—	—	—	—
86-87—New York Rangers		NHL	37	6	7	13	21	—	—	—	—	—
—New Haven		AHL	14	4	9	13	41	—	—	—	—	—
87-88—New York Rangers		NHL	7	0	1	1	2	—	—	—	—	—
—Colorado		IHL	43	10	23	33	68	10	3	7	10	8
88-89—Hershey		AHL	45	27	31	58	66	10	4	5	9	29
89-90—Philadelphia		NHL	1	0	0	0	2	—	—	—	—	—
—Hershey		AHL	43	16	26	42	101	—	—	—	—	—
90-91—Philadelphia		NHL	18	2	1	3	2	—	—	—	—	—
—Hershey		AHL	50	26	20	46	83	6	2	2	4	10
91-92—Hershey		AHL	71	38	33	71	134	6	0	1	1	2
—Philadelphia		NHL	2	0	0	0	0	—	—	—	—	—
NHL totals			74	9	12	21	27	—	—	—	—	—

JERRARD, PAUL
RW, NORTH STARS

PERSONAL: Born April 20, 1965, at Winnipeg, Man.... 5-10/185.... Shoots right.... Full name: Paul C. Jerrard.
HIGH SCHOOL: Institut Collegial Notre-Dame (Notre Dame de Lourdes, Man.).
COLLEGE: Lake Superior State (Mich.).
TRANSACTIONS/CAREER NOTES: Selected by New York Rangers in ninth round (10th Rangers pick, 173rd overall) of NHL entry draft (June 8, 1983).... Fractured cheekbone (October 1987).... Traded by Rangers with D Mark Tinordi, C Mike Sullivan, RW Brett Barnett and third-round pick in 1989 draft (C Murray Garbutt), acquired March 10, 1987, by Rangers from Los Angeles Kings, to Minnesota North Stars for LW Igor Liba, C Brian Lawton and rights to LW Eric Bennett (October 11, 1988).

			REGULAR SEASON					PLAYOFFS				
Season	Team	League	Gms.	G	A	Pts.	Pen.	Gms.	G	A	Pts.	Pen.
82-83—Notre Dame H.S.		Sask. H.S.	60	34	37	71	150	—	—	—	—	—
83-84—Lake Superior State		CCHA	40	8	18	26	48	—	—	—	—	—
84-85—Lake Superior State		CCHA	43	9	25	34	61	—	—	—	—	—
85-86—Lake Superior State		CCHA	40	13	11	24	34	—	—	—	—	—
86-87—Lake Superior State		CCHA	34	10	17	27	54	—	—	—	—	—
87-88—Colorado		IHL	77	20	28	48	182	11	2	4	6	40
88-89—Denver		IHL	2	1	1	2	21	—	—	—	—	—
—Kalamazoo		IHL	68	15	25	40	195	6	2	1	3	37
—Minnesota		NHL	5	0	0	0	4	—	—	—	—	—
89-90—Kalamazoo		IHL	60	9	18	27	134	7	1	1	2	11
90-91—Albany		IHL	7	0	3	3	30	—	—	—	—	—
—Kalamazoo		IHL	62	10	23	33	111	7	0	0	0	13
91-92—Kalamazoo		IHL	76	4	24	28	123	12	1	7	8	31
NHL totals			5	0	0	0	4	—	—	—	—	—

JIRANEK, MARTIN
C, CAPITALS

PERSONAL: Born October 3, 1969, at Bashaw, Alta.... 5-11/170.... Shoots left.
COLLEGE: Bowling Green State.
TRANSACTIONS/CAREER NOTES: Selected by Washington Capitals in NHL supplemental draft (June 15, 1990).
HONORS: Named to CCHA All-Star second team (1991-92).

			REGULAR SEASON					PLAYOFFS				
Season Team	League	Gms.	G	A	Pts.	Pen.	Gms.	G	A	Pts.	Pen.
88-89—Bowling Green State	CCHA	41	9	18	27	36	—	—	—	—	—
89-90—Bowling Green State	CCHA	41	13	21	34	38	—	—	—	—	—
90-91—Bowling Green State	CCHA	39	31	23	54	33	—	—	—	—	—
91-92—Bowling Green State	CCHA	34	25	28	53	46	—	—	—	—	—
—Baltimore	AHL	8	2	8	10	0	—	—	—	—	—

JOHANNSON, JIM
C, BLACKHAWKS

PERSONAL: Born March 10, 1964, at Rochester, Minn.... 6-1/195.... Shoots right.... Full name: James Johannson.
COLLEGE: Wisconsin.
TRANSACTIONS/CAREER NOTES: Signed as free agent by Calgary Flames (February 1988).... Signed as free agent by Chicago Blackhawks (July 6, 1989).
HONORS: Won Iron Man Award (June 1991).

			REGULAR SEASON					PLAYOFFS				
Season Team	League	Gms.	G	A	Pts.	Pen.	Gms.	G	A	Pts.	Pen.
82-83—University of Wisconsin	WCHA	43	12	9	21	16	—	—	—	—	—
83-84—University of Wisconsin	WCHA	35	17	21	38	52	—	—	—	—	—
84-85—University of Wisconsin	WCHA	40	16	24	40	54	—	—	—	—	—
85-86—University of Wisconsin	WCHA	30	18	13	31	44	—	—	—	—	—
86-87—Landsberg	W. Germany	57	46	56	102	90	—	—	—	—	—
87-88—U.S. National Team	Int'l	47	16	14	30	64	—	—	—	—	—
—U.S. Olympic Team	Int'l	4	0	1	1	4	—	—	—	—	—
—Salt Lake City	IHL	18	14	7	21	50	19	8	+15	23	55
88-89—Salt Lake City	IHL	82	35	40	75	87	13	2	5	7	13
89-90—Indianapolis	IHL	82	22	41	63	74	14	1	4	5	6
90-91—Indianapolis	IHL	82	28	41	69	116	7	1	2	3	8
91-92—U.S. National Team	Int'l	50	9	8	17	79	—	—	—	—	—
—U.S. Olympic Team	Int'l	8	1	0	1	2	—	—	—	—	—
—Indianapolis	IHL	11	2	2	4	4	—	—	—	—	—

JOHANSSON, CALLE
D, CAPITALS

PERSONAL: Born February 14, 1967, at Goteborg, Sweden. ... 5-11/205.... Shoots left.
TRANSACTIONS/CAREER NOTES: Selected by Buffalo Sabres in first round (first Sabres pick, 14th overall) of NHL entry draft (June 15, 1985).... Dislocated thumb (October 9, 1988).... Traded by Sabres with second-round pick in 1989 draft (G Byron Dafoe) to Washington Capitals for D Grant Ledyard, G Clint Malarchuk and sixth-round 1991 draft pick (March 6, 1989).... Injured back (October 7, 1989); missed 10 games.
HONORS: Named to NHL All-Rookie team (1987-88).

			REGULAR SEASON					PLAYOFFS				
Season Team	League	Gms.	G	A	Pts.	Pen.	Gms.	G	A	Pts.	Pen.
83-84—Vastra Frolunda	Sweden	34	5	10	15	20	—	—	—	—	—
84-85—Vastra Frolunda	Sweden	36	14	15	29	20	6	1	2	3	4
85-86—Bjorkloven	Sweden	17	1	1	2	14	—	—	—	—	—
86-87—Bjorkloven	Sweden	30	2	13	15	18	6	1	3	4	6
87-88—Buffalo	NHL	71	4	38	42	37	6	0	1	1	0
88-89—Buffalo	NHL	47	2	11	13	33	—	—	—	—	—
—Washington	NHL	12	1	7	8	4	6	1	2	3	0
89-90—Washington	NHL	70	8	31	39	25	15	1	6	7	4
90-91—Washington	NHL	80	11	41	52	23	10	2	7	9	8
91-92—Washington	NHL	80	14	42	56	49	7	0	5	5	4
NHL totals		360	40	170	210	171	44	4	21	25	16

JOHANSSON, MATHIAS
C, FLAMES

PERSONAL: Born February 22, 1974, at Oskarshamn, Sweden.... 6-2/187. ... Shoots left.
TRANSACTIONS/CAREER NOTES: Selected by Calgary Flames in third round (third Flames pick, 54th overall) of NHL entry draft (June 20, 1992).

			REGULAR SEASON					PLAYOFFS				
Season Team	League	Gms.	G	A	Pts.	Pen.	Gms.	G	A	Pts.	Pen.
90-91—Farjestad	Sweden	3	0	0	0	0	—	—	—	—	—
91-92—Farjestad	Sweden	16	0	0	0	2	—	—	—	—	—

JOHNSON, CRAIG
LW, BLUES

PERSONAL: Born March 18, 1972, at St. Paul, Minn.... 6-2/185.... Shoots left.
HIGH SCHOOL: Hill-Murray (St. Paul, Minn.).
COLLEGE: Minnesota.
TRANSACTIONS/CAREER NOTES: Suffered stress fracture of vertebrae (February 1987). ... Selected by St. Louis Blues in second round (first Blues pick, 33rd overall) of NHL entry draft (June 16, 1990).... Separated shoulder (December 1990).
HONORS: Named to WCHA All-Rookie Team (1990-91).

Season	Team	League	Gms.	G	A	Pts.	Pen.	Gms.	G	A	Pts.	Pen.
				REGULAR SEASON					PLAYOFFS			
87-88—Hill Murray H.S.		Minn. H.S.	28	14	20	34	4	—	—	—	—	—
88-89—Hill Murray H.S.		Minn. H.S.	24	22	30	52	10	—	—	—	—	—
89-90—Hill Murray H.S.		Minn. H.S.	23	15	36	51		—	—	—	—	—
90-91—University of Minnesota ...		WCHA	33	13	18	31	34	—	—	—	—	—
91-92—University of Minnesota ...		WCHA	44	19	39	58	70	—	—	—	—	—

JOHNSON, GREGORY

C, FLYERS

PERSONAL: Born March 16, 1971, at Thunder Bay, Ont. . . . 5-11/180. . . . Shoots left.

COLLEGE: North Dakota.

TRANSACTIONS/CAREER NOTES: Selected by Philadelphia Flyers in second round (first Flyers pick, 33rd overall) of NHL entry draft (June 17, 1989). . . . Separated right shoulder (November 24, 1990).

HONORS: Named to USHL All-Star first team (1988-89). . . . Named Canadian Junior A Player of the Year (1989). . . . Named to Centennial Cup All-Star first team (1989). . . . Named to NCAA All-America West first team (1990-91). . . . Named to WCHA All-Star first team (1990-91 and 1991-92).

Season	Team	League	Gms.	G	A	Pts.	Pen.	Gms.	G	A	Pts.	Pen.
				REGULAR SEASON					PLAYOFFS			
88-89—Thunder Bay Jrs.		USHL	47	32	64	96	4	12	5	13	18	
89-90—Univ. of North Dakota		WCHA	44	17	38	55	11	—	—	—	—	—
90-91—Univ. of North Dakota		WCHA	38	18	*61	79	6	—	—	—	—	—
91-92—Univ. of North Dakota		WCHA	39	20	54	74	8	—	—	—	—	—

JOHNSON, JIM

D, NORTH STARS

PERSONAL: Born August 9, 1962, at New Hope, Minn. . . . 6-1/190. . . . Shoots left. . . . Full name: James Erik Johnson.

HIGH SCHOOL: Cooper (New Hope, Minn.).

COLLEGE: Minnesota-Duluth.

TRANSACTIONS/CAREER NOTES: Signed as free agent by Pittsburgh Penguins (June 1985). . . . Tore cartilage in right knee (January 1988). . . . Suffered back pain (October 1990). . . . Injured neck (November 12, 1990); missed three games. . . . Traded by Penguins with D Chris Dahlquist to Minnesota North Stars for D Peter Taglianetti and D Larry Murphy (December 11, 1990). . . . Sprained back (February 12, 1991); missed two games. . . . Bruised hip (April 1991). . . . Injured groin (December 7, 1991); missed five games. . . . Strained hamstring (March 10, 1992); missed two games.

Season	Team	League	Gms.	G	A	Pts.	Pen.	Gms.	G	A	Pts.	Pen.
				REGULAR SEASON					PLAYOFFS			
81-82—Minnesota-Duluth		WCHA	40	0	10	10	62	—	—	—	—	—
82-83—Minnesota-Duluth		WCHA	44	3	18	21	118	—	—	—	—	—
83-84—Minnesota-Duluth		WCHA	43	3	13	16	116	—	—	—	—	—
84-85—Minnesota-Duluth		WCHA	47	7	29	36	49	—	—	—	—	—
85-86—Pittsburgh		NHL	80	3	26	29	115	—	—	—	—	—
86-87—Pittsburgh		NHL	80	5	25	30	116	—	—	—	—	—
87-88—Pittsburgh		NHL	55	1	12	13	87	—	—	—	—	—
88-89—Pittsburgh		NHL	76	2	14	16	163	11	0	5	5	44
89-90—Pittsburgh		NHL	75	3	13	16	154	—	—	—	—	—
90-91—Pittsburgh		NHL	24	0	5	5	23	—	—	—	—	—
—Minnesota		NHL	44	1	9	10	100	14	0	1	1	52
91-92—Minnesota		NHL	71	4	10	14	102	7	1	3	4	18
NHL totals..			505	19	114	133	860	32	1	9	10	114

JOHNSON, MIKE

D, NORTH STARS

PERSONAL: Born May 29, 1974, at Halifax, N.S. . . . 6-3/172. . . . Shoots left. . . . Full name: Michael Johnson.

HIGH SCHOOL: Hillcrest (Thunder Bay, Ont.).

TRANSACTIONS/CAREER NOTES: Selected by Minnesota North Stars in sixth round (fourth North stars pick, 130th overall) of NHL entry draft (June 20, 1992).

Season	Team	League	Gms.	G	A	Pts.	Pen.	Gms.	G	A	Pts.	Pen.
				REGULAR SEASON					PLAYOFFS			
91-92—Ottawa.............................		OHL	63	1	8	9	49	11	1	0	1	14

JOHNSTON, GREG

RW/C, MAPLE LEAFS

PERSONAL: Born January 14, 1965, at Barrie, Ont. . . . 6-1/190. . . . Shoots right.

TRANSACTIONS/CAREER NOTES: Broke ankle (September 1982). . . . Selected by Boston Bruins as underage junior in second round (second Bruins pick, 42nd overall) of NHL entry draft (June 8, 1983). . . . Strained abdominal muscles (November 1988). . . . Traded by Bruins with future considerations to New York Rangers for RW Chris Nilan (June 28, 1990). . . . Traded by Rangers to Toronto Maple Leafs for RW Tie Domi and G Mark Laforest (June 28, 1990).

Season	Team	League	Gms.	G	A	Pts.	Pen.	Gms.	G	A	Pts.	Pen.
				REGULAR SEASON					PLAYOFFS			
82-83—Toronto............................		OHL	58	18	19	37	58	4	1	0	1	4
83-84—Toronto............................		OHL	57	38	35	73	67	9	4	2	6	13
—Boston		NHL	15	2	1	3	2	—	—	—	—	—
84-85—Boston		NHL	6	0	0	0	0	—	—	—	—	—
—Hershey		AHL	3	1	0	1	0	—	—	—	—	—
—Toronto............................		OHL	42	22	28	50	55	5	1	3	4	4
85-86—Moncton		AHL	60	19	26	45	56	10	4	6	10	4
—Boston		NHL	20	0	2	2	0	—	—	—	—	—

Season Team	League	REGULAR SEASON Gms.	G	A	Pts.	Pen.	PLAYOFFS Gms.	G	A	Pts.	Pen.
86-87—Boston	NHL	76	12	15	27	79	4	0	0	0	0
87-88—Maine	AHL	75	21	32	53	105	10	6	4	10	23
—Boston	NHL	—	—	—	—	—	3	0	1	1	2
88-89—Boston	NHL	57	11	10	21	32	10	1	0	1	6
—Maine	AHL	15	5	7	12	31	—	—	—	—	—
89-90—Maine	AHL	52	16	26	42	45	—	—	—	—	—
—Boston	NHL	9	1	1	2	6	5	1	0	1	4
90-91—Newmarket	AHL	73	32	50	82	54	—	—	—	—	—
—Toronto	NHL	1	0	0	0	0	—	—	—	—	—
91-92—St. John's	AHL	63	28	45	73	33	16	8	6	14	10
—Toronto	NHL	3	0	1	1	5	—	—	—	—	—
NHL totals		187	26	30	56	124	22	2	1	3	12

J

JONES, BRAD
RW, FLYERS

PERSONAL: Born June 26, 1965, at Sterling Heights, Mich. . . . 6-0/ 195. . . . Shoots left. . . . Full name: Brad Scott Jones.
COLLEGE: Michigan.
TRANSACTIONS/CAREER NOTES: Selected by Winnipeg Jets in eighth round (eighth Jets pick, 156th overall) of NHL entry draft (June 9, 1984). . . . Injured knee (November 1984). . . . Traded by Jets to Los Angeles Kings for LW Phil Sykes (November 1989). . . . Injured shoulder (February 1991). . . . Signed as free agent by Philadelphia Flyers (August 6, 1991) . . . Tore ligament and chipped bone in ankle (January 28, 1991); missed 29 games.
HONORS: Named to CCHA All-Star second team (1985-86). . . . Named to NCAA All-America West second team (1986-87). . . . Named to CCHA All-Star first team (1986-87).

Season Team	League	REGULAR SEASON Gms.	G	A	Pts.	Pen.	PLAYOFFS Gms.	G	A	Pts.	Pen.
83-84—University of Michigan	CCHA	37	8	26	34	32	—	—	—	—	—
84-85—University of Michigan	CCHA	34	21	27	48	69	—	—	—	—	—
85-86—University of Michigan	CCHA	36	28	39	67	40	—	—	—	—	—
86-87—University of Michigan	CCHA	40	32	46	78	64	—	—	—	—	—
—Winnipeg	NHL	4	1	0	1	0	—	—	—	—	—
87-88—Winnipeg	NHL	19	2	5	7	15	1	0	0	0	0
—U.S. Olympic Team	Int'l	50	27	23	50	59	—	—	—	—	—
88-89—Winnipeg	NHL	22	6	5	11	6	—	—	—	—	—
—Moncton	AHL	44	20	19	39	62	7	0	1	1	22
89-90—Winnipeg	NHL	2	0	0	0	0	—	—	—	—	—
—Moncton	AHL	15	5	6	11	47	—	—	—	—	—
—New Haven	AHL	36	8	11	19	71	—	—	—	—	—
90-91—Los Angeles	NHL	53	9	11	20	57	8	1	1	2	5
91-92—Philadelphia	NHL	48	7	10	17	44	—	—	—	—	—
NHL totals		148	25	31	56	122	9	1	1	2	2

JONES, KEITH
RW, CAPITALS

PERSONAL: Born November 8, 1968, at Brantford, Ont. . . . 6-2/ 190. . . . Shoots left.
COLLEGE: Western Michigan.
TRANSACTIONS/CAREER NOTES: Selected by Washington Capitals in seventh round (seventh Capitals pick, 141st overall) of NHL entry draft (June 11, 1988).

Season Team	League	REGULAR SEASON Gms.	G	A	Pts.	Pen.	PLAYOFFS Gms.	G	A	Pts.	Pen.
87-88—Niagara Falls	OHA	40	50	80	130		—	—	—	—	—
88-89—Western Michigan Univ.	CCHA	37	9	12	21	51	—	—	—	—	—
89-90—Western Michigan Univ.	CCHA	40	19	18	37	82	—	—	—	—	—
90-91—Western Michigan Univ.	CCHA	41	30	19	49	106	—	—	—	—	—
91-92—Western Michigan Univ.	CCHA	35	25	31	56	77	—	—	—	—	—
—Baltimore	AHL	6	2	4	6	0	—	—	—	—	—

JOSEPH, CHRIS
D, OILERS

PERSONAL: Born September 10, 1969, at Burnaby, B.C. . . . 6-2/210. . . . Shoots right. . . . Full name: Robin Christopher Joseph.
TRANSACTIONS/CAREER NOTES: Selected by Pittsburgh Penguins in first round (first Penguins pick, fifth overall) of NHL entry draft (June 13, 1987). . . . Traded by Penguins with C Craig Simpson, C Dave Hannan and D Moe Mantha to Edmonton Oilers for D Paul Coffey, LW Dave Hunter and RW Wayne Van Dorp (November 24, 1987). . . . Strained knee ligaments (January 1989).

Season Team	League	REGULAR SEASON Gms.	G	A	Pts.	Pen.	PLAYOFFS Gms.	G	A	Pts.	Pen.
85-86—Seattle	WHL	72	4	8	12	50	5	0	3	3	12
86-87—Seattle	WHL	67	13	45	58	155	—	—	—	—	—
87-88—Canadian Olympic Team	Int'l	7	0	0	0	6	—	—	—	—	—
—Pittsburgh	NHL	17	0	4	4	12	—	—	—	—	—
—Edmonton	NHL	7	0	4	4	6	—	—	—	—	—
—Nova Scotia	AHL	8	0	2	2	8	4	0	0	0	9
—Seattle	WHL	23	5	14	19	49	—	—	—	—	—
88-89—Cape Breton	AHL	5	1	1	2	18	—	—	—	—	—
—Edmonton	NHL	44	4	5	9	54	—	—	—	—	—
89-90—Edmonton	NHL	4	0	2	2	2	—	—	—	—	—
—Cape Breton	AHL	61	10	20	30	69	6	2	1	3	4

Season Team	League	REGULAR SEASON					PLAYOFFS				
		Gms.	G	A	Pts.	Pen.	Gms.	G	A	Pts.	Pen.
90-91—Edmonton	NHL	49	5	17	22	59	—	—	—	—	—
91-92—Edmonton	NHL	7	0	0	0	8	5	1	3	4	2
—Cape Breton	AHL	63	14	29	43	72	5	0	2	2	8
NHL totals		128	9	32	41	141	5	1	3	4	2

JOSEPH, CURTIS
G, BLUES

PERSONAL: Born April 29, 1967, at Keswick, Ont. . . . 5-11/182. . . . Shoots left. . . . Full name: Curtis Shayne Joseph.
COLLEGE: Wisconsin.
TRANSACTIONS/CAREER NOTES: Signed as free agent by St. Louis Blues (June 16, 1989). . . . Dislocated left shoulder (April 11, 1990). . . . Underwent surgery to left shoulder (May 10, 1990). . . . Sprained right knee (February 26, 1991); missed remainder of season. . . . Injured ankle (March 12, 1992); missed seven games.
HONORS: Named OHA Most Valuable Player (1986-87). . . . Won WCHA Most Valuable Player Award (1988-89). . . . Won WCHA Rookie of the Year Award (1988-89). . . . Named to NCAA All-America West second team (1988-89). . . . Named to WCHA All-Star first team (1988-89).

Season Team	League	REGULAR SEASON							PLAYOFFS						
		Gms.	Min.	W	L	T	GA	SO	Avg.	Gms.	Min.	W	L	GA	SO	Avg.
86-87—Richmond Hill	OHA	—	—	—	—	—	—	—	—	—	—	—	—	—	—	—
87-88—Notre Dame	SCMHL	36	2174	25	4	7	94	1	2.59	—	—	—	—	—	—	—
88-89—Univ. of Wisconsin	WCHA	38	2267	21	11	5	94	1	2.49	—	—	—	—	—	—	—
89-90—Peoria	IHL	23	1241	10	8	2	80	0	3.87	—	—	—	—	—	—	—
—St. Louis	NHL	15	852	9	5	1	48	0	3.38	6	327	4	1	18	0	3.30
90-91—St. Louis	NHL	30	1710	16	10	2	89	0	3.12	—	—	—	—	—	—	—
91-92—St. Louis	NHL	60	3494	27	20	10	175	2	3.01	6	379	2	4	23	0	3.64
NHL totals		105	6056	52	35	13	312	2	3.09	12	706	6	5	41	0	3.48

JOSEPH, TONY
RW, JETS

PERSONAL: Born March 1, 1969, at Cornwall, Ont. . . . 6-4/203. . . . Shoots right. . . . Full name: Anthony Joseph.
TRANSACTIONS/CAREER NOTES: Selected by Winnipeg Jets in fifth round (fifth Jets pick, 94th overall) of NHL entry draft (June 11, 1988). . . . Traded by Jets to Minnesota North Stars C Tyler Larter (October 15, 1991). . . . Traded by North Stars with future considerations to Jets for LW Warren Rychel (December 30, 1991).

Season Team	League	REGULAR SEASON					PLAYOFFS				
		Gms.	G	A	Pts.	Pen.	Gms.	G	A	Pts.	Pen.
85-86—Oshawa	OHL	41	3	1	4	28	—	—	—	—	—
86-87—Oshawa	OHL	44	2	5	7	93	—	—	—	—	—
87-88—Oshawa	OHL	49	9	18	27	126	7	0	0	0	9
88-89—Winnipeg	NHL	2	1	0	1	0	—	—	—	—	—
—Oshawa	OHL	52	20	16	36	106	6	4	2	6	22
89-90—Tappara	Finland	5	0	0	0	2	—	—	—	—	—
—Moncton	AHL	61	9	9	18	74	—	—	—	—	—
90-91—Moncton	AHL	16	4	2	6	79	8	0	1	1	31
91-92—Moncton	AHL	42	6	5	11	118	6	0	1	1	25
—Kalamazoo	IHL	15	2	0	2	51	—	—	—	—	—
NHL totals		2	1	0	1	0					

JOYCE, BOB
LW, JETS

PERSONAL: Born July 11, 1966, at St. Johns, N.B. . . . 6-1/195. . . . Shoots left. . . . Full name: Robert Thomas Joyce.
HIGH SCHOOL: Athol Murray College of Notre Dame (Wilcox, Sask.).
COLLEGE: North Dakota.
TRANSACTIONS/CAREER NOTES: Selected by Boston Bruins in fourth round (fourth Bruins pick, 82nd overall) of NHL entry draft (June 9, 1984). . . . Sprained right knee in training camp (September 1988). . . . Suffered concussion and laceration to lip (October 6, 1988). . . . Pulled groin muscle (March 1989). . . . Dislocated shoulder (November 23, 1989). . . . Traded by Bruins to Washington Capitals for RW/C Dave Christian (December 13, 1989). . . . Sprained right knee and underwent surgery (January 3, 1990); missed 17 games. . . . Sprained left ankle (October 1990). . . . Traded by Capitals with D Kent Paynter and C Tyler Larter to Winnipeg Jets for LW Brent Hughes, LW Craig Duncanson and C Simon Wheeldon (May 21, 1991).
HONORS: Named to NCAA All-America West first team (1986-87). . . . Named to WCHA All-Star first team (1986-87).

Season Team	League	REGULAR SEASON					PLAYOFFS				
		Gms.	G	A	Pts.	Pen.	Gms.	G	A	Pts.	Pen.
83-84—Wilcox Notre Dame H.S.	Sask. H.S.	30	33	37	70		—	—	—	—	—
84-85—Univ. of North Dakota	WCHA	41	18	16	34	10	—	—	—	—	—
85-86—Univ. of North Dakota	WCHA	38	31	28	59	40	—	—	—	—	—
86-87—Univ. of North Dakota	WCHA	48	*52	37	89	42	—	—	—	—	—
87-88—Canadian Olympic Team	Int'l	50	13	10	23	28	—	—	—	—	—
—Boston	NHL	15	7	5	12	10	23	8	6	14	18
88-89—Boston	NHL	77	18	31	49	46	9	5	2	7	2
89-90—Boston	NHL	23	1	2	3	22	—	—	—	—	—
—Washington	NHL	24	5	8	13	4	14	2	1	3	9
90-91—Baltimore	AHL	36	10	8	18	14	6	1	0	1	4
—Washington	NHL	17	3	3	6	8	—	—	—	—	—
91-92—Moncton	AHL	66	19	29	48	51	10	0	5	5	9
—Winnipeg	NHL	1	0	0	0	0	—	—	—	—	—
NHL totals		157	34	49	83	90	46	15	9	24	29

JUDSON, RICK
LW, RED WINGS

PERSONAL: Born August 13, 1969, at Lambentville, Mich. . . . 5-11/180. . . . Shoots left. . . . Full name: Rick Lee Judson.
COLLEGE: Illinois-Chicago.
TRANSACTIONS/CAREER NOTES: Selected by Detroit Red Wings in 10th round (11th Red Wings pick, 204th overall) of NHL entry draft (June 17, 1989).
HONORS: Named to USHL All-Star first team (1987-88).

Season Team	League	REGULAR SEASON					PLAYOFFS				
		Gms.	G	A	Pts.	Pen.	Gms.	G	A	Pts.	Pen.
87-88—Rochester	USHL		56	35	91		—	—	—	—	—
88-89—Illinois-Chicago	CCHA	42	14	20	34	20	—	—	—	—	—
89-90—Illinois-Chicago	CCHA	38	19	22	41	18	—	—	—	—	—
90-91—Illinois-Chicago	CCHA	38	24	26	50	12	—	—	—	—	—
91-92—Illinois-Chicago	CCHA	36	17	19	36	26	—	—	—	—	—
—Toledo	ECHL	2	1	0	1	2	—	—	—	—	—

JUNEAU, JOE
C, BRUINS

PERSONAL: Born January 5, 1968, at Pont-Rouge, Que. . . . 6-0/175. . . . Shoots right.
COLLEGE: Rensselaer Polytechnic Institute (N.Y.).
TRANSACTIONS/CAREER NOTES: Selected by Boston Bruins in fourth round (third Bruins pick, 81st overall) of NHL entry draft (June 11, 1988). . . . Suffered ligament problem in back (November 1990).
HONORS: Named to NCAA All-America East first team (1989-90). . . . Named to ECAC All-Star first team (1989-90). . . . Named to NCAA All-America East second team (1990-91). . . . Named to ECAC All-Star second team (1990-91).
MISCELLANEOUS: Member of 1992 silver medal-winning Canadian Olympic team.

Season Team	League	REGULAR SEASON					PLAYOFFS				
		Gms.	G	A	Pts.	Pen.	Gms.	G	A	Pts.	Pen.
87-88—R.P.I.	ECAC	31	16	29	45	18	—	—	—	—	—
88-89—R.P.I.	ECAC	30	12	23	35	40	—	—	—	—	—
89-90—R.P.I.	ECAC	34	18	*52	*70	31	—	—	—	—	—
90-91—R.P.I.	ECAC	29	23	40	63	70	—	—	—	—	—
91-92—Canadian National Team	Int'l	60	20	49	69	35	—	—	—	—	—
—Canadian Olympic Team	Int'l	8	6	9	15	4	—	—	—	—	—
—Boston	NHL	14	5	14	19	4	15	4	8	12	21
NHL totals		14	5	14	19	4	15	4	8	12	21

KACHOWSKI, MARK
LW, PENGUINS

PERSONAL: Born February 20, 1965, at Edmonton, Alta. . . . 5-11/200. . . . Shoots left. . . . Full name: Mark Edward Kachowski.
TRANSACTIONS/CAREER NOTES: Signed as free agent by Pittsburgh Penguins (August 1987).

Season Team	League	REGULAR SEASON					PLAYOFFS				
		Gms.	G	A	Pts.	Pen.	Gms.	G	A	Pts.	Pen.
83-84—Kamloops	WHL	57	6	9	15	156	—	—	—	—	—
84-85—Kamloops	WHL	68	22	15	37	185	—	—	—	—	—
85-86—Kamloops	WHL	61	21	31	52	182	—	—	—	—	—
86-87—Flint	IHL	75	18	13	31	273	6	1	1	2	21
87-88—Pittsburgh	NHL	38	5	3	8	126	—	—	—	—	—
—Muskegon	IHL	25	3	6	9	72	5	0	2	2	11
88-89—Pittsburgh	NHL	12	1	1	2	43	—	—	—	—	—
—Muskegon	IHL	57	8	8	16	167	8	1	2	3	17
89-90—Pittsburgh	NHL	14	0	1	1	40	—	—	—	—	—
—Muskegon	IHL	62	23	8	31	129	12	2	4	6	21
90-91—Muskegon	IHL	80	19	21	40	108	5	1	1	2	9
91-92—Muskegon	IHL	6	0	0	0	9	4	2	0	2	16
NHL totals		64	6	5	11	209					

KAISER, KEVIN
LW, NORDIQUES

PERSONAL: Born July 26, 1970, at Winnipeg, Man. . . . 6-0/185. . . . Shoots left. . . . Full name: Kevin Michael Kaiser.
COLLEGE: Minnesota-Duluth.
TRANSACTIONS/CAREER NOTES: Selected by Quebec Nordiques in fifth round (seventh Nordiques pick, 85th overall) of NHL entry draft (June 17, 1989).

Season Team	League	REGULAR SEASON					PLAYOFFS				
		Gms.	G	A	Pts.	Pen.	Gms.	G	A	Pts.	Pen.
87-88—Winnipeg	MJHL	74	69	52	121	80	—	—	—	—	—
88-89—Minnesota-Duluth	WCHA	40	2	5	7	26	—	—	—	—	—
89-90—Minnesota-Duluth	WCHA	39	9	11	20	24	—	—	—	—	—
90-91—Minnesota-Duluth	WCHA	39	15	17	32	52	—	—	—	—	—
91-92—Minnesota-Duluth	WCHA	37	18	19	37	66	—	—	—	—	—

KAMENSKY, VALERI
LW, NORDIQUES

PERSONAL: Born April 18, 1966, at Voskresensk, U.S.S.R. . . . 6-2/198. . . . Shoots right.
TRANSACTIONS/CAREER NOTES: Selected by Quebec Nordiques in seventh round (eighth Nordiques pick, 129th overall) of NHL entry draft (June 11, 1988). . . . Fractured leg (October 1991); missed 57 games.
MISCELLANEOUS: Member of 1988 gold-medal-winning U.S.S.R. Olympic team.

Season	Team	League		Gms.	G	A	Pts.	Pen.		Gms.	G	A	Pts.	Pen.
				REGULAR SEASON						**PLAYOFFS**				
82-83	Khimik	USSR		5	0	0	0	0		—	—	—	—	—
83-84	Khimik	USSR		20	2	2	4	6		—	—	—	—	—
84-85	Khimik	USSR		45	9	3	12	24		—	—	—	—	—
85-86	Red Army	USSR		40	15	9	24	6		—	—	—	—	—
86-87	Red Army	USSR		37	13	8	21	16		—	—	—	—	—
87-88	Red Army	USSR		51	26	20	46	40		—	—	—	—	—
88-89	Red Army	USSR		40	18	10	28	30		—	—	—	—	—
89-90	Red Army	USSR		45	19	18	37	38		—	—	—	—	—
90-91	Red Army	USSR		46	20	26	46	66		—	—	—	—	—
91-92	Quebec	NHL		23	7	14	21	14		—	—	—	—	—
	NHL totals			23	7	14	21	14		—	—	—	—	—

KAMINSKI, KEVIN
C, NORDIQUES

PERSONAL: Born March 13, 1969, at Churchbridge, Sask.... 5-9/170.... Shoots left.
TRANSACTIONS/CAREER NOTES: Selected by Minnesota North Stars as an underage junior in third round (third North Stars pick, 48th overall) of NHL entry draft (June 13, 1987). .... Suspended 12 games by WHL for cross-checking (November 4, 1987).... Traded by North Stars to Quebec Nordiques for LW Gaetan Duchesne (June 18, 1989).... Separated shoulder in training camp (September 1989).... Suspended two games by AHL for head-butting (January 26, 1990).

Season	Team	League		Gms.	G	A	Pts.	Pen.		Gms.	G	A	Pts.	Pen.
				REGULAR SEASON						**PLAYOFFS**				
84-85	Saskatoon	WHL		5	0	1	1	17		—	—	—	—	—
85-86	Saskatoon	WHL		4	1	1	2	35		—	—	—	—	—
86-87	Saskatoon	WHL		67	26	44	70	235		11	5	6	11	45
87-88	Saskatoon	WHL		55	38	61	99	247		10	5	7	12	37
88-89	Saskatoon	WHL		52	25	43	68	199		8	4	9	13	25
	Minnesota	NHL		1	0	0	0	0		—	—	—	—	—
89-90	Quebec	NHL		1	0	0	0	0		—	—	—	—	—
	Halifax	AHL		19	3	4	7	128		2	0	0	0	5
90-91	Halifax	AHL		7	1	0	1	44		—	—	—	—	—
	Fort Wayne	IHL		56	9	15	24	*455		19	4	2	6	*169
91-92	Halifax	AHL		63	18	27	45	329		—	—	—	—	—
	Quebec	NHL		5	0	0	0	45		—	—	—	—	—
	NHL totals			7	0	0	0	45		—	—	—	—	—

KAMINSKY, JAN
LW, JETS

PERSONAL: Born July 28, 1971, at Penza, U.S.S.R.... 6-2/176.... Shoots left.
TRANSACTIONS/CAREER NOTES: Selected by Winnipeg Jets in fifth round (fourth Jets pick, 99th overall) of NHL entry draft (June 22, 1991).

Season	Team	League		Gms.	G	A	Pts.	Pen.		Gms.	G	A	Pts.	Pen.
				REGULAR SEASON						**PLAYOFFS**				
89-90	Dynamo Moscow	USSR		6	1	0	1	4		—	—	—	—	—
90-91	Dynamo Moscow	USSR		25	10	5	15	2		—	—	—	—	—
91-92	Dynamo Moscow	CIS		42	9	7	16	22		—	—	—	—	—

KANE, SHAUN
D, SHARKS

PERSONAL: Born February 24, 1970, at Holyoke, Mass.... 6-3/195.... Shoots left.... Full name: Shaun Joseph Kane.
HIGH SCHOOL: Holyoke (Mass.).
COLLEGE: Providence.
TRANSACTIONS/CAREER NOTES: Selected by Minnesota North Stars in third round (third North Stars pick, 43rd overall) of NHL entry draft (June 11, 1988).... Selected by San Jose Sharks in NHL dispersal draft (May 10, 1991).
HONORS: Named to Hockey East All-Rookie team (1988-89).... Named to Hockey East All-Star second team (1990-91).

Season	Team	League		Gms.	G	A	Pts.	Pen.		Gms.	G	A	Pts.	Pen.
				REGULAR SEASON						**PLAYOFFS**				
86-87	Springfield Jr. B	NEJHL			20	36	56			—	—	—	—	—
87-88	Springfield Jr. B	NEJHL			23	40	63			—	—	—	—	—
88-89	Providence College	Hockey East		37	2	9	11	54		—	—	—	—	—
89-90	Providence College	Hockey East		31	9	8	17	46		—	—	—	—	—
90-91	Providence College	Hockey East		36	5	20	25	86		—	—	—	—	—
91-92	Providence College	Hockey East		36	11	11	22	59		—	—	—	—	—

KAPUSTA, THOMAS
C, OILERS

PERSONAL: Born February 23, 1967, at Gottwaldov, Czechoslovakia.... 6-0/187. ... Shoots left.
TRANSACTIONS/CAREER NOTES: Selected by Edmonton Oilers in fifth round (fourth Oilers pick, 104th overall) of NHL entry draft (June 15, 1985).

Season	Team	League		Gms.	G	A	Pts.	Pen.		Gms.	G	A	Pts.	Pen.
				REGULAR SEASON						**PLAYOFFS**				
84-85	Gottwaldov	Czech.		36	5	7	12	14		—	—	—	—	—
85-86	Gottwaldov	Czech.		—	—	—	—	—		—	—	—	—	—
86-87	Gottwaldov	Czech.		—	—	—	—	—		—	—	—	—	—
87-88	Dukla Trencin	Czech.		—	—	—	—	—		—	—	—	—	—
88-89	Dukla Trencin	Czech.		44	8	25	33			—	—	—	—	—

Season Team	League	REGULAR SEASON					PLAYOFFS				
		Gms.	G	A	Pts.	Pen.	Gms.	G	A	Pts.	Pen.
89-90—Zlin	Czech.	—	—	—	—	—	—	—	—	—	—
—Cape Breton	AHL	55	12	37	49	56	6	2	7	9	4
90-91—Cape Breton	AHL	73	21	46	67	47	4	0	2	2	21
91-92—Cape Breton	AHL	67	18	33	51	55	5	1	2	3	2

KARAMNOV, VITALI
LW, BLUES

PERSONAL: Born July 6, 1968, at Moscow, U.S.S.R. . . . 6-2/185. . . . Shoots left.
TRANSACTIONS/CAREER NOTES: Selected by St. Louis Blues in third round (second Blues pick, 62nd overall) of NHL entry draft (June 20, 1992).

Season Team	League	REGULAR SEASON					PLAYOFFS				
		Gms.	G	A	Pts.	Pen.	Gms.	G	A	Pts.	Pen.
86-87—Dynamo Moscow	USSR	4	0	0	0	0	—	—	—	—	—
87-88—Dynamo Moscow	USSR	2	0	1	1	0	—	—	—	—	—
88-89—Dynamo Kharkov	USSR	23	4	1	5	19	—	—	—	—	—
89-90—Torpedo Yaroslavl	USSR	47	6	7	13	32	—	—	—	—	—
90-91—Torpedo Yaroslavl	USSR	45	14	7	21	30	—	—	—	—	—
91-92—Dynamo Moscow	CIS	40	13	19	32	25	—	—	—	—	—

KARJALAINEN, KYOSTI
RW, KINGS

PERSONAL: Born June 19, 1967, at Gavle, Sweden. . . . 6-1/190. . . . Shoots right.
TRANSACTIONS/CAREER NOTES: Selected by Los Angeles Kings in seventh round (sixth Kings pick, 132nd overall) of NHL entry draft (June 13, 1987).

Season Team	League	REGULAR SEASON					PLAYOFFS				
		Gms.	G	A	Pts.	Pen.	Gms.	G	A	Pts.	Pen.
86-87—Brynas	Sweden	11	3	2	5	0	—	—	—	—	—
87-88—Brynas	Sweden	20	2	1	3	10	—	—	—	—	—
88-89—Brynas	Sweden	39	20	17	37	16	—	—	—	—	—
89-90—Brynas	Sweden	39	17	15	32	16	5	0	3	3	0
90-91—Phoenix	IHL	70	14	35	49	10	6	2	3	5	6
91-92—Phoenix	IHL	43	14	22	36	30	—	—	—	—	—
—Los Angeles	NHL	28	1	8	9	12	3	0	1	1	2
NHL totals		28	1	8	9	12	3	0	1	1	2

KARPA, DAVID
D, NORDIQUES

PERSONAL: Born May 7, 1971, at Regina, Sask. . . . 6-1/193. . . . Shoots right. . . . Full name: David James Karpa.
COLLEGE: Ferris State (Mich.).
TRANSACTIONS/CAREER NOTES: Selected by Quebec Nordiques in fourth round (fourth Nordiques pick, 68th overall) of NHL entry draft (June 22, 1991).

Season Team	League	REGULAR SEASON					PLAYOFFS				
		Gms.	G	A	Pts.	Pen.	Gms.	G	A	Pts.	Pen.
88-89—Notre Dame	SCMHL		16	37	53		—	—	—	—	—
89-90—Notre Dame	SCMHL	43	9	19	28	271	—	—	—	—	—
90-91—Ferris State	CCHA	41	6	19	25	109	—	—	—	—	—
91-92—Ferris State	CCHA	34	7	12	19	124	—	—	—	—	—
—Halifax	AHL	2	0	0	0	4	—	—	—	—	—
—Quebec	NHL	4	0	0	0	14	—	—	—	—	—
NHL totals		4	0	0	0	14					

KASATONOV, ALEXEI
D, DEVILS

PERSONAL: Born October 14, 1959, at Leningrad, U.S.S.R. . . . 6-1/215. . . . Shoots left.
TRANSACTIONS/CAREER NOTES: Selected by New Jersey Devils in 12th round (ninth Devils pick, 225th overall) of NHL entry draft (June 8, 1983). . . . Broke toe on right foot (February 1990). . . . Suffered from hemorrhoids (December 1991); missed three games.
HONORS: Named to Soviet League All-Star first team (1979-80 through 1987-88).
MISCELLANEOUS: Member of 1980 silver-medal-winning and 1984 and 1988 gold-medal-winning U.S.S.R. Olympic teams.

Season Team	League	REGULAR SEASON					PLAYOFFS				
		Gms.	G	A	Pts.	Pen.	Gms.	G	A	Pts.	Pen.
76-77—Leningrad SKA	USSR	7	0	0	0	0	—	—	—	—	—
77-78—Leningrad SKA	USSR	35	4	7	11	15	—	—	—	—	—
78-79—CSKA Moscow	USSR	40	5	14	19	30	—	—	—	—	—
79-80—CSKA Moscow	USSR	37	5	8	13	26	—	—	—	—	—
80-81—CSKA Moscow	USSR	47	10	12	22	38	—	—	—	—	—
81-82—CSKA Moscow	USSR	46	12	27	39	45	—	—	—	—	—
82-83—CSKA Moscow	USSR	44	12	19	31	37	—	—	—	—	—
83-84—CSKA Moscow	USSR	39	12	24	36	20	—	—	—	—	—
84-85—CSKA Moscow	USSR	40	18	18	36	26	—	—	—	—	—
85-86—CSKA Moscow	USSR	40	6	17	23	27	—	—	—	—	—
86-87—CSKA Moscow	USSR	40	13	17	30	16	—	—	—	—	—
87-88—CSKA Moscow	USSR	43	8	12	20	8	—	—	—	—	—
88-89—CSKA Moscow	USSR	41	8	14	22	8	—	—	—	—	—

K

Season Team	League	REGULAR SEASON					PLAYOFFS				
		Gms.	G	A	Pts.	Pen.	Gms.	G	A	Pts.	Pen.
89-90—New Jersey	NHL	39	6	15	21	16	6	0	3	3	14
—Utica	AHL	3	0	2	2	7	—	—	—	—	—
90-91—New Jersey	NHL	78	10	31	41	76	7	1	3	4	8
91-92—New Jersey	NHL	76	12	28	40	70	7	1	1	2	12
NHL totals		193	28	74	102	162	20	2	7	9	34

KASPARAITIS, DARIUS
D, ISLANDERS

PERSONAL: Born October 16, 1972, at Elektrenai, U.S.S.R. . . . . 5-11/187. . . . Shoots left.
TRANSACTIONS/CAREER NOTES: Selected by New York Islanders in first round (first Islanders pick, fifth overall) of NHL entry draft (June 20, 1992).
MISCELLANEOUS: Member of 1992 gold-medal-winning Unified Olympic team.

Season Team	League	REGULAR SEASON					PLAYOFFS				
		Gms.	G	A	Pts.	Pen.	Gms.	G	A	Pts.	Pen.
89-90—Dynamo Moscow	USSR	1	0	0	0	0	—	—	—	—	—
90-91—Dynamo Moscow	USSR	17	0	1	1	10	—	—	—	—	—
91-92—Dynamo Moscow	CIS	31	2	10	12	14	—	—	—	—	—
—Unified Olympic Team	Int'l	8	0	2	2		—	—	—	—	—

KASPER, STEVE
C, FLYERS

PERSONAL: Born September 28, 1961, at Montreal. . . . 5-8/175. . . . Shoots left. . . . Full name: Stephen Neil Kasper.
TRANSACTIONS/CAREER NOTES: Selected by Boston Bruins in fourth round (third Bruins pick, 81st overall) of NHL entry draft (June 11, 1980). . . . Suffered hip pointer (October 17, 1981). . . . Underwent surgery to remove torn shoulder cartilage (November 9, 1982). . . . Underwent surgery to left shoulder for a torn capsule (December 7, 1982). . . . Suffered concussion (April 1983). . . . Separated left shoulder (November 1983). . . . Underwernt surgery to shoulder (January 7, 1984). . . . Reinjured shoulder (February 1984). . . . Traded by Bruins with LW Jay Miller to Los Angeles Kings for C Bobby Carpenter (January 23, 1989). . . . Ruptured sinus cavity and fractured eye socket (January 2, 1991); missed 10 games. . . . Traded by Kings with D Steve Duchesne and fourth-round pick in 1991 draft (D Aris Brimanis) to Philadelphia Flyers for D Jeff Chychrun and rights to RW Jari Kurri (May 30, 1991). . . . Tore knee ligaments (November 20, 1991); missed remainder of season.
HONORS: Won Frank J. Selke Trophy (1981-82).

Season Team	League	REGULAR SEASON					PLAYOFFS				
		Gms.	G	A	Pts.	Pen.	Gms.	G	A	Pts.	Pen.
77-78—Verdun	QMJHL	63	26	45	71	16	—	—	—	—	—
78-79—Verdun	QMJHL	67	37	67	104	53	11	7	6	13	22
79-80—Sorel	QMJHL	70	57	65	122	117	—	—	—	—	—
80-81—Sorel	QMJHL	2	5	2	7	0	—	—	—	—	—
—Boston	NHL	76	21	35	56	94	3	0	1	1	0
81-82—Boston	NHL	73	20	31	51	72	11	3	6	9	22
82-83—Boston	NHL	24	2	6	8	24	12	2	1	3	10
83-84—Boston	NHL	27	3	11	14	19	3	0	0	0	7
84-85—Boston	NHL	77	16	24	40	33	5	1	0	1	9
85-86—Boston	NHL	80	17	23	40	73	3	1	0	1	4
86-87—Boston	NHL	79	20	30	50	51	3	0	2	2	0
87-88—Boston	NHL	79	26	44	70	35	23	7	6	13	10
88-89—Boston	NHL	49	10	16	26	49	—	—	—	—	—
—Los Angeles	NHL	29	9	15	24	14	11	1	5	6	10
89-90—Los Angeles	NHL	77	17	28	45	27	10	1	1	2	2
90-91—Los Angeles	NHL	67	9	19	28	33	10	4	6	10	8
91-92—Philadelphia	NHL	16	3	2	5	10	—	—	—	—	—
NHL totals		753	173	284	457	534	94	20	28	48	82

KASTELIC, ED
RW, WHALERS

PERSONAL: Born January 29, 1964, at Toronto. . . . 6-4/215. . . . Shoots right. . . . Full name: Edward Kastelic.
TRANSACTIONS/CAREER NOTES: Selected by Washington Capitals as an underage junior in sixth round (fourth Capitals pick, 110th overall) of NHL entry draft (June 9, 1982). . . . Fractured left cheekbone in preseason game (September 30, 1985). . . . Suspended by Capitals (January 20, 1986). . . . Traded by Capitals with D Grant Jennings to Hartford Whalers for D Neil Sheehy and RW Mike Millar (July 1988). . . . Suspended 20 games by AHL for biting linesman during a fight (December 30, 1988). . . . Cracked rib (October 1990); missed seven games. . . . Injured rotator cuff of right shoulder (February 3, 1991). . . . Suspended 10 games by NHL for fighting (February 10, 1991).
MISCELLANEOUS: Played defense prior to 1981-82 season.

Season Team	League	REGULAR SEASON					PLAYOFFS				
		Gms.	G	A	Pts.	Pen.	Gms.	G	A	Pts.	Pen.
81-82—London	OHL	68	5	18	23	63	4	0	1	1	4
82-83—London	OHL	68	12	11	23	96	3	0	0	0	5
83-84—London	OHL	68	17	16	33	218	8	0	2	2	41
84-85—Fort Wayne	IHL	5	1	0	1	37	—	—	—	—	—
—Binghamton	AHL	4	0	0	0	7	—	—	—	—	—
—Moncton	AHL	62	5	11	16	187	—	—	—	—	—
85-86—Washington	NHL	15	0	0	0	73	—	—	—	—	—
—Binghamton	AHL	23	7	9	16	76	—	—	—	—	—
86-87—Binghamton	AHL	48	17	11	28	124	—	—	—	—	—
—Washington	NHL	23	1	1	2	83	5	1	0	1	13

K

Season	Team	League	REGULAR SEASON					PLAYOFFS				
			Gms.	G	A	Pts.	Pen.	Gms.	G	A	Pts.	Pen.
87-88—Binghamton		AHL	6	4	1	5	6	—	—	—	—	—
—Washington		NHL	35	1	0	1	78	1	0	0	0	19
88-89—Hartford		NHL	10	0	2	2	15	—	—	—	—	—
—Binghamton		AHL	35	9	6	15	124	—	—	—	—	—
89-90—Hartford		NHL	67	6	2	8	198	2	0	0	0	0
90-91—Hartford		NHL	45	2	2	4	211	—	—	—	—	—
91-92—Hartford		NHL	25	1	3	4	61	—	—	—	—	—
NHL totals			220	11	10	21	719	8	1	0	1	32

KEANE, MIKE

RW, CANADIENS

PERSONAL: Born May 29, 1967, at Winnipeg, Man.... 5-10/178.... Shoots right.
TRANSACTIONS/CAREER NOTES: Signed as free agent by Montreal Canadiens (March 1987).... Separated right shoulder (December 21, 1988).... Suffered laceration of left kneecap (October 31, 1990); missed seven games.... Injured neck (March 1991).... Sprained ankle (January 16, 1992); missed four games.... Resprained ankle (February 1, 1992); missed 10 games.... Bruised ankle (March 11, 1992); missed one game.

Season	Team	League	REGULAR SEASON					PLAYOFFS				
			Gms.	G	A	Pts.	Pen.	Gms.	G	A	Pts.	Pen.
83-84—Winnipeg		WHL	1	0	0	0	0	—	—	—	—	—
84-85—Moose Jaw		WHL	65	17	26	43	141	—	—	—	—	—
85-86—Moose Jaw		WHL	67	34	49	83	162	13	6	8	14	9
86-87—Moose Jaw		WHL	53	25	45	70	107	9	3	9	12	11
—Sherbrooke		AHL	—	—	—	—	—	9	2	2	4	16
87-88—Sherbrooke		AHL	78	25	43	68	70	6	1	1	2	18
88-89—Montreal		NHL	69	16	19	35	69	21	4	3	7	17
89-90—Montreal		NHL	74	9	15	24	78	11	0	1	1	8
90-91—Montreal		NHL	73	13	23	36	50	12	3	2	5	6
91-92—Montreal		NHL	67	11	30	41	64	8	1	1	2	16
NHL totals			283	49	87	136	261	52	8	7	15	47

KECZMER, DAN

D, WHALERS

PERSONAL: Born May 25, 1968, at Mt. Clemens, Mich.... 6-1/190.... Shoots left.... Full name: Daniel Leonard Keczmer.
COLLEGE: Lake Superior State (Mich.).
TRANSACTIONS/CAREER NOTES: Selected by Minnesota North Stars in 10th round (11th North Stars pick, 201st overall) of NHL entry draft (June 21, 1986).... Injured shoulder (February 2, 1990).... Claimed by San Jose Sharks as part of ownership change with North Stars (October 1990).... Traded by Sharks to Hartford Whalers for C Dean Evason (October 2, 1991).... Released by U.S. National team prior to Olympics (January 1992).
HONORS: Named to CCHA All-Star second team (1989-90).

Season	Team	League	REGULAR SEASON					PLAYOFFS				
			Gms.	G	A	Pts.	Pen.	Gms.	G	A	Pts.	Pen.
86-87—Lake Superior State		CCHA	38	3	5	8	28	—	—	—	—	—
87-88—Lake Superior State		CCHA	41	2	15	17	34	—	—	—	—	—
88-89—Lake Superior State		CCHA	46	3	26	29	70	—	—	—	—	—
89-90—Lake Superior State		CCHA	43	13	23	36	48	—	—	—	—	—
90-91—Minnesota		NHL	9	0	1	1	6	—	—	—	—	—
—Kalamazoo		IHL	60	4	20	24	60	9	1	2	3	10
91-92—U.S. National Team		Int'l	51	3	11	14	56	—	—	—	—	—
—Springfield		AHL	18	3	4	7	10	4	0	0	0	6
—Hartford		NHL	1	0	0	0	0	—	—	—	—	—
NHL totals			10	0	1	1	6					

KEENAN, CORY

D, WHALERS

PERSONAL: Born March 19, 1970, at St. Louis.... 6-2/185.... Shoots left.... Son of Larry Keenan, left winger, four NHL teams (1961-62 and 1967-68 through 1971-72).
TRANSACTIONS/CAREER NOTES: Selected by Hartford Whalers in sixth round (fifth Whalers pick, 120th overall) of NHL entry draft (June 16, 1990).
HONORS: Named to OUAA All-Star second team (1990-91).

Season	Team	League	REGULAR SEASON					PLAYOFFS				
			Gms.	G	A	Pts.	Pen.	Gms.	G	A	Pts.	Pen.
86-87—St. Mary's Jr. B		OHA	29	3	8	11	52	—	—	—	—	—
87-88—Kitchener		OHL	66	2	18	20	32	—	—	—	—	—
88-89—Kitchener		OHL	66	15	35	50	69	—	—	—	—	—
89-90—Kitchener		OHL	66	13	35	48	88	17	2	11	13	14
90-91—University of Waterloo		OUAA	41	8	14	22	14	—	—	—	—	—
91-92—University of Waterloo		OUAA	22	3	24	27	50	—	—	—	—	—

KELLOGG, ROBERT

D, BLACKHAWKS

PERSONAL: Born February 16, 1971, at Springfield, Mass.... 6-4/210.... Shoots left. ... Full name: Robert Edward Kellogg.
COLLEGE: Northeastern.
TRANSACTIONS/CAREER NOTES: Selected by Chicago Blackhawks in third round (third Blackhawks pick, 48th overall) of NHL entry draft (June 17, 1989).... Suffered mononucleosis (November 1990); missed 30 games.

Season Team	League	REGULAR SEASON Gms.	G	A	Pts.	Pen.	PLAYOFFS Gms.	G	A	Pts.	Pen.
87-88—Springfield Jr. B..............	NEJHL	38	8	36	44	54	—	—	—	—	—
88-89—Springfield Jr. B..............	NEJHL		13	34	47		—	—	—	—	—
89-90—Northeastern University...	Hockey East	36	3	12	15	30	—	—	—	—	—
90-91—Northeastern University...	Hockey East	2	0	0	0	6	—	—	—	—	—
91-92—Northeastern University...	Hockey East	27	2	3	5	34	—	—	—	—	—

KENNEDY, DEAN
D, JETS

PERSONAL: Born January 18, 1963, at Redvers, Sask.... 6-2/200.... Shoots right.... Full name: Edward Dean Kennedy.
TRANSACTIONS/CAREER NOTES: Selected by Los Angeles Kings as underage junior in second round (second Kings pick, 39th overall) of NHL entry draft (June 10, 1981).... Suspended four games by NHL for off-ice altercation (February 18, 1983).... Injured knee; missed part of 1981-82 season.... Suffered hip pointer (March 1987).... Broke finger (November 1987).... Injured groin (March 1988).... Suffered concussion (November 10, 1988).... Traded by Kings with D Denis Larocque to New York Rangers for LW Igor Liba, C Todd Elik, D Michael Boyce and future considerations (December 12, 1988).... Traded by Rangers to Los Angeles Kings for fifth-round pick in 1990 draft (February 3, 1989).... Traded by Kings to Buffalo Sabres for fourth-round pick in 1990 draft (October 4, 1989).... Suffered hip pointer (January 31, 1991); missed nine games.... Broke jaw (April 5, 1991).... Traded by Sabres with LW Darrin Shannon and D Dean Kennedy to Winnipeg Jets for RW Dave McIlwain, D Gordon Donnelly, sixth-round pick in 1992 draft and future considerations (October 11, 1991).... Injured knee (November 20, 1991).

Season Team	League	REGULAR SEASON Gms.	G	A	Pts.	Pen.	PLAYOFFS Gms.	G	A	Pts.	Pen.
79-80—Weyburn Red Wings........	SJHL	57	12	20	32	64	—	—	—	—	—
—Brandon..............................	WHL	1	0	0	0	0	—	—	—	—	—
80-81—Brandon..............................	WHL	71	3	29	32	157	5	0	2	2	7
81-82—Brandon..............................	WHL	49	5	38	43	103	—	—	—	—	—
82-83—Brandon..............................	WHL	14	2	15	17	22	—	—	—	—	—
—Los Angeles.....................	NHL	55	0	12	12	97	—	—	—	—	—
—Saskatoon	WHL	—	—	—	—	—	4	0	3	3	0
83-84—New Haven	AHL	26	1	7	8	23	—	—	—	—	—
—Los Angeles.....................	NHL	37	1	5	6	50	—	—	—	—	—
84-85—New Haven	AHL	76	3	14	17	104	—	—	—	—	—
85-86—Los Angeles......................	NHL	78	2	10	12	132	—	—	—	—	—
86-87—Los Angeles......................	NHL	66	6	14	20	91	5	0	2	2	10
87-88—Los Angeles......................	NHL	58	1	11	12	158	4	0	1	1	10
88-89—New York Rangers	NHL	16	0	1	1	40	—	—	—	—	—
—Los Angeles.....................	NHL	51	3	10	13	63	11	0	2	2	8
89-90—Buffalo...............................	NHL	80	2	12	14	53	6	1	1	2	12
90-91—Buffalo...............................	NHL	64	4	8	12	119	2	0	1	1	17
91-92—Winnipeg............................	NHL	18	2	4	6	21	2	0	0	0	0
NHL totals..		523	21	87	108	824	30	1	7	8	57

KENNEDY, SHELDON
RW, RED WINGS

PERSONAL: Born June 15, 1969, at Brandon, Man.... 5-11/170.... Shoots right.
TRANSACTIONS/CAREER NOTES: Broke ankle (January 18, 1987); missed six weeks. ... Selected by Detroit Red Wings in fourth round (fifth Red Wings pick, 80th overall) of NHL entry draft (June 11, 1988).... Separated shoulder (December 5, 1989).... Injured thumb (March 2, 1990).... Took leave of absence to attend alcohol treatment program (March 21, 1990). ... Injured left arm in automobile accident (Summer 1990); missed 48 games.... Suffered from tonsilitis (February 8, 1991); missed two games.... Suffered from food poisoning (February 19, 1991).... Sent to alchohol treatment center for evaluation (March 27, 1991).

Season Team	League	REGULAR SEASON Gms.	G	A	Pts.	Pen.	PLAYOFFS Gms.	G	A	Pts.	Pen.
86-87—Swift Current...................	WHL	49	23	41	64	64	4	0	3	3	4
87-88—Swift Current...................	WHL	59	53	64	117	45	10	8	9	17	12
88-89—Swift Current...................	WHL	51	58	48	106	92	—	—	—	—	—
89-90—Detroit	NHL	20	2	7	9	10	—	—	—	—	—
—Adirondack	AHL	26	11	15	26	35	—	—	—	—	—
90-91—Adirondack	AHL	11	1	3	4	8	—	—	—	—	—
—Detroit	NHL	7	1	0	1	12	—	—	—	—	—
91-92—Adirondack	AHL	46	25	24	49	56	16	5	9	14	12
—Detroit	NHL	27	3	8	11	24	—	—	—	—	—
NHL totals..		54	6	15	21	46					

KERR, ALAN
RW, RED WINGS

PERSONAL: Born March 28, 1964, at Hazelton, B.C.... 5-11/195.... Shoots right.... Cousin of Reg Kerr, left winger, Cleveland Barons, Chicago Blackhawks and Edmonton Oilers (1977-78 through 1983-84).
TRANSACTIONS/CAREER NOTES: Selected by New York Islanders as underage junior in fourth round (fourth Islanders pick, 84th overall) of NHL entry draft (June 9, 1982).... Lacerated face (April 1988).... Sprained left knee (December 1988).... Bruised left knee (April 1990).... Bruised kidney (September 23, 1990).... Lacerated eyelid (October 15, 1990).... Underwent surgery to left eye (October 31, 1990).... Traded by Islanders to Detroit Red Wings for D Rick Green and future considerations (May 28, 1991).... Injured ankle (February 1992); missed 10 games.
HONORS: Named to WHL All-Star first team (1983-84).

Season	Team	League	REGULAR SEASON Gms.	G	A	Pts.	Pen.	PLAYOFFS Gms.	G	A	Pts.	Pen.
81-82	Seattle	WHL	68	15	18	33	107	10	6	6	12	32
82-83	Seattle	WHL	71	38	53	91	183	4	2	3	5	0
83-84	Seattle	WHL	66	46	66	112	141	5	1	4	5	12
84-85	Springfield	AHL	62	32	27	59	140	4	1	2	3	2
	New York Islanders	NHL	19	3	1	4	24	4	1	0	1	4
85-86	Springfield	AHL	71	35	36	71	127	—	—	—	—	—
	New York Islanders	NHL	7	0	1	1	16	1	0	0	0	0
86-87	New York Islanders	NHL	72	7	10	17	175	14	1	4	5	25
87-88	New York Islanders	NHL	80	24	34	58	198	6	1	0	1	14
88-89	New York Islanders	NHL	71	20	18	38	144	—	—	—	—	—
89-90	New York Islanders	NHL	75	15	20	35	129	4	0	0	0	10
90-91	Capital District	AHL	43	11	21	32	131	—	—	—	—	—
	New York Islanders	NHL	2	0	0	0	5	—	—	—	—	—
91-92	Detroit	NHL	58	3	8	11	133	9	2	0	2	17
NHL totals			384	72	92	164	824	38	5	4	9	70

KERR, TIM
RW, WHALERS

PERSONAL: Born January 5, 1960, at Windsor, Ont. . . . 6-3/228. . . . Shoots right. . . . Full name: Timothy Kerr.

TRANSACTIONS/CAREER NOTES: Signed as free agent by Philadelphia Flyers (January 1980). . . . Injured shoulder (November 1, 1980). . . . Injured knee cartilage (October 1981). . . . Underwent hernia surgery (September 1982). . . . Stretched knee ligaments and underwent surgery (November 10, 1982). . . . Broke fibula of left leg (March 1983). . . . Strained knee ligaments (March 1985). . . . Strained right knee (May 5, 1985). . . . Suffered viral infection of the brain lining (September 1985). . . . Pulled hamstring (November 29, 1986); missed three games. . . . Tore ligaments and damaged cartilage in left shoulder (May 1987); missed six playoff games. . . . Underwent five operations to repair left shoulder (June 1987-November 1987); missed 66 games. . . . Served as assistant coach behind Flyer's bench during rehabilitation (December 1987). . . . Pulled muscle in left shoulder (December 27, 1988). . . . Bruised left shoulder (October 6, 1989); missed four games. . . . Tore rotator cuff in left shoulder and underwent surgery to remove bone chips and scar tissue (November 12, 1989); missed 33 games. . . . Separated left shoulder and underwent surgery (March 18, 1990). . . . Missed four games after death of wife (October 17, 1990). . . . Tore cartilage in right knee (November 11, 1990); missed 22 games. . . . Reinjured right knee (January 7, 1991); missed eight games. . . . Injured groin (February 5, 1991); missed 16 games. . . . Selected by San Jose Sharks in NHL expansion draft (May 30, 1991). . . . Traded by Sharks to New York Rangers for LW Brian Mullen and future considerations. (May 30, 1991). . . . Injured shoulder (October 11, 1991); missed 39 games. . . . Underwent shoulder surgery (November 13, 1991). . . . Irritated right knee (February 17, 1992); missed four games. . . . Strained back (March 14, 1992); missed three games. . . . Traded by Rangers to Hartford Whalers for conditional pick in 1993 draft (July 8, 1992).

HONORS: Named to THE SPORTING NEWS All-Star first team (1986-87). . . . Named to NHL All-Star second team (1986-87). . . . Won Bill Masterton Memorial Trophy (1988-89).

RECORDS: Holds NHL single-season record for most power-play goals—34 (1985-86). . . . Holds NHL single-game playoff record for most power-play goals in one period—3 (April 13, 1985). . . . Shares NHL single-game playoff records in power-play goals—3; goals in one period—4; and points in one period—4 (April 13, 1985).

Season	Team	League	REGULAR SEASON Gms.	G	A	Pts.	Pen.	PLAYOFFS Gms.	G	A	Pts.	Pen.
76-77	Windsor	OMJHL	9	2	4	6	7	—	—	—	—	—
77-78	Kingston	OMJHL	67	14	25	39	33	—	—	—	—	—
78-79	Kingston	OMJHL	57	17	25	42	27	6	1	1	2	2
79-80	Kingston	OMJHL	63	40	33	73	39	3	0	1	1	16
	Maine	AHL	7	2	4	6	2	—	—	—	—	—
80-81	Philadelphia	NHL	68	22	23	45	84	10	1	3	4	2
81-82	Philadelphia	NHL	61	21	30	51	138	4	0	2	2	2
82-83	Philadelphia	NHL	24	11	8	19	6	2	2	0	2	0
83-84	Philadelphia	NHL	79	54	39	93	29	3	0	0	0	0
84-85	Philadelphia	NHL	74	54	44	98	57	12	10	4	14	13
85-86	Philadelphia	NHL	76	58	26	84	79	5	3	3	6	8
86-87	Philadelphia	NHL	75	58	37	95	57	12	8	5	13	2
87-88	Philadelphia	NHL	8	3	2	5	12	6	1	3	4	4
88-89	Philadelphia	NHL	69	48	40	88	73	19	14	11	25	27
89-90	Philadelphia	NHL	40	24	24	48	34	—	—	—	—	—
90-91	Philadelphia	NHL	27	10	14	24	8	—	—	—	—	—
91-92	New York Rangers	NHL	32	7	11	18	12	8	1	0	1	0
NHL totals			633	370	298	668	589	81	40	31	71	58

KETTERER, MARKUS
G, SABRES

PERSONAL: Born August 23, 1967, at Helsinki, Finland. . . . 5-11/169. . . . Shoots left.

TRANSACTIONS/CAREER NOTES: Selected by Buffalo Sabres in fifth round (sixth Sabres pick, 107th overall) of NHL entry draft (June 20, 1992).

Season	Team	League	REGULAR SEASON Gms.	Min.	W	L	T	GA	SO	Avg.	PLAYOFFS Gms.	Min.	W	L	GA	SO	Avg.
87-88	Jokerit	Finland	21					61	0		—	—	—	—	—	—	—
88-89	TPS Turku	Finland	34	2021				95	2	2.82	3	139			6	0	2.59
89-90	TPS Turku	Finland	29	1709				68	1	2.39	7	422			15	1	2.13
90-91	TPS Turku	Finland	36	2022				85	2	2.52	8	440			13	2	1.77
91-92	Finland Olympic Team	Int'l	3	180				8	0	2.67	—	—	—	—	—	—	—
	Jokerit	Finland	37	2128				97	0	2.73	—	—	—	—	—	—	—

KHARIN, SERGEI
RW, NORDIQUES

PERSONAL: Born February 20, 1963, at Odintsovo, U.S.S.R. . . . 5-8/165. . . . Shoots right.
. . . Full name: Sergei Anatoljevich Kharin.
TRANSACTIONS/CAREER NOTES: Selected by Winnipeg Jets in 12th round (15th Jets pick, 240th overall) of NHL entry draft (June 1989). . . . Traded by Jets to Quebec Nordiques for D Shawn Anderson (October 22, 1991).

Season Team	League	REGULAR SEASON					PLAYOFFS				
		Gms.	G	A	Pts.	Pen.	Gms.	G	A	Pts.	Pen.
80-81—Soviet Wings	USSR	2	0	0	0	0	—	—	—	—	—
81-82—Soviet Wings	USSR	34	4	3	7	10	—	—	—	—	—
82-83—Soviet Wings	USSR	49	5	5	10	20	—	—	—	—	—
83-84—Soviet Wings	USSR	33	5	3	8	18	—	—	—	—	—
84-85—Soviet Wings	USSR	34	12	8	20	6	—	—	—	—	—
85-86—Soviet Wings	USSR	38	15	14	29	19	—	—	—	—	—
86-87—Soviet Wings	USSR	40	16	11	27	14	—	—	—	—	—
87-88—Soviet Wings	USSR	45	17	13	30	20	—	—	—	—	—
88-89—Soviet Wings	USSR	44	15	9	24	14	—	—	—	—	—
89-90—Soviet Wings	USSR	47	12	5	17	28	—	—	—	—	—
90-91—Winnipeg	NHL	7	2	3	5	2	—	—	—	—	—
—Moncton	AHL	66	22	18	40	38	5	1	0	1	2
91-92—Halifax	AHL	40	10	12	22	15	—	—	—	—	—
NHL totals		7	2	3	5	2	—	—	—	—	—

KHMYLEV, YURI
LW, SABRES

PERSONAL: Born August 9, 1964, at Moscow, U.S.S.R. . . . 6-1/196. . . . Shoots right.
TRANSACTIONS/CAREER NOTES: Selected by Buffalo Sabres in fifth round (seventh Sabres pick, 108th overall) of NHL entry draft (June 20, 1992).
MISCELLANEOUS: Member of 1992 gold-medal-winning Unified Olympic team.

Season Team	League	REGULAR SEASON					PLAYOFFS				
		Gms.	G	A	Pts.	Pen.	Gms.	G	A	Pts.	Pen.
81-82—Krylja Sovetov	USSR	8	2	2	4	2	—	—	—	—	—
82-83—Krylja Sovetov	USSR	51	9	7	16	14	—	—	—	—	—
83-84—Krylja Sovetov	USSR	43	7	8	15	10	—	—	—	—	—
84-85—Krylja Sovetov	USSR	30	11	4	15	24	—	—	—	—	—
85-86—Krylja Sovetov	USSR	40	24	9	33	22	—	—	—	—	—
86-87—Krylja Sovetov	USSR	40	15	15	30	48	—	—	—	—	—
87-88—Krylja Sovetov	USSR	48	21	8	29	46	—	—	—	—	—
88-89—Krylja Sovetov	USSR	44	16	18	34	38	—	—	—	—	—
89-90—Krylja Sovetov	USSR	44	14	13	27	30	—	—	—	—	—
90-91—Krylja Sovetov	USSR	45	25	14	39	26	—	—	—	—	—
91-92—Unified Olympic Team	Int'l	8	4	6	10		—	—	—	—	—
—Krylja Sovetov	CIS	42	19	17	36	20	—	—	—	—	—

KHRISTICH, DIMITRI
C, CAPITALS

PERSONAL: Born July 23, 1969, at Kiev, U.S.S.R. . . . 6-2/190. . . . Shoots right.
TRANSACTIONS/CAREER NOTES: Selected by Washington Capitals in sixth round (sixth Capitals pick, 120th overall) of NHL entry draft (June 11, 1988). . . . Injured hip (February 16, 1990); missed six games.

Season Team	League	REGULAR SEASON					PLAYOFFS				
		Gms.	G	A	Pts.	Pen.	Gms.	G	A	Pts.	Pen.
88-89—Sokol Kiev	USSR	42	17	8	25	15	—	—	—	—	—
89-90—Sokol Kiev	USSR	47	14	22	36	32	—	—	—	—	—
90-91—Sokol Kiev	USSR	28	10	12	22	20	—	—	—	—	—
—Baltimore	AHL	3	0	0	0	0	—	—	—	—	—
—Washington	NHL	40	13	14	27	21	11	1	3	4	6
91-92—Washington	NHL	80	36	37	73	35	7	3	2	5	15
NHL totals		120	49	51	100	56	18	4	5	9	21

KIDD, IAN
D, CANUCKS

PERSONAL: Born May 11, 1964, at Gresham, Ore. . . . 6-0/197. . . . Shoots right.
COLLEGE: North Dakota.
TRANSACTIONS/CAREER NOTES: Selected first overall in NHL supplemental draft by Detroit Red Wings (October 1986); choice was later voided by NHL. . . . Signed as free agent by Vancouver Canucks (August 1987).
HONORS: Named to NCAA All-America West first team (1986-87).

Season Team	League	REGULAR SEASON					PLAYOFFS				
		Gms.	G	A	Pts.	Pen.	Gms.	G	A	Pts.	Pen.
85-86—Univ. of North Dakota	WCHA	37	6	16	22	65	—	—	—	—	—
86-87—Univ. of North Dakota	WCHA	47	13	47	60	58	—	—	—	—	—
87-88—Fredericton	AHL	53	1	21	22	70	12	0	4	4	22
—Vancouver	NHL	19	4	7	11	25	—	—	—	—	—
88-89—Vancouver	NHL	1	0	0	0	0	—	—	—	—	—
—Milwaukee	IHL	76	13	40	53	124	4	0	2	2	7
89-90—Milwaukee	IHL	65	11	36	47	86	6	2	5	7	0
90-91—Milwaukee	IHL	72	5	26	31	41	6	0	1	1	2
91-92—Milwaukee	IHL	80	9	24	33	75	5	0	1	1	11
NHL totals		20	4	7	11	25					

KIDD, TREVOR
G, FLAMES

PERSONAL: Born March 26, 1972, at St. Boniface, Man.... 6-2/ 176.... Shoots left.
TRANSACTIONS/CAREER NOTES: Broke finger (December 1987).... Selected by Calgary Flames in first round (first Flames pick, 11th overall) of NHL entry draft (June 16, 1990).... Traded by Brandon Wheat Kings with D Bart Cote to Spokane Chiefs for RW Bobby House, C Marty Murray and G Don Blishen (January 21, 1991).
HONORS: Won Del Wilson Trophy (1989-90).... Named to WHL All-Star first team (1989-90).
MISCELLANEOUS: Member of 1992 silver-medal-winning Canadian Olympic team.

					REGULAR SEASON						PLAYOFFS					
Season	Team	League	Gms.	Min.	W	L	T	GA	SO	Avg.	Gms.	Min.	W	L	GA	SO	Avg.
88-89—Brandon		WHL	32	1509				102	0	4.06	—	—	—	—	—	—	—
89-90—Brandon		WHL	*63	*3676	24	32	2	254	2	4.15	—	—	—	—	—	—	—
90-91—Brandon		WHL	30	1730	10	19	1	117	0	4.06	—	—	—	—	—	—	—
—Spokane Chiefs		WHL	14	749	8	3	0	44	0	3.52	15	926	*14	1	32	*2	*2.07
91-92—Can. National Team		Int'l	28	1349	18	4	4	79	2	3.51	—	—	—	—	—	—	—
—Can. Olympic Team		Int'l	1	60	1	0	0	0	1	0.00	—	—	—	—	—	—	—
—Calgary		NHL	2	120	1	1	0	8	0	4.00	—	—	—	—	—	—	—
NHL totals			2	120	1	1	0	8	0	4.00							

KIMBLE, DARIN
RW, LIGHTNING

PERSONAL: Born November 22, 1968, at Lucky Lake, Sask.... 6-2/205.... Shoots right.
TRANSACTIONS/CAREER NOTES: Traded by Brandon Wheat Kings with Kerry Angus to Prince Albert Raiders for C Graham Garden, C Ryan Stewart and Kim Rasmussen (September 1986).... Selected by Quebec Nordiques in fourth round (fifth Nordiques pick, 66th overall) of NHL entry draft (June 11, 1988).... Suspended eight games by NHL for slashing (March 23, 1989); missed final four games of 1988-89 season and first four games of 1989-90.... Sprained right wrist (September 1989).... Bruised ribs (November 5, 1989).... Pulled abdominal muscle (December 1990).... Bruised right hand (January 24, 1991).... Traded by Nordiques to St. Louis Blues for RW Herb Raglan, D Tony Twist and LW Andy Rymsha (February 4, 1991).... Broke nose (February 1992). ... Traded by Blues with D Rob Robinson, G Pat Jablonski and RW Steve Tuttle to Tampa Bay Lightning for future considerations (June 19, 1992).

			REGULAR SEASON					PLAYOFFS				
Season	Team	League	Gms.	G	A	Pts.	Pen.	Gms.	G	A	Pts.	Pen.
84-85—Swift Current Jr. A		SAJHL	59	28	32	60	264	—	—	—	—	—
—Calgary		WHL	—	—	—	—	—	1	0	0	0	0
85-86—Calgary		WHL	37	14	8	22	93	—	—	—	—	—
—New Westminster		WHL	11	1	1	2	22	—	—	—	—	—
—Brandon		WHL	15	1	6	7	39	—	—	—	—	—
86-87—Prince Albert		WHL	68	17	13	30	190	—	—	—	—	—
87-88—Prince Albert		WHL	67	35	36	71	307	10	3	2	5	4
88-89—Halifax		AHL	39	8	6	14	188	—	—	—	—	—
—Quebec		NHL	26	3	1	4	149	—	—	—	—	—
89-90—Quebec		NHL	44	5	5	10	185	—	—	—	—	—
—Halifax		AHL	18	6	6	12	37	6	1	1	2	61
90-91—Halifax		AHL	7	1	4	5	20	—	—	—	—	—
—Quebec		NHL	35	2	5	7	114	—	—	—	—	—
—St. Louis		NHL	26	1	1	2	128	13	0	0	0	38
91-92—St. Louis		NHL	46	1	3	4	166	5	0	0	0	7
NHL totals			177	12	15	27	742	18	0	0	0	45

KING, DEREK
LW, ISLANDERS

PERSONAL: Born February 11, 1967, at Hamilton, Ont.... 6-1/210.... Shoots left.
TRANSACTIONS/CAREER NOTES: Selected by New York Islanders as underage junior in first round (second Islanders pick, 13th overall) of NHL entry draft (June 15, 1985).... Sprained right knee (September 1985).... Fractured left wrist (December 12, 1987).... Separated shoulder (November 23, 1988).... Suffered concussion (November 2, 1990).... Separated right shoulder (February 14, 1991).
HONORS: Won Emms Family Award (1984-85).... Named to OHL All-Star first team (1986-87).

			REGULAR SEASON					PLAYOFFS				
Season	Team	League	Gms.	G	A	Pts.	Pen.	Gms.	G	A	Pts.	Pen.
83-84—Hamilton Jr. A		OHA	37	10	14	24	142	—	—	—	—	—
84-85—Sault Ste. Marie		OHL	63	35	38	73	106	16	3	13	16	11
85-86—Sault Ste. Marie		OHL	25	12	17	29	33	—	—	—	—	—
—Oshawa		OHL	19	8	13	21	15	6	3	2	5	13
86-87—Oshawa		OHL	57	53	53	106	74	17	14	10	24	40
—New York Islanders		NHL	2	0	0	0	0	—	—	—	—	—
87-88—New York Islanders		NHL	55	12	24	36	30	5	0	2	2	2
—Springfield		AHL	10	7	6	13	6	—	—	—	—	—
88-89—Springfield		AHL	4	4	0	4	0	—	—	—	—	—
—New York Islanders		NHL	60	14	29	43	14	—	—	—	—	—
89-90—Springfield		AHL	21	11	12	23	33	—	—	—	—	—
—New York Islanders		NHL	46	13	27	40	20	4	0	0	0	4
90-91—New York Islanders		NHL	66	19	26	45	44	—	—	—	—	—
91-92—New York Islanders		NHL	80	40	38	78	46	—	—	—	—	—
NHL totals			309	98	144	242	154	9	0	2	2	6

KING, KRIS
LW/C, RANGERS

PERSONAL: Born February 18, 1966, at Bracebridge, Ont.... 5-11/208.... Shoots left.
TRANSACTIONS/CAREER NOTES: Selected by Washington Capitals as underage junior in fourth round (fourth pick, 80th overall) of NHL entry draft (June 9, 1984).... Signed as free agent by Detroit Red Wings (June 1987).... Traded by Red Wings to New York Rangers for LW Chris McRae and fifth-round pick in 1990 draft (September 7, 1989).... Sprained knee (January 7, 1991); missed six games.

K

Season Team	League	REGULAR SEASON					PLAYOFFS				
		Gms.	G	A	Pts.	Pen.	Gms.	G	A	Pts.	Pen.
82-83—Gravenhurst	SOJHL	32	72	53	125	115	—	—	—	—	—
83-84—Peterborough	OHL	62	13	18	31	168	8	3	3	6	14
84-85—Peterborough	OHL	61	18	35	53	222	16	2	8	10	28
85-86—Peterborough	OHL	58	19	40	59	254	8	4	0	4	21
86-87—Peterborough	OHL	46	23	33	56	160	12	5	8	13	41
—Binghamton	AHL	7	0	0	0	18	—	—	—	—	—
87-88—Adirondack	AHL	78	21	32	53	337	10	4	4	8	53
—Detroit	NHL	3	1	0	1	2	—	—	—	—	—
88-89—Detroit	NHL	55	2	3	5	168	2	0	0	0	2
89-90—New York Rangers	NHL	68	6	7	13	286	10	0	1	1	38
90-91—New York Rangers	NHL	72	11	14	25	154	6	2	0	2	36
91-92—New York Rangers	NHL	79	10	9	19	224	13	4	1	5	14
NHL totals		277	30	33	63	834	31	6	2	8	90

KING, SCOTT
G, RED WINGS

PERSONAL: Born June 25, 1967, at Thunder Bay, Ont. . . . 6-1/170. . . . Shoots left. . . . Full name: Scott Glenndale Martin King.
COLLEGE: Maine.
TRANSACTIONS/CAREER NOTES: Selected by Detroit Red Wings in 10th round (10th Red Wings pick, 190th overall) of NHL entry draft (June 21, 1986).
HONORS: Named to Hockey East All-Star first team (1987-88 and 1989-90). . . . Named to Hockey East All-Star second team (1988-89).

Season Team	League	REGULAR SEASON							PLAYOFFS						
		Gms.	Min.	W	L	T	GA	SO	Avg.	Gms.	Min.	W	L	GA SO	Avg.
85-86—Vernon	BCJHL	29	1718	17	9	0	134	0	4.68	—	—	—	—	— —	—
86-87—University of Maine	Hoc. East	21	1111	11	6	1	58	0	3.13	—	—	—	—	— —	—
87-88—University of Maine	Hoc. East	33	1762	25	5	1	91	0	3.10	—	—	—	—	— —	—
88-89—University of Maine	Hoc. East	27	1394	13	8	1	83		3.57	—	—	—	—	— —	—
89-90—University of Maine	Hoc. East	29	1526	17	7	2	67	1	2.63	—	—	—	—	— —	—
90-91—Adirondack	AHL	24	1287	8	10	2	91	0	4.24	1	32	0	0	4 0	7.50
—Hampton Roads	ECHL	15	819	8	4	1	57	0	4.18	—	—	—	—	— —	—
—Detroit	NHL	1	45	0	0	0	2	0	2.67	—	—	—	—	— —	—
91-92—Toledo	ECHL	7	424	4	2	1	25	0	3.54	—	—	—	—	— —	—
—Detroit	NHL	1	16	0	0	0	1	0	3.75	—	—	—	—	— —	—
—Adirondack	AHL	33	1904	14	14	3	112	0	3.53	—	—	—	—	— —	—
NHL totals		2	61	0	0	0	3	0	2.95						

KINISKY, AL
LW, FLYERS

PERSONAL: Born May 31, 1972, at Coquitlan, B.C. . . . 6-4/220. . . . Shoots left.
TRANSACTIONS/CAREER NOTES: Selected by Philadelphia Flyers in third round (seventh Flyers pick, 52nd overall) of NHL entry draft (June 16, 1990).

Season Team	League	REGULAR SEASON					PLAYOFFS				
		Gms.	G	A	Pts.	Pen.	Gms.	G	A	Pts.	Pen.
89-90—Nipawin	SJHL	28	2	4	6	92	—	—	—	—	—
—Seattle	WHL	72	9	29	38	103	13	2	3	5	13
90-91—Seattle	WHL	70	16	26	42	128	—	—	—	—	—
91-92—Seattle	WHL	7	2	1	3	27	—	—	—	—	—
—Lethbridge	WHL	56	9	24	33	121	4	0	0	0	0

KISIO, KELLY
C, SHARKS

PERSONAL: Born September 18, 1959, at Peace River, Alta. . . . 5-9/183. . . . Shoots right. . . . Full name: Kelvin W. Kisio.
HIGH SCHOOL: Lindsay Thurber (Red Deer, Alta.).
TRANSACTIONS/CAREER NOTES: Traded by Toledo Goaldiggers to Kalamazoo Wings for LW/C Jean Chouinard (February 1981). . . . Signed as free agent by Detroit Red Wings (February 1983). . . . Suspended five games by NHL for stick-swinging incident (February 1985). . . . Traded by Red Wings with RW Lane Lambert, D Jim Leavins and fifth-round pick in 1988 draft to New York Rangers for G Glen Hanlon, third-round picks in 1987 (C Dennis Holland) and 1988 drafts and future considerations (July 1986). . . . Dislocated left shoulder (October 1986). . . . Underwent surgery on shoulder (April 1987). . . . Bruised and twisted left knee (February 1988). . . . Fractured left hand (October 1988); missed five games. . . . Suffered back spasms (November 1988). . . . Bruised left thigh and suffered back spasms (November 9, 1989); missed 11 games. . . . Tore ligaments and suffered chip fracture of right ankle (October 6, 1990); missed 18 games. . . . Suffered bruised thigh (December 7, 1990). . . . Injured groin (January 17, 1991). . . . Selected by Minnesota North Stars in NHL expansion draft (May 30, 1991). . . . Traded by North Stars to San Jose Sharks for RW Shane Churla (June 3, 1991). . . . Injured ankle (October 17, 1991); missed 18 games. . . . Strained abdominal muscle (February 4, 1992); missed two games. . . . Injured shoulder (March 19, 1992).
HONORS: Named to AJHL All-Star first team (1977-78).

Season Team	League	REGULAR SEASON					PLAYOFFS				
		Gms.	G	A	Pts.	Pen.	Gms.	G	A	Pts.	Pen.
76-77—Red Deer	AJHL	60	53	48	101	101	—	—	—	—	—
77-78—Red Deer	AJHL	58	74	68	142	66	—	—	—	—	—
78-79—Calgary	WHL	70	60	61	121	73	—	—	—	—	—
79-80—Calgary	WHL	71	65	73	138	64	—	—	—	—	—
80-81—Adirondack	AHL	41	10	14	24	43	—	—	—	—	—
—Kalamazoo	IHL	31	27	16	43	48	8	7	7	14	13

— 434 —

Season Team	League	REGULAR SEASON					PLAYOFFS				
		Gms.	G	A	Pts.	Pen.	Gms.	G	A	Pts.	Pen.
81-82—Dallas	CHL	78	*62	39	101	59	16	*12	†17	*29	38
82-83—Davos HC	Switzerland	40	49	38	87		—	—	—	—	—
—Detroit	NHL	15	4	3	7	0	—	—	—	—	—
83-84—Detroit	NHL	70	23	37	60	34	4	1	0	1	4
84-85—Detroit	NHL	75	20	41	61	56	3	0	2	2	2
85-86—Detroit	NHL	76	21	48	69	85	—	—	—	—	—
86-87—New York Rangers	NHL	70	24	40	64	73	4	0	1	1	2
87-88—New York Rangers	NHL	77	23	55	78	88	—	—	—	—	—
88-89—New York Rangers	NHL	70	26	36	62	91	4	0	0	0	9
89-90—New York Rangers	NHL	68	22	44	66	105	10	2	8	10	8
90-91—New York Rangers	NHL	51	15	20	35	58	—	—	—	—	—
91-92—San Jose	NHL	48	11	26	37	54	—	—	—	—	—
NHL totals		620	189	350	539	644	25	3	11	14	25

KJELLBERG, PATRIK
LW, CANADIENS

PERSONAL: Born June 17, 1969, at Falun, Sweden. . . . 6-2/196. . . . Shoots left.
TRANSACTIONS/CAREER NOTES: Selected by Montreal Canadiens in fourth round (fourth Canadiens pick, 83rd overall) of NHL entry draft (June 11, 1988).

Season Team	League	REGULAR SEASON					PLAYOFFS				
		Gms.	G	A	Pts.	Pen.	Gms.	G	A	Pts.	Pen.
86-87—Falun	Sweden	27	11	13	24	14	—	—	—	—	—
87-88—Falun	Sweden	29	15	10	25	18	—	—	—	—	—
88-89—AIK Solna	Sweden	25	7	9	16	8	—	—	—	—	—
89-90—AIK Solna	Sweden	33	8	16	24	6	3	1	0	1	0
90-91—AIK Solna	Sweden	38	4	11	15	18	—	—	—	—	—
91-92—AIK Solna	Sweden	40	20	13	33	16	—	—	—	—	—

KLASSEN, TODD
D/RW, PENGUINS

PERSONAL: Born April 17, 1974, at Saskatoon, Sask. . . . 6-0/205. . . . Shoots right.
HIGH SCHOOL: Kamiakin (Kennewick, Wash.).
TRANSACTIONS/CAREER NOTES: Selected by Pittsburgh Penguins in fourth round (fourth Penguins pick, 91st overall) of NHL entry draft (June 20, 1992).
HONORS: Named to WHL (West) All-Star second team (1991-92).

Season Team	League	REGULAR SEASON					PLAYOFFS				
		Gms.	G	A	Pts.	Pen.	Gms.	G	A	Pts.	Pen.
90-91—Tri-City Americans	WHL	67	6	27	33	72	7	0	1	1	2
91-92—Tri-City Americans	WHL	69	23	42	65	60	5	0	0	0	2

KLATT, TRENT
RW, NORTH STARS

PERSONAL: Born January 30, 1971, at Robbinsdale, Minn. . . . 6-1/205. . . . Shoots right. . . . Full name: Trent Thomas Klatt.
HIGH SCHOOL: Osseo (Minn.).
COLLEGE: Minnesota.
TRANSACTIONS/CAREER NOTES: Selected by Washington Capitals in fourth round (fifth Capitals pick, 82nd overall) of NHL entry draft (June 17, 1989). . . . Rights traded by Capitals with LW Steve Maltais to Minnesota North Stars for D Sean Chambers (June 21, 1991).

Season Team	League	REGULAR SEASON					PLAYOFFS				
		Gms.	G	A	Pts.	Pen.	Gms.	G	A	Pts.	Pen.
87-88—Ossea H.S.	Minn. H.S.	22	19	17	36		—	—	—	—	—
88-89—Ossea H.S.	Minn. H.S.	22	24	39	63		—	—	—	—	—
89-90—University of Minnesota	WCHA	38	22	14	36	16	—	—	—	—	—
90-91—University of Minnesota	WCHA	39	16	28	44	58	—	—	—	—	—
91-92—University of Minnesota	WCHA	44	30	36	66	78	—	—	—	—	—
—Minnesota	NHL	1	0	0	0	0	6	0	0	0	2
NHL totals		1	0	0	0	0	6	0	0	0	2

KLEMM, JON
D, NORDIQUES

PERSONAL: Born January 6, 1970, at Cranbrook, B.C. . . . 6-3/200. . . . Shoots right. . . . Full name: Jonathan Darryl Klemm.
TRANSACTIONS/CAREER NOTES: Signed as free agent by Quebec Nordiques (May 1991).
HONORS: Named to WHL All-Star second team (1990-91).

Season Team	League	REGULAR SEASON					PLAYOFFS				
		Gms.	G	A	Pts.	Pen.	Gms.	G	A	Pts.	Pen.
87-88—Seattle	WHL	68	6	7	13	24	—	—	—	—	—
88-89—Seattle	WHL	2	1	1	2	0	—	—	—	—	—
—Spokane Chiefs	WHL	66	6	34	40	42	—	—	—	—	—
89-90—Spokane Chiefs	WHL	66	3	28	31	100	6	1	1	2	5
90-91—Spokane Chiefs	WHL	72	7	58	65	65	15	3	6	9	8
91-92—Halifax	AHL	70	6	13	19	40	—	—	—	—	—
—Quebec	NHL	4	0	1	1	0	—	—	—	—	—
NHL totals		4	0	1	1	0					

KLIMA, PETR

LW/RW, OILERS

PERSONAL: Born December 23, 1964, at Chaomutov, Czechoslovakia. . . . 6-0/190. . . . Shoots right.

TRANSACTIONS/CAREER NOTES: Selected by Detroit Red Wings in fifth round (fifth Red Wings pick, 88th overall) of NHL entry draft (June 8, 1983). . . . Broke right thumb (May 1988). . . . Sprained right ankle (November 12, 1988). . . . Pulled groin (December 1988). . . . Injured back (February 1989). . . . Traded by Red Wings with C/RW Joe Murphy, C/LW Adam Graves and D Jeff Sharples to Edmonton Oilers for C Jimmy Carson, C Kevin Mc-Clelland and fifth-round pick in 1991 draft (November 2, 1989). . . . Suspended four games by NHL for butt-ending player (October 25, 1990). . . . Pulled groin (March 15, 1991). . . . Scratched cornea in right eye (November 18, 1991); missed one game. . . . Strained groin (February 2, 1992); missed six games.

Season Team	League	REGULAR SEASON					PLAYOFFS				
		Gms.	G	A	Pts.	Pen.	Gms.	G	A	Pts.	Pen.
82-83—Czech. National Team.......	Int'l	44	19	17	36	74	—	—	—	—	—
83-84—Dukla Jihlava...................	Czech.	41	20	16	36	46	—	—	—	—	—
—Czech. National Team.......	Int'l	7	6	5	11		—	—	—	—	—
84-85—Dukla Jihlava...................	Czech.	35	23	22	45		—	—	—	—	—
85-86—Detroit	NHL	74	32	24	56	16	—	—	—	—	—
86-87—Detroit	NHL	77	30	23	53	42	13	1	2	3	4
87-88—Detroit	NHL	78	37	25	62	46	12	10	8	18	10
88-89—Adirondack	AHL	5	5	1	6	4	—	—	—	—	—
—Detroit	NHL	51	25	16	41	44	6	2	4	6	19
89-90—Detroit	NHL	13	5	5	10	6	—	—	—	—	—
—Edmonton	NHL	63	25	28	53	66	21	5	0	5	8
90-91—Edmonton	NHL	70	40	28	68	113	18	7	6	13	16
91-92—Edmonton	NHL	57	21	13	34	52	15	1	4	5	8
NHL totals..................................		483	215	162	377	385	85	26	24	50	65

KLIMOVICH, SERGEI

C, BLACKHAWKS

PERSONAL: Born May 8, 1974, at Novosibirsk, U.S.S.R. . . . 6-2/183. . . . Shoots right.

TRANSACTIONS/CAREER NOTES: Selected by Chicago Blackhawks in second round (third Blackhawks pick, 41st overall) of NHL entry draft (June 20, 1992).

Season Team	League	REGULAR SEASON					PLAYOFFS				
		Gms.	G	A	Pts.	Pen.	Gms.	G	A	Pts.	Pen.
91-92—Dynamo Moscow	CIS	3	0	0	0	0	—	—	—	—	—

KLIMT, TOMAS

C, ISLANDERS

PERSONAL: Born December 26, 1973, at Plzen, Czechoslovakia. . . . 6-1/185. . . . Shoots left.

TRANSACTIONS/CAREER NOTES: Selected by New York Islanders in fifth round (third Islanders pick, 104th overall) of NHL entry draft (June 20, 1992).

Season Team	League	REGULAR SEASON					PLAYOFFS				
		Gms.	G	A	Pts.	Pen.	Gms.	G	A	Pts.	Pen.
91-92—Skoda Plzen.....................	Czech.	40	3	6	9	4	—	—	—	—	—

KNUBLE, MICHAEL

RW, RED WINGS

PERSONAL: Born July 4, 1972, at Toronto. . . . 6-3/200. . . . Shoots right.

HIGH SCHOOL: East Kentwood (Kentwood, Mich.).

COLLEGE: Michigan.

TRANSACTIONS/CAREER NOTES: Selected by Detroit Red Wings in fourth round (fourth Red Wings pick, 76th overall) of NHL entry draft (June 22, 1991).

Season Team	League	REGULAR SEASON					PLAYOFFS				
		Gms.	G	A	Pts.	Pen.	Gms.	G	A	Pts.	Pen.
88-89—East Kentwood H.S.	Mich. H.S.	28	52	37	89	60	—	—	—	—	—
89-90—East Kentwood H.S.	Mich. H.S.	29	63	40	103	40	—	—	—	—	—
90-91—Kalamazoo	NAJHL	36	18	24	42	30	—	—	—	—	—
91-92—University of Michigan	CCHA	43	7	8	15	48	—	—	—	—	—

KOCUR, JOEY

RW, RANGERS

PERSONAL: Born December 21, 1964, at Calgary, Alta. . . . 6-0/209. . . . Shoots right. . . . Full name: Joe Kocur. . . . Cousin of Kory Kocur, right winger in Detroit Red Wings system.

TRANSACTIONS/CAREER NOTES: Stretched knee ligaments (December 1981). . . . Selected by Detroit Red Wings as underage junior in fifth round (sixth Red Wings pick, 88th overall) of NHL entry draft (June 8, 1983). . . . Lacerated right hand (January 1985). . . . Sprained thumb (December 11, 1985). . . . Strained ligaments (March 26, 1986). . . . Suffered sore right elbow (October 1987). . . . Strained sternum and collarbone (November 1987). . . . Injured shoulder (December 1987). . . . Separated shoulder (May 1988). . . . Injured knee (November 1988). . . . Injured back (February 1989). . . . Bruised right foot (February 16, 1990). . . . Strained right knee ligaments (March 1990). . . . Injured right hand and arm (December 1, 1990); missed three weeks. . . . Traded by Red Wings with D Per Djoos to New York Rangers for C Kevin Miller, D Dennis Vial and RW Jim Cummins (March 5, 1991). . . . Suspended four games by NHL for high-sticking (March 10, 1991). . . . Suspended additional four games by NHL for high-sticking during appeal of March 10 incident (March 14, 1991); missed final eight games of 1990-91 season and first game of 1991-92 season. . . . Underwent surgery to middle knuckle of right hand (May 10, 1991). . . . Injured hip flexor (October 1991); missed first five games of season. . . . Separated shoulder (January 28, 1992); missed 13 games. . . . Slightly sprained right knee (March 5, 1992); missed six games.

Season Team	League	REGULAR SEASON					PLAYOFFS				
		Gms.	G	A	Pts.	Pen.	Gms.	G	A	Pts.	Pen.
80-81—Yorkton	SJHL	48	6	9	15	307	—	—	—	—	—
81-82—Yorkton	SJHL	47	20	21	41	199	—	—	—	—	—
82-83—Saskatoon	WHL	62	23	17	40	289	6	2	3	5	25

K

Season Team	League	REGULAR SEASON Gms.	G	A	Pts.	Pen.	PLAYOFFS Gms.	G	A	Pts.	Pen.
83-84—Saskatoon	WHL	69	40	41	81	258	—	—	—	—	—
84-85—Detroit	NHL	17	1	0	1	64	3	1	0	1	5
—Adirondack	AHL	47	12	7	19	171	—	—	—	—	—
85-86—Adirondack	AHL	9	6	2	8	34	—	—	—	—	—
—Detroit	NHL	59	9	6	15	*377	—	—	—	—	—
86-87—Detroit	NHL	77	9	9	18	276	16	2	3	5	71
87-88—Detroit	NHL	64	7	7	14	263	10	0	1	1	13
88-89—Detroit	NHL	60	9	9	18	213	3	0	1	1	6
89-90—Detroit	NHL	71	16	20	36	268	—	—	—	—	—
90-91—Detroit	NHL	52	5	4	9	253	—	—	—	—	—
—New York Rangers	NHL	5	0	0	0	36	6	0	2	2	21
91-92—New York Rangers	NHL	51	7	4	11	121	12	1	1	2	38
NHL totals		456	63	59	122	1871	50	4	8	12	154

KOCUR, KORY
RW, RED WINGS

PERSONAL: Born March 6, 1969, at Kelvington, Sask. . . . 5-11/188. . . . Shoots right. . . . Cousin of Joey Kocur, right winger, New York Rangers.
TRANSACTIONS/CAREER NOTES: Selected by Detroit Red Wings in first round (first Red Wings pick, 17th overall) of NHL entry draft (June 11, 1988).

Season Team	League	REGULAR SEASON Gms.	G	A	Pts.	Pen.	PLAYOFFS Gms.	G	A	Pts.	Pen.
86-87—Saskatoon	WHL	62	13	17	30	98	4	0	0	0	7
87-88—Saskatoon	WHL	69	34	37	71	95	10	5	4	9	18
88-89—Saskatoon	WHL	66	45	57	102	111	8	7	11	18	15
89-90—Adirondack	AHL	79	18	37	55	36	6	2	1	3	2
90-91—Adirondack	AHL	65	8	13	21	83	2	0	0	0	12
91-92—Fort Wayne	IHL	69	25	40	65	68	7	3	3	6	49

KOLSTAD, DEAN
D, SHARKS

PERSONAL: Born June 16, 1968, at Edmonton, Alta. . . . 6-6/220. . . . Shoots left.
TRANSACTIONS/CAREER NOTES: Selected by Minnesota North Stars as underage junior in second round (third North Stars pick, 33rd overall) of NHL entry draft (June 21, 1986). . . . Selected by San Jose Sharks in NHL dispersal draft (May 30, 1991).
HONORS: Named to WHL All-Star first team (1986-87). . . . Named to IHL All-Star second team (1989-90).

Season Team	League	REGULAR SEASON Gms.	G	A	Pts.	Pen.	PLAYOFFS Gms.	G	A	Pts.	Pen.
84-85—New Westminster	WHL	13	0	0	0	16	—	—	—	—	—
—Langley Eagles	BCJHL	25	3	11	14	61	—	—	—	—	—
85-86—New Westminster	WHL	16	0	5	5	19	—	—	—	—	—
—Prince Albert	WHL	54	2	15	17	80	20	5	3	8	26
86-87—Prince Albert	WHL	72	17	37	54	112	8	1	5	6	8
87-88—Prince Albert	WHL	72	14	37	51	121	10	0	9	9	20
88-89—Minnesota	NHL	25	1	5	6	42	—	—	—	—	—
—Kalamazoo	IHL	51	10	23	33	91	6	1	0	1	23
89-90—Kalamazoo	IHL	77	10	40	50	172	10	3	4	7	14
90-91—Minnesota	NHL	5	0	0	0	15	—	—	—	—	—
—Kalamazoo	IHL	33	4	8	12	50	9	1	6	7	4
91-92—Kansas City	IHL	74	9	20	29	83	15	3	6	9	8
NHL totals		30	1	5	6	57					

KOLZIG, OLAF
G, CAPITALS

PERSONAL: Born April 6, 1970, at Johannesburg, South Africa. . . . 6-3/205. . . . Shoots left.
TRANSACTIONS/CAREER NOTES: Underwent surgery to right knee (November 1988). . . . Selected by Washington Capitals in first round (first Capitals pick, 19th overall) of NHL entry draft (June 17, 1989).

Season Team	League	REGULAR SEASON Gms.	Min.	W	L	T	GA	SO	Avg.	PLAYOFFS Gms.	Min.	W	L	GA	SO	Avg.
87-88—New Westminster	WHL	15	650	6	5	0	48	1	4.43	—	—	—	—	—	—	—
88-89—Tri-City Americans	WHL	30	1671	16	10	2	97	1	*3.48	—	—	—	—	—	—	—
89-90—Washington	NHL	2	120	0	2	0	12	0	6.00	—	—	—	—	—	—	—
—Tri-City Americans	WHL	48	2504	27	27	3	187	1	4.48	6	318	4	0	27	0	5.09
90-91—Baltimore	AHL	26	1367	10	12	1	72	0	3.16	—	—	—	—	—	—	—
—Hampton Roads	ECHL	21	1248	11	9	1	71	2	3.41	3	180	1	2	14	0	4.69
91-92—Baltimore	AHL	28	1503	5	17	2	105	1	4.19	—	—	—	—	—	—	—
—Hampton Roads	ECHL	14	847	11	3	0	41	0	2.90	—	—	—	—	—	—	—
NHL totals		2	120	0	2	0	12	0	6.00							

KONOWALCHUK, BRIAN
C, SHARKS

PERSONAL: Born October 14, 1971, at Prince Albert, Sask. . . . 5-11/180. . . . Shoots left.
COLLEGE: Denver.
TRANSACTIONS/CAREER NOTES: Selected by San Jose Sharks in NHL supplemental draft (June 19, 1992).

Season Team	League	Gms.	G	A	Pts.	Pen.	Gms.	G	A	Pts.	Pen.
		REGULAR SEASON					PLAYOFFS				
90-91—University of Denver	WCHA	38	8	19	27		—	—	—	—	—
91-92—University of Denver	WCHA	33	8	17	25	53	—	—	—	—	—

KONOWALCHUK, STEVE
C, CAPITALS

PERSONAL: Born November 11, 1972, at Salt Lake City. . . . 6-0/180. . . . Shoots left.
TRANSACTIONS/CAREER NOTES: Selected by Washington Capitals in third round (fifth Capitals pick, 58th overall) of NHL entry draft (June 22, 1991).
HONORS: Won Four Broncos Memorial Trophy (1991-92). . . . Named to Can.HL All-Star second team (1991-92). . . . Named to WHL (West) All-Star first team (1991-92).

Season Team	League	Gms.	G	A	Pts.	Pen.	Gms.	G	A	Pts.	Pen.
		REGULAR SEASON					PLAYOFFS				
90-91—Portland	WHL	72	43	49	92	78	—	—	—	—	—
91-92—Portland	WHL	64	51	53	104	95	6	3	6	9	12
—Baltimore	AHL	3	1	1	2	0	—	—	—	—	—
—Washington	NHL	1	0	0	0	0	—	—	—	—	—
NHL totals		1	0	0	0	0					

K

KONROYD, STEVE
D, WHALERS

PERSONAL: Born February 10, 1961, at Scarborough, Ont. . . . 6-1/195. . . . Shoots left. . . . Full name: Stephen Mark Konroyd.
TRANSACTIONS/CAREER NOTES: Selected by Calgary Flames as underage junior in second round (fourth Flames pick, 39th overall) of NHL entry draft (June 11, 1980). . . . Dislocated elbow (December 1984). . . . Pulled chest muscle (February 1986). . . . Traded by Flames with LW Richard Kromm to New York Islanders for LW/C John Tonelli (March 1986). . . . Bruised collarbone (December 1986). . . . Suspended four games by NHL for stick-swinging incident (January 1988). . . . Traded by Islanders with C Bob Bassen to Chicago Blackhawks for D Gary Nylund and D Marc Bergevin (November 25, 1988). . . . Bruised thigh (January 1990). . . . Suffered back spasms (February 10, 1991). . . . Broke knuckle on little finger of right hand (March 10, 1991); missed 18 days. . . . Traded by Blackhawks to Hartford Whalers for RW Rob Brown (January 24, 1992).
HONORS: Won Bobby Smith Trophy (1979-80). . . . Named to OHL All-Star second team (1980-81).

Season Team	League	Gms.	G	A	Pts.	Pen.	Gms.	G	A	Pts.	Pen.
		REGULAR SEASON					PLAYOFFS				
78-79—Oshawa	OMJHL	65	4	19	23	63	—	—	—	—	—
79-80—Oshawa	OMJHL	62	11	23	34	133	7	0	2	2	14
80-81—Calgary	NHL	4	0	0	0	4	—	—	—	—	—
—Oshawa	OMJHL	59	19	49	68	232	11	3	11	14	35
81-82—Oklahoma City	CHL	14	2	3	5	15	—	—	—	—	—
—Calgary	NHL	63	3	14	17	78	3	0	0	0	12
82-83—Calgary	NHL	79	4	13	17	73	9	2	1	3	18
83-84—Calgary	NHL	80	1	13	14	94	8	1	2	3	8
84-85—Calgary	NHL	64	3	23	26	73	4	1	4	5	2
85-86—Calgary	NHL	59	7	20	27	64	—	—	—	—	—
—New York Islanders	NHL	14	0	5	5	16	3	0	0	0	6
86-87—New York Islanders	NHL	72	5	16	21	70	14	1	4	5	10
87-88—New York Islanders	NHL	62	2	15	17	99	6	1	0	1	4
88-89—New York Islanders	NHL	21	1	5	6	2	—	—	—	—	—
—Chicago	NHL	57	5	7	12	40	16	2	0	2	10
89-90—Chicago	NHL	75	3	14	17	34	20	1	3	4	19
90-91—Chicago	NHL	70	0	12	12	40	6	1	0	1	8
91-92—Chicago	NHL	49	2	14	16	65	—	—	—	—	—
—Hartford	NHL	33	2	10	12	32	7	0	1	1	2
NHL totals		802	38	181	219	784	96	10	15	25	99

KONSTANTINOV, VLADIMIR
D, RED WINGS

PERSONAL: Born March 19, 1967, at Murmansk, U.S.S.R. . . . 5-11/185. . . . Shoots right.
TRANSACTIONS/CAREER NOTES: Selected by Detroit Red Wings in 11th round (12th Red Wings pick, 221st overall) of NHL entry draft (June 17, 1989).
HONORS: Named to NHL All-Rookie team (1991-92).

Season Team	League	Gms.	G	A	Pts.	Pen.	Gms.	G	A	Pts.	Pen.
		REGULAR SEASON					PLAYOFFS				
84-85—CSKA	USSR	40	1	4	5	10	—	—	—	—	—
85-86—CSKA	USSR	26	4	3	7	12	—	—	—	—	—
86-87—CSKA	USSR	35	2	2	4	19	—	—	—	—	—
87-88—CSKA	USSR	50	3	6	9	32	—	—	—	—	—
88-89—CSKA	USSR	37	7	8	15	20	—	—	—	—	—
89-90—CSKA	USSR	47	14	13	27	44	—	—	—	—	—
90-91—CSKA	USSR	45	5	12	17	42	—	—	—	—	—
91-92—Detroit	NHL	79	8	26	34	172	11	0	1	1	16
NHL totals		79	8	26	34	172	11	0	1	1	16

IN MEMORIAM

KOPOT, ARTEM
D, PENGUINS

PERSONAL: Born July 25, 1972, at Chelyabinsk, U.S.S.R. . . . Died July 1992, in Russia. . . . 6-0/187. . . . Shoots right.
TRANSACTIONS/CAREER NOTES: Selected by Pittsburgh Penguins in sixth round (sixth Penguins pick, 139th overall) of NHL entry draft (June 20, 1992).

Season Team	League	REGULAR SEASON					PLAYOFFS				
		Gms.	G	A	Pts.	Pen.	Gms.	G	A	Pts.	Pen.
90-91—Traktor Chelyabinsk........	USSR	27	1	0	1	14	—	—	—	—	—
91-92—Traktor Chelyabinsk........	CIS	36	0	0	0	20	—	—	—	—	—

KORDIC, DAN
D, FLYERS

PERSONAL: Born April 18, 1971, at Edmonton, Alta. . . . 6-5/220. . . . Shoots left. . . . Brother of John Kordic, right winger, four NHL teams (1985-86 through 1991-92).
TRANSACTIONS/CAREER NOTES: Selected by Philadelphia Flyers in fifth round (eighth Flyers pick, 88th overall) of NHL entry draft (June 16, 1990). . . . Suffered from the flu (January 1992); missed five games.

Season Team	League	REGULAR SEASON					PLAYOFFS				
		Gms.	G	A	Pts.	Pen.	Gms.	G	A	Pts.	Pen.
87-88—Medicine Hat	WHL	63	1	5	6	75	—	—	—	—	—
88-89—Modioino Ilat	WHL	70	1	13	14	190	—	—	—	—	—
89-90—Medicine Hat ....:	WHL	59	4	12	16	182	3	0	0	0	9
90-91—Medicine Hat	WHL	67	8	15	23	150	12	2	6	8	42
91-92—Philadelphia	NHL	46	1	3	4	126	—	—	—	—	—
NHL totals.................		46	1	3	4	126					

KORDIC, JOHN
RW

PERSONAL: Born March 22, 1965, at Edmonton, Alta. . . . 6-2/210. . . . Shoots right. . . . Brother of Dan Kordic, defenseman, Philadelphia Flyers.
TRANSACTIONS/CAREER NOTES: Selected by Montreal Canadiens as underage junior in fourth round (sixth Canadiens pick, 78th overall) of NHL entry draft (June 8, 1983). . . . Suspended five games and fined $100 by NHL for fighting before a game (February 26, 1988). . . . Traded by Canadiens with sixth-round pick in 1989 draft (RW Michael Doers) to Toronto Maple Leafs for C Russ Courtnall (November 7, 1988). . . . Suspended 10 games by NHL for cross-checking (December 14, 1988). . . . Suspended one game by NHL after third game misconduct of season (November 23, 1989). . . . Suspended four games and fined $500 by NHL for attacking another player (January 24, 1990). . . . Suspended two games by AHL for fan abuse (November 1, 1990). . . . Suspended two games by AHL for spitting at referee (November 1990). . . . Suspended by the Newmarket Saints (December 5, 1990). . . . Traded by Maple Leafs with C Paul Fenton to Washington Capitals for fifth-round pick in 1991 draft (C Alexei Kudashov) (January 24, 1991). . . . Suspended by Capitals (March 2, 1991). . . . Signed as free agent by Quebec Nordiques (September 1991). . . . Suffered from the flu (December 1991); missed two games.
HONORS: Named to WHL All-Star second team (1984-85).

Season Team	League	REGULAR SEASON					PLAYOFFS				
		Gms.	G	A	Pts.	Pen.	Gms.	G	A	Pts.	Pen.
82-83—Portland	WHL	72	3	22	25	235	14	1	6	7	30
83-84—Portland	WHL	67	9	50	59	232	14	0	13	13	56
84-85—Portland	WHL	25	6	22	28	73	—	—	—	—	—
—Seattle	WHL	46	17	36	53	154	—	—	—	—	—
—Sherbrooke.....................	AHL	4	0	0	0	4	4	0	0	0	11
85-86—Sherbrooke.....................	AHL	68	3	14	17	238	—	—	—	—	—
—Montreal........................	NHL	5	0	1	1	12	18	0	0	0	53
86-87—Sherbrooke.....................	AHL	10	4	4	8	49	—	—	—	—	—
—Montreal........................	NHL	44	5	3	8	151	11	2	0	2	19
87-88—Montreal........................	NHL	60	2	6	8	159	7	2	2	4	26
88-89—Montreal........................	NHL	6	0	0	0	13	—	—	—	—	—
—Toronto	NHL	46	1	2	3	185	—	—	—	—	—
89-90—Toronto	NHL	55	9	4	13	252	5	0	1	1	33
90-91—Newmarket	AHL	8	1	1	2	79	—	—	—	—	—
—Toronto	NHL	3	0	0	0	9	—	—	—	—	—
—Washington	NHL	7	0	0	0	101	—	—	—	—	—
91-92—Cape Breton	AHL	12	2	1	3	141	5	0	1	1	53
—Quebec	NHL	18	0	2	2	115	—	—	—	—	—
NHL totals.................................		244	17	18	35	997	41	4	3	7	131

KOROLEV, IGOR
RW, BLUES

PERSONAL: Born September 6, 1970, at Moscow, U.S.S.R. . . . 6-1/176. . . . Shoots left.
TRANSACTIONS/CAREER NOTES: Selected by St. Louis Blues in second round (first Blues pick, 38th overall) of NHL entry draft (June 20, 1992).

Season Team	League	REGULAR SEASON					PLAYOFFS				
		Gms.	G	A	Pts.	Pen.	Gms.	G	A	Pts.	Pen.
88-89—Dynamo Moscow	USSR	1	0	0	0	2	—	—	—	—	—
89-90—Dynamo Moscow	USSR	17	3	2	5	2	—	—	—	—	—
90-91—Dynamo Moscow	USSR	38	12	4	16	12	—	—	—	—	—
91-92—Dynamo Moscow	CIS	39	15	12	27	16	—	—	—	—	—

KOVACS, FRANK
RW, NORTH STARS

PERSONAL: Born June 3, 1971, at Regina, Sask. . . . 6-2/205. . . . Shoots left.
TRANSACTIONS/CAREER NOTES: WHL rights traded by Seattle Thunderbirds with RW Craig Endean, C Ray Savard and Grant Chorney to Regina Pats for RW Ken McIntyre, RW Brent Fedyk, LW Grant Kazuik, D Gerald Bzdel and rights to LW Kevin Kowalchuk (November

K

1986).... Selected by Minnesota North Stars in fourth round (fourth North Stars pick, 71st overall) of NHL entry draft (June 16, 1990).
HONORS: Named to WHL (East) All-Star second team (1991-92).

Season Team	League	REGULAR SEASON					PLAYOFFS				
		Gms.	G	A	Pts.	Pen.	Gms.	G	A	Pts.	Pen.
87-88—Regina	WHL	70	10	8	18	48	4	0	1	1	4
88-89—Regina	WHL	70	16	27	43	90	—	—	—	—	—
89-90—Regina	WHL	71	26	32	58	165	11	4	4	8	10
90-91—Regina	WHL	72	50	51	101	148	8	10	3	13	15
91-92—Regina	WHL	69	46	45	91	274	—	—	—	—	—

KOVALEV, ALEXEI
RW, RANGERS

PERSONAL: Born February 24, 1973, at Moscow, U.S.S.R. ... 6-1/189.... Shoots left.
TRANSACTIONS/CAREER NOTES: Selected by New York Rangers in first round (first Rangers pick, 15th overall) of NHL entry draft (June 22, 1991).

Season Team	League	REGULAR SEASON					PLAYOFFS				
		Gms.	G	A	Pts.	Pen.	Gms.	G	A	Pts.	Pen.
89-90—Dynamo Moscow	USSR	1	0	0	0	0	—	—	—	—	—
90-91—Dynamo Moscow	USSR	18	1	2	3	4	—	—	—	—	—
91-92—Dynamo Moscow	CIS	33	16	9	25	20	—	—	—	—	—

KOZLOV, VYACHESLAV
C, RED WINGS

PERSONAL: Born May 3, 1972, at Voskresensk, U.S.S.R. ... 5-10/172. ... Shoots left.
TRANSACTIONS/CAREER NOTES: Selected by Detroit Red Wings in third round (second Red Wings pick, 45th overall) of NHL entry draft (June 16, 1990).

Season Team	League	REGULAR SEASON					PLAYOFFS				
		Gms.	G	A	Pts.	Pen.	Gms.	G	A	Pts.	Pen.
89-90—Khimik	USSR	45	14	12	26	38	—	—	—	—	—
90-91—Khimik	USSR	45	11	13	24	46	—	—	—	—	—
91-92—Red Army	CIS	11	6	5	11	12	—	—	—	—	—
—Detroit	NHL	7	0	2	2	2	—	—	—	—	—
NHL totals		7	0	2	2	2	—	—	—	—	—

KRAMER, TED
RW, KINGS

PERSONAL: Born October 29, 1969, at Findlay, O. ... 6-0/190. ... Shoots right. ... Full name: Ted H. Kramer.
HIGH SCHOOL: Findlay (O.).
COLLEGE: Michigan.
TRANSACTIONS/CAREER NOTES: Underwent surgery to repair stretched knee ligaments (June 1988).... Selected by Los Angeles Kings in seventh round (sixth Kings pick, 144th overall) of NHL entry draft (June 17, 1989).

Season Team	League	REGULAR SEASON					PLAYOFFS				
		Gms.	G	A	Pts.	Pen.	Gms.	G	A	Pts.	Pen.
87-88—St. Michael's Jr. B	ODHA	35	36	25	61	54	—	—	—	—	—
88-89—University of Michigan	CCHA	40	17	15	32	78	—	—	—	—	—
89-90—University of Michigan	CCHA	42	21	24	45	111	—	—	—	—	—
90-91—University of Michigan	CCHA	47	15	17	32	107	—	—	—	—	—
91-92—University of Michigan	CCHA	44	17	14	31	52	—	—	—	—	—

KRAVCHUK, IGOR
D, BLACKHAWKS

PERSONAL: Born September 13, 1966, at Ufa, U.S.S.R. ... 6-1/200. ... Shoots left.
TRANSACTIONS/CAREER NOTES: Selected by Chicago Blackhawks in fourth round (fifth Blackhawks pick, 71st overall) of NHL entry draft (June 22, 1991).
MISCELLANEOUS: Member of 1988 gold-medal-winning U.S.S.R. Olympic team and 1992 gold-medal-winning Unified Olympic team.

Season Team	League	REGULAR SEASON					PLAYOFFS				
		Gms.	G	A	Pts.	Pen.	Gms.	G	A	Pts.	Pen.
90-91—Red Army	USSR	41	6	5	11	16	—	—	—	—	—
91-92—Central Red Army	CIS	30	3	7	10	2	—	—	—	—	—
—Unified Olympic Team	Int'l	8	3	2	5		—	—	—	—	—
—Chicago	NHL	18	1	8	9	4	18	2	6	8	8
NHL totals		18	1	8	9	4	18	2	6	8	8

KRAVETS, MIKHAIL
LW, SHARKS

PERSONAL: Born November 12, 1963, at Leningrad, U.S.S.R. ... 5-10/182. ... Shoots left.
TRANSACTIONS/CAREER NOTES: Selected by San Jose Sharks in 12th round (13th Sharks pick, 243rd overall) of NHL entry draft (June 22, 1991).

Season Team	League	REGULAR SEASON					PLAYOFFS				
		Gms.	G	A	Pts.	Pen.	Gms.	G	A	Pts.	Pen.
88-89—SKA Leningrad	USSR	44	9	5	14	36	—	—	—	—	—
89-90—SKA Leningrad	USSR	43	8	18	26	20	—	—	—	—	—
90-91—SKA Leningrad	USSR	25	8	6	14	28	—	—	—	—	—
91-92—Kansas City	IHL	74	10	32	42	172	15	6	8	14	12
—San Jose	NHL	1	0	0	0	0	—	—	—	—	—
NHL totals		1	0	0	0	0	—	—	—	—	—

KRIVOKRASOV, SERGEI
RW, BLACKHAWKS

PERSONAL: Born April 15, 1974, at Angarsk, U.S.S.R. .... 5-11/175. .... Shoots left.

TRANSACTIONS/CAREER NOTES: Selected by Chicago Blackhawks in first round (first Blackhawks pick, 12th overall) of NHL entry draft (June 20, 1992).

Season Team	League	REGULAR SEASON					PLAYOFFS				
		Gms.	G	A	Pts.	Pen.	Gms.	G	A	Pts.	Pen.
90-91—CSKA Moscow	USSR	41	4	0	4	8	—	—	—	—	—
91-92—CSKA Moscow	CIS	42	10	8	18	35	—	—	—	—	—

KROMM, RICH
LW, ISLANDERS

PERSONAL: Born March 29, 1964, at Trail, B.C. .... 6-1/192. .... Shoots left. .... Full name: Richard Gordon Kromm. .... Son of Bobby Kromm, coach, Winnipeg Jets of WHA (1975-76 through 1976-77) and Detroit Red Wings (1977-78 through 1979-80).

TRANSACTIONS/CAREER NOTES: Broke ankle (October 1981). .... Selected by Calgary Flames as underage junior in second round (second Flames pick, 37th overall) of NHL entry draft (June 9, 1982). .... Pinched nerve (February 1985). .... Traded by Calgary with LW Steve Konroyd to New York Islanders for LW/C John Tonelli (March 1986). ... Sprained left knee (December 2, 1986); missed seven games. .... Reinjured knee (March 1987). .... Fractured rib (February 1988).

Season Team	League	REGULAR SEASON					PLAYOFFS				
		Gms.	G	A	Pts.	Pen.	Gms.	G	A	Pts.	Pen.
80-81—Windsor Jr. B	OHA	39	22	31	53	40	—	—	—	—	—
81-82—Portland	WHL	60	16	38	54	30	14	0	3	3	17
82-83—Portland	WHL	72	35	68	103	64	14	7	13	20	12
83-84—Portland	WHL	10	10	4	14	13	—	—	—	—	—
—Calgary	NHL	53	11	12	23	27	11	1	1	2	9
84-85—Calgary	NHL	73	20	32	52	32	3	0	1	1	4
85-86—Calgary	NHL	63	12	17	29	31	—	—	—	—	—
—New York Islanders	NHL	14	7	7	14	4	3	0	1	1	0
86-87—New York Islanders	NHL	70	12	17	29	20	14	1	3	4	4
87-88—New York Islanders	NHL	71	5	10	15	20	5	0	0	0	5
88-89—New York Islanders	NHL	20	1	6	7	4	—	—	—	—	—
—Springfield	AHL	48	21	26	47	15	—	—	—	—	—
89-90—Leksand	Sweden	40	8	16	24	28	3	3	1	4	0
—Springfield	AHL	9	3	4	7	4	16	1	5	6	4
90-91—Capital District	AHL	76	19	36	55	18	—	—	—	—	—
91-92—Capital District	AHL	76	16	39	55	36	7	2	3	5	6
—New York Islanders	NHL	1	0	0	0	0	—	—	—	—	—
NHL totals		365	68	101	169	138	36	2	6	8	22

KRON, ROBERT
LW, CANUCKS

PERSONAL: Born February 27, 1967, at Brno, Czechoslovakia. .... 5-10/175. .... Shoots right.

TRANSACTIONS/CAREER NOTES: Selected by Vancouver Canucks in fourth round (fifth Canucks pick, 88th overall) of NHL entry draft (June 15, 1985). .... Played entire season with a broken bone in his left wrist (1990-91). .... Underwent surgery to repair torn knee ligaments and wrist fracture (March 22, 1991). .... Fractured ankle (January 28, 1992); missed 22 games.

Season Team	League	REGULAR SEASON					PLAYOFFS				
		Gms.	G	A	Pts.	Pen.	Gms.	G	A	Pts.	Pen.
86-87—Zetor Brno	Czech.	28	14	11	25		—	—	—	—	—
87-88—Zetor Brno	Czech.	32	12	6	18		—	—	—	—	—
88-89—Zetor Brno	Czech.	43	28	19	47		—	—	—	—	—
89-90—Dukla Trencin	Czech.	39	22	22	44		—	—	—	—	—
90-91—Vancouver	NHL	76	12	20	32	21	—	—	—	—	—
91-92—Vancouver	NHL	36	2	2	4	2	11	1	2	3	2
NHL totals		112	14	22	36	23	11	1	2	3	2

KRUPP, UWE
D, ISLANDERS

PERSONAL: Born June 24, 1965, at Cologne, West Germany. .... 6-6/235. .... Shoots right.

TRANSACTIONS/CAREER NOTES: Selected by Buffalo Sabres in 11th round (13th Sabres pick, 214th overall) of NHL entry draft (June 8, 1983). .... Bruised hip (November 1987). .... Injured head (April 1988). .... Broke rib (January 6, 1989). .... Banned from international competition for 18 months by IIHF after failing random substance test (April 20, 1990). .... Suffered from cyst on foot (January 2, 1991); missed NHL All-Star Game. .... Traded by Sabres with C Pierre Turgeon, RW Benoit Hogue and C Dave McLlwain to New York Islanders for C Pat LaFontaine, LW Randy Wood, D Randy Hillier and future considerations (October 25, 1991). .... Sprained left knee (December 28, 1991); missed five games. .... Bruised thigh (February 7, 1992).

Season Team	League	REGULAR SEASON					PLAYOFFS				
		Gms.	G	A	Pts.	Pen.	Gms.	G	A	Pts.	Pen.
83-84—KEC	W. Germany	40	0	4	4	22	—	—	—	—	—
84-85—KEC	W. Germany	39	11	8	19	36	—	—	—	—	—
85-86—KEC	W. Germany	45	10	21	31	83	—	—	—	—	—
—Rochester	AHL	42	3	19	22	50	17	1	11	12	16
86-87—Buffalo	NHL	26	1	4	5	23	—	—	—	—	—
—Buffalo	NHL	75	2	9	11	151	6	0	0	0	15
87-88—Buffalo	NHL	70	5	13	18	55	5	0	1	1	4
88-89—Buffalo	NHL	74	3	20	23	85	6	0	0	0	4
89-90—Buffalo	NHL	74	12	32	44	66	6	1	1	2	6
90-91—Buffalo	NHL	8	2	0	2	6	—	—	—	—	—
91-92—New York Islanders	NHL	59	6	29	35	43	—	—	—	—	—
NHL totals		386	31	107	138	429	23	1	2	3	29

KRUPPKE, GORD

D, RED WINGS

PERSONAL: Born April 2, 1969, at Edmonton, Alta. . . . 6-1/200. . . . Shoots right. . . . Full name: Gordon Kruppke.
TRANSACTIONS/CAREER NOTES: Underwent surgery to have spleen removed (December 1986). . . . Selected by Detroit Red Wings as underage junior in second round (second Red Wings pick, 32nd overall) of NHL entry draft (June 13, 1987). . . . Injured left knee ligaments (October 1987).
HONORS: Named to WHL All-Star second team (1988-89).

Season Team	League	REGULAR SEASON					PLAYOFFS				
		Gms.	G	A	Pts.	Pen.	Gms.	G	A	Pts.	Pen.
85-86—Prince Albert	WHL	62	1	8	9	81	20	4	4	8	22
86-87—Prince Albert	WHL	49	2	10	12	129	8	0	0	0	9
87-88—Prince Albert	WHL	54	8	8	16	113	10	0	0	0	46
88-89—Prince Albert	WHL	62	6	26	32	254	3	0	0	0	11
89-90—Adirondack	AHL	59	2	12	14	103	—	—	—	—	—
90-91—Adirondack	AHL	45	1	8	9	153	—	—	—	—	—
—Detroit	NHL	4	0	0	0	0	—	—	—	—	—
91-92—Adirondack	AHL	65	3	9	12	208	16	0	1	1	52
NHL totals		4	0	0	0	0					

KRUSE, PAUL

LW, FLAMES

PERSONAL: Born March 15, 1970, at Merritt, B.C. . . . 6-0/202. . . . Shoots left.
TRANSACTIONS/CAREER NOTES: Selected by Calgary Flames in fourth round (sixth Flames pick, 83rd overall) of NHL entry draft (June 16, 1990). . . . Injured eye (March 8, 1992); missed four games.

Season Team	League	REGULAR SEASON					PLAYOFFS				
		Gms.	G	A	Pts.	Pen.	Gms.	G	A	Pts.	Pen.
86-87—Merritt	BCJHL	35	8	15	23	120	—	—	—	—	—
87-88—Merritt	BCJHL	44	12	32	44	227	4	1	4	5	18
—Moose Jaw	WHL	1	0	0	0	0	—	—	—	—	—
88-89—Kamloops	WHL	68	8	15	23	209	—	—	—	—	—
89-90—Kamloops	WHL	67	22	23	45	291	17	3	5	8	†79
90-91—Salt Lake City	IHL	83	24	20	44	313	4	1	1	2	4
—Calgary	NHL	1	0	0	0	7	—	—	—	—	—
91-92—Salt Lake City	IHL	57	14	15	29	267	5	1	2	3	19
—Calgary	NHL	16	3	1	4	65	—	—	—	—	—
NHL totals		17	3	1	4	72					

KRUSHELNYSKI, MIKE

C/LW, MAPLE LEAFS

PERSONAL: Born April 27, 1960, at Montreal. . . . 6-2/200. . . . Shoots left. . . . Full name: Michael Krushelnyski.
TRANSACTIONS/CAREER NOTES: Started 1978-79 season at St. Louis University but left to return to junior hockey. . . . Selected by Boston Bruins as an underage junior in sixth round (seventh Bruins pick, 120th overall) of NHL entry draft (August 9, 1979). . . . Separated right shoulder (January 1984). . . . Traded by Bruins to Edmonton Oilers for C Ken Linseman (June 1984). . . . Sprained right knee (December 10, 1985); missed 17 games. . . . Twisted knee (February 14, 1986); missed nine games. . . . Suspended by Oilers for not reporting to training camp (September 1987). . . . Traded by Oilers with C Wayne Gretzky and RW/D Marty McSorley to Los Angeles Kings for C Jimmy Carson, LW Martin Gelinas, first-round picks in 1989 (traded to New Jersey), 1991 and 1993 drafts and cash (August 9, 1988). . . . Fractured left wrist (October 5, 1989); missed 17 games. . . . Traded by Kings to Toronto Maple Leafs for C John McIntyre (November 9, 1990).

Season Team	League	REGULAR SEASON					PLAYOFFS				
		Gms.	G	A	Pts.	Pen.	Gms.	G	A	Pts.	Pen.
78-79—Montreal	QMJHL	46	15	29	44	42	11	3	4	7	8
79-80—Montreal	QMJHL	72	39	61	100	78	6	2	3	5	2
80-81—Springfield	AHL	80	25	38	63	47	7	1	1	2	29
81-82—Erie	AHL	62	31	52	83	44	—	—	—	—	—
—Boston	NHL	17	3	3	6	2	1	0	0	0	2
82-83—Boston	NHL	79	23	42	65	43	17	8	6	14	12
83-84—Boston	NHL	66	25	20	45	55	2	0	0	0	0
84-85—Edmonton	NHL	80	43	45	88	60	18	5	8	13	22
85-86—Edmonton	NHL	54	16	24	40	22	10	4	5	9	16
86-87—Edmonton	NHL	80	16	35	51	67	21	3	4	7	18
87-88—Edmonton	NHL	76	20	27	47	64	19	4	6	10	12
88-89—Los Angeles	NHL	78	26	36	62	110	11	1	4	5	4
89-90—Los Angeles	NHL	63	16	25	41	50	10	1	3	4	12
90-91—Los Angeles	NHL	15	1	5	6	10	—	—	—	—	—
—Toronto	NHL	59	17	22	39	48	—	—	—	—	—
91-92—Toronto	NHL	72	9	15	24	72	—	—	—	—	—
NHL totals		739	215	299	514	603	109	26	36	62	98

KRYGIER, TODD

C, CAPITALS

PERSONAL: Born October 12, 1965, at Northville, Mich. . . . 5-11/180. . . . Shoots left. . . . Full name: Todd Andrew Krygier.
COLLEGE: Connecticut.
TRANSACTIONS/CAREER NOTES: Selected by Hartford Whalers in NHL supplemental draft (June 10, 1988). . . . Bruised heel (March 13, 1990). . . . Traded by Whalers to Washington Capitals for fourth-round pick in 1993 draft (October 3, 1991).
MISCELLANEOUS: Suffers from asthma.

Season Team	League	Gms.	G	A	Pts.	Pen.	Gms.	G	A	Pts.	Pen.
		REGULAR SEASON					PLAYOFFS				
84-85—University of Connecticut.	ECAC-II	14	14	11	25	12	—	—	—	—	—
85-86—University of Connecticut.	ECAC-II	32	29	27	56	46	—	—	—	—	—
86-87—University of Connecticut.	ECAC-II	28	24	24	48	44	—	—	—	—	—
87-88—University of Connecticut.	ECAC-II	27	32	39	71	38	—	—	—	—	—
—New Haven	AHL	13	1	5	6	34	—	—	—	—	—
88-89—Binghamton	AHL	76	26	42	68	77	—	—	—	—	—
89-90—Binghamton	AHL	12	1	9	10	16	—	—	—	—	—
—Hartford	NHL	58	18	12	30	52	7	2	1	3	4
90-91—Hartford	NHL	72	13	17	30	95	6	0	2	2	0
91-92—Washington	NHL	67	13	17	30	107	5	2	1	3	4
NHL totals		197	44	46	90	254	18	4	4	8	8

KUCERA, FRANTISEK
D, BLACKHAWKS

PERSONAL: Born February 3, 1968, at Prague, Czechoslovakia. . . . 6-2/205. . . . Shoots right.
TRANSACTIONS/CAREER NOTES: Selected by Chicago Blackhawks in fourth round (third Blackhawks pick, 77th overall) of NHL entry draft (June 21, 1986).

Season Team	League	Gms	G	A	Pts.	Pen.	Gms.	G	A	Pts.	Pen.
		REGULAR SEASON					PLAYOFFS				
85-86—Sparta Prague	Czech.	15	0	0	0		—	—	—	—	—
86-87—Sparta Prague	Czech.	33	7	2	9		—	—	—	—	—
87-88—Sparta Prague	Czech.	34	4	2	6		—	—	—	—	—
88-89—Dukla Jihlava	Czech.	45	10	9	19		—	—	—	—	—
89-90—Dukla Jihlava	Czech.	43	9	10	19		—	—	—	—	—
90-91—Chicago	NHL	40	2	12	14	32	—	—	—	—	—
—Indianapolis	IHL	35	8	19	27	23	7	0	1	1	15
91-92—Chicago	NHL	61	3	10	13	36	6	0	0	0	0
—Indianapolis	IHL	7	1	2	3	4					
NHL totals		101	5	22	27	68	6	0	0	0	0

KUDELSKI, BOB
C, KINGS

PERSONAL: Born March 3, 1964, at Springfield, Mass. . . . 6-1/200. . . . Shoots right. . . . Full name: Robert R. Kudelski.
HIGH SCHOOL: Cathedral (Springfield, Mass.).
COLLEGE: Yale.
TRANSACTIONS/CAREER NOTES: Selected by Los Angeles Kings in NHL supplemental draft (October 1986). . . . Broke knuckle on left hand (November 22, 1989); missed 15 games. . . . Strained medial collateral knee ligament (April 24, 1991).

Season Team	League	Gms.	G	A	Pts.	Pen.	Gms.	G	A	Pts.	Pen.
		REGULAR SEASON					PLAYOFFS				
83-84—Yale University	ECAC	21	14	12	26	12	—	—	—	—	—
84-85—Yale University	ECAC	32	21	23	44	38	—	—	—	—	—
85-86—Yale University	ECAC	31	18	23	41	48	—	—	—	—	—
86-87—Yale University	ECAC	30	25	22	47	34	—	—	—	—	—
87-88—New Haven	AHL	50	15	19	34	41	—	—	—	—	—
—Los Angeles	NHL	26	0	1	1	8	—	—	—	—	—
88-89—New Haven	AHL	60	32	19	51	43	17	8	5	13	12
—Los Angeles	NHL	14	1	3	4	17	—	—	—	—	—
89-90—Los Angeles	NHL	62	23	13	36	49	8	1	2	3	2
90-91—Los Angeles	NHL	72	23	13	36	46	8	3	2	5	2
91-92—Los Angeles	NHL	80	22	21	43	42	6	0	0	0	0
NHL totals		254	69	51	120	162	22	4	4	8	4

KUMMU, AL
D, JETS

PERSONAL: Born January 21, 1969, at Kitchener, Ont. . . . 6-4/195. . . . Shoots right. . . . Full name: Allen Arnold Kummu.
COLLEGE: Rensselaer Polytechnic Institute (N.Y.).
TRANSACTIONS/CAREER NOTES: Selected by Philadelphia Flyers in 10th round (eighth Flyers pick, 201st overall) of NHL entry draft (June 17, 1989).
HONORS: Named to ECAC All-Rookie team (1989-90).

Season Team	League	Gms.	G	A	Pts.	Pen.	Gms.	G	A	Pts.	Pen.
		REGULAR SEASON					PLAYOFFS				
88-89—Humboldt Jr. A	OPJHL	35	7	22	29	115	—	—	—	—	—
89-90—R.P.I.	ECAC	33	9	13	22	50	—	—	—	—	—
90-91—R.P.I.	ECAC	29	6	8	14	86	—	—	—	—	—
91-92—R.P.I.	ECAC	31	6	14	20	54	—	—	—	—	—

KUMPEL, MARK
RW, JETS

PERSONAL: Born March 7, 1961, at Wakefield, Mass. . . . 6-0/190. . . . Shoots right. . . . Full name: Mark Alan Kumpel.
COLLEGE: Lowell (Mass.).
TRANSACTIONS/CAREER NOTES: Selected by Quebec Nordiques in sixth round (fourth Nordiques pick, 108th overall) of NHL entry draft (June 11, 1980). . . . Suffered knee ligament damage (October 1980); missed 20 games. . . . Separated shoulder (February 16, 1986). . . . Traded by Nordiques with LW Brent Ashton and D Gilbert Delorme to Detroit Red Wings for LW John Ogrodnick, RW Doug Shedden and LW Basil McRae (January 1987). . . . Broke wrist (March 1987). . . . Dislocated left thumb (December 1987). . . . Traded by Red Wings to Winnipeg Jets for RW Jim Nill (January 1988).

. . . Sprained left ankle (November 6, 1989); missed eight games. . . . Separated shoulder (January 1990). . . . Bruised wrist (September 1990). . . . Pulled groin (March 8, 1991).

Season Team	League	REGULAR SEASON					PLAYOFFS				
		Gms.	G	A	Pts.	Pen.	Gms.	G	A	Pts.	Pen.
79-80—University of Lowell..........	ECAC-II	30	18	18	36	12	—	—	—	—	—
80-81—University of Lowell..........	ECAC-II	1	2	0	2	0	—	—	—	—	—
81-82—University of Lowell..........	ECAC-II	35	17	13	30	23	—	—	—	—	—
82-83—University of Lowell..........	ECAC-II	7	8	5	13	0	—	—	—	—	—
—U.S. National Team..........	Int'l	30	14	18	32	6	—	—	—	—	—
83-84—U.S. National Team..........	Int'l	61	14	19	33	19	—	—	—	—	—
—U.S. Olympic Team	Int'l	6	1	0	1	2	—	—	—	—	—
—Fredericton	AHL	16	1	1	2	5	3	0	0	0	15
84-85—Fredericton	AHL	18	9	6	15	17	—	—	—	—	—
—Quebec	NHL	42	8	7	15	26	18	3	4	7	4
85-86—Fredericton	AHL	7	4	2	6	4	—	—	—	—	—
—Quebec	NHL	47	10	12	22	17	2	1	0	1	0
86-87—Quebec	NHL	40	1	8	9	16	—	—	—	—	—
—Detroit	NHL	5	0	1	1	0	8	0	0	0	4
—Adirondack	AHL	7	2	3	5	0	1	1	0	1	0
87-88—Adirondack	AHL	4	5	0	5	2	—	—	—	—	—
—Detroit	NHL	13	0	2	2	4	—	—	—	—	—
—Winnipeg	NHL	32	4	4	8	19	4	0	0	0	4
88-89—Moncton	AHL	53	22	23	45	25	10	3	4	7	0
89-90—Winnipeg	NHL	56	8	9	17	21	7	2	0	2	2
90-91—Winnipeg	NHL	53	7	3	10	10	—	—	—	—	—
91-92—Moncton	AHL	41	11	18	29	12	2	0	0	0	0
NHL totals.............................		**288**	**38**	**46**	**84**	**113**	**39**	**6**	**4**	**10**	**14**

KUNTAR, LES
G, CANADIENS

PERSONAL: Born July 28, 1969, at Buffalo, N.Y. . . . 6-2/195. . . . Shoots left. . . . Full name: Leslie Steven Kuntar.
COLLEGE: St. Lawrence (N.Y.).
TRANSACTIONS/CAREER NOTES: Selected by Montreal Canadiens in sixth round (sixth Canadiens pick, 122nd overall) of NHL entry draft (June 13, 1987)
HONORS: Named to NCAA All-America East first team (1990-91). . . . Named to ECAC All-Star first team (1990-91).

Season Team	League	REGULAR SEASON							PLAYOFFS					
		Gms.	Min.	W	L	T	GA	SO	Avg.	Gms.	Min.	W	L	GA SO	Avg.
86-87—Nichols School	N.Y. H.S.	22	1585				56	3	2.12	—	—	—	—	—	—
87-88—St. Lawrence Univ.	ECAC	10	488	6	1	0	27	0	3.32	—	—	—	—	—	—
88-89—St. Lawrence Univ.	ECAC	14	786	11	2	0	31	0	2.37	—	—	—	—	—	—
89-90—St. Lawrence Univ.	ECAC	19	1076	7	11	1	76	1	4.24	—	—	—	—	—	—
90-91—St. Lawrence Univ.	ECAC	*33	*1794	*19	11	1	97	2	*3.24	—	—	—	—	—	—
91-92—Fredericton	AHL	11	638	7	3	0	26	0	2.45	—	—	—	—	—	—
—U.S. National Team.....	Int'l	2	100				4	0	2.40	—	—	—	—	—	—

KURRI, JARI
RW, KINGS

PERSONAL: Born May 18, 1960, at Helsinki, Finland. . . . 6-1/195. . . . Shoots right.
TRANSACTIONS/CAREER NOTES: Selected by Edmonton Oilers in fourth round (third Oilers pick, 69th overall) of NHL entry draft (June 11, 1980). . . . Pulled groin (November 24, 1981). . . . Pulled groin muscle (January 1984); missed 16 games. . . . Sprained medial collateral ligament in left knee (February 12, 1989). . . . Signed two-year contract to play for Milan Devils in Italian Hockey League (July 30, 1990). . . . Injured knee (January 1991). . . . NHL rights traded by Oilers with RW Dave Brown and D Corey Foster to Philadelphia Flyers for RW Scott Mellanby, LW Craig Berube and C Craig Fisher (May 30, 1991). . . . Rights traded by Flyers to Los Angeles Kings for D Steve Duchesne, C Steve Kasper and fourth-round pick in 1991 draft (D Aris Brimanis). . . . Sprained shoulder (November 12, 1991); missed three games. . . . Suffered from the flu (January 1992); missed two games.
HONORS: Named to NHL All-Star second team (1983-84, 1985-86 and 1988-89). . . . Won Lady Byng Memorial Trophy (1984-85). . . . Named to THE SPORTING NEWS All-Star first team (1984-85). . . . Named to NHL All-Star first team (1984-85 and 1986-87). . . . Named to THE SPORTING NEWS All-Star second team (1985-86 and 1988-89).
RECORDS: Shares NHL career record for most overtime goals—7. . . . Shares NHL career playoff record for most three-or-more-goal games—7. . . . Holds NHL single-season playoff record for most three-or-more-goal games—4 (1985). . . . Shares NHL single-season playoff records for most goals—19 (1985); and most game-winning goals—5 (1987). . . . Holds NHL one-series playoff records for most goals—12 (1985); and most three-or-more-goal games—3 (1985). . . . Shares NHL single-game playoff records for most shorthanded goals—2 (April 24, 1983); most shorthanded goals in one period—2 (April 24, 1983); and most power-play goals—3 (April 9, 1987).

Season Team	League	REGULAR SEASON					PLAYOFFS				
		Gms.	G	A	Pts.	Pen.	Gms.	G	A	Pts.	Pen.
77-78—Jokerit	Finland	29	2	9	11	12	—	—	—	—	—
78-79—Jokerit	Finland	33	16	14	30	12	—	—	—	—	—
79-80—Finland Olympic Team......	Int'l	7	2	1	3	6	—	—	—	—	—
—Jokerit	Finland	33	23	16	39	22	6	7	2	9	13
80-81—Edmonton	NHL	75	32	43	75	40	9	5	7	12	4
81-82—Edmonton	NHL	71	32	54	86	32	5	2	5	7	10
82-83—Edmonton	NHL	80	45	59	104	22	16	8	15	23	8
83-84—Edmonton	NHL	64	52	61	113	14	19	*14	14	28	13
84-85—Edmonton	NHL	73	71	64	135	30	18	*19	12	31	6
85-86—Edmonton	NHL	78	*68	63	131	22	10	2	10	12	4

Season	Team	League	REGULAR SEASON					PLAYOFFS				
			Gms.	G	A	Pts.	Pen.	Gms.	G	A	Pts.	Pen.
86-87	Edmonton	NHL	79	54	54	108	41	21	*15	10	25	20
87-88	Edmonton	NHL	80	43	53	96	30	19	*14	17	31	12
88-89	Edmonton	NHL	76	44	58	102	69	7	3	5	8	6
89-90	Edmonton	NHL	78	33	60	93	48	22	10	15	25	18
90-91	Milan	Italy	40	37	60	97	8	10	10	12	22	2
91-92	Los Angeles	NHL	73	23	37	60	24	4	1	2	3	4
NHL totals			827	497	606	1103	372	150	93	112	205	105

KURVERS, TOM
D, ISLANDERS

PERSONAL: Born September 14, 1962, at Minneapolis. . . . 6-0/197. . . . Shoots left. . . . Full name: Thomas James Kurvers.
COLLEGE: Minnesota-Duluth.
TRANSACTIONS/CAREER NOTES: Selected by Montreal Canadiens as underage player in seventh round (10th Canadiens pick, 145th overall) of NHL entry draft (June 10, 1981). . . . Suffered facial injuries (October 23, 1984); missed five games. . . . Traded by Canadiens to Buffalo Sabres for second-round pick in 1988 draft (LW Martin St. Amour) (November 18, 1986). . . . Traded by Sabres to New Jersey Devils for third-round pick in 1988 draft (LW Andrew MacVicar) (June 13, 1987). . . . Fractured left index finger (November 1987). . . . Pulled groin (February 1988). . . . Injured right thumb (May 1988). . . . Pulled groin (November 17, 1988). . . . Traded by Devils to Toronto Maple Leafs for first-round pick in 1991 draft (D Scott Niedermayer) (October 16, 1989). . . . Injured knee (March 0, 1990). . . . Underwent arthroscopic knee surgery (November 15, 1990). . . . Traded by Maple Leafs to Canucks for C Brian Bradley (January 12, 1991). . . . Traded by Canucks to the New York Islanders as part of a three-way trade that saw D Dave Babych go from Minnesota North Stars to Canucks and D Craig Ludwig go from the Islanders to North Stars (June 22, 1991).
HONORS: Won Hobey Baker Memorial Trophy (1983-84). . . . Named to NCAA All-America West team (1983-84). . . . Named to WCHA All-Star first team (1983-84).

K

Season	Team	League	REGULAR SEASON					PLAYOFFS				
			Gms.	G	A	Pts.	Pen.	Gms.	G	A	Pts.	Pen.
80-81	Minnesota-Duluth	WCHA	39	6	24	30	48	—	—	—	—	—
81-82	Minnesota-Duluth	WCHA	37	11	31	42	18	—	—	—	—	—
82-83	Minnesota-Duluth	WCHA	45	8	36	44	42	—	—	—	—	—
83-84	Minnesota-Duluth	WCHA	43	18	58	76	46	—	—	—	—	—
84-85	Montreal	NHL	75	10	35	45	30	12	0	6	6	6
85-86	Montreal	NHL	62	7	23	30	36	—	—	—	—	—
86-87	Montreal	NHL	1	0	0	0	0	—	—	—	—	—
	Buffalo	NHL	55	6	17	23	24	—	—	—	—	—
87-88	New Jersey	NHL	56	5	29	34	46	19	6	9	15	38
88-89	New Jersey	NHL	74	16	50	66	38	—	—	—	—	—
89-90	New Jersey	NHL	1	0	0	0	0	—	—	—	—	—
	Toronto	NHL	70	15	37	52	29	5	0	3	3	4
90-91	Toronto	NHL	19	0	3	3	8	—	—	—	—	—
	Vancouver	NHL	32	4	23	27	20	6	2	2	4	12
91-92	New York Islanders	NHL	74	9	47	56	30	—	—	—	—	—
NHL totals			519	72	264	336	261	42	8	20	28	60

KUSHNER, DALE
RW, FLYERS

PERSONAL: Born June 13, 1966, at Terrace, B.C. . . . 6-1/195. . . . Shoots left.
TRANSACTIONS/CAREER NOTES: Signed as free agent by New York Islanders (March 1987). . . . Suspended six games by AHL for leaving penalty box to fight (December 30, 1988). . . . Suspended eight games by AHL for leaving penalty box to fight (November 24, 1989). . . . Signed as free agent by Philadelphia Flyers (August 1, 1990).

Season	Team	League	REGULAR SEASON					PLAYOFFS				
			Gms.	G	A	Pts.	Pen.	Gms.	G	A	Pts.	Pen.
83-84	Fort McMurray	AJHL	44	15	6	21	139	—	—	—	—	—
	Prince Albert	WHL	1	0	0	0	5	—	—	—	—	—
84-85	Prince Albert	WHL	2	0	0	0	2	—	—	—	—	—
	Moose Jaw	WHL	17	5	2	7	23	—	—	—	—	—
	Medicine Hat	WHL	48	23	17	40	173	10	3	3	6	18
85-86	Medicine Hat	WHL	66	25	19	44	218	25	0	5	5	*114
86-87	Medicine Hat	WHL	65	34	34	68	250	20	8	13	21	57
87-88	Springfield	AHL	68	13	23	36	201	—	—	—	—	—
88-89	Springfield	AHL	45	5	8	13	132	—	—	—	—	—
89-90	New York Islanders	NHL	2	0	0	0	2	—	—	—	—	—
	Springfield	AHL	45	14	11	25	163	7	2	3	5	61
90-91	Philadelphia	NHL	63	7	11	18	195	—	—	—	—	—
	Hershey	AHL	5	3	4	7	14	—	—	—	—	—
91-92	Hershey	AHL	46	9	7	16	98	6	0	2	2	23
	Philadelphia	NHL	19	3	2	5	18	—	—	—	—	—
NHL totals			84	10	13	23	215					

KUWABARA, RYAN
RW/D, CANADIENS

PERSONAL: Born March 23, 1972, at Hamilton, Ont. . . . 6-0/205. . . . Shoots right.
TRANSACTIONS/CAREER NOTES: Selected by Montreal Canadiens in second round (second Canadiens pick, 39th overall) of NHL entry draft (June 16, 1990).
HONORS: Won Bobby Smith Trophy (1989-90).

Season Team	League	REGULAR SEASON					PLAYOFFS				
		Gms.	G	A	Pts.	Pen.	Gms.	G	A	Pts.	Pen.
88-89—Hamilton Jr. B	OHA	39	13	23	36	128	—	—	—	—	—
89-90—Ottawa	OHL	66	30	38	68	62	4	0	0	0	0
90-91—Ottawa	OHL	64	34	38	72	67	17	12	15	27	25
91-92—Ottawa	OHL	66	43	57	100	84	10	6	5	11	9

KVARTALNOV, DMITRI
LW/RW, BRUINS

PERSONAL: Born March 25, 1966, at Voskresensk, U.S.S.R. . . . 5-11/180. . . . Shoots left.

TRANSACTIONS/CAREER NOTES: Selected by Boston Bruins in first round (first Bruins pick, 16th overall) of NHL entry draft (June 20, 1992).

HONORS: Won James Gatschene Memorial Trophy (1991-92). . . . Won Leo P. Lamoureux Memorial Trophy (1991-92). . . . Won Garry F. Longman Memorial Trophy (1991-92). . . . Named to IHL All-Star first team (1991-92).

Season Team	League	REGULAR SEASON					PLAYOFFS				
		Gms.	G	A	Pts.	Pen.	Gms.	G	A	Pts.	Pen.
82-83—Khimik Voskresensk	USSR	7	0	0	0	0	—	—	—	—	—
83-84—Khimik Voskresensk	USSR	2	0	0	0	0	—	—	—	—	—
84-85—SKA MVO Kalinin	USSR	—	—	—	—	—	—	—	—	—	—
85-86—SKA MVO Kalinin	USSR	—	—	—	—	—	—	—	—	—	—
86-87—Khimik Voskresensk	USSR	40	11	6	17	28	—	—	—	—	—
87-88—Khimik Voskresensk	USSR	43	16	11	27	16	—	—	—	—	—
88-89—Khimik Voskresensk	USSR	44	20	12	32	18	—	—	—	—	—
89-90—Khimik Voskresensk	USSR	46	25	28	53	33	—	—	—	—	—
90-91—Khimik Voskresensk	USSR	42	12	10	22	18	—	—	—	—	—
91-92—San Diego	IHL	77	*60	58	*118	16	4	2	0	2	2

KYPREOS, NICK
LW, WHALERS

PERSONAL: Born June 4, 1966, at Toronto. . . . 6-0/195. . . . Shoots left. . . . Full name: Nicholas George Kypreos.

TRANSACTIONS/CAREER NOTES: Signed as free agent by Philadelphia Flyers (September 30, 1984). . . . Underwent surgery to right knee (Summer 1988); missed first 52 games of 1988-89 season. . . . Selected by Washington Capitals in NHL waiver draft for $20,000 (October 2, 1989). . . . Underwent surgery to right knee (February 8, 1990).

HONORS: Named to OHL All-Star first team (1985-86). . . . Named to OHL All-Star second team (1986-87).

Season Team	League	REGULAR SEASON					PLAYOFFS				
		Gms.	G	A	Pts.	Pen.	Gms.	G	A	Pts.	Pen.
83-84—North Bay	OHL	51	12	11	23	36	4	3	2	5	9
84-85—North Bay	OHL	64	41	36	77	71	8	2	2	4	15
85-86—North Bay	OHL	64	62	35	97	112	—	—	—	—	—
86-87—North Bay	OHL	46	49	41	90	54	24	11	5	16	78
—Hershey	AHL	10	0	1	1	4	—	—	—	—	—
87-88—Hershey	AHL	71	24	20	44	101	12	0	2	2	17
88-89—Hershey	AHL	28	12	15	27	19	12	4	5	9	11
89-90—Washington	NHL	31	5	4	9	82	7	1	0	1	15
—Baltimore	AHL	14	6	5	11	6	7	4	1	5	17
90-91—Washington	NHL	79	9	9	18	196	9	0	1	1	38
91-92—Washington	NHL	65	4	6	10	206	—	—	—	—	—
NHL totals		175	18	19	37	484	16	1	1	2	53

KYTE, JIM
D, FLAMES

PERSONAL: Born March 21, 1964, at Ottawa. . . . 6-5/220. . . . Shoots left.

TRANSACTIONS/CAREER NOTES: Broke left wrist (March 1980). . . . Selected by Winnipeg Jets as underage junior in first round (first Jets pick, 12th overall) of NHL entry draft (June 9, 1982). . . . Suffered stress fracture in lower back (February 1988). . . . Sprained shoulder (March 1989). . . . Traded by Jets with RW Andrew McBain and LW Randy Gilhen to Pittsburgh Penguins for C/LW Randy Cunneyworth, G Richard Tabaracci and RW Dave McLlwain (June 17, 1989). . . . Traded by Penguins to Calgary Flames for C Jiri Hrdina (December 13, 1990). . . . Fractured bone in left hand during preseason (September 1991). . . . Fractured right ankle (January 27, 1991); missed remainder of season.

Season Team	League	REGULAR SEASON					PLAYOFFS				
		Gms.	G	A	Pts.	Pen.	Gms.	G	A	Pts.	Pen.
80-81—Hawkesbury	COJHL	42	2	24	26	133	—	—	—	—	—
81-82—Cornwall	OHL	52	4	13	17	148	5	0	0	0	10
82-83—Cornwall	OHL	65	6	30	36	195	8	0	2	2	24
—Winnipeg	NHL	2	0	0	0	0	—	—	—	—	—
83-84—Winnipeg	NHL	58	1	2	3	55	3	0	0	0	11
84-85—Winnipeg	NHL	71	0	3	3	111	8	0	0	0	14
85-86—Winnipeg	NHL	71	1	3	4	126	3	0	0	0	12
86-87—Winnipeg	NHL	72	5	5	10	162	10	0	4	4	36
87-88—Winnipeg	NHL	51	1	3	4	128	—	—	—	—	—
88-89—Winnipeg	NHL	74	3	9	12	190	—	—	—	—	—
89-90—Pittsburgh	NHL	56	3	1	4	125	—	—	—	—	—
90-91—Muskegon	IHL	25	2	5	7	157	—	—	—	—	—
—Pittsburgh	NHL	1	0	0	0	2	—	—	—	—	—
—Calgary	NHL	42	0	9	9	153	7	0	0	0	7
91-92—Calgary	NHL	21	0	1	1	107	—	—	—	—	—
—Salt Lake City	IHL	6	0	1	1	9	—	—	—	—	—
NHL totals		519	14	36	50	1159	31	0	4	4	80

LACHANCE, BOB
RW, BLUES

PERSONAL: Born February 1, 1974, at North Hampton, Mass. .... 5-11/175. .... Shoots right.

TRANSACTIONS/CAREER NOTES: Selected by St. Louis Blues in sixth round (fifth Blues pick, 134th overall) of NHL entry draft (June 20, 1992).

Season Team	League	REGULAR SEASON					PLAYOFFS				
		Gms.	G	A	Pts.	Pen.	Gms.	G	A	Pts.	Pen.
91-92—Springfield Jr. B	NEJHL	46	40	98	138	87	—	—	—	—	—

LACHANCE, SCOTT
D, ISLANDERS

PERSONAL: Born October 22, 1972, at Charlottesville, Va. .... 6-2/197. .... Shoots left. .... Full name: Scott Joseph Lachance.

COLLEGE: Boston University.

TRANSACTIONS/CAREER NOTES: Selected by New York Islanders in first round (first Islanders pick, fourth overall) of NHL entry draft (June 22, 1991).

HONORS: Named to Hockey East All-Rookie team (1990-91).

Season Team	League	REGULAR SEASON					PLAYOFFS				
		Gms.	G	A	Pts.	Pen.	Gms.	G	A	Pts.	Pen.
88-89—Springfield Jr. B	NEJHL	36	8	28	36	20	—	—	—	—	—
89-90—Springfield Jr. B	NEJHL	34	25	41	66	62	—	—	—	—	—
90-91—Boston University	Hockey East	31	5	19	24	48	—	—	—	—	—
91-92—U.S. National Team	Int'l	36	1	10	11	34	—	—	—	—	—
—U.S. Olympic Team	Int'l	8	0	1	1	6	—	—	—	—	—
—New York Islanders..........	NHL	17	1	4	5	9	—	—	—	—	—
NHL totals................................		17	1	4	5	9					

LACROIX, DANIEL
LW, ISLANDERS

PERSONAL: Born March 11, 1969, at Montreal. .... 6-2/188. .... Shoots left.

TRANSACTIONS/CAREER NOTES: Selected as underage junior by New York Rangers in second round (second Rangers pick, 31st overall) of NHL entry draft (June 13, 1987). .... Signed as free agent by New York Islanders (June 19, 1992).

HONORS: Won Marcel Robert Trophy (1988-89).

Season Team	League	REGULAR SEASON					PLAYOFFS				
		Gms.	G	A	Pts.	Pen.	Gms.	G	A	Pts.	Pen.
86-87—Granby............................	QMJHL	54	9	16	25	311	8	1	2	3	22
87-88—Granby............................	QMJHL	58	24	50	74	468	5	0	4	4	12
88-89—Granby............................	QMJHL	70	45	49	94	320	4	1	1	2	57
—Denver............................	IHL	2	0	1	1	0	2	0	1	1	0
89-90—Flint	IHL	61	12	16	28	128	4	2	0	2	24
90-91—Binghamton	AHL	54	7	12	19	237	5	1	0	1	24
91-92—Binghamton	AHL	52	12	20	32	149	11	2	4	6	28

LADOUCEUR, RANDY
D, WHALERS

PERSONAL: Born June 30, 1960, at Brockville, Ont. .... 6-2/220. .... Shoots left.

TRANSACTIONS/CAREER NOTES: Signed as free agent by Detroit Red Wings (November 1, 1979). .... Suffered back spasms (March 1986). .... Traded by Red Wings to Hartford Whalers for C Dave Barr (January 12, 1987). .... Sprained right knee (March 1990). .... Sprained knee (January 10, 1991); missed 10 games.

Season Team	League	REGULAR SEASON					PLAYOFFS				
		Gms.	G	A	Pts.	Pen.	Gms.	G	A	Pts.	Pen.
78-79—Brantford........................	OMJHL	64	3	17	20	141	—	—	—	—	—
79-80—Brantford........................	OMJHL	37	6	15	21	125	8	0	5	5	18
80-81—Kalamazoo	IHL	80	7	30	37	52	8	1	3	4	10
81-82—Adirondack	AHL	78	4	28	32	78	5	1	1	2	6
82-83—Adirondack	AHL	48	11	21	32	54	—	—	—	—	—
—Detroit	NHL	27	0	4	4	16	—	—	—	—	—
83-84—Adirondack	AHL	11	3	5	8	12	—	—	—	—	—
—Detroit	NHL	71	3	17	20	58	4	1	0	1	6
84-85—Detroit	NHL	80	3	27	30	108	3	1	0	1	0
85-86—Detroit	NHL	78	5	13	18	196	—	—	—	—	—
86-87—Detroit	NHL	34	3	6	9	70	—	—	—	—	—
—Hartford..........................	NHL	36	2	3	5	51	6	0	2	2	12
87-88—Hartford..........................	NHL	68	1	7	8	91	6	1	1	2	4
88-89—Hartford..........................	NHL	75	2	5	7	95	1	0	0	0	10
89-90—Hartford..........................	NHL	71	3	12	15	126	7	1	0	1	10
90-91—Hartford..........................	NHL	67	1	3	4	118	6	1	4	5	6
91-92—Hartford..........................	NHL	74	1	9	10	127	7	0	1	1	11
NHL totals................................		681	24	106	130	1056	40	5	8	13	59

LAFAYETTE, JUSTIN
LW, BLACKHAWKS

PERSONAL: Born January 23, 1970, at Vancouver, B.C. .... 6-6/220. .... Shoots left.

COLLEGE: Ferris State (Mich.).

TRANSACTIONS/CAREER NOTES: Selected by Chicago Blackhawks in sixth round (fifth Blackhawks pick, 113th overall) of NHL entry draft (June 11, 1988).

Season Team	League	REGULAR SEASON					PLAYOFFS				
		Gms.	G	A	Pts.	Pen.	Gms.	G	A	Pts.	Pen.
87-88—Ferris State	CCHA	36	1	2	3	20	—	—	—	—	—
88-89—Ferris State	CCHA	36	3	4	7	59	—	—	—	—	—
89-90—Ferris State	CCHA	34	4	5	9	38	—	—	—	—	—
90-91—Ferris State	CCHA	41	11	9	20	76	—	—	—	—	—
91-92—Indianapolis	IHL	51	7	10	17	37	—	—	—	—	—

LAFAYETTE, NATHAN
C, BLUES

PERSONAL: Born February 17, 1973, at New Westminster, B.C. . . . . 6-1/194. . . . Shoots right.

TRANSACTIONS/CAREER NOTES: Traded by Kingston Fronenacs with Joel Sandie to Cornwall Royals for D Rod Pasma and Shawn Caplice (January 6, 1991). . . . Selected by St. Louis Blues in third round (third Blues pick, 65th overall) of NHL entry draft (June 22, 1991).

HONORS: Won Canadian Airlines Can.HL Scholastic Player of the Year Award (1991-92). . . . Won Bobby Smith Trophy (1990-91 and 1991-92).

Season Team	League	REGULAR SEASON					PLAYOFFS				
		Gms.	G	A	Pts.	Pen.	Gms.	G	A	Pts.	Pen.
89-90—Kingston	OHL	53	6	8	14	14	7	0	1	1	0
90-91—Kingston	OHL	35	13	13	26	10	—	—	—	—	—
—Cornwall	OHL	28	16	22	38	25	—	—	—	—	—
91-92—Cornwall	OHL	66	28	45	73	26	6	2	5	7	16

LaFONTAINE, PAT
C, SABRES

PERSONAL: Born February 22, 1965, at St. Louis. . . . 5-10/177. . . . Shoots right.

TRANSACTIONS/CAREER NOTES: Selected by New York Islanders as underage junior in first round (first Islanders pick, third overall) of NHL entry draft (June 8, 1983). . . . Damaged ligaments in left knee (August 16, 1984). . . . Suffered from mononucleosis (January 1985). . . . Separated right shoulder (January 25, 1986). . . . Bruised knee (March 1988). . . . Broke nose (October 7, 1988); played entire season with injury. . . . Sprained ligaments in right wrist (November 5, 1988). . . . Strained left hamstring (October 13, 1990); missed three games. . . . Traded by Islanders with LW Randy Wood, D Randy Hillier and future consider-ations to Buffalo Sabres for C Pierre Turgeon, RW Benoit Hogue, D Uwe Krupp and C Dave McIlwain (October 25, 1991). . . . Fractured jaw (November 16, 1991); missed 13 games.

HONORS: Won Can.HL Player of the Year Award (1982-83). . . . Won Michel Briere Trophy (1982-83). . . . Won Jean Beliveau Trophy (1982-83). . . . Won Frank J. Selke Trophy (1982-83). . . . Won Des Instructeurs Trophy (1982-83). . . . Won Guy Lafleur Trophy (1982-83). . . . Named to QMJHL All-Star first team (1982-83). . . . Won Dodge Performer of the Year Award (1989-90). . . . Named to THE SPORTING NEWS All-Star second team (1989-90).

RECORDS: Holds NHL playoff record for fastest two goals from the start of a period—35 seconds (May 19, 1984).

Season Team	League	REGULAR SEASON					PLAYOFFS				
		Gms.	G	A	Pts.	Pen.	Gms.	G	A	Pts.	Pen.
82-83—Verdun	QMJHL	70	*104	*130	*234	10	15	11	*24	*35	4
83-84—U.S. National Team	Int'l	58	56	55	111	22	—	—	—	—	—
—U.S. Olympic Team	Int'l	6	5	5	10	0	—	—	—	—	—
—New York Islanders	NHL	15	13	6	19	6	16	3	6	9	8
84-85—New York Islanders	NHL	67	19	35	54	32	9	1	2	3	4
85-86—New York Islanders	NHL	65	30	23	53	43	3	1	0	1	0
86-87—New York Islanders	NHL	80	38	32	70	70	14	5	7	12	10
87-88—New York Islanders	NHL	75	47	45	92	52	6	4	5	9	8
88-89—New York Islanders	NHL	79	45	43	88	26	—	—	—	—	—
89-90—New York Islanders	NHL	74	54	51	105	38	2	0	1	1	0
90-91—New York Islanders	NHL	75	41	44	85	42	—	—	—	—	—
91-92—Buffalo	NHL	57	46	47	93	98	7	8	3	11	4
NHL totals		587	333	326	659	407	57	22	24	46	34

LAFOREST, MARK
G, SENATORS

PERSONAL: Born July 10, 1962, at Welland, Ont. . . . 5-11/190. . . . Shoots left. . . . Full name: Mark Andrew Laforest.

TRANSACTIONS/CAREER NOTES: Signed as free agent by Detroit Red Wings (September 1983). . . . Traded by Red Wings to Philadelphia Flyers for second-round pick in 1987 draft (D Bob Wilkie) (June 1987). . . . Sprained knee (March 16, 1989). . . . Traded by Flyers to Toronto Maple Leafs for sixth-and seventh-round picks in 1991 draft (September 8, 1989). . . . Twisted left ankle (January 11, 1990); missed five weeks. . . . Traded with by Maple Leafs with RW Tie Domi to New York Rangers for RW Greg Johnston (June 18, 1990). . . . Selected by Ottawa Senators in NHL expansion draft (June 18, 1992).

HONORS: Won Baz Bastien Trophy (1986-87 and 1990-91). . . . Named to AHL All-Star second team (1990-91).

Season Team	League	REGULAR SEASON							PLAYOFFS						
		Gms.	Min.	W	L	T	GA	SO	Avg.	Gms.	Min.	W	L	GA	SO	Avg.
81-82—Niagara Falls	OHL	24	1365	10	13	1	105	0	4.62	5	300	1	2	19	0	3.80
82-83—North Bay	OHL	54	3140	34	17	1	195	0	3.73	8	474	4	4	31	0	3.92
83-84—Adirondack	AHL	7	351	3	3	1	29	0	4.96	—	—	—	—	—	—	—
—Kalamazoo	IHL	13	718	4	5	2	48	1	4.01	—	—	—	—	—	—	—
84-85—Mohawk Valley Stars	ACHL	8	420				60	0	8.57	—	—	—	—	—	—	—
—Adirondack	AHL	11	430	2	3	1	35	0	4.88	—	—	—	—	—	—	—
85-86—Adirondack	AHL	19	1142	13	5	1	57	0	2.99	*17	*1075	12	5	*58	0	3.24
—Detroit	NHL	28	1383	4	21	0	114	1	4.95	—	—	—	—	—	—	—
86-87—Adirondack	AHL	37	2229	23	8	0	105	3	2.83	—	—	—	—	—	—	—
—Detroit	NHL	5	219	2	1	0	12	0	3.29	—	—	—	—	—	—	—
87-88—Hershey	AHL	5	309	2	1	2	13	0	2.52	—	—	—	—	—	—	—
—Philadelphia	NHL	21	972	5	9	2	60	1	3.70	2	48	1	0	1	0	1.25

Season Team	League	REGULAR SEASON							PLAYOFFS						
		Gms.	Min.	W	L	T	GA	SO	Avg.	Gms.	Min.	W	L	GA	SO	Avg.
88-89—Philadelphia	NHL	17	933	5	7	2	64	0	4.12	—	—	—	—	—	—	—
—Hershey	AHL	3	185	2	0	0	9	0	2.92	12	744	7	5	27	1	*2.18
89-90—Toronto	NHL	27	1343	9	14	0	87	0	3.89	—	—	—	—	—	—	—
—Newmarket	AHL	10	604	6	4	0	33	1	3.28	—	—	—	—	—	—	—
90-91—Binghamton	AHL	45	2452	25	14	2	129	0	3.16	9	442	3	4	28	*1	3.80
91-92—Binghamton	AHL	43	2559	25	15	3	146	1	3.42	11	662	7	4	34	0	3.08
NHL totals		98	4850	25	52	4	337	2	4.17	2	48	1	0	1	0	1.25

LAFORGE, MARC
LW, OILERS

PERSONAL: Born January 3, 1968, at Sudbury, Ont. . . . 6-2/210. . . . Shoots left.
TRANSACTIONS/CAREER NOTES: Selected by Hartford Whalers as underage junior in second round (second Whalers pick, 32nd overall) of NHL entry draft (June 21, 1986). . . . Suspended nine games by OHL (October 1986). . . . Suspended two years by OHL for attacking several members of opposing team in game-ending fight (November 6, 1987). . . . Suspended three games by AHL for head-butting (November 26, 1988). . . . Suspended six games for leaving bench to start fight (December 8, 1988). . . . Suspended by Whalers for refusing to report to Indianapolis (December 28, 1988). . . . Whalers lifted suspension when he reported to Indianapolis (January 19, 1989). . . . Suffered sore back (November 1989). . . . Suspended five games by AHL for head-butting (February 5, 1990). . . . Traded by Whalers to Edmonton Oilers for rights to D Cam Brauer (March 6, 1990). . . . Suspended 10 games by AHL for cross-checking and kneeing (December 3, 1990). . . . Suspended 10 games by AHL for cross-checking (January 13, 1991). . . . Suspended six games by AHL for leaving the bench to start fight (February 1991). . . . Suspended 10 games by NHL (September 26, 1991).

Season Team	League	REGULAR SEASON					PLAYOFFS				
		Gms.	G	A	Pts.	Pen.	Gms.	G	A	Pts.	Pen.
84-85—Kingston	OHL	57	1	5	6	214	—	—	—	—	—
85-86—Kingston	OHL	60	1	13	14	248	10	0	1	1	30
86-87—Kingston	OHL	53	2	10	12	224	12	1	0	1	79
—Binghamton	AHL	—	—	—	—	—	4	0	0	0	7
87-88—Sudbury	OHL	14	0	2	2	68	—	—	—	—	—
88-89—Indianapolis	IHL	14	0	2	2	138	—	—	—	—	—
—Binghamton	AHL	38	2	2	4	179	—	—	—	—	—
89-90—Hartford	NHL	9	0	0	0	43	—	—	—	—	—
—Binghamton	AHL	25	2	6	8	111	—	—	—	—	—
—Cape Breton	AHL	3	0	1	1	24	3	0	0	0	27
90-91—Cape Breton	AHL	49	1	7	8	217	—	—	—	—	—
91-92—Cape Breton	AHL	59	0	14	14	341	4	0	0	0	24
NHL totals		9	0	0	0	43					

LaGRAND, SCOTT
G, FLYERS

PERSONAL: Born February 11, 1970, at Potsdam, N.Y. . . . 6-1/170. . . . Shoots right.
HIGH SCHOOL: Hotchkiss (Lakeville, Conn.).
COLLEGE: Boston College.
TRANSACTIONS/CAREER NOTES: Selected by Philadelphia Flyers in fourth round (fifth Flyers pick, 77th overall) of NHL entry draft (June 11, 1988).
HONORS: Named to Hockey East All-Star first team (1990-91).

Season Team	League	REGULAR SEASON							PLAYOFFS						
		Gms.	Min.	W	L	T	GA	SO	Avg.	Gms.	Min.	W	L	GA	SO	Avg.
86-87—Hotchkiss	N.Y. H.S.	17	1020				36	0	2.12	—	—	—	—	—	—	—
87-88—Hotchkiss	N.Y. H.S.	—	—	—	—	—	—	—	—	—	—	—	—	—	—	—
88-89—Hotchkiss	N.Y. H.S.	—	—	—	—	—	—	—	—	—	—	—	—	—	—	—
89-90—Boston College	Hoc. East	24	1268	17	4	0	57	0	2.70	7	377	5	1	17	0	2.71
90-91—Boston College	Hoc. East	12	557	7	2	0	39	0	4.20	—	—	—	—	—	—	—
91-92—Boston College	Hoc. East	30	1750	11	16	2	108	1	3.70	—	—	—	—	—	—	—

LALOR, MIKE
D, JETS

PERSONAL: Born March 8, 1963, at Fort Erie, Ont. . . . 6-0/190. . . . Shoots left. . . . Full name: John Michael Lalor.
TRANSACTIONS/CAREER NOTES: Signed as free agent by Nova Scotia Voyageurs (September 1983). . . . Signed as free agent by Montreal Canadiens (September 1983). . . . Suffered from bursitis in right ankle (September 1987). . . . Suffered stress fracture of left ankle (November 1, 1988). . . . Traded by Canadiens to St. Louis Blues for the option to flip first-round picks in 1990 draft and second or third-round picks in 1991 draft (January 16, 1989). . . . Traded by Blues with C Peter Zezel to Washington Capitals for LW Geoff Courtnall (July 13, 1990). . . . Traded by Capitals to Winnipeg Jets for RW Paul MacDermid (March 2, 1992).

Season Team	League	REGULAR SEASON					PLAYOFFS				
		Gms.	G	A	Pts.	Pen.	Gms.	G	A	Pts.	Pen.
81-82—Brantford	OHL	64	3	13	16	114	11	0	6	6	11
82-83—Brantford	OHL	65	10	30	40	113	6	1	3	4	20
83-84—Nova Scotia	AHL	67	5	11	16	80	12	0	2	2	13
84-85—Sherbrooke	AHL	79	9	23	32	114	17	3	5	8	36
85-86—Montreal	NHL	62	3	5	8	56	17	1	2	3	29
86-87—Montreal	NHL	57	0	10	10	47	13	2	1	3	29
87-88—Montreal	NHL	66	1	10	11	113	11	0	0	0	11
88-89—Montreal	NHL	12	1	4	5	15	—	—	—	—	—
—St. Louis	NHL	36	1	14	15	54	10	1	1	2	14
89-90—St. Louis	NHL	78	0	16	16	81	12	0	2	2	31

Season Team	League	REGULAR SEASON					PLAYOFFS				
		Gms.	G	A	Pts.	Pen.	Gms.	G	A	Pts.	Pen.
90-91—Washington	NHL	68	1	5	6	61	10	1	2	3	22
91-92—Washington	NHL	64	5	7	12	64	—	—	—	—	—
—Winnipeg	NHL	15	2	3	5	14	7	0	0	0	19
NHL totals		458	14	74	88	505	80	5	8	13	155

LAMB, MARK
C, SENATORS

PERSONAL: Born August 3, 1964, at Swift Current, Sask.... 5-9/180.... Shoots left.
TRANSACTIONS/CAREER NOTES: Selected by Calgary Flames as underage junior in fourth round (fifth Flames pick, 72nd overall) of NHL entry draft (June 9, 1982).... Refused to dress for a game after Nanaimo Islanders released coach Les Calder; asked to be traded (December 1982). ... Traded by Islanders to Medicine Hat Tigers for Glen Kulka and G Daryl Reaugh (December 1982).... Signed as free agent by Detroit Red Wings (July 1, 1986).... Selected by Edmonton Oilers in NHL waiver draft (October 5, 1987). ...Pinched nerve in neck (October 21, 1990).... Selected by Ottawa Senators in NHL expansion draft (June 18, 1992).
HONORS: Won Frank Boucher Memorial Trophy (1983-84).... Named to WHL All-Star first team (1983-84).

Season Team	League	REGULAR SEASON					PLAYOFFS				
		Gms.	G	A	Pts.	Pen.	Gms.	G	A	Pts.	Pen.
80-81—Billings	WHL	24	1	8	9	12	—	—	—	—	—
81-82—Billings	WHL	72	45	56	101	46	5	4	6	10	4
82-83—Colorado	CHL	—	—	—	—	—	6	0	2	2	0
—Nanaimo	WHL	30	14	37	51	16	—	—	—	—	—
—Medicine Hat	WHL	46	22	43	65	33	5	3	2	5	4
83-84—Medicine Hat	WHL	72	59	77	136	30	14	12	11	23	6
84-85—Medicine Hat	WHL	—	—	—	—	—	6	3	2	5	2
—Moncton	AHL	80	23	49	72	53	—	—	—	—	—
85-86—Calgary	NHL	1	0	0	0	0	—	—	—	—	—
—Moncton	AHL	79	26	50	76	51	10	2	6	8	17
86-87—Detroit	NHL	22	2	1	3	8	11	0	0	0	11
—Adirondack	AHL	49	14	36	50	45	—	—	—	—	—
87-88—Nova Scotia	AHL	69	27	61	88	45	5	0	5	5	6
—Edmonton	NHL	2	0	0	0	0	—	—	—	—	—
88-89—Cape Breton	AHL	54	33	49	82	29	—	—	—	—	—
—Edmonton	NHL	20	2	8	10	14	6	0	2	2	8
89-90—Edmonton	NHL	58	12	16	28	42	22	6	11	17	2
90-91—Edmonton	NHL	37	4	8	12	25	15	0	5	5	20
91-92—Edmonton	NHL	59	6	22	28	46	16	1	1	2	10
NHL totals		199	26	55	81	135	70	7	19	26	51

LAMBERT, DAN
D, NORDIQUES

PERSONAL: Born January 12, 1970, at St. Boniface, Man.... 5-8/177.... Shoots left.... Full name: Daniel Lambert.
TRANSACTIONS/CAREER NOTES: Selected by Quebec Nordiques in sixth round (eighth Nordiques pick, 106th overall) of NHL entry draft (June 17, 1989).... Suffered facial paralysis (December 4, 1991); missed two games.
HONORS: Won Bill Hunter Trophy (1988-89).... Named to WHL All-Star first team (1988-89 and 1989-90).

Season Team	League	REGULAR SEASON					PLAYOFFS				
		Gms.	G	A	Pts.	Pen.	Gms.	G	A	Pts.	Pen.
86-87—Swift Current	WHL	68	13	53	66	95	4	1	1	2	9
87-88—Swift Current	WHL	69	20	63	83	120	10	2	10	12	45
88-89—Swift Current	WHL	57	25	77	102	158	12	9	19	28	12
89-90—Swift Current	WHL	50	17	51	68	119	4	2	3	5	12
90-91—Fort Wayne	IHL	49	10	27	37	65	19	4	10	14	20
—Halifax	AHL	30	7	13	20	20	—	—	—	—	—
—Quebec	NHL	1	0	0	0	0	—	—	—	—	—
91-92—Halifax	AHL	47	3	28	31	33	—	—	—	—	—
—Quebec	NHL	28	6	9	15	22	—	—	—	—	—
NHL totals		29	6	9	15	22					

LAMOTHE, MARC
G, CANADIENS

PERSONAL: Born February 27, 1974, at New Liskeard, Ont.... 6-2/186.... Shoots left.
TRANSACTIONS/CAREER NOTES: Selected by Montreal Canadiens in fourth round (sixth Canadiens pick, 92nd overall) of NHL entry draft (June 20, 1992).

Season Team	League	REGULAR SEASON							PLAYOFFS					
		Gms.	Min.	W	L	T	GA	SO	Avg.	Gms.	Min.	W	L	GA	SO	Avg.
90-91—Ottawa	OHA Mj Jr.A	25	1220				82	1	4.03	—	—	—	—	—	—	—
91-92—Kingston	OHL	42	2378	10	25	2	189	1	4.77	—	—	—	—	—	—	—

LANGWAY, ROD
D, CAPITALS

PERSONAL: Born May 3, 1957, at Maag, Formosa.... 6-3/225.... Shoots left.... Full name: Rod Corry Langway.
COLLEGE: New Hampshire.
TRANSACTIONS/CAREER NOTES: Bruised left foot (January 5, 1982).... Selected by Montreal Canadiens from University of New Hampshire in second round (third Canadiens pick, 36th overall) of NHL amateur draft (June 14, 1977).... Selected by Birmingham Bulls in WHA amateur players' draft (May 1977).... Signed as free agent by Canadiens (October 1978).... Injured left knee (February 9, 1982).... Traded by Canadiens with D Brian Engblom, C Doug Jarvis and

RW Craig Laughlin to Washington Capitals for LW Ryan Walter and D Rick Green (September 9, 1982).... Bruised right knee (October 23, 1985); missed eight games. ... Ruptured disc in back (November 1987).... Pulled thigh muscle (February 1988).... Bruised thigh (April 1988).... Bruised left knee (November 1988).... Strained left knee ligaments (October 7, 1989); missed six games.... Underwent surgery to both knees (December 23, 1989); missed 10 games.... Suffered back spasms (January 11, 1991); missed 18 games.... Suffered slight concussion (November 13, 1991); missed two games.... Fractured two toes on left foot (December 5, 1991); missed eight games. ... Injured groin (March 20, 1992); missed five games.

HONORS: Won James Norris Memorial Trophy (1982-83 and 1983-84).... Named to THE SPORTING NEWS All-Star first team (1982-83 and 1983-84).... Named to NHL All-Star first team (1982-83 and 1983-84).... Named to THE SPORTING NEWS All-Star second team (1984-85).... Named to NHL All-Star second team (1984-85).

MISCELLANEOUS: Does not wear a helmet.

Season	Team	League	REGULAR SEASON Gms.	G	A	Pts.	Pen.	PLAYOFFS Gms.	G	A	Pts.	Pen.
75-76	Univ. of New Hampshire ...	ECAC	—	—	—	—	—	—	—	—	—	—
76-77	Univ. of New Hampshire ...	ECAC	34	10	43	53	52	—	—	—	—	—
77-78	Hampton	AHL	30	6	16	22	50	—	—	—	—	—
	—Birmingham	WHA	52	3	18	21	52	4	0	0	0	9
78-79	Montreal	NHL	45	3	4	7	30	8	0	0	0	16
	—Nova Scotia	AHL	18	6	13	19	29	—	—	—	—	—
79-80	Montreal	NHL	77	7	29	36	81	10	3	3	6	2
80-81	Montreal	NHL	80	11	34	45	120	3	0	0	0	6
81-82	Montreal	NHL	66	5	34	39	116	5	0	3	3	18
82-83	Washington	NHL	80	3	29	32	75	4	0	0	0	0
83-84	Washington	NHL	80	9	24	33	61	8	0	5	5	7
84-85	Washington	NHL	79	4	22	26	54	5	0	1	1	6
85-86	Washington	NHL	71	1	17	18	61	9	1	2	3	6
86-87	Washington	NHL	78	2	25	27	53	7	0	1	1	2
87-88	Washington	NHL	63	3	13	16	28	6	0	0	0	8
88-89	Washington	NHL	76	2	19	21	67	6	0	0	0	6
89-90	Washington	NHL	58	0	8	8	39	15	1	4	5	12
90-91	Washington	NHL	56	1	7	8	24	11	0	2	2	6
91-92	Washington	NHL	64	0	13	13	22	7	0	1	1	2
WHA totals			52	3	18	21	52	4	0	0	0	9
NHL totals			973	51	278	329	831	104	5	22	27	97

LANZ, RICK

D

PERSONAL: Born September 16, 1961, at Karlovy Vary, Czechoslovakia.... 6-2/203.... Shoots right. ... Full name: Rick Roman Lanz.

TRANSACTIONS/CAREER NOTES: Selected by Vancouver Canucks as underage junior in first round (first Canucks pick, seventh overall) of NHL entry draft (June 11, 1980).... Underwent surgery to repair torn knee ligaments (January 1982).... Dislocated disk in neck (December 1984); missed 23 games.... Fractured jaw (October 16, 1986).... Traded by Canucks to Toronto Maple Leafs for D Jim Benning and C Dan Hodgson (December 2, 1986). ...Suffered from asthma (January 1988).... Sprained neck (April 1988).... Sprained shoulder (October 1988).... Suffered from the flu (December 1988).... Injured knee (January 1989).... Bruised shoulder (March 1989).... Signed as free agent by Chicago Blackhawks (September 13, 1990).... Traded by Blackhawks to Los Angeles Kings for D Jeff Rohlicek (December 2, 1991).

Season	Team	League	REGULAR SEASON Gms.	G	A	Pts.	Pen.	PLAYOFFS Gms.	G	A	Pts.	Pen.
77-78	Oshawa	OMJHL	65	1	41	42	51	—	—	—	—	—
78-79	Oshawa	OMJHL	65	12	47	59	88	5	1	3	4	14
79-80	Oshawa	OMJHL	52	18	38	56	51	7	2	3	5	6
80-81	Vancouver	NHL	76	7	22	29	40	3	0	0	0	4
81-82	Vancouver	NHL	39	3	11	14	48	—	—	—	—	—
82-83	Vancouver	NHL	74	10	38	48	46	4	2	1	3	0
83-84	Vancouver	NHL	79	18	39	57	45	4	0	4	4	2
84-85	Vancouver	NHL	57	2	17	19	69	—	—	—	—	—
85-86	Vancouver	NHL	75	15	38	53	73	3	0	0	0	0
86-87	Vancouver	NHL	17	1	6	7	10	—	—	—	—	—
	—Toronto	NHL	44	2	19	21	32	13	1	3	4	27
87-88	Toronto	NHL	75	6	22	28	65	1	0	0	0	2
88-89	Toronto	NHL	32	1	9	10	18	—	—	—	—	—
89-90	Ambri Piotta	Switzerland	36	4	14	18		—	—	—	—	—
90-91	Indianapolis	IHL	8	0	5	5	18	—	—	—	—	—
91-92	Chicago	NHL	1	0	0	0	2	—	—	—	—	—
	—Phoenix	IHL	38	7	14	21	21	—	—	—	—	—
NHL totals			569	65	221	286	448	28	3	8	11	35

LAPERRIERE, DAN

D, BLUES

PERSONAL: Born March 28, 1969, at Laval, Que.... 6-1/180. ... Shoots left.... Full name: Daniel Jacques Laperriere.... Son of Jacques Laperriere, Hall of Fame defenseman, Montreal Canadiens (1962-63 through 1973-74).

COLLEGE: St. Lawrence (N.Y.).

TRANSACTIONS/CAREER NOTES: Selected by St. Louis Blues in fifth round (fourth Blues pick, 93rd overall) of NHL entry draft (June 17, 1989).

HONORS: Named to ECAC All-Star second team (1990-91).... Named ECAC Player of the Year (1991-92).... Named ECAC Playoff Most Valuable Player (1991-92).... Named to ECAC All-Star first team (1991-92).

Season	Team	League	Gms.	G	A	Pts.	Pen.	Gms.	G	A	Pts.	Pen.
			REGULAR SEASON					PLAYOFFS				
88-89—St. Lawrence University...		ECAC	34	1	11	12	14	—	—	—	—	—
89-90—St. Lawrence University...		ECAC	29	6	19	25	16	—	—	—	—	—
90-91—St. Lawrence University...		ECAC	34	7	32	39	18	—	—	—	—	—
91-92—St. Lawrence University...		ECAC	32	8	*45	53	36	—	—	—	—	—

LAPOINTE, CLAUDE
C, NORDIQUES

PERSONAL: Born October 11, 1968, at Ville Emard, Que.... 5-9/173.... Shoots left.
TRANSACTIONS/CAREER NOTES: Traded by Trois-Rivieres Draveurs with G Alain Dubeau and third-round draft pick (D Patrice Brisebois) to Laval Titans for D Raymond Saumier, LW Mike Gober, D Eric Gobeil and second-round draft pick (D Eric Charron) (May 1987).... Selected by Quebec Nordiques in 12th round (12th Nordiques pick, 234th overall) of NHL entry draft (June 11, 1988).... Tore groin muscle (February 9, 1991).... Injured groin (October 23, 1991); missed one game.

Season	Team	League	Gms.	G	A	Pts.	Pen.	Gms.	G	A	Pts.	Pen.
			REGULAR SEASON					PLAYOFFS				
85-86—Trois-Rivieres		QMJHL	72	19	38	57	74	—	—	—	—	—
86-87—Trois-Rivieres		QMJHL	70	47	57	104	123	—	—	—	—	—
87-88—Laval		QMJHL	69	37	83	120	143	13	2	17	19	53
88-89—Laval		QMJHL	63	32	72	104	158	17	5	14	19	66
89-90—Halifax		AHL	63	18	19	37	51	6	1	1	2	34
90-91—Quebec		NHL	13	2	2	4	4	—	—	—	—	—
—Halifax		AHL	43	17	17	34	46	—	—	—	—	—
91-92—Quebec		NHL	78	13	20	33	86	—	—	—	—	—
NHL totals			91	15	22	37	90					

LAPOINTE, MARTIN
RW, RED WINGS

PERSONAL: Born September 12, 1973, at Lachine, Que.... 5-11/197.... Shoots right.
TRANSACTIONS/CAREER NOTES: Selected by Detroit Red Wings in first round (first Red Wings pick, 10th overall) of NHL entry draft (June 22, 1991).... Fractured wrist (October 9, 1991); missed 22 games.
HONORS: Won Michel Bergeron Trophy (1989-90).... Named to QMJHL All-Star first team (1989-90).... Named to QMJHL All-Star second team (1990-91).

Season	Team	League	Gms.	G	A	Pts.	Pen.	Gms.	G	A	Pts.	Pen.
			REGULAR SEASON					PLAYOFFS				
89-90—Laval		QMJHL	65	42	54	96	77	14	8	17	25	54
90-91—Laval		QMJHL	64	44	54	98	66	13	7	14	21	26
91-92—Detroit		NHL	4	0	1	1	5	3	0	1	1	4
—Laval		QMJHL	31	25	30	55	84	10	4	10	14	32
—Adirondack		AHL	—	—	—	—	—	8	2	2	4	4
NHL totals			4	0	1	1	5	3	0	1	1	4

LAPOINTE, SYLVAIN
D, CANADIENS

PERSONAL: Born March 14, 1973, at Anjou, Que.... 6-0/190.... Shoots left.
COLLEGE: Clarkson (N.Y.).
TRANSACTIONS/CAREER NOTES: Selected by Montreal Canadiens in fourth round (sixth Canadiens pick, 83rd overall) of NHL entry draft (June 22, 1991).

Season	Team	League	Gms.	G	A	Pts.	Pen.	Gms.	G	A	Pts.	Pen.
			REGULAR SEASON					PLAYOFFS				
90-91—Clarkson		ECAC	40	2	12	14	30	—	—	—	—	—
91-92—Hull		QMJHL	67	0	11	11	65	6	1	1	2	10

LAPPIN, PETER
RW, SHARKS

PERSONAL: Born December 31, 1965, at St. Charles, Ill.... 5-11/180.... Shoots right.... Full name: Peter John Lappin.
COLLEGE: St. Lawrence (N.Y.).
TRANSACTIONS/CAREER NOTES: Selected by Calgary Flames in NHL supplemental draft (June 1987).... Injured knee (January 1988).... Traded by Flames to Minnesota North Stars for second-round pick in 1990 draft (later traded to New Jersey) (RW Chris Gotziaman) (September 4, 1989).... Selected by San Jose Sharks in NHL dispersal draft (May 30, 1991).
HONORS: Named to ECAC All-Star second team (1986-87).... Named to NCAA All-America East second team (1986-87).... Named to NCAA All-America East first team (1987-88).... Named to NCAA All-Tournament team (1987-88).... Named ECAC Player of the Year (1987-88).... Named to ECAC All-Star first team (1987-88).... Named Turner Cup Playoff Most Valuable Player (1987-88).... Named to IHL All-Star second team (1989-90).

Season	Team	League	Gms.	G	A	Pts.	Pen.	Gms.	G	A	Pts.	Pen.
			REGULAR SEASON					PLAYOFFS				
84-85—St. Lawrence University...		ECAC	32	10	12	22	22	—	—	—	—	—
85-86—St. Lawrence University...		ECAC	30	20	26	46	64	—	—	—	—	—
86-87—St. Lawrence University...		ECAC	35	34	24	58	32	—	—	—	—	—
87-88—St. Lawrence University...		ECAC	34	21	39	60	30	—	—	—	—	—
—Salt Lake City		IHL	3	1	1	2	0	17	*16	12	*28	11
88-89—Salt Lake City		IHL	81	48	42	90	50	14	†9	9	18	4
89-90—Kalamazoo		IHL	74	45	35	80	42	8	5	2	7	4
—Minnesota		NHL	6	0	0	0	2	—	—	—	—	—
90-91—Kalamazoo		IHL	73	20	47	67	74	11	5	4	9	8
91-92—Kansas City		IHL	78	28	30	58	41	4	2	1	3	0
—San Jose		NHL	1	0	0	0	0	—	—	—	—	—
NHL totals			7	0	0	0	2					

L

LARIONOV, IGOR
C

PERSONAL: Born December 3, 1960, at Voskresensk, U.S.S.R. . . . 5-9/165. . . . Shoots left.
TRANSACTIONS/CAREER NOTES: Selected by Vancouver Canucks in 11th round (11th Canucks pick, 214th overall) of NHL entry draft (June 15, 1985). . . . Suffered groin injury (October 25, 1990); missed four games. . . . Sprained ankle (January 8, 1991). . . . Reinjured ankle (January 30, 1991); missed seven games. . . . Signed to play with Lugano of Switzerland (July 14, 1992).
MISCELLANEOUS: Member of 1984 and 1988 gold-medal-winning U.S.S.R. Olympic teams.

			REGULAR SEASON					PLAYOFFS			
Season	Team	League	Gms.	G	A	Pts.	Pen.	Gms.	G	A	Pts.	Pen.
77-78—Khimik Voskresensk	USSR	6	3	0	3	4	—	—	—	—	—
78-79—Khimik Voskresensk	USSR	25	3	4	7	12	—	—	—	—	—
79-80—Khimik Voskresensk	USSR	42	11	7	18	24	—	—	—	—	—
80-81—Khimik Voskresensk	USSR	56	22	23	45	36	—	—	—	—	—
81-82—Central Red Army	USSR	46	31	22	53	6	—	—	—	—	—
82-83—Central Red Army	USSR	44	20	19	39	20	—	—	—	—	—
83-84—Central Red Army	USSR	43	15	26	41	30	—	—	—	—	—
84-85—Central Red Army	USSR	40	18	28	46	20	—	—	—	—	—
85-86—Central Red Army	USSR	40	21	31	52	33	—	—	—	—	—
86-87—Central Red Army	USSR	39	20	26	46	34	—	—	—	—	—
87-88—Central Red Army	USSR	51	25	32	57	54	—	—	—	—	—
88-89—Central Red Army	USSR	31	15	12	27	22	—	—	—	—	—
89-90—Vancouver	NHL	74	17	27	44	20	—	—	—	—	—
90-91—Vancouver	NHL	64	13	21	34	14	6	1	0	1	6
91-92—Vancouver	NHL	72	21	44	65	54	13	3	7	10	4
NHL totals		210	51	92	143	88	19	4	7	11	10

LARKIN, JIM
LW, KINGS

PERSONAL: Born April 15, 1970, at South Weymouth, Mass. . . . 6-0/175. . . . Shoots left. . . . Full name: James Dodd Larkin III.
HIGH SCHOOL: Mount St. Joseph Academy (Rutland, Vt.).
COLLEGE: Vermont.
TRANSACTIONS/CAREER NOTES: Selected by Los Angeles Kings in ninth round (10th Kings pick, 175th overall) of NHL entry draft (June 11, 1988).

			REGULAR SEASON					PLAYOFFS			
Season	Team	League	Gms.	G	A	Pts.	Pen.	Gms.	G	A	Pts.	Pen.
86-87—Mount St. Joseph H.S.	Vt. H.S.		30	26	56		—	—	—	—	—
87-88—Mount St. Joseph H.S.	Vt. H.S.		44	41	85		—	—	—	—	—
88-89—University of Vermont	ECAC	34	16	19	35	8	—	—	—	—	—
89-90—University of Vermont	ECAC	28	20	15	35	14	—	—	—	—	—
90-91—University of Vermont	ECAC	27	6	22	28	22	—	—	—	—	—
91-92—University of Vermont	ECAC	29	15	16	31	32	—	—	—	—	—

LARMER, STEVE
RW, BLACKHAWKS

PERSONAL: Born June 16, 1961, at Peterborough, Ont. . . . 5-10/189. . . . Shoots left. . . . Full name: Steve Donald Larmer. . . . Brother of Jeff Larmer, left winger, Colorado Rockies, New Jersey Devils and Chicago Blackhawks (1981-82 through 1985-86).
TRANSACTIONS/CAREER NOTES: Selected by Chicago Blackhawks as underage junior in sixth round (11th Blackhawks pick, 120th overall) of NHL entry draft (June 11, 1980).
HONORS: Named to OHL All-Star second team (1980-81). . . . Named to AHL All-Star second team (1981-82). . . . Named NHL Rookie of the Year by THE SPORTING NEWS (1982-83). . . . Won Calder Memorial Trophy (1982-83). . . . Named to NHL All-Rookie team (1982-83).

			REGULAR SEASON					PLAYOFFS			
Season	Team	League	Gms.	G	A	Pts.	Pen.	Gms.	G	A	Pts.	Pen.
77-78—Peterborough	OMJHL	62	24	17	41	51	18	5	7	12	27
78-79—Niagara Falls	OMJHL	66	37	47	84	108	—	—	—	—	—
79-80—Niagara Falls	OMJHL	67	45	69	114	71	10	5	9	14	15
80-81—Niagara Falls	OMJHL	61	55	78	133	73	12	13	8	21	24
—Chicago	NHL	4	0	1	1	0	—	—	—	—	—
81-82—New Brunswick	AHL	74	38	44	82	46	15	6	6	12	0
—Chicago	NHL	3	0	0	0	0	—	—	—	—	—
82-83—Chicago	NHL	80	43	47	90	28	11	5	7	12	8
83-84—Chicago	NHL	80	35	40	75	34	5	2	2	4	7
84-85—Chicago	NHL	80	46	40	86	16	15	9	13	22	14
85-86—Chicago	NHL	80	31	45	76	47	3	0	3	3	4
86-87—Chicago	NHL	80	28	56	84	22	4	0	0	0	2
87-88—Chicago	NHL	80	41	48	89	42	5	1	6	7	0
88-89—Chicago	NHL	80	43	44	87	54	16	8	9	17	22
89-90—Chicago	NHL	80	31	59	90	40	20	7	15	22	8
90-91—Chicago	NHL	80	44	57	101	79	6	5	1	6	4
91-92—Chicago	NHL	80	29	45	74	65	18	8	7	15	6
NHL totals		807	371	482	853	427	103	45	63	108	75

LAROSE, GUY
C/LW, MAPLE LEAFS

PERSONAL: Born July 31, 1967, at Hull, Que. . . . 5-10/175. . . . Shoots left. . . . Son of Claude Larose, right winger, Montreal Canadiens, Minnesota North Stars and St. Louis Blues (1962-63 through 1977-78).
TRANSACTIONS/CAREER NOTES: Fractured third left metacarpal (February 22, 1985). . . . Selected

by Buffalo Sabres as underage junior in 11th round (11th Sabres pick, 224th overall) of NHL entry draft (June 15, 1985). . . . Signed as free agent by Winnipeg Jets (July 21, 1987). . . . Traded by Jets to New York Rangers for D Rudy Poeschek (January 22, 1991). . . . Traded by Rangers to Toronto Maple Leafs for C/LW Mike Stevens (December 26, 1991).

Season Team	League	REGULAR SEASON					PLAYOFFS				
		Gms.	G	A	Pts.	Pen.	Gms.	G	A	Pts.	Pen.
83-84—Ottawa	COJHL	54	37	66	103	66	—	—	—	—	—
84-85—Guelph	OHL	58	30	30	60	63	—	—	—	—	—
85-86—Guelph	OHL	37	12	36	48	55	—	—	—	—	—
—Ottawa	OHL	28	19	25	44	63	—	—	—	—	—
86-87—Ottawa	OHL	66	28	49	77	77	11	2	8	10	27
87-88—Moncton	AHL	77	22	31	53	127	—	—	—	—	—
88-89—Winnipeg	NHL	3	0	1	1	6	—	—	—	—	—
—Moncton	AHL	72	32	27	59	176	10	4	4	8	37
89-90—Moncton	AHL	79	44	26	70	232	—	—	—	—	—
90-91—Moncton	AHL	35	14	10	24	60	—	—	—	—	—
—Binghamton	AHL	34	21	15	36	48	10	8	5	13	37
—Winnipeg	NHL	7	0	0	0	8	—	—	—	—	—
91-92—Binghamton	AHL	30	10	11	21	36	—	—	—	—	—
—St. John's	AHL	15	7	7	14	26	—	—	—	—	—
—Toronto	NHL	34	9	5	14	27	—	—	—	—	—
NHL totals		44	9	6	15	41					

LAROUCHE, STEVE
C, CANADIENS

PERSONAL: Born April 14, 1971, at Rouyn, Que. . . . 5-11/180. . . . Shoots right.
TRANSACTIONS/CAREER NOTES: Selected by Montreal Canadiens in second round (third Canadiens pick, 41st overall) of NHL entry draft (June 17, 1989). . . . Injured shoulder (October 8, 1989). . . . QMJHL rights traded by Trois-Rivieres Draveurs with C Sabastien Parent and sixth-round pick in 1990 draft to Chicoutimi Sagueneens for Paul Brosseau and Jasmin Ouellet (May 26, 1990). . . . Tore left knee ligaments (October 5, 1990); missed two months. . . . Sent home by Chicoutimi coach Joe Canale for indifferent play (January 1991).
HONORS: Named to QMJHL All-Star second team (1989-90).

Season Team	League	REGULAR SEASON					PLAYOFFS				
		Gms.	G	A	Pts.	Pen.	Gms.	G	A	Pts.	Pen.
87-88—Trois-Rivieres	QMJHL	66	11	29	40	25	—	—	—	—	—
88-89—Trois-Rivieres	QMJHL	70	51	102	153	53	4	4	2	6	6
89-90—Trois-Rivieres	QMJHL	60	55	90	145	40	7	3	5	8	8
90-91—Chicoutimi	QMJHL	45	35	41	76	64	17	†13	*20	*33	20
91-92—Fredericton	AHL	74	21	35	56	41	7	1	0	1	0

LARTER, TYLER
C, JETS

PERSONAL: Born March 12, 1968, at Charlottetown, P.E.I. . . . 5-10/180. . . . Shoots left.
TRANSACTIONS/CAREER NOTES: Selected by Washington Capitals in fourth round (third Capitals pick, 78th overall) of NHL entry draft (June 13, 1987). . . . Traded by Capitals with LW Bob Joyce and D Kent Paynter to Winnipeg Jets for LW Brent Hughes, LW Craig Duncanson and C Simon Wheeldon (May 21, 1991). . . . Selected by Minnesota North Stars in NHL expansion draft (May 30, 1991). . . . Traded by North Stars to Jets for RW Tony Joseph (October 15, 1991).

Season Team	League	REGULAR SEASON					PLAYOFFS				
		Gms.	G	A	Pts.	Pen.	Gms.	G	A	Pts.	Pen.
83-84—Charlottetown	PEIJHL	26	24	32	56		—	—	—	—	—
84-85—Sault Ste. Marie	OHL	64	14	26	40	48	—	—	—	—	—
85-86—Sault Ste. Marie	OHL	60	15	40	55	137	—	—	—	—	—
86-87—Sault Ste. Marie	OHL	59	34	59	93	122	4	0	2	2	8
87-88—Sault Ste. Marie	OHL	65	44	65	109	155	4	3	9	12	8
88-89—Baltimore	AHL	71	9	19	28	189	—	—	—	—	—
89-90—Baltimore	AHL	79	31	36	67	104	12	5	6	11	57
—Washington	NHL	1	0	0	0	0	—	—	—	—	—
90-91—Baltimore	AHL	62	21	21	42	84	6	1	0	1	13
91-92—Kalamazoo	IHL	3	0	2	2	4	—	—	—	—	—
—Moncton	AHL	68	25	51	76	156	10	5	5	10	33
NHL totals		1	0	0	0	0					

LATAL, JIRI
D

PERSONAL: Born February 2, 1967, at Olomouc, Czechoslovakia. . . . 6-0/190. . . . Shoots left.
TRANSACTIONS/CAREER NOTES: Selected by Toronto Maple Leafs in sixth round (sixth Maple Leafs pick, 106th overall) of NHL entry draft (June 15, 1985). . . . Rights traded by Maple Leafs to Philadelphia Flyers for seventh-round pick in 1991 draft (LW Al Kinisky) (August 28, 1989). . . . Fractured rib (December 19, 1989); missed 13 games. . . . Separated shoulder (January 25, 1990); missed five games. . . . Bruised shoulder (February 28, 1990); missed five games. . . . Separated left shoulder (November 1, 1990); missed 17 games. . . . Bruised ankle (January 24, 1991); missed seven games. . . . Tore tendon in right knee (February 16, 1991); missed 13 games. . . . Bruised back (November 1991). . . . Strained knee (December 10, 1991); missed 19 games. . . . Released by Flyers (February 4, 1992).

Season Team	League	REGULAR SEASON					PLAYOFFS				
		Gms.	G	A	Pts.	Pen.	Gms.	G	A	Pts.	Pen.
84-85—Sparta Prague	Czech.	26	2	2	4	10	—	—	—	—	—
85-86—Sparta Prague	Czech.	27	3	2	5		—	—	—	—	—
86-87—Sparta Prague	Czech.	9	1	0	1	2	—	—	—	—	—

Season	Team	League	REGULAR SEASON Gms.	G	A	Pts.	Pen.	PLAYOFFS Gms.	G	A	Pts.	Pen.
87-88	Dukla Trencin	Czech.	43	8	12	20	27	—	—	—	—	—
88-89	Dukla Trencin	Czech.	45	6	17	23		—	—	—	—	—
89-90	Philadelphia	NHL	32	6	13	19	6	—	—	—	—	—
	Hershey	AHL	22	10	18	28	10	—	—	—	—	—
90-91	Philadelphia	NHL	50	5	21	26	14	—	—	—	—	—
91-92	Philadelphia	NHL	10	1	2	3	4	—	—	—	—	—
	NHL totals		92	12	36	48	24					

LATTA, DAVE

LW, NORDIQUES

PERSONAL: Born January 3, 1967, at Thunder Bay, Ont. . . . 6-1/190. . . . Shoots left. . . . Full name: David Allan Latta.
TRANSACTIONS/CAREER NOTES: Injured shoulder (December 1984). . . . Selected by Quebec Nordiques as underage junior in first round (first Nordiques pick, 15th overall) of NHL entry draft (June 15, 1985). . . . Separated shoulder (October 1987). . . . Underwent shoulder surgery (May 1989). . . . Sprained left knee ligament (September 22, 1989).

Season	Team	League	REGULAR SEASON Gms.	G	A	Pts.	Pen.	PLAYOFFS Gms.	G	A	Pts.	Pen.
82-83	Orillia	OHA	43	16	25	41	26	—	—	—	—	—
83-84	Kitchener	OHL	66	17	26	43	54	16	3	6	9	9
84-85	Kitchener	OHL	52	38	27	65	26	4	2	4	6	4
85-86	Kitchener	OHL	55	36	34	70	60	5	7	1	8	15
	Fredericton	AHL	3	1	0	1	0	5	0	3	3	0
	Quebec	NHL	1	0	0	0	0	—	—	—	—	—
86-87	Kitchener	OHL	50	32	46	78	46	4	0	3	3	2
87-88	Fredericton	AHL	34	11	21	32	28	15	9	4	13	24
	Quebec	NHL	10	0	0	0	0	—	—	—	—	—
88-89	Halifax	AHL	42	20	26	46	36	4	0	2	2	2
	Quebec	NHL	24	4	8	12	4	—	—	—	—	—
89-90	Halifax	AHL	34	11	5	16	45	—	—	—	—	—
90-91	Canadian National Team	Int'l	30	5	14	19	24	—	—	—	—	—
	Quebec	NHL	1	0	0	0	0	—	—	—	—	—
	Halifax	AHL	22	4	7	11	12	—	—	—	—	—
91-92	New Haven	AHL	76	18	27	45	100	5	1	1	2	4
	NHL totals		36	4	8	12	4					

LAUER, BRAD

RW, BLACKHAWKS

PERSONAL: Born October 27, 1966, at Humbolt, Sask. . . . 6-0/195. . . . Shoots left.
TRANSACTIONS/CAREER NOTES: Selected by New York Islanders as underage junior in second round (third Islanders pick, 34th overall) of NHL entry draft (June 15, 1985). . . . Fractured left kneecap (October 1988). . . . Reinjured left knee (March 1989). . . . Suffered abdominal strain (February 1990). . . . Bruised right quadricep (April 1990). . . . Traded by Islanders with C Brent Sutter to Chicago Blackhawks for C Adam Creighton and LW Steve Thomas (October 25, 1991).

Season	Team	League	REGULAR SEASON Gms.	G	A	Pts.	Pen.	PLAYOFFS Gms.	G	A	Pts.	Pen.
83-84	Regina	WHL	60	5	7	12	51	16	0	1	1	24
84-85	Regina	WHL	72	33	46	79	57	8	6	6	12	9
85-86	Regina	WHL	57	36	38	74	69	10	4	5	9	2
86-87	New York Islanders	NHL	61	7	14	21	65	6	2	0	2	4
87-88	New York Islanders	NHL	69	17	18	35	67	5	3	1	4	4
88-89	Springfield	AHL	8	1	5	6	0	—	—	—	—	—
	New York Islanders	NHL	14	3	2	5	2	—	—	—	—	—
89-90	New York Islanders	NHL	63	6	18	24	19	4	0	2	2	10
	Springfield	AHL	7	4	2	6	0	—	—	—	—	—
90-91	New York Islanders	NHL	44	4	8	12	45	—	—	—	—	—
	Capital District	AHL	11	5	11	16	14	—	—	—	—	—
91-92	New York Islanders	NHL	8	1	0	1	2	—	—	—	—	—
	Indianapolis	IHL	57	24	30	54	46	—	—	—	—	—
	Chicago	NHL	6	0	0	0	0	7	1	1	2	2
	NHL totals		265	38	60	98	204	22	6	4	10	20

LAUKKANEN, JANNE

D, NORDIQUES

PERSONAL: Born March 19, 1970, at Lahti, Finland. . . . 6-0/180. . . . Shoots left.
TRANSACTIONS/CAREER NOTES: Selected by Quebec Nordiques in eighth round (eighth Nordiques pick, 156th overall) of NHL entry draft (June 22, 1991).

Season	Team	League	REGULAR SEASON Gms.	G	A	Pts.	Pen.	PLAYOFFS Gms.	G	A	Pts.	Pen.
89-90	Ilves Tampere	Finland	39	5	6	11	10	—	—	—	—	—
90-91	Reipas	Finland	44	8	14	22	56	—	—	—	—	—
91-92	Helsinki HPK	Finland	43	5	14	19	62	—	—	—	—	—

LAUS, PAUL

D, PENGUINS

PERSONAL: Born September 26, 1970, at Grimsby, Ont. . . . 6-1/212. . . . Shoots right.
TRANSACTIONS/CAREER NOTES: Suffered inflamed knuckles (September 1988). . . . Suspended three playoff games by OHL for spearing (April 28, 1989). . . . Selected by Pittsburgh Penguins in second round (second Penguins pick, 37th overall) of NHL entry draft (June 17, 1989).

Season Team	League	Gms.	G	A	Pts.	Pen.	Gms.	G	A	Pts.	Pen.
				REGULAR SEASON					PLAYOFFS		
86-87—St. Catharines Jr. B..........	OHA	40	1	8	9	56	—	—	—	—	—
87-88—Hamilton......................	OHL	56	1	9	10	171	14	0	0	0	28
88-89—Niagara Falls	OHL	49	1	10	11	225	15	0	5	5	56
89-90—Niagara Falls	OHL	60	13	35	48	231	16	6	16	22	71
90-91—Muskegon....................	IHL	35	3	4	7	103	4	0	0	0	13
—Albany	IHL	7	0	0	0	7	—	—	—	—	—
—Knoxville	ECHL	20	6	12	18	83	—	—	—	—	—
91-92—Muskegon....................	IHL	75	0	21	21	248	14	2	5	7	70

LAVIGNE, ERIC
D, CAPITALS

PERSONAL: Born November 14, 1972, at Victoriaville, Que.... 6-3/194.... Shoots left.
TRANSACTIONS/CAREER NOTES: Selected by Washington Capitals in second round (third Capitals pick, 25th overall) of NHL entry draft (June 22, 1991).

Season Team	League	Gms.	G	A	Pts.	Pen.	Gms.	G	A	Pts.	Pen.
				REGULAR SEASON					PLAYOFFS		
89-90—Hull	QMJHL	69	7	11	18	203	11	0	0	0	32
90-91—Hull	QMJHL	66	11	11	22	153	4	0	1	1	16
91-92—Hull	QMJHL	46	4	17	21	101	6	0	0	0	32

LAVIOLETTE, PETER
D, RANGERS

PERSONAL: Born December 7, 1964, at Franklin, Mass.... 6-2/200.... Shoots left.
TRANSACTIONS/CAREER NOTES: Signed as free agent by New York Rangers (June 1987).

Season Team	League	Gms.	G	A	Pts.	Pen.	Gms.	G	A	Pts.	Pen.
				REGULAR SEASON					PLAYOFFS		
86-87—Indianapolis	IHL	72	10	20	30	146	5	0	2	2	12
87-88—U.S. Olympic Team	Int'l	56	3	22	25		—	—	—	—	—
—Colorado......................	IHL	19	2	5	7	27	9	3	5	8	7
88-89—Denver	IHL	57	6	19	25	120	3	0	0	0	4
—New York Rangers	NHL	12	0	0	0	6	—	—	—	—	—
89-90—Flint	IHL	62	6	18	24	82	4	0	0	0	4
90-91—Binghamton	AHL	65	12	24	36	72	10	2	7	9	30
91-92—Binghamton	AHL	50	4	10	14	50	11	2	7	9	9
NHL totals...................................		12	0	0	0	6					

LAVISH, JAMES
RW, BRUINS

PERSONAL: Born October 13, 1970, at Albany, N.Y.... 5-11/175.... Shoots right.... Full name: James Alexander Lavish.
HIGH SCHOOL: Deerfield Academy (Mass.).
COLLEGE: Yale.
TRANSACTIONS/CAREER NOTES: Selected by Boston Bruins in ninth round (ninth Bruins pick, 185th overall) of NHL entry draft (June 17, 1989).

Season Team	League	Gms.	G	A	Pts.	Pen.	Gms.	G	A	Pts.	Pen.
				REGULAR SEASON					PLAYOFFS		
88-89—Deerfield Academy	Mass. H.S.		16	18	34		—	—	—	—	—
89-90—Yale University	ECAC	27	6	11	17	40	—	—	—	—	—
90-91—Yale University	ECAC	29	13	6	19	42	—	—	—	—	—
91-92—Yale University	ECAC	26	16	13	29	44	—	—	—	—	—

LAVOIE, DOMINIC
D, SENATORS

PERSONAL: Born November 21, 1967, at Montreal... 6-2/205.... Shoots right.
TRANSACTIONS/CAREER NOTES: Signed as free agent by St. Louis Blues (September 22, 1986).... Dislocated shoulder (January 1991).... Suffered hairline fracture to foot during preseason (September 1991); missed first seven games of season.... Selected by Ottawa Senators in NHL expansion draft (June 18, 1992).
HONORS: Named to IHL All-Star first team (1990-91).... Named to IHL All-Star second team (1991-92).

Season Team	League	Gms.	G	A	Pts.	Pen.	Gms.	G	A	Pts.	Pen.
				REGULAR SEASON					PLAYOFFS		
84-85—St. Jean	QMJHL	30	1	1	2	10	—	—	—	—	—
85-86—St. Jean	QMJHL	70	12	37	49	99	10	2	3	5	20
86-87—St. Jean	QMJHL	64	12	42	54	97	8	2	7	9	2
87-88—Peoria	IHL	65	7	26	33	54	7	2	2	4	8
88-89—St. Louis	NHL	1	0	0	0	0	—	—	—	—	—
—Peoria	IHL	69	11	31	42	98	4	0	0	0	4
89-90—St. Louis	NHL	13	1	1	2	16	—	—	—	—	—
—Peoria	IHL	58	19	23	42	32	5	2	2	4	16
90-91—St. Louis	NHL	6	1	2	3	2	—	—	—	—	—
—Peoria	IHL	46	15	25	40	72	16	5	7	12	22
91-92—Peoria	IHL	58	20	32	52	87	10	3	4	7	12
—St. Louis	NHL	6	0	1	1	10	—	—	—	—	—
NHL totals...................................		26	2	4	6	28					

LAWTON, BRIAN
C, SHARKS

PERSONAL: Born June 29, 1965, at New Brunswick, N.J.... 6-0/180.... Shoots left.
HIGH SCHOOL: Mount St. Charles Academy (Woonsocket, R.I.).
TRANSACTIONS/CAREER NOTES: Selected by Minnesota North Stars in first round (first North Stars pick, first overall) of NHL entry draft (June 8, 1983).... Separated shoulder

(November 1983).... Injured shoulder (October 1984).... Broke thumb (October 1987).... Bruised ribs (February 1988). ...Suspended by North Stars for refusing to report to Kalamazoo Wings (October 8, 1988).... Traded by North Stars with LW Igor Liba and rights to LW Eric Bennett to New York Rangers for D Mark Tinordi and D Paul Jerrard and the rights to C Mike Sullivan and RW Brett Barnett and the Los Angeles Kings' third-round draft pick (C Murray Garbutt) in 1989 (acquired March 10, 1987, by North Stars) (October 11, 1988).... Traded by Rangers with D Norm Maciver and LW Don Maloney to Hartford Whalers for C Carey Wilson and fifth-round pick in 1990 draft (Rob Lubos) (December 26, 1988).... Suffered facial and jaw injuries (January 27, 1989).... Broke left wrist (January 28, 1989).... Sprained ankle (March 25, 1989).... Fractured bone in left foot (September 1989).... Acquired by Quebec Nordiques on waivers for $12,500 (December 1, 1989).... Released by Nordiques (February 1, 1990).... Signed as free agent by Boston Bruins (February 6, 1990).... Signed as free agent by Kings (July 27, 1990).... Signed as free agent by San Jose Sharks (August 9, 1991).... Injured foot (October 4, 1991); missed three games.... Injured knee (November 27, 1991); missed eight games.

Season	Team	League	REGULAR SEASON					PLAYOFFS				
			Gms.	G	A	Pts.	Pen.	Gms.	G	A	Pts.	Pen.
81-82	Mount St. Charles H.S.	R.I.H.S.	26	45	43	88		—	—	—	—	—
82-83	Mount St. Charles H.S.	R.I.H.S.	23	40	43	83		—	—	—	—	—
	U.S. National Team	Int'l	7	3	2	5	6	—	—	—	—	—
83-84	Minnesota	NHL	58	10	21	31	33	5	0	0	0	10
84-85	Springfield	AHL	42	14	28	42	37	4	1	1	2	2
	Minnesota	NHL	40	5	6	11	24	—	—	—	—	—
85-86	Minnesota	NHL	65	18	17	35	36	3	0	1	1	?
86-87	Minnesota	NHL	66	21	20	44	86	—	—	—	—	—
87-88	Minnesota	NHL	74	17	24	41	71	—	—	—	—	—
88-89	New York Rangers	NHL	30	7	10	17	39	—	—	—	—	—
	Hartford	NHL	35	10	16	26	28	3	1	0	1	0
89-90	Hartford	NHL	13	2	1	3	6	—	—	—	—	—
	Quebec	NHL	14	5	6	11	10	—	—	—	—	—
	Boston	NHL	8	0	0	0	14	—	—	—	—	—
	Maine	AHL	5	0	0	0	14	—	—	—	—	—
90-91	Phoenix	IHL	63	26	40	66	108	11	4	9	13	40
91-92	San Jose	NHL	59	15	22	37	42	—	—	—	—	—
	NHL totals		462	110	146	256	389	11	1	1	2	12

LAXDAL, DEREK
RW, ISLANDERS

PERSONAL: Born February 21, 1966, at St. Boniface, Man.... 6-1/200.... Shoots right. **TRANSACTIONS/CAREER NOTES:** Selected by Toronto Maple Leafs as underage junior in eighth round (seventh Maple Leafs pick, 151st overall) of NHL entry draft (June 1984).... Broke hand (January 1985).... Injured back (October 22, 1988).... Bruised knee (November 1988).... Injured finger (January 1989).... Traded by Maple Leafs with LW Paul Gagne and D Jack Capuano to New York Islanders for C Gilles Thibaudeau and C Mike Stevens (December 20, 1989).... Hyperextended elbow (April 1990).

Season	Team	League	REGULAR SEASON					PLAYOFFS				
			Gms.	G	A	Pts.	Pen.	Gms.	G	A	Pts.	Pen.
82-83	Portland	WHL	39	4	9	13	27	14	0	2	2	2
83-84	Brandon	WHL	70	23	20	43	86	12	0	4	4	10
84-85	Brandon	WHL	69	61	41	102	72	—	—	—	—	—
	St. Catharines	AHL	5	3	2	5	2	—	—	—	—	—
	Toronto	NHL	3	0	0	0	6	—	—	—	—	—
85-86	Brandon	WHL	42	34	35	69	62	—	—	—	—	—
	New Westminster	WHL	18	9	6	15	14	—	—	—	—	—
	St. Catharines	AHL	7	0	1	1	15	12	1	1	2	24
86-87	Newmarket	AHL	78	24	20	44	89	—	—	—	—	—
	Toronto	NHL	2	0	0	0	7	—	—	—	—	—
87-88	Toronto	NHL	5	0	0	0	6	—	—	—	—	—
	Newmarket	AHL	67	18	25	43	81	—	—	—	—	—
88-89	Toronto	NHL	41	9	6	15	65	—	—	—	—	—
	Newmarket	AHL	34	22	22	44	53	2	0	2	2	5
89-90	Newmarket	AHL	23	7	8	15	52	—	—	—	—	—
	New York Islanders	NHL	12	3	1	4	4	1	0	2	2	2
	Springfield	AHL	28	13	12	25	42	13	8	6	14	47
90-91	Capital District	AHL	65	14	25	39	75	—	—	—	—	—
	New York Islanders	NHL	4	0	0	0	0	—	—	—	—	—
91-92	Capital District	AHL	49	7	7	14	61	4	1	1	2	10
	NHL totals		67	12	7	19	88	1	0	2	2	2

LAZARO, JEFF
LW, SENATORS

PERSONAL: Born March 21, 1968, at Waltham, Mass.... 5-10/180.... Shoots left.... Full name: Jeffrey Lazaro. **HIGH SCHOOL:** Waltham (Mass.). **COLLEGE:** New Hampshire. **TRANSACTIONS/CAREER NOTES:** Signed as free agent by Boston Bruins (September 26, 1990).... Bruised back (February 9, 1991).... Suffered concussion (February 23, 1991).... Sprained knee (January 23, 1992); missed 14 games.... Sprained knee (March 11, 1992).... Selected by Ottawa Senators in NHL expansion draft (June 18, 1992). **MISCELLANEOUS:** Played defense prior to 1989-90 season.

Season	Team	League	REGULAR SEASON					PLAYOFFS				
			Gms.	G	A	Pts.	Pen.	Gms.	G	A	Pts.	Pen.
86-87	Univ. of New Hampshire	Hockey East	38	7	14	21	38	—	—	—	—	—
87-88	Univ. of New Hampshire	Hockey East	30	4	13	17	48	—	—	—	—	—

Season Team	League	REGULAR SEASON					PLAYOFFS				
		Gms.	G	A	Pts.	Pen.	Gms.	G	A	Pts.	Pen.
88-89—Univ. of New Hampshire ...	Hockey East	31	8	14	22	38	—	—	—	—	—
89-90—Univ. of New Hampshire ...	Hockey East	39	16	19	35	34	—	—	—	—	—
90-91—Maine	AHL	26	8	11	19	18	—	—	—	—	—
—Boston	NHL	49	5	13	18	67	19	3	2	5	30
91-92—Boston	NHL	27	3	6	9	31	9	0	1	1	2
—Maine	AHL	21	8	4	12	32	—	—	—	—	—
NHL totals		76	8	19	27	98	28	3	3	6	32

LEACH, JAMIE
RW, PENGUINS

PERSONAL: Born August 25, 1969, at Winnipeg, Man. . . . 6-1/205. . . . Shoots right. . . . Full name: William Leach. . . . Son of Reggie Leach, right winger, four NHL teams (1970-71 through 1982-83).
HIGH SCHOOL: Cherry Hill East (N.J.).
TRANSACTIONS/CAREER NOTES: Suffered hip injury (February 1986). . . . Selected by Pittsburgh Penguins as underage junior in third round (third Penguins pick, 47th overall) of NHL entry draft (June 13, 1987). . . . Tore left knee ligaments (September 30, 1990).

Season Team	League	REGULAR SEASON					PLAYOFFS				
		Gms.	G	A	Pts.	Pen.	Gms.	G	A	Pts.	Pen.
84-85—Cherry Hill East H.S.	N.J. H.S.	60	48	51	99	68	—	—	—	—	—
85-86—New Westminster	WHL	58	8	7	15	20	—	—	—	—	—
86-87—Hamilton	OHL	64	12	19	31	67	—	—	—	—	—
87-88—Hamilton	OHL	64	24	19	43	79	14	6	7	13	12
88-89—Niagara Falls	OHL	58	45	62	107	47	17	9	11	20	25
89-90—Muskegon	IHL	72	22	36	58	39	15	9	4	13	14
—Pittsburgh	NHL	10	0	3	3	0	—	—	—	—	—
90-91—Pittsburgh	NHL	7	2	0	2	0	—	—	—	—	—
—Muskegon	IHL	43	33	22	55	26	—	—	—	—	—
91-92—Pittsburgh	NHL	38	5	4	9	8	—	—	—	—	—
—Muskegon	IHL	3	1	1	2	2	—	—	—	—	—
NHL totals		55	7	7	14	8	—	—	—	—	—

LEACH, STEVE
RW, BRUINS

PERSONAL: Born January 16, 1966, at Cambridge, Mass. . . . 5-11/200. . . . Shoots right. . . . Full name: Steven Leach.
HIGH SCHOOL: Matignon (Cambridge, Mass.).
COLLEGE: New Hampshire.
TRANSACTIONS/CAREER NOTES: Selected by Washington Capitals in second round (second Capitals pick, 34th overall) of NHL entry draft (June 9, 1984). . . . Strained left knee (February 1989). . . . Injured thumb (March 1990). . . . Suffered concussion (October 10, 1990). . . . Separated right shoulder (February 2, 1991); missed four games. . . . Traded by Capitals to Boston Bruins for LW Randy Burridge (June 21, 1991).

Season Team	League	REGULAR SEASON					PLAYOFFS				
		Gms.	G	A	Pts.	Pen.	Gms.	G	A	Pts.	Pen.
83-84—Matignon H.S.	Mass. H.S.	21	27	22	49	49	—	—	—	—	—
84-85—Univ. of New Hampshire ...	Hockey East	41	12	25	37	53	—	—	—	—	—
85-86—Univ. of New Hampshire ...	Hockey East	25	22	6	28	30	—	—	—	—	—
—Washington	NHL	11	1	1	2	2	6	0	1	1	0
86-87—Binghamton	AHL	54	18	21	39	39	13	3	1	4	6
—Washington	NHL	15	1	0	1	6	—	—	—	—	—
87-88—U.S. Olympic Team	Int'l	53	26	20	46		—	—	—	—	—
—Washington	NHL	8	1	1	2	17	9	2	1	3	0
88-89—Washington	NHL	74	11	19	30	94	6	1	0	1	12
89-90—Washington	NHL	70	18	14	32	104	14	2	2	4	6
90-91—Washington	NHL	68	11	19	30	99	9	1	2	3	8
91-92—Boston	NHL	78	31	29	60	147	15	4	0	4	10
NHL totals		324	74	83	157	469	59	10	6	16	36

LEBEAU, PATRICK
LW, CANADIENS

PERSONAL: Born March 17, 1970, at St. Jerome, Que. . . . 5-10/173. . . . Shoots left. . . . Brother of Stephan Lebeau, center, Montreal Canadiens.
TRANSACTIONS/CAREER NOTES: Traded by Shawinigan Cataractes with QMJHL rights to G Eric Metivier to St. Jean Castors for LW Steve Cadieux and D Pierre Cote (November 5, 1988). . . . Selected by Montreal Canadiens in eighth round (eighth Canadiens pick, 147th overall) of NHL entry draft (June 17, 1989). . . . Traded by St. Jean Lynx with D Francois Leroux and LW Jean Blouin to Victoriaville Tigres for RW Trevor Duhaime, second- and third-round draft picks and future considerations (February 15, 1990).
HONORS: Won Jean Beliveau Trophy (1989-90). . . . Named to QMJHL All-Star first team (1989-90). . . . Won Dudley (Red) Garrett Memorial Trophy (1990-91). . . . Named to AHL All-Star second team (1990-91).
MISCELLANEOUS: Member of 1992 silver-medal-winning Canadian Olympic team.

Season Team	League	REGULAR SEASON					PLAYOFFS				
		Gms.	G	A	Pts.	Pen.	Gms.	G	A	Pts.	Pen.
86-87—Shawinigan	QMJHL	66	26	52	78	90	13	2	6	8	17
87-88—Shawinigan	QMJHL	53	43	56	99	116	11	3	9	12	16
88-89—Shawinigan/St. Jean	QMJHL	66	62	87	149	89	4	4	3	7	6
89-90—St. Jean/Victoriaville	QMJHL	72	68	*106	*174	109	16	7	15	22	12

Season Team	League	REGULAR SEASON Gms.	G	A	Pts.	Pen.	PLAYOFFS Gms.	G	A	Pts.	Pen.
90-91—Montreal	NHL	2	1	1	2	0	—	—	—	—	—
—Fredericton	AHL	69	50	51	101	32	9	4	7	11	8
91-92—Fredericton	AHL	55	33	38	71	48	7	4	5	9	10
—Canadian National Team..	Int'l	7	4	1	5	6	—	—	—	—	—
—Canadian Olympic Team ..	Int'l	8	1	3	4	4	—	—	—	—	—
NHL totals		2	1	1	2	0					

LEBEAU, STEPHAN
C, CANADIENS

PERSONAL: Born February 28, 1968, at Sherbrooke, Que. . . . 5-10/172. . . . Shoots right. . . . Brother of Patrick Lebeau, left winger, Montreal Canadiens.
TRANSACTIONS/CAREER NOTES: Signed as free agent by Montreal Canadiens (September 27, 1986). . . . Injured thigh (January 25, 1992); missed one game.
HONORS: Named to QMJHL All-Star first team (1986-87). . . . Won Frank J. Selke Trophy (1987-88). . . . Named to QMJHL All-Star second team (1986-87 and 1987-88). . . . Won Les Cunningham Plaque (1988-89). . . . Won John B. Sollenberger Trophy (1988-89). . . . Won Dudley (Red) Garrett Memorial Trophy (1988-89). . . . Named to AHL All-Star first team (1988-89).

Season Team	League	REGULAR SEASON Gms.	G	A	Pts.	Pen.	PLAYOFFS Gms.	G	A	Pts.	Pen.
84-85—Shawinigan	QMJHL	66	41	38	79	18	9	4	5	9	4
85-86—Shawinigan	QMJHL	72	69	77	146	22	5	4	2	6	4
86-87—Shawinigan	QMJHL	65	*77	90	167	60	14	9	20	29	20
87-88—Shawinigan	QMJHL	67	*94	94	188	66	11	†17	9	26	10
—Sherbrooke	AHL	—	—	—	—	—	1	0	1	1	0
88-89—Sherbrooke	AHL	78	*70	64	*134	47	6	1	4	5	8
—Montreal	NHL	1	0	1	1	2	—	—	—	—	—
89-90—Montreal	NHL	57	15	20	35	11	2	3	0	3	0
90-91—Montreal	NHL	73	22	31	53	24	7	2	1	3	2
91-92—Montreal	NHL	77	27	31	58	14	8	1	3	4	4
NHL totals		208	64	83	147	51	17	6	4	10	6

LeBLANC, JOHN
LW/RW, JETS

PERSONAL: Born January 21, 1964, at Campbellton, N.B. . . . 6-1/195. . . . Shoots left. . . . Full name: John Glenn LeBlanc.
TRANSACTIONS/CAREER NOTES: Suffered ankle contusion (February 1992); missed three games. . . . Signed as free agent by Vancouver Canucks (April 12, 1986). . . . Traded by Canucks with fifth-round pick in 1989 draft (LW Peter White) to Edmonton Oilers for C Doug Smith and LW Greg C. Adams (March 7, 1989). . . . Traded by Oilers with 10th-round pick in 1992 draft to Winnipeg Jets for fifth-round pick (C Ryan Haggerty) in 1991 draft (June 12, 1991).
HONORS: Won Senator Joseph A. Sullivan Trophy (1985-86).

Season Team	League	REGULAR SEASON Gms.	G	A	Pts.	Pen.	PLAYOFFS Gms.	G	A	Pts.	Pen.
83-84—Hull	QMJHL	69	39	35	74	32	—	—	—	—	—
84-85—New Brunswick	AHL	24	25	34	59	32	—	—	—	—	—
85-86—New Brunswick	AHL	24	38	28	66	35	—	—	—	—	—
86-87—Vancouver	NHL	2	1	0	1	0	—	—	—	—	—
—Fredericton	AHL	75	40	30	70	27	—	—	—	—	—
87-88—Vancouver	NHL	41	12	10	22	18	—	—	—	—	—
—Fredericton	AHL	35	26	25	51	54	15	6	7	13	34
88-89—Milwaukee	IHL	61	39	31	70	42	—	—	—	—	—
—Edmonton	NHL	2	1	0	1	0	1	0	0	0	0
—Cape Breton	AHL	3	4	0	4	0	—	—	—	—	—
89-90—Cape Breton	AHL	77	*54	34	88	50	6	4	0	4	4
90-91—Cape Breton	AHL	—	—	—	—	—	—	—	—	—	—
91-92—Moncton	AHL	56	31	22	53	24	10	3	2	5	8
—Winnipeg	NHL	16	6	1	7	6	—	—	—	—	—
NHL totals		61	20	11	31	24	1	0	0	0	0

LeBLANC, RAY
G, BLACKHAWKS

PERSONAL: Born October 24, 1964, at Fitchburg, Mass. . . . 5-10/170. . . . Shoots left. . . . Full name: Raymond LeBlanc.
TRANSACTIONS/CAREER NOTES: Signed as free agent by Chicago Blackhawks (September 1989).
HONORS: Named to ACHL All-Star second team (1984-85). . . . Won Ken McKenzie Trophy (1986-87). . . . Named to IHL All-Star second team (1986-87).

Season Team	League	REGULAR SEASON Gms.	Min.	W	L	T	GA	SO	Avg.	PLAYOFFS Gms.	Min.	W	L	GA	SO	Avg.
82-83—Dixie Flyers	OPJHL	30	1705				111	0	3.91	—	—			—	—	—
83-84—Kitchener	OHL	*54	2965				185	1	3.74	†16	914			*79	0	5.19
84-85—Pinebridge	ACHL	40	2178				150	0	4.13	—	—			—	—	—
85-86—Carolina	ECHL	*42	*2505				133	*3	3.19	*11	*669			42	0	*3.77
86-87—Flint	IHL	64	3417				222	1	3.90	—	—			—	—	—
87-88—Flint	IHL	60	3269	27	19	8	*239	1	4.39	16	925	10	6	55	†1	3.57
88-89—Flint	IHL	15	852	5	9	0	67	0	4.72	—	—			—	—	—
—Saginaw	IHL	29	1655	19	7	2	99	0	3.59	1	59	0	1	3	0	3.05

Season	Team	League	Gms.	Min	W	L	T	GA	SO	Avg.	Gms.	Min	W	L	T	GA	SO	Avg.
—New Haven	AHL		1	20				3	0	9.00	—	—	—	—	—	—	—	—
89-90—Fort Wayne	IHL		15	680	3	3	3	44	0	3.88	3	139	0	2		11	0	4.75
—Indianapolis	IHL		23	1334	15	6	2	71	2	3.19	—	—	—	—	—	—	—	—
90-91—Fort Wayne	IHL		21	1072	10	8	0	69	0	3.86	—	—	—	—	—	—	—	—
—Indianapolis	IHL		3	145	2	0	0	8	0	3.31	—	—	—	—	—	—	—	—
91-92—Indianapolis	IHL		25	1468	14	9	2	84	2	3.43	—	—	—	—	—	—	—	—
—U.S. National Team	Int'l		17	891	5	10	1	54	0	3.64	—	—	—	—	—	—	—	—
—U.S. Olympic Team	Int'l		8	463	5	2	1	17	2	2.20	—	—	—	—	—	—	—	—
—Chicago	NHL		1	60	1	0	0	1	0	1.00	—	—	—	—	—	—	—	—
NHL totals			1	60	1	0	0	1	0	1.00	—	—	—	—	—	—	—	—

LeBRUN, SEAN
LW, ISLANDERS

PERSONAL: Born May 2, 1969, at Prince George, B.C.... 6-2/205.... Shoots left. **TRANSACTIONS/CAREER NOTES:** Selected by New York Islanders in third round (third Islanders pick, 37th overall) of NHL entry draft (June 11, 1988).... Broke wrist (March 26, 1989). **HONORS:** Named to WHL All-Star second team (West) (1987-88).

Season	Team	League	REGULAR SEASON Gms.	G	A	Pts.	Pen.	PLAYOFFS Gms.	G	A	Pts.	Pen.
85-86—Spokane Chiefs	WHL		70	6	11	17	41	—	—	—	—	—
86-87—Spokane Chiefs	WHL		6	2	5	7	9	—	—	—	—	—
—New Westminster	WHL		55	21	32	53	47	—	—	—	—	—
87-88—New Westminster	WHL		72	36	53	89	59	5	1	3	4	2
88-89—Tri-City Americans	WHL		71	52	73	125	92	5	0	4	4	13
89-90—Springfield	AHL		63	9	33	42	20	—	—	—	—	—
90-91—Capital District	AHL		56	14	26	40	35	—	—	—	—	—
91-92—Capital District	AHL		14	0	2	2	15	—	—	—	—	—
—Richmond	ECHL		2	0	0	0	2	—	—	—	—	—

LeCLAIR, JOHN
LW, CANADIENS

PERSONAL: Born July 5, 1969, at St. Albans, Vt.... 6-2/205.... Shoots left.... Full name: John Clark LeClair. **HIGH SCHOOL:** Bellows Free Academy (St. Albans, Vt.). **COLLEGE:** Vermont. **TRANSACTIONS/CAREER NOTES:** Selected by Montreal Canadiens in second round (second Canadiens pick, 33rd overall) of NHL entry draft (June 13, 1987).... Injured thigh; missed 16 games during 1988-89 season.... Injured knee and underwent surgery (January 20, 1990); missed remainder of season.... Injured shoulder (January 15, 1992); missed four games. **HONORS:** Named to ECAC All-Star second team (1990-91).

Season	Team	League	REGULAR SEASON Gms.	G	A	Pts.	Pen.	PLAYOFFS Gms.	G	A	Pts.	Pen.
85-86—Bellows Free Academy	Vt. H.S.		22	41	28	69	14	—	—	—	—	—
86-87—Bellows Free Academy	Vt. H.S.		23	44	40	84	25	—	—	—	—	—
87-88—University of Vermont	ECAC		31	12	22	34	62	—	—	—	—	—
88-89—University of Vermont	ECAC		19	9	12	21	40	—	—	—	—	—
89-90—University of Vermont	ECAC		10	10	6	16	38	—	—	—	—	—
90-91—University of Vermont	ECAC		33	25	20	45	58	—	—	—	—	—
—Montreal	NHL		10	2	5	7	2	3	0	0	0	0
91-92—Montreal	NHL		59	8	11	19	14	8	1	1	2	0
—Fredericton	AHL		8	7	7	14	10	2	0	0	0	4
NHL totals			69	10	16	26	16	11	1	1	2	4

LEDYARD, GRANT
D, SABRES

PERSONAL: Born November 19, 1961, at Winnipeg, Man.... 6-2/200.... Shoots left. **TRANSACTIONS/CAREER NOTES:** Signed as free agent by New York Rangers (July 7, 1982).... Suffered hip injury (October 1984).... Traded by Rangers to Los Angeles Kings for LW Brian MacLellan and fourth-round pick in 1987 draft (C Michael Sullivan); Rangers also sent second-round pick in 1986 (D Neil Wilkinson) and fourth-round pick in 1987 draft (RW John Weisbrod) to Minnesota and the North Stars sent G Roland Melanson to the Kings as part of the same deal (December 1986).... Sprained ankle (October 1987).... Traded by Kings to Washington Capitals for RW Craig Laughlin (February 9, 1988).... Traded by Capitals with G Clint Malarchuk and sixth-round pick in 1991 draft to Buffalo Sabres for D Calle Johansson and second-round pick in 1989 draft (G Byron Dafoe) (March 6, 1989).... Injured knee (February 12, 1991).... Injured shoulder (March 2, 1991).... Bruised ankle (March 14, 1992); missed four games. **HONORS:** Named Manitoba Junior Hockey League Most Valuable Player (1981-82).... Named to MJHL All-Star first team (1981-82).... Won Bob Gassoff Award (1983-84).... Won Max McNab Trophy (1983-84).

Season	Team	League	REGULAR SEASON Gms.	G	A	Pts.	Pen.	PLAYOFFS Gms.	G	A	Pts.	Pen.
79-80—Fort Garry	MJHL		49	13	24	37	90	—	—	—	—	—
80-81—Saskatoon	WHL		71	9	28	37	148	—	—	—	—	—
81-82—Fort Garry	MJHL		63	25	45	70	150	—	—	—	—	—
82-83—Tulsa	CHL		80	13	29	42	115	—	—	—	—	—
83-84—Tulsa	CHL		58	9	17	26	71	9	5	4	9	10
84-85—New Haven	AHL		36	6	20	26	18	—	—	—	—	—
—New York Rangers	NHL		42	8	12	20	53	3	0	2	2	4
85-86—New York Rangers	NHL		27	2	9	11	20	—	—	—	—	—
—Los Angeles	NHL		52	7	18	25	78	—	—	—	—	—

Season	Team	League	REGULAR SEASON Gms.	G	A	Pts.	Pen.	PLAYOFFS Gms.	G	A	Pts.	Pen.
86-87	Los Angeles	NHL	67	14	23	37	93	5	0	0	0	10
87-88	New Haven	AHL	3	2	1	3	4	—	—	—	—	—
	Los Angeles	NHL	23	1	7	8	52	—	—	—	—	—
	Washington	NHL	21	4	3	7	14	14	1	0	1	30
88-89	Washington	NHL	61	3	11	14	43	—	—	—	—	—
	Buffalo	NHL	13	1	5	6	8	5	1	2	3	2
89-90	Buffalo	NHL	67	2	13	15	37	—	—	—	—	—
90-91	Buffalo	NHL	60	8	23	31	46	6	3	3	6	10
91-92	Buffalo	NHL	50	5	16	21	45	—	—	—	—	—
	NHL totals		483	55	140	195	489	33	5	7	12	56

LEEMAN, GARY
RW/D, FLAMES

PERSONAL: Born February 19, 1964, at Toronto. . . . 6-0/175. . . . Shoots right.
TRANSACTIONS/CAREER NOTES: Selected by Toronto Maple Leafs as underage junior in second round (second Maple Leafs pick, 24th overall) of NHL entry draft (June 9, 1982). . . . Broke finger (January 1984). . . . Broke wrist (March 1984). . . . Separated shoulder (March 1985). . . . Cracked kneecap (April 14, 1987). . . . Cracked bone in right hand (April 1988). . . . Fractured bone behind left ear (October 22, 1988). . . . Injured back (January 1988). . . . Separated right shoulder (November 10, 1990); missed 21 games. . . . Suffered back spasms (November 18, 1991); missed one game. . . . Traded by Maple Leafs with D Alexander Godynyuk, LW Craig Berube, D Michel Petit and G Jeff Reese to Calgary Flames for C Doug Gilmour, D Jamie Macoun, LW Kent Manderville, D Ric Nattress and G Rick Wamsley (January 2, 1992). . . . Bruised thigh (February 1992). . . . Sprained ankle (February 21, 1992); missed eight games.
HONORS: Won Top Defenseman Trophy (1982-83). . . . Named to WHL All-Star first team (1982-83).

Season	Team	League	REGULAR SEASON Gms.	G	A	Pts.	Pen.	PLAYOFFS Gms.	G	A	Pts.	Pen.
81-82	Regina	WHL	72	19	41	60	112	3	2	2	4	0
82-83	Regina	WHL	63	24	62	86	88	5	1	5	6	4
	Toronto	NHL	—	—	—	—	—	2	0	0	0	0
83-84	Toronto	NHL	52	4	8	12	31	—	—	—	—	—
84-85	St. Catharines	AHL	7	2	2	4	11	—	—	—	—	—
	Toronto	NHL	53	5	26	31	72	—	—	—	—	—
85-86	St. Catharines	AHL	25	15	13	28	6	—	—	—	—	—
	Toronto	NHL	53	9	23	32	20	10	2	10	12	2
86-87	Toronto	NHL	80	21	31	52	66	5	0	1	1	14
87-88	Toronto	NHL	80	30	31	61	62	2	2	0	2	2
88-89	Toronto	NHL	61	32	43	75	66	—	—	—	—	—
89-90	Toronto	NHL	80	51	44	95	63	5	3	3	6	16
90-91	Toronto	NHL	52	17	12	29	39	—	—	—	—	—
91-92	Toronto	NHL	34	7	13	20	44	—	—	—	—	—
	Calgary	NHL	29	2	7	9	27	—	—	—	—	—
	NHL totals		574	178	238	416	490	24	7	14	21	34

LEETCH, BRIAN
D, RANGERS

PERSONAL: Born March 3, 1968, at Corpus Christi, Tex. . . . 5-11/190. . . . Shoots left. . . . Full name: Brian Joseph Leetch.
HIGH SCHOOL: Avon Old Farms School For Boys (Avon, Conn.).
COLLEGE: Boston College.
TRANSACTIONS/CAREER NOTES: Selected by New York Rangers in first round (first Rangers pick, ninth overall) of NHL entry draft (June 21, 1986). . . . Suffered sprained ligaments in left knee at U.S. Olympic Festival (July 1987). . . . Fractured bone in left foot (December 1988). . . . Suffered hip pointer (March 15, 1989). . . . Fractured left ankle (March 14, 1990).
HONORS: Named Hockey East Player of the Year (1986-87). . . . Named Hockey East Rookie of the Year (1986-87). . . . Named to NCAA All-America East first team (1986-87). . . . Named to Hockey East All-Star first team (1986-87). . . . Named NHL Rookie of the Year by THE SPORTING NEWS (1988-89). . . . Won Calder Memorial Trophy (1988-89). . . . Named to NHL All-Rookie team (1988-89). . . . Named to THE SPORTING NEWS All-Star second team (1990-91). . . . Named to NHL All-Star second team (1990-91). . . . Won James Norris Memorial Trophy (1991-92). . . . Named to THE SPORTING NEWS All-Star first team (1991-92). . . . Named to NHL All-Star first team (1991-92).
RECORDS: Holds NHL single-season record for most goals by a rookie defenseman—23 (1988-89).

Season	Team	League	REGULAR SEASON Gms.	G	A	Pts.	Pen.	PLAYOFFS Gms.	G	A	Pts.	Pen.
84-85	Avon Old Farms H.S.	Conn. H.S.	26	30	46	76	15	—	—	—	—	—
85-86	Avon Old Farms H.S.	Conn. H.S.	28	40	44	84	18	—	—	—	—	—
86-87	Boston College	Hockey East	37	9	38	47	10	—	—	—	—	—
87-88	U.S. National Team	Int'l	60	13	61	74	38	—	—	—	—	—
	U.S. Olympic Team	Int'l	6	1	5	6	4	—	—	—	—	—
	New York Rangers	NHL	17	2	12	14	0	—	—	—	—	—
88-89	New York Rangers	NHL	68	23	48	71	50	4	3	2	5	2
89-90	New York Rangers	NHL	72	11	45	56	26	—	—	—	—	—
90-91	New York Rangers	NHL	80	16	72	88	42	6	1	3	4	0
91-92	New York Rangers	NHL	80	22	80	102	26	13	4	11	15	4
	NHL totals		317	74	257	331	144	23	8	16	24	6

LEFEBVRE, SYLVAIN
D, CANADIENS

PERSONAL: Born October 14, 1967, at Richmond, Que. . . . 6-2/204. . . . Shoots left.
TRANSACTIONS/CAREER NOTES: Signed as free agent by Montreal Canadiens (September 24, 1986).
HONORS: Named to AHL All-Star second team (1988-89).

Season Team	League	Gms.	G	A	Pts.	Pen.	Gms.	G	A	Pts.	Pen.
		REGULAR SEASON					**PLAYOFFS**				
84-85—Laval	QMJHL	66	7	5	12	31	—	—	—	—	—
85-86—Laval	QMJHL	71	8	17	25	48	14	1	0	1	25
86-87—Laval	QMJHL	70	10	36	46	44	15	1	6	7	12
87-88—Sherbrooke	AHL	79	3	24	27	73	6	2	3	5	4
88-89—Sherbrooke	AHL	77	15	32	47	119	6	1	3	4	4
89-90—Montreal	NHL	68	3	10	13	61	6	0	0	0	2
90-91—Montreal	NHL	63	5	18	23	30	11	1	0	1	6
91-92—Montreal	NHL	69	3	14	17	91	2	0	0	0	2
NHL totals		200	11	42	53	182	19	1	0	1	10

LEHTINEN, JERE
RW, NORTH STARS

PERSONAL: Born June 24, 1973, at Espoo, Finland.... 6-0/180.... Shoots right.
TRANSACTIONS/CAREER NOTES: Selected by Minnesota North Stars in fourth round (third North Stars pick, 88th overall) of NHL entry draft (June 20, 1992).

Season Team	League	Gms.	G	A	Pts.	Pen.	Gms.	G	A	Pts.	Pen.
		REGULAR SEASON					**PLAYOFFS**				
90-91—Kiekko-Espoo	Finland	32	15	9	24	12	—	—	—	—	—
91-92—Kiekko-Espoo	Finland	43	32	17	49	6	—	—	—	—	—

LEHTO, JONI
D, ISLANDERS

PERSONAL: Born July 15, 1970, at Turku, Finland.... 6-0/205.... Shoots left.
TRANSACTIONS/CAREER NOTES: Selected by New York Islanders in sixth round (fifth Islanders pick, 11th overall) of NHL entry draft (June 16, 1990).... Damaged ligaments in left knee (December 1990); while sidelined, served as an assistant coach for Ottawa 67's; became acting head coach on December 2 when head coach Brian Kilrea was ejected and suspended for the following two games; coached the team to a 2-1 record as head coach.
HONORS: Named to OHL All-Star second team (1989-90).

Season Team	League	Gms.	G	A	Pts.	Pen.	Gms.	G	A	Pts.	Pen.
		REGULAR SEASON					**PLAYOFFS**				
87-88—TPS Turku	Finland	30	9	14	23	42	—	—	—	—	—
88-89—Ottawa	OHL	63	9	25	34	26	—	—	—	—	—
91-92—Richmond	ECHL	18	2	9	11	10	—	—	—	—	—
—Capital District	AHL	26	2	5	7	6	—	—	—	—	—

LEMELIN, REGGIE
G, BRUINS

PERSONAL: Born November 19, 1954, at Sherbrooke, Que.... 5-11/170.... Shoots left. ... Full name: Rejean Lemelin.
TRANSACTIONS/CAREER NOTES: Selected by Philadelphia Flyers from Sherbrooke Beavers in sixth round (sixth Flyers pick, 125th overall) of NHL entry draft (May 28, 1974).... Signed as free agent by Atlanta Flames (August 1978).... Broke thumb on right hand (February 8, 1981).... Flames franchise moved to Calgary (May 21, 1980).... Injured back (January 1984).... Signed as free agent by Boston Bruins (August 1987).... Strained hamstring (January 2, 1992); missed 29 games.... Reinjured hamstring (March 23, 1992).
HONORS: Named to AHL All-Star first team (1977-78).... Shared William M. Jennings Trophy with Andy Moog (1989-90).

Season Team	League	Gms.	Min.	W	L	T	GA	SO	Avg.	Gms.	Min.	W	L	GA	SO	Avg.
		REGULAR SEASON								**PLAYOFFS**						
72-73—Sherbrooke	QMJHL	28	1681				146	0	5.21	2	120			12	0	6.00
73-74—Sherbrooke	QMJHL	35	2061				158	0	4.60	1	60			3	0	3.00
74-75—Philadelphia	NAHL	43	2277				131	3	3.45	—	—	—	—	—	—	—
75-76—Richmond	AHL	7	402				30	0	4.48	—	—	—	—	—	—	—
—Philadelphia	NAHL	29	1601				97	1	3.64	3	171			15	0	5.26
76-77—Philadelphia	NAHL	51	2763	26	19	1	170	1	3.69	3	191			14	0	4.40
—Springfield	AHL	3	180	2	1	0	10	0	3.33	—	—	—	—	—	—	—
77-78—Philadelphia	AHL	*60	*3585	31	21	7	177	4	2.96	2	119	0	2	12	0	6.05
78-79—Atlanta	NHL	18	994	8	8	1	55	0	3.32	1	20	0	0	0	0	0.00
—Philadelphia	AHL	13	780	3	9	1	36	0	2.77	—	—	—	—	—	—	—
79-80—Birmingham	CHL	38	2188	13	21	2	137	0	3.76	2	79	0	1	5	0	3.80
—Atlanta	NHL	3	150	0	2	0	15	0	6.00	—	—	—	—	—	—	—
80-81—Birmingham	CHL	13	757	3	8	2	56	0	4.44	—	—	—	—	—	—	—
—Calgary	NHL	29	1629	14	6	7	88	2	3.24	6	366	3	3	22	0	3.61
81-82—Calgary	NHL	34	1866	10	5	6	135	0	4.34	—	—	—	—	—	—	—
82-83—Calgary	NHL	39	2211	16	12	8	133	0	3.61	7	327	3	3	27	0	4.95
83-84—Calgary	NHL	51	2568	21	12	9	150	3	3.50	8	448	4	4	32	0	4.29
84-85—Calgary	NHL	56	3176	30	12	10	183	1	3.46	4	248	1	3	15	1	3.63
85-86—Calgary	NHL	60	3369	29	24	4	229	1	4.08	3	109	0	1	7	0	3.85
86-87—Calgary	NHL	34	1735	16	9	1	94	2	3.25	2	101	0	1	6	0	3.56
87-88—Boston	NHL	49	2828	24	17	6	138	3	2.93	17	1027	11	6	45	†1	*2.63
88-89—Boston	NHL	40	2392	19	15	6	120	0	3.01	4	252	1	3	16	0	3.81
89-90—Boston	NHL	43	2310	22	15	2	108	2	2.81	3	135	0	1	13	0	5.78
90-91—Boston	NHL	33	1829	17	10	3	111	1	3.64	2	32	0	0	0	0	0.00
91-92—Boston	NHL	8	407	5	1	0	23	0	3.39	2	54	0	0	3	0	3.33
NHL totals		497	27464	231	148	63	1582	12	3.46	59	3119	23	25	186	2	3.58

LEMIEUX, CLAUDE
RW, DEVILS

PERSONAL: Born July 16, 1965, at Buckingham, Que.... 6-1/215.... Shoots right.... Brother of Jocelyn Lemieux, right winger, Chicago Blackhawks.
TRANSACTIONS/CAREER NOTES: Selected by Montreal Canadiens as underage junior in second round (second Canadiens pick, 26th overall) of NHL entry draft (June 8,

1983).... Tore ankle ligaments (October 1987).... Fractured orbital bone above right eye (January 14, 1988).... Pulled groin (March 1989).... Underwent surgery to repair torn stomach muscle (November 1, 1989); missed 41 games.... Traded by Canadiens to New Jersey Devils for LW Sylvain Turgeon (September 4, 1990).... Suffered contusion of right eye retina (February 25, 1991).... Suffered sore back (November 27, 1991); missed four games.... Injured ankle (March 11, 1992); missed two games.
HONORS: Named to QMJHL All-Star second team (1983-84).... Won Guy Lafleur Trophy (1984-85).... Named to QMJHL All-Star first team (1984-85).

			REGULAR SEASON					PLAYOFFS				
Season	Team	League	Gms.	G	A	Pts.	Pen.	Gms.	G	A	Pts.	Pen.
82-83—Trois-Rivieres.................		QMJHL	62	28	38	66	187	4	1	0	1	30
83-84—Verdun............................		QMJHL	51	41	45	86	225	9	8	12	20	63
—Montreal........................		NHL	8	1	1	2	12	—	—	—	—	—
—Nova Scotia...................		AHL	—	—	—	—	—	2	1	0	1	0
84-85—Verdun............................		QMJHL	52	58	66	124	152	14	*23	17	*40	38
—Montreal........................		NHL	1	0	1	1	7	—	—	—	—	—
85-86—Sherbrooke.....................		AHL	58	21	32	53	145	—	—	—	—	—
—Montreal........................		NHL	10	1	2	3	22	20	10	6	16	68
86-87—Montreal.........................		NHL	76	27	26	53	156	17	4	9	13	41
87-88—Montreal.........................		NHL	80	31	30	61	137	11	3	2	5	20
88-89—Montreal.........................		NHL	69	29	22	51	136	18	4	3	7	58
89-90 Montreal.........................		NHL	39	8	10	18	106	11	1	3	4	38
90-91—New Jersey.....................		NHL	78	30	17	47	105	7	4	0	4	34
91-92—New Jersey.....................		NHL	74	41	27	68	109	7	4	3	7	26
NHL totals............................			435	168	136	304	790	91	30	26	56	285

LEMIEUX, JOCELYN
RW, BLACKHAWKS

PERSONAL: Born November 18, 1967, at Mont Laurier, Que.... 5-10/200.... Shoots left.... Brother of Claude Lemieux, right winger, New Jersey Devils.
TRANSACTIONS/CAREER NOTES: Selected by St. Louis Blues as underage junior in first round (first Blues pick, 10th overall) of NHL entry draft (June 21, 1986).... Severed tendon in little finger of left hand (December 1986).... Broke left leg and tore ligaments (January 1988).... Traded by Blues with G Darrell May and second-round pick in 1989 draft (D Patrice Brisebois) to Montreal Canadiens for LW Sergio Momesso and G Vincent Riendeau (August 9, 1988).... Traded by Canadiens to Chicago Blackhawks for third-round pick in 1990 draft (D Charles Poulin) (January 5, 1990).... Suffered concussion and cracked orbital bone above right eye (February 26, 1991); missed a month.
HONORS: Named to QMJHL All-Star first team (1985-86).

			REGULAR SEASON					PLAYOFFS				
Season	Team	League	Gms.	G	A	Pts.	Pen.	Gms.	G	A	Pts.	Pen.
84-85—Laval		QMJHL	68	13	19	32	92	—	—	—	—	—
85-86—Laval		QMJHL	71	57	68	125	131	14	9	15	24	37
86-87—St. Louis		NHL	53	10	8	18	94	5	0	1	1	6
87-88—Peoria		IHL	8	0	5	5	35	—	—	—	—	—
—St. Louis		NHL	23	1	0	1	42	5	0	0	0	0
88-89—Montreal		NHL	1	0	1	1	0	—	—	—	—	—
—Sherbrooke		AHL	73	25	28	53	134	4	3	1	4	6
89-90—Montreal		NHL	34	4	2	6	61	—	—	—	—	—
—Chicago		NHL	39	10	11	21	47	18	1	8	9	28
90-91—Chicago		NHL	67	6	7	13	119	4	0	0	0	0
91-92—Chicago		NHL	78	6	10	16	80	18	3	1	4	33
NHL totals............................			295	37	39	76	443	50	4	10	14	67

LEMIEUX, MARIO
C, PENGUINS

PERSONAL: Born October 5, 1965, at Montreal.... 6-4/210.... Shoots right.... Brother of Alain Lemieux, center, St. Louis Blues, Quebec Nordiques and Pittsburgh Penguins (1981-82 through 1986-87).
TRANSACTIONS/CAREER NOTES: Selected by Pittsburgh Penguins as underage junior in first round (first Penguins pick, first overall) of NHL entry draft (June 9, 1984).... Sprained left knee (September 1984).... Reinjured knee (December 2, 1984).... Sprained right knee (December 20, 1986).... Bruised right shoulder (November 1987).... Sprained right wrist (November 3, 1988).... Suffered herniated disk (February 14, 1990); missed 21 games.... Underwent surgery to remove part of herniated disk (July 11, 1990); missed first 50 games of season.... Suffered back spasms (October 1991); missed three games.... Suffered back spasms (January 4, 1992); missed three games.... Injured back (January 29, 1992); missed six games.... Suffered from the flu (February 1992); missed one game.... Fractured bone in hand (May 5, 1992).
HONORS: Named to QMJHL All-Star second team (1982-83).... Won Can.HL Player of the Year Award (1983-84).... Won Michel Briere Trophy (1983-84).... Won Jean Beliveau Trophy (1983-84).... Won Michael Bossy Trophy (1983-84).... Won Guy Lafleur Trophy (1983-84).... Named to QMJHL All-Star first team (1983-84).... Named QMJHL Most Valuable Player (1983-84).... Named Can.HL Player of the Year (1983-84).... Named NHL Rookie of the Year by THE SPORTING NEWS (1984-85).... Won Calder Memorial Trophy (1984-85).... Named to NHL All-Rookie team (1984-85).... Won Lester B. Pearson Award (1985-86 and 1987-88).... Named to THE SPORTING NEWS All-Star second team (1985-86).... Named to NHL All-Star second team (1985-86, 1986-87 and 1991-92).... Named NHL Player of the Year by THE SPORTING NEWS (1987-88 and 1988-89).... Won Hart Memorial Trophy (1987-88).... Won Art Ross Memorial Trophy (1987-88, 1988-89 and 1991-92).... Won Dodge Performer of the Year Award (1987-88).... Won Dodge Performer of the Year Award (1987-88 and 1988-89).... Named to THE SPORTING NEWS All-Star first team (1987-88 and 1988-89).... Named to NHL All-Star first team (1987-88 and 1988-89).... Won Dodge Ram Tough Award (1988-89).... Won the Conn Smythe Trophy (1990-91 and 1991-92).... Won Pro Set NHL Player of the Year Award (1991-92).
RECORDS: Holds NHL career record for most overtime points—14.... Shares NHL career record for most overtime goals—7....

Holds NHL single-season record for most shorthanded goals—13 (1988-89).... Shares NHL single-game playoff records for most goals—5 (April 25, 1989); most points—8 (April 25, 1989); most goals in one period—4 (April 25, 1989); and most points in one period—4 (April 25, 1989).... Holds NHL All-Star single-game record for most points—6 (1988).... Shares NHL All-Star single-game record for most goals—4 (1990).

Season Team	League	REGULAR SEASON					PLAYOFFS				
		Gms.	G	A	Pts.	Pen.	Gms.	G	A	Pts.	Pen.
81-82—Laval	QMJHL	64	30	66	96	22	18	5	9	14	31
82-83—Laval	QMJHL	66	84	100	184	76	12	†14	18	32	18
83-84—Laval	QMJHL	70	*133	*149	*282	92	14	*29	*23	*52	29
84-85—Pittsburgh	NHL	73	43	57	100	54	—	—	—	—	—
85-86—Pittsburgh	NHL	79	48	93	141	43	—	—	—	—	—
86-87—Pittsburgh	NHL	63	54	53	107	57	—	—	—	—	—
87-88—Pittsburgh	NHL	77	*70	98	*168	92	—	—	—	—	—
88-89—Pittsburgh	NHL	76	*85	†114	*199	100	11	12	7	19	16
89-90—Pittsburgh	NHL	59	45	78	123	78	—	—	—	—	—
90-91—Pittsburgh	NHL	26	19	26	45	30	23	16	*28	*44	16
91-92—Pittsburgh	NHL	64	44	87	*131	94	15	*16	18	*34	2
NHL totals		517	408	606	1014	548	49	44	53	97	34

LENARDUZZI, MIKE
G, WHALERS

PERSONAL: Born September 14, 1972, at Mississauga, Ont.... 6-0/165.... Shoots left.

TRANSACTIONS/CAREER NOTES: Traded by Oshawa 67's with RW Mike DeCoff, RW Jason Denomme, second-round picks in 1990 (D Drew Bannister) and 1991 drafts and cash to Sault Ste. Marie Greyhounds for C Eric Lindros (December 17, 1989).... Selected by Hartford Whalers in third round (third Whalers pick, 57th overall) of NHL entry draft (June 16, 1990).

HONORS: Shared Dave Pinkney Trophy with Kevin Hodson (1990-91).

Season Team	League	REGULAR SEASON							PLAYOFFS					
		Gms.	Min.	W	L	T	GA	SO	Avg.	Gms.	Min.	W	L	GA	SO	Avg.
88-89—Markham Jr. B	OHA	20	1149				111	0	5.80	—	—	—	—	—	—	—
—Oshawa	OHL	6	166				9	0	3.25	—	—	—	—	—	—	—
89-90—Oshawa	OHL	12	444	6	3	1	32	0	4.32	—	—	—	—	—	—	—
—Sault Ste. Marie	OHL	20	1117				66	0	3.55	—	—	—	—	—	—	—
90-91—Sault Ste. Marie	OHL	35	1966	19	8	3	107	0	3.27	5	268	3	1	13	*1	2.91
91-92—Sault Ste. Marie	OHL	9	486	5	3	0	33	0	4.07	—	—	—	—	—	—	—
—Sudbury	OHL	22	1201	11	5	4	84	2	4.20	11	651	4	7	38	0	3.50
—Springfield	AHL	—	—	—	—	—	—	—	—	1	39	0	0	2	0	3.08

LEROUX, FRANCOIS
D, OILERS

PERSONAL: Born April 18, 1970, at St. Adele, Que.... 6-6/221.... Shoots left.

TRANSACTIONS/CAREER NOTES: Selected by Edmonton Oilers in first round (first Oilers pick, 19th overall) of NHL entry draft (June 11, 1988).... Separated shoulder (March 20, 1989).... Traded by St. Jean Lynx with LW Patrick Lebeau and LW Jean Blouin to Victoriaville Tigres for RW Trevor Duhaime, second- and third-round draft picks and future considerations (February 15, 1990).... Tore left knee ligaments (March 18, 1990).... Underwent surgery to left knee (March 22, 1990).

Season Team	League	REGULAR SEASON					PLAYOFFS				
		Gms.	G	A	Pts.	Pen.	Gms.	G	A	Pts.	Pen.
87-88—St. Jean	QMJHL	58	3	8	11	143	7	2	0	2	21
88-89—Edmonton	NHL	2	0	0	0	0	—	—	—	—	—
—St. Jean	QMJHL	57	8	34	42	185	—	—	—	—	—
89-90—Edmonton	NHL	3	0	1	1	0	—	—	—	—	—
—St. Jean/Victoriaville	QMJHL	54	4	33	37	160	—	—	—	—	—
90-91—Cape Breton	AHL	71	2	7	9	124	4	0	1	1	19
—Edmonton	NHL	1	0	2	2	0	—	—	—	—	—
91-92—Cape Breton	AHL	61	7	22	29	114	5	0	0	0	8
—Edmonton	NHL	4	0	0	0	7	—	—	—	—	—
NHL totals		10	0	3	3	7					

LESCHYSHYN, CURTIS
D, NORDIQUES

PERSONAL: Born September 21, 1969, at Thompson, Man.... 6-1/205.... Shoots left.... Full name: Curtis Michael Leschyshyn.

TRANSACTIONS/CAREER NOTES: Selected by Quebec Nordiques in first round (first Nordiques pick, third overall) of NHL entry draft (June 11, 1988).... Separated shoulder (January 10, 1989).... Sprained left knee (November 1989).... Damaged knee ligaments (February 18, 1991) and underwent surgery (February 20, 1991); missed final 19 games of 1990-91 season and first 30 games of 1991-92 season.

HONORS: Named to WHL All-Star first team (1987-88).

Season Team	League	REGULAR SEASON					PLAYOFFS				
		Gms.	G	A	Pts.	Pen.	Gms.	G	A	Pts.	Pen.
85-86—Saskatoon	WHL	1	0	0	0	0	—	—	—	—	—
86-87—Saskatoon	WHL	70	14	26	40	107	11	1	5	6	14
87-88—Saskatoon	WHL	56	14	41	55	86	10	2	5	7	16
88-89—Quebec	NHL	71	4	9	13	71	—	—	—	—	—
89-90—Quebec	NHL	68	2	6	8	44	—	—	—	—	—
90-91—Quebec	NHL	55	3	7	10	49	—	—	—	—	—
91-92—Quebec	NHL	42	5	12	17	42	—	—	—	—	—
—Halifax	AHL	6	0	2	2	4	—	—	—	—	—
NHL totals		236	14	34	48	206					

LESLIE, LEE
LW, BLUES

PERSONAL: Born August 15, 1972, at Prince George, B.C. . . . 6-4/193. . . . Shoots left. . . . Full name: Lee J. Leslie.
HIGH SCHOOL: Carlton Comprensive (Prince Albert, Sask.).
TRANSACTIONS/CAREER NOTES: Selected by St. Louis Blues in fourth round (fourth Blues pick, 86th overall) of NHL entry draft (June 20, 1992).

			REGULAR SEASON					PLAYOFFS			
Season Team	League	Gms.	G	A	Pts.	Pen.	Gms.	G	A	Pts.	Pen.
88-89—Prince George	BCJHL	50	19	23	42	62	—	—	—	—	—
89-90—Prince Albert	WHL	62	14	16	30	13	14	2	3	5	4
90-91—Prince Albert	WHL	72	29	42	71	68	3	0	0	0	5
91-92—Prince Albert	WHL	72	52	48	100	70	10	6	6	12	12

LESSARD, RICK
D, SHARKS

PERSONAL: Born January 9, 1968, at Timmons, Ont. . . . 6-2/206. . . . Shoots left. . . . Full name: Richard Lessard.
TRANSACTIONS/CAREER NOTES: Selected by Calgary Flames as underage junior in seventh round (sixth Flames pick, 142nd overall) of NHL entry draft (June 21, 1986). . . . Selected by San Jose Sharks in NHL expansion draft (May 30, 1991). . . . Punctured ear drum (October 23, 1991).
HONORS: Named to IHL All-Star first team (1988-89).

			REGULAR SEASON					PLAYOFFS			
Season Team	League	Gms.	G	A	Pts.	Pen.	Gms.	G	A	Pts.	Pen.
84-85—Ottawa	OHL	60	2	13	15	128	—	—	—	—	—
85-86—Ottawa	OHL	64	1	20	21	231	—	—	—	—	—
86-87—Ottawa	OHL	66	5	36	41	188	11	1	7	8	30
87-88—Ottawa	OHL	58	5	34	39	210	16	1	0	1	31
88-89—Caigary	NHL	6	0	1	1	2	—	—	—	—	—
—Salt Lake City	IHL	76	10	42	52	239	14	1	6	7	35
89-90—Salt Lake City	IHL	66	3	18	21	169	10	1	2	3	64
90-91—Calgary	NHL	1	0	1	1	0	—	—	—	—	—
—Salt Lake City	IHL	80	8	27	35	272	4	0	1	1	12
91-92—San Jose	NHL	8	0	2	2	16	—	—	—	—	—
—Kansas City	IHL	46	3	16	19	117	3	0	0	0	2
NHL totals		15	0	4	4	18					

LETOURNEAU, RAY
G, FLYERS

PERSONAL: Born January 14, 1969, at Lewistown, N.H. . . . 5-11/190. . . . Shoots left.
TRANSACTIONS/CAREER NOTES: Selected by Philadelphia Flyers in NHL supplemental draft (June 15, 1990).

			REGULAR SEASON							PLAYOFFS					
Season Team	League	Gms.	Min.	W	L	T	GA	SO	Avg.	Gms.	Min.	W	L	GA	SO	Avg.
87-88—Yale University	ECAC	4	175	0	3	0	24	0	8.23	—	—	—	—	—	—	—
88-89—Yale University	ECAC	7	378	1	5	0	42	0	6.67	—	—	—	—	—	—	—
89-90—Yale University	ECAC	28	1631	8	19	1	125	0	4.60	—	—	—	—	—	—	—
90-91—Yale University	ECAC	27	1572	11	14	2	106	0	4.05	—	—	—	—	—	—	—
91-92—Hershey	AHL	15	791	4	8	1	67	0	5.08	—	—	—	—	—	—	—
—Roanoke Valley	ECHL	5	245	2	3	0	33	0	8.08	—	—	—	—	—	—	—

LEVEQUE, GUY
C, KINGS

PERSONAL: Born December 28, 1972, at Kingston, Ont. . . . 5-11/170. . . . Shoots right. . . . Cousin of Mike Murray, center, Philadelphia Flyers (1987-88).
TRANSACTIONS/CAREER NOTES: Selected by Los Angeles Kings in second round (first Kings pick, 42nd overall) of NHL entry draft (June 22, 1991).

			REGULAR SEASON					PLAYOFFS			
Season Team	League	Gms.	G	A	Pts.	Pen.	Gms.	G	A	Pts.	Pen.
89-90—Cornwall	OHL	62	10	15	25	30	3	0	0	0	4
90-91—Cornwall	OHL	66	41	56	97	34	—	—	—	—	—
91-92—Cornwall	OHL	37	23	36	59	40	6	3	5	8	2

LEVINS, SCOTT
RW, JETS

PERSONAL: Born January 30, 1970, at Portland, Ore. . . . 6-3/200. . . . Shoots right.
TRANSACTIONS/CAREER NOTES: Selected by Winnipeg Jets in fourth round (fourth Jets pick, 75th overall) of NHL entry draft (June 16, 1990).
HONORS: Named to WHL All-Star second team (1989-90).

			REGULAR SEASON					PLAYOFFS			
Season Team	League	Gms.	G	A	Pts.	Pen.	Gms.	G	A	Pts.	Pen.
88-89—Penticton	BCJHL	50	27	58	85	154	—	—	—	—	—
89-90—Tri-City Americans	WHL	71	25	37	62	132	6	2	3	5	18
90-91—Moncton	AHL	74	12	26	38	133	4	0	0	0	4
91-92—Moncton	AHL	69	15	18	33	271	11	3	4	7	30

LEVY, JEFF
G, NORTH STARS

PERSONAL: Born December 9, 1970, at Salt Lake City. . . . 5-11/160. . . . Shoots left.
COLLEGE: New Hampshire.
TRANSACTIONS/CAREER NOTES: Selected by Minnesota North Stars in seventh round (seventh North Stars pick, 134th overall) of NHL entry draft (June 16, 1990).
HONORS: Named Hockey East Rookie of the Year (1990-91). . . . Named to NCAA All-America East second team (1990-91). . . . Named to Hockey East All-Star second team (1990-91).

Season Team	League	Gms.	Min.	W	L	T	GA	SO	Avg.	Gms.	Min.	W	L	GA	SO	Avg.
89-90—Rochester	USHL	32	1823	24	7	0	97	3	3.19	—	—	—	—	—	—	—
90-91—U. of New Hampshire	Hoc. East	24	1490	15	7	2	80	0	3.22	—	—	—	—	—	—	—
91-92—U. of New Hampshire	Hoc. East	35	2030	20	13	2	111		3.28	—	—	—	—	—	—	—

LIDSTER, DOUG
D, CANUCKS

PERSONAL: Born October 18, 1960, at Kamloops, B.C. . . . 6-1/200. . . . Shoots right. . . . Full name: John Douglas Andrew Lidster.
COLLEGE: Colorado College.
TRANSACTIONS/CAREER NOTES: Selected by Vancouver Canucks in seventh round (sixth Canucks pick, 133rd overall) of NHL entry draft (June 11, 1980). . . . Strained left knee (January 1988). . . . Hyperextended elbow (October 1988). . . . Broke hand (November 13, 1988). . . . Fractured cheekbone (March 1989). . . . Separated shoulder (March 1, 1992); missed 13 games.
HONORS: Named to WCHA All-Star first team (1981-82).

Season Team	League	Gms.	G	A	Pts.	Pen.	Gms.	G	A	Pts.	Pen.
78-79—Kamloops	BCJHL	59	36	47	83	50	—	—	—	—	—
79-80—Colorado College	WCHA	39	18	25	43	52	—	—	—	—	—
80-81—Colorado College	WCHA	36	10	30	40	54	—	—	—	—	—
81-82—Colorado College	WCHA	36	13	22	35	32	—	—	—	—	—
82-83—Colorado College	WCHA	34	15	41	56	30	—	—	—	—	—
83-84—Canadian Olympic Team	Int'l	59	6	20	26	28	—	—	—	—	—
—Vancouver	NHL	8	0	0	0	4	2	0	1	1	0
84-85—Vancouver	NHL	78	6	24	30	55	—	—	—	—	—
85-86—Vancouver	NHL	78	12	16	28	56	3	0	1	1	2
86-87—Vancouver	NHL	80	12	51	63	40	—	—	—	—	—
87-88—Vancouver	NHL	64	4	32	36	105	—	—	—	—	—
88-89—Vancouver	NHL	63	5	17	22	78	7	1	1	2	9
89-90—Vancouver	NHL	80	8	28	36	36	—	—	—	—	—
90-91—Vancouver	NHL	78	6	32	38	77	6	0	2	2	6
91-92—Vancouver	NHL	66	6	23	29	39	11	1	2	3	11
NHL totals		595	59	223	282	490	29	2	7	9	28

LIDSTROM, NICKLAS
D, RED WINGS

PERSONAL: Born April 28, 1970, at Vasteras, Sweden. . . . 6-2/180. . . . Shoots left.
TRANSACTIONS/CAREER NOTES: Selected by Detroit Red Wings in third round (third Red Wings pick, 53rd overall) of NHL entry draft (June 17, 1989).
HONORS: Named to NHL All-Rookie team (1991-92).

Season Team	League	Gms.	G	A	Pts.	Pen.	Gms.	G	A	Pts.	Pen.
88-89—Vasteras	Sweden	19	0	2	2	4	—	—	—	—	—
89-90—Vasteras	Sweden	39	8	8	16	14	—	—	—	—	—
90-91—Vasteras	Sweden	20	2	12	14	14	—	—	—	—	—
91-92—Detroit	NHL	80	11	49	60	22	11	1	2	3	0
NHL totals		80	11	49	60	22	11	1	2	3	0

LINDBERG, CHRIS
LW, FLAMES

PERSONAL: Born April 16, 1967, at Fort Francis, Ont. . . . 6-1/185. . . . Shoots left.
TRANSACTIONS/CAREER NOTES: Signed as free agent by Hartford Whalers (March 17, 1989). . . . Signed as free agent by Calgary Flames (August 1991). . . . Selected by Ottawa Senators in NHL expansion draft (June 18, 1992). . . . Traded by Senators to Flames for D Mark Osiecki (June 23, 1992).
MISCELLANEOUS: Member of 1992 silver-medal-winning Canadian Olympic team.

Season Team	League	Gms.	G	A	Pts.	Pen.	Gms.	G	A	Pts.	Pen.
87-88—Minnesota-Duluth	WCHA	35	12	10	22	36	—	—	—	—	—
88-89—Minnesota-Duluth	WCHA	36	15	18	33	51	—	—	—	—	—
89-90—Binghamton	AHL	32	4	4	8	36	—	—	—	—	—
90-91—Canadian National Team	Int'l	55	25	31	56	53	—	—	—	—	—
—Springfield	AHL	1	0	0	0	2	1	0	0	0	0
91-92—Canadian National Team	Int'l	56	33	35	68	63	—	—	—	—	—
—Canadian Olympic Team	Int'l	8	1	4	5	4	—	—	—	—	—
—Calgary	NHL	17	2	5	7	17	—	—	—	—	—
NHL totals		17	2	5	7	17					

LINDEN, TREVOR
C, CANUCKS

PERSONAL: Born April 11, 1970, at Medicine Hat, Alta. . . . 6-4/185. . . . Shoots right.
TRANSACTIONS/CAREER NOTES: Selected by Vancouver Canucks in first round (first Canucks pick, second overall) of NHL entry draft (June 11, 1988). . . . Hyperextended elbow (October 1989). . . . Separated shoulder (March 17, 1990).
HONORS: Named to WHL All-Star second team (1987-88). . . . Named to NHL All-Rookie team (1988-89).

Season Team	League	Gms.	G	A	Pts.	Pen.	Gms.	G	A	Pts.	Pen.
85-86—Medicine Hat	WHL	5	2	0	2	0	—	—	—	—	—
86-87—Medicine Hat	WHL	72	14	22	36	59	20	5	4	9	17

Season	Team	League	REGULAR SEASON					PLAYOFFS				
			Gms.	G	A	Pts.	Pen.	Gms.	G	A	Pts.	Pen.
87-88—Medicine Hat		WHL	67	46	64	110	76	16	†13	12	25	19
88-89—Vancouver		NHL	80	30	29	59	41	7	3	4	7	8
89-90—Vancouver		NHL	73	21	30	51	43	—	—	—	—	—
90-91—Vancouver		NHL	80	33	37	70	65	6	0	7	7	2
91-92—Vancouver		NHL	80	31	44	75	101	13	4	8	12	6
NHL totals			313	115	140	255	250	26	7	19	26	16

LINDROS, ERIC
C, FLYERS

PERSONAL: Born February 28, 1973, at London, Ont. . . . 6-5/225. . . . Shoots right.
TRANSACTIONS/CAREER NOTES: Selected by Sault Ste. Marie Greyhounds in OHL priority draft; refused to report (August 30, 1989). OHL rights traded by Greyhounds to Oshawa Generals for RW Mike DeCoff, RW Jason Denomme, G Mike Lenarduzzi, second-round picks in 1991 and 1992 drafts and cash (December 17, 1989). . . . Suspended two games by OHL for fighting (February 7, 1990). . . . Selected by Quebec Nordiques in first round (first Nordiques pick, first overall) of NHL entry draft (June 22, 1991). . . . Traded by Nordiques to Philadelphia Flyers for G Ron Hextall, C Mike Ricci, C Peter Forsberg, D Steve Duchesne, D Kerry Huffman, first-round pick in 1993 draft, cash and future considerations (June 20, 1992); Flyers sent LW Chris Simon and first-round pick in 1994 draft to Nordiques to complete deal (July 21, 1992).
HONORS: Named to Memorial Cup All-Star Team (1989-90). . . . Won Can.HL Player of the Year Award (1990-91). . . . Won the Can.HL Plus/Minus Award (1990-91). . . . Won the Can.HL Top Draft Prospect Award (1990-91). . . . Won the Red Tilson Trophy (1990-91). . . . Won the Eddie Powers Memorial Trophy (1990-91). . . . Named to OHL All-Star first team (1990-91).
MISCELLANEOUS: Member of 1992 silver-medal-winning Canadian Olympic team.

Season	Team	League	REGULAR SEASON					PLAYOFFS				
			Gms.	G	A	Pts.	Pen.	Gms.	G	A	Pts.	Pen.
88-89—St. Michaels		MTHL	36	25	42	67		—	—	—	—	—
89-90—Detroit Compuware		NAJHL	14	25	27	52		—	—	—	—	—
—Oshawa		OHL	25	17	19	36	61	17	*18	18	36	*76
90-91—Oshawa		OHL	57	*71	78	*149	189	16	*18	20	*38	*93
91-92—Oshawa		OHL	13	9	22	31	54	—	—	—	—	—
—Canadian National Team..		Int'l	24	19	16	35	34	—	—	—	—	—
—Canadian Olympic Team ..		Int'l	8	5	6	11	6	—	—	—	—	—

LINDSAY, BILL
LW, NORDIQUES

PERSONAL: Born May 17, 1971, at Big Fork, Mont. . . . 5-11/185. . . . Shoots left. . . . Full name: William Hamilton Lindsay.
TRANSACTIONS/CAREER NOTES: Selected by Quebec Nordiques in fifth round (sixth Nordiques pick, 103rd overall) of NHL entry draft (June 22, 1991).
HONORS: Named to WHL (West) All-Star second team (1991-92).

Season	Team	League	REGULAR SEASON					PLAYOFFS				
			Gms.	G	A	Pts.	Pen.	Gms.	G	A	Pts.	Pen.
89-90—Tri-City Americans		WHL	72	40	45	85	84	—	—	—	—	—
90-91—Tri-City Americans		WHL	63	46	47	93	151	—	—	—	—	—
91-92—Tri-City Americans		WHL	42	34	59	93	111	3	2	3	5	16
—Quebec		NHL	23	2	4	6	14	—	—	—	—	—
NHL totals			23	2	4	6	14					

LINSEMAN, KEN
C

PERSONAL: Born August 11, 1958, at Kingston, Ont. . . . 5-11/175. . . . Shoots left.
TRANSACTIONS/CAREER NOTES: Selected as underage junior by Birmingham Bulls in WHA amateur player draft (June 1977). . . . Selected by Philadelphia Flyers from Bulls (with choice obtained from N.Y. Rangers) in first round (first Flyers pick, seventh overall) of NHL amateur draft (June 15, 1978). . . . Broke tibia bone in leg (September 1980). . . . Traded by Flyers with LW Greg Adams and first- and third-round picks in 1983 draft to Hartford Whalers for LW/D Mark Howe and Whalers third-round pick in 1983 (August 19, 1982). . . . Traded by Whalers with C Don Nachbaur to Edmonton Oilers for D Risto Siltanen and LW Brent Loney (August 19, 1982). . . . Suspended four games by NHL for fighting in stands (February 1983). . . . Traded by Oilers to Boston Bruins for LW/C Mike Krushelnyski (June 1984). . . . Injured shoulder (November 1984). . . . Broke right hand (November 21, 1985); missed 10 games. . . . Injured hand (December 28, 1985); missed six games. . . . Sprained right ankle (March 1988). . . . Tore ligament in left knee (March 27, 1989). . . . Underwent surgery to left arm to correct a circulatory problem (September 28, 1989); missed 14 games. . . . Traded by Bruins to Flyers for C Dave Poulin (January 16, 1990). . . . Signed as free agent by Oilers (August 1990). . . . Tore iris in right eye (February 20, 1991); missed nine games. . . . Traded by Oilers to Toronto Maple Leafs for future considerations (October 2, 1991).
HONORS: Named to OMJHL All-Star second team (1976-77).
RECORDS: Shares NHL single-game playoff record for most points in one period—4 (April 14, 1985).

Season	Team	League	REGULAR SEASON					PLAYOFFS				
			Gms.	G	A	Pts.	Pen.	Gms.	G	A	Pts.	Pen.
74-75—Kingston		OHA Mj. Jr. A	59	19	28	47	70	—	—	—	—	—
75-76—Kingston		OHA Mj. Jr. A	65	61	51	112	92	7	5	0	5	18
76-77—Kingston		OMJHL	63	53	74	127	210	10	9	12	21	54
77-78—Birmingham		WHA	71	38	38	76	126	5	2	2	4	15
78-79—Maine		AHL	38	17	23	40	106	—	—	—	—	—
—Philadelphia		NHL	30	5	20	25	23	8	2	6	8	22
79-80—Philadelphia		NHL	80	22	57	79	107	17	4	*18	22	40
80-81—Philadelphia		NHL	51	17	30	47	150	12	4	16	20	67
81-82—Philadelphia		NHL	79	24	68	92	275	4	1	2	3	6
82-83—Edmonton		NHL	72	33	42	75	181	16	6	8	14	22
83-84—Edmonton		NHL	72	18	49	67	119	19	10	4	14	65

Season Team	League	REGULAR SEASON					PLAYOFFS				
		Gms.	G	A	Pts.	Pen.	Gms.	G	A	Pts.	Pen.
84-85—Boston	NHL	74	25	49	74	126	5	4	6	10	8
85-86—Boston	NHL	64	23	58	81	97	3	0	1	1	17
86-87—Boston	NHL	64	15	34	49	126	4	1	1	2	22
87-88—Boston	NHL	77	29	45	74	167	23	11	14	25	56
88-89—Boston	NHL	78	27	45	72	164	—	—	—	—	—
89-90—Boston	NHL	32	6	16	22	66	—	—	—	—	—
—Philadelphia	NHL	29	5	9	14	30	—	—	—	—	—
90-91—Edmonton	NHL	56	7	29	36	94	2	0	1	1	0
91-92—Toronto	NHL	2	0	0	0	2	—	—	—	—	—
WHA totlas		71	38	38	76	126	5	2	2	4	15
NHL totals		860	256	551	807	1727	113	43	77	120	325

LITTMAN, DAVID

G, SABRES

PERSONAL: Born June 13, 1967, at Cranston, R.I.... 6-0/175.... Shoots left.
COLLEGE: Boston College.
TRANSACTIONS/CAREER NOTES: Selected by Buffalo Sabres in 11th round (12th Sabres pick, 211th overall) of NHL entry draft (June 13, 1987).... Separated shoulder (December 1989); missed six games.
HONORS: Named to NCAA All-America East second team (1988-89).... Named to Hockey East All-Star first team (1988-89). ... Shared Harry (Hap) Holmes Memorial Trophy with Darcy Wakaluk (1990-91).... Named to AHL All-Star first team (1990-91).... Won Harry (Hap) Holmes Memorial Trophy (1991-92).... Named to AHL All-Star second team (1991-92).

Season Team	League	REGULAR SEASON							PLAYOFFS					
		Gms.	Min.	W	L	T	GA	SO	Avg.	Gms.	Min.	W	L	GA	SO	Avg.
85-86—Boston College	Hoc. East	9	442	4	0	1	22	1	2.99	—	—	—	—	—	—	—
86-87—Boston College	Hoc. East	21	1182	15	5	0	68	0	3.45	—	—	—	—	—	—	—
87-88—Boston College	Hoc. East	30	1726	11	16	2	116	0	4.03	—	—	—	—	—	—	—
88-89—Boston College	Hoc. East	32	1945	19	9	4	107	0	3.30	—	—	—	—	—	—	—
89-90—Rochester	AHL	14	681	5	6	1	37	0	3.26	1	33			4	0	7.27
—Phoenix	IHL	18	1047	8	7	2	64	0	3.67	—	—	—	—	—	—	—
90-91—Buffalo	NHL	1	36	0	0	0	3	0	5.00	—	—	—	—	—	—	—
—Rochester	AHL	*56	*3155	*33	13	5	160	3	3.04	8	378	4	2	16	0	2.54
91-92—Rochester	AHL	*61	*3558	*29	20	9	174	†3	2.93	15	879	8	†7	43	1	2.94
—Buffalo	NHL	1	60	0	1	0	4	0	4.00	—	—	—	—	—	—	—
NHL totals		2	96	0	1	0	7	0	4.38							

LIUT, MIKE

G, CAPITALS

PERSONAL: Born January 7, 1956, at Weston, Ont.... 6-2/195.... Shoots left.... Full name: Michael Dennis Liut.... Cousin of Ron Francis, center, Pittsburgh Penguins.
COLLEGE: Bowling Green State.
TRANSACTIONS/CAREER NOTES: Selected by St. Louis Blues from Bowling Green State University in fourth round (fifth Blues pick, 56th overall) of NHL entry draft (June 1, 1976).... Selected by New England Whalers in WHA amateur player draft (May 1976).... WHA rights traded by Whalers to Cincinnati Stingers with second-round pick in 1979 draft for C Greg Carroll and D Bryan Maxwell (May 1977).... Tore cartilage in left knee; missed part of 1977-78 season.... Selected by Blues in NHL reclaim draft (June 1979).... Suffered groin injury (January 10, 1981).... Strained knee ligaments (March 1984).... Traded by Blues with future considerations (LW Jorgen Pettersson) to Hartford Whalers for G Greg Millen and LW/C Mark Johnson (February 1985).... Suffered back spasms (October 1987); missed 13 games.... Twisted knee (March 1988).... Sprained shoulder (April 1988).... Suffered inflamed rotator cuff in right shoulder (November 1988); missed two weeks.... Twisted knee (March 1989).... Underwent surgery to left knee (December 20, 1989); missed 16 games. ... Traded by Whalers to Washington Capitals for LW Yvon Corriveau (March 5, 1990).... Strained groin (November 28, 1990); missed five games.... Suffered herniated disk (February 17, 1992); missed final 22 games of season.
HONORS: Named to CCHA All-Star first team (1974-75 and 1976-77).... Named to CCHA All-Star second team (1975-76).... Named CCHA Player of the Year (1976-77).... Won Lester B. Pearson Award (1980-81).... Named to THE SPORTING NEWS All-Star first team (1980-81 and 1986-87).... Named to NHL All-Star first team (1980-81).... Named to NHL All-Star second team (1986-87).
STATISTICAL NOTES: Led NHL with 2.527 goals-against average and four shutouts in 1989-90.

Season Team	League	REGULAR SEASON							PLAYOFFS					
		Gms.	Min.	W	L	T	GA	SO	Avg.	Gms.	Min.	W	L	GA	SO	Avg.
73-74—Bowling Green State	CCHA	24	1272	10	12	0	88	0	4.15	—	—	—	—	—	—	—
74-75—Bowling Green State	CCHA	20	1174	12	6	1	78	00	3.99	—	—	—	—	—	—	—
75-76—Bowling Green State	CCHA	21	1171	13	5	0	50	2	2.56	—	—	—	—	—	—	—
76-77—Bowling Green State	CCHA	24	1346	18	4	0	61	2	2.72	—	—	—	—	—	—	—
77-78—Cincinnati	WHA	27	1215	8	12	0	86	0	4.25	—	—	—	—	—	—	—
78-79—Cincinnati	WHA	54	3181	23	27	4	*184	†3	3.47	3	179	1	2	12	0	*4.02
79-80—St. Louis	NHL	64	3661	32	23	9	194	2	3.18	3	193	0	3	12	0	3.73
80-81—St. Louis	NHL	61	3570	33	14	13	199	1	3.34	11	685	5	6	50	0	4.38
81-82—St. Louis	NHL	*64	*3691	28	28	7	*250	2	4.06	10	494	5	3	27	0	3.28
82-83—St. Louis	NHL	*68	*3794	21	27	13	235	1	3.72	4	240	1	3	15	0	3.75
83-84—St. Louis	NHL	58	3425	25	29	4	197	3	3.45	11	714	6	5	29	1	2.44
84-85—St. Louis	NHL	32	1869	12	12	6	119	1	3.82	—	—	—	—	—	—	—
—Hartford	NHL	12	731	4	7	1	36	1	2.95	—	—	—	—	—	—	—
85-86—Hartford	NHL	57	3282	27	23	4	197	2	3.60	8	441	5	2	14	†1	*1.90
86-87—Hartford	NHL	59	3476	31	22	5	187	*4	3.23	6	332	2	4	25	0	4.52
87-88—Hartford	NHL	60	3532	25	28	5	187	2	3.18	3	160	1	1	11	0	4.13
88-89—Hartford	NHL	35	2006	13	19	1	142	1	4.25	—	—	—	—	—	—	—

Season Team	League	REGULAR SEASON								PLAYOFFS						
		Gms.	Min.	W	L	T	GA	SO	Avg.	Gms.	Min.	W	L	GA	SO	Avg.
89-90—Hartford	NHL	29	1683	15	12	1	74	*3	*2.64	—	—	—	—	—	—	—
—Washington	NHL	8	478	4	4	0	17	*1	*2.13	9	507	4	4	28	0	3.31
90-91—Washington	NHL	35	1834	13	16	3	114	0	3.73	2	48	0	1	4	0	5.00
91-92—Washington	NHL	21	1123	10	7	2	70	1	3.74	—	—	—	—	—	—	—
WHA totals		81	4396	31	39	4	270	4	3.69	3	179	1	2	12	0	4.02
NHL totals		663	38155	293	271	74	2218	25	3.49	67	3814	29	32	215	2	3.38

LOACH, LONNIE
LW, SENATORS

PERSONAL: Born April 14, 1968, at New Liskeard, Ont.... 5-10/180.... Shoots left.
TRANSACTIONS/CAREER NOTES: Selected by Chicago Blackhawks as underage junior in fifth round (fourth Blackhawks pick, 98th overall) of NHL entry draft (June 21, 1986).... Signed as free agent by Fort Wayne Komets after being released by Blackhawks (August 1990).... Signed as free agent by Detroit Red Wings (April 20, 1991).... Selected by Ottawa Senators in NHL expansion draft (June 18, 1992).
HONORS: Won Emms Family Award (1985-86).... Won Leo P. Lamoureux Memorial Trophy (1990-91).... Named to IHL All-Star second team (1990-91).

Season Team	League	REGULAR SEASON					PLAYOFFS				
		Gms.	G	A	Pts.	Pen.	Gms.	G	A	Pts.	Pen.
84-85—St. Mary's Jr. B	OHA	44	26	36	62	113	—	—	—	—	—
85-86—Guelph	OHL	65	41	42	83	63	20	7	8	15	16
86-87—Guelph	OHL	56	31	24	55	42	5	2	1	3	2
87-88—Guelph	OHL	66	43	49	92	75	—	—	—	—	—
88-89—Saginaw	IHL	32	7	6	13	27	—	—	—	—	—
—Flint	IHL	41	22	26	48	30	—	—	—	—	—
89-90—Indianapolis	IHL	3	0	1	1	0	—	—	—	—	—
—Fort Wayne	IHL	54	15	33	48	40	5	4	2	6	15
90-91—Fort Wayne	IHL	81	55	76	*131	45	19	5	11	16	13
91-92—Adirondack	AHL	67	37	49	86	69	†19	*13	4	17	10

LOEWEN, DARCY
LW, SENATORS

PERSONAL: Born February 26, 1969, at Calgary, Alta.... 5-10/192.... Shoots left.
TRANSACTIONS/CAREER NOTES: Selected by Buffalo Sabres in third round (second Sabres pick, 55th overall) of NHL entry draft (June 11, 1988).... Selected by Ottawa Senators in NHL expansion draft (June 18, 1992).

Season Team	League	REGULAR SEASON					PLAYOFFS				
		Gms.	G	A	Pts.	Pen.	Gms.	G	A	Pts.	Pen.
85-86—Spokane Chiefs	WHL	8	2	1	3	19	—	—	—	—	—
86-87—Spokane Chiefs	WHL	68	15	25	40	129	5	0	0	0	0
87-88—Spokane Chiefs	WHL	72	30	44	74	231	15	7	5	12	54
88-89—Spokane Chiefs	WHL	60	31	27	58	194	—	—	—	—	—
—Canadian National Team..	Int'l	2	0	0	0	0	—	—	—	—	—
89-90—Rochester	AHL	50	7	11	18	193	5	1	0	1	6
—Buffalo	NHL	4	0	0	0	4	—	—	—	—	—
90-91—Buffalo	NHL	6	0	0	0	8	—	—	—	—	—
—Rochester	AHL	71	13	15	28	130	15	1	5	6	14
91-92—Buffalo	NHL	2	0	0	0	2	—	—	—	—	—
—Rochester	AHL	73	11	20	31	193	4	0	1	1	8
NHL totals		12	0	0	0	14					

LOISELLE, CLAUDE
C, ISLANDERS

PERSONAL: Born May 29, 1963, at Ottawa.... 5-11/195.... Shoots left.
TRANSACTIONS/CAREER NOTES: Selected as underage junior by Detroit Red Wings in second round (first Red Wings pick, 23rd overall) of NHL entry draft (June 10, 1981).... Suspended six games by NHL for stick-swinging incident (January 7, 1984).... Injured knee (December 17, 1985); missed 11 games.... Traded by Red Wings to New Jersey Devils for RW Tim Higgins (June 25, 1986).... Separated right shoulder (February 1988).... Traded by Devils with D Joe Cirella and eighth-round pick (D Alexander Karpovtsev) in 1990 draft to Quebec Nordiques for C Walt Poddubny and fourth-round pick (RW Mike Bodnarchuk) in 1990 draft (June 17, 1989).... Broke finger on left hand (February 1990).... Traded by Nordiques to Calgary Flames for LW Bryan Deasley (March 2, 1991); trade voided when Loiselle claimed on waivers by Toronto Maple Leafs (March 4, 1991).... Traded by Maple Leafs with RW Daniel Marois to New York Islanders for LW Ken Baumgartner and C Dave McLlwain (March 10, 1992).

Season Team	League	REGULAR SEASON					PLAYOFFS				
		Gms.	G	A	Pts.	Pen.	Gms.	G	A	Pts.	Pen.
79-80—Gloucester	OPJHL	50	21	38	59	26	—	—	—	—	—
80-81—Windsor	OMJHL	68	38	56	94	103	11	3	3	6	40
81-82—Windsor	OHL	68	36	73	109	192	9	2	10	12	42
—Detroit	NHL	4	1	0	1	2	—	—	—	—	—
82-83—Detroit	NHL	18	2	0	2	15	—	—	—	—	—
—Windsor	OHL	46	39	49	88	75	—	—	—	—	—
—Adirondack	AHL	6	1	7	8	0	6	2	4	6	0
83-84—Adirondack	AHL	29	13	16	29	59	—	—	—	—	—
—Detroit	NHL	28	4	6	10	32	—	—	—	—	—
84-85—Adirondack	AHL	47	22	29	51	24	—	—	—	—	—
—Detroit	NHL	30	8	1	9	45	3	0	2	2	0

Season Team	League	REGULAR SEASON					PLAYOFFS				
		Gms.	G	A	Pts.	Pen.	Gms.	G	A	Pts.	Pen.
85-86—Adirondack	AHL	21	15	11	26	32	16	5	10	15	38
—Detroit	NHL	48	7	15	22	142	—	—	—	—	—
86-87—New Jersey	NHL	75	16	24	40	137	—	—	—	—	—
87-88—New Jersey	NHL	68	17	18	35	121	20	4	6	10	50
88-89—New Jersey	NHL	74	7	14	21	209	—	—	—	—	—
89-90—Quebec	NHL	72	11	14	25	104	—	—	—	—	—
90-91—Quebec	NHL	59	5	10	15	86	—	—	—	—	—
—Toronto	NHL	7	1	1	2	2	—	—	—	—	—
91-92—Toronto	NHL	64	6	9	15	102	—	—	—	—	—
—New York Islanders	NHL	11	1	1	2	13	—	—	—	—	—
NHL totals		558	86	113	199	1010	23	4	8	12	50

LOMAKIN, ANDREI
LW, FLYERS

PERSONAL: Born April 3, 1964, at Voskresensk, U.S.S.R.... 5-10/176.... Shoots left.
TRANSACTIONS/CAREER NOTES: Selected by Philadelphia Flyers in seventh round (sixth Flyers pick, 107th overall) of NHL entry draft (June 22, 1991).... Fractured thumb (January 23, 1992); missed 15 games.
MISCELLANEOUS: Member of 1988 gold-medal-winning U.S.S.R. Olympic team.

Season Team	League	REGULAR SEASON					PLAYOFFS				
		Gms.	G	A	Pts.	Pen.	Gms.	G	A	Pts.	Pen.
81-82—Khimik Voskresensk	USSR	8	1	1	2	2	—	—	—	—	—
82-83—Khimik Voskresensk	USSR	56	15	8	23	32	—	—	—	—	—
83-84—Khimik Voskresensk	USSR	44	10	8	18	26	—	—	—	—	—
84-85—Khimik Voskresensk	USSR	52	13	10	23	24	—	—	—	—	—
86-87—Dynamo Moscow	USSR	40	15	14	29	30	—	—	—	—	—
87-88—Dynamo Moscow	USSR	45	10	15	25	24	—	—	—	—	—
88-89—Dynamo Moscow	USSR	44	9	16	25	22	—	—	—	—	—
89-90—Dynamo Moscow	USSR	48	11	15	26	36	—	—	—	—	—
90-91—Dynamo Moscow	USSR	45	16	17	33	22	—	—	—	—	—
91-92—Philadelphia	NHL	57	14	16	30	26	—	—	—	—	—
NHL totals		57	14	16	30	26	—	—	—	—	—

LONEY, BRIAN
RW, CANUCKS

PERSONAL: Born August 9, 1972, at Winnipeg, Man.... 6-2/195.... Shoots right.
COLLEGE: Ohio State.
TRANSACTIONS/CAREER NOTES: Selected by Vancouver Canucks in fifth round (sixth Canucks pick, 110th overall) of NHL entry draft (June 20, 1992).
HONORS: Named CCHA Rookie of the Year (1991-92).

Season Team	League	REGULAR SEASON					PLAYOFFS				
		Gms.	G	A	Pts.	Pen.	Gms.	G	A	Pts.	Pen.
91-92—Ohio State	CCHA	37	21	34	55	109	—	—	—	—	—

LONEY, TROY
LW, PENGUINS

PERSONAL: Born September 21, 1963, at Bow Island, Alta.... 6-3/209.... Shoots left.
TRANSACTIONS/CAREER NOTES: Selected by Pittsburgh Penguins as underage junior in third round (third Penguins pick, 52nd overall) of NHL entry draft (June 9, 1982).... Suspended by AHL (December 1986).... Sprained right shoulder (January 17, 1987).... Underwent knee surgery (October 1987).... Suspended 10 games by NHL for leaving bench to fight (November 13, 1988).... Broke right hand (November 24, 1989); missed 12 games.... Underwent surgery to right knee (June 1990); missed first two months of season.

Season Team	League	REGULAR SEASON					PLAYOFFS				
		Gms.	G	A	Pts.	Pen.	Gms.	G	A	Pts.	Pen.
80-81—Lethbridge	WHL	71	18	13	31	100	9	2	3	5	14
81-82—Lethbridge	WHL	71	26	31	57	152	12	3	3	6	10
82-83—Lethbridge	WHL	72	33	34	67	156	20	10	7	17	43
83-84—Baltimore	AHL	63	18	13	31	147	10	0	2	2	19
—Pittsburgh	NHL	13	0	0	0	9	—	—	—	—	—
84-85—Baltimore	AHL	15	4	2	6	25	—	—	—	—	—
—Pittsburgh	NHL	46	10	8	18	59	—	—	—	—	—
85-86—Baltimore	AHL	33	12	11	23	84	—	—	—	—	—
—Pittsburgh	NHL	47	3	9	12	95	—	—	—	—	—
86-87—Baltimore	AHL	40	13	14	27	134	—	—	—	—	—
—Pittsburgh	NHL	23	8	7	15	22	—	—	—	—	—
87-88—Pittsburgh	NHL	65	5	13	18	151	—	—	—	—	—
88-89—Pittsburgh	NHL	69	10	6	16	165	11	1	3	4	24
89-90—Pittsburgh	NHL	67	11	16	27	168	—	—	—	—	—
90-91—Muskegon	IHL	2	0	0	0	5	—	—	—	—	—
—Pittsburgh	NHL	44	7	9	16	85	24	2	2	4	41
91-92—Pittsburgh	NHL	76	10	16	26	127	†21	4	5	9	32
NHL totals		450	64	84	148	881	56	7	10	17	97

LONGO, CHRIS
RW, CAPITALS

PERSONAL: Born January 5, 1972, at Belleville, Ont. ... 5-10/180. ... Shoots right. ... Full name: Chris Anthony Longo.
TRANSACTIONS/CAREER NOTES: Selected by Washington Capitals in third round (third Capitals pick, 51st overall) of NHL entry draft (June 16, 1990).
HONORS: Won Emms Family Award (1989-90).

Season	Team	League	REGULAR SEASON					PLAYOFFS				
			Gms.	G	A	Pts.	Pen.	Gms.	G	A	Pts.	Pen.
87-88—Kingston Jr. A	MTHL	37	15	16	31		—	—	—	—	—
88-89—Kingston Jr. A	MTHL	40	28	29	57	54	—	—	—	—	—
89-90—Peterborough	OHL	66	33	42	75	48	11	2	3	5	14
90-91—Peterborough	OHL	64	30	38	68	68	4	1	0	1	9
91-92—Peterborough	OHL	25	5	14	19	16	10	5	6	11	16

LORENZ, DANNY
G, ISLANDERS

PERSONAL: Born December 12, 1969, at Murrayville, B.C. . . . 5-10/183. . . . Shoots left. . . . Full name: Daniel Lorenz.

TRANSACTIONS/CAREER NOTES: Selected by New York Islanders in third round (fourth Islanders pick, 58th overall) of NHL entry draft (June 11, 1988).

HONORS: Won Del Wilson Trophy (1988-89). . . . Named to WHL All-Star first team (1988-89).

Season	Team	League	REGULAR SEASON								PLAYOFFS						
			Gms.	Min.	W	L	T	GA	SO	Avg.	Gms.	Min.	W	L	GA	SO	Avg.
86-87—Seattle	WHL	38	2103	12	21	2	199	0	5.68	—	—	—	—	—	—	—
87-88—Seattle	WHL	62	3302	20	37	2	*314	0	5.71	—	—	—	—	—	—	—
88-89—Seattle	WHL	*68	*4003	31	33	4	240	*3	3.60	—	—	—	—	—	—	—
—Springfield	AHL	4	210	2	1	0	12	0	3.43	—	—	—	—	—	—	—
89-90—Seattle	WHL	50	3226	37	15	2	221	0	4.11	13	751	6	7	40	0	*3.20
90-91—New York Islanders	NHL	2	80	0	1	0	5	0	3.75	—	—	—	—	—	—	—
—Capital District	AHL	17	940	5	9	2	70	0	4.47	—	—	—	—	—	—	—
—Richmond	ECHL	20	1020	6	9	2	75	0	4.41	—	—	—	—	—	—	—
91-92—Capital District	AHL	53	3050	22	22	7	*181	2	3.56	7	442	3	4	25	0	3.39
—New York Islanders	NHL	2	120	0	2	0	10	0	5.00	—	—	—	—	—	—	—
NHL totals		4	200	0	3	0	15	0	4.50							

LOVSIN, KEN
D

PERSONAL: Born December 3, 1966, at Peace River, Alta. . . . 6-0/195. . . . Shoots left.

COLLEGE: Saskatchewan.

TRANSACTIONS/CAREER NOTES: Selected by Hartford Whalers in 1987 NHL supplemental draft (June 1987). . . . Signed as free agent by Washington Capitals (June 27, 1990).

Season	Team	League	REGULAR SEASON					PLAYOFFS				
			Gms.	G	A	Pts.	Pen.	Gms.	G	A	Pts.	Pen.
86-87—Univ. of Saskatchewan	CWUAA	28	3	13	16	14	—	—	—	—	—
87-88—Univ. of Saskatchewan	CWUAA	28	14	24	38	20	—	—	—	—	—
88-89—Canadian National Team	Int'l	59	0	10	10	59	—	—	—	—	—
89-90—Canadian National Team	Int'l	66	7	15	22	60	—	—	—	—	—
90-91—Washington	NHL	1	0	0	0	0	—	—	—	—	—
—Baltimore	AHL	79	8	28	36	54	6	1	1	2	4
91-92—Baltimore	AHL	77	11	24	35	60	—	—	—	—	—
NHL totals		1	0	0	0	0					

LOWE, KEVIN
D, OILERS

PERSONAL: Born April 15, 1959, at Lachute, Que. . . . 6-2/195. . . . Shoots left. . . . Full name: Kevin Hugh Lowe. . . . Husband of Karen Percy, Canadian Olympic bronze-medal-winning downhill skier (1988).

TRANSACTIONS/CAREER NOTES: Selected by Edmonton Oilers in first round (first Oilers pick, 21st overall) of NHL entry draft (August 9, 1979). . . . Broke index finger (March 7, 1986); missed six games. . . . Broke left wrist (March 9, 1988). . . . Pulled rib muscle (September 1988). . . . Suffered concussion (October 14, 1988). . . . Suffered back spasms (April 8, 1990). . . . Bruised back (December 28, 1991); missed one game. . . . Strained rotator cuff (January 28, 1992); missed three games. . . . Restrained rotator cuff (February 5, 1992); missed 21 games. . . . Strained groin (April 12, 1992); missed playoffs.

HONORS: Named to QMJHL All-Star second team (1978-79). . . . Won King Clancy Memorial Trophy (1989-90). . . . Named Budweiser/NHL Man of the Year (1989-90).

Season	Team	League	REGULAR SEASON					PLAYOFFS				
			Gms.	G	A	Pts.	Pen.	Gms.	G	A	Pts.	Pen.
76-77—Quebec	QMJHL	69	3	19	22	39	—	—	—	—	—
77-78—Quebec	QMJHL	64	13	52	65	86	4	1	2	3	6
78-79—Quebec	QMJHL	68	26	60	86	120	6	1	7	8	36
79-80—Edmonton	NHL	64	2	19	21	70	3	0	1	1	0
80-81—Edmonton	NHL	79	10	24	34	94	9	0	2	2	11
81-82—Edmonton	NHL	80	9	31	40	63	5	0	3	3	0
82-83—Edmonton	NHL	80	6	34	40	43	16	1	8	9	10
83-84—Edmonton	NHL	80	4	42	46	59	19	3	7	10	16
84-85—Edmonton	NHL	80	4	22	26	104	16	0	5	5	8
85-86—Edmonton	NHL	74	2	16	18	90	10	1	3	4	15
86-87—Edmonton	NHL	77	8	29	37	94	21	2	4	6	22
87-88—Edmonton	NHL	70	9	15	24	89	19	0	2	2	26
88-89—Edmonton	NHL	76	7	18	25	98	7	1	2	3	4
89-90—Edmonton	NHL	78	7	26	33	140	20	0	2	2	10
90-91—Edmonton	NHL	73	3	13	16	113	14	1	1	2	14
91-92—Edmonton	NHL	55	2	8	10	107	11	0	3	3	16
NHL totals		966	73	297	370	1164	170	9	43	52	152

LOWRY, DAVE
LW, BLUES

PERSONAL: Born January 14, 1965, at Sudbury, Ont. . . . 6-1/195. . . . Shoots left.
TRANSACTIONS/CAREER NOTES: Underwent arthroscopic knee surgery (December 1982). . . . Selected as underage junior by Vancouver Canucks in sixth round (fourth Canucks pick, 110th overall) of NHL entry draft (June 8, 1983). . . . Traded by Canucks to St. Louis Blues for C Ernie Vargas (September 29, 1988). . . . Suffered groin injury (March 1990). . . . Sprained shoulder (October 1991); missed two games.
HONORS: Named to OHL All-Star first team (1984-85).

Season Team	League	REGULAR SEASON					PLAYOFFS				
		Gms.	G	A	Pts.	Pen.	Gms.	G	A	Pts.	Pen.
82-83—London	OHL	42	11	16	27	48	3	0	0	0	14
83-84—London	OHL	66	29	47	76	125	8	6	6	12	41
84-85—London	OHL	61	60	60	120	94	8	6	5	11	10
85-86—Vancouver	NHL	73	10	8	18	143	3	0	0	0	0
86-87—Vancouver	NHL	70	8	10	18	176	—	—	—	—	—
87-88—Fredericton	AHL	46	18	27	45	59	14	7	3	10	72
—Vancouver	NHL	22	1	3	4	38	—	—	—	—	—
88-89—Peoria	IHL	58	31	35	66	45	—	—	—	—	—
—St. Louis	NHL	21	3	3	6	11	10	0	5	5	4
89-90—St. Louis	NHL	78	19	6	25	75	12	2	1	3	39
90-91—St. Louis	NHL	79	19	21	40	168	13	1	4	5	35
91-92—St. Louis	NHL	75	7	13	20	77	6	0	1	1	20
NHL totals		418	67	64	131	688	44	3	11	14	98

LUDWIG, CRAIG
D, NORTH STARS

PERSONAL: Born March 15, 1961, at Rhinelander, Wis. . . . 6-3/217. . . . Shoots left. . . . Full name: Craig Lee Ludwig.
COLLEGE: North Dakota.
TRANSACTIONS/CAREER NOTES: Selected by Montreal Canadiens in third round (fifth Canadiens pick, 61st overall) of NHL entry draft (June 11, 1980). . . . Fractured knuckle in left hand (October 1984). . . . Broke hand (December 2, 1985); missed nine games. . . . Broke right facial bone (January 1988); missed five games. . . . Suspended five games by NHL for elbowing (November 19, 1988). . . . Separated right shoulder (March 21, 1990). . . . Traded by Canadiens to New York Islanders for D Gerald Diduck (September 4, 1990). . . . Traded by Islanders to Minnesota North Stars as part of a three-way trade in which North Stars sent D Dave Babych to Vancouver Canucks and Canucks sent D Tom Kurvers to Islanders (June 22, 1991). . . . Injured foot (December 8, 1991); missed six games.
HONORS: Named to WCHA All-Star second team (1981-82).

Season Team	League	REGULAR SEASON					PLAYOFFS				
		Gms.	G	A	Pts.	Pen.	Gms.	G	A	Pts.	Pen.
79-80—Univ. of North Dakota	WCHA	33	1	8	9	32	—	—	—	—	—
80-81—Univ. of North Dakota	WCHA	34	4	8	12	48	—	—	—	—	—
81-82—Univ. of North Dakota	WCHA	47	5	26	31	70	—	—	—	—	—
82-83—Montreal	NHL	80	0	25	25	59	3	0	0	0	2
83-84—Montreal	NHL	80	7	18	25	52	15	0	3	3	23
84-85—Montreal	NHL	72	5	14	19	90	12	0	2	2	6
85-86—Montreal	NHL	69	2	4	6	63	20	0	1	1	48
86-87—Montreal	NHL	75	4	12	16	105	17	2	3	5	30
87-88—Montreal	NHL	74	4	10	14	69	11	1	1	2	6
88-89—Montreal	NHL	74	3	13	16	73	21	0	2	2	24
89-90—Montreal	NHL	73	1	15	16	108	11	0	1	1	16
90-91—New York Islanders	NHL	75	1	8	9	77	—	—	—	—	—
91-92—Minnesota	NHL	73	2	9	11	54	7	0	1	1	19
NHL totals		745	29	128	157	750	117	3	14	17	174

LUDZIK, STEVE
C, SABRES

PERSONAL: Born April 3, 1962, at Toronto. . . . 5-11/195. . . . Shoots left. . . . Full name: Steven Ludzik.
TRANSACTIONS/CAREER NOTES: Selected by Chicago Blackhawks as underage junior in second round (third Blackhawks pick, 28th overall) of NHL entry draft (June 11, 1980). . . . Broke left foot (October 19, 1985). . . . Broke collarbone (January 26, 1987). . . . Traded by Blackhawks with sixth-round pick in 1990 draft (C Derek Edgerly) to Buffalo Sabres to complete earlier deal involving G Jacques Cloutier (September 28, 1989). . . . Suffered eye injury (November 12, 1989); missed 10 games. . . . Suspended six games by AHL for a pre-game fight (November 25, 1990).

Season Team	League	REGULAR SEASON					PLAYOFFS				
		Gms.	G	A	Pts.	Pen.	Gms.	G	A	Pts.	Pen.
77-78—Markham Waxers	OPJHL	34	15	24	39	20	—	—	—	—	—
78-79—Niagara Falls	OMJHL	68	32	65	97	138	—	—	—	—	—
79-80—Niagara Falls	OMJHL	67	43	76	119	102	10	6	6	12	16
80-81—Niagara Falls	OMJHL	58	50	92	142	108	12	5	9	14	40
81-82—Chicago	NHL	8	2	1	3	2	—	—	—	—	—
—New Brunswick	AHL	75	21	41	62	142	15	3	7	10	6
82-83—Chicago	NHL	66	6	19	25	63	13	3	5	8	20
83-84—Chicago	NHL	80	9	20	29	73	4	0	1	1	9
84-85—Chicago	NHL	79	11	20	31	86	15	1	1	2	16
85-86—Chicago	NHL	49	6	5	11	21	3	0	0	0	12
86-87—Chicago	NHL	52	5	12	17	34	4	0	0	0	0
87-88—Chicago	NHL	73	6	15	21	40	5	0	1	1	13
88-89—Chicago	NHL	6	1	0	1	8	—	—	—	—	—
—Saginaw	IHL	65	21	57	78	129	6	0	1	1	17

Season	Team	League	REGULAR SEASON					PLAYOFFS				
			Gms.	G	A	Pts.	Pen.	Gms.	G	A	Pts.	Pen.
89-90	Rochester	AHL	54	25	29	54	71	16	5	6	11	57
	Buffalo	NHL	11	0	1	1	6	—	—	—	—	—
90-91	Rochester	AHL	65	22	29	51	137	8	3	5	8	6
91-92	Rochester	AHL	45	6	22	28	88	14	2	1	3	8
	NHL totals		424	46	93	139	333	44	4	8	12	70

LUMME, JYRKI
D, CANUCKS

PERSONAL: Born July 16, 1967, at Tampere, Finland.... 6-1/207.... Shoots left.
TRANSACTIONS/CAREER NOTES: Selected by Montreal Canadiens in third round (third Canadiens pick, 57th overall) of NHL entry draft (June 21, 1986).... Strained left knee ligaments (December 1988).... Stretched knee ligaments (February 21, 1989).... Bruised right foot (November 1989).... Traded by Canadiens to Vancouver Canucks for second-round pick in 1991 draft (C Craig Darby) (March 6, 1990).... Lacerated eye (November 19, 1991); missed three games.
MISCELLANEOUS: Member of 1988 silver-medal-winning Finnish Olympic team.

Season	Team	League	REGULAR SEASON					PLAYOFFS				
			Gms.	G	A	Pts.	Pen.	Gms.	G	A	Pts.	Pen.
84-85	Koo Vee	Finland	30	6	4	10	44	—	—	—	—	—
85-86	Ilves Tampere	Finland	31	1	5	6	4	—	—	—	—	—
86-87	Ilves Tampere	Finland	43	12	12	24	52	4	0	1	1	0
87-88	Ilves Tampere	Finland	43	8	22	30	75	—	—	—	—	—
88-89	Montreal	NHL	21	1	3	4	10	—	—	—	—	—
	Sherbrooke	AHL	26	4	11	15	10	6	1	3	4	4
89-90	Montreal	NHL	54	1	19	20	41	—	—	—	—	—
	Vancouver	NHL	11	3	7	10	8	—	—	—	—	—
90-91	Vancouver	NHL	80	5	27	32	59	6	2	3	5	0
91-92	Vancouver	NHL	75	12	32	44	65	13	2	3	5	4
	NHL totals		241	22	88	110	183	19	4	6	10	4

LUONGO, CHRISTOPHER
D, RED WINGS

PERSONAL: Born March 17, 1967, at Detroit.... 6-0/180.... Shoots right.... Full name: Christopher John Luongo.
COLLEGE: Michigan State.
TRANSACTIONS/CAREER NOTES: Selected by Detroit Red Wings in fifth round (fifth Red Wings pick, 92nd overall) of NHL entry draft (June 15, 1985).
HONORS: Named to NCAA All-Tournament team (1986-87).... Named to CCHA All-Star second team (1988-89).

Season	Team	League	REGULAR SEASON					PLAYOFFS				
			Gms.	G	A	Pts.	Pen.	Gms.	G	A	Pts.	Pen.
84-85	St. Clair Shores	NAJHL	41	2	25	27		—	—	—	—	—
85-86	Michigan State	CCHA	38	1	5	6	29	—	—	—	—	—
86-87	Michigan State	CCHA	27	4	16	20	38	—	—	—	—	—
87-88	Michigan State	CCHA	45	3	15	18	49	—	—	—	—	—
88-89	Michigan State	CCHA	47	4	21	25	42	—	—	—	—	—
89-90	Adirondack	AHL	53	9	14	23	37	3	0	0	0	0
	Phoenix	IHL	23	5	9	14	41	—	—	—	—	—
90-91	Detroit	NHL	4	0	1	1	4	—	—	—	—	—
	Adirondack	AHL	76	14	25	39	71	2	0	0	0	7
91-92	Adirondack	AHL	80	6	20	26	60	19	3	5	8	10
	NHL totals		4	0	1	1	4					

LYONS, COREY
LW, FLAMES

PERSONAL: Born June 1, 1970, at Calgary, Alta.... 5-10/186.... Shoots left.
TRANSACTIONS/CAREER NOTES: Selected by Calgary Flames in third round (fourth Flames pick, 63rd overall) of NHL entry draft (June 17, 1989).

Season	Team	League	REGULAR SEASON					PLAYOFFS				
			Gms.	G	A	Pts.	Pen.	Gms.	G	A	Pts.	Pen.
87-88	Lethbridge	WHL	2	0	0	0	0	—	—	—	—	—
88-89	Lethbridge	WHL	71	53	59	112	36	8	4	9	13	7
89-90	Lethbridge	WHL	72	63	79	142	26	19	11	15	26	4
	Salt Lake City	IHL	—	—	—	—	—	1	0	0	0	0
90-91	Salt Lake City	IHL	51	15	12	27	22	3	0	2	2	0
91-92	Salt Lake City	IHL	26	3	3	6	4	—	—	—	—	—
	Roanoke Valley	ECHL	22	10	13	23	13	7	4	3	7	4

MacDERMID, PAUL
RW, CAPITALS

PERSONAL: Born April 14, 1963, at Chesley, Ont.... 6-1/205.... Shoots right.
TRANSACTIONS/CAREER NOTES: Selected by Hartford Whalers as underage junior in third round (second Whalers pick, 61st overall) of NHL entry draft (June 10, 1981).... Injured knee (December 1982).... Injured neck and shoulder (December 6, 1988).... Sprained right knee ligament (February 4, 1989).... Traded by Whalers to Winnipeg Jets for C/LW Randy Cunneyworth (December 13, 1989).... Suffered back spasms (November 3, 1990); missed six games.... Strained knee (December 1990).... Traded by Jets to Washington Capitals for D Mike Lalor (March 2, 1992).

Season	Team	League	REGULAR SEASON					PLAYOFFS				
			Gms.	G	A	Pts.	Pen.	Gms.	G	A	Pts.	Pen.
79-80	Port Elgin Jr. C	OHA	30	23	20	43	87	—	—	—	—	—
80-81	Windsor	OMJHL	68	15	17	32	106	—	—	—	—	—

LM

Season Team	League	REGULAR SEASON					PLAYOFFS				
		Gms.	G	A	Pts.	Pen.	Gms.	G	A	Pts.	Pen.
81-82—Windsor	OHL	65	26	45	71	179	9	6	4	10	17
—Hartford	NHL	3	1	0	1	2	—	—	—	—	—
82-83—Windsor	OHL	42	35	45	80	90	—	—	—	—	—
—Hartford	NHL	7	0	0	0	2	—	—	—	—	—
83-84—Hartford	NHL	3	0	1	1	0	—	—	—	—	—
—Binghamton	AHL	70	31	30	61	130	—	—	—	—	—
84-85—Binghamton	AHL	48	9	31	40	87	—	—	—	—	—
—Hartford	NHL	31	4	7	11	299	—	—	—	—	—
85-86—Hartford	NHL	74	13	10	23	160	10	2	1	3	20
86-87—Hartford	NHL	72	7	11	18	202	6	2	1	3	34
87-88—Hartford	NHL	80	20	15	35	139	6	0	5	5	14
88-89—Hartford	NHL	74	17	27	44	141	4	1	1	2	16
89-90—Hartford	NHL	29	6	12	18	69	—	—	—	—	—
—Winnipeg	NHL	44	7	10	17	100	7	0	2	2	8
90-91—Winnipeg	NHL	69	15	21	36	128	—	—	—	—	—
91-92—Winnipeg	NHL	59	10	11	21	151	—	—	—	—	—
—Washington	NHL	15	2	5	7	43	7	0	1	1	22
NHL totals		560	102	130	232	1436	40	5	11	16	114

MacDONALD, DOUG
LW, SABRES

PERSONAL: Born February 8, 1969, at Point Moody, B.C. . . . 6-0/192. . . . Shoots left. . . . Full name: Douglas Bruce MacDonald.
COLLEGE: Wisconsin.
TRANSACTIONS/CAREER NOTES: Selected by Buffalo Sabres in fourth round (third Sabres pick, 77th overall) of NHL entry draft (June 17, 1989). . . . Injured knee (December 29, 1990).

Season Team	League	REGULAR SEASON					PLAYOFFS				
		Gms.	G	A	Pts.	Pen.	Gms.	G	A	Pts.	Pen.
85-86—Langley Eagles	BCJHL	42	19	37	56	16	—	—	—	—	—
86-87—Delta	BCJHL	51	28	49	77	61	—	—	—	—	—
87-88—Delta	BCJHL	51	50	54	104	70	9	5	9	14	16
88-89—University of Wisconsin	WCHA	44	23	25	48	50	—	—	—	—	—
89-90—University of Wisconsin	WCHA	44	16	35	51	52	—	—	—	—	—
90-91—University of Wisconsin	WCHA	31	20	26	46	50	—	—	—	—	—
91-92—University of Wisconsin	WCHA	33	16	28	44	76	—	—	—	—	—

MacDONALD, GARRETT
D, FLYERS

PERSONAL: Born January 12, 1971, at Burnaby, B.C. . . . 6-0/183. . . . Shoots right. . . . Full name: Garrett Robert MacDonald.
HIGH SCHOOL: Burnaby North Secondary School (Burnaby, B.C.).
COLLEGE: Northern Michigan.
TRANSACTIONS/CAREER NOTES: Selected by Philadelphia Flyers in NHL supplemental draft (June 19, 1992).

Season Team	League	REGULAR SEASON					PLAYOFFS				
		Gms.	G	A	Pts.	Pen.	Gms.	G	A	Pts.	Pen.
90-91—Northern Michigan Univ.	WCHA	41	2	8	10	56	—	—	—	—	—
91-92—Northern Michigan Univ.	WCHA	36	0	6	6	86	—	—	—	—	—

MacDONALD, JASON
RW, RED WINGS

PERSONAL: Born April 1, 1974, at Charlettetown, P.E.I. . . . 6-0/195. . . . Shoots right.
HIGH SCHOOL: St. Mary's (Owen Sound, Ont.).
TRANSACTIONS/CAREER NOTES: Selected by Detroit Red Wings in sixth round (fifth Red Wings pick, 142nd overall) of NHL entry draft (June 20, 1992).

Season Team	League	REGULAR SEASON					PLAYOFFS				
		Gms.	G	A	Pts.	Pen.	Gms.	G	A	Pts.	Pen.
89-90—Charlottetown	PEIJHL	25	11	29	40	206	—	—	—	—	—
90-91—North Bay	OHL	57	12	15	27	126	10	3	3	6	15
91-92—North Bay	OHL	17	5	8	13	50	—	—	—	—	—
—Owen Sound	OHL	42	17	19	36	129	5	0	2	2	8

MacINNIS, AL
D, FLAMES

PERSONAL: Born July 11, 1963, at Inverness, N.S. . . . 6-2/196. . . . Shoots right. . . . Full name: Allan MacInnis.
TRANSACTIONS/CAREER NOTES: Selected by Calgary Flames as underage junior in first round (first Flames pick, 15th overall) of NHL entry draft (June 10, 1981). . . . Twisted knee (February 1985). . . . Lacerated hand (March 23, 1986). . . . Stretched ligaments of knee (April 8, 1990). . . . Separated shoulder (November 22, 1991); missed eight games.
HONORS: Named to OHL All-Star first team (1981-82 and 1982-83). . . . Won Max Kaminsky Trophy (1982-83). . . . Named to NHL All-Star second team (1986-87 and 1988-89). . . . Won Conn Smythe Trophy (1988-89). . . . Named to THE SPORTING NEWS All-Star first team (1989-90 and 1990-91). . . . Named to NHL All-Star first team (1989-90 and 1990-91).

Season Team	League	REGULAR SEASON					PLAYOFFS				
		Gms.	G	A	Pts.	Pen.	Gms.	G	A	Pts.	Pen.
79-80—Regina Blues	SJHL	59	20	28	48	110	—	—	—	—	—
80-81—Kitchener	OMJHL	47	11	28	39	59	18	4	12	16	20

Season Team	League	REGULAR SEASON					PLAYOFFS				
		Gms.	G	A	Pts.	Pen.	Gms.	G	A	Pts.	Pen.
81-82—Kitchener	OHL	59	25	50	75	145	15	5	10	15	44
—Calgary	NHL	2	0	0	0	0	—	—	—	—	—
82-83—Kitchener	OHL	51	38	46	84	67	8	3	8	11	9
—Calgary	NHL	14	1	3	4	9	—	—	—	—	—
83-84—Colorado	CHL	19	5	14	19	22	—	—	—	—	—
—Calgary	NHL	51	11	34	45	42	11	2	12	14	13
84-85—Calgary	NHL	67	14	52	66	75	4	1	2	3	8
85-86—Calgary	NHL	77	11	57	68	76	21	4	*15	19	30
86-87—Calgary	NHL	79	20	56	76	97	4	1	0	1	0
87-88—Calgary	NHL	80	25	58	83	114	7	3	6	9	18
88-89—Calgary	NHL	79	16	58	74	126	22	7	*24	*31	46
89-90—Calgary	NHL	79	28	62	90	82	6	2	3	5	8
90-91—Calgary	NHL	78	28	75	103	90	7	2	3	5	8
91-92—Calgary	NHL	72	20	57	77	83					
NHL totals		678	174	512	686	794	82	22	65	87	131

MacINTYRE, ANDY
LW, BLACKHAWKS

PERSONAL: Born April 16, 1974, at Thunder Bay, Ont. . . . 6-2/195. . . . Shoots left.
HIGH SCHOOL: Marion Graham (Saskatoon, Sask.).
TRANSACTIONS/CAREER NOTES: Selected by Chicago Blackhawks in fourth round (fourth Blackhawks pick, 89th overall) of NHL entry draft (June 20, 1992).

Season Team	League	REGULAR SEASON					PLAYOFFS				
		Gms.	G	A	Pts.	Pen.	Gms.	G	A	Pts.	Pen.
89-90—Elk Valley	BCJHL	40	24	22	46	14	—	—	—	—	—
90-91—Seattle	WHL	71	16	13	29	52	6	0	0	0	2
91-92—Seattle	WHL	12	6	2	8	18	—	—	—	—	—
—Saskatoon	WHL	55	22	13	35	66	22	10	2	12	17

MACIVER, NORM
D, OILERS

PERSONAL: Born September 8, 1964, at Thunder Bay, Ont. . . . 5-11/180. . . . Shoots left. . . . Full name: Norman Steven Maciver.
COLLEGE: Minnesota-Duluth.
TRANSACTIONS/CAREER NOTES: Signed as free agent by New York Rangers (September 8, 1986). . . . Dislocated right shoulder (March 1988). . . . Suffered hip pointer (November 1988). . . . Traded by Rangers with LW Don Maloney and C Brian Lawton to Hartford Whalers for C Carey Wilson and a fifth-round pick in 1990 draft (December 26, 1988). . . . Traded by Whalers to Edmonton Oilers for D Jim Ennis (October 9, 1989).
HONORS: Named to WCHA All-Star second team (1983-84). . . . Named to WCHA All-Star first team (1984-85 and 1985-86). . . . Won Eddie Shore Plaque (1990-91). . . . Named to AHL All-Star first team (1990-91).

Season Team	League	REGULAR SEASON					PLAYOFFS				
		Gms.	G	A	Pts.	Pen.	Gms.	G	A	Pts.	Pen.
82-83—Minnesota-Duluth	WCHA	45	1	26	27	40	6	0	2	2	2
83-84—Minnesota-Duluth	WCHA	31	13	28	41	28	8	1	10	11	8
84-85—Minnesota-Duluth	WCHA	47	14	47	61	63	10	3	3	6	6
85-86—Minnesota-Duluth	WCHA	42	11	51	62	36	4	2	3	5	2
86-87—New Haven	AHL	71	6	30	36	73	7	0	0	0	9
—New York Rangers	NHL	3	0	1	1	0	—	—	—	—	—
87-88—Colorado	IHL	27	6	20	26	22	—	—	—	—	—
—New York Rangers	NHL	37	9	15	24	14	—	—	—	—	—
88-89—New York Rangers	NHL	26	0	10	10	14	—	—	—	—	—
—Hartford	NHL	37	1	22	23	24	1	0	0	0	2
89-90—Binghamton	AHL	2	0	0	0	0	—	—	—	—	—
—Cape Breton	AHL	68	13	37	50	55	6	0	7	7	10
—Edmonton	NHL	1	0	0	0	0	—	—	—	—	—
90-91—Cape Breton	AHL	56	13	46	59	60	—	—	—	—	—
—Edmonton	NHL	21	2	5	7	14	18	0	4	4	8
91-92—Edmonton	NHL	57	6	34	40	38	13	1	2	3	10
NHL totals		182	18	87	105	104	32	1	6	7	20

MACKEY, DAVID
LW, BLUES

PERSONAL: Born July 24, 1966, at New Westminster, B.C. . . . 6-4/210. . . . Shoots left.
TRANSACTIONS/CAREER NOTES: Selected by Chicago Blackhawks as underage junior in 11th round (12th Blackhawks pick, 224th overall) of NHL entry draft (June 9, 1984). . . . Traded by Kamloops Blazers with C Rob Dimaio and C Kalvin Knibbs to Medicine Hat Tigers for LW Doug Pickel and LW Sean Pass (December 1986). . . . Selected by Minnesota North Stars in 1989 NHL waiver draft for $40,000 (October 2, 1989). . . . Torn right thumb ligaments (November 6, 1989); missed 10 games. . . . Suspended five games and fined $500 by NHL for fighting (December 28, 1989). . . . Sprained knee and ankle (January 24, 1990); missed 15 games. . . . Traded by North Stars to Vancouver Canucks for future considerations (September 6, 1990). . . . Signed as free agent by St. Louis Blues (July 1991).

Season Team	League	REGULAR SEASON					PLAYOFFS				
		Gms.	G	A	Pts.	Pen.	Gms.	G	A	Pts.	Pen.
82-83—Victoria	WHL	69	16	16	32	53	12	1	1	2	4
83-84—Victoria	WHL	69	15	15	30	97	—	—	—	—	—
84-85—Victoria	WHL	16	5	6	11	45	—	—	—	—	—
—Portland	WHL	56	28	32	60	122	6	2	1	3	13

M

Season Team	League	REGULAR SEASON					PLAYOFFS				
		Gms.	G	A	Pts.	Pen.	Gms.	G	A	Pts.	Pen.
85-86—Kamloops	WHL	9	3	4	7	13	—	—	—	—	—
—Medicine Hat	WHL	60	25	32	57	167	25	6	3	9	72
86-87—Saginaw	IHL	81	26	49	75	173	10	5	6	11	22
87-88—Saginaw	IHL	62	29	22	51	211	10	3	7	10	44
—Chicago	NHL	23	1	3	4	71	—	—	—	—	—
88-89—Chicago	NHL	23	1	2	3	78	—	—	—	—	—
—Saginaw	IHL	57	22	23	45	223	—	—	—	—	—
89-90—Minnesota	NHL	16	2	0	2	28	—	—	—	—	—
90-91—Milwaukee	IHL	82	28	30	58	226	6	7	2	9	6
91-92—Peoria	IHL	35	20	17	37	90	—	—	—	—	—
—St. Louis	NHL	19	1	0	1	49	1	0	0	0	0
NHL totals		81	5	5	10	226	1	0	0	0	0

MacLEAN, JOHN
RW, DEVILS

PERSONAL: Born November 20, 1964, at Oshawa, Ont.... 6-0/200.... Shoots right. **TRANSACTIONS/CAREER NOTES:** Selected by New Jersey Devils as underage junior in first round (first Devils pick, sixth overall) of NHL entry draft (June 8, 1983).... Bruised shoulder (November 1984).... Injured right knee (January 25, 1985).... Reinjured knee and underwent arthroscopic surgery (January 31, 1985).... Bruised ankle (November 2, 1986).... Sprained right elbow (December 1988).... Bruised ribs (March 1, 1989).... Suffered concussion and stomach contusions (October 1990).... Suffered concussion (December 11, 1990).... Tore ligament in right knee (September 30, 1991); missed entire 1991-92 season. ... Underwent surgery to right knee (November 23, 1991).

Season Team	League	REGULAR SEASON					PLAYOFFS				
		Gms.	G	A	Pts.	Pen.	Gms.	G	A	Pts.	Pen.
81-82—Oshawa	OHL	67	17	22	39	197	12	3	6	9	63
82-83—Oshawa	OHL	66	47	51	98	138	17	*18	20	†38	35
83-84—New Jersey	NHL	23	1	0	1	10	—	—	—	—	—
—Oshawa	OHL	30	23	36	59	58	7	2	5	7	18
84-85—New Jersey	NHL	61	13	20	33	44	—	—	—	—	—
85-86—New Jersey	NHL	74	21	37	58	112	—	—	—	—	—
86-87—New Jersey	NHL	80	31	36	67	120	—	—	—	—	—
87-88—New Jersey	NHL	76	23	16	39	145	20	7	11	18	60
88-89—New Jersey	NHL	74	42	45	87	127	—	—	—	—	—
89-90—New Jersey	NHL	80	41	38	79	80	6	4	1	5	12
90-91—New Jersey	NHL	78	45	33	78	150	7	5	3	8	20
91-92—New Jersey	NHL	Did not play—injured.									
NHL totals		546	217	225	442	788	33	16	15	31	92

MacLELLAN, BRIAN
LW, RED WINGS

M

PERSONAL: Born October 27, 1958, at Guelph, Ont.... 6-3/220.... Shoots left.... Full name: Brian John MacLellan. **COLLEGE:** Bowling Green State. **TRANSACTIONS/CAREER NOTES:** Signed as free agent by Los Angeles Kings (April 1982).... Traded by Kings with fourth-round pick in 1987 draft (C Michael Sullivan) to New York Rangers for G Roland Melanson and D Grant Ledyard (December 9, 1985).... Traded by Rangers to Minnesota North Stars for third-round pick in 1987 draft (RW Simon Gagne) (September 8, 1986).... Traded by North Stars with fourth-round pick in 1989 draft (C Robert Reichel) to Calgary Flames for RW Shane Churla and C Perry Berezan (March 4, 1989).... Injured neck (October 29, 1990); missed eight games.... Traded by Flames to Detroit Red Wings for C/RW Marc Habscheid (June 11, 1991).

Season Team	League	REGULAR SEASON					PLAYOFFS				
		Gms.	G	A	Pts.	Pen.	Gms.	G	A	Pts.	Pen.
78-79—Bowling Green State	CCHA	44	34	29	63	94	—	—	—	—	—
79-80—Bowling Green State	CCHA	38	8	15	23	46	—	—	—	—	—
80-81—Bowling Green State	CCHA	37	11	14	25	96	—	—	—	—	—
81-82—Bowling Green State	CCHA	41	11	21	32	109	—	—	—	—	—
82-83—Los Angeles	NHL	8	0	3	3	7	—	—	—	—	—
—New Haven	AHL	71	11	15	26	40	12	5	3	8	4
83-84—New Haven	AHL	2	0	2	2	0	—	—	—	—	—
—Los Angeles	NHL	72	25	29	54	45	—	—	—	—	—
84-85—Los Angeles	NHL	80	31	54	85	53	3	0	1	1	0
85-86—Los Angeles	NHL	27	5	8	13	19	—	—	—	—	—
—New York Rangers	NHL	51	11	21	32	47	16	2	4	6	15
86-87—Minnesota	NHL	76	32	31	63	69	—	—	—	—	—
87-88—Minnesota	NHL	75	16	32	48	74	—	—	—	—	—
88-89—Minnesota	NHL	60	16	23	39	104	—	—	—	—	—
—Calgary	NHL	12	2	3	5	14	21	3	2	5	19
89-90—Calgary	NHL	65	20	18	38	26	6	0	2	2	8
90-91—Calgary	NHL	57	13	14	27	55	1	0	0	0	0
91-92—Detroit	NHL	23	1	5	6	38	—	—	—	—	—
NHL totals		606	172	241	413	551	47	5	9	14	42

MacLEOD, PAT
D, SHARKS

PERSONAL: Born June 15, 1969, at Melfort, Sask.... 5-11/190.... Shoots left. **TRANSACTIONS/CAREER NOTES:** Injured knee (March 1989).... Selected by Minnesota North Stars in fifth round (fifth North Stars pick, 87th overall) of NHL entry draft (June 17, 1989). ... Selected by San Jose Sharks in NHL dispersal draft (May 30, 1991). **HONORS:** Named to WHL All-Star first team (1988-89).... Named to IHL All-Star second team (1991-92).

Season Team	League	REGULAR SEASON					PLAYOFFS				
		Gms.	G	A	Pts.	Pen.	Gms.	G	A	Pts.	Pen.
87-88—Kamloops	WHL	50	13	33	46	27	18	2	7	9	6
88-89—Kamloops	WHL	37	11	34	45	14	15	7	18	25	24
89-90—Kalamazoo	IHL	82	9	38	47	27	10	1	6	7	2
90-91—Kalamazoo	IHL	59	10	30	40	16	11	1	2	3	5
—Minnesota	NHL	1	0	1	1	0	—	—	—	—	—
91-92—San Jose	NHL	37	5	11	16	4	—	—	—	—	—
—Kansas City	IHL	45	9	21	30	19	11	1	4	5	4
NHL totals		38	5	12	17	4					

MACOUN, JAMIE
D, MAPLE LEAFS

PERSONAL: Born August 17, 1961, at Newmarket, Ont. . . . . 6-2/200. . . . Shoots left.
COLLEGE: Ohio State.
TRANSACTIONS/CAREER NOTES: Signed as free agent by Calgary Flames (January 30, 1983). . . . Fractured cheekbone (December 26, 1984). . . . Suffered nerve damage to left arm in automobile accident (May 1987). . . . Suffered concussion (January 23, 1989). . . . Traded by Flames with C Doug Gilmour, LW Kent Manderville, D Ric Nattress and G Rick Wamsley to Toronto Maple Leafs for LW Craig Berube, D Alexander Godynyuk, LW Gary Leeman, D Michel Petit and G Jeff Reese (January 2, 1992).
HONORS: Named to NHL All-Rookie team (1983-84).

Season Team	League	REGULAR SEASON					PLAYOFFS				
		Gms.	G	A	Pts.	Pen.	Gms.	G	A	Pts.	Pen.
80-81—Ohio State	CCHA	38	9	20	29	83	—	—	—	—	—
81-82—Ohio State	CCHA	25	2	18	20	89	—	—	—	—	—
82-83—Ohio State	CCHA	—	—	—	—	—	—	—	—	—	—
—Calgary	NHL	22	1	4	5	25	9	0	2	2	8
83-84—Calgary	NHL	72	9	23	32	97	11	1	0	1	0
84-85—Calgary	NHL	70	9	30	39	67	4	1	0	1	4
85-86—Calgary	NHL	77	11	21	32	81	22	1	6	7	23
86-87—Calgary	NHL	79	7	33	40	111	3	0	1	1	8
87-88—Calgary	NHL	—	—	—	—	—	—	—	—	—	—
88-89—Calgary	NHL	72	8	19	27	78	22	3	6	9	30
89-90—Calgary	NHL	78	8	27	35	70	6	0	3	3	10
90-91—Calgary	NHL	79	7	15	22	84	7	0	1	1	4
91-92—Calgary	NHL	37	2	12	14	53	—	—	—	—	—
—Toronto	NHL	39	3	13	16	18	—	—	—	—	—
NHL totals		625	65	197	262	684	84	6	19	25	87

MacTAVISH, CRAIG
C, OILERS

PERSONAL: Born August 15, 1958, at London, Ont. . . . . 6-1/195. . . . Shoots left.
COLLEGE: Lowell (Mass.).
TRANSACTIONS/CAREER NOTES: Selected by Boston Bruins in ninth round (ninth Bruins pick, 153rd overall) of NHL amateur draft (June 15, 1978). . . . Involved in automobile accident in which another driver was killed (January 25, 1984); pleaded guilty to vehicular homicide, driving while under the influence of alcohol and reckless driving and sentenced to a year in prison (May 1984); missed 1984-85 season. . . . Signed as free agent by Edmonton Oilers (February 1, 1985).
HONORS: Named ECAC Division II Rookie of the Year (1977-1978). . . . Named to ECAC All-Star second team (1977-78). . . . Named ECAC Division II Player of the Year (1978-1979). . . . Named to ECAC-II All-Star first team (1978-79).
MISCELLANEOUS: Does not wear a helmet.

Season Team	League	REGULAR SEASON					PLAYOFFS				
		Gms.	G	A	Pts.	Pen.	Gms.	G	A	Pts.	Pen.
77-78—University of Lowell	ECAC-II	24	26	19	45		—	—	—	—	—
78-79—University of Lowell	ECAC-II	31	36	52	*88		—	—	—	—	—
79-80—Binghamton	AHL	34	17	15	32	20	—	—	—	—	—
—Boston	NHL	46	11	17	28	8	10	2	3	5	7
80-81—Boston	NHL	24	3	5	8	13	—	—	—	—	—
—Springfield	AHL	53	19	24	43	89	7	5	4	9	8
81-82—Erie	AHL	72	23	32	55	37	—	—	—	—	—
—Boston	NHL	2	0	1	1	0	—	—	—	—	—
82-83—Boston	NHL	75	10	20	30	18	17	3	1	4	18
83-84—Boston	NHL	70	20	23	43	35	1	0	0	0	0
84-85—Boston	NHL				Did not play.						
85-86—Edmonton	NHL	74	23	24	47	70	10	4	4	8	11
86-87—Edmonton	NHL	79	20	19	39	55	21	1	9	10	16
87-88—Edmonton	NHL	80	15	17	32	47	19	0	1	1	31
88-89—Edmonton	NHL	80	21	31	52	55	7	0	1	1	8
89-90—Edmonton	NHL	80	21	22	43	89	22	2	6	8	29
90-91—Edmonton	NHL	80	17	15	32	76	18	3	3	6	20
91-92—Edmonton	NHL	80	12	18	30	98	16	3	0	3	28
NHL totals		770	173	212	385	564	141	18	28	46	168

MADELEY, DARRIN
G, SENATORS

PERSONAL: Born February 25, 1968, at Holland Landing, Ont. . . . . 5-11/165. . . . Shoots right.
HIGH SCHOOL: Aurora (Ont.).
COLLEGE: Lake Superior State (Mich.).

Season Team	League	REGULAR SEASON								PLAYOFFS						
		Gms.	Min.	W	L	T	GA	SO	Avg.	Gms.	Min.	W	L	GA	SO	Avg.
89-90—Lake Superior State.....	CCHA	30	1683	21	7	1	68		2.42	—	—	—	—	—	—	—
90-91—Lake Superior State.....	CCHA	36	2137	29	3	3	93		2.61	—	—	—	—	—	—	—
91-92—Lake Superior State.....	CCHA	35	2144	25	6	4	74		2.07	—	—	—	—	—	—	—

MADILL, JEFF
RW, SHARKS

PERSONAL: Born June 21, 1965, at Oshawa, Ont. ... 5-11/212. ... Shoots right. ... Son of former NHL referee Greg Madill.
COLLEGE: Ohio State.
TRANSACTIONS/CAREER NOTES: Selected by New Jersey Devils in NHL supplemental draft (June 1987). ... Suspended three games by AHL for abusing an official (April 11, 1990). ... Suspended by Utica Devils for being overweight (December 6, 1990). ... Selected by San Jose Sharks in NHL expansion draft (May 30, 1991).
HONORS: Named to AHL All-Star second team (1990-91).

Season Team	League	REGULAR SEASON					PLAYOFFS				
		Gms.	G	A	Pts.	Pen.	Gms.	G	A	Pts.	Pen.
84-85—Ohio State	CCHA	12	5	6	11	18	—	—	—	—	—
85-86—Ohio State	CCHA	41	32	25	57	65	—	—	—	—	—
86-87—Ohio State	CCHA	43	38	32	70	139	—	—	—	—	—
87-88—Utica	AHL	58	18	15	33	127	—	—	—	—	—
88-89—Utica	AHL	69	23	25	48	225	4	1	0	1	35
89-90—Utica	AHL	74	43	26	69	233	4	1	2	3	33
90-91—New Jersey	NHL	14	4	0	4	46	7	0	2	2	8
—Utica	AHL	54	42	35	77	151	—	—	—	—	—
91-92—Kansas City	IHL	62	32	20	52	167	6	2	2	4	30
NHL totals		14	4	0	4	46	7	0	2	2	8

MAGNUSSON, STEVEN
C, FLAMES

PERSONAL: Born November 15, 1972, at Anoka, Minn. ... 5-11/175. ... Shoots left.
HIGH SCHOOL: Anoka (Minn.).
TRANSACTIONS/CAREER NOTES: Selected by Calgary Flames in fourth round (fifth Flames pick, 85th overall) of NHL entry draft (June 22, 1991).

Season Team	League	REGULAR SEASON					PLAYOFFS				
		Gms.	G	A	Pts.	Pen.	Gms.	G	A	Pts.	Pen.
88-89—Anoka H.S.	Minn. H.S.	26	19	21	40	22	—	—	—	—	—
89-90—Anoka H.S.	Minn. H.S.	29	22	34	56	20	—	—	—	—	—
90-91—Anoka H.S.	Minn. H.S.	23	37	35	72	40	—	—	—	—	—
91-92—University of Minnesota ...	WCHA	41	9	24	33	56	—	—	—	—	—

MAGUIRE, KEVIN
RW

PERSONAL: Born January 5, 1963, at Toronto. ... 6-2/200. ... Shoots right.
TRANSACTIONS/CAREER NOTES: Signed as free agent by Toronto Maple Leafs (September 1984). ... Fractured ankle (February 1988). ... Bruised ribs (September 1988). ... Acquired by Buffalo Sabres in 1987 NHL waiver draft (October 1988). ... Sprained ankle (December 1988). ... Lacerated hand (March 1989). ... Traded by Sabres with second-round pick in 1990 draft (LW Mikael Renberg) to Philadelphia Flyers for D Jay Wells and fourth-round pick in 1991 draft (LW Peter Ambroziak) (March 5, 1990). ... Sprained right knee (March 18, 1990). ... Traded by Flyers with eighth-round pick in 1991 draft (D Dimitri Mironov) to Maple Leafs for third-round pick in 1990 draft (LW Al Kinisky) (June 16, 1990). ... Strained back (January 7, 1992); missed 24 games. ... Placed on waivers by Maple Leafs (July 28, 1992).

Season Team	League	REGULAR SEASON					PLAYOFFS				
		Gms.	G	A	Pts.	Pen.	Gms.	G	A	Pts.	Pen.
83-84—Orillia	OHA		35	42	77		—	—	—	—	—
84-85—St. Catharines	AHL	76	10	15	25	112	—	—	—	—	—
85-86—St. Catharines	AHL	61	6	9	15	161	1	0	0	0	0
86-87—Newmarket	AHL	51	4	2	6	131	—	—	—	—	—
—Toronto	NHL	17	0	0	0	74	1	0	0	0	0
87-88—Buffalo	NHL	46	4	6	10	162	5	0	0	0	50
88-89—Buffalo	NHL	60	8	10	18	241	5	0	0	0	36
89-90—Buffalo	NHL	61	6	9	15	115	—	—	—	—	—
—Philadelphia	NHL	5	1	0	1	6	—	—	—	—	—
90-91—Toronto	NHL	63	9	5	14	180	—	—	—	—	—
91-92—St. John's	AHL	30	11	15	26	112	11	3	7	10	43
—Toronto	NHL	8	1	0	1	4	—	—	—	—	—
NHL totals		260	29	30	59	782	11	0	0	0	86

MAHER, JAMES
D, KINGS

PERSONAL: Born June 10, 1970, at Warren, Mich. ... 6-1/205. ... Shoots left. ... Full name: James M. Maher.
COLLEGE: Illinois-Chicago.
TRANSACTIONS/CAREER NOTES: Selected by Los Angeles Kings in fourth round (second Kings pick, 81st overall) of NHL entry draft (June 17, 1989).

M

Season Team	League	REGULAR SEASON Gms.	G	A	Pts.	Pen.	PLAYOFFS Gms.	G	A	Pts.	Pen.
87-88—Detroit Junior Red Wings	NAJHL	24	6	11	17	26	—	—	—	—	—
88-89—Illinois-Chicago	CCHA	41	1	5	6	40	—	—	—	—	—
89-90—Illinois-Chicago	CCHA	38	4	12	16	64	—	—	—	—	—
90-91—Illinois-Chicago	CCHA	37	6	8	14	49	—	—	—	—	—
91-92—Illinois-Chicago	CCHA	34	5	9	14	52	—	—	—	—	—
—Phoenix	IHL	9	0	3	3	21	—	—	—	—	—

MAJOR, BRUCE
C, NORDIQUES

PERSONAL: Born January 3, 1967, at Vernon, B.C.... 6-3/180.... Shoots left.... Full name: Bruce Alan Major.
COLLEGE: Maine.
TRANSACTIONS/CAREER NOTES: Selected by Quebec Nordiques in fifth round (sixth Nordiques pick, 99th overall) of NHL entry draft (June 15, 1985).... Broke leg (February 28, 1987).

Season Team	League	REGULAR SEASON Gms.	G	A	Pts.	Pen.	PLAYOFFS Gms.	G	A	Pts.	Pen.
84-85—Richmond	BCJHL	48	43	56	99	56	—	—	—	—	—
85-86—University of Maine	Hockey East	38	14	14	28	39	—	—	—	—	—
86-87—University of Maine	Hockey East	37	14	10	24	12	—	—	—	—	—
87-88—University of Maine	Hockey East	26	0	5	5	14	—	—	—	—	—
88-89—University of Maine	Hockey East	42	13	11	24	22	—	—	—	—	—
89-90—Halifax	AHL	32	5	6	11	23	—	—	—	—	—
—Greensboro	ECHL	12	4	3	7	6	10	2	2	4	12
90-91—Quebec	NHL	4	0	0	0	0	—	—	—	—	—
—Halifax	AHL	9	2	0	2	9	—	—	—	—	—
—Fort Wayne	IHL	62	11	25	36	48	18	1	3	4	6
91-92—Halifax	AHL	16	1	3	4	11	—	—	—	—	—
NHL totals		4	0	0	0	0					

MAJOR, MARK
LW, PENGUINS

PERSONAL: Born March 20, 1970, at Toronto.... 6-3/223.... Shoots left.
TRANSACTIONS/CAREER NOTES: Selected by Pittsburgh Penguins in second round (second Penguins pick, 25th overall) of NHL entry draft (June 11, 1988).... Broke hand (September 1989); missed training camp.

Season Team	League	REGULAR SEASON Gms.	G	A	Pts.	Pen.	PLAYOFFS Gms.	G	A	Pts.	Pen.
87-88—North Bay	OHL	57	16	17	33	272	4	0	2	2	8
88-89—North Bay	OHL	11	3	2	5	58	—	—	—	—	—
—Kingston	OHL	53	22	29	51	193	—	—	—	—	—
89-90—Kingston	OHL	62	29	32	61	168	6	3	3	6	12
90-91—Muskegon	IHL	60	8	10	18	160	5	0	0	0	0
91-92—Muskegon	IHL	80	13	18	31	302	12	1	3	4	29

MAKAROV, SERGEI
RW, FLAMES

PERSONAL: Born June 19, 1958, at Chelyabinsk, U.S.S.R.... 5-11/185.... Shoots left.
TRANSACTIONS/CAREER NOTES: Selected by Calgary Flames in 12th round (14th Flames pick, 231st overall) of NHL entry draft (June 8, 1983).
HONORS: Won Soviet Player of the Year Award (1979-80, 1984-85 and 1988-89).... Won Izvestia Trophy (1979-82 and 1983-89).... Named to Soviet League All-Star team (1978-79 and 1980-88).... Won Calder Memorial Trophy (1989-90).... Named to NHL All-Rookie team (1989-90).
MISCELLANEOUS: Member of 1980 silver-medal-winning and 1984 and 1988 gold-medal-winning U.S.S.R. Olympic teams.

Season Team	League	REGULAR SEASON Gms.	G	A	Pts.	Pen.	PLAYOFFS Gms.	G	A	Pts.	Pen.
76-77—Traktor Chelyabinsk	USSR	11	1	0	1	4	—	—	—	—	—
77-78—Traktor Chelyabinsk	USSR	36	18	13	31	10	—	—	—	—	—
78-79—Central Red Army	USSR	44	18	21	39	12	—	—	—	—	—
79-80—Central Red Army	USSR	44	29	39	68	16	—	—	—	—	—
80-81—Central Red Army	USSR	49	42	37	79	22	—	—	—	—	—
81-82—Central Red Army	USSR	46	32	43	75	18	—	—	—	—	—
82-83—Central Red Army	USSR	30	25	17	42	6	—	—	—	—	—
83-84—Central Red Army	USSR	44	36	37	73	28	—	—	—	—	—
84-85—Central Red Army	USSR	40	26	39	65	28	—	—	—	—	—
85-86—Central Red Army	USSR	40	30	32	62	28	—	—	—	—	—
86-87—Central Red Army	USSR	40	21	32	53	26	—	—	—	—	—
87-88—Central Red Army	USSR	51	23	45	68	50	—	—	—	—	—
88-89—Central Red Army	USSR	44	21	33	54	42	—	—	—	—	—
89-90—Calgary	NHL	80	24	62	86	55	6	0	6	6	0
90-91—Calgary	NHL	78	30	49	79	44	3	1	0	1	0
91-92—Calgary	NHL	68	22	48	70	60	—	—	—	—	—
NHL totals		226	76	159	235	159	9	1	6	7	0

MALAKHOV, VLADIMIR
D, ISLANDERS

PERSONAL: Born August 30, 1968, at Sverdlovsk, U.S.S.R.... 6-2/207.
TRANSACTIONS/CAREER NOTES: Selected by New York Islanders in 10th round (12th Islanders pick, 191st overall) of NHL entry draft (June 17, 1989).
MISCELLANEOUS: Member of 1992 gold-medal-winning Unified Olympic team.

M

Season	Team	League	REGULAR SEASON Gms.	G	A	Pts.	Pen.	PLAYOFFS Gms.	G	A	Pts.	Pen.
86-87	Spartak Moscow	USSR	22	0	1	1	12	—	—	—	—	—
87-88	Spartak Moscow	USSR	28	2	2	4	26	—	—	—	—	—
88-89	CSKA	USSR	34	6	2	8	16	—	—	—	—	—
89-90	CSKA	USSR	48	2	10	12	34	—	—	—	—	—
90-91	CSKA	USSR	46	5	13	18	22	—	—	—	—	—
91-92	Unified Olympic Team	Int'l	8	3	0	3		—	—	—	—	—

MALARCHUK, CLINT
G, SABRES

PERSONAL: Born May 1, 1961, at Grande, Alta.... 6-0/185.... Shoots left.
TRANSACTIONS/CAREER NOTES: Signed as free agent by Quebec Nordiques (October 1980).... Traded by Nordiques with C Dale Hunter to Washington Capitals for C Alan Haworth, LW Gaeten Duchesne and first-round pick in 1987 draft (C Joe Sakic) (June 1987).... Traded by Capitals with D Grant Ledyard and sixth-round pick in 1991 draft to Buffalo Sabres for D Calle Johansson and second-round pick in 1989 draft (G Byron Dafoe) (March 6, 1989).... Suffered severed jugular vein (March 22, 1989).... Strained neck and shoulder (January 23, 1991); missed 14 games.... Suffered from strep throat (November 2, 1991); missed three games.... Suffered from medicine reaction (January 27, 1992); missed six games.
HONORS: Shared Harry (Hap) Holmes Memorial Trophy with Brian Ford (1982-83).

Season	Team	League	REGULAR SEASON Gms.	Min.	W	L	T	GA	SO	Avg.	PLAYOFFS Gms.	Min.	W	L	GA	SO	Avg.
78-79	Portland	WHL	2	120				4	0	2.00	—	—	—	—	—	—	—
79-80	Portland	WHL	37	1948	21	10	0	147	0	4.53	1	40	0	0	3	0	4.50
80-81	Portland	WHL	38	2235	28	8	0	142	3	3.81	4	307	0	0	21	0	4.10
81-82	Quebec	NHL	2	120	0	1	1	14	0	7.00	—	—	—	—	—	—	—
	Fredericton	AHL	51	2962	15	34	2	*253	0	5.12	—	—	—	—	—	—	—
82-83	Quebec	NHL	15	900	8	5	2	71	0	4.73	—	—	—	—	—	—	—
	Fredericton	AHL	25	1506	0	0	0	78	1	*3.11	—	—	—	—	—	—	—
83-84	Fredericton	AHL	11	663	5	5	1	40	0	3.62	—	—	—	—	—	—	—
	Quebec	NHL	23	1215	10	9	2	80	0	3.95	—	—	—	—	—	—	—
84-85	Fredericton	AHL	*56	*3347	26	25	4	*198	2	3.55	6	379	2	4	20	0	3.17
85-86	Quebec	NHL	46	2657	26	12	4	142	4	3.21	3	143	0	2	11	0	4.62
86-87	Quebec	NHL	54	3092	18	26	9	175	1	3.40	3	140	0	2	8	0	3.43
87-88	Washington	NHL	54	2926	24	20	4	154	+4	3.16	4	193	0	2	15	0	4.66
88-89	Washington	NHL	42	2428	16	18	7	141	1	3.48	1	59	0	1	5	0	5.08
	Buffalo	NHL	7	326	3	1	1	13	1	2.39	—	—	—	—	—	—	—
89-90	Buffalo	NHL	29	1596	14	11	2	89	0	3.35	—	—	—	—	—	—	—
90-91	Buffalo	NHL	37	2131	12	14	10	119	1	3.35	4	246	2	2	17	0	4.15
91-92	Buffalo	NHL	29	1639	10	13	3	102	0	3.73	—	—	—	—	—	—	—
	Rochester	AHL	2	120	2	0	0	3	1	1.50	—	—	—	—	—	—	—
NHL totals			338	19030	141	130	45	1100	12	3.47	15	781	2	9	56	0	4.30

MALEY, DAVID
C, OILERS
M

PERSONAL: Born April 24, 1963, at Beaver Dam, Wis.... 6-3/200.... Shoots left.... Full name: David Joseph Maley.
HIGH SCHOOL: Edina (Minn.).
COLLEGE: Wisconsin.
TRANSACTIONS/CAREER NOTES: Selected by Montreal Canadiens as underage player in second round (fourth Canadiens pick, 33rd overall) of NHL entry draft (June 9, 1982).... Suspended by AHL (May 1987).... Traded by Canadiens to New Jersey Devils for a third-round pick in 1987 draft (D Mathieu Schneider) (June 13, 1987).... Injured back (December 1988).... Tore right knee cartilage (January 16, 1990).... Underwent surgery to right knee (January 24, 1990); missed eight games.... Injured knee (February 22, 1990).... Injured left hand ligaments (September 22, 1990).... Sprained left ankle (November 28, 1990); missed 11 games.... Fractured left wrist (March 27, 1991).... Traded by Devils to Edmonton Oilers for LW Troy Mallette (January 12, 1991).... Twisted knee (March 4, 1992); missed 12 games.

Season	Team	League	REGULAR SEASON Gms.	G	A	Pts.	Pen.	PLAYOFFS Gms.	G	A	Pts.	Pen.
81-82	Edina High School	Minn. H.S.	26	22	28	50	26	—	—	—	—	—
82-83	University of Wisconsin	WCHA	47	17	23	40	24	—	—	—	—	—
83-84	University of Wisconsin	WCHA	38	10	28	38	56	—	—	—	—	—
84-85	University of Wisconsin	WCHA	35	19	9	28	86	—	—	—	—	—
85-86	University of Wisconsin	WCHA	42	20	40	60	*135	—	—	—	—	—
	Montreal	NHL	3	0	0	0	0	7	1	3	4	2
86-87	Sherbrooke	AHL	11	1	5	6	25	12	7	7	14	10
	Montreal	NHL	48	6	12	18	55	—	—	—	—	—
87-88	Utica	AHL	9	5	3	8	40	—	—	—	—	—
	New Jersey	NHL	44	4	2	6	65	20	3	1	4	80
88-89	New Jersey	NHL	68	5	6	11	249	—	—	—	—	—
89-90	New Jersey	NHL	67	8	17	25	160	6	0	0	0	25
90-91	New Jersey	NHL	64	8	14	22	151	—	—	—	—	—
91-92	New Jersey	NHL	37	7	11	18	58	—	—	—	—	—
	Edmonton	NHL	23	3	6	9	46	10	1	1	2	4
NHL totals			354	41	68	109	784	43	5	5	10	111

MALGUNAS, STEWART
D, RED WINGS

PERSONAL: Born April 21, 1970, at Prince George, B.C.... 5-11/190.... Shoots left.
TRANSACTIONS/CAREER NOTES: Selected by Detroit Red Wings in fourth round (third Red Wings pick, 66th overall) of NHL entry draft (June 16, 1990).
HONORS: Named to WHL All-Star first team (1989-90).

Season	Team	League	REGULAR SEASON					PLAYOFFS				
			Gms.	G	A	Pts.	Pen.	Gms.	G	A	Pts.	Pen.
87-88	Prince George	BCJHL	54	12	34	46	99	—	—	—	—	—
	New Westminster	WHL	6	0	0	0	0	—	—	—	—	—
88-89	Seattle	WHL	72	11	41	52	51	—	—	—	—	—
89-90	Seattle	WHL	63	15	48	63	116	13	2	9	11	32
90-91	Adirondack	AHL	78	5	19	24	70	2	0	0	0	4
91-92	Adirondack	AHL	69	4	28	32	82	18	2	6	8	28

MALKOC, DEAN
D, DEVILS

PERSONAL: Born January 26, 1970, at Vancouver, B.C. . . . 6-3/200. . . . Shoots left.
TRANSACTIONS/CAREER NOTES: Selected by New Jersey Devils in fifth round (seventh Devils pick, 95th overall) of NHL entry draft (June 16, 1990). . . . Traded by Kamloops Blazers with LW Todd Esselmont to Swift Current Broncos for RW Eddie Patterson (October 17, 1990).

Season	Team	League	REGULAR SEASON					PLAYOFFS				
			Gms.	G	A	Pts.	Pen.	Gms.	G	A	Pts.	Pen.
87-88	Williams Lake	PCJHL		6	32	38	215	—	—	—	—	—
88-89	Powell River	BCJHL	55	10	32	42	370	—	—	—	—	—
89-90	Kamloops	WHL	48	3	18	21	209	17	0	3	3	56
90-91	Kamloops	WHL	8	1	4	5	47	—	—	—	—	—
	Swift Current	WHL	50	10	23	33	248	3	0	2	2	5
	Utica	AHL	1	0	0	0	0	—	—	—	—	—
91-92	Utica	AHL	66	1	11	12	274	4	0	2	2	6

MALLETTE, TROY
C/LW, DEVILS

PERSONAL: Born February 25, 1970, at Sudbury, Ont. . . . 6-2/190. . . . Shoots left. . . . Full name: Troy Matthew Mallette.
TRANSACTIONS/CAREER NOTES: Selected by New York Rangers in second round (first Rangers pick, 22nd overall) of NHL entry draft (June 11, 1988). . . . Fined $500 by NHL for head-butting (March 19, 1990). . . . Sprained left knee ligaments (September 1990). . . . Fined $500 by NHL for attempting to injure another player (October 28, 1990). . . . Reinjured knee (October 29, 1990). . . . Injured shoulder (January 13, 1991). . . . Awarded to Edmonton Oilers as compensation for Rangers signing free agent C/LW Adam Graves (September 9, 1991). . . . Strained knee ligament (November 1991); missed two games. . . . Traded by Oilers to New Jersey Devils for LW David Maley (January 12, 1992). . . . Sprained right ankle (January 24, 1992); missed four games.

Season	Team	League	REGULAR SEASON					PLAYOFFS				
			Gms.	G	A	Pts.	Pen.	Gms.	G	A	Pts.	Pen.
86-87	Sault Ste. Marie	OHL	65	20	25	45	157	4	0	2	2	2
87-88	Sault Ste. Marie	OHL	62	18	30	48	186	6	1	3	4	12
88-89	Sault Ste. Marie	OHL	64	39	37	76	172	—	—	—	—	—
89-90	New York Rangers	NHL	79	13	16	29	305	10	2	2	4	81
90-91	New York Rangers	NHL	71	12	10	22	252	5	0	0	0	18
91-92	Edmonton	NHL	15	1	3	4	36	—	—	—	—	—
	New Jersey	NHL	17	3	4	7	43	—	—	—	—	—
NHL totals			182	29	33	62	636	15	2	2	4	99

MALLGRAVE, MATTHEW
RW, MAPLE LEAFS

PERSONAL: Born May 3, 1970, at Washington. . . . 6-0/180. . . . Shoots right. . . . Full name: Matthew Francis X. Mallgrave.
HIGH SCHOOL: St. Paul's School For Boys (Brooklandville, Md.).
COLLEGE: Harvard.
TRANSACTIONS/CAREER NOTES: Selected by Toronto Maple Leafs in seventh round (sixth Maple Leafs pick, 132nd overall) of NHL entry draft (June 11, 1988).

Season	Team	League	REGULAR SEASON					PLAYOFFS				
			Gms.	G	A	Pts.	Pen.	Gms.	G	A	Pts.	Pen.
87-88	St. Paul's H.S.	Md. H.S.		21	22	43		—	—	—	—	—
88-89	St. Paul's H.S.	Md. H.S.		24	14	38		—	—	—	—	—
89-90	Harvard University	ECAC	26	3	3	6	33	—	—	—	—	—
90-91	Harvard University	ECAC	27	5	13	18	14	—	—	—	—	—
91-92	Harvard University	ECAC	27	12	15	27	20	—	—	—	—	—

MALTAIS, STEVE
LW, LIGHTNING

PERSONAL: Born January 25, 1969, at Arvida, Ont. . . . 6-2/210. . . . Shoots left.
TRANSACTIONS/CAREER NOTES: Selected by Washington Capitals as underage junior in third round (second Capitals pick, 57th overall) of NHL entry draft (June 13, 1987). . . . Traded by Capitals with C Trent Klatt to Minnesota North Stars for D Shawn Chambers (June 21, 1991). . . . Traded by North Stars to Quebec Nordiques for C Kip Miller (March 8, 1992). . . . Selected by Tampa Bay Lightning in NHL expansion draft (June 18, 1992).

Season	Team	League	REGULAR SEASON					PLAYOFFS				
			Gms.	G	A	Pts.	Pen.	Gms.	G	A	Pts.	Pen.
85-86	Wexford Jr. B	MTHL	33	35	19	54	38	—	—	—	—	—
86-87	Cornwall	OHL	65	32	12	44	29	5	0	0	0	2
87-88	Cornwall	OHL	59	39	46	85	30	11	9	6	15	33
88-89	Cornwall	OHL	58	53	70	123	67	18	14	16	30	16
	Fort Wayne	IHL	—	—	—	—	—	4	2	1	3	0
89-90	Washington	NHL	8	0	0	0	2	1	0	0	0	0
	Baltimore	AHL	67	29	37	66	54	12	6	10	16	6

Season Team	League	REGULAR SEASON					PLAYOFFS				
		Gms.	G	A	Pts.	Pen.	Gms.	G	A	Pts.	Pen.
90-91—Baltimore	AHL	73	36	43	79	97	6	1	4	5	10
—Washington	NHL	7	0	0	0	2	—	—	—	—	—
91-92—Kalamazoo	IHL	48	25	31	56	51	—	—	—	—	—
—Minnesota	NHL	12	2	1	3	2	—	—	—	—	—
—Halifax	AHL	10	3	3	6	0	—	—	—	—	—
NHL totals		27	2	1	3	6	1	0	0	0	0

MALTBY, KIRK
RW, OILERS

PERSONAL: Born December 22, 1972, at Guelph, Ont.... 6-0/180.... Shoots right.
COLLEGE: Georgian (Ont.).
TRANSACTIONS/CAREER NOTES: Selected by Edmonton Oilers in third round (fourth Oilers pick, 65th overall) of NHL entry draft (June 20, 1992).

Season Team	League	REGULAR SEASON					PLAYOFFS				
		Gms.	G	A	Pts.	Pen.	Gms.	G	A	Pts.	Pen.
88-89—Cambridge Jr. B	OHA	48	28	18	46	138	—	—	—	—	—
89-90—Owen Sound	OHL	61	12	15	27	90	12	1	6	7	15
90-91—Owen Sound	OHL	66	34	32	66	100	—	—	—	—	—
91-92—Owen Sound	OHL	64	50	41	91	99	5	3	3	6	18

MANDERVILLE, KENT
LW, MAPLE LEAFS

PERSONAL: Born April 12, 1971, at Edmonton, Alta.... 6-3/195.... Shoots left. ... Full name: Kent Stephen Manderville.
COLLEGE: Cornell.
TRANSACTIONS/CAREER NOTES: Selected by Calgary Flames in second round (first Flames pick, 24th overall) of NHL entry draft (June 17, 1989).... Traded by Flames with C Doug Gilmour, D Jamie Macoun, D Ric Nattress and G Rick Wamsley to Toronto Maple Leafs for LW Craig Berube, D Alexander Godynyuk, RW Gary Leeman, D Michel Petit and G Jeff Reese (Janaury 2, 1992).
HONORS: Named ECAC Rookie of the Year (1989-90).... Named to ECAC All-Rookie team (1989-90).
MISCELLANEOUS: Member of 1992 silver-medal-winning Canadian Olympic team.

Season Team	League	REGULAR SEASON					PLAYOFFS				
		Gms.	G	A	Pts.	Pen.	Gms.	G	A	Pts.	Pen.
88-89—Notre Dame	SJHL	58	39	36	75	165	—	—	—	—	—
89-90—Cornell University	ECAC	26	11	15	26	28	—	—	—	—	—
90-91—Cornell University	ECAC	28	17	14	31	60	—	—	—	—	—
—Canadian National Team..	Int'l	3	1	2	3	0	—	—	—	—	—
91-92—Canadian National Team..	Int'l	63	16	23	39	75	—	—	—	—	—
—Canadian Olympic Team ..	Int'l	8	1	2	3	0	—	—	—	—	—
—Toronto	NHL	15	0	4	4	0	—	—	—	—	—
—St. John's	AHL	—	—	—	—	—	12	5	9	14	14
NHL totals		15	0	4	4	0					

MANELUK, GEORGE
G, ISLANDERS

PERSONAL: Born July 25, 1967, at Winnipeg, Man.... 5-11/193.... Shoots left.
COLLEGE: Manitoba.
TRANSACTIONS/CAREER NOTES: Selected by New York Islanders in fourth round (fourth Islanders pick, 57th overall) of NHL entry draft (June 13, 1987).

Season Team	League	REGULAR SEASON							PLAYOFFS						
		Gms.	Min.	W	L	T	GA	SO	Avg.	Gms.	Min.	W	L	GA SO	Avg.
86-87—Brandon	WHL	*58	*3258	16	35	4	*315	0	5.80	—	—	—	—	— —	—
87-88—Brandon	WHL	64	3651	24	33	3	297	0	4.88	4	271	1	3	22 0	4.87
—Springfield	AHL	2	125	0	1	1	9	0	4.32	—	—	—	—	— —	—
—Peoria	IHL	3	148	1	2	0	14	0	5.68	1	60	0	1	5 0	5.00
88-89—Springfield	AHL	24	1202	7	13	0	84	0	4.19	—	—	—	—	— —	—
89-90—Springfield	AHL	27	1382	11	9	1	94	1	4.08	4	174	2	1	9 0	3.10
90-91—New York Islanders	NHL	4	140	1	1	0	15	0	6.43	—	—	—	—	— —	—
—Capital District	AHL	29	1524	10	14	1	103	1	4.06	—	—	—	—	— —	—
91-92—New Haven	AHL	54	2863	25	22	0	175	1	3.67	3	216	1	2	13 0	3.61
NHL totals		4	140	1	1	0	15	0	6.43						

MANSON, DAVE
D, OILERS

PERSONAL: Born January 27, 1967, at Prince Albert, Sask.... 6-2/192.... Shoots left.
TRANSACTIONS/CAREER NOTES: Selected by Chicago Blackhawks as underage junior in first round (first Blackhawks pick, 11th overall) of NHL entry draft (June 15, 1985).... Suspended three games by NHL for pushing linesman (October 8, 1989).... Bruised right thigh (December 8, 1989).... Suspended 13 games by NHL for abusing linesman and returning to the ice to fight (December 23, 1989).... Suspended three games by NHL for biting (February 27, 1990).... Suspended four games by NHL for attempting to injure another player (October 20, 1990).... Traded by Blackhawks with third-round pick in 1993 draft to Edmonton Oilers for D Steve Smith (October 2, 1991).
HONORS: Named to WHL All-Star second team (1985-86).

Season Team	League	REGULAR SEASON					PLAYOFFS				
		Gms.	G	A	Pts.	Pen.	Gms.	G	A	Pts.	Pen.
83-84—Prince Albert	WHL	70	2	7	9	233	5	0	0	0	4
84-85—Prince Albert	WHL	72	8	30	38	247	13	1	0	1	34

Season Team	League	REGULAR SEASON Gms.	G	A	Pts.	Pen.	PLAYOFFS Gms.	G	A	Pts.	Pen.
85-86—Prince Albert	WHL	70	14	34	48	177	20	1	8	9	63
86-87—Chicago	NHL	63	1	8	9	146	3	0	0	0	10
87-88—Saginaw	IHL	6	0	3	3	37	—	—	—	—	—
—Chicago	NHL	54	1	6	7	185	5	0	0	0	27
88-89—Chicago	NHL	79	18	36	54	352	16	0	8	8	*84
89-90—Chicago	NHL	59	5	23	28	301	20	2	4	6	46
90-91—Chicago	NHL	75	14	15	29	191	6	0	1	1	36
91-92—Edmonton	NHL	79	15	32	47	220	16	3	9	12	44
NHL totals		409	54	120	174	1395	66	5	22	27	247

MANTHA, MOE
D, FLYERS

PERSONAL: Born January 21, 1961, at Lakewood, O. . . . 6-2/197. . . . Shoots right. . . . Full name: Maurice William Mantha.
TRANSACTIONS/CAREER NOTES: Selected by Winnipeg Jets as underage junior in second round (second Jets pick, 23rd overall) of NHL entry draft (June 11, 1980). . . . Suffered recurring back problems; missed 20 games of 1980-81 season. . . . Injured eye (October 1981). . . . Underwent surgery for injured shoulder (October 1982). . . . Traded by Jets to Pittsburgh Penguins to complete March 1984 trade of D Randy Carlyle from Penguins to Jets (May 1, 1984). . . . Broke nose (December 7, 1984). . . . Bruised spine (February 1985). . . . Sprained knee (February 16, 1986). . . . Fractured right wrist (November 26, 1986). . . . Injured eye (February 26, 1987); missed four games. . . . Sprained left knee (March 24, 1987). . . . Traded by Penguins with C Craig Simpson, C Dave Hannan and D Chris Joseph to Edmonton Oilers for D Paul Coffey, LW Dave Hunter and RW Wayne Van Dorp (November 24, 1987). . . . Traded by Oilers to Minnesota North Stars for C Keith Acton (January 22, 1988). . . . Bruised kneecap (February 29, 1988). . . . Separated left shoulder (September 1988). . . . Traded by North Stars to Philadelphia Flyers for fifth-round pick in 1989 draft (D Pat MacLeod) (December 8, 1988). . . . Pulled groin (January 1989). . . . Selected by Jets in NHL waiver draft for $5,000 (October 2, 1989). . . . Pulled groin (March 1990). . . . Bruised ankle (November 1990). . . . Suffered back spasms (March 1991). . . . Injured shoulder (November 23, 1991); missed one game. . . . Injured elbow (December 19, 1991); missed five games. . . . Left Jets to join Team USA (December 30, 1991). . . . Traded by Jets to Flyers for future considerations (February 27, 1992).

Season Team	League	REGULAR SEASON Gms.	G	A	Pts.	Pen.	PLAYOFFS Gms.	G	A	Pts.	Pen.
78-79—Toronto	OMJHL	68	10	38	48	57	4	0	2	2	11
79-80—Toronto	OMJHL	58	8	38	46	86	—	—	—	—	—
80-81—Winnipeg	NHL	58	2	23	25	35	—	—	—	—	—
81-82—Tulsa	CHL	33	8	15	23	56	4	1	3	4	16
—Winnipeg	NHL	25	0	12	12	28	—	—	—	—	—
82-83—Sherbrooke	AHL	13	1	4	5	13	2	2	2	4	0
—Winnipeg	NHL	21	2	7	9	6	—	—	—	—	—
83-84—Sherbrooke	AHL	7	1	1	2	10	3	1	0	1	0
—Winnipeg	NHL	72	16	38	54	67	—	—	—	—	—
84-85—Pittsburgh	NHL	71	11	40	51	54	—	—	—	—	—
85-86—Pittsburgh	NHL	78	15	52	67	102	—	—	—	—	—
86-87—Pittsburgh	NHL	62	9	31	40	44	—	—	—	—	—
87-88—Pittsburgh	NHL	21	2	8	10	23	—	—	—	—	—
—Edmonton	NHL	25	0	6	6	26	—	—	—	—	—
—Minnesota	NHL	30	9	13	22	4	—	—	—	—	—
88-89—Minnesota	NHL	16	1	6	7	10	—	—	—	—	—
—Philadelphia	NHL	30	3	8	11	33	1	0	0	0	0
89-90—Winnipeg	NHL	73	2	26	28	28	7	1	5	6	2
90-91—Winnipeg	NHL	57	9	15	24	33	—	—	—	—	—
91-92—Winnipeg	NHL	12	0	4	4	6	—	—	—	—	—
—U.S. National Team	Int'l	13	0	2	2	29	—	—	—	—	—
—U.S. Olympic Team	Int'l	8	1	1	2	4	—	—	—	—	—
—Philadelphia	NHL	5	0	0	0	2	—	—	—	—	—
NHL totals		656	81	289	370	501	17	5	10	15	18

MARCHMENT, BRYAN
D, BLACKHAWKS

PERSONAL: Born May 1, 1969, at Scarborough, Ont. . . . 6-1/198. . . . Shoots left.
TRANSACTIONS/CAREER NOTES: Suspended three games by OHL (October 1, 1986). . . . Selected by Winnipeg Jets as underage junior in first round (first Jets pick, 16th overall) of NHL entry draft (June 13, 1987). . . . Suspended six games by AHL for fighting (December 10, 1989). . . . Sprained shoulder (March 1990). . . . Suffered back spasms (March 13, 1991). . . . Traded by Jets with D Chris Norton to Chicago Blackhawks for C Troy Murray and LW Warren Rychel (July 22, 1991). . . . Fractured cheekbone (December 12, 1991); missed 12 games.
HONORS: Named to OHL All-Star second team (1988-89).

Season Team	League	REGULAR SEASON Gms.	G	A	Pts.	Pen.	PLAYOFFS Gms.	G	A	Pts.	Pen.
84-85—Toronto Nationals	MTHL		14	35	49	229	21	0	7	7	*83
85-86—Belleville Bulls	OHL	57	5	15	20	225	6	0	4	4	17
86-87—Belleville Bulls	OHL	52	6	38	44	238	6	1	3	4	19
87-88—Belleville Bulls	OHL	56	7	51	58	200	5	0	1	1	12
88-89—Belleville Bulls	OHL	43	14	36	50	198	—	—	—	—	—
—Winnipeg	NHL	2	0	0	0	2	—	—	—	—	—
89-90—Winnipeg	NHL	7	0	2	2	28	—	—	—	—	—
—Moncton	AHL	56	4	19	23	217	—	—	—	—	—

M

Season Team	League	REGULAR SEASON					PLAYOFFS				
		Gms.	G	A	Pts.	Pen.	Gms.	G	A	Pts.	Pen.
90-91—Winnipeg	NHL	28	2	2	4	91	—	—	—	—	—
—Moncton	AHL	33	2	11	13	101	—	—	—	—	—
91-92—Chicago	NHL	58	5	10	15	168	16	1	0	1	36
NHL totals		95	7	14	21	289	16	1	0	1	36

MARCINYSHYN, DAVID
D, NORDIQUES

PERSONAL: Born February 4, 1967, at Edmonton, Alta. . . . 6-3/210. . . . Shoots left.

TRANSACTIONS/CAREER NOTES: Signed as free agent by New Jersey Devils (September 26, 1986). . . . Traded by Devils to Quebec Nordiques for D Brent Severyn (June 3, 1991).

Season Team	League	REGULAR SEASON					PLAYOFFS				
		Gms.	G	A	Pts.	Pen.	Gms.	G	A	Pts.	Pen.
84-85—Fort Saskatchewan	AJHL	55	11	41	52	311	—	—	—	—	—
85-86—Kamloops	WHL	57	2	7	9	111	16	1	3	4	12
86-87—Kamloops	WHL	68	5	27	32	106	13	0	3	3	35
87-88—Utica	AHL	73	2	7	9	179	—	—	—	—	—
—Flint	IHL	3	0	0	0	4	16	0	2	2	31
88-89—Utica	AHL	74	4	14	18	101	5	0	0	0	13
89-90—Utica	AHL	74	6	18	24	164	5	0	2	2	21
90-91—Utica	AHL	52	4	9	13	81	—	—	—	—	—
—New Jersey	NHL	9	0	1	1	21	—	—	—	—	—
91-92—Halifax	AHL	74	10	42	52	138	—	—	—	—	—
—Quebec	NHL	5	0	0	0	26	—	—	—	—	—
NHL totals		14	0	1	1	47					

MARINUCCI, CHRIS
C, ISLANDERS

PERSONAL: Born December 29, 1971, at Grand Rapids, Minn. . . . 6-0/175. . . . Shoots left. . . . Full name: Christopher Jon Marinucci.

HIGH SCHOOL: Grand Rapids (Minn.).

COLLEGE: Minnesota-Duluth.

TRANSACTIONS/CAREER NOTES: Selected by New York Islanders in fifth round (fourth Islanders pick, 90th overall) of NHL entry draft (June 16, 1990).

Season Team	League	REGULAR SEASON					PLAYOFFS				
		Gms.	G	A	Pts.	Pen.	Gms.	G	A	Pts.	Pen.
88-89—Grand Rapids H.S.	Minn. H.S.	25	24	18	42		—	—	—	—	—
89-90—Grand Rapids H.S.	Minn. H.S.	28	24	39	63	0	—	—	—	—	—
90-91—Minnesota-Duluth	WCHA	36	6	10	16	20	—	—	—	—	—
91-92—Minnesota-Duluth	WCHA	37	6	13	19	41	—	—	—	—	—

MARKOVICH, MIKE
D, PENGUINS

PERSONAL: Born April 25, 1969, at Grand Forks, N.D. . . . 6-3/200. . . . Shoots left. . . . Full name: Michael A. Markovich.

HIGH SCHOOL: Central (Devils Lake, N.D.).

COLLEGE: Denver.

TRANSACTIONS/CAREER NOTES: Suffered subflexation of left shoulder (September 1988). . . . Selected by Pittsburgh Penguins in sixth round (sixth Penguins pick, 121st overall) of NHL entry draft (June 17, 1989).

Season Team	League	REGULAR SEASON					PLAYOFFS				
		Gms.	G	A	Pts.	Pen.	Gms.	G	A	Pts.	Pen.
84-85—Central High School	N.D. H.S.	23	8	11	19	12	—	—	—	—	—
85-86—Central High School	N.D. H.S.	23	19	18	37	20	—	—	—	—	—
86-87—Central High School	N.D. H.S.	23	26	25	51	24	—	—	—	—	—
87-88—Rochester	USHL	48	13	41	54	38	—	—	—	—	—
88-89—University of Denver	WCHA	43	5	13	18	38	—	—	—	—	—
89-90—University of Denver	WCHA	42	4	17	21	34	—	—	—	—	—
90-91—University of Denver	WCHA	37	5	15	20	41	—	—	—	—	—
91-92—University of Denver	WCHA	3	0	1	1	10	—	—	—	—	—

MARKWART, NEVIN
LW, FLAMES

PERSONAL: Born December 9, 1964, at Toronto. . . . 5-11/175. . . . Shoots left.

TRANSACTIONS/CAREER NOTES: Separated shoulder (January 1983). . . . Selected by Boston Bruins as underage junior in first round (first Bruins pick, 21st overall) of NHL entry draft (June 8, 1983). . . . Bruised hip (October 1984). . . . Suffered hip-pointer (December 28, 1985); missed four games. . . . Sprained right knee (March 22, 1986). . . . Dislocated left shoulder (October 1987). . . . Strained groin (April 1988). . . . Strained abdominal muscle (October 1988); missed remainder of season. . . . Underwent abdominal surgery (July 1989); missed training camp and first three games of season. . . . Dislocated left shoulder (October 29, 1989). . . . Reinjured left shoulder (November 13, 1989). . . . Underwent surgery to dislocated and fractured left shoulder (November 18, 1989); missed remainder of season. . . . Underwent additional shoulder surgery (February 20, 1990). . . . Tore abdominal muscle (November 1990). . . . Acquired on waivers by Calgary Flames (February 18, 1992). . . . Twisted knee (February 1992); missed seven games.

Season Team	League	REGULAR SEASON					PLAYOFFS				
		Gms.	G	A	Pts.	Pen.	Gms.	G	A	Pts.	Pen.
81-82—Regina Blues	SJHL	—	—	—	—	—	—	—	—	—	—
—Regina	WHL	25	2	12	14	56	20	2	2	4	82

Season Team	League	REGULAR SEASON					PLAYOFFS				
		Gms.	G	A	Pts.	Pen.	Gms.	G	A	Pts.	Pen.
82-83—Regina	WHL	43	27	39	66	91	1	0	0	0	0
83-84—Boston	NHL	70	14	16	30	121	—	—	—	—	—
84-85—Hershey	AHL	38	13	18	31	79	—	—	—	—	—
—Boston	NHL	26	0	4	4	36	1	0	0	0	0
85-86—Boston	NHL	65	7	15	22	207	—	—	—	—	—
86-87—Boston	NHL	64	10	9	19	225	4	0	0	0	9
—Moncton	AHL	3	3	3	6	11	—	—	—	—	—
87-88—Boston	NHL	25	1	12	13	85	2	0	0	0	2
88-89—Maine	AHL	1	0	1	1	0	—	—	—	—	—
89-90—Boston	NHL	8	1	2	3	15	—	—	—	—	—
90-91—Maine	AHL	21	5	5	10	22	—	—	—	—	—
—Boston	NHL	23	3	3	6	36	12	1	0	1	22
91-92—Boston	NHL	18	3	6	9	44	—	—	—	—	—
—Maine	AHL	17	4	7	11	32	—	—	—	—	—
—Calgary	NHL	10	2	1	3	25	—	—	—	—	—
NHL totals		309	41	68	109	794	19	1	0	1	33

MAROIS, DANIEL
RW, ISLANDERS

PERSONAL: Born October 3, 1968, at Montreal. . . . 6-0/190. . . . Shoots right.
TRANSACTIONS/CAREER NOTES: Selected by Toronto Maple Leafs as underage junior in second round (second Maple Leafs pick, 28th overall) of NHL entry draft (June 13, 1987). . . . Suffered from the flu (January 1989). . . . Damaged ligaments in right knee and underwent surgery (April 2, 1989). . . . Bruised left shoulder (November 12, 1989); missed 11 games. . . . Injured wrist (October 25, 1991); missed two games. . . . Traded by Maple Leafs with C Claude Loiselle to New York Islanders for LW Ken Baumgartner and C Dave McIlwain (March 10, 1992).

Season Team	League	REGULAR SEASON					PLAYOFFS				
		Gms.	G	A	Pts.	Pen.	Gms.	G	A	Pts.	Pen.
85-86—Verdun	QMJHL	58	42	35	77	110	5	4	2	6	6
86-87—Chicoutimi	QMJHL	40	22	26	48	143	16	7	14	21	25
87-88—Toronto	NHL	—	—	—	—	—	3	1	0	1	0
—Verdun	QMJHL	67	52	36	88	153	—	—	—	—	—
—Newmarket	AHL	8	4	4	8	4	—	—	—	—	—
88-89—Toronto	NHL	76	31	23	54	76	5	2	2	4	12
89-90—Toronto	NHL	68	39	37	76	82	—	—	—	—	—
90-91—Toronto	NHL	78	21	9	30	112	—	—	—	—	—
91-92—Toronto	NHL	63	15	11	26	76	—	—	—	—	—
—New York Islanders	NHL	12	2	5	7	18	—	—	—	—	—
NHL totals		297	108	85	193	364	8	3	2	5	12

MAROIS, MARIO
D

PERSONAL: Born December 15, 1957, at Ancienne Lorette, Que. . . . 5-11/197. . . . Shoots right. . . . Full name: Mario Joseph Marois.
TRANSACTIONS/CAREER NOTES: Selected by New York Rangers from Quebec Remparts in fourth round (sixth Rangers pick, 62nd overall) of 1977 NHL amateur draft (June 14, 1977). . . . Broke ankle; missed part of 1977-78 season. . . . Traded by Rangers with RW Jim Mayer to Vancouver Canucks for LW Jere Gillis and D Jeff Bandura (November 11, 1980). . . . Traded by Canucks to Quebec Nordiques for D Garry Lariviere (March 10, 1981). . . . Broke right wrist (March 27, 1982). . . . Broke right leg (December 30, 1982). . . . Traded by Nordiques to Winnipeg Jets for D Robert Picard (November 27, 1985). . . . Traded by Jets to Nordiques for D Gord Donnelly (December 6, 1988). . . . Fractured collarbone (January 28, 1989). . . . Sprained right shoulder (November 9, 1989); missed 12 games. . . . Claimed by St. Louis Blues in 1990 NHL waiver draft (October 1, 1990). . . . Traded by Blues to Jets for future considerations (November 26, 1991). . . . Released by Jets (July 28, 1992).
HONORS: Named to QMJHL All-Star second team (1976-77).

Season Team	League	REGULAR SEASON					PLAYOFFS				
		Gms.	G	A	Pts.	Pen.	Gms.	G	A	Pts.	Pen.
75-76—Quebec	QMJHL	67	11	42	53	270	15	2	3	5	86
76-77—Quebec	QMJHL	72	17	67	84	249	14	1	17	18	75
77-78—New Haven	AHL	52	8	23	31	147	12	5	3	8	31
—New York Rangers	NHL	8	1	1	2	15	1	0	0	0	0
78-79—New York Rangers	NHL	71	5	26	31	153	18	0	6	6	29
79-80—New York Rangers	NHL	79	8	23	31	142	9	0	2	2	8
80-81—New York Rangers	NHL	8	1	2	3	46	—	—	—	—	—
—Vancouver	NHL	50	4	12	16	115	5	0	1	1	6
—Quebec	NHL	11	0	7	7	20	13	1	2	3	44
81-82—Quebec	NHL	71	11	32	43	161	—	—	—	—	—
82-83—Quebec	NHL	36	2	12	14	108	9	1	4	5	6
83-84—Quebec	NHL	80	13	36	49	151	18	0	8	8	12
84-85—Quebec	NHL	76	6	37	43	91	—	—	—	—	—
85-86—Quebec	NHL	20	1	12	13	42	3	1	4	5	6
—Winnipeg	NHL	56	4	28	32	110	10	1	3	4	23
86-87—Winnipeg	NHL	79	4	40	44	106	5	0	4	4	6
87-88—Winnipeg	NHL	79	7	44	51	111	—	—	—	—	—
88-89—Winnipeg	NHL	7	1	1	2	17	—	—	—	—	—
—Quebec	NHL	42	2	11	13	101	—	—	—	—	—
89-90—Quebec	NHL	67	3	15	18	104	—	—	—	—	—

M

Season Team	League	REGULAR SEASON					PLAYOFFS				
		Gms.	G	A	Pts.	Pen.	Gms.	G	A	Pts.	Pen.
90-91—St. Louis	NHL	64	2	14	16	81	9	0	0	0	37
91-92—St. Louis	NHL	17	0	1	1	38	—	—	—	—	—
—Winnipeg	NHL	34	1	3	4	34	—	—	—	—	—
NHL totals		955	76	357	433	1746	100	4	34	38	177

MARSH, BRAD

D, SENATORS

PERSONAL: Born March 31, 1958, at London, Ont. . . . 6-3/220. . . . Shoots left. . . . Full name: Charles Bradley Marsh.

TRANSACTIONS/CAREER NOTES: Selected by Atlanta Flames from London Knights in first round (first Flames pick, 11th overall) of 1978 NHL amateur draft (June 15, 1978). . . . Flames franchise moved to Calgary (May 21, 1980). . . . Traded by Flames to Philadelphia Flyers for C Mel Bridgman (November 11, 1981). . . . Bruised knee tendon (January 2, 1983). . . . Broke fibula (March 24, 1983). . . . Suffered concussion (December 1987). . . . Bruised knee (February 1988). . . . Selected by Toronto Maple Leafs in 1988 NHL waiver draft for $2,500 (October 3, 1988). . . . Injured groin (October 31, 1989). . . . Suffered back spasms (December 27, 1990); missed 19 games. . . . Traded by Maple Leafs to Detroit Red Wings for eighth-round pick in 1991 draft (LW Robb McIntyre) (February 4, 1991). . . . Traded by Red Wings to Maple Leafs for future considerations (June 15, 1992). . . . Traded by Maple Leafs to Ottawa Senators for future considerations (July 20, 1992).

HONORS: Shared Max Kaminsky Memorial Trophy with D Rob Ramage (1977-78). . . . Named to OMJHL All-Star first team (1977-78).

MISCELLANEOUS: Does not wear a helmet.

Season Team	League	REGULAR SEASON					PLAYOFFS				
		Gms.	G	A	Pts.	Pen.	Gms.	G	A	Pts.	Pen.
74-75—London	OHA Mj. Jr. A	70	4	17	21	160	—	—	—	—	—
75-76—London	OHA Mj. Jr. A	61	3	26	29	184	—	—	—	—	—
76-77—London	OMJHL	63	7	33	40	121	20	3	5	8	47
77-78—London	OMJHL	62	8	55	63	192	11	2	10	12	21
78-79—Atlanta	NHL	80	0	19	19	101	2	0	0	0	17
79-80—Atlanta	NHL	80	2	9	11	119	4	0	1	1	2
80-81—Calgary	NHL	80	1	12	13	87	16	0	5	5	8
81-82—Calgary	NHL	17	0	1	1	10	—	—	—	—	—
—Philadelphia	NHL	66	2	22	24	106	4	0	0	0	2
82-83—Philadelphia	NHL	68	2	11	13	52	2	0	1	1	0
83-84—Philadelphia	NHL	77	3	14	17	83	3	1	1	2	2
84-85—Philadelphia	NHL	77	2	18	20	91	19	0	6	6	65
85-86—Philadelphia	NHL	79	0	13	13	123	5	0	0	0	2
86-87—Philadelphia	NHL	77	2	9	11	124	26	3	4	7	16
87-88—Philadelphia	NHL	70	3	9	12	57	7	1	0	1	8
88-89—Toronto	NHL	80	1	15	16	79	—	—	—	—	—
89-90—Toronto	NHL	79	1	13	14	95	5	1	0	1	2
90-91—Toronto	NHL	22	0	0	0	15	—	—	—	—	—
—Detroit	NHL	20	1	3	4	16	1	0	0	0	0
91-92—Detroit	NHL	55	3	4	7	53	3	0	0	0	0
NHL totals		1027	23	172	195	1211	97	6	18	24	124

MARSHALL, GRANT

LW/RW/D, MAPLE LEAFS

PERSONAL: Born June 9, 1973, at Toronto. . . . 6-1/185. . . . Shoots right.

HIGH SCHOOL: Hillcrest (Thunder Bay, Ont.).

TRANSACTIONS/CAREER NOTES: Selected by Toronto Maple Leafs in first round (second Maple Leafs pick, 23rd overall) of NHL entry draft (June 20, 1992).

Season Team	League	REGULAR SEASON					PLAYOFFS				
		Gms.	G	A	Pts.	Pen.	Gms.	G	A	Pts.	Pen.
90-91—Ottawa	OHL	26	6	11	17	25	1	0	0	0	0
91-92—Ottawa	OHL	61	32	51	83	132	11	6	11	17	11

MARSHALL, JASON

D, BLUES

PERSONAL: Born February 22, 1971, at Cranbrook, B.C. . . . 6-2/190. . . . Shoots right.

TRANSACTIONS/CAREER NOTES: WHL rights traded by Regina Pats with RW Devin Derksen to Tri-City Americans for RW Mark Cipriano (August 1988). . . . Selected by St. Louis Blues in first round (first Blues pick, ninth overall) of NHL entry draft (June 17, 1989).

Season Team	League	REGULAR SEASON					PLAYOFFS				
		Gms.	G	A	Pts.	Pen.	Gms.	G	A	Pts.	Pen.
87-88—Columbia Valley	KIJHL	40	4	28	32	150	—	—	—	—	—
88-89—Vernon	BCJHL	48	10	30	40	197	31	6	6	12	141
—Canadian National Team	Int'l	2	0	1	1	0	—	—	—	—	—
89-90—Canadian National Team	Int'l	72	1	11	12	57	—	—	—	—	—
90-91—Tri-City Americans	WHL	59	10	34	44	236	7	1	2	3	20
—Peoria	IHL	—	—	—	—	—	18	0	1	1	48
91-92—Peoria	IHL	78	4	18	22	178	10	0	1	1	16
—St. Louis	NHL	2	1	0	1	4	—	—	—	—	—
NHL totals		2	1	0	1	4					

MARTIN, CRAIG

RW, JETS

PERSONAL: Born January 21, 1971, at Amherst, N.S. . . . 6-2/219. . . . Shoots right.

TRANSACTIONS/CAREER NOTES: Suspended by QMJHL for opening game of 1990-91 season for fighting in a playoff game (April 14, 1990). . . . Selected by Winnipeg Jets in fifth round (sixth Jets pick, 98th overall) of NHL entry draft (June 16, 1990). . . . Suspended by QMJHL for striking referee with stick (December 9, 1990).

Season Team	League	REGULAR SEASON					PLAYOFFS				
		Gms.	G	A	Pts.	Pen.	Gms.	G	A	Pts.	Pen.
87-88—Hull	QMJHL	66	5	5	10	137	—	—	—	—	—
88-89—Hull	QMJHL	70	14	29	43	260	—	—	—	—	—
89-90—Hull	QMJHL	66	14	31	45	299	11	2	1	3	65
90-91—St. Hyacinthe	QMJHL	54	13	16	29	257	—	—	—	—	—
91-92—Fort Wayne	IHL	24	0	0	0	115	—	—	—	—	—
—Moncton	AHL	11	1	1	2	70	—	—	—	—	—

MARTINI, DARCY
D, OILERS

PERSONAL: Born January 30, 1969, at Castlegar, B.C.... 6-4/220.... Shoots left.... Full name: Darcy R. Martini.
COLLEGE: Michigan Tech.
TRANSACTIONS/CAREER NOTES: Selected by Edmonton Oilers in eighth round (eighth Oilers pick, 162nd overall) of NHL entry draft (June 17, 1989).

Season Team	League	REGULAR SEASON					PLAYOFFS				
		Gms.	G	A	Pts.	Pen.	Gms.	G	A	Pts.	Pen.
84-85—Castlegar	KIJHL	38	4	17	21	58	—	—	—	—	—
85-86—Castlegar	KIJHL	38	8	28	36	180	—	—	—	—	—
86-87—Castlegar	KIJHL	40	12	53	65	260	—	—	—	—	—
87-88—Vernon	BCJHL	48	9	26	35	193	12	2	0	11	20
88-89—Michigan Tech	WCHA	37	1	2	3	107	—	—	—	—	—
89-90—Michigan Tech	WCHA	36	3	16	19	150	—	—	—	—	—
90-91—Michigan Tech	WCHA	34	10	13	23	*186	—	—	—	—	—
91-92—Michigan Tech	WCHA	17	5	13	18	58	—	—	—	—	—

MARTINSON, STEVE
LW, NORTH STARS

PERSONAL: Born June 21, 1957, at Minnetonka, Minn.... 6-1/205.... Shoots left.
TRANSACTIONS/CAREER NOTES: Traded by Salt Lake Golden Eagles with C Kurt Kleinendorst to Toledo Goaldiggers for Kevin Conway, Blake Stephan, C Grant Rezansoff and D Steve Harrison (February 1985).... Signed as free agent by Philadelphia Flyers (September 1985).... Underwent surgery on disk (May 1986).... Signed as free agent by Adirondack Red Wings (March 1987).... Suspended six games by AHL for fighting (March 12, 1988).... Signed as free agent by Montreal Canadiens (August 1988).... Suffered back spasms (October 10, 1989); missed 10 games.

Season Team	League	REGULAR SEASON					PLAYOFFS				
		Gms.	G	A	Pts.	Pen.	Gms.	G	A	Pts.	Pen.
81-82—Toledo	IHL	35	12	18	30	128	—	—	—	—	—
82-83—Birmingham	CHL	43	4	5	9	184	13	1	2	3	*80
—Toledo	IHL	32	9	10	19	111	—	—	—	—	—
83-84—Tulsa	CHL	42	3	6	9	*240	6	0	0	0	*43
84-85—Salt Lake City	IHL	32	4	7	11	140	—	—	—	—	—
—Toledo	IHL	22	0	3	3	160	2	0	0	0	21
—New Haven	AHL	4	0	0	0	17	—	—	—	—	—
85-86—Hershey	AHL	69	3	6	9	*432	3	0	0	0	56
86-87—Hershey	AHL	17	0	3	3	85	—	—	—	—	—
—Adirondack	AHL	14	1	1	2	78	11	2	0	2	*108
87-88—Adirondack	AHL	32	6	8	14	146	6	1	2	3	66
—Detroit	NHL	10	1	1	2	84	—	—	—	—	—
88-89—Sherbrooke	AHL	10	5	7	12	61	—	—	—	—	—
—Montreal	NHL	25	1	0	1	87	1	0	0	0	10
89-90—Montreal	NHL	13	0	0	0	64	—	—	—	—	—
—Sherbrooke	AHL	37	6	20	26	111	—	—	—	—	—
90-91—San Diego	IHL	53	16	24	40	268	—	—	—	—	—
91-92—San Diego	IHL	70	18	15	33	279	4	1	1	2	15
—Minnesota	NHL	1	0	0	0	9	—	—	—	—	—
NHL totals		49	2	1	3	244	1	0	0	0	10

MARTTILA, JUKKA
D, JETS

PERSONAL: Born April 15, 1968, at Tampere, Finland.... 6-0/185.... Shoots left.
TRANSACTIONS/CAREER NOTES: Selected by Winnipeg Jets in seventh round (ninth Jets pick, 136th overall) of NHL entry draft (June 11, 1988).

Season Team	League	REGULAR SEASON					PLAYOFFS				
		Gms.	G	A	Pts.	Pen.	Gms.	G	A	Pts.	Pen.
86-87—Tappara	Finland	33	4	1	5	18	—	—	—	—	—
87-88—Tappara	Finland	39	5	7	12	16	—	—	—	—	—
88-89—Tappara	Finland	43	11	20	31	32	—	—	—	—	—
89-90—Tappara	Finland	44	12	14	26	14	—	—	—	—	—
90-91—Tappara	Finland	42	10	21	31	32	—	—	—	—	—
91-92—Tappara	Finland	17	2	4	6	14	—	—	—	—	—

MASON, BOB
G, CANUCKS

PERSONAL: Born April 22, 1961, at International Falls, Minn.... 6-1/180.... Shoots right.... Full name: Robert Thomas Mason.
COLLEGE: Minnesota-Duluth.
TRANSACTIONS/CAREER NOTES: Signed as free agent by Washington Capitals (February 21, 1984). ... Signed as free agent by Chicago Blackhawks (June 12, 1987).... Traded by Blackhawks to Quebec Nordiques for C Mike Eagles (July 5, 1988).... Traded by Nordiques to Capitals for future considerations (June 17, 1989).... Signed as free agent by Vancouver Canucks (November 1990).

M

Season	Team	League	Gms.	Min.	W	L	T	GA	SO	Avg.	Gms.	Min.	W	L	GA	SO	Avg.
			REGULAR SEASON								PLAYOFFS						
81-82—Minnesota-Duluth		WCHA	26	1521				115		4.54	—	—	—	—	—	—	—
82-83—Minnesota-Duluth		WCHA	43	2594				151		3.49	—	—	—	—	—	—	—
83-84—U.S. National Team		Int'l	33	1895				89		2.82	—	—	—	—	—	—	—
—U.S. Olympic Team		Int'l	3	160				10	0	3.75	—	—	—	—	—	—	—
—Washington		NHL	2	120	2	0	0	3	0	1.50	—	—	—	—	—	—	—
—Hershey		AHL	5	282	1	4	0	26	0	5.53	—	—	—	—	—	—	—
84-85—Washington		NHL	12	661	8	2	1	31	1	2.81	—	—	—	—	—	—	—
—Binghamton		AHL	20	1052	10	6	1	58	1	3.31	—	—	—	—	—	—	—
85-86—Binghamton		AHL	34	1940	20	11	2	126	0	3.90	3	124	1	1	9	0	4.35
—Washington		NHL	1	16	1	0	0	0	0	0.00	—	—	—	—	—	—	—
86-87—Binghamton		AHL	2	119	1	1	0	4	0	2.02	—	—	—	—	—	—	—
—Washington		NHL	45	2536	20	18	5	137	0	3.24	4	309	2	2	9	1	1.75
87-88—Chicago		NHL	41	2312	13	18	8	160	0	4.15	1	60	0	1	3	0	3.00
88-89—Quebec		NHL	22	1168	5	14	1	92	0	4.73	—	—	—	—	—	—	—
—Halifax		AHL	23	1278	11	7	1	73	1	3.43	2	97	0	2	9	0	5.57
89-90—Washington		NHL	16	822	4	9	1	48	0	3.50	—	—	—	—	—	—	—
—Baltimore		AHL	13	770	9	2	2	44	0	3.43	6	373	2	4	20	0	3.22
90-91—Vancouver		NHL	6	353	2	4	0	29	0	4.93	—	—	—	—	—	—	—
—Milwaukee		IHL	22	1199	8	12	1	82	0	4.10	—	—	—	—	—	—	—
91-92—Milwaukee		IHL	51	3024	27	18	4	171	1	3.39	3	179	1	2	15	0	5.03
NHL totals			145	7988	55	65	16	500	1	3.76	5	369	2	3	12	1	1.95

MATHIESON, JIM
D, CAPITALS

PERSONAL: Born January 24, 1970, at Kindersley, Sask. . . . 6-1/209. . . . Shoots left. . . . Full name: James Johnson Mathieson.
TRANSACTIONS/CAREER NOTES: Selected by Washington Capitals in third round (third Capitals pick, 59th overall) of NHL entry draft (June 17, 1989).

Season	Team	League	Gms.	G	A	Pts.	Pen.	Gms.	G	A	Pts.	Pen.
			REGULAR SEASON					PLAYOFFS				
86-87—Regina		WHL	40	0	9	9	40	3	0	1	1	2
87-88—Regina		WHL	72	3	12	15	115	4	0	2	2	4
88-89—Regina		WHL	62	5	22	27	151	—	—	—	—	—
89-90—Regina		WHL	67	1	26	27	158	11	0	7	7	16
—Baltimore		AHL	—	—	—	—	—	3	0	0	0	4
—Washington		NHL	2	0	0	0	4	—	—	—	—	—
90-91—Baltimore		AHL	65	3	5	8	168	4	1	0	1	6
91-92—Baltimore		AHL	74	2	9	11	206	—	—	—	—	—
NHL totals			2	0	0	0	4					

MATTEAU, STEPHANE
LW, BLACKHAWKS

PERSONAL: Born September 2, 1969, at Rouyn, Que. . . . 6-3/195. . . . Shoots left.
TRANSACTIONS/CAREER NOTES: Selected by Calgary Flames as underage junior in second round (second Flames pick, 25th overall) of NHL entry draft (June 13, 1987). . . . Bruised thigh (October 10, 1991); missed 43 games. . . . Traded by Flames to Chicago Blackhawks for D Trent Yawney (December 16, 1991). . . . Fractured left foot (January 27, 1992); missed 12 games.

Season	Team	League	Gms.	G	A	Pts.	Pen.	Gms.	G	A	Pts.	Pen.
			REGULAR SEASON					PLAYOFFS				
85-86—Hull		QMJHL	60	6	8	14	19	4	0	0	0	0
86-87—Hull		QMJHL	69	27	48	75	113	8	3	7	10	8
87-88—Hull		QMJHL	57	17	40	57	179	18	5	14	19	84
88-89—Hull		QMJHL	59	44	45	89	202	9	8	6	14	30
—Salt Lake City		IHL	—	—	—	—	—	9	0	4	4	13
89-90—Salt Lake City		IHL	81	23	35	58	130	10	6	3	9	38
90-91—Calgary		NHL	78	15	19	34	93	5	0	1	1	0
91-92—Calgary		NHL	4	1	0	1	19	—	—	—	—	—
—Chicago		NHL	20	5	8	13	45	18	4	6	10	24
NHL totals			102	21	27	48	157	23	4	7	11	24

MATTHEWS, JAMIE
C, BLACKHAWKS

PERSONAL: Born May 25, 1973, at Amherst, N.S. . . . 6-1/190. . . . Shoots right.
TRANSACTIONS/CAREER NOTES: Selected by Chicago Blackhawks in second round (third Blackhawks pick, 44th overall) of NHL entry draft (June 22, 1991).

Season	Team	League	Gms.	G	A	Pts.	Pen.	Gms.	G	A	Pts.	Pen.
			REGULAR SEASON					PLAYOFFS				
88-89—Amherst Jr. A		NSJHL	38	39	43	82	9	—	—	—	—	—
89-90—Sudbury		OHL	60	16	17	33	25	7	1	0	1	4
90-91—Sudbury		OHL	66	14	38	52	41	5	3	5	8	8
91-92—Sudbury		OHL	64	26	69	95	30	11	2	11	13	4

MATUSOVICH, SCOTT
D, FLAMES

PERSONAL: Born January 31, 1969, at Derby, Conn. . . . 6-2/205. . . . Shoots left. . . . Full name: Charles Scott Matusovich.
HIGH SCHOOL: Canterbury (New Milford, Conn.).
COLLEGE: Yale.

TRANSACTIONS/CAREER NOTES: Selected by Calgary Flames in fifth round (fifth Flames pick, 90th overall) of NHL entry draft (June 11, 1988).

			REGULAR SEASON					PLAYOFFS				
Season	Team	League	Gms.	G	A	Pts.	Pen.	Gms.	G	A	Pts.	Pen.
86-87—Canterbury School		Conn. H.S.		10	22	32		—	—	—	—	—
87-88—Canterbury School		Conn. H.S.		20	31	51		—	—	—	—	—
88-89—Yale University		ECAC	25	3	11	14	40	—	—	—	—	—
89-90—Yale University		ECAC	28	1	15	16	55	—	—	—	—	—
90-91—Yale University		ECAC	29	3	8	11	48	—	—	—	—	—
91-92—Yale University		ECAC	27	3	13	16	52	—	—	—	—	—

MATVICHUK, RICHARD
D, NORTH STARS

PERSONAL: Born February 5, 1973, at Edmonton, Alta. . . . 6-2/190. . . . Shoots left.
TRANSACTIONS/CAREER NOTES: Selected by Minnesota North Stars in first round (first North Stars pick, eighth overall) of 1991 NHL entry draft (June 22, 1991).
HONORS: Won Bill Hunter Trophy (1991-92). . . . Named to Can.HL All-Star second team (1991-92). . . . Named to WHL (East) All-Star first team (1991-92).

			REGULAR SEASON					PLAYOFFS				
Season	Team	League	Gms.	G	A	Pts.	Pen.	Gms.	G	A	Pts.	Pen.
88-89—Fort Saskatchewan		AJHL	58	7	36	43	147	—	—	—	—	—
89-90—Saskatoon		WHL	56	8	24	32	126	10	2	8	10	16
90-91—Saskatoon		WHL	68	13	36	49	117	—	—	—	—	—
91-92—Saskatoon		WHL	58	14	40	54	126	22	1	9	10	61

MAY, ALAN
RW, CAPITALS

PERSONAL: Born January 14, 1965, at Swan Hills, Alta. . . . 6-1/200. . . . Shoots right. . . . Full name: Alan Randy May.
TRANSACTIONS/CAREER NOTES: Signed as free agent by Boston Bruins (September 1987). . . . Traded by Bruins to Edmonton Oilers for LW Moe Lemay (March 8, 1988). . . . Traded by Oilers with D Jim Wiemer to Los Angeles Kings for C Brian Wilks and D John English (March 7, 1989). . . . Traded by Kings to Washington Capitals for fifth-round pick in 1989 draft (G Tom Newman) (June 17, 1989). . . . Fractured knuckle on left hand (October 20, 1990). . . . Strained shoulder (December 8, 1990). . . . Underwent surgery to nose (March 1992); missed two games.

			REGULAR SEASON					PLAYOFFS				
Season	Team	League	Gms.	G	A	Pts.	Pen.	Gms.	G	A	Pts.	Pen.
84-85—Estevan		SAJHL	64	51	47	98	409	—	—	—	—	—
85-86—Medicine Hat		WHL	6	1	0	1	25	—	—	—	—	—
86-87—New Westminster		WHL	32	8	9	17	81	—	—	—	—	—
—Springfield		AHL	4	0	2	2	11	—	—	—	—	—
—Carolina		ECHL	42	23	14	37	310	5	2	2	4	57
87-88—Maine		AHL	61	14	11	25	357	—	—	—	—	—
—Boston		NHL	3	0	0	0	15	—	—	—	—	—
—Nova Scotia		AHL	12	4	1	5	54	4	0	0	0	51
88-89—Edmonton		NHL	3	1	0	1	7	—	—	—	—	—
—Cape Breton		AHL	50	12	13	25	214	—	—	—	—	—
—New Haven		AHL	12	2	8	10	99	16	6	3	9	*105
89-90—Washington		NHL	77	7	10	17	339	15	0	0	0	37
90-91—Washington		NHL	67	4	6	10	264	11	1	1	2	37
91-92—Washington		NHL	75	6	9	15	221	7	0	0	0	0
NHL totals			225	18	25	43	846	33	1	1	2	74

MAY, BRAD
LW, SABRES

PERSONAL: Born November 29, 1971, at Toronto. . . . 6-0/209. . . . Shoots left.
TRANSACTIONS/CAREER NOTES: Selected by Buffalo Sabres in first round (first Sabres pick, 14th overall) of NHL entry draft (June 16, 1990). . . . Injured knee (August 1990). . . . Injured left knee ligaments (November 1990).
HONORS: Named to OHL All-Star second team (1989-90 and 1990-91).

			REGULAR SEASON					PLAYOFFS				
Season	Team	League	Gms.	G	A	Pts.	Pen.	Gms.	G	A	Pts.	Pen.
87-88—Markham Jr. B		OHA	6	1	1	2	21	—	—	—	—	—
88-89—Niagara Falls		OHL	65	8	14	22	304	17	0	1	1	55
89-90—Niagara Falls		OHL	61	33	58	91	223	16	9	13	22	64
90-91—Niagara Falls		OHL	34	37	32	69	93	14	11	14	25	53
91-92—Buffalo		NHL	69	11	6	17	309	7	1	4	5	2
NHL totals			69	11	6	17	309	7	1	4	5	2

MAZUR, JAY
C, CANUCKS

PERSONAL: Born January 22, 1965, at Hamilton, Ont. . . . 6-2/205. . . . Shoots right. . . . Full name: Jay John Mazur.
HIGH SCHOOL: Breck (Minneapolis).
COLLEGE: Maine.
TRANSACTIONS/CAREER NOTES: Selected by Vancouver Canucks in 12th round (12th Canucks pick, 230th overall) of NHL entry draft (June 8, 1983). . . . Strained rib cartilage (October 12, 1990). . . . Injured right calf and underwent emergency surgery to relieve circulatory problem (February 21, 1991); missed 11 games.

M

Season	Team	League	Gms.	G	A	Pts.	Pen.	Gms.	G	A	Pts.	Pen.
82-83—Breck H.S.	Minn. H.S.	—	—	—	—	—	—	—	—	—	—	
83-84—University of Maine	ECAC	34	14	9	23	14	—	—	—	—	—	
84-85—University of Maine	Hockey East	31	0	6	6	20	—	—	—	—	—	
85-86—University of Maine	Hockey East	35	5	7	12	18	—	—	—	—	—	
86-87—University of Maine	Hockey East	39	16	10	26	61	—	—	—	—	—	
87-88—Flint	IHL	43	17	11	28	36	—	—	—	—	—	
—Fredericton	AHL	31	14	6	20	28	15	4	2	6	38	
88-89—Milwaukee	IHL	73	33	31	64	86	11	6	5	11	2	
—Vancouver	NHL	1	0	0	0	0	—	—	—	—	—	
89-90—Milwaukee	IHL	70	20	27	47	63	6	3	0	3	6	
—Vancouver	NHL	5	0	0	0	4	—	—	—	—	—	
90-91—Milwaukee	IHL	7	2	3	5	21	—	—	—	—	—	
—Vancouver	NHL	36	11	7	18	14	6	0	1	1	8	
91-92—Milwaukee	IHL	56	17	20	37	49	5	2	3	5	0	
—Vancouver	NHL	5	0	0	0	2	—	—	—	—	—	
NHL totals		47	11	7	18	20	6	0	1	1	8	

McAMMOND, DEAN
C, BLACKHAWKS

PERSONAL: Born June 15, 1973, at Grand Cache, Alta.... 5-11/185.... Shoots left.
TRANSACTIONS/CAREER NOTES: Selected by Chicago Blackhawks in first round (first Blackhawks pick, 22nd overall) of NHL entry draft (June 22, 1991).
HONORS: Won Can.HL Plus/Minus Award (1991-92).

Season	Team	League	Gms.	G	A	Pts.	Pen.	Gms.	G	A	Pts.	Pen.
89-90—Prince Albert	WHL	53	11	11	22	49	14	2	3	5	18	
90-91—Prince Albert	WHL	71	33	35	68	108	2	0	1	1	6	
91-92—Prince Albert	WHL	63	37	54	91	189	10	12	11	23	26	
—Chicago	NHL	5	0	2	2	0	3	0	0	0	2	
NHL totals		5	0	2	2	0	3	0	0	0	2	

McBAIN, ANDREW
RW, SENATORS

PERSONAL: Born January 18, 1965, at Toronto.... 6-1/205.... Shoots right.
TRANSACTIONS/CAREER NOTES: Fractured cheekbone (November 1982).... Separated sterno clavicular joint (March 1983).... Selected by Winnipeg Jets as underage junior in first round (first Jets pick, eighth overall) of NHL entry draft (June 8, 1983).... Suffered from mononucleosis (April 25, 1985).... Injured knee (December 8, 1985).... Suspended four games by NHL for stick-swinging incident (March 1987).... Traded by Jets with D Jim Kyte and LW Randy Gilhen to Pittsburgh Penguins for C/LW Randy Cunneyworth, G Richard Tabaracci and RW Dave McLlwain (June 17, 1989).... Traded by Penguins with C Dan Quinn and C Dave Capuano to Vancouver Canucks for RW Tony Tanti, C Barry Pederson and D Rod Buskas (January 8, 1990). ...Suffered sore ribs (February 1990).... Signed as free agent by Ottawa Senators (June 23, 1992).
HONORS: Named to OHL All-Star second team (1982-83).

Season	Team	League	Gms.	G	A	Pts.	Pen.	Gms.	G	A	Pts.	Pen.
81-82—Niagara Falls	OHL	68	19	25	44	35	5	0	3	3	4	
82-83—North Bay	OHL	67	33	87	120	61	8	2	6	8	17	
83-84—Winnipeg	NHL	78	11	19	30	37	3	2	0	2	0	
84-85—Winnipeg	NHL	77	7	15	22	45	7	1	0	1	0	
85-86—Winnipeg	NHL	28	3	3	6	17	—	—	—	—	—	
86-87—Winnipeg	NHL	71	11	21	32	106	9	0	2	2	10	
87-88—Winnipeg	NHL	74	32	31	63	145	5	2	5	7	29	
88-89—Winnipeg	NHL	80	37	40	77	71	—	—	—	—	—	
89-90—Pittsburgh	NHL	41	5	9	14	51	—	—	—	—	—	
—Vancouver	NHL	26	4	5	9	22	—	—	—	—	—	
90-91—Vancouver	NHL	13	0	5	5	32	—	—	—	—	—	
—Milwaukee	IHL	47	27	24	51	69	6	2	5	7	12	
91-92—Milwaukee	IHL	65	24	54	78	132	5	1	2	3	10	
—Vancouver	NHL	6	1	0	1	0	—	—	—	—	—	
NHL totals		494	111	148	259	526	24	5	7	12	39	

McBAIN, JASON
D, WHALERS

PERSONAL: Born April 12, 1974, at Ilion, N.Y.... 6-2/185.... Shoots right.
TRANSACTIONS/CAREER NOTES: Selected by Hartford Whalers in fourth round (fifth Whalers pick, 81st overall) of NHL entry draft (June 20, 1992).

Season	Team	League	Gms.	G	A	Pts.	Pen.	Gms.	G	A	Pts.	Pen.
90-91—Lethbridge	WHL	52	2	7	9	39	1	0	0	0	0	
91-92—Lethbridge	WHL	13	0	1	1	12	—	—	—	—	—	
—Portland	WHL	54	9	23	32	95	6	1	0	1	13	

McBEAN, WAYNE
D, ISLANDERS

PERSONAL: Born February 21, 1969, at Calgary, Alta.... 6-2/185.... Shoots left.
TRANSACTIONS/CAREER NOTES: Selected by Los Angeles Kings as underage junior in first round (first Kings pick, fourth overall) of NHL entry draft (June 13, 1987).... Traded by Kings with G Mark Fitzpatrick and future considerations to New York Islanders for G

M

Kelly Hrudey (February 22, 1989); D Doug Crossman was sent to Islanders to complete deal. . . . Injured left knee (December 23, 1991); missed final 47 games of season. . . . Underwent arthroscopic surgery to left knee (December 31, 1991).
HONORS: Won Top Defenseman Trophy (East) (1986-87). . . . Named to WHL All-Star first team (1986-87).

			REGULAR SEASON				PLAYOFFS				
Season Team	League	Gms.	G	A	Pts.	Pen.	Gms.	G	A	Pts.	Pen.
85-86—Medicine Hat	WHL	67	1	14	15	73	25	1	5	6	36
86-87—Medicine Hat	WHL	71	12	41	53	163	20	2	8	10	40
87-88—Los Angeles	NHL	27	0	1	1	26	—	—	—	—	—
—Medicine Hat	WHL	30	15	30	45	48	16	6	17	23	50
88-89—New Haven	AHL	7	1	1	2	2	—	—	—	—	—
—Los Angeles	NHL	33	0	5	5	23	—	—	—	—	—
—New York Islanders	NHL	19	0	1	1	12	—	—	—	—	—
89-90—Springfield	AHL	68	6	33	39	48	17	4	11	15	31
—New York Islanders	NHL	5	0	1	1	2	2	1	1	2	0
90-91—Capital District	AHL	22	9	9	18	19	—	—	—	—	—
—New York Islanders	NHL	52	5	14	19	47	—	—	—	—	—
91-92—New York Islanders	NHL	25	2	4	6	18	—	—	—	—	—
NHL totals		161	7	26	33	128	2	1	1	2	0

McCABE, SCOTT
D, DEVILS

PERSONAL: Born May 28, 1974, at St. Claire Shores, Mich. . . . 6-4/189. . . . Shoots left.
TRANSACTIONS/CAREER NOTES: Selected by New Jersey Devils in fourth round (fifth Devils pick, 94th overall) of NHL entry draft (June 20, 1992).

McCARTHY, BRIAN
C, SABRES

PERSONAL: Born December 6, 1971, at Salem, Mass. . . . 6-2/190. . . . Shoots left. . . . Full name: Brian Edward McCarthy.
HIGH SCHOOL: Pingree (South Hamilton, Mass.).
COLLEGE: Providence.

TRANSACTIONS/CAREER NOTES: Selected by Buffalo Sabres in fourth round (second Sabres pick, 82nd overall) of NHL entry draft (June 16, 1990).

			REGULAR SEASON				PLAYOFFS				
Season Team	League	Gms.	G	A	Pts.	Pen.	Gms.	G	A	Pts.	Pen.
86-87—Pingree School	Mass. H.S.	20	15	16	31		—	—	—	—	—
87-88—Pingree School	Mass. H.S.	24	22	36	58	24	—	—	—	—	—
88-89—Pingree School	Mass. H.S.	26	37	43	80	24	—	—	—.	—	—
89-90—Pingree School	Mass. H.S.		25	40	65		—	—	—	—	—
90-91—Providence College	Hockey East	33	7	6	13	33	—	—	—	—	—
91-92—St. Lawrence University	ECAC	—	—	—	—	—	—	—	—	—	—

McCARTHY, SANDY
RW, FLAMES

PERSONAL: Born June 15, 1972, at Toronto. . . . 6-3/224. . . . Shoots right.
TRANSACTIONS/CAREER NOTES: Suspended one game by QMJHL for attempting to injure another player (October 2, 1989). . . . Suspended one playoff game by QMJHL for a pre-game fight (March 19, 1990). . . . Selected by Calgary Flames in third round (third Flames pick, 52nd overall) of NHL entry draft (June 22, 1991).

			REGULAR SEASON				PLAYOFFS				
Season Team	League	Gms.	G	A	Pts.	Pen.	Gms.	G	A	Pts.	Pen.
89-90—Laval	QMJHL	65	10	11	21	269	—	—	—	—	—
90-91—Laval	QMJHL	68	21	19	40	297	—	—	—	—	—
91-92—Laval	QMJHL	62	39	51	90	326	8	4	5	9	81

McCARTY, DARREN
RW, RED WINGS

PERSONAL: Born April 1, 1972, at Burnaby, B.C. . . . 6-1/211. . . . Shoots right.
HIGH SCHOOL: Quinte Secondary School (Belleville, Ont.).
TRANSACTIONS/CAREER NOTES: Selected by Detroit Red Wings in second round (second Red Wings pick, 46th overall) of NHL entry draft (June 20, 1992).
HONORS: Won Jim Mahon Memorial Trophy (1991-92). . . . Named to Can.HL All-Star first team (1991-92). . . . Named to OHL All-Star first team (1991-92).

			REGULAR SEASON				PLAYOFFS				
Season Team	League	Gms.	G	A	Pts.	Pen.	Gms.	G	A	Pts.	Pen.
88-89—Peterborough Jr. B	OHA	34	18	17	35	135	—	—	—	—	—
89-90—Belleville	OHL	63	12	15	27	142	11	1	1	2	21
90-91—Belleville	OHL	60	30	37	67	151	6	2	2	4	13
91-92—Belleville	OHL	65	*55	72	127	177	5	1	4	5	13

McCLELLAND, KEVIN
RW, MAPLE LEAFS

PERSONAL: Born July 4, 1962, at Oshawa, Ont. . . . 6-2/205. . . . Shoots right. . . . Full name: Kevin William McClelland.
TRANSACTIONS/CAREER NOTES: Selected by Hartford Whalers as underage junior in fourth round (fourth Whalers pick, 71st overall) of NHL entry draft (June 11, 1980). . . . Acquired by Pittsburgh Penguins with C/LW Pat Boutette as compensation from Whalers for Whalers signing free-agent G Greg Millen. Decision required by NHL Arbitrator Judge Joseph John Kane when Hartford and Pittsburgh were unable to agree on compensation (July 1981). . . . Dislocated shoulder (September 21, 1981). . . . Dislocated shoulder and underwent surgery (January 24, 1983); missed remainder of season. . . . Traded by Penguins with sixth-round pick in 1984 draft (D Emanuel Viveiros) to Edmonton Oilers for C Tom Roulston (December 5, 1983). . . . Sprained left knee (January 1985). . . .

Suspended three games by NHL for being first off the bench during a fight (December 10, 1986).... Sprained knee (November 1987).... Bruised right knee (February 1988).... Traded by Oilers with C Jimmy Carson and fifth-round pick in 1991 draft to Detroit Red Wings for C/RW Joe Murphy, C/LW Adam Graves, LW Petr Klima and D Jeff Sharples (November 2, 1989).... Suffered sore left shoulder (September 1990).... Released by Red Wings (April 21, 1991).

Season Team	League	REGULAR SEASON Gms.	G	A	Pts.	Pen.	PLAYOFFS Gms.	G	A	Pts.	Pen.
79-80—Niagara Falls	OMJHL	67	14	14	28	71	—	—	—	—	—
80-81—Niagara Falls	OMJHL	68	36	72	108	184	—	—	—	—	—
81-82—Niagara Falls	OHL	46	36	47	83	184	12	8	13	21	42
—Pittsburgh	NHL	10	1	4	5	4	—	—	—	—	—
82-83—Pittsburgh	NHL	38	5	4	9	73	5	1	1	2	5
83-84—Baltimore	AHL	3	1	1	2	0	—	—	—	—	—
—Pittsburgh	NHL	24	2	4	6	62	—	—	—	—	—
—Edmonton	NHL	52	8	20	28	127	18	4	6	10	42
84-85—Edmonton	NHL	62	8	15	23	205	18	1	3	4	75
85-86—Edmonton	NHL	79	11	25	36	266	10	1	0	1	32
86-87—Edmonton	NHL	72	12	13	25	238	21	2	3	5	43
87-88—Edmonton	NHL	74	10	6	16	281	19	2	3	5	68
88-89—Edmonton	NHL	79	6	14	20	161	7	0	2	2	16
89-90—Edmonton	NHL	10	1	1	2	13	—	—	—	—	—
—Detroit	NHL	61	4	5	9	183	—	—	—	—	—
90-91—Adirondack	AHL	27	5	14	19	125	—	—	—	—	—
—Detroit	NHL	3	0	0	0	7	—	—	—	—	—
91-92—St. John's	AHL	34	7	15	22	199	5	0	1	1	9
—Toronto	NHL	18	0	1	1	33	—	—	—	—	—
NHL totals		582	68	112	180	1653	98	11	18	29	281

McCOSH, SHAWN
C, KINGS

PERSONAL: Born June 5, 1969, at Oshawa, Ont.... 6-0/188.... Shoots right.
TRANSACTIONS/CAREER NOTES: Selected by Detroit Red Wings in fifth round (fifth Red Wings pick, 95th overall) of NHL entry draft (June 17, 1989).... Traded by Red Wings to Los Angeles Kings for 10th-round pick in 1992 draft (August 1990).

Season Team	League	REGULAR SEASON Gms.	G	A	Pts.	Pen.	PLAYOFFS Gms.	G	A	Pts.	Pen.
86-87—Hamilton	OHL	50	11	17	28	49	6	1	0	1	2
87-88—Hamilton	OHL	64	17	36	53	96	14	6	8	14	14
88-89—Niagara Falls	OHL	56	41	62	103	75	14	4	13	17	23
89-90—Niagara Falls	OHL	9	6	10	16	24	—	—	—	—	—
—Dukes of Hamilton	OHL	39	24	28	52	65	—	—	—	—	—
90-91—New Haven	AHL	66	16	21	37	104	—	—	—	—	—
91-92—Phoenix	IHL	71	21	32	53	118	—	—	—	—	—
—Los Angeles	NHL	4	0	0	0	4	—	—	—	—	—
NHL totals		4	0	0	0	4					

McCRIMMON, BRAD
D, RED WINGS

PERSONAL: Born March 29, 1959, at Dodsland, Sask.... 5-11/197.... Shoots left. ...Full name: Byron Brad McCrimmon.
TRANSACTIONS/CAREER NOTES: Selected by Boston Bruins in first round (second Bruins pick, 15th overall) of NHL entry draft (August 9, 1979).... Traded by Bruins to Philadelphia Flyers for G Pete Peeters (June 1982).... Broke bone in right hand (February 2, 1985); missed 13 games. ...Separated left shoulder and underwent surgery (May 9, 1985).... Missed start of 1986-87 season due to contract dispute. ...Traded by Flyers to Calgary Flames for first-round pick in 1989 draft and third-round pick in 1988 draft (G Dominic Roussel) (August 1987).... Suffered from skin rash (February 1989).... Fractured ankle (March 1989).... Traded by Flames to Detroit Red Wings for second-round pick in 1990 draft (later traded to New Jersey Devils) (June 16, 1990).... Fractured right ankle (January 12, 1991); missed 16 games.
HONORS: Named to WCHL All-Star second team (1976-77).... Won Top Defenseman Trophy (1977-78).... Named to WCHL All-Star first team (1977-78).... Named to WHL All-Star first team (1978-79).... Won Emery Edge Award (1987-88).... Named to THE SPORTING NEWS All-Star second team (1987-88).... Named to NHL All-Star second team (1987-88)....

Season Team	League	REGULAR SEASON Gms.	G	A	Pts.	Pen.	PLAYOFFS Gms.	G	A	Pts.	Pen.
76-77—Brandon	WCHL	72	18	66	84	96	—	—	—	—	—
77-78—Brandon	WCHL	65	19	78	97	245	8	2	11	13	20
78-79—Brandon	WHL	66	24	74	98	139	22	9	19	28	34
79-80—Boston	NHL	72	5	11	16	94	10	1	1	2	28
80-81—Boston	NHL	78	11	18	29	148	3	0	1	1	2
81-82—Boston	NHL	78	1	8	9	83	2	0	0	0	2
82-83—Philadelphia	NHL	79	4	21	25	61	3	0	0	0	4
84-85—Philadelphia	NHL	66	8	25	33	81	11	2	1	3	15
85-86—Philadelphia	NHL	80	13	42	55	85	5	2	0	2	2
86-87—Philadelphia	NHL	71	10	29	39	52	26	3	5	8	30
87-88—Calgary	NHL	80	7	35	42	98	9	2	3	5	22
88-89—Calgary	NHL	72	5	17	22	96	22	0	3	3	30
89-90—Calgary	NHL	79	4	15	19	78	6	0	2	2	8
90-91—Detroit	NHL	64	0	13	13	81	7	1	1	2	21
91-92—Detroit	NHL	79	7	22	29	118	11	0	1	1	8
NHL totals		898	75	256	331	1075	115	11	18	29	172

McDONOUGH, HUBIE
C, ISLANDERS

PERSONAL: Born July 8, 1963, at Manchester, N.H. . . . . 5-9/173. . . . Shoots left. . . . Full name: Hubert B. McDonough III. **HIGH SCHOOL:** Memorial (Manchester, N.H.). **COLLEGE:** St. Anselm (N.H.).

TRANSACTIONS/CAREER NOTES: Signed as free agent by Los Angeles Kings (October 1987). . . . Traded by Kings with D Ken Baumgartner to New York Islanders for RW Mikko Makela (November 29, 1989). . . . Injured knee (September 1990). . . . Fractured left thumb (October 22, 1991).

			REGULAR SEASON					PLAYOFFS			
Season Team	League	Gms.	G	A	Pts.	Pen.	Gms.	G	A	Pts.	Pen.
82-83—St. Anselm College	ECAC-II	27	24	21	45	12	—	—	—	—	—
83-84—St. Anselm College	ECAC-II	26	37	15	52	20	—	—	—	—	—
84-85—St. Anselm College	ECAC-II	26	41	30	71	48	—	—	—	—	—
85-86—St. Anselm College	ECAC-II	25	22	20	42	16	—	—	—	—	—
86-87—Flint	IHL	82	27	52	79	59	6	3	2	5	0
87-88—New Haven	AHL	78	30	29	59	43	—	—	—	—	—
88-89—New Haven	AHL	74	37	55	92	41	17	10	*21	*31	6
—Los Angeles	NHL	4	0	1	1	0	—	—	—	—	—
89-90—Los Angeles	NHL	22	3	4	7	10	—	—	—	—	—
—New York Islanders	NHL	54	18	11	29	26	5	1	0	1	4
90-91—Capital District	AHL	17	9	9	18	4	—	—	—	—	—
—New York Islanders	NHL	52	6	6	12	10	—	—	—	—	—
91-92—Capital District	AHL	21	11	18	29	14	—	—	—	—	—
—New York Islanders	NHL	33	7	2	9	15	—	—	—	—	—
NHL totals		165	34	24	58	61	5	1	0	1	4

McDOUGALL, BILL
C, OILERS

PERSONAL: Born August 10, 1966, at Mississauga, Ont. . . . 6-0/180. . . . Shoots right. . . . Full name: William Henry McDougall. **TRANSACTIONS/CAREER NOTES:** Signed as free agent by Detroit Red Wings (March 1990). . . . Traded by Red Wings to Edmonton Oilers for C Max Middendorf (February 22, 1992).
HONORS: Won ECHL Most Valuable Player Award (1989-90). . . . Won ECHL Rookie of the Year Award (1989-90). . . . Named to ECHL All-Star first team (1989-90).

			REGULAR SEASON					PLAYOFFS			
Season Team	League	Gms.	G	A	Pts.	Pen.	Gms.	G	A	Pts.	Pen.
89-90—Erie	ECHL	57	*80	68	*148	226	7	5	5	10	20
—Adirondack	AHL	11	10	7	17	4	2	1	1	2	2
90-91—Detroit	NHL	2	0	1	1	0	1	0	0	0	0
—Adirondack	AHL	71	47	53	100	192	2	1	2	3	2
91-92—Adirondack	AHL	45	28	24	52	112	—	—	—	—	—
—Cape Breton	AHL	22	8	18	26	36	4	0	1	1	8
NHL totals		2	0	1	1	0	1	0	0	0	0

McEACHERN, SHAWN
C/LW, PENGUINS

PERSONAL: Born February 28, 1969, at Waltham, Mass. . . . 6-0/190. . . . Shoots left. . . . Full name: Shawn K. McEachern. **HIGH SCHOOL:** Matignon (Cambridge, Mass.). **COLLEGE:** Boston University.

TRANSACTIONS/CAREER NOTES: Selected by Pittsburgh Penguins in sixth round (sixth Penguins pick, 110th overall) of NHL entry draft (June 13, 1987).
HONORS: Named to Hockey East All-Star second team (1989-90). . . . Named Hockey East Playoff Most Valuable Player (1990-91). . . . Named to NCAA All-America East first team (1990-91). . . . Named to Hockey East All-Star first team (1990-91).

			REGULAR SEASON					PLAYOFFS			
Season Team	League	Gms.	G	A	Pts.	Pen.	Gms.	G	A	Pts.	Pen.
85-86—Matignon H.S.	Mass. H.S.	20	32	20	52		—	—	—	—	—
86-87—Matignon H.S.	Mass. H.S.	16	29	28	57		—	—	—	—	—
87-88—Matignon H.S.	Mass. H.S.		52	40	92		—	—	—	—	—
88-89—Boston University	Hockey East	36	20	28	48	32	—	—	—	—	—
89-90—Boston University	Hockey East	43	25	31	56	78	—	—	—	—	—
90-91—Boston University	Hockey East	41	34	48	82	43	—	—	—	—	—
91-92—U.S. National Team	Int'l	57	26	23	49	38	—	—	—	—	—
—U.S. Olympic Team	Int'l	8	1	0	1	10	—	—	—	—	—
—Pittsburgh	NHL	15	0	4	4	0	19	2	7	9	4
NHL totals		15	0	4	4	0	19	2	7	9	4

McGILL, BOB
D, LIGHTNING

PERSONAL: Born April 27, 1962, at Edmonton, Alta. . . . 6-1/193. . . . Shoots right. . . . Full name: Robert Paul McGill.

TRANSACTIONS/CAREER NOTES: Selected by Toronto Maple Leafs as underage junior in second round (second Maple Leafs pick, 26th overall) of NHL entry draft (June 11, 1980). . . . Suspended three games by NHL (January 1985). . . . Suspended seven games by NHL (March 1, 1986). . . . Injured ankle (October 1986). . . . Traded by Maple Leafs with RW Rick Vaive and LW Steve Thomas to Chicago Blackhawks for LW Al Secord and RW Ed Olczyk (September 3, 1987). . . . Broke cheekbone (November 4, 1989). . . . Fined $500 by NHL for fighting (December 28, 1989). . . . Bruised left foot (May 1990). . . . Broke right foot in preparation for training camp (August 30, 1990; missed six weeks. . . . Selected by San Jose Sharks in NHL expansion draft (May 30, 1991). . . . Traded by Sharks with eighth-round pick in 1992 draft previously acquired form Vancouver Canucks to Detroit Red Wings for LW Johan Garpenlov (March 10, 1992). . . . Selected by Tampa Bay Lightning in NHL expansion draft (June 18, 1992).

M

Season Team	League	REGULAR SEASON Gms.	G	A	Pts.	Pen.	PLAYOFFS Gms.	G	A	Pts.	Pen.
78-79—Abbotsford	BCJHL	46	3	20	23	242	—	—	—	—	—
79-80—Victoria	WHL	70	3	18	21	230	15	0	5	5	64
80-81—Victoria	WHL	66	5	36	41	295	11	1	5	6	67
81-82—Toronto	NHL	68	1	10	11	263	—	—	—	—	—
82-83—Toronto	NHL	30	0	0	0	146	—	—	—	—	—
—St. Catharines	AHL	32	2	5	7	95	—	—	—	—	—
83-84—Toronto	NHL	11	0	2	2	51	—	—	—	—	—
—St. Catharines	AHL	55	1	15	16	217	6	0	0	0	26
84-85—Toronto	NHL	72	0	5	5	250	—	—	—	—	—
85-86—Toronto	NHL	61	1	4	5	141	9	0	0	0	35
86-87—Toronto	NHL	56	1	4	5	103	3	0	0	0	0
87-88—Chicago	NHL	67	4	7	11	131	3	0	0	0	2
88-89—Chicago	NHL	68	0	4	4	155	16	0	0	0	33
89-90—Chicago	NHL	69	2	10	12	204	5	0	0	0	2
90-91—Chicago	NHL	77	4	5	9	151	5	0	0	0	2
91-92—San Jose	NHL	62	3	1	4	70	—	—	—	—	—
—Detroit	NHL	12	0	0	0	21	8	0	0	0	14
NHL totals		653	16	52	68	1686	49	0	0	0	88

McGILL, RYAN
D, FLYERS

PERSONAL: Born February 28, 1969, at Prince Albert, Sask.... 6-2/198.... Shoots right. **TRANSACTIONS/CAREER NOTES:** Sprained ankle (January 1986).... Underwent knee surgery (July 1986).... Selected by Chicago Blackhawks as underage junior in second round (second Blackhawks pick, 29th overall) of NHL entry draft (June 13, 1987).... Traded by Swift Current Broncos to Medicine Hat Tigers for G Kelly Hitching (September 1987).... Traded by Blackhawks with C Mike McNeil to Quebec Nordiques for LW Dan Vincelette and C Paul Gillis (March 5, 1991).... Traded by Nordiques to Blackhawks for C Mike Dagenais (September 26, 1991).... Traded by Blackhawks to Philadelphia Flyers for LW Tony Horacek (February 7, 1992). **HONORS:** Named to IHL All-Star second team (1990-91).

Season Team	League	REGULAR SEASON Gms.	G	A	Pts.	Pen.	PLAYOFFS Gms.	G	A	Pts.	Pen.
85-86—Lethbridge	WHL	64	5	10	15	171	10	0	1	1	9
86-87—Swift Current	WHL	71	12	36	48	226	4	1	0	1	9
87-88—Medicine Hat	WHL	67	5	30	35	224	15	7	3	10	47
88-89—Medicine Hat	WHL	57	26	45	71	172	3	0	2	2	15
—Saginaw	IHL	8	2	0	2	12	6	0	0	0	42
89-90—Indianapolis	IHL	77	11	17	28	215	14	2	2	4	29
90-91—Indianapolis	IHL	63	11	40	51	200	—	—	—	—	—
—Halifax	AHL	7	0	4	4	6	—	—	—	—	—
91-92—Indianapolis	IHL	40	7	19	26	170	—	—	—	—	—
—Chicago	NHL	9	0	2	2	20	—	—	—	—	—
—Hershey	AHL	17	3	5	8	67	6	1	1	2	4
NHL totals		9	0	2	2	20					

McGOWAN, CAL
C, NORTH STARS

PERSONAL: Born June 19, 1970, at Sidney, Neb.... 6-1/185.... Shoots left. **TRANSACTIONS/CAREER NOTES:** Selected by Minnesota North Stars in fourth round (third North Stars pick, 70th overall) of NHL entry draft (June 16, 1990). **HONORS:** Named to WHL All-Star first team (1990-91).

Season Team	League	REGULAR SEASON Gms.	G	A	Pts.	Pen.	PLAYOFFS Gms.	G	A	Pts.	Pen.
86-87—Merritt	BCJHL	50	18	30	48	60	—	—	—	—	—
87-88—Merritt	BCJHL	50	24	62	86	40	4	2	7	9	14
88-89—Kamloops	WHL	72	21	31	52	44	—	—	—	—	—
89-90—Kamloops	WHL	71	33	44	77	78	17	4	5	9	42
90-91—Kamloops	WHL	71	58	81	139	147	12	7	7	14	24
91-92—Kalamazoo	IHL	77	13	30	43	62	1	0	0	0	2

McHUGH, MIKE
LW, WHALERS

PERSONAL: Born August 16, 1965, at Bowdoin, Mass.... 5-10/190.... Shoots left.... Full name: Michael McHugh. **COLLEGE:** Maine. **TRANSACTIONS/CAREER NOTES:** Selected by Minnesota North Stars in NHL supplemental draft (June 10, 1988).... Selected by San Jose Sharks in NHL dispersal draft (May 30, 1991).... Traded by Sharks to Hartford Whalers for LW Paul Fenton (October 18, 1991). **HONORS:** Named to NCAA All-America East second team (1987-88).

Season Team	League	REGULAR SEASON Gms.	G	A	Pts.	Pen.	PLAYOFFS Gms.	G	A	Pts.	Pen.
84-85—University of Maine	Hockey East	25	9	8	17	9	—	—	—	—	—
85-86—University of Maine	Hockey East	38	9	10	19	24	—	—	—	—	—
86-87—University of Maine	Hockey East	42	21	29	50	40	—	—	—	—	—
87-88—University of Maine	Hockey East	44	29	37	66	90	—	—	—	—	—
88-89—Kalamazoo	IHL	70	17	29	46	89	6	3	1	4	17
—Minnesota	NHL	3	0	0	0	2	—	—	—	—	—
89-90—Kalamazoo	IHL	73	14	17	31	96	10	0	6	6	16
—Minnesota	NHL	3	0	0	0	0	—	—	—	—	—

M

Season	Team	League	REGULAR SEASON Gms.	G	A	Pts.	Pen.	PLAYOFFS Gms.	G	A	Pts.	Pen.
90-91—Kalamazoo		IHL	69	27	38	65	82	11	3	8	11	6
—Minnesota		NHL	6	0	0	0	0	—	—	—	—	—
91-92—San Jose		NHL	8	1	0	1	14	—	—	—	—	—
—Springfield		AHL	70	23	31	54	51	11	4	7	11	25
NHL totals			20	1	0	1	16					

McINNIS, MARTY
C/LW, ISLANDERS

PERSONAL: Born June 2, 1970, at Weymouth, Mass. . . . 5-10/165. . . . Shoots right. . . . Full name: Martin Edward McInnis. **HIGH SCHOOL:** Milton Academy (Mass.). **COLLEGE:** Boston College.
TRANSACTIONS/CAREER NOTES: Selected by New York Islanders in eighth round (10th Islanders pick, 163rd overall) of NHL entry draft (June 11, 1988).

Season	Team	League	REGULAR SEASON Gms.	G	A	Pts.	Pen.	PLAYOFFS Gms.	G	A	Pts.	Pen.
86-87—Milton Academy		Mass. H.S.		21	19	40		—	—	—	—	—
87-88—Milton Academy		Mass. H.S.		26	25	51		—	—	—	—	—
88-89—Boston College		Hockey East	39	13	19	32	8	—	—	—	—	—
89-90—Boston College		Hockey East	41	24	29	53	43	—	—	—	—	—
90-91—Boston College		Hockey East	38	21	36	57	40	—	—	—	—	—
91-92—U.S. National Team		Int'l	54	15	19	34	20	—	—	—	—	—
—U.S. Olympic Team		Int'l	8	5	2	7	4	—	—	—	—	—
—New York Islanders		NHL	15	3	5	8	0	—	—	—	—	—
NHL totals			15	3	5	8	0					

McINTYRE, IAN
LW, NORDIQUES

PERSONAL: Born February 12, 1974, at Montreal. . . . 6-0/184. . . . Shoots left. **TRANSACTIONS/CAREER NOTES:** Selected by Quebec Nordiques in fourth round (fifth Nordiques pick, 76th overall) of NHL entry draft (June 20, 1992). **HONORS:** Named to Can.HL All-Rookie team (1991-92). . . . Named to QMJHL All-Rookie team (1991-92).

Season	Team	League	REGULAR SEASON Gms.	G	A	Pts.	Pen.	PLAYOFFS Gms.	G	A	Pts.	Pen.
91-92—Beauport		QMJHL	63	29	32	61	250	—	—	—	—	—

McINTYRE, JOHN
C/LW, KINGS

PERSONAL: Born April 29, 1969, at Ravenswood, Ont. . . . 6-1/175. . . . Shoots left. **TRANSACTIONS/CAREER NOTES:** Broke ankle (November 1985). . . . Severed nerve in right leg (February 1987). . . . Selected by Toronto Maple Leafs as underage junior in third round (third Maple Leafs pick, 49th overall) of NHL entry draft (June 13, 1987). . . . Traded by Maple Leafs to Los Angeles Kings for LW/C Mike Krushelnyski (November 9, 1990). . . . Sprained left thumb (October 22, 1991); missed two games. . . . Broke nose (March 9, 1992); missed five games.
HONORS: Won Bobby Smith Trophy (1986-87).

Season	Team	League	REGULAR SEASON Gms.	G	A	Pts.	Pen.	PLAYOFFS Gms.	G	A	Pts.	Pen.
84-85—Strathroy Jr. B		OHA	48	21	23	44	49	—	—	—	—	—
85-86—Guelph		OHL	30	4	6	10	25	20	1	5	6	31
86-87—Guelph		OHL	47	8	22	30	95	—	—	—	—	—
87-88—Guelph		OHL	39	24	18	42	109	—	—	—	—	—
88-89—Guelph		OHL	52	30	26	56	129	7	5	4	9	25
—Newmarket		AHL	3	0	2	2	7	5	1	1	2	20
89-90—Newmarket		AHL	6	2	2	4	12	—	—	—	—	—
—Toronto		NHL	59	5	12	17	117	2	0	0	0	2
90-91—Toronto		NHL	13	0	3	3	25	—	—	—	—	—
—Los Angeles		NHL	56	8	5	13	115	12	0	1	1	24
91-92—Los Angeles		NHL	73	5	19	24	100	6	0	4	4	12
NHL totals			201	18	39	57	357	20	0	5	5	38

McKAY, RANDY
RW, DEVILS

PERSONAL: Born January 25, 1967, at Montreal. . . . 6-1/185. . . . Shoots right. . . . Full name: Hugh Randall McKay. **COLLEGE:** Michigan Tech. **TRANSACTIONS/CAREER NOTES:** Selected by Detroit Red Wings in sixth round (sixth Red Wings pick, 113th overall) of NHL entry draft (June 15, 1985). . . . Injured knee (February 1989). . . . Lacerated forearm (February 23, 1991). . . . Sent by Red Wings with C Dave Barr to New Jersey Devils as compensation for Red Wings signing free-agent RW Troy Crowder (September 1991).

Season	Team	League	REGULAR SEASON Gms.	G	A	Pts.	Pen.	PLAYOFFS Gms.	G	A	Pts.	Pen.
84-85—Michigan Tech		WCHA	25	4	5	9	32	—	—	—	—	—
85-86—Michigan Tech		WCHA	40	12	22	34	46	—	—	—	—	—
86-87—Michigan Tech		WCHA	39	5	11	16	46	—	—	—	—	—
87-88—Michigan Tech		WCHA	41	17	24	41	70	—	—	—	—	—
—Adirondack		AHL	10	0	3	3	12	6	0	4	4	0

M

Season Team	League	REGULAR SEASON					PLAYOFFS				
		Gms.	G	A	Pts.	Pen.	Gms.	G	A	Pts.	Pen.
88-89—Adirondack	AHL	58	29	34	63	170	14	4	7	11	60
—Detroit	NHL	3	0	0	0	0	2	0	0	0	2
89-90—Detroit	NHL	33	3	6	9	51	—	—	—	—	—
—Adirondack	AHL	36	16	23	39	99	6	3	0	3	35
90-91—Detroit	NHL	47	1	7	8	183	5	0	1	1	41
91-92—New Jersey	NHL	80	17	16	33	246	7	1	3	4	10
NHL totals		163	21	29	50	480	14	1	4	5	53

McKENZIE, JIM
LW, WHALERS

PERSONAL: Born November 3, 1969, at Gull Lake, Sask.... 6-3/210.... Shoots left.
TRANSACTIONS/CAREER NOTES: Selected by Hartford Whalers in fourth round (third Whalers pick, 73rd overall) of NHL entry draft (June 17, 1989).... Injured elbow (January 31, 1992); missed two games.

Season Team	League	REGULAR SEASON					PLAYOFFS				
		Gms.	G	A	Pts.	Pen.	Gms.	G	A	Pts.	Pen.
85-86—Moose Jaw	WHL	3	0	2	2	0	—	—	—	—	—
86-87—Moose Jaw	WHL	65	5	3	8	125	9	0	0	0	7
87-88—Moose Jaw	WHL	62	1	17	18	134	—	—	—	—	—
88-89—Victoria	WHL	67	15	27	42	176	8	1	4	5	30
89-90—Binghamton	AHL	56	4	12	16	149	—	—	—	—	—
—Hartford	NHL	5	0	0	0	4	—	—	—	—	—
90-91—Springfield	AHL	24	3	4	7	102	—	—	—	—	—
—Hartford	NHL	41	4	3	7	108	6	0	0	0	8
91-92—Hartford	NHL	67	5	1	6	87	—	—	—	—	—
NHL totals		113	9	4	13	199	6	0	0	0	8

McKIM, ANDREW
C

PERSONAL: Born July 6, 1970, at St. Johns, N.B.... 5-7/170.... Shoots right.... Full name: Andrew Harry McKim.
TRANSACTIONS/CAREER NOTES: Traded by Verdun Jr. Canadiens with C Trevor Boland to Hull Olympiques for third-round pick in 1989 draft (G Martin Brodeur) (May 26, 1989). ...Signed as free agent by Calgary Flames (October 5, 1990).
HONORS: Won Can.HL Most Sportsmanlike Player of the Year Award (1989-1990).... Won Frank J. Selke Trophy (1989-90). ... Won Michel Briere Trophy (1989-90).... Named to QMJHL All-Star first team (1989-90).

Season Team	League	REGULAR SEASON					PLAYOFFS				
		Gms.	G	A	Pts.	Pen.	Gms.	G	A	Pts.	Pen.
86-87—Verdun	QMJHL	70	28	59	87	12	—	—	—	—	—
87-88—Verdun	QMJHL	62	27	32	59	27	—	—	—	—	—
88-89—Verdun	QMJHL	68	50	56	106	36	—	—	—	—	—
89-90—Hull	QMJHL	70	66	64	130	44	11	8	10	18	8
90-91—Salt Lake City	IHL	74	30	30	60	48	4	0	2	2	6
91-92—St. John's	AHL	79	43	50	93	79	16	11	12	23	4

McLAUGHLIN, MIKE
LW, SABRES

PERSONAL: Born March 29, 1970, at Springfield, Mass.... 6-1/175.... Shoots left. ... Full name: Michael Sean McLaughlin.
HIGH SCHOOL: Choate Rosemary Hall (Wallingford, Conn.).
COLLEGE: Vermont.
TRANSACTIONS/CAREER NOTES: Selected by Buffalo Sabres in sixth round (seventh Sabres pick, 118th overall) of NHL entry draft (June 11, 1988).

Season Team	League	REGULAR SEASON					PLAYOFFS				
		Gms.	G	A	Pts.	Pen.	Gms.	G	A	Pts.	Pen.
86-87—Choate Rosemary Hall	Conn. H.S.		19	18	37		—	—	—	—	—
87-88—Choate Rosemary Hall	Conn. H.S.		17	18	35		—	—	—	—	—
88-89—University of Vermont	ECAC	32	5	6	11	12	—	—	—	—	—
89-90—University of Vermont	ECAC	29	11	12	23	37	—	—	—	—	—
90-91—University of Vermont	ECAC	32	12	14	26	26	—	—	—	—	—
91-92—University of Vermont	ECAC	30	9	9	18	34	—	—	—	—	—

McLEAN, KIRK
G, CANUCKS

PERSONAL: Born June 26, 1966, at Willowdale, Ont.... 6-0/185.... Shoots left.
TRANSACTIONS/CAREER NOTES: Selected by New Jersey Devils as underage junior in sixth round (sixth Devils pick, 107th overall) of NHL entry draft (June 9, 1984).... Traded by Devils with C Greg Adams to Vancouver Canucks for C Patrik Sundstrom and fourth-round pick in 1988 draft (LW Matt Ruchty) (September 1987).... Suffered tendinitis in left wrist (February 25, 1991).
HONORS: Named to THE SPORTING NEWS All-Star second team (1991-92).... Named to NHL All-Star second team (1991-92).

Season Team	League	REGULAR SEASON							PLAYOFFS						
		Gms.	Min.	W	L	T	GA	SO	Avg.	Gms.	Min.	W	L	GA	SO	Avg.
83-84—Oshawa	OHL	17	940	5	9	0	67	0	4.28	—	—	—	—	—	—	—
84-85—Oshawa	OHL	47	2581	23	17	2	143	1	*3.32	5	271	1	3	21	0	4.65
85-86—Oshawa	OHL	51	2830	24	21	2	169	1	3.58	4	201	1	2	18	0	5.37
—New Jersey	NHL	2	111	1	1	0	11	0	5.95	—	—	—	—	—	—	—

Season Team	League	REGULAR SEASON							PLAYOFFS						
		Gms.	Min.	W	L	T	GA	SO	Avg.	Gms.	Min.	W	L	GA	SO	Avg.
86-87—New Jersey	NHL	4	160	1	1	0	10	0	3.75	—	—	—	—	—	—	—
—Maine	AHL	45	2606	15	23	4	140	1	3.22	—	—	—	—	—	—	—
87-88—Vancouver	NHL	41	2380	11	27	3	147	1	3.71	—	—	—	—	—	—	—
88-89—Vancouver	NHL	42	2477	20	17	3	127	4	3.08	5	302	2	3	18	0	3.58
89-90—Vancouver	NHL	*63	*3739	21	30	10	*216	0	3.47	—	—	—	—	—	—	—
90-91—Vancouver	NHL	41	1969	10	22	3	131	0	3.99	2	123	1	1	7	0	3.41
91-92—Vancouver	NHL	65	3852	†38	17	9	176	†5	2.74	13	785	6	7	33	†2	2.52
NHL totals		258	14688	102	115	28	818	10	3.34	20	1210	9	11	58	2	2.88

McLENNAN, JAMIE
G, ISLANDERS

PERSONAL: Born June 30, 1971, at Edmonton, Alta. . . . 6-0/ 190. . . . Shoots left.
TRANSACTIONS/CAREER NOTES: Selected by New York Islanders in third round (third Islanders pick, 48th overall) of NHL entry draft (June 22, 1991).
HONORS: Won Del Wilson Trophy (1990-91). . . . Named to WHL All-Star first team (1990-91).

Season Team	League	REGULAR SEASON							PLAYOFFS						
		Gms.	Min.	W	L	T	GA	SO	Avg.	Gms.	Min.	W	L	GA	SO	Avg.
88-89—Spokane Chiefs	WHL	11	578				63	0	6.54	—	—	—	—	—	—	—
—Lethbridge	WHl	7	368				22	0	3.50	—	—	—	—	—	—	—
89-90—Lethbridge	WHL	34	1690	20	4	2	110	1	3.91	13	677	6	5	44	0	3.90
90-91—Lethbridge	WHL	56	3230	32	18	4	205	0	3.81	*16	*970	8	8	*56	0	3.46
91-92—Capital District	AHL	18	952	4	10	2	60	1	3.78	—	—	—	—	—	—	—
—Richmond	ECHL	32	1837	16	12	2	114	0	3.72	—	—	—	—	—	—	—

McLLWAIN, DAVID
RW/C, MAPLE LEAFS

PERSONAL: Born January 9, 1967, at Seaforth, Ont. . . . 6-0/ 190. . . . Shoots right.
TRANSACTIONS/CAREER NOTES: Traded by Kitchener Rangers with D John Keller and RW Todd Stromback to North Bay Centennials for RW Ron Sanko, RW Peter Lisy, Richard Hawkins and D Brett MacDonald (November 1985). . . . Selected by Pittsburgh Penguins as underage junior in ninth round (ninth Penguins pick, 172nd overall) of NHL entry draft (June 21, 1986). . . . Traded by Penguins with C/LW Randy Cunneyworth and G Richard Tabaracci to Winnipeg Jets for RW Andrew McBain, D Jim Kyte and LW Randy Gilhen (June 17, 1989). . . . Injured wrist (October 28, 1990). . . . Tore medial collateral ligament of right knee (December 3, 1990); missed 16 games. . . . Traded by Jets with D Gord Donnelly, sixth-round pick in 1992 draft and future considerations to Buffalo Sabres for LW Darrin Shannon, LW Mike Hartman and D Dean Kennedy (October 11, 1991). . . . Traded by Sabres with C Pierre Turgeon, RW Benoit Hogue and D Uwe Krupp to New York Islanders for C Pat LaFontaine, LW Randy Wood, D Randy Hillier and future considerations (October 25, 1991). . . . Traded by Islanders with LW Ken Baumgartner to Toronto Maple Leafs for C Claude Loiselle and RW Daniel Marois (March 10, 1992).
HONORS: Named to OHL All-Star second team (1986-87).

Season Team	League	REGULAR SEASON				PLAYOFFS			
		Gms.	G	A	Pts.	Pen.	Gms.	G	A	Pts.	Pen.
84-85—Kitchener	OHL	61	13	21	34	29	—	—	—	—	—
85-86—Kitchener	OHL	13	7	7	14	12	—	—	—	—	—
—North Bay	OIIL	51	30	28	58	25	10	4	4	8	2
86-87—North Bay	OHL	60	46	73	119	35	24	7	18	25	40
87-88—Muskegon	IHL	9	4	6	10	23	6	2	3	5	8
—Pittsburgh	NHL	66	11	8	19	40	—	—	—	—	—
88-89—Muskegon	IHL	46	37	35	72	51	7	8	2	10	6
—Pittsburgh	NHL	24	1	2	3	4	3	0	1	1	0
89-90—Winnipeg	NHL	80	25	26	51	60	7	0	1	1	2
90-91—Winnipeg	NHL	60	14	11	25	46	—	—	—	—	—
91-92—Winnipeg	NHL	3	1	1	2	2	—	—	—	—	—
—Buffalo	NHL	5	0	0	0	2	—	—	—	—	—
—New York Islanders	NHL	54	8	15	23	28	—	—	—	—	—
—Toronto	NHL	11	1	2	3	4	—	—	—	—	—
NHL totals		303	61	65	126	186	10	0	2	2	2

McNEILL, MIKE
RW, NORDIQUES

PERSONAL: Born July 22, 1966, at Winona, Minn. . . . 6-1/ 175. . . . Shoots right. . . . Full name: Michael McNeill.
TRANSACTIONS/CAREER NOTES: Selected by St. Louis Blues in NHL supplemental draft (June 10, 1988). . . . Signed as free agent by Chicago Blackhawks (September 1989). . . . Traded by Blackhawks with D Ryan McGill to Quebec Nordiques for LW Daniel Vincelette and C Paul Gillis (March 5, 1991). . . . Separated shoulder (February 15, 1992).
HONORS: Won N.R. (Bud) Poile Trophy (1989-90).

Season Team	League	REGULAR SEASON				PLAYOFFS			
		Gms.	G	A	Pts.	Pen.	Gms.	G	A	Pts.	Pen.
84-85—University of Notre Dame	Indep.	28	16	26	42	12	—	—	—	—	—
85-86—University of Notre Dame	Indep.	34	18	29	47	32	—	—	—	—	—
86-87—University of Notre Dame	Indep.	30	21	16	37	24	—	—	—	—	—
87-88—University of Notre Dame	Indep.	32	28	44	72	12	—	—	—	—	—
88-89—Fort Wayne	IHL	75	27	35	62	12	11	1	5	6	2
—Moncton	AHL	1	0	0	0	0	—	—	—	—	—
89-90—Indianapolis	IHL	74	17	24	41	15	14	6	4	10	21

M

Season Team	League	REGULAR SEASON					PLAYOFFS				
		Gms.	G	A	Pts.	Pen.	Gms.	G	A	Pts.	Pen.
90-91—Indianapolis	IHL	33	16	9	25	19	—	—	—	—	—
—Chicago	NHL	23	2	2	4	6	—	—	—	—	—
—Quebec	NHL	14	2	5	7	4	—	—	—	—	—
91-92—Quebec	NHL	26	1	4	5	8	—	—	—	—	—
—Halifax	AHL	30	10	8	18	20	—	—	—	—	—
NHL totals		63	5	11	16	18					

McPHEE, MICHAEL
LW, CANADIENS

PERSONAL: Born February 14, 1960, at Sydney, N.S. . . . . 6-1/203. . . . Shoots left. . . . Full name: Michael Joseph McPhee.
COLLEGE: Rensselaer Polytechnic Institute (N.Y.).
TRANSACTIONS/CAREER NOTES: Selected by Montreal Canadiens in sixth round (eighth Canadiens pick, 124th overall) of NHL entry draft (June 11, 1980). . . . Broke hand (September 1982). . . . Injured ankle (January 10, 1986); missed 10 games. . . . Broke little toe on left foot (February 1989). . . . Pulled muscle in rib cage (April 8, 1989). . . . Tore abdominal muscle (October 7, 1989); missed 13 games. . . . Injured groin, knee and thumb (November 13, 1990); missed 16 games. . . . Bruised thigh (February 26, 1992); missed one game.

Season Team	League	REGULAR SEASON					PLAYOFFS				
		Gms.	G	A	Pts.	Pen.	Gms.	G	A	Pts.	Pen.
78-79—R.P.I.	ECAC	26	14	19	33	16	—	—	—	—	—
79-80—R.P.I.	ECAC	27	15	21	36	22	—	—	—	—	—
80-81—R.P.I.	ECAC	29	28	18	46	22	—	—	—	—	—
81-82—R.P.I.	ECAC	6	0	3	3	4	—	—	—	—	—
82-83—Nova Scotia	AHL	42	10	15	25	29	7	1	1	2	14
83-84—Nova Scotia	AHL	67	22	33	55	101	—	—	—	—	—
—Montreal	NHL	14	5	2	7	41	15	1	0	1	31
84-85—Montreal	NHL	70	17	22	39	120	12	4	1	5	32
85-86—Montreal	NHL	70	19	21	40	69	20	3	4	7	45
86-87—Montreal	NHL	79	18	21	39	58	17	7	2	9	13
87-88—Montreal	NHL	77	23	20	43	53	11	4	3	7	8
88-89—Montreal	NHL	73	19	22	41	74	20	4	7	11	30
89-90—Montreal	NHL	56	23	18	41	47	9	1	1	2	16
90-91—Montreal	NHL	64	22	21	43	56	13	1	7	8	12
91-92—Montreal	NHL	78	16	15	31	63	8	1	1	2	4
NHL totals		581	162	162	324	581	125	26	26	52	191

McRAE, BASIL
LW, LIGHTNING

PERSONAL: Born January 5, 1961, at Beaverton, Ont. . . . 6-2/205. . . . Shoots left. . . . Full name: Basil Paul McRae. . . . Brother of Chris McRae, left winger, Toronto Maple Leafs and Detroit Red Wings (1987-88 through 1989-90).
TRANSACTIONS/CAREER NOTES: Selected by Quebec Nordiques as underage junior in fifth round (third Nordiques pick, 87th overall) of NHL entry draft (June 11, 1980). . . . Traded by Nordiques to Toronto Maple Leafs for D Richard Turmel (August 12, 1983). . . . Signed as free agent by Detroit Red Wings (August 1985). . . . Traded by Red Wings with LW John Ogrodnick and RW Doug Shedden to Nordiques for LW Brent Ashton, RW Mark Kumpel and D Gilbert Delorme (January 17, 1987). . . . Signed as free agent by Minnesota North Stars (July 1987). . . . Strained right knee ligaments (October 10, 1989); missed nine games. . . . Suspended five games and fined $500 by NHL for fighting (December 28, 1989). . . . Strained abdominal muscle (October 1990). . . . Underwent abdominal surgery (November 29, 1990); missed 35 games. . . . Severed tendon (February 29, 1992); missed final 17 games of regular season. . . . Selected by Tampa Bay Lightning in NHL expansion draft (June 18, 1992).

Season Team	League	REGULAR SEASON					PLAYOFFS				
		Gms.	G	A	Pts.	Pen.	Gms.	G	A	Pts.	Pen.
77-78—Seneca Jr. B	OHA	36	21	38	59	80	—	—	—	—	—
78-79—London	OMJHL	66	13	28	41	79	—	—	—	—	—
79-80—London	OMJHL	67	23	35	58	116	5	0	0	0	18
80-81—London	OMJHL	65	29	23	52	266	—	—	—	—	—
81-82—Fredericton	AHL	47	11	15	26	175	—	—	—	—	—
—Quebec	NHL	20	4	3	7	69	9	1	0	1	34
82-83—Fredericton	AHL	53	22	19	41	146	12	1	5	6	75
—Quebec	NHL	22	1	1	2	59	—	—	—	—	—
83-84—Toronto	NHL	3	0	0	0	19	—	—	—	—	—
—St. Catharines	AHL	78	14	25	39	187	6	0	0	0	40
84-85—St. Catharines	AHL	72	30	25	55	186	—	—	—	—	—
—Toronto	NHL	1	0	0	0	0	—	—	—	—	—
85-86—Detroit	NHL	4	0	0	0	5	—	—	—	—	—
—Adirondack	AHL	69	22	30	52	259	17	5	4	9	101
86-87—Detroit	NHL	36	2	2	4	193	—	—	—	—	—
—Quebec	NHL	33	9	5	14	149	13	3	1	4	*99
87-88—Minnesota	NHL	80	5	11	16	378	—	—	—	—	—
88-89—Minnesota	NHL	78	12	19	31	365	5	0	0	0	58
89-90—Minnesota	NHL	66	9	17	26	*351	7	1	0	1	22
90-91—Minnesota	NHL	40	1	3	4	224	22	1	1	2	*94
91-92—Minnesota	NHL	59	5	8	13	245	—	—	—	—	—
NHL totals		442	48	69	117	2057	56	6	2	8	307

McRAE, KEN
C, MAPLE LEAFS

PERSONAL: Born April 23, 1968, at Finch, Ont. . . . 6-1/195. . . . Shoots right. . . . Full name: Kenneth Duncan McRae.
TRANSACTIONS/CAREER NOTES: Selected by Quebec Nordiques as underage junior in first round (first Nordiques pick, 18th overall) of NHL entry draft (June 21, 1986). . . . Traded by Sudbury Wolves

with C Andy Paquette and D Ken Alexander to Hamilton Steelhawks for C Dan Hie, C Joe Simon, RW Steve Locke, C Shawn Heaphy and D Jordan Fois (December 1986).... Lacerated right elbow (December 26, 1989); missed seven games.... Bruised shoulder (March 10, 1990).... Traded by Nordiques to Toronto Maple Leafs for D Leonard Esau (July 21, 1992).

Season Team	League	REGULAR SEASON					PLAYOFFS				
		Gms.	G	A	Pts.	Pen.	Gms.	G	A	Pts.	Pen.
84-85—Hawkesbury	COJHL	51	38	50	88	77	—	—	—	—	—
85-86—Sudbury	OHL	66	25	40	65	127	4	2	1	3	12
86-87—Sudbury	OHL	21	12	15	27	40	—	—	—	—	—
—Hamilton	OHL	20	7	12	19	25	7	1	1	2	12
87-88—Fredericton	AHL	—	—	—	—	—	3	0	0	0	8
—Quebec	NHL	1	0	0	0	0	—	—	—	—	—
—Hamilton	OHL	62	30	55	85	158	14	13	9	22	35
88-89—Halifax	AHL	41	20	21	41	87	—	—	—	—	—
—Quebec	NHL	37	6	11	17	68	—	—	—	—	—
89-90—Quebec	NHL	66	7	8	15	191	—	—	—	—	—
90-91—Quebec	NHL	12	0	0	0	36	—	—	—	—	—
—Halifax	AHL	60	10	36	46	193	—	—	—	—	—
91-92—Halifax	AHL	52	30	41	71	184	—	—	—	—	—
—Quebec	NHL	10	0	1	1	31	—	—	—	—	—
NHL totals		126	13	20	33	326					

McREYNOLDS, BRIAN
C, RANGERS

PERSONAL: Born January 5, 1965, at Penetanguishene, Ont.... 6-1/180.... Shoots left.
COLLEGE: Michigan State.
TRANSACTIONS/CAREER NOTES: Selected by New York Rangers as underage junior in sixth round (sixth Rangers pick, 112th overall) of NHL entry draft (June 15, 1985).... Signed as free agent by Winnipeg Jets (July 1989).... Traded by Jets to Rangers for C Simon Wheeldon (July 10, 1990).

Season Team	League	REGULAR SEASON					PLAYOFFS				
		Gms.	G	A	Pts.	Pen.	Gms.	G	A	Pts.	Pen.
84-85—Orillia	OHA	48	40	54	94		—	—	—	—	—
85-86—Michigan State	CCHA	45	14	24	38	78	—	—	—	—	—
86-87—Michigan State	CCHA	45	16	24	40	68	—	—	—	—	—
87-88—Michigan State	CCHA	43	10	24	34	50	—	—	—	—	—
88-89—Canadian National Team	Int'l	58	5	25	30	59	—	—	—	—	—
89-90—Winnipeg	NHL	9	0	2	2	4	—	—	—	—	—
—Moncton	AHL	72	18	41	59	87	10	0	4	4	6
90-91—Binghamton	AHL	77	30	42	72	74	—	—	—	—	—
—New York Rangers	NHL	1	0	0	0	0	7	2	2	4	12
91-92—Binghamton	AHL	48	19	28	47	22					
NHL totals		10	0	2	2	4					

McSORLEY, MARTY
RW/D, KINGS

PERSONAL: Born May 18, 1963, at Hamilton, Ont.... 6-1/225.... Shoots right.... Full name: Martin J. McSorley.
TRANSACTIONS/CAREER NOTES: Signed as free agent by Pittsburgh Penguins (April 1983).... Traded by Penguins with C Tim Hrynewich to Edmonton Oilers for G Gilles Meloche (August 1985).... Suspended by NHL for an AHL incident (March 1987).... Sprained knee (November 1987).... Suspended three playoff games by NHL for spearing (April 23, 1988).... Traded by Oilers with C Wayne Gretzky and LW/C Mike Krushelnyski to Los Angeles Kings for C Jimmy Carson, LW Martin Gelinas, first-round picks in 1989 (traded to New Jersey), 1991 and 1993 drafts and cash (August 9, 1988).... Injured shoulder (December 31, 1988).... Sprained knee (February 1989).... Suspended four games by NHL for game-misconduct penalties (1989-90).... Twisted right knee (October 14, 1990); missed four games.... Twisted ankle (February 9, 1991).... Suspended three games by NHL for striking another player with a gloved hand (March 2, 1991).... Suffered from throat virus (November 23, 1991); missed six games.... Sprained shoulder (February 19, 1992); missed three games.
HONORS: Shared Alka-Seltzer Plus Award with Theoren Fleury (1990-91).

Season Team	League	REGULAR SEASON					PLAYOFFS				
		Gms.	G	A	Pts.	Pen.	Gms.	G	A	Pts.	Pen.
81-82—Belleville Bulls	OHL	58	6	13	19	234	—	—	—	—	—
82-83—Belleville Bulls	OHL	70	10	41	51	183	4	0	0	0	7
—Baltimore	AHL	2	0	0	0	22	—	—	—	—	—
83-84—Pittsburgh	NHL	72	2	7	9	224	—	—	—	—	—
84-85—Baltimore	AHL	58	6	24	30	154	14	0	7	7	47
—Pittsburgh	NHL	15	0	0	0	15	—	—	—	—	—
85-86—Edmonton	NHL	59	11	12	23	265	8	0	2	2	50
—Nova Scotia	AHL	9	2	4	6	34	—	—	—	—	—
86-87—Edmonton	NHL	41	2	4	6	159	21	4	3	7	65
—Nova Scotia	AHL	7	2	2	4	48	—	—	—	—	—
87-88—Edmonton	NHL	60	9	17	26	223	16	0	3	3	67
88-89—Los Angeles	NHL	66	10	17	27	350	11	0	2	2	33
89-90—Los Angeles	NHL	75	15	21	36	322	10	1	3	4	18
90-91—Los Angeles	NHL	61	7	32	39	221	12	0	0	0	58
91-92—Los Angeles	NHL	71	7	22	29	268	6	1	0	1	21
NHL totals		520	63	132	195	2047	84	6	13	19	312

McSWEEN, DON
D, SABRES

PERSONAL: Born June 9, 1964, at Detroit. . . . 5-11/197. . . . Shoots left. . . . Full name: Donald Kennedy McSween.
COLLEGE: Michigan State.
TRANSACTIONS/CAREER NOTES: Selected by Buffalo Sabres in eighth round (10th Sabres pick, 154th overall) of NHL entry draft (June 8, 1983).
HONORS: Named to CCHA All-Star first team (1986-87). . . . Named to NCAA All-America West second team (1986-87). . . . Named to NCAA All-Tournament team (1986-87). . . . Named to AHL All-Star first team (1989-90).

			REGULAR SEASON					PLAYOFFS				
Season Team	League	Gms.	G	A	Pts.	Pen.	Gms.	G	A	Pts.	Pen.
83-84—Michigan State	CCHA	46	10	26	36	30	—	—	—	—	—
84-85—Michigan State	CCHA	44	2	23	25	52	—	—	—	—	—
85-86—Michigan State	CCHA	45	9	29	38	18	—	—	—	—	—
86-87—Michigan State	CCHA	45	7	23	30	34	—	—	—	—	—
87-88—Rochester	AHL	63	9	29	38	108	6	0	1	1	15
—Buffalo	NHL	5	0	1	1	4	—	—	—	—	—
88-89—Rochester	AHL	66	7	22	29	45	—	—	—	—	—
89-90—Buffalo	NHL	4	0	0	0	6	—	—	—	—	—
—Rochester	AHL	70	16	43	59	43	17	3	10	13	12
90-91—Rochester	AHL	74	7	44	51	57	15	2	5	7	8
91-92—Rochester	AHL	75	6	32	38	60	16	5	6	11	18
NHL totals		9	0	1	1	10					

MEARS, GLEN
D, FLAMES

PERSONAL: Born July 14, 1972, at Anchorage, Alaska. . . . 6-3/215. . . . Shoots right. . . . Full name: Glen Anthony Mears.
COLLEGE: Bowling Green State.
TRANSACTIONS/CAREER NOTES: Selected by Calgary Flames in third round (fifth Flames pick, 62nd overall) of NHL entry draft (June 16, 1990).

			REGULAR SEASON					PLAYOFFS				
Season Team	League	Gms.	G	A	Pts.	Pen.	Gms.	G	A	Pts.	Pen.
88-89—Rochester	USHL	39	2	7	9	56	—	—	—	—	—
89-90—Rochester	USHL	46	5	20	25	95	—	—	—	—	—
90-91—Bowling Green State	CCHA	40	0	7	7	54	—	—	—	—	—
91-92—Bowling Green State	CCHA	32	1	2	3	38	—	—	—	—	—

MELANSON, DEAN
D, SABRES

PERSONAL: Born November 19, 1973, at Antigonish, N.S. . . . 6-0/213. . . . Shoots right.
TRANSACTIONS/CAREER NOTES: Selected by Buffalo Sabres in fourth round (fourth Sabres pick, 80th overall) of NHL entry draft (June 20, 1992).

			REGULAR SEASON					PLAYOFFS				
Season Team	League	Gms.	G	A	Pts.	Pen.	Gms.	G	A	Pts.	Pen.
90-91—St. Hyacinthe	QMJHL	69	10	17	27	110	4	0	1	1	2
91-92—St. Hyacinthe	QMJHL	42	8	19	27	158	6	1	2	3	25

MELANSON, ROLLIE
G, CANADIENS

PERSONAL: Born June 28, 1960, at Moncton, N.B. . . . 5-10/185. . . . Shoots left. . . . Full name: Roland Joseph Melanson.
TRANSACTIONS/CAREER NOTES: Selected by New York Islanders as underage junior in third round (fourth Islanders pick, 59th overall) of NHL entry draft (August 9, 1979). . . . Traded by Islanders to Minnesota North Stars for first-round pick in 1985 draft (RW Brad Dalgarno) (November 1984). . . . Pulled groin (November 19, 1985); missed three weeks before being traded. . . . Traded by North Stars to New York Rangers for second-round pick in 1986 draft (D Neil Wilkinson) and fourth-round pick in 1987 draft (C John Weisbrod) (December 9, 1985). . . . Traded by Rangers with D Grant Ledyard to Los Angeles Kings for LW Brian MacLellan and fourth-round pick in 1987 draft (C Michael Sullivan) (December 9, 1985). . . . Injured groin (January 15, 1986); missed 13 games. . . . Sprained left knee (October 6, 1988). . . . Signed as free agent by New Jersey Devils (August 1989). . . . Traded by Devils with LW Kirk Muller to Montreal Canadiens for RW Stephane Richer and RW Tom Chorske (September 20, 1991). . . . Injured groin (January 11, 1992).
HONORS: Named to OMJHL All-Star second team (1978-79). . . . Won Ken McKenzie Trophy (1980-81). . . . Named to CHL All-Star first team (1980-81). . . . Shared William M. Jennings Trophy with Billy Smith (1982-83). . . . Named to NHL All-Star second team (1982-83).

			REGULAR SEASON							PLAYOFFS					
Season Team	League	Gms.	Min.	W	L	T	GA	SO	Avg.	Gms.	Min.	W	L	GA	SO	Avg.
77-78—Windsor	OMJHL	44	2592				195	1	4.51	—	—	—	—	—	—	—
78-79—Windsor	OMJHL	*62	*3461				254	1	4.40	7	392			31	0	4.74
79-80—Windsor	OMJHL	†22	1099	11	8	0	90	0	4.91	—	—	—	—	—	—	—
—Oshawa	OMJHL	38	2240	26	12	0	136	*3	3.64	7	420	3	4	32	0	4.57
80-81—Indianapolis	CHL	*52	3056	31	16	3	131	2	*2.57	—	—	—	—	—	—	—
—New York Islanders	NHL	11	*620	8	1	1	32	0	3.10	3	92	1	0	6	0	3.91
81-82—New York Islanders	NHL	36	2115	22	7	6	114	0	3.23	3	64	0	1	5	0	4.69
82-83—New York Islanders	NHL	44	2460	24	12	5	109	1	2.66	5	238	2	2	10	0	2.52
83-84—New York Islanders	NHL	37	2019	20	11	2	110	0	3.27	6	87	0	1	5	0	3.45
84-85—New York Islanders	NHL	8	425	3	3	0	35	0	4.94	—	—	—	—	—	—	—
—Minnesota	NHL	20	1142	5	10	3	78	0	4.10	—	—	—	—	—	—	—
85-86—New Haven	AHL	3	179	1	2	0	13	0	4.36	—	—	—	—	—	—	—
—Minnesota	NHL	6	325	2	1	2	24	0	4.43	—	—	—	—	—	—	—
—Los Angeles	NHL	22	1246	4	16	1	87	0	4.19	—	—	—	—	—	—	—

Season	Team	League		REGULAR SEASON								PLAYOFFS					
			Gms.	Min.	W	L	T	GA	SO	Avg.	Gms.	Min.	W	L	GA	SO	Avg.
86-87	Los Angeles	NHL	46	2734	18	21	6	168	1	3.69	5	260	1	4	24	0	5.54
87-88	Los Angeles	NHL	47	2676	17	20	7	195	2	4.37	1	60	0	1	9	0	9.00
88-89	Los Angeles	NHL	4	178	1	1	0	19	0	6.40	—	—	—	—	—	—	—
	New Haven	AHL	29	1734	11	15	3	106	1	3.67	*17	*1019	9	8	*74	1	4.36
89-90	Utica	AHL	48	2737	24	19	3	167	1	3.66	5	298	1	4	20	0	4.03
90-91	Utica	AHL	54	3058	23	28	1	*208	0	4.08	—	—	—	—	—	—	—
	New Jersey	NHL	1	20	0	0	0	2	0	6.00	—	—	—	—	—	—	—
91-92	Montreal	NHL	9	492	5	3	0	22	2	2.68	—	—	—	—	—	—	—
NHL totals			291	16452	129	106	33	995	6	3.63	23	801	4	9	59	0	4.42

MELLANBY, SCOTT
RW, OILERS

PERSONAL: Born June 11, 1966, at Montreal. . . . 6-1/205. . . . Shoots right. . . . Full name: Scott Edgar Mellanby.
HIGH SCHOOL: Henry Carr (Rexdale, Ont.).
COLLEGE: Wisconsin.
TRANSACTIONS/CAREER NOTES: Selected by Philadelphia Flyers as underage junior in second round (first Flyers pick, 27th overall) of NHL entry draft (June 9, 1984). . . . Lacerated index finger on right hand (October 1987). . . . Severed nerve and damaged tendon in left forearm (August 1989); missed first 20 games of season. Suffered viral infection (November 1989). . . . Traded by Flyers with LW Craig Berube and C Craig Fisher to Edmonton Oilers for RW Dave Brown, D Corey Foster and rights to RW Jari Kurri (May 30, 1991).

Season	Team	League		REGULAR SEASON					PLAYOFFS			
			Gms.	G	A	Pts.	Pen.	Gms.	G	A	Pts.	Pen.
83-84	Henry Carr H.S.	MTHL	39	37	37	74	97	—	—	—	—	—
84-85	University of Wisconsin	WCHA	40	14	24	38	60	—	—	—	—	—
85-86	University of Wisconsin	WCHA	32	21	23	44	89	—	—	—	—	—
	Philadelphia	NHL	2	0	0	0	0	—	—	—	—	—
86-87	Philadelphia	NHL	71	11	21	32	94	24	5	5	10	46
87-88	Philadelphia	NHL	75	25	26	51	185	7	0	1	1	16
88-89	Philadelphia	NHL	76	21	29	50	183	19	4	5	9	28
89-90	Philadelphia	NHL	57	6	17	23	77	—	—	—	—	—
90-91	Philadelphia	NHL	74	20	21	41	155	—	—	—	—	—
91-92	Edmonton	NHL	80	23	27	50	197	16	2	1	3	29
NHL totals			435	106	141	247	891	66	11	12	23	119

MELROSE, KEVAN
D, FLAMES

PERSONAL: Born March 28, 1966, at Calgary, Alta. . . . 5-10/185. . . . Shoots left. . . . Full name: Kevan Greg Melrose.
COLLEGE: Harvard.
TRANSACTIONS/CAREER NOTES: Selected by Calgary Flames in seventh round (seventh Flames pick, 138th overall) of NHL entry draft (June 9, 1984). . . . Underwent knee surgery (Summer 1984).

Season	Team	League		REGULAR SEASON					PLAYOFFS			
			Gms.	G	A	Pts.	Pen.	Gms.	G	A	Pts.	Pen.
84-85	Red Deer	AJHL	42	9	26	35	89	—	—	—	—	—
	Penticton	BCJHL	24	15	10	25	42	—	—	—	—	—
85-86	Penticton	BCJHL	22	18	15	33	56	—	—	—	—	—
86-87	Canadian National Team	Int'l	8	1	0	1	4	—	—	—	—	—
	Red Deer	AJHL	29	15	15	30	171	19	8	16	24	60
87-88	Harvard University	ECAC	31	4	6	10	50	—	—	—	—	—
88-89	Harvard University	ECAC	32	2	13	15	126	—	—	—	—	—
89-90	Harvard University	ECAC	16	1	6	7	124	—	—	—	—	—
90-91	Salt Lake City	IHL	60	6	14	20	82	4	1	2	3	10
91-92	Salt Lake City	IHL	82	5	14	19	187	5	0	0	0	4

MENDEL, ROBERT
D, MAPLE LEAFS

PERSONAL: Born September 19, 1968, at Los Angeles. . . . 6-1/195. . . . Shoots left. . . . Full name: Robert Fritz Mendel.
HIGH SCHOOL: Edina (Minn.).
COLLEGE: Wisconsin.
TRANSACTIONS/CAREER NOTES: Selected by Quebec Nordiques in fifth round (fifth Nordiques pick, 93rd overall) of NHL entry draft (June 13, 1987). . . . Signed as free agent by Washington Capitals (May 24, 1990). . . . Traded by Capitals to Toronto Maple Leafs for C Bob Reynolds (March 5, 1991).

Season	Team	League		REGULAR SEASON					PLAYOFFS			
			Gms.	G	A	Pts.	Pen.	Gms.	G	A	Pts.	Pen.
85-86	Edina High School	Minn. H.S.	21	2	27	29		—	—	—	—	—
86-87	University of Wisconsin	WCHA	42	1	7	8	26	—	—	—	—	—
87-88	University of Wisconsin	WCHA	40	0	7	7	22	—	—	—	—	—
88-89	University of Wisconsin	WCHA	44	1	14	15	37	—	—	—	—	—
89-90	University of Wisconsin	WCHA	44	1	13	14	30	—	—	—	—	—
90-91	Hampton Roads	ECHL	2	0	2	2	0	—	—	—	—	—
	Baltimore	AHL	43	0	7	7	20	—	—	—	—	—
	Newmarket	AHL	13	1	0	1	6	—	—	—	—	—
91-92	St. John's	AHL	39	1	4	5	26	—	—	—	—	—
	Raleigh	ECHL	10	0	3	3	12	4	0	0	0	2

M

MESSIER, JOBY

D, RANGERS

PERSONAL: Born March 2, 1970, at Regina, Sask. . . . 6-0/193. . . . Shoots right. . . . Full name: Marcus Cyril Messier. . . . Brother of Mitch Messier, center/right winger in Minnesota North Stars system; and cousin of Mark Messier, center, New York Rangers.
COLLEGE: Michigan State.

TRANSACTIONS/CAREER NOTES: Broke right arm (December 1984). . . . Broke right arm (September 1987). . . . Selected by New York Rangers in sixth round (seventh Rangers seventh pick, 118th overall) of NHL entry draft (June 17, 1989).
HONORS: Named to CCHA All-Star first team (1991-92).

Season Team	League	Gms.	G	A	Pts.	Pen.	Gms.	G	A	Pts.	Pen.
				REGULAR SEASON					PLAYOFFS		
87-88—Notre Dame	SJHL	53	9	22	31	208	—	—	—	—	—
88-89—Michigan State	CCHA	46	2	10	12	70	—	—	—	—	—
89-90—Michigan State	CCHA	42	1	11	12	58	—	—	—	—	—
90-91—Michigan State	CCHA	39	5	11	16	71	—	—	—	—	—
91-92—Michigan State	CCHA	44	13	16	29	85	—	—	—	—	—

MESSIER, MARK

C, RANGERS

PERSONAL: Born January 18, 1961, at Edmonton, Alta. . . . 6-1/202. . . . Shoots left. . . . Full name: Mark Douglas Messier. . . . Brother of Paul Messier, center, Colorado Rockies (1978-79); cousin of Mitch Messier, center/right winger in Minnesota North Stars system; cousin of Joby Messier, defenseman in New York Rangers system; and brother-in-law of John Blum, defenseman, Boston Bruins.

TRANSACTIONS/CAREER NOTES: Given five-game trial by Indianapolis Racers (November 1978). . . . Signed as free agent by Cincinnati Stingers (January 1979). . . . Selected by Edmonton Oilers in third round (second Oilers pick, 48th overall) of NHL entry draft (August 9, 1979). . . . Injured ankle (November 7, 1981). . . . Chipped bone in wrist (March 1983). . . . Suspended six games by NHL for hitting another player with his stick (January 18, 1984). . . . Sprained knee ligaments (November 1984). . . . Suspended 10 games by NHL for injuring another player (December 26, 1984). . . . Bruised left foot (December 3, 1985); missed 17 games. . . . Suspended and fined by Oilers after refusing to report to training camp (October 1987); missed three weeks of camp. . . . Suspended six games by NHL for injuring another player with his stick (October 23, 1988). . . . Twisted left knee (January 28, 1989). . . . Strained right knee (February 3, 1989). . . . Bruised left knee (February 12, 1989). . . . Sprained left knee ligaments (October 16, 1990); missed 10 games. . . . Reinjured left knee (December 12, 1990); missed three games. . . . Reinjured knee (December 22, 1990); missed nine games. . . . Broke left thumb (February 11, 1991); missed eight games. . . . Missed one game due to contract dispute (October 1991). . . . Traded by Oilers with future considerations to New York Rangers for C Bernie Nicholls, LW Louie DeBrusk, RW Steven Rice and future considerations (October 4, 1991); Oilers traded D Jeff Beukeboom to Rangers for D David Shaw to complete deal (November 12, 1991).

HONORS: Named to THE SPORTING NEWS All-Star first team (1981-82, 1982-83, 1989-90 and 1991-92). . . . Named to NHL All-Star first team (1981-82, 1982-83, 1989-90 and 1991-92). . . . Won Conn Smythe Trophy (1983-84). . . . Named to NHL All-Star second team (1983-84). . . . Named to THE SPORTING NEWS All-Star second team (1986-87). . . . Named NHL Player of the Year by THE SPORTING NEWS (1989-90 and 1991-92). . . . Won Hart Memorial Trophy (1989-90 and 1991-92). . . . Won Lester B. Pearson Award (1989-90 and 1991-92).

RECORDS: Holds NHL career playoff record for most shorthanded goals—11. . . . Holds NHL All-Star single-game record for most assists in one period—3 (1983).

Season Team	League	Gms.	G	A	Pts.	Pen.	Gms.	G	A	Pts.	Pen.
				REGULAR SEASON					PLAYOFFS		
76-77—Spruce Grove	AJHL	57	27	39	66	91	—	—	—	—	—
77-78—St. Albert	AJHL	—	—	—	—	—	—	—	—	—	—
—Portland	WHL	—	—	—	—	—	7	4	1	5	2
78-79—Indianapolis	WHA	5	0	0	0	0	—	—	—	—	—
—Cincinnati	WHA	47	1	10	11	58	—	—	—	—	—
79-80—Houston	CHL	4	0	3	3	4	—	—	—	—	—
—Edmonton	NHL	75	12	21	33	120	3	1	2	3	2
80-81—Edmonton	NHL	72	23	40	63	102	9	2	5	7	13
81-82—Edmonton	NHL	78	50	38	88	119	5	1	2	3	8
82-83—Edmonton	NHL	77	48	58	106	72	15	15	6	21	14
83-84—Edmonton	NHL	73	37	64	101	165	19	8	18	26	19
84-85—Edmonton	NHL	55	23	31	54	57	18	12	13	25	12
85-86—Edmonton	NHL	63	35	49	84	68	10	4	6	10	18
86-87—Edmonton	NHL	77	37	70	107	73	21	12	16	28	16
87-88—Edmonton	NHL	77	37	74	111	103	19	11	23	34	29
88-89—Edmonton	NHL	72	33	61	94	130	7	1	11	12	8
89-90—Edmonton	NHL	79	45	84	129	79	22	9	*22	†31	20
90-91—Edmonton	NHL	53	12	52	64	34	18	4	11	15	16
91-92—New York Rangers	NHL	79	35	72	107	76	11	7	7	14	6
WHA totals		52	1	10	11	58					
NHL totals		930	427	714	1141	1198	177	87	142	229	181

MESSIER, MITCH

C/RW, NORTH STARS

PERSONAL: Born August 21, 1965, at Regina, Sask. . . . 6-2/200. . . . Shoots right. . . . Full name: Mitch Ron Messier. . . . Brother of Joby Messier, defenseman in New York Rangers system; and cousin of Mark Messier, center, New York Rangers.
COLLEGE: Michigan State.

TRANSACTIONS/CAREER NOTES: Selected by Minnesota North Stars in third round (fourth North Stars pick, 56th overall) of NHL entry draft (June 8, 1983). . . . Bruised knee (November 1987).
HONORS: Named to NCAA All-America East first team (1986-87). . . . Named to CCHA All-Star first team (1986-87).

Season Team	League	Gms.	G	A	Pts.	Pen.	Gms.	G	A	Pts.	Pen.
				REGULAR SEASON					PLAYOFFS		
81-82—Notre Dame H.S.	Sask. H.S.	26	8	20	28		—	—	—	—	—
82-83—Notre Dame H.S.	Sask. H.S.	60	108	73	181	160	—	—	—	—	—

Season Team	League	REGULAR SEASON					PLAYOFFS				
		Gms.	G	A	Pts.	Pen.	Gms.	G	A	Pts.	Pen.
83-84—Michigan State	CCHA	37	6	15	21	22	—	—	—	—	—
84-85—Michigan State	CCHA	42	12	21	33	46	—	—	—	—	—
85-86—Michigan State	CCHA	38	24	40	64	36	—	—	—	—	—
86-87—Michigan State	CCHA	45	44	48	92	89	—	—	—	—	—
87-88—Kalamazoo	IHL	69	29	37	66	42	4	2	1	3	0
—Minnesota	NHL	13	0	1	1	11	—	—	—	—	—
88-89—Minnesota	NHL	3	0	1	1	0	—	—	—	—	—
—Kalamazoo	IHL	67	34	46	80	71	6	4	3	7	0
89-90—Minnesota	NHL	2	0	0	0	0	—	—	—	—	—
—Kalamazoo	IHL	65	26	58	84	56	8	4	3	7	25
90-91—Minnesota	NHL	2	0	0	0	0	—	—	—	—	—
—Kalamazoo	IHL	73	30	46	76	34	11	4	8	12	2
91-92—Kalamazoo	IHL	77	43	33	76	42	12	3	3	6	25
NHL totals		20	0	2	2	11					

METLYUK, DENIS
C, FLYERS

PERSONAL: Born January 30, 1972, at Togliatti, U.S.S.R. . . . 5-10/183. . . . Shoots left.
TRANSACTIONS/CAREER NOTES: Selected by Philadelphia Flyers in second round (third Flyers pick, 31st overall) of NHL entry draft (June 20, 1992).

Season Team	League	REGULAR SEASON					PLAYOFFS				
		Gms.	G	A	Pts.	Pen.	Gms.	G	A	Pts.	Pen.
90-91—Lada Togliatti	USSR	25	5	6	11	8	—	—	—	—	—
91-92—Lada Togliatti	CIS	26	0	1	1	6	—	—	—	—	—

MICHAYLUK, DAVE
LW, PENGUINS

PERSONAL: Born May 18, 1962, at Wakaw, Sask. . . . 5-10/189. . . . Shoots left. . . . Full name: David Michayluk.
TRANSACTIONS/CAREER NOTES: Selected by Philadelphia Flyers as underage junior in fourth round (fifth Flyers pick, 65th overall) of NHL entry draft (June 10, 1981). . . . Lacerated right arm (May 1989). . . . Signed as free agent by Pittsburgh Penguins (May 24, 1989).
HONORS: Won Stewart (Butch) Paul Memorial Trophy (1980-81). . . . Named to WHL All-Star second team (1980-81 and 1981-82). . . . Named to IHL All-Star second team (1984-85). . . . Named to IHL All-Star first team (1986-87 through 1989-90). . . . Won James Gatschene Memorial Trophy (1988-89). . . . Won Leo P. Lamoureux Memorial Trophy (1988-89). . . . Named Turner Cup Playoff Most Valuable Player (1988-89).

Season Team	League	REGULAR SEASON					PLAYOFFS				
		Gms.	G	A	Pts.	Pen.	Gms.	G	A	Pts.	Pen.
79-80—Prince Albert	AJHL	60	46	67	113	49	—	—	—	—	—
80-81—Regina	WHL	72	62	71	133	39	11	5	12	17	8
81-82—Regina	WHL	72	62	111	173	128	12	16	24	*40	23
—Philadelphia	NHL	1	0	0	0	0	—	—	—	—	—
82-83—Philadelphia	NHL	13	2	6	8	8	—	—	—	—	—
—Maine	AHL	69	32	40	72	16	8	0	2	2	0
83-84—Springfield	AHL	79	18	44	62	37	4	0	0	0	2
84-85—Hershey	AHL	3	0	2	2	2	—	—	—	—	—
—Kalamazoo	IHL	82	*66	33	99	49	11	7	7	14	0
85-86—Nova Scotia	AHL	3	0	1	1	0	—	—	—	—	—
—Muskegon	IHL	77	52	52	104	73	14	6	9	15	12
86-87—Muskegon	IHL	82	47	53	100	69	15	2	14	16	8
87-88—Muskegon	IHL	81	*56	81	137	46	6	2	0	2	18
88-89—Muskegon	IHL	80	50	72	*122	84	13	†9	12	†21	24
89-90—Muskegon	IHL	79	*51	51	102	80	15	8	†14	*22	10
90-91—Muskegon	IHL	83	40	62	102	116	5	2	2	4	4
91-92—Muskegon	IHL	82	39	63	102	154	13	9	8	17	4
—Pittsburgh	NHL	—	—	—	—	—	7	1	1	2	0
NHL totals		14	2	6	8	8	7	1	1	2	0

MICK, TROY
LW, PENGUINS

PERSONAL: Born March 30, 1969, at Burnaby, B.C. . . . 5-11/192. . . . Shoots left.
TRANSACTIONS/CAREER NOTES: Selected by Pittsburgh Penguins in seventh round (sixth Penguins pick, 130th overall) of NHL entry draft (June 11, 1988). . . . Underwent left knee surgery (March 1987). . . . Traded by Portland Winter Hawks to Regina Pats for D Jeff Sebastien (October 5, 1989). . . . Underwent surgery to remove bone chips from right knee (December 29, 1990); missed 14 games.
HONORS: Named to WHL (West) All-Star first team (1987-88 and 1988-89). . . . Named to WHL (East) All-Star first team (1989-90). . . . Named to ECHL All-Star second team (1990-91).

Season Team	League	REGULAR SEASON					PLAYOFFS				
		Gms.	G	A	Pts.	Pen.	Gms.	G	A	Pts.	Pen.
85-86—Portland	WHL	6	2	5	7	2	—	—	—	—	—
—Merritt	BCJHL	42	44	23	67	33	4	3	2	5	0
86-87—Portland	WHL	57	30	33	63	60	20	8	2	10	40
87-88—Portland	WHL	72	63	84	147	78	—	—	—	—	—
88-89—Portland	WHL	66	49	*87	136	70	19	15	19	34	17
89-90—Regina	WHL	66	60	53	113	67	11	7	10	17	17
90-91—Knoxville	ECHL	38	35	48	83	24	—	—	—	—	—
—Albany	IHL	1	0	0	0	2	—	—	—	—	—
91-92—Knoxville	ECHL	48	23	38	61	24	—	—	—	—	—

M

MIDDENDORF, MAX
RW, RED WINGS

PERSONAL: Born August 18, 1967, at Syracuse, N.Y. . . . 6-4/210. . . . Shoots right. **TRANSACTIONS/CAREER NOTES:** Selected by Quebec Nordiques as underage junior in third round (third Nordiques pick, 57th overall) of NHL entry draft (June 15, 1985). . . . Dislocated thumb (February 1, 1987). . . . Suspended five games by AHL for stick-fighting (January 26, 1990). . . . Traded by Nordiques to Edmonton Oilers for a ninth-round pick in 1991 draft (D Brent Brekke) (November 10, 1990). . . . Traded by Oilers to Detroit Red Wings for C Bill McDougall (February 22, 1992).

			REGULAR SEASON					PLAYOFFS			
Season	Team	League	Gms.	G	A	Pts.	Pen.	Gms.	G	A	Pts.	Pen.
84-85—Sudbury	OHL	63	16	28	44	106	—	—	—	—	—
85-86—Sudbury	OHL	61	40	42	82	71	4	4	2	6	11
86-87—Quebec	NHL	6	1	4	5	4	—	—	—	—	—
—Sudbury	OHL	31	31	29	60	7	—	—	—	—	—
—Kitchener	OHL	17	7	15	22	6	4	2	5	7	5
87-88—Fredericton	AHL	38	11	13	24	57	12	4	4	8	18
—Quebec	NHL	1	0	0	0	0	—	—	—	—	—
88-89—Halifax	AHL	72	41	39	80	85	4	1	2	3	6
89-90—Quebec	NHL	3	0	0	0	0	—	—	—	—	—
—Halifax	AHL	48	20	17	37	60	—	—	—	—	—
90-91—Fort Wayne	IHL	15	9	11	20	12	—	—	—	—	—
—Cape Breton	AHL	44	14	21	35	82	4	0	1	1	6
—Edmonton	NHL	3	1	0	1	2	—	—	—	—	—
91-92—Cape Breton	AHL	51	20	19	39	108	—	—	—	—	—
—Adirondack	AHL	6	3	5	8	12	5	0	1	1	16
NHL totals		13	2	4	6	6					

MIEHM, KEVIN
C, BLUES

PERSONAL: Born September 10, 1969, at Kitchener, Ont. . . . 6-2/197. . . . Shoots left. **TRANSACTIONS/CAREER NOTES:** Selected by St. Louis Blues as underage junior in third round (second Blues pick, 54th overall) of NHL entry draft (June 13, 1987). **HONORS:** Won William Hanley Trophy (1988-89).

			REGULAR SEASON					PLAYOFFS			
Season	Team	League	Gms.	G	A	Pts.	Pen.	Gms.	G	A	Pts.	Pen.
85-86—Kitchener Jr. B	OHA	1	0	0	0	0	—	—	—	—	—
86-87—Oshawa	OHL	61	12	27	39	19	26	1	8	9	12
87-88—Oshawa	OHL	52	16	36	52	30	7	2	5	7	0
88-89—Oshawa	OHL	63	43	79	122	19	6	6	6	12	0
—Peoria	IHL	3	1	1	2	0	4	0	2	2	0
89-90—Peoria	IHL	76	23	38	61	20	3	0	0	0	4
90-91—Peoria	IHL	73	25	39	64	14	16	5	7	12	2
91-92—Peoria	IHL	66	21	53	74	22	10	3	4	7	2

MILLEN, COREY
C, KINGS

PERSONAL: Born April 29, 1964, at Cloquet, Minn. . . . 5-7/168. . . . Shoots right. **HIGH SCHOOL:** Cloquet (Minn.). **COLLEGE:** Minnesota. **TRANSACTIONS/CAREER NOTES:** Selected by New York Rangers as underage player in third round (third Rangers pick, 57th overall) of NHL entry draft (June 9, 1982). . . . Injured knee and underwent surgery (November 1982). . . . Injured shoulder (October 1984). . . . Tested positive for a non-anabolic steroid in a random test at World Cup Tournament and was banned from play (April 1989). . . . Sprained left knee ligaments and underwent surgery (September 18, 1989); missed four months. . . . Underwent surgery to left knee (August 1990); missed four months. . . . Traded by Rangers to Los Angeles Kings for C Randy Gilhen (December 23, 1991). . . . Suffered shoulder contusion (February 29, 1992); missed one game. **HONORS:** Named to WCHA All-Star second team (1984-85 through 1986-87). . . . Named to NCAA All-America West second team (1985-86). . . . Named to NCAA All-Tournament team (1986-87).

			REGULAR SEASON					PLAYOFFS			
Season	Team	League	Gms.	G	A	Pts.	Pen.	Gms.	G	A	Pts.	Pen.
81-82—Cloquet H.S.	Minn. H.S.	18	46	35	81		—	—	—	—	—
82-83—University of Minnesota	WCHA	21	14	15	29	18	—	—	—	—	—
83-84—U.S. National Team	Int'l	45	15	11	26	10	—	—	—	—	—
—U.S. Olympic Team	Int'l	6	0	0	0	2	—	—	—	—	—
84-85—University of Minnesota	WCHA	38	28	36	64	60	—	—	—	—	—
85-86—University of Minnesota	WCHA	48	41	42	83	64	—	—	—	—	—
86-87—University of Minnesota	WCHA	42	36	29	65	62	—	—	—	—	—
87-88—U.S. Olympic Team	Int'l	51	46	45	91		—	—	—	—	—
88-89—Ambri Piotta	Switzerland	36	32	22	54	18	6	4	3	7	0
89-90—New York Rangers	NHL	4	0	0	0	2	—	—	—	—	—
—Flint	IHL	11	4	5	9	2	—	—	—	—	—
90-91—Binghamton	AHL	40	19	37	56	68	6	0	7	7	8
—New York Rangers	NHL	4	3	1	4	0	6	1	2	3	0
91-92—New York Rangers	NHL	11	1	4	5	10	—	—	—	—	—
—Binghamton	AHL	15	8	7	15	44	—	—	—	—	—
—Los Angeles	NHL	46	20	21	41	44	6	0	1	1	6
NHL totals		65	24	26	50	56	12	1	3	4	6

MILLEN, GREG
G, RED WINGS

PERSONAL: Born June 25, 1957, at Toronto. . . . 5-9/160. . . . Shoots right. . . . Full name: Greg H. Millen. **TRANSACTIONS/CAREER NOTES:** Selected by Pittsburgh Penguins in sixth round (fourth Penguins pick, 102nd overall) of NHL entry draft (June 14, 1977). . . . Pulled hamstring muscle

(October 1979); missed 18 games. . . . Signed as free agent by Hartford Whalers (June 1981); NHL arbitrator awarded C/LW Pat Boutette and RW Kevin McClelland to Penguins as compensation. . . . Traded by Whalers with LW/C Mark Johnson to St. Louis Blues for G Mike Liut and future considerations (LW Jorgen Pettersson) (February 1985). . . . Traded by Blues with C Tony Hrkac to Quebec Nordiques for D Jeff Brown (December 13, 1989); did not report to Quebec until December 26. . . . Traded by Nordiques with LW Michel Goulet and sixth-round pick in 1991 draft to Chicago Blackhawks for LW Everett Sanipass, LW Dan Vincelette and D Mario Doyon (March 5, 1990). . . . Pulled hamstring (March 10, 1991). . . . Traded by Blackhawks to New York Rangers for future considerations (September 25, 1991). . . . Loaned by Rangers to San Diego Gulls (October 17, 1991); returned (November 5, 1991). . . . Loaned by Rangers to Maine Mariners (November 10, 1991); returned (December 24, 1991). . . . Traded by Rangers to Detroit Red Wings for undisclosed pick in 1992 draft (December 26, 1991).

				REGULAR SEASON								PLAYOFFS					
Season	Team	League	Gms.	Min.	W	L	T	GA	SO	Avg.	Gms.	Min.	W	L	GA	SO	Avg.
74-75—Peterborough		OHA Mj Jr.A	27	1584				90	2	*3.41	—	—	—	—	—	—	—
75-76—Peterborough		OHA Mj Jr.A	†58	3282				233	0	4.26	—	—	—	—	—	—	—
76-77—Peterborough		OMJHL	*59	*3457				244	0	4.23	4	240			23	0	5.75
77-78—Sault Ste. Marie		OMJHL	25	1469				105	1	4.29	13	774			61	0	4.73
—Kalamazoo		IHL	3	180				14	0	4.67	—	—	—	—	—	—	—
78-79—Pittsburgh		NHL	28	1532	14	11	1	86	2	3.37	—	—	—	—	—	—	—
79-80—Pittsburgh		NHL	44	2586	18	18	7	157	2	3.64	5	300	2	3	21	0	4.20
80-81—Pittsburgh		NHL	63	3721	25	27	10	*258	0	4.16	5	325	2	3	19	0	3.51
81-82—Hartford		NHL	55	3201	11	30	12	229	0	4.29	—	—	—	—	—	—	—
82-83—Hartford		NHL	60	3520	14	38	6	*282	1	4.81	—	—	—	—	—	—	—
83-84—Hartford		NHL	*60	*3583	21	30	9	*221	2	3.70	—	—	—	—	—	—	—
84-85—Hartford		NHL	44	2659	16	22	6	187	1	4.22	—	—	—	—	—	—	—
—St. Louis		NHL	10	607	2	7	1	35	0	3.46	1	60	0	1	2	0	2.00
85-86—St. Louis		NHL	36	2168	14	16	6	129	1	3.57	10	586	6	3	29	0	2.97
86-87—St. Louis		NHL	42	2482	15	18	9	146	0	3.53	4	250	1	3	10	0	2.40
87-88—St. Louis		NHL	48	2854	21	19	7	167	1	3.51	10	600	5	5	38	0	3.80
88-89—St. Louis		NHL	52	3019	22	20	7	170	*6	3.38	10	649	5	5	34	0	3.14
89-90—St. Louis		NHL	21	1245	11	7	3	61	1	2.94	—	—	—	—	—	—	—
—Quebec		NHL	18	1080	3	14	1	95	0	5.28	—	—	—	—	—	—	—
—Chicago		NHL	10	575	5	4	1	32	0	3.34	14	613	6	6	40	0	3.92
90-91—Chicago		NHL	3	58	0	1	0	4	0	4.14	—	—	—	—	—	—	—
91-92—San Diego		IHL	5	296	2	3	0	20	0	4.05	—	—	—	—	—	—	—
—Maine		AHL	11	599	2	5	2	37	0	3.71	—	—	—	—	—	—	—
—Detroit		NHL	10	487	3	2	3	22	0	2.71	—	—	—	—	—	—	—
NHL totals			604	35377	215	284	89	2281	17	3.87	59	3383	27	29	193	0	3.42

MILLER, AARON
D, NORDIQUES

PERSONAL: Born August 11, 1971, at Buffalo, N.Y. . . . 6-3/197. . . . Shoots right. . . . Full name: Aaron Michael Miller.
COLLEGE: Vermont.
TRANSACTIONS/CAREER NOTES: Selected by New York Rangers in fifth round (sixth Rangers pick, 88th overall) of NHL entry draft (June 17, 1989). . . . Traded by Rangers with fifth-round pick in 1991 draft (LW Bill Lindsay) to Quebec Nordiques for D Joe Cirella (January 17, 1991).
HONORS: Named to ECAC All-Rookie team (1989-90).

			REGULAR SEASON					PLAYOFFS			
Season	Team	League	Gms.	G	A	Pts.	Pen.	Gms.	G	A	Pts.	Pen.
87-88—Niagara Scenic		NAJHL	30	4	9	13	2	—	—	—	—	—
88-89—Niagara Scenic		NAJHL	59	24	38	62	60	—	—	—	—	—
89-90—University of Vermont		ECAC	31	1	15	16	24	—	—	—	—	—
90-91—University of Vermont		ECAC	30	3	7	10	22	—	—	—	—	—
91-92—University of Vermont		ECAC	31	3	16	19	36	—	—	—	—	—

MILLER, BRAD
D, SENATORS

PERSONAL: Born July 23, 1969, at Edmonton, Alta. . . . 6-4/226. . . . Shoots left.
TRANSACTIONS/CAREER NOTES: Selected by Buffalo Sabres as underage junior in second round (second Sabres pick, 22nd overall) of NHL entry draft (June 13, 1987). . . . Suspended three games by AHL for abusing an official (February 23, 1990). . . . Suspended nine games by AHL for abuse of officials and continuing to fight (April 11, 1990). . . . Selected by Ottawa Senators in NHL expansion draft (June 18, 1992).

			REGULAR SEASON					PLAYOFFS			
Season	Team	League	Gms.	G	A	Pts.	Pen.	Gms.	G	A	Pts.	Pen.
85-86—Regina		WHL	71	2	14	16	99	10	1	1	2	4
86-87—Regina		WHL	67	10	38	48	154	3	0	0	0	6
87-88—Regina		WHL	61	9	34	43	148	4	1	1	2	12
—Rochester		AHL	3	0	0	0	4	2	0	0	0	2
88-89—Buffalo		NHL	7	0	0	0	6	—	—	—	—	—
—Rochester		AHL	3	0	0	0	4	—	—	—	—	—
—Regina		WHL	34	8	18	26	95	—	—	—	—	—
89-90—Buffalo		NHL	1	0	0	0	0	—	—	—	—	—
—Rochester		AHL	60	2	10	12	273	8	1	0	1	52
90-91—Buffalo		NHL	13	0	0	0	67	—	—	—	—	—
—Rochester		AHL	49	0	9	9	248	12	0	4	4	67
91-92—Buffalo		NHL	42	1	4	5	192	—	—	—	—	—
—Rochester		AHL	27	0	4	4	113	11	0	0	0	61
NHL totals			63	1	4	5	265					

MILLER, JASON
C, DEVILS

PERSONAL: Born March 1, 1971, at Edmonton, Alta.... 6-1/190.... Shoots left.
TRANSACTIONS/CAREER NOTES: Separated shoulder (May 1986).... Selected by New Jersey Devils in first round (second Devils pick, 18th overall) of NHL entry draft (June 17, 1989).
HONORS: Named to WHL (East) All-Star second team (1990-91).

Season Team	League	REGULAR SEASON					PLAYOFFS				
		Gms.	G	A	Pts.	Pen.	Gms.	G	A	Pts.	Pen.
87-88—Medicine Hat	WHL	71	11	18	29	28	15	0	1	1	2
88-89—Medicine Hat	WHL	72	51	55	106	44	3	1	2	3	2
89-90—Medicine Hat	WHL	66	43	56	99	40	3	3	2	5	0
90-91—New Jersey	NHL	1	0	0	0	0	—	—	—	—	—
—Medicine Hat	WHL	66	60	76	136	31	12	9	10	19	8
91-92—Utica	AHL	71	23	32	55	31	4	1	3	4	0
—New Jersey	NHL	3	0	0	0	0	—	—	—	—	—
NHL totals		4	0	0	0	0					

MILLER, JAY
LW/D, KINGS

PERSONAL: Born July 16, 1960, at Wellesley, Mass.... 6-2/210.... Shoots left.
COLLEGE: New Hampshire.
TRANSACTIONS/CAREER NOTES: Broke bone in right hand (November 1984).... Signed as free agent by Boston Bruins (September 1985).... Strained right knee ligaments (April 1988).... Traded by Bruins to Los Angeles Kings for future considerations (January 22, 1989); deal completed when Bruins traded C Steve Kasper to Kings for C Bobby Carpenter (January 24, 1989).... Suffered sore left knee (October 1990).... Suffered from the flu (December 1991); missed three games.

Season Team	League	REGULAR SEASON					PLAYOFFS				
		Gms.	G	A	Pts.	Pen.	Gms.	G	A	Pts.	Pen.
79-80—Univ. of New Hampshire ...	ECAC	28	7	12	19	53	—	—	—	—	—
81-82—Univ. of New Hampshire ...	ECAC	10	4	8	12	14	—	—	—	—	—
82-83—Univ. of New Hampshire ...	ECAC	24	6	4	10	34	—	—	—	—	—
83-84—Toledo	IHL	2	0	0	0	4	—	—	—	—	—
—Mohawk Valley Stars	ACHL	48	15	36	51	167	—	—	—	—	—
—Maine	AHL	15	1	1	2	27	—	—	—	—	—
84-85—Muskegon	IHL	56	5	29	34	177	17	1	1	2	56
85-86—Moncton	AHL	18	4	6	10	113	—	—	—	—	—
—Boston	NHL	46	3	0	3	178	2	0	0	0	17
86-87—Boston	NHL	55	1	4	5	208	—	—	—	—	—
87-88—Boston	NHL	78	7	12	19	304	12	0	0	0	*124
88-89—Los Angeles	NHL	29	5	3	8	133	11	0	1	1	63
—Boston	NHL	37	2	4	6	168	—	—	—	—	—
89-90—Los Angeles	NHL	68	10	2	12	224	10	1	1	2	10
90-91—Los Angeles	NHL	66	8	12	20	259	8	0	0	0	17
91-92—Los Angeles	NHL	67	4	7	11	249	5	1	1	2	12
NHL totals		446	40	44	84	1723	48	2	3	5	243

MILLER, KELLY
LW, CAPITALS

PERSONAL: Born March 3, 1963, at Lansing, Mich. ... 5-11/195. ... Shoots left. ... Full name: Kelly David Miller.... Brother of Kevin Miller, right winger, Washington Capitals; and brother of Kip Miller, center, Minnesota North Stars.
COLLEGE: Michigan State.
TRANSACTIONS/CAREER NOTES: Selected by New York Rangers in ninth round (ninth Rangers pick, 183rd overall) of NHL entry draft (June 9, 1982).... Injured ankle (September 1985).... Sprained knee (January 27, 1986); missed five games.... Traded by Rangers with C Mike Ridley and RW Bobby Crawford to Washington Capitals for C Bobby Carpenter and second-round pick in 1989 draft (RW Jason Prosofsky) (January 1, 1987).... Pulled groin (November 1988).... Sprained knee (September 22, 1990).
HONORS: Named to NCAA All-America West first team (1984-85).... Named to CCHA All-Star first team (1984-85).

Season Team	League	REGULAR SEASON					PLAYOFFS				
		Gms.	G	A	Pts.	Pen.	Gms.	G	A	Pts.	Pen.
81-82—Michigan State	CCHA	40	11	19	30	21	—	—	—	—	—
82-83—Michigan State	CCHA	36	16	19	35	12	—	—	—	—	—
83-84—Michigan State	CCHA	46	28	21	49	12	—	—	—	—	—
84-85—Michigan State	CCHA	43	27	23	50	21	—	—	—	—	—
—New York Rangers	NHL	5	0	2	2	2	3	0	0	0	2
85-86—New York Rangers	NHL	74	13	20	33	52	16	3	4	7	4
86-87—New York Rangers	NHL	38	6	14	20	22	—	—	—	—	—
—Washington	NHL	39	10	12	22	26	7	2	2	4	0
87-88—Washington	NHL	80	9	23	32	35	14	4	4	8	10
88-89—Washington	NHL	78	19	21	40	45	6	1	0	1	2
89-90—Washington	NHL	80	18	22	40	49	15	3	5	8	23
90-91—Washington	NHL	80	24	26	50	29	11	4	2	6	10
91-92—Washington	NHL	78	14	38	52	49	7	1	2	3	4
NHL totals		552	113	178	291	309	79	18	19	37	51

MILLER, KEVIN
RW, CAPITALS

PERSONAL: Born August 9, 1965, at Lansing, Mich. ... 5-9/170. ... Shoots right. ... Full name: Kevin Bradley Miller.... Brother of Kelly Miller, left winger, Washington Capitals; and brother of Kip Miller, center, Minnesota North Stars.
COLLEGE: Michigan State.

TRANSACTIONS/CAREER NOTES: Selected by New York Rangers in 10th round (10th Rangers pick, 202nd overall) of NHL entry draft (June 9, 1984).... Pulled groin (September 1990).... Sprained shoulder (December 1990).... Traded by Rangers with D Dennis Vial and RW Jim Cummings to Detroit Red Wings for RW Joe Kocur and D Per Djoos (March 5, 1991).... Traded by Red Wings to Washington Capitals for RW Dino Ciccarelli (June 20, 1992).

			REGULAR SEASON					PLAYOFFS			
Season Team	League	Gms.	G	A	Pts.	Pen.	Gms.	G	A	Pts.	Pen.
84-85—Michigan State	CCHA	44	11	29	40	84	—	—	—	—	—
85-86—Michigan State	CCHA	45	19	52	71	112	—	—	—	—	—
86-87—Michigan State	CCHA	42	25	56	81	63	—	—	—	—	—
87-88—Michigan State	CCHA	9	6	3	9	18	—	—	—	—	—
—U.S. Olympic Team	Int'l	50	32	34	66		—	—	—	—	—
88-89—New York Rangers	NHL	24	3	5	8	2	—	—	—	—	—
—Denver	IHL	55	29	47	76	19	4	2	1	3	2
89-90—New York Rangers	NHL	16	0	5	5	2	1	0	0	0	0
—Flint	IHL	48	19	23	42	41	—	—	—	—	—
90-91—New York Rangers	NHL	63	17	27	44	63	—	—	—	—	—
—Detroit	NHL	11	5	2	7	4	7	3	2	5	20
91-92—Detroit	NHL	80	20	26	46	53	9	0	2	2	4
NHL totals		194	45	65	110	124	17	3	4	7	24

MILLER, KIP

C, NORTH STARS

PERSONAL: Born June 11, 1060, at Lansing, Mich.... 5-10/185.... Shoots left.... Full name: Kip Charles Miller.... Brother of Kelly Miller, left winger, Washington Capitals; and brother of Kevin Miller, right winger, Washington Capitals.
COLLEGE: Michigan State.
TRANSACTIONS/CAREER NOTES: Selected by Quebec Nordiques in fourth round (fourth Nordiques pick, 72nd overall) of NHL entry draft (June 13, 1987).... Suffered hand and forearm injuries in off-ice accident (November 1987).... Traded by Nordiques to Minnesota North Stars for LW Steve Maltais (March 8, 1992).
HONORS: Named to NCAA All-America West first team (1988-89 and 1989-90).... Named to CCHA All-Star first team (1988-89 and 1989-90).... Won Hobey Baker Memorial Trophy (1989-90).... Named CCHA Player of the Year (1989-90).

			REGULAR SEASON					PLAYOFFS			
Season Team	League	Gms.	G	A	Pts.	Pen.	Gms.	G	A	Pts.	Pen.
86-87—Michigan State	CCHA	45	22	19	41	96	—	—	—	—	—
87-88—Michigan State	CCHA	39	16	25	41	51	—	—	—	—	—
88-89—Michigan State	CCHA	47	32	45	77	94	—	—	—	—	—
89-90—Michigan State	CCHA	45	*48	53	*101	60	—	—	—	—	—
90-91—Quebec	NHL	15	4	3	7	7	—	—	—	—	—
—Halifax	AHL	66	36	33	69	40	—	—	—	—	—
91-92—Quebec	NHL	36	5	10	15	12	—	—	—	—	—
—Halifax	AHL	24	9	17	26	8	—	—	—	—	—
—Minnesota	NHL	3	1	2	3	2	—	—	—	—	—
—Kalamazoo	IHL	6	1	8	9	4	12	3	9	12	12
NHL totals		54	10	15	25	21					

MILLER, KURTIS

LW, BLUES

PERSONAL: Born June 1, 1970, at Bemidji, Minn.... 5-11/180.... Shoots left.... Full name: Kurtis Michael Miller.
COLLEGE: Lake Superior State (Mich.).
TRANSACTIONS/CAREER NOTES: Injured back (December 1986).... Injured back and shoulder (January 1989).... Suffered hip pointer (June 1989).... Selected by St. Louis Blues in sixth round (fourth Blues pick, 117th overall) of NHL entry draft (June 16, 1990).
HONORS: Named USHL Most Valuable Player (1989-90).... Won USHL Best Forward Trophy (1989-90).... Named to USHL All-Star first team (1989-90).

			REGULAR SEASON					PLAYOFFS			
Season Team	League	Gms.	G	A	Pts.	Pen.	Gms.	G	A	Pts.	Pen.
88-89—Rochester	USHL	48	28	21	49	50	—	—	—	—	—
89-90—Rochester	USHL	50	50	39	89	56	—	—	—	—	—
90-91—Lake Superior State	CCHA	45	10	12	22	48	—	—	—	—	—
91-92—Lake Superior State	CCHA	15	6	7	13	32	—	—	—	—	—

MIRONOV, BORIS

D, JETS

PERSONAL: Born March 21, 1972, at Moscow, U.S.S.R.... 6-3/196.... Shoots right.... Brother of Dimitri Mironov, defenseman, Toronto Maple Leafs.
TRANSACTIONS/CAREER NOTES: Selected by Winnipeg Jets in second round (second Jets pick, 27th overall) of NHL entry draft (June 20, 1992).

			REGULAR SEASON					PLAYOFFS			
Season Team	League	Gms.	G	A	Pts.	Pen.	Gms.	G	A	Pts.	Pen.
88-89—CSKA Moscow	USSR	1	0	0	0	0	—	—	—	—	—
89-90—CSKA Moscow	USSR	7	0	0	0	0	—	—	—	—	—
90-91—CSKA Moscow	USSR	36	1	5	6	16	—	—	—	—	—
91-92—CSKA Moscow	CIS	36	2	1	3	22	—	—	—	—	—

MIRONOV, DIMITRI

D, MAPLE LEAFS

PERSONAL: Born December 25, 1965, at Moscow, U.S.S.R.... 6-2/191.... Shoots right.... Brother of Boris Mironov, defenseman in Winnipeg Jets system.
TRANSACTIONS/CAREER NOTES: Selected by Toronto Maple Leafs in eighth round (seventh Maple Leafs pick, 160th overall) of NHL entry draft (June 22, 1991).... Broke

M

nose (March 23, 1992).
MISCELLANEOUS: Member of 1992 gold-medal-winning Unified Olympic team.

			REGULAR SEASON					PLAYOFFS				
Season	Team	League	Gms.	G	A	Pts.	Pen.	Gms.	G	A	Pts.	Pen.
90-91—Soviet Wings		USSR	44	16	12	28	22	—	—	—	—	—
91-92—Soviet Wings		USSR	30	11	16	27	44	—	—	—	—	—
—Unified Olympic Team		Int'l	8	3	1	4	4	—	—	—	—	—
—Toronto		NHL	7	1	0	1	0	—	—	—	—	—
NHL totals			7	1	0	1	0					

MITCHELL, ROY
D, NORTH STARS

PERSONAL: Born March 14, 1969, at Edmonton, Alta. . . . 6-1/196. . . . Shoots right.
TRANSACTIONS/CAREER NOTES: Selected by Montreal Canadiens in ninth round (Canadiens ninth pick, 188th overall) of 1989 NHL entry draft (June 17, 1989). . . . Signed as free agent by Minnesota North Stars (July 25, 1991).

			REGULAR SEASON					PLAYOFFS				
Season	Team	League	Gms.	G	A	Pts.	Pen.	Gms.	G	A	Pts.	Pen.
85-86—St. Albert		AJHL	39	2	18	20	32	—	—	—	—	—
86-87—Portland		WHL	68	7	32	39	103	20	0	3	3	23
87-88—Portland		WHL	72	5	42	47	219	—	—	—	—	—
88-89—Portland		WHL	72	9	34	43	177	19	1	8	9	38
89-90—Sherbrooke		AHL	77	5	12	17	98	12	0	2	2	31
90-91—Fredericton		AHL	71	2	15	17	137	9	0	1	1	11
91-92—Kalamazoo		IHL	69	3	26	29	102	11	1	4	5	18

MODANO, MIKE
RW/C, NORTH STARS

PERSONAL: Born June 7, 1970, at Livonia, Mich. . . . 6-3/190. . . . Shoots left. . . . Full name: Michael Modano.
TRANSACTIONS/CAREER NOTES: Selected by Minnesota North Stars in first round (first North Stars pick, first overall) of NHL entry draft (June 11, 1988). . . . Fractured scaphoid bone in left wrist (January 24, 1989). . . . Broke nose (March 4, 1990).
HONORS: Named to WHL All-Star first team (1988-89). . . . Named to NHL All-Rookie team (1989-90).

			REGULAR SEASON					PLAYOFFS				
Season	Team	League	Gms.	G	A	Pts.	Pen.	Gms.	G	A	Pts.	Pen.
86-87—Prince Albert		WHL	70	32	30	62	96	8	1	4	5	4
87-88—Prince Albert		WHL	65	47	80	127	80	9	7	11	18	18
88-89—Prince Albert		WHL	41	39	66	105	74	—	—	—	—	—
—Minnesota		NHL	—	—	—	—	—	2	0	0	0	0
89-90—Minnesota		NHL	80	29	46	75	63	7	1	1	2	12
90-91—Minnesota		NHL	79	28	36	64	61	23	8	12	20	16
91-92—Minnesota		NHL	76	33	44	77	46	7	3	2	5	4
NHL totals			235	90	126	216	170	39	12	15	27	32

M

MOGER, SANDY
RW, CANUCKS

PERSONAL: Born March 21, 1969, at 100 Mile House, B.C. . . . 6-2/190. . . . Shoots right. . . . Full name: Alexander Sandy Moger.
COLLEGE: Lake Superior State (Mich.).
TRANSACTIONS/CAREER NOTES: Broke wrist (September 1988). . . . Selected by Vancouver Canucks in ninth round (seventh Canucks pick, 176th overall) of NHL entry draft (June 17, 1989).
HONORS: Named to CCHA All-Star second team (1991-92).

			REGULAR SEASON					PLAYOFFS				
Season	Team	League	Gms.	G	A	Pts.	Pen.	Gms.	G	A	Pts.	Pen.
86-87—Vernon		BCJHL	13	5	4	9	10	—	—	—	—	—
87-88—Yorkton		SJHL	60	39	41	80	144	—	—	—	—	—
88-89—Lake Superior State		CCHA	31	4	6	10	28	—	—	—	—	—
89-90—Lake Superior State		CCHA	46	17	15	32	76	—	—	—	—	—
90-91—Lake Superior State		CCHA	45	27	21	48	*172	—	—	—	—	—
91-92—Lake Superior State		CCHA	42	26	25	51	111	—	—	—	—	—

MOGILNY, ALEXANDER
RW, SABRES

PERSONAL: Born February 18, 1969, at Khabarovsk, U.S.S.R. . . . 5-11/187. . . . Shoots left.
TRANSACTIONS/CAREER NOTES: Selected by Buffalo Sabres in fifth round (fourth Sabres pick, 89th overall) of NHL entry draft (June 11, 1988). . . . Suffered from the flu (November 26, 1989). . . . Missed games due to fear of flying (January 22, 1990); spent remainder of season traveling on ground. . . . Separated shoulder (February 8, 1991); missed six games. . . . Suffered from the flu (November 1991); missed two games. . . . Suffered from the flu (December 18, 1991); missed one game.
MISCELLANEOUS: Member of 1988 gold-medal-winning U.S.S.R. Olympic team.

			REGULAR SEASON					PLAYOFFS				
Season	Team	League	Gms.	G	A	Pts.	Pen.	Gms.	G	A	Pts.	Pen.
86-87—Central Red Army		USSR	28	15	1	16	4	—	—	—	—	—
87-88—Central Red Army		USSR	39	12	8	20	20	—	—	—	—	—
88-89—Central Red Army		USSR	31	11	11	22	24	—	—	—	—	—
89-90—Buffalo		NHL	65	15	28	43	16	4	0	1	1	2
90-91—Buffalo		NHL	62	30	34	64	16	6	0	6	6	2
91-92—Buffalo		NHL	67	39	45	84	73	2	0	2	2	0
NHL totals			194	84	107	191	105	12	0	9	9	4

MOKOSAK, JOHN

D, RANGERS

PERSONAL: Born September 7, 1963, at Edmonton, Alta.... 5-11/185.... Shoots left.... Brother of Carl Mokosak, left winger, five NHL teams (1981-82, 1982-83, 1984-85 through 1986-87 and 1988-89).

TRANSACTIONS/CAREER NOTES: Selected by Hartford Whalers as underage junior in seventh round (sixth Whalers pick, 130th overall) of NHL entry draft (June 10, 1981).... Signed as free agent by Detroit Red Wings (August 29, 1988).... Signed as free agent by Boston Bruins (July 11, 1990).... Signed as free agent by New York Rangers (August 28, 1991).

			REGULAR SEASON				PLAYOFFS			
Season Team	League	Gms.	G	A	Pts.	Pen.	Gms.	G	A	Pts.	Pen.
79-80—Fort Saskatchewan	SJHL	58	5	13	18	57	—	—	—	—	—
80-81—Victoria.............................	WHL	71	2	18	20	59	15	0	3	3	53
81-82—Victoria.............................	WHL	69	6	45	51	102	4	1	1	2	0
82-83—Victoria.............................	WHL	70	10	33	43	102	12	0	0	0	8
83-84—Binghamton	AHL	79	3	21	24	80	—	—	—	—	—
84-85—Salt Lake City..................	IHL	22	1	10	11	41	—	—	—	—	—
—Binghamton	AHL	54	1	13	14	109	7	0	0	0	12
85-86—Binghamton	AHL	64	0	9	9	196	6	0	0	0	6
86-87—Binghamton	AHL	72	2	15	17	187	9	0	2	2	42
87-88—Springfield........................	AHL	77	1	16	17	178	—	—	—	—	—
88-89—Adirondack	AHL	65	4	31	35	195	17	0	5	5	49
—Detroit	NHL	8	0	1	1	14	—	—	—	—	—
09-90—Detroit	NHL	33	0	1	1	82	—	—	—	—	—
—Adirondack	AHL	29	2	6	8	80	6	1	3	4	13
90-91—Maine	AHL	68	1	12	13	194	2	0	1	1	4
91-92—Binghamton	AHL	28	0	2	2	123	9	0	1	1	14
NHL totals..................................		41	0	2	2	96					

MOLLER, RANDY

D, SABRES

PERSONAL: Born August 23, 1963, at Red Deer, Alta.... 6-2/207.... Shoots right.... Brother of Mike Moller, right winger, Buffalo Sabres and Edmonton Oilers (1980-81 through 1986-87).

TRANSACTIONS/CAREER NOTES: Tore knee ligaments and underwent surgery (December 1980).... Selected by Quebec Nordiques in first round (first Nordiques pick, 11th overall) of NHL entry draft (June 10, 1981).... Broke hand (October 28, 1986).... Suffered lingering neck problem (November 1987).... Injured knee (January 1988).... Suffered back spasms (March 1988).... Separated shoulder (October 29, 1988).... Broke toe (September 1989).... Traded by Nordiques to New York Rangers for D Michel Petit (October 5, 1989).... Dislocated right shoulder (December 13, 1989).... Suffered back spasms (March 21, 1990); missed six games. ... Dislocated left shoulder (November 7, 1990); missed 15 games.... Separated shoulder (January 22, 1992); missed four games.... Traded by Rangers to Buffalo Sabres for D Jay Wells (March 9, 1992).

HONORS: Named to WHL All-Star second team (1981-82).

			REGULAR SEASON				PLAYOFFS			
Season Team	League	Gms.	G	A	Pts.	Pen.	Gms.	G	A	Pts.	Pen.
79-80—Red Deer	AJHL	56	3	34	37	253	—	—	—	—	—
80-81—Lethbridge........................	WHL	46	4	21	25	176	9	0	4	4	24
81-82—Lethbridge........................	WHL	60	20	55	75	249	12	4	6	10	65
—Quebec	NHL	—	—	—	—	—	1	0	0	0	2
82-83—Quebec	NHL	75	2	12	14	145	4	1	0	1	4
83-84—Quebec	NHL	74	4	14	18	147	9	1	0	1	45
84-85—Quebec	NHL	79	7	22	29	120	18	2	2	4	40
85-86—Quebec	NHL	69	5	18	23	141	3	0	0	0	26
86-87—Quebec	NHL	71	5	9	14	144	13	1	4	5	23
87-88—Quebec	NHL	66	3	22	25	169	—	—	—	—	—
88-89—Quebec	NHL	74	7	22	29	136	—	—	—	—	—
89-90—New York Rangers	NHL	60	1	12	13	139	10	1	6	7	32
90-91—New York Rangers	NHL	61	4	19	23	161	6	0	2	2	11
91-92—New York Rangers	NHL	43	2	7	9	78	—	—	—	—	—
—Binghamton	AHL	3	0	1	1	0	—	—	—	—	—
—Buffalo..............................	NHL	13	1	2	3	59	7	0	0	0	8
NHL totals..................................		685	41	159	200	1439	71	6	14	20	191

MOMESSO, SERGIO

LW, CANUCKS

PERSONAL: Born September 4, 1965, at Montreal.... 6-3/215.... Shoots left.

TRANSACTIONS/CAREER NOTES: Selected by Montreal Canadiens as underage junior in second round (third Canadiens pick, 27th overall) of NHL entry draft (June 8, 1983). ... Tore cruciate ligament in left knee and underwent surgery (December 5, 1985); missed remainder of season.... Tore ligaments, injured cartilage and fractured left knee (December 5, 1986).... Lacerated leg (February 1988).... Traded by Canadiens with G Vincent Riendeau to St. Louis Blues for LW Jocelyn Lemieux, G Darrell May and second-round pick in 1989 draft (D Patrice Brisebois) (August 9, 1988).... Fractured right ankle (November 12, 1988).... Traded by Blues with LW Geoff Courtnall, D Robert Dirk, C Cliff Ronning and future draft pick to Vancouver Canucks for C Dan Quinn and D Garth Butcher (March 5, 1991).... Separated shoulder (December 3, 1991); missed 22 games.

HONORS: Named to QMJHL All-Star first team (1984-85).

			REGULAR SEASON				PLAYOFFS			
Season Team	League	Gms.	G	A	Pts.	Pen.	Gms.	G	A	Pts.	Pen.
82-83—Shawinigan	QMJHL	70	27	42	69	93	10	5	4	9	55
83-84—Nova Scotia	AHL	—	—	—	—	—	8	0	2	2	4
—Shawinigan	QMJHL	68	42	88	130	235	6	4	4	8	13

M

Season	Team	League	REGULAR SEASON					PLAYOFFS				
			Gms.	G	A	Pts.	Pen.	Gms.	G	A	Pts.	Pen.
	—Montreal	NHL	1	0	0	0	0	—	—	—	—	—
84-85	—Shawinigan	QMJHL	64	56	90	146	216	8	7	8	15	17
85-86	—Montreal	NHL	24	8	7	15	46	—	—	—	—	—
86-87	—Montreal	NHL	59	14	17	31	96	11	1	3	4	31
	—Sherbrooke	AHL	6	1	6	7	10	—	—	—	—	—
87-88	—Montreal	NHL	53	7	14	21	101	6	0	2	2	16
88-89	—St. Louis	NHL	53	9	17	26	139	10	2	5	7	24
89-90	—St. Louis	NHL	79	24	32	56	199	12	3	2	5	63
90-91	—St. Louis	NHL	59	10	18	28	131	—	—	—	—	—
	—Vancouver	NHL	11	6	2	8	43	6	0	3	3	25
91-92	—Vancouver	NHL	58	20	23	43	198	13	0	5	5	30
	NHL totals		397	98	130	228	953	58	6	20	26	189

MONGEAU, MICHEL
C, LIGHTNING

PERSONAL: Born February 9, 1965, at Nun's Island, Que. . . . 5-9/190. . . . Shoots left.
TRANSACTIONS/CAREER NOTES: Signed as free agent by St. Louis Blues (August 21, 1989). . . . Selected by Tampa Bay Lightning in NHL expansion draft (June 18, 1992).

HONORS: Won Garry F. Longman Memorial Trophy (1986-87). . . . Won James Gatschene Memorial Trophy (1989-90). . . . Won Leo P. Lamoureux Memorial Trophy (1989-90). . . . Named to IHL All-Star first team (1989-90). . . . Won N.R. (Bud) Poile Trophy (1990-91). . . . Named to IHL All-Star second team (1990-91).

Season	Team	League	REGULAR SEASON					PLAYOFFS				
			Gms.	G	A	Pts.	Pen.	Gms.	G	A	Pts.	Pen.
83-84	—Laval	QMJHL	60	45	49	94	30	—	—	—	—	—
84-85	—Laval	QMJHL	67	60	84	144	56	—	—	—	—	—
85-86	—Laval	QMJHL	72	71	109	180	45	—	—	—	—	—
86-87	—Saginaw	IHL	76	42	53	95	34	10	3	6	9	10
87-88	—Played in France	France	30	31	21	52		—	—	—	—	—
88-89	—Flint	IHL	82	41	*76	117	57	—	—	—	—	—
89-90	—St. Louis	NHL	7	1	5	6	2	2	0	1	1	0
	—Peoria	IHL	73	39	*78	*117	53	5	3	4	7	6
90-91	—St. Louis	NHL	7	1	1	2	0	—	—	—	—	—
	—Peoria	IHL	73	41	65	106	114	19	10	*16	26	32
91-92	—Peoria	IHL	32	21	34	55	77	10	5	14	19	8
	—St. Louis	NHL	36	3	12	15	6	—	—	—	—	—
	NHL totals		50	5	18	23	8	2	0	1	1	0

MOOG, ANDY
G, BRUINS

PERSONAL: Born February 18, 1960, at Penticton, B.C. . . . 5-8/170. . . . Shoots left. . . . Full name: Donald Andrew Moog.
TRANSACTIONS/CAREER NOTES: Selected by Edmonton Oilers in seventh round (sixth Oilers pick, 132nd overall) of NHL entry draft (June 11, 1980). . . . Suffered viral infection (December 1983). . . . Injured ligaments in both knees (March 1, 1985). . . . Traded by Oilers to Boston Bruins for LW Geoff Courtnall and G Bill Ranford (March 1988). . . . Hyperextended right knee (January 31, 1991); missed three weeks.
HONORS: Named to WHL All-Star second team (1979-80). . . . Named to CHL All-Star second team (1981-82). . . . Named to THE SPORTING NEWS All-Star second team (1982-83). . . . Shared William M. Jennings Trophy with Rejean Lemelin (1989-90).

Season	Team	League	REGULAR SEASON							PLAYOFFS						
			Gms.	Min.	W	L	T	GA	SO	Avg.	Gms.	Min.	W	L	GA	SO	Avg.
76-77	—Kamloops	BCJHL	44	2735				173	0	3.80	—	—	—	—	—	—	—
	—Kamloops Chiefs	WCHL	1	35				6	0	10.29	—	—	—	—	—	—	—
77-78	—Penticton	BCJHL	39	2243				191	0	5.11	—	—	—	—	—	—	—
78-79	—Billings	WHL	26	1306	13	5	4	90	*3	4.13	5	229	1	3	21	0	5.50
79-80	—Billings	WHL	46	2435	23	14	1	149	1	3.67	3	190	2	1	10	0	3.16
80-81	—Wichita	CHL	29	1602	14	13	1	89	0	3.33	5	300	3	2	16	0	3.20
	—Edmonton	NHL	7	313	3	3	0	20	0	3.83	9	526	5	4	32	0	3.65
81-82	—Edmonton	NHL	8	399	3	5	0	32	0	4.81	—	—	—	—	—	—	—
	—Wichita	CHL	40	2391	23	13	3	119	1	2.99	7	434	3	4	23	0	3.18
82-83	—Edmonton	NHL	50	2833	33	8	7	167	1	3.54	16	949	11	5	48	0	3.03
83-84	—Edmonton	NHL	38	2212	27	8	1	139	1	3.77	7	263	4	0	12	0	2.74
84-85	—Edmonton	NHL	39	2019	22	9	3	111	1	3.30	2	20	0	0	0	0	0.00
85-86	—Edmonton	NHL	47	2664	27	9	7	164	1	3.69	1	60	1	0	1	0	1.00
86-87	—Edmonton	NHL	46	2461	28	11	3	144	0	3.51	2	120	2	0	8	0	4.00
87-88	—Can. National Team	Int'l	27	1438	10	7	5	86	0	3.59	—	—	—	—	—	—	—
	—Can. Olympic Team	Int'l	4	240	4	0	0	9	1	2.25	—	—	—	—	—	—	—
	—Boston	NHL	6	360	4	2	0	17	1	2.83	7	354	1	4	25	0	4.24
88-89	—Boston	NHL	41	2482	18	14	8	133	1	3.22	6	359	4	2	14	0	2.34
89-90	—Boston	NHL	46	2536	24	10	7	122	3	2.89	20	1195	13	7	44	*2	*2.21
90-91	—Boston	NHL	51	2844	25	13	9	136	4	2.87	19	1133	10	9	60	0	3.18
91-92	—Boston	NHL	62	3640	28	22	9	196	1	3.23	15	866	8	7	46	1	3.19
	NHL totals		441	24763	242	114	54	1381	14	3.35	104	5845	59	38	290	3	2.98

MORAN, IAN
D, PENGUINS

PERSONAL: Born August 24, 1972, at Cleveland. . . . 5-11/170. . . . Shoots right.
HIGH SCHOOL: Belmont Hill (Mass.).
TRANSACTIONS/CAREER NOTES: Underwent knee surgery (June 1988). . . . Separated shoulder (March 1989). . . . Selected by Pittsburgh Penguins in sixth round (fifth Penguins pick, 107th

overall) of NHL entry draft (June 16, 1990).
HONORS: Named Hockey East co-Rookie of the Year with Chad Quenneville (1991-92).

Season Team	League	REGULAR SEASON					PLAYOFFS				
		Gms.	G	A	Pts.	Pen.	Gms.	G	A	Pts.	Pen.
87-88—Belmont Hill H.S.	Mass. H.S.	25	3	13	16	15	—	—	—	—	—
88-89—Belmont Hill H.S.	Mass. H.S.	23	7	25	32	8	—	—	—	—	—
89-90—Belmont Hill H.S.	Mass. H.S.	—	10	36	46	0	—	—	—	—	—
90-91—Belmont Hill H.S.	Mass. H.S.	23	7	44	51	12	—	—	—	—	—
91-92—Boston College	Hockey East	30	2	16	18	44	—	—	—	—	—

MORE, JAY
D, SHARKS

PERSONAL: Born January 12, 1969, at Souris, Man. . . . 6-1/190. . . . Shoots right. . . . Full name: Jay-son More.

TRANSACTIONS/CAREER NOTES: Selected by New York Rangers as underage junior in first round (first Rangers pick, 10th overall) of NHL entry draft (June 13, 1987). . . . Traded by Rangers to Minnesota North Stars for C Dave Archibald (November 1, 1989). . . . Traded by North Stars to Montreal Canadiens for G Brian Hayward (November 7, 1990). . . . Selected by San Jose Sharks in NHL expansion draft (May 30, 1991). . . . Injured foot during pre-season (September 1991); missed 16 games. . . . Injured knee (March 1992).
HONORS: Named to WHL All-Star first team (1987-88).

Season Team	League	REGULAR SEASON					PLAYOFFS				
		Gms.	G	A	Pts.	Pen.	Gms.	G	A	Pts.	Pen.
84-85—Lethbridge......................	WHL	71	3	9	12	101	4	1	0	1	7
85-86—Lethbridge......................	WHL	61	7	18	25	155	9	0	2	2	36
86-87—New Westminster	WHL	64	8	29	37	217	—	—	—	—	—
87-88—New Westminster	WHL	70	13	47	60	270	5	0	2	2	26
88-89—Denver	IHL	62	7	15	22	138	3	0	1	1	26
—New York Rangers	NHL	1	0	0	0	0	—	—	—	—	—
89-90—Flint	IHL	9	1	5	6	41	—	—	—	—	—
—Kalamazoo	IHL	64	9	25	34	216	10	0	3	3	13
—Minnesota	NHL	5	0	0	0	16	—	—	—	—	—
90-91—Kalamazoo....................	IHL	10	0	5	5	46	—	—	—	—	—
—Fredericton	AHL	57	7	17	24	152	9	1	1	2	34
91-92—San Jose.......................	NHL	46	4	13	17	85	—	—	—	—	—
—Kansas City......................	IHL	2	0	2	2	4	—	—	—	—	—
NHL totals...................................		52	4	13	17	101					

MORIN, STEPHANE
C, NORDIQUES

PERSONAL: Born March 27, 1969, at Montreal. . . . 6-0/175. . . . Shoots left.
TRANSACTIONS/CAREER NOTES: Traded by Shawinigan Cataractes with second-round draft pick to Chicoutimi Sagueneens for D Daniel Bock (December 1987). . . . Selected by Quebec Nordiques in third round (third Nordiques pick, 43rd overall) of NHL entry draft (June 17, 1989). . . . Stretched right knee ligaments (January 8, 1991); missed six games. . . . Broke finger on right hand (February 20, 1991); missed eight games. . . . Sprained knee (October 12, 1991); missed nine games.
HONORS: Won Michel Briere Trophy (1988-1989). . . . Won Jean Beliveau Trophy (1988-1989). . . . Named to QMJHL All-Star first team (1988-89).

Season Team	League	REGULAR SEASON					PLAYOFFS				
		Gms.	G	A	Pts.	Pen.	Gms.	G	A	Pts.	Pen.
86-87—Shawinigan	QMJHL	65	9	14	23	28	14	1	3	4	27
87-88—Shawinigan/Chicoutimi ...	QMJHL	68	38	45	83	18	6	3	8	11	2
88-89—Chicoutimi	QMJHL	70	77	*109	*186	71	—	—	—	—	—
89-90—Quebec	NHL	6	0	2	2	2	—	—	—	—	—
—Halifax..............................	AHL	65	28	32	60	60	6	3	4	7	6
90-91—Halifax...........................	AHL	17	8	14	22	18	—	—	—	—	—
—Quebec	NHL	48	13	27	40	30	—	—	—	—	—
91-92—Quebec	NHL	30	2	8	10	14	—	—	—	—	—
—Halifax..............................	AHL	30	17	13	30	29	—	—	—	—	—
NHL totals...................................		84	15	37	52	46					

MORRIS, JON
C, DEVILS

PERSONAL: Born May 6, 1966, at Lowell, Mass. . . . 6-0/175. . . . Shoots right.
HIGH SCHOOL: Chelmsford (North Chelmsford, Mass.).
COLLEGE: Lowell (Mass.).
TRANSACTIONS/CAREER NOTES: Selected by New Jersey Devils in fifth round (fifth Devils pick, 86th overall) of NHL entry draft (June 9, 1984). . . . Missed most of 1988-89 season while attending school. . . . Strained rib cage (October 7, 1990).
HONORS: Named to NCAA All-America East second team (1986-87). . . . Named to Hockey East All-Star first team (1986-87).

Season Team	League	REGULAR SEASON					PLAYOFFS				
		Gms.	G	A	Pts.	Pen.	Gms.	G	A	Pts.	Pen.
83-84—Chelmsford H.S.	Mass. H.S.	24	31	50	81		—	—	—	—	—
84-85—University of Lowell...........	Hockey East	42	29	31	60	16	—	—	—	—	—
85-86—University of Lowell...........	Hockey East	39	25	31	56	52	—	—	—	—	—
86-87—University of Lowell...........	Hockey East	36	28	33	61	48	—	—	—	—	—
87-88—University of Lowell...........	Hockey East	37	15	39	54	39	—	—	—	—	—
88-89—New Jersey......................	NHL	4	0	2	2	0	—	—	—	—	—
89-90—Utica................................	AHL	49	27	37	64	6	—	—	—	—	—
—New Jersey......................	NHL	20	6	7	13	8	6	1	3	4	23

M

Season Team	League	REGULAR SEASON					PLAYOFFS				
		Gms.	G	A	Pts.	Pen.	Gms.	G	A	Pts.	Pen.
90-91—New Jersey	NHL	53	9	19	28	27	5	0	4	4	2
—Utica	AHL	6	4	2	6	5	—	—	—	—	—
91-92—New Jersey	NHL	7	1	2	3	6	—	—	—	—	—
—Utica	AHL	7	1	4	5	0	—	—	—	—	—
NHL totals		84	16	30	46	41	11	1	7	8	25

MORRISON, JUSTIN
C, CAPITALS

PERSONAL: Born February 9, 1972, at Newmarket, Ont. . . . 5-10/180. . . . Shoots right. . . . Full name: Justin George Morrison.
TRANSACTIONS/CAREER NOTES: Selected by Washington Capitals in fourth round (sixth Capitals pick, 80th overall) of NHL entry draft (June 22, 1991).

Season Team	League	REGULAR SEASON					PLAYOFFS				
		Gms.	G	A	Pts.	Pen.	Gms.	G	A	Pts.	Pen.
86-87—King City Jr. B.	OHA	34	15	20	35	95	—	—	—	—	—
87-88—Richmond Hill Jr. B	OHA	36	16	33	49	155	—	—	—	—	—
88-89—Kingston	OHL	44	13	13	26	101	—	—	—	—	—
89-90—Kingston	OHL	65	27	40	67	201	—	—	—	—	—
90-91—Kingston	OHL	61	44	57	101	222	—	—	—	—	—
91-92—Kingston	OHL	23	18	21	39	63	—	—	—	—	—
—Owen Sound	OHL	36	9	43	52	106	5	3	2	5	11

MORROW, SCOTT
LW, WHALERS

PERSONAL: Born June 18, 1969, at Chicago. . . . 6-1/180. . . . Shoots left. . . . Brother of Steve Morrow, defenseman in Philadelphia Flyers system.
HIGH SCHOOL: Northwood School (Lake Placid, N.Y.).
COLLEGE: New Hampshire.
TRANSACTIONS/CAREER NOTES: Selected by Hartford Whalers in fifth round (fourth Whalers pick, 95th overall) of NHL entry draft (June 11, 1988). . . . Broke ankle (November 18, 1988).
HONORS: Named to Hockey East All-Star second team (1991-92).

Season Team	League	REGULAR SEASON					PLAYOFFS				
		Gms.	G	A	Pts.	Pen.	Gms.	G	A	Pts.	Pen.
87-88—Northwood School	N.Y. H.S.	24	10	13	23		—	—	—	—	—
88-89—Univ. of New Hampshire	Hockey East	19	6	7	13	14	—	—	—	—	—
89-90—Univ. of New Hampshire	Hockey East	29	10	11	21	35	—	—	—	—	—
90-91—Univ. of New Hampshire	Hockey East	31	11	11	22	52	—	—	—	—	—
91-92—Univ. of New Hampshire	Hockey East	35	30	23	53	65	—	—	—	—	—
—Springfield	AHL	2	0	1	1	0	5	0	0	0	9

M

MORROW, STEVE
D, FLYERS

PERSONAL: Born April 3, 1968, at Plano, Tex. . . . 6-2/220. . . . Shoots left. . . . Full name: Steven Morrow. . . . Brother of Scott Morrow, left winger in Hartford Whalers system.
HIGH SCHOOL: Northwood School (Lake Placid, N.Y.).
COLLEGE: New Hampshire.
TRANSACTIONS/CAREER NOTES: Selected by Philadelphia Flyers in 10th round (10th Flyers pick, 209th overall) of NHL entry draft (June 13, 1987).

Season Team	League	REGULAR SEASON					PLAYOFFS				
		Gms.	G	A	Pts.	Pen.	Gms.	G	A	Pts.	Pen.
86-87—Westminster H.S.	Mass. H.S.	20	10	18	28	30	—	—	—	—	—
87-88—Northwood School	N.Y. H.S.	27	4	20	24		—	—	—	—	—
88-89—Univ. of New Hampshire	Hockey East	30	0	0	0	28	—	—	—	—	—
89-90—Univ. of New Hampshire	Hockey East	35	2	7	9	40	—	—	—	—	—
90-91—Univ. of New Hampshire	Hockey East	33	2	14	16	58	1	0	0	0	0
91-92—Univ. of New Hampshire	Hockey East	35	30	23	53	65	—	—	—	—	—
—Hershey	AHL	31	1	2	3	6	—	—	—	—	—

MOYLAN, DAVE
D, NORTH STARS

PERSONAL: Born August 13, 1967, at Tillsonburg, Ont. . . . 6-1/195. . . . Shoots left. . . . Full name: David Moylan.
TRANSACTIONS/CAREER NOTES: Separated shoulder (November 1983). . . . Selected by Buffalo Sabres as underage junior in fourth round (Sabres fourth pick, 77th overall) of NHL entry draft (June 15, 1985). . . . Signed as free agent by Minnesota North Stars (July 25, 1991).

Season Team	League	REGULAR SEASON					PLAYOFFS				
		Gms.	G	A	Pts.	Pen.	Gms.	G	A	Pts.	Pen.
83-84—St. Mary's Jr. B	OHA	46	7	13	20	143	—	—	—	—	—
84-85—Sudbury	OHL	66	1	15	16	108	—	—	—	—	—
85-86—Sudbury	OHL	52	10	25	35	87	4	0	0	0	15
86-87—Sudbury	OHL	13	5	6	11	41	—	—	—	—	—
—Kitchener	OHL	38	1	7	8	57	3	2	0	2	11
87-88—Flint	IHL	9	0	2	2	10	—	—	—	—	—
—Rochester	AHL	16	0	0	0	2	—	—	—	—	—
—Baltimore	AHL	20	4	5	9	35	—	—	—	—	—
88-89—Rochester	AHL	20	0	2	2	15	—	—	—	—	—
—Jokerit	Finland	15	4	4	8	38	5	0	0	0	2
89-90—Jokerit	Finland	42	3	8	11	107	—	—	—	—	—

Season Team	League	REGULAR SEASON					PLAYOFFS				
		Gms.	G	A	Pts.	Pen.	Gms.	G	A	Pts.	Pen.
90-91—New Haven	AHL	8	0	2	2	23	—	—	—	—	—
—Phoenix	IHL	15	1	2	3	8	—	—	—	—	—
—Kalamazoo	IHL	15	1	3	4	8	11	0	0	0	7
91-92—Kalamazoo	IHL	49	2	10	12	59	7	1	4	5	16

MULLEN, BRIAN
RW, SHARKS

PERSONAL: Born March 16, 1962, at New York. . . . 5-10/180. . . . Shoots left. . . . Full name: Brian Patrick Mullen. . . . Brother of Joe Mullen, right winger, Pittsburgh Penguins.
COLLEGE: Wisconsin.
TRANSACTIONS/CAREER NOTES: Selected by Winnipeg Jets in seventh round (seventh Jets pick, 128th overall) of NHL entry draft (June 11, 1980). . . . Traded by Jets with 10th-round pick in 1987 draft (LW Brett Barnett) to New York Rangers for fifth-round pick in 1988 draft (LW Benoit Lebeau) and third-round pick in 1989 draft (later traded to St. Louis Blues) (June 8, 1987). . . . Bruised left knee (January 1988). . . . Traded by Rangers with future considerations to San Jose Sharks for RW/C Tim Kerr (May 30, 1991). . . . Sprained knee (January 3, 1992); missed six games.

Season Team	League	REGULAR SEASON					PLAYOFFS				
		Gms.	G	A	Pts.	Pen.	Gms.	G	A	Pts.	Pen.
77-78—New York Westsiders	NYMJHL	33	21	36	57	38	—	—	—	—	—
78-79—New York Westsiders	NYMJHL	—	—	—	—	—	—	—	—	—	—
79-80—New York Westsiders	NYMJHL	—	—	—	—	—	—	—	—	—	—
80-81—University of Wisconsin	WCHA	38	11	13	24	28	—	—	—	—	—
81-82—University of Wisconsin	WCHA	33	20	17	37	10	—	—	—	—	—
82-83—Winnipeg	NHL	80	24	26	50	14	3	1	0	1	0
83-84—Winnipeg	NHL	75	21	41	62	28	3	0	3	3	6
84-85—Winnipeg	NHL	69	32	39	71	32	8	1	2	3	4
85-86—Winnipeg	NHL	79	28	34	62	38	3	1	2	3	6
86-87—Winnipeg	NHL	69	19	32	51	20	9	4	2	6	0
87-88—New York Rangers	NHL	74	25	29	54	42	—	—	—	—	—
88-89—New York Rangers	NHL	78	29	35	64	60	3	0	1	1	4
89-90—New York Rangers	NHL	76	27	41	68	42	10	2	2	4	8
90-91—New York Rangers	NHL	79	19	43	62	44	6	0	2	2	0
91-92—San Jose	NHL	72	18	28	46	66	—	—	—	—	—
NHL totals		751	242	348	590	386	45	9	14	23	28

MULLEN, JOE
RW, PENGUINS

PERSONAL: Born February 26, 1957, at New York. . . . 5-9/180. . . . Shoots right. . . . Full name: Joseph Patrick Mullen. . . . Brother of Brian Mullen, right winger, San Jose Sharks.
COLLEGE: Boston College.
TRANSACTIONS/CAREER NOTES: Signed as free agent by St. Louis Blues (August 16, 1979). . . . Suffered leg injury (October 18, 1982). . . . Tore ligaments in left knee and underwent surgery (January 29, 1983); missed remainder of season. . . . Traded by Blues with D Terry Johnson and D Rik Wilson to Calgary Flames for LW Eddy Beers, LW Gino Cavallini and D Charles Bourgeois (February 1, 1986). . . . Bruised knee (April 1988). . . . Suffered from the flu (April 1989). . . . Traded by Flames to Pittsburgh Penguins for second-round pick in 1990 draft (D Nicolas Perreault) (June 16, 1990). . . . Injured neck (January 22, 1991). . . . Underwent neck surgery for herniated disk (February 6, 1991); missed remainder of season. . . . Damaged ligament in knee (May 5, 1992); missed remainder of playoffs.
HONORS: Named Most Valuable Player (1974-75). . . . Named to ECAC All-Star first team (1977-78 and 1978-79). . . . Won Ken McKenzie Trophy (1979-80). . . . Named to Can.HL All-Star second team (1979-80). . . . Won Tommy Ivan Trophy (1980-81). . . . Won Phil Esposito Trophy (1980-81). . . . Named to Can.HL All-Star first team (1980-81). . . . Won Lady Byng Memorial Trophy (1986-87 and 1988-89). . . . Named to THE SPORTING NEWS All-Star first team (1988-89). . . . Named to NHL All-Star first team (1988-89). . . . Named to THE SPORTING NEWS All-Star second team (1991-92).

Season Team	League	REGULAR SEASON					PLAYOFFS				
		Gms.	G	A	Pts.	Pen.	Gms.	G	A	Pts.	Pen.
71-72—New York 14th Precinct	NYMJHL	30	13	11	24	2	—	—	—	—	—
72-73—New York Westsiders	NYMJHL	40	14	28	42	8	—	—	—	—	—
73-74—New York Westsiders	NYMJHL	†42	71	49	120	41	7	9	9	18	0
74-75—New York Westsiders	NYMJHL	40	*110	72	*182	20	13	*24	13	*37	2
75-76—Boston College	ECAC	24	16	18	34	4	—	—	—	—	—
76-77—Boston College	ECAC	28	28	26	54	8	—	—	—	—	—
77-78—Boston College	ECAC	34	34	34	68	12	—	—	—	—	—
78-79—Boston College	ECAC	25	32	24	56	8	—	—	—	—	—
79-80—Salt Lake City	IHL	75	40	32	72	21	13	†9	11	20	0
—St. Louis	NHL	—	—	—	—	—	1	0	0	0	0
80-81—Salt Lake City	IHL	80	59	58	*117	8	17	11	9	20	0
81-82—Salt Lake City	IHL	27	21	27	48	12	—	—	—	—	—
—St. Louis	NHL	45	25	34	59	4	10	7	11	18	4
82-83—St. Louis	NHL	49	17	30	47	6	—	—	—	—	—
83-84—St. Louis	NHL	80	41	44	85	19	6	2	0	2	0
84-85—St. Louis	NHL	79	40	52	92	6	3	0	0	0	0
85-86—St. Louis	NHL	48	28	24	52	10	—	—	—	—	—
—Calgary	NHL	29	16	22	38	11	21	*12	7	19	4
86-87—Calgary	NHL	79	47	40	87	14	6	2	1	3	0
87-88—Calgary	NHL	80	40	44	84	30	7	2	4	6	10
88-89—Calgary	NHL	79	51	59	110	16	21	*16	8	24	4
89-90—Calgary	NHL	78	36	33	69	24	6	3	0	3	0
90-91—Pittsburgh	NHL	47	17	22	39	6	22	8	9	17	4
91-92—Pittsburgh	NHL	77	42	45	87	30	9	3	1	4	4
NHL totals		770	400	449	849	176	112	55	41	96	30

MULLER, KIRK

LW, CANADIENS

PERSONAL: Born February 8, 1966, at Kingston, Ont.... 6-0/205.... Shoots left.
TRANSACTIONS/CAREER NOTES: Selected by New Jersey Devils as underage junior in first round (first Devils pick, second overall) of NHL entry draft (June 9, 1984).... Strained knee (January 13, 1986).... Fractured ribs (April 1986).... Traded by Devils with G Roland Melanson to Montreal Canadiens for RW Stephane Richer and RW Tom Chorske (September 1991).... Injured eye (January 21, 1992); missed one game.
HONORS: Won William Hanley Trophy (1982-83).

			REGULAR SEASON					PLAYOFFS				
Season	Team	League	Gms.	G	A	Pts.	Pen.	Gms.	G	A	Pts.	Pen.
80-81—Kingston		OMJHL	2	0	0	0	0	—	—	—	—	—
81-82—Kingston		OHL	67	12	39	51	27	4	5	1	6	4
82-83—Guelph		OHL	66	52	60	112	41	—	—	—	—	—
83-84—Canadian Olympic Team		Int'l	15	2	2	4	6	—	—	—	—	—
—Guelph		OHL	49	31	63	94	27	—	—	—	—	—
84-85—New Jersey		NHL	80	17	37	54	69	—	—	—	—	—
85-86—New Jersey		NHL	77	25	42	67	45	—	—	—	—	—
86-87—New Jersey		NHL	79	26	50	76	75	—	—	—	—	—
87-88—New Jersey		NHL	80	37	57	94	114	20	4	8	12	37
88-89—New Jersey		NHL	80	31	43	74	119	—	—	—	—	—
89-90—New Jersey		NHL	80	30	56	86	74	6	1	3	4	11
90-91—New Jersey		NHL	80	19	51	70	76	7	0	2	2	10
91-92—Montreal		NHL	78	36	41	77	86	11	4	3	7	31
NHL totals			634	221	377	598	658	44	9	16	25	89

MULLER, MIKE

D, JETS

PERSONAL: Born September 18, 1971, at Minneapolis.... 6-2/205.... Shoots left.... Full name: Mike Todd Muller.
HIGH SCHOOL: Wayzata (Plymouth, Minn.).
COLLEGE: Minnesota.
TRANSACTIONS/CAREER NOTES: Selected by Winnipeg Jets in second round (second Jets pick, 35th overall) of NHL entry draft (June 16, 1990).

			REGULAR SEASON					PLAYOFFS				
Season	Team	League	Gms.	G	A	Pts.	Pen.	Gms.	G	A	Pts.	Pen.
88-89—Wayzata H.S.		Minn. H.S.	24	10	11	21	56	—	—	—	—	—
89-90—Wayzata H.S.		Minn. H.S.	23	11	15	26	45	—	—	—	—	—
90-91—University of Minnesota		WCHA	33	4	4	8	44	—	—	—	—	—
91-92—University of Minnesota		WCHA	44	4	12	16	60	—	—	—	—	—

MULVENNA, GLENN

C, PENGUINS

PERSONAL: Born February 18, 1967, at Calgary, Alta.... 5-11/187.... Shoots left.
TRANSACTIONS/CAREER NOTES: Signed by Pittsburgh Penguins as free agent (December 3, 1987).

			REGULAR SEASON					PLAYOFFS				
Season	Team	League	Gms.	G	A	Pts.	Pen.	Gms.	G	A	Pts.	Pen.
86-87—New Westminster		WHL	53	24	44	68	43	—	—	—	—	—
—Kamloops		WHL	18	13	8	21	18	13	4	6	10	10
87-88—Kamloops		WHL	38	21	38	59	35	—	—	—	—	—
88-89—Flint		IHL	32	9	14	23	12	—	—	—	—	—
—Muskegon		IHL	11	3	2	5	0	—	—	—	—	—
—Knoxville		ECHL	2	0	0	0	5	—	—	—	—	—
89-90—Muskegon		IHL	52	14	21	35	17	11	2	3	5	0
—Fort Wayne		IHL	6	2	5	7	2	—	—	—	—	—
90-91—Muskegon		IHL	48	9	27	36	25	5	1	1	2	0
91-92—Pittsburgh		NHL	1	0	0	0	2	—	—	—	—	—
—Muskegon		IHL	70	15	27	42	24	14	5	6	11	11
NHL totals			1	0	0	0	2					

MUNI, CRAIG

D, OILERS

PERSONAL: Born July 19, 1962, at Toronto.... 6-3/200.... Shoots left.... Full name: Craig Douglas Muni.
TRANSACTIONS/CAREER NOTES: Selected by Toronto Maple Leafs as underage junior in second round (first Maple Leafs pick, 25th overall) of NHL entry draft (June 11, 1980).... Tore left knee ligaments (September 1981).... Broke ankle (January 1983).... Signed as free agent by Edmonton Oilers (August 18, 1986). ... Traded by Oilers to Buffalo Sabres for cash (October 2, 1986).... Traded by Sabres to Pittsburgh Penguins for future considerations (October 3, 1986).... Traded by Penguins to Oilers to complete earlier trade for G Gilles Meloche (October 6, 1986).... Bruised kidney (May 1987).... Bruised ankle (January 1988).... Bruised ankle (December 17, 1988).... Strained right shoulder (January 1989).... Broke little finger of right hand (January 27, 1990); missed eight games.... Suffered pinched nerve (January 15, 1992); missed 17 games.... Injured knee (March 19, 1992); missed eight games.... Suspended two games by NHL during playoffs for kneeing (May 22, 1992); missed final 1992 playoff game and scheduled to sit-out first game of 1992-93 regular season.

			REGULAR SEASON					PLAYOFFS				
Season	Team	League	Gms.	G	A	Pts.	Pen.	Gms.	G	A	Pts.	Pen.
79-80—Kingston		OMJHL	66	6	28	34	114	—	—	—	—	—
80-81—Kingston		OMJHL	38	2	14	16	65	—	—	—	—	—
—Windsor		OMJHL	25	5	11	16	41	11	1	4	5	14
—New Brunswick		AHL	—	—	—	—	—	2	0	1	1	10

Season	Team	League	Gms.	G	A	Pts.	Pen.	Gms.	G	A	Pts.	Pen.
81-82—Toronto	NHL	3	0	0	0	2	—	—	—	—	—
—Windsor	OHL	49	5	32	37	92	9	2	3	5	16
—Cincinnati	CHL	—	—	—	—	—	3	0	2	2	2
82-83—Toronto	NHL	2	0	1	1	0	—	—	—	—	—
—St. Catharines	AHL	64	6	32	38	52	—	—	—	—	—
83-84—St. Catharines	AHL	64	4	16	20	79	7	0	1	1	0
84-85—St. Catharines	AHL	68	7	17	24	54	—	—	—	—	—
—Toronto	NHL	8	0	0	0	0	—	—	—	—	—
85-86—Toronto	NHL	6	0	1	1	4	—	—	—	—	—
—St. Catharines	AHL	73	3	34	37	91	13	0	5	5	16
86-87—Edmonton	NHL	79	7	22	29	85	14	0	2	2	17
87-88—Edmonton	NHL	72	4	15	19	77	19	0	4	4	31
88-89—Edmonton	NHL	69	5	13	18	71	7	0	3	3	8
89-90—Edmonton	NHL	71	5	12	17	81	22	0	3	3	16
90-91—Edmonton	NHL	76	1	9	10	77	18	0	3	3	20
91-92—Edmonton	NHL	54	2	5	7	34	3	0	0	0	2
NHL totals		**440**	**24**	**78**	**102**	**431**	**83**	**0**	**15**	**15**	**94**

MURANO, ERIC
C, CANUCKS

PERSONAL: Born May 4, 1967, at LaSalle, Que. . . . 6-0/200. . . . Shoots right. . . . Full name: Eric A. Murano.
COLLEGE: Denver.
TRANSACTIONS/CAREER NOTES: Selected by Vancouver Canucks in fifth round (fourth Canucks pick, 91st overall) of NHL entry draft (June 21, 1986).
HONORS: Named to WCHA All-Star second team (1989-90).

			REGULAR SEASON					PLAYOFFS				
Season	Team	League	Gms.	G	A	Pts.	Pen.	Gms.	G	A	Pts.	Pen.
85-86—Calgary Canucks	AJHL	52	34	47	81	32	—	—	—	—	—
86-87—University of Denver	WCHA	31	5	7	12	12	—	—	—	—	—
87-88—University of Denver	WCHA	37	8	13	21	26	—	—	—	—	—
88-89—University of Denver	WCHA	42	13	16	29	52	—	—	—	—	—
89-90—University of Denver	WCHA	42	33	35	68	52	—	—	—	—	—
—Canadian National Team	Int'l	6	1	0	1	4	—	—	—	—	—
90-91—Milwaukee	IHL	63	32	35	67	63	3	0	1	1	4
91-92—Milwaukee	IHL	80	35	48	83	61	5	3	4	7	0

MURPHY, GORD
D, BRUINS

PERSONAL: Born February 23, 1967, at Willowdale, Ont. . . . 6-1/180. . . . Shoots right. . . . Full name: Gordon Murphy.
TRANSACTIONS/CAREER NOTES: Injured clavicle (January 1985). . . . Selected by Philadelphia Flyers as underage junior in ninth round (10th Flyers pick, 189th overall) of NHL entry draft (June 15, 1985). . . . Chipped point in left foot and suffered hip pointer (March 24, 1990). . . . Traded by Flyers with RW Brian Dobbin and third-round pick in 1992 draft to Boston Bruins for D Garry Galley, C Wes Walz and future considerations (January 2, 1992).

			REGULAR SEASON					PLAYOFFS				
Season	Team	League	Gms.	G	A	Pts.	Pen.	Gms.	G	A	Pts.	Pen.
83-84—Don Mills Flyers	MTHL	65	24	42	66	130	—	—	—	—	—
84-85—Oshawa	OHL	59	3	12	15	25	—	—	—	—	—
85-86—Oshawa	OHL	64	7	15	22	56	6	1	1	2	6
86-87—Oshawa	OHL	56	7	30	37	95	24	6	16	22	22
87-88—Hershey	AHL	62	8	20	28	44	12	0	8	8	12
88-89—Philadelphia	NHL	75	4	31	35	68	19	2	7	9	13
89-90—Philadelphia	NHL	75	14	27	41	95	—	—	—	—	—
90-91—Philadelphia	NHL	80	11	31	42	58	—	—	—	—	—
91-92—Philadelphia	NHL	31	2	8	10	33	—	—	—	—	—
—Boston	NHL	42	3	6	9	51	15	1	0	1	12
NHL totals		**303**	**34**	**103**	**137**	**305**	**34**	**3**	**7**	**10**	**25**

MURPHY, JOE
RW, OILERS

PERSONAL: Born October 16, 1967, at London, Ont. . . . 6-1/190. . . . Shoots left. . . . Full name: Joseph Patrick Murphy.
COLLEGE: Michigan State.
TRANSACTIONS/CAREER NOTES: Selected by Detroit Red Wings in first round (first Red Wings pick, first overall) of NHL entry draft (June 21, 1986). . . . Sprained right ankle (January 1988). . . . Traded by Red Wings with C/LW Adam Graves, LW Petr Klima and D Jeff Sharples to Edmonton Oilers for C Jimmy Carson, C Kevin McClelland and fifth-round pick in 1991 draft (November 2, 1989). . . . Bruised both thighs (March 1990).
HONORS: Named BCJHL Rookie of the Year (1984-85). . . . Named CCHA Rookie of the Year (1985-86).

			REGULAR SEASON					PLAYOFFS				
Season	Team	League	Gms.	G	A	Pts.	Pen.	Gms.	G	A	Pts.	Pen.
84-85—Penticton	BCJHL	51	68	84	*152	92	—	—	—	—	—
85-86—Michigan State	CCHA	35	24	37	61	50	—	—	—	—	—
—Team Canada	Int'l	8	3	3	6	2	—	—	—	—	—
86-87—Adirondack	AHL	71	21	38	59	61	10	2	1	3	33
—Detroit	NHL	5	0	1	1	2	—	—	—	—	—

Season Team	League	REGULAR SEASON					PLAYOFFS				
		Gms.	G	A	Pts.	Pen.	Gms.	G	A	Pts.	Pen.
87-88—Adirondack	AHL	6	5	6	11	4	—	—	—	—	—
—Detroit	NHL	50	10	9	19	37	8	0	1	1	6
88-89—Detroit	NHL	26	1	7	8	28	—	—	—	—	—
—Adirondack	AHL	47	31	35	66	66	16	6	11	17	17
89-90—Detroit	NHL	9	3	1	4	4	—	—	—	—	—
—Edmonton	NHL	62	7	18	25	56	22	6	8	14	16
90-91—Edmonton	NHL	80	27	35	62	35	15	2	5	7	14
91-92—Edmonton	NHL	80	35	47	82	52	16	8	16	24	12
NHL totals		312	83	118	201	214	61	16	30	46	48

MURPHY, LARRY
D, PENGUINS

PERSONAL: Born March 8, 1961, at Scarborough, Ont. . . . 6-1/210. . . . Shoots right. . . . Full name: Lawrence Thomas Murphy.
TRANSACTIONS/CAREER NOTES: Selected by Los Angeles Kings as underage junior in first round (first Kings pick, fourth overall) of NHL entry draft (June 11, 1980). . . . Traded by Kings to Washington Capitals for D Brian Engblom and RW Ken Houston (October 18, 1983). . . . Injured foot (October 29, 1985). . . . Broke ankle (May 1988). . . . Traded by Capitals with RW Mike Gartner to Minnesota North Stars for RW Dino Ciccarelli and D Bob Rouse (March 7, 1989). . . . Traded by North Stars with D Peter Taglianetti to Pittsburgh Penguins for D Jim Johnson and D Chris Dahlquist (December 11, 1990). . . . Fractured right foot (February 22, 1991); played until March 5 then missed five games.
HONORS: Won Max Kaminsky Trophy (1979-80). . . . Named to OMJHL All-Star first team (1979-80). . . . Named to THE SPORTING NEWS All-Star second team (1986-87). . . . Named to NHL All-Star second team (1986-87).
RECORDS: Holds NHL single-season record for most assists by a rookie defenseman—60; and points by a rookie defenseman—76 (1980-81).

Season Team	League	REGULAR SEASON					PLAYOFFS				
		Gms.	G	A	Pts.	Pen.	Gms.	G	A	Pts.	Pen.
78-79—Peterborough	OMJHL	66	6	21	27	82	19	1	9	10	42
79-80—Peterborough	OMJHL	68	21	68	89	88	14	4	13	17	20
80-81—Los Angeles	NHL	80	16	60	76	79	4	3	0	3	2
81-82—Los Angeles	NHL	79	22	44	66	95	10	2	8	10	12
82-83—Los Angeles	NHL	77	14	48	62	81	—	—	—	—	—
83-84—Los Angeles	NHL	6	0	3	3	0	—	—	—	—	—
—Washington	NHL	72	13	33	46	50	8	0	3	3	6
84-85—Washington	NHL	79	13	42	55	51	5	2	3	5	0
85-86—Washington	NHL	78	21	44	65	50	9	1	5	6	6
86-87—Washington	NHL	80	23	58	81	39	7	2	2	4	6
87-88—Washington	NHL	79	8	53	61	72	13	4	4	8	33
88-89—Washington	NHL	65	7	29	36	70	—	—	—	—	—
—Minnesota	NHL	13	4	6	10	12	5	0	2	2	8
89-90—Minnesota	NHL	77	10	58	68	44	7	1	2	3	31
90-91—Minnesota	NHL	31	4	11	15	38	—	—	—	—	—
—Pittsburgh	NHL	44	5	23	28	30	23	5	18	23	44
91-92—Pittsburgh	NHL	77	21	56	77	48	†21	6	10	16	19
NHL totals		937	181	568	749	759	112	26	57	83	167

MURPHY, ROB
C, SENATORS

PERSONAL: Born April 7, 1969, at Hull, Que. . . . 6-3/210. . . . Shoots left. . . . Full name: Robert Murphy.
TRANSACTIONS/CAREER NOTES: Selected by Vancouver Canucks as underage junior in second round (first Canucks pick, 24th overall) of NHL entry draft (June 13, 1987). . . . Separated shoulder (November 13, 1988). . . . Sprained right knee (November 3, 1990). . . . Selected by Ottawa Senators in NHL expansion draft (June 18, 1992).
HONORS: Won Michel Bergeron Trophy (1986-87). . . . Won Garry F. Longman Memorial Trophy (1989-90).

Season Team	League	REGULAR SEASON					PLAYOFFS				
		Gms.	G	A	Pts.	Pen.	Gms.	G	A	Pts.	Pen.
86-87—Laval	QMJHL	70	35	54	89	86	14	3	4	7	15
87-88—Vancouver	NHL	5	0	0	0	2	—	—	—	—	—
—Laval	QMJHL	26	11	25	36	82	—	—	—	—	—
—Drummondville	QMJHL	33	16	28	44	41	17	4	15	19	45
88-89—Drummondville	QMJHL	26	13	25	38	16	4	1	3	4	20
—Vancouver	NHL	8	0	1	1	2	—	—	—	—	—
—Milwaukee	IHL	8	4	2	6	4	11	3	5	8	34
89-90—Milwaukee	IHL	64	24	47	71	87	6	2	6	8	12
—Vancouver	NHL	12	1	1	2	0	—	—	—	—	—
90-91—Vancouver	NHL	42	5	1	6	90	4	0	0	0	2
—Milwaukee	IHL	23	1	7	8	48	—	—	—	—	—
91-92—Milwaukee	IHL	73	26	38	64	141	5	0	3	3	2
—Vancouver	NHL	6	0	1	1	6	—	—	—	—	—
NHL totals		73	6	4	10	100	4	0	0	0	2

MURRAY, GLEN
RW, BRUINS

PERSONAL: Born November 1, 1972, at Halifax, N.S. . . . 6-2/200. . . . Shoots right.
TRANSACTIONS/CAREER NOTES: Selected by Boston Bruins in first round (first Bruins pick, 18th overall) of NHL entry draft (June 22, 1991).

Season Team	League	REGULAR SEASON					PLAYOFFS				
		Gms.	G	A	Pts.	Pen.	Gms.	G	A	Pts.	Pen.
89-90—Sudbury	OHL	62	8	28	36	17	7	0	0	0	4
90-91—Sudbury	OHL	66	27	38	65	82	5	8	4	12	10
91-92—Sudbury	OHL	54	37	47	84	93	11	7	4	11	18
—Boston	NHL	5	3	1	4	0	15	4	2	6	10
NHL totals		5	3	1	4	0	15	4	2	6	10

MURRAY, PAT
RW, FLYERS

PERSONAL: Born August 20, 1969, at Stratford, Ont. . . . 6-3/195. . . . Shoots left. . . . Full name: Patrick Edward Murray.
COLLEGE: Michigan State.
TRANSACTIONS/CAREER NOTES: Selected by Philadelphia Flyers in second round (second Flyers pick, 35th overall) of NHL entry draft (June 11, 1988).
HONORS: Named to CCHA All-Star second team (1989-90).

Season Team	League	REGULAR SEASON					PLAYOFFS				
		Gms.	G	A	Pts.	Pen.	Gms.	G	A	Pts.	Pen.
86-87—Stratford Jr. B	OHA	42	34	75	109	38	—	—	—	—	—
87-88—Michigan State	CCHA	44	14	23	37	26	—	—	—	—	—
88-89—Michigan State	CCHA	46	21	41	62	65	—	—	—	—	—
89-90—Michigan State	CCHA	45	24	60	84	36	—	—	—	—	—
90-91—Philadelphia	NHL	16	2	1	3	15	—	—	—	—	—
—Hershey	AHL	57	15	38	53	8	7	5	2	7	0
91-92—Hershey	AHL	69	19	43	62	25	6	1	2	3	0
—Philadelphia	NHL	9	1	0	1	0	—	—	—	—	—
NHL totals		25	3	1	4	15					

MURRAY, RAYMOND
LW/C, KINGS

PERSONAL: Born October 9, 1972, at Stratford, Ont. . . . 6-1/183. . . . Shoots left.
COLLEGE: Michigan State.
TRANSACTIONS/CAREER NOTES: Selected by Los Angeles Kings in sixth round (fifth Kings pick, 135th overall) of NHL entry draft (June 20, 1992).

Season Team	League	REGULAR SEASON					PLAYOFFS				
		Gms.	G	A	Pts.	Pen.	Gms.	G	A	Pts.	Pen.
90-91—Stratford Jr. B	OHA	48	39	59	98	22	—	—	—	—	—
91-92—Michigan State	CCHA	44	12	36	48	16	—	—	—	—	—

MURRAY, ROB
C, JETS

PERSONAL: Born April 4, 1967, at Toronto. . . . 6-1/185. . . . Shoots right. . . . Full name: Robert Murray.
TRANSACTIONS/CAREER NOTES: Selected by Washington Capitals as underage junior in third round (third Capitals pick, 61st overall) of NHL entry draft (June 15, 1985). . . . Suspended two games by OHL (November 2, 1986). . . . Injured right hip (December 21, 1989); missed 10 games. . . . Selected by Minnesota North Stars in NHL expansion draft (May 30, 1991). . . . Traded by North Stars with future considerations to Winnipeg Jets for seventh-round pick in 1991 draft (G Geoff Finch) and future considerations (May 30, 1991).

Season Team	League	REGULAR SEASON					PLAYOFFS				
		Gms.	G	A	Pts.	Pen.	Gms.	G	A	Pts.	Pen.
83-84—Mississauga	OHA	35	18	36	54	32	—	—	—	—	—
84-85—Peterborough	OHL	63	12	9	21	155	17	2	7	9	45
85-86—Peterborough	OHL	52	14	18	32	125	16	1	2	3	50
86-87—Peterborough	OHL	62	17	37	54	204	3	1	4	5	8
87-88—Fort Wayne	IHL	80	12	21	33	139	6	0	2	2	16
88-89—Baltimore	AHL	80	11	23	34	235	—	—	—	—	—
89-90—Baltimore	AHL	23	5	4	9	63	—	—	—	—	—
—Washington	NHL	41	2	7	9	58	9	0	0	0	18
90-91—Baltimore	AHL	48	6	20	26	177	4	0	0	0	12
—Washington	NHL	17	0	3	3	19	—	—	—	—	—
91-92—Moncton	AHL	60	16	15	31	247	8	0	1	1	56
—Winnipeg	NHL	9	0	1	1	18	—	—	—	—	—
NHL totals		67	2	11	13	95	9	0	0	0	18

MURRAY, TROY
C, JETS

PERSONAL: Born July 31, 1962, at Winnipeg, Man. . . . 6-1/195. . . . Shoots right. . . . Full name: Troy Norman Murray.
COLLEGE: North Dakota.
TRANSACTIONS/CAREER NOTES: Selected by Chicago Blackhawks in third round (sixth Blackhawks pick, 57th overall) of NHL entry draft (June 11, 1980). . . . Injured knee ligaments (November 1983). . . . Lacerated face (December 1988). . . . Injured right elbow and underwent surgery (December 26, 1989); missed 11 games. . . . Developed bursitis on right elbow and hospitalized (February 8, 1990). . . . Traded by Blackhawks with LW Warren Rychel to Winnipeg Jets for D Bryan Marchment and D Chris Norton (July 22, 1991). . . . Separated shoulder (October 23, 1991); missed four games. . . . Lacerated knee (December 14, 1991); missed three games.
HONORS: Won WCHA Freshman of the Year Award (1980-81). . . . Named to WCHA All-Star second team (1980-81 and 1981-82). . . . Won Frank J. Selke Trophy (1985-86).

Season Team	League	REGULAR SEASON					PLAYOFFS				
		Gms.	G	A	Pts.	Pen.	Gms.	G	A	Pts.	Pen.
79-80—St. Albert	AJHL	60	53	47	100	101	—	—	—	—	—
80-81—Univ. of North Dakota	WCHA	38	33	45	78	28	—	—	—	—	—

M

Season Team	League	REGULAR SEASON					PLAYOFFS				
		Gms.	G	A	Pts.	Pen.	Gms.	G	A	Pts.	Pen.
81-82—Univ. of North Dakota	WCHA	42	22	29	51	62	—	—	—	—	—
—Chicago	NHL	1	0	0	0	0	7	1	0	1	5
82-83—Chicago	NHL	54	8	8	16	27	2	0	0	0	0
83-84—Chicago	NHL	61	15	15	30	45	5	1	0	1	7
84-85—Chicago	NHL	80	26	40	66	82	15	5	14	19	24
85-86—Chicago	NHL	80	45	54	99	94	2	0	0	0	2
86-87—Chicago	NHL	77	28	43	71	59	4	0	0	0	5
87-88—Chicago	NHL	79	22	36	58	96	5	1	0	1	8
88-89—Chicago	NHL	79	21	30	51	113	16	3	6	9	25
89-90—Chicago	NHL	68	17	38	55	86	20	4	4	8	22
90-91—Chicago	NHL	75	14	23	37	74	6	0	1	1	12
91-92—Winnipeg	NHL	74	17	30	47	69	7	0	0	0	2
NHL totals		728	213	317	530	745	89	15	25	40	112

MURZYN, DANA
D, CANUCKS

PERSONAL: Born December 9, 1966, at Regina, Sask. . . . 6-2/200. . . . Shoots left.
TRANSACTIONS/CAREER NOTES: Selected by Hartford Whalers as underage junior in first round (first Whalers pick, fifth overall) of NHL entry draft (June 15, 1985). . . . Traded by Whalers with RW Shane Churla to Calgary Flames for C Carey Wilson, D Neil Sheehy and LW Lane MacDonald (January 3, 1988). . . . Strained knee (March 13, 1989). . . . Pulled groin (February 4, 1990). . . . Bruised hip (October 25, 1990); missed 11 games. . . . Separated shoulder (December 1, 1990); missed 34 games. . . . Traded by Flames with fourth-round pick in 1992 draft to Vancouver Canucks for RW Ron Stern, D Kevan Guy and fourth-round pick in 1992 draft (March 5, 1991).
HONORS: Named to WHL All-Star first team (1984-85). . . . Named to NHL All-Rookie team (1985-86).

Season Team	League	REGULAR SEASON					PLAYOFFS				
		Gms.	G	A	Pts.	Pen.	Gms.	G	A	Pts.	Pen.
83-84—Calgary	WHL	65	11	20	31	135	2	0	0	0	0
84-85—Calgary	WHL	72	32	60	92	233	8	1	11	12	16
85-86—Hartford	NHL	78	3	23	26	125	4	0	0	0	10
86-87—Hartford	NHL	74	9	19	28	95	6	2	1	3	29
87-88—Hartford	NHL	33	1	6	7	45	—	—	—	—	—
—Calgary	NHL	41	6	5	11	94	5	2	0	2	13
88-89—Calgary	NHL	63	3	19	22	142	21	0	3	3	20
89-90—Calgary	NHL	78	7	13	20	140	6	2	2	4	2
90-91—Calgary	NHL	19	0	2	2	30	—	—	—	—	—
—Vancouver	NHL	10	1	0	1	8	6	0	1	1	8
91-92—Vancouver	NHL	70	3	11	14	147	1	0	0	0	15
NHL totals		466	33	98	131	826	49	6	7	13	97

MUSIL, FRANTISEK
D, FLAMES

PERSONAL: Born December 17, 1964, at Pardubice, Czechoslovakia. . . . 6-3/215. . . . Shoots left.
TRANSACTIONS/CAREER NOTES: Selected by Minnesota North Stars in second round (third North Stars pick, 38th overall) of NHL entry draft (June 8, 1983). . . . Separated shoulder (December 9, 1986). . . . Fractured foot (December 17, 1988). . . . Suffered concussion (February 9, 1989). . . . Strained lower back muscles (February 18, 1989). . . . Suffered back spasms (November 2, 1989); missed 10 games. . . . Separated right shoulder (April 1990). . . . Traded by North Stars to Calgary Flames for D Brian Glynn (October 26, 1990).

Season Team	League	REGULAR SEASON					PLAYOFFS				
		Gms.	G	A	Pts.	Pen.	Gms.	G	A	Pts.	Pen.
85-86—Dukla Jihlava	Czech.	35	3	7	10	85	—	—	—	—	—
86-87—Minnesota	NHL	72	2	9	11	148	—	—	—	—	—
87-88—Minnesota	NHL	80	9	8	17	213	—	—	—	—	—
88-89—Minnesota	NHL	55	1	19	20	54	5	1	1	2	4
89-90—Minnesota	NHL	56	2	8	10	109	4	0	0	0	14
90-91—Minnesota	NHL	8	0	2	2	23	—	—	—	—	—
—Calgary	NHL	67	7	14	21	160	7	0	0	0	10
91-92—Calgary	NHL	78	4	8	12	103	—	—	—	—	—
NHL totals		416	25	68	93	810	16	1	1	2	28

MUZZATTI, JASON
G, FLAMES

PERSONAL: Born February 3, 1970, at Toronto. . . . 6-1/190. . . . Shoots left. . . . Full name: Jason Mark Muzzatti.
COLLEGE: Michigan State.
TRANSACTIONS/CAREER NOTES: Selected by Calgary Flames in first round (first Flames pick, 21st overall) of NHL entry draft (June 11, 1988).
HONORS: Named to NCAA All-America West second team (1989-90). . . . Named to CCHA All-Star first team (1989-90). . . . Named to CCHA All-Tournament team (1989-90).

Season Team	League	REGULAR SEASON							PLAYOFFS						
		Gms.	Min.	W	L	T	GA	SO	Avg.	Gms.	Min.	W	L	GA	SO	Avg.
86-87—St. Mikes Jr. B	MTHL	20	1054				69	1	3.93	—	—	—	—	—	—	—
87-88—Michigan State	CCHA	33	1916	19	9	3	109	1	3.41	—	—	—	—	—	—	—
88-89—Michigan State	CCHA	42	2515	32	9	1	127	3	3.03	—	—	—	—	—	—	—
89-90—Michigan State	CCHA	33	1976	24	6	0	99	0	3.01	—	—	—	—	—	—	—
90-91—Michigan State	CCHA	22	1204	8	10	2	75	0	3.74	—	—	—	—	—	—	—
91-92—Salt Lake City	IHL	52	3033	24	22	5	167	2	3.30	4	247	1	3	18	0	4.37

MYHRES, BRANTT
LW, LIGHTNING

PERSONAL: Born March 18, 1974, at Edmonton, Alta. . . . 6-3/200. . . . Shoots right.
HIGH SCHOOL: Sir Winston Churchill (Calgary, Alta.).
TRANSACTIONS/CAREER NOTES: Selected by Tampa Bay Lightning in fifth round (fifth Lightning pick, 97th overall) of NHL entry draft (June 20, 1992).

			REGULAR SEASON					PLAYOFFS				
Season	Team	League	Gms.	G	A	Pts.	Pen.	Gms.	G	A	Pts.	Pen.
90-91	Portland	WHL	59	2	7	9	125	—	—	—	—	—
91-92	Portland	WHL	4	0	2	2	22	—	—	—	—	—
	Lethbridge	WHL	53	4	11	15	359	5	0	0	0	36

MYLLYS, JARMO
G, MAPLE LEAFS

PERSONAL: Born May 29, 1965, at Sovanlinna, Finland. . . . 5-8/150. . . . Shoots right.
TRANSACTIONS/CAREER NOTES: Selected by Minnesota North Stars in ninth round (ninth North Stars pick, 172nd overall) of NHL entry draft (June 13, 1987). . . . Injured knee (April 22, 1990). . . . Selected by San Jose Sharks in NHL dispersal draft (May 30, 1991). . . . Injured hand (November 2, 1991); missed 10 games. . . . Traded by Sharks to Toronto Maple Leafs for future considerations (June 15, 1992).
HONORS: Named to IHL All-Star second team (1989-90).
MISCELLANEOUS: Member of 1988 silver-medal-winning Finnish Olympic team.

			REGULAR SEASON							PLAYOFFS						
Season	Team	League	Gms.	Min.	W	L	T	GA	SO	Avg.	Gms.	Min.	W	L	GA	SO	Avg.
87-88	Lukko	Finland	43	2680				160		3.72	—	—			—		—
88-89	Kalamazoo	IHL	28	1523	13	8	4	93	0	3.66	6	419	2	4	22	0	3.15
	Minnesota	NHL	6	238	1	4	0	22	0	5.55	—	—	—	—	—	—	—
89-90	Minnesota	NHL	4	156	0	3	0	16	0	6.15	—	—	—	—	—	—	—
	Kalamazoo	IHL	49	2715	31	9	3	159	1	3.51	5	258	4	0	11	0	2.56
90-91	Kalamazoo	IHL	38	2278	24	13	3	144	1	3.79	10	600	6	4	26	2	2.60
	Minnesota	NHL	2	78	0	2	0	8	0	6.15	—	—	—	—	—	—	—
91-92	San Jose	NHL	27	1374	3	18	1	115	0	5.02	—	—	—	—	—	—	—
	Kansas City	IHL	5	307	5	0	0	15	0	2.93	—	—	—	—	—	—	—
	NHL totals		39	1846	4	27	1	161	0	5.23							

NASLUND, MARKUS
RW, PENGUINS

PERSONAL: Born July 30, 1973, at Harnosand, Sweden. . . . 5-11/174. . . . Shoots left.
TRANSACTIONS/CAREER NOTES: Selected by Pittsburgh Penguins in first round (first Penguins pick, 16th overall) of NHL entry draft (June 22, 1991).

			REGULAR SEASON					PLAYOFFS				
Season	Team	League	Gms.	G	A	Pts.	Pen.	Gms.	G	A	Pts.	Pen.
89-90	MoDo	Sweden Jr.	33	43	35	78	20	—	—	—	—	—
90-91	MoDo	Sweden	32	10	9	19	14	—	—	—	—	—
91-92	MoDo	Sweden	39	22	17	39	52	—	—	—	—	—

NATTRESS, RIC
D, MAPLE LEAFS

PERSONAL: Born May 25, 1962, at Hamilton, Ont. . . . 6-2/208. . . . Shoots right. . . . Full name: Eric Ric Nattress.
TRANSACTIONS/CAREER NOTES: Selected by Montreal Canadiens as underage junior in second round (second Canadiens pick, 27th overall) of NHL entry draft (June 11, 1980). . . . Suspended 40 games by NHL following his conviction in Ontario court for drug possession (September 1983). . . . Fractured finger (March 1984). . . . Traded by Canadiens to St. Louis Blues to complete June deal for RW Mark Hunter (September 1985). . . . Injured shoulder (March 17, 1986). . . . Strained knee (February 1987). . . . Traded by Blues to Calgary Flames for fourth-round pick in 1987 draft (LW Andy Rymsha) and fifth-round pick in 1988 draft (RW Dave Lacouture) (June 13, 1987). . . . Bruised right shoulder (March 1988). . . . Underwent knee surgery (March 1988). . . . Pulled hamstring (November 1988). . . . Injured groin (February 1989). . . . Bruised hand (December 10, 1989); missed six games. . . . Broke right ankle (February 7, 1990); in cast until March 16. . . . Underwent surgery for torn knee cartilage (September 27, 1990). . . . Twisted knee (October 22, 1991); missed 16 games. . . . Underwent arthroscopic knee surgery (November 4, 1991). . . . Bruised left foot (December 21, 1991); missed four games. . . . Traded by Flames with C Doug Gilmour, LW Kent Manderville, D Jamie Macoun and G Rick Wamsley to Toronto Maple Leafs for LW Craig Berube, D Alexander Godynyuk, LW Gary Leeman, D Michel Petit and G Jeff Reese (January 2, 1992).

			REGULAR SEASON					PLAYOFFS				
Season	Team	League	Gms.	G	A	Pts.	Pen.	Gms.	G	A	Pts.	Pen.
79-80	Brantford	OMJHL	65	3	21	24	94	11	1	6	7	38
80-81	Brantford	OMJHL	51	8	34	42	106	6	1	4	5	19
81-82	Brantford	OHL	59	11	50	61	126	11	3	7	10	17
	Nova Scotia	AHL	—	—	—	—	—	5	0	1	1	7
82-83	Nova Scotia	AHL	9	0	4	4	16	—	—	—	—	—
	Montreal	NHL	40	1	3	4	19	3	0	0	0	10
83-84	Montreal	NHL	34	0	12	12	15	—	—	—	—	—
84-85	Sherbrooke	AHL	72	8	40	48	37	16	4	13	17	20
	Montreal	NHL	5	0	1	1	2	2	0	0	0	2
85-86	St. Louis	NHL	78	4	20	24	52	18	1	4	5	24
86-87	St. Louis	NHL	73	6	22	28	24	6	0	0	0	2
87-88	Calgary	NHL	63	2	13	15	37	6	1	3	4	0
88-89	Calgary	NHL	38	1	8	9	47	19	0	3	3	20
89-90	Calgary	NHL	49	1	14	15	26	6	2	0	2	8
90-91	Calgary	NHL	58	5	13	18	63	7	1	0	1	2
91-92	Calgary	NHL	18	0	5	5	31	—	—	—	—	—
	Toronto	NHL	36	2	14	16	32	—	—	—	—	—
	NHL totals		492	22	125	147	348	67	5	10	15	68

MN

NAZAROV, ANDREI
LW, SHARKS

PERSONAL: Born March 21, 1972, at Chelyabinsk, U.S.S.R. .... 6-4/209. .... Shoots right.
TRANSACTIONS/CAREER NOTES: Selected by San Jose Sharks in first round (second Sharks pick, 10th overall) of NHL entry draft (June 20, 1992).

			REGULAR SEASON				PLAYOFFS			
Season Team	League	Gms.	G	A	Pts.	Pen.	Gms.	G	A	Pts.	Pen.
90-91—Mechel Chelyabinsk	USSR	2	0	0	0	0	—	—	—	—	—
91-92—Dynamo Moscow	CIS	2	1	0	1	2	—	—	—	—	—

NEDVED, PETR
C, CANUCKS

PERSONAL: Born December 9, 1971, at Liberec, Czechoslovakia.... 6-3/185.... Shoots left.
TRANSACTIONS/CAREER NOTES: Defected from Czechoslovakian midget team that was playing in Calgary, Alberta (January 1989).... WHL rights traded by Moose Jaw Warriors with D Brian Ilkuf to Seattle Thunderbirds for D Corey Beaulieu (February 3, 1989).... Selected by Vancouver Canucks in first round (first Canucks pick, second overall) of NHL entry draft (June 16, 1990).
HONORS: Won CHL Rookie of the Year Award (1989-90).... Won Jim Piggott Memorial Trophy (1989-90).

			REGULAR SEASON				PLAYOFFS			
Season Team	League	Gms.	G	A	Pts.	Pen.	Gms.	G	A	Pts.	Pen.
89-90—Seattle	WHL	71	65	80	145	80	11	4	9	13	2
90-91—Vancouver	NHL	61	10	6	16	20	6	0	1	1	0
91-92—Vancouver	NHL	77	15	22	37	36	10	1	4	5	16
NHL totals		138	25	28	53	56	16	1	5	6	16

NEEDHAM, MIKE
RW, PENGUINS

PERSONAL: Born April 4, 1970, at Calgary, Alta.... 5-10/185.... Shoots right.
TRANSACTIONS/CAREER NOTES: Selected by Pittsburgh Penguins in sixth round (seventh Penguins pick, 126th overall) of NHL entry draft (June 17, 1989).
HONORS: Shared Most Dedicated Player Trophy with Bob Calhoon (1985-86).... Named to WHL All-Star first team (1989-90).

			REGULAR SEASON				PLAYOFFS			
Season Team	League	Gms.	G	A	Pts.	Pen.	Gms.	G	A	Pts.	Pen.
85-86—Fort Saskatchewan	AJHL	49	19	26	45	97	—	—	—	—	—
86-87—Fort Saskatchewan	AJHL	—	—	—	—	—	—	—	—	—	—
—Kamloops	WHL	3	1	2	3	0	11	2	1	3	5
87-88—Kamloops	WHL	64	31	33	64	93	5	0	1	1	5
88-89—Kamloops	WHL	49	24	27	51	55	16	2	9	11	13
89-90—Kamloops	WHL	60	59	66	125	75	17	11	13	24	10
90-91—Muskegon	IHL	65	14	32	46	17	5	2	2	4	5
91-92—Muskegon	IHL	80	41	37	78	83	8	4	4	8	6
—Pittsburgh	NHL	—	—	—	—	—	5	1	0	1	2
NHL totals							5	1	0	1	2

NEELY, CAM
RW, BRUINS

PERSONAL: Born June 6, 1965, at Comox, B.C.... 6-1/210.... Shoots right.... Full name: Cameron Michael Neely.
TRANSACTIONS/CAREER NOTES: Selected by Vancouver Canucks as underage junior in first round (first Canucks pick, ninth overall) of NHL entry draft (June 8, 1983).... Dislocated kneecap (October 1984).... Traded by Canucks with first-round pick in 1987 draft (D Glen Wesley) to Boston Bruins for C Barry Pederson (June 6, 1986).... Slipped right kneecap (March 1988).... Fractured right thumb and inflamed right knee (December 1988). ... Suffered recurrence of right knee inflammation (March 1989).... Hyperextended knee (October 1989).... Pulled groin (March 1990).... Suspended five games by NHL for high-sticking (November 23, 1990).... Suffered thigh injury (May 11, 1991); missed first 38 games of 1991-92 season.... Suffered knee inflammation (January 1992).... Underwent surgery to knee (February 3, 1992); missed remainder of season.
HONORS: Named to THE SPORTING NEWS All-Star first team (1987-88).... Named to NHL All-Star second team (1987-88, 1989-90 and 1990-91).... Named to THE SPORTING NEWS All-Star second team (1989-90 and 1990-91).
RECORDS: Shares NHL single-season playoff record for most power-play goals—9 (1991).

			REGULAR SEASON				PLAYOFFS			
Season Team	League	Gms.	G	A	Pts.	Pen.	Gms.	G	A	Pts.	Pen.
82-83—Portland	WHL	72	56	64	120	130	14	9	11	20	17
83-84—Portland	WHL	19	8	18	26	29	—	—	—	—	—
—Vancouver	NHL	56	16	15	31	57	4	2	0	2	2
84-85—Vancouver	NHL	72	21	18	39	137	—	—	—	—	—
85-86—Vancouver	NHL	73	14	20	34	126	3	0	0	0	6
86-87—Boston	NHL	75	36	36	72	143	4	5	1	6	8
87-88—Boston	NHL	69	42	27	69	175	23	9	8	17	51
88-89—Boston	NHL	74	37	38	75	190	10	7	2	9	8
89-90—Boston	NHL	76	55	37	92	117	21	12	16	28	51
90-91—Boston	NHL	69	51	40	91	98	19	16	4	20	36
91-92—Boston	NHL	9	9	3	12	16	—	—	—	—	—
NHL totals		573	281	234	515	1059	84	51	31	82	162

NELSON, CHRISTOPHER
D, DEVILS

PERSONAL: Born February 12, 1969, at Philadelphia. .... 6-2/190. .... Shoots right.... Full name: Christopher Viscount Nelson.
COLLEGE: Wisconsin.
TRANSACTIONS/CAREER NOTES: Selected by New Jersey Devils in fifth round (sixth Devils pick, 96th overall) of NHL entry draft (June 11, 1988).

Season	Team	League	REGULAR SEASON Gms.	G	A	Pts.	Pen.	PLAYOFFS Gms.	G	A	Pts.	Pen.
87-88—	Rochester	USHL	48	6	29	35	82	—	—	—	—	—
88-89—	University of Wisconsin ...	WCHA	21	1	4	5	24	—	—	—	—	—
89-90—	University of Wisconsin ...	WCHA	38	1	3	4	38	—	—	—	—	—
90-91—	University of Wisconsin ...	WCHA	42	5	12	17	48	—	—	—	—	—
91-92—	University of Wisconsin ...	WCHA	43	4	12	16	96	—	—	—	—	—

NELSON, JEFF
C, CAPITALS

PERSONAL: Born December 18, 1972, at Prince Albert, Sask. . . . 6-0/180. . . . Shoots left. . . . Full name: Jeffrey Arthur Nelson. . . . Brother of Todd Nelson, defenseman in Pittsburgh Penguins system.
TRANSACTIONS/CAREER NOTES: Selected by Washington Capitals in second round (fourth Capitals pick, 36th overall) of NHL entry draft (June 22, 1991).
HONORS: Won Can.HL Scholastic Player of the Year Award (1988-89 and 1989-90). . . . Named WHL Scholastic Player of the Year (1988-89 and 1989-90). . . . Named WHL (East) Player of the Year (1990-91). . . . Named to WHL All-Star second team (1990-91). . . . Named to WHL (East) All-Star second team (1991-92).

Season	Team	League	REGULAR SEASON Gms.	G	A	Pts.	Pen.	PLAYOFFS Gms.	G	A	Pts.	Pen.
88-89—	Prince Albert	WHL	71	30	57	87	74	4	0	3	3	4
89-90—	Prince Albert	WHL	72	28	69	97	79	14	2	11	13	10
00 01	Prince Albert	WHL	72	46	74	120	58	3	1	1	2	4
91-92—	Prince Albert	WHL	64	48	65	113	84	9	7	14	21	18

NELSON, TODD
D, PENGUINS

PERSONAL: Born May 15, 1969, at Prince Albert, Sask. . . . 6-1/201. . . . Shoots left. . . . Brother of Jeff Nelson, center in Washington Capitals system.
TRANSACTIONS/CAREER NOTES: Dislocated right shoulder (October 1986). . . . Dislocated left shoulder (May 1987). . . . Selected by Pittsburgh Penguins in fourth round (fourth Penguins pick, 79th overall) of NHL entry draft (June 17, 1989).
HONORS: Named to WHL All-Star second team (1988-89 and 1989-90).

Season	Team	League	REGULAR SEASON Gms.	G	A	Pts.	Pen.	PLAYOFFS Gms.	G	A	Pts.	Pen.
85-86—	Prince Albert	WHL	4	0	0	0	0	—	—	—	—	—
86-87—	Prince Albert	WHL	35	1	6	7	10	4	0	0	0	0
87-88—	Prince Albert	WHL	72	3	21	24	59	10	3	2	5	4
88-89—	Prince Albert	WHL	72	14	45	59	72	4	1	3	4	4
89-90—	Prince Albert	WHL	69	13	42	55	88	14	3	12	15	12
90-91—	Muskegon	IHL	79	4	20	24	32	3	0	0	0	4
91-92—	Muskegon	IHL	80	6	35	41	46	14	1	11	12	4
—	Pittsburgh	NHL	1	0	0	0	0	—	—	—	—	—
NHL totals			1	0	0	0	0					

NEMCHINOV, SERGEI
C, RANGERS

PERSONAL: Born January 14, 1964, at Moscow, U.S.S.R. . . . 6-0/199. . . . Shoots left.
TRANSACTIONS/CAREER NOTES: Selected by New York Rangers in 12th round (14th Rangers pick, 244th overall) of NHL entry draft (June 16, 1990). . . . Sprained knee (November 4, 1991); missed seven games.

Season	Team	League	REGULAR SEASON Gms.	G	A	Pts.	Pen.	PLAYOFFS Gms.	G	A	Pts.	Pen.
81-82—	Soviet Wings	USSR	15	1	0	1	0	—	—	—	—	—
82-83—	CSKA Moscow	USSR	11	0	0	0	2	—	—	—	—	—
83-84—	CSKA Moscow	USSR	20	6	5	11	4	—	—	—	—	—
84-85—	CSKA Moscow	USSR	31	2	4	6	4	—	—	—	—	—
85-86—	Soviet Wings	USSR	39	7	12	19	28	—	—	—	—	—
86-87—	Soviet Wings	USSR	40	13	9	22	24	—	—	—	—	—
87-88—	Soviet Wings	USSR	48	17	11	28	26	—	—	—	—	—
88-89—	Soviet Wings	USSR	43	15	14	29	28	—	—	—	—	—
89-90—	Soviet Wings	USSR	48	17	16	33	34	—	—	—	—	—
90-91—	Soviet Wings	USSR	46	21	24	45	30	—	—	—	—	—
91-92—	New York Rangers	NHL	73	30	28	58	15	13	1	4	5	8
NHL totals			73	30	28	58	15	13	1	4	5	8

NESICH, JIM
RW/C, NORTH STARS

PERSONAL: Born February 22, 1966, at Dearborn, Mich. . . . 5-11/160. . . . Shoots right.
TRANSACTIONS/CAREER NOTES: Selected by Montreal Canadiens in sixth round (eighth Canadiens pick, 116th overall) of NHL entry draft (June 9, 1984). . . . Broke ankle (December 10, 1989). . . . Traded by Canadiens to Minnesota North Stars for future considerations (August 9, 1991).

Season	Team	League	REGULAR SEASON Gms.	G	A	Pts.	Pen.	PLAYOFFS Gms.	G	A	Pts.	Pen.
83-84—	Verdun	QMJHL	70	22	24	46	35	10	11	5	16	2
84-85—	Verdun	QMJHL	65	19	33	52	72	14	1	6	7	25
85-86—	Verdun	QMJHL	71	26	55	81	114	5	0	0	0	8
—	Sherbrooke	AHL	4	0	1	1	0	—	—	—	—	—
86-87—	Verdun	QMJHL	62	20	50	70	133					

Season Team	League	Gms.	G	A	Pts.	Pen.	Gms.	G	A	Pts.	Pen.
			REGULAR SEASON					PLAYOFFS			
87-88—Sherbrooke	AHL	53	4	10	14	51	4	1	2	3	20
88-89—Sherbrooke	AHL	74	12	34	46	112	6	1	2	3	10
89-90—Sherbrooke	AHL	62	21	31	52	79	12	2	†13	15	18
90-91—Fredericton	AHL	72	13	30	43	79	9	0	4	4	36
91-92—Kalamazoo	IHL	80	13	19	32	85	12	3	7	10	12

NEWMAN, THOMAS
G, KINGS

PERSONAL: Born February 23, 1971, at Golden Valley, Minn. . . . 6-1/185. . . . Shoots left. . . . Full name: Thomas Dean Newman.
HIGH SCHOOL: Blaine (Minn.).
COLLEGE: Minnesota.
TRANSACTIONS/CAREER NOTES: Broke foot (April 1987). . . . Selected by Los Angeles Kings in fifth round (fourth Kings pick, 103rd overall) of NHL entry draft (June 17, 1989).

Season Team	League	Gms.	Min.	W	L	T	GA	SO	Avg.	Gms.	Min.	W	L	GA	SO	Avg.
			REGULAR SEASON								PLAYOFFS					
87-88—Blaine H.S.	Minn. HS	16	960				32		2.00	—	—	—	—	—	—	—
88-89—Blaine H.S.	Minn. HS	18	810				43	3	3.19	—	—	—	—	—	—	—
89-90—Univ. of Minnesota	WCHA	35	1982	19	13	2	127	0	3.84	—	—	—	—	—	—	—
90-91—Univ. of Minnesota	WCHA	22	942	12	2	2	54	2	3.44	—	—	—	—	—	—	—
91-92—Univ. of Minnesota	WCHA	12	418	5	1	0	17	0	2.44	—	—	—	—	—	—	—

NICHOLLS, BERNIE
C, OILERS

PERSONAL: Born June 24, 1961, at Haliburton, Ont. . . . 6-0/185. . . . Shoots right. . . . Full name: Bernard Irvine Nicholls.
TRANSACTIONS/CAREER NOTES: Selected by Los Angeles Kings as underage junior in fourth round (fourth Kings pick, 73rd overall) of NHL entry draft (June 11, 1980). . . . Suffered partial tear of medial colateral ligament in right knee (November 18, 1982). . . . Suffered broken jaw (February 1984); missed two games. . . . Fractured left index finger in three places (October 8, 1987). . . . Traded by Kings to New York Rangers for RW Tomas Sandstrom and LW Tony Granato (January 20, 1990). . . . Separated left shoulder (January 22, 1991); missed five games. . . . Suspended three games by NHL for stick-swinging incident (February 14, 1991). . . . Traded by Rangers with LW Louie DeBrusk, RW Steven Rice and future considerations to Edmonton Oilers for C Mark Messier and future considerations (October 4, 1991); Rangers traded D David Shaw to Oilers for D Jeff Beukeboom to complete the deal (November 12, 1991). . . . Did not report to Oilers to be with his wife for the birth of their child (October 4, 1991); missed 27 games. . . . Reported to Oilers (December 6, 1991). . . . Strained abdominal muscle (February 16, 1992); missed two games.

Season Team	League	Gms.	G	A	Pts.	Pen.	Gms.	G	A	Pts.	Pen.
			REGULAR SEASON					PLAYOFFS			
78-79—Kingston	OMJHL	2	0	1	1	0	—	—	—	—	—
79-80—Kingston	OMJHL	68	36	43	79	85	3	1	0	1	10
80-81—Kingston	OMJHL	65	63	89	152	109	14	8	10	18	17
81-82—New Haven	AHL	55	41	30	71	31	—	—	—	—	—
—Los Angeles	NHL	22	14	18	32	27	10	4	0	4	23
82-83—Los Angeles	NHL	71	28	22	50	124	—	—	—	—	—
83-84—Los Angeles	NHL	78	41	54	95	83	—	—	—	—	—
84-85—Los Angeles	NHL	80	46	54	100	76	3	1	1	2	9
85-86—Los Angeles	NHL	80	36	61	97	78	—	—	—	—	—
86-87—Los Angeles	NHL	80	33	48	81	101	5	2	5	7	6
87-88—Los Angeles	NHL	65	32	46	78	114	5	2	6	8	11
88-89—Los Angeles	NHL	79	70	80	150	96	11	7	9	16	12
89-90—Los Angeles	NHL	47	27	48	75	66	—	—	—	—	—
—New York Rangers	NHL	32	12	25	37	20	10	7	5	12	16
90-91—New York Rangers	NHL	71	25	48	73	96	5	4	3	7	8
91-92—New York Rangers	NHL	1	0	0	0	0	—	—	—	—	—
—Edmonton	NHL	49	20	29	49	60	16	8	11	19	25
NHL totals		755	384	533	917	941	65	35	40	75	110

NIEDERMAYER, SCOTT
D, DEVILS

PERSONAL: Born August 31, 1973, at Edmonton, Alta. . . . 6-0/200. . . . Shoots left.
TRANSACTIONS/CAREER NOTES: Stretched left knee ligaments (March 12, 1991); missed nine games. . . . Selected by New Jersey Devils in first round (first Devils pick, third overall) of NHL entry draft (June 22, 1991).
HONORS: Won Can.HL Scholastic Player of the Year Award (1990-91). . . . Named WHL Scholastic Player of the Year (1990-91). . . . Named to WHL (West) All-Star first team (1990-91). . . . Won Stafford Smythe Memorial Trophy (1991-92). . . . Named to Can.HL All-Star first team (1991-92). . . . Named to Memorial Cup All-Star team (1991-92). . . . Named to WHL (West) All-Star first team (1991-92).

Season Team	League	Gms.	G	A	Pts.	Pen.	Gms.	G	A	Pts.	Pen.
			REGULAR SEASON					PLAYOFFS			
89-90—Kamloops	WHL	64	14	55	69	64	17	2	14	16	35
90-91—Kamloops	WHL	57	26	56	82	52	—	—	—	—	—
91-92—New Jersey	NHL	4	0	1	1	2	—	—	—	—	—
—Kamloops	WHL	35	7	32	39	61	17	9	14	23	28
NHL totals		4	0	1	1	2					

NIELSEN, JEFFREY
RW, RANGERS

PERSONAL: Born September 20, 1971, at Grand Rapids, Minn. . . . 6-0/170. . . . Shoots right. . . . Full name: Jeffrey Michael Nielsen.
HIGH SCHOOL: Grand Rapids (Minn.).
COLLEGE: Minnesota.

TRANSACTIONS/CAREER NOTES: Selected by New York Rangers in fourth round (fourth Rangers pick, 69th overall) of NHL entry draft (June 16, 1990).

Season Team	League	REGULAR SEASON					PLAYOFFS				
		Gms.	G	A	Pts.	Pen.	Gms.	G	A	Pts.	Pen.
87-88—Grand Rapids H.S............	Minn. H.S.	21	9	11	20	14	—	—	—	—	—
88-89—Grand Rapids H.S............	Minn. H.S.	25	13	17	30	26	—	—	—	—	—
89-90—Grand Rapids H.S............	Minn. H.S.	28	32	25	57		—	—	—	—	—
90-91—University of Minnesota ...	WCHA	45	11	14	25	50	—	—	—	—	—
91-92—University of Minnesota ...	WCHA	44	15	15	30	74	—	—	—	—	—

NIEUWENDYK, JOE
C, FLAMES

PERSONAL: Born September 10, 1966, at Oshawa, Ont.... 6-1/175.... Shoots left.... Full name: Joe T. Nieuwendyk.... Cousin of Jeff Beukeboom, defenseman, New York Rangers.
COLLEGE: Cornell.
TRANSACTIONS/CAREER NOTES: Selected by Calgary Flames in second round (second Flames pick, 27th overall) of NHL entry draft (June 15, 1985).... Suffered concussion (November 1987).... Bruised ribs (May 25, 1989).... Tore anterior cruciate ligament of left knee (April 17, 1990).... Underwent arthroscopic surgery to knee (September 28, 1991); missed 12 games.
HONORS: Won Ivy League Rookie of the Year Trophy (1984-85).... Named to NCAA All-America East first team (1985-86 and 1986-87).... Named to ECAC All-Star first team (1985-86 and 1986-87).... Named ECAC Player of the Year (1986-87).... Named NHL Rookie of the Year by THE SPORTING NEWS (1987-88).... Won Caldor Memorial Trophy (1907-00).... Won Dodge Ram Tough Award (1987-88).... Named to NHL All-Rookie team (1987-88).
RECORDS: Shares NHL single-game record for most goals in one period—4 (January 11, 1989).
STATISTICAL NOTES: Only the third player in NHL history to score 50 goals in each of his first two seasons.

Season Team	League	REGULAR SEASON					PLAYOFFS				
		Gms.	G	A	Pts.	Pen.	Gms.	G	A	Pts.	Pen.
83-84—Pickering Jr. B	MTHL	38	30	28	58	35	—	—	—	—	—
84-85—Cornell University	ECAC	29	21	24	45	30	—	—	—	—	—
85-86—Cornell University	ECAC	29	26	28	54	67	—	—	—	—	—
86-87—Cornell University	ECAC	23	26	26	52	26	—	—	—	—	—
—Calgary.........................	NHL	9	5	1	6	0	6	2	2	4	0
87-88—Calgary.........................	NHL	75	51	41	92	23	8	3	4	7	2
88-89—Calgary.........................	NHL	77	51	31	82	40	22	10	4	14	10
89-90—Calgary.........................	NHL	79	45	50	95	40	6	4	6	10	4
90-91—Calgary.........................	NHL	79	45	40	85	36	7	4	1	5	10
91-92—Calgary.........................	NHL	69	22	34	56	55	—	—	—	—	—
NHL totals................................		388	219	197	416	194	49	23	17	40	26

NIKOLISHIN, ANDREI
LW, WHALERS

PERSONAL: Born March 25, 1973, at Vorkuta, U.S.S.R.... 5-11/189.... Shoots left.
TRANSACTIONS/CAREER NOTES: Selected by Hartford Whalers in second round (second Whalers pick, 47th overall) of NHL entry draft (June 20, 1992).

Season Team	League	REGULAR SEASON					PLAYOFFS				
		Gms.	G	A	Pts.	Pen.	Gms.	G	A	Pts.	Pen.
90-91—Dynamo Moscow	USSR	2	0	0	0	0	—	—	—	—	—
91-92—Dynamo Moscow	CIS	18	1	0	1	4	—	—	—	—	—

NILAN, CHRIS
RW, CANADIENS

PERSONAL: Born February 9, 1958, at Boston.... 6-0/205.... Shoots right.... Full name: Christopher John Nilan.
HIGH SCHOOL: Catholic Memorial (Boston).
COLLEGE: Northeastern.
TRANSACTIONS/CAREER NOTES: Selected by Montreal Canadiens in 19th round (21st Canadiens pick, 231st overall) of 1978 amateur draft (June 15, 1978).... Suspended three games by NHL for throwing puck at another player from penalty box (November 21, 1981).... Suspended eight games by NHL for intentionally injuring another player (October 13, 1985).... Suspended three games by NHL for fighting (November 20, 1986).... Suffered hip injury (March 1987).... Traded by Canadiens to New York Rangers for the option to flip first-round picks in 1989 draft (January 27, 1988).... Sprained medial colateral ligament in right knee (February 2, 1988).... Strained abdominal ligament on front pelvic bone (December 1988).... Broke right forearm (November 4, 1989); missed 35 games.... Sprained right knee (February 14, 1990).... Broke ulnar bone in right arm (April 11, 1990).... Traded by Rangers to Boston Bruins for RW Greg Johnston and future considerations (June 28, 1990).... Fractured left ankle (January 6, 1991); missed 34 games, including NHL All-Star game.... Fractured transverse process of vertebrae (November 9, 1991); missed four games.... Claimed on waivers by Canadiens (February 12, 1992).... Sprained wrist (February 16, 1992); missed one game.
RECORDS: Holds NHL single-game record for most penalties in one game—10 (March 31, 1991).

Season Team	League	REGULAR SEASON					PLAYOFFS				
		Gms.	G	A	Pts.	Pen.	Gms.	G	A	Pts.	Pen.
77-78—Northeastern University...	ECAC	—	—	—	—	—	—	—	—	—	—
78-79—Northeastern University...	ECAC	32	9	13	22		—	—	—	—	—
79-80—Nova Scotia	AHL	49	15	10	25	*304	—	—	—	—	—
—Montreal........................	NHL	15	0	2	2	50	5	0	0	0	2
80-81—Montreal........................	NHL	57	7	8	15	262	2	0	0	0	0
81-82—Montreal........................	NHL	49	7	4	11	204	5	1	1	2	22
82-83—Montreal........................	NHL	66	6	8	14	213	3	0	0	0	5
83-84—Montreal........................	NHL	76	16	10	26	*338	15	1	0	1	*81
84-85—Montreal........................	NHL	77	21	16	37	*358	12	2	1	3	81

Season Team	League	REGULAR SEASON					PLAYOFFS				
		Gms.	G	A	Pts.	Pen.	Gms.	G	A	Pts.	Pen.
85-86—Montreal	NHL	72	19	15	34	274	18	1	2	3	*141
86-87—Montreal	NHL	44	4	16	20	266	17	3	0	3	75
87-88—Montreal	NHL	50	7	5	12	209	—	—	—	—	—
—New York Rangers	NHL	22	3	5	8	96	—	—	—	—	—
88-89—New York Rangers	NHL	38	7	7	14	177	4	0	1	1	38
89-90—New York Rangers	NHL	25	1	2	3	59	4	0	1	1	19
90-91—Boston	NHL	41	6	9	15	277	19	0	2	2	62
91-92—Boston	NHL	39	5	5	10	186	—	—	—	—	—
—Montreal	NHL	17	1	3	4	74	7	0	1	1	15
NHL totals		688	110	115	225	3043	111	8	9	17	541

NOBILI, MARIO
LW, OILERS

PERSONAL: Born February 16, 1971, at Montreal.... 6-1/185.... Shoots left.
TRANSACTIONS/CAREER NOTES: Selected by Edmonton Oilers in fourth round (fourth Oilers pick, 78th overall) of NHL entry draft (June 22, 1991).

Season Team	League	REGULAR SEASON					PLAYOFFS				
		Gms.	G	A	Pts.	Pen.	Gms.	G	A	Pts.	Pen.
88-89—Longueuil	QMJHL	61	8	6	14	32	—	—	—	—	—
89-90—Longueuil	QMJHL	67	11	34	45	64	—	—	—	—	—
90-91—Longueuil	QMJHL	70	33	52	85	115	—	—	—	—	—
91-92—Longueuil	QMJHL	52	27	48	75	184	18	6	9	15	10

NOLAN, OWEN
RW, NORDIQUES

PERSONAL: Born February 12, 1972, at Belfast, Northern Ireland.... 6-1/194.... Shoots right.
TRANSACTIONS/CAREER NOTES: Separated shoulder (February 22, 1990); missed eight games. ... Selected by Quebec Nordiques in first round (first Nordiques pick, first overall) of NHL entry draft (June 16, 1990).... Suffered concussion, sore knee and sore back (October 1990).
HONORS: Won Emms Family Award (1988-89).... Won Jim Mahon Memorial Trophy (1989-90).... Named to OHL All-Star first team (1989-90).

Season Team	League	REGULAR SEASON					PLAYOFFS				
		Gms.	G	A	Pts.	Pen.	Gms.	G	A	Pts.	Pen.
88-89—Cornwall	OHL	62	34	25	59	213	18	5	11	16	41
89-90—Cornwall	OHL	58	51	59	110	240	6	7	5	12	26
90-91—Quebec	NHL	59	3	10	13	109	—	—	—	—	—
—Halifax	AHL	6	4	4	8	11	—	—	—	—	—
91-92—Quebec	NHL	75	42	31	73	183	—	—	—	—	—
NHL totals		134	45	41	86	292					

NOONAN, BRIAN
C/RW, BLACKHAWKS

PERSONAL: Born May 29, 1965, at Boston.... 6-1/180.... Shoots right.
HIGH SCHOOL: Archbishop Williams (Braintree, Mass.).
TRANSACTIONS/CAREER NOTES: Selected by Chicago Blackhawks in ninth round (10th Blackhawks pick, 179th overall) of NHL entry draft (June 8, 1983).... Separated shoulder (April 3, 1988).... Refused to report to Indianapolis (October 18, 1990); returned home and suspended without pay by Blackhawks. ... Suffered death in family (February 28, 1991); missed six games. ... Damaged left knee ligaments (January 30, 1992); missed 12 games.
HONORS: Won Ken McKenzie Trophy (1985-86).... Named to IHL All-Star second team (1989-90).... Named to IHL All-Star first team (1990-91).

Season Team	League	REGULAR SEASON					PLAYOFFS				
		Gms.	G	A	Pts.	Pen.	Gms.	G	A	Pts.	Pen.
82-83—Archbishop Williams H.S.	Mass. H.S.	21	26	17	43		—	—	—	—	—
83-84—Archbishop Williams H.S.	Mass. H.S.	17	14	23	37		—	—	—	—	—
84-85—New Westminster	WHL	72	50	66	116	76	11	8	7	15	4
85-86—Saginaw	IHL	76	39	39	78	69	11	6	3	9	6
—Nova Scotia	AHL	2	0	0	0	0	—	—	—	—	—
86-87—Nova Scotia	AHL	70	25	26	51	30	5	3	1	4	4
87-88—Chicago	NHL	77	10	20	30	44	3	0	0	0	4
88-89—Chicago	NHL	45	4	12	16	28	1	0	0	0	0
—Saginaw	IHL	19	18	13	31	36	1	0	0	0	0
89-90—Chicago	NHL	8	0	2	2	6	—	—	—	—	—
—Indianapolis	IHL	56	40	36	76	85	14	6	9	15	20
90-91—Indianapolis	IHL	59	38	53	91	67	7	6	4	10	18
—Chicago	NHL	7	0	4	4	2	—	—	—	—	—
91-92—Chicago	NHL	65	19	12	31	81	18	6	9	15	30
NHL totals		202	33	50	83	161	22	6	9	15	34

NORRIS, CLAYTON
RW, FLYERS

PERSONAL: Born March 8, 1972, at Edmonton, Alta.... 6-2/200.... Shoots right.
TRANSACTIONS/CAREER NOTES: Selected by Philadelphia Flyers in sixth round (fifth Flyers pick, 116th overall) of NHL entry draft (June 22, 1991).
HONORS: Named to WHL (East) All-Star second team (1991-92).

Season Team	League	REGULAR SEASON					PLAYOFFS				
		Gms.	G	A	Pts.	Pen.	Gms.	G	A	Pts.	Pen.
88-89—Medicine Hat	WHL	66	4	9	13	122	3	0	0	0	2
89-90—Medicine Hat	WHL	72	13	18	31	176	3	0	0	0	15

Season Team	League	REGULAR SEASON					PLAYOFFS				
		Gms.	G	A	Pts.	Pen.	Gms.	G	A	Pts.	Pen.
90-91—Medicine Hat..................	WHL	71	26	27	53	165	12	5	4	9	41
91-92—Medicine Hat..................	WHL	69	26	39	65	300	2	0	0	0	9

NORRIS, DWAYNE
RW, NORDIQUES

PERSONAL: Born January 8, 1970, at St. John's, Nfld.... 5-10/175.... Shoots right.... Full name: Dwayne Carl Norris.
COLLEGE: Michigan State.
TRANSACTIONS/CAREER NOTES: Selected by Quebec Nordiques in seventh round (fifth Nordiques pick, 127th overall) of NHL entry draft (June 16, 1990).
HONORS: Named CCHA Player of the Year (1991-92).... Named to CCHA All-Star first team (1991-92).

Season Team	League	REGULAR SEASON					PLAYOFFS				
		Gms.	G	A	Pts.	Pen.	Gms.	G	A	Pts.	Pen.
88-89—Michigan State.................	CCHA	47	16	23	39	40	—	—	—	—	—
89-90—Michigan State.................	CCHA	36	19	26	45	30	—	—	—	—	—
90-91—Michigan State.................	CCHA	40	26	25	51	60	—	—	—	—	—
91-92—Michigan State.................	CCHA	44	*44	39	83	62	—	—	—	—	—

NORSTROM, MATTIAS
D, RANGERS

PERSONAL. Dorn January 2, 1972, at Mora, Sweden.... 0-1/190.
TRANSACTIONS/CAREER NOTES: Selected by New York Rangers in second round (second Rangers pick, 48th overall) of NHL entry draft (June 20, 1992).

Season Team	League	REGULAR SEASON					PLAYOFFS				
		Gms.	G	A	Pts.	Pen.	Gms.	G	A	Pts.	Pen.
91-92—AIK Solna	Sweden	39	4	4	8	28	—	—	—	—	—

NORTON, CHRIS
D

PERSONAL: Born March 11, 1965, at Oakville, Ont.... 6-2/200.... Shoots right.... Full name: Christopher Thomas Norton.
COLLEGE: Cornell.
TRANSACTIONS/CAREER NOTES: Selected by Winnipeg Jets in 11th round (11th Jets pick, 228th overall) of NHL entry draft (June 15, 1985).... Fractured ankle (July 1988).... Broke foot (December 6, 1989).... Traded by Jets with D Bryan Marchment to Chicago Blackhawks for C Troy Murray and LW Warren Rychel (July 22, 1991).... Traded by Blackhawks with future considerations to Los Angeles Kings for D Rod Buskas (October 28, 1991).
HONORS: Named to ECAC All-Star second team (1985-86 and 1987-88).

Season Team	League	REGULAR SEASON					PLAYOFFS				
		Gms.	G	A	Pts.	Pen.	Gms.	G	A	Pts.	Pen.
84-85—Cornell University	ECAC	29	4	19	23	34	—	—	—	—	—
85-86—Cornell University	ECAC	21	8	15	23	56	—	—	—	—	—
86-87—Cornell University	ECAC	24	10	21	31	79	—	—	—	—	—
87-88—Cornell University	ECAC	27	9	25	34	53	—	—	—	—	—
88-89—Moncton	AHL	60	1	21	22	49	10	3	2	5	15
89-90—Moncton	AHL	62	9	20	29	49	—	—	—	—	—
90-91—Moncton	AHL	72	8	28	36	45	9	1	3	4	12
91-92—Indianapolis	IHL	8	0	1	1	12	—	—	—	—	—
—Phoenix	IHL	62	12	14	26	44	—	—	—	—	—

NORTON, JEFF
D, ISLANDERS

PERSONAL: Born November 25, 1965, at Cambridge, Mass.... 6-2/195.... Shoots left.... Full name: Jeffrey Zaccari Norton.
HIGH SCHOOL: Cushing Academy (Ashburnham, Mass.).
COLLEGE: Michigan.
TRANSACTIONS/CAREER NOTES: Selected by New York Islanders in third round (third Islanders pick, 62nd overall) of NHL entry draft (June 9, 1984).... Bruised ribs (November 16, 1988).... Injured groin (February 1990).... Strained groin and abdominal muscles (March 2, 1990); missed games.... Suffered concussion (April 9, 1990).... Suspended eight games by NHL for intentionally injuring another player in preseason game (September 30, 1990).... Dislocated right shoulder (November 3, 1990); missed four games.... Reinjured shoulder (December 27, 1990); missed five games.... Reinjured shoulder and underwent surgery (February 23, 1991); missed remainder of season.... Suffered concussion (October 26, 1991); missed one game. ... Tore ligaments in left wrist (January 3, 1992); missed final 42 games of season.... Underwent surgery to left wrist (January 8, 1992).
HONORS: Named to CCHA All-Star second team (1986-87).

Season Team	League	REGULAR SEASON					PLAYOFFS				
		Gms.	G	A	Pts.	Pen.	Gms.	G	A	Pts.	Pen.
83-84—Cushing Academy............	Mass. H.S.	21	22	33	55		—	—	—	—	—
84-85—University of Michigan	CCHA	37	8	16	24	103	—	—	—	—	—
85-86—University of Michigan	CCHA	37	15	30	45	99	—	—	—	—	—
86-87—University of Michigan	CCHA	39	12	37	49	92	—	—	—	—	—
87-88—U.S. Olympic Team	Int'l	57	7	25	32		—	—	—	—	—
—New York Islanders..........	NHL	15	1	6	7	14	3	0	2	2	13
88-89—New York Islanders..........	NHL	69	1	30	31	74	—	—	—	—	—
89-90—New York Islanders..........	NHL	60	4	49	53	65	4	1	3	4	17
90-91—New York Islanders..........	NHL	44	3	25	28	16	—	—	—	—	—
91-92—New York Islanders..........	NHL	28	1	18	19	18	—	—	—	—	—
NHL totals...................................		216	10	128	138	187	7	1	5	6	30

N

NORWOOD, LEE
D, BLUES

PERSONAL: Born February 2, 1960, at Oakland, Calif. . . . 6-0/190. . . . Shoots left. . . . Full name: Lee Charles Norwood.

TRANSACTIONS/CAREER NOTES: Selected by Quebec Nordiques as underage junior in third round (third Nordiques pick, 62nd overall) of NHL entry draft (August 9, 1979). . . . Traded by Nordiques to Washington Capitals for C Tim Tookey and seventh-round pick in 1982 draft (D Daniel Poudrier) (January 1982). . . . Traded by Capitals to Toronto Maple Leafs for D Dave Shand (October 6, 1983). . . . Signed as free agent by St. Louis Blues (August 13, 1985). . . . Traded by Blues to Detroit Red Wings for D Larry Trader (August 7, 1986). . . . Pulled stomach muscle (February 1987). . . . Injured groin (October 1987). . . . Injured knee (December 1987). . . . Sprained ankle (November 1988). . . . Pulled hamstring (February 1989). . . . Suffered hip pointer (November 6, 1989); missed six games. . . . Sprained right wrist (March 15, 1990). . . . Traded by Red Wings with future considerations to New Jersey Devils for C Paul Ysebaert (November 27, 1990). . . . Separated left shoulder (January 3, 1991); missed six games. . . . Fractured cheekbone and underwent surgery (February 16, 1991); missed 19 games. . . . Underwent surgery to left shoulder (Summer 1991). . . . Traded by Devils to Hartford Whalers for future considerations (October 3, 1991). . . . Traded by Whalers to Blues for future considerations (November 13, 1991). . . . Injured ankle (January 28, 1992); missed one game.

HONORS: Won Governors Trophy (1984-85). . . . Named to IHL All-Star first team (1984-85).

Season Team	League	REGULAR SEASON					PLAYOFFS				
		Gms.	G	A	Pts.	Pen.	Gms.	G	A	Pts.	Pen.
77-78—Hull	QMJHL	51	3	17	20	83	—	—	—	—	—
78-79—Oshawa	OMJHL	61	23	38	61	171	5	2	2	4	17
79-80—Oshawa	OMJHL	60	13	39	52	143	6	2	7	9	15
80-81—Hershey	AHL	52	11	32	43	78	8	0	4	4	14
—Quebec	NHL	11	1	1	2	9	3	0	0	0	2
81-82—Fredericton	AHL	29	6	13	19	74	—	—	—	—	—
—Quebec	NHL	2	0	0	0	2	—	—	—	—	—
—Washington	NHL	26	7	10	17	125	—	—	—	—	—
82-83—Washington	NHL	8	0	1	1	14	—	—	—	—	—
—Hershey	AHL	67	12	36	48	90	5	0	1	1	2
83-84—St. Catharines	AHL	75	13	46	59	91	7	0	5	5	31
84-85—Peoria	IHL	80	17	60	77	229	18	1	11	12	62
85-86—St. Louis	NHL	71	5	24	29	134	19	2	7	9	64
86-87—Adirondack	AHL	3	0	3	3	0	—	—	—	—	—
—Detroit	NHL	57	6	21	27	163	16	1	6	7	31
87-88—Detroit	NHL	51	9	22	31	131	16	2	6	8	40
88-89—Detroit	NHL	66	10	32	42	100	6	1	2	3	16
89-90—Detroit	NHL	64	8	14	22	95	—	—	—	—	—
90-91—Detroit	NHL	21	3	7	10	50	—	—	—	—	—
—New Jersey	NHL	28	3	2	5	87	4	0	0	0	18
91-92—Hartford	NHL	6	0	0	0	16	—	—	—	—	—
—St. Louis	NHL	44	3	11	14	94	1	0	1	1	0
NHL totals		**455**	**55**	**145**	**200**	**1020**	**65**	**6**	**22**	**28**	**171**

NUMMINEN, TEPPO
D, JETS

PERSONAL: Born July 3, 1968, at Tampere, Finland. . . . 6-1/190. . . . Shoots right. . . . Full name: Teppo Kalevi Numminen.

TRANSACTIONS/CAREER NOTES: Selected by Winnipeg Jets in second round (second Jets pick, 29th overall) of NHL entry draft (June 21, 1986). . . . Separated shoulder (March 5, 1989). . . . Broke thumb (April 14, 1990).

MISCELLANEOUS: Member of 1988 silver-medal-winning Finnish Olympic team.

Season Team	League	REGULAR SEASON					PLAYOFFS				
		Gms.	G	A	Pts.	Pen.	Gms.	G	A	Pts.	Pen.
84-85—Tappara	Finland	30	14	17	31	10	—	—	—	—	—
85-86—Tappara	Finland	39	2	4	6	6	8	0	0	0	0
86-87—Tappara	Finland	44	9	9	18	16	9	4	1	5	4
87-88—Tappara	Finland	44	10	10	20	29	10	6	6	12	6
88-89—Winnipeg	NHL	69	1	14	15	36	—	—	—	—	—
89-90—Winnipeg	NHL	79	11	32	43	20	7	1	2	3	10
90-91—Winnipeg	NHL	80	8	25	33	28	—	—	—	—	—
91-92—Winnipeg	NHL	80	5	34	39	32	7	0	0	0	0
NHL totals		**308**	**25**	**105**	**130**	**116**	**14**	**1**	**2**	**3**	**10**

NYLANDER, MIKAEL
C, WHALERS

PERSONAL: Born October 3, 1972, at Stockholm, Sweden. . . . 5-11/176. . . . Shoots left.

TRANSACTIONS/CAREER NOTES: Selected by Hartford Whalers in third round (fourth Whalers pick, 59th overall) of NHL entry draft (June 22, 1991).

Season Team	League	REGULAR SEASON					PLAYOFFS				
		Gms.	G	A	Pts.	Pen.	Gms.	G	A	Pts.	Pen.
89-90—Huddinge	Sweden	31	7	15	22	4	—	—	—	—	—
90-91—Huddinge	Sweden	33	14	20	34	10	—	—	—	—	—
91-92—AIK Solna	Sweden	40	11	17	28	30	—	—	—	—	—
—Swedish National Jr. Team..	Sweden	7	8	9	17		—	—	—	—	—
—Swedish National Team....	Int'l	6	0	1	1	0	—	—	—	—	—

NYLUND, GARY
D, ISLANDERS

PERSONAL: Born October 28, 1963, at Surrey, B.C. . . . 6-4/192. . . . Shoots left.

TRANSACTIONS/CAREER NOTES: Selected by Toronto Maple Leafs as underage junior in first round (first Maple Leafs pick, third overall) of NHL entry draft (June 9, 1982). . . . Injured left knee and underwent surgery (September 1982). . . . Underwent knee surgery (October

1983). . . . Suffered concussion (November 5, 1984). . . . Signed as free agent by Chicago Blackhawks (August 27, 1986). Blackhawks sent C Ken Yaremchuk, D Jerome Dupont and fourth-round pick in 1987 draft (LW Joe Sacco) to compensate Maple Leafs. . . . Bruised elbow (October 1987). . . . Broke bone in right forearm (September 1988). . . . Traded by Blackhawks with D Marc Bergevin to New York Islanders for D Steve Konroyd and C Bob Bassen (January 11, 1989). . . . Underwent arthroscopic surgery to right knee (January 11, 1989); missed 10 games. . . . Bruised ribs and lung (March 1989). . . . Irritated right knee ligament (March 8, 1990). . . . Dislocated right shoulder (December 29, 1990); missed five games. . . . Fractured left heel (March 25, 1991). . . . Underwent surgery to heel (March 28, 1991); missed final three games of 1990-91 season and first 52 games of 1991-92 season. . . . Pulled groin (February 29, 1992); missed 11 games.
HONORS: Named to WHL All-Star second team (1980-81). . . . Won Top Defenseman Trophy (1981-82). . . . Named to WHL All-Star first team (1981-82).

			REGULAR SEASON					PLAYOFFS				
Season Team	League	Gms.	G	A	Pts.	Pen.	Gms.	G	A	Pts.	Pen.
78-79—Delta	BCJHL	57	6	29	35	107	—	—	—	—	—
—Portland	WHL	2	0	0	0	0	—	—	—	—	—
79-80—Portland	WHL	72	5	21	26	59	8	0	1	1	2
80-81—Portland	WHL	70	6	40	46	186	9	1	7	8	17
81-82—Portland	WHL	65	7	59	66	267	15	3	16	19	74
82-83—Toronto	NHL	16	0	3	3	16	—	—	—	—	—
83-84—Toronto	NHL	47	2	14	16	103	—	—	—	—	—
84-85—Toronto	NHL	76	3	17	20	99	—	—	—	—	—
85-86—Toronto	NHL	70	2	16	18	100	10	0	2	2	25
86-87—Chicago	NHL	80	7	20	27	190	4	0	2	2	11
87-88—Chicago	NHL	76	4	15	19	208	5	0	0	0	10
88-89—Chicago	NHL	23	3	2	5	63	—	—	—	—	—
—New York Islanders	NHL	46	4	8	12	74	—	—	—	—	—
89-90—New York Islanders	NHL	64	4	21	25	144	5	0	2	2	17
90-91—New York Islanders	NHL	72	2	21	23	105	—	—	—	—	—
91-92—New York Islanders	NHL	7	0	1	1	10	—	—	—	—	—
—Capital District	AHL	4	0	0	0	0	—	—	—	—	—
NHL totals		**586**	**31**	**138**	**169**	**1192**	**24**	**0**	**6**	**6**	**63**

OATES, ADAM
C, BRUINS

PERSONAL: Born August 27, 1962, at Weston, Ont. . . . 5-11/190. . . . Shoots right. . . . Full name: Adam R. Oates.
COLLEGE: Rensselaer Polytechnic Institute (N.Y.).
TRANSACTIONS/CAREER NOTES: Signed as free agent by Detroit Red Wings (June 28, 1985). . . . Pulled abdominal muscle (October 1987). . . . Suffered from chicken pox (November 1988). . . . Bruised thigh (December 1988). . . . Traded by Red Wings with RW Paul MacLean to St. Louis Blues for LW Tony McKegney and C Bernie Federko (June 15, 1989). . . . Tore rib and abdominal muscles (November 5, 1990); missed 18 games. . . . Traded by Blues to Boston Bruins for C Craig Janney and D Stephane Quintal (February 7, 1992).
HONORS: Named to ECAC All-Star second team (1983-84). . . . Named to NCAA All-America East team (1984-85). . . . Named to ECAC All-Star first team (1984-85). . . . Named to THE SPORTING NEWS All-Star second team (1990-91). . . . Named to NHL All-Star second team (1990-91).

			REGULAR SEASON					PLAYOFFS				
Season Team	League	Gms.	G	A	Pts.	Pen.	Gms.	G	A	Pts.	Pen.
82-83—R.P.I.	ECAC	22	9	33	42	8	—	—	—	—	—
83-84—R.P.I.	ECAC	38	26	57	83	15	—	—	—	—	—
84-85—R.P.I.	ECAC	38	31	60	91	29	—	—	—	—	—
85-86—Adirondack	AHL	34	18	28	46	4	17	7	14	21	4
—Detroit	NHL	38	9	11	20	10	—	—	—	—	—
86-87—Detroit	NHL	76	15	32	47	21	16	4	7	11	6
87-88—Detroit	NHL	63	14	40	54	20	16	8	12	20	6
88-89—Detroit	NHL	69	16	62	78	14	6	0	8	8	2
89-90—St. Louis	NHL	80	23	79	102	30	12	2	12	14	4
90-91—St. Louis	NHL	61	25	90	115	29	13	7	13	20	10
91-92—St. Louis	NHL	54	10	59	69	12	—	—	—	—	—
—Boston	NHL	26	10	20	30	10	15	5	14	19	4
NHL totals		**467**	**122**	**393**	**515**	**146**	**78**	**26**	**66**	**92**	**32**

O'BRIEN, JAMES
D, FLAMES

PERSONAL: Born May 8, 1970, at Stoney Creek, Ont. . . . 6-0/190. . . . Shoots left. . . . Full name: James J. O'Brien.
HIGH SCHOOL: Cardinal Newman (Hamilton, Ont.).
COLLEGE: Brown.
TRANSACTIONS/CAREER NOTES: Selected by Calgary Flames in NHL supplemental draft (June 19, 1992).

			REGULAR SEASON					PLAYOFFS				
Season Team	League	Gms.	G	A	Pts.	Pen.	Gms.	G	A	Pts.	Pen.
89-90—Brown University	ECAC	29	3	12	15	78	—	—	—	—	—
90-91—Brown University	ECAC	25	3	8	11	50	—	—	—	—	—
91-92—Brown University	ECAC	28	3	11	14	61	—	—	—	—	—

O'CONNOR, MYLES
D, DEVILS

PERSONAL: Born April 2, 1967, at Calgary, Alta. . . . 5-11/165. . . . Shoots left. . . . Full name: Myles Alexander O'Connor.
COLLEGE: Michigan.
TRANSACTIONS/CAREER NOTES: Selected by New Jersey Devils in third round (fourth

Devils pick, 45th overall) of NHL entry draft (June 15, 1985).... Fractured ankle (February 18, 1991).
HONORS: Named to NCAA All-America West first team (1988-89).... Named to CCHA All-Star first team (1988-89).

Season Team	League	REGULAR SEASON					PLAYOFFS				
		Gms.	G	A	Pts.	Pen.	Gms.	G	A	Pts.	Pen.
84-85—Notre Dame H.S.	Sask. H.S.	40	20	35	55	40	—	—	—	—	—
85-86—University of Michigan	CCHA	37	6	19	25	73	—	—	—	—	—
—Team Canada	Int'l	8	0	0	0	0	—	—	—	—	—
86-87—University of Michigan	CCHA	39	15	30	45	111	—	—	—	—	—
87-88—University of Michigan	CCHA	40	9	25	34	78	—	—	—	—	—
88-89—University of Michigan	CCHA	40	3	31	34	91	—	—	—	—	—
—Utica	AHL	1	0	0	0	0	—	—	—	—	—
89-90—Utica	AHL	76	14	33	47	124	5	1	2	3	26
90-91—New Jersey	NHL	22	3	1	4	41	—	—	—	—	—
—Utica	AHL	33	6	17	23	62	—	—	—	—	—
91-92—Utica	AHL	66	9	39	48	184	—	—	—	—	—
—New Jersey	NHL	9	0	2	2	13	—	—	—	—	—
NHL totals		31	3	3	6	54					

ODELEIN, LYLE
D, CANADIENS

PERSONAL: Born July 21, 1968, at Quill Lake, Sask....5-10/206....Shoots right.
TRANSACTIONS/CAREER NOTES: Selected by Montreal Canadiens as underage junior in seventh round (eighth Canadiens pick, 141st overall) of NHL entry draft (June 21, 1986).... Bruised right ankle (January 22, 1991); missed five games.... Twisted right ankle (February 9, 1991).

Season Team	League	REGULAR SEASON					PLAYOFFS				
		Gms.	G	A	Pts.	Pen.	Gms.	G	A	Pts.	Pen.
85-86—Moose Jaw	WHL	67	9	37	46	117	13	1	6	7	34
86-87—Moose Jaw	WHL	59	9	50	59	70	9	2	5	7	26
87-88—Moose Jaw	WHL	63	15	43	58	166	—	—	—	—	—
88-89—Sherbrooke	AHL	33	3	4	7	120	3	0	2	2	5
—Peoria	IHL	36	2	8	10	116	—	—	—	—	—
89-90—Sherbrooke	AHL	68	7	24	31	265	12	6	5	11	79
—Montreal	NHL	8	0	2	2	33	—	—	—	—	—
90-91—Montreal	NHL	52	0	2	2	259	12	0	0	0	54
91-92—Montreal	NHL	71	1	7	8	212	7	0	0	0	11
NHL totals		131	1	11	12	504	19	0	0	0	65

ODGERS, JEFF
LW, SHARKS

PERSONAL: Born May 31, 1969, at Spy Hill, Sask....6-0/195....Shoots right.
TRANSACTIONS/CAREER NOTES: Signed as free agent by San Jose Sharks (September 3, 1991). ... Injured hand (December 21, 1991); missed four games.

Season Team	League	REGULAR SEASON					PLAYOFFS				
		Gms.	G	A	Pts.	Pen.	Gms.	G	A	Pts.	Pen.
86-87—Brandon	WHL	70	7	14	21	150	—	—	—	—	—
87-88—Brandon	WHL	70	17	18	35	202	4	1	1	2	14
88-89—Brandon	WHL	71	31	29	60	277	—	—	—	—	—
89-90—Brandon	WHL	64	37	28	65	209	—	—	—	—	—
90-91—Kansas City	IHL	77	12	19	31	*318	—	—	—	—	—
91-92—Kansas City	IHL	12	2	2	4	56	9	3	0	3	13
—San Jose	NHL	61	7	4	11	217	—	—	—	—	—
NHL totals		61	7	4	11	217					

ODJICK, GINO
LW, CANUCKS

PERSONAL: Born September 7, 1970, at Maniwaki, Que....6-3/220....Shoots left.
TRANSACTIONS/CAREER NOTES: Suspended five games by QMJHL for attempting to attack another player (May 1, 1989).... Suspended one game by QMJHL for fighting (March 19, 1990). ... Suspended one game by QMJHL for fighting (April 14, 1990).... Selected by Vancouver Canucks in fifth round (fifth Canucks pick, 86th overall) of NHL entry draft (June 16, 1990).... Broke cheekbone (February 27, 1991).... Suspended six games by NHL for stick foul (November 26, 1991).

Season Team	League	REGULAR SEASON					PLAYOFFS				
		Gms.	G	A	Pts.	Pen.	Gms.	G	A	Pts.	Pen.
88-89—Laval	QMJHL	50	9	15	24	278	16	0	9	9	*129
89-90—Laval	QMJHL	51	12	26	38	280	13	6	5	11	*110
90-91—Milwaukee	IHL	17	7	3	10	102	—	—	—	—	—
—Vancouver	NHL	45	7	1	8	296	6	0	0	0	18
91-92—Vancouver	NHL	65	4	6	10	348	4	0	0	0	6
NHL totals		110	11	7	18	644	10	0	0	0	24

OGRODNICK, JOHN
LW, RANGERS

PERSONAL: Born June 20, 1959, at Ottawa....6-0/208....Shoots left....Full name: John Alexander Ogrodnick.
TRANSACTIONS/CAREER NOTES: Selected by Detroit Red Wings in fourth round (fourth Red Wings pick, 66th overall) of NHL entry draft (August 9, 1979).... Fractured left wrist (February 26, 1984).... Sprained ankle (October 1986).... Traded by Red Wings with RW Doug Shedden and LW Basil McRae to Quebec Nordiques for LW Brent Ashton, RW Mark Kumpel and D Gilbert Delorme (January 17, 1987).... Traded by

Nordiques with D David Shaw to New York Rangers for LW Jeff Jackson and D Terry Carkner (September 30, 1987).... Suffered ligament damage and cracked bone in left instep (December 1987).... Bruised ribs (February 1988).... Suffered back spasms (February 12, 1992); missed four games.... Bruised wrist (March 4, 1992); missed one game.
HONORS: Shared WCHL Rookie of the Year Award with Keith Brown (1977-78).... Named to NHL All-Star first team (1984-85).

			REGULAR SEASON					PLAYOFFS			
Season Team	League	Gms.	G	A	Pts.	Pen.	Gms.	G	A	Pts.	Pen.
76-77—Maple Ridge Bruins	BCJHL	67	54	56	110	63	—	—	—	—	—
—New Westminster	WCHL	14	2	4	6	0	14	3	3	6	2
77-78—New Westminster	WCHL	72	59	29	88	47	21	14	7	21	14
78-79—New Westminster	WHL	72	48	36	84	38	6	2	0	2	4
79-80—Adirondack	AHL	39	13	20	33	21	—	—	—	—	—
—Detroit	NHL	41	8	24	32	8	—	—	—	—	—
80-81—Detroit	NHL	80	35	35	70	14	—	—	—	—	—
81-82—Detroit	NHL	80	28	26	54	28	—	—	—	—	—
82-83—Detroit	NHL	80	41	44	85	30	—	—	—	—	—
83-84—Detroit	NHL	64	42	36	78	14	4	0	0	0	0
84-85—Detroit	NHL	79	55	50	105	30	3	1	1	2	0
85-86—Detroit	NHL	76	38	32	70	18	—	—	—	—	—
86-87—Detroit	NHL	39	12	28	40	6	—	—	—	—	—
—Quebec	NHL	32	11	16	27	4	13	9	4	13	6
87-88—New York Rangers	NHL	64	22	32	54	16	—	—	—	—	—
88-89—Denver	IHL	3	2	0	2	0	—	—	—	—	—
—New York Rangers	NHL	60	13	29	42	14	3	2	0	2	0
89-90—New York Rangers	NHL	80	43	31	74	44	10	6	3	9	0
90-91—New York Rangers	NHL	79	31	23	54	10	4	0	0	0	0
91-92—New York Rangers	NHL	55	17	13	30	22	3	0	0	0	0
NHL totals		909	396	419	815	258	40	18	8	26	6

OJANEN, JANNE
C, DEVILS

PERSONAL: Born April 9, 1968, at Tampere, Finland.... 6-2/200.... Shoots left.
TRANSACTIONS/CAREER NOTES: Selected by New Jersey Devils in third round (third Devils pick, 45th overall) of NHL entry draft (June 1986).
MISCELLANEOUS: Member of 1988 silver-medal-winning Finnish Olympic team.

			REGULAR SEASON					PLAYOFFS			
Season Team	League	Gms.	G	A	Pts.	Pen.	Gms.	G	A	Pts.	Pen.
84-85—Tappara	Finland	—	—	—	—	—	—	—	—	—	—
85-86—Tappara	Finland	14	5	17	22	14	—	—	—	—	—
86-87—Tappara	Finland	49	22	19	41	28	—	—	—	—	—
87-88—Tappara	Finland	54	25	35	60	42	—	—	—	—	—
88-89—Utica	AHL	72	23	37	60	10	5	0	3	3	0
—New Jersey	NHL	3	0	1	1	2	—	—	—	—	—
89-90—New Jersey	NHL	64	17	13	30	12	—	—	—	—	—
90-91—Tappara	Finland	44	15	23	38		—	—	—	—	—
91-92—Tappara	Finland	44	21	27	48	24	—	—	—	—	—
—New Jersey	NHL	—	—	—	—	—	3	0	2	2	0
NHL totals		67	17	14	31	14	3	0	2	2	0

OLAUSSON, FREDRIK
D, JETS

PERSONAL: Born October 5, 1966, at Vaxsjo, Sweden.... 6-2/200.... Shoots right.
TRANSACTIONS/CAREER NOTES: Selected by Winnipeg Jets in fourth round (fourth Jets pick, 81st overall) of NHL entry draft (June 15, 1985).... Dislocated shoulder (August 1987).... Underwent shoulder surgery (November 1987).... Signed a five-year contract with Farjestads, Sweden (June 19, 1989); Farjestads agreed to allow Olausson to remain in Winnipeg.

			REGULAR SEASON					PLAYOFFS			
Season Team	League	Gms.	G	A	Pts.	Pen.	Gms.	G	A	Pts.	Pen.
83-84—Nybro	Sweden	28	8	14	22	32	—	—	—	—	—
84-85—Farjestad	Sweden	34	6	12	18	24	3	1	0	1	0
85-86—Farjestad	Sweden	33	5	12	17	14	8	3	2	5	6
86-87—Winnipeg	NHL	72	7	29	36	24	10	2	3	5	4
87-88—Winnipeg	NHL	38	5	10	15	18	5	1	1	2	0
88-89—Winnipeg	NHL	75	15	47	62	32	—	—	—	—	—
89-90—Winnipeg	NHL	77	9	46	55	32	7	0	2	2	2
90-91—Winnipeg	NHL	71	12	29	41	24	—	—	—	—	—
91-92—Winnipeg	NHL	77	20	42	62	34	7	1	5	6	4
NHL totals		410	68	203	271	164	29	4	11	15	10

OLCZYK, ED
C/RW/LW, JETS

PERSONAL: Born August 16, 1966, at Chicago.... 6-1/200.... Shoots left.
TRANSACTIONS/CAREER NOTES: Selected by Chicago Blackhawks in first round (first Blackhawks pick, third overall) of NHL entry draft (June 9, 1984).... Hyperextended knee (September 3, 1984).... Broke bone in left foot (December 16, 1984).... Traded by Blackhawks with LW Al Secord to Toronto Maple Leafs for RW Rick Vaive, LW Steve Thomas and D Bob McGill (September 1987).... Pinched nerve in left knee (January 3, 1990).... Traded by Maple Leafs with LW Mark Osborne to Winnipeg Jets for D Dave Ellett and LW Paul Fenton (November 10, 1990).... Dislocated elbow and sprained ankle (January 8, 1992); missed 15 games.

Season	Team	League	REGULAR SEASON Gms.	G	A	Pts.	Pen.	PLAYOFFS Gms.	G	A	Pts.	Pen.
83-84—U.S. National Team		Int'l	56	19	40	59	36	—	—	—	—	—
—U.S. Olympic Team		Int'l	6	2	7	9	0	—	—	—	—	—
84-85—Chicago		NHL	70	20	30	50	67	15	6	5	11	11
85-86—Chicago		NHL	79	29	50	79	47	3	0	0	0	0
86-87—Chicago		NHL	79	16	35	51	119	4	1	1	2	4
87-88—Toronto		NHL	80	42	33	75	55	6	5	4	9	2
88-89—Toronto		NHL	80	38	52	90	75	—	—	—	—	—
89-90—Toronto		NHL	79	32	56	88	78	5	1	2	3	14
90-91—Toronto		NHL	18	4	10	14	13	—	—	—	—	—
—Winnipeg		NHL	61	26	31	57	69	—	—	—	—	—
91-92—Winnipeg		NHL	64	32	33	65	67	6	2	1	3	4
NHL totals			610	239	330	569	590	39	15	13	28	35

OLIMB, LARRY
C, SHARKS

PERSONAL: Born August 11, 1969, at Warroad, Minn. . . . 5-10/155. . . . Shoots left. . . . Full name: Lawrence Olimb.
HIGH SCHOOL: Warroad (Minn.).
COLLEGE: Minnesota.
TRANSACTIONS/CAREER NOTES: Selected by Minnesota North Stars in 10th round (10th North Stars pick, 193rd overall) of NHL entry draft (June 13, 1987). . . . Selected by San Jose Sharks in 1991 NHL dispersal draft (May 30, 1991).
HONORS: Named to WCHA All-Star second team (1990-91). . . . Named to WCHA All-Star first team (1991-92).

Season	Team	League	REGULAR SEASON Gms.	G	A	Pts.	Pen.	PLAYOFFS Gms.	G	A	Pts.	Pen.
86-87—Warroad H.S.		Minn. H.S.	26	23	30	53		—	—	—	—	—
87-88—Warroad H.S.		Minn. H.S.	27	35	31	66		—	—	—	—	—
88-89—University of Minnesota		WCHA	47	10	29	39	50	—	—	—	—	—
89-90—University of Minnesota		WCHA	46	6	36	42	44	—	—	—	—	—
90-91—University of Minnesota		WCHA	45	19	38	57	52	—	—	—	—	—
91-92—University of Minnesota		WCHA	44	24	*56	80	72	—	—	—	—	—

OLSEN, DARRYL
D, FLAMES

PERSONAL: Born October 7, 1966, at Calgary, Alta. . . . 6-0/180. . . . Shoots left. . . . Full name: Darryl M. Olsen.
COLLEGE: Northern Michigan.
TRANSACTIONS/CAREER NOTES: Selected by Calgary Flames in ninth round (10th Flames pick, 185th overall) of NHL entry draft (June 15, 1985).
HONORS: Named to NCAA All-America West second team (1988-89).

Season	Team	League	REGULAR SEASON Gms.	G	A	Pts.	Pen.	PLAYOFFS Gms.	G	A	Pts.	Pen.
84-85—St. Albert		AJHL	57	19	48	67	77	—	—	—	—	—
85-86—Northern Michigan Univ.		WCHA	37	5	20	25	46	—	—	—	—	—
86-87—Northern Michigan Univ.		WCHA	37	5	20	25	96	—	—	—	—	—
87-88—Northern Michigan Univ.		WCHA	35	11	20	31	59	—	—	—	—	—
88-89—Northern Michigan Univ.		WCHA	45	16	26	42	88	—	—	—	—	—
—Canadian National Team		Int'l	3	1	0	1	4	—	—	—	—	—
89-90—Salt Lake City		IHL	72	16	50	66	90	11	3	6	9	2
90-91—Salt Lake City		IHL	76	15	40	55	89	4	1	5	6	2
91-92—Salt Lake City		IHL	59	7	33	40	80	5	2	1	3	4
—Calgary		NHL	1	0	0	0	0	—	—	—	—	—
NHL totals			1	0	0	0	0					

O'NEILL, MIKE
G, JETS

PERSONAL: Born November 3, 1967, at Montreal. . . . 5-7/155. . . . Shoots left. . . . Full name: Michael Anthony O'Neill Jr.
COLLEGE: Yale.
TRANSACTIONS/CAREER NOTES: Selected by Winnipeg Jets in NHL supplemental draft (June 10, 1988). . . . Dislocated shoulder (April 8, 1991); missed remainder of playoffs.
HONORS: Named to ECAC All-Star first team (1986-87 and 1988-89). . . . Named to NCAA All-America East first team (1988-89).

Season	Team	League	REGULAR SEASON Gms.	Min.	W	L	T	GA	SO	Avg.	PLAYOFFS Gms.	Min.	W	L	GA	SO	Avg.
85-86—Yale University		ECAC	6	389	3	1	0	17	0	2.62	—	—	—	—	—	—	—
86-87—Yale University		ECAC	16	964	9	6	1	55	2	3.42	—	—	—	—	—	—	—
87-88—Yale University		ECAC	24	1385	6	17	0	101	0	4.38	—	—	—	—	—	—	—
88-89—Yale University		ECAC	25	1490	10	14	1	93	0	3.74	—	—	—	—	—	—	—
89-90—Tappara		Finland	41	2369	23	13	5	127	2	3.22	—	—	—	—	—	—	—
90-91—Fort Wayne		IHL	8	490	5	2	1	31	0	3.80	—	—	—	—	—	—	—
—Moncton		AHL	30	1613	13	7	6	84	0	3.12	8	435	3	4	29	0	4.00
91-92—Fort Wayne		IHL	33	1858	22	6	3	97	†4	3.13	—	—	—	—	—	—	—
—Moncton		AHL	32	1902	14	16	2	108	1	3.41	11	670	4	†7	43	1	3.85
—Winnipeg		NHL	1	13	0	0	0	1	0	4.62	—	—	—	—	—	—	—
NHL totals			1	13	0	0	0	1	0	4.62							

OSBORNE, KEITH

RW, LIGHTNING

PERSONAL: Born April 2, 1969, at Toronto.... 6-1/180.... Shoots right.
TRANSACTIONS/CAREER NOTES: Selected by St. Louis Blues as underage junior in first round (first Blues pick, 12th overall) of NHL entry draft (June 13, 1987).... Broke wrist (September 1987).... Broke ankle (October 1987).... Traded by Blues to Toronto Maple Leafs for D Darren Veitch (March 5, 1991).... Selected by Tampa Bay Lightning in NHL expansion draft (June 18, 1992).

			REGULAR SEASON					PLAYOFFS			
Season Team	League	Gms.	G	A	Pts.	Pen.	Gms.	G	A	Pts.	Pen.
86-87—North Bay	OHL	61	34	55	89	31	24	11	11	22	25
87-88—North Bay	OHL	30	14	22	36	20	4	1	5	6	8
88-89—North Bay	OHL	15	11	15	26	12	—	—	—	—	—
—Niagara Falls	OHL	50	34	49	83	45	17	12	12	24	36
89-90—St. Louis	NHL	5	0	2	2	8	—	—	—	—	—
—Peoria	IHL	56	23	24	47	58	—	—	—	—	—
90-91—Peoria	IHL	54	10	20	30	79	—	—	—	—	—
—Newmarket	AHL	12	0	3	3	6	—	—	—	—	—
91-92—St. John's	AHL	53	11	16	27	21	4	0	1	1	2
NHL totals		5	0	2	2	8					

OSBORNE, MARK

LW, MAPLE LEAFS

PERSONAL: Born August 13, 1961, at Toronto.... 6-2/200.... Shoots left.... Full name: Mark Anatole Osborne.
TRANSACTIONS/CAREER NOTES: Selected by Detroit Red Wings as underage junior in third round (second Red Wings pick, 46th overall) of NHL entry draft (June 11, 1980)....
Traded by Red Wings with D Willie Huber and RW Mike Blaisdell to New York Rangers for RW Ron Duguay, G Eddie Mio and RW Ed Johnstone (June 13, 1983).... Injured hip (October 1984).... Sprained ankle (February 12, 1986); missed 12 games.... Suffered laceration behind left knee (February 1987).... Traded by Rangers to Toronto Maple Leafs for third-round pick in 1989 draft (C Rob Zamuner) (March 5, 1987).... Separated left shoulder (April 1988).... Traded by Maple Leafs with C/RW Ed Olczyk to Winnipeg Jets for D Dave Ellett and C Paul Fenton (November 10, 1990).... Fractured left thumb and injured ligaments (December 3, 1990); missed 21 games.... Separated shoulder (October 29, 1991); missed three games.... Fractured ankle (January 1992); missed 14 games.... Traded by Jets to Maple Leafs for RW Lucien Deblois (March 10, 1992).

			REGULAR SEASON					PLAYOFFS			
Season Team	League	Gms.	G	A	Pts.	Pen.	Gms.	G	A	Pts.	Pen.
78-79—Niagara Falls	OMJHL	62	17	25	42	53	—	—	—	—	—
79-80—Niagara Falls	OMJHL	52	10	33	43	104	10	2	1	3	23
80-81—Niagara Falls	OMJHL	54	39	41	80	140	12	11	10	21	20
—Adirondack	AHL	—	—	—	—	—	13	2	3	5	2
81-82—Detroit	NHL	80	26	41	67	61	—	—	—	—	—
82-83—Detroit	NHL	80	19	24	43	83	—	—	—	—	—
83-84—New York Rangers	NHL	73	23	28	51	88	5	0	1	1	7
84-85—New York Rangers	NHL	23	4	4	8	33	3	0	0	0	4
85-86—New York Rangers	NHL	62	16	24	40	80	15	2	3	5	26
86-87—New York Rangers	NHL	58	17	15	32	101	—	—	—	—	—
—Toronto	NHL	16	5	10	15	12	9	1	3	4	6
87-88—Toronto	NHL	79	23	37	60	102	6	1	3	4	16
88-89—Toronto	NHL	75	16	30	46	112	—	—	—	—	—
89-90—Toronto	NHL	78	23	50	73	91	5	2	3	5	12
90-91—Toronto	NHL	18	3	3	6	4	—	—	—	—	—
—Winnipeg	NHL	37	8	8	16	59	—	—	—	—	—
91-92—Winnipeg	NHL	43	4	12	16	65	—	—	—	—	—
—Toronto	NHL	11	3	1	4	8	—	—	—	—	—
NHL totals		733	190	287	477	899	43	6	13	19	71

OSGOOD, CHRIS

G, RED WINGS

PERSONAL: Born November 26, 1972, at Peace River, Alta.... 5-10/156.... Shoots left.
TRANSACTIONS/CAREER NOTES: Selected by Detroit Red Wings in third round (third Red Wings pick, 54th overall) of NHL entry draft (June 22, 1991).
HONORS: Named to WHL All-Star second team (1990-91).

			REGULAR SEASON								PLAYOFFS					
Season Team	League	Gms.	Min.	W	L	T	GA	SO	Avg.	Gms.	Min.	W	L	GA	SO	Avg.
89-90—Medicine Hat	WHL	57	3094	24	28	2	228	0	4.42	3	173	3	4	17	0	5.90
90-91—Medicine Hat	WHL	46	2630	23	18	3	173	2	3.95	12	714	7	5	42	0	3.53
91-92—Medicine Hat	WHL	15	819	10	3	0	44	0	3.22	—	—	—	—	—	—	—
—Brandon	WHL	16	890	3	10	1	60	1	4.04	—	—	—	—	—	—	—
—Seattle	WHL	21	1217	12	7	1	65	1	3.20	15	904	9	6	51	0	3.38

OSIECKI, MARK

D, SENATORS

PERSONAL: Born July 23, 1968, at St. Paul, Minn.... 6-2/200.... Shoots right.... Full name: Mark Anthony Osiecki.
COLLEGE: Wisconsin.
TRANSACTIONS/CAREER NOTES: Selected by Calgary Flames in ninth round (10th Flames pick, 187th overall) of NHL entry draft (June 13, 1987).... Traded by Flames to Ottawa Senators for LW Chris Lindberg (June 23, 1992).
HONORS: Named to NCAA All-Tournament team (1989-90).

			REGULAR SEASON					PLAYOFFS			
Season Team	League	Gms.	G	A	Pts.	Pen.	Gms.	G	A	Pts.	Pen.
86-87—University of Wisconsin	WCHA	8	0	1	1	4	—	—	—	—	—
87-88—University of Wisconsin	WCHA	18	0	1	1	22	—	—	—	—	—

O

Season Team	League	REGULAR SEASON Gms.	G	A	Pts.	Pen.	PLAYOFFS Gms.	G	A	Pts.	Pen.
88-89—University of Wisconsin ...	WCHA	44	1	3	4	56	—	—	—	—	—
89-90—University of Wisconsin ...	WCHA	46	5	38	43	78	—	—	—	—	—
90-91—Salt Lake City	IHL	75	1	24	25	36	4	2	0	2	2
91-92—Calgary	NHL	50	2	7	9	24	—	—	—	—	—
—Salt Lake City	IHL	1	0	0	0	0	—	—	—	—	—
NHL totals		50	2	7	9	24					

O'SULLIVAN, CHRIS
D, FLAMES

PERSONAL: Born May 15, 1974, at Dorchester, Mass. ... 6-2/180. ... Shoots left. **HIGH SCHOOL:** Catholic Memorial (Boston). **TRANSACTIONS/CAREER NOTES:** Selected by Calgary Flames in second round (second Flames pick, 30th overall) of NHL entry draft (June 20, 1992).

Season Team	League	REGULAR SEASON Gms.	G	A	Pts.	Pen.	PLAYOFFS Gms.	G	A	Pts.	Pen.
91-92—Catholic Memorial H.S.	Mass. H.S.	26	26	23	49	65	—	—	—	—	—

O'SULLIVAN, KEVIN
D, ISLANDERS

PERSONAL: Born November 13, 1970, at Dorchester, Mass. ... 6-0/180. ... Shoots left. ... Full name: Kevin Patrick O'Sullivan. **HIGH SCHOOL:** Catholic Memorial (Boston). **COLLEGE:** Boston University.

TRANSACTIONS/CAREER NOTES: Selected by New York Islanders in fifth round (seventh Islanders pick, 99th overall) of NHL entry draft (June 17, 1989).

HONORS: Named to Hockey East All-Star second team (1991-92).

Season Team	League	REGULAR SEASON Gms.	G	A	Pts.	Pen.	PLAYOFFS Gms.	G	A	Pts.	Pen.
87-88—Catholic Memorial H.S.	Mass. H.S.		8	24	32		—	—	—	—	—
88-89—Catholic Memorial H.S.	Mass. H.S.	19	6	14	20		—	—	—	—	—
89-90—Boston University	Hockey East	43	0	6	6	42	—	—	—	—	—
90-91—Boston University	Hockey East	37	4	7	11	50	—	—	—	—	—
91-92—Boston University	Hockey East	33	3	18	21	62	—	—	—	—	—

OTTO, JOEL
C, FLAMES

PERSONAL: Born October 29, 1961, at Elk River, Minn. ... 6-4/220. ... Shoots right. ... Full name: Joel Stuart Otto. **COLLEGE:** Bemidji State (Minn.). **TRANSACTIONS/CAREER NOTES:** Signed as free agent by Calgary Flames (September 11, 1984). ... Tore cartilage in right knee (March 10, 1987). ... Strained right knee ligaments (October 8, 1987). ... Bruised ribs (November 1989). ... Hospitalized after being crosschecked from behind (January 13, 1990). ... Injured ankle (March 10, 1992); missed two games.

Season Team	League	REGULAR SEASON Gms.	G	A	Pts.	Pen.	PLAYOFFS Gms.	G	A	Pts.	Pen.
80-81—Bemidji State	NCAA-II	23	5	11	16	10	—	—	—	—	—
81-82—Bemidji State	NCAA-II	31	19	33	52	24	—	—	—	—	—
82-83—Bemidji State	NCAA-II	37	33	28	61	68	—	—	—	—	—
83-84—Bemidji State	NCAA-II	31	32	43	75	32	—	—	—	—	—
84-85—Moncton	AHL	56	27	36	63	89	—	—	—	—	—
—Calgary	NHL	17	4	8	12	30	3	2	1	3	10
85-86—Calgary	NHL	79	25	34	59	188	22	5	10	15	80
86-87—Calgary	NHL	68	19	31	50	185	2	0	2	2	6
87-88—Calgary	NHL	62	13	39	52	194	9	3	2	5	26
88-89—Calgary	NHL	72	23	30	53	213	22	6	13	19	46
89-90—Calgary	NHL	75	13	20	33	116	6	2	2	4	2
90-91—Calgary	NHL	76	19	20	39	183	7	1	2	3	8
91-92—Calgary	NHL	78	13	21	34	161	—	—	—	—	—
NHL totals		527	129	203	332	1270	71	19	32	51	178

OUIMET, MARK
C, CAPITALS

PERSONAL: Born October 2, 1971, at London, Ont. ... 5-10/165. ... Shoots left. ... Full name: Mark Edward Ouimet. **COLLEGE:** Michigan. **TRANSACTIONS/CAREER NOTES:** Pulled groin (August 1989). ... Selected by Washington Capitals in fifth round (fifth Capitals pick, 94th overall) of NHL entry draft (June 16, 1990).

Season Team	League	REGULAR SEASON Gms.	G	A	Pts.	Pen.	PLAYOFFS Gms.	G	A	Pts.	Pen.
87-88—Strathroy Jr. B	OHA	47	28	36	64	12	—	—	—	—	—
88-89—Strathroy Jr. B	OHA	42	43	50	93	20	—	—	—	—	—
89-90—University of Michigan	CCHA	38	15	32	47	14	—	—	—	—	—
90-91—University of Michigan	CCHA	46	18	32	50	22	—	—	—	—	—
91-92—University of Michigan	CCHA	40	10	19	29	30	—	—	—	—	—

OZOLNICH, SANDIS
D, SHARKS

PERSONAL: Born August 3, 1972, at Riga, U.S.S.R. ... 6-1/189. ... Shoots left. **TRANSACTIONS/CAREER NOTES:** Selected by San Jose Sharks in second round (third Sharks pick, 30th overall) of NHL entry draft (June 22, 1991).

Season	Team	League	REGULAR SEASON					PLAYOFFS				
			Gms.	G	A	Pts.	Pen.	Gms.	G	A	Pts.	Pen.
90-91—Dynamo Riga		USSR	44	0	3	3	49	—	—	—	—	—
91-92—Riga		CIS	30	5	0	5	42	—	—	—	—	—
—Kansas City		IHL	34	6	9	15	20	15	2	5	7	22

PAEK, JIM
D, PENGUINS

PERSONAL: Born April 7, 1967, at Seoul, South Korea.... 6-1/194.... Shoots left.
TRANSACTIONS/CAREER NOTES: Selected by Pittsburgh Penguins as underage junior in ninth round (ninth Penguins pick, 170th overall) of NHL entry draft (June 15, 1985).... Suspended two games by OHL for being involved in bench-clearing incident (November 2, 1986).... Dislocated finger on left hand (January 10, 1992); missed 14 games.

Season	Team	League	REGULAR SEASON					PLAYOFFS				
			Gms.	G	A	Pts.	Pen.	Gms.	G	A	Pts.	Pen.
84-85—Oshawa		OHL	54	2	13	15	57	5	1	0	1	9
85-86—Oshawa		OHL	64	5	21	26	122	6	0	1	1	9
86-87—Oshawa		OHL	57	5	17	22	75	26	1	14	15	43
87-88—Muskegon		IHL	82	7	52	59	141	6	0	0	0	29
88-89—Muskegon		IHL	80	3	54	57	96	14	1	10	11	24
89-90—Muskegon		IHL	81	9	41	50	115	15	1	10	11	41
90-91—Canadian National Team..		Int'l	48	2	12	14	24	—	—	—	—	—
—Pittsburgh		NHL	3	0	0	0	0	8	1	0	1	2
91-92—Pittsburgh		NHL	49	1	7	8	36	19	0	4	4	6
NHL totals			52	1	7	8	45	27	1	4	5	8

PALFFY, ZIGMUND
LW, ISLANDERS

PERSONAL: Born May 5, 1972, at Skalica, Czechoslovakia.... 5-10/169.... Shoots left.
TRANSACTIONS/CAREER NOTES: Selected by New York Islanders in second round (second Islanders pick, 26th overall) of NHL entry draft (June 22, 1991).

Season	Team	League	REGULAR SEASON					PLAYOFFS				
			Gms.	G	A	Pts.	Pen.	Gms.	G	A	Pts.	Pen.
90-91—Nitra		Czech.	50	34	16	50	18	—	—	—	—	—
91-92—Dukla Trencin		Czech.	32	23	25	48		—	—	—	—	—

PANTELEYEV, GRIGOR
LW/RW, BRUINS

PERSONAL: Born November 13, 1972, at Riga, U.S.S.R.... 5-9/194.... Shoots left.... Full name: Grigory Panteleyev.
TRANSACTIONS/CAREER NOTES: Selected by Boston Bruins in sixth round (fifth Bruins pick, 136th overall) of NHL entry draft (June 20, 1992).

Season	Team	League	REGULAR SEASON					PLAYOFFS				
			Gms.	G	A	Pts.	Pen.	Gms.	G	A	Pts.	Pen.
90-91—Dynamo Riga		USSR	23	4	1	5	4	—	—	—	—	—
91-92—Riga		CIS	26	4	8	12	4	—	—	—	—	—

PARKS, GREG
C, ISLANDERS

PERSONAL: Born March 25, 1967, at Edmonton, Alta.... 5-9/180.... Shoots right.... Full name: Gregory Roy Parks.
COLLEGE: Bowling Green State.
TRANSACTIONS/CAREER NOTES: Signed as free agent by Springfield Indians (September 1989).... Signed as free agent by New York Islanders (August 13, 1990).
HONORS: Named to CCHA All-Star first team (1988-89).

Season	Team	League	REGULAR SEASON					PLAYOFFS				
			Gms.	G	A	Pts.	Pen.	Gms.	G	A	Pts.	Pen.
84-85—St. Albert		AJHL	48	36	74	110		—	—	—	—	—
85-86—Bowling Green State		CCHA	41	16	26	42	43	—	—	—	—	—
86-87—Bowling Green State		CCHA	45	23	27	50	52	—	—	—	—	—
87-88—Bowling Green State		CCHA	45	30	44	74	86	—	—	—	—	—
88-89—Bowling Green State		CCHA	47	32	42	74	96	—	—	—	—	—
89-90—Springfield		AHL	49	22	32	54	30	18	9	†13	*22	22
—Johnstown		ECHL	8	5	9	14	7	—	—	—	—	—
90-91—Capital District		AHL	48	32	43	75	67	—	—	—	—	—
—New York Islanders		NHL	20	1	2	3	4	—	—	—	—	—
91-92—New York Islanders		NHL	1	0	0	0	2	—	—	—	—	—
—Capital District		AHL	70	36	57	93	84	7	5	8	13	4
NHL totals			21	1	2	3	6					

PARROTT, JEFF
D, NORDIQUES

PERSONAL: Born April 6, 1971, at The Pas, Man.... 6-1/195.... Shoots right.... Full name: Jeffrey E. Parrott.
COLLEGE: Minnesota-Duluth.
TRANSACTIONS/CAREER NOTES: Strained knee ligaments (November 1988).... Selected by Quebec Nordiques in sixth round (fourth Nordiques pick, 106th overall) of NHL entry draft (June 16, 1990).

Season	Team	League	REGULAR SEASON					PLAYOFFS				
			Gms.	G	A	Pts.	Pen.	Gms.	G	A	Pts.	Pen.
88-89—Notre Dame		SJHL	51	6	18	24	143	—	—	—	—	—
89-90—Minnesota-Duluth		WCHA	35	1	6	7	64	—	—	—	—	—
90-91—Minnesota-Duluth		WCHA	39	2	8	10	65	—	—	—	—	—
91-92—Minnesota-Duluth		WCHA	33	1	8	9	78	—	—	—	—	—

OP

PARSON, MIKE
G, BRUINS

PERSONAL: Born March 3, 1970, at Listowel, Ont. . . . 6-0/170. . . . Shoots left.
TRANSACTIONS/CAREER NOTES: Selected by Boston Bruins in second round (second Bruins pick, 38th overall) of NHL entry draft (June 17, 1989).

			REGULAR SEASON							PLAYOFFS						
Season	Team	League	Gms.	Min.	W	L	T	GA	SO	Avg.	Gms.	Min.	W	L	GA	SO	Avg.
86-87	Elmira Jr. B	OHA	24	1380				72	2	3.13	—	—	—	—	—	—	—
87-88	Guelph	OHL	31	1703	9	17	2	135	0	4.76	—	—	—	—	—	—	—
88-89	Guelph	OHL	*53	*3047	25	22	5	194	0	3.82	7	421	3	4	29	0	4.13
89-90	Owen Sound	OHL	49	2735	21	21	4	200	1	4.39	12	722	5	7	51	0	4.24
90-91	Johnstown	ECHL	6	333	4	2	0	23	0	4.14	—	—	—	—	—	—	—
	Maine	AHL	24	1154	6	10	1	79	0	4.11	—	—	—	—	—	—	—
91-92	Maine	AHL	12	645	5	4	1	37	0	3.44	—	—	—	—	—	—	—
	Johnstown	ECHL	17	994	6	7	3	61	1	3.68	5	224	2	1	15	0	4.02

PASCALL, BRAD
D, SABRES

PERSONAL: Born July 29, 1970, at Coquitlam, B.C. . . . 6-2/192. . . . Shoots left. . . . Full name: Brad D. Pascall.
COLLEGE: North Dakota.
TRANSACTIONS/CAREER NOTES: Selected by Buffalo Sabres in fifth round (fifth Sabres pick, 103rd overall) of NHL entry draft (June 16, 1990).

			REGULAR SEASON					PLAYOFFS			
Season	Team	League	Gms.	G	A	Pts.	Pen.	Gms.	G	A	Pts.	Pen.
88-89	Univ. of North Dakota	WCHA	3	0	0	0	0	—	—	—	—	—
89-90	Univ. of North Dakota	WCHA	45	1	9	10	98	—	—	—	—	—
90-91	Univ. of North Dakota	WCHA	38	1	4	5	81	—	—	—	—	—
91-92	Univ. of North Dakota	WCHA	28	0	7	7	85	—	—	—	—	—

PASLAWSKI, GREG
RW, NORDIQUES

PERSONAL: Born August 25, 1961, at Kindersley, Sask. . . . 5-11/190. . . . Shoots right. . . . Full name: Gregory Stephen Paslawski.
TRANSACTIONS/CAREER NOTES: Signed as free agent by Montreal Canadiens (October 5, 1981). . . . Traded by Canadiens with C Doug Wickenheiser and D Gilbert Delorme to St. Louis Blues for LW Perry Turnbull (December 21, 1983). . . . Injured knee (February 20, 1986). . . . Injured knee (December 1986). . . . Pinched nerve in left leg (October 1987). . . . Underwent disk surgery (November 1987). . . . Traded by Blues with third-round pick in 1989 draft (C Kris Draper) to Winnipeg Jets for second-round pick in 1989 draft (LW Denny Felsner) (June 17, 1989). . . . Ruptured bicep muscle in right shoulder (December 13, 1990). . . . Pulled groin (January 21, 1991). . . . Traded by Jets to Buffalo Sabres as future considerations to complete the C Dale Hawerchuk trade of June 1990 (February 4, 1991). . . . Selected by San Jose Sharks in NHL expansion draft (May 30, 1991). . . . Traded by Sharks to Quebec Nordiques for C Tony Hrkac (May 30, 1991).

			REGULAR SEASON					PLAYOFFS			
Season	Team	League	Gms.	G	A	Pts.	Pen.	Gms.	G	A	Pts.	Pen.
80-81	Prince Albert	SJHL	59	55	60	115	106	—	—	—	—	—
81-82	Nova Scotia	AHL	43	15	11	26	31	—	—	—	—	—
82-83	Nova Scotia	AHL	75	46	42	88	32	6	1	3	4	8
83-84	Montreal	NHL	26	1	4	5	4	—	—	—	—	—
	St. Louis	NHL	34	8	6	14	17	9	1	0	1	2
84-85	St. Louis	NHL	72	22	20	42	21	3	0	0	0	2
85-86	St. Louis	NHL	56	22	11	33	18	17	10	7	17	13
86-87	St. Louis	NHL	76	29	35	64	27	6	1	1	2	4
87-88	St. Louis	NHL	17	2	1	3	4	3	1	1	2	2
88-89	St. Louis	NHL	75	26	26	52	18	9	2	1	3	2
89-90	Winnipeg	NHL	71	18	30	48	14	7	1	3	4	0
90-91	Winnipeg	NHL	43	9	10	19	10	—	—	—	—	—
	Buffalo	NHL	12	2	1	3	4	—	—	—	—	—
91-92	Quebec	NHL	80	28	17	45	18	—	—	—	—	—
NHL totals			562	167	161	328	155	54	16	13	29	25

PASMA, ROD
D, CAPITALS

PERSONAL: Born February 26, 1972, at Hespler, Ont. . . . 6-4/207. . . . Shoots left.
TRANSACTIONS/CAREER NOTES: Selected by Washington Capitals in second round (second Capitals pick, 30th overall) of NHL entry draft (June 16, 1990). . . . Traded by Cornwall Royals with Shawn Caplice to Kingston Frontenacs for C Nathan Lafayette and Joel Sandie (January 6, 1991).

			REGULAR SEASON					PLAYOFFS			
Season	Team	League	Gms.	G	A	Pts.	Pen.	Gms.	G	A	Pts.	Pen.
88-89	Georgetown Jr. B	OHA	37	4	14	18	58	—	—	—	—	—
89-90	Cornwall	OHL	64	3	16	19	142	6	0	2	2	15
90-91	Cornwall	OHL	33	3	9	12	64	—	—	—	—	—
	Kingston	OHL	31	1	9	10	39	—	—	—	—	—
91-92	Kingston	OHL	23	2	1	3	68	—	—	—	—	—
	Windsor	OHL	27	3	4	7	59	7	0	1	1	18

PATERSON, JOE
LW, RANGERS

PERSONAL: Born June 25, 1960, at Toronto. . . . 6-2/207. . . . Shoots left. . . . Full name: Joe Andrew Paterson.
TRANSACTIONS/CAREER NOTES: Selected by Detroit Red Wings as underage junior in fifth round (fifth Red Wings pick, 87th overall) of NHL entry draft (August 9, 1979). . . . Pulled groin muscle (October 1982). . . . Traded by Red Wings with C Murray Craven to Philadelphia Flyers for C Darryl Sittler (Octo-

ber 19, 1984).... Traded by Flyers to Los Angeles Kings for Flyers' fourth-round pick in 1986 draft (D Mark Bar) (December 18, 1985).... Pulled groin (October 21, 1987).... Traded by Kings to New York Rangers for RW Mike Siltala and LW Gord Walker (January 1988).

Season	Team	League	REGULAR SEASON					PLAYOFFS				
			Gms.	G	A	Pts.	Pen.	Gms.	G	A	Pts.	Pen.
77-78	London	OMJHL	68	17	16	33	100	—	—	—	—	—
78-79	London	OMJHL	60	22	19	41	158	7	2	3	5	13
79-80	London	OMJHL	65	21	50	71	156	—	—	—	—	—
	Kalamazoo	IHL	4	1	2	3	2	3	2	1	3	11
80-81	Detroit	NHL	38	2	5	7	53	—	—	—	—	—
	Adirondack	AHL	39	9	16	25	68	—	—	—	—	—
81-82	Adirondack	AHL	74	22	28	50	132	5	1	4	5	6
	Detroit	NHL	3	0	0	0	0	—	—	—	—	—
82-83	Adirondack	AHL	36	11	10	21	85	6	1	2	3	21
	Detroit	NHL	33	2	1	3	14	—	—	—	—	—
83-84	Detroit	NHL	41	2	5	7	148	3	0	0	0	7
	Adirondack	AHL	20	10	15	25	43	—	—	—	—	—
84-85	Hershey	AHL	67	26	27	53	173	—	—	—	—	—
	Philadelphia	NHL	6	0	0	0	31	17	3	4	7	70
85-86	Hershey	AHL	20	5	10	15	68	—	—	—	—	—
	Philadelphia	NHL	6	0	0	0	12	—	—	—	—	—
	Los Angeles	NHL	47	9	18	27	153	—	—	—	—	—
86-87	Los Angeles	NHL	45	2	1	3	158	2	0	0	0	0
87-88	Los Angeles	NHL	32	1	3	4	113	—	—	—	—	—
	New York Rangers	NHL	21	1	3	4	63	—	—	—	—	—
88-89	New York Rangers	NHL	20	0	1	1	84	—	—	—	—	—
	Denver	IHL	9	5	4	9	31	—	—	—	—	—
	New Haven	AHL	7	0	0	0	24	—	—	—	—	—
89-90	Flint	IHL	69	21	26	47	198	4	0	1	1	2
90-91	Binghamton	AHL	80	16	35	51	221	10	5	3	8	25
91-92	Binghamton	AHL	49	7	10	17	115	5	0	0	0	4
	Phoenix	IHL	2	0	0	0	2	—	—	—	—	—
NHL totals			291	19	37	56	829	22	3	4	7	77

PATRICK, JAMES
D, RANGERS

PERSONAL: Born June 14, 1963, at Winnipeg, Man.... 6-2/192.... Shoots right.... Full name: James A. Patrick.... Brother of Steve Patrick, right winger, Buffalo Sabres, New York Rangers and Quebec Nordiques (1980-81 through 1985-86).
COLLEGE: North Dakota.

TRANSACTIONS/CAREER NOTES: Selected by New York Rangers as underage junior in first round (first Rangers pick, ninth overall) of NHL entry draft (June 10, 1981).... Injured groin (October 1984).... Pinched nerve (December 15, 1985).... Strained left knee ligaments (March 1988).... Bruised shoulder and chest (December 1988).... Pulled groin (March 13, 1989).
HONORS: Named Player of the Year (1980-81).... Named to SJHL All-Star first team (1980-81).... Won WCHA Rookie of the Year Award (1981-82).... Named to WCHA All-Star second team (1981-82).... Named to NCAA All-Tournament team (1981-82).... Named to NCAA All-America West team (1982-83).... Named to WCHA All-Star first team (1982-83).

Season	Team	League	REGULAR SEASON					PLAYOFFS				
			Gms.	G	A	Pts.	Pen.	Gms.	G	A	Pts.	Pen.
80-81	Prince Albert	SJHL	59	21	61	82	162	4	1	6	7	0
81-82	Univ. of North Dakota	WCHA	42	5	24	29	26	—	—	—	—	—
82-83	Univ. of North Dakota	WCHA	36	12	36	48	29	—	—	—	—	—
83-84	Canadian Olympic Team	Int'l	63	7	24	31	52	—	—	—	—	—
	New York Rangers	NHL	12	1	7	8	2	5	0	3	3	2
84-85	New York Rangers	NHL	75	8	28	36	71	3	0	0	0	4
85-86	New York Rangers	NHL	75	14	29	43	88	16	1	5	6	34
86-87	New York Rangers	NHL	78	10	45	55	62	6	1	2	3	2
87-88	New York Rangers	NHL	70	17	45	62	52	—	—	—	—	—
88-89	New York Rangers	NHL	68	11	36	47	41	4	0	1	1	2
89-90	New York Rangers	NHL	73	14	43	57	50	10	3	8	11	0
90-91	New York Rangers	NHL	74	10	49	59	58	6	0	0	0	6
91-92	New York Rangers	NHL	80	14	57	71	54	13	0	7	7	12
NHL totals			605	99	339	438	478	63	5	26	31	62

PATTERSON, COLIN
C/RW, SABRES

PERSONAL: Born May 11, 1960, at Rexdale, Ont.... 6-2/195.... Shoots right.
COLLEGE: Clarkson (N.Y.).
TRANSACTIONS/CAREER NOTES: Signed as free agent by Calgary Flames (March 24, 1983).... Injured shoulder (March 14, 1984).... Tore knee ligaments (January 1985).... Pulled hamstring (October 1987).... Sprained ankle (December 1987).... Suffered concussion (November 1988).... Bruised foot (January 11, 1989).... Broke nose (April 24, 1989).... Broke right ankle (March 24, 1990).... Tore anterior cruciate ligament of right knee (September 18, 1990).... Underwent knee surgery (October 12, 1990).... Underwent additional surgery (December 7, 1990); missed remainder of regular season.... Traded by Flames to Buffalo Sabres for future considerations (October 24, 1991).... Suffered sore left knee (February 7, 1992); missed six games.... Injured left knee (February 29, 1992); missed seven games.
HONORS: Named to ECAC All-Star second team (1982-83).

Season	Team	League	REGULAR SEASON					PLAYOFFS				
			Gms.	G	A	Pts.	Pen.	Gms.	G	A	Pts.	Pen.
80-81	Clarkson	ECAC	34	20	31	51	8	—	—	—	—	—
81-82	Clarkson	ECAC	35	21	31	52	32	—	—	—	—	—

Season Team	League	Gms.	G	A	Pts.	Pen.	Gms.	G	A	Pts.	Pen.
82-83—Clarkson	ECAC	31	23	29	52	30	—	—	—	—	—
—Colorado	CHL	7	1	1	2	0	3	0	0	0	15
83-84—Colorado	CHL	6	2	3	5	9	—	—	—	—	—
—Calgary	NHL	56	13	14	27	15	11	1	1	2	6
84-85—Calgary	NHL	57	22	21	43	5	4	0	0	0	5
85-86—Calgary	NHL	61	14	13	27	22	19	6	3	9	10
86-87—Calgary	NHL	68	13	13	26	41	6	0	2	2	2
87-88—Calgary	NHL	39	7	11	18	28	9	1	0	1	8
88-89—Calgary	NHL	74	14	24	38	56	22	3	10	13	24
89-90—Calgary	NHL	61	5	3	8	20	—	—	—	—	—
90-91—Calgary	NHL	—	—	—	—	—	1	0	0	0	0
91-92—Buffalo	NHL	52	4	8	12	30	5	1	0	1	0
NHL totals		468	92	107	199	217	77	12	16	28	55

PAVELICH, MARK

C

PERSONAL: Born February 28, 1958, at Eveleth, Minn. . . . 5-8/170. . . . Shoots right.
HIGH SCHOOL: Eveleth Gilbert (Minn.)
COLLEGE: Minnesota-Duluth.
TRANSACTIONS/CAREER NOTES: Signed as free agent by New York Rangers (June 5, 1981). . . . Fractured leg (October 13, 1984). . . . Fractured finger (December 28, 1985); missed five games. . . . Announced retirement (March 1986). . . . Signed with Dundee of the British Elite League (August 1986); Rangers protested and kept him from playing. . . . Traded by Rangers to Minnesota North Stars for fourth-round pick in 1988 draft (C Martin Bergeron) (October 24, 1986). . . . Suspended by North Stars for failure to report to team (October 1986). . . . Signed as free agent by San Jose Sharks (August 9, 1991). . . . Released by Sharks (October 8, 1991).
HONORS: Named to WCHA All-Star first team (1978-79).
MISCELLANEOUS: Member of 1980 gold-medal-winning U.S. Olympic team.

Season Team	League	Gms.	G	A	Pts.	Pen.	Gms.	G	A	Pts.	Pen.
76-77—Minnesota-Duluth	WCHA	37	12	7	19	8	—	—	—	—	—
77-78—Minnesota-Duluth	WCHA	36	14	30	44	44	—	—	—	—	—
78-79—Minnesota-Duluth	WCHA	37	31	48	79	52	—	—	—	—	—
79-80—U.S. National Team	Int'l	53	15	30	45	12	—	—	—	—	—
—U.S. Olympic Team	Int'l	7	1	6	7	2	—	—	—	—	—
80-81—Lugano	Switzerland	60	24	49	73		—	—	—	—	—
81-82—New York Rangers	NHL	79	33	43	76	67	6	1	5	6	0
82-83—New York Rangers	NHL	78	37	38	75	52	9	4	5	9	12
83-84—New York Rangers	NHL	77	29	53	82	96	5	2	4	6	0
84-85—New York Rangers	NHL	48	14	31	45	29	3	0	3	3	2
85-86—New York Rangers	NHL	59	20	20	40	82	—	—	—	—	—
86-87—Minnesota	NHL	12	4	6	10	10	—	—	—	—	—
87-88—Davos HC	Switzerland				Statistics unavailable.						
88-89—Dundee	Ireland				Statistics unavailable.						
89-90—					Did not play.						
90-91—					Did not play.						
91-92—San Jose	NHL	2	0	1	1	4	—	—	—	—	—
NHL totals		355	137	192	329	340	23	7	17	24	14

PAYNE, DAVIS

LW, OILERS

PERSONAL: Born October 24, 1970, at King City, Ont. . . . 6-1/190. . . . Shoots left. . . . Full name: Davis A. Payne.
COLLEGE: Michigan Tech.
TRANSACTIONS/CAREER NOTES: Selected by Edmonton Oilers in seventh round (sixth Oilers pick, 140th overall) of NHL entry draft (June 17, 1989). . . . Lacerated tendons in index and middle fingers of right hand (February 9, 1990); missed remainder of season.

Season Team	League	Gms.	G	A	Pts.	Pen.	Gms.	G	A	Pts.	Pen.
88-89—Michigan Tech	WCHA	35	5	3	8	39	—	—	—	—	—
89-90—Michigan Tech	WCHA	30	11	10	21	81	—	—	—	—	—
90-91—Michigan Tech	WCHA	41	15	20	35	82	—	—	—	—	—
91-92—Michigan Tech	WCHA	24	6	1	7	71	—	—	—	—	—

PAYNTER, KENT

D, SENATORS

PERSONAL: Born April 27, 1965, at Summerside, P.E.I. . . . 6-0/185. . . . Shoots left. . . . Full name: Kent Douglas Paynter.
TRANSACTIONS/CAREER NOTES: Selected by Chicago Blackhawks as underage junior in eighth round (ninth Blackhawks pick, 159th overall) of NHL entry draft (June 8, 1983). . . . Signed as free agent by Washington Capitals (August 21, 1989). . . . Traded by Capitals with LW Bob Joyce and C Tyler Larter to Winnipeg Jets for LW Brent Hughes, LW Craig Duncanson and C Simon Wheeldon (May 21, 1991). . . . Selected by Ottawa Senators in NHL expansion draft (June 18, 1992).

Season Team	League	Gms.	G	A	Pts.	Pen.	Gms.	G	A	Pts.	Pen.
81-82—Western Capitals	PEIJHL	35	7	23	30	66	—	—	—	—	—
82-83—Kitchener	OHL	65	4	11	15	97	12	1	0	1	20
83-84—Kitchener	OHL	65	9	27	36	94	16	4	9	13	18

P

Season	Team	League	REGULAR SEASON Gms.	G	A	Pts.	Pen.	PLAYOFFS Gms.	G	A	Pts.	Pen.
84-85—Kitchener	OHL	58	7	28	35	93	4	2	1	3	4
85-86—Nova Scotia	AHL	23	1	2	3	36	—	—	—	—	—
—Saginaw	IHL	4	0	1	1	2	—	—	—	—	—
86-87—Nova Scotia	AHL	66	2	6	8	57	2	0	0	0	0
87-88—Saginaw	IHL	74	8	20	28	141	10	0	1	1	30
—Chicago	NHL	2	0	0	0	2	—	—	—	—	—
88-89—Chicago	NHL	1	0	0	0	2	—	—	—	—	—
—Saginaw	IHL	69	12	14	26	148	6	2	2	4	17
89-90—Washington	NHL	13	1	2	3	18	3	0	0	0	10
—Baltimore	AHL	60	7	20	27	110	11	5	6	11	34
90-91—Baltimore	AHL	43	10	17	27	64	6	2	1	3	8
—Washington	NHL	1	0	0	0	15	1	0	0	0	0
91-92—Moncton	AHL	62	3	30	33	71	11	2	6	8	25
—Winnipeg	NHL	5	0	0	0	4	—	—	—	—	—
NHL totals		**22**	**1**	**2**	**3**	**41**	**4**	**0**	**0**	**0**	**10**

PEACOCK, SHANE
D, PENGUINS

PERSONAL: Born July 7, 1973, at Edmonton, Alta.... 5-9/198.... Shoots right.
TRANSACTIONS/CAREER NOTES: Selected by Pittsburgh Penguins in third round (third Penguins pick, 60th overall) of NHL entry draft (June 22, 1991).

Season	Team	League	REGULAR SEASON Gms.	G	A	Pts.	Pen.	PLAYOFFS Gms.	G	A	Pts.	Pen.
88-89—Notre Dame	SCMHL	28	8	12	20	160	—	—	—	—	—
89-90—Lethbridge	WHL	65	7	23	30	60	19	2	8	10	42
90-91—Lethbridge	WHL	69	12	50	62	102	16	1	14	15	26
91-92—Lethbridge	WHL	67	35	45	80	217	5	2	5	7	2

PEAKE, PAT
C, CAPITALS

PERSONAL: Born May 28, 1973, at Detroit.... 6-0/195.... Shoots right.... Full name: Patrick Michael Peake.
TRANSACTIONS/CAREER NOTES: Injured wrist (August 31, 1990).... Selected by Washington Capitals in first round (Capitals first pick, 14th overall) of NHL entry draft (June 22, 1991).

Season	Team	League	REGULAR SEASON Gms.	G	A	Pts.	Pen.	PLAYOFFS Gms.	G	A	Pts.	Pen.
89-90—Detroit Compuware	NAJHL	40	36	37	73	57	—	—	—	—	—
90-91—Detroit	OHL	63	39	51	90	54	—	—	—	—	—
91-92—Detroit	OHL	53	41	52	93	44	7	8	9	17	10
—Baltimore	AHL	3	1	0	1	4	—	—	—	—	—

PEARSON, ROB
RW, MAPLE LEAFS

PERSONAL: Born August 3, 1971, at Oshawa, Ont.... 6-1/180.... Shoots right.
TRANSACTIONS/CAREER NOTES: Broke wrist (November 13, 1988).... Selected by Toronto Maple Leafs in first round (second Maple Leafs pick, 12th overall) of NHL entry draft (June 17, 1989).... Dislocated right knee (August 15, 1989).... Suspended five games by OHL for checking from behind (February 7, 1990).... Broke collarbone (August 1990).... Traded by Belleville Bulls to Oshawa Generals for C Jarrod Skalde (November 18, 1990).
HONORS: Won Jim Mahon Memorial Trophy (1990-91).... Named to OHL All-Star first team (1990-91).

Season	Team	League	REGULAR SEASON Gms.	G	A	Pts.	Pen.	PLAYOFFS Gms.	G	A	Pts.	Pen.
88-89—Belleville	OHL	26	8	12	20	51	—	—	—	—	—
89-90—Belleville	OHL	58	48	40	88	174	11	5	5	10	26
90-91—Belleville	OHL	10	6	3	9	27	—	—	—	—	—
—Oshawa	OHL	41	57	52	109	76	16	16	17	33	39
—Newmarket	AHL	3	0	0	0	29	—	—	—	—	—
91-92—Toronto	NHL	47	14	10	24	58	—	—	—	—	—
—St. John's	AHL	27	15	14	29	107	13	5	4	9	40
NHL totals		**47**	**14**	**10**	**24**	**58**					

PEARSON, SCOTT
LW, NORDIQUES

PERSONAL: Born December 19, 1969, at Cornwall, Ont.... 6-1/205.... Shoots left.
TRANSACTIONS/CAREER NOTES: Underwent surgery to left wrist (May 1988).... Selected by Toronto Maple Leafs in first round (first Maple Leafs pick, sixth overall) of NHL entry draft (June 11, 1988).... Traded by Maple Leafs with second-round picks in 1991 (D Eric Lavigne) and 1992 drafts to Quebec Nordiques for C/LW Aaron Broten, D Michel Petit and RW Lucien Deblois (November 17, 1990).

Season	Team	League	REGULAR SEASON Gms.	G	A	Pts.	Pen.	PLAYOFFS Gms.	G	A	Pts.	Pen.
85-86—Kingston	OHL	63	16	23	39	56	—	—	—	—	—
86-87—Kingston	OHL	62	30	24	54	101	9	3	3	6	42
87-88—Kingston	OHL	46	26	32	58	118	—	—	—	—	—
88-89—Kingston	OHL	13	9	8	17	34	—	—	—	—	—
—Niagara Falls	OHL	32	26	34	60	90	17	14	10	24	53
—Toronto	NHL	9	0	1	1	2	—	—	—	—	—
89-90—Newmarket	AHL	18	12	11	23	64	—	—	—	—	—
—Toronto	NHL	41	5	10	15	90	2	2	0	2	10

P

Season Team	League	REGULAR SEASON					PLAYOFFS				
		Gms.	G	A	Pts.	Pen.	Gms.	G	A	Pts.	Pen.
90-91—Toronto	NHL	12	0	0	0	20	—	—	—	—	—
—Quebec	NHL	35	11	4	15	86	—	—	—	—	—
—Halifax	AHL	24	12	15	27	44	—	—	—	—	—
91-92—Quebec	NHL	10	1	2	3	14	—	—	—	—	—
—Halifax	AHL	5	2	1	3	4	—	—	—	—	—
NHL totals		107	17	17	34	212	2	2	0	2	10

PECA, MIKE
RW/C, CANUCKS

PERSONAL: Born March 26, 1974, at Toronto.... 5-11/165.... Shoots right. **HIGH SCHOOL:** LaSalle Secondary School (Kinston, Ont.). **TRANSACTIONS/CAREER NOTES:** Selected by Vancouver Canucks in second round (second Canucks pick, 40th overall) of NHL entry draft (June 20, 1992).

Season Team	League	REGULAR SEASON					PLAYOFFS				
		Gms.	G	A	Pts.	Pen.	Gms.	G	A	Pts.	Pen.
90-91—Sudbury	OHL	62	14	27	41	24	5	1	0	1	7
91-92—Sudbury	OHL	39	16	34	50	61	—	—	—	—	—
—Ottawa	OHL	27	8	17	25	32	11	6	10	16	6

PEDERSEN, ALLEN
D, WHALERS

PERSONAL: Born January 13, 1965, at Edmonton, Alta.... 6-3/210.... Shoots left. **TRANSACTIONS/CAREER NOTES:** Selected by Boston Bruins as underage junior in fifth round (fifth Bruins pick, 102nd overall) of NHL entry draft (June 8, 1983).... Separated right shoulder (November 3, 1988).... Pulled abdominal muscle (December 1988).... Bruised hip (January 1990).... Selected by Minnesota North Stars in NHL expansion draft (May 30, 1991).... Suffered back spasms (October 28, 1991); missed nine games.... Tore abdominal muscles (February 17, 1992); missed 23 games.... Traded by North Stars to Hartford Whalers for future considerations (June 15, 1992).

Season Team	League	REGULAR SEASON					PLAYOFFS				
		Gms.	G	A	Pts.	Pen.	Gms.	G	A	Pts.	Pen.
82-83—Medicine Hat	WHL	63	3	10	13	49	5	0	0	0	7
83-84—Medicine Hat	WHL	44	0	11	11	47	14	0	2	2	24
84-85—Medicine Hat	WHL	72	6	16	22	66	10	0	0	0	9
85-86—Moncton	AHL	59	1	8	9	39	3	0	0	0	0
86-87—Boston	NHL	79	1	11	12	71	4	0	0	0	4
87-88—Boston	NHL	78	0	6	6	90	21	0	0	0	34
88-89—Boston	NHL	51	0	6	6	69	10	0	0	0	2
89-90—Boston	NHL	68	1	2	3	71	21	0	0	0	41
90-91—Maine	AHL	15	0	6	6	18	2	0	1	1	2
—Boston	NHL	57	2	6	8	107	8	0	0	0	10
91-92—Minnesota	NHL	29	0	1	1	10	—	—	—	—	—
NHL totals		362	4	32	36	418	64	0	0	0	91

PEDERSON, BARRY
C

PERSONAL: Born March 13, 1961, at Big River, Sask.... 5-11/171.... Shoots right. ... Full name: Barry Alan Pederson.... Cousin of Brian Skrudland, center, Montreal Canadiens. **TRANSACTIONS/CAREER NOTES:** Selected by Boston Bruins as underage junior in first round (first Bruins pick, 18th overall) of NHL entry draft (June 11, 1980).... Broke knuckle on right hand (October 2, 1984). ... Underwent surgery to remove benign fibrous tumor from rear shoulder muscle of right arm (January 1985); missed remainder of season.... Traded by Bruins to Vancouver Canucks for RW Cam Neely and first-round pick in 1987 draft (D Glen Wesley) (June 6, 1986).... Suffered whiplash (December 12, 1987).... Separated right shoulder (November 18, 1988).... Broke nose (February 12, 1989).... Broke collarbone (March 5, 1989).... Broke thumb (October 28, 1989); missed 15 games.... Traded by Canucks with RW Tony Tanti and D Rod Buskas to Pittsburgh Penguins for C Dan Quinn, RW Andrew McBain and C Dave Capuano (January 8, 1990).... Signed as free agent by Hartford Whalers (September 1991).... Released by Whalers (November 7, 1991).... Signed as free agent by Bruins (November 12, 1991). **HONORS:** Named to WHL All-Star second team (1979-80).... Won WHL Player of the Year Award (1980-81).... Named to WHL All-Star first team (1980-81). **RECORDS:** Shares NHL single-game playoff record for most points in one period—4 (April 8, 1982).

Season Team	League	REGULAR SEASON					PLAYOFFS				
		Gms.	G	A	Pts.	Pen.	Gms.	G	A	Pts.	Pen.
77-78—Nanaimo	BCJHL	63	51	102	153	68	—	—	—	—	—
—Victoria	WCHL	3	1	4	5	2	—	—	—	—	—
78-79—Victoria	WCHL	72	31	53	84	41	—	—	—	—	—
79-80—Victoria	WHL	72	52	88	140	50	16	13	14	27	31
80-81—Victoria	WHL	55	65	82	147	65	15	15	21	36	10
—Boston	NHL	9	1	4	5	6	—	—	—	—	—
81-82—Boston	NHL	80	44	48	92	53	11	7	11	18	2
82-83—Boston	NHL	77	46	61	107	47	17	14	18	32	21
83-84—Boston	NHL	80	39	77	116	64	3	0	1	1	2
84-85—Boston	NHL	22	4	8	12	10	—	—	—	—	—
85-86—Boston	NHL	79	29	47	76	60	3	1	0	1	0
86-87—Vancouver	NHL	79	24	52	76	50	—	—	—	—	—
87-88—Vancouver	NHL	76	19	52	71	92	—	—	—	—	—
88-89—Vancouver	NHL	62	15	26	41	22	—	—	—	—	—
89-90—Vancouver	NHL	16	2	7	9	10	—	—	—	—	—
—Pittsburgh	NHL	38	4	18	22	29	—	—	—	—	—

P

Season Team	League	REGULAR SEASON					PLAYOFFS				
		Gms.	G	A	Pts.	Pen.	Gms.	G	A	Pts.	Pen.
90-91—Pittsburgh	NHL	46	6	8	14	21	—	—	—	—	—
91-92—Hartford	NHL	5	2	2	4	0	—	—	—	—	—
—Boston	NHL	32	3	6	9	8	—	—	—	—	—
—Maine	AHL	14	5	13	18	6	—	—	—	—	—
NHL totals		701	238	416	654	472	34	22	30	52	25

PEDERSON, MARK
LW, FLYERS

PERSONAL: Born January 14, 1968, at Prelate, Sask.... 6-2/196.... Shoots left.
TRANSACTIONS/CAREER NOTES: Injured shoulder (March 1985).... Selected by Montreal Canadiens as underage junior in first round (first Canadiens pick, 15th overall) of NHL entry draft (June 21, 1986).... Traded by Canadiens to Philadelphia Flyers for second-round pick in 1991 draft (C Jim Campbell) and future considerations (March 5, 1991).... Dislocated shoulder (November 23, 1991); missed 10 games.
HONORS: Named to WHL East All-Star first team (1986-87 and 1989-90).... Named to WHL All-Star second team (1987-88). ...Named to AHL All-Star first team (1989-90)

Season Team	League	REGULAR SEASON					PLAYOFFS				
		Gms.	G	A	Pts.	Pen.	Gms.	G	A	Pts.	Pen.
84-85—Medicine Hat	WHL	71	42	40	82	63	10	3	2	5	0
85-86—Medicine Hat	WHL	72	46	60	106	46	25	12	6	18	25
86-87—Medicine Hat	WHL	69	56	46	102	58	20	†19	7	26	14
87-88—Medicine Hat	WHL	62	53	58	111	55	16	†13	6	19	16
88-89—Sherbrooke	AHL	75	43	38	81	53	6	7	5	12	4
89-90—Montreal	NHL	9	0	2	2	2	2	0	0	0	0
—Sherbrooke	AHL	72	53	42	95	60	11	10	8	18	19
90-91—Montreal	NHL	47	8	15	23	18	—	—	—	—	—
—Philadelphia	NHL	12	2	1	3	5	—	—	—	—	—
91-92—Philadelphia	NHL	58	15	25	40	22	—	—	—	—	—
NHL totals		126	25	43	68	47	2	0	0	0	0

PEDERSON, TOM
D, SHARKS

PERSONAL: Born January 14, 1970, at Bloomington, Minn.... 5-9/165.... Shoots right. ...Full name: Thomas Stuart Pederson.
HIGH SCHOOL: Thomas Jefferson (Bloomington, Minn.).
COLLEGE: Minnesota.
TRANSACTIONS/CAREER NOTES: Selected by Minnesota North Stars in 11th round (12th North Stars pick, 217th overall) of NHL entry draft (June 17, 1989).... Selected by San Jose Sharks in NHL dispersal draft (May 30, 1991).

Season Team	League	REGULAR SEASON					PLAYOFFS				
		Gms.	G	A	Pts.	Pen.	Gms.	G	A	Pts.	Pen.
87-88—Bloomington Jefferson HS	Minn. H.S.	22	16	27	43		—	—	—	—	—
88-89—University of Minnesota	WCHA	42	5	24	29	46	—	—	—	—	—
89-90—University of Minnesota	WCHA	43	8	30	38	58	—	—	—	—	—
90-91—University of Minnesota	WCHA	36	12	20	32	46	—	—	—	—	—
91-92—Kansas City	IHL	20	6	9	15	16	13	1	6	7	14

PELLERIN, BRIAN
RW, BLUES

PERSONAL: Born February 20, 1970, at Hinton, Alta.... 5-10/175.... Shoots right.
TRANSACTIONS/CAREER NOTES: Signed as free agent by St. Louis Blues (May 31, 1991).
HONORS: Named to WHL East All-Star first team (1990-91).

Season Team	League	REGULAR SEASON					PLAYOFFS				
		Gms.	G	A	Pts.	Pen.	Gms.	G	A	Pts.	Pen.
87-88—Prince Albert	WHL	62	6	2	8	113	10	0	0	0	17
88-89—Prince Albert	WHL	60	17	16	33	216	3	0	1	1	27
89-90—Prince Albert	WHL	53	6	15	21	175	10	1	3	4	26
90-91—Prince Albert	WHL	68	46	42	88	223	3	0	0	0	12
91-92—Peoria	IHL	70	7	16	23	231	10	1	2	3	49

PELLERIN, SCOTT
LW, DEVILS

PERSONAL: Born January 9, 1970, at Shediac, N.B.... 5-10/185.... Shoots left.... Full name: Jaque-Frederick Scott Pellerin.
COLLEGE: Maine.
TRANSACTIONS/CAREER NOTES: Selected by New Jersey Devils in third round (fourth Devils pick, 47th overall) of NHL entry draft (June 17, 1989).
HONORS: Named to Hockey East All-Rookie team (1988-89).... Named Hockey East co-Rookie of the Year with Rob Gaudreau (1988-89).... Named Hockey East Player of the Year (1991-92).... Named Hockey East Playoff Most Valuable Player (1991-92).... Named to Hockey East All-Star first team (1991-92).

Season Team	League	REGULAR SEASON					PLAYOFFS				
		Gms.	G	A	Pts.	Pen.	Gms.	G	A	Pts.	Pen.
87-88—Notre Dame	SJHL	57	37	49	86	139	—	—	—	—	—
88-89—University of Maine	Hockey East	45	29	33	62	92	—	—	—	—	—
89-90—University of Maine	Hockey East	42	22	34	56	68	—	—	—	—	—
90-91—University of Maine	Hockey East	43	23	25	48	60	—	—	—	—	—
91-92—University of Maine	Hockey East	37	†32	25	57	54	—	—	—	—	—

P

PELTOLA, PEKKA
C/RW, JETS

PERSONAL: Born June 24, 1965, at Helsinki, Finland. . . . 6-2/196. . . . Shoots right.
TRANSACTIONS/CAREER NOTES: Selected by Winnipeg Jets in sixth round (eighth Jets pick, 130th overall) of NHL entry draft (June 17, 1989).

			REGULAR SEASON					PLAYOFFS			
Season Team	League	Gms.	G	A	Pts.	Pen.	Gms.	G	A	Pts.	Pen.
88-89—Helsinki HPK	Finland	43	28	30	58	62	—	—	—	—	—
89-90—Helsinki HPK	Finland	44	25	24	49	42	—	—	—	—	—
90-91—Helsinki HPK	Finland	41	23	18	41	66	8	3	2	5	10
91-92—Helsinki HPK	Finland	37	22	20	42	91	—	—	—	—	—

PELUSO, MIKE
LW, SENATORS

PERSONAL: Born November 8, 1965, at Hibbing, Minn. . . . 6-4/225. . . . Shoots left. . . . Full name: Michael David Peluso.
COLLEGE: Alaska-Anchorage.
TRANSACTIONS/CAREER NOTES: Selected by New Jersey Devils in 10th round (10th Devils pick, 190th overall) of NHL entry draft (June 15, 1985). . . . Signed as free agent by Chicago Blackhawks (September 7, 1989). . . . Bruised jaw and cheek (November 8, 1990); missed five games. . . . Suspended 10 games by NHL for fighting (March 17, 1991). . . . Selected by Ottawa Senators in NHL expansion draft (June 18, 1992).

			REGULAR SEASON					PLAYOFFS			
Season Team	League	Gms.	G	A	Pts.	Pen.	Gms.	G	A	Pts.	Pen.
84-85—Stratford	OPJHL	52	11	45	56	114	—	—	—	—	—
85-86—Alaska-Anchorage	Indep.	32	2	11	13	59	—	—	—	—	—
86-87—Alaska-Anchorage	Indep.	30	5	21	26	68	—	—	—	—	—
87-88—Alaska-Anchorage	Indep.	35	4	33	37	76	—	—	—	—	—
88-89—Alaska-Anchorage	Indep.	33	10	27	37	75	—	—	—	—	—
89-90—Indianapolis	IHL	75	7	10	17	279	14	0	1	1	58
—Chicago	NHL	2	0	0	0	15	—	—	—	—	—
90-91—Indianapolis	IHL	6	2	1	3	21	5	0	2	2	40
—Chicago	NHL	53	6	1	7	320	3	0	0	0	2
91-92—Chicago	NHL	63	6	3	9	*408	17	1	2	3	8
—Indianapolis	IHL	4	0	1	1	15	—	—	—	—	—
NHL totals		118	12	4	16	743	20	1	2	3	10

PENNEY, CHAD
LW, SENATORS

PERSONAL: Born September 18, 1973, at Labrador City, Nfld. . . . 6-0/195. . . . Shoots left.
HIGH SCHOOL: Chippewa Secondary School (North Bay, Ont.).
TRANSACTIONS/CAREER NOTES: Selected by Ottawa Senators in second round (second Senators pick, 25th overall) of NHL entry draft (June 20 1992).

			REGULAR SEASON					PLAYOFFS			
Season Team	League	Gms.	G	A	Pts.	Pen.	Gms.	G	A	Pts.	Pen.
90-91—North Bay	OHL	66	33	34	67	56	10	2	6	8	12
91-92—North Bay	OHL	57	25	27	52	93	21	13	17	30	9
—Can. National Jr. Team	Int'l	7	0	0	0	2	—	—	—	—	—

PERREAULT, NICOLAS
D, FLAMES

PERSONAL: Born April 24, 1972, at Loretteville, Que. . . . 6-3/200. . . . Shoots left. . . . Full name: Nicolas P. Perreault.
COLLEGE: Michigan State.
TRANSACTIONS/CAREER NOTES: Separated shoulder (April 1988). . . . Selected by Calgary Flames in second round (second Flames pick, 26th overall) of NHL entry draft (June 16, 1990).

			REGULAR SEASON					PLAYOFFS			
Season Team	League	Gms.	G	A	Pts.	Pen.	Gms.	G	A	Pts.	Pen.
89-90—Hawksbury Hawks	QJHL	46	22	34	56	188	—	—	—	—	—
90-91—Michigan State	CCHA	34	1	7	8	32	—	—	—	—	—
91-92—Michigan State	CCHA	44	12	11	23	77	—	—	—	—	—

PERREAULT, YANIC
C, MAPLE LEAFS

PERSONAL: Born April 4, 1971, at Sherbrooke, Que. . . . 5-11/182. . . . Shoots left.
TRANSACTIONS/CAREER NOTES: Selected by Toronto Maple Leafs in third round (first Maple Leafs pick, 47th overall) of NHL entry draft (June 22, 1991).
HONORS: Won Can.HL Rookie of the Year Award (1988-89). . . . Won Michel Bergeron Trophy (1988-89). . . . Won Marcel Robert Trophy (1989-90). . . . Won Michel Briere Trophy (1990-91). . . . Won Jean Beliveau Trophy (1990-91). . . . Won Frank J. Selke Trophy (1990-91). . . . Won Shell Cup (1990-91). . . . Named to QMJHL All-Star first team (1990-91).

			REGULAR SEASON					PLAYOFFS			
Season Team	League	Gms.	G	A	Pts.	Pen.	Gms.	G	A	Pts.	Pen.
88-89—Trois-Rivieres	QMJHL	70	53	55	108	48	—	—	—	—	—
89-90—Trois-Rivieres	QMJHL	63	51	63	114	75	7	6	5	11	19
90-91—Trois-Rivieres	QMJHL	67	*87	98	*185	103	6	4	7	11	6
91-92—St. John's	AHL	62	38	38	76	19	16	7	8	15	4

PETERSON, BRETT
D, FLAMES

P

PERSONAL: Born February 1, 1969, at St. Paul, Minn. . . . 6-2/195. . . . Shoots right.
HIGH SCHOOL: Roseville (Minn.).
COLLEGE: Denver.
TRANSACTIONS/CAREER NOTES: Selected by Calgary Flames in ninth round (ninth Flames pick, 189th overall) of NHL entry draft (June 11, 1988).

Season	Team	League	Gms.	G	A	Pts.	Pen.	Gms.	G	A	Pts.	Pen.
			REGULAR SEASON					PLAYOFFS				
86-87—Roseville H.S.		Minn. H.S.	26	7	15	22		—	—	—	—	—
87-88—St. Paul		USHL	37	2	9	11	68	—	—	—	—	—
88-89—St. Paul		USHL				Statistics unavailable.						
—University of Denver		WCHA	19	0	3	3	4	—	—	—	—	—
89-90—University of Denver		WCHA	34	3	6	9	23	—	—	—	—	—
90-91—University of Denver		WCHA	37	2	9	11	28	—	—	—	—	—
91-92—University of Denver		WCHA	36	3	5	8	30	—	—	—	—	—

PETIT, MICHEL
D, FLAMES

PERSONAL: Born February 12, 1964, at St. Malo, Que. . . . 6-1/185. . . . Shoots right.
TRANSACTIONS/CAREER NOTES: Selected by Vancouver Canucks as underage junior in first round (first Canucks pick, 11th overall) of NHL entry draft (June 9, 1982). . . . Separated shoulder (March 1984). . . . Injured knee (February 1987). . . . Traded by Canucks to New York Rangers for D Willie Huber and D Larry Melnyk (November 1987). . . . Pulled groin (December 1987). . . . Fractured right collarbone (December 27, 1988); missed 11 games. . . . Traded by Rangers to Quebec Nordiques for D Randy Moller (October 5, 1989). . . . Traded by Nordiques with C/LW Aaron Broten and RW Lucien DeBlois to Toronto Maple Leafs for LW Scott Pearson and second-round pick in 1991 (D Eric Lavigne) and 1992 draft (November 17, 1990). . . . Sprained knee (February 4, 1991); missed five games. . . . Sprained thumb (November 9, 1991); missed six games. . . . Traded by Maple Leafs with D Alexander Godynyuk, RW Gary Leeman, LW Craig Berube and G Jeff Reese to Calgary Flames for C Doug Gilmour, D Jamie Macoun, LW Kent Manderville, D Ric Nattress and G Rick Wamsley (January 2, 1992). . . . Suffered back spasms (March 3, 1992); missed four games.
HONORS: Won Raymond Lagace Trophy (1981-82). . . . Won Association of Journalists of Hockey Trophy (1981-82). . . . Named to QMJHL All-Star first team (1981-82 and 1982-83).

Season	Team	League	Gms.	G	A	Pts.	Pen.	Gms.	G	A	Pts.	Pen.
			REGULAR SEASON					PLAYOFFS				
81-82—Sherbrooke		QMJHL	63	10	39	49	106	22	5	20	25	24
82-83—St. Jean		QMJHL	62	19	67	86	196	3	0	0	0	35
—Vancouver		NHL	2	0	0	0	0	—	—	—	—	—
83-84—Canadian Olympic Team		Int'l	19	3	10	13	58	—	—	—	—	—
—Vancouver		NHL	44	6	9	15	53	1	0	0	0	0
84-85—Vancouver		NHL	69	5	26	31	127	—	—	—	—	—
85-86—Fredericton		AHL	25	0	13	13	79	—	—	—	—	—
—Vancouver		NHL	32	1	6	7	27	—	—	—	—	—
86-87—Vancouver		NHL	69	12	13	25	131	—	—	—	—	—
87-88—Vancouver		NHL	10	0	3	3	35	—	—	—	—	—
—New York Rangers		NHL	64	9	24	33	223	—	—	—	—	—
88-89—New York Rangers		NHL	69	8	25	33	156	4	0	2	2	27
89-90—Quebec		NHL	63	12	24	36	215	—	—	—	—	—
90-91—Quebec		NHL	19	4	7	11	47	—	—	—	—	—
—Toronto		NHL	54	9	19	28	132	—	—	—	—	—
91-92—Toronto		NHL	34	1	13	14	85	—	—	—	—	—
—Calgary		NHL	36	3	10	13	79	—	—	—	—	—
NHL totals			565	70	179	249	1310	5	0	2	2	27

PETROVICKY, ROBERT
C, WHALERS

PERSONAL: Born October 26, 1973, at Kosice, Czechoslovakia. . . . 5-11/172. . . . Shoots left.
TRANSACTIONS/CAREER NOTES: Selected by Hartford Whalers in first round (first Whalers pick, ninth overall) of NHL entry draft (June 20, 1992).

Season	Team	League	Gms.	G	A	Pts.	Pen.	Gms.	G	A	Pts.	Pen.
			REGULAR SEASON					PLAYOFFS				
90-91—Dukla Trencin		Czech.	33	9	14	23	12	—	—	—	—	—
91-92—Dukla Trencin		Czech.	46	25	36	61		—	—	—	—	—

PICARD, MICHEL
LW, WHALERS

PERSONAL: Born November 7, 1969, at Beauport, Que. . . . 5-11/190. . . . Shoots left.
TRANSACTIONS/CAREER NOTES: Selected by Hartford Whalers in ninth round (eighth Whalers pick, 178th overall) of NHL entry draft (June 17, 1989). . . . Separated shoulder (November 14, 1991); missed seven games.
HONORS: Named to AHL All-Star first team (1990-91).

Season	Team	League	Gms.	G	A	Pts.	Pen.	Gms.	G	A	Pts.	Pen.
			REGULAR SEASON					PLAYOFFS				
86-87—Trois-Rivieres		QMJHL	66	33	35	68	53	—	—	—	—	—
87-88—Trois-Rivieres		QMJHL	69	40	55	95	71	—	—	—	—	—
88-89—Trois-Rivieres		QMJHL	66	59	81	140	107	4	1	3	4	2
89-90—Binghamton		AHL	67	16	24	40	98	—	—	—	—	—
90-91—Hartford		NHL	5	1	0	1	2	—	—	—	—	—
—Springfield		AHL	77	*56	40	96	61	18	8	13	21	18
91-92—Hartford		NHL	25	3	5	8	6	—	—	—	—	—
—Springfield		AHL	40	21	17	38	44	11	2	0	2	34
NHL totals			30	4	5	9	8					

PIETRANGELO, FRANK
G, WHALERS

PERSONAL: Born December 17, 1964, at Niagara Falls, Ont. . . . 5-10/185. . . . Shoots left.
COLLEGE: Minnesota.
TRANSACTIONS/CAREER NOTES: Selected by Pittsburgh Penguins in fourth

P

round (fourth Penguins pick, 63rd overall) of NHL entry draft (June 8, 1983).... Pulled groin (February 1989).... Pulled groin (February 3, 1991); missed eight games.... Injured back (November 9, 1991); missed four games.... Traded by Penguins to Hartford Whalers for conditional draft pick (March 10, 1992).

Season	Team	League	Gms.	Min.	W	L	T	GA	SO	Avg.	Gms.	Min.	W	L	GA	SO	Avg.
82-83—Univ. of Minnesota		WCHA	25	1348	15	6	1	80	1	3.56	—	—	—	—	—	—	—
83-84—Univ. of Minnesota		WCHA	20	1141	13	7	0	66	0	3.47	—	—	—	—	—	—	—
84-85—Univ. of Minnesota		WCHA	17	912	8	3	3	52	0	3.42	—	—	—	—	—	—	—
85-86—Univ. of Minnesota		WCHA	23	1284	15	7	0	76	0	3.55	—	—	—	—	—	—	—
86-87—Muskegon		IHL	35	2090	23	11	0	119	2	3.42	15	923	10	4	46	0	*2.99
87-88—Pittsburgh		NHL	21	1207	9	11	0	80	1	3.98	—	—	—	—	—	—	—
—Muskegon		IHL	15	868	11	3	1	43	2	2.97	—	—	—	—	—	—	—
88-89—Pittsburgh		NHL	15	669	5	3	0	45	0	4.04	—	—	—	—	—	—	—
—Muskegon		IHL	13	760	10	1	0	38	1	3.00	9	566	8	1	29	0	3.07
89-90—Muskegon		IHL	12	691	9	2	1	38	0	3.30	—	—	—	—	—	—	—
—Pittsburgh		NHL	21	1066	8	6	2	77	0	4.33	—	—	—	—	—	—	—
90-91—Pittsburgh		NHL	25	1311	10	11	1	86	0	3.94	5	288	4	1	15	†1	3.13
91-92—Pittsburgh		NHL	5	225	2	1	0	20	0	5.33	—	—	—	—	—	—	—
—Hartford		NHL	5	306	3	1	1	12	0	2.35	7	425	3	4	19	0	2.68
NHL totals			92	4784	37	33	4	320	1	4.01	12	713	7	5	34	1	2.86

PILON, RICH
D, ISLANDERS

PERSONAL: Born April 30, 1968, at Saskatoon, Sask.... 6-1/211.... Shoots left.... Full name: Richard Pilon.

TRANSACTIONS/CAREER NOTES: Selected by New York Islanders as underage junior in seventh round (ninth Islanders pick, 143rd overall) of NHL entry draft (June 21, 1986).... Injured right leg (December 1988).... Injured right eye (November 4, 1989); missed remainder of season.... Injured medial collateral ligament in left knee (February 23, 1991).... Suffered sore left shoulder (January 9, 1992); missed three games.... Lacerated finger (January 30, 1992); missed four games.

HONORS: Named to WHL All-Star second team (1987-88).

Season	Team	League	Gms.	G	A	Pts.	Pen.	Gms.	G	A	Pts.	Pen.
85-86—Prince Albert		WHL	6	0	0	0	0	—	—	—	—	—
86-87—Prince Albert		WHL	68	4	21	25	192	7	1	6	7	17
87-88—Prince Albert		WHL	65	13	34	47	177	9	0	6	6	38
88-89—New York Islanders		NHL	62	0	14	14	242	—	—	—	—	—
89-90—New York Islanders		NHL	14	0	2	2	31	—	—	—	—	—
90-91—New York Islanders		NHL	60	1	4	5	126	—	—	—	—	—
91-92—New York Islanders		NHL	65	1	6	7	183	—	—	—	—	—
NHL totals			201	2	26	28	582					

PITLICK, LANCE
D, FLYERS

PERSONAL: Born November 5, 1967, at Fridley, Minn.... 6-0/190.... Shoots right.
HIGH SCHOOL: Cooper (New Hope, Minn.).
COLLEGE: Minnesota.
TRANSACTIONS/CAREER NOTES: Selected by Minnesota North Stars in ninth round (10th North Stars pick, 180th overall) of NHL entry draft (June 21, 1986).... Suffered severe pull of lower abdominal muscles (December 1, 1989).... Underwent surgery to have tendons sewn onto his abdominal muscle for reinforcement (January 18, 1990).... Signed as free agent by Philadelphia Flyers (September 5, 1990).

Season	Team	League	Gms.	G	A	Pts.	Pen.	Gms.	G	A	Pts.	Pen.
84-85—Cooper H.S.		Minn. H.S.	23	8	4	12		—	—	—	—	—
85-86—Cooper H.S.		Minn. H.S.	21	17	8	25		—	—	—	—	—
86-87—University of Minnesota		WCHA	45	0	9	9	88	10	0	2	2	4
87-88—University of Minnesota		WCHA	38	3	9	12	76	8	1	1	2	14
88-89—University of Minnesota		WCHA	47	4	9	13	95	8	2	1	3	95
89-90—University of Minnesota		WCHA	14	3	2	5	26	—	—	—	—	—
90-91—Hershey		AHL	64	6	15	21	75	3	0	0	0	9
91-92—U.S. National Team		Int'l	19	0	1	1	38	—	—	—	—	—
—Hershey		AHL	4	0	0	0	6	3	0	0	0	4

PIVONKA, MICHAL
C, CAPITALS

PERSONAL: Born January 28, 1966, at Kladno, Czechoslovakia. ... 6-2/198. ... Shoots left.
TRANSACTIONS/CAREER NOTES: Selected by Washington Capitals in third round (third Capitals pick, 59th overall) of NHL entry draft (June 9, 1984).... Strained ankle ligaments (March 1987).... Sprained right wrist (October 1987).... Sprained left ankle (March 1988).... Sprained left knee (March 9, 1990).

Season	Team	League	Gms.	G	A	Pts.	Pen.	Gms.	G	A	Pts.	Pen.
85-86—Dukla Jihlava		Czech.				Statistics unavailable.						
86-87—Washington		NHL	73	18	25	43	41	7	1	1	2	2
87-88—Washington		NHL	71	11	23	34	28	14	4	9	13	4
88-89—Baltimore		AHL	31	12	24	36	19	—	—	—	—	—
—Washington		NHL	52	8	19	27	30	6	3	1	4	10
89-90—Washington		NHL	77	25	39	64	54	11	0	2	2	6

P

Season Team	League	REGULAR SEASON					PLAYOFFS				
		Gms.	G	A	Pts.	Pen.	Gms.	G	A	Pts.	Pen.
90-91—Washington	NHL	79	20	50	70	34	11	2	3	5	8
91-92—Washington	NHL	80	23	57	80	47	7	1	5	6	13
NHL totals		432	105	213	318	234	56	11	21	32	43

PLANTE, DAN
RW, ISLANDERS

PERSONAL: Born October 5, 1971, at St. Louis. . . . 5-11/190. . . . Shoots right. . . . Full name: Daniel Leon Plante.
HIGH SCHOOL: Edina (Minn.).
COLLEGE: Wisconsin.
TRANSACTIONS/CAREER NOTES: Selected by New York Islanders in third round (third Islanders pick, 48th overall) of NHL entry draft (June 16, 1990).

Season Team	League	REGULAR SEASON					PLAYOFFS				
		Gms.	G	A	Pts.	Pen.	Gms.	G	A	Pts.	Pen.
88-89—Edina High School	Minn. H.S.	27	10	26	36	12	—	—	—	—	—
89-90—Edina High School	Minn. H.S.	24	8	18	26		—	—	—	—	—
90-91—University of Wisconsin	WCHA	33	1	2	3	54	—	—	—	—	—
91-92—University of Wisconsin	WCHA	40	15	16	31	113	—	—	—	—	—

PLANTE, DEREK
C, SABRES

PERSONAL: Born January 17, 1971, at Cloquet, Minn. . . . 5-11/160. . . . Shoots left. . . . Full name: Derek John Plante.
HIGH SCHOOL: Cloquet (Minn.).
COLLEGE: Minnesota-Duluth.
TRANSACTIONS/CAREER NOTES: Broke arm (March 1988). . . . Selected by Buffalo Sabres in eighth round (seventh Sabres pick, 161st overall) of NHL entry draft (June 17, 1989). . . . Injured collarbone (December 15, 1989). . . . Reinjured collarbone (January 20, 1990).
HONORS: Named to WCHA All-Star second team (1991-92).

Season Team	League	REGULAR SEASON					PLAYOFFS				
		Gms.	G	A	Pts.	Pen.	Gms.	G	A	Pts.	Pen.
87-88—Cloquet H.S.	Minn. H.S.	23	16	25	41		—	—	—	—	—
88-89—Cloquet H.S.	Minn. H.S.	24	30	33	63		—	—	—	—	—
89-90—Minnesota-Duluth	WCHA	28	10	11	21	12	—	—	—	—	—
90-91—Minnesota-Duluth	WCHA	36	23	20	43	6	—	—	—	—	—
91-92—Minnesota-Duluth	WCHA	37	27	36	63	28	—	—	—	—	—

PLAVSIC, ADRIEN
D, CANUCKS

PERSONAL: Born January 13, 1970, at Montreal. . . . 6-1/190. . . . Shoots left.
COLLEGE: New Hampshire.
TRANSACTIONS/CAREER NOTES: Selected by St. Louis Blues in second round (second Blues pick, 30th overall) of NHL entry draft (June 11, 1988). . . . Suffered concussion (September 25, 1989). . . . Traded by Blues with first-round pick in 1990 draft and second-round pick in 1991 draft to Vancouver Canucks for RW Rich Sutter, D Harold Snepsts and second-round pick in 1990 draft that had been traded to Canucks in an earlier deal (March 6, 1990). . . . Sprained knee (November 9, 1990); missed 15 games.
MISCELLANEOUS: Member of 1992 silver-medal-winning Canadian Olympic team.

Season Team	League	REGULAR SEASON					PLAYOFFS				
		Gms.	G	A	Pts.	Pen.	Gms.	G	A	Pts.	Pen.
87-88—Univ. of New Hampshire	Hockey East	30	5	6	11	45	—	—	—	—	—
88-89—Canadian National Team	Int'l	62	5	10	15	25	—	—	—	—	—
89-90—Peoria	IHL	51	7	14	21	87	—	—	—	—	—
—St. Louis	NHL	4	0	1	1	2	—	—	—	—	—
—Vancouver	NHL	11	3	2	5	8	—	—	—	—	—
—Milwaukee	IHL	3	1	2	3	14	6	1	3	4	6
90-91—Vancouver	NHL	48	2	10	12	62	—	—	—	—	—
91-92—Canadian National Team	Int'l	38	6	9	15	29	—	—	—	—	—
—Canadian Olympic Team	Int'l	8	0	2	2	0	—	—	—	—	—
—Vancouver	NHL	16	1	9	10	14	13	1	7	8	4
NHL totals		79	6	22	28	86	13	1	7	8	4

PODDUBNY, WALT
LW, DEVILS

PERSONAL: Born February 14, 1960, at Thunder Bay, Ont. . . . 6-1/210. . . . Shoots left. . . . Full name: Walter Michael Poddubny.
TRANSACTIONS/CAREER NOTES: Selected by Edmonton Oilers in fifth round (fourth Oilers pick, 90th overall) of NHL entry draft (June 11, 1980). . . . Traded by Oilers with rights to Phil Drouillard to Toronto Maple Leafs for C Laurie Boschman (March 1982). . . . Injured leg (October 1982). . . . Broke ankle (October 1983). . . . Broke thumb (February 1985). . . . Suffered foot infection (September 1985). . . . Traded by Maple Leafs to New York Rangers for C Mike Allison (August 1986). . . . Injured hip (December 1986). . . . Suffered concussion (December 21, 1986). . . . Traded by Rangers with D Bruce Bell and D Jari Gronstrand and fourth-round pick in 1989 draft to Quebec Nordiques for D Normand Rochefort and C Jason Lafreniere (August 1988). . . . Sprained left knee (October 1988). . . . Lacerated face and broke nose (March 23, 1989). . . . Traded by Nordiques to New Jersey Devils for C Claude Loiselle and D Joe Cirella (June 17, 1989). . . . Injured back (October 1989); missed 26 games. . . . Tore cruciate ligament of right knee (February 19, 1990); missed 20 games. . . . Underwent surgery to right knee (December 12, 1990). . . . Injured knee (September 1991); missed first five games of season.

Season Team	League	REGULAR SEASON					PLAYOFFS				
		Gms.	G	A	Pts.	Pen.	Gms.	G	A	Pts.	Pen.
78-79—Brandon	WHL	20	11	11	22	12	—	—	—	—	—
79-80—Kitchener	OMJHL	19	3	9	12	35	—	—	—	—	—
—Kingston	OMJHL	43	30	17	47	36	3	0	2	2	0

P

Season Team	League	REGULAR SEASON					PLAYOFFS				
		Gms.	G	A	Pts.	Pen.	Gms.	G	A	Pts.	Pen.
80-81—Milwaukee	IHL	5	4	2	6	4	—	—	—	—	—
—Wichita	CHL	70	21	29	50	207	11	1	6	7	26
81-82—Edmonton	NHL	4	0	0	0	0	—	—	—	—	—
—Wichita	CHL	60	35	46	81	79	—	—	—	—	—
—Toronto	NHL	11	3	4	7	8	—	—	—	—	—
82-83—Toronto	NHL	72	28	31	59	71	4	3	1	4	0
83-84—Toronto	NHL	38	11	14	25	48	—	—	—	—	—
84-85—St. Catharines	AHL	8	5	7	12	10	—	—	—	—	—
—Toronto	NHL	32	5	15	20	26	—	—	—	—	—
85-86—St. Catharines	AHL	37	28	27	55	52	—	—	—	—	—
—Toronto	NHL	33	12	22	34	25	9	4	1	5	4
86-87—New York Rangers	NHL	75	40	47	87	49	6	0	0	0	8
87-88—New York Rangers	NHL	77	38	50	88	76	—	—	—	—	—
88-89—Quebec	NHL	72	38	37	75	107	—	—	—	—	—
89-90—Utica	AHL	2	1	2	3	0	—	—	—	—	—
—New Jersey	NHL	33	4	10	14	28	—	—	—	—	—
90-91—New Jersey	NHL	14	4	6	10	10	—	—	—	—	—
91-92—New Jersey	NHL	7	1	2	3	6	—	—	—	—	—
NHL totals		468	184	238	422	454	19	7	2	9	12

PODEIN, SHJON
C, OILERS

PERSONAL: Born March 5, 1968, at Rochester, Minn. . . . 6-2/200. . . . Shoots left.
COLLEGE: Minnesota-Duluth.
TRANSACTIONS/CAREER NOTES: Selected by Edmonton Oilers in eighth round (ninth Oilers pick, 166th overall) of NHL entry draft (June 11, 1988).

Season Team	League	REGULAR SEASON					PLAYOFFS				
		Gms.	G	A	Pts.	Pen.	Gms.	G	A	Pts.	Pen.
87-88—Minnesota-Duluth	WCHA	30	4	4	8	48	—	—	—	—	—
88-89—Minnesota-Duluth	WCHA	36	7	5	12	46	—	—	—	—	—
89-90—Minnesota-Duluth	WCHA	35	21	18	39	36	—	—	—	—	—
90-91—Cape Breton	AHL	63	14	15	29	65	4	0	0	0	5
91-92—Cape Breton	AHL	80	30	24	54	46	5	3	1	4	2

POESCHEK, RUDY
D, JETS

PERSONAL: Born September 29, 1966, at Terrace, B.C. . . . 6-2/210. . . . Shoots right. . . . Full name: Rudolph Leopold Poeschek.
TRANSACTIONS/CAREER NOTES: Injured knee (December 1984). . . . Selected by New York Rangers as underage junior in 12th round (12th Rangers pick, 238th overall) of NHL entry draft (June 15, 1985). . . . Injured shoulder (November 1986). . . . Bruised right hand (February 1989). . . . Suspended six games by AHL for a pre-game fight (November 25, 1990). . . . Traded by Rangers to Winnipeg Jets for C Guy Larose (January 22, 1991).

Season Team	League	REGULAR SEASON					PLAYOFFS				
		Gms.	G	A	Pts.	Pen.	Gms.	G	A	Pts.	Pen.
83-84—Kamloops	WHL	47	3	9	12	93	8	0	2	2	7
84-85—Kamloops	WHL	34	6	7	13	100	15	0	3	3	56
85-86—Kamloops	WHL	32	3	13	16	92	16	3	7	10	40
86-87—Kamloops	WHL	54	13	18	31	153	15	2	4	6	37
87-88—New York Rangers	NHL	1	0	0	0	2	—	—	—	—	—
—Colorado	IHL	82	7	31	38	210	12	2	2	4	31
88-89—Denver	IHL	2	0	0	0	6	—	—	—	—	—
—New York Rangers	NHL	52	0	2	2	199	—	—	—	—	—
89-90—Flint	IHL	38	8	13	21	109	4	0	0	0	16
—New York Rangers	NHL	15	0	0	0	55	—	—	—	—	—
90-91—Binghamton	AHL	38	1	3	4	162	—	—	—	—	—
—Moncton	AHL	23	2	4	6	67	9	1	1	2	41
—Winnipeg	NHL	1	0	0	0	5	—	—	—	—	—
91-92—Moncton	AHL	63	4	18	22	170	11	0	2	2	46
—Winnipeg	NHL	4	0	0	0	17	—	—	—	—	—
NHL totals		73	0	2	2	278					

POLASEK, LIBOR
C, CANUCKS

PERSONAL: Born April 22, 1974, at Vitkovice, Czechoslovakia. . . . 6-3/198. . . . Shoots right.
TRANSACTIONS/CAREER NOTES: Selected by Vancouver Canucks in first round (first Canucks pick, 21st overall) of NHL entry draft (June 20, 1992).

Season Team	League	REGULAR SEASON					PLAYOFFS				
		Gms.	G	A	Pts.	Pen.	Gms.	G	A	Pts.	Pen.
91-92—TJ Vitkovice	Czech.	17	2	2	4	2	—	—	—	—	—

POMICHTER, MIKE
C, BLACKHAWKS

PERSONAL: Born September 10, 1973, at New Haven, Conn. . . . 6-1/200. . . . Shoots left.
HIGH SCHOOL: North Haven (Conn.).
TRANSACTIONS/CAREER NOTES: Selected by Chicago Blackhawks in second round (second Blackhawks pick, 39th overall) of NHL entry draft (June 22, 1991).

P

			REGULAR SEASON					PLAYOFFS				
Season Team	League	Gms.	G	A	Pts.	Pen.	Gms.	G	A	Pts.	Pen.
88-89—North Haven H.S.	Conn. H.S.	22	52	22	74		—	—	—	—	—
89-90—Springfield Jr. B	NEJHL	39	37	31	68	8	—	—	—	—	—
90-91—Springfield Jr. B	NEJHL	38	61	64	125	22	—	—	—	—	—
91-92—Boston University	Hockey East	35	11	27	38	14	—	—	—	—	—

PORKKA, TONI
D, FLYERS

PERSONAL: Born February 4, 1970, at Rauma, Finland.... 6-2/190.... Shoots right.
TRANSACTIONS/CAREER NOTES: Selected by Philadelphia Flyers in ninth round (12th Flyers pick, 172nd overall) of NHL entry draft (June 16, 1990).

			REGULAR SEASON					PLAYOFFS				
Season Team	League	Gms.	G	A	Pts.	Pen.	Gms.	G	A	Pts.	Pen.
89-90—Lukko	Finland	41	0	3	3	18	—	—	—	—	—
90-91—Lukko	Finland	34	2	2	4	8	—	—	—	—	—

POTVIN, FELIX
G, MAPLE LEAFS

PERSONAL: Born June 23, 1971, at Anjou, Que.... 6-0/185.... Shoots left.
TRANSACTIONS/CAREER NOTES: Selected by Toronto Maple Leafs in second round (second Maple Leafs pick, 31st overall) of NHL entry draft (June 16, 1990).
HONORS: Named to QMJHL All-Star second team (1989-90).... Won Can.HL Goaltender of the Year Award (1990-91).... Won the Hap Emms Memorial Trophy (1990-91).... Won the Jacques Plante Trophy (1990-91). ... Won the Shell Cup (1990-91).... Won the Guy Lafleur Trophy (1990-91).... Named to Memorial Cup All-Star Team (1990-91).... Named to QMJHL All-Star first team (1990-91).... Won Baz Bastien Trophy (1991-92).... Won Dudley (Red) Garrett Memorial Trophy (1991-92).... Named to AHL All-Star first team (1991-92).

			REGULAR SEASON						PLAYOFFS					
Season Team	League	Gms.	Min.	W	L	T	GA	SO	Avg.	Gms.	Min.	W	L	GA SO Avg.
88-89—Chicoutimi..................	QMJHL	*65	*3489	25	31	1	*271	†2	4.66	—	—	—	—	— — —
89-90—Chicoutimi..................	QMJHL	*62	*3478	31	26	2	231	†2	3.99	—	—	—	—	— — —
90-91—Chicoutimi..................	QMJHL	54	3216	33	15	4	145	*6	†2.71	*16	*992	*11	5	46 0 *2.78
91-92—St. John's	AHL	35	2070	18	10	6	101	2	2.93	11	642	7	4	41 0 3.83
—Toronto.....................	NHL	4	210	0	2	1	8	0	2.29	—	—	—	—	— — —
NHL totals..........................		4	210	0	2	1	8	0	2.29					

POTVIN, MARC
RW, RED WINGS

PERSONAL: Born January 29, 1967, at Ottawa.... 6-1/200.... Shoots right.... Full name: Marc Richard Potvin.
COLLEGE: Bowling Green State.
TRANSACTIONS/CAREER NOTES: Selected by Detroit Red Wings in ninth round (ninth Red Wings pick, 169th overall) of NHL entry draft (June 21, 1986).

			REGULAR SEASON					PLAYOFFS				
Season Team	League	Gms.	G	A	Pts.	Pen.	Gms.	G	A	Pts.	Pen.
85-86—Stratford.........................	OPJHL	63	5	6	11	117	—	—	—	—	—
86-87—Bowling Green State	CCHA	43	5	15	20	74	—	—	—	—	—
87-88—Bowling Green State	CCHA	45	15	21	36	80	—	—	—	—	—
88-89—Bowling Green State	CCHA	46	23	12	35	63	—	—	—	—	—
89-90—Bowling Green State	CCHA	40	19	17	36	72	—	—	—	—	—
—Adirondack	AHL	5	2	1	3	9	4	0	1	1	23
90-91—Adirondack	AHL	63	9	13	22	†365	—	—	—	—	—
—Detroit	NHL	9	0	0	0	55	6	0	0	0	32
91-92—Adirondack	AHL	51	13	16	29	314	†19	5	4	9	57
—Detroit	NHL	5	1	0	1	52	1	0	0	0	0
NHL totals..........................		14	1	0	1	107	7	0	0	0	32

POULIN, DAVE
C, BRUINS

PERSONAL: Born December 17, 1958, at Mississauga, Ont.... 5-11/190.... Shoots left.... Full name: David James Poulin.
COLLEGE: Notre Dame.
TRANSACTIONS/CAREER NOTES: Signed as free agent by Philadelphia Flyers (February 1983). ... Pulled hamstring and groin muscle (November 1986).... Fractured rib (April 16, 1987).... Pulled groin (February 1988). ... Separated shoulder (November 1988).... Sent home due to irregular heartbeat (December 15, 1988).... Bruised right hand (January 1989).... Fractured ring finger of right hand (April 8, 1989).... Suffered multiple fracture of left thumb (May 1989).... Bruised abdomen (October 1989).... Broke left thumb (October 28, 1989).... Traded by Flyers to Boston Bruins for C Ken Linseman (January 16, 1990).... Stretched nerve in neck and left arm (April 21, 1990).... Pulled groin (October 15, 1990); missed 17 games.... Broke jaw (December 28, 1990); missed 14 games.... Broke right shoulder blade (Febraury 2, 1991); missed 15 games.... Strained groin and abdomen during preseason (September 1991); missed first 61 games of season.... Underwent surgery to groin and abdomen (December 6, 1991).
HONORS: Named to CCHA All-Star second team (1981-82).... Won Frank J. Selke Trophy (1986-87).

			REGULAR SEASON					PLAYOFFS				
Season Team	League	Gms.	G	A	Pts.	Pen.	Gms.	G	A	Pts.	Pen.
78-79—University of Notre Dame .	WCHA	37	28	31	59	32	—	—	—	—	—
79-80—University of Notre Dame .	WCHA	24	19	24	43	46	—	—	—	—	—
80-81—University of Notre Dame .	WCHA	35	13	22	35	53	—	—	—	—	—
81-82—University of Notre Dame .	WCHA	39	29	30	59	44	—	—	—	—	—
82-83—Rogle	Sweden	33	35	18	53		—	—	—	—	—
—Maine..............................	AHL	16	7	9	16	2	—	—	—	—	—
—Philadelphia	NHL	2	2	0	2	2	3	1	3	4	9

Season	Team	League	REGULAR SEASON					PLAYOFFS				
			Gms.	G	A	Pts.	Pen.	Gms.	G	A	Pts.	Pen.
83-84	Philadelphia	NHL	73	31	45	76	47	3	0	0	0	2
84-85	Philadelphia	NHL	73	30	44	74	59	11	3	5	8	6
85-86	Philadelphia	NHL	79	27	42	69	49	5	2	0	2	2
86-87	Philadelphia	NHL	75	25	45	70	53	15	3	3	6	14
87-88	Philadelphia	NHL	68	19	32	51	32	7	2	6	8	4
88-89	Philadelphia	NHL	69	18	17	35	49	19	6	5	11	16
89-90	Philadelphia	NHL	28	9	8	17	12	—	—	—	—	—
	Boston	NHL	32	6	19	25	12	18	8	5	13	8
90-91	Boston	NHL	31	8	12	20	25	16	0	9	9	20
91-92	Boston	NHL	18	4	4	8	18	15	3	3	6	22
NHL totals			548	179	268	447	358	112	28	39	67	103

POULIN, PATRICK
LW, WHALERS

PERSONAL: Born April 23, 1973, at Vanier, Que. . . . 6-1/208. . . . Shoots left.
TRANSACTIONS/CAREER NOTES: Broke wrist (January 15, 1991). . . . Selected by Hartford Whalers in first round (first Whalers pick, ninth overall) of NHL entry draft (June 22, 1991).
HONORS: Won Jean Beliveau Trophy (1991-92). . . . Named to Can.HL All-Star first team (1991-92). . . . Named to QMJHL All-Star first team (1991-92).

Season	Team	League	REGULAR SEASON					PLAYOFFS				
			Gms.	G	A	Pts.	Pen.	Gms.	G	A	Pts.	Pen.
89-90	St. Hyacinthe	QMJHL	60	25	26	51	55	12	1	9	10	5
90-91	St. Hyacinthe	QMJHL	56	32	38	70	82	4	0	2	2	23
91-92	St. Hyacinthe	QMJHL	56	52	86	*138	58	5	2	2	4	4
	Springfield	AHL	—	—	—	—	—	1	0	0	0	0
	Hartford	NHL	1	0	0	0	2	7	2	1	3	0
NHL totals			1	0	0	0	2	7	2	1	3	0

PRAJSLER, PETR
D, BRUINS

PERSONAL: Born September 21, 1965, at Hradec Kralove, Czechoslovakia. . . . 6-2/200. . . . Shoots left.
TRANSACTIONS/CAREER NOTES: Selected by Los Angeles Kings in fifth round (fifth Kings pick, 93rd overall) of NHL entry draft (June 15, 1985). . . . Suffered from the flu (March 1990). . . . Signed as free agent by Boston Bruins (August 1991). . . . Sprained knee (February 9, 1992).

Season	Team	League	REGULAR SEASON					PLAYOFFS				
			Gms.	G	A	Pts.	Pen.	Gms.	G	A	Pts.	Pen.
85-86	Pardubice	Czech.	27	5	5	10	34	—	—	—	—	—
86-87	Pardubice	Czech.	41	3	4	7		—	—	—	—	—
87-88	Los Angeles	NHL	7	0	0	0	2	—	—	—	—	—
	New Haven	AHL	41	3	8	11	58	—	—	—	—	—
88-89	New Haven	AHL	43	4	6	10	96	16	3	3	6	34
	Los Angeles	NHL	2	0	3	3	0	1	0	0	0	0
89-90	Los Angeles	NHL	34	3	7	10	47	3	0	0	0	0
	New Haven	AHL	6	1	7	8	2	—	—	—	—	—
90-91	Phoenix	IHL	77	13	34	47	140	9	1	9	10	18
91-92	Maine	AHL	61	12	33	45	88	—	—	—	—	—
	Boston	NHL	3	0	0	0	2	—	—	—	—	—
NHL totals			46	3	10	13	51	4	0	0	0	0

PRESLEY, WAYNE
RW, SABRES

PERSONAL: Born March 23, 1965, at Dearborn, Mich. . . . 5-11/180. . . . Shoots right.
TRANSACTIONS/CAREER NOTES: Selected by Chicago Blackhawks as an underage junior in second round (second Blackhawks pick, 39th overall) of NHL entry draft (June 8, 1983). . . . Traded by Kitchener Rangers to Sault Ste. Marie Greyhounds for RW Shawn Tyers (January 1985). . . . Underwent surgery to repair ligaments and cartilage in right knee (November 1987); missed 36 games. . . . Dislocated shoulder (May 6, 1989). . . . Traded by Blackhawks to San Jose Sharks for third-round pick in 1993 draft (September 20, 1991). . . . Injured knee (November 17, 1991). . . . Injured hand (December 3, 1991); missed eight games. . . . Traded by Sharks to Buffalo Sabres for C Dave Snuggerud (March 9, 1992).
HONORS: Won Jim Mahon Memorial Trophy (1983-84). . . . Named to OHL All-Star first team (1983-84).
RECORDS: Shares NHL single-season and single-series playoff records for most shorthanded goals—3 (1989).

Season	Team	League	REGULAR SEASON					PLAYOFFS				
			Gms.	G	A	Pts.	Pen.	Gms.	G	A	Pts.	Pen.
82-83	Kitchener	OHL	70	39	48	87	99	12	1	4	5	9
83-84	Kitchener	OHL	70	63	76	139	156	16	12	16	28	38
84-85	Kitchener	OHL	31	25	21	46	77	—	—	—	—	—
	Sault Ste. Marie	OHL	11	5	9	14	14	16	13	9	22	13
	Chicago	NHL	3	0	1	1	0	—	—	—	—	—
85-86	Nova Scotia	AHL	29	6	9	15	22	—	—	—	—	—
	Chicago	NHL	38	7	8	15	38	3	0	0	0	0
86-87	Chicago	NHL	80	32	29	61	114	4	1	0	1	9
87-88	Chicago	NHL	42	12	10	22	52	5	0	0	0	4
88-89	Chicago	NHL	72	21	19	40	100	14	7	5	12	18
89-90	Chicago	NHL	49	6	7	13	67	19	9	6	15	29

P

			REGULAR SEASON					PLAYOFFS			
Season Team	League	Gms.	G	A	Pts.	Pen.	Gms.	G	A	Pts.	Pen.
90-91—Chicago	NHL	71	15	19	34	122	6	0	1	1	38
91-92—San Jose	NHL	47	8	14	22	76	—	—	—	—	—
—Buffalo	NHL	12	2	2	4	57	7	3	3	6	14
NHL totals		414	103	109	212	626	58	20	15	35	112

PRIESTLAY, KEN
C, PENGUINS

PERSONAL: Born August 24, 1967, at Vancouver, B.C. . . . 5-10/190. . . . Shoots left. **TRANSACTIONS/CAREER NOTES:** Separated shoulder (November 1984). . . . Selected by Buffalo Sabres as underage junior in fifth round (fifth Sabres pick, 98th overall) of NHL entry draft (June 15, 1985). . . . Traded by Sabres to Pittsburgh Penguins for RW Tony Tanti (March 5, 1991).
HONORS: Named to WHL All-Star second team (1985-86 and 1986-87).

			REGULAR SEASON					PLAYOFFS			
Season Team	League	Gms.	G	A	Pts.	Pen.	Gms.	G	A	Pts.	Pen.
83-84—Victoria	WHL	55	10	18	28	31	—	—	—	—	—
84-85—Victoria	WHL	50	25	37	62	48	—	—	—	—	—
85-86—Victoria	WHL	72	73	72	145	45	—	—	—	—	—
—Rochester	AHL	4	0	2	2	0	—	—	—	—	—
80-87—Victoria	WIIL	33	13	39	82	37	—	—	—	—	—
—Buffalo	NHL	34	11	6	17	8	—	—	—	—	—
—Rochester	AHL	—	—	—	—	—	8	3	2	5	4
87-88—Buffalo	NHL	33	5	12	17	35	6	0	0	0	11
—Rochester	AHL	43	27	24	51	47	—	—	—	—	—
88-89—Rochester	AHL	64	56	37	93	60	—	—	—	—	—
—Buffalo	NHL	15	2	0	2	2	3	0	0	0	2
89-90—Rochester	AHL	40	19	39	58	46	—	—	—	—	—
—Buffalo	NHL	35	7	7	14	14	5	0	0	0	8
90-91—Canadian National Team	Int'l	40	20	26	46	34	—	—	—	—	—
—Pittsburgh	NHL	2	0	1	1	0	—	—	—	—	—
91-92—Pittsburgh	NHL	49	2	8	10	4	—	—	—	—	—
—Muskegon	IHL	13	4	11	15	6	13	5	11	16	10
NHL totals		168	27	34	61	63	14	0	0	0	21

PRIMEAU, KEITH
LW/C, RED WINGS

PERSONAL: Born November 24, 1971, at Toronto. . . . 6-4/225. . . . Shoots left. **TRANSACTIONS/CAREER NOTES:** Selected by Detroit Red Wings in first round (first Red Wings pick, third overall) of NHL entry draft (June 16, 1990). **HONORS:** Won Eddie Powers Memorial Trophy (1989-90). . . . Named to OHL All-Star second team (1989-90).

			REGULAR SEASON					PLAYOFFS			
Season Team	League	Gms.	G	A	Pts.	Pen.	Gms.	G	A	Pts.	Pen.
87-88—Hamilton	OHL	47	6	6	12	69	11	0	2	2	2
88-89—Niagara Falls	OHL	48	20	35	55	56	17	9	6	15	12
89-90—Niagara Falls	OHL	65	*57	70	*127	97	16	*16	17	*33	49
90-91—Detroit	NHL	58	3	12	15	106	5	1	1	2	25
—Adirondack	AHL	6	3	5	8	8	—	—	—	—	—
91-92—Detroit	NHL	35	6	10	16	83	11	0	0	0	14
—Adirondack	AHL	42	21	24	45	89	9	1	7	8	27
NHL totals		93	9	22	31	189	16	1	1	2	39

PROBERT, BOB
RW, RED WINGS

PERSONAL: Born June 5, 1965, at Windsor, Ont. . . . 6-3/225. . . . Shoots left. . . . Full name: Robert Probert. **TRANSACTIONS/CAREER NOTES:** Selected by Detroit Red Wings as underage junior in third round (third Red Wings pick, 46th overall) of NHL entry draft (June 8, 1984). . . . Entered in-patient alchohol abuse treatment center (July 22, 1986). . . . Suspended six games by NHL during the 1987-88 season for game misconduct penalties. . . . Suspended without pay by Red Wings for skipping practice and missing team buses, flights and curfews (September 23, 1988). . . . Reactivated by Red Wings (November 23, 1988). . . . Suspended three games by NHL for hitting another player (December 10, 1988). . . . Removed from team after showing up late for a game (January 26, 1989). . . . Reactivated by Red Wings (February 15, 1989). . . . Charged with smuggling cocaine into the U.S (March 2, 1989). . . . Expelled from the NHL (March 4, 1989). . . . Reinstated by NHL (March 14, 1990). . . . Unable to play any games in Canada while appealing deportation order by U.S. Immigration Department during 1990-91 and 1991-92 seasons. . . . Fractured left wrist (December 1, 1990); missed 12 games.

			REGULAR SEASON					PLAYOFFS			
Season Team	League	Gms.	G	A	Pts.	Pen.	Gms.	G	A	Pts.	Pen.
82-83—Brantford	OHL	51	12	16	28	133	8	2	2	4	23
83-84—Brantford	OHL	65	35	38	73	189	6	0	3	3	16
84-85—Hamilton	OHL	4	0	1	1	21	—	—	—	—	—
—Sault Ste. Marie	OHL	44	20	52	72	172	15	6	11	17	*60
85-86—Adirondack	AHL	32	12	15	27	152	10	2	3	5	68
—Detroit	NHL	44	8	13	21	186	—	—	—	—	—
86-87—Detroit	NHL	63	13	11	24	221	16	3	4	7	63
—Adirondack	AHL	7	1	4	5	15	—	—	—	—	—

P

Season Team	League	REGULAR SEASON					PLAYOFFS				
		Gms.	G	A	Pts.	Pen.	Gms.	G	A	Pts.	Pen.
87-88—Detroit	NHL	74	29	33	62	*398	16	8	13	21	51
88-89—Detroit	NHL	25	4	2	6	106	—	—	—	—	—
89-90—Detroit	NHL	4	3	0	3	21	—	—	—	—	—
90-91—Detroit	NHL	55	16	23	39	315	6	1	2	3	50
91-92—Detroit	NHL	63	20	24	44	276	11	1	6	7	28
NHL totals		328	93	106	199	1523	49	13	25	38	192

PROKHOROV, VITALI
LW, BLUES

PERSONAL: Born December 25, 1966, at Moscow, U.S.S.R. . . . 5-9/185. . . . Shoots left.

TRANSACTIONS/CAREER NOTES: Selected by St. Louis Blues in third round (third Blues pick, 64th overall) of NHL entry draft (June 20, 1992).

MISCELLANEOUS: Member of 1992 gold-medal-winning Unified Olympic team.

Season Team	League	REGULAR SEASON					PLAYOFFS				
		Gms.	G	A	Pts.	Pen.	Gms.	G	A	Pts.	Pen.
83-84—Spartak Moscow	USSR	5	0	0	0	0	—	—	—	—	—
84-85—Spartak Moscow	USSR	31	1	1	2	10	—	—	—	—	—
85-86—Spartak Moscow	USSR	29	3	9	12	4	—	—	—	—	—
86-87—Spartak Moscow	USSR	27	1	6	7	2	—	—	—	—	—
87-88—Spartak Moscow	USSR	19	5	0	5	4	—	—	—	—	—
88-89—Spartak Moscow	USSR	37	11	5	16	10	—	—	—	—	—
89-90—Spartak Moscow	USSR	43	13	8	21	35	—	—	—	—	—
90-91—Spartak Moscow	USSR	43	21	10	31	29	—	—	—	—	—
91-92—Unified Olympic Team	Int'l	8	2	4	6		—	—	—	—	—
—Spartak Moscow	CIS	38	13	19	32	68	—	—	—	—	—

PRONGER, SEAN
C, CANUCKS

PERSONAL: Born November 30, 1972, at Thunder Bay, Ont. . . . 6-3/195. . . . Shoots left. . . . Full name: Sean James Pronger.

COLLEGE: Bowling Green State.

TRANSACTIONS/CAREER NOTES: Selected by Vancouver Canucks in third round (third Canucks pick, 51st overall) of NHL entry draft (June 22, 1991).

Season Team	League	REGULAR SEASON					PLAYOFFS				
		Gms.	G	A	Pts.	Pen.	Gms.	G	A	Pts.	Pen.
89-90—Thunder Bay Flyers	USHL	48	18	34	52	61	—	—	—	—	—
90-91—Bowling Green State	CCHA	40	3	7	10	30	—	—	—	—	—
91-92—Bowling Green State	CCHA	34	9	7	16	28	—	—	—	—	—

PROPP, BRIAN
LW, NORTH STARS

PERSONAL: Born February 15, 1959, at Lanigan, Sask. . . . 5-10/195. . . . Shoots left. . . . Full name: Brian Philip Propp.

TRANSACTIONS/CAREER NOTES: Selected by Philadelphia Flyers in first round (first Flyers pick, 14th overall) of NHL entry draft (August 9, 1979). . . . Suspended four games by NHL (January 1985). . . . Injured eye (March 4, 1986); missed eight games. . . . Fractured left knee (December 7, 1986). . . . Sprained left knee (December 1987). . . . Traded by Flyers to Boston Bruins for second-round pick in 1990 draft (D Terran Sandwith) (March 2, 1990). . . . Signed as free agent by Minnesota North Stars (July 1990). . . . Injured groin (November 29, 1991); missed eight games. . . . Dislocated shoulder (February 9, 1992); missed 13 games. . . . Sprained knee (March 14, 1992); missed two games. . . . Injured shoulder (April 14, 1992).

HONORS: Named WCHL Rookie of the Year (1976-77). . . . Named to WCHL All-Star second team (1976-77). . . . Named to WCHL All-Star first team (1977-78). . . . Won WHL Player of the Year Award (1978-79). . . . Named to WHL All-Star first team (1978-79).

Season Team	League	REGULAR SEASON					PLAYOFFS				
		Gms.	G	A	Pts.	Pen.	Gms.	G	A	Pts.	Pen.
75-76—Melville	SAJHL	57	76	92	168	36	—	—	—	—	—
76-77—Brandon	WCHL	72	55	80	135	47	16	†14	12	26	5
77-78—Brandon	WCHL	70	70	*112	*182	200	8	7	6	13	12
78-79—Brandon	WHL	71	*94	*100	*194	127	22	15	23	*38	40
79-80—Philadelphia	NHL	80	34	41	75	54	19	5	10	15	29
80-81—Philadelphia	NHL	79	26	40	66	110	12	6	6	12	32
81-82—Philadelphia	NHL	80	44	47	91	117	4	2	2	4	4
82-83—Philadelphia	NHL	80	40	42	82	72	3	1	2	3	8
83-84—Philadelphia	NHL	79	39	53	92	37	3	0	1	1	6
84-85—Philadelphia	NHL	76	43	53	96	43	19	8	10	18	6
85-86—Philadelphia	NHL	72	40	57	97	47	5	0	2	2	4
86-87—Philadelphia	NHL	53	31	36	67	45	26	12	16	28	10
87-88—Philadelphia	NHL	74	27	49	76	76	7	4	2	6	8
88-89—Philadelphia	NHL	77	32	46	78	37	18	14	9	23	14
89-90—Philadelphia	NHL	40	13	15	28	31	—	—	—	—	—
—Boston	NHL	14	3	9	12	10	20	4	9	13	2
90-91—Minnesota	NHL	79	26	47	73	58	23	8	15	23	28
91-92—Minnesota	NHL	51	12	23	35	49	1	0	0	0	0
NHL totals		934	410	558	968	786	160	64	84	148	151

PROSOFSKY, JASON
RW, RANGERS

PERSONAL: Born May 4, 1971, at Medicine Hat, Alta.... 6-4/220.... Shoots right.
TRANSACTIONS/CAREER NOTES: Selected by New York Rangers in second round (second Rangers pick, 40th overall) of NHL entry draft (June 17, 1989).

			REGULAR SEASON					PLAYOFFS				
Season Team	League	Gms.	G	A	Pts.	Pen.	Gms.	G	A	Pts.	Pen.
86-87—Medicine Hat	WHL	1	0	0	0	0	—	—	—	—	—
87-88—Medicine Hat	WHL	47	6	1	7	94	14	0	0	0	20
88-89—Medicine Hat	WHL	67	7	16	23	170	3	1	0	1	6
89-90—Medicine Hat	WHL	71	12	13	25	153	3	0	0	0	8
90-91—Medicine Hat	WHL	72	15	15	30	195	12	6	8	14	33
91-92—San Diego	IHL	31	0	0	0	111	—	—	—	—	—
—Binghamton	AHL	4	0	0	0	5	—	—	—	—	—
—Erie	ECHL	7	2	2	4	28	4	1	2	3	18

PUPPA, DAREN
G, SABRES

PERSONAL: Born March 23, 1965, at Kirkland Lake, Ont.... 6-3/205.... Shoots right.... Full name: Daren James Puppa.
COLLEGE: Rensselaer Polytechnic Institute (N.Y.).
TRANSACTIONS/CAREER NOTES: Selected by Buffalo Sabres in fourth round (sixth Sabres pick, 74th overall) of NHL entry draft (June 8, 1983).... Injured knee (February 1986).... Fractured left index finger (October 1987).... Sprained right wrist (January 14, 1989).... Broke right arm (January 27, 1989).... Injured back (November 21, 1990); missed nine games.... Pulled groin and stomach muscles (February 19, 1991).... Fractured arm (November 12, 1991); missed 16 games.
HONORS: Named to AHL All-Star first team (1986-87).... Named to THE SPORTING NEWS All-Star second team (1989-90). ... Named to NHL All-Star second team (1989-90).

			REGULAR SEASON							PLAYOFFS						
Season Team	League	Gms.	Min.	W	L	T	GA	SO	Avg.	Gms.	Min.	W	L	GA	SO	Avg.
83-84—R.P.I.	ECAC	32	1816	24	6	0	89		2.94	—	—	—	—	—	—	—
84-85—R.P.I.	ECAC	32	1830	31	1	0	78	0	2.56	—	—	—	—	—	—	—
85-86—Buffalo	NHL	7	401	3	4	0	21	1	3.14	—	—	—	—	—	—	—
—Rochester	AHL	20	1092	8	11	0	79	0	4.34	—	—	—	—	—	—	—
86-87—Buffalo	NHL	3	185	0	2	1	13	0	4.22	—	—	—	—	—	—	—
—Rochester	AHL	57	3129	33	14	0	146	1	*2.80	*16	*944	10	6	*48	*1	3.05
87-88—Rochester	AHL	26	1415	14	8	2	65	2	2.76	2	108	0	1	5	0	2.78
—Buffalo	NHL	17	874	8	6	1	61	0	4.19	3	142	1	1	11	0	4.65
88-89—Buffalo	NHL	37	1908	17	10	6	107	1	3.36	—	—	—	—	—	—	—
89-90—Buffalo	NHL	56	3241	31	16	6	156	1	2.89	6	370	2	4	15	0	2.43
90-91—Buffalo	NHL	38	2092	15	11	6	118	2	3.38	2	81	0	1	10	0	7.41
91-92—Buffalo	NHL	33	1757	11	14	4	114	0	3.89	—	—	—	—	—	—	—
—Rochester	AHL	2	119	0	2	0	9	0	4.54	—	—	—	—	—	—	—
NHL totals		191	10458	85	63	24	590	5	3.38	11	593	3	6	36	0	3.64

PURVES, JOHN
RW, CAPITALS

PERSONAL: Born February 12, 1968, at Toronto.... 6-1/201.... Shoots right.
TRANSACTIONS/CAREER NOTES: Selected by Washington Capitals as underage junior in fifth round (sixth Capitals pick, 103rd overall) of NHL entry draft (June 21, 1986).... Broke wrist (October 1986).
HONORS: Named to OHL All-Star second team (1988-89).

			REGULAR SEASON					PLAYOFFS				
Season Team	League	Gms.	G	A	Pts.	Pen.	Gms.	G	A	Pts.	Pen.
84-85—Belleville	OHL	55	15	14	29	39	—	—	—	—	—
85-86—Belleville	OHL	16	3	9	12	6	—	—	—	—	—
—Hamilton	OHL	36	13	28	41	36	—	—	—	—	—
86-87—Hamilton	OHL	28	12	11	23	37	9	2	0	2	12
87-88—Hamilton	OHL	64	39	44	83	65	14	7	18	25	4
88-89—Niagara Falls	OHL	5	5	11	16	2	—	—	—	—	—
—North Bay	OHL	42	34	52	86	38	12	14	12	26	16
89-90—Baltimore	AHL	75	29	35	64	12	9	5	7	12	4
90-91—Washington	NHL	7	1	0	1	0	—	—	—	—	—
—Baltimore	AHL	53	22	29	51	27	6	2	3	5	0
91-92—Baltimore	AHL	78	43	46	89	47	—	—	—	—	—
NHL totals		7	1	0	1	0					

PUSHOR, JAMIE
D, RED WINGS

PERSONAL: Born February 11, 1973, at Lethbridge, Alta.... 6-3/192.... Shoots right.... Full name: James Pushor.
TRANSACTIONS/CAREER NOTES: Selected by Detroit Red Wings in second round (second Red Wings pick, 32nd overall) of NHL entry draft (June 22, 1991).

			REGULAR SEASON					PLAYOFFS				
Season Team	League	Gms.	G	A	Pts.	Pen.	Gms.	G	A	Pts.	Pen.
89-90—Lethbridge	WHL	10	0	2	2	2	—	—	—	—	—
90-91—Lethbridge	WHL	71	1	13	14	193	—	—	—	—	—
91-92—Lethbridge	WHL	49	2	15	17	232	5	0	0	0	33

PYE, BILL
G, SABRES

PERSONAL: Born April 4, 1969, at Royal Oak, Mich.... 5-9/170.... Shoots right.... Full name: William Francis Pye III.
COLLEGE: Northern Michigan.
TRANSACTIONS/CAREER NOTES: Selected by Buffalo Sabres in sixth round (fifth Sabres pick, 107th over-

P

all) of NHL entry draft (June 17, 1989).

HONORS: Won WCHA Playoff Most Valuable Player Award (1990-91). . . . Named to NCAA All-America West second team (1990-91). . . . Named to NCAA All-Tournament team (1990-91). . . . Named to WCHA All-Star first team (1990-91).

Season Team	League	REGULAR SEASON								PLAYOFFS						
		Gms.	Min.	W	L	T	GA	SO	Avg.	Gms.	Min.	W	L	GA	SO	Avg.
87-88—N. Michigan U.	WCHA	13	654				49	0	4.50	—	—	—	—	—	—	—
88-89—N. Michigan U.	WCHA	43	2533	26	15	2	133	1	3.15	—	—	—	—	—	—	—
89-90—N. Michigan U.	WCHA	36	2035	20	14	1	149	1	4.39	—	—	—	—	—	—	—
90-91—N. Michigan U.	WCHA	39	2300	32	3	4	109	*4	2.84	—	—	—	—	—	—	—
91-92—Rochester	AHL	7	272	0	4	0	13	0	2.87	1	60	1	0	2	0	2.00
—New Haven	AHL	4	200	0	3	1	19	0	5.70	—	—	—	—	—	—	—
—Fort Wayne	IHL	8	451	5	2	1	29	0	3.86	—	—	—	—	—	—	—
—Erie	ECHL	5	310	5	0	0	22	0	4.26	4	220	1	3	15	0	4.09

QUENNEVILLE, JOEL
D, MAPLE LEAFS

PERSONAL: Born September 15, 1958, at Windsor, Ont. . . . 6-1/200. . . . Shoots left. . . . Full name: Joel Norman Quenneville.

TRANSACTIONS/CAREER NOTES: Selected by Toronto Maple Leafs from Windsor Spitfires in second round (first Maple Leafs pick, 21st overall) of NHL amateur draft (June 15, 1978). . . . Traded by Maple Leafs with RW Lanny McDonald to Colorado Rockies for RW Wilf Paiement and LW Pat Hickey (December 1979). . . . Injured rib cage (March 1980). . . . Underwent surgery to repair torn ligaments in ring finger of left hand (March 1980). . . . Sprained ankle, twisted knee and suffered facial lacerations (January 4, 1982). . . . Rockies franchise moved to New Jersey and became the Devils (June 30, 1982). . . . Traded by Devils with C Steve Tambellini to Calgary Flames for C Mel Bridgman and D Phil Russell (July 1983). . . . Traded by Flames with D Richie Dunn to Hartford Whalers for D Mickey Volcan and third-round pick in 1984 draft (August 1983). . . . Broke right shoulder (December 18, 1986); missed 42 games. . . . Separated left shoulder (January 19, 1989); missed nine games. . . . Traded by Whalers to Washington Capitals for future considerations (October 3, 1990). . . . Signed as free agent by Toronto Maple Leafs (July 30, 1991).

HONORS: Named to OMJHL All-Star second team (1977-78). . . . Named to AHL All-Star second team (1991-92).

Season Team	League	REGULAR SEASON					PLAYOFFS				
		Gms.	G	A	Pts.	Pen.	Gms.	G	A	Pts.	Pen.
75-76—Windsor	OHA Mj. Jr. A	66	15	33	48	61	—	—	—	—	—
76-77—Windsor	OMJHL	65	19	59	78	169	9	6	5	11	112
77-78—Windsor	OMJHL	66	27	76	103	114	6	2	3	5	17
78-79—Toronto	NHL	61	2	9	11	60	6	0	1	1	4
—New Brunswick	AHL	16	1	10	11	10	—	—	—	—	—
79-80—Toronto	NHL	32	1	4	5	24	—	—	—	—	—
—Colorado	NHL	35	5	7	12	26	—	—	—	—	—
80-81—Colorado	NHL	71	10	24	34	86	—	—	—	—	—
81-82—Colorado	NHL	64	5	10	15	55	—	—	—	—	—
82-83—New Jersey	NHL	74	5	12	17	46	—	—	—	—	—
83-84—Hartford	NHL	80	5	8	13	95	—	—	—	—	—
84-85—Hartford	NHL	79	6	16	22	96	—	—	—	—	—
85-86—Hartford	NHL	71	5	20	25	83	10	0	2	2	12
86-87—Hartford	NHL	37	3	7	10	24	6	0	0	0	0
87-88—Hartford	NHL	77	1	8	9	44	6	0	2	2	2
88-89—Hartford	NHL	69	4	7	11	32	4	0	3	3	4
89-90—Hartford	NHL	44	1	4	5	34	—	—	—	—	—
90-91—Washington	NHL	9	1	0	1	0	—	—	—	—	—
—Baltimore	AHL	59	6	13	19	58	6	1	1	2	6
91-92—St. John's	AHL	73	7	23	30	58	16	0	1	1	10
NHL totals		803	54	136	190	705	32	0	8	8	22

QUINN, DAN
C/RW, FLYERS

PERSONAL: Born June 1, 1965, at Ottawa. . . . 5-11/182. . . . Shoots left.

TRANSACTIONS/CAREER NOTES: Selected by Calgary Flames as underage junior in first round (first Flames pick, 13th overall) of NHL entry draft (June 8, 1983). . . . Traded by Flames to Pittsburgh Penguins for C Mike Bullard (November 1986). . . . Broke left wrist (October 1987). . . . Traded by Penguins with RW Andrew McBain and C Dave Capuano to Vancouver Canucks for RW Tony Tanti, C Barry Pederson and D Rod Buskas (January 8, 1990). . . . Bruised shoulder (January 1991). . . . Traded by Canucks with D Garth Butcher to St. Louis Blues for LW Geoff Courtnall, D Robert Dirk, C Cliff Ronning, LW Sergio Mommesso and undisclosed pick in 1992 draft (March 5, 1991). . . . Traded by Blues with C Rod Brind'Amour to Philadelphia Flyers for C Ron Sutter and D Murray Baron (September 22, 1991).

Season Team	League	REGULAR SEASON					PLAYOFFS				
		Gms.	G	A	Pts.	Pen.	Gms.	G	A	Pts.	Pen.
81-82—Belleville	OHL	67	19	32	51	41	—	—	—	—	—
82-83—Belleville	OHL	70	59	88	147	27	4	2	6	8	2
83-84—Belleville	OHL	24	23	36	59	12	—	—	—	—	—
—Calgary	NHL	54	19	33	52	20	8	3	5	8	4
84-85—Calgary	NHL	74	20	38	58	22	3	0	0	0	0
85-86—Calgary	NHL	78	30	42	72	44	18	8	7	15	10
86-87—Calgary	NHL	16	3	6	9	14	—	—	—	—	—
—Pittsburgh	NHL	64	28	43	71	40	—	—	—	—	—
87-88—Pittsburgh	NHL	70	40	39	79	50	—	—	—	—	—
88-89—Pittsburgh	NHL	79	34	60	94	102	11	6	3	9	10
89-90—Pittsburgh	NHL	41	9	20	29	22	—	—	—	—	—
—Vancouver	NHL	37	16	18	34	27	—	—	—	—	—

PQ

Season Team	League	REGULAR SEASON Gms.	G	A	Pts.	Pen.	PLAYOFFS Gms.	G	A	Pts.	Pen.
90-91—Vancouver	NHL	64	18	31	49	46	—	—	—	—	—
—St. Louis	NHL	14	4	7	11	20	13	4	7	11	32
91-92—Philadelphia	NHL	67	11	26	37	26	—	—	—	—	—
NHL totals		658	232	363	595	433	53	21	22	43	56

QUINNEY, KEN
RW

PERSONAL: Born May 23, 1965, at New Westminster, B.C.... 5-10/186.... Shoots right.
TRANSACTIONS/CAREER NOTES: Selected by Quebec Nordiques as underage junior in 10th round (ninth Nordiques pick, 203rd overall) of NHL entry draft (June 9, 1984).... Broke wrist (February 1986).... Strained right thumb ligament (December 31, 1990); missed 12 games.
HONORS: Named to WHL East All-Star first team (1984-85).... Won Tim Horton Award (1988).

Season Team	League	REGULAR SEASON Gms.	G	A	Pts.	Pen.	PLAYOFFS Gms.	G	A	Pts.	Pen.
81-82—Calgary	WHL	63	11	17	28	55	2	0	0	0	15
82-83—Calgary	WHL	71	26	25	51	71	16	6	1	7	46
83-84—Calgary	WHL	71	64	54	118	38	4	5	2	7	0
84-85—Calgary	WHL	56	47	67	114	65	7	6	4	10	15
85-86—Fredericton	AHL	61	11	26	37	34	6	2	2	4	9
86-87—Quebec	NHL	25	2	7	9	16	—	—	—	—	—
—Fredericton	AHL	48	14	27	41	20	—	—	—	—	—
87-88—Fredericton	AHL	58	37	39	76	39	13	3	5	8	35
—Quebec	NHL	15	2	2	4	5	—	—	—	—	—
88-89—Halifax	AHL	72	41	49	90	65	4	3	0	3	0
89-90—Halifax	AHL	44	9	16	25	63	2	0	0	0	2
90-91—Quebec	NHL	19	3	4	7	2	—	—	—	—	—
—Halifax	AHL	44	20	20	40	76	—	—	—	—	—
91-92—Adirondack	AHL	63	31	29	60	33	19	7	12	19	9
NHL totals		59	7	13	20	23					

QUINTAL, STEPHANE
D, BLUES

PERSONAL: Born October 22, 1968, at Boucherville, Que.... 6-3/220.... Shoots right.
TRANSACTIONS/CAREER NOTES: Broke wrist (December 1985).... Selected by Boston Bruins as underage junior in first round (second Bruins pick, 14th overall) of NHL entry draft (June 13, 1987).... Broke bone near eye (October 1988).... Injured knee (January 1989).... Sprained right knee (October 17, 1989); missed eight games.... Fractured left ankle (April 9, 1991); missed remainder of playoffs.... Traded by Bruins with C Craig Janney to St. Louis Blues for C Adam Oates (February 7, 1992).
HONORS: Named to QMJHL All-Star first team (1986-87).

Season Team	League	REGULAR SEASON Gms.	G	A	Pts.	Pen.	PLAYOFFS Gms.	G	A	Pts.	Pen.
85-86—Granby	QMJHL	67	2	17	19	144	—	—	—	—	—
86-87—Granby	QMJHL	67	13	41	54	178	8	0	9	9	10
87-88—Hull	QMJHL	38	13	23	36	138	19	7	12	19	30
88-89—Maine	AHL	16	4	10	14	28	—	—	—	—	—
—Boston	NHL	26	0	1	1	29	—	—	—	—	—
89-90—Boston	NHL	38	2	2	4	22	—	—	—	—	—
—Maine	AHL	37	4	16	20	27	—	—	—	—	—
90-91—Maine	AHL	23	1	5	6	30	—	—	—	—	—
—Boston	NHL	45	2	6	8	89	3	0	1	1	7
91-92—Boston	NHL	49	4	10	14	77	—	—	—	—	—
—St. Louis	NHL	26	0	6	6	32	4	1	2	3	6
NHL totals		184	8	25	33	249	7	1	3	4	13

QUINTIN, J.F.
LW, SHARKS

PERSONAL: Born May 28, 1969, at St. Jean, Que.... 6-0/187.... Shoots left.... Full name: Jean-Francois Quintin.
TRANSACTIONS/CAREER NOTES: Fractured knee (October 1985).... Selected by Minnesota North Stars in fourth round (fourth North Stars pick, 75th overall) of NHL entry draft (June 17, 1989).... Selected by San Jose Sharks in NHL dispersal draft (May 30, 1991).

Season Team	League	REGULAR SEASON Gms.	G	A	Pts.	Pen.	PLAYOFFS Gms.	G	A	Pts.	Pen.
86-87—Shawinigan	QMJHL	43	1	9	10	17	—	—	—	—	—
87-88—Shawinigan	QMJHL	70	28	70	98	143	11	5	8	13	26
88-89—Shawinigan	QMJHL	69	52	100	152	105	10	9	15	24	16
89-90—Kalamazoo	IHL	68	20	18	38	38	10	8	4	12	14
90-91—Kalamazoo	IHL	78	31	43	74	64	9	1	5	6	11
91-92—Kansas City	IHL	21	4	6	10	29	13	2	10	12	29
—San Jose	NHL	8	3	0	3	0	—	—	—	—	—
NHL totals		8	3	0	3	0					

RACICOT, ANDRE
G, CANADIENS

PERSONAL: Born June 9, 1969, at Rouyn-Noranda, Que.... 5-11/165.... Shoots left.
TRANSACTIONS/CAREER NOTES: Selected by Montreal Canadiens in fourth round (fifth Canadiens pick, 83rd overall) of NHL draft (June 17, 1989).
HONORS: Shared Harry (Hap) Holmes Memorial Trophy with Jean-Claude Bergeron (1989-90).

QR

Season Team	League	Gms.	Min.	W	L	T	GA	SO	Avg.	Gms.	Min.	W	L	GA	SO	Avg.
86-87—Longueuil	QMJHL	3	180	1	2	0	19	0	6.33	—	—	—	—	—	—	—
87-88—Hull/Granby	QMJHL	30	1547	15	11	1	105	1	4.07	5	298	1	4	23	0	4.63
88-89—Granby	QMJHL	54	2944	22	24	3	198	0	4.04	4	218	0	4	18	0	4.95
89-90—Sherbrooke	AHL	33	1948	19	11	2	97	1	2.99	5	227	0	4	18	0	4.76
—Montreal	NHL	1	13	0	0	0	3	0	13.85	—	—	—	—	—	—	—
90-91—Fredericton	AHL	22	1252	13	8	1	60	1	2.88	—	—	—	—	—	—	—
—Montreal	NHL	21	975	7	9	2	52	1	3.20	2	12	0	1	2	0	10.00
91-92—Fredericton	AHL	28	1666	14	8	5	86	0	3.10	—	—	—	—	—	—	—
—Montreal	NHL	9	436	0	3	3	23	0	3.17	1	1	0	0	0	0	0.00
NHL totals		31	1424	7	12	5	78	1	3.29	3	13	0	1	2	0	9.23

RACINE, BRUCE
G, PENGUINS

PERSONAL: Born August 9, 1966, at Cornwall, Ont. . . . 6-0/178. . . . Shoots left. . . . Full name: Bruce Michael Racine.
COLLEGE: Northeastern.
TRANSACTIONS/CAREER NOTES: Selected by Pittsburgh Penguins in third round (third Penguins pick, 58th overall) of NHL entry draft (June 15, 1985).
HONORS: Named to Hockey East All-Star second team (1984-85). . . . Named to NCAA All-America East first team (1986-87 and 1987-88). . . . Named to Hockey East All-Star first team (1986-87).

Season Team	League	Gms.	Min.	W	L	T	GA	SO	Avg.	Gms.	Min.	W	L	GA	SO	Avg.
84-85—Northeastern Univ.	Hoc. East	26	1615	11	14	1	103	1	3.83	—	—	—	—	—	—	—
85-86—Northeastern Univ.	Hoc. East	37	2212	17	14	1	171	0	4.64	—	—	—	—	—	—	—
86-87—Northeastern Univ.	Hoc. East	33	1966	12	18	3	133	0	4.06	—	—	—	—	—	—	—
87-88—Northeastern Univ.	Hoc. East	30	1809	15	11	4	108	1	3.58	—	—	—	—	—	—	—
88-89—Muskegon	IHL	51	*3039	37	11	0	184	*3	3.63	5	300	4	1	15	0	3.00
89-90—Muskegon	IHL	49	2911	29	15	4	182	1	3.75	—	—	—	—	—	—	—
90-91—Albany	IHL	29	1567	7	18	1	104	0	3.98	—	—	—	—	—	—	—
—Muskegon	IHL	9	516	4	4	1	40	0	4.65	—	—	—	—	—	—	—
91-92—Muskegon	IHL	27	1559	13	10	3	91	1	3.50	1	60	0	1	6	0	6.00

RACINE, YVES
D, RED WINGS

PERSONAL: Born February 7, 1969, at Matane, Que. . . . 6-0/200. . . . Shoots left.
TRANSACTIONS/CAREER NOTES: Selected by Detroit Red Wings as underage junior in first round (first Red Wings pick, 11th overall) of NHL entry draft (June 13, 1987). . . . Injured shoulder (March 22, 1991); missed four games.
HONORS: Named to QMJHL All-Star first team (1987-88 and 1988-89). . . . Won Emile (Butch) Bouchard Trophy (1988-89).

Season Team	League	Gms.	G	A	Pts.	Pen.	Gms.	G	A	Pts.	Pen.
86-87—Longueuil	QMJHL	70	7	43	50	50	20	3	11	14	14
87-88—Victoriaville	QMJHL	69	10	84	94	150	5	0	0	0	13
—Adirondack	AHL	—	—	—	—	—	9	4	2	6	2
88-89—Victoriaville	QMJHL	63	23	85	108	95	18	3	*30	*33	41
—Adirondack	AHL	—	—	—	—	—	2	1	1	2	0
89-90—Detroit	NHL	28	4	9	13	23	—	—	—	—	—
—Adirondack	AHL	46	8	27	35	31	—	—	—	—	—
90-91—Adirondack	AHL	16	3	9	12	10	—	—	—	—	—
—Detroit	NHL	62	7	40	47	33	7	2	0	2	0
91-92—Detroit	NHL	61	2	22	24	94	11	2	1	3	10
NHL totals		151	13	71	84	150	18	4	1	5	10

RAGLAN, HERB
RW, NORDIQUES

PERSONAL: Born August 5, 1967, at Peterborough, Ont. . . . 6-0/205. . . . Shoots right. . . . Full name: Herbert Raglan. . . . Son of Clare Raglan, defenseman, Detroit Red Wings and Chicago Blackhawks (1950-51 through 1952-53).
TRANSACTIONS/CAREER NOTES: Selected by St. Louis Blues as underage junior in second round (first Blues pick, 37th overall) of NHL entry draft (June 15, 1985). . . . Suffered severe ankle sprain (December 1985). . . . Strained right knee ligaments (November 1987). . . . Sprained right wrist (October 1988). . . . Separated left shoulder (November 1988). . . . Pulled right groin (February 1989). . . . Broke right wrist and underwent surgery (November 4, 1989). . . . Bruised ribs (October 27, 1990). . . . Pulled right groin (December 1990). . . . Sprained left knee (February 2, 1991); missed 11 games. . . . Traded by Blues with D Tony Twist and LW Andy Rymsha to Quebec Nordiques for RW Darin Kimble (February 4, 1991). . . . Broke nose (November 2, 1991); missed 12 games.

Season Team	League	Gms.	G	A	Pts.	Pen.	Gms.	G	A	Pts.	Pen.
84-85—Kingston	OHL	58	20	22	42	166	—	—	—	—	—
85-86—Kingston	OHL	28	10	9	19	88	10	5	2	7	30
—St. Louis	NHL	7	0	0	0	5	10	1	1	2	24
86-87—St. Louis	NHL	62	6	10	16	159	4	0	0	0	2
87-88—St. Louis	NHL	73	10	15	25	190	10	1	3	4	11
88-89—St. Louis	NHL	50	7	10	17	144	8	1	2	3	13
89-90—St. Louis	NHL	11	0	1	1	21	—	—	—	—	—
90-91—St. Louis	NHL	32	3	3	6	52	—	—	—	—	—
—Quebec	NHL	15	1	3	4	30	—	—	—	—	—
91-92—Quebec	NHL	62	6	14	20	120	—	—	—	—	—
NHL totals		312	33	56	89	721	32	3	6	9	50

RAGNARSSON, MARCUS
D, SHARKS

PERSONAL: Born August 13, 1971, at Ostervala, Sweden.... 6-1/200....
Shoots left.
TRANSACTIONS/CAREER NOTES: Selected by San Jose Sharks in fifth round
(fifth Sharks pick, 99th overall) of NHL entry draft (June 20, 1992).

Season Team	League	REGULAR SEASON					PLAYOFFS				
		Gms.	G	A	Pts.	Pen.	Gms.	G	A	Pts.	Pen.
89-90—Djurgarden	Sweden	13	0	2	2	0	1	0	0	0	0
90-91—Djurgarden	Sweden	35	4	1	5	12	7	0	0	0	6
91-92—Djurgarden	Sweden	40	8	5	13	14	—	—	—	—	—

RAITER, MARK
D, MAPLE LEAFS

PERSONAL: Born January 27, 1973, at Calgary, Alta.... 6-4/220.... Shoots right.
HIGH SCHOOL: Marion Graham (Saskatoon, Sask.).
TRANSACTIONS/CAREER NOTES: Selected by Toronto Maple Leafs in fourth round (fourth Maple
Leafs pick, 95th overall) of NHL entry draft (June 20, 1992).

Season Team	League	REGULAR SEASON					PLAYOFFS				
		Gms.	G	A	Pts.	Pen.	Gms.	G	A	Pts.	Pen.
89-90—Saskatoon	WHL	14	1	1	2	51	—	—	—	—	—
90-91—Saskatoon	WHL	35	2	3	5	73	—	—	—	—	—
91-92—Saskatoon	WHL	72	2	12	14	354	22	0	7	7	45

RAMAGE, ROB
D, LIGHTNING

PERSONAL: Born January 11, 1959, at Byron, Ont.... 6-2/205.... Shoots right.... Full name:
George Robert Ramage.
TRANSACTIONS/CAREER NOTES: Signed as underage junior by Birmingham Bulls (July 1978)....
Selected by Colorado Rockies in first round (first Rockies pick, first overall) of NHL entry draft
(August 9, 1979).... Traded by Rockies to St. Louis Blues for first-round picks in 1982 draft (C Rocky Trottier) and 1983 draft
(RW John MacLean) (June 1982).... Sprained knee (March 22, 1986).... Suffered tendinitis around left kneecap (November
24, 1986); missed 21 games.... Traded by Blues with G Rick Wamsley to Calgary Flames for RW Brett Hull and LW Steve Bozek
(March 7, 1988).... Suspended eight games by NHL for high-sticking (February 3, 1989).... Traded by Flames to Toronto
Maple Leafs for second-round pick in 1989 draft (LW Kent Manderville) (June 16, 1989).... Selected by Minnesota North
Stars in NHL expansion draft (May 30, 1991).... Underwent knee surgery (January 23, 1992); missed 38 games.... Selected
by Tampa Bay Lightning in NHL expansion draft (June 18, 1992).
HONORS: Shared Max Kaminsky Trophy with Brad Marsh (1977-78).... Named to OMJHL All-Star first team (1977-78)....
Named to WHA All-Star first team (1978-79).

Season Team	League	REGULAR SEASON					PLAYOFFS				
		Gms.	G	A	Pts.	Pen.	Gms.	G	A	Pts.	Pen.
75-76—London	OHA Mj. Jr. A	65	12	31	43	113	5	0	1	1	11
76-77—London	OMJHL	65	15	58	73	177	20	3	11	14	55
77-78—London	OMJHL	59	17	47	64	162	11	4	5	9	29
78-79—Birmingham	WHA	80	12	36	48	165	—	—	—	—	—
79-80—Colorado	NHL	75	8	20	28	135	—	—	—	—	—
80-81—Colorado	NHL	79	20	42	62	193	—	—	—	—	—
81-82—Colorado	NHL	80	13	29	42	201	—	—	—	—	—
82-83—St. Louis	NHL	78	16	35	51	193	4	0	3	3	22
83-84—St. Louis	NHL	80	15	45	60	121	11	1	8	9	32
84-85—St. Louis	NHL	80	7	31	38	178	3	1	3	4	6
85-86—St. Louis	NHL	77	10	56	66	171	19	1	10	11	66
86-87—St. Louis	NHL	59	11	28	39	106	6	2	2	4	21
87-88—St. Louis	NHL	67	8	34	42	127	—	—	—	—	—
—Calgary	NHL	12	1	6	7	37	9	1	3	4	21
88-89—Calgary	NHL	68	3	13	16	156	20	1	11	12	26
89-90—Toronto	NHL	80	8	41	49	202	5	1	2	3	20
90-91—Toronto	NHL	80	10	25	35	173	—	—	—	—	—
91-92—Minnesota	NHL	34	4	5	9	69	—	—	—	—	—
WHA totals		80	12	36	48	165					
NHL totals		949	134	410	544	2062	77	8	42	50	214

RAMSEY, MIKE
D, SABRES

PERSONAL: Born December 3, 1960, at Minneapolis.... 6-3/195.... Shoots left.... Full name:
Michael Allen Ramsey.
COLLEGE: Minnesota.
TRANSACTIONS/CAREER NOTES: Selected by Buffalo Sabres in first round (first Sabres pick,
11th round) of NHL entry draft (August 9, 1979).... Dislocated thumb (December 4, 1983).... Injured groin (October 1987).
... Fractured bone in right hand (November 2, 1988).... Pulled groin (January 12, 1989).... Pulled rib cage muscle (Novem-
ber 26, 1990); missed seven games.... Injured groin (November 22, 1991); missed five games.... Injured groin (January 31,
1992); missed three games.... Injured groin (March 8, 1992); missed three games.... Injured leg (April 12, 1992).
MISCELLANEOUS: Member of 1980 gold-medal-winning U.S. Olympic team.

Season Team	League	REGULAR SEASON					PLAYOFFS				
		Gms.	G	A	Pts.	Pen.	Gms.	G	A	Pts.	Pen.
78-79—University of Minnesota	WCHA	26	6	11	17	30	—	—	—	—	—
79-80—U.S. Olympic Team	Int'l	63	11	24	35	63	—	—	—	—	—
—Buffalo	NHL	13	1	6	7	6	13	1	2	3	12
80-81—Buffalo	NHL	72	3	14	17	56	8	0	3	3	20
81-82—Buffalo	NHL	80	7	23	30	56	4	1	1	2	14
82-83—Buffalo	NHL	77	8	30	38	55	10	4	4	8	15

Season	Team	League	REGULAR SEASON					PLAYOFFS				
			Gms.	G	A	Pts.	Pen.	Gms.	G	A	Pts.	Pen.
83-84—Buffalo		NHL	72	9	22	31	82	3	0	1	1	6
84-85—Buffalo		NHL	79	8	22	30	102	5	0	1	1	23
85-86—Buffalo		NHL	76	7	21	28	117	—	—	—	—	—
86-87—Buffalo		NHL	80	8	31	39	109	—	—	—	—	—
87-88—Buffalo		NHL	63	5	16	21	77	6	0	3	3	29
88-89—Buffalo		NHL	56	2	14	16	84	5	1	0	1	11
89-90—Buffalo		NHL	73	4	21	25	47	6	0	1	1	8
90-91—Buffalo		NHL	71	6	14	20	46	5	1	0	1	12
91-92—Buffalo		NHL	66	3	14	17	67	7	0	2	2	8
NHL totals			878	71	248	319	904	72	8	18	26	158

RANFORD, BILL
G, OILERS

PERSONAL: Born December 14, 1966, at Brandon, Man.... 5-10/170.... Shoots left.
TRANSACTIONS/CAREER NOTES: Selected by Boston Bruins as underage junior in third round (second Bruins pick, 52nd overall) of NHL entry draft (June 15, 1985).... Traded by Bruins with LW Geoff Courtnall and second-round pick in 1988 draft (C Petro Koivunen) to Edmonton Oilers for G Andy Moog (March 1988).... Sprained ankle (February 14, 1990); missed six games.... Strained groin (January 4, 1992); missed two games.... Strained hamstring (January 29, 1992); missed five games.
HONORS: Named to WHL All-Star second team (1985-86).... Won Conn Smythe Trophy (1989-90).
RECORDS: Shares NHL single-season playoff record for most wins by a goaltender—16 (1990).

Season	Team	League	REGULAR SEASON							PLAYOFFS					
			Gms.	Min.	W	L	T	GA	SO	Avg.	Gms.	Min.	W	L	GA	SO	Avg.
83-84—New Westminster	WHL	27	1450	10	14	0	130	0	5.38	1	27	0	0	2	0	4.44
84-85—New Westminster	WHL	38	2034	19	17	0	142	0	4.19	7	309	2	3	26	0	5.05
85-86—New Westminster	WHL	53	2791	17	29	1	225	1	4.84	—	—	—	—	—	—	—
—Boston	NHL	4	240	3	1	0	10	0	2.50	2	120	0	2	7	0	3.50
86-87—Moncton	AHL	3	180	3	0	0	6	0	2.00	—	—	—	—	—	—	—
—Boston	NHL	41	2234	16	20	2	124	3	3.33	2	123	0	2	8	0	3.90
87-88—Maine	AHL	51	2856	27	16	6	165	1	3.47	—	—	—	—	—	—	—
—Edmonton	NHL	6	325	3	0	2	16	0	2.95	—	—	—	—	—	—	—
88-89—Edmonton	NHL	29	1509	15	8	2	88	1	3.50	—	—	—	—	—	—	—
89-90—Edmonton	NHL	56	3107	24	16	9	165	1	3.19	*22	*1401	*16	6	*59	0	2.53
90-91—Edmonton	NHL	60	3415	27	27	3	182	0	3.20	3	135	1	2	8	0	3.56
91-92—Edmonton	NHL	67	3822	27	26	10	228	1	3.58	16	909	8	*8	51	†2	3.37
NHL totals		263	14652	115	98	28	813	6	3.33	45	2688	25	20	133	2	2.97

RANHEIM, PAUL
LW, FLAMES

PERSONAL: Born January 25, 1966, at St. Louis.... 6-0/195.... Shoots right.... Full name: Paul Stephen Ranheim.
HIGH SCHOOL: Edina (Minn.).
COLLEGE: Wisconsin.
TRANSACTIONS/CAREER NOTES: Selected by Calgary Flames in second round (third Flames pick, 38th overall) of NHL entry draft (June 8, 1983).... Broke right ankle (December 11, 1990); missed 41 games.
HONORS: Named to WCHA All-Star second team (1986-87).... Named to NCAA West All-America first team (1987-88).... Named to WCHA All-Star first team (1987-88).... Won Garry F. Longman Memorial Trophy (1988-89).... Won Ken McKenzie Trophy (1988-89).... Named to IHL All-Star second team (1988-89).

Season	Team	League	REGULAR SEASON					PLAYOFFS				
			Gms.	G	A	Pts.	Pen.	Gms.	G	A	Pts.	Pen.
82-83—Edina High School	Minn. H.S.	26	12	25	37	4	—	—	—	—	—
83-84—Edina High School	Minn. H.S.	26	16	24	40	6	—	—	—	—	—
84-85—University of Wisconsin	WCHA	42	11	11	22	40	—	—	—	—	—
85-86—University of Wisconsin	WCHA	33	17	17	34	34	—	—	—	—	—
86-87—University of Wisconsin	WCHA	42	24	35	59	54	—	—	—	—	—
87-88—University of Wisconsin	WCHA	44	36	26	62	63	—	—	—	—	—
88-89—Calgary	NHL	5	0	0	0	0	—	—	—	—	—
—Salt Lake City	IHL	75	*68	29	97	16	14	5	5	10	8
89-90—Calgary	NHL	80	26	28	54	23	6	1	3	4	2
90-91—Calgary	NHL	39	14	16	30	4	7	2	2	4	0
91-92—Calgary	NHL	80	23	20	43	32	—	—	—	—	—
NHL totals		204	63	64	127	59	13	3	5	8	2

RATHJE, MIKE
D, SHARKS

PERSONAL: Born May 11, 1974, at Manville, Alta.... 6-5/195.... Shoots left.... Full name: Michael Rathje.
HIGH SCHOOL: Medicine Hat (Alta.).
TRANSACTIONS/CAREER NOTES: Selected by San Jose Sharks in first round (first Sharks pick, third overall) of NHL entry draft (June 20, 1992).
HONORS: Named to WHL (East) All-Star second team (1991-92).

Season	Team	League	REGULAR SEASON					PLAYOFFS				
			Gms.	G	A	Pts.	Pen.	Gms.	G	A	Pts.	Pen.
90-91—Medicine Hat	WHL	64	1	16	17	28	12	0	4	4	2
91-92—Medicine Hat	WHL	67	11	23	34	109	4	0	1	1	2

RATUSHNY, DAN
D, JETS

PERSONAL: Born October 29, 1970, at Nepean, Ont. . . . 6-1/185. . . . Shoots right. . . . Full name: Daniel Paul Ratushny.
COLLEGE: Cornell.
TRANSACTIONS/CAREER NOTES: Selected by Winnipeg Jets in second round (second Jets pick, 25th overall) of NHL entry draft (June 17, 1989).
HONORS: Named to NCAA All-America East second team (1989-90). . . . Named to NCAA All-America East first team (1990-91). . . . Named to ECAC All-Star first team (1990-91).
MISCELLANEOUS: Member of 1992 silver-medal-winning Canadian Olympic team.

Season Team	League	Gms.	G	A	Pts.	Pen.	Gms.	G	A	Pts.	Pen.
		REGULAR SEASON					PLAYOFFS				
87-88—Napean	COJHL	54	8	20	28	116	—	—	—	—	—
88-89—Cornell University	ECAC	28	2	13	15	50	—	—	—	—	—
—Canadian National Team..	Int'l	2	0	0	0	2	—	—	—	—	—
89-90—Cornell University	ECAC	26	5	14	19	54	—	—	—	—	—
90-91—Cornell University	ECAC	26	7	24	31	52	—	—	—	—	—
—Canadian National Team..	Int'l	12	0	1	1	6	—	—	—	—	—
91-92—Canadian National Team..	Int'l	58	5	13	18	50	—	—	—	—	—
—Canadian Olympic Team ..	Int'l	8	0	0	0	4	—	—	—	—	—

RAY, ROB
LW, SABRES

PERSONAL: Born June 8, 1968, at Stirling, Ont. . . . 6-0/203. . . . Shoots left.
TRANSACTIONS/CAREER NOTES: Broke jaw (January 1987). . . . Selected by Buffalo Sabres in fifth round (fifth Sabres pick, 97th overall) of NHL entry draft (June 11, 1988).

Season Team	League	Gms.	G	A	Pts.	Pen.	Gms.	G	A	Pts.	Pen.
		REGULAR SEASON					PLAYOFFS				
84-85—Whitby Lawmen	OPJHL	35	5	10	15	318	—	—	—	—	—
85-86—Cornwall	OHL	53	6	13	19	253	6	0	0	0	26
86-87—Cornwall	OHL	46	17	20	37	158	5	1	1	2	16
87-88—Cornwall	OHL	61	11	41	52	179	11	2	3	5	33
88-89—Rochester	AHL	74	11	18	29	*446	—	—	—	—	—
89-90—Buffalo	NHL	27	2	1	3	99	—	—	—	—	—
—Rochester	AHL	43	2	13	15	335	17	1	3	4	*115
90-91—Rochester	AHL	8	1	1	2	15	—	—	—	—	—
—Buffalo	NHL	66	8	8	16	*350	6	1	1	2	56
91-92—Buffalo	NHL	63	5	3	8	354	7	0	0	0	2
NHL totals		156	15	12	27	803	13	1	1	2	58

REAUGH, DARYL
G, WHALERS

PERSONAL: Born February 13, 1965, at Prince George, B.C. . . . 6-4/200. . . . Shoots left.
TRANSACTIONS/CAREER NOTES: Selected by Edmonton Oilers as underage junior in second round (second Oilers pick, 42nd overall) of NHL entry draft (June 9, 1984). . . . Signed as free agent by Hartford Whalers (September 1989). . . . Tore semi-tendinosis muscle (February 26, 1991); missed remainder of season.
HONORS: Named to WHL All-Star second team (1983-84). . . . Named to WHL All-Star first team (1984-85).

Season Team	League	Gms.	Min.	W	L	T	GA	SO	Avg.	Gms.	Min.	W	L	GA	SO	Avg.
		REGULAR SEASON								PLAYOFFS						
83-84—Kamloops	WHL	55	2748				199	1	4.34	17	972			57	0	*3.52
84-85—Kamloops	WHL	49	2749				170	2	3.71	*14	*787			*56	0	4.27
—Edmonton	NHL	1	60	0	1	0	5	0	5.00	—	—	—	—	—	—	—
85-86—Nova Scotia	AHL	38	2205	15	18	4	156	0	4.24	—	—	—	—	—	—	—
86-87—Nova Scotia	AHL	46	2637	19	22	0	163	1	3.71	2	120	0	2	13	0	6.50
87-88—Edmonton	NHL	6	176	1	1	0	14	0	4.77	—	—	—	—	—	—	—
—Nova Scotia	AHL	8	443	2	5	0	33	0	4.47	—	—	—	—	—	—	—
—Milwaukee	IHL	9	493	0	8	0	44	0	5.35	—	—	—	—	—	—	—
88-89—Cape Breton	AHL	13	778	3	10	0	72	0	5.55	—	—	—	—	—	—	—
—Karpat	Finland	13	756				46	2	3.65	—	—	—	—	—	—	—
89-90—Binghamton	AHL	52	2735	8.	31	6	192	0	4.21	—	—	—	—	—	—	—
90-91—Springfield	AHL	16	912	7	6	3	55	0	3.62	—	—	—	—	—	—	—
—Hartford	NHL	20	1010	7	7	1	53	1	3.15	—	—	—	—	—	—	—
91-92—Springfield	AHL	22	1005	3	12	2	63	0	3.76	1	39	0	0	1	0	1.54
NHL totals		27	1246	8	9	1	72	1	3.47							

RECCHI, MARK
RW, FLYERS

PERSONAL: Born February 1, 1968, at Kamloops, B.C. . . . 5-10/185. . . . Shoots left.
TRANSACTIONS/CAREER NOTES: Broke ankle (January 1987). . . . Selected by Pittsburgh Penguins in fourth round (fourth Penguins pick, 67th overall) of NHL entry draft (June 11, 1988). . . . Injured left shoulder (December 23, 1990). . . . Sprained right knee (March 30, 1991). . . . Traded by Penguins with D Brian Benning and first-round pick in 1992 draft (previously acquired from Los Angeles Kings) to Philadelphia Flyers for RW Rick Tocchet, D Kjell Samuelsson, G Ken Wregget and third-round pick in 1992 draft (February 19, 1992).
HONORS: Named to WHL West All-Star team (1987-88). . . . Named to IHL All-Star second team (1988-89). . . . Named to NHL All-Star second team (1991-92).

Season Team	League	Gms.	G	A	Pts.	Pen.	Gms.	G	A	Pts.	Pen.
		REGULAR SEASON					PLAYOFFS				
84-85—Langley Eagles	BCJHL	51	26	39	65	39	—	—	—	—	—
85-86—New Westminster	WHL	72	21	40	61	55	—	—	—	—	—

R

Season	Team	League	Gms.	G	A	Pts.	Pen.	Gms.	G	A	Pts.	Pen.
			REGULAR SEASON					**PLAYOFFS**				
86-87—Kamloops		WHL	40	26	50	76	63	13	3	16	19	17
87-88—Kamloops		WHL	62	61	*93	154	75	17	10	*21	†31	18
88-89—Pittsburgh		NHL	15	1	1	2	0	—	—	—	—	—
—Muskegon		IHL	63	50	49	99	86	14	7	*14	†21	28
89-90—Muskegon		IHL	4	7	4	11	2	—	—	—	—	—
—Pittsburgh		NHL	74	30	37	67	44	—	—	—	—	—
90-91—Pittsburgh		NHL	78	40	73	113	48	24	10	24	34	33
91-92—Pittsburgh		NHL	58	33	37	70	78	—	—	—	—	—
—Philadelphia		NHL	22	10	17	27	18	—	—	—	—	—
NHL totals			247	114	165	279	188	24	10	24	34	33

R

REDDICK, ELDON
G

PERSONAL: Born October 6, 1964, at Halifax, N.S. . . . 5-8/170. . . . Shoots left. **TRANSACTIONS/CAREER NOTES:** Traded by New Westminster Bruins to Brandon Wheat Kings for D Jayson Meyer and D Lee Trim (October 1984). . . . Signed as free agent by Winnipeg Jets (September 1985). . . . Traded by Jets to Edmonton Oilers for future consideration (September 28, 1989).
HONORS: Named to WHL All-Star second team (1983-84). . . . Shared James Norris Memorial Trophy with Rick St. Croix (1985-86).

Season	Team	League	Gms.	Min.	W	L	T	GA	SO	Avg.	Gms.	Min.	W	L	GA	SO	Avg.
			REGULAR SEASON								**PLAYOFFS**						
81-82—Billings		WHL	1	60				7	0	7.00	—	—	—	—	—	—	—
82-83—Nanaimo		WHL	*66	*3549	19	38	1	*383	0	6.48	—	—	—	—	—	—	—
83-84—New Westminster		WHL	50	2930	24	22	2	215	0	4.40	9	542	4	5	53	0	5.87
84-85—Brandon		WHL	47	2585	14	30	1	243	0	5.64	—	—	—	—	—	—	—
—Fort Wayne		IHL	10	491				32	2	3.91	—	—	—	—	—	—	—
85-86—Fort Wayne		IHL	32	1811	15	11	0	92	†3	3.05	—	—	—	—	—	—	—
86-87—Winnipeg		NHL	48	2762	21	21	4	149	0	3.24	3	166	0	2	10	0	3.61
87-88—Winnipeg		NHL	28	1487	9	13	3	102	0	4.12	—	—	—	—	—	—	—
—Moncton		AHL	9	545	2	6	1	26	0	2.86	—	—	—	—	—	—	—
88-89—Winnipeg		NHL	41	2109	11	17	7	144	0	4.10	—	—	—	—	—	—	—
89-90—Edmonton		NHL	11	604	5	4	2	31	0	3.08	1	2	0	0	0	0	0.00
—Cape Breton		AHL	15	821	9	4	1	54	0	3.95	—	—	—	—	—	—	—
—Phoenix		IHL	3	185	2	1	0	7	0	2.27	—	—	—	—	—	—	—
90-91—Edmonton		NHL	2	120	0	2	0	9	0	4.50	—	—	—	—	—	—	—
—Cape Breton		AHL	31	1673	19	10	0	97	2	3.48	2	124	0	2	10	0	4.84
91-92—Cape Breton		AHL	16	765	5	3	3	45	0	3.53	—	—	—	—	—	—	—
—Fort Wayne		IHL	14	787	6	5	2	40	1	3.05	7	369	3	4	18	0	2.93
NHL totals			130	7082	46	57	16	435	0	3.69	4	168	0	2	10	0	3.57

REDMOND, KEITH
LW, KINGS

PERSONAL: Born October 25, 1972, at Richmond Hill, Ont. . . . 6-3/208. . . . Shoots left. . . . Full name: Keith Christopher Redmond.
COLLEGE: Bowling Green State.
TRANSACTIONS/CAREER NOTES: Selected by Los Angeles Kings in fourth round (second Kings pick, 79th overall) of NHL entry draft (June 22, 1991).

Season	Team	League	Gms.	G	A	Pts.	Pen.	Gms.	G	A	Pts.	Pen.
			REGULAR SEASON					**PLAYOFFS**				
88-89—Nepean		COJHL	59	3	12	15	110	—	—	—	—	—
89-90—Nepean		COJHL	40	14	10	24	169	—	—	—	—	—
90-91—Bowling Green State		CCHA	35	1	3	4	72	—	—	—	—	—
91-92—Bowling Green State		CCHA	8	0	0	0	14	—	—	—	—	—
—Belleville		OHL	16	1	7	8	52	—	—	—	—	—
—Detroit		OHL	25	6	12	18	61	7	1	3	4	49

REEKIE, JOE
D, LIGHTNING

PERSONAL: Born February 22, 1965, at Victoria, B.C. . . . 6-3/215. . . . Shoots left. . . . Full name: Joseph James Reekie.
TRANSACTIONS/CAREER NOTES: Selected by Hartford Whalers as underage junior in seventh round (eighth Whalers pick, 124th overall) of NHL entry draft (June 8, 1983). . . . Released by Whalers (June 1984). . . . Selected by Buffalo Sabres in sixth round (sixth Sabres pick, 119th overall) of NHL entry draft (June 15, 1985). . . . Injured ankle (March 14, 1987). . . . Injured shoulder (October 1987). . . . Broke kneecap (November 15, 1987). . . . Underwent surgery to left knee (September 1988). . . . Traded by Sabres to New York Islanders for sixth-round pick in 1989 draft (G Bill Pye) (June 17, 1989). . . . Sprained right knee (November 1989). . . . Broke two bones in left hand and suffered facial cuts in automobile accident and underwent surgery (December 7, 1989). . . . Broke left middle finger (March 21, 1990). . . . Injured eye (January 12, 1991); missed six games. . . . Fractured knuckle on left hand (January 3, 1992); missed 22 games. . . . Selected by Tampa Bay Lightning in NHL expansion draft (June 18, 1992).

Season	Team	League	Gms.	G	A	Pts.	Pen.	Gms.	G	A	Pts.	Pen.
			REGULAR SEASON					**PLAYOFFS**				
81-82—Nepean		COJHL	16	2	5	7	4	—	—	—	—	—
82-83—North Bay		OHL	59	2	9	11	49	8	0	1	1	11
83-84—North Bay		OHL	9	1	0	1	18	—	—	—	—	—
—Cornwall		OHL	53	6	27	33	166	3	0	0	0	4
84-85—Cornwall		OHL	65	19	63	82	134	9	4	13	17	18

Season Team	League	REGULAR SEASON					PLAYOFFS				
		Gms.	G	A	Pts.	Pen.	Gms.	G	A	Pts.	Pen.
85-86—Rochester	AHL	77	3	25	28	178	—	—	—	—	—
—Buffalo	NHL	3	0	0	0	14	—	—	—	—	—
86-87—Buffalo	NHL	56	1	8	9	82	—	—	—	—	—
—Rochester	AHL	22	0	6	6	52	—	—	—	—	—
87-88—Buffalo	NHL	30	1	4	5	68	2	0	0	0	4
88-89—Rochester	AHL	21	1	2	3	56	—	—	—	—	—
—Buffalo	NHL	15	1	3	4	26	—	—	—	—	—
89-90—New York Islanders	NHL	31	1	8	9	43	—	—	—	—	—
—Springfield	AHL	15	1	4	5	24	—	—	—	—	—
90-91—Capital District	AHL	2	1	0	1	0	—	—	—	—	—
—New York Islanders	NHL	66	3	16	19	96	—	—	—	—	—
91-92—New York Islanders	NHL	54	4	12	16	85	—	—	—	—	—
—Capital District	AHL	3	2	2	4	2	—	—	—	—	—
NHL totals		255	11	51	62	414	2	0	0	0	4

REESE, JEFF
G, FLAMES

PERSONAL: Born March 24, 1966, at Brantford, Ont. . . . 5-9/155. . . . Shoots left.
TRANSACTIONS/CAREER NOTES: Selected by Toronto Maple Leafs as underage junior in fourth round (third Maple Leafs pick, 67th overall) of NHL entry draft (June 9, 1984). . . . Broke left kneecap (October 23, 1989); missed two months. . . . Suffered contusion to left kneecap (April 12, 1990). . . . Broke transverse processes (March 23, 1991); missed remainder of season. . . . Traded by Maple Leafs with D Alexander Godynyuk, RW Gary Leeman, D Michel Petit and LW Craig Berube to Calgary Flames for C Doug Gilmour, D Jamie Macoun, LW Kent Manderville, D Ric Nattress and G Rick Wamsley (January 2, 1992).

Season Team	League	REGULAR SEASON							PLAYOFFS					
		Gms.	Min.	W	L	T	GA	SO	Avg.	Gms.	Min.	W	L	GA	SO	Avg.
82-83—Hamilton A's	OJHL	40	2380				176	0	4.44	—	—	—	—	—	—	—
83-84—London	OHL	43	2308	18	19	0	173	0	4.50	6	327	3	3	27	0	4.95
84-85—London	OHL	50	2878	31	15	1	186	1	3.88	8	440	5	2	20	†1	*2.73
85-86—London	OHL	*57	*3281	25	26	3	215	0	3.93	5	299	0	4	25	0	5.02
86-87—Newmarket	AHL	50	2822	11	29	0	193	1	4.10	—	—	—	—	—	—	—
87-88—Newmarket	AHL	28	1587	10	14	3	103	0	3.89	—	—	—	—	—	—	—
—Toronto	NHL	5	249	1	2	1	17	0	4.10	—	—	—	—	—	—	—
88-89—Toronto	NHL	10	486	2	6	1	40	0	4.94	—	—	—	—	—	—	—
—Newmarket	AHL	37	2072	17	14	3	132	0	3.82	—	—	—	—	—	—	—
89-90—Newmarket	AHL	7	431	3	2	2	29	0	4.04	—	—	—	—	—	—	—
—Toronto	NHL	21	1101	9	6	3	81	0	4.41	2	108	1	1	6	0	3.33
90-91—Toronto	NHL	30	1430	6	13	3	92	1	3.86	—	—	—	—	—	—	—
—Newmarket	AHL	3	180	2	1	0	7	0	2.33	—	—	—	—	—	—	—
91-92—Toronto	NHL	8	413	1	5	1	20	1	2.91	—	—	—	—	—	—	—
—Calgary	NHL	12	587	3	2	2	37	0	3.78	—	—	—	—	—	—	—
NHL totals		86	4266	22	34	11	287	2	4.04	2	108	1	1	6	0	3.33

REEVES, KYLE
RW, BLUES

PERSONAL: Born May 12, 1971, at Swan River, Man. . . . 5-11/190. . . . Shoots right.
TRANSACTIONS/CAREER NOTES: Traded by Swift Current Broncos with G Don Blishen to Tri-City Americans for D Kelly Chotowetz (October 4, 1989). . . . Selected by St. Louis Blues in third round (second Blues pick, 64th overall) of NHL entry draft (June 22, 1991).
HONORS: Named to WHL West All-Star second team (1990-91).

Season Team	League	REGULAR SEASON					PLAYOFFS				
		Gms.	G	A	Pts.	Pen.	Gms.	G	A	Pts.	Pen.
88-89—Swift Current	WHL	68	19	21	40	49	—	—	—	—	—
89-90—Swift Current	WHL	2	1	1	2	2	—	—	—	—	—
—Tri-City Americans	WHL	67	67	36	103	94	7	2	1	3	8
90-91—Tri-City Americans	WHL	63	*89	40	129	146	3	1	3	4	10
91-92—Peoria	IHL	60	12	7	19	92	—	—	—	—	—

REICHEL, MARTIN
RW/C, OILERS

PERSONAL: Born November 7, 1973, at Most, Czechoslovakia. . . . 6-1/183. . . . Shoots left. . . . Brother of Robert Reichel, center, Calgary Flames.
TRANSACTIONS/CAREER NOTES: Selected by Edmonton Oilers in second round (second Oilers pick, 37th overall) of NHL entry draft (June 20, 1992).

Season Team	League	REGULAR SEASON					PLAYOFFS				
		Gms.	G	A	Pts.	Pen.	Gms.	G	A	Pts.	Pen.
90-91—Freiburg	Germany	23	7	8	15	19	—	—	—	—	—
91-92—Freiburg	Germany	27	15	16	31	8	4	1	1	2	4

REICHEL, ROBERT
C, FLAMES

PERSONAL: Born June 25, 1971, at Litvinov, Czechoslovakia. . . . 5-10/185. . . . Shoots right. . . . Brother of Martin Reichel, right winger/center in Edmonton Oilers system.
TRANSACTIONS/CAREER NOTES: Selected by Calgary Flames in fourth round (fifth Flames pick, 70th overall) of NHL entry draft (June 17, 1989).

Season Team	League	REGULAR SEASON					PLAYOFFS				
		Gms.	G	A	Pts.	Pen.	Gms.	G	A	Pts.	Pen.
88-89—Litvinov	Czech.		20	31	51		—	—	—	—	—
89-90—Litvinov	Czech.	52	49	34	83		—	—	—	—	—

Season Team	League	REGULAR SEASON					PLAYOFFS				
		Gms.	G	A	Pts.	Pen.	Gms.	G	A	Pts.	Pen.
90-91—Calgary	NHL	66	19	22	41	22	6	1	1	2	0
91-92—Calgary	NHL	77	20	34	54	32	—	—	—	—	—
NHL totals		143	39	56	95	54	6	1	1	2	0

REID, DAVID
LW, BRUINS

PERSONAL: Born May 15, 1964, at Toronto. . . . 6-1/205. . . . Shoots left.
TRANSACTIONS/CAREER NOTES: Selected by Boston Bruins as underage junior in third round (fourth Bruins pick, 60th overall) of NHL entry draft (June 9, 1982). . . . Underwent knee surgery (December 1986). . . . Separated shoulder (November 1987); missed 10 games. . . . Signed as free agent by Toronto Maple Leafs (August 1988). . . . Suffered from pneumonia (March 1992); missed 10 games.

Season Team	League	REGULAR SEASON					PLAYOFFS				
		Gms.	G	A	Pts.	Pen.	Gms.	G	A	Pts.	Pen.
81-82—Peterborough	OHL	68	10	32	42	41	9	2	3	5	11
82-83—Peterborough	OHL	70	23	34	57	33	4	3	1	4	0
83-84—Peterborough	OHL	60	33	64	97	12	—	—	—	—	—
—Boston	NHL	8	1	0	1	2	—	—	—	—	—
84-85—Hershey	AHL	43	10	14	24	6	—	—	—	—	—
—Boston	NHL	35	14	13	27	27	5	1	0	1	0
85-86—Moncton	AHL	26	14	18	32	4	—	—	—	—	—
—Boston	NHL	37	10	10	20	10	—	—	—	—	—
86-87—Boston	NHL	12	3	3	6	0	2	0	0	0	0
—Moncton	AHL	40	12	22	34	23	5	0	1	1	0
87-88—Maine	AHL	63	21	37	58	40	10	6	7	13	0
—Boston	NHL	3	0	0	0	0	—	—	—	—	—
88-89—Toronto	NHL	77	9	21	30	22	—	—	—	—	—
89-90—Toronto	NHL	70	9	19	28	9	3	0	0	0	0
90-91—Toronto	NHL	69	15	13	28	18	—	—	—	—	—
91-92—Maine	AHL	12	1	5	6	4	—	—	—	—	—
—Boston	NHL	43	7	7	14	27	15	2	5	7	4
NHL totals		354	68	86	154	115	25	3	5	8	4

REID, GRAYDEN
C, BLUES

PERSONAL: Born October 7, 1972, at Mississauga, Ont. . . . 6-0/185. . . . Shoots left.
TRANSACTIONS/CAREER NOTES: Bruised kidney (October 1989). . . . Selected by St. Louis Blues in fourth round (third Blues pick, 87th overall) of NHL entry draft (June 22, 1991).

Season Team	League	REGULAR SEASON					PLAYOFFS				
		Gms.	G	A	Pts.	Pen.	Gms.	G	A	Pts.	Pen.
87-88—Toronto Red Wings	MTHL		54	68	122	108	—	—	—	—	—
88-89—Guelph	OHL	66	7	13	20	34	—	—	—	—	—
89-90—Owen Sound	OHL	52	18	36	54	86	—	—	—	—	—
90-91—Owen Sound	OHL	66	23	74	97	58	—	—	—	—	—
91-92—Owen Sound	OHL	8	2	10	12	4	—	—	—	—	—
—Ottawa	OHL	54	10	26	36	18	11	0	2	2	2

REID, JARRET
C, WHALERS

PERSONAL: Born March 10, 1973, at Sault Ste. Marie, Ont. . . . 5-10/180. . . . Shoots right.
HIGH SCHOOL: St. Mary's College High School (Sault Ste. Marie, Ont.).
TRANSACTIONS/CAREER NOTES: Selected by Hartford Whalers in sixth round (sixth Whalers pick, 143rd overall) of NHL entry draft (June 20, 1992).

Season Team	League	REGULAR SEASON					PLAYOFFS				
		Gms.	G	A	Pts.	Pen.	Gms.	G	A	Pts.	Pen.
90-91—Sault Ste. Marie	OHL	63	37	29	66	18	14	5	12	17	14
91-92—Sault Ste. Marie	OHL	61	53	40	93	67	19	5	13	18	17

REISMAN, ERIC
D, BRUINS

PERSONAL: Born May 19, 1968, at Manhattan, N.Y. . . . 6-2/220. . . . Shoots left.
COLLEGE: Ohio State.
TRANSACTIONS/CAREER NOTES: Selected by Boston Bruins in 11th round (eighth Bruins pick, 228th overall) of NHL entry draft (June 11, 1988).

Season Team	League	REGULAR SEASON					PLAYOFFS				
		Gms.	G	A	Pts.	Pen.	Gms.	G	A	Pts.	Pen.
87-88—Ohio State	CCHA	29	0	3	3	45	—	—	—	—	—
88-89—Ohio State	CCHA	38	4	6	10	56	—	—	—	—	—
89-90—Ohio State	CCHA	39	1	2	3	91	—	—	—	—	—
90-91—Ohio State	CCHA	40	2	8	10	105	—	—	—	—	—
91-92—Johnstown	ECHL	32	0	12	12	50	—	—	—	—	—

RENBERG, MIKAEL
RW, FLYERS

PERSONAL: Born May 5, 1972, at Pitea, Sweden. . . . 6-2/183. . . . Shoots left.
TRANSACTIONS/CAREER NOTES: Selected by Philadelphia Flyers in second round (third Flyers pick, 40th overall) of NHL entry draft (June 16, 1990).

Season Team	League	REGULAR SEASON					PLAYOFFS				
		Gms.	G	A	Pts.	Pen.	Gms.	G	A	Pts.	Pen.
88-89—Pitea	Sweden	12	6	3	9		—	—	—	—	—
89-90—Pitea	Sweden	29	15	19	34		—	—	—	—	—

Season	Team	League	Gms.	G	A	Pts.	Pen.	Gms.	G	A	Pts.	Pen.
					REGULAR SEASON					**PLAYOFFS**		
90-91—Lulea		Sweden	29	11	6	17	12	—	—	—	—	—
91-92—Lulea		Sweden	38	8	15	23	20	—	—	—	—	—

REYNOLDS, BOBBY
C/LW, NORTH STARS

PERSONAL: Born July 14, 1967, at Flint, Mich. . . . 5-11/175. . . . Shoots left. . . . Full name: Robert DeHart Reynolds.
COLLEGE: Michigan State.
TRANSACTIONS/CAREER NOTES: Selected by Toronto Maple Leafs in 10th round (10th Maple Leafs pick, 190th overall) of NHL entry draft (June 15, 1985). . . . Traded by Maple Leafs to Washington Capitals for D Robert Mendel (March 5, 1991). . . . Traded by Capitals to Minnesota North Stars for future considerations (March 10, 1992).
HONORS: Named to CCHA All-Star second team (1987-88). . . . Named to NCAA All-America West first team (1988-89).

Season	Team	League	Gms.	G	A	Pts.	Pen.	Gms.	G	A	Pts.	Pen.
					REGULAR SEASON					**PLAYOFFS**		
83-84—St. Clair Shores		NAJHL	60	25	34	59		—	—	—	—	—
84-85—St. Clair Shores		NAJHL	43	20	30	50		—	—	—	—	—
85-86—Michigan State		CCHA	45	9	10	19	26	—	—	—	—	—
86-87—Michigan State		CCHA	40	20	13	33	40	—	—	—	—	—
87-88—Michigan State		CCHA	46	42	25	67	52	—	—	—	—	—
88-89—Michigan State		CCHA	47	36	41	77	78	—	—	—	—	—
89-90—Newmarket		AHL	66	22	28	50	55	—	—	—	—	—
—Toronto		NHL	7	1	1	2	0	—	—	—	—	—
90-91—Newmarket		AHL	65	24	22	46	59	—	—	—	—	—
—Baltimore		AHL	14	4	9	13	8	6	2	2	4	10
91-92—Baltimore		AHL	53	12	18	30	39	—	—	—	—	—
—Kalamazoo		IHL	13	8	10	18	19	12	5	4	9	4
NHL totals			7	1	1	2	0					

RHODES, DAMIAN
G, MAPLE LEAFS

PERSONAL: Born May 28, 1969, at St. Paul, Minn. . . . 6-0/170. . . . Shoots right. . . . Full name: Damian G. Rhodes.
HIGH SCHOOL: Richfield (Minn.).
COLLEGE: Michigan Tech.
TRANSACTIONS/CAREER NOTES: Selected by Toronto Maple Leafs in sixth round (sixth Maple Leafs pick, 112th overall) of NHL entry draft (June 13, 1987).

Season	Team	League	Gms.	Min.	W	L	T	GA	SO	Avg.	Gms.	Min.	W	L	GA	SO	Avg.
						REGULAR SEASON								**PLAYOFFS**			
85-86—Richfield H.S.		Minn. HS	16	720				56	0	4.67	—	—	—	—	—	—	—
86-87—Richfield H.S.		Minn. HS	19	673				51	1	4.55	—	—	—	—	—	—	—
87-88—Michigan Tech		WCHA	29	1623	16	10	1	114	0	4.21	—	—	—	—	—	—	—
88-89—Michigan Tech		WCHA	37	2216	15	22	0	163	0	4.41	—	—	—	—	—	—	—
89-90—Michigan Tech		WCHA	25	1358	6	17	0	119	0	5.26	—	—	—	—	—	—	—
90-91—Toronto		NHL	1	60	1	0	0	1	0	1.00	—	—	—	—	—	—	—
—Newmarket		AHL	38	2154	8	24	3	144	1	4.01	—	—	—	—	—	—	—
91-92—St. John's		AHL	43	2454	20	16	5	148	0	3.62	6	331	4	1	16	0	2.90
NHL totals			1	60	1	0	0	1	0	1.00							

RICCI, MIKE
C, NORDIQUES

PERSONAL: Born October 27, 1971, at Scarborough, Ont. . . . 6-0/190. . . . Shoots left.
TRANSACTIONS/CAREER NOTES: Separated right shoulder (December 1989). . . . Selected by Philadelphia Flyers in first round (first Flyers pick, fourth overall) of NHL entry draft (June 16, 1990). . . . Broke right index finger and thumb (October 4, 1990); missed nine games. . . . Traded by Flyers with G Ron Hextall, C Peter Forsberg, D Steve Duchesne, D Kerry Huffman, first-round pick in 1993 draft, cash and future considerations to Quebec Nordiques for C Eric Lindros (June 20, 1992); Flyers sent LW Chris Simon and first-round pick in 1994 draft to Nordiques to complete deal (July 21, 1992).
HONORS: Named to OHL All-Star second team (1988-89). . . . Won Red Tilson Trophy (1989-90). . . . Won William Hanley Trophy (1989-90). . . . Won Can.HL Player of the Year Award (1989-90). . . . Named to OHL All-Star first team (1989-90).

Season	Team	League	Gms.	G	A	Pts.	Pen.	Gms.	G	A	Pts.	Pen.
					REGULAR SEASON					**PLAYOFFS**		
87-88—Peterborough		OHL	41	24	37	61	20	8	5	5	10	4
88-89—Peterborough		OHL	60	54	52	106	43	17	19	16	35	18
89-90—Peterborough		OHL	60	52	64	116	39	12	5	7	12	26
90-91—Philadelphia		NHL	68	21	20	41	64	—	—	—	—	—
91-92—Philadelphia		NHL	78	20	36	56	93	—	—	—	—	—
NHL totals			146	41	56	97	157					

RICE, STEVE
RW, OILERS

PERSONAL: Born May 26, 1971, at Waterloo, Ont. . . . 6-0/210. . . . Shoots right. . . . Full name: Steven Rice.
TRANSACTIONS/CAREER NOTES: Underwent knee surgery (October 1986). . . . Selected by New York Rangers in first round (first Rangers pick, 20th overall) of NHL entry draft (June 17, 1989). . . . Suffered back spasms (September 14, 1989). . . . Injured left shoulder (October 1990). . . . Traded by Rangers with C Bernie Nicholls, LW Louie DeBrusk and future considerations to Edmonton Oilers for C Mark Messier and future considerations (October 4, 1991); Rangers later traded D David Shaw to Oilers for D Jeff Beukeboom to complete the deal (November 12, 1991).
HONORS: Named to Memorial Cup All-Star team (1989-90). . . . Named to OHL All-Star second team (1990-91).

Season	Team	League	Gms.	G	A	Pts.	Pen.	Gms.	G	A	Pts.	Pen.
87-88	—Kitchener	OHL	59	11	14	25	43	4	0	1	1	0
88-89	—Kitchener	OHL	64	36	31	67	42	5	2	1	3	8
89-90	—Kitchener	OHL	58	39	37	76	102	16	4	8	12	24
90-91	—New York Rangers	NHL	11	1	1	2	4	2	2	1	3	6
	—Binghamton	AHL	8	4	1	5	12	5	2	0	2	2
	—Kitchener	OHL	29	30	30	60	43	6	5	6	11	2
91-92	—Edmonton	NHL	3	0	0	0	2	—	—	—	—	—
	—Cape Breton	AHL	45	32	20	52	38	5	4	4	8	10
NHL totals			14	1	1	2	6	2	2	1	3	6

R

RICHARD, JEAN-MARC
D

PERSONAL: Born October 8, 1966, at St. Raymond, Que. . . . 5-11/178. . . . Shoots left.

TRANSACTIONS/CAREER NOTES: Signed as free agent by Quebec Nordiques (April 1987). . . . Loaned to Fort Wayne Komets (March 1991); became free agent when contract expired with Nordiques at end of season. . . . Signed as free agent by Komets (September 1991).

HONORS: Won Emile (Butch) Bouchard Trophy (1986-87). . . . Named to QMJHL All-Star first team (1985-86 and 1986-87). . . . Won Governors Trophy (1991-92). . . . Named to IHL All-Star first team (1991-92).

Season	Team	League	Gms.	G	A	Pts.	Pen.	Gms.	G	A	Pts.	Pen.
83-84	—Chicoutimi	QMJHL	61	1	20	21	41	—	—	—	—	—
84-85	—Chicoutimi	QMJHL	68	10	61	71	57	—	—	—	—	—
85-86	—Chicoutimi	QMJHL	72	19	88	107	111	9	3	5	8	14
86-87	—Chicoutimi	QMJHL	67	21	81	102	105	16	6	25	31	28
87-88	—Fredericton	AHL	68	14	42	56	52	7	2	1	3	4
	—Quebec	NHL	4	2	1	3	2	—	—	—	—	—
88-89	—Halifax	AHL	57	8	25	33	38	4	1	0	1	4
89-90	—Quebec	NHL	1	0	0	0	0	—	—	—	—	—
	—Halifax	AHL	40	1	24	25	38	—	—	—	—	—
90-91	—Halifax	AHL	80	7	41	48	76	—	—	—	—	—
	—Fort Wayne	IHL	1	0	0	0	0	19	3	9	12	8
91-92	—Fort Wayne	IHL	82	18	68	86	109	7	0	5	5	20
NHL totals			5	2	1	3	2					

RICHARDS, TODD
D, WHALERS

PERSONAL: Born October 20, 1966, at Robbinsdale, Minn. . . . 6-0/190. . . . Shoots right.

HIGH SCHOOL: Armstrong (Plymouth, Minn.).

COLLEGE: Minnesota.

TRANSACTIONS/CAREER NOTES: Selected by Montreal Canadiens in second round (third Canadiens pick, 33rd overall) of NHL entry draft (June 15, 1985). . . . Traded by Canadiens to Hartford Whalers for future considerations (October 1990). . . . Bruised knee (October 14, 1991); missed two games.

HONORS: Named to WCHA All-Star second team (1987-88 and 1988-89). . . . Named to NCAA All-America West second team (1988-89). . . . Named to NCAA All-Tournament team (1988-89).

Season	Team	League	Gms.	G	A	Pts.	Pen.	Gms.	G	A	Pts.	Pen.
84-85	—Armstrong H.S.	Minn. H.S.	24	10	23	33	24	—	—	—	—	—
85-86	—University of Minnesota	WCHA	38	6	23	29	38	—	—	—	—	—
86-87	—University of Minnesota	WCHA	49	8	43	51	70	—	—	—	—	—
87-88	—University of Minnesota	WCHA	34	10	30	40	26	—	—	—	—	—
88-89	—University of Minnesota	WCHA	46	6	32	38	60	—	—	—	—	—
89-90	—Sherbrooke	AHL	71	6	18	24	73	5	1	2	3	6
90-91	—Fredericton	AHL	3	0	1	1	2	—	—	—	—	—
	—Springfield	AHL	71	10	41	51	62	14	2	8	10	2
	—Hartford	NHL	2	0	4	4	2	6	0	0	0	2
91-92	—Hartford	NHL	6	0	0	0	2	5	0	3	3	4
	—Springfield	AHL	43	6	23	29	33	8	0	3	3	2
NHL totals			8	0	4	4	4	11	0	3	3	6

RICHARDSON, LUKE
D, OILERS

PERSONAL: Born March 26, 1969, at Ottawa. . . . 6-4/210. . . . Shoots left. . . . Full name: Luke Glen Richardson.

TRANSACTIONS/CAREER NOTES: Selected by Toronto Maple Leafs as underage junior in first round (first Maple Leafs pick, seventh overall) of NHL entry draft (June 13, 1987). . . . Traded by Maple Leafs with LW Vincent Damphousse, G Peter Ing, C Scott Thornton and future considerations to Edmonton Oilers for G Grant Fuhr, LW Glenn Anderson and LW Craig Berube (September 19, 1991). . . . Strained clavicular joint (February 11, 1992); missed three games.

Season	Team	League	Gms.	G	A	Pts.	Pen.	Gms.	G	A	Pts.	Pen.
84-85	—Ottawa Jr. B	ODHA	35	5	26	31	72	—	—	—	—	—
85-86	—Peterborough	OHL	63	6	18	24	57	16	2	1	3	50
86-87	—Peterborough	OHL	59	13	32	45	70	12	0	5	5	24
87-88	—Toronto	NHL	78	4	6	10	90	2	0	0	0	0
88-89	—Toronto	NHL	55	2	7	9	106	—	—	—	—	—
89-90	—Toronto	NHL	67	4	14	18	122	5	0	0	0	22

Season Team	League	REGULAR SEASON					PLAYOFFS				
		Gms.	G	A	Pts.	Pen.	Gms.	G	A	Pts.	Pen.
90-91—Toronto	NHL	78	1	9	10	238	—	—	—	—	—
91-92—Edmonton	NHL	75	2	19	21	118	16	0	5	5	45
NHL totals		353	13	55	68	674	23	0	5	5	67

RICHER, STEPHANE
D, LIGHTNING

PERSONAL: Born April 28, 1966, at Hull, Que.... 6-2/212.... Shoots right.... Full name: Stephane J.G. Richer.
TRANSACTIONS/CAREER NOTES: Signed as free agent by Montreal Canadiens (January 9, 1988).... Signed as free agent by Los Angeles Kings (July 11, 1990).... Signed as free agent by Canadiens (September 1, 1991).... Signed as free agent by Tampa Bay Lightning (July 29, 1992).

Season Team	League	REGULAR SEASON					PLAYOFFS				
		Gms.	G	A	Pts.	Pen.	Gms.	G	A	Pts.	Pen.
83-84—Hull	QMJHL	70	8	38	46	42	—	—	—	—	—
84-85—Hull	QMJHL	67	21	56	77	98	—	—	—	—	—
85-86—Hull	QMJHL	71	14	52	66	166	—	—	—	—	—
86-87—Hull	QMJHL	33	6	22	28	74	8	3	4	7	17
87-88—Baltimore	AHL	22	0	3	3	6	—	—	—	—	—
—Sherbrooke	AHL	41	4	7	11	46	5	1	0	1	10
88-89—Sherbrooke	AHL	70	7	26	33	158	6	1	2	3	18
89-90—Sherbrooke	AHL	60	10	12	22	85	12	4	0	13	16
90-91—Phoenix	IHL	67	11	38	49	48	11	4	6	10	6
—New Haven	AHL	3	0	1	1	0	—	—	—	—	—
91-92—Fredericton	AHL	80	17	47	64	74	7	0	5	5	18

RICHER, STEPHANE
RW, DEVILS

PERSONAL: Born June 7, 1966, at Buckingham, Que.... 6-2/200.... Shoots right.... Full name: Stephane Joseph Jean Richer.
TRANSACTIONS/CAREER NOTES: Selected by Montreal Canadiens as underage junior in second round (third Canadiens pick, 29th overall) of NHL entry draft (June 9, 1984).... Traded by Granby Bisons with LW Greg Choules to Chicoutimi Sagueneens for C Stephane Roy, RW Marc Bureau, Lee Duhemee, Sylvain Demers and D Rene L'Ecuyer (January 1985).... Sprained ankle (November 18, 1985); missed 13 games.... Bruised right hand (March 12, 1988).... Broke right thumb (April 1988).... Sprained right thumb (September 1988).... Suspended 10 games by NHL for slashing (November 16, 1988).... Suffered from the flu (March 15, 1989).... Bruised right shoulder (September 1989).... Bruised left foot (February 1990).... Injured left ankle (April 21, 1990).... Injured knee (December 12, 1990).... Traded by Canadiens with RW Tom Chorske to New Jersey Devils for LW Kirk Muller and G Roland Melanson (September 20, 1991).... Injured groin (October 22, 1991); missed two games.... Injured left knee (March 24, 1992); missed three games.
HONORS: Named QMJHL Rookie of the Year (1983-84).... Named to QMJHL All-Star second team (1984-85).... Named to AHL All-Star second team (1991-92).

Season Team	League	REGULAR SEASON					PLAYOFFS				
		Gms.	G	A	Pts.	Pen.	Gms.	G	A	Pts.	Pen.
83-84—Granby	QMJHL	67	39	37	76	58	3	1	1	2	4
84-85—Granby/Chicoutimi	QMJHL	57	61	59	120	71	12	13	13	26	25
—Montreal	NHL	1	0	0	0	0	—	—	—	—	—
—Sherbrooke	AHL	—	—	—	—	—	9	6	3	9	10
85-86—Montreal	NHL	65	21	16	37	50	16	4	1	5	23
86-87—Sherbrooke	AHL	12	10	4	14	11	—	—	—	—	—
—Montreal	NHL	57	20	19	39	80	5	3	2	5	0
87-88—Montreal	NHL	72	50	28	78	72	8	7	5	12	6
88-89—Montreal	NHL	68	25	35	60	61	21	6	5	11	14
89-90—Montreal	NHL	75	51	40	91	46	9	7	3	10	2
90-91—Montreal	NHL	75	31	30	61	53	13	9	5	14	6
91-92—New Jersey	NHL	74	29	35	64	25	7	1	2	3	0
NHL totals		487	227	203	430	387	79	37	23	60	51

RICHTER, BARRY
D/RW, WHALERS

PERSONAL: Born September 11, 1970, at Madison, Wis.... 6-2/190.... Shoots left.... Full name: Barron Patrick Richter.... Son of Pat Richter, tight end, Washington Redskins of National Football League (1963-70).
HIGH SCHOOL: Culver Military Academy (Ind.).
COLLEGE: Wisconsin.
TRANSACTIONS/CAREER NOTES: Selected by Hartford Whalers in second round (second Whalers pick, 32nd overall) of NHL entry draft (June 11, 1988).

Season Team	League	REGULAR SEASON					PLAYOFFS				
		Gms.	G	A	Pts.	Pen.	Gms.	G	A	Pts.	Pen.
86-87—Culver Military Academy	Indiana H.S.	35	19	26	45		—	—	—	—	—
87-88—Culver Military Academy	Indiana H.S.	35	24	29	53	18	—	—	—	—	—
88-89—Culver Military Academy	Indiana H.S.	19	21	29	50	16	—	—	—	—	—
89-90—University of Wisconsin	WCHA	42	13	23	36	26	—	—	—	—	—
90-91—University of Wisconsin	WCHA	43	15	20	35	42	—	—	—	—	—
91-92—University of Wisconsin	WCHA	43	10	29	39	62	—	—	—	—	—

RICHTER, MIKE
G, RANGERS

PERSONAL: Born September 22, 1966, at Philadelphia.... 5-11/182.... Shoots left.... Full name: Michael Thomas Richter.
HIGH SCHOOL: Northwood School (Lake Placid, N.Y.).
COLLEGE: Wisconsin.

TRANSACTIONS/CAREER NOTES: Selected by New York Rangers in second round (second Rangers pick, 28th overall) of NHL entry draft (June 15, 1985).... Bruised thigh (January 30, 1992); missed 12 games.
HONORS: Won WCHA Rookie of the Year Award (1985-86).... Named to WCHA All-Star second team (1985-86 and 1986-87).

Season Team	League	Gms.	Min.	W	L	T	GA	SO	Avg.	Gms.	Min.	W	L	GA	SO	Avg.
84-85—Northwood School	N.Y. H.S.	24	1374				52	2	2.27	—	—	—	—	—	—	—
85-86—Univ. of Wisconsin	WCHA	24	1394	14	9	0	92	1	3.96	—	—	—	—	—	—	—
86-87—Univ. of Wisconsin	WCHA	36	2136	19	16	1	126	0	3.54	—	—	—	—	—	—	—
87-88—U.S. Olympic Team	Int'l	33	1789	19	9	3	101	0	3.39	—	—	—	—	—	—	—
—Colorado	IHL	22	1298	16	5	0	68	1	3.14	10	536	5	3	35	0	3.92
88-89—Denver	IHL	*57	3031	23	26	0	*217	4	4.30	4	210	0	4	21	0	6.00
89-90—New York Rangers	NHL	23	1320	12	5	5	66	0	3.00	6	330	3	2	19	0	3.45
—Flint	IHL	13	782	7	4	2	49	0	3.76	—	—	—	—	—	—	—
90-91—New York Rangers	NHL	45	2596	21	13	7	135	0	3.12	6	313	2	4	14	†1	2.68
91-92—New York Rangers	NHL	41	2298	23	12	2	119	3	3.11	7	412	4	2	24	1	3.50
NHL totals		109	6214	56	30	14	320	3	3.09	19	1055	9	8	57	2	3.24

RIDLEY, MIKE
C, CAPITALS

PERSONAL: Born July 8, 1963, at Winnipeg, Man.... 6-1/200.... Shoots left.
COLLEGE: Manitoba.
TRANSACTIONS/CAREER NOTES: Signed as free agent by New York Rangers (September 1985).... Traded by Rangers with LW Kelly Miller and RW Bobby Crawford to Washington Capitals for C Bobby Carpenter and second-round pick in 1989 draft (RW Jason Prosofsky) (January 1987).... Collapsed left lung (March 9, 1990); missed six games.... Bruised ribs (April 5, 1990).
HONORS: Won Senator Joseph A. Sullivan Trophy (1983-84).... Named to NHL All-Rookie team (1985-86).

Season Team	League	Gms.	G	A	Pts.	Pen.	Gms.	G	A	Pts.	Pen.
83-84—University of Manitoba	CWUAA	46	39	41	80		—	—	—	—	—
84-85—University of Manitoba	CWUAA	30	29	38	67	48	—	—	—	—	—
85-86—New York Rangers	NHL	80	22	43	65	69	16	6	8	14	26
86-87—New York Rangers	NHL	38	16	20	36	20	—	—	—	—	—
—Washington	NHL	40	15	19	34	20	7	2	1	3	6
87-88—Washington	NHL	70	28	31	59	22	14	6	5	11	10
88-89—Washington	NHL	80	41	48	89	49	6	0	5	5	2
89-90—Washington	NHL	74	30	43	73	27	14	3	4	7	8
90-91—Washington	NHL	79	23	48	71	26	11	3	4	7	8
91-92—Washington	NHL	80	29	40	69	38	7	0	11	11	0
NHL totals		541	204	292	496	271	75	20	38	58	60

RIENDEAU, VINCE
G, RED WINGS

PERSONAL: Born April 20, 1966, at St. Hyacinthe, Que.... 5-10/185.... Shoots left.... Full name: Vincent Riendeau.
COLLEGE: Sherbrooke (Que.).
TRANSACTIONS/CAREER NOTES: Signed as free agent by Montreal Canadiens (October 1985).... Suffered skin rash (November 1987).... Broke leg (April 10, 1988).... Traded by Canadiens with LW Sergio Momesso to St. Louis Blues for LW Jocelyn Lemieux, G Darrell May and second-round pick in 1989 draft (D Patrice Brisebois) (August 1988).... Suffered compound fracture of little finger of left hand (October 4, 1989); missed 10 games.... Pulled groin (February 17, 1991); missed seven games.... Traded by Blues to Detroit Red Wings for D Rick Zombo (October 18, 1991).... Sprained knee (October 25, 1991); missed 59 games.
HONORS: Named to QMJHL All-Star second team (1985-86).... Won Harry (Hap) Holmes Memorial Trophy (1986-87).... Shared Harry (Hap) Holmes Memorial Trophy with Jocelyn Perreault (1987-88).

Season Team	League	Gms.	Min.	W	L	T	GA	SO	Avg.	Gms.	Min.	W	L	GA	SO	Avg.
83-84—Verdun	QMJHL	41	2133				147	†2	4.14	—	—	—	—	—	—	—
84-85—Univ. of Sherbrooke	Can. Coll.															
85-86—Drummondville	QMJHL	57	3336	33	20	3	215	†2	3.87	*23	*1271	10	13	*106	1	5.00
86-87—Sherbrooke	AHL	41	2363	25	14	0	114	2	2.89	13	742	8	5	47	0	3.80
87-88—Sherbrooke	AHL	44	2521	27	13	3	112	*4	*2.67	2	127	0	2	7	0	3.31
—Montreal	NHL	1	36	0	0	0	5	0	8.33	—	—	—	—	—	—	—
88-89—St. Louis	NHL	32	1842	11	15	5	108	0	3.52	—	—	—	—	—	—	—
89-90—St. Louis	NHL	43	2551	17	19	5	149	1	3.50	8	397	3	4	24	0	3.63
90-91—St. Louis	NHL	44	2671	29	9	6	134	3	3.01	13	687	6	7	35	†1	3.06
91-92—St. Louis	NHL	3	157	1	2	0	11	0	4.20	—	—	—	—	—	—	—
—Detroit	NHL	2	87	2	0	0	2	0	1.38	2	73	1	0	4	0	3.29
—Adirondack	AHL	3	179	2	1	0	8	0	2.68	—	—	—	—	—	—	—
NHL totals		125	7344	60	45	16	409	4	3.34	23	1157	10	11	63	1	3.27

RIVET, CRAIG
D, CANADIENS

PERSONAL: Born September 13, 1974, at North Bay, Ont.... 6-2/172.... Shoots right.
TRANSACTIONS/CAREER NOTES: Selected by Montreal Canadiens in third round (fourth Canadiens pick, 68th overall) of NHL entry draft (June 20, 1992).

Season Team	League	Gms.	G	A	Pts.	Pen.	Gms.	G	A	Pts.	Pen.
90-91—Barrie Jr. B	OHA	42	9	17	26	55	—	—	—	—	—
91-92—Kingston	OHL	66	5	21	26	97	—	—	—	—	—

ROBERGE, MARIO
LW, CANADIENS

PERSONAL: Born January 31, 1964, at Quebec City. . . . 5-11/185. . . . Shoots left. . . . Brother of Serge Roberge, right winger, Quebec Nordiques.
TRANSACTIONS/CAREER NOTES: Signed as free agent by Sherbrooke Canadiens (January 1988). . . . Injured thigh (December 22, 1991).

		REGULAR SEASON					PLAYOFFS				
Season Team	League	Gms.	G	A	Pts.	Pen.	Gms.	G	A	Pts.	Pen.
81-82—Quebec	QMJHL	8	0	3	3	2	—	—	—	—	—
82-83—Quebec	QMJHL	69	3	27	30	153	—	—	—	—	—
83-84—Quebec	QMJHL	60	12	28	40	253	—	—	—	—	—
84-85—						Did not play.					
85-86—						Did not play.					
86-87—						Did not play.					
87-88—Port Aux Basques	Nova Scotia	35	25	64	89	152	—	—	—	—	—
88-89—Sherbrooke	AHL	58	4	9	13	249	6	0	2	2	8
89-90—Sherbrooke	AHL	73	13	27	40	247	12	5	2	7	53
90-91—Fredericton	AHL	68	12	27	39	†365	2	0	2	2	5
—Montreal	NHL	5	0	0	0	21	12	0	0	0	24
91-92—Montreal	NHL	20	2	1	3	62	—	—	—	—	—
—Fredericton	AHL	6	1	2	3	20	7	0	2	2	20
NHL totals		25	2	1	3	83	12	0	0	0	24

ROBERGE, SERGE
RW, NORDIQUES

PERSONAL: Born March 31, 1965, at Quebec City. . . . 6-1/195. . . . Shoots right. . . . Brother of Mario Roberge, left winger, Montreal Canadiens.
TRANSACTIONS/CAREER NOTES: Signed as free agent by Montreal Canadiens (January 25, 1988).

		REGULAR SEASON					PLAYOFFS				
Season Team	League	Gms.	G	A	Pts.	Pen.	Gms.	G	A	Pts.	Pen.
82-83—Quebec	QMJHL	9	0	0	0	30	—	—	—	—	—
—Hull	QMJHL	22	0	4	4	115	—	—	—	—	—
83-84—Drummondville	QMJHL	58	1	7	8	287	10	0	2	2	*105
84-85—Drummondville	QMJHL	45	8	19	27	299	—	—	—	—	—
85-86—						Did not play.					
86-87—Virginia	ACHL	49	9	16	25	*353	12	4	2	6	*104
87-88—Sherbrooke	AHL	30	0	1	1	130	5	0	0	0	21
88-89—Sherbrooke	AHL	65	5	7	12	352	6	0	1	1	10
89-90—Sherbrooke	AHL	66	8	5	13	*343	12	2	0	2	44
90-91—Halifax	AHL	52	0	5	5	152	—	—	—	—	—
—Quebec	NHL	9	0	0	0	24	—	—	—	—	—
91-92—Halifax	AHL	66	2	8	10	319	—	—	—	—	—
NHL totals		9	0	0	0	24					

ROBERTS, DAVID
LW, BLUES

PERSONAL: Born May 28, 1970, at Alameda, Calif. . . . 6-0/185. . . . Shoots left. . . . Full name: David Lance Roberts. . . . Son of Doug Roberts, defenseman, four NHL teams (1965-66 through 1974-75) and New England Whalers of WHA (1975-76 through 1976-77); and nephew of Gordie Roberts, defenseman, Boston Bruins.
HIGH SCHOOL: Avon Old Farms School For Boys (Avon, Conn.).
COLLEGE: Michigan.
TRANSACTIONS/CAREER NOTES: Selected by St. Louis Blues in sixth round (fifth Blues pick, 114th overall) of NHL entry draft (June 17, 1989).
HONORS: Named CCHA Rookie of the Year (1989-90). . . . Named to CCHA All-Rookie team (1989-90). . . . Named to NCAA All-America West second team (1990-91). . . . Named to CCHA All-Star second team (1990-91).

		REGULAR SEASON					PLAYOFFS				
Season Team	League	Gms.	G	A	Pts.	Pen.	Gms.	G	A	Pts.	Pen.
87-88—Avon Old Farms H.S.	Conn. H.S.		18	39	57		—	—	—	—	—
88-89—Avon Old Farms H.S.	Conn. H.S.		28	48	76		—	—	—	—	—
89-90—University of Michigan	CCHA	42	21	32	53	46	—	—	—	—	—
90-91—University of Michigan	CCHA	43	26	45	71	44	—	—	—	—	—
91-92—University of Michigan	CCHA	44	16	42	58	68	—	—	—	—	—

ROBERTS, GARY
LW, FLAMES

PERSONAL: Born May 23, 1966, at North York, Ont. . . . 6-1/190. . . . Shoots left.
TRANSACTIONS/CAREER NOTES: Selected by Calgary Flames as underage junior in first round (first Flames pick, 12th overall) of NHL entry draft (June 9, 1984). . . . Injured back (January 1989). . . . Suffered whiplash (November 9, 1991); missed one game.
HONORS: Named to OHL All-Star second team (1984-85 and 1985-86).

		REGULAR SEASON					PLAYOFFS				
Season Team	League	Gms.	G	A	Pts.	Pen.	Gms.	G	A	Pts.	Pen.
82-83—Ottawa	OHL	53	12	8	20	83	5	1	0	1	19
83-84—Ottawa	OHL	48	27	30	57	144	13	10	7	17	*62
84-85—Ottawa	OHL	59	44	62	106	186	5	2	8	10	10
—Moncton	AHL	7	4	2	6	7	—	—	—	—	—
85-86—Ottawa	OHL	24	26	25	51	83	—	—	—	—	—
—Guelph	OHL	23	18	15	33	65	20	18	13	31	43
86-87—Moncton	AHL	38	20	18	38	72	—	—	—	—	—
—Calgary	NHL	32	5	10	15	85	2	0	0	0	4

R

Season Team	League	REGULAR SEASON					PLAYOFFS				
		Gms.	G	A	Pts.	Pen.	Gms.	G	A	Pts.	Pen.
87-88—Calgary	NHL	74	13	15	28	282	9	2	3	5	29
88-89—Calgary	NHL	71	22	16	38	250	22	5	7	12	57
89-90—Calgary	NHL	78	39	33	72	222	6	2	5	7	41
90-91—Calgary	NHL	80	22	31	53	252	7	1	3	4	18
91-92—Calgary	NHL	76	53	37	90	207	—	—	—	—	—
NHL totals		411	154	142	296	1298	46	10	18	28	149

ROBERTS, GORDIE

D, BRUINS

PERSONAL: Born October 2, 1957, at Detroit.... 6-1/195.... Shoots left.... Full name: Gordon Roberts.... Brother of Doug Roberts, defenseman, four NHL teams (1965-66 through 1974-75) and New England Whalers of WHA (1975-76 through 1976-77); and uncle of David Roberts, left winger in St. Louis Blues system.

TRANSACTIONS/CAREER NOTES: Signed by New England Whalers (September 1975).... Selected by Montreal Canadiens from Whalers in third round (seventh Canadiens pick, 54th overall) of NHL amateur draft (June 14, 1977).... Selected by Hartford Whalers from Canadiens in NHL expansion draft (June 22, 1979).... Traded by Whalers to Minnesota North Stars for LW Mike Fidler (December 16, 1980).... Bruised hip (April 1984).... Injured foot (November 13, 1985); missed four games.... Dislocated shoulder (October 1986).... Bruised shoulder (January 1988).... Traded by North Stars to Philadelphia Flyers for fourth-round pick in 1989 draft (C Jean-Francois Quintin) (February 8, 1988).... Traded by Flyers to St. Louis Blues for fourth-round pick in 1989 draft (LW Reid Simpson) (March 1988).... Traded by Blues to Pittsburgh Penguins for future considerations (October 27, 1990).... Signed as free agent by Boston Bruins (June 19, 1992).

Season Team	League	REGULAR SEASON					PLAYOFFS				
		Gms.	G	A	Pts.	Pen.	Gms.	G	A	Pts.	Pen.
73-74—Detroit Junior Red Wings	SOJHL	70	25	55	80	340	—	—	—	—	—
74-75—Victoria	WCHL	53	19	45	64	145	12	1	9	10	42
75-76—New England	WHA	77	3	19	22	102	17	2	9	11	36
76-77—New England	WHA	77	13	33	46	169	5	2	2	4	6
77-78—New England	WHA	78	15	46	61	118	14	0	5	5	29
78-79—New England	WHA	79	11	46	57	113	10	0	4	4	10
79-80—Hartford	NHL	80	8	28	36	89	3	1	1	2	2
80-81—Hartford	NHL	27	2	11	13	81	—	—	—	—	—
—Minnesota	NHL	50	6	31	37	94	19	1	5	6	17
81-82—Minnesota	NHL	79	4	30	34	119	4	0	3	3	27
82-83—Minnesota	NHL	80	3	41	44	103	9	1	5	6	14
83-84—Minnesota	NHL	77	8	45	53	132	15	3	7	10	23
84-85—Minnesota	NHL	78	6	36	42	112	9	1	6	7	6
85-86—Minnesota	NHL	76	2	21	23	101	5	0	4	4	8
86-87—Minnesota	NHL	67	3	10	13	68	—	—	—	—	—
87-88—Minnesota	NHL	48	1	10	11	103	—	—	—	—	—
—Philadelphia	NHL	11	1	2	3	15	—	—	—	—	—
—St. Louis	NHL	11	1	3	4	25	10	1	2	3	33
88-89—St. Louis	NHL	77	2	24	26	90	10	1	7	8	8
89-90—St. Louis	NHL	75	3	14	17	140	10	0	2	2	26
90-91—Peoria	IHL	6	0	8	8	4	—	—	—	—	—
—St. Louis	NHL	3	0	1	1	8	—	—	—	—	—
—Pittsburgh	NHL	61	3	12	15	70	24	1	2	3	63
91-92—Pittsburgh	NHL	73	2	22	24	87	19	0	2	2	32
WHA totals		311	42	144	186	502	46	4	20	24	81
NHL totals		973	55	341	396	1437	137	10	46	56	259

ROBINSON, LARRY

D

PERSONAL: Born June 2, 1951, at Winchester, Ont.... 6-4/225.... Shoots left.... Full name: Larry Clark Robinson.... Brother of Moe Robinson, defenseman, Montreal Canadiens (1979-80).

TRANSACTIONS/CAREER NOTES: Selected by Montreal Canadiens from Kitchener Rangers in second round (fourth Canadiens pick, 20th overall) of NHL amateur draft (June 10, 1971).... Injured knee; missed part of 1978-79 season.... Separated right shoulder (March 6, 1980).... Injured groin (October 1980).... Separated left shoulder (November 14, 1980).... Broke nose (January 8, 1981).... Injured left shoulder (October 1982).... Suffered skin infection behind right knee (October 1983).... Hyperextended left elbow (March 1985).... Strained ligaments in right ankle (March 9, 1987).... Broke right leg (August 1987).... Sprained right wrist (December 1987).... Hyperextended knee (May 23, 1989). ... Signed as free agent by Los Angeles Kings (July 26, 1989).... Suffered food poisoning (March 1990); missed games.... Injured eye (November 26, 1991); missed two games.

HONORS: Named to NHL All-Star first team (1969-70).... Won James Norris Memorial Trophy (1976-77 and 1979-80).... Named to THE SPORTING NEWS All-Star first team (1976-77 through 1979-80).... Named to NHL All-Star first team (1976-77, 1978-79 and 1979-80).... Won Conn Smythe Trophy (1977-78).... Named to NHL All-Star second team (1977-78, 1980-81 and 1985-86).... Named to THE SPORTING NEWS All-Star second team (1980-81, 1981-82 and 1985-86).

RECORDS: Holds NHL career playoff records for most games—227; and most consecutive years in playoffs—20 (1972-73 through 1991-92).... Shares NHL career playoff record for most years in playoffs—20 (1972-73 through 1991-92).

Season Team	League	REGULAR SEASON					PLAYOFFS				
		Gms.	G	A	Pts.	Pen.	Gms.	G	A	Pts.	Pen.
68-69—Brockville	COJHL	—	—	—	—	—	—	—	—	—	—
69-70—Brockville	COJHL	40	22	29	51	74	—	—	—	—	—
70-71—Kitchener	OHA Jr. A	61	12	39	51	65	—	—	—	—	—
71-72—Nova Scotia	AHL	74	10	14	24	54	15	2	10	12	31
72-73—Nova Scotia	AHL	38	6	33	39	33	—	—	—	—	—
—Montreal	NHL	36	2	4	6	20	11	1	4	5	9

Season	Team	League	Gms.	G	A	Pts.	Pen.	Gms.	G	A	Pts.	Pen.
			REGULAR SEASON					**PLAYOFFS**				
73-74—Montreal	NHL	78	6	20	26	66	6	0	1	1	26
74-75—Montreal	NHL	80	14	47	61	76	11	0	4	4	27
75-76—Montreal	NHL	80	10	30	40	59	13	3	3	6	10
76-77—Montreal	NHL	77	19	66	85	45	14	2	10	12	12
77-78—Montreal	NHL	80	13	52	65	39	15	4	*17	†21	6
78-79—Montreal	NHL	67	16	45	61	33	16	6	9	15	8
79-80—Montreal	NHL	72	14	61	75	39	10	0	4	4	2
80-81—Montreal	NHL	65	12	38	50	37	3	0	1	1	2
81-82—Montreal	NHL	71	12	47	59	41	5	0	1	1	8
82-83—Montreal	NHL	71	14	49	63	33	3	0	0	0	2
83-84—Montreal	NHL	74	9	34	43	39	15	0	5	5	22
84-85—Montreal	NHL	76	14	33	47	44	12	3	8	11	8
85-86—Montreal	NHL	78	19	63	82	39	20	0	13	13	22
86-87—Montreal	NHL	70	13	37	50	44	17	3	17	20	6
87-88—Montreal	NHL	53	6	34	40	30	11	1	4	5	4
88-89—Montreal	NHL	74	4	26	30	22	21	2	8	10	12
89-90—Los Angeles	NHL	64	7	32	39	34	10	2	3	5	10
90-91—Los Angeles	NHL	62	1	22	23	16	12	1	4	5	15
91-92—Los Angeles	NHL	66	3	10	13	37	?	0	0	0	0
NHL totals		1384	208	750	958	793	227	28	116	144	211

ROBINSON, ROB

D, LIGHTNING

PERSONAL: Born April 19, 1967, at St. Catharines, Ont. . . . 6-1/214. . . . Shoots left. . . . Full name: Robert Robinson. . . . Son of Doug Robinson, left winger, Chicago Blackhawks, New York Rangers and Los Angeles Kings (1964-65 through 1970-71).
COLLEGE: Miami of Ohio.
TRANSACTIONS/CAREER NOTES: Selected by St. Louis Blues in sixth round (sixth Blues pick, 117th overall) of NHL entry draft (June 13, 1987). . . . Traded by Blues with G Pat Jablonski, RW Darin Kimble and RW Steve Tuttle to Tampa Bay Lightning for future considerations (June 19, 1992).
HONORS: Named to IHL All-Star second team (1990-91).

Season	Team	League	Gms.	G	A	Pts.	Pen.	Gms.	G	A	Pts.	Pen.
			REGULAR SEASON					**PLAYOFFS**				
85-86—Miami of Ohio	CCHA	38	1	9	10	24	—	—	—	—	—
86-87—Miami of Ohio	CCHA	33	3	5	8	32	—	—	—	—	—
87-88—Miami of Ohio	CCHA	35	1	3	4	56	—	—	—	—	—
88-89—Miami of Ohio	CCHA	30	3	4	7	42	—	—	—	—	—
—Peoria	IHL	11	2	0	2	6	—	—	—	—	—
89-90—Peoria	IHL	60	2	11	13	72	5	0	1	1	10
90-91—Peoria	IHL	79	2	21	23	42	19	0	6	6	8
91-92—St. Louis	NHL	22	0	1	1	8	—	—	—	—	—
—Peoria	IHL	35	1	10	11	29	10	0	2	2	12
NHL totals		22	0	1	1	8					

ROBINSON, SCOTT

RW, NORTH STARS

PERSONAL: Born March 29, 1964, at 100 Mile House, B.C. . . . 6-2/180. . . . Shoots left.
COLLEGE: Calgary.
TRANSACTIONS/CAREER NOTES: Signed as free agent by Minnesota North Stars (September 27, 1988).

Season	Team	League	Gms.	G	A	Pts.	Pen.	Gms.	G	A	Pts.	Pen.
			REGULAR SEASON					**PLAYOFFS**				
82-83—Seattle	WHL	63	14	13	27	151	4	3	0	3	9
83-84—Seattle	WHL	44	17	18	35	105	5	0	1	1	25
84-85—Seattle	WHL	64	44	53	97	106	—	—	—	—	—
85-86—University of Calgary	CWUAA	18	3	9	12	61	—	—	—	—	—
86-87—University of Calgary	CWUAA	19	12	14	26	95	—	—	—	—	—
87-88—University of Calgary	CWUAA	21	14	14	28	64	—	—	—	—	—
88-89—Kalamazoo	IHL	49	14	17	31	129	6	1	2	3	21
89-90—Kalamazoo	IHL	47	13	12	25	97	10	4	7	11	21
—Minnesota	NHL	1	0	0	0	2	—	—	—	—	—
90-91—Kalamazoo	IHL	27	7	9	16	36	11	2	1	3	32
91-92—Kalamazoo	IHL	78	29	27	56	58	11	2	6	8	*86
NHL totals		1	0	0	0	2					

ROBISON, JEFF

D, KINGS

PERSONAL: Born June 3, 1970, at Norwood, Mass. . . . 6-1/183. . . . Shoots left. . . . Full name: Jeffrey Arthur Robison.
HIGH SCHOOL: Mount St. Charles Academy (Woonsocket, R.I.).
COLLEGE: Providence.
TRANSACTIONS/CAREER NOTES: Broke wrist (January 1988). . . . Selected by Los Angeles Kings in fifth round (fifth Kings pick, 91st overall) of NHL entry draft (June 11, 1988).

Season	Team	League	Gms.	G	A	Pts.	Pen.	Gms.	G	A	Pts.	Pen.
			REGULAR SEASON					**PLAYOFFS**				
86-87—Mount St. Charles H.S.	R.I.H.S.	24	11	14	25		—	—	—	—	—
87-88—Mount St. Charles H.S.	R.I.H.S.		5	30	35		—	—	—	—	—

R

Season	Team	League	REGULAR SEASON					PLAYOFFS				
			Gms.	G	A	Pts.	Pen.	Gms.	G	A	Pts.	Pen.
88-89—Providence College		Hockey East	41	0	5	5	36	—	—	—	—	—
89-90—Providence College		Hockey East	35	2	8	10	16	—	—	—	—	—
90-91—Providence College		Hockey East	36	3	8	11	34	—	—	—	—	—
91-92—Providence College		Hockey East	33	0	3	3	20	—	—	—	—	—

ROBITAILLE, LUC
LW, KINGS

PERSONAL: Born February 17, 1966, at Montreal. . . . 6-0/ 190. . . . Shoots left.
TRANSACTIONS/CAREER NOTES: Selected by Los Angeles as underage junior in ninth round (ninth Kings pick, 171st overall) of NHL entry draft (June 9, 1984). . . . Suspended four games by NHL games for cross-checking from behind (November 10, 1990).

HONORS: Named to QMJHL All-Star second team (1984-85). . . . Won Can.HL Player of the Year Award (1985-86). . . . Shared Guy Lafleur Trophy with Sylvain Cote (1985-86). . . . Named to QMJHL All-Star first team (1985-86). . . . Won Calder Memorial Trophy (1986-87). . . . Named to THE SPORTING NEWS All-Star second team (1986-87 and 1991-92). . . . Named to NHL All-Star second team (1986-87 and 1991-92). . . . Named to NHL All-Rookie team (1986-87). . . . Named to THE SPORTING NEWS All-Star first team (1987-88 through 1990-91). . . . Named to NHL All-Star first team (1987-88 through 1990-91).

Season	Team	League	REGULAR SEASON					PLAYOFFS				
			Gms.	G	A	Pts.	Pen.	Gms.	G	A	Pts.	Pen.
83-84—Hull		QMJHL	70	32	53	85	48	—	—	—	—	—
84-85—Hull		QMJHL	64	55	94	149	115	5	4	2	6	27
85-86—Hull		QMJHL	63	68	*123	†191	93	15	17	27	*44	28
86-87—Los Angeles......................		NHL	79	45	39	84	28	5	1	4	5	2
87-88—Los Angeles......................		NHL	80	53	58	111	82	5	2	5	7	18
88-89—Los Angeles......................		NHL	78	46	52	98	65	11	2	6	8	10
89-90—Los Angeles......................		NHL	80	52	49	101	38	10	5	5	10	10
90-91—Los Angeles......................		NHL	76	45	46	91	68	12	12	4	16	22
91-92—Los Angeles......................		NHL	80	44	63	107	95	6	3	4	7	12
NHL totals.................................			473	285	307	592	376	49	25	28	53	74

ROCHEFORT, NORMAND
D, RANGERS

PERSONAL: Born January 28, 1961, at Trois-Rivieres, Que. . . . 6-1/212. . . . Shoots left. . . . Nephew of Leon Rochefort, right winger, seven NHL teams (1960-61 through 1975-76).
TRANSACTIONS/CAREER NOTES: Selected by Quebec Nordiques as underage junior in second round (first Nordiques pick, 24th overall) of NHL entry draft (June 11, 1980). . . . Injured neck (November 1980). . . . Injured knee; missed parts of 1982-83 season. . . . Sprained ankle (October 19, 1985). . . . Separated shoulder (February 8, 1986). . . . Injured neck and upper back (October 1987). . . . Bruised left foot (January 1988). . . . Sprained right knee (February 1988). . . . Traded by Nordiques with C Jason Lafreniere to New York Rangers for C Walt Poddubny, D Bruce Bell, D Jari Gronstrand and fourth-round pick in 1989 draft (August 1, 1988). . . . Sprained right knee (October 1988). . . . Reinjured knee and underwent surgery (November 9, 1988). . . . Reinjured knee and underwent reconstructive surgery (February 5, 1989). . . . Injured left knee cartilage and underwent surgery (October 6, 1990); missed 18 games. . . . Suffered compressed fracture of second lumbar vertebrae (March 13, 1991). . . . Developed tendinitis in right knee (October 1991); missed 14 games. . . . Suffered infection to right elbow (February 25, 1992); missed four games.
HONORS: Named to QMJHL All-Star second team (1979-80).

Season	Team	League	REGULAR SEASON					PLAYOFFS				
			Gms.	G	A	Pts.	Pen.	Gms.	G	A	Pts.	Pen.
77-78—Trois-Rivieres.................		QMJHL	72	9	37	46	36	—	—	—	—	—
78-79—Trois-Rivieres.................		QMJHL	72	17	57	74	80	13	3	11	14	17
79-80—Trois-Rivieres.................		QMJHL	20	5	25	30	22	—	—	—	—	—
—Quebec		QMJHL	52	8	39	47	68	5	1	3	4	8
80-81—Quebec		QMJHL	9	2	6	8	14	—	—	—	—	—
—Quebec		NHL	56	3	7	10	51	5	0	0	0	4
81-82—Quebec		NHL	72	4	14	18	115	16	0	2	2	10
82-83—Quebec		NHL	62	6	17	23	40	1	0	0	0	2
83-84—Quebec		NHL	75	2	22	24	47	6	1	0	1	6
84-85—Quebec		NHL	73	3	21	24	74	18	2	1	3	8
85-86—Quebec		NHL	26	5	4	9	30	—	—	—	—	—
86-87—Quebec		NHL	70	6	9	15	46	13	2	1	3	26
87-88—Quebec		NHL	46	3	10	13	49	—	—	—	—	—
88-89—New York Rangers		NHL	11	1	5	6	18	—	—	—	—	—
89-90—Flint		IHL	7	3	2	5	4	—	—	—	—	—
—New York Rangers		NHL	31	3	1	4	24	10	2	1	3	26
90-91—New York Rangers		NHL	44	3	7	10	35	—	—	—	—	—
91-92—New York Rangers		NHL	26	0	2	2	31	—	—	—	—	—
NHL totals.................................			592	39	119	158	560	69	7	5	12	82

ROENICK, JEREMY
C, BLACKHAWKS

PERSONAL: Born January 17, 1970, at Boston. . . . 6-0/ 170. . . . Shoots right.
HIGH SCHOOL: Thayer Academy (Braintree, Mass.).
TRANSACTIONS/CAREER NOTES: Selected by Chicago Blackhawks in first round (first Blackhawks pick, eighth overall) of NHL entry draft (June 11, 1988). . . . Sprained knee ligaments (January 9, 1989); missed one month.
HONORS: Named to QMJHL All-Star second team (1988-89). . . . Named NHL Rookie of the Year by THE SPORTING NEWS (1989-1990).

Season Team	League	REGULAR SEASON					PLAYOFFS				
		Gms.	G	A	Pts.	Pen.	Gms.	G	A	Pts.	Pen.
86-87—Thayer Academy	Mass. H.S.	24	31	34	65	—	—	—	—	—	—
87-88—Thayer Academy	Mass. H.S.		34	50	84	—	—	—	—	—	—
88-89—Hull	QMJHL	28	34	36	70	14	—	—	—	—	—
—Chicago	NHL	20	9	9	18	4	10	1	3	4	7
89-90—Chicago	NHL	78	26	40	66	54	20	11	7	18	8
90-91—Chicago	NHL	79	41	53	94	80	6	3	5	8	4
91-92—Chicago	NHL	80	53	50	103	98	18	12	10	22	12
NHL totals................................		257	129	152	281	236	54	27	25	52	31

ROHLICEK, JEFF
LW, BLACKHAWKS

R

PERSONAL: Born January 27, 1966, at Park Ridge, Ill. . . . 6-0/180. . . . Shoots left.
HIGH SCHOOL: Maine West (Des Plaines, Ill.).
TRANSACTIONS/CAREER NOTES: Selected by Vancouver Canucks as underage junior in second round (second Canucks pick, 31st overall) of NHL entry draft (June 9, 1984). . . . Traded by Canucks to New York Islanders for D Jack Capuano (March 6, 1990). . . . Released by Islanders (September 10, 1990). . . . Signed as free agent by Los Angeles Kings (October 1990). . . . Traded by Kings to Chicago Blackhawks for D Rick Lanz (December 2, 1991).
HONORS: Named to WHL All-Star second team (1983-84 and 1984-85). . . . Named to IHL All-Star first team (1988-89).

Season Team	League	REGULAR SEASON					PLAYOFFS				
		Gms.	G	A	Pts.	Pen.	Gms.	G	A	Pts.	Pen.
82-83—Main West H.S.	Ill. H.S.	25	60	60	120		—	—	—	—	—
83-84—Portland	WHL	71	44	53	97	22	14	13	8	21	10
84-85—Portland	WHL	16	5	13	18	2	—	—	—	—	—
—Kelowna Wings	WHL	49	34	39	73	24	6	3	6	9	2
85-86—Spokane Chiefs	WHL	57	50	52	102	39	9	6	2	8	16
86-87—Fredericton	AHL	70	19	37	56	22	—	—	—	—	—
87-88—Vancouver........................	NHL	7	0	0	0	4	—	—	—	—	—
—Fredericton	AHL	65	26	31	57	50	—	—	—	—	—
88-89—Vancouver........................	NHL	2	0	0	0	4	—	—	—	—	—
—Milwaukee......................	IHL	78	47	63	110	106	11	6	6	12	8
89-90—Springfield.......................	AHL	12	1	2	3	4	7	3	2	5	6
—Milwaukee......................	IHL	53	22	26	48	37	—	—	—	—	—
90-91—New Haven	AHL	4	1	1	2	6	—	—	—	—	—
—Phoenix	IHL	74	29	31	60	67	10	7	6	13	12
91-92—Phoenix	IHL	23	5	11	16	32	—	—	—	—	—
—Indianapolis	IHL	59	25	32	57	28	—	—	—	—	—
NHL totals................................		9	0	0	0	8					

ROHLOFF, JON
D, BRUINS

PERSONAL: Born October 3, 1969, at Mankato, Minn. . . . 6-0/200. . . . Shoots right. . . . Full name: Jon Richard Rohloff.
HIGH SCHOOL: Grand Rapids (Minn.).
COLLEGE: Minnesota-Duluth.
TRANSACTIONS/CAREER NOTES: Selected by Boston Bruins in ninth round (seventh Bruins pick, 186th overall) of NHL entry draft (June 11, 1988).

Season Team	League	REGULAR SEASON					PLAYOFFS				
		Gms.	G	A	Pts.	Pen.	Gms.	G	A	Pts.	Pen.
86-87—Grand Rapids H.S.............	Minn. H.S.	21	12	23	35	16	—	—	—	—	—
87-88—Grand Rapids H.S.............	Minn. H.S.	23	10	13	23		—	—	—	—	—
88-89—Minnesota-Duluth	WCHA	39	1	2	3	44	—	—	—	—	—
89-90—Minnesota-Duluth	WCHA	5	0	1	1	6	2	0	0	0	2
90-91—Minnesota-Duluth	WCHA	32	6	11	17	38	—	—	—	—	—
91-92—Minnesota-Duluth	WCHA	27	9	9	18	48	—	—	—	—	—

ROLSTON, BRIAN
C, DEVILS

PERSONAL: Born February 21, 1973, at Flint, Mich. . . . 6-1/175. . . . Shoots left.
TRANSACTIONS/CAREER NOTES: Selected by New Jersey Devils in first round (second Devils pick, 11th overall) of NHL entry draft (June 22, 1991).

Season Team	League	REGULAR SEASON					PLAYOFFS				
		Gms.	G	A	Pts.	Pen.	Gms.	G	A	Pts.	Pen.
89-90—Detroit Compuware..........	NAJHL	40	36	37	73	57	—	—	—	—	—
90-91—Detroit Compuware..........	NAJHL	36	49	46	95	14	—	—	—	—	—
91-92—Lake Superior State	CCHA	41	18	28	46	16	—	—	—	—	—

ROMANIUK, RUSS
LW, JETS

PERSONAL: Born June 9, 1970, at Winnipeg, Man. . . . 6-0/185. . . . Shoots left. . . . Full name: Russell James Romaniuk.
COLLEGE: North Dakota.
TRANSACTIONS/CAREER NOTES: Suffered chip fracture of left knee (December 1987). . . . Sprained right shoulder (February 1988). . . . Selected by Winnipeg Jets in second round (second Jets pick, 31st overall) of NHL entry draft (June 11, 1988). . . . Fractured knuckle (October 27, 1991); missed six games. . . . Sprained wrist (December 10, 1991); missed one game.
HONORS: Named to WCHA All-Tournament team (1989-90). . . . Named to WCHA All-Star first team (1990-91).

Season Team	League	Gms.	G	A	Pts.	Pen.	Gms.	G	A	Pts.	Pen.
		REGULAR SEASON					PLAYOFFS				
87-88—St. Boniface	MJHL			Statistics unavailable.							
88-89—Univ. of North Dakota	WCHA	39	17	14	31	32	—	—	—	—	—
89-90—Canadian National Team	Int'l	3	1	0	1	0	—	—	—	—	—
—Univ. of North Dakota	WCHA	45	36	15	51	54	—	—	—	—	—
90-91—Univ. of North Dakota	WCHA	39	40	28	68	30	—	—	—	—	—
91-92—Winnipeg	NHL	27	3	5	8	18	—	—	—	—	—
—Moncton	AHL	45	16	15	31	25	10	5	4	9	19
NHL totals		27	3	5	8	18					

RONAN, ED
RW, CANADIENS

PERSONAL: Born March 21, 1968, at Quincy, Mass. . . . 6-0/197. . . . Shoots right. . . . Full name: Edward Ronan.

TRANSACTIONS/CAREER NOTES: Selected by Montreal Canadiens in 11th round (13th Canadiens pick, 227th overall) of NHL entry draft (June 13, 1987).

Season Team	League	Gms.	G	A	Pts.	Pen.	Gms.	G	A	Pts.	Pen.
		REGULAR SEASON					PLAYOFFS				
87-88—Boston University	Hockey East	31	2	5	7	20	—	—	—	—	—
88-89—Boston University	Hockey East	36	4	11	15	34	—	—	—	—	—
89-90—Boston University	Hockey East	44	17	23	40	50	—	—	—	—	—
90-91—Boston University	Hockey East	41	16	19	35	38	—	—	—	—	—
91-92—Fredericton	AHL	78	25	34	59	82	7	5	1	6	6
—Montreal	NHL	3	0	0	0	0	—	—	—	—	—
NHL totals		3	0	0	0	0					

RONNING, CLIFF
C, CANUCKS

PERSONAL: Born October 1, 1965, at Vancouver, B.C. . . . 5-8/175. . . . Shoots left.

TRANSACTIONS/CAREER NOTES: Selected by St. Louis Blues as underage junior in seventh round (ninth Blues pick, 134th overall) of NHL entry draft (June 9, 1984). . . . Injured groin (November 1988). . . . Agreed to play in Italy for 1989-90 season (August 1989). . . . Fractured right index finger (November 12, 1990); missed 12 games. . . . Traded by Blues with LW Geoff Courtnall, D Robert Dirk, LW Sergio Momesso and fifth-round pick in 1992 draft (RW Brian Loney) to Vancouver Canucks for C Dan Quinn and D Garth Butcher (March 5, 1991).

HONORS: Won Stewart (Butch) Paul Memorial Trophy (1983-84). . . . Named to WHL All-Star second team (1983-84). . . . Won Most Valuable Player Trophy (1984-85). . . . Won Bob Brownridge Memorial Trophy (1984-85). . . . Won Frank Boucher Memorial Trophy (1984-85). . . . Named to WHL All-Star first team (1984-85).

Season Team	League	Gms.	G	A	Pts.	Pen.	Gms.	G	A	Pts.	Pen.
		REGULAR SEASON					PLAYOFFS				
82-83—New Westminster	BCJHL	52	82	68	150	42	—	—	—	—	—
83-84—New Westminster	WHL	71	69	67	136	10	9	8	13	21	10
84-85—New Westminster	WHL	70	*89	108	*197	20	11	10	14	24	4
85-86—Team Canada	Int'l	71	55	63	118	53	—	—	—	—	—
—St. Louis	NHL	—	—	—	—	—	5	1	1	2	2
86-87—Canadian National Team	Int'l	26	16	16	32	12	—	—	—	—	—
—St. Louis	NHL	42	11	14	25	6	4	0	1	1	0
87-88—St. Louis	NHL	26	5	8	13	12	—	—	—	—	—
88-89—St. Louis	NHL	64	24	31	55	18	7	1	3	4	0
—Peoria	IHL	12	11	20	31	8	—	—	—	—	—
89-90—Asiago	Italy	42	76	60	136	30	6	7	12	19	4
90-91—St. Louis	NHL	48	14	18	32	10	—	—	—	—	—
—Vancouver	NHL	11	6	6	12	0	6	6	3	9	12
91-92—Vancouver	NHL	80	24	47	71	42	13	8	5	13	6
NHL totals		271	84	124	208	88	35	16	13	29	20

ROUSE, BOB
D, MAPLE LEAFS

PERSONAL: Born June 18, 1964, at Surrey, B.C. . . . 6-2/210. . . . Shoots right.

TRANSACTIONS/CAREER NOTES: Selected by Minnesota North Stars as underage junior in fourth round (third North Stars pick, 80th overall) of NHL entry draft (June 9, 1982). . . . Suffered hip contusions (January 1988). . . . Traded by North Stars with RW Dino Ciccarelli to Washington Capitals for RW Mike Gartner and D Larry Murphy (March 7, 1989). . . . Sprained right knee (December 12, 1989); missed eight games. . . . Traded by Capitals with C Peter Zezel to Toronto Maple Leafs for D Al Iafrate (January 16, 1991). . . . Broke collarbone (February 16, 1991).

HONORS: Won Top Defenseman Trophy (1983-84). . . . Named to WHL All-Star first team (1983-84).

Season Team	League	Gms.	G	A	Pts.	Pen.	Gms.	G	A	Pts.	Pen.
		REGULAR SEASON					PLAYOFFS				
80-81—Billings	WHL	70	0	13	13	116	5	0	0	0	2
81-82—Billings	WHL	71	7	22	29	209	5	0	2	2	10
82-83—Nanaimo	WHL	29	7	20	27	86	—	—	—	—	—
—Lethbridge	WHL	42	8	30	38	82	20	2	13	15	55
83-84—Lethbridge	WHL	71	18	42	60	101	5	0	1	1	28
—Minnesota	NHL	1	0	0	0	0	—	—	—	—	—
84-85—Springfield	AHL	8	0	3	3	6	—	—	—	—	—
—Minnesota	NHL	63	2	9	11	113	—	—	—	—	—
85-86—Minnesota	NHL	75	1	14	15	151	3	0	0	0	2
86-87—Minnesota	NHL	72	2	10	12	179	—	—	—	—	—

Season Team	League	REGULAR SEASON Gms.	G	A	Pts.	Pen.	PLAYOFFS Gms.	G	A	Pts.	Pen.
87-88—Minnesota	NHL	74	0	12	12	168	—	—	—	—	—
88-89—Minnesota	NHL	66	4	13	17	124	6	2	0	2	4
—Washington	NHL	13	0	2	2	36	15	2	3	5	47
89-90—Washington	NHL	70	4	16	20	123	—	—	—	—	—
90-91—Washington	NHL	47	5	15	20	65	—	—	—	—	—
—Toronto	NHL	13	2	4	6	10	—	—	—	—	—
91-92—Toronto	NHL	79	3	19	22	97	—	—	—	—	—
NHL totals		573	23	114	137	1066	24	4	3	7	53

ROUSSEL, DOMINIC
G, FLYERS

PERSONAL: Born February 22, 1970, at Hull, Que.... 6-1/180.... Shoots left.
TRANSACTIONS/CAREER NOTES: Selected by Philadelphia Flyers as underage junior in third round (fourth Flyers pick, 63rd overall) of NHL entry draft (June 11, 1988).

Season Team	League	REGULAR SEASON Gms.	Min.	W	L	T	GA	SO	Avg.	PLAYOFFS Gms.	Min.	W	L	GA	SO	Avg.
87-88—Trois-Rivieres	QMJHL	51	2905	18	25	4	251	0	5.18	—	—	—	—	—	—	—
88-89—Shawinigan	QMJHL	46	2555	24	15	2	171	0	4.02	10	638	6	4	36	0	3.39
89-90—Shawinigan	QMJHL	37	1985	20	14	1	133	0	4.02	2	120	1	1	12	0	6.00
90-91—Hershey	AHL	45	2507	20	14	7	151	1	3.61	7	366	3	4	21	0	3.44
91-92—Hershey	AHL	35	2040	15	11	6	121	1	3.56	—	—	—	—	—	—	—
—Philadelphia	NHL	17	922	7	8	2	40	1	2.60	—	—	—	—	—	—	—
NHL totals		17	922	7	8	2	40	1	2.60							

ROUSSON, BORIS
G, RANGERS

PERSONAL: Born June 14, 1970, at Val d'Or, Que.... 6-2/195.
TRANSACTIONS/CAREER NOTES: Signed as free agent by New York Rangers (March 31, 1991).

Season Team	League	REGULAR SEASON Gms.	Min.	W	L	T	GA	SO	Avg.	PLAYOFFS Gms.	Min.	W	L	GA	SO	Avg.
87-88—Laval	QMJHL	2	104	0	1	0	14	0	8.08	—	—	—	—	—	—	—
88-89—Laval	QMJHL	22	1187	12	7	0	88	0	4.45	6	295	4	1	15	0	3.05
89-90—Granby	QMJHL	39	2076	10	26	0	158	0	4.57	—	—	—	—	—	—	—
90-91—Granby	QMJHL	*63	*3693	28	25	6	190	2	3.09	—	—	—	—	—	—	—
91-92—Binghamton	AHL	38	2261	16	15	6	123	1	3.26	—	—	—	—	—	—	—

ROY, ALLAIN
G, JETS

PERSONAL: Born February 6, 1970, at Campbelltown, N.B.... 5-10/165.... Shoots left.... Full name: Allain Roland Roy.
COLLEGE: Harvard.
TRANSACTIONS/CAREER NOTES: Selected by Winnipeg Jets in fourth round (sixth Jets pick, 69th overall) of NHL entry draft (June 17, 1989).
HONORS: Named to NCAA All-Tournament team (1988-89).

Season Team	League	REGULAR SEASON Gms.	Min.	W	L	T	GA	SO	Avg.	PLAYOFFS Gms.	Min.	W	L	GA	SO	Avg.
88-89—Harvard University	ECAC	16	952	14	2	0	40	0	2.52	—	—	—	—	—	—	—
89-90—Harvard University	ECAC	15	867	7	8	0	54	1	3.74	—	—	—	—	—	—	—
—Can. National Team	Int'l	3	180				11		3.67	—	—	—	—	—	—	—
90-91—Harvard University	ECAC	14	821	7	5	2	45	*1	3.29	—	—	—	—	—	—	—
91-92—Harvard University	ECAC	15	919	9	4	2	39	1	2.55	—	—	—	—	—	—	—

ROY, JEAN-YVES
RW, RANGERS

PERSONAL: Born February 17, 1969, at Rosemere, Que.... 5-10/185.... Shoots left.
COLLEGE: Maine.
TRANSACTIONS/CAREER NOTES: Signed as free agent by New York Rangers (July 20, 1992).
HONORS: Named to All-America East second team (1989-90).... Named to All-America East first team (1990-91 and 1991-92).... Named to Hockey East All-Star first team (1990-91).... Named to Hockey East All-Star second team (1991-92).

Season Team	League	REGULAR SEASON Gms.	G	A	Pts.	Pen.	PLAYOFFS Gms.	G	A	Pts.	Pen.
89-90—University of Maine	Hockey East	46	39	26	65	52	—	—	—	—	—
90-91—University of Maine	Hockey East	43	37	45	82	26	—	—	—	—	—
91-92—University of Maine	Hockey East	35	32	24	56	62	—	—	—	—	—

ROY, PATRICK
G, CANADIENS

PERSONAL: Born October 5, 1965, at Quebec City.... 6-0/182.... Shoots left.
TRANSACTIONS/CAREER NOTES: Selected by Monteral Canadiens as underage junior in third round (fourth Canadiens pick, 51st overall) of NHL entry draft (June 9, 1984).... Suspended eight games by NHL for slashing (October 19, 1987).... Sprained medial collateral ligaments in left knee (December 12, 1990); missed nine games.... Tore left ankle ligaments (January 27, 1991); missed 14 games.... Reinjured left ankle (March 16, 1991).
HONORS: Won Conn Smythe Trophy (1985-86).... Named to NHL All-Rookie team (1985-86).... Shared William M. Jennings Trophy with Brian Hayward (1986-87 through 1988-89).... Named to NHL All-Star second team (1987-88 and 1990-91).... Named to THE SPORTING NEWS All-Star first team (1988-89, 1989-90, and 1991-92).... Won Trico Goaltender Award (1988-89 and 1989-90).... Named to NHL All-Star first team (1988-89, 1989-90 and 1991-92).... Won Vezina Trophy

R

(1988-89, 1989-90 and 1991-92).... Named to THE SPORTING NEWS All-Star second team (1990-91).... Won William M. Jennings Trophy (1991-92).

Season Team	League	REGULAR SEASON								PLAYOFFS						
		Gms.	Min.	W	L	T	GA	SO	Avg.	Gms.	Min.	W	L	GA	SO	Avg.
82-83—Granby	QMJHL	54	2808				293	0	6.26	—	—	—	—	—	—	—
83-84—Granby	QMJHL	61	3585	29	29	1	265	0	4.44	4	244	0	4	22	0	5.41
84-85—Granby	QMJHL	44	2463	16	25	1	228	0	5.55	—	—	—	—	—	—	—
—Montreal	NHL	1	20	1	0	0	0	0	0.00	—	—	—	—	—	—	—
—Sherbrooke	AHL	1	60	1	0	0	4	0	4.00	*13	*769	10	3	37	0	*2.89
85-86—Montreal	NHL	47	2651	23	18	3	148	1	3.35	20	1218	*15	5	39	†1	1.92
86-87—Montreal	NHL	46	2686	22	16	6	131	1	2.93	6	330	4	2	22	0	4.00
87-88—Montreal	NHL	45	2586	23	12	9	125	3	2.90	8	430	3	4	24	0	3.35
88-89—Montreal	NHL	48	2744	33	5	6	113	4	*2.47	19	1206	13	6	42	2	*2.09
89-90—Montreal	NHL	54	3173	31	16	5	134	3	2.53	11	641	5	6	26	1	2.43
90-91—Montreal	NHL	48	2835	25	15	6	128	1	2.71	13	785	7	5	40	0	3.06
91-92—Montreal	NHL	67	3935	36	22	8	155	†5	*2.36	11	686	4	7	30	1	2.62
NHL totals		356	20630	194	104	43	934	18	2.72	88	5296	51	35	223	5	2.53

ROY, SIMON
D, OILERS

PERSONAL: Born June 14, 1974, at Montreal.... 6-1/181.... Shoots left.
TRANSACTIONS/CAREER NOTES: Selected by Edmonton Oilers in third round (third Oilers pick, 61st overall) of NHL entry draft (June 20, 1992).

Season Team	League	REGULAR SEASON					PLAYOFFS				
		Gms.	G	A	Pts.	Pen.	Gms.	G	A	Pts.	Pen.
91-92—Shawinigan	QMJHL	63	3	24	27	24	10	1	4	5	9

RUBACHUK, BRAD
C, SABRES

PERSONAL: Born June 11, 1970, at Winnipeg, Man.... 5-11/180.... Shoots left.
TRANSACTIONS/CAREER NOTES: Selected by Buffalo Sabres in 12th round (11th Sabres pick, 250th overall) of NHL entry draft (June 16, 1990).

Season Team	League	REGULAR SEASON					PLAYOFFS				
		Gms.	G	A	Pts.	Pen.	Gms.	G	A	Pts.	Pen.
88-89—Lethbridge	WHL	66	19	13	32	161	6	3	1	4	25
89-90—Lethbridge	WHL	67	37	36	73	179	16	3	7	10	51
90-91—Lethbridge	WHL	70	64	68	132	237	16	*14	14	28	55
91-92—Rochester	AHL	70	18	16	34	201	13	4	0	4	19

RUCHTY, MATT
LW, DEVILS

PERSONAL: Born November 27, 1969, at Kitchener, Ont.... 6-1/210.... Shoots left.... Full name: Matthew Kerry Ruchty.
COLLEGE: Bowling Green State.
TRANSACTIONS/CAREER NOTES: Selected by New Jersey Devils in fourth round (fourth Devils pick, 65th overall) of NHL entry draft (June 11, 1988).

Season Team	League	REGULAR SEASON					PLAYOFFS				
		Gms.	G	A	Pts.	Pen.	Gms.	G	A	Pts.	Pen.
87-88—Bowling Green State	CCHA	41	6	15	21	78	—	—	—	—	—
88-89—Bowling Green State	CCHA	43	11	21	32	110	—	—	—	—	—
89-90—Bowling Green State	CCHA	42	28	21	49	135	—	—	—	—	—
90-91—Bowling Green State	CCHA	38	13	18	31	147	—	—	—	—	—
91-92—Utica	AHL	73	9	14	23	250	4	0	0	0	25

RUCINSKY, MARTIN
LW, NORDIQUES

PERSONAL: Born March 11, 1971, at Most, Czechoslovakia.... 5-11/178.... Shoots left.
TRANSACTIONS/CAREER NOTES: Selected by Edmonton Oilers in first round (second Oilers pick, 20th overall) of NHL entry draft (June 22, 1991).... Traded by Oilers to Quebec Nordiques for G Ron Tugnutt and LW Brad Zavisha (March 10, 1992).

Season Team	League	REGULAR SEASON					PLAYOFFS				
		Gms.	G	A	Pts.	Pen.	Gms.	G	A	Pts.	Pen.
88-89—CHZ Litvinov	Czech.	3	1	0	1	2	—	—	—	—	—
89-90—CHZ Litvinov	Czech.	47	12	6	18		—	—	—	—	—
90-91—CHZ Litvinov	Czech.	49	23	18	41	79	—	—	—	—	—
—Czechoslovakia Jr.	Czech.	7	9	5	14	2	—	—	—	—	—
91-92—Cape Breton	AHL	35	11	12	23	34	—	—	—	—	—
—Edmonton	NHL	2	0	0	0	0	—	—	—	—	—
—Halifax	AHL	7	1	1	2	6	—	—	—	—	—
—Quebec	NHL	4	1	1	2	2	—	—	—	—	—
NHL totals		6	1	1	2	2					

RUFF, JASON
LW, BLUES

PERSONAL: Born January 27, 1970, at Kelowna, B.C.... 6-3/195.... Shoots left.
TRANSACTIONS/CAREER NOTES: Underwent heel surgery (May 1988).... Selected by St. Louis Blues in fifth round (third Blues pick, 96th overall) of NHL entry draft (June 16, 1990).
HONORS: Named to WHL All-Star first team (1990-91).

Season Team	League	REGULAR SEASON					PLAYOFFS				
		Gms.	G	A	Pts.	Pen.	Gms.	G	A	Pts.	Pen.
86-87—Kelowna	BCJHL	45	25	20	45	70	—	—	—	—	—
87-88—Lethbridge	WHL	69	25	22	47	109	—	—	—	—	—
88-89—Lethbridge	WHL	69	42	38	80	127	—	—	—	—	—
89-90—Lethbridge	WHL	72	55	64	119	114	19	9	10	19	18
90-91—Lethbridge	WHL	66	61	75	136	154	16	12	17	29	18
—Peoria	IHL	—	—	—	—	—	5	0	0	0	2
91-92—Peoria	IHL	67	27	45	72	148	10	7	7	14	19

RUFF, LINDY
D, SABRES

PERSONAL: Born February 17, 1960, at Warburg, Alta.... 6-2/200.... Shoots left.... Full name: Lindy Cameron Ruff.

TRANSACTIONS/CAREER NOTES: Selected by Buffalo Sabres as underage junior in second round (second Sabres pick, 32nd overall) of NHL entry draft (August 9, 1979).... Fractured ankle (December 1980).... Broke hand (March 1983).... Injured shoulder (January 14, 1984).... Separated shoulder (October 26, 1984).... Broke left clavicle (March 5, 1986).... Sprained shoulder (November 1988).... Traded by Sabres to New York Rangers for fifth-round pick in 1990 draft (D Richard Smehlik) (March 7, 1989).... Fractured rib (January 23, 1990); missed seven games.... Broke nose (March 21, 1990).... Bruised left thigh (April 1990).... Signed as free agent by Sabres (September 1991).

Season Team	League	REGULAR SEASON					PLAYOFFS				
		Gms.	G	A	Pts.	Pen.	Gms.	G	A	Pts.	Pen.
76-77—Taber	AJHL	60	13	33	46	112	—	—	—	—	—
—Lethbridge	WCHL	2	0	2	2	0	—	—	—	—	—
77-78—Lethbridge	WCHL	66	9	24	33	219	8	2	8	10	4
78-79—Lethbridge	WHL	24	9	18	27	108	6	0	1	1	0
79-80—Buffalo	NHL	63	5	14	19	38	8	1	1	2	19
80-81—Buffalo	NHL	65	8	18	26	121	6	3	1	4	23
81-82—Buffalo	NHL	79	16	32	48	194	4	0	0	0	28
82-83—Buffalo	NHL	60	12	17	29	130	10	4	2	6	47
83-84—Buffalo	NHL	58	14	31	45	101	3	1	0	1	9
84-85—Buffalo	NHL	39	13	11	24	45	5	2	4	6	15
85-86—Buffalo	NHL	54	20	12	32	158	—	—	—	—	—
86-87—Buffalo	NHL	50	6	14	20	74	—	—	—	—	—
87-88—Buffalo	NHL	77	2	23	25	179	6	0	2	2	23
88-89—Buffalo	NHL	63	6	11	17	86	—	—	—	—	—
—New York Rangers	NHL	13	0	5	5	31	2	0	0	0	17
89-90—New York Rangers	NHL	56	3	6	9	80	8	0	3	3	12
90-91—New York Rangers	NHL	14	0	1	1	27	—	—	—	—	—
91-92—Rochester	AHL	62	10	24	34	110	13	0	4	4	16
NHL totals		691	105	195	300	1264	52	11	13	24	193

RUMBLE, DARREN
D, SENATORS

PERSONAL: Born January 23, 1969, at Barrie, Ont.... 6-1/200.... Shoots left.

TRANSACTIONS/CAREER NOTES: Selected by Philadelphia Flyers as underage junior in first round (first Flyers pick, 20th overall) of NHL entry draft (June 13, 1987).... Stretched knee ligaments (November 27, 1988).... Selected by Ottawa Senators in NHL expansion draft (June 18, 1992).

Season Team	League	REGULAR SEASON					PLAYOFFS				
		Gms.	G	A	Pts.	Pen.	Gms.	G	A	Pts.	Pen.
85-86—Barrie Jr. B	OHA	46	14	32	46	91	—	—	—	—	—
86-87—Kitchener	OHL	64	11	32	43	44	4	0	1	1	9
87-88—Kitchener	OHL	55	15	50	65	64	—	—	—	—	—
88-89—Kitchener	OHL	46	11	29	40	25	5	1	0	1	2
89-90—Hershey	AHL	57	2	13	15	31	—	—	—	—	—
90-91—Philadelphia	NHL	3	1	0	1	0	—	—	—	—	—
—Hershey	AHL	73	6	35	41	48	3	0	5	5	2
91-92—Hershey	AHL	79	12	54	66	118	6	0	3	3	2
NHL totals		3	1	0	1	0					

RUSHFORTH, PAUL
RW, SABRES

PERSONAL: Born April 22, 1974, at Prince George, B.C.... 6-0/188.... Shoots right.

HIGH SCHOOL: Chippewa Secondary School (North Bay, Ont.).

TRANSACTIONS/CAREER NOTES: Selected by Buffalo Sabres in sixth round (eighth Sabres pick, 131st overall) of NHL entry draft (June 20, 1992).

Season Team	League	REGULAR SEASON					PLAYOFFS				
		Gms.	G	A	Pts.	Pen.	Gms.	G	A	Pts.	Pen.
89-90—Ottawa	OHA Mj. Jr. A	50	10	7	17	30	—	—	—	—	—
90-91—Ottawa	OHA Mj. Jr. A	38	14	16	30	58	—	—	—	—	—
91-92—North Bay	OHL	65	8	11	19	24	19	0	2	2	6

RUSSELL, CAM
D, BLACKHAWKS

PERSONAL: Born January 12, 1969, at Halifax, N.S.... 6-4/175.... Shoots left.

TRANSACTIONS/CAREER NOTES: Selected by Chicago Blackhawks as underage junior in third round (third Blackhawks pick, 50th overall) of NHL entry draft (June 13, 1987).

Season	Team	League	REGULAR SEASON					PLAYOFFS				
			Gms.	G	A	Pts.	Pen.	Gms.	G	A	Pts.	Pen.
85-86—Hull		QMJHL	56	3	4	7	24	15	0	2	2	4
86-87—Hull		QMJHL	66	3	16	19	119	8	0	1	1	16
87-88—Hull		QMJHL	53	9	18	27	141	19	2	5	7	39
88-89—Hull		QMJHL	66	8	32	40	109	9	2	6	8	6
89-90—Indianapolis		IHL	46	3	15	18	114	9	0	1	1	24
—Chicago		NHL	19	0	1	1	27	1	0	0	0	0
90-91—Indianapolis		IHL	53	5	9	14	125	6	0	2	2	30
—Chicago		NHL	3	0	0	0	5	1	0	0	0	0
91-92—Indianapolis		IHL	41	4	9	13	78	—	—	—	—	—
—Chicago		NHL	19	0	0	0	34	12	0	2	2	2
NHL totals			41	0	1	1	66	14	0	2	2	2

RUSSELL, KERRY
C, WHALERS

PERSONAL: Born June 23, 1969, at Kamloops, B.C. . . . 5-11/165. . . . Shoots right. . . . Full name: Kerry Bruce Russell.
COLLEGE: Michigan State.
TRANSACTIONS/CAREER NOTES: Selected by Hartford Whalers in seventh round (sixth Whalers pick, 137th overall) of NHL entry draft (June 11, 1988).

Season	Team	League	REGULAR SEASON					PLAYOFFS				
			Gms.	G	A	Pts.	Pen.	Gms.	G	A	Pts.	Pen.
85-86—Kelowna		BCJHL	45	18	22	40	48	10	3	2	5	33
86-87—Kelowna		BCJHL	49	41	61	102	71	12	9	17	26	14
87-88—Michigan State		CCHA	46	16	23	39	50	—	—	—	—	—
88-89—Michigan State		CCHA	46	5	23	28	50	—	—	—	—	—
89-90—Michigan State		CCHA	45	15	12	27	62	—	—	—	—	—
90-91—Michigan State		CCHA	39	20	28	48	36	—	—	—	—	—
91-92—Springfield		AHL	47	10	14	24	44	5	1	1	2	2

RUUTTU, CHRISTIAN
C, JETS

PERSONAL: Born February 20, 1964, at Lappeenranta, Finland. . . . 5-11/192. . . . Shoots left.
TRANSACTIONS/CAREER NOTES: Selected by Buffalo Sabres in seventh round (ninth Sabres pick, 134th overall) of NHL entry draft (June 8, 1983). . . . Injured knee (February 1988). . . . Sprained knee (September 1988). . . . Tore pectoral muscle (October 22, 1988). . . . Separated left shoulder (April 5, 1989). . . . Injured leg (January 21, 1992); missed four games. . . . Suffered from the flu (March 16, 1992); missed three games. . . . Traded by Sabres with future considerations to Winnipeg Jets for G Stephane Beauregard (June 15, 1992).

Season	Team	League	REGULAR SEASON					PLAYOFFS				
			Gms.	G	A	Pts.	Pen.	Gms.	G	A	Pts.	Pen.
82-83—Pori Assat		Finland	36	15	18	33	34	—	—	—	—	—
83-84—Pori Assat		Finland	37	18	42	60	72	9	2	5	7	12
84-85—Pori Assat		Finland	32	14	32	46	34	8	1	6	7	8
85-86—Helsinki IFK		Finland	36	14	42	56	41	10	3	6	9	8
86-87—Buffalo		NHL	76	22	43	65	62	—	—	—	—	—
87-88—Buffalo		NHL	73	26	45	71	85	6	2	5	7	4
88-89—Buffalo		NHL	67	14	46	60	98	2	0	0	0	0
89-90—Buffalo		NHL	75	19	41	60	66	6	0	0	0	4
90-91—Buffalo		NHL	77	16	34	50	96	6	1	3	4	29
91-92—Buffalo		NHL	70	4	21	25	76	3	0	0	0	6
NHL totals			438	101	230	331	483	23	3	8	11	43

RUZICKA, VLADIMIR
C, BRUINS

PERSONAL: Born June 6, 1963, at Most, Czechoslovakia. . . . 6-3/212. . . . Shoots left.
TRANSACTIONS/CAREER NOTES: Selected by Toronto Maple Leafs in fourth round (fifth Maple Leafs pick, 73rd overall) of NHL entry draft (June 9, 1982). . . . Rights traded by Maple Leafs to Edmonton Oilers for fourth-round pick in 1990 draft (C Greg Walters) (December 21, 1989). . . . Traded by Oilers to Boston Bruins for D Greg Hawgood (October 22, 1990). . . . Injured left ankle and developed tendinitis (December 29, 1990). . . . Underwent surgery to left ankle tendon (February 12, 1991).

Season	Team	League	REGULAR SEASON					PLAYOFFS				
			Gms.	G	A	Pts.	Pen.	Gms.	G	A	Pts.	Pen.
86-87—CHZ Litvinov		Czech.	32	24	15	39		—	—	—	—	—
87-88—Dukla Trencin		Czech.	34	32	21	53		—	—	—	—	—
88-89—Dukla Trencin		Czech.	45	46	38	84		—	—	—	—	—
89-90—CHZ Litvinov		Czech.	32	21	23	44		—	—	—	—	—
—Edmonton		NHL	25	11	6	17	10	—	—	—	—	—
90-91—Boston		NHL	29	8	8	16	19	17	2	11	13	0
91-92—Boston		NHL	77	39	36	75	48	13	2	3	5	2
NHL totals			131	58	50	108	77	30	4	14	18	2

RYCHEL, WARREN
LW, NORTH STARS

PERSONAL: Born May 12, 1967, at Tecumseh, Ont. . . . 6-0/190. . . . Shoots left. . . . Full name: Warren Stanley Rychel.
TRANSACTIONS/CAREER NOTES: Signed as free agent by Chicago Blackhawks (September 19, 1986). . . . Hyperextended left knee (February 1989). . . . Traded by Black-

hawks with C Troy Murray to Winnipeg Jets for D Bryan Marchment and D Chris Norton (July 22, 1991).... Traded by Jets to Minnesota North Stars for RW Tony Joseph and future considerations (December 30, 1991).

Season Team	League	REGULAR SEASON					PLAYOFFS				
		Gms.	G	A	Pts.	Pen.	Gms.	G	A	Pts.	Pen.
83-84—Essex Jr. C	OHA	24	11	16	27	86	—	—	—	—	—
84-85—Sudbury	OHL	35	5	8	13	74	—	—	—	—	—
—Guelph	OHL	29	1	3	4	48	—	—	—	—	—
85-86—Guelph	OHL	38	14	5	19	119	—	—	—	—	—
—Ottawa	OHL	29	11	18	29	54	—	—	—	—	—
86-87—Ottawa	OHL	28	11	7	18	57	—	—	—	—	—
—Kitchener	OHL	21	5	5	10	39	4	0	0	0	9
87-88—Saginaw	IHL	51	2	7	9	113	1	0	0	0	0
—Peoria	IHL	7	2	1	3	7	—	—	—	—	—
88-89—Saginaw	IHL	50	15	14	29	226	6	0	0	0	51
—Chicago	NHL	2	0	0	0	17	—	—	—	—	—
89-90—Indianapolis	IHL	77	23	16	39	374	14	1	3	4	64
90-91—Indianapolis	IHL	68	33	30	63	338	5	2	1	3	30
—Chicago	NHL	—	—	—	—	—	3	1	3	4	2
91-92—Moncton	AHL	36	14	15	29	211	—	—	—	—	—
—Kalamazoo	IHL	45	15	20	35	165	8	0	3	3	51
NHL totals		2	0	0	0	17	3	1	3	4	2

RYMSHA, ANDY
D, NORDIQUES

PERSONAL: Born December 10, 1968, at St. Catharines, Ont.... 6-3/210.... Shoots left.... Full name: Andrew Anthony Rymsha.
COLLEGE: Western Michigan.
TRANSACTIONS/CAREER NOTES: Selected by St. Louis Blues in fourth round (fifth Blues pick, 82nd overall) of NHL entry draft (June 13, 1987).... Traded by Blues with RW Herb Raglan and D Tony Twist to Quebec Nordiques for RW Darin Kimble (February 4, 1991).

Season Team	League	REGULAR SEASON					PLAYOFFS				
		Gms.	G	A	Pts.	Pen.	Gms.	G	A	Pts.	Pen.
85-86—St. Catharines Jr. B	OHA	39	6	13	19	170	—	—	—	—	—
86-87—Western Michigan Univ.	CCHA	42	7	10	17	122	—	—	—	—	—
87-88—Western Michigan Univ.	CCHA	42	5	6	11	114	—	—	—	—	—
88-89—Western Michigan Univ.	CCHA	35	3	4	7	139	—	—	—	—	—
89-90—Western Michigan Univ.	CCHA	37	1	10	11	108	—	—	—	—	—
90-91—Peoria	IHL	45	2	9	11	64	—	—	—	—	—
—Halifax	AHL	12	1	2	3	22	—	—	—	—	—
91-92—Halifax	AHL	44	4	7	11	54	—	—	—	—	—
—New Haven	AHL	16	0	5	5	20	—	—	—	—	—
—Quebec	NHL	6	0	0	0	23	—	—	—	—	—
NHL totals		6	0	0	0	23					

SABOL, SHAUN
D, RANGERS

PERSONAL: Born July 13, 1966, at Minneapolis, Minn.... 6-3/203.... Shoots left.... Full name: Shaun Thomas Sabol.
COLLEGE: Wisconsin.
TRANSACTIONS/CAREER NOTES: Selected by Philadelphia Flyers in 10th round (ninth Flyers pick, 209th overall) of NHL entry draft (June 21, 1986).... Traded by Flyers to New York Rangers for future considerations (August 5, 1991).

Season Team	League	REGULAR SEASON					PLAYOFFS				
		Gms.	G	A	Pts.	Pen.	Gms.	G	A	Pts.	Pen.
83-84—St. Paul	USHL	47	6	10	16	32	—	—	—	—	—
84-85—St. Paul	USHL	47	4	13	17	137	—	—	—	—	—
85-86—St. Paul	USHL	46	10	19	29	129	—	—	—	—	—
86-87—University of Wisconsin	WCHA	40	7	16	23	98	—	—	—	—	—
87-88—University of Wisconsin	WCHA	8	4	3	7	10	—	—	—	—	—
—Hershey	AHL	51	1	9	10	66	2	0	0	0	5
88-89—Hershey	AHL	58	7	11	18	134	12	0	2	2	35
89-90—Hershey	AHL	46	6	16	22	49	—	—	—	—	—
—Philadelphia	NHL	2	0	0	0	0	—	—	—	—	—
90-91—Hershey	AHL	59	6	13	19	136	7	0	1	1	34
91-92—Binghamton	AHL	72	5	19	24	123	11	1	2	3	10
NHL totals		2	0	0	0	0					

SABOURIN, KEN
D, CAPITALS

PERSONAL: Born April 28, 1966, at Scarborough, Ont.... 6-3/205.... Shoots left.... Full name: Ken R. Sabourin.
TRANSACTIONS/CAREER NOTES: Selected by Calgary Flames as underage junior in second round (2nd Flames pick, 33rd overall) of NHL entry draft (June 9, 1984).... Traded by Sault Ste. Marie Greyhounds to Cornwall Royals for Kent Trolley and fifth-round pick in OHL priority draft (March 1986). ... Traded by Flames to Washington Capitals for C Paul Fenton (January 24, 1991).

Season Team	League	REGULAR SEASON					PLAYOFFS				
		Gms.	G	A	Pts.	Pen.	Gms.	G	A	Pts.	Pen.
82-83—Sault Ste. Marie	OHL	58	0	8	8	90	10	0	0	0	14
83-84—Sault Ste. Marie	OHL	63	7	13	20	157	9	0	1	1	25

RS

Season Team	League	REGULAR SEASON					PLAYOFFS				
		Gms.	G	A	Pts.	Pen.	Gms.	G	A	Pts.	Pen.
84-85—Sault Ste. Marie	OHL	63	5	19	24	139	16	1	4	5	10
85-86—Sault Ste. Marie	OHL	25	1	5	6	77	—	—	—	—	—
—Cornwall	OHL	37	3	12	15	94	6	1	2	3	6
—Moncton	AHL	3	0	0	0	0	6	0	1	1	2
86-87—Moncton	AHL	75	1	10	11	166	6	0	1	1	27
87-88—Salt Lake City	IHL	71	2	8	10	186	16	1	6	7	57
88-89—Calgary	NHL	6	0	1	1	26	1	0	0	0	0
—Salt Lake City	IHL	74	2	18	20	197	11	0	1	1	26
89-90—Calgary	NHL	5	0	0	0	10	—	—	—	—	—
—Salt Lake City	IHL	76	5	19	24	336	11	0	2	2	40
90-91—Salt Lake City	IHL	28	2	15	17	77	—	—	—	—	—
—Calgary	NHL	16	1	3	4	36	—	—	—	—	—
—Washington	NHL	28	1	4	5	81	11	0	0	0	34
91-92—Baltimore	AHL	30	3	8	11	106	—	—	—	—	—
—Washington	NHL	19	0	0	0	48	—	—	—	—	—
NHL totals		74	2	8	10	201	12	0	0	0	34

SACCO, DAVID
C, MAPLE LEAFS

PERSONAL: Born July 31, 1970, at Medford, Mass. . . . 6-0/190. . . . Shoots right. . . . Full name: David Anthony Sacco. . . . Brother of Joe Sacco, left winger, Toronto Maple Leafs.
HIGH SCHOOL: Medford (Mass.).
COLLEGE: Boston University.
TRANSACTIONS/CAREER NOTES: Selected by Toronto Maple Leafs in 10th round (ninth Maple Leafs pick, 195th overall) of NHL entry draft (June 11, 1988).
HONORS: Named to Hockey East All-Star first team (1991-92).

Season Team	League	REGULAR SEASON					PLAYOFFS				
		Gms.	G	A	Pts.	Pen.	Gms.	G	A	Pts.	Pen.
88-89—Boston University	Hockey East	35	14	29	43	40	—	—	—	—	—
89-90—Boston University	Hockey East	3	0	4	4	2	—	—	—	—	—
90-91—Boston University	Hockey East	40	21	40	61	24	—	—	—	—	—
91-92—Boston University	Hockey East	35	14	33	47	30	—	—	—	—	—

SACCO, JOE
LW, MAPLE LEAFS

PERSONAL: Born February 4, 1969, at Medford, Mass. . . . 6-1/180. . . . Shoots left. . . . Full name: Joseph William Sacco. . . . Brother of David Sacco, center in Toronto Maple Leafs system.
HIGH SCHOOL: Medford (Mass.).
COLLEGE: Boston University.
TRANSACTIONS/CAREER NOTES: Selected by Toronto Maple Leafs in fourth round (fourth Maple Leafs pick, 71st overall) of NHL entry draft (June 13, 1987).

Season Team	League	REGULAR SEASON					PLAYOFFS				
		Gms.	G	A	Pts.	Pen.	Gms.	G	A	Pts.	Pen.
85-86—Medford H.S.	Mass. H.S.	20	30	30	60		—	—	—	—	—
86-87—Medford H.S.	Mass. H.S.	21	22	32	54		—	—	—	—	—
87-88—Boston University	Hockey East	34	14	22	36	38	—	—	—	—	—
88-89—Boston University	Hockey East	33	21	19	40	66	—	—	—	—	—
89-90—Boston University	Hockey East	44	28	24	52	70	—	—	—	—	—
90-91—Newmarket	AHL	49	18	17	35	24	—	—	—	—	—
—Toronto	NHL	20	0	5	5	2	—	—	—	—	—
91-92—U.S. National Team	Int'l	50	11	26	37	51	—	—	—	—	—
—U.S. Olympic Team	Int'l	8	0	2	2	0	—	—	—	—	—
—Toronto	NHL	17	7	4	11	4	—	—	—	—	—
—St. John's	AHL	—	—	—	—	—	1	1	1	2	0
NHL totals		37	7	9	16	6					

SAGISSOR, THOMAS
C, CANADIENS

PERSONAL: Born September 12, 1967, at Hastings, Minn. . . . 5-11/202. . . . Shoots left. . . . Full name: Thomas Steven Sagissor.
HIGH SCHOOL: Hastings (Minn.).
COLLEGE: Wisconsin.
TRANSACTIONS/CAREER NOTES: Selected by Montreal Canadiens in fifth round (seventh Canadiens pick, 96th overall) of NHL entry draft (June 15, 1985).

Season Team	League	REGULAR SEASON					PLAYOFFS				
		Gms.	G	A	Pts.	Pen.	Gms.	G	A	Pts.	Pen.
85-86—Hastings H.S.	Minn. H.S.	25	26	38	64	28	—	—	—	—	—
86-87—University of Wisconsin	WCHA	41	1	4	5	32	—	—	—	—	—
87-88—University of Wisconsin	WCHA	38	4	5	9	65	—	—	—	—	—
88-89—University of Wisconsin	WCHA	40	7	11	18	119	—	—	—	—	—
89-90—University of Wisconsin	WCHA	43	19	28	47	*122	—	—	—	—	—
90-91—Fredericton	AHL	52	8	13	21	99	—	—	—	—	—
91-92—Fredericton	AHL	57	12	15	27	111	3	0	2	2	2

SAKIC, BRIAN
LW, CAPITALS

PERSONAL: Born April 9, 1971, at Burnaby, B.C. . . . 5-10/179. . . . Shoots left. . . . Brother of Joe Sakic, center, Quebec Nordiques.
TRANSACTIONS/CAREER NOTES: Traded by Swift Current Broncos with RW Wade Smith to Tri-City Americans for LW Murray Duval and D Jason Smith (October 18, 1989). . . . Broke jaw

(March 15, 1990).... Selected by Washington Capitals in fifth round (fifth Capitals pick, 93rd overall) of NHL entry draft (June 16, 1990).
HONORS: Named to WHL All-Star second team (1989-90).... Named to WHL All-Star first team (1990-91).

Season Team	League	REGULAR SEASON					PLAYOFFS				
		Gms.	G	A	Pts.	Pen.	Gms.	G	A	Pts.	Pen.
87-88—Swift Current..................	WHL	65	12	37	49	12	—	—	—	—	—
88-89—Swift Current..................	WHL	71	36	64	100	28	—	—	—	—	—
89-90—Swift Current..................	WHL	8	6	7	13	4	—	—	—	—	—
—Tri-City Americans	WHL	58	47	92	139	8	—	—	—	—	—
90-91—Tri-City Americans	WHL	69	40	*122	162	19	—	—	—	—	—
91-92—Tri-City Americans	WHL	72	45	*83	128	55	5	4	4	8	14

SAKIC, JOE
C, NORDIQUES

PERSONAL: Born July 7, 1969, at Burnaby, B.C. ... 5-11/185. ... Shoots left. ... Full name: Joseph Steve Sakic. ... Brother of Brian Sakic, left winger in Washington Capitals system.
TRANSACTIONS/CAREER NOTES: Selected by Quebec Nordiques as underage junior in first round (second Nordiques pick, 15th overall) of NHL entry draft (June 13, 1987). ... Sprained right ankle (November 28, 1988). ... Developed bursitis in left ankle (January 21, 1992); missed three games. ... Suffered recurrance of bursitis in left ankle (January 30, 1992); missed eight games.
HONORS: Won WHL East Most Valuable Player Trophy (1986-87). ... Won WHL East Stewart (Butch) Paul Memorial Trophy (1986-87). ... Named to WHL All-Star second team (1986-87). ... Won Can.HL Player of the Year Award (1987-88). ... Won Four Broncos Memorial Trophy (1987-88). ... Shared Bob Clarke Trophy with Theoren Fleury (1987-88). ... Won WHL Player of the Year Award (1986-87 and 1987-88). ... Named to WHL All-Star first team (East) (1987-88). ... Named Canadian Major Junior Player of the Year (1987-88).

Season Team	League	REGULAR SEASON					PLAYOFFS				
		Gms.	G	A	Pts.	Pen.	Gms.	G	A	Pts.	Pen.
86-87—Swift Current..................	WHL	72	60	73	133	31	4	0	1	1	0
87-88—Swift Current..................	WHL	64	†78	82	†160	64	10	11	13	24	12
88-89—Quebec	NHL	70	23	39	62	24	—	—	—	—	—
89-90—Quebec	NHL	80	39	63	102	27	—	—	—	—	—
90-91—Quebec	NHL	80	48	61	109	24	—	—	—	—	—
91-92—Quebec	NHL	69	29	65	94	20	—	—	—	—	—
NHL totals............................		299	139	228	367	95					

SAMUELSSON, KJELL
D, PENGUINS

PERSONAL: Born October 18, 1958, at Tyngsryd, Sweden. ... 6-6/235. ... Shoots right.
TRANSACTIONS/CAREER NOTES: Selected by New York Rangers in sixth round (fifth Rangers pick, 119th overall) of NHL entry draft (June 9, 1984). ... Traded by Rangers with second-round pick in 1989 draft (LW Patrik Juhlin) to Philadelphia Flyers for G Bob Froese (December 18, 1986). ... Pulled groin (February 1988). ... Suffered herniated disc (October 1988). ... Bruised hand (March 1989). ... Bruised right shoulder (November 22, 1989); missed 13 games. ... Underwent shoulder surgery (March 1990). ... Traded by Flyers with RW Rick Tocchet, G Ken Wregget and third-round pick in 1992 draft to Pittsburgh Penguins for RW Mark Recchi, D Brian Benning and first-round pick in 1992 draft previously acquired from Los Angeles Kings (February 19, 1992).

Season Team	League	REGULAR SEASON					PLAYOFFS				
		Gms.	G	A	Pts.	Pen.	Gms.	G	A	Pts.	Pen.
82-83—Tyngsryd..................	Sweden	32	11	6	17	57	—	—	—	—	—
83-84—Leksand..........................	Sweden	36	6	7	13	59	—	—	—	—	—
84-85—Leksand..........................	Sweden	35	9	5	14	34	—	—	—	—	—
85-86—New York Rangers	NHL	9	0	0	0	10	9	0	1	1	8
—New Haven	AHL	56	6	21	27	87	3	0	0	0	10
86-87—New York Rangers	NHL	30	2	6	8	50	—	—	—	—	—
—Philadelphia	NHL	46	1	6	7	86	26	0	4	4	25
87-88—Philadelphia	NHL	74	6	24	30	184	7	2	5	7	23
88-89—Philadelphia	NHL	69	3	14	17	140	19	1	3	4	24
89-90—Philadelphia	NHL	66	5	17	22	91	—	—	—	—	—
90-91—Philadelphia	NHL	78	9	19	28	82	—	—	—	—	—
91-92—Philadelphia	NHL	54	4	9	13	76	—	—	—	—	—
—Pittsburgh	NHL	20	1	2	3	34	15	0	3	3	12
NHL totals...........................		446	31	97	128	753	76	3	16	19	92

SAMUELSSON, ULF
D, PENGUINS

PERSONAL: Born March 26, 1964, at Fagersta, Sweden. ... 6-1/195. ... Shoots left.
TRANSACTIONS/CAREER NOTES: Selected by Hartford Whalers in fourth round (fourth Whalers pick, 67th overall) of NHL entry draft (June 9, 1982). ... Suffered from the flu (December 1988); missed nine games. ... Tore ligaments in right knee and underwent surgery (August 1989); missed part of 1989-90 season. ... Traded by Whalers with C Ron Francis and D Grant Jennings to Pittsburgh Penguins for C John Cullen, D Zarley Zalapski and RW Jeff Parker (March 4, 1991). ... Injured hip flexor (October 29, 1991); missed six games. ... Underwent surgery to right elbow (December 1991); missed four games. ... Bruised left hand (February 8, 1992); missed one game. ... Suffered from the flu (February 1992); missed one game.

Season Team	League	REGULAR SEASON					PLAYOFFS				
		Gms.	G	A	Pts.	Pen.	Gms.	G	A	Pts.	Pen.
83-84—Leksand..........................	Sweden	36	5	10	15	53	—	—	—	—	—
84-85—Binghamton	AHL	36	5	11	16	92	—	—	—	—	—
—Hartford...........................	NHL	41	2	6	8	83	—	—	—	—	—
85-86—Hartford...........................	NHL	80	5	19	24	174	10	1	2	3	38

Season Team	League	REGULAR SEASON					PLAYOFFS				
		Gms.	G	A	Pts.	Pen.	Gms.	G	A	Pts.	Pen.
86-87—Hartford............................	NHL	78	2	31	33	162	5	0	1	1	41
87-88—Hartford............................	NHL	76	8	33	41	159	5	0	0	0	8
88-89—Hartford............................	NHL	71	9	26	35	181	4	0	2	2	4
89-90—Hartford............................	NHL	55	2	11	13	167	7	1	0	1	2
90-91—Hartford............................	NHL	62	3	18	21	174	—	—	—	—	—
—Pittsburgh........................	NHL	14	1	4	5	37	20	3	2	5	34
91-92—Pittsburgh........................	NHL	62	1	14	15	206	21	0	2	2	39
NHL totals..		539	33	162	195	1343	72	5	9	14	166

SANDELIN, SCOTT
D, NORTH STARS

PERSONAL: Born August 8, 1964, at Hibbing, Minn. . . . 6-0/200. . . . Shoots right. . . . Full name: Scott A. Sandelin.
HIGH SCHOOL: Hibbing (Minn.).
COLLEGE: North Dakota.
TRANSACTIONS/CAREER NOTES: Selected by Montreal Canadiens as underage player in second round (fifth Canadiens pick, 40th overall) of NHL entry draft (June 9, 1982). . . . Stretched knee ligaments (October 1984). . . . Traded by Canadiens to Philadelphia Flyers for D J.J. Daigneault (November 7, 1988). . . . Broke right arm (December 11, 1990). . . . Signed as free agent by Boston Bruins (August 12, 1991).
HONORS: Named to WCHA All-Star first team (1985-86). . . . Named to NCAA West All-Star second team (1985-86).

Season Team	League	REGULAR SEASON					PLAYOFFS				
		Gms.	G	A	Pts.	Pen.	Gms.	G	A	Pts.	Pen.
81-82—Hibbing H.S.	Minn. H.S.	20	5	15	20	30	—	—	—	—	—
82-83—Univ. of North Dakota	WCHA	30	1	6	7	10	—	—	—	—	—
83-84—Univ. of North Dakota	WCHA	41	4	23	27	24	—	—	—	—	—
84-85—Univ. of North Dakota	WCHA	38	4	17	21	30	—	—	—	—	—
85-86—Univ. of North Dakota	WCHA	40	7	31	38	38	—	—	—	—	—
—Sherbrooke........................	AHL	6	0	2	2	2	—	—	—	—	—
86-87—Montreal..........................	NHL	1	0	0	0	0	—	—	—	—	—
—Sherbrooke........................	AHL	74	7	22	29	35	16	2	4	6	2
87-88—Montreal..........................	NHL	8	0	1	1	2	—	—	—	—	—
—Sherbrooke........................	AHL	58	8	14	22	35	4	0	2	2	0
88-89—Sherbrooke........................	AHL	12	0	9	9	8	—	—	—	—	—
—Hershey..............................	AHL	39	6	9	15	38	8	2	1	3	4
89-90—Hershey..............................	AHL	70	4	27	31	38	—	—	—	—	—
90-91—Philadelphia........................	NHL	15	0	3	3	0	—	—	—	—	—
—Hershey..............................	AHL	39	3	10	13	21	7	1	2	3	0
91-92—Kalamazoo........................	IHL	49	3	18	21	32	11	1	1	2	2
—Minnesota........................	NHL	1	0	0	0	0	—	—	—	—	—
NHL totals...		25	0	4	4	2					

SANDERSON, GEOFF
C, WHALERS

PERSONAL: Born February 1, 1972, at Hay River, N.W.T. . . . 6-0/185. . . . Shoots left.
TRANSACTIONS/CAREER NOTES: Selected by Hartford Whalers in second round (second Whalers pick, 36th overall) of NHL entry draft (June 16, 1990). . . . Bruised shoulder (October 14, 1991); missed one game. . . . Injured groin (November 13, 1991); missed three games. . . . Bruised knee (December 7, 1991); missed five games.

Season Team	League	REGULAR SEASON					PLAYOFFS				
		Gms.	G	A	Pts.	Pen.	Gms.	G	A	Pts.	Pen.
88-89—Swift Current....................	WHL	58	17	11	28	16	12	3	5	8	6
89-90—Swift Current....................	WHL	70	32	62	94	56	4	1	4	5	8
90-91—Swift Current....................	WHL	70	62	50	112	57	3	1	2	3	4
—Hartford............................	NHL	2	1	0	1	0	3	0	0	0	0
—Springfield........................	AHL	—	—	—	—	—	1	0	0	0	2
91-92—Hartford............................	NHL	64	13	18	31	18	7	1	0	1	2
NHL totals..		66	14	18	32	18	10	1	0	1	2

SANDLAK, JIM
RW, CANUCKS

PERSONAL: Born December 12, 1966, at Kitchener, Ont. . . . 6-3/220. . . . Shoots right. . . . Full name: James Sandlak Jr.
TRANSACTIONS/CAREER NOTES: Selected by Vancouver Canucks as underage junior in first round (first Canucks pick, fourth overall) of NHL entry draft (June 15, 1985). . . . Ruptured ligaments in right thumb (January 1986). . . . Bruised shoulder (October 1988). . . . Suffered sore back (November 5, 1991). . . . Sprained hand (December 1, 1991); missed seven games. . . . Strained groin (December 31, 1991). . . . Sprained knee (March 1992); missed seven games.
HONORS: Named top forward and member of All-Tournament team at 1986 World Junior Championships. . . . Named to NHL All-Rookie team (1986-87).

Season Team	League	REGULAR SEASON					PLAYOFFS				
		Gms.	G	A	Pts.	Pen.	Gms.	G	A	Pts.	Pen.
82-83—Kitchener..........................	OHL	38	26	25	51	100	—	—	—	—	—
83-84—London	OHL	68	23	18	41	143	8	1	11	12	13
84-85—London	OHL	58	40	24	64	128	8	3	2	5	14
85-86—London	OHL	16	7	13	20	36	5	2	3	5	24
—Vancouver........................	NHL	23	1	3	4	10	3	0	1	1	0

Season	Team	League	Gms.	G	A	Pts.	Pen.	Gms.	G	A	Pts.	Pen.
			REGULAR SEASON					PLAYOFFS				
86-87	—Vancouver	NHL	78	15	21	36	66	—	—	—	—	—
87-88	—Vancouver	NHL	49	16	15	31	81	—	—	—	—	—
	—Fredericton	AHL	24	10	15	25	47	—	—	—	—	—
88-89	—Vancouver	NHL	72	20	20	40	99	6	1	1	2	2
89-90	—Vancouver	NHL	70	15	8	23	104	—	—	—	—	—
90-91	—Vancouver	NHL	59	7	6	13	125	—	—	—	—	—
91-92	—Vancouver	NHL	66	16	24	40	176	13	4	6	10	22
	NHL totals		417	90	97	187	661	22	5	8	13	24

SANDSTROM, TOMAS
RW, KINGS

PERSONAL: Born September 4, 1964, at Jakobstad, Finland. . . . 6-2/200. . . . Shoots left.
TRANSACTIONS/CAREER NOTES: Selected by New York Rangers in second round (second Rangers pick, 36th overall) of NHL entry draft (June 9, 1982). . . . Suffered concussion (February 24, 1986). . . . Fractured right ankle (February 11, 1987). . . . Fractured right index finger (November 1987). . . . Traded by Rangers with LW Tony Granato to Los Angeles Kings for C Bernie Nicholls (January 20, 1990). . . . Fractured vertebrae (November 29, 1990); missed 10 games. . . . Partially dislocated shoulder (December 28, 1991); missed 26 games.
HONORS: Named to NHL All-Rookie team (1984-85).

Season	Team	League	Gms.	G	A	Pts.	Pen.	Gms.	G	A	Pts.	Pen.
			REGULAR SEASON					PLAYOFFS				
82-83	—Brynas	Sweden	36	22	14	36	36	—	—	—	—	—
83-84	—Brynas	Sweden	20	10	30			—	—	—	—	—
84-85	—New York Rangers	NHL	74	29	29	58	51	3	0	2	2	0
85-86	—New York Rangers	NHL	73	25	29	54	109	16	4	6	10	20
86-87	—New York Rangers	NHL	64	40	34	74	60	6	1	2	3	20
87-88	—New York Rangers	NHL	69	28	40	68	95	—	—	—	—	—
88-89	—New York Rangers	NHL	79	32	56	88	148	4	3	2	5	12
89-90	—New York Rangers	NHL	48	19	19	38	100	—	—	—	—	—
	—Los Angeles	NHL	28	13	20	33	28	10	5	4	9	19
90-91	—Los Angeles	NHL	68	45	44	89	106	10	4	4	8	14
91-92	—Los Angeles	NHL	49	17	22	39	70	6	0	3	3	8
	NHL totals		552	248	293	541	767	55	17	23	40	93

SANDWITH, TERRAN
D, FLYERS

PERSONAL: Born April 17, 1972, at Edmonton, Alta. . . . 6-4/210. . . . Shoots left.
TRANSACTIONS/CAREER NOTES: Selected by Philadelphia Flyers in second round (fourth Flyers pick, 42nd overall) of NHL entry draft (June 16, 1990). . . . Suffered blood disorder (September 1990).

Season	Team	League	Gms.	G	A	Pts.	Pen.	Gms.	G	A	Pts.	Pen.
			REGULAR SEASON					PLAYOFFS				
87-88	—Hobbema	AJHL	58	5	8	13	106	—	—	—	—	—
88-89	—Tri-City Americans	WHL	31	0	0	0	29	6	0	0	0	4
89-90	—Tri-City Americans	WIIL	70	4	14	18	92	7	0	2	2	14
90-91	—Tri-City Americans	WHL	46	5	17	22	132	7	1	0	1	14
91-92	—Brandon	WHL	41	6	14	20	145	—	—	—	—	—
	—Saskatoon	WHL	18	2	5	7	53	18	2	1	3	28

SANIPASS, EVERETT
LW, NORDIQUES

PERSONAL: Born February 13, 1968, at Big Cove, N.B. . . . 6-2/204. . . . Shoots left.
TRANSACTIONS/CAREER NOTES: Selected by Chicago Blackhawks as underage junior in first round (first Blackhawks pick, 14th overall) of NHL entry draft (June 21, 1986). . . . Suffered back spasms (December 1987). . . . Suffered back spasms and concussion (January 17, 1988). . . . Broke hand (March 1988). . . . Broke right ankle in eight places playing softball (August 1988). . . . Broke jaw (September 5, 1989). . . . Fractured right foot (October 17, 1989). . . . Traded by Blackhawks with LW Dan Vincelette and D Mario Doyon to Quebec Nordiques for LW Michel Goulet, G Greg Millen and sixth-round pick in 1991 draft (March 5, 1990). . . . Injured left ankle (March 17, 1990). . . . Broke left ankle in preseason game (September 26, 1990); missed first 10 games of season. . . . Injured back (January 17, 1991); missed eight games. . . . Reinjured back (March 19, 1991); missed final six games of season.
HONORS: Named to QMJHL All-Star first team (1986-87).

Season	Team	League	Gms.	G	A	Pts.	Pen.	Gms.	G	A	Pts.	Pen.
			REGULAR SEASON					PLAYOFFS				
84-85	—Verdun	QMJHL	38	8	11	19	84	—	—	—	—	—
85-86	—Verdun	QMJHL	67	28	66	94	320	5	0	2	2	16
86-87	—Granby	QMJHL	35	34	48	82	220	8	6	4	10	48
	—Chicago	NHL	7	1	3	4	2	—	—	—	—	—
87-88	—Chicago	NHL	57	8	12	20	126	2	2	0	2	2
88-89	—Chicago	NHL	50	6	9	15	164	3	0	0	0	2
	—Saginaw	IHL	23	9	12	21	76	—	—	—	—	—
89-90	—Indianapolis	IHL	33	15	13	28	121	—	—	—	—	—
	—Chicago	NHL	12	2	2	4	17	—	—	—	—	—
	—Quebec	NHL	9	3	3	6	8	—	—	—	—	—
90-91	—Halifax	AHL	14	11	7	18	41	—	—	—	—	—
	—Quebec	NHL	29	5	5	10	41	—	—	—	—	—
91-92	—Halifax	AHL	7	3	5	8	31	—	—	—	—	—
	NHL totals		164	25	34	59	358	5	2	0	2	4

SARAULT, YVES
LW, CANADIENS

PERSONAL: Born December 23, 1972, at Valleyfield, Que.... 6-1/170.... Shoots left.
TRANSACTIONS/CAREER NOTES: Traded by Victoriaville Tigers with D Jason Downey to St. Jean Lynx for D Sylvain Bourgeois (May 26, 1990).... Selected by Montreal Canadiens in third round (fourth Canadiens pick, 61st overall) of NHL entry draft (June 22, 1991).
HONORS: Named to QMJHL All-Star second team (1991-92).

Season Team	League	REGULAR SEASON					PLAYOFFS				
		Gms.	G	A	Pts.	Pen.	Gms.	G	A	Pts.	Pen.
89-90—Victoriaville	QMJHL	70	12	28	40	140	16	0	3	3	26
90-91—St. Jean	QMJHL	56	22	24	46	113	—	—	—	—	—
91-92—Trois-Rivieres	QMJHL	68	44	52	96	106	15	10	10	20	18

SARJEANT, GEOFF
G

PERSONAL: Born November 30, 1969, at Newmarket, Ont. ... 5-9/175. ... Shoots left. ... Full name: Geoff Ian Sarjeant.
HIGH SCHOOL: Newmarket (Ont.).
COLLEGE: Michigan Tech.
TRANSACTIONS/CAREER NOTES: Selected by St. Louis Blues in NHL supplemental draft (June 15, 1990).

Season Team	League	REGULAR SEASON								PLAYOFFS						
		Gms.	Min.	W	L	T	GA	SO	Avg.	Gms.	Min.	W	L	GA	SO	Avg.
88-89—Michigan Tech	WCHA	6	329	0	3	2	22	0	4.01	—	—	—	—	—	—	—
89-90—Michigan Tech	WCHA	19	1043	4	13	0	94	0	5.41	—	—	—	—	—	—	—
90-91—Michigan Tech	WCHA	28	1540	6	16	3	97	1	3.78	—	—	—	—	—	—	—
91-92—Michigan Tech	WCHA	23	1246	7	13	0	90	1	4.33	—	—	—	—	—	—	—

SAUNDERS, MATT
LW, BLACKHAWKS

PERSONAL: Born July 17, 1970, at Ottawa.... 6-1/190.... Shoots left.... Full name: Matthew Henry Saunders. ... Brother of David Saunders, left winger, Vancouver Canucks (1987-88).
COLLEGE: Northeastern.
TRANSACTIONS/CAREER NOTES: Selected by Chicago Blackhawks in 10th round (eighth Blackhawks pick, 195th overall) of NHL entry draft (June 17, 1989).... Suspended two games by Hockey East for fighting (November 28, 1989).... Bruised thigh (December 1990).

Season Team	League	REGULAR SEASON					PLAYOFFS				
		Gms.	G	A	Pts.	Pen.	Gms.	G	A	Pts.	Pen.
86-87—Nepean	COJHL	55	15	23	38		—	—	—	—	—
87-88—Nepean	COJHL	49	30	27	57	122	—	—	—	—	—
88-89—Northeastern University	Hockey East	27	8	8	16	17	—	—	—	—	—
89-90—Northeastern University	Hockey East	35	19	21	40	51	—	—	—	—	—
90-91—Northeastern University	Hockey East	29	13	12	25	36	—	—	—	—	—
91-92—Northeastern University	Hockey East	35	8	17	25	38	—	—	—	—	—

SAVAGE, JOEL
RW, SABRES

PERSONAL: Born December 25, 1969, at Surrey, B.C.... 5-11/205.... Shoots right.
TRANSACTIONS/CAREER NOTES: Selected by Buffalo Sabres in first round (first Sabres pick, 13th overall) of NHL entry draft (June 11, 1988).... Suffered concussion (October 1985).
HONORS: Named to WHL All-Star second team (1987-88).

Season Team	League	REGULAR SEASON					PLAYOFFS				
		Gms.	G	A	Pts.	Pen.	Gms.	G	A	Pts.	Pen.
85-86—Kelowna	BCJHL	43	10	12	22	76	11	2	1	3	6
86-87—Victoria	WHL	68	14	13	27	48	5	2	0	2	0
87-88—Victoria	WHL	69	37	32	69	73	—	—	—	—	—
88-89—Victoria	WHL	60	17	30	47	95	6	1	1	2	8
89-90—Rochester	AHL	43	6	7	13	39	5	0	1	1	4
90-91—Rochester	AHL	61	25	19	44	45	15	3	3	6	8
—Buffalo	NHL	3	0	1	1	0	—	—	—	—	—
91-92—Rochester	AHL	59	8	14	22	39	9	2	0	2	8
NHL totals		3	0	1	1	0					

SAVAGE, REGGIE
RW, CAPITALS

PERSONAL: Born May 1, 1970, at Montreal. ... 5-10/187. ... Shoots left. ... Full name: Reginald David Savage.
TRANSACTIONS/CAREER NOTES: Selected by Washington Capitals in first round (first Capitals pick, 15th overall) of NHL entry draft (June 11, 1988).... Suspended six games by QMJHL for stick-swinging incident (February 19, 1989).

Season Team	League	REGULAR SEASON					PLAYOFFS				
		Gms.	G	A	Pts.	Pen.	Gms.	G	A	Pts.	Pen.
87-88—Victoriaville	QMJHL	68	68	54	122	77	5	2	3	5	8
88-89—Victoriaville	QMJHL	54	58	55	113	178	16	15	13	28	52
89-90—Victoriaville	QMJHL	63	51	43	94	79	16	13	10	23	40
90-91—Baltimore	AHL	62	32	29	61	10	6	1	1	2	6
—Washington	NHL	1	0	0	0	0	—	—	—	—	—
91-92—Baltimore	AHL	77	42	28	70	51	—	—	—	—	—
NHL totals		1	0	0	0	0					

SAVARD, DENIS
C, CANADIENS

PERSONAL: Born February 4, 1961, at Pointe Gatineau, Que. . . . 5-10/175. . . . Shoots right. . . . Full name: Denis Joseph Savard.
TRANSACTIONS/CAREER NOTES: Selected by Chicago Blackhawks as underage junior in first round (first Blackhawks pick, third overall) of NHL entry draft (June 11, 1980). . . . Strained knee (October 15, 1980). . . . Broke nose (January 7, 1984). . . . Injured ankle (October 13, 1984). . . . Bruised ribs (March 22, 1987). . . . Broke right ankle (January 21, 1989); missed 19 games. . . . Sprained left ankle (January 17, 1990). . . . Broke left index finger (January 26, 1990); missed 17 games. . . . Traded by Blackhawks to Montreal Canadiens for D Chris Chelios and second-round pick in 1991 draft (C Michael Pomichter) (June 29, 1990). . . . Suffered sinus infection (January 17, 1991); missed five games. . . . Injured right thumb (March 16, 1991). . . . Injured eye (October 30, 1991); missed two games.
HONORS: Won Michel Briere Trophy (1979-80). . . . Named to QMJHL All-Star first team (1979-80). . . . Named to THE SPORTING NEWS All-Star second team (1982-83). . . . Named to NHL All-Star second team (1982-83).
RECORDS: Shares NHL record for fastest goal from the start of a period—4 seconds (January 12, 1986).

Season Team	League	REGULAR SEASON					PLAYOFFS				
		Gms.	G	A	Pts.	Pen.	Gms.	G	A	Pts.	Pen.
77-78—Montreal	QMJHL	72	37	79	116	22	—	—	—	—	—
78-79—Montreal	QMJHL	70	46	*112	158	88	11	5	6	11	46
79-80—Montreal	QMJHL	72	63	118	181	93	10	7	16	23	8
80-81—Chicago	NHL	76	28	47	75	47	3	0	0	0	0
81-82—Chicago	NHL	80	32	87	119	82	15	11	7	18	52
82-83—Chicago	NHL	78	35	86	121	99	13	8	9	17	22
83-84—Chicago	NHL	75	37	57	94	71	5	1	3	4	0
84-85—Chicago	NHL	79	38	67	105	56	15	9	20	29	20
85-86—Chicago	NHL	80	47	69	116	111	3	4	1	5	6
86-87—Chicago	NHL	70	40	50	90	108	4	1	0	1	12
87-88—Chicago	NHL	80	44	87	131	95	5	4	3	7	17
88-89—Chicago	NHL	58	23	59	82	110	16	8	11	19	10
89-90—Chicago	NHL	60	27	53	80	56	20	7	15	22	41
90-91—Montreal	NHL	70	28	31	59	52	13	2	11	13	35
91-92—Montreal	NHL	77	28	42	70	73	11	3	9	12	8
NHL totals		**883**	**407**	**735**	**1142**	**960**	**123**	**58**	**89**	**147**	**232**

SCHLEGEL, BRAD
D, CAPITALS

PERSONAL: Born July 22, 1968, at Kitchener, Ont. . . . 5-10/190. . . . Shoots right.
TRANSACTIONS/CAREER NOTES: Selected by Washington Capitals in seventh round (eighth Capitals pick, 144th overall) of NHL entry draft (June 17, 1989).
HONORS: Named to OHL All-Star second team (1987-88).
MISCELLANEOUS: Member of 1992 silver-medal-winning Canadian Olympic team.

Season Team	League	REGULAR SEASON					PLAYOFFS				
		Gms.	G	A	Pts.	Pen.	Gms.	G	A	Pts.	Pen.
86-87—London	OHL	65	4	23	27	24	—	—	—	—	—
87-88—London	OHL	66	13	63	76	49	12	8	17	25	6
88-89—Team Canada	Int'l	60	2	22	24	30	—	—	—	—	—
89-90—Team Canada	Int'l	61	7	25	32	38	—	—	—	—	—
90-91—Team Canada	Int'l	53	8	18	26	62	—	—	—	—	—
91-92—Canadian National Team..	Int'l	61	3	18	21	84	—	—	—	—	—
—Canadian Olympic Team ..	Int'l	8	1	2	3	4	—	—	—	—	—
—Baltimore	AHL	2	0	1	1	0	—	—	—	—	—
—Washington	NHL	15	0	1	1	0	7	0	1	1	2
NHL totals		**15**	**0**	**1**	**1**	**0**	**7**	**0**	**1**	**1**	**2**

SCHNEIDER, MATHIEU
D, CANADIENS

PERSONAL: Born June 12, 1969, at New York. . . . 5-11/189. . . . Shoots left.
HIGH SCHOOL: Mount St. Charles Academy (Woonsocket, R.I.).
TRANSACTIONS/CAREER NOTES: Selected by Montreal Canadiens in third round (fourth Canadiens pick, 44th overall) of NHL entry draft (June 13, 1987). . . . Bruised left shoulder (February 1990). . . . Sprained left ankle (January 26, 1991); missed nine games.
HONORS: Named to OHL All-Star first team (1987-88).

Season Team	League	REGULAR SEASON					PLAYOFFS				
		Gms.	G	A	Pts.	Pen.	Gms.	G	A	Pts.	Pen.
85-86—Mount St. Charles H.S.	R.I.H.S.	19	3	27	30		—	—	—	—	—
86-87—Cornwall	OHL	63	7	29	36	75	5	0	0	0	22
87-88—Montreal	NHL	4	0	0	0	2	—	—	—	—	—
—Cornwall	OHL	48	21	40	61	85	11	2	6	8	14
—Sherbrooke	AHL	—	—	—	—	—	3	0	3	3	12
88-89—Cornwall	OHL	59	16	57	73	96	18	7	20	27	30
89-90—Sherbrooke	AHL	28	6	13	19	20	—	—	—	—	—
—Montreal	NHL	44	7	14	21	25	9	1	3	4	31
90-91—Montreal	NHL	69	10	20	30	63	13	2	7	9	18
91-92—Montreal	NHL	78	8	24	32	72	10	1	4	5	6
NHL totals		**195**	**25**	**58**	**83**	**162**	**32**	**4**	**14**	**18**	**55**

SCHULTE, PAXTON
LW, NORDIQUES

PERSONAL: Born July 16, 1972, at Edmonton, Alta. . . . 6-2/210. . . . Shoots left.
COLLEGE: North Dakota, then Spokane Falls (Wash.).
TRANSACTIONS/CAREER NOTES: Selected by Quebec Nordiques in sixth round (seventh Nordiques pick, 124th overall) of NHL entry draft (June 20, 1992).

Season Team	League	REGULAR SEASON					PLAYOFFS				
		Gms.	G	A	Pts.	Pen.	Gms.	G	A	Pts.	Pen.
89-90—Sherwood Park	AJHL	56	28	38	66	151	—	—	—	—	—
90-91—North Dakota	WCHA	38	2	4	6	32	—	—	—	—	—
91-92—Spokane Chiefs	WHL	70	42	42	84	222	10	2	8	10	48

SCISSONS, SCOTT
C, ISLANDERS

PERSONAL: Born October 29, 1971, at Saskatoon, Sask. . . . 6-1/201. . . . Shoots left.
TRANSACTIONS/CAREER NOTES: Selected by New York Islanders in first round (first Islanders pick, sixth overall) of NHL entry draft (June 16, 1990). . . . Injured right arm in preseason game (October 29, 1990); missed 11 games.

Season Team	League	REGULAR SEASON					PLAYOFFS				
		Gms.	G	A	Pts.	Pen.	Gms.	G	A	Pts.	Pen.
88-89—Saskatoon	WHL	71	30	56	86	65	7	0	4	4	16
89-90—Saskatoon	WHL	61	40	47	87	81	10	3	8	11	6
90-91—Saskatoon	WHL	57	24	53	77	61	—	—	—	—	—
—New York Islanders	NHL	1	0	0	0	0	—	—	—	—	—
91-92—Canadian National Team	Int'l	27	4	8	12	23	—	—	—	—	—
NHL totals		1	0	0	0	0					

SCREMIN, CLAUDIO
D, SHARKS

PERSONAL: Born May 28, 1968, at Burnaby, B.C. . . . 6-2/200. . . . Shoots right. . . . Full name: Claudio Francesco Scremin.
COLLEGE: Maine.
TRANSACTIONS/CAREER NOTES: Selected by Washington Capitals in 12th round (12th Capitals pick, 204th overall) in NHL entry draft (June 11, 1988). . . . Traded by Capitals to Minnesota North Stars for G Don Beaupre (November 1, 1988). . . . Signed as free agent by San Jose Sharks (September 3, 1991).

Season Team	League	REGULAR SEASON					PLAYOFFS				
		Gms.	G	A	Pts.	Pen.	Gms.	G	A	Pts.	Pen.
86-87—University of Maine	Hockey East	15	0	1	1	2	—	—	—	—	—
87-88—University of Maine	Hockey East	44	6	18	24	22	—	—	—	—	—
88-89—University of Maine	Hockey East	45	5	24	29	42	—	—	—	—	—
89-90—University of Maine	Hockey East	45	4	26	30	14	—	—	—	—	—
90-91—Kansas City	IHL	77	7	14	21	60	—	—	—	—	—
91-92—Kansas City	IHL	70	5	23	28	44	15	1	6	7	14
—San Jose	NHL	13	0	0	0	25	—	—	—	—	—
NHL totals		13	0	0	0	25					

SEARS, SVERRE
D, FLYERS

PERSONAL: Born October 17, 1970, at Boston. . . . 6-2/185. . . . Shoots left. . . . Full name: Sverre Frederick Sears.
HIGH SCHOOL: Belmont Hill (Belmont, Mass.).
COLLEGE: Princeton.
TRANSACTIONS/CAREER NOTES: Selected by Philadelphia Flyers in eighth round (sixth Flyers pick, 159th overall) of NHL entry draft (June 17, 1989).

Season Team	League	REGULAR SEASON					PLAYOFFS				
		Gms.	G	A	Pts.	Pen.	Gms.	G	A	Pts.	Pen.
87-88—Belmont Hill H.S.	Mass. H.S.		2	8	10		—	—	—	—	—
88-89—Belmont Hill H.S.	Mass. H.S.	23	5	19	24	34	—	—	—	—	—
89-90—Princeton University	ECAC	18	0	1	1	14	—	—	—	—	—
90-91—Princeton University	ECAC	27	2	9	11	56	—	—	—	—	—
91-92—Princeton University	ECAC	25	3	9	12	62	—	—	—	—	—

SEFTEL, STEVE
LW, CAPITALS

PERSONAL: Born May 14, 1968, at Kitchener, Ont. . . . 6-3/200. . . . Shoots left. . . . Full name: Steven Jerome Seftel.
TRANSACTIONS/CAREER NOTES: Broke ankle (September 1985). . . . Selected by Washington Capitals as underage junior in second round (second Capitals pick, 40th overall) of NHL entry draft (June 21, 1986).

Season Team	League	REGULAR SEASON					PLAYOFFS				
		Gms.	G	A	Pts.	Pen.	Gms.	G	A	Pts.	Pen.
85-86—Kingston	OHL	42	11	16	27	53	—	—	—	—	—
86-87—Kingston	OHL	54	21	43	64	55	12	1	4	5	9
87-88—Kingston	OHL	66	32	43	75	51	—	—	—	—	—
—Binghamton	AHL	3	0	0	0	2	—	—	—	—	—
88-89—Baltimore	AHL	58	12	15	27	70	—	—	—	—	—
89-90—Baltimore	AHL	74	10	19	29	52	12	4	3	7	10
90-91—Baltimore	AHL	66	22	22	44	46	6	0	0	0	14
—Washington	NHL	4	0	0	0	2	—	—	—	—	—
91-92—Baltimore	AHL	18	2	6	8	27	—	—	—	—	—
NHL totals		4	0	0	0	2					

SEJBA, JIRI
RW/LW, SABRES

PERSONAL: Born July 22, 1962, at Pardubice, Czechoslovakia. . . . 5-10/193. . . . Shoots left.
TRANSACTIONS/CAREER NOTES: Selected by Buffalo Sabres in ninth round (ninth Sabres pick, 182nd overall) of NHL entry draft (June 15, 1985).

Season Team	League	REGULAR SEASON Gms.	G	A	Pts.	Pen.	PLAYOFFS Gms.	G	A	Pts.	Pen.
86-87—Pardubice	Czech.	34	23	11	34	—	—	—	—	—	—
87-88—Pardubice	Czech.	23	10	15	25	—	—	—	—	—	—
88-89—Pardubice	Czech.	44	38	21	59	68	—	—	—	—	—
89-90—Pardubice	Czech.	26	11	14	25	—	—	—	—	—	—
90-91—Buffalo	NHL	11	0	2	2	8	—	—	—	—	—
—Rochester	AHL	31	15	13	28	54	14	6	7	13	29
91-92—Rochester	AHL	59	27	31	58	36	2	0	0	0	0
NHL totals		11	0	2	2	8					

SELANNE, TEEMU
RW, JETS

PERSONAL: Born March 7, 1970, at Helsinki, Finland.... 6-0/180.... Shoots right. **TRANSACTIONS/CAREER NOTES:** Selected by Winnipeg Jets in first round (first Jets pick, 10th overall) of NHL entry draft (June 11, 1988).... Broke left leg (October 19, 1989).

Season Team	League	REGULAR SEASON Gms.	G	A	Pts.	Pen.	PLAYOFFS Gms.	G	A	Pts.	Pen.
87-88—Jokerit	Finland	33	42	23	65	18	5	4	3	7	2
88-89—Jokerit	Finland	34	35	33	68	12	5	7	3	10	4
89-90—Jokerit	Finland	11	4	8	12	0	—	—	—	—	—
90-91—Jokerit	Finland	42	*33	25	58	12	—	—	—	—	—
91-92—Jokerit	Finland	44	39	23	62	20	—	—	—	—	—
—Finland Olympic Team	Int'l	8	7	4	11						

SEMAK, ALEXANDER
C, DEVILS

PERSONAL: Born February 11, 1966, at Ufa, U.S.S.R.... 5-9/190.... Shoots left. **TRANSACTIONS/CAREER NOTES:** Selected by New Jersey Devils in 10th round (12 Devils pick, 207th overall) of NHL entry draft (June 11, 1988).... Injured shoulder (February 8, 1992); missed seven games.

Season Team	League	REGULAR SEASON Gms.	G	A	Pts.	Pen.	PLAYOFFS Gms.	G	A	Pts.	Pen.
87-88—Dynamo Moscow	USSR	47	21	14	35	40	—	—	—	—	—
88-89—Dynamo Moscow	USSR	44	18	10	28	22	—	—	—	—	—
89-90—Dynamo Moscow	USSR	43	23	11	34	33	—	—	—	—	—
90-91—Dynamo Moscow	USSR	46	17	21	38	48	—	—	—	—	—
91-92—Dynamo Moscow	CIS	18	6	11	17	18	—	—	—	—	—
—Utica	AHL	7	3	2	5	0	—	—	—	—	—
—New Jersey	NHL	25	5	6	11	0	1	0	0	0	0
NHL totals		25	5	6	11	0	1	0	0	0	0

SEMCHUK, BRANDY
RW/LW, KINGS

PERSONAL: Born September 22, 1971, at Calgary, Alta.... 6-1/187.... Shoots right.... Full name: Thomas Semchuk. **TRANSACTIONS/CAREER NOTES:** Selected by Los Angeles Kings in second round (second Kings pick, 28th overall) of NHL entry draft (June 16, 1990).... Bruised thigh (December 1989).... Strained hip flexor (March 1990).

Season Team	League	REGULAR SEASON Gms.	G	A	Pts.	Pen.	PLAYOFFS Gms.	G	A	Pts.	Pen.
87-88—Calgary Canucks	AJHL	90	44	42	86	120	—	—	—	—	—
88-89—Canadian National Team	Int'l	42	11	11	22	60	—	—	—	—	—
89-90—Canadian National Team	Int'l	60	9	14	23	14	—	—	—	—	—
90-91—Lethbridge	WHL	14	9	8	17	10	15	8	5	13	18
—New Haven	AHL	21	1	4	5	6	—	—	—	—	—
91-92—Phoenix	IHL	15	1	5	6	6	—	—	—	—	—
—Raleigh	ECHL	5	1	2	3	16	2	1	0	1	4

SEMENOV, ANATOLI
LW/C, LIGHTNING

PERSONAL: Born March 5, 1962, at Moscow, U.S.S.R.... 6-2/190.... Shoots left. **TRANSACTIONS/CAREER NOTES:** Selected by Edmonton Oilers in sixth round (fifth Oilers pick, 120th overall) of 1989 NHL entry draft (June 17, 1989).... Bruised ribs (March 1, 1991); missed five games.... Suffered hairline fracture in left foot (October 1991); missed four games.... Suffered concussion (November 1991); missed two games.... Injured shoulder (January 4, 1992); missed six games.... Sprained ankle (February 28, 1992); missed one game.... Selected by Tampa Bay Lightning in NHL expansion draft (June 18, 1992).
MISCELLANEOUS: Member of 1988 gold-medal-winning U.S.S.R. Olympic team.

Season Team	League	REGULAR SEASON Gms.	G	A	Pts.	Pen.	PLAYOFFS Gms.	G	A	Pts.	Pen.
79-80—Dynamo Moscow	USSR	8	3	0	3	2	—	—	—	—	—
80-81—Dynamo Moscow	USSR	47	18	14	32	18	—	—	—	—	—
81-82—Dynamo Moscow	USSR	44	12	14	26	28	—	—	—	—	—
82-83—Dynamo Moscow	USSR	44	22	18	40	26	—	—	—	—	—
83-84—Dynamo Moscow	USSR	19	10	5	15	14	—	—	—	—	—
84-85—Dynamo Moscow	USSR	30	17	12	29	32	—	—	—	—	—
85-86—Dynamo Moscow	USSR	32	18	17	35	19	—	—	—	—	—
86-87—Dynamo Moscow	USSR	40	15	29	44	32	—	—	—	—	—
87-88—Dynamo Moscow	USSR	32	17	8	25	22	—	—	—	—	—
88-89—Dynamo Moscow	USSR	31	9	12	21	24	—	—	—	—	—

Season Team	League	REGULAR SEASON Gms.	G	A	Pts.	Pen.	PLAYOFFS Gms.	G	A	Pts.	Pen.
89-90—Dynamo Moscow	USSR	48	13	20	33	16	—	—	—	—	—
—Edmonton	NHL	—	—	—	—	—	2	0	0	0	0
90-91—Edmonton	NHL	57	15	16	31	26	12	5	5	10	6
91-92—Edmonton	NHL	59	20	22	42	16	8	1	1	2	6
NHL totals....................		116	35	38	73	42	22	6	6	12	12

SEROWIK, JEFF
D, MAPLE LEAFS

PERSONAL: Born October 1, 1967, at Manchester, N.H. . . . . 6-0/190. . . . Shoots right. . . . Full name: Jeff Michael Serowik.
HIGH SCHOOL: Lawrence Academy (Groton, Mass.).
COLLEGE: Providence.
TRANSACTIONS/CAREER NOTES: Broke left ankle (April 1982). . . . Broke right ankle (March 1983). . . . Selected by Toronto Maple Leafs in fifth round (fifth Maple Leafs pick, 85th overall) of NHL entry draft (June 15, 1985).
HONORS: Named to Hockey East All-Star second team (1989-90).

Season Team	League	REGULAR SEASON Gms.	G	A	Pts.	Pen.	PLAYOFFS Gms.	G	A	Pts.	Pen.
83-84—Manchester West H.S.......	N.H. H.S.	21	12	12	24		—	—	—	—	—
84-85—Lawrence Academy	Mass. H.S.	24	8	25	33		—	—	—	—	—
85-86—Lawrence Academy	Mass. H.S.			Statistics unavailable.			—	—	—	—	—
86-87—Providence College	Hockey East	33	3	8	11	22	—	—	—	—	—
87-88—Providence College	Hockey East	33	3	9	12	44	—	—	—	—	—
88-89—Providence College	Hockey East	35	3	14	17	48	—	—	—	—	—
89-90—Providence College	Hockey East	35	6	19	25	34	—	—	—	—	—
90-91—Toronto........................	NHL	1	0	0	0	0	—	—	—	—	—
—Newmarket......................	AHL	60	8	15	23	45	—	—	—	—	—
91-92—St. John's	AHL	78	11	34	45	60	16	4	9	13	22
NHL totals....................		1	0	0	0	0					

SEVERYN, BRENT
D, DEVILS

PERSONAL: Born February 22, 1966, at Vegreville, Alta. . . . 6-2/210. . . . Shoots left. . . . Full name: Brent Leonard Severyn.
COLLEGE: Alberta.
TRANSACTIONS/CAREER NOTES: Selected by Winnipeg Jets in fifth round (fifth Jets pick, 99th overall) of NHL entry draft (June 9, 1984). . . . Injured knee (October 1985). . . . Signed as free agent by Quebec Nordiques (July 15, 1988). . . . Traded by Nordiques to New Jersey Devils for D Dave Marcinyshyn (June 3, 1991).

Season Team	League	REGULAR SEASON Gms.	G	A	Pts.	Pen.	PLAYOFFS Gms.	G	A	Pts.	Pen.
82-83—Vegreville	CAJHL	21	20	22	42	10	—	—	—	—	—
83-84—Seattle	WHL	72	14	22	36	49	5	2	1	3	2
84-85—Seattle	WHL	38	8	32	40	54	—	—	—	—	—
—Brandon............................	WHL	26	7	16	23	57	—	—	—	—	—
85-86—Seattle.............................	WHL	33	11	20	31	164	5	0	4	4	4
—Saskatoon	WHL	9	1	4	5	38	—	—	—	—	—
86-87—University of Alberta	CWUAA	43	7	19	26	171	—	—	—	—	—
87-88—University of Alberta	CWUAA	46	21	29	50	178	—	—	—	—	—
88-89—Halifax............................	AHL	47	2	12	14	141	—	—	—	—	—
89-90—Quebec	NHL	35	0	2	2	42	—	—	—	—	—
—Halifax............................	AHL	43	6	9	15	105	6	1	2	3	49
90-91—Halifax............................	AHL	50	7	26	33	202	—	—	—	—	—
91-92—Utica................................	AHL	80	11	33	44	211	4	0	1	1	4
NHL totals....................		35	0	2	2	42					

SEVIGNY, PIERRE
LW, CANADIENS

PERSONAL: Born September 8, 1971, at Trois-Rivieres, Que. . . . 6-0/189. . . . Shoots left.
TRANSACTIONS/CAREER NOTES: Selected by Montreal Canadiens in third round (fourth Canadiens pick, 51st overall) of NHL entry draft (June 17, 1989). . . . Severed knee ligament in off-ice accident (March 25, 1991).
HONORS: Named to QMJHL All-Star second team (1989-90 and 1990-91).

Season Team	League	REGULAR SEASON Gms.	G	A	Pts.	Pen.	PLAYOFFS Gms.	G	A	Pts.	Pen.
88-89—Verdun..............................	QMJHL	67	27	43	70	88	—	—	—	—	—
89-90—St. Hyacinthe	QMJHL	67	47	72	119	205	12	8	8	16	42
90-91—St. Hyacinthe	QMJHL	60	36	46	82	203	—	—	—	—	—
91-92—Fredericton	AHL	74	22	37	59	145	7	1	1	2	26

SHANAHAN, BRENDAN
RW/LW, BLUES

PERSONAL: Born January 23, 1969, at Mimico, Ont. . . . 6-3/210. . . . Shoots right.
TRANSACTIONS/CAREER NOTES: Bruised tendons in shoulder (January 1987). . . . Selected by New Jersey Devils as underage junior in first round (first Devils pick, second overall) of NHL entry draft (June 13, 1987). . . . Broke nose (December 1987). . . . Suffered back spasms (March 1989). . . . Suspended five games by NHL for stick-fighting (January 13, 1990). . . . Suffered lower abdominal strain (February 1990). . . . Suffered lacerations to lower right side of face and underwent surgery (January 8, 1991); missed five games. . . . Signed as free agent by St. Louis Blues (July 25, 1991); D Scott Stevens awarded to New Jersey Devils as compensation (September 3, 1991).

Season Team	League	REGULAR SEASON					PLAYOFFS				
		Gms.	G	A	Pts.	Pen.	Gms.	G	A	Pts.	Pen.
84-85—Mississauga	MTHL	36	20	21	41	26	—	—	—	—	—
85-86—London	OHL	59	28	34	62	70	5	5	5	10	5
86-87—London	OHL	56	39	53	92	128	—	—	—	—	—
87-88—New Jersey	NHL	65	7	19	26	131	12	2	1	3	44
88-89—New Jersey	NHL	68	22	28	50	115	—	—	—	—	—
89-90—New Jersey	NHL	73	30	42	72	137	6	3	3	6	20
90-91—New Jersey	NHL	75	29	37	66	141	7	3	5	8	12
91-92—St. Louis	NHL	80	33	36	69	171	6	2	3	5	14
NHL totals		361	121	162	283	695	31	10	12	22	90

SHANK, DANIEL
RW, WHALERS

PERSONAL: Born May 12, 1967, at Montreal.... 5-10/190.... Shoots right. **TRANSACTIONS/CAREER NOTES:** Signed as free agent by Detroit Red Wings (July 13, 1988). ... Traded by Red Wings to Hartford Whalers for C/LW Chris Tancill (December 18, 1991).

Season Team	League	REGULAR SEASON					PLAYOFFS				
		Gms.	G	A	Pts.	Pen.	Gms.	G	A	Pts.	Pen.
85-86—Shawinigan	QMJHL	51	34	38	72	184	—	—	—	—	—
86-87—Hull	QMJHL	46	26	43	69	325	—	—	—	—	—
87-88—Hull	QMJHL	52	31	42	73	343	19	10	19	29	*106
88-89—Adirondack	AHL	42	5	20	25	113	17	11	8	19	102
89-90—Detroit	NHL	57	11	13	24	143	—	—	—	—	—
—Adirondack	AHL	14	8	8	16	36	—	—	—	—	—
90-91—Detroit	NHL	7	0	1	1	14	—	—	—	—	—
—Adirondack	AHL	60	26	49	75	278	—	—	—	—	—
91-92—Adirondack	AHL	27	13	21	34	112	—	—	—	—	—
—Hartford	NHL	13	2	0	2	18	5	0	0	0	22
—Springfield	AHL	31	9	19	28	83	8	8	0	8	48
NHL totals		77	13	14	27	175	5	0	0	0	22

SHANNON, DARRIN
LW, JETS

PERSONAL: Born December 8, 1969, at Barrie, Ont.... 6-2/200.... Shoots left.... Full name: Darrin A. Shannon.... Brother of Darryl Shannon, defenseman, Toronto Maple Leafs. **TRANSACTIONS/CAREER NOTES:** Separated right shoulder (November 1986).... Dislocated left elbow (November 1987).... Separated left shoulder (January 1988).... Selected by Pittsburgh Penguins in first round (first Penguins pick, fourth overall) of NHL entry draft (June 11, 1988).... Traded by Penguins with D Doug Bodger to Buffalo Sabres for G Tom Barrasso and third-round pick in 1990 draft (LW Joe Dziedzic) (November 12, 1988).... Strained knee ligaments (May 1990).... Injured jaw (January 8, 1991); missed five games.... Traded by Sabres with LW Mike Hartman and D Dean Kennedy to Winnipeg Jets for RW Dave McLlwain, D Gordon Donnelly, sixth-round pick in 1992 draft and future considerations (October 11, 1991).... Injured knee (November 20, 1991).... Injured eye (November 25, 1991); missed one game.... Sprained leg (December 31, 1991); missed seven games. **HONORS:** Named to OHL All-Scholastic team (1986-87).... Won Bobby Smith Trophy (1987-88).... Named to OHL All-Star first team (1987-88).

Season Team	League	REGULAR SEASON					PLAYOFFS				
		Gms.	G	A	Pts.	Pen.	Gms.	G	A	Pts.	Pen.
85-86—Barrie Jr. B	OHA	40	13	22	35	21	—	—	—	—	—
86-87—Windsor	OHL	60	16	67	83	116	14	4	6	10	8
87-88—Windsor	OHL	43	33	41	74	49	12	6	12	18	9
88-89—Windsor	OHL	54	33	48	81	47	4	1	6	7	2
—Buffalo	NHL	3	0	0	0	0	2	0	0	0	0
89-90—Buffalo	NHL	17	2	7	9	4	6	0	1	1	4
—Rochester	AHL	50	20	23	43	25	9	4	1	5	2
90-91—Rochester	AHL	49	26	34	60	56	10	3	5	8	22
—Buffalo	NHL	34	8	6	14	12	6	1	2	3	4
91-92—Buffalo	NHL	1	0	1	1	0	—	—	—	—	—
—Winnipeg	NHL	68	13	26	39	41	7	0	1	1	10
NHL totals		123	23	40	63	57	21	1	4	5	18

SHANNON, DARRYL
D, MAPLE LEAFS

PERSONAL: Born June 21, 1968, at Barrie, Ont.... 6-2/195.... Shoots left.... Brother of Darrin Shannon, left winger, Winnipeg Jets. **TRANSACTIONS/CAREER NOTES:** Selected by Toronto Maple Leafs in second round (second Maple Leafs pick, 36th overall) of NHL entry draft (June 21, 1986).... Broke right leg and right thumb, bruised chest and suffered slipped disk in automobile accident (June 20, 1990). **HONORS:** Named to OHL All-Star second team (1986-87).... Won Max Kaminsky Trophy (1987-88).... Named to OHL All-Star first team (1987-88).

Season Team	League	REGULAR SEASON					PLAYOFFS				
		Gms.	G	A	Pts.	Pen.	Gms.	G	A	Pts.	Pen.
84-85—Barrie Jr. B	OHA	39	5	23	28	50	—	—	—	—	—
85-86—Windsor	OHL	57	6	21	27	52	16	5	6	11	22
86-87—Windsor	OHL	64	23	27	50	83	14	4	8	12	18
87-88—Windsor	OHL	60	16	70	86	116	12	3	8	11	17
88-89—Toronto	NHL	14	1	3	4	6	—	—	—	—	—
—Newmarket	AHL	61	5	24	29	37	5	0	3	3	10

Season Team	League	REGULAR SEASON					PLAYOFFS				
		Gms.	G	A	Pts.	Pen.	Gms.	G	A	Pts.	Pen.
89-90—Newmarket......................	AHL	47	4	15	19	58	—	—	—	—	—
—Toronto.............................	NHL	10	0	1	1	12	—	—	—	—	—
90-91—Toronto.............................	NHL	10	0	1	1	0	—	—	—	—	—
—Newmarket......................	AHL	47	2	14	16	51	—	—	—	—	—
91-92—Toronto.............................	NHL	48	2	8	10	23	—	—	—	—	—
NHL totals..................................		82	3	13	16	41					

SHANTZ, JEFF
C, BLACKHAWKS

PERSONAL: Born October 10, 1973, at Edmonton, Alta.... 6-0/185.... Shoots right.
HIGH SCHOOL: R. Usher Collegiate (Regina, Sask.).
TRANSACTIONS/CAREER NOTES: Selected by Chicago Blackhawks in second round (second Blackhawks pick, 36th overall) of NHL entry draft (June 20, 1992).

Season Team	League	REGULAR SEASON					PLAYOFFS				
		Gms.	G	A	Pts.	Pen.	Gms.	G	A	Pts.	Pen.
89-90—Regina	WHL	1	0	0	0	0	—	—	—	—	—
90-91—Regina	WHL	69	16	21	37	22	8	2	2	4	2
91-92—Regina	WHL	72	39	50	89	75	—	—	—	—	—

SHARPLES, WARREN
G, FLAMES

PERSONAL: Born March 1, 1968, at Calgary, Alta.... 6-0/180.... Shoots left....
Full name: Warren Scott Sharples.
COLLEGE: Michigan.
TRANSACTIONS/CAREER NOTES: Selected by Calgary Flames in ninth round (eighth Flames pick, 184th overall) of NHL entry draft (June 21, 1986).

Season Team	League	REGULAR SEASON							PLAYOFFS						
		Gms.	Min.	W	L	T	GA	SO	Avg.	Gms.	Min.	W	L	GA	SO	Avg.
85-86—Penticton......................	BCJHL	28	1522	20	6		94	0	3.71	—	—	—	—	—	—	—
86-87—University of Michigan .	CCHA	32	1728	12	16	1	148	1	5.14	—	—	—	—	—	—	—
87-88—University of Michigan .	CCHA	33	1930	18	15	0	132		4.10	—	—	—	—	—	—	—
88-89—University of Michigan .	CCHA	33	1887	17	11	2	116		3.69	—	—	—	—	—	—	—
89-90—University of Michigan .	CCHA	39	2165	20	10	6	117		3.24	—	—	—	—	—	—	—
—Salt Lake City..............	IHL	3	178	0	3	0	13	0	4.38	—	—	—	—	—	—	—
90-91—Salt Lake City..............	IHL	37	2097	21	11	1	124	2	3.55	4	188	0	3	14	0	4.47
91-92—Salt Lake City..............	IHL	35	1936	9	18	4	121	0	3.75	1	60	0	1	7	0	7.00
—Calgary........................	NHL	1	65	0	0	1	4	0	3.69	—	—	—	—	—	—	—
NHL totals..................................		1	65	0	0	1	4	0	3.69							

SHAW, BRAD
D, SENATORS

PERSONAL: Born April 28, 1964, at Cambridge, Ont.... 6-0/190.... Shoots right.
TRANSACTIONS/CAREER NOTES: Selected by Detroit Red Wings as underage junior in fifth round (fifth Red Wings pick, 86th overall) of NHL entry draft (June 9, 1982).... Traded by Red Wings to Hartford Whalers for eighth-round pick in 1984 draft (LW Lars Karlsson) (May 29, 1984)....
Fractured finger on left hand (February 1988).... Broke nose (October 21, 1989).... Suffered back spasms (November 12, 1989).... Bruised right foot (February 28, 1990).... Injured groin (October 28, 1991); missed two games.... Injured knee (January 31, 1992); missed four games.... Bruised knee (February 29, 1992); missed four games.... Injured groin (March 14, 1992); missed three games.... Traded by Whalers to New Jersey Devils for future considerations (June 15, 1992).... Selected by Ottawa Senators in NHL expansion draft (June 18, 1992).
HONORS: Won Max Kaminsky Trophy (1983-84).... Named to OHL All-Star first team (1983-84).... Won Eddie Shore Plaque (1986-87).... Named to AHL All-Star first team (1986-87 and 1987-88).... Named to NHL All-Rookie team (1989-90).

Season Team	League	REGULAR SEASON					PLAYOFFS				
		Gms.	G	A	Pts.	Pen.	Gms.	G	A	Pts.	Pen.
81-82—Ottawa.............................	OHL	68	13	59	72	24	15	1	13	14	4
82-83—Ottawa.............................	OHL	63	12	66	78	24	9	2	9	11	4
83-84—Ottawa.............................	OHL	68	11	71	82	75	13	2	*27	29	9
84-85—Salt Lake City..................	IHL	44	3	29	32	25	—	—	—	—	—
—Binghamton	AHL	24	1	10	11	4	8	1	8	9	6
85-86—Hartford.........................	NHL	8	0	2	2	4	—	—	—	—	—
—Binghamton	AHL	64	10	44	54	33	5	0	2	2	6
86-87—Hartford.........................	NHL	2	0	0	0	0	—	—	—	—	—
—Binghamton	AHL	77	9	30	39	43	12	1	8	9	2
87-88—Binghamton	AHL	73	12	50	62	50	4	0	5	5	4
—Hartford........................	NHL	1	0	0	0	0	—	—	—	—	—
88-89—Verice	Italy	35	10	30	40	44	11	4	8	12	13
—Hartford........................	NHL	3	1	0	1	0	3	1	0	1	0
—Canadian National Team..	Int'l	4	1	0	1	2	—	—	—	—	—
89-90—Hartford.........................	NHL	64	3	32	35	40	7	2	5	7	0
90-91—Hartford.........................	NHL	72	4	28	32	29	6	1	2	3	2
91-92—Hartford.........................	NHL	62	3	22	25	44	3	0	1	1	4
NHL totals..................................		212	11	84	95	117	19	4	8	12	6

SHAW, DAVID
D, NORTH STARS

PERSONAL: Born May 25, 1964, at St. Thomas, Ont.... 6-2/204.... Shoots right.
TRANSACTIONS/CAREER NOTES: Selected by Quebec Nordiques as underage junior in first round (first Nordiques pick, 13th overall) of NHL entry draft (June 9, 1982).... Sprained wrist (December 18, 1985).... Traded by Nordiques with LW John Ogrodnick to New York Rangers for

LW Jeff Jackson and D Terry Carkner (September 30, 1987).... Separated shoulder (October 1987).... Suspended 12 games by NHL for slashing (October 27, 1988).... Bruised shoulder (March 15, 1989).... Dislocated right shoulder (November 2, 1989).... Reinjured right shoulder (November 22, 1989); missed 10 games.... Underwent surgery to right shoulder (February 7, 1990).... Bruised finger (September 1990).... Bruised left big toe (October 31, 1990).... Sprained knee (October 20, 1991).... Traded by Rangers to Edmonton Oilers for D Jeff Beukeboom (November 12, 1991) to complete deal in which Rangers traded C Bernie Nicholls, LW Louie DeBrusk, RW Steven Rice and future considerations to Oilers for C Mark Messier and future considerations (October 4, 1991).... Traded by Oilers to Minnesota North Stars for D Brian Glynn (January 21, 1992).
HONORS: Named to OHL All-Star first team (1983-84).

			REGULAR SEASON					PLAYOFFS				
Season	Team	League	Gms.	G	A	Pts.	Pen.	Gms.	G	A	Pts.	Pen.
80-81	—Stratford Jr. B	OHA	41	12	19	31	30	—	—	—	—	—
81-82	—Kitchener	OHL	68	6	25	31	99	15	2	2	4	51
82-83	—Kitchener	OHL	57	18	56	74	78	12	2	10	12	18
	—Quebec	NHL	2	0	0	0	0	—	—	—	—	—
83-84	—Kitchener	OHL	58	14	34	48	73	16	4	9	13	12
	—Quebec	NHL	3	0	0	0	0	—	—	—	—	—
84-85	—Guelph	OHL	2	0	0	0	0	—	—	—	—	—
	—Fredericton	AHL	48	7	6	13	73	2	0	0	0	7
	—Quebec	NHL	14	0	0	0	11	—	—	—	—	—
85-86	—Quebec	NHL	73	7	19	26	78	—	—	—	—	—
86-87	—Quebec	NHL	75	0	19	19	69	—	—	—	—	—
87-88	—New York Rangers	NHL	68	7	25	32	100	—	—	—	—	—
88-89	—New York Rangers	NHL	63	6	11	17	88	4	0	2	2	30
89-90	—New York Rangers	NHL	22	2	10	12	22	—	—	—	—	—
90-91	—New York Rangers	NHL	77	2	10	12	89	6	0	0	0	11
91-92	—New York Rangers	NHL	10	0	1	1	15	—	—	—	—	—
	—Edmonton	NHL	12	1	1	2	8	—	—	—	—	—
	—Minnesota	NHL	37	0	7	7	49	7	2	2	4	10
NHL totals			456	25	103	128	529	17	2	4	6	51

SHEEHY, NEIL
D, FLAMES

PERSONAL: Born February 9, 1960, at International Falls, Minn.... 6-2/214.... Shoots right.... Full name: Neil Kane Sheehy.... Brother of Tim Sheehy, right winger, Detroit Red Wings and Hartford Whalers (1977-78 and 1979-80) and New England Whalers, Edmonton Oilers and Birmingham Bulls of WHA (1972-73 through 1977-78); and nephew of Bronko Nagurski, Hall of Fame fullback/tackle, Chicago Bears of the National Football League (1930-37 and 1943).
COLLEGE: Harvard.
TRANSACTIONS/CAREER NOTES: Signed as free agent by Calgary Flames (August 16, 1983).... Dislocated shoulder (October 1986).... Suffered from recurring shoulder problems (December 1986); missed games.... Suffered deep thigh bruise (March 10, 1987).... Traded by Flames with C Carey Wilson and LW Lane MacDonald to Hartford Whalers for D Dana Murzyn and RW Shane Churla (January 3, 1988).... Injured hip (January 1988).... Traded by Whalers with RW Mike Millar to Washington Capitals for RW Ed Kastelic and D Grant Jennings (July 6, 1988).... Bruised left shin (March 9, 1990).... Broke left leg and ankle in preseason game, injured back and developed herniated disk in a team practice and underwent surgery (September 20, 1990); missed entire regular season and nine playoff games.... Signed as free agent by Flames (September 1991).

			REGULAR SEASON					PLAYOFFS				
Season	Team	League	Gms.	G	A	Pts.	Pen.	Gms.	G	A	Pts.	Pen.
79-80	—Harvard University	ECAC	13	0	0	0	10	—	—	—	—	—
80-81	—Harvard University	ECAC	26	4	8	12	22	—	—	—	—	—
81-82	—Harvard University	ECAC	30	7	11	18	46	—	—	—	—	—
82-83	—Harvard University	ECAC	34	5	13	18	48	—	—	—	—	—
83-84	—Colorado	CHL	74	5	18	23	151	—	—	—	—	—
	—Calgary	NHL	1	1	0	1	2	4	0	0	0	4
84-85	—Moncton	AHL	34	6	9	15	101	—	—	—	—	—
	—Calgary	NHL	31	3	4	7	109	—	—	—	—	—
85-86	—Moncton	AHL	4	1	1	2	21	—	—	—	—	—
	—Calgary	NHL	65	2	16	18	271	22	0	2	2	79
86-87	—Calgary	NHL	54	4	6	10	151	6	0	0	0	21
87-88	—Calgary	NHL	36	2	6	8	73	—	—	—	—	—
	—Hartford	NHL	26	1	4	5	116	1	0	0	0	7
88-89	—Washington	NHL	72	3	4	7	179	6	0	0	0	19
89-90	—Washington	NHL	59	1	5	6	291	13	0	1	1	*92
90-91	—Washington	NHL	—	—	—	—	—	2	0	0	0	19
91-92	—Calgary	NHL	35	1	2	3	119	—	—	—	—	—
	—Salt Lake City	IHL	6	0	0	0	34	—	—	—	—	—
NHL totals			379	18	47	65	1311	54	0	3	3	241

SHEPPARD, RAY
RW, RED WINGS

PERSONAL: Born May 27, 1966, at Pembroke, Ont.... 6-1/190.... Shoots right.
TRANSACTIONS/CAREER NOTES: Selected by Buffalo Sabres as underage junior in third round (third Sabres pick, 60th overall) of NHL entry draft (June 9, 1984).... Injured left knee (September 1986); missed Sabres training camp.... Bruised back during training camp (September 1988).... Suffered facial lacerations (November 25, 1988).... Suffered facial lacerations (November 27, 1988). ... Suffered from the flu (December 1988).... Sprained ankle (January 30, 1989).... Injured left knee (March 16, 1990).... Traded by Sabres to New York Rangers for future considerations and cash (July 10, 1990).... Sprained medial collateral ligaments of right knee (February 18, 1991); missed 13 games.... Dislocated left shoulder (March 24, 1991).... Signed as free agent by Detroit Red Wings (August 5, 1991).... Strained lower abdomen (March 20, 1992); missed five games.

HONORS: Won Red Tilson Trophy (1985-86).... Won Eddie Powers Memorial Trophy (1985-86).... Won Jim Mahon Memorial Trophy (1985-86).... Named to OHL All-Star first team (1985-86).... Named to NHL All-Rookie team (1987-88).

			REGULAR SEASON					PLAYOFFS			
Season Team	League	Gms.	G	A	Pts.	Pen.	Gms.	G	A	Pts.	Pen.
82-83—Brockville	COJHL	48	27	36	63	81	—	—	—	—	—
83-84—Cornwall	OHL	68	44	36	80	69	—	—	—	—	—
84-85—Cornwall	OHL	49	33	33	58	51	9	2	12	14	4
85-86—Cornwall	OHL	63	*81	61	*142	25	6	7	4	11	0
86-87—Rochester	AHL	55	18	13	31	11	15	12	3	15	2
87-88—Buffalo	NHL	74	38	27	65	14	6	1	1	2	2
88-89—Buffalo	NHL	67	22	21	43	15	1	0	1	1	0
89-90—Buffalo	NHL	18	4	2	6	0	—	—	—	—	—
—Rochester	AHL	5	3	5	8	2	17	8	7	15	9
90-91—New York Rangers	NHL	59	24	23	47	21	—	—	—	—	—
91-92—Detroit	NHL	74	36	26	62	27	11	6	2	8	4
NHL totals		292	124	99	223	77	18	7	4	11	6

SHEVALIER, JEFF
LW/C, KINGS

PERSONAL: Born March 14, 1974, at Mississauga, Ont.... 5-11/178.... Shoots left.
HIGH SCHOOL: Chippewa Secondary School (North Bay, Ont.).
TRANSACTIONS/CAREER NOTES: Selected by Los Angeles Kings in fifth round (fourth Kings pick, 111th overall) of NHL entry draft (June 20, 1992).

			REGULAR SEASON					PLAYOFFS			
Season Team	League	Gms.	G	A	Pts.	Pen.	Gms.	G	A	Pts.	Pen.
90-91—Oakville Jr.B	OHA	5	1	4	5	0	—	—	—	—	—
—Georgetown Jr. B	OHA	12	11	11	22	8	—	—	—	—	—
—Acton Jr. C	OHA	28	29	31	60	62	—	—	—	—	—
91-92—North Bay	OHL	64	28	29	57	26	21	5	11	16	25

SHOEBOTTOM, BRUCE
D

PERSONAL: Born August 20, 1965, at Windsor, Ont.... 6-2/200.... Shoots left.
TRANSACTIONS/CAREER NOTES: Broke leg (December 1982).... Selected by Los Angeles Kings as underage junior in third round (first Kings pick, 47th overall) of NHL entry draft (June 8, 1983).... Traded by Kings to Washington Capitals for RW Bryan Erickson (October 31, 1985).... Suspended by IHL for going into stands (January 24, 1987).... Signed as free agent by Boston Bruins (July 20, 1987).... Broke collarbone (April 1988).... Suffered facial lacerations (November 29, 1989).... Suspended 10 games by AHL for physically abusing linesman (November 17, 1990); suspension later reduced to five games.

			REGULAR SEASON					PLAYOFFS			
Season Team	League	Gms.	G	A	Pts.	Pen.	Gms.	G	A	Pts.	Pen.
81-82—Peterborough	OHL	51	0	4	4	67	—	—	—	—	—
82-83—Peterborough	OHL	34	2	10	12	106	—	—	—	—	—
83-84—Peterborough	OHL	16	0	5	5	73	—	—	—	—	—
84-85—Peterborough	OHL	60	2	15	17	143	17	0	4	4	26
85-86—New Haven	AHL	6	2	0	2	12	—	—	—	—	—
—Binghamton	AHL	62	7	5	12	249	—	—	—	—	—
86-87—Fort Wayne	IHL	75	2	10	12	309	10	0	0	0	31
87-88—Maine	AHL	70	2	12	14	138	—	—	—	—	—
—Boston	NHL	3	0	1	1	0	4	1	0	1	42
88-89—Maine	AHL	44	0	8	8	265	—	—	—	—	—
—Boston	NHL	29	1	3	4	44	10	0	2	2	35
89-90—Maine	AHL	66	3	11	14	228	—	—	—	—	—
—Boston	NHL	2	0	0	0	4	—	—	—	—	—
90-91—Maine	AHL	71	2	8	10	238	1	0	0	0	14
—Boston	NHL	1	0	0	0	5	—	—	—	—	—
91-92—Peoria	IHL	79	4	12	16	234	10	0	0	0	33
NHL totals		35	1	4	5	53	14	1	2	3	77

SHUCHUK, GARY
C, RED WINGS

PERSONAL: Born February 17, 1967, at Edmonton, Alta.... 5-10/191.... Shoots right.... Full name: Gary Robert Shuchuk.
COLLEGE: Wisconsin.
TRANSACTIONS/CAREER NOTES: Selected by Detroit Red Wings in NHL supplemental draft (June 10, 1988).
HONORS: Named to NCAA All-America West first team (1989-90).... Won WCHA Most Valuable Player Award (1989-90).... Named to WCHA All-Star first team (1989-90).

			REGULAR SEASON					PLAYOFFS			
Season Team	League	Gms.	G	A	Pts.	Pen.	Gms.	G	A	Pts.	Pen.
86-87—University of Wisconsin	WCHA	42	19	11	30	72	—	—	—	—	—
87-88—University of Wisconsin	WCHA	44	7	22	29	70	—	—	—	—	—
88-89—University of Wisconsin	WCHA	46	18	19	37	102	—	—	—	—	—
89-90—University of Wisconsin	WCHA	45	*41	39	*80	70	—	—	—	—	—
90-91—Detroit	NHL	6	1	2	3	6	3	0	0	0	0
—Adirondack	AHL	59	23	24	47	32	—	—	—	—	—
91-92—Adirondack	AHL	79	32	48	80	48	†19	4	9	13	18
NHL totals		6	1	2	3	6	3	0	0	0	0

SHULMISTRA, RICH
G, NORDIQUES

PERSONAL: Born April 1, 1971, at Sudbury, Ont. . . . 6-2/186. . . . Full name: Richard Shulmistra.
HIGH SCHOOL: LaSalle Secondary School (Kingston, Ont.).
COLLEGE: Miami of Ohio.
TRANSACTIONS/CAREER NOTES: Selected by Quebec Nordiques in NHL supplemental draft (June 19, 1992).

					REGULAR SEASON							PLAYOFFS				
Season	Team	League	Gms.	Min.	W	L	T	GA	SO	Avg.	Gms.	Min.	W	L	GA SO	Avg.
90-91—Miami of Ohio		CCHA	15	920	2	12	2	80	0	5.22	—	—	—	—	— —	—
91-92—Miami of Ohio		CCHA	19	850	3	5	2	67	0	4.73	—	—	—	—	— —	—

SHUTE, DAVE
LW/C, PENGUINS

PERSONAL: Born February 10, 1971, at Carlyle, Penn. . . . 5-11/188. . . . Shoots left.
HIGH SCHOOL: Richfield (Minn.).
TRANSACTIONS/CAREER NOTES: Dislocated shoulder (February 1987). . . . Selected by Pittsburgh Penguins in eighth round (ninth Penguins pick, 163rd overall) of NHL entry draft (June 17, 1989).

					REGULAR SEASON					PLAYOFFS			
Season	Team	League	Gms.	G	A	Pts.	Pen.	Gms.	G	A	Pts.	Pen.
86-87—Richfield H.S.		Minn. H.S.	23	17	15	32	26	—	—	—	—	—
87-88—Richfield H.S.		Minn. H.S.	13	7	9	16	38	—	—	—	—	—
88-89—Victoria		WHL	69	5	11	16	26	8	0	1	1	10
89-90—Victoria		WHL	14	4	5	9	25	—	—	—	—	—
—Medicine Hat		WHL	48	13	15	28	56	—	—	—	—	—
90-91—Medicine Hat		WHL	72	31	28	59	91	11	6	2	8	9
91-92—Muskegon		IHL	7	1	2	3	6	—	—	—	—	—
—Knoxville		ECHL	57	18	35	53	91	—	—	—	—	—

SIDORKIEWICZ, PETER
G, SENATORS

PERSONAL: Born June 29, 1963, at Dabrown Bialostocka, Poland. . . . 5-9/180. . . . Shoots left.
TRANSACTIONS/CAREER NOTES: Selected by Washington Capitals as underage junior in fifth round (fifth Capitals pick, 91st overall) of NHL entry draft (June 10, 1981). . . . Sprained right ankle (March 3, 1991). . . . Traded by Capitals with C Dean Evason to Hartford Whalers for LW David Jensen (March 1985). . . . Selected by Ottawa Senators in NHL expansion draft (June 18, 1992).
HONORS: Shared Dave Pinkney Trophy with Jeff Hogg (1982-83). . . . Named to AHL All-Star second team (1986-87). . . . Named to NHL All-Rookie team (1988-89).

					REGULAR SEASON						PLAYOFFS					
Season	Team	League	Gms.	Min.	W	L	T	GA	SO	Avg.	Gms.	Min.	W	L	GA SO	Avg.
80-81—Oshawa		OMJHL	7	308	3	3	0	24	0	4.68	5	266	2	2	20 0	4.51
81-82—Oshawa		OHL	29	1553	14	11	1	123	*2	4.75	1	13	0	0	1 0	4.62
82-83—Oshawa		OHL	60	3536	36	20	3	213	0	3.61	*17	*1020	15	1	*60 0	3.53
83-84—Oshawa		OHL	52	2966	28	21	1	205	1	4.15	7	420	3	4	27 +1	3.86
84-85—Fort Wayne		IHL	10	590	4	4	2	43	0	4.37	—	—	—	—	— —	—
—Binghamton		AHL	45	2691	31	9	5	137	3	3.05	8	481	4	4	31 0	3.87
85-86—Binghamton		AHL	49	2819	21	22	3	150	2	*3.19	4	235	1	3	12 0	3.06
86-87—Binghamton		AHL	57	3304	23	16	0	161	4	2.92	13	794	6	7	36 0	*2.72
87-88—Hartford		NHL	1	60	0	1	0	6	0	6.00	—	—	—	—	— —	—
—Binghamton		AHL	42	2346	19	17	3	144	0	3.68	3	147	0	2	8 0	3.27
88-89—Hartford		NHL	44	2635	22	18	4	133	4	3.03	2	124	0	2	8 0	3.87
89-90—Hartford		NHL	46	2703	19	19	7	161	1	3.57	7	429	3	4	23 0	3.22
90-91—Hartford		NHL	52	2953	21	22	7	164	1	3.33	6	359	2	4	24 0	4.01
91-92—Hartford		NHL	35	1995	9	19	6	111	2	3.34	—	—	—	—	— —	—
NHL totals			178	10346	71	79	24	575	8	3.33	15	912	5	10	55 0	3.62

SILLINGER, MIKE
C, RED WINGS

PERSONAL: Born June 29, 1971, at Regina, Sask. . . . 5-10/191. . . . Shoots right.
TRANSACTIONS/CAREER NOTES: Selected by Detroit Red Wings in first round (first Red Wings pick, 11th overall) of NHL entry draft (June 17, 1989). . . . Fractured rib in training camp (September 1990).
HONORS: Named to WHL All-Star second team (1989-90). . . . Named to WHL All-Star first team (1990-91).

					REGULAR SEASON					PLAYOFFS			
Season	Team	League	Gms.	G	A	Pts.	Pen.	Gms.	G	A	Pts.	Pen.
87-88—Regina		WHL	67	18	25	43	17	4	2	2	4	0
88-89—Regina		WHL	72	53	78	131	52	—	—	—	—	—
89-90—Regina		WHL	70	57	72	129	41	11	12	10	22	2
—Adirondack		AHL	—	—	—	—	—	1	0	0	0	0
90-91—Regina		WHL	57	50	66	116	42	8	6	9	15	4
—Detroit		NHL	3	0	1	1	0	3	0	1	1	0
91-92—Adirondack		AHL	64	25	41	66	26	15	9	*19	*28	12
—Detroit		NHL	—	—	—	—	—	8	2	2	4	2
NHL totals			3	0	1	1	0	11	2	3	5	2

SIMARD, MARTIN
RW, LIGHTNING

PERSONAL: Born June 25, 1966, at Montreal. . . . 6-3/215. . . . Shoots right.
TRANSACTIONS/CAREER NOTES: Signed as free agent by Calgary Flames (May 1987). . . . Underwent surgery to right knee (September 26, 1988). . . . Suspended 10 games by IHL for fighting (December 11, 1988). . . . Underwent appendectomy (November 28, 1989).

... Strained right knee (November 21, 1991).... Traded by Flames to Quebec Nordiques for D Greg Smyth (March 10, 1992). ... Traded by Nordiques to Tampa Bay Lightning for RW Tim Hunter (June 22, 1992).

			REGULAR SEASON					PLAYOFFS			
Season Team	League	Gms.	G	A	Pts.	Pen.	Gms.	G	A	Pts.	Pen.
83-84—Quebec	QMJHL	59	6	10	16	26	—	—	—	—	—
84-85—Granby	QMJHL	58	22	31	53	78	—	—	—	—	—
85-86—Granby	QMJHL	54	32	28	60	129	—	—	—	—	—
—Hull	QMJHL	14	8	8	16	55	14	8	19	27	19
86-87—Granby	QMJHL	41	30	47	77	105	8	3	7	10	21
87-88—Salt Lake City	IHL	82	8	23	31	281	19	6	3	9	100
88-89—Salt Lake City	IHL	71	13	15	28	221	14	4	0	4	45
89-90—Salt Lake City	IHL	59	22	23	45	151	11	5	8	13	10
90-91—Calgary	NHL	16	0	2	2	53	—	—	—	—	—
—Salt Lake City	IHL	54	24	25	49	113	4	3	0	3	20
91-92—Salt Lake City	IHL	11	3	7	10	51					
—Calgary	NHL	21	1	3	4	119					
—Halifax	AHL	10	5	3	8	26					
NHL totals		37	1	5	6	172					

SIMON, CHRIS
LW, NORDIQUES

PERSONAL: Born January 30, 1972, at Wawa, Ont.... 6-3/230.... Shoots left. **TRANSACTIONS/CAREER NOTES:** Suspended six games by OHL for shooting the puck in frustration and striking another player (January 20, 1990).... Selected by Philadelphia Flyers in second round (second Flyers pick, 25th overall) of NHL entry draft (June 16, 1990).... Underwent surgery to repair left rotator cuff and a torn muscle (September 1990).... Traded by Flyers with first-round pick in 1994 draft to Quebec Nordiques (July 21, 1992) to complete deal in which Flyers sent G Ron Hextall, C Mike Ricci, C Peter Forsberg, D Steve Duchesne, first-round pick in 1993 draft, cash and future considerations to Nordiques for C Eric Lindros (June 20, 1992).

			REGULAR SEASON					PLAYOFFS			
Season Team	League	Gms.	G	A	Pts.	Pen.	Gms.	G	A	Pts.	Pen.
87-88—Sault Ste. Marie	OHA	55	42	36	78	172	—	—	—	—	—
88-89—Ottawa	OHL	36	4	2	6	31	—	—	—	—	—
89-90—Ottawa	OHL	57	36	38	74	146	3	2	1	3	4
90-91—Ottawa	OHL	20	16	6	22	69	17	5	9	14	59
91-92—Ottawa	OHL	2	1	1	2	24	—	—	—	—	—
—Sault Ste. Marie	OHL	31	19	25	44	143	11	5	8	13	49

SIMPSON, CRAIG
LW, OILERS

PERSONAL: Born February 15, 1967, at London, Ont.... 6-2/195.... Shoots right.... Full name: Craig Andrew Simpson. **COLLEGE:** Michigan State. **TRANSACTIONS/CAREER NOTES:** Selected by Pittsburgh Penguins in first round (first Penguins pick, second overall) of NHL entry draft (June 15, 1985).... Pulled muscle in right hip (March 1987).... Sprained right wrist (March 14, 1987).... Traded by Penguins with C Dave Hannan, D Chris Joseph and D Moe Mantha to Edmonton Oilers for D Paul Coffey, LW Dave Hunter and RW Wayne Van Dorp (November 1987).... Broke right ankle (December 4, 1988).... Suspended three games by NHL for injuring an opposing player (January 23, 1991).... Bruised chest (November 1991); missed one game.... Bruised shoulder (April 18, 1992). **HONORS:** Named to NCAA All-America West first team (1984-85).... Named to CCHA All-Star first team (1984-85).

			REGULAR SEASON					PLAYOFFS			
Season Team	League	Gms.	G	A	Pts.	Pen.	Gms.	G	A	Pts.	Pen.
82-83—London Jr. B	OHA		48	63	*111		—	—	—	—	—
83-84—Michigan State	CCHA	30	8	28	36	22	—	—	—	—	—
84-85—Michigan State	CCHA	42	31	53	84	33	—	—	—	—	—
85-86—Pittsburgh	NHL	76	11	17	28	49	—	—	—	—	—
86-87—Pittsburgh	NHL	72	26	25	51	57	—	—	—	—	—
87-88—Pittsburgh	NHL	21	13	13	26	34	—	—	—	—	—
—Edmonton	NHL	59	43	21	64	43	19	13	6	19	26
88-89—Edmonton	NHL	66	35	41	76	80	7	2	0	2	10
89-90—Edmonton	NHL	80	29	32	61	180	22	*16	15	†31	8
90-91—Edmonton	NHL	75	30	27	57	66	18	5	11	16	12
91-92—Edmonton	NHL	79	24	37	61	80	1	0	0	0	0
NHL totals		528	211	213	424	589	67	36	32	68	56

SIMPSON, GEOFF
D, BRUINS

PERSONAL: Born March 6, 1969, at Victoria, B.C.... 6-1/180.... Shoots right.... Full name: Geoffrey Ronald Simpson. **COLLEGE:** Northern Michigan. **TRANSACTIONS/CAREER NOTES:** Broke ankle (February 1988).... Selected by Boston Bruins in 10th round (10th Bruins pick, 206th overall) of NHL entry draft (June 17, 1989).

			REGULAR SEASON					PLAYOFFS			
Season Team	League	Gms.	G	A	Pts.	Pen.	Gms.	G	A	Pts.	Pen.
86-87—Estevan	SJHL	62	5	16	21	145	—	—	—	—	—
87-88—Estevan	SJHL	58	9	28	37	151	—	—	—	—	—
88-89—Estevan	SJHL	63	20	53	73	57	—	—	—	—	—
89-90—Northern Michigan Univ.	WCHA	39	4	9	13	40	—	—	—	—	—
90-91—Northern Michigan Univ.	WCHA	44	2	15	17	27	—	—	—	—	—
91-92—Northern Michigan Univ.	WCHA	25	1	3	4	20	—	—	—	—	—

SIMPSON, REID
LW, FLYERS

PERSONAL: Born May 21, 1969, at Flin Flon, Man. . . . 6-1/210. . . . Shoots left.
TRANSACTIONS/CAREER NOTES: Selected by Philadelphia Flyers in fourth round (third Flyers pick, 72nd overall) of NHL entry draft (June 17, 1989).

			REGULAR SEASON					PLAYOFFS				
Season	Team	League	Gms.	G	A	Pts.	Pen.	Gms.	G	A	Pts.	Pen.
85-86—Flin Flon		MJHL	40	20	21	41	200	—	—	—	—	—
—New Westminster		WHL	2	0	0	0	0	—	—	—	—	—
86-87—Prince Albert		WHL	47	3	8	11	105	—	—	—	—	—
87-88—Prince Albert		WHL	72	13	14	27	164	10	1	0	1	43
88-89—Prince Albert		WHL	59	26	29	55	264	4	2	1	3	30
89-90—Prince Albert		WHL	29	15	17	32	121	14	4	7	11	34
—Hershey		AHL	28	2	2	4	175	—	—	—	—	—
90-91—Hershey		AHL	54	9	15	24	183	1	0	0	0	0
91-92—Hershey		AHL	60	11	7	18	145	—	—	—	—	—
—Philadelphia		NHL	1	0	0	0	0	—	—	—	—	—
NHL totals			1	0	0	0	0					

SINCLAIR, AL
D, SENATORS

PERSONAL: Born April 3, 1973, at Mississauga, Ont. . . . 6-3/210. . . . Shoots right. . . . Full name: Alan Sinclair.
COLLEGE: Michigan.
TRANSACTIONS/CAREER NOTES: Selected by Ottawa Senators in sixth round (sixth Senators pick, 121st overall) of NHL entry draft (June 20, 1992).

			REGULAR SEASON					PLAYOFFS				
Season	Team	League	Gms.	G	A	Pts.	Pen.	Gms.	G	A	Pts.	Pen.
90-91—Wexford Jr. B		MTHL	43	4	15	19	46	—	—	—	—	—
91-92—University of Michigan		CCHA	22	0	4	4	40	—	—	—	—	—

SINISALO, ILKKA
RW

PERSONAL: Born July 10, 1958, at Valeskoski, Finland. . . . 6-0/200. . . . Shoots left.
TRANSACTIONS/CAREER NOTES: Signed as free agent by Philadelphia Flyers (February 1981). . . . Broke collarbone (September 1982). . . . Suffered back spasms (December 1984); missed 10 games. . . . Strained left knee and underwent surgery (December 1986). . . . Suffered back spasms (December 1987). . . . Bruised knee (February 1988). . . . Twisted left knee (March 1988). . . . Sprained right ankle (November 1988). . . . Fractured left wrist in three places (January 17, 1989). . . . Reinjured left wrist (February 1989). . . . Sprained right knee (December 27, 1989); missed 10 games. . . . Bruised collarbone (March 17, 1990). . . . Signed as free agent by Minnesota North Stars (July 3, 1990). . . . Traded by North Stars to Los Angeles Kings for eighth-round pick in 1991 draft (LW Michael Burkett) (March 5, 1991).

			REGULAR SEASON					PLAYOFFS				
Season	Team	League	Gms.	G	A	Pts.	Pen.	Gms.	G	A	Pts.	Pen.
78-79—Helsinki IFK		Finland	30	6	4	10	16	6	0	6	6	25
79-80—Helsinki IFK		Finland	35	16	9	25	16	7	1	3	4	12
80-81—Helsinki IFK		Finland	36	27	17	44	14	6	5	3	8	4
81-82—Philadelphia		NHL	66	15	22	37	22	4	0	2	2	0
82-83—Philadelphia		NHL	61	21	29	50	16	3	1	1	2	0
83-84—Philadelphia		NHL	73	29	17	46	29	2	2	0	2	0
84-85—Philadelphia		NHL	70	36	37	73	16	19	6	1	7	0
85-86—Philadelphia		NHL	74	39	37	76	31	5	2	2	4	2
86-87—Philadelphia		NHL	42	10	21	31	8	18	5	1	6	4
87-88—Philadelphia		NHL	68	25	17	42	30	7	4	2	6	0
88-89—Philadelphia		NHL	13	1	6	7	2	8	1	1	2	0
89-90—Philadelphia		NHL	59	23	23	46	26	—				
90-91—Minnesota		NHL	46	5	12	17	24	—				
—Los Angeles		NHL	7	0	0	0	2	2	0	1	1	0
91-92—Los Angeles		NHL	3	0	1	1	2	—				
—Phoenix		IHL	42	19	21	40	32	—				
NHL totals			582	204	222	426	208	68	21	11	32	6

SIRKKA, JEFF
D, BLACKHAWKS

PERSONAL: Born June 17, 1968, at Copper Cliff, Ont. . . . 6-1/204. . . . Shoots left.
TRANSACTIONS/CAREER NOTES: Traded by North Bay Centennials to Toronto Marlboros for sixth-round pick in 1989 draft (Michael Murray) (November 28, 1988). . . . Signed as free agent by Boston Bruins (September 1989). . . . Traded by Bruins to Hartford Whalers for D Steve Dykstra (March 3, 1990). . . . Signed as free agent by Chicago Blackhawks (September 1990).

			REGULAR SEASON					PLAYOFFS				
Season	Team	League	Gms.	G	A	Pts.	Pen.	Gms.	G	A	Pts.	Pen.
85-86—Kingston		OHL	34	1	6	7	51	—	—	—	—	—
86-87—Kingston		OHL	64	0	5	5	156	—	—	—	—	—
87-88—Kingston		OHL	59	1	16	17	114	—	—	—	—	—
88-89—North Bay		OHL	12	0	3	3	66	—	—	—	—	—
—Toronto		OHL	29	1	14	15	71	—	—	—	—	—
89-90—Maine		AHL	56	0	9	9	110	—	—	—	—	—
—Binghamton		AHL	16	0	1	1	38	—	—	—	—	—
90-91—Indianapolis		IHL	69	6	12	18	203	6	0	0	0	6
91-92—Indianapolis		IHL	71	3	17	20	146	—	—	—	—	—

SITTLER, RYAN
LW/C, FLYERS

PERSONAL: Born January 28, 1974, at London, Ont. . . . 6-2/185. . . . Shoots left. . . . Son of Darryl Sittler, Hall of Fame center, Toronto Maple Leafs, Philadelphia Flyers and Detroit Red Wings (1970-71 through 1984-85).
HIGH SCHOOL: Nichols (Buffalo, N.Y.).
TRANSACTIONS/CAREER NOTES: Selected by Philadelphia Flyers in first round (first Flyers pick, seventh overall) of NHL entry draft (June 20, 1992).

Season Team	League	REGULAR SEASON					PLAYOFFS				
		Gms.	G	A	Pts.	Pen.	Gms.	G	A	Pts.	Pen.
90-91—Nichols School	N.Y. H.S.	7	8	9	17	8	—	—	—	—	—
91-92—Nichols School	N.Y. H.S.	21	19	29	48	38	—	—	—	—	—

SJODIN, TOMMY
D, NORTH STARS

PERSONAL: Born August 13, 1965, at Sundsvall, Sweden. . . . 5-11/190. . . . Shoots right.
TRANSACTIONS/CAREER NOTES: Selected by Minnesota North Stars in 12th round (10th North Stars pick, 237th overall) of NHL entry draft (June 15, 1985).

Season Team	League	REGULAR SEASON					PLAYOFFS				
		Gms.	G	A	Pts.	Pen.	Gms.	G	A	Pts.	Pen.
87-88—Brynas	Sweden	40	6	9	15	28	—	—	—	—	—
88-89—Brynas	Sweden	40	8	11	19	54	—	—	—	—	—
89-90—Brynas	Sweden	40	14	14	28	46	5	0	0	0	2
90-91—Brynas	Sweden	38	12	17	29	79	—	—	—	—	—
91-92—Brynas	Sweden	40	6	16	22	46	—	—	—	—	—

SKALDE, JARROD
C, DEVILS

PERSONAL: Born February 26, 1971, at Niagara Falls, Ont. . . . 6-0/170. . . . Shoots left.
TRANSACTIONS/CAREER NOTES: Selected by New Jersey Devils in second round (third Devils pick, 26th overall) of NHL entry draft (June 17, 1989). . . . Traded by Oshawa Generals to Belleville Bulls for RW Rob Pearson (November 18, 1990).
HONORS: Named to OHL All-Star second team (1990-91).

Season Team	League	REGULAR SEASON					PLAYOFFS				
		Gms.	G	A	Pts.	Pen.	Gms.	G	A	Pts.	Pen.
86-87—Fort Erie Jr. B	OHA	41	27	34	61	36	—	—	—	—	—
87-88—Oshawa	OHL	60	12	16	28	24	7	2	1	3	2
88-89—Oshawa	OHL	65	38	38	76	36	6	1	5	6	2
89-90—Oshawa	OHL	62	40	52	92	66	17	10	7	17	6
90-91—New Jersey	NHL	1	0	1	1	0	—	—	—	—	—
—Utica	AHL	3	3	2	5	0	—	—	—	—	—
—Oshawa	OHL	15	8	14	22	14	—	—	—	—	—
—Belleville	OHL	40	30	52	82	21	6	9	6	15	10
91-92—Utica	AHL	62	20	20	40	56	4	3	1	4	8
—New Jersey	NHL	15	2	4	6	4	—	—	—	—	—
NHL totals		16	2	5	7	4					

SKARDA, RANDY
D, BLUES

PERSONAL: Born May 5, 1968, at St. Paul, Minn. . . . 6-1/205. . . . Shoots right. . . . Full name: Randall Skarda.
HIGH SCHOOL: St. Thomas Academy (St. Paul, Minn.).
COLLEGE: Minnesota.
TRANSACTIONS/CAREER NOTES: Selected by St. Louis Blues in eighth round (eighth Blues pick, 157th overall) of NHL entry draft (June 21, 1986).
HONORS: Named to NCAA All-America West second team (1987-88).

Season Team	League	REGULAR SEASON					PLAYOFFS				
		Gms.	G	A	Pts.	Pen.	Gms.	G	A	Pts.	Pen.
84-85—St. Thomas Academy	Minn. H.S.	23	14	42	56		—	—	—	—	—
85-86—St. Thomas Academy	Minn. H.S.	23	15	27	42		—	—	—	—	—
86-87—University of Minnesota	WCHA	43	3	10	13	77	—	—	—	—	—
87-88—University of Minnesota	WCHA	42	19	26	45	102	—	—	—	—	—
88-89—University of Minnesota	WCHA	43	6	24	30	91	—	—	—	—	—
89-90—St. Louis	NHL	25	0	5	5	11	—	—	—	—	—
—Peoria	IHL	38	7	17	24	40	4	0	0	0	0
90-91—Peoria	IHL	78	8	34	42	126	19	3	5	8	22
91-92—St. Louis	NHL	1	0	0	0	0	—	—	—	—	—
—Peoria	IHL	57	8	24	32	64	7	0	0	0	14
NHL totals		26	0	5	5	11					

SKRIKO, PETRI
RW, JETS

PERSONAL: Born March 12, 1962, at Laapeenranta, Finland. . . . 5-10/172. . . . Shoots left.
TRANSACTIONS/CAREER NOTES: Selected by Vancouver Canucks in seventh round (seventh Canucks pick, 157th overall) of NHL entry draft (June 10, 1981). . . . Broke thumb (October 1984). . . . Bruised knee (October 1987). . . . Sprained ankle (January 1988). . . . Strained knee (December 1988). . . . Twisted knee (February 12, 1989). . . . Suffered from the flu (March 1990). . . . Traded by Canucks to Boston Bruins for second-round pick in 1991 draft (January 16, 1991). . . . Traded by Bruins to Winnipeg Jets for LW Brent Ashton (October 29, 1991).

Season Team	League	REGULAR SEASON					PLAYOFFS				
		Gms.	G	A	Pts.	Pen.	Gms.	G	A	Pts.	Pen.
80-81—Saipa	Finland	36	20	13	33	14	—	—	—	—	—
81-82—Saipa	Finland	33	19	27	46	24	—	—	—	—	—
82-83—Saipa	Finland	36	23	12	35	12	—	—	—	—	—

Season Team	League	REGULAR SEASON					PLAYOFFS				
		Gms.	G	A	Pts.	Pen.	Gms.	G	A	Pts.	Pen.
83-84—Saipa	Finland	32	25	26	51	13	—	—	—	—	—
84-85—Vancouver	NHL	72	21	14	35	10	—	—	—	—	—
85-86—Vancouver	NHL	80	38	40	78	34	3	0	0	0	0
86-87—Vancouver	NHL	76	33	41	74	44	—	—	—	—	—
87-88—Vancouver	NHL	73	30	34	64	32	—	—	—	—	—
88-89—Vancouver	NHL	74	30	36	66	57	7	1	5	6	0
89-90—Vancouver	NHL	77	15	33	48	36	—	—	—	—	—
90-91—Vancouver	NHL	20	4	4	8	8	—	—	—	—	—
—Boston	NHL	28	5	14	19	9	18	4	4	8	4
91-92—Finland Olympic Team	Int'l	8	1	4	5		—	—	—	—	—
—Boston	NHL	9	1	0	1	6	—	—	—	—	—
—Winnipeg	NHL	15	2	3	5	4	—	—	—	—	—
NHL totals		524	179	219	398	240	28	5	9	14	4

SKRUDLAND, BRIAN
C, CANADIENS

PERSONAL: Born July 31, 1963, at Peace River, Alta.... 6-0/196.... Shoots left.... Cousin of Barry Pederson, center, four NHL teams (1980-81 through 1991-92).

TRANSACTIONS/CAREER NOTES: Signed as free agent by Montreal Canadiens (August 1983).... Injured groin (February 1988).... Strained left knee ligaments (December 27, 1988).... Bruised right foot (January 1989).... Sprained right ankle (October 7, 1989); missed 21 games.... Pulled hip muscle (November 4, 1990), missed six games.... Broke foot (January 17, 1991); missed 14 games including All-Star game.... Broke left thumb (October 5, 1991); missed five games. ... Sprained knee (October 26, 1991); missed 25 games.... Broke nose (January 25, 1992); missed eight games.

HONORS: Won Jack Butterfield Trophy (1984-85).

Season Team	League	REGULAR SEASON					PLAYOFFS				
		Gms.	G	A	Pts.	Pen.	Gms.	G	A	Pts.	Pen.
80-81—Saskatoon	WHL	66	15	27	42	97	—	—	—	—	—
81-82—Saskatoon	WHL	71	27	29	56	135	5	0	1	1	2
82-83—Saskatoon	WHL	71	35	59	94	42	6	1	3	4	19
83-84—Nova Scotia	AHL	56	13	12	25	55	12	2	8	10	14
84-85—Sherbrooke	AHL	70	22	28	50	109	17	9	8	17	23
85-86—Montreal	NHL	65	9	13	22	57	20	2	4	6	76
86-87—Montreal	NHL	79	11	17	28	107	14	1	5	6	29
87-88—Montreal	NHL	79	12	24	36	112	11	1	5	6	24
88-89—Montreal	NHL	71	12	29	41	84	21	3	7	10	40
89-90—Montreal	NHL	59	11	31	42	56	11	3	5	8	30
90-91—Montreal	NHL	57	15	19	34	85	13	3	10	13	42
91-92—Montreal	NHL	42	3	3	6	36	11	1	1	2	20
NHL totals		452	73	136	209	537	101	14	37	51	261

SKRYPEC, GERRY
D, BLACKHAWKS

PERSONAL: Born June 21, 1974, at Kitchener, Ont.... 6-0/190.... Shoots left.
HIGH SCHOOL: Hillcrest (Thunder Bay, Ont.).
TRANSACTIONS/CAREER NOTES: Selected by Chicago Blackhawks in sixth round (sixth Blackhawks pick, 137th overall) of NHL entry draft (June 20, 1992).

Season Team	League	REGULAR SEASON					PLAYOFFS				
		Gms.	G	A	Pts.	Pen.	Gms.	G	A	Pts.	Pen.
90-91—Ottawa	OHL	61	2	7	9	53	17	0	4	4	2
91-92—Ottawa	OHL	65	6	21	27	105	5	0	1	1	8

SLANEY, JOHN
D, CAPITALS

PERSONAL: Born February 7, 1972, at St. John's, Nfld. ... 5-11/180.... Shoots left.... Full name: John G. Slaney.
TRANSACTIONS/CAREER NOTES: Selected by Washington Capitals in first round (first Capitals pick, ninth overall) of NHL entry draft (June 16, 1990).

HONORS: Won Max Kaminsky Trophy (1989-90).... Named to OHL All-Star first team (1989-90).... Named to OHL All-Star second team (1990-91).

Season Team	League	REGULAR SEASON					PLAYOFFS				
		Gms.	G	A	Pts.	Pen.	Gms.	G	A	Pts.	Pen.
88-89—Cornwall	OHL	66	16	43	59	23	18	8	16	24	10
89-90—Cornwall	OHL	64	38	59	97	60	6	0	8	8	11
90-91—Cornwall	OHL	34	21	25	46	28	—	—	—	—	—
91-92—Cornwall	OHL	34	19	41	60	43	6	3	8	11	0
—Baltimore	AHL	6	2	4	6	0	—	—	—	—	—

SLEGR, JIRI
D, CANUCKS

PERSONAL: Born May 30, 1971, at Litvinov, Czechoslovakia.... 5-11/190.... Shoots left.... Son of Jiri Bubla, defenseman, Vancouver Canucks (1981-82 through 1985-86).
TRANSACTIONS/CAREER NOTES: Selected by Vancouver Canucks in second round (third Canucks pick, 23rd overall) of NHL entry draft (June 16, 1990).

Season Team	League	REGULAR SEASON					PLAYOFFS				
		Gms.	G	A	Pts.	Pen.	Gms.	G	A	Pts.	Pen.
88-89—Litvinov	Czech.	8	0	0	0		—	—	—	—	—
89-90—Litvinov	Czech.	51	4	15	19		—	—	—	—	—

Season Team	League	REGULAR SEASON					PLAYOFFS				
		Gms.	G	A	Pts.	Pen.	Gms.	G	A	Pts.	Pen.
90-91—Litvinov	Czech.	39	10	33	43	26	—	—	—	—	—
91-92—Litvinov	Czech.	38	7	22	29	30	—	—	—	—	—
—Czech. Olympic Team	Int'l	8	1	1	2		—	—	—	—	—

SMAIL, DOUG

LW, NORDIQUES

PERSONAL: Born September 2, 1957, at Moose Jaw, Sask. . . . 5-9/175. . . . Shoots left. . . . Full name: Douglas D. Smail.

COLLEGE: North Dakota.

TRANSACTIONS/CAREER NOTES: Signed as free agent by Winnipeg Jets (May 1980). . . . Fractured jaw in practice (November 1980). . . . Fractured jaw (January 10, 1981). . . . Stretched knee ligaments (December 1983). . . . Pulled leg muscle (October 25, 1985); missed seven games. . . . Underwent arthroscopic knee surgery (September 1987). . . . Lacerated left calf (December 1988). . . . Fractured orbital bone near eye (February 13, 1989). . . . Traded by Jets to Minnesota North Stars for LW Don Barber and future draft considerations (November 7, 1990). . . . Signed as free agent by Quebec Nordiques (September 1991). . . . Pulled ligaments during preseason (September 1991); missed first 10 games of season. . . . Injured knee (February 22, 1992).

HONORS: Won NCAA Tournament Most Valuable Player Award (1979-80). . . . Named to NCAA Tournament All-Star team (1979-80). . . . Named to WCHA All-Star second team (1979-80).

RECORDS: Shares NHL record for fastest goal at the start of a game—5 seconds (December 20, 1981).

Season Team	League	REGULAR SEASON					PLAYOFFS				
		Gms.	G	A	Pts.	Pen.	Gms.	G	A	Pts.	Pen.
77-78—Univ. of North Dakota	WCHA	38	22	28	50	52	—	—	—	—	—
78-79—Univ. of North Dakota	WCHA	35	24	34	58	46	—	—	—	—	—
79-80—Univ. of North Dakota	WCHA	40	43	44	87	70	—	—	—	—	—
80-81—Winnipeg	NHL	30	10	8	18	45	—	—	—	—	—
81-82—Winnipeg	NHL	72	17	18	35	55	4	0	0	0	0
82-83—Winnipeg	NHL	80	15	29	44	32	3	0	0	0	6
83-84—Winnipeg	NHL	66	20	17	37	62	3	0	1	1	7
84-85—Winnipeg	NHL	80	31	35	66	45	8	2	1	3	4
85-86—Winnipeg	NHL	73	16	26	42	32	3	1	0	1	0
86-87—Winnipeg	NHL	78	25	18	43	36	10	4	0	4	10
87-88—Winnipeg	NHL	71	15	16	31	34	5	1	0	1	22
88-89—Winnipeg	NHL	47	14	15	29	52	—	—	—	—	—
89-90—Winnipeg	NHL	79	25	24	49	63	5	1	0	1	0
90-91—Winnipeg	NHL	15	1	2	3	10	—	—	—	—	—
—Minnesota	NHL	57	7	13	20	38	1	0	0	0	0
91-92—Quebec	NHL	46	10	18	28	47	—	—	—	—	—
NHL totals		794	206	239	445	551	42	9	2	11	49

SMART, JASON

C, PENGUINS

PERSONAL: Born January 23, 1970, at Prince George, B.C. . . . 6-4/212. . . . Shoots left.

TRANSACTIONS/CAREER NOTES: Injured shoulder (November 1986); missed 10 days. . . . Underwent shoulder surgery (May 1987). . . . Traded by Prince Albert Raiders to Brandon Wheat Kings for Graham Garden (December 1, 1988); refused to report to Wheat Kings and later dealt to Saskatoon Blades. . . . Selected by Pittsburgh Penguins in 12th round (13th pick Penguins pick, 247th overall) of NHL entry draft (June 17, 1989).

Season Team	League	REGULAR SEASON					PLAYOFFS				
		Gms.	G	A	Pts.	Pen.	Gms.	G	A	Pts.	Pen.
86-87—Prince Albert	WHL	57	9	22	31	62	8	3	3	6	8
87-88—Prince Albert	WHL	72	16	29	45	79	10	1	2	3	11
88-89—Prince Albert	WHL	12	1	3	4	31	—	—	—	—	—
—Saskatoon	WHL	36	6	17	23	33	8	1	6	7	16
89-90—Saskatoon	WHL	66	27	48	75	187	10	1	5	6	19
90-91—Albany	IHL	15	4	2	6	28	—	—	—	—	—
—Muskegon	IHL	36	12	27	39	55	5	0	3	3	11
91-92—Muskegon	IHL	45	10	14	24	49	—	—	—	—	—

SMITH, BOBBY

C, NORTH STARS

PERSONAL: Born February 12, 1958, at North Sydney, N.S. . . . 6-4/210. . . . Shoots left. . . . Full name: Robert David Smith.

TRANSACTIONS/CAREER NOTES: Selected by Minnesota North Stars from Ottawa 67's in first round (first North Stars pick, first overall) of NHL amateur draft (June 15, 1978). . . . Fractured ankle; missed part of 1979-80 season. . . . Traded by North Stars to Montreal Canadiens for RW Mark Napier, C Keith Acton and third-round pick in 1984 draft (C Kenneth Hodge) (October 1983). . . . Fractured jaw (December 1984). . . . Lost tooth (December 1, 1988). . . . Separated right shoulder (January 6, 1990); missed seven games. . . . Fractured jaw (February 4, 1990); missed 18 games. . . . Traded by Canadiens to North Stars for fourth-round pick in 1992 draft (D Louis Bernard) (August 7, 1990).

HONORS: Won George Parsons Trophy (1976-77). . . . Named to OMJHL All-Star second team (1976-77). . . . Won Can.HL Player of the Year Award (1977-78). . . . Won Albert (Red) Tilson Memorial Trophy (1977-78). . . . Won Eddie Powers Memorial Trophy (1977-78). . . . Named to OMJHL All-Star first team (1977-78). . . . Won Calder Memorial Trophy (1978-79). . . . Named NHL Rookie of the Year by THE SPORTING NEWS (1978-79).

RECORDS: Shares NHL single-season playoff record for most game-winning goals—5 (1991).

Season Team	League	REGULAR SEASON					PLAYOFFS				
		Gms.	G	A	Pts.	Pen.	Gms.	G	A	Pts.	Pen.
75-76—Ottawa	OHA Mj. Jr. A	62	24	34	58	21	—	—	—	—	—
76-77—Ottawa	OMJHL	64	*65	70	135	52	19	16	16	32	29

Season Team	League	REGULAR SEASON Gms.	G	A	Pts.	Pen.	PLAYOFFS Gms.	G	A	Pts.	Pen.
77-78—Ottawa	OMJHL	61	69	*123	*192	44	16	15	15	30	10
78-79—Minnesota	NHL	80	30	44	74	39	—	—	—	—	—
79-80—Minnesota	NHL	61	27	56	83	24	15	1	13	14	9
80-81—Minnesota	NHL	78	29	64	93	73	19	8	17	25	13
81-82—Minnesota	NHL	80	43	71	114	82	4	2	4	6	5
82-83—Minnesota	NHL	77	24	53	77	81	9	6	4	10	17
83-84—Minnesota	NHL	10	3	6	9	9	—	—	—	—	—
—Montreal	NHL	70	26	37	63	62	15	2	7	9	8
84-85—Montreal	NHL	65	16	40	56	59	12	5	6	11	30
85-86—Montreal	NHL	79	31	55	86	55	20	7	8	15	22
86-87—Montreal	NHL	80	28	47	75	72	17	9	9	18	19
87-88—Montreal	NHL	78	27	66	93	78	11	3	4	7	8
88-89—Montreal	NHL	80	32	51	83	69	21	11	8	19	46
89-90—Montreal	NHL	53	12	14	26	35	11	1	4	5	6
90-91—Minnesota	NHL	73	15	31	46	60	23	8	8	16	56
91-92—Minnesota	NHL	68	9	37	46	109	7	1	4	5	6
NHL totals		1032	352	672	1024	907	184	64	96	160	245

SMITH, DENNIS
D, CAPITALS

PERSONAL: Born July 27, 1964, at Livonia, Mich. . . . 5-11/192. . . . Shoots left.
TRANSACTIONS/CAREER NOTES: Signed as free agent by Detroit Red Wings (September 1986). . . . Signed as free agent by Washington Capitals (June 29, 1989). . . . Signed as free agent by Los Angeles Kings (July 11, 1990). . . . Signed as free agent by Boston Bruins (August 2, 1991). . . . Traded by Bruins with RW John Byce to Capitals for LW Brent Hughes and 12th-round pick in 1992 draft (February 24, 1992).
HONORS: Named to AHL All-Star second team (1989-90).

Season Team	League	REGULAR SEASON Gms.	G	A	Pts.	Pen.	PLAYOFFS Gms.	G	A	Pts.	Pen.
81-82—Kingston	OHL	48	2	23	25	83	4	0	2	2	0
82-83—Kingston	OHL	65	6	24	30	90	—	—	—	—	—
83-84—Kingston	OHL	62	10	40	50	136	—	—	—	—	—
84-85—Erie	ACHL	19	5	20	25	67	—	—	—	—	—
85-86—Peoria	IHL	70	5	15	20	102	10	0	2	2	18
86-87—Adirondack	AHL	64	4	24	28	120	6	0	0	0	8
87-88—Adirondack	AHL	75	6	24	30	213	11	2	2	4	47
88-89—Adirondack	AHL	75	4	35	40	176	17	1	6	7	47
89-90—Baltimore	AHL	74	8	25	33	103	12	0	3	3	65
—Washington	NHL	4	0	0	0	0	—	—	—	—	—
90-91—New Haven	AHL	61	7	25	32	148	—	—	—	—	—
—Los Angeles	NHL	4	0	0	0	4	—	—	—	—	—
91-92—Maine	AHL	59	2	32	34	63	—	—	—	—	—
—Baltimore	AHL	17	1	4	5	23	—	—	—	—	—
NHL totals		8	0	0	0	4	—	—	—	—	—

SMITH, DERRICK
LW, NORTH STARS

PERSONAL: Born January 22, 1965, at Scarborough, Ont. . . . 6-2/215. . . . Shoots left.
TRANSACTIONS/CAREER NOTES: Selected by Philadelphia Flyers as underage junior in third round (second Flyers pick, 44th overall) of NHL entry draft (June 8, 1983). . . . Bruised back (November 1987). . . . Bruised left shoulder (February 1989). . . . Fractured left foot during training camp (September 1989). . . . Sprained right ankle and developed an infected toe (October 30, 1989). . . . Injured ribs (February 20, 1990); missed six games. . . . Claimed by Minnesota North Stars on waivers (October 26, 1991). . . . Injured ankle (December 8, 1991); missed 20 games. . . . Separated shoulder (March 19, 1992); missed five games.

Season Team	League	REGULAR SEASON Gms.	G	A	Pts.	Pen.	PLAYOFFS Gms.	G	A	Pts.	Pen.
82-83—Peterborough	OHL	70	16	19	35	47	—	—	—	—	—
83-84—Peterborough	OHL	70	30	36	66	31	8	4	4	8	7
84-85—Philadelphia	NHL	77	17	22	39	31	19	2	5	7	16
85-86—Philadelphia	NHL	69	6	6	12	57	4	0	0	0	10
86-87—Philadelphia	NHL	71	11	21	32	34	26	6	4	10	26
87-88—Philadelphia	NHL	76	16	8	24	104	7	0	0	0	6
88-89—Philadelphia	NHL	74	16	14	30	43	19	5	2	7	12
89-90—Philadelphia	NHL	55	3	6	9	32	—	—	—	—	—
90-91—Philadelphia	NHL	72	11	10	21	37	7	1	0	1	9
91-92—Minnesota	NHL	33	2	4	6	33	—	—	—	—	—
—Kalamazoo	IHL	6	1	5	6	4	—	—	—	—	—
NHL totals		527	82	91	173	371	82	14	11	25	79

SMITH, GEOFF
D, OILERS

PERSONAL: Born March 7, 1969, at Edmonton, Alta. . . . 6-3/200. . . . Shoots left. . . . Full name: Geoff Arthur Smith.
COLLEGE: North Dakota.
TRANSACTIONS/CAREER NOTES: Selected by Edmonton Oilers in third round (third Oilers pick, 63rd overall) of NHL entry draft (June 13, 1987). . . . Fractured ankle (October 1988); missed first 10 games. . . . Left University of North Dakota and signed to play with Kamloops Blazers (January 1989). . . . Broke jaw (March 1989). . . . Pulled back

muscle (February 8, 1991); missed eight games. . . . Bruised shoulder (April 26, 1992).
HONORS: Named to WHL All-Star first team (1988-89). . . . Named to NHL All-Rookie team (1989-90).

Season Team	League	REGULAR SEASON					PLAYOFFS				
		Gms.	G	A	Pts.	Pen.	Gms.	G	A	Pts.	Pen.
86-87—St. Albert	AJHL	57	7	28	35	101	—	—	—	—	—
87-88—Univ. of North Dakota	WCHA	42	4	12	16	34	—	—	—	—	—
88-89—Kamloops	WHL	32	4	31	35	29	6	1	3	4	12
89-90—Edmonton	NHL	74	4	11	15	52	3	0	0	0	0
90-91—Edmonton	NHL	59	1	12	13	55	4	0	0	0	0
91-92—Edmonton	NHL	74	2	16	18	43	5	0	1	1	6
NHL totals		207	7	39	46	150	12	0	1	1	6

SMITH, JASON
D, DEVILS

PERSONAL: Born November 2, 1973, at Calgary, Alta. . . . 6-3/185. . . . Shoots right.
TRANSACTIONS/CAREER NOTES: Selected by New Jersey Devils in first round (first Devils pick, 18th overall) of NHL entry draft (June 20, 1992).

Season Team	League	REGULAR SEASON					PLAYOFFS				
		Gms.	G	A	Pts.	Pen.	Gms.	G	A	Pts.	Pen.
90-91—Calgary Canucks	AJHL	45	3	15	18	69	—	—	—	—	—
—Regina	WHL	2	0	0	0	7	—	—	—	—	—
91-92—Regina	WHL	62	9	29	38	168	—	—	—	—	—

SMITH, SANDY
RW, PENGUINS

PERSONAL: Born October 23, 1967, at Brainerd, Minn. . . . 5-11/200. . . . Shoots right. . . . Full name: James Sanford Smith.
HIGH SCHOOL: Brainerd (Minn.).
COLLEGE: Minnesota-Duluth.
TRANSACTIONS/CAREER NOTES: Tore knee ligaments (September 1985). . . . Selected by Pittsburgh Penguins in fifth round (fifth Penguins pick, 88th overall) of NHL entry draft (June 21, 1986).

Season Team	League	REGULAR SEASON					PLAYOFFS				
		Gms.	G	A	Pts.	Pen.	Gms.	G	A	Pts.	Pen.
84-85—Brainerd H.S.	Minn. H.S.	21	30	20	50		—	—	—	—	—
85-86—Brainerd H.S.	Minn. H.S.	17	28	22	50		—	—	—	—	—
86-87—Minnesota-Duluth	WCHA	35	3	3	6	26	—	—	—	—	—
87-88—Minnesota-Duluth	WCHA	41	22	9	31	47	—	—	—	—	—
88-89—Minnesota-Duluth	WCHA	40	6	16	22	75	—	—	—	—	—
89-90—Minnesota-Duluth	WCHA	39	15	16	31	53	—	—	—	—	—
—Muskegon	IHL	3	1	0	1	0	—	—	—	—	—
90-91—Muskegon	IHL	82	25	29	54	51	5	1	1	2	6
91-92—Muskegon	IHL	64	15	18	33	109	14	7	2	9	4

SMITH, STEVE
D/RW, BLACKHAWKS

PERSONAL: Born April 30, 1963, at Glasgow, Scotland. . . . 6-4/215. . . . Shoots left. . . . Full name: James Stephen Smith.
TRANSACTIONS/CAREER NOTES: Selected by Edmonton Oilers as underage junior in sixth round (fifth Oilers pick, 111th overall) of NHL entry draft (June 10, 1981). . . . Strained right shoulder (November 1, 1985). . . . Pulled stomach muscle (February 1986). . . . Separated left shoulder (September 20, 1988). . . . Aggravated shoulder injury (October 1988). . . . Dislocated left shoulder and tore cartilage (January 2, 1989). . . . Underwent surgery to left shoulder (January 23, 1989); missed 45 games. . . . Traded by Oilers to Chicago Blackhawks for D Dave Manson and third-round pick in 1993 draft (September 26, 1991). . . . Pulled ribcage muscle (December 31, 1991); missed three games.

Season Team	League	REGULAR SEASON					PLAYOFFS				
		Gms.	G	A	Pts.	Pen.	Gms.	G	A	Pts.	Pen.
80-81—London	OMJHL	62	4	12	16	141	—	—	—	—	—
81-82—London	OHL	58	10	36	46	207	4	1	2	3	13
82-83—London	OHL	50	6	35	41	133	3	1	0	1	10
—Moncton	AHL	2	0	0	0	0	—	—	—	—	—
83-84—Moncton	AHL	64	1	8	9	176	—	—	—	—	—
84-85—Nova Scotia	AHL	68	2	28	30	161	5	0	3	3	40
—Edmonton	NHL	2	0	0	0	2	—	—	—	—	—
85-86—Nova Scotia	AHL	4	0	2	2	11	—	—	—	—	—
—Edmonton	NHL	55	4	20	24	166	6	0	1	1	14
86-87—Edmonton	NHL	62	7	15	22	165	15	1	3	4	45
87-88—Edmonton	NHL	79	12	43	55	286	19	1	11	12	55
88-89—Edmonton	NHL	35	3	19	22	97	7	2	2	4	20
89-90—Edmonton	NHL	75	7	34	41	171	22	5	10	15	37
90-91—Edmonton	NHL	77	13	41	54	193	18	1	2	3	45
91-92—Chicago	NHL	76	9	21	30	304	18	1	11	12	16
NHL totals		461	55	193	248	1384	105	11	40	51	232

SMOLINSKI, BRYAN
C, BRUINS

PERSONAL: Born December 27, 1971, at Toledo, O. . . . 6-0/185. . . . Shoots right. . . . Full name: Bryan Anthony Smolinski.
COLLEGE: Michigan State.
TRANSACTIONS/CAREER NOTES: Selected by Boston Bruins in first round (first Bruins pick, 21st overall) of NHL entry draft (June 16, 1990).
HONORS: Named to CCHA All-Rookie team (1989-90).

Season Team	League	REGULAR SEASON					PLAYOFFS				
		Gms.	G	A	Pts.	Pen.	Gms.	G	A	Pts.	Pen.
87-88—Detroit Little Caesars	MNHL	80	43	77	120		—	—	—	—	—
88-89—Stratford Jr. B	OHA	46	32	62	94	132	—	—	—	—	—
89-90—Michigan State................	CCHA	39	10	17	27	45	—	—	—	—	—
90-91—Michigan State................	CCHA	35	9	12	21	24	—	—	—	—	—
91-92—Michigan State................	CCHA	44	30	35	65	59	—	—	—	—	—

SMYTH, GREG
D, FLAMES

PERSONAL: Born April 23, 1966, at Oakville, Ont.... 6-3/195.... Shoots right.
TRANSACTIONS/CAREER NOTES: Selected by Philadelphia Flyers as underage junior in second round (first Flyers pick, 22nd overall) of NHL entry draft (June 9, 1984).... Suspended 10 games by OHL for fighting with fans (December 1984).... Suspended by London Knights (October 1985).... Suspended eight games by OHL (November 7, 1985).... Traded by Flyers with third-round pick in 1989 draft (G John Tanner) to Quebec Nordiques for D Terry Carkner (July 1988).... Broke two bones in right hand during training camp (September 1988).... Suspended eight games by AHL for fighting (December 17, 1988).... Injured back (February 15, 1990).... Recalled from Halifax by Quebec and refused to report (February 10, 1991).... Traded by Nordiques to Calgary Flames for RW Martin Simard (March 10, 1992).
HONORS: Named to OHL All-Star second team (1985-86).

Season Team	League	REGULAR SEASON					PLAYOFFS				
		Gms.	G	A	Pts.	Pen.	Gms.	G	A	Pts.	Pen.
83-84—London	OHL	64	4	21	25	*252	6	1	0	1	24
84-85—London	OHL	47	7	16	23	188	8	2	2	4	27
85-86—London	OHL	46	12	42	54	197	4	1	2	3	28
—Hershey	AHL	2	0	1	1	5	8	0	0	0	60
86-87—Hershey	AHL	35	0	2	2	158	2	0	0	0	19
—Philadelphia	NHL	1	0	0	0	0	1	0	0	0	2
87-88—Hershey	AHL	21	0	10	10	102	—	—	—	—	—
—Philadelphia	NHL	48	1	6	7	192	5	0	0	0	38
88-89—Halifax	AHL	43	3	9	12	310	4	0	1	1	35
—Quebec	NHL	10	0	1	1	70	—	—	—	—	—
89-90—Quebec	NHL	13	0	0	0	57	—	—	—	—	—
—Halifax	AHL	49	5	14	19	235	6	1	0	1	52
90-91—Quebec	NHL	1	0	0	0	0	—	—	—	—	—
—Halifax	AHL	56	6	23	29	340	—	—	—	—	—
91-92—Quebec	NHL	29	0	2	2	138	—	—	—	—	—
—Halifax	AHL	9	1	3	4	35	—	—	—	—	—
—Calgary	NHL	7	1	1	2	15	—	—	—	—	—
NHL totals.................		109	2	10	12	472	6	0	0	0	40

SMYTH, KEVIN
LW, WHALERS

PERSONAL: Born November 22, 1973, at Banff, Alta.... 6-2/217.... Shoots left.
TRANSACTIONS/CAREER NOTES: Selected by Hartford Whalers in fourth round (fourth Whalers pick, 79th overall) of NHL entry draft (June 20, 1992).

Season Team	League	REGULAR SEASON					PLAYOFFS				
		Gms.	G	A	Pts.	Pen.	Gms.	G	A	Pts.	Pen.
90-91—Moose Jaw	WHL	66	30	45	75	96	6	1	1	2	0
91-92—Moose Jaw	WHL	71	30	55	85	114	4	1	3	4	6

SNUGGERUD, DAVE
LW, SHARKS

PERSONAL: Born June 20, 1966, at Minnetonka, Minn.... 6-0/170.... Shoots left.
COLLEGE: Minnesota.
TRANSACTIONS/CAREER NOTES: Selected by Buffalo Sabres in NHL supplemental draft (June 1987).... Injured knee (January 3, 1992); missed eight games.... Traded by Sabres to San Jose Sharks for RW Wayne Presley (March 9, 1992).
HONORS: Named to USHL All-Star second team (1984-85).... Named to NCAA All-America West second team (1988-89).... Named to WCHA All-Star second team (1988-89).

Season Team	League	REGULAR SEASON					PLAYOFFS				
		Gms.	G	A	Pts.	Pen.	Gms.	G	A	Pts.	Pen.
84-85—Minneapolis......................	USHL	48	38	35	73	26	—	—	—	—	—
85-86—University of Minnesota ...	WCHA	42	14	18	32	47	—	—	—	—	—
86-87—University of Minnesota ...	WCHA	39	30	29	59	38	—	—	—	—	—
87-88—U.S. National Team..........	Int'l	51	14	21	35	26	—	—	—	—	—
—U.S. Olympic Team	Int'l	6	3	2	5	4	—	—	—	—	—
88-89—University of Minnesota ...	WCHA	45	29	20	49	39	—	—	—	—	—
89-90—Buffalo.............................	NHL	80	14	16	30	41	6	0	0	0	2
90-91—Buffalo.............................	NHL	80	9	15	24	32	6	1	3	4	4
91-92—Buffalo.............................	NHL	55	3	15	18	36	—	—	—	—	—
—San Jose	NHL	11	0	1	1	4	—	—	—	—	—
NHL totals.................................		226	26	47	73	113	12	1	3	4	6

SODERSTROM, TOMMY
G, FLYERS

PERSONAL: Born July 17, 1969, at Stockholm, Sweden.... 5-9/163.... Full name: Thomas Soderstrom.
TRANSACTIONS/CAREER NOTES: Selected by Philadelphia Flyers in 11th round (14th Flyers pick, 214th overall) of NHL entry draft (June 16, 1990).

| | | REGULAR SEASON | | | | | | | | PLAYOFFS | | | | | | |
Season Team	League	Gms.	Min.	W	L	T	GA	SO	Avg.	Gms.	Min.	W	L	GA	SO	Avg.
89-90—Djurgarden	Sweden	4	240				14	0	3.50	—	—	—	—	—	—	—
90-91—Djurgarden	Sweden	39	2340	22	12	6	104	3	2.67	7	423			10	2	1.42
91-92—Djurgarden	Sweden	31														

SOULES, JASON
D, OILERS

PERSONAL: Born March 14, 1971, at Hamilton, Ont. . . . 6-2/212. . . . Shoots left. . . . Full name: Jason Kenneth Soules.
TRANSACTIONS/CAREER NOTES: Fractured clavicle (July 1987). . . . Selected by Edmonton Oilers in first round (first Oilers pick, 15th overall) of NHL entry draft (June 17, 1989). . . . Traded by Dukes of Hamilton to Belleville Bulls for RW Ken Ruddick (November 28, 1990).

| | | REGULAR SEASON | | | | | PLAYOFFS | | | | |
Season Team	League	Gms.	G	A	Pts.	Pen.	Gms.	G	A	Pts.	Pen.
87-88—Hamilton Jr. B	OHA	27	3	10	13	99	—	—	—	—	—
—Hamilton	OHL	19	1	1	2	56	4	0	0	0	13
88-89—Niagara Falls	OHL	57	3	8	11	187	—	—	—	—	—
89-90—Niagara Falls	OHL	9	2	8	10	20	—	—	—	—	—
—Dukes of Hamilton	OHL	18	0	2	2	42	—	—	—	—	—
90-91—Dukes of Hamilton	OHL	25	3	16	19	50	—	—	—	—	—
—Belleville	OHL	37	5	26	31	94	6	1	2	3	4
—Cape Breton	AHL	1	0	0	0	0	—	—	—	—	—
91-92—Cape Breton	AHL	51	0	9	9	44	—	—	—	—	—

SPEER, MICHAEL
D, BLACKHAWKS

PERSONAL: Born March 26, 1971, at Toronto. . . . 6-2/202. . . . Shoots left.
TRANSACTIONS/CAREER NOTES: Selected by Chicago Blackhawks in second round (second Blackhawks pick, 27th overall) of NHL entry draft (June 17, 1989). . . . Traded by Owen Sound Platers to Windsor Spitfires for D Rick Morton (January 10, 1991).

| | | REGULAR SEASON | | | | | PLAYOFFS | | | | |
Season Team	League	Gms.	G	A	Pts.	Pen.	Gms.	G	A	Pts.	Pen.
87-88—Guelph	OHL	53	4	10	14	60	—	—	—	—	—
88-89—Guelph	OHL	65	9	31	40	185	7	2	4	6	23
89-90—Owen Sound	OHL	61	18	39	57	176	12	3	7	10	21
90-91—Owen Sound	OHL	32	13	19	32	86	—	—	—	—	—
—Windsor	OHL	25	8	28	36	40	11	2	7	9	15
—Indianapolis	IHL	1	0	1	1	0	1	0	0	0	5
91-92—Indianapolis	IHL	54	0	6	6	67	—	—	—	—	—

SPENRATH, GREG
LW, NORTH STARS

PERSONAL: Born September 27, 1969, at Edmonton, Alta. . . . 6-1/212. . . . Shoots left.
TRANSACTIONS/CAREER NOTES: Selected by New York Rangers in eighth round (ninth Rangers pick, 160th overall) of NHL entry draft (June 17, 1989). . . . Signed as free agent by Minnesota North Stars (July 25, 1991).

| | | REGULAR SEASON | | | | | PLAYOFFS | | | | |
Season Team	League	Gms.	G	A	Pts.	Pen.	Gms.	G	A	Pts.	Pen.
87-88—New Westminster	WHL	72	18	24	42	210	5	0	4	4	16
88-89—Tri-City	WHL	64	26	35	61	213	7	4	2	6	23
89-90—Tri-City	WHL	67	36	32	68	256	7	1	0	1	15
90-91—Binghamton	AHL	2	0	0	0	14	—	—	—	—	—
—Erie	ECHL	61	29	36	65	*407	4	1	2	3	46
91-92—Kalamazoo	IHL	69	4	7	11	237	—	—	—	—	—

SRSEN, THOMAS
RW, OILERS

PERSONAL: Born August 25, 1966, at Olomouc, Czechoslovakia. . . . 5-11/180. . . . Shoots left.
TRANSACTIONS/CAREER NOTES: Selected by Edmonton Oilers in seventh round (seventh Oilers pick, 147th overall) of NHL entry draft (June 13, 1987).

| | | REGULAR SEASON | | | | | PLAYOFFS | | | | |
Season Team	League	Gms.	G	A	Pts.	Pen.	Gms.	G	A	Pts.	Pen.
87-88—Zetor Brno	Czech.	34	14	5	19		—	—	—	—	—
88-89—Zetor Brno	Czech.	42	19	11	30		—	—	—	—	—
89-90—Zetor Brno	Czech.	30	7	15	22		—	—	—	—	—
90-91—Cape Breton	AHL	72	32	26	58	100	4	3	1	4	6
—Edmonton	NHL	2	0	0	0	0	—	—	—	—	—
91-92—Cape Breton	AHL	68	19	27	46	79	5	2	2	4	4
NHL totals		2	0	0	0	0					

ST. LAURENT, SAM
G, RANGERS

PERSONAL: Born February 16, 1959, at Arvida, Que. . . . 5-10/190. . . . Shoots left.
TRANSACTIONS/CAREER NOTES: Signed as free agent by Philadelphia Flyers (September 1979). . . . Traded by Flyers to New Jersey Devils for future considerations (August 1984). . . . Traded by Devils to Detroit Red Wings for D Steve Richmond (August 1986). . . . Pulled muscle (January 1989); missed 30 days. . . . Sold by Red Wings to New York Rangers (June 26, 1990).
HONORS: Named to AHL All-Star second team (1984-85). . . . Shared Harry (Hap) Holmes Memorial Trophy with Karl Friesen (1985-86). . . . Won Baz Bastien Trophy (1985-86). . . . Named to AHL All-Star second team (1985-86). . . . Won Jack Butterfield Trophy (1988-89).
MISCELLANEOUS: Member of 1992 silver-medal-winning Canadian Olympic team.

		REGULAR SEASON								PLAYOFFS						
Season Team	League	Gms.	Min.	W	L	T	GA	SO	Avg.	Gms.	Min.	W	L	GA	SO	Avg.
75-76—Chicoutimi	QMJHL	17	889				81	0	5.47	—	—	—	—	—	—	—
76-77—Chicoutimi	QMJHL	21	901				81	0	5.39	—	—	—	—	—	—	—
77-78—Chicoutimi	QMJHL	60	3251				*351	0	6.48	—	—	—	—	—	—	—
78-79—Chicoutimi	QMJHL	70	3806				290	0	4.57	1	47			8	0	10.21
79-80—Toledo	IHL	38	2145				138	2	3.86	4	239			24	0	6.03
—Maine	AHL	4	201	2	1	0	15	0	4.48	—	—	—	—	—	—	—
80-81—Maine	AHL	7	363	3	3	0	28	0	4.63	—	—	—	—	—	—	—
—Toledo	IHL	30	1614				113	1	4.20	—	—	—	—	—	—	—
81-82—Maine	AHL	25	1396	15	7	1	76	0	3.27	4	240	1	3	18	0	4.50
—Toledo	IHL	4	248				11	0	2.66	—	—	—	—	—	—	—
82-83—Toledo	IHL	13	785				52	0	3.97	—	—	—	—	—	—	—
—Maine	AHL	30	1739				109	0	3.76	*17	*1012			*54	0	3.20
83-84—Maine	AHL	38	2158	14	18	4	145	0	4.03	12	708	9	2	32	*1	*2.71
84-85—Maine	AHL	55	3245	26	22	7	168	†4	3.11	10	656	5	5	*45	0	4.12
85-86—New Jersey	NHL	4	188	2	1	0	13	1	4.15	—	—	—	—	—	—	—
—Maine	AHL	50	2862	24	20	4	161	1	3.38	—	—	—	—	—	—	—
86-87—Adirondack	AHL	25	1397	7	13	0	98	1	4.21	3	105	0	2	10	0	5.71
—Detroit	NHL	6	342	1	2	2	16	0	2.81	—	—	—	—	—	—	—
87-88—Adirondack	AHL	32	1826	12	14	4	104	2	3.42	1	59	0	1	6	0	6.10
—Detroit	NHL	6	294	2	2	0	16	0	3.27	1	10	0	0	1	0	6.00
88-89—Detroit	NHL	4	141	0	1	1	9	0	3.83	—	—	—	—	—	—	—
—Adirondack	AHL	34	2054	20	11	3	113	0	3.30	16	956	*11	5	47	*2	*2.95
89-90—Detroit	NHL	14	607	2	6	1	38	0	3.76	—	—	—	—	—	—	—
—Adirondack	AHL	13	785	10	2	1	40	0	3.06	—	—	—	—	—	—	—
90-91—Binghamton	AHL	45	2379	19	16	4	138	1	3.48	3	160	1	2	11	0	4.13
91-92—Can. National Team	Int'l	1	60	0	1	0	3	0	3.00	—	—	—	—	—	—	—
—Can. Olympic Team	Int'l						Member of team—did not play.									
—Binghamton	AHL	1	20	0	0	0	2	0	6.00	—	—	—	—	—	—	—
NHL totals		34	1572	7	12	4	92	1	3.51	1	10	0	0	1	0	6.00

STAIOS, STEVE
D, BLUES

PERSONAL: Born July 28, 1973, at Hamilton, Ont. . . . 6-0/ 183. . . . Shoots right.
TRANSACTIONS/CAREER NOTES: Selected by St. Louis Blues in second round (first Blues pick, 27th overall) of NHL entry draft (June 22, 1991).

		REGULAR SEASON					PLAYOFFS				
Season Team	League	Gms.	G	A	Pts.	Pen.	Gms.	G	A	Pts.	Pen.
89-90—Hamilton Jr. B	OHA	40	9	27	36	66	—	—	—	—	—
90-91—Niagara Falls	OHL	66	17	29	46	115	12	2	3	5	10
91-92—Niagara Falls	OHL	65	11	42	53	122	17	7	8	15	27

STANTON, PAUL
D, PENGUINS

PERSONAL: Born June 22, 1967, at Boston. . . . 6-0/200. . . . Shoots right. . . . Full name: Paul Fredrick Stanton.
HIGH SCHOOL: Catholic Memorial (Boston).
COLLEGE: Wisconsin.
TRANSACTIONS/CAREER NOTES: Selected by Pittsburgh Penguins in eighth round (eighth Penguins pick, 149th overall) of NHL entry draft (June 15, 1985). . . . Injured knee ligament (October 31, 1991); missed 16 games.
HONORS: Named to NCAA All-America West first team (1987-88). . . . Named to WCHA All-Star first team (1988-89).

		REGULAR SEASON					PLAYOFFS				
Season Team	League	Gms.	G	A	Pts.	Pen.	Gms.	G	A	Pts.	Pen.
83-84—Catholic Memorial H.S.	Mass. H.S.		15	20	35		—	—	—	—	—
84-85—Catholic Memorial H.S.	Mass. H.S.	20	16	21	37	17	—	—	—	—	—
85-86—University of Wisconsin	WCHA	36	4	6	10	16	—	—	—	—	—
86-87—University of Wisconsin	WCHA	41	5	17	22	70	—	—	—	—	—
87-88—University of Wisconsin	WCHA	45	9	38	47	98	—	—	—	—	—
88-89—University of Wisconsin	WCHA	45	7	29	36	126	—	—	—	—	—
89-90—Muskegon	IHL	77	5	27	32	61	15	2	4	6	21
90-91—Pittsburgh	NHL	75	5	18	23	40	22	1	2	3	24
91-92—Pittsburgh	NHL	54	2	8	10	62	†21	1	7	8	42
NHL totals		129	7	26	33	102	43	2	9	11	66

STAPLETON, MIKE
C, BLACKHAWKS

PERSONAL: Born May 5, 1966, at Sarnia, Ont. . . . 5-10/ 183. . . . Shoots right. . . . Son of Pat Stapleton, defenseman, Boston Bruins and Chicago Blackhawks (1961-62 through 1972-73); and Chicago Cougars, Indianapolis Racers and Cincinnati Stingers of WHA (1973-74 through 1977-78).
TRANSACTIONS/CAREER NOTES: Selected by Chicago Blackhawks in seventh round (seventh Blackhawks pick, 132nd overall) of NHL entry draft (June 9, 1984).

		REGULAR SEASON					PLAYOFFS				
Season Team	League	Gms.	G	A	Pts.	Pen.	Gms.	G	A	Pts.	Pen.
82-83—Strathroy Jr. B	OHA	40	39	38	77	99	—	—	—	—	—
83-84—Cornwall	OHL	70	24	45	69	94	3	1	2	3	4
84-85—Cornwall	OHL	56	41	44	85	68	9	2	4	6	23
85-86—Cornwall	OHL	56	39	65	104	74	6	2	3	5	2

Season Team	League	REGULAR SEASON					PLAYOFFS				
		Gms.	G	A	Pts.	Pen.	Gms.	G	A	Pts.	Pen.
86-87—Canadian National Team..	Int'l	21	2	4	6	4	—	—	—	—	—
—Chicago	NHL	39	3	6	9	6	4	0	0	0	2
87-88—Saginaw	IHL	31	11	19	30	52	10	5	6	11	10
—Chicago	NHL	53	2	9	11	59	—	—	—	—	—
88-89—Chicago	NHL	7	0	1	1	7	—	—	—	—	—
—Saginaw	IHL	69	21	47	68	162	6	1	3	4	4
89-90—Arvika	Sweden	30	15	18	33		—	—	—	—	—
—Indianapolis	IHL	16	5	10	15	6	13	9	10	19	38
90-91—Chicago	NHL	7	0	1	1	2	—	—	—	—	—
—Indianapolis	IHL	75	29	52	81	76	7	1	4	5	0
91-92—Indianapolis	IHL	59	18	40	58	65	—	—	—	—	—
—Chicago	NHL	19	4	4	8	8	—	—	—	—	—
NHL totals		125	9	21	30	82	4	0	0	0	2

STAROSTENKO, DIMITRI
RW, RANGERS

PERSONAL: Born March 18, 1973, at Minsk, U.S.S.R. .... 6-0/185. .... Shoots left.
TRANSACTIONS/CAREER NOTES: Selected by New York Rangers in fifth round (fifth Rangers pick, 120th overall) of NHL entry draft (June 20, 1992).

Season Team	League	REGULAR SEASON					PLAYOFFS				
		Gms.	G	A	Pts.	Pen.	Gms.	G	A	Pts.	Pen.
89-90—Dynamo Minsk	USSR	7	0	0	0	2	—	—	—	—	—
90-91—CSKA Moscow	USSR	20	2	1	3	4	—	—	—	—	—
91-92—CSKA Moscow	CIS	32	3	1	4	12	—	—	—	—	—

STASTNY, PETER
C, DEVILS

PERSONAL: Born September 18, 1956, at Bratislava, Czechoslovakia. .... 6-1/200. .... Shoots left. ... Brother of Anton Stastny, left winger, Quebec Nordiques (1980-81 through 1988-89); and brother of Marian Stastny, right winger, Quebec Nordiques and Toronto Maple Leafs (1981-82 through 1985-86).
TRANSACTIONS/CAREER NOTES: Signed as free agent by Quebec Nordiques (August 1980). .... Injured knee (December 18, 1982). .... Suspended five games by NHL (October 1984). .... Injured lower back (November 1987). .... Sprained left shoulder (December 1988). .... Suffered sore left knee (December 1989). .... Traded by Nordiques to New Jersey Devils for D Craig Wolanin and future considerations (D Randy Velischek was sent to Quebec in August, 1990) (March 6, 1990). .... Suffered from digestive virus (February 29, 1992); missed eight games. ... Suffered from minor knee sprain and the flu (March 21, 1992); missed five games.
HONORS: Named to Czechoslovakian League All-Star second team (1977-78). .... Named to Czechoslovakian League All-Star first team (1978-79). .... Named Czechoslovakian League Player of the Year (1979-80). .... Named NHL Rookie of the Year by THE SPORTING NEWS (1980-81). .... Won Calder Memorial Trophy (1980-81).
RECORDS: Holds NHL single-season record for most assists by a rookie—70 (1980-81); and most points by a rookie—109 (1980-81). .... Shares NHL single-game record for most points by a rookie—8 (February 22, 1981).
STATISTICAL NOTES: One of only three players to score 100 points in each of their first six NHL seasons (Wayne Gretzky and Mario Lemieux).

Season Team	League	REGULAR SEASON					PLAYOFFS				
		Gms.	G	A	Pts.	Pen.	Gms.	G	A	Pts.	Pen.
77-78—Slovan Bratislava	Czech.	44	29	24	53		—	—	—	—	—
—Czech. National Team	Int'l	16	5	2	7		—	—	—	—	—
78-79—Slovan Bratislava	Czech.	44	32	23	55		—	—	—	—	—
—Czech. National Team	Int'l	18	12	9	21		—	—	—	—	—
79-80—Slovan Bratislava	Czech.	40	28	30	58		—	—	—	—	—
—Czech. Olympic Team	Int'l	6	7	7	14	6	—	—	—	—	—
80-81—Quebec	NHL	77	39	70	109	37	5	2	8	10	7
81-82—Quebec	NHL	80	46	93	139	91	12	7	11	18	10
82-83—Quebec	NHL	75	47	77	124	78	4	3	2	5	10
83-84—Quebec	NHL	80	46	73	119	73	9	2	7	9	31
84-85—Quebec	NHL	75	32	68	100	95	18	4	19	23	24
85-86—Quebec	NHL	76	41	81	122	60	3	0	1	1	2
86-87—Quebec	NHL	64	24	53	77	43	13	6	9	15	12
87-88—Quebec	NHL	76	46	65	111	69	—	—	—	—	—
88-89—Quebec	NHL	72	35	50	85	117	—	—	—	—	—
89-90—Quebec	NHL	62	24	38	62	24	—	—	—	—	—
—New Jersey	NHL	12	5	6	11	16	6	3	2	5	4
90-91—New Jersey	NHL	77	18	42	60	53	7	3	4	7	2
91-92—New Jersey	NHL	66	24	38	62	42	7	3	7	10	19
NHL totals		892	427	754	1181	798	84	33	70	103	121

STAUBER, PETE
LW, RED WINGS

PERSONAL: Born May 10, 1966, at Duluth, Minn. .... 5-11/185. .... Shoots left. .... Full name: Peter A. Stauber. .... Brother of Robb Stauber, goaltender in Los Angeles Kings system.
COLLEGE: Lake Superior State (Mich.).
TRANSACTIONS/CAREER NOTES: Signed as free agent by Detroit Red Wings (June 21, 1990).

Season Team	League	REGULAR SEASON					PLAYOFFS				
		Gms.	G	A	Pts.	Pen.	Gms.	G	A	Pts.	Pen.
86-87—Lake Superior State	CCHA	40	22	13	35	80	—	—	—	—	—
87-88—Lake Superior State	CCHA	45	25	33	58	103	—	—	—	—	—

Season	Team	League	Gms.	G	A	Pts.	Pen.	Gms.	G	A	Pts.	Pen.
88-89—Lake Superior State		CCHA	46	25	13	38	115	—	—	—	—	—
89-90—Lake Superior State		CCHA	46	25	31	56	90	—	—	—	—	—
90-91—Adirondack		AHL	26	7	11	18	2	—	—	—	—	—
91-92—Adirondack		AHL	25	2	5	7	14	—	—	—	—	—
—Toledo		ECHL	25	7	21	28	46	5	2	3	5	46

STAUBER, ROBB
G, KINGS

PERSONAL: Born November 25, 1967, at Duluth, Minn. . . . 5-11/180. . . . Shoots left. . . . Brother of Pete Stauber, left winger in Detroit Red Wings system.
HIGH SCHOOL: Denfeld (Duluth, Minn.).
COLLEGE: Minnesota.
TRANSACTIONS/CAREER NOTES: Selected by Los Angeles Kings in fifth round (fifth Kings pick, 107th overall) of NHL entry draft (June 21, 1986). . . . Twisted left knee and ankle (December 3, 1988); missed 14 games. . . . Injured groin and back (October 1989). . . . Underwent knee surgery (March 1991).
HONORS: Won Hobey Baker Memorial Trophy (1987-88). . . . Named to NCAA All-America West first team (1987-88). . . . Named to WCHA All-Star first team (1987-88). . . . Won WCHA Goaltender of the Year Award (1988-89). . . . Named to WCHA All-Star second team (1988-89).

					REGULAR SEASON						PLAYOFFS					
Season	Team	League	Gms.	Min.	W	L	T	GA	SO	Avg.	Gms.	Min.	W	L	GA SO	Avg.
84-85	Duluth Denfeld H.S.	Minn. HS	22	990				37	0	2.24	—	—	—	—	—	—
85-86	Duluth Denfeld H.S.	Minn. HS	27	1215				66	0	3.26	—	—	—	—	—	—
86-87—Univ. of Minnesota		WCHA	20	1072	13	5	0	63	0	3.53	—	—	—	—	—	—
87-88—Univ. of Minnesota		WCHA	44	2621	34	10	0	119	5	2.72	—	—	—	—	—	—
88-89—Univ. of Minnesota		WCHA	34	2024	26	8	0	82	0	2.43	—	—	—	—	—	—
89-90—New Haven		AHL	14	851	6	6	2	43	0	3.03	5	302	2	3	24 0	4.77
—Los Angeles		NHL	2	83	0	1	0	11	0	7.95	—	—	—	—	—	—
90-91—Phoenix		IHL	4	160	1	2	0	11	0	4.13	—	—	—	—	—	—
—New Haven		AHL	33	1882	13	16	4	115	1	3.67	—	—	—	—	—	—
91-92—Phoenix		IHL	22	1242	8	12	1	80	0	3.86	—	—	—	—	—	—
NHL totals			2	83	0	1	0	11	0	7.95						

STEEN, THOMAS
C, JETS

PERSONAL: Born June 8, 1960, at Tocksmark, Sweden. . . . 5-10/195. . . . Shoots left.
TRANSACTIONS/CAREER NOTES: Selected by Winnipeg Jets in fifth round (fifth Jets pick, 103rd overall) of NHL entry draft (June 11, 1980). . . . Lacerated elbow during Canada Cup (September 1981). . . . Injured knee in training camp (October 1981). . . . Suffered protruding disk (December 1989); missed 22 games. . . . Fractured right ankle (November 28, 1990); missed 20 games. . . . Suffered lower back spasms during preseason (September 1991); missed first 24 games of season. . . . Suffered ankle contusion (December 1991); missed 10 games. . . . Suffered recurrance of back spasms (January 1992); missed six games.
HONORS: Named Player of the Year in Swedish League (1980-81).

				REGULAR SEASON					PLAYOFFS			
Season	Team	League	Gms.	G	A	Pts.	Pen.	Gms.	G	A	Pts.	Pen.
76-77—Leksand		Sweden	2	1	1	2	2	—	—	—	—	—
77-78—Leksand		Sweden	35	5	6	11	30	—	—	—	—	—
78-79—Leksand		Sweden	25	13	4	17	35	2	0	0	0	0
—Swedish National Team		Int'l	2	0	0	0	0	—	—	—	—	—
79-80—Leksand		Sweden	18	7	7	14	14	2	0	0	0	6
80-81—Farjestad		Sweden	32	16	23	39	30	7	4	2	6	8
—Swedish National Team		Int'l	19	2	5	7	12	—	—	—	—	—
81-82—Winnipeg		NHL	73	15	29	44	42	4	0	4	4	2
82-83—Winnipeg		NHL	75	26	33	59	60	3	0	2	2	0
83-84—Winnipeg		NHL	78	20	45	65	69	3	0	1	1	9
84-85—Winnipeg		NHL	79	30	54	84	80	8	2	3	5	17
85-86—Winnipeg		NHL	78	17	47	64	76	3	1	1	2	4
86-87—Winnipeg		NHL	75	17	33	50	59	10	3	4	7	8
87-88—Winnipeg		NHL	76	16	38	54	53	5	1	5	6	2
88-89—Winnipeg		NHL	80	27	61	88	80	—	—	—	—	—
89-90—Winnipeg		NHL	53	18	48	66	35	7	2	5	7	16
90-91—Winnipeg		NHL	58	19	48	67	49	—	—	—	—	—
91-92—Winnipeg		NHL	38	13	25	38	29	7	2	4	6	2
NHL totals			763	218	461	679	632	50	11	29	40	60

STEINER, ONDREJ
C, SABRES

PERSONAL: Born February 12, 1974, at Plzen, Czechoslovakia. . . . 6-1/176. . . . Shoots left.
TRANSACTIONS/CAREER NOTES: Selected by Buffalo Sabres in third round (third Sabres pick, 59th overall) of NHL entry draft (June 20, 1992).

				REGULAR SEASON					PLAYOFFS			
Season	Team	League	Gms.	G	A	Pts.	Pen.	Gms.	G	A	Pts.	Pen.
91-92—Skoda Plzen		Czech.	4	0	1	1	0	—	—	—	—	—

STERN, RONNIE
RW, FLAMES

PERSONAL: Born January 11, 1967, at Ste. Agatha Des Mont, Que. . . . 6-0/195. . . . Shoots right. . . . Full name: Ronald Stern.
TRANSACTIONS/CAREER NOTES: Selected by Vancouver Canucks as underage junior in fourth round (third Canucks pick, 70th overall) of NHL entry draft (June 21, 1986). . . . Bruised

shoulder (April 1989).... Suffered laceration near eye and dislocated shoulder (March 19, 1990).... Fractured wrist (October 30, 1990); missed 10 weeks. ... Traded by Canucks with D Kevan Guy and fourth-round pick in 1992 draft to Calgary Flames for D Dana Murzyn and fourth-round pick in 1992 draft (March 5, 1991).

Season Team	League	REGULAR SEASON					PLAYOFFS				
		Gms.	G	A	Pts.	Pen.	Gms.	G	A	Pts.	Pen.
84-85—Longueuil	QMJHL	67	6	14	20	176	—	—	—	—	—
85-86—Longueuil	QMJHL	70	39	33	72	317	—	—	—	—	—
86-87—Longueuil	QMJHL	56	32	39	71	266	19	11	9	20	55
87-88—Fredericton	AHL	2	1	0	1	4	—	—	—	—	—
—Flint	IHL	55	14	19	33	294	16	8	8	16	94
—Vancouver	NHL	15	0	0	0	52	—	—	—	—	—
88-89—Milwaukee	IHL	45	19	23	42	280	5	1	0	1	11
—Vancouver	NHL	17	1	0	1	49	3	0	1	1	17
89-90—Milwaukee	IHL	26	8	9	17	165	—	—	—	—	—
—Vancouver	NHL	34	2	3	5	208	—	—	—	—	—
90-91—Milwaukee	IHL	7	2	2	4	81	—	—	—	—	—
—Vancouver	NHL	31	2	3	5	171	—	—	—	—	—
—Calgary	NHL	13	1	3	4	69	7	1	3	4	14
91-92—Calgary	NHL	72	13	9	22	338	—	—	—	—	—
NHL totals		182	19	18	37	887	10	1	4	5	31

S

STEVENS, JOHN
D, WHALERS

PERSONAL: Born May 4, 1966, at Completon, N.B. ... 6-1/195. ... Shoots left.
TRANSACTIONS/CAREER NOTES: Selected by Chicago Blackhawks as underage junior in third round (second Blackhawks pick, 45th overall) of NHL entry draft (June 9, 1984). ... Underwent knee surgery (September 1984). ... Signed as free agent by Philadelphia Flyers (September 1987). ... Signed as free agent by Hartford Whalers (July 16, 1990).

Season Team	League	REGULAR SEASON					PLAYOFFS				
		Gms.	G	A	Pts.	Pen.	Gms.	G	A	Pts.	Pen.
82-83—Newmarket	OHA	48	2	9	11	111	—	—	—	—	—
83-84—Oshawa	OHL	70	1	10	11	71	7	0	1	1	6
84-85—Oshawa	OHL	45	2	10	12	61	5	0	2	2	4
—Hershey	AHL	3	0	0	0	2	—	—	—	—	—
85-86—Oshawa	OHL	65	1	7	8	146	6	0	2	2	14
—Kalamazoo	IHL	6	0	1	1	8	6	0	3	3	9
86-87—Hershey	AHL	63	1	15	16	131	3	0	0	0	7
—Philadelphia	NHL	6	0	2	2	14	—	—	—	—	—
87-88—Philadelphia	NHL	3	0	0	0	0	—	—	—	—	—
—Hershey	AHL	59	1	15	16	108	—	—	—	—	—
88-89—Hershey	AHL	78	3	13	16	129	12	1	1	2	29
89-90—Hershey	AHL	79	3	10	13	193	—	—	—	—	—
90-91—Hartford	NHL	14	0	1	1	11	—	—	—	—	—
—Springfield	AHL	65	0	12	12	139	18	0	6	6	35
91-92—Springfield	AHL	45	1	12	13	73	11	1	3	4	27
—Hartford	NHL	21	0	4	4	19	—	—	—	—	—
NHL totals		44	0	7	7	44					

STEVENS, KEVIN
LW, PENGUINS

PERSONAL: Born April 15, 1965, at Brockton, Mass. ... 6-3/215. ... Shoots left. ... Full name: Kevin Michael Stevens.
HIGH SCHOOL: Silver Lake (Minn.).
COLLEGE: Boston College.
TRANSACTIONS/CAREER NOTES: Selected by Los Angeles Kings in sixth round (sixth Kings pick, 108th overall) of NHL entry draft (June 8, 1983). ... Traded by Kings to Pittsburgh Penguins for LW Anders Hakansson (September 1983).
HONORS: Named to NCAA All-America East second team (1986-87). ... Named to Hockey East All-Star first team (1986-87). ... Named to THE SPORTING NEWS All-Star second team (1990-91). ... Named to NHL All-Star second team (1990-91). ... Named to THE SPORTING NEWS All-Star first team (1991-92). ... Named to NHL All-Star first team (1991-92).
RECORDS: Holds NHL single-season records for most points by a left winger—123 (1991-92); and most assists by a left-winger—69 (1991-92).

Season Team	League	REGULAR SEASON					PLAYOFFS				
		Gms.	G	A	Pts.	Pen.	Gms.	G	A	Pts.	Pen.
82-83—Silver Lake H.S.	Minn. H.S.	18	24	27	51		—	—	—	—	—
83-84—Boston College	ECAC	37	6	14	20	36	—	—	—	—	—
84-85—Boston College	Hockey East	40	13	23	36	36	—	—	—	—	—
85-86—Boston College	Hockey East	42	17	27	44	56	—	—	—	—	—
86-87—Boston College	Hockey East	39	*35	35	70	54	—	—	—	—	—
87-88—U.S. National Team	Int'l	44	22	23	45	52	—	—	—	—	—
—U.S. Olympic Team	Int'l	5	1	3	4	2	—	—	—	—	—
—Pittsburgh	NHL	16	5	2	7	8	—	—	—	—	—
88-89—Pittsburgh	NHL	24	12	3	15	19	11	3	7	10	16
—Muskegon	IHL	45	24	41	65	113	—	—	—	—	—
89-90—Pittsburgh	NHL	76	29	41	70	171	—	—	—	—	—
90-91—Pittsburgh	NHL	80	40	46	86	133	24	*17	16	33	53
91-92—Pittsburgh	NHL	80	54	69	123	254	†21	13	15	28	28
NHL totals		276	140	161	301	585	56	33	38	71	97

STEVENS, MIKE
C/LW, RANGERS

PERSONAL: Born December 30, 1965, at Kitchener, Ont. . . . . 5-11/195. . . . Shoots left. . . . Brother of Scott Stevens, defenseman, New Jersey Devils.

TRANSACTIONS/CAREER NOTES: Selected by Vancouver Canucks as underage junior in third round (fourth Canucks pick, 58th overall) of NHL entry draft (June 9, 1984). . . . Underwent arthroscopic knee surgery (October 1984). . . . Traded by Canucks to Boston Bruins for future considerations (October 1987). . . . Signed as free agent by New York Islanders (August 1988). . . . Traded by Islanders with C Gilles Thibaudeau to Toronto Maple Leafs for LW Paul Gagne, RW Derek Laxdal and D Jack Capuano (December 20, 1989). . . . Traded by Maple Leafs to New York Rangers for C Guy Larose (December 26, 1991).

Season Team	League	REGULAR SEASON					PLAYOFFS				
		Gms.	G	A	Pts.	Pen.	Gms.	G	A	Pts.	Pen.
82-83—Kitchener Jr. B	OHA	29	5	18	23	86	—	—	—	—	—
—Kitchener	OHL	13	0	4	4	16	12	0	1	1	9
83-84—Kitchener	OHL	66	19	21	40	109	16	10	7	17	40
84-85—Kitchener	OHL	37	17	18	35	121	4	1	1	2	8
—Vancouver	NHL	6	0	3	3	6	—	—	—	—	—
85-86—Fredericton	AHL	79	12	19	31	208	6	1	1	2	35
86-87—Fredericton	AHL	71	7	18	25	258	—	—	—	—	—
87-88—Maine	AHL	63	30	25	55	265	7	1	2	3	37
—Boston	NHL	7	0	1	1	9	—	—	—	—	—
88-89—Springfield	AHL	42	17	13	30	120	—	—	—	—	—
—New York Islanders	NHL	9	1	0	1	14	—	—	—	—	—
89-90—Springfield	AHL	28	12	10	22	75	—	—	—	—	—
—Toronto	NHL	1	0	0	0	0	—	—	—	—	—
—Newmarket	AHL	46	16	28	44	86	—	—	—	—	—
90-91—Newmarket	AHL	68	24	23	47	229	—	—	—	—	—
91-92—St. John's	AHL	30	13	11	24	65	—	—	—	—	—
—Binghamton	AHL	44	15	15	30	87	11	7	6	13	45
NHL totals		23	1	4	5	29					

STEVENS, SCOTT
D, DEVILS

PERSONAL: Born April 1, 1964, at Kitchener, Ont. . . . 6-2/215. . . . Shoots left. . . . Brother of Mike Stevens, center/left winger in New York Rangers system.

TRANSACTIONS/CAREER NOTES: Selected by Washington Capitals as underage junior in first round (first Capitals pick, fifth overall) of NHL entry draft (June 9, 1982). . . . Bruised right knee (November 6, 1985); missed seven games. . . . Broke right index finger (December 14, 1986). . . . Bruised shoulder (April 1988). . . . Suffered from poison oak (November 1988). . . . Suffered facial lacerations during World Cup (April 21, 1989). . . . Broke left foot (December 29, 1989); missed 17 games. . . . Suspended three games by NHL for scratching (February 27, 1990). . . . Bruised left shoulder (March 27, 1990). . . . Dislocated left shoulder (May 3, 1990). . . . Signed as free agent by St. Louis Blues (July 9, 1990); Blues owed Capitals two first-round draft picks among the top seven over next two years and $100,000 cash; upon failing to get a pick in the top seven in 1991, Blues forfeited their first-round pick in 1991 (LW Trevor Halverson), 1992 (D Sergei Gonchar), 1993, 1994 and 1995 draft to Capitals (July 9, 1990). . . . Awarded to New Jersey Devils as compensation for Blues signing free agent RW/LW Brendan Shanahan (September 1, 1991). . . . Strained right knee (February 20, 1992); missed 12 games.

HONORS: Named to NHL All-Rookie team (1982-83). . . . Named to NHL All-Star first team (1987-88). . . . Named to NHL All-Star second team (1991-92).

Season Team	League	REGULAR SEASON					PLAYOFFS				
		Gms.	G	A	Pts.	Pen.	Gms.	G	A	Pts.	Pen.
80-81—Kitchener Jr. B	OHA	39	7	33	40	82	—	—	—	—	—
—Kitchener	OHL	1	0	0	0	0	—	—	—	—	—
81-82—Kitchener	OHL	68	6	36	42	158	15	1	10	11	71
82-83—Washington	NHL	77	9	16	25	195	4	1	0	1	26
83-84—Washington	NHL	78	13	32	45	201	8	1	8	9	21
84-85—Washington	NHL	80	21	44	65	221	5	0	1	1	20
85-86—Washington	NHL	73	15	38	53	165	9	3	8	11	12
86-87—Washington	NHL	77	10	51	61	283	7	0	5	5	19
87-88—Washington	NHL	80	12	60	72	184	13	1	11	12	46
88-89—Washington	NHL	80	7	61	68	225	6	1	4	5	11
89-90—Washington	NHL	56	11	29	40	154	15	2	7	9	25
90-91—St. Louis	NHL	78	5	44	49	150	13	0	3	3	36
91-92—New Jersey	NHL	68	17	42	59	124	7	2	1	3	29
NHL totals		747	120	417	537	1902	87	11	48	59	245

STEVENSON, JEREMY
LW/C, JETS

PERSONAL: Born July 28, 1974, at San Bernardino, Calif. . . . 6-1/212. . . . Shoots left.

HIGH SCHOOL: St. Lawrence (Cornwall, Ont.).

TRANSACTIONS/CAREER NOTES: Selected by Winnipeg Jets in third round (third Jets pick, 60th overall) of NHL entry draft (June 20, 1992).

Season Team	League	REGULAR SEASON					PLAYOFFS				
		Gms.	G	A	Pts.	Pen.	Gms.	G	A	Pts.	Pen.
90-91—Cornwall	OHL	58	13	20	33	124	—	—	—	—	—
91-92—Cornwall	OHL	63	15	23	38	176	6	3	1	4	4

STEVENSON, SHAYNE
RW, LIGHTNING

PERSONAL: Born October 26, 1970, at Newmarket, Ont. . . . 6-1/190. . . . Shoots right.

TRANSACTIONS/CAREER NOTES: Selected by Boston Bruins in first round (first Bruins pick, 17th overall) of NHL entry draft (June 17, 1989). . . . Selected by Tampa Bay Lightning in NHL expansion draft (June 18, 1992).

Season Team	League	REGULAR SEASON					PLAYOFFS				
		Gms.	G	A	Pts.	Pen.	Gms.	G	A	Pts.	Pen.
85-86—Barrie Jr. B	OHA	38	14	23	37	75	—	—	—	—	—
86-87—London	OHL	61	7	15	22	56	—	—	—	—	—
87-88—London	OHL	36	14	25	39	56	—	—	—	—	—
—Kitchener	OHL	30	10	25	35	48	4	1	1	2	4
88-89—Kitchener	OHL	56	25	51	76	86	5	2	3	5	4
89-90—Kitchener	OHL	56	28	62	90	115	17	16	21	*37	31
90-91—Maine	AHL	58	22	28	50	112	—	—	—	—	—
—Boston	NHL	14	0	0	0	26	—	—	—	—	—
91-92—Maine	AHL	54	10	23	33	150	—	—	—	—	—
—Boston	NHL	5	0	1	1	2	—	—	—	—	—
NHL totals		19	0	1	1	28					

STEVENSON, TURNER
RW, CANADIENS

PERSONAL: Born May 18, 1972, at Port Alberni, B.C. . . . 6-3/200. . . . Shoots right.
TRANSACTIONS/CAREER NOTES: Underwent surgery to remove growth in chest (August 1987). . . . Injured shoulder (December 1987). . . . Selected by Montreal Canadiens in first round (first Canadiens pick, 12th overall) of NHL entry draft (June 16, 1990).
HONORS: Named to Can.HL All-Star second team (1991-92). . . . Named to Memorial Cup All-Star team (1991-92). . . . Named to WHL West All-Star first team (1991-92).

Season Team	League	REGULAR SEASON					PLAYOFFS				
		Gms.	G	A	Pts.	Pen.	Gms.	G	A	Pts.	Pen.
88-89—Seattle	WHL	69	15	12	27	84	—	—	—	—	—
89-90—Seattle	WHL	62	29	32	61	276	13	3	2	5	35
90-91—Seattle	WHL	57	36	27	63	222	6	1	5	6	15
—Fredericton	AHL	—	—	—	—	—	4	0	0	0	5
91-92—Seattle	WHL	58	20	32	52	304	15	9	3	12	55

STEWART, ALAN
LW

PERSONAL: Born January 31, 1964, at Fort St. John, B.C. . . . 5-11/173. . . . Shoots left.
TRANSACTIONS/CAREER NOTES: Selected by New Jersey Devils as underage junior in 11th round (ninth Devils pick, 205th overall) of NHL entry draft (June 8, 1983). . . . Underwent hernia surgery (October 1987); missed two months. . . . Broke left leg in four places during practice (September 21, 1989); missed first 79 games of season. . . . Traded by Devils to Boston Bruins for future considerations (October 16, 1991). . . . Retired (November 1991).

Season Team	League	REGULAR SEASON					PLAYOFFS				
		Gms.	G	A	Pts.	Pen.	Gms.	G	A	Pts.	Pen.
81-82—Prince Albert	WHL	46	9	25	34	53	—	—	—	—	—
82-83—Prince Albert	WHL	70	25	34	59	272	—	—	—	—	—
83-84—Prince Albert	WHL	67	44	39	83	216	5	1	2	3	29
—Maine	AHL	—	—	—	—	—	3	0	0	0	4
84-85—Maine	AHL	75	8	11	19	241	11	1	2	3	58
85-86—Maine	AHL	58	7	12	19	181	—	—	—	—	—
—New Jersey	NHL	4	0	0	0	21	—	—	—	—	—
86-87—Maine	AHL	74	14	24	38	143	—	—	—	—	—
—New Jersey	NHL	7	1	0	1	26	—	—	—	—	—
87-88—New Jersey	NHL	1	0	0	0	0	—	—	—	—	—
—Utica	AHL	49	8	17	25	129	—	—	—	—	—
88-89—New Jersey	NHL	6	0	2	2	15	—	—	—	—	—
—Utica	AHL	72	9	23	32	110	5	1	0	1	4
89-90—Utica	AHL	1	0	0	0	0	1	0	0	0	11
90-91—Utica	AHL	9	2	0	2	9	—	—	—	—	—
—New Jersey	NHL	41	5	2	7	159	—	—	—	—	—
91-92—New Jersey	NHL	1	0	0	0	5	—	—	—	—	—
—Boston	NHL	4	0	0	0	17	—	—	—	—	—
NHL totals		64	6	4	10	243					

STEWART, CAMERON
C, BRUINS

PERSONAL: Born September 18, 1971, at Kitchener, Ont. . . . 5-10/188. . . . Shoots left. . . . Full name: Cameron G. Stewart.
COLLEGE: Michigan.
TRANSACTIONS/CAREER NOTES: Strained knee ligaments (June 1989). . . . Selected by Boston Bruins in third round (second Bruins pick, 63rd overall) of NHL entry draft (June 16, 1990).

Season Team	League	REGULAR SEASON					PLAYOFFS				
		Gms.	G	A	Pts.	Pen.	Gms.	G	A	Pts.	Pen.
88-89—Elmira Jr. B	OHA	43	38	50	88	138	—	—	—	—	—
89-90—Elmira Jr. B	OHA	46	44	95	139	172	—	—	—	—	—
90-91—University of Michigan	CCHA	44	8	24	32	122	—	—	—	—	—
91-92—University of Michigan	CCHA	44	13	15	28	106	—	—	—	—	—

STEWART, MICHAEL
D, RANGERS

PERSONAL: Born March 30, 1972, at Calgary, Alta. . . . 6-2/197. . . . Shoots left. . . . Full name: Michael Donald Stewart.
COLLEGE: Michigan State.
TRANSACTIONS/CAREER NOTES: Selected by New York Rangers in first round (first

Rangers pick, 13th overall) of NHL entry draft (June 16, 1990).
HONORS: Named to CCHA All-Rookie team (1989-90).

Season Team	League	REGULAR SEASON					PLAYOFFS				
		Gms.	G	A	Pts.	Pen.	Gms.	G	A	Pts.	Pen.
89-90—Michigan State	CCHA	45	2	6	8	45	—	—	—	—	—
90-91—Michigan State	CCHA	37	3	12	15	58	—	—	—	—	—
91-92—Michigan State	CCHA	8	1	3	4	6	—	—	—	—	—

STILLMAN, CORY
C, FLAMES

PERSONAL: Born December 20, 1973, at Peterborough, Ont. . . . 6-0/174. . . . Shoots left.
HIGH SCHOOL: Herman E. Fawcett (Brantford, Ont.).
TRANSACTIONS/CAREER NOTES: Selected by Calgary Flames in first round (first Flames pick, sixth overall) of NHL entry draft (June 20, 1992).
HONORS: Won Emms Family Award (1990-91).

Season Team	League	REGULAR SEASON					PLAYOFFS				
		Gms.	G	A	Pts.	Pen.	Gms.	G	A	Pts.	Pen.
89-90—Peterborough Jr. B	OHA	41	30	54	84	76	—	—	—	—	—
90-91—Windsor	OHL	64	31	70	101	31	11	3	6	9	8
91-92—Windsor	OHL	53	29	61	90	59	7	2	4	6	8

STOJANOV, ALEX
LW, CANUCKS

PERSONAL: Born April 25, 1973, at Windsor, Ont. . . . 6-4/225. . . . Shoots left. . . . Full name: Aleksander Stojanov.
TRANSACTIONS/CAREER NOTES: Dislocated shoulder (July 1989). . . . Selected by Vancouver Canucks in first round (first Canucks pick, seventh overall) of NHL entry draft (June 22, 1991).

Season Team	League	REGULAR SEASON					PLAYOFFS				
		Gms.	G	A	Pts.	Pen.	Gms.	G	A	Pts.	Pen.
89-90—Dukes of Hamilton	OHL	37	4	4	8	91	—	—	—	—	—
90-91—Dukes of Hamilton	OHL	62	25	20	45	179	4	1	1	2	14
91-92—Guelph	OHL	33	12	15	27	91	—	—	—	—	—

STOLP, JEFF
G, NORTH STARS

PERSONAL: Born June 20, 1970, at Grand Rapids, Minn. . . . 6-0/180. . . . Shoots left. . . . Full name: Jeffery Stolp.
HIGH SCHOOL: Greenway (Coleraine, Minn.).
COLLEGE: Minnesota.
TRANSACTIONS/CAREER NOTES: Selected by Minnesota North Stars in fourth round (fourth North Stars pick, 64th overall) of NHL entry draft (June 11, 1988).
HONORS: Named to WCHA All-Tournament team (1990-91). . . . Named to WCHA All-Star second team (1991-92).

Season Team	League	REGULAR SEASON								PLAYOFFS						
		Gms.	Min.	W	L	T	GA	SO	Avg.	Gms.	Min.	W	L	GA	SO	Avg.
86-87—Greenway H.S.	Minn. HS	24	1080				39	1	2.17	—	—	—	—	—	—	—
87-88—Greenway H.S.	Minn. HS	23	1035				57	1	3.30	—	—	—	—	—	—	—
88-89—Univ. of Minnesota	WCHA	16	742	7	2	3	45	0	3.64	—	—	—	—	—	—	—
89-90—Univ. of Minnesota	WCHA	10	417	5	1	0	33	1	4.75	—	—	—	—	—	—	—
90-91—Univ. of Minnesota	WCHA	32	1766	18	8	3	82	2	*2.79	—	—	—	—	—	—	—
91-92—Univ. of Minnesota	WCHA	†36	2017	*26	9	0	98	*2	*2.92	—	—	—	—	—	—	—

STORM, JIM
LW, WHALERS

PERSONAL: Born February 5, 1971, at Detroit. . . . 6-2/200. . . . Shoots left. . . . Full name: James David Storm.
COLLEGE: Michigan Tech.
TRANSACTIONS/CAREER NOTES: Selected by Hartford Whalers in fourth round (fifth Whalers pick, 75th overall) of NHL entry draft (June 22, 1991).

Season Team	League	REGULAR SEASON					PLAYOFFS				
		Gms.	G	A	Pts.	Pen.	Gms.	G	A	Pts.	Pen.
88-89—Detroit Compuware	NAJHL	60	30	45	75	50	—	—	—	—	—
89-90—Detroit Compuware	NAJHL	55	38	73	111	58	—	—	—	—	—
90-91—Michigan Tech	WCHA	36	16	17	33	46	—	—	—	—	—
91-92—Michigan Tech	WCHA	39	25	33	58	12	—	—	—	—	—

STOTHERS, MIKE
D, FLYERS

PERSONAL: Born February 22, 1962, at Toronto. . . . 6-4/210. . . . Shoots left. . . . Full name: Michael Patrick Stothers.
TRANSACTIONS/CAREER NOTES: Selected by Philadelphia Flyers as underage junior in first round (first Flyers pick, 21st overall) of NHL entry draft (June 11, 1980). . . . Injured ankle (December 1984). . . . Traded by Flyers to Toronto Maple Leafs for fifth-round pick in 1989 draft (December 4, 1987). . . . Traded by Maple Leafs to Flyers for Bill Root (June 21, 1988). . . . Injured hand (October 1989). . . . Named player/assistant coach for Hershey Bears (September 30, 1990).

Season Team	League	REGULAR SEASON					PLAYOFFS				
		Gms.	G	A	Pts.	Pen.	Gms.	G	A	Pts.	Pen.
79-80—Kingston	OMJHL	66	4	23	27	137	—	—	—	—	—
80-81—Kingston	OMJHL	65	4	22	26	237	14	0	3	3	27
81-82—Kingston	OHL	61	1	20	21	203	4	0	1	1	8
—Maine	AHL	5	0	0	0	4	1	0	0	0	0

Season Team	League	REGULAR SEASON Gms.	G	A	Pts.	Pen.	PLAYOFFS Gms.	G	A	Pts.	Pen.
82-83—Maine	AHL	80	2	16	18	139	12	0	0	0	21
83-84—Maine	AHL	61	2	10	12	109	17	0	1	1	34
84-85—Philadelphia	NHL	1	0	0	0	0	—	—	—	—	—
—Hershey	AHL	59	8	18	26	142	—	—	—	—	—
85-86—Hershey	AHL	66	4	9	13	221	13	0	3	3	88
—Philadelphia	NHL	6	0	1	1	6	3	0	0	0	4
86-87—Philadelphia	NHL	2	0	0	0	4	2	0	0	0	7
—Hershey	AHL	75	5	11	16	283	5	0	0	0	10
87-88—Philadelphia	NHL	3	0	0	0	13	—	—	—	—	—
—Toronto	NHL	18	0	1	1	42	—	—	—	—	—
—Hershey	AHL	13	3	2	5	55	—	—	—	—	—
—Newmarket	AHL	38	1	9	10	69	—	—	—	—	—
88-89—Hershey	AHL	76	4	11	15	262	9	0	2	2	29
89-90—Hershey	AHL	56	1	6	7	170	—	—	—	—	—
90-91—Hershey	AHL	72	5	6	11	234	7	0	1	1	9
91-92—Hershey	AHL	70	3	8	11	152	6	0	1	1	6
NHL totals		30	0	2	2	65	5	0	0	0	11

STRAKA, MARTIN
C, PENGUINS

PERSONAL: Born September 3, 1972, at Plzen, Czechoslovakia. . . . 5-9/172. . . . Shoots left.

TRANSACTIONS/CAREER NOTES: Selected by Pittsburgh Penguins in first round (first Penguins pick, 19th overall) of NHL entry draft (June 20, 1992).

Season Team	League	REGULAR SEASON Gms.	G	A	Pts.	Pen.	PLAYOFFS Gms.	G	A	Pts.	Pen.
89-90—Skoda Plzen	Czech.	1	0	3	3		—	—	—	—	—
90-91—Skoda Plzen	Czech.	47	7	24	31	6	—	—	—	—	—
91-92—Skoda Plzen	Czech.	50	27	28	55		—	—	—	—	—

STUMPEL, JOZEF
RW

PERSONAL: Born June 20, 1972, at Nitra, Czechoslovakia. . . . 6-1/190. . . . Shoots right.

TRANSACTIONS/CAREER NOTES: Selected by Boston Bruins in second round (second Bruins pick, 40th overall) of NHL entry draft (June 22, 1991).

Season Team	League	REGULAR SEASON Gms.	G	A	Pts.	Pen.	PLAYOFFS Gms.	G	A	Pts.	Pen.
89-90—Nitra	Czech.	38	12	11	23	0	—	—	—	—	—
90-91—Nitra	Czech.	49	23	22	45	14	—	—	—	—	—
91-92—Boston	NHL	4	1	0	1	0	—	—	—	—	—
—Koln	Germany	33	19	18	37	35	—	—	—	—	—
NHL totals		4	1	0	1	0					

SULLIVAN, BRIAN
LW, DEVILS

PERSONAL: Born April 23, 1969, at South Windsor, Conn. . . . 6-4/195. . . . Shoots right. . . . Brother of Kevin Sullivan, right winger in San Jose Sharks system.

HIGH SCHOOL: South Windsor (Conn.).

COLLEGE: Northeastern.

TRANSACTIONS/CAREER NOTES: Selected by New Jersey Devils in fourth round (third Devils pick, 65th overall) of NHL entry draft (June 13, 1987). . . . Bruised shoulder (November 1989).

Season Team	League	REGULAR SEASON Gms.	G	A	Pts.	Pen.	PLAYOFFS Gms.	G	A	Pts.	Pen.
85-86—South Windsor H.S.	Conn. H.S.		39	50	89		—	—	—	—	—
86-87—Springfield Jr. B	NEJHL		30	35	65		—	—	—	—	—
87-88—Northeastern University	Hockey East	37	20	12	32	18	—	—	—	—	—
88-89—Northeastern University	Hockey East	34	13	14	27	65	—	—	—	—	—
89-90—Northeastern University	Hockey East	34	24	21	45	72	—	—	—	—	—
90-91—Northeastern University	Hockey East	32	17	23	40	75	—	—	—	—	—
91-92—Utica	AHL	70	23	24	47	58	4	0	4	4	6

SULLIVAN, KEVIN
RW, SHARKS

PERSONAL: Born May 16, 1968, at South Windsor, Conn. . . . 6-3/188. . . . Shoots right. . . . Full name: Kevin Patrick Sullivan. . . . Brother of Brian Sullivan, left winger in New Jersey Devils system.

COLLEGE: Princeton.

TRANSACTIONS/CAREER NOTES: Selected by Hartford Whalers in 11th round (ninth Whalers pick, 228th overall) of NHL entry draft (June 13, 1987). . . . Traded by Whalers to Minnesota North Stars for D Mike Berger (October 7, 1989). . . . Signed as free agent by San Jose Sharks (September 3, 1991).

Season Team	League	REGULAR SEASON Gms.	G	A	Pts.	Pen.	PLAYOFFS Gms.	G	A	Pts.	Pen.
86-87—Princeton University	ECAC	25	1	0	1	10	—	—	—	—	—
87-88—Princeton University	ECAC	22	0	3	3	8	—	—	—	—	—
88-89—Princeton University	ECAC	26	7	7	14	58	—	—	—	—	—
89-90—Princeton University	ECAC	27	12	13	25	28	—	—	—	—	—
90-91—Kansas City	IHL	24	0	4	4	15	—	—	—	—	—
—Nashville	ECHL	33	14	14	28	29	—	—	—	—	—

Season Team	League	Gms.	G	A	Pts.	Pen.	Gms.	G	A	Pts.	Pen.
		REGULAR SEASON					**PLAYOFFS**				
91-92—Kansas City	IHL	5	0	1	1	0	—	—	—	—	—
—Nashville	ECHL	26	7	11	18	33	—	—	—	—	—
—Richmond	ECHL	30	14	8	22	33	7	3	4	7	4

SULLIVAN, MIKE
C, SHARKS

PERSONAL: Born February 28, 1968, at Marshfield, Mass. . . . 6-2/193. . . . Shoots left. . . . Full name: Michael Barry Sullivan.
HIGH SCHOOL: Boston College High School (Boston).
COLLEGE: Boston University.
TRANSACTIONS/CAREER NOTES: Selected by New York Rangers in fourth round (fourth Rangers pick, 69th overall) of NHL entry draft (June 13, 1987). . . . Traded by Rangers with D Mark Tinordi, D Paul Jerrard, RW Brett Barnett and Los Angeles Kings third-round pick in 1989 draft (C Murray Garbutt) to Minnesota North Stars for LW Igor Liba, C Brian Lawton and NHL rights to LW Eric Bennett (October 11, 1988). . . . Signed as free agent by San Jose Sharks (August 9, 1991).

Season Team	League	Gms.	G	A	Pts.	Pen.	Gms.	G	A	Pts.	Pen.
		REGULAR SEASON					**PLAYOFFS**				
85-86—Boston College H.S.	Mass. H.S.	22	26	33	59		—	—	—	—	—
86-87—Boston College H.S.	Mass. H.S.	37	13	18	31	18	—	—	—	—	—
87-88—Boston College H.S.	Mass. H.S.	30	18	22	40	30	—	—	—	—	—
88-89—Boston College H.S.	Mass. H.S.	36	19	17	36	30	—	—	—	—	—
—Virginia	ECHL	2	0	0	0	0	—	—	—	—	—
89-90—Boston University	Hockey East	38	11	20	31	26	—	—	—	—	—
90-91—San Diego	IHL	74	12	23	35	27	—	—	—	—	—
91-92—Kansas City	IHL	10	2	8	10	8	—	—	—	—	—
—San Jose	NHL	64	8	11	19	15	—	—	—	—	—
NHL totals		64	8	11	19	15					

SULLIVAN, MIKE
C, RED WINGS

PERSONAL: Born October 16, 1973, at Woburn, Mass. . . . 6-1/190. . . . Shoots left.
HIGH SCHOOL: Reading Memorial (Reading, Mass.).
TRANSACTIONS/CAREER NOTES: Selected by Detroit Red Wings in fifth round (fourth Red Wings pick, 118th overall) of NHL entry draft (June 20, 1992).

Season Team	League	Gms.	G	A	Pts.	Pen.	Gms.	G	A	Pts.	Pen.
		REGULAR SEASON					**PLAYOFFS**				
91-92—Reading H.S.	Mass. H.S.	24	39	41	80	0	—	—	—	—	—

SUNDIN, MATS
RW, NORDIQUES

PERSONAL: Born February 13, 1971, at Sollentuna, Sweden. . . . 6-2/190. . . . Shoots right. . . . Full name: Mats Johan Sundin.
TRANSACTIONS/CAREER NOTES: Selected by Quebec Nordiques in first round (first Nordiques pick, first overall) of NHL entry draft (June 17, 1989).

Season Team	League	Gms.	G	A	Pts.	Pen.	Gms.	G	A	Pts.	Pen.
		REGULAR SEASON					**PLAYOFFS**				
88-89—Nacka	Sweden	25	10	8	18	18	—	—	—	—	—
89-90—Djurgarden	Sweden	34	10	8	18	16	8	7	0	7	4
90-91—Quebec	NHL	80	23	36	59	58	—	—	—	—	—
91-92—Quebec	NHL	80	33	43	76	103	—	—	—	—	—
NHL totals		160	56	79	135	161					

SUNDSTROM, PATRIK
C, DEVILS

PERSONAL: Born December 14, 1961, at Skelleftea, Sweden. . . . 6-1/200. . . . Shoots left.
TRANSACTIONS/CAREER NOTES: Selected by Vancouver Canucks in ninth round (eighth Canucks pick, 175th overall) of NHL entry draft (June 11, 1980). . . . Separated shoulder (November 1982). . . . Broke left wrist in final game of Canada Cup (September 1985). . . . Tore rotator cuff (January 1987); missed six games. . . . Traded by Canucks with fourth-round pick in 1988 draft (LW Matt Ruchty) to New Jersey Devils for G Kirk McLean and C Greg Adams (September 1987). . . . Suffered abdominal strain (March 1988). . . . Strained lower back (October 1988). . . . Bruised right thigh (December 1988). . . . Bruised left knee (March 1989). . . . Injured back (October 8, 1991); missed two games. . . . Suffered recurring sore back (November 1991); missed seven games. . . . Bruised thigh (December 29, 1991); missed final 43 games of season.
HONORS: Won Viking Award (1983-84).
RECORDS: Shares NHL single-game playoff record for most points—8 (April 22, 1988).

Season Team	League	Gms.	G	A	Pts.	Pen.	Gms.	G	A	Pts.	Pen.
		REGULAR SEASON					**PLAYOFFS**				
79-80—Umea Bjorkloven IF	Sweden	26	5	7	12	20	3	1	0	1	4
80-81—Umea Bjorkloven IF	Sweden	36	10	18	28	30	3	1	0	1	4
—Swedish National Team	Int'l	15	4	2	6	6	—	—	—	—	—
81-82—Umea Bjorkloven IF	Sweden	36	22	13	35	38	7	3	4	7	6
—Swedish National Team	Int'l	36	17	7	24	24	—	—	—	—	—
82-83—Vancouver	NHL	74	23	23	46	30	4	0	0	0	2
83-84—Vancouver	NHL	78	38	53	91	37	4	0	1	1	7
84-85—Vancouver	NHL	71	25	43	68	46	—	—	—	—	—
85-86—Vancouver	NHL	79	18	48	66	28	3	1	0	1	0
86-87—Vancouver	NHL	72	29	42	71	40	—	—	—	—	—
87-88—New Jersey	NHL	78	15	36	51	42	18	7	13	20	14

S

Season Team	League	REGULAR SEASON					PLAYOFFS				
		Gms.	G	A	Pts.	Pen.	Gms.	G	A	Pts.	Pen.
88-89—New Jersey	NHL	65	28	41	69	36	—	—	—	—	—
89-90—New Jersey	NHL	74	27	49	76	34	6	1	3	4	2
90-91—New Jersey	NHL	71	15	31	46	48	2	0	0	0	0
91-92—New Jersey	NHL	17	1	3	4	8	—	—	—	—	—
—Utica	AHL	1	0	0	0	0	—	—	—	—	—
NHL totals		679	219	369	588	349	37	9	17	26	25

SUTER, GARY
D, FLAMES

PERSONAL: Born June 24, 1964, at Madison, Wis. . . . 6-0/190. . . . Shoots left. . . . Full name: Gary Lee Suter.

COLLEGE: Wisconsin.

TRANSACTIONS/CAREER NOTES: Selected by Calgary Flames in ninth round (ninth Flames pick, 180th overall) of NHL entry draft (June 9, 1984). . . . Stretched ligament in knee (December 1986). . . . Suspended for first four games of regular season and next six international games in which NHL participates for high-sticking during Canada Cup (September 4, 1987). . . . Injured left knee (February 1988). . . . Pulled hamstring (February 1989). . . . Ruptured appendix (February 22, 1989); missed 16 games. . . . Broke jaw (April 11, 1989). . . . Bruised knee (December 12, 1991); missed 10 games.

HONORS: Named USHL Top Defenseman (1982-83). . . . Named to USHL All-Star first team (1982-83). . . . Won Calder Memorial Trophy (1985-86). . . . Named to NHL All-Rookie team (1985-86). . . . Named to THE SPORTING NEWS All-Star first team (1987-88). . . . Named to NHL All-Star second team (1987-88). . . . Named to THE SPORTING NEWS All-Star second team (1988-89).

RECORDS: Shares NHL single-game record for most assists by a defenseman—6 (April 4, 1986).

Season Team	League	REGULAR SEASON					PLAYOFFS				
		Gms.	G	A	Pts.	Pen.	Gms.	G	A	Pts.	Pen.
81-82—Dubuque	USHL	18	3	4	7	32	—	—	—	—	—
82-83—Dubuque	USHL	41	9	10	19	112	—	—	—	—	—
83-84—University of Wisconsin ...	WCHA	35	4	18	22	68	—	—	—	—	—
84-85—University of Wisconsin ...	WCHA	39	12	39	51	110	—	—	—	—	—
85-86—Calgary	NHL	80	18	50	68	141	10	2	8	10	8
86-87—Calgary	NHL	68	9	40	49	70	6	0	3	3	10
87-88—Calgary	NHL	75	21	70	91	124	9	1	9	10	6
88-89—Calgary	NHL	63	13	49	62	78	5	0	3	3	10
89-90—Calgary	NHL	76	16	60	76	97	6	0	1	1	14
90-91—Calgary	NHL	79	12	58	70	102	7	1	6	7	12
91-92—Calgary	NHL	70	12	43	55	128	—	—	—	—	—
NHL totals		511	101	370	471	740	43	4	30	34	60

SUTTER, BRENT
C, BLACKHAWKS

PERSONAL: Born June 10, 1962, at Viking, Alta. . . . 5-11/180. . . . Shoots right. . . . Full name: Brent Colin Sutter. . . . Brother of Brian Sutter, left winger, St. Louis Blues (1976-77 through 1987-88) and current head coach, Boston Bruins; brother of Darryl Sutter, left winger, Chicago Blackhawks (1979-80 through 1986-87) and current head coach, Blackhawks; brother of Duane Sutter, right winger, New York Islanders and Blackhawks (1979-80 through 1989-90) and current head coach, Medicine Hat of WHL; brother of Rich Sutter, right winger, Blues; and brother of Ron Sutter, center, Blues.

TRANSACTIONS/CAREER NOTES: Selected by New York Islanders as underage junior in first round (first Islanders pick, 17th overall) of NHL entry draft (June 11, 1980). . . . Damaged tendon and developed infection in right hand (January 1984); missed 11 games. . . . Separated shoulder (March 1985). . . . Bruised left shoulder (October 19, 1985); missed 12 games. . . . Bruised shoulder (December 21, 1985); missed seven games. . . . Strained abductor muscle in right leg (March 1987). . . . Suffered non-displaced fracture of right thumb (December 1987). . . . Lacerated right leg (January 19, 1990). . . . Hospitalized upon developing an infection in right leg after stitches were removed (January 28, 1990); missed seven games. . . . Traded by Islanders with RW Brad Lauer to Chicago Blackhawks for C Adam Creighton and LW Steve Thomas (October 25, 1991). . . . Injured abdomen (March 11, 1992).

Season Team	League	REGULAR SEASON					PLAYOFFS				
		Gms.	G	A	Pts.	Pen.	Gms.	G	A	Pts.	Pen.
77-78—Red Deer	AJHL	60	12	18	30	33	—	—	—	—	—
78-79—Red Deer	AJHL	60	42	42	84	79	—	—	—	—	—
79-80—Red Deer	AJHL	59	70	101	171	131	—	—	—	—	—
—Lethbridge	WHL	5	1	0	1	2	—	—	—	—	—
80-81—New York Islanders	NHL	3	2	2	4	0	—	—	—	—	—
—Lethbridge	WHL	68	54	54	108	116	9	6	4	10	51
81-82—Lethbridge	WHL	34	46	34	80	162	—	—	—	—	—
—New York Islanders	NHL	43	21	22	43	114	19	2	6	8	36
82-83—New York Islanders	NHL	80	21	19	40	128	20	10	11	21	26
83-84—New York Islanders	NHL	69	34	15	49	69	20	4	10	14	18
84-85—New York Islanders	NHL	72	42	60	102	51	10	3	3	6	14
85-86—New York Islanders	NHL	61	24	31	55	74	3	0	1	1	2
86-87—New York Islanders	NHL	69	27	36	63	73	5	1	0	1	4
87-88—New York Islanders	NHL	70	29	31	60	55	6	2	1	3	18
88-89—New York Islanders	NHL	77	29	34	63	77	—	—	—	—	—
89-90—New York Islanders	NHL	67	33	35	68	65	5	2	3	5	2
90-91—New York Islanders	NHL	75	21	32	53	49	—	—	—	—	—
91-92—New York Islanders	NHL	8	4	6	10	6	—	—	—	—	—
—Chicago	NHL	61	18	32	50	30	18	3	5	8	22
NHL totals		755	305	355	660	791	106	27	40	67	142

SUTTER, RICH
RW, BLUES

PERSONAL: Born December 2, 1963, at Viking, Alta. . . . 5-11/188. . . . Shoots right. . . . Full name: Richard Sutter. . . . Brother of Brian Sutter, left winger, St. Louis Blues (1976-77 through 1987-88) and current head coach, Boston Bruins; brother of Brent Sutter, center, Chicago Blackhawks; brother of Darryl Sutter, left winger, Blackhawks (1979-80 through 1986-87) and current head coach, Blackhawks; brother of Duane Sutter, right winger, New York Islanders and Blackhawks (1979-80 through 1989-90) and current head coach, Medicine Hat of WHL; and twin brother of Ron Sutter, center, Blues.

TRANSACTIONS/CAREER NOTES: Selected as underage junior by Pittsburgh Penguins in first round (first Penguins pick, 10th overall) of NHL entry draft (June 9, 1982). . . . Traded by Penguins with second-round pick (D Greg Smyth) and third-round pick (LW David McLay) in 1984 draft to Philadelphia Flyers for C Ron Flockhart, C/LW Mark Taylor, LW Andy Brickley, first-round pick (RW/C Roger Belanger) and third-round pick in 1984 draft (October 1983). . . . Traded by Flyers with D Dave Richter and third-round pick in 1986 draft to Vancouver Canucks for D J.J. Daigneault, second-round pick in 1986 draft (C Kent Hawley) and fifth-round pick in 1987 draft (June 1986). . . . Lost four teeth (October 23, 1988). . . . Injured lower back (January 17, 1989). . . . Broke nose (March 24, 1989). . . . Suspended five games by NHL for slashing (January 27, 1990). . . . Traded by Canucks with D Harold Snepsts and second-round pick in 1990 draft (previously acquired from St. Louis Blues) to Blues for D Adrien Plavsic, first-round pick in 1990 draft (later traded to Montreal Canadiens) (March 6, 1990) and second-round pick in 1991 draft. . . . Suffered concussion (November 1, 1991); missed two games.

Season Team	League	REGULAR SEASON					PLAYOFFS				
		Gms.	G	A	Pts.	Pen.	Gms.	G	A	Pts.	Pen.
79-80—Red Deer	AJHL	60	13	19	32	157	—	—	—	—	—
80-81—Lethbridge	WHL	72	23	18	41	255	9	3	1	4	35
81-82—Lethbridge	WHL	57	38	31	69	263	12	3	3	6	55
82-83—Lethbridge	WHL	64	37	30	67	200	17	14	9	23	43
—Pittsburgh	NHL	4	0	0	0	0	—	—	—	—	—
83-84—Baltimore	AHL	2	0	1	1	0	—	—	—	—	—
—Pittsburgh	NHL	5	0	0	0	0	—	—	—	—	—
—Philadelphia	NHL	70	16	12	28	93	3	0	0	0	15
84-85—Hershey	AHL	13	3	7	10	14	—	—	—	—	—
—Philadelphia	NHL	56	6	10	16	89	11	3	0	3	10
85-86—Philadelphia	NHL	78	14	25	39	199	5	2	0	2	19
86-87—Vancouver	NHL	74	20	22	42	113	—	—	—	—	—
87-88—Vancouver	NHL	80	15	15	30	165	—	—	—	—	—
88-89—Vancouver	NHL	75	17	15	32	122	7	2	1	3	12
89-90—Vancouver	NHL	62	9	9	18	133	—	—	—	—	—
—St. Louis	NHL	12	2	0	2	22	12	2	1	3	39
90-91—St. Louis	NHL	77	16	11	27	122	13	4	2	6	16
91-92—St. Louis	NHL	77	9	16	25	107	6	0	0	0	8
NHL totals		670	124	135	259	1165	57	13	4	17	119

SUTTER, RON
C, BLUES

PERSONAL: Born December 2, 1963, at Viking, Alta. . . . 6-0/180. . . . Shoots right. . . . Full name: Ronald Sutter. . . . Brother of Brian Sutter, left winger, St. Louis Blues (1976-77 through 1987-88) and current head coach, Boston Bruins; brother of Brent Sutter, center, Chicago Blackhawks; brother of Darryl Sutter, left winger, Blackhawks (1979-80 through 1986-87) and current head coach, Blackhawks; brother of Duane Sutter, right winger, New York Islanders and Blackhawks (1979-80 through 1989-90) and current head coach, Medicine Hat of WHL; and twin brother of Rich Sutter, right winger, Blues.

TRANSACTIONS/CAREER NOTES: Selected by Philadelphia Flyers as underage junior in first round (first Flyers pick, fourth overall) of NHL entry draft (June 9, 1982). . . . Broke ankle (November 27, 1981). . . . Bruised ribs (March 1985). . . . Suffered stress fracture in lower back (January 1987). . . . Tore rib cartilage (March 1988). . . . Fractured jaw (October 29, 1988). . . . Pulled groin (March 1989). . . . Traded by Flyers with D Murray Baron to St. Louis Blues for C Rod Brind'Amour and C Dan Quinn (September 22, 1991). . . . Strained ligament in right knee (February 1, 1992); missed 10 games.

Season Team	League	REGULAR SEASON					PLAYOFFS				
		Gms.	G	A	Pts.	Pen.	Gms.	G	A	Pts.	Pen.
79-80—Red Deer	AJHL	60	12	33	45	44	—	—	—	—	—
80-81—Lethbridge	WHL	72	13	32	45	152	9	2	5	7	29
81-82—Lethbridge	WHL	59	38	54	92	207	12	6	5	11	28
82-83—Lethbridge	WHL	58	35	48	83	98	20	*22	†19	*41	45
—Philadelphia	NHL	10	1	1	2	9	—	—	—	—	—
83-84—Philadelphia	NHL	79	19	32	51	101	3	0	0	0	22
84-85—Philadelphia	NHL	73	16	29	45	94	19	4	8	12	28
85-86—Philadelphia	NHL	75	18	42	60	159	5	0	2	2	10
86-87—Philadelphia	NHL	39	10	17	27	69	16	1	7	8	12
87-88—Philadelphia	NHL	69	8	25	33	146	7	0	1	1	26
88-89—Philadelphia	NHL	55	26	22	48	80	19	1	9	10	51
89-90—Philadelphia	NHL	75	22	26	48	104	—	—	—	—	—
90-91—Philadelphia	NHL	80	17	28	45	92	—	—	—	—	—
91-92—St. Louis	NHL	68	19	27	46	91	6	1	3	4	8
NHL totals		623	156	249	405	945	75	7	30	37	157

SUTTON, KEN
D, SABRES

PERSONAL: Born May 11, 1969, at Edmonton, Alta. . . . 6-0/198. . . . Shoots left. . . . Full name: Kenneth Sutton.

TRANSACTIONS/CAREER NOTES: Selected by Buffalo Sabres in fifth round (fourth Sabres pick, 98th overall) of NHL entry draft (June 17, 1989). . . . Separated shoulder (March 3, 1992); missed six games.

Season Team	League	REGULAR SEASON					PLAYOFFS				
		Gms.	G	A	Pts.	Pen.	Gms.	G	A	Pts.	Pen.
87-88—Calgary Canucks	AJHL	53	13	43	56	228	—	—	—	—	—
88-89—Saskatoon	WHL	71	22	31	53	104	8	2	5	7	12

Season Team	League	REGULAR SEASON					PLAYOFFS				
		Gms.	G	A	Pts.	Pen.	Gms.	G	A	Pts.	Pen.
89-90—Rochester	AHL	57	5	14	19	83	11	1	6	7	15
90-91—Buffalo	NHL	15	3	6	9	13	6	0	1	1	2
—Rochester	AHL	62	7	24	31	65	3	1	1	2	14
91-92—Buffalo	NHL	64	2	18	20	71	7	0	2	2	4
NHL totals		79	5	24	29	84	13	0	3	3	6

SVEHLA, ROBERT
D, FLAMES

PERSONAL: Born January 2, 1969, at Martin, Czechoslovakia. . . . 6-0/185. . . . Shoots left.

TRANSACTIONS/CAREER NOTES: Selected by Calgary Flames in fourth round (fourth Flames pick, 78th overall) of NHL entry draft (June 20, 1992).

MISCELLANEOUS: Member of 1992 bronze-medal-winning Czechoslovakian Olympic team.

Season Team	League	REGULAR SEASON					PLAYOFFS				
		Gms.	G	A	Pts.	Pen.	Gms.	G	A	Pts.	Pen.
89-90—Dukla Trencin	Czech.	29	4	3	7		—	—	—	—	—
90-91—Dukla Trencin	Czech.	58	16	9	25		—	—	—	—	—
91-92—Czech. Olympic Team	Int'l	8	2	1	3		—	—	—	—	—
—Dukla Trencin	Czech.	51	23	28	51	0	—	—	—	—	—

SVOBODA, PETR
D, SABRES

PERSONAL: Born February 14, 1966, at Most, Czechoslovakia. . . . 6-1/175. . . . Shoots left.

TRANSACTIONS/CAREER NOTES: Selected by Montreal Canadiens in first round (first Canadiens pick, fifth overall) of NHL entry draft (June 9, 1984). . . . Suffered back spasms (January 1988). . . . Suffered hip pointer (March 1988). . . . Sprained right wrist (November 21, 1988); missed five games. . . . Injured back (March 1989). . . . Separated shoulder (November 1989). . . . Pulled groin (November 22, 1989). . . . Aggravated groin injury (December 11, 1989); missed 15 games. . . . Bruised left foot (March 11, 1990). . . . Suffered stomach disorder (November 28, 1990); missed five games. . . . Suffered broken left foot (January 15, 1991); missed 15 games. . . . Injured mouth (December 14, 1991). . . . Sprained ankle (February 17, 1992); missed seven games. . . . Traded by Canadiens to Buffalo Sabres for D Kevin Haller (March 10, 1992).

Season Team	League	REGULAR SEASON					PLAYOFFS				
		Gms.	G	A	Pts.	Pen.	Gms.	G	A	Pts.	Pen.
83-84—Czechoslovakia Jr.	Czech.	40	15	21	36	14	—	—	—	—	—
84-85—Montreal	NHL	73	4	27	31	65	7	1	1	2	12
85-86—Montreal	NHL	73	1	18	19	93	8	0	0	0	21
86-87—Montreal	NHL	70	5	17	22	63	14	0	5	5	10
87-88—Montreal	NHL	69	7	22	29	149	10	0	5	5	12
88-89—Montreal	NHL	71	8	37	45	147	21	1	11	12	16
89-90—Montreal	NHL	60	5	31	36	98	10	0	5	5	2
90-91—Montreal	NHL	60	4	22	26	52	2	0	1	1	2
91-92—Montreal	NHL	58	5	16	21	94	—	—	—	—	—
—Buffalo	NHL	13	1	6	7	52	7	1	4	5	6
NHL totals		547	40	196	236	813	79	3	32	35	81

SWEENEY, BOB
C/RW, BRUINS

PERSONAL: Born January 25, 1964, at Boxborough, Mass. . . . 6-3/200. . . . Shoots right. . . . Full name: Robert Emmett Sweeney. . . . Brother of Tim Sweeney, left winger, Calgary Flames.

HIGH SCHOOL: Acton-Boxborough (Mass.).

COLLEGE: Boston College.

TRANSACTIONS/CAREER NOTES: Selected by Boston Bruins in sixth round (sixth Bruins pick, 123rd overall) of NHL entry draft (June 9, 1982). . . . Pulled rib muscle (November 1989); missed six games. . . . Injured left shoulder (April 23, 1991). . . . Sprained knee (February 4, 1992); missed 11 games.

Season Team	League	REGULAR SEASON					PLAYOFFS				
		Gms.	G	A	Pts.	Pen.	Gms.	G	A	Pts.	Pen.
82-83—Boston College	ECAC	30	17	11	28	10	—	—	—	—	—
83-84—Boston College	ECAC	23	14	7	21	10	—	—	—	—	—
84-85—Boston College	Hockey East	44	32	32	64	43	—	—	—	—	—
85-86—Boston College	Hockey East	41	15	24	39	52	—	—	—	—	—
86-87—Boston	NHL	14	2	4	6	21	3	0	0	0	0
—Moncton	AHL	58	29	26	55	81	4	0	2	2	13
87-88—Boston	NHL	80	22	23	45	73	23	6	8	14	66
88-89—Boston	NHL	75	14	14	28	99	10	2	4	6	19
89-90—Boston	NHL	70	22	24	46	93	20	0	2	2	30
90-91—Boston	NHL	80	15	33	48	115	17	4	2	6	45
91-92—Boston	NHL	63	6	14	20	103	14	1	0	1	25
—Maine	AHL	1	1	0	1	0	—	—	—	—	—
NHL totals		382	81	112	193	504	87	13	16	29	185

SWEENEY, DON
D, BRUINS

PERSONAL: Born August 17, 1966, at St. Stephen, N.B. . . . 5-11/170. . . . Shoots left. . . . Full name: Donald Clark Sweeney.

COLLEGE: Harvard.

TRANSACTIONS/CAREER NOTES: Selected by Boston Bruins in eighth round (eighth Bruins pick, 166th overall) of NHL entry draft (June 9, 1984). . . . Bruised left heel (February 22, 1990). . . . Injured knee (October 12, 1991); missed four games.

HONORS: Named to NCAA All-America East second team (1987-88).

Season Team	League	REGULAR SEASON					PLAYOFFS				
		Gms.	G	A	Pts.	Pen.	Gms.	G	A	Pts.	Pen.
83-84—St. Paul N.B. H.S.	N.B. H.S.	22	33	26	59		—	—	—	—	—
84-85—Harvard University	ECAC	29	3	7	10	30	—	—	—	—	—
85-86—Harvard University	ECAC	31	4	5	9	29	—	—	—	—	—
86-87—Harvard University	ECAC	34	7	14	21	22	—	—	—	—	—
87-88—Harvard University	ECAC	30	6	23	29	37	—	—	—	—	—
—Maine................................	AHL	—	—	—	—	—	6	1	3	4	0
88-89—Maine................................	AHL	42	8	17	25	24	—	—	—	—	—
—Boston................................	NHL	36	3	5	8	20	—	—	—	—	—
89-90—Boston................................	NHL	58	3	5	8	58	21	1	5	6	18
—Maine................................	AHL	11	0	8	8	8	—	—	—	—	—
90-91—Boston................................	NHL	77	8	13	21	67	19	3	0	3	25
91-92—Boston................................	NHL	75	3	11	14	74	15	0	0	0	10
NHL totals................................		246	17	34	51	219	55	4	5	9	53

SWEENEY, TIM
LW, FLAMES

PERSONAL: Born April 12, 1967, at Boston. . . . 5-11/180. . . . Shoots left. . . . Full name: Timothy Paul Sweeney. . . . Brother of Bob Sweeney, center/right winger, Boston Bruins.
HIGH SCHOOL: Weymouth (East Weymouth, Mass.).
COLLEGE: Boston College.
TRANSACTIONS/CAREER NOTES: Selected by Calgary Flames in sixth round (seventh Flames pick, 122nd overall) of NHL entry draft (June 15, 1985). . . . Fractured index finger (January 20, 1990). . . . Bruised ankle (May 1990).
HONORS: Named to NCAA All-America East second team (1988-89). . . . Named to Hockey East All-Star first team (1988-89). . . . Won Ken McKenzie Trophy (1989-90). . . . Named to IHL All-Star second team (1989-90).

Season Team	League	REGULAR SEASON					PLAYOFFS				
		Gms.	G	A	Pts.	Pen.	Gms.	G	A	Pts.	Pen.
83-84—Weymouth North H.S.......	Mass. H.S.	23	33	26	59		—	—	—	—	—
84-85—Weymouth North H.S.......	Mass. H.S.	22	32	56	88		—	—	—	—	—
85-86—Boston College	Hockey East	32	8	4	12	8	—	—	—	—	—
86-87—Boston College	Hockey East	38	31	16	47	28	—	—	—	—	—
87-88—Boston College	Hockey East	18	9	11	20	18	—	—	—	—	—
88-89—Boston College	Hockey East	39	29	44	73	26	—	—	—	—	—
89-90—Salt Lake City..................	IHL	81	46	51	97	32	11	5	4	9	4
90-91—Calgary............................	NHL	42	7	9	16	8	—	—	—	—	—
—Salt Lake City..................	IHL	31	19	16	35	8	4	3	3	6	0
91-92—Calgary............................	NHL	11	1	2	3	4	—	—	—	—	—
—U.S. National Team.........	Int'l	21	9	11	20	10	—	—	—	—	—
—U.S. Olympic Team	Int'l	8	3	4	7	6	—	—	—	—	—
NHL totals................................		53	8	11	19	12					

SYCHRA, MARTIN
C, CANADIENS

PERSONAL: Born June 19, 1974, at Brno, Czechoslovakia. . . . 6-0/176. . . . Shoots right.
TRANSACTIONS/CAREER NOTES: Selected by Montreal Canadiens in sixth round (eighth Canadiens pick, 140th overall) of NHL entry draft (June 20, 1992).

Season Team	League	REGULAR SEASON					PLAYOFFS				
		Gms.	G	A	Pts.	Pen.	Gms.	G	A	Pts.	Pen.
91-92—Zetor Brno	Czech.	13	1	2	3	2	—	—	—	—	—

SYDOR, DARRYL
D, KINGS

PERSONAL: Born March 13, 1972, at Edmonton, Alta. . . . 6-0/205. . . . Shoots left.
TRANSACTIONS/CAREER NOTES: Selected by Los Angeles Kings in first round (first Kings pick, seventh overall) of NHL entry draft (June 16, 1990).
HONORS: Named to WHL All-Star first team (1989-90 and 1990-91). . . . Won Bill Hunter Trophy (1990-91). . . . Named to Can.HL All-Star second team (1991-92). . . . Named to WHL West All-Star first team (1991-92).

Season Team	League	REGULAR SEASON					PLAYOFFS				
		Gms.	G	A	Pts.	Pen.	Gms.	G	A	Pts.	Pen.
88-89—Kamloops	WHL	65	12	14	26	86	15	1	4	5	19
89-90—Kamloops	WHL	67	29	66	95	129	17	2	9	11	28
90-91—Kamloops	WHL	66	27	78	105	88	12	3	*22	25	10
91-92—Kamloops	WHL	29	9	39	48	43	17	3	15	18	18
—Los Angeles.....................	NHL	18	1	5	6	22	—	—	—	—	—
NHL totals................................		18	1	5	6	22					

SYKES, PHIL
LW, JETS

PERSONAL: Born May 18, 1959, at Dawson Creek, B.C. . . . 6-0/175. . . . Shoots left. . . . Full name: Phil Max Sykes.
COLLEGE: North Dakota.
TRANSACTIONS/CAREER NOTES: Signed as free agent by Los Angeles Kings (April 1982). . . . Injured left wrist during world championships (May 1986); underwent surgery (October 2, 1986). . . . Sprained knee (February 24, 1987); missed seven games. . . . Partially tore groin muscle (October 1987); missed 38 games. . . . Injured neck (March 1988); missed two games. . . . Strained knee (March 1988). . . . Left Kings for two weeks (October 4, 1988). . . . Pulled groin (March 1989). . . . Traded by Kings to Winnipeg Jets for C Brad Jones (November 30, 1989). . . . Suffered from virus (October 1991). . . . Suffered hamstring contusion (March 1992).
HONORS: Named to NCAA All-America West team (1981-82).

S

Season Team	League	REGULAR SEASON					PLAYOFFS				
		Gms.	G	A	Pts.	Pen.	Gms.	G	A	Pts.	Pen.
78-79—Univ. of North Dakota......	WCHA	41	9	5	14	16	—	—	—	—	—
79-80—Univ. of North Dakota......	WCHA	37	22	27	49	34	—	—	—	—	—
80-81—Univ. of North Dakota......	WCHA	38	28	34	62	22	—	—	—	—	—
81-82—Univ. of North Dakota......	WCHA	45	39	24	63	20	—	—	—	—	—
82-83—Los Angeles..................	NHL	7	2	0	2	2	—	—	—	—	—
—New Haven..................	AHL	71	19	26	45	111	12	2	2	4	21
83-84—New Haven..................	AHL	77	29	37	66	101	—	—	—	—	—
—Los Angeles..................	NHL	3	0	0	0	2	—	—	—	—	—
84-85—Los Angeles..................	NHL	79	17	15	32	38	3	0	1	1	4
85-86—Los Angeles..................	NHL	76	20	24	44	97	—	—	—	—	—
86-87—Los Angeles..................	NHL	58	6	15	21	133	5	0	1	1	8
87-88—Los Angeles..................	NHL	40	9	12	21	82	4	0	0	0	0
88-89—New Haven..................	AHL	34	9	17	26	23	—	—	—	—	—
—Los Angeles..................	NHL	23	0	1	1	8	3	0	0	0	8
89-90—New Haven..................	AHL	25	3	12	15	32	—	—	—	—	—
—Winnipeg..................	NHL	48	9	6	15	26	4	0	0	0	0
—Moncton..................	AHL	5	0	1	1	20	—	—	—	—	—
90-91—Winnipeg..................	NHL	70	12	10	22	59	—	—	—	—	—
91-92—Winnipeg..................	NHL	52	4	2	6	72	7	0	1	1	9
NHL totals..................		456	79	85	164	519	26	0	3	3	29

SYKORA, MICHAL
D, SHARKS

PERSONAL: Born July 5, 1973, at Pardubice, Czechoslovakia. . . . 6-3/195. . . . Shoots left.

TRANSACTIONS/CAREER NOTES: Selected by San Jose Sharks in sixth round (sixth Sharks pick, 123rd overall) of NHL entry draft (June 20, 1992).

Season Team	League	REGULAR SEASON					PLAYOFFS				
		Gms.	G	A	Pts.	Pen.	Gms.	G	A	Pts.	Pen.
90-91—Pardubice..................	Czech.	2	0	0	0	0	—	—	—	—	—
91-92—Tacoma	WHL	61	13	23	36	66	4	0	2	2	2

TABARACCI, RICK
G, JETS

PERSONAL: Born January 2, 1969, at Toronto. . . . 5-10/185. . . . Shoots left. . . . Full name: Richard Stephen Tabaracci.

TRANSACTIONS/CAREER NOTES: Selected by Pittsbrgh Penguins as underage junior in second round (second Penguins pick, 26th overall) of NHL entry draft (June 13, 1987). . . . Traded by Penguins with C/LW Randy Cunneyworth and RW Dave McIlwain to Winnipeg Jets for RW Andrew McBain, D Jim Kyte and LW Randy Gilhen (June 17, 1989). . . . Pulled right hamstring (December 11, 1990); missed seven games.

HONORS: Named to OHL All-Star first team (1987-88). . . . Named to OHL All-Star second team (1988-89).

Season Team	League	REGULAR SEASON							PLAYOFFS						
		Gms.	Min.	W	L	T	GA	SO	Avg.	Gms.	Min.	W	L	GA	SO	Avg.
85-86—Markham Jr. B	OHA	40	2176				188	1	5.18	—	—	—	—	—		—
86-87—Cornwall..................	OHL	*59	*3347	23	32	3	*290	1	5.20	5	303	1	4	26	0	5.15
87-88—Cornwall..................	OHL	58	3448	33	18	6	200	†3	3.48	11	642	5	6	37	0	3.46
—Muskegon..................	IHL	—	—	—	—	—	—	—	—	1	13	0	1	0		4.62
88-89—Cornwall..................	OHL	50	2974	24	20	5	*210	1	4.24	18	1080	10	8	65	†1	3.61
—Pittsburgh..................	NHL	1	33	0	0	0	4	0	7.27	—	—	—	—	—		—
89-90—Moncton..................	AHL	27	1580	10	15	2	107	2	4.06	—	—	—	—	—		—
—Fort Wayne	IHL	22	1064	8	9	1	73	0	4.12	3	159	1	2	19	0	7.17
90-91—Moncton..................	AHL	11	645	4	5	2	41	0	3.81	—	—	—	—	—		—
—Winnipeg..................	NHL	24	1093	4	9	4	71	1	3.90	—	—	—	—	—		—
91-92—Moncton..................	AHL	23	1313	10	11	1	80	0	3.66	—	—	—	—	—		—
—Winnipeg..................	NHL	18	966	6	7	3	52	0	3.23	7	387	3	4	26	0	4.03
NHL totals..................		43	2092	10	16	7	127	1	3.64	7	387	3	4	26	0	4.03

TAGLIANETTI, PETER
D, LIGHTNING

PERSONAL: Born August 15, 1963, at Framingham, Mass. . . . 6-2/195. . . . Shoots left. . . . Full name: Peter Anthony Taglianetti.

COLLEGE: Providence.

TRANSACTIONS/CAREER NOTES: Selected by Winnipeg Jets in third round (fourth Jets pick, 43rd overall) of NHL entry draft (June 8, 1983). . . . Dislocated shoulder during training camp (October 1985). . . . Dislocated shoulder (February 20, 1986). . . . Underwent surgery to correct recurring shoulder dislocations (March 1986). . . . Damaged right knee cartilage during training camp and underwent surgery (September 1988). . . . Injured knee and underwent surgery (October 6, 1989). . . . Suspended five games by NHL for attempting to injure opposing player (February 20, 1990). . . . Bruised ribs (April 1990). . . . Traded by Jets to Minnesota North Stars for future considerations (September 23, 1990). . . . Traded by North Stars with D Larry Murphy to Pittsburgh Penguins for D Jim Johnson and D Chris Dahlquist (December 11, 1990). . . . Suffered collapsed lung (February 11, 1991); missed nine games. . . . Injured back (December 21, 1991); missed two games. . . . Injured back (March 7, 1992); missed final 15 games of season. . . . Underwent back surgery (April 5, 1992). . . . Selected by Tampa Bay Lightning in NHL expansion draft (June 18, 1992).

HONORS: Named to Hockey East All-Star first team (1984-85).

Season Team	League	REGULAR SEASON					PLAYOFFS				
		Gms.	G	A	Pts.	Pen.	Gms.	G	A	Pts.	Pen.
81-82—Providence College	ECAC	2	0	0	0	2	—	—	—	—	—
82-83—Providence College	ECAC	43	4	17	21	68	—	—	—	—	—
83-84—Providence College	ECAC	30	4	25	29	68	—	—	—	—	—

Season Team	League	REGULAR SEASON					PLAYOFFS				
		Gms.	G	A	Pts.	Pen.	Gms.	G	A	Pts.	Pen.
84-85—Providence College	Hockey East	43	8	21	29	114	—	—	—	—	—
—Winnipeg	NHL	1	0	0	0	0	1	0	0	0	0
85-86—Sherbrooke	AHL	24	1	8	9	75	—	—	—	—	—
—Winnipeg	NHL	18	0	0	0	48	3	0	0	0	2
86-87—Winnipeg	NHL	3	0	0	0	12	—	—	—	—	—
—Sherbrooke	AHL	54	5	14	19	104	10	2	5	7	25
87-88—Winnipeg	NHL	70	6	17	23	182	5	1	1	2	12
88-89—Winnipeg	NHL	66	1	14	15	226	—	—	—	—	—
89-90—Moncton	AHL	3	0	2	2	2	—	—	—	—	—
—Winnipeg	NHL	49	3	6	9	136	5	0	0	0	6
90-91—Minnesota	NHL	16	0	1	1	14	—	—	—	—	—
—Pittsburgh	NHL	39	3	8	11	93	19	0	3	3	49
91-92—Pittsburgh	NHL	44	1	3	4	57	—	—	—	—	—
NHL totals................................		306	14	49	63	768	33	1	4	5	69

TAMER, CHRIS
D, PENGUINS

PERSONAL: Born November 17, 1970, at Dearborn, Mich. . . . 6-2/185. . . . Shoots left. . . . Full name: Chris Thomas Tamer.
COLLEGE: Michigan.
TRANSACTIONS/CAREER NOTES: Selected by Pittsburgh Penguins in fourth round (third Penguins pick, 00th overall) of NHL entry draft (June 16, 1990).

Season Team	League	REGULAR SEASON					PLAYOFFS				
		Gms.	G	A	Pts.	Pen.	Gms.	G	A	Pts.	Pen.
87-88—Redford	NAJHL	40	10	20	30	217	—	—	—	—	—
88-89—Redford	NAJHL	31	6	13	19	79	—	—	—	—	—
89-90—University of Michigan	CCHA	42	2	7	9	147	—	—	—	—	—
90-91—University of Michigan	CCHA	45	8	19	27	130	—	—	—	—	—
91-92—University of Michigan	CCHA	43	4	15	19	*125	—	—	—	—	—

TAMMINEN, JOE
C, PENGUINS

PERSONAL: Born January 23, 1973, at Virginia, Minn. . . . 6-1 . . . Shoots left.
HIGH SCHOOL: Virginia (Minn.).
TRANSACTIONS/CAREER NOTES: Selected by Pittsburgh Penguins in fourth round (fourth Penguins pick, 82nd overall) of NHL entry draft (June 22, 1991).

Season Team	League	REGULAR SEASON					PLAYOFFS				
		Gms.	G	A	Pts.	Pen.	Gms.	G	A	Pts.	Pen.
87-88—Virginia H.S.	Minn. H.S.	20	1	1	2	4	—	—	—	—	—
88-89—Virginia H.S.	Minn. H.S.	25	7	15	22	39	—	—	—	—	—
89-90—Virginia H.S.	Minn. H.S.	23	20	21	41	33	—	—	—	—	—
90-91—Virginia H.S.	Minn. H.S.	22	20	18	38	40	—	—	—	—	—
91-92—Minnesota-Duluth	WCHA	23	1	3	4	12	—	—	—	—	—

TANCILL, CHRIS
C, RED WINGS

PERSONAL: Born February 7, 1968, at Livonia, Mich. . . . 5-10/185. . . . Shoots left. . . . Full name: Christopher William Tancill.
COLLEGE: Wisconsin.
TRANSACTIONS/CAREER NOTES: Selected by Hartford Whalers in NHL supplemental draft (June 16, 1989). . . . Traded by Whalers to Detroit Red Wings for RW Daniel Shank (December 18, 1991).
HONORS: Named to NCAA All-Tournament team (1990). . . . Won NCAA Tournament Most Valuable Player Award (1990). . . . Named to AHL All-Star first team (1991-92).

Season Team	League	REGULAR SEASON					PLAYOFFS				
		Gms.	G	A	Pts.	Pen.	Gms.	G	A	Pts.	Pen.
87-88—University of Wisconsin ...	WCHA	44	13	14	27	48	—	—	—	—	—
88-89—University of Wisconsin ...	WCHA	44	20	23	43	50	—	—	—	—	—
89-90—University of Wisconsin ...	WCHA	45	39	32	71	44	—	—	—	—	—
90-91—Hartford.......................	NHL	9	1	1	2	4	—	—	—	—	—
—Springfield.......................	AHL	72	37	35	72	46	17	8	4	12	32
91-92—Springfield....................	AHL	17	12	7	19	20	—	—	—	—	—
—Hartford.........................	NHL	10	0	0	0	2	—	—	—	—	—
—Adirondack	AHL	50	36	34	70	42	19	7	9	16	31
—Detroit	NHL	1	0	0	0	0	—	—	—	—	—
NHL totals...............................		20	1	1	2	6					

TANGUAY, MARTIN
C, LIGHTNING

PERSONAL: Born January 12, 1973, at Ste.-Julie, Que. . . . 6-0/185. . . . Shoots left.
TRANSACTIONS/CAREER NOTES: Selected by Tampa Bay Lightning in sixth round (sixth Lightning pick, 122nd overall) of NHL entry draft (June 20, 1992).

Season Team	League	REGULAR SEASON					PLAYOFFS				
		Gms.	G	A	Pts.	Pen.	Gms.	G	A	Pts.	Pen.
89-90—Longueuil	QMJHL	61	11	16	27	35	7	1	4	5	9
90-91—Longueuil	QMJHL	69	27	34	61	14	8	3	4	7	6
91-92—Verdun........................	QMJHL	67	41	50	91	117	19	8	13	21	32

TANNER, JOHN
G, NORDIQUES

PERSONAL: Born March 17, 1971, at Cambridge, Ont. . . . 6-3/182. . . . Shoots left.
TRANSACTIONS/CAREER NOTES: Selected by Quebec Nordiques in third round (fourth Nordiques pick, 54th overall) of NHL entry draft (June 17, 1989). . . . Traded by Peterborough Petes to London Knights for second-round pick in 1990 draft they had acquired earlier from Windsor, and second- and third-round picks in 1991 draft (January 1990). . . . Traded by Knights to Sudbury Wolves for fourth-round pick in 1991 draft (December 1990).
HONORS: Shared Dave Pinkney Trophy with G Todd Bojcun (1987-88 and 1988-89).

Season Team	League	REGULAR SEASON								PLAYOFFS					
		Gms.	Min.	W	L	T	GA	SO	Avg.	Gms.	Min.	W	L	GA	SO	Avg.
86-87—New Hamburg Jr. C	OHA	15	889				83	0	5.60	—	—	—	—	—	—	—
87-88—Peterborough	OHL	26	1532	18	4	3	88	0	3.45	2	98	1	0	3	0	1.84
88-89—Peterborough	OHL	34	1923	22	10	0	107	†2	*3.34	8	369	4	3	23	0	3.74
89-90—Quebec	NHL	1	60	0	1	0	3	0	3.00	—	—	—	—	—	—	—
—Peterborough	OHL	18	1037	6	8	2	70	0	4.05	—	—	—	—	—	—	—
—London	OHL	19	1097	12	5	1	53	1	2.90	6	341	2	4	24	0	4.22
90-91—Quebec	NHL	6	228	1	3	1	16	0	4.21	—	—	—	—	—	—	—
—London	OHL	7	427	3	3	1	29	0	4.07	—	—	—	—	—	—	—
—Sudbury	OHL	19	1043	10	8	0	60	0	3.45	5	274	1	4	21	0	4.60
91-92—Halifax	AHL	12	672	6	5	1	29	2	2.59	—	—	—	—	—	—	—
—New Haven	AHL	16	908	7	6	2	57	0	3.77	—	—	—	—	—	—	—
—Quebec	NHL	14	796	1	7	4	46	1	3.47	—	—	—	—	—	—	—
NHL totals		21	1084	2	11	5	65	1	3.60							

TANTI, TONY
RW, SABRES

PERSONAL: Born September 7, 1963, at Toronto. . . . 5-9/180. . . . Shoots left. . . . Full name: Antony Tanti.
TRANSACTIONS/CAREER NOTES: Selected by Chicago Blackhawks in first round (first Blackhawks pick, 12th overall) of NHL entry draft (June 10, 1981). . . . Separated shoulder (November 1981). . . . Traded by Blackhawks to Vancouver Canucks for LW Curt Fraser (January 1983). . . . Strained knee (November 1984). . . . Broke foot (December 8, 1987). . . . Twisted knee (March 24, 1989). . . . Traded by Canucks with C Barry Pederson and D Rod Buskas to Pittsburgh Penguins for C Dan Quinn, RW Andrew McBain and C Dave Capuano (January 8, 1990). . . . Traded by Penguins to Buffalo Sabres for rights to C Ken Priestlay (March 4, 1991).
HONORS: Won Emms Family Award (1980-81). . . . Named to OMJHL All-Star first team (1980-81). . . . Won Jim Mahon Memorial Trophy (1980-81 and 1981-82). . . . Named to OHL All-Star second team (1981-82).

Season Team	League	REGULAR SEASON					PLAYOFFS				
		Gms.	G	A	Pts.	Pen.	Gms.	G	A	Pts.	Pen.
79-80—St. Michael's Jr. B	ODHA	37	31	27	58	67	—	—	—	—	—
80-81—Oshawa	OMJHL	67	81	69	150	197	11	7	8	15	41
81-82—Oshawa	OHL	57	62	64	126	138	12	14	12	26	15
—Chicago	NHL	2	0	0	0	0	—	—	—	—	—
82-83—Oshawa	OHL	30	34	28	62	35	—	—	—	—	—
—Chicago	NHL	1	1	0	1	0	—	—	—	—	—
—Vancouver	NHL	39	8	8	16	16	4	0	1	1	0
83-84—Vancouver	NHL	79	45	41	86	50	4	1	2	3	0
84-85—Vancouver	NHL	68	39	20	59	45	—	—	—	—	—
85-86—Vancouver	NHL	77	39	33	72	85	3	0	1	1	11
86-87—Vancouver	NHL	77	41	38	79	84	—	—	—	—	—
87-88—Vancouver	NHL	73	40	37	77	90	—	—	—	—	—
88-89—Vancouver	NHL	77	24	25	49	69	7	0	5	5	4
89-90—Vancouver	NHL	41	14	18	32	50	—	—	—	—	—
—Pittsburgh	NHL	37	14	18	32	22	—	—	—	—	—
90-91—Pittsburgh	NHL	46	6	12	18	44	—	—	—	—	—
—Buffalo	NHL	10	1	7	8	6	5	2	0	2	8
91-92—Buffalo	NHL	70	15	16	31	100	7	0	3	3	4
NHL totals		697	287	273	560	661	30	3	12	15	27

TARDIF, PATRICE
C, BLUES

PERSONAL: Born October 30, 1970, at Thetford Mines, Que. . . . 6-2/175. . . . Shoots left.
COLLEGE: Champlain Regional College (Lennoxville, Que.), then Maine.
TRANSACTIONS/CAREER NOTES: Selected by St. Louis Blues in third round (second Blues pick, 54th overall) of NHL entry draft (June 16, 1990).

Season Team	League	REGULAR SEASON					PLAYOFFS				
		Gms.	G	A	Pts.	Pen.	Gms.	G	A	Pts.	Pen.
89-90—Champlain Junior College	Can. Coll.	27	58	36	94	36	—	—	—	—	—
90-91—University of Maine	Hockey East	36	13	12	25	18	—	—	—	—	—
91-92—University of Maine	Hockey East	31	18	20	38	14	—	—	—	—	—

TATARINOV, MIKHAIL
D, NORDIQUES

PERSONAL: Born July 16, 1966, at Penza, U.S.S.R. . . . 5-10/194. . . . Shoots left.
TRANSACTIONS/CAREER NOTES: Selected by Washington Capitals in 11th round (10th Capitals pick, 225th overall) of NHL entry draft (June 9, 1984). . . . Traded by Capitals to Quebec Nordiques for second-round pick in 1991 draft (D Eric Lavigne) (June 22, 1991). . . . Injured ribs (November 16, 1991); missed six games. . . . Bruised ribs (February 18, 1992); missed five games.

Season Team	League	REGULAR SEASON					PLAYOFFS				
		Gms.	G	A	Pts.	Pen.	Gms.	G	A	Pts.	Pen.
83-84—Sokol Kiev	USSR	38	7	3	10	46	—	—	—	—	—
84-85—Sokol Kiev	USSR	34	3	6	9	54	—	—	—	—	—

Season Team	League	REGULAR SEASON					PLAYOFFS				
		Gms.	G	A	Pts.	Pen.	Gms.	G	A	Pts.	Pen.
85-86—Sokol Kiev	USSR	37	7	5	12	41	—	—	—	—	—
86-87—Dynamo Moscow	USSR	40	10	8	18	43	—	—	—	—	—
87-88—Dynamo Moscow	USSR	30	2	2	4	8	—	—	—	—	—
88-89—Dynamo Moscow	USSR	4	1	0	1	2	—	—	—	—	—
89-90—Dynamo Moscow	USSR	44	11	10	21	34	—	—	—	—	—
90-91—Washington	NHL	65	8	15	23	82	—	—	—	—	—
91-92—Quebec	NHL	66	11	27	38	72	—	—	—	—	—
NHL totals		131	19	42	61	154					

TAYLOR, CHRIS
C, ISLANDERS

PERSONAL: Born March 6, 1972, at Stratford, Ont. . . . 6-1/190. . . . Shoots left. . . . Brother of Tim Taylor, center in Washington Capitals system.
TRANSACTIONS/CAREER NOTES: Tore knee ligaments when checked by Scott Pearson vs. Niagara Falls (March 1989). . . . Selected by New York Islanders in second round (second Islanders pick, 27th overall) of NHL entry draft (June 16, 1990).

Season Team	League	REGULAR SEASON					PLAYOFFS				
		Gms.	G	A	Pts.	Pen.	Gms.	G	A	Pts.	Pen.
88-89—London	OHL	62	7	16	23	52	15	0	2	2	15
89-90—London	OHL	66	45	60	105	60	6	3	2	5	6
90-91—London	OIIL	65	50	78	128	60	7	4	8	12	6
91-92—London	OHL	66	48	74	122	57	10	8	16	24	9

TAYLOR, DAVE
RW, KINGS

PERSONAL: Born December 4, 1955, at Levack, Ont. . . . 6-0/195. . . . Shoots right. . . . Full name: David Andrew Taylor.
HIGH SCHOOL: Levack District (Ont.).
COLLEGE: Clarkson, N.Y. (degree, 1977).
TRANSACTIONS/CAREER NOTES: Selected by Los Angeles Kings in 15th round (14th Kings pick, 210th overall) of NHL amateur draft (June 3, 1975). . . . Pulled back muscle and sprained left knee; missed parts of 1979-80 season. . . . Sprained shoulder (November 5, 1980). . . . Broke right wrist (October 29, 1982); missed 33 games. . . . Injured right knee (January 1983). . . . Broke wrist at World Championships and underwent surgery (May 28, 1983); missed games. . . . Sprained knee (November 1986). . . . Injured groin (December 1987). . . . Tore knee cartilage (January 1989). . . . Pulled groin (December 13, 1989); missed 15 games. . . . Suffered knee inflamation (January 1990). . . . Strained shoulder (April 1990).
HONORS: Named ECAC Player of the Year (1976-77). . . . Named to NCAA All-America East team (1976-77). . . . Named to THE SPORTING NEWS All-Star second team (1980-81). . . . Named to NHL All-Star second team (1980-81). . . . Won King Clancy Memorial Trophy (1990-91). . . . Won Bill Masterton Trophy (1990-91).

Season Team	League	REGULAR SEASON					PLAYOFFS				
		Gms.	G	A	Pts.	Pen.	Gms.	G	A	Pts.	Pen.
74-75—Clarkson	ECAC		20	34	54		—	—	—	—	—
75-76—Clarkson	ECAC		26	33	59		—	—	—	—	—
76-77—Clarkson	ECAC	34	41	67	108		—	—	—	—	—
—Fort Worth	CHL	7	2	4	6	6	—	—	—	—	—
77-78—Los Angeles	NHL	64	22	21	43	47	2	0	0	0	5
78-79—Los Angeles	NHL	78	43	48	91	124	2	0	0	0	2
79-80—Los Angeles	NHL	61	37	53	90	72	4	2	1	3	4
80-81—Los Angeles	NHL	72	47	65	112	130	4	2	2	4	10
81-82—Los Angeles	NHL	78	39	67	106	130	10	4	6	10	20
82-83—Los Angeles	NHL	46	21	37	58	76	—	—	—	—	—
83-84—Los Angeles	NHL	63	20	49	69	91	—	—	—	—	—
84-85—Los Angeles	NHL	79	41	51	92	132	3	2	2	4	8
85-86—Los Angeles	NHL	76	33	38	71	110	—	—	—	—	—
86-87—Los Angeles	NHL	67	18	44	62	84	5	2	3	5	6
87-88—Los Angeles	NHL	68	26	41	67	129	5	3	3	6	6
88-89—Los Angeles	NHL	70	26	37	63	80	11	1	5	6	19
89-90—Los Angeles	NHL	58	15	26	41	96	6	4	4	8	2
90-91—Los Angeles	NHL	73	23	30	53	148	12	2	1	3	12
91-92—Los Angeles	NHL	77	10	19	29	63	6	1	1	2	20
NHL totals		1030	421	626	1047	1512	70	23	28	51	114

TAYLOR, TIM
C, CAPITALS

PERSONAL: Born February 6, 1969, at Stratford, Ont. . . . 6-1/180. . . . Shoots left. . . . Full name: Tim Robertson Taylor. . . . Brother of Chris Taylor, center in New York Islanders system.
TRANSACTIONS/CAREER NOTES: Suffered from mononucleosis (October 1986). . . . Selected by Washington Capitals in second round (second Capitals pick, 36th overall) of NHL entry draft (June 11, 1988).

Season Team	League	REGULAR SEASON					PLAYOFFS				
		Gms.	G	A	Pts.	Pen.	Gms.	G	A	Pts.	Pen.
86-87—London	OHL	34	7	9	16	11	—	—	—	—	—
87-88—London	OHL	64	46	50	96	66	12	9	9	18	26
88-89—London	OHL	61	34	80	114	93	21	*21	25	*46	58
89-90—Baltimore	AHL	74	22	21	43	63	9	2	2	4	13
90-91—Baltimore	AHL	79	25	42	67	75	5	0	1	1	4
91-92—Baltimore	AHL	65	9	18	27	131	—	—	—	—	—

TEPPER, STEPHEN
RW, BLACKHAWKS

PERSONAL: Born March 10, 1969, at Santa Ana, Calif.... 6-4/215.... Shoots right.... Full name: Stephen Christopher Tepper.
HIGH SCHOOL: Westborough (Mass.).
COLLEGE: Maine.
TRANSACTIONS/CAREER NOTES: Selected by Chicago Blackhawks in seventh round (seventh Blackhawks pick, 134th overall) of NHL entry draft (June 13, 1987).

Season Team	League	REGULAR SEASON					PLAYOFFS				
		Gms.	G	A	Pts.	Pen.	Gms.	G	A	Pts.	Pen.
85-86—Westborough H.S............	Mass. H.S.		18	26	44		—	—	—	—	—
86-87—Westborough H.S............	Mass. H.S.		34	18	52		—	—	—	—	—
87-88—Westborough H.S............	Mass. H.S.	24	39	24	63		—	—	—	—	—
88-89—University of Maine	Hockey East	26	3	9	12	32	—	—	—	—	—
89-90—University of Maine	Hockey East	41	10	6	16	68	—	—	—	—	—
90-91—University of Maine	Hockey East	38	6	11	17	58	—	—	—	—	—
91-92—University of Maine	Hockey East	16	0	3	3	20	—	—	—	—	—

TERRERI, CHRIS
G, DEVILS

PERSONAL: Born November 15, 1964, at Warwick, R.I.... 5-8/155.... Shoots left.... Full name: Christopher Arnold Terreri.
COLLEGE: Providence.
TRANSACTIONS/CAREER NOTES: Selected by New Jersey Devils in fifth round (third Devils pick, 87th overall) of NHL entry draft (June 8, 1983).... Strained knee (October 1986).... Strained lower back (March 21, 1992); missed five games.
HONORS: Named to NCAA All-America East first team (1984-85).... Named Hockey East Most Valuable Player (1984-85).... Named to Hockey East All-Star team (1984-85).

Season Team	League	REGULAR SEASON								PLAYOFFS						
		Gms.	Min.	W	L	T	GA	SO	Avg.	Gms.	Min.	W	L	GA	SO	Avg.
82-83—Providence College	ECAC	11	529	7	1	0	17	2	1.93	—	—	—	—	—	—	—
83-84—Providence College	ECAC	10	391	4	2	0	20	0	3.07	—	—	—	—	—	—	—
84-85—Providence College	Hoc. East	41	2515	15	13	5	131	1	3.13	—	—	—	—	—	—	—
85-86—Providence College	Hoc. East	27	1540	6	16	0	96	0	3.74	—	—	—	—	—	—	—
86-87—Maine..........................	AHL	14	765	4	9	1	57	0	4.47	—	—	—	—	—	—	—
—New Jersey...................	NHL	7	286	0	3	1	21	0	4.41	—	—	—	—	—	—	—
87-88—Utica..........................	AHL	7	399	5	1	0	18	0	2.71	—	—	—	—	—	—	—
—U.S. Olympic Team	Int'l	29	1558	18	8	2	95	0	3.66	—	—	—	—	—	—	—
88-89—New Jersey...................	NHL	8	402	0	4	2	18	0	2.69	—	—	—	—	—	—	—
—Utica..........................	AHL	39	2314	20	15	3	132	0	3.42	2	80	0	1	6	0	4.50
89-90—New Jersey...................	NHL	35	1931	15	12	3	110	0	3.42	4	238	2	2	13	0	3.28
90-91—New Jersey...................	NHL	53	2970	24	21	7	144	1	2.91	7	428	3	4	21	0	2.94
91-92—New Jersey...................	NHL	54	3186	22	22	10	169	1	3.18	7	386	3	3	23	0	3.58
NHL totals.................		157	8775	61	62	23	462	2	3.16	18	1052	8	9	57	0	3.25

THIESSEN, TRAVIS
D, PENGUINS

PERSONAL: Born November 7, 1972, at North Battleford, Sask.... 6-3/204.... Shoots left.
TRANSACTIONS/CAREER NOTES: Selected by Pittsburgh Penguins in third round (third Penguins pick, 67th overall) of NHL entry draft (June 20, 1992).

Season Team	League	REGULAR SEASON					PLAYOFFS				
		Gms.	G	A	Pts.	Pen.	Gms.	G	A	Pts.	Pen.
90-91—Moose Jaw	WHL	69	4	14	18	80	8	0	0	0	10
91-92—Moose Jaw	WHL	72	9	50	59	112	4	0	2	2	8

THOMAS, SCOTT
RW, SABRES

PERSONAL: Born January 18, 1970, at Buffalo, N.Y.... 6-2/195.... Shoots right.... Full name: John Scott Thomas.
HIGH SCHOOL: Nichols (Buffalo, N.Y.).
COLLEGE: Clarkson (N.Y.).
TRANSACTIONS/CAREER NOTES: Selected by Buffalo Sabres in third round (second Sabres pick, 56th overall) of NHL entry draft (June 17, 1989).... Broke left thumb (December 1990).
HONORS: Named to ECAC All-Rookie team (1989-90).

Season Team	League	REGULAR SEASON					PLAYOFFS				
		Gms.	G	A	Pts.	Pen.	Gms.	G	A	Pts.	Pen.
87-88—Nichols School	N.Y. H.S.	16	23	39	62	82	—	—	—	—	—
88-89—Nichols School	N.Y. H.S.		38	52	90		—	—	—	—	—
89-90—Clarkson.......................	ECAC	34	19	13	32	95	—	—	—	—	—
90-91—Clarkson.......................	ECAC	40	28	14	42	90	—	—	—	—	—
91-92—Clarkson.......................	ECAC	30	†25	21	46	62	—	—	—	—	—
—Rochester.......................	AHL	—	—	—	—	—	9	0	1	1	17

THOMAS, STEVE
LW/RW, ISLANDERS

PERSONAL: Born July 15, 1963, at Stockport, England.... 5-11/185.... Shoots left.
TRANSACTIONS/CAREER NOTES: Signed as free agent by Toronto Maple Leafs (June 1984).... Broke wrist during training camp (September 1984).... Traded by Toronto Maple Leafs with RW Rick Vaive and D Bob McGill to Chicago Blackhawks for LW Al Secord and RW Ed Olczyk (September 1987).... Pulled stomach muscle (October 1987).... Separated left shoulder (February 20, 1988); underwent surgery (May 1988).... Pulled back muscle (October 18, 1988).... Separated right shoulder (December 21,

1988).... Underwent surgery to repair chronic shoulder separation problem (January 25, 1989).... Strained knee ligaments during training camp (September 1990); missed first 11 games of season.... Traded by Blackhawks with C Adam Creighton to New York Islanders for C Brent Sutter and RW Brad Lauer (October 25, 1991).... Bruised ribs (March 10, 1992); missed one game.
HONORS: Won Dudley (Red) Garrett Memorial Trophy (1984-85).... Named to AHL All-Star first team (1984-85).

Season Team	League	REGULAR SEASON					PLAYOFFS				
		Gms.	G	A	Pts.	Pen.	Gms.	G	A	Pts.	Pen.
81-82—Markham Tier II Jr. A	OHA	48	68	57	125	113	—	—	—	—	—
82-83—Toronto	OHL	61	18	20	38	42	—	—	—	—	—
83-84—Toronto	OHL	70	51	54	105	77	—	—	—	—	—
84-85—Toronto	NHL	18	1	1	2	2	—	—	—	—	—
—St. Catharines	AHL	64	42	48	90	56	—	—	—	—	—
85-86—St. Catharines	AHL	19	18	14	32	35	—	—	—	—	—
—Toronto	NHL	65	20	37	57	36	10	6	8	14	9
86-87—Toronto	NHL	78	35	27	62	114	13	2	3	5	13
87-88—Chicago	NHL	30	13	13	26	40	3	1	2	3	6
88-89—Chicago	NHL	45	21	19	40	69	12	3	5	8	10
89-90—Chicago	NHL	76	40	30	70	91	20	7	6	13	33
90-91—Chicago	NHL	69	19	35	54	129	6	1	2	3	15
91-92—Chicago	NHL	11	2	6	8	26	—	—	—	—	—
—New York Islanders	NHL	71	28	42	70	71	—	—	—	—	—
NHL totals		463	179	210	389	578	64	20	26	46	86

THOMLINSON, DAVE
LW, BRUINS

PERSONAL: Born October 22, 1966, at Edmonton, Alta.... 6-1/195.... Shoots left. **TRANSACTIONS/CAREER NOTES:** Separated shoulder (November 1983).... Separated shoulder (November 1984).... Selected by Toronto Maple Leafs as underage junior in third round (third Maple Leafs pick, 43rd overall) of NHL entry draft (June 15, 1985).... Signed as free agent by St. Louis Blues (July 1987).... Bruised foot (February 1990).... Signed as free agent by Boston Bruins; Bruins and Blues later arranged a trade in which Bruins received Thomlinson and D Glen Featherstone, whom they had also previously signed as free agent, for RW Dave Christian, whom the Blues had previously signed as free agent, third-round pick in 1992 draft and either seventh-round pick in 1992 draft or sixth-round pick in 1993 draft (July 1991).... Suffered sore back (December 1991).

Season Team	League	REGULAR SEASON					PLAYOFFS				
		Gms.	G	A	Pts.	Pen.	Gms.	G	A	Pts.	Pen.
83-84—Brandon	WHL	41	17	12	29	62	—	—	—	—	—
84-85—Brandon	WHL	26	13	14	27	70	—	—	—	—	—
85-86—Brandon	WHL	53	25	20	45	116	—	—	—	—	—
86-87—Brandon	WHL	2	0	1	1	9	—	—	—	—	—
—Moose Jaw	WHL	69	44	36	80	126	9	7	3	10	19
87-88—Peoria	IHL	74	27	30	57	56	7	4	3	7	11
88-89—Peoria	IHL	64	27	29	56	154	3	0	1	1	8
89-90—St. Louis	NHL	19	1	2	3	12	—	—	—	—	—
—Peoria	IHL	59	27	40	67	87	5	1	1	2	15
90-91—Peoria	IHL	80	53	54	107	107	11	6	7	13	28
—St. Louis	NHL	3	0	0	0	0	9	3	1	4	4
91-92—Boston	NHL	12	0	1	1	17	—	—	—	—	—
—Maine	AHL	25	9	11	20	36	—	—	—	—	—
NHL totals		34	1	3	4	29	9	3	1	4	4

THOMPSON, BRENT
D, KINGS

PERSONAL: Born January 9, 1971, at Calgary, Alta.... 6-2/175.... Shoots left. **TRANSACTIONS/CAREER NOTES:** Stretched knee ligaments and separated shoulder (September 1987).... Selected by Los Angeles Kings in second round (first Kings pick, 39th overall) of NHL entry draft (June 17, 1989).

HONORS: Named to WHL All-Star second team (1990-91).

Season Team	League	REGULAR SEASON					PLAYOFFS				
		Gms.	G	A	Pts.	Pen.	Gms.	G	A	Pts.	Pen.
88-89—Medicine Hat	WHL	72	3	10	13	160	3	0	0	0	2
89-90—Medicine Hat	WHL	68	10	35	45	167	3	0	1	1	14
90-91—Medicine Hat	WHL	51	5	40	45	87	12	1	7	8	16
—Phoenix	IHL	—	—	—	—	—	4	0	1	1	6
91-92—Phoenix	IHL	42	4	13	17	139	—	—	—	—	—
—Los Angeles	NHL	27	0	5	5	89	4	0	0	0	4
NHL totals		27	0	5	5	89	4	0	0	0	4

THOMSON, JIM
RW, SENATORS

PERSONAL: Born December 30, 1965, at Edmonton, Alta.... 6-1/205.... Shoots right. **TRANSACTIONS/CAREER NOTES:** Selected by Washington Capitals as underage junior in ninth round (eighth Capitals pick, 185th overall) of NHL entry draft (June 9, 1984).... Traded by Capitals to Hartford Whalers for D Scot Kleinendorst (March 6, 1989).... Traded by Whalers to New Jersey Devils for RW Chris Cichocki (October 31, 1989).... Signed as free agent by Los Angeles Kings (July 11, 1990).... Fractured foot (January 19, 1991).... Selected by Minnesota North Stars in NHL expansion draft (May 30, 1991). ... Traded by North Stars with D Charlie Huddy, LW Randy Gilhen and fourth-round pick in 1991 draft (D Alexei Zhitnik) to Kings for C Todd Elik (June 22, 1991).... Hyperextended elbow (November 11, 1991); missed four games.... Selected by Ottawa Senators in NHL expansion draft (June 18, 1992).

Season	Team	League	REGULAR SEASON					PLAYOFFS				
			Gms.	G	A	Pts.	Pen.	Gms.	G	A	Pts.	Pen.
82-83—	Markham Waxers	OPJHL	35	6	7	13	81	—	—	—	—	—
83-84—	Toronto	OHL	60	10	18	28	68	9	1	0	1	26
84-85—	Toronto	OHL	63	23	28	51	122	5	3	1	4	25
—	Binghamton	AHL	4	0	0	0	2	—	—	—	—	—
85-86—	Binghamton	AHL	59	15	9	24	195	—	—	—	—	—
86-87—	Binghamton	AHL	57	13	10	23	*360	10	0	1	1	40
—	Washington	NHL	10	0	0	0	35	—	—	—	—	—
87-88—	Binghamton	AHL	25	8	9	17	64	4	1	2	3	7
88-89—	Baltimore	AHL	41	25	16	41	129	—	—	—	—	—
—	Washington	NHL	14	2	0	2	53	—	—	—	—	—
—	Hartford	NHL	5	0	0	0	14	—	—	—	—	—
89-90—	Binghamton	AHL	8	1	2	3	30	—	—	—	—	—
—	Utica	AHL	60	20	23	43	124	4	1	0	1	19
—	New Jersey	NHL	3	0	0	0	31	—	—	—	—	—
90-91—	New Haven	AHL	27	5	8	13	121	—	—	—	—	—
—	Los Angeles	NHL	8	1	0	1	19	—	—	—	—	—
91-92—	Los Angeles	NHL	45	1	2	3	162	—	—	—	—	—
—	Phoenix	IHL	2	1	0	1	0	—	—	—	—	—
NHL totals			85	4	2	6	314					

THORNTON, SCOTT
C, OILERS

PERSONAL: Born January 9, 1971, at London, Ont. . . . 6-2/200. . . . Shoots left. . . . Full name: Scott C. Thornton.

TRANSACTIONS/CAREER NOTES: Selected by Toronto Maple Leafs in first round (first Maple Leafs pick, third overall) of NHL entry draft (June 17, 1989). . . . Suspended 12 games by OHL for refusing to leave ice following penalty (February 7, 1990). . . . Separated shoulder (January 24, 1991); missed eight games. . . . Traded by Maple Leafs with LW Vincent Damphousse, D Luke Richardson, G Peter Ing and future considerations to Edmonton Oilers for G Grant Fuhr, RW/LW Glenn Anderson and LW Craig Berube (September 19, 1991). . . . Suffered concussion (November 23, 1991); missed one game.

Season	Team	League	REGULAR SEASON					PLAYOFFS				
			Gms.	G	A	Pts.	Pen.	Gms.	G	A	Pts.	Pen.
86-87—	London	OPJHL	31	10	7	17	10	—	—	—	—	—
87-88—	Belleville	OHL	62	11	19	30	54	6	0	1	1	2
88-89—	Belleville	OHL	59	28	34	62	103	5	1	1	2	6
89-90—	Belleville	OHL	47	21	28	49	91	11	2	10	12	15
90-91—	Belleville	OHL	3	2	1	3	2	6	0	7	7	14
—	Newmarket	AHL	5	1	0	1	4	—	—	—	—	—
—	Toronto	NHL	33	1	3	4	30	—	—	—	—	—
91-92—	Edmonton	NHL	15	0	1	1	43	1	0	0	0	0
—	Cape Breton	AHL	49	9	14	23	40	5	1	0	1	8
NHL totals			48	1	4	5	73	1	0	0	0	0

THYER, MARIO
C, NORTH STARS

PERSONAL: Born September 29, 1966, at Montreal. . . . 5-11/170. . . . Shoots left.
COLLEGE: Maine.

TRANSACTIONS/CAREER NOTES: Broke leg (November 1988). . . . Signed as free agent by Minnesota North Stars (July 12, 1989). . . . Traded by North Stars with third-round pick in 1993 draft to New York Rangers for C Mark Janssens (March 10, 1992). . . . Traded by Rangers to North Stars for future considerations (July 16, 1992).

Season	Team	League	REGULAR SEASON					PLAYOFFS				
			Gms.	G	A	Pts.	Pen.	Gms.	G	A	Pts.	Pen.
86-87—	St. Laurent College	QCAAA				Statistics unavailable.						
87-88—	University of Maine	Hockey East	44	24	42	66	4	—	—	—	—	—
88-89—	University of Maine	Hockey East	9	9	7	16	0	—	—	—	—	—
89-90—	Minnesota	NHL	5	0	0	0	0	1	0	0	0	2
—	Kalamazoo	IHL	68	19	42	61	12	10	2	6	8	4
90-91—	Kalamazoo	IHL	75	15	51	66	15	10	4	5	9	2
91-92—	Kalamazoo	IHL	46	17	28	45	0	—	—	—	—	—
—	Binghamton	AHL	9	2	7	9	0	3	0	0	0	0
NHL totals			5	0	0	0	0	1	0	0	0	2

TIKKANEN, ESA
LW, OILERS

PERSONAL: Born January 25, 1965, at Helsinki, Finland. . . . 6-1/200. . . . Shoots left. . . . Full name: Esa Kalervo Tikkanen.

TRANSACTIONS/CAREER NOTES: Selected by Edmonton Oilers in fourth round (fourth Oilers pick, 82nd overall) of NHL entry draft (August 8, 1983). . . . Lacerated elbow, developed bursitis and underwent surgery (December 9, 1986). . . . Fractured left wrist (January 1989). . . . Injured right knee (October 28, 1989). . . . Underwent left knee surgery (August 1990); missed first 10 days of training camp. . . . Sprained wrist (December 1, 1991); missed one game. . . . Sprained wrist (December 20, 1991); missed two games. . . . Fractured shoulder (January 4, 1992); missed 37 games.

Season	Team	League	REGULAR SEASON					PLAYOFFS				
			Gms.	G	A	Pts.	Pen.	Gms.	G	A	Pts.	Pen.
81-82—	Regina	WHL	2	0	0	0	0	—	—	—	—	—
82-83—	Helsinki Junior IFK	Finland	30	34	31	65	104	4	4	3	7	10
—	Helsinki IFK	Finland	—	—	—	—	—	1	0	0	0	2

Season Team	League	REGULAR SEASON					PLAYOFFS				
		Gms.	G	A	Pts.	Pen.	Gms.	G	A	Pts.	Pen.
83-84—Helsinki IFK	Finland	36	19	11	30	30	2	0	0	0	0
—Helsinki Junior IFK	Finland	6	5	9	14	13	4	4	3	7	8
84-85—Helsinki IFK	Finland	36	21	33	54	42					
—Edmonton	NHL	—	—	—	—	—	3	0	0	0	2
85-86—Nova Scotia	AHL	15	4	8	12	17	—	—	—	—	—
—Edmonton	NHL	35	7	6	13	28	8	3	2	5	7
86-87—Edmonton	NHL	76	34	44	78	120	21	7	2	9	22
87-88—Edmonton	NHL	80	23	51	74	153	19	10	17	27	72
88-89—Edmonton	NHL	67	31	47	78	92	7	1	3	4	12
89-90—Edmonton	NHL	79	30	33	63	161	22	13	11	24	26
90-91—Edmonton	NHL	79	27	42	69	85	18	12	8	20	24
91-92—Edmonton	NHL	40	12	16	28	44	16	5	3	8	8
NHL totals		456	164	239	403	683	114	51	46	97	173

TILEY, BRAD
D, BRUINS

PERSONAL: Born July 5, 1971, at Markdale, Ont. . . . 6-1/185. . . . Shoots left.
TRANSACTIONS/CAREER NOTES: Selected by Boston Bruins in fourth round (fourth Bruins pick, 84th overall) of NHL entry draft (June 22, 1991).
HONORS: Named to Memorial Cup All-Star Team (1990-91).

Season Team	League	REGULAR SEASON					PLAYOFFS				
		Gms.	G	A	Pts.	Pen.	Gms.	G	A	Pts.	Pen.
87-88—Owen Sound Jr. B	OHA	40	19	25	44	68	—	—	—	—	—
88-89—Sault Ste. Marie	OHL	50	4	11	15	31	—	—	—	—	—
89-90—Sault Ste. Marie	OHL	66	9	32	41	47	—	—	—	—	—
90-91—Sault Ste. Marie	OHL	66	11	55	66	29	—	—	—	—	—
91-92—Maine	AHL	62	7	22	29	36	—	—	—	—	—

TINORDI, MARK
D, NORTH STARS

PERSONAL: Born May 9, 1966, at Red Deer, Alta. . . . 6-4/205. . . . Shoots left.
TRANSACTIONS/CAREER NOTES: Signed as free agent by New York Rangers (January 1987). . . . Suffered abdominal pains (January 1988). . . . Underwent left knee surgery (October 6, 1988). . . . Traded by Rangers with D Paul Jerrard, C Mike Sullivan, RW Brett Barnett and Los Angeles Kings' third-round pick in 1989 draft (C Murray Garbutt) to Minnesota North Stars for LW Igor Liba, C Brian Lawton and rights to LW Eric Bennett (October 11, 1988). . . . Bruised ribs (December 1988). . . . Underwent knee surgery (April 1989). . . . Suspended four games by NHL for cross-checking in a preseason game (September 27, 1989). . . . Bruised shoulder (December 1989). . . . Fined $500 by NHL for fighting (December 28, 1989). . . . Suffered concussion (January 17, 1990); missed six games. . . . Suspended 10 games by NHL for leaving the penalty box to fight during a pre-season game (September 26, 1990). . . . Suffered from foot palsy (October 15, 1991); missed 17 games.
HONORS: Named to WHL All-Star first team (1986-87).

Season Team	League	REGULAR SEASON					PLAYOFFS				
		Gms.	G	A	Pts.	Pen.	Gms.	G	A	Pts.	Pen.
82-83—Lethbridge	WHL	64	0	4	4	50	20	1	1	2	6
83-84—Lethbridge	WHL	72	5	14	19	53	5	0	1	1	7
84-85—Lethbridge	WHL	58	10	15	25	134	4	0	2	2	12
85-86—Lethbridge	WHL	58	8	30	38	139	8	1	3	4	15
86-87—Calgary	WHL	61	29	37	66	148	—	—	—	—	—
—New Haven	AHL	2	0	0	0	2	2	0	0	0	0
87-88—New York Rangers	NHL	24	1	2	3	50	—	—	—	—	—
—Colorado	IHL	41	8	19	27	150	11	1	5	6	31
88-89—Minnesota	NHL	47	2	3	5	107	5	0	0	0	0
—Kalamazoo	IHL	10	0	0	0	35	—	—	—	—	—
89-90—Minnesota	NHL	66	3	7	10	240	7	0	1	1	16
90-91—Minnesota	NHL	69	5	27	32	189	23	5	6	11	78
91-92—Minnesota	NHL	63	4	24	28	179	7	1	2	3	11
NHL totals		269	15	63	78	765	42	6	9	15	105

TIPPETT, DAVE
C/LW, CAPITALS

PERSONAL: Born August 25, 1961, at Moosomin, Sask. . . . 5-10/180. . . . Shoots left. . . . Full name: David G. Tippett.
COLLEGE: North Dakota.
TRANSACTIONS/CAREER NOTES: Signed as free agent by Hartford Whalers (February 1984). . . . Injured right thumb tendons (October 8, 1989). . . . Traded by Whalers to Washington Capitals for sixth-round pick in 1992 draft (September 30, 1990). . . . Separated shoulder (November 28, 1990); missed 11 games.
MISCELLANEOUS: Member of 1992 silver-medal-winning Canadian Olympic team.

Season Team	League	REGULAR SEASON					PLAYOFFS				
		Gms.	G	A	Pts.	Pen.	Gms.	G	A	Pts.	Pen.
79-80—Prince Albert	SJHL	85	72	95	167		—	—	—	—	—
80-81—Prince Albert	SJHL	84	62	93	155		—	—	—	—	—
81-82—Univ. of North Dakota	WCHA	43	13	28	41	24	—	—	—	—	—
82-83—Univ. of North Dakota	WCHA	36	15	31	46	44	—	—	—	—	—
83-84—Canadian Olympic Team	Int'l	66	14	19	33	24	—	—	—	—	—
—Hartford	NHL	17	4	2	6	2	—	—	—	—	—
84-85—Hartford	NHL	80	7	12	19	12	—	—	—	—	—

Season Team	League	REGULAR SEASON					PLAYOFFS				
		Gms.	G	A	Pts.	Pen.	Gms.	G	A	Pts.	Pen.
85-86—Hartford	NHL	80	14	20	34	18	10	2	2	4	4
86-87—Hartford	NHL	80	9	22	31	42	6	0	2	2	4
87-88—Hartford	NHL	80	16	21	37	32	6	0	0	0	2
88-89—Hartford	NHL	80	17	24	41	45	4	0	1	1	0
89-90—Hartford	NHL	66	8	19	27	32	7	1	3	4	2
90-91—Washington	NHL	61	6	9	15	24	10	2	3	5	8
91-92—Washington	NHL	30	2	10	12	16	7	0	1	1	0
—Canadian National Team	Int'l	1	0	0	0	4	—	—	—	—	—
—Canadian Olympic Team	Int'l	6	1	2	3	10	—	—	—	—	—
NHL totals		574	83	139	222	223	50	5	12	17	20

TKACHUK, KEITH
C/LW, JETS

PERSONAL: Born March 28, 1972, at Melrose, Mass. . . . 6-2/200. . . . Shoots left. . . . Full name: Keith Matthew Tkachuk.

HIGH SCHOOL: Malden Catholic (Malden, Mass.).

COLLEGE: Boston University.

TRANSACTIONS/CAREER NOTES: Selected by Winnipeg Jets in first round (first Jets pick, 19th overall) of NHL entry draft (June 16, 1990).

HONORS: Named to Hockey East All-Rookie team (1990-91).

Season Team	League	REGULAR SEASON					PLAYOFFS				
		Gms.	G	A	Pts.	Pen.	Gms.	G	A	Pts.	Pen.
88-89—Malden Catholic H.S.	Mass. H.S.	21	30	16	46		—	—	—	—	—
89-90—Malden Catholic H.S.	Mass. H.S.	6	12	14	26		—	—	—	—	—
90-91—Boston University	Hockey East	36	17	23	40	70	—	—	—	—	—
91-92—U.S. National Team	Int'l	45	10	10	20	141	—	—	—	—	—
—U.S. Olympic Team	Int'l	8	1	1	2	12	—	—	—	—	—
—Winnipeg	NHL	17	3	5	8	28	7	3	0	3	30
NHL totals		17	3	5	8	28	7	3	0	3	30

TOCCHET, RICK
RW, PENGUINS

PERSONAL: Born April 9, 1964, at Scarborough, Ont. . . . 6-0/205. . . . Shoots right.

TRANSACTIONS/CAREER NOTES: Selected by Philadelphia Flyers as underage junior in sixth round (fifth Flyers pick, 121st overall) of NHL entry draft (June 8, 1983). . . . Bruised right knee (November 23, 1985); missed seven games. . . . Separated left shoulder (February 1988). . . . Suspended 10 games by NHL for injuring an opposing player during a fight (October 27, 1988). . . . Hyperextended right knee (April 21, 1989). . . . Suffered viral infection (November 1989). . . . Tore tendon in left groin area (January 26, 1991); missed five games. . . . Reinjured groin (March 1991); missed five games. . . . Sprained knee (November 29, 1991); missed five games. . . . Bruised heel (January 18, 1991); missed 10 games. . . . Traded by Flyers with G Ken Wregget, D Kjell Samuelsson and third-round pick in 1992 draft to Pittsburgh Penguins for RW Mark Recchi, D Brian Benning and first-round pick in 1992 draft previously acquired from Los Angeles Kings (February 19, 1992). . . . Fractured jaw (March 15, 1992); missed three games.

Season Team	League	REGULAR SEASON					PLAYOFFS				
		Gms.	G	A	Pts.	Pen.	Gms.	G	A	Pts.	Pen.
81-82—Sault Ste. Marie	OHL	59	7	15	22	184	11	1	1	2	28
82-83—Sault Ste. Marie	OHL	66	32	34	66	146	16	4	13	17	*67
83-84—Sault Ste. Marie	OHL	64	44	64	108	209	16	*22	14	†36	41
84-85—Philadelphia	NHL	75	14	25	39	181	19	3	4	7	72
85-86—Philadelphia	NHL	69	14	21	35	284	5	1	2	3	26
86-87—Philadelphia	NHL	69	21	26	47	288	26	11	10	21	72
87-88—Philadelphia	NHL	65	31	33	64	301	5	1	4	5	55
88-89—Philadelphia	NHL	66	45	36	81	183	16	6	6	12	69
89-90—Philadelphia	NHL	75	37	59	96	196	—	—	—	—	—
90-91—Philadelphia	NHL	70	40	31	71	150	—	—	—	—	—
91-92—Philadelphia	NHL	42	13	16	29	102	—	—	—	—	—
—Pittsburgh	NHL	19	14	16	30	49	14	6	13	19	24
NHL totals		550	229	263	492	1734	85	28	39	67	318

TODD, KEVIN
C, DEVILS

PERSONAL: Born May 4, 1968, at Winnipeg, Man. . . . 5-10/175. . . . Shoots left. . . . Full name: Kevin L. Todd.

TRANSACTIONS/CAREER NOTES: Stretched knee ligaments (December 1985). . . . Selected by New Jersey Devils as underage junior in seventh round (seventh Devils pick, 129th overall) of NHL entry draft (June 21, 1986).

HONORS: Won Les Cunningham Plaque (1990-91). . . . Won the John B. Sollenberger Trophy (1990-91). . . . Named to AHL All-Star first team (1990-91). . . . Named to NHL All-Rookie team (1991-92).

Season Team	League	REGULAR SEASON					PLAYOFFS				
		Gms.	G	A	Pts.	Pen.	Gms.	G	A	Pts.	Pen.
85-86—Prince Albert	WHL	55	14	25	39	19	20	7	6	13	29
86-87—Prince Albert	WHL	71	39	46	85	92	8	2	5	7	17
87-88—Prince Albert	WHL	72	49	72	121	83	10	8	11	19	27
88-89—New Jersey	NHL	1	0	0	0	0	—	—	—	—	—
—Utica	AHL	78	26	45	71	62	4	2	0	2	6
89-90—Utica	AHL	71	18	36	54	72	5	2	4	6	2
90-91—Utica	AHL	75	37	*81	*118	75	—	—	—	—	—
—New Jersey	NHL	1	0	0	0	0	1	0	0	0	6
91-92—New Jersey	NHL	80	21	42	63	69	7	3	2	5	8
NHL totals		82	21	42	63	69	8	3	2	5	14

TOMILIN, VITLAI
LW/RW, DEVILS

PERSONAL: Born January 15, 1974, at Elektrostal, U.S.S.R.... 6-0/183.... Shoots left.
TRANSACTIONS/CAREER NOTES: Selected by New Jersey Devils in fourth round (fourth Devils pick, 90th overall) of NHL entry draft (June 20, 1992).

		REGULAR SEASON					PLAYOFFS				
Season Team	League	Gms.	G	A	Pts.	Pen.	Gms.	G	A	Pts.	Pen.
90-91—Kristall Elektrostal..........	USSR	18	3	3	6	8	—	—	—	—	—
—Krylja Sovetov.................	USSR	1	0	0	0	0	—	—	—	—	—
91-92—Krylja Sovetov.................	CIS	37	1	1	2	8	—	—	—	—	—

TOMLAK, MIKE
LW, WHALERS

PERSONAL: Born October 17, 1964, at Thunder Bay, Ont.... 6-3/205.... Shoots left.... Full name: Michael Ronald Tomlak.
COLLEGE: Western Ontario.
TRANSACTIONS/CAREER NOTES: Selected by Toronto Maple Leafs in 11th round (10th Maple Leafs pick, 208th overall) of NHL entry draft (June 8, 1983).... Signed as free agent by Hartford Whalers (May 28, 1989).... Sprained right wrist (February 9, 1990).... Bruised left foot (January 26, 1992); missed 15 games.... Fractured left leg (March 6, 1992); missed remainder of season and playoffs.
HONORS: Named to CIAU All-Canada team (1986-87).... Named to OUAA All-Star first team (1988-89).

		REGULAR SEASON					PLAYOFFS				
Season Team	League	Gms.	G	A	Pts.	Pen.	Gms.	G	A	Pts.	Pen.
81-82—Thunder Bay	TDJIIL	25	10	26	45	30	—	—	—	—	—
82-83—Cornwall	OHL	70	18	49	67	26	—	—	—	—	—
83-84—Cornwall	OHL	64	24	64	88	21	—	—	—	—	—
84-85—Cornwall	OHL	66	30	70	100	9	—	—	—	—	—
85-86—Univ. of Western Ontario..	OUAA	38	28	20	48	45	—	—	—	—	—
86-87—Univ. of Western Ontario..	OUAA	38	16	30	46	10	—	—	—	—	—
87-88—Univ. of Western Ontario..	OUAA	39	24	52	76		—	—	—	—	—
88-89—Univ. of Western Ontario..	OUAA	35	16	34	50		—	—	—	—	—
89-90—Hartford.........................	NHL	70	7	14	21	48	7	0	1	1	2
90-91—Springfield.....................	AHL	15	4	9	13	15	—	—	—	—	—
—Hartford.........................	NHL	64	8	8	16	55	3	0	0	0	2
91-92—Springfield.....................	AHL	39	16	21	37	24	—	—	—	—	—
—Hartford.........................	NHL	6	0	0	0	0	—	—	—	—	—
NHL totals...............................		140	15	22	37	103	10	0	1	1	4

TOMLINSON, DAVE
C, MAPLE LEAFS

PERSONAL: Born May 8, 1968, at North Vancouver, B.C.... 5-11/190.... Shoots left.... Full name: David H. Tomlinson.
COLLEGE: Boston University.
TRANSACTIONS/CAREER NOTES: Selected by Toronto Maple Leafs in NHL supplemental draft (June 16, 1989).

		REGULAR SEASON					PLAYOFFS				
Season Team	League	Gms.	G	A	Pts.	Pen.	Gms.	G	A	Pts.	Pen.
87-88—Boston University	Hockey East	34	16	20	36	28	—	—	—	—	—
88-89—Boston University	Hockey East	34	16	30	46	40	—	—	—	—	—
89-90—Boston University	Hockey East	43	15	22	37	53	—	—	—	—	—
90-91—Boston University	Hockey East	41	30	30	60	55	—	—	—	—	—
91-92—St. John's	AHL	75	23	34	57	75	12	4	5	9	6
—Toronto............................	NHL	3	0	0	0	2	—	—	—	—	—
NHL totals...............................		3	0	0	0	2	—	—	—	—	—

TONELLI, JOHN
LW/C, NORDIQUES

PERSONAL: Born March 23, 1957, at Hamilton, Ont.... 6-1/190.... Shoots left.
TRANSACTIONS/CAREER NOTES: Signed by Houston Aeros (March 1975).... Selected by New York Islanders from Aeros in second round (second Islanders pick, 33rd overall) of NHL amateur draft (June 14, 1977).... Injured shoulder (February 1981).... Injured knee (December 1983).... Missed 22 days of training camp due to contract dispute (Fall 1985).... Traded by Islanders to Calgary Flames for LW Richard Kromm and D Steve Konroyd (March 1986).... Suffered from the flu (April 1988); missed four playoff games.... Signed as free agent by Los Angeles Kings (July 1988).... Strained knee (April 1989).... Suffered from sinus infection (March 1990).... Signed as free agent by Chicago Blackhawks (June 28, 1991).... Bruised cheek (March 11, 1992); missed one game.... Injured heel (March 15, 1992); missed two games.... Claimed on waivers by Quebec Nordiques (February 18, 1992).
HONORS: Named to OHA Major Junior A All-Star first team (1974-75).... Named to THE SPORTING NEWS All-Star second team (1981-82).... Named to NHL All-Star second team (1981-82 and 1984-85).

		REGULAR SEASON					PLAYOFFS				
Season Team	League	Gms.	G	A	Pts.	Pen.	Gms.	G	A	Pts.	Pen.
73-74—Toronto............................	OHA Mj. Jr. A	69	18	37	55	62	—	—	—	—	—
74-75—Toronto............................	OHA Mj. Jr. A	70	49	86	135	85	—	—	—	—	—
75-76—Houston.........................	WHA	79	17	14	31	66	17	7	7	14	18
76-77—Houston.........................	WHA	80	24	31	55	109	11	3	4	7	12
77-78—Houston.........................	WHA	65	23	41	64	103	6	1	3	4	8
78-79—New York Islanders.........	NHL	73	17	39	56	44	10	1	6	7	0
79-80—New York Islanders.........	NHL	77	14	30	44	49	21	7	9	16	18
80-81—New York Islanders.........	NHL	70	20	32	52	57	16	5	8	13	16
81-82—New York Islanders.........	NHL	80	35	58	93	57	19	6	10	16	18
82-83—New York Islanders.........	NHL	76	31	40	71	55	20	7	11	18	20

Season Team	League	REGULAR SEASON Gms.	G	A	Pts.	Pen.	PLAYOFFS Gms.	G	A	Pts.	Pen.
83-84—New York Islanders	NHL	73	27	40	67	66	17	1	3	4	31
84-85—New York Islanders	NHL	80	42	58	100	95	10	1	8	9	10
85-86—New York Islanders	NHL	65	20	41	61	50	—	—	—	—	—
—Calgary	NHL	9	3	4	7	10	22	7	9	16	49
86-87—Calgary	NHL	78	20	31	51	72	3	0	0	0	4
87-88—Calgary	NHL	74	17	41	58	84	6	2	5	7	8
88-89—Los Angeles	NHL	77	31	33	64	110	6	0	0	0	8
89-90—Los Angeles	NHL	73	31	37	68	62	10	1	2	3	6
90-91—Los Angeles	NHL	71	14	16	30	49	12	2	4	6	12
91-92—Chicago	NHL	33	1	7	8	37	—	—	—	—	—
—Quebec	NHL	19	2	4	6	14	—	—	—	—	—
WHA totals		224	64	86	150	278	34	11	14	25	38
NHL totals		1028	325	511	836	911	172	40	75	115	200

TOPOROWSKI, KERRY
RW, BLACKHAWKS

PERSONAL: Born April 9, 1971, at Prince Albert, Sask. . . . 6-2/212. . . . Shoots right.

TRANSACTIONS/CAREER NOTES: Selected by San Jose Sharks in fourth round (fourth Sharks pick, 67th overall) of NHL entry draft (June 22, 1991). . . . Traded by Sharks with second-round pick in 1992 draft to Chicago Blackhawks for D Doug Wilson (September 6, 1991).

Season Team	League	REGULAR SEASON Gms.	G	A	Pts.	Pen.	PLAYOFFS Gms.	G	A	Pts.	Pen.
89-90—Spokane Chiefs	WHL	65	1	13	14	*384	6	0	0	0	37
90-91—Spokane Chiefs	WHL	65	11	16	27	*505	15	2	2	4	*108
91-92—Indianapolis	IHL	18	1	2	3	206	—	—	—	—	—

TORCHIA, MIKE
G, NORTH STARS

PERSONAL: Born February 23, 1972, at Toronto. . . . 5-11/215. . . . Shoots left.

TRANSACTIONS/CAREER NOTES: Broke ankle (July 1989). . . . Selected by Minnesota North Stars in fourth round (second North Stars pick, 74th overall) of NHL entry draft (June 22, 1991).

HONORS: Won Hap Emms Memorial Trophy (1989-90). . . . Named to OHL All-Star first team (1990-91). . . . Named to Memorial Cup All-Star team (1989-90).

Season Team	League	REGULAR SEASON Gms.	Min.	W	L	T	GA	SO	Avg.	PLAYOFFS Gms.	Min.	W	L	GA	SO	Avg.
88-89—Kitchener	OHL	30	1672	14	9	4	112	0	4.02	2	126	0	2	8	0	3.81
89-90—Kitchener	OHL	40	2280	25	11	2	136	1	3.58	*17	*1023	*11	6	60	0	3.52
90-91—Kitchener	OHL	57	*3317	25	24	7	219	0	3.96	6	382	2	4	30	0	4.71
91-92—Kitchener	OHL	55	3042	25	24	3	203	1	4.00	14	900	7	7	47	0	3.13

TORREL, DOUGLAS
LW, CANUCKS

PERSONAL: Born April 29, 1969, at Hibbing, Minn. . . . 6-2/180. . . . Shoots right. . . . Full name: Douglas James Torrel.

HIGH SCHOOL: Hibbing (Minn.).

COLLEGE: Minnesota-Duluth.

TRANSACTIONS/CAREER NOTES: Broke hand (January 1987). . . . Selected by Vancouver Canucks in fourth round (third Canucks pick, 66th overall) of NHL entry draft (June 13, 1987).

Season Team	League	REGULAR SEASON Gms.	G	A	Pts.	Pen.	PLAYOFFS Gms.	G	A	Pts.	Pen.
85-86—Hibbing H.S.	Minn. H.S.	26	13	18	31		—	—	—	—	—
86-87—Hibbing H.S.	Minn. H.S.	20	22	21	43		—	—	—	—	—
87-88—Hibbing H.S.	Minn. H.S.	20	22	16	38	38	—	—	—	—	—
88-89—Minnesota-Duluth	WCHA	40	4	6	10	36	—	—	—	—	—
89-90—Minnesota-Duluth	WCHA	39	11	11	22	48	—	—	—	—	—
90-91—Minnesota-Duluth	WCHA	40	17	18	35	78	—	—	—	—	—
91-92—Minnesota-Duluth	WCHA	37	22	22	44	84	—	—	—	—	—

TOWNSHEND, GRAEME
RW, ISLANDERS

PERSONAL: Born October 2, 1965, at Kingston, Jamaica. . . . 6-2/225. . . . Shoots right. . . . Full name: Graeme Scott Townshend.

COLLEGE: Rensselaer Polytechnic Institute (N.Y.).

TRANSACTIONS/CAREER NOTES: Signed as free agent by Boston Bruins (May 12, 1989). . . . Suspended six games by AHL for a pre-game fight (December 15, 1990). . . . Signed as free agent by New York Islanders (September 3, 1991).

Season Team	League	REGULAR SEASON Gms.	G	A	Pts.	Pen.	PLAYOFFS Gms.	G	A	Pts.	Pen.
85-86—R.P.I.	ECAC	29	1	7	8	52	—	—	—	—	—
86-87—R.P.I.	ECAC	31	7	1	8	56	—	—	—	—	—
87-88—R.P.I.	ECAC	32	6	14	20	64	—	—	—	—	—
88-89—R.P.I.	ECAC	31	6	16	22	50	—	—	—	—	—
—Maine	AHL	5	2	1	3	11	—	—	—	—	—
89-90—Boston	NHL	4	0	0	0	7	—	—	—	—	—
—Maine	AHL	64	15	13	28	162	—	—	—	—	—
90-91—Maine	AHL	46	16	10	26	119	2	2	0	2	4
—Boston	NHL	18	2	5	7	12	—	—	—	—	—
91-92—Capital District	AHL	61	14	23	37	94	4	0	2	2	0
—New York Islanders	NHL	7	1	2	3	0	—	—	—	—	—
NHL totals		29	3	7	10	19					

TRAVERSE, PATRICK

D, SENATORS

PERSONAL: Born March 14, 1974, at Montreal. . . . 6-3/173. . . . Shoots left.
TRANSACTIONS/CAREER NOTES: Selected by Ottawa Senators in third round (third Senators pick, 50th overall) of NHL entry draft (June 20, 1992).

			REGULAR SEASON				PLAYOFFS			
Season Team	League	Gms.	G	A	Pts.	Pen.	Gms.	G	A	Pts.	Pen.
91-92—Shawinigan	QMJHL	59	3	11	14	12	10	0	0	0	4

TREBIL, DANIEL

D, DEVILS

PERSONAL: Born April 10, 1974, at Edina, Minn. . . . 6-3/185. . . . Shoots right.
HIGH SCHOOL: Thomas Jefferson (Bloomington, Minn.).
TRANSACTIONS/CAREER NOTES: Selected by New Jersey Devils in sixth round (seventh Devils pick, 138th overall) of NHL entry draft (June 20, 1992).

			REGULAR SEASON				PLAYOFFS			
Season Team	League	Gms.	G	A	Pts.	Pen.	Gms.	G	A	Pts.	Pen.
89-90—Bloomington Jefferson HS	Minn. H.S.	22	3	6	9	10	—	—	—	—	—
90-91—Bloomington Jefferson HS	Minn. H.S.	23	4	12	16	8	—	—	—	—	—
91-92—Bloomington Jefferson HS	Minn. H.S.	28	7	26	33	6	—	—	—	—	—

TRETOWICZ, DAVE

D, KINGS

PERSONAL: Born March 15, 1969, at Pittsfield, Mass. . . . 5-11/195. . . . Shoots left.
COLLEGE: Clarkson (N.Y.).
TRANSACTIONS/CAREER NOTES: Selected by Calgary Flames in 11th round (11th Flames pick, 231st overall) of NHL entry draft (June 11, 1988). . . . Signed as free agent by Los Angeles Kings (March 2, 1992).
HONORS: Named to NCAA All-Tournament team (1989-90). . . . Named to ECAC All-Star second team (1989-90). . . . Named to ECAC All-Star first team (1990-91).

			REGULAR SEASON				PLAYOFFS			
Season Team	League	Gms.	G	A	Pts.	Pen.	Gms.	G	A	Pts.	Pen.
87-88—Clarkson	ECAC	35	8	14	22	28	—	—	—	—	—
88-89—Clarkson	ECAC	32	6	17	23	22	—	—	—	—	—
89-90—Clarkson	ECAC	35	2	27	29	12	—	—	—	—	—
90-91—Clarkson	ECAC	40	4	31	35	18	—	—	—	—	—
91-92—Phoenix	IHL	16	3	2	5	14	—	—	—	—	—
—U.S. National Team	Int'l	57	1	7	8	4	—	—	—	—	—
—U.S. Olympic Team	Int'l	8	0	0	0	0	—	—	—	—	—

TROTTIER, BRYAN

C, PENGUINS

PERSONAL: Born July 17, 1956, at Val Marie, Sask. . . . 5-11/195. . . . Shoots left. . . . Full name: Bryan John Trottier.
TRANSACTIONS/CAREER NOTES: Selected by New York Islanders from Swift Current Broncos in second round (second Islanders pick, 22nd overall) of NHL amateur draft (May 28, 1974). . . . Sprained left knee (April 1983). . . . Injured left knee (January 1984). . . . Injured knee (October 1984). . . . Fined $1,000 by NHL for being critical of officiating (March 1987). . . . Suffered back spasms (March 1989); missed seven games. . . . Broke little toe on left foot (September 23, 1989). . . . Broke rib at New Jersey (December 19, 1989); missed 12 games. . . . Released by Islanders (July 3, 1990). . . . Signed as free agent by Pittsburgh Penguins (July 20, 1990). . . . Suffered lower back pain (September 1990); missed five preseason games (September 1990); missed 13 games (November 1990); missed 13 games (January 1991). . . . Sprained right knee (November 30, 1991); missed 14 games. . . . Bruised lower back (March 15, 1992); missed two games.
HONORS: Named to WCHL All-Star first team (1974-75). . . . Named NHL Rookie of the Year by THE SPORTING NEWS (1975-76). . . . Won Calder Memorial Trophy (1975-76). . . . Named to THE SPORTING NEWS All-Star first team (1977-78 and 1978-79). . . . Named to NHL All-Star first team (1977-78 and 1978-79). . . . Named NHL Player of the Year by THE SPORTING NEWS (1978-79). . . . Won Hart Memorial Trophy (1978-79). . . . Won Art Ross Trophy (1978-79). . . . Won Conn Smythe Trophy (1979-80). . . . Named to THE SPORTING NEWS All-Star second team (1981-82 and 1983-84). . . . Named to NHL All-Star second team (1981-82 and 1983-84). . . . Won Budweiser/NHL Man of the Year (1987-88). . . . Won King Clancy Memorial Trophy (1988-89).
RECORDS: Holds NHL record for most points in one period—6 (December 23, 1978). . . . Shares NHL record for most goals in one period—4 (February 13, 1982). . . . Holds NHL career playoff record for scoring points in most consecutive games—27 (1980-82). . . . Shares NHL record for fastest goal from the start of a game—5 seconds (March 22, 1984). . . . Holds NHL single-season playoff record for scoring points in most consecutive games—18 (1981). . . . Shares NHL single-game playoff records for most shorthanded goals in one period—2; and most shorthanded goals—2 (April 8, 1980).

			REGULAR SEASON				PLAYOFFS			
Season Team	League	Gms.	G	A	Pts.	Pen.	Gms.	G	A	Pts.	Pen.
72-73—Swift Current	WCHL	67	16	29	45	10	—	—	—	—	—
73-74—Swift Current	WCHL	68	41	71	112	76	13	7	8	15	8
74-75—Lethbridge	WCHL	67	46	*98	144	103	6	2	5	7	14
75-76—New York Islanders	NHL	80	32	63	95	21	13	1	7	8	8
76-77—New York Islanders	NHL	76	30	42	72	34	12	2	8	10	2
77-78—New York Islanders	NHL	77	46	*77	123	46	7	0	3	3	4
78-79—New York Islanders	NHL	76	47	*87	*134	50	10	2	4	6	13
79-80—New York Islanders	NHL	78	42	62	104	68	21	†12	17	*29	16
80-81—New York Islanders	NHL	73	31	72	103	74	18	11	†18	29	34
81-82—New York Islanders	NHL	80	50	79	129	88	19	6	*23	*29	40
82-83—New York Islanders	NHL	80	34	55	89	68	17	8	12	20	18
83-84—New York Islanders	NHL	68	40	71	111	59	21	8	6	14	49
84-85—New York Islanders	NHL	68	28	31	59	47	10	4	2	6	8
85-86—New York Islanders	NHL	78	37	59	96	72	3	1	1	2	2
86-87—New York Islanders	NHL	80	23	64	87	50	14	8	5	13	12

Season	Team	League	REGULAR SEASON					PLAYOFFS				
			Gms.	G	A	Pts.	Pen.	Gms.	G	A	Pts.	Pen.
87-88—New York Islanders	NHL	77	30	52	82	48	6	0	0	0	10
88-89—New York Islanders	NHL	73	17	28	45	44	—	—	—	—	—
89-90—New York Islanders	NHL	59	13	11	24	29	4	1	0	1	4
90-91—Pittsburgh	NHL	52	9	19	28	24	23	3	4	7	49
91-92—Pittsburgh	NHL	63	11	18	29	54	21	4	3	7	8
NHL totals		1238	520	890	1410	876	219	71	113	184	277

TUCKER, CHRIS
C, BLACKHAWKS

PERSONAL: Born February 9, 1972, at White Plains, N.Y. . . . 5-11/183. . . . Shoots left. . . . Full name: Christopher Matthew Tucker.
HIGH SCHOOL: Thomas Jefferson (Bloomington, Minn.).
COLLEGE: Wisconsin.
TRANSACTIONS/CAREER NOTES: Selected by Chicago Blackhawks in fourth round (third Blackhawks pick, 79th overall) of NHL entry draft (June 16, 1990).

Season	Team	League	REGULAR SEASON					PLAYOFFS				
			Gms.	G	A	Pts.	Pen.	Gms.	G	A	Pts.	Pen.
88-89—Bloomington Jefferson HS	Minn. H.S.	25	41	23	64		—	—	—	—	—
89-90—Bloomington Jefferson HS	Minn. H.S.	24	24	24	48		—	—	—	—	—
90-91—University of Wisconsin	WCHA	35	5	6	11	6	—	—	—	—	—
91-92—University of Wisconsin	WCHA	38	13	10	23	23	—	—	—	—	—

TUGNUTT, RON
G, OILERS

PERSONAL: Born October 22, 1967, at Scarborough, Ont. . . . 5-11/155. . . . Shoots left. . . . Full name: Ronald Frederick Bradley Tugnutt.
TRANSACTIONS/CAREER NOTES: Selected by Quebec Nordiques as underage junior in fourth round (fourth Nordiques pick, 81st overall) of NHL entry draft (June 21, 1986). . . . Sprained ankle (March 1989). . . . Sprained knee (January 13, 1990). . . . Injured hamstring (January 29, 1991); missed 11 games. . . . Traded by Nordiques with LW Brad Zavisha to Edmonton Oilers for LW Martin Rucinsky (March 10, 1992).
HONORS: Won F.W. (Dinty) Moore Trophy (1984-85). . . . Shared Dave Pinkney Trophy with Kay Whitmore (1985-86). . . . Named to OHL All-Star first team (1986-87).

Season	Team	League	REGULAR SEASON							PLAYOFFS						
			Gms.	Min.	W	L	T	GA	SO	Avg.	Gms.	Min.	W	L	GA	SO	Avg.
84-85—Peterborough	OHL	18	938	7	4	2	59	0	3.77	—	—	—	—	—	—	—
85-86—Peterborough	OHL	26	1543	18	7	0	74	1	2.88	3	133	2	0	6	0	2.71
86-87—Peterborough	OHL	31	1891	21	7	2	88	2	*2.79	6	374	3	3	21	1	3.37
87-88—Quebec	NHL	6	284	2	3	0	16	0	3.38	—	—	—	—	—	—	—
—Fredericton	AHL	34	1962	20	9	4	118	1	3.61	4	204	1	2	11	0	3.24
88-89—Quebec	NHL	26	1367	10	10	3	82	0	3.60	—	—	—	—	—	—	—
—Halifax	AHL	24	1368	14	7	2	79	1	3.46	—	—	—	—	—	—	—
89-90—Quebec	NHL	35	1978	5	24	3	152	0	4.61	—	—	—	—	—	—	—
—Halifax	AHL	6	366	1	5	0	23	0	3.77	—	—	—	—	—	—	—
90-91—Halifax	AHL	2	100	0	1	0	8	0	4.80	—	—	—	—	—	—	—
—Quebec	NHL	56	3144	12	†29	10	212	0	4.05	—	—	—	—	—	—	—
91-92—Quebec	NHL	30	1583	6	17	3	106	1	4.02	—	—	—	—	—	—	—
—Halifax	AHL	8	447	3	3	1	30	0	4.03	—	—	—	—	—	—	—
—Edmonton	NHL	3	124	1	1	0	10	0	4.84	2	60	0	0	3	0	3.00
NHL totals		156	8480	36	84	19	578	1	4.09	2	60	0	0	3	0	3.00

TULLY, BRENT
D, CANUCKS

PERSONAL: Born March 26, 1974, at Peterborough, Ont. . . . 6-3/185. . . . Shoots right.
HIGH SCHOOL: Thomas A. Stewart (Peterborough, Ont.).
TRANSACTIONS/CAREER NOTES: Selected by Vancouver Canucks in fourth round (fifth Canucks pick, 93rd overall) of NHL entry draft (June 20, 1992).

Season	Team	League	REGULAR SEASON					PLAYOFFS				
			Gms.	G	A	Pts.	Pen.	Gms.	G	A	Pts.	Pen.
90-91—Peterborough Jr. B	OHA	9	3	0	3	23	—	—	—	—	—
—Peterborough	OHL	45	3	5	8	35	2	0	0	0	0
91-92—Peterborough	OHL	65	9	23	32	65	10	0	0	0	2

TURCOTTE, DARREN
C, RANGERS

PERSONAL: Born March 2, 1968, at Boston. . . . 6-0/178. . . . Shoots left.
TRANSACTIONS/CAREER NOTES: Selected by New York Rangers as underage junior in sixth round (sixth Rangers pick, 114th overall) of NHL entry draft (June 21, 1986). . . . Separated shoulder (October 1987); missed 34 games. . . . Suffered concussion (March 1989). . . . Sprained left ankle (October 1989). . . . Injured knee (April 11, 1990). . . . Broke left foot (April 27, 1990). . . . Suffered contusion above left ankle (November 13, 1991); missed two games. . . . Bruised right foot (March 4, 1992); missed one game. . . . Reinjured right foot (March 9, 1992); missed two games.

Season	Team	League	REGULAR SEASON					PLAYOFFS				
			Gms.	G	A	Pts.	Pen.	Gms.	G	A	Pts.	Pen.
84-85—North Bay	OHL	62	33	32	65	28	8	0	2	2	0
85-86—North Bay	OHL	62	35	37	72	35	10	3	4	7	8
86-87—North Bay	OHL	55	30	48	78	20	18	12	8	20	6
87-88—Colorado	IHL	8	4	3	7	9	6	2	6	8	8
—North Bay	OHL	32	30	33	63	16	4	3	0	3	4

Season Team	League	REGULAR SEASON					PLAYOFFS				
		Gms.	G	A	Pts.	Pen.	Gms.	G	A	Pts.	Pen.
88-89—Denver	IHL	40	21	28	49	32	—	—	—	—	—
—New York Rangers	NHL	20	7	3	10	4	1	0	0	0	0
89-90—New York Rangers	NHL	76	32	34	66	32	10	1	6	7	4
90-91—New York Rangers	NHL	74	26	41	67	37	6	1	2	3	0
91-92—New York Rangers	NHL	71	30	23	53	57	8	4	0	4	6
NHL totals		241	95	101	196	130	25	6	8	14	10

TURGEON, PIERRE
C, ISLANDERS

PERSONAL: Born August 29, 1969, at Rouyn, Que. ... 6-1/203. ... Shoots left. ... Brother of Sylvain Turgeon, left winger/center, Ottawa Senators.
TRANSACTIONS/CAREER NOTES: Underwent knee surgery (June 1985). ... Selected by Buffalo Sabres as underage junior in first round (first Sabres pick, first overall) of NHL entry draft (June 13, 1987). ... Traded by Sabres with RW Benoit Hogue, D Uwe Krupp and C Dave McLlwain to New York Islanders for C Pat LaFontaine, LW Randy Wood, D Randy Hillier and future considerations (October 25, 1991). ... Injured right knee (January 3, 1992); missed three games.
HONORS: Won Michel Bergeron Trophy (1985-86). ... Won Michael Bossy Trophy (1986-87).

Season Team	League	REGULAR SEASON					PLAYOFFS				
		Gms.	G	A	Pts.	Pen.	Gms.	G	A	Pts.	Pen.
85-86—Granby	QMJHL	69	47	67	114	31	—	—	—	—	—
86-87—Granby	QMJHL	58	69	85	154	8	7	0	6	15	15
87-88—Buffalo	NHL	76	14	28	42	34	6	4	3	7	4
88-89—Buffalo	NHL	80	34	54	88	26	5	3	5	8	2
89-90—Buffalo	NHL	80	40	66	106	29	6	2	4	6	2
90-91—Buffalo	NHL	78	32	47	79	26	6	3	1	4	6
91-92—Buffalo	NHL	8	2	6	8	4	—	—	—	—	—
—New York Islanders	NHL	69	38	49	87	16	—	—	—	—	—
NHL totals		391	160	250	410	135	23	12	13	25	14

TURGEON, SYLVAIN
LW/C, SENATORS

PERSONAL: Born January 17, 1965, at Noranda, Que. ... 6-0/195. ... Shoots left. ... Brother of Pierre Turgeon, center, New York Islanders.
TRANSACTIONS/CAREER NOTES: Selected by Hartford Whalers as underage junior in first round (first Whalers pick, second overall) of NHL entry draft (June 8, 1983). ... Pulled abdominal muscles (October 1984). ... Underwent surgery to repair torn abdominal muscle (November 14, 1986); missed 39 games. ... Broke left arm during Team Canada practice (August 11, 1987). ... Sprained right knee during training camp (September 1988). ... Separated left shoulder (December 21, 1988); missed 36 games. ... Burned both eyes from ultraviolet light produced by welder's torch while working on car (February 28, 1989). ... Traded by Whalers to New Jersey Devils for RW/LW Pat Verbeek (June 17, 1989). ... Aggravated groin injury (March 20, 1990). ... Underwent hernia surgery (August 23, 1990); missed first 33 games of season. ... Traded by Devils to Montreal Canadiens for RW Claude Lemieux (September 4, 1990). ... Broke right kneecap (February 6, 1991); missed remainder of regular season and returned during playoffs. ... Selected by Ottawa Senators in NHL expansion draft (June 18, 1992).
HONORS: Won Des Instructeurs Trophy (1981-82). ... Won Association of Journalists of Hockey Trophy (1982-83). ... • Named to QMJHL All-Star first team (1982-83). ... Named to NHL All-Rookie team (1983-84).

Season Team	League	REGULAR SEASON					PLAYOFFS				
		Gms.	G	A	Pts.	Pen.	Gms.	G	A	Pts.	Pen.
81-82—Hull	QMJHL	57	33	40	73	78	14	11	11	22	16
82-83—Hull	QMJHL	67	54	109	163	103	7	8	7	15	10
83-84—Hartford	NHL	76	40	32	72	55	—	—	—	—	—
84-85—Hartford	NHL	64	31	31	62	67	—	—	—	—	—
85-86—Hartford	NHL	76	45	34	79	88	9	2	3	5	4
86-87—Hartford	NHL	41	23	13	36	45	6	1	2	3	4
87-88—Hartford	NHL	71	23	26	49	71	6	0	0	0	4
88-89—Hartford	NHL	42	16	14	30	40	4	0	2	2	4
89-90—New Jersey	NHL	72	30	17	47	81	1	0	0	0	0
90-91—Montreal	NHL	19	5	7	12	20	5	0	0	0	2
91-92—Montreal	NHL	56	9	11	20	39	5	1	0	1	4
NHL totals		517	222	185	407	506	36	4	7	11	22

TURNER, BRAD
D, ISLANDERS

PERSONAL: Born May 25, 1968, at Winnipeg, Man. ... 6-2/205. ... Shoots right.
TRANSACTIONS/CAREER NOTES: Selected by Minnesota North Stars in third round (sixth North Stars pick, 58th overall) of NHL entry draft (June 21, 1986).

Season Team	League	REGULAR SEASON					PLAYOFFS				
		Gms.	G	A	Pts.	Pen.	Gms.	G	A	Pts.	Pen.
86-87—University of Michigan	CCHA	40	3	10	13	40	—	—	—	—	—
87-88—University of Michigan	CCHA	39	3	11	14	52	—	—	—	—	—
88-89—University of Michigan	CCHA	33	3	8	11	38	—	—	—	—	—
89-90—University of Michigan	CCHA	32	8	9	17	34	—	—	—	—	—
90-91—Capital District	AHL	31	1	2	3	8	—	—	—	—	—
—Richmond	ECHL	40	16	25	41	31	—	—	—	—	—
91-92—New Haven	AHL	32	6	11	17	58	—	—	—	—	—
—Capital District	AHL	35	3	6	9	17	—	—	—	—	—
—New York Islanders	NHL	3	0	0	0	0	—	—	—	—	—
NHL totals		3	0	0	0	0					

TUTTLE, STEVE
RW, LIGHTNING

PERSONAL: Born January 5, 1966, at Vancouver, B.C. . . . . 6-1/200. . . . Shoots right. . . . Full name: Steven Walter Tuttle.
COLLEGE: Wisconsin.
TRANSACTIONS/CAREER NOTES: Selected by St. Louis Blues in sixth round (eighth Blues pick, 113th overall) of NHL entry draft (June 9, 1984). . . . Sprained left knee (December 1988); missed 15 games. . . . Sprained shoulder (February 1989). . . . Traded by Blues with D Rob Robinson, RW Darin Kimble and G Pat Jablonski to Tampa Bay Lightning for future considerations (June 19, 1992).
HONORS: Named to NCAA All-America West second team (1987-88). . . . Named to IHL All-Star first team (1991-92).

Season Team	League	REGULAR SEASON					PLAYOFFS				
		Gms.	G	A	Pts.	Pen.	Gms.	G	A	Pts.	Pen.
83-84—Richmond	BCJHL	46	46	34	80	22	—	—	—	—	—
84-85—University of Wisconsin	WCHA	28	3	4	7	0	—	—	—	—	—
85-86—University of Wisconsin	WCHA	32	2	10	12	2	—	—	—	—	—
86-87—University of Wisconsin	WCHA	42	31	21	52	14	—	—	—	—	—
87-88—University of Wisconsin	WCHA	45	27	39	66	18	—	—	—	—	—
88-89—St. Louis	NHL	53	13	12	25	6	6	1	2	3	0
89-90—St. Louis	NHL	71	12	10	22	4	5	0	1	1	2
90-91—St. Louis	NHL	20	3	6	9	2	6	0	3	3	0
—Peoria	IHL	42	24	32	56	8	—	—	—	—	—
91-92—Peoria	IHL	71	43	46	89	22	10	4	8	12	4
NHL totals		144	28	28	56	12	17	1	6	7	2

TWIST, TONY
LW, NORDIQUES

PERSONAL: Born May 9, 1968, at Sherwood Park, Alta. . . . 6-1/212. . . . Shoots left. . . . Full name: Anthony Rory Twist.
TRANSACTIONS/CAREER NOTES: Suspended three games and fined $250 by WHL for leaving the penalty box to fight (January 28, 1988). . . . Selected by St. Louis Blues in ninth round (ninth Blues pick, 177th overall) of NHL entry draft (June 11, 1988). . . . Suspended 13 games by IHL for checking goaltender after play had been blown dead (December 15, 1990). . . . Traded by Blues with RW Herb Raglan and LW Andy Rymsha to Quebec Nordiques for RW Darin Kimble (February 4, 1991).

Season Team	League	REGULAR SEASON					PLAYOFFS				
		Gms.	G	A	Pts.	Pen.	Gms.	G	A	Pts.	Pen.
86-87—Saskatoon	WHL	64	0	8	8	181	—	—	—	—	—
87-88—Saskatoon	WHL	55	1	8	9	226	10	1	1	2	6
88-89—Peoria	IHL	67	3	8	11	312	—	—	—	—	—
89-90—St. Louis	NHL	28	0	0	0	124	—	—	—	—	—
—Peoria	IHL	36	1	5	6	200	5	0	1	1	8
90-91—Peoria	IHL	38	2	10	12	244	—	—	—	—	—
—Quebec	NHL	24	0	0	0	104	—	—	—	—	—
91-92—Quebec	NHL	44	0	1	1	164	—	—	—	—	—
NHL totals		96	0	1	1	392	—	—	—	—	—

ULANOV, IGOR
D, JETS

PERSONAL: Born October 1, 1969, at Perm, U.S.S.R. . . . 6-1/198. . . . Shoots right.
TRANSACTIONS/CAREER NOTES: Selected by Winnipeg Jets in 10th round (eighth Jets pick, 203rd overall) in NHL entry draft (June 22, 1991).

Season Team	League	REGULAR SEASON					PLAYOFFS				
		Gms.	G	A	Pts.	Pen.	Gms.	G	A	Pts.	Pen.
90-91—Khimik	USSR	41	2	2	4	52	—	—	—	—	—
91-92—Winnipeg	NHL	27	2	9	11	67	7	0	0	0	39
—Moncton	AHL	3	0	1	1	16	—	—	—	—	—
NHL totals		27	2	9	11	67	7	0	0	0	39

USTORF, STEFAN
C, CAPITALS

PERSONAL: Born January 3, 1974, at Kaufbeuren, West Germany. . . . 5-11/172. . . . Shoots left.
TRANSACTIONS/CAREER NOTES: Selected by Washington Capitals in third round (third Capitals pick, 53rd overall) of NHL entry draft (June 20, 1992).

Season Team	League	REGULAR SEASON					PLAYOFFS				
		Gms.	G	A	Pts.	Pen.	Gms.	G	A	Pts.	Pen.
91-92—Kaufbeuren	Germany	41	2	22	24	46	—	—	—	—	—

VAIVE, RICK
RW, SABRES

PERSONAL: Born May 14, 1959, at Ottawa. . . . 6-1/198. . . . Shoots right. . . . Full name: Rick Claude Vaive.
TRANSACTIONS/CAREER NOTES: Signed by Birmingham Bulls as underage junior (July 1978). . . . Selected by Vancouver Canucks in first round (first Canucks pick, fifth overall) of NHL entry draft (June 9, 1979). . . . Traded by Canucks with C Bill Derlago to Toronto Maple Leafs for LW Dave Williams and RW Jerry Butler (February 1980). . . . Suffered slight groin pull (February 1981). . . . Injured ankle (February 25, 1984). . . . Injured knee (December 1984). . . . Injured hand (December 23, 1985); missed 12 games. . . . Pinched nerve in neck (October 1986). . . . Traded by Maple Leafs with LW Steve Thomas and D Bob McGill to Chicago Blackhawks for LW Al Secord and RW Ed Olczyk (September 1987). . . . Traded by Blackhawks to Buffalo Sabres for C Adam Creighton (December 26, 1988). . . . Injured stomach muscle (January 27, 1989). . . . Pinched nerve in neck (February 19, 1989). . . . Pulled groin (November 22, 1989). . . . Pinched knee cartilage during training camp and underwent surgery (September 7, 1990). . . . Bruised left shoulder (October 31, 1990); missed six games. . . . Lacerated hand (February 8, 1992); missed four games.
HONORS: Won Rookie of the Year Award (1976-77).

Season	Team	League	REGULAR SEASON					PLAYOFFS				
			Gms.	G	A	Pts.	Pen.	Gms.	G	A	Pts.	Pen.
76-77—Sherbrooke	QMJHL	68	51	59	110	91	18	10	13	23	78
77-78—Sherbrooke	QMJHL	68	76	79	155	199	9	8	4	12	38
78-79—Birmingham	WHA	75	26	33	59	†248	—	—	—	—	—
79-80—Vancouver	NHL	47	13	8	21	111					
—Toronto	NHL	22	9	7	16	77	3	1	0	1	11
80-81—Toronto	NHL	75	33	29	62	229	3	1	0	1	4
81-82—Toronto	NHL	77	54	35	89	157					
82-83—Toronto	NHL	78	51	28	79	105	4	2	5	7	6
83-84—Toronto	NHL	76	52	41	93	114					
84-85—Toronto	NHL	72	35	33	68	112					
85-86—Toronto	NHL	61	33	31	64	85	9	6	2	8	9
86-87—Toronto	NHL	73	32	34	66	61	13	4	2	6	23
87-88—Chicago	NHL	76	43	26	69	108	5	6	2	8	38
88-89—Chicago	NHL	30	12	13	25	60					
—Buffalo	NHL	28	19	13	32	64	5	2	1	3	8
89-90—Buffalo	NHL	70	29	19	48	74	6	4	2	6	6
90-91—Buffalo	NHL	71	25	27	52	74	6	1	2	3	6
91-92—Buffalo	NHL	20	1	3	4	14					
—Rochester	AHL	12	4	9	13	4	16	4	4	8	10
WHA totals		75	20	00	50	248					
NHL totals		876	441	347	788	1445	54	27	16	43	111

VALIMONT, CARL
D, CANUCKS

PERSONAL: Born March 1, 1966, at Southington, Conn. . . . 6-1/200. . . . Shoots left. . . . Full name: Carl A. Valimont.
COLLEGE: Lowell (Mass.).
TRANSACTIONS/CAREER NOTES: Selected by Vancouver Canucks in 10th round (10th Canucks pick, 193rd overall) of NHL entry draft (June 15, 1985).

Season	Team	League	REGULAR SEASON					PLAYOFFS				
			Gms.	G	A	Pts.	Pen.	Gms.	G	A	Pts.	Pen.
84-85—University of Lowell	Hockey East	40	4	11	15	24	—	—	—	—	—
85-86—University of Lowell	Hockey East	26	1	9	10	12	—	—	—	—	—
86-87—University of Lowell	Hockey East	36	8	9	17	36	—	—	—	—	—
87-88—University of Lowell	Hockey East	38	6	26	32	59	—	—	—	—	—
88-89—Milwaukee	IHL	79	4	33	37	56	11	2	8	10	12
89-90—Milwaukee	IHL	78	13	28	41	48	3	0	1	1	6
90-91—Milwaukee	IHL	80	10	21	31	66	6	2	1	3	2
91-92—Milwaukee	IHL	71	14	31	45	81	5	0	2	2	4

VALK, GARRY
LW/RW, CANUCKS

PERSONAL: Born November 27, 1967, at Edmonton, Alta. . . . 6-1/190. . . . Shoots left. . . . Full name: Garry P. Valk.
COLLEGE: North Dakota.
TRANSACTIONS/CAREER NOTES: Selected by Vancouver Canucks in sixth round (fifth Canucks pick, 108th overall) of NHL entry draft (June 13, 1987). . . . Sprained thumb (November 24, 1991); missed one game. . . . Sprained shoulder (January 21, 1992); missed eight games.

Season	Team	League	REGULAR SEASON					PLAYOFFS				
			Gms.	G	A	Pts.	Pen.	Gms.	G	A	Pts.	Pen.
85-86—Sherwood Park	AJHL	40	20	26	46	116	—	—	—	—	—
86-87—Sherwood Park	AJHL	59	42	44	86	204	—	—	—	—	—
87-88—Univ. of North Dakota	WCHA	38	23	12	35	64	—	—	—	—	—
88-89—Univ. of North Dakota	WCHA	40	14	17	31	71	—	—	—	—	—
89-90—Univ. of North Dakota	WCHA	43	22	17	39	92	—	—	—	—	—
90-91—Vancouver	NHL	59	10	11	21	67	5	0	0	0	20
—Milwaukee	IHL	10	12	4	16	13	3	0	0	0	2
91-92—Vancouver	NHL	65	8	17	25	56	4	0	0	0	5
NHL totals		124	18	28	46	123	9	0	0	0	25

VALLIS, LINDSAY
RW, CANADIENS

PERSONAL: Born January 12, 1971, at Winnipeg, Man. . . . 6-3/207. . . . Shoots right.
TRANSACTIONS/CAREER NOTES: Selected by Montreal Canadiens in first round (first Canadiens pick, 13th overall) of NHL entry draft (June 17, 1989).

Season	Team	League	REGULAR SEASON					PLAYOFFS				
			Gms.	G	A	Pts.	Pen.	Gms.	G	A	Pts.	Pen.
87-88—Seattle	WHL	68	31	45	76	65	—	—	—	—	—
88-89—Seattle	WHL	63	21	32	53	48	—	—	—	—	—
89-90—Seattle	WHL	65	34	43	77	68	13	6	5	11	14
90-91—Seattle	WHL	72	41	38	79	119	6	1	3	4	17
—Fredericton	AHL	—	—	—	—	—	7	0	0	0	6
91-92—Fredericton	AHL	71	10	19	29	84	4	0	1	1	7

VAN ALLEN, SHAUN
C, OILERS

PERSONAL: Born August 29, 1967, at Shaunavon, Sask. . . . 6-1/200. . . . Shoots left.
TRANSACTIONS/CAREER NOTES: Selected by Edmonton Oilers in fifth round (fifth Oilers pick, 105th overall) of NHL entry draft (June 13, 1987).

Named to AHL All-Star second team (1990-91).... Won John B. Sollenberger Trophy (1991-92).... Named to AHL All-Star first team (1991-92).

Season Team	League	REGULAR SEASON					PLAYOFFS				
		Gms.	G	A	Pts.	Pen.	Gms.	G	A	Pts.	Pen.
84-85—Swift Current	SAJHL	61	12	20	32	136	—	—	—	—	—
85-86—Saskatoon	WHL	55	12	11	23	43	13	4	8	12	28
86-87—Saskatoon	WHL	72	38	59	97	116	11	4	6	10	24
87-88—Nova Scotia	AHL	19	4	10	14	17	4	1	1	2	4
—Milwaukee	IHL	40	14	28	42	34	—	—	—	—	—
88-89—Cape Breton	AHL	76	32	42	74	81	—	—	—	—	—
89-90—Cape Breton	AHL	61	25	44	69	83	4	0	2	2	8
90-91—Edmonton	NHL	2	0	0	0	0	—	—	—	—	—
—Cape Breton	AHL	76	25	75	100	182	4	0	1	1	8
91-92—Cape Breton	AHL	77	29	*84	*113	80	5	3	7	10	14
NHL totals		2	0	0	0	0					

VANBIESBROUCK, JOHN
G, RANGERS

PERSONAL: Born September 4, 1963, at Detroit.... 5-8/172.... Shoots left.

TRANSACTIONS/CAREER NOTES: Selected by New York Rangers in fourth round (fifth Rangers pick, 72nd overall) of NHL entry draft (June 10, 1981).... Fractured jaw (October 1987).... Severely lacerated wrist (June 1988).... Underwent knee surgery (May 11, 1990).... Suffered lower back spasms (February 25, 1992); missed 11 games.

HONORS: Won F.W. (Dinty) Moore Trophy (1980-81).... Shared Dave Pinkney Trophy with Marc D'Amour (1981-82).... Named to OHL All-Star second team (1982-83).... Shared Tommy Ivan Trophy with D Bruce Affleck (1983-84).... Shared Terry Sawchuk Trophy with Ron Scott (1983-84).... Named to CHL All-Star first team (1983-84).... Won Vezina Trophy (1985-86).... Named to THE SPORTING NEWS All-Star first team (1985-86).... Named to NHL All-Star first team (1985-86).

Season Team	League	REGULAR SEASON								PLAYOFFS						
		Gms.	Min.	W	L	T	GA	SO	Avg.	Gms.	Min.	W	L	GA	SO	Avg.
80-81—Sault Ste. Marie	OMJHL	56	2941	31	16	1	203	0	4.14	11	457	3	3	24	1	3.15
81-82—Sault Ste. Marie	OHL	31	1686	12	12	2	102	0	3.63	7	276	1	4	20	0	4.35
—New York Rangers	NHL	1	60	1	0	0	1	0	1.00	—	—	—	—	—	—	—
82-83—Sault Ste. Marie	OHL	*62	3471	39	21	1	209	0	3.61	16	944	7	6	56	†1	3.56
83-84—New York Rangers	NHL	3	180	2	1	0	10	0	3.33	1	1	0	0	0	0	0.00
—Tulsa	CHL	37	2153	20	13	2	124	*3	3.46	4	240	4	0	10	0	*2.50
84-85—New York Rangers	NHL	42	2358	12	24	3	166	1	4.22	1	20	0	0	0	0	0.00
85-86—New York Rangers	NHL	61	3326	31	21	5	184	3	3.32	16	899	8	8	49	†1	3.27
86-87—New York Rangers	NHL	50	2656	18	20	5	161	0	3.64	4	195	1	3	11	1	3.38
87-88—New York Rangers	NHL	56	3319	27	22	7	187	2	3.38	—	—	—	—	—	—	—
88-89—New York Rangers	NHL	56	3207	28	21	4	197	0	3.69	2	107	0	1	6	0	3.36
89-90—New York Rangers	NHL	47	2734	19	19	7	154	1	3.38	6	298	2	3	15	0	3.02
90-91—New York Rangers	NHL	40	2257	15	18	6	126	3	3.35	1	52	0	0	1	0	1.15
91-92—New York Rangers	NHL	45	2526	27	13	3	120	2	2.85	7	368	2	5	23	0	3.75
NHL totals		401	22623	180	159	40	1306	12	3.46	38	1940	13	20	105	2	3.25

VAN DORP, WAYNE
LW, NORDIQUES

PERSONAL: Born May 19, 1961, at Vancouver, B.C.... 6-4/225.... Shoots right.

TRANSACTIONS/CAREER NOTES: Traded by Buffalo Sabres with RW Norm Lacombe and future considerations to Edmonton Oilers for D Lee Fogolin and RW Mark Napier (March 1987).... Traded by Oilers with D Paul Coffey and LW Dave Hunter to Pittsburgh Penguins for D Chris Joseph, C Craig Simpson, C Dave Hannan and D Moe Mantha (November 1987).... Injured right knee during team practice (February 1988).... Traded by Penguins to Buffalo Sabres for future considerations (October 3, 1988).... Suspended two games by AHL (December 2, 1988).... Traded by Sabres to Chicago Blackhawks for future considerations (February 16, 1989).... Suspended 10 games and fined $500 by NHL for fighting (December 28, 1989).... Tore right shoulder muscle during training camp (September 1990); missed first 21 games of season.... Selected by Quebec Nordiques in NHL waiver draft for $50,000 (October 1, 1990).... Reinjured shoulder and underwent surgery (November 24, 1990); missed remainder of season.... Separated shoulder (October 23, 1991); missed seven games.... Injured groin (November 22, 1991); missed ten games.... Bruised ankle (February 13, 1992); missed four games.

HONORS: Named Playoff Most Valuable Player (1985-86).

Season Team	League	REGULAR SEASON					PLAYOFFS				
		Gms.	G	A	Pts.	Pen.	Gms.	G	A	Pts.	Pen.
78-79—Billington	BCJHL	61	18	30	48	66	—	—	—	—	—
79-80—Seattle	WHL	68	8	13	21	195	12	3	1	4	33
80-81—Seattle	WHL	63	22	30	52	242	5	1	0	1	10
81-82—						Did not play.					
82-83—						Did not play.					
83-84—Erie	AHL	45	19	18	37	131	—	—	—	—	—
84-85—Gronigen	Holland	29	38	46	84	112	6	6	2	8	23
—Erie	AHL	7	9	8	17	21	10	0	2	2	2
85-86—Gronigen	Holland	29	19	24	43	81	8	9	*12	21	6
86-87—Rochester	AHL	47	7	3	10	192	—	—	—	—	—
—Nova Scotia	AHL	11	2	3	5	37	5	0	0	0	56
—Edmonton	NHL	3	0	0	0	25	3	0	0	0	2
87-88—Pittsburgh	NHL	25	1	3	4	75	—	—	—	—	—
—Nova Scotia	AHL	12	2	2	4	87	—	—	—	—	—

Season Team	League	REGULAR SEASON Gms.	G	A	Pts.	Pen.	PLAYOFFS Gms.	G	A	Pts.	Pen.
88-89—Rochester	AHL	28	3	6	9	202	—	—	—	—	—
—Chicago	NHL	8	0	0	0	23	16	0	1	1	17
—Saginaw	IHL	11	4	3	7	60	—	—	—	—	—
89-90—Chicago	NHL	61	7	4	11	303	8	0	0	0	23
90-91—Quebec	NHL	4	1	0	1	30	—	—	—	—	—
91-92—Quebec	NHL	24	3	5	8	109	—	—	—	—	—
—Halifax	AHL	15	5	5	10	54	—	—	—	—	—
NHL totals		125	12	12	24	565	27	0	1	1	42

VAN KESSEL, JOHN
RW, SENATORS

PERSONAL: Born December 19, 1969, at Bridgewater, Ont. . . . 6-4/193. . . . Shoots right.
TRANSACTIONS/CAREER NOTES: Selected by Los Angeles Kings in third round (third Kings pick, 49th overall) of NHL entry draft (June 11, 1988). . . . Selected by Ottawa Senators in NHL expansion draft (June 18, 1992).

Season Team	League	REGULAR SEASON Gms.	G	A	Pts.	Pen.	PLAYOFFS Gms.	G	A	Pts.	Pen.
86-87—Belleville Bulls	OHL	61	1	10	11	58	—	—	—	—	—
87-88—North Bay	OHL	50	13	10	29	214	4	1	1	2	16
88-89—North Bay	OHL	50	7	13	20	218	11	2	4	6	31
89-90—North Bay	OHL	40	7	21	28	127	5	0	3	3	16
—New Haven	AHL	6	1	1	2	9	—	—	—	—	—
90-91—Phoenix	IHL	65	15	15	30	246	3	1	1	2	16
91-92—Phoenix	IHL	44	2	6	8	247	—	—	—	—	—
NHL totals		125	12	12	24	565	27	0	1	1	42

VARGA, JOHN
LW, CAPITALS

PERSONAL: Born January 31, 1974, at Chicago. . . . 5-10/170. . . . Shoots left.
HIGH SCHOOL: Clover Park (Tacoma, Wash.).
TRANSACTIONS/CAREER NOTES: Selected by Washington Capitals in fifth round (fifth Capitals pick, 119th overall) of NHL entry draft (June 20, 1992).

Season Team	League	REGULAR SEASON Gms.	G	A	Pts.	Pen.	PLAYOFFS Gms.	G	A	Pts.	Pen.
91-92—Tacoma	WHL	72	25	34	59	93	4	1	2	3	0

VARVIO, JARKKO
RW, NORTH STARS

PERSONAL: Born April 28, 1972, at Tampere, Finland. . . . 5-9/172. . . . Shoots right.
TRANSACTIONS/CAREER NOTES: Selected by Minnesota North Stars in second round (first North Stars pick, 34th overall) of NHL entry draft (June 20, 1992).

Season Team	League	REGULAR SEASON Gms.	G	A	Pts.	Pen.	PLAYOFFS Gms.	G	A	Pts.	Pen.
89 90—Ilves Tampere	Finland	1	0	0	0	0	—	—	—	—	—
90-91—Ilves Tampere	Finland	37	10	7	17	6	—	—	—	—	—
91-92—HPK Hameenlinna	Finland	41	25	9	34	6	—	—	—	—	—

VARY, JOHN
D, RANGERS

PERSONAL: Born February 11, 1972, at Owen Sound, Ont. . . . 6-1/207. . . . Shoots right.
TRANSACTIONS/CAREER NOTES: Injured knee during 1988-89 season. . . . Selected by New York Rangers in third round (third Rangers pick, 55th overall) of NHL entry draft (June 16, 1990).

Season Team	League	REGULAR SEASON Gms.	G	A	Pts.	Pen.	PLAYOFFS Gms.	G	A	Pts.	Pen.
87-88—Owen Sound Jr. B	OHA	43	16	25	41	171	—	—	—	—	—
88-89—North Bay	OHL	45	2	7	9	38	3	0	0	0	0
89-90—North Bay	OHL	59	7	39	46	79	5	0	2	2	8
90-91—North Bay	OHL	39	5	21	26	108	—	—	—	—	—
—Kingston	OHL	31	5	15	20	16	—	—	—	—	—
91-92—Kingston	OHL	54	11	38	49	102	—	—	—	—	—
—Binghamton	AHL	1	0	0	0	0	—	—	—	—	—

VASKE, DENNIS
D, ISLANDERS

PERSONAL: Born October 11, 1967, at Rockford, Ill. . . . 6-2/210. . . . Shoots left. . . . Full name: Dennis James Vaske.
HIGH SCHOOL: Armstrong (Plymouth, Minn.).
COLLEGE: Minnesota-Duluth.
TRANSACTIONS/CAREER NOTES: Selected by New York Islanders in second round (second Islanders pick, 38th overall) of NHL entry draft (June 21, 1986).

Season Team	League	REGULAR SEASON Gms.	G	A	Pts.	Pen.	PLAYOFFS Gms.	G	A	Pts.	Pen.
84-85—Armstrong H.S.	Minn. H.S.	22	5	18	23		—	—	—	—	—
85-86—Armstrong H.S.	Minn. H.S.	20	9	13	22		—	—	—	—	—
86-87—Minnesota-Duluth	WCHA	33	0	2	2	40	—	—	—	—	—
87-88—Minnesota-Duluth	WCHA	39	1	6	7	90	—	—	—	—	—
88-89—Minnesota-Duluth	WCHA	37	9	19	28	86	—	—	—	—	—
89-90—Minnesota-Duluth	WCHA	37	5	24	29	72	—	—	—	—	—

Season Team	League	REGULAR SEASON					PLAYOFFS				
		Gms.	G	A	Pts.	Pen.	Gms.	G	A	Pts.	Pen.
90-91—New York Islanders..........	NHL	5	0	0	0	2	—	—	—	—	—
—Capital District................	AHL	67	10	10	20	65	—	—	—	—	—
91-92—Capital District................	AHL	31	1	11	12	59	—	—	—	—	—
—New York Islanders..........	NHL	39	0	1	1	39	—	—	—	—	—
NHL totals................................		44	0	1	1	41					

VEILLEUX, STEVE
D, CANADIENS

PERSONAL: Born March 9, 1969, at Montreal. . . . 6-0/190. . . . Shoots right.
TRANSACTIONS/CAREER NOTES: Selected by Vancouver Canucks as underage junior in third round (second Canucks pick, 45th overall) of NHL entry draft (June 13, 1987). . . . Signed as free agent by Montreal Canadiens (August 6, 1991).
HONORS: Named to QMJHL All-Star second team (1987-88).

Season Team	League	REGULAR SEASON					PLAYOFFS				
		Gms.	G	A	Pts.	Pen.	Gms.	G	A	Pts.	Pen.
85-86—Trois-Rivieres................	QMJHL	67	1	20	21	132	5	0	0	0	13
86-87—Trois-Rivieres................	QMJHL	62	6	22	28	227	—	—	—	—	—
87-88—Trois-Rivieres................	QMJHL	63	7	25	32	150	—	—	—	—	—
88-89—Trois-Rivieres................	QMJHL	49	5	28	33	149	4	0	0	0	10
—Milwaukee......................	IHL	1	0	0	0	0	4	0	0	0	13
89-90—Milwaukee......................	IHL	76	4	12	16	195	2	0	0	0	2
90-91—Milwaukee......................	IHL	58	0	9	9	152	—	—	—	—	—
—Indianapolis..................	IHL	11	1	3	4	30	7	0	3	3	13
91-92—Fredericton	AHL	53	3	7	10	122					

VELISCHEK, RANDY
D, NORDIQUES

PERSONAL: Born February 10, 1962, at Montreal. . . . 6-0/200. . . . Shoots left. . . . Full name: Randolph John Velischek.
COLLEGE: Providence.
TRANSACTIONS/CAREER NOTES: Selected by Minnesota North Stars as underage player in third round (third North Stars pick, 53rd overall) of NHL entry draft (June 11, 1980). . . . Acquired by New Jersey Devils in NHL waiver draft (1985-86). . . . Sprained left knee during training camp (September 1988). . . . Suffered concussion (March 20, 1990). . . . Traded by Devils to Quebec Nordiques to complete trade of C Peter Stastny from Nordiques to Devils for D Craig Wolanin and future considerations on March 6, 1990 (August 1990). . . . Fractured foot (October 24, 1991); missed 13 games. . . . Suffered from the flu (December 1991); missed two games.
HONORS: Named to ECAC All-Star second team (1981-82). . . . Named ECAC Player of the Year (1982-83). . . . Named to NCAA All-America East team (1982-83). . . . Named to ECAC All-Star first team (1982-83).

Season Team	League	REGULAR SEASON					PLAYOFFS				
		Gms.	G	A	Pts.	Pen.	Gms.	G	A	Pts.	Pen.
79-80—Providence College	ECAC	31	5	5	10	20	—	—	—	—	—
80-81—Providence College	ECAC	33	3	12	15	26	—	—	—	—	—
81-82—Providence College	ECAC	33	1	14	15	34	—	—	—	—	—
82-83—Providence College	ECAC	41	18	34	52	50	—	—	—	—	—
—Minnesota	NHL	3	0	0	0	2	9	0	0	0	0
83-84—Salt Lake City................	IHL	43	7	21	28	54	5	0	3	3	2
—Minnesota	NHL	33	2	2	4	10	1	0	0	0	0
84-85—Springfield....................	AHL	26	2	7	9	22	—	—	—	—	—
—Minnesota	NHL	52	4	9	13	26	9	2	3	5	8
85-86—New Jersey....................	NHL	47	2	7	9	39	—	—	—	—	—
—Maine............................	AHL	21	0	4	4	4	—	—	—	—	—
86-87—New Jersey....................	NHL	64	2	16	18	52	—	—	—	—	—
87-88—New Jersey....................	NHL	51	3	9	12	66	19	0	2	2	20
88-89—New Jersey....................	NHL	80	4	14	18	70	—	—	—	—	—
89-90—New Jersey....................	NHL	62	0	6	6	72	6	0	0	0	4
90-91—Quebec	NHL	79	2	10	12	42	—	—	—	—	—
91-92—Quebec	NHL	38	2	3	5	22	—	—	—	—	—
—Halifax..........................	AHL	16	3	6	9	0	—	—	—	—	—
NHL totals...........................		509	21	76	97	401	44	2	5	7	32

VERBEEK, PAT
LW, WHALERS

PERSONAL: Born May 24, 1964, at Sarnia, Ont. . . . 5-9/190. . . . Shoots right.
TRANSACTIONS/CAREER NOTES: Selected by New Jersey Devils as underage junior in third round (third Devils pick, 43rd overall) of NHL entry draft (June 9, 1982). . . . Suffered severed left thumb between knuckles in a corn-planting machine on his farm and underwent surgery to have thumb reconnected (May 15, 1985). . . . Pulled side muscle (March 1987). . . . Bruised chest (October 28, 1988). . . . Traded by Devils to Hartford Whalers for LW Sylvain Turgeon (June 17, 1989). . . . Missed first three games of 1991-92 season due to contract dispute.
HONORS: Won Emms Family Award (1981-82).
STATISTICAL NOTES: Only NHL player ever to lead his team in goals scored and penalty minutes. (1989-90 and 1990-91).

Season Team	League	REGULAR SEASON					PLAYOFFS				
		Gms.	G	A	Pts.	Pen.	Gms.	G	A	Pts.	Pen.
80-81—Petrolia Jr. B.	OPJHL	42	44	44	88	155	—	—	—	—	—
81-82—Sudbury........................	OHL	66	37	51	88	180	—	—	—	—	—
82-83—Sudbury........................	OHL	61	40	67	107	184	—	—	—	—	—
—New Jersey......................	NHL	6	3	2	5	8	—	—	—	—	—

Season Team	League	REGULAR SEASON					PLAYOFFS				
		Gms.	G	A	Pts.	Pen.	Gms.	G	A	Pts.	Pen.
83-84—New Jersey	NHL	79	20	27	47	158	—	—	—	—	—
84-85—New Jersey	NHL	78	15	18	33	162	—	—	—	—	—
85-86—New Jersey	NHL	76	25	28	53	79	—	—	—	—	—
86-87—New Jersey	NHL	74	35	24	59	120	—	—	—	—	—
87-88—New Jersey	NHL	73	46	31	77	227	20	4	8	12	51
88-89—New Jersey	NHL	77	26	21	47	189	—	—	—	—	—
89-90—Hartford	NHL	80	44	45	89	228	7	2	2	4	26
90-91—Hartford	NHL	80	43	39	82	246	6	3	2	5	40
91-92—Hartford	NHL	76	22	35	57	243	7	0	2	2	12
NHL totals		699	279	270	549	1660	40	9	14	23	129

VERMETTE, MARK

RW, NORDIQUES

PERSONAL: Born October 3, 1967, at Cochenour, Ont. . . . 6-1/203. . . . Shoots right. . . . Full name: Mark A. Vermette.
COLLEGE: Lake Superior State (Mich.).
TRANSACTIONS/CAREER NOTES: Selected by Quebec Nordiques in seventh round (eighth Nordiques pick, 134th overall) of NHL entry draft (June 21, 1986).

Season Team	League	REGULAR SEASON					PLAYOFFS				
		Gms.	G	A	Pts.	Pen.	Gms.	G	A	Pts.	Pen.
85-86—Lake Superior State	CCHA	32	1	4	5	7	—	—	—	—	—
86-87—Lake Superior State	CCHA	38	19	17	36	59	—	—	—	—	—
87-88—Lake Superior State	CCHA	46	45	29	74	154	—	—	—	—	—
88-89—Quebec	NHL	12	0	4	4	7	—	—	—	—	—
—Halifax	AHL	52	12	16	28	30	1	0	0	0	0
89-90—Quebec	NHL	11	1	5	6	8	—	—	—	—	—
—Halifax	AHL	47	20	17	37	44	6	1	5	6	6
90-91—Halifax	AHL	46	26	22	48	37	—	—	—	—	—
—Quebec	NHL	34	3	4	7	10	—	—	—	—	—
91-92—Quebec	NHL	10	1	0	1	8	—	—	—	—	—
—Halifax	AHL	44	21	18	39	39	—	—	—	—	—
NHL totals		67	5	13	18	33					

VERNER, ANDREW

G, OILERS

PERSONAL: Born November 10, 1972, at Weston, Ont. . . . 6-0/194. . . . Shoots left.
TRANSACTIONS/CAREER NOTES: Selected by Edmonton Oilers in second round (second Oilers pick, 34th overall) of NHL entry draft (June 22, 1991).
HONORS: Named to OHL All-Star second team (1990-91 and 1991-92).

Season Team	League	REGULAR SEASON							PLAYOFFS						
		Gms.	Min.	W	L	T	GA	SO	Avg.	Gms.	Min.	W	L	GA	SO	Avg.
89-90—Peterborough	OHL	13	624	7	3	0	38	0	3.65	—	—	—	—	—	—	—
90-91—Peterborough	OHL	46	2523	22	14	7	148	0	3.52	3	185	0	3	15	0	4.86
91-92—Peterborough	OHL	53	3123	*34	13	6	190	1	3.65	10	539	5	5	30	0	3.34

VERNON, MIKE

G, FLAMES

PERSONAL: Born February 24, 1963, at Calgary, Alta. . . . 5-9/170. . . . Shoots left.
TRANSACTIONS/CAREER NOTES: Selected by Calgary Flames in third round (second Flames pick, 56th overall) of NHL entry draft (June 10, 1981). . . . Injured hip (March 2, 1988). . . . Suffered back spasms (February 1989). . . . Suffered back spasms (March 1990); missed 10 games.
HONORS: Won Most Valuable Player Trophy (1981-82 and 1982-83). . . . Won Top Goaltender Trophy (1981-82 and 1982-83). . . . Won WHL Player of the Year Award (1981-82). . . . Named to WHL All-Star first team (1982-83). . . . Named to CHL All-Star second team (1983-84). . . . Named to THE SPORTING NEWS All-Star second team (1988-89). . . . Named to NHL All-Star second team (1988-89).
RECORDS: Shares NHL single-season playoff record for most wins by a goaltender—16 (1989).

Season Team	League	REGULAR SEASON							PLAYOFFS						
		Gms.	Min.	W	L	T	GA	SO	Avg.	Gms.	Min.	W	L	GA	SO	Avg.
80-81—Calgary	WHL	59	3154	33	17	1	198	1	3.77	22	1271			82	1	3.87
81-82—Oklahoma City	CHL	—	—	—	—	—	—	—	—	1	70	0	1	4	0	3.43
—Calgary	WHL	42	2329	22	14	2	143	*3	*3.68	9	527			30	0	*3.42
82-83—Calgary	WHL	50	2856	19	18	2	155	*3	*3.26	16	925	9	7	60	0	3.89
—Calgary	NHL	2	100	0	2	0	11	0	6.60	—	—	—	—	—	—	—
83-84—Calgary	NHL	1	11	0	1	0	4	0	21.82	—	—	—	—	—	—	—
—Colorado	CHL	*46	*2648	30	13	2	148	1	*3.35	6	347	2	4	21	0	3.63
84-85—Moncton	AHL	41	2050	10	20	4	134	0	3.92	—	—	—	—	—	—	—
85-86—Salt Lake City	IHL	10	601				34	1	3.39	—	—	—	—	—	—	—
—Moncton	AHL	6	374	3	1	2	21	0	3.37	—	—	—	—	—	—	—
—Calgary	NHL	18	921	9	3	3	52	1	3.39	*21	*1229	12	*9	*60	0	2.93
86-87—Calgary	NHL	54	2957	30	21	1	178	1	3.61	5	263	2	3	16	0	3.65
87-88—Calgary	NHL	64	3565	39	16	7	210	1	3.53	9	515	4	4	34	0	3.96
88-89—Calgary	NHL	52	2938	*37	6	5	130	0	2.65	*22	*1381	*16	5	*52	*3	2.26
89-90—Calgary	NHL	47	2795	23	14	9	146	0	3.13	6	342	2	3	19	0	3.33
90-91—Calgary	NHL	54	3121	31	19	3	172	1	3.31	7	427	3	4	21	0	2.95
91-92—Calgary	NHL	63	3640	24	30	9	217	0	3.58	—	—	—	—	—	—	—
NHL totals		355	20048	193	112	37	1120	4	3.35	70	4157	39	28	202	3	2.92

— 629 —

VESEY, JIM

C, BRUINS

PERSONAL: Born September 29, 1965, at Charlestown, Mass. . . . 6-1/200. . . . Shoots right. . . . Full name: James Edward Vesey.
COLLEGE: Merrimack (Mass.).
TRANSACTIONS/CAREER NOTES: Selected by St. Louis Blues in eighth round (11th Blues pick, 155th overall) of NHL entry draft (June 9, 1984). . . . Broke two bones above right wrist (April 20, 1990). . . . Traded by Blues to Winnipeg Jets to complete February 28, 1991 deal in which Jets traded G Tom Draper to Blues (May 24, 1991). . . . Traded by Jets to Boston Bruins for future considerations (June 20, 1991). . . . Injured shoulder (November 14, 1991). . . . Underwent shoulder surgery (January 6, 1992); missed remainder of season.
HONORS: Named to IHL All-Star first team (1988-89).

Season Team	League	—REGULAR SEASON—					—PLAYOFFS—				
		Gms.	G	A	Pts.	Pen.	Gms.	G	A	Pts.	Pen.
84-85—Merrimack College	ECAC-II	33	19	11	30	28	—	—	—	—	—
85-86—Merrimack College	ECAC-II	32	29	32	61	67	—	—	—	—	—
86-87—Merrimack College	ECAC-II	35	22	36	58	57	—	—	—	—	—
87-88—Merrimack College	ECAC-II	40	40	55	95	95	—	—	—	—	—
88-89—St. Louis	NHL	5	1	1	2	7	—	—	—	—	—
—Peoria	IHL	76	47	46	93	137	4	1	2	3	6
89-90—St. Louis	NHL	6	0	1	1	0	—	—	—	—	—
—Peoria	IHL	60	47	44	91	75	5	1	3	4	21
90-91—Peoria	IHL	58	32	41	73	69	19	4	14	18	26
91-92—Maine	AHL	10	6	7	13	13	—	—	—	—	—
—Boston	NHL	4	0	0	0	0	—	—	—	—	—
NHL totals		15	1	2	3	7					

VIAL, DENNIS

D, RED WINGS

PERSONAL: Born April 10, 1969, at Sault Ste. Marie, Ont. . . . 6-1/200. . . . Shoots left.
TRANSACTIONS/CAREER NOTES: Suspended three games by OHL for spearing (October 1986). . . . Selected by New York Rangers in sixth round (fifth Rangers pick, 110th overall) of NHL entry draft (June 11, 1988). . . . Suspended indefinitely by OHL for leaving the bench to fight (March 23, 1989). . . . Traded by Rangers with C Kevin Miller and RW Jim Cummins to Detroit Red Wings for RW Joe Kocur and D Per Djoos (March 5, 1991). . . . Injured right knee and ankle (December 7, 1991); missed two games.

Season Team	League	—REGULAR SEASON—					—PLAYOFFS—				
		Gms.	G	A	Pts.	Pen.	Gms.	G	A	Pts.	Pen.
85-86—Hamilton	OHL	31	1	1	2	66	—	—	—	—	—
86-87—Hamilton	OHL	53	1	8	9	194	8	0	0	0	8
87-88—Hamilton	OHL	52	3	17	20	229	13	2	2	4	49
88-89—Niagara Falls	OHL	50	10	27	37	230	15	1	7	8	44
89-90—Flint	IHL	79	6	29	35	351	4	0	0	0	10
90-91—Binghamton	AHL	40	2	7	9	250	—	—	—	—	—
—New York Rangers	NHL	21	0	0	0	61	—	—	—	—	—
—Detroit	NHL	9	0	0	0	16	—	—	—	—	—
91-92—Detroit	NHL	27	1	0	1	72	—	—	—	—	—
—Adirondack	AHL	20	2	4	6	107	17	1	3	4	43
NHL totals		57	1	0	1	149					

VILGRAIN, CLAUDE

RW, DEVILS

PERSONAL: Born March 1, 1963, at Port-au-Prince, Haiti. . . . 6-1/205. . . . Shoots right.
COLLEGE: Moncton (N.B.).
TRANSACTIONS/CAREER NOTES: Selected by Detroit Red Wings in sixth round (sixth Red Wings pick, 107th overall) of NHL entry draft (June 9, 1982). . . . Signed as free agent by Vancouver Canucks (June 1987). . . . Traded by Canucks to New Jersey Devils for C Tim Lenardon (March 7, 1989). . . . Suffered concussion (December 10, 1991); missed two games. . . . Injured groin (January 24, 1992); missed one game.

Season Team	League	—REGULAR SEASON—					—PLAYOFFS—				
		Gms.	G	A	Pts.	Pen.	Gms.	G	A	Pts.	Pen.
80-81—Laval	QMJHL	72	20	31	51	65	—	—	—	—	—
81-82—Laval	QMJHL	58	26	29	55	64	17	14	10	24	22
82-83—Laval	QMJHL	69	46	80	126	72	12	10	4	14	4
83-84—University of Moncton	AUAA	20	11	20	31	8	—	—	—	—	—
84-85—University of Moncton	AUAA	24	35	28	63	20	—	—	—	—	—
85-86—University of Moncton	AUAA	19	17	20	37	25	—	—	—	—	—
86-87—Canadian National Team	Int'l	78	28	42	70	38	—	—	—	—	—
87-88—Canadian National Team	Int'l	61	21	20	41	41	—	—	—	—	—
—Canadian Olympic Team	Int'l	6	0	0	0	0	—	—	—	—	—
—Vancouver	NHL	6	1	1	2	0	—	—	—	—	—
88-89—Milwaukee	IHL	23	9	13	22	26	—	—	—	—	—
—Utica	AHL	55	23	30	53	41	5	0	2	2	2
89-90—New Jersey	NHL	6	1	2	3	4	4	0	0	0	0
—Utica	AHL	73	37	52	89	32	—	—	—	—	—
90-91—Utica	AHL	59	32	46	78	26	—	—	—	—	—
91-92—New Jersey	NHL	71	19	27	46	74	7	1	1	2	17
NHL totals		83	21	30	51	78	11	1	1	2	17

VINCELETTE, DAN

LW, LIGHTNING

PERSONAL: Born August 1, 1967, at Verdun, Que. . . . 6-2/202. . . . Shoots left. . . . Full name: Daniel Vincelette.
TRANSACTIONS/CAREER NOTES: Underwent knee surgery (December 1983). . . . Selected by Chicago Blackhawks as underage junior in fourth round (third Blackhawks pick,

74th overall) of NHL entry draft (June 15, 1985).... Bruised ribs (February 1988).... Traded by Blackhawks with LW Everett Sanipass and D Mario Doyon to Quebec Nordiques for LW Michel Goulet, G Greg Millen and sixth-round pick in 1991 draft (March 5, 1990).... Separated left shoulder (October 7, 1990); missed 11 games.... Sprained right knee (November 17, 1990).... Traded by Nordiques with C Paul Gillis to Blackhawks for C Mike McNeil and D Ryan McGill (March 5, 1991).... Pulled groin (November 29, 1991); missed four games.... Sprained knee ligaments (January 26, 1992); missed 12 games.... Fractured foot (April 14, 1992).... Selected by Tampa Bay Lightning in NHL expansion draft (June 18, 1992).

			REGULAR SEASON					PLAYOFFS			
Season	Team	League	Gms.	G	A	Pts.	Pen.	Gms.	G	A	Pts.	Pen.
84-85—Drummondville.................		QMJHL	64	11	24	35	124	12	0	1	1	11
85-86—Drummondville.................		QMJHL	70	37	47	84	234	22	11	14	25	40
86-87—Drummondville.................		QMJHL	50	34	35	69	288	8	6	5	11	17
—Chicago		NHL	—	—	—	—	—	3	0	0	0	0
87-88—Chicago		NHL	69	6	11	17	109	4	0	0	0	0
88-89—Chicago		NHL	66	11	4	15	119	5	0	0	0	4
—Saginaw		IHL	2	0	0	0	14	—	—	—	—	—
89-90—Indianapolis		IHL	49	16	13	29	262	—	—	—	—	—
—Chicago		NHL	2	0	0	0	4	—	—	—	—	—
—Quebec		NHL	11	0	1	1	25	—	—	—	—	—
—Halifax		AHL	—	—	—	—	—	2	0	0	0	4
90-91—Halifax		AHL	24	4	9	13	85	—	—	—	—	—
—Quebec		NHL	16	0	1	1	38	—	—	—	—	—
—Indianapolis		IHL	15	5	3	8	51	7	2	1	3	62
91-92—Chicago		NHL	29	3	5	8	56	—	—	—	—	—
—Indianapolis		IHL	16	5	3	8	84	—	—	—	—	—
NHL totals..			193	20	22	42	351	12	0	0	0	4

VISHEAU, MARK
D, JETS

PERSONAL: Born June 27, 1973, at Burlington, Ont.... 6-5/200.... Shoots right.
HIGH SCHOOL: Saunders Secondary School (London, Ont.).
TRANSACTIONS/CAREER NOTES: Selected by Winnipeg Jets in fourth round (fourth Jets pick, 84th overall) of NHL entry draft (June 20, 1992).

			REGULAR SEASON					PLAYOFFS			
Season	Team	League	Gms.	G	A	Pts.	Pen.	Gms.	G	A	Pts.	Pen.
89-90—Burlington Jr. B...............		OHA	42	11	22	33	53	—	—	—	—	—
90-91—London		OHL	59	4	11	15	40	7	0	1	1	6
91-92—London		OHL	66	5	31	36	104	10	0	4	4	27

VOLEK, DAVID
LW/RW, ISLANDERS

PERSONAL: Born August 16, 1966, at Prague, Czechoslovakia.... 6-0/190.... Shoots right.
TRANSACTIONS/CAREER NOTES: Selected by New York Islanders in 10th round (11th Islanders pick, 208th overall) of NHL entry draft (June 9, 1984).... Suspended six months by International Ice Hockey Federation for steroid use (August 1988).... Separated right shoulder (October 1988).... Injured back (November 16, 1991); missed three games.... Strained lower back (February 17, 1992); missed one game.... Pulled rib cage muscles (March 7, 1992); missed two games.
HONORS: Named to NHL All-Rookie team (1988-89).

			REGULAR SEASON					PLAYOFFS			
Season	Team	League	Gms.	G	A	Pts.	Pen.	Gms.	G	A	Pts.	Pen.
86-87—Sparta Prague.................		Czech.	39	27	25	52		—	—	—	—	—
87-88—Sparta Prague.................		Czech.	30	18	12	30		—	—	—	—	—
88-89—New York Islanders..........		NHL	77	25	34	59	24	—	—	—	—	—
89-90—New York Islanders..........		NHL	80	17	22	39	41	5	1	4	5	0
90-91—New York Islanders..........		NHL	77	22	34	56	57	—	—	—	—	—
91-92—New York Islanders..........		NHL	74	18	42	60	35	—	—	—	—	—
NHL totals..			308	82	132	214	157	5	1	4	5	0

VON STEFENELLI, PHIL
D, CANUCKS

PERSONAL: Born April 10, 1969, at Vancouver, B.C.... 6-1/183.... Shoots left.... Full name: Philip Von Stefenelli.
COLLEGE: Boston University.
TRANSACTIONS/CAREER NOTES: Selected by Vancouver Canucks in 6th round (5th Canucks pick, 122nd overall) of NHL entry draft (June 11, 1988).

			REGULAR SEASON					PLAYOFFS			
Season	Team	League	Gms.	G	A	Pts.	Pen.	Gms.	G	A	Pts.	Pen.
85-86—Richmond		BCJHL	41	6	11	17	28	12	1	1	2	14
86-87—Richmond		BCJHL	52	5	32	37	51	—	—	—	—	—
87-88—Boston University		Hockey East	34	3	13	16	38	—	—	—	—	—
88-89—Boston University		Hockey East	33	2	6	8	34	—	—	—	—	—
89-90—Boston University		Hockey East	44	8	20	28	40	—	—	—	—	—
90-91—Boston University		Hockey East	41	7	23	30	32	—	—	—	—	—
91-92—Milwaukee		IHL	80	2	34	36	40	5	1	2	3	2

VOPAT, JAN
D, WHALERS

PERSONAL: Born March 22, 1973, at Most, Czechoslovakia.... 6-0/200.... Shoots left.
TRANSACTIONS/CAREER NOTES: Selected by Hartford Whalers in third round (third Whalers pick, 57th overall) of NHL entry draft (June 20, 1992).

Season Team	League	REGULAR SEASON					PLAYOFFS				
		Gms.	G	A	Pts.	Pen.	Gms.	G	A	Pts.	Pen.
90-91—CHZ Litvinov	Czech.	25	1	4	5	4	—	—	—	—	—
91-92—Chemopetrol Litvinov	Czech.	46	4	2	6	6	—	—	—	—	—

VUJTEK, VLADIMIR
LW, CANADIENS

PERSONAL: Born February 17, 1972, at Ostrava, Severomoravsky, Czechoslovakia. . . . 5-11/175. . . . Shoots left.

TRANSACTIONS/CAREER NOTES: Selected by Montreal Canadiens in fourth round (fifth Canadiens pick, 73rd overall) of NHL entry draft (June 22, 1991).

HONORS: Named to WHL West All-Star first team (1991-92).

Season Team	League	REGULAR SEASON					PLAYOFFS				
		Gms.	G	A	Pts.	Pen.	Gms.	G	A	Pts.	Pen.
90-91—Tri-City Americans	WHL	37	26	18	44	25	—	—	—	—	—
91-92—Tri-City Americans	WHL	53	41	61	102	114	—	—	—	—	—
—Montreal...........................	NHL	2	0	0	0	0	—	—	—	—	—
NHL totals.................................		2	0	0	0	0					

VUKONICH, MIKE
C, KINGS

PERSONAL: Born November 5, 1968, at Duluth, Minn. . . . 6-1/185. . . . Shoots left. . . . Full name: Michael William Vukonich.

HIGH SCHOOL: Denfeld (Duluth, Minn.).

COLLEGE: Harvard.

TRANSACTIONS/CAREER NOTES: Selected by Los Angeles Kings in fifth round (fourth Kings pick, 90th overall) of NHL entry draft (June 13, 1987). . . . Suffered from mononucleosis (November 1988).

HONORS: Named to ECAC All-Star first team (1989-90).

Season Team	League	REGULAR SEASON					PLAYOFFS				
		Gms.	G	A	Pts.	Pen.	Gms.	G	A	Pts.	Pen.
85-86—Duluth Denfeld H.S.	Minn. H.S.	24	14	20	34		—	—	—	—	—
86-87—Duluth Denfeld H.S.	Minn. H.S.	22	30	23	53		—	—	—	—	—
87-88—Harvard University	ECAC	32	9	14	23	24	—	—	—	—	—
88-89—Harvard University	ECAC	27	11	8	19	12	—	—	—	—	—
89-90—Harvard University	ECAC	27	22	29	51	18	—	—	—	—	—
90-91—Harvard University	ECAC	28	32	22	54	28	—	—	—	—	—
91-92—Phoenix	IHL	68	17	11	28	21	—	—	—	—	—

VUKOTA, MICK
RW, ISLANDERS

PERSONAL: Born September 14, 1966, at Saskatoon, Sask. . . . 6-2/215. . . . Shoots right.

TRANSACTIONS/CAREER NOTES: Signed as free agent by New York Islanders (September 1987). . . . Suspended six games by AHL for returning from locker room to fight (November 20, 1987). . . . Suffered sore back (February 1990). . . . Separated left shoulder (March 18, 1990). . . . Suspended 10 games by NHL for fighting (April 5, 1990); missed final four games of 1989-90 season and first six games of 1990-91 season.

Season Team	League	REGULAR SEASON					PLAYOFFS				
		Gms.	G	A	Pts.	Pen.	Gms.	G	A	Pts.	Pen.
83-84—Winnipeg	WHL	3	1	1	2	10	—	—	—	—	—
84-85—Kelowna Wings	WHL	66	10	6	16	247	—	—	—	—	—
85-86—Spokane Chiefs	WHL	64	19	14	33	369	9	6	4	10	68
86-87—Spokane Chiefs	WHL	61	25	28	53	*337	4	0	0	0	40
87-88—New York Islanders..........	NHL	17	1	0	1	82	2	0	0	0	23
—Springfield......................	AHL	52	7	9	16	372	—	—	—	—	—
88-89—Springfield......................	AHL	3	1	0	1	33	—	—	—	—	—
—New York Islanders..........	NHL	48	2	2	4	237	—	—	—	—	—
89-90—New York Islanders..........	NHL	76	4	8	12	290	1	0	0	0	17
90-91—Capital District................	AHL	2	0	0	0	9	—	—	—	—	—
—New York Islanders..........	NHL	60	2	4	6	238	—	—	—	—	—
91-92—New York Islanders..........	NHL	74	0	6	6	293	—	—	—	—	—
NHL totals..		275	9	20	29	1140	3	0	0	0	40

VYKOUKAL, JIRI
D, CAPITALS

PERSONAL: Born March 11, 1971, at Olomouc, Severomoravsky, Czechoslovakia. . . . 5-11/176. . . . Shoots right.

TRANSACTIONS/CAREER NOTES: Selected by Washington Capitals in ninth round (ninth Capitals pick, 208th overall) of NHL entry draft (June 17, 1989).

Season Team	League	REGULAR SEASON					PLAYOFFS				
		Gms.	G	A	Pts.	Pen.	Gms.	G	A	Pts.	Pen.
89-90—Sparta Prague..................	Czech.	47	5	12	17		—	—	—	—	—
90-91—Baltimore.........................	AHL	60	4	22	26	41	—	—	—	—	—
91-92—Baltimore.........................	AHL	56	1	21	22	47	—	—	—	—	—
—Hampton Roads	ECHL	9	3	9	12	12	—	—	—	—	—

WAITE, JIMMY
G, BLACKHAWKS

PERSONAL: Born April 15, 1969, at Sherbrooke, Que. . . . 6-0/163. . . . Shoots right.

TRANSACTIONS/CAREER NOTES: Selected by Chicago Blackhawks as underage junior in first round (first Blackhawks pick, eighth overall) of NHL entry draft (June 13, 1987). . . . Broke collarbone (December 6, 1988). . . . Sprained ankle (October 12, 1991); missed one game. . . .

VW

Loaned to Hershey Bears for part of 1991-92 season.
HONORS: Won Raymond Lagace Trophy (1986-87).... Named to QMJHL All-Star second team (1986-87).... Won James Norris Memorial Trophy (1989-90).... Named to IHL All-Star first team (1989-90).

Season Team	League	REGULAR SEASON								PLAYOFFS						
		Gms.	Min.	W	L	T	GA	SO	Avg.	Gms.	Min.	W	L	GA	SO	Avg.
86-87—Chicoutimi	QMJHL	50	2569	23	17	3	209	†2	4.88	11	576	4	6	54	*1	5.63
87-88—Chicoutimi	QMJHL	36	2000	17	16	1	150	0	4.50	4	222	1	2	17	0	4.59
88-89—Chicago	NHL	11	494	0	7	1	43	0	5.22	—	—	—	—	—	—	—
—Saginaw	IHL	5	304	3	1	0	10	0	1.97	—	—	—	—	—	—	—
89-90—Indianapolis	IHL	54	*3207	34	14	5	135	*5	*2.53	†10	*602	9	1	19	†1	*1.89
—Chicago	NHL	4	183	2	0	0	14	0	4.59	—	—	—	—	—	—	—
90-91—Indianapolis	IHL	49	2888	26	18	4	167	3	3.47	6	369	2	4	20	0	3.25
—Chicago	NHL	1	60	1	0	0	2	0	2.00	—	—	—	—	—	—	—
91-92—Chicago	NHL	17	877	4	7	4	54	0	3.69	—	—	—	—	—	—	—
—Indianapolis	IHL	13	702	4	7	1	53	0	4.53	—	—	—	—	—	—	—
—Hershey	AHL	11	631	6	4	1	44	0	4.18	6	360	2	4	19	0	3.17
NHL totals		33	1614	7	14	5	113	0	4.20							

WAKALUK, DARCY
G, NORTH STARS

PERSONAL: Born March 14, 1966, at Pincher Creek, Alta....5-11/180....Shoots left.
TRANSACTIONS/CAREER NOTES: Selected by Buffalo Sabres as underage junior in seventh round (seventh Sabres pick, 144th overall) of NHL entry draft (June 9, 1984). Traded by Sabres to Minnesota North Stars for eighth-round pick in 1991 draft (D Jiri Kuntos) and future considerations (May 26, 1991).
HONORS: Shared Harry (Hap) Holmes Memorial Trophy with David Littman (1990-91).

Season Team	League	REGULAR SEASON								PLAYOFFS						
		Gms.	Min.	W	L	T	GA	SO	Avg.	Gms.	Min.	W	L	GA	SO	Avg.
83-84—Kelowna Wings	WHL	31	1555				163	0	6.29	—	—	—	—	—	—	—
84-85—Kelowna Wings	WHL	54	3094	19	30	4	244	0	4.73	5	282	1	4	22	0	4.68
85-86—Spokane Chiefs	WHL	47	2562	21	22	1	224	1	5.25	7	419	3	4	37	0	5.30
86-87—Rochester	AHL	11	545	2	2	0	26	0	2.86	5	141	2	0	11	0	4.68
87-88—Rochester	AHL	55	2763	27	16	3	159	0	3.45	6	328	3	3	22	0	4.02
88-89—Buffalo	NHL	6	214	1	3	0	15	0	4.21	—	—	—	—	—	—	—
—Rochester	AHL	33	1566	11	14	0	97	1	3.72	—	—	—	—	—	—	—
89-90—Rochester	AHL	56	3095	31	16	4	173	2	3.35	†17	*1001	10	6	50	0	*3.00
90-91—Buffalo	NHL	16	630	4	3	3	35	0	3.33	—	—	—	—	—	—	—
—Rochester	AHL	26	1363				68	*4	*2.99	—	—	—	—	—	—	—
91-92—Minnesota	NHL	36	1905	13	19	1	104	1	3.28	—	—	—	—	—	—	—
—Kalamazoo	IHL	1	60	1	0	0	7	0	7.00	—	—	—	—	—	—	—
NHL totals		58	2749	18	25	4	154	1	3.36							

WALTER, RYAN
C/LW, CANUCKS

PERSONAL: Born April 23, 1958, at New Westminster, B.C....6-0/200....Shoots left.... Full name: Ryan William Walter.
TRANSACTIONS/CAREER NOTES: Selected by Washington Capitals from Seattle Breakers in first round (first Capitals pick, second overall) of NHL amateur draft (June 15, 1978).... Traded by Capitals with D Rick Green to Montreal Canadiens for D Rod Langway, D Brian Engblom, C Doug Jarvis and RW Craig Laughlin (September 1982).... Injured groin muscle (November 1983).... Suffered concussion and twisted knee (October 27, 1984).... Suffered back spasms (March 8, 1986).... Broke ankle (March 1986); missed remainder of regular season and 15 playoff games.... Bruised ribs (October 1987).... Suffered back spasms (November 1987).... Suffered concussion (December 9, 1989).... Broke right wrist (October 13, 1990); missed 42 games.... Signed as free agent by Vancouver Canucks (July 26, 1991).
HONORS: Won WCHL Most Valuable Player Award (1977-78).... Won WCHL Player of the Year Award (1977-78).... Named to WCHL All-Star first team (1977-78).... Named Bud Light/NHL Man of the Year (1991-92).

Season Team	League	REGULAR SEASON					PLAYOFFS				
		Gms.	G	A	Pts.	Pen.	Gms.	G	A	Pts.	Pen.
73-74—Langley Lords	BCJHL		40	62	102		—	—	—	—	—
—Kamloops Chiefs	WCHL	2	0	0	0	0	—	—	—	—	—
74-75—Langley Lords	BCJHL		32	60	92	111	—	—	—	—	—
—Kamloops Chiefs	WCHL	9	8	4	12	2	2	1	1	2	2
75-76—Kamloops Chiefs	WCHL	72	35	49	84	96	12	3	9	12	10
76-77—Kamloops Chiefs	WCHL	71	41	58	99	100	5	1	3	4	11
77-78—Seattle	WCHL	62	54	71	125	148	—	—	—	—	—
78-79—Washington	NHL	69	28	28	56	70	—	—	—	—	—
79-80—Washington	NHL	80	24	42	66	106	—	—	—	—	—
80-81—Washington	NHL	80	24	44	68	150	—	—	—	—	—
81-82—Washington	NHL	78	38	49	87	142	—	—	—	—	—
82-83—Montreal	NHL	80	29	46	75	40	3	0	0	0	11
83-84—Montreal	NHL	73	20	29	49	83	15	2	1	3	4
84-85—Montreal	NHL	72	19	19	38	59	12	2	7	9	13
85-86—Montreal	NHL	69	15	34	49	45	5	0	1	1	2
86-87—Montreal	NHL	76	23	23	46	34	17	7	12	19	10
87-88—Montreal	NHL	61	13	23	36	39	11	2	4	6	6
88-89—Montreal	NHL	78	14	17	31	48	21	3	5	8	6
89-90—Montreal	NHL	70	8	16	24	59	11	0	2	2	0
90-91—Montreal	NHL	25	0	1	1	12	5	0	0	0	2
91-92—Vancouver	NHL	67	6	11	17	49	13	0	3	3	8
NHL totals		978	261	382	643	936	113	16	35	51	62

W

WALTERS, GREG
C, MAPLE LEAFS

PERSONAL: Born August 8, 1970, at Calgary, Alta. . . . 6-1/195. . . . Shoots left.
TRANSACTIONS/CAREER NOTES: Broke leg (December 1989). . . . Selected by Toronto Maple Leafs in fourth round (third Maple Leafs pick, 80th overall) of NHL entry draft (June 16, 1990).

			REGULAR SEASON					PLAYOFFS			
Season	Team	League	Gms.	G	A	Pts.	Pen.	Gms.	G	A	Pts.	Pen.
87-88—Ottawa		OHL	63	11	25	36	52	—	—	—	—	—
88-89—Ottawa		OHL	28	17	21	38	20	—	—	—	—	—
89-90—Ottawa		OHL	63	36	54	90	57	—	—	—	—	—
90-91—Newmarket		AHL	54	7	14	21	58	—	—	—	—	—
91-92—St. John's		AHL	10	0	2	2	20	—	—	—	—	—
—Raleigh		ECHL	18	9	13	22	30	4	1	2	3	8

WALZ, WES
C, FLYERS

PERSONAL: Born May 15, 1970, at Calgary, Alta. . . . 5-10/181. . . . Shoots right.
TRANSACTIONS/CAREER NOTES: Selected by Boston Bruins in third round (third Bruins pick, 57th overall) of NHL entry draft (June 17, 1989). . . . Traded by Bruins with D Garry Galley and future considerations to Philadelphia Flyers for D Gord Murphy, RW Brian Dobbin and third-round pick in 1992 draft (January 2, 1992).
HONORS: Won Jim Piggott Memorial Trophy (1988-89). . . . Won WHL Player of the Year Award (1989-90). . . . Named to WHL East All-Star first team (1989-90).

			REGULAR SEASON					PLAYOFFS			
Season	Team	League	Gms.	G	A	Pts.	Pen.	Gms.	G	A	Pts.	Pen.
87-88—Prince Albert		WHL	1	1	1	2	0	—	—	—	—	—
88-89—Lethbridge		WHL	63	29	75	104	32	8	1	5	6	6
89-90—Boston		NHL	2	1	1	2	0	—	—	—	—	—
—Lethbridge		WHL	56	54	86	140	69	19	13	*24	†37	33
90-91—Maine		AHL	20	8	12	20	19	2	0	0	0	21
—Boston		NHL	56	8	8	16	32	2	0	0	0	0
91-92—Boston		NHL	15	0	3	3	12	—	—	—	—	—
—Maine		AHL	21	13	11	24	38	—	—	—	—	—
—Hershey		AHL	41	13	28	41	37	6	1	2	3	0
—Philadelphia		NHL	2	1	0	1	0	—	—	—	—	—
NHL totals			75	10	12	22	44	2	0	0	0	0

WAMSLEY, RICK
G, MAPLE LEAFS

PERSONAL: Born May 25, 1959, at Simcoe, Ont. . . . 5-11/185. . . . Shoots left. . . . Full name: Richard Wamsley.
TRANSACTIONS/CAREER NOTES: Selected by Montreal Canadiens in third round (fifth Canadiens pick, 58th overall) of NHL entry draft (August 9, 1979). . . . Traded by Canadiens with second-round (D Brian Benning) and third-round (D Robert Dirk) picks in 1984 draft to St. Louis Blues for first-round (C Shayne Corson) and second-round (C Stephane Richer) picks in 1984 draft (June 1984). . . . Bruised right hand (October 16, 1985); missed nine games. . . . Traded by Blues with D Rob Ramage to Calgary Flames for RW Brett Hull and LW Steve Bozek (March 1988). . . . Pulled groin (March 1988). . . . Broke two bones in left hand (October 10, 1990). . . . Traded by Flames with C Doug Gilmour, LW Kent Manderville, D Jamie Macoun and D Ric Nattress to Toronto Maple Leafs for LW Craig Berube, D Alexander Godynyuk, LW Gary Leeman, D Michel Petit and G Jeff Reese (January 2, 1992). . . . Strained knee (March 5, 1992).
HONORS: Shared Dave Pinkney Trophy with Al Jensen (1977-78). . . . Shared William M. Jennings Trophy with Denis Herron (1981-82).

			REGULAR SEASON						PLAYOFFS					
Season	Team	League	Gms.	Min.	W	L	T	GA	SO	Avg.	Gms.	Min.	W	L	GA	SO	Avg.
76-77—St. Catharines		OMJHL	12	647				36	0	3.34	—	—	—	—	—	—	—
77-78—Hamilton Fincups		OMJHL	25	1495				74	2	*2.97	—	—	—	—	—	—	—
78-79—Brantford		OMJHL	24	1444				128	0	5.32	—	—	—	—	—	—	—
79-80—Nova Scotia		AHL	40	2305	19	16	2	125	2	3.25	3	143	1	1	12	0	5.03
80-81—Nova Scotia		AHL	43	2372	17	19	3	155	0	3.92	4	199	2	1	6	†1	*1.81
—Montreal		NHL	5	253	3	0	1	8	1	1.90	—	—	—	—	—	—	—
81-82—Montreal		NHL	38	2206	23	7	7	101	2	2.75	5	300	2	3	11	0	*2.20
82-83—Montreal		NHL	46	2583	27	12	5	151	2	3.51	3	152	0	3	7	0	2.76
83-84—Montreal		NHL	42	2333	19	17	3	144	2	3.70	1	32	0	0	0	0	0.00
84-85—St. Louis		NHL	40	2319	23	12	5	126	0	3.26	2	120	0	2	7	0	3.50
85-86—St. Louis		NHL	42	2517	22	16	3	144	1	3.43	10	569	4	6	37	0	3.90
86-87—St. Louis		NHL	41	2410	17	15	6	142	0	3.54	2	120	1	1	5	0	2.50
87-88—St. Louis		NHL	31	1818	13	16	1	103	2	3.40	—	—	—	—	—	—	—
—Calgary		NHL	2	73	1	0	0	5	0	4.11	1	33	0	1	2	0	3.64
88-89—Calgary		NHL	35	1927	17	11	4	95	2	2.96	1	20	0	1	2	0	6.00
89-90—Calgary		NHL	36	1969	18	8	6	107	2	3.26	1	49	0	1	9	0	11.02
90-91—Calgary		NHL	29	1670	14	7	5	85	0	3.05	1	2	0	0	1	0	30.00
91-92—Calgary		NHL	9	457	3	4	0	34	0	4.46	—	—	—	—	—	—	—
—Toronto		NHL	8	428	4	3	0	27	0	3.79	—	—	—	—	—	—	—
NHL totals			404	22963	204	128	46	1272	12	3.32	27	1397	7	18	81	0	3.48

WARD, AARON
D, JETS

PERSONAL: Born January 17, 1973, at Windsor, Ont. . . . 6-2/200. . . . Shoots right. . . . Full name: Aaron Christian Ward.
COLLEGE: Michigan.
TRANSACTIONS/CAREER NOTES: Selected by Winnipeg Jets in first round (first Jets pick, fifth

W

overall) of NHL entry draft (June 22, 1991).
HONORS: Named to CCHA All-Rookie Team (1990-91).... Named to CCHA All-Tournament Team (1990-91).

Season	Team	League	REGULAR SEASON					PLAYOFFS				
			Gms.	G	A	Pts.	Pen.	Gms.	G	A	Pts.	Pen.
88-89—Nepean		COJHL	56	2	17	19	44	—	—	—	—	—
89-90—Nepean		COJHL	52	6	33	39	85	—	—	—	—	—
90-91—University of Michigan		CCHA	46	8	11	19	126	—	—	—	—	—
91-92—University of Michigan		CCHA	42	7	12	19	64	—	—	—	—	—

WARD, DIXON
RW, CANUCKS

PERSONAL: Born September 23, 1968, at Edmonton, Alta.... 6-1/195.... Shoots right.... Full name: Dixon M. Ward Jr.
COLLEGE: North Dakota.
TRANSACTIONS/CAREER NOTES: Selected by Vancouver Canucks in seventh round (sixth Canucks pick, 128th overall) of NHL entry draft (June 11, 1988).... Separated left shoulder (December 1990).
HONORS: Named to WCHA All-Star second team (1990-91 and 1991-92).

Season	Team	League	REGULAR SEASON					PLAYOFFS				
			Gms.	G	A	Pts.	Pen.	Gms.	G	A	Pts.	Pen.
86-87—Red Deer		AJHL	59	46	40	86	153	—	—	—	—	—
87-88—Red Deer		AJHL	51	60	71	131	167	—	—	—	—	—
88-89—Univ. of North Dakota		WCHA	37	8	9	17	26	—	—	—	—	—
89-90—Univ. of North Dakota		WCHA	45	35	34	69	44	—	—	—	—	—
90-91—Univ. of North Dakota		WCHA	43	34	35	69	84	—	—	—	—	—
91-92—Univ. of North Dakota		WCHA	38	33	31	64	90	—	—	—	—	—

WARRINER, TODD
LW/C, NORDIQUES

PERSONAL: Born January 3, 1974, at Chatham, Ont.... 6-1/172.... Shoots left.
HIGH SCHOOL: Herman E. Fawcett (Brantfor, Ont.).
TRANSACTIONS/CAREER NOTES: Selected by Quebec Nordiques in first round (first Nordiques pick, fourth overall) of NHL entry draft (June 20, 1992).
HONORS: Won Can.HL Top Draft Prospect Award (1991-92).... Won OHL Top Draft Prospect Award (1991-92).... Named to Can.HL All-Star second team (1991-92).

Season	Team	League	REGULAR SEASON					PLAYOFFS				
			Gms.	G	A	Pts.	Pen.	Gms.	G	A	Pts.	Pen.
88-89—Blenheim Jr. C		OHA	10	1	4	5	0	—	—	—	—	—
89-90—Chatham Jr. B		OHA	40	24	21	45	12	—	—	—	—	—
90-91—Windsor		OHL	57	36	28	64	26	11	6	5	11	12
91-92—Windsor		OHL	50	41	42	83	66	7	5	4	9	6

WASLEY, CHARLEY
D, NORDIQUES

PERSONAL: Born April 4, 1974, at Minneapolis.... 6-2/173.... Shoots left.
TRANSACTIONS/CAREER NOTES: Selected by Quebec Nordiques in fifth round (sixth Nordiques pick, 100th overall) of NHL entry draft (June 20, 1992).

Season	Team	League	REGULAR SEASON					PLAYOFFS				
			Gms.	G	A	Pts.	Pen.	Gms.	G	A	Pts.	Pen.
91-92—St. Paul Jr. A		Tier II	44	3	6	9	144	—	—	—	—	—

WATTERS, TIMOTHY
D, KINGS

PERSONAL: Born July 25, 1959, at Kamloops, B.C.... 5-11/185.... Shoots left. ... Full name: Timothy J. Watters.
COLLEGE: Michigan Tech.
TRANSACTIONS/CAREER NOTES: Selected by Winnipeg Jets in sixth round (sixth Jets pick, 124th overall) of NHL draft (August 9, 1979).... Pulled hamstring (October 1983).... Broke wrist (December 1984).... Suffered back spasms (February 1986).... Strained knee (December 1987).... Signed as free agent by Los Angeles Kings (July 1988).... Bruised calf (March 1989).... Bruised ankle (December 23, 1989); missed nine games.... Bruised ankle (April 1990).... Bruised ribs (October 14, 1990); missed six games.... Twisted right knee (January 12, 1991).... Injured ankle (October 28, 1991); missed 14 games.... Injured ankle (December 1991).
HONORS: Named to NCAA All-America West team (1980-81).... Name to NCAA All-Tournament team (1980-81).... Named to WCHA All-Star first team (1980-81).

Season	Team	League	REGULAR SEASON					PLAYOFFS				
			Gms.	G	A	Pts.	Pen.	Gms.	G	A	Pts.	Pen.
76-77—Kamloops		BCJHL	60	10	38	48		—	—	—	—	—
77-78—Michigan Tech		WCHA	37	1	15	16	47	—	—	—	—	—
78-79—Michigan Tech		WCHA	31	6	21	27	48	—	—	—	—	—
79-80—Canadian National Team		Int'l	56	8	21	29	43	—	—	—	—	—
—Canadian Olympic Team		Int'l	6	1	1	2	0	—	—	—	—	—
80-81—Michigan Tech		WCHA	43	12	38	50	36	—	—	—	—	—
81-82—Tulsa		CHL	5	1	2	3	0	—	—	—	—	—
—Winnipeg		NHL	69	2	22	24	97	4	0	1	1	8
82-83—Winnipeg		NHL	77	5	18	23	98	3	0	0	0	2
83-84—Winnipeg		NHL	74	3	20	23	169	3	1	0	1	2
84-85—Winnipeg		NHL	63	2	20	22	74	8	0	1	1	16
85-86—Winnipeg		NHL	56	6	8	14	97	—	—	—	—	—
86-87—Winnipeg		NHL	63	3	13	16	119	10	0	0	0	21
87-88—Winnipeg		NHL	36	0	0	0	106	4	0	0	0	4
—Canadian Olympic Team		Int'l	10	0	3	3	2	—	—	—	—	—

Season Team	League	REGULAR SEASON					PLAYOFFS				
		Gms.	G	A	Pts.	Pen.	Gms.	G	A	Pts.	Pen.
88-89—Los Angeles	NHL	76	3	18	21	168	11	0	1	1	6
89-90—Los Angeles	NHL	62	1	10	11	92	4	0	0	0	6
90-91—Los Angeles	NHL	45	0	4	4	92	7	0	0	0	12
91-92—Los Angeles	NHL	37	0	7	7	92	6	0	0	0	8
—Phoenix	IHL	5	0	3	3	6	—	—	—	—	—
NHL totals		658	25	140	165	1204	60	1	3	4	85

WEEKS, STEVE
G, KINGS

PERSONAL: Born June 30, 1958, at Scarborough, Ont. . . . 5-11/170. . . . Shoots left. . . . Full name: Steve K. Weeks.
COLLEGE: Northern Michigan.
TRANSACTIONS/CAREER NOTES: Selected by New York Rangers in 11th round (12th Rangers pick, 176th overall) of NHL entry draft (June 15, 1978). . . . Traded by Rangers to Hartford Whalers for future considerations (September 1984). . . . Traded by Whalers to Vancouver Canucks for G Richard Brodeur (March 1988). . . . Traded by Canucks to Buffalo Sabres for cash and future considerations (March 5, 1991); remained in Milwaukee through IHL playoffs. . . . Signed as free agent by New York Islanders (October 1991). . . . Traded by Islanders to Los Angeles Kings for seventh-round pick in 1992 draft (February 18, 1992). . . . Suffered back spasms (March 3, 1992); missed three games.
HONORS: Named CCHA Most Valuable Player (1979-80). . . . Named to CCHA All-Star first team (1979-80). . . . Named to NCAA Tournament All-Star team (1979-80).

Season Team	League	REGULAR SEASON							PLAYOFFS						
		Gms.	Min.	W	L	T	GA	SO	Avg.	Gms.	Min.	W	L	GA	SO	Avg.
75-76—Toronto	OHA Mj Jr.A	18	873				73	0	5.02	—	—	—	—	—	—	—
76-77—N. Michigan U.	WCHA	16	811				58	0	4.29	—	—	—	—	—	—	—
77-78—N. Michigan U.	WCHA	19	1015				56	1	3.31	—	—	—	—	—	—	—
78-79—N. Michigan U.	WCHA	25	1437				82	0	3.42	—	—	—	—	—	—	—
79-80—N. Michigan U.	WCHA	36	2133	29	6	1	105	0	*2.95	—	—	—	—	—	—	—
80-81—New Haven	AHL	36	2065	14	17	3	142	1	4.13	—	—	—	—	—	—	—
—New York Rangers	NHL	1	60	0	1	0	2	0	2.00	1	14	0	0	1	0	4.29
81-82—New York Rangers	NHL	49	2852	23	16	9	179	1	3.77	4	127	1	2	9	0	4.25
82-83—Tulsa	CHL	19	1116	8	10	0	60	0	3.23	—	—	—	—	—	—	—
—New York Rangers	NHL	18	1040	9	5	3	68	0	3.92	—	—	—	—	—	—	—
83-84—New York Rangers	NHL	26	1361	10	11	2	90	0	3.97	—	—	—	—	—	—	—
—Tulsa	CHL	3	180	3	0	0	7	0	2.33	—	—	—	—	—	—	—
84-85—Binghamton	AHL	5	303	5	0	0	13	0	2.57	—	—	—	—	—	—	—
—Hartford	NHL	24	1457	10	12	2	93	2	3.83	—	—	—	—	—	—	—
85-86—Hartford	NHL	27	1544	13	13	0	99	1	3.85	3	169	1	2	8	0	2.84
86-87—Hartford	NHL	25	1367	12	8	2	78	1	3.42	1	36	0	0	1	0	1.67
87-88—Hartford	NHL	18	918	6	7	2	55	0	3.59	—	—	—	—	—	—	—
—Vancouver	NHL	9	550	4	3	2	31	0	3.38	—	—	—	—	—	—	—
88-89—Vancouver	NHL	35	2056	11	19	5	102	0	2.98	3	140	1	1	8	0	3.43
89-90—Vancouver	NHL	21	1142	4	11	4	79	0	4.15	—	—	—	—	—	—	—
90-91—Milwaukee	IHL	37	2014	16	19	0	127	0	3.78	3	210	1	2	13	0	3.71
—Vancouver	NHL	1	59	0	1	0	6	0	6.10	—	—	—	—	—	—	—
91-92—New York Islanders	NHL	23	1032	9	4	2	62	0	3.60	—	—	—	—	—	—	—
—Los Angeles	NHL	7	252	1	3	0	17	0	4.05	—	—	—	—	—	—	—
NHL totals		284	15690	112	114	33	961	5	3.67	12	486	3	5	27	0	3.33

WEIGHT, DOUG
C, RANGERS

PERSONAL: Born January 21, 1971, at Warren, Mich. . . . 5-11/196. . . . Shoots left. . . . Full name: Douglas D. Weight.
COLLEGE: Lake Superior State (Mich.).
TRANSACTIONS/CAREER NOTES: Selected by New York Rangers in second round (second Rangers pick, 34th overall) of NHL entry draft (June 16, 1990). . . . Sprained elbow (October 14, 1991); missed three games. . . . Damaged ligaments (January 11, 1991).
HONORS: Named to CCHA All-Rookie team (1989-90). . . . Named to NCAA All-America West second team (1990-91). . . . Named to CCHA All-Star first team (1990-91).

Season Team	League	REGULAR SEASON					PLAYOFFS				
		Gms.	G	A	Pts.	Pen.	Gms.	G	A	Pts.	Pen.
88-89—Bloomfield	NAJHL	34	26	53	79	105	—	—	—	—	—
89-90—Lake Superior State	CCHA	46	21	48	69	44	—	—	—	—	—
90-91—Lake Superior State	CCHA	42	29	46	75	86	—	—	—	—	—
91-92—New York Rangers	NHL	53	8	22	30	23	7	2	2	4	0
—Binghamton	AHL	9	3	14	17	2	4	1	4	5	6
NHL totals		53	8	22	30	23	7	2	2	4	0

WEINRICH, ERIC
D, DEVILS

PERSONAL: Born December 19, 1966, at Roanoke, Va. . . . 6-1/210. . . . Shoots left. . . . Full name: Eric John Weinrich.
HIGH SCHOOL: North Yarmouth Academy (Yarmouth, Maine).
COLLEGE: Maine.
TRANSACTIONS/CAREER NOTES: Dislocated shoulder (December 1984). . . . Selected by New Jersey Devils in second round (third Devils pick, 32nd overall) of NHL entry draft (June 15, 1985).
HONORS: Named to NCAA All-America East second team (1986-87). . . . Named to Hockey East All-Star first team (1986-87). . . . Won Eddie Shore Plaque (1989-90). . . . Named to AHL All-Star first team (1989-90). . . . Named to NHL All-Rookie team (1990-91).

W

Season	Team	League	REGULAR SEASON					PLAYOFFS				
			Gms.	G	A	Pts.	Pen.	Gms.	G	A	Pts.	Pen.
83-84—North Yarmouth Acad.		Mass. H.S.	17	23	33	56		—	—	—	—	—
84-85—North Yarmouth Acad.		Mass. H.S.	20	6	21	27		—	—	—	—	—
85-86—University of Maine		Hockey East	34	0	15	15	26	—	—	—	—	—
86-87—University of Maine		Hockey East	41	12	32	44	59	—	—	—	—	—
87-88—U.S. Olympic Team		Int'l	39	3	9	12	24	—	—	—	—	—
—University of Maine		Hockey East	8	4	7	11	22	—	—	—	—	—
88-89—Utica...........................		AHL	80	17	27	44	70	5	0	1	1	8
—New Jersey......................		NHL	2	0	0	0	0	—	—	—	—	—
89-90—Utica...........................		AHL	57	12	48	60	38	—	—	—	—	—
—New Jersey......................		NHL	19	2	7	9	11	6	1	3	4	17
90-91—New Jersey......................		NHL	76	4	34	38	48	7	1	2	3	6
91-92—New Jersey......................		NHL	76	7	25	32	55	7	0	2	2	4
NHL totals..............			173	13	66	79	114	20	2	7	9	27

WELLS, JAY
D, RANGERS

PERSONAL: Born May 18, 1959, at Paris, Ont. . . . 6-1/210. . . . Shoots left. . . . Full name: Gordon Jay Wells.

TRANSACTIONS/CAREER NOTES: Selected by Los Angeles Kings in first round (first Kings pick, 16th overall) of NHL entry draft (August 9, 1979). . . . Broke right hand in team practice (October 16, 1981). . . . Tore medial collateral ligament in right knee (December 14, 1982). . . . Sprained ankle (December 1983). . . . Struck in eye during team practice (February 1987). . . . Strained lower back (November 1987). . . . Traded by Kings to Philadelphia Flyers for D Doug Crossman (September 29, 1988). . . . Bruised right shoulder (October 1988). . . . Broke knuckle on right hand (January 1989). . . . Broke toe (November 1989). . . . Traded by Flyers with fourth-round pick in 1991 draft to Buffalo Sabres for RW Kevin Maguire and second-round pick in 1990 draft (RW Mikael Renberg) (March 5, 1990). . . . Fractured right ankle (March 6, 1990). . . . Tore medial collateral ligament of right knee (October 13, 1990); missed 18 games. . . . Traded by Sabres to New York Rangers for D Randy Moller (March 9, 1992).
HONORS: Named to OMJHL All-Star first team (1978-79).

Season	Team	League	REGULAR SEASON					PLAYOFFS				
			Gms.	G	A	Pts.	Pen.	Gms.	G	A	Pts.	Pen.
76-77—Kingston...........................		OMJHL	59	4	7	11	90	—	—	—	—	—
77-78—Kingston...........................		OMJHL	68	9	13	22	195	5	1	2	3	6
78-79—Kingston...........................		OMJHL	48	6	21	27	100	11	2	7	9	29
79-80—Los Angeles......................		NHL	43	0	0	0	113	4	0	0	0	11
—Binghamton		AHL	28	0	6	6	48	—	—	—	—	—
80-81—Los Angeles......................		NHL	72	5	13	18	155	4	0	0	0	27
81-82—Los Angeles......................		NHL	60	1	8	9	145	10	1	3	4	41
82-83—Los Angeles......................		NHL	69	3	12	15	167	—	—	—	—	—
83-84—Los Angeles......................		NHL	69	3	18	21	141	—	—	—	—	—
84-85—Los Angeles......................		NHL	77	2	9	11	185	3	0	1	1	0
85-86—Los Angeles......................		NHL	79	11	31	42	226	—	—	—	—	—
86-87—Los Angeles......................		NHL	77	7	29	36	155	5	1	2	3	10
87-88—Los Angeles......................		NHL	58	2	23	25	159	5	1	2	3	21
88-89—Philadelphia......................		NHL	67	2	19	21	184	18	0	2	2	51
89-90—Philadelphia......................		NHL	59	3	16	19	129	—	—	—	—	—
—Buffalo............................		NHL	1	0	1	1	0	6	0	0	0	12
90-91—Buffalo............................		NHL	43	1	2	3	86	1	0	1	1	0
91-92—Buffalo............................		NHL	41	2	9	11	157	—	—	—	—	—
—New York Rangers		NHL	11	0	0	0	24	13	0	2	2	10
NHL totals.................			826	42	190	232	2026	69	3	13	16	183

WERENKA, BRAD
D, OILERS

PERSONAL: Born February 12, 1969, at Two Hills, Alta. . . . 6-2/204. . . . Shoots left. . . . Full name: John Bradley Werenka.
COLLEGE: Northern Michigan.
TRANSACTIONS/CAREER NOTES: Selected by Edmonton Oilers as underage junior in second round (second Oilers pick, 42nd overall) of NHL entry draft (June 13, 1987). . . . Tore stomach muscles (October 1988). . . . Sprained right knee (November 3, 1989).
HONORS: Named to NCAA All-America West first team (1990-91). . . . Named to NCAA All-Tournament team (1990-91). . . . Named to WCHA All-Star first team (1990-91).

Season	Team	League	REGULAR SEASON					PLAYOFFS				
			Gms.	G	A	Pts.	Pen.	Gms.	G	A	Pts.	Pen.
85-86—Fort Saskatchewan		AJHL	29	12	23	35	24	—	—	—	—	—
86-87—Northern Michigan Univ...		WCHA	30	4	4	8	35	—	—	—	—	—
87-88—Northern Michigan Univ...		WCHA	34	7	23	30	26	—	—	—	—	—
88-89—Northern Michigan Univ...		WCHA	28	7	13	20	16	—	—	—	—	—
89-90—Northern Michigan Univ...		WCHA	8	2	5	7	8	—	—	—	—	—
90-91—Northern Michigan Univ...		WCHA	47	20	43	63	36	—	—	—	—	—
91-92—Cape Breton		AHL	66	6	21	27	95	5	0	3	3	6

WERENKA, DARCY
D, RANGERS

PERSONAL: Born May 13, 1973, at Edmonton, Alta. . . . 6-1/210. . . . Shoots right.
TRANSACTIONS/CAREER NOTES: Selected by New York Rangers in second round (second Rangers pick, 37th overall) of NHL entry draft (June 22, 1991).
HONORS: Named to WHL East All-Star second team (1990-91).

Season	Team	League	REGULAR SEASON					PLAYOFFS				
			Gms.	G	A	Pts.	Pen.	Gms.	G	A	Pts.	Pen.
89-90—Lethbridge		WHL	63	1	18	19	16	19	0	2	2	4
90-91—Lethbridge		WHL	72	13	37	50	39	16	1	7	8	4
91-92—Lethbridge		WHL	69	17	58	75	56	5	2	1	3	0

WESLEY, GLEN
D, BRUINS

PERSONAL: Born October 2, 1968, at Red Deer, Alta.... 6-1/195.... Shoots left.
TRANSACTIONS/CAREER NOTES: Selected by Boston Bruins as underage junior in first round (first Bruins pick, third overall) of NHL entry draft (June 13, 1987).... Sprained left knee (October 1988).
HONORS: Won WHL West Top Defenseman Trophy (1985-86 and 1986-87).... Named to WHL All-Star first team (1985-86 and 1986-87).... Named to NHL All-Rookie team (1987-88).

Season	Team	League	REGULAR SEASON					PLAYOFFS				
			Gms.	G	A	Pts.	Pen.	Gms.	G	A	Pts.	Pen.
83-84—Red Deer		AJHL	57	9	20	29	40	—	—	—	—	—
—Portland		WHL	3	1	2	3	0	—	—	—	—	—
84-85—Portland		WHL	67	16	52	68	76	6	1	6	7	8
85-86—Portland		WHL	69	16	75	91	96	15	3	11	14	29
86-87—Portland		WHL	63	16	46	62	72	20	8	18	26	27
87-88—Boston		NHL	79	7	30	37	69	23	6	8	14	22
88-89—Boston		NHL	77	19	35	54	61	10	0	2	2	4
89-90—Boston		NHL	78	9	27	36	48	21	2	6	8	36
90-91—Boston		NHL	80	11	32	43	78	19	2	9	11	19
91-92—Boston		NHL	78	9	37	46	54	15	2	4	6	16
NHL totals			392	55	161	216	310	88	12	29	41	97

WHEELDON, SIMON
C, CAPITALS

PERSONAL: Born August 30, 1966, at Vancouver, B.C.... 5-11/170.... Shoots left.
TRANSACTIONS/CAREER NOTES: Selected by Edmonton Oilers as underage junior in 11th round (11th Oilers pick, 229th overall) of NHL entry draft (June 9, 1984).... Signed as free agent by New York Rangers (August 1987).... Traded by Rangers to Winnipeg Jets for C Brian McReynolds (July 10, 1990).... Traded by Jets with LW Brent Hughes and LW Craig Duncanson to Washington Capitals for LW Bob Joyce, D Kent Paynter and C Tyler Larter (May 1991).
HONORS: Named to WHL West All-Star second team (1984-85 and 1985-86).... Named to IHL All-Star second team (1987-88 and 1988-89).

Season	Team	League	REGULAR SEASON					PLAYOFFS				
			Gms.	G	A	Pts.	Pen.	Gms.	G	A	Pts.	Pen.
82-83—Kelowna		BCJHL	55	30	44	74	74	—	—	—	—	—
83-84—Victoria		WHL	56	14	24	38	43	—	—	—	—	—
84-85—Victoria		WHL	67	50	76	126	78	—	—	—	—	—
—Nova Scotia		AHL	4	0	1	1	0	1	0	0	0	0
85-86—Victoria		WHL	70	61	96	157	85	—	—	—	—	—
86-87—Flint		IHL	41	17	53	70	67	—	—	—	—	—
—New Haven		AHL	38	11	28	39	39	5	0	0	0	6
87-88—New York Rangers		NHL	5	0	1	1	4	—	—	—	—	—
—Colorado		IHL	69	45	54	99	80	13	8	11	19	12
88-89—New York Rangers		NHL	6	0	1	1	2	—	—	—	—	—
—Denver		IHL	74	50	56	106	77	4	0	2	2	6
89-90—Flint		IHL	76	34	49	83	61	4	1	2	3	2
90-91—Moncton		AHL	66	30	38	68	38	8	4	3	7	2
—Winnipeg		NHL	4	0	0	0	4	—	—	—	—	—
91-92—Baltimore		AHL	78	38	53	91	62	—	—	—	—	—
NHL totals			15	0	2	2	10					

WHITE, PETER
LW, OILERS

PERSONAL: Born March 15, 1969, at Montreal.... 5-11/201.... Shoots left.... Full name: Peter Toby White.
COLLEGE: Michigan State.
TRANSACTIONS/CAREER NOTES: Selected by Edmonton Oilers in fifth round (fourth Oilers pick, 92nd overall) of NHL entry draft (June 17, 1989).
HONORS: Named to CCHA All-Rookie Team (1988-89).... Named CCHA Playoff Most Valuable Player (1989-90).... Named to CCHA All-Tournament team (1989-90).

Season	Team	League	REGULAR SEASON					PLAYOFFS				
			Gms.	G	A	Pts.	Pen.	Gms.	G	A	Pts.	Pen.
87-88—Pembroke		COJHL	56	90	136	226	32	—	—	—	—	—
88-89—Michigan State		CCHA	46	20	33	53	17	—	—	—	—	—
89-90—Michigan State		CCHA	45	22	40	62	6	—	—	—	—	—
90-91—Michigan State		CCHA	37	7	31	38	28	—	—	—	—	—
91-92—Michigan State		CCHA	44	26	51	77	32	—	—	—	—	—

WHITMORE, KAY
G, WHALERS

PERSONAL: Born April 10, 1967, at Sudbury, Ont.... 5-11/165.... Shoots left.
TRANSACTIONS/CAREER NOTES: Selected by Hartford Whalers as underage junior in second round (second Whalers pick, 26th overall) of NHL entry draft (June 15, 1985).
HONORS: Shared Dave Pinkney Trophy with Ron Tugnutt (1985-86).... Named to OHL All-Star first team (1985-86).... Won Jack Butterfield Trophy (1990-91).

Season Team	League	Gms.	Min.	W	L	T	GA	SO	Avg.	Gms.	Min.	W	L	GA	SO	Avg.
				REGULAR SEASON								**PLAYOFFS**				
83-84—Peterborough	OHL	29	1471	17	8	0	110	0	4.49	—	—	—	—	—	—	—
84-85—Peterborough	OHL	*53	*3077	35	16	2	172	†2	3.35	*17	*1020	10	4	58	0	3.41
85-86—Peterborough	OHL	41	2467	27	12	2	114	†3	*2.77	14	837	8	5	40	0	2.87
86-87—Peterborough	OHL	36	2159	14	17	5	118	1	3.28	7	366	3	3	17	1	2.79
87-88—Binghamton	AHL	38	2137	17	15	4	121	3	3.40	2	118	0	2	10	0	5.08
88-89—Binghamton	AHL	*56	3200	21	29	4	*241	1	4.52	—	—	—	—	—	—	—
—Hartford	NHL	3	*180	2	1	0	10	0	3.33	2	135	0	2	10	0	4.44
89-90—Binghamton	AHL	24	1386	3	19	2	109	0	4.72	—	—	—	—	—	—	—
—Hartford	NHL	9	442	4	2	1	26	0	3.53	—	—	—	—	—	—	—
90-91—Hartford	NHL	18	850	3	9	3	52	0	3.67	—	—	—	—	—	—	—
—Springfield	AHL	33	1916	22	9	1	98	1	3.07	*15	*926	11	4	*37	0	*2.40
91-92—Hartford	NHL	45	2567	14	21	6	155	3	3.62	1	19	0	0	1	0	3.16
NHL totals		75	4039	23	33	10	243	3	3.61	3	154	0	2	11	0	4.29

WHITNEY, RAY
C, SHARKS

PERSONAL: Born May 8, 1972, at Edmonton, Alta. . . . 5-9/160. . . . Shoots right.
TRANSACTIONS/CAREER NOTES: Selected by San Jose Sharks in second round (second Sharks pick, 23rd overall) of NHL entry draft (June 22, 1991).
HONORS: Won Four Broncos Memorial Trophy (1990-91). . . . Won Bob Clarke Trophy (1990-91). . . . Won WHL West Player of the Year Award (1990-91). . . . Won George Parsons Trophy (1990-91). . . . Named to Memorial Cup All-Star Team (1990-91). . . . Named to WHL All-Star first team (1990-91).

Season Team	League	Gms.	G	A	Pts.	Pen.	Gms.	G	A	Pts.	Pen.
			REGULAR SEASON					**PLAYOFFS**			
88-89—Spokane Chiefs	WHL	71	17	33	50	16	—	—	—	—	—
89-90—Spokane Chiefs	WHL	71	57	56	113	50	6	3	4	7	6
90-91—Spokane Chiefs	WHL	72	67	118	*185	36	15	13	18	*31	12
91-92—San Diego	IHL	63	36	54	90	12	4	0	0	0	0
—San Jose	NHL	2	0	3	3	0	—	—	—	—	—
NHL totals		2	0	3	3	0					

WHYTE, SEAN
RW, KINGS

PERSONAL: Born May 4, 1970, at Sudbury, Ont. . . . 6-0/198. . . . Shoots right.
TRANSACTIONS/CAREER NOTES: Stretched left knee ligaments (October 2, 1988). . . . Selected by Los Angeles Kings in eighth round (seventh Kings pick, 165th overall) of NHL entry draft (June 17, 1989).

Season Team	League	Gms.	G	A	Pts.	Pen.	Gms.	G	A	Pts.	Pen.
			REGULAR SEASON					**PLAYOFFS**			
86-87—Guelph	OHL	41	1	3	4	13	—	—	—	—	—
87-88—Guelph	OHL	62	6	22	28	71	—	—	—	—	—
88-89—Guelph	OHL	53	20	44	64	57	—	—	—	—	—
89-90—Owen Sound	OHL	54	23	30	53	90	3	0	1	1	10
90-91—Phoenix	IHL	60	18	17	35	61	4	1	0	1	2
91-92—Phoenix	IHL	72	24	30	54	113	—	—	—	—	—
—Los Angeles	NHL	3	0	0	0	0	—	—	—	—	—
NHL totals		3	0	0	0	0					

WIEMER, JIM
D, BRUINS

PERSONAL: Born January 9, 1961, at Sudbury, Ont. . . . 6-4/210. . . . Shoots left. . . . Full name: James Duncan Wiemer.
TRANSACTIONS/CAREER NOTES: Selected by Buffalo Sabres as underage junior in fourth round (fifth Sabres pick, 83rd overall) of NHL entry draft (June 11, 1980). . . . Traded by Sabres with RW Steve Patrick to New York Rangers for D Chris Renaud and D Dave Maloney (December 1984). . . . Traded by Rangers with rights to D Reijo Ruotsalainen, LW Ville Kentala and LW Clark Donatelli to Edmonton Oilers to complete earlier deal in which the Rangers acquired D Don Jackson, D Miroslav Horava and C Mike Golden (October 1986). . . . Traded by Oilers with RW Alan May to Los Angeles Kings for C Brian Wilks and D John English (March 7, 1989). . . . Signed as free agent by Boston Bruins (July 1989). . . . Bruised right leg (November 1989). . . . Pulled groin (January 27, 1992); missed 10 games. . . . Reinjured groin (March 19, 1992); missed six games.
HONORS: Won Eddie Shore Plaque (1985-86). . . . Named to AHL All-Star first team (1985-86).

Season Team	League	Gms.	G	A	Pts.	Pen.	Gms.	G	A	Pts.	Pen.
			REGULAR SEASON					**PLAYOFFS**			
78-79—Peterborough	OMJHL	63	15	12	27	50	18	4	4	8	15
79-80—Peterborough	OMJHL	53	17	32	49	63	14	6	9	15	19
80-81—Peterborough	OMJHL	65	41	54	95	102	5	1	2	3	15
81-82—Rochester	AHL	74	19	26	45	57	9	0	4	4	2
82-83—Rochester	AHL	74	15	44	59	43	15	5	15	20	22
—Buffalo	NHL	—	—	—	—	—	1	0	0	0	0
83-84—Buffalo	NHL	64	5	15	20	48	—	—	—	—	—
—Rochester	AHL	12	4	11	15	11	18	3	13	16	20
84-85—Rochester	AHL	13	1	9	10	24	—	—	—	—	—
—New Haven	AHL	33	9	27	36	39	—	—	—	—	—
—Buffalo	NHL	10	3	2	5	4	—	—	—	—	—
—New York Rangers	NHL	22	4	3	7	30	1	0	0	0	0
85-86—New Haven	AHL	73	24	49	73	108	—	—	—	—	—
—New York Rangers	NHL	7	3	0	3	2	8	1	0	1	6

W

Season Team	League	REGULAR SEASON Gms.	G	A	Pts.	Pen.	PLAYOFFS Gms.	G	A	Pts.	Pen.
86-87—New Haven	AHL	6	0	7	7	6	—	—	—	—	—
—Nova Scotia	AHL	59	9	25	34	72	5	0	4	4	2
87-88—Nova Scotia	AHL	57	11	32	43	99	5	1	1	2	14
—Edmonton	NHL	12	1	2	3	15	2	0	0	0	2
88-89—Cape Breton	AHL	51	12	29	41	80	—	—	—	—	—
—Los Angeles	NHL	9	2	3	5	20	10	2	1	3	19
—New Haven	AHL	3	1	1	2	2	7	2	3	5	2
89-90—Maine	AHL	6	3	4	7	27	—	—	—	—	—
—Boston	NHL	61	5	14	19	63	8	0	1	1	4
90-91—Boston	NHL	61	4	19	23	62	16	1	3	4	14
91-92—Maine	AHL	3	0	1	1	4	—	—	—	—	—
—Boston	NHL	47	1	8	9	84	15	1	3	4	14
NHL totals		293	28	66	94	328	61	5	8	13	59

WILKIE, BOB
D, RED WINGS

PERSONAL: Born February 11, 1969, at Calgary, Alta.... 6-2/200.... Shoots right.
TRANSACTIONS/CAREER NOTES: Selected by Detroit Red Wings as underage junior in second round (third Red Wings pick, 41st overall) of NHL entry draft (June 13, 1987).... Fractured kneecap (January 1990).

Season Team	League	REGULAR SEASON Gms.	G	A	Pts.	Pen.	PLAYOFFS Gms.	G	A	Pts.	Pen.
85-86—Calgary	WHL	63	8	19	27	56	—	—	—	—	—
86-87—Swift Current	WHL	65	12	38	50	50	4	1	3	4	2
87-88—Swift Current	WHL	67	12	68	80	124	10	4	12	16	8
88-89—Swift Current	WHL	62	18	67	85	89	12	1	11	12	47
89-90—Adirondack	AHL	58	5	33	38	64	6	1	4	5	2
90-91—Detroit	NHL	8	1	2	3	2	—	—	—	—	—
—Adirondack	AHL	43	6	18	24	71	2	1	0	1	2
91-92—Adirondack	AHL	7	1	4	5	6	16	2	5	7	12
NHL totals		8	1	2	3	2					

WILKIE, DAVID
D, CANADIENS

PERSONAL: Born May 30, 1974, at Ellensburg, Wash.... 6-2/202.... Shoots right.
COLLEGE: Cariboo (B.C.).
TRANSACTIONS/CAREER NOTES: Selected by Montreal Canadiens in first round (first Canadiens pick, 20th overall) of NHL entry draft (June 20, 1992).

Season Team	League	REGULAR SEASON Gms.	G	A	Pts.	Pen.	PLAYOFFS Gms.	G	A	Pts.	Pen.
89-90—Northwest Americans Jr. B.	WCHL	41	21	27	48	59	—	—	—	—	—
90-91—Seattle	WHL	25	1	1	2	22	—	—	—	—	—
91-92—Kamloops	WHL	71	12	28	40	153	16	6	5	11	19

WILKINSON, NEIL
D, SHARKS

PERSONAL: Born August 15, 1967, at Selkirk, Man.... 6-3/180.... Shoots right.... Full name: Neil John Wilkinson.
COLLEGE: Michigan State.
TRANSACTIONS/CAREER NOTES: Suffered concussion and broke nose (January 1986). ... Selected by Minnesota North Stars in second round (second North Stars pick, 30th overall) of NHL entry draft (June 21, 1986).... Twisted knee ligaments during training camp (September 1988).... Bruised left instep (November 9, 1989).... Strained back (January 1990).... Tore left thumb ligaments (March 6, 1991); missed five games.... Selected by San Jose Sharks in NHL dispersal draft (May 30, 1991).... Injured groin (December 16, 1991); missed four games.... Injured eye (Janaury 8, 1992); missed three games.... Strained back (February 4, 1992); missed 13 games.

Season Team	League	REGULAR SEASON Gms.	G	A	Pts.	Pen.	PLAYOFFS Gms.	G	A	Pts.	Pen.
85-86—Selkirk	MJHL	42	14	35	49	91	—	—	—	—	—
86-87—Michigan State	CCHA	19	3	4	7	18	—	—	—	—	—
87-88—Medicine Hat	WHL	55	11	21	32	157	5	1	0	1	2
88-89—Kalamazoo	IHL	39	5	15	20	96	—	—	—	—	—
89-90—Kalamazoo	IHL	20	6	7	13	62	—	—	—	—	—
—Minnesota	NHL	36	0	5	5	100	7	0	2	2	11
90-91—Kalamazoo	IHL	10	0	3	3	38	—	—	—	—	—
—Minnesota	NHL	50	2	9	11	117	22	3	3	6	12
91-92—San Jose	NHL	60	4	15	19	107	—	—	—	—	—
NHL totals		146	6	29	35	324	29	3	5	8	23

WILLIAMS, DARRYL
LW, KINGS

PERSONAL: Born February 9, 1968, at Mount Pearl, Nfld.... 5-11/185.... Shoots left.
TRANSACTIONS/CAREER NOTES: Traded by Hamilton Steelhawks with future considerations to Belleville Bulls for C Keith Gretzky (December 1986).... Signed as free agent by Los Angeles Kings (September 1989).

Season Team	League	REGULAR SEASON					PLAYOFFS				
		Gms.	G	A	Pts.	Pen.	Gms.	G	A	Pts.	Pen.
85-86—Victoria	WHL	38	3	2	5	66	—	—	—	—	—
86-87—Hamilton	OHL	24	2	4	6	36	—	—	—	—	—
—Belleville	OHL	34	7	6	13	72	—	—	—	—	—
87-88—Belleville	OHL	63	29	39	68	169	—	—	—	—	—
88-89—New Haven	AHL	15	5	5	10	24	—	—	—	—	—
—Belleville	OHL	45	24	21	45	137	—	—	—	—	—
89-90—New Haven	AHL	51	9	13	22	124	—	—	—	—	—
90-91—New Haven	AHL	57	14	11	25	278	—	—	—	—	—
—Phoenix	IHL	12	2	1	3	53	—	—	—	—	—
91-92—New Haven	AHL	13	0	2	2	69	—	—	—	—	—
—Phoenix	IHL	48	8	19	27	219	—	—	—	—	—

WILLIAMS, DAVID
D, SHARKS

PERSONAL: Born August 25, 1967, at Plainfield, N.J. . . . 6-2/195. . . . Shoots right. . . . Full name: David Andrew Williams.
HIGH SCHOOL: Choate Rosemary Hall (Wallingford, Conn.).
COLLEGE: Dartmouth.
TRANSACTIONS/CAREER NOTES: Selected by New Jersey Devils as underage junior in 12th round (12th Devils pick, 234th overall) of NHL entry draft (June 15, 1985). . . . Signed as free agent by San Jose Sharks (August 9, 1991).
HONORS: Named to ECAC All-Star first team (1988-89). . . . Named to NCAA All-America East second team (1988-89).

Season Team	League	REGULAR SEASON					PLAYOFFS				
		Gms.	G	A	Pts.	Pen.	Gms.	G	A	Pts.	Pen.
86-87—Dartmouth College	ECAC	23	2	19	21	20	—	—	—	—	—
87-88—Dartmouth College	ECAC	25	8	14	22	30	—	—	—	—	—
88-89—Dartmouth College	ECAC	25	4	11	15	28	—	—	—	—	—
89-90—Dartmouth College	ECAC	26	3	12	15	32	—	—	—	—	—
90-91—Knoxville	ECHL	38	12	15	27	40	3	0	0	0	4
—Muskegon	IHL	14	1	2	3	4	—	—	—	—	—
91-92—Kansas City	IHL	18	2	3	5	22	—	—	—	—	—
—San Jose	NHL	56	3	25	28	40	—	—	—	—	—
NHL totals		56	3	25	28	40					

WILLIAMS, SEAN
C, BLACKHAWKS

PERSONAL: Born January 28, 1968, at Oshawa, Ont. . . . 6-1/182. . . . Shoots left.
TRANSACTIONS/CAREER NOTES: Selected by Minnesota North Stars as underage junior in 12th round (11th North Stars pick, 245th overall) of NHL entry draft (June 21, 1986).
HONORS: Won Jim Mahon Memorial Trophy (1987-88). . . . Named to OHL All-Star first team (1987-88).

Season Team	League	REGULAR SEASON					PLAYOFFS				
		Gms.	G	A	Pts.	Pen.	Gms.	G	A	Pts.	Pen.
84-85—Oshawa	OHL	40	6	7	13	28	5	1	0	1	0
85-86—Oshawa	OHL	55	15	23	38	23	6	2	3	5	4
86-87—Oshawa	OHL	62	21	23	44	32	25	7	5	12	19
87-88—Oshawa	OHL	65	58	65	123	38	7	3	3	6	6
88-89—Saginaw	IHL	77	32	27	59	75	6	0	3	3	0
89-90—Indianapolis	IHL	78	27	31	58	25	14	8	5	13	12
90-91—Indianapolis	IHL	82	46	52	98	59	7	1	2	3	12
91-92—Indianapolis	IHL	79	29	36	65	89	—	—	—	—	—
—Chicago	NHL	2	0	0	0	4	—	—	—	—	—
NHL totals		2	0	0	0	4					

WILLIS, RICK
LW, RANGERS

PERSONAL: Born January 9, 1972, at Lynn, Mass. . . . 6-0/185. . . . Shoots left. . . . Full name: Richard Bancroft Willis Jr.
HIGH SCHOOL: Pingree (South Hamilton, Mass.).
COLLEGE: Michigan.
TRANSACTIONS/CAREER NOTES: Selected by New York Rangers in fourth round (fifth Rangers pick, 76th overall) of NHL entry draft (June 16, 1990).

Season Team	League	REGULAR SEASON					PLAYOFFS				
		Gms.	G	A	Pts.	Pen.	Gms.	G	A	Pts.	Pen.
86-87—Pingree H.S.	Mass. H.S.	22	14	17	31		—	—	—	—	—
87-88—Pingree H.S.	Mass. H.S.	22	25	30	55		—	—	—	—	—
88-89—Pingree H.S.	Mass. H.S.	24	23	30	53		—	—	—	—	—
89-90—Pingree H.S.	Mass. H.S.		17	30	47		—	—	—	—	—
90-91—Pingree H.S.	Mass. H.S.				Statistics unavailable.						
91-92—University of Michigan	CCHA	32	1	4	5	42	—	—	—	—	—

WILLNER, BRAD
D, DEVILS

PERSONAL: Born January 6, 1973, at Edina, Minn. . . . 6-3/190. . . . Shoots right. . . . Full name: Bradley Willner.
HIGH SCHOOL: Richfield (Minn.).
TRANSACTIONS/CAREER NOTES: Selected by New Jersey Devils in fourth round (fifth Devils pick, 77th overall) of NHL entry draft (June 22, 1991).

W

Season	Team	League	REGULAR SEASON					PLAYOFFS				
			Gms.	G	A	Pts.	Pen.	Gms.	G	A	Pts.	Pen.
88-89—Richfield H.S.	Minn. H.S.	22	1	6	7	16	—	—	—	—	—
89-90—Richfield H.S.	Minn. H.S.	23	7	14	21	26	—	—	—	—	—
90-91—Richfield H.S.	Minn. H.S.	25	7	18	25	24	—	—	—	—	—
91-92—Lake Superior State	CCHA	16	0	0	0	8	—	—	—	—	—

WILSON, CAREY
C/RW, FLAMES

PERSONAL: Born May 19, 1962, at Winnipeg, Man. . . . 6-2/205. . . . Shoots right. . . . Full name: Carey John Wilson. . . . Son of Dr. Gerry Wilson, former vice-president and team doctor of Winnipeg Jets of WHA.
COLLEGE: Dartmouth.

TRANSACTIONS/CAREER NOTES: Selected by Chicago Blackhawks in fourth round (eighth Blackhawks pick, 67th overall) of NHL entry draft (June 11, 1980). . . . Traded by Blackhawks to Calgary Flames for RW Denis Cyr (November 1982). . . . Suffered ruptured spleen (April 28, 1986); missed remainder of playoffs. . . . Traded by Flames with D Neil Sheehy and rights to LW Lane MacDonald to Hartford Whalers for RW Shane Churla and D Dana Murzyn (January 1987). . . . Strained shoulder (October 1987). . . . Traded by Whalers with fifth-round pick in 1990 draft to New York Rangers for C Brian Lawton, LW Don Maloney and D Norm Maciver (December 26, 1988). . . . Bruised wrist (February 1989). . . . Sprained left knee ligaments (October 28, 1989); missed 26 games. . . . Sprained right knee (March 3, 1990); missed eight games. . . . Traded by Rangers with future considerations to C/RW Jody Hull (July 9, 1990). . . . Pulled groin in informal skate prior to training camp (September 6, 1990). . . . Reinjured groin (November 17, 1990); missed eight games. . . . Tore cartilage (February 15, 1991); missed seven games. . . . Traded by Whalers to Flames for RW Mark Hunter (March 5, 1991). . . . Irritated shoulder and ribs (October 20, 1991); missed 14 games. . . . Suffered reactive tissue irritation (December 1991); missed 17 games.

Season	Team	League	REGULAR SEASON					PLAYOFFS				
			Gms.	G	A	Pts.	Pen.	Gms.	G	A	Pts.	Pen.
78-79—Calgary Chinooks	AJHL	60	30	34	64		—	—	—	—	—
79-80—Dartmouth College	ECAC	31	16	22	38	20	—	—	—	—	—
80-81—Dartmouth College	ECAC	21	9	13	22	52	—	—	—	—	—
81-82—Helsinki IFK	Finland	39	15	17	32	58	7	1	4	5	6
82-83—Helsinki IFK	Finland	36	16	24	40	62	9	1	3	4	12
83-84—Canadian Olympic Team	Int'l	59	21	24	45	34	—	—	—	—	—
—Calgary	NHL	15	2	5	7	2	6	3	1	4	2
84-85—Calgary	NHL	74	24	48	72	27	4	0	0	0	0
85-86—Calgary	NHL	76	29	29	58	24	9	0	2	2	2
86-87—Calgary	NHL	80	20	36	56	42	6	1	1	2	6
87-88—Calgary	NHL	34	9	21	30	18	—	—	—	—	—
—Hartford	NHL	36	18	20	38	22	6	2	4	6	2
88-89—Hartford	NHL	34	11	11	22	14	—	—	—	—	—
—New York Rangers	NHL	41	21	34	55	45	4	1	2	3	2
89-90—New York Rangers	NHL	41	9	17	26	57	10	2	1	3	0
90-91—Hartford	NHL	45	8	15	23	16	—	—	—	—	—
—Calgary	NHL	12	3	3	6	2	7	2	2	4	0
91-92—Calgary	NHL	42	11	12	23	37	—	—	—	—	—
NHL totals			530	165	251	416	306	52	11	13	24	14

WILSON, DOUG
D, SHARKS

W

PERSONAL: Born July 5, 1957, at Ottawa. . . . 6-1/187. . . . Shoots left. . . . Full name: Douglas Wilson Jr.
TRANSACTIONS/CAREER NOTES: Underwent knee surgery; missed part of 1976-77 season. . . . Selected by Chicago Blackhawks from Ottawa 67's in first round (first Blackhawks pick, sixth overall) of NHL amateur draft (June 14, 1977). . . . Injured shoulder and underwent surgery; missed part of 1978-79 season. . . . Broke jaw (November 25, 1981). . . . Injured ankle (November 1983). . . . Broke nose (February 3, 1984). . . . Fractured skull (March 4, 1984); missed remainder of season. . . . Sprained right knee (March 8, 1987). . . . Underwent shoulder surgery (December 1987). . . . Fractured right hand (January 25, 1989). . . . Bruised left shoulder (March 4, 1989). . . . Pulled left groin (April 9, 1989). . . . Bruised toe (January 1990). . . . Pulled groin (March 1990). . . . Bruised forearm (April 1990). . . . Underwent surgery to right ankle ligaments (July 27, 1990); missed first 25 games of season. . . . Aggravated right ankle at Toronto (December 8, 1990); missed four games. . . . Traded by Blackhawks to San Jose Sharks for RW Kerry Toporowski and second-round pick in 1992 draft (September 6, 1991). . . . Dislocated thumb (October 26, 1991); missed 10 games. . . . Strained back (January 24, 1992); missed three games. . . . Sprained knee (February 23, 1992).
HONORS: Named to OHA Major Junior A All-Star second team (1975-76). . . . Named to OMJHL All-Star first team (1976-77). . . . Won James Norris Memorial Trophy (1981-82). . . . Named to THE SPORTING NEWS All-Star first team (1981-82). . . . Named to NHL All-Star first team (1981-82). . . . Named to THE SPORTING NEWS All-Star second team (1984-85 and 1989-90). . . . Named to NHL All-Star second team (1984-85 and 1989-90).
MISCELLANEOUS: Does not wear a helmet.

Season	Team	League	REGULAR SEASON					PLAYOFFS				
			Gms.	G	A	Pts.	Pen.	Gms.	G	A	Pts.	Pen.
74-75—Ottawa	OHA Mj. Jr. A	55	29	58	87	75	—	—	—	—	—
75-76—Ottawa	OHA Mj. Jr. A	58	26	62	88	142	12	5	10	15	24
76-77—Ottawa	OMJHL	43	25	54	79	85	19	4	20	24	34
77-78—Chicago	NHL	77	14	20	34	72	4	0	0	0	0
78-79—Chicago	NHL	56	5	21	26	37	—	—	—	—	—
79-80—Chicago	NHL	73	12	49	61	70	7	2	8	10	6
80-81—Chicago	NHL	76	12	39	51	80	3	0	3	3	2
81-82—Chicago	NHL	76	39	46	85	54	15	3	10	13	32
82-83—Chicago	NHL	74	18	51	69	58	13	4	11	15	12
83-84—Chicago	NHL	66	13	45	58	64	5	0	3	3	0

			REGULAR SEASON					PLAYOFFS			
Season Team	League	Gms.	G	A	Pts.	Pen.	Gms.	G	A	Pts.	Pen.
84-85—Chicago	NHL	78	22	54	76	44	12	3	10	13	12
85-86—Chicago	NHL	79	17	47	64	80	3	1	1	2	2
86-87—Chicago	NHL	69	16	32	48	36	4	0	0	0	0
87-88—Chicago	NHL	27	8	24	32	28	—	—	—	—	—
88-89—Chicago	NHL	66	15	47	62	69	4	1	2	3	0
89-90—Chicago	NHL	70	23	50	73	40	20	3	12	15	18
90-91—Chicago	NHL	51	11	29	40	32	5	2	1	3	2
91-92—San Jose	NHL	44	9	19	28	26	—	—	—	—	—
NHL totals		982	234	573	807	790	95	19	61	80	86

WILSON, RON

C, BLUES

PERSONAL: Born May 13, 1956, at Toronto. . . . 5-9/180. . . . Shoots left. . . . Full name: Ronald Lee Wilson.
TRANSACTIONS/CAREER NOTES: Selected by Montreal Canadiens from St. Catharines Blackhawks in 15th round (15th Canadiens pick, 133rd overall) of NHL amateur draft (June 1, 1976). . . . Sold by Canadiens to Winnipeg Jets (June 1979). . . . Named player/assistant coach of Moncton Golden Flames (May 1988). . . . Traded by Jets to St. Louis Blues for C Doug Evans (January 22, 1990).
HONORS: Named to AHL All-Star second team (1988-89).

			REGULAR SEASON					PLAYOFFS			
Season Team	League	Gms.	G	A	Pts.	Pen.	Gms.	G	A	Pts.	Pen.
74-75—Markham Waxers	OPJHL	43	26	28	54	24	—	—	—	—	—
—Toronto	OHA Mj. Jr. A	16	6	12	18	6	23	9	17	26	6
75-76—St. Catharines	OHA Mj. Jr. A	64	37	62	99	44	4	1	6	7	7
76-77—Nova Scotia	AHL	67	15	21	36	18	6	0	0	0	0
77-78—Nova Scotia	AHL	59	15	25	40	17	11	4	4	8	9
78-79—Nova Scotia	AHL	77	33	42	75	91	10	5	6	11	14
79-80—Winnipeg	NHL	79	21	36	57	28	—	—	—	—	—
80-81—Winnipeg	NHL	77	18	33	51	55	—	—	—	—	—
81-82—Tulsa	CHL	41	20	38	58	22	3	1	0	1	2
—Winnipeg	NHL	39	3	13	16	49	—	—	—	—	—
82-83—Sherbrooke	AHL	65	30	55	85	71	—	—	—	—	—
—Winnipeg	NHL	12	6	3	9	4	3	2	2	4	2
83-84—Winnipeg	NHL	51	3	12	15	12	—	—	—	—	—
—Sherbrooke	AHL	22	10	30	40	16	—	—	—	—	—
84-85—Winnipeg	NHL	75	10	9	19	31	8	4	2	6	2
85-86—Winnipeg	NHL	54	6	7	13	16	1	0	0	0	0
—Sherbrooke	AHL	10	9	8	17	9	—	—	—	—	—
86-87—Winnipeg	NHL	80	3	13	16	13	10	1	2	3	0
87-88—Winnipeg	NHL	69	5	8	13	28	1	0	0	0	2
88-89—Moncton	AHL	80	31	61	92	110	8	1	4	5	20
89-90—Moncton	AHL	47	16	37	53	64	—	—	—	—	—
—St. Louis	NHL	33	3	17	20	23	12	3	5	8	18
90-91—St. Louis	NHL	73	10	27	37	54	7	0	0	0	28
91-92—St. Louis	NHL	64	12	17	29	46	6	0	1	1	0
NHL totals		706	100	195	295	359	48	10	12	22	52

WILSON, ROSS

RW

PERSONAL: Born June 26, 1969, at The Pas, Man. . . . 6-3/197. . . . Shoots right.
TRANSACTIONS/CAREER NOTES: Selected by Los Angeles as underage junior in third round (third Kings pick, 43rd overall) of NHL entry draft (June 13, 1987).

			REGULAR SEASON					PLAYOFFS			
Season Team	League	Gms.	G	A	Pts.	Pen.	Gms.	G	A	Pts.	Pen.
86-87—Peterborough	OHL	66	28	11	39	91	12	3	5	8	16
87-88—Peterborough	OHL	66	29	30	59	114	12	2	9	11	15
88-89—Peterborough	OHL	64	48	41	89	90	15	10	13	23	23
89-90—New Haven	AHL	61	19	14	33	39	—	—	—	—	—
90-91—New Haven	AHL	68	29	17	46	28	—	—	—	—	—
91-92—Phoenix	IHL	28	9	9	18	81	—	—	—	—	—
—Kalamazoo	IHL	31	18	6	24	38	11	9	1	10	6

WINCH, JASON

LW, SABRES

PERSONAL: Born May 23, 1971, at Listowel, Ont. . . . 6-1/215. . . . Shoots left.
TRANSACTIONS/CAREER NOTES: Selected by Buffalo Sabres in ninth round (eighth Sabres pick, 187th overall) of NHL entry draft (June 16, 1990).

			REGULAR SEASON					PLAYOFFS			
Season Team	League	Gms.	G	A	Pts.	Pen.	Gms.	G	A	Pts.	Pen.
86-87—St. Catharines Jr. B	OHA	39	21	33	54	10	—	—	—	—	—
87-88—Toronto	OHL	64	14	25	39	14	4	1	2	3	0
88-89—Toronto	OHL	66	33	50	83	8	6	3	3	6	0
89-90—Dukes of Hamilton	OHL	18	6	16	22	17	—	—	—	—	—
—Niagara Falls	OHL	46	25	46	71	6	16	9	12	21	4
90-91—Niagara Falls	OHL	66	40	82	122	16	14	14	12	26	6
91-92—Rochester	AHL	73	23	35	58	24	12	2	6	8	0

W

WINNES, CHRIS
RW, BRUINS

PERSONAL: Born February 12, 1968, at Ridgefield, Conn. . . . 6-0/170. . . . Shoots right. . . . Full name: Christopher Winnes.
HIGH SCHOOL: Ridgefield (Conn.), then Northwood School (Lake Placid, N.Y.).
COLLEGE: New Hampshire.
TRANSACTIONS/CAREER NOTES: Selected by Boston Bruins in eighth round (ninth Bruins pick, 161st overall) of NHL entry draft (June 13, 1987). . . . Broke nose (February 23, 1992).

			REGULAR SEASON					PLAYOFFS				
Season	Team	League	Gms.	G	A	Pts.	Pen.	Gms.	G	A	Pts.	Pen.
85-86—Ridgefield H.S.	Conn. H.S.		24	40	30	70	—	—	—	—	—	—
86-87—Northwood School	N.Y. H.S.		27	25	25	50	—	—	—	—	—	—
87-88—Univ. of New Hampshire	Hockey East		30	17	19	36	28	—	—	—	—	—
88-89—Univ. of New Hampshire	Hockey East		30	11	20	31	22	—	—	—	—	—
89-90—Univ. of New Hampshire	Hockey East		24	10	13	23	12	—	—	—	—	—
90-91—Univ. of New Hampshire	Hockey East		33	15	16	31	24	—	—	—	—	—
—Maine	AHL		7	3	1	4	0	1	0	2	2	0
—Boston	NHL		—	—	—	—	—	1	0	0	0	0
91-92—Maine	AHL		45	12	35	47	30	—	—	—	—	—
—Boston	NHL		24	1	3	4	6	—	—	—	—	—
NHL totals			24	1	3	4	6	1	0	0	0	0

WOHLERS, NICK
D, MAPLE LEAFS

PERSONAL: Born July 12, 1970, at Stillwater, Minn. . . . 6-1/210. . . . Shoots right.
HIGH SCHOOL: Stillwater (Minn.).
COLLEGE: St. Thomas (Minn.).
TRANSACTIONS/CAREER NOTES: Selected by Toronto Maple Leafs in NHL supplemental draft (June 19, 1992).

			REGULAR SEASON					PLAYOFFS				
Season	Team	League	Gms.	G	A	Pts.	Pen.	Gms.	G	A	Pts.	Pen.
88-89—University of St. Thomas	MIAC		25	1	9	10		—	—	—	—	—
89-90—University of St. Thomas	MIAC		24	0	11	11	48	—	—	—	—	—
90-91—University of St. Thomas	MIAC		28	11	8	19	69	—	—	—	—	—
91-92—University of St. Thomas	MIAC		30	25	34	*59		—	—	—	—	—

WOLANIN, CRAIG
D, NORDIQUES

PERSONAL: Born July 27, 1967, at Grosse Point, Mich. . . . 6-3/205. . . . Shoots left.
TRANSACTIONS/CAREER NOTES: Selected by New Jersey Devils as underage junior in first round (first Devils pick, third overall) of NHL entry draft (June 15, 1985). . . . Bruised left shoulder (October 31, 1985). . . . Broke ring finger on left hand (February 1, 1986). . . . Underwent surgery to finger (February 19, 1986). . . . Suffered sore left hip (December 1987). . . . Sprained right knee (November 15, 1988). . . . Underwent surgery to right knee (December 1988). . . . Injured finger (November 22, 1989). . . . Traded by Devils with future considerations to Quebec Nordiques for C Peter Stastny (March 6, 1990); D Randy Velischek sent to Nordiques in August 1990 to complete deal. . . . Injured knee (April 1, 1990). . . . Injured groin (October 17, 1991); missed three games. . . . Injured knee (January 8, 1992); missed four games.

			REGULAR SEASON					PLAYOFFS				
Season	Team	League	Gms.	G	A	Pts.	Pen.	Gms.	G	A	Pts.	Pen.
84-85—Kitchener	OHL		60	5	16	21	95	4	1	1	2	2
85-86—New Jersey	NHL		44	2	16	18	74	—	—	—	—	—
86-87—New Jersey	NHL		68	4	6	10	109	—	—	—	—	—
87-88—New Jersey	NHL		78	6	25	31	170	18	2	5	7	51
88-89—New Jersey	NHL		56	3	8	11	69	—	—	—	—	—
89-90—Utica	AHL		6	2	4	6	2	—	—	—	—	—
—New Jersey	NHL		37	1	7	8	47	—	—	—	—	—
—Quebec	NHL		13	0	3	3	10	—	—	—	—	—
90-91—Quebec	NHL		80	5	13	18	89	—	—	—	—	—
91-92—Quebec	NHL		69	2	11	13	80	—	—	—	—	—
NHL totals			445	23	89	112	648	18	2	5	7	51

WOOD, RANDY
RW/LW, SABRES

PERSONAL: Born October 12, 1963, at Princeton, NJ. . . . 6-0/195. . . . Shoots left. . . . Full name: Randolph B. Wood.
COLLEGE: Yale.
TRANSACTIONS/CAREER NOTES: Signed as free agent by New York Islanders (August 1986). . . . Suspended four games by NHL for stick-swinging incident (October 17, 1989). . . . Strained right shoulder (March 17, 1990). . . . Traded by Islanders with C Pat LaFontaine, D Randy Hillier and future considerations to Buffalo Sabres for C Pierre Turgeon, RW Benoit Hogue, D Uwe Krupp and C Dave McLlwain (October 25, 1991).

			REGULAR SEASON					PLAYOFFS				
Season	Team	League	Gms.	G	A	Pts.	Pen.	Gms.	G	A	Pts.	Pen.
82-83—Yale University	ECAC		26	5	14	19	10	—	—	—	—	—
83-84—Yale University	ECAC		18	7	7	14	10	—	—	—	—	—
84-85—Yale University	ECAC		32	25	28	53	23	—	—	—	—	—
85-86—Yale University	ECAC		31	25	30	55	26	—	—	—	—	—
86-87—Springfield	AHL		75	23	24	47	57	—	—	—	—	—
—New York Islanders	NHL		6	1	0	1	4	13	1	3	4	14
87-88—New York Islanders	NHL		75	22	16	38	80	5	1	0	1	6
—Springfield	AHL		1	0	1	1	0	—	—	—	—	—

			REGULAR SEASON					PLAYOFFS				
Season Team	League	Gms.	G	A	Pts.	Pen.		Gms.	G	A	Pts.	Pen.
88-89—Springfield....................	AHL	1	1	1	2	0		—	—	—	—	—
—New York Islanders.........	NHL	77	15	13	28	44		—	—	—	—	—
89-90—New York Islanders.........	NHL	74	24	24	48	39		5	1	1	2	4
90-91—New York Islanders.........	NHL	76	24	18	42	45		—	—	—	—	—
91-92—New York Islanders.........	NHL	8	2	2	4	21		—	—	—	—	—
—Buffalo........................	NHL	70	20	16	36	65		7	2	1	3	6
NHL totals.................		386	108	89	197	298		30	5	5	10	30

WOODCROFT, CRAIG
LW, BLACKHAWKS

PERSONAL: Born December 3, 1969, at Toronto. . . . 6-1/195. . . . Shoots left. . . . Full name: Craig Patrick Woodcroft.
COLLEGE: Colgate.
TRANSACTIONS/CAREER NOTES: Selected by Chicago Blackhawks in seventh round (sixth Blackhawks pick, 134th overall) of NHL entry draft (June 11, 1988).
HONORS: Named ECAC Playoff Most Valuable Player (1989-90). . . . Named to ECAC All-Tournament team (1989-90).

			REGULAR SEASON					PLAYOFFS				
Season Team	League	Gms.	G	A	Pts.	Pen.		Gms.	G	A	Pts.	Pen.
86-87—Pickering Jr. B	OHA	37	21	21	42	42		—	—	—	—	—
87-88—Colgate University	ECAC	29	7	10	17	28		—	—	—	—	—
88-89—Colgate University	ECAC	29	20	29	49	62		—	—	—	—	—
—Canadian National Team..	Int'l	2	0	0	0	4		—	—	—	—	—
89-90—Colgate University	ECAC	37	20	26	46	108		—	—	—	—	—
90-91—Colgate University	ECAC	32	26	30	56	50		—	—	—	—	—
91-92—Indianapolis	IHL	75	21	17	38	67		—	—	—	—	—

WOODWARD, ROBERT
LW, CANUCKS

PERSONAL: Born January 15, 1971, at Evanston, Ill. . . . 6-4/225. . . . Shoots left. . . . Full name: Robert Fairfield Woodward.
HIGH SCHOOL: Deerfield (Ill.).
COLLEGE: Michigan State.
TRANSACTIONS/CAREER NOTES: Bruised kidney playing football (October 1987). . . . Selected by Vancouver Canucks in second round (second Canucks pick, 29th overall) of NHL entry draft (June 17, 1989).

			REGULAR SEASON					PLAYOFFS				
Season Team	League	Gms.	G	A	Pts.	Pen.		Gms.	G	A	Pts.	Pen.
87-88—Deerfield H.S.	Ill. H.S.	25	36	55	91			—	—	—	—	—
88-89—Deerfield H.S.	Ill. H.S.	29	46	71	117	12		—	—	—	—	—
89-90—Michigan State................	CCHA	44	17	9	26	8		—	—	—	—	—
90-91—Michigan State................	CCHA	32	5	13	18	16		—	—	—	—	—
91-92—Michigan State................	CCHA	43	14	16	30	64		—	—	—	—	—

WOOLLEY, JASON
D, CAPITALS

PERSONAL: Born July 27, 1969, at Toronto. . . . 6-0/190. . . . Shoots left. . . . Full name: Jason Douglas Woolley.
COLLEGE: Michigan State.
TRANSACTIONS/CAREER NOTES: Selected by Washington Capitals in third round (fourth Capitals pick, 61st overall) of NHL entry draft (June 17, 1989).
HONORS: Named to CCHA All-Rookie Team (1988-89). . . . Named to CCHA All-Star first team (1990-91). . . . Named to NCAA All-America West first team (1990-91).
MISCELLANEOUS: Member of 1992 silver-medal-winning Canadian Olympic team.

			REGULAR SEASON					PLAYOFFS				
Season Team	League	Gms.	G	A	Pts.	Pen.		Gms.	G	A	Pts.	Pen.
87-88—St. Michael's Jr. B............	ODHA	31	19	37	56	22		—	—	—	—	—
88-89—Michigan State................	CCHA	47	12	25	37	26		—	—	—	—	—
89-90—Michigan State................	CCHA	45	10	38	48	26		—	—	—	—	—
90-91—Michigan State................	CCHA	40	15	44	59	24		—	—	—	—	—
91-92—Canadian National Team..	Int'l	60	14	30	44	36		—	—	—	—	—
—Canadian Olympic Team ..	Int'l	8	0	5	5	4		—	—	—	—	—
—Baltimore........................	AHL	15	1	10	11	6		—	—	—	—	—
—Washington	NHL	1	0	0	0	0		—	—	—	—	—
NHL totals.................		1	0	0	0	0						

WREGGET, KEN
G, PENGUINS

PERSONAL: Born March 25, 1964, at Brandon, Man. . . . 6-1/195. . . . Shoots left.
TRANSACTIONS/CAREER NOTES: Selected by Toronto Maple Leafs as underage junior in third round (fourth Maple Leafs pick, 45th overall) of NHL entry draft (June 9, 1982). . . . Injured knee (December 26, 1985). . . . Traded by Maple Leafs to Philadelphia Flyers for two first-round picks in 1989 draft (RW Rob Pearson and D Steve Bancroft) (March 6, 1989). . . . Tore hamstring (November 1, 1989); missed seven games. . . . Pulled hamstring (March 24, 1990). . . . Strained right hip flexor (November 4, 1990); missed 15 games. . . . Traded by Flyers with RW Rick Tocchet, D Kjell Samuelsson and third-round pick in 1992 draft to Pittsburgh Penguins for RW Mark Recchi, D Brian Benning and first-round pick in 1992 draft previously acquired from Los Angeles Kings (February 19, 1992).
HONORS: Won Top Goaltender Trophy (1983-84). . . . Named to WHL East All-Star first team (1983-84).

			REGULAR SEASON						PLAYOFFS						
Season Team	League	Gms.	Min.	W	L	T	GA	SO	Avg.	Gms.	Min.	W	L	GA	SO	Avg.
81-82—Lethbridge....................	WHL	36	1713	19	12	0	118	1	4.13	3	84			3	0	2.14
82-83—Lethbridge....................	WHL	48	2696	26	17	1	157	1	3.49	*20	*1154	14	5	58	*1	*3.02

Season Team	League	REGULAR SEASON								PLAYOFFS					
		Gms.	Min.	W	L	T	GA	SO	Avg.	Gms.	Min.	W	L	GA SO	Avg.
83-84—Lethbridge	WHL	53	3053	32	20	0	161	0	*3.16	4	210	1	3	18 0	5.14
—Toronto	NHL	3	*165	1	1	1	14	0	5.09	—	—	—	—	— —	—
84-85—Toronto	NHL	23	1278	2	15	3	103	0	4.84	—	—	—	—	— —	—
—St. Catharines	AHL	12	688	2	8	1	48	0	4.19	—	—	—	—	— —	—
85-86—St. Catharines	AHL	18	1058	8	9	0	78	1	4.42	—	—	—	—	— —	—
—Toronto	NHL	30	1566	9	13	4	113	0	4.33	10	607	6	4	32 †1	3.16
86-87—Toronto	NHL	56	3026	22	28	3	200	0	3.97	13	761	7	6	29 1	*2.29
87-88—Toronto	NHL	56	3000	12	35	4	222	2	4.44	2	108	0	1	11 0	6.11
88-89—Toronto	NHL	32	1888	9	20	2	139	0	4.42	—	—	—	—	— —	—
—Philadelphia	NHL	3	130	1	1	0	13	0	6.00	5	268	2	2	10 0	2.24
89-90—Philadelphia	NHL	51	2961	22	24	3	169	0	3.42	—	—	—	—	— —	—
90-91—Philadelphia	NHL	30	1484	10	14	3	88	0	3.56	—	—	—	—	— —	—
91-92—Philadelphia	NHL	23	1259	9	8	3	75	0	3.57	—	—	—	—	— —	—
—Pittsburgh	NHL	9	448	5	3	0	31	0	4.15	1	40	0	0	4 0	6.00
NHL totals		316	17205	102	162	26	1167	2	4.07	31	1784	15	13	86 2	2.89

WRIGHT, TYLER
C, OILERS

PERSONAL: Born April 6, 1973, at Canora, Sask. . . . 5-11/175. . . . Shoots right.
TRANSACTIONS/CAREER NOTES: Selected by Edmonton Oilers in first round (first Oilers pick, 12th overall) of NHL entry draft (June 22, 1991).

Season Team	League	REGULAR SEASON					PLAYOFFS				
		Gms.	G	A	Pts.	Pen.	Gms.	G	A	Pts.	Pen.
89-90—Swift Current	WHL	67	14	18	32	119	4	0	0	0	12
90-91—Swift Current	WHL	66	41	51	92	157	3	0	0	0	6
91-92—Swift Current	WHL	63	36	46	82	295	8	2	5	7	16

YAKE, TERRY
C, WHALERS

PERSONAL: Born October 22, 1968, at New Westminister, B.C. . . . 5-11/175. . . . Shoots right.
TRANSACTIONS/CAREER NOTES: Selected by Hartford Whalers in fourth round (third Whalers pick, 81st overall) of NHL entry draft (June 13, 1987).

Season Team	League	REGULAR SEASON					PLAYOFFS				
		Gms.	G	A	Pts.	Pen.	Gms.	G	A	Pts.	Pen.
84-85—Brandon	WHL	11	1	1	2	0	—	—	—	—	—
85-86—Brandon	WHL	72	26	26	52	49	—	—	—	—	—
86-87—Brandon	WHL	71	44	58	102	64	—	—	—	—	—
87-88—Brandon	WHL	72	55	85	140	59	3	4	2	6	7
88-89—Hartford	NHL	2	0	0	0	0	—	—	—	—	—
—Binghamton	AHL	75	39	56	95	57	—	—	—	—	—
89-90—Hartford	NHL	2	0	1	1	0	—	—	—	—	—
—Binghamton	AHL	77	13	42	55	37	—	—	—	—	—
90-91—Hartford	NHL	19	1	4	5	10	6	1	1	2	16
—Springfield	AHL	60	35	42	77	56	15	9	9	18	10
91-92—Hartford	NHL	15	1	1	2	4	—	—	—	—	—
—Springfield	AHL	53	21	34	55	63	8	3	4	7	2
NHL totals		38	2	6	8	14	6	1	1	2	16

YAKUBOV, RAVIL
C, FLAMES

PERSONAL: Born July 26, 1970, at Moscow, U.S.S.R. . . . 6-1/187. . . . Shoots left.
TRANSACTIONS/CAREER NOTES: Selected by Calgary Flames in sixth round (sixth Flames pick, 126th overall) of NHL entry draft (June 20, 1992).

Season Team	League	REGULAR SEASON					PLAYOFFS				
		Gms.	G	A	Pts.	Pen.	Gms.	G	A	Pts.	Pen.
90-91—Dynamo Moscow	USSR	31	4	4	8	6	—	—	—	—	—
91-92—Dynamo Moscow	CIS	39	14	1	15	29	—	—	—	—	—

YASHIN, ALEXEI
C, SENATORS

PERSONAL: Born November 5, 1973, at Sverdlovsk, U.S.S.R. . . . 6-2/189. . . . Shoots right.
TRANSACTIONS/CAREER NOTES: Selected by Ottawa Senators in first round (first Senators pick, second overall) of NHL entry draft (June 20, 1992).

Season Team	League	REGULAR SEASON					PLAYOFFS				
		Gms.	G	A	Pts.	Pen.	Gms.	G	A	Pts.	Pen.
90-91—Automobilist Sverdlovsk	USSR	26	2	1	3	10	—	—	—	—	—
91-92—Dynamo Moscow	CIS	35	7	5	12	19	—	—	—	—	—

YAWNEY, TRENT
D, FLAMES

PERSONAL: Born September 29, 1965, at Hudson Bay, Sask. . . . 6-3/185. . . . Shoots left.
TRANSACTIONS/CAREER NOTES: Selected by Chicago Blackhawks as underage junior in third round (second Blackhawks pick, 45th overall) of NHL entry draft (June 9, 1984). . . . Bruised left shoulder (March 1989). . . . Strained right knee (April 24, 1989). . . . Bruised kidney (November 11, 1989). . . . Bruised thigh (January 1990). . . . Strained knee (October 1990). . . . Traded by Blackhawks to Calgary Flames for LW Stephane Matteau (December 16, 1991).

Season Team	League	REGULAR SEASON					PLAYOFFS				
		Gms.	G	A	Pts.	Pen.	Gms.	G	A	Pts.	Pen.
81-82—Saskatoon	WHL	6	1	0	1	0	—	—	—	—	—
82-83—Saskatoon	WHL	59	6	31	37	44	6	0	2	2	0
83-84—Saskatoon	WHL	72	13	46	59	81	—	—	—	—	—
84-85—Saskatoon	WHL	72	16	51	67	158	3	1	6	7	7
85-86—Team Canada	Int'l	73	6	15	21	60	—	—	—	—	—
86-87—Team Canada	Int'l	51	4	15	19	37	—	—	—	—	—
87-88—Canadian National Team	Int'l	60	4	12	16	81	—	—	—	—	—
—Canadian Olympic Team	Int'l	8	1	1	2	6	—	—	—	—	—
—Chicago	NHL	15	2	8	10	15	5	0	4	4	8
88-89—Chicago	NHL	69	5	19	24	116	15	3	6	9	20
89-90—Chicago	NHL	70	5	15	20	82	20	3	5	8	27
90-91—Chicago	NHL	61	3	13	16	77	1	0	0	0	0
91-92—Indianapolis	IHL	9	2	3	5	12	—	—	—	—	—
—Calgary	NHL	47	4	9	13	45	—	—	—	—	—
NHL totals		262	19	64	83	335	41	6	15	21	55

YORK, JASON
D, RED WINGS

PERSONAL: Born May 20, 1970, at Nepean, Ont. . . . 6-2/195. . . . Shoots right.
TRANSACTIONS/CAREER NOTES: Selected by Detroit Red Wings in seventh round (sixth Red Wings pick, 129th overall) of NHL entry draft (June 16, 1990).

Season Team	League	REGULAR SEASON					PLAYOFFS				
		Gms.	G	A	Pts.	Pen.	Gms.	G	A	Pts.	Pen.
89-90—Windsor	OHL	39	9	30	39	38	—	—	—	—	—
—Kitchener	OHL	25	11	25	36	17	17	3	19	22	10
90-91—Windsor	OHL	66	13	80	93	40	11	3	10	13	12
91-92—Adirondack	AHL	49	4	20	24	32	5	0	1	1	0

YOUNG, C.J.
RW, FLAMES

PERSONAL: Born January 1, 1968, at Waban, Mass. . . . 5-10/180. . . . Shoots right. . . . Full name: Carl Joshua Young.
COLLEGE: Harvard.
TRANSACTIONS/CAREER NOTES: Selected by New Jersey Devils in NHL supplemental draft (June 16, 1989). . . . Signed as free agent by Calgary Flames (September 9, 1990).
HONORS: Named to ECAC All-Star second team (1988-89). . . . Named to NCAA All-America East second team (1989-90). . . . Named to ECAC All-Star first team (1989-90). . . . Won Ken McKenzie Trophy (1990-91).

Season Team	League	REGULAR SEASON					PLAYOFFS				
		Gms.	G	A	Pts.	Pen.	Gms.	G	A	Pts.	Pen.
86-87—Harvard University	ECAC	34	17	12	29	30	—	—	—	—	—
87-88—Harvard University	ECAC	28	13	16	29	40	—	—	—	—	—
88-89—Harvard University	ECAC	34	33	22	55	24	—	—	—	—	—
89-90—Harvard University	ECAC	28	21	28	49	32	—	—	—	—	—
90-91—Salt Lake City	IHL	80	31	36	67	43	4	1	2	3	2
91-92—U.S. National Team	Int'l	49	17	17	34	38	—	—	—	—	—
—U.S. Olympic Team	Int'l	8	1	3	4	4	—	—	—	—	—

YOUNG, JASON
LW, SABRES

PERSONAL: Born December 16, 1972, at Sudbury, Ont. . . . 5-10/197. . . . Shoots left.
TRANSACTIONS/CAREER NOTES: Suspended remainder of season by OHL for checking opposing player from behind and breaking his neck (December 4, 1990); reinstated due to career record of 86 penalty minutes in 99 games and also due to the fact that he had no penalties in 71 of the 99 games (March 4, 1991). . . . Selected by Buffalo Sabres in third round (third Sabres pick, 57th overall) of NHL entry draft (June 22, 1991).

Season Team	League	REGULAR SEASON					PLAYOFFS				
		Gms.	G	A	Pts.	Pen.	Gms.	G	A	Pts.	Pen.
89-90—Sudbury	OHL	62	26	47	73	64	—	—	—	—	—
90-91—Sudbury	OHL	37	21	38	59	22	5	0	4	4	10
91-92—Sudbury	OHL	55	26	56	82	49	11	3	2	5	14

YOUNG, SCOTT
D, NORDIQUES

PERSONAL: Born October 1, 1967, at Clinton, Mass. . . . 6-0/190. . . . Shoots right. . . . Full name: Scott Allen Young.
HIGH SCHOOL: St. Mark's (Southborough, Mass.).
COLLEGE: Boston University.
TRANSACTIONS/CAREER NOTES: Selected by Hartford Whalers in first round (first Whalers pick, 11th overall) of NHL entry draft (June 21, 1986). . . . Suffered lacerations above right eye (October 8, 1988). . . . Suffered facial lacerations (February 18, 1990). . . . Traded by Whalers to Pittsburgh Penguins for RW Rob Brown (December 21, 1990). . . . Traded by Penguins to Quebec Nordiques for D Bryan Fogarty (March 10, 1992).
HONORS: Named Hockey East Rookie of the Year (1985-85).

Season Team	League	REGULAR SEASON					PLAYOFFS				
		Gms.	G	A	Pts.	Pen.	Gms.	G	A	Pts.	Pen.
84-85—St. Marks H.S.	Mass. H.S.	23	28	41	69		—	—	—	—	—
85-86—Boston University	Hockey East	38	16	13	29	31	—	—	—	—	—
86-87—Boston University	Hockey East	33	15	21	36	24	—	—	—	—	—
87-88—U.S. Olympic Team	Int'l	59	13	53	66		—	—	—	—	—
—Hartford	NHL	7	0	0	0	2	4	1	0	1	0

Y

Season Team	League	REGULAR SEASON					PLAYOFFS				
		Gms.	G	A	Pts.	Pen.	Gms.	G	A	Pts.	Pen.
88-89—Hartford	NHL	76	19	40	59	27	4	2	0	2	4
89-90—Hartford	NHL	80	24	40	64	47	7	2	0	2	2
90-91—Hartford	NHL	34	6	9	15	8					
—Pittsburgh	NHL	43	11	16	27	33	17	1	6	7	2
91-92—U.S. National Team	Int'l	10	2	4	6	21	—	—	—	—	—
—U.S. Olympic Team	Int'l	8	2	1	3	2	—	—	—	—	—
NHL totals		240	60	105	165	117	32	6	6	12	8

YOUNG, WENDELL
G, LIGHTNING

PERSONAL: Born August 1, 1963, at Halifax, N.S. . . . 5-8/181. . . . Shoots left.
TRANSACTIONS/CAREER NOTES: Selected by Vancouver Canucks as underage junior in fourth round (third Canucks pick, 73rd overall) of NHL entry draft (June 10, 1981). . . . Traded by Canucks with third-round pick in 1990 draft (C Kimbi Daniels) to Philadelphia Flyers for D Daryl Stanley and G Darren Jensen (August 28, 1987). . . . Traded by Flyers with seventh-round pick in 1990 draft (C Mike Valila) to Pittsburgh Penguins for Flyers third-round pick in 1990 NHL draft (D Chris Therien) (September 1, 1988). . . . Strained ankle (October 1988). . . . Dislocated right shoulder (February 26, 1991); missed remainder of season. . . . Fractured right hand (February 5, 1992); missed six games. . . . Selected by Tampa Bay Lightning in NHL expansion draft (June 18, 1992).
HONORS: Won Baz Bastien Trophy (1987-88). . . . Won Jack Butterfield Trophy (1987-88). . . . Named to AHL All-Star first team (1987-88).

Season Team	League	REGULAR SEASON								PLAYOFFS						
		Gms.	Min.	W	L	T	GA	SO	Avg.	Gms.	Min.	W	L	GA	SO	Avg.
79-80—Cole Harbour	NSJHL		1446				94	0	3.90	—	—	—	—	—	—	—
80-81—Kitchener	OMJHL	42	2215	19	15	0	164	1	4.44	14	800	9	1	42	1	3.15
81-82—Kitchener	OHL	*60	*3470	38	17	2	195	1	3.37	15	900	12	1	35	*1	*2.33
82-83—Kitchener	OHL	61	*3611	41	19	0	231	1	3.84	12	720	6	5	43	0	3.58
83-84—Salt Lake City	IHL	20	1094	11	6	0	80	0	4.39	4	122	0	2	11	0	5.41
—Fredericton	AHL	11	569	7	3	0	39	1	4.11	—	—	—	—	—	—	—
—Milwaukee	IHL	6	339				17	0	3.01	—	—	—	—	—	—	—
84-85—Fredericton	AHL	22	1242	7	11	3	83	0	4.01	—	—	—	—	—	—	—
85-86—Fredericton	AHL	24	1457	12	8	4	78	0	3.21	—	—	—	—	—	—	—
—Vancouver	NHL	22	1023	4	9	3	61	0	3.58	1	60	0	1	5	0	5.00
86-87—Fredericton	AHL	30	1676	11	16	0	118	0	4.22	—	—	—	—	—	—	—
—Vancouver	NHL	8	420	1	6	1	35	0	5.00	—	—	—	—	—	—	—
87-88—Philadelphia	NHL	6	320	3	2	0	20	0	3.75	—	—	—	—	—	—	—
—Hershey	AHL	51	2922	33	15	1	135	1	2.77	†12	*767	12	0	28	*1	*2.19
88-89—Pittsburgh	NHL	22	1150	12	9	0	92	0	4.80	1	39	0	0	1	0	1.54
—Muskegon	IHL	2	125				7	0	3.36	—	—	—	—	—	—	—
89-90—Pittsburgh	NHL	43	2318	16	20	3	161	1	4.17	—	—	—	—	—	—	—
90-91—Pittsburgh	NHL	18	773	4	6	2	52	0	4.04	—	—	—	—	—	—	—
91-92—Pittsburgh	NHL	18	838	7	6	0	53	0	3.79	—	—	—	—	—	—	—
NHL totals		137	6842	47	58	9	474	1	4.16	2	99	0	1	6	0	3.64

YSEBAERT, PAUL
LW, RED WINGS

PERSONAL: Born May 15, 1966, at Sarnia, Ont. . . . 6-1/190. . . . Shoots left. . . . Full name: Paul Robert Ysebaert.
COLLEGE: Bowling Green State.
TRANSACTIONS/CAREER NOTES: Selected by New Jersey Devils in fourth round (fourth Devils pick, 74th overall) of NHL entry draft (June 9, 1984). . . . Pulled stomach and groin muscles (December 1988). . . . Suffered contusion to left thigh (March 1989). . . . Traded by New Jersey Devils to Detroit Red Wings for D Lee Norwood and future considerations (November 27, 1990). . . . Injured knee (December 1991); missed one game.
HONORS: Named to CCHA All-Star second team (1985-86 and 1986-87). . . . Won Les Cunningham Plaque (1989-90). . . . Won John B. Sollenberger Trophy (1989-90). . . . Named to AHL All-Star first team (1989-90). . . . Won Alka-Seltzer Plus Award (1991-92).

Season Team	League	REGULAR SEASON					PLAYOFFS				
		Gms.	G	A	Pts.	Pen.	Gms.	G	A	Pts.	Pen.
83-84—Petrolia Jr. B	OHA	33	35	42	77	20	—	—	—	—	—
84-85—Bowling Green State	CCHA	42	23	32	55	54	—	—	—	—	—
85-86—Bowling Green State	CCHA	42	23	45	68	50	—	—	—	—	—
86-87—Bowling Green State	CCHA	45	27	58	85	44	—	—	—	—	—
—Canadian National Team	Int'l	5	1	0	1	4	—	—	—	—	—
87-88—Utica	AHL	78	30	49	79	60	—	—	—	—	—
88-89—Utica	AHL	56	36	44	80	22	5	0	1	1	4
—New Jersey	NHL	5	0	4	4	0	—	—	—	—	—
89-90—New Jersey	NHL	5	1	2	3	0	—	—	—	—	—
—Utica	AHL	74	53	52	*105	61	5	2	4	6	0
90-91—New Jersey	NHL	11	4	3	7	6	—	—	—	—	—
—Detroit	NHL	51	15	18	33	16	2	0	2	2	0
91-92—Detroit	NHL	79	35	40	75	55	10	1	0	1	10
NHL totals		151	55	67	122	77	12	1	2	3	10

YUSHKEVICH, DIMITRI
D, FLYERS

PERSONAL: Born November 19, 1971, at Yaroslavl, U.S.S.R. . . . 5-11/187. . . . Shoots left.
TRANSACTIONS/CAREER NOTES: Selected by Philadelphia Flyers in sixth round (sixth Flyers pick, 122nd overall) of NHL entry draft (June 22, 1991).

Y

Season Team	League	REGULAR SEASON					PLAYOFFS				
		Gms.	G	A	Pts.	Pen.	Gms.	G	A	Pts.	Pen.
89-90—Torpedo Yaroslavl	USSR	40	2	3	5		—	—	—	—	—
90-91—Torpedo Yaroslavl	USSR	41	10	4	14		—	—	—	—	—
91-92—Dynamo Moscow	CIS	41	6	7	13	14	—	—	—	—	—

YZERMAN, STEVE
C, RED WINGS

PERSONAL: Born May 9, 1965, at Cranbrook, B.C. . . . 5-11/183. . . . Shoots right.
TRANSACTIONS/CAREER NOTES: Selected by Detroit Red Wings as underage junior in first round (first Red Wings pick, fourth overall) of NHL entry draft (June 8, 1983). . . . Became youngest person (18) to ever play in NHL All-Star Game (January 31, 1984). . . . Fractured collarbone (January 31, 1986). . . . Injured ligaments of right knee and underwent surgery (March 1, 1988). . . . Injured right knee in playoff game (April 8, 1991).
HONORS: Named NHL Rookie of the Year by THE SPORTING NEWS (1983-84). . . . Named to NHL All-Rookie team (1983-84). . . . Won Lester B. Pearson Award (1988-89).

Season Team	League	REGULAR SEASON					PLAYOFFS				
		Gms.	G	A	Pts.	Pen.	Gms.	G	A	Pts.	Pen.
81-82—Peterborough	OHL	58	21	43	64	65	6	0	1	1	16
82-83—Peterborough	OHL	56	42	49	91	33	4	1	4	5	0
83-84—Detroit	NHL	80	39	48	87	33	4	3	3	6	0
84-85—Detroit	NHL	80	30	59	89	58	3	2	1	3	2
85-86—Detroit	NHL	51	14	28	42	16	—	—	—	—	—
86-87—Detroit	NHL	80	31	59	90	43	16	5	13	18	0
87-88—Detroit	NHL	64	50	52	102	44	3	1	3	4	6
88-89—Detroit	NHL	80	65	90	155	61	6	5	5	10	2
89-90—Detroit	NHL	79	62	65	127	79	—	—	—	—	—
90-91—Detroit	NHL	80	51	57	108	34	7	3	3	6	4
91-92—Detroit	NHL	79	45	58	103	64	11	3	5	8	12
NHL totals		673	387	516	903	432	50	22	33	55	34

ZALAPSKI, ZARLEY
D, WHALERS

PERSONAL: Born April 22, 1968, at Edmonton, Alta. . . . 6-1/210. . . . Shoots left.
TRANSACTIONS/CAREER NOTES: Selected by Pittsburgh Penguins in first round (first Penguins pick, fourth overall) of NHL entry draft (June 21, 1986). . . . Suffered from Spondylosis, deterioration of the structure of the spine (October 1987). . . . Tore ligaments in right knee (December 29, 1988). . . . Broke right collarbone (October 25, 1989). . . . Sprained right knee (February 24, 1990); missed 13 games. . . . Traded by Penguins with C John Cullen and RW Jeff Parker to Hartford Whalers for C Ron Francis, D Ulf Samuelsson and D Grant Jennings (March 4, 1991).
HONORS: Named to NHL All-Rookie team (1988-89).

Season Team	League	REGULAR SEASON					PLAYOFFS				
		Gms.	G	A	Pts.	Pen.	Gms.	G	A	Pts.	Pen.
84-85—Fort Saskatchewan	AJHL	23	17	30	47	14	—	—	—	—	—
85-86—Fort Saskatchewan	AJHL	27	20	33	53	46	—	—	—	—	—
—Team Canada	Int'l	32	2	4	6	10	—	—	—	—	—
86-87—Team Canada	Int'l	74	11	29	40	28	—	—	—	—	—
87-88—Canadian National Team	Int'l	47	3	13	16	32	—	—	—	—	—
—Canadian Olympic Team	Int'l	8	1	3	4	2	—	—	—	—	—
—Pittsburgh	NHL	15	3	8	11	7	11	1	8	9	13
88-89—Pittsburgh	NHL	58	12	33	45	57	—	—	—	—	—
89-90—Pittsburgh	NHL	51	6	25	31	37	—	—	—	—	—
90-91—Pittsburgh	NHL	66	12	36	48	59	6	1	3	4	8
—Hartford	NHL	11	3	3	6	6	7	2	3	5	6
91-92—Hartford	NHL	79	20	37	57	120					
NHL totals		280	56	142	198	286	24	4	14	18	27

ZAMUNER, ROB
LW/C, LIGHTNING

PERSONAL: Born September 17, 1969, at Oakville, Ont. . . . 6-2/202. . . . Shoots left.
TRANSACTIONS/CAREER NOTES: Selected by New York Rangers in third round (third Rangers pick, 45th overall) of NHL entry draft (June 17, 1989). . . . Signed as free agent by Tampa Bay Lightning (July 14, 1992); Rangers awarded third-round pick in 1993 draft as compensation (July 23, 1992).

Season Team	League	REGULAR SEASON					PLAYOFFS				
		Gms.	G	A	Pts.	Pen.	Gms.	G	A	Pts.	Pen.
86-87—Guelph	OHL	62	6	15	21	8	—	—	—	—	—
87-88—Guelph	OHL	58	20	41	61	18	—	—	—	—	—
88-89—Guelph	OHL	66	46	65	111	38	7	5	5	10	9
89-90—Flint	IHL	77	44	35	79	32	4	1	0	1	6
90-91—Binghamton	AHL	80	25	58	83	50	9	7	6	13	35
91-92—Binghamton	AHL	61	19	53	72	42	11	8	9	17	8
—New York Rangers	NHL	9	1	2	3	2	—	—	—	—	—
NHL totals		9	1	2	3	2					

ZAVISHA, BRAD
LW/C, OILERS

PERSONAL: Born January 4, 1972, at Hines Creek, Alta. . . . 6-1/195. . . . Shoots left.
TRANSACTIONS/CAREER NOTES: Selected by Quebec Nordiques in third round (third Nordiques pick, 43rd overall) of NHL entry draft (June 16, 1990). . . . Traded by Nordiques with G Ron Tugnutt to Edmonton Oilers for LW Martin Rucinsky (March 10, 1992).
HONORS: Named to WHL East All-Star first team (1991-92).

Season Team	League	REGULAR SEASON					PLAYOFFS				
		Gms.	G	A	Pts.	Pen.	Gms.	G	A	Pts.	Pen.
88-89—Seattle	WHL	52	8	13	21	43	—	—	—	—	—
89-90—Seattle	WHL	69	22	38	60	124	13	1	6	7	16
90-91—Seattle	WHL	24	15	12	27	40	—	—	—	—	—
—Portland	WHL	48	25	22	47	41	—	—	—	—	—
91-92—Portland	WHL	11	7	4	11	18	—	—	—	—	—
—Lethbridge	WHL	59	44	40	84	160	5	3	1	4	18

ZELEPUKIN, VALERI
RW, DEVILS

PERSONAL: Born September 17, 1968, at Voskresensk, U.S.S.R. . . . 5-11/180. . . . Shoots left.

TRANSACTIONS/CAREER NOTES: Selected by New Jersey Devils in 11th round (13th Devils pick, 221st overall) of NHL entry draft (June 22, 1991).

Season Team	League	REGULAR SEASON					PLAYOFFS				
		Gms.	G	A	Pts.	Pen.	Gms.	G	A	Pts.	Pen.
84-85—Khimik	USSR	5	0	0	0	2	—	—	—	—	—
85-86—Khimik	USSR	33	2	2	4	10	—	—	—	—	—
86-87—Khimik	USSR	19	1	0	1	4	—	—	—	—	—
87-88—SKA Leningrad	USSR	18	18	6	24		—	—	—	—	—
—CSKA	USSR	19	3	1	4	8	—	—	—	—	—
88-89—CSKA	USSR	17	2	3	5	2	—	—	—	—	—
89-90—Khimik	USSR	46	17	14	31	26	—	—	—	—	—
90-91—Khimik	USSR	46	12	19	31	22	—	—	—	—	—
91-92—Utica	AHL	22	20	9	29	8	—	—	—	—	—
—New Jersey	NHL	44	13	18	31	28	4	1	1	2	2
NHL totals		44	13	18	31	28	4	1	1	2	2

ZEMLAK, RICHARD
C, FLAMES

PERSONAL: Born March 3, 1963, at Wynard, Sask. . . . 6-2/190. . . . Shoots right. . . . Full name: Richard Andrew Zemlak.

TRANSACTIONS/CAREER NOTES: Selected by St. Louis Blues as underage junior in 10th round (ninth Blues pick, 209th overall) of NHL entry draft (June 10, 1981). . . . Selected by Medicine Hat Tigers in special WHL draft of players from defunct Spokane Flyers (December 1981). . . . Sold by Blues to Quebec Nordiques (August 1984). . . . Acquired by the New York Rangers in the 1987 NHL waiver draft as compensation for Nordiques drafting of RW Stu Kulak; subsequently selected by Minnesota North Stars from Rangers list (October 1987). . . . Traded by North Stars to Pittsburgh Penguins for RW Rob Gaudreau (November 1, 1988). . . . Sprained right knee (November 1988). . . . Injured shoulder (February 1989). . . . Signed as free agent by Calgary Flames (November 8, 1990). . . . Twisted right knee (December 19, 1991).

Season Team	League	REGULAR SEASON					PLAYOFFS				
		Gms.	G	A	Pts.	Pen.	Gms.	G	A	Pts.	Pen.
79-80—Regina Pat Blues	SJHL	30	4	7	11	80	—	—	—	—	—
80-81—Spokane Flyers	WHL	72	19	19	38	132	4	1	1	2	6
81-82—Spokane Flyers	WHL	28	10	22	32	113	—	—	—	—	—
—Medicine Hat	WHL	41	11	20	31	70	—	—	—	—	—
—Salt Lake City	IHL	6	0	0	0	2	1	0	0	0	0
82-83—Medicine Hat	WHL	51	20	17	37	119	—	—	—	—	—
—Nanaimo	WHL	18	2	8	10	50	—	—	—	—	—
83-84—Montana	CHL	14	2	2	4	17	—	—	—	—	—
—Toledo	IHL	45	8	19	27	101	—	—	—	—	—
84-85—Fredericton	AHL	16	3	4	7	59	—	—	—	—	—
—Muskegon	IHL	64	19	18	37	221	17	5	4	9	68
85-86—Muskegon	IHL	3	1	2	3	36	—	—	—	—	—
—Fredericton	AHL	58	6	5	11	305	3	0	0	0	49
86-87—Fredericton	AHL	28	9	6	15	201	—	—	—	—	—
—Quebec	NHL	20	0	2	2	47	—	—	—	—	—
87-88—Minnesota	NHL	54	1	4	5	307	—	—	—	—	—
88-89—Kalamazoo	IHL	2	1	3	4	22	—	—	—	—	—
—Minnesota	NHL	3	0	0	0	13	—	—	—	—	—
—Pittsburgh	NHL	31	0	0	0	135	1	0	0	0	10
—Muskegon	IHL	18	5	4	9	55	8	1	1	2	35
89-90—Muskegon	IHL	61	17	39	56	263	14	3	4	7	*105
—Pittsburgh	NHL	19	1	5	6	43	—	—	—	—	—
90-91—Salt Lake City	IHL	59	14	20	34	194	3	0	1	1	14
91-92—Salt Lake City	IHL	60	5	14	19	204	3	0	0	0	0
—Calgary	NHL	5	0	1	1	42	—	—	—	—	—
NHL totals		132	2	12	14	587	1	0	0	0	10

ZENT, JASON
LW, ISLANDERS

PERSONAL: Born April 15, 1971, at Buffalo, N.Y. . . . 5-11/180. . . . Shoots left. . . . Full name: Jason William Zent.

HIGH SCHOOL: Nichols (Buffalo, N.Y.).

COLLEGE: Wisconsin.

TRANSACTIONS/CAREER NOTES: Selected by New York Islanders in third round (third Islanders pick, 44th overall) of NHL entry draft (June 17, 1989). . . . Sprained ankle while playing racquetball (January 1991).

HONORS: Named to WCHA All-Rookie team (1990-91).

Season	Team	League	REGULAR SEASON					PLAYOFFS				
			Gms.	G	A	Pts.	Pen.	Gms.	G	A	Pts.	Pen.
87-88	Nichols School	N.Y. H.S.	21	20	16	36	28	—	—	—	—	—
88-89	Nichols School	N.Y. H.S.	29	49	32	81	26	—	—	—	—	—
89-90	Nichols School	N.Y. H.S.			Statistics unavailable.							
90-91	University of Wisconsin	WCHA	39	19	18	37	51	—	—	—	—	—
91-92	University of Wisconsin	WCHA	43	27	17	44	134	—	—	—	—	—

ZETTLER, ROB
D, SHARKS

PERSONAL: Born March 8, 1968, at Sept Iles, Que. . . . 6-3/195. . . . Shoots left.
TRANSACTIONS/CAREER NOTES: Selected by Minnesota North Stars as underage junior in fifth round (fifth North Stars pick, 55th overall) of NHL entry draft (June 21, 1986). . . . Tore hip flexor (January 21, 1991); missed 11 games.

Season	Team	League	REGULAR SEASON					PLAYOFFS				
			Gms.	G	A	Pts.	Pen.	Gms.	G	A	Pts.	Pen.
84-85	Sault Ste. Marie	OHL	60	2	14	16	37	—	—	—	—	—
85-86	Sault Ste. Marie	OHL	57	5	23	28	92	—	—	—	—	—
86-87	Sault Ste. Marie	OHL	64	13	22	35	89	4	0	0	0	0
87-88	Sault Ste. Marie	OHL	64	7	41	48	77	6	2	2	4	9
	Kalamazoo	IHL	2	0	1	1	0	7	0	2	2	2
88-89	Minnesota	NHL	2	0	0	0	0	—	—	—	—	—
	Kalamazoo	IHL	80	5	21	26	79	6	0	1	1	26
89-90	Minnesota	NHL	31	0	8	8	45	—	—	—	—	—
	Kalamazoo	IHL	41	6	10	16	64	7	0	0	0	6
90-91	Kalamazoo	IHL	1	0	0	0	2	—	—	—	—	—
	Minnesota	NHL	47	1	4	5	119	—	—	—	—	—
91-92	San Jose	NHL	74	1	8	9	99	—	—	—	—	—
	NHL totals		154	2	20	22	263					

ZEZEL, PETER
C, MAPLE LEAFS

PERSONAL: Born April 22, 1965, at Toronto. . . . 5-11/200. . . . Shoots left.
TRANSACTIONS/CAREER NOTES: Played three games as a striker for Toronto Blizzard in the North American Soccer League (1982). . . . Selected by Philadelphia Flyers as underage junior in second round (first Flyers pick, 41st overall) of NHL entry draft (June 8, 1983). . . . Broke hand (November 1984). . . . Tore medial cartilage in left knee (March 1987). . . . Sprained right ankle (November 1987). . . . Separated left shoulder (March 1988). . . . Traded by Flyers to St. Louis Blues for C Mike Bullard (November 29, 1988). . . . Pulled groin (December 1988). . . . Bruised sternum (January 1989). . . . Sprained right knee (March 5, 1989). . . . Bruised right hip (March 11, 1990). . . . Traded by Blues with D Mike Lalor to Washington Capitals for LW Geoff Courtnall (July 13, 1990). . . . Sprained left ankle (October 23, 1990); missed 23 games. . . . Reinjured ankle (December 28, 1990); missed two games. . . . Traded by Capitals with D Bob Rouse to Toronto Maple Leafs for D Al Iafrate (January 16, 1991). . . . Sprained knee (November 14, 1991); missed five games. . . . Strained knee (March 5, 1992).

Season	Team	League	REGULAR SEASON					PLAYOFFS				
			Gms.	G	A	Pts.	Pen.	Gms.	G	A	Pts.	Pen.
81-82	Don Mills Flyers	MTHL	40	43	51	94	36	—	—	—	—	—
82-83	Toronto	OHL	66	35	39	74	28	4	2	4	6	0
83-84	Toronto	OHL	68	47	86	133	31	9	7	5	12	4
84-85	Philadelphia	NHL	65	15	46	61	26	19	1	8	9	28
85-86	Philadelphia	NHL	79	17	37	54	76	5	3	1	4	4
86-87	Philadelphia	NHL	71	33	39	72	71	25	3	10	13	10
87-88	Philadelphia	NHL	69	22	35	57	42	7	3	2	5	7
88-89	Philadelphia	NHL	26	4	13	17	15	—	—	—	—	—
	St. Louis	NHL	52	17	36	53	27	10	6	6	12	4
89-90	St. Louis	NHL	73	25	47	72	30	12	1	7	8	4
90-91	Washington	NHL	20	7	5	12	10	—	—	—	—	—
	Toronto	NHL	32	14	14	28	4	—	—	—	—	—
91-92	Toronto	NHL	64	16	33	49	26	—	—	—	—	—
	NHL totals		551	170	305	475	327	78	17	34	51	57

ZHAMNOV, ALEXEI
C, JETS

PERSONAL: Born October 1, 1970, at Moscow, U.S.S.R. . . . 6-1/187. . . . Shoots left.
TRANSACTIONS/CAREER NOTES: Selected by Winnipeg Jets in fourth round (fifth Jets pick, 77th overall) of NHL entry draft (June 16, 1990).

Season	Team	League	REGULAR SEASON					PLAYOFFS				
			Gms.	G	A	Pts.	Pen.	Gms.	G	A	Pts.	Pen.
88-89	Dynamo Moscow	USSR	4	0	0	0	0	—	—	—	—	—
89-90	Dynamo Moscow	USSR	43	11	6	17	23	—	—	—	—	—
90-91	Dynamo Moscow	USSR	46	16	12	28	24	—	—	—	—	—
91-92	Dynamo Moscow	CIS	39	15	21	36	28	—	—	—	—	—

ZHITNIK, ALEXEI
D, KINGS

PERSONAL: Born October 10, 1972, at Kiev, U.S.S.R. . . . 5-10/178. . . . Shoots left.
TRANSACTIONS/CAREER NOTES: Selected by Los Angeles Kings in fourth round (third Kings pick, 81st overall) of NHL entry draft (June 22, 1991).

Season	Team	League	REGULAR SEASON					PLAYOFFS				
			Gms.	G	A	Pts.	Pen.	Gms.	G	A	Pts.	Pen.
90-91	Sokol Kiev	USSR	40	1	4	5	46	—	—	—	—	—
91-92	CSKA Moscow	CIS	36	2	7	9	48	—	—	—	—	—

Z

ZHOLTOK, SERGEI
LW, BRUINS

PERSONAL: Born December 2, 1972, at Riga, U.S.S.R. . . . 6-0/185. . . . Shoots right.
TRANSACTIONS/CAREER NOTES: Selected by Boston Bruins in third round (second Bruins pick, 56th overall) of NHL entry draft (June 20, 1992).

			REGULAR SEASON					PLAYOFFS				
Season Team	League	Gms.	G	A	Pts.	Pen.	Gms.	G	A	Pts.	Pen.
90-91—Dynamo Riga	USSR	39	4	0	4	16	—	—	—	—	—
91-92—Riga	CIS	27	6	3	9	6	—	—	—	—	—

ZMOLEK, DOUG
D, SHARKS

PERSONAL: Born November 3, 1970, at Rochester, Minn. . . . 6-1/195. . . . Shoots left. . . . Full name: Doug Allan Zmolek.
HIGH SCHOOL: John Marshall (Rochester, Minn.).
COLLEGE: Minnesota.
TRANSACTIONS/CAREER NOTES: Selected by Minnesota North Stars in first round (first North Stars pick, seventh overall) of NHL entry draft (June 17, 1989). . . . Selected by San Jose Sharks in NHL dispersal draft (May 30, 1991).
HONORS: Named to WCHA All-Star second team (1991-92).

			REGULAR SEASON					PLAYOFFS				
Season Team	League	Gms.	G	A	Pts.	Pen.	Gms.	G	A	Pts.	Pen.
87-88—Rochester John Marshall HS	Minn. H.S.	27	4	32	36		—	—	—	—	—
88-89—Rochester John Marshall HS	Minn. H.S.	29	17	41	58		—	—	—	—	—
89-90—University of Minnesota	WCHA	40	1	10	11	52	—	—	—	—	—
90-91—University of Minnesota	WCHA	42	3	15	18	94	—	—	—	—	—
91-92—University of Minnesota	WCHA	44	6	21	27	88	—	—	—	—	—

ZOLOTOV, ROMAN
D, FLYERS

PERSONAL: Born February 13, 1974, at Moscow, U.S.S.R. . . . 6-1/183. . . . Shoots left.
TRANSACTIONS/CAREER NOTES: Selected by Philadelphia Flyers in sixth round (fourth Flyers pick, 127th overall) of NHL entry draft (June 20, 1992).

			REGULAR SEASON					PLAYOFFS				
Season Team	League	Gms.	G	A	Pts.	Pen.	Gms.	G	A	Pts.	Pen.
91-92—Dynamo Moscow	CIS	1	0	0	0	2	—	—	—	—	—

ZOMBO, RICK
D, BLUES

PERSONAL: Born May 8, 1963, at Des Plaines, Ill. . . . 6-1/195. . . . Shoots right. . . . Full name: Richard J. Zombo.
COLLEGE: North Dakota.
TRANSACTIONS/CAREER NOTES: Selected by Detroit Red Wings in eighth round (sixth Red Wings pick, 149th overall) of NHL entry draft (June 10, 1981). . . . Injured knee (December 1984). . . . Injured shoulder (December 1987). . . . Strained knee (December 1988). . . . Suspended three games by NHL for high-sticking (December 27, 1989). . . . Traded by Red Wings to St. Louis Blues for G Vincent Riendeau (October 18, 1991). . . . Fractured bone in left foot (March 14, 1992); missed seven games.
HONORS: Named USHL Best Defenseman (1980-81). . . . Named to USHL All-Star first team (1980-81).

			REGULAR SEASON					PLAYOFFS				
Season Team	League	Gms.	G	A	Pts.	Pen.	Gms.	G	A	Pts.	Pen.
80-81—Austin	USHL	43	10	26	36	73	—	—	—	—	—
81-82—Univ. of North Dakota	WCHA	45	1	15	16	31	—	—	—	—	—
82-83—Univ. of North Dakota	WCHA	33	5	11	16	41	—	—	—	—	—
83-84—Univ. of North Dakota	WCHA	34	7	24	31	40	—	—	—	—	—
84-85—Adirondack	AHL	56	3	32	35	70	—	—	—	—	—
—Detroit	NHL	1	0	0	0	0	—	—	—	—	—
85-86—Adirondack	AHL	69	7	34	41	94	17	0	4	4	40
—Detroit	NHL	14	0	1	1	16	—	—	—	—	—
86-87—Adirondack	AHL	25	0	6	6	22	—	—	—	—	—
—Detroit	NHL	44	1	4	5	59	7	0	1	1	9
87-88—Detroit	NHL	62	3	14	17	96	16	0	6	6	55
88-89—Detroit	NHL	75	1	20	21	106	6	0	1	1	16
89-90—Detroit	NHL	77	5	20	25	95	—	—	—	—	—
90-91—Detroit	NHL	77	4	19	23	55	7	1	0	1	10
91-92—Detroit	NHL	3	0	0	0	15	—	—	—	—	—
—St. Louis	NHL	64	3	15	18	46	6	0	2	2	12
NHL totals		417	17	93	110	488	42	1	10	11	102

ZUBOV, SERGEI
D, RANGERS

PERSONAL: Born July 22, 1970, at Moscow, U.S.S.R. . . . 6-0/187. . . . Shoots left.
TRANSACTIONS/CAREER NOTES: Selected by New York Rangers in fifth round (sixth Rangers pick, 85th overall) of NHL entry draft (June 16, 1990).

			REGULAR SEASON					PLAYOFFS				
Season Team	League	Gms.	G	A	Pts.	Pen.	Gms.	G	A	Pts.	Pen.
88-89—CSKA	USSR	29	1	4	5	10	—	—	—	—	—
89-90—CSKA	USSR	48	6	2	8	16	—	—	—	—	—
90-91—CSKA	USSR	41	6	5	11	12	—	—	—	—	—
91-92—CSKA Moscow	CIS	36	4	7	11	6	—	—	—	—	—

Z

ARBOUR, AL
ISLANDERS

PERSONAL: Born November 1, 1932, at Sudbury, Ont. . . . 6-0/180. . . . Shot left. . . . Full name: Alger Arbour.

TRANSACTIONS/CAREER NOTES: Selected by Chicago Blackhawks from Detroit Red Wings in intraleague draft (June 1958). . . . Selected by Toronto Maple Leafs from Blackhawks in intraleague draft (June 1961). . . . Selected by St. Louis Blues from Maple Leafs in NHL expansion draft (June 6, 1967).

HONORS: Won Eddie Shore Plaque (1964-65). . . . Named to THE SPORTING NEWS West Division All-Star second team (1967-68). . . . Named to THE SPORTING NEWS West Division All-Star first team (1968-69 and 1969-70). . . . Won Jack Adams Award (1978-79).

MISCELLANEOUS: Played defense.

			REGULAR SEASON					PLAYOFFS				
Season	Team	League	Gms.	G	A	Pts.	Pen.	Gms.	G	A	Pts.	Pen.
49-50—Detroit		IHL	33	14	8	22	10	—	—	—	—	—
—Windsor		OHA Jr. A	3	0	0	0	0	—	—	—	—	—
50-51—Windsor		OHA Jr. A	31	5	4	9	0	—	—	—	—	—
51-52—Windsor		OHA Jr. A	52	7	12	19	0	—	—	—	—	—
52-53—Windsor		OHA Jr. A	56	5	7	12	0	—	—	—	—	—
—Washington		EHL	4	0	2	2	0	—	—	—	—	—
—Edmonton		WHL	8	0	1	1	2	15	0	5	5	10
53-54—Detroit		NHL	36	0	1	1	18	—	—	—	—	—
—Sherbrooke		QHL	19	1	3	4	24	2	0	0	0	2
54-55—Edmonton		WHL	41	3	9	12	39	—	—	—	—	—
—Quebec		AHL	20	4	5	9	55	4	0	0	0	2
55-56—Edmonton		WHL	70	5	14	19	109	3	0	0	0	4
—Detroit		NHL	—	—	—	—	—	4	0	1	1	0
56-57—Edmonton		WHL	24	2	3	5	24	—	—	—	—	—
—Detroit		NHL	44	1	6	7	38	5	0	0	0	6
57-58—Detroit		NHL	69	1	6	7	104	4	0	1	1	4
58-59—Chicago		NHL	70	2	10	12	86	6	1	2	3	26
59-60—Chicago		NHL	57	1	5	6	66	4	0	0	0	4
60-61—Chicago		NHL	53	3	2	5	40	7	0	0	0	2
61-62—Toronto		NHL	52	1	5	6	68	8	0	0	0	6
62-63—Rochester		AHL	63	6	21	27	97	2	0	2	2	2
—Toronto		NHL	4	1	0	1	4	—	—	—	—	—
63-64—Rochester		AHL	60	3	19	22	62	2	1	0	1	0
—Toronto		NHL	6	0	1	1	0	1	0	0	0	0
64-65—Rochester		AHL	17	1	16	17	88	10	0	1	1	16
—Toronto		NHL	—	—	—	—	—	1	0	0	0	2
65-66—Toronto		NHL	4	0	1	1	2	—	—	—	—	—
—Rochester		AHL	59	2	11	13	86	12	0	2	2	8
66-67—Rochester		AHL	71	3	19	22	48	13	0	1	1	16
67-68—St. Louis		NHL	74	1	10	11	50	14	0	3	3	10
68-69—St. Louis		NHL	67	1	6	7	50	12	0	0	0	10
69-70—St. Louis		NHL	68	0	3	3	85	14	0	1	1	16
70-71—St. Louis		NHL	22	0	2	2	6	6	0	0	0	6
NHL totals			**626**	**12**	**58**	**70**	**617**	**86**	**1**	**8**	**9**	**92**

HEAD COACHING RECORD

BACKGROUND: Vice president of player development, N.Y. Islanders (1986-87 and 1987-88).

HONORS: Shared Lester Patrick Trophy with Lou Lamoriello and Art Berglund (1991-92).

			REGULAR SEASON					PLAYOFFS		
Season	Team	League	W	L	T	Pct.	Finish	W	L	Pct.
70-71—St. Louis		NHL	21	15	14	.560	2nd/West Division	—	—	—
71-72—St. Louis		NHL	19	19	6	.438	3rd/West Division	11	4	.364
72-73—St. Louis		NHL	2	6	5	.346	4th/West Division	—	—	—
73-74—New York Islanders		NHL	19	41	18	.358	8th/East Division	—	—	—
74-75—New York Islanders		NHL	33	25	22	.550	3rd/Patrick Division	9	8	.529
75-76—New York Islanders		NHL	42	21	17	.631	2nd/Patrick Division	7	6	.538
76-77—New York Islanders		NHL	47	21	12	.663	2nd/Patrick Division	8	4	.667
77-78—New York Islanders		NHL	48	17	15	.694	1st/Patrick Division	3	4	.429
78-79—New York Islanders		NHL	51	15	14	.725	1st/Patrick Division	6	4	.600
79-80—New York Islanders		NHL	39	28	13	.569	2nd/Patrick Division	15	6	.714
80-81—New York Islanders		NHL	48	18	14	.688	1st/Patrick Division	15	3	.833
81-82—New York Islanders		NHL	54	16	10	.738	1st/Patrick Division	15	4	.789
82-83—New York Islanders		NHL	42	26	12	.600	2nd/Patrick Division	15	5	.750
83-84—New York Islanders		NHL	50	26	4	.650	1st/Patrick Division	12	9	.571
84-85—New York Islanders		NHL	40	34	6	.538	3rd/Patrick Division	4	6	.400
85-86—New York Islanders		NHL	39	29	12	.563	3rd/Patrick Division	0	3	.000
88-89—New York Islanders		NHL	21	29	3	.425	6th/Patrick Division	—	—	—
89-90—New York Islanders		NHL	31	38	11	.456	4th/Patrick Division	1	4	.200
90-91—New York Islanders		NHL	25	45	10	.375	6th/Patrick Division	—	—	—
91-92—New York Islanders		NHL	34	35	11	.494	5th/Patrick Division	—	—	—
NHL totals (20 years)			**705**	**504**	**229**	**.570**	**NHL totals (14 years)**	**114**	**73**	**.610**

NOTES:

1972— Defeated Minnesota in Stanley Cup quarterfinals; lost to Boston in Stanley Cup semifinals.
1975— Defeated New York Rangers in Stanley Cup preliminary round; defeated Pittsburgh in Stanley Cup quarterfinals; lost to Philadelphia in Stanley Cup semifinals.
1976— Defeated Vancouver in Stanley Cup preliminary round; defeated Buffalo in Stanley Cup quarterfinals; lost to Montreal in Stanley Cup semifinals.
1977— Defeated Chicago in Stanley Cup preliminary round; defeated Buffalo in Stanley Cup quarterfinals; lost to Montreal in Stanley Cup semifinals.
1978— Lost to Toronto in Stanley Cup quarterfinals.
1979— Defeated Chicago in Stanley Cup quarterfinals; lost to New York Rangers in Stanley Cup semifinals.
1980— Defeated Los Angeles in Stanley Cup preliminary round; defeated Boston in quarterfinals; defeated Buffalo in Stanley Cup semifinals; defeated Philadelphia in Stanley Cup finals.
1981— Defeated Toronto in Stanley Cup preliminary round; defeated Edmonton in Stanley Cup quarterfinals; defeated New York Rangers in Stanley Cup semifinals; defeated Minnesota in Stanley Cup finals.
1982— Defeated Pittsburgh in Patrick Division semifinals; defeated New York Rangers in Patrick Division finals; defeated Quebec in Wales Conference finals; defeated Vancouver in Stanley Cup finals.
1983— Defeated Washington in Patrick Division semifinals; defeated New York Rangers in Patrick Division finals; defeated Boston in Wales Conference finals; defeated Edmonton in Stanley Cup finals.
1984— Defeated New York Rangers in Patrick Division semifinals; defeated Washington in Patrick Division finals; defeated Montreal in Wales Conference finals; lost to Edmonton in Stanley Cup finals.
1985— Defeated Washington in Patrick Division semifinals; lost to Philadelphia in Patrick Division finals.
1986— Lost to Washington in Patrick Division semifinals.
1990— Lost to New York Rangers in Patrick Division semifinals.

BOWMAN, SCOTTY
PERSONAL: Born September 18, 1933, at Montreal. . . . Full name: William Scott Bowman.

PENGUINS

HEAD COACHING RECORD

BACKGROUND: Minor league hockey supervisor, Montreal Canadiens organization (1954-55 through 1956-57). . . . Coach, Team Canada (1976, 1981, and 1986). . . . Director of hockey operations/general manager, Buffalo Sabres (1979-80 through 1986-87). . . . Director of player development, Pittsburgh Penguins (1990-91).
HONORS: Won Jack Adams Award (1976-777). . . . Named NHL Executive of the Year by THE SPORTING NEWS (1979-80).

Season Team	League			REGULAR SEASON					PLAYOFFS	
		W	L	T	Pct.	Finish	W	L	Pct.
67-68—St. Louis	NHL	23	21	14	.517	3rd/Western Division	8	10	.444
68-69—St. Louis	NHL	37	25	14	.579	1st/Western Division	8	4	.667
69-70—St. Louis	NHL	37	27	12	.566	1st/Western Division	8	8	.500
70-71—St. Louis	NHL	13	10	5	.554	2nd/West Division	2	4	.333
71-72—Montreal	NHL	46	16	16	.692	3rd/East Division	2	4	.333
72-73—Montreal	NHL	52	10	16	.769	1st/East Division	12	5	.706
73-74—Montreal	NHL	45	24	9	.635	2nd/East Division	2	4	.333
74-75—Montreal	NHL	47	14	19	.706	1st/Adams Division	6	5	.545
75-76—Montreal	NHL	58	11	11	.794	1st/Adams Division	12	1	.923
76-77—Montreal	NHL	60	8	12	.825	1st/Adams Division	12	2	.857
77-78—Montreal	NHL	59	10	11	.806	1st/Adams Division	12	3	.800
78-79—Montreal	NHL	52	17	11	.719	1st/Adams Division	12	4	.750
79-80—Buffalo	NHL	47	17	16	.688	1st/Adams Division	9	5	.643
81-82—Buffalo	NHL	18	10	7	.614	3rd/Adams Division	1	3	.250
82-83—Buffalo	NHL	38	29	13	.556	3rd/Adams Division	6	4	.600
83-84—Buffalo	NHL	48	25	7	.644	2nd/Adams Division	0	3	.000
84-85—Buffalo	NHL	38	28	14	.563	3rd/Adams Division	2	3	.400
85-86—Buffalo	NHL	18	18	1	.500	5th/Adams Division	—	—	—
86-87—Buffalo	NHL	3	7	2	.333	5th/Adams Division	—	—	—
91-92—Pittsburgh	NHL	39	32	9	.544	3rd/Adams Division	16	5	.762
NHL totals (20 years)		778	359	219	.654	**NHL totals (18 years)**	130	81	.616

NOTES:

1968— Defeated Philadelphia in Western Division finals; defeated Minnesota in Stanley Cup semifinals; lost to Montreal in Stanley Cup finals.
1969— Defeated Philadelphia in Stanley Cup quarterfinals; defeated Los Angeles in Stanley Cup semifinals; lost to Montreal in Stanley Cup finals.
1970— Defeated Minnesota in Stanley Cup quarterfinals; defeated Pittsburgh in Stanley Cup quarterfinals; lost to Boston in Stanley Cup finals.
1971— Lost to Minnesota in Stanley Cup quarterfinals.
1972— Lost to New York Rangers in Stanley Cup quarterfinals.
1973— Defeated Buffalo in Stanley Cup quarterfinals; defeated Philadelphia in Stanley Cup semifinals; defeated Chicago in Stanley Cup finals.
1974— Lost to New York Rangers in Stanley Cup quarterfinals.
1975— Defeated Vancouver in Stanley Cup quarterfinals; lost to Buffalo in Stanley Cup semifinals.
1976— Defeated Chicago in Stanley Cup quarterfinals; defeated New York Islanders in Stanley Cup semifinals; defeated Philadelphia in Stanley Cup finals.
1977— Defeated St. Louis in Stanley Cup quarterfinals; defeated New York Islanders in Stanley Cup semifinals; defeated Boston in Stanley Cup finals.
1978— Defeated Detroit in Stanley Cup quarterfinals; defeated Toronto in Stanley Cup semifinals; defeated Boston in Stanley Cup finals.
1979— Defeated Toronto in Stanley Cup quarterfinals; defeated Boston in Stanley Cup semifinals; defeated New York Rangers in Stanley Cup finals.

1980— Defeated Vancouver in Stanley Cup preliminary round; defeated Chicago in Stanley Cup quarterfinals; lost to New York Islanders in Stanley Cup semifinals.
1982— Lost to Boston in Stanley Cup preliminary rounds.
1983— Defeated Montreal in Adams Division semifinals; lost to Boston in Adams Division finals.
1984— Lost to Quebec in Adams Division semifinals.
1985— Lost to Quebec in Adams Division semifinals.
1992— Defeated Washington in Patrick Division semifinals; defeated New York Rangers in Patrick Division finals; defeated Boston in Wales Conference finals; defeated Chicago in Stanley Cup finals.

BOWNESS, RICK
SENATORS

PERSONAL: Born January 25, 1955, at Moncton, N.B. . . . . 6-1/185. . . . Shot right. . . . Full name: Richard Gary Bowness.
HIGH SCHOOL: Halifax (N.S.).
COLLEGE: St. Mary's University.
TRANSACTIONS/CAREER NOTES: Selected by Atlanta Flames from Montreal Juniors in second round (second Flames pick, 26th overall) of NHL amateur draft (June 3, 1975). . . . Sold by Atlanta Flames to Detroit Red Wings (September 1977). . . . Sold by Red Wings to St. Louis Blues (September 1978). . . . Traded by Blues to Winnipeg Jets for D Craig Norwich (June 19, 1980).
MISCELLANEOUS: Played right wing.

			REGULAR SEASON					PLAYOFFS				
Season	Team	League	Gms.	G	A	Pts.	Pen.	Gms.	G	A	Pts.	Pen.
72-73—Quebec		QMJHL	30	2	7	9	2	—	—	—	—	—
73-74—Montreal		QMJHL	67	25	46	71	95	—	—	—	—	—
74-75—Montreal		QMJHL	71	24	76	100	130	—	—	—	—	—
75-76—Tulsa		CHL	64	25	38	63	160	9	4	3	7	12
—Nova Scotia		AHL	2	0	1	1	0	—	—	—	—	—
—Atlanta		NHL	5	0	0	0	0	—	—	—	—	—
76-77—Tulsa		CHL	39	15	15	30	72	8	0	1	1	20
—Atlanta		NHL	28	0	4	4	29	—	—	—	—	—
77-78—Detroit		NHL	61	8	11	19	76	4	0	0	0	2
78-79—St. Louis		NHL	24	1	3	4	30	—	—	—	—	—
—Salt Lake City		CHL	48	25	28	53	92	10	5	4	9	27
79-80—Salt Lake City		CHL	71	25	46	71	135	13	5	9	14	39
—St. Louis		NHL	10	1	2	3	11	—	—	—	—	—
80-81—Tulsa		CHL	35	12	20	32	82	—	—	—	—	—
—Winnipeg		NHL	45	8	17	25	45	1	0	0	0	0
81-82—Tulsa		CHL	79	34	53	87	201	3	0	2	2	2
82-83—Sherbrooke		AHL	65	17	31	48	117	—	—	—	—	—
NHL totals			173	18	37	55	191	5	0	0	0	2

HEAD COACHING RECORD

BACKGROUND: Player/assistant coach, Sherbrooke, Winnipeg Jets organization (1982-83). . . . Assistant coach, Winnipeg Jets (1983-84 through 1986-87). . . . General manager/coach, Moncton, Jets organization (1987-88).

			REGULAR SEASON					PLAYOFFS		
Season	Team	League	W	L	T	Pct.	Finish	W	L	Pct.
87-88—Moncton		AHL	27	45	8	.388	6th/North Division	—	—	—
88-89—Moncton		AHL	37	34	9	.519	3rd/North Division	—	—	—
—Winnipeg		NHL	8	17	3	.339	5th/Smythe Division	—	—	—
89-90—Maine		AHL	31	38	11	.456	5th/North Division	—	—	—
90-91—Maine		AHL	34	34	12	.500	5th/North Division	—	—	—
91-92—Boston		NHL	36	32	12	.525	2nd/Adams Division	8	7	.533
NHL totals (2 years)			44	49	15	.477	**NHL totals (1 year)**	8	7	.533

NOTES:
1992— Defeated Buffalo in Adams Division semifinals; defeated N.Y. Rangers in Adams Division finals; lost to Pittsburgh in Wales Conference finals.

BROOKS, HERB
DEVILS

PERSONAL: Born August 5, 1937, at St. Paul, Minn.
HIGH SCHOOL: Johnson (St. Paul, Minn.).
COLLEGE: Minnesota.
MISCELLANEOUS: Served as commentator on SportsChannel America NHL broadcasts (1988-89 and 1989-90). . . . Played wing and defense.

			REGULAR SEASON					PLAYOFFS				
Season	Team	League	Gms.	G	A	Pts.	Pen.	Gms.	G	A	Pts.	Pen.
56-57—University of Minnesota		WCHA	28	4	7	11	8	—	—	—	—	—
57-58—University of Minnesota		WCHA	22	3	8	11	8	—	—	—	—	—
58-59—University of Minnesota		WCHA	25	11	12	23	8	—	—	—	—	—

HEAD COACHING RECORD

BACKGROUND: Assistant coach, University of Minnesota (1969-70 and 1970-71).
HONORS: Named WCHA Coach of Year (1973-74). . . . Won Lester Patrick Award (1979-80). . . . Named NHL Coach of Year by THE SPORTING NEWS (1981-82). . . . Elected to U.S. Hockey Hall of Fame (1990).

			REGULAR SEASON					PLAYOFFS		
Season	Team	League	W	L	T	Pct.	Finish	W	L	Pct.
72-73—University of Minnesota		WCHA	15	16	3	.485	6th/WCHA	0	2	.000
73-74—University of Minnesota		WCHA	22	12	6	.625	2nd/WCHA	5	0	.917
74-75—University of Minnesota		WCHA	39	11	3	.764	1st/WCHA	4	1	.750

Season	Team	League	W	L	T	Pct.	Finish	W	L	Pct.
						REGULAR SEASON			**PLAYOFFS**	
75-76	University of Minnesota	WCHA	28	14	2	.659	3rd/WCHA	5	0	.917
76-77	University of Minnesota	WCHA	17	22	3	.440	7th/WCHA	1	3	.250
77-78	University of Minnesota	WCHA	22	14	2	.605	4th/WCHA	0	1	.250
78-79	University of Minnesota	WCHA	32	11	1	.739	2nd/WCHA	5	0	1.000
78-79	U.S. National Team	Int'l	42	16	3	.713		—	—	—
79-80	U.S. Olympic Team	Int'l	6	0	1	.929	1st (gold medal)/Winter Olympics			
80-81	Davos	Switz.					Record unavailable.			
81-82	New York Rangers	NHL	39	27	14	.575	2nd/Patrick Division	5	5	.500
82-83	New York Rangers	NHL	35	35	10	.500	4th/Patrick Division	5	4	.556
83-84	New York Rangers	NHL	42	29	9	.581	4th/Patrick Division	2	3	.400
84-85	New York Rangers	NHL	15	22	8	.422	4th/Patrick Division	—	—	—
86-87	St. Cloud	Div. III	25	10	1	.708	1st/NCHA	7	3	.700
87-88	Minnesota	NHL	19	48	13	.319	5th/Norris Division	—	—	—
90-91	Utica	AHL	36	42	2	.463	6th/South Division	—	—	—
91-92	Utica	AHL	34	40	6	.463	4th/Southern Division	0	4	.000
NHL totals (5 years)			150	161	54	.485	**NHL totals (3 years)**	12	12	.500

NOTES:

1973— Lost to Wisconsin in WCHA semifinals.

1974— Defeated Michigan in WCHA semifinals; defeated Denver in WCHA finals; defeated Boston University in NCAA tournament semifinals; defeated Michigan Tech in NCAA tournament finals. Minnesota had one playoff tie.

1975— Defeated Minnesota-Duluth in WCHA semifinals; defeated Michigan in WCHA finals; defeated Harvard in NCAA semifinals; lost to Michigan Tech in NCAA finals. Minnesota had one playoff tie.

1976— Defeated Colorado College in WCHA semifinals; defeated Michigan State in WCHA finals; defeated Boston University in NCAA tournament semifinals; defeated Michigan Tech in NCAA tournament finals. Minnesota had one playoff tie.

1977— Defeated Notre Dame in WCHA semifinals; lost to Wisconsin in WCHA finals.

1978— Lost to Colorado College in WCHA semifinals. Minnesota had one playoff tie.

1979— Defeated Minnesota-Duluth in WCHA finals; defeated Bowling Green in NCAA tournament semifinals; defeated North Dakota in NCAA tournament finals.

1982— Defeated Philadelphia in Patrick Division semifinals; lost to New York Islanders in Patrick Division finals.

1983— Defeated Philadelphia in Patrick Division semifinals; lost to New York Islanders in Patrick Division semifinals.

1984— Lost to New York Islanders in Patrick Division semifinals.

1987— Defeated Wisconsin-River Falls in NCHA semifinals; defeated Bemidji State in NCHA finals; defeated Salem State in NCAA Division III quarterfinals; lost to Oswego State in NCAA Division III semifinals; defeated Bemidji State in NCAA Division III third place game.

1985— Lost to Philadelphia in Patrick Division semifinals.

1992— Lost to Binghamton in Calder Cup preliminary round.

BURNS, PAT

MAPLE LEAFS

PERSONAL: Born April 4, 1952, at St.-Henri, Que.
MISCELLANEOUS: Served 17 years with the Gastineau (Quebec) and Ottawa Police Departments before launching a professional hockey career.

HEAD COACHING RECORD

BACKGROUND: Assistant coach, Team Canada (1986).
HONORS: Named NHL Coach of the Year by THE SPORTING NEWS (1988-89).... Won Jack Adams Award (1988-89).

Season	Team	League	W	L	T	Pct.	Finish	W	L	Pct.
						REGULAR SEASON			**PLAYOFFS**	
83-84	Hull	QMJHL	25	45	0	.357	6th/LeBel Division	—	—	—
84-85	Hull	QMJHL	33	34	1	.493	2nd/LeBel Division	1	4	.200
85-86	Hull	QMJHL	54	18	0	.750	1st/LeBel Division	15	0	1.000
86-87	Hull	QMJHL	26	39	5	.407	4th/LeBel Division	4	4	.500
87-88	Sherbrooke	AHL	42	34	4	.550	3rd/North Division	2	4	.333
88-89	Montreal	NHL	53	18	9	.719	1st/Adams Division	14	7	.667
89-90	Montreal	NHL	41	28	11	.581	3rd/Adams Division	5	6	.455
90-91	Montreal	NHL	39	30	11	.556	2nd/Adams Division	6	7	.462
91-92	Montreal	NHL	41	28	11	.581	1st/Adams Division	4	7	.364
NHL totals (4 years)			174	104	42	.609	**NHL totals (4 years)**	29	27	.518

NOTES:

1985— Lost to Verdun in President Cup quarterfinals.

1986— Defeated Shawinigan in President Cup quarterfinals; defeated St. Jean in President Cup semifinals; defeated Drummondville in President Cup finals.

1987— Eliminated in President Cup quarterfinal round-robin series.

1988— Lost to Fredericton in Calder Cup quarterfinals.

1989— Defeated Hartford in Adams Division semifinals; defeated Boston in Adams Division finals; defeated Philadelphia in Wales Conference finals; lost to Calgary in Stanley Cup finals.

1990— Defeated Buffalo in Adams Division semifinals; lost to Boston in Adams Division finals.

1991— Defeated Buffalo in Adams Division semifinals; lost to Boston in Adams Division finals.

1992— Defeated Hartford in Adams Division semifinals; lost to Boston in Adams Division finals.

CRISP, TERRY

LIGHTNING

PERSONAL: Born May 28, 1943, at Parry Sound, Ont.... 5-10/180.... Shot left.... Full name: Terrance Arthur Crisp.
TRANSACTIONS/CAREER NOTES: Underwent appendectomy and hernia operation; missed part of 1963-64 season.... Selected by St. Louis Blues from Boston Bruins in NHL expansion draft

(June 1967).... Selected by New York Islanders from Blues in expansion draft (June 1972).... Traded by Islanders to Philadelphia Flyers for D Jean Potvin and future considerations (D Glen Irwin) (March 1973).
MISCELLANEOUS: Played center.

Season · Team	League	REGULAR SEASON Gms.	G	A	Pts.	Pen.	PLAYOFFS Gms.	G	A	Pts.	Pen.
60-61—St. Mary's	OHA					Statistics unavailable.					
61-62—Niagara Falls	OHA	50	16	22	38	0	—	—	—	—	—
62-63—Niagara Falls	OHA	50	39	35	74	0	—	—	—	—	—
63-64—Minneapolis	CPHL	42	15	20	35	22	—	—	—	—	—
64-65—Minneapolis	CPHL	70	28	34	62	22	5	0	2	2	0
65-66—Boston	NHL	3	0	0	0	0	—	—	—	—	—
—Oklahoma City	CPHL	61	11	22	33	35	9	1	5	6	0
66-67—Oklahoma City	CPHL	69	31	42	73	37	11	3	7	10	0
67-68—St. Louis	NHL	73	9	20	29	10	18	1	5	6	6
68-69—Kansas City	CHL	4	1	1	2	4	—	—	—	—	—
—St. Louis	NHL	57	6	9	15	14	12	3	4	7	20
69-70—St. Louis	NHL	26	5	6	11	2	16	2	3	5	2
—Buffalo	AHL	51	15	34	49	14	—	—	—	—	—
70-71—St. Louis	NHL	54	5	11	16	13	6	1	0	1	2
71-72—St. Louis	NHL	75	13	18	31	12	11	1	3	4	2
72-73—New York Islanders	NHL	54	4	16	20	6	—	—	—	—	—
—Philadelphia	NHL	12	1	5	6	2	11	0	2	5	2
73-74—Philadelphia	NHL	71	10	21	31	28	17	2	2	4	4
74-75—Philadelphia	NHL	71	8	19	27	20	9	2	4	6	0
75-76—Philadelphia	NHL	38	6	9	15	28	10	0	5	5	2
76-77—Philadelphia	NHL	2	0	0	0	0	—	—	—	—	—
NHL totals		534	67	134	201	125	110	15	28	43	40

HEAD COACHING RECORD

BACKGROUND: Assistant coach, Philadelphia Flyers (1977-78 and 1978-79).... Assistant coach, Canadian National Team (1990 through 1992).
HONORS: Won Matt Leyden Trophy (1982-83 and 1984-85).... Named NHL Coach of the Year by THE SPORTING NEWS (1987-88).

Season Team	League	REGULAR SEASON W	L	T	Pct.	Finish	PLAYOFFS W	L	Pct.
79-80—Sault Ste. Marie	OHL	22	45	1	.331	6th/Leyden Division	—	—	—
80-81—Sault Ste. Marie	OHL	47	19	2	.706	1st/Leyden Division	8	7	.526
81-82—Sault Ste. Marie	OHL	40	25	3	.610	2nd/Emms Division	4	6	.423
82-83—Sault Ste. Marie	OHL	48	21	1	.693	1st/Emms Division	7	6	.531
83-84—Sault Ste. Marie	OHL	38	28	4	.571	3rd/Emms Division	8	4	.625
84-85—Sault Ste. Marie	OHL	54	11	1	.826	1st/Emms Division	12	2	.813
85-86—Moncton	AHL	34	34	12	.500	3rd/North Division	5	5	.500
86-87—Moncton	AHL	43	31	6	.575	3rd/North Division	2	4	.333
87-88—Calgary	NHL	48	23	9	.656	1st/Smythe Division	4	5	.444
88-89—Calgary	NHL	54	17	9	.731	1st/Smythe Division	16	6	.727
89-90—Calgary	NHL	42	23	15	.619	1st/Smythe Division	2	4	.333
NHL totals (3 years)		144	63	33	.669	NHL totals (3 years)	22	15	.595

NOTES:
1981— Sault Ste. Marie had four playoff ties.
1982— Defeated Brantford in Emms Division semifinals; lost to Kitchener in Emms Division finals. Sault Ste. Marie had three playoff ties.
1983— Defeated Brantford in Emms Division semifinals; defeated Kitchener in Emms Division finals; lost to Oshawa in Robertson Cup finals. Sault Ste. Marie had three playoff ties.
1984— Defeated Windsor in Emms Division quarterfinals; defeated Brantford in Emms division semifinals; lost to Kitchener in Emms Division finals. Sault Ste. Marie had four playoff ties.
1985— Defeated Kitchener in Emms Division quarterfinals; defeated Hamilton in Emms Division finals; defeated Peterborough in Robertson Cup finals. Sault Ste. Marie had two playoff ties.
1986— Defeated Maine in Calder Cup quarterfinals; lost to Adirondack in Calder Cup semifinals.
1987— Lost to Adirondack in Calder Cup quarterfinals.
1988— Defeated Los Angeles in Smythe Division semifinals; lost to Edmonton in Smythe Division finals.
1989— Defeated Vancouver in Smythe Division semifinals; defeated Los Angeles in Smythe Division finals; defeated Chicago in Campbell Conference finals; defeated Montreal in Stanley Cup finals.
1990— Lost to Los Angeles in Smythe Division semifinals.

DEMERS, JACQUES
CANADIENS

PERSONAL: Born August 25, 1944, at Montreal.
HEAD COACHING RECORD
BACKGROUND: Director of player personnel, Chicago Cougars (1972-73).
HONORS: Won Louis A.R. Pieri Memorial Award (1982-83).... Named NHL Coach of the Year by THE SPORTING NEWS (1985-86 and 1986-87).... Won Jack Adams Award (1986-87 and 1987-88).

Season Team	League	REGULAR SEASON W	L	T	Pct.	Finish	PLAYOFFS W	L	Pct.
79-80—Quebec	NHL	25	44	11	.381	5th/Adams Division	—	—	—
81-82—Fredericton	AHL	20	55	5	.281	5th/Northern Division			
82-83—Fredericton	AHL	45	27	8	.544	1st/Northern Division	6	6	.500

Season Team	League	W	L	T	Pct.	Finish	W	L	Pct.
83-84—St. Louis	NHL	32	41	7	.444	2nd/Norris Division	6	5	.545
84-85—St. Louis	NHL	37	31	12	.538	1st/Norris Division	0	3	.000
85-86—St. Louis	NHL	37	34	9	.519	3rd/Norris Division	10	9	.526
86-87—Detroit	NHL	34	36	10	.488	2nd/Norris Division	9	7	.563
87-88—Detroit	NHL	41	28	11	.581	1st/Norris Division	9	7	.563
88-89—Detroit	NHL	34	34	12	.500	1st/Norris Division	2	4	.333
89-90—Detroit	NHL	28	38	14	.438	5th/Norris Division	—	—	—
NHL totals (8 years)		268	286	86	.486	**NHL totals (6 years)**	36	35	.507

NOTES:

1983 — Defeated Adirondack in Calder Cup quarterfinals; lost to Maine in Calder Cup semifinals.

1984 — Defeated Detroit in Norris Division semifinals; lost to Minnesota in Norris Division finals.

1985 — Lost to Minnesota in Norris Division semifinals.

1986 — Defeated Minnesota in Norris Division semifinals; defeated Toronto in Norris Division finals; lost to Calgary in Campbell Conference finals.

1987 — Defeated Chicago in Norris Division semifinals; defeated Toronto in Norris Division finals; lost to Edmonton in Campbell Conference finals.

1988 — Defeated Toronto in Norris Division semifinals; defeated St. Louis in Norris Division finals; lost to Edmonton in Campbell Conference finals.

1989 — Lost to Chicago in Norris Division semifinals.

DINEEN, BILL
FLYERS

PERSONAL: Born September 18, 1932, at Arvida, Que. . . . 5-11/180. . . . Shot right. . . . Full name: William Patrick Dineen. . . . Father of Gordon Dineen, defenseman, Pittsburgh Penguins; father of Kevin Dineen, right winger, Philadelphia Flyers; and father of Peter Dineen, defenseman, Los Angeles Kings and Detroit Red Wings (1986-87 and 1989-90).

HIGH SCHOOL: St. Michael Choir (Toronto).

COLLEGE: Ottawa.

TRANSACTIONS/CAREER NOTES: Traded by Detroit Red Wings with C Billy Dea, LW Lorne Ferguson, and C Earl Reibel to Chicago Blackhawks for C Nick Mickoski, RW Bob Bailey, C Hec Lalande, and LW Jack McIntyre (December 17, 1957).

MISCELLANEOUS: Played right wing.

Season Team	League	Gms.	G	A	Pts.	Pen.	Gms.	G	A	Pts.	Pen.
53-54—Detroit	NHL	70	17	8	25	34	12	0	0	0	2
54-55—Detroit	NHL	69	10	9	19	36	11	0	1	1	8
55-56—Detroit	NHL	70	12	7	19	30	10	1	0	1	8
56-57—Detroit	NHL	51	6	7	13	12	4	0	0	0	0
57-58—Detroit	NHL	22	2	4	6	2	—	—	—	—	—
—Chicago	NHL	41	4	9	13	10	—	—	—	—	—
58-59—Buffalo	AHL	49	8	19	27	17	11	3	5	8	10
59-60—Buffalo-Cleveland	AHL	67	26	28	54	19	7	2	3	5	4
60-61—Cleveland	AHL	72	28	31	59	24	4	0	3	3	0
61-62—Rochester	AHL	70	19	19	38	20	2	0	0	0	2
62-63—Quebec	AHL	72	24	17	41	22	—	—	—	—	—
63-64—Quebec	AHL	61	27	25	52	26	9	3	3	6	0
64-65—Seattle	WHL	69	25	17	42	4	7	0	1	1	8
65-66—Seattle	WHL	71	23	16	39	10	—	—	—	—	—
66-67—Seattle	WHL	62	32	33	65	8	10	2	*7	9	4
67-68—Seattle	WHL	72	28	33	61	10	9	3	6	9	4
68-69—Seattle	WHL	74	9	16	25	8	4	0	0	0	0
69-70—Denver	WHL	51	10	8	18	4	—	—	—	—	—
NHL totals		323	51	44	95	124	37	1	1	2	18

HEAD COACHING RECORD

BACKGROUND: Director of scouting, Hartford Whalers (1979-80 through 1982-83). . . . General manager, Adirondack, Detroit Red Wings organization (1989-90). . . . Scout, Detroit Red Wings (1989-90 and 1990-91).

HONORS: Named WHA Coach of the Year (1976-77 and 1977-78). . . . Won Louis A.R. Pieri Memorial Award (1984-85 and 1985-86).

Season Team	League	W	L	T	Pct.	Finish	W	L	Pct.
72-73—Houston	WHA	39	35	4	.526	2nd/Western Division	4	6	.400
73-74—Houston	WHA	48	25	5	.647	1st/Western Division	12	2	.857
74-75—Houston	WHA	53	25	0	.679	1st/Western Division	12	1	.923
75-76—Houston	WHA	53	27	0	.663	1st/Western Division	8	9	.471
76-77—Houston	WHA	50	24	6	.663	1st/Western Division	6	5	.545
77-78—Houston	WHA	42	34	4	.550	3rd/WHA	2	4	.333
78-79—New England	WHA	34	29	9	.535	4th/WHA	—	—	—
83-84—Adirondack	AHL	37	29	14	.550	2nd/North Division	3	4	.429
84-85—Adirondack	AHL	35	37	8	.488	5th/North Division	—	—	—
85-86—Adirondack	AHL	41	31	8	.563	1st/North Division	12	5	.706
86-87—Adirondack	AHL	44	31	5	.581	2nd/North Division	5	6	.455
87-88—Adirondack	AHL	42	27	11	.594	3rd/South Division	4	7	.364
88-89—Adirondack	AHL	47	27	6	.625	1st/South Division	12	5	.706
91-92—Philadelphia	NHL	24	23	9	.509	6th/Patrick Division	—	—	—
WHA totals (7 years)		319	199	28	.610	**WHA totals (6 years)**	44	27	.620
NHL totals (1 year)		24	23	9	.509				

1973— Defeated Los Angeles in Western Division semifinals; lost to Winnipeg in Western Division finals.
1974— Defeated Winnipeg in Western Division semifinals; defeated Minnesota in Western Division finals; defeated Toronto in AVCO World Cup finals.
1975— Defeated Cleveland in AVCO World Cup quarterfinals; defeated San Diego in AVCO World Cup semifinals; defeated Quebec in AVCO World Cup finals.
1976— Defeated San Diego in AVCO World Cup quarterfinals; defeated New England in AVCO World Cup semifinals; lost to Winnipeg in AVCO World Cup finals.
1977— Defeated Edmonton in AVCO World Cup quarterfinals; lost to Winnipeg in AVCO World Cup semifinals.
1978— Lost to Quebec in AVCO World Cup quarterfinals.
1984— Lost to Maine in Calder Cup quarterfinals.
1986— Defeated Fredericton in Calder Cup semifinals; defeated Moncton in Calder Cup semifinals; defeated Hershey in Calder Cup finals.
1987— Defeated Moncton in Calder Cup in quarterfinals; lost to Sherbrooke in Calder Cup semifinals.
1988— Defeated Rochester in Calder Cup quarterfinals; lost to Hershey in Calder Cup semifinals.
1989— Defeated Newmarket in Calder Cup quarterfinals; defeated Hershey in Calder Cup semifinals; defeated New Haven in Calder Cup finals.

GAINEY, BOB
NORTH STARS

PERSONAL: Born December 13, 1953, at Peterborough, Ont. . . . 6-2/195. . . . Shot left. . . . Full name; Robert Michael Gainey.
HIGH SCHOOL: Peterborough Secondaire School (Ont.).
TRANSACTIONS/CAREER NOTES: Selected by Montreal Canadiens from Peterborough TPTs in first round (first Canadiens pick, eighth overall) of NHL amateur draft (May 15, 1973). . . . Injured shoulder (1977-78). . . . Tore ligaments in left knee (October 1986). . . . Pulled groin (March 1987). . . . Bruised ankle (April 1988). . . . Bruised left foot (October 1988). . . . Broke bone in right foot (January 1989) . . . Injured left knee (March 1989). . . . Reinjured left knee (April 1989). . . . Released by Canadiens when he announced he would play the 1989-90 season with Epinal Ecureuils (Squirrels), a second-division team in France.
HONORS: Won Frank J. Selke Award (1977-78 through 1980-81). . . . Won Conn Smythe Trophy (1978-79).
MISCELLANEOUS: Played left wing.

			REGULAR SEASON					PLAYOFFS			
Season Team	League	Gms.	G	A	Pts.	Pen.	Gms.	G	A	Pts.	Pen.
70-71—Peterborough	OHA Jr. A	4	0	0	0	0	—	—	—	—	—
71-72—Peterborough	OHA Mj. Jr. A	4	2	1	3	33	—	—	—	—	—
72-73—Peterborough	OHA Mj. Jr. A	52	22	21	43	99	—	—	—	—	—
73-74—Nova Scotia	AHL	6	2	5	7	4	—	—	—	—	—
—Montreal	NHL	66	3	7	10	34	6	0	0	0	6
74-75—Montreal	NHL	80	17	20	37	49	11	2	4	6	4
75-76—Montreal	NHL	78	15	13	28	57	13	1	3	4	20
76-77—Montreal	NHL	80	14	19	33	41	14	4	1	5	25
77-78—Montreal	NHL	66	15	16	31	57	15	2	7	9	14
78-79—Montreal	NHL	79	20	18	38	44	16	6	10	16	10
79-80—Montreal	NHL	64	14	19	33	32	10	1	2	4	4
80-81—Montreal	NHL	78	23	24	47	36	3	0	0	0	2
81-82—Montreal	NHL	79	21	24	45	24	5	0	1	1	8
82-83—Montreal	NHL	80	12	18	30	43	3	0	0	0	4
83-84—Montreal	NHL	77	17	22	39	41	15	1	5	6	9
84-85—Montreal	NHL	79	19	13	32	40	12	1	3	4	13
85-86—Montreal	NHL	80	20	23	43	20	20	5	5	10	12
86-87—Montreal	NHL	47	8	8	16	19	17	1	3	4	6
87-88—Montreal	NHL	78	11	11	22	14	6	0	1	1	6
88-89—Montreal	NHL	49	10	7	17	34	16	1	4	5	8
NHL totals		1160	239	262	501	585	182	25	48	73	151

HEAD COACHING RECORD

BACKGROUND: Player/coach for Epinal, a second-division team in France (1989-90).

		REGULAR SEASON					PLAYOFFS		
Season Team	League	W	L	T	Pct.	Finish	W	L	Pct.
90-91—Minnesota	NHL	27	39	14	.425	4th/Norris Division	14	9	.609
91-92—Minnesota	NHL	32	42	6	.438	4th/Norris Division	3	4	.429
NHL totals (2 years)		59	81	20	.431	NHL totals (2 years)	17	13	.567

NOTES:
1991— Defeated Chicago in Norris Division semifinals; defeated St. Louis in Norris Division finals; defeated Edmonton in Campbell Conference finals; lost to Pittsburgh in Stanley Cup finals.
1992— Lost to Detroit in Norris Division semifinals.

GREEN, TED
OILERS

PERSONAL: Born March 23, 1940, at St. Boniface, Man. . . . 5-11/195. . . . Shot right. . . . Full name: Edward Joseph Green.
TRANSACTIONS/CAREER NOTES: Selected by Boston Bruins from Montreal Canadiens in intraleague draft (June 1960). . . . Underwent surgery on both knees (1966-67). . . . Sustained skull fracture in preseason game (September 1969); missed entire 1969-70 season. . . . Pulled stomach muscles (1971). . . . Suffered back spasms (1974-75). . . . Selected by Winnipeg Jets in World Hockey Association player selection draft (February 1972). . . . Rights traded to New England Whalers (May 1972). . . . Traded by Whalers to Jets for future considerations (May 1975).
HONORS: Named to NHL All-Star second team (1968-69).
MISCELLANEOUS: Played defense.

Season Team	League	REGULAR SEASON Gms.	G	A	Pts.	Pen.	PLAYOFFS Gms.	G	A	Pts.	Pen.
58-59—St. Boniface	MJHL				Statistics unavailable.						
59-60—Winnipeg	WHL	70	8	20	28	109	—	—	—	—	—
60-61—Kingston	EPHL	11	1	5	6	30	5	1	0	1	2
—Boston	NHL	1	0	0	0	2	—	—	—	—	—
—Winnipeg	WHL	57	1	18	19	127	—	—	—	—	—
61-62—Boston	NHL	66	3	8	11	116	—	—	—	—	—
62-63—Boston	NHL	70	1	11	12	117	—	—	—	—	—
63-64—Boston	NHL	70	4	10	14	145	—	—	—	—	—
64-65—Boston	NHL	70	8	27	35	156	—	—	—	—	—
65-66—Boston	NHL	27	5	13	18	113	—	—	—	—	—
66-67—Boston	NHL	47	6	10	16	67	—	—	—	—	—
67-68—Boston	NHL	72	7	36	43	133	4	1	1	2	11
68-69—Boston	NHL	65	8	38	46	99	10	2	7	9	18
69-70—					Did not play.						
70-71—Boston	NHL	78	5	37	42	60	7	1	0	1	25
71-72—Boston	NHL	54	1	16	17	21	10	0	0	0	0
72-73—New England	WHA	78	16	30	46	47	12	1	5	6	25
73-74—New England	WHA	75	7	26	33	42	7	0	4	4	7
74-75—New England	WHA	57	6	14	20	29	—	—	—	—	—
75-76—Winnipeg	WHA	79	5	23	28	73	11	0	2	2	16
76-77—Winnipeg	WHA	70	4	21	25	45	20	1	3	4	12
77-78—Winnipeg	WHA	73	4	22	26	52	8	0	2	2	2
78-79—Winnipeg	WHA	20	0	2	2	16	—	—	—	—	—
NHL totals		620	48	206	254	1029	31	4	8	12	54
WHA totals		432	42	136	178	288	58	2	16	18	62

HEAD COACHING RECORD

BACKGROUND: Assistant coach, Edmonton Oilers (1981-82 through 1985-86 and 1987-88 through 1990-91).... Assistant coach, Team Canada (1984).

Season Team	League	REGULAR SEASON W	L	T	Pct.	Finish	PLAYOFFS W	L	Pct.
91-92—Edmonton	NHL	36	34	10	.513	3rd/Smythe Division	8	8	.500
NHL totals (1 year)		36	34	10	.513	**NHL totals (1 year)**	8	8	.500

NOTES:

1992—Defeated Los Angeles in Smythe Division semifinals; defeated Vancouver in Smythe Division finals; lost to Chicago in Campbell Conference finals.

HOLMGREN, PAUL

WHALERS

PERSONAL: Born December 2, 1955, at St. Paul, Minn.... 6-3/210.... Shot right.... Full name: Paul Howard Holmgren.

COLLEGE: Minnesota.

TRANSACTIONS/CAREER NOTES: Selected by Edmonton Oilers in fifth round (fifth Oilers pick, 67th overall) of WHA amateur draft (May 1974).... WHA rights traded by Oilers to Minnesota Fighting Saints for future considerations (May 1974).... Selected by Philadelphia Flyers from the University of Minnesota in sixth round (fifth Flyers pick, 108th overall) of NHL amateur draft (June 3, 1975).... Signed by Flyers following demise of Minnesota Fighting Saints (March 1976).... Underwent eye surgery (1976).... Separated right shoulder (1976-77).... Separated right shoulder (1977-78).... Separated shoulder during Team U.S.A. training camp (August 1981).... Suspended five games for assaulting referee (December 12, 1981).... Injured knee (January 1982).... Sprained left knee (October 1983).... Bruised left shoulder (January 1984).... Traded by Flyers to Minnesota North Stars for RW Paul Guay and third-round pick in 1985 draft (G Darryl Gilmour) (February 1984).... Injured shoulder (March 1984).... Underwent shoulder surgery (April 1984).... Separated shoulder (October 1984).... Underwent surgery to left shoulder (December 1984).... Announced retirement as a player to become assistant coach of Flyers (July 1985).

MISCELLANEOUS: Played right wing.

Season Team	League	REGULAR SEASON Gms.	G	A	Pts.	Pen.	PLAYOFFS Gms.	G	A	Pts.	Pen.
73-74—St. Paul Jr. B	OHA	55	22	59	81	183	—	—	—	—	—
74-75—University of Minnesota	WCHA	37	10	21	31	108	—	—	—	—	—
75-76—Johnstown	NAHL	6	3	12	15	12	—	—	—	—	—
—University of Minnesota	WCHA	51	14	16	30	121	—	—	—	—	—
—Richmond	AHL	6	4	4	8	23	—	—	—	—	—
—Philadelphia	NHL	1	0	0	0	2	—	—	—	—	—
76-77—Philadelphia	NHL	59	14	12	26	201	10	1	1	2	25
77-78—Philadelphia	NHL	62	16	18	34	190	12	1	4	5	26
78-79—Philadelphia	NHL	57	19	10	29	168	8	1	5	6	22
79-80—Philadelphia	NHL	74	30	35	65	267	18	10	10	20	47
80-81—Philadelphia	NHL	77	22	37	59	306	12	5	9	14	49
81-82—Philadelphia	NHL	41	9	22	31	183	4	1	2	3	6
82-83—Philadelphia	NHL	77	19	24	43	178	3	0	0	0	6
83-84—Philadelphia	NHL	52	9	13	22	105	—	—	—	—	—
—Minnesota	NHL	11	2	5	7	46	12	0	1	1	6
84-85—Philadelphia	NHL	16	4	3	7	38	3	0	0	0	8
NHL totals		527	144	179	323	1684	82	19	32	51	195

HEAD COACHING RECORD

BACKGROUND: Assistant coach, Philadelphia Flyers (1985-86 through 1987-88).

Season Team	League	REGULAR SEASON W	L	T	Pct.	Finish	PLAYOFFS W	L	Pct.
88-89—Philadelphia .... NHL		36	36	8	.500	4th/Patrick Division	10	9	.526
89-90—Philadelphia .... NHL		30	39	11	.444	6th/Patrick Division	—	—	—
90-91—Philadelphia .... NHL		33	37	10	.475	5th/Patrick Division	—	—	—
91-92—Philadelphia .... NHL		8	14	3	.380		—	—	—
NHL totals (4 years)...............................		107	126	32	.464	NHL totals (1 year).........................	10	9	.526

NOTES:
1989— Defeated Washington in Patrick Division semifinals; defeated Pittsburgh in Patrick Division finals; lost to Montreal in Wales Conference finals.

KING, DAVE
FLAMES

PERSONAL: Born December 22, 1947, at North Battleford, Sask. . . . Full name: W. David King.
HEAD COACHING RECORD
BACKGROUND: Assistant coach, University of Saskatchewan (1972-73). . . . Assistant coach, Team Canada (1982).
HONORS: Won Dunc McCallum Memorial Trophy (1977-78). . . . Named CIAU Coach of the Year (1979-80).

Season Team	League	REGULAR SEASON W	L	T	Pct.	Finish	PLAYOFFS W	L	Pct.
77-78—Billings .... WHL		32	31	9	.507	2nd/Central Division	13	7	.650
78-79—Billings .... WHL		38	23	11	.604	1st/Central Division	3	5	.375
79-80—Univ. of Saskatchewan...CIAU		14	15	0	.483	3rd/Canada West	—	—	—
80-81—Univ. of Saskatchewan...CIAU		15	9	0	.625	2nd/Canada West	4	2	.667
81-82—Univ. of Saskatchewan...CIAU		17	7	0	.708	1st/Canada West	4	1	.800
82-83—Univ. of Saskatchewan...CIAU		16	8	0	.667	1st/Canada West	5	0	1.000
1984—Team Canada................. Int'l		4	3	0	.571	4th/Winter Olympics	—	—	—
1987—Team Canada................. Int'l		3	5	2	.400	7th/World Championships	—	—	—
1988—Team Canada................. Int'l		5	2	1	.688	4th/Winter Olympics	—	—	—
1989—Team Canada................. Int'l		7	3	0	.700	2nd (silver medal)/World Championships	—	—	—
1990—Team Canada................. Int'l		6	3	1	.650	4th/World Championships	—	—	—
—Team Canada................. Int'l		4	2	0	.667	2nd (silver medal)/Goodwill Games	—	—	—
1991—Team Canada................. Int'l		5	2	1	.688	2nd (silver medal)/World Championships	—	—	—
1992—Team Canada................. Int'l		6	2	0	.750	2nd (silver medal)/Winter Olympics	—	—	—
—Team Canada................. Int'l		2	3	1	.417	7th/World Championships	—	—	—

NOTES:
1978— Advanced in Central Division semifinal round-robin tournament; defeated Medicine Hat in Central Division finals; advanced in WHL semifinal round-robin tournament; lost to Westminster in CHL finals.
1981— Defeated Calgary in Canada West Conference finals; defeated Concordia in CIAU tournament finals; defeated Queens in CIAU tournament finals; lost to Moncton in CIAU Championship game.
1982— Defeated Calgary in Canada West Conference finals; defeated Concordia in CIAU tournament finals; defeated Regina in CIAU tournament finals; lost to Moncton in CIAU Championship game.
1983— Defeated Alberta in Canada West Conference finals; defeated Brandon in CIAU tournament finals; defeated Wilfrid Laurier in CIAU tournament finals; defeated Concordia in CIAU Championship game.

KINGSTON, GEORGE
SHARKS

PERSONAL: Born August 20, 1939, at Biggar, Sask. . . . 6-0/195. . . . Shot left.
COLLEGE: Alberta.
MISCELLANEOUS: Played defense.

Season Team	League	REGULAR SEASON Gms.	G	A	Pts.	Pen.	PLAYOFFS Gms.	G	A	Pts.	Pen.
60-61—University of Alberta .... CWUAA		12	2	4	6	8	—	—	—	—	—
62-63—University of Alberta .... CWUAA		23	0	4	4	30	—	—	—	—	—
66-67—University of Alberta .... CWUAA		14	1	3	4	12	—	—	—	—	—

HEAD COACHING RECORD
BACKGROUND: Assistant coach, University of Calgary (1967-68). . . . Coach, Canadian Olympic Team (1979-80). . . . Spotter/analyst, Calgary Flames (1980-81 and 1981-82). . . . Coach, Olympic selection team tour of Czechoslovakia (1982). . . . Assistant coach, Team Canada (1983). . . . Assistant coach, Canadian Olympic Team (1983-84). . . . Coach, Canadian National Team (1984-85 through 1986-87). . . . Tournament chairman, Calgary Cup (1986). . . . Coach, Team Canada (1987). . . . Coach, Canadian Olympic Team (1987-88). . . . Tournament Chairman, XV Winter Olympic Games hockey tournament (1988). . . . Assistant coach, Minnesota North Stars (1988-89). . . . Sports Director, Norwegian Ice Hockey Federation (1989 through 1991). . . . Coach, Norwegian National Team (1989-90 and 1990-91). . . . Consultant, 1994 Winter Olympics Organizing Committee.
HONORS: Named Canadian college Coach of the Year (1973-74 and 1980-81).

Season Team	League	REGULAR SEASON W	L	T	Pct.	Finish	PLAYOFFS W	L	Pct.
68-69—University of Calgary......CIAU		11	9	0	.550	3rd/Canada West	—	—	—
69-70—University of Calgary......CIAU		11	3	0	.765	1st/Canada West	2	2	.500
70-71—University of Calgary......CIAU		13	7	0	.650	3rd/Canada West	1	2	.333
71-72—University of Calgary......CIAU		15	5	0	.700	2nd/Canada West	1	1	.500
72-73—University of Calgary......CIAU		16	8	0	.667	2nd/Canada West	—	—	—
73-74—University of Calgary......CIAU		14	4	0	.778	1st/Canada West	4	2	.667
75-76—University of Calgary......CIAU		17	7	0	.708	1st/Canada West	5	1	.833
78-79—University of Calgary......CIAU		15	9	0	.625	2nd/Canada West	1	2	.333
79-80—University of Calgary......CIAU		18	11	0	.621	2nd/Canada West	2	1	.667
80-81—University of Calgary......CIAU		18	6	0	.750	1st/Canada West	1	2	.333

Season	Team	League	W	L	T	Pct.	Finish	W	L	Pct.
						REGULAR SEASON			PLAYOFFS	
81-82	University of Calgary	CIAU	14	10	0	.583	2nd/Canada West	0	2	.000
82-83	University of Calgary	CIAU	10	14	0	.417	3rd/Canada West	—	—	—
84-85	University of Calgary	CIAU	8	16	0	.333	4th/Canada West	—	—	—
85-86	University of Calgary	CIAU	19	9	0	.679	2nd/Canada West	4	4	.500
86-87	University of Calgary	CIAU	23	5	0	.821	1st/Canada West	3	2	.600
87-88	University of Calgary	CIAU	23	5	0	.821	1st/Canada West	4	2	.667
91-92	San Jose	NHL	17	58	5	.244	6th/Smythe Division	—	—	—
	NHL totals (1 year)		17	58	5	.244				

NOTES:
1970— Defeated British Columbia in Canada West Conference semifinals; lost to Alberta in Canada West finals.
1971— Lost to British Columbia in Canada West Conference semifinals.
1972— Defeated Winnipeg in Canada West Conference Championship tournament semifinals; lost to Alberta in Canada West Conference Championship tournament finals.
1974— Defeated Alberta in Canada West Conference finals; defeated Brandon in CIAU Western Regionals; lost to Waterloo in CIAU semifinals.
1976— Defeated Alberta in Canada West Conference finals; defeated Brandon and Alberta in CIAU Western Regional semifinal tournament; defeated Toronto in Western Regional finals; lost to Guelph in Western Regional finals.
1979— Lost to Alberta in Canada West Conference finals.
1980— Defeated Alberta in Canada West Conference finals; lost to Alberta in Western Regional semifinals.
1981— Lost to Saskatchewan in Canada West Conference finals.
1982— Lost to Saskatchewan in Canada West Conference finals.
1986— Defeated Manitoba in Canada West Conference semifinals; defeated Saskatchewan in Canada West Conference finals; lost to Trois-Rivieres in Quebec Regional.
1987— Defeated British Columbia in Canada West semifinals; lost to Saskatchewan in Canada West finals.
1988— Defeated Manitoba in Canada West Conference semifinals; defeated Alberta in Canada West Conference finals; lost to York in CIAU semifinals.

MELROSE, BARRY

KINGS

PERSONAL: Born July 15, 1956, at Kelvington, Sask. . . . 6-1/201. . . . Shot right. . . . Full name: Barry James Melrose.
TRANSACTIONS/CAREER NOTES: Selected by Montreal Canadiens from Kamloops Chiefs in second round (fourth Canadiens pick, 36th overall) of NHL amateur draft (June 1, 1976). . . . Selected by Cincinnati Stingers in WHA amateur player draft (June 1976). . . . Signed by Stingers (September 1976). . . . Claimed by Quebec Nordiques in WHA dispersal draft (June 1979). . . . Selected by Canadiens in NHL reclaim draft (June 1979). . . . Selected by Winnipeg Jets in NHL expansion draft (June 1979). . . . Claimed by Toronto Maple Leafs on waivers (November 1980). . . . Signed as free agent by Detroit Red Wings (July 1983). . . . Injured knee (March 1986). . . . Underwent leg surgery (September 1986).
MISCELLANEOUS: Played defense.

Season	Team	League	Gms.	G	A	Pts.	Pen.	Gms.	G	A	Pts.	Pen.
					REGULAR SEASON					PLAYOFFS		
73-74	Weyburn	SJHL	50	2	19	21	162	—	—	—	—	—
74-75	Kamloops	WCHL	70	6	18	24	95	6	1	1	2	21
75-76	Kamloops	WCHL	72	12	49	61	112	12	4	6	10	14
76-77	Springfield	AHL	23	0	3	3	17	—	—	—	—	—
	Cincinnati	WHA	29	1	4	5	8	2	0	0	0	0
77-78	Cincinnati	WHA	69	2	9	11	113	—	—	—	—	—
78-79	Cincinnati	WHA	80	2	14	16	222	3	0	1	1	8
79-80	Winnipeg	NHL	74	4	6	10	124	—	—	—	—	—
80-81	Winnipeg	NHL	18	1	1	2	40	—	—	—	—	—
	Toronto	NHL	57	2	5	7	166	3	0	1	1	15
81-82	Toronto	NHL	64	1	5	6	186	—	—	—	—	—
82-83	St. Catharines	AHL	25	1	10	11	106	—	—	—	—	—
	Toronto	NHL	52	2	5	7	68	4	0	1	1	23
83-84	Detroit	NHL	21	0	1	1	74	—	—	—	—	—
	Adirondack	AHL	16	2	1	3	226	—	—	—	—	—
84-85	Adirondack	AHL	72	3	13	16	226	—	—	—	—	—
85-86	Adirondack	AHL	57	4	4	8	204	—	—	—	—	—
	Detroit	NHL	14	0	0	0	70	—	—	—	—	—
86-87	Adirondack	AHL	55	4	9	13	170	1	1	2	3	107
	WHA totals		178	5	27	32	343	5	0	1	1	8
	NHL totals		300	10	23	33	728	7	0	2	2	38

HEAD COACHING RECORD

BACKGROUND: General manager, Adirondack, Detroit Red Wings organization (1990-91 and 1991-92).

Season	Team	League	W	L	T	Pct.	Finish	W	L	Pct.
						REGULAR SEASON			PLAYOFFS	
87-88	Medicine Hat	WHL	44	22	6	.653	2nd/East Division	12	4	.750
88-89	Seattle	WHL	33	35	4	.486	5th/West Division	—	—	—
89-90	Adirondack	AHL	42	27	11	.594	2nd/South Division	2	4	.333
90-91	Adirondack	AHL	33	37	10	.475	5th/South Division	1	1	.500
91-92	Adirondack	AHL	40	36	4	.525	2nd/Northern Division	14	5	.737

NOTES:
1988— Defeated Prince Albert in East Division quarterfinals; defeated Saskatoon in East Division finals; defeated Kamloops in WHL finals.

1990— Lost to Baltimore in Calder Cup quarterfinals.
1991— Lost to Hershey in Calder Cup qualifying round.
1992— Defeated New Haven in Northern Division semifinals; defeated Springfield in Northern Division finals; defeated Roches-
    ter in Calder Cup pre-finals series; defeated St. John's in Calder Cup finals.

MUCKLER, JOHN
SABRES

PERSONAL: Born April 13, 1934, at Midland, Ont. . . . 6-1/200. . . . Shot left. . . . Full name: John Ernest Muckler.
MISCELLANEOUS: Played defense.

| Season Team | League | REGULAR SEASON | | | | | PLAYOFFS | | | |
		Gms.	G	A	Pts.	Pen.	Gms.	G	A	Pts.	Pen.
49-50—Detroit	IHL	32	3	4	7	24	—	—	—	—	—
50-51—Windsor	OJHA				Statistics unavailable.		—	—	—	—	—
51-52—Windsor	OJHA	48	2	3	5		—	—	—	—	—
52-53—Windsor	OJHA				Statistics unavailable.						
53-54—Guelph	OJHA				Statistics unavailable.						
54-55—Chatham	OHA	7	0	1	1		—	—	—	—	—
—Belleville	OHA				Statistics unavailable.						
55-56—Baltimore	EHL	62	11	34	45	82	—	—	—	—	—

HEAD COACHING RECORD

BACKGROUND: Director of player personnel, N.Y. Rangers (1966-67). . . . Scout, Vancouver Canucks (1979-80 and 1980-81) . . . Assistant coach, Edmonton Oilers (1982-83 and 1984-85). . . . Co-coach, Oilers (1985-86 through 1988-89). . . . Director of hockey operations, Buffalo Sabres (1991-92).
HONORS: Named EHL Coach of the Year (1964-65). . . . Won Louis A.R. Pieri Memorial Award (1974-75). . . . Shared Jake Milford Trophy with Jack Evans (1978-79).

| Season Team | League | REGULAR SEASON | | | | | PLAYOFFS | | |
		W	L	T	Pct.	Finish	W	L	Pct.
59-60—N.Y. Rovers	EHL	18	41	1	.308		—	—	—
60-61—N.Y. Rovers	EHL	18	45	1	.289		—	—	—
61-62—Long Island	EHL	26	41	1	.390		—	—	—
62-63—Long Island	EHL					Record unavailable.			
63-64—Long Island	EHL	32	24	6	.565		—	—	—
64-65—Long Island	EHL	42	29	1	.590		—	—	—
65-66—Long Island	EHL	46	23	3	.660		—	—	—
68-69—Memphis	CHL	3	5	1	.389	4th/Northern Division	—	—	—
68-69—Minnesota	NHL	6	23	6	.257	6th/West Division	—	—	—
71-72—Cleveland	AHL	32	34	10	.487	4th/Western Division	2	4	.333
72-73—Cleveland-Jacksonville	AHL	23	44	9	.362	5th/Western Division	—	—	—
73-74—Providence	AHL	38	26	12	.579	2nd/Northern Division	9	6	.600
74-75—Providence	AHL	43	21	12	.645	1st/North Division	2	4	.333
75-76—Providence	AHL	34	34	8	.500	3rd/North Division	0	3	.000
76-77—Rhode Island	AHL	21	30	2	.415	6th/AHL	—	—	—
78-79—Dallas	CHL	45	28	3	.612	2nd/CHL	8	1	.889
81-82—Wichita	CHL	44	33	3	.569	1st/Southern Division	3	4	.429
89-90—Edmonton	NHL	38	28	14	.563	2nd/Smythe Division	16	4	.800
90-91—Edmonton	NHL	37	37	6	.500	3rd/Smythe Division	9	9	.500
91-92—Buffalo	NHL	22	22	8	.500	3rd/Adams Division	3	4	.429
NHL totals (4 years)		**103**	**110**	**34**	**.486**	**NHL totals (3 years)**	**28**	**17**	**.622**

NOTES:
1972— Lost to Baltimore in Calder Cup semifinals.
1974— Defeated Nova Scotia in Calder Cup quarterfinals; defeated New Haven in Calder Cup semifinals; lost to Hershey in
    Calder Cup finals.
1975— Lost to Springfield in Calder Cup quarterfinals.
1976— Lost to Rochester in Calder Cup quarterfinals.
1979— Defeated Kansas City in Adams Cup semifinals; defeated Salt Lake City in Adams Cup finals.
1982— Defeated Nashville in Adams Cup quarterfinals; lost to Indianapolis in Adams Cup semifinals.
1990— Defeated Winnipeg in Smythe Division semifinals; defeated Los Angeles in Smythe Division finals; defeated Chicago in
    Campbell Conference finals; defeated Boston in Stanley Cup finals.
1991— Defeated Calgary in Smythe Division semifinals; defeated Los Angeles in Smythe Division finals; lost to Minnesota in
    Campbell Conference finals.

MURRAY, BRYAN
RED WINGS

PERSONAL: Born December 5, 1942, at Shawville, Que. . . . Full name: Bryan Clarence Murray. . . . Brother of Terry Murray, defenseman, four NHL teams (1972-73 through 1981-82) and current coach, Washington Capitals.
HIGH SCHOOL: Shawville (Que.).
COLLEGE: McGill (Que.).

HEAD COACHING RECORD

BACKGROUND: Athletic director and coach, MacDonald College (1970-71 through 1972-73). . . . General manager, Detroit Red Wings (1990-91 and 1991-92).
HONORS: Named NHL Coach of the Year by THE SPORTING NEWS (1983-84). . . . Won Jack Adams Trophy (1983-84).

| Season Team | League | REGULAR SEASON | | | | | PLAYOFFS | | |
		W	L	T	Pct.	Finish	W	L	Pct.
78-79—Regina	WHL	18	47	7	.299	4th/East Division	—	—	—
79-80—Regina	WHL	47	24	1	.660	1st/East Division	14	4	.778

Season Team	League	W	L	T	Pct.	Finish	W	L	Pct.
80-81—Hershey	AHL	47	24	9	.644	1st/Southern Division	6	4	.600
81-82—Hershey	AHL	6	7	0	.462		—	—	—
81-82—Washington	NHL	25	28	13	.477	5th/Patrick Division	—	—	—
82-83—Washington	NHL	39	25	16	.588	3rd/Patrick Division	1	3	.250
83-84—Washington	NHL	48	27	5	.631	2nd/Patrick Division	4	4	.500
84-85—Washington	NHL	46	25	9	.631	2nd/Patrick Division	2	3	.400
85-86—Washington	NHL	50	23	7	.669	2nd/Patrick Division	5	4	.555
86-87—Washington	NHL	38	32	10	.538	2nd/Patrick Division	3	4	.429
87-88—Washington	NHL	38	33	9	.531	2nd/Patrick Division	7	7	.500
88-89—Washington	NHL	41	29	10	.575	1st/Patrick Division	2	4	.333
89-90—Washington	NHL	18	24	4	.435		—	—	—
90-91—Detroit	NHL	34	38	8	.475	3rd/Norris Division	3	4	.429
91-92—Detroit	NHL	43	25	12	.613	1st/Norris Division	4	7	.364
NHL totals (11 years)		420	309	103	.558	**NHL totals (9 years)**	31	40	.437

NOTES:

1980— Defeated Lethbridge in East Division semifinals; eliminated Brandon in East Division round-robin series; defeated Medicine Hat in East Division finals; defeated Victoria in Monsignor Athol Murray Memorial Trophy finals.

1981— Defeated New Haven in Calder Cup quarterfinals; lost to Adirondack in Calder Cup semifinals.

1983— Lost to N.Y. Islanders in Patrick Division semifinals.

1984— Defeated Philadelphia in Patrick Division semifinals; lost to N.Y. Islanders in Patrick Division finals.

1985— Lost to N.Y. Islanders in Patrick Division semifinals.

1986— Defeated N.Y. Islanders in Patrick Division semifinals; lost to N.Y. Rangers in Patrick Division finals.

1987— Lost to N.Y. Islanders in Patrick Division semifinals.

1988— Defeated Philadelphia in Patrick Division semifinals; lost to New Jersey in Patrick Division finals.

1989— Lost to Philadelphia in Patrick Division semifinals.

1991— Lost to St. Louis in Norris Division semifinals.

1992— Defeated Minnesota in Norris Division semifinals; lost to Chicago in Norris Division finals.

MURRAY, TERRY
CAPITALS

PERSONAL: Born July 20, 1950, at Shawville, Que. ... 6-2/190. ... Shot right. ... Full name: Terry Rodney Murray. ... Brother of Bryan Murray, coach, Detroit Red Wings.

HIGH SCHOOL: Shawville (Que.).

TRANSACTIONS/CAREER NOTES: Selected by Oakland Seals from Ottawa 67s in seventh round (seventh Seals pick, 88th overall) of amateur draft (June 11, 1970). ... Loaned to Boston Braves (February 1972). ... Broke leg (1973-74). ... Traded by Philadelphia Flyers with RW Dave Kelly, RW Steve Coates and LW Bob Ritchie to Detroit Red Wings for D Mike Korney and D Rick LaPointe (February 1977). ... Sold by Red Wings to Flyers (November 1977). ... Acquired by Washington Capitals in NHL waiver draft (October 1981).

HONORS: Won Eddie Shore Plaque (1977-78 and 1978-79).

MISCELLANEOUS: Played defense.

Season Team	League	Gms.	G	A	Pts.	Pen.	Gms.	G	A	Pts.	Pen.
67-68—Ottawa	OHA Jr. A	52	0	4	4	59	—	—	—	—	—
68-69—Ottawa	OHA Jr. A	50	1	16	17	39	—	—	—	—	—
69-70—Ottawa	OHA Jr. A	50	4	24	28	43	—	—	—	—	—
70-71—Providence	AHL	57	1	22	23	47	10	0	1	1	5
71-72—Baltimore	AHL	30	0	5	5	13	—	—	—	—	—
—Boston	AHL	9	0	0	0	0	—	—	—	—	—
—Oklahoma City	CPHL	17	1	1	2	19	6	0	0	0	2
72-73—Salt Lake City	WHL	39	3	8	11	30	9	0	6	6	14
—California	NHL	23	0	3	3	4	—	—	—	—	—
73-74—California	NHL	58	0	12	12	48	—	—	—	—	—
74-75—Salt Lake City	CHL	62	5	30	35	122	11	2	2	4	30
—California	NHL	9	0	2	2	8	—	—	—	—	—
75-76—Richmond	AHL	67	8	48	56	95	6	1	4	5	2
—Philadelphia	NHL	3	0	0	0	2	6	0	1	1	0
76-77—Philadelphia	AHL	36	0	13	13	14	—	—	—	—	—
—Detroit	NHL	23	0	7	7	10	—	—	—	—	—
77-78—Philadelphia	AHL	7	2	1	3	13	—	—	—	—	—
—Maine	AHL	68	9	40	49	53	12	1	7	8	28
78-79—Philadelphia	NHL	5	0	0	0	0	—	—	—	—	—
—Maine	AHL	55	14	23	37	14	10	1	5	6	6
79-80—Maine	AHL	68	3	19	22	26	12	2	2	4	10
80-81—Maine	AHL	2	0	1	1	0	—	—	—	—	—
—Philadelphia	NHL	71	1	17	18	53	12	2	1	3	10
81-82—Washington	NHL	74	3	22	25	60	—	—	—	—	—
NHL totals		302	4	76	80	199	18	2	2	4	10

HEAD COACHING RECORD

BACKGROUND: Assistant coach, Washington Capitals (1982-83 through 1987-1988).

Season Team	League	W	L	T	Pct.	Finish	W	L	Pct.
88-89—Baltimore	AHL	30	46	4	.400	6th/South Division	—	—	—
89-90—Baltimore	AHL	26	17	1	.646		—	—	—
89-90—Washington	NHL	18	14	2	.559	3rd/Patrick Division	8	7	.533

Season Team	League	W	L	T	Pct.	Finish	W	L	Pct.
				REGULAR SEASON			PLAYOFFS		
90-91—Washington	NHL	37	36	7	.506	3rd/Patrick Division	5	6	.455
91-92—Washington	NHL	45	27	8	.613	2nd/Patrick Division	3	4	.429
NHL totals (3 years)		100	77	17	.559	**NHL totals (3 years)**	16	17	.485

NOTES:

1990— Defeated New Jersey in Patrick Division semifinals; defeated N.Y. Rangers in Patrick Division finals; lost to Boston in Wales Conference finals.

1991— Defeated N.Y. Rangers in Patrick Division semifinals; lost to Pittsburgh in Patrick Division finals.

1992— Lost to Pittsburgh in Patrick Division semifinals.

NEILSON, ROGER

RANGERS

PERSONAL: Born June 16, 1934, at Toronto.

HEAD COACHING RECORD

BACKGROUND: Scout, Peterborough, Montreal Canadiens organization (1964-65 through 1966-67).... Assistant coach, Buffalo Sabres (1979-80).... Assistant coach, Vancouver Canucks (1981-82).... Assistant coach, Chicago Blackhawks (1984-85 through 1986-87).... Scout, Blackhawks (1987-88 and 1988-89).

Season Team	League	W	L	T	Pct.	Finish	W	L	Pct.
				REGULAR SEASON			PLAYOFFS		
66-67—Peterborough	OHA	7	8	3	.472		—	—	—
67-68—Peterborough	OHA	13	30	11	.343	8th/OHA	—	—	—
68-69—Peterborough	OHA	27	18	9	.583	3rd/OHA	4	6	.400
69-70—Peterborough	OHA	29	13	12	.648	2nd/OHA	2	4	.333
70-71—Peterborough	OHA	41	13	8	.726	1st/OHA	1	4	.200
71-72—Peterborough	OHA	34	20	9	.611	3rd/OHA	13	2	.824
72-73—Peterborough	OHA	42	13	8	.730	2nd/OHA	9	4	.639
73-74—Peterborough	OHA	35	21	14	.600	3rd/OHA	7	7	.500
74-75—Peterborough	OHA	37	20	13	.621	2nd/OHA	5	4	.545
75-76—Peterborough	OHA	18	37	11	.356	6th/Leyden Division	—	—	—
76-77—Dallas	CHL	35	25	16	.565	2nd/CHL	1	4	.200
77-78—Toronto	NHL	41	29	10	.575	3rd/Adams Division	6	7	.462
78-79—Toronto	NHL	34	33	13	.506	3rd/Adams Division	2	4	.333
79-80—Buffalo	NHL	14	6	6	.654	1st/Adams Division	—	—	—
80-81—Buffalo	NHL	39	20	21	.619	1st/Adams Division	4	4	.500
81-82—Vancouver	NHL	4	0	1	.900	2nd/Smythe Division	11	6	.647
82-83—Vancouver	NHL	30	35	15	.469	3rd/Smythe Division	1	3	.250
83-84—Vancouver	NHL	17	26	5	.406	3rd/Smythe Division	—	—	—
—Los Angeles	NHL	8	17	3	.339	5th/Smythe Division	—	—	—
89-90—N.Y. Rangers	NHL	36	31	13	.531	1st/Patrick Division	5	5	.500
90-91—N.Y. Rangers	NHL	36	31	13	.531	2nd/Patrick Division	2	4	.333
91-92—N.Y. Rangers	NHL	50	25	6	.656	1st/Patrick Division	6	7	.462
NHL totals (10 years)		309	253	105	.542	**NHL totals (8 years)**	37	40	.429

NOTES:

1969— Defeated London in OHA quarterfinals; lost to Montreal in OHA semifinals.

1970— Lost to London in OHA quarterfinals.

1971— Lost to Toronto in OHA quarterfinals.

1972— Defeated St. Catherines in OHA quarterfinals; defeated Toronto in OHA semifinals; defeated Ottawa in OHA finals; lost to Cornwall in Memorial Cup finals. Peterborough had two playoff ties.

1973— Defeated Oshawa in OHA quarterfinals; defeated London in OHA semifinals; lost to Toronto in OHA finals. Peterborough had five playoff ties.

1974— Defeated Oshawa in OHA quarterfinals; defeated Kitchener in OHA semifinals; lost to St. Catherines in OHA finals. Peterborough had four playoff ties.

1975— Defeated Oshawa in OHA quarterfinals; lost to Hamilton in OHA finals. Peterborough had two playoff ties.

1977— Lost to Tulsa in Adams Cup semifinals.

1978— Defeated Los Angeles in Stanley Cup preliminary round; defeated N.Y. Islanders in Stanley Cup quarterfinals; lost to Montreal in Stanley Cup semifinals.

1979— Defeated Atlanta in Stanley Cup preliminary round; lost to Montreal in Stanley Cup quarterfinals.

1981— Defeated Vancouver in Stanley Cup preliminary round; lost to Minnesota in Stanley Cup quarterfinals.

1982— Defeated Calgary in Smythe Division semifinals; defeated Los Angeles in Smythe Division finals; defeated Chicago in Campbell Conference finals; lost to N.Y. Islanders in Stanley Cup finals.

1983— Lost to Calgary in Smythe Division semifinals.

1990— Defeated N.Y. Islanders in Patrick Division semifinals; lost to Washington in Patrick Division finals.

1991— Lost to Washington in Patrick Division semifinals.

1992— Defeated New Jersey in Patrick Division semifinals; lost to Pittsburgh in Patrick Division finals.

PADDOCK, JOHN

JETS

PERSONAL: Born June 9, 1954, at Brandon, Man.... 6-3/192.... Shot right.... Full name: Alvin John Paddock.

HIGH SCHOOL: Rivers Collegiate (Man.).

TRANSACTIONS/CAREER NOTES: Selected by Washington Capitals from Brandon Wheat Kings in third round (third Capitals pick, 37th overall) of NHL amateur draft (May 28, 1974).... Traded by Capitals to Philadelphia Flyers to complete earlier deal for LW Bob Sirois (September 1976).... Dislocated shoulder (1977-78).... Dislocated right elbow (1979-80).... Sold by Flyers to Quebec Nordiques (August 1980).... Signed as free agent by New Jersey Devils (August 1983).

MISCELLANEOUS: Played right wing.

Season Team	League	REGULAR SEASON					PLAYOFFS				
		Gms.	G	A	Pts.	Pen.	Gms.	G	A	Pts.	Pen.
72-73—Brandon	WCHL	11	3	2	5	6	—	—	—	—	—
73-74—Brandon	WCHL	68	34	49	83	228	—	—	—	—	—
74-75—Richmond	AHL	72	26	22	48	206	7	5	3	8	38
75-76—Richmond	AHL	42	11	14	25	98	8	0	3	3	5
—Washington	NHL	8	1	1	2	12	—	—	—	—	—
76-77—Springfield	AHL	61	13	16	29	106	—	—	—	—	—
—Philadelphia	NHL	5	0	0	0	9	—	—	—	—	—
77-78—Maine	AHL	61	8	12	20	152	8	0	0	0	25
78-79—Maine	AHL	79	30	37	67	275	10	*9	1	10	13
79-80—Philadelphia	NHL	32	3	7	10	36	3	2	0	2	0
80-81—Maine	AHL	22	8	7	15	53	8	10	6	16	48
—Quebec	NHL	32	2	5	7	25	2	0	0	0	0
81-82—Maine	AHL	39	6	10	16	123	3	0	1	1	18
82-83—Maine	AHL	69	30	23	53	188	13	2	2	4	18
—Philadelphia	NHL	10	2	1	3	4	—	—	—	—	—
83-84—Maine	AHL	17	3	6	9	34	—	—	—	—	—
NHL totals		87	8	14	22	86	5	2	0	2	0

HEAD COACHING RECORD

BACKGROUND: Assistant general manager, Philadelphia Flyers (1989-90).
HONORS: Shared Louis A.R. Pieri Memorial Award with Mike Milbury (1987-88).

Season Team	League	REGULAR SEASON					PLAYOFFS		
		W	L	T	Pct.	Finish	W	L	Pct.
83-84—Maine	AHL	33	36	11	.481	3rd/North Division	12	5	.706
84-85—Maine	AHL	38	32	10	.538	1st/North Division	5	6	.454
85-86—Hershey	AHL	48	29	3	.619	1st/South Division	10	8	.555
86-87—Hershey	AHL	43	36	1	.544	4th/South Division	1	4	.200
87-88—Hershey	AHL	50	27	3	.644	1st/South Division	12	0	.1000
88-89—Hershey	AHL	40	30	10	.563	2nd/South Division	7	5	.583
90-91—Binghamton	AHL	44	30	6	.588	2nd/South Division	4	6	.400
91-92—Winnipeg	NHL	33	32	15	.506	4th/Smythe Division	3	4	.429
NHL totals (1 year)		33	32	15	.506	**NHL totals (1 year)**	3	4	.429

NOTES:
1984— Defeated Adirondack in Calder Cup quarterfinals; defeated Nova Scotia in Calder Cup semifinals; defeated Rochester in Calder Cup finals.
1985— Defeated Maine in Calder Cup quarterfinals; lost to Sherbrooke in Calder Cup semifinals.
1986— Defeated New Haven in Calder Cup quarterfinals; defeated St. Catherines in Calder Cup semifinals; lost to Adirondack in Calder Cup finals.
1987— Lost to Rochester in Calder Cup quarterfinals.
1988— Defeated Binghamton in Calder Cup quarterfinals; defeated Adirondack in Calder Cup semifinals; defeated Fredericton in Calder Cup finals.
1989— Defeated Utica in Calder Cup quarterfinals; lost to Adirondack in Calder Cup semifinals.
1991— Defeated Adirondack in Calder Cup qualifying round; defeated Baltimore in Calder Cup quarterfinals; lost to Rochester in Calder Cup semifinals.

PAGE, PIERRE
NORDIQUES

PERSONAL: Born April 30, 1948, at St. Hermas, Que.
COLLEGE: Rigaud College, then St. Francis-Xavier (N.S.), then Dalhousie (N.S.).

Season Team	League	REGULAR SEASON					PLAYOFFS				
		Gms.	G	A	Pts.	Pen.	Gms.	G	A	Pts.	Pen.
69-70—St. Francis-Xavier		22	16	33	49		—	—	—	—	—
70-71—St. Francis-Xavier		25	23	54	77		—	—	—	—	—

HEAD COACHING RECORD

BACKGROUND: Consultant, Nova Scotia, Montreal Canadiens organization (1973-74 through 1979-80).... Coach, Canadian Olympic Team (1980).... Assistant coach, Calgary Flames (1980-81 through 1981-82 and 1985-86 through 1987-88).... General manager/coach, Colorado Flames (1982-83 and 1983-84).... General manager/coach, Moncton, Flames organization (1984-85).

Season Team	League	REGULAR SEASON					PLAYOFFS		
		W	L	T	Pct.	Finish	W	L	Pct.
71-72—Dalhousie University	AUAA	10	8	0	.556	3rd/AUAA	—	—	—
72-73—Dalhousie University	AUAA	7	14	0	.333	8th/AUAA	—	—	—
73-74—Dalhousie University	AUAA	6	11	4	.381	4th/Kelly Division	—	—	—
74-75—Dalhousie University	AUAA	12	6	0	.667	3rd/AUAA	—	—	—
75-76—Dalhousie University	AUAA	6	9	1	.406	6th/AUAA	—	—	—
76-77—Dalhousie University	AUAA	6	13	1	.325	6th/AUAA	—	—	—
77-78—Dalhousie University	AUAA	9	9	2	.500	5th/AUAA	—	—	—
78-79—Dalhousie University	AUAA	13	7	0	.650	2nd/AUAA	6	2	.750
79-80—Dalhousie University	AUAA	20	1	1	.932	1st/Kelly Division	2	3	.400
82-83—Colorado	CHL	41	36	3	.531	2nd/CHL	2	4	.333
83-84—Colorado	CHL	48	25	3	.619	1st/CHL	2	4	.333
84-85—Moncton	AHL	32	40	8	.450	6th/North Division	—	—	—
88-89—Minnesota	NHL	27	37	16	.438	4th/Norris Division	1	4	.200

Season Team	League	W	L	T	Pct.	Finish	W	L	Pct.
					REGULAR SEASON		PLAYOFFS		
89-90—Minnesota	NHL	36	40	4	.475	4th/Norris Division	3	4	.429
91-92—Quebec	NHL	17	34	11	.363	5th/Adams Division	—	—	—
NHL totals (3 years)		80	111	31	.430	NHL totals (2 years)	4	8	.333

NOTES:

1979— Defeated Moncton in AUAA semifinals; defeated Saint Mary's in AUAA semifinals; defeated Guelph in CIAU Championship round; defeated Chicoutimi in CIAU Championship round; lost to Alberta in CIAU Championship finals.

1980— Defeated St. Francis-Xavier in AUAA semifinals; lost to Moncton in AUAA finals.

1983— Lost to Birmingham in Adams Cup semifinals.

1984— Lost to Indianapolis in Adams Cup semifinals.

1989— Lost to Chicago in Norris Division semifinals.

1990— Lost to St. Louis in Norris Division semifinals.

PLAGER, BOB
BLUES

PERSONAL: Born March 11, 1943, at Kirkland Lake, Ont. . . . 5-10/205. . . . Shot left. . . . Full name: Robert Bryan Plager. . . . Brother of Barclay Plager, defenseman, St. Louis Blues (1967-68 through 1976-77); and brother of William Plager, defenseman, Minnesota North Stars, Blues and Atlanta Flames (1967-68 through 1975-76).

HIGH SCHOOL: Kirkland Lake Collegiate Vocational Institute (Kirkland Lake, Ont.).

TRANSACTIONS/CAREER NOTES: Traded by New York Rangers with RW Gary Sabourin, D Gordon Kannegieser and RW Tim Ecclestone to St. Louis Blues for LW/D Rod Seiling (June 1967) . . . . Injured rib, hand and knee (1969-70) . . . . Underwent surgery to remove calcium deposit in leg (1972). . . . Tore knee ligaments (1970-71) . . . . Suspended by NHL during training camp and for first two regular season games (October 1973). . . . Suspended for first five games of 1975-76 season for shoving an official.

MISCELLANEOUS: Played defense.

Season Team	League	Gms.	G	A	Pts.	Pen.	Gms.	G	A	Pts.	Pen.
				REGULAR SEASON					PLAYOFFS		
59-60—Guelph	OJHA	44	0	1	1	0	—	—	—	—	—
60-61—Guelph	OJHA	43	3	12	15	0	—	—	—	—	—
61-62—Guelph	OJHA	50	5	22	27	0	—	—	—	—	—
—Kitchener	EPHL	3	0	0	0	2	—	—	—	—	—
62-63—Guelph	OJHA	45	11	28	39	0	—	—	—	—	—
—Baltimore	AHL	4	0	0	0	6	2	0	0	0	10
63-64—St. Paul	CPHL	61	13	35	48	158	8	3	6	9	21
64-65—Vancouver	WHL	31	5	12	17	103	—	—	—	—	—
—Baltimore	AHL	19	2	12	14	27	5	0	0	0	6
—New York Rangers	NHL	10	0	0	0	18	—	—	—	—	—
65-66—New York Rangers	NHL	18	0	5	5	22	—	—	—	—	—
—Minnesota	CPHL	44	7	12	19	145	—	—	—	—	—
66-67—Baltimore	AHL	63	3	16	19	*169	9	0	5	5	15
—New York Rangers	NHL	1	0	0	0	0	—	—	—	—	—
67-68—St. Louis	NHL	53	2	5	7	86	18	1	2	3	69
68-69—Kansas City	CHL	5	1	3	4	16	—	—	—	—	—
—St. Louis	NHL	32	0	7	7	43	9	0	4	4	47
69-70—St. Louis	NHL	64	3	11	14	113	16	0	3	3	46
70-71—St. Louis	NHL	70	1	19	20	114	6	0	2	2	4
71-72—St. Louis	NHL	50	4	7	11	81	11	1	4	5	5
72-73—St. Louis	NHL	77	2	31	33	107	5	0	2	2	2
73-74—St. Louis	NHL	61	3	10	13	48	—	—	—	—	—
74-75—St. Louis	NHL	73	1	14	15	53	2	0	0	0	20
75-76—St. Louis	NHL	63	3	8	11	90	3	0	0	0	2
76-77—Kansas City	CHL	4	0	2	2	15	—	—	—	—	—
—St. Louis	NHL	54	1	9	10	23	4	0	0	0	0
77-78—St. Louis	NHL	18	0	0	0	2	—	—	—	—	—
—Salt Lake City	CHL	11	0	3	3	52	6	0	3	3	6
NHL totals		644	20	126	146	800	74	2	17	19	195

HEAD COACHING RECORD

BACKGROUND: Scout, St. Louis Blues (1978-79 through 1982-83) . . . Special assistant to director of player personnel (1983-84). . . . Special assignment scout/assistant to general manager, Blues (1984-85 through 1986-87). . . . Director of player development, Blues (1987-88 and 1988-89). . . . Vice president/director of player development, Blues (1989-1990 through 1991-1992).

HONORS: Won Commissioner's Trophy (1990-91).

Season Team	League	W	L	T	Pct.	Finish	W	L	Pct.
					REGULAR SEASON		PLAYOFFS		
90-91—Peoria	IHL	58	19	5	.738	1st/West Division	12	7	.632

NOTES:

1991— Defeated Milwaukee in Turner Cup quarterfinals; defeated Phoenix in Turner Cup semifinals; defeated Fort Wayne in Turner Cup finals.

QUINN, PAT
CANUCKS

PERSONAL: Born January 29, 1943, at Hamilton, Ont. . . . 6-3/215. . . . Shot left. . . . Full name: John Brian Patrick Quinn.

HIGH SCHOOL: Central (Hamilton, Ont.).

COLLEGE: UC San Diego, then Delaware (attended law school).

TRANSACTIONS/CAREER NOTES: Suspended eight games for stick-swinging (November 1960). . . . Loaned by Detroit Red Wings to Tulsa Oilers for 1964-65 season. . . . Broke ankle (1965). . . . Selected by Montreal Canadiens from Red Wings in intraleague

draft (June 1966).... Sold by Canadiens to St. Louis Blues (June 1967).... Loaned to Oilers for 1967-68 season.... Sold by Blues to Toronto Maple Leafs for rights to LW Dickie Moore (March 1968).... Selected by Vancouver Canucks in NHL expansion draft (June 1970).... Selected by Atlanta Flames in NHL expansion draft (June 1972).... Broke leg (1976).
MISCELLANEOUS: Played defense.

			REGULAR SEASON					PLAYOFFS				
Season	Team	League	Gms.	G	A	Pts.	Pen.	Gms.	G	A	Pts.	Pen.
58-59—Hamilton Jr. A		OHA	20	0	1	1		—	—	—	—	—
59-60—Hamilton Jr. A		OHA	27	0	1	1		—	—	—	—	—
60-61—Hamilton Jr. B		OHA				Statistics unavailable.		—	—	—	—	—
61-62—						Unknown.						
62-63—Edmonton		CAHL				Statistics unavailable.						
63-64—Knoxville		EHL	72	6	31	37	217	3	0	0	0	9
64-65—Tulsa		CPHL	70	3	32	35	202	—	—	—	—	—
65-66—Memphis		CPHL	67	2	16	18	135	—	—	—	—	—
66-67—Houston		CPHL	15	0	3	3	66	—	—	—	—	—
—Seattle		WHL	35	1	3	4	49	5	0	0	0	2
67-68—Tulsa		CPHL	51	3	15	18	178	11	1	4	5	19
68-69—Tulsa		CHL	17	0	6	6	25	—	—	—	—	—
—Toronto		NHL	40	2	7	9	95	4	0	0	0	13
69-70—Tulsa		CHL	2	0	1	1	6	—	—	—	—	—
—Toronto		NHL	59	0	5	5	88	—	—	—	—	—
70-71—Vancouver		NHL	76	2	11	13	149	—	—	—	—	—
71-72—Vancouver		NHL	57	2	3	5	63	—	—	—	—	—
72-73—Atlanta		NHL	78	2	18	20	113	—	—	—	—	—
73-74—Atlanta		NHL	77	5	27	32	94	4	0	0	0	6
74-75—Atlanta		NHL	80	2	19	21	156	—	—	—	—	—
75-76—Atlanta		NHL	80	2	11	13	134	2	0	1	1	2
76-77—Atlanta		NHL	59	1	12	13	58	1	0	0	0	0
NHL totals			606	18	113	131	950	11	0	1	1	21

HEAD COACHING RECORD

BACKGROUND: Assistant coach, Philadelphia Flyers (1977-78).... Coach, Team Canada (1986).... President/general manager, Vancouver Canucks (1987-88 through 1991-1992).
HONORS: Named NHL Coach of the Year by THE SPORTING NEWS (1979-80 and 1991-92).... Won Jack Adams Award (1979-80 and 1991-92).

			REGULAR SEASON					PLAYOFFS		
Season	Team	League	W	L	T	Pct.	Finish	W	L	Pct.
78-79—Philadelphia		NHL	18	8	4	.667	2nd/Patrick Division	3	5	.375
79-80—Philadelphia		NHL	48	12	20	.725	1st/Patrick Division	13	6	.684
80-81—Philadelphia		NHL	41	24	15	.606	2nd/Patrick Division	6	6	.500
81-82—Philadelphia		NHL	34	29	9	.535	3rd/Patrick Division	—	—	—
84-85—Los Angeles		NHL	34	32	14	.513	4th/Smythe Division	0	3	.000
85-86—Los Angeles		NHL	23	49	8	.338	5th/Smythe Division	—	—	—
86-87—Los Angeles		NHL	18	20	4	.476	4th/Smythe Division	—	—	—
90-91—Vancouver		NHL	9	13	4	.423	4th/Smythe Division	2	4	.333
91-92—Vancouver		NHL	42	26	12	.600	1st/Smythe Division	6	7	.462
NHL totals (9 years)			267	213	90	.547	**NHL totals (6 years)**	30	31	.492

NOTES:
1979— Defeated Vancouver in Stanley Cup preliminary round; lost to N.Y. Rangers in Stanley Cup quarterfinals.
1980— Defeated Edmonton in Stanley Cup preliminary round; defeated N.Y. Rangers in Stanley Cup quarterfinals; defeated Minnesota in Stanley Cup semifinals; lost to N.Y. Islanders in Stanley Cup finals.
1985— Lost to Edmonton in Smythe Division semifinals.
1991— Lost to Los Angeles in Smythe Division semifinals.
1992— Defeated Winnipeg in Smythe Division semifinals; lost to Edmonton in Smythe Division finals.

SUTTER, BRIAN
BRUINS

PERSONAL: Born October 7, 1956, at Viking, Alta.... 5-11/172.... Shot left.... Full name: Brian Louis Allen Sutter.... Brother of Darryl Sutter, left winger, Chicago Blackhawks (1979-80 through 1986-87) and current head coach, Blackhawks; brother of Brent Sutter, center, Blackhawks; brother of Ron Sutter, center, St. Louis Blues; brother of Rich Sutter, right winger, Blues; and brother of Duane Sutter, right winger, New York Islanders and Blackhawks (1979-80 through 1989-90) and current head coach, Medicine Hat of WHL.
TRANSACTIONS/CAREER NOTES: Selected by St. Louis Blues from Lethbridge Broncos in second round (second Blues pick, 20th overall) of NHL amateur draft (June 1, 1976).... Suffered hairline fracture of pelvis (November 3, 1983).... Broke left shoulder (January 16, 1986).... Reinjured left shoulder (March 8, 1986).... Damaged left shoulder muscle (November 1986).... Sprained ankle (November 1987).... Retired as player and signed as head coach of Blues (June 1988).
MISCELLANEOUS: Played left wing.

			REGULAR SEASON					PLAYOFFS				
Season	Team	League	Gms.	G	A	Pts.	Pen.	Gms.	G	A	Pts.	Pen.
72-73—Red Deer		AJHL	51	27	40	67	54	—	—	—	—	—
73-74—Red Deer		AJHL	59	42	54	96	139	—	—	—	—	—
74-75—Lethbridge		WCHL	53	34	47	81	134	6	0	1	1	39
75-76—Lethbridge		WCHL	72	36	56	92	233	7	3	4	7	45
76-77—Kansas City		CHL	38	15	23	38	47	—	—	—	—	—
—St. Louis		NHL	35	4	10	14	82	4	1	0	1	14
77-78—St. Louis		NHL	78	9	13	22	123	—	—	—	—	—
78-79—St. Louis		NHL	77	41	39	80	165	—	—	—	—	—

Season Team	League	REGULAR SEASON						PLAYOFFS				
		Gms.	G	A	Pts.	Pen.		Gms.	G	A	Pts.	Pen.
79-80—St. Louis	NHL	71	23	35	58	156		3	0	0	0	4
80-81—St. Louis	NHL	78	35	34	69	232		11	6	3	9	77
81-82—St. Louis	NHL	74	39	36	75	239		10	8	6	14	49
82-83—St. Louis	NHL	79	46	30	76	254		4	2	1	3	10
83-84—St. Louis	NHL	76	32	51	83	162		11	1	5	6	22
84-85—St. Louis	NHL	77	37	37	74	121		3	2	1	3	2
85-86—St. Louis	NHL	44	19	23	42	87		9	1	2	3	22
86-87—St. Louis	NHL	14	3	3	6	18		—	—	—	—	—
87-88—St. Louis	NHL	76	15	22	37	147		10	0	3	3	49
NHL totals		779	303	333	636	1786		65	21	21	42	249

HEAD COACHING RECORD

BACKGROUND: Assistant coach, Team Canada (1991).
HONORS: Won Jack Adams Trophy (1990-91).

Season Team	League	REGULAR SEASON					PLAYOFFS		
		W	L	T	Pct.	Finish	W	L	Pct.
88-89—St. Louis	NHL	33	35	12	.488	2nd/Norris Division	5	5	.500
89-90—St. Louis	NHL	37	34	9	.519	2nd/Norris Division	7	5	.583
90-91—St. Louis	NHL	47	22	11	.656	2nd/Norris Division	6	7	.462
91-92—St. Louis	NHL	36	33	11	.519	3rd/Norris Division	2	4	.333
NHL totals (4 years)		153	124	43	.545	**NHL totals (4 years)**	20	21	.488

NOTES:
1989— Defeated Minnesota in Norris Division semifinals; lost to Chicago in Norris Division finals.
1990— Defeated Toronto in Norris Division semifinals; lost to Chicago in Norris Division finals.
1991— Defeated Detroit in Norris Division semifinals; lost to Minnesota in Norris Division finals.
1992— Lost to Chicago in Norris Division semifinals.

SUTTER, DARRYL
BLACKHAWKS

PERSONAL: Born August 19, 1958, at Viking, Alta. . . . 5-10/ 163. . . . Shot left. . . . Full name: Darryl John Sutter. . . . Brother of Brian Sutter, left winger, St. Louis Blues (1976-77 through 1987-88) and current head coach, Boston Bruins; brother of Duane Sutter, right winger, New York Islanders and Chicago Blackhawks (1979-80 through 1989-90) and current head coach, Medicine Hat of WHL; brother of Rich Sutter, right winger, Blues; brother of Ron Sutter, center, Blues; and brother of Brent Sutter, center, Blackhawks.
TRANSACTIONS/CAREER NOTES: Selected by Chicago Blackhawks in 11th round (11th Blackhawks pick, 179th overall) of NHL amateur draft (June 1978). . . . Lacerated left elbow, developed infection and underwent surgery (November 27, 1981). . . . Broke nose (November 7, 1982). . . . Broke ribs (November 1983). . . . Fractured left cheekbone and injured left eye (January 2, 1984). . . . Underwent arthroscopic surgery to right knee (September 1984). . . . Bruised ribs (October 1984). . . . Broke left ankle (December 26, 1984). . . . Separated right shoulder and underwent surgery (November 13, 1985); missed 30 games. . . . Injured knee (February 1987). . . . Retired as player and signed as assistant coach of Blackhawks (June 1987).
HONORS: Named top rookie of Japan National League (1978-79). . . . Won Dudley (Red) Garrett Memorial Trophy (1979-80).

Season Team	League	REGULAR SEASON					PLAYOFFS				
		Gms.	G	A	Pts.	Pen.	Gms.	G	A	Pts.	Pen.
74-75—Red Deer	AJHL	60	16	20	36	43	—	—	—	—	—
75-76—Red Deer	AJHL	60	43	93	136	82	—	—	—	—	—
76-77—Red Deer	AJHL	56	55	78	133	131	—	—	—	—	—
—Lethbridge	WCHL	1	1	0	1	0	15	3	7	10	13
77-78—Lethbridge	WCHL	68	33	48	81	119	8	4	9	13	2
78-79—New Brunswick	AHL	19	7	6	13	6	5	1	2	3	0
—Iwakura	Japan	20	28	13	41	0	—	—	—	—	—
79-80—New Brunswick	AHL	69	35	31	66	69	12	6	6	12	8
—Chicago	NHL	8	2	0	2	2	7	3	1	4	2
80-81—Chicago	NHL	76	40	22	62	86	3	3	1	4	2
81-82—Chicago	NHL	40	23	12	35	31	3	0	1	1	2
82-83—Chicago	NHL	80	31	30	61	53	13	4	6	10	8
83-84—Chicago	NHL	59	20	20	40	44	5	1	1	2	0
84-85—Chicago	NHL	49	20	18	38	12	15	12	7	19	12
85-86—Chicago	NHL	50	17	10	27	44	3	1	2	3	0
86-87—Chicago	NHL	44	8	6	14	16	2	0	0	0	0
NHL totals		406	161	118	279	685					

HEAD COACHING RECORD

BACKGROUND: Assistant coach, Chicago Blackhawks (1987-88). . . . Associate coach, Blackhawks (1991-92).
HONORS: Won Commissioner's Trophy (1989-90).

Season Team	League	REGULAR SEASON					PLAYOFFS		
		W	L	T	Pct.	Finish	W	L	Pct.
88-89—Saginaw	IHL	46	26	10	.622	2nd/East Division	2	4	.333
89-90—Indianapolis	IHL	53	21	8	.695	1st/West Division	12	2	.857
90-91—Indianapolis	IHL	48	29	5	.616	2nd/East Division	3	4	.429

NOTES:
1989— Lost to Fort Wayne in Turner Cup quarterfinals.
1990— Defeated Peoria in Turner Cup quarterfinals; defeated Salt Lake City in Turner Cup semifinals; defeated Muskegon in Turner Cup finals.
1991— Lost to Fort Wayne in Turner Cup quarterfinals.

OTHER BOOKS AVAILABLE
FROM THE SPORTING NEWS LIBRARY
Take your pick!

1992 Baseball Guide
Available February 1992. #418...$11.95

1992 Official Baseball Register
Available February 1992. #419...$11.95

The Complete Baseball Record Book — 1992
Available January 1992. #420..$14.95

1992 Official Baseball Rules
Available March 1992. #427 ....$3.95

Official 1991 American League Averages and Box Scores
Available January 1992. #428..$19.95

Official 1991 National League Averages and Box Scores
Available January 1992. #429..$19.95

American League 1992 Red Book
Available March 1992. #421 ....$10.95

National League 1992 Green Book
Available March 1992. #422 ....$10.95

Complete Super Bowl Book — 1992
Available March 1992. #433 ....$11.95

1992 Pro Football Guide
Available July 1992. #434 ....$11.95

1992 Pro Football Register
Available July 1992. #435 ....$11.95

1992-93 Official NBA Guide
Available September 1992. #436 ....$11.95

1992-93 Official NBA Register
Available September 1992. #437 ....$11.95

The Series — 1992
Available November 1992. #444 ....$12.95